DEVELOPMENT
THROUGH THE LIFESPAN

Laura E. Berk

**Custom Edition for
Mt. San Antonio College**

Taken from:

Development Through the Lifespan, Fourth Edition
by Laura E. Berk

PEARSON CUSTOM PUBLISHING
75 Arlington Street, Suite 300, Boston, MA 02116
A Pearson Education Company

About the Author

Laura E. Berk is a distinguished professor of psychology at Illinois State University, where she has taught human development to both undergraduate and graduate students for more than three decades. She received her bachelor's degree in psychology from the University of California, Berkeley, and her master's and doctoral degrees in child development and educational psychology from the University of Chicago. She has been a visiting scholar at Cornell University, UCLA, Stanford University, and the University of South Australia.

Berk has published widely on the effects of school environments on children's development, the development of private speech, and most recently the role of make-believe play in development. Her research has been funded by the U.S. Office of Education and the National Institute of Child Health and Human Development. It has appeared in many prominent journals, including *Child Development, Developmental Psychology, Merrill-Palmer Quarterly, Journal of Abnormal Child Psychology, Development and Psychopathology,* and *Early Childhood Research Quarterly.* Her empirical studies have attracted the attention of the general public, leading to contributions to *Psychology Today* and *Scientific American.*

Berk has served as a research editor for *Young Children* and consulting editor for *Early Childhood Research Quarterly* and the *Journal of Cognitive Education and Psychology.* She is a frequent contributor to edited volumes on early childhood development, having recently authored chapters on the importance of parenting, on make-believe play and self-regulation, and on the kindergarten child. She has also written the chapter on development for *The Many Faces of Psychological Research in the Twenty-First Century* (Society for the Teaching of Psychology), the chapter on social development for *The Chicago Companion to the Child,* the article on Vygotsky for the *Encyclopedia of Cognitive Science,* and the chapter on storytelling as a teaching strategy for *Voices of Experience: Memorable Talks from the National Institute on the Teaching of Psychology* (Association for Psychological Science).

Berk's books include *Private Speech: From Social Interaction to Self-Regulation, Scaffolding Children's Learning: Vygotsky and Early Childhood Education,* and *Landscapes of Development: An Anthology of Readings.* In addition to *Development Through the Lifespan,* she is author of the best-selling texts *Child Development* and *Infants, Children, and Adolescents,* published by Allyn and Bacon. Her book for parents and teachers is *Awakening Children's Minds: How Parents and Teachers Can Make a Difference.*

Berk is active in work for children's causes. In addition to service in her home community, she is a member of the national board of directors of Jumpstart, a nonprofit organization that provides early literacy intervention to thousands of low-income preschoolers across the United States, using college and university students as interveners.

List of Features

Contents

Part I

THEORY AND RESEARCH IN HUMAN DEVELOPMENT *000*

1 History, Theory, and Research Strategies   2

Part II

FOUNDATIONS OF DEVELOPMENT   42

2 Biological and Environmental Foundations   42

3 Prenatal Development, Birth, and the Newborn Baby   78

Part III

INFANCY AND TODDLERHOOD: THE FIRST TWO YEARS 118

4 Physical Development in Infancy and Toddlerhood 118

5 Cognitive Development in Infancy and Toddlerhood 150

6 Emotional and Social Development in Infancy and Toddlerhood 182

Part IV

EARLY CHILDHOOD: TWO TO SIX YEARS 214

7 Physical and Cognitive Development in Early Childhood 214

8 Emotional and Social Development in Early Childhood 254

Part V

MIDDLE CHILDHOOD: SIX TO ELEVEN YEARS 288

9 Physical and Cognitive Development in Middle Childhood 288

10 Emotional and Social Development in Middle Childhood 328

Part VI

ADOLESCENCE: THE TRANSITION TO ADULTHOOD 360

11 Physical and Cognitive Development in Adolescence 360

Part VII

EARLY ADULTHOOD 428

16 Emotional and Social Development in Middle Adulthood   528

Part IX
LATE ADULTHOOD   560

17 Physical and Cognitive Development in Late Adulthood   560

A Personal Note to Students

My more than 30 years of teaching child development have brought me in contact with thousands of students like you—students with diverse college majors, future goals, interests, and needs. Some are affiliated with my own department, psychology, but many come from other related fields—education, sociology, anthropology, family studies, social service, nursing, and biology, to name just a few. Each semester, my students' aspirations have proved to be as varied as their fields of study. Many look toward careers in applied work—counseling, caregiving, nursing, social work, school psychology, and program administration. Some plan to teach, and a few want to do research. Most hope someday to become parents, whereas others are already parents who come with a desire to better understand and rear their children. And almost all arrive with a deep curiosity about how they themselves developed from tiny infants into the complex human beings they are today.

My goal in preparing this fourth edition of *Development Through the Lifespan* is to provide a textbook that meets the instructional goals of your course as well as your personal interests and needs. To achieve these objectives, I have grounded this book in a carefully selected body of classic and current theory and research. In addition, the text highlights the lifespan perspective on development and the interacting contributions of biology and environment to the developing person. It also illustrates commonalities and differences among ethnic groups and cultures, and discusses the broader social contexts in which we develop. I have provided a unique pedagogical program that will assist you in mastering information, integrating various aspects of development, critically examining controversial issues, applying what you have learned, and relating the information to your own life.

I hope that learning about human development will be as rewarding for you as I have found it over the years. I would like to know what you think about both the field of human development and this book. I welcome your comments; please feel free to send them to me at Department of Psychology, Box 4620, Illinois State University, Normal, IL 61790, or care of the publisher, who will forward them to me.

—Laura E. Berk

✦ Preface for Instructors

My decision to write *Development Through the Lifespan* was inspired by a wealth of professional and personal experiences. First and foremost were the interests and concerns of hundreds of students of human development with whom I have worked in over three decades of college teaching. Each semester, their insights and questions have revealed how an understanding of any single period of development is enriched by an appreciation of the entire lifespan. Second, as I moved through adult development myself, I began to think more intensely about factors that have shaped and reshaped my own life course—family, friends, mentors, co-workers, community, and larger society. My career well-established, my marriage having stood the test of time, and my children launched into their adult lives, I felt that a deeper grasp of these multiple, interacting influences would help me better appreciate where I had been and where I would be going in the years ahead. I was also convinced that such knowledge could contribute to my becoming a better teacher, scholar, family member, and citizen. And because teaching has been so central and gratifying to my work life, I wanted to bring to others a personally meaningful understanding of lifespan development.

The years since *Development Through the Lifespan* first appeared have been a period of considerable expansion and change in theory and research. This fourth edition represents these rapidly transforming aspects of the field, with a wealth of new content and teaching tools:

- *Diverse pathways of change are highlighted.* Investigators have reached broad consensus that variations in biological makeup and everyday tasks lead to wide individual differences in paths of change and resulting competencies. This edition pays more attention to variability in development and to recent theories—including ecological, sociocultural, and dynamic systems—that attempt to explain it. Multicultural and cross-cultural findings, including international comparisons, are enhanced throughout the text. Biology and Environment and Cultural Influences boxes also accentuate the theme of diversity in development.

- *The lifespan perspective is emphasized.* As in previous editions, the lifespan perspective—development is lifelong, multidimensional, multidirectional, plastic, and embedded in multiple contexts—continues to serve as a unifying approach to understanding human change and is woven thoroughly into the text. In addition, special Lifespan Vista boxes discuss lifespan-perspective assumptions and consider development across a wide age span.

- *The complex, bidirectional relationship between biology and environment is given greater attention.* Accumulating evidence on development of the brain, motor skills, cog- nitive and language competencies, temperament and personality, and developmental problems underscores the way biological factors emerge in, are modified by, and share power with experience. Interconnections between biology and environment are integral to the lifespan per- spective and are revisited throughout the text narrative and in the Biology and Environment boxes with new and updated topics.

- *Inclusion of interdisciplinary research is expanded.* The move toward viewing thoughts, feelings, and behavior as an integrated whole, affected by a wide array of influences in biology, social context, and culture, has motivated developmental researchers to strengthen their ties with other fields of psychology and with other disciplines. Topics and findings included in this edition increasingly reflect the contributions of educational psychology, social psychology, health psychology, clinical psychology, neuro- psychology, biology, pediatrics, geriatrics, sociology, anthropology, social welfare, and other fields.

- *The links among theory, research, and applications are strengthened.* As researchers intensify their efforts to gen- erate findings relevant to real-life situations, I have placed even greater weight on social policy issues and sound theory- and research-based applications. Further applica- tions are provided in the Applying What We Know tables, which give students concrete ways of building bridges between their learning and the real world.

- *The role of active student learning is made more explicit.* Ask Yourself questions at the end of each major section have been thoroughly revised and expanded to promote four approaches to engaging actively with the subject matter—*Review, Apply, Connect,* and *Reflect.* The new *Reflect* questions help make the study of lifespan develop- ment personally meaningful by encouraging students to take a well-reasoned stand on important issues and to relate theory and research to their own lives. In addition, highlighting of key terms within the text narrative rein- forces student learning in context.

Text Philosophy

The basic approach of this book has been shaped by my own professional and personal history as a teacher, researcher, and parent. It consists of seven philosophical ingredients that I regard as essential for students to emerge from a course with a thorough understanding of lifespan development. Each theme is woven into every chapter:

1. **An understanding of the diverse array of theories in the field and the strengths and shortcomings of each.** The first chapter begins by emphasizing that only knowledge of multiple theories can do justice to the richness of human development. As I take up each age period and domain of development, I present a variety of theoretical perspectives, indicate how each highlights previously overlooked aspects of development, and discuss research that evaluates it. Consideration of contrasting theories also serves as the context for an evenhanded analysis of many controversial issues.

2. **A grasp of the lifespan perspective as an integrative approach to development.** I introduce the lifespan perspective as an organizing framework in the first chapter and refer to and illustrate its assumptions throughout the text, in an effort to help students construct an overall vision of development from conception to death.

3. **Knowledge of both the sequence of human development and the processes that underlie it.** Students are provided with a discussion of the organized sequence of development along with processes of change. An understanding of process—how complex combinations of biological and environmental events produce development—has been the focus of most recent research. Accordingly, the text reflects this emphasis. But new information about the timetable of change has also emerged. In many ways, the very young and the old have proved to be far more competent than they were believed to be in the past. In addition, many milestones of adult development, such as finishing formal education, entering a career, getting married, having children, and retiring, have become less predictable. Current evidence on the sequence and timing of development, along with its implications for process, is presented for all periods of the lifespan.

4. **An appreciation of the impact of context and culture on human development.** A wealth of research indicates that people live in rich physical and social contexts that affect all domains of development. Throughout the book, students travel to distant parts of the world as I review a growing body of cross-cultural evidence. The text narrative also discusses many findings on socioeconomically and ethnically diverse people within the United States and Canada. Furthermore, the impact of historical time period and cohort membership receives continuous attention. In this vein, gender issues—the distinctive but continually evolving experiences, roles, and life paths of males and females—are granted substantial emphasis. Besides highlighting the effects of immediate settings, such as family, neighborhood, and school, I make a concerted effort to underscore the influence of larger social structures—societal values, laws, and government programs—on lifelong well-being.

5. **An understanding of the joint contributions of biology and environment to development.** The field recognizes more powerfully than ever before the joint roles of hereditary/constitutional and environmental factors—that these contributions to development combine in complex ways and cannot be separated in a simple manner. Numerous examples of how biological dispositions can be maintained as well as transformed by social contexts are presented throughout the book.

6. **A sense of the interdependency of all domains of development—physical, cognitive, emotional, and social.** Every chapter emphasizes an integrated approach to human development. I show how physical, cognitive, emotional, and social development are interwoven. Within the text narrative, and in a special series of Ask Yourself questions at the end of major sections, students are referred to other sections of the book to deepen their grasp of relationships among various aspects of change.

7. **An appreciation of the interrelatedness of theory, research, and applications.** Throughout this book, I emphasize that theories of human development and the research stimulated by them provide the foundation for sound, effective practices with children, adolescents, and adults. The link among theory, research, and applications is reinforced by an organizational format in which theory and research are presented first, followed by practical implications. In addition, a current focus in the field—harnessing knowledge of human development to shape social policies that support human needs throughout the lifespan—is reflected in every chapter. The text addresses the current condition of children, adolescents, and adults in the United States, Canada, and around the world and shows how theory and research have combined with public interest to spark successful interventions. Many important applied topics are considered, such as family planning, infant mortality, maternal employment and child care, teenage pregnancy and parenthood, domestic violence, exercise and adult health, lifelong learning, grandparents rearing grandchildren, adjustment to retirement, adapting to widowhood, and palliative care for the dying.

Text Organization

I have chosen a chronological organization for *Development Through the Lifespan*. The book begins with an introductory chapter that describes the history of the field, contemporary theories, and research strategies. It is followed by two chapters on the foundations of development. Chapter 2 combines an overview of biological and environmental contexts into a single, integrated discussion of these multifaceted influences on development. Chapter 3 is devoted to prenatal development, birth, and the newborn baby. With this foundation, students are ready to look closely at seven major age periods: infancy and toddlerhood (Chapters 4, 5, and 6), early childhood (Chapters 7 and 8), middle childhood (Chapters 9 and 10), adolescence (Chapters 11 and 12), early adulthood (Chapters 13 and 14), middle adulthood (Chapters 15 and 16), and late adulthood (Chapters 17 and 18). Topical chapters within each chronological division cover physical development, cognitive development, and emotional and social development. The book concludes with a chapter on death, dying, and bereavement (Chapter 19).

The chronological approach assists students in thoroughly understanding each age period. It also eases the task of integrating the various domains of development because each is discussed in close proximity. At the same time, a chronologically organized book requires that theories covering several age periods be presented piecemeal. This creates a challenge for students, who must link the various parts together. To assist with this task, I frequently remind students of important earlier achievements before discussing new developments, referring back to related sections with page references. Also, chapters or sections devoted to the same topic (for example, cognitive development) are similarly organized, making it easier for students to draw connections across age periods and construct an overall view of developmental change.

New Coverage in the Fourth Edition

Lifespan development is a fascinating and ever-changing field of study, with constantly emerging new discoveries and refinements in existing knowledge. The fourth edition represents this burgeoning contemporary literature, with over 2,200 new citations. Cutting-edge topics throughout the text underscore the book's major themes. Here is a sampling:

- **Chapter 1:** Increased attention to the dynamic systems view of development ● New historical findings on childhood as a separate phase of life in medieval Europe ● Introduction to developmental cognitive neuroscience as a new area of investigation ● New examples of research using systematic observation, structured interviews, and correlational research ● New section on combining experimental and developmental designs, including an illustration in a new Social Issues box answering the question, "Can musical experiences enhance intelligence?"

- **Chapter 2:** Updated discussion of basic genetics ● New evidence on the changing proportion of male to female births ● Inclusion of both germline and somatic mutation, with implications for health over the lifespan ● New evidence on genetic testing and genetic treatments

of disease ● Updated section on development of adopted children ● New section on affluence, family functioning, and development ● Updated research on neighborhood influences on physical and mental health of children and adults ● Expanded consideration of rural versus urban contexts for development in childhood and adulthood ● Updated section on public policies and lifespan development ● New Lifespan Vista box on worldwide education of girls and its transforming impact on current and future generations ● Updated indicators on the status of children and adults in the United States, Canada, and other industrialized nations ● Enhanced discussion of environmental influences on gene expression

- **Chapter 3:** Updated research on fetal sensory and behavioral capacities and on fetal activity level as a predictor of childhood temperament ● Updated Lifespan Vista box on the prenatal environment and health in later life ● Expanded and updated consideration of teratogens ● New evidence on the long-term consequences of emotional stress during pregnancy ● New findings on older maternal age and prenatal and birth complications ● Updated discussion of preterm and low-birth-weight infants ● Enhanced consideration of the benefits of "kangaroo care" for preterm babies ● Updated Biology and Environment box on sudden infant death syndrome, including protective sleeping practices ● New research on fetal and newborn pain perception ● New findings on the impact of the prenatal environment on newborn odor preferences ● Expanded consideration of paternal influences, including teratogenic effects, social support of the mother, and hormonal changes around the time of birth that facilitate paternal caregiving

- **Chapter 4:** Introduction to major methods of assessing brain functioning, including EEG, ERPs, fMRI, and PET ● Updated Lifespan Vista box on brain plasticity over the lifespan ● New research on children adopted from Romanian orphanages, bearing on the question of whether infancy is a sensitive period of development ● New discussion of appropriate stimulation in infancy and early childhood, and the distinction between experience-expectant and experience-dependent brain growth ● Updated Cultural Influences box on cultural variation in infant sleeping arrangements ● Updated section on breastfeeding ● New evidence on infants' and toddlers' eating habits and early risk for obesity ● Revised and updated section on habituation, including using habituation tasks to assess both recent and remote memory ● New findings on newborn imitation in humans and chimpanzees ● New dynamic systems research on development of reaching ● New findings on development of infant speech perception ● Expanded and updated consideration of early face perception ● Expanded and updated section on intermodal perception, including contributions of intermodal perception to all aspects of psychological development

🖉 **Chapter 5:** Expanded coverage of the core knowledge perspective on cognitive development ● New research on imitation in toddlerhood ● Updated findings on development of memory and categorization ● New findings on cultural variations in early attentional strategies ● Revised and updated Biology and Environment box on infantile amnesia ● Inclusion of the most recent edition of the Bayley Scales of Infant Development (Bayley III) ● Updated findings on quality of child care in the United States and Canada, with consequences for cognitive and social competence ● New research on early intervention for poverty-stricken families with infants and toddlers, including Early Head Start ● Expanded section on early language development, including updated presentation of interactionist theories and new research on vocabulary development, SES variations in language progress, and development of babies with hearing impairments ● New Biology and Environment box on impact of parent–child interaction on language and cognitive development of deaf children

🖉 **Chapter 6:** Revised Lifespan Vista box on parental depression and child development, including both maternal and paternal depression ● Expanded treatment of social referencing, including new findings on infants' sensitivity to parents' voice ● New research on the self-regulatory dimension of temperament—effortful control ● Updated section on the stability of temperament ● New research on parents' tendency to emphasize children's temperamental differences ● Expanded attention to methods of assessing attachment, including the Attachment Q-Sort ● Enhanced consideration of cultural variations in sensitive caregiving, with implications for attachment security ● Expanded section on fathers' involvement with infants ● New Cultural Influences box on the powerful role of paternal warmth in development ● Enhanced discussion of the influence of attachment quality in infancy on later development ● Updated Social Issues box on the influence of quality of child care and long child-care hours on attachment and later development

🖉 **Chapter 7:** Updated research on childhood immunization ● New Social Issues box on child health care in the United States and other Western nations ● New section on preschoolers' understanding of symbol–real world relations, including dual representation ● Updated findings on development of the appearance–reality distinction ● New Cultural Influences box on how children in village and tribal cultures learn by observing and participating in adult work ● Expanded consideration of the development of attention, including the role of inhibition ● Enhanced

discussion of development of autobiographical memory, including the influence of the parent–child relationship ● New evidence on cognitive attainments that contribute to mastery of false belief ● Updated research on early development of counting ● Updated Biology and Environment box on "mindblindness" and autism, including explanations for deficient theory of mind among children with autism ● Enhanced consideration of the long-term benefits of preschool intervention for poverty-stricken children ● Expanded section on educational media, including effects of television and computers ● Expanded and updated research on the diverse strategies preschoolers use to figure out word meanings ● New findings on the gradual development of grammatical skills, with implications for theoretical controversies

🖉 **Chapter 8:** Enhanced explanation of the I-self and me-self, with an illustrative figure ● Inclusion of the concept of emotional competence ● Updated consideration of emotional self-regulation in early childhood, including effortful control ● Expanded discussion of peer sociability, including the consequences of nonsocial play for adjustment ● Revised and updated section on parenting and children's peer relations ● Updated research on the impact of harsh punishment on development ● New Cultural Influences box on ethnic differences in the consequences of physical punishment ● Enhanced treatment of positive discipline ● Updated discussion of preschoolers' moral reasoning ● Revised and updated consideration of types of aggression, including physical, verbal, and relational forms ● Updated discussion of violent media and development of aggression ● New evidence on gender-stereotyped learning in early childhood, including the influence of parents and same-sex peer associations ● Updated research on cognitive contributions to gender constancy ● Updated discussion of gender schema theory, noting individual differences among children in gender-schematic processing ● New findings on the harmful impact of parental psychological control on children's adjustment ● Enhanced discussion of cultural variation in parenting beliefs and practices ● Updated section on child maltreatment, including the success of home visitation prevention programs

🖉 **Chapter 9:** Revised and updated section on overweight and obesity ● Updated evidence on outcomes of participation in youth sports programs ● New section on evolutionary influences on children's play, with special attention to rough-and-tumble and its adaptive significance ● Revised Biology and Environment box on children with attention-deficit hyperactivity disorder ● Enhanced consideration of development of metacognition in middle childhood, including second-order false belief ● Updated discussion of learning to read, including the role of phonological awareness ● Expanded section on mathematical development, with implications for math education ● Description of the new Stanford-Binet Intelligence Scales, Fifth Edition, and the WISC-IV, with updated sample intelligence test items ● Updated description of Sternberg's triarchic theory of successful intelligence ● New Lifespan Vista box on social and emotional intelligence ● New research on culture, communication styles, and children's mental test performance ● New section on the impact of stereotype threat on the test taking of ethnic minority children ● New Social Issues box on high-stakes testing ● Expanded treatment of language development in middle childhood, with special attention to narrative ● Revised and updated section on educational philosophies, including constructivist and social constructivist classrooms ● Updated cross-national comparisons of academic achievement, with special attention to family, school, and societal factors that support high achievement

Chapter 10: Increased attention to cultural variations in school-age children's self-concept ● Enhanced attention to emotional self-regulation, including school-age children's use of problem-centered and emotion-centered coping ● Expanded and updated attention to school-age children's moral and social-conventional understanding ● New section on school-age children's grasp of individual rights, with implications for moral understanding ● New section on children's understanding of diversity and inequality, including research on development of racial and ethnic prejudice ● Enhanced consideration of differences in prosocial and aggressive children's friendships ● Updated Biology and Environment box on bullies and their victims ● New evidence on development of gender identity in middle childhood, with implications for emotional adjustment ● Enhanced attention to parenting of school-age children, with emphasis on paternal involvement and children's development ● Updated consideration of common fears of school-age children ● New evidence on children's eyewitness testimony, with emphasis on factors that contribute to children's suggestibility

Chapter 11: New section on adolescent brain development ● Updated research on consequences of adolescent sleep "phase delay" for school performance and high-risk behaviors ● New evidence on implications of pubertal timing for psychological adjustment in adulthood ● New research on parent–adolescent conversations about sex ● Revised and updated Biology and Environment box on development of sexual identity among gay, lesbian, and bisexual youths ● New findings on the link between father absence and early sexual activity ● Enhanced consideration of factors that increase adolescent fathers' involvement in caregiving ● Expanded attention to cultural

influences on adolescent drug and alcohol use ● New section on adolescent decision making ● New evidence on the decline in reading and writing achievement among adolescent boys ● Updated consideration of factors contributing to sex differences in math and spatial reasoning ● New evidence on the impact of school transitions on adjustment ● Updated research on the academic consequences of tracking in secondary school

Chapter 12: Updated and expanded section on adolescents' self-esteem ● Updated Cultural Influences box on identity development among ethnic minority youths ● Revised evaluation of Kohlberg's stages ● New section on adolescents' coordination of moral, social-conventional, and personal concerns ● Enhanced consideration of experiences that promote moral self-relevance ● New section on religious involvement and moral development ● Updated Social Issues box on development of civic responsibility ● Expanded and updated section on parenting and adolescent autonomy ● New section on Internet friendships ● New research on the relationship of parent–child attachment to adolescent romantic ties ● Revised and updated Lifespan Vista box on two routes to adolescent delinquency, with new research on the link between early relational aggression and adolescent antisocial activity

Chapter 13: New section introducing emerging adulthood, an extended transition to full assumption of adult roles ● Updated consideration of theories of biological aging ● New findings on changes in motor performance in adulthood, based on research on outstanding athletes ● Updated and enhanced discussion of SES variations in adult health ● New evidence on substance abuse in early adulthood ● New findings on use of Internet dating services ● Inclusion of research on both male-initiated and female-initiated coercive sexual behavior ● Revised and updated section on Perry's theory and development of epistemic cognition, including experiences that foster its development ● Expanded consideration of Labouvie-Vief's theory and cognitive-affective complexity in early and middle adulthood ● New findings on factors that contribute to dropping out of college and enhanced discussion of preventive measures ● Updated research on factors influencing vocational choice, with special attention to the role of parents and teachers ● New Social Issues box on men who choose nontraditional careers

Chapter 14: Expanded discussion of the relationship of the developmental tasks of identity and intimacy ● Updated research on development of companionate love, with emphasis on constructive conflict resolution ● New evidence on changing relationships with parents after leaving home • New findings on sex differences in marital satisfaction • Discussion of parental adjustment to both a first and a second birth • Updated section on parent education • New research on intergenerational transmission of risk for divorce • Updated research on gay and lesbian parents • New evidence on unique workplace challenges faced by women and ethnic minority young adults • Enhanced discussion of workplace policies that help adults meet both work and family responsibilities • New Social Issues box on women in "fast-track" careers who opt to stay home

✐ **Chapter 15:** Updated coverage of menopausal symptoms • New research on risks and benefits of hormone therapy and alternative treatments for menopausal symptoms • Enhanced consideration of women's psychological reactions to menopause, including ethnic variations • Updated section on reproductive changes in men • Updated statistics on the age-related incidence of chronic diseases • Expanded discussion of genetic, biological-aging, and environmental contributions to cancer • Enhanced attention to osteoporosis in men, including the need for widespread screening and treatment • Updated consideration of age-related declines in processing speed and inhibition • New research on middle-aged adults' memory in pressured, classroomlike contexts versus self-paced contexts • Enhanced consideration of challenges faced by nontraditional college students, including gender and ethnic stereotypes

✐ **Chapter 16:** New findings on middle-aged men's and women's emotional reactions to their aging appearance • Updated section addressing the question, Is there a midlife crisis?, including research asking middle-aged adults about life regrets • New evidence on age-related changes in psychological stressors from early through middle adulthood • New findings on men's and women's expressed reasons for midlife divorce • Updated section on the sandwich generation and caring for aging parents • Updated Social Issues box on grandparents rearing grandchildren: the skipped-generation family • New findings on women, ethnic minorities, and the "glass ceiling" in the workplace

✐ **Chapter 17:** Updated North American statistics on average life expectancy and active lifespan • Updated Lifespan Vista box on centenarians, with biographical information about Jeanne Louise Calment, the longest-lived person on record • Expanded and updated discussion of stereotypes of aging and their impact on elders, including stereotype threat and media portrayals of older adults • Enhanced attention to compression of morbidity, with special emphasis on the importance of a healthy lifestyle • New findings on the impact of nutrition and exercise on health status in late adulthood • New evidence on factors that

contribute to frailty in old age • Updated statistics on leading causes of death in late adulthood • New findings on neurological changes associated with Alzheimer's disease • Updated research on genetic and environmental risks for Alzheimer's disease, including the link between diabetes and Alzheimer's • Updated Social Issues box on interventions for caregivers of elders with dementia, including the effectiveness of REACH intervention programs • New research on memory changes, including deficient recall of the context of events, memory for remote events (very long-term recall), and prospective memory • New findings on language processing, including elders' more frequent experience of tip-of-the-tongue states • Updated evidence on factors related to cognitive change, including education, cigarette smoking, chronic conditions, and complex, stimulating work • Discussion of the age-related rise in inconsistency of cognitive performance as predictive of cognitive declines • Enhanced consideration of cognitive training programs for the elderly, including ACTIVE, a large-scale intervention demonstrating impressive gains in trained skills

✐ **Chapter 18:** Discussion of Joan Erikson's additional psychosocial stage of gerotranscendence • Expanded treatment of emotional expertise in late adulthood, including Labouvie-Vief's research on affect optimization • Enhanced consideration of possible selves in old age • New findings on spirituality and religiosity in late adulthood • New section on continuity theory and related research • Updated evidence relevant to socioemotional selectivity theory • Consideration of cohabitation in late adulthood • Updated findings on adaptation to widowhood • Discussion of elder abandonment as a form of elder abuse

✐ **Chapter 19:** Updated research on children's understanding of death • New evidence on the relationship between religiosity and death anxiety • Updated evidence on terminally ill patients' varied reactions to dying • New illustrations of cultural influences on the experiences of dying people • New Biology and Environment box on music as palliative care for dying patients • The Terry Schiavo case and public debate over right-to-die issues • Updated Social Issues box on voluntary active euthanasia, with special attention to legalization in the Netherlands • New statistics on public approval of assisted suicide • Updated consideration of the Oregon Death with Dignity Act • Inclusion of Worden's view of grieving as a set of tasks to be accomplished • Increased attention to finding meaning in loss as an effective bereavement coping strategy • Inclusion of disenfranchised grief, induced by lack of opportunity to mourn publicly • Coverage of public tragedies and risk of bereavement overload • Enhanced consideration of self-help groups as bereavement interventions

Pedagogical Features

Maintaining a highly accessible writing style—one that is lucid and engaging without being simplistic—continues to be one of my major goals. I frequently converse with students, encouraging them to relate what they read to their own lives. In doing so, I hope to make the study of human development involving and pleasurable.

Stories and Vignettes about Real People. To help students construct a clear image of development and to enliven the text narrative, each chronological age division is unified by case examples woven throughout that set of chapters. For example, the middle childhood section highlights the experiences and concerns of 10-year-old Joey; 8-year-old Lizzie; their divorced parents, Rena and Drake; and their classmates. In the chapters on late adulthood, students get to know Walt and Ruth, a vibrant retired couple, along with Walt's older brother Dick and his wife Goldie and Ruth's sister Ida, a victim of Alzheimer's disease. Besides a set of main characters who bring unity to each age period, many additional vignettes offer vivid examples of development and diversity among children, adolescents, and adults.

Chapter Introductions and End-of-Chapter Summaries. To provide a helpful preview, I include an outline and overview of chapter content in each chapter introduction. Especially comprehensive end-of-chapter summaries, organized according to the major divisions of each chapter and highlighting important terms, remind students of key points in the text discussion. Review questions are included in the summaries to encourage active study.

Ask Yourself Questions. Active engagement with the subject matter is also supported by study questions at the end of each major section. Four types of questions prompt students to think about human development in diverse ways: *Review* questions help students recall and comprehend information they have just read; *Apply* questions encourage the application of knowledge to controversial issues and problems faced by children, adolescents, adults, and professionals who work with them; *Connect* questions help students build an image of the whole person by integrating what they have learned across age periods and domains of development. *Reflect* questions help make the study of human development personally meaningful by asking students to reflect on their own development and life experiences. Each question is answered on the text's companion website where students can compare their reasoning to a model response. A URL to the site (*www.ablongman.com/berk*) is included below each set of questions.

Four types of thematic boxes accentuate the philosophical themes of this book:

A Lifespan Vista boxes are devoted to topics that have long-term implications for development or involve intergenerational issues. Examples include: *Worldwide Education of Girls: Transforming Current and Future Generations, The Prenatal Environment and Health in Later Life, Social and Emotional Intelligence, Childhood Attachment Patterns and Adult Romantic Relationships, Generative Adults Tell Their Life Stories,* and *What Can We Learn about Aging from Centenarians?*

Social Issues boxes discuss the impact of social conditions on children, adolescents, and adults and emphasize the need for sensitive social policies to ensure their well-being— for example, *Can Musical Experiences Enhance Intelligence?, Child Health Care in the United States and Other Western Nations, High-Stakes Testing, Masculinity at Work: Men Who Choose Nontraditional Careers, Women in "Fast-Track" Careers Who Opt to Stay Home,* and *Interventions for Caregivers of Elders with Dementia*

Cultural Influences boxes have been expanded and updated to deepen attention to culture threaded throughout the text. They highlight both cross-cultural and multicultural variations in human development—for example, *Immigrant Youths: Amazing Adaptation, The African-American Extended Family, Cultural Variation in Infant Sleeping Arrangements, The Powerful Role of Paternal Warmth in Development, Children in Village and Tribal Cultures Observe and Participate in Adult Work,* and *Cultural Variations in the Experience of Aging.*

Biology and Environment boxes highlight the growing attention to the complex, bidirectional relationship between biology and environment during development. Examples include *Parent–Child Interaction: Impact on Language and Cognitive Development of Deaf Children, Development of Shyness and Sociability, "Mindblindness" and Autism, Bullies and Their Victims, Antiaging Effects of Dietary Calorie Restriction: Relevant to Humans?, What Factors Promote Psychological Well-Being in Midlife?,* and *Music as Palliative Care for Dying Patients.*

Applying What We Know Tables. To accentuate the link between theory and research and applications, Applying What We Know tables provide easily accessible practical advice on the importance of caring for oneself and others throughout the lifespan. The tables also speak directly to students as parents or future parents and to those pursuing child- and family-related careers or areas of study, such as teaching, health care, counseling, or social work. They include: *Signs of Developmentally Appropriate Infant and Toddler Child Care, Supporting Early Language Learning, Using Positive Discipline, Helping Children Adjust to Their Parents' Divorce, Communicating with Adolescents about Sexual Issues, Strategies That Help Dual-Earner Couples Combine Work and Family Roles, Relieving the Stress of Caring for an Aging Parent,* and *Fostering Adaptation to Widowhood in Late Adulthood.*

🍂 **Milestones Tables.** A Milestones table appears at the end of each age division of the text. These tables summarize major physical, cognitive, language, emotional, and social attainments, providing a convenient aid for reviewing the chronology of lifespan development.

🍂 **Enhanced Art and Photo Program.** A thoroughly revised art style presents concepts and research findings with clarity and attractiveness, thereby greatly aiding student understanding and retention. The illustration program increases the number of photos in the previous edition. Each has been carefully selected to portray human development and to represent the diversity of people in the United States, Canada, and around the world.

🍂 **In-Text Key Terms with Definitions, End-of-Chapter Term List, and End-of-Book Glossary.** Mastery of terms that make up the central vocabulary of the field is promoted through in-text highlighting of key terms and concept definitions, which encourages students to review the terminology of the field in greater depth by rereading related information. Key terms also appear in an end-of-chapter page-referenced term list and an end-of-book page-referenced glossary.

Acknowledgments

The dedicated contributions of many individuals helped make this book a reality and contributed to refinements and improvements in this fourth edition. An impressive cast of reviewers provided many helpful suggestions, constructive criticisms, and enthusiasm for the organization and content of the text. I am grateful to each one of them.

● **Reviewers for the Fourth Edition**
Gerald Adams, University of Guelph
Jackie Adamson, S.D. School of Mines and Technology
Cheryl Anagnopoulos, Black Hills State University
Sherry Beaumont, University of Northern British Columbia
Kimberly Blair, University of Pittsburgh
Tracie L. Blumentritt, University of Wisconsin La Crosse
Lanthan Camblin, University of Cincinnati
Byron Egeland, University of Minnesota
Karen Fingerman, Purdue University
Laurie Gottlieb, McGill University
Dan Grangaard, Austin Community College
Marlene Groomes, Miami Dade College
Laura Gruntmeir, Redlands Community College
Deb Hollister, Valencia Community College
Hui-Chin Hsu, University of Georgia
Marita Kloseck, University of Western Ontario
Karen Kopera-Frye, University of Nevada, Reno
Valerie Kuhlmeier, Queens University
Deanna Kuhn, Teachers College, Columbia University
Dale Lund, University of Utah
Ashley Maynard, University of Hawaii
Kate McLean, University of Toronto at Mississauga

Carol Miller, Anne Arundel Community College
Ulrich Mueller, University of Victoria
Marion Perlmutter, University of Michigan
Dolores Pushkar, Concordia University
David Shwalb, Southeastern Louisiana University
Judi Smetana, University of Rochester
JoNell Strough, West Virginia University
Mojisola Tiamiyu, University of Toledo
Ruth Tincoff, Harvard University
Laura Thompson, New Mexico State University

● **Reviewers for Previous Editions**
Paul C. Amrhein, University of New Mexico
Doreen Arcus, University of Massachusetts, Lowell
René L. Babcock, Central Michigan University
W. Keith Berg, University of Florida
James A. Bird, Weber State University
Joyce Bishop, Golden West College
Ed Brady, Belleville Area College
Michele Y. Breault, Truman State University
Dilek Buchholz, Weber State University
Lanthan D. Camblin Jr., University of Cincinnati
Judith W. Cameron, Ohio State University
Joan B. Cannon, University of Massachusetts, Lowell
Michael Caruso, University of Toledo
Susan L. Churchill, University of Nebraska-Lincoln
Gary Creasey, Illinois State University
Rhoda Cummings, University of Nevada, Reno
Rita M. Curl, Minot State University
Carol Lynn Davis, University of Maine
Maria P. Fracasso, Towson University
Elizabeth E. Garner, University of North Florida
Clifford Gray, Pueblo Community College
Laurie Gottlieb, McGill University
Laura Hanish, Arizona State University
Traci Haynes, Columbus State Community College
Vernon Haynes, Youngstown State University
Karl Hennig, St. Francis Xavier University
Paula Hillman, University of Wisconsin, Whitewater
Lera Joyce Johnson, Centenary College of Louisiana
Janet Kalinowski, Ithaca College
Kevin Keating, Broward Community College

Wendy Kliewer, Virginia Commonwealth University
Rebecca A. López, California State University-Long Beach
Dale A. Lund, University of Utah
Pamela Manners, Troy State University
Robert B. McLaren, California State University, Fullerton
Randy Mergler, California State University
Karla K. Miley, Black Hawk College
Teri Miller, Milwaukee Area Technical College
Steve Mitchell, Somerset Community College
Gary T. Montgomery, University of Texas, Pan American
Feleccia Moore-Davis, Houston Community College
Karen Nelson, Austin College
Bob Newby, Tarleton State University
Jill Norvilitis, Buffalo State College
Patricia O'Brien, University of Illinois at Chicago
Nancy Ogden, Mount Royal College
Peter Oliver, University of Hartford
Verna C. Pangman, University of Manitoba
Robert Pasnak, George Mason University
Ellen Pastorino, Gainesville College
Warren H. Phillips, Iowa State University
Leslee K. Polina, Southeast Missouri State University
Dana Plude, University of Maryland
Dolores Pushkar, Concordia University
Leon Rappaport, Kansas State University
Pamela Roberts, California State University, Long Beach
Stephanie J. Rowley, University of North Carolina
Elmer Ruhnke, Manatee Community College
Randall Russac, University of North Florida
Marie Saracino, Stephen F. Austin State University
Edythe H. Schwartz, California State University-Sacramento
Bonnie Seegmiller, City University of New York, Hunter College
Richard Selby, Southeast Missouri State University
Paul S. Silverman, University of Montana
Glenda Smith, North Harris College
Jeanne Spaulding, Houston Community College
Thomas Spencer, San Francisco State University
Bruce Stam, Chemeketa Community College
Vince Sullivan, Pensacola Junior College
Mojisola F. Tiamiyu, University of Toledo
Joe Tinnin, Richland College
Catya von Károlyi, University of Wisconsin-Eau Claire
L. Monique Ward, University of Michigan
Rob Weisskirch, California State University, Fullerton
Nancy White, Youngstown State University
Ursula M. White, El Paso Community College
Carol L. Wilkinson, Whatcom Community College
Lois J. Willoughby, Miami-Dade Community College
Deborah R. Winters, New Mexico State University

In addition, I thank the following individuals for responding to a survey comparing a chapter from this text to their current textbook, providing encouraging feedback, and seriously considering adopting *Development Through the Lifespan*, Fourth Edition, for their upcoming courses.

Marna Burns, Mercer University
Kathy Canter, Pennsylvania State University-Fayette
Aileen M. Collins, Chemeketa Community College
Susan Durr, Macon State College
Martha Frank, Sage Graduate School
Karen N. Hayes, Guilford College

Art Houser, Fort Scott Community College
Joyce K. Jones, Texas State University
Joanne Kaminski, Alvernia College
Tara LaCasta-Revell, Glendale Community College
Brenda Levine, Broward Community College
Elizabeth Mazur, Pennsylvania State University-McKeesport
Victoria L. Nackley, Utica College
Carilyn Ott, University of Montevallo
Michele S. Parker, Glendale Community College
Jean Poppei, Russell Sage College
Rochelle Robbins, Holy Family University
Denise Simonsen, Fort Lewis College
Perle Slavik Cowen, University of Iowa
Maureen Vandermaas-Peeler, Elon University
Christine Wale, University of Northern Colorado

Colleagues and students at Illinois State University aided my research and contributed significantly to the text's supplements. Richard Payne, Department of Politics and Government, is a kind and devoted friend with whom I have shared many profitable discussions about the writing process, the condition of children and the elderly, and other topics that significantly influenced my perspective on lifespan development and social policy. Sara Harris joined me in preparing the Instructor's Resource Manual, the Lifespan Development in Action Observation Video Guide and A Window on Lifespan Development Video Guide, bringing to these tasks enthusiasm, imagination, depth of knowledge, and impressive writing skill. Trisha Mann's dedicated work in conducting literature searches and in revising the Grade Aid study guide is much appreciated. Courtney Cooper spent countless hours gathering and organizing library materials.

The supplements package also benefited from the talents and diligence of several other individuals. Gabrielle F. Principe of Ursinus College and Naomi Tyler of Vanderbilt University authored a superb Test Bank. Richard Wilcox wrote the excellent Companion Website and Grade Aid practice texts, Michael Sonntag of Lander University contributed to the Companion Website links, Sheralee Connors prepared the PowerPoint slides, and Susan Messer authored the informative biographies of major figures in the field that appear in *MyDevelopmentLab*.

I have been fortunate to work with a highly capable editorial team at Allyn and Bacon. Susan Hartman, Editor in Chief, provided helpful advice and oversight from initial planning to publication, generously taking time from her busy schedule to join in many weekly meetings. Mirella Misiaszek, Managing Editor, brought skillful and caring attention to the multifaceted task of coordinating all aspects of the project—arranging for expert reviews, overseeing supplements, organizing video shoots that greatly expanded my ability to illustrate important developmental concepts and milestones, contributing uniquely to the book's photo illustrations, and much, much more. Mirella's interest in human development has added to my pleasure in working with her this year.

Judy Ashkenaz, Development Editor, worked closely with me as I wrote each chapter, making sure that every thought and concept would be precisely expressed and well-developed. Her keen writing and editing skills and her impressive knowledge of developmental issues made the editing an exceptional learning experience and pleasure. I am grateful also for Susan Messer's fine contributions to the photo captions and Judy Hauck's keen eye for enhancing the artwork.

Patrick Cash-Peterson coordinated the complex production tasks that resulted in an exquisitely beautiful fourth edition. I am grateful for his keen aesthetic sensibilities, attention to detail, flexibility, efficiency, and thoughtfulness. I thank Sarah Evertson and Laurie Frankenthaler for obtaining the exceptional photographs that so aptly illustrate the text narrative. Margaret Pinette and Bill Heckman provided outstanding copyediting and proofreading.

I would like to express a heartfelt thank-you to Pam Laskey, Executive Marketing Manager, for her enthusiasm, creativity, frequent consultation and communication, and warm friendship. Pam has made sure that accurate and clear information about my books and their ancillaries reached Allyn and Bacon's sales force and that the needs of prospective and current adopters were met. Words cannot do justice to everything she has contributed to the quality and broad distribution of *Development Through the Lifespan.*

A final word of gratitude goes to my family, whose love, patience, and understanding have enabled me to be wife, mother, teacher, researcher, and text author at the same time. My sons, David and Peter, have taken a special interest in this project. Their reflections on events and progress in their own lives, conveyed over telephone and e-mail and during family gatherings, helped mold the early adulthood chapters. My husband, Ken, willingly made room for yet another time-consuming endeavor in our life together and communicated his belief in its importance in a great many unspoken, caring ways.

—*Laura E. Berk*

Supplementary Materials

Instructor Supplements

A variety of teaching tools are available for qualified instructors in organizing lectures, planning demonstrations and examinations, and ensuring student comprehension.

- **MyDevelopmentLab.** This interactive and instructive multimedia resource can be used as a supplement to a classroom course or to completely administer an online course. Prepared in collaboration with Laura E. Berk, MyDevelopmentLab includes a variety of assessments that enable continuous evaluation of students' learning. Extensive video footage, multimedia simulations, biographies of major figures in the field, and interactive activities that are unique to *Development Through the Lifespan* are also included. The power of MyDevelopmentLab lies in its design as an all-inclusive teaching and learning tool. For a sampling of its rich content, contact your Allyn and Bacon publisher's representative.

- **Instructor's Classroom Kit, Volume I and II and CD-ROM.** A comprehensive and unparalleled instructional resource, this classroom kit includes all print supplements. Supplements for Chapters 1–10 are available in Volume I, and those for Chapters 11–19 are in Volume II. Organized by chapter, each volume contains the Instructor's Manual, Test Bank, Grade Aid Study Guide with Practice Tests, and slides from the PowerPoint presentation.

  - **Instructor's Resource Manual (IRM).** This thoroughly revised IRM can be used by first-time or experienced instructors to enrich classroom experiences. Each chapter includes a Chapter-at-a-Glance grid, Brief Chapter Summary, Learning Objectives, detailed Lecture Outline, Lecture Enhancements, Learning Activities, Ask Yourself questions with answers, Suggested Student Readings, a Transparency Listing, and Media Materials list.

  - **Test Bank.** The Test Bank contains over 2,000 multiple-choice questions, each of which is page-referenced to chapter content and classified by type (factual, applied, or conceptual). Each chapter also includes a selection of essay questions and sample answers.

  - **Grade Aid with Practice Tests.** This helpful guide offers Chapter Summaries, Learning Objectives, Study Questions organized according to major headings in the text, Crossword Puzzles for mastering important terms, and two multiple-choice Practice Tests per chapter.

  - **PowerPoint Presentation.** The PowerPoint presentation contains illustrations and outlines of key topics for each chapter from the text, presented in a clear and visually attractive format.

  - **Instructor's Resource CD-ROM.** Electronic versions of all the resources in the Instructor's Classroom Kit are made available on this easy-to-use CD.

- **Computerized Test Bank.** This computerized version of the Test Bank, in easy-to-use TestGen software, lets you prepare tests for printing as well as for network and online testing. It has full editing capability. Test items are also available in CourseCompass, Blackboard, and WebCT formats.

- **"Development Through the Lifespan in Action" Observation Program.** This revised and expanded real-life videotape is over two hours in length and contains hundreds of observation segments that illustrate the many theories, concepts, and milestones of human development. New additions include understanding of false belief, emerging adulthood, retirement and volunteering, centenarians, elder caregiving, and bereavement and meaning-making after losing a child. An Observation Guide helps students use the video in conjunction with the textbook, deepening their understanding and applying what they have learned to everyday life.

- **"A Window on Lifespan Development" Running Observational Footage Video.** This video complements the Observation Program described above through more than two hours of unscripted footage on many aspects of human development. An accompanying Video Guide is also available.

🖋 **Transparencies.** Two hundred full-color transparencies taken from the text and other sources are referenced in the IRM for the most appropriate use in your classroom presentations.

Student Supplements

Beyond the study aids found in the textbook, Allyn and Bacon offers a number of supplements for students:

🖋 **MyDevelopment Lab.** This interactive and instructive multimedia resource is an all-inclusive learning tool. Prepared in collaboration with Laura E. Berk, MyDevelopmentLab engages users and reinforces learning through controlled assessments, extensive video footage, multimedia simulations, biographies of major figures in the field, and interactive activities that are unique to *Development Through the Lifespan.* Easy to use, MyDevelopmentLab meets the individual learning needs of every student. For a sampling of its rich content, visit *www.mydevelopmentlab.com.*

🖋 **Grade Aid with Practice Tests.** This helpful study guide offers Chapter Summaries, Learning Objectives, Study Questions organized according to major headings in the text, Crossword Puzzles for mastering important terms, and two multiple-choice Practice Tests per chapter.

🖋 **Companion Website.** The companion website, *http://www.ablongman.com/berk,* offers support for stu-dents through chapter-specific learning objectives, anno-tated Web resources, flashcard vocabulary building activi-ties, and model answers to the text's Ask Yourself questions.

🖋 **Milestones Study Cards.** Adapted from the popular Milestones tables featured in the text, these colorfully illustrated study cards outline key developmental attain-ments. Easy-to-use, they assist students in integrating the various domains of development and constructing a vision of the whole developing person.

🖋 **ResearchNavigator™—Now Included in MyDevelop-mentLab.** Through three exclusive databases, this intu-itive search interface provides extensive help with the research process, enabling students to make the most of their research time. EBSCO's *ContentSelect* Academic Journal Database permits a discipline-specific search through professional and popular journals. Also included are the *New York Times* Search-by-Subject Archive and *Best of the Web* Link Library. To examine the features of Research Navigator, visit *www.researchnavigator.com.*

🖋 **Tutor Center—Now Included in MyDevelopmentLab.** The Tutor Center provides students free, one-on-one, interactive tutoring from qualified instructors on all material in the text. Tutoring assistance is available by phone, FAX, Internet, and e-mail during peak study hours, 5 P.M. to 12 P.M. (EST), Sunday through Thursday during the academic year. Visit *www.ablongman.com/ tutorcenter.*

Legend for Photos Accompanying Sofie's Story Sofie's story is told in Chapters 1 and 19, from her birth to her death. The photos that appear at the beginning of Chapter 1 follow her through her lifespan and include family members of two succeeding generations.

Page 2
1. Sofie as a baby, with her mother in 1908.
2. Sofie, age 6, with her brother, age 8, in 1914.
3. Sophie, age 18, high school graduation in 1926.
4. Sofie's German passport.
5. Sofie, age 60, and daughter Laura on Laura's wedding day in 1968.
6. Sofie and Phil in 1968, less than two years before Sofie died.
7. Laura, Ken, and sons Peter and David, ages 10 and 13, on the occasion of David's Bar Mitzvah in 1985.
8. Sofie's grandsons, David and Peter, ages 5 and 2, children of Laura and Ken.
9. Laura, Ken, and son Peter as a young adult, in 2005.
10. Ken and sons David and Peter as young adults, in 2005.

Page 3
11. Sofie, age 61, and her first grandchild, Ellen, October 1969, less than 3 months before Sofie died.

Page 4
12. Sofie and Phil in their midthirties, during World War II, when they became engaged.

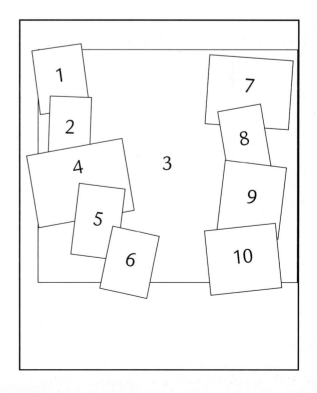

Development Through the Lifespan

PHOTOS COURTESY OF LAURA E. BERK

*T*his photo essay chronicles the life course and
family legacy of Sofie Lentschner. It begins in 1908
with Sofie's infancy and concludes in 2005, 35 years
after Sofie's death, with her young adult grandsons,
Peter and David. For a description of each photo,
see the legend on page xxix.

History, Theory, and Research Strategies

COURTESY OF LAURA E. BERK

Sofie Lentschner was born in 1908, the second child of Jewish parents who made their home in Leipzig, Germany, a city of thriving commerce and cultural vitality. Her father was a successful businessman and community leader. Her mother was a socialite well known for her charm, beauty, and hospitality. As a baby, Sofie displayed the determination and persistence that would be sustained throughout her life. She sat for long periods inspecting small objects with her eyes and hands. The single event that consistently broke her gaze was the sound of the piano in the parlor. As soon as Sofie could crawl, she steadfastly pulled herself up to finger its keys and marveled at the tinkling sound.

By the time Sofie entered elementary school, she was an introspective child, often ill at ease at the festive parties that girls of her family's social standing were expected to attend. She immersed herself in her schoolwork, especially in mastering the foreign languages that were a regular part of German elementary and secondary education. Twice a week, she took piano lessons from the finest teacher in Leipzig. By the time Sofie graduated from high school, she spoke English and French fluently and had become an accomplished pianist. Whereas most German girls of her time married by age 20, Sofie postponed serious courtship in favor of entering the university. Her parents began to wonder whether their intense, studious daughter would ever settle into family life.

Sofie wanted marriage as well as education, but her plans were thwarted by the political turbulence of her times. When Hitler rose to power in the early 1930s, Sofie's father, fearing for the safety of his wife and children, moved the family to Belgium. Conditions for Jews in Europe quickly worsened. The Nazis plundered Sofie's family home and confiscated her father's business. By the end of the 1930s, Sofie had lost contact with all but a handful of her aunts, uncles, cousins, and childhood friends, many of whom (she later learned) were herded into cattle cars and transported to the slave labor and death camps at Auschwitz-Birkenau. In 1939, as anti-Jewish laws and atrocities intensified, Sofie's family fled to the United States.

3

As Sofie turned 30, her parents concluded she would never marry and would need a career for financial security. They agreed to support her return to school, and Sofie earned two master's degrees, one in music and the other in librarianship. Then, on a blind date, she met Philip, a U.S. army officer. Philip's calm, gentle nature complemented Sofie's intensity and worldliness. Within 6 months they married. During the next 4 years, two daughters and a son were born. Soon Sofie's father became ill. The strain of uprooting his family and losing his home and business had shattered his health. After months of being bedridden, he died of heart failure.

When World War II ended, Philip left the army and opened a small men's clothing store. Sofie divided her time between caring for the children and helping Philip in the store. Now in her forties, she was a devoted mother, but few women her age were still rearing young children. As Philip struggled with the business, he spent longer hours at work, and Sofie often felt lonely. She rarely touched the piano, which brought back painful memories of youthful life plans shattered by war. Sofie's sense of isolation and lack of fulfillment frequently left her short-tempered. Late at night, she and Philip could be heard arguing.

As Sofie's children grew older and parenting took less time, she returned to school once more, this time to earn a teaching credential. Finally, at age 50, she launched a career. For the next decade, Sofie taught German and French to high school students and English to newly arrived immigrants. Besides easing her family's financial difficulties, she felt a gratifying sense of accomplishment and creativity. These years were among the most energetic and satisfying of Sofie's life. She had an unending enthusiasm for teaching—for transmitting her facility with language, her first-hand knowledge of the consequences of hatred and oppression, and her practical understanding of how to adapt to life in a new land. She watched her children, whose young lives were free of the trauma of war, adopt many of her values and commitments and begin their marital and vocational lives at the expected time.

Sofie approached age 60 with an optimistic outlook. As she and Philip were released from the financial burden of paying for their children's college education, they looked forward to greater leisure. Their affection and respect for one another deepened. Once again, Sofie began to play the piano. But this period of contentment was short-lived.

One morning, Sofie awoke and felt a hard lump under her arm. Several days later, her doctor diagnosed cancer. Sofie's spirited disposition and capacity to adapt to radical life changes helped her meet the illness head on. She defined it as an enemy—to be fought and overcome. As a result, she lived 5 more years. Despite the exhaustion of chemotherapy, Sofie maintained a full schedule of teaching duties and continued to visit and run errands for her elderly mother. But as she weakened physically, she no longer had the stamina to meet her classes. Gradually, she gave in to the ravaging illness. Bedridden for the last few weeks, she slipped quietly into death with Philip at her side. The funeral chapel overflowed with hundreds of Sofie's students. She had granted each a memorable image of a woman of courage and caring.

One of Sofie's three children, Laura, is the author of this book. Married a year before Sofie died, Laura and her husband, Ken, often think of Sofie's message, spoken privately to them on the eve of their wedding day: "I learned from my own life and marriage that you must build a life together but also a life apart. You must grant each other the time, space, and support to forge your own identities, your own ways of expressing yourselves and giving to others. The most important ingredient of your relationship must be respect."

Laura and Ken settled in a small Midwestern city, near Illinois State University, where they continue to teach today—Laura in the Department of Psychology, Ken in the Department of Mathematics. They have two sons, David and Peter, to whom Laura has related many stories about Sofie's life and who carry her legacy forward. David shares his grandmother's penchant for teaching; he is a second-grade teacher of mostly immigrant children. Peter, a lawyer, shares his grandmother's love of music, playing violin, viola, and mandolin in his spare time. Sofie also had a lifelong impact on many of her students. Recently, a professor of human development wrote to Laura:

> I have been meaning to contact you for a while. I teach a class in lifespan development. When I opened the textbook and saw the pictures of your mother, I was very surprised. From 1962 to 1966, I took high school German classes from your mother. . . . I remember her as a very tough teacher who both held her students accountable and cared about each and every one of us. That she was an incredible teacher did not really sink in until I went to Germany during my [college] years and was able to both understand German and speak it.
>
> . . .

Sofie's story raises a wealth of fascinating issues about human life histories:

- What determines the features that Sofie shares with others and those that make her unique—in physical characteristics, mental capacities, interests, and behaviors?
- What led Sofie to retain the same persistent, determined disposition throughout her life but to change in other essential ways?
- How do historical and cultural conditions—for Sofie, the persecution that destroyed her childhood home, caused the death of family members and friends, and led her family to flee to the United States—affect well-being throughout life?
- How does the timing of events—for example, Sofie's early exposure to foreign languages and her delayed entry into marriage, parenthood, and career—affect development?
- What factors—both personal and environmental—led Sofie to die sooner than expected?

These are central questions addressed by **human development**, a field of study devoted to understanding constancy and change throughout the lifespan. Great diversity characterizes the interests and concerns of investigators who study human development. But all share a single goal: to identify those factors that influence consistencies and transformations in people from conception to death.

Human Development as a Scientific, Applied, and Interdisciplinary Field

The questions just listed are not merely of scientific interest. Each has *applied*, or practical, importance as well. In fact, scientific curiosity is just one factor that led human development to become the exciting field of study it is today. Research about development has also been stimulated by social pressures to improve people's lives. For example, the beginning of public education in the early twentieth century led to a demand for knowledge about what and how to teach children of different ages. The interest of the medical profession in improving people's health required an understanding of physical development, nutrition, and disease. The social service profession's desire to treat emotional problems and to help people adjust to major life events, such as divorce, job loss, war, natural disasters, or the death of loved ones, required information about personality and social development. And parents have continually sought expert advice about child-rearing practices and experiences that would foster happy and successful lives for their children.

Our large storehouse of information about human development is *interdisciplinary*. It grew through the combined efforts of people from many fields of study. Because of the need for solutions to everyday problems at all ages, researchers from psychology, sociology, anthropology, biology, and neuroscience have joined forces in research with professionals from education, family studies, medicine, public health, and social service, to name just a few. Together, they have created the field as it exists today—a body of knowledge that is not just scientifically important but also relevant and useful.

Basic Issues

Research on human development is a relatively recent endeavor. Studies of children did not begin until the late nineteenth and early twentieth centuries. Investigations into adult development, aging, and change over the life course emerged only in the 1960s and 1970s (Elder, 1998). But speculations about how people grow and change have existed for centuries. As they combined with research, they inspired the construction of *theories* of development. A **theory** is an orderly, integrated set of statements that describes, explains, and predicts behavior. For example, a good theory of infant–caregiver attachment would (1) *describe* the behaviors of babies of 6 to 8 months of age as they seek the affection and comfort of a familiar adult, (2) *explain* how and why infants develop this strong desire to bond with a caregiver, and (3) *predict* the consequences of this emotional bond for relationships throughout life.

Theories are vital tools for two reasons. First, they provide organizing frameworks for our observations of people. In other words, they *guide and give meaning to what we see*. Second, theories that are verified by research provide a sound basis for practical action. Once a theory helps us *understand* development, we are in a much better position to know *how to improve* the welfare and treatment of children and adults.

As we will see, theories are influenced by the cultural values and belief systems of their times. But theories differ in one important way from mere opinion or belief: A theory's continued existence depends on *scientific verification*. All theories must be tested using a fair set of research procedures agreed on by the scientific community, and findings must endure, or be replicated, over time.

The field of human development contains many theories offering different ideas about what people are like and how they change. Humans are complex beings; they change physically, mentally, emotionally, and socially. And investigators do not always agree on the meaning of what they see. No single theory has been able to explain every aspect of human development. But the existence of many theories helps advance knowledge as researchers continually try to support, contradict, and integrate these different points of view.

This chapter introduces you to major theories of human development and research strategies used to test them. We will return to each theory in greater detail, as well as introduce other important but less grand theories, in later chapters. Although there are many theories, we can easily organize them, since almost all take a stand on three basic issues: (1) Is the course of development continuous or discontinuous? (2) Does one course of development characterize all people, or are there many possible courses? (3) Are genetic or environmental factors more important in influencing development? Let's look closely at each of these issues.

Continuous or Discontinuous Development?

How can we best describe the differences in capacities between infants, children, adolescents, and adults? As Figure 1.1 illustrates, major theories recognize two possibilities.

One view holds that infants and preschoolers respond to the world in much the same way as adults do. The difference between the immature and mature being is simply one of *amount or complexity*. For example, when Sofie was a baby, her perception of a piano melody, memory for past events, and ability to sort objects into categories may have been much like our own. Perhaps her only limitation was that she could not perform these skills with as much information and precision as we can. If this is so, then change in her thinking must be **continuous**—a process of gradually augmenting the same types of skills that were there to begin with.

According to a second view, infants and children have *unique ways of thinking, feeling and behaving*, ones quite different from adults'. If so, then development is **discontinuous**—a process in which new and different ways of understanding and responding to the world emerge at specific times. From this perspective, Sofie could not yet perceive, remember, and organize experiences as a mature person can. Rather, she moved through a series of developmental steps, each of which has unique features, until she reached the highest level of functioning.

Theories that accept the discontinuous perspective regard development as taking place in **stages**—*qualitative* changes in thinking, feeling, and behaving that characterize specific periods of development. In stage theories, development is like climbing a staircase, with each step corresponding to a more mature, reorganized way of functioning. The stage concept also assumes that people undergo periods of rapid transformation as they step up from one stage to the next. In other words, change is fairly sudden rather than gradual and ongoing.

Does development actually take place in a neat, orderly sequence of stages? In fact, this ambitious assumption has faced significant challenges. We will review some influential stage theories later in this chapter.

One Course of Development or Many?

Stage theorists assume that people everywhere follow the same sequence of development. Yet the field of human development

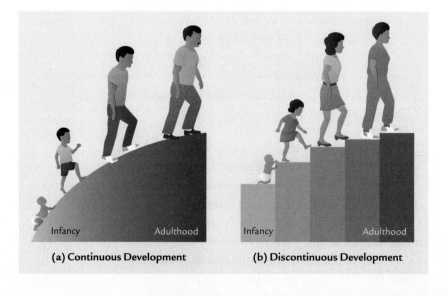

▨ FIGURE 1.1 Is development continuous or discontinuous? (a) Some theorists believe that development is a smooth, continuous process. Individuals gradually add more of the same types of skills. (b) Other theorists think that development takes place in discontinuous stages. People change rapidly as they step up to a new level and then change very little for a while. With each new step, the person interprets and responds to the world in a qualitatively different way.

(a) Continuous Development

Infancy · Adulthood

(b) Discontinuous Development

Infancy · Adulthood

is becoming increasingly aware that children and adults live in distinct **contexts**—unique combinations of personal and environmental circumstances that can result in different paths of change. For example, a shy individual who fears social encounters develops in very different contexts from those of an outgoing agemate who readily seeks out other people (Kagan, 2003). Children and adults in non-Western village societies have experiences in their families and communities that differ sharply from those of people in large Western cities. These different circumstances result in markedly different intellectual capacities, social skills, and feelings about the self and others (Rogoff, 2003).

As you will see, contemporary theorists regard the contexts that shape development as many-layered and complex. On the personal side, they include heredity and biological makeup. On the environmental side, they include immediate settings, such as home, school, and neighborhood, as well as circumstances more remote from people's everyday lives—community resources, societal values, and historical time period. Finally, researchers have become increasingly conscious of cultural diversity in development.

Relative Influence of Nature and Nurture?

In addition to describing the course of human development, each theory takes a stand on a major question about its underlying causes: Are genetic or environmental factors more important? This is the age-old **nature–nurture controversy**. By *nature*, we mean inborn biological givens—the hereditary information we receive from our parents at the moment of conception. By *nurture*, we mean the complex forces of the physical and social world that influence our biological makeup and psychological experiences before and after birth.

Although all theories grant at least some role to both nature and nurture, they vary in emphasis. Consider the following questions: Is the developing person's ability to think in more complex ways largely the result of an inborn timetable of growth? Or is it primarily influenced by stimulation from parents and teachers? Do children acquire language rapidly because they are genetically predisposed to do so or because parents tutor them from an early age? And what accounts for the vast individual differences among people—in height, weight, physical coordination, intelligence, personality, and social skills? Is nature or nurture more responsible?

A theory's position on the roles of nature and nurture affects how it explains individual differences. Theorists who emphasize *stability*—that individuals who are high or low in a characteristic (such as verbal ability, anxiety, or sociability) will remain so at later ages—typically stress the importance of *heredity*. If they do regard environment as important, they usually point to *early experiences* as establishing a lifelong pattern of behavior. Powerful negative events in the first few years, they argue, cannot be fully overcome by later, more positive ones (Bowlby, 1980; Johnson, 2000; Sroufe, Egeland, & Kreutzer, 1990). Other theorists take a more optimistic view (Greenspan & Shanker, 2004; Masten & Reed, 2002; Nelson, 2002; Werner

Early research on human development focused only on children. Since the 1960s, researchers have also investigated how adults develop over the life course. These three bird watchers, all in their seventies, continue to undergo important changes, physically, mentally, and socially. Their expressions convey the satisfactions and pleasures that many elders experience in the final decades.

& Smith, 2001). They emphasize *plasticity*—that change is possible and even likely if new experiences support it.

Throughout this book, we will see that investigators disagree, at times sharply, on the question of *stability versus plasticity*. Their answers often vary across *domains*, or aspects, of development. Think back to Sofie's story, and you will see that her linguistic ability and persistent approach to challenges were stable over the lifespan. In contrast, her psychological well-being and life satisfaction fluctuated considerably.

The Lifespan Perspective: A Balanced Point of View

So far, we have discussed basic issues of human development in terms of extremes—solutions favoring one side or the other. But as we trace the unfolding of the field, you will see that the positions of many theorists have softened. Some contemporary theorists believe that both continuous and discontinuous changes occur. Some recognize that development has both universal features and features unique to the individual and his or her contexts. And a growing number regard heredity and environment as inseparably interwoven, each affecting the potential of the other to modify the child's traits and capacities (Huttenlocher, 2002; Reiss, 2003; Rutter, 2002).

These balanced visions owe much to the expansion of research from a nearly exclusive focus on the first two decades of life to include development during adulthood. In the first half of the twentieth century, it was widely assumed that development stopped at adolescence. Infancy and childhood were viewed as periods of rapid transformation, adulthood as a plateau, and aging as a period of decline. The changing character of the North American population awakened researchers to the idea that gains in functioning are lifelong.

Because of improvements in nutrition, sanitation, and medical knowledge, the *average life expectancy* (the number of years an individual born in a particular year can expect to live) gained more in the twentieth century than in the preceding five thousand years. In 1900, it was just under age 50; today, it is 77.7 years in the United States and 80.1 years in Canada. Life expectancy continues to increase; in North America, it is predicted to reach 84 years in 2050. Consequently, there are more older adults—a trend that characterizes most of the world but that is especially striking in industrialized nations. People age 65 and older accounted for about 4 percent of the North American population in 1900, 7 percent in 1950, and 13 percent in 2005 (Statistics Canada, 2005e; U.S. Census Bureau, 2006a).

Older adults are not only more numerous but also healthier and more active. Challenging the earlier stereotype of the withering person, they have contributed to a profound shift in our view of human change and the factors that underlie it. Increasingly, researchers are envisioning *development as a dynamic system*—a perpetually ongoing process extending from conception to death that is molded by a complex network of biological, psychological, and social influences (Lerner, Theokas, & Bobek, 2005). A leading dynamic systems approach is the **lifespan perspective**. Four assumptions make up this broader view: that development is (1) lifelong, (2) multidimensional and multidirectional, (3) highly plastic, and (4) affected by multiple interacting forces (Baltes, Lindenberger, & Staudinger, 1998; Smith & Baltes, 1999; Staudinger & Lindenberger, 2003).

Development Is Lifelong

According to the lifespan perspective, no age period is supreme in its impact on the life course. Instead, events occurring during each major period, summarized in Table 1.1, can have equally powerful effects on future change. Within each period, change occurs in three broad domains: *physical, cognitive,* and *emotional/social,* which we separate for convenience of discussion (see Figure 1.2 on the following page for a description of each). Yet, as you are already aware from reading the first part of this chapter, these domains are not really distinct; they overlap and interact.

Every age period has its own agenda, its unique demands and opportunities that yield some similarities in development across many individuals. Nevertheless, throughout life, the challenges people face and the adjustments they make are highly diverse in timing and pattern, as the remaining assumptions make clear.

Table 1.1	Major Periods of Human Development	
Period	**Approximate Age Range**	**Brief Description**
Prenatal	Conception to birth	The one-celled organism transforms into a human baby with remarkable capacities to adjust to life outside the womb.
Infancy and toddlerhood	Birth–2 years	Dramatic changes in the body and brain support the emergence of a wide array of motor, perceptual, and intellectual capacities and first intimate ties to others.
Early childhood	2–6 years	During the "play years," motor skills are refined, thought and language expand at an astounding pace, a sense of morality is evident, and children begin to establish ties to peers.
Middle childhood	6–11 years	The school years are marked by advances in athletic abilities; logical thought processes; basic literacy skills; understanding of self, morality, and friendship; and peer-group membership.
Adolescence	11–18 years	Puberty leads to an adult-sized body and sexual maturity. Thought becomes abstract and idealistic and school achievement more serious. Adolescents focus on defining personal values and goals and establishing autonomy from the family.
Early adulthood	18–40 years	Most young people leave home, complete their education, and begin full-time work. Major concerns are developing a career; forming an intimate partnership; and marrying, rearing children, or establishing other lifestyles.
Middle adulthood	40–65 years	Many people are at the height of their careers and attain leadership positions. They must also help their children begin independent lives and their parents adapt to aging. They become more aware of their own mortality.
Late adulthood	65 years–death	People adjust to retirement, to decreased physical strength and health, and often to the death of a spouse. They reflect on the meaning of their lives.

Development Is Multidimensional and Multidirectional

Think back to Sofie's life and how she continually faced new demands and opportunities. From a lifespan perspective, the challenges and adjustments of development are *multidimensional*—affected by an intricate blend of biological, psychological, social forces.

Lifespan development is also *multidirectional,* in at least two ways. First, development is not limited to improved performance. Rather, at every period, it is a joint expression of growth and decline. When Sofie directed her energies toward mastering languages and music as a school-age child, she gave up refining other skills to their full potential. Later, when she chose to become a teacher, she let go of other career options. Although gains are especially evident early in life, and losses during the final years, people of all ages can improve current skills and develop new ones, including skills that compensate for reduced functioning (Freund & Baltes, 2000). Most older adults, for example, devise compensatory techniques for dealing with their increasing memory failures. They may rely more on external aids, such as calendars and lists, or generate new internal strategies, such as visualizing exactly where they will be and what they will be doing when they must keep an appointment or take medication (Chazottes, 2004).

Second, besides being multidirectional over time, change is multidirectional within each domain of development. Although some qualities of Sofie's cognitive functioning (such as memory) probably declined in her mature years, her knowledge of both English and French undoubtedly grew throughout her life. And she also developed new forms of thinking. For example, Sofie's wealth of experience and ability to cope with diverse problems led her to become expert in practical matters—a quality of reasoning called *wisdom.* Recall Sofie's wise advice to Laura and Ken on the eve of their wedding day. We will consider the development of wisdom in Chapter 17. Notice, in these examples, how the lifespan perspective includes both continuous and discontinuous change.

Development Is Plastic

Lifespan researchers emphasize that development is plastic at all ages. For example, consider Sofie's social reserve in childhood and her decision to study rather than marry as a young adult. As new opportunities arose, Sofie moved easily into marriage and childbearing in her thirties. And although parenthood and financial difficulties posed challenges to Sofie's and Philip's happiness, their relationship gradually became richer and more fulfilling. In Chapter 17, we will see that intellectual performance also remains flexible with advancing age. Elderly

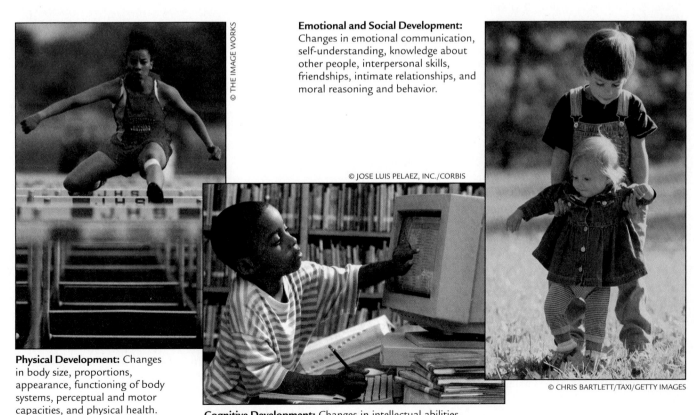

Emotional and Social Development: Changes in emotional communication, self-understanding, knowledge about other people, interpersonal skills, friendships, intimate relationships, and moral reasoning and behavior.

© THE IMAGE WORKS

© JOSE LUIS PELAEZ, INC./CORBIS

© CHRIS BARTLETT/TAXI/GETTY IMAGES

Physical Development: Changes in body size, proportions, appearance, functioning of body systems, perceptual and motor capacities, and physical health.

Cognitive Development: Changes in intellectual abilities, including attention, memory, academic and everyday knowledge, problem solving, imagination, creativity, and language.

■ **FIGURE 1.2 Major domains of development.** The three domains are not really distinct. Rather, they overlap and interact.

Biology and Environment

Resilience

John and his best friend Gary grew up in a rundown, crime-ridden, inner-city neighborhood. By age 10, each had experienced years of family conflict followed by parental divorce. Reared for the rest of childhood and adolescence in mother-headed households, John and Gary rarely saw their fathers. Both dropped out of high school and were in and out of trouble with the police.

Then John's and Gary's paths diverged. By age 30, John had fathered two children with women he never married, had spent time in prison, was unemployed, and drank alcohol heavily. In contrast, Gary had returned to finish high school, had studied auto mechanics at a community college, and became manager of a gas station and repair shop. Married with two children, he had saved his earnings and bought a home. He was happy, healthy, and well-adapted to life.

A wealth of evidence shows that environmental risks—poverty, negative family interactions and parental divorce, job loss, mental illness, and drug abuse—predispose children to future problems (Masten & Coatsworth, 1998). Why did

Gary "beat the odds" and come through unscathed?

New evidence on **resilience**—the ability to adapt effectively in the face of threats to development—is receiving increased attention because investigators want to find ways to protect young people from the damaging effects of stressful life conditions (Masten & Powell, 2003). This interest has been inspired by several long-term studies on the relationship of life stressors in childhood to competence and adjustment in adolescence and adulthood (Fergusson & Horwood, 2003; Garmezy, 1993; Masten et al., 1995; Werner & Smith, 2001). In each study, some individuals were shielded from negative outcomes, whereas others had lasting problems. Four broad factors seemed to offer protection from the damaging effects of stressful life events.

Personal Characteristics. A child's biologically endowed characteristics can reduce exposure to risk or lead to experiences that compensate for early stressful events. High intelligence and socially valued tal-

This boy's special relationship with his grandmother promotes resilience. By providing social support, she helps him cope with stress and solve problems constructively.

ents (in music or athletics, for example) are protective factors. They increase the chances that a child will have rewarding experiences in school and in the community that offset the impact of a stressful home life. Temperament is particularly powerful. Children with easygoing, sociable dispositions have an optimistic outlook on life and a special capacity to adapt to change—qualities that elicit

---

people respond to special training with substantial (but not unlimited) gains in a wide variety of mental abilities (Nyberg, 2005; Thompson & Foth, 2005).

Evidence on plasticity makes it clear that aging is not an eventual "shipwreck," as has often been assumed. Instead, the metaphor of a "butterfly"—of metamorphosis and continued potential—provides a far more accurate picture of lifespan change (Lemme, 2006). Still, development gradually becomes less plastic, as both capacity and opportunity for change are reduced. And plasticity varies greatly across individuals. Some children and adults experience more diverse life circumstances. And as the Biology and Environment box above reveals, some adapt more easily than others to changing conditions.

Development Is Influenced by Multiple, Interacting Forces

According to the lifespan perspective, pathways of change are highly diverse because *development is influenced by multiple*

forces: biological, historical, social, and cultural. Although these wide-ranging influences can be organized into three categories, they work together, combining in unique ways to fashion each life course.

■ **Age-Graded Influences.** Events that are strongly related to age and therefore fairly predictable in when they occur and how long they last are called **age-graded influences**. For example, most individuals walk shortly after their first birthday, acquire their native language during the preschool years, reach puberty around ages 12 to 14, and (for women) experience menopause in their late forties or early fifties. These milestones are influenced by biology, but social customs can create age-graded influences as well. Starting school around age 6, getting a driver's license at age 16, and entering college around age 18 are good examples. Age-graded influences are especially prevalent in childhood and adolescence, when biological changes are rapid and cultures impose many age-related experiences to ensure that young people acquire the skills they need to participate in their society.

positive responses from others. In contrast, emotionally reactive, irritable, and impulsive children often tax the patience of people around them (Masten & Reed, 2002; Masten et al., 1999). For example, both John and Gary moved several times during their childhoods. Each time, John became anxious and angry. Gary looked forward to making new friends and exploring a new neighborhood.

A Warm Parental Relationship. A close relationship with at least one parent who provides warmth, appropriately high expectations, monitoring of the child's activities, and an organized home environment fosters resilience. But note that this factor (as well as the next one) is not independent of children's personal characteristics. Children who are relaxed, socially responsive, and able to deal with change are easier to rear and more likely to enjoy positive relationships with parents and other people. At the same time, some children may develop more attractive dispositions as a result of parental warmth and attention (Conger & Conger, 2002).

Social Support Outside the Immediate Family. The most consistent asset of resilient children is a strong bond to a competent, caring adult, who need not be a parent. A grandparent, aunt, uncle, or teacher who forms a special relationship with the child can promote resilience (Masten & Reed, 2002). Gary received support in adolescence from his grandfather, who listened to Gary's concerns and helped him solve problems. In addition, Gary's grandfather had a stable marriage and work life and handled stressors skillfully. Consequently, he served as a model of effective coping.

Associations with rule-abiding peers who value school achievement are also linked to resilience. But children who have positive relationships with adults are far more likely to establish these supportive peer ties.

Community Resources and Opportunities. Community supports—good schools, convenient and affordable health care and social services, libraries, and recreation centers—foster both parents' and children's well-being. In addition, opportunities to participate in community life help older children and adolescents overcome adversity. Extracurricular activities at school, religious youth groups, scouting, and other organizations teach important social skills, such

as cooperation, leadership, and contributing to others' welfare. As a result, participants gain in self-esteem, responsibility, and community commitment. As a high school student, Gary volunteered for Habitat for Humanity, a nonprofit organization that builds affordable housing in low-income neighborhoods. Community involvement offered Gary opportunities to form meaningful relationships and develop new competencies, which further strengthened his resilience (Seccombe, 2002).

Research on resilience highlights the complex connections between heredity and environment. Armed with positive characteristics, which stem from innate endowment, favorable rearing experiences, or both, children and adolescents take action to reduce stressful situations.

Nevertheless, when many risks pile up, they are increasingly difficult to overcome (Quyen et al., 1998). Therefore, interventions must reduce risks and enhance relationships at home, in school, and in the community that protect young people against the negative effects of risk. This means attending to both the person and the environment—strengthening the individual's capacities as well as fixing problems.

■ **History-Graded Influences.** Development is also profoundly affected by forces unique to a particular historical era. Examples include epidemics, wars, and periods of economic prosperity or depression; technological advances, such as the introduction of television, computers, and the Internet; and changing cultural values, such as revised attitudes toward women and ethnic minorities. These **history-graded influences** explain why people born around the same time—called a *cohort*—tend to be alike in ways that set them apart from people born at other times.

■ **Nonnormative Influences.** *Normative* means typical, or average. Age-graded and history-graded influences are normative because each affects large numbers of people in a similar way. **Nonnormative influences** are events that are irregular—they happen to just one person or a few people and do not follow a predictable timetable. Consequently, they enhance the multidirectionality of development. Nonnormative influences that had a major impact on the direction of Sofie's life were

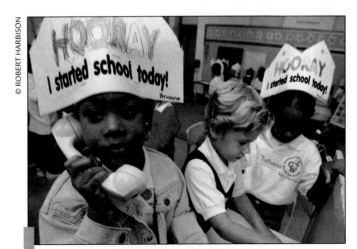

For these 5- and 6-year-olds, starting kindergarten marks a major life transition. In industrialized nations, the first day of school is an *age-graded influence*—one that occurs at about the same age for most children.

piano lessons in childhood with an inspiring teacher; a blind date with Philip; delayed marriage, parenthood, and career entry; and a battle with cancer. Because they occur haphazardly, nonnormative events are difficult for researchers to capture and study. Yet, as each of us can attest from our own experiences, they can affect us in powerful ways.

Lifespan investigators point out that nonnormative influences have become more powerful and age-graded influences less so in contemporary adult development. Compared with Sofie's era, today the ages at which people finish their education, enter careers, get married, have children, and retire are much more diverse. Indeed, Sofie's "off-time" accomplishments would have been less unusual had she been born a generation or two later! Age remains a powerful organizer of everyday experiences, and age-related expectations have certainly not disappeared. But age markers have blurred, and they vary across ethnic groups and cultures. The increasing role of nonnormative events in the life course adds to the fluid nature of lifespan development.

Notice that instead of a single line of development, the lifespan perspective emphasizes many potential pathways and outcomes—an image more like fibers extending in diverse directions, which may undergo both continuous and stagewise transformations (see Figure 1.3). Now let's turn to the historical foundations of the field as a prelude to major theories that address various aspects of change.

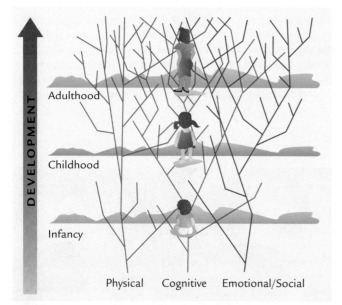

■ FIGURE 1.3 The lifespan view of development. Rather than envisioning a single line of stagewise or continuous change (see Figure 1.1 on page 6), lifespan theorists conceive of development as more like tree branches extending in diverse directions. Many potential pathways are possible, depending on the contexts that influence the individual's life course. Each branch in this treelike image represents a possible skill within one of the major domains of development. The crossing of the branches signifies that the domains—physical, cognitive, emotional, and social—are interrelated.

Historical Foundations

Contemporary theories of human development are the result of centuries of change in Western cultural values, philosophical thinking, and scientific progress. To understand the field as it exists today, we must return to its beginnings—to influences that long preceded scientific study. We will see that many early ideas linger on as important forces in current theory and research.

Philosophies of Childhood

As early as medieval Europe (the sixth through the fifteenth centuries), childhood was regarded as a separate period from adulthood. Medieval painters often depicted children in loose, comfortable gowns while playing games and looking up to adults. Written texts contained terms that distinguished children from other people, and manuals offering advice on child care, including health, feeding, clothing, and games, had become common by the fourteenth century (Alexandre-Bidon & Lett, 1997). Laws recognized that children needed protection from people who might mistreat them, and courts exercised leniency with lawbreaking youths because of their tender years. Medieval religious writings, however, contained contradictory beliefs about children's basic nature, sometimes portraying them as possessed by the devil and in need of purification, at other times as innocent and close to angels (Hanawalt, 2003). Both ideas foreshadowed later views of childhood.

In the sixteenth century, the Puritan belief in original sin gave rise to a view of children as inherently evil and stubborn. Harsh, restrictive parenting practices were recommended as the most efficient means of taming the depraved child. Although a punitive approach was the prevailing child-rearing philosophy, affection for their children prevented most Puritan parents from using extremely repressive measures. Instead, they tried to teach their sons and daughters to use reason to distinguish right from wrong (Clarke-Stewart, 1998). As they trained their children in self-reliance and self-control, Puritan parents gradually adopted a moderate balance between severity and permissiveness.

■ **John Locke.** The philosophies of the seventeenth-century Enlightenment emphasized ideals of human dignity and respect. The writings of British philosopher John Locke (1632–1704) served as the forerunner of a twentieth-century perspective that we will discuss shortly: behaviorism. Locke viewed the child as a **tabula rasa**—Latin for "blank slate." According to this idea, children are, to begin with, nothing at all; their characters are shaped by experience. Locke (1690/1892) described parents as rational tutors who can mold the child in any way they wish through careful instruction, effec-

tive example, and rewards for good behavior. His philosophy led to a change from harshness toward children to kindness and compassion.

Look carefully at Locke's ideas, and you will see that he regarded development as *continuous:* Adultlike behaviors are gradually built up through the warm, consistent teachings of parents. His view of the child as a tabula rasa led him to champion *nurture*—the power of the environment to shape the child. And his faith in nurture suggests the possibility of *many courses of development* and of *change at later ages* due to new experiences. Finally, in Locke's philosophy, children did little to shape their own destiny, which was written on blank slates by others. This vision of a passive child has been discarded. All contemporary theories view developing individuals as active, purposeful beings who contribute substantially to their own development.

■ **Jean-Jacques Rousseau.** In the eighteenth century, French philosopher Jean-Jacques Rousseau (1712–1778) claimed that children are not blank slates to be filled by adult instruction. Instead, Rousseau (1762/1955) viewed children as **noble savages**, naturally endowed with a sense of right and wrong and with an innate plan for orderly, healthy growth. Unlike Locke, Rousseau thought children's built-in moral sense and unique ways of thinking and feeling would only be harmed by adult training. His was a child-centered philosophy in which adults should be receptive to children's needs at each of four stages: infancy, childhood, late childhood, and adolescence.

Rousseau's philosophy includes two influential concepts: (1) *stage,* which we discussed earlier in this chapter, and (2) **maturation**, which refers to a genetically determined, naturally unfolding course of growth. Unlike Locke, Rousseau saw children as determining their own destinies. And he saw development as a *discontinuous, stagewise* process that follows a *single, unified course* mapped out by *nature*.

Philosophies of Adulthood and Aging

Soon after Rousseau devised his conception of childhood, the first lifespan views appeared. In the eighteenth and early nineteenth centuries, two German philosophers—John Nicolaus Tetens (1736–1807) and Friedrich August Carus (1770–1808)—urged that attention to development be extended through adulthood. Each asked important questions about aging.

Tetens (1777) addressed the origins and extent of individual differences, the degree to which behavior can be changed in adulthood, and the impact of historical eras on the life course. He was ahead of his time in recognizing that older people can compensate for intellectual declines that, at times, may reflect hidden gains. For example, Tetens suggested that some memory difficulties are due to searching for a word or name among a lifetime of accumulated information—a possibility acknowledged by current research (Perfect & Maylor, 2000).

Carus (1808) moved beyond Rousseau's stages by identifying four periods that span the life course: childhood, youth,

As early as medieval times, adults viewed childhood as a distinct developmental period and were sensitive to children's needs. The children in this fourteenth-century image, painted in a book of songs, are dressed in loose, comfortable gowns as they play a lively game of Blind Man's Bluff in a garden.

adulthood, and senescence. Like Tetens, Carus viewed aging not only as decline but also as progression. His writings reflect a remarkable awareness of multidirectionality and plasticity, which are at the heart of the lifespan perspective.

Scientific Beginnings

The study of development evolved quickly during the late nineteenth and early twentieth centuries. Early observations of human change were soon followed by improved methods and theories. Each advance contributed to the firm foundation on which the field rests today.

■ **Darwin: Forefather of Scientific Child Study.** British naturalist Charles Darwin (1809–1882) observed the infinite variation among plant and animal species. He also saw that within a species, no two individuals are exactly alike. From these observations, he constructed his famous *theory of evolution.*

The theory emphasized two related principles: *natural selection* and *survival of the fittest.* Darwin explained that certain species survive in particular environments because they have characteristics that fit with, or are adapted to, their surroundings. Other species die off because they are not well suited to their environments. Individuals within a species who best meet the survival requirements of the environment live long enough to reproduce and pass their more beneficial characteristics to future generations. Darwin's (1859/1936) emphasis on the adaptive value of physical characteristics and behavior found its way into important developmental theories.

During his explorations, Darwin discovered that early prenatal growth is strikingly similar in many species. Other scientists concluded from Darwin's observation that the development of the human child follows the same general plan as the evolution of the human species. Although this belief eventually proved inaccurate, efforts to chart parallels between child growth and human evolution prompted researchers to make careful observations of all aspects of children's behavior. Out of these first attempts to document an idea about development, scientific child study was born.

■ **The Normative Period.** G. Stanley Hall (1844–1924), one of the most influential American psychologists of the early twentieth century, is generally regarded as the founder of the child study movement (Hogan, 2003). He also foreshadowed lifespan research by writing one of the few books of his time on aging. Inspired by Darwin's work, Hall and his well-known student Arnold Gesell (1880–1961) devised theories based on evolutionary ideas. They regarded development as a genetically determined process that unfolds automatically, much like a flower (Gesell, 1933; Hall, 1904).

Hall and Gesell are remembered less for their one-sided theories than for their intensive efforts to describe all aspects of development. They launched the **normative approach**, in which measures of behavior are taken on large numbers of individuals, and age-related averages are computed to represent typical development. Using this procedure, Hall con-

Darwin's theory of evolution emphasizes the adaptive value of physical characteristics and behavior. Affection and care in families is adaptive throughout the lifespan, promoting survival and psychological well-being. Here a daughter helps her elderly mother with medication.

structed elaborate questionnaires asking children of different ages almost everything they could tell about themselves—interests, fears, imaginary playmates, dreams, friendships, everyday knowledge, and more. And through careful observations and interviews with parents, Gesell collected detailed normative information on infants' and children's motor achievements, social behaviors, and personality characteristics.

Gesell was also among the first to make knowledge about child development meaningful to parents. If, as he believed, the timetable of development is the product of millions of years of evolution, then children are naturally knowledgeable about their needs. His child-rearing advice, in the tradition of Rousseau, recommended sensitivity to children's cues (Thelen & Adolph, 1992). Along with Benjamin Spock's *Baby and Child Care,* Gesell's books became a central part of a rapidly expanding child development literature for parents.

■ **The Mental Testing Movement.** While Hall and Gesell were developing their theories and methods in the United States, French psychologist Alfred Binet (1857–1911) was also taking a normative approach to child development, but for a different reason. In the early 1900s, Binet and his colleague Theodore Simon were asked to find a way to identify children with learning problems who needed to be placed in special classes. To address these practical educational concerns, they constructed the first successful intelligence test.

In 1916, Binet's test was adapted for use with English-speaking children at Stanford University. Since then, the English version has been known as the Stanford-Binet Intelligence Scale. Besides providing a score that could successfully predict school achievement, the Binet test sparked tremendous interest in individual differences in development. Comparisons of the scores of people who vary in gender, ethnicity, birth order, family background, and other characteristics became a major focus of research. And intelligence tests moved quickly to the forefront of the nature–nurture controversy.

Ask Yourself

Review

Explain how central assumptions of the lifespan perspective are reflected in Tetens's and Carus's philosophies of adulthood and aging.

Apply

Imagine a debate between John Locke and Jean-Jacques Rousseau on the nature–nurture controversy. Summarize the argument each historical figure would be likely to present.

Connect

What do the ideas of Rousseau, Darwin, and Hall have in common?

Reflect

Find out whether your parents read child-rearing advice books when you were growing up. What questions most concerned them? Do you think the concerns of today's parents differ from those of your parents? Explain.

www.ablongman.com/berk

Mid-Twentieth-Century Theories

In the mid-twentieth century, human development expanded into a legitimate discipline. As it attracted increasing interest, a variety of theories emerged, each of which continues to have followers today.

The Psychoanalytic Perspective

In the 1930s and 1940s, as more people sought help from professionals to deal with emotional difficulties, a new question had to be addressed: How and why did people become the way they are? To treat psychological problems, psychiatrists and social workers turned to an approach to personality development that emphasized each individual's unique life history.

According to the **psychoanalytic perspective**, people move through a series of stages in which they confront conflicts between biological drives and social expectations. The way these conflicts are resolved determines the individual's ability to learn, to get along with others, and to cope with anxiety. Although many individuals contributed to the psychoanalytic perspective, two were especially influential: Sigmund Freud, founder of the psychoanalytic movement, and Erik Erikson.

■ **Freud's Theory.** Freud (1856–1939), a Viennese physician, sought a cure for emotionally troubled adults by having them talk freely about painful events of their childhoods. On the basis of these recollections, he examined the unconscious motivations of his patients and constructed his **psychosexual theory**, which emphasized that how parents manage their child's sexual and aggressive drives in the first few years is crucial for healthy personality development.

Three Parts of the Personality. In Freud's theory, three parts of the personality—id, ego, and superego—become integrated during five stages, summarized in Table 1.2 on page 16. The *id*, the largest portion of the mind, is the source of basic biological needs and desires. The *ego*—the conscious, rational part of personality—emerges in early infancy to redirect the id's impulses so they are discharged on appropriate objects at acceptable times and places. For example, aided by the ego, the hungry baby stops crying when he sees his mother preparing to feed him. And the more competent preschooler gets a snack from the kitchen on her own.

Between 3 and 6 years of age, the *superego*, or conscience, develops through interactions with parents, who insist that children conform to the values of society. Now the ego faces the increasingly complex task of reconciling the demands of the id, the external world, and conscience (Freud, 1923/1974). For example, when the ego is tempted to gratify an id impulse by hitting a playmate to get an attractive toy, the superego may warn that such behavior is wrong. The ego must decide which of the two forces (id or superego) will win this inner struggle, or it must work out a compromise, such as asking for a turn with the toy. According to Freud, the relations established among the id, ego, and superego during the preschool years determine the individual's basic personality.

Psychosexual Development. Freud (1938/1973) believed that during childhood, sexual impulses shift their focus from the oral to the anal to the genital regions of the body. In each stage, parents walk a fine line between permitting too much or too little gratification of their child's basic needs. If parents strike an appropriate balance, then children grow into well-adjusted adults with the capacity for mature sexuality and investment in family life.

Freud's theory was the first to stress the influence of the early parent–child relationship on development. But his theory was eventually criticized. First, it overemphasized the influence of sexual feelings in development. Second, because it was based on the problems of sexually repressed, well-to-do adults, it did not apply in cultures differing from nineteenth-century Victorian society. Finally, Freud had not studied children directly.

■ **Erikson's Theory.** Several of Freud's followers took what was useful from his theory and improved on his vision. The most important of these neo-Freudians is Erik Erikson (1902–1994).

Although Erikson (1950) accepted Freud's basic psychosexual framework, he expanded the picture of development at each stage. In his **psychosocial theory**, Erikson emphasized that the ego does not just mediate between id impulses and superego demands. At each stage, it also acquires attitudes and

Table 1.2		Freud's Psychosexual Stages
Psychosexual Stage	**Period of Development**	**Description**
Oral	Birth–1 year	The new ego directs the baby's sucking activities toward breast or bottle. If oral needs are not met appropriately, the individual may develop such habits as thumb sucking, fingernail biting, and pencil chewing in childhood and overeating and smoking in later life.
Anal	1–3 years	Toddlers and preschoolers enjoy holding and releasing urine and feces. Toilet training becomes a major issue between parent and child. If parents insist that children be trained before they are ready, or if they make too few demands, conflicts about anal control may appear in the form of extreme orderliness and cleanliness or messiness and disorder.
Phallic	3–6 years	As preschoolers take pleasure in genital stimulation, Freud's Oedipus conflict for boys and Electra conflict for girls arise: Children feel a sexual desire for the other-sex parent. To avoid punishment, they give up this desire and adopt the same-sex parent's characteristics and values. As a result, the superego is formed, and children feel guilty each time they violate its standards.
Latency	6–11 years	Sexual instincts die down, and the superego develops further. The child acquires new social values from adults and same-sex peers outside the family.
Genital	Adolescence	With puberty, the sexual impulses of the phallic stage reappear. If development has been successful during earlier stages, it leads to marriage, mature sexuality, and the birth and rearing of children. This stage extends through adulthood.

Erik Erikson believed that child rearing can be understood only in relation to the competencies valued and needed by the individual's society. This boy fishing with his father in the Inle Lake in Myanmar is learning skills that he will need as an adult in his culture.

skills that make the individual an active, contributing member of society. A basic psychological conflict, which is resolved along a continuum from positive to negative, determines healthy or maladaptive outcomes at each stage. As Table 1.3 on the following page shows, Erikson's first five stages parallel Freud's stages, but Erikson added three adult stages.

Finally, unlike Freud, Erikson pointed out that normal development must be understood in relation to each culture's life situation. For example, in the 1940s, he observed that Yurok Indians of the northwest coast of the United States deprived babies of breastfeeding for the first 10 days after birth and instead fed them a thin soup. At age 6 months, infants were abruptly weaned—if necessary, by having the mother leave for a few days. These experiences, from our cultural vantage point, might seem cruel. But Erikson explained that the Yurok lived in a world in which salmon filled the river just once a year, a circumstance requiring considerable self-restraint for survival. In this way, he showed that child rearing can be understood only in relation to the competencies valued and needed by the individual's society.

■ **Contributions and Limitations of Psychoanalytic Theory.**
A special strength of the psychoanalytic perspective is its emphasis on the individual's unique life history as worthy of study and understanding. Consistent with this view, psychoanalytic theorists accept the *clinical,* or *case study, method,* which synthesizes information from a variety of sources into a detailed picture of the personality of a single person. (We will discuss the clinical method further at the end of this chapter.) Psychoanalytic theory has also inspired a wealth of research on many

Table 1.3	Erikson's Psychosocial Stages, with Corresponding Psychosexual Stages Indicated	

Psychosocial Stage	Period of Development	Description
Basic trust versus mistrust (Oral)	Birth–1 year	From warm, responsive care, infants gain a sense of trust, or confidence, that the world is good. Mistrust occurs when infants have to wait too long for comfort and are handled harshly.
Autonomy versus shame and doubt (Anal)	1–3 years	Using new mental and motor skills, children want to choose and decide for themselves. Autonomy is fostered when parents permit reasonable free choice and do not force or shame the child.
Initiative versus guilt (Phallic)	3–6 years	Through make-believe play, children explore the kind of person they can become. Initiative—a sense of ambition and responsibility—develops when parents support their child's new sense of purpose. When parents demand too much self-control, they induce excessive guilt.
Industry versus inferiority (Latency)	6–11 years	At school, children develop the capacity to work and cooperate with others. Inferiority develops when negative experiences at home, at school, or with peers lead to feelings of incompetence.
Identity versus role confusion (Genital)	Adolescence	The adolescent tries to answer the question, Who am I, and what is my place in society? By exploring values and vocational goals, the young person forms a personal identity. The negative outcome is confusion about future adult roles.
Intimacy versus isolation	Early adulthood	Young adults work on establishing intimate ties to others. Because of earlier disappointments, some individuals cannot form close relationships and remain isolated.
Generativity versus stagnation	Middle adulthood	Middle-aged adults contribute to the next generation through child rearing, caring for other people, or productive work. The person who fails in these ways feels an absence of meaningful accomplishment.
Ego integrity versus despair	Late adulthood	Elders reflect on the kind of person they have been. Integrity results from feeling that life was worth living as it happened. Those who are dissatisfied with their lives fear death.

© OLIVE PIERCE/BLACK STAR

Erik Erikson

aspects of emotional and social development, including infant–caregiver attachment, aggression, sibling relationships, child-rearing practices, morality, gender roles, and adolescent identity.

Despite its extensive contributions, the psychoanalytic perspective is no longer in the mainstream of human development research. Psychoanalytic theorists may have become isolated from the rest of the field because they were so strongly committed to the clinical approach that they failed to consider other methods. In addition, many psychoanalytic ideas, such as psychosexual stages and ego functioning, are so vague that they are difficult or impossible to test empirically (Crain, 2005; Thomas, 2005).

Nevertheless, Erikson's broad outline of lifespan change captures the essence of personality development during each major period of the life course, so we will return to it in later chapters. We will also encounter perspectives inspired by Erikson's theory that clarify the attainments of early, middle, and late adulthood and that are within the tradition of stage models of psychosocial development (Levinson, 1978, 1996; Vaillant, 1977, 2002).

Behaviorism and Social Learning Theory

As psychoanalytic theory gained in prominence, human development was also influenced by a very different perspective. According to **behaviorism**, directly observable events—stimuli and responses—are the appropriate focus of study. North American behaviorism began in the early twentieth century with the work of psychologist John Watson (1878–1958). He rejected the psychoanalytic concern with the unseen workings of the mind. Instead, he wanted to create an objective science of psychology.

■ **Traditional Behaviorism.** Watson was inspired by Russian physiologist Ivan Pavlov's studies of animal learning. Pavlov knew that dogs release saliva as an innate reflex when they are given food. But he noticed that his dogs were salivating before they tasted any food—when they saw the trainer who usually fed them. The dogs, Pavlov reasoned, must have learned to associate a neutral stimulus (the trainer) with another stimulus (food) that produces a reflexive response (salivation). As a result of this association, the neutral stimulus could bring about a response resembling the reflex. Eager to test this idea, Pavlov successfully taught dogs to salivate at the sound of a bell by pairing it with the presentation of food. He had discovered *classical conditioning.*

Watson wanted to find out if classical conditioning could be applied to children's behavior. In a historic experiment, he taught Albert, an 11-month-old infant, to fear a neutral stimulus—a soft white rat—by presenting it several times with a sharp, loud sound, which naturally scared the baby. Little Albert, who at first had reached out eagerly to touch the furry rat, began to cry and turn his head away when he caught sight of it (Watson & Raynor, 1920). In fact, Albert's fear was so intense that researchers eventually challenged the ethics of studies like this one. Consistent with Locke's tabula rasa, Watson concluded that environment is the supreme force in development. Adults can mold children's behavior, he thought, by carefully controlling stimulus–response associations. And development is a continuous process, consisting of a gradual increase in the number and strength of these associations.

Another form of behaviorism is B. F. Skinner's (1904–1990) *operant conditioning theory.* According to Skinner, the frequency of a behavior can be increased by following it with a wide variety of *reinforcers,* such as food, praise, or a friendly smile. It can also be decreased through *punishment,* such as disapproval or withdrawal of privileges. As a result of Skinner's work, operant conditioning became a broadly applied learning principle. We will consider these conditioning techniques further in Chapter 4.

■ **Social Learning Theory.** Psychologists quickly became interested in whether behaviorism might explain the development of social behavior better than the less precise concepts of psychoanalytic theory. This sparked the emergence of approaches that built on the principles of conditioning, offering expanded views of how children and adults acquire new responses.

Several kinds of **social learning theory** emerged. The most influential, devised by Albert Bandura, emphasizes *modeling,* also known as *imitation* or *observational learning,* as a powerful source of development. The baby who claps her hands after her mother does so, the child who angrily hits a playmate in the same way that he has been punished at home, and the teenager who wears the same clothes and hairstyle as her friends at school are all displaying observational learning. By the 1950s, social learning theory had become a major force in developmental research.

Bandura's work continues to influence much research on social development. Today, however, like the field of human development as a whole, his theory stresses the importance of *cognition,* or thinking. In fact, the most recent revision of Bandura's (1992, 2001) theory places such strong emphasis on how we think about ourselves and other people that he calls it a *social-cognitive* rather than a social learning approach.

According to Bandura's revised view, children gradually become more selective in what they imitate. From watching others engage in self-praise and self-blame and through feedback about the worth of their own actions, children develop *personal standards* for behavior and *a sense of self-efficacy*—the belief that their own abilities and characteristics will help them succeed. These cognitions guide responses in particular situations (Bandura, 1999, 2001). For example, imagine a parent who often remarks, "I'm glad I kept working on that task, even though it was hard," who explains the value of persistence, and who encourages it by saying, "I know you can do a good job on that homework!" Soon the child starts to view himself as hardworking and high-achieving and selects people with these characteristics as models. In this way, as individuals acquire attitudes, values, and convictions about themselves, they control their own learning and behavior.

■ **Contributions and Limitations of Behaviorism and Social Learning Theory.** Behaviorism and social learning theory have been helpful in treating a wide range of adjustment problems. **Behavior modification** consists of procedures that combine conditioning and modeling to eliminate undesirable behaviors and increase desirable responses. It has been used to relieve a difficulties in children and adults, such as persistent aggression, language delays, and extreme fears (Conyers et al., 2004; Wolpe & Plaud, 1997).

Nevertheless, many theorists believe that behaviorism and social learning theory offer too narrow a view of important environmental influences, which extend beyond immediate reinforcement, punishment, and modeled behaviors to people's rich physical and social worlds. Finally, behaviorism and social learning theory have been criticized for neglecting people's contributions to their own development. In emphasizing cognition, Bandura is unique among theorists whose work grew out of the behaviorist tradition in granting children and adults an active role in their own learning.

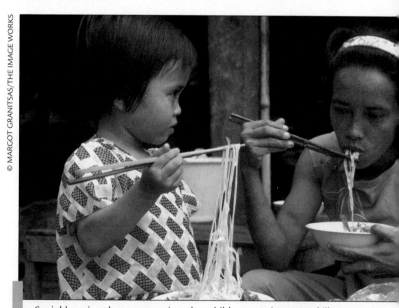

Social learning theory recognizes that children acquire many skills through modeling. By observing and imitating her mother's behavior, this Vietnamese preschooler is becoming a skilled user of chopsticks.

Piaget's Cognitive-Developmental Theory

If one individual has influenced research on child development more than any other, it is Swiss cognitive theorist Jean Piaget (1896–1980). North American investigators had been aware of Piaget's work since 1930. Not until the 1960s, however, did they grant it much attention, mainly because Piaget's ideas were at odds with behaviorism, which dominated North American psychology in the mid-twentieth century (Zigler & Gilman, 1998). Piaget did not believe that children's learning depends on reinforcers, such as rewards from adults. According to his **cognitive-developmental theory**, children actively construct knowledge as they manipulate and explore their world.

■ **Piaget's Stages.** Piaget's view of development was greatly influenced by his early training in biology. Central to his theory is the biological concept of adaptation (Piaget, 1971). Just as structures of the body are adapted to fit with the environment, so structures of the mind develop to better fit with, or represent, the external world. In infancy and early childhood, Piaget claimed, children's understanding is different from adults'. For example, he believed that young babies do not realize that an object hidden from view—a favorite toy or even the mother—continues to exist. He also concluded that preschoolers' thinking is full of faulty logic. For example, children younger than age 7 commonly say that the amount of a liquid changes when it is poured into a differently shaped container. According to Piaget, children eventually revise these incorrect ideas in their ongoing efforts to achieve an *equilibrium,* or balance, between internal structures and information they encounter in their everyday worlds.

In Piaget's theory, as the brain develops and children's experiences expand, they move through four broad stages, each characterized by qualitatively distinct ways of thinking. Table 1.4 on page 20 provides a brief description of Piaget's stages. In the *sensorimotor stage,* cognitive development begins with the baby's use of the senses and movements to explore the world. These action patterns evolve into the symbolic but illogical thinking of the preschooler in the *preoperational stage.* Next comes the *concrete operational stage,* when cognition is transformed into the more organized reasoning of the school-age child. Finally, in the *formal operational stage,* thought becomes the complex, abstract reasoning system of the adolescent and adult.

■ **Piaget's Methods of Study.** Piaget devised special methods for investigating how children think. Early in his career, he carefully observed his three infant children and also presented them with everyday problems, such as an attractive object that could be grasped, mouthed, kicked, or searched for. From their responses, Piaget derived his ideas about cognitive changes during the first two years. In studying childhood and adolescent thought, Piaget took advantage of children's ability to describe their thinking. Adapting the clinical method of psychoanalysis, he conducted open-ended *clinical interviews* in which a child's initial response to a task served as the basis for Piaget's next question. We will look more closely at this technique when we discuss research methods later in this chapter.

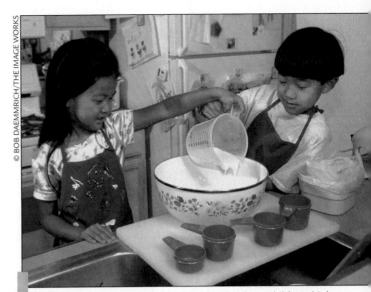

In Piaget's concrete operational stage, school-age children think in an organized, logical fashion about concrete objects. This 6-year-old girl and 7-year-old boy understand that the amount of milk remains the same after being poured into a differently shaped container, even though its appearance changes.

■ **Contributions and Limitations of Piaget's Theory.** Piaget's cognitive-developmental perspective convinced the field that children are active learners whose minds consist of rich structures of knowledge. Besides investigating children's understanding of the physical world, Piaget explored their reasoning about the social world. His stages have sparked a wealth of research on children's conceptions of themselves, other people, and human relationships. Practically speaking, Piaget's theory encouraged the development of educational philosophies and programs that emphasize discovery learning and direct contact with the environment.

Despite Piaget's overwhelming contributions, his theory has been challenged. Research indicates that Piaget underestimated the competencies of infants and preschoolers. When young children are given tasks scaled down in difficulty and relevant to their everyday experiences, their understanding appears closer to that of the older child and adult than Piaget assumed. Furthermore, many studies show that children's performance on Piagetian problems can be improved with training. This finding calls into question his assumption that discovery learning rather than adult teaching is the best way to foster development (Klahr & Nigam, 2004). Critics also point out that Piaget's stagewise account pays insufficient attention to social and cultural influences on development. Finally, some lifespan theorists disagree with Piaget's conclusion that no major cognitive changes occur after adolescence. Several have proposed important transformations in adulthood (Arlin, 1989; Labouvie-Vief, 1985; Perry, 1981).

Today, the field of human development is divided over its loyalty to Piaget's ideas. Those who continue to find merit in Piaget's stage approach accept a modified view—one in which changes in thinking take place more gradually than Piaget

Table 1.4		Piaget's Stages of Cognitive Development

Stage	Period of Development	Description
Sensorimotor	Birth–2 years	Infants "think" by acting on the world with their eyes, ears, hands, and mouth. As a result, they invent ways of solving simple problems, such as pulling a lever to hear the sound of a music box, finding hidden toys, and putting objects in and taking them out of containers.
Preoperational	2–7 years	Preschool children use symbols to represent their earlier sensorimotor discoveries. Development of language and make-believe play takes place. However, thinking lacks the logic of the two remaining stages.
Concrete operational	7–11 years	Children's reasoning becomes logical. School-age children understand that a certain amount of lemonade or play dough remains the same even after its appearance changes. They also organize objects into hierarchies of classes and subclasses. However, thinking falls short of adult intelligence. It is not yet abstract.
Formal operational	11 years on	The capacity for abstract, systematic thinking enables adolescents, when faced with a problem, to start with a hypothesis, deduce testable inferences, and isolate and combine variables to see which inferences are confirmed. Adolescents can also evaluate the logic of verbal statements without referring to real-world circumstances.

© BETTMANN/CORBIS

Jean Piaget

believed (Case, 1998; Demetriou et al., 2002; Fischer & Bidell, 1998). Others have embraced an approach that emphasizes continuous gains in children's cognition: information processing. And still others have been drawn to theories that focus on the role of children's social and cultural contexts. We take up these approaches in the next section.

Recent Theoretical Perspectives

New ways of understanding the developing person are constantly emerging—questioning, building on, and enhancing the discoveries of earlier theories. Today, a burst of fresh approaches and research emphases is broadening our understanding of the lifespan.

Information Processing

In the 1970s and 1980s, researchers turned to the field of cognitive psychology for ways to understand the development of thinking. The design of digital computers that use mathematically specified steps to solve problems suggested to psychologists that the human mind might also be viewed as a symbol-manipulating system through which information flows—a perspective called **information processing** (Klahr & MacWhinney, 1998). From the time information is presented to the senses at input until it emerges as a behavioral response at output, information is actively coded, transformed, and organized.

Information-processing researchers often use flowcharts to map the precise series of steps individuals use to solve problems and complete tasks, much like the plans devised by programmers to get computers to perform a series of "mental operations." Let's look at an example to clarify the usefulness of this approach. In a study of problem solving, a researcher provided a pile of blocks varying in size, shape, and weight and asked school-age children to build a bridge across a "river" (painted on a floor mat) that was too wide for any single block

■ **FIGURE 1.4 Information-processing flowchart showing the steps that a 5-year-old used to solve a bridge-building problem.** Her task was to use blocks varying in size, shape, and weight, some of which were planklike, to construct a bridge across a "river" (painted on a floor mat) too wide for any single block to span. The child discovered how to counterweight and balance the bridge. The arrows reveal that, even after building a successful counterweight, she returned to earlier, unsuccessful strategies, which seemed to help her understand why the counterweight approach worked. (Adapted from Thornton, 1999.)

to span (Thornton, 1999). Figure 1.4 shows one solution to the problem: Two planklike blocks span the water, each held in place by the counterweight of heavy blocks on the bridge's towers. Whereas older children easily built successful bridges, only one 5-year-old did. Careful tracking of her efforts revealed that she repeatedly tried unsuccessful strategies, such as pushing two planks together and pressing down on their ends to hold them in place. But eventually, her experimentation triggered the idea of using the blocks as counterweights. Her mistaken procedures helped her understand why the counterweight approach worked.

Many information-processing models exist. Some, like the one just considered, track children's mastery of one or a few tasks. Others describe the human cognitive system as a whole (Atkinson & Shiffrin, 1968; Lockhart & Craik, 1990). These general models are used as guides for asking questions about broad changes in thinking: Does a child's ability to solve problems become more organized and "planful" with age? Why is information processing slower among older than younger adults? Are declines in memory during old age evident on all types of tasks or only some?

Like Piaget's cognitive-developmental theory, the information-processing approach regards people as active, sense-making beings (Halford, 2002). But unlike Piaget's theory, it does not divide development into stages. Rather, the thought processes studied—perception, attention, memory, planning strategies, categorization of information, and comprehension of written and spoken prose—are regarded as similar at all ages but present to a lesser or greater extent. Therefore, the view of development is one of continuous change.

A great strength of the information-processing approach is its commitment to rigorous research methods. Because it has provided precise accounts of how children and adults tackle many cognitive tasks, its findings have important implications for education (Siegler, 1998). But information processing has fallen short in some respects. Although good at analyzing thinking into its components, information processing has had difficulty putting them back together into a comprehensive theory. In addition, this approach all but ignores aspects of cognition that are not linear and logical (Birney et al., 2005). Furthermore, much information-processing research has been conducted in laboratories rather than in real-life situations. Recently, investigators have addressed this concern by studying conversations, stories, memory for everyday events, and academic problem solving.

Over the past two decades, information-processing research has expanded in another way: A new area of investigation has arisen, called **developmental cognitive neuroscience.** It brings together researchers from psychology, biology, neuroscience, and medicine to study the relationship between changes in the brain and the developing person's cognitive processing and behavior patterns. Improved methods for analyzing activity within the brain while children and adults perform various tasks have greatly enhanced knowledge of relationships between brain functioning and behavior (Cabeza, Nyberg, & Park, 2005; Johnson, 2005). Armed with these brain-imaging techniques (which we will consider in Chapter 4), neuroscientists are tackling questions like these: How do early experiences influence the growth and organization of the young child's brain? What transformations in the brain make it harder for adolescents and adults than for children to acquire a second language? What neurological changes are related to declines in speed of thinking, memory, and other aspects of cognitive processing in old age?

During the first 5 years, the brain is highly plastic—especially open to growth as a result of experience. But it retains considerable plasticity throughout life. Neuroscientists are making rapid progress in identifying the types of experiences to which the brain is sensitive at various ages. They are also clarifying the brain bases of many learning and behavior disorders, and they are contributing to the design of effective interventions by examining their impact on both behavior and brain functioning (Munakata, Casey, & Diamond, 2004). Although much remains to be discovered, developmental cognitive neuroscience is already transforming our understanding of development and yielding major practical applications throughout the lifespan.

An advantage of having many theories is that they encourage researchers to attend to previously neglected dimensions of people's lives. The final three perspectives we will discuss focus on *contexts* for development. The first of these views emphasizes that development of many capacities is influenced by our long evolutionary history.

Ethology and Evolutionary Developmental Psychology

Ethology is concerned with the adaptive, or survival, value of behavior and its evolutionary history (Hinde, 1992). Its roots can be traced to the work of Darwin. Two European zoologists, Konrad Lorenz and Niko Tinbergen, laid its modern foundations. Watching diverse animal species in their natural habitats, Lorenz and Tinbergen observed behavior patterns that promote survival. The best known of these is *imprinting,* the early following behavior of certain baby birds, such as geese, that ensures that the young will stay close to the mother and be fed and protected from danger. Imprinting takes place during an early, restricted period of development. If the mother goose is absent during this time but an object resembling her in important features is present, young goslings may imprint on it instead (Lorenz, 1952).

Observations of imprinting led to a major concept in human development: the *critical period.* It is a limited time span during which the individual is biologically prepared to acquire certain adaptive behaviors but needs the support of an appropriately stimulating environment. Many researchers have investigated whether complex cognitive and social behaviors must be learned during certain time periods. For example, if children are deprived of adequate food or physical and social stimulation during their early years, will their intelligence be impaired? If language is not mastered in early childhood, is the capacity to acquire it reduced?

In later chapters, we will see that the term *sensitive period* applies better to human development than does the strict notion of a critical period (Bornstein, 1989). A **sensitive period** is a time that is optimal for certain capacities to emerge and in which the individual is especially responsive to environmental influences. However, its boundaries are less well defined than those of a critical period. Development can occur later, but it is harder to induce.

Ethology focuses on the adaptive, or survival, value of behavior and on similarities between human behavior and that of other species, especially our primate relatives. Observing this mother cuddling her 8-day-old infant helps us understand the human-infant caregiver relationship.

Inspired by observations of imprinting, British psychoanalyst John Bowlby (1969) applied ethological theory to the understanding of the human infant–caregiver relationship. He argued that infant smiling, babbling, grasping, and crying are built-in social signals that encourage the caregiver to approach, care for, and interact with the baby. By keeping the parent near, these behaviors help ensure that the infant will be fed, protected from danger, and provided with stimulation and affection necessary for healthy growth. The development of attachment in humans is a lengthy process that leads the baby to form a deep affectionate tie with the caregiver (van den Boom, 2002). Bowlby believed that this bond has lifelong consequences for human relationships. In later chapters, we will consider research that evaluates this assumption.

Observations by ethologists have shown that many aspects of social behavior, including emotional expressions, aggression, cooperation, and social play, resemble those of our primate relatives. Recently, researchers have extended this effort in a new area of research called **evolutionary developmental psychology**. It seeks to understand the adaptive value of specieswide cognitive, emotional, and social competencies as those competencies change with age. Evolutionary developmental psychologists ask such questions as: What role does the newborn's visual preference for facelike stimuli play in survival? Does it support older infants' capacity to distinguish familiar caregivers from unfamiliar people? Why do children play in sex-segregated groups? What do they learn from such play that might lead to adult gender-typed behaviors, such as male dominance and female investment in caregiving?

As these examples suggest, evolutionary psychologists are not just concerned with the biological basis of development. They realize that humans' large brain and extended childhood resulted from the need to master an increasingly complex social and technological environment, so they are also interested in learning (Blasi & Bjorklund, 2003). The evolutionary selection benefits of behavior are believed to be strongest in the first half of life—to ensure survival, reproduction, and effective parenting. As people age, social and cultural factors become increasingly important in promoting and maintaining high levels of functioning (Smith & Baltes, 1999; Staudinger & Lindenberger, 2003). The next contextual perspective we will discuss, Vygotsky's sociocultural theory, serves as an excellent complement to ethology because it highlights social and cultural contexts for development.

Vygotsky's Sociocultural Theory

The field of human development has recently seen a dramatic increase in studies addressing the cultural context of people's lives. Investigations that make comparisons across cultures, and among ethnic groups within cultures, provide insight into whether developmental pathways apply to all people or are limited to particular environmental conditions (Cole, 2005). As a result, cross-cultural and multicultural research helps us untangle the contributions of biological and environmental factors to the timing, order of appearance, and diversity of children's and adults' behaviors.

In the past, cross-cultural studies focused on broad cultural differences in development—for example, whether children in one culture are more advanced in motor development or do better on intellectual tasks than children in another. However, this approach can lead us to conclude incorrectly that some cultures are superior to others in enhancing development. In addition, it does not help us understand the precise experiences that contribute to cultural differences in behavior.

Today, more research is examining the relationship of *culturally specific beliefs and practices* to development. The contributions of Russian psychologist Lev Vygotsky (1896–1934) have played a major role in this trend. Vygotsky's (1934/1987) perspective, called **sociocultural theory**, focuses on how *culture*—the values, beliefs, customs, and skills of a social group—is transmitted to the next generation. According to Vygotsky, *social interaction*—in particular, cooperative dialogues with more knowledgeable members of society—is necessary for children to acquire the ways of thinking and behaving that make up a community's culture (Rowe & Wertsch, 2002). Vygotsky believed that as adults and more expert peers help children master culturally meaningful activities, the communication between them becomes part of children's thinking. As children internalize the essential features of these dialogues, they can use the language within them to guide their own thought and actions and to acquire new skills (Berk, 2003).

Vygotsky's theory has been especially influential in the study of cognitive development. Vygotsky agreed with Piaget that children are active, constructive beings. But unlike Piaget,

Through her grandmother's guidance, a Navajo girl learns to use a vertical weaving loom. According to Vygotsky's sociocultural theory, social interaction between children and more knowledgeable members of their culture leads to ways of thinking and behaving essential for success in that culture.

who emphasized children's independent efforts to make sense of their world, Vygotsky viewed cognitive development as a *socially mediated process*—dependent on the support that adults and more mature peers provide as children try new tasks.

In Vygotsky's theory, children undergo certain stagewise changes. For example, when they acquire language, their ability to participate in dialogues with others is greatly enhanced, and mastery of culturally valued competencies surges forward. When children enter school, they spend much time discussing language, literacy, and other academic concepts—experiences that encourage them to reflect on their own thinking. As a result, they gain dramatically in reasoning and problem solving.

Although most research inspired by Vygotsky's theory focuses on children, his ideas apply to people of any age. A central theme is that cultures select tasks for their members, and social interaction surrounding those tasks leads to competencies essential for success in a particular culture. For example, in industrialized nations, teachers help people learn to read, drive a car, or use a computer. Among the Zinacanteco Indians of southern Mexico, adult experts guide young girls as they master complicated weaving techniques (Greenfield, Maynard, & Childs, 2000). In Brazil, child candy sellers with little or no schooling develop sophisticated mathematical abilities as the result of buying candy from wholesalers, pricing it in collaboration with adults and experienced peers, and bargaining with customers on city streets (Saxe, 1988).

Research stimulated by Vygotsky's theory reveals that people in every culture develop unique strengths. But his emphasis on culture and social experience led Vygotsky to neglect the biological side of development. Although he recognized the importance of heredity and brain growth, he said little about their role in cognitive change. Furthermore, Vygotsky's emphasis on social transmission of knowledge meant that he placed less emphasis than other theorists on children's capacity to shape their own development. Followers of Vygotsky grant the individual and society more balanced roles (Karpov, 2005; Rogoff, 1998, 2003).

Ecological Systems Theory

Urie Bronfenbrenner (1917–2005) is responsible for an approach to human development that has moved to the forefront of the field because it offers the most differentiated and complete account of contextual influences on development. **Ecological systems theory** views the person as developing within a complex *system* of relationships affected by multiple levels of the surrounding environment. Since the child's biologically influenced dispositions join with environmental forces to mold development, Bronfenbrenner recently characterized his perspective as a *bioecological model* (Bronfenbrenner & Evans, 2000).

Bronfenbrenner envisioned the environment as a series of nested structures, including but extending beyond the home, school, neighborhood, and workplace settings in which people spend their everyday lives (see Figure 1.5). Each layer of the environment is viewed as having a powerful impact on development.

■ **The Microsystem.** The innermost level of the environment is the **microsystem**, which consists of activities and interaction patterns in the person's immediate surroundings. Bronfenbrenner emphasized that to understand development at this level, we must keep in mind that all relationships are *bidirectional*. For example, adults affect children's behavior, but children's biologically and socially influenced characteristics—their physical attributes, personalities, and capacities—also affect adults' behavior. A friendly, attentive child is likely to evoke positive and patient reactions from parents, whereas an active, distractible youngster is more likely to be a target of parental restriction and punishment. Bidirectional interactions that occur often over time have an enduring impact on development (Collins et al., 2000; Crockenberg & Leerkes, 2003).

Other individuals in the microsystem affect the quality of any two-person relationship. If they are supportive, then interaction is enhanced. For example, when parents encourage each other in their child-rearing roles, each engages in more effective parenting. In contrast, marital conflict is associated with inconsistent discipline and hostile reactions toward children. In response, children typically become hostile, and both parent and child adjustment suffers (Hetherington & Stanley-Hagen, 2002).

■ **The Mesosystem.** The second level of Bronfenbrenner's model, the **mesosystem**, encompasses connections between microsystems. For example, a child's academic progress depends not just on activities that take place in classrooms but also on parent involvement in school life and on the extent to which academic learning is carried over into the home (Epstein & Sanders, 2002). Among adults, how well a person functions as spouse and parent at home is affected by relationships in the workplace, and vice versa (Gottfried, Gottfried, & Bathurst, 2002).

■ **FIGURE 1.5 Structure of the environment in ecological systems theory.** The *microsystem* concerns relations between the developing person and the immediate environment; the *mesosystem*, connections among immediate settings; the *exosystem*, social settings that affect but do not contain the developing person; and the *macrosystem*, the values, laws, customs, and resources of the culture that affect activities and interactions at all inner layers. The *chronosystem* (not pictured) is not a specific context. Instead, it refers to the dynamic, ever-changing nature of the person's environment.

In ecological systems theory, development occurs within a complex system of relationships affected by multiple levels of the environment. This father greets his daughter at the end of the school day. The girl's experiences at school (microsystem) and the father's experiences at work (exosystem) affect father–daughter interaction.

■ **A Dynamic, Ever-Changing System.** According to Bronfenbrenner, the environment is not a static force that affects people in a uniform way. Instead, it is dynamic and ever-changing. Whenever individuals add or let go of roles or settings in their lives, the breadth of their microsystems changes. Throughout life, these shifts in contexts—or *ecological transitions,* as Bronfenbrenner called them—are often important turning points in development. Starting school, entering the workforce, marrying, becoming a parent, getting divorced, moving, and retiring are examples.

Bronfenbrenner referred to the temporal dimension of his model as the **chronosystem** (the prefix *chrono* means "time"). Life changes can be imposed externally. Alternatively, they can arise from within the person, since individuals select, modify, and create many of their own settings and experiences. How they do so depends on their age; their physical, intellectual, and personality characteristics; and their environmental opportunities. Therefore, in ecological systems theory, development is neither controlled by environmental circumstances nor driven by inner dispositions. Instead, people are products and producers of their environments, so both people and their environments form a network of interdependent effects. Our discussion of resilience on page 10 illustrates this idea. We will see many more examples in later chapters.

■ **The Exosystem.** The **exosystem** is made up of social settings that do not contain the developing person but nevertheless affect experiences in immediate settings. These can be formal organizations, such as the board of directors in the individual's workplace or community health and welfare services. For example, flexible work schedules, paid maternity and paternity leave, and sick leave for parents whose children are ill are ways that work settings can help parents rear children and, indirectly, enhance the development of both adult and child. Exosystem supports can also be informal. Children are affected by their parents' social networks—friends and extended-family members who provide advice, companionship, and even financial assistance. Research confirms the negative impact of a breakdown in exosystem activities. Families who are socially isolated, with few personal or community-based ties, or who are affected by unemployment show increased rates of conflict and child abuse (Emery & Laumann-Billings, 1998).

■ **The Macrosystem.** The outermost level of Bronfenbrenner's model, the **macrosystem**, is not a specific context but, rather, consists of cultural values, laws, customs, and resources. The priority that the macrosystem gives to the needs of children and adults affects the support they receive at inner levels of the environment. For example, in countries that set high standards for child care and workplace benefits for employed parents, children are more likely to have favorable experiences in their immediate settings. And when the government provides a generous pension plan for retirees, it supports the well-being of the elderly.

Ask Yourself

Review

Explain how each recent theoretical perspective regards children and adults as active contributors to their own development.

Apply

Mario wants to find out precisely how children of different ages recall stories. Anna is interested in how adult–child communication in different cultures influences children's storytelling. Which theoretical perspective has Mario probably chosen? How about Anna? Explain.

Connect

Is ecological systems theory compatible with assumptions of the lifespan perspective—that development is lifelong, multidirectional, highly plastic, and influenced by multiple, interacting forces? Explain.

Reflect

To illustrate the chronosystem in ecological systems theory, select an important event from your childhood, such as the birth of a sibling or a class with an inspiring teacher. How did the event affect you? How might its impact have differed had you been five years younger? How about five years older?

Comparing and Evaluating Theories

In the preceding sections, we reviewed major theoretical perspectives in human development research. They differ in many respects. First, they focus on different domains of development. Some, such as the psychoanalytic perspective and ethology, emphasize emotional and social development. Others, such as Piaget's cognitive-developmental theory, informa-tion processing, and Vygotsky's sociocultural theory, stress changes in thinking. The remaining approaches—behavior-ism, social learning theory, evolutionary developmental psychology, ecological systems theory, and the lifespan per-spective—discuss many aspects of human functioning. Sec-ond, every theory contains a point of view about development. As we conclude our review of theoretical perspectives, identify the stand each theory takes on the controversial issues pre-sented at the beginning of this chapter. Then check your analy-sis against Table 1.5.

Table 1.5	Stances of Major Theories on Basic Issues in Human Development		
Theory	**Continuous or Discontinuous Development?**	**One Course of Development or Many?**	**Relative Influence of Nature and Nurture**
Psychoanalytic perspective	*Discontinuous:* Psychosexual and psychosocial development takes place in stages.	*One course:* Stages are assumed to be universal.	*Both nature and nurture:* Innate impulses are channeled and controlled through child-rearing experiences. *Early experiences* set the course of later development.
Behaviorism and social learning theory	*Continuous:* Development involves an increase in learned behaviors.	*Many possible courses:* Behaviors reinforced and modeled may vary from person to person.	*Emphasis on nurture:* Development is the result of conditioning and modeling. *Both early and later experiences* are important.
Piaget's cognitive-developmental theory	*Discontinuous:* Cognitive develop-ment takes place in stages.	*One course:* Stages are assumed to be universal.	*Both nature and nurture:* Development occurs as the brain grows and children exercise their innate drive to discover reality in a generally stimulating environment. *Both early and later experiences* are important.
Information processing	*Continuous:* Children and adults gradually improve in perception, attention, memory, and problem-solving skills.	*One course:* Changes studied characterize most or all children and adults.	*Both nature and nurture:* Children and adults are active, sense-making beings who modify their thinking as the brain grows and they confront new environmental demands. *Both early and later experiences* are important.
Ethology and evolutionary developmental psychology	*Both continuous and discontinuous:* Children and adults gradually develop a wider range of adap-tive behaviors. Sensitive periods occur, in which qualitatively distinct capacities emerge fairly suddenly.	*One course:* Adaptive behaviors and sensitive periods apply to all members of a species.	*Both nature and nurture:* Evolution and heredity influence behavior, and learning lends greater adaptiveness to it. In sensitive periods, *early experiences* set the course of later development.
Vygotsky's sociocultural theory	*Both continuous and discontinuous:* Language development and schooling lead to stagewise changes. Dialogues with more expert members of society also lead to continuous changes that vary from culture to culture.	*Many possible courses:* Socially mediated changes in thought and behavior vary from culture to culture.	*Both nature and nurture:* Heredity, brain growth, and dialogues with more expert members of society jointly contribute to development. *Both early and later experiences* are important.
Ecological systems theory	*Not specified.*	*Many possible courses:* Biological dispositions join with environ-mental forces at multiple levels to mold development in unique ways.	*Both nature and nurture:* The individual's characteristics and the reactions of others affect each other in a bidirectional fashion. *Both early and later experiences* are important.
Lifespan perspective	*Both continuous and discontinuous:* Continuous gains and declines and discontinuous, stagewise emergence of new skills occur.	*Many possible courses:* Develop-ment is influenced by multiple, interacting biological, psycho-logical, and social forces, many of which vary from person to person, leading to diverse pathways of change.	*Both nature and nurture:* Development is multidimensional, affected by an intricate blend of hereditary and environmental factors. Emphasizes plasticity at all ages. *Both early and later experiences* are important.

Finally, all theories have strengths and limitations. Perhaps you found that you were attracted to some theories, but you have doubts about others. As you read more about development in later chapters, you may find it useful to keep a notebook in which you test your theoretical likes and dislikes against the evidence. Don't be surprised if you revise your ideas many times, just as theorists have done since scientific study of development began.

Studying Development

In every science, research is usually based on a prediction about behavior drawn from a theory, or what we call a *hypothesis*. Theories and hypotheses, however, merely initiate the many activities that result in sound evidence on human development. Conducting research according to scientifically accepted procedures involves many steps and choices. Investigators must decide which participants, and how many, to include. Then they must figure out what the participants will be asked to do and when, where, and how many times each will be seen. Finally, they must examine and draw conclusions from their data.

In the following sections, we look at research strategies commonly used to study human development. We begin with *research methods*—participants' specific activities, such as taking tests, answering questionnaires, responding to interviews, or being observed. Then we turn to *research designs*—overall plans for research studies that permit the best possible test of the investigator's hypothesis. Finally, we discuss ethical issues involved in doing research with human participants.

Why learn about research strategies? Why not leave these matters to research specialists and concentrate, instead, on what is known about the developing person and how this knowledge can be applied? There are two reasons. First, each of us must be a wise and critical consumer of knowledge. Knowing the strengths and limitations of various research strategies is important in separating dependable information from misleading results. Second, individuals who work directly with children or adults may be in a unique position to build bridges between research and practice by carrying out research, either on their own or in partnership with experienced investigators. Community agencies, such as schools, mental health facilities, and parks and recreation programs, sometimes collaborate with researchers in designing, implementing, and evaluating interventions aimed at enhancing development (Lerner, Fisher, & Weinberg, 2000). To broaden these efforts, a basic understanding of the research process is essential.

Common Research Methods

How does a researcher choose a basic approach to gathering information? Common methods include systematic observation, self-reports (such as questionnaires and interviews), clinical or case studies of a single individual, and ethnographies of the life circumstances of a specific group of people. Table 1.6 on page 28 summarizes the strengths and limitations of each of these methods.

■ **Systematic Observation.** Observations of the behavior of children and adults can be made in different ways. One approach is to go into the field, or natural environment, and record the behavior of interest—a method called **naturalistic observation**.

A study of preschoolers' responses to their peers' distress provides a good example (Farver & Branstetter, 1994). Observing 3- and 4-year-olds in child-care centers, the researchers recorded each instance of crying and the reactions of nearby children—whether they ignored, watched, commented on the child's unhappiness, scolded or teased, or shared, helped, or expressed sympathy. Caregiver behaviors—explaining why a child was crying, mediating conflict, or offering comfort—were noted to see if adult sensitivity was related to children's caring responses. A strong relationship emerged. The great strength of naturalistic observation is that investigators can see directly the everyday behaviors they hope to explain.

Naturalistic observation also has a major limitation: Not all individuals have the same opportunity to display a particular behavior in everyday life. In the study just described, some children might have witnessed a child crying more often than others or received more direct prompting from caregivers to respond positively. For these reasons, they might have displayed more compassion.

Researchers commonly deal with this difficulty by making **structured observations**, in which the investigator sets up a laboratory situation that evokes the behavior of interest so that every participant has an equal opportunity to display the response. In one study, 2-year-olds' emotional reactions to harm that they thought they had caused were observed by asking them to take care of a rag doll that had been modified so its leg would fall off when the child picked it up. To make the child feel at fault, once the leg detached, an adult "talked for" the doll by saying, "Ow!" Researchers recorded children's facial expressions of sadness and concern for the injured doll, efforts to help the doll, and body tension—responses that indicated remorse and a desire to make amends for the mishap. In addition, mothers were asked to engage in brief conversations about emotions with their children (Garner, 2003). Toddlers whose mothers more often explained the causes and consequences of emotion were more likely to express concern for the injured doll.

The procedures used to collect systematic observations vary, depending on the research problem posed. Some investigators must describe the entire stream of behavior—everything said and done over a certain time period. In one of my own studies, I wanted to find out how sensitive, responsive, and verbally stimulating caregivers were when they interacted with children in child-care centers. In this case, everything each caregiver said and did—even the amount of time she spent away from the children, taking coffee breaks and talking on the phone—was important. In other studies, only one or a few kinds of behavior are needed, so researchers can use more efficient procedures in which they record only specified events or mark off behaviors on checklists.

Researchers have devised ingenious ways of observing difficult-to-capture behaviors. For example, to record instances

Table 1.6	Strengths and Limitations of Common Research Methods		
Method	**Description**	**Strengths**	**Limitations**
Systematic Observation			
Naturalistic observation	Observation of behavior in natural contexts	Reflects participants' everyday lives.	Cannot control conditions under which participants are observed.
Structured observation	Observation of behavior in a laboratory, which conditions are the same for all participants	Grants each participant an equal opportunity to display the behavior of interest.	May not yield observations typical of participants' behavior in everyday life.
Self-Reports			
Clinical interview	Flexible interviewing procedure in which the investigator obtains a complete account of the participant's thoughts	Comes as close as possible to the way participants think in everyday life. Great breadth and depth of information can be obtained in a short time.	May not result in accurate reporting of information. Flexible procedure makes comparing individuals' responses difficult.
Structured interview, questionnaires, and tests	Self-report instruments in which each participant is asked the same questions in the same way	Permits comparisons of participants' responses and efficient data collection. Researchers can specify answer alternatives that participants might not think of in an open-ended interview.	Does not yield the same depth of information as a clinical interview. Responses are still subject to inaccurate reporting.
Clinical, or Case Study, Method			
	A full picture of one individual's psychological functioning, obtained by combining interviews, observations, and test scores	Provides rich, descriptive insights into factors that affect development.	May be biased by researchers' theoretical preferences. Findings cannot be applied to individuals other than the participant.
Ethnography			
	Participant observation of a culture or distinct social group; by making extensive field notes, the researcher tries to capture the culture's unique values and social processes	Provides a more thorough and accurate description than can be derived from a single observational visit, interview, or questionnaire.	May be biased by researchers' values and theoretical preferences. Findings cannot be applied to individuals and settings other than the ones studied.

of bullying, a group of investigators set up video cameras overlooking a classroom and a playground and had fourth to sixth graders wear small, remote microphones and pocket-sized transmitters (Craig, Pepler, & Atlas, 2000). Results revealed that bullying occurred often—at rates of 2.4 episodes per hour in the classroom and 4.5 episodes per hour on the playground. Yet only 15 to 18 percent of the time did teachers take steps to stop the harassment.

Systematic observation provides invaluable information on how children and adults actually behave, but it tells us little about the reasoning behind their responses. For that information, researchers must turn to self-report techniques.

■ **Self-Reports.** Self-reports ask research participants to provide information on their perceptions, thoughts, abilities, feelings, attitudes, beliefs, and past experiences. They range from relatively unstructured interviews to highly structured interviews, questionnaires, and tests.

In a **clinical interview**, researchers use a flexible, conversational style to probe for the participant's point of view. In the following example, Piaget questioned a 5-year-old child about his understanding of dreams:

Where does the dream come from?—I think you sleep so well that you dream.—*Does it come from us or from outside?*—From outside.—*When you are in bed and you dream, where is the dream?*—In my bed, under the blanket. I don't really know. If it was in my stomach, the bones would be in the way and I shouldn't see it.—*Is the dream there when you sleep?*—Yes, it is in the bed beside me. (Piaget, 1926/1930, pp. 97–98)

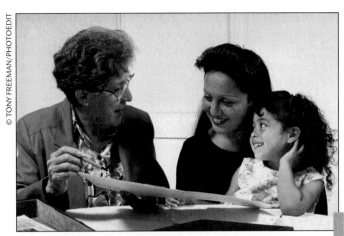

Using the clinical interview, this researcher asks a mother to describe her child's development. The method permits a large amount of information to be gathered in a relatively short period, but a drawback is that participants do not always report information accurately.

Notice how Piaget encouraged the child to expand his ideas. Although a researcher conducting clinical interviews with more than one participant would typically ask the same first question to ensure a common task, individualized prompts are given to evoke a fuller picture of each person's reasoning (Ginsburg, 1997).

The clinical interview has two major strengths. First, it permits people to display their thoughts in terms that are as close as possible to the way they think in everyday life. Second, it can provide a large amount of information in a fairly brief period. For example, in an hour-long session, we can obtain a wide range of information on child rearing from a parent or on life circumstances from an elder—much more than we could capture by observing for the same amount of time.

A major limitation of the clinical interview has to do with the accuracy with which people report their thoughts, feelings, and experiences. Some participants, wishing to please the interviewer, may make up answers that do not represent their actual thinking. When asked about past events, some may have trouble recalling exactly what happened. And because the clinical interview depends on verbal ability and expressiveness, it may underestimate the capacities of individuals who have difficulty putting their thoughts into words.

The clinical interview has also been criticized because of its flexibility. When each participant is asked different questions, responses may reflect the manner of interviewing rather than real differences in the way people think about a topic. **Structured interviews**, in which each participant is asked the same set of questions in the same way, eliminate this problem. These instruments are also much more efficient. Answers are briefer, and researchers can obtain written responses from an entire group of children or adults simultaneously. Also, by listing answer alternatives, researchers can specify the activities and behaviors of interest—ones that participants might not think of in an open-ended clinical interview. For example, in a study in which parents were asked what they considered "the

most important thing for children to prepare them for life," 62 percent checked "to think for themselves" when this choice appeared on a list. Yet only 5 percent thought of it during a clinical interview (Schwarz, 1999).

Nevertheless, structured interviews do not yield the same depth of information as clinical interviews. And they can still be affected by the problem of inaccurate reporting.

■ **The Clinical, or Case Study, Method.** An outgrowth of psychoanalytic theory, the **clinical, or case study, method** brings together a wide range of information on one person, including interviews, observations, and sometimes test scores. The aim is to obtain as complete a picture as possible of that individual's psychological functioning and the experiences that led up to it.

The clinical method is well suited to studying the development of types of individuals who are few in number and who vary widely in characteristics. For example, it has been used to find out what contributes to the accomplishments of *prodigies*—extremely gifted children who attain adult competence in a field before age 10 (Gardner, 1998b). Consider Adam, a boy who read, wrote, and composed musical pieces before he was out of diapers. By age 4, Adam was deeply involved in mastering human symbol systems—French, German, Russian, Sanskrit, Greek, the computer programming language BASIC, ancient hieroglyphs, music, and mathematics. Adam's parents provided a home rich in stimulation and reared him with affection, firmness, and humor. They searched for schools in which he could both develop his abilities and form rewarding social relationships. He graduated from college at age 18 and continued to pursue musical composition. Would Adam have realized his abilities without the chance combination of his special gift with nurturing, committed parents? Probably not, researchers concluded (Goldsmith, 2000).

The clinical method yields richly detailed case narratives that offer valuable insights into the many factors that affect development. Like all other methods, however, it has drawbacks. Information is often collected unsystematically and subjectively, permitting too much leeway for researchers' theoretical preferences to bias their observations and interpretations. In addition, investigators cannot assume that their conclusions apply, or generalize, to anyone other than the person studied (Stanovich, 2004). Even when patterns emerge across several cases, it is wise to confirm these with other research strategies.

■ **Methods for Studying Culture.** A growing interest in the impact of culture has led researchers to adjust the methods just considered or tap procedures specially devised for cross-cultural and multicultural research (Triandis, 1998). Which approach investigators choose depends on their research goals.

Sometimes researchers are interested in characteristics that are believed to be universal but that vary in degree from one society to the next: Are parents warmer or more directive in some cultures than others? How strong are gender stereotypes in different nations? In each instance, several cultural groups will be compared, and all participants must be questioned or

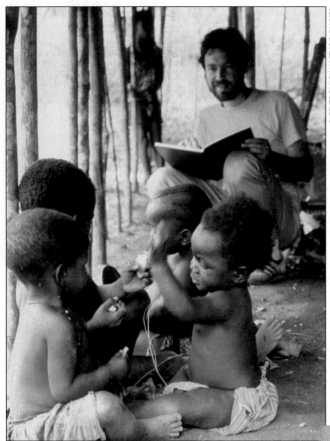

© ED TRONICK/ANTHRO-PHOTO

This Western ethnographer is spending months living among the Efe people of the Republic of Congo. Here he observes a group of young children sharing food. Among the Efe, cooperation and generosity are highly valued and encouraged at an early age.

observed in the same way. Therefore, researchers draw on the self-report and observational procedures we have already considered, adapting them through translation so they can be understood in each cultural context. For example, to study cultural variation in parenting practices, the same questionnaire, asking for ratings on such items as "I often hug and kiss my child" or "I scold my child when his/her behavior does not meet my expectations," is given to all participants (Wu et al., 2002).

At other times, researchers want to uncover the *cultural meanings* of children's and adults' behaviors by becoming as familiar as possible with their way of life. To achieve this goal, researchers rely on a method borrowed from the field of anthropology—**ethnography.** Like the clinical method, ethnographic research is largely a descriptive, qualitative technique. But instead of aiming to understand a single individual, it is directed toward understanding a culture or a distinct social group through *participant observation.* Typically, the researcher spends months, and sometimes years, in the cultural community, participating in its daily life. Extensive field notes are made, consisting of a mix of observations, self-reports from members of the culture, and careful interpretations by the investigator (Miller, Hengst, & Wang, 2003; Shweder, 1996). Later, these notes are put together into a description of

the community that tries to capture its unique values and social processes.

The ethnographic method assumes that by entering into close contact with a social group, researchers can understand the beliefs and behaviors of its members in a way not possible with an observational visit, interview, or questionnaire. In some ethnographies, investigators look at many aspects of experience, as one team of researchers did in describing what it is like to grow up in a small American town. Others focus on one or a few settings, such as home, school, or neighborhood life (LeVine et al., 1994; Peshkin, 1978, 1997; Valdés, 1998). Researchers may supplement traditional self-report and observational methods with ethnography if they suspect that unique meanings underlie cultural differences, as the Cultural Influences box on the following page reveals.

Ethnographers strive to minimize their influence on the culture they are studying by becoming part of it. Nevertheless, as with clinical studies, investigators' cultural values and theoretical commitments sometimes lead them to observe selectively or misinterpret what they see. In addition, the findings of ethnographic studies cannot be assumed to generalize beyond the people and settings in which the research was conducted.

Ask Yourself

Review

Why might a researcher choose structured observation over naturalistic observation? How about the reverse? What might lead the researcher to opt for clinical interviewing over systematic observation?

Apply

A researcher is interested in how elders experience daily life in different cultures. Which method should she use? Explain.

Connect

What strengths and limitations do the clinical, or case study, method and ethnography have in common?

Reflect

Reread the description of nonnormative influences on pages 11–12 and cite an example from your own life. Which method would be best-suited to studying the impact of such a nonnormative event on development?

www.ablongman.com/berk

General Research Designs

In deciding on a research design, investigators choose a way of setting up a study that permits them to test their hypotheses with the greatest certainty possible. Two main types of designs are used in all research on human behavior: *correlational* and *experimental.*

■ **Correlational Design.** In a **correlational design**, researchers gather information on individuals, generally in

Cultural Influences

Immigrant Youths: Amazing Adaptation

Over the past several decades, a rising tide of immigrants has come to North America, fleeing war and persecution in their homelands or seeking greater life chances. Today, one-fifth of the U.S. youth population has foreign-born parents; nearly one-third of these youths are foreign-born themselves. Similarly, immigrant youths are the fastest-growing segment of the Canadian population (Fuligni, 2001; Service Canada, 2005). In the United States, most come from Asia and Latin America; in Canada, from Asia, Africa, the Middle East, and Europe.

To find out how well immigrant youths are adapting to their new country, researchers use multiple research methods, including academic testing, questionnaires assessing psychological adjustment, and in-depth ethnographic research.

Academic Achievement and Adjustment.
Despite a widespread belief that the transition to a new country has a negative impact on psychological well-being, recent evidence reveals that children of immigrant parents adapt amazingly well. Both first-generation (foreign-born) or second-generation (American- or Canadian-born, with immigrant parents) students achieve in school as well as or better than students of native-born parents (Fuligni, 1997; Saucier et al., 2002).

Findings on psychological adjustment are similar. Adolescents from immigrant families are less likely than their agemates to commit delinquent and violent acts, to use drugs and alcohol, or to have early sex. They are also less likely to be obese or to have missed school because of illness. And they feel as positively about themselves as young people with native-born parents, and report less emotional distress. These successes do not depend on having extensive time to adjust to a new way of life. Recently arrived high school students do as well in school and report just as favorable self-esteem as students who came at younger ages (Fuligni, 1998; Saucier et al., 2002).

The outcomes just described are strongest for Chinese, Japanese, Korean, and East Indian youths, less dramatic for other ethnicities (Fuligni, 1997; Kao & Tienda, 1995; Louie, 2001). Variations in parental education and income account for these differences. Still, even first- and second-generation youths from ethnic groups that face considerable economic hardship (such as Mexican and Vietnamese) are remarkably successful (Fuligni & Yoshikawa, 2003). Factors other than income are responsible.

Family and Community Influences.
Ethnographies reveal that immigrant parents uniformly express the belief that education is the surest way to improve life chances. Consequently, they highly value academic achievement (Goldenberg et al., 2001; Louie, 2001). Aware of the challenges their children face, immigrant parents underscore the importance of trying hard. They remind their children that educational opportunities were not available in their native countries and that as a result, they themselves are often limited to menial jobs.

Adolescents from immigrant families internalize their parents' valuing of education, endorsing it more strongly than agemates with native-born parents (Asakawa, 2001; Fuligni, 1997). Because minority ethnicities usually stress allegiance to family and community over individual goals, first- and second-generation young people feel a strong sense of obligation to their parents. They view school success as one of the most important ways to repay their parents for the hardships they endured in coming to a new land (Fuligni, Yip, & Tseng, 2002; Suárez-Orozco & Suárez-Orozco, 2001). Both family relationships and school achievement protect these youths from risky behaviors, such as delinquency, early pregnancy, and drug use (see the Biology and Environment box on resilience on pages 10–11).

Immigrant parents typically develop close ties to an ethnic community. It exerts additional control through a high consensus on values and constant monitoring of young people's activities. The following comments capture the power of these family and community forces:

Immigrant youths from central and south Asia in Toronto, Canada, enjoy lunch together in their school cafeteria. Cultural values that foster allegiance to family and community and that emphasize the importance of achievement play a vital role in these young peoples' academic success and favorable psychological adjustment.

A New York City cab driver from Ghana, father of three teenage boys who later enrolled at prestigious universities: "I make sure I know my children's friends and if they want to come to my house they have to follow my rules . . . and I never let my children work. . . . Who knows what influences they will be exposed to?" (Suárez-Orozco & Suárez-Orozco, 2001, p. 89)

Elizabeth, age 16, straight-A student, like her two older sisters: "My parents know pretty much all the kids in the neighborhood. . . . Everybody here knows everybody else. It's hard to get away with much." (Zhou & Bankston, 1998, pp. 93, 130)

Immigrant youths' experiences are not problem-free. In interviews with adolescents who had arrived in Canada within the previous five years, the majority found that their first year was "very difficult" because they did not yet speak one of the country's two official languages (English and French) and felt socially isolated (Hanvey & Kunz, 2000). And tensions between family values and the new culture often create identity conflicts—challenges we will take up in Chapter 12. But family and community cohesion, supervision, and expectations for academic and social maturity powerfully shape long-term positive outcomes for these young people.

natural life circumstances, without altering their experiences. Then they look at relationships between participants' characteristics and their behavior or development. Suppose we want to answer the following question: Do parents' styles of interacting with children have any bearing on children's intelligence? Does the arrival of a baby influence a couple's marital satisfaction? Does the death of a spouse in old age affect the surviving partner's physical health and psychological well-being? In these and many other instances, the conditions of interest are difficult or impossible to arrange and control and must be studied as they currently exist.

Correlational studies have one major limitation: We cannot infer cause and effect. For example, suppose we find that parental interaction is related to children's intelligence. But we would not know whether parents' behavior actually *causes* intellectual differences among children. In fact, the opposite is possible: The behaviors of highly intelligent children may be so attractive that they cause parents to interact more favorably. Or a third variable that we did not even consider, such as the amount of noise and distraction in the home, may cause changes in both maternal interaction and children's intelligence.

In correlational studies and in other types of research designs, investigators often examine relationships by using a **correlation coefficient**, a number that describes how two measures, or variables, are associated with one another. We will encounter the correlation coefficient in discussing research findings throughout this book, so let's look at what it is and how it is interpreted. A correlation coefficient can range in value from +1.00 to −1.00. The *magnitude,* or *size, of the number* shows the *strength of the relationship.* A zero correlation indicates no relationship, but the closer the value is to +1.00 or −1.00, the stronger the relationship (see Figure 1.6). For instance, a correlation of −.78 is high, −.52 is moderate, and −.18 is low. Note, however, that correlations of +.52 and −.52 are equally strong. The *sign of the number* (+ or −) refers to the *direction of the relationship.* A positive sign (+) means that as one variable *increases,* the other also *increases.* A negative sign (−) indicates that as one variable *increases,* the other *decreases.*

Let's look at some examples of how a correlation coefficient works. One researcher reported a +.55 correlation between a measure of maternal language stimulation and the size of children's vocabularies at 2 years of age (Hoff, 2003). This is a moderate correlation, which indicates that mothers who verbalized more had children who were more advanced in language development. In two other studies, maternal sensitivity was modestly associated with children's cooperativeness in consistent ways. First, maternal warmth and encouragement during play correlated positively with 2-year-olds' willingness to comply with their mother's directive to clean up toys, at +.34 (Feldman & Klein, 2003). Second, the extent to which mothers interrupted and controlled their 3-year-old's play correlated negatively with children's compliance, at −.23 (Whiteside-Mansell et al., 2003).

All these investigations found correlations between parenting and young children's behavior. Are you tempted to conclude that the maternal behaviors influenced children's responses? Although the researchers suspected this was so, none of the studies revealed cause and effect. But finding a relationship in a correlational study suggests that tracking down its cause—using a more powerful experimental strategy, if possible—would be worthwhile.

■ **Experimental Design.** An **experimental design** permits inferences about cause and effect because researchers use an evenhanded procedure to assign people to two or more treatment conditions. In an experiment, the events and behaviors of interest are divided into two types, independent and dependent variables. The **independent variable** is the one the investigator expects to cause changes in another variable. The **dependent variable** is the one the investigator expects to be influenced by the independent variable. Cause-and-effect relationships can be detected because the researcher directly *controls* or *manipulates* changes in the independent variable by exposing participants to the treatment conditions. Then the researcher compares their performance on measures of the dependent variable.

In one *laboratory experiment,* investigators explored the impact of adults' angry interactions on children's adjustment (El-Sheikh, Cummings, & Reiter, 1996). They hypothesized that the way angry encounters end (independent variable) affects children's emotional reactions (dependent variable). Four- and 5-year-olds were brought to a laboratory one at a time, accompanied by their mothers. One group was exposed to an *unresolved-anger treatment,* in which two adult actors entered the room and argued but did not work out their disagreements. The other group witnessed a *resolved-anger treatment,* in which the adults ended their disputes by apologizing and compromising. During a follow-up adult conflict, chil-

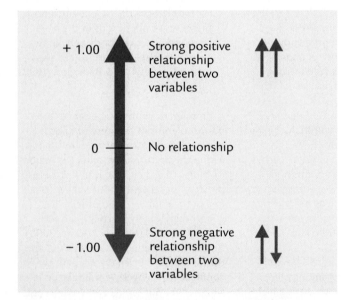

■ **FIGURE 1.6 The meaning of correlation coefficients.** The magnitude of the number indicates the *strength* of the relationship. The sign of the number (+ or −) indicates the *direction* of the relationship.

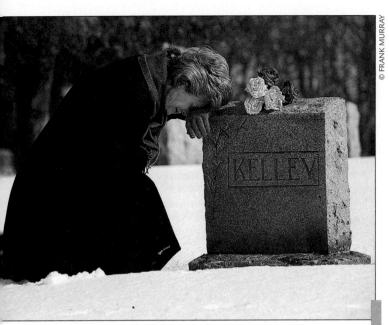

Does the death of a spouse in old age affect the surviving partner's physical health and psychological well-being? A correlational design can be used to answer this question, but it does not permit researchers to determine the precise cause of their findings.

dren in the resolved-anger treatment showed less distress, as measured by fewer anxious facial expressions, less freezing in place, and less seeking of closeness to their mothers. The experiment revealed that anger resolution can reduce the stressful impact of adult conflict on children.

In experimental studies, investigators must take special precautions to control for participants' characteristics that could reduce the accuracy of their findings. For example, in the study just described, if more children from homes high in parental conflict ended up in the unresolved-anger treatment, we would not be able to tell whether the independent variable or the children's backgrounds produced the results. To protect against this problem, researchers engage in **random assignment** of participants to treatment conditions. By using an unbiased procedure, such as drawing numbers out of a hat or flipping a coin, investigators increase the chances that participants' characteristics will be equally distributed across treatment conditions.

■ **Modified Experimental Designs: Field and Natural Experiments.** Most experiments are conducted in laboratories, where researchers can achieve the maximum possible control over treatment conditions. But, as we have already indicated, findings obtained in laboratories may not always apply to everyday situations. In *field experiments,* investigators capitalize on opportunities to assign participants randomly to treatment conditions in natural settings. In the experiment just described, we can conclude that the emotional climate established by adults affects children's behavior in the laboratory. But does it also do so in daily life?

Another study helps answer this question (Yarrow, Scott, & Waxler, 1973). This time, the research was carried out in a child-care center. A caregiver deliberately interacted differently with two groups of preschoolers. In one condition (the *nurturant treatment*), she modeled many instances of warmth and helpfulness. In the second condition (the *control,* since it involved no treatment), she behaved as usual, with no special emphasis on concern for others. Two weeks later, the researchers created several situations that called for helpfulness. For example, a visiting mother asked each child to watch her baby for a few moments, but the baby's toys had fallen out of the playpen. The investigators found that children exposed to the nurturant treatment were much more likely than those in the control condition to return toys to the baby.

Often researchers cannot randomly assign participants and manipulate conditions in the real world. Sometimes they can compromise by conducting *natural, or quasi-, experiments.* Treatments that already exist, such as different family environments, schools, workplaces, or retirement villages, are compared. These studies differ from correlational research only in that groups of participants are carefully chosen to ensure that their characteristics are as much alike as possible. In this way, investigators rule out as best they can alternative explanations for their treatment effects. But, despite these efforts, natural experiments cannot achieve the precision and rigor of true experimental research.

To help you compare correlational and experimental designs, Table 1.7 on page 34 summarizes their strengths and limitations. It also includes an overview of designs for studying development, to which we now turn.

Designs for Studying Development

Scientists interested in human development require information about the way research participants change over time. To answer questions about development, they must extend correlational and experimental approaches to include measurements at different ages. Longitudinal and cross-sectional designs are special *developmental* research strategies. In each, age comparisons form the basis of the research plan.

■ **The Longitudinal Design.** In a **longitudinal design**, participants are studied repeatedly, and changes are noted as they get older. The time spanned may be relatively short (a few months to several years) or very long (a decade or even a lifetime). The longitudinal approach has two major strengths. First, because it tracks the performance of each person over time, researchers can identify common patterns as well as individual differences in development. Second, longitudinal studies permit investigators to examine relationships between early and later events and behaviors. Let's illustrate these ideas.

A group of researchers wondered whether children who display extreme personality styles—either angry and explosive or shy and withdrawn—retain the same dispositions as adults. In addition, the researchers wanted to know what kinds of experiences promote stability or change in personality and

Table 1.7	Strengths and Limitations of Research Designs		
Design	**Description**	**Strengths**	**Limitations**
General			
Correlational	The investigator obtains information on participants without altering their experiences.	Permits study of relationships between variables.	Does not permit inferences about cause-and-effect relationships.
Experimental	Through random assignment of participants to treatment conditions, the investigator manipulates an independent variable and examines its effect on a dependent variable. Can be conducted in the laboratory or the natural environment.	Permits inferences about cause-and-effect relationships.	When conducted in the laboratory, findings may not generalize to the real world. In *field experiments*, control over the treatment is usually weaker than in the laboratory. In *natural*, or *quasi-*, *experiments*, lack of random assignment substantially reduces the precision of research.
Developmental			
Longitudinal	The investigator studies the same group of participants repeatedly at different ages.	Permits study of common patterns and individual differences in development and relationships between early and later events and behaviors.	Age-related changes may be distorted because of participant dropout, practice effects, and cohort effects.
Cross-sectional	The investigator studies groups of participants differing in age at the same point in time.	More efficient than the longitudinal design. Not plagued by such problems as participant dropout and practice effects.	Does not permit study of individual developmental trends. Age differences may be distorted because of cohort effects.
Sequential	The investigator conducts several similar cross-sectional or longitudinal studies (called sequences) at varying times.	Permits longitudinal and cross-sectional comparisons. Reveals cohort effects.	May have the same problems as longitudinal and cross-sectional strategies, but the design itself helps identify difficulties.

what consequences explosiveness and shyness have for long-term adjustment. To answer these questions, the researchers delved into the archives of the Guidance Study, a well-known longitudinal investigation initiated in 1928 at the University of California, Berkeley, and continued for several decades (Caspi, Elder, & Bem, 1987, 1988).

Results revealed that the two personality styles were moderately stable. Between ages 8 and 30, a good number of individuals remained the same, whereas others changed substantially. When stability did occur, it appeared to be due to a "snowballing effect," in which children evoked responses from adults and peers that acted to maintain their dispositions. Explosive youngsters were likely to be treated with anger, whereas shy children were apt to be ignored. As a result, the two types of children came to view their social worlds differently. Explosive children regarded others as hostile; shy children regarded them as unfriendly (Caspi & Roberts, 2001). Together these factors led explosive children to sustain or increase their unruliness and shy children to continue to withdraw.

Persistence of extreme personality styles affected many areas of adult adjustment. For men, the results of early explo-

siveness were most apparent in their work lives, in the form of conflicts with supervisors, frequent job changes, and unemployment. Since few women in this sample of an earlier generation worked after marriage, their family lives were most affected. Explosive girls grew up to be hotheaded wives and mothers who were especially prone to divorce. Sex differences in the long-term consequences of shyness were even greater. Men who had been withdrawn in childhood were delayed in marrying, becoming fathers, and developing stable careers. However, because a withdrawn, unassertive style was socially acceptable for females, women with shy personalities showed no special adjustment problems.

■ **Problems in Conducting Longitudinal Research.** Despite their strengths, longitudinal investigations pose a number of problems. For example, participants may move away or drop out of the research for other reasons. This changes the original sample so that it no longer represents the population to whom researchers would like to generalize their findings. Also, from repeated study, people may become more aware of their own thoughts, feelings, and actions and revise

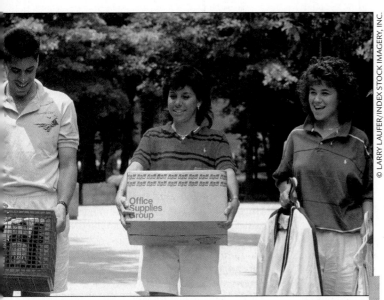

Cohort effects are the particular historical and cultural conditions that affect individuals born in the same time period. What cohort effects make the experiences of today's college students different from the experiences of these college students of the 1980s?

them in ways that have little to do with age-related change. In addition, they may become "test-wise." Their performance may improve as a result of *practice effects*—better test-taking skills and increased familiarity with the test—not because of factors commonly associated with development.

The most widely discussed threat to longitudinal findings is **cohort effects** (see page 11): Individuals born in the same time period are influenced by a particular set of historical and cultural conditions. Results based on one cohort may not apply to people developing in other times. For example, unlike the findings on female shyness described in the preceding section, which were gathered in the 1950s, today's shy young women tend to be poorly adjusted—a difference that may be due to changes in gender roles in Western societies. Shy adults, whether male or female, feel more depressed, have fewer social supports, and may do less well in educational and career attainment than their agemates (Caspi, 2000; Caspi et al., 2003). Similarly, a longitudinal study of lifespan development would probably result in quite different findings if it were carried out in the first decade of the twenty-first century, around the time of World War II, or during the Great Depression of the 1930s. (See the Lifespan Vista box on page 36.)

Cohort effects do not just operate broadly on an entire generation. They also occur when specific experiences influence some groups of individuals but not others in the same generation. For example, children who witnessed the terrorist attacks of September 11, 2001, either because they were near Ground Zero or because they saw injury and death on TV, were far more likely than other children to display persistent emotional problems, including intense fear, anxiety, and depression (Saylor et al., 2003). A study of one New York City sample suggested that as many as one-fourth of the city's children were affected (Hoven, Mandell, & Duarte, 2003).

The Cross-Sectional Design. The length of time it takes for many behaviors to change, even in limited longitudinal studies, has led researchers to turn toward a more convenient strategy for studying development. In the **cross-sectional design**, groups of people differing in age are studied at the same point in time. The cross-sectional design is an efficient strategy for describing age-related trends. Because participants are measured only once, researchers need not be concerned about such difficulties as participant dropout or practice effects.

A study in which students in grades 3, 6, 9, and 12 filled out a questionnaire about their sibling relationships provides a good illustration (Buhrmester & Furman, 1990). Findings revealed that sibling interaction was characterized by greater equality and less power assertion with age. Also, feelings of sibling companionship declined during adolescence. The researchers thought that several factors contributed to these age differences. As later-born children become more competent and independent, they no longer need, and are probably less willing to accept, direction from older siblings. And as adolescents move from psychological dependence on the family to greater involvement with peers, they may have less time and emotional need to invest in siblings. As we will see in Chapter 12, subsequent research has confirmed these intriguing ideas about the development of sibling relationships.

Problems in Conducting Cross-Sectional Research. Despite its convenience, cross-sectional research does not provide evidence about development at the level at which it actually occurs: the individual (Kraemer et al., 2000). For example, in the cross-sectional study of sibling relationships just discussed, comparisons are limited to age-group averages. We cannot tell if important individual differences exist. Indeed, longitudinal findings reveal that adolescents vary considerably in the changing quality of their sibling relationships. Although many become more distant, others become more supportive and intimate, and still others more rivalrous and antagonistic (Branje et al., 2004; Dunn, Slomkowski, & Beardsall, 1994).

Cross-sectional studies—especially those that cover a wide age span—have another problem. Like longitudinal research, they can be threatened by cohort effects. For example, comparisons of 10-year-old cohorts, 20-year-old cohorts, and 30-year-old cohorts—groups born and reared in different years—may not really represent age-related changes. Instead, they may reflect unique experiences associated with the historical period in which the age groups were growing up.

Improving Developmental Designs. Researchers have devised ways of building on the strengths and minimizing the weaknesses of longitudinal and cross-sectional approaches. Several modified developmental designs have resulted.

Sequential Designs. To overcome some of the limitations of traditional developmental designs, investigators sometimes use **sequential designs,** in which they conduct several similar cross-sectional or longitudinal studies (called *sequences*) at varying times. As the illustration in Figure 1.7 on page 37

A Lifespan Vista

Impact of Historical Times on the Life Course: The Great Depression and World War II

Cataclysmic events, such as economic disaster, wars, and rapid social change, shake the foundations of life, inducing shared adaptations among people born at the same time (Rogler, 2002). Glen Elder (1999) examined the hardships that families experienced during the Great Depression of the 1930s to study its influence on lifespan development. He delved into the vast archives of two major longitudinal studies: (1) the Oakland Growth Study, an investigation of individuals born in the early 1920s, who were adolescents when the Depression took its toll; and (2) the Guidance Study, whose participants were born in the late 1920s and were young children when their families faced severe financial losses.

In both cohorts, relationships changed when economic deprivation struck. As unemployed fathers lost status, mothers took greater control over family affairs. This reversal of traditional gender roles often sparked conflict. Fathers sometimes became explosive and punitive toward their children. At other times, they withdrew into passivity and depression. Mothers often became frantic with worry over their family's well-being and sought work to make ends meet (Elder, Liker, & Cross, 1984).

Outcomes for Adolescents. Although unusual burdens were placed on them as family lives changed, the Oakland Growth Study cohort—especially the boys—weathered economic hardship well. As adolescents, they were too old to be wholly dependent on their highly stressed parents. Boys spent less time at home as they searched for part-time jobs, and many turned toward adults and peers outside the family for emotional support. Girls took over household chores and cared for younger siblings. Their greater involvement in family affairs exposed them to more parental conflict and unhappiness. Consequently, adolescent girls' adjustment in economically deprived homes was somewhat less favorable than that of adolescent boys (Elder, Nguyen, & Caspi, 1985).

These changes had major consequences for adolescents' future aspirations and adult lives. As girls focused on home and family, they were less likely to think about college and careers and more likely to marry early. Boys learned that economic resources could not be taken for granted, and they tended to make an early commitment to an occupational choice. And the chance to become a parent was especially important to men whose lives had been disrupted by the Depression. Perhaps because they believed that a rewarding career could not be guaranteed, they viewed children as the most enduring benefit of their adult lives.

Outcomes for Children. Unlike the Oakland Growth Study cohort, the Guidance Study participants were within the years of intense family dependency when the Depression struck. For young boys (who, as you will see in later chapters, are especially prone to adjustment problems in the face of family stress), the impact of economic strain was severe. They showed emotional difficulties and poor attitudes toward school and work that persisted through the teenage years (Elder & Caspi, 1988).

But as the Guidance Study sample became adolescents, another major historical event occurred: World War II. Thousands of men left their communities for military bases, leading to dramatic life changes. Some combat veterans came away with symptoms of emotional trauma that persisted for decades. Yet for most young soldiers, war mobilization broadened their range of knowledge and experience. It also granted time out from civilian responsibilities, giving many soldiers a chance to consider where their lives were going. And the U.S. GI Bill of Rights, which provided government subsides for college education, enabled veterans to expand their education and acquire new skills after the war. By middle adulthood, the Guidance Study veterans had reversed the early negative impact of the Great Depression. They were more successful educationally and occupationally than their counterparts who had not entered the service (Elder & Hareven, 1993).

Clearly, cultural-historical change does not have a uniform impact on development. Outcomes can vary considerably, depending on the pattern of historical events and the age at which people experience them.

Historical time period has profound implications for development. These U.S. World War II veterans, entering college in 1945 under the GI Bill of Rights, benefited from educational opportunities that made them more successful, as a group, than their agemates who had not entered the service. Here ex-soldier students wait to be issued books, notes, and tuition checks for a new term.

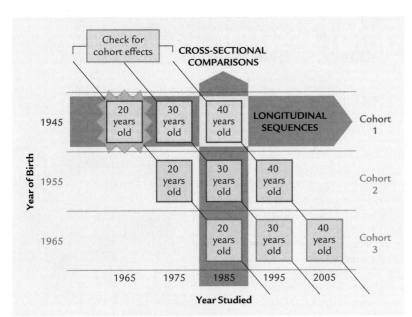

■ **FIGURE 1.7 Example of a sequential design.** Three cohorts, born in 1945 (blue), 1955 (pink), and 1965 (green), are followed longitudinally from 20 to 40 years of age. The design permits the researcher to check for cohort effects by comparing people of the same age who were born in different years. In a study that used this design, the 20-year-olds in Cohort 1 differed substantially from the 20-year-olds in Cohorts 2 and 3, indicating powerful history-graded influences. This design also permits longitudinal and cross-sectional comparisons. Similar findings lend additional confidence in the results.

reveals, some sequential designs combine longitudinal and cross-sectional strategies, an approach that has two advantages:

⬛ We can find out whether cohort effects are operating by comparing participants of the same age who were born in different years. In the example in Figure 1.7, for example, we can compare the three longitudinal samples at ages 20, 30, and 40. If they do not differ, we can rule out cohort effects.

⬛ We can make longitudinal and cross-sectional comparisons. If outcomes are similar in both, then we can be especially confident about our findings.

In a study that used the design in Figure 1.7, researchers wanted to find out whether adult personality development progresses as Erikson's psychosocial theory predicts (Whitbourne et al., 1992). Questionnaires measuring Erikson's stages were given to three cohorts of 20-year-olds, each born a decade apart. The cohorts were reassessed at 10-year intervals. Consistent with Erikson's theory, longitudinal and cross-sectional gains in identity and intimacy occurred between ages 20 and 30—a trend unaffected by historical time period. But a powerful cohort effect emerged for consolidation of the sense of industry: At age 20, Cohort 1 scored substantially below Cohorts 2 and 3. Look at Figure 1.7 again and notice that members of Cohort 1 reached age 20 in the mid-1960s. As college students, they were part of an era of political protest that reflected disenchantment with the work ethic. Once out of college, they caught up with the other cohorts, perhaps as a result of experiencing the pressures of the work world.

By uncovering cohort effects, sequential designs help explain diversity in development. Yet to date only a small number of sequential studies have been conducted.

Combining Experimental and Developmental Designs. Perhaps you noticed that all the examples of longitudinal and cross-sectional research we have considered permit only corre-

lational, not causal, inferences. Yet causal information is desirable, both for testing theories and for finding ways to enhance development. Sometimes researchers can explore the causal link between experiences and development by experimentally manipulating the experiences. If, as a result, development improves, then we have strong evidence for a causal association. Today, research that combines an experimental strategy with either a longitudinal or a cross-sectional approach is increasingly common. For an example, refer to the Social Issues box on page 38.

Ask Yourself

Review

Explain how cohort effects can affect the findings of both longitudinal and cross-sectional studies. How do sequential designs reveal cohort effects?

Apply

A researcher compares older adults with chronic heart disease to those with no major health problems and finds that the first group scores lower on mental tests. Can the researcher conclude that heart disease causes a decline in intellectual functioning in late adulthood? Explain.

Apply

A researcher wants to find out if aggressive preschoolers tend to have problems with peer relationships in elementary school. Which developmental design is appropriate for answering this question? Why?

Reflect

Suppose a researcher asks you to enroll your baby in a 10-year longitudinal study. What factors would lead you to agree and stay involved? Do your answers shed light on why longitudinal studies often have biased samples?

Social Issues

Can Musical Experiences Enhance Intelligence?

In a 1993 experiment, researchers reported that college students who listened to a Mozart sonata for a few minutes just before taking a test of spatial reasoning abilities did better on the test than students who took the test after listening to relaxation instructions or sitting in silence (Rauscher, Shaw, & Ky, 1993). Strains of Mozart, the investigators concluded, seem to induce changes in the brain that "warm up" neural connections, thereby improving thinking. But the gain in performance, widely publicized as the "Mozart effect," lasted only 15 minutes and proved difficult to replicate. Rather than involving a real change in ability, Mozart seemed to improve

Children who take music lessons over many weeks gain in mental test performance compared to children who take drama lessons or who receive no lessons at all. To make music, children must use diverse intellectual skills, including extended focused attention, reading muscial notation, memorizing lengthy passages, analyzing musical structures, and mastering technical skills.

arousal and mood, yielding better concentration on the test (Husain, Thompson, & Schellenberg, 2002; Thompson, Schellenberg, & Husain, 2001).

Despite mounting evidence that the Mozart effect was uncertain at best, the media and politicians were enthralled with the idea that a brief exposure of the brain to classical music in infancy, when neural connections are forming rapidly,

might yield lifelong intellectual benefits. Soon, Georgia, Tennessee, and South Dakota began providing free CDs for every newborn baby leaving the hospital. Yet no studies of the Mozart effect have ever been conducted on infants! And an experiment with school-age children failed to yield any intellectual gains as a result of simply listening to music (McKelvie & Low, 2002).

Research suggests that to produce lasting gains in mental test scores, interventions must be long-lasting and involve children's active participation. Consequently, Glenn Schellenberg (2004) wondered, Can music lessons enhance intelligence? Children who take music lessons must practice regularly, engage in extended focused attention, read music, memorize lengthy musical passages, understand diverse musical structures, and master technical skills. These experiences might foster cognitive processing, particularly during childhood, when regions of the brain are taking on specialized functions and are highly plastic—sensitive to environmental influences.

Schellenberg recruited 132 6-year-olds—children just old enough for formal lessons. First, the children took an intelligence test and were rated on social maturity, permitting the researchers to see whether music lessons would affect one aspect of development but not the others. Next, the children were randomly assigned to one of four experimental conditions. Two were music groups; one received piano lessons and the other voice lessons. The third group took drama lessons—a condition that shed light on whether intellectual gains were unique to musical experiences. The fourth group—a no-lessons control—was offered music lessons the following year. Music and drama instruction took place at the prestigious Royal Conservatory of Music in Toronto, where experienced teachers taught the children in small groups. After 36 weeks of lessons, a longitudinal follow-up was conducted: The children's intelligence and social maturity were assessed again.

All four groups showed gains in mental test performance, probably because the participants had just entered grade school, which usually leads to an

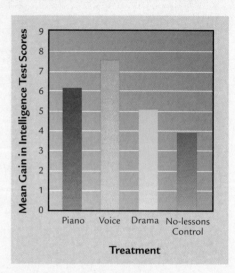

■ **FIGURE 1.8 Music lessons promote gains in intelligence.** In a study that combined experimental and longitudinal research strategies, children's mental test performance was tracked longitudinally, before and after they experienced one of four conditions: (1) piano lessons, (2) voice lessons, (3) drama lessons, and (4) no lessons. Children in the two groups receiving music lessons showed greater gains in test scores.

increase in intelligence test scores. But the two music groups consistently gained more than the drama and no-lessons groups (see Figure 1.8). Their advantage, though just a few points, extended across many mental abilities, including verbal and spatial skills and speed of thinking. At the same time, only the drama group improved in social maturity.

In sum, active, sustained musical experiences can lead to small increases in intelligence among 6-year-olds that do not arise from comparable drama lessons. But other enrichment activities with similar properties, such as reading, science, math, and chess programs, may confer similar benefits. All demand that children invest far more time and effort than they would in listening to a Mozart sonata. Nevertheless—despite the absence of evidence to support these claims—music companies persist in selling CDs entitled, "Tune Your Brain with Mozart," "Music for Accelerating Learning," and "Mozart for Newborns: A Bright Beginning."

Ethics in Lifespan Research

Research into human behavior creates ethical issues because, unfortunately, the quest for scientific knowledge can sometimes exploit people. For this reason, special guidelines for research have been developed by the federal government, by funding agencies, and by research-oriented associations, such as the American Psychological Association (2002), the Canadian Psychological Association (2000), and the Society for Research in Child Development (1993). Table 1.8 presents a summary of basic research rights drawn from these guidelines. After examining them, read about the following research situations, each of which poses a serious ethical dilemma. What precautions do you think should be taken in each instance?

◢ In a study of moral development, an investigator wants to assess children's ability to resist temptation by videotaping their behavior without their knowledge. She promises 7-year-olds a prize for solving difficult puzzles but tells them not to look at a classmate's correct solutions, which are deliberately placed at the back of the room. Informing children ahead of time that cheating is being studied or that their behavior is being monitored will destroy the purpose of the study.

◢ A researcher wants to study the impact of mild daily exercise on the physical and mental health of elderly patients in nursing homes. He consults each resident's doctor to make sure that the exercise routine will not be harmful. But when he seeks the residents' consent, he finds that many do not comprehend the purpose of the research. And some appear to agree simply to relieve feelings of isolation and loneliness.

As these examples indicate, when children or the aged take part in research, the ethical concerns are especially complex. Immaturity makes it difficult or impossible for children to evaluate for themselves what participation in research will mean. And because mental impairment rises with very advanced age, some older adults cannot make voluntary and informed choices. The life circumstances of others make them unusually vulnerable to pressure for participation (Kim et al., 2004; Society for Research in Child Development, 1993).

Virtually every organization that has devised ethical principles for research has concluded that conflicts arising in research situations often cannot be resolved with simple right-or-wrong answers. The ultimate responsibility for the ethical integrity of research lies with the investigator. However, researchers are advised—and usually required—to seek advice from others. Colleges, universities, and other institutions have special committees for this purpose. These *institutional review*

Table 1.8	Rights of Research Participants
Research Right	**Description**
Protection from harm	Participants have the right to be protected from physical or psychological harm in research. If in doubt about the harmful effects of research, investigators should seek the opinion of others. When harm seems possible, investigators should find other means for obtaining the desired information or abandon the research.
Informed consent	All participants, including children and the elderly, have the right to have explained to them, in language appropriate to their level of understanding, all aspects of the research that may affect their willingness to participate. When children are participants, informed consent of parents as well as of others who act on the child's behalf (such as school officials) should be obtained, preferably in writing. Older adults who are cognitively impaired should be asked to appoint a surrogate decision maker. If they cannot do so, then someone should be named by an institutional review board (IRB) after careful consultation with relatives and professionals who know the person well. All participants have the right to discontinue participation in the research at any time.
Privacy	Participants have the right to concealment of their identity on all information collected in the course of research. They also have this right with respect to written reports and any informal discussions about the research.
Knowledge of results	Participants have the right to be informed of the results of research in language that is appropriate to their level of understanding.
Beneficial treatments	If experimental treatments believed to be beneficial are under investigation, participants in control groups have the right to alternative beneficial treatments if they are available.

Sources: American Psychological Association, 2002; Canadian Psychological Association, 2000; Society for Research in Child Development, 1993.

boards (IRBs) weigh the costs of the research to participants in terms of inconvenience and possible psychological or physical injury against the study's value for advancing knowledge and improving conditions of life. If there are any risks to participants' safety and welfare that the research does not justify, then preference is always given to the participants' interests.

The ethical principle of *informed consent* requires special interpretation when participants cannot fully appreciate the research goals and activities. Parental consent is meant to protect the safety of children, whose ability to decide is not yet mature. By age 7, children's own informed consent should be obtained in addition to parental consent. Around this age,

© DAVID YOUNG-WOLFF/GETTY IMAGES

Older adults should not be arbitrarily excluded from research. Most require only the typical informed-consent procedures, and their participation brings both personal and scientific benefits. For elders who are cognitively impaired—like this man with Alzheimer's disease—informed consent may not be possible without the assistance of a surrogate decision maker.

changes in children's thinking permit them to better understand simple scientific principles and the needs of others. Researchers should respect and enhance these new capacities by giving school-age children a full explanation of research activities in language they can understand (Fisher, 1993). Extra care must be taken when telling children that the information they provide will be kept confidential and that they can end their participation at any time. Even adolescents may not understand, and sometimes do not believe, these promises (Bruzzese & Fisher, 2003; Ondrusek et al., 1998).

Most older adults require no more than the usual informed-consent procedures. Yet many investigators set upper age limits in studies relevant to the elderly, thereby excluding the oldest adults (Bayer & Tadd, 2000). The elderly should not be stereotyped as incompetent to decide about their own participation or to engage in research activities. Nevertheless, extra measures must be taken to protect those who are cognitively impaired or who reside in settings for the chronically ill. As noted, some individuals may agree to participate simply to engage in rewarding social interaction. Yet participation should not be automatically withheld, since it can result in personal as well as scientific benefits. In these instances, potential participants should be asked to appoint a surrogate decision maker. If they cannot do so, then someone should be named by an IRB after careful consultation with relatives and professionals who know the person well. As an added precaution, if the elderly person is incapable of consenting and the risks of the research are more than minimal, then the study should not be done unless it is likely to directly benefit the participant (Kim et al., 2004).

Finally, all ethical guidelines advise that special precautions be taken in the use of deception and concealment, as occurs when researchers observe people from behind one-way mirrors, give them false feedback about their performance, or do not tell them the truth regarding what the research is about. When these kinds of procedures are used, *debriefing,* in which the investigator provides a full account and justification of the activities, occurs after the research session is over. Debriefing should also be done with children, but it rarely works well. Despite explanations, children may leave the research situation with their belief in the honesty of adults undermined. Ethical standards permit deception if investigators satisfy institutional committees that such practices are necessary. Nevertheless, because deception may have serious emotional consequences for some youngsters, investigators should try to come up with other research strategies when children are involved.

Summary

Human Development as a Scientific, Applied, and Interdisciplinary Field

What is human development, and what factors stimulated expansion of the field?

■ **Human development** is an interdisciplinary field devoted to understanding human constancy and change throughout the lifespan. Research on human development has been stimulated by both scientific curiosity and social pressures to improve people's lives.

Basic Issues

Identify three basic issues on which theories of human development take a stand.

■ Each **theory** of human development takes a stand on three basic issues: (1) Is development a **continuous** process, or does it proceed in a series of **discontinuous stages**? (2) Does one general course of development characterize all individuals, or do many possible courses exist, depending on children's and adult's **contexts**? (3) Is development determined primarily by **nature** or by **nurture,** and is it stable or open to change?

The Lifespan Perspective: A Balanced Point of View

Describe the lifespan perspective on development.

■ The **lifespan perspective** is a balanced view that recognizes great complexity in human change and the factors that underlie it. In this view, development is lifelong, multidimensional (affected by biological, psychological, and social forces), multidirectional (a joint expression of growth and decline), and plastic (open to change through new experiences), as research on **resilience** illustrates.

■ Furthermore, the lifespan perspective regards the life course as influenced by multiple, interacting forces that can be organized into three categories: (1) **age-graded influences** that are predictable in timing and duration; (2) **history-graded influences,** unique to a particular historical era; and (3) **nonnormative influences,** which are unique to one or a few individuals.

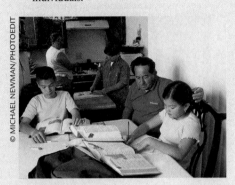

© MICHAEL NEWMAN/PHOTOEDIT

Historical Foundations

Describe major historical influences on theories of development.

■ Contemporary theories of human development have roots in the distant past. As early as medieval Europe, childhood was viewed as a distinct phase of life, separate from adulthood. The sixteenth-century Puritan belief in original sin led to a harsh philosophy of child rearing, but in the seventeenth century, the ideas of the Enlightenment promoted more humane child treatment.

■ Locke's view of the child as a **tabula rasa** ("blank slate") formed the basis of twentieth-century behaviorism, while Rousseau's idea of children as **noble savages** foreshadowed the concepts of stage and **maturation.**

■ In the eighteenth and early nineteenth centuries, German philosophers Tetens and Carus extended conceptions of development through adulthood, anticipating many aspects of today's lifespan perspective.

■ Darwin's theory of evolution influenced important modern theories and inspired scientific child study. In the early twentieth century, Hall and Gesell introduced the **normative approach,** which produced a large body of descriptive facts about development. Binet and Simon constructed the first successful intelligence test, initiating the mental testing movement.

Mid-Twentieth-Century Theories

What theories influenced human development research in the mid-twentieth century?

■ In the 1930s and 1940s, psychiatrists and social workers turned to the **psychoanalytic perspective** for help in treating people's emotional problems. In Freud's **psychosexual theory,** the individual moves through five stages, during which three portions of the personality—id, ego, and superego—become integrated. Erikson's **psychosocial theory** expands Freud's theory by emphasizing the development of culturally relevant attitudes and skills and the lifespan nature of development.

■ As psychoanalytic theory gained in prominence, **behaviorism** and **social learning theory** emerged, emphasizing principles of conditioning and modeling and practical procedures of **behavior modification** to eliminate undesirable behaviors and increase desirable responses.

■ In contrast to behaviorism, Piaget's **cognitive-developmental theory** emphasizes an active individual whose mind consists of rich structures of knowledge. According to Piaget, children move through four stages, from the baby's sensorimotor action patterns to the elaborate, abstract reasoning system of the adolescent. Although some of Piaget's conclusions have been challenged, his work has had an overwhelming impact, stimulating a wealth of research on children's thinking and encouraging educational philosophies and programs that emphasize discovery learning.

Recent Theoretical Perspectives

Describe recent theoretical perspectives on human development.

■ **Information processing** views the mind as a complex, symbol-manipulating system much like a computer and views development as a matter of continuous change. This approach helps investigators achieve a detailed understanding of what individuals of different ages do when faced with tasks and problems. Its findings have important implications for education.

■ Over the past two decades, researchers in **developmental cognitive neuroscience,** who study the relationship between changes in the brain and the development of cognitive processing and behavior patterns, have made progress in identifying the types of experiences to which the brain is sensitive at various ages.

■ Three contemporary perspectives emphasize contexts of development. **Ethology,** which stresses the evolutionary origins and adaptive value of behavior, inspired the **sensitive period** concept. In **evolutionary developmental psychology,** researchers have extended this emphasis, seeking to understand the adaptiveness of specieswide competencies as they change over time.

■ Vygotsky's **sociocultural theory** has enhanced our understanding of cultural influences, especially in the area of cognitive development. Through cooperative dialogues with more expert members of society, children come to use language to guide their own thought and actions and acquire culturally relevant knowledge and skills.

■ In **ecological systems theory,** nested layers of the environment—**microsystem, mesosystem, exosystem,** and **macrosystem**—are seen as major influences on the developing person. The **chronosystem** represents the dynamic, ever-changing nature of individuals and their experiences.

Comparing and Evaluating Theories

Identify the stand taken by each major theory on the three basic issues of human development.

■ Theories vary in their focus on different domains of development, in their view of development, and in their strengths and limitations. (For a full summary, see Table 1.5 on page 26.)

Studying Development

Describe methods commonly used in research on human development.

■ **Naturalistic observations,** gathered in everyday environments, permit researchers to see directly the everyday behaviors they hope to explain. In contrast, **structured observations** take place in laboratories, where every participant has an equal opportunity to display the behaviors of interest.

■ Self-report methods can be flexible and open-ended, as in the **clinical interview.** Alternative methods include **structured interviews,** tests, and questionnaires, which permit efficient administration and scoring. Investigators use the **clinical,** or **case study, method** to gain an in-depth understanding of a single individual.

■ A growing interest in the impact of culture has prompted researchers to adapt observational and self-report methods to permit cultural comparisons. **Ethnography,** a method borrowed from the field of anthropology, uses participant observation to understand the unique values and social processes of a culture or distinct social group.

Distinguish correlational and experimental research designs, noting the strengths and limitations of each.

■ The **correlational design** examines relationships between variables as they occur, without altering people's experiences. The **correlation coefficient** is often used to measure the association between variables. Correlational studies do not permit inferences about cause and effect. Their use is justified when it is difficult or impossible to control the variables of interest.

■ An **experimental design** permits inferences about cause and effect. Researchers manipulate an **independent variable** by exposing participants to two or more treatment conditions. Then they determine what effect this variable has on a **dependent variable.** **Random assignment** reduces the chances that participant characteristics will affect the accuracy of experimental findings.

■ To achieve high degrees of control, most experiments are conducted in laboratories, but their findings may not apply to everyday life. Field and natural experiments compare treatments in natural environments. These approaches, however, are less rigorous than laboratory experiments.

Describe designs for studying development, noting the strengths and limitations of each.

■ The **longitudinal design** permits study of common patterns as well as individual differences in development and of the relationship between early and later events and behaviors. Longitudinal research poses several problems for researchers, including biased samples, participant dropout, practice effects, and **cohort effects**—difficulty generalizing to people developing in other historical times.

■ The **cross-sectional design** is an efficient way to study development, but it is limited to comparisons of age-group averages. Findings of cross-sectional studies also can be distorted by cohort effects, especially when they cover a wide age span.

■ To overcome some of the limitations of these designs, investigators sometimes combine the two approaches. The **sequential design,** in which researchers conduct several similar cross-sectional or longitudinal studies at varying times, permits investigators to test for cohort effects and to compare longitudinal and cross-sectional findings. When researchers combine experimental and developmental designs, they can examine causal influences on development.

Ethics in Lifespan Research

What special ethical concerns arise in research on human development?

■ Research creates ethical issues, since the quest for scientific knowledge has the potential to exploit people. The ethical principle of informed consent requires special safeguards for children and for elderly people who are cognitively impaired or who live in settings for the care of the chronically ill. The use of deception in research with children is especially risky because it may undermine their basic faith in the trustworthiness of adults.

Important Terms and Concepts

age-graded influences (p. 10)
behavior modification (p. 18)
behaviorism (p. 17)
chronosystem (p. 25)
clinical interview (p. 28)
clinical, or case study, method (p. 29)
cognitive-developmental theory (p. 19)
cohort effects (p. 35)
contexts (p. 7)
continuous development (p. 6)
correlation coefficient (p. 32)
correlational design (p. 30)
cross-sectional design (p. 35)
dependent variable (p. 32)
developmental cognitive neuroscience
    (p. 21)
discontinuous development (p. 6)
ecological systems theory (p. 24)

ethnography (p. 30)
ethology (p. 22)
evolutionary developmental psychology
    (p. 22)
exosystem (p. 25)
experimental design (p. 32)
history-graded influences (p. 11)
human development (p. 5)
independent variable (p. 32)
information processing (p. 20)
lifespan perspective (p. 8)
longitudinal design (p. 33)
macrosystem (p. 25)
maturation (p. 13)
mesosystem (p. 24)
microsystem (p. 24)
naturalistic observation (p. 27)
nature–nurture controversy (p. 7)

noble savage (p. 13)
nonnormative influences (p. 11)
normative approach (p. 14)
psychoanalytic perspective (p. 15)
psychosexual theory (p. 15)
psychosocial theory (p. 15)
random assignment (p. 33)
resilience (p. 10)
sensitive period (p. 22)
sequential design (p. 35)
social learning theory (p. 18)
sociocultural theory (p. 23)
stage (p. 6)
structured interview (p. 29)
structured observation (p. 27)
tabula rasa (p. 13)
theory (p. 5)

*E*ach new individual is the product of a complex blend of genetic and environmental influences. This toddler resembles her parents and grandparents in some physical characteristics and behaviors while differing from them in others.

Biological and Environmental Foundations

"*I*t's a girl!" announces the doctor, holding up the squalling little creature as her parents gaze with amazement at their miraculous creation.

"A girl! We've named her Sarah!" exclaims the proud father to eager relatives waiting for news of their new family member.

As we join these parents in thinking about how this wondrous being came into existence and imagining her future, we are struck by many questions. How could this baby, equipped with everything necessary for life outside the womb, have developed from the union of two tiny cells? What ensures that Sarah will, in due time, roll over, reach for objects, walk, talk, make friends, learn, imagine, and create—just like other typical children born before her? Why is she a girl and not a boy, dark-haired rather than blond, calm and cuddly instead of wiry and energetic? What difference will it make that Sarah is given a name and place in one family, community, nation, and culture rather than another?

© RUBBERBALL PRODUCTIONS/JUPITERIMAGES

To answer these questions, this chapter takes a close look at the foundations of development: heredity and environment. Because nature has prepared us for survival, all humans have features in common. Yet each of us is also unique. Jot down the most obvious physical and behavioral similarities and differences for several of your friends and their parents. Did you find that one person shows combined features of both parents, another resembles just one parent, whereas a third is not like either parent? These directly observable characteristics are called **phenotypes**. They depend in part on the individual's **genotype**—the complex blend of genetic information that determines our species and influences all our unique characteristics. Yet phenotypes are also affected by each person's lifelong history of experiences.

We begin our discussion at the moment of conception, an event that establishes the hereditary makeup of the new individual. First we review basic genetic principles that help explain similarities and differences among us in appearance and behavior. Then we turn to aspects of the environment that play powerful roles throughout the lifespan. Finally, we consider the question of how nature and nurture *work together* to shape the course of development.

Genetic Foundations

Each of us is made up of trillions of separate units called *cells*. Inside each cell (except red blood cells) is a control center, or *nucleus*, that contains rodlike structures called **chromosomes**, which store and transmit genetic information. Human chromosomes come in 23 matching pairs (an exception is the XY pair in males, which we will discuss shortly). Each pair member corresponds to the other in size, shape, and genetic functions. One is inherited from the mother and one from the father (see Figure 2.1).

The Genetic Code

Chromosomes are made up of a chemical substance called **deoxyribonucleic acid**, or **DNA**. As Figure 2.2 shows, DNA is a long, double-stranded molecule that looks like a twisted ladder. Each rung of the ladder consists of a specific pair of chemical substances called *bases*, joined together between the two sides. It is this sequence of bases that provides genetic instructions. A **gene** is a segment of DNA along the length of the chromosome. Genes can be of different lengths—perhaps 100 to several thousand ladder rungs long. An estimated 20,000 to 25,000 genes lie along the human chromosomes (International Human Genome Sequencing Consortium, 2004).

We share some of our genetic makeup with even the simplest organisms, such as bacteria and molds, and most of it with other mammals, especially primates. Between 98 and 99 percent of chimpanzee and human DNA is identical. This means that only a small portion of our heredity is responsible for the traits that make us human, from our upright gait to our extraordinary language and cognitive capacities. And overall variation in DNA sequences from one human to the next is even less (Gibbons et al., 2004; Human Genome Program, 2004). But it takes a change in only a single base pair to influence human traits and capacities. And such tiny changes can combine in unique ways across multiple genes, thereby amplifying variability within the human species (National Center for Biotechnology Information, 2004).

A unique feature of DNA is that it can duplicate itself through a process called **mitosis**. This special ability permits the one-celled fertilized ovum to develop into a complex human being composed of a great many cells. Refer again to Figure 2.2 and you will see that during mitosis, the chromosomes copy themselves. As a result, each new body cell contains the same number of chromosomes and identical genetic information.

Genes accomplish their task by sending instructions for making a rich assortment of proteins to the *cytoplasm*, the area surrounding the cell nucleus. Proteins, which trigger chemical reactions throughout the body, are the biological foundation on which our characteristics are built. How do humans, with far fewer genes than scientists once thought (only twice as many as the worm or fly), manage to develop into such complex beings? The answer lies in the proteins our genes make, which break up and reassemble in staggering variety—about 10 to 20 million altogether. Simpler species have far fewer proteins. Furthermore, the communication system between the cell nucleus and cytoplasm, which fine-tunes gene activity, is more intricate in humans than in simpler organisms. Within the cell, a wide range of environmental factors modify gene expression (Strachan & Read, 2004). So even at this microscopic level, biological events are the result of *both* genetic and nongenetic forces.

The Sex Cells

New individuals are created when two special cells called **gametes**, or sex cells—the sperm and ovum—combine. A gamete contains only 23 chromosomes, half as many as a regular body cell. Gametes are formed through a cell division process called **meiosis**, which halves the number of chromosomes normally present in body cells. When sperm and ovum unite at conception, the cell that results, called a **zygote**, will again have 46 chromosomes. Meiosis ensures that a constant

■ **FIGURE 2.1 A karyotype, or photograph, of human chromosomes.** The 46 chromosomes shown on the left were isolated from a body cell (shown on the right), stained, greatly magnified, and arranged in pairs according to decreasing size of the upper "arm" of each chromosome. Note the twenty-third pair, XY. The cell donor is a male. In a female, the twenty-third pair would be XX. (© CNRI/Science Photo Library/Photo Researchers)

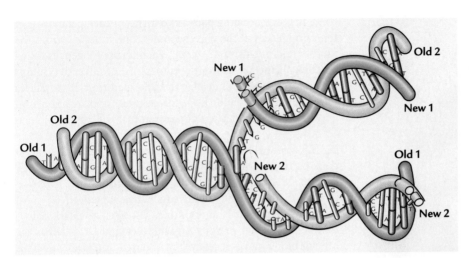

■ **FIGURE 2.2 DNA's ladderlike structure.** This figure shows that the pairings of bases across the rungs of the ladder are very specific: Adenine (A) always appears with thymine (T), and cytosine (C) always appears with guanine (G). Here, the DNA ladder duplicates by splitting down the middle of its ladder rungs. Each free base picks up a new complementary partner from the area surrounding the cell nucleus.

quantity of genetic material is transmitted from one generation to the next.

In *meiosis,* the chromosomes pair up and exchange segments, so that genes from one are replaced by genes from another. Then chance determines which member of each pair will gather with others and end up in the same gamete. These events make the likelihood extremely low—about 1 in 700 trillion—that nontwin siblings will be genetically identical (Gould & Keeton, 1996). Thus, meiosis contributes to genetic variability, which is adaptive: It increases the chances that at least some members of a species will cope with ever-changing environments and survive.

In the male, four sperm are produced when meiosis is complete. Also, the cells from which sperm arise are produced continuously throughout life. For this reason, a healthy man can father a child at any age after sexual maturity. In the female, meiosis results in just one ovum. In addition, the female is born with all her ova already present in her ovaries, and she can bear children for only three to four decades. Still, there are plenty of female sex cells. About 1 to 2 million are present at birth, 40,000 remain at adolescence, and approximately 350 to 450 will mature during a woman's childbearing years (Moore & Persaud, 2003).

Boy or Girl?

Return to Figure 2.1 and note that 22 of the 23 pairs of chromosomes are matching pairs, called **autosomes.** The twenty-third pair consists of **sex chromosomes.** In females, this pair is called XX; in males, it is called XY. The X is a relatively large chromosome, whereas the Y is short and carries little genetic material. When gametes form in males, the X and Y chromosomes separate into different sperm cells. The gametes that form in females all carry an X chromosome. Therefore, the sex of the new organism is determined by whether an X-bearing or a Y-bearing sperm fertilizes the ovum.

Multiple Births

Ruth and Peter, a couple I know well, tried for several years to have a child, without success. When Ruth reached age 33, her

doctor prescribed a fertility drug, and twins—Jeannie and Jason—were born. Jeannie and Jason are **fraternal,** or **dizygotic, twins,** the most common type of multiple birth, resulting from the release and fertilization of two ova. Therefore, Jeannie and Jason are genetically no more alike than ordinary siblings. Older maternal age, fertility drugs, and in vitro fertilization (to be discussed shortly) are major causes of the doubling of fraternal twinning and the even greater rise in other multiple births in North America since 1970 (Russell et al., 2003; SOGC, 2005). As Table 2.1 shows, other genetic and environmental factors are also involved.

Table 2.1	Maternal Factors Linked to Fraternal Twinning
Factor	**Description**
Ethnicity	Occurs in 4 per 1,000 births among Asians, 8 per 1,000 births among whites, 12 to 16 per 1,000 births among blacks[a]
Family history of twinning	Occurs more often among women whose mothers and sisters gave birth to fraternal twins
Age	Rises with maternal age, peaking between 35 and 39 years, and then rapidly falls
Nutrition	Occurs less often among women with poor diets; occurs more often among women who are tall and overweight or of normal weight as opposed to slight body build
Number of births	Is more likely with each additional birth
Fertility drugs and in vitro fertilization	Is more likely with fertility hormones and in vitro fertilization (see page 54), which also increase the chances of triplets to quintuplets

[a]Worldwide rates, not including multiple births resulting from use of fertility drugs.

Sources: Bortolus et al., 1999; Mange & Mange, 1998.

These identical, or monozygotic, twins were created when a duplicating zygote separated into two clusters of cells, and two individuals with the same genetic makeup developed. Identical twins not only look alike but also resemble each other in a variety of psychological characteristics.

Twins can be created in another way. Sometimes a zygote that has started to duplicate separates into two clusters of cells that develop into two individuals. These are called **identical**, or **monozygotic, twins** because they have the same genetic makeup. The frequency of identical twins is the same around the world—about 1 in every 285 births (Zach, Pramanik, & Ford, 2001). Animal research has uncovered a variety of environmental influences that prompt this type of twinning, including temperature changes, variation in oxygen levels, and late fertilization of the ovum.

In infancy and early childhood, children of single births are often healthier and develop more rapidly than twins (Mogford-Bevan, 1999). Jeannie and Jason, like most twins, were born early—three weeks before Ruth's due date. And, like other premature infants—as you will see in Chapter 3—they required special care after birth. When the twins came home from the hospital, Ruth and Peter had to divide time between them. Perhaps because neither baby received as much attention as the average single infant, Jeannie and Jason walked and talked several months later than most other children their age, although both caught up by middle childhood (Lytton & Gallagher, 2002). Parental energies are further strained after the birth of triplets, whose early development is slower than that of twins (Feldman, Eidelman, & Rotenberg, 2004).

Patterns of Genetic Inheritance

Jeannie has her parents' dark, straight hair; Jason is curly-haired and blond. Patterns of genetic inheritance—the way genes from each parent interact—explain these outcomes. Recall that, except for the XY pair in males, all chromosomes

come in corresponding pairs. Two forms of each gene occur at the same place on the chromosomes, one inherited from the mother and one from the father. Each form of a gene is called an **allele**. If the alleles from both parents are alike, the child is **homozygous** and will display the inherited trait. If the alleles differ, then the child is **heterozygous**, and relationships between the alleles determine the trait that will appear.

■ **Dominant–Recessive Inheritance.** In many heterozygous pairings, **dominant–recessive inheritance** occurs: Only one allele affects the child's characteristics. It is called *dominant*; the second allele, which has no effect, is called *recessive*. Hair color is an example. The allele for dark hair is dominant (we can represent it with a capital *D*), whereas the one for blond hair is recessive (symbolized by a lowercase *b*). A child who inherits a homozygous pair of dominant alleles *(DD)* and a child who inherits a heterozygous pair *(Db)* will both be dark-haired, even though their genotypes differ. Blond hair (like Jason's) can result only from having two recessive alleles *(bb)*. Still, heterozygous individuals with just one recessive allele *(Db)* can pass that trait to their children. Therefore, they are called **carriers** of the trait.

Some human characteristics that follow the rules of dominant–recessive inheritance are listed in Tables 2.2 and 2.3. As you can see, many disabilities and diseases are the product

Table 2.2	Examples of Dominant and Recessive Characteristics

Dominant	Recessive
Dark hair	Blond hair
Normal hair	Pattern baldness
Curly hair	Straight hair
Nonred hair	Red hair
Facial dimples	No dimples
Normal hearing	Some forms of deafness
Normal vision	Nearsightedness
Farsightedness	Normal vision
Normal vision	Congenital eye cataracts
Normally pigmented skin	Albinism
Double-jointedness	Normal joints
Type A blood	Type O blood
Type B blood	Type O blood
Rh-positive blood	Rh-negative blood

Note: Many normal characteristics that were previously thought to result from dominant–recessive inheritance, such as eye color, are now regarded as due to multiple genes. For the characteristics listed here, most experts agree that the simple dominant–recessive relationship holds.

Source: McKusick, 2002.

Table 2.3	Examples of Dominant and Recessive Diseases

Disease	Description	Mode of Inheritance	Incidence	Treatment
Autosomal Diseases				
Cooley's anemia	Pale appearance, retarded physical growth, and lethargic behavior begin in infancy.	Recessive	1 in 500 births to parents of Mediterranean descent	Frequent blood transfusion; death from complications usually occurs by adolescence.
Cystic fibrosis	Lungs, liver, and pancreas secrete large amounts of thick mucus, leading to breathing and digestive difficulties.	Recessive	1 in 2,000 to 2,500 Caucasian births; 1 in 16,000 births to North Americans of African descent	Bronchial drainage, prompt treatment of respiratory infection, dietary management. Advances in medical care allow survival with good life quality into middle adulthood.
Phenylketonuria (PKU)	Inability to metabolize the amino acid phenylalanine, contained in many proteins, causes severe central nervous system damage in the first year of life.	Recessive	1 in 8,000 births	Placing the child on a special diet results in average intelligence and normal lifespan. Subtle difficulties with planning and problem solving are often present.
Sickle cell anemia	Abnormal sickling of red blood cells causes oxygen deprivation, pain, swelling, and tissue damage. Anemia and susceptibility to infections, especially pneumonia, occur.	Recessive	1 in 600 births to North Americans of African descent	Blood transfusions, painkillers, prompt treatment of infection. No known cure; 50 percent die by age 20.
Tay-Sachs disease	Central nervous system degeneration, with onset at about 6 months, leads to poor muscle tone, blindness, deafness, and convulsions.	Recessive	1 in 3,600 births to Jews of European descent and to French Canadians	None; death occurs by 3 to 4 years of age.
Huntington disease	Central nervous system degeneration leads to muscular coordination difficulties, mental deterioration, and personality changes. Symptoms usually do not appear until age 35 or later.	Dominant	1 in 18,000 to 25,000 births	None; death occurs 10 to 20 years after symptom onset.
Marfan syndrome	Symptoms include a tall, slender build; thin, elongated arms and legs; and heart defects and eye abnormalities, especially of the lens. Excessive lengthening of the body results in a variety of skeletal defects.	Dominant	1 in 20,000 births	Correction of heart and eye defects is sometimes possible. Death from heart failure in young adulthood is common.
X-Linked Diseases				
Duchenne muscular dystrophy	This degenerative muscle disease causes abnormal gait, with loss of ability to walk between 7 and 13 years of age.	Recessive	1 in 3,000 to 5,000 male births	None; death from respiratory infection or weakening of the heart muscle usually occurs in adolescence.
Hemophilia	Blood fails to clot normally; can lead to severe internal bleeding and tissue damage.	Recessive	1 in 4,000 to 7,000 male births	Blood transfusions. Safety precautions may prevent injury.
Diabetes insipidus	Insufficient production of the hormone vasopressin results in excessive thirst and urination. Dehydration can cause central nervous system damage.	Recessive	1 in 2,500 male births	Hormone replacement.

Note: For recessive disorders listed, carrier status can be detected in prospective parents through a blood test or genetic analyses. For all disorders listed, prenatal diagnosis is available (see page 56).

Sources: Behrman, Kliegman, & Arvin, 1996; Chodirker et al., 2001; Gott, 1998; Grody, 1999; Knoers et al., 1993; McKusick, 2002; Schulman & Black, 1997.

of recessive alleles. One of the most frequently occurring recessive disorders is *phenylketonuria*, or *PKU*, which affects the way the body breaks down proteins contained in many foods. Infants born with two recessive alleles lack an enzyme that converts one of the basic amino acids that make up proteins (phenylalanine) into a byproduct essential for body functioning (tyrosine). Without this enzyme, phenylalanine quickly builds to toxic levels that damage the central nervous system. By 1 year, infants with PKU are permanently mentally retarded.

Despite its potentially damaging effects, PKU provides an excellent illustration of the fact that inheriting unfavorable genes does not always lead to an untreatable condition. All U.S. states and Canadian provinces require that each newborn be given a blood test for PKU. If the disease is found, doctors place the baby on a diet low in phenylalanine. Children who receive this treatment nevertheless show mild deficits in certain cognitive skills, such as memory, planning, and problem solving, because even small amounts of phenylalanine interfere with brain functioning (Antshel, 2003; Luciana, Sullivan, & Nelson, 2001). But as long as dietary treatment begins early and continues, children with PKU usually attain an average level of intelligence and have a normal lifespan.

In dominant–recessive inheritance, if we know the genetic makeup of the parents, we can predict the percentage of children in a family who are likely to display or carry a trait. Figure 2.3 illustrates this for PKU. Notice that for a child to inherit the condition, each parent must have a recessive allele.

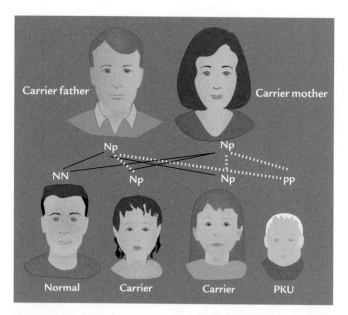

■ **FIGURE 2.3 Dominant–recessive mode of inheritance, as illustrated by PKU.** When both parents are heterozygous carriers of the recessive gene (p), we can predict that 25 percent of their offspring are likely to be normal (NN), 50 percent are likely to be carriers (Np), and 25 percent are likely to inherit the disorder (pp). Notice that the PKU-affected child, in contrast to his siblings, has light hair. The recessive gene for PKU affects more than one trait. It also leads to fair coloring.

Only rarely are serious diseases due to dominant alleles. Think about why this is so. Children who inherit the dominant allele always develop the disorder. They seldom live long enough to reproduce, so the harmful dominant allele is eliminated from the family's heredity in a single generation. Some dominant disorders, however, do persist. One of them is *Huntington disease*, a condition in which the central nervous system degenerates. Why has this disorder endured? Its symptoms usually do not appear until age 35 or later, after the person has passed on the dominant gene to his or her children.

■ **Incomplete dominance.** In some heterozygous circumstances, the dominant–recessive relationship does not hold completely. Instead, we see **incomplete dominance**, a pattern of inheritance in which both alleles are expressed, resulting in a combined trait, or one that is intermediate between the two.

The *sickle cell trait,* a heterozygous condition present in many black Africans, provides an example. *Sickle cell anemia* (see Table 2.3) occurs in full form when a child inherits two recessive genes. They cause the usually round red blood cells to become sickle (crescent-moon) shaped, especially under low-oxygen conditions. The sickled cells clog the blood vessels and block the flow of blood, causing intense pain, swelling, and tissue damage. Despite medical advances that today allow 85 percent of affected children to survive to adulthood, North Americans with sickle cell anemia have an average life expectancy of only 55 years (Quinn, Rogers, & Buchanan, 2004; Wierenga, Hambleton, & Lewis, 2001). Heterozygous individuals are protected from the disease under most circumstances. However, when they experience oxygen deprivation—for example, at high altitudes or after intense physical exercise—the single recessive allele asserts itself, and a temporary, mild form of the illness occurs.

The sickle cell allele is common among black Africans for a special reason. Carriers of it are more resistant to malaria than are individuals with two alleles for normal red blood cells. In Africa, where malaria is common, these carriers survived and reproduced more frequently than others, leading the gene to be maintained in the black population.

■ **X-Linked Inheritance.** Males and females have an equal chance of inheriting recessive disorders carried on the autosomes, such as PKU and sickle cell anemia. But when a harmful allele is carried on the X chromosome, **X-linked inheritance** applies. Males are more likely to be affected because their sex chromosomes do not match. In females, any recessive allele on one X chromosome has a good chance of being suppressed by a dominant allele on the other X. But the Y chromosome is only about one-third as long and therefore lacks many corresponding genes to override those on the X. A well-known example is *hemophilia*, a disorder in which the blood fails to clot normally. Figure 2.4 shows its greater likelihood of inheritance by male children whose mothers carry the abnormal allele.

Besides X-linked disorders, many sex differences reveal the male to be at a disadvantage. Rates of miscarriage, infant and

FIGURE 2.4 X-linked inheritance. In the example shown here, the allele on the father's X chromosome is normal. The mother has one normal and one abnormal recessive allele on her X chromosomes. By looking at the possible combinations of the parents' alleles, we can predict that 50 percent of these parents' male children are likely to have the disorder and 50 percent of their female children are likely to be carriers of it.

childhood deaths, birth defects, learning disabilities, behavior disorders, and mental retardation all are higher for boys (Halpern, 1997). It is possible that these sex differences can be traced to the genetic code. The female, with two X chromosomes, benefits from a greater variety of genes. Nature, however, seems to have adjusted for the male's disadvantage. Worldwide, about 105 boys are born for every 100 girls, and judging from miscarriage and abortion statistics, an even greater number of males are conceived (Pyeritz, 1998).

Nevertheless, in recent decades the proportion of male births has declined in many industrialized countries, including the United States, Canada, and European nations (Jongbloet et al., 2001). Some researchers attribute the trend to a rise in stressful living conditions, which heighten spontaneous abortions, especially of male fetuses. In one test of this hypothesis, male-to-female birth ratios in East Germany were examined between 1946 and 1999. The ratio was lowest in 1991, the year that the country's economy collapsed (Catalano, 2003).

■ **Genetic Imprinting.** More than 1,000 human characteristics follow the rules of dominant–recessive and incomplete-dominance inheritance (McKusick, 2002). In these cases, whichever parent contributes a gene to the new individual, the gene responds in the same way. Geneticists, however, have identified some exceptions. In **genetic imprinting**, alleles are *imprinted*, or chemically *marked*, in such a way that one member of the pair (either the mother's or the father's) is activated, regardless of its makeup. The imprint is often temporary; it

may be erased in the next generation, and it may not occur in all individuals (Everman & Cassidy, 2000).

Imprinting helps us understand certain puzzling genetic patterns. For example, children are more likely to develop diabetes if their father, rather than their mother, suffers from it. And people with asthma or hay fever tend to have mothers, not fathers, with the illness. Imprinting is involved in several childhood cancers. And it may explain why Huntington disease, when inherited from the father, tends to emerge at an earlier age and to progress more rapidly (Navarrete, Martinez, & Salamanca, 1994).

Genetic imprinting can also operate on the sex chromosomes, as *fragile X syndrome*—the most common inherited cause of mental retardation—reveals. In this disorder, an abnormal repetition of a sequence of DNA bases occurs on the X chromosome, damaging a particular gene. Fragile X has been linked to 2 to 3 percent of cases of *autism*, a serious disorder usually diagnosed in early childhood that involves impaired social interaction, delayed or absent language and communication, and repetitive motor behavior (Goodlin-Jones et al., 2004). Research reveals that the defective gene at the fragile site is expressed only when it is passed from mother to child (Reiss & Dant, 2003).

■ **Mutation.** How are harmful genes created in the first place? The answer is **mutation**, a sudden change in a segment of DNA. A mutation may affect only one or two genes, or it may involve many genes, as in the chromosomal disorders we will discuss shortly. Some mutations occur spontaneously, simply by chance. Others are caused by hazardous environmental agents.

Although nonionizing forms of radiation—electromagnetic waves and microwaves—have no demonstrated impact on DNA, ionizing (high-energy) radiation is an established cause of mutation. Women who receive repeated doses before conception are more likely to miscarry or to give birth to children with hereditary defects. The incidence of genetic abnormalities, such as physical malformations and childhood cancer, is also higher in children whose fathers are exposed to radiation in their occupation. However, infrequent and mild exposure to radiation does not cause genetic damage (Jacquet, 2004). Rather, high doses over a long period impair DNA.

The examples just given illustrate *germline mutation*, which takes place in the cells that give rise to gametes. When the affected individual mates, the defective DNA is passed on to the next generation. In a second type, called *somatic mutation*, normal body cells mutate, an event that can occur at any time of life. The DNA defect appears in every cell derived from the affected body cell, eventually becoming widespread enough to cause disease or disability. Many cancers, including lung, colon, and prostate, originate this way. Other diseases, such as epilepsy and heart disease, are also believed to be due to somatic mutation (Gottlieb, Beitel, & Trifiro, 2001; Steinlein, 2004).

It is easy to see how disorders that run in families can result from germline mutation. But somatic mutation may be involved in these disorders as well. Some people may harbor a genetic susceptibility that causes certain body cells to mutate easily in the presence of triggering events (Weiss, 2005). This helps explain why some individuals develop serious illnesses as a result of smoking, exposure to pollutants, or psychological stress, while others do not.

Somatic mutation shows that each of us does not have a single, permanent genotype. Rather, the genetic makeup of each cell can change over time. Somatic mutation increases with age, raising the possibility that it contributes to the age-related rise in disease and to the aging process itself (Vijg, 2000).

■ **Polygenic Inheritance.** So far, we have focused on patterns of inheritance in which people either display a particular trait or do not. These cut-and-dried individual differences are easier to trace to their genetic origins than are characteristics that vary on a continuum among people, such as height, weight, intelligence, and personality. These traits are due to **polygenic inheritance**, in which many genes influence the characteristic in question. Polygenic inheritance is complex, and much about it is still unknown. In the final section of this chapter, we will discuss how researchers infer the influence of heredity on human attributes when they do not know the precise patterns of inheritance.

Chromosomal Abnormalities

Besides harmful recessive alleles, abnormalities of the chromosomes are a major cause of serious developmental problems. Most chromosomal defects result from mistakes during meiosis, when the ovum and sperm are formed. A chromosome pair does not separate properly, or part of a chromosome breaks off. Because these errors involve far more DNA than problems due to single genes, they usually produce many physical and mental symptoms.

■ **Down Syndrome.** The most common chromosomal disorder, occurring in 1 out of every 800 live births, is *Down syndrome*. In 95 percent of cases, it results from a failure of the twenty-first pair of chromosomes to separate during meiosis, so the new individual inherits three of these chromosomes rather than the normal two. In other, less frequent forms, an extra broken piece of a twenty-first chromosome is present. Or an error occurs during the early stages of mitosis, causing some but not all body cells to have the defective chromosomal makeup (called a *mosaic* pattern) (Tocci, 2000). Because less genetic material is involved in the mosaic type, symptoms of the disorder are less extreme.

The consequences of Down syndrome include mental retardation, memory and speech problems, limited vocabulary, and slow motor development. Affected individuals also have distinct physical features—a short, stocky build, a flattened face, a protruding tongue, almond-shaped eyes, and an unusual crease running across the palm of the hand. In addition, infants with Down syndrome are often born with eye

The boy on the right has facial features typical of children with Down syndrome. Despite his impaired intellectual development, he is doing well because he is growing up in a stimulating home where he is loved and accepted and receives attention from family members, including his older, typically developing brother.

cataracts and heart and intestinal defects. Three decades ago, most died by early adulthood. Today, because of medical advances, many survive into their fifties, and a few into their sixties to eighties (Roizen & Patterson, 2003).

Infants with Down syndrome smile less readily, show poor eye-to-eye contact, and explore objects less persistently. But when parents encourage them to engage with their surroundings, Down syndrome children develop more favorably (Sigman, 1999). They also benefit from infant and preschool intervention programs, although emotional, social, and motor skills improve more than intellectual performance (Carr, 2002). Clearly, environmental factors affect how well children with Down syndrome fare.

The risk of bearing a Down syndrome baby rises dramatically with maternal age, from 1 in 1,900 births at age 20, to 1 in 300 at age 35, to 1 in 30 at age 45 (Halliday et al., 1995; Meyers et al., 1997). Why is this so? Geneticists believe that the ova, present in the woman's body since her own prenatal period, weaken over time. As a result, chromosomes do not separate properly as they complete the process of meiosis at conception. But in about 5 to 10 percent of cases, the extra genetic material originates with the father. The reasons for this mutation are unknown. Some studies suggest a role for advanced paternal age, while others show no age effects (Fisch et al., 2003; Muller et al., 2000; Savage et al., 1998).

■ **Abnormalities of the Sex Chromosomes.** Disorders of the autosomes other than Down syndrome usually disrupt development so severely that miscarriage occurs. When such babies are born, they rarely survive beyond early childhood. In contrast, abnormalities of the sex chromosomes usually lead to fewer problems. In fact, sex chromosome disorders often are not recognized until adolescence when, in some of the deviations, puberty is delayed. The most common problems involve the presence of an extra chromosome (either X or Y) or the absence of one X in females.

Research has discredited a variety of popular beliefs about individuals with sex chromosome disorders. For example, males with *XYY syndrome* are not necessarily more aggressive and antisocial than XY males. And most children with sex chromosome disorders do not suffer from mental retardation. Rather, their intellectual problems usually are very specific. Verbal difficulties—for example, with reading and vocabulary—are common among girls with *triple X syndrome* and boys with *Klinefelter syndrome,* both of whom inherit an extra X chromosome. In contrast, girls with *Turner syndrome,* who are missing an X, have trouble with spatial relationships—for example, drawing pictures, telling right from left, following travel directions, and noticing changes in facial expressions (Geschwind et al., 2000; Lawrence et al., 2003; Simpson et al., 2003). These findings tell us that adding to or subtracting from the usual number of X chromosomes results in particular intellectual deficits. At present, geneticists do not know why.

Ask Yourself

Review
Explain the genetic origins of PKU and Down syndrome. Cite evidence that both heredity and environment contribute to the development of individuals with these disorders.

Apply
Gilbert's genetic makeup is homozygous for dark hair. Jan's is homozygous for blond hair. What color is Gilbert's hair? How about Jan's? What proportion of their children are likely to be dark-haired? Explain.

Connect
Referring to ecological systems theory (Chapter 1, pages 24–25), explain why parents of children with genetic disorders often experience increased stress. What factors, within and beyond the family, can help these parents support their children's development?

www.ablongman.com/berk

Reproductive Choices

Two years after they married, Ted and Marianne gave birth to their first child. Kendra appeared to be a healthy infant, but by 4 months her growth slowed, and she was diagnosed as having Tay-Sachs disease (see Table 2.3 on page 49). When Kendra died at 2 years of age, Ted and Marianne were devastated. Although they did not want to bring another infant into the world who would endure such suffering, they badly wanted to have a child. They began to avoid family get-togethers, where little nieces and nephews were constant reminders of the void in their lives.

In the past, many couples with genetic disorders in their families chose not to bear a child at all rather than risk the birth of an abnormal baby. Today, genetic counseling and prenatal diagnosis help people make informed decisions about conceiving, carrying a pregnancy to term, or adopting a child.

Genetic Counseling

Genetic counseling is a communication process designed to help couples assess their chances of giving birth to a baby with a hereditary disorder and choose the best course of action in view of risks and family goals (Hodgson & Spriggs, 2005). Individuals likely to seek counseling are those who have had difficulties bearing children, such as repeated miscarriages, or who know that genetic problems exist in their families. In addition, women who delay childbearing past age 35 are candidates for genetic counseling. After this time, the overall rate of chromosomal abnormalities rises sharply, from 1 in every 190 to as many as 1 in every 20 pregnancies at age 43 (Wille et al., 2004).

If a family history of mental retardation, physical defects, or inherited diseases exists, the genetic counselor interviews the couple and prepares a *pedigree,* a picture of the family tree in which affected relatives are identified. The pedigree is used to estimate the likelihood that parents will have an abnormal child, using the genetic principles discussed earlier in this chapter. For many disorders, blood tests or genetic analyses can reveal whether the parent is a carrier of the harmful gene. Carrier detection is possible for all of the recessive disorders listed in Table 2.3 on page 49, as well as others, and for fragile X syndrome.

When all the relevant information is in, the genetic counselor helps people consider appropriate options. These include taking a chance and conceiving, choosing from among a variety of reproductive technologies (see the Social Issues box on pages 54–55), or adopting a child.

Prenatal Diagnosis and Fetal Medicine

If couples who might bear an abnormal child decide to conceive, several **prenatal diagnostic methods**—medical procedures that permit detection of problems before birth—are

Social Issues

The Pros and Cons of Reproductive Technologies

Some couples decide not to risk pregnancy because of a history of genetic disease. Many others—in fact, one-sixth of all couples who try to conceive—discover that they are sterile. And some never-married adults and gay and lesbian partners want to bear children. Today, increasing numbers of individuals are turning to alternative methods of conception—technologies that, although they fulfill the wish for parenthood, have become the subject of heated debate.

Donor Insemination and In Vitro Fertilization. For several decades, *donor insemination*—injection of sperm from an anonymous man into a woman—has been used to overcome male reproductive difficulties. In recent years, it has also permitted women without a male partner to become pregnant. Donor insemination is 70 to 80 percent successful, resulting in 30,000 to 50,000 births in North America each year (Reynolds et al., 2003; Wright et al., 2004).

In vitro fertilization is another reproductive technology that has become increasingly common. Since the first "test tube" baby was born in England in 1978, 1 percent of all children in developed countries—about 40,000 babies in the United States and 3,500 babies in Canada—have been conceived through this technique annually (Jackson, Gibson, & Wu, 2004; Sutcliffe, 2002). With in vitro fertilization, hormones are given to a woman, stimulating ripening of several ova. These are removed surgically and placed in a dish of nutrients, to which sperm are added. Once an ovum is fertilized and begins to duplicate into several cells, it is injected into the mother's uterus.

By mixing and matching gametes, pregnancies can be brought about when either or both partners have a reproductive problem. Usually, in vitro fertilization is used to treat women whose fallopian tubes are permanently damaged. But a recently developed technique permits a single sperm to be injected directly into an ovum, thereby overcoming most male fertility problems. And a "sex sorter" method helps ensure that couples who carry X-linked diseases (which usually affect males) have a daughter. Fertilized ova and sperm can even be frozen and stored in embryo banks for use at some future time, thereby guaranteeing healthy zygotes should age or illness lead to fertility problems.

The overall success rate of in vitro fertilization is about 30 percent. However, success declines steadily with age, from 40 percent in women younger than age 35 to 7 percent in women age 43 and older (Wright et al., 2004). Furthermore, the resulting children may be genetically unrelated to one or both of their parents. In addition, most parents who have used in vitro fertilization do not tell their children about their origins, even though health professionals now encourage them to do so. Does lack of genetic ties or secrecy surrounding these techniques interfere with parent–child relationships? Perhaps because of a strong desire for parenthood, caregiving is actually somewhat warmer for young children conceived through donor insemination or in vitro fertilization. And in vitro infants are as securely attached to their parents, and in vitro children and adolescents as well-adjusted, as their counterparts who were naturally conceived (Golombok & MacCallum, 2003).

Although donor insemination and in vitro fertilization have many benefits, serious questions have arisen about their use. Most U.S. states and Canadian provinces have few legal guidelines for these procedures. As a result, donors are not always screened for genetic or sexually transmitted diseases. Furthermore, in many countries (including the United States and Canada), doctors are not required to keep records of donor characteristics. Canada, however, does retain a file on donor identities, permitting contact only in cases of serious disease, where knowledge of the child's genetic background might have medical value (Bioethics Consultative Committee, 2003). Another concern is that the in vitro "sex sorter" method will lead to parental sex selection, thereby eroding the moral value that children of both sexes are equally precious.

Finally, more than 50 percent of in vitro procedures result in multiple births. Most are twins, but 9 percent are triplets and higher-order multiples. Consequently, among in vitro babies, the rate of low birth weight is 2.6 times higher than in the general population (Jackson, Gibson, & Wu, 2004). Risk of major birth defects also doubles because of many factors, including drugs used to induce ripening of ova and delays in fertilizing the ova outside the womb (Hansen et al., 2002). In sum, in vitro fertilization poses greater risks than natural conception to infant survival and healthy development.

Surrogate Motherhood. An even more controversial form of medically assisted conception is *surrogate motherhood*. Typically in this procedure, sperm from a man whose wife is infertile are used to inseminate a woman, called a surrogate, who is paid a fee for her childbearing services. In return, the surrogate agrees to turn the baby over to the man (who is the natural father). The child is then adopted by his wife.

Although most of these arrangements proceed smoothly, those that end up in court highlight serious risks for all concerned. In one case, both parties rejected the infant with severe disabilities that resulted from the pregnancy. In several others, the surrogate mother wanted to keep the baby, or the couple changed their mind during the pregnancy. These children came into the world in the midst of conflict that threatened to last for years.

Because surrogacy favors the wealthy as contractors for infants and the less economically advantaged as surrogates, it may promote exploitation of financially needy women (Sureau, 1997). In addition, most surrogates already have children of their own who may be deeply affected by the pregnancy. Knowledge that their mother would give away a baby for profit may cause these youngsters to worry about the security of their own family circumstances.

New Reproductive Frontiers. Reproductive technologies are evolving faster than societies can weigh the ethics of these procedures. Doctors have used donor ova from younger women in combination with in vitro fertilization to help postmenopausal women become pregnant. Most recipients are in their forties, but several women in their fifties and sixties have given birth. These cases raise questions about bringing children into the world whose parents may not live to see them reach adulthood. Based on U.S. life expectancy data, 1 in 3 mothers and 1 in 2 fathers having a baby at age 55 will die before their child enters college (U.S. Census Bureau, 2006b).

Currently, experts are debating other reproductive options. In one instance, a woman with a busy stage career who could have become pregnant naturally chose to combine in vitro fertilization (using her own ova and her husband's sperm) and surrogate motherhood. This permitted the woman to continue her career while the surrogate carried her biological child (Wood, 2001). At donor banks, customers can select ova or sperm on the basis of physical characteristics and even IQ. Some worry that this practice is a dangerous step toward selective breeding through "designer babies"—controlling offspring characteristics by manipulating the genetic makeup of fertilized ova.

Finally, scientists have successfully cloned (made multiple copies of) fertilized ova in sheep, cattle, and monkeys, and they are working on effective ways to do so in humans. By providing extra ova for injection, cloning might improve the success rate of in vitro fertilization. But it also opens the possibility of mass-

This German couple are parents of quintuplets. Although the babies are now in good condition, at birth, they averaged only 2 pounds, or 940 grams each. Reproductive technologies can pose grave ethical dilemmas. In vitro fertilization and fertility drugs often lead to multiple fetuses, with higher risks of low birth weight and major birth defects than in natural conception. When severe pregnancy complications are likely, doctors may even recommend aborting one or more fetuses to save the others.

producing genetically identical people. Therefore, it is widely condemned (Fasouliotis & Schenker, 2000).

Although reproductive technologies permit many barren couples to rear healthy newborn babies, laws are needed to regulate such practices. In Australia, New Zealand, Sweden, and Switzerland, individuals conceived with donated gametes have a right to information about their genetic origins (Frith, 2001). Pressure from those working in the field of assisted reproduction may soon lead to similar policies in the United States and Canada.

In the case of surrogate motherhood, the ethical problems are so complex that 18 U.S. states have sharply restricted the

practice. Australia, Canada, and many European nations have banned it, arguing that the status of a baby should not be a matter of commercial arrangement and that a part of the body should not be rented or sold (Chen, 2003; McGee, 1997). Denmark, France, and Great Britain have prohibited in vitro fertilization for women past menopause (Bioethics Consultative Committee, 2003). At present, nothing is known about the psychological consequences of being a product of these procedures. Research on how such children grow up, including later-appearing medical conditions and knowledge and feelings about their origins, is important for weighing the pros and cons of these techniques.

Table 2.4	Prenatal Diagnostic Methods

Method	Description
Amniocentesis	The most widely used technique. A hollow needle is inserted through the abdominal wall to obtain a sample of fluid in the uterus. Cells are examined for genetic defects. This test can be performed by 11–14 weeks after conception but is safest after 15 weeks; 1 to 2 more weeks are required for test results. There is a small risk of miscarriage.
Chorionic villus sampling	This procedure can be used if results are desired or needed very early in pregnancy. A thin tube is inserted into the uterus through the vagina, or a hollow needle is inserted through the abdominal wall. A small plug of tissue is removed from the end of one or more chorionic villi, the hairlike projections on the membrane surrounding the developing organism. Cells are examined for genetic defects. This test can be performed at 6–8 weeks after conception, and results are available within 24 hours. It entails a slightly greater risk of miscarriage than does amniocentesis and is also associated with a small risk of limb deformities, which increases the earlier the procedure is performed.
Fetoscopy	A small tube with a light source at one end is inserted into the uterus to inspect the fetus for defects of the limbs and face. This also allows a sample of fetal blood to be obtained, permitting diagnosis of such disorders as hemophilia and sickle cell anemia as well as neural defects (see below). Usually performed 15–18 weeks after conception, fetoscopy can be done as early as 5 weeks. It entails some risk of miscarriage.
Ultrasound	High-frequency sound waves are beamed at the uterus; their reflection is translated into a picture on a video screen that reveals the size, shape, and placement of the fetus. By itself, ultrasound permits assessment of fetal age, detection of multiple pregnancies, and identification of gross physical defects. It is also used to guide amniocentesis, chorionic villus sampling, and fetoscopy. When used five or more times, it may increase the chances of low birth weight.
Maternal blood analysis	By the second month of pregnancy, some of the developing organism's cells enter the maternal bloodstream. An elevated level of alpha-fetoprotein may indicate kidney disease, abnormal closure of the esophagus, or neural tube defects, such as anencephaly (absence of most of the brain) and spina bifida (bulging of the spinal cord from the spinal column). Isolated cells can be examined for genetic defects, such as Down syndrome.
Preimplantation genetic diagnosis	After in vitro fertilization and duplication of the zygote into a cluster of about eight to ten cells, one or two cells are removed and examined for hereditary defects. Only if that sample is free of detectable genetic disorders is the fertilized ovum implanted in the woman's uterus.

Sources: Kumar & O'Brien, 2004; Moore & Persaud, 2003; Newnham et al., 1993; Sermon, Van Steirteghem, & Liebaers, 2004.

available (see Table 2.4). Women of advanced maternal age are prime candidates for *amniocentesis* or *chorionic villus sampling* (see Figure 2.5). Except for *ultrasound* and *maternal blood analysis,* prenatal diagnosis should not be used routinely, as other methods have some chance of injuring the developing organism.

Prenatal diagnosis has led to advances in fetal medicine. For example, by inserting a needle into the uterus, doctors can administer drugs to the fetus. Surgery has been performed to repair such problems as heart, lung, and diaphragm malformations, urinary tract obstructions, and neural defects. Fetuses with blood disorders have been given blood transfusions. And those with immune deficiencies have received bone marrow transplants that succeeded in creating a normally functioning immune system (Flake, 2003).

These techniques frequently result in complications, the most common being premature labor and miscarriage (James, 1998). Yet parents may be willing to try almost any option, even one with only a slim chance of success. Currently, the medical profession is struggling with how to help parents make informed decisions about fetal surgery. One suggestion is that advice be provided by an independent counselor—a doctor or nurse who is not involved in performing or doing research on the procedure.

Advances in *genetic engineering* also offer hope for correcting hereditary defects. As part of the Human Genome Project—an ambitious international research program aimed at deciphering the chemical makeup of human genetic material (genome)—researchers have mapped the sequence of all human DNA base pairs. Using that information, they are "annotating" the genome—identifying all its genes and their functions, including their protein products and what they do. A major goal is to understand the estimated 4,000 human disorders, those due to single genes and those resulting from a complex interplay of multiple genes and environmental factors.

Already, thousands of genes have been identified, including those involved in hundreds of diseases, such as cystic fibrosis, Huntington disease, Duchenne muscular dystrophy, Marfan syndrome, and many forms of cancer (National Institutes of Health, 2005). As a result, new treatments are being explored, such as *gene therapy*—correcting genetic abnormalities by delivering DNA carrying a functional gene to the cells.

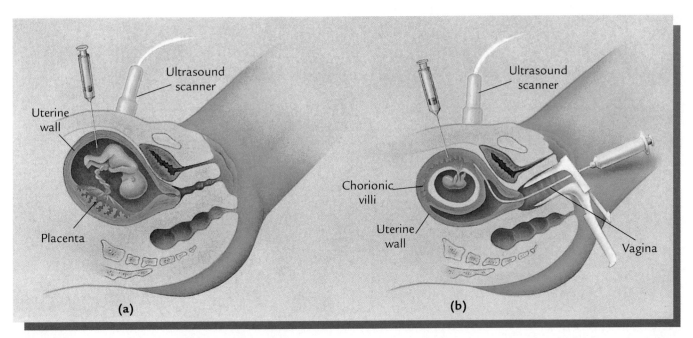

■ FIGURE 2.5 Amniocentesis and chorionic villus sampling. Today, hundreds of defects and diseases can be detected before birth using these two procedures. (a) In amniocentesis, a hollow needle is inserted through the abdominal wall into the uterus during the fourteenth week after conception, or later. Fluid is withdrawn, and fetal cells are cultured, a process that takes one to two weeks. (b) Chorionic villus sampling can be performed much earlier in pregnancy, at nine weeks after conception, and results are available within 24 hours. Two approaches to obtaining a sample of chorionic villus are shown: inserting a thin tube through the vagina into the uterus and inserting a needle through the abdominal wall. In both amniocentesis and chorionic villus sampling, an ultrasound scanner is used for guidance. (From K. L. Moore & T. V. N. Persaud, 2003, *Before We Are Born*, 6th ed., Philadelphia: Saunders, p. 87. Adapted by permission of the publisher and author.)

In recent experiments, gene therapy relieved symptoms in hemophilia patients and in patients with severe immune system dysfunction. A few, however, experienced serious side effects (Ralph, Harrington, & Pandha, 2004). In another approach, called *proteomics,* scientists modify gene-specified proteins involved in biological aging and disease (Bradshaw & Burlingame, 2005).

Genetic treatments are still some distance away for most single-gene defects—and far off for diseases involving multiple genes that combine in complex ways with each other and the environment. Applying What We Know on page 58 summarizes steps that prospective parents can take before conception to protect the genetic health of their child.

Genetic Testing

Fortunately, over 90 percent of pregnancies in North America result in the birth of healthy infants (Moore & Persaud, 2003). For those who harbor genes that might lead to later-emerging illness, a few tests exist that involve scanning an individual's DNA for mutations associated with such diseases as breast cancer, colon cancer, kidney disease, and severe, chronic anemia. By the year 2010, many more such tests are likely to be available, permitting people to find out about their genetic risks and, hopefully, take steps to reduce them—through medical monitoring, lifestyle changes, or drug therapy (Collins, 2003).

Although its potential benefits are great, genetic testing raises serious social, ethical, and legal concerns. A major controversy involves testing children and adults who are at risk but who do not yet show disease symptoms. Delay between the availability of predictive tests and effective interventions means that people must live with the knowledge that they might become seriously ill.

The mother of this girl with cystic fibrosis has learned to provide the time-consuming physical care her daughter needs. Here, she pounds on the child's chest with open palms to clear the child's lungs of thick mucus. In the future, such children may benefit from the discovery of new gene-based treatments for hereditary disorders.

Steps Prospective Parents Can Take Before Conception to Increase the Chances of a Healthy Baby

Suggestion	Rationale
Arrange for a physical exam.	A physical exam before conception permits detection of diseases and other medical problems that might reduce fertility, be difficult to treat after the onset of pregnancy, or affect the developing organism.
Consider your genetic makeup.	Find out if anyone in your family has had a child with a genetic disease or disability. If so, seek genetic counseling before conception.
Reduce or eliminate toxins under your control.	Since the developing organism is highly sensitive to damaging environmental agents during the early weeks of pregnancy (see Chapter 3), couples trying to conceive should avoid drugs, alcohol, cigarette smoke, radiation, pollution, chemical substances in the home and workplace, and infectious diseases. Furthermore, stay away from ionizing radiation and some industrial chemicals which are known to cause mutations.
Ensure proper nutrition.	A doctor-recommended vitamin-mineral supplement, begun before conception, helps prevent many prenatal problems. It should include folic acid, which reduces the chances of neural tube defects, prematurity, and low birth weight (see Chapter 3, page 93).
Consult your doctor after 12 months of unsuccessful efforts at conception.	Long periods of infertility may be due to undiagnosed spontaneous abortions, which can be caused by genetic defects in either partner. If a physical exam reveals a healthy reproductive system, seek genetic counseling.

A related concern is the need for greater knowledge of genetics, on the part of both health professionals and the general public. Without this understanding, doctors and patients may misinterpret genetic risk. For example, genes associated with breast cancer were first identified in families with a high incidence of the disease. In those families, 85 percent of individuals harboring the genes developed cancer. But in the general population, the risk is reduced to 35 to 50 percent (Burke et al. 2002). Furthermore, some Americans whose tests revealed abnormal genes have encountered discrimination in the workplace, where they lost their health insurance and even their jobs (National Human Genome Research Institute, 2005).

Experts in medical ethics recommend that genetic testing be offered only to high-risk individuals who undergo extensive education and counseling and agree to close medical and psychological follow-up if they test positive. And procedures have been devised in the United States and Canada to ensure the privacy of genetic information and to prohibit mandatory genetic testing by employers (Privacy Commissioner of Canada, 2005; U.S. Department of Health and Human Services, 2005i). As the Human Genome Project continues to make invaluable contributions to human health, scientists are debating the best ways to protect the public interest while reaping the project's monumental rewards.

Adoption

Adults who are infertile, who are likely to pass along a genetic disorder, or who are older and single but want a family are turning to adoption in increasing numbers. Those who have children by birth, too, sometimes choose to expand their families through adoption. Adoption agencies try to ensure a good fit by seeking parents of the same ethnic and religious background as the child and, where possible, trying to choose parents who are the same age as most biological parents. Because the availability of healthy babies has declined (fewer young unwed mothers give up their babies than in the past), more people in North America and Western Europe are adopting from other countries or accepting children who are past infancy or who have known developmental problems (Schweiger & O'Brien, 2005).

Adopted children and adolescents—whether or not they are born in their adoptive parents' country—have more learning and emotional difficulties than other children, a difference that increases with the child's age at time of adoption (Brodzinsky & Pinderhughes, 2002; Nickman, Rosenfeld, & Fine, 2005). There are many possible reasons for adoptees' more problematic childhoods. The biological mother may have been unable to care for the child because of problems believed to be partly genetic, such as alcoholism or severe depression. She may have passed this tendency to her offspring. Or perhaps she experienced stress, poor diet, or inadequate medical care during pregnancy—factors that can affect the child (as we will see in Chapter 3). Furthermore, children adopted after infancy often have a preadoptive history of conflict-ridden family relationships, lack of parental affection, or neglect and abuse. Finally, adoptive parents and children, who are genetically unrelated, are less alike in intelligence and personality than biological relatives—differences that may threaten family harmony.

Despite these risks, most adopted children fare well, and those with preexisting problems usually make rapid progress

(Johnson, 2002; Kim, 2002). In a Swedish study, researchers followed more than 600 infant candidates for adoption into adolescence. Some were adopted shortly after birth; some were reared in foster homes; and some were reared by their biological mothers, who changed their minds about giving them up. As Figure 2.6 shows, adoptees developed much more favorably than children reared in foster families or returned to their birth mothers (Bohman & Sigvardsson, 1990). And in a study of internationally adopted children in the Netherlands, sensitive maternal care and secure attachment in infancy predicted cognitive and social competence at age 7 (Stams, Juffer, & van IJzendoorn, 2002). So even when parents and children are not genetically related, an early warm, trusting parent–child relationship fosters development. Children with troubled family histories also develop trust and affection for their adoptive parents as they come to feel loved and supported by them (Sherrill & Pinderhughes, 1999).

By adolescence, however, adoptees' lives are often complicated by unresolved curiosity about their roots. Some have difficulty accepting the possibility that they may never know their birth parents. Others worry about what they would do if their birth parents suddenly reappeared. Nevertheless, the decision to search for birth parents is usually postponed until early adulthood, when marriage and childbirth may trigger it. Despite concerns about their origins, most adoptees appear well-adjusted as adults. And as long as their parents took steps to help them learn about their heritage in childhood, young people adopted into a different ethnic group or culture generally develop identities that are healthy blends of their birth and rearing backgrounds (Brooks & Barth, 1999; Yoon, 2004).

As we conclude our discussion of reproductive choices, perhaps you are wondering how things turned out for Ted and Marianne. Through genetic counseling, Marianne discovered a history of Tay-Sachs disease on her mother's side of the family. Ted had a distant cousin who died of the disorder. The genetic counselor explained that the chances of giving birth to another affected baby were 1 in 4. Ted and Marianne took that risk. Their son Douglas is now 12 years old. Although Douglas is a carrier of the recessive allele, he is a normal, healthy boy. In a few years, Ted and Marianne will tell Douglas about his genetic history and explain the importance of genetic counseling and testing before he has children of his own.

Ask Yourself

Review

Why is genetic counseling called a *communication process*? Who should seek it?

Apply

Imagine that you must counsel a couple considering in vitro fertilization using the wife's ova and sperm from an anonymous man to overcome the husband's infertility. What medical and ethical risks would you raise?

Connect

How does research on adoption reveal resilience? Which factor related to resilience (see Chapter 1, pages 10–11) is central in positive outcomes for adoptees?

Reflect

Imagine that you are a woman who is a carrier of fragile X syndrome but who wants to have children. Would you become pregnant, adopt, use a surrogate mother, or give up your desire for parenthood? If you became pregnant, would you seek prenatal diagnosis? Explain your decisions.

www.ablongman.com/berk

Environmental Contexts for Development

Just as complex as genetic inheritance is the surrounding environment—a many-layered set of influences that combine to help or hinder physical and psychological well-being. Take a moment to reflect on your own childhood and jot down a brief description of events and people that you believe significantly influenced your development. Next, do the same for your adult life. When I ask my students to do this, most entries on their list involve their families. This emphasis is not surprising, since the family is the first and longest-lasting context for development. But other settings turn out to be important

■ **FIGURE 2.6 Relationship of type of rearing to maladjustment among a sample of Swedish adolescents who had been candidates for adoption at birth.** Compared with the other two groups, adopted youths were rated by teachers as having far fewer problems, including anxiety, withdrawal, aggression, inability to concentrate, peer difficulties, and poor school motivation. (Adapted from Bohman & Sigvardsson, 1990.)

as well. Friends, neighbors, school, workplace, community organizations, and church, synagogue, or mosque generally make the top ten.

Think back to Bronfenbrenner's ecological systems theory, discussed in Chapter 1. It emphasizes that the environments extending beyond the *microsystem,* or the immediate settings just mentioned, powerfully affect development. Indeed, my students rarely mention one important context. Its impact is so pervasive that we seldom stop to think about it in our daily lives. This is the *macrosystem,* or broad social climate of society—its values and programs that support and protect human development. All people need help with the demands of each period of the lifespan—through affordable housing and health care, safe neighborhoods, good schools, well-equipped recreational facilities, and high-quality child care and other services that permit them to meet both work and family responsibilities. And some people, because of poverty or special tragedies, need considerably more help than others.

In the following sections, we take up these contexts for development. Because they affect every age and aspect of change, we will return to them in later chapters. For now, our discussion emphasizes that environments, as well as heredity, can enhance or create risks for development. And when a vulnerable child or adult—an individual with physical or psychological problems—is exposed to unfavorable contexts, development is seriously threatened.

The Family

In power and breadth of influence, no other context equals the family. The family creates bonds among people that are unique. Attachments to parents and siblings usually last a lifetime and serve as models for relationships in the wider world of neighborhood, school, and community. Within the family, children learn the language, skills, and social and moral values of their culture. And at all ages, people turn to family members for information, assistance, and pleasurable interaction. Warm, gratifying family ties predict physical and psychological health throughout development. In contrast, isolation or alienation from the family is often associated with developmental problems (Deković & Buist, 2005; Parke & Buriel, 1998).

Contemporary researchers view the family as a *social system.* Recall from ecological systems theory that *bidirectional influences* exist, in which family members mutually influence one another. Indeed, the very term *system* implies a network of interdependent relationships (Lerner et al., 2002). These system influences operate both directly and indirectly.

■ **Direct Influences.** The next time you have a chance to observe family members interacting, watch carefully. You are likely to see that kind, patient communication evokes cooperative, harmonious responses, whereas harshness and impatience engender angry, resistive behavior. Each of these reactions, in turn, forges a new link in the interactive chain. In the first

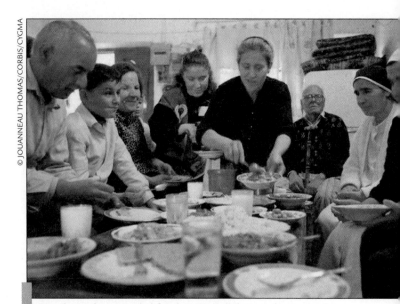

Members of an extended family in Baghdad, Iraq, share a meal. The family is a complex system of interdependent relationships in which each person's behavior influences the behavior of other family members, both directly and indirectly.

instance, a positive message tends to follow; in the second, a negative or avoidant one tends to occur.

These observations fit with a wealth of research on the family system. For example, studies of families of diverse ethnicities show that when parents' requests are accompanied by warmth, children tend to cooperate. And when children willingly comply, their parents are likely to be warm and gentle in the future. In contrast, parents who discipline with harshness and impatience are likely to have children who refuse and rebel. And because children's misbehavior is stressful for parents, they may increase their use of punishment, leading to more unruliness by the child (Stormshak et al., 2000; Whiteside-Mansell et al., 2003). This principle also applies to other two-person family relationships—brother and sister, husband and wife, parent and adult child. In each case, the behavior of one family member helps sustain a form of interaction in the other that either promotes or undermines psychological well-being.

■ **Indirect Influences.** The impact of family relationships on development becomes even more complicated when we consider that interaction between any two members is affected by others present in the setting. Bronfenbrenner calls these indirect influences the effect of *third parties.*

Third parties can serve as supports for or barriers to development. For example, parents with a warm, considerate marital relationship praise and stimulate their children more. In contrast, parents whose marriage is tense and hostile tend to be less responsive to their children's needs and more likely to criticize, express anger, and punish (Cox, Paley, & Harter, 2001; McHale et al., 2002). Children chronically exposed to angry, unresolved parental conflict have serious emotional problems (Harold et al., 2004). These include both *internalizing difficulties* (especially among girls), such as feeling worried and afraid and trying to repair their parents' relationship, and *externalizing difficulties* (especially among boys), including verbal and physical aggression (Davies & Lindsay, 2004). These child problems can further disrupt parents' marital relationship.

Yet even when third parties strain family ties, other members may help restore effective interaction. Grandparents are a case in point. They can promote children's development in many ways—both directly, by responding warmly to the child, and indirectly, by providing parents with child-rearing advice, models of child-rearing skill, and even financial assistance. Of course, as with any indirect influence, grandparents can sometimes be harmful. When quarrelsome relations exist between grandparents and parents, parent–child communication may suffer.

◼ **Adapting to Change.** Think back to the *chronosystem* in Bronfenbrenner's theory (see page 25 in Chapter 1). The interplay of forces within the family is dynamic and ever-changing. Important events, such as the birth of a baby, a change of jobs, or the addition to the household of an elderly parent in declining health, create challenges that modify existing relationships. The way such events affect family interaction depends on the support other family members provide and on the developmental status of each participant. For example, the arrival of a new baby prompts very different reactions in a toddler than in a school-age child. And caring for an ill elderly parent is more stressful for a middle-aged adult still rearing young children than for an adult of the same age who has no child-rearing responsibilities.

Historical time period also contributes to a dynamic family system. In recent decades, a declining birth rate, a high divorce rate, and expansion of women's roles have led to a smaller family size. This, combined with a longer lifespan, means that more generations are alive, with fewer members in the youngest ones, leading to a "top-heavy" family structure. Young people today are more likely to have older relatives than at any time in history—a circumstance that can be enriching as well as a source of tension. In sum, as this complex intergenerational system moves through time, relationships are constantly revised as members adjust to their own and others' development as well as to external pressures.

Despite these variations, some general patterns in family functioning do exist. In the United States, Canada, and other Western nations, one important source of these consistencies is socioeconomic status.

Socioeconomic Status and Family Functioning

People in industrialized nations are stratified on the basis of what they do at work and how much they earn for doing it—factors that determine their social position and economic well-being. Researchers assess a family's standing on this continuum through an index called **socioeconomic status (SES)**, which combines three related, but not completely overlapping, variables: (1) years of education and (2) the prestige of and skill required by one's job, both of which measure social status, and (3) income, which measures economic status. As SES rises and falls, people face changing circumstances that profoundly affect family functioning.

SES affects the timing and duration of phases of the family life cycle. People who work in skilled and semiskilled manual occupations (for example, machinists, truck drivers, and custodians) tend to marry and have children earlier as well as give birth to more children than people in white-collar and professional occupations. The two groups also differ in values and expectations. For example, when asked about personal qualities they desire for their children, lower-SES parents tend to emphasize external characteristics, such as obedience, politeness, neatness, and cleanliness. In contrast, higher-SES parents emphasize psychological traits, such as curiosity, happiness, self-direction, and cognitive and social maturity (Duncan & Magnuson, 2003; Hoff, Laursen, & Tardif, 2002; Tudge et al., 2000).

These differences are reflected in family interaction. Parents higher in SES talk to, read to, and otherwise stimulate their infants and preschoolers more. When their children are older, higher-SES parents use more warmth, explanations, and verbal praise. Commands ("You do that because I told you to"), criticism, and physical punishment all occur more often in low-SES households (Bradley & Corwyn, 2003).

Education contributes substantially to these variations in child rearing. Higher-SES parents' interest in providing verbal stimulation and nurturing inner traits is supported by years of schooling, during which they learned to think about abstract, subjective ideas. In diverse cultures around the world, as the Lifespan Vista box on page 62 makes clear, education of women in particular fosters patterns of thinking that greatly improve quality of life, for both parents and children.

Because of limited education and low social status, many lower-SES parents feel a sense of powerlessness and lack of influence in their relationships beyond the home. At work, for example, they must obey rules of others in positions of power and authority. When they get home, their parent–child interaction seems to duplicate these experiences—but now they are in the authority role. Higher levels of stress combined with a stronger belief in the value of physical punishment contribute to low-SES parents' greater use of coercive discipline (Pinderhughes et al., 2000). Higher-SES parents, in contrast, have more control over their own lives. At work, they are used to making independent decisions and convincing others of their point of view. At home, they teach these skills to their children (Greenberger, O'Neil, & Nagel, 1994).

Affluence

Despite their advanced education and great material wealth, affluent parents—those in highly prestigious occupations with six-figure annual incomes—too often fail to engage in family interaction and parenting that promote favorable development.

A Lifespan Vista

Worldwide Education of Girls: Transforming Current and Future Generations

When a new school opened in the Egyptian village of Beni Shara'an, some villagers complained that the school would deprive them of their children's help in the wheat fields and small businesses. Ahmen, an illiterate shopkeeper, heard an elderly merchant, who had donated space for the school, say, "I have come to believe that a girl's education is even more important than a boy's." Immediately, Ahmen enrolled his 8-year-old daughter Rawia (Bellamy, 2004, p. 19). Until that day, Rawia had divided her days between backbreaking farming and confinement to her home.

Before long, Rawia's advancing language, literacy, and reasoning skills transformed her family's quality of life. "My store accounts were in a mess, but soon Rawia started straightening out the books," Ahmen recalled. She also began helping her older sister learn to read and write and explaining to her family the instructions on prescription medicines and the news on television. In addition, Rawia began to envision a better life for herself. "When I grow up," she told her father, "I want to be a doctor. Or maybe a teacher."

Over the past century, the percentage of children in the developing world who go to school has increased from a small minority of boys to a majority of all children in most regions. Still, some 135 million 7- to 18-year-olds, most of them poverty-stricken girls, receive no education at all (see Figure 2.7). Millions of others, again mostly girls, drop out before completing the first three grades (Gordon, 2003).

Although schooling is vital for all children, educating girls has an especially powerful impact on the welfare of families, societies, and future generations. The diverse benefits of girls' schooling largely accrue in two ways: (1) through enhanced verbal skills—reading, writing, and oral communication; and (2) through empowerment—a growing desire to improve their life conditions. In studies carried out on three continents, in three cultures, and in three community settings—rural Nepal, a small Mexican town, and a large city in Zambia—the more education women obtained, the better their language and literacy skills and the higher their aspirations for a better life. Their knowledge and attitudes, in turn, dramatically influenced family health, relationships, and parenting (LeVine, LeVine, & Schnell, 2001).

Family Health. Education equips people with the communicative skills and confidence to seek health services and to benefit from public health information. As a result, years of schooling strongly predicts women's preventive health behavior: prenatal visits, child immunizations, healthy diet, and sanitary practices (Dexter, LeVine, & Velasco, 1998; LeVine et al., 2004; Peña, Wall, & Person, 2000). In addition, because educated women have more life opportunities, they are more likely to take advantage of family planning services, delay childbearing, and have more widely spaced and fewer children (Caldwell, 1999). All these practices are linked to increased maternal and child survival and family health.

Family Relationships and Parenting. In developed and developing nations alike, the empowerment that springs from education is associated with more equitable husband–wife relationships and a reduction in harsh disciplining of children (LeVine et al., 1991; LeVine, LeVine, & Schnell, 2001). Also, educated mothers engage in more verbal stimulation and teaching of literacy skills to their children, which fosters success in school, higher educational attainment, and economic gains in the next generation. Regions of the world that have invested more in girls' education, such as southeast Asia and Latin America, tend to have higher levels of economic development (King & Mason, 2001).

According to a recent United Nations report, the education of girls is the most effective means of combating the most profound, global threats to human development: poverty, maternal and child mortality, and disease. As a result, the United Nations is encouraging all developing nations to make education a high priority and to take special steps to enable girls to go to school (Bellamy, 2004).

Rawia got the chance to go to school because of an Egyptian national initiative, which led to the establishment of several thousand one-classroom schools in rural areas with the poorest record in educating girls. Because of cultural beliefs about gender roles or reluctance to give up a

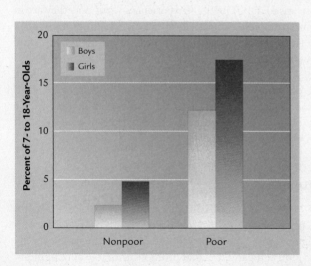

■ **FIGURE 2.7** **Percentage of children age 7 to 18 in the developing world who have never attended school.** Many more poor than nonpoor children have not had a chance to go to school. And far more girls than boys—especially poverty-stricken girls—are affected. (From D. Gordon, 2003, *The Distribution of Child Poverty in the Developing World: Report to UNICEF.* Bristol, U.K.: Centre for International Poverty Research, University of Bristol. Adapted by permission.)

daughter's work at home, parents sometimes resist. But when governments create employment possibilities for women and provide information about the benefits of education for girls, the overwhelming majority of parents—including the very poor—choose to send their daughters to school, and some make great sacrifices to do so (Narayan et al., 2000).

For these girls in the Taza region of Mauritania, attending school will dramatically improve their life opportunities and the welfare of their nation. In both developed and developing nations, education of girls leads to changes in family income and relationships that carry over to health, education, and economic gains in the next generation.

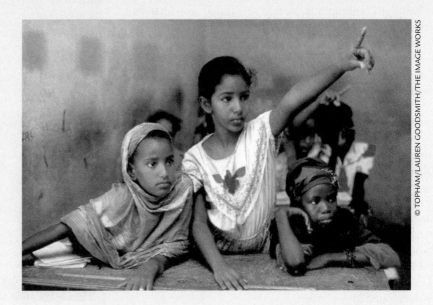

In several studies, researchers tracked the adjustment of youths growing up in wealthy suburbs (Luthar & Latendresse, 2005a). By seventh grade, many showed serious problems that worsened in high school. Their school grades were poor, and they were more likely to engage in alcohol and drug use and to report high levels of anxiety and depression than low-SES youths (Luthar & Becker, 2002). Furthermore, among affluent (but not low-SES) teenagers, substance use was correlated with anxiety and depression, suggesting that wealthy youths took drugs to self-medicate—a practice that predicts persistent abuse (Luthar & Sexton, 2004).

Why are so many affluent youths troubled? Compared to their better-adjusted counterparts, poorly adjusted affluent young people report less emotional closeness and supervision from their parents, who lead professionally and socially demanding lives. And like their parents, many of these teenagers are overscheduled: An excessive number of activities keep them busy but disconnected from their families. Overall, wealthy parents are nearly as physically and emotionally unavailable to their youngsters as parents coping with serious financial strain. At the same time, these parents often make excessive demands for achievement (Luthar & Becker, 2002). Adolescents whose parents value their accomplishments more than their character are more likely to have academic and emotional problems.

For both affluent and low-SES youths, a simple routine—eating dinner with parents—is associated with a reduction in adjustment difficulties, even after many other aspects of parenting are controlled (see Figure 2.8) (Luthar & Latendresse, 2005b). Interventions that make wealthy parents aware of the high costs of a competitive, overscheduled lifestyle and minimal family time are badly needed.

■ FIGURE 2.8 Relationship of regularly eating dinner with parents to affluent youths' adjustment problems. Compared with sixth graders who often ate dinner with their parents, those who rarely did so were far more likely to display anxiety and depression, delinquency and substance use, and poor school grades, even after many other aspects of parenting were controlled. In this study, frequent family mealtimes also protected low-SES youths from delinquency and substance use and from classroom learning problems. (Adapted from Luthar & Latendresse, 2005b.)

Poverty

When families slip into poverty, development is seriously threatened. Consider the case of Zinnia Mae, who grew up in a close-knit black community located in a small southeastern American city (Heath, 1990). As unemployment struck in the 1980s and citizens moved away, 16-year-old Zinnia Mae caught a ride to Atlanta. Two years later, she was the mother of a daughter and twin boys and had moved into a high-rise in public housing.

All of Zinnia Mae's days were much the same. She worried constantly about scraping together enough money to put food on the table, finding baby-sitters so she could go to the laundry or grocery, freeing herself from a cycle of rising debt, and finding the twins' father, who had stopped sending money. To relieve loneliness and anxiety, she watched TV and talked with a few friends on the phone. Her most frequent words were "I'm so tired." The children had only one set meal (breakfast); otherwise, they ate whenever they were hungry or bored. Their play space was limited to the living room sofa and a mattress on the floor. Toys consisted of scraps of a blanket, spoons and food cartons, a small rubber ball, a few plastic cars, and a roller skate abandoned in the building.

At the researcher's request, Zinnia Mae agreed to tape record her interactions with her children. Cut off from family and community ties and overwhelmed by financial strains and feelings of helplessness, she found herself unable to join in activities with her children. In 500 hours of tape, she started a conversation with her children only 18 times.

Although poverty rates in the United States and Canada declined slightly in the 1990s, in recent years they have risen (UNICEF, 2005a). Today, about 12 percent of people in Canada and 13 percent in the United States are affected. Those hit hardest are parents under age 25 with young children and elderly people who live alone. Poverty is also magnified among ethnic minorities and women. For example, 16 percent of Canadian and 18 percent of American children are poor, rates that climb to 32 percent for Native-American children, 34 percent for African-American and Hispanic children, and 60 percent for Canadian Aboriginal children.[1] For single mothers with preschool children and elderly women on their own, the poverty rate in both countries is nearly 50 percent (Canada Campaign 2000, 2003b, 2004; U.S. Census Bureau, 2006b).

Joblessness, a high divorce rate, a lower remarriage rate among women than men, widowhood, and (as we will see later) inadequate government programs to meet family needs are responsible for these disheartening statistics. The poverty rate is higher among children than any other age group. And of all Western nations, the United States has the highest percentage of extremely poor children. More than 6 percent of American children live in deep poverty (well below the poverty

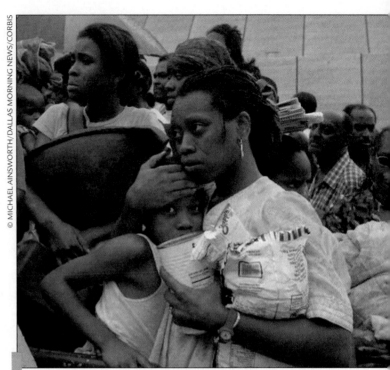

This mother and child were evacuated in the aftermath of Hurricane Katrina, which devastated the southern Gulf Coast of the United States in 2005. For low-income families, the destruction and dislocation caused by a natural disaster is especially likely to result in long-term homelessness, impoverishment, and emotional stress.

© MICHAEL AINSWORTH/DALLAS MORNING NEWS/CORBIS

threshold, the income level judged necessary for a minimum living standard), compared with 2.5 percent of Canadian children. However, these circumstances are worrisome in both countries because the earlier poverty begins, the deeper it is, and the longer it lasts, the more devastating are its effects. Children of poverty are more likely than other children to suffer from lifelong poor physical health, persistent deficits in cognitive development and academic achievement, high school dropout, mental illness, and antisocial behavior (Children's Defense Fund, 2005; Poulton et al., 2002; Seccombe, 2002).

The constant stressors that accompany poverty gradually weaken the family system. Poor families have many daily hassles—bills to pay, the car breaking down, loss of welfare and unemployment payments, something stolen from the house, to name just a few. When daily crises arise, family members become depressed, irritable, and distracted, and hostile interactions increase (Evans, 2004). These outcomes are especially severe in single-parent families and families that must live in poor housing and dangerous neighborhoods—conditions that make everyday existence even more difficult, while reducing social supports that help people cope with economic hardship (Leventhal & Brooks-Gunn, 2003).

Besides poverty, another problem—one that has become more common in the past 25 years—has reduced the life chances of many children and adults. On any given night, approximately 35,000 people in Canada and 350,000 people in the United States have no place to live. The majority are adults

---

[1]Aboriginal peoples in Canada include three groups: (1) First Nations, or Native Canadian peoples; (2) Inuit, most of whom live in northern Canada; and (3) Métis, or mixed-blood people of both Native Canadian and European descent.

on their own, many of whom suffer from serious mental illness. But an estimated 25 to 40 percent of the homeless are families with children (Kidd & Scrimenti, 2004). The rise in homelessness is mostly due to two factors: a decline in the availability of government-supported, low-cost housing and the release of large numbers of mentally ill people from institutions, without an increase in community treatment programs to help them adjust to ordinary life and get better.

Most homeless families consist of women with children under age 5. Besides health problems (which affect most homeless people), many homeless children suffer from chronic emotional stress due to their harsh, insecure daily lives (Bratt, 2002; Pardeck, 2005). An estimated 25 to 30 percent who are old enough do not go to school. Those who do enroll achieve less well than other poverty-stricken children due to poor attendance and health and emotional difficulties (Vostanis, Grattan, & Cumella, 1997).

Beyond the Family: Neighborhoods, Towns, and Cities

As the concepts of *mesosystem* and *exosystem* in ecological systems theory make clear, connections between family and community are vital for psychological well-being. From our discussion of poverty, perhaps you can see why. In poverty-stricken urban areas, community life is usually disrupted. Families move often, parks and playgrounds are in disarray, and community centers providing organized leisure time activities do not exist. In such neighborhoods, family violence, child abuse and neglect, children's problem behavior, youth antisocial activity, and adult criminal behavior are especially high (Brody et al., 2003; Kohen et al., 2002). In contrast, strong family ties to the surrounding social context—as indicated by frequent contact with friends and relatives and regular church, synagogue, or mosque attendance—reduce family stress and enhance adjustment (Boardman, 2004; Magnuson & Duncan, 2002).

■ **Neighborhoods.** Let's look closely at the functions of communities in the lives of children and adults by beginning with the neighborhood. What were your childhood experiences like in the yards, streets, and parks surrounding your home? How did you spend your time, whom did you get to know, and how important were these moments to you?

Neighborhoods offer resources and social ties that play an important part in children's development. In several studies, low-SES families were randomly assigned vouchers to move out of public housing into neighborhoods varying widely in affluence. Compared with their peers who remained in poverty-stricken areas, children and youths who moved into low-poverty neighborhoods showed substantially better physical and mental health and school achievement (Goering, 2003; Leventhal & Brooks-Gunn, 2003).

Neighborhood resources have a greater impact on economically disadvantaged than well-to-do young people. Higher-SES families are less dependent on their immediate

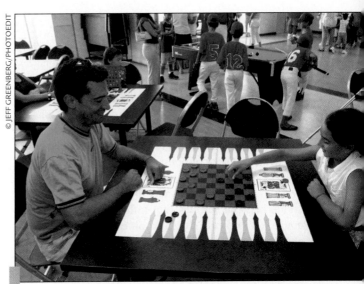

A girl and her father enjoy a game of checkers at the grand opening of a community center in Florida. Community resources like this gathering place play a vital role in development, especially for economically disadvantaged young people whose families depend on the immediate neighborhood for social support.

surroundings for social support, education, and leisure pursuits. They can afford to reach beyond the streets near their homes, transporting their children to lessons and entertainment and, if necessary, to better-quality schools in distant parts of the community (Elliott et al., 1996). In low-income neighborhoods, in-school and after-school programs that substitute for lack of resources by providing enrichment activities are associated with improved academic performance and a reduction in emotional and behavior problems in middle childhood (Peters, Petrunka, & Arnold, 2003; Vandell & Posner, 1999). Neighborhood organizations and informal social activities predict favorable development in adolescence, including increased self-confidence, school achievement, and educational aspirations (Gonzales et al., 1996).

Neighborhoods also affect adults' well-being. An employed parent who can rely on a neighbor to assist her school-age child in her absence and who lives in an area safe for walking to and from school gains the peace of mind essential for productive work. In low-SES areas with high resident stability and social cohesion, where neighbors collaborate in keeping the environment clean and watching out for vandalism and other crimes, adults report less stress, which in turn predicts substantially better physical health (Boardman, 2004; Feldman & Steptoe, 2004).

During late adulthood, neighborhoods become increasingly important because people spend more time in their homes. Despite the availability of planned housing for elders, about 90 percent remain in regular housing, usually in the same neighborhood where they lived during their working lives (Health Canada, 2002; U.S. Census Bureau, 2006). Proximity to relatives and friends is a significant factor in the decision to move or stay put late in life. In the absence of nearby family members, the elderly mention neighbors and nearby friends as resources they rely on most for physical and social support (Hooyman & Kiyak, 2005).

■ **Towns and Cities.** Neighborhoods are embedded in towns and cities, which also mold children's and adults' daily lives. In rural areas and small towns, children and youths are more likely to be given important work tasks—caring for live-stock, operating the snowplow, or playing in the town band. They usually perform these tasks alongside adults, who instill in them a strong sense of responsibility and teach them practi-cal and social skills needed to sustain their community. Com-pared with large urban areas, small towns also offer stronger connections between settings that influence children's lives. For example, because most citizens know each other and schools serve as centers of community life, contact between teachers and parents occurs often—an important factor in promoting children's academic achievement (Hill & Taylor, 2004).

Adults in small towns participate in more civic groups, such as town council, school board, and volunteer fire brigade. And they are more likely to occupy positions of leadership because a greater proportion of residents are needed to meet community needs (Elder & Conger, 2000). In late adulthood, people residing in small towns and suburbs have neighbors who are more willing to provide assistance. As a result, they develop a greater number of warm relationships with nonrela-tives. As one 99-year-old resident of a small Midwestern com-munity, living alone and leading an active life, commented, "I don't think I could get along if I didn't have good neighbors." The family next door helps him with grocery shopping, checks each night to make sure his basement light is off (the signal that he is out of the shower and into bed), and looks out in the morning to see that his garage door is raised (the signal that he is up and OK) (Fergus, 1995).

Of course, children and adults in small towns cannot visit museums, go to professional baseball games, or attend orches-tra concerts on a regular basis. The variety of settings is not as great as in a large city. In small towns, however, active involve-ment in the community is likely to be greater throughout the lifespan. Also, public places in small towns are relatively safe and secure. Responsible adults are present in almost all settings to keep an eye on children. And the elderly feel safer—a strong contributor to how satisfied they are with their place of resi-dence (Parmelee & Lawton, 1990; Shields et al., 2002). These conditions are hard to match in today's urban environments.

The Cultural Context

Our discussion in Chapter 1 emphasized that human develop-ment can be fully understood only when viewed in its larger cultural context. In the following sections, we expand on this theme by taking up the role of the *macrosystem* in develop-ment. First, we discuss ways that cultural values and practices affect environmental contexts for development. Second, we consider how healthy development depends on laws and gov-ernment programs that shield people from harm and foster their well-being.

■ **Cultural Values and Practices.** Cultures shape family interaction and community settings beyond the home—in short, all aspects of daily life. Many of us remain blind to aspects of our own cultural heritage until we see them in rela-tion to the practices of others.

Each semester, I ask my students to think about the ques-tion, Who should be responsible for rearing young children? Here are some typical answers: "If parents decide to have a baby, then they should be ready to care for it." "Most people are not happy about others intruding into family life." These state-ments reflect a widely held opinion in North America—that the care and rearing of children, and paying for that care, are the duty of parents, and only parents. This view has a long his-tory—one in which independence, self-reliance, and the pri-vacy of family life emerged as central North American values (Halfon & McLearn, 2002). It is one reason, among others, that the public has been slow to endorse government-supported benefits for all families, such as high-quality child care. And it has also contributed to the large number of American and Canadian families that remain poor, even though family mem-bers are gainfully employed (Pohl, 2002; UNICEF, 2005a).

Although the culture as a whole may value independence and privacy, not all citizens share the same values. Some belong to **subcultures**—groups of people with beliefs and customs that differ from those of the larger culture. Many ethnic minority groups in the United States and Canada have coop-erative family structures, which help protect their members from the harmful effects of poverty. As the Cultural Influences box on the following page indicates, the African-American tra-dition of **extended family households**, in which three or more generations live together, is a vital feature of black family life that has enabled its members to survive, despite a long history of prejudice and economic deprivation. Within the extended family, grandparents play meaningful roles in guiding younger generations; adults with employment, marital, or child-rearing difficulties receive assistance and emotional support; and care-giving is enhanced for children and the elderly. Active and involved extended families also characterize other minorities, such as Asian, Native-American, Hispanic, and Canadian Abo-riginal subcultures (Becker et al., 2003; Harrison et al., 1994).

Our discussion so far reflects a broad dimension on which cultures and subcultures differ: the extent to which *collectivism* versus *individualism* is emphasized. In **collectivist societies**, people define themselves as part of a group and stress group goals over individual goals. In **individualistic societies**, people think of themselves as separate entities and are largely con-cerned with their own personal needs (Triandis, 1995). As these definitions suggest, the two cultural patterns are associ-ated with two distinct views of the self. Collectivist societies value an *interdependent self*, which stresses social harmony, obligations and responsibility to others, and collaborative endeavors. In contrast, individualistic societies value an *independent self*, which emphasizes personal exploration, dis-covery, and achievement and individual choice in relation-ships. Both interdependence and independence are part of the makeup of every person and occur in varying mixtures

Cultural Influences

The African-American Extended Family

The African-American extended family can be traced to the African heritage of most black Americans. In many African societies, newly married couples do not start their own households. Instead, they live with a large extended family, which assists its members with all aspects of daily life. This tradition of maintaining a broad network of kin ties traveled to North America during the period of slavery. Since then, it has served as a protective shield against the destructive impact of poverty and racial prejudice on African-American family life. Today, more black than white adults have relatives other than their own children living in the same household. African-American parents also live closer to kin, often establish familylike relationships with friends and neighbors, see more relatives during the week, and perceive relatives as more important figures in their lives (Kane, 2000).

By providing emotional support and sharing essential resources, the African-American extended family helps reduce the stress of poverty and single parenthood. Extended-family members often help with child rearing, and adolescent mothers living in extended families are more likely to complete high school and get a job and less likely to be on welfare than mothers living on their own—factors that in turn benefit children's well-being (Gordon, Chase-Lansdale, & Brooks-Gunn, 2004; Trent & Harlan, 1994).

For single mothers who were very young at the time of their child's birth, extended-family living continues to be associated with more positive mother–child interaction during the preschool years. Otherwise, establishing an independent household with the help of nearby relatives is related to improved child rearing. Perhaps this arrangement permits the more mature teenage mother who has developed effective parenting skills to implement them (Chase-Lansdale, Brooks-Gunn, & Zamsky, 1994). In families rearing adolescents, kinship support increases the likelihood of effective parenting, which is related to adolescents' self-reliance, emotional well-being, and reduced delinquency (Hamilton, 2005; Taylor & Roberts, 1995).

Finally, the extended family plays an important role in transmitting African-American culture. Compared with nuclear-family households (which include only parents and their children), extended-family arrangements place more emphasis on cooperation and on moral and religious values. And older black adults, such as grandparents and great-grandparents, regard educating children about their African heritage as especially important (Mosely-Howard & Evans, 2000; Taylor, 2000). These influences strengthen family bonds, protect children's development, and increase the chances that the extended-family lifestyle will carry over to the next generation.

Strong bonds with extended-family members have helped protect many African-American children growing up under conditions of poverty and single parenthood. This extended family gathers to celebrate the eighty-fifth birthday of their oldest member.

© MICHAEL SCHWARTZ/THE IMAGE WORKS

(Greenfield et al., 2003; Keller, 2003). But societies vary greatly in the extent to which they emphasize each alternative and—as later chapters will reveal—instill it in their young.

Although individualism tends to increase as cultures become more complex, cross-national differences remain. The United States is strongly individualistic, while Canada falls in between the United States and most Western European countries, which lean toward collectivism. As we will see next, collectivist versus individualistic values have a powerful impact on a nation's approach to protecting the well-being of its children, families, and aging citizens.

■ **Public Policies and Lifespan Development.** When widespread social problems arise, such as poverty, homelessness, hunger, and disease, nations attempt to solve them through **public policies**—laws and government programs aimed at improving current conditions. For example, when poverty increases and families become homeless, a country might decide to build more low-cost housing, raise the minimum wage, and increase welfare benefits. When reports indicate that many children are not achieving well in school, federal and state or provincial governments might grant more tax money to school districts, strengthen teacher preparation, and make sure that help reaches children who need it most. And when senior citizens have difficulty making ends meet because of inflation, a nation might increase its social security benefits.

Nevertheless, American and Canadian public policies safeguarding children and youths have lagged behind policies for the elderly. And both sets of policies have been especially slow to emerge in the United States.

Policies for Children, Youths, and Families. We have already seen that although many North American children fare well, a large number grow up in environments that threaten their development. As Table 2.5 reveals, the United States does not rank well on any key measure of children's health and well-being. Canada, which devotes considerably more of its resources to education and health, fares somewhat better. For example, Canada grants all its citizens government-funded health care.

The problems of children and youths extend beyond the indicators in the table. For example, approximately 11 percent of American children—most of them in low-income families—have no health insurance, making children the largest segment of the U.S. uninsured population (U.S. Census Bureau, 2006b). Furthermore, the United States and Canada have been slow to move toward national standards and funding for child care. In both countries, much child care is substandard in quality (Goelman et al., 2000; NICHD Early Child Care Research Network, 2000a). In families affected by divorce, weak enforcement of child support payments heightens poverty in mother-headed families. By the time they finish high school, many non-college-bound young people in North America do not have the vocational preparation they need to contribute fully to society. And about 11 percent of U.S. and Canadian adolescents leave high school without a diploma (Bushnik, Barr-Telford, & Bussiére, 2004; U.S. Department of Education, 2005).

Why have attempts to help children and youths been especially difficult to realize in the United States and (to a lesser extent) Canada? A complex set of political and economic forces is involved. North American values of self-reliance and privacy have made government hesitant to become involved in family matters. Furthermore, good social programs are expensive, and they must compete for a fair share of a country's economic resources. Children can easily remain unrecognized in this process because they cannot vote or speak out to protect their own interests, as adult citizens do (Ripple & Zigler, 2003). Instead, they must rely on the goodwill of others to become an important government priority.

Policies for the Elderly. Until well into the twentieth century, the United States had few policies in place to protect its aging population. For example, Social Security benefits, which address the income needs of retired citizens who contributed to society through prior employment, were not awarded until the late 1930s. Yet most Western nations had social security systems in place a decade or more earlier; Canada's began in 1927 (DiNitto & Cummins, 2005). In the 1960s, U.S. federal spending on programs for the elderly expanded rapidly. Medicare, a national health insurance program for older people that pays partial health care costs, was initiated. But it mainly covers acute care services and requires participants to pay part of those costs, leaving about half of elderly health spending to be covered by supplemental private insurance, government health insurance for the poor, or out-of-pocket payments (National

| Table 2.5 | How Do the United States and Canada Compare to Other Nations on Indicators of Children's Health and Well-Being? |

Indicator	U.S. Rank[a]	Canadian Rank[a]	Some Countries the United States and Canada Trail
Childhood poverty (among 23 industrialized nations considered)	23rd	16th	Australia, Czech Republic, Germany, Norway, Sweden, Taiwan
Infant deaths in the first year of life (worldwide)	26th	16th	Hong Kong, Ireland, Singapore, Spain
Teenage pregnancy rate (among 45 industrialized nations considered)	28th	21st	Albania, Australia, Czech Republic, Denmark, Poland, Netherlands
Expenditures on education as percentage of gross domestic product[b] (among 22 industrialized nations considered)	10th	6th	*For Canada:* Israel, Sweden *For the United States:* Australia, France, New Zealand, Sweden
Expenditures on health as a percentage of gross domestic product (among 22 industrialized nations considered)	16th	3rd	*For Canada:* Iceland, Switzerland *For the United States:* Austria, Australia, Hungary, New Zealand

[a]1 = highest rank
[b]Gross domestic product is the value of all goods and services produced by a nation during a specified time period. It provides an overall measure of a nation's wealth.

Sources: Luxembourg Income Study, 2005; Perie et al., 2000; UNICEF, 2001; U.S. Census Bureau, 2006b; U.S. Department of Education, 2005.

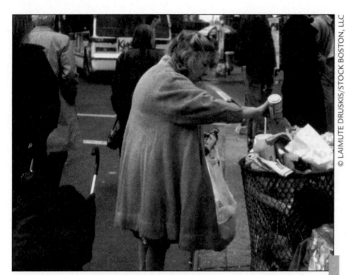

Overall, senior citizens in the United States are better off economically than are children. But many older adults—especially women and ethnic minorities—are poverty-stricken. And American elders are less well off than Canadian elders, who benefit from Canada's more generous income supplements and full health-care coverage.

Coalition on Health Care, 2005). Canadian elders, like other residents of Canada, benefit from a government-supported full health coverage system, initiated in the 1950s (also called Medicare).

Social Security and Medicare consume 96 percent of the U.S. federal budget for the elderly; only 4 percent is devoted to other programs. Consequently, U.S. programs for the elderly have been criticized for neglecting social services (Hooyman & Kiyak, 2005). To meet this need, a national network for planning, coordinating, and delivering assistance to the aged has been established. Approximately 700 Area Agencies on Aging operate at regional and local levels, assessing community needs and offering communal and home-delivered meals, self-care education, elder abuse prevention, and a wide range of other social services. But limited funding means that the Area Agencies help far too few people in need.

As noted earlier, many senior citizens—especially women, ethnic minorities, and those living alone—remain in dire economic straits. Those who had interrupted employment histories, held jobs without benefits, or suffered lifelong poverty are not eligible for Social Security. Although all Americans age 65 and older are guaranteed a minimum income, it is less than the poverty line—the amount judged necessary for bare subsistence by the federal government. Furthermore, Social Security benefits are rarely enough to serve as a sole source of retirement income; they must be supplemented through other pensions and family savings. But a substantial percentage of U.S. aging citizens do not have access to these resources. Therefore, they are more likely to be among the "near poor" than are other age groups (Greenberg, 2005). Because Canada provides more generous income supplements as part of its Old Age Security Program, far fewer Canadian than U.S. elders are poverty-stricken.

Nevertheless, the U.S. aging population is financially much better off now than in the past. Today, the elderly are a large, powerful, well-organized constituency, far more likely than children or low-income families to attract the support of politicians. As a result, the number of aging poor has declined from 1 out of 3 people in 1960 to 1 out of 10 in the early twenty-first century (U.S. Census Bureau, 2006b). And senior citizens are healthier and more independent than ever before. Still, as Figure 2.9 shows, the elderly in the United States are not as well off as those in many other Western nations.

■ **Looking Toward the Future.** Despite the worrisome state of many children, families, and aging citizens, efforts are being made to improve their condition. Throughout this book, we will discuss many successful programs that could be expanded. Also, growing awareness of the gap between what we know and what we do to better people's lives has led experts in human development to join with concerned citizens as advocates for more effective policies. As a result, several influential interest groups devoted to the well-being of children or the elderly have emerged.

In the United States, the Children's Defense Fund—a private, nonprofit organization founded by Marian Wright Edelman in 1973—engages in research, public education, legal action, drafting of legislation, congressional testimony, and community organizing. Each year, it publishes *The State of America's Children*, which provides a comprehensive analysis of children's condition, government-sponsored programs that serve children and families, and proposals for improving those programs. To learn more about the Children's Defense Fund, visit its website at *www.childrensdefense.org*

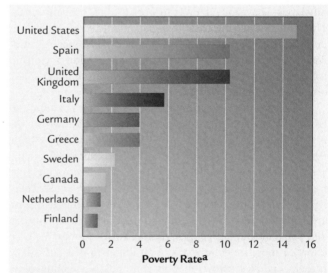

a Percentage of citizens age 65 and older earning 40 percent or less of the country's median income, adjusted for number of persons in household.

■ **FIGURE 2.9 Percentage of elderly living in poverty in ten industrialized nations.** Among the countries listed, the United States has the highest rate of elderly living in poverty. Public expenditures on social security and other income guarantees for senior citizens are highest in Finland, the Netherlands, and Canada and lowest in the United States. (Adapted from Luxembourg Income Study, 2005.)

Organizations such as the Children's Defense Fund in the United States and Campaign 2000 in Canada advocate for the needs of children. Policy-relevant research helps child advocates make the case for expanding programs like the Thomas J. Pappas School in Phoenix, Arizona, where all the students are homeless. Each receives vital supports for learning through health services, stimulating classroom experiences, and frequent teacher–parent contact. Here the students gather for an assembly.

In 1991, Canada initiated a public education movement, called Campaign 2000, to build nationwide awareness of the extent and consequences of child poverty and to lobby government representatives for improved policies benefiting children. Diverse organizations—including professional, religious, health, and labor groups at national, provincial, and community levels—have joined forces to work toward campaign goals. These include raising basic living standards so no child lives in poverty and strengthening child care and other community resources that assist families in rearing children. Consult *www.campaign2000.ca* to explore the work of Campaign 2000, including its annual *Report Card on Child Poverty in Canada.*

Nearly half of Americans over age 50, both retired and employed, are members of AARP (originally known as the American Association of Retired Persons). Founded by Ethel Percy Andrus in 1958, AARP has a large and energetic lobbying staff that works for increased government benefits of all kinds for the aged. Each year, it releases the *AARP Public Policy Agenda,* which forms the basis for advocacy activities in diverse areas, including income, health care, social services, housing, and personal and legal rights. Among AARP's programs is an effort to mobilize elderly voters, an initiative that keeps lawmakers highly sensitive to policy proposals affecting older Americans. A description of AARP and its activities can be found at *www.aarp.org*

Besides strong advocacy, public policies that enhance human development depend on policy-relevant research that documents needs and evaluates programs to spark improvements. Today, more researchers are collaborating with community and government agencies to enhance the social relevance of their investigations. They are also doing a better job of dis-

seminating their findings to the public, through television documentaries, newspaper stories, magazine articles, websites, and direct reports to government officials. As a result, they are helping to create a sense of immediacy about the condition of children, families, and the aged that is necessary to spur a society into action.

Ask Yourself

Review

Links between family and community foster development throughout the lifespan. Cite several examples from our discussion that support this idea.

Apply

Check your local newspaper or one or two national news magazines to see how often articles on the condition of children, families, and the aged appear. Why is it important for researchers to communicate with the general public about the well-being of these sectors of the population?

Connect

How does poverty affect the family system, placing all aspects of development at risk?

Reflect

Review the discussion of cultural values and practices on page 66. Under what circumstances do you believe government should become involved in family life?

www.ablongman.com/berk

Understanding the Relationship Between Heredity and Environment

So far in this chapter, we have discussed a wide variety of genetic and environmental influences, each of which has the power to alter the course of development. Yet people who are born into the same family (and who therefore share genes and environments) are often quite different in characteristics. We also know that some individuals are affected more than others by their homes, neighborhoods, and communities. Cases exist in which a person provided with all the advantages in life does poorly, whereas another exposed to the worst of rearing conditions does well. How do scientists explain the impact of heredity and environment when they seem to work in so many different ways?

All contemporary researchers agree that both heredity and environment are involved in every aspect of development. But for polygenic traits (those due to many genes) such as intelligence and personality, scientists are a long way from knowing the precise hereditary influences involved. Although they are making progress in identifying the multiple variations in DNA sequences associated with complex traits, so far these genetic markers explain only a small amount of variation in human behavior, and a minority of cases of most psychological disorders (Plomin, 2005; Plomin et al., 2003). For the most part, scientists are still limited to investigating the impact of genes on complex characteristics indirectly.

Some believe that it is useful and possible to answer the question of *how much each factor contributes* to differences among people. A growing consensus, however, regards that question as unanswerable. These investigators believe that genetic and environmental influences are inseparable. The important question, they maintain, is *how nature and nurture work together.* Let's consider each position in turn.

The Question, "How Much?"

Researchers use two methods—heritability estimates and concordance rates—to infer the role of heredity in complex human characteristics. Let's look closely at the information these procedures yield, along with their limitations.

■ **Heritability. Heritability estimates** measure the extent to which individual differences in complex traits in a specific population are due to genetic factors. We will take a brief look at heritability findings on intelligence and personality here and will return to them in later chapters, when we consider these topics in greater detail. Heritability estimates are obtained from **kinship studies,** which compare the characteristics of family members. The most common type of kinship study compares identical twins, who share all their genes, with fraternal twins, who share only some. If people who are genetically more alike are also more similar in intelligence and personality, then the researcher assumes that heredity plays an important role.

Kinship studies of intelligence provide some of the most controversial findings in the field of human development. Some experts claim a strong genetic influence, whereas others believe that heredity is barely involved. Currently, most kinship findings support a moderate role for heredity. When many twin studies are examined, correlations between the scores of identical twins are consistently higher than those of fraternal twins. In a summary of more than 13,000 twin pairs, the correlation for intelligence was .86 for identical twins and .60 for fraternal twins (Plomin & Spinath, 2004).

Researchers use a complex statistical procedure to compare these correlations, arriving at a heritability estimate ranging from 0 to 1.00. The value for intelligence is about .50 for child and adolescent twin samples in Western industrialized nations. This suggests that differences in genetic makeup explain half the variation in intelligence. However, heritability increases in adulthood, with some estimates as high as .80. As we will see later, one explanation is that, compared to children, adults exert greater personal control over their intellectual experiences—for example, how much time they spend reading or solving challenging problems (McClearn et al.,

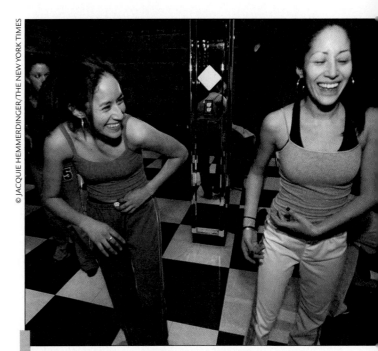

Adriana and Tamara, identical twins born in Mexico, were separated at birth and adopted into different homes in the New York City area. They were unaware of each other until a mutual acquaintance noted resemblances between them. When they decided to meet, at age 20, they discovered many similarities: Both like the same styles of clothing, were B students, prefer to stay up late at night, and love to dance. The study of identical twins reared apart reveals that heredity contributes to many personality characteristics. But not all separated twins match up as well as this pair, and generalizing from twin evidence to the broader population is controversial.

1997; McGue & Christensen, 2002). Adopted children's mental test scores are more strongly related to their biological parents' scores than to those of their adoptive parents, offering further support for the role of heredity (Plomin et al., 1997).

Heritability research also reveals that genetic factors are important in personality. For frequently studied traits, such as sociability, emotional expressiveness, agreeableness, and activity level, heritability estimates obtained on child, adolescent, and young adult twins are moderate, at .40 to .50 (Bouchard & McGue, 2003; Rothbart & Bates, 1998). Unlike intelligence, however, heritability of personality does not increase over the lifespan (Loehlin et al., 2005; Heiman et al., 2003).

■ **Concordance.** A second measure used to infer the contribution of heredity to complex characteristics is the **concordance rate.** It refers to the percentage of instances in which both twins show a trait when it is present in one twin. Researchers typically use concordance to study the contribution of heredity to emotional and behavior disorders, which can be judged as either present or absent.

A concordance rate ranges from 0 to 100 percent. A score of 0 indicates that if one twin has the trait, the other twin never has it. A score of 100 means that if one twin has the trait, the other one always has it. When a concordance rate is much higher for identical twins than for fraternal twins, heredity is believed to play a major role. Twin studies of schizophrenia (a disorder involving delusions and hallucinations, difficulty distinguishing fantasy from reality, and irrational and inappropriate behaviors) and severe depression show this pattern. In the case of schizophrenia, the concordance rate for identical twins is 50 percent, that for fraternal twins only 18 percent. For severe depression, the figures are 69 percent and 25 percent (Gottesman, 1991; McGuffin & Sargeant, 1991). Again, adoption studies support these results. Biological relatives of schizophrenic and depressed adoptees are more likely than adoptive relatives to share the same disorder (Plomin et al., 2001; Tienari et al., 2003).

Taken together, concordance and adoption research suggests that the tendency for schizophrenia and depression to run in families is partly due to genetic factors. However, we also know that environment is involved: If heredity were the only influence, the concordance rate for identical twins would be 100 percent.

■ **Limitations of Heritability and Concordance.** Serious questions have been raised about the accuracy of heritability estimates and concordance rates. First, each value refers only to the particular population studied and its unique range of genetic and environmental influences. For example, imagine a country in which people's home, school, and community experiences are very similar. Under these conditions, individual differences in behavior would be largely genetic, and heritability estimates would be close to 1.00. Conversely, the more environments vary, the greater their opportunity to account for individual differences, and the lower heritability estimates are likely to be.

Second, the accuracy of heritability estimates and concordance rates depends on the extent to which the twin pairs used reflect genetic and environmental variation in the population. Yet most twins studied are reared together under highly similar conditions. Even when separated twins are available for study, social service agencies often place them in advantaged homes that are alike in many ways (Rutter et al., 2001). Because the environments of most twin pairs are less diverse than those of the general population, heritability estimates are likely to exaggerate the role of heredity.

Heritability estimates are controversial because they can easily be misapplied. For example, high heritabilities have been used to suggest that ethnic differences in intelligence, such as the poorer performance of black children compared to white children, have a genetic basis (Jensen, 1969, 1985, 1998). Yet this line of reasoning is widely regarded as incorrect. Heritabilities computed on mostly white twin samples do not tell us what is responsible for test score differences between ethnic groups. We have already seen that large economic and cultural differences are involved. In Chapter 9, we will discuss research indicating that, when black children are adopted into economically advantaged homes at an early age, their scores are well above average and substantially higher than those of children growing up in impoverished families.

Perhaps the most serious criticism of heritability estimates and concordance rates has to do with their limited usefulness.

They are interesting statistics but give us no precise information on how intelligence and personality develop or how children might respond to environments designed to help them develop as far as possible (Rutter, 2002; Wachs, 1999). Indeed, the heritability of children's intelligence increases as parental education and income increase—that is, as children grow up in conditions that allow them to make the most of their genetic endowment. In disadvantaged environments, children are prevented from realizing their potential. Consequently, enhancing their experiences through interventions—such as parent education and high-quality preschool or child care—has a greater impact on development (Bronfenbrenner & Morris, 1998; Turkheimer et al., 2003).

According to one group of experts, heritability estimates have too many problems to yield any firm conclusions about the relative strength of nature and nurture (Collins et al., 2000). Although these statistics confirm that heredity contributes to complex traits, they do not tell us how environment can modify genetic influences.

The Question, "How?"

Today, most researchers view development as the result of a dynamic interplay between heredity and environment. How do nature and nurture work together? Several concepts shed light on this question.

■ **Reaction Range.** The first of these ideas is **range of reaction,** each person's unique, genetically determined response to the environment (Gottesman, 1963). Let's explore this idea in Figure 2.10. Reaction range can apply to any characteristic;

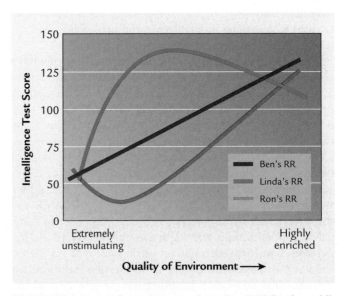

■ **FIGURE 2.10 Intellectual ranges of reaction (RR) for three children in environments that vary from extremely unstimulating to highly enriched.** Each child, due to his or her genetic makeup, responds differently as quality of the environment changes. Ben's intelligence test score increases steadily, Linda's rises sharply and then falls off, and Ron's begins to increase only after the environment becomes modestly stimulating. (Adapted from Wahlsten, 1994.)

here it is illustrated for intelligence. Notice that when environments vary from extremely unstimulating to highly enriched, Ben's intelligence increases steadily, Linda's rises sharply and then falls off, and Ron's begins to increase only after the environment becomes modestly stimulating.

Reaction range highlights two important points. First, it shows that because each of us has a unique genetic makeup, we respond differently to the same environment. Notice in Figure 2.10 how a poor environment results in similarly low scores for all three individuals. But Linda is by far the best-performing child when environments provide an intermediate level of stimulation. And when environments are highly enriched, Ben does best, followed by Ron, both of whom now outperform Linda. Second, sometimes different genetic–environmental combinations can make two people look the same! For example, if Linda is reared in a minimally stimulating environment, her score will be about 100—average for people in general. Ben and Ron can also obtain this score, but to do so, they must grow up in a fairly enriched home. In sum, range of reaction reveals that unique blends of heredity and environment lead to both similarities and differences in behavior (Wahlsten, 1994).

■ **Canalization.** The concept of canalization provides another way of understanding how heredity and environment combine. **Canalization** is the tendency of heredity to restrict the development of some characteristics to just one or a few outcomes. A behavior that is strongly canalized develops similarly in a wide range of environments; only strong environmental forces can change it (Waddington, 1957). For example, infant perceptual and motor development seems to be strongly canalized because all normal human babies eventually roll over, reach for objects, sit up, crawl, and walk. It takes extreme circumstances to modify these behaviors. In contrast, intelligence and personality are less strongly canalized, since they vary much more with changes in the environment.

When we look at the behaviors constrained by heredity, we can see that canalization is highly adaptive. Through it, nature ensures that children will develop certain species-typical skills under many rearing conditions, thereby promoting survival.

■ **Genetic–Environmental Correlation.** A major problem in trying to separate heredity and environment is that they are often correlated (Plomin et al., 2001; Scarr & McCartney, 1983). According to the concept of **genetic–environmental correlation,** our genes influence the environments to which we are exposed. The way this happens changes with age.

Passive and Evocative Correlation. At younger ages, two types of genetic–environmental correlation are common. The first is called *passive* correlation because the child has no control over it. Early on, parents provide environments influenced by their own heredity. For example, parents who are good athletes emphasize outdoor activities and enroll their children in activities like swimming and gymnastics. Besides being exposed to an "athletic environment," the children may have inherited their parents' athletic ability. As a result, they are

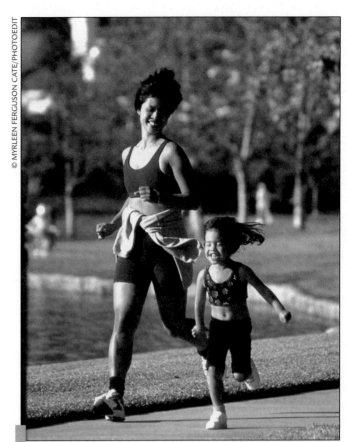

This mother shares her love of running with her daughter. In addition, her child may have inherited her mother's athletic ability. When heredity and environment are correlated, they jointly foster the same capacities, and the influence of one cannot be separated from the influence of the other.

likely to become good athletes for both genetic and environmental reasons.

The second type of genetic–environmental correlation is *evocative.* Children evoke responses that are influenced by the child's heredity, and these responses strengthen the child's original style. For example, an active, friendly baby is likely to receive more social stimulation than a passive, quiet infant. And a cooperative, attentive child probably receives more patient and sensitive interactions from parents than an inattentive, distractible child. In support of this idea, the less genetically alike siblings are, the more their parents treat them differently, in both warmth and negativity. Thus, parents' treatment of identical twins is highly similar, whereas their treatment of fraternal twins and nontwin biological siblings is only moderately so. And little resemblance exists in parents' warm and negative interactions with unrelated stepsiblings (Reiss, 2003).

Active Correlation. At older ages, *active* genetic–environmental correlation becomes common. As children extend their experiences beyond the immediate family and are given the freedom to make more choices, they actively seek environments that fit with their genetic tendencies. The well-coordinated, muscular child spends more time at after-school sports, the musically talented youngster joins the school orchestra and practices his violin, and the intellectually curious child is a familiar patron at her local library.

This tendency to actively choose environments that complement our heredity is called **niche-picking** (Scarr & McCartney, 1983). Infants and young children cannot do much niche-picking because adults select environments for them. In contrast, older children, adolescents, and adults are increasingly in charge of their environments.

The niche-picking idea explains why pairs of identical twins reared apart during childhood and later reunited may find, to their great surprise, that they have similar hobbies, food preferences, and vocations—a trend that is especially marked when twins' environmental opportunities are similar (Plomin, 1994). Niche-picking also helps us understand why identical twins become somewhat more alike, and fraternal twins and adopted siblings less alike, in intelligence with age (Loehlin, Horn, & Willerman, 1997; McGue & Bouchard, 1998). And niche-picking sheds light on why identical twins, compared to fraternal twins and other adults, select more similar spouses and best friends—in height, weight, personality, political attitudes, and other characteristics (Rushton & Bons, 2005).

The influence of heredity and environment is not constant but changes over time. With age, genetic factors may become more important in influencing the environments we experience and choose for ourselves.

■ **Environmental Influences on Gene Expression.** Notice how, in the concepts just considered, heredity is granted priority. In range of reaction, it *limits* responsiveness to varying environments. In canalization, it *restricts* the development of certain behaviors. Similarly, some theorists regard genetic–environmental correlation as entirely driven by genetics (Harris, 1998; Rowe, 1994). They believe that children's genetic

makeup causes them to receive, evoke, or seek experiences that actualize their inborn tendencies.

Others argue that heredity does not dictate children's experiences or development in a rigid way. Parents and other caring adults can provide children with experiences that modify the expression of heredity, yielding favorable outcomes. For example, in a study that tracked the development of 5-year-old identical twins, pair members tended to resemble each other in antisocial behavior. And the more antisocial behavior they displayed, the more maternal criticism and hostility they received (a genetic–environmental correlation). Nevertheless, some mothers treated their twins differently. When followed up at age 7, twins who had been targets of more maternal negativity engaged in even more antisocial behavior. In contrast, their better-treated, genetically identical counterparts showed a reduction in hostility (Caspi et al., 2004). Good parenting protected them from a spiraling, antisocial course of development.

Investigations extending over a longer time span reveal similar findings. In adoption research, children with a genetic risk for criminality (their biological mothers were imprisoned offenders) showed a high rate of antisocial behavior in adolescence only when reared in unfavorable homes, as indicated by adoptive parents or siblings with severe adjustment problems. In families free of psychological disturbance, adoptees with a predisposition to criminality did not differ from adoptees without this genetic risk (Bohman, 1996; Yates, Cadoret, & Troughton, 1999).

Accumulating evidence reveals that the relationship between heredity and environment is not a one-way street, from genes to environment to behavior. Rather, like other system influences considered in this and the previous chapter, it is *bidirectional*: Genes affect people's behavior and experiences, but their experiences and behavior also affect gene expression (Gottlieb, 2000, 2003; Ryff & Singer, 2005).

■ **FIGURE 2.11 The epigenetic framework.** Development takes place through ongoing, bidirectional exchanges between heredity and all levels of the environment. Genes affect behavior and experiences. Experiences and behavior also affect gene expression. (Adapted from Gottlieb, 2000.)

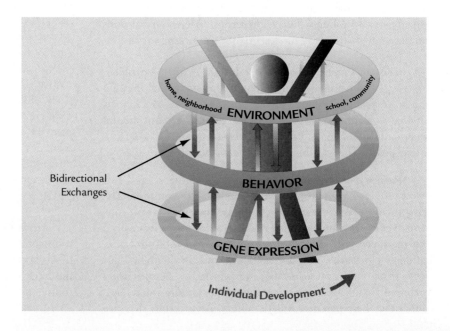

Researchers call this view of the relationship between heredity and environment the *epigenetic framework* (Gottlieb, 1998, 2002). It is depicted in Figure 2.11. **Epigenesis** means development resulting from ongoing, bidirectional exchanges between heredity and all levels of the environment. To illustrate, providing a baby with a healthy diet increases brain growth, leading to new connections between nerve cells, which transform gene expression. This opens the door to new gene–environment exchanges—for example, advanced exploration of objects and interaction with caregivers, which further enhance brain growth and gene expression. These ongoing, bidirectional influences foster cognitive and social development. In contrast, harmful environments can dampen gene expression, at times so profoundly that later experiences can do little to change characteristics (such as intelligence and personality) that were flexible to begin with.

A major reason that researchers are interested in the nature–nurture issue is that they want to improve environments so that people can develop as far as possible. The concept of epigenesis reminds us that development is best understood as a series of complex exchanges between nature and nurture. Although people cannot be changed in any way we might desire, environments can modify genetic influences. The success of any attempt to improve development depends on the characteristics we want to change, the genetic makeup of the individual, and the type and timing of our intervention.

Ask Yourself

Review

What is epigenesis, and how does it differ from range of reaction and genetic–environmental correlation? Provide an example of epigenesis.

Apply

Bianca's parents are accomplished musicians. At age 4, Bianca began taking piano lessons. By age 10, she was accompanying the school choir. At age 14, she asked if she could attend a special music high school. Explain how genetic-environmental correlation promoted Bianca's talent.

Connect

Explain how each of the following concepts supports the conclusion that genetic influences on human characteristics are not constant but change over time: somatic mutation (page 51), niche-picking (page 74), and epigenesis (page 75).

Reflect

What aspects of your own development—for example, interests, hobbies, college major, or vocational choice—are probably due to niche-picking? Explain.

www.ablongman.com/berk

Summary

Genetic Foundations

What are genes, and how are they transmitted from one generation to the next?

- Each individual's **phenotype**, or directly observable characteristics, is a product of both **genotype** and environment. **Chromosomes**, rodlike structures within the cell nucleus, contain our hereditary endowment. Along their length are **genes**, segments of **DNA** that send instructions for making a rich assortment of proteins to the cell's cytoplasm—a process that makes us distinctly human and influences our development and characteristics. We share most of our genetic makeup with other mammals, especially primates.

- **Gametes**, or sex cells, are produced by a process of cell division called **meiosis**, in which each individual receives a unique set of genes from each parent. Once sperm and ovum unite, the resulting **zygote** starts to

develop into a complex human being through cell duplication, or **mitosis**.

- If the fertilizing sperm carries an X chromosome, the child will be a girl; if it contains a Y chromosome, a boy. **Fraternal**, or **dizygotic**, **twins** result when two ova are released from the mother's ovaries and each is fertilized. **Identical**, or **monozygotic**,

© ELLEN SENISI/THE IMAGE WORKS

twins develop when a zygote divides in two during the early stages of cell duplication.

Describe various patterns of genetic inheritance.

- Traits controlled by single genes follow **dominant–recessive** and **incomplete-dominance** patterns of inheritance. **Homozygous** individuals have two identical **alleles**, or forms of a gene. **Heterozygous** individuals with one dominant and recessive allele are **carriers** of the recessive trait.

- Recessive disorders carried on the X chromosome (**X-linked**) are more likely to affect males. In **genetic imprinting**, one parent's gene is activated, regardless of its makeup.

- Unfavorable genes arise from **mutations**, which can occur spontaneously or be induced by hazardous environmental agents. Mutations can be either germline, affecting cells that give rise to gametes, or somatic, occurring in body cells at any time of life.

■ **Polygenic** human traits, such as intelligence and personality, are influenced by many genes. For such characteristics, scientists must study the influence of heredity indirectly.

Describe major chromosomal abnormalities, and explain how they occur.

■ Most chromosomal abnormalities are due to errors in meiosis. The most common is Down syndrome, which results in physical defects and mental retardation. Disorders of the **sex chromosomes** are generally milder than defects of the **autosomes**. Specific intellectual problems result when a child has either more or fewer X chromosomes than usual, as in triple X, Klinefelter, and Turner syndromes.

Reproductive Choices

What procedures can assist prospective parents in having healthy children?

■ **Genetic counseling** helps couples at risk for giving birth to children with genetic abnormalities decide whether or not to conceive. **Prenatal diagnostic methods** permit early detection of genetic problems.

■ Reproductive technologies such as donor insemination, in vitro fertilization, surrogate motherhood, and postmenopausal-assisted childbirth permit many individuals to become parents who otherwise would

not, but they raise serious legal and ethical concerns.

■ Many parents who cannot conceive or who are at high risk of transmitting a genetic disorder decide to adopt. Although adopted children have more learning and emotional problems than children in general, warm, sensitive parenting predicts favorable development. In the long run, most adopted children fare well.

Environmental Contexts for Development

Describe the social systems perspective on family functioning, along with aspects of the environment that support family well-being and development.

■ Just as complex as heredity are the environments in which human development takes place. The family is the first and foremost context for development. The family system is dynamic, constantly adjusting to new events, to developmental changes in its members, and to societal change. Ecological systems theory emphasizes that the behaviors of each family member affect those of others.

■ One source of consistency in family functioning is **socioeconomic status (SES)**. Higher-SES families tend to be smaller, to emphasize nurturing psychological traits, and to promote warm, verbally stimulating interaction with children. Lower-SES families often stress external characteristics and engage in more restrictive child rearing. Further, poverty and homelessness can seriously undermine development.

■ Supportive communities—those that encourage constructive leisure activities, warm interactions among residents, connections between settings, and children and adults' active participation—foster well-being throughout the lifespan.

■ The values and practices of cultures and **subcultures** affect all aspects of daily life. **Extended family households** including three or more generations are common among ethnic minorities. They protect

development under stressful life conditions.

■ In our complex world, favorable development depends on **public policies**. Factors promoting effective social programs include cultural values that stress **collectivism** over **individualism**, a nation's economic resources, and organizations and individuals that work to improve quality of life.

■ American and Canadian policies safeguarding children and their families are less well developed than those safeguarding the elderly.

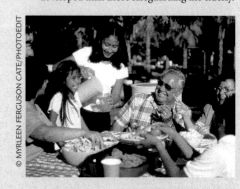

Understanding the Relationship Between Heredity and Environment

Explain the various ways heredity and environment may combine to influence complex traits.

■ Some researchers attempt to determine how much heredity and environment, respectively, contribute to individual differences by computing **heritability estimates** and **concordance rates** from **kinship studies**. Although these measures show that genetic factors influence such traits as intelligence and personality, their accuracy and usefulness have been challenged.

■ Most researchers view development as the result of a dynamic interplay between nature and nurture. The concepts of **range of reaction, canalization, genetic–environmental correlation, niche-picking**, and **epigenesis** remind us that development is best understood as a series of complex exchanges between nature and nurture that change over the lifespan.

Important Terms and Concepts

allele (p. 48)
autosomes (p. 47)
canalization (p. 73)
carrier (p. 48)
chromosomes (p. 46)
collectivist societies (p. 66)
concordance rate (p. 71)
deoxyribonucleic acid (DNA) (p. 46)
dominant–recessive inheritance (p. 48)
epigenesis (p. 75)
extended family household (p. 66)
fraternal, or dizygotic, twins (p. 47)
gametes (p. 46)

gene (p. 46)
genetic counseling (p. 53)
genetic–environmental correlation (p. 73)
genetic imprinting (p. 51)
genotype (p. 45)
heritability estimate (p. 71)
heterozygous (p. 48)
homozygous (p. 48)
identical, or monozygotic, twins (p. 48)
incomplete dominance (p. 50)
individualistic societies (p. 66)
kinship studies (p. 71)
meiosis (p. 46)

mitosis (p. 46)
mutation (p. 51)
niche-picking (p. 74)
phenotype (p. 45)
polygenic inheritance (p. 52)
prenatal diagnostic methods (p. 53)
public policies (p. 67)
range of reaction (p. 72)
sex chromosomes (p. 47)
socioeconomic status (SES) (p. 61)
subculture (p. 66)
X-linked inheritance (p. 50)
zygote (p. 46)

© JOSE LUIS PELAEZ, INC./CORBIS

As these parents share a joyful, intimate moment with their children, they convey a sense of delight in their growing family and help older siblings welcome the new baby.

Prenatal Development, Birth, and the Newborn Baby

When I met Yolanda and Jay one fall in my child development class, Yolanda was just two months pregnant. After months of wondering if the time in their own lives was right, they had decided to have a baby. Both were full of questions: "How does the baby grow before birth? When are different organs formed? Has its heart begun to beat? Can it hear, feel, or sense our presence?"

Most of all, Yolanda and Jay wanted to do everything possible to make sure their baby would be born healthy. At first, they believed that the uterus completely shielded the developing organism from any dangers in the environment. All babies born with problems, they thought, had unfavorable genes. After browsing through several pregnancy books, Yolanda and Jay realized they were wrong. Yolanda started to wonder about her diet. And she asked me whether an aspirin for a headache, a glass of wine at dinner, or a few cups of coffee during study hours might be harmful.

© PHOTODISC/GREEN/RF/GETTY IMAGE

In this chapter, we answer Yolanda's and Jay's questions, along with a great many more that scientists have asked about the events before birth. First, we trace prenatal development, paying special attention to environmental supports for healthy growth, as well as damaging influences that threaten the child's health and survival. Next, we turn to the events of childbirth. Today, women in industrialized nations have many more choices than ever before about where and how they give birth, and hospitals often go to great lengths to make the arrival of a new baby a rewarding, family-centered event.

Yolanda and Jay's son Joshua reaped the benefits of their careful attention to his needs during pregnancy. He was strong, alert, and healthy at birth. Nevertheless, the birth process does not always go smoothly. We will consider the pros and cons of medical interventions, such as pain-relieving drugs and surgical deliveries, designed to ease a difficult birth and protect the health of mother and baby. Our discussion also addresses the development of infants born underweight or too early, before the prenatal period is complete. We conclude with a close look at the remarkable capacities of newborns.

Prenatal Development

The sperm and ovum that unite to form the new individual are uniquely suited for the task of reproduction. The ovum is a tiny sphere, measuring 1/175 inch in diameter, that is barely visible to the naked eye as a dot the size of the period at the end of this sentence. But in its microscopic world, it is a giant—the largest cell in the human body. The ovum's size makes it a perfect target for the much smaller sperm, which measure only 1/500 inch.

Conception

About once every 28 days, in the middle of a woman's menstrual cycle, an ovum bursts from one of her *ovaries*, two walnut-sized organs located deep inside her abdomen, and is drawn into one of two *fallopian tubes*—long, thin structures that lead to the hollow, soft-lined uterus (see Figure 3.1). While the ovum travels, the spot on the ovary from which it was released, now called the *corpus luteum*, secretes hormones that prepare the lining of the uterus to receive a fertilized ovum. If pregnancy does not occur, the corpus luteum shrinks, and the lining of the uterus is discarded two weeks later with menstruation.

The male produces sperm in vast numbers—an average of 300 million a day—in the *testes*, two glands located in the *scrotum*, a sac that lies just behind the penis. In the final process

© JACK BURNS/ACE/PHOTOTAKE

In this photo taken with the aid of a powerful microscope, sperm have completed their journey up the female reproductive tract and are beginning to penetrate the surface of the enormous-looking ovum, the largest cell in the human body. When one of the sperm is successful at fertilizing the ovum, the resulting zygote will begin to duplicate.

of maturation, each sperm develops a tail that permits it to swim long distances upstream in the female reproductive tract, through the *cervix* (opening of the uterus) and into the fallopian tube, where fertilization usually takes place. The journey is difficult, and many sperm die. Only 300 to 500 reach the

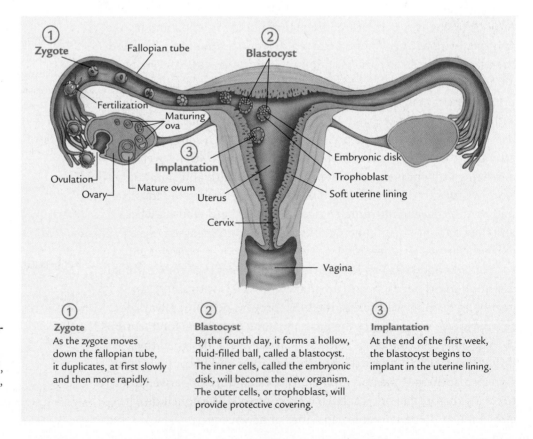

① Zygote
Fallopian tube
② Blastocyst
Fertilization
Maturing ova
Embryonic disk
③
Implantation
Trophoblast
Soft uterine lining
Ovulation
Mature ovum
Ovary
Uterus
Cervix
Vagina

■ **FIGURE 3.1 Female reproductive organs, showing fertilization, early cell duplication, and implantation.** (Adapted from K. L. Moore and T. V. N. Persaud, 2003, *Before We Are Born*, 6th ed., Philadelphia: Saunders, p. 36. Reprinted by permission of the publisher and authors.)

① Zygote
As the zygote moves down the fallopian tube, it duplicates, at first slowly and then more rapidly.

② Blastocyst
By the fourth day, it forms a hollow, fluid-filled ball, called a blastocyst. The inner cells, called the embryonic disk, will become the new organism. The outer cells, or trophoblast, will provide protective covering.

③ Implantation
At the end of the first week, the blastocyst begins to implant in the uterine lining.

Table 3.1			Milestones of Prenatal Development	

Trimester	Period	Weeks	Length and Weight	Major Events
First	Zygote	1		The one-celled zygote multiplies and forms a blastocyst.
		2		The blastocyst burrows into the uterine lining. Structures that feed and protect the developing organism begin to form—*amnion, chorion, yolk sac, placenta,* and *umbilical cord.*
	Embryo	3–4	¼ inch (6 mm)	A primitive brain and spinal cord appear. Heart, muscles, ribs, backbone, and digestive tract begin to develop.
		5–8	1 inch (2.5 cm); ½ ounce (4 g)	Many external body structures (face, arms, legs, toes, fingers) and internal organs form. The sense of touch begins to develop, and the embryo can move.
	Fetus	9–12	3 inches (7.6 cm); less than 1 ounce (28 g)	Rapid increase in size begins. Nervous system, organs, and muscles become organized and connected, and new behavioral capacities (kicking, thumb sucking, mouth opening, and rehearsal of breathing) appear. External genitals are well-formed, and the fetus's sex is evident.
Second		13–24	12 inches (30 cm); 1.8 pounds (820 g)	The fetus continues to enlarge rapidly. In the middle of this period, fetal movements can be felt by the mother. Vernix and lanugo keep the fetus's skin from chapping in the amniotic fluid. Most of the brain's neurons are present by 24 weeks. Eyes are sensitive to light, and the fetus reacts to sound.
Third		25–38	20 inches (50 cm); 7.5 pounds (3,400 g)	The fetus has a chance of survival if born during this time. Size increases. Lungs mature. Rapid brain development causes sensory and behavioral capacities to expand. In the middle of this period, a layer of fat is added under the skin. Antibodies are transmitted from mother to fetus to protect against disease. Most fetuses rotate into an upside-down position in preparation for birth.

Source: Moore & Persaud, 2003.

Photos (from top to bottom): © Claude Cortier/Photo Researchers, Inc.; © G. Moscoso/Photo Researchers, Inc.; © John Watney/Photo Researchers, Inc.; © James Stevenson/Photo Researchers, Inc.; © Lennart Nilsson, *A Child is Born*/Bonniers.

ovum, if one happens to be present. Sperm live for up to 6 days and can lie in wait for the ovum, which survives for only 1 day after being released into the fallopian tube. However, most conceptions result from intercourse occurring during a 3-day period—on the day of ovulation or during the 2 days preceding it (Wilcox, Weinberg, & Baird, 1995).

With conception, the story of prenatal development begins to unfold. The vast changes that take place during the 38 weeks of pregnancy are usually divided into three phases: (1) the period of the zygote, (2) the period of the embryo, and (3) the period of the fetus. As we look at what happens in each, you may find it useful to refer to Table 3.1, which summarizes the milestones of prenatal development.

Period of the Zygote

The period of the zygote lasts about 2 weeks, from fertilization until the tiny mass of cells drifts down and out of the fallopian tube and attaches itself to the wall of the uterus. The zygote's first cell duplication is long and drawn out; it is not complete until about 30 hours after conception. Gradually, new cells are added at a faster rate. By the fourth day, 60 to 70 cells exist that form a hollow, fluid-filled ball called a *blastocyst* (refer again to Figure 3.1). The cells on the inside, called the *embryonic disk*, will become the new organism; the outer ring of cells, termed the *trophoblast*, will provide protective covering and nourishment.

© LENNART NILSSON, *A CHILD IS BORN*/BONNIERS

Period of the zygote: seventh to ninth day. The fertilized ovum duplicates at an increasingly rapid rate, forming a hollow ball of cells, or blastocyst, by the fourth day after fertilization. Here the blastocyst, magnified thousands of times, burrows into the uterine lining between the seventh and ninth day.

■ **Implantation.** Between the seventh and ninth days after fertilization, **implantation** occurs: the blastocyst burrows deep into the uterine lining. Surrounded by the woman's nourishing blood, it starts to grow in earnest. At first, the trophoblast (protective outer layer) multiplies fastest. It forms a membrane, called the **amnion**, that encloses the developing organism in *amniotic fluid*, which helps keep the temperature of the prenatal world constant and provides a cushion against any jolts caused by the woman's movements. A *yolk sac* emerges that produces blood cells until the liver, spleen, and bone marrow are mature enough to take over this function (Moore & Persaud, 2003).

The events of these first 2 weeks are delicate and uncertain. As many as 30 percent of zygotes do not survive this period. In some, the sperm and ovum do not join properly. In others, cell duplication never begins. By preventing implantation in these cases, nature quickly eliminates most prenatal abnormalities (Sadler, 2003).

■ **The Placenta and Umbilical Cord.** By the end of the second week, cells of the trophoblast form another protective membrane—the **chorion**, which surrounds the amnion. From the chorion, tiny hairlike *villi*, or blood vessels, begin to emerge.[1] As these villi burrow into the uterine wall, a special organ called the placenta starts to develop. By bringing the embryo's and mother's blood close together, the **placenta** per-

mits food and oxygen to reach the organism and waste products to be carried away. A membrane forms that allows these substances to be exchanged but prevents the blood of the mother and that of the embryo from mixing directly.

The placenta is connected to the developing organism by the **umbilical cord**, which first appears as a tiny stalk and eventually grows to a length of one to three feet. The umbilical cord contains one large vein, which delivers blood loaded with nutrients, and two arteries, which remove waste products. The force of blood flowing through the cord keeps it firm, so it seldom tangles while the embryo, like a space-walking astronaut, floats freely in its fluid-filled chamber (Moore & Persaud, 2003).

By the end of the period of the zygote, the developing organism has found food and shelter. These dramatic beginnings take place before most mothers know they are pregnant.

Period of the Embryo

The period of the **embryo** lasts from implantation through the eighth week of pregnancy. During these brief 6 weeks, the most rapid prenatal changes take place as the groundwork is laid for all body structures and internal organs.

■ **Last Half of the First Month.** In the first week of this period, the embryonic disk forms three layers of cells: (1) the *ectoderm*, which will become the nervous system and skin; (2) the *mesoderm*, from which will develop the muscles, skeleton, circulatory system, and other internal organs; and (3) the *endoderm*, which will become the digestive system, lungs, urinary tract, and glands. These three layers give rise to all parts of the body.

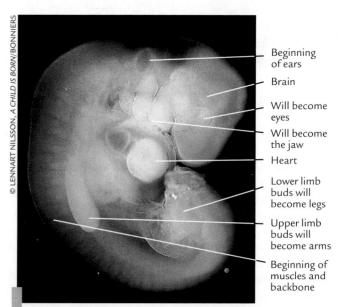

© LENNART NILSSON, *A CHILD IS BORN*/BONNIERS

- Beginning of ears
- Brain
- Will become eyes
- Will become the jaw
- Heart
- Lower limb buds will become legs
- Upper limb buds will become arms
- Beginning of muscles and backbone

Period of the embryo: fourth week. In actual size, this 4-week-old embryo is only ¼-inch long, but many body structures have begun to form. The primitive tail will disappear by the end of the embryonic period.

---

[1]Recall from Table 2.4 on page 56 that *chorionic villus sampling* is the prenatal diagnostic method that can be performed earliest, by 6 to 8 weeks after conception.

Period of the embryo: seventh week. The embryo's posture is more upright. Body structures—eyes, nose, arms, legs, and internal organs—are more distinct. An embryo of this age responds to touch. It can also move, although at less than one inch long and one ounce in weight, it is still too tiny to be felt by the mother.

At first, the nervous system develops fastest. The ectoderm folds over to form a **neural tube**, which will become the spinal cord and brain. At 3½ weeks, production of neurons (nerve cells that store and transmit information) begins deep inside the neural tube at the astounding pace of more than 250,000 per minute. Once formed, neurons travel along tiny threads to their permanent locations, where they will form the major parts of the brain (Huttenlocher, 2002).

While the nervous system is developing, the heart begins to pump blood, and the muscles, backbone, ribs, and digestive tract appear. At the end of the first month, the curled embryo—only ¼ inch long—consists of millions of organized groups of cells with specific functions.

■ **The Second Month.** Growth continues rapidly in the second month. The eyes, ears, nose, jaw, and neck form. Tiny buds become arms, legs, fingers, and toes. Internal organs are more distinct: The intestines grow, the heart develops separate chambers, and the liver and spleen take over production of blood cells so that the yolk sac is no longer needed. Changing body proportions cause the embryo's posture to become more upright. Now 1 inch long and ⅐ of an ounce in weight, the embryo can sense its world. It responds to touch, particularly in the mouth area and on the soles of the feet. And it can move, although its tiny flutters are still too light to be felt by the mother (Moore & Persaud, 2003).

Period of the Fetus

The period of the **fetus**, from the ninth week to the end of pregnancy, is the longest prenatal period. During this "growth and finishing" phase, the organism increases rapidly in size.

■ **The Third Month.** In the third month, the organs, muscles, and nervous system start to become organized and connected. When the brain signals, the fetus kicks, bends its arms, forms a fist, curls its toes, opens its mouth, and even sucks its thumb. The tiny lungs begin to expand and contract in an early rehearsal of breathing movements. By the twelfth week, the external genitals are well-formed, and the sex of the fetus can be detected with ultrasound. Other finishing touches appear, such as fingernails, toenails, tooth buds, and eyelids that open and close. The heartbeat can now be heard through a stethoscope.

Prenatal development is sometimes divided into **trimesters**, or three equal time periods. At the end of the third month, the *first trimester* is complete.

■ **The Second Trimester.** By the middle of the second trimester, between 17 and 20 weeks, the new being has grown large enough that the mother can feel its movements. A white, cheeselike substance called **vernix** protects its skin from chapping during the long months spent bathing in the amniotic

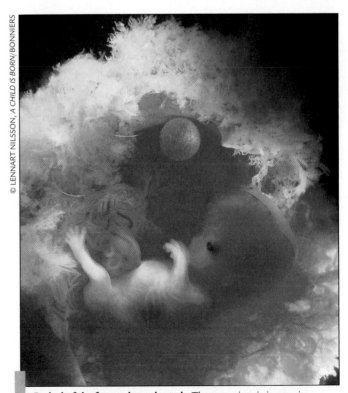

Period of the fetus: eleventh week. The organism is increasing rapidly in size. At 11 weeks, the brain and muscles are better connected. The fetus can kick, bend its arms, open and close its hands and mouth, and suck its thumb. Notice the yolk sac, which shrinks as pregnancy advances. The internal organs have taken over its function of producing blood cells.

fluid. White, downy hair called **lanugo** also appears over the entire body, helping the vernix stick to the skin.

At the end of the second trimester, many organs are well developed. And most of the brain's billions of neurons are in place; few will be produced after this time. However, *glial cells*, which support and feed the neurons, continue to increase at a rapid rate throughout pregnancy, as well as after birth. Consequently, brain weight increases tenfold from the 20th week until birth (Roelfsema et al., 2004).

Brain growth means new behavioral capacities. The 20-week-old fetus can be stimulated as well as irritated by sounds. And if a doctor looks inside the uterus with fetoscopy (see Table 2.4 on page 56), fetuses try to shield their eyes from the light with the hands, indicating that sight has begun to emerge (Moore & Persaud, 2003). Still, a fetus born at this time cannot survive. Its lungs are immature, and the brain cannot yet control breathing and body temperature.

◾ **The Third Trimester.** During the final trimester, a fetus born early has a chance for survival. The point at which the fetus can first survive, called the **age of viability**, occurs sometime between 22 and 26 weeks (Moore & Persaud, 2003). If born between the seventh and eighth month, however, the baby usually needs oxygen assistance to breathe. Although the brain's respiratory center is now mature, tiny air sacs in the lungs are not yet ready to inflate and exchange carbon dioxide for oxygen.

The brain continues to make great strides. The *cerebral cortex*, the seat of human intelligence, enlarges. As neurological organization improves, the fetus spends more time awake. At 20 weeks, heart rate variability reveals no periods of alertness. But by 28 weeks, fetuses are awake about 11 percent of the time, a figure that rises to 16 percent just before birth (DiPietro et al., 1996).

The fetus also takes on the beginnings of a personality. Fetal activity is linked to infant temperament. Higher fetal activity in the last weeks of pregnancy predicts a more active infant in the first month of life—a relationship that, for boys, persists into early childhood. And in one study, more active fetuses during the third trimester became 1-year-olds who could better handle frustration and 2-year-olds who were less fearful, in that they interacted more readily with toys and with an unfamiliar adult in a laboratory (DiPietro et al., 2002). Perhaps fetal activity is an indicator of healthy neurological development, which fosters adaptability in childhood. The relationships just described, however, are only modest. As you will see in Chapter 10, sensitive caregiving can modify the temperaments of children who have difficulty adapting to new experiences.

The third trimester brings greater responsiveness to stimulation. As we will see later, when we take up newborn

Period of the fetus: twenty-second week. This fetus is almost a foot long and weighs slightly more than one pound. Its movements can be felt easily by the mother and by other family members who place a hand on her abdomen. The fetus has reached the age of viability. If born, it has a slim chance of surviving.

Period of the fetus: thirty-sixth week. This fetus fills the uterus. To support its need for nourishment, the umbilical cord and placenta have grown large. Notice the vernix (cheeselike substance) on the skin, which protects it from chapping. The fetus has accumulated a layer of fat to assist with temperature regulation after birth. In two more weeks, it will be full-term.

© LENNART NILSSON, *A CHILD IS BORN*/BONNIERS
© LENNART NILSSON, *A CHILD IS BORN*/BONNIERS

capacities, from bathing in and swallowing amniotic fluid, fetuses acquire taste and odor preferences. Between 23 and 30 weeks, connections form between the cerebral cortex and brain regions involved in pain sensitivity. By this time, painkillers should be used in any surgical procedures (Lee et al., 2005). Around 25 weeks, fetuses react to nearby sounds with body movements (Kisilevsky & Low, 1998). Soon they distinguish the tone and rhythm of different voices. They show systematic heart rate changes to a male versus a female speaker and to the mother versus a stranger (Kisilevsky et al., 2003; Lecanuet et al., 1993). And in one clever study, mothers read aloud Dr. Seuss's lively book *The Cat in the Hat* for the last 6 weeks of pregnancy. After birth, their infants learned to turn on recordings of the mother's voice by sucking on nipples. They showed a preference for the familiar poem by sucking harder to hear *The Cat in the Hat* than other rhyming stories (DeCasper & Spence, 1986).

During the final 3 months, the fetus gains more than 5 pounds and grows 7 inches. In the eighth month, a layer of fat is added to assist with temperature regulation. The fetus also receives antibodies from the mother's blood that protect against illnesses, since the newborn's own immune system will not work well until several months after birth. In the last weeks, most fetuses assume an upside-down position, partly because of the shape of the uterus and also because the head is heavier than the feet. Growth slows, and birth is about to take place.

Ask Yourself

Review

Why is the period of the embryo regarded as the most dramatic prenatal phase? Why is the period of the fetus called the "growth and finishing" phase?

Apply

Amy, 2 months pregnant, wonders how the embryo is being fed. "I don't look pregnant yet, so does that mean not much development has occurred?" How would you respond to Amy?

Connect

How does brain development relate to fetal behavior?

www.ablongman.com/berk

Prenatal Environmental Influences

Although the prenatal environment is far more constant than the world outside the womb, many factors can affect the embryo and fetus. Yolanda and Jay learned that there is much that parents—and society as a whole—can do to create a safe environment for development before birth.

Teratogens

The term **teratogen** refers to any environmental agent that causes damage during the prenatal period. It comes from the Greek word *teras*, meaning "malformation" or "monstrosity." Scientists selected this label because they first learned about harmful prenatal influences from cases in which babies had been profoundly damaged. Yet the harm done by teratogens is not always simple and straightforward. It depends on the following factors:

- *Dose.* As we discuss particular teratogens, you will see that larger doses over longer time periods usually have more negative effects.

- *Heredity.* The genetic makeup of the mother and that of the developing organism play an important role. Some individuals are better able than others to withstand harmful environments.

- *Other negative influences.* The presence of several negative factors at once, such as poor nutrition, lack of medical care, and additional teratogens, can worsen the impact of a single harmful agent.

- *Age.* The effects of teratogens vary with the age of the organism at time of exposure. We can best understand this last idea if we think of the *sensitive period* concept introduced in Chapter 1. A sensitive period is a limited time span in which a part of the body or a behavior is biologically prepared to develop rapidly. During that time, it is especially sensitive to its surroundings. If the environment is harmful, then damage occurs, and recovery is difficult and sometimes impossible.

Figure 3.2 on page 86 summarizes prenatal sensitive periods. In the *period of the zygote*, before implantation, teratogens rarely have any impact. If they do, the tiny mass of cells is usually so badly damaged that it dies. The *embryonic period* is the time when serious defects are most likely to occur because the foundations for all body parts are being laid down. During the *fetal period*, teratogenic damage is usually minor. However, organs such as the brain, eyes, and genitals can still be strongly affected.

The effects of teratogens are not limited to immediate physical damage. Some health effects are subtle and delayed. As the Lifespan Vista box on pages 88–89 illustrates, they may not show up for decades. Furthermore, psychological consequences may occur indirectly, as a result of physical damage. For example, a defect resulting from drugs the mother took during pregnancy can change the reactions of others to the child as well as the child's ability to explore the environment. Over time, parent–child interaction, peer relations, and cognitive, emotional, and social development may suffer.

Notice how an important idea about development that we discussed in earlier chapters is at work here: *bidirectional influences* between child and environment. Now let's take a look at what scientists have discovered about a variety of teratogens.

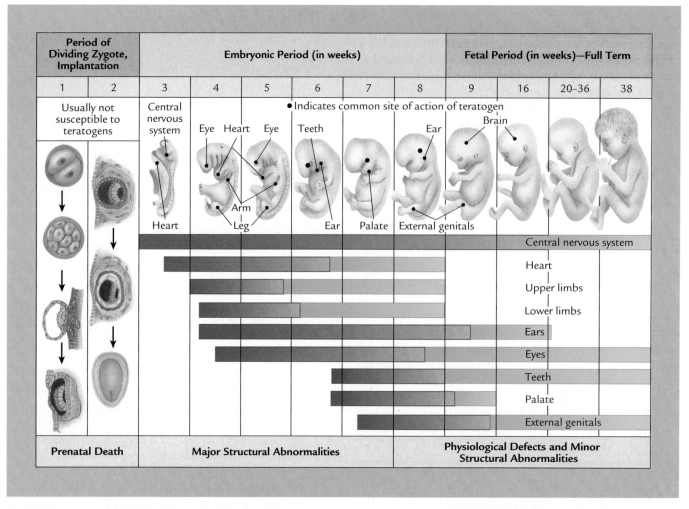

FIGURE 3.2 Sensitive periods in prenatal development. Each organ or structure has a sensitive period, during which its development may be disturbed. Blue horizontal bars indicate highly sensitive periods. Green horizontal bars indicate periods that are somewhat less sensitive to teratogens, although damage can occur. (Adapted from K. L. Moore & T. V. N. Persaud, 2003, *Before We Are Born*, 6th ed., Philadelphia: Saunders, p. 130. Reprinted by permission of the publisher and authors.)

■ **Prescription and Nonprescription Drugs.** In the early 1960s, the world learned a tragic lesson about drugs and prenatal development. At that time, a sedative called *thalidomide* was widely available in Canada, Europe, and South America. When taken by mothers 4 to 6 weeks after conception, thalidomide produced gross deformities of the embryo's arms and legs and, less frequently, damage to the ears, heart, kidneys, and genitals. About 7,000 infants worldwide were affected (Moore & Persaud, 2003). As children exposed to thalidomide grew older, many scored below average in intelligence. Perhaps the drug damaged the central nervous system directly. Or perhaps the child-rearing conditions of these severely deformed youngsters impaired their intellectual development.

Another medication, a synthetic hormone called *diethylstilbestrol (DES)*, was widely prescribed between 1945 and 1970 to prevent miscarriages. As daughters of these mothers reached adolescence and young adulthood, they showed unusually high rates of cancer of the vagina, malformations of the uterus, and infertility. When they tried to have children, their pregnancies more often resulted in prematurity, low birth weight, and mis-

carriage than those of non-DES-exposed women. Young men showed an increased risk of genital abnormalities and cancer of the testes (Hammes & Laitman, 2003; Palmer et al., 2001).

Currently, *Accutane*, a vitamin A derivative used to treat severe acne (also known by the generic name *isotretinoin*), is the most widely used, potent teratogen. Hundreds of thousands of U.S. and Canadian women of childbearing age take it. Exposure during the first trimester results in eye, ear, skull, brain, heart, and immune system abnormalities (Honein, Paulozzi, & Erickson, 2001). Accutane's packaging warns users to avoid pregnancy by using two methods of birth control, but many women do not heed this advice (Honein, Paulozzi, & Erickson, 2001).

Indeed, any drug with a molecule small enough to penetrate the placental barrier can enter the embryonic or fetal bloodstream. Yet many pregnant women continue to take over-the-counter medications without consulting their doctors. Aspirin is one of the most common. Several studies suggest that regular aspirin use is linked to low birth weight, infant death around the time of birth, poorer motor development, and lower intelligence scores in early childhood, although other research fails to confirm these findings (Barr et al., 1990; Hauth et al., 1995; Streissguth et al., 1987). Heavy caffeine intake (more than three cups of coffee per day) is associated with low birth weight, miscarriage, and newborn withdrawal symptoms, such as irritability and vomiting (Klebanoff et al., 2002; Vik et al., 2003). And antidepressant medication taken during the third trimester is linked to increased risk of birth complications, including respiratory distress (Costei et al., 2002).

Because children's lives are involved, we must take findings like these seriously. At the same time, we cannot be sure that these frequently used drugs actually cause the problems mentioned. Often mothers take more than one drug. If the embryo or fetus is injured, it is hard to tell which drug might be responsible or whether other factors correlated with drug taking are at fault. Until we have more information, the safest course of action is the one Yolanda took: Avoid these drugs entirely.

■ **Illegal Drugs.** The use of highly addictive mood-altering drugs, such as cocaine and heroin, has become more widespread, especially in poverty-stricken inner cities, where these drugs provide a temporary escape from a daily life of hopelessness. As many as 3 to 7 percent of American and Canadian babies born in large cities, and 1 to 2 percent of all North American newborns, have been exposed to cocaine prenatally (British Columbia Reproductive Care Program, 2003; Lester et al., 2001).

Babies born to users of cocaine, heroin, or methadone (a less addictive drug used to wean people away from heroin) are at risk for a wide variety of problems, including prematurity, low birth weight, physical defects, breathing difficulties, and death around the time of birth (Behnke et al., 2001; Walker, Rosenberg, & Balaban-Gil, 1999). In addition, these infants are born drug-addicted. They are often feverish and irritable and have trouble sleeping, and their cries are abnormally shrill and piercing—a common symptom among stressed newborns (Bauer et al., 2005). When mothers with many problems of their own must take care of these babies, who are difficult to calm down, cuddle, and feed, behavior problems are likely to persist.

Throughout the first year, heroin- and methadone-exposed infants are less attentive to the environment than nonexposed babies, and their motor development is slow. After infancy, some children get better, while others remain jittery and inattentive. The kind of parenting they receive may explain why problems persist for some but not for others (Cosden, Peerson, & Elliott, 1997).

Evidence on cocaine suggests that some prenatally exposed babies have lasting difficulties. Cocaine constricts the blood vessels, causing oxygen delivered to the developing organism to fall dramatically for 15 minutes following a high dose. Cocaine also alters the production and functioning of neurons and the chemical balance in the fetus's brain. These effects may contribute to any array of cocaine-associated physical defects, including eye, bone, genital, urinary tract, kidney, and heart deformities; hemorrhages and seizures; and severe

growth retardation (Covington et al., 2002; Feng, 2005; Mayes, 1999). Some studies report perceptual, motor, attention, memory, and language problems that persist into the preschool years (Lester et al., 2003; Noland et al., 2005; Singer et al., 2002, 2004).

But other investigations reveal no major negative effects of prenatal cocaine exposure (Frank et al., 2005; Hurt et al., 2005). These contradictory findings indicate how difficult it is to isolate the precise damage caused by illegal drugs. Cocaine users vary greatly in the amount, potency, and purity of the cocaine they ingest. Also, they often take several drugs, display other high-risk behaviors, suffer from poverty and other stresses, and engage in insensitive caregiving. The joint impact of these factors worsens outcomes for children (Alessandri, Bendersky, & Lewis, 1998; Carta et al., 2001). But researchers have yet to determine exactly what accounts for findings of cocaine-related damage in some studies but not in others.

Another illegal drug, marijuana, is used more widely than heroin and cocaine. Studies examining its relationship to low birth weight and prematurity reveal mixed findings (Fried, 1993). Several researchers have linked prenatal marijuana exposure to smaller head size (a measure of brain growth); to sleep, attention, memory, and academic achievement difficulties and to depression in childhood; and to poorer problem-solving performance in adolescence (Dahl et al., 1995; Gray et al., 2005; Goldschmidt et al., 2004). As with cocaine, however, lasting effects have not been established.

■ **Tobacco.** Although smoking has declined in Western nations, an estimated 12 percent of American women and 17 percent of Canadian women smoke during their pregnancies (Martin et al., 2005; Millar & Hill, 2004). The best-known

This 3-day-old infant, who was born many weeks before his due date and is underweight, breathes with the aid of a respirator. Prematurity and low birth weight can result from a variety of environmental influences during pregnancy, including maternal drug use and cigarette smoking. Babies born prematurely are at increased risk for later physical, emotional, and behavioral problems and school learning deficits.

A Lifespan Vista

The Prenatal Environment and Health in Later Life

When Michael entered the world 55 years ago, 6 weeks premature and weighing only 4 pounds, the doctor delivering him wasn't sure he would make it. Michael not only survived but enjoyed good health until his mid-forties when, during a routine medical checkup, he was diagnosed with high blood pressure and adult-onset diabetes. Michael had no apparent risk factors for these conditions: He wasn't overweight, didn't smoke, and didn't eat high-fat foods. Nor did the illnesses run in his family. Could the roots of Michael's health problems date back to his prenatal development?

Increasing evidence suggests that prenatal environmental factors—ones not toxic (as are tobacco or alcohol) but rather fairly subtle, such as the flow of nutrients and hormones across the placenta—can affect an individual's health decades later.

Low Birth Weight and Heart Disease, Stroke, and Diabetes. Carefully controlled animal experiments reveal that a poorly nourished, underweight fetus experiences changes in body structure and function

that result in cardiovascular disease in adulthood (Franco et al., 2002). To explore this relationship in humans, researchers tapped public records, gathering information on the birth weights of 15,000 British men and women and the occurrence of disease in middle adulthood. Those weighing less than 5 pounds at birth had a 50 percent greater chance of dying of heart disease and stroke, after SES and a variety of other health risks were controlled. The connection between birth weight and cardiovascular disease was strongest for people whose weight-to-length ratio at birth was very low—a sign of prenatal growth stunting (Godfrey & Barker, 2000; Martyn, Barker, & Osmond, 1996).

In other large-scale studies, a consistent link between low birth weight and heart disease, stroke, and diabetes in middle adulthood has emerged—for both sexes and in diverse countries, including Finland, India, Jamaica, and the United States (Barker, 2002; Fowden, Giussani, & Forhead, 2005; Godfrey & Barker, 2001). Smallness itself does not cause later health problems; rather, researchers believe, complex factors associated with it are involved.

Some speculate that a poorly nourished fetus diverts large amounts of blood to the brain, causing organs in the

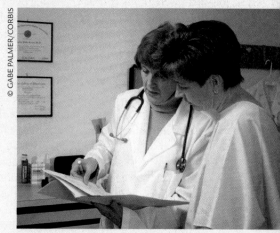

Prenatal influences resulting in unusually low or high birth weight can increase the risk of later-life illnesses, such as heart disease, diabetes, or breast cancer. As part of regular preventive health care, adults should make sure their health care providers have birth-weight information. Here, a woman talks with her physician about the results of a mammogram.

abdomen such as the liver and kidney (involved in controlling cholesterol and blood pressure) to be undersized (Hales & Ozanne, 2003). The result is heightened later risk for heart disease and stroke. In the case of diabetes, inadequate prenatal nutrition may permanently impair functioning of the pancreas,

effect of smoking during the prenatal period is low birth weight. But the likelihood of other serious consequences, such as miscarriage, prematurity, impaired heart rate and breathing during sleep, infant death, and asthma and cancer later in childhood, is also increased (Franco et al., 2000; Jaakkola & Gissler, 2004). The more cigarettes a mother smokes, the greater the chances that her baby will be affected. If a pregnant woman decides to stop smoking at any time, even during the last trimester, she reduces the likelihood that her infant will be born underweight and suffer from future problems (Klesges et al., 2001).

Even when a baby of a smoking mother appears to be born in good physical condition, slight behavioral abnormalities may threaten the child's development. Newborns of smoking mothers are less attentive to sounds, display more muscle tension, are more excitable when touched and visually stimulated, and more often have colic (persistent crying)—findings that

suggest lasting negative effects on brain development (Law et al., 2003; Sondergaard et al., 2002). Some studies report that prenatally exposed children have shorter attention spans, poorer memories, lower mental test scores, and more behavior problems in childhood and adolescence (Cornelius et al., 2001; Fried, Watkinson, & Gray, 2003; Thapar et al., 2003). However, other factors closely associated with smoking, such as lower maternal education and income levels, may contribute to these outcomes (Ernst, Moolchan, & Robinson, 2001).

Exactly how can smoking harm the fetus? Nicotine, the addictive substance in tobacco, constricts blood vessels, lessens blood flow to the uterus, and causes the placenta to grow abnormally. This reduces transfer of nutrients, so the fetus gains weight poorly. Also, nicotine raises the concentration of carbon monoxide in the bloodstreams of both mother and fetus. Carbon monoxide displaces oxygen from red blood cells, damaging the central nervous system and slowing body growth leading glucose intolerance to rise as the person ages (Wu et al., 2004). Yet another hypothesis, supported by both animal and human research, is that the malfunctioning placentas of some expectant mothers permit high levels of stress hormones to reach the fetus, which retards fetal growth, increases fetal blood pressure, and promotes hyperglycemia (excess blood sugar), predisposing the developing person to later disease (Stocker, Arch, & Cawthorne, 2005). Finally, prenatally growth-stunted babies often gain excessive weight in childhood, once they have access to plentiful food. This excess weight usually persists, greatly magnifying the risk of diabetes (Hyppönen, Power, & Smith, 2003).

High Birth Weight and Cancer. The other prenatal growth extreme—high birth weight—is linked to breast cancer, the most common malignancy in adult women (Ahlgren et al., 2004; Vatten et al., 2002). In one sample of over 2,000 British women, high birth weight—especially more than 8.8 pounds—was associated with a greatly increased incidence of breast cancer, even after other cancer risks were controlled (see Figure 3.3) (Silva et al., 2004). Researchers suspect that the culprit is excessive maternal estrogen during pregnancy, which pro-

motes large fetal size and alters beginning breast tissue so that it may respond to estrogen in adulthood by becoming malignant.

High birth weight is also associated with increases in digestive and lymphatic cancers in both men and women (McCormack et al., 2005). As yet, the reasons are unclear.

Prevention. The relationships between prenatal development and later-life illnesses emerging in research do not mean that the illnesses are inevitable. Rather, prenatal environmental conditions *influence* adult health, and the steps we take to protect our health can prevent prenatal risks from becoming reality. Researchers advise individuals who were low-weight at birth to get regular medical checkups and to be attentive to diet, weight, fitness, and stress—controllable factors that contribute to heart disease and adult-onset diabetes. And high-birth-weight women should be conscientious about breast self-exams and mammograms, which permit early detection—and, in many cases, cure—of breast cancer.

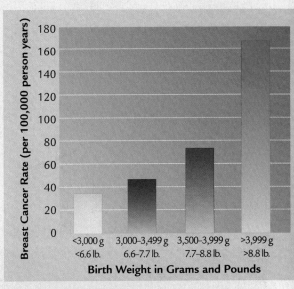

■ **FIGURE 3.3 Relationship of birth weight to breast cancer risk in adulthood.** In a study of over 2,000 British births with follow-ups in adulthood, birth weight predicted breast cancer incidence after many other prenatal and postnatal health risks were controlled. The breast cancer risk was especially high for women whose birth weights were greater than 3,999 grams, or 8.8 pounds. (Adapted from Silva et al., 2004.)

in the fetuses of laboratory animals (Friedman, 1996). Similar effects may occur in humans.

Finally, from one-third to one-half of nonsmoking pregnant women are "passive smokers" because their husbands, relatives, or co-workers use cigarettes. Passive smoking is also related to low birth weight, infant death, and possible long-term impairments in attention and learning (Hanke, Sobala, & Kalinka, 2004; Makin, Fried, & Watkinson, 1991). Clearly, expectant mothers should avoid smoke-filled environments.

■ **Alcohol.** In his book *The Broken Cord*, Michael Dorris (1989), a Dartmouth College anthropology professor, described what it was like to raise his adopted son, Abel (called Adam in the book), whose biological mother drank heavily throughout pregnancy and died of alcohol poisoning shortly after his birth. A Sioux Indian, Abel was born with **fetal alcohol syndrome (FAS).** Mental retardation; impaired motor coordi-

nation, attention, memory, and language; and overactivity are typical of children with the disorder (Connor et al., 2001; Sokol, Delaney-Black, & Nordstrom, 2003). Distinct physical symptoms also accompany FAS, including slow physical growth and a particular pattern of facial abnormalities: widely spaced eyes, short eyelid openings, a small upturned nose, a thin upper lip, and a small head, indicating that the brain has not developed fully. Other defects—of the eyes, ears, nose, throat, heart, genitals, urinary tract, or immune system—may also be present.

In a related condition, known as **fetal alcohol effects (FAE)**—seen in children of mothers who generally drank alcohol in smaller quantities—affected individuals display only some of these abnormalities. The particular defects vary with the timing and length of alcohol exposure during pregnancy. New evidence suggests that paternal alcohol use around the time of conception may alter gene expression (see page 74 in

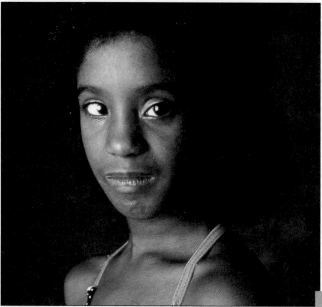

(Top) The mother of these two baby girls drank heavily during pregnancy. Their widely spaced eyes, thin upper lip, and short eyelid openings are typical of fetal alcohol syndrome (FAS). (Bottom) The adolescent girl shown here also has symptoms of FAS.

Chapter 2), thereby contributing to symptoms of low birth weight, heart defects, mild cognitive impairments, and overactivity (Abel, 2004).

Even when provided with enriched diets, FAS babies fail to catch up in physical size during infancy and childhood. Mental impairment is also permanent: In his teens and twenties, Abel Dorris had trouble concentrating and keeping a routine job. He also suffered from poor judgment: He would buy something and not wait for change or wander off in the middle of a task. He died in 1991, at age 23, after being hit by a car. The more alcohol a woman consumes during pregnancy, the poorer the child's motor coordination, speed of information processing, reasoning, and intelligence and achievement test scores during the preschool and school years (Korkman, Kettunen, & Autti-Raemoe, 2003; Streissguth et al., 1994). In adolescence, FAS is associated with poor school performance, trouble with the law, inappropriate sexual behavior, alcohol and drug abuse, depression, and other lasting mental health problems (Baer et al., 2003; Kelly, Day, & Streissguth, 2000).

How does alcohol produce its devastating effects? First, it interferes with the production and migration of neurons in the primitive neural tube. Brain-imaging research reveals arrested brain growth, structural damage, and abnormalities in the electrical and chemical activity involved in transferring messages from one part of the brain to another (Bookstein et al., 2002; Riley, McGee, & Sowell, 2004). Second, the body uses large quantities of oxygen to metabolize alcohol. A pregnant woman's heavy drinking draws away oxygen that the developing organism needs for cell growth.

About 25 percent of American and Canadian mothers reported drinking at some time during their pregnancies. As with heroin and cocaine, alcohol abuse is higher in poverty-stricken women (Health Canada, 2003b; U.S. Department of Health and Human Services, 2005f). On some Native American and Canadian First Nations reservations, the incidence of FAS is as high as 10 percent (Silverman et al., 2003). Unfortunately, when affected girls later become pregnant, the poor judgment caused by the syndrome often prevents them from understanding why they themselves should avoid alcohol. Thus, the tragic cycle is likely to be repeated in the next generation.

How much alcohol is safe during pregnancy? Even mild drinking, less than one drink per day, is associated with FAS-like facial features, reduced head size and body growth, and lower mental test scores (Day et al., 2002; Jacobson et al., 2004). Recall that other factors—both genetic and environmental—can make some fetuses more vulnerable to teratogens. Therefore, no amount of alcohol is safe. Couples planning a pregnancy and expectant mothers should avoid alcohol entirely.

■ **Radiation.** Defects due to radiation were tragically apparent in children born to pregnant women who survived the bombing of Hiroshima and Nagasaki during World War II. Similar abnormalities surfaced in the nine months following the 1986 Chernobyl, Ukraine, nuclear power plant accident. After each disaster, the incidence of miscarriage, small head size (indicating an underdeveloped brain), physical deformities, and slow physical growth rose dramatically (Hoffmann, 2001; Schull, 2003).

Even when a radiation-exposed baby appears normal, problems may appear later. For example, even low-level radiation, resulting from industrial leakage or medical X-rays, can increase the risk of childhood cancer (Fattibene et al., 1999). In middle childhood, prenatally exposed Chernobyl children had abnormal brain-wave activity, lower intelligence test scores, and rates

This child's mother was just a few weeks pregnant during the Chernobyl nuclear power plant disaster. Radiation exposure is probably responsible for his limb deformities. He is also at risk for low intelligence and language and emotional disorders.

threatening diseases and health problems later on (Houlihan et al., 2005).

In the 1950s, an industrial plant released waste containing high levels of *mercury* into a bay providing seafood and water for the town of Minamata, Japan. Many children born at the time displayed physical deformities, mental retardation, abnormal speech, difficulty in chewing and swallowing, and uncoordinated movements. High levels of prenatal mercury exposure disrupt production and migration of neurons, causing widespread brain damage (Clarkson, Magos, & Myers, 2003). Pregnant women are wise to avoid eating long-lived predatory fish, such as swordfish, albacore tuna, and shark, which are heavily contaminated with mercury.

For many years, *polychlorinated biphenyls (PCBs)* were used to insulate electrical equipment until research showed that, like mercury, they entered waterways and the food supply. In Taiwan, prenatal exposure to high levels of PCBs in rice oil resulted in low birth weight, discolored skin, deformities of the gums and nails, brain-wave abnormalities, and delayed cognitive development (Chen & Hsu, 1994; Chen et al., 1994). Steady, low-level PCB exposure is also harmful. Women who frequently ate Great Lakes PCB-contaminated fish, compared with those who ate little or no fish, had infants with lower birth weights, smaller heads, persisting attention and memory difficulties, and lower intelligence test scores in childhood (Jacobson & Jacobson, 2003; Stewart et al., 2000; Walkowiak et al., 2001).

Another teratogen, *lead,* is present in paint flaking off the walls of old buildings and in certain materials used in industrial occupations. High levels of prenatal lead exposure are related to prematurity, low birth weight, brain damage, and a wide variety of physical defects. Even low levels seem to be dangerous. Affected babies show slightly poorer mental and motor development (Bellinger, 2005).

Finally, prenatal exposure to dioxins—toxic compounds resulting from incineration—is linked to brain, immune system, and thyroid damage in babies and an increased incidence of breast and uterine cancers in women, perhaps through altering hormone levels (ten Tusscher & Koppe, 2004). Furthermore, even tiny amounts of dioxin in the paternal bloodstream cause a dramatic change in sex ratio of offspring: Affected men father nearly twice as many girls as boys (Mocarelli et al., 2000). The reasons are not yet clear.

■ **Infectious Disease.** During her first prenatal visit, Yolanda's doctor asked her if she and Jay had already had measles, mumps, chicken pox, and several other illnesses. Although most infectious diseases seem to have no impact, a few—as Table 3.2 on page 92 illustrates—can cause extensive damage.

In the mid-1960s, a worldwide epidemic of *rubella* (3-day, or German, measles) led to the birth of more than 20,000 North American babies with serious defects. Consistent with the sensitive period concept, the greatest damage occurs when rubella strikes during the embryonic period. Over 50 percent of infants whose mothers become ill during that time show eye cataracts; deafness; heart, genital, urinary, and intestinal

of language and emotional disorders two to three times greater than those of nonexposed Russian children (Kolominsky, Igumnov, & Drozdovitch, 1999; Loganovskaja & Loganovsky, 1999). Furthermore, the more tension parents reported, due to forced evacuation from their homes and worries about living in irradiated areas, the poorer their children's emotional functioning (Kolominsky, Igumnov, & Drozdovitch, 1999). Stressful rearing conditions seemed to combine with the damaging effects of prenatal radiation to impair children's development.

■ **Environmental Pollution.** In industrialized nations, an astounding number of potentially dangerous chemicals are released into the environment. More than 75,000 are in common use in the United States, and many new pollutants are introduced each year. When ten newborns were randomly selected from U.S. hospitals in different locales for analysis of umbilical cord blood, researchers uncovered a startling array of industrial contaminants—287 in all! They concluded that many babies are "born polluted" by chemicals that not only impair prenatal development but increase the chances of life-

Table 3.2	Effects of Some Infectious Diseases During Pregnancy			
Disease	Miscarriage	Physical Malformations	Mental Retardation	Low Birth Weight and Prematurity
Viral				
Acquired immune deficiency syndrome (AIDS)	0	?	+	?
Chicken pox	0	+	+	+
Cytomegalovirus	+	+	+	+
Herpes simplex 2 (genital herpes)	+	+	+	+
Mumps	+	?	0	0
Rubella (German measles)	+	+	+	+
Bacterial				
Chlamydia	+	?	0	+
Syphilis	+	+	+	?
Tuberculosis	+	?	+	+
Parasitic				
Malaria	+	0	0	+
Toxoplasmosis	+	+	+	+

+ = established finding, 0 = no present evidence, ? = possible effect that is not clearly established.

Sources: Behrman, Kliegman, & Jenson, 2000; Jones, Lopez, & Wilson, 2003; Mardh, 2002; O'Rahilly & Müller, 2001.

abnormalities; and mental retardation (Eberhart-Phillips, Frederick, & Baron, 1993). Infection during the fetal period is less harmful, but low birth weight, hearing loss, and bone defects may still occur. And the brain abnormalities resulting from prenatal rubella increase the risk of severe mental illness in adulthood (Brown & Susser, 2002). Although vaccination in infancy and childhood is now routine, about 10 to 20 percent of women in North America and Western Europe lack the rubella antibody, so new disease outbreaks are possible (Health Canada, 2002d; Pebody et al., 2000).

The *human immunodeficiency virus (HIV)*, which leads to *acquired immune deficiency syndrome (AIDS)*, a disease that destroys the immune system, has infected increasing numbers of women over the past two decades. When they become pregnant, HIV-infected women pass the deadly virus to the developing organism about 20 to 30 percent of the time. AIDS progresses rapidly in infants. By 6 months, weight loss, diarrhea, and repeated respiratory illnesses are common. The virus also causes brain damage. Most prenatal AIDS babies survive for only 5 to 8 months after the appearance of these symptoms (O'Rahilly & Müller, 2001). The antiviral drug zidovudine (ZDV) reduces prenatal AIDS transmission as much as 95 percent, with no harmful consequences of drug treatment for children (Culnane et al., 1999). It has led to a dramatic decline in prenatally acquired AIDS in Western nations, but it is not widely available in impoverished regions of the world, where 95 percent of new infections occur, more than half of which affect women. In Africa, for example, one-fourth of all pregnant women are HIV-positive (United Nations, 2004a).

As Table 3.2 reveals, the developing organism is especially sensitive to the family of herpes viruses, for which there is no vaccine or treatment. Among these, *cytomegalovirus* (the most frequent prenatal infection, transmitted through respiratory or sexual contact) and *herpes simplex 2* (which is sexually transmitted) are especially dangerous. In both, the virus invades the mother's genital tract, infecting babies either at birth or during pregnancy.

Table 3.2 also includes several bacterial and parasitic diseases. Among the most common is *toxoplasmosis,* caused by a parasite found in many animals. Pregnant women may become infected from eating raw or undercooked meat or from contact with the feces of infected cats. About 40 percent of women who have the disease transmit it to the developing organism. If it strikes during the first trimester, it is likely to cause eye and brain damage. Later infection is linked to mild visual and cognitive impairments (Jones, Lopez, & Wilson, 2003). Expectant mothers can avoid toxoplasmosis by making sure that the meat they eat is well-cooked, having pet cats checked for the disease, and turning over the care of litter boxes to other family members.

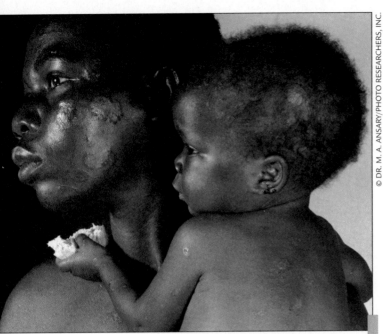

© DR. M. A. ANSARY/PHOTO RESEARCHERS, INC.

This South African mother and infant who are suffering from AIDS both have extensive ringworm skin rashes. Their weakened immune systems make normally harmless infections life threatening. Because AIDS progresses rapidly in infants, the baby may live only a few months. The antiviral drugs that have dramatically reduced prenatal AIDS transmission in Western nations are not yet widely available in impoverished regions of the world.

Other Maternal Factors

Besides avoiding teratogens, expectant parents can support the development of the embryo and fetus in other ways. In healthy, physically fit women, regular moderate exercise, such as walking, swimming, biking, or an aerobic workout, is related to increased birth weight (Leiferman & Evenson, 2003). However, very frequent, vigorous exercise predicts the opposite outcome—lower birth weight than in healthy, nonexercising controls (Clapp et al., 2002; Pivarnik, 1998). (Pregnant women with health problems, such as circulatory difficulties or previous miscarriages, should consult their doctors about a physical fitness routine.)

In the following sections, we examine other maternal factors—nutrition, emotional stress, blood type, age, and previous births.

■ **Nutrition.** During the prenatal period, when children are growing more rapidly than at any other time, they depend totally on the mother for nutrients. A healthy diet that results in a weight gain of 25 to 30 pounds (10 to 13.5 kilograms) helps ensure the health of mother and baby.

Prenatal malnutrition can cause serious damage to the central nervous system. The poorer the mother's diet, the greater the loss in brain weight, especially if malnutrition occurs during the last trimester. During that time, the brain is increasing rapidly in size, and a maternal diet high in all the basic nutrients is necessary for it to reach its full potential (Morgane et al., 1993). An inadequate diet during pregnancy

can also distort the structure of other organs, including the liver, kidney, and pancreas, resulting in lifelong health problems (refer again to the Lifespan Vista box on pages 88–89).

Because poor nutrition suppresses development of the immune system, prenatally malnourished babies frequently catch respiratory illnesses (Chandra, 1991). In addition, they are often irritable and unresponsive to stimulation. In poverty-stricken families, these effects quickly combine with a stressful home life. With age, low intelligence and serious learning problems become more apparent (Pollitt, 1996).

Many studies show that providing pregnant women with adequate food has a substantial impact on the health of their newborn babies. Yet the growth demands of the prenatal period require more than just increasing the quantity of a typical diet. Vitamin–mineral enrichment is also crucial.

For example, taking a folic acid supplement around the time of conception greatly reduces abnormalities of the neural tube, such as *anencephaly* and *spina bifida* (see Table 2.4 on page 56). In addition, adequate folate intake during the last 10 weeks of pregnancy cuts in half the risk of premature delivery and low birth weight (MCR Vitamin Study Research Group, 1991; Scholl, Heidiger, & Belsky, 1996). Because of these findings, U.S. and Canadian government guidelines recommend that all women of childbearing age consume at least 0.4 but not more than 1 milligram of folic acid per day (excessive intake can be harmful). Currently, bread, flour, rice, pasta, and other grain products are being fortified with folic acid.

When poor nutrition persists throughout pregnancy, infants usually require more than dietary improvement. Successful interventions must also break the cycle of apathetic mother–baby interactions. Some do so by teaching parents how to interact effectively with their infants, while others focus on stimulating infants to promote active engagement with their physical and social surroundings (Grantham-McGregor et al., 1994; Grantham-McGregor, Schofield, & Powell, 1987).

Although prenatal malnutrition is highest in poverty-stricken regions of the world, it is not limited to developing countries. The U.S. Special Supplemental Food Program for Women, Infants, and Children (WIC) provides food packages to low-income pregnant women, reaching about 90 percent of those who qualify because of their extremely low incomes (U.S. Department of Agriculture, 2005c), although many U.S. women who need nutrition intervention are not eligible. The Canadian Prenatal Nutrition Program (CPNP), which provides counseling, social support, access to health care, and shelter, as well as food, to all pregnant women in need, regardless of income, reaches nearly 10 percent of expectant mothers in Canada (Health Canada, 2005a).

■ **Emotional Stress.** When women experience severe emotional stress during pregnancy, their babies are at risk for a wide variety of difficulties. Intense anxiety is associated with a higher rate of miscarriage, prematurity, low birth weight, and infant respiratory illness and digestive disturbances (Mulder et al., 2002; Wadhwa, Sandman, & Garite, 2001). It is also related to several commonly occurring physical defects—namely, cleft lip and palate and pyloric stenosis (tightening of the infant's stomach outlet, which often must be treated surgically) (Carmichael & Shaw, 2000).

When we experience fear and anxiety, stimulant hormones released into our bloodstream cause us to be "poised for action." Large amounts of blood are sent to parts of the body involved in the defensive response—the brain, the heart, and muscles in the arms, legs, and trunk. Blood flow to other organs, including the uterus, is reduced. As a result, the fetus is deprived of a full supply of oxygen and nutrients.

Stress hormones also cross the placenta, causing a dramatic rise in fetal heart rate (Monk et al., 2000, 2004). They may also alter fetal neurological functioning, thereby heightening stress reactivity in later life. In one study, researchers identified mothers who had been directly exposed to the September 11, 2001, World Trade Center collapse during their pregnancies. At 9 months of age, their babies were tested for saliva concentrations of *cortisol*, a hormone involved in regulating the stress response. Infants whose mothers had reacted to the disaster with severe anxiety had cortisol levels that were abnormally low—a symptom of reduced physiological capacity to manage stress (Yehuda et al., 2005). Consistent with this finding, maternal emotional stress during pregnancy predicts anxiety, anger and aggression, and overactivity among school-age children, above and beyond the impact of other risks, such as maternal smoking during pregnancy, low birth weight, postnatal maternal anxiety, and low SES (Van den Bergh, 2004).

But stress-related prenatal complications are greatly reduced when mothers have husbands, other family members, and friends who offer social support (Federenko & Wadhwa, 2004). The link between social support and positive pregnancy outcomes is particularly strong for low-income women, who often lead highly stressful daily lives (Hoffman & Hatch, 1996).

■ **Rh Factor Incompatibility.** When the inherited blood types of mother and fetus differ, serious problems sometimes result. The most common cause of these difficulties is **Rh factor incompatibility.** When the mother is Rh-negative (lacks the Rh blood protein) and the father is Rh-positive (has the protein), the baby may inherit the father's Rh-positive blood type. If even a little of a fetus's Rh-positive blood crosses the placenta into the Rh-negative mother's bloodstream, she begins to form antibodies to the foreign Rh protein. If these enter the fetus's system, they destroy red blood cells, reducing the oxygen supply to organs and tissues. Mental retardation, miscarriage, heart damage, and infant death can occur.

It takes time for the mother to produce Rh antibodies, so firstborn children are rarely affected. The danger increases with each additional pregnancy. Fortunately, Rh incompatibility can be prevented in most cases. After the birth of each Rh-positive baby, Rh-negative mothers are routinely given a vaccine to prevent the buildup of antibodies.

■ **Maternal Age and Previous Births.** In Chapter 2, we noted that women who delay childbearing until their thirties

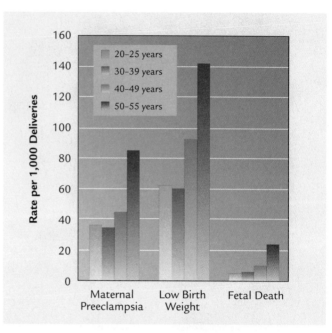

■ **FIGURE 3.4 Relationship of maternal age to prenatal and birth complications.** Complications increase after age 40, with a sharp rise between 50 and 55 years. See page 95 for a description of toxemia. (Adapted from Salihu et al., 2003.)

or forties face increased risk of infertility, miscarriage, and babies born with chromosomal defects. Are other pregnancy complications more common for older mothers? Research consistently indicates that healthy women in their thirties have about the same rates of prenatal and birth complications as those in their twenties (Bianco et al., 1996; Dildy et al., 1996; Prysak, Lorenz, & Kisly, 1995). Thereafter, as Figure 3.4 reveals, complication rates increase, with a sharp rise among women age 50 to 55—an age at which because of menopause (end of menstruation) and aging reproductive organs, few women can conceive naturally (Salihu et al., 2003).

In the case of teenage mothers, does physical immaturity cause prenatal complications? As we will see in Chapter 11, nature tries to ensure that once a girl can conceive, she is physically ready to carry and give birth to a baby. Infants of teenagers are born with a higher rate of problems, but not directly because of maternal age. Most pregnant teenagers come from low-income backgrounds, where stress, poor nutrition, and health problems are common. Also, many are afraid to seek medical care or, in the United States, do not have access to it because they lack health insurance (U.S. Department of Health and Human Services, 2005n).

The Importance of Prenatal Health Care

Yolanda had her first prenatal appointment 3 weeks after missing her menstrual period. After that, she visited the doctor's office once a month until she was 7 months pregnant, then twice during the eighth month. As birth grew near, Yolanda's appointments increased to once a week. The doctor kept track

During a routine prenatal visit, this doctor uses ultrasound to show an expectant mother an image of her fetus and to evaluate its development. All pregnant women should receive early and regular prenatal care to protect their own health and the health of their babies.

of her general health, her weight gain, and the capacity of her uterus and cervix to support the fetus. The fetus's growth was also carefully monitored.

Yolanda's pregnancy, like most others, was free of complications. But unexpected difficulties can arise, especially when mothers have health problems to begin with. For example, women with diabetes need careful monitoring. Extra sugar in the mother's bloodstream causes the fetus to grow larger than average, making pregnancy and birth problems more common. Another complication, *toxemia* (sometimes called *pre-eclampsia*), in which blood pressure increases sharply and the face, hands, and feet swell in the last half of pregnancy, is experienced by 5 to 10 percent of pregnant women. If untreated, toxemia can cause convulsions in the mother and fetal death. Usually, hospitalization, bed rest, and drugs can lower blood pressure to a safe level (Vidaeff, Carroll, & Ramin, 2005). If not, the baby must be delivered at once.

Unfortunately, 17 percent of pregnant women in the United States receive late or no prenatal care. Most are adolescents, unmarried, or members of poverty-stricken ethnic minorities. Their infants are three times as likely to be born underweight and five times as likely to die as are babies of mothers who receive early medical attention (Child Trends, 2005b). Why do these mothers delay going to the doctor? One reason is a lack of health insurance. Although the very poorest of these mothers are eligible for government-sponsored health services, many low-income women do not qualify. As we will see when we take up birth complications, in nations where affordable medical care is universally available, such as Australia, Canada, Japan, and Western Europe, late-care pregnancies and maternal and infant health problems are greatly reduced.

Besides financial hardship, some mothers have other reasons for not seeking prenatal care. These include situational barriers (difficulty finding a doctor, getting an appointment, and arranging transportation) and personal barriers (psychological stress, the demands of taking care of other young children, ambivalence about the pregnancy, and family crises). Many also engage in high-risk behaviors, such as smoking and drug abuse (Maupin et al., 2004; Rogers & Shiff, 1996). These women, who had no medical attention for most of their pregnancies, were among those who need it most!

Clearly, public education about the importance of early and sustained prenatal care for all pregnant women is badly needed. Refer to Applying What We Know on page 96, which lists "do's and don'ts" for a healthy pregnancy, based on our discussion of the prenatal environment.

Ask Yourself

Review

Why is it difficult to determine the prenatal effects of some environmental agents, such as drugs and pollution?

Apply

Nora, pregnant for the first time, believes that a few cigarettes and an occasional glass of wine won't be harmful. Provide Nora with research-based reasons for not smoking or drinking.

Connect

How do teratogens illustrate the notion of *epigenesis*, presented in Chapter 2, that environments can affect gene expression (see page 75 to review)? Cite an example.

Reflect

If you had to choose five environmental influences to publicize in a campaign aimed at promoting healthy prenatal development, which ones would you choose, and why?

www.ablongman.com/berk

Childbirth

Although Yolanda and Jay completed my course three months before their baby was born, both agreed to return the following spring to share their experiences with my next class. Two-week-old Joshua came along as well. Yolanda and Jay's story revealed that the birth of a baby is one of the most dramatic and emotional events in human experience. Jay was present throughout Yolanda's labor and delivery. Yolanda explained:

By morning, we knew I was in labor. It was Thursday, so we went in for my usual weekly appointment. The doctor

Applying What We Know

Do's and Don'ts for a Healthy Pregnancy

Do	Don't
Do make sure that, before you get pregnant, you have been vaccinated against infectious diseases that are dangerous to the embryo and fetus, such as rubella. Most vaccinations are unsafe during pregnancy.	Don't take any drugs without consulting your doctor.
Do see a doctor as soon as you suspect that you are pregnant, and continue to get regular medical checkups throughout pregnancy.	Don't smoke. If you are a smoker, cut down or, better yet, quit. Avoid secondhand smoke. If other members of your family are smokers, ask them to quit or to smoke outside.
Do eat a well-balanced diet and take vitamin–mineral supplements, as prescribed by your doctor, both prior to and during pregnancy. Gain 25 to 30 pounds gradually.	Don't drink alcohol from the time you decide to get pregnant.
Do keep physically fit through mild exercise. If possible, join an exercise class for expectant mothers.	Don't engage in activities that might expose the developing organism to environmental hazards, such as radiation or pollutants.
Do avoid emotional stress. If you are a single expectant mother, find a relative or friend on whom you can count for emotional support.	Don't eat undercooked meat, handle cat litter, or garden in areas frequented by cats—behaviors that increase the risk of toxoplasmosis.
Do get plenty of rest. An overtired mother is at risk for complications.	Don't choose pregnancy as a time to go on a diet.
Do obtain literature from your doctor, library, or bookstore about prenatal development, and ask your doctor about anything that concerns you.	Don't gain too much weight during pregnancy. An excessive weight gain is associated with complications.
Do enroll in a prenatal and childbirth education class with your partner or other companion. When you know what to expect, the nine months before birth can be one of the most joyful times of life.	

said, yes, the baby was on the way, but it would be a while. He told us to go home, relax, and come to the hospital in three or four hours. We checked in at 3 in the afternoon; Joshua arrived at 2 o'clock the next morning. When, finally, I was ready to deliver, it went quickly; a half hour or so and some good hard pushes, and there he was! His face was red and puffy, and his head was misshapen, but I thought, "Oh! He's beautiful. I can't believe he's really here!"

Jay was also elated by Joshua's birth. "I wanted to support Yolanda and to experience as much as I could. It was awesome, indescribable," he said, holding Joshua over his shoulder and patting and kissing him gently. In the following sections, we explore the experience of childbirth, from both the parents' and the baby's point of view.

The Stages of Childbirth

It is not surprising that childbirth is often referred to as *labor*. It is the hardest physical work a woman may ever do. A complex series of hormonal changes between the mother and the fetus initiates the process, which naturally divides into three stages (see Figure 3.5).

1. *Dilation and effacement of the cervix.* This is the longest stage of labor, lasting, on the average, 12 to 14 hours in a first birth and 4 to 6 hours in later births. Contractions of the uterus gradually become more frequent and powerful, causing the cervix, or uterine opening, to widen and thin to nothing, forming a clear channel from the uterus into the birth canal, or vagina.

2. *Delivery of the baby.* This stage is much shorter, lasting about 50 minutes in a first birth and 20 minutes in later births. Strong contractions of the uterus continue, but the mother also feels a natural urge to squeeze and push with her abdominal muscles. As she does so with each contraction, she forces the baby down and out.

3. *Delivery of the placenta.* Labor comes to an end with a few final contractions and pushes. These cause the placenta to separate from the wall of the uterus and be delivered in about 5 to 10 minutes.

To accommodate the well-developed brain, a newborn's head is large in relation to the trunk and legs. In addition, the round face, with its chubby cheeks and big eyes, induces adults to approach, pick up, and cuddle the newborn.

Stage 1

(a) Dilation and Effacement of the Cervix
Contractions of the uterus cause dilation and effacement of the cervix.

(b) Transition
Transition is reached when the frequency and strength of the contractions are at their peak and the cervix opens completely.

Stage 2

(c) Pushing
The mother pushes with each contraction, forcing the baby down the birth canal, and the head appears.

(d) Birth of the Baby
Near the end of Stage 2, the shoulders emerge and are followed quickly by the rest of the baby's body.

Stage 3

(e) Delivery of the Placenta
With a few final pushes, the placenta is delivered.

■ **FIGURE 3.5 The three stages of labor.**

The Baby's Adaptation to Labor and Delivery

At first glance, labor and delivery seem like a dangerous ordeal for the baby. The strong contractions exposed Joshua's head to a great deal of pressure, and they squeezed the placenta and the umbilical cord repeatedly. Each time, Joshua's supply of oxygen was temporarily reduced.

Fortunately, healthy babies are well-equipped to withstand these traumas. The force of the contractions causes the infant to produce high levels of stress hormones. Recall that during pregnancy, maternal stress can endanger the baby. In contrast, during childbirth the infant's production of cortisol and other stress hormones is adaptive. It helps the baby withstand oxygen deprivation by sending a rich supply of blood to the brain and heart (Gluckman, Sizonenko, & Bassett, 1999). In addition, it prepares the baby to breathe effectively by causing the lungs to absorb any remaining fluid and by expanding the bronchial tubes (passages leading to the lungs). Finally, stress hormones arouse the infant into alertness. Joshua was born wide awake, ready to interact with the surrounding world (Lagercrantz & Slotkin, 1986).

The Newborn Baby's Appearance

What do babies look like after birth? When my students asked this question, Jay smiled. "Yolanda and I are probably the only people in the world who thought Joshua was beautiful!" The average newborn is 20 inches long and 7½ pounds in weight; boys tend to be slightly longer and heavier than girls. The head is large in comparison to the trunk and legs, which are short and bowed. This combination of a big head (with its well-developed brain) and a small body means that human infants learn quickly in the first few months of life. But unlike most other mammals, they cannot get around on their own until much later.

Even though newborn babies may look strange, some features do make them attractive. Their round faces, chubby cheeks, large foreheads, and big eyes make adults feel like picking them up and cuddling them (Berman, 1980).

Assessing the Newborn's Physical Condition: The Apgar Scale

Infants who have difficulty making the transition to life outside the uterus must be given special help at once. To assess the newborn's physical condition quickly, doctors and nurses use the **Apgar Scale.** As Table 3.3 shows, a rating of 0, 1, or 2 on each of five characteristics is made at one minute and again at five minutes after birth. A combined Apgar score of 7 or better indicates that the infant is in good physical condition. If the score is between 4 and 6, the baby requires assistance in establishing breathing and other vital signs. If the score is 3 or below, the infant is in serious danger and requires emergency medical attention. Two Apgar ratings are given because some babies have trouble adjusting at first but do quite well after a few minutes (Apgar, 1953).

Approaches to Childbirth

Childbirth practices, like other aspects of family life, are molded by the society of which mother and baby are a part. In many village and tribal cultures, expectant mothers are well-acquainted with the childbirth process. For example, the Jarara of South America and the Pukapukans of the Pacific Islands treat birth as a vital part of daily life. The Jarara mother gives birth in full view of the entire community, including small children. The Pukapukan girl is so familiar with the events of labor and delivery that she can frequently be seen playing at it. Using a coconut to represent the baby, she stuffs it inside her dress, imitates the mother's pushing, and lets the nut fall at the proper moment. In most nonindustrialized cultures, women are assisted during the birth process. Among the Mayans of the Yucatán, the mother leans against the body of a woman called the "head helper," who supports her weight and breathes with her during each contraction (Jordan, 1993; Mead & Newton, 1967).

In Western nations, childbirth has changed dramatically over the centuries. Before the late 1800s, birth usually took place at home and was a family-centered event. The industrial revolution brought greater crowding to cities, along with new health problems. As a result, childbirth moved from home to the hospital, where the health of mothers and babies could be protected. Once doctors assumed responsibility for childbirth, women's knowledge of it declined, and relatives and friends were no longer welcome to participate (Borst, 1995).

By the 1950s and 1960s, women were starting to question the medical procedures that had come to be used routinely during labor and delivery. Many felt that routine use of strong drugs and delivery instruments had robbed them of a precious

Table 3.3	The Apgar Scale		
		Rating	
Sign[a]	**0**	**1**	**2**
Heart rate	No heartbeat	Under 100 beats per minute	100 to 140 beats per minute
Respiratory effort	No breathing for 60 seconds	Irregular, shallow breathing	Strong breathing and crying
Reflex irritability (sneezing, coughing, and grimacing)	No response	Weak reflexive response	Strong reflexive response
Muscle tone	Completely limp	Weak movements of arms and legs	Strong movements of arms and legs
Color[b]	Blue body, arms, and legs	Body pink with blue arms and legs	Body, arms, and legs completely pink

[a]To remember these signs, you may find it helpful to use a technique in which the original labels are reordered and renamed as follows: color = **A**ppearance, heart rate = **P**ulse, reflex irritability = **G**rimace, muscle tone = **A**ctivity, and respiratory effort = **R**espiration. Together, the first letters of the new labels spell **Apgar**.

[b]The skin tone of nonwhite babies makes it difficult to apply the "pink" color criterion. However, newborns of all races can be rated for pinkish glow resulting from the flow of oxygen through body tissues.

Source: Apgar, 1953.

In a hospital birth center, this mother and father welcome their newborn baby, delivered by the midwife just moments before. The father's support is part of widespread use of natural childbirth techniques in Western nations. Natural childbirth is associated with shorter labors and fewer birth complications and offers parents a more rewarding birth experience.

experience and were often neither necessary nor safe for the baby. Gradually, a natural childbirth movement arose in Europe and spread to North America. Its purpose was to make hospital birth as comfortable and rewarding for mothers as possible. Today, most hospitals carry this theme further by offering birth centers that are family-centered and homelike. *Freestanding birth centers,* which permit greater maternal control over labor and delivery, including choice of delivery positions, presence of family members and friends, and early contact between parents and baby, also exist. And a small number of North American women are rejecting institutional birth entirely and choosing to have their babies at home.

Natural, or Prepared, Childbirth

Yolanda and Jay chose **natural**, or **prepared, childbirth**—a group of techniques aimed at reducing pain and medical intervention and making childbirth as rewarding an experience as possible. Although many natural childbirth programs exist, most draw on methods developed by Grantly Dick-Read (1959) in England and Fernand Lamaze (1958) in France. These physicians recognized that cultural attitudes had taught women to fear the birth experience. An anxious, frightened woman in labor tenses her muscles, turning the mild pain that sometimes accompanies strong contractions into a great deal of pain.

In a typical natural childbirth program, the expectant mother and a companion (a partner, a relative, or a friend) participate in three activities:

- *Classes.* Yolanda and Jay attended a series of classes in which they learned about the anatomy and physiology of labor and delivery. Knowledge about the birth process reduces a mother's fear.

- *Relaxation and breathing techniques.* During each class, Yolanda was taught relaxation and breathing exercises aimed at counteracting the pain of uterine contractions.

- *Labor coach.* Jay learned how to help Yolanda during childbirth by reminding her to relax and breathe, massaging her back, supporting her body, and offering words of encouragement and affection.

Social support is an important part of the success of natural childbirth techniques. In Guatemalan and American hospitals that routinely isolated patients during childbirth, some mothers were randomly assigned a companion who stayed with them throughout labor and delivery, talking to them, holding their hands, and rubbing their backs to promote relaxation. These mothers had fewer birth complications and shorter labors than women with no companionship. Guatemalan mothers who received support also interacted more positively with their babies after delivery, talking, smiling, and gently stroking (Kennell et al., 1991; Sosa et al., 1980). Other studies indicate that mothers who are supported during labor and delivery less often have cesarean (surgical) deliveries, and their babies' Apgar scores are higher (Sauls, 2002). Social support also makes Western hospital-birth customs more acceptable to women from parts of the world where assistance from family and community members is the norm (Granot et al., 1996).

Home Delivery

Home birth has always been popular in certain industrialized nations, such as England, the Netherlands, and Sweden. The number of North American women choosing to have their babies at home rose during the 1970s and 1980s but nevertheless remains small, at about 1 percent (Curtin & Park, 1999). Although some home births are attended by doctors, many more are handled by certified *nurse-midwives,* who have degrees in nursing and additional training in childbirth management.

The joys and perils of home delivery are well-illustrated by the story that Don, who painted my house as I worked on this book, related to me. "Our first child was delivered in the hospital," he said. "Even though I was present, Kathy and I found the atmosphere to be rigid and insensitive. We wanted a warmer, more personal birth environment." With the coaching of a nurse-midwife, Don delivered their second child, Cindy, at their farmhouse, 3 miles out of town. Three years later, when Kathy went into labor with Marnie, a heavy snowstorm prevented the midwife from reaching the house on time, and Don delivered the baby alone. The birth was difficult. Marnie failed to breathe for several minutes; with great effort, Don revived her. The frightening memory of Marnie's limp, blue body convinced Don and Kathy to return to the hospital to have their

Unlike women in the developed world, who usually give birth in hospitals or freestanding birth centers, most women in nonindustrialized cultures give birth at home. This woman of Uzbekistan, in central Asia, is attended by a midwife as she prepares for childbirth, with her own mother also present to support her.

last child. By then, hospital practices had changed, and the event was a rewarding one for both parents.

Don and Kathy's experience raises the question: Is it just as safe to give birth at home as in a hospital? For healthy women who are assisted by a well-trained doctor or midwife, the answer is yes, since complications rarely occur (Janssen et al., 2002; Vedam, 2003). However, if attendants are not carefully trained and prepared to handle emergencies, the rate of infant death is high (Mehlmadrona & Madrona, 1997). And when mothers are at risk for any kind of complication, the appropriate place for labor and delivery is the hospital, where life-saving treatment is available.

Medical Interventions

Two-year-old Melinda walks with a halting, lumbering gait and has difficulty keeping her balance. She has *cerebral palsy,* a general term for a variety of impairments in muscle coordination that result from brain damage before, during, or just after birth.

Melinda is among the 10 percent of children with cerebral palsy whose brain damage resulted from **anoxia,** or inadequate oxygen supply, during labor and delivery (Anslow, 1998). Her mother got pregnant accidentally, was frightened and alone, and arrived at the hospital at the last minute. Melinda was in **breech position,** turned so that the buttocks or feet would be delivered first, and the umbilical cord was wrapped around her neck. Had her mother come to the hospital earlier, doctors could have monitored Melinda's condition and delivered her surgically as soon as squeezing of the umbilical cord led to distress, thereby reducing the damage or preventing it entirely.

In cases like Melinda's, medical interventions are clearly justified. But in others, they can interfere with delivery and even pose new risks. In the following sections, we examine some commonly used medical procedures during childbirth.

Fetal Monitoring

Fetal monitors are electronic instruments that track the baby's heart rate during labor. An abnormal heartbeat may indicate that the baby is in distress due to anoxia and needs to be delivered immediately. Most U.S. hospitals require continuous fetal monitoring; it is used in over 80 percent of American births. In Canada, continuous monitoring is usually reserved for babies at risk for birth complications (Banta & Thacker, 2001; Liston et al., 2002). The most popular type of monitor is strapped across the mother's abdomen throughout labor. A second, more accurate method involves threading a recording device through the cervix and placing it directly under the baby's scalp.

Fetal monitoring is a safe medical procedure that has saved the lives of many babies in high-risk situations. Nevertheless, the practice is controversial. In healthy pregnancies, it does not reduce the already low rates of infant brain damage and death. Furthermore, most infants have some heartbeat irregularities during labor, and critics worry that fetal monitors identify many babies as in danger who, in fact, are not. Monitoring is linked to an increase in the number of cesarean (surgical) deliveries, which we will discuss shortly (Thacker & Stroup, 2003). In addition, some women complain that the devices are uncomfortable, prevent them from moving easily, and interfere with the normal course of labor.

Still, fetal monitors will probably continue to be used routinely in the United States, even though they are not necessary in most cases. Doctors fear that they will be sued for malpractice if an infant dies or is born with problems and they cannot show that they did everything possible to protect the baby.

Labor and Delivery Medication

Some form of medication is used in more than 80 percent of North American births (Sharma & Leveno, 2003). *Analgesics,* drugs used to relieve pain, may be given in mild doses during labor to help a mother relax. *Anesthetics* are a stronger type of painkiller that blocks sensation. Currently, the most common approach to controlling pain during labor is *epidural analgesia,* in which a regional pain-relieving drug is delivered continuously through a catheter into a small space in the lower spine. Unlike older spinal block procedures, which numb the entire lower half of the body, epidural analgesia limits pain reduction to the pelvic region. Because the mother retains the capacity to feel the pressure of the contractions and to move her trunk and legs, she can push during the second stage of labor.

Although pain-relieving drugs help women cope with childbirth and enable doctors to perform essential medical interventions, they also can cause problems. Epidural analgesia, for example, weakens uterine contractions. As a result, labor is prolonged. And because drugs rapidly cross the placenta, exposed newborns tend to have lower Apgar scores, to be sleepy and withdrawn, to suck poorly during feedings, and to be irritable when awake (Caton et al., 2002; Eltzschig, Lieberman, & Camann, 2003; Emory, Schlackman, & Fiano, 1996).

Do heavy doses of childbirth medication have a lasting impact on physical and mental development? Some researchers have claimed so (Brackbill, McManus, & Woodward, 1985), but their findings have been challenged (Golub, 1996; Riordan et al., 2000). Use of medication may be related to other risk factors that could account for long-term consequences in some studies, but more research is needed to sort out these effects. Meanwhile, the negative impact of these drugs on the newborn's adjustment supports the current trend to limit their use.

Cesarean Delivery

A **cesarean delivery** is a surgical birth; the doctor makes an incision in the mother's abdomen and lifts the baby out of the uterus. Forty years ago, cesarean delivery was rare. Since then, cesarean rates have climbed internationally, reaching 15 percent in Finland, 19 percent in Canada and New Zealand, 21 percent in Australia, and 29 percent in the United States (Canadian Institute for Health Information, 2005; Martin et al., 2005).

Cesareans have always been warranted by medical emergencies, such as Rh incompatibility, premature separation of the placenta from the uterus, or serious maternal illness or infection (for example, the herpes simplex 2 virus, which can infect the baby during a vaginal delivery). Cesareans are also justified in breech births, in which the baby risks head injury or anoxia (as in Melinda's case). But the infant's exact position makes a difference. Certain breech babies fare just as well with a normal delivery as with a cesarean (Giuliani et al., 2002). Sometimes the doctor can gently turn the baby into a head-down position during the early part of labor.

Until recently, many women who have had a cesarean have been offered the option of a vaginal birth in subsequent pregnancies. But new evidence indicates that compared with repeated cesareans, a natural labor after a cesarean is associated with slightly increased rates of rupture of the uterus and infant death (Gerten et al., 2005). As a result, the rule, "Once a cesarean, always a cesarean," is making a comeback.

Repeated cesareans, however, do not explain the worldwide rise in cesarean deliveries. Instead, medical control over childbirth is largely responsible. Because many needless cesareans are performed, pregnant women should ask questions about the procedure before choosing a doctor. Although the operation itself is safe, mother and baby require more time for recovery. Anesthetic may have crossed the placenta, making cesarean newborns sleepy and unresponsive and at increased risk for breathing difficulties (McDonagh, Osterweil, & Guise, 2005).

Preterm and Low-Birth-Weight Infants

Babies born 3 weeks or more before the end of a full 38-week pregnancy or who weigh less than 5½ pounds (2,500 grams) have for many years been referred to as "premature." A wealth of research indicates that premature babies are at risk for many problems. Birth weight is the best available predictor of infant survival and healthy development. Many newborns who weigh less than 3½ pounds (1,500 grams) experience difficulties that are not overcome, an effect that becomes stronger as birth weight decreases (see Figure 3.6 on page 102). Frequent illness, inattention, overactivity, language delays, low intelligence test scores, deficits in school learning, and emotional and behavior problems are some of the difficulties that persist through childhood and adolescence and extend into adulthood (Bhutta et al., 2002; Davis, 2003; Johnson et al., 2003).

About 1 in 13 American infants and 1 in 18 Canadian infants are born underweight. Although the problem can strike unexpectedly, it is highest among poverty-stricken women, including many ethnic minority and teenage mothers (Children's Defense Fund, 2005; Statistics Canada, 2004a). These mothers, as noted earlier, are more likely to be undernourished and to be exposed to other harmful environmental influences. In addition, they often do not receive adequate prenatal care.

Recall from Chapter 2 that prematurity is also common among twins. On average, twins are born about three weeks early. And because space inside the uterus is restricted, twins gain less weight than singletons after the twentieth week of pregnancy.

■ **FIGURE 3.6 Incidence of major and minor disabilities by birth weight, obtained from studies of low-birth-weight children at school age.** *Major disabilities* include cerebral palsy, mental retardation, and vision and hearing impairments. *Minor disabilities* include slightly below-average intelligence, learning disabilities (usually in reading, spelling, and math), mild difficulties in motor control, and behavior problems (including poor attention and impulse control, aggressiveness, noncompliance, depression, passivity, anxiety, and difficulty separating from parents). (Adapted from D'Agostino & Clifford, 1998.)

Preterm versus Small for Date

Although low-birth-weight infants face many obstacles to healthy development, most go on to lead normal lives; half of those who weighed only a couple of pounds at birth have no disability (refer again to Figure 3.6). To better understand why some babies do better than others, researchers divide them into two groups. **Preterm** infants are those born several weeks or more before their due date. Although they are small, their weight may still be appropriate, based on time spent in the uterus. **Small-for-date** babies are below their expected weight considering length of the pregnancy. Some small-for-date infants are actually full-term. Others are preterm infants who are especially underweight.

Of the two types of babies, small-for-date infants usually have more serious problems. During the first year, they are more likely to die, catch infections, and show evidence of brain damage. By middle childhood, they have lower intelligence test scores, are less attentive, achieve less well in school, and are socially immature (Hediger et al., 2002; O'Keefe et al., 2003). Small-for-date infants probably experienced inadequate nutrition before birth. Perhaps their mothers did not eat properly, the placenta did not function normally, or the babies themselves had defects that prevented them from growing as they should. Recall that an abnormally functioning placenta is associated with ready transfer of stress hormones from mother to fetus. Consequently,

small-for-date infants are especially likely to suffer from prenatal neurological impairments that permanently weaken their capacity to manage stress (Wust et al., 2005).

Consequences for Caregiving

Imagine a scrawny, thin-skinned infant whose body is only a little larger than the size of your hand. You try to play with the baby by stroking and talking softly, but he is sleepy and unresponsive. When you feed him, he sucks poorly. He is usually irritable during the short, unpredictable periods in which he is awake.

The appearance and behavior of preterm babies can lead parents to be less sensitive and responsive in caring for them. Compared with full-term infants, preterm babies—especially those who are very ill at birth—are less often held close, touched, and talked to gently. At times, mothers of these infants resort to interfering pokes and verbal commands in an effort to obtain a higher level of response from the baby (Barratt, Roach, & Leavitt, 1996). This may explain why preterm babies as a group are at risk for child abuse. When they are born to isolated, poverty-stricken mothers who cannot provide good nutrition, health care, and parenting, the likelihood of unfavorable outcomes increases. In contrast, parents with stable life circumstances and social supports usually can overcome the stresses of caring for a preterm infant. In these cases, even sick preterm babies have a good chance of catching up in development by middle childhood (Ment et al., 2003).

These findings suggest that how well preterm infants develop has a great deal to do with the parent–child relationship. Consequently, interventions directed at supporting both sides of this tie are more likely to help these infants recover.

Interventions for Preterm Infants

A preterm baby is cared for in a special Plexiglas-enclosed bed called an *isolette*. Temperature is carefully controlled because these babies cannot yet regulate their own body temperature effectively. To help protect the baby from infection, air is filtered before it enters the isolette. Infants born more than 6 weeks early commonly have a disorder called *respiratory distress syndrome* (otherwise known as *hyaline membrane disease*). Their tiny lungs are so poorly developed that the air sacs collapse, causing serious breathing difficulties. When a preterm infant breathes with the aid of a respirator, is fed through a stomach tube, and receives medication through an intravenous needle, the isolette can be very isolating indeed! Physical needs that otherwise would lead to close contact and other human stimulation are met mechanically.

■ **Special Infant Stimulation.** At one time, doctors believed that stimulating such a fragile baby could be harmful. Now we know that in proper doses, certain kinds of stimulation can help preterm infants develop. In some intensive care nurseries, preterm babies can be seen rocking in suspended hammocks or lying on waterbeds designed to replace the gentle motion they would have received while still in the mother's uterus. Other forms of stimulation have also been used—an attractive mobile or a tape recording of a heartbeat, soft music, or the mother's voice. These experiences promote faster weight gain, more predictable sleep patterns, and greater alertness (Marshall-Baker, Lickliter, & Cooper, 1998; Standley, 1998).

Touch is an especially important form of stimulation. In baby animals, touching the skin releases certain brain chemicals that support physical growth—effects believed to occur in humans as well. When preterm infants were massaged several times each day in the hospital, they gained weight faster and, at the end of the first year, were advanced in mental and motor development over preterm babies not given this stimulation (Field, 2001; Field, Hernandez-Reif, & Freedman, 2004).

In developing countries where hospitalization is not always possible, skin-to-skin "kangaroo care" is the most readily available intervention for promoting the survival and recovery of preterm babies. It involves placing the infant in a vertical position between the mother's breasts or next to the father's chest (under the parent's clothing) so the parent's body functions as a human incubator. Kangaroo care offers fathers a unique opportunity to increase their involvement in caring for the preterm newborn. Because of its many physical and psychological benefits, the technique is used often in Western nations as a supplement to hospital intensive care.

Kangaroo skin-to-skin contact fosters improved oxygenation of the baby's body, temperature regulation, sleep, breastfeeding, weight gain, and infant survival (Feldman & Eidelman, 2003). In addition, the kangaroo position provides the baby with gentle stimulation of all sensory modalities: hearing (through the parent's voice), smell (through proximity of the parent's body), touch (through skin-to-skin contact), and visual (through the upright position). Mothers and fathers

This mother practices "kangaroo care" with her preterm baby in the intensive care nursery. By holding the infant close to her chest, she promotes oxygenation of the baby's body, temperature regulation, feeding, alertness, and more favorable development. At the same time, she gains confidence in her ability to meet her fragile newborn's needs.

© KNUT-MUELLER/DAS FOTOARCHIV/PETER ARNOLD, INC.

practicing kangaroo care feel more confident about caring for their fragile babies and interact more sensitively and affectionately with them (Feldman et al., 2002, 2003). Together, these factors may explain why preterm babies given many hours of kangaroo care in their early weeks, compared to those given little or no such care, score higher on measures of mental and motor development during the first year (Charpak et al., 2005; Tessier et al., 2003).

■ **Training Parents in Infant Caregiving Skills.** Interventions that support parents of preterm infants generally teach them about the infant's characteristics and promote caregiving skills. For parents who have the economic and personal resources to care for a low-birth-weight infant, just a few sessions of coaching in recognizing and responding to the baby's needs are linked to steady gains in mental test performance that, after several years, equal those of full-term children (Achenbach et al., 1990). Warm parenting that helps preterm infants sustain attention (for example, gently commenting on and showing the baby features of a toy) is especially helpful in promoting favorable early cognitive and language development (Smith et al., 1996).

When preterm infants live in stressed, low-income households, long-term, intensive intervention is necessary to reduce developmental problems. In the Infant Health and Development Project, preterm babies born into poverty received a comprehensive intervention that combined medical follow-up, weekly parent training sessions, and enrollment in cognitively stimulating child care. More than four times as many intervention children as controls (39 versus 9 percent) were within normal range at age 3 in intelligence, psychological adjustment, and physical growth (Bradley et al., 1994). In addition, mothers in the intervention group were more affectionate and more often encouraged play and cognitive mastery in their children—one reason their 3-year-olds may have been developing so favorably (McCarton, 1998).

At ages 5 and 8, children who had attended the child-care program regularly—for more than 350 days over the 3-year period—continued to show better intellectual functioning. The more they attended, the higher they scored, with greater gains among those whose birth weights were higher—between 4½ and 5½ pounds (2,001 to 2,500 grams). In contrast, children who attended only sporadically gained little or even lost ground (Hill, Brooks-Gunn, & Waldfogel, 2003). These findings confirm that babies who are both preterm and economically disadvantaged require *intensive* intervention. And special strategies, such as extra adult–child interaction, may be necessary to achieve lasting changes in children with the lowest birth weights.

Finally, the high rate of underweight babies in the United States—one of the worst in the industrialized world—could be greatly reduced by improving the health and social conditions described in the Social Issues box on pages 104–105. Fortunately, today we can save many preterm infants, but an even better course of action would be to prevent this serious threat to infant survival and development before it happens.

Social Issues

A Cross-National Perspective on Health Care and Other Policies for Parents and Newborn Babies

Infant mortality is an index used around the world to assess the overall health of a nation's children. It refers to the number of deaths in the first year of life per 1,000 live births. Although the United States has the most up-to-date health care technology in the world, it has made less progress in reducing infant deaths than many other countries. Over the past three decades, it has slipped in the international rankings, from seventh in the 1950s to twenty-sixth in 2003.

Members of America's poor ethnic minorities are at greatest risk. African-American and Native-American babies are twice as likely as white infants to die in the first year of life (U.S. Census Bureau, 2006b). Canada, in contrast, has achieved one of the lowest infant mortality rates in the world. It ranks sixteenth and falls only slightly behind top-ranked countries. Still, infant mortality among Canada's lowest-income groups is much higher than the national figure. First Nations babies die at twice the rate, and Inuit babies at three times the rate, of Canadian babies in general (Smylie, 2001; Statistics Canada, 2005d).

Neonatal mortality, the rate of death within the first month of life, accounts for 67 percent of the infant death rate in the United States and 80 percent in Canada. Two factors are largely responsible for neonatal mortality. The first is serious physical defects, most of which cannot be prevented. The percentage of babies born with physical defects is about the same in all ethnic and income groups. The second leading cause of neonatal mortality is low

birth weight, which is largely preventable. African-American, Native-American, and Canadian-Aboriginal babies are more than twice as likely as white infants to be born early and underweight (Health Canada, 2004b; U.S. Census Bureau, 2006b).

Widespread poverty and, in the United States, weak health care programs for mothers and young children are largely responsible for these trends. Each country in Figure 3.7 that outranks the United States in infant survival provides all its citizens with government-sponsored health care benefits. And each takes extra steps to make sure that pregnant mothers and babies have access to good nutrition, high-quality medical care, and social and economic supports that promote effective parenting.

For example, all Western European nations guarantee women a certain number of prenatal visits at very low or no cost. After a baby is born, a health professional routinely visits the home to provide counseling about infant care and to arrange continuing medical services. Home assistance is especially extensive in the Netherlands. For a token fee, each mother is granted a specially trained maternity helper, who assists with infant care, shopping, housekeeping, meal preparation, and the care of other children during the days after delivery (Bradley & Bray, 1996; Kamerman, 1993).

Paid, job-protected employment leave is another vital societal intervention for new parents. Canadian mothers are eligible for 15 weeks' maternity leave at 55 percent of prior earnings, and Canadian mothers or fathers are eligible for an additional 35 weeks of parental leave at the same rate. Paid leave is widely available in other industrialized nations as well. Sweden has the most generous parental leave program in the world. Parents have the right to paid birth leave of 2 weeks for fathers plus 18 months of leave to share between them—the first 12 months at 80 percent of prior earnings,

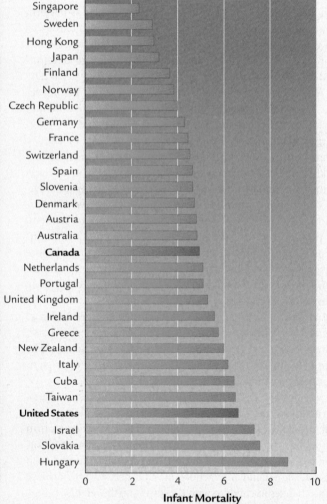

Infant Mortality
(number of deaths per 1,000 births)

FIGURE 3.7 Infant mortality in 29 nations. Despite its advanced health care technology, the United States ranks poorly. It is twenty-sixth in the world, with a death rate of 6.6 infants per 1,000 births. Canada, which provides all its citizens government-funded health care, ranks fifteenth. Its infant death rate is 4.8 per 1,000 births. (Adapted from U.S. Census Bureau, 2006b.)

the next 3 months at a modest flat rate, and the final 3 months unpaid (Seward, Yeats, & Zottarelli, 2002). Even less-developed nations provide parental leave benefits. For example, in the People's Republic of China, a new mother is granted 3 months' leave at regular pay. Furthermore, many countries supplement basic paid leave. In Germany, for example, after a fully paid 3-month leave, a parent may take 2 more years at a modest flat rate and a third year at no pay (Waldfogel, 2001).

Yet in the United States, the federal government mandates *only 12 weeks of unpaid leave* for employees in businesses with at least 50 workers. In 2002, California became the first state to guarantee a mother or father paid leave—up to 6 weeks at half salary, regardless of the size of the company. Nevertheless, research indicates that 6 weeks of childbirth leave (the norm in the United States) is too short. When a family is stressed by a baby's arrival, leaves of

6 weeks or less are linked to increased maternal anxiety, depression, marital dissatisfaction, sense of role overload (conflict between work and family responsibilities), and negative interactions with the baby. Longer leaves of 12 weeks or more predict favorable maternal mental health and sensitive, responsive caregiving (Clark et al., 1997; Hyde et al., 2001). Single women and their babies are most hurt by the absence of a generous national paid-leave policy. These mothers are usually the sole source of support for their families and can least afford to take time from their jobs.

In countries with low infant mortality rates, expectant parents need not wonder how they will get health care and other resources to support their baby's development. The powerful impact of universal, high-qual-

This Inuit mother, from Baffin Island in northernmost Canada, experienced pregnancy complications and had to be flown 190 miles to deliver her son. Limited access to health care and social services in remote areas compromises the futures of many Inuit newborns.

ity health care, generous parental leave, and other social services on maternal and infant well-being provides strong justification for these policies.

Birth Complications, Parenting, and Resilience

In the preceding sections, we discussed a variety of birth complications. Now let's try to put the evidence together. Can any general principles help us understand how infants who survive a traumatic birth are likely to develop? A landmark study carried out in Hawaii provides answers to this question.

In 1955, Emmy Werner and Ruth Smith began to follow the development of nearly 700 infants on the island of Kauai who had experienced mild, moderate, or severe birth complications. Each was matched, on the basis of SES and ethnicity, with a healthy newborn (Werner & Smith, 1982). Findings revealed that the likelihood of long-term difficulties increased if birth trauma was severe. Among mildly to moderately stressed children, however, the best predictor of how well they did in later years was the quality of their home environments. Children growing up in stable families did almost as well on measures of intelligence and psychological adjustment as those with no birth problems. Those exposed to poverty, family disorganization, and mentally ill parents often developed serious learning difficulties, behavior problems, and emotional disturbance.

The Kauai study tells us that as long as birth injuries are not overwhelming, a supportive home environment can restore children's growth. But the most intriguing cases in this study were the handful of exceptions. A few children with both fairly serious birth complications and troubled family environments grew into competent adults who fared as well as controls in career attainment and psychological adjustment. Werner and Smith found that these children relied on factors outside the family and within themselves to overcome stress. Some had attractive personalities that caused them to receive positive responses from relatives, neighbors, and peers. In other instances, a grandparent, aunt, uncle, or baby-sitter provided the needed emotional support (Werner, 1989, 2001; Werner & Smith, 1992).

Do these outcomes remind you of the characteristics of resilient children, discussed in Chapter 1? The Kauai study—and other similar investigations—reveal that the impact of early biological risks often wanes as children's personal characteristics and social experiences increasingly contribute to their functioning (Laucht, Esser, & Schmidt, 1997; Resnick et al., 1999). In sum, when the overall balance of life events tips toward the favorable side, children with serious birth problems can develop successfully.

Ask Yourself

Review

Sensitive care can help preterm infants recover, but they are less likely than full-term newborns to receive such care. Explain why.

Apply

Cecilia and Adena each gave birth to a 3-pound baby 7 weeks preterm. Cecilia is single and on welfare. Adena and her husband are happily married and earn a good income. Plan an intervention for helping each baby develop.

Connect

List factors discussed in this chapter that increase the chances that an infant will be born underweight. How many of these factors could be prevented by better health care for expectant mothers?

Reflect

Extremely low-birth-weight babies (less than 2.2 pounds, or 1,000 grams) who survive are at high risk for serious physical, cognitive, and emotional problems. Do you agree or disagree with the use of extraordinary medical measures to save these babies? Explain.

www.ablongman.com/berk

The Newborn Baby's Capacities

Newborn infants have a remarkable set of capacities that are crucial for survival and for evoking attention and care from parents. In relating to the physical world and building their first social relationships, babies are active from the very start.

Newborn Reflexes

A **reflex** is an inborn, automatic response to a particular form of stimulation. Reflexes are the newborn baby's most obvious organized patterns of behavior. As Jay placed Joshua on a table in my classroom, we saw several. When Jay bumped the side of the table, Joshua reacted by flinging his arms wide and bringing them back toward his body. As Yolanda stroked Joshua's cheek, he turned his head in her direction. When she put her finger in Joshua's palm, he grabbed on tightly. Look at Table 3.4 and see if you can name the newborn reflexes that Joshua displayed.

Some reflexes have survival value. The rooting reflex helps a breastfed baby find the mother's nipple. Babies display it only when hungry and touched by another person, not when they touch themselves (Rochat & Hespos, 1997). And if newborns

Table 3.4	**Some Newborn Reflexes**			
Reflex	**Stimulation**	**Response**	**Age of Disappearance**	**Function**
Eye blink	Shine bright light at eyes or clap hand near head.	Infant quickly closes eyelids.	Permanent	Protects infant from strong stimulation
Rooting	Stroke cheek near corner of mouth.	Head turns toward source of stimulation.	3 weeks (becomes voluntary turning at this time)	Helps infant find the nipple
Sucking	Place finger in infant's mouth.	Infant sucks finger rhythmically.	Replaced by voluntary sucking after 4 months	Permits feeding
Moro	Hold infant horizontally on back and let head drop slightly, or produce a sudden loud sound against surface supporting infant.	Infant makes an "embracing" motion by arching back, extending legs, throwing arms outward, and then bringing arms in toward the body.	6 months	In human evolutionary past, may have helped infant cling to mother
Palmar grasp	Place finger in infant's hand and press against palm.	Infant spontaneously grasps finger.	3–4 months	Prepares infant for voluntary grasping
Tonic neck	Turn baby's head to one side while lying awake on back.	Infant lies in a "fencing position." One arm is extended in front of eyes on side to which head is turned, other arm is flexed.	4 months	May prepare infant for voluntary reaching
Stepping	Hold infant under arms and permit bare feet to touch a flat surface.	Infant lifts one foot after another in stepping response.	2 months in infants who gain weight quickly; sustained in lighter infants.	Prepares infant for voluntary walking
Babinski	Stroke sole of foot from toe toward heel.	Toes fan out and curl as foot twists in.	8–12 months	Unknown

Sources: Knobloch & Pasamanick, 1974; Prechtl & Beintema, 1965; Thelen, Fisher, & Ridley-Johnson, 1984.

could not suck, our species would be unlikely to survive for a single generation! At birth, babies adjust their sucking pressure to how easily milk flows from the nipple (Craig & Lee, 1999).

A few reflexes form the basis for complex motor skills that will develop later. The stepping reflex looks like a primitive walking response. In infants who gain weight quickly in the weeks after birth, the stepping reflex drops out because thigh and calf muscles are not strong enough to lift the baby's chubby legs. But if the lower part of the infant's body is dipped in water, the reflex reappears because the buoyancy of the water lightens the load on the baby's muscles (Thelen, Fisher, & Ridley-Johnson, 1984). When the stepping reflex is exercised regularly, babies make more reflexive stepping movements and are likely to walk several weeks earlier than if stepping is not practiced (Zelazo et al., 1993). However, there is no special need for infants to practice the stepping reflex because all normal babies walk in due time.

Some reflexes help parents and infants establish gratifying interaction. A baby who searches for and successfully finds the nipple, sucks easily during feedings, and grasps when the hand is touched encourages parents to respond lovingly and feel competent as caregivers. Reflexes can also help caregivers comfort the baby because they permit infants to control distress and amount of stimulation. For example, on short trips with Joshua to the grocery store, Yolanda brought along a pacifier. If he became fussy, sucking helped quiet him until she could feed, change, or hold him.

Look at Table 3.4 again, and you will see that most newborn reflexes disappear during the first 6 months. Researchers believe that this is due to a gradual increase in voluntary control over behavior as the cerebral cortex develops. Pediatricians test reflexes carefully because reflexes can reveal the health of the baby's nervous system. Weak or absent reflexes, overly rigid or exaggerated reflexes, and reflexes that persist beyond the

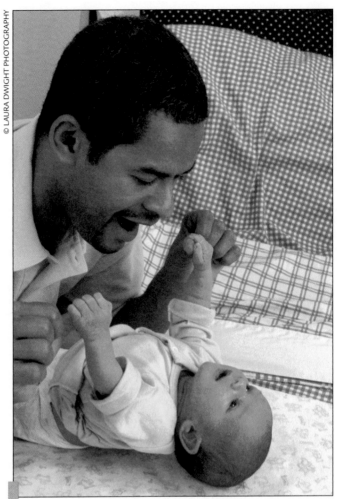

The palmar grasp reflex is so strong during the first week after birth that many infants can use it to support their entire weight.

point in development when they should normally disappear can signal brain damage (Schott & Rossor, 2003; Zafeiriou, 2000).

Newborn States

Throughout the day and night, newborn infants move in and out of five **states of arousal**, or degrees of sleep and wakefulness, described in Table 3.5 on page 108. During the first month, these states alternate frequently. The most fleeting is quiet alertness, which usually moves quickly toward fussing and crying. Much to the relief of their fatigued parents, newborns spend the greatest amount of time asleep—about 16 to 18 hours a day. Although newborns sleep more at night than during the day, their sleep–wake cycles are affected more by fullness–hunger than by darkness–light (Davis, Parker, & Montgomery, 2004; Goodlin-Jones, Burnham, & Anders, 2000).

However, striking individual differences in daily rhythms exist that affect parents' attitudes toward and interaction with the baby. A few newborns sleep for long periods, increasing the energy their well-rested parents have for sensitive, responsive care. Other babies cry a great deal, and their parents must exert

In the Moro reflex, loss of support or a sudden loud sound causes this baby to arch her back, extend her arms outward, and then bring them in toward her body.

Table 3.5	Infant States of Arousal	
State	**Description**	**Daily Duration in Newborn**
Regular sleep	The infant is at full rest and shows little or no body activity. The eyelids are closed, no eye movements occur, the face is relaxed, and breathing is slow and regular.	8–9 hours
Irregular sleep	Gentle limb movements, occasional stirring, and facial grimacing occur. Although the eyelids are closed, occasional rapid eye movements can be seen beneath them. Breathing is irregular.	8–9 hours
Drowsiness	The infant is either falling asleep or waking up. Body is less active than in irregular sleep but more active than in regular sleep. The eyes open and close; when open, they have a glazed look. Breathing is even but somewhat faster than in regular sleep.	Varies
Quiet alertness	The infant's body is relatively inactive, with eyes open and attentive. Breathing is even.	2–3 hours
Waking activity and crying	The infant shows frequent bursts of uncoordinated body activity. Breathing is very irregular. Face may be relaxed or tense and wrinkled. Crying may occur.	1–4 hours

Source: Wolff, 1966.

great effort to soothe them. If these parents do not succeed, they may feel less competent and less positive toward their infant. Babies who spend more time alert probably receive more social stimulation and opportunities to explore and, therefore, may have a slight advantage in mental development (Gertner et al., 2002)

Of the states listed in Table 3.5, the two extremes of sleep and crying have been of greatest interest to researchers. Each tells us something about normal and abnormal early development.

■ **Sleep.** One day, Yolanda and Jay watched Joshua while he slept and wondered why his eyelids and body twitched and his rate of breathing varied. Sleep is made up of at least two states. During irregular, or **rapid-eye-movement (REM), sleep**, brainwave activity is remarkably similar to that of the waking state. The eyes dart beneath the lids; heart rate, blood pressure, and breathing are uneven; and slight body movements occur. In contrast, during regular, or **non-rapid-eye-movement (NREM) sleep**, the body is almost motionless, and heart rate, breathing, and brain-wave activity are slow and even.

Like children and adults, newborns alternate between REM and NREM sleep. However, they spend far more time in the REM state than they ever will again. REM sleep accounts for 50 percent of a newborn baby's sleep time. By 3 to 5 years, it has declined to an adultlike level of 20 percent (Louis et al., 1997).

Why do young infants spend so much time in REM sleep? In older children and adults, the REM state is associated with dreaming. Babies probably do not dream, at least not in the same way we do. But researchers believe that the stimulation of REM sleep is vital for growth of the central nervous system. Young infants seem to have a special need for this stimulation because they spend little time in an alert state, when they can

get input from the environment. In support of this idea, the percentage of REM sleep is especially great in the fetus and in preterm babies, who are even less able than full-term newborns to take advantage of external stimulation (DiPietro et al., 1996; de Weerd & van den Bossche, 2003).

Because the normal sleep behavior of a newborn baby is organized and patterned, observations of sleep states can help identify central nervous system abnormalities. In infants who are brain-damaged or who have experienced serious birth trauma, disturbed REM–NREM sleep cycles are often present. Babies with poor sleep organization are likely to be behaviorally disorganized and, therefore, to have difficulty learning and evoking caregiver interactions that enhance their development (de Weerd & van den Bossche, 2003; Groome et al., 1997). And the brain-functioning problems that underlie newborn sleep irregularities may culminate in sudden infant death syndrome, a major cause of infant mortality (see the Biology and Environment box on the following page).

■ **Crying.** Crying is the first way that babies communicate, letting parents know they need food, comfort, or stimulation. During the weeks after birth, all infants have some fussy periods when they are difficult to console. But most of the time, the nature of the cry, combined with the experiences leading up to it, helps guide parents toward its cause. The baby's cry is a complex stimulus that varies in intensity, from a whimper to a message of all-out distress (Gustafson, Wood, & Green, 2000). As early as the first few weeks, individual infants can be identified by the unique vocal "signature" of their cry, which helps parents locate their baby from a distance (Gustafson, Green, & Cleland, 1994).

Young infants usually cry because of physical needs, most commonly hunger, but babies may also cry in response to

Biology and Environment

The Mysterious Tragedy of Sudden Infant Death Syndrome

Millie awoke with a start one morning and looked at the clock. It was 7:30, and Sasha had missed both her night waking and her early morning feeding. Wondering if she was all right, Millie and her husband Stuart tiptoed into the room. Sasha lay still, curled up under her blanket. She had died silently during her sleep.

Sasha was a victim of **sudden infant death syndrome (SIDS)**, the unexpected death, usually during the night, of an infant under 1 year of age that remains unexplained after thorough investigation. In industrialized nations, SIDS is the leading cause of infant mortality between 1 and 12 months of age (Health Canada, 2004d; Hamilton et al., 2005).

Although the precise cause of SIDS is not known, its victims usually show physical problems from the very beginning. Early medical records of SIDS babies reveal higher rates of prematurity and low birth weight, poor Apgar scores, and limp muscle tone. Abnormal heart rate and respiration and disturbances in sleep–wake activity are also involved (Daley, 2004; Kato et al., 2003). At the time of death, many SIDS babies have a mild respiratory infection (Samuels, 2003). This seems to increase the chances of respiratory failure in an already vulnerable baby.

One hypothesis about the cause of SIDS is that impaired brain functioning prevents these infants from learning how to respond when their survival is threatened—for example, when respiration is suddenly interrupted. Between 2 and 4 months, when SIDS is most likely, reflexes decline and are replaced by voluntary, learned responses. Respiratory and muscular weaknesses may stop SIDS babies from acquiring behaviors that replace defensive reflexes (Lipsitt, 2003). As a result, when breathing difficulties occur during sleep, infants do not wake up, shift their position, or cry out for help. Instead, they simply give in to oxygen deprivation and death. In support of this interpretation, autopsies reveal that SIDS babies, more often than other infants, show abnormalities in brain centers controlling breathing (Kinney et al., 2003).

In an effort to reduce the occurrence of SIDS, researchers are studying environmental factors related to it. Maternal cigarette smoking, both during and after pregnancy, as well as smoking by other caregivers, strongly predicts the disorder. Babies exposed to cigarette smoke have more respiratory infections and are twice as likely as nonexposed infants to die of SIDS (Anderson, Johnson, & Batal, 2005). Prenatal abuse of drugs that depress central nervous system functioning (opiates and barbiturates) increases the risk of SIDS tenfold (Kandall et al., 1993). SIDS babies are also more likely to sleep on their stomachs than on their backs and often are wrapped very warmly in clothing and blankets (Hauck et al., 2003).

Researchers suspect that nicotine, depressant drugs, excessive body warmth, and respiratory infection all lead to physiological stress, which disrupts the normal sleep pattern. When sleep-deprived infants experience a sleep "rebound," they sleep more deeply, which results in loss of muscle tone in the airway passages. In at-risk babies, the airway may collapse, and the infant may fail to arouse sufficiently to reestablish breathing (Simpson, 2001). In other cases, healthy babies sleeping face down in soft bedding may die from continually breathing their own exhaled breath.

Quitting smoking, changing an infant's sleeping position, and removing a few bedclothes can reduce the incidence of SIDS. For example, if women refrained from smoking while pregnant, an estimated 30 percent of SIDS cases would be prevented. Public education campaigns that encourage parents to put their infants down on their backs have cut the incidence of SIDS in half in many Western nations (Byard & Krous, 2003). Another protective measure is pacifier

Public education campaigns encouraging parents to put their infants down on their backs to sleep have helped to reduce the incidence of SIDS, which has dropped by half in many Western nations. Research also confirms the value of using a pacifier. If breathing or heart-rate irregularities occur, infants who suck wake from sleep more easily.

use: Sleeping babies who suck arouse more easily in response to breathing and heart-rate irregularities (Hauck, Omojokun, & Siadaty, 2005). Nevertheless, compared with white infants, SIDS rates are two to six times higher in poverty-stricken minority groups, where parental stress, substance abuse, reduced access to health care, and lack of knowledge about preventive sleep practices are widespread (Pickett, Luo, & Lauderdale, 2005).

When SIDS does occur, surviving family members require a great deal of help to overcome a sudden and unexpected death. As Millie commented 6 months after Sasha's death, "It's the worst crisis we've ever been through. What's helped us most are the comforting words of others who've experienced the same tragedy."

temperature change when undressed, a sudden noise, or a painful stimulus. Newborns (as well as older babies) often cry at the sound of another crying baby (Dondi, Simion, & Caltran, 1999). Some researchers believe that this response reflects an inborn capacity to react to the suffering of others. Furthermore, crying typically increases during the early weeks, peaks at about 6 weeks, and then declines. Because this trend appears in many cultures with vastly different infant care practices, researchers believe that normal readjustments of the central nervous system underlie it (Barr, 2001).

The next time you hear an infant cry, notice your own reaction. The sound stimulates strong feelings of arousal and discomfort in just about anyone (Murray, 1985). This powerful response is probably innately programmed in humans to make sure that babies receive the care and protection they need to survive.

Soothing a Crying Infant. Although parents do not always interpret their baby's cry correctly, their accuracy improves with experience (Thompson & Leger, 1999). Fortunately, there are many ways to soothe a crying baby when feeding and diaper changing do not work (see Applying What We Know below). The technique that Western parents usually try first, lifting the baby to the shoulder and rocking or walking, is the most effective.

Another common soothing method is swaddling—wrapping the baby snugly in a blanket. The Quechua, who live in the cold, high-altitude desert regions of Peru, dress young babies in layers of clothing and blankets that cover the head and body. The result—a warm pouch placed on the mother's back that

To soothe her crying infant, this mother holds her baby upright against her gently moving body. Besides encouraging infants to stop crying, this technique causes them to become quietly alert and attentive to the environment.

Ways to Soothe a Crying Newborn

Applying What We Know

Method	Explanation
Lift the baby to the shoulder and rock or walk.	This provides a combination of physical contact, upright posture, and motion. It is the most effective soothing technique, causing young infants to become quietly alert.
Swaddle the baby.	Restricting movement and increasing warmth often soothe a young infant.
Offer a pacifier, preferably sweetened with a sugar solution.	Sucking helps babies control their own level of arousal. Sucking a sweetened pacifier relieves pain and quiets a crying infant.
Talk softly or play rhythmic sounds.	Continuous, monotonous, rhythmic sounds (such as a clock ticking, a fan whirring, or peaceful music) are more effective than intermittent sounds.
Take the baby for a short car ride or a walk in a baby carriage; swing the baby in a cradle.	Gentle, rhythmic motion of any kind helps lull the baby to sleep.
Massage the baby's body by stroking the baby's torso and limbs with continuous, gentle motions.	This technique is used in some non-Western cultures to relax the baby's muscles.
Combine several of the methods just listed.	Stimulating several of the baby's senses at once is often more effective than stimulating only one.
If these methods do not work, let the baby cry for a short period.	Occasionally, a baby responds well to just being put down and will, after a few minutes, fall asleep.

Sources: Blass, 1999; Campos, 1989; Lester, 1985; Reisman, 1987.

Some cultures routinely swaddle young infants, restricting movement and increasing warmth by wrapping blankets tightly around the body. This Navajo baby rests on a traditional cradle board that can be strapped to the mother's back. Swaddling reduces crying and promotes sleep.

© STEVE MAINES/STOCK BOSTON, LLC.

moves rhythmically as she walks—reduces crying and promotes sleep. It also allows the baby to conserve energy for early growth in the harsh Peruvian highlands (Tronick, Thomas, & Daltabuit, 1994).

In many tribal and village societies and non-Western developed nations, infants spend most of the day and night in close physical contact with their caregivers. Among the !Kung of the desert regions of Botswana, Africa, mothers sling their young babies on their hips, so infants can see their surroundings and nurse at will. The Gusii, an agricultural and herding society of Kenya, care for infants by placing them on the backs of their mothers, who respond to crying with ready feeding. Japanese mothers and babies also spend much time in close body contact (Small, 1998). Infants in these cultures show shorter bouts of crying than their North American counterparts (Barr, 2001).

But not all research indicates that rapid parental responsiveness reduces infant crying (van IJzendoorn & Hubbard, 2000). Parents must make reasoned choices about what to do on the basis of culturally accepted practices, the suspected reason for the cry, and the context in which it occurs—for example, in the privacy of their own home or while having dinner at a restaurant. Fortunately, with age, crying declines. Virtually all researchers agree that parents can lessen older babies' need to cry by encouraging more mature ways of expressing their desires, such as gestures and vocalizations.

Abnormal Crying. Like reflexes and sleep patterns, the infant's cry offers a clue to central nervous system distress. The cries of brain-damaged babies and those who have experienced prenatal and birth complications are often shrill, piercing, and shorter in duration than the cries of healthy infants (Boukydis & Lester, 1998; Green, Irwin, & Gustafson, 2000). Even newborns with a fairly common problem—*colic*, or persistent crying—tend to have high-pitched, harsh-sounding cries (Zeskind & Barr, 1997). Although the cause of colic is unknown, certain newborns, who react especially strongly to unpleasant stimuli, are susceptible. Because their crying is intense, they have more difficulty calming down than other babies. Colic generally subsides between 3 and 6 months of age (Barr & Gunnar, 2000; St James-Roberts et al., 2003).

Most parents try to respond to a crying baby with extra care and sensitivity, but sometimes the cry is so unpleasant and the infant so difficult to soothe that parents become frustrated, resentful, and angry. Preterm and ill babies are more likely to be abused by highly stressed parents, who frequently mention a high-pitched, grating cry as one factor that caused them to lose control and harm the baby (Zeskind & Lester, 2001). We will discuss a host of additional influences on child abuse in Chapter 8.

Sensory Capacities

On his visit to my class, Joshua looked wide-eyed at my bright pink blouse and turned to the sound of his mother's voice. During feedings, he lets Yolanda know through his sucking rhythm that he prefers the taste of breast milk to a bottle of plain water. Clearly, Joshua has some well-developed sensory capacities. In the following sections, we explore the newborn's responsiveness to touch, taste, smell, sound, and visual stimulation.

■ **Touch.** In our discussion of preterm infants, we saw that touch helps stimulate early physical growth. As we will see in Chapter 6, it is vital for emotional development as well. Therefore, it is not surprising that sensitivity to touch is well-developed at birth. The reflexes listed in Table 3.4 reveal that the newborn baby responds to touch, especially around the mouth, on the palms, and on the soles of the feet. During the prenatal period, these areas, along with the genitals, are the first to become sensitive to touch (Humphrey, 1978).

At birth, infants are highly sensitive to pain. If male newborns are circumcised, anesthetic is sometimes not used because of the risk of giving drugs to a very young infant. Babies often respond with a high-pitched, stressful cry and a dramatic rise in heart rate, blood pressure, palm sweating, pupil dilation, and muscle tension (Jorgensen, 1999; Warnock & Sandrin, 2004). Recent research establishing the safety of certain local anesthetics for newborns promises to ease the pain of these procedures. Offering a nipple that delivers a sugar solution is also helpful; it quickly reduces crying and discomfort in young babies. And combining the sweet liquid with gentle holding by the parent lessens pain even more. Research on infant mammals indicates that physical touch releases *endorphins*—painkilling chemicals in the brain (Gormally et al., 2001). Allowing a newborn to endure severe pain overwhelms the nervous system with stress hormones, which can disrupt the child's developing capacity to handle common, everyday stressors. The result is heightened pain sensitivity, sleep disturbances, feeding problems, and difficulty calming down when upset (Mitchell & Boss, 2002).

◼ **Taste and Smell.** Facial expressions reveal that newborns can distinguish several basic tastes. Like adults, they relax their facial muscles in response to sweetness, purse their lips when the taste is sour, and show a distinct archlike mouth opening when it is bitter (Steiner, 1979; Steiner et al., 2001). These reactions are important for survival: The food that best supports the infant's early growth is the sweet-tasting milk of the mother's breast. Not until 4 months do babies prefer a salty taste to plain water, a change that may prepare them to accept solid foods (Mennella & Beauchamp, 1998).

Nevertheless, newborns can readily learn to like a taste that at first evoked either a neutral or a negative response. For

(a) Responses by newborns of anise-consuming mothers

(b) Responses by newborns of non-anise-consuming mothers

◼ **FIGURE 3.8 Examples of facial expressions of newborns exposed to the odor of anise whose mothers' diets differed in anise-flavored foods during late pregnancy.** (a) Babies of anise-consuming mothers spent more time turning toward the odor and sucking, licking, and chewing. (b) Babies of non-anise-consuming mothers more often turned away with a negative facial expression. (From B. Schaal, L. Marlier, & R. Soussignan, 2000, "Human Foetuses Learn Odours from Their Pregnant Mother's Diet," *Chemical Senses, 25,* p. 731. Reprinted by permission of the authors.)

example, babies allergic to cow's-milk formula who are given a soy or other vegetable-based substitute (typically very strong and bitter-tasting) soon prefer it to regular formula. A taste previously disliked can come to be preferred when it is paired with relief of hunger (Harris, 1997).

As with taste, certain odor preferences are present at birth. For example, the smell of bananas or chocolate causes a relaxed, pleasant facial expression, whereas the odor of rotten eggs makes the infant frown (Steiner, 1979). During pregnancy, the amniotic fluid is rich in tastes and smells that vary with the mother's diet—early experiences that influence newborns' preferences. In a study carried out in the Alsatian region of France, where anise is frequently used to flavor foods, researchers tested newborns for their reaction to the anise odor (Schaal, Marlier, & Soussignan, 2000). The mothers of some babies had regularly consumed anise during the last 2 weeks of pregnancy; the other mothers had never consumed it. When presented with the anise odor on the day of birth, the babies of non-anise-consuming mothers were far more likely to turn away than the babies of anise-consuming mothers (see Figure 3.8). These different reactions were still apparent 4 days later, even though all mothers had refrained from consuming anise during this time.

In many mammals, the sense of smell plays an important role in feeding and in protecting the young from predators by helping mothers and babies identify each other. Although smell is less well-developed in humans, traces of its survival value remain. Newborns given a choice between the smell of their own mother's amniotic fluid and that of another mother spend more time oriented toward the familiar fluid (Marlier, Schaal, & Soussignan, 1998). The smell of the mother's amniotic fluid is comforting; babies exposed to it cry less than babies who are not (Varendi et al., 1998).

Immediately after birth, babies placed face down between their mother's breasts spontaneously latch on to a nipple and begin sucking within an hour. If one breast is washed to remove its natural scent, most newborns grasp the unwashed breast, indicating that they are guided by smell (Varendi & Porter, 2001). At 4 days of age, breastfed babies prefer the smell of their own mother's breast to that of an unfamiliar lactating mother (Cernoch & Porter, 1985). Bottle-fed babies orient to the smell of any lactating woman over the smell of formula or of a nonlactating woman (Marlier & Schaal, 1997; Porter et al., 1992). Newborns' dual attraction to the odors of their mother and of the lactating breast helps them locate an appropriate food source and, in the process, begin to distinguish their caregiver from other people.

◼ **Hearing.** Newborn infants can hear a wide variety of sounds, although their sensitivity improves greatly over the first few months (Tharpe & Ashmead, 2001). At birth, infants prefer complex sounds, such as noises and voices, to pure tones. And babies only a few days old can tell the difference between a few sound patterns—a series of tones arranged in ascending versus descending order, utterances with two versus three syllables, the stress patterns of words, such as *ma*-ma versus ma-*ma*, and happy-sounding speech as opposed to speech with negative or neutral emotional qualities (Mastropieri &

Turkewitz, 1999; Sansavini, Bertoncini, & Giovanelli, 1997; Trehub, 2001).

Young infants listen longer to human speech than structurally similar nonspeech sounds (Vouloumanos & Werker, 2004). And they can detect the sounds of any human language. Newborns make fine-grained distinctions among many speech sounds. For example, when given a nipple that turns on a recording of the "ba" sound, babies suck vigorously and then slow down as the novelty wears off. When the sound switches to "ga," sucking picks up, indicating that infants detect this subtle difference. Using this method, researchers have found only a few speech sounds that newborn infants cannot discriminate (Aldridge, Stillman, & Bower, 2001; Jusczyk & Luce, 2002). These capacities reveal that the baby is marvelously prepared for the awesome task of acquiring language.

Listen carefully to yourself the next time you talk to a young infant. You will probably speak in ways that highlight important parts of the speech stream—use a slow, high-pitched, expressive voice and a rising tone at the ends of phrases and sentences, and pause before continuing. Adults probably communicate this way because they notice that infants are more attentive when they do so. Indeed, newborns prefer speech with these characteristics (Aslin, Jusczyk, & Pisoni, 1998). They will also suck more on a nipple to hear a recording of their mother's voice than that of an unfamiliar woman and to hear their native language as opposed to a foreign language (Moon, Cooper, & Fifer, 1993; Spence & DeCasper, 1987). These preferences may have developed from hearing the muffled sounds of the mother's voice before birth.

■ **Vision.** Vision is the least developed of the newborn baby's senses. Visual structures in both the eye and the brain are not yet fully formed. For example, cells in the *retina*, a membrane lining the inside of the eye that captures light and transforms it into messages that are sent to the brain, are not as mature or densely packed as they will be in several months. The optic nerve and other pathways that relay these messages, and the visual centers in the brain that receive them, will not be adultlike for several years. And the muscles of the *lens*, which permit us to adjust our visual focus to varying distances, are weak (Atkinson, 2000).

As a result, newborn babies cannot focus their eyes well, and **visual acuity**, or fineness of discrimination, is limited. At birth, infants perceive objects at a distance of 20 feet about as clearly as adults do at 600 feet (Slater, 2001). In addition, unlike adults (who see nearby objects most clearly), newborn babies see unclearly across a wide range of distances (Banks, 1980; Hainline, 1998). As a result, images such as the parent's face, even from close up, look quite blurred.

Although newborns cannot see well, they actively explore their environment by scanning it for interesting sights and tracking moving objects. However, their eye movements are slow and inaccurate (Aslin, 1993). Joshua's captivation with my pink blouse reveals that he is attracted to bright objects. Although newborns prefer to look at colored rather than gray stimuli, they are not yet good at discriminating colors. It will take a month or two for color vision to improve (Teller, 1998).

Neonatal Behavioral Assessment

A variety of instruments permit doctors, nurses, and researchers to assess the behavior of newborn babies. The most widely used of these tests, T. Berry Brazelton's **Neonatal Behavioral Assessment Scale (NBAS)**, evaluates the newborn's reflexes, state changes, responsiveness to physical and social stimuli, and other reactions (Brazelton & Nugent, 1995). A major goal is to understand each infant's capacity to initiate caregiver support and to adjust his or her behavior to avoid being overwhelmed by stimulation.

The NBAS has been given to many infants around the world. As a result, researchers have learned about individual and cultural differences in newborn behavior and how child-rearing practices can maintain or change a baby's reactions. For example, NBAS scores of Asian and Native-American babies reveal that they are less irritable than Caucasian infants. Mothers in these cultures often encourage their babies' calm dispositions through holding and nursing at the first signs of discomfort (Chisholm, 1989; Muret-Wagstaff & Moore, 1989).

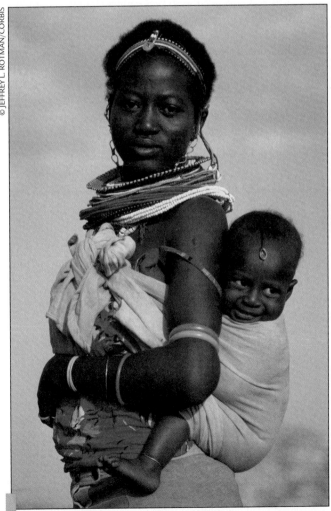

Similar to women in the Zambian culture, this mother of the El Molo people of northern Kenya carries her baby around all day, providing close physical contact, a rich variety of stimulation, and ready feeding.

In contrast, maternal care seems to quickly change the poor NBAS scores of undernourished newborns in Zambia, Africa. The Zambian mother carries her baby about all day, providing a rich variety of sensory stimulation. When reassessed at 1 week of age, a once unresponsive newborn appears alert and contented (Brazelton, Koslowski, & Tronick, 1976).

Can you tell from these examples why a single NBAS score is not a good predictor of later development? Because newborn behavior and parenting styles combine to shape development, *changes in NBAS scores* over the first week or two of life (rather than a single score) provide the best estimate of the baby's ability to recover from the stress of birth. NBAS "recovery curves" predict intelligence and absence of emotional and behavior problems with moderate success well into the preschool years (Brazelton, Nugent, & Lester, 1987; Ohgi et al., 2003a, 2003b).

The NBAS has also been used to help parents get to know their infants. In some hospitals, health professionals discuss with or demonstrate to parents the newborn capacities assessed by the NBAS. Parents of both preterm and full-term newborns who participate in these programs interact more confidently and effectively with their babies (Eiden & Reifman, 1996). In one study, Brazilian mothers who experienced a 50-minute NBAS-based discussion a few days after delivery were more likely than controls who received only health care information to establish eye contact, smile, vocalize, and soothe in response to infant signals a month later (Wendland-Carro, Piccinini, & Millar, 1999). Although lasting effects on development have not been demonstrated, NBAS-based interventions are useful in helping the parent–infant relationship get off to a good start.

Ask Yourself

Review

What functions does REM sleep serve in young infants? Can sleep tell us anything about the health of the newborn's central nervous system? Explain.

Apply

Jackie, who had a difficult delivery, observes her 2-day-old daughter Kelly being given the NBAS. Kelly scores poorly on many items. Jackie wonders if this means Kelly will not develop normally. How would you respond to Jackie's concern?

Connect

How do the diverse capacities of newborn babies contribute to their first social relationships? Provide as many examples as you can.

Reflect

Are newborns more competent than you thought they were before you read this chapter? Which of their capacities most surprised you?

Adjusting to the New Family Unit

Because effective parental care is crucial for infant survival and optimal development, nature helps prepare expectant mothers and fathers for their new role. Toward the end of pregnancy, mothers begin producing the hormone *oxytocin*, which stimulates uterine contractions; causes the breasts to "let down" milk; induces a calm, relaxed mood; and promotes responsiveness to the baby (Russell, Douglas, & Ingram, 2001). And in several studies, first-time fathers enrolled in prenatal classes showed hormonal changes around the time of birth that were compatible with those of mothers—specifically, slight increases in *prolactin* (a hormone that stimulates milk production in females) and *estrogens* (sex hormones produced in larger quantities in females) and a drop in *androgens* (sex hormones produced in larger quantities in males). In animal and human research, these changes are associated with positive emotional reactions to infants and with paternal caregiving (Storey et al., 2000; Wynne-Edwards, 2001).

Although birth-related hormones can facilitate caregiving, their release and effects may depend on experiences, such as a positive couple relationship and paternal close contact with the pregnant mother. Furthermore, humans can parent effectively without experiencing birth-related hormonal changes, as successful adoption reveals. And as we have already seen, a great many factors—from family functioning to social policies—are involved in good infant care.

Indeed, the early weeks after the baby's arrival are full of profound challenges. The mother needs to recuperate from childbirth. If she is breastfeeding, energies must be devoted to working out this intimate relationship. The father needs to support the mother in her recovery and become a part of this new threesome. At times, he may feel ambivalent about the baby, who constantly demands and gets the mother's attention. And as we will see in Chapter 6, siblings—especially those who are young and firstborn—understandably feel displaced. They sometimes react with jealousy and anger.

While all this is going on, the tiny infant is very assertive about his urgent physical needs, demanding to be fed, changed, and comforted at odd times of the day and night. A family schedule that was once routine and predictable is now irregular and uncertain. Yolanda spoke candidly about the changes that she and Jay experienced:

When we brought Joshua home, we had to deal with the realities of our new responsibility. Joshua seemed so small and helpless, and we worried about whether we would be able to take proper care of him. It took us 20 minutes to change the first diaper! I rarely feel rested because I'm up two to four times every night, and I spend a good part of my waking hours trying to anticipate Joshua's rhythms and needs. If Jay weren't so willing to help by holding and walking Joshua, I think I'd find it much harder.

How long does this time of adjustment to parenthood last? In Chapter 14, we will see that when parents support each other's needs, the stress caused by the birth of a baby remains manageable. Nevertheless, as one pair of counselors who have worked with many new parents point out, "As long as children are dependent on their parents, those parents find themselves preoccupied with thoughts of their children. This does not keep them from enjoying other aspects of their lives, but it does mean that they never return to being quite the same people they were before they became parents" (Colman & Colman, 1991, p. 198).

Summary

Prenatal Development

List the three phases of prenatal development, and describe the major milestones of each.

■ The first prenatal phase, the period of the zygote, lasts about 2 weeks, from fertilization until **implantation** of the blastocyst in the uterine lining. During this time, structures that will support prenatal growth begin to form. The embryonic disk is surrounded by the **amnion**, which fills with amniotic fluid to regulate temperature and cushion against the mother's movements. From the **chorion**, villi emerge that burrow into the uterine wall, and the **placenta** starts to develop. The developing organism is connected to the placenta by the **umbilical cord**.

■ The period of the **embryo** lasts from 2 to 8 weeks, during which the foundations for all body structures are laid down. In the first week of this period, the **neural tube** forms, and the nervous system starts to develop. Other organs follow and grow rapidly. At the end of this phase, the embryo responds to touch and can move.

■ The period of the **fetus**, lasting until the end of pregnancy, involves a dramatic increase in body size and the completion of physical structures. By the middle of the second **trimester**, the mother can feel movement. The fetus becomes covered with **vernix**, which protects the skin from chapping. White, downy hair called **lanugo** helps the vernix stick to the skin. At the end of the second trimester, production of neurons in the brain is complete.

■ At the beginning of the third trimester, between 22 and 26 weeks, the fetus reaches the **age of viability**. The brain continues to develop rapidly, and new sensory and behavioral capacities emerge. The lungs gradually mature, the fetus fills the uterus, and birth is near.

Prenatal Environmental Influences

What are teratogens, and what factors influence their impact?

■ **Teratogens** are environmental agents that cause damage during the prenatal period.

Their effects conform to the sensitive period concept. The impact of teratogens varies with the amount and length of exposure, the genetic makeup of mother and fetus, the presence or absence of other harmful agents, and the age of the organism at time of exposure. The developing organism is especially vulnerable during the embryonic period because all essential body structures are emerging. Immediate physical damage is easy to notice, but serious health and psychological consequences may not show up until later in development.

List agents that are known or suspected teratogens, and discuss evidence supporting the harmful impact of each.

■ Currently, the most widely used potent teratogen is Accutane, a drug used to treat acne. The prenatal impact of many other commonly used medications, such as aspirin and caffeine, is hard to separate from other factors correlated with drug taking. Babies whose mothers used heroin, methadone, or cocaine during pregnancy have withdrawal symptoms after birth and are jittery and inattentive. Some babies exposed to cocaine prenatally have lasting difficulties, but others show no major negative effects. Studies of the effects of marijuana use also show contradictory findings.

© SIMON FRASER/PRINCESS MARY HOSPITAL/SCIENCE PHOTO LIBRARY/ PHOTO RESEARCHERS, INC.

■ Infants of parents who use tobacco are often born underweight and may have attention, learning, and behavior problems in childhood. When mothers consume alcohol in large quantities, **fetal alcohol syndrome**

(**FAS**), a disorder involving mental retardation, poor attention, overactivity, slow physical growth, and facial abnormalities, often results. Babies whose mothers consumed smaller amounts of alcohol may experience some of these problems, a condition known as **fetal alcohol effects (FAE)**.

■ Prenatal exposure to high levels of radiation, mercury, lead, dioxins, and PCBs leads to physical malformations and severe brain damage. Low-level exposure has also been linked to diverse impairments, including lower intelligence test scores and, in the case of radiation, language and emotional disorders.

■ Among infectious diseases, rubella (German measles) causes a wide variety of abnormalities, which vary with the time the disease strikes during pregnancy. The human immunodeficiency virus (HIV), responsible for AIDS, results in brain damage, delayed mental and motor development, and early death. The developing organism is especially sensitive to the herpes viruses, including cytomegalovirus and herpes simplex 2. The parasitic disease toxoplasmosis, in the first trimester, may lead to eye and brain damage.

Describe the impact of other maternal factors on prenatal development.

■ In healthy, physically fit women, regular moderate exercise is related to increased birth weight. However, very frequent, vigorous exercise results in lower birth weight. When the mother's diet is inadequate, low birth weight and damage to the brain and other organs are major concerns.

■ Severe emotional stress is linked to many pregnancy complications, although its impact can be reduced by providing the mother with emotional support. **Rh factor incompatibility**—an Rh-negative mother carrying an Rh-positive fetus—can lead to oxygen deprivation, brain and heart damage, and infant death.

■ Aside from the risk of chromosomal abnormalities in older women, maternal age and number of previous births are not major causes of prenatal problems. Rather, poor health and environmental risks associated with poverty are the strongest predictors of pregnancy complications.

Why is early and regular health care vital during the prenatal period?

- Unexpected difficulties, such as toxemia, can arise, especially when mothers have health problems to begin with. Prenatal health care is especially critical for women unlikely to seek it—in particular, those who are young, single, and poor.

Childbirth

Describe the three stages of childbirth, the baby's adaptation to labor and delivery, and the newborn baby's appearance.

- Childbirth takes place in three stages, beginning with contractions that open the cervix so the mother can push the baby through the birth canal and ending with delivery of the placenta. During labor, infants produce high levels of stress hormones, which help them withstand oxygen deprivation, clear the lungs for breathing, and arouse them into alertness at birth.

- Newborn infants have large heads, small bodies, and facial features that make adults feel like cuddling them. The **Apgar Scale** assesses the baby's physical condition at birth.

Approaches to Childbirth

Describe natural childbirth and home delivery, noting any benefits and concerns associated with each.

- **Natural**, or **prepared, childbirth** involves classes in which prospective parents learn about labor and delivery, relaxation and breathing techniques to counteract pain, and coaching during childbirth. The method helps reduce use of medication. Social support, a vital part of natural childbirth, is linked to fewer birth complications and shorter labors. Home birth is safe for

healthy mothers who are assisted by a well-trained doctor or midwife, but mothers at risk for any kind of complication are safer giving birth in a hospital.

Medical Interventions

List common medical interventions during childbirth, circumstances that justify their use, and any dangers associated with each.

- When pregnancy and birth complications make **anoxia** likely, **fetal monitors** help save the lives of many babies. However, when used routinely, they may identify infants as in danger who, in fact, are not.

- Medication to relieve pain is necessary in complicated deliveries. When given in large doses, it may prolong labor and produce a depressed state in the newborn that affects the early mother–infant relationship.

- **Cesarean deliveries** are justified in cases of medical emergency and serious maternal illness and sometimes when babies are in **breech position**. Cesarean delivery has climbed internationally. Many unnecessary cesareans are performed, especially in the United States.

Preterm and Low-Birth-Weight Infants

What are the risks of preterm birth and low birth weight, and what factors can help infants who survive a traumatic birth?

- **Preterm** and low-birth-weight babies are especially likely to be born to poverty-stricken mothers. Compared with preterm babies whose weight is appropriate for time spent in the uterus, **small-for-date** infants are more likely to develop poorly. The fragile appearance and unresponsive, irritable behavior of preterm infants can lead parents to be less sensitive and responsive in caring for them.

- Some interventions provide special stimulation in the intensive care nursery. Others teach parents how to care for and interact with their babies. When preterm infants live in stressed, low-income households, long-term, intensive intervention is required. A major cause of **infant mortality** is low birth weight.

Birth Complications, Parenting, and Resilience

- When infants experience birth trauma, a supportive home environment can help restore their growth. Even children with

fairly serious birth complications can recover with the help of favorable life events.

The Newborn Baby's Capacities

Describe the newborn baby's reflexes and states of arousal, including sleep characteristics and ways to soothe a crying baby.

- Infants begin life with remarkable skills for relating to their physical and social worlds. **Reflexes** are the newborn baby's most obvious organized patterns of behavior. Some have survival value, others provide the foundation for voluntary motor skills, and still others contribute to early social relationships.

- Although newborns move in and out of five different **states of arousal**, they spend most of their time asleep. Sleep consists of at least two states, **rapid-eye-movement (REM)** sleep and **non-rapid-eye-movement (NREM)** sleep. REM sleep provides young infants with stimulation essential for central nervous system development. Disturbed REM–NREM cycles are a sign of central nervous system abnormalities, which may contribute to **sudden infant death syndrome (SIDS)**.

- A crying baby stimulates strong feelings of discomfort in nearby adults. The intensity of the cry and the experiences that led up to it help parents identify what is wrong. Once feeding and diaper changing have been tried, lifting the baby to the shoulder is the most effective soothing technique. In societies where babies spend most of the day and night in close physical contact with their caregivers, crying is greatly reduced.

Describe the newborn baby's sensory capacities.

- The senses of touch, taste, smell, and sound are well-developed at birth. Newborns are sensitive to pain, prefer sweet tastes and smells, and orient toward the odor of their own mother's amniotic fluid and the lactating breast. Already they can distinguish a few sound patterns as well as almost all speech sounds. They are especially responsive to high-pitched, expressive voices, their own mother's voice, and speech in their native tongue.

■ Vision is the least mature of the newborn's senses. At birth, focusing ability and **visual acuity** are limited. In exploring the visual field, newborn babies are attracted to bright objects but have difficulty discriminating colors.

Why is neonatal behavioral assessment useful?

■ The most widely used instrument for assessing the behavior of the newborn infant is Brazelton's **Neonatal Behavioral Assessment Scale (NBAS)**. The NBAS has helped researchers understand individual and cultural differences in newborn behavior. Sometimes it is used to teach parents about their baby's capacities.

Adjusting to the New Family Unit

Describe typical changes in the family after the birth of a new baby.

■ The new baby's arrival is exciting but stressful. When parents are sensitive to each other's needs, adjustment problems are usually temporary, and the transition to parenthood goes well.

Important Terms and Concepts

age of viability (p. 84)
amnion (p. 82)
anoxia (p. 100)
Apgar Scale (p. 98)
breech position (p. 100)
cesarean delivery (p. 101)
chorion (p. 82)
embryo (p. 82)
fetal alcohol effects (FAE) (p. 89)
fetal alcohol syndrome (FAS) (p. 89)
fetal monitors (p. 100)
fetus (p. 83)

implantation (p. 82)
infant mortality (p. 104)
lanugo (p. 84)
natural, or prepared, childbirth (p. 99)
Neonatal Behavioral Assessment Scale (NBAS) (p. 113)
neural tube (p. 83)
non-rapid-eye-movement (NREM) sleep (p. 108)
placenta (p. 82)
preterm (p. 102)
rapid-eye-movement (REM) sleep (p. 108)

reflex (p. 106)
Rh factor incompatibility (p. 94)
small-for-date (p. 102)
states of arousal (p. 107)
sudden infant death syndrome (SIDS) (p. 109)
teratogen (p. 85)
trimesters (p. 83)
umbilical cord (p. 82)
vernix (p. 83)
visual acuity (p. 113)

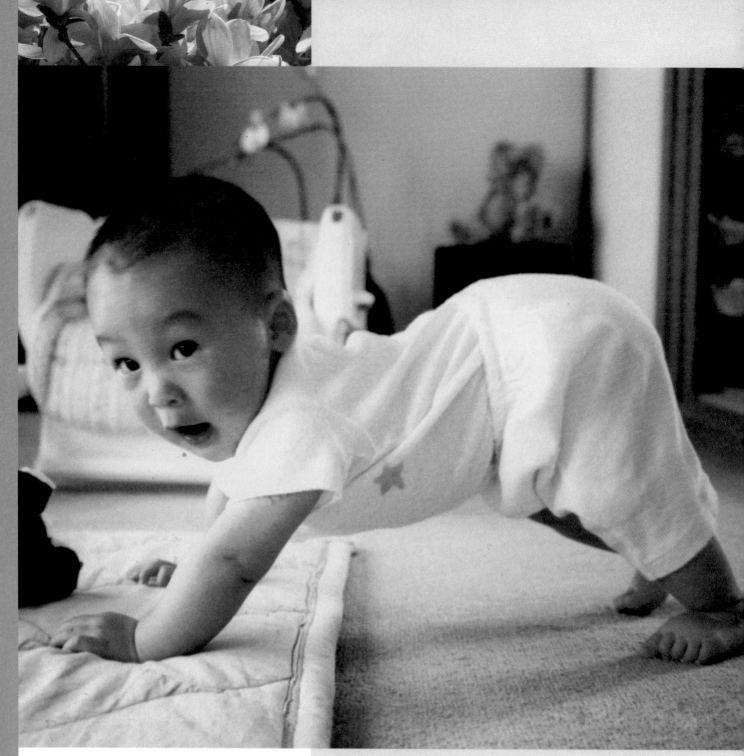

*B*abies acquire new motor skills in individual ways, by building on previously acquired capacities. Eager to explore a tantalizing world of objects and spaces, this 7-month-old is on the verge of crawling. Once he figures out how to move on his own, he will make dramatic strides understanding his surroundings.

Physical Development in Infancy and Toddlerhood

© ELIZABETH CREWS/THE IMAGE WORKS

On a brilliant June morning, 16-month-old Caitlin emerged from her front door, ready for the short drive to the child-care home where she spent her weekends while her mother, Carolyn, and her father, David, worked. Clutching a teddy bear in one hand and her mother's arm with the other, Caitlin descended the steps. "One! Two! Threeee!" Carolyn counted as she helped Caitlin down. "How much she's changed," Carolyn thought to herself, looking at the child who, not long ago, had been a newborn cradled in her arms. With her first steps, Caitlin had passed from infancy to toddlerhood—a period spanning the second year of life. At first, Caitlin did, indeed, "toddle" with an awkward gait, rocking from side to side and tipping over frequently. But her face reflected the thrill of conquering a new skill.

As they walked toward the car, Carolyn and Caitlin spotted 3-year-old Eli and his father, Kevin, in the neighboring yard. Eli dashed toward them, waving a bright yellow envelope. Carolyn bent down to open the envelope and took out a card. It read, "Announcing the arrival of Grace Ann. Born: Cambodia. Age: 16 months." Carolyn turned toward Kevin and Eli. "That's wonderful news! When can we see her?"

"Let's wait a few days," Kevin suggested. "Monica's taken Grace to the doctor this morning. She's underweight and malnourished." Kevin described Monica's first night with Grace in a hotel room in Phnom Penh before they flew to the United States. Grace lay on the bed, withdrawn and fearful. Eventually she fell asleep, clutching crackers in both hands.

Carolyn felt Caitlin's impatient tug at her sleeve. Off they drove to child care, where Vanessa had just dropped off her 18-month-old son, Timmy. Within moments, Caitlin and Timmy were in the sandbox, shoveling sand into plastic cups and buckets with the help of their caregiver, Ginette.

A few weeks later, Grace joined Caitlin and Timmy at Ginette's child-care home. Although still tiny and unable to crawl or walk, she had grown taller and heavier, and her sad, vacant gaze had given way to an alert expression, a ready smile, and an enthusiastic desire to imitate and explore. When Caitlin headed for the sandbox, Grace stretched out her arms, asking Ginette to carry her there, too. Soon Grace was pulling herself up at every opportunity. Finally, at age 18 months, she walked!

This chapter traces physical growth during the first 2 years—one of the most remarkable and busiest times of development. We will see how rapid changes in the infant's body and brain support learning, motor skills, and perceptual capacities. Caitlin, Grace, and Timmy will join us along the way to illustrate individual differences and environmental influences on physical development.

Body Growth

The next time you're walking in your neighborhood or at a shopping center, observe the contrast between the capabilities of infants and those of toddlers. One reason for the vast changes in what children can do over the first 2 years is that their bodies change enormously—faster than at any other time after birth.

Changes in Body Size and Muscle–Fat Makeup

By the end of the first year, a typical infant's height is about 32 inches, more than 50 percent greater than at birth; by 2 years, it is nearly 75 percent greater (36 inches). Similarly, by 5 months of age, birth weight has doubled (to about 15 pounds), at 1 year it has tripled (to 22 pounds), and at 2 years it has quadrupled (to about 30 pounds).

Figure 4.1 illustrates this dramatic increase in body size. But rather than making steady gains, infants and toddlers grow in little spurts. In one study, children who were followed over the first 21 months of life went for periods of 7 to 63 days with no growth, then added as much as half an inch in a 24-hour period! Almost always, parents described their babies as irritable and very hungry on the day before the spurt (Lampl, 1993; Lampl, Veldhuis, & Johnson, 1992).

One of the most obvious changes in infants' appearance is their transformation into round, plump babies by the middle of the first year. This early rise in "baby fat," which peaks at

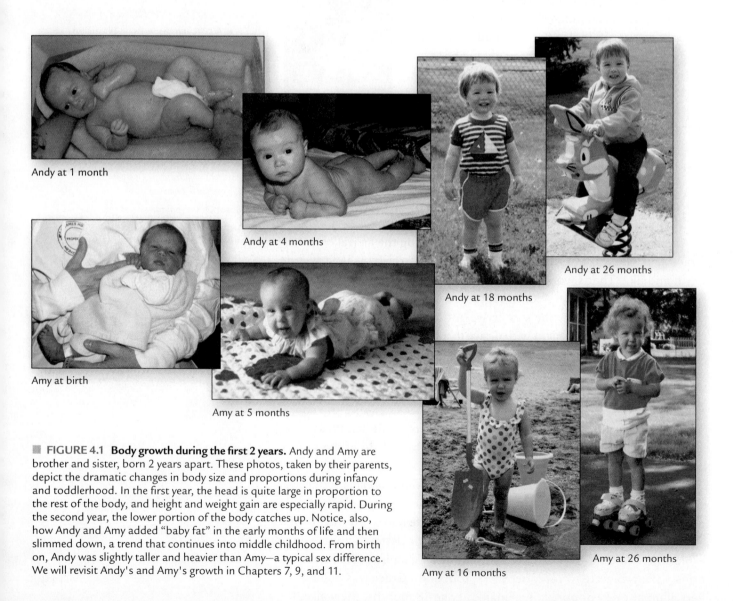

Andy at 1 month

Andy at 4 months

Andy at 18 months

Andy at 26 months

Amy at birth

Amy at 5 months

Amy at 16 months

Amy at 26 months

■ **FIGURE 4.1 Body growth during the first 2 years.** Andy and Amy are brother and sister, born 2 years apart. These photos, taken by their parents, depict the dramatic changes in body size and proportions during infancy and toddlerhood. In the first year, the head is quite large in proportion to the rest of the body, and height and weight gain are especially rapid. During the second year, the lower portion of the body catches up. Notice, also, how Andy and Amy added "baby fat" in the early months of life and then slimmed down, a trend that continues into middle childhood. From birth on, Andy was slightly taller and heavier than Amy—a typical sex difference. We will revisit Andy's and Amy's growth in Chapters 7, 9, and 11.

about 9 months, helps the small infant keep a constant body temperature. In the second year, most toddlers slim down, a trend that continues into middle childhood (Fomon & Nelson, 2002). In contrast, muscle tissue increases very slowly during infancy and will not reach a peak until adolescence. Babies are not very muscular creatures; their strength and physical coordination are limited.

Individual and Group Differences

As with all aspects of development, children vary in body size and muscle–fat makeup. In infancy, girls are slightly shorter and lighter than boys, with a higher ratio of fat to muscle. These small sex differences persist throughout early and middle childhood and are greatly magnified at adolescence. Ethnic differences in body size are apparent as well. Grace was below the *growth norms* (height and weight averages for children her age). Although early malnutrition contributed, even after substantial catch-up Grace remained below North American norms, a trend typical for Asian children. In contrast, Timmy is slightly above average, as African-American children tend to be (Bogin, 2001).

Children of the same age also differ in *rate* of physical growth; some progress more rapidly than others. Current body size does not tell us how quickly a child's physical growth is moving along. For example, Timmy is larger and heavier than either Caitlin or Grace, but he is not physically more mature. In a moment, you will see why.

The best way of estimating a child's physical maturity is to use *skeletal age*, a measure of bone development. It is determined by X-raying the long bones of the body to see the extent to which soft, pliable cartilage has hardened into bone, a gradual process that is completed in adolescence. When skeletal ages are examined, African-American children tend to be slightly ahead of Caucasian children at all ages, and girls considerably ahead of boys. At birth, the sexes differ by about 4 to 6 weeks, a gap that widens over infancy and childhood and accounts for the fact that girls reach their full body size several years before boys (Tanner, Healy, & Cameron, 2001). This greater physical maturity may contribute to girls' greater resistance to harmful environmental influences. As noted in Chapter 2, girls experience fewer developmental problems than boys and have lower infant and childhood mortality rates.

Changes in Body Proportions

As the child's overall size increases, different parts of the body grow at different rates. Two growth patterns describe these changes. The first is the **cephalocaudal trend**—from the Latin for "head to tail." During the prenatal period, the head develops more rapidly than the lower part of the body. At birth, the head takes up one-fourth of total body length, the legs only one-third. Notice how, in Figure 4.1, the lower portion of the body catches up. By age 2, the head accounts for only one-fifth and the legs for nearly one-half of body length.

In the second pattern, the **proximodistal trend**, growth proceeds, literally, from "near to far," from the center of the body outward. In the prenatal period, the head, chest, and trunk grow first, then the arms and legs, and finally the hands and feet. During infancy and childhood, the arms and legs continue to grow somewhat ahead of the hands and feet. As we will see later, motor development—with some exceptions—also follows these general trends.

Brain Development

At birth, the brain is nearer to its adult size than any other physical structure, and it continues to develop at an astounding pace throughout infancy and toddlerhood. We can best understand brain growth by looking at it from two vantage points: (1) the microscopic level of individual brain cells and (2) the larger level of the cerebral cortex, which is responsible for the highly developed intelligence of our species.

Development of Neurons

The human brain has 100 to 200 billion **neurons**, or nerve cells that store and transmit information, many of which have thousands of direct connections with other neurons. Neurons differ from other body cells in that they are not tightly packed together. Between them are tiny gaps, or **synapses**, where fibers from different neurons come close together but do not touch (see Figure 4.2). Neurons send messages to one another by releasing chemicals called **neurotransmitters**, which cross the synapse.

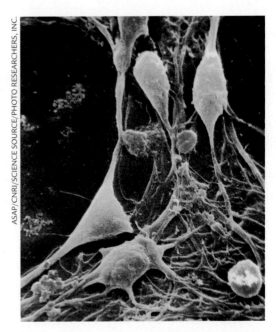

ASAP/CNRI/SCIENCE SOURCE/PHOTO RESEARCHERS, INC.

■ **FIGURE 4.2 Neurons and their connective fibers.** This photograph of several neurons, taken with the aid of a powerful microscope, shows the elaborate synaptic connections that form with neighboring cells.

The basic story of brain growth concerns how neurons develop and form this elaborate communication system. Figure 4.3 summarizes the major milestones of brain development. In the prenatal period, neurons are produced in the embryo's primitive neural tube. From there, they migrate to form the major parts of the brain, traveling along threads produced by a network of guiding cells. By the end of the second trimester of pregnancy, production and migration of neurons are largely complete.

Once neurons are in place, they differentiate, establishing their unique functions by extending their fibers to form synaptic connections with neighboring cells. During the first two years, neural fibers and synapses increase at an astounding pace (Huttenlocher, 2002; Moore & Persaud, 2003). Because developing neurons require space for these connective structures, a surprising aspect of brain growth is that as synapses form, many surrounding neurons die—20 to 80 percent depending on the brain region (de Haan & Johnson, 2003; Stiles, 2001a). Fortunately, during the prenatal period, the neural tube produces far more neurons than the brain will ever need.

As neurons form connections, *stimulation* becomes vital to their survival. Neurons that are stimulated by input from the surrounding environment continue to establish synapses, forming increasingly elaborate systems of communication that support more complex abilities. Neurons that are seldom stimulated soon lose their synapses, in a process called **synaptic pruning** that returns neurons not needed at the moment to an uncommitted state so they can support future development (Webb, Monk, & Nelson, 2001). In all, about 40 percent of synapses are pruned during childhood and adoles-

cence to reach the adult level (refer again to Figure 4.3) (Webb, Monk, & Nelson, 2001). For this process to go forward, appropriate stimulation of the child's brain is vital during periods in which the formation of synapses is at its peak (Greenough et al., 1993; Huttenlocher, 2002).

If few neurons are produced after the prenatal period, what causes the dramatic increase in brain size during the first two years? About half the brain's volume is made up of **glial cells**, which are responsible for **myelination**, the coating of neural fibers with an insulating fatty sheath (called *myelin*) that improves the efficiency of message transfer. Glial cells multiply dramatically from the end of pregnancy through the second year of life, a process that slows through middle childhood and accelerates again in adolescence. Dramatic increases in neural fibers and myelination are responsible for the swift gain in overall size of the brain. At birth, the brain is nearly 30 percent of its adult weight; by age 2, it reaches 70 percent (Thatcher et al., 1996).

In sum, brain development can be compared to molding a "living sculpture." After neurons and synapses are overproduced, cell death and synaptic pruning sculpt away excess building material to form the mature brain—a process jointly influenced by genetically programmed events and the child's experiences. The resulting sculpture is a set of interconnected regions, each with specific functions—much like countries on a globe that communicate with one another (Johnston et al., 2001).

This "geography" of the brain permits researchers to study its developing organization and the activity of its regions using various physiological techniques, described in Table 4.1. For example, EEG brain-wave patterns can be examined for stability and organization—signs of mature cortical functioning. As a

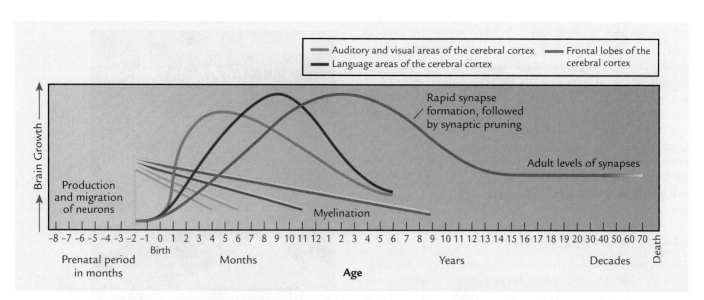

■ **FIGURE 4.3 Major milestones of brain development.** Formation of synapses is rapid during the first two years, especially in the auditory, visual, and language areas of the cerebral cortex. The frontal lobes undergo more extended synaptic growth. In each area, overproduction of synapses is followed by synaptic pruning. The frontal lobes are among the last regions to attain adult levels of synaptic connections—in mid- to late adolescence. Myelination occurs at a dramatic pace during the first two years and then at a slower pace through childhood and adolescence. The multiple yellow lines indicate that the timing of myelination varies among different brain areas. For example, neural fibers continue to myelinate over a longer period in the language areas, and especially in the frontal lobes, than in the visual and auditory areas. (Adapted from Thompson & Nelson, 2001).

Table 4.1	Methods for Measuring Brain Functioning
Method	**Description**
Electroencephalogram (EEG)	Electrodes are taped to the scalp to record electrical brain-wave activity in the brain's outer layers—the cerebral cortex.
Event-related potentials (ERPs)	Using the EEG, the frequency and amplitude of brain waves in response to particular stimuli (such as a picture, music, or speech) are recorded in specific areas of the cerebral cortex.
Functional magnetic resonance imaging (fMRI)	While the person lies inside an apparatus that creates a magnetic field, a scanner magnetically detects increased blood flow and oxygen metabolism in areas of the brain in response to particular stimuli. The result is a computerized image of activity anywhere in the brain (not just its outer layers).
Positron emission tomography (PET)	After injection or inhalation of a radioactive substance, the person lies inside an apparatus with a scanner that emits fine streams of X-rays, which detect increased blood flow and oxygen metabolism in areas of the brain in response to particular stimuli. As with fMRI, the result is a computerized image of activity anywhere in the brain.

Note: Reactions of children and adults to the elaborate equipment affect the accuracy of these measures. Taking participants through a simulated experience prior to testing can ease apprehension.

child processes a stimulus, ERPs can detect the location of brain-wave activity in the cerebral cortex. Functional brain-imaging techniques, which yield three-dimensional pictures of the entire brain, provide the most precise information on which brain regions are specialized for certain capacities. The most promising of these methods is fMRI. Unlike PET, fMRI does not depend on X-ray photography, which requires injection of a radioactive substance. Rather, when a child is exposed to a stimulus, fMRI detects changes in blood flow magnetically, producing a computerized image of active areas (see Figure 4.4 for an example).

Development of the Cerebral Cortex

Surrounding the brain is the **cerebral cortex**, which resembles a half-shelled walnut. It is the largest, most complex brain structure—accounting for 85 percent of the brain's weight, containing the greatest number of neurons and synapses, and responsible for the unique intelligence of our species. Because the cerebral cortex is the last brain structure to stop growing, it is sensitive to environmental influences for a much longer period than any other part of the brain.

(a)   (b)

▧ **FIGURE 4.4 Measuring brain activity using functional magnetic resonance imaging (fMRI).** (a) This 6-year-old is part of a study that uses fMRI to find out how his brain processes light and motion. (b) The fMRI image shows which areas of the boy's brain are active while he views changing visual stimuli.

■ **Regions of the Cortex.** Figure 4.5 shows specific functions of regions of the cerebral cortex, such as receiving information from the senses, instructing the body to move, and thinking. The general order in which cortical regions develop corresponds to the order in which various capacities emerge in the infant and growing child. For example, ERP and fMRI measures reveal a burst of activity (signifying synaptic growth and myelination) in the auditory and visual cortexes and in areas responsible for body movement over the first year—a period of dramatic gains in auditory and visual perception and mastery of motor skills (Johnson, 2005). Language areas are especially active from late infancy through the preschool years, when language development flourishes (Thompson, 2000).

The cortical regions with the most extended period of development are the *frontal lobes*, which are responsible for thought—in particular, consciousness, inhibition of impulses, integration of information, and regulation of behavior through planning. From age 2 months on, these areas function more effectively. Formation and pruning of synapses in the frontal lobes continue for many years, yielding an adult level of synaptic connections around mid- to late adolescence (Nelson, 2002; Sowell et al., 2002; Thompson et al., 2000a).

■ **Lateralization and Plasticity of the Cortex.** The cerebral cortex has two *hemispheres*, or sides—left and right—that differ in their functions. Some tasks are done mostly by one hemisphere and some by the other. For example, each hemisphere receives sensory information from the side of the body opposite to it and controls only that side.[1] For most of us, the left hemisphere is largely responsible for verbal abilities (such as

spoken and written language) and positive emotion (for example, joy). The right hemisphere handles spatial abilities (judging distances, reading maps, and recognizing geometric shapes) and negative emotion (such as distress) (Banish & Heller, 1998; Nelson & Bosquet, 2000). This pattern may be reversed in left-handed people, but more often, the cerebral cortex of left-handers is less clearly specialized than that of right-handers.

Specialization of the two hemispheres is called **lateralization**. Why are abilities and behaviors lateralized? fMRI studies reveal that the left hemisphere is better at processing information in a sequential, analytic (piece-by-piece) way, a good approach for dealing with communicative information—both verbal (language) and emotional (a joyful smile). In contrast, the right hemisphere is specialized for processing information in a holistic, integrative manner, ideal for making sense of spatial information and regulating negative emotion. A lateralized brain may have evolved because it enabled humans to cope more successfully with changing environmental demands (Rogers, 2000). It permits a wider array of functions to be carried out effectively than if both sides processed information in the same way.

Researchers study when brain lateralization occurs to learn more about **brain plasticity**. In a highly *plastic* cortex, many areas are not yet committed to specific functions. Consequently, the cortex has a high capacity for learning. In addition, if a part of the brain is damaged, other parts can take over tasks that it would have handled. But once the hemispheres lateralize, damage to a specific region means that the abilities it controls cannot be recovered to the same extent or as easily as earlier.

At birth, the hemispheres have already begun to specialize. Most newborns show greater ERP brain-wave activity in the left hemisphere while listening to speech sounds or displaying a positive state of arousal. In contrast, the right hemisphere reacts more strongly to nonspeech sounds or to stimuli (such as a sour-tasting fluid) that evoke a negative reaction (Davidson, 1994; Fox & Davidson, 1986).

Nevertheless, research on brain-damaged children and adults offers dramatic evidence for substantial plasticity in the young brain, summarized in the Lifespan Vista box on the following page. Furthermore, early experience greatly influences the organization of the cerebral cortex. For example, deaf adults who, as infants and children, learned sign language (a spatial skill) depend more than hearing individuals on the right hemisphere for language processing (Neville & Bavelier, 2002). And toddlers who are advanced in language development show greater left-hemispheric specialization for language

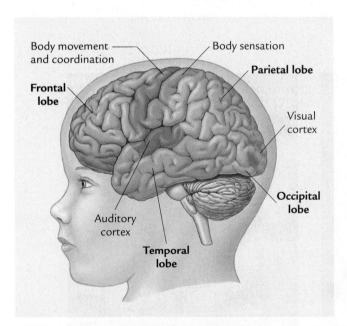

■ **FIGURE 4.5 The left side of the human brain, showing the cerebral cortex.** The cortex is divided into different lobes, each of which contains a variety of regions with specific functions. Some major regions are labeled here.

---

[1]The eyes are an exception. Messages from the right half of each retina go to the right hemisphere; messages from the left half of each retina go to the left hemisphere. Thus, visual information from *both* eyes is received by *both* hemispheres.

A Lifespan Vista

Brain Plasticity: Insights from Research on Brain-Damaged Children and Adults

In the first few years of life, the brain is highly plastic. It can reorganize areas committed to specific functions in ways that the mature brain cannot. Consistently, adults who suffered brain injuries in infancy and early childhood show fewer cognitive impairments than adults with later-occurring injuries (Huttenlocher, 2002). Nevertheless, the young brain is not totally plastic. When it is injured, its functioning is compromised. The extent of plasticity depends on several factors, including age at time of injury, site of damage, and skill area. Furthermore, plasticity is not restricted to childhood. Some reorganization after injury also occurs in the mature brain.

Brain Plasticity in Infancy and Early Childhood.

In a large study of children with injuries to the cerebral cortex that occurred before birth or in the first 6 months of life, language and spatial skills were assessed repeatedly into adolescence (Akshoomoff et al., 2002; Stiles, 2001a). All the children had experienced early brain seizures or hemorrhages. fMRI and PET techniques revealed the precise site of damage.

Regardless of whether injury occurred in the left or right cerebral hemisphere, the children showed delays in language development that persisted until about 3½ years of age. That damage to either hemisphere affected early language competence indicates that at first, language functioning is broadly distributed in the brain. But by age 5, the children caught up in vocabulary and grammatical skills. Undamaged areas—either in the left or the right hemisphere—had taken over these language functions.

Compared with language, spatial skills were more impaired after early brain injury. When preschool through adolescent-age youngsters were asked to copy designs, those with early right-hemispheric damage had trouble with holistic processing—accurately representing the overall shape. In contrast, those with left-hemispheric damage captured the basic shape but omitted fine-grained details. Nevertheless, the children showed improvements in their drawings with age—gains that did not occur in brain-injured adults (Akshoomoff et al., 2002; Stiles et al., 2003).

Clearly, recovery after early brain injury is greater for language than spatial skills. Why is this so? Researchers speculate that spatial processing is the older of the two capacities in our evolutionary history and, therefore, more lateralized at birth (Stiles, 2001b; Stiles et al., 2002). But early brain injury has far less impact than later injury on *both* language and spatial skills. In sum, the young brain is remarkably plastic.

The Price of High Plasticity in the Young Brain.

Despite impressive recovery of language and (to a lesser extent) spatial skills, children with early brain injuries show deficits in many complex mental abilities during the school years. For example, their progress in reading and math is slow. And in telling stories, they produce simpler narratives than age-mates without early brain injuries (Reilly, Bates, & Marchman, 1998).

High brain plasticity, researchers explain, comes at a price. When healthy brain regions take over the functions of damaged areas, a "crowding effect" occurs: Multiple tasks must be done by a smaller-than-usual volume of brain tissue. Consequently, the brain processes information less quickly and accurately than it would if it were intact. Complex mental abilities suffer because performing them requires considerable space in the cerebral cortex (Huttenlocher, 2002).

Brain Plasticity in Adulthood.

Although it is more limited, brain plasticity can occur in adulthood. For example, adult stroke victims often display considerable recovery, especially in response to stimulation of language and motor skills. Brain-imaging techniques reveal that structures adjacent to the permanently damaged area or in the opposite cerebral hemisphere reorganize to support the impaired ability (Bach-y-Rita, 2001; Hallett, 2000).

In infancy and childhood, the goal of brain growth is to form neural connections that ensure mastery of essential skills. Plasticity is greatest while the brain is forming many new synapses (Kolb & Gibb, 2001). At older ages, specialized brain structures are in place, but after injury they can still reorganize to some degree. The adult brain can produce a small number of new neurons (Gould et al., 1999). And when an individual practices relevant tasks, the brain strengthens existing synapses and generates new ones.

Plasticity seems to be a basic property of the nervous system. Researchers hope to discover how experience and brain plasticity work together throughout life so they can help people of all ages—with and without brain injuries—develop at their best.

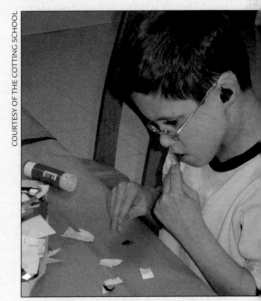

COURTESY OF THE COTTING SCHOOL

This 8-year-old, who experienced brain damage in infancy, has well-developed language skills but has difficulty with spatial tasks. Still, because of early, high brain plasticity, he has been spared massive impairments. The boy's teachers strengthen his spatial skills by providing him with activities in which he copies and creates designs.

than their more slowly developing agemates (Mills, Coffey-Corina, & Neville, 1997). Apparently, the very process of acquiring language and other skills promotes lateralization (Casey et al., 2002; Luna et al., 2001).

In sum, the brain is more plastic during the first few years than at any later time of life (Nelson, 2000). An overabundance of synaptic connections supports brain plasticity and, therefore, young children's ability to learn, which is fundamental to their survival. And although the cortex is programmed from the start for hemispheric specialization, experience greatly influences the rate and success of its advancing organization.

Sensitive Periods in Brain Development

Stimulation of the brain is vital during periods in which it is growing most rapidly. Animal studies confirm that early, extreme sensory deprivation results in permanent brain damage and loss of functions—findings that verify the existence of sensitive periods in brain development. For example, early, varied visual experiences are essential for the brain's visual centers to develop normally. If a 1-month-old kitten is deprived of light for as brief a time as 3 or 4 days, these areas of the brain degenerate. If the kitten is kept in the dark during the fourth week of life and beyond, the damage is severe and permanent (Crair, Gillespie, & Stryker, 1998).

The general quality of the early environment affects overall brain growth. When animals reared from birth in physically and socially stimulating surroundings are compared with those reared in isolation, the brains of the stimulated animals have much denser synaptic connections (Greenough & Black, 1992).

■ **Human Evidence: Orphanage Children.** For ethical reasons, we cannot deliberately deprive some infants of normal rearing experiences and observe the impact on their brains and competencies. Instead, we must turn to natural experiments, in which children were victims of deprived early environments but were later exposed to stimulating sensitive care.

In one study, researchers followed the progress of a large sample of children transferred between birth and 3½ years from extremely deprived Romanian orphanages to adoptive families in Great Britain (O'Connor et al., 2000; Rutter et al., 1998, 2004). On arrival, most were impaired in all domains of development. By the preschool years, catch-up in physical size was dramatic. Cognitive catch-up, though also impressive, was not as great for children adopted after 6 months of age. And the longer infants had been institutionalized, the more severe and persistent their deficits. As Figure 4.6 shows, those adopted after age 2 were profoundly affected. Even among babies who had experienced adequate early nutrition, both time spent in the institution and poor cognitive functioning were correlated with below-average head size, suggesting that early lack of stimulation damaged the brain.

Additional evidence shows that the chronic stress of early, deprived orphanage rearing disrupts the brain's capacity to manage stress, with long-term consequences for physical and

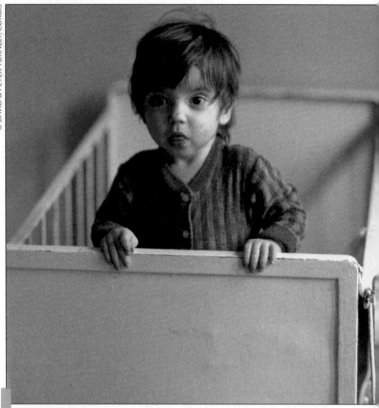

This child, who has spent his first two years in a Romanian orphanage with little adult contact and stimulation, is likely to be profoundly impaired in all domains of development.

emotional health. In another investigation, researchers followed the development of children adopted into Canadian homes, who had spent their first 8 months or more in Romanian institutions (Gunnar et al., 2001; Gunnar & Cheatham, 2003). Compared with agemates adopted shortly after birth, these children showed extreme stress reactivity, as indicated by high concentrations of the stress hormone *cortisol* in their saliva—a physiological response linked to illness, retarded physical growth, and learning and behavior problems, including deficits in attention and control of anger and other impulses. The longer the children spent in orphanage care, the higher their cortisol levels, even 6½ years after adoption.

The adoption research just described, and other similar studies, indicate that exposing babies to understimulating institutional care for 6 months to 2 years permanently undermines all aspects of psychological development (Ames & Chisholm, 2001; MacLean, 2003). The longer the deprivation, the more profound the effects.

■ **Appropriate Stimulation.** Unlike the orphanage children just described, Grace, whom Monica and Kevin had adopted in Cambodia at 16 months of age, showed favorable progress. Two years earlier, they had adopted Grace's older brother, Eli. When Eli was 2 years old, Monica and Kevin sent a letter and a photo of Eli to his biological mother, describing a bright,

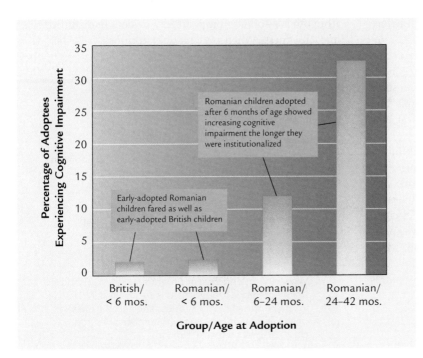

■ FIGURE 4.6 **Relationship of age at adoption to cognitive impairment at age 6 years among British and Romanian adoptees.** Children transferred from Romanian orphanages to British adoptive homes in the first 6 months of life fared as well as British early-adopted children, suggesting that they had fully recovered from extreme early deprivation. Romanian children adopted after 6 months of age showed increasing cognitive impairment with time spent institutionalized. Those adopted after 2 years of age were profoundly affected; 30 percent scored below 80 on an intelligence test. (Adapted from Rutter et al., 2004.)

happy child. The next day, she tearfully asked an adoption agency to send her baby daughter to join Eli and his American family. Although Grace's early environment was very depleted, her biological mother's loving care—holding gently, speaking softly, and breastfeeding—may have prevented irreversible damage to her brain.

In addition to impoverished environments, ones that overwhelm children with expectations beyond their current capacities also undermine the brain's potential. In recent years, expensive early-learning centers have sprung up, in which infants are trained with letter and number flash cards, and slightly older toddlers are given a full curriculum of reading, math, science, art, music, gym, and more. There is no evidence that these programs yield smarter, better "superbabies" (Hirsh-Pasek & Golinkoff, 2003). Instead, trying to prime infants with stimulation for which they are not ready can cause them to withdraw, thereby threatening their interest in learning and creating conditions much like stimulus deprivation!

How, then, can we characterize appropriate stimulation during the early years? To answer this question, researchers distinguish between two types of brain development. The first, **experience-expectant brain growth**, refers to the young brain's rapidly developing organization, which depends on ordinary experiences—opportunities to see and touch objects, to hear language and other sounds, and to move about and explore the environment. As a result of millions of years of evolution, the brains of all infants, toddlers, and young children expect to encounter these experiences and, if they do, grow normally. The second type of brain development—**experience-dependent brain growth**—occurs throughout our lives. It consists of additional growth and refinement of established brain structures as a result of specific learning ex-

periences that vary widely across individuals and cultures (Greenough & Black, 1992). Reading and writing, playing computer games, weaving an intricate rug, and practicing the violin are examples. The brain of a violinist differs in certain ways from the brain of a poet because each has exercised different brain regions for a long time (Thompson & Nelson, 2001).

Experience-expectant brain growth takes place early and naturally, as caregivers offer babies and preschoolers age-appropriate play materials and engage them in enjoyable daily

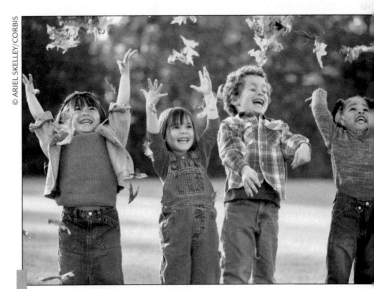

Experience-expectant brain growth takes place naturally, through ordinary, stimulating experiences. These young children exuberantly playing in the autumn leaves enjoy the type of activity that is best for promoting brain development in the early years.

routines—a shared meal, a game of peek-a-boo, a bath before bed, a picture book to talk about, or a song to sing. The resulting growth provides the foundation for later-occurring experience-dependent development (Huttenlocher, 2002; Shonkoff & Phillips, 2001). No evidence exists for a sensitive period in the first few years of life for mastering skills that depend on extensive training, such as reading, musical performance, or gymnastics (Bruer, 1999).

As we have seen, the young, rapidly growing brain is vulnerable in many ways—to hazardous drug exposure, environmental toxins, poor diet, stimulus deprivation, and chronic stress. Researchers speculate that rushing early learning also harms the brain by overwhelming its neural circuits, thereby reducing the brain's sensitivity to the everyday experiences it needs for a healthy start in life. In addition, when "mind-building" lessons do not produce young geniuses, disappointed parents may come to view their children as failures at a tender age.

Changing States of Arousal

Rapid brain growth means that the organization of sleep and wakefulness changes substantially between birth and age 2, and fussiness and crying also decline. The newborn baby takes round-the-clock naps totaling about 16 to 18 hours (Davis, Parker & Montgomery, 2004). Total sleep time declines slowly; the average 2-year-old still needs 12 to 13 hours. But periods of sleep and wakefulness become fewer and longer, and the sleep–wake pattern increasingly conforms to a night–day schedule. Between 6 and 9 months, daytime sleep typically declines to two naps. By 1½, most infants take just one nap (Iglowstein et al., 2003).

These changing arousal patterns are due to brain development, but they are affected by the social environment. In Western nations, many parents try to get their babies to sleep through the night around 4 months of age by feeding solid foods before bedtime—a practice that may be at odds with young infants' neurological development. Not until the middle of the first year is the secretion of *melatonin*, a hormone within the brain that promotes drowsiness, much greater at night than during the day (Sadeh, 1997).

As the Cultural Influences box on the following page reveals, the practice of isolating infants to promote sleep is rare elsewhere in the world. When babies sleep with their parents, their average sleep period remains constant at 3 hours from 1 to 8 months of age. Only at the end of the first year, as REM sleep (the state that usually prompts waking) declines, do infants move in the direction of an adultlike sleep–waking schedule (Ficca et al., 1999).

Even after infants sleep through the night, they continue to wake occasionally. In sleep observations and in surveys of parents in Australia, Great Britain, and Israel, night wakings increased between 1½ and 2 years (Scher, Epstein, & Tirosh, 2004; Scher et al., 1995). As Chapter 6 will reveal, the challenges of toddlerhood—ability to range farther from the familiar caregiver and a clearer awareness of the self as separate

from others—often prompt anxiety, evident in disturbed sleep and clinginess. When parents offer comfort, these behaviors subside.

Ask Yourself

Review
How does stimulation affect early brain development? Cite evidence at the level of neurons and at the level of the cerebral cortex.

Review
How do overproduction of synapses and synaptic pruning support infants' and children's ability to learn?

Apply
Which infant enrichment program would you choose: one that emphasizes gentle talking and touching, exposure to sights and sounds, and social games, or one that includes reading and number drills and classical music lessons? Explain.

Reflect
What is your attitude toward parent–infant cosleeping? Is it influenced by your cultural background? Explain.

www.ablongman.com/berk

Influences on Early Physical Growth

Physical growth, like other aspects of development, results from the continuous and complex interplay between genetic and environmental factors. Heredity, nutrition, and emotional well-being all affect early physical growth.

Heredity

Because identical twins are much more alike in body size than fraternal twins, we know that heredity is important in physical growth. When diet and health are adequate, height and rate of physical growth are largely determined by heredity. In fact, as long as negative environmental influences such as poor nutrition and illness are not severe, children and adolescents typically show *catch-up growth*—a return to a genetically influenced growth path—once conditions improve. Still, many organs, from the brain to the heart and digestive system, may be permanently compromised (Hales & Ozanne, 2003). (Recall the consequences of inadequate prenatal nutrition for long-term health, discussed on page 93 in Chapter 3.)

Genetic makeup also affects body weight: The weights of adopted children correlate more strongly with those of their biological than of their adoptive parents (Sørensen, Holst, & Stunkard, 1998). At the same time, environment—in particular, nutrition—plays an especially important role.

Cultural Influences

Cultural Variation in Infant Sleeping Arrangements

While awaiting the birth of a new baby, North American parents typically furnish a room as the infant's sleeping quarters. For decades, child-rearing advice from experts has strongly encouraged the nighttime separation of baby from parent. For example, the most recent edition of Benjamin Spock's *Baby and Child Care* recommends that infants be moved into their own room by 3 months of age, explaining, "By 6 months, a child who regularly sleeps in her parents' room may become dependent on this arrangement" (Spock & Needlman, 2004, p. 60).

Yet parent–infant "cosleeping" is the norm for approximately 90 percent of the world's population. Cultures as diverse as the Japanese, the Guatemalan Maya, the Inuit of northwestern Canada, and the !Kung of Botswana, Africa, practice it. Japanese and Korean children usually lie next to their mothers throughout infancy and early childhood, and many continue to sleep with a parent or other family member until adolescence (Takahashi, 1990; Yang & Hahn, 2002). Among the Maya, mother–infant cosleeping is interrupted only by the birth of a new baby, at which time the older child is moved next to the father or to another bed in the same room (Morelli et al., 1992). Cosleeping is also common in some North American subcultures. African-American children frequently fall asleep with their parents and remain with them for part or all of the night (Brenner et al., 2003). Appalachian children of eastern Kentucky typically sleep with their parents for the first 2 years (Abbott, 1992).

Cultural values—specifically, collectivism versus individualism (see Chapter 2, page 66)—strongly influence infant sleeping arrangements. In one study, researchers interviewed Guatemalan Mayan mothers and American middle-SES mothers about their sleeping practices. Mayan mothers stressed a collectivist perspective, explaining that cosleeping helps build a close parent–

child bond, which is essential for children to learn the ways of people around them. In contrast, American mothers conveyed an individualistic perspective, mentioning the importance of early independence, preventing bad habits, and protecting their own privacy (Morelli et al., 1992).

Over the past 15 years, cosleeping has increased dramatically in North America and other Western nations, perhaps because more mothers are breast-feeding. Today, the rate of bedsharing among U.S. mothers of young babies may be as high as 50 percent (Willinger et al., 2003). Research suggests that cosleeping evolved to protect infants' survival and health. During the night, cosleeping babies breastfeed three times longer than infants who sleep alone. Because infants arouse to nurse more often when sleeping next to their mothers, some researchers believe that co-sleeping may actually help safeguard babies at risk for sudden infant death syndrome (SIDS) (see page 109 in Chapter 3). In Asian cultures where cosleeping is widespread, including Cambodia, China, Japan, Korea, Thailand, and Vietnam, SIDS is rare (McKenna, 2002; McKenna & McDade, 2005). And contrary to popular belief, cosleeping does not reduce mothers' total sleep time, although they experience a great number of brief awakenings, which permits them to check on their baby (Mosko, Richard, & McKenna, 1997).

Infant sleeping practices affect other aspects of family life. Sleep problems are not an issue for Mayan parents. Babies doze off in the midst of ongoing family activities and are carried to bed by their mothers. In contrast, for many North American parents, getting young children ready for bed often requires an elaborate ritual that takes a good part of the evening. Perhaps bedtime struggles, so common in Western homes but rare elsewhere in the world, are related to the stress young children feel when they are required to fall asleep without assistance (Latz, Wolf, & Lozoff, 1999).

Critics of cosleeping warn that cosleeping children will develop emotional problems, especially excessive dependency. Yet a longitudinal study following children from the end of pregnancy through age 18 showed that young people who had bedshared in the early years were no different from others in any aspect of adjustment (Okami, Weisner, & Olmstead, 2002). Another concern is that infants might become trapped under the parent's body or in soft covers and suffocate. Parents who are obese or who use alcohol, tobacco, or illegal drugs do pose a serious risk to their sleeping babies. Use of quilts and comforters is also dangerous (Willinger et al., 2003).

But with appropriate precautions, parents and infants can cosleep safely. In cultures where cosleeping is widespread, parents and infants usually sleep with light covering on hard surfaces, such as firm mattresses, floor mats, and wooden planks, or infants sleep in a cradle or hammock next to the parents' bed (McKenna, 2001, 2002; Nelson, Schiefenhoevel, & Haimerl, 2000). Also, infants lie on their backs, which promotes arousal if breathing is threatened and helps ensure frequent, easy communication between parent and baby.

© STEPHEN L. RAYMER/NATIONAL GEOGRAPHIC IMAGE COLLECTION

This Cambodian father and child sleep together—a practice common in their culture and around the globe. The family sleeps on hard wooden surfaces, which protect cosleeping children from entrapment in soft bedding.

Nutrition

Nutrition is especially crucial for development in the first 2 years because the baby's brain and body are growing so rapidly. Pound for pound, an infant's energy needs are twice those of an adult. Twenty-five percent of infants' total caloric intake is devoted to growth, and babies need extra calories to keep rapidly developing organs functioning properly (Trahms & Pipes, 1997).

■ **Breastfeeding versus Bottle-Feeding.** Babies not only need sufficient food; they need the right kind of food. In early infancy, breastfeeding is ideally suited to their needs, and bottled formulas try to imitate it. Applying What We Know below summarizes the major nutritional and health advantages of breastfeeding.

Because of these benefits, breastfed babies in poverty-stricken regions of the world are much less likely to be malnourished and 6 to 14 times more likely to survive the first year of life. The World Health Organization recommends breastfeeding until age 2 years, with solid foods added at 6 months. These practices, if widely followed, would save the lives of more than a million infants annually. Even breastfeeding for just a few weeks offers some protection against respiratory and intestinal infections, which are devastating to young children in developing countries. Also, because a nursing mother is less likely to get pregnant, breastfeeding helps increase spacing among siblings, a major factor in reducing infant and childhood deaths in nations with widespread poverty (Bellamy, 2005). (Note, however, that breastfeeding is not a reliable method of birth control.)

Yet many mothers in the developing world do not know about the benefits of breastfeeding. Instead, they give their babies commercial formula or low-grade nutrients, such as rice water or highly diluted cow or goat milk. Contamination of these foods as a result of poor sanitation is common and often leads to illness. The United Nations has encouraged all hospitals and maternity units in developing countries to promote breastfeeding as long as mothers do not have viral or bacterial infections (such as HIV or tuberculosis) that can be transmitted to the baby. Today, most developing countries have banned the practice of giving free or subsidized formula to new mothers.

Partly as a result of the natural childbirth movement, breastfeeding has become more common in industrialized nations, especially among well-educated women. Today, 68 per-

Reasons to Breastfeed

Applying What We Know

Nutritional and Health Advantages	Explanation
Provides the correct balance of fat and protein	Compared with the milk of other mammals, human milk is higher in fat and lower in protein. This balance, as well as the unique proteins and fats contained in human milk, is ideal for a rapidly myelinating nervous system.
Ensures nutritional completeness	A mother who breastfeeds need not add other foods to her infant's diet until the baby is 6 months old. The milks of all mammals are low in iron, but the iron contained in breast milk is much more easily absorbed by the baby's system. Consequently, bottle-fed infants need iron-fortified formula.
Helps ensure healthy physical growth	In the first few months, breastfed infants add weight and length slightly faster than bottle-fed infants, who catch up by the end of the first year. One-year-old breastfed babies are leaner (have a higher percentage of muscle to fat), a growth pattern that may help prevent later overweight and obesity.
Protects against many diseases	Breastfeeding transfers antibodies and other infection-fighting agents from mother to child and enhances functioning of the immune system. As a result, compared with bottle-fed infants, breastfed babies have far fewer allergic reactions and respiratory and intestinal illnesses. Breast milk also has anti-inflammatory effects, which reduce the severity of illness symptoms.
Protects against faulty jaw development and tooth decay	Sucking the mother's nipple instead of an artificial nipple helps avoid malocclusion, a condition in which the upper and lower jaws do not meet properly. It also protects against tooth decay due to sweet liquid remaining in the mouths of infants who fall asleep while sucking on a bottle.
Ensures digestibility	Because breastfed babies have a different kind of bacteria growing in their intestines than do bottle-fed infants, they rarely suffer from constipation or other gastrointestinal problems.
Smoothes the transition to solid foods	Breastfed infants accept new solid foods more easily than bottle-fed infants, perhaps because of their greater experience with a variety of flavors, which pass from the maternal diet into the mother's milk.

Sources: Buescher, 2001; Fulhan, Collier, & Duggan, 2003; Kramer et al., 2002, 2003.

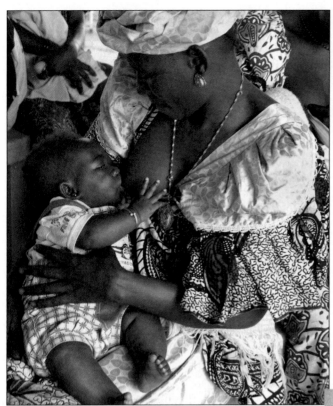

Breastfeeding is especially important in developing countries, where infants are at risk for malnutrition and early death due to wide-spread poverty. This baby from Gambia is likely to grow normally during the first year because his mother decided to breastfeed.

© SEAN SPRAGUE/THE IMAGE WORKS

cent of American mothers and 73 percent of Canadian mothers breastfeed. However, about two-thirds of breastfeeding American mothers and nearly half of Canadian mothers stop after a few months (Health Canada, 2003e; U.S. Department of Health and Human Services, 2004a). Not surprisingly, mothers who return to work sooner wean their babies from the breast earlier (Arora et al., 2000).

A mother who cannot be with her baby all the time can still combine breastfeeding with bottle-feeding. U.S. and Canadian national health agencies advise exclusive breastfeeding for the first 6 months. In the United States, recommendations also suggest including breast milk in the baby's diet until at least 1 year; in Canada, until 2 years and beyond (Health Canada, 2004c; U.S. Department of Health and Human Services, 2004a).

Women who do not breastfeed sometimes worry that they are depriving their baby of an experience essential for healthy psychological development. Yet breastfed and bottle-fed children in industrialized nations do not differ in emotional adjustment (Fergusson & Woodward, 1999). As noted in Applying What We Know, breast milk contains nutrients ideally suited for early brain development. Some studies report a slight advantage in intelligence test performance for children and adolescents who were breastfed, after controlling for many factors, but other studies find no cognitive benefits (Gómez-Sanchiz et al., 2003; Jain, Concat, & Leventhal, 2002).

■ Are Chubby Babies at Risk for Later Overweight and Obesity? From early infancy, Timmy was an enthusiastic eater who nursed vigorously and gained weight quickly. By 5 months, he began reaching for food on his parents' plates. Vanessa wondered: Was she overfeeding Timmy and increasing his chances of being permanently overweight?

Most chubby babies thin out during toddlerhood and early childhood, as weight gain slows and they become more active. Infants and toddlers can eat nutritious foods freely without risk of becoming overweight. But recent evidence does indicate a strengthening relationship between rapid weight gain in infancy and later obesity (Stettler et al., 2005; Yanovski, 2003). This trend may be due to the growing number of overweight and obese parents, who promote unhealthful eating habits in their young children. Interviews with more than 3,000 U.S. parents of 4- to 24-month-olds revealed that many routinely served them french fries, pizza, candy, sugary fruit drinks, and soda. On average, infants consumed 20 percent and toddlers 30 percent more calories than they needed. At the same time, one-third ate no fruits or vegetables (Briefel et al., 2004).

How can concerned parents prevent their infants from becoming overweight children and adults? One way is to breastfeed for the first 6 months, which is associated with slower early weight gain (Baker et al., 2004; Kalies et al., 2005). Another is to avoid foods loaded with sugar, salt, and saturated fats. When young children eat such foods regularly, they start to prefer them (Birch & Fisher, 1995). Physical exercise is an additional safeguard against excessive weight gain. Once toddlers learn to walk, climb, and run, parents should provide opportunities for energetic play.

Malnutrition

Osita is an Ethiopian 2-year-old whose mother has never had to worry about his gaining too much weight. When she weaned him at 1 year, there was little for him to eat besides starchy rice-flour cakes. Soon his belly enlarged, his feet swelled, his hair fell out, and a rash appeared on his skin. His bright-eyed curiosity vanished, and he became irritable and listless.

In developing countries and war-torn areas where food resources are limited, malnutrition is widespread. Recent evidence indicates that about one-third of the world's children suffer from malnutrition before age 5 (Bellamy, 2005). The 4 to 7 percent who are severely affected suffer from two dietary diseases.

Marasmus is a wasted condition of the body caused by a diet low in all essential nutrients. It usually appears in the first year of life when a baby's mother is too malnourished to produce enough breast milk and bottle-feeding is also inadequate. Her starving baby becomes painfully thin and is in danger of dying.

Osita has **kwashiorkor**, caused by an unbalanced diet very low in protein. The disease usually strikes after weaning, between 1 and 3 years of age. It is common in regions where children get just enough calories from starchy foods, but little

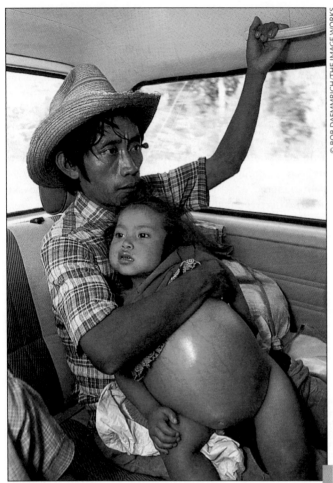

The swollen abdomen and listless behavior of this Honduran child are classic symptoms of kwashiorkor, a nutritional illness that results from a diet very low in protein.

protein. The child's body responds by breaking down its own protein reserves, which causes the swelling and other symptoms that Osita experienced.

Children who survive these extreme forms of malnutrition grow to be smaller in all body dimensions (Galler, Ramsey, & Solimano, 1985). When their diets improve, however, they often gain excessive weight. Studies in many poverty-stricken regions of the world reveal that growth-stunted children have a higher percentage of body fat and are far more likely to be overweight than their nonstunted agemates (Branca & Ferrari, 2002; Martins et al., 2004). A malnourished body protects itself by establishing a low basal metabolism rate, which may endure after nutrition improves. Also, malnutrition may disrupt appetite control centers in the brain, causing the child to overeat when food becomes plentiful.

Learning and behavior are also seriously affected. One long-term study of marasmic children revealed that an improved diet did not result in catch-up in head size (Stoch et al., 1982). The malnutrition probably interfered with growth of

neural fibers and myelination, causing a permanent loss in brain weight. These children score low on intelligence tests, show poor fine-motor coordination, and have difficulty paying attention (Galler et al., 1990; Liu et al., 2003). They also display a more intense stress response to fear-arousing situations, perhaps caused by the constant, gnawing pain of hunger (Fernald & Grantham-McGregor, 1998).

Inadequate nutrition is not confined to developing countries. Because government-supported supplementary food programs do not reach all families in need, an estimated 13 percent of Canadian children and 16 percent of American children suffer from *food insecurity*—uncertain access to enough food for a healthy, active life. Food insecurity is especially high among single-parent families (30 percent) and low-income ethnic minority families—for example, Hispanics and African Americans (22 percent) and Canadian Aboriginals (31 percent) (Government of Canada, 2004; U.S. Department of Agriculture, 2005b). Although few of these children have marasmus or kwashiorkor, their physical growth and ability to learn are still affected.

Emotional Well-Being

We may not think of affection and stimulation as necessary for healthy physical growth, but they are just as vital as food. **Nonorganic failure to thrive**, a growth disorder that results from lack of parental love, is usually present by 18 months of age. Infants who have it show all the signs of marasmus—their bodies look wasted, and they are withdrawn and apathetic. But no organic (or biological) cause for the baby's failure to grow can be found. The baby is offered enough food and has no serious illness.

Lana, an observant nurse at a public health clinic, became concerned about 8-month-old Melanie, who was 3 pounds lighter than she had been at her last checkup. Her mother claimed to feed her often. Lana observed Melanie's behavior and noted that she showed little interest in toys but, instead, kept her eyes on nearby adults, anxiously watching their every move. She rarely smiled when her mother came near or cuddled when picked up (Steward, 2001).

Family circumstances surrounding failure to thrive help explain these typical reactions. During feeding, diaper changing, and play, Melanie's mother sometimes seemed cold and distant, at other times impatient and hostile (Hagekull, Bohlin, & Rydell, 1997). Melanie tried to protect herself by tracking her mother's whereabouts and, when she approached, avoiding her gaze. Often an unhappy marriage and parental psychological disturbance contribute to these serious caregiving problems (Drotar, Pallotta, & Eckerle, 1994; Duniz et al., 1996). Sometimes the baby is irritable and displays abnormal feeding behaviors, such as poor sucking or vomiting—circumstances that stress the parent–child relationship further (Wooster, 1999).

In Melanie's case, her alcoholic father was out of work, and her parents argued constantly. Melanie's mother had little energy to meet Melanie's psychological needs. When treated early, by helping parents or placing the baby in a caring foster home, failure-to-thrive infants show quick catch-up growth. But if the disorder is not corrected in infancy, most children remain small and show lasting cognitive and emotional difficulties (Dykman et al., 2001).

Ask Yourself

Review

Explain why breastfeeding can have lifelong consequences for the development of babies born in poverty-stricken regions of the world.

Apply

Ten-month-old Shaun is below average in height and painfully thin. He has one of two serious growth disorders. Name them, and indicate what clues you would look for to tell which one Shaun has.

Connect

How are bidirectional influences between parent and child involved in the negative impact of malnutrition on psychological development?

Reflect

Imagine that you are the parent of a newborn baby. Describe some feeding practices you would use, and some you would avoid, to prevent overweight and obesity.

www.ablongman.com/berk

Learning Capacities

*L*earning refers to changes in behavior as the result of experience. Babies come into the world with built-in learning capacities that permit them to profit from experience immediately. Infants are capable of two basic forms of learning, which were introduced in Chapter 1: classical and operant conditioning. They also learn through their natural preference for novel stimulation. Finally, shortly after birth, babies learn by observing others; they can soon imitate the facial expressions and gestures of adults.

Classical Conditioning

Newborn reflexes, discussed in Chapter 3, make **classical conditioning** possible in the young infant. In this form of learning, a neutral stimulus is paired with a stimulus that leads to a reflexive response. Once the baby's nervous system makes the connection between the two stimuli, the neutral stimulus will produce the behavior by itself.

Classical conditioning helps infants recognize which events usually occur together in the everyday world, so they can anticipate what is about to happen next. As a result, the environment becomes more orderly and predictable. Let's take a closer look at the steps of classical conditioning.

As Carolyn settled down in the rocking chair to nurse Caitlin, she often stroked her baby's forehead. Soon Carolyn noticed that each time she did this, Caitlin made sucking movements. Caitlin had been classically conditioned. Here is how it happened (see Figure 4.7 on page 134):

1. Before learning takes place, an **unconditioned stimulus (UCS)** must consistently produce a reflexive, or **unconditioned, response (UCR)**. In Caitlin's case, sweet breast milk (UCS) resulted in sucking (UCR).

2. To produce learning, a *neutral stimulus* that does not lead to the reflex is presented just before, or at about the same time as, the UCS. Carolyn stroked Caitlin's forehead as each nursing period began. The stroking (neutral stimulus) was paired with the taste of milk (UCS).

3. If learning has occurred, the neutral stimulus by itself produces a response similar to the reflexive response. The neutral stimulus is then called a **conditioned stimulus (CS)**, and the response it elicits is called a **conditioned response (CR)**. We know that Caitlin has been classically conditioned because stroking her forehead outside the feeding situation (CS) results in sucking (CR).

If the CS is presented alone enough times, without being paired with the UCS, the CR will no longer occur, an outcome called *extinction*. In other words, if Carolyn repeatedly strokes Caitlin's forehead without feeding her, Caitlin will gradually stop sucking in response to stroking.

Young infants can be classically conditioned most easily when the association between two stimuli has survival value. Learning which stimuli regularly accompany feeding improves the infant's ability to get food and survive (Blass, Ganchrow, & Steiner, 1984). In contrast, some responses, such as fear, are very difficult to classically condition in young babies. Until infants have the motor skills to escape unpleasant events, they have no biological need to form these associations. After 6 months of age, however, fear is easy to condition. In Chapter 6, we will discuss the development of fear and other emotional reactions.

Operant Conditioning

In classical conditioning, babies build expectations about stimulus events in the environment, but they do not influence the stimuli that occur. In **operant conditioning**, infants act, or *operate*, on the environment, and stimuli that follow their behavior change the probability that the behavior will occur again. A stimulus that increases the occurrence of a response is called a **reinforcer**. For example, sweet liquid *reinforces* the sucking response in newborns. Removing a desirable stimulus

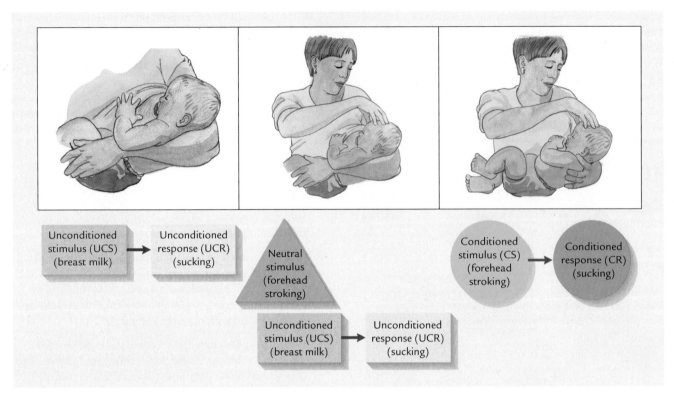

■ **FIGURE 4.7 The steps of classical conditioning.** This example shows how Caitlin's mother classically conditioned her to make sucking movements by stroking her forehead at the beginning of feedings.

or presenting an unpleasant one to decrease the occurrence of a response is called **punishment**. A sour-tasting fluid *punishes* newborns' sucking response. It causes them to purse their lips and stop sucking entirely.

In very young infants, who can control only a few behaviors, successful operant conditioning is limited to sucking and head-turning responses. However, many stimuli besides food can serve as reinforcers. For example, researchers have created special laboratory conditions in which the baby's rate of sucking on a nipple produces a variety of interesting sights and sounds. Newborns will suck faster to see visual designs or hear music and human voices (Floccia, Christophe, & Bertoncini, 1997). As these findings suggest, operant conditioning has become a powerful tool for finding out what stimuli babies can perceive and which ones they prefer.

As infants get older, operant conditioning includes a wider range of responses and stimuli. For example, special mobiles have been hung over the cribs of 2- to 6-month-olds. When the baby's foot is attached to the mobile with a long cord, the infant can, by kicking, make the mobile turn. Under these conditions, it takes only a few minutes for infants to start kicking vigorously (Rovee-Collier, 1999; Rovee-Collier & Barr, 2001).

As you will see in Chapter 5, operant conditioning with mobiles is frequently used to study infants' memory and ability to group similar stimuli into categories. Once babies learn the response, researchers see how long and under what conditions they retain it when exposed again to the original mobile or to mobiles with varying features. Operant conditioning also plays a vital role in the formation of social relationships. As the baby gazes into the adult's eyes, the adult looks and smiles back, and then the infant looks and smiles again. The behavior of each partner reinforces the other, and both continue their pleasurable interaction. In Chapter 6, we will see that this contingent responsiveness contributes to the development of infant–caregiver attachment.

Habituation

At birth, the human brain is set up to be attracted to novelty. Infants tend to respond more strongly to a new element that has entered their environment. **Habituation** refers to a gradual reduction in the strength of a response due to repetitive stimulation. Looking, heart rate, and respiration rate may all decline, indicating a loss of interest. Once this has occurred, a new stimulus—a change in the environment—causes responsiveness to return to a high level, an increase called **recovery**. For example, when you walk through a familiar space, you notice things that are new and different— a recently hung picture on the wall or a piece of furniture that has been moved. Habituation and recovery make learning more efficient by enabling us to focus our attention on those aspects of the environment we know the least about.

Researchers investigating infants' understanding of the world rely on habituation and recovery more than any other learning capacity. For example, a baby who first *habituates* to a visual pattern (a photo of a baby) and then *recovers* to a new one (a photo of a bald man) appears to remember the first stimulus and perceive the second one as new and different from it. This method of studying infant perception and cognition, illustrated in Figure 4.8, can be used with newborns, including preterm infants. It has even been used to study the fetus's sensitivity to external stimuli in the third trimester of pregnancy—for example, by measuring changes in fetal heart rate when various repeated sounds are presented (Doherty & Hepper, 2000).

Recovery to a new stimulus, or *novelty preference*, assesses infants' *recent memory*. Think about what happens when you return to a place you have not seen for a long time. Instead of attending to novelty, you are likely to focus on aspects that are familiar: "I recognize that—I've been here before!" Similarly, with passage of time, infants shift from a novelty preference to a *familiarity preference*. That is, they *recover to the familiar stimulus* rather than to a novel stimulus (see Figure 4.8) (Bahrick & Pickens, 1995; Courage & Howe, 1998). By focusing on that shift, researchers can also use habituation to assess *remote memory*, or memory for stimuli to which infants were exposed weeks or months earlier.

As Chapter 5 will reveal, habituation research has greatly enriched our understanding of how long babies remember a wide range of stimuli. And by varying stimulus features, researchers can use habituation and recovery to study babies' ability to categorize stimuli as well.

Imitation

Newborn babies come into the world with a primitive ability to learn through **imitation**—by copying the behavior of another person. Figure 4.9 on page 136 shows infants and a chimp from 2 days to several weeks old imitating adult facial expressions (Field et al., 1982; Meltzoff & Moore, 1977). The newborn's capacity to imitate extends to certain gestures, such as head movements, and has been demonstrated in many ethnic groups and cultures (Meltzoff & Kuhl, 1994). As the figure reveals, even newborn chimpanzees, our closest evolutionary ancestors, imitate some facial expressions (Myowa-Yamakoshi et al., 2004).

Because a few studies (for example, Anisfeld et al., 2001) have failed to reproduce the human findings, some researchers regard the imitative capacity as little more than an automatic response, similar to a reflex. But others claim that newborns imitate many facial expressions with apparent effort and determination, even shortly after the adult stops demonstrating the behavior (Hayne, 2002; Meltzoff & Moore, 1999). According to Andrew Meltzoff, newborns imitate much as older children and adults do—by trying to match body movements they see with ones they feel themselves make (Meltzoff & Decety, 2003). Later we will encounter evidence that young infants are remarkably adept at coordinating information across sensory systems.

Furthermore, scientists have identified specialized cells in many areas of cerebral cortex of primates—called *mirror neurons*—that underlie these capacities (Rizzolatti & Craighero, 2004). Mirror neurons fire identically when a primate hears or

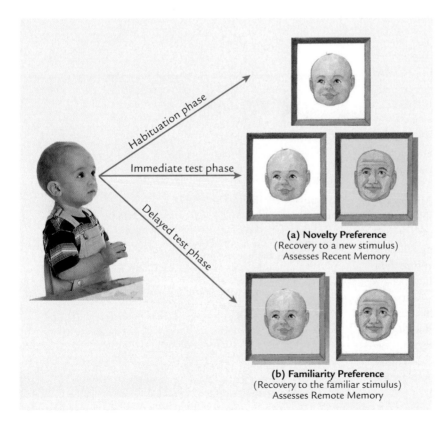

■ **FIGURE 4.8 Using habituation to study infant memory and knowledge.** In the habituation phase, infants view a photo of a baby until their looking declines. In the test phase, infants are again shown the baby photo, but this time it appears alongside a photo of a bald-headed man. (a) When the test phase occurs soon after the habituation phase (within minutes, hours, or days, depending on the age of the infants), participants who remember the baby face and distinguish it from the man's face show a *novelty preference*; they recover to the new stimulus. (b) When the test phase is delayed for weeks or months, infants who continue to remember the baby face shift to a *familiarity preference*; they recover to the familiar baby face rather than to the novel man's face.

Habituation phase

Immediate test phase

Delayed test phase

(a) Novelty Preference
(Recovery to a new stimulus)
Assesses Recent Memory

(b) Familiarity Preference
(Recovery to the familiar stimulus)
Assesses Remote Memory

■ **FIGURE 4.9 Imitation by human and chimpanzee newborns.** The human infants in the center row imitating (a) tongue protrusion and (b) mouth opening are 2 to 3 weeks old. The human infant imitating (c) lip protrusion is 2 days old. The chimpanzee imitating all three facial expressions, (d), (e), and (f), is 2 weeks old. (From A. N. Meltzoff & M. K. Moore, 1977, "Imitation of Facial and Manual Gestures by Human Neonates," *Science, 198,* p. 75; T. M. Field et al., 1992, "Discrimination and Imitation of Facial Expressions by Neonates," *Science, 218,* p. 180; and M. Myowa-Yamakoshi et al., 2004, "Imitation in neonatal chimpanzees (Pan troglodytes)," *Developmental Science, 7,* p. 440. Copyright 1997 and 1982 by the AAAS, copyright 2004 by Blackwell Publishing Ltd. Reprinted by permission.)

sees an action and when it carries out that action on its own. Humans have particularly elaborate systems of mirror neurons, which enable us to observe another's behavior (such as smiling or throwing a ball) while simulating the behavior in our own brain. Mirror neurons are believed to be the biological basis of a variety of interrelated, complex social abilities, including imitation, empathic sharing of emotions, and understanding others' intentions (Iocaboni et al., 2005).

Meltzoff's view of newborn imitation as a voluntary capacity remains controversial. Mirror neurons probably require an extended period of development. But however limited imitation is at birth, it is a powerful means of learning (Blasi & Bjorklund, 2003). Using imitation, young infants explore their social world, getting to know people by matching their behavioral states. As babies notice similarities between their own actions and those of others, they learn about themselves. By tapping into infants' ability to imitate, adults can get infants to express desirable behaviors. Finally, caregivers take great pleasure in a baby who imitates their facial gestures and actions. Imitation seems to be one of those capacities that help get the infant's relationship with parents off to a good start.

Ask Yourself

Review

Provide an example of classical conditioning, of operant conditioning, and of habituation/recovery in young infants. Why is each type of learning useful?

Apply

Nine-month-old Byron has a toy with large, colored push buttons on it. Each time he pushes a button, he hears a nursery tune. Which learning capacity is the toy's manufacturer taking advantage of? What can Byron's play with the toy reveal about his perception of sound patterns?

Connect

Infants with nonorganic failure to thrive rarely smile at friendly adults. Also, they anxiously keep track of nearby adults. Explain these reactions using the learning capacities discussed in the preceding sections.

Motor Development

Carolyn, Monica, and Vanessa each kept a baby book, filled with proud notations about when their children first held up their heads, reached for objects, sat by themselves, and walked alone. Parents are understandably excited about these new motor skills, which allow babies to master their bodies and the environment in a new way. For example, sitting upright gives infants a new perspective on the world. Reaching enables babies to find out about objects by acting on them. And when infants can move on their own, their opportunities for exploration multiply.

Babies' motor achievements have a powerful effect on their social relationships. When Caitlin crawled at 7½ months, Carolyn and David began to restrict her movements by saying no and expressing mild impatience. When Caitlin walked three days after her first birthday, the first "testing of wills" occurred (Biringen et al., 1995). Despite her mother's warnings, she sometimes pulled items from shelves that were off limits. "I said, 'Don't do that!'" Carolyn would say firmly, taking Caitlin by the hand and redirecting her attention.

At the same time, Carolyn and David increased their expressions of affection and playful activities as Caitlin sought them out for greetings, hugs, and a gleeful game of hide-and-seek (Campos, Kermoian, & Zumbahlen, 1992). Soon after, Caitlin turned the pages of a book while she and her parents named the pictures. Caitlin's delight as she worked on new motor competencies triggered pleasurable reactions in others, which encouraged her efforts further (Mayes & Zigler, 1992). Motor skills, social competencies, cognition, and language developed together and supported one another.

The Sequence of Motor Development

Gross motor development refers to control over actions that help infants get around in the environment, such as crawling, standing, and walking. In contrast, *fine motor development* has to do with smaller movements, such as reaching and grasping. Table 4.2 shows the average age at which North American infants and toddlers achieve a variety of gross and fine motor skills. Most (but not all) children follow this sequence.

Table 4.2 also presents the age ranges during which the majority of babies accomplish each skill. Although the *sequence*

Table 4.2	Gross and Fine Motor Development in the First Two Years	
Motor Skill	**Average Age Achieved**	**Age Range in Which 90 Percent of Infants Achieve the Skill**
When held upright, holds head erect and steady	6 weeks	3 weeks–4 months
When prone, lifts self by arms	2 months	3 weeks–4 months
Rolls from side to back	2 months	3 weeks–5 months
Grasps cube	3 months, 3 weeks	2–7 months
Rolls from back to side	4½ months	2–7 months
Sits alone	7 months	5–9 months
Crawls	7 months	5–11 months
Pulls to stand	8 months	5–12 months
Plays pat-a-cake	9 months, 3 weeks	7–15 months
Stands alone	11 months	9–16 months
Walks alone	11 months, 3 weeks	9–17 months
Builds tower of two cubes	11 months, 3 weeks	10–19 months
Scribbles vigorously	14 months	10–21 months
Walks up stairs with help	16 months	12–23 months
Jumps in place	23 months, 2 weeks	17–30 months
Walks on tiptoe	25 months	16–30 months

Note: These milestones represent overall age trends. Individual differences exist in the precise age at which each milestone is attained.

Sources: Bayley, 1969, 1993, 2005.

of motor development is fairly uniform, large individual differences exist in *rate* of motor progress. We would be concerned about a child's development only if many motor skills were seriously delayed.

Table 4.2 reveals organization and direction in infants' motor achievements. A *cephalocaudal trend* is evident: Motor control of the head comes before control of the arms and trunk, which precedes control of the legs. You can also see a *proximodistal trend:* Head, trunk, and arm control precedes coordination of the hands and fingers. The similarities between physical and motor development suggest a genetic contribution to motor progress. But as we will see, some motor milestones deviate sharply from these trends.

We must be careful not to think of motor skills as unrelated accomplishments that follow a fixed maturational timetable. Rather, each skill is a product of earlier motor attainments and a contributor to new ones. And children acquire motor skills in highly individual ways. For example, Grace, who had spent most of her days lying in a hammock before her adoption, did not try to crawl because she rarely spent time on firm surfaces that enabled her to move on her own. As a result, she pulled to a stand and walked before she crawled! Many influences—both internal and external to the child—join together to support the vast transformations in motor competencies of the first 2 years.

Motor Skills as Dynamic Systems

According to **dynamic systems theory of motor development**, mastery of motor skills involves acquiring increasingly complex *systems of action*. When motor skills work as a *system*, separate abilities blend together, each cooperating with others to produce more effective ways of exploring and controlling the environment. For example, control of the head and upper chest are combined into sitting with support. Kicking, rocking on all fours, and reaching combine to become crawling. Then crawling, standing, and stepping are united into walking (Thelen, 1989).

Each new skill is a joint product of four factors: (1) central nervous system development, (2) the body's movement capacities, (3) the goal the child has in mind, and (4) environmental supports for the skill. Change in any element makes the system less stable, and the child starts to explore and select new, more effective motor patterns. The broader physical environment also has a profound impact on motor skills. If children were reared on the moon with its reduced gravity, they would prefer jumping to walking or running!

When a skill is first acquired, infants must refine it. For example, one baby just starting to crawl often collapsed on her tummy and moved backward instead of forward. Soon she figured out how to propel herself forward by alternately pulling with her arms and pushing with her feet. As she experimented, she perfected the crawling motion (Adolph, Vereijken, & Denny, 1998). In learning to walk, toddlers practice six or more hours a day, traveling the length of 29 football fields! Gradually their small, unsteady steps change to a longer stride, their feet move closer together, their toes point to the front,

and their legs become symmetrically coordinated (Adolph, Vereijken, & Shrout, 2003). As movements are repeated thousands of times, they promote new connections in the brain that govern motor patterns.

Dynamic systems theory shows us why motor development cannot be genetically determined. Because exploration and the desire to master new tasks motivate it, heredity can map it out only at a general level (Hopkins & Butterworth, 1997; Thelen & Smith, 1998). Each skill is acquired by combining early accomplishments into a more complex system that permits the child to reach a goal. Consequently, different paths to the same motor skill exist.

■ **Dynamic Motor Systems in Action.** To find out how babies acquire motor capacities, some studies have tracked their first attempts at a skill until it became smooth and effortless. In one investigation, researchers held sounding toys alternately in front of infants' hands and feet, from the time they showed interest until they engaged in well-coordinated reaching and grasping (Galloway & Thelen, 2004). As Figure 4.10 shows, the infants, violating the cephalocaudal trend, first reached for the toys with their feet—as early as 8 weeks of age, at least a month before reaching with their hands!

Why did babies reach "feet first"? Because the hip joint constrains the legs to move less freely than the shoulder constrains the arms, infants could more easily control their leg movements. When they first tried reaching with their hands, their arms actually moved *away* from the object! Consequently, hand reaching required far more practice than foot reaching. As these findings confirm, rather than following a

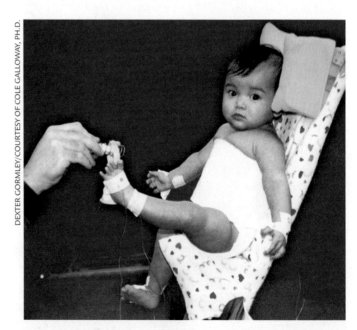

DEXTER GORMLEY/COURTESY OF COLE GALLOWAY, PH.D.

■ **FIGURE 4.10 Reaching "feet first."** When sounding toys were held in front of babies' hands and feet, they reached with their feet as early as 8 weeks of age, a month or more before they reached with their hands—a clear violation of the cephalocaudal pattern. This 2½-month-old skillfully explores an object with her foot.

strict cephalocaudal pattern, the order in which motor skills develop depends on the anatomy of the body part being used, the surrounding environment, and the baby's efforts.

■ **Cultural Variations in Motor Development.** Cross-cutural research further illustrates how early movement opportunities and a stimulating environment contribute to motor development. Nearly half a century ago, Wayne Dennis (1960) observed infants in Iranian orphanages who were deprived of the tantalizing surroundings that induce infants to acquire motor skills. These babies spent their days lying on their backs in cribs, without toys to play with. As a result, most did not move on their own until after 2 years of age. When they finally did move, the constant experience of lying on their backs led them to scoot in a sitting position rather than crawl on their hands and knees. Because babies who scoot come up against furniture with their feet, not their hands, they are far less likely to pull themselves to a standing position in preparation for walking. Indeed, by 3 to 4 years of age, only 15 percent of the Iranian orphans were walking.

Cultural variations in infant-rearing practices also affect motor development. Take a quick survey of several parents you know: Should sitting, crawling, and walking be deliberately encouraged? Answers vary widely from culture to culture. Japanese mothers and mothers from rural India, for example, believe such efforts are unnecessary (Seymour, 1999). Among the Zinacanteco Indians of Southern Mexico, rapid motor progress is actively discouraged. Babies who walk before they know enough to keep away from cooking fires and weaving looms are viewed as dangerous to themselves and disruptive to others (Greenfield, 1992).

In contrast, among the Kipsigis of Kenya and the West Indians of Jamaica, babies hold their heads up, sit alone, and walk considerably earlier than North American infants. Kipsigi parents deliberately teach these motor skills. In the first few months, babies are seated in holes dug in the ground, with rolled blankets used to keep them upright. Walking is promoted by frequently bouncing babies on their feet (Super, 1981). As Figure 4.11 shows, West Indian mothers use a highly stimulating, formal handling routine. They believe that exercise helps babies grow up strong, healthy, and physically attractive (Hopkins & Westra, 1988).

Finally, because it decreases exposure to "tummy time," the current Western practice of having babies sleep on their backs to protect them from SIDS (see page 109 in Chapter 3) delays gross motor milestones of rolling, sitting, and crawling (Majnemer & Barr, 2005; Scrutton, 2005). To prevent these delays, caregivers can regularly expose babies to the tummy-lying position during waking hours.

Fine Motor Development: Reaching and Grasping

Of all motor skills, reaching may play the greatest role in infant cognitive development because it opens up a whole new way of exploring the environment. By grasping things, turning them over, and seeing what happens when they are released, infants learn a great deal about the sights, sounds, and feel of objects.

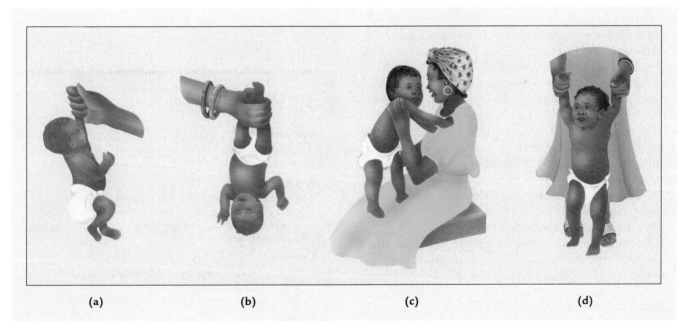

(a) (b) (c) (d)

■ **FIGURE 4.11 West Indians of Jamaica use a formal handling routine with their babies.** Exercises practiced in the first few months include (a) stretching each arm while suspending the baby and (b) holding the infant upside-down by the ankles. Later in the first year, the baby is (c) "walked" up the mother's body and (d) encouraged to take steps on the floor while supported. (Adapted from B. Hopkins & T. Westra, 1988, "Maternal Handling and Motor Development: An Intracultural Study," *Genetic, Social and General Psychology Monographs, 14,* pp. 385, 388, 389. Reprinted by permission of the Helen Dwight Reid Educational Foundation. Published by Heldref Publications, 1319 Eighteenth St., N.W., Washington, DC 20036-1802.)

| Prereaching | Reaching with ulnar grasp | Transfer of object from hand to hand | Pincer grasp |
| Newborn | 3–4 months | 4–5 months | 9 months |

■ **FIGURE 4.12 Some milestones of voluntary reaching.** The average age at which each skill is attained is given. (Ages from Bayley, 1969; Rochat, 1989.)

Reaching and grasping, like many other motor skills, start out as gross, diffuse activity and move toward mastery of fine movements. Figure 4.12 illustrates some milestones of voluntary reaching over the first 9 months. Newborns make poorly coordinated swipes or swings, called *prereaching*, toward an object in front of them. Because they cannot control their arms and hands, they seldom contact the object. Like newborn reflexes, prereaching eventually drops out, around 7 weeks of age. Yet these early behaviors suggest that babies are biologically prepared to coordinate hand with eye in the act of exploring (Thelen, 2001; von Hofsten, 2004).

At about 3 months, as infants develop the necessary eye-gaze and head and shoulder control, reaching reappears and gradually improves in accuracy (Spencer et al., 2000). By 5 to 6 months, infants reach for an object in a room that has been darkened during the reach by switching off the lights—a skill that improves over the next few months (Clifton et al., 1994; McCarty & Ashmead, 1999). Early on, vision is freed from the basic act of reaching so it can focus on more complex adjustments. By 7 months, the arms become more independent; infants can reach for objects by extending just one arm, rather than both (Fagard & Pezé, 1997). During the next few months, infants become better at reaching for moving objects—ones that spin, change direction, or move closer or farther away (Wentworth, Benson, & Haith, 2000).

Once infants can reach, they modify their grasp. The newborn's grasp reflex is replaced by the *ulnar grasp*, a clumsy motion in which the fingers close against the palm. Still, even 3-month-olds readily adjust their grasp to the size and shape of objects—a capacity that improves over the first year (Newman, Atkinson, & Braddick, 2001). Around 4 to 5 months, when infants begin to sit up, they coordinate both hands in exploring objects. They can hold an object in one hand while the other scans it with the fingertips, and they frequently transfer objects from hand to hand (Rochat & Goubet, 1995). By the end of the first year, infants use the thumb and index finger opposably in

a well-coordinated *pincer grasp*. Then the ability to manipulate objects greatly expands. The 1-year-old can pick up raisins and blades of grass, turn knobs, and open and close small boxes.

Between 8 and 11 months, reaching and grasping are well practiced, so that attention is released from the motor skill to events that occur before and after attaining the object. For example, 10-month-olds easily adjust their reach to anticipate their next action. They reach for a ball faster when they intend to throw it than when they intend to drop it carefully through an opening (Claxton, Keen, & McCarty, 2003). Around this time, too, infants begin to solve simple problems that involve reaching, such as searching for and finding hidden toys.

Ask Yourself

Review

Cite evidence that motor development is a joint product of biological, psychological, and environmental factors.

Apply

List everyday experiences that support mastery of reaching, grasping, sitting, and crawling. Why should caregivers place young infants in a variety of waking-time body positions?

Connect

Provide several examples of how motor development influences infants' social experiences. How do social experiences, in turn, influence motor development?

Reflect

Do you favor early, systematic training of infants in motor skills such as crawling, walking, and stair climbing? Why or why not?

www.ablongman.com/berk

Perceptual Development

In Chapter 3, you learned that the senses of touch, taste, smell, and hearing—but not vision—are remarkably well-developed at birth. Now let's turn to a related question: How does perception change over the first year of life?

Our discussion will focus on hearing and vision because almost all research addresses these two aspects of perceptual development. Recall that in Chapter 3, we used the word *sensation* to talk about these capacities. Now we use the word *perception*. "Sensation" suggests a fairly passive process—what the baby's receptors detect when they are exposed to stimulation—whereas "perception" is active: When we perceive, we organize and interpret what we see.

As we review the perceptual achievements of infancy, you may find it hard to tell where perception leaves off and thinking begins. The research we are about to discuss provides an excellent bridge to the topic of Chapter 5—cognitive development during the first 2 years.

Hearing

On Timmy's first birthday, Vanessa bought several tapes of nursery songs, and she turned one on each afternoon at naptime. Soon Timmy let her know his favorite tune. If she put on "Twinkle, Twinkle," he stood up in his crib and whimpered until she replaced it with "Jack and Jill." Timmy's behavior illustrates the greatest change in hearing over the first year of life: Babies organize sounds into increasingly complex patterns.

Between 4 and 7 months, infants have a sense of musical phrasing: They prefer Mozart minuets with pauses between phrases to those with awkward breaks (Krumhansl & Jusczyk, 1990). And at the end of the first year, they recognize the same melody when it is played in different keys. When the tone sequence is changed only slightly, they can tell that the melody is no longer the same (Trehub, 2001).

Responsiveness to sound provides support for the young baby's exploration of the environment through sight and touch. Infants as young as 3 days old turn their eyes and head in the general direction of a sound, an ability that improves greatly over the first 6 months and shows further gains into the second year (Litovsky & Ashmead, 1997).

As we will see in the next chapter, throughout the first year babies are preparing to acquire language. Recall from Chapter 3 that newborns can distinguish nearly all sounds in human languages and that they prefer listening to their native tongue. As infants continue to listen to the talk of people around them, they learn to focus on meaningful sound variations. ERP brain-wave recordings reveal that around 5 months, infants become sensitive to syllable stress patterns in their own language (Weber et al., 2004). Between 6 and 8 months, they start to "screen out" sounds not used in their native tongue (Anderson, Morgan, & White, 2003; Polka & Werker, 1994).

Soon after, infants focus on larger speech segments. Between 7 and 9 months, they recognize familiar words in spoken passages, begin to perceive the speech stream in wordlike units, and listen longer to speech with clear clause and phrase boundaries (Jusczyk, 2002; Soderstrom et al., 2003).

How do infants make such rapid progress in perceiving the structure of language? Research shows that babies are impressive *statistical analyzers* of sound patterns. In detecting words, for example, they distinguish syllables that frequently occur together (indicating they belong to the same word) from those that seldom occur together (indicating a word boundary) (Saffran, Aslin, & Newport, 1996; Saffran & Thiessen, 2003).

Clearly, babies have a powerful ability to extract regularities from continuous verbal stimulation. Some researchers believe that infants are innately equipped with a general learning mechanism for detecting structure in the environment, which they also apply to visual stimulation (Kirkham, Slemmer, & Johnson, 2002). Indeed, because communication is often multisensory (simultaneously verbal, visual, and tactile), infants receive much support from other senses in analyzing speech. Perhaps you have observed parents name objects while demonstrating—for example, saying "doll" while moving a doll and, sometimes, having the doll touch the infant. By doing this, caregivers increase the chances that babies will remember the association between the word and the object (Gogate & Bahrick, 2001).

Vision

For exploring the environment, humans depend on vision more than any other sense. Although at first a baby's visual world is fragmented, it undergoes extraordinary changes during the first 7 to 8 months of life.

Visual development is supported by rapid maturation of the eye and visual centers in the cerebral cortex. Recall from Chapter 3 that the newborn baby focuses and perceives color poorly. Around 2 months, infants can focus on objects and discriminate colors about as well as adults can (Teller, 1998). *Visual acuity* (fineness of discrimination) improves steadily throughout the first year, reaching a near-adult level of about 20/20 by 6 months (Slater, 2001). Scanning the environment and tracking moving objects improve over the first half-year as infants better control their eye movements and build an organized perceptual world (Johnson, Slemmer, & Amso, 2004; von Hofsten & Rosander, 1998).

As babies explore their visual field, they figure out the characteristics of objects and how they are arranged in space. To understand how they do so, let's examine the development of two aspects of vision: depth and pattern perception.

■ **Depth Perception.** *Depth perception* is the ability to judge the distance of objects from one another and from ourselves. It is important for understanding the layout of the environment and for guiding motor activity. To reach for objects, babies must have some sense of depth. Later, when infants crawl, depth perception helps prevent them from bumping into furniture and falling down stairs.

Figure 4.13 shows the *visual cliff*, designed by Eleanor Gibson and Richard Walk (1960) and used in the earliest studies of depth perception. It consists of a Plexiglas-covered table with a platform at the center, a "shallow" side with a checkerboard pattern just under the glass, and a "deep" side with a checkerboard several feet below the glass. The researchers found that crawling babies readily crossed the shallow side, but most reacted with fear to the deep side. They concluded that around the time infants crawl, most distinguish deep and shallow surfaces and avoid drop-offs.

The research of Gibson and Walk shows that crawling and avoidance of drop-offs are linked, but it does not tell us how they are related or when depth perception first appears. To better understand the development of depth perception, researchers have turned to babies' ability to detect specific depth cues, using methods that do not require that they crawl.

Motion is the first depth cue to which infants are sensitive. Babies 3 to 4 weeks of age blink their eyes defensively when an object is moved toward their face as though it is going to hit (Nánez & Yonas, 1994). *Binocular* depth cues arise because our two eyes have slightly different views of the visual field. The

brain blends these two images, resulting in perception of depth. Research in which two overlapping images are projected before the baby, who wears special goggles to ensure that each eye receives one image, reveals that sensitivity to binocular cues emerges between 2 and 3 months and improves rapidly over the first year (Birch, 1993; Brown & Miracle, 2003). Finally, around 6 to 7 months, babies become sensitive to *pictorial* depth cues—the ones artists use to make a painting look three-dimensional. Examples include receding lines that create the illusion of perspective, changes in texture (nearby textures are more detailed than faraway ones), and overlapping objects (an object partially hidden by another object is perceived to be more distant) (Sen, Yonas, & Knill, 2001; Yonas et al., 1986).

Why does perception of depth cues emerge in the order just described? Researchers speculate that motor development is involved. For example, control of the head during the early weeks of life may help babies notice motion and binocular cues. Around 5 to 6 months, the ability to turn, poke, and feel the surface of objects may promote perception of pictorial cues (Bushnell & Boudreau, 1993). And as we will see next, one aspect of motor progress—independent movement—plays a vital role in refinement of depth perception.

■ **Independent Movement and Depth Perception.** At 6 months, Timmy started crawling. "He's fearless!" exclaimed Vanessa. "If I put him down in the middle of our bed, he crawls right over the edge. The same thing's happened by the stairs." Will Timmy become more wary of the side of the bed and the staircase as he becomes a more experienced crawler? Research suggests that he will. Infants with more crawling experience (regardless of when they start to crawl) are far more likely to refuse to cross the deep side of the visual cliff (Campos et al., 2000).

From extensive everyday experience, babies gradually figure out how to use depth cues to detect the danger of falling. But because the loss of body control that leads to falling differs greatly for each body position, babies must undergo this learning separately for each posture. In one study, 9-month-olds who were experienced sitters but novice crawlers were placed on the edge of a shallow drop-off that could be widened (Adolph, 2000). While in the familiar sitting position, infants avoided leaning out for an attractive toy at distances likely to result in falling. But in the unfamiliar crawling posture, they headed over the edge, even when the distance was extremely wide! Later, when babies walk, they must again learn to perceive surfaces in new ways to remain upright (Adolph & Eppler, 1999).

Independent movement promotes additional aspects of three-dimensional understanding. For example, seasoned crawlers are better than their inexperienced agemates at remembering object locations and finding hidden objects (Bai & Bertenthal, 1992; Campos et al., 2000). Why does crawling make such a difference? Compare your own experience of the environment when you are driven from one place to another as opposed to walking or driving yourself. When you move on your own, you are more aware of landmarks and routes of travel, and you take more careful note of what things look like

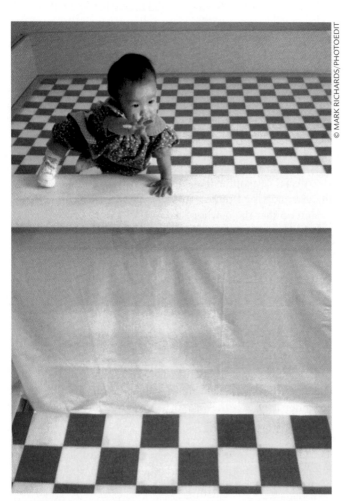

© MARK RICHARDS/PHOTOEDIT

■ **FIGURE 4.13 The visual cliff.** Plexiglas covers the deep and shallow sides. By refusing to cross the deep side and showing a preference for the shallow side, this infant demonstrates the ability to perceive depth.

Crawling promotes three-dimensional understanding, including wariness of drop-offs and ability to find hidden objects. As this Sri Lankan baby becomes adept at crawling, she takes note of how to get from place to place, where objects are in relation to herself and to other objects, and what they look like from different points of view.

more complex patterns, so they prefer to look at the large, bold checkerboard. Around 2 months of age, when detection of fine-grained detail has improved, infants become sensitive to the contrast in complex patterns and spend more time looking at them (Gwiazda & Birch, 2001).

In the early weeks of life, infants respond to the separate parts of a pattern. They stare at single, high-contrast features and have difficulty shifting their gaze away toward other interesting stimuli (Hunnius & Geuze, 2004a, 2004b). In exploring drawings of human faces, for example, 1-month-olds focus on the edges of the stimulus—the hairline or chin. At 2 to 3 months, when scanning ability and contrast sensitivity improve, infants thoroughly explore a pattern's internal features, pausing briefly to look at each part (Bronson, 1994).

Once babies can take in all aspects of a pattern, they integrate them into a unified whole. Around 4 months, they are so good at detecting pattern organization that they even perceive subjective boundaries that are not really present. For example, they perceive a square in the center of Figure 4.15a on page 145, just as you do (Ghim, 1990). Older infants carry this responsiveness to subjective form even further. For example, 9-month-olds look much longer at an organized series of

from different points of view. The same is true for infants. In fact, crawling promotes a new level of brain organization, as indicated by more organized EEG brain-wave activity in the cerebral cortex. Perhaps it strengthens certain neural connections, especially those involved in vision and understanding of space (Bell & Fox, 1996). As the Biology and Environment box on page 144 reveals, the link between independent movement and spatial knowledge is also evident in a population with a very different perceptual experience: infants with severe visual impairments.

■ **Pattern and Face Perception.** Even newborns prefer to look at patterned rather than plain stimuli—for example, a drawing of the human face or one with scrambled facial features rather than a black-and-white oval (Fantz, 1961). As infants get older, they prefer more complex patterns. Three-week-old infants look longest at black-and-white checkerboards with a few large squares, whereas 8- and 14-week-olds prefer those with many squares (Brennan, Ames, & Moore, 1966).

A general principle, called **contrast sensitivity**, explains these early pattern preferences (Banks & Ginsburg, 1985). *Contrast* refers to the difference in the amount of light between adjacent regions in a pattern. If babies *are sensitive to* (can detect) the contrast in two or more patterns, they prefer the one with more contrast. To understand this idea, look at the checkerboards in the top row of Figure 4.14. To us, the one with many small squares has more contrasting elements. Now look at the bottom row, which shows how these checkerboards appear to infants in the first few weeks of life. Because of their poor vision, very young babies cannot resolve the features in

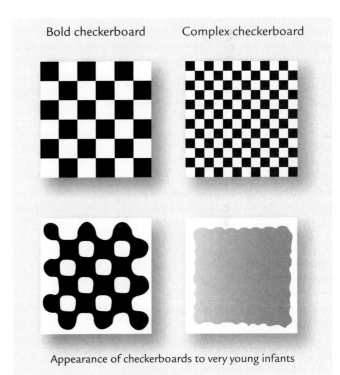

Appearance of checkerboards to very young infants

■ FIGURE 4.14 **The way two checkerboards differing in complexity look to infants in the first few weeks of life.** Because of their poor vision, very young infants cannot resolve the fine detail in the *complex checkerboard*. It appears blurred, like a gray field. The large, *bold checkerboard* appears to have more contrast, so babies prefer to look at it. (Adapted from M. S. Banks & P. Salapatek, 1983, "Infant Visual Perception," in M. M. Haith & J. J. Campos [Eds.], *Handbook of Child Psychology: Vol 2. Infancy and Developmental Psychobiology* [4th ed.], New York: Wiley, p. 504. Copyright © 1983 by John Wiley & Sons. Reprinted by permission.)

Biology and Environment

Development of Infants with Severe Visual Impairments

Research on infants who can see little or nothing at all dramatically illustrates the interdependence of vision, motor exploration, social interaction, and understanding of the world. In a longitudinal study, infants with a visual acuity of 20/800 or worse (they had only dim light perception or were blind) were followed through the preschool years. Compared to agemates with less severe visual impairments, they showed serious delays in all aspects of development. Motor and cognitive functioning suffered the most; with age, performance in both domains became increasingly distant from that of other children (Hatton et al., 1997).

What explains these profound developmental delays? Minimal or absent vision seems to alter the child's experiences in at least two crucial, interrelated ways.

Impact on Motor Exploration and Spatial Understanding. Infants with severe visual impairments attain gross and fine motor milestones many months later than their sighted counterparts (Levtzion-Korach et al., 2000). For example, on average, blind infants do not reach for and manipulate objects until 12 months, crawl until 13 months, or walk until 19 months (compare these averages to the norms in Table 4.2 on page 137). Why is this so?

Infants with severe visual impairments must rely on sound to identify the whereabouts of objects. But sound does not function as a precise clue to object location until much later than vision—around the middle of the first year (Litovsky & Ashmead, 1997). And because infants who cannot see have difficulty engaging their caregivers, adults may not provide them with rich, early exposure to sounding objects. As a result, the baby comes to understand relatively late that there is a world of interesting objects to explore.

Until "reaching on sound" is achieved, infants with severe visual impairments are not motivated to move indepen-

dently. Because of their own uncertainty coupled with parents' protection and restraint to prevent injury, blind infants are typically tentative in their movements. These factors delay motor development further.

Motor and cognitive development are closely linked, especially for infants with little or no vision. These babies build an understanding of the location and arrangement of objects in space only after reaching and crawling (Bigelow, 1992). Inability to imitate the motor actions of others presents additional challenges as these children get older, contributing to declines in motor and cognitive progress relative to peers with better vision (Hatton et al., 1997).

Impact on the Caregiver–Infant Relationship. Infants who see poorly have great difficulty evoking stimulating caregiver interaction. They cannot make eye contact, imitate, or pick up nonverbal social cues. Their emotional expressions are muted; for example, their smile is fleeting and unpredictable. And because they cannot gaze in the same direction as a partner, they are greatly delayed in establishing a shared focus of attention on objects as the basis for play (Bigelow, 2003). Consequently, these infants may receive little adult attention and other stimulation vital for all aspects of development.

When a visually impaired child does not learn how to participate in social interaction during infancy, communication is compromised in early childhood. In an observational study of blind children enrolled in preschools with sighted agemates, the blind children seldom initiated contact with peers and teachers. When they did interact, they had trouble interpreting the meaning of others' reactions and responding appropriately (Preisler, 1991, 1993).

Interventions. Parents, teachers, and professional caregivers can help infants with minimal vision overcome early developmental delays through stimulating, responsive interaction. Until a close emotional bond with an adult is forged,

visually impaired babies cannot establish vital links with their environments.

Techniques that help infants become aware of their physical and social surroundings include heightened sensory input through combining sound and touch (holding, touching, or bringing the baby's hands to the adult's face while talking or singing), engaging in many repetitions, and consistently reinforcing the infant's efforts to make contact. Manipulative play with objects that make sounds is also vital.

Finally, rich language stimulation can compensate for visual loss (Conti-Ramsden & Pérez-Pereira, 1999). It gives young children a ready means of finding out about objects, events, and behaviors they cannot see. Once language emerges, many children with limited or no vision show impressive rebounds. Some acquire a unique capacity for abstract thinking, and most master social and practical skills that permit them to lead productive, independent lives (Warren, 1994).

COURTESY OF RICH KENNEY, FOUNDATION FOR BLIND CHILDREN

As a result of complications from prematurity, this 2-year-old experienced nearly complete detachment of her retinas and has only minimal light perception. By guiding the child's exploration of a zither through touch and sound, a caregiver helps prevent the developmental delays often associated with severely impaired vision.

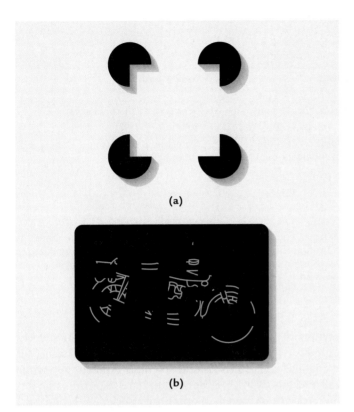

FIGURE 4.15 Subjective boundaries in visual patterns. Do you perceive a square in the middle of image (a)? By 4 months of age, infants do, too. What does image (b), missing two-thirds of its outline, look like to you? By 12 months, infants detect the image of a motorcycle. After habituating to the incomplete motorcycle image, they were shown an intact motorcycle figure paired with a novel form. Twelve-month-olds recovered to (looked longer at) the novel figure, indicating that they recognized the motorcycle pattern on the basis of very little visual information. (Adapted from Ghim, 1990; Rose, Jankowski, & Senior, 1997.)

moving lights that resembles a human being walking than at an upside-down or scrambled version (Bertenthal, 1993). At 12 months, infants can detect objects represented by incomplete drawings, even when as much as two-thirds of the drawing is missing (see Figure 4.15b) (Rose, Jankowski, & Senior, 1997). As these findings reveal, infants' increasing knowledge of objects and actions supports pattern perception.

The tendency to search for structure in a patterned stimulus also applies to face perception. Newborns prefer to look at simple, facelike stimuli with features arranged naturally (upright) rather than unnaturally (upside-down or sideways) (see Figure 4.16a) (Mondloch et al., 1999). They also track a facial pattern moving across their visual field farther than they track other stimuli (Johnson, 1999). And although their ability to distinguish real faces on the basis of inner features is limited, shortly after birth babies prefer photos of faces with eyes open and a direct gaze. Yet another amazing capacity is their tendency to look longer at faces judged by adults as attractive, compared with less attractive ones—a preference that may be the origin of the widespread social bias favoring physically attractive people (Slater et al., 2000).

Some researchers claim that these behaviors reflect newborns' built-in capacity to orient toward members of one's own species, just as many baby animals do (Johnson, 2001; Slater & Quinn, 2001). But others assert that newborns prefer any stimulus in which the most salient elements are arranged horizontally in the upper part of a pattern—like the "eyes" in Figure 4.16a (Turati, 2004). Possibly, however, a bias favoring the facial pattern promotes such preferences. Still other researchers argue that newborns are exposed to faces more often than to other stimuli—early experiences that could quickly "wire" the brain to detect faces and prefer attractive ones (Nelson, 2001).

Although newborns respond to a general facelike structure, they cannot discriminate a complex facial pattern from other, equally complex patterns (see Figure 4.16b). But from repeated exposures to their mother's face, they quickly learn to prefer her face to that of an unfamiliar woman, although they are sensitive only to its broad outlines. Around 2 months, when they can scan an entire stimulus and combine its elements into an organized whole, babies recognize and prefer their mothers' detailed facial features (Bartrip, Morton, & de Schonen, 2001). And they prefer a drawing of the human face to other stimulus arrangements (Dannemiller & Stephens, 1988).

Around 3 months, infants make fine distinctions among the features of different faces. For example, they can tell the difference between the photos of two strangers, even when the

FIGURE 4.16 Early face perception. (a) Newborns prefer to look at the simple pattern resembling a face on the left over the upside-down version on the right. (b) When the complex drawing of a face on the left and the equally complex, scrambled version on the right are moved across newborns' visual field, they follow the face longer. But if the two stimuli are stationary, infants show no preference for the face until 2 to 3 months of age. (From Johnson, 1999; Mondloch et al., 1999.)

Table 4.3	Development of Visual Perception		
	Birth–1 Month	**2–4 Months**	**5–12 Months**
Depth perception	Sensitivity to motion cues	Sensitivity to binocular cues	Sensitivity to pictorial cues; wariness of heights
Pattern perception	Preference for patterns with large elements	Visual exploration of entire stimulus, including internal features	Detection of increasingly complex, meaningful patterns
	Visual exploration limited to border of a stimulus and single, high-contrast features	Combining pattern elements into an organized whole	
Face perception	Preference for a simple, facelike pattern	Preference for a complex facial pattern over other, equally complex patterns and for mother's facial features over those of an unfamiliar woman	More fine-grained discrimination of faces, including ability to perceive emotional expressions as organized wholes

faces are moderately similar. At 5 months—and strengthening over the second half of the first year—infants perceive emotional expressions as meaningful wholes. They treat positive faces (happy and surprised) as different from negative ones (sad and fearful) (Bornstein & Arterberry, 2003; Ludemann, 1991). Extensive face-to-face interaction with caregivers undoubtedly contributes to infants' refinement of face perception. And as babies recognize and respond to the expressive behavior of others, face perception supports their earliest social relationships.

Table 4.3 summarizes the development of depth and pattern perception. Up to this point, we have considered the infant's sensory systems one by one. Now let's examine their coordination.

Intermodal Perception

Our world provides rich, continuous *intermodal stimulation*—simultaneous input from more than one modality, or sensory system. In **intermodal perception**, we make sense of these running streams of light, sound, tactile, odor, and taste information by perceiving objects and events as unified wholes.

Recall that newborns turn in the general direction of a sound and reach for objects in a primitive way. These behaviors suggest that infants expect sight, sound, and touch to go together. Research reveals that babies perceive input from different sensory systems in a unified way by detecting *amodal sensory properties*—information that overlaps two or more sensory systems, such as rate, rhythm, duration, intensity, and temporal synchrony. Consider the sight and sound of a bouncing ball or the face and voice of a speaking person. In each event, visual and auditory information occur simultaneously and with the same rate, rhythm, duration, and intensity.

Early on, both animal and human babies are impressive perceivers of amodal properties (Lickliter & Bahrick, 2000). In one study, the day before they hatched, quail chicks were exposed to a light flashing in synchrony with the rate and

rhythm of a typical maternal call. After birth, the chicks exposed to this amodal information developed a preference for the familiar call much faster than chicks exposed only to the call (Lickliter, Bahrich, & Honeycutt, 2002). Similarly, after just one exposure, human newborns learn associations between the sights and sounds of toys, such as a rhythmically jangling rattle (Morrongiello, Fenwick, & Chance, 1998).

Within the first half-year, infants master a remarkable range of intermodal relationships. For example, 3- and 4-month-olds can relate a child's or adult's moving lips to the corresponding sounds in speech. They can also link the age of a voice (child versus adult) and its emotional tone (happy or angry) with the appropriate face of a person (Bahrick, Netto, & Hernandez-Reif, 1998; Walker-Andrews, 1997). Between 4 and 6 months, infants can perceive and remember the unique face–voice pairings of unfamiliar adults (Bahrick, Hernandez-Reif, & Flom, 2005). And by 8 months, they can even match voices and faces on the basis of gender (Patterson & Werker, 2002).

How does intermodal perception develop so quickly? Young infants seem biologically primed to focus on amodal information. Their detection of amodal relations—for example, the common tempo and rhythm in sights and sounds—may provide the basis for detecting more specific intermodal matches, such as the relation between a particular person's face and the sound of her voice or between an object and its verbal label (Bahrick, 2001).

Intermodal sensitivity is crucial for perceptual development. In the first few months, when much stimulation is unfamiliar and confusing, it enables babies to notice meaningful correlations between sensory inputs and rapidly make sense of their surroundings (Bahrick, Lickliter, & Flom, 2004). And as the examples just reviewed suggest, intermodal perception also facilitates social and language processing. Recall, also, the evidence presented in our discussion of hearing—that in their earliest efforts to make sense of language, infants profit from temporal synchrony between a speech sound and the motion of an object (page 141).

Finally, early parent–infant interaction presents the baby with a rich context—consisting of many concurrent sights, sounds, touches, and smells—for expanding intermodal knowledge (Lickliter & Bahrick, 2000). Intermodal perception is a fundamental ability that fosters all aspects of psychological development.

Understanding Perceptual Development

Now that we have reviewed the development of infant perceptual capacities, how can we put together this diverse array of amazing achievements? Widely accepted answers come from the work of Eleanor and James Gibson. According to the Gibsons' **differentiation theory**, infants actively search for **invariant features** of the environment—those that remain stable—in a constantly changing perceptual world. For example, in pattern perception, at first babies are confronted with a confusing mass of stimulation. Very quickly, however, they search for features that stand out along the border of a stimulus and orient toward images that crudely represent a face. Soon they explore internal features and notice *stable relationships* among those features. As a result, they detect patterns, such as complex designs and faces. The development of intermodal perception also reflects this principle. Babies seek out invariant relationships—for example, amodal properties, such as rhythm, in concurrent sights and sounds. Gradually, they perceive more detailed intermodal associations.

The Gibsons describe their theory as *differentiation* (where "differentiate" means to analyze or break down) because, over time, the baby detects finer and finer invariant features among stimuli. In addition to pattern perception and intermodal perception, differentiation applies to depth perception. Recall how sensitivity to motion and binocular cues precedes detection of fine-grained pictorial features. So one way of understanding perceptual development is to think of it as a built-in tendency to search for order and consistency, a capacity that becomes more fine-tuned with age (Gibson, 1970; Gibson, 1979).

Acting on the environment is vital in perceptual differentiation. Think back to the links between motor milestones and perceptual development discussed in this chapter. Infants constantly look for ways in which the environment affords opportunities for action (Gibson, 2000, 2003). By moving about and exploring the environment, they figure out which objects can be grasped, squeezed, bounced, or stroked and when a surface is safe to cross or presents the possibility of falling. As a result, they differentiate the world in new ways and act more competently (Adolph & Eppler, 1998, 1999).

As we conclude this chapter, it is only fair to note that some researchers believe that babies do more than make sense of experience by searching for invariant features. Instead, they *impose meaning* on what they perceive, constructing categories of objects and events in the surrounding environment. We have seen the glimmerings of this *cognitive* point of view in this chapter. For example, older babies *interpret* a familiar face as a source of pleasure and affection and a pattern of blinking lights as a moving human being. This cognitive perspective also has merit in understanding the achievements of infancy. In fact, many researchers combine these two positions, regarding infant development as proceeding from a perceptual to a cognitive emphasis over the first year of life.

Ask Yourself

Review

What gains in pattern perception contribute to infants' improved perception of faces during the first year?

Review

Using examples, show how intermodal perception supports all aspects of infant psychological development.

Apply

After several weeks of crawling, Ben learned to avoid going headfirst down a steep incline. Now he has started to walk. Can his parents trust him not to try walking down the steep surface? Explain. (Hint: Reread page 142.)

Connect

According to differentiation theory, perceptual development reflects infants' active search for invariant features. Provide examples from research on hearing, pattern perception, and intermodal perception.

www.ablongman.com/berk

Summary

Body Growth

Describe major changes in body growth over the first 2 years.

- Changes in height and weight are rapid during the first 2 years. In the first 9 months, body fat is laid down quickly, while muscle development is slow and gradual. Skeletal age is the best way to estimate a child's physical maturity, which tends to vary by ethnic group and sex. Body proportions change as growth follows **cephalocaudal** and **proximodistal trends**.

© RICHARD HUTCHINGS/PHOTOEDIT

Brain Development

What changes in brain development occur during infancy and toddlerhood both at the level of individual brain cells and at the level of the cerebral cortex?

- Early in development, the brain grows faster than any other organ of the body. Once **neurons**, or nerve cells, are in place, they rapidly form **synapses**. To communicate, neurons release **neurotransmitters**, which cross synapses. As synapses form, to make room for new synaptic connections, many surrounding neurons die. Neurons that are seldom stimulated lose their synapses in a process called **synaptic pruning**. **Glial cells**, responsible for **myelination**, multiply rapidly into the second year, contributing to large gains in brain weight.

- The **cerebral cortex** is the largest, most complex brain structure and the last to stop growing. Its regions develop in the general order in which various capacities emerge in the growing child. The hemispheres of the cerebral cortex specialize, a process called **lateralization**. In the first few years of life, there is high **brain plasticity**, with many areas not yet committed to specific functions.

- Both heredity and early experience contribute to brain organization. Stimulation of the brain is essential during sensitive peri-

ods in brain development—periods in which the brain is growing most rapidly. Prolonged early deprivation, as in some babies reared in orphanages, can undermine all aspects of psychological development.

- Appropriate early stimulation promotes **experience-expectant brain growth**, which depends on ordinary experiences. No evidence exists for a sensitive period in the first few years for **experience-dependent brain growth**, which relies on specific learning experiences. In fact, environments that overwhelm children with inappropriately advanced expectations can undermine the brain's potential.

How does the organization of sleep and wakefulness change over the first 2 years?

- The infant's changing arousal patterns are primarily affected by brain growth, but the social environment also plays a role. Periods of sleep and wakefulness become fewer but longer, increasingly conforming to a night–day schedule. Parents in Western nations try to get their babies to sleep through the night much earlier than parents throughout most of the world, who are more likely to sleep with their babies.

Influences on Early Physical Growth

Cite evidence that heredity, nutrition, and affection and stimulation contribute to early physical growth.

- Twin and adoption studies reveal the contribution of heredity to body size and rate of physical growth.

- Nutrition is also important. Breast milk is ideally suited to infants' growth needs. Breastfeeding also offers protection against disease and prevents malnutrition and infant death in poverty-stricken areas of the world. Although breast- and bottle-fed babies do not differ in emotional adjustment, some studies report a slight advantage in mental test performance for children and adolescents who were breastfed.

- Most chubby babies slim down during toddlerhood and early childhood. Infants and toddlers can eat nutritious foods freely, without risk of becoming overweight. However, recent evidence shows a relationship between rapid weight gain in infancy and later obesity. Breastfeeding, limiting sugary and fatty foods, and encouraging energetic

play are ways parents can help children maintain desirable weight.

© LAURA DWIGHT PHOTOGRAPHY

- **Marasmus** and **kwashiorkor** are dietary diseases caused by malnutrition that affect many children in developing countries and, if prolonged, can permanently stunt body growth and brain development.

- **Nonorganic failure to thrive**, which occurs in infants who are adequately nourished but lack affection and stimulation, illustrates the importance of these factors in normal physical growth.

Learning Capacities

Describe four infant learning capacities, the conditions under which they occur, and the unique value of each.

- **Classical conditioning** is based on the infant's ability to associate events that usually occur together in the everyday world. Infants can be classically conditioned most easily when the pairing of an **unconditioned stimulus** (UCS) and a **conditioned stimulus** (CS) has survival value—for example, learning which stimuli regularly accompany feeding.

- In **operant conditioning**, infants act on their environment, and their behavior is followed by either **reinforcers** (stimuli that increase the occurrence of a response) or **punishment**, which either removes a desirable stimulus or presents an unpleasant one to decrease the occurrence of a response. In young infants, interesting sights and sounds serve as effective reinforcers. Operant conditioning also plays a role in early social relationships as infant and caregiver reinforce each other with pleasurable interaction.

- **Habituation** and **recovery** reveal that at birth, babies are attracted to novelty. Novelty preference (recovery to a novel stimulus) assesses recent memory, whereas familiarity preference (recovery to the familiar stimulus) assesses remote memory.

■ Newborns have a primitive ability to imitate adults' facial expressions and gestures. Another powerful means of learning, **imitation** contributes to the parent–infant bond.

Motor Development

Describe the general course of motor development during the first 2 years, along with factors that influence it.

■ Like physical development, motor development follows the cephalocaudal and proximodistal trends. According to **dynamic systems theory of motor development**, new motor skills are achieved by combining existing skills into increasingly complex systems of action. Each new skill is a joint product of central nervous system development, movement possibilities of the body, the child's goals, and environmental supports for the skill.

■ Movement opportunities and a stimulating environment profoundly affect motor development, as shown by research on infants raised in institutions. Cultural values and child-rearing customs contribute to the emergence and refinement of early motor skills.

■ During the first year, infants perfect reaching and grasping. The poorly coordinated prereaching of the newborn period drops out. Voluntary reaching gradually becomes more accurate and flexible, and the clumsy ulnar grasp is transformed into a refined pincer grasp.

© LAURA DWIGHT PHOTOGRAPHY

Perceptual Development

What changes in hearing, depth and pattern perception, and intermodal perception take place during infancy?

■ Over the first year, infants organize sounds into more complex patterns and can identify their precise location. Infants also become more sensitive to the sounds of their own language. During the second half of the first year, they are able to detect meaningful speech units.

■ Rapid development of the eye and visual centers in the brain supports the development of focusing, color discrimination, and visual acuity during the first half-year. The ability to scan the environment and track moving objects also improves.

■ Research on depth perception reveals that responsiveness to motion cues develops first, followed by sensitivity to binocular and then to pictorial cues. Experience in crawling enhances depth perception and other aspects of three-dimensional understand-

ing, but babies must learn to avoid drop-offs for each body position.

■ **Contrast sensitivity** accounts for infants' early pattern preferences. At first, babies stare at single, high-contrast features and often focus on the edges of a pattern. At 2 to 3 months, they explore a pattern's internal features and start to detect pattern organization. Over time, they discriminate increasingly complex, meaningful patterns.

■ Newborns prefer to look at and track simple, facelike stimuli. However, researchers disagree on whether they have an innate tendency to orient toward human faces. Around 2 months, they recognize and prefer their mother's facial features, and at 3 months, they distinguish the features of different faces. In the second half-year, they perceive emotional expressions as meaningful wholes.

■ From the start, infants are capable of **intermodal perception**—combining information across sensory modalities. Detection of amodal relations (such as common tempo or rhythm) precedes and may provide a basis for detecting other intermodal matches.

Explain differentiation theory of perceptual development.

■ According to **differentiation theory**, perceptual development is a matter of detecting **invariant features** in a constantly changing perceptual world. Acting on the world plays a major role in perceptual differentiation. According to a more cognitive view, at an early age, infants impose meaning on what they perceive. Many researchers combine these two ideas.

Important Terms and Concepts

This grandfather in Shanghai, China, shares his grandson's curiosity and delight in discovery. With the sensitive support of caring adults, infants' and toddlers' cognition and language develop rapidly.

Cognitive Development in Infancy and Toddlerhood

When Caitlin, Grace, and Timmy gathered at Ginette's child-care home, the playroom was alive with activity. The three spirited explorers, each nearly 18 months old, were bent on discovery. Grace dropped shapes through holes in a plastic box that Ginette held and adjusted so the harder ones would fall smoothly into place. Once a few shapes were inside, Grace grabbed the box and shook it, squealing with delight as the lid fell open and the shapes scattered around her. The clatter attracted Timmy, who picked up a shape, carried it to the railing at the top of the basement steps, and dropped it overboard, then followed with a teddy bear, a ball, his shoe, and a spoon. Meanwhile, Caitlin pulled open a drawer, unloaded a set of wooden bowls, stacked them in a pile, knocked it over, and then banged two bowls together.

As the toddlers experimented, I could see the beginnings of language—a whole new way of influencing the world. "All gone baw!" Caitlin exclaimed as Timmy tossed the bright red ball down the basement steps. "Bye-bye," Grace chimed in, waving as the ball disappeared from sight. Later that day, Grace revealed that she could use words and gestures to pretend. "Night-night," she said, putting her head down and closing her eyes, ever so pleased that in make-believe, she could decide for herself when and where to go to bed.

Over the first two years, the small, reflexive newborn baby becomes a self-assertive, purposeful being who solves simple problems and has started to master the most amazing human ability: language. Parents often wonder, How does all this happen so quickly? This question has also captivated researchers, yielding a wealth of findings along with vigorous debate over how to explain the astonishing pace of infant and toddler cognition.

In this chapter, we take up three perspectives on early cognitive development: *Piaget's cognitive-developmental theory, information processing,* and *Vygotsky's sociocultural theory.* We also consider the usefulness of tests that measure infants' and toddlers' intellectual progress. Our discussion concludes with the beginnings of language. We will see how toddlers' first words build on early cognitive achievements and how, very soon, new words and expressions greatly increase the speed and flexibility of their thinking. Throughout development, cognition and language mutually support each other.

© MYRLEEN FERGUSON CATE/PHOTOEDIT

Piaget's Cognitive-Developmental Theory

Swiss theorist Jean Piaget inspired a vision of children as busy, motivated explorers whose thinking develops as they act directly on the environment. Influenced by his background in biology, he believed that the child's mind forms and modifies psychological structures so they achieve a better fit with external reality. Recall from Chapter 1 that in Piaget's theory, children move through four stages between infancy and adolescence. According to Piaget, all aspects of cognition develop in an integrated fashion, changing in a similar way at about the same time.

Piaget's first stage, the **sensorimotor stage,** spans the first 2 years of life. Piaget believed that infants and toddlers "think" with their eyes, ears, hands, and other sensorimotor equipment. They cannot yet carry out many activities inside their heads. But by the end of toddlerhood, children can solve practical, everyday problems and represent their experiences in speech, gesture, and play. To appreciate Piaget's view of how these vast changes take place, let's consider some important concepts.

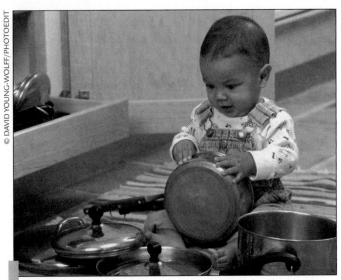

In Piaget's theory, the first schemes are motor action patterns. As this 8-month-old takes apart, turns, and bangs these pots and pans, he discovers that his movements have predictable effects on objects and that objects influence one another in predictable ways.

Piaget's Ideas About Cognitive Change

According to Piaget, specific psychological structures—organized ways of making sense of experience called **schemes**—change with age. At first, schemes are sensorimotor action patterns. For example, at 6 months, Timmy dropped objects in a fairly rigid way, simply by letting go of a rattle or teething ring and watching with interest. By 18 months, his "dropping scheme" had become deliberate and creative. In tossing objects down the basement stairs, he threw some in the air, bounced others off walls, released some gently and others forcefully. Soon, instead of just acting on objects, he will show evidence of thinking before he acts. For Piaget, this change marks the transition from sensorimotor to preoperational thought.

In Piaget's theory, two processes, *adaptation* and *organization,* account for changes in schemes.

■ **Adaptation.** The next time you have a chance, notice how infants and toddlers tirelessly repeat actions that lead to interesting effects. **Adaptation** involves building schemes through direct interaction with the environment. It consists of two complementary activities, *assimilation* and *accommodation.* During **assimilation,** we use our current schemes to interpret the external world. For example, when Timmy dropped objects, he was assimilating them to his sensorimotor "dropping scheme." In **accommodation,** we create new schemes or adjust old ones after noticing that our current way of thinking does not capture the environment completely. When Timmy dropped objects in different ways, he modified his dropping scheme to take account of the varied properties of objects.

According to Piaget, the balance between assimilation and accommodation varies over time. When children are not changing much, they assimilate more than they accommodate. Piaget called this a state of cognitive *equilibrium,* implying a steady, comfortable condition. During rapid cognitive change, however, children are in a state of *disequilibrium,* or cognitive discomfort. They realize that new information does not match their current schemes, so they shift away from assimilation toward accommodation. Once they modify their schemes, they move back toward assimilation, exercising their newly changed structures until they are ready to be modified again.

Each time this back-and-forth movement between equilibrium and disequilibrium occurs, more effective schemes are produced. Because the times of greatest accommodation are the earliest ones, the sensorimotor stage is Piaget's most complex period of development.

■ **Organization.** Schemes also change through **organization,** a process that takes place internally, apart from direct contact with the environment. Once children form new schemes, they rearrange them, linking them with other schemes to create a strongly interconnected cognitive system. For example, eventually Timmy will relate "dropping" to "throwing" and to his developing understanding of "nearness" and "farness." According to Piaget, schemes reach a true state of equilibrium when they become part of a broad network of structures that can be jointly applied to the surrounding world (Piaget, 1936/1952).

In the following sections, we will first consider infant development as Piaget saw it, noting research that supports his observations. Then we will consider evidence demonstrating that, in some ways, babies' cognitive competence is more advanced than Piaget believed it to be.

The Sensorimotor Stage

The difference between the newborn baby and the 2-year-old child is so vast that the sensorimotor stage is divided into six substages (see Table 5.1 for a summary). Piaget's observations of his own three children—a very small sample—served as the basis for this sequence of development. But Piaget watched carefully and also presented his son and two daughters with everyday problems (such as hidden objects) that helped reveal their understanding of the world.

According to Piaget, at birth infants know so little about the world that they cannot purposefully explore it. The **circular reaction** provides a special means of adapting their first schemes. It involves stumbling onto a new experience caused by the baby's own motor activity. The reaction is "circular" because, as the infant tries to repeat the event again and again, a sensorimotor response that first occurred by chance becomes strengthened into a new scheme. Consider Caitlin, who at age 2 months accidentally made a smacking sound after a feeding. Finding the sound intriguing, she tried to repeat it until she became quite expert at smacking her lips.

At first, the circular reaction centers around the infant's own body. Later, it turns outward, toward manipulation of objects. Then, in the second year, it becomes experimental and creative, aimed at producing novel outcomes. Infants' difficulty inhibiting new and interesting behaviors may underlie the circular reaction. This immaturity in inhibition seems to be adaptive, helping to ensure that new skills will not be interrupted before they consolidate (Carey & Markman, 1999). Piaget considered revisions in the circular reaction so important that he named the sensorimotor substages after them (refer again to Table 5.1).

■ **Repeating Chance Behaviors.** Piaget saw newborn reflexes as the building blocks of sensorimotor intelligence. In Substage 1, babies suck, grasp, and look in much the same way,

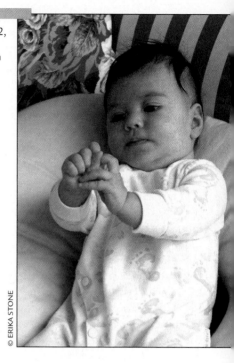

During Piaget's Substage 2, infants' adaptations are oriented toward their own bodies. This young baby carefully watches the movements of her hands, a primary circular reaction that helps her gain voluntary control over her behavior.

© ERIKA STONE

no matter what experiences they encounter. In one amusing example, Carolyn described how 2-week-old Caitlin lay on the bed next to her sleeping father. Suddenly, he awoke with a start. Caitlin had latched on and begun to suck on his back!

Around 1 month, as babies enter Substage 2, they start to gain voluntary control over their actions through the *primary circular reaction,* by repeating chance behaviors largely motivated by basic needs. This leads to some simple motor habits, such as sucking their fists or thumbs. Babies of this substage also begin to vary their behavior in response to environmental demands. For example, they open their mouths differently for a nipple than for a spoon. Young infants also start to anticipate

Table 5.1	Summary of Piaget's Sensorimotor Stage
Sensorimotor Substage	**Typical Adaptive Behaviors**
1. Reflexive schemes (birth–1 month)	Newborn reflexes (see Chapter 3, page 106)
2. Primary circular reactions (1–4 months)	Simple motor habits centered around the infant's own body; limited anticipation of events
3. Secondary circular reactions (4–8 months)	Actions aimed at repeating interesting effects in the surrounding world; imitation of familiar behaviors
4. Coordination of secondary circular reactions (8–12 months)	Intentional, or goal-directed, behavior; ability to find a hidden object in the first location in which it is hidden (object permanence); improved anticipation of events; imitation of behaviors slightly different from those the infant usually performs
5. Tertiary circular reactions (12–18 months)	Exploration of the properties of objects by acting on them in novel ways; imitation of novel behaviors; ability to search in several locations for a hidden object (accurate A–B search)
6. Mental representation (18 months–2 years)	Internal depictions of objects and events, as indicated by sudden solutions to problems, ability to find an object that has been moved while out of sight (invisible displacement), deferred imitation, and make-believe play

events. At 3 months, when Timmy awoke from his nap, he cried out with hunger. But as soon as Vanessa entered the room, his crying stopped. He knew that feeding time was near.

During Substage 3, from 4 to 8 months, infants sit up and reach for and manipulate objects. These motor achievements play a major role in turning their attention outward toward the environment. Using the *secondary circular reaction,* they try to repeat interesting events caused by their own actions. For example, 4-month-old Caitlin accidentally knocked a toy hung in front of her, producing a fascinating swinging motion. Over the next 3 days, Caitlin tried to repeat this effect, and when she succeeded, gleefully repeated her new hitting scheme. Improved control over their own behavior permits infants to imitate others' behavior more effectively. However, 4- to 8-month-olds cannot adapt flexibly and quickly enough to imitate novel behaviors (Kaye & Marcus, 1981). Although they enjoy watching an adult demonstrate a game of pat-a-cake, they are not yet able to participate.

■ **Intentional Behavior.** In Substage 4, 8- to 12-month-olds combine schemes into new, more complex action sequences. Now, behaviors that lead to new schemes no longer have a hit-or-miss quality—*accidentally* bringing the thumb to the mouth or *happening* to hit the toy. Instead, 8- to 12-month-olds can engage in **intentional,** or **goal-directed, behavior,** coordinating schemes deliberately to solve simple problems. Consider Piaget's famous object-hiding task, in which he shows the baby an attractive toy and then hides it behind his hand or under a cover. Infants of this substage can find the object by coordinating two schemes—"pushing" aside the obstacle and "grasping" the toy. Piaget regarded these action sequences as the foundation for all problem solving.

The capacity to search for and find hidden objects between 8 and 12 months of age marks a major advance in cognitive development. This infant displays intentional, or goal-directed, behavior and coordinates schemes in obtaining a toy—capacities that are the foundation for all problem solving.

Retrieving hidden objects reveals that infants have begun to master **object permanence,** the understanding that objects continue to exist when out of sight. But awareness of object permanence is not yet complete. If the baby reaches several times for an object at a first hiding place (*A*) and sees it moved to a second (*B*), she will still search for it in the first hiding place (*A*). Because babies make this *A-not-B search error,* Piaget concluded, they do not have a clear image of the object as persisting when hidden from view.

Infants of Substage 4, who can better anticipate events, sometimes use their capacity for intentional behavior to try to change those events. At 10 months, Timmy crawled after Vanessa when she put on her coat, whimpering to keep her from leaving. Also, babies can now imitate behaviors slightly different from those they usually perform. After watching someone else, they try to stir with a spoon, push a toy car, or drop raisins into a cup. Again, they draw on intentional behavior, purposefully modifying schemes to fit an observed action (Piaget, 1945/1951).

In Substage 5, from 12 to 18 months, the *tertiary circular reaction,* in which toddlers repeat behaviors with variation, emerges. Recall how Timmy dropped objects over the basement steps, trying first this action, then that, then another. Because they approach the world in this deliberately exploratory way, 12- to 18-month-olds become better problem solvers. For example, Grace figured out how to fit a shape through a hole in a container by turning and twisting it until it fell through, and she used a stick to get toys that were out of reach. According to Piaget, this capacity to experiment leads to a more advanced understanding of object permanence. Toddlers look for a hidden toy in several locations, displaying an accurate *A–B* search. Their more flexible action patterns also permit them to imitate many more behaviors, such as stacking blocks, scribbling on paper, and making funny faces.

■ **Mental Representation.** Substage 6 brings the ability to create **mental representations**—internal depictions of information that the mind can manipulate. Our most powerful mental representations are of two kinds: (1) *images,* or mental pictures of objects, people, and spaces; and (2) *concepts,* or categories in which similar objects or events are grouped together. We can use a mental image to retrace our steps when we've misplaced something or to imitate someone's behavior long after we've observed it. And by thinking in concepts and labeling them (for example, "ball" for all rounded, movable objects used in play), we become more efficient thinkers, organizing our diverse experiences into meaningful, manageable, and memorable units.

Piaget noted that 18- to 24-month-olds arrive at solutions suddenly rather than through trial-and-error behavior. In doing so, they seem to experiment with actions inside their heads—evidence that they can mentally represent their experiences. For example, at 19 months, Grace—after bumping her new push toy against a wall—paused for a moment as if to "think," then immediately turned the toy in a new direction.

Representation also enables older toddlers to solve advanced object permanence problems involving *invisible dis-*

placement—finding a toy moved while out of sight, such as into a small box while under a cover. It permits **deferred imitation**—the ability to remember and copy the behavior of models who are not present. And it makes possible **make-believe play,** in which children act out everyday and imaginary activities. As the sensorimotor stage draws to a close, mental symbols have become major instruments of thinking.

Follow-Up Research on Infant Cognitive Development

Many studies suggest that infants display a wide array of understandings earlier than Piaget believed. Recall the operant conditioning research reviewed in Chapter 4, in which newborns sucked vigorously on a nipple to gain access to interesting sights and sounds. This behavior, which closely resembles Piaget's secondary circular reaction, indicates that babies try to explore and control the external world long before 4 to 8 months. In fact, they do so as soon as they are born.

A major method used to find out what infants know about hidden objects and other aspects of physical reality capitalizes on habituation, discussed in Chapter 4. In the **violation-of-expectation method,** researchers *habituate* babies to a physical event (expose them to the event until their looking declines). Then they determine whether infants *recover* to (look longer at) an *expected event* (a variation of the first event that follows physical laws) or an *unexpected event* (a variation that violates physical laws). Recovery to the *unexpected event* suggests that the infant is "surprised" by a deviation from physical reality, as indicted by heightened attention, and therefore is aware of that aspect of the physical world.

The violation-of-expectation method is controversial. Some researchers believe that it indicates only limited, implicit (nonconscious) detection of physical events, not the full-blown, conscious understanding that was Piaget's focus in requiring infants to act on their surroundings, as in searching for hidden objects (Munakata, 2001; Thelen & Smith, 1994). Others maintain that the method reveals only babies' perceptual preference for novelty, not their understanding of experience (Bremner & Mareschal, 2004; Hood, 2004; Schilling, 2000). Let's examine this debate in light of recent evidence.

■ **Object Permanence.** In a series of studies using the violation-of-expectation method, Renée Baillargeon and her collaborators claimed to have found evidence for object permanence in the first few months of life. One of Baillargeon's studies is illustrated in Figure 5.1 (Aguiar & Baillargeon, 1999, 2002; Baillargeon & DeVos, 1991). After habituating to a short and a tall carrot moving behind a screen, infants were given two test events: (1) an *expected event,* in which the short carrot moved behind a screen, could not been seen in its window, and reappeared on the other side, and (2) an *unexpected event,* in which the tall carrot moved behind a screen, could not be seen in its window (although it was taller than the window's lower edge), and then reappeared. Infants as young as 2½ to 3½ months looked longer at the unexpected event, suggesting that they had some awareness that an object that was moved behind a screen should continue to exist.

Additional violation-of-expectation studies yielded similar results (Baillargeon, 2004; Wang, Baillargeon, & Paterson, 2005). But several researchers using similar procedures failed to confirm some of Baillargeon's findings (Bogartz, Shinskey, &

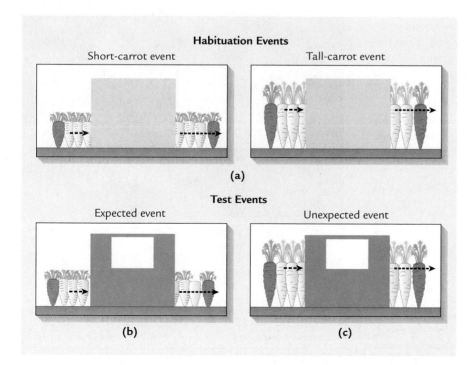

Habituation Events

Short-carrot event | Tall-carrot event

(a)

Test Events

Expected event | Unexpected event

(b) | **(c)**

■ **FIGURE 5.1 Testing young infants for understanding of object permanence using the violation-of-expectation method.** (a) First, infants were habituated to two events: a short carrot and a tall carrot moving behind a yellow screen, on alternate trials. Next, the researchers presented two test events. The color of the screen was changed to help infants notice its window. (b) In the *expected event,* the carrot shorter than the window's lower edge moved behind the blue screen and reappeared on the other side. (c) In the *unexpected event,* the carrot taller than the window's lower edge moved behind the screen and did not appear in the window, but then emerged intact on the other side. Infants as young as 2½ to 3½ months recovered to (looked longer at) the *unexpected event,* suggesting that they had some understanding of object permanence. (Adapted from R. Baillargeon & J. DeVos, 1991, "Object Permanence in Young Infants: Further Evidence," *Child Development, 62,* p. 1230. © The Society for Research in Child Development. Reprinted with permission.)

Schilling, 2000; Cashon & Cohen, 2000; Rivera, Wakeley, & Langer, 1999). Baillargeon and others answer that these opposing investigations did not include crucial controls. And they emphasize that infants look longer at a wide variety of unexpected events involving hidden objects (Baillargeon, 2000; Newcombe, Sluzenski, & Huttenlocher, 2005). Still, critics question what babies' looking preferences actually tell us about their understanding.

If 2½- to 3½-month-olds do have some notion of object permanence, how do we explain Piaget's finding that much older infants (who are quite capable of reaching) do not try to search for hidden objects? Consistent with Piaget's theory, research suggests that searching for hidden objects represents a true advance in understanding of object permanence because infants solve some object-hiding tasks before others. Ten-month-olds search for an object placed on a table and covered by a cloth before they search for an object that a hand deposits under a cloth (Moore & Meltzoff, 1999). In the second, more difficult task, infants seem to expect the object to reappear in the hand from which it initially disappeared. When the hand emerges without the object, they conclude that there is no other place the object could be. Not until 14 months can most babies infer that the hand deposited the object under the cloth.

Once 8- to 12-month-olds search for hidden objects, they make the *A-not-B* search error. Some research suggests that they search at *A* (where they found the object previously) instead of *B* (its most recent location) because they have trouble inhibiting a previously rewarded response (Diamond, Cruttenden, & Neiderman, 1994). Another possibility is that after finding the object several times at *A*, they do not attend closely when it is hidden at *B* (Ruffman & Langman, 2002). A more comprehensive explanation is that a complex, dynamic system of factors—having built a habit of reaching toward *A*, continuing to look at *A*, having the hiding place at *B* appear similar to the one at *A*, and maintaining a constant body posture—increases the chances that the baby will make the *A-not-B* search error. Research shows that disrupting any one of these factors increases 10-month-olds' accurate searching at *B* (Smith et al., 1999).

In sum, before 12 months, infants have difficulty translating what they know about object location into a successful search strategy. The ability to engage in an accurate *A–B* search coincides with rapid development of the frontal lobes of the cerebral cortex at the end of the first year (Bell, 1998). Also crucial are a wide variety of experiences perceiving, acting on, and remembering objects.

■ **Mental Representation.** In Piaget's theory, infants lead purely sensorimotor lives; they cannot represent experience until about 18 months of age. Yet 8-month-olds' ability to recall the location of a hidden object after delays of more than a minute, and 14-month-olds' recall after delays of a day or more, indicate that babies construct mental representations of objects and their whereabouts (McDonough, 1999; Moore & Meltzoff, 2004). And new studies of deferred imitation and

problem solving reveal that representational thought is evident even earlier.

Deferred Imitation. Piaget studied imitation by noting when his three children demonstrated it in their everyday behavior. Under these conditions, a great deal must be known about the infant's daily life to be sure that deferred imitation—which requires infants to represent a model's past behavior—has occurred.

Laboratory research suggests that deferred imitation is present at 6 weeks of age! In one study, infants who watched an unfamiliar adult's facial expression imitated it when exposed to the same adult the next day (Meltzoff & Moore, 1994). As motor capacities improve, infants copy actions with objects. In one study, an adult showed 6-month-olds a novel series of actions with a puppet: taking its glove off, shaking the glove to ring a bell inside, and replacing the glove. When tested a day later, infants who had seen the novel actions were far more likely to imitate them. Furthermore, by merely pairing a second, motionless puppet with the first puppet during the demonstration, the researchers induced the infants to generalize the novel actions to a new, very different-looking puppet (Barr, Marrott, & Rovee-Collier, 2003).

Between 12 and 18 months, toddlers use deferred imitation skillfully to enrich their range of sensorimotor schemes. They retain modeled behaviors for at least several months, copy the actions of peers as well as adults, and imitate across situational changes—for example, enact at home a behavior

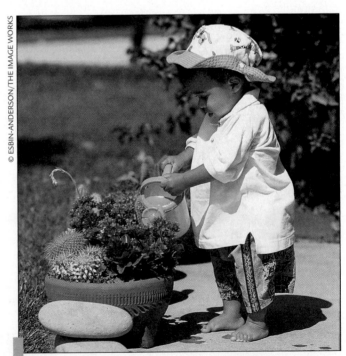

Deferred imitation greatly enriches young children's adaptations to their surrounding world. This toddler probably learned the function of sprinkling cans by watching an adult water flowers. Later, he imitates that behavior.

© ESBIN-ANDERSON/THE IMAGE WORKS

learned at child care or on TV (Barr & Hayne, 1999; Hayne, Boniface, & Barr, 2000; Klein & Meltzoff, 1999).

Toddlers even imitate rationally, by inferring others' intentions! Fourteen-month-olds are more likely to imitate purposeful than accidental behaviors (Carpenter, Akhtar, & Tomasello, 1998). And they adapt their imitative acts to a model's goal. If 14-month-olds see an adult perform an unusual action for fun (turn on a light with her head, even though her hands are free), they copy the behavior after a week's delay. But if the adult engages in the odd behavior because she *must* (her hands are otherwise occupied), toddlers imitate using a more efficient action (turning on the light with their hand) (Gergely, Bekkering, & Király, 2003).

Around 18 months, toddlers can imitate actions an adult *tries* to produce, even if these are not fully realized (Meltzoff, 1995). For example, one mother attempted to pour some raisins into a small bag but missed, spilling them. A moment later, her 18-month-old son began dropping the raisins into the bag, indicating that he had inferred his mother's goal. By age 2, children mimic entire social roles—mommy, daddy, baby—during make-believe play.

Problem Solving. As Piaget indicated, around 7 to 8 months, infants develop intentional action sequences, which they use to solve simple problems, such as pulling on a cloth to obtain a toy resting on its far end (Willatts, 1999). Soon after, infants' representational skills permit more effective problem solving than Piaget's theory suggests.

By 10 to 12 months, infants can *solve problems by analogy*—take a solution strategy from one problem and apply it to other relevant problems. In one study, babies of this age were given three similar problems, each requiring them to overcome a barrier, grasp a string, and pull it to get an attractive toy. The problems differed in all aspects of their specific features (see Figure 5.2). For the first problem, the parent demonstrated the solution and encouraged the baby to imitate. Infants obtained the toy more readily with each additional problem (Chen, Sanchez, & Campbell, 1997). In another study, 12-month-olds who were repeatedly presented with a spoon in the same orientation (handle to one side) readily adapted their motor actions when the spoon was presented in the opposite orientation (handle to the other side), successfully transporting food to their mouths most of the time (McCarty & Keen, 2005). These findings suggest that at the end of the first year, infants form flexible mental representations of how to use tools to get objects.

With age, children become better at reasoning by analogy, applying relevant strategies across increasingly dissimilar situations (Goswami, 1996). But even in the first year, infants have some ability to move beyond trial-and-error experimentation, represent solutions mentally, and use them in new contexts.

Evaluation of the Sensorimotor Stage

Table 5.2 on page 158 summarizes the remarkable cognitive attainments we have just considered. Compare this table with the description of Piaget's sensorimotor substages in Table 5.1. You will see that infants anticipate events, actively search for hidden objects, master the A–B object search, flexibly vary their sensorimotor schemes, and engage in make-believe play

■ **FIGURE 5.2 Analogical problem solving by 10- to 12-month-olds.** After the parent demonstrated the solution to problem (a), infants solved problems (b) and (c) with increasing efficiency, even though these problems differed from problem (a) in all aspects of their superficial features. (From Z. Chen, R. P. Sanchez, & T. Campbell, 1997, "From Beyond to Within Their Grasp: The Rudiments of Analogical Problem Solving in 10- to 13-Month-Olds," *Developmental Psychology, 33,* p. 792. Copyright © 1997 by the American Psychological Association. Reprinted by permission of the publisher and author.)

(a)　　　　　(b)　　　　　(c)

Table 5.2	Some Cognitive Attainments of Infancy and Toddlerhood
Age	**Cognitive Attainments**
Birth–1 month	Secondary circular reactions using limited motor skills, such as sucking a nipple to gain access to interesting sights and sounds
1–4 months	Awareness of many object properties, including object permanence, object solidity, and gravity, as suggested by violation-of-expectation findings; deferred imitation of an adult's facial expression over a short delay (1 day)
4–8 months	Improved physical knowledge and basic numerical knowledge, as suggested by violation-of-expectation findings; deferred imitation of an adult's novel actions on objects over a short delay (1 day)
8–12 months	Ability to search for a hidden object in diverse situations—when covered by a cloth, when a hand deposits it under a cloth, and when it is moved from one location to another (accurate A–B search); ability to solve sensorimotor problems by analogy to a previous problem
12–18 months	Deferred imitation of an adult's novel actions on an object over a long delay (at least several months) and across a change in situation (from child care to home, from TV to everyday life); rational imitation, taking into account the model's intentions
18 months–2 years	Deferred imitation of actions an adult tries to produce, again indicating a capacity to infer others' intentions; imitation of everyday behaviors in make-believe play

Note: Which of the capacities listed in the table indicate that mental representation emerges earlier than Piaget believed?

within Piaget's time frame. Yet other capacities—including secondary circular reactions, understanding of object properties, first signs of object permanence, deferred imitation, and problem solving by analogy—emerge earlier than Piaget expected. These findings show that the cognitive attainments of infancy do not develop together in the neat, stepwise fashion that Piaget assumed.

Disagreements between Piaget's observations and those of recent research raise controversial questions about how infant development takes place. Consistent with Piaget's ideas, sensorimotor action helps infants construct some forms of knowledge. For example, in Chapter 4, we saw that experience in crawling enhances depth perception and ability to find hidden objects. Yet we have also seen that infants comprehend a great deal before they are capable of the motor behaviors that Piaget assumed led to those understandings. How can we account for babies' amazing cognitive accomplishments?

■ **Alternative Explanations.** Unlike Piaget, who thought young babies constructed all mental representations out of sensorimotor activity, most researchers now believe that infants have some built-in cognitive equipment for making sense of experience. But intense disagreement exists over the extent of this initial understanding. As we have seen, much evidence on young infants' cognition rests on the violation-of-expectation method. Researchers who lack confidence in this method argue that babies' cognitive starting point is limited. For example, some believe that newborns begin life with a set of biases for attending to certain information and with general-purpose learning procedures, such as powerful techniques for analyzing complex perceptual information. Together, these capacities enable infants to construct a wide variety of schemes

(Bahrick, Lickliter, & Flom, 2004; Huttenlocher, 2002; Kirkham, Slemmer, & Johnson, 2002; Mandler, 2004).

Others, convinced by violation-of-expectation findings, believe that infants start out with impressive understandings. According to this **core knowledge perspective,** babies are born with a set of innate knowledge systems, or *core domains of thought.* Each of these prewired understandings permits a ready grasp of new, related information and therefore supports early, rapid development (Carey & Markman, 1999; Spelke & Newport, 1998). Core knowledge theorists argue that infants could not make sense of the complex stimulation around them without having been genetically "set up" in the course of evolution to comprehend crucial aspects of it.

The core knowledge perspective asserts that an inherited foundation *of linguistic knowledge* enables swift language acquisition in early childhood—a possibility we will consider later in this chapter. Further, core knowledge theorists argue, infants' early orientation toward people initiates swift development of *psychological knowledge*—in particular, understanding of mental states, such as intentions, emotions, desires, and beliefs, which we will address further in Chapter 6. Furthermore, researchers have conducted many studies of infants' *physical knowledge*, including object permanence, object solidity (that one object cannot move through another object), and gravity (that an object will fall without support). Violation-of-expectation findings suggest that in the first few months, infants have some awareness of all these basic object properties and quickly build on this knowledge (Baillargeon, 2004; Hespos & Baillargeon, 2001; Luo & Baillargeon, 2005; Spelke, 2000).

Researchers have even examined infants' *numerical knowledge!* In the best-known of these investigations, 5-month-olds saw a screen raised to hide a single toy animal, then watched a

Did this toddler figure out that each block placed on the tower will fall without support through extensive sensorimotor activity, as Piaget assumed? Or did she begin life with prewired physical knowledge—a core domain of thought that promotes early, rapid understanding?

© LAURA DWIGHT/CORBIS

findings and those of similar studies suggest that infants discriminate quantities up to three and use that knowledge to perform simple arithmetic—both addition and subtraction (in which two objects are covered and one object is removed) (Kobayashi et al., 2004; Kobayashi, Hiraki, & Hasegawa, 2005; Wynn, Bloom, & Chiang, 2002).

But like other violation-of-expectation results, babies' numerical capacities are controversial. In experiments similar to those just described, infants' looking preferences were inconsistent (Langer, Gillette, & Arriaga, 2003; Wakeley, Rivera, & Langer, 2000). Critics also note that claims for number concepts in infants are surprising, in view of other research indicating that children have difficulty with less-than and greater-than relationships between small sets of items before 14 to 16 months and do not add and subtract correctly until the preschool years.

Finally, although the core knowledge perspective emphasizes native endowment, it acknowledges that experience is essential for children to extend this initial knowledge. But so far, it has said little about which experiences are most important in each core domain of thought and how those experiences advance children's thinking. Despite these limitations, core knowledge research has sharpened the field's focus on clarifying the starting point for human cognition and on carefully tracking the changes that build on it.

■ **Piaget's Legacy.** Current research on infant cognition yields broad agreement on two issues: First, many cognitive changes of infancy are gradual and continuous rather than

hand place a second, identical toy behind the screen. Finally the screen was removed to reveal either one or two toys. If infants kept track of and represented the two objects (requiring them to add one object to another), then they should look longer at the unexpected, one-toy display—which is what they did (see Figure 5.3) (Wynn, Bloom, & Chiang, 2002). These

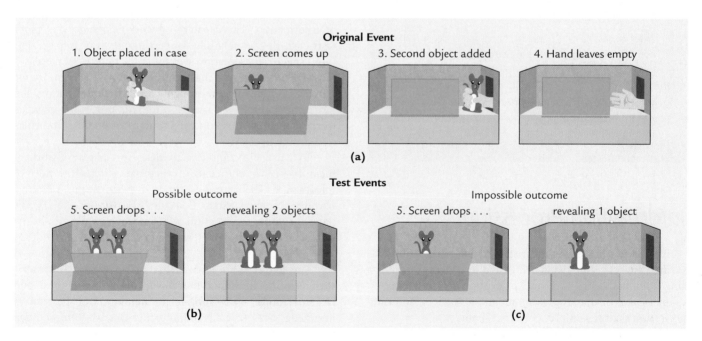

Original Event

1. Object placed in case   2. Screen comes up   3. Second object added   4. Hand leaves empty

(a)

Test Events

Possible outcome

5. Screen drops . . .   revealing 2 objects

Impossible outcome

5. Screen drops . . .   revealing 1 object

(b)   (c)

■ **FIGURE 5.3 Testing infants for basic number concepts.** (a) First, infants saw a screen raised in front of a toy animal. Then an identical toy was added behind the screen. Next, the researchers presented two outcomes. (b) In the *expected outcome*, the screen dropped to reveal two toy animals. (c) In the *unexpected outcome*, the screen dropped to reveal one toy animal. Five-months-olds shown the unexpected outcome looked longer than did 5-month-olds shown the expected outcome. The researchers concluded that infants can discriminate the quantities "one" and "two" and use that knowledge to perform simple addition: 1 + 1 = 2. A variation of this procedure suggested that 5-month-olds could also do simple subtraction: 2 − 1 = 1. (From K. Wynn, 1992, "Addition and Subtraction by Human Infants," *Nature, 358*, p. 749. Reprinted by permission.)

abrupt and stagelike (Bjorklund, 2004; Courage & Howe, 2002). Second, rather than developing together, various aspects of infant cognition change unevenly because of the challenges posed by different types of tasks and infants' varying experience with those tasks. These ideas serve as the basis for another major approach to cognitive development—*information processing.*

Before turning to this alternative point of view, let's conclude our discussion of the sensorimotor stage by recognizing Piaget's enormous contributions. Piaget's work inspired a wealth of research on infant cognition, including studies that challenged his theory. Although his account of development is no longer fully accepted, contemporary theorists are far from consensus on how to modify or replace it. Piaget's observations also have been of great practical value. Teachers and caregivers continue to look to the sensorimotor stage for guidelines on how to create developmentally appropriate environments for infants and toddlers.

Ask Yourself

Review

Using the text discussion on pages 155–159, construct an age-related list of infant and toddler cognitive attainments. Which ones are consistent with Piaget's sensorimotor stage? Which ones develop earlier than Piaget anticipated?

Apply

Several times, after Mimi's father hid a teething biscuit under a red cup, 12-month-old Mimi retrieved it easily. Then Mimi's father hid the biscuit under a nearby yellow cup. Why did Mimi persist in searching for the biscuit under the red cup?

Reflect

Which explanation of infants' cognitive competencies do you prefer, and why?

www.ablongman.com/berk

Information Processing

Information-processing theorists agree with Piaget that children are active, inquiring beings. But instead of providing a single, unified theory of cognitive development, they focus on many aspects of thinking, from attention, memory, and categorization skills to complex problem solving.

Recall from Chapter 1 that the information-processing approach frequently relies on computerlike flowcharts to describe the human cognitive system. Information-processing theorists are not satisfied with general concepts, such as assimilation and accommodation, to describe how children think. Instead, they want to know exactly what individuals of different ages do when faced with a task or problem (Birney et al., 2005; Halford, 2002). The computer model of human thinking is attractive because it is explicit and precise.

Structure of the Information-Processing System

Most information-processing researchers assume that we hold information in three parts of the mental system for processing: *the sensory register; working,* or *short-term, memory;* and *long-term memory* (see Figure 5.4). As information flows through each, we can use **mental strategies** to operate on and transform it, increasing the chances that we will retain information, use it efficiently, and think flexibly, adapting the information to changing circumstances. To understand this more clearly, let's look at each aspect of the mental system.

First, information enters the **sensory register,** where sights and sounds are represented directly and stored briefly. Look around you and then close your eyes. An image of what you saw persists for a few seconds, but then it decays, or disappears, unless you use mental strategies to preserve it. For example, by *attending to* some information more carefully than to other information, you increase the chances that it will transfer to the next step of the information-processing system.

The second part of the mind is **working,** or **short-term, memory,** where we actively apply mental strategies as we "work" on a limited amount of information. For example, if you are studying this book effectively, you are taking notes, repeating information to yourself, or grouping pieces of information together. Why do you apply these strategies? The sensory register, though limited, can take in a wide panorama of information. The capacity of working memory is more restricted. By meaningfully connecting pieces of information into a single representation, we reduce the number of pieces we must attend to, thereby making room in working memory for more. Also, the more thoroughly we learn information, the more *automatically* we use it. Automatic processing expands working memory by permitting us to focus on other information simultaneously.

To manage its complex activities, a special part of working memory—called the **central executive**—directs the flow of information. The central executive is the conscious, reflective part of our mental system. It decides what to attend to, coordinates incoming information with information already in the system, and selects, applies, and monitors strategies (Baddeley, 1993, 2000).

The longer we hold information in working memory, the greater the likelihood that it will transfer to the third, and largest, storage area—**long-term memory,** our permanent knowledge base, which is unlimited. In fact, we store so much in long-term memory that we sometimes have problems with *retrieval,* or getting information back from the system. To aid retrieval, we apply strategies, just as we do in working memory. Information in long-term memory is *categorized* according to a master plan based on content, much like a library shelving system that allows us to retrieve items easily by

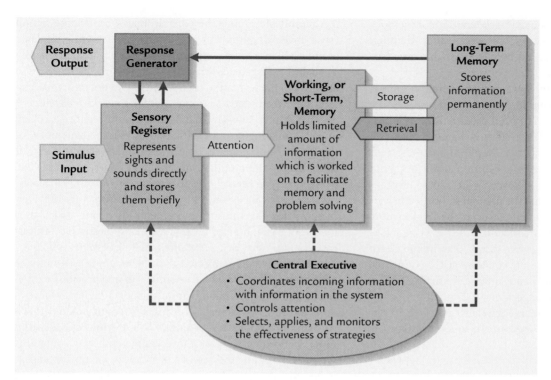

■ FIGURE 5.4 **Model of the human information-processing system.** Information flows through three parts of the mental system: the *sensory register;* *working,* or *short-term, memory;* and *long-term memory.* In each, mental strategies can be used to manipulate information, increasing the efficiency and flexibility of thinking and the chances that information will be retained. The *central executive* is the conscious, reflective part of working memory. It coordinates incoming information already in the system, decides what to attend to, and oversees the use of strategies.

following the same network of associations used to store them in the first place.

Information-processing researchers believe that the basic structure of the mental system is similar throughout life. However, the *capacity* of the system—the amount of information that can be retained and processed at once and the speed with which it can be processed—increases, making more complex forms of thinking possible with age (Case, 1998; Kail, 2003). Gains in information-processing capacity are due in part to brain development and in part to improvements in strategies—such as attending to information and categorizing it effectively—that are already developing in the first two years of life.

Attention

Recall from Chapter 4 that between 1 and 2 months of age, infants shift from focusing on single, high-contrast features to exploring objects and patterns more thoroughly. Besides attending to more aspects of the environment, infants gradually take in information more quickly. Habituation research reveals that preterm and newborn babies require a long time to habituate and recover to novel visual stimuli—about 3 or 4 minutes. But by 4 or 5 months, infants require as little as 5 to 10 seconds to take in a complex visual stimulus and recognize it as different from a previous one (Slater et al., 1996).

One reason that very young babies' habituation times are so long is that they have difficulty disengaging their attention from interesting stimuli (Colombo, 2002). When Carolyn held up a doll dressed in red-and-white checked overalls, 2-month-

old Caitlin stared intently until, unable to break her gaze, she burst into tears. The ability to shift attention from one stimulus to another is just as important as attending to a stimulus. By 4 months, infants' attention becomes more flexible (Hood, Atkinson, & Braddick, 1998).

During the first year, infants attend to novel and eye-catching events (Richards & Holley, 1999). With the transition to toddlerhood, children become increasingly capable of intentional behavior (refer back to Piaget's Substage 4). Consequently, attraction to novelty declines (but does not disappear) and *sustained attention* improves, especially when children play with toys. A toddler who engages even in simple goal-directed behavior, such as stacking blocks or putting them in a container, must maintain attention to reach the goal. As plans and activities become more complex, so does the duration of attention (Ruff & Capozzoli, 2003).

Memory

Operant conditioning and habituation provide windows into early memory. Both methods show that retention of visual events increases dramatically over infancy and toddlerhood.

Using operant conditioning, researchers study infant memory by teaching 2- to 6-month-olds to move a mobile by kicking a foot tied to it with a long cord. Two- to 3-month-olds still remember how to activate the mobile one week after training. By 6 months, memory increases to two weeks (Rovee-Collier, 1999; Rovee-Collier & Bhatt, 1993). Around the middle of the first year, babies can manipulate switches or buttons to control stimulation. When 6- to 18-month-olds pressed a lever to make a toy train move around a track, duration of memory continued to increase with age; 13 weeks after training, 18-month-olds still remembered how to press the lever (see Figure 5.5) (Hartshorn et al., 1998).

Even after 2- to 6-month-olds forget an operant response, they need only a brief prompt—an adult who shakes the mobile—to reinstate the memory (Hildreth & Rovee-Collier, 2002). And when 6-month-olds are given a chance to reactivate the response themselves for just a couple of minutes, their memory not only returns but extends dramatically, to about 17 weeks (Hildreth, Sweeney, & Rovee-Collier, 2003). Perhaps permitting the baby to generate the previously learned behavior strengthens memory because it reexposes the child to more aspects of the original learning situation.

Habituation/recovery research shows that infants learn and retain a wide variety of information just by watching objects and events, without being physically active. Sometimes, they do so for much longer time spans than in operant conditioning studies. Babies are especially attentive to the movements of objects and people. In one investigation,

$5\frac{1}{2}$-month-olds remembered a woman's captivating action (such as blowing bubbles or brushing hair) seven weeks later, as indicated by a *familiarity preference* (see page 135 in Chapter 4) (Bahrick, Gogate, & Ruiz, 2002). In fact, the babies were so attentive to the woman's action that they did not remember her face, even when tested 1 minute later for a *novelty preference*.

In Chapter 4 we saw that 3- to 5-month-olds are excellent at discriminating faces in static photos. But their memory for the faces of unfamiliar people and for other static patterns is short-lived—at 3 months, only about 24 hours, and at the end of the first year, several days to a few weeks (Fagan, 1973; Pascalis, de Haan, & Nelson, 1998). In comparison, 3-month-olds' memory for the unusual movements of objects (such as a metal nut swinging on the end of a string) persists for at least three months (Bahrick, Hernandez-Reif, & Pickens, 1997).

So far, we have discussed only **recognition**—noticing when a stimulus is identical or similar to one previously experienced. It is the simplest form of memory: All babies have to do is indicate (by kicking, pressing a lever, or looking) that a new stimulus is identical or similar to a previous one. **Recall** is more challenging because it involves remembering something not present. But by the end of the first year, infants can engage in recall, as indicated by their ability to find hidden objects and to imitate others' actions long after observing the behavior (see page 156). Yet as adults, we no longer recall our earliest experiences. The Lifespan Vista box on the following page helps explain this puzzling finding.

Categorization

Even young infants can categorize, grouping similar objects and events into a single representation. Categorization helps infants make sense of experience—reduce the enormous amount of new information they encounter every day so they can learn and remember (Cohen, 2003; Oakes & Madole, 2003).

Some creative variations of operant conditioning research with mobiles have been used to find out about infant categorization. One such study, of 3-month-olds, is described and illustrated in Figure 5.7 on page 164. Similar investigations reveal that in the first few months, babies categorize stimuli on the basis of shape, size, color, and other physical properties (Wasserman & Rovee-Collier, 2001). And by 6 months of age, they can categorize on the basis of two correlated features—for example, the shape and color of the alphabet letter (Bhatt et al., 2004). Being able to categorize using clusters of features prepares babies for acquiring many complex everyday categories.

Habituation/recovery has also been used to study infant categorization. Researchers show babies a series of pictures belonging to one category and then see whether they recover to (look longer at) a picture that is not a member of the category. Findings reveal that 7- to 12-month-olds structure objects into an impressive array of meaningful categories, including food items, furniture, birds, animals, vehicles, kitchen utensils, plants, and spatial location ("above" and "below," "on" and "in")

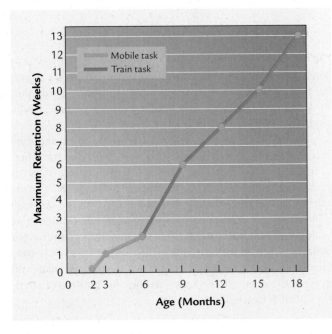

■ **FIGURE 5.5 Increase in retention in two operant conditioning tasks from 2 to 18 months.** Two- to 6-month-olds were trained to make a kicking response that turned a mobile. Six- to 18-month-olds were trained to press a lever that made a toy train move around a track. Six-month-olds learned both responses and retained them for an identical length of time, indicating that the tasks are comparable. Consequently, researchers could plot a single line tracking gains in retention of operant responses from 2 to 18 months of age. The line shows that memory improves dramatically. (From C. Rovee-Collier & R. Barr, 2001, "Infant Learning and Memory," in G. Bremner & A. Fogel, eds., *Blackwell Handbook of Infant Development*, Oxford, U.K.: Blackwell, p. 150. Reprinted by permission.)

A Lifespan Vista

Infantile Amnesia

If infants and toddlers remember many aspects of their everyday lives, how do we explain **infantile amnesia**—that most of us cannot retrieve events that happened to us before age 3? The reason we forget cannot be merely the passage of time, because we can recall many personally meaningful one-time events from both the recent and the distant past: the day a sibling was born, a birthday party, or a move to a new house—recollections known as **autobiographical memory.**

Several complementary explanations of infantile amnesia exist. In one theory, vital changes in the frontal lobes of the cerebral cortex may pave the way for an *explicit* memory system—one in which children remember deliberately rather than *implicitly,* without conscious awareness (Boyer & Diamond, 1992; Rovee-Collier & Barr, 2001). A related conjecture is that older children and adults often use verbal means to store information, whereas infants' and toddlers' memory processing is largely nonverbal—an incompatibility that may prevent long-term retention of their experiences.

To test this idea, researchers sent two adults to the homes of 2- to 4-year-olds with an unusual toy that the children were likely to remember: The Magic Shrinking Machine, shown in Figure 5.6.

One of the adults showed the child how, after inserting an object in an opening on top of the machine and turning a crank that activated flashing lights and musical sounds, the child could retrieve a smaller, identical object from behind a door on the front of the machine. (The second adult discreetly dropped the smaller object down a chute leading to the door.) The child was encouraged to participate as the machine "shrunk" additional objects.

A day later, the researchers tested the children to see how well they recalled the event. Their nonverbal memory—based on acting out the "shrinking" event and recognizing the "shrunken" objects in photos—was excellent. But even when they had the vocabulary, children younger than age 3 had trouble describing features of the "shrinking" experience. Verbal recall increased sharply between ages 3 and 4—the period during which children "scramble over the amnesia barrier" (Simcock & Hayne, 2003, p. 813). In a second study, preschoolers could not translate their nonverbal memory for the game into language 6 months to 1 year later, when their language had improved dramatically. Their verbal reports were "frozen in time," reflecting their limited language skill at the time they played the game (Simcock & Hayne, 2002).

These findings help us reconcile infants' and toddlers' remarkable memory skills with infantile amnesia. In the first few years, children rely on nonverbal memory techniques, such as visual images and motor actions. As language develops, children first use words to talk about the here and now. Only after age 3 do they often represent events verbally and discuss them in elaborate conversations with adults. As children encode autobiographical events in verbal form, they increase the later accessibility of those memories because they can use language-based cues to retrieve them (Hayne, 2004).

Other findings suggest that the advent of a clear self-image contributes to the end of infantile amnesia. In longitudinal research, toddlers who were advanced in development of a sense of self demonstrated better verbal memories a year later while conversing about past events with their mothers (Harley & Reese, 1999). Very likely, both biology and social experience contribute to the decline of infantile amnesia. Brain development and adult–child interaction may jointly foster self-awareness and language, which enable children to talk with adults about significant past experiences (Nelson & Fivush, 2004). As a result, preschoolers begin to construct a long-lasting autobiographical narrative of their lives and enter into the history of their family and community.

(a)

(b)

(c)

■ **FIGURE 5.6 The Magic Shrinking Machine, used to test young children's verbal and nonverbal memory of an unusual event.** After being shown how the machine worked, the child participated in selecting objects from a polka-dot bag, dropping them into the top of the machine (a) and turning a crank, which produced a "shrunken" object (b). When tested the next day, 2- to 4-year-olds' nonverbal memory for the event was excellent. But below 36 months, verbal recall was poor, based on the number of features recalled about the game during an open-ended interview (c). Recall improved between 36 and 48 months, the period during which infantile amnesia subsides. (From G. Simcock & H. Hayne, 2003, "Age-Related Changes in Verbal and Nonverbal Memory During Early Childhood," *Developmental Psychology, 39,* pp. 806, 808. Copyright © by the American Psychological Association. Reprinted by permission.) *Photos:* Ross Coombes/Courtesy of Harlene Hayne.

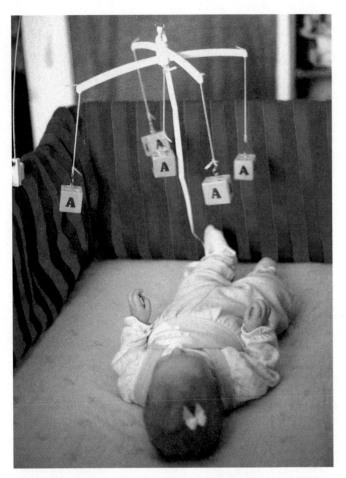

■ **FIGURE 5.7 Investigating infant categorization using operant conditioning.** Three-month-olds were taught to kick to move a mobile that was made of small blocks, all with the letter A on them. After a delay, kicking returned to a high level only if the babies were shown a mobile whose elements were labeled with the same form (the letter A). If the form was changed (from As to 2s), infants no longer kicked vigorously. While making the mobile move, the babies had grouped together its features. They associated the kicking response with the category A and, at later testing, distinguished it from the category 2 (Bhatt, Rovee-Collier, & Weiner, 1994; Hayne, Rovee-Collier, & Perris, 1987.)

(Casasola, Cohen, & Chiarello, 2003; Mandler & McDonough, 1998; Oakes, Coppage, & Dingel, 1997). Besides organizing the physical world, infants of this age categorize their emotional and social worlds. They sort people and their voices by gender and age, have begun to distinguish emotional expressions, and can separate people's natural movements from other motions (see Chapter 4, pages 144 and 145–146).

Babies' earliest categories are *perceptual*—based on similar overall appearance or prominent object parts (legs for animals and wheels for vehicles). But by the end of the first year, more categories are *conceptual*—based on common functions or behaviors (Cohen, 2003; Mandler, 2004). For example, 1-year-olds group together kitchen utensils because each is used to prepare or eat food.

In the second year, toddlers become active categorizers. Around 12 months, they touch objects that go together but do not group them. At 16 months, they can group objects into a single category. For example, when given four balls and four boxes, they put all the balls together but not the boxes. Around 18 months, they sort objects into two classes (Gopnik & Meltzoff, 1987). Compared with habituation/recovery, touching, sorting, and other play behaviors better reveal the meanings that toddlers attach to categories. After watching an adult give a toy dog a drink from a cup, 14-month-olds shown a rabbit and a motorcycle usually offer the drink only to the rabbit (Mandler & McDonough, 1998). They clearly understand that certain actions are appropriate for some categories of items (animals) and not others (vehicles).

How does this perceptual-to-conceptual change take place? Although researchers disagree on whether this shift requires a new approach to analyzing experience, most acknowledge that exploration of objects and expanding knowledge of the world contribute to older infants' capacity to group objects by their functions and behaviors (Mandler, 2004; Oakes & Madole, 2003). In addition, language both builds on and facilitates categorization. Adult labeling of objects ("This one's a car, and that one's a bicycle") helps toddlers refine their earliest categories. Toddlers' advancing vocabulary, in turn, fosters categorization (Waxman, 2003). Korean toddlers, who learn a language in which object names are often omitted from sentences, develop object-sorting skills later than their English-speaking counterparts (Gopnik & Choi, 1990).

Evaluation of Information-Processing Findings

The information-processing perspective underscores the continuity of human thinking from infancy into adult life. In attending to the environment, remembering everyday events, and categorizing objects, Caitlin, Grace, and Timmy think in ways that are remarkably similar to our own, though their mental processing is far from proficient. Findings on infant memory and categorization join with other research in challenging Piaget's view of early cognitive development. If 3-month-olds can remember events for as long as 3 months and can categorize stimuli, then they must have some ability to represent their experiences.

Information-processing research has contributed greatly to our view of young babies as sophisticated cognitive beings. But its central strength—analyzing cognition into its components, such as perception, attention, and memory—is also its greatest drawback. Information processing has had difficulty putting these components back together into a broad, comprehensive theory. One approach to overcoming this weakness has been to combine Piaget's theory with the information-processing approach, an effort we will explore in Chapter 9. A more recent trend has been the application of a *dynamic systems view* to early cognition (see Chapter 4, page 138). Researchers analyze each cognitive attainment to see how it results from a complex system of prior accomplishments and the child's current goals (Courage & Howe, 2002; Spencer & Schöner, 2003; Thelen & Smith, 1998). These ideas, once they are fully tested, may move the field closer to a more powerful view of how the mind of the infant and child develops.

The Social Context of Early Cognitive Development

Look back at the short episode at the beginning of this chapter in which Grace dropped shapes into a container. Notice that she learns about the toy with Ginette's help. With adult support, Grace will gradually become better at matching shapes to openings and dropping them into the container. Then she will be able to perform the activity (and others like it) on her own.

Vygotsky's sociocultural theory has helped researchers realize that children live in rich social contexts that affect the way their cognitive world is structured (Rogoff, 2003; Tudge & Scrimsher, 2003). Vygotsky believed that complex mental activities have their origins in social interaction. Through joint activities with more mature members of their society, children come to master activities and think in ways that have meaning in their culture.

A special Vygotskian concept explains how this happens. The **zone of proximal** (or potential) **development** refers to a range of tasks that the child cannot yet handle alone but can do with the help of more skilled partners. To understand this idea, think about how a sensitive adult (such as Ginette) introduces a child to a new activity. The adult picks a task that the child can master but that is challenging enough that the child cannot do it by herself, or perhaps capitalizes on an activity that the child has chosen. Then, as the adult guides and supports, the child joins in the interaction and picks up mental strategies. As her competence increases, the adult steps back, permitting the child to take more responsibility for the task.

Vygotsky's ideas have been applied mostly to older children, who are more skilled in language and social communication. Recently, however, his theory has been extended to infancy and toddlerhood. Recall that babies are equipped with capacities that ensure that caregivers will interact with them. Then adults adjust the environment and their communication in ways that promote learning adapted to their cultural circumstances.

A study by Barbara Rogoff and her collaborators illustrates this process. Placing a jack-in-the-box nearby, the researchers watched how several adults played with Rogoff's son and daughter over the first two years. In the early months, the adults tried to focus the baby's attention by working the toy and, as the bunny popped out, saying something like "My, what happened?" By the end of the first year, when the baby's cognitive and motor skills had improved, interaction centered on how to use the toy. The adults guided the baby's hand in turning the crank and putting the bunny back in the box. During the second year, adults helped from a distance, using gestures and verbal prompts, such as making a turning motion with the hand near the crank. Research indicates that this fine-

With simple words and gentle physical support, this father helps his young son put together a puzzle. By bringing the task within the child's zone of proximal development and adjusting his communication to suit the child's needs, the father transfers mental strategies to the child and promotes his cognitive development.

tuned support is related to advanced play, language, and problem solving in toddlerhood and early childhood (Bornstein et al., 1992; Charman et al., 2001; Tamis-LeMonda & Bornstein, 1989).

As early as the first year, cultural variations in social experiences affect mental strategies. In the jack-in-the-box example, adults and children focused their attention on a single activity. This strategy, common in Western middle-SES homes, is well-suited to lessons in which children master skills apart from the everyday situations in which they will later use those skills. In contrast, Guatemalan Mayan adults and babies often attend to several events at once. For example, one 12-month-old skillfully put objects in a jar while also watching a passing truck and blowing a toy whistle (Chavajay & Rogoff, 1999). Processing several competing events simultaneously may be vital in cultures where children learn largely through keen observation of others' ongoing activities. Mexican children from low-SES families continue to display this style of attention well into middle childhood (Correa-Chavez, Rogoff, & Arauz, 2005).

Earlier we saw how infants and toddlers create new schemes by acting on the physical world (Piaget) and how certain skills become better developed as children represent their experiences more efficiently and meaningfully (information processing). Vygotsky adds a third dimension to our understanding by emphasizing that many aspects of cognitive development are socially mediated. The Cultural Influences box on the following page presents additional evidence for this idea, and we will see even more in the next section.

Cultural Influences

Caregiver–Toddler Interaction and Early Make-Believe Play

One of the activities my husband, Ken, used to do with our two sons when they were young was to bake pineapple upside-down cake, a favorite treat. One Sunday afternoon when a cake was in the making, 21-month-old Peter stood on a chair at the kitchen sink, busily pouring water from one cup to another.

"He's in the way, Dad!" complained 4-year-old David, trying to pull Peter away from the sink.

"Maybe if we let him help, he'll give us room," Ken suggested. As David stirred the batter, Ken poured some into a small bowl for Peter, moved his chair to the side of the sink, and handed him a spoon.

"Here's how you do it, Petey," instructed David, with an air of superiority. Peter watched as David stirred, then tried to copy his motion. When it was time to pour the batter, Ken helped Peter hold and tip the small bowl.

"Time to bake it," said Ken.

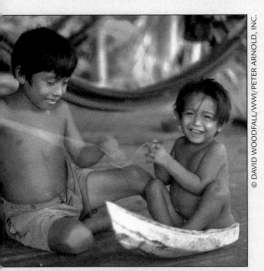

In cultures where sibling caregiving is common, make-believe play is more frequent and complex with older siblings than with mothers. As these Venezuelan brothers play with a balsa-wood boat, the older boy provides his younger sibling with enjoyable and challenging stimulation.

"Bake it, bake it," repeated Peter, watching Ken slip the pan into the oven.

Several hours later, we observed one of Peter's earliest instances of make-believe play. He got his pail from the sandbox and, after filling it with a handful of sand, carried it into the kitchen and put it down on the floor in front of the oven. "Bake it, bake it," Peter called to Ken. Together, father and son placed the pretend cake in the oven.

Until recently, most researchers studied make-believe play apart from the social environment in which it occurs, by observing children while they played alone. Probably for this reason, Piaget and his followers concluded that toddlers discover make-believe independently, once they are capable of representational schemes. Vygotsky's theory has challenged this view. He believed that society provides children with opportunities to represent culturally meaningful activities in play. Make-believe, like other complex mental activities, is first learned under the guidance of experts (Berk, 2006a). In the example just described, Peter extended his capacity to represent daily events when Ken drew him into the baking task and helped him act it out in play.

Current evidence supports the idea that early make-believe is the combined result of children's readiness to engage in it and social experiences that promote it. In one observational study of middle-SES American toddlers, 75 to 80 percent of make-believe involved mother–child interaction (Haight & Miller, 1993). At 12 months, make-believe was fairly one-sided: Almost all play episodes were initiated by mothers. By the end of the second year, mothers and children displayed mutual interest in getting make-believe started; half of pretend episodes were initiated by each.

Toddlers' make-believe is more elaborate when adults participate (Keren et al., 2005). Toddlers are more likely to combine schemes into complex sequences, as Peter did when he put sand in the bucket ("making the batter"), carried it into the kitchen, and, with Ken's help, put it in the oven ("baking the cake"). The more parents pretend with their toddlers, the more time their children devote to make-believe. In some collectivist societies, such as Argentina and Japan, mother–toddler other-directed pretending (feeding or putting a doll to sleep) is particularly frequent and rich in maternal expressions of affection and praise (Bornstein et al., 1999).

In some cultures, such as those of Indonesia and Mexico, where extended-family households and sibling caregiving are common, make-believe is more frequent and more complex with older siblings than with mothers. As early as age 3 to 4, children provide rich, challenging stimulation to their younger brothers and sisters, take these teaching responsibilities seriously, and, with age, become better at them (Zukow-Goldring, 2002). In a study of Zinacanteco Indian children of southern Mexico, by age 8, sibling teachers were highly skilled at showing 2-year-olds how to play at everyday tasks, such as washing and cooking. They often guided toddlers verbally and physically through the task and provided feedback (Maynard, 2002).

Older siblings in Western middle-SES families less often teach deliberately, but they are still serve as influential models of playful behavior. In a study of New Zealand families of Western European descent, when both a parent and older sibling were available, toddlers more often imitated the actions of the sibling, especially when siblings engaged in make-believe or in routines (like answering the phone or raking leaves) that could inspire pretending (Barr & Hayne, 2003).

As we will see in Chapter 7, make-believe is a major means through which children extend their cognitive skills and learn about important activities in their culture. Vygotsky's theory, and the findings that support it, tell us that providing a stimulating physical environment is not enough to promote early cognitive development. In addition, toddlers must be invited and encouraged by more skilled members of their culture to participate in the social world around them. Parents and teachers can enhance early make-believe by playing often with toddlers, guiding and elaborating on their make-believe themes.

we can do is present them with stimuli, coax them to respond, and observe their behavior. As a result, most infant tests emphasize perceptual and motor responses. But new tests are being developed that increasingly tap early language, cognition, and social behavior, especially with older infants and toddlers.

One commonly used test, the Bayley Scales of Infant Development, is suitable for children between 1 month and 3½. The most recent edition, the Bayley-III, has three main subtests: (1) the Cognitive Scale, which includes such items as attention to familiar and unfamiliar objects, looking for a fallen object, and pretend play; (2) the Language Scale, which taps understanding and expression of language—for example, recognition of objects and people, following simple directions, and naming objects and pictures; and (3) the Motor Scale, which includes gross and fine motor skills, such as grasping, sitting, stacking blocks, and climbing stairs (Bayley, 2005).

In addition, the Bayley-III has two scales that depend on parental report: (4) the Social-Emotional Scale, which asks caregivers about such behaviors as ease of calming, social responsiveness, and imitation in play; and (5) the Adaptive Behavior Scale, which asks about adaptation to the demands of daily life, including communication, self-control, following rules, and getting along with others.

Individual Differences in Early Mental Development

Because of Grace's deprived early environment, Kevin and Monica had a psychologist give her one of many tests available for assessing mental development in infants and toddlers. Worried about Timmy's progress, Vanessa also arranged for him to be tested. At age 22 months, he had only a handful of words in his vocabulary, played in a less mature way than Caitlin and Grace, and seemed restless and overactive.

The cognitive theories we have just discussed try to explain the *process* of development—how children's thinking changes. Mental tests, in contrast, focus on cognitive *products*. Their goal is to measure behaviors that reflect development and to arrive at scores that *predict* future performance, such as later intelligence, school achievement, and adult vocational success. This concern with prediction arose nearly a century ago, when French psychologist Alfred Binet designed the first successful intelligence test, which predicted school achievement (see Chapter 1). It inspired the design of many new tests, including ones that measure intelligence at very early ages.

Infant and Toddler Intelligence Tests

Accurately measuring infants' intelligence is a challenge because young babies cannot answer questions or follow directions. All

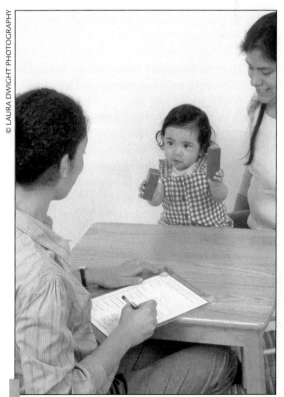

A trained examiner administers a test based on the Bayley Scales of Infant Development to a baby while her mother looks on. Unlike tests for older children, which assess verbal, conceptual, and problem-solving skills, most infant tests emphasize perceptual and motor responses, which predict later intelligence poorly.

■ **Computing Intelligence Test Scores.** Intelligence tests for infants, children, and adults are scored in much the same way—by computing an **intelligence quotient (IQ),** which indicates the extent to which the raw score (number of items passed) deviates from the typical performance of same-age individuals. In constructing a test, designers engage in **standardization**—giving the test to a large, representative sample and using the results as the *standard* for interpreting scores. The standardization sample for the Bayley-III included 1,700 infants, toddlers, and young preschoolers, representing the U.S. population in SES and ethnic diversity.

Within the standardization sample, performances at each age level form a **normal distribution** in which most scores cluster around the mean, or average, and progressively fewer fall toward the extremes (see Figure 5.8). This bell-shaped distribution results whenever researchers measure individual differences in large samples. When intelligence tests are standardized, the mean IQ is set at 100. An individual's IQ is higher or lower than 100 by an amount that reflects how much his or her test performance deviates from the standardization-sample mean.

The IQ offers a way of finding out whether an individual is ahead, behind, or on time (average) in mental development in relation to others of the same age. For example, if Timmy did better than 50 percent of his agemates, his score will be 100. A child who does better than only 16 percent has an IQ of 85; one who outperforms 98 percent has an IQ of 130. The IQs of 96 percent of individuals fall between 70 and 130; only a few achieve higher or lower scores.

■ **Predicting Later Performance from Infant Tests.** Despite careful construction, most infant tests predict later intelligence poorly. Longitudinal research reveals that the majority of children show substantial fluctuations in IQ between toddlerhood and adolescence—10 to 20 points in most cases and sometimes much more (McCall, 1993; Weinert & Hany, 2003).

Because infants and toddlers are especially likely to become distracted, fatigued, or bored during testing, their scores often do not reflect their true abilities. In addition, the items on infant tests differ from the tasks given to older children, which emphasize increasingly complex verbal, conceptual, and problem-solving skills. Because of concerns that infant test scores do not tap the same dimensions of intelligence measured at older ages, they are conservatively labeled **developmental quotients,** or **DQs,** rather than IQs.

Infant tests are somewhat better at making long-term predictions for extremely low-scoring babies. Today, they are largely used for *screening*—helping to identify for further observation and intervention babies who are likely to have developmental problems.

Because infant tests do not predict later IQ for most children, some researchers have turned to information-processing measures, such as habituation, to assess early mental progress. Their findings show that speed of habituation and recovery to novel visual stimuli are among the best available infant predictors of IQ from early childhood through adolescence (McCall & Carriger, 1993; Sigman, Cohen, & Beckwith, 1997). Habituation and recovery seem to be an especially effective early index of intelligence because they assess memory as well as quickness and flexibility of thinking, which underlie intelligent behavior at all ages (Colombo, 1995; Rose & Feldman, 1997). The consistency of these findings has prompted designers of the Bayley-III to include items that tap such cognitive skills as habituation/recovery, object permanence, and categorization.

Early Environment and Mental Development

In Chapter 2, we indicated that intelligence is a complex blend of hereditary and environmental influences. Many studies have examined the relationship of environmental factors to infant and toddler mental test scores. As we consider this evidence, you will encounter findings that highlight the role of heredity as well.

■ **Home Environment.** The **Home Observation for Measurement of the Environment (HOME)** is a checklist for gathering information about the quality of children's home lives through observation and interviews with parents (Caldwell & Bradley, 1994). Refer to Applying What We Know on the following page for factors measured by HOME during the first three years. Each is positively related to toddlers' mental test performance. Regardless of SES and ethnicity, an organized, stimulating physical setting and parental encouragement, involvement, and affection repeatedly predict better language and IQ scores in toddlerhood and early childhood (Espy, Molfese, & DiLalla, 2001; Klebanov et al., 1998; Roberts, Burchinal, & Durham, 1999). The extent to which parents talk to infants and toddlers is particularly important. It contributes strongly

■ **FIGURE 5.8 Normal distribution of intelligence test scores.** To determine what percentage of same-age individuals in the population a person with a certain IQ outperformed, add the figures to the left of that IQ score. For example, an 8-year-old child with an IQ of 115 scored better than 84 percent of the population of 8-year-olds.

to early language progress, which, in turn, predicts intelligence and academic achievement in elementary school (Hart & Risley, 1995).

Yet we must interpret these correlational findings cautiously. In all the studies, children were reared by their biological parents, with whom they share not just a common environment but also a common heredity. Parents who are genetically more intelligent may provide better experiences while also giving birth to genetically brighter children, who evoke more stimulation from their parents. This hypothesis, which refers to *genetic–environmental correlation* (see Chapter 2, page 73), is supported by research (Saudino & Plomin, 1997). But heredity does not account for all the association between home environment and mental test scores. Family living conditions continue to predict children's IQ beyond the contribution of parental IQ and education (Chase-Lansdale et al., 1997; Klebanov et al., 1998). In one study, infants and children growing up in less crowded homes had parents who were far more verbally responsive to them—a major contributor to language, intellectual, and academic progress (Evans, Maxwell, & Hart, 1999).

How can the research summarized so far help us understand Vanessa's concern about Timmy's development? Ben, the psychologist who tested Timmy, found that he scored only slightly below average. Ben talked with Vanessa about her child-rearing practices and watched her play with Timmy. A single parent, Vanessa worked long hours and had little energy for Timmy at the end of the day. Ben also noticed that Vanessa, anxious about how well Timmy was doing, tended to pressure him, dampening his active behavior and bombarding him with directions: "That's enough ball play. Stack these blocks."

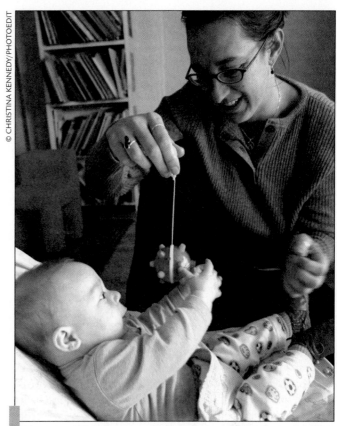

A mother talks affectionately while playing with her 6-month-old baby. Parental warmth, sensitive attention, and verbal communication contribute greatly to early language development.

Applying What We Know

Features of a High-Quality Home Life for Infants and Toddlers: The HOME Infant–Toddler Subscales

Home Subscale	Sample Item
Emotional and verbal responsiveness of the parent	Parent caresses or kisses child at least once during observer's visit.
	Parent spontaneously speaks to child twice or more (excluding scolding) during observer's visit.
Parental acceptance of the child	Parent does not interfere with child's actions or restrict child's movements more than three times during observer's visit.
Organization of the physical environment	Child's play environment appears safe and free of hazards.
Provision of appropriate play materials	Parent provides toys or interesting activities for child during observer's visit.
Parental involvement with the child	Parent tends to keep child within visual range and to look at child often during observer's visit.
Opportunities for variety in daily stimulation	Child eats at least one meal per day with mother and/or father, according to parental report.
	Child frequently has a chance to get out of house (for example, accompanies parent on trips to grocery store).

Source: Bradley, 1994; Bradley et al., 2001.

Ben explained that when parents are intrusive in these ways, infants and toddlers are likely to be distractible, play immaturely, and do poorly on mental tests (Bono & Stifter, 2003; Stilson & Harding, 1997). He coached Vanessa in how to interact sensitively with Timmy. At the same time, he assured her that Timmy's current performance need not forecast his future development. Warm, responsive parenting that builds on toddlers' current capacities is a much better indicator of how they will do later than early mental test scores.

■ **Infant and Toddler Child Care.** Today, more than 60 percent of North American mothers with a child under age 2 are employed (Statistics Canada, 2003g; U.S. Census Bureau, 2006b). Child care for infants and toddlers has become common, and its quality has a major impact on mental development. Research consistently shows that infants and young children exposed to poor-quality child care, regardless of whether they come from middle- or low-SES homes, score lower on measures of cognitive and social skills (Hausfather et al., 1997; Kohen et al., 2000; NICHD Early Child Care Research Network, 2000b, 2001, 2003b).

In contrast, good child care can reduce the negative impact of a stressed, poverty-stricken home life, and it sustains the benefits of growing up in an economically advantaged family (Lamb, 1998; NICHD Early Child Care Research Network, 2003b). In Swedish longitudinal research, entering high-quality child care in infancy and toddlerhood was associated with cognitive, emotional, and social competence in middle childhood and adolescence (Andersson, 1989, 1992; Broberg et al., 1997).

Visit some child-care settings and take notes on what you see. In contrast to most European countries and to Australia and New Zealand, where child care is nationally regulated and funded to ensure its quality, reports on U.S. and Canadian child care are cause for concern. Standards are set by the individual states and provinces and vary widely. In studies of child-care quality in each nation, only 20 to 25 percent of child-care centers and family child-care settings (in which a caregiver cares for children in her home) provided infants and toddlers with sufficiently positive, stimulating experiences to promote healthy psychological development; most settings offered substandard care (Doherty et al., 2000; Goelman et al., 2000; NICHD Early Childhood Research Network, 2000a). Unfortunately, children from low-income families are especially likely to have inadequate child care (Brooks-Gunn, 2004).

See Applying What We Know on the following page for signs of high-quality care that can be used in choosing a child-care setting for an infant or toddler, based on standards for **developmentally appropriate practice.** These standards, devised by the U.S. National Association for the Education of Young Children, specify program characteristics that meet the developmental and individual needs of young children, based on both current research and expert consensus. When child care meets these standards, children's learning opportunities and the warmth, sensitivity, and stability of their caregivers are especially high (Helburn, 1995).

Child care in the United States and Canada is affected by a macrosystem of individualistic values and weak government regulation and funding. Furthermore, many parents are unable to identify good care and do not demand it: They think that their children's child-care experiences are better than they really are (Helburn, 1995). In recent years, recognizing that child care is in a state of crisis, the U.S. and Canadian federal governments, and some states and provinces, have allocated additional funds to subsidize its cost, especially for low-income families. Though far from meeting the need, this increase in resources has had a positive impact on child-care quality and accessibility (Canada Campaign 2000, 2003a; Children's Defense Fund, 2005). In Canada, the province of Québec leads the nation with universal, good-quality child care for infants and preschoolers. Every Québec family pays the same minimal daily fee for government-supported services.

These developments are hopeful signs because good child care is a cost-effective means of protecting children's well-being. Much like the programs we are about to consider, excellent child care can also serve as effective early intervention for children whose development is at risk.

Early Intervention for At-Risk Infants and Toddlers

Many studies indicate that children living in poverty are likely to show gradual declines in intelligence test scores and to achieve poorly when they reach school age (Bradley et al., 2001; Gutman, Sameroff, & Cole, 2003). These problems are largely due to stressful home environments that undermine children's ability to learn and increase their likelihood of remaining poor throughout their lives. A variety of intervention programs have been developed to break this tragic cycle of

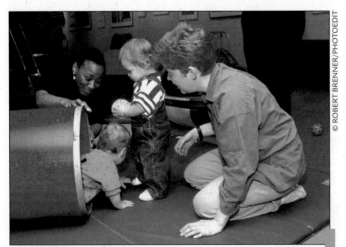

As child care for infants and toddlers has become common, the prevalence of poor-quality care is cause for concern. But a high-quality child-care setting like this one, where well-trained caregivers provide positive, developmentally appropriate stimulation, can be especially beneficial for children from low-SES homes.

Signs of Developmentally Appropriate Infant and Toddler Child Care

Applying What We Know

Program Characteristics	Signs of Quality
Physical setting	Indoor environment is clean, in good repair, well lighted, and well ventilated. Fenced outdoor play space is available. Setting does not appear overcrowded when children are present.
Toys and equipment	Play materials are appropriate for infants and toddlers and are stored on low shelves within easy reach. Cribs, highchairs, infant seats, and child-sized tables and chairs are available. Outdoor equipment includes small riding toys, swings, slide, and sandbox.
Caregiver–child ratio	In child-care centers, caregiver–child ratio is no greater than 1 to 3 for infants and 1 to 6 for toddlers. Group size (number of children in one room) is no greater than 6 infants with 2 caregivers and 12 toddlers with 2 caregivers. In family child care, caregiver is responsible for no more than 6 children; within this group, no more than 2 are infants and toddlers. Staffing is consistent, so infants and toddlers can form relationships with particular caregivers.
Daily activities	Daily schedule includes times for active play, quiet play, naps, snacks, and meals. It is flexible rather than rigid, to meet the needs of individual children. Atmosphere is warm and supportive, and children are never left unsupervised.
Interactions among adults and children	Caregivers respond promptly to infants' and toddlers' distress; hold, talk to, sing to, and read to them; and interact with them in a manner that respects the individual child's interests and tolerance for stimulation.
Caregiver qualifications	Caregiver has some training in child development, first aid, and safety.
Relationships with parents	Parents are welcome anytime. Caregivers talk frequently with parents about children's behavior and development.
Licensing and accreditation	Child-care setting, whether a center or a home, is licensed by the state or province. In the United States, voluntary accreditation by the National Academy of Early Childhood Programs (*www.naeyc.org/accreditation*) or the National Association for Family Child Care (*www.nafcc.org*) is evidence of an especially high-quality program. Canada is working on a voluntary accreditation system, under the leadership of the Canadian Child Care Federation (*www.cccf-fcsge.ca.*)

Sources: Bredekamp & Copple, 1997; National Association for the Education of Young Children, 1998.

poverty. Although most begin in the preschool years (we will discuss these in Chapter 7), a few start during infancy and continue through early childhood.

Some interventions are center-based: Children attend an organized child-care or preschool program where they receive educational, nutritional, and health services, and child-rearing and other social-service supports are provided to parents as well. In other, home-based interventions, a skilled adult visits the home and works with parents, teaching them how to stimulate their child's development. In most programs, participating children score higher than untreated controls on mental tests by age 2. And the earlier intervention begins and the longer it lasts, the better participants' cognitive and academic performance is throughout childhood and adolescence (Brooks-Gunn, 2003; Nelson, Westhues, & MacLeod, 2003).

The Carolina Abecedarian Project illustrates these favorable outcomes. In the 1970s, more than 100 infants from poverty-stricken families, ranging in age from 3 weeks to 3 months, were randomly assigned to either a treatment group or a control group. Treatment infants were enrolled in full-time, year-round child care through the preschool years. There they received stimulation aimed at promoting motor, cognitive, language, and social skills and, after age 3, prereading and math concepts. At all ages, special emphasis was placed on rich, responsive adult–child verbal communication. All children received nutrition and health services; the primary difference between treatment and controls was the child-care experience.

As Figure 5.9 on page 172 shows, by 12 months of age, the IQs of the two groups diverged, and the treatment group sustained its IQ advantage until last tested—at age 21. In addition, throughout their years of schooling, treatment youths achieved considerably better in reading and math. These gains translated into more years of schooling completed and higher rates of college enrollment and employment in skilled jobs (Campbell et al., 2001, 2002; Ramey & Ramey, 1999).

Without some form of early intervention, many children born into economically disadvantaged families will not reach their potential. Recognition of this reality led the U.S. Congress to provide limited funding for intervention directed at infants and toddlers at risk for developmental problems. *Early Head Start,* begun in 1995, currently has 700 sites serving 62,000

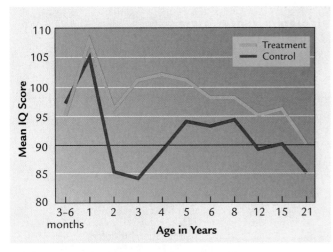

FIGURE 5.9 IQ scores of treatment and control children from infancy to 21 years in the Carolina Abecedarian Project. At 1 year, treatment children outperformed controls, an advantage consistently maintained through age 21. The IQ scores of both groups declined gradually during childhood and adolescence—a trend probably due to the damaging impact of poverty on mental development. (Adapted from Campbell et al., 2001.)

low-income families. A recent evaluation, conducted when children reached age 3, showed that intervention led to warmer, more stimulating parenting, a reduction in harsh discipline, gains in cognitive and language development, and lessening of child aggression. The strongest effects occurred at sites offering a mix of center- and home-based services (Love et al., 2005). Though not yet plentiful enough to meet the need, such programs are a promising beginning.

Ask Yourself

Review

What probably accounts for the finding that speed of habituation and recovery to novel visual stimuli are good predictors of later IQ?

Apply

Fifteen-month-old Joey's developmental quotient (DQ) is 115. His mother wants to know exactly what this means and what she should do to support his mental development. How would you respond?

Connect

Using what you learned about brain development in Chapter 4, explain why it is best to initiate intervention for poverty-stricken children in the first two years.

Reflect

Suppose you were seeking a child-care setting for your baby. What would you want it to be like, and why?

Language Development

As perception and cognition improve during infancy, they pave the way for an extraordinary human achievement—language. In Chapter 4, we saw that by the second half of the first year, infants make dramatic progress in distinguishing the basic sounds of their language and in segmenting the flow of speech in to word and phrase units. They also start to comprehend some word meanings and, around 12 months of age, say their first word. Sometime between 1½ and 2 years, toddlers combine two words (MacWhinney, 2005). By age 6, children have a vocabulary of about 10,000 words, speak in elaborate sentences, and are skilled conversationalists.

To appreciate this awesome task, think about the many abilities involved in your own flexible use of language. When you speak, you must select words that match the underlying concepts you want to convey. Next, you must pronounce words correctly, or you will not be understood. Then you must combine them into phrases and sentences using a complex set of grammatical rules. Finally, you must follow the rules of everyday conversation—for example, make comments relevant to what your partner just said and use an appropriate tone of voice.

How do infants and toddlers make such remarkable progress in getting these skills under way? To address this question, let's examine several prominent theories of language development.

Theories of Language Development

In the 1950s, researchers did not take seriously the idea that very young children might be able to figure out important properties of language. As a result, the first two theories of how children acquire language were extreme views. One, *behaviorism*, regards language development as entirely due to environmental influences. The second, *nativism*, assumes that children are "prewired" to master the intricate rules of their language.

■ **The Behaviorist Perspective.** Behaviorist B. F. Skinner (1957) proposed that language, like any other behavior, is acquired through *operant conditioning* (see Chapter 4, page 133). As the baby makes sounds, parents reinforce those that are most like words with smiles, hugs, and speech in return. For example, at 12 months, my older son, David, often babbled like this: "book-a-book-a-dook-a-dook-a-book-a-nook-a-book-aaa." One day while he babbled away, I held up his picture book and said, "Book!" Very soon, David was saying "book-aaa" in the presence of books.

Some behaviorists believe that children rely on *imitation* to rapidly acquire complex utterances, such as whole phrases and sentences (Moerk, 1992). Imitation can combine with reinforcement to promote language, as when a parent coaxes, "Say, 'I want a cookie,'" and delivers praise and a treat after the toddler responds, "Wanna cookie!"

Although reinforcement and imitation contribute to early language development, they are best viewed as supporting rather than fully explaining it. "It's amazing how creative Caitlin is with language," Carolyn remarked one day. "She combines words in ways she's never heard before, such as 'needle it' when she wants me to sew up her teddy bear and 'all-gone outside' when she has to come in."

Carolyn's observations are accurate: Young children create many novel utterances that are not reinforced by or copied from others. And when they do imitate others' language, they do so selectively, focusing mainly on building their vocabularies and on refining aspects of language that they are working on at the moment (Owens, 2005).

The Nativist Perspective. Linguist Noam Chomsky (1957) proposed a nativist theory that regards the young child's amazing language skill as etched into the structure of the human brain. Focusing on grammar, Chomsky reasoned that the rules of sentence organization are too complex to be directly taught to or discovered by even a cognitively adept young child. Instead, he argued, all children are born with a **language acquisition device (LAD),** an innate system that contains a set of rules common to all languages. It permits children, no matter which language they hear, to understand and speak in a rule-oriented fashion as soon as they pick up enough words.

Are children biologically primed to acquire language? Recall from Chapter 4 that newborn babies are remarkably sensitive to speech sounds and prefer to listen to the human voice. In addition, children the world over reach major language milestones in a similar sequence (Gleitman & Newport, 1996). Also, the ability to master a grammatically complex language system seems unique to humans, as efforts to teach language to nonhuman primates—using either specially devised artificial symbol systems or sign language—have met with limited success. Even after extensive training, chimpanzees (who are closest to humans in the evolutionary hierarchy) master only a basic vocabulary and short word combinations and produce these far less consistently than a human preschooler (Tomasello, Call, & Hare, 2003).

Furthermore, evidence that childhood is a *sensitive period* for language acquisition is consistent with Chomsky's idea of a biologically based language program. Researchers have examined the language competence of deaf adults who acquired their first language—American Sign Language (ASL), a gestural system used by the deaf—at different ages. The late learners, whose parents chose to educate them through speech and lip reading, did not acquire spoken language because of their profound deafness. Consistent with the sensitive period notion, those who learned ASL in adolescence or adulthood never became as proficient as those who learned in childhood (Mayberry, 1994; Newport, 1991; Singleton & Newport, 2004).

At the same time, challenges to Chomsky's theory suggest that it, too, provides only a partial account of language development. First, researchers have had great difficulty identifying the single system of grammar that Chomsky believes underlies all languages (Maratsos, 1998; Tomasello, 2003). Second, children do not acquire language quite as quickly as nativist theory

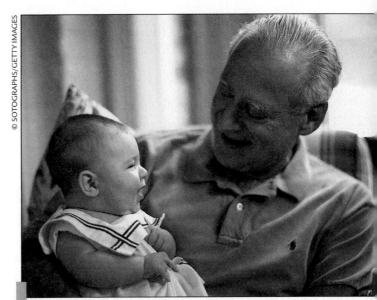

Infants are communicative beings from the start, as this interchange between a 6-month-old and his grandfather illustrates. How will this child accomplish the awesome task of becoming a fluent speaker of his native tongue within the next few years? Theorists disagree sharply on answers to this question.

suggests. Their progress in mastering many sentence constructions is not immediate but gradual, indicating more learning and discovery than Chomsky assumed (Tager-Flusberg, 2005).

Finally, recall from Chapter 4 that for most people, language is housed largely in the left hemisphere of the cerebral cortex, consistent with Chomsky's notion of a brain specialized from the start to process language. But our discussion also revealed that language areas in the cortex *develop* as children acquire language. And although the left hemisphere is biased for language processing, if it is injured in the first few years, other regions take over (see page 125 in Chapter 4). So localization of language in the left hemisphere is not necessary for effective language use. Furthermore, brain-imaging research shows that many regions of the cortex support language activities (Dick et al., 2004).

The Interactionist Perspective. In recent years, new ideas about language development have arisen, emphasizing *interactions* between inner capacities and environmental influences. One type of interactionist theory applies *the information-processing perspective* to language development. A second type emphasizes social interaction.

Some information-processing theorists assume that children make sense of their complex language environments by applying powerful cognitive capacities of a general kind (Bates, 1999; Elman, 2001). These theorists note that regions of the brain housing language also govern similar perceptual and cognitive abilities, such the capacity to analyze musical and visual patterns (Bates et al., 2003; Saygin et al., 2004). Other theorists blend this information-processing view with Chomsky's nativist perspective. They agree that infants are amazing analyzers of speech and other information. But, they

Table 5.3	Milestones of Language Development During the First Two Years

Approximate Age	Milestone
2 months	Infants coo, making pleasant vowel sounds.
4 months on	Infants babble, adding consonants to their cooing sounds and repeating syllables. By 7 months, babbling starts to include many sounds of spoken languages.
	Infants observe with interest as the caregiver plays turn-taking games, such as pat-a-cake and peekaboo.
8–12 months	Infants comprehend some words.
	Infants become more accurate at establishing joint attention with the caregiver, who often verbally labels what the baby is looking at.
	Infants actively participate in turn-taking games, trading roles with the caregiver.
	Infants use preverbal gestures, such as showing and pointing, to influence the behavior of others.
12 months	Babbling includes sound and intonation patterns of the child's language community.
	Toddlers say their first recognizable word.
18–24 months	Vocabulary expands from about 50 to 200 spoken words.
	Toddlers combine two words.

argue, these capacities probably are not sufficient to account for mastery of higher-level aspects of language, such as intricate grammatical structures (Newport & Aslin, 2000).

Still other interactionists emphasize that children's social skills and language experiences are centrally involved in language development. In this social interactionist view, an active child, well endowed for making sense of language, strives to communicate. In doing so, she cues her caregivers to provide appropriate language experiences, which help her relate the content and structure of language to its social meanings (Bohannon & Bonvillian, 2005; Chapman, 2000).

Among social interactionists, disagreement continues over whether or not children are equipped with specialized language abilities (Bloom, 1999; Tomasello, 2003). But as we chart the course of language development, we will encounter much support for their central premise—that children's social competencies and language experiences greatly affect their language progress. In reality, native endowment, cognitive-processing strategies, and social experience may operate in different balances with respect to each aspect of language. Table 5.3 provides an overview of early language milestones that we will take up in the next few sections.

Getting Ready to Talk

Before babies say their first word, they make impressive progress toward understanding and speaking their native tongue. They listen closely for meaningful speech units, and they make speechlike sounds. As adults, we can hardly help but respond.

■ **Cooing and Babbling.** Around 2 months, babies begin to make vowel-like noises, called **cooing** because of their pleasant "oo" quality. Gradually, consonants are added, and around 4 months, **babbling** appears, in which infants repeat consonant–vowel combinations in long strings, such as "babababa" or "nanananana."

Babies everywhere start babbling at about the same age and produce a similar range of early sounds. But for babbling to develop further, infants must be able to hear human speech. In hearing-impaired babies, these speechlike sounds are greatly delayed; in deaf infants, they are totally absent (Oller, 2000).

As infants listen to spoken language, babbling expands to include a broader range of sounds. At around 7 months, it starts to include many sounds of mature spoken languages. By 10 months, it reflects the sound and intonation patterns of infants' language community, some of which are transferred to their first words (Boysson-Bardies & Vihman, 1991).

Deaf infants exposed to sign language from birth babble with their hands much as hearing infants do through speech (Petitto & Marentette, 1991). Furthermore, hearing babies of deaf, signing parents produce babblelike hand motions with the rhythmic patterns of natural sign languages (Petitto et al., 2001, 2004). This sensitivity to language rhythm—evident in both spoken and signed babbling—supports both discovery and production of meaningful language units.

■ **Becoming a Communicator.** At birth, infants are prepared for some aspects of conversational behavior. For example, they initiate interaction through eye contact and terminate it by looking away. Around 4 months, infants start to display **joint attention,** gazing in the same direction adults are looking, a skill that becomes more accurate around 10 to 11 months as babies realize that others' focus provides information about their communicative intentions (Brooks & Meltzoff, 2005).

Adults also follow the baby's line of vision and comment on what the infant sees, labeling the baby's environment. Infants and toddlers who often experience this *joint attention* comprehend more language, produce meaningful gestures and words earlier, and show faster vocabulary development (Carpenter, Nagell, & Tomasello, 1998; Flom & Pick, 2003; Silvén, 2001).

Around 4 to 6 months, interaction between parent and baby begins to include *give-and-take,* as in pat-a-cake and peekaboo games. At first, the parent starts the game, and the baby is an amused observer. But even 4-month-olds are sensitive to the structure and timing of these interactions, smiling more to an organized than a disorganized peekaboo exchange (Rochat, Querido, & Striano, 1999). By 12 months, babies participate actively, trading roles with the parent. As they do so, they practice the turn-taking pattern of conversation, a vital context for acquiring language and communication skills. Infants' play maturity and vocalizations during games predict advanced language progress in the second year (Rome-Flanders & Cronk, 1995).

At the end of the first year, as infants become capable of intentional behavior, they use *preverbal gestures* to influence the behavior of others (Carpenter, Nagell, & Tomasello, 1998). For example, Caitlin held up a toy to show it and pointed to the cupboard when she wanted a cookie. Carolyn responded to her gestures and also labeled them ("Oh, you want a cookie!"). In this way, toddlers learn that using language leads to desired results. Soon they integrate words with gestures, using the gesture to expand their verbal message, as in pointing to a toy

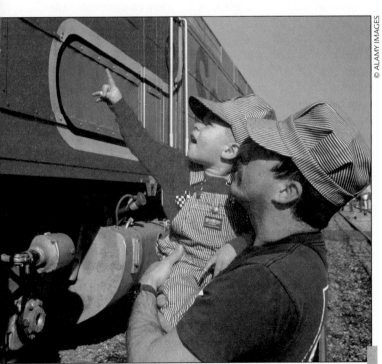

This 1-year-old baby uses a preverbal gesture to draw his father's attention to the train. His father's verbal response promotes the baby's transition to spoken language.

while saying "give" (Namy & Waxman, 1998). Gradually, gestures recede, and words become dominant. Nevertheless, the earlier toddlers produce these word–gesture combinations, the sooner they combine words later in the second year (Goldin-Meadow & Butcher, 2003).

First Words

In the second half of the first year, infants begin to understand word meanings. When 6-month-olds listened to the word "Mommy" or "Daddy" while looking at side-by-side videos of their parents, they looked longer at the video of the named parent (Tincoff & Jusczyk, 1999). First spoken words, around 1 year, build on the sensorimotor foundations Piaget described and on categories children form during their first 2 years. Usually they refer to important people ("Mama," "Dada"), animals ("doggie," "kitty,"), objects that move ("car," "ball,"), foods ("milk," "apple"), familiar actions ("bye-bye," "more"), or outcomes of familiar actions ("wet," "hot") (Hart, 2004; Nelson, 1973). In their first 50 words, toddlers rarely name things that just *sit there,* like "table" or "vase."

Some early words are linked to specific cognitive achievements. For example, about the time toddlers master advanced object permanence problems, they use disappearance words ("all gone"). And success and failure expressions ("There!" "Uh-oh!") appear when toddlers can solve sensorimotor problems suddenly (Gopnik & Meltzoff, 1986).

Besides cognition, emotion influences early word learning. At first, when acquiring a new word, 1½-year-olds say it neutrally. To learn, they need to listen carefully, and strong emotion would divert their attention. But as words become better learned, toddlers integrate talking and expressing feelings (Bloom, 1998). "Shoe!" said one enthusiastic 22-month-old as her mother tied her shoelaces before an outing. At the end of the second year, children begin to label their emotions, using words like "happy," "mad," and "sad."

When toddlers first learn words, they sometimes apply them too narrowly, an error called **underextension.** For example, at 16 months, Caitlin used "bear" to refer only to the worn and tattered bear that she carried around much of the day. A more common error is **overextension**—applying a word to a wider collection of objects and events than is appropriate. For example, Grace used "car" for buses, trains, trucks, and fire engines. Toddlers' overextensions reflect their sensitivity to categories. They apply a new word to a group of similar experiences: "car" to wheeled objects, "open" to opening a door, peeling fruit, and undoing shoelaces. This suggests that children sometimes overextend deliberately because they have difficulty recalling or have not acquired a suitable word (Bloom, 2000). As their vocabularies enlarge, overextensions disappear.

Overextensions illustrate another important feature of language development: the distinction between language *production* (the words children use) and language *comprehension* (the words they understand). At all ages, comprehension develops ahead of production. As a result, children overextend many more words in production than they do in comprehension. A 2-year-old who refers to trucks, trains, and bikes as "car" may look at or point to these objects correctly when given their names (Naigles & Gelman, 1995). Failure to say a word does not mean that toddlers do not understand it. If we rely only on what children say, we will underestimate their knowledge of language.

The Two-Word Utterance Phase

Young toddlers add to their vocabularies at a rate of 1 to 3 words per week. Gradually, the number of words learned accelerates (Caselli et al., 1995). Because rate of word learning between 18 and 24 months is so impressive (1 or 2 words per day), many researchers concluded that toddlers undergo a spurt in vocabulary—a transition between a slower and faster learning phase. Recent evidence, however, indicates that most show a steady, continuous increase in rate of word learning that persists through the preschool years (Ganger & Brent, 2004).

How do toddlers build their vocabularies so quickly? In the second year, they improve in ability to categorize experience, to remember words, and to grasp others' intentions, which helps them figure out what others are talking about (Dapretto & Bjork, 2000; Gershoff-Stowe & Smith, 1997; Tomasello, 2003). In Chapter 7, we will consider young children's specific strategies for word learning.

Once toddlers produce about 200 words, they start to combine two words: "Mommy shoe," "go car," "more cookie." These two-word utterances are called **telegraphic speech** because, like a telegram, they leave out smaller and less important words. Children the world over use them to express an impressive variety of meanings.

Two-word speech consists largely of simple formulas, such as "more + *X*" and "eat + *X*," with different words inserted in the *X* position. Toddlers rarely make gross grammatical errors, such as saying "chair my" instead of "my chair." But their word-order regularities are usually copies of adult word pairings, as when the parent says, "How about *more sandwich?*" or "Let's see if you can *eat the berries*" (Tomasello & Brooks, 1999). As we will see in Chapter 7, children acquire word-order and other basic grammatical rules steadily over the preschool years.

Individual and Cultural Differences

Although, on average, children produce their first word around their first birthday, the range is large, from 8 to 18 months—variation that results from a complex blend of genetic and environmental influences. For example, earlier we saw that Timmy's spoken language was delayed, in part because of Vanessa's tense, directive communication with him. But Timmy is also a boy, and many studies show that girls are slightly ahead of boys in early vocabulary growth (Fenson et al., 1994). The most common explanation is girls' faster rate of physical maturation, believed to promote earlier development of the left cerebral hemisphere. The child's personality makes a differ-

ence, too. Shy toddlers often wait until they understand a great deal before trying to speak. When they finally do speak, their vocabularies increase rapidly, although they remain slightly behind their agemates (Spere et al., 2004).

The surrounding environment also plays a role: The more words caregivers use, the more children learn (Weizman & Snow, 2001). Mothers talk much more to toddler-age girls than to boys, and parents converse less often with shy than with sociable children (Leaper, Anderson, & Sanders, 1998; Patterson & Fisher, 2002). Because low-SES children receive less verbal stimulation in their homes than higher-SES children, their vocabularies are usually smaller (Hoff, 2004). Limited parent–child book reading contributes greatly this difference. On average, a middle-SES child is read to for 1,000 hours between 1 and 5 years, a low-SES child for only 25 hours (Neuman, 2003). As a result, the vocabularies of low-SES kindergartners are only one-fourth as large as their higher SES agemates' (Lee & Burkam, 2002).

Young children have unique styles of early language learning. Caitlin and Grace, like most toddlers, used a **referential style;** their vocabularies consisted mainly of words that referred to objects. A smaller number of toddlers use an **expressive style;** compared with referential children, they produce many more pronouns and social formulas: "Stop it," "Thank you," "I want it." These styles reflect early ideas about the functions of language. Grace, for example, thought words were for naming things. In contrast, expressive-style children believe words are for talking about people's feelings and needs. The vocabularies of referential-style toddlers grow faster because all languages contain many more object labels than social phrases (Bates et al., 1994).

What accounts for a toddler's language style? Rapidly developing referential-style children often have an especially active interest in exploring objects. They also eagerly imitate their parents' frequent naming of objects, and their parents imitate back—a strategy that supports swift vocabulary growth by helping children remember new labels (Masur & Rodemaker, 1999). Expressive-style children tend to be highly sociable, and their parents more often use verbal routines ("How are you?" "It's no trouble") that support social relationships (Goldfield, 1987). The two language styles are also linked to culture. Whereas object words (nouns) are particularly common in the vocabularies of English-speaking toddlers, action words (verbs) are more numerous among Chinese and Korean toddlers. When mothers' speech is examined, it reflects these differences (Choi & Gopnik, 1995; Tardif, Gelman, & Xu, 1999).

At what point should parents be concerned if their child does not talk or says very little? If a toddler's language is greatly delayed when compared with the norms in Table 5.3 (page 174), then parents should consult the child's doctor or a speech and language therapist. Late babbling may be a sign of slow language development that can be prevented with early intervention (Oller et al., 1999). Some toddlers who do not follow simple directions or who, after age 2, have difficulty putting their thoughts into words may suffer from a hearing impairment or a language disorder that requires immediate treatment.

This mother speaks to her baby in short, clearly pronounced sentences with high-pitched, exaggerated intonation. The use of this child-directed speech, common in many cultures, eases early language learning.

Supporting Early Language Development

Consistent with the interactionist view, a rich social environment builds on young children's natural readiness to acquire language. For a summary of how caregivers can consciously support early language development, see Applying What We Know below. Caregivers also do so unconsciously—through a special style of speech.

Adults in many cultures speak to young children in **child-directed speech (CDS),** a form of communication made up of short sentences with high-pitched, exaggerated expression, clear pronunciation, distinct pauses between speech segments, and repetition of new words in a variety of contexts ("See the ball," "The ball bounced!") (Fernald et al., 1989; Kuhl, 2000). Deaf parents use a similar style of communication when signing to their deaf babies (Masataka, 1996). CDS builds on several communicative strategies we have already considered: joint attention, turn-taking, and caregivers' sensitivity to children's preverbal gestures. Here is an example of Carolyn using CDS with 18-month-old Caitlin:

Caitlin: "Go car."

Carolyn: "Yes, time to go in the car. Where's your jacket?"

Caitlin: *[Looks around, walks to the closet.]* "Dacket!" *[Pointing to her jacket]*

Carolyn: "There's that jacket! *[She helps Caitlin into the jacket.]* On it goes! Let's zip up. *[Zips up the jacket.]* Now, say bye-bye to Grace and Timmy."

Caitlin: "Bye-bye, G-ace."

Carolyn: "What about Timmy? Bye to Timmy?"

Caitlin: "Bye-bye, Te-te."

Carolyn: "Where's your bear?"

Caitlin: *[Looks around.]*

Carolyn: *[Pointing]* "See? Go get the bear. By the sofa." *[Caitlin gets the bear.]*

From birth on, infants prefer to listen to CDS over other adult talk, and by 5 months they are more emotionally responsive to it (Aslin, Jusczyk, & Pisoni, 1998). And parents constantly fine-tune the length and content of their utterances to fit their children's needs—adjustments that foster word learning and enable toddlers to join in (Cameron-Faulkner, Lieven, & Tomasello, 2003). As we saw earlier, parent–toddler conversation—especially, reading and talking about picture books—strongly predicts language development and academic

Supporting Early Language Learning

Applying What We Know

Strategy	Consequence
Respond to coos and babbles with speech sounds and words.	Encourages experimentation with sounds that can later be blended into first words. Provides experience with turn-taking pattern of human conversation.
Establish joint attention and comment on what child sees.	Predicts earlier onset of language and faster vocabulary development.
Play social games, such as pat-a-cake and peekaboo.	Provides experience with the turn-taking pattern of human conversation.
Engage toddlers in joint make-believe play.	Promotes all aspects of conversational dialogue.
Engage toddlers in frequent conversations.	Predicts faster early language development and academic success during the school years.
Read to toddlers often, engaging them in dialogues about picture books.	Provides exposure to many aspects of language, including vocabulary, grammar, communication skills, and information about written symbols and story structures.

Biology and Environment

Parent–Child Interaction: Impact on Language and Cognitive Development of Deaf Children

About one in every 1,000 North American infants is born profoundly or fully deaf (Deafness Research Foundation, 2005). When a deaf child cannot participate fully in communication with caregivers, development is severely compromised. Yet the consequences of deafness for children's language and cognition vary with social context, as comparisons of deaf children of hearing parents with deaf children of deaf parents reveal.

Over 90 percent of deaf children have hearing parents who are not fluent in sign language. In toddlerhood and early childhood, these children often are delayed in development of language and make-believe play. In middle childhood, many achieve poorly in school and are deficient in social skills. Yet deaf children of deaf parents escape these difficulties! Their language (use of sign) and play maturity are on a par with hearing children's. After school entry, deaf children of deaf parents learn easily and get along well with adults and peers (Bornstein et al., 1999; Spencer & Lederberg, 1997).

These differences can be traced to early parent–child communication. Beginning in infancy, hearing parents of deaf children are less positive, less responsive to the child's efforts to communicate, less effective at achieving joint attention and turn-taking, less involved in play, and more directive and intrusive (Spencer, 2000; Spencer & Meadow-Orlans, 1996). In contrast, the quality of interaction between deaf children and deaf parents is similar to that of hearing children and hearing parents.

Children with limited and less sensitive parental communication lag behind their agemates in achieving verbal control over their behavior—in thinking before they act and in planning. Deaf children of hearing parents frequently display impulse-control problems (Arnold, 1999).

Hearing parents are not at fault for their deaf child's problems. Rather, they lack experience with visual communication, which enables deaf parents to respond readily to a deaf child's needs. Deaf parents know they must wait for the child to turn toward them before interacting (Loots & Devise, 2003). Hearing parents tend to speak or gesture while the child's attention is directed elsewhere—a strategy that works with a hearing but not with a deaf partner. When the child is confused or unresponsive, hearing parents often feel overwhelmed and become overly controlling (Jamieson, 1995).

The impact of deafness on language and cognitive development can best be understood by considering its impact on parents and other significant people in the child's life. Deaf children need access to language models—deaf adults and peers—to experience natural language learning. And their hearing parents benefit from social support along with training in how to interact sensitively with a nonhearing partner.

On average, deafness is not diagnosed until age 2½. Yet a prenatal diagnostic test can identify inherited deafness (Santoro et al., 2003). Other screening techniques can identify deaf babies shortly after birth, enabling immediate enrollment in programs aimed at fostering effective parent–child interaction. When children with profound hearing loss are identified and start to receive intervention within the first year of life, they show much better language, cognitive, and social development (Yoshinaga-Itano, 2003).

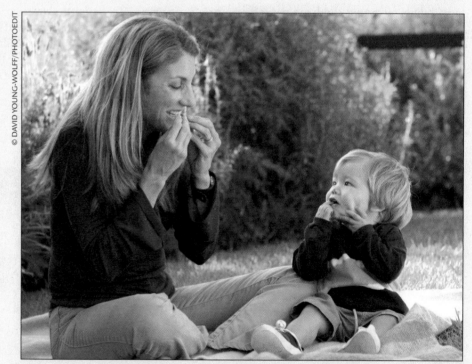

© DAVID YOUNG-WOLFF/PHOTOEDIT

When this mother signs "eat" to her 11-month-old child, who is deaf, he responds with babblelike hand motions, similar to the babbling that hearing infants do through speech. This "babbling" supports his production of meaningful language.

success during the school years. And as the Biology and Environment box on the previous page makes clear, when a child's disability makes it difficult for parents to engage in the sensitive communication of CDS, language and cognitive development are drastically delayed.

Do social experiences that promote language development remind you of those that strengthen cognitive development in general? CDS and parent–child conversation create a *zone of proximal development* in which children's language skills expand. In contrast, impatience with and rejection of children's efforts to talk lead them to stop trying and result in immature language skills (Baumwell, Tamis-LeMonda, & Bornstein, 1997). In the next chapter, we will see that sensitivity to children's needs and capacities supports their emotional and social development as well.

Ask Yourself

Review

Why is the social interactionist perspective attractive to many investigators of language development? Cite evidence that supports it.

Apply

Prepare a list of research-based recommendations for supporting language development during the first two years.

Connect

Cognition and language are interrelated. List examples of how cognition fosters language development. Next, list examples of how language fosters cognitive development.

Reflect

Find an opportunity to speak to an infant or toddler. How did your manner of speaking differ from the way you typically speak to an adult? What features of your speech are likely to promote early language development, and why?

www.ablongman.com/berk

Summary

Piaget's Cognitive-Developmental Theory

According to Piaget, how do schemes change over the course of development?

■ In Piaget's theory, by acting directly on the environment, children move through four stages in which psychological structures, or **schemes,** achieve a better fit with external reality.

■ Schemes change in two ways: through **adaptation,** which is made up of two complementary activities—**assimilation** and **accommodation**—and through **organization,** the internal rearrangement of schemes into a strongly interconnected cognitive system.

Describe the major cognitive achievements of the sensorimotor stage.

■ Piaget's **sensorimotor stage** is divided into six substages. Through the **circular reaction,** the newborn baby's reflexes are gradually transformed into the more flexible action patterns of the older infant. During Substage 4, infants develop **intentional,**

© SPENCER GRANT/PHOTOEDIT

or **goal-directed, behavior** and begin to understand **object permanence.** By Substage 6, toddlers become capable of **mental representation,** as seen in sudden solutions to sensorimotor problems, mastery of object permanence problems involving invisible displacement, **deferred imitation,** and **make-believe play.**

What does recent research reveal about the accuracy of Piaget's sensorimotor stage?

■ Many studies suggest that infants display certain understandings earlier than Piaget believed. Some awareness of object permanence, as revealed by the **violation-of-expectation method,** may be evident in the first few months. In addition, young infants display deferred imitation and analogical problem solving, which suggests that they are capable of mental representation in the first year.

■ Today, researchers believe that newborns have more built-in equipment for making sense of their world than Piaget assumed, although they disagree on how much initial understanding infants have. According to the **core knowledge perspective,** infants begin life with core domains of thought that support early, rapid cognitive development. Although findings on early, ready-made knowledge are mixed, there is broad agreement that many cognitive changes of infancy are continuous rather than stagelike and that various aspects of cognition develop unevenly rather than in an integrated fashion.

Information Processing

Describe the information-processing view of cognitive development and the general structure of the information-processing system.

■ Information-processing researchers regard development as gradual and continuous and study many aspects of thinking. They want to know exactly what individuals of different ages do when faced with a task or problem.

■ Most information-processing researchers assume that we hold information in three parts of the system, the **sensory register; working,** or **short-term, memory;** and **long-term memory.** As information flows through the system, **mental strategies** operate on it so that it can be retained and used efficiently. To manage the complex activities of working memory, the **central executive** directs the flow of information.

What changes in attention, memory, and categorization take place during the first 2 years?

■ With age, infants attend to more aspects of the environment and take information in more quickly. In the second year, attention to novelty declines and sustained attention improves, especially during play with toys.

■ Young infants are capable of **recognition** memory; by the end of the first year, they can **recall** past events. Both brain development and social experience probably contribute to the end of **infantile amnesia** and the emergence of **autobiographical memory.**

■ During the first year, infants group stimuli into increasingly complex categories, and categorization shifts from a *perceptual* to a *conceptual* basis. By the second year, children become active categorizers, spontaneously sorting objects during play.

Describe contributions and limitations of the information-processing approach to our understanding of early cognitive development.

■ Information-processing findings challenge Piaget's view of babies as purely sensorimotor beings who cannot mentally represent experiences. But information processing has not yet provided a broad, comprehensive theory of children's thinking.

The Social Context of Early Cognitive Development

How does Vygotsky's concept of the zone of proximal development expand our understanding of early cognitive development?

■ According to Vygotsky's sociocultural theory, complex mental activities originate in social interaction. Through the support and guidance of more skilled partners, infants

master tasks within the **zone of proximal development**—that is, tasks just ahead of their current capacities. As early as the first year, cultural variations in social experiences affect mental strategies.

Individual Differences in Early Mental Development

Describe the mental testing approach, the meaning of intelligence test scores, and the extent to which infant tests predict later performance.

■ The mental testing approach measures intellectual development in an effort to predict future performance. Scores are arrived at by computing an **intelligence quotients (IQ).** It compares an individual's test performance with that of a **standardization sample** of same-age individuals, which forms a **normal,** or bell-shaped, **distribution.** IQ is higher or lower, depending on how much the test-taker's performance deviates from the mean of the standardization sample.

■ Infant tests, which consist largely of perceptual and motor responses, predict later intelligence poorly. As a result, scores on infant tests are called **developmental quotients,** or **DQs,** rather than IQs. Speed of habituation and recovery to visual stimuli are better predictors of future performance.

Discuss environmental influences on early mental development, including home, child care, and early intervention for at-risk infants and toddlers.

■ Research with the **Home Observation for Measurement of the Environment (HOME)** shows that an organized, stimulating home environment and parental encouragement, involvement, and affection repeatedly predict early mental test scores. Although the HOME–IQ relationship is partly due to heredity, family living conditions also affect mental development.

■ Infant and toddler child care is increasingly common, and its quality has a major impact on mental development. Standards for **developmentally appropriate practice** specify program characteristics that meet young children's developmental needs.

■ Intensive early intervention can prevent the gradual declines in intelligence and poor academic performance seen in many poverty-stricken children. Findings of the Carolina Abecedarian Project reveal an IQ advantage still evident at age 21, along with better school achievement, which translated into higher educational attainment and skilled employment rates for the treatment group than the control group.

Language Development

Describe theories of language development, and indicate how much emphasis each places on innate abilities and environmental influences.

■ According to the *behaviorist* perspective, parents train children in language skills through operant conditioning and imitation. Behaviorism, however, has difficulty accounting for children's novel utterances.

■ In contrast, Chomsky's *nativist* view regards children as naturally endowed with a **language acquisition device (LAD).** Although evidence that mastery of a complex language system is unique to humans and that childhood is a *sensitive period* for language acquisition is supportive, Chomsky's theory provides only a partial account of language development.

■ Recent theories suggest that language development results from *interactions* between inner capacities and environmental influences. Some interactionists apply the information-processing perspective to language development. Others emphasize the importance of children's social skills and language experiences.

Describe major language milestones in the first two years, individual differences, and ways adults can support early language development.

■ Infants begin **cooing** at 2 months and **babbling** at around 4 months. Around 10 to 11 months, their skill at establishing **joint attention** improves. Adults can encourage language progress by responding to infants' coos and babbles, establishing joint attention and labeling what babies see, playing turn-taking games, and acknowledging infants' preverbal gestures.

■ In the second half of the first year, infants begin to understand word meanings. At the end of the first year, they use *preverbal gestures,* such as pointing, to influence others' behavior.

■ Around 12 months, toddlers say their first word. Young children often make errors of **underextension** and **overextension.** Rate of word learning increases steadily, and once vocabulary reaches about 200 words, two-word utterances called **telegraphic speech** appear. At all ages, language *comprehension* is ahead of *production.*

■ Individual and cultural differences in early language development exist. Girls show faster progress than boys, and reserved, cautious toddlers may wait before trying to speak. Most toddlers use a **referential style** of language learning; their early words consist largely of names for objects. A few use an **expressive style,** in which pronouns and social formulas are common and vocabulary grows more slowly.

■ Adults in many cultures speak to young children in **child-directed speech (CDS),** a simplified form of language that is well suited to their learning needs. Conversation between parent and toddler is one of the best predictors of early language development and academic success during the school years.

Important Terms and Concepts

accommodation (p. 152)

adaptation (p. 152)

assimilation (p. 152)

autobiographical memory (p. 163)

babbling (p. 174)

central executive (p. 160)

child-directed speech (CDS) (p. 177)

circular reaction (p. 153)

cooing (p. 174)

core knowledge perspective (p. 158)

deferred imitation (p. 155)

developmental quotient, or DQ (p. 168)

developmentally appropriate practice
    (p. 170)

expressive style of language learning
    (p. 176)

Home Observation for Measurement of
    the Environment (HOME) (p. 168)

infantile amnesia (p. 163)

intelligence quotient, or IQ (p. 168)

intentional, or goal-directed, behavior
    (p. 154)

joint attention (p. 174)

language acquisition device (LAD)
    (p. 173)

long-term memory (p. 160)

make-believe play (p. 155)

mental representation (p. 154)

mental strategies (p. 160)

normal distribution (p. 168)

object permanence (p. 154)

organization (p. 152)

overextension (p. 175)

recall (p. 162)

recognition (p. 162)

referential style of language learning
    (p. 176)

scheme (p. 152)

sensorimotor stage (p. 152)

sensory register (p. 160)

standardization (p. 168)

telegraphic speech (p. 176)

underextension (p. 175)

violation-of-expectation method
    (p. 155)

working, or short-term, memory
    (p. 160)

zone of proximal development (p. 165)

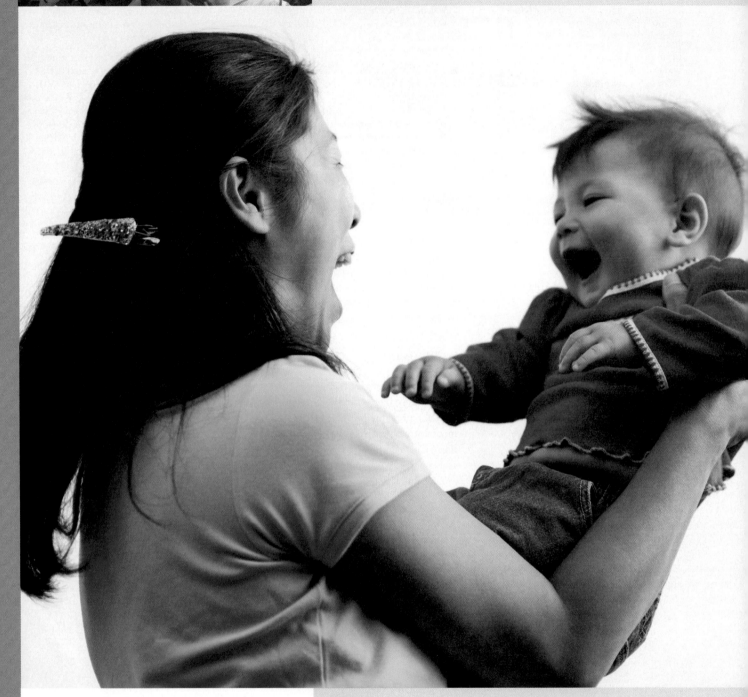

*T*his mother and infant gaze at each other with mutual delight, suggesting that they have formed a deeply affectionate bond. The baby's sense of trust in his caregivers is fundamental to all aspects of early development.

Emotional and Social Development in Infancy and Toddlerhood

As Caitlin reached 8 months of age, her parents noticed that she had become more fearful. One evening, when Carolyn and David left her with a babysitter, she wailed when they headed for the door—an experience she had accepted easily a few weeks earlier. Caitlin and Timmy's caregiver Ginette also observed an increasing wariness of strangers. When Ginette turned to go to another room, both babies dropped their play to crawl after her. And a knock at the door from the mail carrier prompted them to cling to Ginette's legs and reach out to be picked up.

© GAVIN HELLIER/NATURE PICTURE LIBRARY

At the same time, each baby seemed more willful. Removing an object from the hand produced little response at 5 months, but at 8 months Timmy resisted when his mother, Vanessa, took away a table knife he had managed to reach. He burst into angry screams and could not be consoled by the toys she offered in its place.

Monica and Kevin knew little about Grace's development during her first year, except that she had been deeply loved by her destitute, homeless mother. Separation from her, followed by a long journey to an unfamiliar home, had left Grace in shock. At first she was extremely sad, turning away when Monica or Kevin picked her up. She did not smile for over a week.

But as Grace's new parents held her close, spoke gently, and satisfied her craving for food, Grace returned their affection. Two weeks after her arrival, her despondency gave way to a sunny, easygoing disposition. She burst into a wide grin, reached out at the sight of Monica and Kevin, and laughed at her brother Eli's funny faces. As her second birthday approached, she pointed to herself, exclaiming "Gwace!" and laid claim to treasured possessions. "Gwace's chicken!" she would announce at mealtimes, sucking the marrow from the drumstick, a practice she brought with her from Cambodia.

Taken together, Caitlin's, Timmy's, and Grace's reactions reflect two related aspects of personality development during the first two years: close ties to others and a sense of self. We begin with Erikson's psychosocial theory, which provides an overview of personality development during infancy and toddlerhood. Then we chart the course of emotional development. As we do so, we will discover why fear and anger became more apparent in Caitlin's and Timmy's range of emotions by the end of the first year. Our attention then turns to individual differences in temperament. We will examine biological and environmental contributions to these differences and their consequences for future development.

Next, we take up attachment to the caregiver, the child's first affectionate tie. We will see how the feelings of security that grow out of this important bond provide support for the child's sense of independence and expanding social relationships.

Finally, we focus on early self-development. By the end of toddlerhood, Grace recognized herself in mirrors and photographs, labeled herself as a girl, and showed the beginnings of self-control. "Don't touch!" she instructed herself one day as she resisted the desire to pull a lamp cord out of its socket. Cognitive advances combine with social experiences to produce these changes during the second year.

Erikson's Theory of Infant and Toddler Personality

Our discussion of major theories in Chapter 1 revealed that psychoanalytic theory is no longer in the mainstream of human development research. But one of its lasting contributions is its ability to capture the essence of personality during each period of development. Recall that Sigmund Freud, founder of the psychoanalytic movement, believed that psychological health and maladjustment could be traced to the early years—in particular, to the quality of the child's relationships with parents. Although Freud's preoccupation with the channeling of instincts and his neglect of important experiences beyond infancy and early childhood came to be heavily criticized, the basic outlines of his theory were accepted and elaborated in several subsequent theories. The leader of these neo-Freudian perspectives is Erik Erikson's *psychosocial theory*, also introduced in Chapter 1.

Basic Trust versus Mistrust

Erikson accepted Freud's emphasis on the importance of the parent–infant relationship during feeding, but he expanded and enriched Freud's view. A healthy outcome during infancy, Erikson believed, does not depend on the *amount* of food or oral stimulation offered but rather on the *quality* of caregiving: relieving discomfort promptly and sensitively, holding the infant gently, waiting patiently until the baby has had enough milk, and weaning when the infant shows less interest in breast or bottle.

Erikson recognized that no parent can be perfectly in tune with the baby's needs. Many factors affect parental responsiveness—feelings of personal happiness, current life conditions (for example, additional young children in the family), and culturally valued child-rearing practices. But when the *balance of care* is sympathetic and loving, the psychological conflict of the first year—**basic trust versus mistrust**—is resolved on the positive side. The trusting infant expects the world to be good and gratifying, so he feels confident about venturing out and exploring it. The mistrustful baby cannot count on the kindness and compassion of others, so she protects herself by withdrawing from people and things around her.

Autonomy versus Shame and Doubt

With the transition to toddlerhood, Freud viewed toilet training as decisive for psychological health. Although Erikson agreed that the parent's manner of toilet training is important, he viewed it as only one of many influential experiences. The familiar refrains of newly walking, talking toddlers—"No!" "Do it myself!"—reveal that they have entered a period of budding selfhood. They want to decide for themselves not just in toileting but also in other situations. The conflict of toddlerhood, **autonomy versus shame and doubt,** is resolved favorably when parents provide young children with suitable guidance and reasonable choices. A self-confident, secure 2-year-old has been encouraged not only to use the toilet but also to eat with a spoon and to help pick up his toys. His parents do not criticize or attack him when he fails at these new skills. And they meet his assertions of independence with tolerance and understanding. For example, before leaving for the grocery store, they give him an extra five minutes to finish his play and wait patiently while he tries to zip his jacket.

According to Erikson, the parent who is over- or undercontrolling in toileting is likely to be so in other aspects of the toddler's life as well. The outcome is a child who feels forced and shamed or who doubts his ability to control his impulses and act competently on his own.

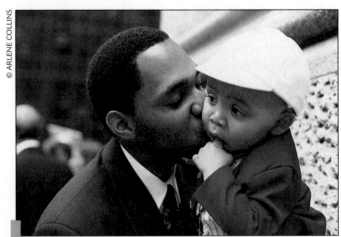

© ARLENE COLLINS

According to Erikson, basic trust grows out of the quality of the early caregiving relationship. A parent who relieves the baby's discomfort promptly and holds the baby tenderly, during feeding and at other times, promotes basic trust—the feeling that the world is good and gratifying.

In sum, basic trust and autonomy grow out of warm, sensitive parenting and reasonable expectations for impulse control starting in the second year. If children emerge from the first few years without sufficient trust in caregivers and without a healthy sense of individuality, the seeds are sown for adjustment problems. Adults who have difficulty establishing intimate ties, who are overly dependent on a loved one, or who continually doubt their own ability to meet new challenges may not have fully mastered the tasks of trust and autonomy during infancy and toddlerhood.

Emotional Development

Observe several infants and toddlers, noting the emotions each displays, the cues you rely on to interpret the baby's emotional state, and how caregivers respond. Researchers have conducted many such observations to find out how babies convey their emotions and interpret those of others. They have discovered that emotions play powerful roles in organizing the attainments that Erikson regarded as so important: social relationships, exploration of the environment, and discovery of the self (Frijda, 2000; Halle, 2003; Saarni, Mumme, & Campos, 1998).

Because infants cannot describe their feelings, determining exactly which emotions they are experiencing is a challenge. Although vocalizations and body movements provide some information, facial expressions offer the most reliable cues. Cross-cultural evidence reveals that people around the world associate photographs of different facial expressions with emotions in the same way (Ekman, 2003; Ekman & Friesen, 1972). These findings, which suggest that emotional expressions are built-in social signals, inspired researchers to analyze infants' facial patterns to determine the range of emotions they display at different ages.

Development of Some Basic Emotions

Basic emotions—happiness, interest, surprise, fear, anger, sadness, and disgust—are universal in humans and other primates, have a long evolutionary history of promoting survival, and can be directly inferred from facial expressions. Do infants come into the world with the ability to express basic emotions? Although signs of some emotions are present, babies' earliest emotional life consists of little more than two global arousal states: attraction to pleasant stimulation and withdrawal from unpleasant stimulation. Only gradually do emotions become clear, well-organized signals (Camras et al., 2003; Fox, 1991).

According to one view, sensitive, contingent caregiver communication, in which parents selectively mirror aspects of the baby's diffuse emotional behavior, helps infants construct discrete emotional expressions that more closely resemble those of adults (Gergely & Watson, 1999). Around 6 months, face, voice, and posture form well-organized signals that vary meaningfully with environmental events. For example, Caitlin typically responded to her parents' playful interaction with a joyful face, pleasant cooing, and a relaxed posture, as if to say, "This is fun!" In contrast, an unresponsive parent often evokes a sad face, fussy vocalizations, and a drooping body (sending the message, "I'm despondent") or an angry face, crying, and "pick-me-up" gestures (as if to say, "Change this unpleasant event!") (Weinberg & Tronick, 1994; Yale et al., 1999). By the middle of the first year, emotional expressions are well-organized and specific and therefore able to tell us a great deal about the infant's internal state.

Four emotions—happiness, anger, sadness, and fear—have received the most research attention. Refer to Table 6.1 for an overview of changes in these emotions and others we will take up in this chapter.

Table 6.1	Milestones of Emotional Development During the First Two Years
Approximate Age	**Milestone**
Birth	Infants' emotions consist largely of two global arousal states: attraction to pleasant stimulation and withdrawal from unpleasant stimulation.
2–3 months	Infants engage in social smiling and respond in kind to adults' facial expressions.
3–5 months	Laughter at active stimuli emerges. Infants perceive facial expressions as organized patterns and can match the emotion in voices and faces.
6–8 months	Expressions of basic emotions are well-organized and vary meaningfully with environmental events. Infants start to become angry more often and in a wider range of situations. Fear, especially stranger anxiety, begins to rise.
	Attachment to familiar caregivers is clearly evident, and separation anxiety appears. Infants use familiar caregivers as a secure base for exploration.
8–12 months	Understanding of the meaning of others' emotional expressions improves, and social referencing appears. Infants laugh at subtle elements of surprise.
18–24 months	Self-conscious emotions of shame, embarrassment, guilt, and pride emerge. A vocabulary for talking about feelings develops rapidly, and emotional self-regulation improves. Toddlers appreciate that others' emotional reactions may differ from their own. First signs of empathy appear.

■ **Happiness.** Happiness—first expressed in blissful smiles and later through exuberant laughter—contributes to many aspects of development. When infants achieve new skills, they smile and laugh, displaying their delight in motor and cognitive mastery. As the smile encourages caregivers to be affectionate and stimulating, the baby smiles even more. Happiness binds parent and baby into a warm, supportive relationship that fosters the infant's developing competences.

During the early weeks, newborn babies smile when full, during REM sleep, and in response to gentle touches and sounds, such as stroking of the skin, rocking, and the mother's soft, high-pitched voice. By the end of the first month, infants smile at interesting sights that are dynamic and eye-catching, such as a bright object jumping suddenly across their field of vision. Between 6 and 10 weeks, the human face evokes a broad grin called the **social smile** (Sroufe & Waters, 1976). These changes in smiling parallel the development of infant perceptual capacities—in particular, babies' increasing sensitivity to visual patterns, including the human face (see Chapter 4).

Laughter, which first occurs around 3 to 4 months, reflects faster processing of information than does smiling. As with smiling, the first laughs occur in response to very active stimuli, such as the parent saying playfully, "I'm gonna get you!" and kissing the baby's tummy. As infants understand more about their world, they laugh at events with subtler elements of surprise, such as a silent game of peekaboo (Sroufe & Wunsch, 1972).

Around the middle of the first year, infants smile and laugh more when interacting with familiar people, a preference that strengthens the parent–child bond. Like adults, 10- to 12-month-olds have several smiles, which vary with context. They show a broad, "cheek-raised" smile in response to a parent's greeting; a reserved, muted smile to a friendly stranger; and a "mouth-open" smile during stimulating play (Bolzani et al., 2002; Dickson, Fogel, & Messinger, 1998).

■ **Anger and Sadness.** Newborn babies respond with generalized distress to a variety of unpleasant experiences, including hunger, painful medical procedures, changes in body temperature, and too much or too little stimulation. From 4 to 6 months into the second year, angry expressions increase in frequency and intensity. Older infants react with anger in a wider range of situations—when an object is taken away, their arms are restrained, the caregiver leaves for a brief time, or they are put down for a nap (Camras et al., 1992; Stenberg & Campos, 1990; Sullivan & Lewis, 2003).

Why do angry reactions increase with age? Cognitive and motor development are involved. As infants become capable of intentional behavior (see Chapter 5), they want to control their own actions (Alessandri, Sullivan, & Lewis, 1990). Older infants are also better at identifying who caused them pain or removed a toy. The rise in anger is also adaptive. New motor capacities enable an angry infant to defend herself or overcome an obstacle (Izard & Ackerman, 2000). Finally, anger motivates caregivers to relieve the infant's distress and, in the case of separation, may discourage them from leaving again soon.

Although expressions of sadness also occur in response to pain, removal of an object, and brief separations, they are less frequent than anger (Alessandri, Sullivan, & Lewis, 1990; Izard, Hembree, & Huebner, 1987). But when caregiver–infant communication is seriously disrupted, infant sadness is common—a condition that impairs all aspects of development (see the Lifespan Vista box on the following page).

■ **Fear.** Like anger, fear rises during the second half of the first year. Older infants often hesitate before playing with a new toy, and newly crawling infants soon show fear of heights (see Chapter 4). But the most frequent expression of fear is to unfamiliar adults, a response called **stranger anxiety.** Many infants and toddlers are quite wary of strangers, although the reaction does not always occur. It depends on several factors: the infant's temperament (some babies are generally more fearful), past experiences with strangers, and the current situation (Thompson & Limber, 1991). When an unfamiliar adult picks up the infant in a new setting, stranger anxiety is likely. But if the adult sits still while the baby moves around and a parent is nearby, infants often show positive and curious behavior (Horner, 1980). The stranger's style of interaction—expressing warmth, holding out an attractive toy, playing a familiar game, and approaching slowly rather than abruptly—reduces the baby's fear.

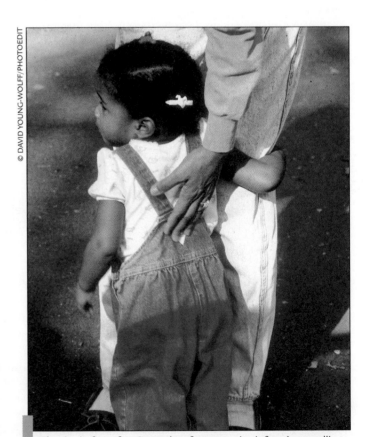

© DAVID YOUNG-WOLFF/PHOTOEDIT

The rise in fear after 6 months of age restrains infants' compelling drive to set out on their own. But this 1-year-old will be able to venture off confidently, as long as her mother remains near as a secure base to which she can return should she become too frightened.

A Lifespan Vista

Parental Depression and Children's Development

Approximately 8 to 10 percent of women experience chronic depression—mild to severe feelings of sadness and withdrawal that continue for months or years. Often the beginnings of this emotional state cannot be pinpointed; it simply becomes part of the person's daily life. In other instances, depression emerges or strengthens after childbirth but fails to subside as the new mother adjusts to hormonal changes in her body and gains confidence in caring for her baby. Julia experienced this type—called *postpartum depression*.

Although less recognized and studied, about 4 percent of fathers also report depression after the birth of a child (Deater-Deckard et al., 1998). Either maternal or paternal depression can interfere with effective parenting and seriously impair children's development. Although genetic makeup increases the risk of depressive illness, social and cultural factors are also involved.

Maternal Depression. During Julia's pregnancy, her husband, Kyle, showed so little interest in the baby that Julia worried that having a child might be a mistake. Then, shortly after Lucy was born, Julia's mood plunged. She became anxious and weepy, overwhelmed by Lucy's needs, and angry that she no longer had control over her own schedule. When Julia approached Kyle about her own fatigue and his unwillingness to help with the baby, he snapped that she overreacted to every move he made. Julia's childless friends stopped by just once to see Lucy but did not call again.

Julia's depressed mood quickly affected her baby. In the weeks after birth, infants of depressed mothers sleep poorly, are less attentive to their surroundings, and have elevated levels of the stress hormone cortisol (Field, 1998). The more extreme the depression and the greater the number of stressors in a mother's life (such as marital discord, little or no social support, and poverty), the more the parent–child relationship suffers (Simpson et al., 2003). Julia, for example, rarely smiled at, comforted, or talked to Lucy, who responded to her mother's sad, vacant gaze by turning away, crying, and often looking sad or angry herself (Herrera, Reissland, & Shepherd, 2004; Stanley, Murray, & Stein, 2004). Each time this happened, Julia felt guilty and inadequate, and her depression deepened. By age 6 months, Lucy showed mental and emotional symptoms common in babies of depressed mothers—delays in development, an irritable mood, and attachment difficulties (Martins & Gaffan, 2000).

When maternal depression persists, the parent–child relationship worsens. Depressed mothers view their infants more negatively than do independent observers (Hart, Field, & Roitfarb, 1999). And they use inconsistent discipline—sometimes lax, at other times too forceful. As we will see in later chapters, children who experience these maladaptive parenting practices often have serious adjustment problems. Some withdraw into a depressive mood themselves; others become impulsive and aggressive (Hay et al., 2003).

Paternal Depression. In a study of a large representative sample of British parents and babies, researchers assessed depressive symptoms in both mothers and fathers shortly after birth and again the following year. Then they tracked the development of their children into the preschool years. Like findings on children of depressed mothers, paternal depression was strongly associated with children's behavior problems—especially overactivity, defiance, and aggression in boys—even after many other factors, including family SES and maternal depression, had been controlled (Ramchandani et al., 2005).

Although little is known about the precise effects of paternal depression on parenting, well-adjusted fathers are more positive, attentive, and involved with their babies. At older ages, paternal depression is linked to frequent father–child conflict (Kane & Garber, 2004). Over time, children subjected to parental negativity develop a pessimistic worldview—one in which they lack self-confidence and perceive their parents and other people as threatening. Children who constantly feel in danger are likely to become overly aroused in stressful situations, easily losing control in the face of cognitive and social challenges (Cummings & Davies, 1994). Although children of depressed mothers or fathers may inherit a tendency toward emotional and behavior problems, quality of parenting is a major factor in their adjustment.

Interventions. Early treatment of parental depression is vital to prevent the disorder from interfering with the parent–child relationship. Julia's doctor referred her to a counselor, who helped Julia and Kyle with their marital problems and encouraged them to interact more sensitively with Lucy. Therapy that teaches depressed mothers to engage in emotionally positive, responsive caregiving reduces young children's attachment and developmental problems (Van Doesum, Hosman, & Riksen-Walraven, 2005). At times, antidepressant medication is prescribed. In most cases of postpartum depression, mothers bounce back after short-term treatment (Steinberg & Bellavance, 1999). When a depressed parent does not respond easily to treatment, a warm relationship with the other parent or another caregiver can safeguard children's development (Mezulis, Hyde, & Clark, 2004).

© JANINE WIEDEL PHOTOLIBRARY/ALAMY

This depressed mother appears overwhelmed and unresponsive to her infant. If her disengagement continues, the baby is likely to become negative and irritable, and eventually to withdraw. Over time, this disruption in the parent–child relationship leads to serious emotional and behavior problems.

Infant-rearing practices can modify stranger anxiety, as cross-cultural research reveals. Among the Efe hunters and gatherers of Congo, West Africa, where the maternal death rate is high, infant survival is safeguarded by a collective caregiving system in which, starting at birth, Efe babies are passed from one adult to another. Consequently, Efe infants show little stranger anxiety (Tronick, Morelli, & Ivey, 1992). In contrast, in Israeli kibbutzim (cooperative agricultural settlements), living in an isolated community vulnerable to terrorist attacks has led to widespread wariness of strangers. By the end of the first year, when infants look to others for cues about how to respond emotionally, kibbutz babies display greater stranger anxiety than their city-reared counterparts (Saarni, Mumme, & Campos, 1998).

The rise in fear after 6 months keeps newly mobile babies' enthusiasm for exploration in check. Once wariness develops, babies use the familiar caregiver as a **secure base,** or point from which to explore, venturing into the environment and then returning for emotional support. As part of this adaptive system, encounters with strangers lead to two conflicting tendencies: approach (indicated by interest and friendliness) and avoidance (indicated by fear). The infant's behavior is a balance between the two.

Eventually, as cognitive development permits toddlers to discriminate more effectively between threatening and nonthreatening people and situations, stranger anxiety and other fears of the first 2 years decline. Fear also wanes as toddlers acquire more strategies for coping with it, as you will see when we discuss emotional self-regulation.

Understanding and Responding to the Emotions of Others

Infants' emotional expressions are closely tied to their ability to interpret the emotional cues of others. We have seen that within the first few months, babies match the feeling tone of the caregiver in face-to-face communication. Early on, infants detect others' emotions through a fairly automatic process of *emotional contagion,* just as we tend to feel happy or sad when we sense these emotions in others. Around 4 months, infants become sensitive to the structure and timing of face-to-face interactions. When they gaze, smile, or vocalize, they now expect their social partner to respond in kind (Rochat, Striano, & Blatt, 2002). Within these exchanges, babies become increasingly aware of the range of emotional expressions (Montague & Walker-Andrews, 2001).

Around 5 months, infants perceive facial expressions as organized patterns and can match the emotion in a voice with the appropriate face of a speaking person (see Chapter 4). Responding to emotional expressions as organized wholes indicates that these signals have become meaningful to babies. As skill at grasping others' intentions and establishing joint attention improves, infants realize that an emotional expression not only has meaning but is also a meaningful reaction to a specific object or event (Moses et al., 2001; Tomasello, 1999a).

Once these understandings are in place, infants engage in **social referencing,** in which they actively seek emotional information from a trusted person in an uncertain situation. Many studies show that the caregiver's emotional expression (happy, angry, or fearful) influences whether a 1-year-old will be wary of strangers, play with an unfamiliar toy, or cross the deep side of the visual cliff (Repacholi, 1998; Stenberg, 2003; Striano & Rochat, 2000).

Mothers and fathers serve as equally effective sources of emotional information. In both parents' absence, babies turn to other familiar caregivers (Camras & Sachs, 1991; Hirshberg & Svejda, 1990). The adult's voice, either alone or combined with a facial expression, is more effective than a facial expression alone in guiding the baby's behavior (Vaish & Striano, 2004). By relying on the adult's voice, the baby need not turn toward the adult but can focus on evaluating the novel event. The voice also offers both emotional and verbal information.

Parents can capitalize on social referencing to teach their youngster how to react to many everyday events. And social referencing lets toddlers compare their own assessments of events with those of others. Around the middle of the second year, they appreciate that others' emotional reactions may differ from their own. In one study, an adult showed 14- and 18-month-olds broccoli and crackers and acted delighted with one food but disgusted with the other. When asked to share the food, 18-month-olds gave the adult whichever food she appeared to like, regardless of their own preferences (Repacholi & Gopnik, 1997).

In sum, social referencing helps young children move beyond simply reacting to others' emotional messages. They use those signals to guide their own actions and to find out about others' internal states and preferences.

Emergence of Self-Conscious Emotions

Besides basic emotions, humans are capable of a second, higher-order set of feelings, including guilt, shame, embarrassment, envy, and pride. These are called **self-conscious emotions** because each involves injury to or enhancement of our sense of self. We feel guilt when we have harmed someone and want to correct the wrongdoing. When we are ashamed or embarrassed, our negative feelings about our behavior make us want to retreat so others will no longer notice our failings. In contrast, pride reflects delight in the self's achievements, and we are inclined to tell others what we have accomplished (Saarni, Mumme, & Campos, 1998).

Self-conscious emotions appear in the second half of the second year, as 18- to 24-month-olds become firmly aware of the self as a separate, unique individual. Toddlers show shame and embarrassment by lowering their eyes, hanging their heads, and hiding their faces with their hands. They show guiltlike reactions, too: One 22-month-old returned a toy she had grabbed, then patted her upset playmate. Pride also emerges around this time, and envy by age 3 (Barrett, 1998; Garner, 2003; Lewis et al., 1989).

Besides self-awareness, self-conscious emotions require an additional ingredient: adult instruction in *when* to feel proud,

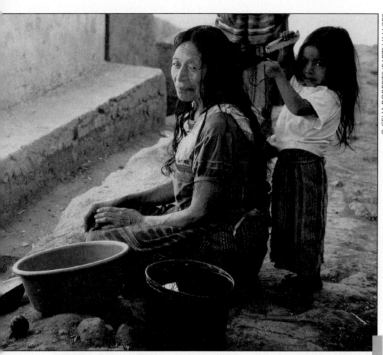

Self-conscious emotions appear at the end of the second year. This Guatemalan 2-year-old undoubtedly feels a sense of pride as she helps care for her elderly grandmother—an activity highly valued in her culture.

ashamed, or guilty. Parents begin this tutoring early when they say, "Look how far you can throw that ball!" or "You should feel ashamed for grabbing that toy!"

Self-conscious emotions play important roles in children's achievement-related and moral behaviors. The situations in which adults encourage these feelings vary from culture to culture. In most of the United States, children are taught to feel pride about personal achievement—throwing a ball the farthest, winning a game, and (later on) getting good grades. But in collectivist cultures, such as China and Japan, calling attention to purely personal success evokes embarrassment and self-effacement. And violating cultural standards by failing to show concern for others—a parent, a teacher, or an employer—sparks intense shame (Akimoto & Sanbonmatsu, 1999; Lewis, 1992).

Beginnings of Emotional Self-Regulation

Besides expressing a wider range of emotions, infants and toddlers begin to manage their emotional experiences. **Emotional self-regulation** refers to the strategies we use to adjust our emotional state to a comfortable level of intensity so we can accomplish our goals (Eisenberg et al., 1995; Eisenberg & Spinrad, 2004). When you remind yourself that an anxiety-provoking event will be over soon, suppress your anger at a friend's behavior, or decide not to see a scary horror film, you are engaging in emotional self-regulation.

Emotional self-regulation requires voluntary, effortful management of emotions. This capacity for *effortful control* improves gradually, as a result of development of the cerebral

cortex and the assistance of caregivers, who help children manage intense emotion and teach them strategies for doing so (Eisenberg & Morris, 2002; Fox & Calkins, 2003). Individual differences in control of emotion are evident in infancy and, by early childhood, play such a vital role in children's adjustment that—as we will see later—effortful control is regarded as a major dimension of temperament. A good start in regulating emotion during the first 2 years contributes greatly to autonomy and mastery of cognitive and social skills (Crockenberg & Leerkes, 2000).

In the early months of life, infants have only a limited capacity to regulate their emotional states. Although they can turn away from unpleasant stimulation and can mouth and suck when their feelings get too intense, they are easily overwhelmed. They depend on the soothing interventions of caregivers—lifting the distressed baby to the shoulder, rocking, and talking softly.

Rapid development of the frontal lobes of the cerebral cortex increases the baby's tolerance for stimulation. Between 2 and 4 months, caregivers build on this capacity by initiating face-to-face play and attention to objects. In these interactions, parents arouse pleasure in the baby while adjusting the pace of their behavior so the infant does not become overwhelmed and distressed. As a result, the baby's tolerance for stimulation increases further (Kopp & Neufeld, 2003). By 4 months, the ability to shift attention helps infants control emotion. Babies who more readily turn away from unpleasant events are less prone to distress (Axia, Bonichini, & Benini, 1999). At the end of the first year, crawling and walking enable infants to regulate feelings by approaching or retreating from various situations.

Infants whose parents "read" and respond sympathetically to their emotional cues tend to be less fussy, more easily soothed, and more interested in exploration. In contrast, parents who wait to intervene until the infant has become extremely agitated reinforce the baby's rapid rise to intense distress. When caregivers do not regulate stressful experiences for babies, brain structures that buffer stress may fail to develop properly, resulting in an anxious, reactive child with a reduced capacity for regulating emotion (Crockenberg & Leerkes, 2000; Nelson & Bosquet, 2000).

Caregivers also provide lessons in socially approved ways of expressing feelings. From the first few months, parents encourage infants to suppress negative emotion by imitating their expressions of interest, happiness, and surprise more often than their expressions of anger and sadness. Infant boys get more of this training than girls, in part because boys have a harder time regulating negative emotion (Malatesta et al., 1986; Weinberg et al., 1999). As a result, the well-known sex difference—females as emotionally expressive and males as emotionally controlled—is promoted at a tender age. Collectivist cultures place particular emphasis on socially appropriate emotional behavior. Compared with North Americans, Japanese and Chinese adults discourage the expression of strong emotion in babies (Fogel, 1993; Kuchner, 1989). By the end of the first year, Chinese and Japanese infants smile and cry less than American infants (Camras et al., 1998).

Toward the end of the second year, a vocabulary for talking about feelings—"happy," "surprised," "scary," "yucky," and "mad"—develops rapidly (Bretherton et al., 1986). Although 2-year-olds can redirect their attention for short periods when they are distressed, they are better able to do so in the presence of a supportive adult (Grolnick, Bridges, & Connell, 1996). And once they can describe their internal states, they can guide caregivers to help them. For example, while listening to a story about monsters, Grace whimpered, "Mommy, scary." Monica put the book down and gave Grace a comforting hug.

Ask Yourself

Review

Why do many infants show stranger anxiety in the second half of the first year? What factors can increase or decrease wariness of strangers?

Apply

At age 14 months, Reggie built a block tower and gleefully knocked it down. But at age 2, he called to his mother and pointed proudly at his tall block tower. What explains this change in Reggie's emotional behavior?

Connect

Why do children of depressed mothers have difficulty regulating emotion (see page 187)? What implications do their weak self-regulatory skills have for their response to cognitive and social challenges?

Reflect

Describe several recent events in your own life that required you to manage negative emotion. How did you react in each case? How might your early experiences, gender, and cultural background have influenced your style of emotional self-regulation?

www.ablongman.com/berk

Temperament and Development

From early infancy, Caitlin's sociability was unmistakable. She smiled and laughed while interacting with adults and, in her second year, readily approached other children. Meanwhile, Monica marveled at Grace's calm, relaxed disposition. At 19 months, she sat contented in a highchair through a two-hour family celebration at a restaurant. In contrast, Timmy was active and distractible. Vanessa found herself chasing him as he dropped one toy, moved on to the next, and climbed on chairs and tables.

When we describe one person as cheerful and "upbeat," another as active and energetic, and still others as calm, cautious, or prone to angry outbursts, we are referring to **temperament**—early-appearing, stable individual differences in reactivity and self-regulation. *Reactivity* refers to quickness and intensity of emotional arousal, attention, and motor activity. *Self-regulation*, as we have seen, refers to strategies that modify that reactivity (Rothbart, 2004; Rothbart & Bates, 1998). The psychological traits that make up temperament are believed to form the cornerstone of the adult personality.

In 1956, Alexander Thomas and Stella Chess initiated the New York Longitudinal Study, a groundbreaking investigation of the development of temperament that followed 141 children from early infancy well into adulthood. Results showed that temperament can increase a child's chances of experiencing psychological problems or, alternatively, protect a child from the negative effects of a highly stressful home life. At the same time, Thomas and Chess (1977) discovered that parenting practices can modify children's temperaments considerably.

These findings stimulated a growing body of research on temperament, including its stability, biological roots, and interaction with child-rearing experiences. Let's begin to explore these issues by looking at the structure, or makeup, of temperament and how it is measured.

The Structure of Temperament

Thomas and Chess's nine dimensions, listed in Table 6.2 on the following page, served as the first influential model of temperament. When detailed descriptions of infants' and children's behavior obtained from parent interviews were rated on these dimensions, certain characteristics clustered together, yielding three types of children:

- The **easy child** (40 percent of the sample) quickly establishes regular routines in infancy, is generally cheerful, and adapts easily to new experiences.

- The **difficult child** (10 percent of the sample) is irregular in daily routines, is slow to accept new experiences, and tends to react negatively and intensely.

- The **slow-to-warm-up child** (15 percent of the sample) is inactive, shows mild, low-key reactions to environmental stimuli, is negative in mood, and adjusts slowly to new experiences.

Note that 35 percent of the children did not fit any of these categories. Instead, they showed unique blends of temperamental characteristics.

The "difficult" pattern has sparked the most interest because it places children at high risk for adjustment problems—both anxious withdrawal and aggressive behavior in early and middle childhood (Bates, Wachs, & Emde, 1994; Ramos et al., 2005; Thomas, Chess, & Birch, 1968). Compared with difficult children, slow-to-warm-up children present fewer problems in the early years. However, they tend to show excessive fearfulness and slow, constricted behavior in the late preschool and school years, when they are expected to respond actively and quickly in classrooms and peer groups (Chess & Thomas, 1984; Schmitz et al., 1999).

Table 6.2 also shows a second model of temperament, devised by Mary Rothbart, which combines overlapping dimensions of Thomas and Chess and other researchers. For

Table 6.2	Two Models of Temperament

Thomas and Chess		Rothbart	
Dimension	**Description**	**Dimension**	**Description**
		Reactivity	
Activity level	Ratio of active periods to inactive ones	Activity level	Level of gross motor activity
Rhythmicity	Regularity of body functions, such as sleep, wakefulness, hunger, and excretion	Attention span/ persistence	Duration of orienting or interest
Distractibility	Degree to which stimulation from the environment alters behavior—for example, whether crying stops when a toy is offered	Fearful distress	Wariness and distress in response to intense or novel stimuli, including time to adjust to new situations
Approach/ withdrawal	Response to a new object, food, or person	Irritable distress	Extent of fussing, crying, and distress when desires are frustrated
Adaptability	Ease with which child adapts to changes in the environment, such as sleeping or eating in a new place	Positive affect	Frequency of expression of happiness and pleasure
Attention span and persistence	Amount of time devoted to an activity, such as watching a mobile or playing with a toy	**Self-regulation**	
Intensity of reaction	Energy level of response, such as laughing, crying, talking, or gross motor activity	Effortful control	Capacity to voluntarily suppress a dominant, reactive response in order to plan and execute a more adaptive response
Threshold of responsiveness	Intensity of stimulation required to evoke a response		
Quality of mood	Amount of friendly, joyful behavior as opposed to unpleasant, unfriendly behavior		

Sources: Left: Thomas & Chess, 1977; Right: Rothbart, Ahadi, & Evans, 2000; Rothbart & Mauro, 1990.

example, "distractibility" and "attention span and persistence" are considered opposite ends of the same dimension, labeled "attention span/persistence." This model also includes a dimension not identified by Thomas and Chess, "irritable distress," which distinguishes between reactivity triggered by frustration and reactivity due to fear. And it omits overly broad dimensions such as "rhythmicity," "intensity of reaction," and "threshold of responsiveness" (Rothbart, Ahadi, & Evans, 2000; Rothbart & Mauro, 1990). A child who is rhythmic in sleeping is not necessarily rhythmic in eating or bowel habits. And a child who smiles and laughs quickly and intensely is not necessarily quick and intense in fear, irritability, or motor activity.

According to Rothbart, individuals differ not just in their reactivity on each dimension, but also in the self-regulatory dimension of temperament, **effortful control**—the capacity to voluntarily suppress a dominant response in order to plan and execute a more adaptive response (Rothbart, 2003; Rothbart & Bates, 1998). Variations in effortful control are evident in how effectively a child can focus and shift attention, inhibit impulses, and manage negative emotion.

Measuring Temperament

Temperament is often assessed through interviews or questionnaires given to parents. Behavior ratings by pediatricians,

teachers, and others familiar with the child and laboratory observations by researchers have also been used. Parental reports are convenient and take advantage of parents' depth of knowledge about the child (Gartstein & Rothbart, 2003). Although information from parents has been criticized as biased, parental reports are moderately related to researchers' observations of children's behavior (Mangelsdorf, Schoppe, & Buur, 2000). And parent perceptions are useful for understanding the way parents view and respond to their child.

Although observations by researchers in the home or laboratory avoid the subjectivity of parental reports, they can lead to other inaccuracies. In homes, observers find it hard to capture rare but important events, such as infants' response to frustration. And in an unfamiliar lab, fearful children who calmly avoid certain experiences at home may become too upset to complete the session (Wachs & Bates, 2001). Still, researchers can better control children's experiences in the lab. And they can conveniently combine observations of behavior with physiological measures to gain insight into the biological bases of temperament.

Most physiological research has focused on children who fall at opposite extremes of the positive-affect and fearful-distress dimensions of temperament (refer again to Table 6.2): **inhibited,** or **shy, children,** who react negatively to and withdraw from novel stimuli, and **uninhibited,** or **sociable, chil-**

dren, who display positive emotion to and approach novel stimuli. As the Biology and Environment box on the following page reveals, biologically based reactivity—evident in heart rate, hormone levels, and EEG brain waves—differentiates children with inhibited and uninhibited temperaments. Nevertheless, parenting practices are crucially important in whether an inhibited style is sustained over time.

Stability of Temperament

Many studies indicate that young children who score low or high on attention span, irritability, sociability, shyness, or effortful control tend to respond similarly when assessed again several months to a few years later and, occasionally, even into the adult years (Caspi et al., 2003; Kochanska & Knaack, 2003; Pedlow et al., 1993; Rothbart, Ahadi, & Evans, 2000; Ruff & Rothbart, 1996). However, the overall stability of temperament is low to moderate (Putnam, Samson, & Rothbart, 2000).

A major reason is that temperament itself develops with age. To illustrate, let's look at irritability and activity level. Recall from Chapter 3 that the early months are a period of fussing and crying for most babies. As infants can better regulate their attention and emotions, many who initially seemed irritable become calm and content. In the case of activity level, the meaning of the behavior changes. At first, an active, wriggling infant tends to be highly aroused and uncomfortable, whereas an inactive baby is often alert and attentive. As infants begin to move on their own, the reverse is so! An active crawler is usually alert and interested in exploration, whereas an inactive baby might be fearful and withdrawn.

These discrepancies help us understand why long-term predictions from early temperament are most accurately made after age 2, when styles of responding are better established (Caspi, 1998; Lemery et al., 1999). In line with this idea, between 2½ and 3, children perform more consistently across a wide range of tasks that require effortful control, such as waiting for a reward, lowering their voice to a whisper, and selectively attending to one stimulus while ignoring competing stimuli. Researchers believe that around this time, areas in frontal lobes involved in suppressing impulses develop rapidly (Gerardi-Caulton, 2000; Rothbart et al., 2003).

Furthermore, 2- and 3-year-olds with fearful or negative, irritable temperaments who experience patient, supportive parenting are better at managing their reactivity (Warren & Simmens, 2005). They are especially likely to decline in difficultness during the preschool years—findings demonstrating that child rearing plays an important role in modifying biologically based temperamental traits.

When we consider the evidence as a whole, the low to moderate stability of temperament makes sense. Many factors affect the extent to which a temperamental style persists, including development of the biological systems on which temperament is based, the child's capacity for effortful control, and rearing experiences. But children's temperaments rarely change from one extreme to another—that is, shy toddlers seldom become highly sociable, and irritable toddlers seldom become easy-going. With these ideas in mind, let's turn to genetic and environmental contributions to temperament and personality.

Genetic Influences

The word *temperament* implies a genetic foundation for individual differences in personality. Research indicates that identical twins are more similar than fraternal twins across a wide range of temperamental and personality traits (Caspi, 1998; DiLalla, Kagan, & Reznick, 1994; Emde et al., 1992; Goldsmith et al., 1999; Saudino & Cherny, 2001). In Chapter 2, we noted that heritability estimates suggest a moderate role for heredity in temperament and personality: On average, half of individual differences have been attributed to differences in genetic makeup.

Consistent ethnic and sex differences in early temperament exist, again implying a role for heredity. Compared with North American Caucasian infants, Japanese and Chinese babies tend to be less active, irritable, and vocal, more easily soothed when upset, and better at quieting themselves (Kagan et al., 1994; Lewis, Ramsay, & Kawakami, 1993). Grace's capacity to remain contentedly seated in her highchair through a long family dinner certainly fits with this evidence. And Timmy's high rate of activity is consistent with sex differences (Gartstein & Rothbart, 2003). From an early age, boys tend to be more active and daring and girls more anxious and timid—a difference reflected in boys' higher injury rates throughout childhood and adolescence.

Nevertheless, genetic influences vary with the temperamental trait and with the age of individuals studied. For example, heritability estimates are higher for expressions of negative emotion than for positive emotion. And the role of heredity is considerably less in infancy than in childhood and later years, when temperament becomes more stable (Wachs & Bates, 2001).

Environmental Influences

Environment also has a powerful influence on temperament. For example, persistent nutritional and emotional deprivation profoundly alters temperament, resulting in maladaptive emotional reactivity. Recall from Chapter 4 that even after dietary improvement, children exposed to severe, early malnutrition remain more distractible and fearful than their agemates. And infants reared in deprived orphanages are easily overwhelmed by stressful events. Their poor regulation of emotion results in inattention and weak impulse control, including frequent expressions of anger (see pages 126 and 132).

Other research shows that heredity and environment often combine to influence temperament, since a child's approach to the world affects the experiences to which she is exposed. To see how this works, let's take a second look at ethnic and sex differences in temperament.

Japanese mothers usually say that babies come into the world as independent beings who must learn to rely on their

Biology and Environment

Development of Shyness and Sociability

Two 4-month-old babies, Larry and Mitch, visited the laboratory of Jerome Kagan, who observed their reactions to various unfamiliar experiences. When exposed to new sights and sounds, such as a moving mobile decorated with colorful toys, Larry tensed his muscles, moved his arms and legs with agitation, and began to cry. In contrast, Mitch remained relaxed and quiet, smiling and cooing.

As toddlers, Larry and Mitch returned to the laboratory, where they experienced procedures designed to induce uncertainty. Electrodes were placed on their bodies and blood pressure cuffs on their arms to measure heart rate; toy robots, animals, and puppets moved before their eyes; and unfamiliar people behaved in unexpected ways or wore novel costumes. While Larry whimpered and quickly withdrew, Mitch watched with interest, laughed, and approached the toys and strangers.

On a third visit, at age 4½, Larry barely talked or smiled during an interview with an unfamiliar adult. In contrast, Mitch asked questions and communicated his pleasure at each new activity. In a playroom with two unfamiliar peers, Larry pulled back and watched, while Mitch made friends quickly.

In longitudinal research on several hundred Caucasian children, Kagan (1998) found that about 20 percent of 4-month-old babies were, like Larry, easily upset by novelty; 40 percent, like Mitch, were comfortable, even delighted, with new experiences. About 20 to 30 percent of these groups retained their temperamental styles as they grew older (Kagan, 2003; Kagan & Saudino, 2001). But most children's dispositions became less extreme over time. Biological makeup and child-rearing experiences jointly influenced stability and change in temperament.

Physiological Correlates of Shyness and Sociability. Kagan believes that individual differences in arousal of the *amygdala*, an inner brain structure that controls avoidance reactions, contribute to these contrasting temperaments. In shy, inhibited children, novel stimuli easily excite the amygdala and its connections to the cerebral cortex and the sympathetic nervous system, which prepares the body to act in the face of threat. In sociable, uninhibited children, the same level of stimulation evokes minimal neural excitation. While viewing photos of unfamiliar faces, adults who had been classified as inhibited in the second year of life showed greater fMRI activity in the amygdala than adults who had been uninhibited as toddlers (Schwartz et al., 2003). And the two emotional styles are distinguished by additional physiological responses that are known to be mediated by the amygdala:

- *Heart rate.* From the first few weeks of life, the heart rates of shy children are consistently higher than those of sociable youngsters, and they speed up further in response to unfamiliar events (Snidman et al., 1995).

- *Cortisol.* Saliva concentration of the stress hormone cortisol tends to be higher in shy than in sociable children (Gunnar & Nelson, 1994).

- *Pupil dilation, blood pressure, and skin surface temperature.* Compared with sociable children, shy children show greater pupil dilation, rise in blood pressure, and cooling of the fingertips when faced with novelty (Kagan et al., 1999).

Another physiological correlate of approach–withdrawal to people and objects is the pattern of brain waves in the frontal lobes of the cerebral cortex. Shy infants and preschoolers show greater EEG activity in the right frontal lobe, which is associated with negative emotional reactivity; sociable children show the opposite pattern (Calkins, Fox, & Marshall, 1996). Neural activity in the amygdala is transmitted to the frontal lobes, probably contributing to these differences. Inhibited children also show greater generalized activation of the cerebral cortex, an indicator of high emotional arousal and monitoring of new situations for potential threats (Henderson et al., 2004).

Child-Rearing Practices. According to Kagan (1998), extremely shy or sociable children inherit a physiology that biases them toward a particular temperamental style. Yet heritability research indicates that genes contribute only modestly to shyness and sociability. Experience, too, has a powerful impact.

Child-rearing practices affect the chances that an emotionally reactive baby will become a fearful child. Warm, supportive parenting reduces shy infants' and preschoolers' intense physiological reaction to novelty, whereas cold, intrusive parenting heightens anxiety (Rubin, Burgess, & Hastings, 2002). And if parents protect infants who dislike novelty from minor stresses, they make it harder for the child to overcome an urge to retreat. Parents who make appropriate demands for their baby to approach new experiences help the child overcome fear (Rubin et al., 1997).

When inhibition persists, it leads to excessive cautiousness, low self-esteem, and loneliness. In adolescence, persistent shyness increases the risk of severe anxiety, especially social phobia—intense fear of being humiliated in social situations (Prior et al., 2000). For inhibited children to acquire effective social skills, parenting must be tailored to their temperaments—a theme we will encounter again in this and later chapters.

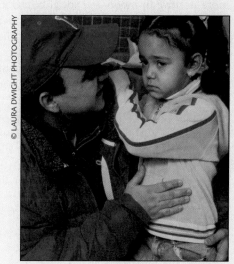

A strong physiological response to uncertain situations prompts this child to cling to her father. With patient but insistent encouragement, he can modify her reactivity and help her overcome her urge to retreat from unfamiliar events.

mothers through close physical contact. North American mothers typically believe just the opposite—that they must wean babies away from dependence toward autonomy (Kojima, 1986). Consistent with these beliefs, Asian mothers interact gently and soothingly, relying heavily on gestures and (as we saw earlier) discouraging strong emotion in their babies, whereas Caucasian mothers use a more active, stimulating, verbal approach (Rothbaum et al., 2000a). These differences enhance early ethnic differences in temperament.

A similar process seems to contribute to sex differences in temperament. Within 24 hours after birth (before they have had much experience with the baby), parents perceive boys and girls differently. They rate sons as larger, better coordinated, more alert, and stronger, daughters as softer, weaker, and more delicate and awkward (Stern & Karraker, 1989; Vogel et al., 1991). These gender-stereotyped beliefs influence parents' treatment of infants and toddlers. Parents more often encourage their young sons to be physically active and their daughters to seek help and physical closeness (Ruble & Martin, 1998).

In families with several children, an additional influence on temperament is at work. Listen to the comments parents make, and you will see that they often look for personality differences in their children: "She's a lot more active," "He's more sociable," "She's far more persistent." As a result, parents often regard siblings as more distinct than other observers do. In a large study of 1- to 3-year-old twin pairs, parents rated identical twins as resembling each other less in temperament than researchers' ratings indicated. And whereas researchers rated fraternal twins as moderately similar, parents viewed them as somewhat opposite in temperamental style (see Figure 6.1) (Saudino, 2003).

Parents' tendency to emphasize each child's unique qualities affects their child-rearing practices. In an investigation of identical-twin toddlers, mothers treated each twin differently. The twin who received more warmth and less harshness was more positive in mood and social behavior (Deater-Deckard et al., 2001). Each child, in turn, evokes responses from caregivers that are consistent with parental beliefs and the child's developing temperament.

Besides different experiences within the family, siblings have distinct experiences with teachers, peers, and others in their community that affect development. And in middle childhood and adolescence, they often seek ways to differ from one another. In adulthood, both identical and fraternal twins tend to become increasingly dissimilar (Loehlin & Martin, 2001; McCartney, Harris, & Bernieri, 1990). The less contact twins have with each other, the stronger this effect. In sum, temperament and personality can be understood only in terms of complex interdependencies between genetic and environmental factors.

Temperament and Child Rearing: The Goodness-of-Fit Model

As we have seen, the temperaments of many children change with age. This suggests that if a child's disposition interferes

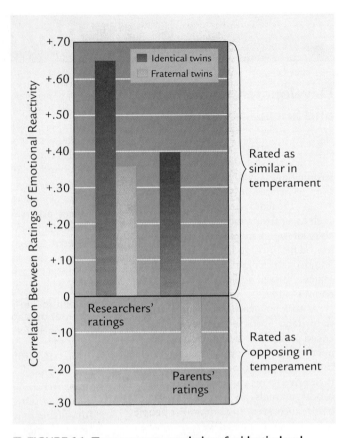

■ **FIGURE 6.1 Temperament correlations for identical and fraternal twin pairs, as rated by researchers and parents.** Parents rated 1- to 3-year-old identical twins as resembling each other less in temperament than did researchers. And whereas researchers rated fraternal twins as moderately similar, parents rated them as somewhat opposing in temperament. The correlations depicted here are for emotional reactivity. Activity level, shyness, and attention span/persistence yielded a similar pattern of findings. (Adapted from Saudino, 2003.)

with learning or getting along with others, adults can counteract the child's maladaptive behavior.

Thomas and Chess (1977) proposed a **goodness-of-fit model** to describe how temperament and environment can together produce favorable outcomes. Goodness of fit involves creating child-rearing environments that recognize each child's temperament while encouraging more adaptive functioning.

Difficult children (who withdraw from new experiences and react negatively and intensely) frequently experience parenting that fits poorly with their dispositions, putting them at high risk for later adjustment problems. By the second year, parents of difficult children often resort to angry, punitive discipline, which undermines the development of effortful control. As the child reacts with defiance and disobedience, parents become increasingly stressed (Coplan, Bowker, & Cooper, 2002). As a result, they continue their coercive tactics and also discipline inconsistently, at times rewarding the child's noncompliance by giving in to it (Calkins, 2002). These practices maintain and even increase the child's irritable, conflict-ridden style. In contrast, as we have seen, when parents are positive

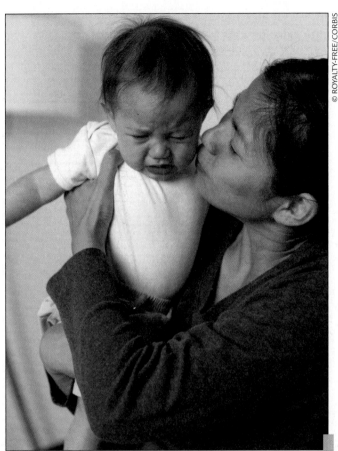

"Goodness-of-fit" describes the interaction between a child's biologically based temperament and the child-rearing environment. This mother's calm, soothing response to her baby's fussiness will help the child regulate intense emotional reactions and develop more adaptive responses to frustration.

and sensitive, which helps infants and toddlers regulate emotion, difficultness declines.

Effective parenting, however, depends on life conditions. In a comparison of Russian and U.S. babies, Russian infants were more emotionally negative, fearful, and upset when frustrated (Garstein, Slobodskaya, & Kinsht, 2003). Faced with a depressed national economy, which resulted in financial worries and longer work hours, Russian parents may have lacked time and energy for the patient parenting that protects against difficultness.

Cultural values also affect the fit between parenting and child temperament, as research in China illustrates. In the past, collectivist values, which discourage self-assertion, led Chinese adults to evaluate shy children positively, and several studies showed that Chinese children of a decade or two ago appeared well-adjusted, academically and socially (Chen, Rubin, & Li, 1995; Chen et al., 1998).

But rapid expansion of a competitive economy in China, which requires assertiveness and sociability for success, may be responsible for a recent reversal in Chinese parents' and teacher's attitudes toward childhood shyness (Xu & Peng, 2001; Yu, 2002). Among Shanghai fourth graders, the association

between shyness and adjustment also changed over time. Whereas shyness was positively correlated with teacher-rated competence, peer acceptance, leadership, and academic achievement in 1990, these relationships weakened in 1998 and reversed in 2002, at which time they mirrored findings of Western research (see Figure 6.2) (Chen et al., 2005). Cultural context makes a difference in whether shy children receive support or disapproval and whether they adjust well or poorly.

An effective match between rearing conditions and child temperament is best accomplished early, before unfavorable temperament–environment relationships produce maladjustment. Both difficult and shy children benefit from warm, accepting parenting that makes firm but reasonable demands for mastering new experiences. With reserved, inactive toddlers, highly stimulating parental behavior—encouraging, questioning, and pointing out objects—fosters exploration. Yet for highly active babies, these same parental behaviors are too directive, dampening their play and curiosity (Gandour, 1989; Miceli et al., 1998).

The goodness-of-fit model reminds us that infants have unique dispositions that adults must accept. Parents can neither take full credit for their children's virtues nor be blamed for all their faults. But parents can transform an environment that exaggerates a child's problems into one that builds on the child's strengths. As we will see, goodness of fit is also at the heart of infant–caregiver attachment. This first intimate relationship grows out of interaction between parent and baby, to which the emotional styles of both partners contribute.

■ **FIGURE 6.2 Changes over time in correlations between shyness and adjustment among Chinese fourth graders.** In 1990, shy Chinese children appeared well-adjusted. But as China's market economy expanded and valuing of self-assertion and sociability increased, the direction of the correlations shifted. In 2002, shyness was negatively associated with adjustment. These findings are for teacher-rated competence and peer acceptance. Those for leadership (holding offices in student organizations) and academic achievement changed similarly. (Adapted from Chen et al., 2005.)

Ask Yourself

Review

How do genetic and environmental factors work together to influence temperament? Cite several examples from research.

Apply

At 18 months, highly active Jake climbed out of his highchair and had a tantrum when his father insisted that he sit at the table until the meal was finished. Using the concept of goodness of fit, suggest another way of handling Jake.

Connect

Do findings on ethnic and sex differences in temperament illustrate genetic–environmental correlation, discussed on page 73 in Chapter 2? Explain.

Reflect

How would you describe your temperament as a young child? Do you think your temperament has remained stable, or has it changed? What factors might be involved?

www.ablongman.com/berk

Development of Attachment

Attachment is the strong affectionate tie we have with special people in our lives that leads us to feel pleasure when we interact with them and to be comforted by their nearness in times of stress. By the second half of the first year, infants have become attached to familiar people who have responded to their needs, and they single out their parents for special attention. When the mother enters the room, the baby breaks into a broad, friendly smile. When she picks him up, he pats her face, explores her hair, and snuggles against her. When he feels anxious or afraid, he crawls into her lap and clings closely.

Freud first suggested that the infant's emotional tie to the mother is the foundation for all later relationships. Contemporary research indicates that—although the quality of the infant–parent bond is vitally important—later development is influenced not just by early attachment experiences, but also by the continuing quality of the parent–child relationship.

Attachment has also been the subject of intense theoretical debate. Turn back to the description of Erikson's theory at the beginning of this chapter and notice how the *psychoanalytic perspective* regards feeding as the primary context in which caregivers and babies build this emotional bond. *Behaviorism*, too, emphasizes the importance of feeding, but for different reasons. According to a well-known behaviorist account, as the mother satisfies the baby's hunger, infants learn to prefer her soft caresses, warm smiles, and tender words of comfort because these events have been paired with tension relief.

Although feeding is an important context for building a close relationship, attachment does not depend on hunger sat-

isfaction. In the 1950s, a famous experiment showed that rhesus monkeys reared with terrycloth and wire-mesh "surrogate mothers" clung to the soft terrycloth substitute, even though the wire-mesh "mother" held the bottle and infants had to climb on it to be fed (Harlow & Zimmerman, 1959). Similarly, human infants become attached to family members who seldom feed them, including fathers, siblings, and grandparents. And toddlers in Western cultures who sleep alone and experience frequent daytime separations from their parents sometimes develop strong emotional ties to cuddly objects, such as blankets and teddy bears, that have never played a role in infant feeding!

Ethological Theory of Attachment

Today, **ethological theory of attachment,** which recognizes the infant's emotional tie to the caregiver as an evolved response that promotes survival, is the most widely accepted view. John Bowlby (1969), who first applied this idea to the infant–caregiver bond, was inspired by Konrad Lorenz's studies of imprinting in baby geese (see Chapter 1). Bowlby believed that the human infant, like the young of other animal species, is endowed with a set of built-in behaviors that help keep the parent nearby to protect the infant from danger and to provide

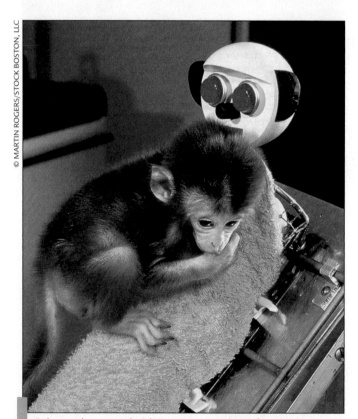

© MARTIN ROGERS/STOCK BOSTON, LLC

Baby monkeys reared with "surrogate mothers" from birth preferred to cling to a soft terrycloth "mother" instead of a wire-mesh "mother" that held a bottle. These findings reveal that attachment—the emotional bond between baby and caregiver—is not simply based on hunger satisfaction, as earlier theorists had assumed.

support for exploring and mastering the environment (Waters & Cummings, 2000). Contact with the parent also ensures that the baby will be fed, but Bowlby pointed out that feeding is not the basis for attachment. Rather, the attachment bond can best be understood in an evolutionary context in which survival of the species—through ensuring both safety and competence—is of utmost importance.

According to Bowlby, the infant's relationship with the parent begins as a set of innate signals that call the adult to the baby's side. Over time, a true affectionate bond develops, supported by new cognitive and emotional capacities as well as by a history of warm, sensitive care. Attachment develops in four phases:

1. *Preattachment phase* (birth to 6 weeks). Built-in signals—grasping, smiling, crying, and gazing into the adult's eyes—help bring newborn babies into close contact with other humans, who comfort them. Although babies of this age recognize their own mother's smell and voice (see Chapter 3), they are not yet attached to her, since they do not mind being left with an unfamiliar adult.

2. *"Attachment-in-the-making" phase* (6 weeks to 6–8 months). During this phase, infants respond differently to a familiar caregiver than to a stranger. For example, at 4 months, Timmy smiled, laughed, and babbled more freely when interacting with his mother and quieted more quickly when she picked him up. As infants learn that their own actions affect the behavior of those around them, they begin to develop a *sense of trust*—the expectation that the caregiver will respond when signaled—but they still do not protest when separated from her.

3. *"Clear-cut" attachment phase* (6–8 months to 18 months–2 years). Now attachment to the familiar caregiver is evident. Babies display **separation anxiety,** becoming upset when the adult whom they have come to rely on leaves. Separation anxiety does not always occur; like stranger anxiety (see page 186), it depends on infant temperament and the current situation. But in many cultures, separation anxiety increases between 6 and 15 months. Besides protesting the parent's departure, older infants and toddlers try hard to maintain her presence. They approach, follow, and climb on her in preference to others. And they use the familiar caregiver as a *secure base* from which to explore.

4. *Formation of a reciprocal relationship* (18 months–2 years and on). By the end of the second year, rapid growth in representation and language permits toddlers to understand some of the factors that influence the parent's coming and going and to predict her return. As a result, separation protest declines. Now children start to negotiate with the caregiver, using requests and persuasion to alter her goals. For example, at age 2, Caitlin asked Carolyn and David to read a story before leaving her with a baby-sitter. The extra time with her parents, along with a better understanding of where they were going ("to have

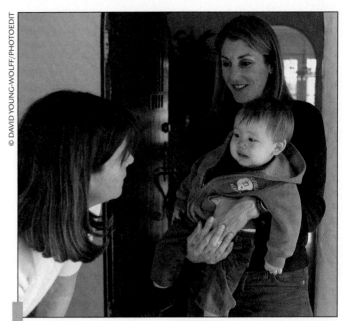

Separation anxiety increases between 6 and 15 months, when clear-cut infant–caregiver attachment develops. But the occurrence of separation anxiety depends on infant temperament, context, and adult behavior. Here, the child's distress at his mother's departure will probably be short-lived because his caregiver is supportive and sensitive.

dinner with Uncle Sean") and when they would be back ("right after you go to sleep"), helped Caitlin withstand her parents' absence.

According to Bowlby (1980), out of their experiences during these four phases, children construct an enduring affectionate tie to the caregiver that they can use as a secure base in the parents' absence. This image serves as an **internal working model,** or set of expectations about the availability of attachment figures and their likelihood of providing support during times of stress. The internal working model becomes a vital part of personality, serving as a guide for all future close relationships (Bretherton & Munholland, 1999). Children continually revise and expand the internal working model as their cognitive, emotional, and social capacities increase; as they interact with parents; and as they form other close bonds with adults, siblings, and friends.

Measuring the Security of Attachment

Although virtually all family-reared babies become attached to a familiar caregiver by the second year, the quality of this relationship varies. Some children appear secure—certain that the caregiver will provide affection and support. Others seem anxious and uncertain.

A widely used laboratory procedure for assessing the quality of attachment between 1 and 2 years of age is the **Strange Situation,** which takes the baby through eight short episodes in which brief separations from and reunions with the parent occur (see Table 6.3 on page 198). In designing it, Mary

Ainsworth and her colleagues reasoned that securely attached infants and toddlers should use the parent as a secure base from which to explore an unfamiliar playroom, and that, when the parent leaves, an unfamiliar adult should be less comforting than the parent.

Observing infants' responses to these episodes, researchers have identified a secure attachment pattern and three patterns of insecurity; a few babies cannot be classified (Ainsworth et al., 1978; Barnett & Vondra, 1999; Main & Solomon, 1990). From the description at the beginning of this chapter, which pattern do you think Grace displayed after adjusting to her adoptive family?

✏ **Secure attachment.** These infants use the parent as a secure base. When separated, they may or may not cry, but if they do, it is because the parent is absent and they prefer her to the stranger. When the parent returns, they actively seek contact, and their crying is reduced immediately. About 65 percent of North American infants show this pattern.

✏ **Avoidant attachment.** These infants seem unresponsive to the parent when she is present. When she leaves, they usually are not distressed, and they react to the stranger in much the same way as to the parent. During reunion, they avoid or are slow to greet the parent, and when picked up, they often fail to cling. About 20 percent of North American infants show this pattern.

✏ **Resistant attachment.** Before separation, these infants seek closeness to the parent and often fail to explore. When she leaves, they are usually distressed, and on her return they display angry, resistive behavior, sometimes hitting and pushing. Many continue to cry after being picked up and cannot be comforted easily. About 10 to 15 percent of North American infants show this pattern.

✏ **Disorganized/disoriented attachment.** This pattern reflects the greatest insecurity. At reunion, these infants show confused, contradictory behaviors. They might look away while being held by the parent or approach her with flat, depressed emotion. Most communicate their emotion with a dazed facial expression. A few cry out after having calmed down or display odd, frozen postures. About 5 to 10 percent of North American infants show this pattern.

An alternative method, the **Attachment Q-Sort,** suitable for children between 1 and 4 years, depends on home observation (Waters et al., 1995). Either the parent or a highly trained observer sorts 90 behaviors ("Child greets mother with a big smile when she enters the room," "If mother moves very far, child follows along") into categories ranging from highly descriptive to not at all descriptive of the child. Then a score, ranging from high to low in security, is computed.

The Q-Sort is time-consuming, requiring a nonparent observer to spend several hours observing the child before sorting. And it does not indicate patterns of insecurity. But it may better reflect the parent–infant relationship in everyday life. Expert observers' Q-Sorts correspond well with babies' secure-base behavior in the Strange Situation. Parents' Q-Sorts, however, show little relationship with the Strange Situation (van IJzendoorn et al., 2004). Parents of insecure children, especially, may have difficulty accurately reporting their child's attachment behaviors.

Stability of Attachment

Research on the stability of attachment patterns between 1 and 2 years of age yields a wide range of findings (Thompson, 1998, 2000). A close look at which babies stay the same and which ones change yields a more consistent picture. Quality of attachment is usually secure and stable for middle-SES babies

Table 6.3	Episodes in the Strange Situation	
Episode	**Events**	**Attachment Behavior Observed**
1	Researcher introduces parent and baby to playroom and then leaves.	
2	Parent is seated while baby plays with toys.	Parent as a secure base
3	Stranger enters, is seated, and talks to parent.	Reaction to unfamiliar adult
4	Parent leaves room. Stranger responds to baby and offers comfort if baby is upset.	Separation anxiety
5	Parent returns, greets baby, and offers comfort if necessary. Stranger leaves room.	Reaction to reunion
6	Parent leaves room.	Separation anxiety
7	Stranger enters room and offers comfort.	Ability to be soothed by stranger
8	Parent returns, greets baby, offers comfort if necessary, and tries to reinterest baby in toys.	Reaction to reunion

Note: Episode 1 lasts about 30 seconds; each of the remaining episodes lasts about 3 minutes. Separation episodes are cut short if the baby becomes very upset. Reunion episodes are extended if the baby needs more time to calm down and return to play.
Source: Ainsworth et al., 1978.

experiencing favorable life conditions. And infants who move from insecurity to security typically have well-adjusted mothers with positive family and friendship ties. Perhaps many became parents before they were psychologically ready but, with social support, grew into the role. In contrast, in low-SES families with many daily stresses, attachment generally moves away from security or changes from one insecure pattern to another (Belsky et al., 1996; Vondra, Hommerding, & Shaw, 1999; Vondra et al., 2001).

These findings indicate that securely attached babies more often maintain their attachment status than insecure babies—a trend also evident in long-term assessments of attachment stability, based on follow-up interviews with adolescents and young adults (Waters et al., 2000; Weinfield, Sroufe, & Egeland, 2000). The exception is disorganized/disoriented attachment—an insecure pattern that remains highly stable (Hesse & Main, 2000; Weinfield, Whaley, & Egeland, 2004). As you will soon see, many disorganized/disoriented babies experience extremely negative caregiving, which may disrupt emotional self-regulation so severely that confused, ambivalent feelings toward parents persist for many years.

Cultural Variations

Cross-cultural evidence indicates that attachment patterns may have to be interpreted differently in certain cultures. For example, as Figure 6.3 reveals, German infants show consider-

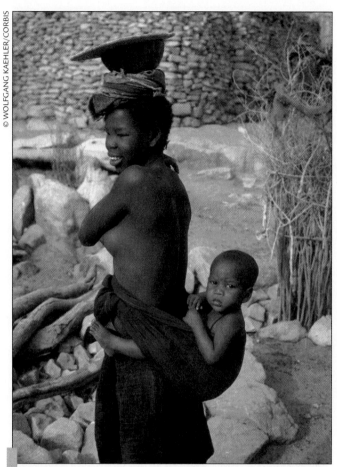

Among the Dogon people of Mali, Africa, mothers stay close to their babies and respond promptly and gently to infant distress. Dogon mothers are almost never overly stimulating or intrusive—practices linked to avoidant attachment. And in Dogon culture, none of the infants were avoidantly attached to their mothers.

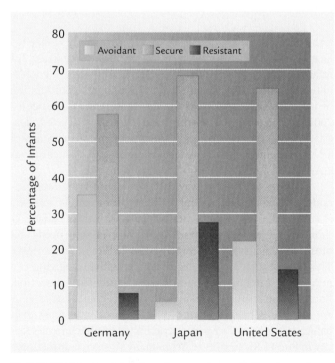

■ **FIGURE 6.3 A cross-cultural comparison of infants' reactions in the Strange Situation.** A high percentage of German babies seem avoidantly attached, whereas a substantial number of Japanese infants appear resistantly attached. Note that these responses may not reflect true insecurity. Instead, they are probably due to cultural differences in values and child-rearing practices. (Adapted from van IJzendoorn & Kroonenberg, 1988.)

ably more avoidant attachment than American babies do. But German parents value independence and encourage their infants to be nonclingy (Grossmann et al., 1985). In contrast, a study of infants of the Dogon people of Mali, Africa, revealed that none showed avoidant attachment to their mothers (True, Pisani, & Oumar, 2001). Even when grandmothers are primary caregivers (as they are with firstborn sons), Dogon mothers remain available, holding their babies close and nursing promptly in response to hunger and distress.

Japanese infants, as well, rarely show avoidant attachment (refer again to Figure 6.3) An unusually high number are resistantly attached, but this reaction may not represent true insecurity. Japanese mothers rarely leave their babies in others' care, so the Strange Situation probably creates greater stress for them than for infants who frequently experience maternal separations (Takahashi, 1990). Also, Japanese parents view the infant attention seeking that is part of resistant attachment as a normal indicator of infant dependency (Rothbaum et al., 2000b). Despite such cultural variations, the secure pattern is still the most common attachment quality in all societies studied (van IJzendoorn & Sagi, 1999).

Factors That Affect Attachment Security

What factors might influence attachment security? Researchers have looked closely at four important influences: (1) opportunity to establish a close relationship, (2) quality of caregiving, (3) the baby's characteristics, and (4) family context.

■ **Opportunity for Attachment.** What happens when a baby does not have the opportunity to establish an affectional tie to a caregiver? In a series of studies, René Spitz (1946) observed institutionalized infants whose mothers had given them up between 3 and 12 months of age. After being placed in a large ward where each shared a nurse with at least seven others, the babies lost weight and withdrew from their surroundings. If a consistent caregiver did not replace the mother, the depression deepened rapidly.

These institutionalized babies had emotional difficulties because they were prevented from forming a bond with one or a few adults (Rutter, 1996). Another study supports this conclusion. Researchers followed the development of infants in an institution with a good caregiver–child ratio and a rich selection of books and toys. However, staff turnover was so rapid that the average child had 50 caregivers by age 4½! Many of these children became "late adoptees" who were placed in homes after age 4. Most developed deep ties with their adoptive parents, indicating that a first attachment bond can develop as late as 4 to 6 years of age (Tizard & Rees, 1975).

But these youngsters were more likely to display emotional and social problems, including an excessive desire for adult attention, "overfriendliness" to unfamiliar adults and peers, and few friendships. Adopted children who spent their first eight months or more in deprived Romanian orphanages often display these same difficulties (Hodges & Tizard, 1989; O'Connor et al., 2003). These findings suggest that fully normal development depends on establishing a close, caregiver bond during the early years of life.

■ **Quality of Caregiving.** Dozens of studies report that **sensitive caregiving**—responding promptly, consistently, and appropriately to infants and holding them tenderly and carefully—is moderately related to attachment security in diverse cultures and SES groups (De Wolff & van IJzendoorn, 1997; Posada et al., 2002, 2004; van IJzendoorn et al., 2004). In contrast, insecurely attached infants tend to have mothers who engage in less physical contact, handle them awkwardly or "routinely," and are sometimes resentful and rejecting (Ainsworth et al., 1978; Isabella, 1993; Pederson & Moran, 1996).

Also, in several studies of North American babies, a special form of communication called **interactional synchrony** separated the experiences of secure and insecure babies. It is best described as a sensitively tuned "emotional dance," in which the caregiver responds to infant signals in a well-timed, rhythmic, appropriate fashion. In addition, both partners match emotional states, especially the positive ones (Feldman, 2003;

This mother and baby are engaging in a sensitively tuned form of communication called interactional synchrony in which they match emotional states, especially positive ones. Interactional synchrony may support secure attachment, but it does not characterize mother-infant interaction in all cultures.

Isabella & Belsky, 1991). Earlier we saw that sensitive face-to-face play, in which interactional synchrony occurs, helps infants regulate emotion. But moderate adult–infant coordination predicts attachment security, not "tight" coordination in which the adult responds to most infant cues (Jaffee et al., 2001). Perhaps warm, sensitive caregivers use a relaxed, flexible style of communication in which they comfortably accept and repair emotional mismatches, returning to a synchronous state.

Cultures vary in the way they view sensitivity toward infants. Among the Gusii people of Kenya, for example, mothers rarely cuddle, hug, or interact playfully with their babies, although they are very responsive to their infants' needs. Yet most Gusii infants appear securely attached (LeVine et al., 1994). This suggests that security depends on attentive caregiving, not necessarily on moment-by-moment contingent interaction. Puerto Rican mothers, who highly value obedience and socially appropriate behavior, often physically direct and limit their babies' actions—a caregiving style linked to attachment security in Puerto Rican culture. Yet in many Western cultures, such physical control predicts insecurity (Carlson & Harwood, 2003).

Compared with securely attached infants, avoidant babies tend to receive overly stimulating, intrusive care. Their mothers might, for example, talk energetically to them while they are looking away or falling asleep. By avoiding the mother, these infants try to escape from overwhelming interaction. Resistant infants often experience inconsistent care. Their mothers are unresponsive to infant signals. Yet when the baby begins to explore, these mothers interfere, shifting the infant's attention back to themselves. As a result, the baby is overly dependent as well as angry at the mother's lack of involvement (Cassidy & Berlin, 1994; Isabella & Belsky, 1991).

Highly inadequate caregiving is a powerful predictor of disruptions in attachment. Child abuse and neglect (topics we will consider in Chapter 8) are associated with all three forms of attachment insecurity. Among maltreated infants, disorganized/disoriented attachment is especially high (van IJzendoorn, Schuengel, & Bakermans-Kranenburg, 1999). Persistently depressed mothers and parents suffering from a traumatic event, such as loss of a loved one, also tend to promote the uncertain behaviors of this pattern (Campbell et al., 2004; van IJzendoorn, 1995). Observations reveal that they often display frightening, contradictory, and unpleasant behaviors, such as looking scared, teasing the baby, holding the baby stiffly at a distance, or seeking reassurance from the upset child (Goldberg et al., 2003; Lyons-Ruth, Bronfman, & Parsons, 1999).

■ **Infant Characteristics.** Because attachment is the result of a *relationship* that builds between two partners, infant characteristics should affect how easily it is established. In Chapter 3, we saw that prematurity, birth complications, and newborn illness make caregiving more taxing. In stressed, poverty-stricken families, these difficulties are linked to attachment insecurity (Wille, 1991). But when parents have the time and patience to care for a baby with special needs and view their infants positively, at-risk newborns fare quite well in attachment security (Cox, Hopkins, & Hans, 2000; Pederson & Moran, 1995).

Babies whose temperament is emotionally reactive and difficult are more likely to develop later insecure attachments (van IJzendoorn et al., 2004; Vaughn & Bost, 1999). Again, however, caregiving is involved. In a study extending from birth to age 2, difficult infants more often had highly anxious mothers, a combination that, by the second year, often resulted in a "disharmonious relationship" characterized by both maternal insensitivity and attachment insecurity (Symons, 2001).

If children's temperaments determined attachment quality, we would expect attachment, like temperament, to be at least moderately heritable. Yet the heritability of attachment is virtually nil (O'Connor & Croft, 2001). In fact, about two-thirds of siblings establish similar attachment patterns with their parents, although the siblings often differ in temperament (Dozier et al., 2001). This suggests that most parents try to adjust their caregiving to each child's individual needs.

Why don't infant characteristics show strong relationships with attachment quality? Their influence probably depends on goodness of fit. From this perspective, *many* child attributes can lead to secure attachment as long as the caregiver behaves sensitively (Seifer & Schiller, 1995). Interventions that teach parents to interact with difficult-to-care-for infants are highly successful in enhancing both sensitive care and attachment security (Bakermans-Kranenburg, van IJzendoorn, & Juffer, 2003). But when parents' capacity is strained—by their own personalities or by stressful living conditions—then infants with illnesses, disabilities, and difficult temperaments are at risk for attachment problems.

■ **Family Circumstances.** Shortly after Timmy's birth, his parents divorced and his father moved to a distant city. Anxious and distracted, Vanessa placed 1-month-old Timmy in Ginette's child-care home and began working 50- to 60-hour weeks to make ends meet. When Vanessa stayed late at the office, a baby-sitter picked Timmy up, gave him dinner, and put him to bed. Once or twice a week, Vanessa went to get Timmy from child care. As he neared his first birthday, Vanessa noticed that unlike the other children, who reached out, crawled, or ran to their parents, Timmy ignored her.

Timmy's behavior reflects a repeated finding: Job loss, a failing marriage, and financial difficulties can undermine attachment by interfering with parental sensitivity. These stressors can also affect babies' sense of security directly, by exposing them to angry adult interactions or unfavorable child-care arrangements (Thompson & Raikes, 2003). (See the Social Issues box on pages 202–203 to find out how child care affects early emotional development.) Social support, especially assistance with parenting, reduces parental stress and fosters attachment security. Ginette's sensitivity was helpful, as was the advice Vanessa received from Ben, a psychologist. As Timmy turned 2, his relationship with his mother seemed warmer.

Parents bring to the family context their own history of attachment experiences, from which they construct internal working models that they apply to the bonds they establish with their babies. Monica, who recalled her mother as tense and preoccupied, expressed regret that they had not had a closer relationship. Is her image of parenthood likely to affect Grace's attachment security?

To assess parents' internal working models, researchers have asked them to evaluate childhood memories of attachment experiences (Main & Goldwyn, 1998). In studies in several Western nations, parents who showed objectivity and balance in discussing childhood experiences, regardless of whether they were positive or negative, tended to have securely attached infants. In contrast, parents who either dismissed the importance of early relationships or described them in angry, confused ways usually had insecurely attached babies (Slade et al., 1999; van IJzendoorn, 1995).

But we must not assume any direct transfer of parents' childhood experiences to quality of attachment with their own children. Internal working models are *reconstructed memories* affected by many factors, including relationship experiences over the life course, personality, and current life satisfaction. Longitudinal research shows that negative life events can weaken the link between an individual's own attachment security in

Social Issues

Does Child Care in Infancy Threaten Attachment Security and Later Adjustment?

Research suggests that infants placed in full-time child care before 12 months of age are more likely than infants who remain at home to display insecure attachment—especially avoidance—in the Strange Situation (Belsky, 1992, 2001). Does this mean that infants who experience daily separations from their employed parents and early placement in child care are at risk for developmental problems? Let's look closely at the evidence.

Attachment Quality. In studies reporting an association between child care and attachment quality, the rate of insecurity among child-care infants is somewhat greater than among non-child-care infants—about 36 versus 29 percent (Lamb, Sternberg, & Prodromidis, 1992). But not all investigations report that babies in child care differ in attachment quality from those cared for solely by parents (NICHD Early Child Care Research Network, 1997; Roggman et al., 1994). The relationship between child care and emotional well-being depends on both family and child-care experiences.

Family Circumstances. We have seen that family conditions affect attachment security. Many employed women find the pressures of handling two full-time jobs—work and motherhood—stressful. Some mothers, fatigued and harried because they receive little help from the child's father, may respond less sensitively to their babies, thereby risking the infants' security (Stifter, Coulehan, & Fish, 1993). Other employed parents probably value and encourage their infants' independence. Or their babies may be unfazed by the Strange Situation because they are used to separating from their parents. In these cases, avoidance in the Strange Situation may represent healthy autonomy rather than insecurity (Clarke-Stewart, Althusen, & Goosens, 2001).

Quality and Extent of Child Care. Long periods spent in poor-quality child care may contribute to a higher rate of insecure attachment. In the U.S. National Institute of Child Health and Human Development (NICHD) Study of Early Child Care—the largest longitudinal study to date, including more than 1,300

infants and their families—child care alone did not contribute to attachment insecurity. But when babies were exposed to combined home and child-care risk factors—insensitive caregiving at home along with insensitive caregiving in child care, long hours in child care, or more than one child-care arrangement—the rate of insecurity increased. Overall, mother–child interaction was more favorable when children attended higher-quality child care and were in child care for fewer hours (NICHD Early Child Care Research Network, 1997, 1999).

Furthermore, when the NICHD sample reached 3 years of age, a history of higher-quality child care predicted better social skills (NICHD Early Child Care Research Network, 2002b). At the same time, at age 4½ to 5, children averaging more than 30 child-care hours per week displayed more behavior problems, especially defiance, disobedience, and aggression (NICHD Early Child Care Research Network, 2003). This does not necessarily mean that child care causes behavior problems. Rather, heavy exposure to substandard care, which is widespread in the United States, may promote these difficulties. In Australia, infants enrolled full-time in government-funded, high-

---

infancy and a secure internal working model in adulthood. And insecurely attached babies who become adults with insecure internal working models often have lives that, based on self-reports in adulthood, are filled with family crises (Waters et al., 2000; Weinfield, Sroufe, & Egeland, 2000).

In sum, our early rearing experiences do not destine us to become sensitive or insensitive parents. Rather, the way we *view* our childhoods—our ability to come to terms with negative events, to integrate new information into our working models, and to look back on our own parents in an understanding, forgiving way—is much more influential in how we rear our children than the actual history of care we received (Main, 2000).

Multiple Attachments

We have already indicated that babies develop attachments to a variety of familiar people—not just mothers but also fathers, siblings, grandparents, and professional caregivers. Although

Bowlby (1969) acknowledged the existence of multiple attachments, he believed that infants are predisposed to direct their attachment behaviors to a single special person, especially when they are distressed. When anxious or unhappy, most babies do prefer to be comforted by their mother. But this preference typically declines over the second year. And when babies are not distressed, they approach, vocalize to, and smile at both parents equally (Lamb, 1997).

■ **Fathers.** Like that of mothers, fathers' sensitive caregiving and synchronous interaction with infants predict attachment security (Lundy, 2003; van IJzendoorn et al., 2004). Nevertheless, mothers and fathers in many cultures—Australia, India, Israel, Italy, Japan, and the United States—tend to interact with babies in different ways. Mothers devote more time to physical care and expressing affection. Fathers spend more time in playful interaction (Roopnarine et al., 1990).

Mothers and fathers also play differently. Mothers more often provide toys, talk to infants, and gently engage in convenquality child care have a higher rate of secure attachment than infants informally cared for by relatives, friends, or baby-sitters. And amount of time in child care is unrelated to behavior problems in Australian preschoolers (Love et al., 2003).

Still, some children may be particularly stressed by long child-care hours. Many infants, toddlers, and preschoolers who attend child-care centers for full days show a mild increase in saliva concentrations of the stress hormone cortisol across the day—a pattern that does not occur on days they spend at home. In one study, children rated as highly fearful by their caregivers experienced an especially sharp increase in cortisol levels (Watamura et al., 2003). Inhibited children may find the social context of child care—constantly being in the company of large numbers of peers—particularly stressful.

Conclusions. Taken together, research suggests that some infants may be at risk for attachment insecurity and adjustment problems due to inadequate child care, long hours in child care, and the joint pressures their mothers experience from full-time employment and parenthood. But it is inappropriate to use

these findings to justify a reduction in child-care services. When family incomes are limited or mothers who want to work are forced to stay at home, children's emotional security is not promoted.

Instead, it makes sense to increase the availability of high-quality child care, to provide paid employment leave so parents can limit the hours their children spend in child care (see pages 104–105), and to educate parents about the vital role of sensitive caregiving and child-care quality in early emotional development. Return to Chapter 5, page 171, to review signs of developmentally appropriate child care for infants and toddlers. For child care to foster attachment security, the professional caregiver's relationship with the baby is vital. When caregiver–child ratios are generous, group sizes are small, and caregivers are educated about child development and child rearing, caregivers' interactions are more positive and children develop more favorably (NICHD Early Child Care Research Network, 2002a, 2000b). Child care with these characteristics can become part of an ecological system that relieves rather than intensifies parental and child stress, thereby promoting healthy attachment and development.

At the end of her day in child care, a toddler eagerly greets her mother. High-quality child care and fewer hours in child care are associated with favorable mother–child interaction, which contributes to attachment security.

tional games like pat-a-cake and peekaboo. In contrast, fathers tend to engage in highly arousing physical play with bursts of excitement that increase as play progresses, especially with their infant sons (Yogman, 1981; Feldman, 2003). Perhaps such play helps prepare babies to venture confidently into their surrounding world (Paquette, 2004). Through a stimulating, surprising play style, fathers teach children how to approach unfamiliar situations, such as play with peers.

In cultures such as Japan's, where long work hours prevent most fathers from sharing in infant caregiving, play is a vital context in which fathers build secure attachments (Hewlett, 2004; Schwalb et al., 2004). In many Western nations, however, a strict division of parental roles—mother as caregiver, father as playmate—has changed over the past quarter century in response to women's workforce participation and to cultural valuing of gender equality. Recent surveys indicate that in dual-earner families, U.S. fathers devote 85 percent as much time, and Canadian fathers 75 percent as much time, as mothers do to children—on average, about 3½ hours per day (Sandberg & Hof-

ferth, 2001; Zuzanek, 2000; Pleck & Masciadrelli, 2004). Paternal time engaged with or accessible to children is fairly similar across SES and ethnic groups, with one exception: Hispanic fathers spend more time engaged, probably due to the particularly high value that Hispanic cultures place on family involvement (Cabrera & Garcia-Coll, 2004; Parke et al., 2004; Wilcox, 2002).

Mothers in dual-earner families tend to engage in more playful stimulation of their babies (Cox et al., 1992). When fathers are primary caregivers, they retain their arousing play style (Lamb & Oppenheim, 1989). Such highly involved fathers typically are less gender-stereotyped in their beliefs; have sympathetic, friendly personalities; often had fathers who were more involved in rearing them; and regard parenthood as an especially enriching experience (Cabrera et al., 2000; Levy-Shiff & Israelashvili, 1988).

Fathers' involvement with babies unfolds within a complex system of family attitudes and relationships. When both mothers and fathers believe that men are capable of nurturing infants, fathers devote more time to caregiving (Beitel & Parke,

Cultural Influences

The Powerful Role of Paternal Warmth in Development

Research in diverse cultures demonstrates that fathers' warmth contributes greatly to children's long-term favorable development. In studies of many societies and ethnic groups around the world, researchers coded paternal expressions of love and nurturance—evident in such behaviors as cuddling, hugging, comforting, playing, verbally expressing love, and praising the child's behavior. Fathers' affectionate involvement predicted later cognitive, emotional, and social competence as strongly, and occasionally more strongly, than did mothers' warmth (Rohner & Veneziano, 2001; Veneziano, 2003). And in Western cultures, paternal warmth protected children against a wide range of difficulties, including childhood emotional and behavior problems and adolescent substance abuse and delinquency (Grant et al., 2000; Rohner & Brothers, 1999; Tacon & Caldera, 2001).

In families where fathers devote little time to physical caregiving, they express warmth through play. In a German study, fathers' play sensitivity—accepting toddlers' play initiatives, adapting play behaviors to toddlers' capacities, and responding appropriately to toddlers' expressions of emotion—predicted a secure father–child relationship in childhood and adolescence (Grossmann et al., 2002). Through play, fathers seemed

to transfer to young children a sense of confidence about parental support, which may strengthen their capacity to master many later challenges.

What factors promote paternal warmth? Cross-cultural research reveals a consistent association between the amount of time fathers spend near infants and toddlers and their expressions of caring and affection (Rohner & Veneziano, 2001). Consider the Aka hunters and gatherers of Central Africa, where fathers spend more time in physical proximity to their babies than in any other known society. Observations reveal that Aka fathers are within arm's reach of infants more than half the day. They pick up, cuddle, and play with their babies at least five times as often as fathers in other hunting-and-gathering societies. Why are Aka fathers so involved? The bond between Aka husband and wife is unusually cooperative and intimate. Throughout the day, couples share hunting, food preparation, and social and leisure activities. The more time Aka parents spend together, the greater the father's loving interaction with his baby (Hewlett, 1992).

In Western cultures as well, fathers in gratifying marriages spend more time with and interact more effectively with infants. In contrast, marital dissatisfaction is associated with insensitive paternal care (Grych & Clark, 1999; Lundy, 2002). Clearly mothers' and fathers' warm interactions with each other and with their babies are closely linked. But paternal warmth promotes long-term favorable development, beyond the influ-

© RONNIE KAUFMAN/CORBIS

This Japanese father engages in the exciting, active play typical of fathers in many cultures. In both Western and non-Western nations, fathers' warmth predicts long-term favorable development. And in Western societies, it protects against a range of adjustment problems in childhood and adolescence.

ence of maternal warmth (Rohner & Veneziano, 2001). Evidence for the power of fathers' affection, reported in virtually every culture and ethnic group studied, is reason to encourage more men to engage in nurturing care of young children.

1998). A warm marital relationship supports both parents' involvement with babies, but it is especially important for fathers (Lamb & Lewis, 2004). See the Cultural Influences box above for cross-cultural evidence documenting this conclusion—and also highlighting the powerful role of paternal warmth in children's development.

■ **Siblings.** Despite a smaller family size, 80 percent of North American and European children grow up with at least one sibling (Dunn, 2004). The arrival of a baby brother or sister is a difficult experience for most preschoolers, who, realizing that they must now share their parents' attention and affection, often become demanding, clingy, and deliberately

naughty for a time. Security of attachment also typically declines, especially for children over age 2 (old enough to feel threatened and displaced) and for those with mothers under stress (Baydar, Greek, & Brooks-Gunn, 1997; Teti et al., 1996).

Yet resentment is only one feature of a rich emotional relationship that starts to build between siblings after a baby's birth. Older children also show affection and concern—kissing and patting the baby, and calling out, "Mom, he needs you," when the infant cries. By the end of the first year, babies typically spend much time with older siblings and are comforted by the presence of a preschool-age brother or sister during short parental absences. And in the second year, toddlers often imitate and join in play with older siblings (Barr & Hayne, 2003).

Applying What We Know

Encouraging Affectionate Ties Between Infants and Their Preschool Siblings

Suggestion	Description
Spend extra time with the older child.	To minimize the older child's feelings of being deprived of affection and attention, set aside time to spend with her. Fathers can be especially helpful in this regard, planning special outings with the preschooler and taking over care of the baby so the mother can be with the older child.
Handle sibling misbehavior with patience.	Respond patiently to the older sibling's misbehavior and demands for attention, recognizing that these reactions are temporary. Give the preschooler opportunities to feel proud of being more grown-up than the baby. For example, encourage the older child to assist with feeding, bathing, dressing, and offering toys and show appreciation for these efforts.
Discuss the baby's wants and needs.	By helping the older sibling understand the baby's point of view, parents can promote friendly, considerate behavior. Say, for example, "He's so little that he just can't wait to be fed," or "He's trying to reach his rattle and can't."

Nevertheless, individual differences in sibling relationships emerge soon after the new baby's arrival. Temperament plays an important role. For example, conflict is greater when one sibling is emotionally intense or highly active (Brody, Stoneman, & McCoy, 1994; Dunn, 1994). And maternal warmth toward both children is related to positive sibling interaction and to preschoolers' support of a distressed younger sibling (Volling, 2001; Volling & Belsky, 1992). Mothers who frequently play with their young children and explain the toddler's wants and needs to the preschool sibling foster sibling cooperation. In contrast, maternal harshness and lack of involvement are linked to antagonistic sibling relationships (Howe, Aquan-Assee, & Bukowski, 2001).

Refer to Applying What We Know above for ways to promote positive sibling relationships between babies and preschoolers. Siblings offer a rich social context in which young children learn and practice a wide range of skills, including affectionate caring, conflict resolution, and control of hostile and envious feelings.

Attachment and Later Development

According to psychoanalytic and ethological theories, the inner feelings of affection and security that result from a healthy attachment relationship support all aspects of psychological development. Consistent with this view, an extensive longitudinal study found that preschoolers who were securely attached as babies were rated by their teachers as higher in self-esteem, social skills, and empathy than were their insecurely attached counterparts. Studied again at age 11 in summer camp, children who had been secure infants continued to be more socially competent, as judged by camp counselors (Elicker, Englund, & Sroufe, 1992; Matas, Arend, & Sroufe, 1978; Shulman, Elicker, & Sroufe, 1994).

For some researchers, these findings seem to indicate that secure attachment in infancy causes better development in later years. Yet contrary evidence exists. In other longitudinal research, secure infants sometimes developed more favorably than insecure infants, but not always (Lewis, 1997; Schneider, Atkinson, & Tardif, 2001; Stams, Juffer, & van IJzendoorn, 2002). The exception is disorganized/disoriented attachment, which is uniformly related to high hostility and aggression during the preschool and school years (Lyons-Ruth, 1996; Lyons-Ruth, Easterbrooks, & Cibelli, 1997).

What accounts for this inconsistency in findings? Mounting evidence indicates that *continuity of caregiving* determines whether attachment security is linked to later development

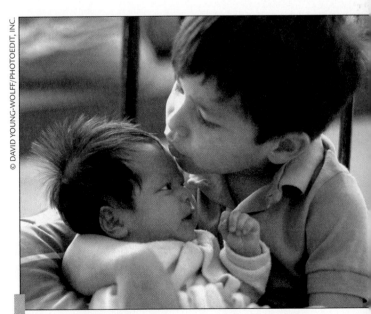

© DAVID YOUNG-WOLFF/PHOTOEDIT, INC.

The arrival of a baby brother or sister is a difficult experience for most preschoolers, but it also offers practice in expressing affectionate caring. As this boy holds and tenderly kisses his newborn sister, he begins to build a rich emotional relationship.

(Lamb et al., 1985; Thompson, 2000). Much research shows that parents who respond sensitively not just in infancy but also during later years promote many aspects of development: a more confident self-concept, more advanced emotional understanding, more favorable relationships with teachers and peers, a stronger sense of moral responsibility, and higher motivation to achieve in school (Thompson, Easterbrooks, & Padilla-Walker, 2003). In contrast, children of parents who react insensitively over a long period are at risk for a wide array of developmental difficulties.

In sum, a secure attachment in infancy launches the parent–child relationship on a positive path. But the effects of early attachment security are *conditional*—dependent on the quality of the baby's future relationships. A child who experiences tender care in infancy but lacks sympathetic ties later is at risk for problems. In contrast, a child whose parental caregiving improves or who has other compensating ties outside the immediate family is likely to display *resilience*, or recovery from adversity (Belsky & Fearon, 2002).

As we conclude our discussion of attachment, consider the diverse factors that affect the parent–child bond: infant and parent characteristics, parents' marital relationship, outside-the-family stressors, the availability of social supports, parents' views of their own attachment history, and child-care arrangements. Although attachment builds within the warmth and intimacy of caregiver–infant interactions, it can be fully understood only from an ecological systems perspective (Cummings & Cummings, 2002). Return to Chapter 1, page 24, to review ecological systems theory. Notice how research confirms the contribution of each level of the environment to attachment security.

Ask Yourself

Review
> What factors explain stability in attachment pattern for some children and change for others? Are these factors also involved in the link between attachment in infancy and later development? Explain.

Apply
> What attachment pattern did Timmy display when Vanessa picked him up from child care? What factors probably contributed to his response?

Connect
> Review research on emotional self-regulation on page 189. How do the caregiving experiences of securely attached infants promote development of emotional self-regulation?

Reflect
> How would you characterize your internal working model? What factors, in addition to your relationship with your parents, might have influenced it?

Self-Development During the First Two Years

Infancy is a rich, formative period for the development of physical and social understanding. In Chapter 5, you learned that infants develop an appreciation of the permanence of objects. And in this chapter, we have seen that over the first year, infants recognize and respond appropriately to others' emotions and distinguish familiar from unfamiliar people. That both objects and people achieve an independent, stable existence for the infant implies that knowledge of the self as a separate, permanent entity is also emerging.

Self-Awareness

After Caitlin's bath, Carolyn often held her in front of the bathroom mirror. As early as the first few months, Caitlin smiled and returned friendly behaviors to her image. At what age did she realize that the charming baby gazing and grinning back was herself?

■ **Beginnings of Self-Awareness.** At birth, infants sense that they are physically distinct from their surroundings. For example, newborns display a stronger rooting reflex in response to external stimulation (an adult's finger touching their cheek) than to self-stimulation (their own hand contacting their cheek) (Rochat & Hespos, 1997). Newborns' remarkable capacity for *intermodal perception* (see page 146 in Chapter 4) supports the beginnings of self-awareness (Rochat, 2003). As they feel their own touch, feel and watch their limbs move, and feel and hear themselves cry, babies experience intermodal matches that differentiate their own body from surrounding bodies and objects.

Over the first few months, infants distinguish their own visual image from other stimuli, although self-awareness is still limited—expressed only in perception and action. When showed two side-by-side video images of their kicking legs, one from their own perspective (camera behind the baby) and one from an observer's perspective (camera in front of the baby), 3-month-olds looked longer at the unfamiliar, observer's view (Rochat, 1998). By 4 months, infants look and smile more at video images of others than at video images of themselves, indicating that they treat another person (as opposed to the self) as a social partner (Rochat & Striano, 2002).

■ **Self-Recognition.** During the second year, toddlers become consciously aware of the self's physical features. Seeing their image in a mirror, they may act silly or coy, playfully experimenting with the way the self looks (Bullock & Lutkenhaus, 1990). In one study, 9- to 24-month-olds were placed in front of a mirror. Then, under the pretext of wiping the baby's face, each mother rubbed red dye on her infant's nose. Younger infants touched the mirror as if the red mark had nothing to do with them. But 15-month-olds rubbed their strange-looking red noses, a response indicating awareness of their unique appearance (Lewis & Brooks-Gunn, 1979).

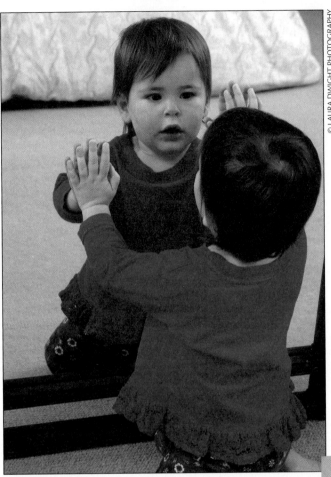

This 1-year-old notices the correspondence between her own movements and the movements of the image in the mirror, a cue that helps her figure out that the baby is really herself.

2001). For example, batting a mobile and seeing it swing in a pattern different from the infant's own actions gives the baby information about the relation between self and physical world. Smiling and vocalizing at a caregiver who smiles and vocalizes back helps clarify the relation between self and social world. The contrast between these experiences helps infants build an image of the self as separate from, but vitally connected to, external reality.

■ **Self-Awareness and Early Emotional and Social Development.** Self-awareness quickly becomes a central part of children's emotional and social lives. Recall that self-conscious emotions depend on a strengthening sense of self. Self-awareness also supports initial efforts to appreciate others' perspectives. It is associated with the beginnings of **empathy**— the ability to understand another's emotional state and *feel with* that person, or respond emotionally in a similar way. For example, toddlers start to give to others what they themselves find comforting—a hug, a reassuring comment, or a favorite doll or blanket (Hoffman, 2000). At the same time, they demonstrate clearer awareness of how to upset others. One 18-month-old heard her mother talking to another adult about an older sibling: "Anny is really frightened of spiders" (Dunn, 1989, p. 107). The innocent-looking toddler ran to the bedroom, returned with a toy spider, and pushed it in front of Anny's face!

Around age 2, **self-recognition**—identification of the self as a physically unique being—is well under way. Children point to themselves in photos and refer to themselves by name or with a personal pronoun ("I" or "me"). But it will take another year before children grasp the self as extending over time. When shown a live video of themselves, 2- and 3-year-olds quickly reached for a Post-It note stuck on top of their head as they saw it on the screen. But when they saw the note in a video that was replayed a few minutes later, not until age 4 did children remove the note and, when asked who was on TV, say with certainty, "Me" (Povinelli, 2001).

According to many theorists, self-awareness develops as infants and toddlers increasingly realize that their own actions cause objects and people to react in predictable ways (Harter, 1998). In support of this idea, babies whose parents encourage exploration and respond sensitively to their signals tend to be advanced in self-development (Pipp, Easterbrooks, & Harmon, 1992).

As infants act on the environment, they notice effects that help them sort out self, other people, and objects (Rochat,

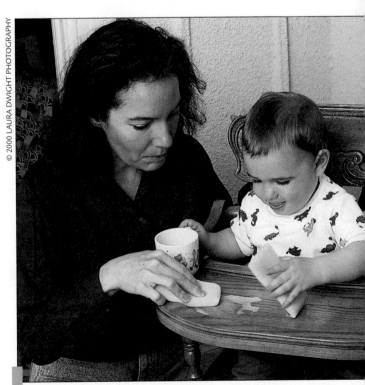

Encouraging this toddler to help wipe up spilled milk fosters compliance and the beginnings of self-control. He joins in the clean-up task with an eager, willing spirit, suggesting that he is beginning to adopt the adult's directive as his own.

Categorizing the Self

By the end of the second year, language becomes a powerful tool in self-development. Because it permits children to represent the self more clearly, it greatly enhances self-awareness.

Between 18 and 30 months, children develop a **categorical self** as they categorize themselves and others on the basis of age ("baby," "boy," or "man"), sex ("boy" or "girl"), physical characteristics ("big," "strong"), and even goodness versus badness ("I a good girl," "Tommy mean!") (Stipek, Gralinski, & Kopp, 1990). Toddlers use their limited understanding of these social categories to organize their own behavior. For example, children's ability to label their own gender is associated with a sharp rise in gender-stereotyped responses. As early as 18 months, toddlers select and play in a more involved way with toys that are stereotyped for their own gender—dolls and tea sets for girls, trucks and cars for boys. Parents then encourage these preferences by responding positively when toddlers display them (Fagot, Leinbach, & O'Boyle, 1992). As we will see in Chapter 8, gender-typed behavior increases dramatically in early childhood.

Self-Control

Self-awareness also contributes to *effortful control*, the extent to which children can inhibit impulses, manage negative emotion, and behave in socially acceptable ways. Indeed, a firmer sense of self may underlie the increasing stability and organization of effortful control after age 2 (see page 192). To behave in a self-controlled fashion, children must have some ability to think of themselves as separate, autonomous beings who can direct their own actions. And they must have the representational and memory capacities to recall a caregiver's directive ("Caitlin, don't touch that light socket!") and apply it to their own behavior.

As these capacities emerge between 12 and 18 months, toddlers first become capable of **compliance.** They show clear awareness of caregivers' wishes and expectations and can obey simple requests and commands. And as every parent knows, they can also decide to do just the opposite! One way toddlers assert their autonomy is by resisting adult directives. But for most, opposition is far less common than compliance with an eager, willing spirit, which suggests that the child is beginning to adopt the adult's directives as his own (Kochanska, Murray, & Harlan, 2000). Compliance quickly leads to toddlers' first consciencelike verbalizations—for example, correcting the self by saying "No, can't" before reaching for a treat or jumping on the sofa (Kochanska, 1993).

Researchers often study the early emergence of self-control by giving children tasks that, like the situations just mentioned, require **delay of gratification**—waiting for an appropriate time and place to engage in a tempting act. Between ages 1½ and 3, children show an increasing capacity to wait before eating a treat, opening a present, or playing with a toy (Vaughn, Kopp, & Krakow, 1984).

Applying What We Know

Helping Toddlers Develop Compliance and Self-Control

Suggestion	Rationale
Respond to the toddler with sensitivity and encouragement.	Toddlers whose parents are sensitive and supportive are more compliant and self-controlled.
Provide advance notice when the toddler must stop an enjoyable activity.	Toddlers find it more difficult to stop a pleasant activity already under way than to wait before engaging in a desired action.
Offer many prompts and reminders.	Toddlers' ability to remember and comply with rules is limited; they need continuous adult oversight.
Respond to self-controlled behavior with verbal and physical approval.	Praise and hugs reinforce appropriate behavior, increasing its likelihood of occurring again.
Encourage sustained attention (see Chapter 5, page 161).	Development of attention is related to self-control. Children who can shift attention from a captivating stimulus and focus on a less attractive alternative are better at controlling their impulses.
Support language development (see Chapter 5, page 171).	Early language development is related to self-control. In the second year, children begin to use language to remind themselves of adult expectations and to delay gratification.
Gradually increase rules in accord with the toddler's developing capacities.	As cognition and language improve, toddlers can follow more rules related to safety, respect for people and property, family routines, manners, and simple chores.

Children who are advanced in development of attention and language tend to be better at delaying gratification—findings that help explain why girls are typically more self-controlled than boys (Cournoyer, Solomon, & Trudel, 1998; Kochanska & Knaack, 2003). Some toddlers already use verbal and other attention-diverting techniques—talking to themselves, singing, or looking away—to keep from engaging in prohibited acts. And toddlers who experience parental warmth and gentle encouragement are advanced in self-control (Kochanska, Murray, & Harlan, 2000; Lehman et al., 2002). Such parenting seems to encourage as well as model patient, nonimpulsive behavior.

As self-control improves, parents gradually expand the rules they expect toddlers to follow, from safety and respect for property and people to family routines, manners, and responsibility for simple chores (Gralinski & Kopp, 1993). Still, toddlers' control over their own actions depends on constant parental oversight and reminders. Several prompts ("Remember, we're going to go in just a minute") and gentle insistence were usually necessary to get Caitlin to stop playing so that she and her parents could go on an errand. Applying What We Know on the previous page summarizes ways to help toddlers develop compliance and self-control.

As the second year of life drew to a close, Carolyn, Monica, and Vanessa were delighted at their children's readiness to learn the rules of social life. As we will see in Chapter 8, advances in cognition and language, along with parental warmth and reasonable maturity demands, lead preschoolers to make tremendous strides in this area.

Ask Yourself

Review

Why is insisting that infants comply with parental directives inappropriate? What competencies are necessary for the emergence of compliance and self-control?

Apply

Len, a caregiver of 1- and 2-year-olds, wonders whether toddlers recognize themselves. List signs of self-recognition in the second year that Len can observe.

Connect

What type of parenting fosters development of emotional self-regulation, secure attachment, and self-control? Why, in each instance, is it effective?

www.ablongman.com/berk

Summary

Erikson's Theory of Infant and Toddler Personality

What personality changes occur during Erikson's stages of basic trust versus mistrust and autonomy versus shame and doubt?

■ According to Erikson, warm, responsive caregiving leads infants to resolve the psychological conflict of **basic trust versus mistrust** on the positive side. During toddlerhood, the conflict of **autonomy versus shame and doubt** is resolved favorably when parents provide appropriate guidance and reasonable choices. If children emerge from the first few years without sufficient trust and autonomy, the seeds are sown for adjustment problems.

Emotional Development

Describe changes in happiness, anger, and fear over the first year, noting the adaptive function of each.

■ During the first half-year, **basic emotions** gradually become clear, well-organized signals. The **social smile** appears between 6 and 10 weeks, laughter around 3 to 4 months. Happiness strengthens the parent–child bond and both reflects and supports physical and cognitive mastery.

■ Anger and fear, especially in the form of **stranger anxiety,** increase in the second half of the first year. Newly mobile babies use the familiar caregiver as a **secure base,** or point from which to explore. Sadness, while less frequent than anger, is common when care-giver–infant communication is seriously disrupted. These reactions have survival value as infants' motor capacities improve.

Summarize changes during the first two years in understanding others' emotions, expression of self-conscious emotions, and emotional self-regulation.

■ The ability to understand the feelings of others expands over the first year. Around 5 months, babies perceive facial expressions as organized patterns. Toward the end of the first year, **social referencing** appears; in uncertain situations, infants actively seek emotional information from caregivers, relying especially on the caregiver's voice. By the middle of the second year, infants appreciate that others' emotional reactions may differ from their own.

■ During toddlerhood, self-awareness and adult instruction provide the foundation for **self-conscious emotions,** such as guilt, shame, embarrassment, envy, and pride. Caregivers help infants with **emotional self-regulation** by relieving distress, engaging in stimulating play, and discouraging negative emotion. During the second year, growth in representation and language leads to more effective ways of regulating emotion.

Temperament and Development

What is temperament, and how is it measured?

■ Children differ greatly in **temperament**—early-appearing, stable individual differences in reactivity and self-regulation. Three patterns of temperament—the **easy child,** the **difficult child,** and the **slow-to-warm-up child**—were identified in the New York Longitudinal Study. Difficult children, especially, are likely to display adjustment problems. Another model of temperament, devised by Mary Rothbart, includes **effortful control,** the ability to regulate one's reactivity.

■ Temperament is assessed using parental reports, behavior ratings by others familiar with the child, and laboratory observations. A combination of laboratory and physiological measures has been used to distinguish **inhibited,** or **shy, children** from **uninhibited,** or **sociable, children.**

Discuss the role of heredity and environment in the stability of temperament, including the goodness-of-fit model.

■ Stability of temperament is generally low to moderate. Temperament has a genetic foundation, but child rearing and cultural beliefs and practices have much to do with main-

taining or changing it. The **goodness-of-fit model** describes how temperament and environment work together to affect later development. Parenting practices that create a good fit with the child's temperament help difficult and shy children achieve more adaptive functioning.

Development of Attachment

Describe ethological theory of attachment and the development of attachment during the first 2 years.

■ The most widely accepted perspective on development of **attachment** is **ethological theory.** It views babies as biologically prepared to contribute actively to ties established with their caregivers, which promote survival by ensuring both safety and competence.

■ In early infancy, a set of built-in behaviors encourages the parent to remain close to the baby. Around 6 to 8 months, **separation anxiety** and use of the parent as a secure base indicate that a true attachment bond has formed. As representation and language develop, toddlers try to alter the parent's coming and going through requests and persuasion. Out of early caregiving experiences, children construct an **internal working model** that serves as a guide for all future close relationships.

Describe the Strange Situation and the Attachment Q-Sort, along with factors that affect attachment security.

■ The **Strange Situation** is a laboratory technique for assessing the quality of attachment between 1 and 2 years. Using it, researchers have identified four attachment patterns: **secure attachment, avoidant attachment, resistant attachment,** and **disorganized/disoriented attachment.** The **Attachment Q-Sort,** an alternative method based on home observations, yields a score ranging from low to high security and is suitable for 1- to 4-year-olds.

■ Securely attached babies in middle-SES families experiencing favorable life conditions more often maintain their attachment pattern than do insecure babies. An exception is the disorganized/disoriented pattern, which is highly stable. Cultural conditions must be considered in interpreting the meaning of attachment patterns.

■ Attachment quality is influenced by the infant's opportunity to develop a close affectional tie with one or a few adults, **sensitive caregiving,** the fit between the baby's temperament and parenting practices, and fam-

ily circumstances. In some (but not all) cultures, **interactional synchrony** characterizes the experiences of securely attached babies. Parents' internal working models are good predictors of infant attachment patterns, but parents' childhood experiences do not transfer directly to quality of attachment with their own children.

Discuss infants' attachments to fathers and siblings.

■ Infants develop strong affectionate ties to fathers, whose sensitive caregiving predicts secure attachment. Fathers in a variety of cultures engage in more exciting, physical play with babies than do mothers. Early in the first year, infants begin to build rich emotional relationships with siblings that mix affection and caring with rivalry and resentment. Individual differences in the quality of sibling relationships are influenced by temperament and parenting practices.

Describe and interpret the relationship between secure attachment in infancy and later development.

■ Continuity of caregiving is the crucial factor that determines whether attachment security is linked to later development. Children can recover from an insecure attachment history if caregiving improves. Nevertheless, a secure attachment in infancy is important because it launches the parent–child relationship on a positive path.

Self-Development During the First Two Years

Describe the development of self-awareness in infancy and toddlerhood, along with the emotional and social capacities it supports.

■ At birth, infants sense that they are physically distinct from their surroundings, an awareness that is promoted by their capacity for intermodal perception. Around age 2, **self-recognition**—identification of the self as a physically unique being—is well under way. Two-year-olds refer to themselves by name or with a personal pronoun and point to themselves in photos.

■ Self-awareness leads to toddlers' first efforts to appreciate others' perspectives. It is associated with the beginnings of **empathy,** the ability to *feel with* another person. As language strengthens and toddlers compare themselves to others, between 18 and 30 months they develop a **categorical self** based on age, sex, physical characteristics, and goodness and badness.

■ Self-awareness also provides the foundation for the emergence of **compliance** between 12 and 18 months, and an increasing capacity for **delay of gratification** between ages 1½ and 3. Children who are advanced in development of attention and language and who have warm, encouraging parents tend to be more self-controlled.

Important Terms and Concepts

attachment (p. 196)
Attachment Q-Sort (p. 198)
autonomy versus shame and doubt (p. 184)
avoidant attachment (p. 198)
basic emotions (p. 185)
basic trust versus mistrust (p. 184)
categorical self (p. 208)
compliance (p. 208)
delay of gratification (p. 208)
difficult child (p. 190)
disorganized/disoriented attachment (p. 198)

easy child (p. 190)
effortful control (p. 191)
emotional self-regulation (p. 189)
empathy (p. 207)
ethological theory of attachment (p. 196)
goodness-of-fit model (p. 194)
inhibited, or shy, child (p. 191)
interactional synchrony (p. 200)
internal working model (p. 197)
resistant attachment (p. 198)
secure attachment (p. 198)
secure base (p. 188)

self-conscious emotions (p. 188)
self-recognition (p. 207)
sensitive caregiving (p. 200)
separation anxiety (p. 197)
slow-to-warm-up child (p. 190)
social referencing (p. 188)
social smile (p. 186)
Strange Situation (p. 197)
stranger anxiety (p. 186)
temperament (p. 190)
uninhibited, or sociable, child (p. 191)

Milestones

Development in Infancy and Toddlerhood

Age	Physical	Cognitive	Language	Emotional/Social
BIRTH– 6 MONTHS	• Height and weight increase rapidly (120–121) • Reflexes decline (186–187) • Synaptic growth and myelination of neural fibers in the brain occur rapidly (121) • Sleep is organized into a day-night schedule (128) • Holds head up, rolls over, and reaches for objects (137–138, 139) • By end of this period, is sensitive to syllable stress patterns of own language (141) • Depth and pattern perception improve (141–146)	• Engages in immediate and deferred imitation of adults' facial expressions (135–136, 155) • Prefers faces and facelike visual stimuli (145) • Repeats chance behaviors leading to interesting results (153–154) • Has some awareness of many physical properties (including object permanence) and basic numerical knowledge (155) • Attention becomes more efficient and flexible (161) • Recognition memory for people, places, and objects improves (161–162) • Forms perceptual categories based on objects' similar features (162–164)	• Is sensitive to speech sounds and prefers human voice to other sounds (173) • Coos, then babbles (174) • Engages in vocal exchanges with caregiver (177) • Begins to establish joint attention with caregiver, who labels objects and events (177)	• Social smile and laughter emerge (300) • Matches adults' feeling tone in face-to-face interaction (285) • Emotional expressions become well-organized and meaningfully related to environmental events (185) • Awareness of self as physically distinct from surroundings increases (206–207)
7–12 MONTHS	• Sits alone, crawls, and walks (118) • Shows pincer grasp (140) • "Screens out" sounds not used in own language; perceives meaningful speech units (141) • Depth perception improves further (146–149) • Has mastered many intermodal relationships (146)	• Engages in intentional, or goal-directed, behavior (161) • Able to find object hidden in one place (154) • Engages in deferred imitation of adults' actions with objects (155) • Recall memory for people, places, and objects improves (162) • Categorizes objects conceptually, by similar function and behavior (154) • Solves simple problems by analogy (157)	• Babbling expands to include sounds of spoken languages and the child's language community (174–175) • Comprehends some words (174) • Uses preverbal gestures to communicate (174–175) 	• Anger and fear increase (186) • Stranger anxiety and separation anxiety appear (186) • Uses caregiver as a secure base (188) • Detects the meaning of others' emotional expressions and engages in social referencing (188) • Regulates emotion by approaching and retreating from stimulation (189) • Shows "clear-cut" attachment to familiar caregivers (197)

Age	Physical	Cognitive	Language	Emotional/Social
13–18 MONTHS	• Height and weight gain rapid, but not as great as in first year; babies slim down (120) • Walking is better coordinated (137) • Manipulates small objects with improved coordination (139–140)	• Explores the properties of objects by acting on them in novel ways (153) • Searches in several locations for a hidden object (154) • Sorts objects into categories (162, 164)	• Joint attention with caregiver becomes more accurate (174) • Takes turns in games, such as pat-a-cake and peekaboo (175) • Says first words (175) 	• Joins in play with familiar adults and siblings (202–206) • Recognizes image of self in mirror (207) • Shows signs of empathy (207) • Complies with simple directives (208–209)
19–24 MONTHS	• Brain reaches 70 percent of its adult weight (122) • Jumps and climbs (137) • Manipulates small objects with good coordination (139–140) 	• Solves simple problems suddenly, through representation (154–155) • Finds hidden object moved while out of sight (154) • Engages in deferred imitation of actions an adult tries to produce, even if not fully realized (155) • Engages in make-believe play, using simple actions (155) • Sustained attention improves (161) • Sorts objects into categories more effectively (162, 164) • Recall memory improves further (165)	• Produces about 200 words (176) 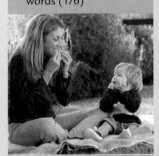 • Combines two words (172–173)	• Self-conscious emotions (shame, embarrassment, guilt, and pride) emerge (188–189) • Begins using language to assist with emotional self-regulation (189) • Acquires a vocabulary for talking about feelings (190) • Begins to tolerate caregiver's absences more easily (204) • Uses own name or personal pronoun to label self (206) • Categorizes self and others on the basis of age, sex, physical characteristics, and goodness and badness (208) • Shows gender-stereotyped toy preferences (208) • Self-control emerges (208–209)

Note: Numbers in parentheses indicate the page or pages on which each milestone is discussed.

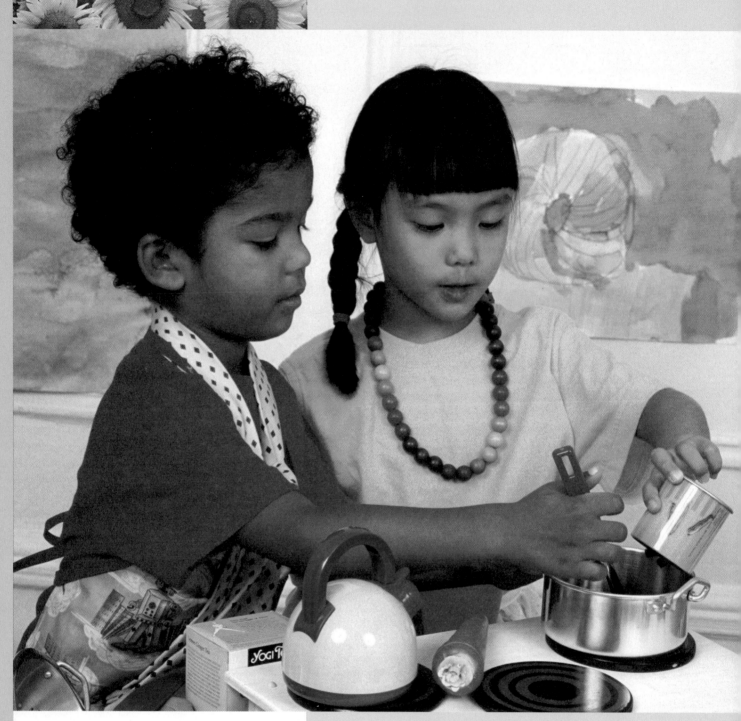

Make-believe play is an engrossing, enjoyable activity for preschoolers, who draw on their rich array of everyday experiences to create elaborate scenes and story lines. Children's make-believe contributes greatly to their rapidly advancing cognitive and language skills.

Physical and Cognitive Development in Early Childhood

For more than a decade, my fourth-floor office window over-looked the preschool and kindergarten play yard of our university laboratory school. On mild fall and spring mornings, the doors of the classrooms swung open, and sand table, easels, and large blocks spilled out into a small courtyard. Alongside the building was a grassy area with jungle gyms, swings, a playhouse, and a flower garden planted by the children; beyond it, a circular path lined with tricycles and wagons. Each day, the setting was alive with activity.

© LAURA DWIGHT PHOTOGRAPHY

The years from 2 to 6 are often called "the play years"—aptly so, since play blossoms during this time and supports every aspect of development. Our discussion opens with the physical achievements of early childhood—growth in body size, improvements in motor coordination, and refinements in perception. We look at biological and environmental factors that support physical changes and at their intimate connection with other domains of development.

Then we explore early childhood cognition, beginning with Piaget's preoperational stage. Recent research, along with Vygotsky's sociocultural theory and information processing, extends our understanding of preschoolers' cognitive competencies. Next, we turn to factors that contribute to early childhood mental development—the home environment, the quality of preschool and child care, and educational media. We conclude with the most awesome achievement of early childhood—language development.

🌿 Physical Development

Body Growth

In early childhood, body growth tapers off from the rapid rate of the first 2 years. On average, children add two to three inches in height and about five pounds in weight each year; boys continue to be slightly larger than girls. As "baby fat" drops off further, children gradually become thinner, although girls retain somewhat more body fat than boys, who are slightly more muscular. As Figure 7.1 shows, by age 5 the top-heavy, bowlegged, potbellied toddler has become a more streamlined, flat-tummied, longer-legged child with body proportions similar to those of adults. Consequently, posture and balance improve—changes that support gains in motor coordination.

Individual differences in body size are even more apparent during early childhood than in infancy and toddlerhood. Speeding around the bike path in the play yard, 5-year-old Darryl—at 48 inches tall and 55 pounds—towered over his kindergarten classmates. (The average North American 5-year-old boy is 43 inches tall and weighs 42 pounds.) Priti, an Asian-Indian child, was unusually small because of genetic factors linked to her cultural ancestry. Lynette and Hal, two Caucasian children with impoverished home lives, were well below average for reasons we will discuss shortly.

Andy at 3 years

Andy at 4 years

Andy at 5 years

Andy at 5¾ years

Amy at 3 years

Amy at 3½ years

Amy at 4½ years

Amy at 5½ years

■ **FIGURE 7.1 Body growth during early childhood.** During the preschool years, Andy and Amy grew more slowly than in infancy and toddlerhood (see Chapter 4, page 120). By age 5, their bodies became more streamlined, flat-tummied, and longer-legged. Boys continue to be slightly taller, heavier, and more muscular than girls. But generally, the two sexes are similar in body proportions and physical capacities.

Skeletal Growth

The skeletal changes of infancy continue throughout early childhood. Between ages 2 and 6, approximately 45 new *epiphyses*—or growth centers in which cartilage hardens into bone—emerge in various parts of the skeleton. X-rays of these growth centers enable doctors to estimate children's *skeletal age,* or progress toward physical maturity (see page 121 in Chapter 4)—information helpful in diagnosing growth disorders.

By the end of the preschool years, children start to lose their primary, or "baby," teeth. The age at which they do so is heavily influenced by genetic factors. For example, girls, who are ahead of boys in physical development, lose teeth sooner. Environmental influences, especially prolonged malnutrition, can delay the appearance of permanent teeth.

Care of primary teeth is essential because diseased baby teeth can affect the health of permanent teeth. Brushing consistently, avoiding sugary foods, drinking fluoridated water, and getting topical fluoride treatments and sealants (plastic coatings that protect tooth surfaces) prevent cavities. Another factor is exposure to tobacco smoke, which suppresses children's immune system, including the ability to fight bacteria responsible for tooth decay. Young children in homes with regular smokers are three times more likely than their agemates to have decayed teeth, even after other factors that influence dental health have been controlled (Shenkin et al., 2004).

Unfortunately, an estimated 40 percent of North American 5-year-olds have tooth decay, a figure that rises to 80 percent by age 18 (World Health Organization, 2003). Causes include poor diet, lack of fluoridation in some communities, and inadequate health care—factors that are more likely to affect low-SES children.

Asynchronies in Physical Growth

As Figure 7.2 shows, physical growth is *asynchronous;* body systems differ in their patterns of growth. Body size (as measured by height and weight) and a variety of internal organs follow the **general growth curve:** rapid growth during infancy, slower gains in early and middle childhood, and rapid growth again during adolescence. The genitals develop slowly from birth to age 4, change little throughout middle childhood, and then grow rapidly during adolescence. In contrast, the lymph glands grow at an astounding pace in infancy and childhood; in adolescence, lymph tissue declines. The lymph system helps fight infection and assists with absorption of nutrients, thereby supporting children's health and survival.

Figure 7.2 illustrates another growth trend with which you are already familiar: During the first few years, the brain grows faster than any other body structure.

Brain Development

Between ages 2 and 6, the brain increases from 70 percent of its adult weight to 90 percent. By age 4, many parts of the cerebral cortex have overproduced synapses, and fMRI evidence indicates that cerebral blood flow peaks, signifying a

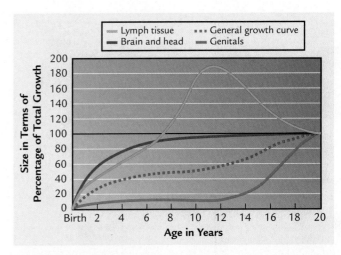

■ **FIGURE 7.2 Growth of three different organ systems and tissues contrasted with the body's general growth.** Growth is plotted in terms of percentage of change from birth to 20 years. Note that the growth of lymph tissue rises to nearly twice its adult level by the end of childhood. Then it declines. (Reprinted by permission of the publisher from J. M. Tanner, 1990, *Foetus into Man,* 2nd ed., Cambridge, MA: Harvard University Press, p. 16. Copyright © 1990 by J. M. Tanner. All rights reserved.)

high energy need (Huttenlocher, 2002). As *formation of synapses, cell death, myelination,* and *synaptic pruning* occur (see Chapter 4), preschoolers improve in a wide variety of skills—physical coordination, perception, attention, memory, language, logical thinking, and imagination.

EEG and fMRI measures of neural activity in various cortical regions reveal especially rapid growth from 3 to 6 years in frontal-lobe areas devoted to planning and organizing behavior. Furthermore, for most children, the left cerebral hemisphere is especially active between 3 and 6 years and then levels off. In contrast, activity in the right hemisphere increases steadily throughout early and middle childhood (Thatcher, Walker, & Giudice, 1987; Thompson et al., 2000a).

These findings fit nicely with what we know about several aspects of cognitive development. Early childhood is a time of marked gains on tasks that depend on the frontal cortex—ones that require inhibiting impulses and substituting thoughtful responses (Diamond, 2004). Further, language skills (typically housed in the left hemisphere) increase at an astonishing pace in early childhood, and they support children's increasing control over behavior. In contrast, spatial skills (usually located in the right hemisphere), such as giving directions, drawing pictures, and recognizing geometric shapes, develop gradually over childhood and adolescence. Differences in rate of development between the two hemispheres suggest that they are continuing to *lateralize* (specialize in cognitive functions). Let's take a closer look at brain lateralization in early childhood by focusing on handedness.

Handedness

On one visit to the preschool, I observed 3-year-old Moira drawing pictures, eating a snack, and playing outside. Unlike most of her classmates, Moira does most things—drawing,

© LAURA DWIGHT PHOTOGRAPHY

Twins are more likely than ordinary siblings to differ in handedness, perhaps because they usually lie in opposite orientations in the uterus. Although left-handedness is associated with developmental problems, most left-handed children are normal, and some develop outstanding verbal and mathematical talents.

eating, zipping her jacket—with her left hand. But she uses her right hand for a few activities, such as throwing a ball. Research on handedness, along with other evidence covered in Chapter 4, supports the joint contribution of nature and nurture to brain lateralization.

By the end of the first year, children typically display a hand preference that, over the next few years, gradually extends to a wider range of skills (Hinojosa, Sheu, & Michael, 2003). Handedness reflects the greater capacity of one side of the brain—often referred to as the individual's **dominant cerebral hemisphere**—to carry out skilled motor action. Other important abilities are generally located on the dominant side as well. For right-handed people, who make up 90 percent of the population in Western nations, language is housed with hand control in the left hemisphere. For the left-handed 10 percent, language is occasionally located in the right hemisphere or, more often, shared between the hemispheres (Szaflarski et al., 2002). This indicates that the brains of left-handers tend to be less strongly lateralized than those of right-handers.

Left-handed parents show only a weak tendency to have left-handed children. One genetic theory proposes that most children inherit a gene that *biases* them for right-handedness and a left-dominant cerebral hemisphere, but the bias is not strong enough to overcome experiences that might sway children toward a left-hand preference (Annett, 2002). Even prenatal events may profoundly affect handedness. Both identical and fraternal twins are more likely than ordinary siblings to differ in hand preference, probably because twins usually lie in opposite orientations in the uterus (Derom et al., 1996). And the way most singleton fetuses orient—toward the left—is believed to promote greater control over movements on the body's right side (Previc, 1991).

Handedness also involves practice. Newborns' bias in head position causes them to spend more time looking at and using

one hand, which contributes to greater skillfulness of that hand (Hinojosa, Sheu, & Michael, 2003). Also, wide cultural differences exist in rates of left-handedness. In Tanzania, Africa, where children are physically restrained and punished for favoring their left hand, less than 1 percent of adults are left-handed (Provins, 1997).

You may have heard that left-handedness is more frequent among severely retarded and mentally ill people than in the general population. Although this is true, atypical lateralization is probably not responsible for these individuals' problems. Rather, early damage to the left hemisphere may have caused their disabilities while also leading to a shift in handedness. In support of this idea, left-handedness is associated with prenatal and birth difficulties that can result in brain damage, including prolonged labor, prematurity, Rh incompatibility, and breech delivery (O'Callaghan et al., 1993; Powls et al., 1996).

Most left-handers have no developmental problems. In fact, unusual lateralization may have certain advantages. Left- and mixed-handed youngsters are more likely than their right-handed agemates to develop outstanding verbal and mathematical talents (Flannery & Liederman, 1995). More even distribution of cognitive functions across both hemispheres may be responsible.

Other Advances in Brain Development

Besides the cortex, other parts of the brain make strides during early childhood (see Figure 7.3). These changes involve establishing links between different parts of the brain, increasing the coordinated functioning of the central nervous system.

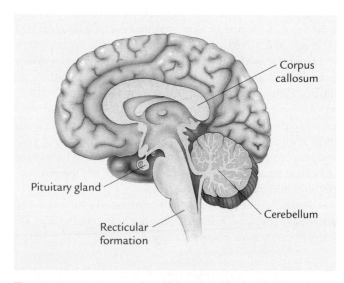

■ **FIGURE 7.3 Cross section of the human brain, showing the location of the cerebellum, the reticular formation, and the corpus callosum.** These structures undergo considerable development during early childhood. Also shown is the pituitary gland, which secretes hormones that control body growth (see page 219).

At the rear and base of the brain is the **cerebellum,** a structure that aids in balance and control of body movement. Fibers linking the cerebellum to the cerebral cortex grow and myelinate from birth through the preschool years. This change contributes to dramatic gains in motor coordination: By the end of the preschool years, children can play hopscotch, throw a ball with a well-organized set of movements, and print letters of the alphabet. Connections between the cerebellum and cerebral cortex also support thinking (Diamond, 2000): Children with damage to the cerebellum usually display both motor and cognitive deficits, including problems with memory, planning, and language (Noterdaeme et al., 2002; Riva & Giorgi, 2000).

The **reticular formation,** a structure in the brain stem that maintains alertness and consciousness, myelinates throughout childhood and into adolescence. Neurons in the reticular formation send out fibers to the frontal lobes of the cortex, contributing to improvements in sustained, controlled attention.

The **corpus callosum** is a large bundle of fibers connecting the two cortical hemispheres. Production of synapses and myelination of the corpus callosum peak between 3 and 6 years, then continue at a slower pace through adolescence (Thompson et al., 2000a). The corpus callosum supports smooth coordination of movements on both sides of the body and integration of many aspects of thinking, including perception, attention, memory, language, and problem solving. The more complex the task, the more critical is communication between the hemispheres.

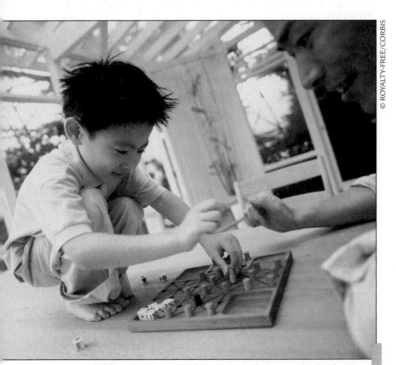

In early childhood, changes in the corpus callosum and other brain structures enhance communication between different parts of the brain, enabling children to perform increasingly complex tasks—like this board game—that require integration of attention, memory, language, and problem solving.

Ask Yourself

Review

What aspects of brain development underlie the tremendous gains in language, thinking, and motor control of early childhood?

Connect

What stand on the nature–nurture issue do findings on development of handedness support? Explain, using research findings.

Reflect

How early, and to what extent, did you experience tooth decay in childhood? What factors might have been responsible?

www.ablongman.com/berk

Influences on Physical Growth and Health

As we consider factors that affect growth and health in early childhood, you will encounter some familiar themes. Heredity remains important, but environmental factors—including emotional well-being, good nutrition, relative freedom from disease, and physical safety— also play crucial roles.

Heredity and Hormones

The impact of heredity on physical growth is evident throughout childhood. Children's physical size and rate of growth are related to those of their parents (Bogin, 2001). Genes influence growth by controlling the body's production of hormones. The **pituitary gland,** located at the base of the brain, plays a critical role by releasing two hormones that induce growth.

The first is **growth hormone (GH),** which from birth on is necessary for development of all body tissues except the central nervous system and genitals. Children who lack GH reach an average mature height of only four feet, four inches. When treated early with injections of GH, such children show catch-up growth and then grow at a normal rate, becoming much taller than they would have without treatment (Saenger, 2003).

A second pituitary hormone, **thyroid-stimulating hormone (TSH),** prompts the thyroid gland (in the neck) to release *thyroxine,* which is necessary for brain development and for GH to have its full impact on body size. Infants born with a deficiency of thyroxine must receive it at once, or they will be mentally retarded. Once the most rapid period of brain development is complete, children with too little thyroxine grow at a below-average rate, but the central nervous system is no longer affected. With prompt treatment, such children catch up in body growth and eventually reach normal size (Salerno et al., 2001).

Emotional Well-Being

In childhood as in infancy, emotional well-being can have a profound effect on growth and health. Children with stressful home lives (due to divorce, financial difficulties, or parental job loss) suffer more respiratory and intestinal illnesses and more unintentional injuries than others (Cohen & Herbert, 1996; Kemeny, 2003).

Extreme emotional deprivation can interfere with the production of GH and lead to **psychosocial dwarfism,** a growth disorder that usually appears between ages 2 and 15. Typical characteristics include very short stature, decreased GH secretion, immature skeletal age, and serious adjustment problems, which help distinguish psychosocial dwarfism from normal shortness (Doeker et al., 1999; Voss, Mulligan, & Betts, 1998). Lynette, the very small 4-year-old mentioned earlier in this chapter, was diagnosed with this condition. She had been placed in foster care after child welfare authorities discovered that she spent most of the day home alone, unsupervised, and might also have been physically abused. When such children are removed from their emotionally inadequate environments, their GH levels quickly return to normal, and they grow rapidly. But if treatment is delayed, the dwarfism can be permanent.

Nutrition

With the transition to early childhood, many children become unpredictable, picky eaters. One father I know wistfully recalled how his son, as a toddler, eagerly sampled Chinese food: "Now, at age 3, the only thing he'll try is the ice cream!"

Preschoolers' appetites decline because their growth has slowed. Their wariness of new foods is also adaptive. If they stick to familiar foods, they are less likely to swallow dangerous substances when adults are not around to protect them (Birch & Fisher, 1995). Parents need not worry about variations in amount eaten from meal to meal. Preschoolers compensate for eating little at one meal by eating more at a later one (Hursti, 1999).

Though they eat less, preschoolers require a high-quality diet, including the same foods adults need, but in smaller amounts. Fats, oils, and salt should be kept to a minimum because of their link to high blood pressure and heart disease in adulthood. Foods high in sugar should also be avoided to prevent tooth decay and protect against overweight and obesity—a topic we will take up in Chapter 9.

Children tend to imitate the food choices of people they admire, both adults and peers. For example, in Mexico, where children often see family members delighting in the taste of peppery foods, preschoolers enthusiastically eat chili peppers, whereas most North American children reject them (Birch, Zimmerman, & Hind, 1980). Repeated, unpressured exposure to a new food also increases acceptance. Children served broccoli or tofu come to like these nutritious foods. In contrast, children who are routinely offered sweet fruit or soft drinks may develop "milk avoidance" (Black et al., 2002).

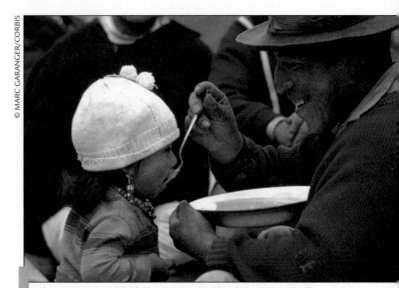

This Quechua child of the Peruvian highlands enthusiastically shares a soup made from bitter-tasting potatoes with her father. She has already acquired a taste for the foods that are commonly served in her culture.

Healthy eating depends on a wholesome food environment, but too much parental control limits children's opportunities to develop self-control. Offering bribes ("Finish your vegetables, and you can have an extra cookie") causes children to like the healthy food less and the treat more (Birch, Fisher, & Davison, 2003).

Finally, as indicated in earlier chapters, many children in North America and in developing countries lack access to sufficient high-quality food to support healthy growth. Five-year-old Hal rode a bus from a poor neighborhood to our laboratory preschool. His mother's welfare check barely covered her rent, let alone food. Hal's diet was deficient in protein and in essential vitamins and minerals—iron (to prevent anemia), calcium (to support development of bones and teeth), vitamin A (to help maintain eyes, skin, and a variety of internal organs), and vitamin C (to facilitate iron absorption and wound healing). These are the most common deficiencies of the preschool years (Kennedy, 1998). Not surprisingly, Hal was thin, pale, and tired. By age 7, low-SES North American children are, on average, about one inch shorter than their economically advantaged counterparts (Yip, Scanlon, & Trowbridge, 1993).

Infectious Disease

One day, I noticed that Hal had been absent from the play yard for several weeks, so I asked Leslie, his preschool teacher, what was wrong. "Hal's been hospitalized with the measles," she explained. "He's had difficulty recovering—lost weight when there wasn't much to lose in the first place." In well-nourished children, ordinary childhood illnesses have no effect on physical growth. But when children are poorly fed, disease interacts with malnutrition in a vicious spiral, with potentially severe consequences.

Infectious Disease and Malnutrition. Hal's reaction to the measles would be typical in developing nations, where a large proportion of the population lives in poverty and children do not receive routine immunizations. Illnesses such as measles and chicken pox, which typically do not appear until after age 3 in industrialized nations, occur much earlier. Poor diet depresses the body's immune system, making children far more susceptible to disease. Of the 10 million annual deaths of children under age 5 worldwide, 98 percent are in developing countries and 70 percent are due to infectious diseases (World Health Organization, 2005a).

Disease, in turn, is a major contributor to malnutrition, hindering both physical growth and cognitive development. Illness reduces appetite and limits the body's ability to absorb foods, especially in children with intestinal infections. In developing countries, widespread diarrhea, resulting from unsafe water and contaminated foods, leads to growth stunting and several million childhood deaths each year (Tharpar & Sanderson, 2004).

Most growth retardation and deaths due to diarrhea can be prevented with nearly cost-free *oral rehydration therapy (ORT)*, in which sick children are given a solution of glucose, salt, and water that quickly replaces fluids the body loses. Since 1990, public health workers have taught nearly half the families in the developing world how to administer ORT. Also, supplements of zinc, a mineral essential for immune system functioning, substantially reduce the incidence of severe diarrhea (Bhandari et al., 2002). Through these interventions, the lives of millions of children are saved each year.

Immunization. In industrialized nations, widespread immunization of infants and young children has led to a dramatic decline in childhood diseases during the past half-century. Hal got the measles because, unlike classmates from advantaged homes, he did not receive a full program of immunizations. Among American preschoolers, 24 percent lack essential immunizations, a rate that rises to 40 percent for poverty-stricken children, who do not receive full protection until age 5 or 6, when it is required for school entry (U.S. Department of Health and Human Services, 2005j). In contrast, fewer than 10 percent of preschoolers lack immunizations in Denmark and Norway, and fewer than 7 percent in Canada, Great Britain, the Netherlands, and Sweden (United Nations, 2002).

Why does the United States lag behind these countries in immunization? In earlier chapters, we noted that many U.S. children do not have access to the health care they need. The Social Issues box on page 222 compares child health care in the United States with that in other Western nations.

Inability to pay for vaccines is only one cause of inadequate immunization. Parents with stressful daily lives often fail to schedule vaccination appointments, and those without a primary care physician do not want to endure long waits in crowded U.S. public health clinics. Misconceptions about vaccine safety also contribute: Some parents have been influenced by media reports suggesting a link between the measles–mumps–rubella vaccine and a rise in the number of children diagnosed with autism, although large-scale studies show no such association (Dales, Hammer, & Smith, 2001; Stehr-Green et al., 2003). In areas where many parents have refused to immunize their children, disease outbreaks of whooping cough and rubella have occurred, with life-threatening consequences (Tuyen & Bisgard, 2003). Public education programs directed at increasing parental knowledge about the importance of timely immunizations are badly needed.

Childhood Injuries

More than any other child in the preschool classroom, 3-year-old Tommy had trouble sitting still and paying attention. Instead, he darted from one place and one activity to another. One day, I read in our local newspaper that Tommy had narrowly escaped serious injury when he put his mother's car into gear while she was outside scraping ice from its windows. The vehicle rolled through a guardrail and over the side of a 10-foot concrete underpass, where it hung until rescue workers arrived. Police charged Tommy's mother with failure to use a restraint seat for a child younger than age 8.

Unintentional injuries are the leading cause of childhood mortality in industrialized countries (Agran et al., 2001). As Figure 7.4 reveals, the United States and, to a lesser extent,

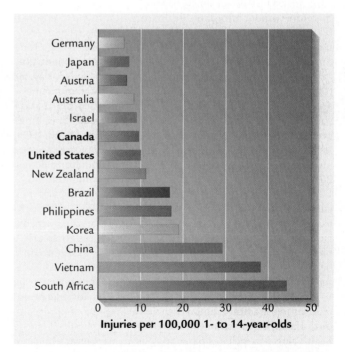

■ **FIGURE 7.4 International rates of unintentional injury among 1- to 14-year-olds.** Compared with other industrialized nations, the United States and Canada have high injury rates, due to widespread childhood poverty and shortages of high-quality child care. Injury rates are many times higher in developing nations, where poverty, rapid population growth, overcrowding in cities, and inadequate safety measures endanger children's lives. (Adapted from Safe Kids Worldwide, 2002; Health Canada, 2005b.)

Social Issues

Child Health Care in the United States and Other Western Nations

In the United States, health insurance is generally an optional, employment-related fringe benefit. Strongly individualistic values, which emphasize parental responsibility for the care and rearing of children, join with powerful economic interests in the medical community to prevent government-sponsored health services from being offered to all American children. Businesses that rely on low-wage and part-time help often do not insure their employees; others do not cover employees' family members, including children.

The largest U.S. public health insurance program, Medicaid, serves only very-low-income people. This leaves about 8.5 million children (11 percent of the child population), many of whom have working parents, uninsured and therefore without affordable health care (U.S. Census Bureau, 2006b). In the United States, uninsured children are three times as likely to go without needed doctor visits as insured children (Newachek et al., 2002). Consequently, an estimated one-third of children younger than age 5 who come from economically disadvantaged families are in less than optimal health (U.S. Department of Health and Human Services, 2004b).

The inadequacies of U.S. child health care stand in sharp contrast to services in Australia, Canada, Western Europe, New Zealand, and other industrialized nations, where government-sponsored health insurance is available to all citizens. Let's look at two examples.

In the Netherlands, every child receives free medical examinations from birth through adolescence. Children's health care also includes parental counseling in nutrition, disease prevention, and child development (de Winter, Balledux, & de Mare, 1997). The Netherlands achieves its high childhood immunization rate by giving parents of every newborn baby a written schedule that shows exactly when and where the child should

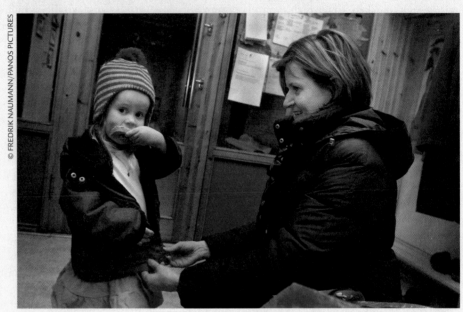

© FREDRIK NAUMANN/PANOS PICTURES

Child health care in the United States compares poorly with services universally available to children in other industrialized nations. In Norway, for example, well baby and child clinics like this one in Oslo provide free, regular preventive care to all young children.

be immunized. If a parent does not bring the child, a public health nurse calls the family. In instances of repeated missed appointments, the nurse goes to the home to ensure that the child receives the recommended immunizations (de Pree-Geerlings, de Pree, & Bulk-Bunschoten, 2001).

In Norway, federal law requires that all communities establish well-baby and child clinics and that health checkups occur three times in the first year, then at ages 2 and 4. On other occasions, children are seen by specialized nurses who monitor their development, provide immunizations, and counsel parents on physical and mental health (AWC Oslo, 2005). Although citizens pay a small fee for routine medical visits, hospital services are free.

Currently, many organizations, government officials, and concerned citizens are working to guarantee every American child basic health care. Under the State Children's Health Insurance Program (SCHIP), launched in 1997, the states receive $4 billion a year in federal matching funds for upgrading children's health insurance. State control over program implementation enables each state to adapt insurance coverage to meet its unique needs. But it also means that child advocates must exert pressure for family-friendly policies. For example, a

state can require that families share health costs, although even a small premium or copayment makes SCHIP unaffordable for low-income families.

Even many insured U.S. children do not see a doctor regularly. Parents who have no health benefits of their own are less inclined to make appointments for their children. Furthermore, because of low insurance-reimbursement rates, many doctors refuse to take public-aid patients. As a result, children with public insurance frequently do not have a primary care physician. Instead, they endure long waits in crowded public health clinics, and their parents often say they cannot gain access to needed services (Dombrowski, Lantz, & Freed, 2004; Hughes & Ng, 2003).

Finally, millions of eligible children are not enrolled in SCHIP because their parents either do not understand the eligibility requirements or find the application process confusing. Clearly, the United States has a long way to go to ensure that all its children receive excellent health care.

Canada rank poorly in these largely preventable events. In North America, nearly 40 percent of childhood deaths and 70 percent of adolescent deaths result from injuries (Children's Defense Fund, 2005; Health Canada, 2005b). And among injured children and youths who survive, thousands suffer pain, brain damage, and permanent physical disabilities.

Auto and traffic accidents, drownings, and burns are the most common injuries during early childhood. Motor vehicle collisions are by far the most frequent source of injury across all ages, ranking as the leading cause of death among children more than 1 year old.

■ **Factors Related to Childhood Injuries.** The common view of childhood injuries as "accidental" suggests they are due to chance and cannot be prevented (Sleet & Mercy, 2003). In fact, these injuries occur within a complex *ecological system* of individual, family, community, and societal influences—and we can do something about them.

Because of their higher activity level and greater willingness to take risks, boys are 1.5 times more likely to be injured than girls (National Safe Kids Campaign, 2005). Children with certain temperamental characteristics—irritability, inattentiveness, and negative mood—are also at greater risk. As we saw in Chapter 6, these are the children most likely to protest when placed in auto seat restraints or to refuse to take a companion's hand when crossing the street—even after repeated instruction and discipline (Matheny, 1991).

Poverty and low parental education are also strongly associated with injury (Ramsay et al., 2003). Parents who must cope with many daily stresses often have little energy to monitor the safety of their children. And their noisy, crowded, run-down homes and neighborhoods pose further risks (Dal Santo et al., 2004).

Childhood injury rates are high in the United States and Canada because of extensive poverty, shortages of high-quality child care (to supervise children in their parents' absence), and—especially in the United States—a high rate of births to teenagers, who are not ready for parenthood. But North American children from advantaged families are also at somewhat greater risk for injury than children in Western Europe (Safe Kids Worldwide, 2002). This indicates that besides reducing poverty and teenage pregnancy and upgrading the status of child care, additional steps are needed to ensure children's safety.

■ **Preventing Childhood Injuries.** Because childhood injuries have many causes, a variety of approaches are needed to reduce them. Laws prevent many injuries by requiring car safety seats, child-resistant caps on medicine bottles, flame-proof clothing, and fencing around backyard swimming pools (the site of 50 percent of early childhood drownings) (Brenner et al., 2003).

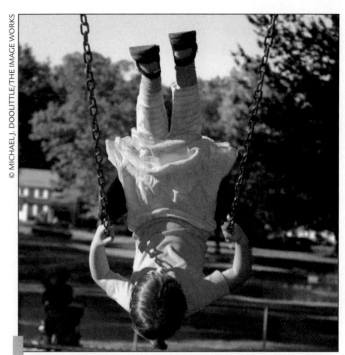

Unintentional injuries—the leading cause of childhood mortality in industrialized nations—occur within a complex ecological system of individual, family, and societal influences. Communities can help by designing playgrounds and other physical environments to lessen the danger of injury.

Communities can take steps to modify their physical environments. Playgrounds, a common site of injury, can be covered with protective surfaces (National Safe Kids Campaign, 2005). Free, easily installed window guards can be given to families in high-rise apartment buildings to prevent falls. And media campaigns can inform parents and children about safety issues.

But even though they know better, many parents and children behave in ways that compromise safety. About 10 percent of Canadian parents and 40 percent of American parents (like Tommy's mother) fail to place their preschoolers in car safety seats. And when parents do use safety seats, 82 percent either install or use them incorrectly (Howard, 2002; National Safe Kids Campaign, 2005). Yet without consistent parental commitment to safety, young children are seriously at risk. Preschoolers need frequent prompting to remember their parents' home safety rules and supervision to ensure that they follow them (Morrongiello, Midgett, & Shields, 2001).

Programs based on *behavior modification* (modeling and reinforcement) have been used to improve parent and child safety practices. But such efforts focus narrowly on specific risks. Attention must also be paid to family conditions that can prevent childhood injury: relieving crowding in the home, providing social supports to ease parental stress, and teaching parents to use effective discipline, a topic we take up in Chapter 8.

Motor Development

Observe several 2- to 6-year-olds at play in a neighborhood park, preschool, or child-care center. You will see that an explosion of new motor skills occurs in early childhood, each of which builds on the simpler movement patterns of toddlerhood.

During the preschool years, children continue to integrate previously acquired skills into more complex, *dynamic systems.* Then they revise each new skill as their bodies grow larger and stronger, their central nervous systems develop, and their environments present new challenges.

Gross Motor Development

As children's bodies become more streamlined and less top-heavy, their center of gravity shifts downward, toward the trunk. As a result, balance improves greatly, paving the way for new motor skills involving large muscles of the body (Haywood & Getchell, 2001). By age 2, preschoolers' gaits become smooth and rhythmic—secure enough that soon they leave the ground, at first by running and later by jumping, hopping, galloping, and skipping.

As children become steadier on their feet, their arms and torsos are freed to experiment with new skills—throwing and catching balls, steering tricycles, and swinging on horizontal bars and rings. Then upper- and lower-body skills combine into more refined actions. Five- and 6-year-olds simultaneously steer and pedal a tricycle and flexibly move their whole body when throwing, catching, hopping, and jumping. By the end of the preschool years, all skills are performed with greater speed and endurance. Table 7.1 provides a closer look at gross motor development in early childhood.

Fine Motor Development

As Table 7.1 shows, fine motor skills, too, take a giant leap forward in the preschool years. As control of the hands and fingers improves, young children put puzzles together, build with small blocks, cut and paste, and string beads. To parents, fine motor progress is most apparent in two areas: (1) children's care of their own bodies, and (2) the drawings and paintings that fill the walls at home, child care, and preschool.

■ **Self-Help Skills.** Table 7.1 illustrates how young children gradually become self-sufficient at dressing and feeding. But parents must be patient about these abilities: When tired and in a hurry, young children often revert to eating with their fingers. And the 3-year-old who dresses himself may end up with his shirt on inside out, his pants on backward, and his left snow boot on his right foot! Perhaps the most complex self-help skill of early childhood is shoe tying, mastered around age 6. Success requires a longer attention span, memory for an intricate series of hand movements, and the dexterity to perform them. Shoe tying illustrates the close connection between motor and cognitive development, as do two other skills: drawing and writing.

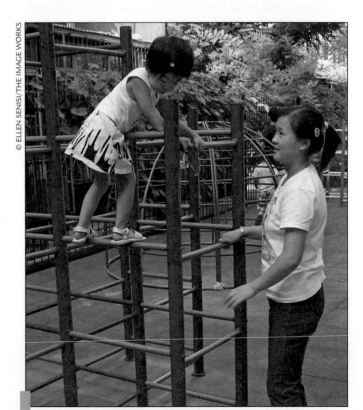

As children's bodies become more streamlined, they become steadier on their feet, freeing their arms and torsos to experiment with new upper- and lower-body skills, like this 3-year-old in Beijing, China, who takes her first, tentative steps on a climbing structure.

Table 7.1	Changes in Gross and Fine Motor Skills During Early Childhood	
Age	**Gross Motor Skills**	**Fine Motor Skills**
2–3 years	Walks more rhythmically; hurried walk changes to run Jumps, hops, throws, and catches with rigid upper body Pushes riding toy with feet; little steering	Puts on and removes simple items of clothing Zips and unzips large zippers Uses spoon effectively

3–4 years	Walks up stairs, alternating feet, and downstairs, leading
	  with one foot
	Jumps and hops, flexing upper body
	Throws and catches with slight involvement of upper
	  body; still catches by trapping ball against chest
	Pedals and steers tricycle
		Fastens and unfastens large buttons
		Serves self food without assistance
		Uses scissors
		Copies vertical line and circle
		Draws first picture of person, using tadpole image

4–5 years	Walks downstairs, alternating feet Runs more smoothly Gallops and skips with one foot Throws ball with increased body rotation and transfer of weight on feet; catches ball with hands Rides tricycle rapidly, steers smoothly	Uses fork effectively Cuts with scissors following line Copies triangle, cross, and some letters
5–6 years	Increases running speed Gallops more smoothly; engages in true skipping Displays mature throwing and catching patterns Rides bicycle with training wheels	Uses knife to cut soft food Ties shoes Draws person with six parts Copies some numbers and simple words

Sources: Cratty, 1986; Malina & Bouchard, 1991; Newborg, Stock, & Wnek, 1984; Roberton, 1984.

■ **Drawing.** When given crayon and paper, even toddlers scribble in imitation of others. As preschoolers' ability to mentally represent the world expands, marks on the page take on meaning. A variety of factors combine with fine motor control to influence changes in children's artful representations (Golomb, 2004). These include the realization that pictures can serve as symbols, improved planning and spatial understanding, and the emphasis that the child's culture places on artistic expression.

Typically, drawing progresses through the following sequence:

1. *Scribbles.* At first, the intended representation is contained in gestures rather than the resulting marks on the page. For example, one 18-month-old made her crayon hop and, as it produced a series of dots, explained, "Rabbit goes hop-hop" (Winner, 1986).

2. *First representational forms.* Around age 3, children's scribbles start to become pictures. Often children make a gesture with the crayon, notice that they have drawn a recognizable shape, and then label it (Winner, 1986). Few 3-year-olds spontaneously draw so others can tell what their picture represents. But when adults draw with children and point out the resemblances between drawings and objects, preschoolers' pictures become more comprehensible and detailed (Braswell & Callanan, 2003).

A major milestone in drawing occurs when children use lines to represent the boundaries of objects. This enables 3- and 4-year-olds to draw their first picture of a person. Look at the tadpole image—a circular shape with lines attached—on the left in Figure 7.5 on page 226. It is a universal one in which fine motor and cognitive limitations lead the preschooler to reduce the figure to the simplest form that still looks human.

3. *More realistic drawings.* Greater realism in drawings occurs gradually, as perception, language (ability to describe visual details), memory, and fine motor capacities improve (Toomela, 2002). Five- and 6-year-olds create more complex drawings, like the one on the right in Figure 7.5, which contains more conventional human and animal figures, with the head and body differentiated. Older preschoolers' drawings still contain perceptual distortions because they have just begun to represent depth (Cox & Littlejohn, 1995). This free depiction of reality makes children's artwork look fanciful and inventive. Accomplished artists often must work hard to do deliberately what they achieved without effort as 5- and 6-year-olds.

■ **Cultural Variations in Development of Drawing.** In cultures with rich artistic traditions, children create elaborate drawings that reflect the conventions of their culture. In cultures with little interest in art, even older children and adolescents produce simple forms. In the Jimi Valley—a remote region of Papua New Guinea with no indigenous pictorial art—many children do not go to school and therefore have little opportunity to develop drawing skills. When a Western researcher asked nonschooled Jimi 10- to 15-year-olds to draw a human figure for the first time, most produced nonrepresentational scribbles and shapes or simple "stick" or "contour"

■ **FIGURE 7.5 Examples of young children's drawings.** The universal tadpolelike shape that children use to draw their first picture of a person is shown on the left. The tadpole soon becomes an anchor for greater details that sprout from the basic shape. By the end of the preschool years, children produce more complex, differentiated pictures like the one on the right, drawn by a 6-year-old child. (Tadpole drawings from H. Gardner, 1980, *Artful Scribbles: The Significance of Children's Drawings*, New York: Basic Books, p. 64. Reprinted by permission of Basic Books, a division of HarperCollins Publishers, Inc. Six-year-old's picture from E. Winner, August 1986, "Where Pelicans Kiss Seals," *Psychology Today, 20*[8], p. 35. Reprinted with permission from *Psychology Today* magazine. Copyright © 1986 Sussex Publishers, Inc.)

images resembling those of preschoolers (see Figure 7.6) (Martlew & Connolly, 1996). These forms seem to be a universal beginning in drawing. Once children realize that lines must evoke human features, they find solutions to figure drawing that vary somewhat from culture to culture but, overall, follow the sequence described earlier.

■ **Early Printing.** At first, preschoolers do not distinguish writing from drawing. When they try to write, they scribble, just as they do when they draw. Around age 4, writing shows some distinctive features of print, such as separate forms arranged in a line on the page. But children often include picturelike devices in their writing—for example, using a circular shape to write "sun" (Levin & Bus, 2003). Only gradually, between ages 4 and 6, do children realize that writing stands for language.

■ **FIGURE 7.6 Drawings produced by nonschooled 10- to 15-year-old children of the Jimi Valley of Papua New Guinea when asked to draw a human figure for the first time.** Many produced nonrepresentational scribbles and shapes (a), "stick" figures (b), or "contour" figures (c). Compared with the Western tadpole form, the Jimi "stick" and "contour" figures emphasize the hands and feet. Otherwise, the drawings of these older children resemble those of young preschoolers. (From M. Martlew & K. J. Connolly, 1996, "Human Figure Drawings by Schooled and Unschooled Children in Papua New Guinea," *Child Development, 67,* pp. 2750–2751. © The Society for Research in Child Development, Inc. Adapted by permission.)

Preschoolers' first attempts to print often involve their name, generally using a single letter. "How do you make a *D*?" my older son David asked at age 3. When I printed a large uppercase *D,* he tried to copy. "*D* for David," he said as he wrote, quite satisfied with his backward, imperfect creation. By age 5, David wrote his name clearly enough that others could read it, but like many children, he continued to reverse some letters in his printing until well into second grade. Until children start to read, they do not find it useful to distinguish between mirror-image forms, such as *b* and *d* and *p* and *q* (Bornstein & Arterberry, 1999; Casey, 1986).

Individual Differences in Motor Skills

Wide individual differences exist in the ages at which children reach motor milestones. A child with a tall, muscular body tends to move more quickly and to acquire certain skills earlier than a short, stocky youngster. And as in other domains, parents and teachers probably provide more encouragement to children with biologically based motor-skill advantages.

Sex differences in motor skills are evident in early childhood. Boys are ahead of girls in skills that emphasize force and power. By age 5, they can jump slightly farther, run slightly faster, and throw a ball about five feet farther. Girls have an edge in fine motor skills and in certain gross motor skills that require a combination of good balance and foot movement, such as hopping and skipping (Fischman, Moore, & Steele, 1992; Thomas & French, 1985). Boys' greater muscle mass and (in the case of throwing) slightly longer forearms contribute to their skill advantages. And girls' greater overall physical maturity is partly responsible for their better balance and precision of movement.

From an early age, boys and girls are usually channeled into different physical activities. Fathers are more likely to play catch with their sons than with their daughters. And though differences in physical capacity remain small until adolescence, sex differences in motor skills increase as children get older. This suggests that social pressures for boys to be active and physically skilled and for girls to play quietly at fine motor activities exaggerate small, genetically based sex differences (Greendorfer, Lewko, & Rosengren, 1996).

Children master the motor skills of early childhood during everyday play. Aside from throwing (where direct instruction is helpful), preschoolers exposed to gymnastics, tumbling, and other formal lessons do not make faster progress. When children have access to play spaces appropriate for running, climbing, jumping, and throwing and are encouraged to use them, they respond eagerly to these challenges. Similarly, fine motor skills can be supported through daily routines, such as pouring juice and dressing, and through play that involves puzzles, construction sets, drawing, painting, sculpting, cutting, and pasting.

Finally, the social climate created by adults can enhance or dampen preschoolers' motor development. When parents and teachers criticize a child's performance, push specific motor skills, or promote a competitive attitude, they risk undermining children's self-confidence and, in turn, their motor progress (Berk, 2006b). Adults involved in young children's motor activities should focus on fun, not on perfecting the "correct" technique.

Ask Yourself

Review
Describe typical changes in children's drawings during early childhood. What factors contribute to those changes?

Apply
Mabel and Chad want to do everything they can to support their 3-year-old daughter's motor development. What advice would you give them?

Connect
How are experiences that best support preschoolers' motor development consistent with experience-expectant brain growth of the early years? (Return to page 127 in Chapter 4 to review.)

www.ablongman.com/berk

🍂 Cognitive Development

One rainy morning, as I observed in our laboratory preschool, Leslie, the children's teacher, joined me at the back of the room for a moment. "Preschoolers' minds are such a blend of logic, fantasy, and faulty reasoning," Leslie reflected. "Every day, I'm startled by the maturity and originality of what they say and do. Yet at other times, their thinking seems limited and inflexible."

Leslie's comments sum up the puzzling contradictions of early childhood cognition. That day, for example, 3-year-old Sammy looked up, startled, after a loud crash of thunder outside. "A magic man turned on the thunder!" he pronounced. Even when Leslie patiently explained that thunder is caused by lightning, not by a person turning it on or off, Sammy persisted: "Then a magic lady did it."

In other respects, Sammy's thinking was surprisingly advanced. At snack time, he accurately counted, "One, two, three, four!" and then got four cartons of milk, one for each child at his table. But when more than four children joined his snack group, Sammy's counting broke down. And some of his notions about quantity seemed as fantastic as his understanding of thunder. Across the snack table, Priti dumped out her raisins, which scattered in front of her. "How come you got lots, and I only got this little bit?" asked Sammy, not realizing that he had just as many; they were simply all bunched up in a tiny red box.

To understand Sammy's reasoning, we turn first to Piaget's and Vygotsky's theories and evidence highlighting the strengths and limitations of each. Then we consider additional research on young children's cognition, inspired by the information-processing perspective, and look at the dramatic expansion of language in early childhood.

Piaget's Theory: The Preoperational Stage

As children move from the sensorimotor to the **preoperational stage,** which spans the years 2 to 7, the most obvious change is an extraordinary increase in representational, or symbolic, activity. Recall that infants and toddlers have some ability to represent their world. During early childhood, this capacity blossoms.

Mental Representation

Piaget acknowledged that language is our most flexible means of mental representation. By detaching thought from action, language permits far more efficient thinking than was possible earlier. When we think in words, we overcome the limits of our momentary experiences. We can deal with past, present, and future at once and combine concepts in unique ways, as when we think about a hungry caterpillar eating bananas or monsters flying through the forest at night.

Despite the power of language, Piaget did not regard it as the primary ingredient in childhood cognitive change. Instead, he believed that sensorimotor activity leads to internal images of experience, which children then label with words (Piaget, 1936/1952). In support of Piaget's view, recall from Chapter 5 that the first words toddlers use have a strong sensorimotor basis. In addition, toddlers acquire an impressive range of categories long before they use words to label them (see page 162). But as we will see, other theorists regard Piaget's account of the link between language and thought as incomplete.

Make-Believe Play

Make-believe play is another excellent example of the development of representation in early childhood. Piaget believed that through pretending, young children practice and strengthen newly acquired representational schemes. Drawing on his

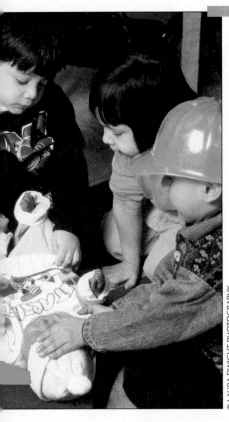

These 3- and 4-year-olds coordinate several make-believe roles as they jointly care for a sick baby. Sociodramatic play contributes to cognitive, emotional, and social development.

© LAURA DWIGHT PHOTOGRAPHY

ideas, several investigators have traced the development of make-believe during the preschool years.

■ **Development of Make-Believe.** One day, Sammy's 18-month-old brother, Dwayne, came to visit the classroom. Dwayne wandered around, picked up a toy telephone receiver, said, "Hi, Mommy," and then dropped it. In the housekeeping area, he found a cup, pretended to drink, and then toddled off again. Meanwhile, Sammy joined a group of children in the block area for a space shuttle launch.

"That can be our control tower," Sammy suggested to Vance and Lynette, pointing to a corner by a bookshelf. "Countdown!" he announced, speaking into a small wooden block, his pretend walkie-talkie. "Five, six, two, four, one, blastoff!" Lynette made a doll push a pretend button, and the rocket was off!

Comparing Dwayne's pretend play with Sammy's, we see three important changes that reflect the preschool child's growing symbolic mastery:

🔹 *Play detaches from the real-life conditions associated with it.* In early pretending, toddlers use only realistic objects—a toy telephone to talk into, a cup to drink from. Their first pretend acts imitate adults' actions and are not yet flexible. Children younger than age 2, for example, will pretend to drink from a cup but refuse to pretend a cup is a hat (Tomasello, Striano, & Rochat, 1999). They have trouble using an object (cup) that already has an obvious use as a symbol of another object (hat).

After age 2, children pretend with less realistic toys—a block might stand for a telephone receiver. Gradually, they can flexibly imagine objects and events without any support from the real world, as Sammy's imaginary control tower illustrates (O'Reilly, 1995; Striano, Tomasello, & Rochat, 2001).

🔹 *Play becomes less self-centered.* At first, make-believe is directed toward the self—for example, Dwayne pretends to feed only himself. Soon, children begin to direct pretend actions toward other objects, as when a child feeds a doll. And early in the third year, they become detached participants who make a doll feed itself or (in Lynette's case) push a button to launch a rocket. Make-believe becomes less self-centered as children realize that agents and recipients of pretend actions can be independent of themselves (McCune, 1993).

🔹 *Play includes more complex combinations of schemes.* Dwayne can pretend to drink from a cup, but he does not yet combine pouring and drinking. Later, children combine schemes with those of peers in **sociodramatic play,** the make-believe with others that is under way by age 2½ and increases rapidly during the next few years (Haight & Miller, 1993). Already, Sammy and his classmates can create and coordinate several roles in an elaborate plot. By the end of early childhood, children have a sophisticated understanding of story lines (Göncü, 1993).

With the appearance of sociodramatic play, children display awareness that make-believe is a representational activity—an understanding that improves steadily over early childhood (Lillard, 1998, 2001; Rakoczy, Tomasello, & Striano, 2004). Listen closely to preschoolers as they assign roles and negotiate make-believe plans: "You *pretend to be* the astronaut, I'll *act like* I'm operating the control tower!" In communicating about pretend, children think about their own and others' fanciful representations—evidence that they have begun to reason about people's mental activities.

■ **Benefits of Make-Believe.** Today, Piaget's view of make-believe as mere practice of representational schemes is regarded as too limited. Play not only reflects but also contributes to children's cognitive and social skills. Compared with social nonpretend activities (such as drawing or putting puzzles together), during sociodramatic play preschoolers' interactions last longer, show more involvement, draw larger numbers of children into the activity, and are more cooperative (Creasey, Jarvis, & Berk, 1998).

It is not surprising, then, that preschoolers who spend more time at sociodramatic play are seen as more socially competent by their teachers (Connolly & Doyle, 1984). And many studies reveal that make-believe strengthens a wide variety of mental abilities, including attention, memory, logical reasoning, language and literacy, imagination, creativity, and the ability to reflect on one's own thinking, control one's own behavior, and take another's perspective (Bergen & Mauer, 2000; Berk, 2001; Elias & Berk, 2002; Kavanaugh & Engel, 1998;

Lindsey & Colwell, 2003; Ruff & Capozzoli, 2003). We will return to the topic of early childhood play in this and the next chapter.

Symbol–Real World Relations

To make believe and draw—and to understand other forms of representation, such as photographs, models, and maps—preschoolers must realize that each symbol corresponds to a specific state of affairs in everyday life. When do children comprehend symbol–real world relations?

In one study, 2½- and 3-year-olds, after watching an adult hide a small toy (Little Snoopy) in a scale model of a room, were asked to retrieve it. Next, they had to find a larger toy (Big Snoopy) hidden in the room that the model represented. Not until age 3 could most children use the model as a guide to finding Big Snoopy in the real room (DeLoache, 1987). The 2½-year-olds did not realize that the model could be both a toy room and a symbol of another room. They had trouble with **dual representation**—viewing a symbolic object as both an object in its own right and a symbol. In support of this interpretation, when researchers decreased the prominence of the model room as an object, by placing it behind a window and preventing children from touching it, more 2½-year-olds succeeded at the search task (DeLoache, 2000, 2002).

Recall a similar limitation in early pretending—that 1½- to 2-year-olds cannot use an object with an obvious use (cup) to stand for another object (hat). Likewise, 2-year-olds do not yet grasp that a drawing—an object in its own right—also represents real-world objects.

How do children grasp the dual representation of symbolic objects? When adults point out similarities between models and real-world spaces, 2½-year-olds perform better on the find-Snoopy task (Peralta de Mendoza & Salsa, 2003). Also, insight into one type of symbol–real world relation promotes mastery of others. For example, children regard photos as symbols early, around 1½ to 2 years, because a picture's primary purpose is to stand for something; it is not an interesting object in its own right (Preissler & Carey, 2004). And 3-year-olds who can use a model of a room to locate Big Snoopy readily transfer their understanding to a simple map (Marzolf & DeLoache, 1994). In sum, experiences with diverse symbols—photos, picture books, make-believe, and maps—help preschoolers appreciate that one object can stand for another.

Limitations of Preoperational Thought

Aside from gains in representation, Piaget described preschoolers in terms of their limitations—what they *cannot* understand (Beilin, 1992). As the term *pre*operational suggests, he compared them to older, more competent children who have reached the concrete operational stage. According to Piaget, young children are not capable of *operations*—mental actions that obey logical rules. Rather, their thinking is rigid, limited to one aspect of a situation at a time, and strongly influenced by the way things appear at the moment.

■ **Egocentrism.** For Piaget, the most fundamental deficiency of preoperational thinking is **egocentrism**—failure to distinguish the symbolic viewpoints of others from one's own. He believed that when children first mentally represent the world, they tend to focus on their own viewpoint and simply assume that others perceive, think, and feel the same way they do.

Piaget's most convincing demonstration of egocentrism involves his *three-mountains problem*, described in Figure 7.7. Egocentrism is responsible for preoperational children's **animistic thinking**—the belief that inanimate objects have lifelike qualities, such as thoughts, wishes, feelings, and intentions

Children who experience a variety of symbols come to understand that one object, such as the birdhouse this daughter and her father are making, can stand for another—a full-sized house that people live in.

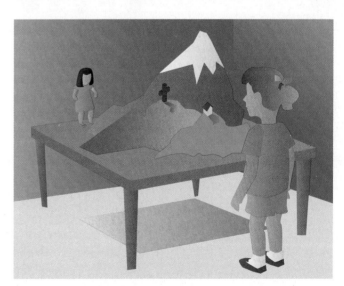

■ **FIGURE 7.7 Piaget's three-mountains problem.** Each mountain is distinguished by its color and by its summit. One has a red cross, another a small house, and the third a snow-capped peak. Children at the preoperational stage respond egocentrically. They cannot select a picture that shows the mountains from the doll's perspective. Instead, they simply choose the photo that reflects their own vantage point.

(Piaget, 1926/1930). Recall Sammy's firm insistence that someone must have turned on the thunder. According to Piaget, because young children egocentrically assign human purposes to physical events, magical thinking is common during the preschool years.

Piaget argued that preschoolers' egocentric bias prevents them from *accommodating*, or reflecting on and revising their faulty reasoning in response to their physical and social worlds. To appreciate their shortcomings fully, let's consider some additional tasks that Piaget gave to children.

■ **Inability to Conserve.** Piaget's famous conservation tasks reveal a variety of deficiencies of preoperational thinking. **Conservation** refers to the idea that certain physical characteristics of objects remain the same, even when their outward appearance changes. At snack time, Priti and Sammy each had identical boxes of raisins, but when Priti spread her raisins out on the table, Sammy was convinced that she had more.

In another conservation task involving liquid, the child is shown two identical tall glasses of water and asked if they contain equal amounts. Once the child agrees that they do, the water in one glass is poured into a short, wide container, changing the appearance of the water but not its amount. Then the child is asked whether the amount of water is the same or has changed. Preoperational children think the quantity has changed. They explain, "There is less now because the water is way down here" (that is, its level is so low) or, "There is more now because it is all spread out." Figure 7.8 illustrates other conservation tasks that you can try with children.

The inability to conserve highlights several related aspects of preoperational children's thinking. First, their understanding is *centered*, or characterized by **centration.** They focus on one aspect of a situation, neglecting other important features. In conservation of liquid, the child *centers* on the height of the water, failing to realize that all changes in height are compensated for by changes in width. Second, children are easily distracted by the perceptual appearance of objects. Third, children treat the initial and final states of the water as unrelated events, ignoring the *dynamic transformation* (pouring of water) between them.

The most important illogical feature of preoperational thought is its **irreversibility,** an inability to mentally go through a series of steps in a problem and then reverse direction, returning to the starting point. *Reversibility* is part of every logical operation. After Priti spills her raisins, Sammy cannot reverse by thinking, "I know that Priti doesn't have more raisins than I do. If we put them back in that little box, her raisins and my raisins would look just the same."

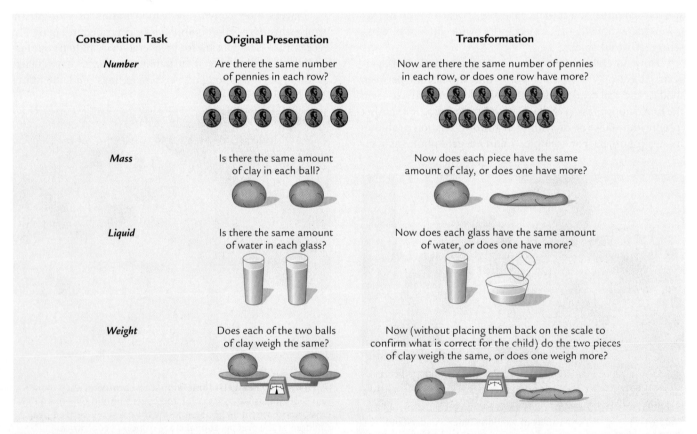

Conservation Task	Original Presentation	Transformation
Number	Are there the same number of pennies in each row?	Now are there the same number of pennies in each row, or does one row have more?
Mass	Is there the same amount of clay in each ball?	Now does each piece have the same amount of clay, or does one have more?
Liquid	Is there the same amount of water in each glass?	Now does each glass have the same amount of water, or does one have more?
Weight	Does each of the two balls of clay weigh the same?	Now (without placing them back on the scale to confirm what is correct for the child) do the two pieces of clay weigh the same, or does one weigh more?

■ **FIGURE 7.8 Some Piagetian conservation tasks.** Children at the preoperational stage cannot yet conserve. These tasks are mastered gradually over the concrete operational stage. Children in Western nations typically acquire conservation of number, mass, and liquid sometime between 6 and 7 years and of weight between 8 and 10 years.

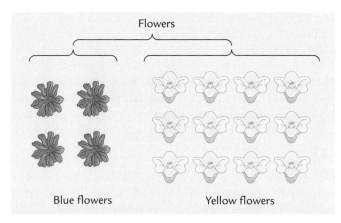

■ **FIGURE 7.9 A Piagetian class inclusion problem.** Children are shown 16 flowers, 4 of which are blue and 12 of which are yellow. Asked, "Are there more yellow flowers or flowers?" the preoperational child responds, "More yellow flowers," failing to realize that both yellow and blue flowers are included in the category "flowers."

■ **Lack of Hierarchical Classification.** Lacking logical operations, preschoolers have difficulty with **hierarchical classification**—the organization of objects into classes and subclasses on the basis of similarities and differences. Piaget's famous *class inclusion problem*, illustrated in Figure 7.9, demonstrates this limitation. Preoperational children center on the overriding feature, yellow. They do not think reversibly by moving from the whole class (flowers) to the parts (yellow and blue) and back again.

Follow-Up Research on Preoperational Thought

Over the past three decades, researchers have challenged Piaget's view of a cognitively deficient preschooler. Because many Piagetian problems contain unfamiliar elements or too many pieces of information for young children to handle at once, preschoolers' responses do not reflect their true abilities. Piaget also missed many naturally occurring instances of effective reasoning by preschoolers.

■ **Egocentric, Animistic, and Magical Thinking.** Do young children really believe that a person standing elsewhere in a room sees the same thing they see? When researchers change the nature of the three-mountains problem to include familiar objects and use methods other than picture selection (which is difficult even for 10-year-olds), 4-year-olds show clear awareness of others' vantage points (Borke, 1975; Newcombe & Huttenlocher, 1992).

Young children's conversations also include nonegocentric responses. For example, preschoolers adapt their speech to fit the needs of their listeners. Four-year-olds use shorter, simpler expressions when talking to 2-year-olds than to agemates or adults (Gelman & Shatz, 1978). And in describing objects, children do not use such words as "big" and "little" in a rigid, egocentric fashion. Rather, they *adjust* their descriptions to allow for context. By age 3, children judge a 2-inch shoe as "small"

when seen by itself (because it is much smaller than most shoes) but as "big" for a tiny 5-inch-tall doll (Ebeling & Gelman, 1994).

In Chapter 5, we saw that toddlers have already begun to infer others' intentions (see page 157). And in his later writings, Piaget (1945/1951) did describe preschoolers' egocentrism as a tendency rather than an inability. As we revisit the topic of perspective taking, we will see that it develops gradually throughout childhood and adolescence.

Piaget also overestimated preschoolers' animistic beliefs. Beginning in infancy, children distinguish animate from inanimate, as indicated by babies' remarkable categorical distinctions among living and nonliving things (see pages 162–164). By age 2½, children give psychological explanations—"He likes to" or "She wants to"—for people and occasionally for animals but rarely for objects (Hickling & Wellman, 2001). They do make errors when questioned about vehicles, such as trains and airplanes, which appear to be self-moving and have other lifelike features—for example, headlights that look like eyes (Gelman & Opfer, 2002). But their responses result from incomplete knowledge, not from a belief that inanimate objects are alive.

The same is true for other fantastic beliefs of the preschool years. Most 3- and 4-year-olds believe in the supernatural powers of fairies, goblins, and other enchanted creatures. They think that magic accounts for events that they cannot explain, as in 3-year-old Sammy's magical explanation of thunder in the opening to this chapter (Rosengren & Hickling, 2000). But they deny that magic can alter their everyday experiences—for example, turn a picture into a real object (Subbotsky, 1994).

Between ages 4 and 8, as children gain familiarity with physical events and principles, their magical beliefs decline. They figure out who is really behind Santa Claus and the Tooth Fairy, and they realize that the antics of magicians are due to trickery (Subbotsky, 2004). Religion and culture also play a role. Jewish children are more likely than their Christian agemates to express disbelief in Santa Claus and the Tooth Fairy. Having heard at home that Santa is unreal, they seem to generalize this attitude to other mythical figures (Woolley, 1997). And cultural myths about wishing—for example, the custom of making a wish before blowing out birthday candles—probably underlie the conviction of most 3- to 6-year-olds that by wishing, you can sometimes make your desires come true (Woolley, 2000).

■ **Illogical Thought.** Many studies have reexamined the illogical characteristics that Piaget saw in the preoperational stage. Results show that when preschoolers are given tasks that are simplified and relevant to their everyday lives, they do better than Piaget might have expected.

For example, when a conservation-of-number task is scaled down to include only three items instead of six or seven, 3-year-olds perform well (Gelman, 1972). And when preschoolers are asked carefully worded questions about what happens to substances (such as sugar) after they are dissolved in water, they give accurate explanations. Most 3- to 5-year-olds know that the substance is conserved—that it continues to exist, can be tasted, and makes the liquid heavier, even though it is invisible in the water (Au, Sidle, & Rollins, 1993; Rosen & Rozin, 1993).

Preschoolers' ability to reason about transformations is evident on other problems. They can engage in impressive *reasoning by analogy* about physical changes. Presented with the picture-matching problem, "Play dough is to cut-up play dough as apple is to ?," even 3-year-olds choose the correct answer (a cut-up apple) from a set of alternatives, several of which share physical features with the right choice (a bitten apple, a cut-up loaf of bread) (Goswami, 1996). These findings indicate that in familiar contexts, preschoolers can overcome appearances and think logically.

Finally, even without detailed biological knowledge, preschoolers understand that the insides of animals are responsible for cause–effect sequences (such as willing oneself to move) that are not possible for nonliving things (Keil & Lockhart, 1999). Illogical reasoning seems to occur only when preschoolers grapple with unfamiliar topics, too much information, or contradictory facts that they have trouble reconciling (Ruffman, 1999).

■ **Categorization.** Although preschoolers have difficulty with Piagetian class inclusion tasks, they organize their everyday knowledge into nested categories at an early age. Recall that by the second half of the first year, children have formed a variety of global categories, such as furniture, animals, vehicles, and plants. Each category includes objects that vary widely in perceptual features but have common functions or behaviors, challenging Piaget's assumption that preschoolers' thinking is wholly governed by the way things appear. Indeed, 2- to 5-year-olds readily draw inferences about nonobservable characteristics shared by category members (Gopnik & Nazzi, 2003). For example, after being told that a bird has warm blood and that a stegosaurus (dinosaur) has cold blood, preschoolers infer that a pterodactyl (labeled a dinosaur) has cold blood, even though it closely resembles a bird.

Children's global categories quickly differentiate. Preschoolers form many *basic-level categories*—ones at an intermediate level of generality, such as "chairs," "tables," and "beds." By the third year, children easily move back and forth between basic-level categories and *superordinate categories,* such as "furniture." And they break down basic-level categories into *subcategories,* such as "rocking chairs" and "desk chairs" (Mervis, Pani, & Pani, 2003).

Preschoolers' rapidly increasing vocabularies and general knowledge support their impressive skill at categorizing (Gelman & Koenig, 2003). As they learn more about their world, they expand their understanding of characteristics that category members share—for example, that a combination of physical features, internal organs, and behaviors determines an animal's identity (Krascum & Andrews, 1998). Also, adults label and explain categories to children, and picture-book reading seems to be a rich context for doing so (Gelman et al., 1998). While looking at books, parents make categorical statements ("Penguins live at the South Pole, swim, catch fish, and have thick layers of fat and feathers that help them stay warm") that guide children's construction of categories.

In sum, preschoolers' category systems are not yet very complex. But the capacity to classify hierarchically is present in early childhood.

■ **Appearance versus Reality.** What happens when preschoolers encounter objects that have two identities—a real one and an apparent one? Can they distinguish appearance from reality? In a series of studies, John Flavell and his colleagues presented children with objects that were disguised in various ways and asked what each "looks like" and what each "is really and truly." Preschoolers had difficulty. For example, when asked whether a candle that looks like a crayon "is really and truly" a crayon, they often responded, "Yes!" Not until age 6 or 7 did children do well on these tasks (Flavell, Green, & Flavell, 1987).

Younger children's poor performance, however, is not due to a general difficulty in distinguishing appearance from reality, as Piaget suggested. Rather, they have trouble with the *language* of these tasks (Deák, Ray, & Brenneman, 2003). When permitted to solve appearance–reality problems nonverbally, by choosing from an array of objects the one that "really" has a particular identity, most 3-year-olds perform well (Sapp, Lee, & Muir 2000).

Note how the appearance–reality distinction involves an attainment discussed earlier: dual representation—the realization that an object can be one thing (a candle) while symbolizing another (a crayon). At first, however, children's understanding is fragile. After putting on a Halloween mask,

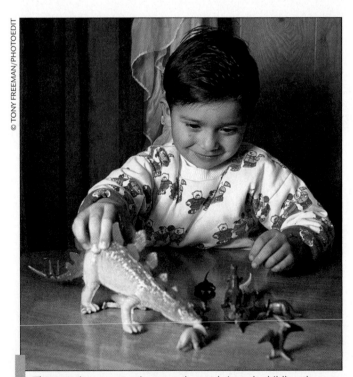

The capacity to categorize expands greatly in early childhood. Children form many categories based on underlying characteristics rather than perceptual features. Guided by knowledge that "dinosaurs have cold blood," this 4-year-old categorizes the pterodactyl (in the foreground) as a dinosaur rather than a bird, even though pterodactyls have wings and can fly.

© TONY FREEMAN/PHOTOEDIT

young preschoolers may be wary and even frightened when they see themselves in a mirror. Performing well on verbal appearance–reality tasks signifies a more secure understanding and is related to further progress in representational ability (Bialystok & Senman, 2004).

Evaluation of the Preoperational Stage

Table 7.2 provides an overview of the cognitive attainments of early childhood. Compare them with Piaget's description of the preoperational child on pages 227–231. The evidence as a whole indicates that Piaget was partly right and partly wrong about young children's cognitive capacities. When given simplified tasks based on familiar experiences, preschoolers do show the beginnings of logical thinking.

That preschoolers have some logical understanding suggests that they attain logical operations gradually. Over time, children rely on increasingly effective mental (as opposed to perceptual) approaches to solving problems. For example, children who cannot use counting to compare two sets of items do not conserve number (Sophian, 1995). Once preschoolers can count, they apply this skill to conservation-of-number tasks involving only a few items. As counting improves, they extend the strategy to problems with more items. By age 6, they understand that number remains the same after a transformation as long as nothing is added or taken away. Consequently, they no longer need to count to verify their answer (Klahr & MacWhinney, 1998).

Evidence that logical operations develop gradually poses yet another challenge to Piaget's stage concept, which assumes abrupt change toward logical reasoning around age 6 or 7. Does a preoperational stage really exist? Some no longer think

so. Recall from Chapter 5 that according to the information-processing perspective, children work out their understanding of each type of task separately. According to this view, children's thought processes are basically the same at all ages—just present to a greater or lesser extent.

Other experts think the stage concept is valid but must be modified. For example, some *neo-Piagetian theorists* combine Piaget's stage approach with the information-processing emphasis on task-specific change (Case, 1998; Halford, 2002). They believe that Piaget's strict stage definition must be transformed into a less tightly knit concept, one in which a related set of competencies develops over an extended time period, depending on brain development and specific experiences. These investigators point to findings indicating that as long as the complexity of tasks and children's exposure to them are carefully controlled, children approach those tasks in similar, stage-consistent ways (Andrews & Halford, 2002; Case & Okamoto, 1996). For example, in drawing pictures, preschoolers depict objects separately, ignoring their spatial arrangement. In understanding stories, they grasp a single story line but have trouble with a main plot plus one or more subplots.

This flexible stage notion recognizes the unique qualities of early childhood thinking. At the same time, it provides a better account of why, as Leslie put it, "Preschoolers' minds are such a blend of logic, fantasy, and faulty reasoning."

Piaget and Education

Three educational principles derived from Piaget's theory continue to have a major impact on both teacher training and classroom practices, especially during early childhood:

Table 7.2	Some Cognitive Attainments of Early Childhood

Approximate Age		Cognitive Attainments
2–4 years	© ELLEN B. SENISI/ THE IMAGE WORKS	Shows a dramatic increase in representational activity, as reflected in the development of language, make-believe play, drawing, and understanding of dual representation
		Takes the perspective of others in simplified, familiar situations and in everyday, face-to-face communication
		Distinguishes animate beings from inanimate objects; denies that magic can alter everyday experiences
		Grasps conservation, notices transformations, reverses thinking, and understands many cause-and-effect relationships in familiar contexts
		Categorizes objects on the basis of common function and behavior and devises ideas about underlying characteristics that category members share
		Sorts familiar objects into hierarchically organized categories
		Distinguishes appearance from reality
4–7 years	© PETER HVIZDAK/ THE IMAGE WORKS	Becomes increasingly aware that make-believe (and other thought processes) are representational activities.
		Replaces magical beliefs about fairies, goblins, and events that violate expectations with plausible explanations.
		Solves verbal appearance-reality problems, signifying a more secure understanding

🖋 *Discovery learning.* In a Piagetian classroom, children are encouraged to discover for themselves through spontaneous interaction with the environment. Instead of simply presenting ready-made knowledge, teachers provide a rich variety of materials designed to promote exploration—art supplies, puzzles, table games, dress-up clothing, building blocks, books, measuring tools, musical instruments, and more.

🖋 *Sensitivity to children's readiness to learn.* In a Piagetian classroom, teachers introduce activities that build on children's current thinking, challenging their incorrect ways of viewing the world and enabling them to practice newly discovered schemes. But they do not try to speed up development by imposing new skills before children indicate they are interested and ready.

🖋 *Acceptance of individual differences.* Piaget's theory assumes that all children go through the same sequence of development, but at different rates. Therefore, teachers must plan activities for individual children and small groups rather than just for the whole class. In addition, teachers evaluate each child's educational progress in relation to that child's previous development. They are less interested in evaluating children on the basis of normative standards, or average performance of same-age peers.

Like his stages, educational applications of Piaget's theory have met with criticism. Perhaps the greatest challenge has to do with his insistence that young children learn mainly through acting on the environment (Brainerd, 2003). In the next section, we will see that young children also rely on language-based routes to knowledge.

Ask Yourself

Review

Select two of the following features of preoperational thought: egocentrism, a focus on perceptual appearances, difficulty reasoning about transformations, and lack of hierarchical classification. Present evidence indicating that preschoolers are more capable thinkers than Piaget assumed.

Apply

Three-year-old Will understands that his tricycle isn't alive and can't feel or move on its own. Yet on a trip to the beach, as the sun dipped below the horizon, Will exclaimed, "The sun is tired. It's going to sleep!" What explains this apparent contradiction in Will's reasoning?

Connect

Make-believe play promotes both cognitive and social development (see page 228). Explain why this is so.

Reflect

On the basis of what you have read, do you accept Piaget's claim for a preoperational stage of cognitive development? Explain.

www.ablongman.com/berk

Vygotsky's Sociocultural Theory

Piaget's deemphasis on language as a source of cognitive development brought on yet another challenge, this time from Vygotsky's sociocultural theory, which stresses the social context of cognitive development. During early childhood, rapid growth of language broadens preschoolers' participation in social dialogues with more knowledgeable individuals, who encourage them to master culturally important tasks. Soon children start to communicate with themselves in much the same way they converse with others. This greatly enhances their thinking and ability to control their own behavior. Let's see how this happens.

Private Speech

Watch preschoolers going about their daily activities, and you will see that they frequently talk out loud to themselves. For example, as Sammy worked a puzzle, he said, "Where's the red piece? Now, a blue one. No, it doesn't fit. Try it here."

Piaget (1923/1926) called these utterances *egocentric speech*, reflecting his belief that young children have difficulty taking the perspectives of others. Their talk, he said, is often "talk for self" in which they run off thoughts in whatever form they happen to occur, regardless of whether a listener can understand. Piaget believed that cognitive maturity and certain social experiences—namely, disagreements with peers—eventually bring an end to egocentric speech. Through arguments with agemates, children repeatedly see that others hold viewpoints different from their own. As a result, egocentric speech declines.

Vygotsky (1934/1987) disagreed with Piaget's conclusions. Because language helps children think about their mental activities and behavior and select courses of action, Vygotsky regarded it as the foundation for all higher cognitive processes, including controlled attention, deliberate memorization and recall, categorization, planning, problem solving, and self-reflection. In Vygotsky's view, children speak to themselves for self-guidance. As children get older and find tasks easier, their self-directed speech is internalized as silent, *inner speech*—the verbal dialogues we carry on with ourselves while thinking and acting in everyday situations.

Over the past three decades, almost all studies have supported Vygotsky's perspective (Berk & Harris, 2003). As a result, children's self-directed speech is now called **private speech** instead of egocentric speech. Research shows that children use more of it when tasks are difficult and they are confused about how to proceed. Also, as Vygotsky predicted, private speech goes underground with age, changing into whispers and silent lip movements (Patrick & Abravanel, 2000; Winsler & Naglieri, 2003). Furthermore, children who freely use private speech during a challenging activity are more attentive and involved and do better than their less talkative agemates (Berk & Spuhl, 1995; Winsler, Diaz, & Montero, 1997).

Social Origins of Early Childhood Cognition

Where does private speech come from? Recall from Chapter 5 that Vygotsky believed that children's learning takes place within the *zone of proximal development*—a range of tasks too difficult for the child to do alone but possible with the help of adults and more skilled peers. Consider the joint activity of Sammy and his mother, who helps him put together a difficult puzzle:

> *Sammy:* I can't get this one in. *[Tries to insert a piece in the wrong place.]*
>
> *Mother:* Which piece might go down here? *[Points to the bottom of the puzzle.]*
>
> *Sammy:* His shoes. *[Looks for a piece resembling the clown's shoes but tries the wrong one.]*
>
> *Mother:* Well, what piece looks like this shape? *[Pointing again to the bottom of the puzzle.]*
>
> *Sammy:* The brown one. *[Tries it, and it fits; then attempts another piece and looks at his mother.]*
>
> *Mother:* Try turning it just a little. *[Gestures to show him.]*
>
> *Sammy:* There! *[Puts in several more pieces while his mother watches.]*

Sammy's mother keeps the puzzle within his zone of proximal development, at a manageable level of difficulty. To do so, she engages in **scaffolding**—adjusting the support offered during a teaching session to fit the child's current level of performance. When the child has little notion of how to proceed, the adult uses direct instruction and breaks the task into manageable units. As the child's competence increases, effective scaffolders gradually and sensitively withdraw support, turning over responsibility to the child. Then children take the language of these dialogues, make it part of their private speech, and use that speech to organize their independent efforts.

What evidence supports Vygotsky's ideas on the social origins of cognitive development? In several studies, children whose parents were effective scaffolders used more private speech and were more successful when attempting difficult tasks on their own (Berk & Spuhl, 1995; Conner & Cross, 2003). Adult cognitive support—teaching in small steps and offering strategies—predicts gains in children's thinking. And adult emotional support—offering encouragement and allowing the child to take over the task—predicts children's effort (Neitzel & Stright, 2003).

Other research shows that although children benefit from working on tasks with same-age peers, their planning and problem solving improve more when their partner is either an "expert" peer (especially capable at the task) or an adult. And peer disagreement (emphasized by Piaget) seems less important in fostering cognitive development than the extent to which children resolve differences of opinion and cooperate (Kobayashi, 1994; Tudge, 1992).

Vygotsky and Education

Both Piagetian and Vygotskian classrooms emphasize active participation and acceptance of individual differences. But a

This 3-year-old makes a sculpture from play dough and plastic sticks with the aid of private speech. During the preschool years, children frequently talk to themselves as they play and tackle other challenging tasks. Research supports Vygotsky's theory that children use private speech to guide their own thinking and behavior.

© LAURA DWIGHT PHOTOGRAPHY

Vygotskian classroom goes beyond independent discovery to promote *assisted discovery*. Teachers guide children's learning, tailoring their interventions to each child's zone of proximal development. Assisted discovery is also aided by *peer collaboration* as children of varying abilities work in groups, teaching and helping one another.

Vygotsky (1933/1978) saw make-believe play as the ideal social context for fostering cognitive development in early childhood. As children create imaginary situations, they learn to follow internal ideas and social rules rather than their immediate impulses. For example, a child pretending to go to sleep follows the rules of bedtime behavior. A child imagining himself as a father and a doll as a child conforms to the rules of parental behavior. According to Vygotsky, make-believe play is a unique, broadly influential zone of proximal development in which children try out a wide variety of challenging activities and acquire many new competencies.

Turn back to page 228 to review findings that make-believe play enhances a diverse array of cognitive and social skills. Pretending is also rich in private speech—a finding that supports its role in helping children bring action under the control of thought (Krafft & Berk, 1998). And preschoolers who spend more time engaged in sociodramatic play are better at taking personal responsibility for following classroom rules and regulating emotion (Berk, Mann, & Ogan, 2006; Lemche et al., 2003). These findings support the role of make-believe in children's increasing self-control.

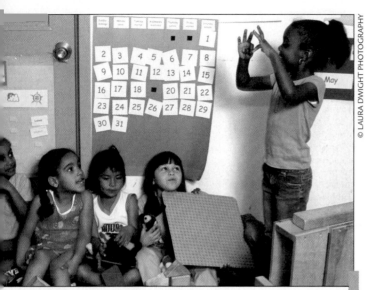

© LAURA DWIGHT PHOTOGRAPHY

In this Vygotskian classroom, 4- and 5-year-olds benefit from peer collaboration as they work together in groups, teaching and helping one another.

Evaluation of Vygotsky's Theory

In granting social experience a fundamental role in cognitive development, Vygotsky's theory underscores the vital role of teaching and helps us understand the wide cultural variation in children's cognitive skills. Nevertheless, it has not gone challenged. Verbal communication may not be the only means through which children's thinking develops—or even, in some cultures, the most important means. When Western parents scaffold their young children's mastery of challenging tasks, their verbal communication resembles the teaching that takes place in school, where their children will spend years preparing for adult life. In cultures that place less emphasis on schooling and literacy, parents often expect children to take greater responsibility for acquiring new skills through keen observation and participation in community activities (see the Cultural Influences box on the following page).

To account for children's diverse ways of learning through involvement with others, Barbara Rogoff (1998, 2003) suggests the term **guided participation,** a broader concept than scaffolding. It refers to shared endeavors between more expert and less expert participants, without specifying the precise features of communication. Consequently, it allows for variations across situations and cultures.

Finally, Vygotsky's theory says little about how basic motor, perceptual, attention, memory, and problem-solving skills, discussed in Chapters 4 and 5, contribute to socially transmitted higher cognitive processes. For example, his theory does not address how these elementary capacities spark changes in children's social experiences, from which more advanced cognition springs (Moll, 1994). Piaget paid far more attention than Vygotsky to the development of basic cognitive processes. It is intriguing to speculate about the broader theory that might exist today if Piaget and Vygotsky—the two twentieth-century giants of cognitive development—had had a chance to meet and weave together their extraordinary accomplishments.

Ask Yourself

Review

Describe characteristics of social interaction that support children's cognitive development. How does such interaction create a zone of proximal development?

Apply

Tanisha sees her 5-year-old son Toby talking aloud to himself as he plays. She wonders whether she should discourage this behavior. Using Vygotsky's theory and related research, explain why Toby talks to himself. How would you advise Tanisha?

Connect

Explain how Piaget's and Vygotsky's theories complement each other. That is, what aspects of development does one emphasize that the other downplays or overlooks?

Reflect

When do you use private speech? Does it serve a self-guiding function for you, as it does for children? Explain.

www.ablongman.com/berk

Information Processing

Return to the model of information processing discussed on page 161 of Chapter 5. Recall that information processing focuses on *mental strategies* that children use to transform stimuli flowing into their mental systems. During early childhood, advances in representation and in children's ability to guide their own behavior lead to more efficient ways of attending, manipulating information, and solving problems. Preschoolers also become more aware of their own mental life and begin to acquire academically relevant knowledge important for school success.

Attention

Parents and teachers are quick to notice that compared with school-age children, preschoolers spend relatively short times involved in tasks and are easily distracted. But recall from Chapter 5 that sustained attention improves in toddlerhood, a trend that continues during the preschool years.

A major reason is a steady gain in children's ability to inhibit impulses and keep their mind on a competing goal. Consider a task in which the child must tap once when the adult taps twice and tap twice when the adult taps once, or

Cultural Influences

Children in Village and Tribal Cultures Observe and Participate in Adult Work

In Western societies, the role of equipping children with the skills they need to become competent workers is assigned to school. In early childhood, middle-class parents' interactions with children dwell on preparing the children for school success through child-focused activities—especially adult–child conversations and play that enhance language, literacy, and other academic knowledge. In village and tribal cultures, children receive little or no schooling, spend their days in contact with adult work, and start to assume mature responsibilities in early childhood (Rogoff et al., 2003). Consequently, parents have little need to rely on conversation and play to teach children.

A study comparing 2- and 3-year-olds' daily lives in four cultures—two U.S. middle-SES suburbs, the Efe hunters and gatherers of the Republic of Congo, and a Mayan agricultural town in Guatemala—documented these differences (Morelli, Rogoff, & Angelillo, 2003). In the U.S. communities, young children had little access to adult work and spent much time conversing and playing with adults. In contrast, the Efe and Mayan children rarely engaged in these child-focused activities. Instead, they spent their days close to—and frequently observing—adult work, which often took place in or near the Efe campsite or the Mayan family home.

An ethnography of a remote Mayan village in Yucatán, Mexico, shows that when young children are legitimate onlookers and participants in a daily life structured around adult work, their competencies differ from those of Western preschoolers (Gaskins, 1999). Yucatec Mayan adults are subsistence farmers. Men tend cornfields, aided by sons age 8 and older. Women oversee the household and yard; they prepare meals, wash clothes, and care for the livestock and garden, assisted by daughters and by sons not yet old enough to work in the fields. Children join in these activities from the second year on. When not participating, they are expected to be self-sufficient. Young children make many nonwork decisions for themselves—how much to sleep and eat, what to wear, and even when to start school. As a result, Yucatec Mayan preschoolers are highly competent at self-care. In contrast, their make-believe play is limited; when it occurs, they usually enact adult work. Otherwise, they watch others—for hours each day.

Yucatec Mayan parents rarely converse or play with preschoolers or scaffold their learning. Rather, when children imitate adult tasks, parents conclude that they are ready for more responsibility. Then they assign chores, selecting tasks the child can do with little help so that adult work is not disturbed. If a child cannot do a task, the adult takes over and the child observes, reengaging when able to contribute.

Expected to be autonomous and helpful, Yucatec Mayan children seldom ask others for something interesting to do. From an early age, they can sit quietly for long periods—through a long religious service or a ride to town. And when an adult directs them to do a chore, they respond eagerly to the type of command that Western children frequently resent. By age 5, Yucatec Mayan children spontaneously take responsibility for tasks beyond those assigned.

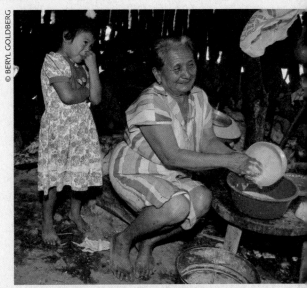

© BERYL GOLDBERG

In Yucatec Mayan culture, adults rarely converse with children or scaffold their learning. And rather than engaging in make-believe, children join in the work of their community from an early age, spending many hours observing adults. This Mayan preschooler watches intently as her grandmother washes dishes. When the child begins to imitate adult tasks, she will be given additional responsibilities.

---

must say "night" to a picture of the sun and "day" to a picture of the moon with stars. As Figure 7.10 on page 238 shows, 3- and 4-year-olds make many errors. But by age 6 to 7, children find such tasks easy (Diamond & Taylor, 1996; Kirkham, Cruess, & Diamond, 2003; Zelazo et al., 2003). They can resist the "pull" of their attention toward a dominant stimulus.

During early childhood, children also become better at *planning*—thinking out a sequence of acts ahead of time and allocating attention accordingly to reach a goal. As long as tasks are familiar and not too complex, preschoolers can generate and follow a plan. For example, they can search for a lost object in a play yard systematically and exhaustively (Wellman, Somerville, & Haake, 1979). Still, planning has a long way to go. When asked to compare detailed pictures, preschoolers fail to search thoroughly. And on tasks with several steps, they rarely decide what to do first and what to do next in an orderly fashion (Friedman & Scholnick, 1997; Ruff & Rothbart, 1996).

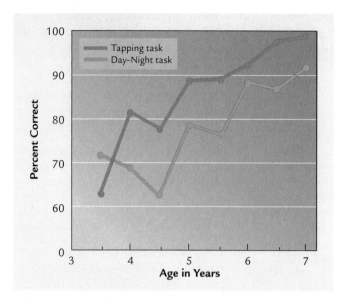

FIGURE 7.10 Gains between ages 3 and 7 in performance on tasks requiring children to inhibit an impulse and focus on a competing goal. In the tapping task, children had to tap once when the adult tapped twice and tap twice when the adult tapped once. In the day-night task, children had to say "night" to a picture of the sun and "day" to a picture of the moon with stars. (From A. Diamond, 2004, "Normal Development of Prefrontal Cortex from Birth to Young Adulthood: Cognitive Functions, Anatomy, and Biochemistry," in D. T. Stuff & R. T. Knight, eds., *Principles of Frontal Lobe Function*, New York: Oxford University Press, p. 474. Reprinted by permission.)

Children learn much from cultural tools that support planning—directions for playing games, patterns for construction, recipes for cooking—especially when they collaborate with more expert planners. When 4- to 7-year-olds were observed jointly constructing a toy with their mothers, the mothers gave preschoolers basic information about the usefulness of plans and suggestions for implementing specific steps: "Do you want to look at the picture and see what goes where? What piece do you need first?" After working with their mothers, younger children more often referred to the plan when building on their own (Gauvain, 2004; Gauvain, de la Ossa, & Hurtado-Ortiz, 2001). When parents encourage planning in everyday activities, from loading the dishwasher to packing for a vacation, they help children plan more effectively.

Memory

Unlike infants and toddlers, preschoolers have the language skills to describe what they remember, and they can follow directions on memory tasks. As a result, memory becomes easier to study in early childhood.

■ **Recognition and Recall.** Try showing a young child a set of 10 pictures or toys. Then mix them up with some unfamiliar items and ask the child to point to the ones in the original set. You will find that preschoolers' *recognition* memory—ability to tell whether a stimulus is the same as or similar to one they

have seen before—is remarkably good. In fact, 4- and 5-year-olds perform nearly perfectly.

Now keep the items out of view and ask the child to name the ones she saw. This more demanding task requires *recall*—that the child generate a mental image of an absent stimulus. Young children's recall is much poorer than their recognition. At age 2, they can recall no more than one or two of the items, at age 4 only about three or four (Perlmutter, 1984).

Better recall in early childhood is strongly associated with language development, which greatly enhances long-lasting representations of past experiences (Simcock & Hayne, 2003). But even preschoolers with good language skills recall poorly because they are not skilled at using **memory strategies,** deliberate mental activities that improve our chances of remembering. Preschoolers do not yet rehearse, or repeat items over and over to remember. Nor do they organize, grouping together items that are alike (all the animals together, all the vehicles together) so they can easily retrieve the items by thinking of their similar characteristics. Even when they are trained to do so, their memory performance rarely improves, and they do not apply these strategies in new situations (Gathercole, Adams, & Hitch, 1994).

Why do young children seldom use memory strategies? One reason is that strategies tax their limited working memories. *Digit span* tasks, in which children try to repeat an adult-provided string of numbers, assess the size of working memory, which improves slowly, from an average of two digits at age 2½ to five digits at age 7 (Kail, 2003). With such limits, preschoolers have difficulty holding on to pieces of information and applying a strategy at the same time.

■ **Memory for Everyday Experiences.** Think about the difference between your recall of listlike information and your memory for everyday experiences. In remembering lists, you recall isolated bits, reproducing them exactly as you originally learned them. In remembering everyday experiences, you recall complex, meaningful events.

Memory for Familiar Events. Like adults, preschoolers remember familiar, repeated events—what you do when you go to preschool or have dinner—in terms of **scripts,** general descriptions of what occurs and when it occurs in a particular situation. Young children's scripts begin as a structure of main acts. For example, when asked to tell what happens when you go to a restaurant, a 3-year-old might say, "You go in, get the food, eat, and then pay." Although children's first scripts contain only a few acts, they are almost always recalled in correct sequence (Bauer, 1997, 2002). With age, scripts become more elaborate, as in this 5-year-old's account of eating at a restaurant: "You go in. You can sit in a booth or at a table. Then you tell the waitress what you want. You eat. If you want dessert, you can have some. Then you pay and go home" (Hudson, Fivush, & Kuebli, 1992).

Scripts are a basic means through which children (and adults) organize and interpret everyday experiences. Once formed, they can be used to predict what will happen in the future. Children rely on scripts in make-believe play and when

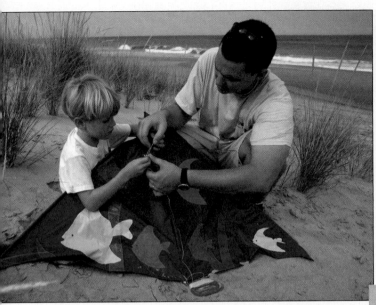

A preschooler enjoys a special day assembling and flying a kite with his father. If the father later reminisces about the event with the child in an elaborative style, the boy's autobiographical recall is likely to be more organized and detailed.

listening to and telling stories. Scripts also support children's earliest efforts at planning by helping them represent sequences of actions that lead to desired goals (Hudson, Sosa, & Shapiro, 1997).

Memory for One-Time Events. In Chapter 5, we considered a second type of everyday memory—*autobiographical memory,* or representations of personally meaningful, one-time events. As preschoolers' cognitive and conversational skills improve, their descriptions of special events become better organized in time, more detailed, and related to the larger context of their lives (Haden, Haine, & Fivush, 1997).

Adults use two styles to elicit children's autobiographical narratives. Parents who use the *elaborative style* ask varied questions, add information to children's statements, and volunteer their own recollections and evaluations of events. For example, after a trip to the zoo, the parent might say, "What was the first thing we did? Why weren't the parrots in their cages? I thought the lion was scary. What did you think?" In contrast, parents who use the *repetitive style* provide little information and ask the same short-answer questions over and over: "Do you remember the zoo? What did we do at the zoo?" These differences depend, in part, on the emotional quality of the parent–child relationship. Parents and preschoolers with secure attachment bonds engage in more elaborate reminiscing (Fivush & Reese, 2002). Preschoolers who experience elaborative dialogues produce more organized and detailed personal stories when followed up one to two years later (Farrant & Reese, 2000; Reese, Haden, & Fivush, 1993).

Girls produce more detailed narratives than boys. And compared with Asian children, Western children include more comments about their own thoughts, emotions, and preferences. These differences fit with variations in parent–child conversations. Parents reminisce more with daughters (Bruce, Dolan, & Phillips-Grant, 2000). And collectivist cultural values lead Asian parents to discourage children from talking about themselves (Han, Leichtman, & Wang, 1998). In line with Vygotsky's theory, social experiences influence children's memory skills.

The Young Child's Theory of Mind

As representation of the world, memory, and problem solving improve, children start to reflect on their own thought processes. They begin to construct a *theory of mind,* or coherent set of ideas about mental activities. This understanding is also called **metacognition.** The prefix *meta-* means "beyond or higher," and *metacognition* means "thinking about thought." As adults, we have a complex appreciation of our inner mental worlds, which we use to interpret our own and others' behavior and to improve our performance on various tasks. How early are children aware of their mental lives, and how complete and accurate is their knowledge?

■ **Awareness of Mental Life.** At the end of the first year, babies view people as intentional beings who can share and influence one another's mental states, a milestone that opens the door to new forms of communication—joint attention, social referencing, preverbal gestures, and spoken language. These interactive skills, in turn, enhance toddlers' mental understandings (Tomasello & Rakoczy, 2003). As they approach age 2, children display a clearer grasp of others' emotions and desires, evident in their realization that others' perspectives can differ from their own ("Daddy like carrots. I no like carrots.").

As 2-year-olds' vocabularies expand, their first verbs include such words as *think, remember,* and *pretend* (Wellman, 1990). By age 3, children realize that thinking takes place inside their heads and that a person can think about something without seeing it, talking about it, or touching it (Flavell, Green, & Flavell, 1995). But 2- to 3-year-olds have only a beginning grasp of the distinction between mental life and behavior. They think that people always behave in ways consistent with their *desires* and do not understand that less obvious, more interpretive mental states, such as *beliefs,* also affect behavior.

Between ages 3 and 4, children use *think* and *know* to refer to their own and others' thoughts and beliefs (Wellman, 2002). And from age 4 on, they realize that both *beliefs* and *desires* determine behavior. Dramatic evidence for this new understanding comes from games that test whether preschoolers realize that *false beliefs*—ones that do not represent reality accurately—can guide people's actions.

For example: Show a child two small closed boxes—a familiar Band-Aid box and a plain, unmarked box (see Figure 7.11 on page 240)—and say, "Pick the box you think has the Band-Aids in it." Almost always, children pick the marked container. Next, open the boxes and show the child that, contrary to her own belief, the marked one is empty and the unmarked one contains the Band-Aids. Finally, introduce the child to a hand puppet and ask, "Here's Pam. She has a cut, see? Where do you think she'll look for Band-Aids? Why would she look in

■ **FIGURE 7.11 Example of a false-belief task.**
(a) An adult shows a child the contents of a
Band-Aid box and of an unmarked box. The
Band-Aids are in the unmarked container.
(b) The adult introduces the child to a hand
puppet named Pam and asks the child to predict where Pam would look for the Band-Aids
and to explain Pam's behavior. The task reveals
whether children understand that without
having seen that the Band-Aids are in the
unmarked container, Pam will hold a false
belief.

there? Before you looked inside, did you think that the plain box contained Band-Aids? Why?" (Bartsch & Wellman, 1995). Only a handful of 3-year-olds can explain Pam's—and their own—false beliefs, but many 4-year-olds can.

Among children of diverse cultural and SES backgrounds, false-belief understanding strengthens between ages 4 and 6 (Callaghan et al., 2005; Wellman, Cross, & Watson, 2001). During that time, it becomes a powerful tool for understanding oneself and others and a good predictor of social skills (Jenkins & Astington, 2000; Watson et al., 1999).

■ **Factors Contributing to Preschoolers' Theory of Mind.** How do children manage to develop a theory of mind at such a young age? Language, cognitive abilities, make-believe play, and social experiences all contribute.

Understanding the mind requires the ability to reflect on thoughts, which is made possible by language. Children who spontaneously use, or who are trained to use, complex sentences with mental-state words are more likely to pass false-belief tasks (de Villiers & de Villiers, 2000; Hale & Tager-Flusberg, 2003). Among the Quechua of the Peruvian highlands, whose language lacks mental-state terms, children have difficulty with false-belief tasks for years after children in industrialized nations have mastered them (Vinden, 1996). Chinese languages, in contrast, have verb markers that can label the word *believe* as decidedly false. When adults use those markers within false-belief tasks, Chinese preschoolers perform better (Tardif et al., 2004).

The ability to inhibit inappropriate responses, think flexi-bly, and plan predicts current false-belief understanding and improvements over time (Carlson & Moses, 2001; Hughes, 1998). Gains in inhibition are strongly related to mastery of false belief, perhaps because to do well on false-belief tasks, children must suppress a competing response—the tendency to assume that others' knowledge and beliefs are the same as their own (Birch & Bloom, 2003; Carlson, Moses, & Claxton, 2004).

Social experience also promotes understanding of the mind. In longitudinal research, mothers of securely attached babies were more likely to comment appropriately on their infants' mental states: "Do you *remember* Grandma?" "You really *like* that swing!" This maternal "mind-mindedness" was positively associated with later performance on false belief and

other theory-of-mind tasks (Meins et al., 1998, 2002). Also, preschoolers with siblings—especially those with older sib-lings—tend to be more aware of false belief because of expo-sure to more family talk about others' perspectives (Jenkins et al., 2003; Peterson, 2001).

Similarly, preschoolers who often engage in mental-state talk with friends, as children do during make-believe play, are ahead in false-belief understanding (Harris & Leevers, 2000). Interacting with more mature members of society contributes, too. In a study of Greek preschoolers, daily contact with many adults and older children predicted mastery of false belief (Lewis et al., 1996). These encounters offer extra opportunities to observe different viewpoints and talk about inner states.

Core knowledge theorists (see Chapter 5, page 158) believe that to profit from the social experiences just described, children must be biologically prepared to develop a theory of mind. They claim that children with *autism,* who do not grasp false belief, are deficient in the brain mechanism that enables humans to detect mental states. See the Biology and Environ-ment box on the following page to find out more about the biological basis of reasoning about the mind.

■ **Limitations of the Young Child's Understanding of Mental Life.** Though surprisingly advanced, preschoolers' awareness of mental activities is far from complete. For exam-ple, 3- and 4-year-olds are unaware that people continue to think while they wait, look at pictures, listen to stories, or read books. They conclude that mental activity stops when there are no obvious cues to indicate a person is thinking (Flavell, Green, & Flavell, 1993, 1995). And children younger than age 5 pay little attention to the *process* of thinking. When questioned about subtle distinctions between mental states, such as *know* and *forget,* they express confusion (Lyon & Flavell, 1994). And they believe that all events must be directly observed to be known. They do not understand that *mental inferences* can be a source of knowledge (Miller, Hardin, & Montgomery, 2003).

These findings suggest that preschoolers view the mind as a passive container of information. Consequently, they greatly underestimate the amount of mental activity that people engage in and are poor at inferring what people know or are thinking about. In contrast, older children view the mind as an active, constructive agent—a change we will consider further in Chapter 9.

Biology and Environment

"Mindblindness" and Autism

Sidney stood at the water table in his preschool classroom, repeatedly filling a plastic cup and dumping out its contents—dip–splash, dip–splash—until his teacher came over and redirected his actions. Without looking at his teacher's face, Sidney moved to a new repetitive pursuit: pouring water from one cup into another and back again. As other children entered the play space and conversed, Sidney hardly noticed. He rarely spoke, and when he did, he usually used words to get things he wanted, not to exchange ideas.

Sidney has *autism*, the most severe behavior disorder of childhood. The term *autism*, which means "absorbed in the self," is an apt description of Sidney. Like other children with the disorder, by age 3 he displayed deficits in three core areas of functioning: First, he had only limited ability to engage in nonverbal behaviors required for successful social interaction, such as eye gaze, facial expressions, gestures, imitation, and give-and-take. Second, his language was delayed and stereotyped. He used words to echo what others said and to get things he wanted, not to exchange ideas. Third, he engaged in much less make-believe play than other children (Frith, 2003). And Sidney showed another typical feature of autism: His interests were narrow and overly intense. For example, one day he sat for more than an hour spinning a toy Ferris wheel.

Researchers agree that autism stems from abnormal brain functioning, usually due to genetic or prenatal environmental causes. From the first year on, children with the disorder have larger-than-average brains, perhaps due to massive overgrowth of synapses and lack of synaptic pruning, which accompanies normal development of cognitive and language skills (Courchesne, Carper, & Akshoomoff, 2003). Furthermore, fMRI studies reveal that autism is associated with reduced activity in areas of the cerebral cortex known to mediate emotional and social responsiveness and thinking

about mental activities, including mirror neurons, discussed in Chapter 4 (see page 135) (Mundy, 2003; Théoret et al., 2005).

Growing evidence reveals that children with autism have a deficient theory of mind. Long after they reach the intellectual level of an average 4-year-old, they have great difficulty with false-belief tasks. Most find it hard to attribute mental states to themselves or others (Steele, Joseph, & Tager-Flusberg, 2003). Such words as *believe, think, know, feel,* and *pretend* are rarely part of their vocabularies.

As early as the second year, children with autism show deficits in capacities believed to contribute to an understanding of mental life. Compared with other children, they less often establish joint attention, engage in social referencing, or imitate an adult's novel behaviors (Mundy & Stella, 2000). Furthermore, they are relatively insensitive to eye gaze as a cue to what a speaker is talking about. Instead, they often assume that another person's language refers to what they themselves are looking at (Baron-Cohen, Baldwin, & Crowson, 1997).

Do these findings indicate that autism is due to impairment of an innate, core brain function, which leaves the child "mindblind" and therefore deficient in human sociability? Some researchers think so (Baron-Cohen & Belmonte, 2005; Scholl & Leslie, 2000). But others point out that nonautistic, mentally retarded individuals also do poorly on tasks assessing mental understanding (Yirmiya et al., 1998). This suggests that some kind of general intellectual impairment may be involved.

One conjecture is that children with autism are impaired in *executive processing* (refer to the central executive in the information-processing model on page

This child, who has autism, is hardly aware of his mother's voice or touch as she tries to direct his attention to the computer. Researchers disagree on whether autistic children's "mindblindness" results from a specific deficit in social understanding or from a general intellectual impairment involving executive processing.

161 in Chapter 5). This leaves them deficient in a variety of cognitive abilities that result in flexible, goal-oriented thinking, including shifting attention to relevant aspects of a situation, inhibiting irrelevant responses, applying strategies to hold information in working memory, and generating plans (Geurts et al., 2004; Joseph & Tager-Flusberg, 2004). An inability to think flexibly would interfere with understanding the social world, since social interaction requires quick integration of information from various sources and evaluation of alternative possibilities.

It is not clear which of these hypotheses is correct. Some research suggests that impairments in social awareness, integrative thinking, and verbal ability contribute independently to autism (Morgan, Maybery, & Durkin, 2003). Perhaps several biologically based deficits underlie the tragic social isolation of children like Sidney.

Early Childhood Literacy

One week, Leslie's students created a make-believe grocery store. They brought empty food boxes from home, placed them on shelves in the classroom, labeled items with prices, made shopping lists, and wrote checks at the cash register. A sign at the entrance announced the daily specials: "APLS BNS 5¢" ("apples bananas 5¢").

As such play reveals, preschoolers understand a great deal about written language long before they learn to read or write in conventional ways. This is not surprising when we consider that children in industrialized nations live in a world filled with written symbols. Each day, they observe and participate in activities involving storybooks, calendars, lists, and signs. As part of these informal experiences, they try to figure out how written symbols convey meaning—active efforts known as **emergent literacy.**

Young preschoolers search for units of written language as they "read" memorized versions of stories and recognize familiar signs ("PIZZA"). But they do not yet understand the symbolic function of the elements of print (Bialystok & Martin, 2003). Many preschoolers think that a single letter stands for a whole word or that each letter in a person's signature represents a separate name. Children revise these ideas as their cognitive capacities improve, as they encounter writing in many contexts, and as adults help them with written communication. Gradually, they notice more features of written language and depict writing that varies in function, as in the "story" and "grocery list" in Figure 7.12.

Eventually, children figure out that letters are parts of words and are linked to sounds in systematic ways, as seen in the invented spellings that are typical between ages 5 and 7. At first, children rely on sounds in the names of letters, as in "ADE LAFWTS KRMD NTU A LAVATR" ("eighty elephants crammed into a[n] elevator"). Over time, they grasp sound–letter correspondences and learn that some letters have more than one common sound (McGee & Richgels, 2004).

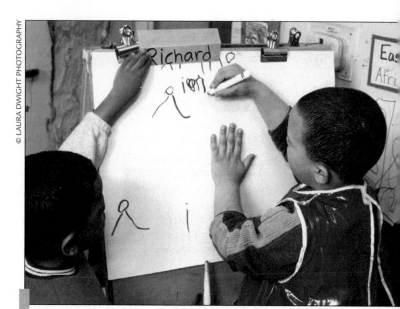

Preschoolers acquire a great deal of literacy knowledge informally through participating in everyday activities involving written symbols. This 4-year-old tries to write his name while a classmate helps by holding up his name card so he can easily see the letters.

The more informal literacy-related experiences young children have, the better their language and emergent literacy development (Dickinson & McCabe, 2001). Pointing out letter–sound correspondences and playing language–sound games enhance children's awareness of the sound structure of language and how it is represented in print (Foy & Mann, 2003). *Interactive* storybook reading, in which adults discuss story content with preschoolers, promotes many aspects of language and literacy development. And adult-supported writing activities that focus on narrative, such as preparing a letter or a story, also have wide-ranging benefits (Purcell-Gates, 1996; Wasik & Bond, 2001).

Preschoolers from low-SES families have fewer home and preschool language and literacy learning opportunities—a major reason that they are behind in reading achievement throughout the school years (Serpell et al., 2002). In a program that "flooded" child-care centers with children's books and provided training to caregivers on how to get 3- and 4-year-olds to spend time with books, children showed much greater gains in emergent literacy than a no-intervention control group (Neuman, 1999). Providing low-SES parents with children's books, along with guidance in how to stimulate literacy learning in preschoolers, greatly enhances literacy activities in the home (High et al., 2000).

Young Children's Mathematical Reasoning

Mathematical reasoning, like literacy, builds on informally acquired knowledge. Between 14 and 16 months, toddlers display a beginning grasp of **ordinality,** or order relationships between quantities—for example, three is more than two, and two is more than one. Soon they attach verbal labels (such as *lots, little, big, small*) to amounts and sizes. Sometime in the

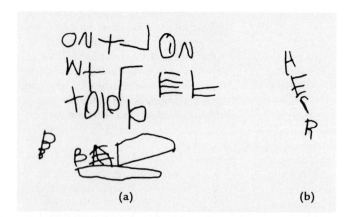

(a)   (b)

■ **FIGURE 7.12 A story (a) and a grocery list (b) written by a 4-year-old child.** This child's writing has many features of real print. It also reveals an awareness of different kinds of written expression. (From L. M. McGee & D. J. Richgels, 2004, *Literacy's Beginnings* (4th ed.), Boston: Allyn and Bacon, p. 76. Reprinted by permission.)

third year, they begin to count. By the time children turn 3, they can count rows of about five objects, although they do not yet know what the words mean. For example, when asked for "one," they give one item, but when asked for "two," "three," "four," or "five," they usually give a larger, but incorrect, amount. Nevertheless, 2½- to 3½-year-olds realize that a number word refers to a unique quantity—that when a number label changes (for example, from five to six), the number of items should also change (Sarnecka & Gelman, 2004).

By age 3½ to 4, most children have mastered the meaning of numbers up to ten, count correctly, and grasp the vital principle of **cardinality**—that the last number in a counting sequence indicates the quantity of items in a set (Zur & Gelman, 2004). Mastery of cardinality increases the efficiency of children's counting.

Around age 4, children start to solve arithmetic problems. At first, their strategies are tied to the order of numbers as presented; to add 2 + 4, they count on from 2 (Bryant & Nunes, 2002). But they soon experiment with other strategies—for example, holding up four fingers on one hand and two on the other, then recognizing 6 as the total; or starting with the higher digit, 4, and counting on (Siegler, 1996). Gradually, children select the most efficient, accurate strategy—in this example, beginning with the higher digit. Then they generalize the strategy to subtraction and soon realize that subtraction reverses addition. Knowing, for example, that 4 + 3 = 7, they can infer without counting that 7 − 3 = 4 (Rasmussen, Ho, & Bisanz, 2003). Grasping basic arithmetic rules facilitates rapid computation, and with enough practice, children recall answers automatically.

In homes and preschools where adults provide many meaningful occasions and requests for counting, comparing quantities, and adding and subtracting, children acquire these understandings sooner. For example, low-income 4-year-olds exposed to a math intervention program in which teachers included math activities in almost all classroom routines scored higher in math concepts and enjoyed math activities more than children in other classrooms (Arnold et al., 2002). Solid, secure early childhood math knowledge is essential for the wide variety of mathematical skills children will be taught in school.

Individual Differences in Mental Development

Five-year-old Hal sat in a testing room while Sarah gave him an intelligence test. Some of Sarah's questions were *verbal*. For example, she showed him a picture of a shovel and said, "Tell me what this is"—an item measuring vocabulary. She tested his memory by asking him to repeat sentences and lists of numbers back to her. To assess Hal's spatial reasoning, Sarah used *nonverbal* tasks: Hal copied designs with special blocks, figured out the pattern in a series of shapes, and indicated what a piece of paper folded and cut would look like when unfolded (Roid, 2003; Wechsler, 2002).

Sarah knew that Hal came from an economically disadvantaged family. When low-SES and certain ethnic minority preschoolers are faced with an unfamiliar adult who bombards them with questions, they sometimes react with anxiety. Also, such children may not define the testing situation in achievement terms. Often they look for attention and approval from the examiner and may settle for lower performance than their abilities allow. Sarah spent time playing with Hal before she began testing and encouraged him while testing was in progress. Under these conditions, low-SES preschoolers improve in performance (Bracken, 2000).

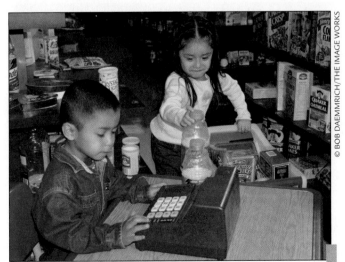

It's time for this shopper to count and pay for her items at a preschool play grocery store. Children who are exposed to rich, informal mathematical activities acquire a solid foundation of math concepts and skills—while also learning that math is interesting, enjoyable, and useful.

© BOB DAEMMRICH/THE IMAGE WORKS

The questions Sarah asked Hal tap knowledge and skills that not all children have equal opportunity to learn. In Chapter 9, we will take up the hotly debated issue of *cultural bias* in mental testing. For now, keep in mind that intelligence tests do not sample all human abilities, and performance is affected by cultural and situational factors (Sternberg, 2003a). Nevertheless, test scores remain important: By age 6 to 7, they are good predictors of later IQ and academic achievement, which are related to vocational success in industrialized societies. Let's see how the environments in which preschoolers spend their days—home, preschool, and child care—affect mental test performance.

Home Environment and Mental Development

A special version of the *Home Observation for Measurement of the Environment (HOME),* covered in Chapter 5, assesses aspects of 3- to 6-year-olds' home lives that support mental development (see Applying What We Know below). Preschoolers who develop well intellectually tend to be those who have homes rich in educational toys and books. Their parents are warm and affectionate, stimulate language and academic knowledge, and arrange outings to places with interesting things to see and do. They also make reasonable demands for socially mature behavior—for example, that the child perform simple chores and act courteously toward others. And these parents resolve conflicts with reason instead of physical force and punishment (Bradley & Caldwell, 1982; Espy, Molfese, & DiLalla, 2001; Roberts, Burchinal, & Durham, 1999).

As we saw in Chapter 2, these characteristics are less likely to be found in poverty-stricken families. When low-SES parents manage, despite daily pressures, to obtain high HOME scores, preschoolers do substantially better on intelligence tests

(Klebanov et al., 1998). These findings highlight the vital role of home environmental quality in children's performance.

Preschool, Kindergarten, and Child Care

Children between ages 2 and 6 spend even more time away from their homes and parents than infants and toddlers do. Largely because of the rise in maternal employment, over the past several decades the number of young children enrolled in preschool or child care has steadily increased, reaching nearly 75 percent in the United States and in some Canadian provinces (Federal Interagency Forum on Child and Family Statistics, 2005; Statistics Canada, 2005a).

A *preschool* is a program with planned educational experiences aimed at enhancing the development of 2- to 5-yearolds. In contrast, *child care* identifies a variety of arrangements for supervising children. With age, children tend to transition from home care (either in the child's own home or in someone else's home) to center care. Many children, however, experience several types of care and frequently switch settings (NICHD Early Child Care Research Network, 2004).

The line between preschool and child care is fuzzy. Responding to the needs of employed parents, many North American preschools—and public school kindergartens as well—have increased their hours from half to full days (U.S. Department of Education, 2005b). At the same time, good child care is not simply a matter of keeping children safe and adequately fed. It should provide the same high-quality educational experiences that an effective preschool does.

■ **Types of Preschool and Kindergarten.** Preschool and kindergarten programs range along a continuum, from childcentered to teacher-directed. In **child-centered programs,** teachers provide a wide variety of activities from which children

Features of a High-Quality Home Life for Preschoolers: The HOME Early Childhood Subscales

Subscale	Sample Item
Stimulation through toys, games, and reading material	Home includes toys that teach colors, sizes, and shapes.
Language stimulation	Parent teaches child about animals through books, games, and puzzles.
Organization of the physical environment	All visible rooms are reasonably clean and minimally cluttered.
Pride, affection, and warmth	Parent spontaneously praises child's qualities once or twice during observer's visit.
Stimulation of academic behavior	Child is encouraged to learn colors.
Modeling and encouragement of social maturity	Parent introduces interviewer to child.
Variety in daily stimulation	Family member takes child on one outing at least every other week (picnic, shopping).
Avoidance of physical punishment	Parent neither slaps nor spanks child during observer's visit.

Sources: Bradley, 1994; Bradley et al., 2001.

select, and much learning takes place through play. In contrast, in **academic programs,** teachers structure children's learning, teaching letters, numbers, colors, shapes, and other academic skills through formal lessons, often using repetition and drill.

Despite grave concern about the appropriateness of the approach, preschool and kindergarten teachers have felt increased pressure to stress formal academic training. Yet doing so undermines motivation and emotional well-being. When preschoolers and kindergartners spend much time passively sitting and completing worksheets as opposed to being actively engaged in learning centers, they display more stress behaviors (such as wiggling and rocking), have less confidence in their abilities, prefer less challenging tasks, and are less advanced in motor, academic, language, and social skills at the end of the school year (Marcon, 1999a; Stipek et al., 1995). Follow-ups reveal lasting effects through elementary school in poorer study habits and achievement (Burts et al., 1992; Hart et al., 1998, 2003). These outcomes are strongest for low-SES children.

■ **Early Intervention for At-Risk Preschoolers.** In the 1960s, when the United States launched a "War on Poverty," many preschool intervention programs, aimed at offsetting the declines in IQ and achievement common among low-SES children, were initiated. The most extensive of these programs is **Project Head Start,** begun by the U.S. federal government in 1965. A typical Head Start center provides children with a year or two of preschool, along with nutritional and health services. Parent involvement is central to the Head Start philosophy. Parents serve on policy councils and contribute to program planning. They also work directly with children in classrooms, attend special programs on parenting and child development, and receive services directed at their own emotional, social, and vocational needs. Currently, more than 20,000 U.S. Head Start centers serve about 906,000 children (Head Start Bureau, 2005).

In 1995, Canada initiated **Aboriginal Head Start** for First Nations, Inuit, and Métis children younger than age 6, 60 percent of whom live in poverty. Like Project Head Start, the program provides children with preschool education and nutritional and health services and encourages parent involvement. Currently, Aboriginal Head Start has about 120 sites and serves more than 3,900 children (Health Canada, 2004a).

More than two decades of research have established the long-term benefits of preschool intervention. The most extensive of these studies combined data from seven interventions implemented by universities or research foundations. Results showed that children who attended programs scored higher in IQ and achievement than controls during the first two to three years of elementary school. After that time, differences declined (Lazar & Darlington, 1982). Nevertheless, children and adolescents who received intervention remained ahead on real-life measures of school adjustment. They were less likely to be placed in special education or retained in grade, and a greater number graduated from high school.

A separate report on one program—the High/Scope Perry Preschool Project—revealed benefits lasting well into adult-

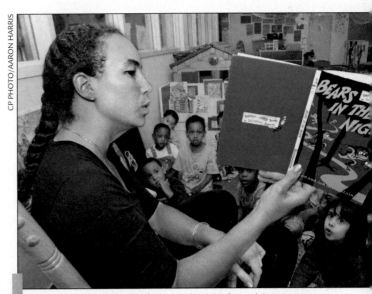

These 4-year-olds benefit from an Aboriginal Head Start program in Nunavut, Canada. Like U.S. Head Start children, they receive rich, stimulating educational experiences and nutritional and health services, and their parents participate. In the classroom, the children have many opportunities to engage in activities with special cultural meaning.

hood. Two years' exposure to cognitively enriching preschool was associated with increased employment and reduced pregnancy and delinquency rates in adolescence. At age 27, those who had attended preschool were more likely than no-preschool counterparts to have graduated from high school and college, have higher earnings, be married, and own their own home—and less likely to have been involved with the criminal justice system (see Figure 7.13 on page 246) (Weikart, 1998). In the most recent follow-up, at age 40, the intervention group sustained its advantage on all measures of life success, including education, income, family life, and law-abiding behavior (Schweinhart et al., 2004).

Do the effects of these well-designed and well-delivered programs generalize to Head Start and other community-based preschool interventions? Gains in school adjustment are similar, though not as strong. Head Start preschoolers are more economically disadvantaged than children in university-based programs and hence have more severe learning and behavior problems. And quality of services is more variable across community programs (NICHD Early Child Care Research Network, 2001; Ramey & Ramey, 1999).

A consistent finding is that gains in IQ and achievement test scores from attending Head Start and other interventions quickly dissolve. One reason is that these children typically enter inferior public schools in poverty-stricken neighborhoods, an experience that undermines the benefits of preschool education (Brooks-Gunn, 2003). But the gains in school adjustment that result from attending a one- or two-year Head Start program are still impressive. They may be partly due to program effects on parents. The more involved parents are in Head Start, the better their child-rearing practices and the more stimulating their home learning environments. These

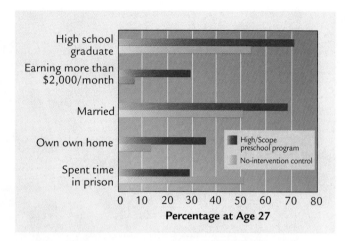

■ **FIGURE 7.13 Some outcomes of the High/Scope Perry Preschool Project on follow-up at age 27.** Although two years of a cognitively enriching preschool program did not eradicate the effects of growing up in poverty, children who received intervention were advantaged over no-intervention controls on all measures of life success when they reached adulthood. (Adapted from Schweinhart et al., 2004.)

factors are positively related to preschoolers' task persistence in the classroom and to their year-end academic, language, and social skills (Marcon, 1999b; Parker et al., 1999).

Head Start is highly cost-effective when compared with the cost of providing special education, treating criminal behavior, and supporting unemployed adults. Economists estimate that the lifetime return to society is more than $250,000 on an investment of $15,000 per preschool child—a total savings of many billions of dollars were every poverty-stricken preschooler in the United States and Canada to be enrolled (Heckman & Masterov, 2004). Because of funding shortages, however, many eligible children do not receive services.

■ **Child Care.** We have seen that high-quality early intervention can enhance the development of economically disadvantaged children. As noted in Chapter 5, however, much North American child care lacks quality. Preschoolers exposed to substandard child care, regardless of family SES, score lower in cognitive and social skills (Howes & James, 2002; NICHD Early Child Care Research Network, 2003b). And when children experience the instability of several child-care settings, their psychological well-being declines. The emotional and behavior problems of temperamentally difficult preschoolers worsen considerably (De Schipper, van IJzendoorn, & Tavecchio, 2004; De Schipper et al., 2004).

In contrast, good child care enhances development, especially among low-SES children. In an investigation that followed very-low-income children over the preschool years, center-based care was more strongly associated with cognitive gains than other child-care arrangements, probably because centers are more likely to provide a systematic educational program. At the same time, better-quality experiences in all types of child care predicted modest improvements in cognitive,

emotional, and social development (Loeb et al., 2004). In other research, these effects persisted into the early school years (Peisner-Feinberg et al., 2001).

Consult Applying What We Know on the following page for characteristics of high-quality early childhood programs, based on standards for developmentally appropriate practice devised by the U.S. National Association for the Education of Young Children. These standards offer a set of worthy goals as the United States and Canada strive to upgrade child-care and educational services for young children.

Educational Media

Besides home and preschool, children are introduced early to another learning context: electronic media, especially television but also computers. Exposure to television is almost universal in the United States, Canada, and other industrialized nations. Nearly all homes have at least one television set, and most have two or more. Similarly, computers are familiar fixtures in the everyday lives of today's children. About 85 percent of North American children live in homes with one or more computers, two-thirds of which have an Internet connection (Roberts, Foehr, & Rideout, 2005; Statistics Canada, 2004c).

■ **Educational Television.** Each afternoon, Sammy looked forward to his favorite TV program, *Sesame Street.* It uses lively visual and sound effects to stress basic literacy and number concepts and engaging puppet and human characters to teach general knowledge, emotional and social understanding, and social skills. Today, more than two-thirds of North American preschoolers watch *Sesame Street,* and it is broadcast in more than 120 countries (Sesame Workshop, 2005).

The more children watch *Sesame Street,* the higher they score on tests designed to measure the program's learning goals (Fisch, Truglio, & Cole, 1999). One study reported a link between preschool viewing of *Sesame Street* and other similar educational programs and getting higher grades, reading more books, and placing more value on achievement in high school (Anderson et al., 2001). In recent years, *Sesame Street* has reduced its rapid-paced format in favor of more leisurely episodes with a clear story line. Watching children's programs with slow-paced action and easy-to-follow narratives, such as *Mister Rogers' Neighborhood* and *Barney and Friends,* leads to more elaborate make-believe play than viewing programs that present quick, disconnected bits of information (Singer & Singer, 2005).

Despite the spread of computers, television remains the dominant youth media. The average North American 2- to 6-year-old watches TV from 1½ to 2 hours a day—a long time in a young child's life. In middle childhood, viewing time increases to an average of 3½ hours a day for U.S. children and 2½ hours a day for Canadian children, then declines slightly in adolescence (Scharrer & Comstock, 2003; Statistics Canada, 2005f). Low-SES children are more frequent viewers, perhaps because few alternative forms of entertainment are available

Applying What We Know

Signs of Developmentally Appropriate Early Childhood Programs

Program Characteristics	Signs of Quality
Physical setting	Indoor environment is clean, in good repair, and well-ventilated. Classroom space is divided into richly equipped activity areas, including make-believe play, blocks, science, math, games and puzzles, books, art, and music. Fenced outdoor play space is equipped with swings, climbing equipment, tricycles, and sandbox.
Group size	In preschools and child-care centers, group size is no greater than 18 to 20 children with 2 teachers.
Caregiver–child ratio	In child-care centers, teacher is responsible for no more than 8 to 10 children. In child-care homes, caregiver is responsible for no more than 6 children.
Daily activities	Most of the time, children work individually or in small groups. Children select many of their own activities and learn through experiences relevant to their own lives. Teachers facilitate children's involvement, accept individual differences, and adjust expectations to children's developing capacities.
Interactions among adults and children	Teachers move among groups and individuals, asking questions, offering suggestions, and adding more complex ideas. Teachers use positive guidance techniques, such as modeling and encouraging expected behavior and redirecting children to more acceptable activities.
Teacher qualifications	Teachers have college-level specialized preparation in early childhood development, early childhood education, or a related field.
Relationships with parents	Parents are encouraged to observe and participate. Teachers talk frequently with parents about children's behavior and development.
Licensing and accreditation	Child-care setting, whether a center or a home, is licensed by the state or province. In the United States, voluntary accreditation by the National Academy of Early Childhood Programs, *www.naeyc. org/accreditation*, or the National Association for Family Child Care, *www.nafcc.org*, is evidence of a high-quality program. Canada is working on a voluntary accreditation system, under the leadership of the Canadian Child Care Federation, *www.cccf-fcsge.ca*.

Sources: Bredekamp & Copple, 1997; National Association for the Education of Young Children, 1998.

in their neighborhoods or affordable for their parents. And if parents watch a lot of TV, their children do, too (Roberts, Foehr, & Rideout, 2005).

Does extensive TV viewing take children away from worthwhile activities? The more preschool and school-age children watch prime-time TV and cartoons, the less time they spend reading and interacting with others and the poorer their academic skills (Huston et al., 1999; Wright et al., 2001). Whereas educational programs can be beneficial, watching entertainment TV—especially heavy viewing—detracts from children's school success and social experiences.

■ **Learning with Computers.** Because computers can have rich educational benefits, many early childhood classrooms include computer learning centers. Children as young as age 3 enjoy computer activities and can type simple keyboard commands. Word-processing programs can support emergent literacy, enabling preschool and young school-age children to experiment with letters and words without having to struggle with handwriting and to easily revise their text and check their spelling. When children worry less about making mistakes,

their written products tend to be longer and of higher quality (Clements & Sarama, 2003).

Computer games that enable young children to practice basic skills, such as letter–sound correspondences, counting, and arithmetic operations, result in learning gains (Clements, 1995). Simplified computer languages that children can use to make designs or build structures introduce them to programming skills. As long as adults support children's efforts, computer programming promotes improved problem solving and metacognition (awareness of thought processes) because children must plan and reflect on their thinking to get their programs to work. Furthermore, while programming, children are especially likely to help one another and to persist in the face of challenge (Nastasi & Clements, 1994). In classrooms, small groups often gather around computers, and children more often collaborate than in other pursuits (Svensson, 2000).

As with television, children spend much time using computers for entertainment purposes, especially game playing. Both media are rife with gender stereotypes and violence. We will look at their impact on emotional and social development in the next chapter.

Ask Yourself

Review

What findings indicate that child-centered rather than academic preschools and kindergartens are better suited to fostering academic development?

Apply

Your senator has heard that IQ gains resulting from Head Start do not last, so he plans to vote against additional funding. Write a letter explaining why he should support Head Start.

Connect

Compare outcomes resulting from preschool intervention programs with those from interventions beginning in infancy (see pages 170–172 in Chapter 5). Which are more likely to lead to lasting gains in IQ? Explain.

Reflect

How much and what kinds of TV viewing and computer use did you engage in as a child? How do you think your home media environment influenced your development?

www.ablongman.com/berk

Language Development

Language is intimately related to virtually all the cognitive changes discussed in this chapter. Between ages 2 and 6, children make momentous advances in language. Their remarkable achievements, as well as their mistakes along the way, reveal their active, rule-oriented approach to mastering language.

Vocabulary

At age 2, Sammy had a vocabulary of 200 words. By age 6, he will have acquired around 10,000 words (Bloom, 1998). To accomplish this feat, Sammy will learn about five new words each day. How do children build their vocabularies so quickly? Research shows that they can connect new words with their underlying concepts after only a brief encounter, a process called **fast-mapping.** Preschoolers can even fast-map two or more new words encountered in the same situation (Wilkinson, Ross, & Diamond, 2003).

■ **Types of Words.** Western children fast-map labels for objects especially rapidly because these refer to concepts that are easy to perceive. When adults point to and label an object, they help the child figure out the word's meaning. Soon children add verbs (*go, run, broke*), which require more complex understandings of relationships between objects and actions. Chinese-, Japanese-, and Korean-speaking children acquire verbs especially quickly. In these languages, nouns are often omitted from adult sentences, and verbs are stressed (Kim, McGregor, & Thompson, 2000; Tardif, Gelman, & Xu, 1999). Gradually, preschoolers add modifiers (*red, round, sad*).

Among those that are related in meaning, general distinctions (which are easier) appear before specific ones, Thus, children first acquire *big–small,* then *tall–short, high–low,* and *wide–narrow* (Stevenson & Pollitt, 1987).

To fill in for words they have not yet learned, children as young as age 3 coin new words using ones they already know. For example, Sammy created a compound word, "plant-man," for a gardener, and added the ending *-er* to make "crayoner" for a child using crayons (Clark, 1995). Preschoolers also extend language meanings through metaphor—like the 3-year-old who described a stomachache as a "fire engine in my tummy" (Winner, 1988). Young preschoolers' metaphors involve concrete sensory comparisons: "Clouds are pillows," "Leaves are dancers." Once vocabulary and general knowledge expand, children also appreciate nonsensory comparisons: "Friends are like magnets" (Karadsheh, 1991; Keil, 1986). As a result, young children sometimes communicate in amazingly vivid and memorable ways.

■ **Strategies for Word Learning.** Preschoolers figure out the meanings of new words by contrasting them with words they already know. But exactly how they discover which concept each word picks out is not yet fully understood. One speculation is that early in vocabulary growth, children adopt a *mutual exclusivity bias;* they assume that words refer to entirely separate (nonoverlapping) categories (Markman, 1992). Consistent with this idea, when 2-year-olds are told the names of two very different novel objects (a clip and a horn), they assign each word correctly, to the whole object and not just a part of it (Waxman & Senghas, 1992).

But mutual exclusivity cannot account for what preschoolers do when objects have more than one name. In these instances, children often call on other components of language. According to one proposal, they figure out many word meanings by observing how words are used in the structure of sentences (Hoff & Naigles, 2002). Consider an adult who says, "This is a *citron* one," while showing the child a yellow car. Two- and 3-year-olds interpret a new word used as an adjective as referring to a property of the object (Hall & Graham, 1999).

Young children also take advantage of the rich social information that adults frequently provide when they introduce new words. For example, they often draw on their expanding ability to infer others' intentions and perspectives (Akhtar & Tomasello, 2000). In one study, an adult performed an action on an object and then used a new label while looking back and forth between the child and the object, as if inviting the child to play. Two-year-olds concluded that the label referred to the action, not the object (Tomasello & Akhtar, 1995). And when an adult first designates the whole object ("See the bird") and then points to a part of it ("That's a beak"), 3-year-olds realize that *beak* is a certain part, not the whole bird (Saylor, Sabbagh, & Baldwin, 2002).

Adults also inform children directly about which of two or more words to use—by saying, for example, "It looks like a car, but actually it's a truck," or "You can call it a sea creature, but it's better to say dolphin." Parents who provide such clarifying

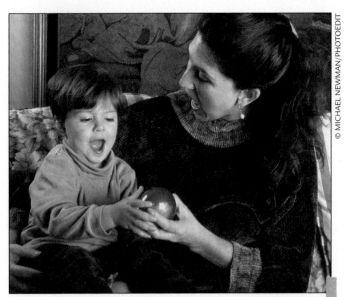

Young children rely on any useful information available to figure out the meanings of new words. This boy might be attending to how his mother uses the word *apple* in the structure of sentences. Or he might be noticing social cues—the direction of his mother's gaze and her actions on the object.

information have preschoolers whose vocabularies grow more quickly (Callanan & Sabbagh, 2004).

If no social cues or direct information is available, children as young as 2 are remarkably flexible in their word-learning strategies. They simply treat a new word applied to an already-labeled object as a second name for the object (Deák, 2000).

■ **Explaining Vocabulary Development.** Children acquire vocabulary so efficiently and accurately that some theorists believe they are innately biased to induce word meanings using certain principles, such as mutual exclusivity (Woodward & Markman, 1998). But critics point out that a small set of built-in, fixed principles is not sufficient to account for the varied, flexible manner in which children master vocabulary (Deák, 2000).

An alternative view is that word learning is governed by the same cognitive strategies that children apply to nonlinguistic information. These strategies become more effective as children's knowledge of categories, vocabulary size, and sensitivity to social cues improve (Hollich, Hirsh-Pasek, & Golinkoff, 2000; Markson & Bloom, 1997). Preschoolers are most successful at figuring out new word meanings when several kinds of information are available (Saylor, Baldwin, & Sabbagh, 2005). Researchers have just begun to study the multiple cues that children use for different kinds of words and how they change with development.

Grammar

Between ages 2 and 3, English-speaking children use simple sentences that follow a subject–verb–object word order. Children learning other languages adopt the word orders of the adult speech to which they are exposed (Maratsos, 1998).

■ **Basic Rules.** Studies of children acquiring diverse languages reveal that their first use of grammatical rules is piecemeal—limited to just a few verbs. As children listen for familiar verbs in adults' speech, they expand their own utterances containing those verbs, relying on adult speech as their model (Gathercole, Sebastián, & Soto, 1999; Lieven, Pine, & Baldwin, 1997). Sammy, for example, added the preposition *with* to the verb *open* ("You open with scissors") but not to the word *stick* ("He hit me stick").

To test preschoolers' ability to generate novel sentences that conform to basic English grammar, researchers had them use a new verb in the subject–verb–object form after hearing it in a different construction, such as passive: "Ernie is getting *gorped* by the dog." The percentage of children who, when asked what the dog was doing, could respond, "He's *gorping* Ernie," rose steadily with age. But not until 3½ to 4 could the majority of children apply the subject–verb–object structure broadly, to newly acquired verbs (Tomasello, 2000, 2003).

As these examples suggest, once children form three-word sentences, they also make small additions and changes to words that enable us to express meanings flexibly and efficiently. For example, they add *-s* for plural ("cats"), use prepositions ("in" and "on"), and form various tenses of the verb *to be* ("is," "are," "were," "has been," "will"). All English-speaking children master these grammatical markers in a regular sequence, starting with those that involve the simplest meanings and structures (Brown, 1973; de Villiers & de Villiers, 1973).

Once children acquire these markers, they apply them so consistently that they sometimes overextend the rules to words that are exceptions—a type of error called **overregularization.** "My toy car *breaked*" and "We each have two *feets*" are expressions that appear between ages 2 and 3 (Maratsos, 2000; Marcus, 1995).

■ **Complex Structures.** Gradually, preschoolers master more complex grammatical structures, although they make errors. In first creating questions, for example, 2- to 3-year-olds use many formulas: "Where's *X*?" "Can I *X*?" (Dabrowska, 2000; Tomasello, 1992). Question asking remains variable for the next couple of years. An analysis of one child's questions revealed that he inverted the subject and verb when asking certain questions but not others ("What she will do?" "Why he can go?") The correct expressions were the ones he heard most often in his mother's speech (Rowland & Pine, 2000).

Similarly, children have trouble with some passive sentences. When told, "The car was pushed by the truck," young preschoolers often make a toy car push a truck. By age 5, they understand such expressions, but full mastery of the passive form is not complete until the end of middle childhood (Horgan, 1978; Lempert, 1990).

Nevertheless, preschoolers' grasp of grammar is remarkable. By age 4 to 5, they form embedded sentences ("I think *he will come*"), tag questions ("Dad's going to be home soon, *isn't he?*"), and indirect objects ("He showed *his friend* the present"). As the preschool years draw to a close, children use most of the grammatical constructions of their language competently (Tager-Flusberg, 2005).

■ **Explaining Grammatical Development.** Evidence that grammatical development is an extended process has raised questions about Chomsky's nativist theory (to review, see page 173 in Chapter 5). Some experts believe that grammar is a product of general cognitive development—children's tendency to search the environment for consistencies and patterns of all sorts (Bloom, 1999; MacWhinney, 2005; Tomasello, 2003). These *information-processing theorists* believe that children notice which words appear in the same positions in sentences and are similarly combined with other words. Over time, they group words into grammatical categories and use them appropriately in sentences.

Still other theorists, while also focusing on how children process language, agree with Chomsky that children are specially tuned to acquire grammar. One idea proposes that the grammatical categories into which children group word meanings are innate—present at the outset (Pinker, 1999). But critics point out that children's early word combinations do not show a grasp of grammar. According to another view, rather than starting with innate knowledge, children have built-in procedures for analyzing language that support discovery of grammatical regularities (Slobin, 1985, 1997). Controversy persists over whether this universal language-processing device exists or whether children hearing different languages devise unique strategies (de Villiers & de Villiers, 1999; Marchman & Thal, 2005).

Conversation

Besides acquiring vocabulary and grammar, children must learn to engage in effective and appropriate communication. This practical, social side of language is called **pragmatics,** and preschoolers make considerable headway in mastering it.

As early as age 2, children are skilled conversationalists. In face-to-face interaction, they take turns and respond appropriately to their partners' remarks (Pan & Snow, 1999). With age, the number of turns over which children can sustain interaction and their ability to maintain a topic over time increase.

By age 4, children adjust their speech to fit the age, sex, and social status of their listeners. For example, in acting out roles with hand puppets, they use more commands when playing socially dominant and male roles (teacher, doctor, father) but speak more politely and use more indirect requests when playing less dominant and female roles (student, patient, mother) (Anderson, 1992, 2000).

Preschoolers' conversational skills occasionally do break down—for example, when talking on the phone. Here is an excerpt of one 4-year-old's phone conversation with his grandfather:

Grandfather: How old will you be?

John: Dis many. [*Holding up four fingers.*]

Grandfather: Huh?

John: Dis many. [*Again holding up four fingers.*] (Warren & Tate, 1992, pp. 259–260)

Young children's conversations appear less mature in highly demanding situations in which they cannot see their listeners' reactions or rely on typical conversational aids, such as gestures and objects to talk about. But when asked to tell a listener how to solve a simple puzzle, 3- to 6-year-olds give more specific directions over the phone than in person, indicating that they realize more verbal description is necessary on the phone (Cameron & Lee, 1997). Between ages 4 and 8, both conversing and giving directions over the phone improve greatly. Telephone talk provides yet another example of how preschoolers' competencies depend on the demands of the situation.

Supporting Language Development in Early Childhood

How can adults foster preschoolers' language development? Interaction with more skilled speakers, which is so important during toddlerhood, remains vital in early childhood. Conversational give-and-take with adults, either at home or in preschool, is consistently related to general measures of language progress (Hart & Risley, 1995; NICHD Early Child Care Research Network, 2000).

Sensitive, caring adults use additional techniques that promote early language skills. When children use words incorrectly or communicate unclearly, they give helpful, explicit feedback, such as, "I can't tell which ball you want. Do you mean the large red one?" But they do not overcorrect, especially when children make grammatical mistakes. Criticism discourages children from freely using language in ways that lead to new skills.

Instead, adults often provide indirect feedback about grammar by using two strategies, often in combination: **recasts**—restructuring inaccurate speech into correct form, and **expansions**—elaborating on children's speech, increasing its complexity (Bohannon & Stanowicz, 1988; Chouinard & Clark, 2003). For example, if a child says, "I gotted new red shoes," the parent might respond, "Yes, you got a pair of new red shoes." However, some researchers question whether

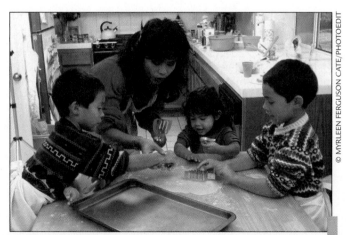

Vital support for children's language progress comes from conversational give-and-take with adults, through which children rapidly acquire vocabulary and grammar and learn how to engage in effective and appropriate communication with others.

expansions and recasts are as important in children's mastery of grammar as mere exposure to a rich language environment. The techniques are not used in all cultures and do not consistently affect children's usage (Strapp & Federico, 2000; Valian, 1996). Rather than eliminating errors, perhaps expansions and recasts model grammatical alternatives and encourage children to experiment with them.

Do the findings just described remind you once again of Vygotsky's theory? In language, as in other aspects of intellectual growth, parents and teachers gently prompt children to take the next step forward. Children strive to master language because they want to connect with other people. Adults, in turn, respond to children's desire to become competent speakers by listening attentively, elaborating on what children say, modeling correct usage, and stimulating children to talk further. In the next chapter, we will see that this combination of warmth and encouragement of mature behavior is at the heart of early childhood emotional and social development as well.

Ask Yourself

Review

Provide a list of recommendations for supporting language development in early childhood, noting research that supports each.

Apply

Sammy's mother explained to him that the family would take a vacation in Miami. The next morning, Sammy announced, "I gotted my bags packed. When are we going to Your-ami?" What explains Sammy's errors?

Connect

Explain how children's strategies for word learning support the interactionist perspective on language development, described on pages 173–174 in Chapter 5.

www.ablongman.com/berk

Summary

🍂 Physical Development

Body Growth

Describe major trends in body growth during early childhood.

■ Children grow more slowly in early childhood than they did in the first 2 years. As body fat declines, they become longer and leaner. New growth centers appear in the skeleton, and by the end of early childhood, children start to lose their primary teeth.

■ Different parts of the body grow at different rates. Changes in body size follow the **general growth curve**—rapid in infancy, slower in early and middle childhood, rapid again in adolescence—except for the genitals, the lymph tissue, and the brain.

Brain Development

Describe brain development during early childhood.

■ In early childhood, frontal-lobe areas of the cerebral cortex devoted to planning and organizing behavior develop rapidly. Also, the left cerebral hemisphere shows more neural activity than the right, supporting young children's expanding language skills.

■ Hand preference strengthens during early and middle childhood, indicating that lateralization is increasing. Handedness reflects an individual's **dominant cerebral hemisphere.** One theory proposes that most children are genetically biased for right-handedness but that experience can sway

them toward a left-hand preference. Although left-handedness is correlated with developmental problems, such problems are rare, and unusual lateralization may have certain advantages.

■ In early childhood, connections are established among different brain structures. Fibers linking the **cerebellum** to the cerebral cortex myelinate, enhancing balance and motor control. The **reticular formation,** responsible for alertness and consciousness, and the **corpus callosum,** which connects the two cerebral hemispheres, also myelinate rapidly.

Influences on Physical Growth and Health

Explain how heredity influences physical growth.

■ Heredity influences physical growth by controlling the release of hormones from the **pituitary gland.** Two hormones are especially influential: **growth hormone (GH)** and **thyroid-stimulating hormone (TSH).**

Describe the effects of emotional well-being, nutrition, and infectious disease on physical growth in early childhood.

■ Emotional well-being continues to influence body growth in middle childhood. An emotionally inadequate home life can lead to a growth disorder called **psychosocial dwarfism.**

■ As preschoolers' growth rate slows, their appetites decline, and they may become picky eaters. Repeated exposure to new

foods (without pressure to eat them) and a positive atmosphere at mealtimes can encourage healthy, varied eating.

■ Many children in North America and in developing countries do not have access to enough high-quality food to support healthy growth. Dietary deficiencies, especially in protein and essential vitamins and minerals, can affect children's growth and resistance to disease.

■ Infectious diseases affect children who do not receive routine immunizations, both in the developing world and in industrialized nations. Illness, especially intestinal infections, can lead to malnutrition.

■ Immunization rates are lower in the United States than in other industrialized nations because many economically disadvantaged children do not have access to health care. Also, because of misconceptions about vaccine safety, some parents refuse to immunize their children.

What factors increase the risk of unintentional injuries, and how can childhood injuries be prevented?

■ Unintentional injuries are the leading cause of childhood mortality in industrialized countries. Injury victims are more likely to be boys; to be temperamentally irritable, inattentive, and negative; and to be growing up in stressed, poverty-stricken inner-city families.

■ Injury deaths are especially high in developing nations, but they are also high in North

America because of poverty and lack of high-quality child care to provide supervision for young children in their parents' absence.

■ Approaches to preventing childhood injuries should include reducing poverty and other sources of family stress; passing laws that promote child safety; creating safer home, travel, child-care, and play environments; improving public education; and changing parent and child behaviors.

Motor Development

Cite major milestones of gross and fine motor development in early childhood.

■ During early childhood, the child's center of gravity shifts toward the trunk, and balance improves, paving the way for many gross motor achievements. Preschoolers run, jump, hop, gallop, eventually skip, throw and catch, and generally become better coordinated.

■ Increasing control of the hands and fingers leads to dramatic improvements in fine motor skills. Preschoolers gradually become self-sufficient at dressing and using a knife and fork.

■ By age 3, children's scribbles become pictures. With age, their drawings increase in complexity and realism, influenced by schooling and by their culture's artistic traditions. Preschoolers also try to print letters of the alphabet and, later, words.

■ Body build and opportunity for physical play affect early childhood motor development. Sex differences that favor boys in skills requiring force and power and girls in skills requiring good balance and fine movements are partly genetic, but environmental pressures exaggerate them. Children master the motor skills of early childhood through informal play experiences.

🍂 Cognitive Development

Piaget's Theory: The Preoperational Stage

Describe advances in mental representation and limitations of thinking during the preoperational stage.

■ Rapid advances in mental representation, notably language and make-believe play, mark the beginning of Piaget's **preoperational stage.** With age, make-believe becomes increasingly complex, evolving into **sociodramatic play** with others. Preschoolers' make-believe supports many aspects of development. Gradually, children become capable of **dual representation**—viewing a symbolic object, such as a model or map, as both an object in its own right and a symbol.

■ Aside from representation, Piaget described the young child in terms of deficits. According to his theory, preoperational children are **egocentric,** often failing to imagine others' perspectives. By preventing children from reflecting on their own thinking and accommodating, egocentrism contributes to **animistic thinking, centration,** a focus on perceptual appearances, and **irreversibility.** These difficulties cause preschoolers to fail **conservation** and **hierarchical classification** tasks.

What are the implications of recent research for the accuracy of the preoperational stage?

■ When young children are given simplified problems relevant to their everyday lives, their performance appears more mature than Piaget assumed. Preschoolers recognize differing perspectives, distinguish animate and inanimate objects, reason by analogy about physical transformations, understand cause-and-effect relationships, and organize knowledge into hierarchical categories, including categories based on nonobvious features.

■ Evidence that operational thinking develops gradually over the preschool years, rather than abruptly around age 6 or 7, challenges Piaget's stage concept. Some theorists propose a more flexible view of stages.

What educational principles can be derived from Piaget's theory?

■ A Piagetian classroom promotes discovery learning, sensitivity to children's readiness to learn, and acceptance of individual differences.

Vygotsky's Sociocultural Theory

Explain Vygotsky's perspective on the origins and significance of children's private speech, and describe applications of his theory to education.

■ Unlike Piaget, Vygotsky regarded language as the foundation for all higher cognitive processes. According to Vygotsky, **private speech,** or language used for self-guidance, emerges out of social communication as adults and more skilled peers help children master challenging tasks. Eventually private speech is internalized as inner, verbal thought. **Scaffolding** is a form of social interaction that promotes the transfer of cognitive processes to children.

■ A Vygotskian classroom emphasizes assisted discovery. Verbal guidance from teachers and peer collaboration are vitally important. Make-believe play serves as a vital zone of proximal development that enhances many new competencies.

■ **Guided participation,** a broader term than scaffolding, recognizes cultural and situational variations in adult support of children's efforts.

Information Processing

How do attention and memory change during early childhood?

■ Attention gradually becomes more sustained, and planning improves. Nevertheless, compared with older children, preschoolers spend relatively short periods involved in tasks and are less systematic in planning.

■ Preschoolers' recognition memory is very accurate, but their recall for listlike information is much poorer than that of older children and adults because they use **memory strategies** less effectively. Like adults, preschoolers remember recurring experiences in terms of **scripts,** which become more elaborate with age. When adults use an elaborative style of conversing with children about the past, their autobiographical memory becomes better organized and detailed.

Describe the young child's theory of mind.

■ Preschoolers begin to construct a theory of mind, indicating that they are capable of **metacognition,** or thinking about thought. Around age 4, they understand that people can hold false beliefs. Factors contributing to young children's appreciation of mental life include cognitive and language development, having older siblings, interactions with friends, make-believe play, and contact with more mature members of society. Preschoolers regard the mind as a passive container of information rather than as an active, constructive agent.

Summarize children's literacy and mathematical knowledge during early childhood.

■ Young children in industrialized nations attempt to figure out how written symbols convey meaning—an active effort known as **emergent literacy.** Preschoolers gradually revise incorrect ideas about the meaning of written symbols as their perceptual and cognitive capacities improve, as they encounter writing in many different contexts, and as adults help them make sense of written information.

■ In the second year, children have a beginning grasp of **ordinality,** which serves as the basis for more complex understandings. Soon they discover additional mathematical principles, including **cardinality,** and experiment with counting strategies, selecting the most efficient, accurate techniques. Both literacy and mathematical reasoning build on a foundation of informally acquired knowledge.

Individual Differences in Mental Development

Describe early childhood intelligence tests and the impact of home, educational programs, child care, and media on mental development in early childhood.

■ Intelligence tests in early childhood sample a wide variety of verbal and nonverbal skills. By age 5 to 6, test scores are good predictors of later IQ and academic achievement. Children growing up in warm, stimulating homes with parents who make reasonable demands for mature behavior score higher on mental tests.

■ Preschool and kindergarten programs range along a continuum. In **child-centered programs,** much learning takes place through play. In **academic programs,** teachers promote academic skills through formal lessons, often using repetition and drill. This stress on formal academic training actually undermines young children's motivation and negatively influences later school achievement.

■ **Project Head Start** is the largest U.S. federally funded preschool program for low-income children. In Canada, **Aboriginal Head Start** serves First Nations, Inuit, and Métis preschoolers. High-quality preschool intervention results in immediate test score gains and long-term improvements in school adjustment. The more parents are involved in Head Start, the higher children's year-end academic, language, and social skills. Regardless of SES, poor-quality child care undermines children's cognitive and social development.

■ Children pick up many cognitive skills from educational television programs like *Sesame Street.* Programs with slow-paced action and easy-to-follow story lines foster more elaborate make-believe play. But heavy TV viewing, especially entertainment shows and cartoons, takes children away from reading and interacting with others and is related to weaker academic skills.

■ Computer word-processing programs can support preschoolers' emergent literacy, and computer games are available that provide practice in basic academic skills. Introducing young children to simplified computer languages fosters problem solving and metacognition. In classrooms, children more often collaborate in computer activities than in other pursuits.

Language Development

Trace the development of vocabulary, grammar, and conversational skills in early childhood.

■ Supported by **fast-mapping,** children's vocabularies grow dramatically during early childhood. On hearing a new word, children contrast it with words they know and often assume the word refers to an entirely separate category. When adults call an object by

© LAURA DWIGHT/PHOTOEDIT

more than one name, children figure out word meanings from sentence structure or social cues. Once preschoolers have sufficient vocabulary, they extend language meanings, coining new words and creating metaphors.

■ Between ages 2 and 3, children adopt the basic word order of their language. As they master grammatical rules, they may overextend them in a type of error called **overregularization.** By the end of early childhood, children have acquired complex grammatical forms.

■ To communicate effectively, children must master the practical, social side of language, known as **pragmatics.** Two-year-olds are already skilled conversationalists in face-to-face interaction. By age 4, children adapt their speech to their listeners in culturally accepted ways. In highly demanding contexts, preschoolers' communication skills may appear less mature.

Cite factors that support language learning in early childhood.

■ Conversational give-and-take with more skilled speakers fosters language progress. Adults often provide explicit feedback on the clarity of children's language and indirect feedback about grammar through **recasts** and **expansions.** However, some researchers believe these strategies may be less important than exposure to a rich language environment.

Important Terms and Concepts

Initiative—a spirited, enterprising purpose-fulness—is a landmark attainment of early childhood. Children also make great strides in understanding the thoughts and feelings of others, and they build on these skills as they form first friendships—special relationships marked by attachment and common interests.

Emotional and Social Development in Early Childhood

*A*s the children in Leslie's classroom moved through the pre-school years, their personalities took on clearer definition. By age 3, they voiced firm likes and dislikes as well as new ideas about themselves. "Stop bothering me," Sammy said to Mark, who was reach-ing for Sammy's beanbag as Sammy aimed it toward the mouth of a large clown face. "See, I'm great at this game," Sammy announced with confidence, an attitude that kept him trying, even though he missed most of the throws.

The children's conversations also revealed early notions about morality. Often they combined adults' statements about right and wrong with forceful attempts to defend their own desires. "You're 'posed to share," stated Mark, grab-bing the beanbag out of Sammy's hand.

"I was here first! Gimme it back," demanded Sammy, pushing Mark. The two boys struggled until Leslie intervened, provided another beanbag, and showed them how both could play.

As the interaction between Sammy and Mark reveals, preschoolers quickly become complex social beings. Young children argue, grab, and push, but cooperative exchanges are far more frequent. Between ages 2 and 6, first friendships form, in which children converse, act out com-plementary roles, and learn that their own desires for companionship and toys are best met when they consider others' needs and interests.

The children's developing understanding of their social world was especially evident in their growing attention to the dividing line between male and female. Already, the children preferred same-sex peers and, in their play, mirrored their culture's gender stereotypes. While Lynette and Karen cared for a sick baby doll in the housekeeping area, Sammy, Vance, and Mark transformed the block corner into a busy intersection. "Green light, go!" shouted police officer Sammy as Vance and Mark pushed large wooden cars and trucks across the floor.

This chapter is devoted to the many facets of early childhood emo-tional and social development. We begin with Erik Erikson's theory, which provides an overview of personality change in the preschool

255

years. Then we consider children's concepts of themselves, their insights into their social and moral worlds, their gender typing, and their increasing ability to manage their emotional and social behaviors. Finally, we ask, What is effective child rearing? And we consider the complex conditions that support good parenting or lead it to break down, including the serious and widespread problems of child abuse and neglect.

Erikson's Theory: Initiative versus Guilt

Erikson (1950) described early childhood as a period of "vigorous unfolding." Once children have a sense of autonomy, they become less contrary than they were as toddlers. Their energies are freed for tackling the psychological conflict of the preschool years: **initiative versus guilt.** As the word *initiative* suggests, young children have a new sense of purposefulness. They are eager to tackle new tasks, join in activities with peers, and discover what they can do with the help of adults. They also make strides in conscience development.

Erikson regarded play as a means through which young children learn about themselves and their social world. Play

This 3-year-old girl plays at washing clothes on the washing stone in her family's backyard in Otavalo, Ecuador. Children around the world act out highly visible occupations in their culture during play, developing a sense of initiative as they gain insight into what they can do.

permits preschoolers to try out new skills with little risk of criticism and failure. It also creates a small social organization of children who must cooperate to achieve common goals. Around the world, children act out family scenes and highly visible occupations—police officer, doctor, and nurse in Western societies, rabbit hunter and potter among the Hopi Indians, hut builder and spear maker among the Baka of West Africa (Roopnarine et al., 1998).

Recall that Erikson's theory builds on Freud's psychosexual stages (see Chapter 1, page 15). In Freud's Oedipus and Electra conflicts, to avoid punishment and maintain the affection of parents, children form a *superego,* or conscience, by *identifying* with the same-sex parent. As a result, they adopt the moral and gender-role standards of their society. Each time the child disobeys standards of conscience, painful feelings of guilt occur. For Erikson, the negative outcome of early childhood is an overly strict superego that causes children to feel too much guilt because they have been threatened, criticized, and punished excessively by adults. When this happens, preschoolers' exuberant play and bold efforts to master new tasks break down.

Although Freud's ideas are no longer accepted as satisfactory explanations of conscience development, Erikson's image of initiative captures the diverse changes in young children's emotional and social lives. Early childhood is, indeed, a time when children develop a confident self-image, more effective control over their emotions, new social skills, the foundations of morality, and a clear sense of themselves as boy or girl.

Self-Understanding

Virtually all investigators agree that the self has two distinct aspects, identified by American philosopher and psychologist William James (1890/1963) more than a century ago:

🖊 The **I-self,** or *self as knower and actor,* includes the realization that the self is separate from the surrounding world; remains the same person over time; has a private, inner life not accessible to others; and controls its own thoughts and actions.

🖊 The **me-self,** or *self as object of knowledge,* consists of all qualities that make the self unique—physical characteristics and possessions; psychological characteristics, including desires, attitudes, beliefs, and personality traits; and social characteristics, such as roles and relationships with others.

The I-self can be thought of as the active observer, the me-self as developing from the observing process (see Figure 8.1). Both aspects of the self emerge in the first 2 years, as babies become self-aware (I-self), recognize the self's physical features, and start to categorize themselves on the basis of age, sex, and other characteristics (me-self).

During early childhood, language enables children to talk about the I-self—their own subjective experience of being (Harter, 1998). In Chapter 7, we noted that preschoolers acquire a vocabulary for talking about their inner mental lives

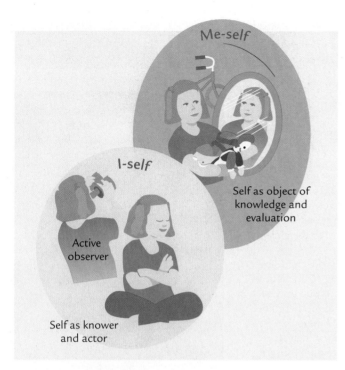

■ **FIGURE 8.1 The I-self and the me-self.** The I-self is a sense of self as knower and actor. It is the active observer. The me-self is a sense of self as object of knowledge and evaluation. It results from the observing process.

and refine their understanding of mental states. As the I-self becomes more firmly established, preschoolers focus more intently on the me-self. They begin to develop a **self-concept,** the set of attributes, abilities, attitudes, and values that an individual believes defines who he or she is.

Foundations of Self-Concept

Ask a 3- to 5-year-old to tell you about himself, and you are likely to hear something like this: "I'm Tommy. See, I got this new red T-shirt. I'm 4 years old. I can brush my teeth, and I can wash my hair all by myself. I have a new Tinkertoy set, and I made this big, big tower." Preschoolers' self-concepts are very concrete. Usually, they mention observable characteristics, such as their name, physical appearance, possessions, and everyday behaviors (Harter, 1996; Watson, 1990).

By age 3½, preschoolers also describe themselves in terms of typical emotions and attitudes—"I'm happy when I play with my friends"; "I don't like being with grown-ups"—suggesting a beginning understanding of their unique psychological characteristics (Eder & Mangelsdorf, 1997). Furthermore, when given a trait label, such as "shy" or "mean," 4-year-olds infer appropriate motives and feelings. For example, they know that a shy person doesn't like to be with unfamiliar people (Heyman & Gelman, 1999). But preschoolers do not say, "I'm helpful" or "I'm shy." Direct references to personality traits must wait for greater cognitive maturity.

In fact, very young preschoolers' concepts of themselves are so bound up with specific possessions and actions that they

spend much time asserting their rights to objects, as Sammy did in the beanbag incident at the beginning of this chapter. The stronger children's self-definition, the more possessive they tend to be, claiming objects as "Mine!" (Fasig, 2000; Levine, 1983). A firmer sense of self also enables children to cooperate in resolving disputes over objects, playing games, and solving simple problems (Brownell & Carriger, 1990; Caplan et al., 1991). Accordingly, when trying to promote friendly peer interaction, rather than simply insisting on sharing, parents and teachers can accept young children's possessiveness as a sign of self-assertion ("Yes, that's your toy") and then encourage compromise ("but in a little while, would you give someone else a turn?")

Recall from Chapter 7 that adult–child conversations about personally experienced events contribute to the development of an autobiographical memory, in which children represent the self in relation to their social context and, eventually, as extending over time (see page 239). Parents also use these discussions to impart evaluative information about the child, as when they say, "You were a big boy when you did that!" Consequently, narratives serve as a rich source of early self-knowledge and—as the Cultural Influences box on page 258 reveals—as a major means of imbuing the self-concept with cultural values.

Emergence of Self-Esteem

Another aspect of self-concept emerges in early childhood: **self-esteem,** the judgments we make about our own worth and the feelings associated with those judgments. Take a moment

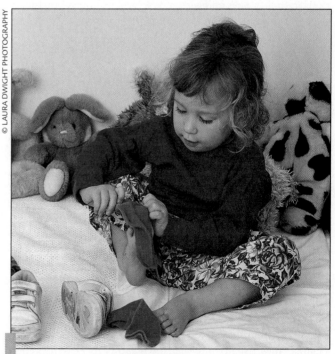

In their early self-descriptions, children usually emphasize observable characteristics—physical appearance, possessions, and everyday behaviors. When asked to tell about herself, this 4-year-old might say proudly, "I can put my socks and shoes on all by myself!"

Cultural Influences

Cultural Variations in Personal Storytelling: Implications for Early Self-Concept

Preschoolers of many cultural backgrounds participate in personal storytelling with their parents. Striking cultural differences exist in parents' selection and interpretation of events in these narratives, affecting the way children view themselves.

In one study, researchers spent hundreds of hours studying the storytelling practices of six middle-SES Irish-American families in Chicago and six middle-SES Chinese families in Taiwan. From extensive videotapes of adults' conversations with 2½-year-olds, the investigators identified personal stories and coded them for content, quality of their endings, and evaluation of the child (Miller, Fung, & Mintz, 1996; Miller et al., 1997).

Parents in both cultures discussed pleasurable holidays and family excursions in similar ways and with similar frequency. But Chinese parents more often told long stories about the child's misdeeds—using impolite language, writing on the wall, or playing in an overly rowdy

way. These narratives were conveyed with warmth and caring, stressed the impact of misbehavior on others ("You made Mama lose face"), and often ended with direct teaching of proper behavior ("Saying dirty words is not good"). By contrast, in the few instances in which Irish-American stories referred to transgressions, parents downplayed their seriousness, attributing them to the child's spunk and assertiveness.

Early narratives about the child seem to launch preschoolers' self-concepts on culturally distinct paths. Influenced by Confucian traditions of strict discipline and social obligations, Chinese parents integrated these values into their stories, affirming the importance of not disgracing the family and explicitly conveying expectations in the story's conclusion. Although Irish-American parents disciplined their children, they rarely dwelt on misdeeds in storytelling. Rather, they cast the child's shortcomings in a positive light, perhaps to promote self-esteem. Whereas most North Americans believe that favorable self-esteem is crucial for healthy development, Chinese adults generally regard it as unimportant or even negative—as impeding the child's willingness to listen and be corrected (Miller et al., 2002). Consistent with these cultural differences, the Chinese

© PETER TURNLEY/CORBIS

This Chinese mother speaks gently to her child about proper behavior on an outing. Chinese parents often tell preschoolers stories that point out the negative impact on others of the child's misdeeds. The Chinese child's self-concept, in turn, emphasizes social obligations.

child's self-image emphasizes obligations to others; the North American child's is more autonomous.

---

to think about your own self-esteem. Besides a global appraisal of your worth as a person, you have a variety of separate self-judgments concerning how well you perform at different activities. These evaluations are among the most important aspects of self-development because they affect emotional experiences, future behavior, and long-term psychological adjustment.

By age 4, preschoolers have several self-judgments—for example, about learning things well in school, making friends, getting along with parents, and treating others kindly (Marsh, Ellis, & Craven, 2002). Compared with that of older children, however, their understanding is limited. Because preschoolers cannot distinguish between their desired and their actual competence, they usually rate their own ability as extremely high and underestimate task difficulty, as in Sammy's announcement that he was great at beanbag throwing despite his many misses (Harter, 1990, 1998).

High self-esteem contributes greatly to preschoolers' initiative during a period in which they must master many new skills. By age 3, children with a history of parental criticism of their worth and performance give up easily when faced with a challenge and express shame and despondency after failing (Kelley, Brownell, & Campbell, 2000). When preschool nonpersisters use dolls to act out an adult's reaction to failure, they anticipate disapproval, saying for example, "He's punished because he can't do the puzzle." They also report that their parents berate them for small mistakes (Burhans & Dweck, 1995; Heyman, Dweck, & Cain, 1992). Adults can avoid promoting these self-defeating reactions by adjusting their expectations to children's capacities, scaffolding children's attempts at difficult tasks (see Chapter 7, page 235), and pointing out effort and increasing skill in children's behavior.

Emotional Development

Gains in representation, language, and self-concept support emotional development in early childhood. Between ages 2 and 6, children make strides in emotional abilities that, collectively, researchers refer to as *emotional competence* (Halberstadt, Denham, & Dunsmore, 2001; Saarni, 2000). First, preschoolers gain in emotional understanding. As a result, they are better able to talk about feelings and to respond appropriately to others' emotional signals. Second, they become better at emotional self-regulation—in particular, at coping with intense negative emotion. Finally, preschoolers more often experience *self-conscious emotions* and *empathy,* which contribute to their developing sense of morality.

Parenting strongly influences preschoolers' emotional competence. Emotional competence, in turn, is vital for successful peer relationships and overall mental health.

Understanding Emotion

Early in the preschool years, children refer to causes, consequences, and behavioral signs of emotion—understandings that increase rapidly in accuracy and complexity (Stein & Levine, 1999). By age 4 to 5, children correctly judge the causes of many basic emotions ("He's happy because he's swinging very high"; "He's sad because he misses his mother"). Preschoolers' explanations tend to emphasize external factors over internal states, a balance that changes with age (Levine, 1995). After age 4, children better understand how beliefs motivate behavior (see page 239 in Chapter 7). Then their grasp of how internal factors can trigger emotion expands.

Preschoolers can also predict what a playmate expressing a certain emotion might do next. Four-year-olds know that an angry child might hit someone and that a happy child is more likely to share (Russell, 1990). And they realize that thinking and feeling are interconnected—that a person reminded of a previous sad experience is likely to feel sad (Lagattuta, Wellman, & Flavell, 1997). Furthermore, they come up with effective ways to relieve others' negative feelings, such as hugging to reduce sadness (Fabes et al., 1988). Overall, preschoolers have an impressive ability to interpret, predict, and change others' feelings.

At the same time, preschoolers have difficulty interpreting situations that offer conflicting cues about how a person is feeling. When shown a picture of a happy-faced child with a broken bicycle, 4- and 5-year-olds tended to rely on the emotional expression: "He's happy because he likes to ride his bike." Older children more often reconciled the two cues: "He's happy because his father promised to help fix his broken bike" (Gnepp, 1983; Hoffner & Badzinski, 1989). As in their approach to Piagetian tasks, preschoolers focus on the most obvious aspect of an emotional situation to the neglect of other relevant information.

Preschoolers whose parents frequently acknowledge their emotional reactions and talk about diverse emotions are better able to judge others' emotions when tested at later ages (Denham & Kochanoff, 2002). In one study, mothers who explained feelings and who negotiated and compromised during conflicts with their 2½-year-olds had children who, at age 3, were advanced in emotional understanding and used similar strategies to resolve disagreements (Laible & Thompson, 2002). Furthermore, 3- to 5-year-olds who are securely attached to their mothers better understand emotion, perhaps because secure attachment is related to richer mother–child conversations about feelings (Laible & Thompson, 2000).

As preschoolers learn about emotion from interacting with adults, they engage in more emotion talk with siblings and friends, especially during make-believe (Brown, Donelan-McCall, & Dunn, 1996; Hughes & Dunn, 1998). Make-believe, in turn, contributes to emotional understanding, especially when children play with siblings (Youngblade & Dunn, 1995). The intense nature of the sibling relationship, combined with frequent acting out of feelings in make-believe, makes pretending an excellent context for learning about emotions. Also, the more preschoolers refer to feelings when interacting with playmates, the better liked they are by their peers (Fabes et al., 2001). Children seem to recognize that acknowledging others' emotions and explaining their own enhance the quality of relationships.

Emotional Self-Regulation

Language also contributes to preschoolers' improved *emotional self-regulation.* By age 3 to 4, children verbalize a variety of strategies for adjusting their emotional arousal to a more comfortable level. For example, they know they can blunt emotions by restricting sensory input (covering their eyes or ears to block out an unpleasant sight or sound), talking to themselves ("Mommy said she'll be back soon"), or changing their goals (deciding, after being excluded from a game, that they don't want to play anyway) (Thompson, 1990). As children use these strategies, emotional outbursts decline. *Effortful control*—in particular, inhibiting impulses and shifting attention—also continues to be vital in managing emotion during early childhood. Three-year-olds who can distract themselves when frustrated tend to become cooperative school-age children who are low in problem behaviors (Gilliom et al., 2002).

Preschoolers learn strategies for regulating emotion by watching adults handle their own feelings. Warm, patient parents who suggest and explain strategies for controlling feelings strengthen children's capacity to handle stress (Gottman, Katz, & Hooven, 1997). In contrast, when parents rarely express positive emotion, dismiss children's feelings as unimportant, and have difficulty controlling their own anger, children have continuing problems managing emotion (Eisenberg et al., 2001; Gilliom et al., 2002; Katz & Windecker-Nelson, 2004).

Temperament also affects emotional self-regulation. Children who experience negative emotion intensely find it harder to inhibit feelings and shift attention away from disturbing events. Consequently, they are more likely to respond with irritation to others' distress, to react angrily or aggressively when frustrated, and to get along poorly with teachers and peers

Helping Children Manage Common Fears of Early Childhood

Fear	Suggestion
Monsters, ghosts, and darkness	Reduce exposure to frightening stories in books and on TV until the child is better able to sort out appearance from reality. Make a thorough "search" of the child's room for monsters, showing him that none are there. Leave a night-light burning, sit by the child's bed until he falls asleep, and tuck in a favorite toy for protection.
Preschool or child care	If the child resists going to preschool but seems content once there, then the fear is probably separation. Under these circumstances, provide a sense of warmth and caring while gently encouraging independence. If the child fears being at preschool, find out what is frightening—the teacher, the children, or perhaps a crowded, noisy environment. Provide extra support by accompanying the child and gradually lessening the amount of time you are present.
Animals	Do not force the child to approach a dog, cat, or other animal that arouses fear. Let the child move at her own pace. Demonstrate how to hold and pet the animal, showing the child that when treated gently, the animal is friendly. If the child is larger than the animal, emphasize this: "You're so big. That kitty is probably afraid of *you*!"
Intense fears	If a child's fear is intense, persists for a long time, interferes with daily activities, and cannot be reduced in any of the ways just suggested, it has reached the level of a *phobia*. Sometimes phobias are linked to family problems, and counseling is needed to reduce them. At other times, phobias diminish without treatment as the child's capacity for emotional self-regulation improves.

(Chang et al., 2003; Denham et al., 2002; Shields et al., 2001). Because these emotionally reactive children become increasingly difficult to rear, they are often targets of ineffective parenting, which compounds their poor emotional self-regulation.

Even children with good emotion-regulation skills sometimes have difficulty managing their feelings. Preschoolers' vivid imaginations, combined with their incomplete grasp of the distinction between appearance and reality, make fears common in early childhood. Consult Applying What We Know above for ways adults can help children manage fears.

Self-Conscious Emotions

One morning in Leslie's classroom, a group of children crowded around for a bread-baking activity. Leslie asked them to wait patiently while she got a baking pan. But Sammy reached over to feel the dough, and the bowl tumbled over the side of the table. When Leslie returned, Sammy looked at her, then covered his eyes with his hands and said, "I did something bad." He felt ashamed and guilty.

As children's self-concepts become better developed, they more often experience *self-conscious emotions*—feelings that involve injury to or enhancement of their sense of self (see Chapter 6). By age 3, self-conscious emotions are clearly linked to self-evaluation. But because preschoolers are still developing standards of excellence and conduct, they depend on adults' messages to know when to feel proud, ashamed, or guilty (Lewis, 1995; Stipek, 1995). Parents whose feedback labels the worth of the child and her performance ("That's a bad job! I thought you were a good girl!") have children who experience self-conscious emotions intensely—more pride after success, more shame after failure. In contrast, parents who focus on how to improve performance ("You did it this way; now try

doing it that way") induce moderate, more adaptive levels of shame and pride and greater persistence on difficult tasks (Kelley, Brownell, & Campbell, 2000; Lewis, 1998).

Among Western children, intense shame is associated with feelings of personal inadequacy ("I'm stupid"; "I'm a terrible person") and with maladjustment—withdrawal and depression as well as intense anger and aggression at those who participated in the shame-evoking situation (Lindsay-Hartz, de Rivera, & Mascolo, 1995; Mills, 2005). In contrast, guilt—when it occurs in appropriate circumstances and is not accompanied by shame—is related to good adjustment. Guilt may help children resist harmful impulses, and it motivates a misbehaving child to repair the damage and behave more considerately (Ferguson et al., 1999; Tangney, 2001).

The consequences of shame for children's adjustment, however, may vary across cultures. As illustrated in the Cultural Influences box on page 258 and on page 189 in Chapter 6, people in Asian collectivist societies, who define themselves in relation to their social group, view shame as an adaptive reminder of an interdependent self and of the importance of others' judgments (Bedford, 2004).

Empathy

In early childhood, another emotional capacity, *empathy*, becomes more common and serves as an important motivator of **prosocial,** or **altruistic, behavior**—actions that benefit another person without any expected reward for the self (Eisenberg, 2005). Compared with toddlers, preschoolers rely more on words to communicate their empathic feelings, a change that indicates a more reflective level of empathy. And as the ability to take another's perspective improves, empathic responding increases.

Yet empathy, or *feeling with* another person and responding emotionally in a similar way, does not always yield acts of kindness and helpfulness. For some children, empathizing with an upset adult or peer escalates into personal distress. In trying to reduce these feelings, the child focuses on her own anxiety rather than the person in need. As a result, empathy does not give way to **sympathy**—feelings of concern or sorrow for another's plight.

Temperament plays a role in whether empathy prompts sympathetic, prosocial behavior or self-focused personal distress. Children who are sociable, assertive, and good at regulating emotion are more likely to help, share, and comfort others in distress. But poor emotion regulators less often display sympathetic concern and prosocial behavior (Bengtsson, 2005; Eisenberg et al., 1998). When faced with someone in need, they react with facial and physiological distress—frowning, lip biting, a rise in heart rate, and a sharp increase in EEG brain-wave activity in the right cerebral hemisphere (which houses negative emotion)—indications that they are overwhelmed by their feelings (Miller et al., 1996; Pickens, Field, & Nawrocki, 2001).

As with emotional self-regulation, parenting affects empathy and sympathy. When parents are warm, encourage emotional expressiveness, and show sensitive, sympathetic concern for their preschoolers, their children are likely to react in a concerned way to the distress of others—relationships that persist into adolescence and young adulthood (Eisenberg & McNally, 1993; Koestner, Franz, & Weinberger, 1990; Strayer & Roberts, 2004). Besides modeling sympathy, parents can teach the importance of kindness and can intervene when a child displays inappropriate emotion. These parenting behaviors predict high levels of sympathetic responding in children (Eisenberg, 2003).

© LAWRENCE MIGDALE/PIX

Outside the playhouse at preschool, a young boy comforts his friend. As children's language skills expand and their ability to take the perspective of others improves, empathy also increases, motivating prosocial, or altruistic, behavior.

In contrast, angry, punitive parenting disrupts empathy and sympathy at an early age. In one study, physically abused preschoolers at a child-care center rarely showed signs of concern at a peer's unhappiness but, rather, reacted with fear, anger, and physical attacks (Klimes-Dougan & Kistner, 1990). The children's behavior resembled their parents' insensitive responses to the suffering of others.

Peer Relations

As children become increasingly self-aware and better at communicating and understanding the thoughts and feelings of others, their skill at interacting with peers improves. Peers provide young children with learning experiences they can get in no other way. Because peers interact on an equal footing, children must work at keeping a conversation going, cooperating, and setting goals in play. With peers, children form friendships—special relationships marked by attachment and common interests. Let's look at how peer interaction changes over the preschool years.

Advances in Peer Sociability

Mildred Parten (1932), one of the first to study peer sociability among 2- to 5-year-olds, noticed a dramatic rise with age in joint, interactive play. She concluded that social development proceeds in a three-step sequence. It begins with **nonsocial activity**—unoccupied, onlooker behavior and solitary play. Then it shifts to **parallel play,** in which a child plays near other children with similar materials but does not try to influence their behavior. At the highest level are two forms of true social interaction. One is **associative play,** in which children engage in separate activities but exchange toys and comment on one another's behavior. The other is **cooperative play,** a more advanced type of interaction in which children orient toward a common goal, such as acting out a make-believe theme.

■ **Follow-Up Research on Peer Sociability.** Longitudinal evidence indicates that these play forms emerge in the order suggested by Parten, but that later-appearing ones do not replace earlier ones in a developmental sequence (Howes & Matheson, 1992). Rather, all types coexist in early childhood.

Watch children move from one play type to another, and you will see that they often transition from onlooker to parallel to cooperative play and back again (Robinson et al., 2003). Preschoolers seem to use parallel play as a way station—a respite from the demands of complex social interaction and a crossroad to new activities. And although nonsocial activity declines with age, it is still the most frequent form among 3- to 4-year-olds and accounts for a third of kindergartners' free-play time. Also, solitary and parallel play remain fairly stable from 3 to 6 years, accounting for as much of the child's play as cooperative interaction (Rubin, Fein, & Vandenberg, 1983).

We now understand that the *type,* not the amount, of solitary and parallel play changes in early childhood. In studies of

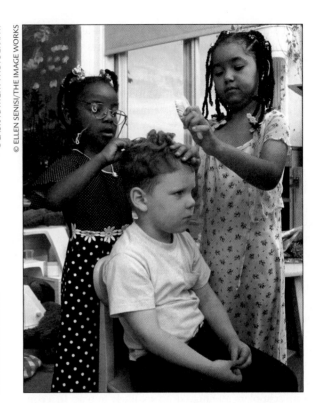

These 3-year-olds stringing wooden beads (left) are engaging in parallel play. Cooperative play, like that of the two 5-year-olds fixing their classmate's hair (right), develops later than parallel play, but preschool children continue to move back and forth between the two types of sociability. Parallel play often serves as a respite from the demands of complex social interaction.

preschoolers' play in Taiwan and the United States, researchers rated the *cognitive maturity* of nonsocial, parallel, and cooperative play, using the categories shown in Table 8.1. Within each play type, older children displayed more cognitively mature behavior than younger children (Pan, 1994; Rubin, Watson, & Jambor, 1978).

Often parents wonder if a preschooler who spends much time playing alone is developing normally. But only *certain kinds* of nonsocial activity—aimless wandering, hovering near peers, and functional play involving repetitive motor action— are cause for concern. Children who watch peers without playing are usually temperamentally inhibited—high in social fearfulness (Coplan et al., 2004; Rubin, Burgess, & Hastings, 2002). And preschoolers who engage in solitary, repetitive

behavior (banging blocks, making a doll jump up and down) tend to be immature, impulsive children who find it difficult to regulate anger and aggression (Coplan et al., 2001). As a result, peers usually ostracize them.

But most preschoolers with low rates of peer interaction are not socially anxious. They simply like to play by themselves, and their solitary activities are positive and constructive. Children who prefer solitary play with art materials, puzzles, and building toys are typically well-adjusted youngsters who, when they do play with peers, show socially skilled behavior (Rubin & Coplan, 1998). Still, a few preschoolers who engage in such age-appropriate solitary play (mostly boys) are rebuffed by peers. Perhaps because their behavior is inconsistent with the "masculine" gender role, boys who play quietly are at risk for

Table 8.1	Developmental Sequence of Cognitive Play Categories	
Play Category	**Description**	**Examples**
Functional play	Simple, repetitive motor movements with or without objects, especially common during the first 2 years of life	Running around a room, rolling a car back and forth, kneading clay with no intent to make something
Constructive play	Creating or constructive something, especially common between 3 and 6 years	Making a house out of toy blocks, drawing a picture, putting together a puzzle
Make-believe play	Acting out everyday and imaginary roles, especially common between 2 and 6 years	Playing house, school, or police officer; acting out storybook or television characters

Source: Rubin, Fein, & Vandenberg, 1983.

negative reactions from both parents and peers and, eventually, for adjustment problems (Coplan et al., 2001, 2004).

■ **Cultural Variations.** Peer sociability takes different forms in collectivist societies than in individualistic cultures. For example, children in India generally play in large groups. Much of their behavior is imitative, occurs in unison, involves close physical contact—a play style requiring high levels of cooperation. In Bhatto Bhatto, children act out a script about a trip to the market, touching each other's elbows and hands as they pretend to cut and share a tasty vegetable (Roopnarine et al., 1994).

Cultural beliefs about the importance of play also affect early peer associations. Adults who view play as mere entertainment are less likely to provide props or to encourage pretend than those who value its cognitive and social benefits (Farver & Wimbarti, 1995). Preschoolers of Korean-American parents, who emphasize task persistence as vital for learning, spend less time than Caucasian-American children in joint make-believe and more time unoccupied and in parallel play (Farver, Kim, & Lee, 1995).

Recall the description of children's daily lives in village and tribal cultures, described on page 237 in Chapter 7. Mayan parents, for example, do not promote children's play—yet

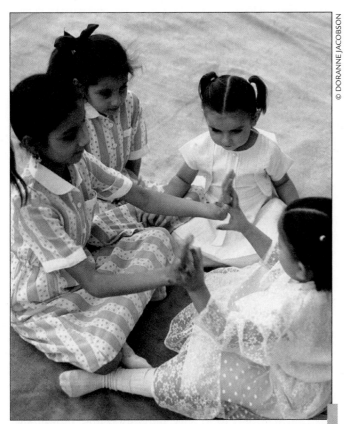

These cousins at a family birthday party in a village in central India play an intricate hand-clapping game, called *Chapte,* in which they clap in unison, clapping faster as the game proceeds. The game is played to a jingle with eleven verses, which take the girls through their lifespan and conclude with their turning into ghosts. Their play reflects the value their culture places on group harmony.

Mayan children are socially competent (Gaskins, 2000). Perhaps Western-style sociodramatic play, with its elaborate materials and wide-ranging themes, is particularly important for social development in societies where child and adult worlds are distinct. It may be less crucial when children participate in adult activities from an early age.

First Friendships

As preschoolers interact, first friendships form that serve as important contexts for emotional and social development. To adults, friendship is a mutual relationship involving companionship, sharing, understanding of thoughts and feelings, and caring for one another in times of need. In addition, mature friendships endure over time and survive occasional conflicts.

Preschoolers understand something about the uniqueness of friendship. They say that a friend is someone "who likes you" and with whom you spend a lot of time playing. Yet their ideas about friendship are far from mature. Four- to 7-year-olds regard friendship as pleasurable play and sharing of toys. As yet, friendship does not have a long-term, enduring quality based on mutual trust (Hartup & Abecassis, 2004; Selman, 1980). Indeed, Sammy would declare, "Mark's my best friend," on days when the boys got along well. But when a dispute arose, he would reverse himself: "Mark, you're not my friend!"

Nevertheless, interactions between young friends are unique. Preschoolers give far more reinforcement—greetings, praise, and compliance—to children they identify as friends and also receive more from them. Friends are also more emotionally expressive, talking, laughing, and looking at each other more often than nonfriends do (Hartup & Stevens, 1999; Vaughn et al., 2001). Furthermore, early childhood friendships offer social support. Children who begin kindergarten with friends in their class or readily make new friends adjust to school more favorably (Ladd, Birch, & Buhs, 1999; Ladd & Price, 1987). Through friendships, children seem to integrate themselves into the learning environment in ways that foster both academic and social competence.

Parental Influences on Early Peer Relations

Children first acquire skills for interacting with peers within the family. Parents influence children's peer sociability both *directly,* through attempts to influence children's peer relations, and *indirectly,* through their child-rearing practices and play behaviors (Ladd & Pettit, 2002; Rubin et al., 2005).

■ **Direct Parental Influences.** Preschoolers whose parents frequently arrange informal peer play activities tend to have larger peer networks and to be more socially skilled (Ladd, LeSieur, & Profilet, 1993). In providing play opportunities, parents show children how to initiate their own peer contacts. And parents' skillful guidance for how to enter play groups and manage conflict are associated with preschoolers' social competence and peer acceptance (Mize & Pettit, 1997; Parke et al., 2004).

© MICHAEL NEWMAN/PHOTOEDIT

Parents influence children's peer interaction skills by offering advice, guidance, and examples of how to behave. These boys receive a gentle lesson in how to greet a friend by shaking hands.

■ **Indirect Parental Influences.** Many parenting behaviors not directly aimed at promoting peer sociability nevertheless influence it. For example, secure attachments to parents are linked to more responsive, harmonious peer interaction; larger peer networks; and warmer, more supportive friendships during the preschool and school years (Coleman, 2003; Wood, Emmerson, & Cowan, 2004). The sensitive, emotionally expressive communication that contributes to attachment security may be responsible.

Furthermore, highly involved, emotionally positive, cooperative play between parents and preschoolers is associated with social skills and peer acceptance. Perhaps because parents play more with children of their own sex, mothers' play is more strongly linked to daughters' social competence, fathers' play to sons' competence (Lindsey & Mize, 2000; Pettit et al., 1998).

Some preschoolers already have great difficulty with peer relations. In Leslie's classroom, Robbie was one of them. Wherever he happened to be, comments like "Robbie ruined our block tower" and "Robbie hit me for no reason" could be heard. As we take up moral development in the next section, you will learn more about how parenting contributed to Robbie's peer problems.

Ask Yourself

Review

Among children who spend much time playing alone, what factors distinguish those who are likely to have adjustment difficulties from those who are well-adjusted and socially skilled?

Apply

Reread the description of Sammy and Mark's argument at the beginning of this chapter. On the basis of what you know about self-development, why was it a good idea for Leslie to resolve the dispute by providing an extra beanbag?

Connect

How does emotional self-regulation affect the development of empathy and sympathy? Why are these emotional capacities vital for positive peer relations?

Reflect

Think back to your first friendship. How old were you? Describe the quality of your relationship. What did your parents do, directly and indirectly, that might have influenced your earliest peer associations?

www.ablongman.com/berk

Foundations of Morality

Children's conversations and behavior provide many examples of their developing moral sense. By age 2, they use words to evaluate behavior as "good" or "bad" and react with distress to acts that are aggressive or that otherwise might do harm (Kochanska, Casey, & Fukumoto, 1995).

Throughout the world, adults take note of this budding capacity to distinguish right from wrong. Some cultures have special words for it. The Utku Indians of Hudson Bay say the child develops *ihuma* (reason). The Fijians believe that *vakayalo* (sense) appears. In response, parents hold children more responsible for their behavior (Kagan, 1998). By the end of early childhood, children can state a great many moral rules: "You're not supposed to take things without asking!" "Tell the truth!" In addition, they argue over matters of justice: "You sat there last time, so it's my turn." "It's not fair. He got more!"

All theories of moral development recognize that conscience begins to take shape in early childhood. And most agree that at first, the child's morality is *externally controlled* by adults. Gradually, it becomes regulated by *inner standards*. Truly moral individuals do not just do the right thing for the sake of conformity or to obey authority figures. Instead, they have developed compassionate concerns and principles of good conduct, which they follow in a wide variety of situations.

Although points of agreement exist, each major theory emphasizes a different aspect of morality. Psychoanalytic theory stresses the *emotional side* of conscience development—in particular, identification and guilt as motivators of good conduct. Social learning theory focuses on *moral behavior* and how it is learned through reinforcement and modeling. And the cognitive-developmental perspective emphasizes *thinking*—children's ability to reason about justice and fairness.

The Psychoanalytic Perspective

Recall that according to Freud, young children form a *superego,* or conscience, by *identifying* with the same-sex parent, whose moral standards they adopt. Children obey the superego to avoid *guilt,* a painful emotion that arises each time they are tempted to misbehave. Moral development, Freud believed, is largely complete by 5 to 6 years of age.

Today, most researchers disagree with Freud's view of conscience development. In his theory (see page 15), fear of punishment and loss of parental love motivate conscience formation and moral behavior (Tellings, 1999). Yet children whose parents frequently use threats, commands, or physical force tend to violate standards often and feel little guilt (Kochanska et al., 2002). And if a parent withdraws love after misbehavior—for example, refuses to speak to or states a dislike for the child—children often respond with high levels of self-blame, thinking "I'm no good," or "Nobody loves me." Eventually, to protect themselves from overwhelming feelings of guilt, these children may deny the emotion and, as a result, develop a weak conscience (Kochanska, 1991; Zahn-Waxler et al., 1990).

■ **Inductive Discipline.** In contrast, a type of discipline called **induction,** in which an adult helps the child notice feelings by pointing out the effects of the child's misbehavior on others, supports conscience formation. For example, a parent might say, "She's crying because you won't give back her doll" (Hoffman, 2000). When generally warm parents provide explanations that match the child's capacity to understand while firmly insisting that the child listen and comply, induction is effective as early as 2 years of age. Preschoolers whose parents use it are more likely to refrain from wrongdoing, confess and repair damages after misdeeds, and display prosocial behavior (Kerr et al., 2004; Zahn-Waxler, Radke-Yarrow, & King, 1979).

The success of induction may lie in its power to motivate children's active commitment to moral standards. Induction gives children information about how to behave that they can use in future situations. By emphasizing the impact of the child's actions on others, it encourages empathy and sympathy (Krevans & Gibbs, 1996). And giving children reasons for changing their behavior encourages them to adopt moral standards because they make sense. In contrast, discipline that relies too heavily on threats of punishment or withdrawal of love makes children so anxious and afraid that they cannot think clearly enough to figure out what they should do. As a result, these practices do not get children to internalize moral rules.

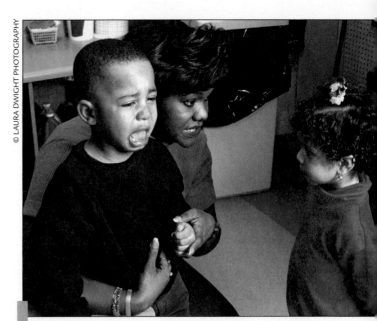

This teacher uses inductive discipline to explain to a child the impact of her transgression on others. Induction supports conscience development by indicating how the child should behave, encouraging empathy and sympathetic concern, and clarifying the reasons behind adult expectations.

■ **The Child's Contribution.** Although good discipline is crucial, children's characteristics can affect the success of parenting techniques. Twin studies suggest a modest genetic contribution to empathy (Zahn-Waxler et al., 2001). A more empathic child requires less power assertion and is more responsive to induction.

Temperament is also influential. Mild, patient tactics—requests, suggestions, and explanations—are sufficient to prompt guilt reactions in anxious, fearful preschoolers (Kochanska et al., 2002). But with fearless, impulsive children, gentle discipline has little impact. Power assertion also works poorly, undermining the child's capacity for impulse control (Kochanska & Knaack, 2003). Instead, parents of impulsive children can foster conscience development by ensuring a secure attachment relationship and combining firm correction with induction (Fowles & Kochanska, 2000). When children are so low in anxiety that parental disapproval causes them little discomfort, a close parent–child bond provides an alternative foundation for morality. It motivates children to listen to parents as a means of preserving an affectionate, supportive relationship.

■ **The Role of Guilt.** Although little support exists for Freudian ideas about conscience development, Freud was correct that guilt is an important motivator of moral action. Inducing *empathy-based guilt* (expressions of personal responsibility and regret, such as "I'm sorry I hurt him") by explaining that the child is harming someone and has disappointed the parent is a means of influencing children without using coercion (Baumeister, 1998).

But contrary to Freud's belief, guilt is not the only force that compels us to act morally. Nor is moral development complete by the end of early childhood. Rather, it is a gradual process, extending into adulthood.

Social Learning Theory

According to social learning theory, morality does not have a unique course of development. Rather, moral behavior is acquired just like any other set of responses: through reinforcement and modeling.

■ The Importance of Modeling.

Operant conditioning—reinforcement for good behavior, in the form of approval, affection, and other rewards—is not enough for children to acquire moral responses. For a behavior to be reinforced, it must first occur spontaneously. Yet many prosocial acts, such as sharing, helping, or comforting an unhappy playmate, do not occur often enough at first for reinforcement to explain their rapid development in early childhood. Instead, social learning theorists believe that children learn to behave morally largely through *modeling*—by observing and imitating people who demonstrate appropriate behavior (Bandura, 1977; Grusec, 1988). Once children acquire a moral response, such as sharing or telling the truth, reinforcement in the form of praise increases its frequency (Mills & Grusec, 1989).

Many studies show that having helpful or generous models increases young children's prosocial responses. And certain characteristics of models affect children's willingness to imitate:

- *Warmth and responsiveness.* Preschoolers are more likely to copy the prosocial actions of a warm, responsive adult than those of a cold, distant adult (Yarrow, Scott, & Waxler, 1973). Warmth seems to make children more attentive and receptive to the model, and it is itself a model of a prosocial response.

- *Competence and power.* Children admire and therefore tend to imitate competent, powerful models—especially older peers and adults (Bandura, 1977).

- *Consistency between assertions and behavior.* When models say one thing and do another—for example, announce, "It's important to help others," but rarely engage in helpful acts—children generally choose the most lenient standard of behavior that adults demonstrate (Mischel & Liebert, 1966).

Models are most influential in the preschool years. By the end of early childhood, children who have had consistent exposure to caring adults have internalized prosocial rules and follow them whether or not a model is present (Mussen & Eisenberg-Berg, 1977).

■ The Effects of Punishment.

Many parents know that yelling at, slapping, and spanking children for misbehavior are ineffective disciplinary tactics. A sharp reprimand or use of physical force to restrain or move a child is justified when immediate obedience is necessary—for example, when a 3-year-old is about to run into the street. In fact, parents are most likely to use forceful methods under these conditions. When they want to foster long-term goals, such as acting kindly toward others, they tend to rely on warmth and reasoning (Kuczynski, 1984). And they often combine power assertion with reasoning in response to very serious transgressions, such as lying and stealing (Grusec & Goodnow, 1994).

When used frequently, however, punishment promotes only momentary compliance, not lasting changes in behavior. For example, Robbie's parents often hit, criticized, and shouted at him. But as soon as they were out of sight, Robbie usually engaged in the unacceptable behavior again. The more harsh threats, angry physical control, and physical punishment children experience, the more likely they are to develop serious, lasting mental health problems. These include weak internalization of moral rules; depression, aggression, antisocial behavior, and poor academic performance in childhood and adolescence; and criminality and partner and child abuse in adulthood (Brezina, 1999; Gershoff, 2002a; Kochanska, Aksan, & Nichols, 2003).

Harsh punishment has several undesirable side effects:

- Parents often spank in response to children's aggression (Holden, Coleman, & Schmidt, 1995). Yet the punishment itself models aggression!

- Harshly treated children develop a chronic sense of being personally threatened, which prompts a focus on their own distress rather than a sympathetic orientation to others' needs.

- Children who are frequently punished soon learn to avoid the punishing adult, who, as a result, has little opportunity to teach desirable behaviors.

- By stopping children's misbehavior temporarily, harsh punishment offers immediate relief to adults. For this reason, a punitive adult is likely to punish with greater frequency over time, a course of action that can spiral into serious abuse.

- Adults whose parents used corporal punishment are more accepting of such discipline (Bower-Russa, Knutson, & Winebarger, 2001; Deater-Deckard et al., 2003). In this way, use of physical punishment may transfer to the next generation.

In view of these findings, the widespread use of corporal punishment by North American parents is cause for concern. A survey of a nationally representative sample of U.S. households revealed that although corporal punishment increases from infancy to age 5 and then declines, it is high at all ages (see Fig-

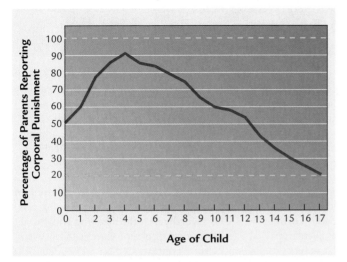

FIGURE 8.2 Prevalence of corporal punishment by child's age. Estimates are based on the percentage of parents in a nationally representative U. S. sample of nearly 1,000 reporting one or more instances of spanking, slapping, pinching, shaking, or hitting with a hard object in the past year. Physical punishment increases sharply during early childhood and then declines, but it is high at all ages. (From M. A. Straus & J. H. Stewart, 1999, "Corporal Punishment by American Parents: National Data on Prevalence, Chronicity, Severity, and Duration in Relation to Child and Family Characteristics," *Clinical Child and Family Psychology Review, 2*, p. 59. Adapted by permission of Kluwer Academic/Plenum Publishers and the author.)

ure 8.2). Similarly, more than 70 percent of Canadian parents admit to having hit or spanked their children (Durrant, Broberg, & Rose-Krasnor, 2000; Straus & Stewart, 1999). Repeated use of physical punishment is more common with toddlers and preschoolers. And more than one-fourth of physically punishing parents report having used a hard object, such as a brush or a belt, to hit their children (Gershoff, 2002b).

A prevailing North American belief is that corporal punishment, if implemented by caring parents, is harmless, perhaps even beneficial. But as the Cultural Influences box on page 268 reveals, this assumption is valid only under conditions of limited use in certain social contexts.

■ **Alternatives to Harsh Punishment.** Alternatives to criticism, slaps, and spankings can reduce the undesirable side effects of punishment. A technique called **time out** involves removing children from the immediate setting—for example, by sending them to their rooms—until they are ready to act appropriately. When a child is out of control, a few minutes in time out can be enough to change behavior while also giving angry parents a cooling-off period. Another approach is *withdrawal of privileges,* such as watching a favorite TV program. Like time out, removing privileges allows parents to avoid harsh techniques that can easily intensify into violence.

When parents decide to use punishment, they can increase its effectiveness in three ways:

🍃 *Consistency.* Permitting children to act inappropriately on some occasions but scolding them on others confuses children, and the unacceptable act persists (Acker & O'Leary, 1996).

🍃 *A warm parent–child relationship.* Children of involved, caring parents find the interruption in parental affection that accompanies punishment especially unpleasant. They want to regain parental warmth and approval as quickly as possible.

🍃 *Explanations.* Providing reasons for mild punishment helps children relate the misdeed to expectations for future behavior. This approach leads to a far greater reduction in misbehavior than using punishment alone (Larzelere et al., 1996).

■ **Positive Discipline.** The most effective forms of discipline encourage good conduct—by building a mutually respectful bond with the child, letting the child know ahead of time how to act, and praising mature behavior (Zahn-Waxler & Robinson, 1995). When sensitivity, cooperation, and shared positive emotion are evident in joint activities between parents and preschoolers, children show firmer conscience development—expressing empathy after transgressions, playing fairly in games, and behaving responsibly and kindly (Kochanska & Murray, 2000). Parent–child closeness leads children to want to heed parental demands because children feel a sense of commitment to the relationship.

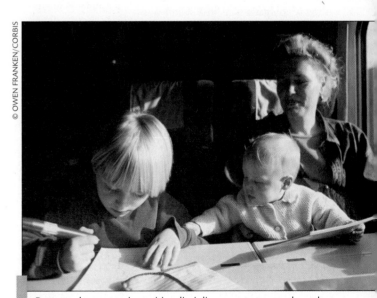

Parents who engage in positive discipline encourage good conduct and reduce opportunities for misbehavior. This mother brought along plenty of quiet activities to keep her children occupied during a long train ride.

Cultural Influences

Ethnic Differences in the Consequences of Physical Punishment

In an African-American community, six elders, all of whom had volunteered to serve as mentors for parents facing child-rearing challenges, met to discuss parenting issues at a social service agency. Their attitudes toward discipline were strikingly different from those of the white social workers who had brought them together. Each elder argued that successful child rearing required the use of appropriate physical tactics. At the same time, they voiced strong disapproval of screaming or cursing at children, calling such out-of-control parental behavior "abusive." Ruth, the oldest and most respected member of the group, characterized good parenting as a complex combination of warmth, teaching, talking nicely, and disciplining physically. She related how an older neighbor advised her to handle her own children when she was a young parent:

> She said to me says, don't scream . . . you talk to them real nice and sweet and when they do something ugly . . . she say you get a nice little switch and you won't have any trouble with them and from that day that's the way I raised 'em.

The others chimed in, emphasizing *mild* punishment. "Just tap 'em a little bit." "When you do things like [get too harsh] you're wronging yourself" (Mosby et al., 1999, pp. 511–512).

Use of physical punishment is highest among low-SES ethnic minority parents, who are more likely than middle-SES white parents to advocate slaps and spankings (Pinderhughes et al., 2000;

Straus & Stewart, 1999). And although corporal punishment is linked to a wide array of negative child outcomes, exceptions do exist.

In one longitudinal study, researchers followed several hundred families for 12 years, collecting information from mothers on disciplinary strategies in early and middle childhood and from both mothers and their children on youth problem behaviors in adolescence. Even after many child and family characteristics were controlled, the findings were striking: In Caucasian-American families, physical punishment was positively associated with adolescent aggression and antisocial behavior. In African-American families, by contrast, the more mothers had disciplined physically in childhood, the less their teenagers displayed angry, acting-out behavior and got in trouble at school and with the police (Lansford et al., 2004).

African-American and Caucasian-American parents seem to mete out physical punishment differently. In black families, such discipline is culturally approved, generally mild, delivered in a context of parental warmth, and aimed at helping children become responsible adults. White parents, in contrast, typically consider physical punishment to be wrong, so when they resort to it, they are usually highly agitated and rejecting of the child (Graziano & Hamblen, 1996). As a result, black children may view spanking as a practice carried out with their best interests in mind, whereas white children may regard it as an "act of personal aggression" (Gunnoe & Mariner, 1997, p. 768).

In support of this view, when several thousand ethnically diverse children were followed from the preschool through the early school years, spanking was associ-

ated with a rise in behavior problems if parents were cold and rejecting, but not if they were warm and supportive (McLoyd & Smith, 2002). These findings are not an endorsement of physical punishment. Other forms of discipline, including time out, withdrawal of privileges, and the positive strategies listed on page 269, are far more effective. But it is noteworthy that the meaning and impact of physical discipline varies sharply with cultural context.

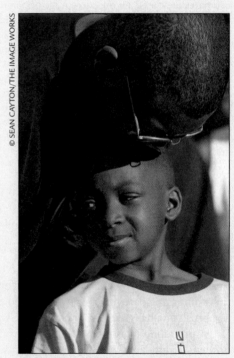

To discipline children, many African-American parents use mild physical punishment. Because the practice is culturally approved and delivered in an overall context of parental warmth, African-American children may view spanking as something that is done with their best interests in mind, rather than an act of personal aggression.

Consult Applying What We Know on the following page for ways to discipline positively. Parents who use these strategies focus on long-term social and life skills—cooperation, problem solving, and consideration for others' welfare. As a result, they greatly reduce the need for punishment.

The Cognitive-Developmental Perspective

The psychoanalytic and behaviorist approaches to morality focus on how children acquire ready-made standards of good conduct from adults. In contrast, the cognitive-developmental perspective regards children as *active thinkers* about social

Applying What We Know

Using Positive Discipline

Strategy	Explanation
Use transgressions as opportunities to teach.	When a child engages in harmful or unsafe behavior, use induction, which motivates children to make amends and behave prosocially.
Reduce opportunities for misbehavior.	On a long car trip, bring back-seat activities that relieve children's restlessness. At the super-market, converse with children and permit them to assist with shopping. As a result, children learn to occupy themselves constructively when options are limited.
Provide reasons for rules.	When children appreciate that rules are fair to all concerned, not arbitrary, they strive to follow the rules because these are reasonable and rational.
Arrange for children to participate in family routines and duties.	By joining with adults in preparing a meal, washing dishes, or raking leaves, children develop a sense of responsible participation in family and community life and acquire many practical skills.
When children are obstinate, try compromising and problem solving.	When a child refuses to obey, express understanding of the child's feelings ("I know it's not fun to clean up"), suggest a compromise ("You put those away, I'll take care of these"), and help the child think of ways to avoid the problem in the future. Responding firmly but kindly and respectfully increases the likelihood of willing cooperation.
Encourage mature behavior.	Express confidence in children's capacity to learn and appreciation for effort and cooperation, as in "You gave that your best!" "Thanks for helping!" Adult encouragement fosters pride and satisfaction in succeeding, thereby inspiring children to improve further.

rules. As early as the preschool years, children make moral judgments, deciding what is right or wrong on the basis of concepts they construct about justice and fairness (Gibbs, 1991, 2003).

Young children have some well-developed ideas about morality. As long as researchers emphasize people's intentions, 3-year-olds say that a person with bad intentions—someone who deliberately frightens, embarrasses, or otherwise hurts another—is more deserving of punishment than a well-intentioned person (Helwig, Zelazo, & Wilson, 2001; Jones & Thompson, 2001). Around age 4, children can tell the difference between truthfulness and lying. They approve of telling the truth and disapprove of lying, even when a lie remains undetected (Bussey, 1992).

Furthermore, preschoolers distinguish **moral impera-tives,** which protect people's rights and welfare, from two other types of action: **social conventions,** customs determined solely by consensus, such as table manners; and **matters of personal choice,** which do not violate rights, are not socially regulated, and are up to the individual, such as choice of friends and color of clothing (Ardila-Rey & Killen, 2001; Nucci, 1996; Yan & Smetana, 2003). Interviews with 3- and 4-year-olds reveal that they consider moral violations (stealing an apple) as more wrong than violations of social conventions (eating ice cream with your fingers) (Smetana, 1995; Turiel, 1998). And pre-schoolers' concern with personal choice, conveyed through such statements as "I'm gonna wear *this* shirt," serves as the springboard for moral concepts of individual rights, which will expand greatly in middle childhood and adolescence (Killen & Smetana, 1999).

Within the moral domain, however, preschool and young school-age children tend to reason *rigidly,* making judgments based on salient features and consequences while neglecting other important information. For example, they are more likely than older children to claim that stealing and lying are always wrong, even when a person has a morally sound reason for engaging in these acts (Lourenco, 2003). And although they disapprove of undetected lies, they also judge lies that lead to punishment more negatively than lies that do not (Bussey, 1992).

Still, preschoolers' ability to distinguish moral imperatives from social conventions is impressive. How do they do so? According to cognitive-developmental theorists, they *actively make sense* of their experiences. They observe that after a moral offense, peers respond with strong negative emotion, describe their own injury or loss, tell another child to stop, or retaliate. And an adult who intervenes is likely to call attention to the rights and feelings of the victim. In contrast, peers react less intensely to violations of social convention. And in these situations, adults usually demand obedience without explanation or point to the importance of obeying rules or keeping order (Turiel, Smetana, & Killen, 1991).

Cognition and language support preschoolers' moral understanding, but social experiences are vital. Disputes with siblings and peers over rights, possessions, and property allow preschoolers to work out their first ideas about justice and fair-ness (Killen & Nucci, 1995). Children also learn by observing the way adults handle rule violations and discuss moral issues. Children who are advanced in moral thinking tend to have parents who adapt their communications about fighting, honesty, and ownership to what their children can understand, tell stories with moral implications, encourage prosocial behavior, and gently stimulate the child to think further, without being hostile or critical (Janssens & Deković, 1997; Walker & Taylor, 1991a).

Preschool children who verbally and physically assault others, often with little or no provocation, are already delayed in moral reasoning (Helwig & Turiel, 2002a; Sanderson & Siegal, 1988). Without special help, such children show long-term disruptions in moral development.

The Other Side of Morality: Development of Aggression

Beginning in late infancy, all children display aggression at times. As interactions with siblings and peers increase, so do aggressive outbursts (Tremblay, 2002). By the early preschool years, two general types of aggression emerge. The most common is **instrumental aggression,** in which children want an object, privilege, or space and, in trying to get it, push, shout at, or otherwise attack a person who is in the way. The other type, **hostile aggression,** is meant to hurt another person.

Hostile aggression comes in at least three varieties:

- **Physical aggression** harms others through physical injury—pushing, hitting, kicking, or punching others or destroying another's property.

- **Verbal aggression** harms others through threats of physical aggression, name-calling, or hostile teasing.

- **Relational aggression** damages another's peer relationships through social exclusion, malicious gossip, or friendship manipulation.

Although verbal aggression is always direct, physical and relational aggression can be either *direct* or *indirect*. For example, hitting injures a person directly, whereas destroying property indirectly inflicts physical harm. Similarly, saying, "Do what I say, or I won't be your friend," conveys relational aggression directly, while spreading rumors, refusing to talk to a peer, or manipulating friendship by saying behind someone's back, "Don't play with her; she's a nerd," does so indirectly.

In early childhood, physical aggression is gradually replaced by verbal aggression (Tremblay et al., 1999), and instrumental aggression declines as preschoolers' improved capacity to delay gratification enables them to avoid grabbing others' possessions. But hostile aggression increases (Tremblay, 2000). Older children are better able to recognize malicious intentions and, as a result, more often retaliate in hostile ways.

By the late preschool years, boys in many cultures are more physically aggressive than girls (Coie & Dodge, 1998). This sex difference is due in part to biology—in particular, to androgens, or male sex hormones. Androgens contribute to boys' greater physical activity, which is likely to change into aggression in certain situations. Boys also spend more time than girls playing competitively in large groups, a context that promotes bossy, belligerent acts (Benenson et al., 2001). Gen-

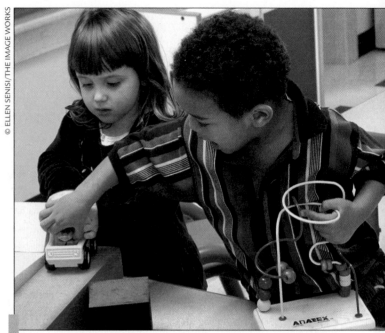

This preschool boy displays instrumental aggression as he grabs his classmate's toy. Instrumental aggression declines with age as children learn to compromise and share, and as their capacity to delay gratification improves.

der typing (a topic we will take up shortly) is important, too. Once preschoolers are aware of gender stereotypes—that males and females are expected to behave differently—physical aggression drops off more sharply in girls than in boys (Fagot & Leinbach, 1989). Parents also respond much more negatively to physical fighting in girls than boys (Arnold, McWilliams, & Harvey-Arnold, 1998).

Although girls have a reputation for being both more verbally and relationally aggressive than boys, the sex difference is small (Salmivalli, Kaukiainen, & Lagerspetz, 2000; Underwood, Galen, & Paquette, 2001). Beginning in the preschool years, girls concentrate most of their aggressive acts in the relational category. Boys inflict harm in more variable ways and, therefore, display overall rates of aggression that are much higher than girls' (see Figure 8.3).

At the same time, girls more often select indirect relational tactics that—in disrupting intimate bonds especially important to girls—can be particularly mean. And whereas physical attacks are usually brief, acts of indirect relational aggression may extend for hours, weeks, or even months (Nelson, Robinson, & Hart, 2005; Underwood, 2003). In one instance, a 6-year-old girl formed a "pretty-girls club" and—for nearly an entire school year—convinced its members to exclude several classmates by saying they were "dirty and smelly."

An occasional aggressive exchange between preschoolers is normal. But some children—especially those who are emotionally negative, impulsive, and disobedient—are prone to early, high rates of physical or relational aggression that often persist, resulting in serious conduct problems in middle childhood and adolescence (Brame, Nagin, & Tremblay, 2001; Coté

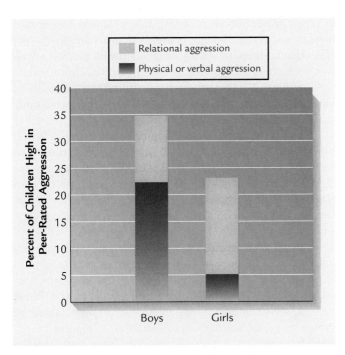

FIGURE 8.3 Types of aggression by gender. More than 1,100 school-age children identified classmates who often engage in physical or verbal aggression (hitting, kicking, punching, or insulting) and relational aggression (spreading rumors, gossiping, or manipulating friendships). Boys engage in higher overall rates and more varied types of aggression than girls, who concentrate most of their aggression in the relational category. (Adapted from Crick, 1996.)

et al., 2001; Vaillancourt et al., 2003) These negative outcomes, however, depend on child-rearing conditions.

■ **The Family as Training Ground for Aggressive Behavior.** "I can't control him, he's impossible," complained Nadine, Robbie's mother, to Leslie one day. When Leslie asked if Robbie might be troubled by something happening at home, she discovered that Robbie's parents fought constantly and resorted to harsh, inconsistent discipline. The same child-rearing practices that undermine moral internalization—love withdrawal, power assertion, physical punishment, and inconsistency—are linked to aggression from early childhood through adolescence, in children of both sexes and in many cultures (Bradford et al., 2003; Capaldi et al., 2002; Rubin et al., 2003; Yang et al., 2003).

In families like Robbie's, anger and punitiveness quickly lead to a conflict-ridden family atmosphere and an "out-of-control" child. The pattern begins with forceful discipline, which occurs more often with stressful life experiences, a parent with an unstable personality, or a difficult child. Typically, the parent threatens, criticizes, and punishes, and the child whines, yells, and refuses until the parent "gives in." As these cycles become more frequent, they generate anxiety and irritability among other family members, who soon join in the hostile interactions. Compared with siblings in typical fami-

lies, preschool siblings who have critical, punitive parents are more verbally and physically aggressive to one another. Destructive sibling conflict, in turn, contributes to poor impulse control and antisocial behavior by the early school years (Garcia et al., 2000).

Boys are more likely than girls to be targets of harsh, inconsistent discipline because they are more active and impulsive and therefore harder to control. Children who are products of these family processes come to view the world from a violent perspective, seeing hostile intent where it does not exist (Lochman & Dodge, 1998; Orbio de Castro et al., 2002). As a result, they make many unprovoked attacks and soon conclude that aggression "works" to control others.

Highly aggressive children tend to be rejected by peers, to fail in school, and (by adolescence) to seek out deviant peer groups that lead them toward violent delinquency and adult criminality. We will consider this life-course path of antisocial activity in Chapter 12.

■ **Violent Media and Aggression.** In the United States, 57 percent of television programs between 6 A.M. and 11 P.M. contain violent scenes, often in the form of repeated aggressive acts that go unpunished. Most TV violence does not show victims experiencing any serious harm, and few programs condemn violence or depict other ways of solving problems. Violent content is 9 percent above average in children's programming, and cartoons are the most violent (Center for Communication and Social Policy, 1998). Although Canadian broadcasters follow a code that sharply restricts televised violence, Canadians devote two-thirds of their viewing time to U.S. channels (Statistics Canada, 2005f).

Reviewers of thousands of studies have concluded that TV violence increases the likelihood of hostile thoughts and emotions and of verbally and physically aggressive behavior (Anderson et al., 2003; Comstock & Scharrer, 1999). And a growing number of studies show that playing violent video and computer games has similar effects (Anderson et al., 2003). Although young people of all ages are susceptible, preschool and young school-age children are especially likely to imitate TV violence because they believe much TV fiction is real and accept what they see uncritically.

Violent programming creates short-term difficulties in parent and peer relations as well as lasting negative consequences. In several longitudinal studies, time spent watching TV in childhood and adolescence predicted aggressive behavior in adulthood, after other factors linked to TV viewing (such as prior child and parent aggression, IQ, parental education, family income, and neighborhood crime) were controlled (see Figure 8.4 on page 272) (Huesmann, 1986; Huesmann et al., 2003; Johnson et al., 2002). Aggressive children and adolescents have a greater appetite for violent TV. And boys watch more violent programming than girls, in part because violent shows cater to male audiences by using males as lead characters. But violent TV sparks hostile thoughts and behavior even in nonaggressive children; its impact is simply less intense (Bushman & Huesmann, 2001).

FIGURE 8.4 **Relationship of television viewing in childhood and early adolescence to aggressive acts in adolescence and early adulthood.** Interviews with more than 700 parents and youths revealed that the more TV watched in childhood and early adolescence, the greater the annual number of aggressive acts committed by the young person, as reported in follow-up interviews at ages 16 and 22. (Adapted from Johnson et al., 2002.)

Furthermore, television violence "hardens" children to aggression. Viewers quickly habituate, responding with reduced arousal to real-world instances and tolerating more aggression in others (Anderson et al., 2003). Heavy viewers believe that there is much more violence in society than actually exists—an effect that is especially strong for children who perceive television violence to be relevant to their own lives (Donnerstein, Slaby, & Eron, 1994). As these responses indicate, exposure to violent media modifies children's attitudes toward social reality so they increasingly match media images.

The ease with which television can manipulate children's beliefs and behavior has led to strong public pressure to improve its content. In the United States, the First Amendment right to free speech has hampered efforts to regulate TV content. Instead, all programs must be rated for violent and sexual content, and all new TV sets are required to contain the V-chip, which allows parents to block undesired material.

Canada also mandates both the V-chip and program ratings. In addition, Canada's broadcasting code bans from children's shows realistic scenes of violence that minimize consequences and cartoons in which violence is the central theme. Further, violent programming intended for adults cannot be shown on Canadian channels before 9 P.M. (Canadian Broadcast Standards, 2003). Still, Canadian children have access to violent TV fare on U.S. channels.

Until children's television improves, it is largely up to parents to take steps to regulate children's media exposure. See Applying What We Know below for some effective strategies.

■ **Helping Children and Parents Control Aggression.** Treatment for aggressive children is best begun early, before their antisocial behavior becomes well-practiced and difficult to change. Breaking the cycle of hostilities between family members and promoting effective ways of relating to others is crucial.

Leslie suggested that Robbie's parents see a family therapist, who observed their inept practices and coached them in

Regulating TV and Computer Use

Applying What We Know

Strategy	Description
Limit TV viewing and computer use.	Provide clear rules that limit what children can view on TV and do on the computer, and stick to the rules. Avoid using the TV or the computer as a baby-sitter for children. Do not place a TV or a computer in a child's bedroom; doing so increases use substantially and makes the child's activity hard to monitor.
Refrain from using TV or computer time to reward or punish children.	When TV or computer access is used to reward or punish, children become increasingly attracted to it.
View TV with children, helping them understand what they see.	When adults express disapproval of on-screen behavior, raise questions about its realism, and encourage children to discuss it, they teach children to evaluate TV content rather than accepting it uncritically.
Link TV content to everyday learning experiences.	Building on TV programs in constructive ways enhances learning by encouraging children into active engagement with their surroundings. For example, a program on animals might spark a trip to the zoo, a visit to the library for a book about animals, or new ways of observing and caring for the family pet.
Model good TV and computer practices.	Avoid excess television viewing and computer use and exposure to violent media content yourself. Parental viewing patterns influence children's viewing patterns.

alternatives. They learned not to give in to Robbie, to pair commands with reasons, and to replace verbal insults and harsh physical punishment with more effective strategies, such as time out and withdrawal of privileges. After several weeks of such training, children's aggression declines, and parents view their children more positively—benefits still evident one to four years later (Patterson & Fisher, 2002).

Leslie also began coaching Robbie in emotional competence (see page 259) and in how to interact successfully with peers. When opportunities arose, she encouraged Robbie to talk about a playmate's emotions and express his own. As Robbie practiced taking the perspective of others and feeling sympathetic concern, his angry lashing out at peers declined (Izard et al., 2004). Robbie participated in *social problem-solving training* as well. Over several months, he met with Leslie and a small group of classmates to act out common conflicts using puppets, discuss alternatives for resolving disputes, and practice successful strategies. Children who receive such training show gains in social competence still present several months later (Shure, 2001).

Finally, Robbie's parents sought counseling for their marital problems. When parents receive help in coping with stressors in their own lives, interventions aimed at reducing children's aggression are even more effective (Kazdin & Whitley, 2003).

Ask Yourself

Review

What experiences help children differentiate moral imperatives, social conventions, and matters of personal choice?

Apply

Alice and Wayne want their two children to become morally mature, caring individuals. List some parenting practices they should use and some they should avoid.

Connect

What must parents do to foster conscience development in fearless, impulsive children? Does this remind you of the concept of goodness of fit (see page 194 in Chapter 6)? Explain.

Reflect

Which types of punishment for a misbehaving preschooler do you endorse, and which types do you reject? Why?

www.ablongman.com/berk

Gender Typing

Gender typing refers to any association of objects, activities, roles, or traits with one sex or the other in ways that conform to cultural stereotypes (Liben & Bigler, 2002). In Leslie's classroom, girls spent more time in the housekeeping, art, and reading corners, while boys gathered more often in spaces devoted to blocks, woodworking, and active play. Already, the children had acquired many gender-linked beliefs and preferences and tended to play with peers of their own sex.

The same theories that provide accounts of morality have been used to explain children's gender typing: *social learning theory*, with its emphasis on modeling and reinforcement, and *cognitive-developmental theory*, with its focus on children as active thinkers about their social world. We will see that neither is adequate by itself. *Gender schema theory*, a third perspective that combines elements of both, has gained favor. In the following sections, we consider the early development of gender typing.

Gender-Stereotyped Beliefs and Behavior

Even before children can label their own sex consistently, they have begun to acquire common associations with gender—men as rough and sharp, women as soft and round. In one study, 18-month-olds linked such items as fir trees and hammers with males, although they had not yet learned comparable feminine associations (Eichstedt et al., 2002). Recall from Chapter 6 that around age 2, children use such words as "boy" and "girl" and "lady" and "man" appropriately. As soon as gender categories are established, children sort out what they mean in terms of activities and behavior.

Preschoolers associate toys, articles of clothing, tools, household items, games, occupations, and colors (pink and blue) with one sex or the other (Poulin-Dubois et al., 2002; Ruble & Martin, 1998). And their actions reflect their beliefs, not only in play preferences but in personality traits as well. As we have seen, boys tend to be more active, assertive, and directly aggressive. Girls tend to be more fearful, dependent, emotionally sensitive, and skilled at understanding self-conscious emotions and at inflicting indirect relational aggression (Bosacki & Moore, 2004; Eisenberg & Fabes, 1998; Underwood, 2003).

During early childhood, children's gender-stereotyped beliefs become stronger, operating more like blanket rules than as flexible guidelines. When children were asked whether gender stereotypes could be violated, half or more of 3- and 4-year-olds answered "no" to clothing, hairstyle, and play with certain toys (such as Barbie dolls and G.I. Joes). Although they were less insistent about other types of play and occupations, many said a girl can't play roughly or be a doctor (Blakemore, 2003).

The rigidity of preschoolers' gender stereotypes helps us understand some commonly observed everyday behaviors. When Leslie showed her class a picture of a Scottish bagpiper wearing a kilt, the children insisted, "Men don't wear skirts!" During free play, they often exclaimed that girls can't be police officers and boys don't take care of babies. These one-sided judgments are a joint product of gender stereotyping in the environment and young children's cognitive limitations. Most preschoolers do not yet realize that characteristics *associated* with one's sex—activities, toys, occupations, hairstyle, and clothing—do not *determine* whether a person is male or female.

Genetic Influences on Gender Typing

The sex differences just described appear in many cultures around the world (Whiting & Edwards, 1988). And certain ones—male activity level and overt aggression, female emotional sensitivity, and the preference for same-sex playmates as well—are widespread among mammalian species (Beatty, 1992; de Waal, 1993). According to an evolutionary perspective, the adult life of our male ancestors was largely oriented toward competing for mates, that of our female ancestors toward rearing children. Therefore, males became genetically primed for dominance and females for intimacy, responsiveness, and cooperativeness. Evolutionary theorists claim that although family and cultural forces can influence the intensity of biologically based sex differences, experience cannot eradicate those aspects of gender typing that served adaptive functions in human history (Geary, 1999; Maccoby, 2002).

Experiments with animals reveal that prenatally administered androgens increase active play and aggression and suppress maternal caregiving in many mammals. Eleanor Maccoby (1998) argues that hormones also affect human play styles, leading to rough, noisy movements among boys and calm, gentle actions among girls. Then, as children interact with peers, they choose partners whose interests and behaviors are compatible with their own. Preschool girls increasingly seek out other girls and like to play in pairs because they share preference for quieter activities involving cooperative roles. In contrast, boys come to prefer larger-group play with other boys, who share a desire to run, climb, play-fight, compete, and build up and knock down (Fabes, Martin, & Hanish, 2003). At age 4, children spend three times as much time with same-sex as with other-sex playmates. By age 6, this ratio has climbed to 11 to 1 (Martin & Fabes, 2001).

Additional evidence for the role of biology in gender typing comes from a case study of a boy who experienced serious sexual-identity and adjustment problems because his biological makeup and sex of rearing were at odds. Turn to the Lifespan Vista box on the following page to find out about David's development. But note, also, that David's reflections on his upbringing caution us against minimizing the role of experience in gender typing.

Environmental Influences on Gender Typing

A wealth of evidence reveals that environmental forces—at home, at school, and in the community—build on genetic influences to promote the vigorous gender typing of early childhood.

■ **Parents.** Beginning at birth, parents have different expectations of sons than of daughters. Many parents state that they want their children to play with "gender-appropriate" toys. And they tend to describe achievement, competition, and control of emotion as important for sons and warmth, "ladylike" behavior, and closely supervised activities as important for daughters (Brody, 1999; Turner & Gervai, 1995).

Early in the preschool years, gender typing is well under way. Girls tend to play with girls and are drawn to toys and activities that emphasize nurturance, cooperation, and physical attractiveness.

Actual parenting practices reflect these beliefs. Parents give their sons toys that stress action and competition (guns, cars, tools, footballs) and give their daughters toys that emphasize nurturance, cooperation, and physical attractiveness (dolls, tea sets, jewelry) (Leaper, 1994). Parents also actively reinforce independence in boys and dependency in girls. For example, parents react more positively when a son plays with cars and trucks, demands attention, runs and climbs, or tries to take toys from others. When interacting with daughters, they more often direct play activities, provide help, encourage participation in household tasks, and refer to emotions (Fagot & Hagan, 1991; Kuebli, Butler, & Fivush, 1995; Leaper et al., 1995). Gender-typed play contexts amplify these communication differences. For example, when playing housekeeping, mothers engage in high rates of supportive, emotional talk with girls (Leaper, 2000).

Furthermore, parents provide children with indirect cues about gender categories and stereotypes through the language they use. In one study, researchers observed mothers talking about picture books with their 2- to 6-year-olds (Gelman, Taylor, & Nguyen, 2004). Mothers often labeled gender, even when they did not have to do so ("That's a boy." "Is that a she?"). And they frequently expressed *generic utterances,* referring to many, or nearly all, males and females: "Boys can be sailors." "Most girls don't like trucks." With age, both mothers and children produced an increasing number of these generic statements. And 4- to 6-year-olds frequently voiced stereotypes, which their mothers often affirmed (*Child:* "Only boys can be sailors." *Mother:* "OK.").

Parents who consciously avoid behaving in these ways have children who are less gender-typed (Weisner & Wilson-Mitchell,

A Lifespan Vista

David: A Boy Who Was Reared as a Girl

As a married man and father in his mid-thirties, David Reimer talked freely about his everyday life: his interest in auto mechanics, his problems at work, and the challenges of child rearing. But when asked about his first 15 years, he distanced himself, speaking as if the child of his early life were another person. In essence, she was.

David—named Bruce at birth—underwent the first infant sex reassignment ever reported on a genetically and hormonally normal child. To find out about David's development, researchers interviewed him intensively and studied his medical and psychotherapy records (Colapinto, 2001; Diamond & Sigmundson, 1999).

When Bruce was 8 months old, his penis was accidentally severed during circumcision. Soon afterward, his desperate parents heard about psychologist John Money's success in assigning a sex to children born with ambiguous genitals. They traveled from their home in Canada to Johns Hopkins University in Baltimore, where, under Money's oversight, 22-month-old Bruce had surgery to remove his testicles and sculpt his genitals to look like those of a girl. The operation complete, Bruce's parents named their daughter Brenda.

Brenda's upbringing was tragic. From the outset, she resisted her parents' efforts to steer her in a "feminine" direction. Brian (Brenda's identical twin brother) recalled that Brenda looked like a delicate, pretty girl—until she moved or spoke: "She walked like a guy. Sat with her legs apart. She talked about guy things. . . . She played with my toys: Tinkertoys, dump trucks" (Colapinto, 2001, p. 57). Brian was quiet and gentle in personality. Brenda, in contrast, was a dominant, rough-and-tumble child who picked fights with other children and usually won. Former teachers and classmates agreed that Brenda was the more traditionally masculine of the two children.

At school, Brenda's boyish behavior led classmates to taunt and tease her. When she played with girls, she tried organizing large-group, active games, but they weren't interested. Friendless and uncomfortable as a girl, Brenda increasingly displayed behavior problems. During periodic medical follow-ups, she drew pictures of herself as a boy and refused additional surgery to create a vagina. Reflecting back on Brenda's

COURTESY OF DAVID REIMER

Because of a medical accident when he was a baby, David Reimer underwent the first sex reassignment on a genetically and hormonally normal child: He was reared as a girl. David's case shows the overwhelming impact of biology on gender identity. At age 36, as seen here, he was a married man and father. But two years later, the troubled life that sprang from David's childhood ended tragically, in suicide.

elementary school years, David explained that she realized she was not a girl and never would be.

As adolescence approached, Brenda's parents moved her from school to school and from therapist to therapist in an effort to help her fit in socially and accept a female identity. But Brenda reacted with anxiety and insecurity, and conflict with her parents increased. At puberty, when Brenda's shoulders broadened and her body added muscle, her parents insisted that she begin estrogen therapy to feminize her appearance. Soon she grew breasts and added fat around her waist and hips. Repelled by

her own feminizing shape, Brenda began overeating to hide it. Her classmates reacted to her confused appearance with stepped-up brutality.

At last, Brenda was transferred to a therapist who recognized her despair and encouraged her parents to tell her about her infancy. When Brenda was 14, her father explained the circumcision accident. David recalled reacting with relief. Deciding to return to his biological sex immediately, he chose for himself the name David, after the biblical lad who slew a giant and overcame adversity. David soon started injections of the androgen hormone testosterone to masculinize his body, and he underwent surgery to remove his breasts and to construct a penis. Although his adolescence continued to be troubled, in his twenties he fell in love with Jane, a single mother of three children, and married her.

David's case confirms the impact of genetic sex and prenatal hormones on a person's sense of self as male or female. At the same time, his childhood highlights the importance of experience. David expressed outrage at adult encouragement of dependency in girls—after all, he had experienced it firsthand. In adulthood, David worked in a slaughterhouse with all male employees, who were extreme in their gender stereotyping. At one point he wondered, if he had had a typical childhood, would he have become like them? He could never know the answer to that question, of course, but his case does clarify one issue: His gender reassignment failed because his male biology overwhelmingly demanded a consistent sexual identity.

Although David tried to surmount his tragic childhood, the troubled life that sprang from it persisted. When he was in his mid-thirties, his twin brother, Brian, committed suicide. Then, after David had lost his job and had been swindled out of his life savings in a shady investment deal, his wife left him, taking the children with her. Grief-stricken, David sank into a deep depression. On May 4, 2004, at age 38, he shot himself.

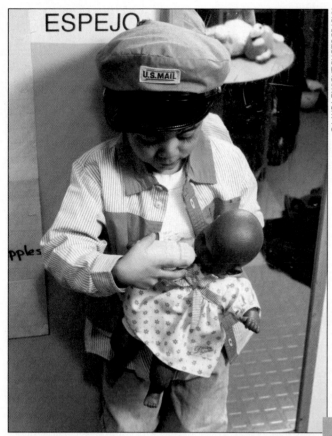

Perhaps because this 3-year-old boy has observed family members engaged in non-gender-stereotyped activities, he enacts a similar role as he pretends to feed a doll in his preschool classroom.

1990). And in nontraditional homes where fathers devote as much or more time to caregiving as mothers, children tend to be less gender-typed in emotional style—sons more emotionally sensitive, daughters more self-confident (Brody, 1997).

Overall, boys are the more gender-typed of the two sexes. Fathers, especially, are more insistent that boys conform to gender roles. They place more pressure to achieve on sons than on daughters and are less tolerant of "cross-gender" behavior in sons—more concerned when a boy acts like a "sissy" than when a girl acts like a tomboy (Sandnabba & Ahlberg, 1999; Wood, Desmarais, & Gugula, 2002).

■ **Teachers.** Teachers often act in ways that extend gender-role learning. Several times, Leslie caught herself emphasizing gender distinctions when she called out, "Will the girls line up on one side and the boys on the other?" "Boys, I wish you'd quiet down like the girls!"

Like parents, preschool teachers give girls more encouragement to participate in adult-structured activities. Girls frequently cluster around the teacher, following directions, while boys are attracted to areas of the classroom where teachers are minimally involved (Carpenter, 1983; Powlishta, Serbin, & Moller, 1993). As a result, boys and girls engage in different social behaviors. Compliance and bids for help occur more often in adult-structured contexts; assertiveness, leadership, and creative use of materials in unstructured pursuits.

Teachers also use more disapproval and controlling discipline with boys. When girls misbehave, teachers tend to negotiate, coming up with a joint plan to improve behavior (Erden & Wolfgang, 2004). Teachers seem to expect boys to misbehave more often—a belief based partly on boys' actual behavior and partly on gender stereotypes.

■ **Peers.** Children's same-sex peer associations make the peer context a potent source of gender-role learning. In a study that followed preschoolers and kindergartners over the school year, children who spent more time playing with same-sex partners in the fall showed greater gains in gender typing in the spring—in terms of toy choices, activity level, aggression, and extent of play near adults (Martin & Fabes, 2001).

By age 3, same-sex peers positively reinforce one another for "gender-appropriate" play by praising, imitating, or joining in. In contrast, when preschoolers engage in "cross-gender" activities—for example, when boys play with dolls or girls with cars and trucks—peers criticize them. Boys are especially intolerant of cross-gender play in other boys (Fagot, 1984). A boy who frequently crosses gender lines is likely to be ignored by other boys even when he does engage in "masculine" activities!

Children also develop different styles of social influence in gender-segregated peer groups. To get their way in large-group play, boys often rely on commands, threats, and physical force. Girls' preference for playing in pairs leads to greater concern with a partner's needs, evident in girls' use of polite requests, persuasion, and acceptance. Girls soon find that these tactics succeed with other girls but not with boys, who ignore their courteous overtures (Leaper, 1994; Leaper, Tenenbaum, & Shaffer, 1999). Thus, boys' unresponsiveness gives girls another reason to stop interacting with them.

Over time, children come to believe in the "correctness" of gender-segregated play, which further strengthens gender segregation and gender-stereotyped activities (Martin et al., 1999). As boys and girls separate, *in-group favoritism*—more positive evaluations of members of one's own gender—becomes another factor that sustains the separate social worlds of boys and girls, resulting in "two distinct subcultures" of knowledge, beliefs, interests, and behaviors (Maccoby, 2002).

■ **The Broader Social Environment.** Finally, although children's everyday environments have changed to some degree, they continue to present many examples of gender-typed behavior—in occupations, leisure activities, entertainment TV, and achievements of men and women. As we will see in the next section, children soon come to view not just their social surroundings but also themselves through a "gender-biased lens"—a perspective that can seriously restrict their interests and learning opportunities.

Gender Identity

As adults, each of us has a **gender identity**—an image of oneself as relatively masculine or feminine in characteristics. By middle childhood, researchers can measure gender identity by asking children to rate themselves on personality traits. A child or adult with a "masculine" identity scores high on traditionally masculine items (such as *ambitious, competitive,* and *self-sufficient*) and low on traditionally feminine items (such as *affectionate, cheerful,* and *soft-spoken*). Someone with a "feminine" identity does the reverse. And a substantial minority (especially females) have a gender identity called **androgyny,** scoring high on *both* masculine and feminine personality characteristics.

Gender identity is a good predictor of psychological adjustment. "Masculine" and androgynous children and adults have a higher sense of self-esteem, whereas "feminine" individuals often think poorly of themselves, perhaps because many of their traits are not highly valued by society (Alpert-Gillis & Connell, 1989; Boldizar, 1991). Also, androgynous individuals are more adaptable—able to show masculine independence or feminine sensitivity, depending on the situation (Taylor & Hall, 1982). The existence of an androgynous identity demonstrates that children can acquire a mixture of positive qualities traditionally associated with each gender—an orientation that may best help them realize their potential.

■ **Emergence of Gender Identity.** How do children develop a gender identity? According to *social learning theory,* behavior comes before self-perceptions. Preschoolers first acquire gender-typed responses through modeling and reinforcement and only later organize these behaviors into gender-linked ideas about themselves. In contrast, *cognitive-developmental theory* maintains that self-perceptions come before behavior. Over the preschool years, children acquire a cognitive appreciation of the permanence of their sex. They develop **gender constancy**—the understanding that sex is biologically based and remains the same even if clothing, hairstyle, and play activities change. Then children use this idea to guide their behavior (Kohlberg, 1966).

Children younger than age 6 who watch an adult dressing a doll in "other-gender" clothing typically insist that the doll's sex has also changed (Fagot, 1985; McConaghy, 1979). Mastery of gender constancy is associated with attainment of conservation (De Lisi & Gallagher, 1991). It is also strongly related to the ability to pass verbal appearance–reality tasks (see page 232 in Chapter 7) (Trautner, Gervai, & Nemeth, 2003). Indeed, gender constancy tasks can be considered a type of appearance–reality problem, in that children must distinguish what a person looks like from who he or she really is (Trautner, Gervai, & Nemeth, 2003).

In many cultures, young children do not have access to basic biological knowledge about gender because they rarely see members of the other sex naked. But providing preschoolers with information about genital differences does not result in gender constancy. Preschoolers who have such knowledge usually say changing a doll's clothing will not change its sex, but when asked to justify their responses, they do not refer to sex as an innate, unchanging quality of people (Szkrybalo & Ruble, 1999). This suggests that cognitive immaturity, not social experience, is responsible for preschoolers' difficulty grasping the permanence of sex.

Is cognitive-developmental theory correct that gender constancy is responsible for children's gender-typed behavior? Evidence for this assumption is weak. "Gender-appropriate" behavior appears so early in the preschool years that its initial appearance must result from modeling and reinforcement, as social learning theory suggests. Researchers disagree on just how gender constancy contributes to gender-role development. But they do know that once children begin to reflect on gender roles, their gender-typed self-image and behavior strengthen.

■ **Gender Schema Theory. Gender schema theory** is an information-processing approach to gender typing that combines social learning and cognitive-developmental features. It explains how environmental pressures and children's cognitions work together to shape gender-role development (Martin & Halverson, 1987; Martin, Ruble, & Szkrybalo, 2002). At an early age, children pick up gender-typed preferences and behaviors from others. At the same time, they organize their experiences into *gender schemas,* or masculine and feminine categories, that they use to interpret their world. As soon as preschoolers can label their own sex, they select gender schemas consistent with it ("Only boys can be doctors" or "Cooking is a girl's job") and apply those categories to themselves. Their self-perceptions then become gender-typed and serve as additional schemas that children use to process information and guide their own behavior.

We have seen that individual differences exist in the extent to which children endorse gender-typed views. Figure 8.5 on page 278 shows different cognitive pathways for children who often apply gender schemas to their experiences and children who rarely do (Liben & Bigler, 2002). Consider Billy, who encounters a doll. If Billy is a *gender-schematic child,* his *gender-salience filter* immediately makes gender highly relevant. Drawing on his prior learning, he asks himself, "Should boys play with dolls?" If he answers "yes" and the toy interests him, he will approach it, explore it, and learn more about it. If he answers "no," he will respond by avoiding the "gender-inappropriate" toy. But if Billy is a *gender-aschematic child*—one who seldom views the world in gender-linked terms—he will simply ask himself, "Do I like this toy?" and respond on the basis of his interests.

Gender schemas are powerful: When children see others behaving in "gender-inconsistent" ways, they often cannot remember the information or distort it to make it "gender-consistent." For example, when shown a picture of a male nurse, they may remember him as a doctor (Liben & Signorella, 1993). And because gender-schematic preschoolers typically conclude that whatever they like, children of their own sex will also like, they often use their own preferences to add to their gender biases! For example, a girl who dislikes oysters may conclude that only boys like oysters even though she has never actually been given information promoting such a stereotype (Liben & Bigler, 2002).

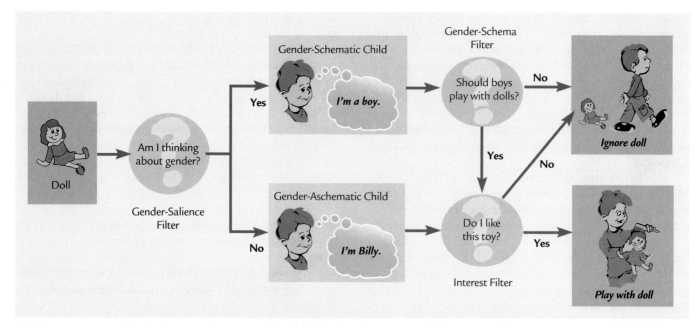

FIGURE 8.5 Cognitive pathways for gender-schematic and gender-aschematic children. In *gender-schematic children*, the gender-salience filter immediately makes gender highly relevant: Billy sees a doll and thinks, "I'm a boy. Should boys play with dolls?" Drawing on his experiences, he answers "yes" or "no." If he answers "yes" and the doll interests him, he plays with the doll. If he answers "no," he avoids the "gender–inappropriate" toy. *Gender-aschematic children* rarely view the world in gender-linked terms: Billy simply asks, "Do I like this toy?" and responds on the basis of his interests. (Reprinted by permission of Rebecca Bigler, University of Texas, Austin.)

Reducing Gender Stereotyping in Young Children

How can we help young children avoid developing rigid gender schemas that restrict their behavior and learning opportunities? No easy recipe exists. Biology clearly affects children's gender typing, channeling boys, on average, toward active, competitive play and girls toward quieter, more intimate interaction. But most aspects of gender typing are not built into human nature (Maccoby, 2000).

Because young children's cognitive limitations lead them to assume that cultural practices determine gender, parents and teachers are wise to try to delay preschoolers' exposure to gender-stereotyped messages. Adults can begin by limiting traditional gender roles in their own behavior and by providing nontraditional alternatives for children—for example, taking turns making dinner, bathing children, and driving the family car. They can give their sons and daughters both trucks and dolls, both pink and blue clothing. Teachers can ensure that all children spend time in both adult-structured and unstructured activities. Finally, adults can avoid language that conveys gender stereotypes, and they can shield children from media presentations that do so.

Once children notice the vast array of gender stereotypes in their society, parents and teachers can point out exceptions. For example, they can arrange for children to see men and women pursuing nontraditional careers and can explain that interests and skills, not sex, should determine a person's occupation. Research shows that such reasoning is highly effective in reducing children's tendency to view the world in a gender-biased fashion. By middle childhood, children who hold flexible beliefs about what boys and girls can do are more likely to notice instances of gender discrimination (Bigler & Liben, 1992; Brown & Bigler, 2004). And, as we will see next, a rational approach to child rearing promotes healthy, adaptable functioning in many other areas as well.

Ask Yourself

Review

Explain how the social environment and young children's cognitive limitations contribute to rigid gender stereotyping in early childhood.

Apply

While looking at a book, 4-year-old Roger saw a picture of a boy cooking at a stove. Later, he recalled the person in the picture as a girl. Using gender schema theory, explain Roger's memory error.

Connect

What other cognitive changes are associated with gender constancy? What do these attainments have in common?

Reflect

Would you describe your own gender identity as "masculine," "feminine," or androgynous? What biological and social factors might have influenced your gender identity?

www.ablongman.com/berk

Child Rearing and Emotional and Social Development

In this and previous chapters, we have seen how parents can foster children's competence—by building a parent–child relationship based on affection and cooperation, by serving as models and reinforcers of mature behavior, by using reasoning and inductive discipline, and by guiding and encouraging children's mastery of new skills. Now let's put these practices together into an overall view of effective parenting.

Child-Rearing Styles

Child-rearing styles are combinations of parenting behaviors that occur over a wide range of situations, creating an enduring child-rearing climate. In a landmark series of studies, Diana Baumrind gathered information on child rearing by watching parents interact with their preschoolers (Baumrind, 1971). Her findings, and those of others who have extended her work, reveal three features that consistently differentiate an effective style from less effective ones: (1) acceptance and involvement, (2) control, and (3) autonomy granting (Gray & Steinberg, 1999; Hart, Newell, & Olsen, 2003). Table 8.2 shows how child-rearing styles differ in each of these features.

■ **Authoritative Child Rearing.** The **authoritative child-rearing style**—the most successful approach to child rearing—involves high acceptance and involvement, adaptive control techniques, and appropriate autonomy granting. Authoritative parents are warm, attentive, and sensitive to their child's needs.

They establish an enjoyable, emotionally fulfilling parent–child relationship that draws the child into close connection. At the same time, authoritative parents exercise firm, reasonable control; they insist on mature behavior and give reasons for their expectations. Finally, authoritative parents engage in gradual, appropriate autonomy granting, allowing the child to make decisions in areas where he is ready to do so (Kuczynski & Lollis, 2002; Russell, Mize, & Bissaker, 2004).

Throughout childhood and adolescence, authoritative parenting is linked to many aspects of competence—an upbeat mood, self-control, task persistence, cooperativeness, high self-esteem, social and moral maturity, and favorable school performance (Amato & Fowler, 2002; Aunola, Stattin, & Nurmi, 2000; Luster & McAdoo, 1996; Mackey, Arnold, & Pratt, 2001; Steinberg, Darling, & Fletcher, 1995).

■ **Authoritarian Child Rearing.** The **authoritarian child-rearing style** is low in acceptance and involvement, high in coercive control, and low in autonomy granting. Authoritarian parents appear cold and rejecting. To exert control, they yell, command, criticize, and threaten. "Do it because I said so!" is their attitude. They make decisions for their child and expect the child to accept their word unquestioningly. If the child resists, authoritarian parents resort to force and punishment.

Children of authoritarian parents are anxious, unhappy, and low in self-esteem and self-reliance and tend to react with hostility when frustrated. Boys, especially, show high rates of anger and defiance. Although girls also engage in acting-out behavior, they are more likely to be dependent, lacking interest in exploration, and overwhelmed by challenging tasks (Hart, Newell, & Olsen, 2003; Nix et al., 1999; Thompson, Hollis, & Richards, 2003).

Table 8.2	**Features of Child-Rearing Styles**		
Child-Rearing Style	Acceptance and Involvement	Control	Autonomy Granting
Authoritative	Is warm, responsive, attentive, and sensitive to the child's needs	Makes reasonable demands for maturity, and consistently enforces and explains them	Permits the child to make decisions in accord with readiness Encourages the child to express thoughts, feelings, and desires When parent and child disagree, engages in joint decision making when possible
Authoritarian	Is cold and rejecting and frequently degrades the child	Makes many demands coercively, using force and punishment; often uses psychological control, withdrawing love and intruding on the child's individuality	Makes decisions for the child Rarely listens to the child's point of view
Permissive	Is warm but over-indulgent or inattentive	Makes few or no demands	Permits the child to make many decisions before the child is ready
Uninvolved	Is emotionally detached and withdrawn	Makes few or no demands	Is indifferent to the child's decision making and point of view

This father uses an authoritative style as he allows his son to assemble the outfit he will wear on a family outing. He engages in appropriate autonomy granting, encouraging the child to express his thoughts and opinions.

© MYRLEEN FERGUSON CATE/PHOTOEDIT

In addition to unwarranted direct control, authoritarian parents engage in a more subtle type called **psychological control,** in which they intrude on and manipulate children's verbal expression, individuality, and attachments to parents (Barber, 1996). These parents, wishing to decide virtually everything for the child, frequently interrupt or put down the child's ideas, decisions, and choice of friends. When they are dissatisfied, they withdraw love, making their affection contingent on the child's compliance. They also hold excessively high expectations that do not fit the child's developing capacities. Children subjected to psychological control exhibit adjustment problems involving both anxious, withdrawn and defiant, aggressive behaviors (Barber & Harmon, 2002; Silk et al., 2003).

■ **Permissive Child Rearing.** The **permissive child-rearing style** is warm and accepting, but uninvolved. Permissive parents are either overindulging or inattentive. They engage in little control of their child's behavior, and they allow children to make many of their own decisions at an age when they are not yet capable of doing so. Their children can eat meals and go to bed whenever they wish and can watch as much television as they want. They do not have to learn good manners or do any household chores. Although some permissive parents truly believe in this approach, many others simply lack confidence in their ability to influence their child's behavior.

Children of permissive parents are impulsive, disobedient, and rebellious. Compared with children whose parents exert more control, they are also overly demanding and dependent on adults, and they show less persistence on tasks. The link between permissive parenting and dependent, nonachieving behavior is especially strong for boys (Barber & Olsen, 1997; Baumrind, 1991, 1997).

■ **Uninvolved Parenting.** The **uninvolved child-rearing style** combines low acceptance and involvement with little control and general indifference to autonomy granting. Often these parents are emotionally detached and depressed, so overwhelmed by life stress that they have little time and energy for children. At its extreme, uninvolved parenting is a form of child maltreatment called *neglect.* Especially when it begins early, it disrupts virtually all aspects of development, including attachment, cognition, and emotional and social skills (see Chapter 6, page 187). Even with less extreme parental disengagement, children and adolescents display many problems—poor emotional self-regulation, school achievement difficulties, and antisocial behavior (Aunola, Stattin, & Nurmi, 2000; Kurdek & Fine, 1994).

What Makes Authoritative Child Rearing Effective?

Like all correlational findings, the relationship between parenting and children's development is open to interpretation. Perhaps parents of well-adjusted children are authoritative because their youngsters have especially cooperative, obedient dispositions. But longitudinal research indicates that authoritative child rearing promotes maturity in children of diverse temperaments (Hart, Newell, & Olson, 2003; Olson et al., 2000; Rubin, Burgess, & Coplan, 2002). It seems to create an emotional context for positive parental influence in the following ways:

- Warm, involved parents who are secure in the standards they hold for their children provide models of caring concern as well as confident, self-controlled behavior.

- Children are far more likely to comply with and internalize control that appears fair and reasonable, not arbitrary.

- Authoritative parents make demands and engage in autonomy granting that matches children's ability to take responsibility for their own behavior. By letting children know that they are competent individuals who can do things successfully for themselves, these parents foster high self-esteem and cognitive and social maturity.

- Supportive aspects of the authoritative style, including parental acceptance, involvement, and rational control, help protect children from the negative effects of family stress and poverty (Beyers et al., 2003).

Over time, the relationship between parenting and children's attributes becomes increasingly bidirectional (Kuczynski, 2003). When parents intervene patiently but firmly, they promote favorable adjustment, setting the stage for a positive parent–child relationship.

Cultural Variations

Although authoritative child rearing is broadly advantageous, ethnic groups often have distinct parenting beliefs and practices reflecting cultural values. Let's take some examples.

Compared with Western parents, Chinese parents describe their parenting as more controlling (Chao, 1994; Wu et al., 2002). They are more directive in teaching and scheduling their children's time, as a way of fostering self-control and high achievement. Chinese parents may appear less warm than Western parents because they think frequent praise results in self-satisfied, poorly motivated children (Chen et al., 2001). But several studies report that Chinese fathers, though high in control, display as much warmth as Caucasian-American fathers (Jose et al., 2000; Schwalb et al., 2004). When Chinese parents engage in harsh, excessive control, however, their children display the same negative outcomes seen in Western children: anxiety, depression, and aggression (Nelson et al., 2005; Yang et al., 2003).

In Hispanic and Asian Pacific Island families, firm insistence on respect for parental authority, particularly that of the father, is paired with high parental warmth. Hispanic fathers typically spend much time with their children and are warm and sensitive (Cabrera & Garcia-Coll, 2004; Jambunathan, Burts, & Pierce, 2000).

Although wide variation exists, low-SES African-American parents tend to expect immediate obedience, regarding strictness as fostering self-control and a watchful attitude in risky surroundings. Consistent with these beliefs, African-American parents who use more controlling strategies tend to have more cognitively and socially competent children (Brody & Flor, 1998). Recall, also, that a history of physical punishment is associated with a reduction in childhood behavior problems and youth antisocial activity among African Americans, but with an increase among Caucasian Americans (see page 268). Most African-American parents who use "no-nonsense" discipline use physical punishment sparingly and combine strictness with warmth and reasoning (Bluestone & Tamis-LeMonda, 1999).

These cultural variations remind us that child-rearing styles must be viewed in their larger context. As we have seen, many factors contribute to good parenting: personal characteristics of the child and parent, SES, access to extended family and community supports, cultural values and practices, and public policies.

As we turn to the topic of child maltreatment, our discussion will underscore, once again, that effective child rearing is sustained not just by the desire of mothers and fathers to be good parents. Almost all want to be. Unfortunately, when vital supports for parenting break down, children—as well as parents—can suffer terribly.

Child Maltreatment

Child maltreatment is as old as human history, but only recently has the problem been widely acknowledged and research aimed at understanding it. Perhaps public concern has increased because child maltreatment is especially common in large industrialized nations. In the most recently reported year, 906,000 American children (12 out of every 1,000) and 136,000 Canadian children (10 out of every 1,000) were identified as victims (Hovdestad et al., 2005; U.S. Department of Health and Human Services, 2005c). Most cases go unreported, so the true figures are much higher.

Child maltreatment takes the following forms:

- *Physical abuse:* Assaults on children, such as kicking, biting, shaking, punching, or stabbing, that inflict physical injury

- *Sexual abuse:* Fondling, intercourse, exhibitionism, commercial exploitation through prostitution or production of pornography, and other forms of exploitation

- *Neglect:* Failure to meet a child's basic needs for food, clothing, medical attention, or supervision

- *Emotional abuse:* Acts that could cause serious mental or behavioral disorders, including social isolation, repeated unreasonable demands, ridicule, humiliation, intimidation, or terrorizing

Parents commit more than 80 percent of abusive incidents. Other relatives account for about 7 percent. The remainder are perpetrated by parents' unmarried partners, school officials, camp counselors, and other adults. Mothers engage in neglect more often than fathers, whereas fathers engage in sexual abuse more often than mothers. Maternal and paternal rates of physical and emotional abuse are fairly similar. Infants and young preschoolers are at greatest risk for neglect, preschool and school-age children for physical, emotional, and sexual abuse (Trocomé & Wolfe, 2002; U.S. Department of Health and Human Services, 2005c). Because most sexual abuse victims are identified in middle childhood, we will pay special attention to this form of maltreatment in Chapter 10.

■ **Origins of Child Maltreatment.** Early findings suggested that child maltreatment was rooted in adult psychological disturbance (Kempe et al., 1962). But although child maltreatment is more common among disturbed parents, no single "abusive personality type" exists. Parents who were abused as children do not necessarily become abusers (Buchanan, 1996; Simons et al., 1991). And even "normal" parents sometimes harm their children!

For help in understanding child maltreatment, researchers turned to ecological systems theory (see Chapters 1 and 2). They discovered that many interacting variables—at the family, community, and cultural levels—that contribute. The more risks that are present, the greater the likelihood of abuse or neglect (see Table 8.3 on page 282). Let's examine each set of influences in turn.

The Family. Within the family, children whose characteristics make them more of a challenge to rear are at increased risk for abuse. These include premature or very sick babies and children who are temperamentally difficult, are inattentive and overactive, or have other developmental problems (Sidebotham et al., 2003). But whether such children actually are maltreated depends on parents' characteristics.

Table 8.3	Factors Related to Child Maltreatment

Factor	Description
Parent characteristics	Psychological disturbance; alcohol and drug abuse; history of abuse as a child; belief in harsh physical discipline; desire to satisfy unmet emotional needs through the child; unreasonable expectations for child behavior; young age (most under 30); low educational level
Child characteristics	Premature or very sick baby; difficult temperament; inattentiveness and overactivity; other developmental problems
Family characteristics	Low income; poverty; homelessness; marital instability; social isolation; physical abuse of mother by husband or boyfriend; frequent moves; large families with closely spaced children; overcrowded living conditions; disorganized household; lack of steady employment; other signs of high life stress
Community	Characterized by violence and social isolation; few parks, childcare centers, preschool programs, recreation centers, or churches to serve as family supports
Culture	Approval of physical force and violence as ways to solve problems

Sources: Cicchetti & Toth, 2000; Wekerle & Wolfe, 2003.

Maltreating parents are less skillful than other parents in handling discipline confrontations. They also suffer from biased thinking about their child. For example, they often evaluate transgressions as worse than they are, attribute their child's misdeeds to a bad disposition, and feel powerless in parenting—perspectives that lead them to move quickly toward physical force (Bugental & Happaney, 2004; Haskett et al., 2003).

Once abuse starts, it quickly becomes part of a self-sustaining relationship. The small irritations to which abusive parents react—a fussy baby, a preschooler who knocks over her milk, a child who will not mind immediately—soon become bigger ones. Then the harshness increases. By the preschool years, abusive and neglectful parents seldom interact with their children. When they do, the communication is almost always negative (Wolfe, 1999).

Most parents, however, have enough self-control not to respond with abuse to their child's misbehavior or developmental problems. Other factors, such as unmanageable parental stress, must combine with these conditions to prompt an extreme parental response. Abusive parents react to stressful situations with high emotional arousal. And low income, unemployment, young maternal age, alcohol and drug use, marital conflict, overcrowded living conditions, frequent moves, and extreme household disorganization are common in abusive homes (Wekerle & Wolfe, 2003). These conditions increase the chances that parents will be too overwhelmed to meet basic child-rearing responsibilities or will vent their frustrations by lashing out at their children.

The Community. The majority of abusive and neglectful parents are isolated from both formal and informal social supports. Some of these parents, because of their own life histories, have learned to mistrust and avoid others and are poorly skilled at establishing and maintaining positive relationships. Also, maltreating parents are more likely to live in unstable, rundown neighborhoods that provide few links between fam-

ily and community, such as parks, child-care centers, preschool programs, recreation centers, and religious institutions (Coulton, Korbin, & Su, 1999). They lack "lifelines" to others and have no one to turn to for help during stressful times.

The Larger Culture. Cultural values, laws, and customs profoundly affect the chances that child maltreatment will occur when parents feel overburdened. Societies that view violence as an appropriate way to solve problems set the stage for child abuse. Although the United States and Canada have laws to protect children from maltreatment, widespread support exists for use of physical force with children (refer back to page 267).

The U.S. Supreme Court has twice upheld the right of school officials to use corporal punishment. Likewise, the Canadian federal criminal code states that physical disciplining of children is justified, as long as such force is "reasonable under the circumstances." The vagueness of this definition encourages adults to assault children and provides a ready defense for those who do (Justice for Children and Youth, 2003). Every industrialized nation except the United States and Canada now prohibits school corporal punishment (Center for Effective Discipline, 2005). Fortunately, some U.S. states and Canadian provinces have passed laws that ban it.

◼ **Consequences of Child Maltreatment.** The family circumstances of maltreated children impair the development of emotional self-regulation, empathy and sympathy, self-concept, social skills, and academic motivation. Over time, these youngsters show serious learning and adjustment problems, including academic failure, severe depression, aggressive behavior, peer difficulties, substance abuse, and delinquency, including violent crime (Shonk & Cicchetti, 2001; Wolfe et al., 2001).

How do these damaging consequences occur? Think back to our earlier discussion of hostile cycles of parent–child interaction, which are especially severe for abused children. Indeed, within families, spouse abuse is strongly associated with child abuse (Cox, Kotch, & Everson, 2003). Clearly, the home lives of abused children overflow with opportunities to learn to use aggression as a way of solving problems.

Furthermore, demeaning parental messages, in which children are ridiculed, humiliated, rejected, or terrorized, result in low self-esteem, high anxiety, self-blame, depression, and efforts to escape from extreme psychological pain—at times severe enough to lead to attempted suicide in adolescence (Wolfe, 1999). At school, maltreated children are serious discipline problems. Their noncompliance, poor motivation, and cognitive immaturity interfere with academic achievement—an outcome that further undermines their chances for life success (Wekerle & Wolfe, 2003).

Finally, the trauma of repeated abuse is associated with central nervous system damage, including abnormal EEG brain-wave activity, fMRI-detected reduced size and impaired functioning of the cerebral cortex and corpus callosum, and heightened production of stress hormones (Cicchetti, 2003; Kaufman & Charney, 2001). These effects increase the chances that cognitive and emotional problems will endure.

■ Preventing Child Maltreatment.

Because child maltreatment is embedded in families, communities, and society as a whole, efforts to prevent it must be directed at each of these levels. Suggested approaches include teaching high-risk parents effective child-rearing strategies, providing direct experience with children in high school child development courses, and developing broad social programs aimed at improving economic conditions for low-SES families.

We have seen that providing social supports to families is effective in easing parental stress, and this approach also sharply reduces child maltreatment. A trusting relationship with another person is the most important factor in preventing mothers with childhood histories of abuse from repeating the cycle with their own children (Egeland, Jacobvitz, & Sroufe, 1988). Parents Anonymous, a North American organization that has as its main goal helping child-abusing parents learn constructive parenting practices, does so largely through social supports. Its local chapters offer self-help group meetings, daily phone calls, and regular home visits to relieve social isolation and teach child-rearing skills.

Home-visitation programs starting during pregnancy are especially effective in preventing child maltreatment. The *Nurse-Family Partnership (NFP)*, funded by the U.S. federal government, has sites operating in 22 states (U.S. Department of Health and Human Services, 2005m). High-risk expectant mothers receive two years of regular home visits by a trained nurse, who helps the mother manage crises, engage in effective child rearing, and access community agencies to meet family needs. A 15-year follow-up showed that NFP, compared with other services, led to better parenting and a 79 percent reduction in child abuse and neglect (Eckenrode et al., 2001).

Even with intensive treatment, some adults persist in their abusive acts. An estimated 1,500 American children and 100 Canadian children, most of them infants and preschoolers, die from maltreatment each year (Trocomé & Wolfe, 2002; U.S. Department of Health and Human Services, 2005a). When

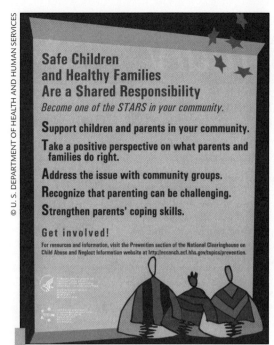

By educating people about the needs of children and families, communities can simultaneously prevent child abuse and promote effective parenting. This poster, from the U.S. Department of Health and Human Services, reminds us that protecting children is the responsibility of each and every adult.

parents are unlikely to change their behavior, the drastic step of separating parent from child and legally terminating parental rights is the only justifiable course of action.

Child maltreatment is a sad note on which to end our discussion of a period of childhood that is so full of excitement, awakening, and discovery. But there is reason to be optimistic. Great strides have been made over the past several decades in understanding and preventing child maltreatment.

Ask Yourself

Review
Summarize findings on ethnic variations in child-rearing styles. Is the concept of authoritative parenting useful for understanding effective parenting across cultures? Explain.

Apply
Chandra heard a news report about ten severely neglected children, living in squalor in an inner-city tenement. She wondered, "Why would parents mistreat their children?" How would you answer Chandra?

Connect
Which child-rearing style is most likely to be associated with inductive discipline, and why?

Reflect
How would you classify your parents' child-rearing styles? What factors might have influenced their approach to parenting?

Summary

Erikson's Theory: Initiative versus Guilt

What personality changes take place during Erikson's stage of initiative versus guilt?

■ Erikson's image of **initiative versus guilt** captures the emotional and social changes of early childhood. A healthy sense of initiative depends on exploring the social world through play, forming a conscience through identification with the same-sex parent, and receiving supportive child rearing.

Self-Understanding

Describe preschoolers' self-concepts and self-esteem.

■ During early childhood, language enables children to talk about the two aspects of the self—the **I-self** (the self as active observer) and the **me-self** (the self as object of knowledge)—from which they develop a **self-concept.**

■ Preschoolers' self-concepts consist largely of observable characteristics and typical emotions and attitudes. Their increasing self-awareness underlies struggles over objects as well as first efforts to cooperate.

■ During early childhood, **self-esteem** differentiates into several self-judgments. Preschoolers' high self-esteem contributes to their mastery-oriented approach to the environment. But even a little adult disapproval can undermine a young child's self-esteem and enthusiasm for learning.

Emotional Development

Cite changes in understanding and expression of emotion during early childhood, along with factors that influence those changes.

■ Preschoolers have an impressive understanding of the causes, consequences, and behavioral signs of basic emotions, supported by secure attachment and conversations about feelings. By age 3 to 4, children are aware of various strategies for emotional self-regulation. Temperament and parental modeling influence preschoolers' capacity to handle negative emotion.

■ As their self-concepts become better developed, preschoolers experience self-conscious emotions more often. Parental messages affect the intensity of these emotions and the situations in which they occur. Empathy also becomes more common. Temperament and parenting affect the extent to which

empathy leads to **sympathy** and to **prosocial**, or **altruistic, behavior.**

Peer Relations

Describe peer sociability and friendship in early childhood, along with cultural and parental influences on early peer relations.

■ During early childhood, peer interaction increases, as children move from **nonsocial activity** to **parallel play,** then to **associative** and **cooperative play.** But even as associative and cooperative play increase, both solitary and parallel play remain common.

■ In collectivist societies, play occurs in large groups and is highly cooperative. Sociodramatic play seems especially important in societies where child and adult worlds are distinct.

■ Preschoolers view friendship in concrete, activity-based terms. Their interactions with friends are especially positive and cooperative. Parents affect peer sociability both directly, through attempts to influence their child's peer relations, and indirectly, through their child-rearing practices. Secure attachment and emotionally positive parent–child conversations are linked to favorable peer interaction.

Foundations of Morality

What are the central features of psychoanalytic, social learning, and cognitive-developmental approaches to moral development?

■ Psychoanalytic and social learning approaches to morality focus on how children acquire ready-made standards held by adults. Contrary to the claims of Freud's psychoanalytic theory, discipline based on fear of punishment and loss of parental love does not foster conscience development. Instead, **induction** is far more effective in encouraging self-control and prosocial behavior.

■ Social learning theory regards reinforcement and modeling as the basis for moral action. Adults who are warm, powerful, and practice what they preach provide effective models of morality. Alternatives such as **time out** and withdrawal of privileges can help parents avoid the undesirable side effects of harsh punishment. Punishment is more effective when parents are consistent, have a warm relationship with the child, and offer explanations.

■ The cognitive-developmental perspective views children as active thinkers about social rules. Although preschoolers tend to reason rigidly about moral matters, by age 4 they can consider people's intentions in making moral judgments and can distinguish truthfulness from lying. Preschoolers also distinguish **moral imperatives** from **social conventions** and **matters of personal choice.**

■ Through sibling and peer interaction, children work out their first ideas about justice and fairness. Parents who discuss moral issues foster children's moral understanding.

Describe the development of aggression in early childhood, including family and television as major influences.

■ All children display aggression from time to time. During early childhood, **instrumental aggression** declines, while **hostile aggression** increases. Three types of hostile aggression appear: **physical aggression,** more common among boys; **verbal aggression;** and **relational aggression.**

■ Ineffective discipline and a conflict-ridden family atmosphere promote and sustain aggression in children. Media violence, both on TV and in computer games, also triggers childhood aggression. Teaching parents effective child-rearing practices, providing children with social problem-solving training, reducing family hostility, and shielding children from violent media can reduce aggressive behavior.

Gender Typing

Discuss genetic and environmental influences on preschoolers' gender-stereotyped beliefs and behavior.

■ **Gender typing** is well under way in the preschool years. Preschoolers acquire many gender stereotypes and behaviors. Heredity, through prenatal hormones, contributes to boys' higher activity level and overt aggression and to children's preference for same-sex playmates. But parents, teachers, peers, and the broader social environment also encourage many gender-typed responses.

Describe and evaluate the accuracy of major theories that explain the emergence of gender identity.

■ Although most people have a traditional **gender identity,** some exhibit **androgyny,** combining both masculine and feminine characteristics. Masculine and androgynous identities are linked to better psychological adjustment.

■ According to social learning theory, preschoolers first acquire gender-typed responses through modeling and reinforcement and then organize them into gender-linked ideas about themselves. Cognitive-developmental theory suggests that **gender constancy** must be mastered before children develop gender-typed behavior. In contrast to cognitive-developmental predictions, gender-role behavior is acquired long before gender constancy.

■ **Gender schema theory** combines features of social learning and cognitive-developmental perspectives. As children acquire gender-stereotyped preferences and behaviors, they form masculine and feminine categories, or gender schemas, that they apply to themselves and use to interpret their world.

© LAURA DWIGHT PHOTOGRAPHY

Child Rearing and Emotional and Social Development

Describe the impact of child-rearing styles on children's development, explain why authoritative parenting is effective, and note cultural variations in child rearing.

■ Three features distinguish major **child-rearing styles:** (1) acceptance and involvement, (2) control, and (3) autonomy granting. Compared with the **authoritarian, permissive,** and **uninvolved** styles, the **authoritative style** promotes cognitive, emotional, and social competence. Warmth, explanations, and reasonable demands for mature behavior account for the effectiveness of this style.

■ **Psychological control,** in which parents intrude on children's individuality and make affection contingent on the child's compliance, is associated with authoritarian parenting and contributes to adjustment problems.

■ Certain ethnic groups, including Chinese, Hispanic, Asian Pacific Island, and African-American, combine parental warmth with high levels of control. But when control becomes harsh and excessive, it impairs academic and social competence.

Discuss the multiple origins of child maltreatment, its consequences for development, and effective prevention.

■ Child maltreatment is related to factors within the family, community, and larger culture. Maltreating parents use ineffective discipline, hold a negatively biased view of their child, and feel powerless in parenting. Unmanageable parental stress and social isolation greatly increase the chances of abuse and neglect. When a society approves of physical force as a means of solving problems, child abuse is promoted.

■ Maltreated children are impaired in emotional self-regulation, empathy and sympathy, self-concept, social skills, and academic motivation. The trauma of repeated abuse is associated with central nervous system damage and serious adjustment problems. Successful prevention requires efforts at the family, community, and societal levels.

Important Terms and Concepts

androgyny (p. 277)
associative play (p. 261)
authoritarian child-rearing style (p. 279)
authoritative child-rearing style (p. 279)
child-rearing styles (p. 279)
cooperative play (p. 261)
gender constancy (p. 277)
gender identity (p. 276)
gender schema theory (p. 277)
gender typing (p. 273)
hostile aggression (p. 270)

I-self (p. 256)
induction (p. 265)
initiative versus guilt (p. 256)
instrumental aggression (p. 270)
matters of personal choice (p. 269)
me-self (p. 256)
moral imperatives (p. 269)
nonsocial activity (p. 261)
parallel play (p. 261)
permissive child-rearing style (p. 280)
physical aggression (p. 270)

prosocial, or altruistic, behavior (p. 260)
psychological control (p. 280)
relational aggression (p. 270)
self-concept (p. 257)
self-esteem (p. 257)
social conventions (p. 269)
sympathy (p. 261)
time out (p. 267)
uninvolved child-rearing style (p. 280)
verbal aggression (p. 270)

Milestones

Development in Early Childhood

Age	Physical	Cognitive	Language	Emotional/Social

2 YEARS

Physical
- Height and weight increase more slowly than in toddlerhood (217)

- Rapid synaptic growth and myelination in the brain continue, especially in the frontal lobes (219)
- Walks more rhythmically; run (225)
- Jumps, hops, throws, and catches with rigid upper body (225)
- Puts on and removes simple items of clothing (225)
- Uses spoon effectively (225)

Cognitive
- Make-believe becomes less dependent on realistic toys, less self-centered, and more complex (227–228)

- Can take the perspective of others in simplified situations (233)
- Recognition memory is well developed (238)
- Shows awareness of the difference between inner mental and outer physical events (239)

Language
- Vocabulary increases rapidly (248)
- Can figure out word meanings from sentence structure and social cues (249)
- Sentences follow basic word order of native language; adds grammatical markers (249)
- Displays effective conversational skills (250)

Emotional/Social
- Begins to develop self-concept and self-esteem (257–258)

- Cooperation and instrumental aggression appear (244, 257)
- Understands causes, consequences, behavioral signs of basic emotions (259)
- Empathy increases (260)
- Gender-stereotyped beliefs and behavior increase (262)

3–4 YEARS

Physical
- Rapid synaptic growth and myelination of neural fibers in the brain continue, especially in the frontal lobes (217)
- Running, jumping, hopping, throwing, and catching become better coordinated (225)
- Galloping and one-foot skipping appear (225)
- Pedals and steers tricycle (225)
- Can feed self without help (224)

Cognitive
- Masters dual representation (229)
- Notices transformations, can reverse thinking, and has a basic understanding of causality in familiar situations (232)
- Sorts familiar objects into hierarchically organized categories (233)
- Distinguishes appearance from reality (233)

Language
- Masters increasingly complex grammatical structures (249)
- Occasionally overextends grammatical rules to exceptions (249)
- Adjusts speech to fit the age, sex, and social status of speakers and listeners (250)

Emotional/Social
- Emotional self-regulation improves (259)
- Experiences self-conscious emotions more often (259)
- Interactive play (associative and cooperative) increases (261)
- Instrumental aggression declines, while hostile aggression (verbal and relational) increases (270)
- Forms first friendships (263)

Age	Physical	Cognitive	Language	Emotional/Social
3–4 YEARS (continued)	• Uses scissors, draws first picture of a person (225)	• Uses private speech to guide behavior in challenging tasks (234) • Attention becomes more sustained and planful (236) • Uses scripts to recall familiar experiences (238) • Understands that both beliefs and desires can determine behavior (239) • Aware of some meaningful features of written language (242) • Counts small numbers of objects and grasps cardinality (243)		• Distinguishes truthfulness from lying (269) • Distinguishes moral rules from social conventions and matters of personal choice (264) • Preference for same-sex playmates strengthens (274)
5–6 YEARS	• Brain reaches 90 percent of its adult weight (217) • Body is streamlined and longer-legged (217) • First permanent tooth erupts (217) • Gallops more smoothly and engages in true skipping (224) • Shows mature throwing and catching patterns (225) • Ties shoes (225) • Draws more complex pictures, copies some numbers and simple words (225–226)	• Ability to distinguish appearance from reality improves (231) • Attention continues to improve (236) • Recognition, recall, scripted memory, and autobiographical memory improve (238–239) • Understanding of false belief improves (239) • Counts on and counts down, engaging in simple addition and subtraction (243)	• Vocabulary reaches about 10,000 words (248) • Uses many complex grammatical forms (249) • Understands that letters and sounds are linked in systematic ways (242) • Uses invented spellings (242)	• Ability to interpret and predict others' emotional reactions improves (259) • Relies more on language to express empathy (260) • Has acquired many morally relevant rules and behaviors (268–269) • Gender-stereotyped beliefs and behavior continue to increase (273) • Understands gender constancy (277)

Note: Numbers in parentheses indicate the page or pages on which each milestone is discussed.

*A*n improved capacity to remember, reason, and reflect on one's own thinking makes middle childhood a time of dramatic advances in academic learning and problem solving. Here, fourth graders collaborate in a quilt-making project.

Physical and Cognitive Development in Middle Childhood

I'm on my way, Mom!" hollered 10-year-old Joey as he stuffed the last bite of toast into his mouth, slung his book bag over his shoulder, dashed out the door, jumped on his bike, and headed down the street for school. Joey's 8-year-old sister Lizzie followed, kissing her mother good-bye and pedaling furiously until she caught up with Joey. Rena, the children's mother and one of my colleagues at the university, watched from the front porch as her son and daughter disappeared in the distance.

"They're branching out," Rena told me over lunch that day, as she described the children's expanding activities and relationships. Homework, household chores, soccer teams, music lessons, scouting, friends at school and in the neighborhood, and Joey's new paper route were all part of the children's routine. "It seems as if the basics are all there," Rena said. "I don't have to monitor Joey and Lizzie constantly anymore. Being a parent is still very challenging, but it's more a matter of refinements—helping them become independent, competent, and productive individuals."

Joey and Lizzie have entered middle childhood—the years from 6 to 11. Around the world, children of this age are assigned new responsibilities. For children in industrialized nations, middle childhood is often called the "school years," since its onset is marked by the start of formal schooling. In village and tribal cultures, the school may be a field or a jungle. But universally, children in this period are guided by mature members of society toward real-world tasks that increasingly resemble those they will perform as adults (Rogoff, 1996).

This chapter focuses on physical and cognitive development in middle childhood. By age 6, the brain has reached 90 percent of its adult size, and the body continues to grow slowly. In this way, nature gives school-age children the mental powers to master challenging tasks as well as added time to acquire the knowledge and skills essential for life in a complex social world.

We begin by reviewing typical growth trends, gains in motor skills, and special health concerns. Then we return to Piaget's theory and the information-processing approach for an overview of cognitive changes

© CELIA MANNING/ALAMY

during the school years. Next, we examine the genetic and environmental roots of IQ scores, which often enter into educational decisions. Our discussion continues with the further blossoming of language in middle childhood. Finally, we turn to the importance of schools in children's learning and development.

🌱 Physical Development

Body Growth

Physical growth during the school years continues at the slow, regular pace of early childhood. At age 6, the average North American child weighs about 45 pounds and is 3½ feet tall. Over the next few years, children add about 2 to 3 inches in height and 5 pounds in weight each year (see Figure 9.1). Between ages 6 and 8, girls are slightly shorter and lighter than boys. By age 9, this trend reverses. Already, Rena noticed, Lizzie was starting to catch up with Joey in size as she approached the dramatic adolescent growth spurt, which occurs two years earlier in girls than in boys.

Because the lower portion of the body is growing fastest, Joey and Lizzie appeared longer-legged than they had in early childhood. They grew out of their jeans more quickly than their jackets and frequently needed larger shoes. As in early childhood, girls have slightly more body fat and boys more muscle. After age 8, girls begin accumulating fat at a faster rate, and they will add even more during adolescence (Siervogel et al., 2000).

During middle childhood, the bones of the body lengthen and broaden. But ligaments are not yet firmly attached to bones, and this, combined with increasing muscle strength, gives children the unusual flexibility needed to turn cartwheels and perform handstands. As their bodies become stronger, many children experience a greater desire for physical exercise. Nighttime "growing pains"—stiffness and aches in the legs—are common as muscles adapt to an enlarging skeleton (Wall, 2000).

Between ages 6 and 12, all 20 primary teeth are lost and replaced by permanent ones, with girls losing their teeth slightly earlier than boys. For a while, the permanent teeth seem much too large. Gradually, growth of facial bones, especially the jaw and chin, causes the child's face to lengthen and mouth to widen, accommodating the newly erupting teeth.

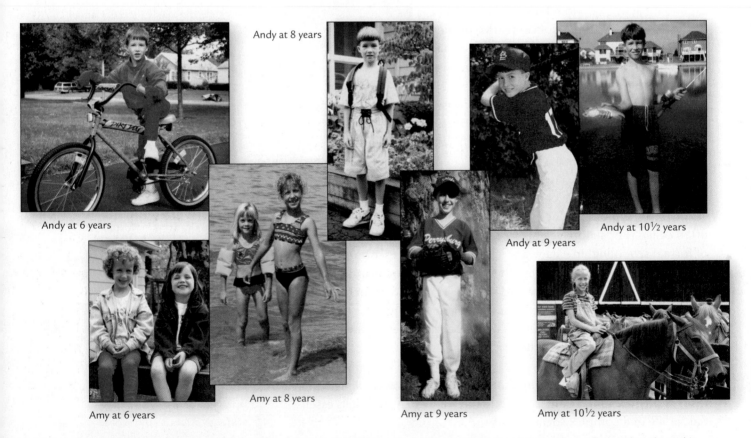

Andy at 8 years

Andy at 6 years

Amy at 8 years

Andy at 9 years

Andy at 10½ years

Amy at 6 years

Amy at 9 years

Amy at 10½ years

■ **FIGURE 9.1 Body growth during middle childhood.** Andy and Amy continued the slow, regular pattern of growth that they showed in early childhood (see Chapter 7, page 216). But around age 9, Amy began to grow at a faster rate than Andy. At age 10½, she was taller, heavier, and more mature looking.

These young bowlers are similar in age but vary greatly in body size. They illustrate faster growth of the lower portion of the body in middle childhood, appearing longer-legged than they did as preschoolers.

Common Health Problems

Children from economically advantaged homes, like Joey and Lizzie, are at their healthiest in middle childhood, full of energy and play. The cumulative effects of good nutrition, combined with rapid development of the body's immune system, offer greater protection against disease. At the same time, growth in lung size permits more air to be exchanged with each breath, so children are better able to exercise vigorously without tiring.

Not surprisingly, poverty continues to be a powerful predictor of ill health during the school years. Because economically disadvantaged U.S. families often lack health insurance (see Chapter 7), many children do not have regular access to a doctor. A substantial number also lack such basic necessities as a comfortable home and regular meals.

Vision and Hearing

The most common vision problem in middle childhood is *myopia,* or nearsightedness. By the end of the school years, it affects nearly 25 percent of children—a rate that rises to 60 percent by early adulthood. Heredity plays a role: Identical twins are more likely than fraternal twins to share the condition (Pacella et al., 1999). And it occurs far more frequently in Asian than in Caucasian populations worldwide (Feldkámper & Schaeffel, 2003). Early biological trauma also can induce myopia. School-age children with low birth weights show an especially high rate, believed to result from immaturity of visual structures, slower eye growth, and a greater incidence of eye disease (O'Connor et al., 2002).

In warning their children not to read in dim light or sit too close to the TV or computer screen, parents often exclaim, "You'll ruin your eyes!" Their concern is well-founded. In diverse cultures, the more time children spend reading, writing, using the computer, and doing other close work, the more likely they are to be myopic (Mutti et al., 2002; Saw et al., 2002). Consequently, myopia is one of the few health conditions to increase with SES. Fortunately, myopia can be overcome easily with corrective lenses.

During middle childhood, the eustachian tube (the canal that runs from the inner ear to the throat) becomes longer, narrower, and more slanted, preventing fluid and bacteria from traveling so easily from the mouth to the ear. As a result, middle-ear infections, common in infancy and early childhood, become less frequent. Still, about 3 to 4 percent of the school-age population, and as many as 20 percent of low-SES children, develop permanent hearing loss as a result of repeated infections (Ryding et al., 2002). With regular screening for both vision and hearing, defects can be corrected before they lead to serious learning difficulties.

Malnutrition

School-age children need a well-balanced, plentiful diet to provide energy for successful learning in school and increased physical activity. With their increasing focus on play, friendships, and new activities, many children spend little time at the table, and the percentage who eat dinner with their families drops sharply between ages 9 and 14 years. Family dinnertimes have waned in general over the past decade. Yet eating an evening meal with parents leads to a diet higher in fruits and vegetables and lower in fried foods and soft drinks (Neumark-Sztainer et al., 2003).

As long as parents encourage healthy eating, mild nutritional deficits resulting from the child's busy daily schedule have no impact on development. But as we have seen, many poverty-stricken children in developing countries and in North America suffer from serious and prolonged malnutrition. By middle childhood, the effects are apparent in retarded physical growth, low intelligence test scores, poor motor coordination, and inattention.

Unfortunately, malnutrition that persists from infancy or early childhood into the school years usually leads to permanent physical and mental damage (Grantham-McGregor, Walker, & Chang, 2000; Liu et al., 2003). Government-sponsored food programs from the early years through adolescence can prevent these effects. In studies carried out in Egypt, Kenya, and Mexico, quality of food (protein, vitamin, and mineral content) strongly predicted favorable cognitive development in middle childhood (Sigman, 1995; Watkins & Pollitt, 1998).

Obesity

Mona, a very heavy child in Lizzie's class, often watched from the sidelines during recess. When she did join in games, she was slow and clumsy, the target of unkind comments: "Move it, Tubs!"

Most afternoons, she walked home from school alone while the other children gathered in groups, talking, laughing, and chasing. At home, Mona sought comfort in high-calorie snacks.

Mona suffers from **obesity,** a greater-than-20-percent increase over average body weight, based on an individual's age, sex, and physical build. During the past several decades, a rise in overweight and obesity has occurred in many Western nations, with large increases in Canada, Finland, Greece, Great Britain, Ireland, New Zealand, and especially the United States. Today, 15 percent of Canadian and 16 percent of American children are obese (U.S. Department of Health and Human Services, 2005g; Willms, Tremblay, & Katzmarzyk, 2003). Obesity rates are also increasing rapidly in developing countries, as urbanization shifts the population toward sedentary lifestyles and diets high in meats and refined foods (World Press Review, 2004; Wrotniak et al., 2004).

More than 80 percent of affected children become overweight adults (Oken & Lightdale, 2000). Besides serious emotional and social difficulties, obese children are at risk for lifelong health problems. High blood pressure, high cholesterol levels, respiratory abnormalities, and insulin resistance begin to appear in the early school years—symptoms that are powerful predictors of heart disease, adult-onset diabetes, gallbladder disease, sleep and digestive disorders, many forms of cancer, and early death (Calle et al., 2003; Krebs & Jacobson, 2003). Furthermore, obesity has caused a dramatic rise in cases of diabetes in children, sometimes leading to early, severe complications, including stroke, kidney failure, and circulatory problems that heighten the risk of blindness and leg amputation (Hannon, Rao, & Arslanian, 2005).

■ **Causes of Obesity.** Not all children are equally at risk for obesity. Overweight children tend to have overweight parents, and identical twins are more likely to share the disorder than fraternal twins. But heredity accounts only for a *tendency* to gain weight (Salbe et al., 2002). The importance of environment is seen in the consistent relationship between low SES and obesity in industrialized nations, especially among ethnic minorities, including African-American, Hispanic, Native-American, and Canadian-Aboriginal children and adults (Anand et al., 2001; Kim et al., 2002). Factors responsible include lack of knowledge about healthy diet; a tendency to buy high-fat, low-cost foods; and family stress, which can prompt overeating. Recall, also, that children who were malnourished early in life are at increased risk for becoming overweight later.

Parental feeding practices also play a role. Some parents anxiously overfeed, interpreting almost all their child's discomforts as hunger. Others are overly controlling, constantly monitoring what their child eats and worrying about weight gain (Spruijt-Metz et al., 2002). Both types of parents fail to help children learn to regulate their own energy intake. Furthermore, parents of obese children often use food as a reward to reinforce other behaviors—a practice that leads children to attach greater value to treats (Sherry et al., 2004).

Because of these experiences, obese children soon develop maladaptive eating habits. They are more responsive than normal-weight individuals to external stimuli associated with

food—taste, sight, smell, time of day, and food-related words—and less responsive to internal hunger cues (Braet & Crombez, 2003; Jansen et al., 2003). They also eat faster and chew their food less thoroughly, a behavior pattern that appears as early as age 18 months (Drabman et al., 1979).

Overweight children are less physically active than their normal-weight peers. Inactivity is both cause and consequence of excessive weight gain. Research reveals that the rise in childhood obesity is due in part to the many hours North American children spend watching television. In a study that tracked children's TV viewing from ages 4 to 11, the more TV children watched, the more body fat they added: Children who devoted more than 3 hours per day to TV accumulated 40 percent more fat than those devoting less than 1¾ hours (see Figure 9.2) (Proctor et al., 2003). Watching TV reduces time spent in physical exercise, and TV ads encourage children to eat fattening, unhealthy snacks. As children get heavier, they increasingly replace active play with sedentary pursuits, including eating (Salbe et al., 2002).

Finally, the broader food environment affects the incidence of obesity. The Pima Indians of Arizona, who recently changed from a traditional diet of plant foods to a high-fat, typically American diet, have one of the highest rates of obesity in the world. Compared with descendants of their ancestors living in the remote Sierra Madre region of Mexico, the Arizona Pima have body weights 50 percent greater. Half the population has diabetes (8 times the national average), with many in their twenties and thirties already disabled by the disease—blind, in wheelchairs, and on kidney dialysis (Gladwell, 1998). Although the Pima have a genetic susceptibility to overweight, it emerges only under Western dietary conditions.

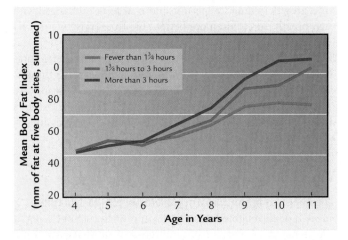

■ **FIGURE 9.2 Relationship of television viewing to gains in body fat from ages 4 to 11.** Researchers followed children longitudinally, collecting information on hours per day of television viewing and on body fat, measured in millimeters of skinfold thickness at five body sites (upper arms, shoulders, abdomen, trunk, and thighs). The more TV children watched, the greater the gain in body fat. At ages 10 to 11, the difference between children watching fewer than 1¾ hours and those watching more than 3 hours had become large. (Adapted from M. H. Proctor et al., 2003, "Television Viewing and Change in Body Fat from Preschool to Early Adolescence: The Framingham Children's Study," *International Journal of Obesity, 27,* p. 831. © Nature Publishing Group. Adapted by permission.)

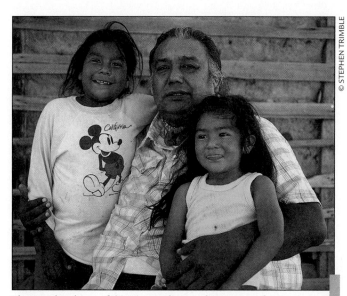

The two daughters of this Pima Indian medicine man of Arizona are likely to become obese, like their father, by the time they reach adolescence. The rate of obesity among the Pima residing in the southwestern United States, who have a high-fat diet, is one of the highest in the world. In contrast, the Pima living in the remote Sierra Madre region of Mexico, who have a low-fat vegetarian diet, are average weight and rarely suffer from diabetes and its life-threatening complications.

■ **Consequences of Obesity.** Unfortunately, physical attractiveness is a powerful predictor of social acceptance. In Western societies, both children and adults rate obese youngsters as unlikable, stereotyping them as lazy, sloppy, ugly, stupid, self-doubting, and deceitful (Kilpatrick & Sanders, 1978; Tiggemann & Anesbury, 2000). In school, obese children are often socially isolated (Strauss & Pollack, 2003). By middle childhood, they report more emotional, social, and school difficulties and display more behavior problems than normal-weight peers. Persistent obesity from childhood into adolescence predicts serious disorders, including defiance, aggression, and severe depression (Mustillo et al., 2003; Schwimmer, Burwinkle, & Varni, 2003). As we will see in Chapter 13, these psychological consequences combine with continuing discrimination to result in reduced life chances in close relationships and employment.

■ **Treating Obesity.** In Mona's case, the school nurse suggested that Mona and her obese mother enter a weight-loss program together. But Mona's mother, unhappily married for many years, had her own reasons for overeating and rejected this idea. In one study, only one-fourth of overweight parents judged their overweight children to have a weight problem (Jeffrey, 2004). Consistent with these findings, less than 20 percent of obese children get any treatment.

Because childhood obesity is often a family disorder, the most effective interventions are family-based. In one study, both parent and child revised eating patterns, exercised daily, and reinforced each other with praise and points for progress, which they exchanged for special activities and times together. The more weight parents lost, the more their children lost

(Wrotniak et al., 2004). Follow-ups after 5 and 10 years showed that children maintained their weight loss more effectively than adults, a finding that underscores the importance of early intervention (Epstein, Roemmich, & Raynor, 2001). Treatment programs that focus on diet and lifestyle can yield substantial, long-lasting weight reduction among children and adolescents. But these interventions work best when parents' and children's weight problems are not severe (Eliakim et al., 2004; Nemet et al., 2005).

Children consume one-third of their daily caloric intake at school. Therefore, schools can also help reduce obesity by serving healthier meals and ensuring regular physical activity.

Illnesses

Children experience a somewhat higher rate of illness during the first two years of elementary school than later, because of exposure to sick children and an immune system that is still developing. About 15 to 20 percent of North American children have chronic diseases and conditions (including physical disabilities). By far the most common—accounting for about one-third of childhood chronic illness and the most frequent cause of school absence and childhood hospitalization—is *asthma,* in which the bronchial tubes (passages that connect the throat and lungs) are highly sensitive. In response to a variety of stimuli, such as cold weather, infection, exercise, allergies, and emotional stress, they fill with mucus and contract, leading to coughing, wheezing, and serious breathing difficulties (Akinbami & Schoendorf, 2002).

During the past three decades, the number of children with asthma has more than doubled, and asthma-related deaths have also risen. Although heredity contributes to asthma, researchers believe that environmental factors are necessary to spark the illness. Boys, African-American children, and children who were born underweight, whose parents smoke, or who live in poverty are at greatest risk (Federico & Liu, 2003). The higher rate and greater severity of asthma among African-American and poverty-stricken youngsters may be the result of pollution in inner-city areas (which triggers allergic reactions), stressful home lives, and lack of access to good health care. Childhood obesity is also related to asthma in middle childhood, perhaps due to high levels of blood-circulating inflammatory substances associated with body fat (Saha, Riner, & Liu, 2005).

About 2 percent of North American youngsters have more severe chronic illnesses, such as sickle cell anemia, cystic fibrosis, diabetes, arthritis, cancer, and acquired immune deficiency syndrome (AIDS). Painful medical treatments, physical discomfort, and changes in appearance often disrupt the sick child's daily life, making it difficult to concentrate in school and separating the child from peers. As the illness worsens, family stress increases (LeBlanc, Goldsmith, & Patel, 2003). For these reasons, chronically ill children are at risk for academic, emotional, and social difficulties. A strong link between good family functioning and child well-being exists for chronically ill children, just as it does for physically healthy children (Barakat & Kazak, 1999). Interventions that foster positive family relationships help parent and child cope with the disease and improve children's adjustment. These include health education, counseling, social support, and disease-specific summer camps, which teach children self-help skills and give parents time off from the demands of caring for a chronically ill youngster.

Unintentional Injuries

As we conclude our discussion of threats to school-age children's health, let's return to the topic of unintentional injuries (discussed in detail in Chapter 7). As Figure 9.3 shows, injury fatalities increase from middle childhood into adolescence, with rates for boys rising considerably above those for girls.

Motor vehicle accidents, involving children as passengers or pedestrians, continue to be the leading cause of injury, followed by bicycle accidents (Pless & Millar, 2000; U.S. Department of Health and Human Services, 2005q). Pedestrian injuries most often result from midblock dart-outs, bicycle accidents from disobeying traffic signals and rules. When many stimuli impinge on them at once, young school-age children often fail to think before they act (Tuchfarber, Zins, & Jason, 1997). They need frequent reminders, supervision, and prohibitions against venturing into busy traffic on their own—especially as they begin to range farther from home.

School-based intervention programs with lasting effects use extensive modeling and rehearsal of safety practices, give children feedback about their performance along with praise and tangible rewards for acquiring safety skills, and provide occasional booster sessions (Zins et al., 1994). Parents, who often overestimate their child's safety knowledge and physical

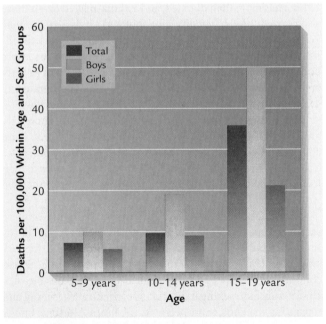

■ FIGURE 9.3 Rate of injury mortality in North America from middle childhood to adolescence. Injury fatalities increase with age, and the gap between boys and girls expands. Motor vehicle (passenger and pedestrian) accidents are the leading cause, with bicycle injuries next in line. American and Canadian injury rates are nearly identical. (From U.S. Department of Health and Human Services, 2005g.)

abilities, must be educated about children's age-related safety capacities (Schwebel & Bounds, 2003). One vital safety measure is insisting that children wear protective helmets while bicycling, in-line skating, skateboarding, or using scooters. This simple precaution leads to an 85 percent reduction in risk of head injury, a leading cause of permanent disability and death in school-age children (Schieber & Sacks, 2001).

By middle childhood, the greatest risk-takers tend to be children whose parents either do not act as safety-conscious models or try to enforce rules with punitive or inconsistent discipline. As we saw in Chapter 8, these child-rearing techniques spark defiance in children and may promote high-risk behavior. Highly active impulsive children, many of whom are boys, and poverty-stricken children remain especially susceptible to injury (Schwebel et al., 2004). The greatest challenge for injury control programs is reaching these children and reducing the dangers to which they are exposed.

Motor Development and Play

Visit a park on a pleasant weekend afternoon and watch several preschool and school-age children at play. You will see that gains in body size and muscle strength support improved motor coordination in middle childhood. And greater cognitive and social maturity permit older children to use their new motor skills in more complex ways. A major change in children's play takes place at this time.

Gross Motor Development

During the school years, running, jumping, hopping, and ball skills become more refined. Third to sixth graders burst into sprints as they race across the playground, jump quickly over rotating ropes, engage in intricate patterns of hopscotch, kick and dribble soccer balls, bat at balls pitched by their classmates, and balance adeptly as they walk heel-to-toe across narrow ledges. These diverse skills reflect gains in four basic motor capacities:

- *Flexibility.* Compared with preschoolers, school-age children are physically more pliable and elastic, a difference that can be seen as children swing a bat, kick a ball, jump over a hurdle, and execute tumbling routines.

- *Balance.* Improved balance supports many athletic skills, including running, hopping, skipping, throwing, kicking, and the rapid changes of direction required in many team sports.

- *Agility.* Quicker and more accurate movements are evident in the fancy footwork of dance and cheerleading and in the forward, backward, and sideways motions older children use as they dodge opponents in tag and soccer.

- *Force.* Older youngsters can throw and kick a ball harder and propel themselves farther off the ground when running and jumping than they could at earlier ages (Haywood & Getchell, 2001).

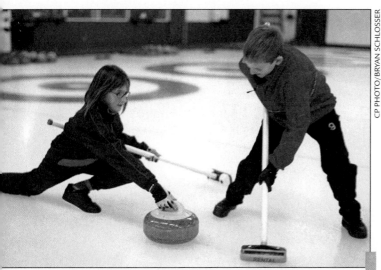

This 10-year-old boy and his older sister in Regina, Saskatchewan, go curling. Improved flexibility, balance, agility, and force along with more efficient information processing support the athletic skills needed to play this precision team sport, popular in Canada, which requires a high degree of strategic thinking.

Along with body growth, more efficient information processing plays a vital role in improved motor performance. Younger children often have difficulty with skills that require rapid responding, such as batting and dribbling. Steady gains in reaction time occur, with 11-year-olds responding twice as quickly as 5-year-olds. The capacity to react only to relevant information also increases (Band et al., 2000; Kail, 2003). Because 6- and 7-year-olds are seldom successful at batting a thrown ball, T-ball is more appropriate than baseball at this

age. Likewise, handball, four-square, and kickball should precede instruction in tennis, basketball, and football.

Fine Motor Development

Fine motor development also improves over the school years. On rainy afternoons, Joey and Lizzie experimented with yo-yos, built model airplanes, and wove potholders on small looms. Like many children, they took up musical instruments, which demand considerable fine motor control.

By age 6, most children can print the alphabet, their first and last names, and the numbers from 1 to 10 with reasonable clarity. Their writing is large, however, because they make strokes with the entire arm rather than just the wrist and fingers. Children usually master uppercase letters first because their horizontal and vertical motions are easier to control than the small curves of the lowercase alphabet. Legibility of writing gradually increases as children produce more accurate letters with uniform height and spacing. These improvements prepare children for mastering cursive writing by third grade.

Children's drawings show dramatic gains in middle childhood. By the end of the preschool years, children can accurately copy many two-dimensional shapes, and they integrate these into their drawings. Some depth cues have also begun to appear, such as making distant objects smaller than near ones (Braine et al., 1993). Around 9 to 10 years, the third dimension is clearly evident through overlapping objects, diagonal placement, and converging lines. Furthermore, as Figure 9.4 shows, school-age children not only depict objects in considerable detail but also relate them to one another as part of an organized whole (Case, 1998; Case & Okamoto, 1996).

■ **FIGURE 9.4 Increase in organization, detail, and depth cues in school-age children's drawings.** Compare both drawings to the one by a 6-year-old on page 226. In the drawing on the left, an 8-year-old depicts her family—father, mother, and three children. Notice how all parts are depicted in relation to one another, and the human figures are given much more detail. (The artist is your author, as a third grader. In the drawing, Laura can be found between her older sister and younger brother.) Integration of depth cues increases dramatically over the school years, as shown in the drawing on the right, by a 10-year-old artist from Singapore. Here, depth is indicated by overlapping objects, diagonal placement, and converging lines, as well as by making distant objects smaller than near ones.

Sex Differences

Sex differences in motor skills that appeared during the pre-school years extend into middle childhood and, in some instances, become more pronounced. Girls remain ahead in the fine motor area, including handwriting and drawing. They also maintain an edge in skipping, jumping, and hopping, which depend on balance and agility. But boys outperform girls on all other gross motor skills, and in throwing and kicking, the gender gap is large (Cratty, 1986; Haywood & Getchell, 2001).

School-age boys' genetic advantage in muscle mass is not large enough to account for their gross motor superiority. Rather, the social environment plays a larger role. Research confirms that parents hold higher expectations for boys' athletic performance, and children readily absorb these messages. From first through twelfth grades, girls are less positive than boys about the value of sports and their own sports ability—differences explained in part by parental beliefs (Fredricks & Eccles, 2002). In one study, boys more often stated that it was vital to their parents that they participate in athletics. These attitudes affected children's self-confidence and behavior. Girls saw themselves as having less talent at sports and, by sixth grade, devoted less time than boys to athletics (Eccles & Harold, 1991). At the same time, girls and older school-age children regard boys' advantage in sports as unjust. They indicate, for example, that coaches should spend equal time with children of each sex and that female sports should command just as much media attention as male sports (Solomon & Bredemeier, 1999).

Clearly, steps must be taken to increase girls' self-confidence, participation, and sense of fair treatment in athletics. Educating parents about the minimal differences between school-age boys' and girls' physical capacities and sensitizing them to unfair biases against promotion of girls' athletic ability may help. And greater emphasis on skill training for girls, along with increased attention to their athletic achievements, is likely to increase their involvement and performance. As a positive sign, compared with a generation ago, many more girls now participate in individual and team sports such as gymnastics and soccer (National Council of Youth Sports, 2002; Sport Canada, 2003). Middle childhood is a crucial time to encourage girls' sports participation because during this time, children start to discover what they are good at and make some definite skill commitments.

Games with Rules

The physical activities of school-age children reflect an important advance in the quality of their play: Games with rules become common. Children around the world engage in an enormous variety of informally organized games, including variants on popular sports such as soccer, baseball, and basketball. In addition to the best-known childhood games, such as tag, jacks, and hopscotch, children have also invented hundreds of other games, including red rover, statues, leapfrog, kick the can, and prisoner's base (Kirchner, 2000).

Is this Little League coach careful to encourage rather than criticize? Does he emphasize teamwork, fair play, courtesy, and skill development over winning? These factors determine whether or not adult-organized sports are pleasurable, constructive experiences for children.

Children's gains in perspective taking—in particular, the ability to understand the roles of several players in a game—permit this transition to rule-oriented games. These play experiences, in turn, contribute greatly to emotional and social development. Child-invented games usually rely on simple physical skills and a sizable element of luck. As a result, they rarely become contests of individual ability. Instead, they permit children to try out different styles of cooperating, competing, winning, and losing with little personal risk. Also, in their efforts to organize a game, children discover why rules are necessary and which ones work well. In fact, children often spend as much time working out how a game should proceed as playing the game itself! As we will see in Chapter 10, these experiences help children construct more mature concepts of fairness and justice.

Partly because of parents' concerns about safety and the attractions of TV and video and computer games, today's children devote less time to informal outdoor play. At the same time, organized sports, such as Little League baseball and soccer and hockey leagues, have expanded tremendously, filling many hours that children used to spend gathering on sidewalks and playgrounds. About half of North American children—60 percent of boys and 40 percent of girls—participate in organized sports at some time between ages 5 and 14 (National Council of Youth Sports, 2002; Sport Canada, 2003).

Research indicates that for most children, playing on a community athletic team is associated with greater social competence (Fletcher, Nickerson, & Wright, 2003). In some cases, though, the arguments of critics—that youth sports overemphasize competition and substitute adult control for children's natural experimentation with rules and strategies—are valid. Children who join teams so early that the necessary skills are

Providing Developmentally Appropriate Organized Sports in Middle Childhood

Applying What We Know

Build on children's interests.	Permit children to select from among appropriate activities the ones that suit them best. Do not push children into sports they do not enjoy.
Teach age-appropriate skills.	For children younger than age 9, emphasize basic skills, such as kicking, throwing, and batting, and simplified games that grant all participants adequate playing time.
Emphasize enjoyment.	Permit children to progress at their own pace and to play for the fun of it, whether or not they become expert athletes.
Limit the frequency and length of practices.	Adjust practice time to children's attention spans and need for unstructured time with peers, with family, and for homework. Two practices a week, each no longer than 30 minutes for younger school-age children and 60 minutes for older school-age children, are sufficient.
Focus on personal and team improvement.	Emphasize effort, skill gains, and teamwork rather than winning. Avoid criticism for errors and defeat, which promotes anxiety and avoidance of athletics.
Discourage unhealthy competition.	Avoid all-star games and championship ceremonies that recognize individuals. Instead, acknowledge all participants.
Permit children to contribute to rules and strategies.	Involve children in decisions aimed at ensuring fair play and teamwork. To strengthen desirable responses, reinforce compliance rather than punishing noncompliance.

beyond their abilities soon lose interest. Coaches and parents who criticize rather than encourage and who react angrily to defeat can prompt intense anxiety in some children, setting the stage for emotional difficulties and early athletic dropout, not elite performance (Marsh & Daigneault, 1999; Tofler, Knapp, & Drell, 1998). See Applying What We Know above for ways to ensure that athletic leagues provide children with positive learning experiences.

Shadows of Our Evolutionary Past

While watching children in your city park, notice how they sometimes wrestle, roll, hit, and run after one another, alternating roles while smiling and laughing. This friendly chasing and play-fighting is called **rough-and-tumble play.** It emerges in the preschool years and peaks in middle childhood, and children in many cultures engage in it with peers whom they like especially well (Pellegrini, 2004).

Children's rough-and-tumble play resembles the social behavior of many other young mammals. It seems to originate in parents' physical play with babies, especially fathers with sons (see page 203 in Chapter 6). Rough-and-tumble play is also more common among boys, probably because prenatal exposure to androgens (male sex hormones) predisposes boys toward active play (see Chapter 8).

In our evolutionary past, rough-and-tumble play may have been important for developing fighting skill (Power, 2000). It also helps children establish a **dominance hierarchy**—a stable ordering of group members that predicts who will win when conflict arises. Observations of arguments, threats, and physical attacks between children reveal a consistent lineup of winners and losers that becomes increasingly stable in middle childhood, especially among boys. Children seem to use play-fighting as a safe context to assess the strength

of a peer before challenging that peer's dominance (Pellegrini & Smith, 1998).

As children reach puberty, individual differences in strength become apparent, and rough-and-tumble play declines. When it does occur, its meaning changes: Adolescent boys' rough-and-tumble is linked to aggression (Pellegini, 2003). Unlike children, teenage rough-and-tumble players "cheat," hurting their opponent. In explanation, boys often say that they are retaliating, apparently to reestablish dominance among their peers. Thus, a play behavior that limits aggression in childhood becomes a context for hostility in adolescence.

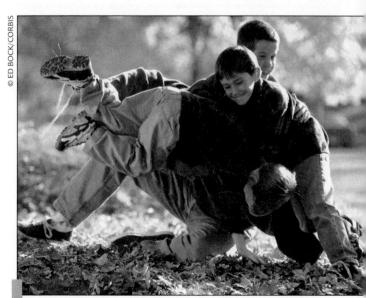

© ED BOCK/CORBIS

This father and his sons engage in rough-and-tumble play, which can be distinguished from aggression by its good-natured quality. In our evolutionary past, rough-and-tumble may have been important for promoting fighting skill and dominance hierarchies.

Physical Education

Physical activity and games support many aspects of children's development—health, sense of self-worth, and the cognitive and social skills necessary for getting along with others. Yet only 50 percent of U.S. elementary schools require physical education, a figure that drops to 25 percent in middle school and to less than 10 percent in high school. The average American school-age child gets only 20 minutes of physical education a week. Canadian children fare better, averaging 2 hours per week (Canadian Fitness & Lifestyle Research Institute, 2003; U.S. Department of Health and Human Services, 2005q). But in both nations, physical inactivity is pervasive. Among North American 5- to 17-year-olds, only about 40 percent of girls and 50 percent of boys are active enough for good health—that is, engage in at least 30 minutes of vigorous aerobic activity and 1 hour of walking per day.

Many experts believe that schools should not only offer more frequent physical education classes but also change the content of these programs. Training in competitive sports, often a high priority, is unlikely to reach the least physically fit youngsters, who hang back from activities demanding a high level of skill. Instead, programs should emphasize enjoyable, informal games and individual exercise—pursuits most likely to endure. Furthermore, children of varying skill levels are more likely to sustain physical activities when teachers focus on each child's personal progress and contribution to team accomplishment (Connor, 2003). Then physical education fosters a healthy sense of self while satisfying school-age children's need for relatedness.

Physically fit children tend to become active adults who reap many benefits (Dennison et al., 1998; Tammelin et al., 2003). These include greater physical strength; resistance to many illnesses, from colds and flu to cancer, diabetes, and heart disease; enhanced psychological well-being; and a longer life.

Ask Yourself

Review
What aspects of physical growth account for the long-legged appearance of many 8- to 12-year-olds?

Connect
Select one of the following health problems of middle childhood: myopia, obesity, asthma, or unintentional injuries. Explain how both genetic and environmental factors contribute to it.

Apply
Nine-year-old Allison thinks she isn't good at sports, and she doesn't like physical education class. Suggest some strategies her teacher can use to improve her pleasure and involvement in physical activity.

Reflect
Did you participate in organized sports as a child? What kind of climate for learning did coaches and parents create? What impact do you think your experiences had on your development?

🍂 Cognitive Development

Finally!" Lizzie exclaimed the day she entered first grade. "Now I get to go to real school, just like Joey!" Rena remembered how 6-year-old Lizzie had walked confidently into her classroom, pencils, crayons, and writing pad in hand, ready for a more disciplined approach to learning than she had experienced in early childhood.

Lizzie was entering a whole new world of challenging mental activities. In a single morning, she and her classmates wrote in journals, met in reading groups, worked on addition and subtraction, and sorted leaves gathered on the playground for a science project. As Lizzie and Joey moved through the elementary school grades, they tackled increasingly complex tasks and became more accomplished at reading, writing, math skills, and general knowledge of the world. To understand the cognitive attainments of middle childhood, we turn to research inspired by Piaget's theory and by the information-processing perspective. And we look at expanding definitions of intelligence that help us appreciate individual differences.

Piaget's Theory: The Concrete Operational Stage

When Lizzie visited my child development class as a 4-year-old, Piaget's conservation problems easily confused her (see Chapter 7, page 230). For example, when water was poured from a tall, narrow container into a short, wide one, she insisted that the amount of water had changed. But when Lizzie returned at age 8, she found these tasks easy. "Of course it's the same!" she exclaimed. "The water's shorter but it's also wider. Pour it back," she instructed the college student who was interviewing her. "You'll see, it's the same amount!"

Concrete Operational Thought

Lizzie has entered Piaget's **concrete operational stage,** which extends from about 7 to 11 years and marks a major turning point in cognitive development. Thought is far more logical, flexible, and organized than it was earlier.

■ **Conservation.** The ability to pass *conservation tasks* provides clear evidence of *operations*—mental actions that obey logical rules. Notice how Lizzie is capable of *decentration*, focusing on several aspects of a problem and relating them, rather than centering on just one. Lizzie also demonstrates **reversibility,** the capacity to think through a series of steps and then mentally reverse direction, returning to the starting point. Recall from Chapter 7 that reversibility is part of every logical operation. It is solidly achieved in middle childhood.

■ **Classification.** Between ages 7 and 10, children pass Piaget's *class inclusion problem* (see page 231). This indicates that they are more aware of classification hierarchies and can

An improved ability to categorize underlies children's interest in collecting objects during middle childhood. These four older school-age boys enjoy trading baseball cards from their extensive, carefully sorted collections.

focus on relations between a general category and two specific categories at the same time—that is, three relations at once (Hodges & French, 1988; Ni, 1998). Collections—stamps, coins, baseball cards, rocks, bottle caps, and more—become common in middle childhood. At age 10, Joey spent hours sorting and resorting his large box of baseball cards. At times he grouped them by league and team, at other times by playing position and batting average. He could separate the players into a variety of classes and subclasses and easily rearrange them.

■ **Seriation.** The ability to order items along a quantitative dimension, such as length or weight, is called **seriation.** To test for it, Piaget asked children to arrange sticks of different lengths from shortest to longest. Older preschoolers can put the sticks in a row, but they do so haphazardly, making many errors. In contrast, 6- to 7-year-olds create the series efficiently, according to an orderly plan—beginning with the smallest stick, then moving to the next largest, and so on.

The concrete operational child can also seriate mentally, an ability called **transitive inference.** In a well-known transitive inference problem, Piaget showed children pairings of differently colored sticks. From observing that Stick A is longer than Stick B and Stick B is longer than Stick C, children must make the mental inference that A is longer than C. Like Piaget's class inclusion task, transitive inference requires children to integrate three relations at once—in this instance, A–B, B–C, and A–C. When researchers take steps to ensure that children remember the premises (A–B and B–C), 7- to 8-year-olds can grasp transitive inference (Andrews & Halford, 1998; Wright & Dowker, 2002).

■ **Spatial Reasoning.** Piaget found that school-age youngsters have a more accurate understanding of space than preschoolers. Let's consider children's **cognitive maps**—their mental representations of familiar large-scale spaces, such as neighborhood or school. Drawing a map of a large-scale space

requires considerable perspective-taking skill. Because the entire space usually cannot be seen at once, children must infer its overall layout by relating its separate parts.

Preschoolers and young school-age children display *landmarks* on the maps they draw, but their placement is fragmented. They do better when asked to place stickers showing the location of desks and people on a map of their classroom. But if the map is rotated relative to the orientation of the classroom, they have difficulty (Liben & Downs, 1993). Around age 8 to 10, maps become better organized, showing landmarks along an *organized route of travel.* At the same time, children become able to give clear, well-organized instructions for getting from one place to another by using a "mental walk" strategy—imagining another person's movements along a route (Gauvain & Rogoff, 1989). At the end of middle childhood, children form an *overall view of a large-scale space.* And they readily draw and read maps when the orientation of the map and the space it represents do not match (Liben, 1999).

Cultural frameworks also influence children's map making. In many non-Western communities, people rarely use maps for way-finding but rely on information from neighbors, street vendors, and shopkeepers. Also, compared to their Western agemates, non-Western children less often ride in cars and more often walk, which results in intimate neighborhood knowledge. When a researcher had older school-age children in small cities in India and in the United States draw maps of their neighborhoods, the Indian children represented a rich array of landmarks and aspects of social life, such as people and vehicles, in a small area surrounding their home. The American children, in contrast, drew a more formal, extended space and highlighted main streets and key directions (north–south, east–west) but included few landmarks (see Figure 9.5 on page 300) (Parameswaran, 2003). Although the American children's maps scored higher in cognitive maturity, cultural interpretations of the task accounted for this difference. When asked to create a map to "help people find their way," the Indian children drew spaces as far-reaching and organized as the American children's.

Limitations of Concrete Operational Thought

Although school-age children are far more capable problem solvers than they were as preschoolers, concrete operational thinking suffers from one important limitation: Children think in an organized, logical fashion only when dealing with concrete information they can perceive directly. Their mental operations work poorly with abstract ideas—ones not apparent in the real world. Children's solutions to transitive inference problems provide a good illustration. When shown pairs of sticks of unequal length, Lizzie easily figured out that if stick A is longer than stick B and stick B is longer than stick C, then stick A is longer than stick C. But she had great difficulty with a hypothetical version of this task: "Susan is taller than Sally and Sally is taller than Mary. Who is the tallest?" Not until age 11 or 12 can children solve this problem.

■ **FIGURE 9.5 Maps drawn by older school-age children from India and the United States.** (a) The Indian child depicted many landmarks and features of social life in a small area near her home. (b) The U.S. child drew a more extended space and highlighted main streets and key directions but included few landmarks and people. (From G. Parameswaran, 2003, "Experimenter Instructions as a Mediator in the Effects of Culture on Mapping One's Neighborhood," *Journal of Environmental Psychology, 23*, pp. 415–416. © 2003 Elsevier Ltd. Reprinted by permission.)

(a) (b)

That logical thought is at first tied to immediate situations helps account for a special feature of concrete operational reasoning: School-age children master Piaget's concrete operational tasks step by step, not all at once. For example, they usually grasp conservation of number before conservation of length, mass, and liquid. This *continuum of acquisition* (or gradual mastery) of logical concepts is another indication of the limitations of concrete operational thinking (Fischer & Bidell, 1991). School-age children do not come up with general logical principles and then apply them to all relevant situations. Instead, they seem to work out the logic of each problem separately.

Follow-Up Research on Concrete Operational Thought

According to Piaget, brain development combined with experience in a rich and varied external world should lead children everywhere to reach the concrete operational stage. Yet recent evidence indicates that specific cultural and school practices have much to do with mastery of Piagetian tasks (Rogoff, 2003; Rogoff & Chavajay, 1995). And information-processing research helps explain the gradual mastery of logical concepts in middle childhood.

■ **The Impact of Culture and Schooling.** In tribal and village societies, conservation is often delayed. For example, among the Hausa of Nigeria, who live in small agricultural settlements and rarely send their children to school, even the most basic conservation tasks—number, length, and liquid—are not understood until age 11 or later (Fahrmeier, 1978). This suggests that taking part in relevant everyday activities helps children master conservation and other Piagetian problems (Light & Perrett-Clermont, 1989). Joey and Lizzie, for example, think of fairness in terms of equal distribution—a value emphasized in their culture. They frequently divide materials, such as

crayons, Halloween treats, and lemonade, equally among their friends. Because they often see the same quantity arranged in different ways, they grasp conservation early.

The very experience of going to school seems to promote mastery of Piagetian tasks. When children of the same age are tested, those who have been in school longer do better on transitive inference problems (Artman & Cahan, 1993). Opportunities to seriate objects, to learn about order relations, and to remember the parts of complex problems are probably responsible. Yet certain informal nonschool experiences can also foster operational thought. Around age 7 to 8, Zinacanteco Indian girls of southern Mexico, who learn to weave elaborately

This Zinacanteco Indian girl of southern Mexico learns the centuries-old practice of backstrap weaving. Although North American children perform better on Piaget's tasks, Zinacanteco children are far more adept at the complex mental transformations required to figure out how warp strung on a loom will turn out as woven cloth.

designed fabrics as an alternative to schooling, engage in mental transformations to figure out how a warp strung on a loom will turn out as woven cloth—reasoning expected at the concrete operational stage. North American children of the same age, who do much better than Zinacanteco children on Piagetian tasks, have great difficulty with these weaving problems (Maynard & Greenfield, 2003).

On the basis of such findings, some investigators have concluded that the forms of logic required by Piagetian tasks do not emerge spontaneously but, rather, are heavily influenced by training, context, and cultural conditions. Does this view remind you of Vygotsky's sociocultural theory, discussed in earlier chapters?

■ **An Information-Processing View of Concrete Operational Thought.** The gradual mastery of logical concepts in middle childhood raises a familiar question about Piaget's theory: Is an abrupt stagewise transition to logical thought the best way to describe cognitive development in middle childhood?

Some *neo-Piagetian theorists* argue that the development of operational thinking can best be understood in terms of gains in information-processing speed rather than a sudden shift to a new stage. For example, Robbie Case (1992, 1998) proposed that, with practice, cognitive schemes demand less attention and become more automatic. This frees up space in *working memory* (see page 160) so children can focus on combining old schemes and generating new ones. For instance, the child confronted with water poured from one container to another recognizes that the height of the liquid changes. As this understanding becomes routine, the child notices that the width of the water changes as well. Soon children coordinate these observations, and they conserve liquid. Then, as this logical idea becomes well-practiced, the child transfers it to more demanding situations.

Once the schemes of a Piagetian stage are sufficiently automatic, enough working memory is available to integrate them into an improved representation. As a result, children acquire *central conceptual structures*—networks of concepts and relations that permit them to think more effectively about a wide range of situations (Case, 1996, 1998). The central conceptual structures that emerge from integrating concrete operational schemes are broadly applicable principles that result in increasingly complex, systematic reasoning, which we will discuss in Chapter 11 in the context of formal operational thought.

Case and his colleagues—along with other information-processing researchers—have examined children's performance on a wide variety of tasks, including solving arithmetic problems, understanding stories, drawing pictures, and interpreting social situations. In each task, preschoolers typically focus on only one dimension. In understanding stories, for example, they grasp only a single story line. In drawing pictures, they depict objects separately. By the early school years, children coordinate two dimensions—two story lines in a single plot and drawings that show both the features of objects and their relationships. Around 9 to 11 years, children integrate multiple dimensions (Case, 1998; Halford & Andrews, 2006). Children tell coherent stories with a main plot and several subplots. And

their drawings follow a set of rules for representing perspective and, therefore, include several points of reference, such as near, midway, and far.

Case's theory helps explain why many understandings appear in specific situations at different times rather than being mastered all at once. First, different forms of the same logical insight, such as the various conservation tasks, vary in their processing demands, with those acquired later requiring more space in working memory. Second, children's experiences vary widely. A child who often listens to and tells stories but rarely draws pictures displays more advanced central conceptual structures in storytelling. Compared with Piaget's, Case's theory better accounts for unevenness in cognitive development.

Evaluation of the Concrete Operational Stage

Piaget was correct that school-age children approach many problems in organized, rational ways not possible in early childhood. But disagreement continues over whether this difference occurs because of *continuous* improvement in logical skills or *discontinuous* restructuring of children's thinking (as Piaget's stage idea assumes). Many researchers think that both types of change may be involved (Carey, 1999; Case, 1998; Demetriou et al., 2002; Fischer & Bidell, 1998; Halford, 2002). During the school years, children apply logical schemes to many more tasks. In the process, their thought seems to undergo qualitative change—toward a comprehensive grasp of the underlying principles of logical thought. Piaget himself seems to have recognized this possibility in evidence for gradual mastery of conservation and other tasks. So perhaps some blend of Piagetian and information-processing ideas holds the greatest promise for understanding cognitive development in middle childhood.

Ask Yourself

Review

Children's performance on conservation tasks illustrates a continuum of acquisition of logical concepts. Review the preceding sections and list additional examples of gradual development of logical reasoning.

Apply

Nine-year-old Adrienne spends many hours helping her father build furniture in his woodworking shop. How might this experience facilitate Adrienne's performance on Piagetian seriation problems?

Connect

Explain how advances in perspective taking contribute to school-age children's improved ability to draw and use maps.

Reflect

Which aspects of Piaget's description of the concrete operational child do you accept? Which do you doubt? Explain, citing research evidence.

Information Processing

In contrast to Piaget's focus on overall cognitive change, the information-processing perspective examines separate aspects of thinking. Attention and memory, which underlie every act of cognition, are central concerns in middle childhood, just as they were during infancy and the preschool years. Also, increased understanding of how school-age children process information is being applied to their academic learning—in particular, to reading and mathematics.

Researchers believe that brain development contributes to the following basic changes in information processing that facilitate diverse aspects of thinking:

🖋 *Increases in information-processing speed and capacity.* Time needed to process information on a wide variety of cognitive tasks declines rapidly between ages 6 and 12 (Kail & Park, 1992, 1994). This suggests a biologically based gain in speed of thinking, possibly due to myelination and synaptic pruning in the brain (Kail, 2003). Some researchers believe this greater efficiency contributes to more complex, effective thinking because a faster thinker can hold on to and operate on more information in working memory (Halford & Andrews, 2006; Luna et al., 2004). Indeed, *digit span,* which assesses the basic capacity of working memory (see page 238), improves from about 4 digits at age 7 to 7 digits at age 12 (Kail, 2003).

🖋 *Gains in inhibition.* As indicated in earlier chapters, inhibition—the ability to control internal and external distracting stimuli—improves from infancy on. But additional strides occur in middle childhood as the frontal lobes of the cerebral cortex develop further (Dempster & Corkill, 1999; Luna et al., 2004). Individuals skilled at inhibition can prevent their minds from straying to irrelevant thoughts, a capacity that supports many information-processing skills.

Besides brain development, strategy use contributes to more effective information processing. As we will see, school-age children think far more strategically than preschoolers.

Attention

In middle childhood, attention becomes more selective, adaptable, and planful. First, children become better at deliberately attending to just those aspects of a situation that are relevant to their goals. Researchers study this increasing selectivity of attention by introducing irrelevant stimuli into a task and seeing how well children attend to its central elements. Performance improves sharply between ages 6 and 10 (Goldberg, Maurer, & Lewis, 2001; Lin, Hsiao, & Chen, 1999; Smith et al., 1998).

Second, older children flexibly adapt their attention to task requirements. For example, when asked to sort cards with pictures that vary in both color and shape, children age 5 and older can switch their basis of sorting from color to shape when asked to do so; younger children typically persist in sort-

ing in just one way (Brooks et al., 2003; Zelazo, Frye, & Rapus, 1996). And when given lists of items to learn and allowed to select half for further study, first graders do not choose systematically. But by third grade, children select items they had previously missed (Masur, McIntyre, & Flavell, 1973).

Finally, *planning* improves greatly in middle childhood (Gauvain, 2004; Scholnick, 1995). School-age children scan detailed pictures and written materials for similarities and differences more thoroughly than preschoolers. And on tasks with many parts, they make decisions about what to do first and what to do next in an orderly fashion. As Chapter 7 revealed, children learn much about planning by collaborating with more expert planners. In one study of family interactions, discussions involving planning at ages 4 and 9 predicted planning competence in adolescence (Gauvain & Huard, 1999). The demands of school tasks—and teachers' explanations of how to plan—also contribute to gains in planning.

The selective, adaptable, and planful strategies just considered are crucial for success in school. Unfortunately, however, some children have great difficulty paying attention. See the Biology and Environment box on page 304 for a discussion of the serious learning and behavior problems of children with attention-deficit hyperactivity disorder.

Memory Strategies

As attention improves, so do *memory strategies,* deliberate mental activities we use to store and retain information. When Lizzie had a list of things to learn, such as a phone number or the state capitals of the United States, she immediately used **rehearsal**—repeating the information to herself, a memory strategy that first appears in the early grade school years. Soon after, a second strategy becomes common: **organization**—grouping related items together (for example, all the cities in the same part of the country), an approach that improves recall dramatically (Schneider, 2002).

Perfecting memory strategies requires time and effort. For example, 8-year-old Lizzie rehearsed in a piecemeal fashion. After being given the word *cat* in a list of items, she said, "Cat, cat, cat." But 10-year-old Joey combined previous words with each new item, saying, "Desk, man, yard, cat, cat"—a more effective approach (Kunzinger, 1985). Joey also organized more skillfully, grouping items into fewer categories. And he used organization in a wide range of memory tasks, whereas Lizzie used it only when categorical relations among items were obvious (Bjorklund et al., 1994).

Furthermore, Joey often combined several strategies—for example, organizing items, then stating the category names, and finally rehearsing. The more strategies children use simultaneously and consistently, the better they remember (Hock, Park, & Bjorklund, 1998). Younger school-age children often try out various memory strategies, but they use them less systematically and with less success than older children. Still, the tendency to experiment allows younger children to discover which strategies work best on certain tasks and how to combine strategies effectively. Indeed, children experiment with strategies when faced with many cognitive challenges—an approach that enables them to gradually "home in" on the most effective techniques (Siegler, 1996).

By the end of middle childhood, children start to use **elaboration**—creating a relationship, or shared meaning, between two or more pieces of information that are not members of the same category. For example, if two of the words you must learn are *fish* and *pipe,* you might generate the verbal statement or mental image, "The fish is smoking a pipe." This highly effective memory technique, which requires considerable effort and space in working memory, becomes increasingly common in adolescence and early adulthood (Schneider & Pressley, 1997).

Because organization and elaboration combine items into *meaningful chunks,* they permit children to hold onto much more information and, as a result, further expand working memory. In addition, when children link a new item to information they already know, they can *retrieve* it easily by thinking of other items associated with it. As we will see, this also contributes to improved memory during the school years.

The Knowledge Base and Memory Performance

During middle childhood, the long-term knowledge base grows larger and becomes organized into increasingly elaborate, hierarchically structured networks. This rapid growth of knowledge helps children use strategies and remember (Schneider, 2002). In other words, knowing more about a topic makes new information more meaningful and familiar so it is easier to store and retrieve.

To test this idea, researchers classified fourth graders as either experts or novices in knowledge of soccer, then gave both groups lists of soccer and nonsoccer items to learn. Experts remembered far more items on the soccer list (but not on the nonsoccer list) than nonexperts. And during recall, experts' listing of items was better organized, as indicated by clustering of items into categories (Schneider & Bjorklund, 1992). These findings suggest that highly knowledgeable children organize information in their area of expertise with little or no effort. Consequently, experts can devote more working-memory resources to using recalled information for reasoning and problem solving (Bjorklund & Douglas, 1997).

But knowledge is not the only important factor in children's strategic memory processing. Children who are expert in an area are usually highly motivated. As a result, they not only acquire knowledge more quickly but also *actively use what they know* to add more. In contrast, academically unsuccessful children fail to ask how previously stored information can clarify new material. This, in turn, interferes with the development of a broad knowledge base (Schneider & Bjorklund, 1998). So by the end of the school years, extensive knowledge and use of memory strategies support one another.

Culture, Schooling, and Memory Strategies

Rehearsal, organization, and elaboration are techniques that people usually use when they need to remember information

A father in Kabul, Afghanistan, draws water from a well, and his son distributes it among ceramic pitchers. As the boy engages in this meaningful work, he demonstrates keen memory for relevant information—how to pour without spilling, how much water each pitcher can hold. Nevertheless, he may not perform well on a list-memory task of the kind often given in schools.

for its own sake. On many other occasions, memory occurs as a natural byproduct of participation in daily activities (Rogoff, 2003).

A repeated finding is that people in non-Western cultures who have no formal schooling do not use or benefit from instruction in memory strategies (Rogoff & Chavajay, 1995). Tasks that require children to recall isolated bits of information, which are common in classrooms, motivate children to use memory strategies. In fact, Western children get so much practice with this type of learning that they do not refine other techniques for remembering that rely on cues available in everyday life, such as spatial location and arrangement of objects. Australian-Aboriginal and Guatemalan Mayan children are considerably better at these memory skills (Kearins, 1981; Rogoff, 1986). The development of memory strategies, then, is not just a product of a more competent information-processing system. It also depends on task demands and cultural circumstances.

Biology and Environment

Children with Attention-Deficit Hyperactivity Disorder

While the other fifth graders worked quietly at their desks, Calvin squirmed in his seat, dropped his pencil, looked out the window, fiddled with his shoelaces, and talked aloud. "Hey Joey," he yelled over the heads of several classmates, "wanna play ball after school?" But Joey and the other children weren't eager to play with Calvin. On the playground, Calvin was physically awkward and a poor listener who failed to follow the rules of the game. He had trouble taking turns at bat. In the outfield, he tossed his mitt up in the air and looked elsewhere when the ball came his way. Calvin's desk at school and his room at home were chaotic messes. He often lost pencils, books, and other materials he needed to complete his work, and he had difficulty remembering assignments and when they were due.

Symptoms of ADHD. Calvin is one of 3 to 5 percent of school-age children with **attention-deficit hyperactivity disorder (ADHD)**, which involves inattention, impulsivity, and excessive motor activity resulting in academic and social problems (American Psychiatric Association, 1994). Boys are diagnosed 3 to 9 times more often than girls. However, most girls with ADHD seem to be overlooked, either because their symptoms are less flagrant or because of a gender bias: A difficult, disruptive boy is more likely to be referred for treatment (Abikoff et al., 2002; Biederman et al., 2005).

Children with ADHD cannot stay focused on a task that requires mental effort for more than a few minutes. In addition, they often act impulsively, ignoring social rules and lashing out with hostility when frustrated. Many (but not all) are *hyperactive*. Their excessive motor activity is exhausting for parents and teachers and so irritating to other children that they are quickly rejected. For a child to be diagnosed with ADHD, these symptoms must have appeared before age 7 as a persistent problem.

Because of their difficulty concentrating, children with ADHD score 7 to 15 points lower than other children on intelligence tests (Barkley, 2002a). According to one view that has amassed substantial research support, two related deficits underlie ADHD symptoms: (1) an impairment in executive processing (see page 161 in Chapter 5), which interferes with the child's ability to use thought to guide behavior; and (2) an impairment in inhibition, which makes it difficult to delay action in favor of thought. Consequently, such children do poorly on tasks requiring sustained attention, find it hard to ignore irrelevant information, and have difficulty with memory, planning, reasoning, and problem solving in academic and social situations (Barkley, 2003b).

Origins of ADHD. ADHD runs in families and is highly heritable: Identical twins share it more often than fraternal twins (Rasmussen et al., 2004; Rietvelt et al., 2004). Children with ADHD show abnormal brain functioning, including reduced electrical and blood-flow activity in the frontal lobes of the cerebral cortex and in other areas involved in attention, inhibition of behavior, and other aspects of motor control (Castellanos et al., 2003; Sowell et al., 2002). Also, the brains of children with ADHD grow more slowly and are about 3 percent smaller in overall volume than those of unaffected agemates (Castellanos et al., 2002; Durston et al., 2004). Several genes that affect neural communication have been implicated in the disorder (Biederman & Spencer, 2000; Quist & Kennedy, 2001).

At the same time, ADHD is associated with environmental factors. Exposure to prenatal teratogens—particularly those involving long-term exposure, such as illegal drugs, alcohol, and tobacco—are linked to inattention and hyperactivity (Milberger et al, 1997). Furthermore, children with ADHD are more likely to come from homes in which marriages are unhappy and family stress is high (Bernier & Siegel, 1994). But a stressful home life rarely causes ADHD. Rather,

The School-Age Child's Theory of Mind

During middle childhood, children's *theory of mind*, or set of ideas about mental activities, becomes more elaborate and refined. Recall from Chapter 7 that this awareness of thought is often called *metacognition*. School-age children's improved ability to reflect on their own mental life is another reason that their thinking advances.

Unlike preschoolers, who view the mind as a passive container of information, older children regard it as an active, constructive agent that selects and transforms information (Kuhn, 2000). Consequently, they have a much better understanding of the process of thinking and the impact of psychological factors on performance. School-age children, for example, know that doing well on a task depends on focusing attention—concentrating, wanting to do it, and not being tempted by anything else (Miller & Bigi, 1979). With age, they also become increasingly aware of effective memory strategies and why they work (Alexander et al., 2003). And children gradually grasp relationships between mental activities—for example, that remembering is crucial for understanding and that understanding strengthens memory (Schwanenflugel, Henderson, & Fabricius, 1998).

Furthermore, school-age children's understanding of sources of knowledge expands. They realize that people can extend their knowledge not only by directly observing events the behaviors of these children can contribute to family problems, which intensify the child's preexisting difficulties.

Treating ADHD. Calvin's doctor eventually prescribed stimulant medication, the most common treatment for ADHD. As long as dosage is carefully regulated, these drugs reduce symptoms in 70 percent of children who take them, with benefits for academic performance and peer relations (Greenhill, Halperin, & Abikoff, 1999). Stimulant medication seems to increase activity in the frontal lobes, thereby improving the child's capacity to sustain attention and to inhibit off-task behavior.

In 2006, an advisory panel convened by the U.S. Food and Drug Administration warned that stimulants might impair heart functioning, even causing sudden death in a few individuals, and advocated warning labels describing these potential risks. Debate over the safety of medication for ADHD is likely to intensify. In any case, medication is not enough. Drugs cannot teach children how to compensate for inattention and impulsivity. The most effective treatment approach combines medication with interventions that model and reinforce appropriate academic and social behavior (American Academy of Pediatrics, 2005a). Family intervention is also important. Inattentive, overactive children strain the patience of parents, who

are likely to react punitively and inconsistently—a child-rearing style that strengthens inappropriate behavior. Breaking this cycle through training parents in effective child-rearing skills is as important for children with ADHD as it is for the defiant, aggressive youngsters discussed in Chapter 8. In fact, in 45 to 65 percent of cases, these two sets of behavior problems occur together (Barkley, 2002b).

Some media reports suggest that the number of North American children diagnosed with ADHD has increased greatly. But two large surveys yielded similar overall prevalence rates 20 years ago and today. Nevertheless, the incidence of ADHD is much higher in some communities than others. At times, children are overdiagnosed and unnecessarily medicated because their parents and teachers are impatient with inattentive, active behavior within normal range. In Hong Kong, where academic success is particularly prized, children are diagnosed at more than twice the rate seen in North America. At other times, children are underdiagnosed and do not receive the treatment they need, as occurs in Great Britain, where doctors are hesitant to label a child with ADHD or to prescribe medication (Taylor, 2004).

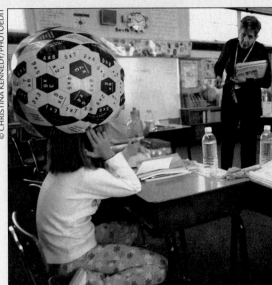

This girl frequently engages in disruptive behavior at school. Children with ADHD have great difficulty staying on task and often act impulsively, ignoring social rules.

ADHD is a lifelong disorder. Affected individuals are at risk for persistent antisocial behavior, depression, and other problems (Barkley, 2003a; Fisher et al., 2002). Adults with ADHD continue to need help structuring their environments, regulating negative emotion, choosing appropriate careers, and understanding their condition as a biological deficit rather than a character flaw.

and talking to others but also by making *mental inferences* (Carpendale & Chandler, 1996; Miller, Hardin, & Montgomery, 2003). This grasp of inference enables knowledge of *false belief* to expand. In several studies, researchers told children complex stories involving one character's belief about a second character's belief. Then the children answered questions about what the first character thought the second character would do (see Figure 9.6 on page 306). By age 7, children were aware that people form beliefs about other people's beliefs and that these second-order beliefs can be wrong! Once children appreciate *second-order false belief,* they can better pinpoint the reasons that another person arrived at a certain belief (Astington, Pelletier, & Homer, 2002). This assists them greatly in understanding others' perspectives.

School-age children's capacity for more complex thinking contributes greatly to their more reflective, process-oriented view of the mind. But experiences that foster awareness of mental activities are also involved. In a study of rural children of Cameroon, Africa, those who attended school performed much better on theory-of-mind tasks (Vinden, 2002). In school, teachers often call attention to the workings of the mind when they remind children to pay attention, remember mental steps, and evaluate their reasoning. And as children engage in reading, writing, and math, they often use *private speech*, at first speaking out loud and then silently to themselves. As they "hear themselves think," they probably detect many aspects of mental life (Flavell, Green, & Flavell, 1995).

(a)	(b)	(c)
Jason has a letter from a friend. Lisa wants to read the letter, but Jason doesn't want her to. Jason puts the letter under his pillow.	Jason leaves the room to help his mother.	While Jason is gone, Lisa takes the letter and reads it. Jason returns and watches Lisa, but Lisa doesn't see Jason. Then Lisa puts the letter in Jason's desk.

■ **FIGURE 9.6   A second-order false-belief task.** After relating the story in the sequence of pictures, the researcher asks a second-order false-belief question: "Where does Lisa think Jason will look for the letter? Why?" Around age 7, children answer correctly—that Lisa thinks Jason will look under his pillow because Lisa doesn't know that Jason saw her put the letter in the desk. (Adapted form Astington, Pelletier, & Homer, 2002.)

Cognitive Self-Regulation

Although metacognition expands, school-age children often have difficulty putting what they know about thinking into action. They are not yet good at **cognitive self-regulation,** the process of continuously monitoring progress toward a goal, checking outcomes, and redirecting unsuccessful efforts. For example, Lizzie knows she should group items when memorizing and that she should reread a complicated paragraph to make sure she understands. But she does not always engage in these activities.

To study cognitive self-regulation, researchers sometimes look at the impact that children's awareness of memory strategies has on how well they remember. By second grade, the more children know about memory strategies, the more they recall—a relationship that strengthens over middle childhood (Pierce & Lange, 2000). And when children apply a strategy consistently, their knowledge of strategies strengthens, resulting in a bidirectional association between metacognition and strategy use that enhances self-regulation (Schlagmüller & Schneider, 2002).

Why does cognitive self-regulation develop gradually? Monitoring learning outcomes is cognitively demanding, requiring constant evaluation of effort and progress. By adolescence, self-regulation is a strong predictor of academic success (Joyner & Kurtz-Costes, 1997). Students who do well in school know when their learning is going well and when it is not. If they encounter obstacles—poor study conditions, a confusing text passage, or an unclear class presentation—they take steps to organize the learning environment, review the material, or turn to other sources of support. This active, purposeful approach contrasts sharply with the passive orientation of students who achieve poorly (Zimmerman & Risemberg, 1997).

Parents and teachers can foster self-regulation. In one study, researchers observed parents instructing their children in problem solving during the summer before third grade. Parents who patiently pointed out important features of the task and suggested strategies had children who, in the classroom, more often discussed ways to approach problems and monitored their own performance (Stright et al., 2002). Explaining the effectiveness of strategies is particularly helpful because it provides a rationale for future action.

Children who acquire effective self-regulatory skills develop a sense of *academic self-efficacy*—confidence in their own ability, which supports future self-regulation (Schunk & Zimmerman, 2003). Unfortunately, some children receive messages from parents and teachers that seriously undermine their academic self-esteem and self-regulatory skills. We will consider these *learned-helpless* children, along with ways to help them, in Chapter 10.

Applications of Information Processing to Academic Learning

Fundamental discoveries about the development of information processing have been applied to children's learning of reading and mathematics. Researchers are identifying the cognitive ingredients of skilled performance, tracing their development, and distinguishing good from poor learners by pinpointing differences in cognitive skills. They hope, as a result, to design teaching methods that will improve children's learning.

■ **Reading.** Reading makes use of many skills at once, taxing all aspects of our information-processing systems. Joey and Lizzie must perceive single letters and letter combinations, translate them into speech sounds, recognize the visual appearance of many common words, hold chunks of text in working memory while interpreting their meaning, and combine the meanings of various parts of a text passage into an understandable whole. In fact, reading is so demanding that most or all of these skills must be done automatically. If one or more are poorly developed, they will compete for space in our limited working memories, and reading performance will decline.

As children make the transition from emergent literacy to conventional reading, language development continues to facilitate their progress. **Phonological awareness**—the ability to reflect on and manipulate the sound structure of spoken language, as indicated by sensitivity to changes in sounds within words and to incorrect pronunciation—strongly predicts reading (and spelling) achievement (Dickinson et al., 2003). It enables children to isolate speech segments and link them with their written symbols. Vocabulary, grammar, and narrative skills are also vital.

Other information-processing activities also contribute to reading proficiency. Gains in speed of information processing permit children to rapidly convert visual symbols into sounds (McBride-Chang & Kail, 2002). And visual scanning and discrimination play important roles and improve with reading experience (Rayner, Pollatsek, & Starr, 2003). Performing all these skills efficiently releases working memory for higher-level activities involved in comprehending the text's meaning.

Until recently, researchers were involved in an intense debate over how to teach beginning reading. On one side were those who take a **whole-language approach.** They argued that reading should be taught in a way that parallels natural language learning. From the beginning, children should be exposed to text in its complete form—stories, poems, letters, posters, and lists—so that they can appreciate the communicative function of written language. According to these experts, as long as reading is kept whole and meaningful, children will be motivated to discover the specific skills they need (Watson, 1989). On the other side were those who advocated a **phonics approach.** In their view, children should be given simplified reading materials and, at first, should be coached on *phonics*—the basic rules for translating written symbols into sounds. Only later, after they have mastered these skills, should they get complex reading material (Rayner & Pollatsek, 1989).

Many studies have resolved this debate by showing that children learn best with a mixture of both approaches. In kindergarten, first, and second grades, teaching that includes phonics boosts reading scores, especially for children who are behind in reading progress (Berninger et al., 2003; Xue & Meisels, 2004). And when teachers combine real reading and writing with teaching of phonics and engage in other excellent teaching practices—encouraging children to tackle reading challenges and integrating reading into all school subjects—first graders show far greater literacy progress (Pressley et al., 2002).

Why might combining phonics with whole language work best? Learning the relationships between letters and sounds enables children to decipher words they have never seen before. Yet if practice in basic skills is overemphasized, children may lose sight of the goal of reading—understanding. Children who read aloud fluently without registering meaning know little about effective reading strategies—for example, that they must read more carefully if they will be tested than if they are reading for pleasure, or that explaining a passage in their own words is a good way to assess comprehension. Providing instruction aimed at increasing knowledge and use of reading strategies enhances reading performance from third grade on (Dickson et al., 1998; Van Keer, 2004).

■ **Mathematics.** Mathematics teaching in elementary school builds on and greatly enriches children's informal knowledge of number concepts and counting. Written notation systems and formal computational procedures enhance children's ability to represent numbers and compute. Over the early elementary school years, children acquire basic math facts through a combination of frequent practice, reasoning about number concepts, and teaching that conveys effective strategies (Alibali, 1999; Canobi, Reeve, & Pattison, 1998). For example, when first graders realize that regardless of the order in which two sets are combined, they yield the same result (2 + 6 = 8 and 6 + 2 = 8), they more often start with the higher digit (6) and count on (7, 8), a strategy that minimizes the work involved. Eventually children retrieve answers automatically and apply this knowledge to more complex problems.

Arguments about how to teach mathematics resemble those about reading. Extensive speeded practice of computational skills is pitted against "number sense," or understanding. Again, a blend of these two approaches is most beneficial. In learning basic math, poorly performing students tend to use cumbersome techniques or try to retrieve answers from memory too soon. Their responses are often wrong because they have not experimented with strategies sufficiently to see which ones are most effective. And on tasks that assess their understanding of math concepts, their performance is weak (Canobi, 2004; Canobi, Reeve, & Pattison, 2003). This suggests that encouraging students to apply strategies and making sure they know why certain strategies work well are essential for solid mastery of basic math.

A similar picture emerges for more complex skills, such as carrying in addition, borrowing in subtraction, and operating with decimals and fractions. When taught by rote, children

Culture and language-based factors contribute to Asian children's skill at mathematics. The abacus supports these Japanese students' understanding of place value. Ones, tens, hundreds, and thousands are each represented by a different column of beads, and calculations are performed by moving the beads to different positions. As children become skilled at using the abacus, they learn to think in ways that help them solve complex arithmetic problems.

cannot apply the procedure to new problems. Instead, they persistently make mistakes, using a "math rule" that they recall incorrectly because they do not understand it (Carpenter et al., 1999). Consider the following subtraction errors:

$$
\begin{array}{r}
427 \\
-\,138 \\
\hline
311
\end{array}
\qquad
\begin{array}{r}
7{,}002 \\
-\,5{,}445 \\
\hline
1{,}447
\end{array}
$$

In the first problem, the child subtracts a smaller from a larger digit, regardless of which is on top. In the second, columns with zeros are skipped in a borrowing operation, and the bottom digit is written as the answer.

When provided with rich opportunities to experiment with problem solving, to grasp the reasons behind strategies, and to evaluate solution techniques, children seldom make such errors. In one study, second graders taught in these ways not only mastered correct procedures but even invented their own successful strategies, some of which were superior to standard, school-taught methods (Fuson & Burghard, 2003).

In Asian countries, students receive a variety of supports for acquiring mathematical knowledge and often excel at math computation and reasoning. For example, use of the metric system helps Asian children grasp place value. The consistent structure of number words in Asian languages (*ten-two* for 12, *ten-three* for 13) also makes this idea clear (Miura & Okamoto, 2003). Furthermore, Asian number words are shorter and more quickly pronounced, thereby increasing the speed of thinking (Geary et al., 1996). Finally, as we will see later in this chapter, compared with lessons in North America, those in Asian classrooms devote more time to exploring math concepts and less to computational drill.

Ask Yourself

Review

Cite evidence that school-age children view the mind as an active, constructive agent.

Apply

After viewing a slide show on endangered species, second and fifth graders were asked to remember as many animals as they could. Explain why fifth graders recalled much more than second graders.

Apply

Lizzie knows that if you have difficulty learning part of a task, you should devote extra attention to that part. But she plays each of her piano pieces from beginning to end instead of practicing the hard parts. What explains Lizzie's failure to engage in cognitive self-regulation?

Reflect

In your own elementary school math education, how much emphasis was placed on computational drill and how much on understanding of concepts? How do you think that balance affected your interest and performance in math?

Individual Differences in Mental Development

In middle childhood, educators rely heavily on intelligence tests for assessing individual differences in mental development. Around age 6, IQ becomes more stable than it was at earlier ages, and it correlates moderately well with academic achievement, typically around .50 to .60 (Brody, 1997). Because IQ predicts school performance, it often enters into educational decisions.

Do intelligence tests accurately assess the school-age child's ability to profit from academic instruction? Let's look closely at this controversial issue.

Defining and Measuring Intelligence

Virtually all intelligence tests provide an overall score (the IQ), along with an array of separate scores measuring specific mental abilities (see page 167 in Chapter 5). But intelligence is a collection of many capacities, not all of which are included on currently available tests (Sternberg et al., 2000). Test designers use a complicated statistical technique called *factor analysis* to identify the various abilities that intelligence tests measure. It identifies which sets of test items cluster together, meaning that test-takers who do well on one item in the cluster tend to do well on the others. Distinct clusters are called *factors,* each of which represents an ability. See Figure 9.7 for items typically included in intelligence tests for children.

The intelligence tests given from time to time in classrooms are *group-administered tests.* They permit large numbers of students to be tested at once and are useful for instructional planning and for identifying children who require more extensive evaluation with *individually administered tests.* Unlike group tests, which teachers can give with minimal training, individually administered tests demand considerable training and experience to give well. The examiner not only considers the child's answers but also observes the child's behavior, noting such reactions as attention to and interest in the tasks and wariness of the adult. These observations provide insight into whether the test score accurately reflects the child's abilities. Two individual tests—the Stanford-Binet and the Wechsler—are often used to identify highly intelligent children and to diagnose children with learning problems.

The modern descendant of Alfred Binet's first successful intelligence test is the *Stanford-Binet Intelligence Scales, Fifth Edition,* for individuals from age 2 to adulthood. In addition to general intelligence, this latest edition assesses five intellectual factors: general knowledge, quantitative reasoning, visual–spatial processing, working memory, and basic information processing (such as speed of analyzing information). Each factor includes both a verbal mode and a nonverbal mode of testing, yielding 10 subtests in all (Roid, 2003). The nonverbal subtests, which do not require spoken language, are especially useful when assessing individuals with limited English, with hearing impairments, or with communication disorders. The

TYPICAL VERBAL ITEMS

Vocabulary	Tell me what *carpet* means.
General Information	What day of the week comes right after Thursday?
Verbal Comprehension	Why do we need police officers?
Similarities	How are a ship and a train alike?
Arithmetic	If a $60 jacket is 25% off, how much does it cost?

TYPICAL PERCEPTUAL- AND SPATIAL-REASONING ITEMS

Block Design — Make these blocks look just like the picture.

Picture Concepts — Choose one object from each row to make a group of objects that goes together.

Spatial Visualization — Which of the boxes on the right can be made from the pattern on the left?

a   b   c   d   e

TYPICAL WORKING-MEMORY ITEMS

Digit Span — Repeat these digits in the same order. Now repeat these digits (a similar series) backward.
2, 6, 4, 7, 1, 8

Letter–Number Sequencing — Repeat these numbers and letters, first giving the numbers, then the letters, each in correct sequence.
8 G 4 B 5 N 2

TYPICAL PROCESSING-SPEED ITEM

Symbol Search — If the shape on the left is the same as any of those on the right, mark YES. If the shape is not the same, mark NO. Work as quickly as you can without making mistakes.

YES   NO

FIGURE 9.7 Test items like those on commonly used intelligence tests for children. The verbal items emphasize culturally loaded, fact-oriented information. The perceptual- and spatial-reasoning, working-memory, and processing-speed items emphasize aspects of information processing and are assumed to assess more biologically based skills.

knowledge and quantitative reasoning factors emphasize culturally loaded, fact-oriented information, such as vocabulary and arithmetic problems. In contrast, the basic information processing, visual–spatial processing, and working-memory factors are assumed to be less culturally biased because they require little specific information (see the spatial visualization item in Figure 9.7).

The *Wechsler Intelligence Scale for Children (WISC-IV)* is the fourth edition of a widely used test for 6- through 16-year-olds (Wechsler, 2003). It measures general intelligence and four broad factors: verbal reasoning, perceptual (or visual–spatial) reasoning, working memory, and processing speed. Each factor is made up of two or three subtests, yielding 10 separate scores

in all. The WISC-IV was designed to downplay culturally dependent knowledge, which is emphasized on only one factor (verbal reasoning). According to the test designers, the result is the most "culture-fair" intelligence test available (Williams, Weis, & Rolfhus, 2003).

The WISC was the first test to be standardized on children representing the total population of the United States, including ethnic minorities. Previous editions have been adapted for children in Canada, where both English and French versions are available.

Recent Efforts to Define Intelligence

As we have seen, mental tests now tap important aspects of information processing. In line with this trend, some researchers are combining the factor-analytic approach to defining intelligence with the information-processing approach. They believe that identifying the cognitive processes responsible for intellectual factors will yield a better understanding of why a particular child does well or poorly and what capacities must be worked on to improve performance. These investigators conduct *componential analyses* of children's mental test scores. This means that they look for relationships between aspects (or components) of information processing and children's intelligence test scores.

Many studies reveal that speed of processing is modestly related to IQ (Deary, 2001). This suggests that individuals whose nervous systems function more efficiently, permitting them to take in and manipulate information quickly, have an edge in intellectual skills. But flexible attention, memory, and reasoning strategies are just as important as efficient thinking in predicting IQ, and they explain some of the association between response speed and good test performance (Lohman, 2000; Miller & Vernon, 1992). Children who apply strategies effectively acquire more knowledge and can retrieve that knowledge rapidly—advantages that seem to carry over to performance on intelligence tests.

The componential approach has one major shortcoming: It regards intelligence as entirely due to causes within the child. Yet throughout this book, we have seen how cultural and situational factors affect children's thinking. Robert Sternberg has expanded the componential approach into a comprehensive theory that regards intelligence as a product of both inner and outer forces.

■ **Sternberg's Triarchic Theory of Successful Intelligence.** As Figure 9.8 on page 310 shows, Sternberg's (1997, 1999, 2002) **triarchic theory of successful intelligence** identifies three broad, interacting intelligences: (1) *analytical intelligence,* or information-processing skills; (2) *creative intelligence,* the capacity to solve novel problems; and (3) *practical intelligence,* application of intellectual skills in everyday situations. Intelligent behavior involves balancing all three intelligences to achieve success in life according to one's personal goals and the requirements of one's cultural community.

Analytical Intelligence. *Analytical intelligence* consists of the information-processing components that underlie all intelligent

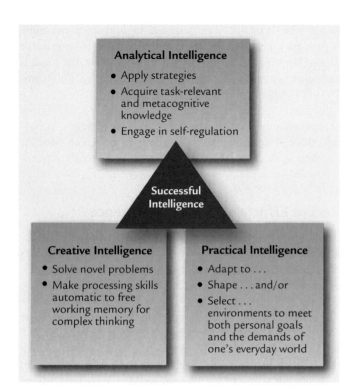

FIGURE 9.8 Sternberg's triarchic theory of successful intelligence. People who behave intelligently balance three interrelated intelligences—analytical, creative, and practical—to achieve success in life, defined by their personal goals and the requirements of their cultural communities.

acts: applying strategies, acquiring task-relevant and metacognitive knowledge, and engaging in self-regulation. On mental tests, however, processing skills are used in only a few of their potential ways, resulting in a far too narrow view of intelligent behavior. As we have seen, children in tribal and village societies do not necessarily perform well on measures of "school" knowledge but thrive when processing information in out-of-school situations that most Westerners would find highly challenging.

Creative Intelligence. In any context, success depends not only on processing familiar information but also on generating useful solutions to new problems. People who are *creative* think more skillfully than others when faced with novelty. Given a new task, they apply their information-processing skills in exceptionally effective ways, rapidly making these skills automatic so that working memory is freed for more complex aspects of the situation; they quickly move to high-level performance. Although all of us are capable of some creativity, only a few individuals excel at generating novel solutions.

Practical Intelligence. Finally, intelligence is a *practical*, goal-oriented activity aimed at *adapting to, shaping,* or *selecting environments.* Intelligent people skillfully *adapt* their thinking to fit with both their desires and the demands of their everyday worlds. When they cannot adapt to a situation, they try to *shape,* or change, it to meet their needs. If they cannot shape it, they *select* new contexts that better match their skills, values, or

goals. Practical intelligence reminds us that intelligent behavior is never culture-free. Children with certain life histories do well at the behaviors required for success on intelligence tests and adapt easily to the testing conditions and tasks. Others, with different life histories, may misinterpret or reject the testing context. Yet such children often display sophisticated abilities in daily life—for example, telling stories, engaging in complex artistic activities, or interacting skillfully with other people.

The triarchic theory highlights the complexity of intelligent behavior and the limitations of current intelligence tests in assessing that complexity. For example, out-of-school, practical forms of intelligence are vital for life success, and they help explain why cultures vary widely in the behaviors they regard as intelligent (Sternberg et al., 2000). When researchers asked ethnically diverse parents for their idea of an intelligent first grader, Caucasian Americans mentioned cognitive traits. In contrast, ethnic minorities (Cambodian, Filipino, Vietnamese, and Mexican immigrants) saw noncognitive capacities—motivation, self-management, and social skills—as particularly important (Okagaki & Sternberg, 1993). According to Sternberg, mental tests can easily underestimate, and even overlook, the intellectual strengths of some children, especially ethnic minorities.

■ **Gardner's Theory of Multiple Intelligences.** In yet another view of how information-processing skills underlie intelligent behavior, Howard Gardner's (1983, 1993, 2000) **theory of multiple intelligences** defines intelligence in terms of distinct sets of processing operations that permit individuals to engage in a wide range of culturally valued activities. Dismissing the idea of general intelligence, Gardner proposes at least eight independent intelligences (see Table 9.1).

Gardner believes that each intelligence has a unique biological basis, a distinct course of development, and different expert, or "end-state," performances. At the same time, he emphasizes that a lengthy process of education is required to transform any raw potential into a mature social role (Torff & Gardner, 1999). Cultural values and learning opportunities

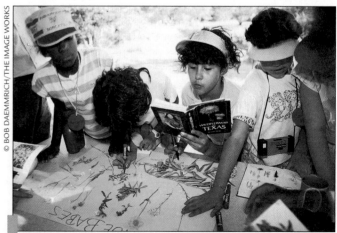

According to Gardner, children are capable of at least eight distinct intelligences. As these children classify wildflowers they collected on a walk through a forest and meadow, they enrich their naturalist intelligence.

Table 9.1	Gardner's Multiple Intelligences	
Intelligence	**Processing Operations**	**End-State Performance Possibilities**
Linguistic	Sensitivity to the sounds, rhythms, and meaning of words and the functions of language	Poet, journalist
Logico-mathematical	Sensitivity to, and capacity to detect, logical or numerical patterns; ability to handle long chains of logical reasoning	Mathematician
Musical	Ability to produce and appreciate pitch, rhythm (or melody), and aesthetic quality of the forms of musical expressiveness	Instrumentalist, composer
Spatial	Ability to perceive the visual–spatial world accurately, to perform transformations on those perceptions, and to re-create aspects of visual experience in the absence of relevant stimuli	Sculptor, navigator
Bodily-kinesthetic	Ability to use the body skillfully for expressive as well as goal-directed purposes; ability to handle objects skillfully	Dancer, athlete
Naturalist	Ability to recognize and classify all varieties of animals, minerals, and plants	Biologist
Interpersonal	Ability to detect and respond appropriately to the moods, temperaments, motivations, and intentions of others	Therapist, salesperson
Intrapersonal	Ability to discriminate complex inner feelings and to use them to guide one's own behavior; knowledge of one's own strengths, weaknesses, desires, and intelligences	Person with detailed, accurate self-knowledge

Sources: Gardner, 1993, 1998a, 2000.

affect the extent to which a child's intellectual strengths are realized and the ways they are expressed.

Gardner's list of abilities has yet to be firmly grounded in research. Neurological evidence for the independence of his abilities is weak. Some exceptionally gifted individuals have abilities that are broad rather than limited to a particular domain (Goldsmith, 2000). And research with mental tests suggests that several of Gardner's intelligences (linguistic, logico-mathematical, and spatial) have common features. Nevertheless, Gardner calls attention to several abilities not measured by intelligence tests. For example, his interpersonal and intrapersonal intelligences include a set of capacities for dealing with people and understanding oneself. As the Lifespan Vista box on page 312 indicates, researchers are attempting to define, measure, and foster these abilities, which are vital for a satisfying, successful life.

Explaining Individual and Group Differences in IQ

When we compare individuals in terms of academic achievement, years of education, and occupational status, it quickly becomes clear that certain sectors of the population are advantaged over others. In trying to explain these differences, researchers have compared the IQ scores of ethnic and SES groups. North American black children score, on average, 15 IQ points below white children, although the difference has been shrinking (Hedges & Nowell, 1995; Loehlin, 2000; Rushton & Jensen, 2003). Hispanic children fall midway between black and white children (Ceci, Rosenblum, & Kumpf, 1998).

The IQ gap between middle-SES and low-SES children is about 9 points. SES accounts for some, but not all, of the black–white IQ difference. Controlling for parental education and income reduces the black–white IQ gap by one-third to one-half (Brooks-Gunn et al., 2003; Smith, Duncan, & Lee, 2003). Of course, considerable variation exists *within* each ethnic and SES group. Still, these group differences in IQ are large enough and their consequences serious enough that they cannot be ignored.

In the 1970s, the IQ nature–nurture controversy escalated after psychologist Arthur Jensen (1969) published a controversial monograph entitled, "How Much Can We Boost IQ and Scholastic Achievement?" Jensen argued—and still maintains—that heredity is largely responsible for individual, ethnic, and SES variations in intelligence (Jensen, 1998, 2001). His work sparked an outpouring of responses and research studies. The controversy was rekindled by Richard Herrnstein and Charles Murray in *The Bell Curve* (1994). Like Jensen, these authors argued that the contribution of heredity to individual and SES differences in IQ is substantial. And although they did not arrive at a firm conclusion, they implied that heredity plays a sizable role in the black–white IQ gap. Let's look closely at some important evidence.

■ **Nature versus Nurture.** In Chapter 2, we introduced the *heritability estimate*. Recall that heritabilities are obtained from *kinship studies,* which compare family members. The most powerful evidence on the role of heredity in IQ involves twin comparisons. The IQ scores of identical twins (who share all their genes) are more similar than those of fraternal twins (who are genetically no more alike than ordinary siblings). On the basis of this and other kinship evidence, researchers estimate that about half the differences in IQ among children can be traced to their genetic makeup.

A Lifespan Vista

Social and Emotional Intelligence

During recess, Muriel handed a birthday party invitation to every fifth-grade girl except Claire, who looked on sadly as her classmates chattered about the party. But one of Muriel's friends, Jessica, appeared troubled. Pulling Muriel aside, she exclaimed, "Why'd you do that? You hurt Claire's feelings—you embarrassed her! If you bring invitations to school, you've got to give everybody one!" And after school, Jessica offered these comforting words to Claire: "If you aren't invited, I'm not going, either!"

Jessica's IQ is only slightly above average, but she excels at acting wisely in social situations. Although early theorists of mental abilities recognized the existence of *social intelligence,* they gave it scant attention. Only in the 1960s did researchers construct the first tests of social aptitude. Test items assessed the capacity of adolescents and adults to detect others' thoughts and feelings and to come up with effective solutions to social problems. Although studies reported positive correlations between social scores and IQ, these were modest. And factor analyses revealed that social intelligence, like nonsocial intelligence, is made up of diverse abilities (Kihlstrom & Cantor, 2000). Jessica, for example, takes Claire's perspective, communicates sensitively, displays mature morality, and expresses herself confidently.

Today, abilities formerly called social intelligence are labeled *emotional intelligence*—a term that has captured public attention because of popular books suggesting that it is an overlooked set of skills that can greatly improve life success (Goleman, 1995, 1998). According to one influential definition, **emotional intelligence** refers to individual differences in the capacity to process and adapt to emotional information (Salovey & Pizzaro, 2003). To measure it, researchers have devised items that tap various aspects of emotional competence. One test requires people to identify and rate the strength of emotions expressed in photographs of faces (perceiving emotions), to reason about emotions in social situations (understanding emotions), and to evaluate the effectiveness of strategies for controlling negative emotions (regulating emotions). Factor analyses of the scores of hundreds of test-takers identified several emotional abilities as well as a higher-order general factor (Mayer, Salovey, & Caruso, 2003).

Like social intelligence, emotional intelligence is modestly related to IQ. It also is positively associated with self-esteem, empathy, prosocial behavior, and life satisfaction and negatively associated with aggression and drug taking among adolescents and adults (Bohnert, Crnic, & Lim, 2003; Law et al, 2004; Wilhelm, 2005). In the workplace, emotional intelligence predicts many aspects of success, including leadership, work-group cooperation, and job performance (Abraham, 2005).

Only a few assessments of emotional intelligence are available for children. These require careful training of teachers in observing and recording children's emotional skills during everyday activities, gathering information from parents, and taking ethnic backgrounds into account (Denham, 2005; Denham & Burton, 2003). As more and better measures are devised, they may help identify children with weak social and emotional competencies who would profit from intervention. But some researchers worry that emotional ability scores will lead psychologists and educators to make simplistic comparisons between children and to lose sight of the fact that the adaptiveness of emotional and social behavior often varies across situations (Saarni, 2000).

The concepts of social and emotional intelligence have increased teachers' awareness that providing experiences that meet students' social and emotional needs can improve their adjustment (Graczyk et al., 2000). Lessons that teach emotion understanding, respect and caring for others, strategies for regulating emotion, and resistance to unfavorable peer pressure—using active learning techniques that provide skill practice both in and out of the classroom—are becoming more common (Goetz et al., 2005).

© DAVID YOUNG-WOLFF/PHOTOEDIT

The child on the left displays high emotional intelligence as she accurately reads her friend's sadness and offers comfort. Because emotional intelligence is positively associated with self-esteem and prosocial behavior, teachers are increasingly providing lessons aimed at promoting emotional and social skills.

Recall, however, that heritabilities risk overestimating genetic influences and underestimating environmental influences. Although these measures offer convincing evidence that genes contribute to IQ, disagreement persists over how large the role of heredity really is (Grigorenko, 2000; Plomin, 2003). And heritability estimates do not reveal the complex processes through which genes and experiences influence intelligence as children develop.

Compared with heritabilities, adoption studies offer a wider range of information. In one investigation, children of two extreme groups of biological mothers—those with IQs below 95 and those with IQs above 120—were adopted at birth by parents well above average in income and education. During the school years, the children of the low-IQ biological mothers scored above average in IQ, indicating that test performance can be greatly improved by an advantaged home life. But they did not do as well as children of high-IQ biological mothers placed in similar adoptive families (Loehlin, Horn, & Willerman, 1997). Adoption research confirms that heredity and environment contribute jointly to IQ.

Some intriguing adoption research sheds light on the black–white IQ gap. When African-American children were placed in economically well-off homes during the first year of life, they scored high on intelligence tests. In two such studies, adopted black children attained mean IQs of 110 and 117 by middle childhood—20 to 30 points higher than the typical scores of children growing up in low-income black communities (Moore, 1986; Scarr & Weinberg, 1983). The IQs of black adoptees declined in adolescence, perhaps because of the challenges faced by minority teenagers in forming an ethnic identity that blends their birth and adoptive backgrounds. When this process is filled with emotional turmoil, it can dampen motivation on tests and in school (DeBerry, Scarr, & Weinberg, 1996; Waldman, Weinberg, & Scarr, 1994). Still, the black adoptees remained above the IQ average for low-SES African Americans.

Adoption findings do not completely resolve questions about ethnic differences in IQ. Nevertheless, the IQ gains of black children "reared in the culture of the tests and schools" are consistent with a wealth of evidence that poverty severely depresses the intelligence of ethnic minority children.

■ **Cultural Influences.** A controversial question raised about ethnic differences in IQ has to do with whether they result from *test bias*. If a test samples knowledge and skills that not all groups of children have had equal opportunity to learn, or if the testing situation impairs the performance of some groups but not others, then the resulting score is a biased, or unfair, measure.

Some experts reject the idea that intelligence tests are biased, claiming that they are intended to represent success in the common culture. According to this view, because IQ predicts academic achievement equally well for majority and minority children, IQ tests are fair to both groups (Brown, Reynolds, & Whitaker, 1999; Jensen, 2002). Others take a broader view of test bias. They believe that lack of exposure to certain communication styles and knowledge, and negative stereotypes about the test-taker's ethnic group, can undermine children's performance (Ceci & Williams, 1997; Sternberg, 2002).

Communication Styles. Ethnic minority families often foster unique language skills that do not match the expectations of most classrooms and testing situations. In one study, a researcher spent many hours observing in low-SES black homes in a southeastern U.S. city (Heath, 1990). She found that African-American parents rarely asked their children knowledge-training questions ("What color is it?" "What's this story about?") that resemble the questioning style of middle-SES white parents and of tests and classrooms. Instead, the

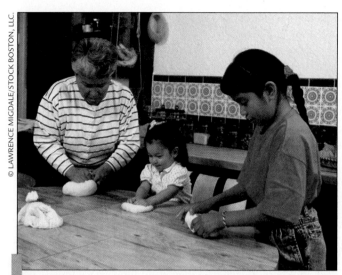

An American Pueblo grandmother and her granddaughters work smoothly and efficiently on the same aspect of a task—making bread—until it is complete. Like many ethnic minority parents with little education, this grandmother uses a collaborative style of communication with her granddaughters. Because these children are not accustomed to the hierarchical style of communication typical of classrooms, they may do poorly on tests and assignments.

black parents asked only "real" questions, ones that they themselves could not answer. Often these were analogy questions ("What's that like?") or story-starter questions ("Didja hear Miss Sally this morning?") that called for elaborate responses about personal experiences and had no "right" answer.

These experiences lead low-SES black children to develop complex verbal skills at home, such as storytelling and exchanging quick-witted remarks. But their language emphasizes emotional and social concerns rather than facts about the world. Not surprisingly, black children may be confused by the "objective" questions they encounter on tests and in classrooms.

Furthermore, many ethnic minority parents without extensive schooling prefer a *collaborative style of communication* when completing tasks with children. They work together in a coordinated, fluid way, each focused on the same aspect of the problem. This pattern of adult–child engagement has been observed in Native-American, Canadian Inuit, Hispanic, and Guatemalan Mayan cultures (Chavajay & Rogoff, 2002; Crago, Annahatak, & Ningiuruvik, 1993; Delgado-Gaitan, 1994). With increasing education, parents establish a *hierarchical style of communication,* like that of classrooms. The parent directs each child to carry out an aspect of the task, and children work independently. This sharp discontinuity between home and school practices may contribute to low-SES minority children's lower IQ and school performance (Greenfield, Quiroz, & Raeff, 2000).

Test Content. Many researchers argue that IQ scores are affected by specific information acquired as part of majority-culture upbringing. Consistent with this view, low-SES African-American children often miss vocabulary words on mental tests that have alternative meanings in their cultural community—for example, *frame* refers to "physique" and wrapping, which can be interpreted as "rapping," a popular style of music (Champion, 2003a).

Unfortunately, attempts to change tests by eliminating verbal, fact-oriented items and relying only on spatial reasoning and performance items (believed to be less culturally loaded) have not raised the scores of low-SES minority children (Reynolds & Kaiser, 1990). Yet even these nonverbal test items depend on learning opportunities. For example, using small blocks to duplicate designs and playing video games increase success on spatial test items (Dirks, 1982; Subrahmanyam & Greenfield, 1996). Low-income minority children, who often grow up in more "people-oriented" than "object-oriented" homes, may lack toys and games that promote certain intellectual skills.

Furthermore, the sheer amount of time a child spends in school is a strong predictor of IQ. When children of the same age enrolled in different grades are compared, those who have been in school longer score higher on intelligence tests (Ceci, 1991, 1999). Taken together, these findings indicate that children's exposure to the factual knowledge and ways of thinking valued in classrooms has a sizable impact on their intelligence test performance.

Stereotypes. Imagine trying to succeed at an activity when the prevailing attitude is that members of your group are incompetent. **Stereotype threat**—the fear of being judged on the basis of a negative stereotype—can trigger anxiety that interferes with performance (Steele, 1997). Mounting evidence confirms that stereotype threat undermines test taking in children and adults. For example, researchers gave African-American, Hispanic-American, and Caucasian 6- to 10-year-olds verbal tasks. Some children were told that the tasks "were not a test," whereas others were told they were "a test of how good children are at school problems" (McKown & Weinstein, 2003). Among children who were aware of ethnic stereotypes (such as "black people aren't smart"), African Americans and Hispanics performed far worse in the "test" condition than in the "not a test" condition. Caucasian children, in contrast, performed similarly in both conditions (see Figure 9.9).

Over middle childhood, children become increasingly conscious of ethnic stereotypes, and those from stigmatized groups are especially mindful of them. By junior high school, many low-SES minority students start to say that doing well in school is not important to them (Major et al., 1998; Osborne, 1994). Self-protective disengagement, sparked by stereotype threat, may be responsible. This undermining of motivation can have serious, long-term consequences. Research shows that self-discipline—effort and delay of gratification—predicts school performance at least as well as, and sometimes better than, IQ does (Duckworth & Seligman, 2005).

Reducing Cultural Bias in Testing. Although not all experts agree, many acknowledge that IQ scores can underestimate the intelligence of culturally different children. A special concern exists about incorrectly labeling minority children as slow learners and assigning them to remedial classes, which are far less stimulating than regular school experiences. Because of this danger, test scores need to be combined with assessments

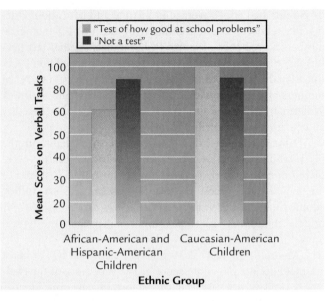

■ **FIGURE 9.9 Effect of stereotype threat on test performance.** Among African-American and Hispanic-American children who were aware of ethnic stereotypes, being told that verbal tasks were a "test of how good children are at school problems" led to far worse performance than being told the tasks "were not a test." These statements had little impact on the performance of Caucasian-American children. (Adapted from McKown & Weinstein, 2003.)

of children's adaptive behavior—their ability to cope with the demands of their everyday environments. The child who does poorly on an IQ test yet plays a complex game on the playground or figures out how to rewire a broken TV is unlikely to be mentally deficient.

In addition, culturally relevant testing procedures enhance minority children's test performance. In an approach called **dynamic assessment,** an innovation consistent with Vygotsky's zone of proximal development, the adult introduces purposeful teaching into the testing situation to find out what the child can attain with social support. Research shows that children's receptivity to teaching and their capacity to transfer what they have learned to novel problems contribute substantially to gains in test performance (Lidz, 2001; Sternberg & Grigorenko, 2002). As yet, however, dynamic assessment is not more effective than traditional tests in predicting academic achievement. Better correspondence may emerge in classrooms where teaching interactions resemble the dynamic testing approach—namely, individualized assistance on tasks carefully selected to help the child move beyond her current level of development (Grigorenko & Sternberg, 1998).

But rather than adapting testing to support high-quality classroom learning experiences, North American education is placing greater emphasis on traditional test scores. Efforts to upgrade the academic achievement of poorly performing students have led to a *high-stakes testing* movement that makes progress through school contingent on test performance. As the Social Issues box on page 316 indicates, this stepped-up emphasis on passing standardized tests has narrowed the focus of instruction, and it may widen SES and ethnic differences in educational attainment.

This teacher uses dynamic assessment in a classroom of Inuit children in Nunavik, Canada. In this approach, the teacher introduces purposeful teaching into the testing situation, creating a zone of proximal development to better assess what a child can attain with social support. Many ethnic minority children perform better under dynamic assessment than in traditional testing.

In view of its many problems, should intelligence testing in schools be suspended? Most experts regard this solution as unacceptable. Without testing, important educational decisions would be based only on subjective impressions—a policy that could increase the discriminatory placement of minority children. Intelligence tests are useful when interpreted carefully by psychologists and educators who are sensitive to cultural influences on test performance. And despite their limitations, IQ scores continue to be fairly accurate measures of school learning potential for the majority of Western children.

Ask Yourself

Review

Using Sternberg's triarchic theory and Gardner's theory of multiple intelligences, explain the limitations of current intelligence tests in assessing the diversity of human of intelligence.

Apply

Lonnie, an African-American fourth grader, does well on homework assignments. But when his teacher announces, "It's time for a test to see how much you've learned," Lonnie usually does poorly. How might stereotype threat explain this inconsistency?

Connect

Explain how dynamic assessment is consistent with Vygotsky's zone of proximal development and with scaffolding. (See Chapter 7, pages 235–236.)

Reflect

Do you think that intelligence tests are culturally biased? What observations and evidence influenced your conclusions?

Language Development

Vocabulary, grammar, and pragmatics continue to develop in middle childhood, although less obviously than at earlier ages. In addition, school-age children's attitude toward language undergoes a fundamental shift. They develop *language awareness.*

Schooling contributes greatly to these language competencies. Reflecting on language is extremely common during reading instruction. And fluent reading is a major new source of language learning (Ravid & Tolchinsky, 2002). In the following sections, we will see how an improved ability to reflect on language grows out of literacy and supports language skills.

Vocabulary

During the elementary school years, vocabulary increases fourfold, eventually exceeding 40,000 words. On average, children learn about 20 new words each day, a rate of growth exceeding that in early childhood. In addition to the word-learning strategies discussed in Chapter 7, school-age children add to their vocabularies by analyzing the structure of complex words. From *happy* and *decide,* they quickly derive the meanings of *happiness* and *decision* (Anglin, 1993). They also figure out many more word meanings from context (Nagy & Scott, 2000).

As at earlier ages, children benefit from conversation with more expert speakers, especially when their partners use and explain complex words (Weizman & Snow, 2001). But because written language contains a far more diverse and complex vocabulary than spoken language, reading contributes enormously to vocabulary growth in middle childhood and adolescence. Children who engage in as little as 21 minutes of independent reading per day are exposed to nearly 2 million words per year (Cunningham & Stanovich, 1998).

As their knowledge becomes better organized, school-age children think about and use words more precisely, as reflected in their word definitions. Five- and 6-year-olds offer concrete descriptions referring to functions or appearance—for example, *knife:* "when you're cutting carrots"; *bicycle:* "it's got wheels, a chain, and handlebars." By the end of elementary school, synonyms and explanations of categorical relationships appear—for example, *knife:* "something you could cut with. A saw is like a knife. It could also be a weapon" (Wehren, De Lisi, & Arnold, 1981). This advance reflects older children's ability to deal with word meanings on an entirely verbal plane. They can add new words to their vocabulary simply by being given a definition.

The school-age child's more reflective and analytical approach to language permits appreciation of the multiple meanings of words. For example, children now recognize that many words, such as *cool* or *neat,* have psychological as well as physical meanings: "What a cool shirt!" or "That movie was really neat!" This grasp of double meanings permits 8- to 10-year-olds to comprehend subtle metaphors, such as "sharp as a

Social Issues

High-Stakes Testing

To better hold schools accountable for educating students, during the past two decades many U.S. states and Canadian provinces have mandated that students pass exams for high school graduation. As these high-stakes achievement tests spread, schools stepped up their testing programs, extending them downward to elementary school. Some U.S. states and school districts also made grade promotion (in New York City, as early as the third grade) and secondary-school academic course credits contingent on test scores (Gootman, 2005).

The U.S. No Child Left Behind Act, authorized by Congress in 2002, broadens high-stakes testing to the identification of "passing" and "failing" schools. The law mandates that each state evaluate every public school's performance through annual achievement testing and publicize the results. Schools that consistently perform poorly (have a high percentage of failing students) must give parents options for upgrading their children's education, such as transfers to nearby, higher-performing schools or enrollment in remedial classes. In some states, schoolwide rewards for high scores and penalties for low scores are in place. These include, on the positive side, official praise and financial bonuses to school staff and, on the negative side, withdrawal of accreditation, state takeover, and closure.

Proponents of high-stakes testing believe that it will introduce greater rigor into classroom teaching, improve student motivation and achievement, and either turn around poor-performing schools or protect students from being trapped in them. But accumulating evidence indicates that high-stakes testing often undermines, rather than upgrades, the quality of education.

For example, in a Canadian study, researchers examined the impact of requiring students to pass British Columbia's high school exit exam on eighth-, tenth-, and twelfth-grade science teaching. Observing classes and interviewing teachers, they found that 12th-grade teachers narrowed the scope of what they taught to strings of facts to be memorized for the test. As a result, 8th and 10th graders, in some respects, were doing more advanced work than 12th graders—conducting more experiments, exploring topics in greater depth, and engaging in more critical thinking (Wideen et al., 1997).

An additional concern is that high-stakes testing promotes fear—a poor motivator for upgrading teaching and learning. Principals and teachers worry about losing funding and their jobs if students do poorly. And many students who get passing grades, even high grades, fail exams because a time-limited test with several dozen multiple-choice questions can tap only a small sample of skills covered in the classroom (Sacks, 1999). Students most likely to score poorly are minority youths living in poverty. When they are punished with course failure and grade retention, their self-esteem and motivation drop sharply, and they are likely to drop out (Kornhaber, Orfield, & Kurlaender, 2001). A Massachusetts study demonstrated that relying solely on test scores while ignoring teacher-assigned grades (which take into account effort and a broad range of skills) amplifies achievement gaps between white and black students and between boys and girls in math and science (Brennan et al., 2001).

The trend toward teaching to tests induced by high-stakes testing contrasts sharply with the emphasis on teaching for deeper understanding in countries that rank at the top in cross-cultural

The current high-stakes testing movement emphasizes standardized tests as the means of assessing and improving student performance. In response, many classrooms have narrowed the focus of instruction to preparing children for these tests.

comparisons of academic achievement (see pages 323–324). Even after hundreds of hours of class time devoted to test preparation, tens of thousands of Canadian and U.S. students fail school-exit exams and do not graduate. As just one example, in the Canadian province of Ontario, more than 60,000 high school seniors—mostly low-SES minorities, immigrants not yet proficient in English, or students with learning problems—were in danger of not graduating in 2005 because they had failed the grade 10 literacy exam (OSSTF, 2005). Most try these tests again, but some fail repeatedly and never graduate, with potentially dire consequences for the course of their lives. Clearly, many issues remain to be resolved about high-stakes tests, including their ethnic and gender fairness and their questionable power to spark school reforms that make children and adolescents better learners.

---

tack" and "spilling the beans" (Nippold, Taylor, & Baker, 1996; Wellman & Hickling, 1994). It also leads to a change in children's humor. Riddles and puns that go back and forth between different meanings of a key word are common: "Hey, did you take a bath?" "Why, is one missing?"

Grammar

During the school years, mastery of complex grammatical constructions improves. For example, English-speaking children use the passive voice more frequently, and they more often extend it from an abbreviated form ("It broke") into full statements

("The glass was broken by Mary") (Horgan, 1978; Pinker, Lebeaux, & Frost, 1987). Although the passive form is challenging, language input makes a difference. When adults speak a language that emphasizes full passives, such as Inukitut (spoken by the Inuit people of Arctic Canada), children produce them earlier (Allen & Crago, 1996).

Another grammatical achievement of middle childhood is advanced understanding of infinitive phrases—the difference between "John is eager to please" and "John is easy to please" (Chomsky, 1969). Like gains in vocabulary, appreciation of these subtle grammatical distinctions is supported by an improved ability to analyze and reflect on language.

Pragmatics

Improvements in *pragmatics,* the communicative side of language, also occur. Children adapt to the needs of listeners in challenging communicative situations, such as describing one object among a group of very similar objects. Whereas preschoolers tend to give ambiguous descriptions ("the red one"), school-age children are precise: "the round red one with stripes on it" (Deutsch & Pechmann, 1982). Conversational strategies also become more refined. For example, older children are better at phrasing things to get their way. When faced with an adult who refuses to hand over a desired object, 9-year-olds, but not 5-year-olds, state their second requests more politely (Axia & Baroni, 1985).

In middle childhood, as a result of improved memory and ability to take the perspective of listeners, children's narratives increase in organization, detail, and expressiveness. A typical 4- or 5-year-old's narrative states what happened: "We went to the lake. We fished and waited. Paul caught a huge catfish." Six- and 7-year-olds, in contrast, include orienting information (time, place, and participants) and many connectives that lend coherence to the story ("next," "then," "so," "finally"). Gradually, narratives lengthen into a *classic form* in which events not only build to a high point but resolve: "After Paul reeled in the catfish, Dad cleaned and cooked it. Then we ate it all up!" Evaluative comments also increase, becoming common by age 8 to 9: "The catfish tasted great. Paul was so proud!" (Bliss, McCabe, & Miranda, 1998; Ely, 2005).

Because children pick up the narrative styles of significant adults in their lives, their narratives vary widely across cultures. For example, instead of the *topic-focused style* of most North American school-age children, who describe an experience from beginning to end, African-American children often use a *topic-associating style* in which they blend several similar experiences. One 9-year-old related having a tooth pulled, then described seeing her sister's tooth pulled, next told how she had removed one of her baby teeth, and concluded, "I'm a pullin-teeth expert . . . call me, and I'll be over" (McCabe, 1997, p. 164). As a result, African-American children's narratives are usually longer and more complex than those of white children (Champion, 2003b).

The ability to generate clear oral narratives enhances reading comprehension and prepares children for producing

A boy tells a story to an elderly relative wearing the traditional Bedouin costume of the nomadic Al Murrah tribe in Saudi Arabia. Children's narratives vary widely across cultures, reflecting the styles of significant adults in their lives.

© WAYNE EASTEP/GETTY IMAGES/STONE

longer, more explicit written narratives. In families who regularly eat meals together, children are advanced in language and literacy development, perhaps because mealtimes offer many opportunities to relate personal stories (Beals, 2001).

Learning Two Languages at a Time

Joey and Lizzie speak only one language—English, their native tongue. Yet throughout the world, many children grow up *bilingual,* learning two languages, and sometimes more than two, in childhood. An estimated 15 percent of American children—6 million in all—speak a language other than English at home (U.S. Census Bureau, 2006b). Similarly, the native languages of 12 percent of Canadian children—nearly 700,000—are neither English nor French, the country's two official languages. In the French-speaking province of Québec, 41 percent of the population are French–English bilinguals. In the remaining English-speaking provinces, the French–English bilingualism rate is about 10 percent (Statistics Canada, 2003d).

■ **Bilingual Development.** Children can become bilingual in two ways: (1) by acquiring both languages at the same time in early childhood or (2) by learning a second language after mastering the first. Children of bilingual parents who teach them both languages in early childhood acquire normal native ability in the language of their surrounding community and good-to-native ability in the second language, depending on their exposure to it (Genessee, 2001). When school-age children acquire a second language after they already speak a first language, they generally take 3 to 5 years to become as fluent as native-speaking agemates (Hakuta, 1999).

As with first-language development, a *sensitive period* for second-language development exists. Mastery must begin sometime in childhood for most second-language learners to attain full proficiency. But a precise age cutoff for a decline in second-language learning has not been established. Rather, a continuous age-related decrease from childhood to adulthood occurs (Hakuta, Bialystok, & Wiley, 2003).

A large body of research shows that bilingualism has positive consequences for development. Children who are fluent in two languages do better than others on tests of selective attention, analytical reasoning, concept formation, and cognitive flexibility (Bialystok, 1999, 2001). They are also advanced in certain aspects of language awareness, such as detection of errors in grammar and meaning. And children readily transfer their phonological awareness skills in one language to the other (Bialystok & Herman, 1999; Bialystok, McBride-Chang, & Luk, 2005). These capacities, as noted earlier, enhance reading achievement.

■ **Bilingual Education.** The advantages of bilingualism provide strong justification for bilingual education programs in schools. In Canada, about 7 percent of elementary school students are enrolled in *language immersion programs,* in which English-speaking children are taught entirely in French for several years. This strategy has been successful in developing children who are proficient in both languages and who, by grade 6, achieve as well as their counterparts in the regular English program (Harley & Jean, 1999; Holobow, Genesee, & Lambert, 1991; Turnbull, Hart, & Lapkin, 2003). Canadian schools are also encouraged to provide programs that maintain the languages and cultures of immigrants and to promote First Nations languages. Although such programs are in short supply, funding for them is increasing.

In the United States, fierce disagreement exists over the question of how best to educate ethnic minority children with limited English proficiency. Some believe that time spent communicating in the child's native tongue detracts from English-language achievement, which is crucial for success in school and at work. Other educators, committed to developing minority children's native language while fostering mastery of English, note that providing instruction in the native tongue lets minority children know that their heritage is respected. In addition, it prevents *semilingualism*—inadequate proficiency in both languages. Minority children who gradually lose the first language as a result of being taught the second end up limited in both languages for a time, a circumstance that leads to serious academic difficulties (Ovando & Collier, 1998). Semilingualism is believed to contribute to high rates of school failure and dropout among low-SES Hispanic youngsters, who make up 50 percent of the U.S. language-minority population.

At present, public opinion and educational practice favor English-only instruction. Many U.S. states have passed laws declaring English to be their official language, creating conditions in which schools have no obligation to teach minority students in languages other than English. Yet in classrooms where both languages are integrated into the curriculum, minority children are more involved in learning and acquire the second language more easily. In contrast, when teachers speak only in a language children can barely understand, the

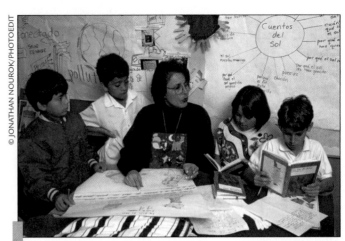

In this English–Spanish bilingual classroom serving low-SES third graders who have recently immigrated to the United States, children's first and second languages are both integrated into the curriculum. As a result, the children are more involved in learning, participate more actively in class discussions, and acquire the second language more easily.

children display frustration, boredom, and withdrawal (Crawford, 1997).

Supporters of U.S. English-only education often point to the success of Canadian language immersion programs, in which classroom lessons are conducted in the second language. But Canadian parents enroll their children in immersion classrooms voluntarily, and both French and English are majority languages—equally valued in Canada. For American non-English-speaking minority children, whose native languages are not valued by the larger society, a different strategy seems necessary: one that promotes children's native-language skills while they learn English (Cloud, Genesee, & Humayan, 2000).

Ask Yourself

Review

Cite examples of how language awareness fosters school-age children's language progress.

Apply

Ten-year-old Shana arrived home from soccer practice and remarked, "I'm wiped out!" Megan, her 5-year-old sister, looked puzzled. "What did'ya wipe out, Shana?" Megan asked. Explain Shana's and Megan's different understandings of this expression.

Connect

How can bilingual education promote ethnic minority children's cognitive and academic development?

Reflect

Did you acquire a second language at home or study one in school? When did you start, and how proficient are you in the second language? Considering research on bilingualism, what changes would you make in your own second-language learning, and why?

www.ablongman.com/berk

Learning in School

Evidence cited throughout this chapter indicates that schools are vital forces in children's cognitive development. How do schools exert such a powerful influence? Research looking at schools as complex social systems—class size, educational philosophies, teacher–student relationships, and larger cultural context—provides important insights. As you read about these topics, refer to Applying What We Know below, which summarizes characteristics of high-quality education in elementary school.

Class Size

As each school year began, Rena telephoned the principal's office to ask, "How large will Joey's and Lizzie's classes be?" Her concern is well-founded. In a large field experiment, more than 6,000 Tennessee kindergartners were randomly assigned to three class types: "small" (13 to 17 students), "regular" (22 to 25 students) with only a teacher, and regular with a teacher plus a full-time teacher's aide. These arrangements continued into third grade. Small-class students—especially minority children—scored higher in reading and math achievement each year (Mosteller, 1995). Placing teacher's aides in regular-size classes had no impact. Rather, being in small classes from kindergarten through third grade predicted substantially higher achievement from fourth through ninth grades, after

children had returned to regular-size classes (Nye, Hedges, & Konstantopoulos, 2001).

Why is small class size beneficial? With fewer children, teachers spend less time disciplining and more time giving individual attention. Also, children who learn in smaller groups show better concentration, higher-quality class participation, and more favorable attitudes toward school (Blatchford et al., 2003; Finn, Pannozzo, & Achilles, 2003).

Educational Philosophies

Each teacher brings to the classroom an educational philosophy that plays a major role in children's learning. Two philosophical approaches have received most research attention. They differ in what children are taught, the way they are believed to learn, and how their progress is evaluated.

■ **Traditional versus Constructivist Classrooms.** In a **traditional classroom,** the teacher is the sole authority for knowledge, rules, and decision making and does most of the talking. Students are relatively passive—listening, responding when called on, and completing teacher-assigned tasks. Their progress is evaluated by how well they keep pace with a uniform set of standards for their grade.

A **constructivist classroom,** in contrast, encourages students to *construct* their own knowledge. Although constructivist classrooms vary, many are grounded in Piaget's theory, which views children as active agents, who reflect on and coordinate

Signs of High-Quality Education in Elementary School

Applying What We Know

Classroom Characteristics	Signs of Quality
Class size	Optimum class size is no larger than 18 children.
Physical setting	Space is divided into richly equipped activity centers—for reading, writing, playing math or language games, exploring science, working on construction projects, using computers, and engaging in other academic pursuits. Spaces are used flexibly for individual and small-group activities and whole-class gatherings.
Curriculum	The curriculum helps children both achieve academic standards and make sense of their learning. Subjects are integrated so children apply knowledge in one area to others. The curriculum is implemented through activities responsive to children's interests, ideas, and everyday lives, including their cultural backgrounds.
Daily activities	Teachers provide challenging activities that include opportunities for small-group and independent work. Groupings vary in size and makeup of children, depending on the activity and children's learning needs. Teachers encourage cooperative learning and guide children in attaining it.
Interactions between teachers and children	Teachers foster each child's progress and use intellectually engaging strategies, including posing problems, asking thought-provoking questions, discussing ideas, and adding complexity to tasks. They also demonstrate, explain, coach, and assist in other ways, depending on each child's learning needs.
Evaluations of progress	Teachers regularly evaluate children's progress through written observations and work samples, which they use to individualize teaching. They help children reflect on their work and decide how to improve it. They also seek information and perspectives from parents on how well children are learning and include parents' views in evaluations.
Relationship with parents	Teachers forge partnerships with parents. They hold periodic conferences and encourage parents to visit the classroom anytime, to observe and volunteer.

Source: Bredekamp & Copple, 1997.

their own thoughts, rather than absorbing those of others. A glance inside a constructivist classroom reveals richly equipped learning centers, small groups and individuals solving problems they choose themselves, and a teacher who guides and supports in response to children's needs. Students are evaluated by considering their progress in relation to their own prior development.

In North America, the pendulum has swung back and forth between these two views. In the 1960s and early 1970s, constructivist classrooms gained in popularity. Then, as concern arose over the academic progress of children and youths, a "back-to-basics" movement arose. Classrooms returned to traditional instruction, a style still prevalent today.

Although older elementary school children in traditional classrooms have a slight edge in achievement test scores, constructivist settings are associated with many other benefits—gains in critical thinking, greater social and moral maturity, and more positive attitudes toward school (DeVries, 2001; Walberg, 1986). And as noted in Chapter 7, when teacher-directed instruction is emphasized in preschool and kindergarten, it actually undermines academic motivation and achievement, especially in low-SES children.

The heavy emphasis on knowledge absorption in many kindergarten and primary classrooms has contributed to a growing trend among parents to delay their child's school entry—especially if the child is boy with a birth date close to the cutoff for kindergarten enrollment. But research has not revealed any advantages, either academic or social, for delaying kindergarten (Graue & DiPerna, 2000; Stipek, 2002). To the contrary, younger first graders reap academic gains from on-time enrollment; they outperform same-age children a year behind them in school (Stipek & Byler, 2001). An alternative perspective is that school readiness can be cultivated through classroom experiences that foster children's individual progress.

■ **New Philosophical Directions.** New approaches to education, grounded in Vygotsky's sociocultural theory, capitalize on the rich social context of the classroom to spur children's learning. In these **social-constructivist classrooms,** children participate in a wide range of challenging activities with teachers and peers, with whom they jointly construct understandings. As children acquire knowledge and strategies from working together, they become competent, contributing members of their classroom community and advance in cognitive and social development (Palincsar, 2003). Vygotsky's emphasis on the social origins of higher cognitive processes has inspired the following educational themes:

▰ *Teachers and children as partners in learning.* A classroom rich in both teacher–child and child–child collaboration transfers culturally valued ways of thinking to children.

▰ *Experiences with many types of symbolic communication in meaningful activities.* As children master reading, writing, and mathematics, they become aware of their culture's communication systems, reflect on their own thinking, and bring it under voluntary control. (Can you identify

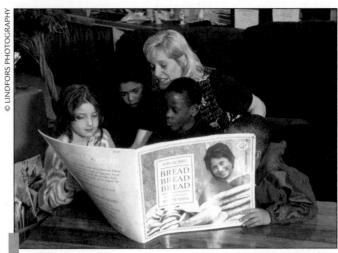

In social-constructivist classrooms, which are grounded in Vygotsky's sociocultural theory, children engage in rich literacy activities with teachers and peers. As students jointly construct understandings, they advance in cognitive and social development.

research presented earlier in this chapter that supports this theme?)

▰ *Teaching adapted to each child's zone of proximal development.* Assistance that both responds to current understandings and encourages children to take the next step helps ensure that each child makes the best progress possible.

A growing number of teaching approaches translate these ideas into action. For example, in **reciprocal teaching,** a teacher and two to four students form a collaborative group and take turns leading dialogues on the content of a text passage. Within the dialogues, group members apply four cognitive strategies: questioning, summarizing, clarifying, and predicting. The dialogue leader (at first the teacher, later a student) begins by *asking questions* about the content of the text passage. Students offer answers, raise additional questions, and, in case of disagreement, reread the original text. Next, the leader *summarizes* the passage, and children discuss the summary and *clarify* unfamiliar ideas. Finally, the leader encourages pupils to *predict* upcoming content based on prior knowledge and clues in the passage (Palincsar & Herrenkohl, 1999).

Elementary and junior high school students exposed to reciprocal teaching show impressive gains in reading comprehension in many subjects compared with controls taught in other ways (Lederer, 2000; Rosenshine & Meister, 1994). Notice how reciprocal teaching creates a zone of proximal development in which children gradually assume more responsibility for comprehending text passages. Also, by collaborating with others, children forge group expectations for high-level thinking and acquire skills vital for learning and success in everyday life.

Teacher–Student Interaction

Elementary school students describe good teachers as caring, helpful, and stimulating—behaviors associated with gains in motivation, achievement, and positive peer relations (Daniels, Kalkman, & McCombs, 2001; Davis, 2003). But too many U.S.

teachers emphasize rote, repetitive drill over higher-level thinking, such as grappling with ideas and applying knowledge to new situations (Campbell, Hombo, & Mazzeo, 2000). In a longitudinal investigation of middle-school students, those in more academically demanding classrooms showed better attendance and larger gains in math achievement over the following two years (Phillips, 1997).

Of course, teachers do not interact in the same way with all children. Well-behaved, high-achieving students typically get more encouragement and praise, whereas unruly students have more conflicts with teachers and receive more criticism from them (Henricsson & Rydell, 2004). Caring teacher–student relationships have an especially strong impact on the achievement and social behavior of low-SES minority students (Crosno, Kirkpatrick, & Elder, 2004; Meehan, Hughes, & Cavell, 2003). But overall, higher-SES students—who tend to be higher-achieving and to have fewer discipline problems—have more sensitive and supportive relationships with teachers (Pianta, Hamre, & Stuhlman, 2003).

Unfortunately, once teachers' attitudes toward students are established, they can become more extreme than is warranted by students' behavior. A special concern is **educational self-fulfilling prophecies:** Children may adopt teachers' positive or negative views and start to live up to them. This effect is especially strong when teachers emphasize competition and publicly compare children, regularly favoring the best students (Kuklinski & Weinstein, 2001; Weinstein, 2002).

Teacher expectations have a greater impact on low-achieving than high-achieving students (Madon, Jussim, & Eccles, 1997). High achievers have less room to improve when teachers think well of them, and when a teacher is critical, they can fall back on their history of success. Low-achieving students' sensitivity to self-fulfilling prophecies can be beneficial when teachers believe in them. But biased teacher judgments are usually slanted in a negative direction. In one study, African-American children were especially responsive to negative teacher expectations in reading, and girls were especially responsive to negative teacher expectations in math (McKown & Weinstein, 2002). Recall our discussion of *stereotype threat.* A child in the position of confirming a negative stereotype may respond with anxiety and reduced motivation, increasing the likelihood of a negative self-fulfilling prophecy.

Grouping Practices

In many schools, students are assigned to *homogeneous* groups or classes in which children of similar ability levels are taught together. Homogeneous grouping can be a potent source of self-fulfilling prophecies. Low-group students get more drill on basic facts and skills, engage in less discussion, and progress at a slower pace. Gradually, they show a drop in self-esteem and are viewed by themselves and others as "not smart." Not surprisingly, homogeneous grouping widens the gap between high and low achievers (Dornbusch, Glasgow, & Lin, 1996).

Partly because of this finding, some schools have increased the *heterogeneity* of classes by combining two or three adjacent grades. In *multigrade classrooms,* academic achievement, self-

These second and third graders learn together during a visit to their school library. Compared to children in single-grade classrooms, children in multigrade classrooms are usually advantaged in academic achievement, self-esteem, and attitudes toward school.

esteem, and attitudes toward school are usually more favorable than in the single-grade arrangement (Lloyd, 1999; Ong, Allison, & Haladyna, 2000). Perhaps multigrade grouping decreases competition and promotes *cooperative learning,* in which small, heterogeneous groups of students share responsibility and consider one another's ideas while working toward common goals. When teachers explain, model, and have children role-play how to work together, cooperative learning promotes greater student enjoyment and higher achievement across a wide range of school subjects (Gillies, 2003; Terwel et al., 2001).

Teaching Children with Special Needs

We have seen that effective teachers flexibly adjust their teaching strategies to accommodate students with a wide range of characteristics. These adjustments are especially challenging at the very low and high ends of the ability distribution. How do schools serve children with special learning needs?

■ **Children with Learning Difficulties.** American and Canadian legislation mandates that schools place children who require special supports for learning in the "least restrictive" (as close to normal as possible) environments that meet their educational needs. In **mainstreaming,** students with learning difficulties are placed in regular classrooms for part of the school day, a practice designed to prepare them for participation in society. Largely as the result of parental pressures, mainstreaming has been extended to **full inclusion**—placement in regular classrooms full time.

Some mainstreamed students have **mild mental retardation:** Their IQs fall between 55 and 70, and they also show problems in adaptive behavior, or skills of everyday living (American Psychiatric Association, 1994). But the largest number—5 to 10 percent of school-age children—have **learning disabilities,** great difficulty with one or more aspects of learning, usually reading. As a result, their achievement is considerably

© PAUL CONKLIN/PHOTOEDIT

The girl in the blue shirt, who has mild mental retardation, is fully included in this regular classroom. She is likely to do well if she receives support from a special education teacher, and if her classroom teacher minimizes comparisons with classmates and encourages cooperative learning—as in this card game.

behind what would be expected on the basis of their IQ. The problems of these students cannot be traced to any obvious physical or emotional difficulty or to environmental disadvantage. Instead, subtle deficits in brain functioning seem to be involved (Lyon, Fletcher, & Barnes, 2002). In many instances, the cause is unknown.

Although some mainstreamed and fully included students benefit academically, many do not. Achievement gains depend on both the severity of the disability and the support services available (Klingner et al., 1998). Furthermore, children with disabilities are often rejected by regular-classroom peers. Students with mental retardation are overwhelmed by the social skills of their classmates; they cannot interact adeptly in a conversation or game. And the processing deficits of some students with learning disabilities lead to problems in social awareness and responsiveness (Gresham & MacMillan, 1997; Sridhar & Vaughn, 2001).

Does this mean that students with special needs cannot be served in regular classrooms? Not necessarily. Children with mild to moderate learning difficulties do best under one of two conditions: (1) They are fully included but receive consistent support from a special education teacher, who consults with their regular teacher and spends time in their classroom each day, or (2) they receive instruction from a special education teacher in a resource room for part of the day and are mainstreamed for the remainder (Vaughn & Klingner, 1998; Weiner & Tardif, 2004).

Special steps must to be taken to promote peer acceptance of mainstreamed children. Cooperative learning and peer-tutoring experiences in which teachers guide children with learning difficulties and their classmates in working together lead to friendly interaction, improved peer acceptance, and achievement gains (Fuchs et al., 2002a, 2002b). Teachers can also prepare children for the arrival of a student with special needs. Under these conditions, mainstreaming and full inclusion may foster emotional sensitivity and prosocial behavior among regular classmates.

■ **Gifted Children.** In Joey and Lizzie's school, some children are **gifted,** displaying exceptional intellectual strengths. Their characteristics are diverse. One or two students in every grade have IQ scores above 130, the standard definition of giftedness based on intelligence test performance (Gardner, 1998b). High-IQ children, as we have seen, have keen memories and an exceptional capacity to solve challenging academic problems. Yet recognition that intelligence tests do not sample the entire range of human mental skills has led to an expanded conception of giftedness.

Creativity and Talent. **Creativity** is the ability to produce work that is original yet appropriate—something others have not thought of that is useful in some way (Lubart, 2003; Sternberg, 2003b). A child with high potential for creativity can be designated as gifted. Tests of creative capacity tap **divergent thinking**—the generation of multiple and unusual possibilities when faced with a task or problem. Divergent thinking contrasts with **convergent thinking,** which involves arriving at a single correct answer and is emphasized on intelligence tests (Guilford, 1985).

Because highly creative children (like high-IQ children) are often better at some tasks than others, a variety of tests of divergent thinking are available (Runco, 1992; Torrance, 1988). A verbal measure might ask children to name uses for common objects (such as a newspaper). A figural measure might ask them to create drawings based on a circular motif (see Figure 9.10). A "real-world problem" measure requires students to suggest solutions to everyday problems. Responses can be scored for the number of ideas generated and their originality.

Yet critics point out that these measures are poor predictors of creative accomplishment in everyday life because they tap only one of the complex cognitive contributions to creativity. Also involved are defining new and important problems, evaluating divergent ideas, choosing the most promising, and calling on relevant knowledge to understand and solve problems (Sternberg, 2003b; Sternberg & Lubart, 1996).

Consider these ingredients, and you will see why people usually demonstrate creativity in only one or a few related areas. Even individuals designated as gifted by virtue of high IQ often show uneven ability across academic subjects. Partly for this reason, definitions of giftedness have been extended to include **talent**—outstanding performance in a specific field. Case studies reveal that excellence in writing, mathematics, science, music, visual arts, athletics, or leadership has roots in specialized interests and skills that first appear in childhood (Winner, 2003). Highly talented children are biologically prepared to master their domain of interest, and they display a passion for doing so.

But talent must be nurtured. Studies of the backgrounds of talented children and highly accomplished adults often reveal parents who are warm and sensitive, provide a stimulating home life, are devoted to developing their child's abilities, and provide models of hard work. Rather than being driving and overambitious, these parents are reasonably demanding (Winner, 1996, 2000). They arrange for caring teachers while the child is young and for more rigorous master teachers as the talent develops.

FIGURE 9.10 Responses of an 8-year-old who scored high on a figural measure of divergent thinking. This child was asked to make as many pictures as she could from the circles on the page. The titles she gave her drawings, from left to right, are as follows: "Dracula," "one-eyed monster," "pumpkin," "Hula-Hoop," "poster," "wheelchair," "earth," "stop-light," "planet," "movie camera," "sad face," "picture," "beach ball," "the letter O," "car," "glasses." Tests of divergent thinking tap only one of the complex cognitive contributions to creativity. (Reprinted by permission of Laura Berk.)

Extreme giftedness often results in social isolation. Many gifted children and adolescents spend much time alone, partly because their highly driven, nonconforming, and independent styles leave them out of step with peers and partly because they enjoy solitude, which is necessary to develop their talents. Still, gifted children desire gratifying peer relationships and some—more often girls than boys—try to hide their abilities to become better liked. Compared with their ordinary agemates, gifted youths, especially girls, report more emotional and social difficulties, including low self-esteem and depression (Gross, 1993; Winner, 2000).

Finally, whereas many talented youths become experts in their fields, few become highly creative. Rapidly mastering an existing field requires different skills than innovating in that field (Csikszentmihalyi, 1999). The world, however, needs both experts and creators.

Educating the Gifted. Although many schools offer programs for the gifted, debate about their effectiveness usually focuses on factors irrelevant to giftedness—whether to provide enrichment in regular classrooms, pull children out for special instruction (the most common practice), or advance brighter students to a higher grade. Overall, gifted children fare well academically and socially within each of these models (Moon & Feldhusen, 1994). Yet the extent to which programs foster creativity and talent depends on opportunities to acquire relevant skills.

Gardner's theory of multiple intelligences has inspired several model programs that provide enrichment to all students in diverse disciplines. Meaningful activities, each tapping a specific intelligence or set of intelligences, serve as contexts for assessing strengths and weaknesses and, on that basis, teaching new knowledge and original thinking (Gardner, 1993, 2000). For example, linguistic intelligence might be fostered through storytelling or playwriting, and spatial intelligence through drawing, sculpting, or taking apart and reassembling objects.

Evidence is still needed on how effectively these programs nurture children's talent and creativity. But they have already succeeded in one way—by highlighting the strengths of some students who previously had been considered unexceptional or even at risk for school failure (Kornhaber, 2004). Consequently, they may be especially useful in identifying talented, low-SES ethnic minority children, who are underrepresented in school programs for the gifted.

How Well Educated Are North American Children?

Our discussion of schooling has largely focused on how teachers can support the education of children. Yet many factors—both within and outside schools—affect children's learning. Societal values, school resources, quality of teaching, and parental encouragement all play important roles. Nowhere are these multiple influences more apparent than when schooling is examined in cross-cultural perspective.

In international studies of reading, mathematics, and science achievement, young people in Hong Kong, Korea, and Japan are consistently top performers. Among Western nations, Canada is also in the top tier, but U.S. students typically perform at the international average, and sometimes below it (see Figure 9.11 on page 324) (Programme for International Student Assessment, 2000, 2003).

Why do U.S. children fall behind in academic accomplishment? According to international comparisons, instruction in the United States is not as challenging and focused as it is in other countries. In the Programme for International Student Assessment, which assessed the academic achievement of 15-year-olds in many countries, students were asked about their study habits. Compared with students in the top-achieving nations listed in Figure 9.11, many more U.S. students reported studying by memorizing rather than relating information to previously acquired knowledge. And achievement varies much more among U.S. schools, suggesting that the United States is less equitable in the quality of education it provides (Programme for International Student Assessment, 2005).

Researchers have conducted in-depth research on learning environments in Asian nations, such as Japan, Korea, and Taiwan, to clarify the factors that support high achievement. Except for the influence of language on early counting skills (see page 308), Asian students do not start school with cognitive advantages. Instead, a variety of social forces combine to foster a strong commitment to learning in Asian families and schools:

🖋 *Cultural valuing of academic achievement.* Compared to Western countries, Japan, Korea, and Taiwan invest more

Country		Average Math Achievement Score
High-Performing Nations	Hong Kong	550
	Finland	544
	Korea, Republic of	542
	Netherlands	538
	Japan	534
	Canada	**532**
	Belgium	529
	United Kingdom	529
	Switzerland	527
	Australia	524
	New Zealand	523
Intermediate-Performing Nations	Czech Republic	516
	Iceland	515
	Denmark	514
	France	511
	Sweden	509
	Austria	505
	Germany	503
International Average = 500	Ireland	503
	Norway	495
	Luxembourg	493
	Hungary	490
	Poland	490
	Spain	485
	United States	**483**
Low-Performing Nations	Italy	466
	Portugal	466
	Greece	445
	Mexico	385

■ **FIGURE 9.11 Average mathematics scores of 15-year-olds by country.** The Programme for International Student Assessment assessed achievement in many nations around the world. Japan, Korea, and Canada were among the top performers in mathematics, whereas the United States performed below the international average. Similar outcomes occurred in reading and science. (Adapted from Programme for International Student Assessment, 2005.)

in education, including higher salaries for teachers. In these countries, where natural resources are limited, progress in science and technology is essential for economic well-being (United Nations Development Programme, 2002).

● *Emphasis on effort.* North American parents and teachers tend to regard native ability as key to academic success. In contrast, Japanese, Korean, and Taiwanese parents and teachers believe that all children can succeed academically with enough effort, and these Asian parents devote many more hours to helping their children with homework (Stevenson, Lee, & Mu, 2000). Furthermore, Asian youths, influenced by collectivist values, typically view striving to achieve as a moral obligation—part of their responsibility to family and community. North American young people view working hard in individualistic terms—as a personal choice (Bempechat & Drago-Severson, 1999).

● *High-quality education for all.* No ability groups exist in Japanese, Korean, and Taiwanese elementary schools. Instead, all students receive the same nationally mandated education. Academic lessons are particularly well-organized and presented in ways that capture children's attention and encourage high-level thinking (Grow-Maienza, Hahn, & Joo, 2001). And Japanese elementary school teachers are three times as likely as U.S. teachers to work outside class with students who need extra help (Woodward & Ono, 2004).

● *More time devoted to instruction.* In Japan, Korea, and Taiwan, the school year is more than 50 days longer than in the United States and about 30 days longer than in Canada (World Education Services, 2005). And on a day-to-day basis, Asian teachers devote more time to academic pursuits (Stevenson, Lee, & Mu, 2000).

The Asian examples underscore the need for families, schools, and the larger society to work together to upgrade education. Currently, the United States is investing more tax dollars in elementary and secondary education and strengthening teacher preparation. In addition, many schools are taking steps to increase parent involvement. Children whose parents create stimulating learning environments at home, monitor their child's academic progress, help with homework, and communicate often with teachers consistently show superior achievement (Christenson & Sheridan, 2001). The results of these efforts can be seen in recent national assessments of educational progress (U.S Department of Education, 2003, 2005h). After two decades of decline, overall academic achievement in the United States has risen, although not enough to enhance its standing internationally.

Ask Yourself

Review

List some teaching practices that foster children's achievement and some that undermine it. Provide a brief explanation of each practice.

Apply

Sandy wonders whether she should enroll her child in a multigrade class of first and second graders. How would you advise Sandy, and why?

Connect

Review research on child-rearing styles on pages 279–280 in Chapter 8. What style do gifted children who realize their potential typically experience? Explain.

Reflect

What grouping practices were used in your elementary education—homogeneous, heterogeneous, or a combination? What impact do you think those practices had on your motivation and achievement?

Summary

🍂 *Physical Development*

Body Growth

Describe major trends in body growth during middle childhood.

- Gains in body size during middle childhood extend the pattern of slow, regular growth established during the preschool years. Bones continue to lengthen and broaden, and all 20 primary teeth are replaced by permanent ones. By age 9, girls overtake boys in physical size.

Common Health Problems

What vision and hearing problems are common in middle childhood?

- During middle childhood, children from economically advantaged homes are at their healthiest, as a result of good nutrition and rapid development of the immune system. But a variety of health problems do occur, many of which are more prevalent among low-SES children.

- The most common vision problem in middle childhood is myopia, or nearsightedness. It is influenced by heredity, early biological trauma, and time spent reading and doing other close work. Myopia is one of the few health conditions that increase with SES.

- Middle-ear infections become less frequent in middle childhood. But repeated, untreated infections lead to permanent hearing loss in as many as 20 percent of low-SES children.

Describe the causes and consequences of serious nutritional problems in middle childhood, giving special attention to obesity.

- Poverty-stricken children in developing countries and North America continue to suffer from malnutrition in middle childhood. When it persists for many years, malnutrition has a permanent negative impact on physical growth, intelligence, motor coordination, and attention.

- Overweight and **obesity** are growing problems in Western nations. Although heredity contributes to obesity, parental feeding practices, maladaptive eating habits, and lack of exercise also play important roles. Obese children are disliked by peers and adults and have serious adjustment problems. They are also at risk for serious health difficulties, including early-onset diabetes. Family-based interventions to change parents' and children's eating patterns and

lifestyles, including time spent watching TV, are the most effective treatment approaches.

What factors contribute to illness during the school years, and how can these health problems be reduced?

- Children experience more illnesses during the first two years of elementary school than later because of exposure to sick children and an immune system that is not yet mature.

- The most common cause of school absence and childhood hospitalization is asthma. Although heredity contributes to asthma, environmental factors—pollution, exposure to tobacco smoke, stressful home lives, lack of access to good health care, and the rise in childhood obesity—have led to an increase in the disease, especially among African-American and poverty-stricken children.

- Children with severe chronic illnesses are at risk for academic, emotional, and social difficulties. Positive family relationships predict favorable adjustment among chronically ill children.

Describe changes in unintentional injuries in middle childhood.

- Unintentional injuries increase over middle childhood and adolescence, especially for boys, with auto and bicycle accidents accounting for most of the rise. School-based programs can prevent injury by teaching safety practices through modeling and rehearsal and rewarding children for following them.

Motor Development and Play

Cite major changes in motor development and play during middle childhood.

- Gains in flexibility, balance, agility, and force, along with more efficient information processing, contribute to school-age children's improved motor performance.

- Fine motor development also improves. Children's writing becomes more legible, and their drawings increase in organization, detail, and representation of depth.

- Gender stereotyping, which affects parental encouragement, largely accounts for boys' superior performance on a wide range of gross

motor skills. However, more girls participate in both individual and team sports than in the past.

- Games with rules become common during the school years. Children, especially boys, also engage in **rough-and-tumble play,** friendly play-fighting that helps establish a **dominance hierarchy** among group members. Children's spontaneous games support emotional and social development.

- Many school-age children are not physically fit. More frequent physical education classes emphasizing individual exercise rather than competition could help ensure that all children have access to the benefits of regular exercise and play.

🍂 *Cognitive Development*

Piaget's Theory: The Concrete Operational Stage

What are the major characteristics of concrete operational thought?

- Children in the **concrete operational stage** can reason logically about concrete, tangible information. Mastery of conservation demonstrates **reversibility** in thinking. School-age youngsters are also better at hierarchical classification and **seriation,** including **transitive inference.** Their spatial reasoning improves, as seen in their ability to give directions and to create **cognitive maps** representing familiar large-scale spaces.

- School-age children master logical ideas gradually. Concrete operational thought is limited in that children do not come up with general logical principles.

Discuss recent research on concrete operational thought.

- Specific cultural practices, especially those associated with schooling, affect children's mastery of Piagetian tasks.

- Some researchers believe that the gradual development of operational thought can best be understood within an information-processing framework. According to Case's neo-Piagetian theory, with practice, cognitive schemes demand less attention, freeing up space in working memory for combining old schemes and generating new ones. Eventually, children consolidate schemes into highly efficient, central conceptual structures. On a wide variety of tasks, children move from a focus on only one dimension to coordinating two dimensions to integrating multiple dimensions.

Information Processing

Cite basic changes in information processing, and describe the development of attention and memory in middle childhood.

■ Brain development contributes to increases in processing speed and capacity and to gains in inhibition, which facilitate many aspects of thinking.

■ During the school years, attention becomes more selective, adaptable, and planful, and memory strategies improve. The serious symptoms of **attention-deficit hyperactivity disorder (ADHD)** lead to both academic and social problems.

■ Memory strategies improve during the school years. **Rehearsal** appears first, followed by **organization** and then **elaboration.** With age, children use several memory strategies at once.

■ Development of the long-term knowledge base makes new information easier to store and retrieve. Children's motivation to use what they know also contributes to memory development. Memory strategies are promoted by learning activities in school.

Describe the school-age child's theory of mind and capacity to engage in self-regulation.

■ Metacognition expands over middle childhood. School-age children regard the mind as an active, constructive agent. **Cognitive self-regulation**—putting what one knows about thinking into action—develops slowly over middle childhood and adolescence. It improves with instructions to monitor cognitive activity.

Discuss current controversies in teaching reading and mathematics to elementary school children.

■ Skilled reading draws on all aspects of the information-processing system, including **phonological awareness**—the ability to reflect on the sound structure of spoken language. The debate over whether a **whole-language approach** or a **phonics approach** should be used to teach beginning reading has been largely resolved by research showing that a mixture of both is most effective. Teaching that blends practice in basic skills with conceptual understanding also is best in mathematics.

Individual Differences in Mental Development

Describe major approaches to defining and measuring intelligence.

■ Most intelligence tests yield an overall score as well as scores for separate intellectual factors. During the school years, IQ becomes more stable, and it correlates well with academic achievement. The Stanford-Binet Intelligence Scale and the Wechsler Intelligence Scale for Children (WISC-IV) are widely used individually administered intelligence tests.

■ Aspects of information processing that are related to IQ include speed of thinking and effective strategy use. Sternberg's **triarchic theory of successful intelligence** views intelligence as an interaction of information-processing skills, specific experiences, and contextual (or cultural) influences.

■ Gardner's **theory of multiple intelligences**—which identifies at least eight mental abilities, each with a unique biological basis and distinct course of development—has been especially helpful in understanding and nurturing children's talents. It has also stimulated efforts to define, measure, and foster **emotional intelligence.**

Describe evidence indicating that both heredity and environment contribute to intelligence.

■ Heritability estimates and adoption research indicate that intelligence is a product of both heredity and environment. Studies of black children adopted into well-to-do homes indicate that the black–white IQ gap is substantially influenced by environment.

■ IQ scores are affected by specific learning experiences, including exposure to certain communication styles and to knowledge sampled by the test. Cultural bias in intelligence testing can lead test scores to underestimate minority children's intelligence, and **stereotype threat** may trigger anxiety that interferes with test performance. **Dynamic assessment** helps many minority children perform more competently on mental tests.

Language Development

Describe changes in school-age children's vocabulary, grammar, and pragmatics, and cite the advantages of bilingualism for development.

■ During middle childhood, vocabulary continues to grow rapidly, and children have a more precise and flexible understanding of word meanings. They also use complex grammatical constructions and conversational strategies, and their narratives increase in organization, detail, and expressiveness. Language awareness contributes to school-age children's language progress.

■ Mastery of a second language must begin in childhood for full development to occur. Bilingualism has positive consequences for cognitive development and certain aspects of language awareness. In Canada, language immersion programs are highly successful in making children proficient in both English and French. In the United States, bilingual education that combines instruction in the native tongue and in English supports ethnic minority children's academic learning.

Learning in School

Describe the impact of class size and educational philosophies on children's motivation and academic achievement.

■ As class size declines, academic achievement improves. Older students in **traditional classrooms** have a slight edge in academic achievement over those in **constructivist classrooms,** who are more likely to be critical thinkers, respect individual differences, and to have more positive attitudes toward school.

■ Students in **social-constructivist classrooms** benefit from working collaboratively in meaningful activities and from teaching adapted to each child's zone of proximal development. **Reciprocal teaching** results in impressive gains in reading comprehension.

Discuss the role of teacher–student interaction and grouping practices in academic achievement.

■ Instruction that encourages high-level thinking fosters children's interest and academic progress. **Educational self-fulfilling prophecies** are most likely to occur in classrooms that emphasize competition and public evaluation. Teachers' inaccurate views have a greater impact on poorly achieving students. Heterogeneous grouping in multi-grade classrooms promotes favorable self-esteem and school attitudes and higher achievement.

Under what conditions is placement of children with mild mental retardation and learning disabilities in regular classrooms successful?

■ Students with **mild mental retardation** and **learning disabilities** are often placed in regular classrooms, usually through **mainstreaming** but also through **full inclusion.** The success of regular-classroom placement depends on meeting individual learning needs and positive peer relations.

Describe the characteristics of gifted children and current efforts to meet their educational needs.

■ **Giftedness** includes high IQ, **creativity,** and **talent.** Tests of creativity that tap **divergent** rather than **convergent thinking** focus on only one of the ingredients of creativity. Highly talented children have parents and teachers who nurture their exceptional abilities. Gifted children are best served by educational programs that build on their special strengths.

How well are North American children achieving compared with children in other industrialized nations?

■ In international studies, young people in Asian nations are consistently top performers. Canadian students generally score high, whereas American students typically display an average or below-average performance. A strong commitment to learning in families and schools underlies the high academic success of Asian students.

Important Terms and Concepts

attention-deficit hyperactivity disorder (ADHD) (p. 304)
cognitive maps (p. 299)
cognitive self-regulation (p. 306)
concrete operational stage (p. 298)
constructivist classroom (p. 319)
convergent thinking (p. 322)
creativity (p. 322)
divergent thinking (p. 322)
dominance hierarchy (p. 297)
dynamic assessment (p. 314)
educational self-fulfilling prophecy (p. 321)
elaboration (p. 303)

emotional intelligence (p. 312)
full inclusion (p. 321)
gifted (p. 322)
learning disabilities (p. 321)
mainstreaming (p. 321)
mild mental retardation (p. 321)
obesity (p. 292)
organization (p. 302)
phonics approach (p. 307)
phonological awareness (p. 307)
reciprocal teaching (p. 320)
rehearsal (p. 302)
reversibility (p. 298)

rough-and-tumble play (p. 297)
seriation (p. 299)
social-constructivist classroom (p. 320)
stereotype threat (p. 314)
talent (p. 322)
theory of multiple intelligences (p. 310)
traditional classroom (p. 319)
transitive inference (p. 299)
triarchic theory of successful intelligence (p. 309)
whole-language approach (p. 307)

*A*s social understanding expands in middle childhood, friendship becomes more complex and psychologically based. Children rely on their close friends for understanding and emotional support, and one-to-one friendships contribute to the development of trust and sensitivity.

Emotional and Social Development in Middle Childhood

*L*ate one afternoon, Rena heard her son Joey burst through the front door, run upstairs, and phone his best friend Terry. "Terry, gotta talk to you," Joey pleaded breathlessly. "Everything was going great until that word I got—*porcupine,*" Joey went on, referring to the fifth-grade spelling bee at school that day. "Just my luck! *P-o-r-k,* that's how I spelled it! I can't believe it. Maybe I'm not so good at social studies," Joey confided, "but I *know* I'm better at spelling than that stuck-up Belinda Brown. I knocked myself out studying those spelling lists. Then *she* got all the easy words. If I *had* to lose, why couldn't it be to a nice person?"

Joey's conversation reflects his new emotional and social capacities. By entering the spelling bee, he shows *industriousness,* the energetic pursuit of meaningful achievement in his culture—a major change of middle childhood. Joey's social understanding has also expanded: He can size up strengths, weaknesses, and personality characteristics. Furthermore, friendship means something different to Joey than it did earlier—he counts on his best friend, Terry, for understanding and emotional support.

For an overview of personality change in middle childhood, we return to Erikson's theory. Then we look at children's views of themselves and of others and at their peer relationships. Each increases in complexity as children reason more effectively and spend more time in school and with agemates.

Despite changing parent–child relationships, the family remains powerfully influential in middle childhood—and family lifestyles today are more diverse than ever before. Through Joey's and Lizzie's experiences with parental divorce, we will see that family functioning is far more important than family structure in ensuring children's well-being. Finally, we look at some common emotional problems of middle childhood.

Erikson's Theory: Industry versus Inferiority

Self-Understanding

Self-Concept • Development of Self-Esteem • Influences on Self-Esteem

Emotional Development

Self-Conscious Emotions • Emotional Understanding • Emotional Self-Regulation

Understanding Others: Perspective Taking

Moral Development

Learning About Justice Through Sharing • Moral and Social-Conventional Understanding • Understanding Individual Rights • Understanding Diversity and Inequality

Peer Relations

Peer Groups • Friendships • Peer Acceptance

   • Biology and Environment: Bullies and Their Victims

Gender Typing

Gender-Stereotyped Beliefs • Gender Identity and Behavior

Family Influences

Parent–Child Relationships • Siblings • Only Children • Divorce • Blended Families • Maternal Employment and Dual-Earner Families

Some Common Problems of Development

Fears and Anxieties • Child Sexual Abuse • Fostering Resilience in Middle Childhood

   • A Lifespan Vista: Children of War

   • Social Issues: Children's Eyewitness Testimony

Erikson's Theory: Industry versus Inferiority

According to Erikson (1950), children whose previous experiences have been positive enter middle childhood prepared to redirect their energies from the make-believe of early childhood into realistic accomplishment. Erikson believed that the combination of adult expectations and children's drive toward mastery sets the stage for the psychological conflict of middle childhood, **industry versus inferiority,** which is resolved positively when children develop a sense of competence at useful skills and tasks. In cultures everywhere, adults respond to children's improved physical and cognitive capacities by making new demands, and children are ready to benefit from those challenges.

In industrialized nations, the beginning of formal schooling marks the transition to middle childhood. With it comes literacy training, which prepares children for a vast array of specialized careers. In school, children discover their own and others' unique capacities, learn the value of division of labor, and develop a sense of moral commitment and responsibility. The danger at this stage is *inferiority,* reflected in the pessimism of children who have little confidence in their ability to do things well. This sense of inadequacy can develop when family life has not prepared children for school life or when teachers and peers destroy children's feelings of competence and mastery with negative responses.

Erikson's sense of industry combines several developments of middle childhood: a positive but realistic self-concept, pride in accomplishment, moral responsibility, and cooperative participation with agemates. How do these aspects of self and social relationships change over the school years?

© TOM & DEE ANN MCCARTHY/CORBIS

The industriousness of middle childhood involves mastery of useful skills and tasks. As these young musicians participate in their school orchestra, they become more aware of one another's unique capacities and come to view themselves as responsible, capable, and cooperative.

Self-Understanding

In middle childhood, children become able to describe themselves in terms of psychological traits, to compare their own characteristics with those of their peers, and to speculate about the causes of their strengths and weaknesses. These transformations in self-understanding have a major impact on children's self-esteem.

Self-Concept

During the school years, children refine their *me-self,* or self-concept, organizing their observations of behaviors and internal states into general dispositions, with a major change taking place between ages 8 and 11. Consider the following self-description by an 11-year-old:

> My name is A. I'm a human being. I'm a girl. I'm a truthful person. I'm not pretty. I do so-so in my studies. I'm a very good cellist. I'm a very good pianist. I'm a little bit tall for my age. I like several boys. I like several girls. I'm old-fashioned. I play tennis. I am a very good swimmer. I try to be helpful. I'm always ready to be friends with anybody. Mostly I'm good, but I lose my temper. I'm not well-liked by some girls and boys. I don't know if I'm liked by boys or not. (Montemayor & Eisen, 1977, pp. 317–318)

Instead of specific behaviors, this child emphasizes competencies: "I'm a very good cellist" (Damon & Hart, 1988). She also clearly describes her personality, mentioning both positive and negative traits: "truthful" but short-tempered, "a good cellist [and] pianist" but only "so-so in my studies." Older school-age children are far less likely than younger children to describe themselves in extreme, all-or-none ways (Harter, 2003).

These qualified self-descriptions result from school-age children's frequent **social comparisons**—judgments of their appearance, abilities, and behavior in relation to those of others. For example, Joey observed that he was better than his peers at spelling but not so good at social studies. Whereas 4- to 6-year-olds can compare their own performance to that of one peer, older children can compare multiple individuals, including themselves (Butler, 1998).

What factors are responsible for revisions in self-concept during middle childhood? Cognitive development affects the changing *structure* of the self. School-age children, as we saw in Chapter 9, can better coordinate several aspects of a situation when they reason about their physical world. Similarly, in the social realm, they combine typical experiences and behaviors into psychological dispositions, blend positive and negative characteristics, and compare their own characteristics with those of many other peers (Harter, 1999, 2003).

The changing *content* of self-concept is a product of both cognitive capacities and feedback from others. Sociologist George Herbert Mead (1934) proposed that a well-organized psychological self emerges when the child's I-self adopts a view of the me-self that resembles others' attitudes toward the child.

Mead's ideas indicate that *perspective-taking skills*—in particular, an improved ability to infer what other people are thinking—are crucial for the development of a self-concept based on personality traits. School-age children become better at "reading" others' messages and incorporating these into their self-definitions. As they internalize others' expectations, children form an *ideal self* that they use to evaluate their *real self*. As we will see, a large discrepancy between the two can undermine self-esteem, leading to sadness, hopelessness, and depression.

In middle childhood, as children enter a wider range of settings in school and community, they look to more people for information about themselves. Their self-descriptions now include frequent reference to social groups: "I'm a Boy Scout, a paperboy, and a Prairie City soccer player," said Joey. And as children move into adolescence, although parents and other adults remain influential, self-concept is increasingly vested in feedback from close friends (Oosterwegel & Oppenheimer, 1993).

But recall that the content of self-concept varies from culture to culture. In earlier chapters, we noted that Asian parents stress harmonious interdependence, whereas Western parents stress independence and self-assertion. These differences are also evident in many subcultures in Western nations. In one study, researchers gathered children's self-descriptions in a Puerto Rican fishing village and an American small town (Damon, 1988). Whereas the Puerto Rican children often described themselves as "polite," "respectful," and "obedient," the American small-town children mostly mentioned individual interests, preferences, and skills.

Development of Self-Esteem

Recall that most preschoolers have extremely high self-esteem. But as children enter school and receive much more feedback about how well they perform compared with their peers, self-esteem differentiates, and it also adjusts to a more realistic level.

■ **A Hierarchically Structured Self-Esteem.** Researchers have asked children to indicate the extent to which statements such as, "I am good at homework" or "I'm usually the one chosen for games," are true of themselves. By age 6 to 7, children have formed at least four broad self-evaluations—academic competence, social competence, physical/athletic competence, and physical appearance. Within these are more refined categories that become increasingly distinct with age (Marsh, 1990; Marsh & Ayotte, 2003; Van den Bergh & De Rycke, 2003). Furthermore, the capacity to view the self in terms of stable dispositions permits school-age children to combine their separate self-evaluations into a general psychological image of themselves—an overall sense of self-esteem (Harter, 1999, 2003). As a result, self-esteem takes on the hierarchical structure shown in Figure 10.1.

Children attach greater importance to certain self-evaluations than to others. Although individual differences exist, during childhood and adolescence, perceived physical appearance correlates more strongly with overall self-worth than any other self-esteem factor (Hymel et al., 1999; Klomsten, Skaalvik, & Espnes, 2004). Emphasis on appearance, in the media and in society, has major implications for young people's overall satisfaction with themselves.

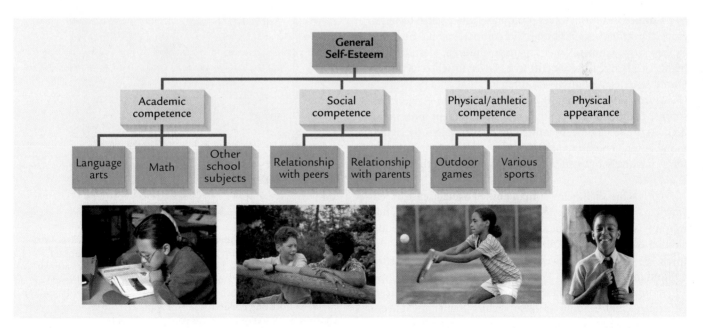

■ **FIGURE 10.1 Hierarchical structure of self-esteem in the mid-elementary school years.** From their experiences in different settings, children form at least four separate self-esteems: academic competence, social competence, physical/athletic competence, and physical appearance. These differentiate into additional self-evaluations and combine to form a general sense of self-esteem. (Photo credits: *Far left:* © Mary Kate Denny/PhotoEdit; *Middle left:* © Myrleen Ferguson Cate/PhotoEdit; *Middle right:* © Mitch Wojnarowicz/The Image Works; *Far right:* Charles Gupton/Stock Boston, LLC)

Changes in Level of Self-Esteem. Self-esteem declines during the first few years of elementary school as children evaluate themselves in various areas (Marsh, Craven, & Debus, 1998; Wigfield et al., 1997). Typically, the drop is not great enough to be harmful. Most (but not all) children appraise their characteristics and competencies realistically while maintaining an attitude of self-respect. Then, from fourth grade on, self-esteem rises for the majority of young people, who feel especially good about their peer relationships and athletic capabilities (Cole et al., 2001; Twenge & Campbell, 2001).

Influences on Self-Esteem

From middle childhood on, individual differences in self-esteem become increasingly stable (Trzesniewski, Donnellan, & Robins, 2003). And positive relationships emerge between self-esteem, valuing of various activities, and success at those activities. Academic self-esteem predicts how important, useful, and enjoyable children judge school subjects to be, their willingness to try hard, and their achievement (Jacobs et al., 2002; Valentine, DuBois, & Cooper, 2004). In one study, school-age children's academic self-worth was associated with educational attainment in early adulthood (Guay, La Rose, & Boivin, 2004). Children with high social self-esteem are consistently better-liked by classmates (Harter, 1999). And as we saw in Chapter 9, sense of athletic competence is positively associated with investment and performance in sports.

A profile of low self-esteem in all areas is linked to anxiety, depression, and increasing antisocial behavior (DuBois et al., 1999; Robins et al., 2001). What social influences might lead self-esteem to be high for some children and low for others?

Culture. Cultural forces profoundly affect self-esteem. An especially strong emphasis on social comparison in school may explain why Chinese and Japanese children, despite their higher academic achievement, score lower in self-esteem than North American children—a difference that widens with age (Hawkins, 1994; Twenge & Crocker, 2002). In Asian classrooms, competition is tough, and achievement pressure is high. At the same time, because their culture values social harmony, Asian children tend to be reserved about judging themselves positively but generous in their praise of others (Falbo et al., 1997).

Girls score slightly lower than boys in overall sense of self-worth, partly because they feel less confident about their physical appearance, academic competence, and athletic abilities (Marsh & Ayotte, 2003; Young & Mroczek, 2003). Girls may think less well of themselves because they internalize negative cultural messages.

Compared with their Caucasian agemates, African-American children tend to have slightly higher self-esteem, possibly because of warm, extended families and a strong sense of ethnic pride (Gray-Little & Hafdahl, 2000). Finally, children and adolescents who attend schools or live in neighborhoods where their SES and ethnic groups are well-represented feel a

stronger sense of belonging and have fewer self-esteem problems (Gray-Little & Carels, 1997).

Child-Rearing Practices. Children whose parents use an *authoritative* child-rearing style (see Chapter 8) feel especially good about themselves (Carlson, Uppal, & Prosser, 2000; Feiring & Taska, 1996). Warm, positive parenting lets children know that they are accepted as competent and worthwhile. And firm but appropriate expectations, backed up with explanations, seem to help children evaluate their own behavior against reasonable standards.

Controlling parents—those who too often help or make decisions for their child—communicate a sense of inadequacy to children that is linked to low self-esteem, as are repeated disapproval and parental insults (Kernis, 2002; Pomerantz & Eaton, 2000). In contrast, overindulgent parenting is correlated with unrealistically high self-esteem, which also undermines development. These children tend to lash out at challenges to their overblown self-images and to have adjustment problems, including meanness and aggression (Hughes, Cavell, & Grossman, 1997).

North American cultural values have increasingly emphasized a focus on the self that may lead parents to indulge children and boost their self-esteem too much. As Figure 10.2 illustrates, the self-esteem of American young people has risen sharply over the past few decades—a period in which much popular parenting literature advised promoting children's self-esteem (Twenge & Campbell, 2001). Yet compared with

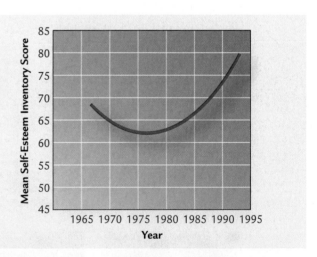

■ **FIGURE 10.2 Cohort effects for U.S. junior high school students' self-esteem from 1965 to 1995.** Self-esteem dropped slightly during the late 1960s and 1970s as the divorce rate skyrocketed, schools became larger and more impersonal, and poverty increased. From 1980 on, a period of considerable public focus on boosting children's self-esteem, average self-esteem rose sharply. Self-esteem scores for younger and older students showed a similar rise. (From J. M. Twenge & W. K. Campbell, 2001, "Age and Birth Cohort Differences in Self-Esteem: A Cross-Temporal Meta-Analysis," *Personality and Social Psychology Review, 5,* p. 337. Adapted by permission.)

previous generations, American youths are achieving less well and displaying more antisocial behavior and other adjustment problems (Berk, 2005). Research confirms that children do not benefit from compliments ("You're terrific") that have no basis in real attainment (Damon, 1995). Rather, the best way to foster a positive, secure self-image is to encourage children to strive for worthwhile goals. Over time, a bidirectional relationship emerges: Achievement fosters self-esteem, and self-esteem, in turn, promotes good performance (Guay, Marsh, & Boivin, 2003).

What can adults do to promote, and to avoid undermining, this mutually supportive relationship between motivation and self-esteem? Some answers come from research on the precise content of adults' messages to children in achievement situations.

■ **Making Achievement-Related Attributions.** *Attributions* are our common, everyday explanations for the causes of behavior—our answers to the question "Why did I [or another person] do that?" Notice how Joey, in talking about the spelling bee at the beginning of this chapter, attributes his disappointing performance to *luck* (Belinda got all the easy words) and his usual success to *ability* (he *knows* he's a better speller than Belinda). Joey also appreciates that *effort* matters: "I knocked myself out studying those spelling lists."

Cognitive development permits school-age children to separate all these variables in explaining performance (Dweck, 2002). Those who are high in academic self-esteem and motivation make **mastery-oriented attributions,** crediting their successes to ability—a characteristic they can improve through trying hard and can count on when facing new challenges. And they attribute failure to factors that can be changed or controlled, such as insufficient effort or a very difficult task (Heyman & Dweck, 1998). So whether these children succeed or fail, they take an industrious, persistent approach to learning.

In contrast, children who develop **learned helplessness** attribute their failures, not their successes, to ability. When they succeed, they conclude that external factors, such as luck, are responsible. Unlike their mastery-oriented counterparts, they believe that ability is fixed and cannot be changed by trying hard (Cain & Dweck, 1995). When a task is difficult, these children experience an anxious loss of control—in Erikson's terms, a pervasive sense of inferiority. They give up without really trying.

Over time, the ability of learned-helpless children no longer predicts their performance. Because they fail to make the connection between effort and success, these children do not develop the metacognitive and self-regulatory skills necessary for high achievement (see Chapter 9). Lack of effective learning strategies, reduced persistence, and a sense of loss of control sustain one another in a vicious cycle (Pomerantz & Saxon, 2001).

■ **Influences on Achievement-Related Attributions.** What accounts for the different attributions of mastery-oriented and

Repeated negative evaluations of their ability can cause children to develop learned helplessness—the belief that ability cannot be improved by trying hard. When faced with a challenging task, this learned-helpless child is overwhelmed by negative thoughts and anxiety.

© MARY KATE DENNY/PHOTOEDIT

learned-helpless children? Adult communication plays a key role. Parents of children with a learned-helpless style tend to set unusually high standards while believing that their child is not very capable and must work harder than others to succeed. When these children fail, the parent might say, "You can't do that, can you? It's OK if you quit" (Hokoda & Fincham, 1995). When the child succeeds, the parent might give feedback that evaluates the child's traits ("You're so smart"). Trait statements promote a fixed view of ability, leading children to question their competence in the face of setbacks and to retreat from challenge (Mueller & Dweck, 1998).

Teachers' messages also affect children's attributions. Teachers who are caring and helpful and emphasize learning over getting good grades tend to have mastery-oriented students (Anderman et al., 2001). In a study of 1,600 third to eighth graders, students who viewed their teachers as providing positive, supportive learning conditions worked harder and participated more in class—factors that predicted high achievement, which sustained children's belief in the role of effort. In contrast, students with unsupportive teachers regarded their performance as externally controlled (by their teachers or by luck). This attitude predicted withdrawal from learning activities and declining achievement—outcomes that led children to doubt their ability (Skinner, Zimmer-Gembeck, & Connell, 1998).

For some children, performance is especially likely to be undermined by adult feedback. Girls tend to receive messages from teachers and parents that their ability is at fault when they do not do well, and negative stereotypes (for example, that girls are weak at math) undermine their interest and performance (Bleeker & Jacobs, 2004; Cole et al., 1999). Despite their higher achievement, girls more often than boys blame poor performance on ability. And as Chapter 9 revealed, low-SES ethnic minority students often receive less favorable feedback from teachers, especially when assigned to homogeneous groups of poorly achieving students—conditions that result in a drop in academic self-esteem and achievement.

■ **Fostering a Mastery-Oriented Approach.** Attribution research suggests that well-intended messages from adults sometimes undermine children's competence. An intervention called *attribution retraining* encourages learned-helpless children to believe that they can overcome failure by exerting more effort. Most often, children are first given tasks that are hard enough that they will experience some failure, followed by repeated feedback that helps them revise their attributions: "You can do it if you try harder." After they succeed, children receive additional feedback—"You're really good at this" or "You really tried hard on that one"—so that they view their success as due to both ability and effort, not to chance. Another approach is to encourage low-effort children to focus less on grades and more on mastering a task for its own sake (Hilt, 2004; Horner & Gaither, 2004).

Attribution retraining is best begun early, before children's views of themselves become hard to change. An even better approach is to prevent learned helplessness, using the strategies summarized in Applying What We Know below.

Emotional Development

Greater self-awareness and social sensitivity support gains in emotional competence in middle childhood. Changes take place in experience of self-conscious emotions, emotional understanding, and emotional self-regulation.

Ways to Foster a Mastery-Oriented Approach to Learning

Applying What We Know

Strategy	Description
Provision of tasks	Select tasks that are meaningful, responsive to a diversity of student interests, and appropriately matched to current competence so that the child is challenged but not overwhelmed.
Parent and teacher encouragement	Communicate warmth, confidence in the child's abilities, the value of achievement, and the importance of effort in success.
	Model high effort in overcoming failure.
	(For teachers) Communicate often with parents, suggesting ways to foster children's effort and progress.
	(For parents) Monitor schoolwork; provide scaffolded assistance that promotes knowledge of effective strategies and self-regulation.
Performance evaluations	Make evaluations private; avoid publicizing success or failure through wall posters, stars, privileges to "smart" children, and prizes for "best" performance.
	Stress individual progress and self-improvement.
School environment	Offer small classes, which permit teachers to provide individualized support for mastery.
	Provide for cooperative learning and peer tutoring, in which children assist each other; avoid ability grouping, which makes evaluations of children's progress public.
	Accommodate individual and cultural differences in styles of learning.
	Create an atmosphere that sends a clear message that all students can learn.

Sources: Hilt, 2004; Eccles, Wigfield, & Schiefele, 1998.

Self-Conscious Emotions

In middle childhood, the self-conscious emotions of pride and guilt become clearly governed by a sense of personal responsibility. An adult need not be present for a new accomplishment to spark pride or for a transgression to arouse guilt (Harter & Whitesell, 1989). Also, children no longer report guilt for any mishap, as they did earlier, but only for intentional wrongdoing, such as ignoring responsibilities, cheating, or lying (Ferguson, Stegge, & Damhuis, 1991).

Pride motivates children to take on further challenges. And guilt prompts them to make amends and to strive for self-improvement. But harsh, insensitive reprimands from adults ("Everyone else can do it! Why can't you?") can lead to intense shame, which (as noted in Chapter 8) is particularly destructive. As children form an overall sense of self-esteem, they may take one or two unworthy acts to be the whole of self-worth. A shame-induced, sharp drop in self-esteem can trigger withdrawal, depression, and intense anger at those who participated in the shame-evoking situation (Lindsay-Hartz, de Rivera, & Mascolo, 1995; Mills, 2005).

Emotional Understanding

School-age children's understanding of mental activity means that, unlike preschoolers, they are likely to explain emotion by referring to internal states, such as happy or sad thoughts, rather than to external events (Flavell, Flavell, & Green, 2001). Also, around age 8, children become aware that they can experience more than one emotion at a time, each of which may be positive or negative and differ in intensity (Pons et al., 2003). For example, recalling the birthday present he received from his grandmother, Joey reflected, "I was very happy that I got something but a little sad that I didn't get just what I wanted."

Appreciating mixed emotions helps children realize that people's expressions may not reflect their true feelings (Saarni, 1999). It also fosters awareness of self-conscious emotions. For example, 8- and 9-year-olds understand that pride combines two sources of happiness—joy in accomplishment and joy that a significant person recognized that accomplishment (Harter, 1999). Furthermore, children of this age can reconcile contradictory facial and situational cues in figuring out another's feelings, whereas younger children rely only on the emotional expression (Hoffner & Badzinski, 1989).

As with self-understanding, gains in emotional understanding are supported by cognitive development and social experiences, especially adults' sensitivity to children's feelings and willingness to discuss emotions. Together, these factors lead to a rise in empathy as well. As children move closer to adolescence, advances in perspective taking permit an empathic response not just to people's immediate distress but also to their general life condition (Hoffman, 2000). As Joey and Lizzie imagined how people who are chronically ill or hungry feel and evoked those emotions in themselves, they gave part of their allowance to charity and joined in fundraising projects through school, community center, and scouting.

Emotional Self-Regulation

Rapid gains in emotional self-regulation occur in middle childhood. As children engage in social comparison and care more about peer approval, they must learn to manage negative emotion that threatens their self-esteem.

By age 10, most children shift adaptively between two general strategies for managing emotion. In **problem-centered coping,** they appraise the situation as changeable, identify the difficulty, and decide what to do about it. If this does not work, they engage in **emotion-centered coping,** which is internal, private, and aimed at controlling distress when little can be done about an outcome (Kliewer, Fearnow, & Miller, 1996; Lazarus & Lazarus, 1994). For example, when faced with an anxiety-provoking test or an angry friend, older school-age children view problem solving and seeking social support as the best strategies. But when outcomes are beyond their control—for example, after receiving a bad grade—they opt for distraction or try to redefine the situation: "Things could be worse. There'll be another test." Compared with preschoolers, school-age children more often use these internal strategies to manage emotion, due to an improved ability to reflect on thoughts and feelings (Brenner & Salovey, 1997).

Furthermore, through interacting with parents, teachers, and peers, school-age children become more knowledgeable about socially approved ways to display negative emotion. They increasingly prefer verbal strategies ("Please stop pushing and wait your turn") to crying, sulking, or aggression (Shipman et al., 2003). Young school-age children justify these more mature displays of emotion by mentioning avoidance of punishment or adult approval, but by third grade, they begin to emphasize concern for others' feelings. Children with this awareness are rated as especially helpful, cooperative, and

These children are conducting a fundraiser to help the thousands of pets who were injured or left homeless by Hurricane Katrina in 2005. Their efforts are an adaptive strategy for managing the intense fear they may have felt after witnessing on television the widespread destruction caused by the hurricane.

© JOURNAL-COURIER/TIFFANY M. HERMON/THE IMAGE WORKS

socially responsive by teachers and as better-liked by peers (Garner, 1996; McDowell & Parke, 2000).

When emotional self-regulation has developed well, school-age children acquire a sense of *emotional self-efficacy*— a feeling of being in control of their emotional experience (Saarni, 2000). This fosters a favorable self-image and an optimistic outlook, which further help children face emotional challenges. Emotionally well-regulated children are upbeat in mood, empathic, and prosocial (Zeman, Shipman, & Suveg, 2002). In contrast, poorly regulated children impulsively unleash negative emotion, a response that interferes with prosocial behavior and peer acceptance.

Understanding Others: Perspective Taking

We have seen that middle childhood brings major advances in **perspective taking,** the capacity to imagine what other people may be thinking and feeling. These changes support self-concept and self-esteem, understanding of others, and a wide variety of social skills. Robert Selman's five-stage sequence describes changes in perspective-taking skill, based on children's and adolescents' responses to social dilemmas in which characters have differing information and opinions about an event.

As Table 10.1 indicates, at first children have only a limited idea of what other people might be thinking and feeling. Over time, they become more aware that people can interpret the same event quite differently. Soon, they can "step into another person's shoes" and reflect on how that person might regard their own thoughts, feelings, and behavior, as when they say something like, "I *thought you would think* I was just kidding when I said that." (Note that this level of perspective taking is similar to second-order false belief, described on page 305 in Chapter 9.) Finally, older children and adolescents can evaluate two people's perspectives simultaneously, at first from the vantage point of a disinterested spectator and later by referring to societal values. The following explanation reflects this ability: "I know why Joey hid the stray kitten in the basement, even though his mom was against keeping it. He believes in not hurting animals. If you put the kitten outside or give it to the pound, it might die."

Experiences in which adults and peers explain their viewpoints contribute greatly to children's perspective taking. Good perspective takers, in turn, are more likely to display empathy and sympathy and to handle difficult social situations in effective ways—among the reasons they are better-liked by peers (FitzGerald & White, 2003). Children with poor social skills, especially the angry, aggressive styles discussed in Chapter 8, have great difficulty imagining others' thoughts and feelings. They often mistreat adults and peers without feeling the guilt and remorse prompted by awareness of another's viewpoint. Interventions that provide coaching and practice in perspective taking help reduce antisocial behavior and increase empathy and prosocial responding (Chalmers & Townsend, 1990).

Moral Development

Recall from Chapter 8 that preschoolers pick up many morally relevant behaviors through modeling and reinforcement. By middle childhood, they have had time to internalize rules for good conduct: "It's good to help others in trouble" or "It's wrong to take something that doesn't belong to you." This change leads children to become considerably more independent and trustworthy. They can take on many more responsibilities, from running errands at the supermarket to watching younger siblings (Weisner, 1996). Of course, these

Table 10.1	Selman's Stages of Perspective Taking	
Stage	**Approximate Age Range**	**Description**
Level 0: Undifferentiated perspective taking	3–6	Children recognize that self and other can have different thoughts and feelings, but they frequently confuse the two.
Level 1: Social-informational perspective taking	4–9	Children understand that different perspectives may result because people have access to different information.
Level 2: Self-reflective perspective taking	7–12	Children can "step into another person's shoes" and view their own thoughts, feelings, and behavior from the other person's perspective. They also recognize that others can do the same.
Level 3: Third-party perspective taking	10–15	Children can step outside a two-person situation and imagine how the self and other are viewed from the point of view of a third, impartial party.
Level 4: Societal perspective taking	14–adult	Individuals understand that third-party perspective taking can be influenced by one or more systems of larger societal values.

Sources: Selman, 1976; Selman & Byrne, 1974.

advances occur only when children have had the consistent guidance and example of caring adults.

In Chapter 8, we also saw that children do not just copy their morality from others. As the cognitive-developmental approach emphasizes, they actively think about right and wrong. An expanding social world, the capacity to consider more information when reasoning, and perspective taking lead moral understanding to advance greatly in middle childhood.

Learning About Justice Through Sharing

In everyday life, children frequently experience situations involving **distributive justice**—beliefs about how to divide material goods fairly. Heated debate arises over how much weekly allowance is appropriate for siblings of different ages, who should sit where on a long car trip, or how six hungry playmates should share an eight-slice pizza. William Damon (1977, 1988) has traced children's concepts of distributive justice over early and middle childhood.

Even 4-year-olds recognize the importance of sharing, but their reasons often seem self-serving: "I shared because if I didn't, she wouldn't play with me" or "I let her have some, but most are for me because I'm older." In middle childhood, children express more mature notions of distributive justice. Their reasoning develops in an age-related, three-step sequence:

1. *Strict equality* (5 to 6 years). Children in the early school grades focus on making sure each person gets the same amount of a treasured resource, such as money, turns in a game, or a treat.

2. *Merit* (6 to 7 years). Slightly older children say extra rewards should go to someone who has worked especially hard or otherwise performed in an exceptional way.

3. *Equity and benevolence* (around 8 years). Finally, children believe that special consideration should be given to those at a disadvantage—for example, that a child who cannot produce as much or who does not get any allowance should be given more. Older children also adapt their basis of fairness to fit the situation, relying more on equality when interacting with strangers and more on benevolence with friends (McGillicuddy-De Lisi, Watkins, & Vinchur, 1994).

According to Damon (1988), the give-and-take of peer interaction makes children more sensitive to others' perspectives, which in turn supports their developing ideas of justice. Advanced distributive justice reasoning is associated with a greater willingness to help, share, and cooperate with others (Blotner & Bearison, 1984; McNamee & Peterson, 1986).

Moral and Social-Conventional Understanding

During the school years, children construct a flexible appreciation of moral rules. By age 7 to 8, they no longer say truth telling is always good and lying is always bad but also consider

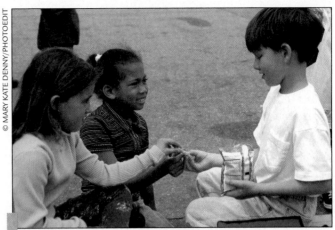

Children's ideas about distributive justice—how to divide material goods fairly—develop gradually in middle childhood. The child on the right understands that fairness should include benevolence. He shares with two younger children who do not have access to a special treat.

prosocial and antisocial intentions. They evaluate very negatively certain types of truthfulness, such as bluntly telling a classmate that you don't like her drawing (Bussey, 1999). And although both Chinese and Canadian schoolchildren consider lying about antisocial acts "very naughty," Chinese children—influenced by collectivist values—are more likely than their North American agemates to rate lying favorably when the intention is modesty, as when a student who has thoughtfully picked up litter from the playground says, "I didn't do it" (Lee et al., 1997).

As their ideas about justice advance, children take into account an increasing number of variables. As a result, they start to clarify and link moral imperatives and social conventions. School-age children, for example, distinguish social conventions with a clear *purpose* (not running in the school hallways to prevent injuries) from ones with no obvious justification (crossing a "forbidden" line on the playground). They regard violations of purposeful social conventions as closer to moral transgressions (Buchanan-Barrow & Barrett, 1998). With age, children also realize that people's *intentions* and the *contexts* of their actions affect the moral implications of violating a social convention. In a Canadian study, 8- to 10-year-olds stated that because of a flag's symbolic value, burning it to express disapproval of a country or to start a cooking fire is worse than burning it accidentally. They also stated that public flag burning is worse than private flag burning because of the emotional harm inflicted on others. But they recognized that flag burning is a form of freedom of expression, and most agreed that it would be acceptable in a country that treated its citizens unfairly (Helwig & Prencipe, 1999).

Children in Western and non-Western cultures reason similarly about moral and social-conventional concerns (Neff & Helwig, 2002; Nucci, 2002). When a directive is fair and caring, such as telling children to stop fighting or to share candy, school-age children view it as right, regardless of who states it—a principal, a teacher, or a child with no authority. Even in

Korean culture, which places a high value on deference to authority, 7- to 11-year-olds evaluate negatively a teacher's or principal's order to engage in immoral acts, such as stealing or refusing to share—a response that strengthens with age (Kim, 1998; Kim & Turiel, 1996).

Understanding Individual Rights

When children do challenge adult authority, they typically do so within the personal domain. As their grasp of moral imperatives and social conventions strengthens, so does their conviction that certain choices, such as hairstyle, friends, and leisure activities, are up to the individual (Nucci, 1996).

Notions of personal choice, in turn, enhance children's moral understanding. As early as age 6, children view freedom of speech and religion as individual rights, even if laws exist that deny those rights (Helwig & Turiel, 2002b). And they regard laws that discriminate against individuals—for example, denying certain people access to medical care or education—as wrong and worthy of violating (Helwig & Jasiobedzka, 2001). In justifying their responses, children appeal to personal privileges and, as they transition to adolescence, to the importance of individual rights for a fair society.

At the same time, older school-age children place limits on individual choice. Fourth graders faced with conflicting moral and personal concerns—such as whether or not to befriend a classmate of a different race or gender—typically decide in favor of kindness and fairness (Killen et al., 2002). Partly for this reason, prejudice usually declines in middle childhood.

Understanding Diversity and Inequality

By the early school years, children associate power and privilege with white people and poverty and inferior status with people of color. They do not necessarily acquire these views directly from parents or friends (Aboud & Doyle, 1996). Rather, they seem to pick up prevailing societal attitudes from implicit messages in the media and elsewhere in their environments.

Studies in diverse Western nations confirm that by age 5 to 7, white children generally evaluate their own racial group favorably and other racial groups less favorably or negatively (Aboud, 2003; Nesdale et al., 2004). Many minority children of this age, in a reverse pattern, assign positive characteristics to the privileged white majority and negative characteristics to their own group. In one study, researchers asked African-American 5- to 7-year-olds to recall information in stories either consistent or inconsistent with stereotypes of blacks. The children recalled more stereotyped traits, especially if they agreed with negative cultural views of African Americans (Averhart & Bigler, 1997). Similarly, Native Canadian children recall more positive attributes about white Canadians and more negative attributes about Native Canadians (Corenblum, 2003).

But recall that with age, children pay more attention to inner traits. The capacity to classify the social world in multiple ways enables school-age children to understand that people can be both "the same" and "different"—that those who look different need not think, feel, or act differently (Aboud & Amato, 2001). Consequently, negative attitudes toward minorities decline. After age 7 or 8, both majority and minority children express in-group favoritism, and white children's prejudice against out-group members often weakens (Ruble et al., 2004).

Nevertheless, the extent to which children hold racial and ethnic biases varies, depending on the following factors:

- *A fixed view of personality traits.* Children who believe that people's personality traits are fixed rather than changeable often judge others as either "good" or "bad." Ignoring people's motives and circumstances, they readily form prejudices on the basis of limited information. For example, they might infer that "a new child at school who tells a lie to get other kids to like her" is simply a bad person (Levy & Dweck, 1999).

- *Overly high self-esteem.* Children (and adults) with very high self-esteem are more likely to hold racial and ethnic prejudices (Baumeister et al., 2003; Bigler, Brown, & Markell, 2001). These individuals seem to put down disadvantaged individuals or groups as a way of justifying their own extremely favorable self-evaluation.

- *A social world in which people are sorted into groups.* The more adults highlight group distinctions for children, the more likely white children are to display prejudice (Bigler, Brown, & Markell, 2001).

These findings offer guidance in how to reduce racial and ethnic prejudices. One promising approach involves inducing children to view others' traits as changeable, by discussing with them the many possible influences on those traits. Intergroup

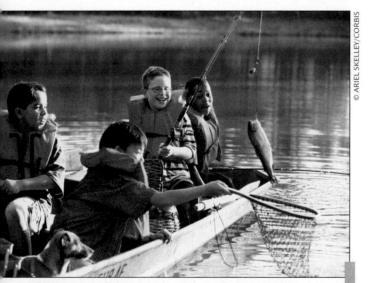

© ARIEL SKELLEY/CORBIS

Children who collaborate with members of other racial and ethnic groups are more likely to develop positive attitudes toward those who differ from themselves. These boys have many opportunities to work toward common goals at a summer camp.

contact, in which racially and ethnically different children become personally acquainted by collaborating on projects, is also helpful (Pettigrew, 1998). And long-term contact in neighborhoods, schools, and communities seems most effective. In support of this view, 5- and 6-year-olds attending a racially mixed school held generally positive out-group attitudes based on their everyday experiences (Aboud, 2003). Classrooms that expose children to diversity early and encourage them to value it prevent them from forming negative biases that are hard to overcome.

Ask Yourself

Review

How does emotional self-regulation improve in middle childhood? What implications do these changes have for children's self-esteem?

Apply

Ten-year-old Marla says her classmate Bernadette will never get good grades because she's lazy. Jane believes that Bernadette tries but can't concentrate because her parents are divorcing. Why is Marla more likely than Jane to develop prejudices?

Connect

Cite examples of how older children's capacity to take more information into account enhances their emotional and moral understanding.

www.ablongman.com/berk

Peer Relations

In middle childhood, the society of peers becomes an increasingly important context for development. Peer contact, as we have seen, contributes to perspective taking and understanding of self and others. These developments, in turn, enhance peer interaction. Compared with preschoolers, school-age children resolve conflicts more effectively, using persuasion and compromise (Mayeux & Cillessen, 2003). Sharing, helping, and other prosocial acts also increase. In line with these changes, aggression declines. But the drop is greatest for physical attacks (Tremblay, 2000). As we will see, other types of hostile aggression continue as children form peer groups.

Peer Groups

Watch children in the schoolyard or neighborhood, and notice how often they gather in groups of three to a dozen or more. By the end of middle childhood, children display a strong desire for group belonging. They form **peer groups,** collectives that generate unique values and standards for behavior and a social structure of leaders and followers. Peer groups organize on the basis of proximity (being in the same classroom) and similarity in sex, ethnicity, and popularity (Cairns, Xie, & Leung, 1998).

Peer groups first form in middle childhood. These girls have probably established a social structure of leader and followers as they gather for joint activities. Their body language suggests that they feel a strong sense of group belonging.

The practices of these informal groups lead to a "peer culture" that typically consists of a specialized vocabulary, dress code, and place to "hang out." As children develop these exclusive associations, the codes of dress and behavior that grow out of them become more broadly influential. At school, children who deviate are often rebuffed. "Kissing up" to teachers, wearing the wrong kind of shirt or shoes, or tattling on classmates can be grounds for critical glances and comments. These customs bind peers together, creating a sense of group identity. Within the group, children acquire many social skills—cooperation, leadership, followership, and loyalty to collective goals.

Most school-age children believe a group is wrong to exclude a peer (Killen et al., 2002). Nevertheless, children do exclude, often using relationally aggressive tactics. And peer groups—at the instigation of their leaders, who can be skillfully aggressive—frequently oust no longer "respected" children. These cast-outs are profoundly wounded, and many find new group ties hard to establish. Their previous behavior toward outsiders may reduce their chances of being included elsewhere. Excluded children often turn to other low-status peers for group belonging (Bagwell et al., 2001). By associating with peers who have poor social skills, they reduce their opportunities to learn socially competent behavior.

School-age children's desire for group membership can also be satisfied through formal group ties such as scouting, 4-H, and religious youth groups. Adult involvement holds in check the negative behaviors associated with children's informal peer groups. And through working on joint projects and helping in their communities, children gain in social and moral maturity (Vandell & Shumow, 1999).

Friendships

Whereas peer groups provide children with insight into larger social structures, one-to-one friendships contribute to the development of trust and sensitivity. During the school years, friendship becomes more complex and psychologically based. Consider the following 8-year-old's ideas:

> *Why is Shelly your best friend?* Because she helps me when I'm sad, and she shares. . . . *What makes Shelly so special?* I've known her longer, I sit next to her and got to know her better. . . . *How come you like Shelly better than anyone else?* She's done the most for me. She never disagrees, she never eats in front of me, she never walks away when I'm crying, and she helps me with my homework. . . . *How do you get someone to like you?* . . . If you're nice to [your friends], they'll be nice to you. (Damon, 1988, pp. 80–81)

As these responses show, friendship has become a mutually agreed-on relationship in which children like each other's personal qualities and respond to one another's needs and desires. And once a friendship forms, *trust* becomes its defining feature. School-age children state that a good friendship is based on acts of kindness that signify that each person can be counted on to support the other. Consequently, older children regard violations of trust, such as not helping when others need help, breaking promises, and gossiping behind the other's back, as serious breaches of friendship (Hartup & Abecassis, 2004; Selman, 1980).

Because of these features, school-age children's friendships are more selective. Whereas preschoolers say they have lots of friends, by age 8 or 9, children name only a handful of good friends. Girls, who demand greater closeness than boys, are more exclusive in their friendships (Markovitz, Benenson, & Dolensky, 2001).

In addition, children tend to select friends similar to themselves in age, sex, race, ethnicity, and SES. Friends also resemble one another in personality (sociability, aggression), peer popularity, academic achievement, and prosocial behavior (Hartup,

1996). Children probably choose companions much like themselves to increase the supportiveness of friendship. But the friendship opportunities offered by children's environments also affect their choices. In integrated schools and in classrooms with mixed-race collaborative learning groups, students report more cross-race friendships (Slavin & Cooper, 1999).

Over middle childhood, friendships remain fairly stable, usually lasting for several years. Through them, children learn the importance of emotional commitment. They come to realize that close relationships can survive disagreements if friends are secure in their liking for one another (Rose & Asher, 1999). In this way, friendship provides an important context in which children learn to tolerate criticism and resolve disputes.

Yet the impact of friendships on children's development depends on the nature of those friends. Children who bring kindness and compassion to their friendships strengthen each other's prosocial tendencies. When aggressive children make friends, the relationship often magnifies antisocial acts. Aggressive girls' friendships are high in exchange of private feelings but full of jealousy, conflict, and betrayal (Grotpeter & Crick, 1996). Among aggressive boys, friendships involve frequent expressions of anger, coercive statements, physical attacks, and enticements to rule-breaking behavior (Bagwell & Coie, 2004; Crick & Nelson, 2002; Dishion, Andrews, & Crosby, 1995). These findings indicate that the social problems of aggressive children operate within their closest peer ties.

Peer Acceptance

Peer acceptance refers to likability—the extent to which a child is viewed by a group of agemates, such as classmates, as a worthy social partner. Unlike friendship, likability is not a mutual relationship but a one-sided perspective, involving the group's view of an individual. Nevertheless, certain social skills that contribute to friendship also enhance peer acceptance. Better-accepted children tend to have more friends and more positive relationships with them (Gest, Graham-Bermann, & Hartup, 2001).

Researchers usually assess peer acceptance using self-reports that measure *social preferences*—for example, asking children to identify classmates whom they "like very much" or "like very little." Another approach assesses *social prominence*—children's judgments of whom most of their classmates admire. The classmates children identify as prominent (looked up to by many others) show only moderate correspondence with those they say they personally prefer (LaFontana & Cillessen, 1999).

These self-reports yield four general categories of peer acceptance:

- **Popular children,** who get many positive votes
- **Rejected children,** who are actively disliked
- **Controversial children,** who receive many votes, both positive and negative
- **Neglected children,** who are seldom chosen, either positively or negatively

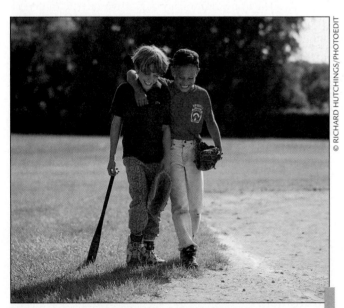

These boys both enjoy playing baseball, but they want to spend time together mainly because they like each other's personal qualities. A defining feature of their friendship is mutual trust. Each child counts on the other for support and assistance.

About two-thirds of students in a typical elementary school classroom fit one of these categories (Coie, Dodge, & Coppotelli, 1982). The remaining one-third are considered *average* in peer acceptance.

Peer acceptance is a powerful predictor of psychological adjustment. Rejected children, especially, are unhappy, alienated, poorly achieving children with low self-esteem. Both teachers and parents rate them as having a wide range of emotional and social problems. Peer rejection in middle childhood is also strongly associated with poor school performance, absenteeism, dropping out, substance use, antisocial behavior, and delinquency in adolescence and with criminality in young adulthood (Bagwell, Newcomb, & Bukowski, 1998; Laird et al., 2001; Parker et al., 1995).

However, earlier influences—children's characteristics combined with parenting practices—may largely explain the link between peer acceptance and adjustment. School-age children with problems in peer relationships are more likely to have experienced family stress due to low income, insensitive child rearing, and coercive discipline (Cowan & Cowan, 2004). Nevertheless, as we will see, rejected children evoke reactions from peers that contribute to their unfavorable development.

■ **Determinants of Peer Acceptance.** Why is one child liked while another is rejected? A wealth of research reveals that social behavior plays a powerful role.

Popular Children. Many popular children are kind and considerate. These **popular-prosocial children** usually combine academic and social competence, performing well in school and communicating with peers in sensitive, friendly, and cooperative ways (Cillessen & Bellmore, 2004). But other popular children are admired for their socially adept yet belligerent behavior. This smaller subtype, **popular-antisocial children,** includes "tough" boys—athletically skilled but poor students who cause trouble and defy adult authority—and relationally aggressive boys and girls who enhance their own status by ignoring, excluding, and spreading rumors about other children (Cillessen & Mayeux, 2004; Rodkin et al., 2000; Rose, Swenson, & Waller, 2004).

Despite their aggressiveness, these youths are viewed as "cool" by peers, perhaps because of their athletic ability and sophisticated though devious social skills. Although peer admiration gives these children some protection against lasting adjustment difficulties, their antisocial acts require intervention (Prinstein & La Greca, 2004). With age, peers like these high-status, aggressive youths less and less and may eventually reject them.

Rejected Children. Rejected children display a wide range of negative social behaviors. The largest subtype, **rejected-aggressive children,** show high rates of conflict, physical and relational aggression, and hyperactive, inattentive, and impulsive behavior. They are more extremely belligerent than popular-aggressive children and are also deficient in perspective taking and emotion regulation. For example, they tend to mis-

interpret the innocent behaviors of peers as hostile and to blame others for their social difficulties (Coie & Dodge, 1998; Crick, Casas, & Nelson, 2002). In contrast, **rejected-withdrawn children** are passive and socially awkward. These timid children are overwhelmed by social anxiety, hold negative expectations for how peers will treat them, and worry about being scorned and attacked (Hart et al., 2000; Ladd & Burgess, 1999).

As early as kindergarten, peers exclude rejected children. Soon rejected children's classroom participation declines, their feelings of loneliness rise, their academic achievement falters, and they want to avoid school (Buhs & Ladd, 2001). Rejected children generally have few friends, and some have none—a circumstance that predicts severe adjustment difficulties (Ladd & Troup-Gordon, 2003). Both types of rejected children are at risk for peer harassment. But as the Biology and Environment box on page 342 reveals, rejected-withdrawn children are especially likely to be targets.

Controversial and Neglected Children. Controversial children display a blend of positive and negative social behaviors that engenders mixed peer opinion. They are hostile and disruptive, but they also engage in positive, prosocial acts. Though some peers dislike them, they have qualities that protect them from social exclusion (Newcomb, Bukowski, & Pattee, 1993). But like their popular-antisocial counterparts, they often bully others and engage in calculated relational aggression to sustain their dominance (DeRosier & Thomas, 2003).

Finally, perhaps the most surprising finding is that neglected children, once thought to be in need of treatment, are usually well-adjusted. Although they engage in low rates of interaction and are considered shy by classmates, they are just as socially skilled as average children. They do not report feeling especially lonely or unhappy, and when they want to, they can break away from their usual pattern of playing by themselves (Harrist et al., 1997; Ladd & Burgess, 1999). Neglected children remind us that an outgoing, gregarious personality style is not the only path to emotional well-being.

■ **Helping Rejected Children.** A variety of interventions exist to improve the peer relations and psychological adjustment of rejected children. Most involve coaching, modeling, and reinforcing positive social skills, such as how to initiate interaction with a peer, cooperate in games, and respond to another child with friendly emotion and approval. Several of these programs have produced lasting gains in social competence and peer acceptance (Asher & Rose, 1997). Combining social-skills training with other treatments increases their effectiveness. Rejected children are often poor students, whose low academic self-esteem magnifies negative reactions to teachers and classmates. Intensive academic tutoring improves both school achievement and social acceptance (O'Neil et al., 1997).

Still another approach focuses on training in perspective taking and solving social problems. Many rejected-aggressive children are unaware of their poor social skills and do not take responsibility for their social failures (Mrug, Hoza, & Gerdes,

Biology and Environment

Bullies and Their Victims

Follow the activities of aggressive children over a school day and you will see that they reserve their hostilities for certain peers. A particularly destructive form of interaction is **peer victimization,** in which certain children become frequent targets of verbal and physical attacks or other forms of abuse. What sustains these repeated assault–retreat cycles between pairs of children?

Research indicates that about 10 to 20 percent of children are bullies, while 15 to 30 percent are repeatedly victimized. Most bullies are boys who use both physical and verbal attacks, but girls

Children who are victimized by bullies tend to be physically weak, rejected by peers, and afraid to defend themselves—characteristics that make them easy targets. Most bullies are boys who use both physical and relational aggression, but some girls are bullies too, bombarding their victims with relational hostility.

sometimes bombard a vulnerable classmate with verbal hostility (Pepler et al., 2004; Rigby, 2004). A substantial number of bullies are high-status youngsters. Some are liked for their leadership or athletic abilities, but most are disliked—or eventually become so—because of their cruelty (Vaillancourt, Hymel, & McDougall, 2003). Nevertheless, peers rarely help victims of bullying, and about 20 to 30 percent of onlookers actually encourage bullies, even joining in (Salmivalli & Voeten, 2004).

Chronic victims are passive when active behavior is expected. On the playground, they hang around chatting or wander on their own. When bullied, they give in, cry, and assume defensive postures (Boulton, 1999). Biologically based traits—an inhibited temperament and a frail physical appearance—contribute to victimization. Victims also have histories of resistant attachment, overly controlling child rearing, and maternal overprotection. These parenting behaviors prompt anxiety, low self-esteem, and dependency, resulting in a fearful demeanor that marks these children as vulnerable (Snyder et al., 2003). Victimization leads to adjustment difficulties that may include depression, loneliness, low self-esteem, poor school performance, disruptive behavior, and school avoidance (Kochenderfer-Ladd & Wardrop, 2001; Paul & Cillessen, 2003).

Aggression and victimization are not polar opposites. One-third to one-half of victims are also aggressive, picking fights or retaliating with relational aggression. Occasionally, they retaliate against powerful bullies, who respond by abusing them again—a cycle that sustains their

victim status (Camodeca et al., 2002; Kochenderfer-Ladd, 2003). Among rejected children, these bully/ victims are the most despised, placing them at severe risk for maladjustment. They often have histories of extremely maladaptive parenting, including child abuse. This combination of highly negative home and peer experiences places them at severe risk for maladjustment (Schwartz, Proctor, & Chien, 2001).

Interventions that change victimized children's negative opinions of themselves and that teach them to respond in nonreinforcing ways to their attackers are helpful. Another way to assist victimized children is to help them acquire the social skills to form and maintain a gratifying friendship. When children have a close friend to whom they can turn for help, bullying episodes usually end quickly. Anxious, withdrawn children with a best friend have fewer adjustment problems than victims with no close friends (Goldbaum et al., 2003).

Although changing the behavior of victimized children can help, this does not mean they are to blame. The best way to reduce bullying is to change youth environments (including school, sports programs, recreation centers, and neighborhoods), promoting prosocial attitudes and behaviors and enlisting young people's cooperation. Effective approaches include developing school and community codes against bullying, teaching child bystanders to intervene, enlisting parents' assistance in changing bullies' behaviors, and (if necessary) moving socially prominent bullies to another class or school (Smith, Ananiadou, & Cowie, 2003).

2001). Rejected-withdrawn children, in contrast, are likely to develop a *learned-helpless* approach to peer difficulties—concluding, after repeated rebuffs, that they will never be liked (Wichmann, Coplan, & Daniels, 2004). Both types of children need help attributing their peer difficulties to internal, changeable causes.

Finally, because rejected children's socially incompetent behaviors often originate in a poor fit between the child's temperament and parenting practices, interventions that focus on the child alone may not be sufficient. If parent–child interaction does not change, children may soon return to their old behavior patterns.

Gender Typing

Children's understanding of gender roles broadens in middle childhood, and their gender-role identities (views of themselves as relatively masculine or feminine) change as well. We will see that development differs for boys and girls, and it can vary considerably across cultures.

Gender-Stereotyped Beliefs

During the school years, children extend the gender-stereotyped beliefs they acquired in early childhood. Research in many countries reveals that stereotyping of personality traits increases steadily, resembling that of adults around age 11 (Best, 2001; Heyman & Legare, 2004). For example, children regard "tough," "aggressive," "rational," and "dominant" as masculine and "gentle," "sympathetic," and "dependent" as feminine (Serbin, Powlishta, & Gulko, 1993).

Children derive these distinctions from observing sex differences in behavior as well as from adult treatment. Adults, for example, tend to demand greater independence from boys. When helping a child with a task, parents (especially fathers) behave in a more mastery-oriented fashion with sons, setting higher standards, explaining concepts, and pointing out important features of tasks—particularly during gender-typed pursuits, such as science activities (Tenenbaum & Leaper, 2003; Tenenbaum et al., 2005). Furthermore, parents less often encourage girls to make their own decisions. And both parents and teachers more often praise boys for knowledge and accomplishment, girls for obedience (Good & Brophy, 2003; Leaper, Anderson, & Sanders, 1998; Pomerantz & Ruble, 1998).

Also in line with adult stereotypes, school-age children quickly figure out which academic subjects and skill areas are "masculine" and which are "feminine." They often regard reading, spelling, art, and music as more for girls and mathematics, athletics, and mechanical skills as more for boys (Eccles, Jacobs, & Harold, 1990; Jacobs & Weisz, 1994). These attitudes influence children's preferences for and sense of competence at certain subjects. For example, boys feel more competent than girls at math and science, whereas girls feel more competent than boys at language arts—even when children of equal skill level are compared (Andre et al., 1999; Freedman-Doan et al., 2000; Hong, Veach, & Lawrenz, 2003). As we will see in Chapter 11, these beliefs become realities for many young people in adolescence.

Although school-age children are aware of many stereotypes, they also develop a more open-minded view of what males and females *can do*. As with racial stereotypes (see page 338), the ability to classify flexibly underlies this change. School-age children realize that a person can belong to more than one social category—for example, be a "boy" yet "like to play house" (Bigler, 1995). Still, acknowledging that people *can* cross gender lines does not mean that children always *approve* of doing so. Children take a harsh view of certain violations—boys playing with dolls and wearing girls' clothing and girls acting noisily and roughly. They are especially intolerant when

boys engage in these "cross-gender" acts, which children regard as nearly as bad as moral transgressions (Blakemore, 2003; Levy, Taylor, & Gelman, 1995). These findings reflect the greater social pressure on boys and men to conform to gender stereotypes.

Gender Identity and Behavior

Boys' and girls' gender identities follow different paths in middle childhood. From third to sixth grade, boys strengthen their identification with "masculine" personality traits, whereas girls' identification with "feminine" traits declines. Girls begin to describe themselves as having some "other-gender" characteristics (Serbin, Powlishta, & Gulko, 1993). Whereas boys usually stick to "masculine" pursuits, girls now experiment with a wider range of options. Besides cooking, sewing, and babysitting, they join organized sports teams and work on science projects. And girls, more often than boys, consider future work roles stereotyped for the other gender, such as firefighter and astronomer (Liben & Bigler, 2002).

These changes reflect a mixture of cognitive and social forces. School-age children of both sexes are aware that society attaches greater prestige to "masculine" characteristics. For example, they rate "masculine" occupations as having higher status than "feminine" occupations (Liben, Bigler, & Krogh, 2001). Messages from adults and peers are also influential. In Chapter 8 we saw that parents (especially fathers) are far less tolerant when sons, as opposed to daughters, cross gender lines. Similarly, a tomboyish girl can make her way into boys' activities without losing the approval of her female peers, but a boy who hangs out with girls is likely to be ridiculed and rejected.

As school-age children characterize themselves in terms of general dispositions, their gender identity expands to include

During middle childhood, girls feel freer than boys to experiment with "cross-gender" activities. This 9-year-old perfects her wood-carving skills.

the following self-evaluations, which greatly affect their adjustment:

🖋 *Gender typicality*—the degree to which the child feels similar to others of the same gender. Although children need not be highly gender typed to view themselves as gender-typical, their psychological well-being depends, to some degree, on feeling that they "fit in" with their same-sex peers (Egan & Perry, 2001).

🖋 *Gender contentedness*—the degree to which the child feels satisfied with his or her gender assignment, which also promotes happiness.

🖋 *Felt pressure to conform to gender roles*—the degree to which the child feels parents and peers disapprove of his or her gender-related traits. Because such pressure reduces the likelihood that children will explore options related to their interests and talents, children who feel gender-typed pressure strongly are often distressed.

In a longitudinal study of third through seventh graders, gender-typical and gender-contented children gained in self-esteem over the following year. In contrast, children who were gender-atypical and gender-discontented declined in self-worth. Furthermore, gender-atypical children who reported intense pressure to conform to gender roles experienced serious difficulties—withdrawal, sadness, disappointment, and anxiety (Yunger, Carver, & Perry, 2004).

Clearly, how children feel about themselves in relation to their gender group becomes vitally important in middle childhood, and those who experience peer rejection because of their gender-atypical traits suffer profoundly. Return to the case of David, the boy who was reared as a girl, on page 275 in Chapter 8, and note how his dissatisfaction with his gender assignment joined with severe peer condemnation to severely impair his adjustment.

Ask Yourself

Review
How does friendship change in middle childhood?

Apply
What changes in parent–child relationships are probably necessary to help rejected children?

Connect
Return to page 277 in Chapter 8 and review the concept of androgyny. Which of the two sexes is more androgynous in middle childhood, and why?

Reflect
As a school-age child, did you have classmates whom you would classify as popular-aggressive? What were they like, and why do you think peers admired them?

Family Influences

As children move into school, peer, and community contexts, the parent–child relationship changes. At the same time, children's well-being continues to depend on the quality of family interaction. In the following sections, we will see that contemporary changes in North American families—high rates of divorce, remarriage, and maternal employment—can have positive as well as negative effects on children. In later chapters, we take up other family structures, including gay and lesbian families, never-married single-parent families, and the increasing numbers of grandparents rearing grandchildren.

Parent–Child Relationships

In middle childhood, the amount of time children spend with parents declines dramatically. The child's growing independence means that parents must deal with new issues. "I've struggled with how many chores to assign, how much allowance to give, whether their friends are good influences, and what to do about problems at school," Rena remarked. "And then there's the challenge of how to keep track of them when they're out of the house or even when they're home and I'm not there to see what's going on."

Despite these new concerns, child rearing becomes easier for those parents who established an authoritative style in the early years. Reasoning is more effective with school-age children because of their greater capacity for logical thinking and their increased respect for parents' expert knowledge (Collins, Madsen, & Susman-Stillman, 2002). When parents communicate openly with children and engage in joint decision making when possible, children are more likely to listen to parents' perspectives in situations where compliance is vital (Kuczynski & Lollis, 2002; Russell, Mize, & Bissaker, 2004).

As children demonstrate that they can manage daily activities and responsibilities, effective parents gradually shift control from adult to child. This does not mean they let go entirely. Instead, they engage in **coregulation,** a transitional form of supervision in which they exercise general oversight while permitting children to be in charge of moment-by-moment decision making. Coregulation grows out of a cooperative relationship between parent and child based on give-and-take and mutual respect. Parents must guide and monitor from a distance and effectively communicate expectations when they are with their children. And children must inform parents of their whereabouts, activities, and problems so parents can intervene when necessary (Maccoby, 1984). Coregulation supports and protects children while preparing them for adolescence, when they will make many important decisions themselves.

As at younger ages, mothers spend more time than fathers with school-age children. Mothers also are more knowledgeable about children's everyday activities. Still, fathers often are highly involved. Each parent, however, tends to devote more time to children of their own sex (Crouter et al., 1999; Lamb & Lewis, 2004). In parents' separate activities with children, mothers are more concerned with caregiving and ensuring that children meet responsibilities in homework, after-school lessons, and chores. Fathers, especially those with sons, focus on achievement-related and recreational pursuits (Collins & Russell, 1991). But when both parents are present, fathers engage in as much caregiving as mothers.

Although school-age children often press for greater independence, they know how much they need their parents' continuing support. In one study, fifth and sixth graders described parents as the most influential people in their lives (Furman & Buhrmester, 1992). They often turned to mothers and fathers for affection, advice, enhancement of self-worth, and assistance with everyday problems.

Siblings

In addition to parents and friends, siblings are important sources of support for school-age children. Yet sibling rivalry tends to increase in middle childhood. As children participate in a wider range of activities, parents often compare siblings' traits and accomplishments. The child who gets less parental affection, more disapproval, or fewer material resources is likely to be resentful (Brody, 2004; Dunn, 2004).

For same-sex siblings who are close in age, parental comparisons are more frequent, resulting in more quarreling and antagonism and poorer adjustment. This effect is particularly strong when parents are under stress as a result of financial worries, marital conflict, or single parenthood (Jenkins, Rasbash, & O'Connor, 2003). Parents whose energies are drained become less careful about being fair. Children react especially intensely when fathers prefer one child. Perhaps because

fathers, overall, spend less time with children than mothers, their favoritism is more noticeable and triggers greater anger (Brody, Stoneman, & McCoy, 1992).

To reduce this rivalry, siblings often strive to be different from one another. For example, two brothers I know deliberately selected different athletic pursuits and musical instruments. If the older one did especially well at an activity, the younger one did not want to try it. Parents can limit these effects by making an effort not to compare children, but some feedback about their competencies is inevitable. As siblings strive to win recognition for their own uniqueness, they shape important aspects of each other's development.

Although conflict rises, school-age siblings continue to rely on each other for companionship and assistance. When researchers asked siblings about shared daily activities, children mentioned that older siblings often helped younger siblings with academic and peer challenges. And both offered each other help with family issues (Tucker, McHale, & Crouter, 2001). When parents are distant and uninvolved, siblings sometimes fill in and become more supportive of one another.

Only Children

Although sibling relationships bring many benefits, they are not essential for healthy development. Contrary to popular belief, only children are not spoiled but are even advantaged in some respects. North American children growing up in one-child families are higher in self-esteem and achievement motivation, do better in school, and attain higher levels of education (Falbo, 1992). One reason may be that only children have somewhat closer relationships with parents, who may exert more pressure for mastery and accomplishment. However, only children tend to be less well-accepted in the peer group, perhaps because they have not had the opportunities that sibling interaction offers in practicing conflict resolution skills (Kitzmann, Cohen, & Lockwood, 2002).

Favorable development also characterizes only children in China, where a one-child family policy has been strictly enforced in urban areas for more than two decades to control overpopulation. Compared with agemates who have siblings, Chinese only children are advanced in cognitive development and academic achievement (Falbo & Poston, 1993; Jiao, Ji, & Jing, 1996). They also feel more emotionally secure, perhaps because government disapproval promotes tension in families with more than one child (Yang et al., 1995). Chinese mothers usually ensure that their children have regular contact with first cousins (who are considered siblings). Perhaps as a result, Chinese only children do not differ from agemates with siblings in social skills and peer acceptance (Hart et al., 2003). The next generation of Chinese only children, however, will have no first cousins.

Divorce

Children's interactions with parents and siblings are affected by other aspects of family life. Joey and Lizzie's relationship,

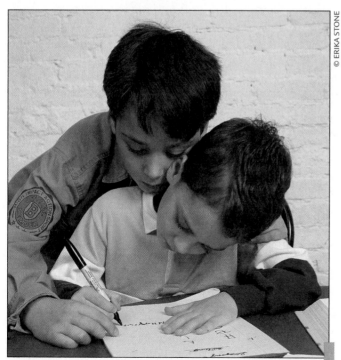

Although sibling rivalry tends to increase in middle childhood, siblings also provide one another with emotional support and help with difficult tasks.

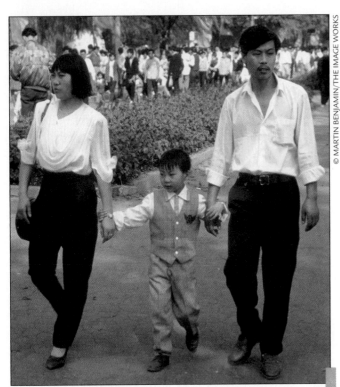

Limiting family size has been a national policy in the People's Republic of China since 1979. In urban areas, the majority of couples have no more than one child.

© MARTIN BENJAMIN/THE IMAGE WORKS

Rena told me, had been particularly negative only a few years before. Joey pushed, hit, and taunted Lizzie and called her names. Although she tried to retaliate, she was no match for Joey's larger size. The arguments usually ended with Lizzie running in tears to her mother. Joey's and Lizzie's fighting coincided with Rena and her husband's growing marital unhappiness. When Joey was 8 and Lizzie 5, their father, Drake, moved out.

The children were not alone in having to weather this traumatic event. Between 1960 and 1985, divorce rates in Western nations rose dramatically before stabilizing in most countries. The United States has the highest divorce rate in the world, Canada the sixth highest (see Figure 10.3). Of the 45 percent of American and 30 percent of Canadian marriages that end in divorce, half involve children. At any given time, one-fourth of American and one-fifth of Canadian children live in single-parent households. Although most reside with their mothers, the percentage in father-headed households has increased steadily, to about 12 percent in both nations (Hetherington & Stanley-Hagan, 2002; Statistics Canada, 2005b).

Children of divorce spend an average of five years in a single-parent home—almost a third of childhood. For many, divorce leads to new family relationships. About two-thirds of divorced parents marry again. Half their children eventually experience a third major change—the end of a parent's second marriage (Hetherington & Kelly, 2002).

These figures reveal that divorce is not a single event in the lives of parents and children. Instead, it is a transition that leads to a variety of new living arrangements, accompanied by changes in housing, income, and family roles and responsibili-

ties. Since the 1960s, many studies have reported that marital breakup is quite stressful for children. But the research also reveals great individual differences (Hetherington, 2003). How well children fare depends on many factors: the custodial parent's psychological health, the child's characteristics, and social supports within the family and surrounding community.

■ **Immediate Consequences.** "Things were worst during the period Drake and I decided to separate," Rena reflected. "We fought over division of our belongings and the custody of the children, and the kids suffered. Sobbing, Lizzie told me she was 'sorry she made Daddy go away.' Joey kicked and threw things at home and didn't do his work at school. In the midst of everything, I could hardly deal with their problems. We had to sell the house; I couldn't afford it alone. And I needed a better-paying job."

Rena's description captures conditions in many newly divorced households. Family conflict often rises as parents try to settle disputes over children and possessions. Once one parent moves out, additional events threaten supportive interactions between parents and children. Mother-headed households typically experience a sharp drop in income. In the United States and Canada, the majority of single mothers with young children live in poverty, getting less than the full amount of child support from the absent father or none at all (Children's Defense Fund, 2005; Statistics Canada, 2005b). They often have to move to lower-cost housing, reducing supportive ties to neighbors and friends.

The transition from marriage to divorce typically leads to high maternal stress, depression, and anxiety and to a disorganized family situation (Hope, Power, & Rodgers, 1999). "Meals and bedtimes were at all hours, the house didn't get cleaned, and I stopped taking Joey and Lizzie on weekend outings," said Rena. As children react with distress and anger to their less secure home lives, discipline may become harsh and inconsistent. Contact with noncustodial fathers often decreases over time (Hetherington & Kelly, 2002). Fathers who see their children only occasionally are inclined to be permissive and indulgent, making the mother's task of managing the child even more difficult.

In view of these changes, it is not surprising that about 20 to 25 percent of children in divorced families display severe problems, compared with about 10 percent in nondivorced families (Greene et al., 2003; Martinez & Forgatch, 2002; Pruett et al., 2003). At the same time, reactions vary with children's age, temperament, and sex.

Children's Age. Five-year-old Lizzie's fear that she had caused her father to leave is not unusual. Preschool and young school-age children often blame themselves for a marital breakup and fear that both parents may abandon them (Pryor & Rodgers, 2001). Even many older children, with the cognitive maturity to understand that they are not responsible for their parents' divorce, react strongly, becoming unruly and escaping into undesirable peer activities, especially when family conflict is high and supervision of children is low (Hetherington & Stanley-Hagan, 1999; Simons & Chao, 1996). But not all older children react this way. Some—especially the oldest child in

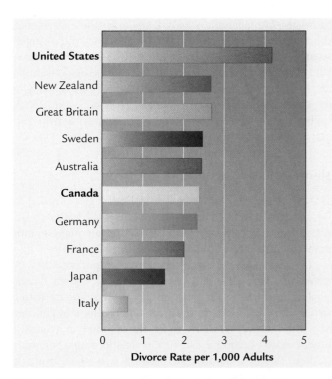

■ FIGURE 10.3 Divorce rates in ten industrialized nations. The U.S. divorce rate is the highest in the industrialized world, far exceeding divorce rates in other countries. The Canadian divorce rate is the sixth highest. (Adapted from Australian Bureau of Statistics, 2004; U.S. Census Bureau, 2006b; United Nations, 2001.)

the family—display more mature behavior, willingly taking on extra family and household tasks as well as emotional support of a depressed, anxious mother. But if these demands are too great, children may eventually become resentful, withdraw from the family, and engage in angry, acting-out behavior (Hetherington, 1999).

Children's Temperament and Sex. When temperamentally difficult children are exposed to stressful life events and inadequate parenting, their problems are magnified. In contrast, easy children are less often targets of parental anger and also cope more effectively with adversity.

These findings help us understand sex differences in response to divorce. Girls sometimes respond as Lizzie did, with internalizing reactions such as crying, self-criticism, and withdrawal or, more often, with demanding, attention-getting behavior. But in mother-custody families, boys are at greater risk for serious adjustment problems (Amato, 2001). Recall from Chapter 8 that boys are more active and noncompliant—behaviors that increase with exposure to parental conflict and inconsistent discipline. Coercive mother–child interaction and impulsive, defiant behavior on the part of sons are common in divorcing households.

Perhaps because their behavior is so unruly, boys receive less emotional support from mothers, teachers, and peers. And as Joey's behavior toward Lizzie illustrates, the coercive cycles of interaction between boys and their divorced mothers soon spread to sibling relations (Hetherington & Kelly, 2002). These

outcomes compound adjustment difficulties. After divorce, children who are challenging to rear generally get worse (Hanson, 1999).

■ Long-Term Consequences. Rena eventually found better-paying work and gained control over the daily operation of the household. Her own feelings of anger and rejection also declined. And after several meetings with a counselor, Rena and Drake realized the harmful impact of their quarreling on Joey and Lizzie. Drake visited regularly and handled Joey's unruliness with firmness and consistency. Soon Joey's school performance improved, his behavior problems subsided, and both children seemed calmer and happier.

Most children show improved adjustment by two years after divorce. Yet overall, children and adolescents of divorced parents continue to show slightly lower academic achievement, self-esteem, and social competence and to have more emotional and behavior problems (Amato, 2001). Children with difficult temperaments are especially likely to drop out of school, to be depressed, and to display antisocial behavior. And divorce is linked to problems with adolescent sexuality and with development of intimate ties. Young people who experienced parental divorce—especially more than once—display higher rates of early sexual activity and adolescent parenthood (Wolfinger, 2000). And other lasting difficulties occur for some, in the form of reduced educational attainment, troubled marriages, poor parent–child relationships, and divorce in adulthood (Amato & Cheadle, 2005).

The overriding factor in positive adjustment following divorce is effective parenting—how well the custodial parent handles stress and shields the child from conflict, and the extent to which each parent uses authoritative child rearing (Leon, 2003; Wolchik et al., 2000). Where the custodial parent is the mother, contact with fathers is important. The more paternal contact and the warmer the father–child relationship, the less children react with defiance and aggression (Dunn et al., 2004). For girls, a good father–child relationship protects against early sexual activity and unhappy romantic involvements. For boys, it seems to affect overall psychological well-being. In fact, several studies indicate that outcomes for sons are better when the father is the custodial parent (Clarke-Stewart & Hayward, 1996; McLanahan, 1999). Fathers' greater economic security and image of authority seem to help them engage in effective parenting with sons. And boys in father-custody families may benefit from greater involvement of both parents because noncustodial mothers participate more than noncustodial fathers in their children's lives.

Although divorce is painful for children, remaining in an intact but high-conflict family is much worse than making the transition to a low-conflict, single-parent household (Greene et al., 2003). Divorcing parents who set aside their disagreements and support one another in their child-rearing roles greatly increase that chances that their children will grow up competent, stable, and happy. Caring extended-family members, teachers, siblings, and friends also reduce the likelihood that divorce will result in long-term difficulties (Hetherington, 2003; Lussier et al., 2002).

■ **Divorce Mediation, Joint Custody, and Child Support.**
Awareness that divorce is highly stressful for children and families has led to community-based services aimed at helping families through this difficult time. One such service is **divorce mediation,** a series of meetings between divorcing adults and a trained professional aimed at reducing family conflict, including legal battles over property division and child custody. Research reveals that mediation increases out-of-court settlements, cooperation and involvement of both parents in child rearing, and parents' and children's feelings of well-being (Emery, 2001).

An increasingly common child custody option is **joint custody,** which grants the mother and father equal say in important decisions about the child's upbringing, as a means of encouraging both to remain involved in their children's lives. In most instances, children reside with one parent and see the other on a fixed schedule, much like the typical sole-custody situation. But in other cases, parents share physical custody, and children move between homes and sometimes schools and peer groups. These transitions can be especially hard on some children. Joint-custody parents report little conflict—fortunately so, since the success of the arrangement depends on parental cooperation. And their children—regardless of living arrangements—tend to be better-adjusted than children in sole-maternal-custody homes (Bauserman, 2002).

Finally, many single-parent families depend on child support from the absent parent to relieve financial strain. All U.S. states and Canadian provinces have procedures for withholding wages from parents who fail to make these payments. Although child support is usually not enough to lift a single-parent family out of poverty, it can ease its burdens substantially. Noncustodial fathers who have generous visitation schedules and who often see their children are more likely to pay child support regularly (Amato & Sobolewski, 2004). Applying What We Know below summarizes ways to help children adjust to their parents' divorce.

Blended Families

"If you get married to Wendell, and Daddy gets married to Carol," Lizzie wondered aloud to Rena, "then I'll have two sisters and one more brother. And let's see, how many grandmothers and grandfathers? A lot!" exclaimed Lizzie.

Life in a single-parent family is often temporary. About 60 percent of divorced parents remarry within a few years. Others cohabit, or share a sexual relationship and a residence with a partner outside of marriage. Parent, stepparent, and children form a new family structure called the **blended,** or **reconstituted, family**—a complex set of new relationships. For some children, this expanded family network is positive, bringing more adult attention. But most have more problems than in stable, first-marriage families. Switching to stepparents' new rules and expectations can be stressful. In addition, children often view steprelatives as intruders. But how well they adapt is, again, related to the quality of family functioning

---

Helping Children Adjust to Their Parents' Divorce

Applying What We Know

Suggestion	Rationale
Shield children from conflict.	Witnessing intense parental conflict is very damaging to children. If one parent insists on expressing hostility, children fare better if the other parent does not respond in kind.
Provide children with as much continuity, familiarity, and predictability as possible.	Children adjust better during the period surrounding divorce when their lives have stability—for example, the same school, bedroom, baby-sitter, playmates, and daily schedule.
Explain the divorce and tell children what to expect.	Children are more likely to develop fears of abandonment if they are not prepared for their parents' separation. They should be told that their mother and father will not be living together anymore, which parent will be moving out, and when they will be able to see that parent. If possible, mother and father should explain the divorce together. Parents should provide a reason for the divorce that the child can understand and assure children that they are not to blame.
Emphasize the permanence of the divorce.	Fantasies of parents getting back together can prevent children from accepting the reality of their current life. Children should be told that the divorce is final and that they cannot change this fact.
Respond sympathetically to children's feelings.	Children need a supportive and understanding response to their feelings of sadness, fear, and anger. For children to adjust well, their painful emotions must be acknowledged, not denied or avoided.
Engage in authoritative parenting.	Provide children with affection and acceptance as well as reasonable demands for mature behavior and consistent, rational discipline. Parents who engage in authoritative parenting greatly reduce their children's risk of maladjustment following divorce.
Promote a continuing relationship with both parents.	When parents disentangle their lingering hostility toward the former spouse from the child's need for a continuing relationship with the other parent, children adjust well. Grandparents and other extended-family members can help by not taking sides.

Source: Teyber, 2001.

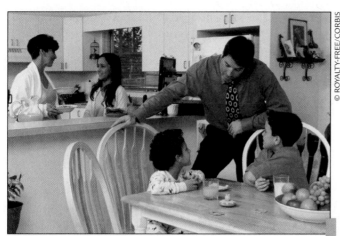

Adapting to life in a blended family is stressful for children. When stepparents build warm relationships with children before moving into their parenting role and form a cooperative "parenting coalition" with their partner, they provide consistency in child rearing, limit loyalty conflicts, and ease children's adjustment.

(Hetherington & Kelly, 2002). This depends on which parent forms a new relationship and on the child's age and sex. As we will see, older children and girls seem to have the hardest time.

■ **Mother–Stepfather Families.** Since mothers generally retain custody of children, the most common form of blended family is a mother–stepfather arrangement. Boys tend to adjust quickly, welcoming a stepfather who is warm, who refrains from exerting his authority too quickly, and who offers relief from coercive cycles of mother–son interaction. Mothers' friction with sons also declines as a result of greater economic security, another adult to share household tasks, and an end to loneliness (Visher, Visher, & Pasley, 2003). In contrast, girls adapt less favorably. Stepfathers disrupt the close ties many girls have established with their mothers, and girls often react with sulky, resistant behavior (Bray, 1999).

Note, however, that age affects these findings. Older school-age children and adolescents of both sexes display more irresponsible, acting-out behavior than their peers in nonstepfamilies (Hetherington & Stanley-Hagan, 2000). Some parents are warmer and more involved with their biological children than with their stepchildren. Older children are more likely to notice and challenge unfair treatment. And adolescents often view the new stepparent as a threat to their freedom, especially if they experienced little parental monitoring in the single-parent family. Still, many teenagers have good relationships with both fathers—a circumstance linked to better adjustment (White & Gilbreth, 2001).

■ **Father–Stepmother Families.** Remarriage of noncustodial fathers often leads to reduced contact with their biological children, as these fathers tend to withdraw from their "previous" families (Dunn, 2002). When fathers have custody, children typically react negatively to remarriage. One reason is that children living with fathers often start out with more problems. Perhaps the biological mother could no longer handle the unruly child (usually a boy), so the father and his new part-

ner are faced with a youngster who has behavior problems. In other instances, the father has custody because of a very close relationship with the child, and his remarriage disrupts this bond (Buchanan, Maccoby, & Dornbusch, 1996).

Girls, especially, have a hard time getting along with their stepmothers, either because the girl's bond with her father is threatened or because she becomes entangled in a loyalty conflict between the two mother figures. But the longer girls live in father–stepmother households, the more positive their interaction with stepmothers becomes (Hetherington & Jodl, 1994). With time and patience, most girls eventually benefit from the support of a second mother figure.

■ **Support for Blended Families.** Family life education and therapy can help parents and children adapt to the complexities of blended families. Effective approaches encourage stepparents to move into their new roles gradually by first building a warm relationship with the child before engaging in more active parenting (Visher, Visher, & Pasley, 2003). Counselors can help couples form a cooperative "parenting coalition" to limit loyalty conflicts and provide consistency in child rearing. This allows children to benefit from the increased diversity that stepparent relationships bring to their lives.

Unfortunately, the divorce rate for second marriages is even higher than for first marriages. Parents with antisocial tendencies and poor child-rearing skills are particularly likely to have several divorces and remarriages. And the more marital transitions children experience, the greater their difficulties (Dunn, 2002). These families usually require prolonged, intensive therapy.

Maternal Employment and Dual-Earner Families

Today, single and married mothers are in the labor market in nearly equal proportions, and more than three-fourths of those

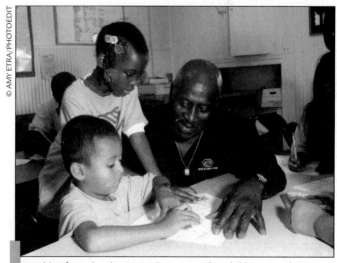

In this after-school program in Los Angeles, children spend time productively and enjoyably while their parents are at work. A community volunteer helps children with learning and completing homework. Children who attend high-quality "after-care" fare better in emotional and social adjustment.

with school-age children are employed (Statistics Canada, 2005b; U.S. Census Bureau, 2006b). In Chapter 6, we saw that the impact of maternal employment on early development depends on the quality of child care and the continuing parent–child relationship. This same is true in later years.

■ **Maternal Employment and Child Development.** When mothers enjoy their work and remain committed to parenting, their children show favorable adjustment—higher self-esteem, more positive family and peer relations, less gender-stereotyped beliefs, and better grades in school. Girls, especially, profit from the image of female competence. Regardless of SES, daughters of employed mothers perceive women's roles as involving more freedom of choice and satisfaction and are more achievement- and career-oriented (Hoffman, 2000).

These benefits reflect parenting practices. Employed mothers who value their parenting role are more likely to use authoritative child rearing and coregulation. Also, children in dual-earner households devote more daily hours to doing homework under parental guidance and participate more in household chores. And maternal employment leads fathers to take on greater child-rearing responsibilities, with a small but increasing number staying home full-time (Gottfried, Gottfried, & Bathurst, 2002; Hoffman & Youngblade, 1999). Paternal involvement is associated with higher intelligence and achievement, more mature social behavior, and a flexible view of gender roles in childhood and adolescence, and with generally better mental health in adulthood (Coltrane, 1996; Pleck & Masciadrelli, 2004).

But when employment places heavy demands on the mother's schedule or is stressful for other reasons, children are at risk for ineffective parenting (Brooks-Gunn, Han, & Waldfogel, 2002; Costigan, Cox, & Cauce, 2003). Negative consequences are magnified when low-SES mothers spend long days at low-paying, physically exhausting jobs—conditions linked to maternal depression and to harsh, inconsistent discipline (Raver, 2003). In contrast, part-time employment and flexible work schedules are associated with good child adjustment. By preventing work–family role conflict, these arrangements help parents meet children's needs (Frederiksen-Goldsen & Sharlach, 2000).

■ **Support for Employed Parents and Their Families.** In dual-earner families, the husband's willingness to share responsibilities is a crucial factor. If the father is uninvolved, the mother carries a double load, at home and at work, leading to fatigue, distress, and little time and energy for children.

Employed mothers and dual-earner parents need assistance from work settings and communities in their child-rearing roles. Part-time employment, flexible schedules, job sharing, and paid leave when children are ill help parents juggle the demands of work and child rearing. Equal pay and employment opportunities for women are also important. Because these policies enhance financial status and morale, they improve the way mothers feel and behave when they arrive home at the end of the working day.

■ **Child Care for School-Age Children.** High-quality child care is vital for parents' peace of mind and children's well-being, even in middle childhood. But not all 5- to 13-year-olds have round-the-clock supervision. An estimated 2.4 million in the United States and several hundred thousand in Canada are **self-care children,** who regularly look after themselves during after-school hours. Self-care increases with age and also with SES, perhaps because of the greater safety of higher-income neighborhoods. But when low-SES parents lack alternatives to self-care, their children spend more hours on their own (Casper & Smith, 2002).

Some studies report that self-care children suffer from low self-esteem, antisocial behavior, poor academic achievement, and fearfulness. Others show no such effects. Children's maturity and the way they spend their time seem to explain these contradictions. Among younger school-age children, those who spend more hours alone have more adjustment difficulties (Vandell & Posner, 1999). As children become old enough to look after themselves, those who have a history of authoritative child rearing, are monitored by parental telephone calls, and have regular after-school chores appear responsible and well-adjusted. In contrast, children left to their own devices are more likely to bend to peer pressures and engage in antisocial behavior (Coley, Morris, & Hernandez, 2004; Steinberg, 1986).

Before age 8 or 9, most children need supervision because they are not yet competent to handle emergencies (Galambos & Maggs, 1991). But throughout middle childhood, attending after-school programs with well-trained staffs, generous adult–child ratios, and stimulating activities is linked to better emotional and social adjustment (Pierce, Hamm, & Vandell, 1999). And low-SES children who participate in "after-care" enrichment activities (scouting, music, or art lessons) show special benefits, including better school grades and fewer behavior problems (Posner & Vandell, 1994; Vandell, 1999).

Ask Yourself

Review

Describe and explain changes in sibling relationships during middle childhood.

Apply

Steve and Marissa are in the midst of an acrimonious divorce. Their 9-year-old son Dennis has become hostile and defiant. How can Steve and Marissa help Dennis adjust?

Connect

How does each level in Bronfenbrenner's ecological systems theory—microsystem, mesosystem, exosystem, and macrosystem—contribute to the effects of maternal employment on children's development?

Reflect

What after-school child-care arrangements did you experience in elementary school? How do you think they influenced your development?

Some Common Problems of Development

We have considered a variety of stressful experiences that place children at risk for future problems. Next, we address two more areas of concern: school-age children's fears and anxieties and the consequences of child sexual abuse. Finally, we sum up factors that help children cope effectively with stress.

Fears and Anxieties

Although fears of the dark, thunder and lightning, and supernatural beings persist into middle childhood, children's anxieties are also directed toward new concerns. As children begin to understand the realities of the wider world, the possibility of personal harm (being robbed, stabbed, or shot) and media events (war and disasters) often trouble them. Other common worries include academic failure, parents' health, physical injuries, and peer rejection (Muris et al., 2000; Silverman, La Greca, & Wasserstein, 1995).

Children in Western nations mention exposure to negative information in the media as the most common source of their fears, followed by direct exposure to frightening events (Muris et al., 2001). Nevertheless, only a minority of parents have rules about what TV programs their school-age children and young teenagers can watch, restrict their activities on the computer, or know what sites they visit on the Web (Media Awareness Network, 2001; Roberts, Foehr, & Rideout, 2005).

As long as fears are not too intense, most children handle them constructively, using the more sophisticated emotional regulation strategies that develop in middle childhood. Consequently, fears decline with age, especially for girls, who express more fears than boys throughout childhood and adolescence (Gullone, 2000). But about 5 percent of school-age children develop an intense, unmanageable fear called a **phobia.** Children with inhibited temperaments are at high risk, displaying phobias five to six times more often than other children (Ollendick, King, & Muris, 2002).

For example, in *school phobia,* children feel severe apprehension about attending school, often accompanied by physical complaints (dizziness, nausea, stomachaches, and vomiting). About one-third of children with school phobia are 5- to 7-year-olds for whom the real fear is separation from their mother. Family therapy helps these children, whose difficulty can often be traced to parental overprotection (Elliott, 1999).

Most cases of school phobia appear around age 11 to 13, during the transition from middle childhood to adolescence. These children usually find a particular aspect of school frightening—an overcritical teacher, a school bully, or too much parental pressure to achieve. A change in school environment or parenting practices may be needed. Firm insistence that the child return to school, along with training in how to cope with difficult situations, is also helpful (Csoti, 2003).

Severe childhood anxieties may arise from harsh living conditions. In inner-city ghettos and war-torn areas of the world, a great many children live in the midst of constant danger, chaos, and deprivation. As the Lifespan Vista box on page 352 reveals, these youngsters are at risk for long-term emotional distress and behavior problems. Finally, as we saw in our discussion of child abuse in Chapter 8, too often violence and other destructive acts become part of adult–child relationships. During middle childhood, child sexual abuse increases.

Child Sexual Abuse

Until recently, child sexual abuse was considered rare, and children's claims of abuse were often dismissed by adults. In the 1970s, efforts by professionals and media attention led to recognition of child sexual abuse as a serious and widespread problem. About 90,000 cases in the United States and 14,000 cases in Canada were confirmed in the most recently reported year (Trocomé & Wolfe, 2002; U.S. Department of Health and Human Services, 2005c).

■ **Characteristics of Abusers and Victims.** Sexual abuse is committed against children of both sexes, but more often against girls. Most cases are reported in middle childhood, but for some victims, abuse begins early in life and continues for many years (Trickett & Putnam, 1998).

Typically, the abuser is male—a parent or someone the parent knows well—often a father, stepfather, or live-in boyfriend, somewhat less often an uncle or older brother. In a few instances, mothers are the offenders, more often with sons (Kolvin & Trowell, 1996). Abusers make the child comply in a variety of distasteful ways, including deception, bribery, verbal intimidation, and physical force.

You may wonder how any adult—especially a parent or close relative—could possibly violate a child sexually. Many offenders deny their own responsibility. They blame the abuse on the willing participation of a seductive youngster. Yet children are not capable of making a deliberate, informed decision to enter into a sexual relationship! Even older children and adolescents are not free to say yes or no. Rather, the responsibility lies with abusers, who tend to have characteristics that predispose them toward sexual exploitation of children. They have great difficulty controlling their impulses and may suffer from psychological disorders, including alcohol and drug abuse. Often they pick out children who are unlikely to defend themselves or to be believed—those who are physically weak, emotionally deprived, socially isolated, or affected by disabilities (Bolen, 2001).

Reported cases of child sexual abuse are linked to poverty, marital instability, and resulting weakening of family ties. Children who live in homes with a constantly changing cast of characters—repeated marriages, separations, and new partners—are especially vulnerable. But children in economically advantaged, stable families are also victims, although their abuse is more likely to escape detection (Putnam, 2003).

A Lifespan Vista

Children of War

Today, half of all casualties of worldwide conflict are children. Around the world, many children live with armed conflict, terrorism, and other acts of violence stemming from ethnic and political tensions. Some children may participate in fighting, either because they are forced or because they want to please adults. Others are kidnapped, assaulted, and tortured. Those who are bystanders often come under direct fire and may be killed or physically maimed. And many watch in horror as family members, friends, and neighbors flee, are wounded, or die. In the past decade, wars have left 4 to 5 million children physically disabled, 20 million homeless, and more than 1 million separated from their parents (UNICEF, 2005).

When war and social crises are temporary, most children can be comforted and do not show long-term emotional difficulties. But chronic danger requires children to make substantial adjustments that can seriously impair their psychological functioning. Many children of war lose their sense of safety, become desensitized to violence, are haunted by terrifying memories, and build a pessimistic view of the future. Anxiety and depression increase, as do aggression and antisocial behavior (Garbarino, Andreas, & Vorrasi, 2002; McIntyre & Ventura, 2003). These outcomes seem to be culturally universal, appearing among children from every war zone studied—from Bosnia, Angola, Rwanda, and the Sudan to the West Bank, Afghanistan, and Iraq (Barenbaum, Ruchkin, & Schwab-Stone, 2004).

Parental affection and reassurance are the best protection against lasting problems. When parents offer security and serve as role models of calm emotional strength, most children can withstand even extreme war-related violence (Smith et al., 2001). Children who are separated from parents must rely on help from their communities. Preschool and school-age orphans in Eritrea who were placed in residential settings where they could form close emotional ties with at least one adult showed less emotional stress five years later than orphans placed in impersonal settings (Wolff & Fesseha, 1999). Education and recreation programs are powerful safeguards, too, providing children with a sense of consistency in their lives along with teacher and peer supports.

With the September 11, 2001, terrorist attacks on the World Trade Center, some American children experienced extreme wartime violence firsthand. Children in Public School 31 in Brooklyn, New York, for example, stared out windows as planes rushed toward the towers and engulfed them in flames, and as the towers crumbled. Many worried about the safety of family members, and some lost them. In the aftermath, most expressed intense fears—for example, that terrorists were infiltrating their neighborhoods and that planes flying overhead might smash into nearby buildings.

Unlike many war-traumatized children in the developing world, Public School 31 students received immediate intervention—a "trauma curriculum" in which they expressed their emotions through writing, drawing, and discussion and participated in experiences aimed at restoring trust and tolerance (Lagnado, 2001). Older children learned about the feelings of their Muslim classmates, the dire condition of children in Afghanistan, and ways to help victims as a means of overcoming a sense of helplessness.

When wartime drains families and communities of resources, international organizations must step in and help children. Efforts to preserve children's physical, psychological, and educational well-being may be the best way to stop transmission of violence to the next generation.

These traumatized victims of air raids in Kabul, Afghanistan, witnessed the destruction of their neighborhoods and the maimings and deaths of family members and friends. During a therapy session at a mental health hospital, this 7-year-old draws a picture of several schoolmates who died. Without special support from caring adults, these children are likely to have lasting emotional problems.

Consequences. The adjustment problems of child sexual abuse victims—including depression, low self-esteem, mistrust of adults, and feelings of anger and hostility—are often severe and can persist for years after the abusive episodes. Younger children frequently react with sleep difficulties, loss of appetite, and generalized fearfulness. Adolescents may run away and show suicidal reactions, substance abuse, and delinquency. At all ages, persistent abuse accompanied by force, violence, and a close relationship to the perpetrator (incest) has a more severe impact (Feiring, Taska, & Lewis, 1999; Trickett et al., 2001).

Sexually abused children frequently display precocious sexual knowledge and behavior. They have learned from their abusers that sexual overtures are acceptable ways to get attention and rewards. In adolescence, abused young people often become promiscuous, and as adults, they show increased arrest rates for sex crimes and prostitution (Friedrich et al., 2001; Salter et al., 2003). Furthermore, women who were sexually abused are likely to choose partners who abuse them and their children. As mothers, they often engage in irresponsible and coercive parenting, including child abuse and neglect (Pianta, Egeland, & Erickson, 1989). In these ways, the harmful impact of sexual abuse is transmitted to the next generation.

Prevention and Treatment. Because child abuse typically appears in the midst of other serious family problems, treatment is difficult. Long-term therapy with both children and parents is usually needed (Olafson & Boat, 2000). The best way

to reduce the suffering of victims is to prevent sexual abuse from continuing. Today, courts are prosecuting abusers more vigorously and taking children's testimony more seriously (see the Social Issues box on page 354).

Educational programs that teach children to recognize inappropriate sexual advances and tell them where to turn for help reduce the risk of abuse. Yet because of controversies over educating children about sexual abuse, few schools offer these interventions. New Zealand is the only country with a national, school-based prevention program targeting sexual abuse. In Keeping Ourselves Safe, children and adolescents learn that abusers are rarely strangers. Parent involvement ensures that home and school collaborate in teaching children self-protection skills. Evaluations reveal that virtually all New Zealand parents and children support the program and that it has helped many children avoid or report abuse (Briggs, 2002).

Fostering Resilience in Middle Childhood

Throughout middle childhood—and other phases of development—children encounter challenging and sometimes threatening situations that require them to cope with psychological stress. In this and the previous chapter, we have look at some of these: chronic illness, learning disabilities, achievement expectations, divorce, and child sexual abuse. Each taxes children's coping resources, creating serious risks for development.

Nevertheless, only a modest relationship exists between stressful life experiences and psychological disturbance in childhood (Masten & Reed, 2002). In our discussion in Chapter 3 of the long-term consequences of birth complications, we noted that some children manage to overcome the combined effects of birth trauma, poverty, and troubled family life. The same is true for school difficulties, family transitions, and child maltreatment. Recall from Chapter 1 that four broad factors protect against maladjustment: (1) the child's personal characteristics, including an easy temperament and a mastery-oriented approach to new situations; (2) a warm parental relationship; (3) an adult outside the immediate family who offers a support system, and (4) community resources, such as good schools, social services, and youth organizations and recreation centers.

Any one of these ingredients of resilience can account for why one child fares well and another poorly. Usually, however, personal and environmental factors are interconnected: Each resource favoring resilience strengthens others. For example, safe, stable neighborhoods with family-friendly community services reduce parents' daily hassles and stress, thereby promoting good parenting (Pinderhughes et al., 2001). In contrast, unfavorable home and neighborhood experiences increase the chances that children will act in ways that expose them to further hardship. And when negative conditions pile up, such as marital discord, poverty, crowded living conditions, neighborhood violence, and abuse, the rate of maladjustment multiplies (Farrington & Loeber, 2000; Wyman et al., 1999).

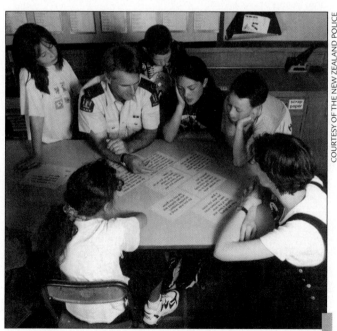

In Keeping Ourselves Safe, New Zealand's national, school-based child abuse prevention program, teachers and police officers collaborate in teaching children to recognize abusive adult behaviors so they can take steps to protect themselves. Parents are informed about children's classroom learning experiences and encouraged to support and extend them at home.

COURTESY OF THE NEW ZEALAND POLICE

Social Issues

Children's Eyewitness Testimony

Increasingly, children are being called on to testify in court cases involving child abuse and neglect, child custody, and similar matters. Providing information on such topics can be difficult and traumatic. Almost always, children must report on highly stressful events, and they may have to speak against a parent or other relative to whom they feel loyal. In some family disputes, they may fear punishment for telling the truth. In addition, child witnesses are faced with an unfamiliar situation—at the very least an interview in the judge's chambers and at most an open courtroom with judge, jury, spectators, and the possibility of unsympathetic cross-examination. Not surprisingly, these conditions can compromise the accuracy of children's recall.

Age Differences. Until recently, children younger than age 5 were rarely asked to testify, and not until age 10 were they assumed fully competent to do so. Yet as a result of societal reactions to rising rates of child abuse and the difficulty of prosecuting perpetrators, legal requirements for child testimony have been relaxed in the United States and Canada. Children as young as age 3 frequently serve as witnesses (Ceci & Bruck, 1998).

Compared with preschoolers, school-age children are better at giving accurate, detailed descriptions of past experiences and correctly inferring others' motives and intentions. Older children are also more resistant to misleading questions of the sort asked by attorneys when they probe for more information or, in cross-examination, try to influence the content of the child's response (Roebers & Schneider, 2001). Nevertheless, when properly questioned, even 3-year-olds can recall recent events accurately, including highly stressful ones (Peterson & Rideout, 1998).

Suggestibility. Court testimony, however, often involves repeated interviews. When adults lead children by suggesting incorrect facts ("He touched you there, didn't he?") or reinforce the child for giving

desired answers, they increase the likelihood of incorrect reporting on the part of preschoolers and school-age children alike (Bruck & Ceci, 2004).

In one study, 4- to 7-year-olds were asked to recall details about a visitor who had come to their classroom a week earlier. Half the children received a low-pressure interview containing leading questions that implied abuse ("He took your clothes off, didn't he?"). The other half received a high-pressure interview in which an adult told the child that her friends had said "yes" to the leading questions, praised the child for agreeing ("You're doing great"), and, if the child did not agree, asked the question again. Children were far more likely to give false information—even to fabricate quite fantastic events—in the high-pressure condition (Finnilä et al., 2003).

By the time children appear in court, weeks, months, or even years have passed since the target events. When a long delay is combined with biased interviewing and with stereotyping of the accused ("He's in jail because he's been bad"), children can easily be misled into giving false information (Ceci, Fitneva, & Gilstrap, 2003).

Special interviewing methods have been devised to ease children's task in providing testimony. In many sexual abuse cases, anatomically correct dolls are used to prompt children's recall. Although this method helps older children provide more detail about experienced events, it increases the suggestibility of preschoolers, who report physical and sexual contact that never happened (Goodman et al., 1999).

Interventions. Adults must prepare child witnesses so they understand the courtroom process and know what to expect. In some places, "court schools" take children through the setting and give them an opportunity to role-play court activities. Practice interviews—in which children learn to provide the most accurate, detailed information possible and to admit not knowing rather than agreeing or guessing—are helpful (Saywitz, Goodman, & Lyon, 2002).

At the same time, legal professionals must use interviewing procedures that

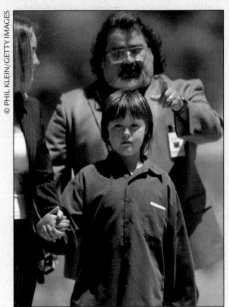

© PHIL KLEIN/GETTY IMAGES

As this 9-year-old's expression suggests, having to testify in court cases involving child maltreatment, child custody, and other matters can be difficult for children. The child is arriving at court to testify for the defense in the 2005 Michael Jackson child molestation trial, accompanied by her mother and the defense attorney. As long as attorneys refrain from using biased interviewing tactics, school-age children are able to provide accurate, detailed descriptions of past experiences.

increase children's accurate reporting. Unbiased, open-ended questions that prompt children to disclose details— "Tell me what happened" or "You said there was a man; tell me about the man"—reduce suggestibility (Holliday, 2003). Also, a warm, supportive interview tone fosters accurate recall, perhaps by easing children's anxiety so they feel freer to disagree with an interviewer's false suggestions (Ceci, Bruck, & Battin, 2000).

If children are likely to experience emotional trauma or later punishment (as in a family dispute), courtroom procedures can be adapted to protect them. For example, children can testify over closed-circuit TV so they do not have to face an abuser. When it is not wise for a child to participate directly, impartial expert witnesses can provide testimony that reports on the child's psychological condition and includes important elements of the child's story.

Rather than a preexisting attribute, *resilience* is a capacity that develops, enabling children to use internal and external resources to cope with adversity (Yates, Egeland, & Sroufe, 2003). Throughout our discussion, we have seen many examples of how families, schools, communities, and society as a whole can enhance or undermine school-age children's supportive relationships and sense of competence. As the next two chapters will reveal, young people whose childhood experiences helped them learn to overcome obstacles, strive for self-direction, and respond considerately and sympathetically to others meet the challenges of the next period—adolescence—quite well.

Ask Yourself

Review

When children must testify in court cases, what factors increase the chances of accurate reporting?

Apply

Claire told her 6-year-old daughter never to talk to or take candy from strangers. Why will Claire's warning not protect her daughter from sexual abuse?

Connect

Explain how factors that promote resilience contribute to favorable adjustment following divorce.

Reflect

Describe a challenging time during your childhood. What aspects of the experience increased stress? What resources helped you cope with adversity?

www.ablongman.com/berk

Summary

Erikson's Theory: Industry versus Inferiority

What personality changes take place during Erikson's stage of industry versus inferiority?

■ According to Erikson, children who successfully resolve the psychological conflict of **industry versus inferiority** develop a sense of competence at skills and tasks, a positive but realistic self-concept, pride in accomplishment, moral responsibility, and the ability to work cooperatively with agemates.

Self-Understanding

Describe school-age children's self-concept and self-esteem, and discuss factors that affect their achievement-related attributions.

■ During middle childhood, children's self-concepts include personality traits, competencies, and **social comparisons** with agemates.

■ Self-esteem differentiates further, becomes hierarchically organized, and declines over the early school years as children adjust their self-judgments to feedback from the environment. Authoritative parenting is linked to favorable self-esteem.

■ Children who make **mastery-oriented attributions** credit their successes to high ability

and failures to insufficient effort. In contrast, children who receive negative feedback about their ability are likely to develop **learned helplessness**, attributing their successes to external factors, such as luck, and failures to low ability.

© SYRACUSE NEWSPAPERS/DICK BLUME/ THE IMAGE WORKS

Emotional Development

Cite changes in understanding and expression of emotion in middle childhood.

■ In middle childhood, the self-conscious emotions of pride and guilt become clearly governed by personal responsibility. Experiencing intense shame can shatter children's overall sense of self-esteem.

■ School-age children recognize that people can experience more than one emotion at a time. They also attend to more cues in inter-

preting another's feelings, and empathy increases.

■ By the end of middle childhood, most children can shift adaptively between **problem-centered coping** and **emotion-centered coping** in regulating emotion. Emotionally well-regulated children are optimistic, prosocial, and well-liked by peers.

Understanding Others: Perspective Taking

How does perspective taking change in middle childhood?

■ **Perspective taking,** the ability to take another person's viewpoint, improves greatly during the school years, as Selman's five-stage sequence indicates. Cognitive maturity and experiences in which adults and peers explain their viewpoints support gains in perspective taking. Good perspective takers have more positive social skills.

Moral Development

Describe changes in moral understanding during middle childhood.

■ By middle childhood, children have internalized a wide variety of moral rules. Their concepts of **distributive justice** change, from equality, to merit, to equity and benevolence. They also clarify and link moral rules and social conventions. In judging the morality of rule violations, they take into account the purpose of the rule, people's intentions, and the context of their actions. School-age children also make strides in understanding individual rights.

■ Children of all races pick up prevailing societal attitudes about race and ethnicity, but by middle childhood, they understand that people can be both "the same" and "different," and prejudice typically declines. Children most likely to hold biases are those who believe that personality traits are fixed, who have inflated self-esteem, and who live among adults who highlight group differences.

Peer Relations

How do peer sociability and friendship change in middle childhood?

■ In middle childhood, peer interaction becomes more prosocial, and aggression, especially physical aggression, declines. By the end of the school years, children organize themselves into **peer groups.** Friendships develop into mutual relationships based on trust. Children tend to select friends similar to themselves in many ways. Kind, compassionate friendships strengthen prosocial behavior, but friendships between aggressive children magnify antisocial acts.

Describe major categories of peer acceptance and ways to help rejected children.

■ On measures of **peer acceptance, popular children** are liked by many agemates; **rejected children** are actively disliked; **controversial children** are both liked and disliked; and **neglected children** are seldom chosen, either positively or negatively.

■ Two subtypes of popular children exist: **popular-prosocial children,** who are academically and socially competent, and **popular-antisocial children**—aggressive youngsters whom peers admire, perhaps because of their sophisticated but devious social skills. Rejected children also divide into two subtypes: **rejected-aggressive children,** who are especially high in conflict and hostility, and **rejected-withdrawn children,** who are passive, socially awkward, and at risk for **peer victimization.**

■ Rejected children often experience lasting adjustment difficulties. Helpful interventions include coaching in social skills; academic tutoring; training in perspective taking and social problem solving and in attributing peer difficulties to internal, changeable causes; and improving parent–child interaction.

Gender Typing

What changes in gender-stereotyped beliefs and gender identity occur during middle childhood?

■ School-age children extend their awareness of gender stereotypes to personality traits and academic subjects. But they also develop a more open-minded view of what males and females can do. Boys strengthen their identification with the masculine role, whereas girls often experiment with "other-gender" activities.

Family Influences

How do parent–child communication and sibling relationships change in middle childhood?

■ Effective parents of school-age youngsters engage in **coregulation,** exerting general oversight while permitting children to be in charge of moment-by-moment decision making. Coregulation depends on a cooperative relationship between parent and child.

■ Sibling rivalry tends to increase as children participate in a wider range of activities and parents compare their traits and accomplishments. Only children are as well-adjusted as children with siblings, and they do better in school and attain higher levels of education.

What factors influence children's adjustment to divorce and remarriage?

■ Although marital breakup is often quite stressful for children, great individual differences exist. Boys and children with difficult temperaments are more likely to show lasting problems in school performance and antisocial behavior. For children of both sexes, divorce is linked to problems with adolescent sexuality and development of intimate ties in adulthood.

■ The overriding factor in positive adjustment following divorce is effective parenting. Contact with noncustodial fathers is important for children of both sexes, and outcomes for sons are better when fathers have

custody. **Divorce mediation,** which helps parents resolve disputes and cooperate in parenting, can be beneficial in the difficult period surrounding divorce. The success of **joint custody** depends on a cooperative relationship between divorcing parents.

■ When divorced parents enter new relationships and form **blended,** or **reconstituted families,** girls, older children, and children in father–stepmother families display the greatest adjustment problems. Stepparents who move into their roles gradually and form a "parenting coalition" help children adjust.

How do maternal employment and life in dual-earner families affect school-age children?

■ When mothers enjoy their work and remain committed to parenting, maternal employment is associated with higher self-esteem in children, more positive family and peer relations, less gender-stereotyped beliefs, and better grades in school. In dual-earner families, the father's willingness to share in child-rearing responsibilities is linked to many positive outcomes for children. Workplace supports, such as part-time employment, flexible schedules, and paid parental leave, help parents meet the demands of work and child rearing.

■ **Self-care children** who are old enough to look after themselves, are monitored from a distance, and experience authoritative parenting appear responsible and well-adjusted. Children in high-quality after-school programs reap academic and social benefits.

Some Common Problems of Development

Cite common fears and anxieties in middle childhood.

■ School-age children's fears are directed toward new concerns, including physical safety, media events, academic failure, parents' health, and peer rejection. Children with inhibited temperaments are at higher risk of developing a **phobia**—an intense, unmanageable fear. Harsh living conditions can also cause severe anxiety.

Discuss factors related to child sexual abuse and its consequences for children's development.

■ Child sexual abuse is generally committed by male family members, more often against girls than boys. Abusers have characteristics that predispose them toward sexual exploi-

tation of children. Reported cases are strongly associated with poverty and marital instability. Abused children often have severe adjustment problems.

Cite factors that foster resilience in middle childhood.

■ Overall, only a modest relationship exists between stressful life experiences and psy-

chological disturbance in childhood. Personal characteristics of children; a warm, well-organized family life; and social supports outside the family are related to childhood resilience in the face of stress. But when negative factors pile up, the rate of maladjustment multiplies.

Important Terms and Concepts

blended, or reconstituted, families (p. 348)
controversial children (p. 340)
coregulation (p. 344)
distributive justice (p. 337)
divorce mediation (p. 348)
emotion-centered coping (p. 335)
industry versus inferiority (p. 330)
joint custody (p. 348)
learned helplessness (p. 333)

mastery-oriented attributions (p. 333)
neglected children (p. 340)
peer acceptance (p. 340)
peer group (p. 339)
peer victimization (p. 342)
perspective taking (p. 336)
phobia (p. 351)
popular children (p. 340)
popular-antisocial children (p. 341)

popular-prosocial children (p. 341)
problem-centered coping (p. 335)
rejected children (p. 340)
rejected-aggressive children (p. 341)
rejected-withdrawn children (p. 341)
self-care children (p. 350)
social comparisons (p. 330)

Milestones

Development in Middle Childhood

Age	Physical	Cognitive	Language	Emotional/Social

6–8
YEARS

Physical

- Slow gains in height and weight continue until adolescent growth spurt (290)

- Lateralization of the cerebral cortex strengthens; brain plasticity declines (125)

- Permanent teeth gradually replace primary teeth (290)

- Writing becomes smaller and more legible (295)

- Drawings become more organized and detailed and include some depth cues (295)

- Games with rules and rough-and-tumble play become common (296–297)

- Dominance hierarchies become more stable, especially among boys (297)

Cognitive

- Thought becomes more logical, as shown by the ability to pass Piagetian conservation, class inclusion, and seriation problems (298–299)

- Understanding of spatial concepts improves, as illustrated by ability to give clear, well-organized directions and to draw and read maps (299)

- Attention becomes more selective, adaptable, and planful (302)

- Uses memory strategies of rehearsal and organization (302)

- Views the mind as an active, constructive agent, capable of transforming information (304)

- Awareness of memory strategies and the impact of psychological factors (such as focusing attention) on task performance improves (304–305)

Language

- Vocabulary increases rapidly throughout middle childhood, eventually exceeding 40,000 words (315)

- Word definitions are concrete, referring to functions and appearance (315)

- Language awareness improves (315)

Emotional/Social

- Self-concept begins to include personality traits and social comparisons (330–331)

- Self-esteem differentiates, is hierarchically organized, and declines to a more realistic level (331–332)

- Self-conscious emotions of pride and guilt are governed by personal responsibility (335)

- Recognizes that individuals can experience more than one emotion at a time (335)

- Attends to facial and situational cues in interpreting another's feelings (335)

- Understands that people may have different perspectives because of access to different information (336)

- Becomes more responsible and independent (336–337)

- Distributive justice reasoning shifts from equality to merit to equity and benevolence (337)

- Peer interaction becomes more prosocial, and aggression declines (339)

358

Age	Physical	Cognitive	Language	Emotional/Social
9–11 YEARS	• Adolescent growth spurt begins two years earlier in girls than in boys (290) • Executes gross motor skills of running, jumping, throwing, catching, kicking, batting, and dribbling more quickly and with better coordination (294) • Reaction time improves, contributing to motor skill development (295) • Representation of depth in drawings expands (295)	• Logical thought remains tied to concrete situations (299) • Continues to master Piagetian tasks in a step-by-step fashion (300) • Memory strategies of rehearsal and organization become more effective; begins to use elaboration (302–303) • Can apply several memory strategies at once (302) • Long-term knowledge base grows larger and becomes better organized (303) • Cognitive self-regulation improves (306)	• Word definitions emphasize synonyms and categorical relations (315) • Grasps double meanings of words, as reflected in understanding of metaphors and humor (315–316) • Use of complex grammatical constructions improves (316) • Adapts messages to the needs of listeners in challenging communicative situations (317) • Develops more refined conversational strategies (317) • Narratives increase in organization, detail, and expressiveness (317)	• Self-esteem tends to rise (332) • Distinguishes ability, effort, and luck in attributions for success and failure (333) • Has an adaptive set of strategies for regulating emotion (335–336) • Can "step into another's shoes" and view the self from that person's perspective (336) • Later, can view the relationship between self and other from the perspective of a third, impartial party (336) • Clarifies and links moral rules and social conventions (337) • Understanding of individual rights expands (338) • Peer groups emerge (339) • Friendships are based on mutual trust (340) • Becomes aware of more gender stereotypes, but has a flexible appreciation of what males and females can do (343) • Sibling rivalry tends to increase (345)

Note: Numbers in parentheses indicate the page or pages on which each milestone is discussed.

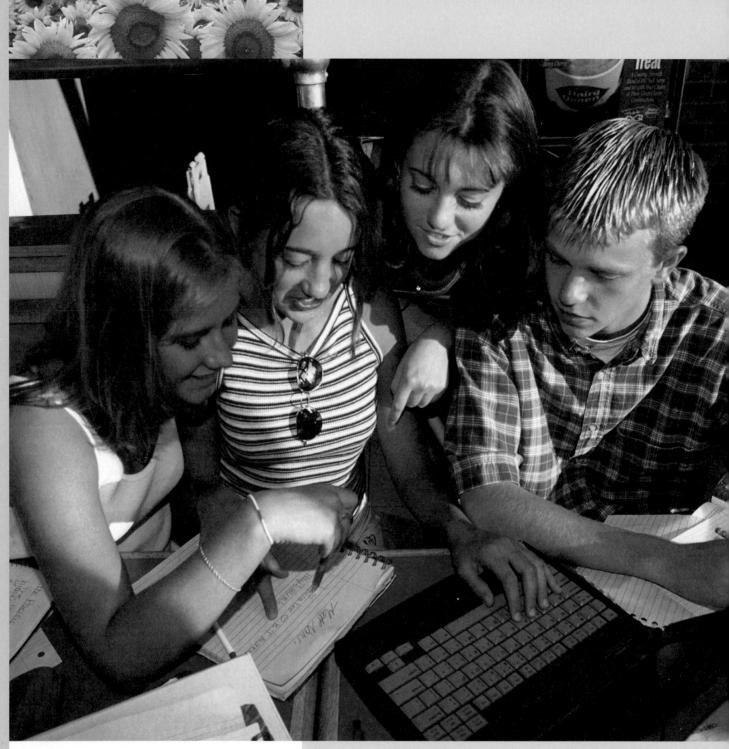

Adolescence brings momentous advances. With puberty, the young person experiences a flood of biological events leading to an adult-sized body and sexual maturity. And cognitive changes allow teenagers to grasp complex scientific principles, grapple with political issues, and detect the deep meaning of a poem or story.

Physical and Cognitive Development in Adolescence

On Sabrina's eleventh birthday, her friend Joyce gave her a surprise party, but Sabrina seemed somber during the celebration. Although Sabrina and Joyce had been close friends since third grade, their relationship was faltering. Sabrina was a head taller and some 20 pounds heavier than most of the other girls in her sixth-grade class. Her breasts were well-developed, her hips and thighs had broadened, and she had begun to menstruate. In contrast, Joyce still had the short, lean, flat-chested body of a school-age child.

© GRACE/ZEFA/CORBIS

Ducking into the bathroom while Joyce and the other girls set the table for cake and ice cream, Sabrina looked herself over in the mirror and frowned. "I feel so big and heavy," she whispered. At church youth group on Sunday evenings, Sabrina broke away from Joyce and spent time with the eighth-grade girls. Around them, she didn't feel so large and awkward.

Once every two weeks, parents gathered at Sabrina's and Joyce's school for discussions about child-rearing concerns. Sabrina's Italian-American parents, Franca and Antonio, attended whenever they could. "How you know they are becoming teenagers is this," volunteered Antonio. "The bedroom door is closed, and they want to be alone. Also, they contradict and disagree. I tell Sabrina, 'You have to go to Aunt Gina's for dinner with the family.' The next thing I know, she is arguing with me."

Sabrina has entered **adolescence,** the transition between childhood and adulthood. In industrialized societies, the skills young people must master are so complex and the choices confronting them so diverse that adolescence is greatly extended. But around the world, the basic tasks of this period are much the same. Sabrina must accept her full-grown body, acquire adult ways of thinking, attain greater independence from her family, develop more mature ways of relating to peers of both sexes, and begin to construct an identity—a secure sense of who she is in terms of sexual, vocational, moral, ethnic, religious, and other life values and goals.

The beginning of adolescence is marked by **puberty,** a flood of biological events leading to an adult-sized body and sexual maturity. As Sabrina's reactions suggest, entry into adolescence can be an

361

especially trying time for some young people. In this chapter, we trace the events of puberty and take up a variety of health concerns—nutrition, sexual activity, substance abuse, and other problems affecting teenagers who encounter difficulties on the path to maturity.

Adolescence brings with it momentous cognitive advances. Teenagers can grasp complex scientific principles, grapple with political issues, and detect the hidden meaning of a poem or story. The second part of this chapter traces these extraordinary changes from both Piaget's and the information-processing perspective. Next we take a close look at sex differences in mental abilities. Finally, we turn to the primary setting in which adolescent thought takes shape: the school.

🌿 Physical Development

Conceptions of Adolescence

Why is Sabrina self-conscious, argumentative, and in retreat from family activities? Historically, theorists explained the impact of puberty on psychological development by resorting to extremes—either a biological or a social explanation. Today, researchers realize that biological and social forces jointly determine adolescent psychological change.

The Biological Perspective

Ask contemporary adults what teenagers are like, and you will probably get answers like these: "rebellious and reckless," or "full of rages and tempers" (Buchanan & Holmbeck, 1998). This widespread view dates back to the writings of eighteenth-century philosopher Jean-Jacques Rousseau (see Chapter 1), who believed that the biological upheaval of puberty triggered heightened emotionality, conflict, and defiance of adults.

In the early twentieth century, major theorists picked up this storm-and-stress perspective. The most influential, G. Stanley Hall, based his ideas about development on Darwin's theory of evolution. Hall (1904) described adolescence as a period so turbulent that it resembled the era in which humans evolved from savages into civilized beings. Similarly, Anna Freud (1969), who expanded the focus on adolescence of her father Sigmund Freud's theory, viewed the teenage years as a biologically based, universal "developmental disturbance." In Freud's *genital stage,* sexual impulses reawaken, triggering psychological conflict and volatile behavior. As adolescents find intimate partners, inner forces gradually achieve a new, mature harmony, and the stage concludes with marriage, birth, and child rearing. In this way, young people fulfill their biological destiny: sexual reproduction and survival of the species.

The Social Perspective

Contemporary research suggests that the storm-and-stress notion of adolescence is exaggerated. Certain problems, such as eating disorders, depression, suicide, and lawbreaking, do occur more often than earlier (Farrington, 2004; Graber, 2004). But the overall rate of psychological disturbance rises only slightly, by about 2 percent, from childhood to adolescence, when it is the same as in the adult population—about 20 percent (Costello & Angold, 1995). Although some teenagers do encounter serious difficulties, emotional turbulence is not routine.

The first researcher to point out the wide variability in adolescent adjustment was anthropologist Margaret Mead (1928). She returned from the Pacific islands of Samoa with a startling conclusion: Because of the culture's relaxed social relationships and openness toward sexuality, adolescence "is perhaps the pleasantest time the Samoan girl (or boy) will ever know" (p. 308). Mead offered an alternative view in which the social environment is entirely responsible for the range of teenage experiences, from erratic and agitated to calm and stress-free. Later researchers found that Samoan adolescence was not as untroubled as Mead had assumed (Freeman, 1983). Still, she showed that to understand adolescent development, researchers must pay greater attention to social and cultural influences.

A Balanced Point of View

Today we know that biological, psychological, and social forces combine to influence adolescent development (Magnusson, 1999; Susman & Rogol, 2004). Biological changes are universal—found in all primates and all cultures. These internal stresses and the social expectations accompanying them—that the young person give up childish ways, develop new interpersonal relationships, and take on greater responsibility—are likely to prompt moments of uncertainty, self-doubt, and disappointment in all teenagers. Adolescents' prior and current experiences affect their success in surmounting these challenges.

At the same time, the demands and pressures of adolescence differ substantially among cultures. Most tribal and village societies have only a brief intervening phase between childhood and full assumption of adult roles (Schlegel & Barry, 1991; Weisfield, 1997). In industrialized nations, where successful participation in economic life requires many years of education, young people face extra years of dependence on parents and postponement of sexual gratification as they prepare for a productive work life. As a result, adolescence is greatly extended—so much so that researchers commonly divide it into three phases:

1. *Early adolescence* (11–12 to 14 years): This is a period of rapid pubertal change.
2. *Middle adolescence* (14 to 16 years): Pubertal changes are now nearly complete.
3. *Late adolescence* (16 to 18 years): The young person achieves full adult appearance and anticipates assumption of adult roles.

The more the social environment supports young people in achieving adult responsibilities, the better they adjust. For all the biological tensions and uncertainties about the future that teenagers feel, most negotiate this period successfully. With this in mind, let's look closely at puberty, the dawning of adolescent development.

Puberty: The Physical Transition to Adulthood

The changes of puberty are dramatic: Within a few years, the body of the school-age child is transformed into that of a full-grown adult. Genetically influenced hormonal processes regulate pubertal growth. Girls, who have been advanced in physical maturity since the prenatal period, reach puberty, on average, 2 years earlier than boys.

Hormonal Changes

The complex hormonal changes that underlie puberty occur gradually and are under way by age 8 or 9. Secretions of *growth hormone (GH)* and *thyroxine* (see Chapter 7, page 219) increase, leading to tremendous gains in body size and to attainment of skeletal maturity.

Sexual maturation is controlled by the sex hormones. Although we think of *estrogens* as female hormones and *androgens* as male hormones, both types are present in each sex but in different amounts. The boy's testes release large quantities of the androgen *testosterone*, which leads to muscle growth, body and facial hair, and other male sex characteristics. Androgens (especially testosterone for boys) also contribute to gains in body size. The testes secrete small amounts of estrogen as well—the reason that 50 percent of boys experience temporary breast enlargement. In both sexes, estrogens also increase GH secretion, adding to the growth spurt and, in combination with androgens, stimulating gains in bone density, which continue into early adulthood (Delemarre-van de Waal, van Coeverden, & Rotteveel, 2001; Styne, 2003).

Estrogens released by girls' ovaries cause the breasts, uterus, and vagina to mature, the body to take on feminine proportions, and fat to accumulate. Estrogens also contribute to regulation of the menstrual cycle. *Adrenal androgens,* released from the adrenal glands on top of each kidney, influence girls' height spurt and stimulate growth of underarm and pubic hair. They have little impact on boys, whose physical characteristics are influenced mainly by androgen and estrogen secretions from the testes.

As you can see, pubertal changes are of two broad types: (1) overall body growth and (2) maturation of sexual characteristics. Although we will discuss these changes separately, they are interrelated. We have seen that the hormones responsible for sexual maturity also affect body growth; boys and girls differ in both aspects. In fact, puberty is the time of greatest sexual differentiation since prenatal life.

Sex differences in pubertal growth are obvious among these sixth graders. Although the children are the same age, the girl is taller and more mature looking than the boys.

Body Growth

The first outward sign of puberty is the rapid gain in height and weight known as the **growth spurt.** On average, it is under way for North American girls shortly after age 10, for boys around age 12½. The typical girl is taller and heavier during early adolescence, but this advantage is short-lived (Bogin, 2001). At age 14, she is surpassed by the typical boy, whose adolescent growth spurt has started, whereas hers is almost finished. Growth in body size is complete for most girls by age 16 and for boys by age 17½, when the epiphyses at the ends of the long bones close completely (see Chapter 7, page 217). Altogether, adolescents add 10 to 11 inches in height and 50 to 75 pounds—nearly 50 percent of adult body weight. Figure 11.1 on page 364 illustrates pubertal changes in general body growth.

■ **Body Proportions.** During puberty, the cephalocaudal growth trend of infancy and childhood reverses. The hands, legs, and feet accelerate first, followed by the torso, which accounts for most of the adolescent height gain (Sheehy et al., 1999). This pattern helps explain why early adolescents often appear awkward and out of proportion—long-legged and with giant feet and hands.

Large sex differences in body proportions also appear, caused by the action of sex hormones on the skeleton. Boys' shoulders broaden relative to the hips, whereas girls' hips broaden relative to the shoulders and waist. Of course, boys also end up larger than girls, and their legs are longer in relation to the rest of the body. The major reason is that boys have two extra years of preadolescent growth, when the legs are growing the fastest.

■ **Muscle–Fat Makeup and Other Internal Changes.** Sabrina worried about her weight because compared with her later-developing girlfriends, she had accumulated much more

Andy at 11 years

Amy at 12 years

Andy at 12 years

Andy at 15 years

Amy at 13 years

Amy at 15 years

▓ **FIGURE 11.1** **Body growth during adolescence.** Because the pubertal growth spurt takes place earlier for girls than for boys, Amy reached her adult body size earlier than Andy. Rapid pubertal growth is accompanied by large sex differences in body proportions that were not present in middle childhood (see Chapter 9, page 290).

fat. Around age 8, girls start to add fat on their arms, legs, and trunk, a trend that accelerates between ages 11 and 16. In contrast, arm and leg fat decreases in adolescent boys. Although both sexes gain in muscle, this increase is much greater in boys, who develop larger skeletal muscles, hearts, and lung capacity (Rogol, Roemmich, & Clark, 2002). Also, the number of red blood cells—and therefore the ability to carry oxygen from the lungs to the muscles—increases in boys but not in girls. Altogether, boys gain far more muscle strength than girls, a difference that contributes to teenage boys' superior athletic performance (Ramos et al., 1998).

Motor Development and Physical Activity

Puberty brings steady improvement in gross motor performance, but changes differ for boys and girls. Girls' gains are slow and gradual, leveling off by age 14. In contrast, boys show a dramatic spurt in strength, speed, and endurance that continues through the teenage years. By midadolescence, few girls perform as well as the average boy in running speed, broad jump, and throwing distance, and practically no boys score as low as the average girl (Malina & Bouchard, 1991).

Because girls and boys are no longer well-matched physically, gender-segregated physical education usually begins in middle or junior high school. At the same time, athletic options for both sexes expand. Many new sports are added to the curriculum—track and field, wrestling, tackle football, weight lifting, floor hockey, archery, tennis, and golf, to name just a few.

Among boys, athletic competence is strongly related to peer admiration and self-esteem. Some adolescents become so obsessed with physical prowess that they turn to performance-enhancing drugs. About 3 percent of North American high school seniors, mostly boys, report having taken anabolic steroids, a powerful prescription medication that boosts muscle mass and strength (Focus on the Family Canada, 2004; U.S. Department of Health and Human Services, 2005l). Teenagers usually obtain steroids illegally, ignoring their side effects, which range from acne, excess body hair, and high blood pressure to mood swings, aggressive behavior, and damage to the liver, circulatory system, and reproductive organs (American Academy of Pediatrics, 2005b). Coaches and health professionals should inform teenagers of the dangers of steroids and other performance-enhancing substances.

In 1972, the U.S. federal government required schools receiving public funds to provide equal opportunities for males and females in all educational programs, including athletics. Since then, high school girls' sports participation has increased

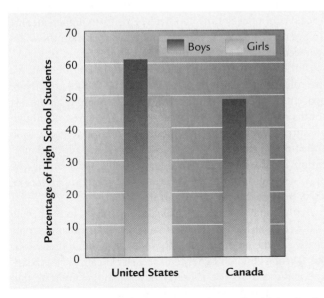

These exuberant young baseball players celebrate each others' hard-won athletic accomplishments. However, some adolescent boys become so obsessed with physical prowess that they turn to performance-enhancing drugs, ignoring their dangerous side effects.

in both the United States and Canada, although it still falls short of boys' (see Figure 11.2). In Chapter 9, we saw that from an early age, girls get less encouragement and recognition for athletic achievement, a pattern that persists into the teenage years. Recall that only about 40 percent of North American girls and 50 percent of boys are active enough for good health (see page 298). And activity rates of U.S. and Canadian youths decline over the teenage years (Canadian Fitness & Lifestyle Research Institute, 2003; U.S. Department of Health and Human Services, 2004d).

■ **FIGURE 11.2 Involvement of U.S. and Canadian high school students in extracurricular school sports.** In both nations, more boys than girls participate. Nevertheless, girls' participation has increased greatly over the past several decades. (From Canadian Fitness and Lifestyle Research Institute, 2005; National Federation of State High School Associations, 2005.)

Besides improving motor performance, sports and exercise influence cognitive and social development. Interschool and intramural athletics provide important lessons in teamwork, problem solving, assertiveness, and competition. And regular, sustained physical activity is associated with lifelong health benefits. Yet in high school, only 55 percent of U.S. and 65 percent of Canadian students are enrolled in physical education (Canadian Fitness & Lifestyle Research Institute, 2003; U.S. Department of Health and Human Services, 2004d). Required daily physical education, aimed at helping all teenagers find pleasure in sports and exercise, is a vital means of promoting adolescent physical and psychological well-being.

Sexual Maturation

Accompanying rapid body growth are changes in physical features related to sexual functioning. Some, called **primary sexual characteristics,** involve the reproductive organs (ovaries, uterus, and vagina in females; penis, scrotum, and testes in males). Others, called **secondary sexual characteristics,** are visible on the outside of the body and serve as additional signs of sexual maturity (for example, breast development in females and the appearance of underarm and pubic hair in both sexes). As Table 11.1 on page 366 shows, these characteristics develop in a fairly standard sequence, although the ages at which each begins and is completed vary greatly. Typically, pubertal development takes 4 years, but some adolescents complete it in 2 years, whereas others take 5 to 6 years.

■ **Sexual Maturation in Girls.** Female puberty usually begins with the budding of the breasts and the growth spurt. **Menarche,** or first menstruation, typically happens around age 12½ for North American girls, 13 for Western Europeans. But the age range is wide, from 10½ to 15½ years. Following menarche, breast and pubic hair growth are completed, and underarm hair appears (Rogol, Roemmich, & Clark, 2002).

Notice in Table 11.1 that nature delays sexual maturity until the girl's body is large enough for childbearing; menarche takes place after the peak of the height spurt. As an extra measure of security, for 12 to 18 months following menarche, the menstrual cycle often takes place without an ovum being released from the ovaries (Bogin, 2001). However, this temporary period of sterility does not occur in all girls, and it cannot be counted on for protection against pregnancy.

■ **Sexual Maturation in Boys.** The first sign of puberty in boys is the enlargement of the testes (glands that manufacture sperm), accompanied by changes in the texture and color of the scrotum. Soon after, pubic hair emerges, and the penis begins to enlarge (Rogol, Roemmich, & Clark, 2002).

Refer again to Table 11.1, and you will see that the growth spurt occurs much later in the sequence of pubertal events for boys than for girls. When it reaches its peak (at about age 14), enlargement of the testes and penis is nearly complete, and underarm hair appears soon after. Facial and body hair also emerge just after the peak in body growth and gradually

Table 11.1	Pubertal Development in North American Girls and Boys

Girls	Average Age Attained	Age Range	Boys	Average Age Attained	Age Range
Breasts begin to "bud"	10	(8–13)	Testes begin to enlarge	11.5	(9.5–13.5)
Height spurt begins	10	(8–13)	Pubic hair appears	12	(10–15)
Pubic hair appears	10.5	(8–14)	Penis begins to enlarge	12	(10.5–14.5)
Peak strength spurt	11.6	(9.5–14)	Height spurt begins	12.5	(10.5–16)
Peak height spurt	11.7	(10–13.5)	Spermarche (first ejaculation) occurs	13.5	(12–16)
Menarche (first menstruation) occurs	12.5	(10.5–14)	Peak height spurt	14	(12.5–15.5)
Peak weight spurt	12.7	(10–14)	Peak weight spurt	14	(12.5–15.5)
Adult stature reached	13	(10–16)	Facial hair begins to grow	14	(12.5–15.5)
Breast growth completed	14	(10–16)	Voice begins to deepen	14	(12.5–15.5)
Pubic hair growth completed	14.5	(14–15)	Penis and testes growth completed	14.5	(12.5–16)
			Peak strength spurt	15.3	(13–17)
			Adult stature reached	15.5	(13.5–17.5)
			Pubic hair growth completed	15.5	(14–17)

Sources: Chumlea et al., 2003; Rogol, Roemmich, & Clark, 2002; Wu, Mendola, & Buck, 2002.

Photos: (left) © Aaron Haupt/Photo Researchers, Inc.; (right) © Bill Aron/PhotoEdit

increase for several years. Another landmark of male physical maturity is the deepening of the voice as the larynx enlarges and the vocal cords lengthen. (Girls' voices also deepen slightly.) Voice change usually takes place at the peak of the male growth spurt and is often not complete until puberty is over.

While the penis is growing, the prostate gland and seminal vesicles (which together produce semen, the fluid containing sperm) enlarge. Then, around age 13½, **spermarche,** or first ejaculation, occurs (Rogol, Roemmich, & Clark, 2002). For a while, the semen contains few living sperm. So, like girls, boys have an initial period of reduced fertility.

Individual Differences in Pubertal Growth

Heredity contributes substantially to the timing of puberty: Identical twins generally reach menarche within a month or two of each other, whereas fraternal twins differ by about 12 months (Kaprio et al., 1995). Nutrition and exercise also contribute. In girls, a sharp rise in body weight and fat may trigger sexual maturation. Fat cells release a protein called *leptin,* which is believed to signal the brain that the girls' energy stores are sufficient for puberty—a likely reason that breast and pubic hair growth and menarche occur earlier for heavier and, especially, obese girls. In contrast, girls who begin serious athletic training at young ages or who eat very little (both of which reduce the percentage of body fat) usually experience later puberty (Anderson, Dallal, & Must, 2003; Delemarre-van de Waal, 2002).

Variations in pubertal growth also exist among regions of the world and among SES and ethnic groups. Physical health plays a major role. In poverty-stricken regions where malnutrition and infectious disease are common, menarche is greatly delayed, occurring as late as age 14 to 16 in many parts of Africa. Within developing countries, girls from higher-income families reach menarche 6 to 18 months earlier than those living in economically disadvantaged homes (Parent et al., 2003).

But in industrialized nations where food is abundant, the joint roles of heredity and environment in pubertal growth are apparent. African-American girls reach menarche about six months earlier than Caucasian-American girls. Although widespread overweight and obesity in the black population contribute, a genetically influenced faster rate of physical maturation is also involved. Black girls usually reach menarche before white girls of the same age and body weight (Anderson, Dallal, & Must, 2003; Chumlea et al., 2003).

Early family experiences may also contribute to the timing of puberty. One theory suggests that humans have evolved to be sensitive to the emotional quality of their childhood environments. When children's safety and security are at risk, it is adaptive for them to reproduce early. Several studies indicate that girls exposed to family conflict tend to reach menarche early, whereas those with warm family ties reach menarche relatively late (Ellis & Garber, 2000; Ellis et al., 1999; Romans et al., 2003).

In the research we have considered, threats to emotional health accelerate puberty, whereas threats to physical health delay it. A **secular trend,** or generational change, in pubertal timing lends added support to the role of physical well-being in pubertal development. In industrialized nations, age of menarche declined steadily—by about three to four months per decade—from 1900 to 1970, a period in which nutrition, health care, sanitation, and control of infectious disease improved greatly. Boys, too, have reached puberty earlier in recent decades (Karpati et al., 2002). In North America and some European countries, soaring rates of overweight and obesity are sustaining this trend (Parent et al., 2003). A worrisome consequence is that girls who reach sexual maturity at age 10 or 11 will feel pressure to act much older than they are. As we will see shortly, early-maturing girls are at risk for unfavorable peer involvements, including sexual activity.

Brain Development

The physical transformations of adolescence include major changes in the brain. Brain-imaging research reveals continued pruning of unused synapses in the cerebral cortex, especially in the frontal lobes—the "governor" of thought and action. In addition, growth and myelination of stimulated neural fibers accelerate, strengthening connections among various brain regions. In particular, linkages between the frontal lobes and other brain areas expand and attain rapid communication (Giedd et al., 1999; Keating, 2004; Sowell et al., 2002). This sculpting of the adolescent brain supports diverse cognitive advances, including attention, planning, capacity to integrate information, and self-regulation.

In addition, sensitivity of neurons to certain chemical messages changes. In humans and other mammals, neurons become more responsive to excitatory neurotransmitters during puberty. As a result, adolescents react more strongly to

Because neurons become more sensitive to certain neurotransmitters during adolescence, young people react more strongly to stressful and pleasurable events than they did as children. You can see this intensity in the elation of these teenagers, completely engaged in the delights of summer.

stressful events, and they also experience pleasurable stimuli more intensely (Spear, 2003). These changes probably play a role in the drive for novel experiences, including drug taking, during this period, especially among teenagers who engage in reward seeking to counteract chronic emotional pain. Alterations in neurotransmitter activity may also be involved in adolescents' increased susceptibility to certain disorders, such as depression and eating disturbances.

To what extent are the hormonal changes of puberty responsible for adolescent brain growth and reorganization? Researchers do not yet have a ready answer. But the transformations that occur—much greater than previously thought—enhance our understanding of teenagers' troubling behaviors and their need for adult patience, oversight, and guidance.

Changing States of Arousal

At puberty, revisions occur in the way the brain regulates the timing of sleep, perhaps because of increased neural sensitivity to evening light. As a result, adolescents go to bed much later than they did as children. Yet they need almost as much sleep as they did in middle childhood—about nine hours. When they must get up early for school, their sleep needs are not satisfied.

This sleep "phase delay" strengthens with pubertal growth. But today's teenagers often have evening social activities and part-time jobs, as well as TVs, computers, and phones in their bedrooms. As a result, they get much less sleep than teenagers of previous generations (Carskadon et al., 2002; Fins & Wohlgemuth, 2001). Sleep-deprived adolescents perform especially poorly on cognitive tasks during morning hours. And they are more likely to achieve less well in school, suffer from depressed mood, and engage in high-risk behaviors, including drinking and reckless driving (Dahl & Lewin, 2002; Hansen et al., 2005). They also engage in sleep rebound on weekends, which sustains the pattern by leading to difficulty falling asleep on subsequent evenings (Laberge et al., 2001). Later school start times ease sleep loss but do not eliminate it. Educating teenagers about the importance of sleep is vital.

The Psychological Impact of Pubertal Events

Think back to your late elementary and junior high school days. As you reached puberty, how did your feelings about yourself and your relationships with others change? Research reveals that pubertal events affect adolescents' self-image, mood, and interaction with parents and peers. Some outcomes are a response to dramatic physical change, regardless of when it occurs. Others have to do with pubertal timing.

Reactions to Pubertal Changes

Two generations ago, menarche was often traumatic. Today, girls commonly react with "surprise," undoubtedly due to the

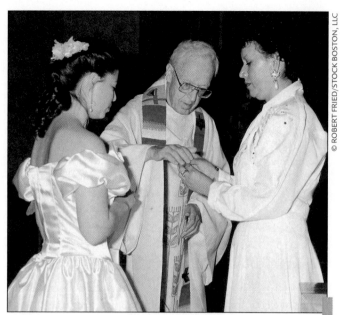

© ROBERT FRIED/STOCK BOSTON, LLC

Quinceañera, the traditional Hispanic fifteenth birthday celebration, is a rite of passage honoring a girl's journey from childhood to maturity. It usually begins with a mass in which the priest blesses gifts presented to the girl.

benefit, especially, from opportunities to ask questions and discuss feelings with a sympathetic parent or health professional.

The larger cultural context affects the experience of puberty. Many tribal and village societies celebrate its onset with an *initiation ceremony*, a ritualized announcement to the community that marks an important change in privilege and responsibility. Consequently, young people know that reaching puberty is valued in their culture. In contrast, Western societies grant little formal recognition to movement from childhood to adolescence or from adolescence to adulthood. Certain ethnic and religious ceremonies, such as the Jewish bar or bat mitzvah and the *quinceañera* in Hispanic communities (celebrating a 15-year-old girl's journey to adulthood) resemble initiation ceremonies. But they usually do not lead to a meaningful change in social status.

Instead, Western adolescents are granted partial adult status at many different ages—for example, an age for starting employment, for driving, for leaving high school, for voting, and for drinking. And in some contexts (at home and at school), they may still be regarded as children. The absence of a widely accepted marker of physical and social maturity makes the process of becoming an adult more confusing.

Pubertal Change, Emotion, and Social Behavior

A common belief is that puberty has something to do with adolescent moodiness and the desire for greater physical and psychological separation from parents. Let's see what research says about these relationships.

■ **Adolescent Moodiness.** Although research reveals that higher pubertal hormone levels are linked to greater moodiness, these relationships are not strong (Buchanan, Eccles, & Becker, 1992). What else might contribute to the common observation that adolescents are moody? In several studies, the moods of children, adolescents, and adults were monitored by having them carry electronic pagers. Over a one-week period, they were beeped at random intervals and asked to write down what they were doing, whom they were with, and how they felt.

As expected, adolescents reported less favorable moods than school-age children and adults (Larson et al, 2002; Larson & Lampman-Petraitis, 1989). But negative moods were linked to a greater number of negative life events, such as difficulties with parents, disciplinary actions at school, and breaking up with a boyfriend or girlfriend. Negative events increased steadily from childhood to adolescence, and teenagers also seemed to react to them with greater emotion than children (Larson & Ham, 1993). (Recall that stress reactivity is heightened by changes in brain neurotransmitter activity during adolescence.)

Compared with adults' moods, those of younger adolescents (ages 12 to 16) were less stable, often shifting from cheerful to sad and back again. These mood swings were strongly related to situational changes. High points of adolescents' days were times spent with peers and in self-chosen leisure activities. Low points tended to occur in adult-structured settings—

sudden onset of the event. Otherwise, they typically report a mixture of positive and negative emotions. Yet wide individual differences exist that depend on prior knowledge and support from family members.

For girls who have no advance information, menarche can be shocking and disturbing. In the 1950s, up to 50 percent received no prior warning, and of those who did, many were given "grin-and-bear-it" messages (Costos, Ackerman, & Paradis, 2002; Shainess, 1961). Today, few are uninformed, a shift that is probably due to modern parents' greater willingness to discuss sexual matters and more widespread health education classes (Omar, McElderry, & Zakharia, 2003). Almost all girls get some information from their mothers. And girls whose fathers know about their pubertal changes adjust especially well. Perhaps a father's involvement reflects a family atmosphere that is highly accepting of physical and sexual matters (Brooks-Gunn & Ruble, 1983).

Like girls' reactions to menarche, boys' responses to spermarche reflect mixed feelings. Virtually all boys know about ejaculation ahead of time, but many say that no one spoke to them before or during puberty about physical changes (Omar, McElderry, & Zakharia, 2003). Usually they get their information from their own reading. Even boys who had advance information often say that their first ejaculation occurred earlier than they expected and that they were unprepared for it. As with girls, boys who feel better prepared tend to react more positively (Stein & Reiser, 1994). But whereas almost all girls eventually tell a friend that they are menstruating, far fewer boys tell anyone about spermarche (Downs & Fuller, 1991). Overall, boys get much less social support than girls for the physical changes of puberty. This suggests that boys might

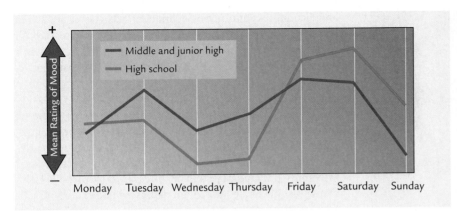

FIGURE 11.3 Younger and older adolescents' emotional experiences across the week. Adolescents' reports revealed that emotional high points are on Fridays and Saturdays. Mood drops on Sunday, before returning to school, and during the week, as students spend much time in adult-structured settings in school. (From R. Larson & M. Richards, 1998, "Waiting for the Weekend: Friday and Saturday Night as the Emotional Climax of the Week." in A. C. Crouter & R. Larson (Eds.), *Temporal Rhythms in Adolescence: Clocks, Calendars, and the Coordination of Daily Life.* San Francisco: Jossey-Bass, p. 41. Reprinted by permission.)

class, job, and religious services. Furthermore, teenagers' emotional highs coincided with Friday and Saturday evenings, especially in high school (see Figure 11.3). Going out with friends and romantic partners increases so dramatically during adolescence that it becomes a "cultural script" for what is *supposed* to happen (Larson & Richards, 1998). Consequently, teenagers who spend weekend evenings at home often feel profoundly lonely.

In sum, biological, psychological, and social forces combine to make adolescence a time of deeper valleys and higher peaks in emotional experience. This explanation is consistent with the balanced view presented earlier in this chapter.

■ **Parent–Child Relationships.** Sabrina's father noticed that as his children entered adolescence, they kept their bedroom doors closed, resisted spending time with the family, and became more argumentative. Sabrina and her mother squabbled over Sabrina's messy room ("It's *my* room, Mom. You don't have to live in it!"). And Sabrina resisted the family's regular weekend visit to Aunt Gina's ("Why do I have to go *every* week?"). Many studies show that puberty is related to a rise in parent–child conflict (Laursen, Coy, & Collins, 1998; Steinberg & Morris, 2001). Frequency of arguing is surprisingly similar across North American subcultures, occurring as often in families of European descent as in immigrant Asian and Hispanic families whose traditions respect parental authority (Fuligni, 1998).

Why should a youngster's more adultlike appearance trigger these disputes? The association may have adaptive value. Among nonhuman primates, the young typically leave the family group around the time of puberty. The same is true in many nonindustrialized cultures (Caine, 1986; Schlegel & Barry, 1991). Departure of young people discourages sexual relations between close blood relatives. But because they are still economically dependent on parents, adolescents in industrialized nation cannot leave the family. Consequently, a modern substitute seems to have emerged: psychological distancing.

As children become physically mature, they demand to be treated in adultlike ways. And as we will see, adolescents' new powers of reasoning may also contribute to a rise in family tensions. Parent–adolescent disagreements focus largely on mundane, day-to-day matters—driving, dating partners, curfews, and the like (Adams & Laursen, 2001). But beneath these disputes lie serious concerns: parental efforts to protect teenagers from substance use, auto accidents, and early sex. The larger the gap between parents' and adolescents' views of teenagers' readiness for new responsibilities, the more quarreling (Deković, Noom, & Meeus, 1997).

Parent–daughter conflict tends to be more intense than conflict with sons, perhaps because parents place more restrictions on girls (Allison & Schultz, 2004). But most disputes are mild. Parents and adolescents display both conflict and affection, and they usually agree on important values, such as honesty and the importance of education. Although separation from parents is adaptive, both generations benefit from warm, protective family bonds throughout the lifespan.

Pubertal Timing

"All our children were early maturers," said Franca during the parents' discussion group. "The three boys were tall by age 12 or 13, but it was easier for them. They felt big and important. Sabrina was skinny as a little girl, but now she says she is too fat and needs to diet. She thinks about boys and doesn't concentrate on her schoolwork."

Findings of several studies match the experiences of Sabrina and her brothers. Both adults and peers viewed early-maturing boys as relaxed, independent, self-confident, and physically attractive. Popular with agemates, they tended to hold leadership positions in school and to be athletic stars. In contrast, late-maturing boys were viewed by both adults and peers as anxious, overly talkative, and attention-seeking (Brooks-Gunn, 1988; Clausen, 1975; Jones, 1965). However, early-maturing boys, though viewed as well-adjusted, report slightly more psychological stress than their later-maturing agemates (Ge, Conger, & Elder, 2001).

In contrast, early-maturing girls were unpopular, withdrawn, lacking in self-confidence, and anxious, and they held few leadership positions (Ge, Conger, & Elder, 1996; Graber et al., 1997; Jones & Mussen, 1958). They were more involved in deviant behavior (getting drunk, participating in early sexual activity) and achieved less well in school (Caspi et al., 1993; Dick et al., 2000). In contrast, their late-maturing counterparts were regarded as physically attractive, lively, sociable, and leaders at school.

These boys are all 13 years old, yet they differ in timing of pubertal maturation. The two in the center are early-maturing boys and, thus, likely have a positive body image. The other two appear to be on-time maturers, about average in progress for their age.

Two factors largely account for these trends: (1) how closely the adolescent's body matches cultural ideals of physical attractiveness and (2) how well young people fit in physically with their peers.

The Role of Physical Attractiveness.

Flip through the pages of your favorite popular magazine. You will see evidence of our society's view of an attractive female as thin and long-legged and a good-looking male as tall, broad-shouldered, and muscular. The female image is a girlish shape that favors the late developer. The male image fits the early-maturing boy.

Consistent with these preferences, early-maturing girls usually report a less positive **body image**—conception of and attitude toward their physical appearance—than their on-time and late-maturing agemates (Williams & Currie, 2000). Although boys are less consistent, early, rapid maturers tend to be more satisfied with their physical characteristics (Alsaker, 1995; Sinkkonen, Anttila, & Siimes, 1998). These conclusions affect young people's self-esteem and psychological well-being.

The Importance of Fitting in with Peers.

Physical status in relation to peers also explains differences in adjustment between early and late maturers. From this perspective, early-maturing girls and late-maturing boys have difficulty because they fall at the extremes of physical development and feel "out of place" when with their agemates. Not surprisingly, adolescents feel most comfortable with peers who match their own level of biological maturity (Stattin & Magnusson, 1990).

Because few agemates of the same pubertal status are available, early-maturing adolescents of both sexes seek out older companions, sometimes with unfavorable consequences. Older peers often encourage them into activities they are not yet ready to handle emotionally, including sexual activity, drug and alcohol use, and minor delinquent acts (Ge et al., 2002). Perhaps because of such involvements, early maturers of both sexes report feeling depressed and show declines in academic performance (Graber, 2003; Kaltiala-Heino, Kosunen, & Rimpelä, 2003).

Long-Term Consequences.

Do the effects of pubertal timing persist? Follow-ups reveal that early-maturing girls, especially, are prone to lasting difficulties. In one study, early-maturing boys' depression subsided by age 13; puberty seemed to be only a temporary stressor. In contrast, depressed early-maturing girls tended to remain depressed (Ge et al., 2003). In another study, which followed young people from age 14 to 24, early-maturing boys again showed good adjustment. Early-maturing girls, however, reported poorer-quality relationships with family and friends, smaller social networks, and lower life satisfaction into early adulthood than did their on-time counterparts (Graber et al., 2004). Similarly, in a Swedish study, achievement and substance use difficulties of early-maturing girls lingered, in the form of greater alcohol abuse and lower educational attainment than their agemates (Andersson & Magnusson, 1990; Stattin & Magnusson, 1990).

Researchers believe that impaired social relationships underlie these negative outcomes. Recall that childhood family conflict is linked to earlier menarche (see page 366). Perhaps many early-maturing girls enter adolescence with emotional and social difficulties. As the stresses of puberty interfere with school performance and lead to unfavorable peer pressures, poor adjustment extends and deepens. Clearly, interventions that target at-risk early-maturing youths are needed. These include educating parents and teachers and providing adolescents with counseling and social supports that prepare them to handle the emotional and social challenges of this transition.

Ask Yourself

Review

Summarize the consequences of pubertal timing for adolescent development.

Apply

As a school-age child, Chloe enjoyed leisure activities with her parents. Now, as a 14-year-old, she spends hours in her room and resists going on weekend family excursions. Explain Chloe's behavior.

Connect

How might adolescent moodiness contribute to psychological distancing between parents and adolescents? (*Hint:* Think about bidirectional influences in parent–child relationships.)

Reflect

Think back to your own reactions to the physical changes of puberty. Are they consistent with research findings? Explain.

Health Issues

The arrival of puberty is accompanied by new health issues related to the young person's striving to meet physical and psychological needs. As adolescents attain greater autonomy, their personal decision making becomes important, in health as well as other areas (Bearison, 1998). Yet none of the health concerns we are about to discuss can be traced to a single cause. Rather, biological, psychological, family, peer, and cultural factors jointly contribute.

Nutritional Needs

When their sons reached puberty, Franca and Antonio reported a "vacuum cleaner effect" in the kitchen as the boys routinely emptied the refrigerator. Rapid body growth leads to a dramatic rise in food intake. During the growth spurt, boys require about 2,700 calories a day and much more protein than they did earlier, girls about 2,200 calories but somewhat less protein than boys because of their smaller size and muscle mass (Cortese & Smith, 2003).

This increase in nutritional requirements comes at a time when the diets of many young people are the poorest. Of all age groups, adolescents are the most likely to skip breakfast (a practice linked to obesity), consume empty calories, and eat on the run (Videon & Manning, 2003). Fast-food restaurants, which are favorite teenage gathering places, have started to offer some healthy menu options. But adolescents need guidance in choosing these alternatives. Fast-food eating and school food purchases from snack bars and vending machines are associated with consumption of high-fat foods and soft drinks, indicating that teenagers often make unhealthy food choices (Bowman et al., 2004; Kubik et al., 2003).

The most common nutritional problem of adolescence is iron deficiency, as iron requirements increase to a maximum during the growth spurt and remain high among girls because of iron loss during menstruation. A tired, irritable teenager may be suffering from anemia rather than unhappiness and should have a medical checkup. Most teenagers do not get enough calcium, and they are also deficient in riboflavin (vitamin B_2) and magnesium, both of which support metabolism (Cavadini, Siega-Riz, & Popkin, 2000). And contrary to what many parents believe, obese children rarely outgrow their weight problem as teenagers (Berkowitz & Stunkard, 2002).

Frequency of family meals is strongly associated with healthy eating in teenagers—greater intake of fruits, vegetables, grains, and calcium-rich foods and reduced soft drink consumption (Neumark-Sztainer et al., 2003). But compared to families with younger children, those with adolescents eat fewer meals together. In addition to their other benefits (see page 63 in Chapter 2 and page 317 in Chapter 9), family meals can greatly improve teenagers' diets.

Adolescents—especially girls concerned about their weight—tend to be attracted to fad diets. Unfortunately, most are too limited in nutrients and calories to be healthy for fast-growing, active teenagers (Donatelle, 2004). When a young person wants to try a special diet, parents should encourage consultation with a doctor or dietician.

Eating Disorders

Sabrina's desire to lose weight worried Franca. She explained to her daughter that Sabrina was really quite average in build for an adolescent girl and reminded her that her Italian ancestors had considered a plump female body more beautiful than a thin one. Girls who reach puberty early, who are very dissatisfied with their body image, and who grow up in homes where concern with weight and thinness is high are at risk for serious eating problems. Severe dieting is the strongest predictor of the onset of an eating disorder in adolescence (Patton et al., 1999). The two most serious are anorexia nervosa and bulimia nervosa.

■ **Anorexia Nervosa.** **Anorexia nervosa** is a tragic eating disturbance in which young people starve themselves because of a compulsive fear of getting fat. About 1 percent of North American and Western European teenage girls are affected. During the past half-century, cases have increased sharply, fueled by cultural admiration of female thinness. Anorexia nervosa is equally common in all SES groups (Rogers et al., 1997), but Asian-American, Caucasian-American, and Hispanic girls are at greater risk than African-American girls, who tend to be more satisfied with their size and shape (Fairburn & Harrison, 2003; Wildes, Emery, & Simons, 2001). Boys account for about 10 percent of cases of anorexia; about half of these are homosexual or bisexual young people who are

Gennifer, an anorexia nervosa patient, is shown in the left photo in the hospital where she received life-saving treatment for malnutrition. After prolonged family therapy, she recovered, and is pictured in the right photo at home, two years after her hospital stay.

uncomfortable with a strong, muscular appearance (Robb & Dadson, 2002).

Anorexics have an extremely distorted body image. Even after they have become severely underweight, they see themselves as too heavy. Most go on self-imposed diets so strict that they struggle to avoid eating in response to hunger. To enhance weight loss, they exercise strenuously.

In their attempt to reach "perfect" slimness, anorexics lose between 25 and 50 percent of their body weight. Because a normal menstrual cycle requires about 15 percent body fat, either menarche does not occur or menstrual periods stop. Malnutrition causes pale skin, brittle discolored nails, fine dark hairs all over the body, and extreme sensitivity to cold. If it continues, the heart muscle can shrink, the kidneys can fail, and irreversible brain damage and loss of bone mass can occur. About 6 percent of anorexics die of the disorder, as a result of either physical complications or suicide (Katzman, 2005).

Forces within the person, the family, and the larger culture give rise to anorexia nervosa. Identical twins share the disorder more often than fraternal twins, indicating a genetic influence. And abnormalities in neurotransmitters in the brain, linked to anxiety and impulse control, may make some individuals more susceptible (Kaye et al., 2005; Klump, Kaye, & Strober, 2001). Many anorexics have extremely high standards for their own behavior and performance, are emotionally inhibited, and avoid intimate ties outside the family. Consequently, these girls are often ideal daughters in many respects—excellent students who are also responsible and well-behaved. But as we have also seen, the societal image of "thin is beautiful" contributes to the poorer body image of early-maturing girls, who are at greatest risk for anorexia (Tyrka, Graber, & Brooks-Gunn, 2000).

In addition, parent–adolescent interactions reveal problems related to adolescent autonomy. Often the mothers of these girls have high expectations for physical appearance, achievement, and social acceptance and are overprotective and controlling. Fathers tend to be emotionally distant. Instead of rebelling openly, anorexic girls do so indirectly—by fiercely pursuing perfection in achievement, respectable behavior, and thinness (Bruch, 2001). Nevertheless, it remains unclear whether maladaptive parent–child relationships precede the disorder, emerge as a response to it, or both.

Because anorexic girls typically deny that any problem exists, treating the disorder is difficult. Hospitalization is often necessary to prevent life-threatening malnutrition. Common treatments include family therapy, as well as medication to reduce anxiety and neurotransmitter imbalances (Fairburn, 2005; Treasure & Schmidt, 2005). But less than 50 percent of patients recover fully.

■ **Bulimia Nervosa.** When Sabrina's 16-year-old brother, Louis, brought his girlfriend, Cassie, to the house, Sabrina admired her good figure. "What willpower!" Sabrina thought. "Cassie hardly touches food. But what in the world is wrong with her teeth?"

Willpower was not the secret to Cassie's slender shape. When it came to food, she actually had great difficulty controlling herself. Cassie suffered from **bulimia nervosa,** an eating disorder in which young people (again, mainly girls, but gay and bisexual boys are also vulnerable) engage in strict dieting and excessive exercise accompanied by binge eating, often followed by deliberate vomiting and purging with laxatives. When she was alone, Cassie often felt anxious and unhappy. She responded with eating rampages, consuming thousands of calories in an hour or two, followed by vomiting that eroded the enamel on her teeth. In some cases, life-threatening damage to the throat and stomach occurs.

Bulimia is more common than anorexia nervosa. About 2 to 3 percent of teenage girls are affected; only 5 percent have previously been anorexic. Twin studies show that bulimia, like anorexia, is influenced by heredity (Klump, Kaye, & Strober, 2001). Overweight and early puberty increase the risk. Some bulimics, like anorexics, are perfectionists. Others lack self-control not just in eating but in other areas of their lives, engaging in petty shoplifting and alcohol abuse. And although bulimics share with anorexics pathological anxiety about gaining weight, they may have experienced their parents as disengaged and emotionally unavailable rather than controlling (Fairburn & Harrison, 2003).

Unlike anorexics, bulimics usually feel depressed and guilty about their abnormal eating habits and are desperate to get help. As a result, bulimia is usually easier to treat than anorexia, through support groups, nutrition education, training in changing eating habits, and anti-anxiety, antidepressant, and appetite-control medication (Hay & Bacaltchuk, 2004).

Sexual Activity

Louis and Cassie hadn't planned to have intercourse—it "just happened." But before and after, a lot of things passed through their minds. Cassie had been dating Louis for three months, and she began to wonder, "Will he think I'm normal if I don't have sex with him? If he wants to and I say no, will I lose him?" Both young people knew their parents wouldn't approve. In fact, when Franca and Antonio noticed how attached Louis was to Cassie, they talked to him about the importance of waiting and the dangers of pregnancy. But that Friday evening, Louis and Cassie's feelings for each other seemed overwhelming. As things went further and further, Louis thought, "If I don't make a move, will she think I'm a wimp?"

With the arrival of puberty, hormonal changes—in particular, the production of androgens in young people of both sexes—lead to an increase in sex drive (Halpern, Udry, & Suchindran, 1997). In response, adolescents become very concerned about how to manage sexuality in social relationships. New cognitive capacities involving perspective taking and self-reflection affect their efforts to do so. Yet like the eating behaviors we have just discussed, adolescent sexuality is heavily influenced by the young person's social context.

■ **The Impact of Culture.** When did you first learn the "facts of life"—and how? Was sex discussed openly in your family, or was it treated with secrecy? Exposure to sex, education about it, and efforts to limit the sexual curiosity of children and adolescents vary widely around the world.

Despite the publicity granted to the image of a sexually free modern adolescent, sexual attitudes in North America are relatively restrictive. Typically, parents give children little or no information about sex, discourage sex play, and rarely talk about sex in their presence. When young people become interested in sex, only about half report talking with their parents about intercourse, pregnancy prevention, and sexually transmitted disease. Many parents avoid meaningful discussions about sex out of fear of embarrassment or concern that the adolescent will not take them seriously. Yet warm, open give-and-take is associated with teenagers' adoption of parents' views and with reduced sexual risk taking (Jaccard, Dodge, & Dittus, 2003; Miller, Forehand, & Kotchick, 1999). Applying What We Know below lists qualities of successful communication.

Adolescents who do not get information about sex from their parents are likely to learn from friends, books, magazines, movies, TV, and the Internet (Jaccard, Dodge, & Dittus, 2002). On prime-time TV shows, which adolescents watch more than other TV offerings, two-thirds of programs contain sexual content. Most depict partners as spontaneous and passionate, having little commitment to each other, taking no steps to avoid pregnancy or sexually transmitted disease, and experiencing no negative consequences (Roberts, Henriksen, & Foehr, 2004).

Consider the contradictory messages delivered by these sources. On one hand, adults emphasize that sex at a young age and outside of marriage is wrong. On the other hand, the broader social environment extols the excitement and romanticism of sex. North American teenagers are left bewildered, poorly informed about sexual facts, and with little sound advice on how to conduct their sex lives responsibly.

© JEFF GREENBERG/PHOTOEDIT

Adolescence is an especially important time for the development of sexuality, as these two young people demonstrate, but North American teenagers often receive contradictory and confusing messages about the appropriateness of sex.

■ **Adolescent Sexual Attitudes and Behavior.** Although differences between subcultural groups exist, the sexual attitudes of North American adolescents and adults have become more liberal over the past 40 years. Compared with a generation ago, more people believe that sexual intercourse before marriage is all right, as long as two people are emotionally committed to one another (Michael et al., 1994). Recently, a slight swing back in the direction of conservative sexual beliefs has occurred, largely due to the risk of sexually transmitted disease, especially AIDS, and to teenage sexual abstinence programs sponsored by schools and religious organizations (Ali & Scelfo, 2002; Cope-Farrar & Kunkel, 2002).

Communicating with Adolescents About Sexual Issues

Strategy	Explanation
Foster open communication.	Let the teenager know you are a willing and trustworthy resource by stating that you are available when questions arise and will answer fully and accurately.
Use correct terms for body parts.	Correct vocabulary provides the young person with a basis for future discussion and also indicates that sex is not a topic that needs to be discussed in secret.
Use effective discussion techniques.	Listen, encourage the adolescent to participate, ask open-ended rather than yes/no questions, and give supportive responses. Avoid dominating and lecturing, which cause teenagers to withdraw. If questions arise that you cannot answer, collaborate with the teenager to gathering further information.
Reflect before speaking.	When the adolescent asks questions or offers opinions about sex, remain nonjudgmental. If you differ with the teenager's views, convey your perspective in a nonthreatening manner, emphasizing that although you disagree, you are not attacking his or her character. Trying to dictate the young person's behavior generally results in alienation.
Keep conversations going.	Many parents regard their job as finished once they have had the "big talk" in early adolescence. But young people are more likely to be influenced by an accumulation of smaller discussions. If open communication is sustained, the teenager is more likely to return with thoughts and questions.

Applying What We Know

Source: Berkowitz, 2004.

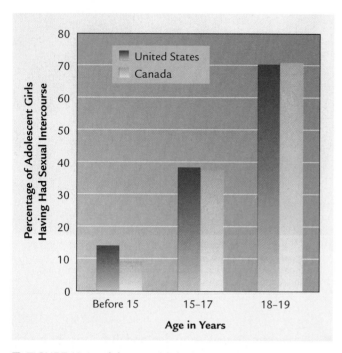

FIGURE 11.4 Adolescent girls in the United States and Canada reporting ever having had sexual intercourse. A greater percentage of U.S. than of Canadian girls engage in sexual activity before age 15. Otherwise, rates of sexual activity are similar in the two countries and resemble those of Western European nations. Boys' sexual activity rates are 3 to 6 percent higher than the rates for girls shown here. (Adapted from Darroch, Frost, & Singh, 2001; Maticka-Tyndale, 2001; U.S. Department of Health and Human Services, 2004d.)

Trends in adolescents' sexual behavior are consistent with their attitudes. After rising for several decades, the rate of premarital sex among U.S. and Canadian young people has declined since 1990 (Dryburgh, 2001; U.S. Department of Health and Human Services, 2004d). Nevertheless, as Figure 11.4 illustrates, a substantial percentage of young people are sexually active quite early, by age 15. Males tend to have their first intercourse earlier than females.

Although the overall rates of teenage sexual activity are similar in the United States, Canada, and other Western countries, the quality of sexual experiences differs. Youths in the United States begin sexual activity at a younger age than their Canadian and Western European counterparts (Boyce et al., 2003; U.S. Department of Health and Human Services, 2004d). And about 12 percent of adolescent boys in the United States, compared with 8 percent in Canada, have had sexual relations with three or more partners in the past year (Alan Guttmacher Institute, 2004; Darroch, Frost, & Singh, 2001). These teenagers, however, are in the minority; most have had only one or two sexual partners by the end of high school.

Characteristics of Sexually Active Adolescents. Early and frequent teenage sexual activity is linked to personal, family, peer, and educational characteristics. These include early pubertal timing, parental divorce, single-parent and stepfamily homes, large family size, little or no religious involvement,

weak parental monitoring, disrupted parent–child communication, sexually active friends and older siblings, poor school performance, lower educational aspirations, and tendency to engage in norm-violating acts, including alcohol and drug use and delinquency (Anaya, Cantwell, & Rothman-Borus, 2003; Howard & Wang, 2004).

Because many of these factors are associated with growing up in a low-income family, it is not surprising that early sexual activity is more common among young people from economically disadvantaged homes. Living in a hazardous neighborhood—one high in physical deterioration, crime, and violence—also increases the likelihood that teenagers will be sexually active (Ge et al., 2002). In such neighborhoods, social ties are weak, adults exert little oversight and control over adolescents' activities, and negative peer influences are widespread. In fact, the high rate of premarital intercourse among African-American teenagers—67 percent compared with 51 percent for all U.S. young people—is largely accounted for by poverty in the black population (Darroch, Frost, & Singh, 2001).

Early and prolonged father absence predicts higher rates of intercourse and pregnancy among adolescent girls, after many family background and personal characteristics are controlled (Ellis et al., 2003). Perhaps father absence exposes young people to their mother's dating and sexual behaviors—modeling that promotes early sex. An alternative, evolutionary view holds that fathers' investment in parenting encourages daughters to delay sexual activity in favor of seeking a similarly committed male partner to ensure their offspring's well-being. Because father-absent girls view male commitment as uncertain, they may readily enter into casual sexual relationships.

Contraceptive Use. Although adolescent contraceptive use has increased in recent years, 27 percent of sexually active teenagers in the United States and 13 percent in Canada are at risk for unintended pregnancy because they do not use contraception consistently (see Figure 11.5) (Alan Guttmacher Institute, 2002; Manlove, Ryan, & Franzetta, 2003). Why do these youths fail to take precautions? As we will see when we take up adolescent cognitive development, adolescents can consider many possibilities when faced with a problem, but they often fail to apply this reasoning to everyday situations. When asked to explain why they did not use contraception, they often give answers like these: "I was waiting until I had a steady boyfriend," or "I wasn't planning to have sex."

One reason for these responses is that advances in perspective taking lead teenagers, for a time, to be extremely concerned about others' opinions of them. Recall how Cassie and Louis each worried about what the other would think if they decided not to have sex. Furthermore, in the midst of everyday social pressures, adolescents often overlook the consequences of engaging in risky behaviors (Beyth-Marom & Fischhoff, 1997).

The social environment also contributes to teenagers' reluctance to use contraception. Those without the rewards of meaningful education and work are especially likely to engage in irresponsible sex, sometimes within relationships characterized by exploitation. About 12 percent of North American girls

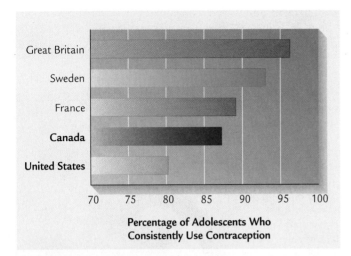

FIGURE 11.5 Adolescent contraceptive use in five industrialized nations. Sexually active U.S. teenagers are less likely to use contraception consistently than teenagers in other industrialized nations. Canadian adolescents, as well, fall below adolescents in Western Europe in contraceptive use. (Adapted from Darroch, Frost, & Singh, 2001; U.S. Department of Health and Human Services, 2004d.)

and 6 percent of boys say they were pressured to have intercourse when they did not want to do so (Boyce et al., 2003; U.S. Department of Health and Human Services, 2004d).

Teenagers who talk openly with parents about sex and contraception are more likely to use birth control (Kirby, 2002a; Whitaker & Miller, 2000). But as noted earlier, many parents do not engage in such discussions. Sex education classes, as well, often leave teenagers with incomplete or incorrect knowledge. Some young people do not know where to get birth control counseling and devices. When they do, they often worry that a doctor or family planning clinic might not keep their visits confidential. About 20 percent of adolescents using health services say that if their parents were notified, they would still have sex but without contraception (Jones et al., 2005).

■ **Sexual Orientation.** Up to this point, our discussion has focused only on heterosexual behavior. About 2 to 3 percent of young people identify as lesbian, gay, or bisexual (Bailey, Dunne, & Martin, 2000; Savin-Williams & Diamond, 2004). An as-yet-unknown number who experience same-sex attraction have not come out to friends or family (see the Social Issues box on page 376). Adolescence is an equally crucial time for the sexual development of these young people, and societal attitudes, once again, loom large in how well they fare.

Heredity makes an important contribution to homosexuality: Identical twins of both sexes are much more likely than fraternal twins to share a homosexual orientation. The same is true for biological as opposed to adoptive relatives (Kendler et al., 2000; Kirk et al., 2000). Furthermore, male homosexuality tends to be more common on the maternal than on the paternal side of families. This suggests that it might be X-linked (see Chapter 2). Indeed, one gene-mapping study found that among 40 pairs of homosexual brothers, 33 (82 percent) had

an identical segment of DNA on the X chromosome. One or several genes in that region might predispose males to become homosexual (Hamer et al., 1993).

How might heredity lead to homosexuality? According to some researchers, certain genes affect the level or impact of prenatal sex hormones, which modify brain structures in ways that induce homosexual feelings and behavior (Bailey et al., 1995; LeVay, 1993). Keep in mind, however, that both genetic and environmental factors can alter prenatal hormones. Girls exposed prenatally to very high levels of androgens or estrogens—either because of a genetic defect or from drugs given to the mother to prevent miscarriage—are more likely to become homosexual or bisexual (Meyer-Bahlburg et al., 1995). Furthermore, homosexual men tend to be later in birth order and to have a higher-than-average number of older brothers (Blanchard & Bogaert, 2004). One possibility is that mothers with several male children sometimes produce antibodies to androgens, which reduce the prenatal impact of male sex hormones on the brains of later-born boys.

Stereotypes and misconceptions about homosexuality continue to be widespread. For example, contrary to common belief, most homosexual adolescents are not "gender-deviant" in dress or behavior. Furthermore, attraction to members of the same sex is not limited to gay and lesbian teenagers. About 50 to 60 percent of adolescents who report having engaged in homosexual acts identify as heterosexual (Savin-Williams & Diamond, 2004).

Sexually Transmitted Diseases

Sexually active adolescents, both homosexual and heterosexual, are at risk for sexually transmitted diseases (STDs). Adolescents have the highest rates of STDs of all age groups. Despite a recent decline in STDs in the United States, one out of six teenagers contracts one of these illnesses each year—a rate three times higher than that of Canada. Canada, however, exceeds many Western nations in incidence of the most common STDs, such as chlamydia and herpes (Maticka-Tyndale, 2001; Weinstock, Berman, & Cates, 2004). When STDs are left untreated, sterility and life-threatening complications can result. Teenagers in greatest danger of STDs are the same ones most likely to engage in irresponsible sexual behavior: poverty-stricken young people who feel a sense of hopelessness about their lives (Niccolai et al., 2004).

The most serious STD is AIDS. In contrast to Canada, where the incidence of AIDS among people under age 30 is low, one-fifth of U.S. AIDS cases occur in young people between ages 20 and 29. Since AIDS symptoms typically take 8 to 10 years to emerge in a person infected with the HIV virus, nearly all of these cases originated in adolescence. Drug-abusing adolescents who share needles and homosexual teenagers who have sex with HIV-positive partners account for most cases, but heterosexual spread of the disease has increased, especially among teenagers who have had more than one partner in the previous 18 months (Kelley et al., 2003). It is at least twice as easy for a male to infect a female with any STD, including AIDS, as for a female to infect a male.

Social Issues

Gay, Lesbian, and Bisexual Youths: Coming Out to Oneself and Others

Cultures vary as much in their acceptance of homosexuality as in their approval of extramarital sex. In North America, homosexuals are stigmatized, as shown by the degrading language often used to describe them. This makes forming a sexual identity a much greater challenge for gay, lesbian, and bisexual youths than for their heterosexual counterparts.

Wide variations in sexual identity formation exist, depending on personal, family, and community factors. Yet interviews with gay and lesbian adolescents and adults reveal that many (though not all) move through a three-phase sequence in coming out to themselves and others.

Feeling Different. Many gay men and lesbians say they felt different from other children when they were young. Typically, this first sense of their biologically determined sexual orientation appears between ages 6 and 12, in play interests more like those of the other gender (Rahman & Wilson, 2003). Boys may find that they are less interested in sports, more drawn to quieter activities, and more emotionally sensitive than other boys; girls that they are more athletic and active than other girls.

By age 10, many of these children start to engage in *sexual questioning*—wondering why the typical heterosexual orientation does not apply to them. Often, they experience their sense of being different as deeply distressing. Compared with children who are confident of their homosexuality, sexual-questioning children report greater anxiety about peer relationships and greater dissatisfaction with their biological gender over time (Carver, Egan, & Perry, 2004).

Confusion. With the arrival of puberty, feeling different clearly encompasses feeling sexually different. In research on ethnically diverse gay, lesbian, and bisexual youths, awareness of a same-sex physical attraction occurred, on average, between ages 11 and 12 for boys and 14 and 15 for girls, perhaps because adolescent social pressures toward heterosexuality

are particularly intense for girls (Diamond, 1998; D'Augelli, 2006).

Realizing that homosexuality has personal relevance sparks additional confusion. A few adolescents resolve their discomfort by crystallizing a gay, lesbian, or bisexual identity quickly, with a flash of insight into their sense of being different. But most experience an inner struggle and a deep sense of isolation—outcomes intensified by lack of role models and social support (D'Augelli, 2002).

Some throw themselves into activities they have come to associate with heterosexuality. Boys may go out for athletic teams; girls may drop softball and basketball in favor of dance. And homosexual youths typically try heterosexual dating, sometimes to hide their sexual orientation and at other times to develop intimacy skills that they later apply to same-sex relationships (Dubé, Savin-Williams, & Diamond, 2001). Those who are extremely troubled and guilt-ridden may escape into alcohol, drugs, and suicidal thinking. Suicide attempts are unusually high among gay, lesbian, and bisexual young people (McDaniel, Purcell, & D'Augelli, 2001).

Self-Acceptance. The majority of gay, lesbian, and bisexual teenagers accept their sexual identity. Then they face another crossroad: whether to tell others. Powerful stigma against their sexual orientation leads some to decide that no disclosure is possible. As a result, they self-define as gay but otherwise "pass" as heterosexual (Savin-Williams, 2001). When homosexual youths do come out, they often face intense hostility. In a study of over 500 gay, lesbian, and bisexual youths in Canada, New Zealand, and the United States, 75 percent reported being verbally abused, and 15 percent physically attacked, because of their sexual orientation (D'Augelli, 2002).

Nevertheless, many young people eventually acknowledge their sexual orientation publicly, usually by telling trusted friends first. Once teenagers establish a same-sex sexual or romantic relationship, many come out to parents. Few parents respond with severe rejection; most are either positive or slightly negative and disbelieving (Savin-Williams & Ream, 2003a). Parental understanding

Teenagers from around Boston join in the annual Gay/Straight Youth Pride March. When family members and peers react with acceptance, coming out strengthens the young person's view of homosexuality as a valid and fulfilling identity.

is the strongest predictor of favorable adjustment (Savin-Williams, 2003).

When people react positively, coming out strengthens the young person's view of homosexuality as a meaningful and fulfilling identity. Contact with other gays and lesbians is important for reaching this phase, and changes in society permit many adolescents in urban areas to attain it earlier than they did several decades ago. Gay and lesbian communities exist in large cities, along with specialized interest groups, social clubs, religious groups, newspapers, and periodicals. Small towns and rural areas remain difficult places to meet other homosexuals and to find a supportive environment. Teenagers in these locales have a special need for caring adults and peers who can help them find self- and social acceptance.

Gay, lesbian, and bisexual youths who succeed in coming out to themselves and others integrate their sexual orientation into a broader sense of identity, a process we will address in Chapter 12. As a result, they no longer need to focus so heavily on their homosexual self, and energy is freed for other aspects of psychological growth. In sum, coming out can foster many aspects of adolescent development, including self-esteem, psychological well-being, and relationships with family and friends.

As the result of school courses and media campaigns, about 60 percent of middle-school students and 90 percent of high school students are aware of basic facts about AIDS. But most have limited understanding of other STDs and their consequences, underestimate their own susceptibility, and are poorly informed about how to protect themselves (Boyce et al., 2003; Coholl et al., 2001; Ethier et al., 2003). Concerted efforts are needed to educate young people about the full range of STDs.

Adolescent Pregnancy and Parenthood

Cassie was lucky not to get pregnant after having sex with Louis, but some of her high school classmates weren't so fortunate. About 900,000 teenage girls in the United States become pregnant annually, 30,000 of them younger than age 15. Despite a steady decline since 1991, the U.S. adolescent pregnancy rate is higher than that of most other industrialized countries (see Figure 11.6). Although the Canadian rate is only about half the U.S. rate, teenage pregnancy in Canada remains a problem. Three factors heighten the incidence of adolescent pregnancy: (1) Effective sex education reaches too few teenagers, (2) convenient, low-cost contraceptive services for adolescents are scarce, and (3) many families live in poverty, which encourages young people to take risks.

Because 40 percent of U.S. and 50 percent of Canadian teenage pregnancies end in abortion, the number of North American teenage births is actually lower than it was 35 years ago (Maticka-Tyndale, 2001; U.S. Department of Health and Human Services, 2004d). But teenage parenthood is a much greater problem today because adolescents are far less likely to marry before childbirth. In 1960, only 15 percent of teenage births were to unmarried females, whereas today, 85 percent

are. And 1 out of 5 births to adolescents are repeat births (Child Trends, 2005a). Increased social acceptance of single motherhood, along with the belief of many teenage girls that a baby might fill a void in their lives, has meant that only a small number of girls give up their infants for adoption.

■ **Correlates and Consequences of Adolescent Parenthood.** Becoming a parent is challenging for anyone, but especially for adolescents. Teenage parents have not yet established a clear sense of direction for their own lives. They have both life conditions and personal attributes that interfere with their ability to parent effectively (Jaffee et al., 2001).

Teenage parents are many times more likely to be poor than agemates who postpone childbearing. Their backgrounds often include low parental warmth and involvement, domestic violence and child abuse, repeated parental divorce and remarriage, adult models of unmarried parenthood, and residence in neighborhoods where other adolescents also display these risks. Girls at risk for early pregnancy do poorly in school, engage in alcohol and drug use, have a childhood history of aggressive and antisocial behavior, associate with deviant peers, and experience high rates of depression (Elfenbein & Felice, 2003; Hillis et al., 2004). A high percentage of out-of-wedlock births are to low-income minority teenagers—African-American, Native-American, Hispanic, and Canadian-Aboriginal. Many turn to early parenthood as a way to move into adulthood when educational and career avenues are unavailable.

After a baby is born, adolescents' lives often worsen in at least three respects:

- *Educational attainment.* Giving birth before age 18 reduces the likelihood of finishing high school. Only about 70 percent of U.S. adolescent mothers graduate, compared with 95 percent of girls who wait to become parents (U.S. Department of Education, 2005a).

- *Marital patterns.* Teenage motherhood reduces the chances of marriage. When these mothers do marry, they are more likely to divorce than their peers who delay childbearing (Moore et al., 1993). Consequently, teenage mothers spend more of their parenting years as single parents.

- *Economic circumstances.* Because of low educational attainment, marital instability, and poverty, many teenage mothers are on welfare. If they are employed, their limited education restricts them to unsatisfying, low-paid jobs. Many adolescent fathers, too, are unemployed or work at unskilled jobs. Usually they earn too little to provide their children with basic necessities. And an estimated 50 percent have committed illegal offenses resulting in imprisonment (Elfenbein & Felice, 2003).

Because many pregnant teenage girls have inadequate diets, smoke, use alcohol and other drugs, and do not receive early prenatal care, their babies often experience prenatal and birth complications—especially low birth weight (Dell, 2001). And compared with adult mothers, adolescent mothers know less about child development, have unrealistically high expectations of infants, perceive their babies as more difficult, and

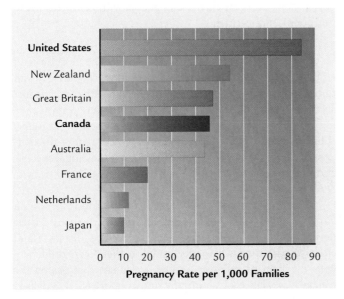

United States
New Zealand
Great Britain
Canada
Australia
France
Netherlands
Japan

0 10 20 30 40 50 60 70 80 90

Pregnancy Rate per 1,000 Families

■ **FIGURE 11.6 Pregnancy rates among 15- to 19-year-olds in eight industrialized nations.** U.S. teenagers have the highest pregnancy rate. The pregnancy rate in Canada is about half the U.S. rate but much higher than that in Western European nations and Japan. (Adapted from Alan Guttmacher Institute, 2001; Singh & Darroch, 2000.)

Although early parenthood imposes lasting hardships on both generations—adolescent and newborn baby—the presence of a caring father and a stable partnership between the parents can improve outcomes for the young family.

© NANCY SHIA

interact less effectively with them (Moore & Florsheim, 2001; Pomerleau, Scuccimarri, & Malcuit, 2003). Their children tend to score low on intelligence tests, achieve poorly in school, and engage in disruptive social behavior. And often the cycle of adolescent pregnancy is repeated in the next generation (Brooks-Gunn, Schley, & Hardy, 2002).

Still, how well adolescent parents and their children fare varies. If the teenager finishes high school, avoids additional births, and finds a stable marriage partner, long-term disruptions in her own and her child's development will be less severe.

■ **Prevention Strategies.** Preventing teenage pregnancy means addressing the many factors underlying early sexual activity and lack of contraceptive use. Too often, sex education courses are given late (after sexual activity has begun), last only a few sessions, and are limited to a catalogue of facts about anatomy and reproduction. Sex education that goes beyond this minimum does not encourage early sex, as some opponents claim (Kirby, 2002c). It does improve awareness of sexual facts—knowledge that is necessary for responsible sexual behavior.

Knowledge, however, is not enough: Sex education must also help teenagers build a bridge between what they know and what they do. Today, more effective sex education programs combine the following key elements:

🪶 Teaching skills for handling sexual situations through creative discussion and role-playing techniques

🪶 Promoting the value of abstinence to teenagers who are not yet sexually active

🪶 Providing information about contraceptives and ready access to them

Many studies show that sex education with these components can delay the initiation of sexual activity, increase contraceptive use, and reduce pregnancy rates (Kirby, 2002b).

Proposals to increase access to contraceptives are the most controversial aspect of adolescent pregnancy prevention. Many adults argue that placing birth control pills or condoms in the hands of teenagers is equivalent to saying that early sex is OK. Yet evaluations reveal that focusing only on abstinence prevents sexual activity only among sexually inexperienced adolescents; it is not effective with those who already have had intercourse (Aten et al., 2002; DiCenso et al., 2002). And in Canada and Western Europe, where community and school-based clinics offer contraceptives and where universal health insurance helps pay for them, teenage sexual activity is no higher than in the United States, but pregnancy, childbirth, and abortion rates are much lower (Alan Guttmacher Institute, 2001).

Efforts to prevent adolescent pregnancy and parenthood must go beyond improving sex education to build social competence. In one study, researchers randomly assigned at-risk high school students either to a year-long community service class, called Teen Outreach, or to regular classroom experiences in health or social studies. In Teen Outreach, adolescents participated in at least 20 hours per week of volunteer work tailored to their interests. They returned to school for discussions that focused on enhancing their community service skills and their ability to cope with everyday challenges. At the end of the school year, pregnancy, school failure, and school suspension were substantially lower in the group enrolled in Teen Outreach, which fostered social skills, connection to the community, and self-respect (Allen et al., 1997).

Finally, teenagers who look forward to a promising future are far less likely to engage in early and irresponsible sex. By expanding educational, vocational, and employment opportunities, society can provide young people with good reasons to postpone childbearing.

■ **Intervening with Adolescent Parents.** The most difficult and costly way to deal with adolescent parenthood is to wait until it has happened. Young parents need health care, encouragement to stay in school, job training, instruction in parenting and life-management skills, and high-quality, affordable child care. Schools that provide these services reduce the incidence of low-birth-weight babies, increase educational success, and prevent additional childbearing (Barnet et al., 2004; Seitz & Apfel, 1993, 1994).

Adolescent mothers also benefit from relationships with family members and other adults who are sensitive to their developmental needs. Older teenage mothers display more effective parenting when they establish their own residences with the help of relatives—an arrangement that grants the teenager a balance of autonomy and support (East & Felice, 1996). In one study, teenage mothers who had a long-term "mentor" relationship—an aunt, neighbor, or teacher who provided emotional support and guidance—were far more likely than those without a mentor to stay in school and graduate (Klaw, Rhodes, & Fitzgerald, 2003).

Programs focusing on fathers are attempting to increase their financial and emotional commitment to the baby. Although nearly half of young fathers visit their children during the first few years after birth, contact usually diminishes. Interventions that legally establish paternity and child support, treat mental health problems, help fathers attain financial self-sufficiency, and provide training in parenting skills increase responsible fatherhood (Smith, Buzi, & Weinman, 2002). Teenage mothers who receive financial and child-care assistance and emotional support from their child's father are less distressed and more likely to sustain a relationship with him (Cutrona et al., 1998; Gee & Rhodes, 2003). A positive mother–father relationship, in turn, predicts greater paternal involvement in caregiving and warmer, more stimulating father–infant interaction. And infants with lasting ties to their teenage fathers show better long-term adjustment (Florsheim & Smith, 2005; Furstenberg & Harris, 1993).

Substance Use and Abuse

At age 14, Louis waited until he was alone at home, took some cigarettes out of his uncle's pack, and smoked. At an unchaperoned party, he and Cassie drank several cans of beer because everyone else was doing it. Louis got little physical charge out of these experiences. He was a good student, was well-liked by peers, and got along well with his parents. He had no need for drugs as an escape valve from daily life. But he knew of others for whom things were different—teenagers who started with alcohol and cigarettes, moved on to harder substances, and eventually were hooked.

In industrialized nations, teenage alcohol and drug use is pervasive. According to the most recent, nationally representative survey of U.S. high school students, by tenth grade, 40 percent of U.S. young people have tried cigarette smoking, 63 percent drinking, and 38 percent at least one illegal drug (usually marijuana). At the end of high school, 14 percent smoke cigarettes regularly, 28 percent have engaged in heavy drinking during the past two weeks, and over 50 percent have experimented with illegal drugs. About 27 percent have tried at least one highly addictive and toxic substance, such as amphetamines, cocaine, phencyclidine (PCP), Ecstasy (MDMA), inhalants, or heroin. Canadian rates of teenage alcohol and drug use are similar (Statistics Canada, 2003d; U.S. Department of Health and Human Services, 2005l).

These figures represent a substantial decline since the mid-1990s, probably resulting from greater parent, school, and media focus on the hazards of drug use. Still, drug use rises steadily over adolescence. Why do so many young people subject themselves to the health risks of these substances? In part, drug taking reflects the sensation seeking of these years. But teenagers also live in drug-dependent cultural contexts. They see adults using caffeine to wake up in the morning, cigarettes to cope with daily hassles, a drink to calm down in the evening, and other remedies to relieve stress, depression, and physical illness. And compared to a decade or two ago, today doctors more often prescribe, and parents frequently seek, medication

to treat children's problems (Brody, 2006). When these young people reach adolescence, they may readily "self-medicate" in the face of stress. Furthermore, an increasing number of cigarette and alcohol ads are designed to appeal to teenagers. Over 90 percent of teenagers are aware of such advertising, and most say the ads influence their behavior (Alcohol Concern, 2004).

The majority of teenagers who dabble in alcohol, tobacco, and marijuana are not headed for a life of decadence and addiction. Rather, these minimal *experimenters* are psychologically healthy, sociable, curious young people (Shedler & Block, 1990). As Figure 11.7 shows, tobacco and alcohol use is much greater among European than U.S. adolescents, perhaps because European adults more often smoke and drink. In contrast, illegal drug use is more prevalent among U.S. teenagers (Hibell, 2001). A greater percentage of American young people live in poverty, which is linked to family and peer contexts that promote illegal drug use. At the same time, use of diverse drugs is lower among African Americans than among Hispanics and Caucasian-Americans; Native American and Canadian-Aboriginal youths rank highest in drug taking (van der Woerd & Cox, 2001; Wallace et al., 2003). Researchers have yet to explain these variations.

Regardless of type of drug, adolescent experimentation should not be taken lightly. Because most drugs impair perception and thought processes, a single heavy dose can lead to permanent injury or death. And a worrisome minority of teenagers move from substance *use* to *abuse*—taking drugs regularly, requiring increasing amounts to achieve the same effect, moving on to harder substances, and using enough to impair their ability to meet school, work, or other responsibilities.

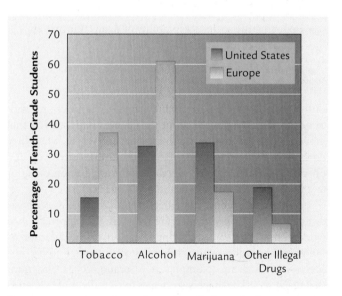

■ **FIGURE 11.7 Tenth-grade students in the United States and Europe who have used various substances.** Rates for tobacco and alcohol are based on any use in the past 30 days. Rates for marijuana and other illegal drugs are based on any lifetime use. Tobacco use and alcohol use are greater for European adolescents, whereas illegal drug use is greater for U.S. adolescents. (Adapted from Hibell, 2001; U.S. Department of Health and Human Services, 2005l.)

■ **Correlates and Consequences of Adolescent Substance Abuse.** In contrast to experimenters, drug abusers are seriously troubled young people who express their unhappiness through antisocial acts. Their impulsive, disruptive style is often evident in early childhood. And compared with other young people, their drug taking starts earlier and may have genetic roots (Chassin & Ritter, 2001; Silberg et al., 2003). But a wide range of environmental factors also promote it. These include low SES, family mental health problems, parental and older sibling drug abuse, lack of parental warmth and involvement, physical and sexual abuse, and poor school performance. Especially among teenagers with family problems, peer encouragement—friends who use and provide access to drugs—increases substance abuse (Prinstein, Boergers, & Spirito, 2001).

Adolescent substance abuse often has lifelong consequences. When teenagers depend on alcohol and hard drugs to deal with daily stresses, they fail to learn responsible decision-making skills and alternative coping techniques. These young people show serious adjustment problems, including chronic anxiety, depression, and antisocial behavior, that are both cause and consequence of heavy drug taking (Simons-Morton & Haynie, 2003). They often enter into marriage, childbearing, and the work world prematurely and fail at them—painful outcomes that encourage further addictive behavior.

■ **Prevention and Treatment.** School and community programs that reduce drug experimentation typically combine several features:

🍂 Promoting effective parenting, including monitoring of teenagers' activities

🍂 Teaching skills for resisting peer pressure

🍂 Reducing the social acceptability of drug taking by emphasizing health and safety risks

🍂 Getting adolescents to commit to not using drugs (Cuijpers, 2002)

But some drug taking seems inevitable. Therefore, interventions that teach teenagers about the dangers of drugs and that prevent them from harming themselves and others when they do experiment are essential. Many communities offer weekend on-call transportation services that any young person can contact for a safe ride home, with no questions asked.

Because drug abuse has different roots than occasional use, different prevention strategies are required. One approach is to work with parents early, reducing family adversity and improving parenting skills, before children are old enough to become involved with drugs (Kumpfer & Alvarado, 2003). Programs that teach at-risk teenagers strategies for handling life stressors and that build competence through community service reduce alcohol and drug use, just as they reduce teenage pregnancy.

When an adolescent becomes a drug abuser, family and individual therapy are generally needed to treat negative parent–child relationships, impulsivity, low self-esteem, anxiety, and depression. Academic and vocational training to improve life success makes a difference as well. But even comprehensive programs have high relapse rates (Cornelius et al., 2003). One

recommendation is to start treatment gradually, through support-group sessions that focus on reducing drug taking (Myers et al., 2001). Modest improvements may increase young people's motivation to make longer-lasting changes through intensive treatment.

Ask Yourself

Review

Compare risk factors for anorexia nervosa and bulimia nervosa. How do treatments and outcomes differ for the two disorders?

Apply

After 17-year-old Veronica gave birth to Ben, her parents told her they didn't have room for the baby. Veronica dropped out of school and moved in with her boyfriend. A few months later, he left. Why are Veronica and Ben likely to experience long-term hardships?

Connect

What unfavorable life experiences do teenagers who engage in early and frequent sexual activity and those who abuse drugs have in common?

Reflect

Describe your experiences with peer pressure to experiment with alcohol and drugs. What factors influenced your response?

www.ablongman.com/berk

🌰 Cognitive Development

One mid-December evening, a knock at the front door announced the arrival of Franca and Antonio's oldest son Jules, home for vacation after the fall semester of his sophomore year at college. The family gathered around the kitchen table. "How did it all go, Jules?" asked Antonio as he passed out slices of apple pie.

"Well, physics and philosophy were awesome," Jules responded with enthusiasm. "The last few weeks, our physics prof introduced us to Einstein's theory of relativity. Boggles my mind, it's so incredibly counterintuitive."

"Counter-what?" asked 11-year-old Sabrina.

"Counterintuitive. Unlike what you'd normally expect," explained Jules. "Imagine you're on a train, going unbelievably fast, like 160,000 miles a second. The faster you go, approaching the speed of light, the slower time passes and the denser and heavier things get relative to on the ground. The theory revolutionized the way we think about time, space, matter—the entire universe."

Sabrina wrinkled her forehead, unable to comprehend Jules's otherworldly reasoning. "Time slows down when I'm bored, like right now, not on a train when I'm going somewhere exciting. No speeding train ever made me heavier, but this apple pie will if I eat any more of it," Sabrina announced, leaving the table.

Sixteen-year-old Louis reacted differently. "Totally cool, Jules. So what'd you do in philosophy?"

"It was a course in philosophy of technology. We studied the ethics of futuristic methods in human reproduction. For example, we argued the pros and cons of a world in which all embryos develop in artificial wombs."

"What do you mean?" asked Louis. "You order your kid at the lab?"

"That's right. I wrote my term paper on it. I had to evaluate it in terms of principles of justice and freedom. I can see some advantages but also lots of dangers. . . ."

As this conversation illustrates, adolescence brings with it vastly expanded powers of reasoning. At age 11, Sabrina finds it difficult to move beyond her firsthand experiences to a world of possibilities. Over the next few years, her thinking will take on the complex qualities that characterize the cognition of her older brothers. Jules considers multiple variables simultaneously and thinks about situations that are not easily detected in the real world or that do not exist at all. As a result, he can grasp advanced scientific and mathematical principles and grapple with social and political issues. Compared with school-age children's thinking, adolescent thought is more enlightened, imaginative, and rational.

Systematic research on adolescent cognitive development began with testing of Piaget's ideas (Keating, 2004). Recently, information-processing research has greatly enhanced our understanding.

Piaget's Theory: The Formal Operational Stage

According to Piaget, around age 11 young people enter the **formal operational stage,** in which they develop the capacity for abstract, systematic, scientific thinking. Whereas concrete operational children can "operate on reality," formal operational adolescents can "operate on operations." In other words, they no longer require concrete things and events as objects of thought. Instead, they can come up with new, more general logical rules through internal reflection (Inhelder & Piaget, 1955/1958). Let's look at two major features of the formal operational stage.

Hypothetico-Deductive Reasoning

Piaget believed that at adolescence, young people first become capable of **hypothetico-deductive reasoning.** When faced with a problem, they start with a *hypothesis,* or prediction about variables that might affect an outcome. Then they *deduce* logical, testable inferences from that hypothesis, systematically isolating and combining variables to see which inferences are confirmed in the real world. Notice how this form of problem solving begins with possibility and proceeds to reality. In contrast, concrete operational children start with reality—with the most obvious predictions about a situation.

■ **FIGURE 11.8 Piaget's pendulum problem.** Adolescents who engage in hypothetico-deductive reasoning think of variables that might possibly affect the speed with which a pendulum swings through its arc. Then they isolate and test each variable, as well as testing the variables in combination. Eventually they deduce that the weight of the object, the height from which it is released, and how forcefully it is pushed have no effect on the speed with which the pendulum swings through its arc. Only string length makes a difference.

When these are not confirmed, they usually cannot think of alternatives and fail to solve the problem.

Adolescents' performance on Piaget's famous *pendulum problem* illustrates this approach. Suppose we present several school-age children and adolescents with strings of different lengths, objects of different weights to attach to the strings, and a bar from which to hang the strings (see Figure 11.8). Then we ask each of them to figure out what influences the speed with which a pendulum swings through its arc.

Formal operational adolescents hypothesize that four variables might be influential: (1) the length of the string, (2) the weight of the object hung on it, (3) how high the object is raised before it is released, and (4) how forcefully the object is pushed. Then, they isolate and test each and, if necessary, test them in combination, eventually discovering that only string length makes a difference.

In contrast, concrete operational children cannot separate the effects of each variable. They may test for the effect of string length without holding weight constant, comparing, for example, a short, light pendulum with a long, heavy one. Also, they typically fail to notice variables that are not immediately suggested by the concrete materials of the task—the height at which and forcefulness with which the pendulum is released.

Propositional Thought

A second important characteristic of Piaget's formal operational stage is **propositional thought**—adolescents' ability to evaluate the logic of propositions (verbal statements) without referring to real-world circumstances. In contrast, children can evaluate the logic of statements only by considering them against concrete evidence in the real world.

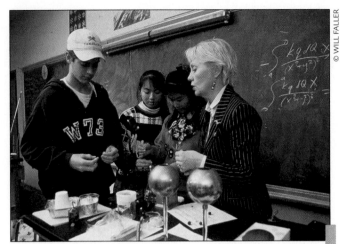

© WILL FALLER

In Piaget's formal operational stage, adolescents engage in hypothetico-deductive reasoning. These high school students solve a complex scientific problem by deducing testable inferences from a hypothesis and then systematically isolating and combining variables to see which inferences are confirmed.

In a study of propositional reasoning, a researcher showed children and adolescents a pile of poker chips and asked whether statements about the chips were true, false, or uncertain (Osherson & Markman, 1975). In one condition, the researcher hid a chip in her hand and presented the following propositions:

"*Either* the chip in my hand is green *or* it is not green."

"The chip in my hand is green *and* it is not green."

In another condition, the experimenter held either a red or a green chip in full view and made the same statements.

School-age children focused on the concrete properties of the poker chips. When the chip was hidden from view, they replied that they were uncertain about both statements. When it was visible, they judged both statements to be true if the chip was green and false if it was red. In contrast, adolescents analyzed the logic of the statements. They understood that the "either-or" statement is always true and the "and" statement is always false, regardless of the poker chip's color.

Although Piaget did not view language as playing a central role in children's cognitive development (see Chapter 7), he acknowledged its importance in adolescence. Formal operations require language-based and other symbolic systems that do not stand for real things, such as those in higher mathematics. Secondary school students use such systems in algebra and geometry. Formal operational thought also involves verbal reasoning about abstract concepts. Jules showed that he could think in this way when he pondered relationships among time, space, and matter in physics and wondered about justice and freedom in philosophy.

Follow-Up Research on Formal Operational Thought

Research on formal operational thought poses questions similar to those we discussed with respect to Piaget's earlier stages:

Does formal operational thinking appear earlier than Piaget expected? Do all individuals reach formal operations during their teenage years?

■ **Are Children Capable of Hypothetico-Deductive and Propositional Thinking?** School-age children show the glimmerings of hypothetico-deductive reasoning, although they are not as competent at it as adolescents. For example, in simplified situations—ones involving no more than two possible causal variables—6-year-olds understand that hypotheses must be confirmed by appropriate evidence (Ruffman et al., 1993). But school-age children cannot sort out evidence that bears on three or more variables at once. And as we will see when we take up information-processing research, children have difficulty explaining why a pattern of observations supports a hypothesis, even when they recognize the connection between the two.

With respect to propositional thought, when a simple set of premises defies real-world knowledge ("All cats bark. Rex is a cat. Does Rex bark?"), 4- to 6-year-olds can reason logically in make-believe play. In justifying their answer, they are likely to say, "We can pretend cats bark!" (Dias & Harris, 1988, 1990). But in an entirely verbal mode, children have great difficulty reasoning from premises that contradict reality or their own beliefs.

Consider the following set of statements: "If dogs are bigger than elephants and elephants are bigger than mice, then dogs are bigger than mice." Children younger than 10 judge such reasoning to be false because not all relations specified occur in real life (Moshman & Franks, 1986; Pillow, 2002). They automatically bring to mind well-learned knowledge ("Elephants are larger than dogs") that casts doubt on the truthfulness of the premises. Children find it more difficult than adolescents to inhibit such knowledge (Klaczynski, Schuneman, & Daniel, 2004; Simoneau & Markovits, 2003). Partly for this reason, they fail to grasp the *logical necessity* of propositional reasoning—that the accuracy of conclusions drawn from premises rests on the rules of logic, not on real-world confirmation.

As with hypothetico-deductive reasoning, in early adolescence, young people become better at analyzing the logic of propositions irrespective of their content. And as they get older, they handle problems with more complex sets of mental operations. Further, in justifying their reasoning, they more often explain the logical rules on which they are based (Müller, Overton, & Reese, 2001; Venet & Markovits, 2001). But these capacities do not appear suddenly, around the time of puberty. Rather, gains occur gradually from childhood on—findings that call into question the emergence of a discrete new stage of cognitive development at adolescence (Keating, 2004; Kuhn & Franklin, 2006; Moshman, 2005).

■ **Do All Individuals Reach the Formal Operational Stage?** Try giving one or two of the formal operational tasks just described to your friends. How well do they do? Even well-educated adults have difficulty with such reasoning! Many fail hypothetico-deductive tasks and have difficulty reasoning with sets of propositions that contradict real-world facts (Keating, 1979; Markovits & Vachon, 1990).

Why are so many adults not fully formal operational? One reason is that people are most likely to think abstractly and systematically in situations in which they have had extensive experience. This conclusion is supported by evidence that taking college courses leads to improvements in formal reasoning related to course content. For example, math and science courses prompt gains in propositional thought, while social science courses foster gains in statistical reasoning (Lehman & Nisbett, 1990). As these findings illustrate, formal operations, like concrete reasoning, are often specific to situation and task (Keating, 1990, 2004).

In many village and tribal societies, formal operational tasks are not mastered at all (Cole, 1990). Piaget acknowledged that without the opportunity to solve hypothetical problems, people in some societies might not display formal operations. Still, these findings raise further questions about Piaget's stage sequence. Does formal operational thought largely result from children's and adolescents' independent efforts to make sense of their world, as Piaget claimed? Or is it a culturally transmitted way of thinking that is specific to literate societies and taught in school? Just how do young people make the transition to formal operational thought? These issues have prompted many investigators to adopt an information-processing view.

An Information-Processing View of Adolescent Cognitive Development

Information-processing theorists refer to a variety of specific mechanisms, supported by brain development and experience, that underlie cognitive change in adolescence. Each was discussed in previous chapters (Case, 1998; Kuhn & Franklin, 2006; Luna et al., 2004). Now let's draw them together:

- *Attention* becomes more selective (focused on relevant information) and better-adapted to the changing demands of tasks.

- *Inhibition*—both of irrelevant stimuli and of well-learned responses in situations where they are inappropriate—improves, supporting gains in attention and reasoning.

- *Strategies* become more effective, improving storage, representation, and retrieval of information.

- *Knowledge* increases, easing strategy use.

- *Metacognition* (awareness of thought) expands, leading to new insights into effective strategies for acquiring information and solving problems.

- *Cognitive self-regulation* improves, yielding better moment-by-moment monitoring, evaluation, and redirection of thinking.

- *Speed of thinking* and *processing capacity* increase. As a result, more information can be held at once in working

memory and combined into increasingly complex, efficient representations, "opening possibilities for growth" in the capacities just listed and also improving as a result of gains in those capacities (Demetriou et al., 2002, p. 97).

As we look at influential findings from an information-processing perspective, we will see some of these mechanisms of change in action. And we will discover that researchers regard one of them—*metacognition*—as central to adolescent cognitive development.

Scientific Reasoning: Coordinating Theory with Evidence

During a free moment in physical education class, Sabrina wondered why more of her tennis serves and returns seemed to pass the net and drop into her opponent's court when she used a particular brand of balls. "Is it something about their color or size?" she asked herself. "Hmm . . . or could it be their surface texture? That might affect their bounce."

The heart of scientific reasoning is coordinating theories with evidence. Deanna Kuhn (2002) has conducted extensive research into the development of scientific reasoning, using problems that resemble Piaget's tasks, in that several variables might affect an outcome. In one series of studies, third, sixth, and ninth graders and adults were provided evidence, sometimes consistent with and sometimes conflicting with theories. Then they were questioned about the accuracy of each theory.

For example, participants were given a problem much like the one Sabrina posed. They were asked to theorize about which of several features of sports balls—size (large or small), color (light or dark), texture (rough or smooth), or presence or absence of ridges on the surface—influences the quality of a player's serve. Next, they were told about the theory of Mr. (or Ms.) S, who believes that the ball's size is important, and the theory of Mr. (or Ms.) C, who thinks color makes a difference. Finally, the interviewer presented evidence by placing balls with certain characteristics in two baskets labeled "good serve" and "bad serve" (see Figure 11.9 on page 384).

The youngest participants often ignored conflicting evidence or distorted it in ways consistent with their preferred theory. Instead of viewing evidence as separate from and bearing on a theory, children might blend the two into a single representation of "the way things are." The ability to distinguish theory from evidence and to use logical rules to examine their relationship in complex, multivariable situations improves steadily from childhood into adolescence and adulthood (Kuhn & Dean, 2004; Kuhn & Pearsall, 2000).

How Scientific Reasoning Develops

What factors support adolescents' skill at coordinating theory with evidence? Greater working-memory capacity, permitting a theory and the effects of several variables to be compared at once, is vital. In addition, adolescents benefit from exposure to increasingly complex problems and instruction that highlights

FIGURE 11.9 **Which features of these sports balls—size, color, surface texture, or presence or absence of ridges—influence the quality of a player's serve?** This set of evidence suggests that color might be important, since light-colored balls are largely in the good-serve basket and dark-colored balls in the bad-serve basket. But the same is true for texture! The good-serve basket has mostly smooth balls; the bad-serve basket, rough balls. Since all light-colored balls are smooth and all dark-colored balls are rough, we cannot tell whether color or texture makes a difference. But we can conclude that size and presence or absence of ridges are not important, since these features are equally represented in the good-serve and bad-serve baskets. (Adapted from Kuhn, Amsel, & O'Loughlin, 1988.)

critical features of tasks and effective strategies. Consequently, scientific reasoning is strongly influenced by years of schooling, whether individuals grapple with traditional scientific tasks (as in the sports-ball problem) or engage in informal reasoning—for example, justifying a theory about what causes children to fail in school (Kuhn, 1993).

Researchers believe that sophisticated *metacognitive understanding* is at the heart of scientific reasoning (Kuhn, 1999; Moshman, 1999). When adolescents regularly pit theory against evidence over many weeks, they experiment with various strategies, reflect on and revise them, and become aware of the nature of logic. Over time, they apply their appreciation of logic to an increasingly wide variety of situations. The ability to *think about* theories, *deliberately isolate* variables, and *actively seek* disconfirming evidence is rarely present before adolescence (Kuhn, 2000; Moshman, 1998).

But adolescents and adults vary widely in scientific reasoning skills. Many show a self-serving bias, in that they apply logic more effectively to ideas they doubt than to ideas they favor (Klaczynski, 1997; Klaczynski & Narasimham, 1998). Reasoning scientifically requires the metacognitive capacity to evaluate one's objectivity—to be fair-minded rather than self-serving (Moshman, 1999). As we will see in Chapter 12, this flexible, open-minded approach is both a cognitive attainment and a personality disposition—one that assists teenagers greatly in forming an identity and developing morally.

Adolescents develop scientific reasoning skills in a similar step-by-step fashion on different types of tasks. In a series of studies, 10- to 20-year-olds were given sets of problems graded in difficulty. For example, one set consisted of quantitative-relational tasks like the pendulum problem in Figure 11.8. Another set contained propositional tasks like the poker chip problem on page 382. And still another set were causal-experimental tasks like the sports-ball problem in Figure 11.9 (Demetriou et al., 1993, 1996, 2002).

In each type of task, adolescents mastered component skills in sequential order by expanding their metacognitive awareness. For example, on causal-experimental tasks, they first became aware of the many variables that could influence an outcome. This enabled them to formulate and test hypotheses. Over time, adolescents combined separate skills into a smoothly functioning system, constructing a general model that they could apply to many instances of a given type of problem. In the researcher's words, young people seem to form a "hypercognitive system," or supersystem, that understands, organizes, and influences other aspects of cognition (Demetriou & Kazi, 2001).

Piaget also underscored the role of metacognition in formal operational thought when he spoke of "operating on operations" (see page 381). However, information-processing findings confirm that scientific reasoning is not the result of an abrupt, stagewise change. Instead, it develops out of many specific experiences that require children and adolescents to match theories against evidence and reflect on and evaluate their thinking.

Consequences of Adolescent Cognitive Changes

The development of increasingly complex, effective thinking leads to dramatic revisions in the way adolescents see themselves, others, and the world in general. But just as adolescents are occasionally awkward in the use of their transformed bodies, they are initially faltering in their abstract thinking. Although teenagers' self-concern, idealism, criticism, and indecisiveness often perplex and worry adults, they are usually beneficial in the long run. Applying What We Know on the following page suggests ways to handle the everyday consequences of teenagers' newfound cognitive capacities.

Self-Consciousness and Self-Focusing

Adolescents' improved ability to reflect on their own thoughts, combined with the physical and psychological changes they are undergoing, means that they start to think more about themselves. Piaget believed that a new form of egocentrism arises, in which adolescents again have difficulty distinguishing their own and others' perspectives (Inhelder & Piaget, 1955/1958). Followers of Piaget suggested that two distorted images of the relation between self and other appear.

The first is called the **imaginary audience,** adolescents' belief that they are the focus of everyone else's attention and concern (Elkind & Bowen, 1979). As a result, they become extremely self-conscious, often going to great lengths to avoid embarrassment. Sabrina, for example, woke up one Sunday morning with a large pimple on her chin. "I can't possibly go to church!" she cried. "Everyone will notice how ugly I look." The imaginary audience helps us understand the hours adolescents spend inspecting every detail of their appearance. It also accounts for their sensitivity to public criticism. To teenagers, who believe that everyone is monitoring their performance, a critical remark from a parent or teacher can be mortifying.

A second cognitive distortion is the **personal fable.** Because teenagers are so sure that others are observing and thinking about them, they develop an inflated opinion of their own importance. They start to feel that they are special and unique. Many adolescents view themselves as reaching great heights of glory as well as sinking to unusual depths of despair—experiences that others could not possibly understand (Elkind, 1994). As one teenager wrote in her diary, "My parents' lives are so ordinary, so stuck in a rut. Mine will be different. I'll realize my hopes and ambitions." When combined with a sensation-seeking personality, the personal fable seems to contribute to adolescent risk taking by convincing teenagers of their invulnerability. In one study, young people with both high personal-fable and high sensation-seeking scores took more sexual risks, more often used drugs, and committed more delinquent acts than their agemates (Greene et al., 2000).

The imaginary audience and personal fable are strongest during early adolescence, after which they gradually decline (Lapsley et al., 1988). Yet these distorted visions of the self do not result from egocentrism, as Piaget suggested. Rather, they are an outgrowth of gains in perspective taking, which cause young teenagers to be more concerned with what others think (Vartanian & Powlishta, 1996). When asked why they worry about the opinions of others, adolescents responded that they do so because others' evaluations have important *real* consequences—for self-esteem, peer acceptance, and social support (Bell & Bromnick, 2003). Adolescents also have emotional reasons for

These adolescents are acting for the camera, but the imaginary audience leads them to think that everyone is monitoring their performance at other times as well. Consequently, young teens are extremely self-conscious and go to great lengths to avoid embarrassment.

clinging to the idea that others are concerned with their appearance and behavior. Doing so helps them maintain a hold on important relationships as they struggle to separate from parents and establish an independent sense of self (Vartanian, 1997).

Idealism and Criticism

Adolescents' capacity to think about possibilities opens up the world of the ideal and of perfection. Teenagers can imagine alternative family, religious, political, and moral systems, and they want to explore them. As a result, they often construct grand visions of a perfect world with no injustice, discrimination, or tasteless behavior. The disparity between adults' and teenagers' worldviews, often called the "generation gap," creates tension between parent and child. Aware of the perfect family

Handling Everyday Consequences of Teenagers' New Cognitive Capacities

Applying What We Know

Thought expressed as . . .	Suggestion
Sensitivity to public criticism	Refrain from finding fault with the adolescent in front of others. If the matter is important, wait until you can speak to the teenager alone.
Exaggerated sense of personal uniqueness	Acknowledge the adolescent's unique characteristics. At opportune times, point out how you felt similarly as a young teenager, encouraging a more balanced perspective.
Idealism and criticism	Respond patiently to the adolescent's grand expectations and critical remarks. Point out positive features of targets, helping the teenager see that all worlds and people are blends of virtues and imperfections.
Difficulty making everyday decisions	Refrain from deciding for the adolescent. Model effective decision making and offer diplomatic suggestions about the pros and cons of alternatives, the likelihood of various outcomes, and learning from poor choices.

against which their real parents and siblings do not measure up, adolescents become fault-finding critics.

Overall, however, teenage idealism and criticism are advantageous. Once adolescents come to see other people as having both strengths and weaknesses, they have a much greater capacity to work constructively for social change and to form positive and lasting relationships (Elkind, 1994).

Decision Making

Although adolescents handle many cognitive tasks more effectively than they did when younger, when they make decisions, they often do not think rationally: (1) identifying the pros and cons of each alternative, (2) assessing the likelihood of various outcomes, (3) evaluating their choice in terms of whether their goals were met and, if not, (4) learning from the mistake and making a better future decision. In one study of decision making, researchers gave adolescents and adults hypothetical dilemmas, such as whether to have cosmetic surgery or which parent to live with after divorce, and asked them to explain how they would decide. Adults outperformed adolescents, more often considering alternatives, weighing the benefits and risks of each, and suggesting advice-seeking (Halpern-Felsher & Cauffman, 2001).

Furthermore, in making decisions, adolescents, more often than adults (who also have difficulty), fall back on well-learned intuitive judgments (Jacobs & Klaczynski, 2002). Consider a hypothetical problem in which you have to choose, on the basis of two arguments, between taking a traditional lecture class and taking a computer-based class. One argument contains large-sample information: course evaluations from 150 students, 85 percent of whom liked the computer class. The other argument contains small-sample personal reports: complaints of two honor-roll students who both hated the computer class and enjoyed the traditional class. Many adolescents knew that selecting the large-sample argument was "more intelligent." Even so, most based their choice on the

small-sample argument, which resembled the informal opinions they depend on in everyday life (Klaczynski, 2001).

Why is decision making so challenging for adolescents? As "first-timers" at many experiences, they do not have sufficient knowledge to predict potential outcomes. They are also confronted with many complex situations involving competing goals, such as how to maintain social status while avoiding getting drunk at a party. Furthermore, teenagers often feel overwhelmed by their expanding range of options—abundant choices of school courses, extracurricular activities, social events, and material goods. As a result, their efforts to choose frequently break down, and they resort to habit, act on impulse, or postpone decisions.

Prompting teenagers to think logically enhances their ability to make rational decisions (Klaczynski, 2001). And over time, as they learn from their successes and failures and reflect on the decision-making process, decision-making confidence and performance improve (Byrnes, 2003; Jacobs & Klaczynski, 2002). Still, errors in decision making remain common in adulthood.

Ask Yourself

Review

Describe research findings that challenge Piaget's notion of a new, discrete stage of cognitive development at adolescence.

Apply

Thirteen-year-old Rosie had a crush on a boy who failed to return her affections. After her mother assured her that there would be other boys, Rosie snapped, "Mom! You don't know what it's like to be in love!" Which cognitive distortion of adolescence does Rosie's thinking illustrate? Explain.

Connect

How does evidence on adolescent decision making help us understand teenagers' risk taking in sexual activity and drug use?

Reflect

Do you recall engaging in idealistic thinking or poor decision making as a teenager? Describe examples.

www.ablongman.com/berk

Sex Differences in Mental Abilities

Sex differences in mental abilities have sparked almost as much controversy as the ethnic and SES differences in IQ considered in Chapter 9. Although boys and girls do not differ in general intelligence, they do vary in specific mental abilities.

Verbal Abilities

Throughout the school years, girls attain higher scores on reading and writing achievement tests and account for a lower

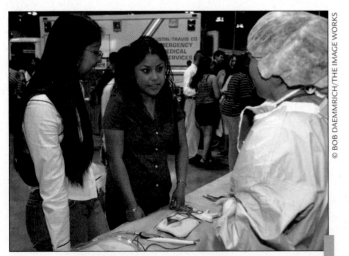

These high school students talk with future employers at a spring job fair. Decision making is challenging for adolescents, as they often feel overwhelmed by their expanding range of options.

© BOB DAEMMRICH/THE IMAGE WORKS

percentage of children referred for remedial reading instruction. Girls continue to score slightly higher on tests of general verbal ability in adolescence (Halpern, 2000, 2004).

But a special concern is that girls' advantage in reading and writing achievement increases over adolescence, with boys doing especially poorly in writing—trends evident in the United States, Canada, and other industrialized nations (see Figure 11.10) (OECD, 2004; Statistics Canada, 2003c; U.S. Department of Education, 2005e, 2005g). These differences in literacy skills are believed to be major contributors to a widening gender gap in college enrollments. Thirty years ago, males accounted for 60 percent of North American undergraduates; today, they are in the minority, at 42 percent (Statistics Canada, 2005g; U.S. Department of Education, 2005b).

Recall from Chapter 5 that girls show a biological advantage in earlier development of the left hemisphere of the cerebral cortex, where language is usually localized. Girls also receive more verbal stimulation from mothers from the preschool years through adolescence (Peterson & Roberts, 2003). Furthermore, children view language arts as a "feminine" subject. And as a result of the high-stakes testing movement, students spend more time at their desks being taught in a regimented, uniform way—an approach particularly at odds with boys' higher activity level, assertiveness, and incidence of learning problems.

Finally, high divorce and out-of-wedlock birth rates mean that more children today grow up without a father who models and encourages good work habits and skill at reading and writing. Both maternal and paternal involvement contributes to the achievement and educational attainment of adolescents of both genders (Flouri & Buchanan, 2004). But some research suggests that high-achieving African-American boys are particularly likely to come from homes in which fathers are warm, verbally communicative, and demanding of achievement

(Grief, Hrabowski, & Maton, 1998). Clearly, reversing boys' weakening literacy skills is a high priority—one that requires a concerted effort on the part of families, schools, and supportive communities.

Mathematics

Sex differences in mathematical skills are apparent by first grade. Girls more often depend on concrete manipulatives to solve basic math problems, whereas boys more often mentally represent numbers and rapidly retrieve answers from memory (Fennema et al., 1998). Girls' better verbal skills and careful approach to problem solving contribute to an advantage in arithmetic computation in the early grades. But boys start to outperform girls around early adolescence, when math concepts become more abstract and spatial, with the difference especially evident on tests of complex reasoning and geometry (Bielinski & Davison, 1998).

When all adolescents are considered, this male advantage is evident in virtually every country where males and females have equal access to secondary education. At the same time, it is small, and it has diminished over the past 30 years (Halpern, Wai, & Saw, 2005; U.S. Department of Education, 2005c). Among the most capable students, however, the gender gap is greater. In widely publicized research on more than 100,000 bright seventh and eighth graders invited to take the Scholastic Assessment Test (SAT), boys outscored girls on the mathematics subtest year after year. Yet even this disparity has been shrinking. A quarter-century ago, 13 times as many boys as girls scored over 700 (out of a possible 800) on the math portion of the SAT; today, the ratio is 2.8 to 1 (Benbow & Stanley, 1983; Monastersky, 2005).

Some researchers believe that heredity contributes substantially to the gender gap in math, especially to the tendency for more boys to be extremely talented. Accumulating evidence suggests that boys' superior spatial reasoning enhances their mathematical problem solving. See the Biology and Environment box on page 388 for discussion of this issue.

Social pressures are also highly influential. Long before sex differences in math achievement appear, both boys and girls view math as a "masculine" subject. In addition, girls regard math as less useful for their future lives and more often blame their errors on lack of ability. These beliefs, in turn, reduce girls' confidence and interest in math and their willingness to consider math- or science-related careers (Bleeker & Jacobs, 2004; Catsambis, 1994). Furthermore, *stereotype threat*—the fear of being judged on the basis of a negative stereotype (see page 314 in Chapter 9)—causes females to do worse than their abilities allow on difficult math problems (Ben-Zeev et al., 2005; Steele, 1997). As a result of all of these influences, girls—even those who are highly talented—are less likely to develop effective math reasoning skills.

A positive sign is that today, boys and girls reach advanced levels of high school math and science study in equal proportions—a crucial factor in reducing sex differences in knowledge and skill (Gallagher & Kaufman, 2005). High school boys and girls also spend about the same amount of

■ **FIGURE 11.10 Reading and writing achievement score gaps favoring girls at grades 4, 8, and 12.** Findings are based on the U.S. National Assessment of Educational Progress. The bars represent the average girls' score minus the average boys' score. The height of the bar thus indicates the extent to which girls outperform boys, a difference that increases over adolescence. By grade 12, girls have an especially large advantage in writing skill. Similar trends are evident in other industrialized nations. (Adapted from U.S. Department of Education, 2005c, 2005e.)

Biology and Environment

Sex Differences in Spatial Abilities

Spatial abilities are a key focus of researchers' efforts to explain sex differences in mathematical reasoning. The gender gap favoring males is large for *mental rotation tasks,* in which individuals must rotate a three-dimensional figure rapidly and accurately inside their heads (see Figure 11.11). Males also do considerably better on *spatial perception tasks,* in which people must determine spatial relationships by considering the orientation of the surrounding environment. Sex differences on *spatial visualization tasks,* involving analysis of complex visual forms, are weak or nonexistent. Because many strategies can be used to solve these tasks, both sexes may come up with effective procedures (Voyer, Voyer, & Bryden, 1995).

Sex differences in spatial abilities emerge in early childhood and persist throughout the lifespan (Levine et al., 1999). The pattern is consistent enough to suggest a biological explanation. One hypothesis is that heredity, perhaps through prenatal exposure to androgen hormones, enhances right hemispheric functioning, giving males a spatial advantage. (Recall that for most people, spatial skills are housed in the right hemisphere of the cerebral cortex.) In support of this idea, girls and women whose prenatal androgen levels were abnormally high show superior performance on spatial rotation tasks (Berenbaum, 2001). And in some studies, spatial performance varies with daily and annual androgen levels in men and women (Temple & Carney, 1995; Van Goozen et al., 1995).

Why might a biologically based sex difference in spatial abilities exist? Evolutionary theorists point out that mental rotation skill predicts rapid, accurate map drawing and interpretation, areas in which boys and men do better than girls and women. During human evolution, the cognitive abilities of males became adapted for hunting, which required generating mental representations of large-

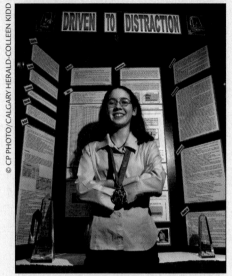

This seventh-grade girl is the gold medal winner in her age category in the Canada-Wide Science Fair. In her project, which examines the hazards of cell phone use while driving, she used advanced mathematical skills, data analysis, and graphing.

scale spaces to find one's way (Choi & Silverman, 2003; Jones, Braithwaite, & Healy, 2003).

Experience also contributes to males' superior spatial performance. Children who engage in manipulative activities, such as block play, model building, and carpentry, do better on spatial tasks (Baenninger & Newcombe, 1995). Furthermore, playing video games that require rapid mental rotation of visual images enhances spatial scores (Okagaki & Frensch, 1996; Subrahmanyam & Greenfield, 1996). Boys spend far more time than girls at these pursuits.

Research confirms that superior spatial skills contribute to the greater ease with which males solve complex math problems. In studies of middle and high school students, both spatial ability and self-confidence at doing math were related to performance on complex math problems, with spatial skills being the stronger predictor (Casey, Nuttall, & Pezaris, 1997, 2001). Boys are advantaged not only in mental rotation but also in math self-confidence, despite the fact that their grades are poorer than those of girls. In sum, biology and environment *jointly* explain variations in spatial and math performance—both within and between the sexes.

■ FIGURE 11.11 **Types of spatial tasks.** Large sex differences favoring males appear on mental rotation, and males do considerably better than females on spatial perception. In contrast, sex differences on spatial visualization are weak or nonexistent. (From M. C. Linn & A. C. Petersen, 1985, "Emergence and Characterization of Sex Differences in Spatial Ability: A Meta-Analysis," *Child Development, 56,* pp. 1482, 1483, 1485. © The Society for Research in Child Development, Inc. Reprinted by permission.)

time with computers. But they tend to use computers differently: Girls focus on e-mail, word processing, and completing homework assignments, whereas boys more often write computer programs, analyze data, and use graphics software. As a result, boys acquire more specialized computer knowledge (Freeman, 2004; Looker & Thiessen, 2003).

Clearly, extra steps must be taken to promote girls' interest in and confidence at math and science. When parents hold nonstereotyped beliefs, daughters are less likely to avoid math and science and more likely to achieve well (Updegraff, McHale, & Crouter, 1996). And a math curriculum beginning in kindergarten that teaches children how to apply effective spatial strategies—drawing diagrams, mentally manipulating visual images, searching for numerical patterns, and graphing—is vital (Nuttal, Casey, & Pezaris, 2005). Because girls are biased toward verbal processing, they may not realize their math and science potential unless they are taught how to think spatially. Exposure to successful women scientists is also likely to improve girls' belief in their own capacity to succeed.

Learning in School

In complex societies, adolescence coincides with entry into secondary school. Most young people move into either a middle or a junior high school and then into a high school. With each change, academic achievement becomes more serious, affecting college choices and job opportunities. In the following sections, we take up a variety of aspects of secondary school life.

School Transitions

When Sabrina started junior high, she left a small, intimate, self-contained sixth-grade classroom for a much larger school. "I don't know most of the kids in my classes, and my teachers don't know me," Sabrina complained to her mother at the end of the first week. "Besides, there's too much homework. I get assignments in all my classes at once. I can't do all this!" she shouted, bursting into tears.

◼ **Impact of School Transitions.** As Sabrina's reactions suggest, school transitions can create adjustment problems. With each school change—from elementary to middle school or junior high and then to high school—adolescents' grades decline. The drop is partly due to tighter academic standards. At the same time, the transition to secondary school often brings with it less personal attention, more whole-class instruction, and less chance to participate in classroom decision making (Seidman, Aber, & French, 2004). In view of these changes, it is not surprising that students rate their middle or junior high school learning experiences less favorably than their elementary school experiences (Wigfield & Eccles, 1994). They also report that their middle school teachers care less about them, are less friendly, grade less fairly, and stress competition more. Consequently, many young people feel less academically competent and decline in motivation (Anderman & Midgley, 1997).

Inevitably, students must readjust their feelings of self-confidence and self-worth as school becomes more impersonal and academic expectations are revised. A study following more than 300 students from sixth to tenth grade revealed that grade point average declined and feelings of anonymity increased after each school change—to junior high and then to high school. But the earlier school transition had a more negative impact, especially on girls' self-esteem, which dropped sharply after transition to junior high school and only gradually rebounded. Girls fared poorest, the researchers argued, because movement to junior high tended to coincide with other life changes—namely, the onset of puberty and dating. Adolescents who face added strains, such as family disruption, poverty, low parental involvement, or learned helplessness on academic tasks, are at greatest risk for self-esteem and academic difficulties (Rudolph et al., 2001; Seidman et al., 2003).

Distressed young people whose school performance drops sharply often show a persisting pattern of poor self-esteem, motivation, and achievement. In another study, researchers compared "multiple-problem" youths (those having both academic and mental health problems), youths having difficulties in just one area (either academic or mental health), and well-adjusted youths (those doing well in both areas) across the transition to high school. Although all groups declined in grade point average, well-adjusted students continued to get high marks and multiple-problem youths low marks, with the others falling in between. And as Figure 11.12 shows, the multiple-problem youths showed a far greater rise in truancy and out-of-school problem behaviors (Roeser, Eccles, & Freedman-Doan, 1999). For some, school transition initiates

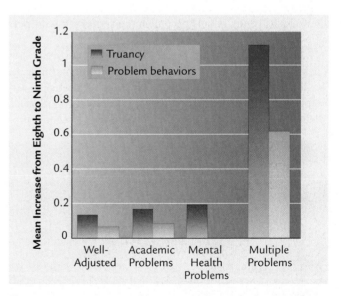

◼ **FIGURE 11.12 Increase in truancy and out-of-school problem behaviors across the transition to high school in four groups of students.** Well-adjusted students, students with only academic problems, and students with only mental health problems showed little change. (Good students with mental health problems actually declined in problem behaviors, so no blue bar is shown for them.) In contrast, multiple-problem students—with both academic and mental health difficulties—increased sharply in truancy and problem behaviors after changing schools from eighth to ninth grade. (Adapted from Roeser, Eccles, & Freedman-Doan, 1999.)

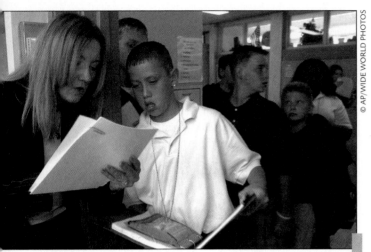

Arriving at their new middle school on the first day of classes, this boy, and the line of students behind him, try to figure out their schedules and the location of their classrooms. Moving from a small, self-contained elementary school classroom to a large, impersonal secondary school is stressful for adolescents.

motes closer relationships with teachers and peers and greater extracurricular involvement (Seidman, Aber, & French, 2004).

Other, less extensive changes are also effective. In the first year after a school transition, homerooms can be provided in which teachers offer academic and personal counseling. Students can also be assigned to classes with several familiar peers or a constant group of new peers—arrangements that promote emotional security and social support. In schools that intervened in these ways, students were less likely to decline in academic performance and to display other adjustment problems, including low self-esteem, substance abuse, delinquency, and dropping out (Felner et al., 2002).

Finally, teenagers' perceptions of the sensitivity and flexibility of their school learning environments contribute substantially to successful school transitions. When schools minimize competition and differential treatment based on ability, students in middle and junior high school are less likely to feel angry and depressed, to be truant, or to show declines in academic values, self-esteem, and achievement (Roeser, Eccles, & Sameroff, 2000).

a downward spiral in academic performance and school involvement that leads to dropping out.

■ **Helping Adolescents Adjust to School Transitions.** As these findings reveal, school transitions often lead to environmental changes that fit poorly with adolescents' developmental needs (Eccles, 2004). They disrupt close relationships with teachers at a time when adolescents need adult support. They emphasize competition during a period of heightened self-focusing. They reduce decision making and choice as the desire for autonomy is increasing. And they interfere with peer networks as young people become more concerned with peer acceptance.

Enhanced support from parents, teachers, and peers eases the strain of school transition. Parent involvement, monitoring, and gradual autonomy granting are associated with better adjustment after entering middle or junior high school (Grolnick et al., 2000). Also, forming smaller units within larger schools pro-

Academic Achievement

Adolescent achievement is the result of a long history of cumulative effects. Early on, positive educational environments, both family and school, lead to personal traits that support achievement—intelligence, confidence in one's own abilities, the desire to succeed, and high educational aspirations. Nevertheless, improving an unfavorable environment can foster resilience among poorly performing young people. See Applying What We Know below for a summary of environmental factors that enhance achievement during the teenage years.

■ **Child-Rearing Practices.** Authoritative parenting is linked to achievement in adolescence, just as it predicts mastery-oriented behavior during the childhood years. Research reveals that the authoritative style is linked to higher grades for young people varying widely in SES. In contrast, authoritarian and permissive styles are associated with lower grades (Steinberg,

Factors That Support High Achievement During Adolescence

Factor	Description
Child-rearing practices	Authoritative parenting
	Joint parent–adolescent decision making
	Parent involvement in the adolescent's education
Peer influences	Peer valuing of and support for high achievement
School characteristics	Teachers who are warm and supportive, develop personal relationships with parents, and show them how to support their teenager's learning
	Learning activities that encourage high-level thinking
	Active student participation in learning activities and classroom decision making
Employment schedule	Job commitment limited to less than 15 hours per week
	High-quality vocational education for non-college-bound adolescents

Applying What We Know

Darling, & Fletcher, 1995; Vazsonyi, Hibbert, & Snider, 2003). Of all parenting approaches, an uninvolved style (low in both warmth and maturity demands) predicts the poorest grades and worsening school performance over time (Glasgow et al., 1997; Kaisa, Stattin, & Nurmi, 2000).

The link between authoritative parenting and adolescents' academic competence has been confirmed in countries with diverse value systems, including Argentina, Australia, China, Hong Kong, Pakistan, and Scotland (Steinberg, 2001). In Chapter 8, we noted that authoritative parents adjust their expectations to children's capacity to take responsibility for their own behavior. Adolescents whose parents engage in joint decision making, gradually permitting more autonomy with age, achieve especially well (Dornbusch et al., 1990; Spera, 2005). Warmth, open discussion, firmness, and monitoring of the adolescents' whereabouts and activities make young people feel cared about and valued, encourage reflective thinking and self-regulation, and increase awareness of the importance of doing well in school. These factors, in turn, are related to mastery-oriented attributions, effort, achievement, and high educational aspirations (Aunola, Stattin, & Nurmi, 2000; Trusty, 1999).

■ **Parent–School Partnerships.** High-achieving students typically have parents who keep tabs on their child's progress, communicate with teachers, and make sure that their child is enrolled in challenging, well-taught classes. These efforts are just as important during middle and high school as they were earlier (Hill & Taylor, 2004). In a longitudinal study of a nationally representative sample of more than 15,000 American adolescents, parents' school involvement in eighth grade strongly predicted students' grade point average in tenth grade, beyond the influence of SES and previous academic achievement. This relationship held for each ethnic group included—black, white, Native-American, and Asian (Keith et al., 1998). Parents who are in frequent contact with the school send a message to their teenager about the value of education, promote wise educational decisions, and model constructive solutions to academic problems.

This parent is involved in his adolescent son's school. By keeping tabs on his progress, the father sends a message to his child about the importance of education and teaches skills for solving academic problems.

Parents living in low-income, high-risk neighborhoods face daily stresses that reduce their energy for school involvement (Bowen, Bowen, & Ware, 2002). Yet stronger home–school links could relieve some of this stress. Schools can build parent–school partnerships by strengthening personal relationships between teachers and parents, tapping parents' talents to increase the quality of school programs, and including parents in school governance so they remain invested in school goals (Epstein, 2001).

■ **Peer Influences.** Peers play an important role in adolescent achievement, in a way that relates to both family and school. Teenagers whose parents value achievement generally choose friends who share those values (Berndt & Keefe, 1995). For example, when Sabrina began to make new friends in junior high, she often studied with her girlfriends. Each girl wanted to do well and reinforced the same desire in the others.

Peer support for high achievement also depends on the overall climate of the peer culture, which, for ethnic minority youths, is powerfully affected by the surrounding social order. African-American minority adolescents, for example, observe that their ethnic group is worse off than the white majority in educational attainment, jobs, income, housing, and political power. And discriminatory treatment by teachers and peers, often resulting from stereotypes that they are "not intelligent," triggers anger, anxiety, self-doubt, declines in achievement, association with peers who are not interested in school, and increases in problem behaviors (Wong, Eccles, & Sameroff, 2003). Under these conditions, even middle-SES black teenagers may react against working hard, convinced that getting good grades will have little future payoff (Ogbu, 2003).

Yet not all economically disadvantaged minority students respond this way. A case study of six inner-city, poverty-stricken African-American adolescents who were high-achieving and optimistic about their futures revealed that they were intensely aware of oppression but believed in striving to alter their social position (O'Connor, 1997). How did they develop this sense of agency? Parents, relatives, and teachers had convinced them through discussion and example that injustice should not be tolerated and that, together, blacks could overcome it—a perspective that encouraged both strong ethnic identity and high academic motivation, even in the face of peer pressures against doing well in school.

■ **School Characteristics.** Adolescents need classroom environments that are responsive to their expanding powers of reasoning and their emotional and social needs. Without appropriate learning experiences, their cognitive potential is unlikely to be realized.

Classroom Learning Experiences. As noted earlier, in large, departmentalized secondary schools, many adolescents report that their classes lack warmth and supportiveness—a circumstance that dampens their motivation. One study tracked changes in students' academic orientation in math classes from seventh to eighth grade. Those who entered classrooms high in teacher support, encouragement of student interaction about academic work, and promotion of mutual respect among classmates gained in academic motivation and cognitive self-regulation (reflected in whether they understood concepts and in their willingness to check their work). In contrast, declines in motivation and self-regulation occurred in classrooms emphasizing competition and public comparison of students (Ryan & Patrick, 2001).

Of course, an important benefit of separate classes in each subject is that adolescents can be taught by experts, who are more likely to encourage high-level thinking, teach effective learning strategies, and emphasize content relevant to students' experiences—factors that promote interest, effort, and achievement (Eccles, 2004). But many secondary school classrooms do not consistently provide interesting, challenging teaching. Because of the uneven quality of instruction, many seniors graduate from high school deficient in basic academic skills. Although the achievement gap separating African-American, Hispanic, Native-American, and Native-Canadian students from white students has declined since the 1970s, mastery of reading, writing, mathematics, and science by low-SES ethnic minority students remains disappointing (Statistics Canada, 1999; U.S. Department of Education, 2005d, 2005f). Too often these young people attend underfunded schools with rundown buildings, outdated equipment, and textbook shortages. In some, crime and discipline problems receive more attention than teaching and learning. By junior high, large numbers of poverty-stricken minority students have been placed in low academic tracks, compounding their learning difficulties.

Tracking. Ability grouping, as we saw in Chapter 9, is detrimental during the elementary school years. At least into middle or junior high school, heterogeneous classes are desirable. They effectively support the motivation and achievement of students who vary widely in academic progress (Gillies, 2003; Gillies & Ashman, 1996).

By high school, some grouping is unavoidable because certain aspects of education must dovetail with the young person's future educational and vocational plans. In the United States and Canada, high school students are counseled into college preparatory, vocational, or general education tracks. Unfortunately, this sorting tends to perpetuate educational inequalities of earlier years: Low-SES minority students are assigned in large numbers to noncollege tracks.

Longitudinal research following thousands of U.S. students from eighth to twelfth grade reveals that assignment to a college preparatory track accelerates academic progress, whereas assignment to a vocational or general education track decelerates it (Hallinan & Kubitschek, 1999). Even in secondary schools that do not have a formal tracking program, low-SES minority students tend to be assigned to lower course levels in most or all of their academic subjects, resulting in de facto (unofficial) tracking (Lucas & Behrends, 2002).

Once a student is assigned to a low track of courses, breaking out is difficult. Track or course enrollment is generally based on past performance, which is limited by history of placement. Interviews with African-American students in one high school revealed that many thought their previous performance did not reflect their ability (Ogbu, 2003). Yet teachers

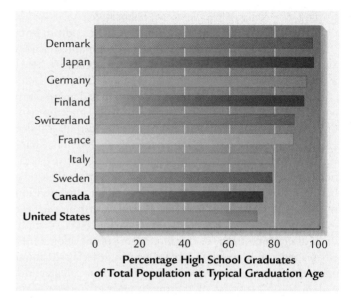

■ **FIGURE 11.13 High school graduation rates in ten industrialized nations.** The United States and Canada rank below many other developed countries. (OECD, 2004.)

and counselors, overburdened with other responsibilities, had little time to reconsider individual cases.

High school students are separated into academic and vocational tracks in virtually all industrialized nations. In China, Japan, and most Western European countries, students take a national examination to determine their placement in high school. The outcome usually fixes future possibilities for the young person. In North America, educational decisions are more fluid. Students who are not assigned to a college preparatory track or who do poorly in high school can still get a college education. Even so, by the adolescent years, SES differences in quality of education and academic achievement have sorted students more drastically than is the case in other countries. In the end, many young people do not benefit from this more open system. Compared with other Western nations, the United States and Canada have a higher percentage of young people who regard themselves as educational failures and drop out of high school (see Figure 11.13).

■ **Part-Time Work.** About half of U.S. and Canadian high school students work part-time during the school year—a greater percentage than in other developed countries (Bowlby & McMullen, 2002; Children's Defense Fund, 2005). Most are middle-SES adolescents in pursuit of spending money rather than vocational exploration and training. Low-income teenagers who need to contribute to family income or to support themselves find it harder to get jobs (U.S. Department of Education, 2005a).

Furthermore, the jobs adolescents hold are limited to low-level repetitive tasks that provide little contact with adult supervisors. A heavy commitment to such jobs is harmful. The more hours students work, the poorer their school attendance, the lower their grades, the less likely they are to participate in extracurricular activities, and the more likely they are to drop out (Marsh & Kleitman, 2005). Students who spend many hours at such jobs also tend to feel more distant from their parents and report more drug and alcohol use and delinquent acts (Kouvonen & Kivivuori, 2001; Staff & Uggen, 2003).

When work experiences are specially designed to meet educational and vocational goals, outcomes are different. Participation in work–study programs or other jobs that provide academic and vocational learning opportunities is related to positive school and work attitudes, improved achievement, and reduced delinquency (Hamilton & Hamilton, 2000; Staff & Uggen, 2003). Yet high-quality vocational preparation for non-college-bound North American adolescents is scarce. Unlike some European nations, the United States and Canada have no widespread training systems to prepare youths for skilled business and industrial occupations and manual trades (Heinz, 1999a). U.S. and Canadian federal, state, and provincial governments support some job-training programs. But most are too brief to make a difference in the lives of poorly skilled adolescents, who need intensive training and academic remediation before they are ready to enter the job market. And at present, these programs serve only a small minority of young people who need assistance.

Dropping Out

Across the aisle from Louis in math class sat Norman, who daydreamed, crumpled his notes into his pocket after class, and rarely did his homework. On test days, he twirled a rabbit's foot for good luck but left most of the questions blank. Louis had been in school with Norman since fourth grade, but the two boys had little to do with one another. To Louis, who was quick at schoolwork, Norman seemed to live in another world. Once or twice each week, Norman cut class; one spring day, he stopped coming altogether.

Norman is one of the 11 percent of American and Canadian young people who leave high school without a diploma (Statistics Canada, 2004d; U.S. Department of Education, 2005b). The dropout rate is particularly high among low-SES ethnic minority youths, especially Hispanic and Canadian-Aboriginal teenagers (see Figure 11.14). The decision to leave school has dire consequences. Youths without upper secondary education have much lower literacy scores than high school graduates; they lack the skills employers value in today's knowledge-based economy. Consequently, employment rates are lower for U.S. and Canadian high school dropouts than for secondary school graduates. Even when they are employed, dropouts are far more likely to remain in menial, low-paying jobs and to be out of work from time to time.

■ **Factors Related to Dropping Out.** Although many dropouts achieve poorly and show high rates of norm-violating acts, a substantial number—like Norman—are young people with few behavior problems who simply experience academic difficulties and quietly disengage from school (Janosz et al., 2000; Newcomb et al., 2002). The pathway to dropping out starts early. Risk factors in first grade predict dropout nearly as well as risk factors in secondary school (Entwisle, Alexander, & Olson, 2005).

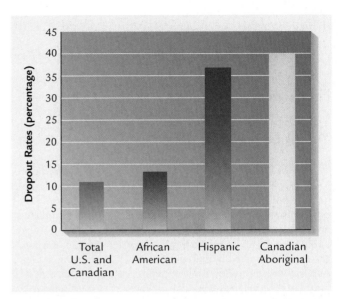

■ **FIGURE 11.14 High school dropout rates by ethnicity, United States and Canada.** Because many African-American, Hispanic, and Canadian-Aboriginal teenagers come from low-income and poverty-stricken families, their dropout rates are above the national average. Rates for Hispanic and Canadian-Aboriginal youths are especially high. (*Source:* Human Resources Development Canada, 2000; U.S. Department of Education, 2005b.)

Norman had a long history of marginal-to-failing school grades and low academic self-esteem. He gave up on tasks that presented the least bit of challenge and counted on luck—his rabbit's foot—to get by. As Norman got older, he attended class less regularly, paid little attention when he was there, and rarely did his homework. He didn't join any school clubs or participate in athletics. Because he was so uninvolved, few teachers or students got to know him well. By the day Norman left, he felt alienated from all aspects of school life.

As with other dropouts, Norman's family background contributed to his problems. Compared with other students, even those with the same grade profile, dropouts are more likely to have parents who are uninvolved in their youngster's education. Many did not finish high school themselves and are unemployed or coping with the aftermath of divorce. When their youngsters bring home poor report cards, these parents are more likely than others to respond with punishment and anger—reactions that cause the young person to rebel further against academic work (Garnier, Stein, & Jacobs, 1997).

Academically marginal students who drop out often have school experiences that undermine their chances for success—large, impersonal schools and classes, unsupportive teachers, and few opportunities for active participation (Croninger & Lee, 2001; Hardre & Reeve, 2003; Lee & Burkam, 2003). Recent reports indicate that over 60 percent of adolescents in some U.S. inner-city high schools do not graduate. Students in general education and vocational tracks, where teaching tends to be the least stimulating, are three times more likely to drop out than those in an a college preparatory track (U.S. Department of Education, 2005b).

A Lifespan Vista

Extracurricular Activities: Contexts for Positive Youth Development

The weekend before graduation, Terrell—a senior at an inner-city high school—attended a cast party celebrating the drama club's final performance of the year. That evening, Terrell had played a leading role in a production written and directed by club members. As Mrs. Meyer, the club's adviser, congratulated Terrell, he responded, "I loved this club. When I joined, I wasn't good at English and math and all that stuff, and I thought I couldn't do anything. Working on the sets and acting was so great—finding out that I could do these things well. Before, I wasn't secure with myself. Now I've got this boost of confidence."

Many studies show that high school extracurricular activities that focus on the arts, community service, and vocational development promote diverse academic and social skills and have a lasting positive impact on adjustment. Outcomes include improved academic performance, reduced antisocial behavior, more favorable self-esteem and initiative, greater peer acceptance, and increased concern for others (Mahoney, 2000; Sandstrom & Coie, 1999). The benefits of extracurricular involvement extend into adult life. After many factors were controlled (including SES and academic performance), young people more involved in high school clubs and organizations achieved more in their occupations and engaged in more community service when they reached their twenties and thirties (Berk, 1992).

How do extracurricular activities produce such wide-ranging benefits? Not just by giving young people something fun to do during leisure hours. In a Swedish study, adolescents who spent many afternoons and evenings in youth recreation centers offering such unstructured pastimes as pool, Ping-Pong, video games, and TV showed repeated and persisting antisocial behavior (Mahoney, Stattin, & Magnusson, 2001). In contrast, highly structured, goal-oriented pursuits that require teenagers to take on challenging roles and responsibilities have a positive impact on development. Such activities also include caring and supportive interactions with peers and adults, who impose high expectations, help with problems, and serve as mentors (Roth et al., 1998).

Youths with academic, emotional, and social problems are especially likely to benefit from extracurricular participation. In a study of teenagers experiencing uninvolved parenting, those who engaged in extracurricular pursuits showed far lower levels of depressed mood. This outcome was strongest for adolescents reporting a trusting relationship with an activity adviser who validated their skills and encouraged them to do their best (Mahoney, Schweder, & Stattin, 2002). Furthermore, activity participation sometimes strengthens connectedness between parent and teenager as family members attend performances and exhibits or otherwise see the fruits of the young person's efforts (Mahoney & Magnuson, 2001).

Students seem to recognize the power of their extracurricular experiences to foster a smooth transition to adulthood. They report enjoyment, increased confidence, valuable relationships with adults,

A group of high school students gather after school to rehearse for a school play. Extracurricular involvement builds many competencies: improved academic performance, more self-esteem, greater peer acceptance, and increased concern for others.

new friendships, and gains in setting goals, managing time, and working with others (Dworkin, Larson, & Hansen, 1993). Unfortunately, extracurricular activities are among the first aspects of school life to be eliminated when budgets are cut. Yet a wealth of evidence indicates that these pursuits should, in fact, be expanded, with special attempts made to reach academically and socially marginal young people. One example is TRUCE (The Renaissance University in Children's Education), a program in New York City's Harlem neighborhood that reaches ethnic minority teenagers through a variety of extracurricular pursuits— publishing a widely circulated community newspaper and producing a TV show for a local cable channel, among other activities. TRUCE's effects included improved academic achievement, reduced dropout, and enhanced leadership skills in participating teenagers.

■ **Prevention Strategies.** Among the diverse strategies available for helping teenagers at risk of dropping out, several common themes are related to success:

🖋 *High-quality vocational training.* For many marginal students, the real-life nature of vocational education is more comfortable and effective than purely academic work. But to work well, vocational education must carefully integrate academic and job-related instruction so students see the relevance of what happens in the classroom to their future goals (Ianni & Orr, 1996).

🖋 *Remedial instruction and counseling that offer personalized attention.* Most potential dropouts need intensive remedial instruction in small classes that permit warm, caring teacher–student relationships to form. To overcome the negative psychological effects of repeated school failure, academic assistance must be combined with social support. One successful approach is to match at-risk students with retired adults, who serve as tutors, mentors, and role models in addressing academic and vocational needs (Prevatt, 2003).

Efforts to address the many factors in students' lives related to leaving school early. Programs that strengthen parent involvement, offer flexible work–study arrangements, and provide on-site child care for teenage parents can make staying in school easier for at-risk adolescents.

Participation in extracurricular activities. Another way of helping marginal students is to draw them into the community life of the school (Mahoney & Stattin, 2000). The most powerful influence on extracurricular involvement is small school size. In smaller high schools (500 to 700 students or less), a greater proportion of the student body is needed to staff and operate activities. Potential dropouts are far more likely to participate, feel needed, gain recognition, and remain until graduation. Consult the Lifespan Vista box on the previous page for research indicating that extracurricular participation has a lasting, favorable impact on development.

As we conclude our discussion of academic achievement, let's place the school dropout problem in historical perspective. Over the past half-century, the percentage of U.S. and Canadian young people completing high school by age 24 increased steadily, from less than 50 percent to nearly 90 percent. During this same period, college attendance also rose. Today, nearly 42 percent of American and 58 percent of Canadian young people earn college degrees. Despite the worrisome decline in male college enrollment noted earlier, U.S. and Canadian higher education rates continue to rank among the highest in the world (OECD, 2005).

Finally, although many dropouts get caught in a vicious cycle in which their lack of self-confidence and skills prevents them from seeking further education and training, about one-third return to finish their secondary education within a few years (U.S. Office of Education, 2005a). And some extend their schooling further. As the end of adolescence approaches, many young people realize how essential education is for a rewarding job and a satisfying adult life.

Ask Yourself

Review

List ways that parents can promote their adolescent's academic achievement, and explain why each is effective.

Apply

Tanisha is finishing sixth grade. She could either continue in her current school through eighth grade or switch to a much larger junior high school. What would you suggest she do, and why?

Connect

How are educational practices that prevent school dropout similar to those that improve learning for adolescents in general?

Reflect

Describe your own experiences in making the transition to middle or junior high school and then to high school. What did you find stressful? What helped you adjust?

www.ablongman.com/berk

Summary

🍁 *Physical Development*

Conceptions of Adolescence

How have conceptions of adolescence changed over the past century?

■ **Adolescence,** initiated by **puberty,** is the period of transition between childhood and adulthood. Early biologically oriented theories viewed adolescence as an inevitable period of storm and stress. An alternative perspective regarded the social environment as entirely responsible for the wide variability in adolescent adjustment. Contemporary research

© CHRIS WARE/THE IMAGE WORKS

shows that adolescence is a product of biological, psychological, and social forces.

Puberty: The Physical Transition to Adulthood

Describe pubertal changes in body size, proportions, sleep patterns, motor performance, and sexual maturity.

■ Hormonal changes beginning in middle childhood initiate puberty, on average, two years earlier for girls than for boys. The first outward sign is the **growth spurt.** As the body enlarges, girls' hips and boys' shoulders broaden. Girls add more fat, boys more muscle.

■ Pubertal changes lead to improvements in gross motor performance, which are much larger for boys than for girls.

Some boys become so preoccupied with physical prowess that they use dangerous, often illegal performance-enhancing drugs.

■ Although girls' involvement in high school sports has increased, they continue to receive less athletic encouragement than boys. The number of adolescents participating in regular physical activity declines from ninth to twelfth grade.

■ Sex hormones regulate changes in **primary** and **secondary sexual characteristics. Menarche** occurs late in the girl's sequence of pubertal events, following the rapid increase in body size. Among boys, as the sex organs and body enlarge and pubic and underarm hair appear, **spermarche** takes place.

What factors influence the timing of puberty?

■ Heredity, nutrition, exercise, and overall physical health contribute to the timing of puberty. In industrialized nations, a

secular trend toward earlier menarche has occurred.

What changes in the brain take place during adolescence?

■ Pruning of unused synapses in the cerebral cortex continues in adolescence, and growth and myelination of stimulated neural fibers accelerate. These changes support adolescents' cognitive advances and may play a role in their drive for novel experiences.

■ Changes occur in the way the brain regulates sleep timing, so that adolescents generally go to bed much later than they did as children. Sleep deprivation contributes to poorer achievement, depressed mood, and behavior problems.

The Psychological Impact of Pubertal Events

Explain adolescents' reactions to the physical changes of puberty.

■ Girls generally react to menarche with surprise and mixed emotions, but whether their feelings lean in a positive or a negative direction depends on prior knowledge and support from family members. Although boys usually know ahead of time about spermarche, they also react with mixed feelings. Boys receive less social support for the physical changes of puberty than girls.

© BRAND X PICTURES/GETTY IMAGES

■ Besides higher hormone levels, negative life events and adult-structured situations are associated with adolescents' negative moods. In contrast, teenagers feel upbeat when with peers and in self-chosen leisure activities.

■ Puberty is accompanied by psychological distancing between parent and child. The reaction may be a modern substitute for physical departure from the family, which typically occurs at sexual maturity in primate species and in nonindustrialized cultures.

Describe the impact of maturational timing on adolescent adjustment, noting sex differences.

■ Early-maturing boys and late-maturing girls, whose appearance closely matches cultural standards of physical attractiveness, have a more positive **body image** and usually adjust well in adolescence. In contrast, early-maturing girls and late-maturing boys, who fit in least well physically with peers,

experience emotional and social difficulties. Early-maturing girls, in particular, may experience lasting difficulties.

Health Issues

Describe nutritional needs, and cite factors related to serious eating disturbances during adolescence.

■ As the body grows, nutritional requirements increase. Because of poor eating habits, many adolescents suffer from iron, vitamin, and mineral deficiencies. Frequency of family meals is associated with healthy eating.

■ Girls who reach puberty early, who are very dissatisfied with their body images, and who grow up in homes where thinness is idealized are at increased risk for eating disorders. **Anorexia nervosa** tends to appear in girls with perfectionist, inhibited personalities; overprotective, controlling mothers; and emotionally distant fathers. The impulsive eating and purging of **bulimia nervosa** is associated with disengaged parenting. Some bulimics are perfectionists; others lack self-control in many areas of their lives.

Discuss social and cultural influences on adolescent sexual attitudes and behavior.

■ The hormonal changes of puberty lead to an increase in sex drive, but social factors affect how teenagers manage their sexuality. North America is fairly restrictive in its attitude toward adolescent sex, but popular culture presents images of spontaneous, uncommitted sexual activity. Adolescents' sexual attitudes and behavior have become more liberal, with a slight swing back recently.

■ Early and frequent sexual activity is linked to a variety of factors associated with economic disadvantage. Also many sexually active teenagers do not practice contraception regularly. Adolescent cognitive processes and a lack of social support for responsible sexual behavior underlie the failure of these young people to protect themselves against pregnancy.

Describe factors involved in the development of homosexuality.

■ About 2 to 3 percent of young people identify as lesbian, gay, or bisexual. Biological factors, including heredity and prenatal hormone levels, play an important role in homosexuality. Lesbian and gay teenagers face special problems in developing a positive sexual identity.

Discuss factors related to sexually transmitted diseases and to teenage pregnancy and parenthood.

■ Early sexual activity combined with inconsistent contraceptive use results in high rates of sexually transmitted diseases (STDs) among U.S. adolescents. Many young adults with AIDS contracted the virus as teenagers.

■ Adolescent pregnancy and parenthood rates are higher in the United States than in most other industrialized nations. Teenage pregnancy in Canada, though lower than in the United States, is still a problem. Adolescent parenthood is associated with school dropout, reduced chances of marriage, greater likelihood of divorce, and poverty—circumstances that jeopardize the well-being of both adolescent and newborn child.

■ Improved sex education, access to contraceptives, programs that build social competence, and expanded educational and vocational opportunities help prevent early pregnancy. Adolescent mothers benefit from school programs that provide job training and child care and from family relationships that are sensitive to their needs. When teenage fathers stay involved, children develop more favorably.

What personal and social factors are related to adolescent substance use and abuse?

■ For most young people in industrialized nations, drug and alcohol experimentation reflects curiosity about these forbidden substances. The minority who move from use to abuse have serious psychological, family, and school problems. Programs that work with parents early to reduce family adversity and improve parenting skills and that build teenagers' competence help prevent substance abuse.

🍂 *Cognitive Development*

Piaget's Theory: The Formal Operational Stage

What are the major characteristics of formal operational thought?

■ During Piaget's **formal operational stage**, adolescents engage in **hypothetico-deductive reasoning.** When faced with a problem, they start with a hypothesis about variables that might affect an outcome, deduce logical, testable inferences, and systematically isolate and combine variables to see which inferences are confirmed.

■ **Propositional thought** also develops. Adolescents can evaluate the logic of verbal statements apart from real-world circumstances.

Discuss recent research on formal operational thought and its implications for the accuracy of Piaget's formal operational stage.

■ Adolescents are capable of more advanced reasoning than school-age children. However, college students and adults often fail Piaget's formal operational tasks and are more likely to think abstractly and systematically in situations in which they have had extensive experience. In village and tribal cultures, formal operational tasks are usually not mastered at all. These findings indicate that Piaget's highest stage is affected by specific learning opportunities typically encountered in school.

An Information-Processing View of Adolescent Cognitive Development

How do information-processing researchers account for cognitive changes in adolescence?

■ Information-processing researchers believe that a variety of specific mechanisms underlie cognitive gains in adolescence: improved attention and inhibition, more effective strategies, greater knowledge, improved cognitive self-regulation, gains in speed of thinking and processing capacity, and, especially, advances in metacognition.

■ Research on scientific reasoning indicates that the ability to coordinate theory with evidence improves as adolescents solve increasingly complex problems and reflect on their thinking, acquiring more mature metacognitive understandings. Adolescents develop formal operational thinking in a similar, step-by-step fashion on different types of tasks, constructing general models that can be applied to many instances of a given type of problem.

Consequences of Adolescent Cognitive Changes

Describe typical reactions of adolescents that result from their advancing cognition.

■ As adolescents reflect on their own thoughts, they think more about themselves, and two distorted images of the relation between self and other appear—the **imaginary audience** and the **personal fable**. Teenagers' capacity to think about possibilities prompts idealistic visions at odds with everyday reality, and they often become fault-finding critics. Compared with adults, adolescents have difficulty with decision making, more often falling back on well-learned, intuitive judgments.

Sex Differences in Mental Abilities

Describe sex differences in mental abilities at adolescence and factors that affect them.

■ During adolescence, girls score slightly better than boys on tests of verbal ability, and their advantage in reading and writing achievement increases. Earlier development of the left hemisphere of the cerebral cortex

and greater maternal verbal stimulation probably contribute to girls' better verbal performance. And gender-stereotyping of language arts as "feminine" and regimented teaching may weaken boys' literacy skills.

■ Boys exceed girls in complex mathematical reasoning. Overall, the gender difference is small, but among the most capable students, it is greater. Boys' biologically based superior spatial skills enhance their mathematical problem solving. At the same time, childhood manipulative play activities, gender stereotyping of math as "masculine," self-confidence and interest in doing math, and specialized computer knowledge contribute to boys' spatial and math advantages.

Learning in School

Discuss the impact of school transitions on adolescent adjustment.

■ School transitions in adolescence can be stressful. Girls experience more adjustment difficulties than boys after the transition from elementary school to junior high because other life changes (puberty and the beginning of dating) tend to occur at the same time. Teenagers who must cope with added stresses—especially young people with both academic and mental health difficulties—are at greatest risk for adjustment problems following school transition.

© CRAIG WITKOWSKI/INDEX STOCK

Discuss family, peer, school, and employment influences on academic achievement during adolescence.

■ Authoritative parenting and parents' school involvement promote high achievement. Teenagers whose parents encourage achievement are likely to choose friends from similar families.

■ Warm, supportive learning environments with activities that emphasize high-level thinking enable adolescents to reach their academic potential.

■ By high school, separate educational tracks that dovetail with students' future plans are necessary. Unfortunately, high school tracking in the United States and Canada usually extends the educational inequalities of earlier years.

■ The more hours students devote to a part-time job, the poorer their school attendance, academic performance, and extracurricular participation. In contrast, work–study programs designed to meet both educational and vocational goals predict positive school and work attitudes and better academic achievement among non-college-bound teenagers.

What factors are related to dropping out of school?

■ Eleven percent of U.S. and Canadian young people, many of whom are low-SES minority youths, leave high school without a diploma. Dropping out is the result of a long, gradual process of disengagement from school. Family and school influences combine to undermine the young person's chances for success. These include poor school performance, lack of parental support for academic achievement, large impersonal classes, and unstimulating teaching.

Important Terms and Concepts

adolescence (p. 361)

anorexia nervosa (p. 371)

body image (p. 370)

bulimia nervosa (p. 372)

formal operational stage (p. 381)

growth spurt (p. 363)

hypothetico-deductive reasoning (p. 381)

imaginary audience (p. 384)

menarche (p. 365)

personal fable (p. 385)

primary sexual characteristics (p. 365)

propositional thought (p. 381)

puberty (p. 361)

secondary sexual characteristics (p. 365)

secular trend (p. 366)

spermarche (p. 366)

*A*s adolescents spend less time with family members, peer groups become more tightly knit into cliques. And as interest in dating increases, boys' and girls' cliques come together. Mixed-sex cliques provide boys and girls with models for how to interact and a chance to do so without having to be intimate.

Emotional and Social Development in Adolescence

L ouis sat on the grassy hillside overlooking the high school, waiting for his best friend, Darryl, to arrive from his fourth-period class. The two boys often met at noontime and then crossed the street to have lunch at a nearby hamburger stand.

Watching as hundreds of students poured onto the school grounds, Louis reflected on what he had learned in government class that day. "Suppose I *had* been born in the People's Republic of China. I'd be sitting here, speaking a different language, being called by a different name, and thinking about the world in different ways. Wow," Louis pondered. "I am who I am through some quirk of fate."

Louis awoke from his thoughts with a start to see Darryl standing in front of him. "Hey, dreamer! I've been shouting and waving from the bottom of the hill for five minutes. How come you're so spaced out lately, Louis?"

"Oh, just wondering about stuff—what I want, what I believe in. My older brother Jules—I envy him. He seems to know more about where he's going. I'm up in the air about it. You ever feel that way?"

"Yeah, a lot," Darryl admitted, looking at Louis seriously as they approached the hamburger stand. "I wonder, What am I really like? Who will I become?"

Louis and Darryl's introspective remarks are signs of a major re-organization of the self at adolescence: the development of identity. Both young people are attempting to formulate who they are—their personal values and the directions they will pursue in life.

We begin this chapter with Erikson's account of identity development and the research it has stimulated on teenagers' thoughts and feelings about themselves. The quest for identity extends to many aspects of development. We will see how a sense of cultural belonging, moral understanding, and masculine and feminine self-images are refined during adolescence. And as parent–child relationships are revised and young people become increasingly independent of the family, friendships and peer networks become crucial contexts for bridging the gap between childhood and adulthood. Our chapter concludes with a discussion of several serious adjustment problems of adolescence: depression, suicide, and delinquency.

Erikson's Theory: Identity versus Role Confusion

E rikson (1950, 1968) was the first to recognize **identity** as the major personality achievement of adolescence and as a crucial step toward becoming a productive, happy adult. Constructing an identity involves defining who you are, what you value, and the directions you choose to pursue in life. One expert described it as an explicit theory of oneself as a rational agent—one who acts on the basis of reason, takes responsibility for those actions, and can explain them (Moshman, 1999). This search for what is true and real about the self drives many choices—vocation, interpersonal relationships, community involvement, ethnic-group membership, and expression of one's sexual orientation, as well as moral, political, and religious ideals.

Erikson called the psychological conflict of adolescence **identity versus role confusion.** Successful outcomes of earlier stages pave the way to its positive resolution. Young people who reach adolescence with a weak sense of *trust* have trouble finding ideals to have faith in. Those with little *autonomy* or *initiative* do not engage in the active exploration required to choose among alternatives. And those who lack a sense of *industry* fail to select a vocation that matches their interests and skills.

Although the seeds of identity formation are planted early, not until late adolescence and early adulthood do young people become absorbed in this task. According to Erikson, in complex societies, teenagers experience an *identity crisis*—a temporary period of distress as they experiment with alternatives before settling on values and goals. They go through a process of inner soul-searching, sifting through characteristics that defined the self in childhood and combining them with emerging traits, capacities, and commitments. Then they mold these into a solid inner core that provides a mature identity—a sense of self-continuity as they move through various roles in daily life. In Erikson's view, a healthy identity is experienced as a sense of physical, psychological, and social well-being—"a feeling of being at home in one's body, a sense of 'knowing where one is going,' and an inner assuredness of anticipated recognition from those who count" (Erikson, 1968, p. 165). Once formed, identity continues to be refined in adulthood as people reevaluate earlier commitments and choices.

Current theorists agree with Erikson that questioning of values, plans, and priorities is necessary for a mature identity, but they no longer describe this process as a "crisis" (Grotevant, 1998; Kroger, 2005). For some young people, identity development is traumatic and disturbing, but the typical experience is, rather, one of *exploration* followed by *commitment*. As young people try out life possibilities, they gather important information about themselves and their environment and move toward making enduring decisions. In the process, they forge an organized self-structure (Arnett, 2000; Moshman, 2005).

Erikson described the negative outcome of adolescence as *role confusion*. If young people's earlier conflicts were resolved negatively or if society limits their choices to ones that do not match their abilities and desires, they may appear shallow, directionless, and unprepared for the psychological challenges of adulthood. For example, young people who lack a firm sense of self (an identity) to which they can return will find it difficult to risk *intimacy*—the self-sharing involved in Erikson's early adulthood stage.

Does research support Erikson's ideas about identity development? In the following sections, we will see that adolescents go about the task of defining the self in ways that closely match Erikson's description.

Self-Understanding

D uring adolescence, the young person's vision of the self becomes more complex, well-organized, and consistent. Compared with younger children, adolescents have more or less positive feelings about an increasing variety of aspects of the self. Over time, they form a balanced, integrated representation of their strengths and limitations (Harter, 2003). Changes in self-concept and self-esteem set the stage for developing a unified personal identity.

Changes in Self-Concept

Recall that by the end of middle childhood, children can describe themselves in terms of personality traits. In early adolescence, they unify separate traits ("smart," "talented") into more abstract descriptors ("intelligent"). But these generalizations are not interconnected and are often contradictory. For example, 12- to 14-year-olds might mention opposing traits— "intelligent" and "airhead," "shy" and "outgoing." These disparities result from the expansion of adolescents' social world, which creates pressure to display different selves in different relationships—with parents, classmates, close friends, and romantic partners. As they become increasingly aware of these inconsistencies, teenagers agonize over "which is the real me" (Harter, 1998, 2003).

From middle to late adolescence, cognitive changes enable teenagers to combine their traits into an organized system. Their use of qualifiers ("I have a *fairly* quick temper," "I'm not *thoroughly* honest") reveals their awareness that psychological qualities can change from one situation to the next. Older adolescents also add integrating principles that make sense out of formerly troublesome contradictions. "I'm very adaptable," said one young person. "When I'm around my friends, who think that what I say is important, I'm talkative; but around my family I'm quiet because they're never interested enough to really listen to me" (Damon, 1990, p. 88).

Compared with school-age children, teenagers place more emphasis on social virtues, such as being friendly, considerate, kind, and cooperative (Damon & Hart, 1988). Their statements about themselves reflect a concern with being viewed positively by others. Among older adolescents, personal and moral values also appear as key themes. As young people revise their views of themselves to include enduring beliefs and plans, they move toward the unity of self that is central to identity development.

Changes in Self-Esteem

Self-esteem, the evaluative side of self-concept, continues to differentiate in adolescence. Young people add several new dimensions of self-evaluation—close friendship, romantic appeal, and job competence—to those of middle childhood (see Chapter 10, page 331) (Harter, 1999, 2003).

Level of self-esteem also changes. Though some adolescents experience temporary declines after school transitions (see Chapter 11, page 389), self-esteem rises for most young people, who report feeling especially good about their peer relationships and athletic capabilities (Cole et al., 2001; Twenge & Campbell, 2001). Teenagers often assert that they have become more mature, capable, personable, and attractive than in the past. In a study of adolescents in 13 industrialized nations, most were optimistic, felt a sense of control over their personal and vocational futures, and expressed confidence in their ability to cope with life's problems (Grob & Flammer, 1999).

At the same time, individual differences in self-esteem become increasingly stable in adolescence (Trzesniewski, Donnellan, & Robins, 2003). And positive relationships among self-esteem, valuing of various activities, and success at those activities strengthen. For example, academic self-esteem is a powerful predictor of teenagers' judgments of the importance and usefulness of school subjects, their willingness to exert effort, their achievement, and their eventual career choice (Bleeker & Jacobs, 2004; Jacobs et al., 2002; Valentine, DuBois, & Cooper, 2004).

Across SES and ethnic groups, individuals with mostly favorable self-esteem profiles tend to be well-adjusted, sociable, and conscientious. In contrast, low self-esteem in all areas is linked to adjustment difficulties (DuBois et al., 1999; Robins et al., 2001). But certain self-esteem factors are more strongly related to adjustment. Teenagers who feel highly dissatisfied with parental relationships often are aggressive and antisocial. Those with poor academic self-esteem tend to be anxious and unfocused, and those with negative peer relationships are anxious and depressed (Leadbeater et al., 1999; Marsh, Parada, & Ayotte, 2004).

In adolescence as in childhood, authoritative parenting predicts high self-esteem, as does encouragement from teachers (Carlson, Uppal, & Prosser, 2000; Feiring & Taska, 1996;

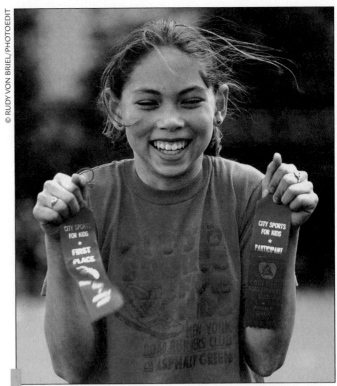

In adolescence, self-esteem usually rises. This 14-year-old girl feels especially good about her athletic abilities.

Steinberg, Darling, Fletcher, 1995). In contrast, teenagers whose parents are critical and insulting have unstable and generally low self-esteem (Kernis, 2002). Feedback that is negative, inconsistent, or not contingent on performance triggers, at best, uncertainty about the self's capacities and, at worst, a sense of being incompetent and unloved. Teenagers who experience such parenting tend to rely only on peers, not on adults, to affirm their self-esteem—a risk factor for adjustment difficulties (DuBois et al., 1999; 2002).

The larger social environment also influences self-esteem. Recall from Chapter 10 that extended family support and ethnic pride may underlie the higher self-esteem of African-American compared with Caucasian children—a trend that extends into adolescence. And Asians' reserve in judging themselves favorably increases at adolescence (see page 332). Furthermore, teenage girls—who worry more about physical appearance and are less confident of their abilities—are more likely than boys to drop in self-esteem. Finally, as we noted in Chapter 10, youths who attend schools and live in neighborhoods with many others of their own ethnicity report higher self-esteem.

Paths to Identity

Adolescents' well-organized self-descriptions and differentiated sense of self-esteem provide the cognitive foundation for forming an identity. Using a clinical interviewing procedure devised by James Marcia (1980) or briefer questionnaire measures, researchers commonly evaluate progress in identity development on two key criteria derived from Erikson's theory: *exploration* and *commitment.* Their various combinations yield four *identity statuses:* **identity achievement,** commitment to values, beliefs, and goals following a period of exploration; **identity moratorium,** exploration without having reached commitment; **identity foreclosure,** commitment in the absence of exploration; and **identity diffusion,** an apathetic state characterized by lack of both exploration and commitment. Table 12.1 summarizes these identity statuses.

Identity development follows many paths. Some young people remain in one status; others experience many status transitions. And the pattern often varies across *identity domains,* such as sexual orientation, vocation, and religious and political values. Most young people change from "lower" statuses (foreclosure or diffusion) to higher ones (moratorium or achievement) between their mid-teens and mid-twenties, but some move in the reverse direction (Kroger, 2001; Meeus, 1996).

Because attending college provides many opportunities to explore career options and lifestyles, college students make more progress toward formulating an identity than they did in high school (Meeus et al., 1999). After college, they often sample a broad range of life experiences before choosing a life course. Those who go to work immediately after high school graduation settle on a self-definition earlier than college-educated youths. But those who have difficulty realizing their occupational goals because of lack of training or vocational choices are at risk for identity diffusion (Eccles et al., 2003).

At one time, researchers thought that adolescent girls postponed establishing an identity and instead focused on Erikson's next stage, intimacy development. Some girls do show more sophisticated reasoning than boys in identity domains related to intimacy, such as sexuality and family versus career priorities. Otherwise, adolescents of both sexes typically make progress on identity concerns before experiencing genuine intimacy in relationships (Kroger, 2000; Meeus et al., 1999).

Identity Status and Psychological Well-Being

A wealth of research verifies that both identity achievement and moratorium are psychologically healthy routes to a mature self-definition. Long-term foreclosure and diffusion, in contrast, are maladaptive.

Although adolescents in moratorium are often anxious about the challenges that lie before them, they resemble identity-achieved individuals in using an active, *information-gathering cognitive style* when making personal decisions and solving problems. That is, they seek out relevant information, evaluate it carefully, and critically reflect on and revise their views (Berzonsky, 2003; Berzonsky & Kuk, 2000). Young people who are identity-achieved or exploring have higher self-esteem, feel more in control of their own lives, are more likely to view school and work as feasible avenues for realizing their aspirations, and are more advanced in moral reasoning (Adams & Marshall, 1996; Kroger, 2002; Serafini & Adams, 2002).

Adolescents who get stuck in either foreclosure or diffusion are passive in the face of identity concerns and have adjustment difficulties. Foreclosed individuals display a *dogmatic, inflexible cognitive style* in which they internalize the values and

Table 12.1	The Four Identity Statuses	
Identity Status	**Description**	**Example**
Identity achievement	Having already explored alternatives, identity-achieved individuals are committed to a clearly formulated set of self-chosen values and goals. They feel a sense of psychological well-being, of sameness through time, and of knowing where they are going.	When asked how willing she would be to give up going into her chosen occupation if something better came along, Darla responded, "Well, I might, but I doubt it. I've thought long and hard about law as a career. I'm pretty certain it's for me."
Identity moratorium	*Identity moratorium* means "delay or holding pattern." These individuals have not yet made definite commitments. They are in the process of exploring—gathering information and trying out activities, with the desire to find values and goals to guide their lives.	When asked whether he had ever had doubts about his religious beliefs, Ramon said, "Yes, I guess I'm going through that right now. I just don't see how there can be a God and yet so much evil in the world."
Identity foreclosure	Identity-foreclosed individuals have committed themselves to values and goals without exploring alternatives. They accept a ready-made identity that authority figures (usually parents but sometimes teachers, religious leaders, or romantic partners) have chosen for them.	When asked if she had ever reconsidered her political beliefs, Hillary answered, "No, not really, our family is pretty much in agreement on these things."
Identity diffusion	Identity-diffused individuals lack clear direction. They are neither committed to values and goals nor actively trying to reach them. They may never have explored alternatives or may have found the task too threatening and overwhelming.	When asked about his attitude toward nontraditional gender roles, Joel responded, "Oh, I don't know. It doesn't make much difference to me. I can take it or leave it."

beliefs of parents and others without deliberate evaluation and are closed to information that may threaten their position (Berzonsky & Kuk, 2000). Most fear rejection by people on whom they depend for affection and self-esteem. A few foreclosed teenagers who are alienated from their families and society may join cults or other extremist groups, uncritically adopting a way of life different from their past.

Long-term diffused individuals are the least mature in identity development. They typically use a *diffuse-avoidant cognitive style* in which they avoid dealing with personal decisions and problems and, instead, allow current situational pressures to dictate their reactions (Berzonsky & Kuk, 2000). Taking an "I don't care" attitude, they entrust themselves to luck or fate and go along with whatever the "crowd" is doing. As a result, they experience time management and academic difficulties and, of all young people, are most likely to use and abuse drugs (Archer & Waterman, 1990). Often at the heart of their apathy is a sense of hopelessness about the future.

Factors Affecting Identity Development

Adolescent identity formation begins a lifelong, dynamic process, influenced by a wide variety of factors related to both personality and context. A change in either the individual or the context opens up the possibility of reformulating identity (Kunnen & Bosma, 2003).

As our discussion of identity and adjustment suggested, identity status is both cause and consequence of personality. Adolescents who assume that absolute truth is always attainable tend to be foreclosed, while those who doubt that they will ever feel certain about anything are more often identity-diffused. Young people who appreciate that they can use rational criteria to choose among alternatives are likely to be in a state of moratorium or identity achievement (Berzonsky & Kuk, 2000; Boyes & Chandler, 1992).

Recall from Chapter 6 that when parents of toddlers provide both emotional support and freedom to explore, their children develop a healthy sense of self. Similarly, identity development is enhanced for teenagers whose families serve as a "secure base" from which they can confidently move out into the wider world. Adolescents who feel attached to their parents but also free to voice their own opinions tend to be in a state of moratorium or identity achievement (Berzonsky, 2004; Grotevant & Cooper, 1998). Foreclosed teenagers usually have close bonds with parents but lack opportunities for healthy separation. And diffused young people report the lowest levels of parental support and of warm, open communication (Reis & Youniss, 2004; Zimmerman & Becker-Stoll, 2002).

Through interaction with a variety of peers, adolescents' exposure to ideas and values expands. Close friends help one another explore options by providing emotional support and role models of identity development. In one study, 15-year-olds with warm, trusting peer ties were more involved in exploring relationship issues—for example, thinking about what they valued in close friends and in a life partner (Meeus, Oosterwegel, & Vollebergh, 2002). In another study, young

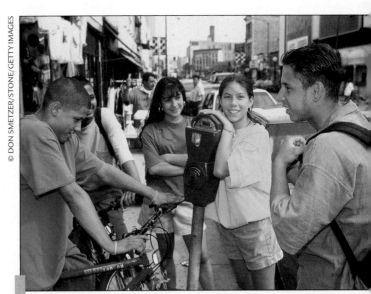

These Hispanic teenagers congregate in a city neighborhood where their ethnicity is well-represented. Schools and communities that are accepting of the young person's cultural heritage promote high self-esteem.

people's attachment to friends predicted career exploration and progress in choosing a career (Felsman & Blustein, 1999).

Schools and communities offering rich and varied opportunities for exploration also support identity development. Schools can help by providing classrooms that promote high-level thinking, extracurricular activities that enable teenagers to take on responsible roles, teachers and counselors who encourage low-SES students to go to college, and vocational training programs that immerse young people in the real world of adult work (Cooper, 1998).

Culture strongly influences the way adolescents deal with a feature of mature identity that the identity-status approach fails to capture: constructing a sense of self-continuity despite major personal changes. In one study, researchers asked Canadian-Aboriginal and cultural-majority 12- to 20-year-olds to describe themselves in the past and in the present and then to justify why they regarded themselves as the same continuous person (Lalonde & Chandler, 2005). Responses of both groups increased in complexity with age, but their strategies differed. Most cultural-majority adolescents used an individualistic approach: They described an *enduring personal essence*, a core self that remained the same despite change. In contrast, Aboriginal youths took an interdependent approach that emphasized a constantly transforming self, resulting from new roles and relationships. They typically constructed a *coherent narrative* in which they linked together various time slices of their life with a thread that explained how they had changed in meaningful ways.

Finally, societal forces also are responsible for the special problems faced by gay, lesbian, and bisexual youths (see Chapter 11) and by some ethnic minority adolescents in forming a secure identity (see the Cultural Influences box on page 404). Applying What We Know on page 405 summarizes ways that adults can support adolescents in their quest for identity.

Cultural Influences

Identity Development Among Ethnic Minority Adolescents

Most adolescents are aware of their cultural ancestry but relatively unconcerned about it. For teenagers who are members of minority groups, however, **ethnic identity**—a sense of ethnic-group membership and attitudes and feelings associated with that membership—is central to the quest for identity, and it presents complex challenges. As they develop cognitively and become more sensitive to feedback from the social environment, minority youths become painfully aware that they are targets of discrimination and inequality. This discovery complicates their efforts to develop a sense of cultural belonging and a set of personally meaningful goals.

Minority youths often feel caught between the standards of the larger society and those of their culture of origin. In many immigrant families from collectivist cultures, adolescents' commitment to obeying their parents and fulfilling family obligations lessens the longer the family has been in the immigrant-receiving country (Phinney, Ong, & Madden, 2000). When immigrant parents tightly restrict their teenagers through fear that assimilation into the larger society will undermine their cultural traditions, their youngsters often rebel, rejecting aspects of their ethnic background.

Other minority teenagers react to years of shattered self-esteem, school failure, and barriers to success in the mainstream by defining themselves in contrast to majority values. A Mexican-American teenager who had given up on school commented, "Mexicans don't have a chance to go on to college and make something of themselves" (Matute-Bianchi, 1986, pp. 250–251). At the same time, discrimination can interfere with the formation of a positive ethnic identity. In one study, Mexican-American youths who had experienced more discrimination were less likely to explore their ethnicity and to report feeling good about it. Those with low ethnic pride showed a sharp drop in self-esteem in the face of discrimination (Romero & Roberts, 2003).

Because it is painful and confusing, minority high school students often dodge the exploring that leads to ethnic-identity achievement. Many are diffused or foreclosed on ethnic-identity issues (Markstrom-Adams & Adams, 1995). Young people with parents of different ethnicities face extra challenges. In a large survey of high school students, part-black biracial teenagers reported as much discrimination as their mono-racial black counterparts, yet they felt less positively about their ethnicity. And compared with monoracial minorities, many biracials—including black–white, black–Asian, white–Asian, black–Hispanic, and white–Hispanic—regarded ethnicity as less central to their identities (Herman, 2004). Perhaps because these adolescents did not feel as if they belonged to any ethnic group, they discounted the significance of ethnic identity and (in the case of part-black biracials) viewed their minority background somewhat negatively.

When family members encourage adolescents to behave proactively by disproving ethnic stereotypes of low achievement or antisocial behavior, young people typically surmount the threat that discrimination poses to a favorable ethnic identity (Phinney & Chavira, 1995). In addition, adolescents whose families have taught them the history, traditions, values, and language of their ethnic group and who frequently interact with same-ethnicity peers are more likely to forge a favorable ethnic identity (Phinney et al., 2001b).

How can society help minority adolescents resolve identity conflicts constructively? Here are some relevant approaches:

- Promote effective parenting, in which children and adolescents benefit from family ethnic pride, yet are encouraged to explore the meaning of ethnicity in their own lives.

- Ensure that schools respect minority youths' native languages, unique learning styles, and right to high-quality education.

- Foster contact with peers of the same ethnicity, along with respect between ethnic groups (García Coll & Magnuson, 1997).

A strong, secure ethnic identity is associated with higher self-esteem, optimism, a sense of mastery over the environment, and more positive attitudes toward one's ethnicity (Carlson, Uppal, & Prosser, 2000; Smith et al., 1999). For these reasons, adolescents with a positive connection to their ethnic group are better adjusted. They cope more effectively with stress, achieve more favorably in school, and have fewer emotional and behavior problems than agemates who identify only weakly with their ethnicity (Chavous et al., 2003; Wong, Eccles, & Sameroff, 2003).

Forming a **bicultural identity**—by exploring and adopting values from both the adolescent's subculture and the dominant culture—offers added benefits. Biculturally identified adolescents tend to be achieved in other areas of identity as well. And their relations with members of other ethnic groups are especially favorable (Phinney et al., 2001a; Phinney & Kohatsu, 1997). In sum, ethnic-identity achievement enhances many aspects of emotional and social development.

© ED KASHI/IPN

High school students on a Chippewa reservation in northern Wisconsin gather at a local gym for a weekly powwow organized to celebrate their culture and language. When minority youths encounter respect for their cultural heritage, they are more likely to retain ethnic values and customs as an important part of their identities.

Supporting Healthy Identity Development

Strategy	Explanation
Engage in warm, open communication.	Provides both emotional support and freedom to explore values and goals
Initiate discussions that promote high-level thinking at home and at school.	Encourages rational and deliberate selection among competing beliefs and values
Provide opportunities to participate in extra-curricular activities and vocational training programs.	Permits young people to explore the real world of adult work
Provide opportunities to talk with adults and peers who have worked through identity questions.	Offers models of identity achievement and advice on how to resolve identity concerns
Provide opportunities to explore ethnic heritage and learn about other cultures in an atmosphere of respect.	Fosters identity achievement in all areas and ethnic tolerance, which supports the identity explorations of others

Ask Yourself

Review

List personal and contextual factors that contribute to identity development.

Apply

Return to the conversation between Louis and Darryl in the opening of this chapter. Which identity status best characterizes each of the two boys, and why?

Connect

Explain how changes in self-concept and self-esteem at adolescence pave the way for constructing an identity.

Reflect

How would you characterize your identity status? Does it vary across the domains of sexuality, close relationships, vocation, religious beliefs, and political values? Describe your identity development in an important domain, along with factors that may have influenced it.

www.ablongman.com/berk

Moral Development

Eleven-year-old Sabrina sat at the kitchen table reading the Sunday newspaper, her eyes wide with interest. "You gotta see this," she said to 16-year-old Louis, who sat munching cereal. Sabrina held up a page of large photos showing a 70-year-old woman standing in her home. The floor and furniture were piled with stacks of newspapers, cardboard boxes, tin cans, glass containers, food, and clothing. The accompanying article described crumbling plaster on the walls, frozen pipes, and nonfunctioning sinks, toilet, and furnace. The headline read: "Loretta Perry: My Life Is None of Their Business."

"Look what they're trying to do to this poor lady," exclaimed Sabrina. "They wanna throw her out of her house and tear it down! Those city inspectors must not care about anyone. Here it says, 'Mrs. Perry has devoted much of her life to doing favors for people.' Why doesn't someone help *her?*"

"Sabrina, you're missing the point," Louis responded. "Mrs. Perry is violating 30 building code standards. The law says you're supposed to keep your house clean and in good repair."

"But Louis, she's old, and she needs help. She says her life will be over if they destroy her home."

"The building inspectors aren't being mean, Sabrina. Mrs. Perry is stubborn. She's refusing to obey the law. And she's not just a threat to herself—she's a danger to her neighbors, too. Suppose her house caught on fire. You can't live around other people and say your life is nobody's business."

"You don't just knock someone's home down," Sabrina replied angrily. "Why aren't her friends and neighbors over there fixing up that house? You're just like those building inspectors, Louis. You've got no feelings!"

As Louis and Sabrina's disagreement over Mrs. Perry's plight illustrates, cognitive development and expanding social experiences permit adolescents to better understand larger social structures—societal institutions and lawmaking systems—that govern moral responsibilities. As their grasp of social arrangements expands, adolescents construct new ideas about what should be done when the needs and desires of people conflict. As a result, they move toward increasingly just, fair, and balanced solutions to moral problems.

Piaget's Theory of Moral Development

Piaget's early work on the moral judgment of the child inspired Lawrence Kohlberg's more recent cognitive-developmental theory of moral development. On the basis of 5- to 13-year-olds' views of the origins of the rules and their moral judgments of

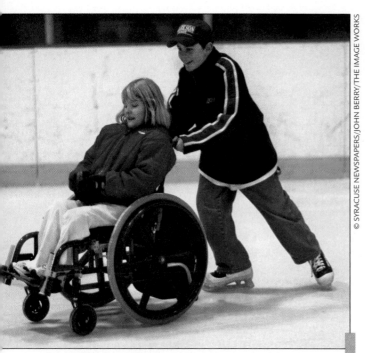

As this teenage boy skates his disabled friend around the ice rink, he demonstrates his understanding of the Golden Rule. A sophisticated grasp of reciprocity—expressing the same concern for others as for oneself—contributes to advances in moral understanding.

characters' behaviors in stories, Piaget (1932/1965) identified two broad stages of morality.

The first stage, **heteronomous morality,** extends from about 5 to 10 years of age. As the word *heteronomous* (meaning "under the authority of another") suggests, children regard rules as handed down by authorities (God, parents, and teachers), as permanent and unchangeable, and as requiring strict obedience. Also, in judging an act's wrongness, they tend to focus on outcomes rather than intent to do harm. When asked to decide who is naughtier—John, who accidentally breaks 15 cups while on his way to dinner, or Henry, who breaks a single cup while stealing some jam—a 6- or 7-year-old chooses John.

As they approach adolescence, young people move into the stage of **autonomous morality.** Now, they no longer view rules as fixed but, rather, as flexible, socially agreed-on principles that can be revised when necessary. Older children and adolescents use a standard of fairness called *ideal reciprocity.* They express the same concern for the welfare of others as they do for themselves. Most of us know this standard in the form of the Golden Rule: "Do unto others as you would have others do unto you." Individuals at this stage realize that intentions, not just outcomes, should serve as the basis for judging behavior. Piaget believed that this advance in moral judgment is based on gains in perspective taking, which result from cognitive development and opportunities to interact with peers.

Think about Piaget's theory in light of what you have already learned about moral development in earlier chapters (return to pages 269 and 336–338). You will see that his account of young children as rigid, external, and focused on

physical consequences underestimates their moral capacities. Nevertheless, Piaget's moral stages do describe the general direction of moral development.

Kohlberg's more comprehensive theory is a direct continuation of Piaget's research. Kohlberg identified six distinct stages of moral development, including three that develop after the first appearance of autonomous morality.

Kohlberg's Extension of Piaget's Theory

To study moral development, Kohlberg used a clinical interviewing procedure in which he presented a sample of 10- to 16-year-old boys with hypothetical *moral dilemmas*—stories presenting a conflict between two moral values—and asked them what the main actor should do and why. Then he followed the participants longitudinally, reinterviewing them at 3- to 4-year intervals over the next 20 years. The best known of Kohlberg's dilemmas, the "Heinz dilemma," pits the value of obeying the law (not stealing) against the value of human life (saving a dying person):

> In Europe a woman was near death from cancer. There was one drug the doctors thought might save her. A druggist in the same town had discovered it, but he was charging ten times what the drug cost him to make. The sick woman's husband, Heinz, went to everyone he knew to borrow the money, but he could only get together half of what it cost. The druggist refused to sell the drug for less or let Heinz pay later. So Heinz got desperate and broke into the man's store to steal the drug for his wife. Should Heinz have done that? Why or why not? (paraphrased from Colby et al., 1983, p. 77)

Kohlberg emphasized that it is *the way an individual reasons* about the dilemma, not *the content of the response* (whether or not to steal), that determines moral maturity. Individuals who believe Heinz should take the drug and those who think he should not can be found at each of Kohlberg's first four stages. Only at the two highest stages do moral reasoning and content come together in a coherent ethical system (Kohlberg, Levine, & Hewer, 1983). Given a choice between obeying the law and preserving individual rights, the most advanced moral thinkers support individual rights (in the Heinz dilemma, stealing the drug to save a life). Does this remind you of adolescents' efforts to formulate a sound, well-organized set of personal values in constructing an identity? According to some theorists, the development of identity and moral understanding are part of the same process (Bergman, 2004; Blasi, 1994).

■ **Kohlberg's Stages of Moral Understanding.** Kohlberg organized his six stages into three general levels of moral development. As in Piaget's theory, Kohlberg's first three stages characterize children as moving from a morality focused on outcomes to one based on ideal reciprocity. Interviews with older adolescents yielded the fourth stage, in which young people view societal rules and laws as vital for ensuring that people treat one another justly. On the basis of the responses of a small minority of adolescents, Kohlberg posited the fifth and sixth stages.

Kohlberg believed that moral understanding is promoted by the same factors Piaget thought were important for cognitive growth: (1) actively grappling with moral issues and noticing weaknesses in one's current reasoning, and (2) gains in perspective taking, which permit individuals to resolve moral conflicts in more effective ways. As we examine Kohlberg's developmental sequence in light of possible responses to the Heinz dilemma, look for changes in perspective taking that each stage assumes.

The Preconventional Level. At the **preconventional level,** morality is externally controlled. As in Piaget's heteronomous stage, children accept the rules of authority figures and judge actions by their consequences. Behaviors that result in punishment are viewed as bad, those that lead to rewards as good.

Stage 1: The punishment and obedience orientation. Children at this stage find it difficult to consider two points of view in a moral dilemma. As a result, they ignore people's intentions and, instead, focus on fear of authority and avoidance of punishment as reasons for behaving morally.

> *Prostealing:* "If you let your wife die, you will . . . be blamed for not spending the money to help her and there'll be an investigation of you and the druggist for your wife's death." (Kohlberg, 1969, p. 381)

> *Antistealing:* "You shouldn't steal the drug because you'll be caught and sent to jail if you do. If you do get away, [you'd be scared that] the police would catch up with you any minute." (Kohlberg, 1969, p. 381)

Stage 2: The instrumental purpose orientation. Children become aware that people can have different perspectives in a moral dilemma, but at first this understanding is very concrete. They view right action as flowing from self-interest and understand reciprocity as equal exchange of favors: "You do this for me and I'll do that for you."

> *Prostealing:* "[I]f Heinz decides to risk jail to save his wife, it's his life he's risking; he can do what he wants with it. And the same goes for the druggist; it's up to him to decide what he wants to do." (Rest, 1979, p. 26)

> *Antistealing:* "[Heinz] is running more risk than it's worth [to save a wife who is near death]." (Rest, 1979, p. 27)

The Conventional Level. At the **conventional level,** individuals continue to regard conformity to social rules as important, but not for reasons of self-interest. They believe that actively maintaining the current social system ensures positive relationships and societal order.

Stage 3: The "good boy–good girl" orientation, or the morality of interpersonal cooperation. The desire to obey rules because they promote social harmony first appears in the context of close personal ties. Stage 3 individuals want to main-

tain the affection and approval of friends and relatives by being a "good person"—trustworthy, loyal, respectful, helpful, and nice. The capacity to view a two-person relationship from the vantage point of an impartial outside observer supports this new approach to morality. At this stage, the individual understands *ideal reciprocity.*

> *Prostealing:* "No one will think you're bad if you steal the drug, but your family will think you're an inhuman husband if you don't. If you let your wife die, you'll never be able to look anyone in the face again." (Kohlberg, 1969, p. 381)

> *Antistealing:* "It isn't just the druggist who will think you're a criminal, everyone else will too. . . . [Y]ou'll feel bad thinking how you've brought dishonor on your family and yourself." (Kohlberg, 1969, p. 381)

Stage 4: The social-order-maintaining orientation. At this stage, the individual takes into account a larger perspective—that of societal laws. Moral choices no longer depend on close ties to others. Instead, rules must be enforced in the same evenhanded fashion for everyone, and each member of society has a personal duty to uphold them. The Stage 4 individual believes that laws should never be disobeyed because they are vital for ensuring societal order and cooperative relations between individuals.

> *Prostealing:* "Heinz has a duty to protect his wife's life; it's a vow he took in marriage. But it's wrong to steal, so he would have to take the drug with the idea of paying the druggist for it and accepting the penalty for breaking the law later."

> *Antistealing:* "Even if his wife is dying, it's still [Heinz's] duty as a citizen to obey the law. . . . If everyone starts breaking the law in a jam, there'd be no civilization, just crime and violence." (Rest, 1979, p. 30)

The Postconventional or Principled Level. Individuals at the **postconventional level** move beyond unquestioning support for their own society's rules and laws. They define morality in terms of abstract principles and values that apply to all situations and societies.

Stage 5: The social contract orientation. At Stage 5, individuals regard laws and rules as flexible instruments for furthering human purposes. They can imagine alternatives to their own social order, and they emphasize fair procedures for interpreting and changing the law. When laws are consistent with individual rights and the interests of the majority, each person follows them because of a *social contract orientation*—free and willing participation in the system because it brings about more good for people than if it did not exist.

> *Prostealing:* "Although there is a law against stealing, the law wasn't meant to violate a person's right to life. . . . If Heinz is prosecuted for stealing, the law needs to be reinterpreted to take into account situations in which it goes against people's natural right to keep on living."

Stage 6: The universal ethical principle orientation. At this highest stage, right action is defined by self-chosen ethical principles of conscience that are valid for all people, regardless of law and social agreement. These values are abstract, not concrete moral rules like the Ten Commandments. Stage 6 individuals typically mention such principles as equal consideration of the claims of all human beings and respect for the worth and dignity of each person.

Prostealing: "It doesn't make sense to put respect for property above respect for life itself. [People] could live together without private property at all. Respect for human life and personality is absolute and accordingly [people] have a mutual duty to save one another from dying." (Rest, 1979, p. 37)

■ **Research on Kohlberg's Stage Sequence.** Kohlberg's original research and other longitudinal studies provide the most convincing evidence for his stage sequence. With few exceptions, individuals move through the first four stages in the predicted order (Colby et al., 1983; Dawson, 2002; Walker & Taylor, 1991b). Moral development is slow and gradual: Reasoning at Stages 1 and 2 decreases in early adolescence, while Stage 3 increases through midadolescence and then declines. Stage 4 reasoning rises over the teenage years until, by early adulthood, it is the typical response.

Few people move beyond Stage 4. In fact, postconventional morality is so rare that no clear evidence exists that Kohlberg's Stage 6 actually follows Stage 5. This poses a key challenge to Kohlberg's theory: If people must reach Stages 5 and 6 to be considered truly morally mature, few individuals anywhere would measure up! According to one reexamination of Kohlberg's stages, moral maturity can be found in a revised understanding of Stages 3 and 4 (Gibbs, 1991, 2003). These stages are not "conventional"—based on social conformity—as Kohlberg assumed. Rather, they require profound moral constructions—an understanding of ideal reciprocity as the basis for relationships (Stage 3) and for widely accepted moral standards, set forth in rules and laws (Stage 4). In this view, "postconventional" morality is a highly reflective endeavor limited to a handful of people who have attained advanced education, usually in philosophy.

In reading the Heinz dilemma, you probably came up with your own solution. Now, think of an actual moral dilemma you faced recently. How did you solve it? Did your reasoning fall at the same stage as your thinking about Heinz? Real-life conflicts often elicit moral reasoning below a person's actual capacity because they involve practical considerations and mix cognition with intense emotion. Although adolescents and adults mention reasoning as their most frequent strategy for resolving these dilemmas, they also refer to other strategies—talking through issues with others, relying on intuition, and calling on notions of religion and spirituality. Especially striking are expressions of anguish in working through everyday dilemmas, a motivational and emotional side of moral judgment not tapped by hypothetical situations. As one person observed, "It's a lot easier to be moral when you have nothing to lose" (Walker, 2004; Walker et al., 1995, p. 381).

The influence of situational factors on moral judgments indicates that like Piaget's cognitive stages, Kohlberg's moral stages are loosely organized. Rather than developing in a neat, stepwise fashion, people draw on a range of moral responses that vary with context. With age, this range shifts upward as less mature moral reasoning is gradually replaced by more advanced moral thought.

Are There Sex Differences in Moral Reasoning?

As we have seen, real-life moral dilemmas often highlight the role of emotion in moral judgment. In the discussion at the beginning of this section, notice how Sabrina's moral argument focuses on caring and commitment to others. Carol Gilligan (1982) is the best-known of those who have argued that Kohlberg's theory—originally formulated on the basis of interviews with males—does not adequately represent the morality of girls and women. Gilligan believes that feminine morality emphasizes an "ethic of care" that Kohlberg's system devalues. For example, Sabrina's reasoning falls at Stage 3 because it is based on mutual trust and affection, whereas Louis's is at Stage 4 because he emphasizes following the law. According to Gilligan, a concern for others is a *different* but no less valid basis for moral judgment than a focus on impersonal rights.

Many studies have tested Gilligan's claim that Kohlberg's approach underestimates the moral maturity of females. Most do not support it (Turiel, 1998). On hypothetical dilemmas as well as everyday moral problems, adolescent and adult females display reasoning at the same or a higher stage as their male agemates. Also, themes of justice and caring appear in the responses of both sexes, and when girls do raise interpersonal

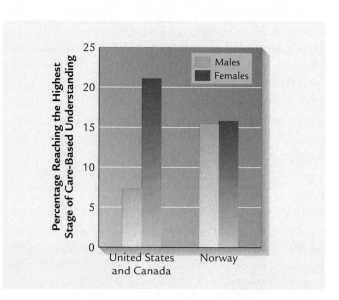

■ **FIGURE 12.1 Complex reasoning about care issues among U.S. and Canadian versus Norwegian males and females.** In this study of 17- to 26-year-olds, North American females scored much higher than males in complex care-based understanding. In contrast, Norwegian males and females displayed equally advanced care-based understanding. (Adapted from Skoe, 1998.)

concerns, they are not downgraded in Kohlberg's system (Jadack et al., 1995; Kahn, 1992; Walker, 1995). These findings suggest that although Kohlberg emphasized justice rather than caring as the highest moral ideal, his theory taps both sets of values.

Still, Gilligan makes a powerful claim that research on moral development has been limited by too much attention to rights and justice (a "masculine" ideal) and too little to care and responsiveness (a "feminine" ideal). Some evidence shows that although the morality of males and females taps both orientations, females do tend to emphasize care, whereas males either stress justice or focus equally on justice and care (Jaffee & Hyde, 2000; Wark & Krebs, 1996; Weisz & Black, 2002).

This difference in emphasis, which appears more often in real-life dilemmas than in hypothetical ones, may reflect women's greater involvement in daily activities involving care and concern for others. In one study, U.S. and Canadian 17- to 26-year-old females exceeded their male counterparts in complex reasoning about care issues. But as Figure 12.1 shows, Norwegian males were just as advanced as Norwegian females in care-based understanding (Skoe, 1998). Perhaps Norwegian culture, which explicitly endorses gender equality, induces boys and men to think deeply about interpersonal obligations.

Coordinating Moral, Social-Conventional, and Personal Concerns

Adolescents' moral advances are also evident in their reasoning about situations that raise competing moral, social-conventional, and personal issues. In diverse Western and non-Western cultures, teenagers express great concern with matters of personal choice—a reflection of their quest for identity and strengthening independence (Neff & Helwig, 2002; Nucci, 2002). More firmly than at younger ages, they assert that dress, hairstyle, diary records, and friendships are solely the province of the individual and not subject to control by authority figures (such as parents) (Nucci, 2001). As adolescents enlarge the range of issues they regard as personal, they think more intently about conflicts between personal choice and community obligation—for example, whether, and under what conditions, it is permissible for laws to restrict speech, religion, marriage, childbearing, group membership, and other individual rights (Helwig, 1995; Wainryb, 1997).

Teenagers display more subtle thinking than school-age children on such issues. For example, when asked if it is OK to exclude a child from a peer group on the basis of race or gender, fourth graders usually say exclusion is unfair in all circumstances. But by tenth grade, young people, though increasingly mindful of fairness, indicate that under certain conditions—within friendship more often than peer groups, and on the basis of gender more often than race—exclusion is OK (Killen et al., 2002). In explaining, they mention the right to personal choice as well as concerns about effective group functioning. Justifying why she thought members of an all-boys music club need not let a girl join, one tenth grader said, "It's not nice . . . but it's their club." Another commented, "[The girl and the boys] probably wouldn't relate on very many things" (p. 62).

These students participate in a program in which they write legislation and meet for a week to debate their proposed laws in the senate chambers of their state capitol building. Their intensity reflects their growing interest in complex moral issues that balance personal choice against community obligation.

As adolescents integrate personal rights with ideal reciprocity, they demand that the protections they want for themselves extend to others. Similarly, they are increasingly mindful of the overlap between moral imperatives and social conventions. Eventually they realize that violating strongly held conventions—showing up at a wedding in a T-shirt, talking out of turn at a student council meeting—can harm others, either by inducing distress or by undermining fair treatment. Over time, as their grasp of fairness deepens, young people realize that social conventions are not just dictates of authority figures but vital for maintaining a just and peaceful society (Nucci, 2001). Notice how this understanding is central to Kohlberg's Stage 4, which is typically attained as adolescence draws to a close.

Influences on Moral Reasoning

Many factors influence moral understanding, including child-rearing practices, schooling, peer interaction, and culture. Growing evidence suggests that, as Kohlberg believed, these experiences work by presenting young people with cognitive challenges, which stimulate them to think about moral problems in more complex ways.

■ **Parenting Practices.** As in childhood, moral understanding in adolescence is fostered by warm parenting and discussion of moral concerns. Teenagers whose parents listen sensitively, ask clarifying questions, and present higher-level reasoning gain most in moral development (Pratt, Skoe, & Arnold, 2004; Wyatt & Carlo, 2002). In contrast, young people whose parents lecture, use threats, or make sarcastic remarks show little or no change (Walker & Taylor, 1991a).

■ **Schooling.** Years of schooling is a powerful predictor of movement to Kohlberg's Stage 4 or higher (Dawson et al., 2003; Speicher, 1994). Attending college introduces young people to social issues that range beyond personal relationships to entire political or cultural groups. Consistent with this idea, college students who report more academic perspective-taking opportunities (for example, classes that emphasize open discussion of opinions) and who indicate that they have become more aware of social diversity tend to be advanced in moral reasoning (Mason & Gibbs, 1993a, 1993b).

■ **Peer Interaction.** Research supports Piaget's belief that interaction among peers, who confront one another with differing viewpoints, promotes moral understanding. When children and adolescents negotiate and compromise with agemates, they realize that social life can be based on cooperation between equals rather than authority relations (Killen & Nucci, 1995). Young people who report more close friendships and who more often participate in conversations with their friends are advanced in moral reasoning (Schonert-Reichl, 1999). The mutuality and intimacy of friendship, which fosters decisions based on consensual agreement, may be particularly important for moral development.

Peer discussions and role playing of moral problems have provided the basis for interventions aimed at improving high school and college students' moral understanding. For these discussions to be effective, young people must be highly engaged, confronting, critiquing, and attempting to clarify one another's viewpoints, as Sabrina and Louis did when they argued over Mrs. Perry's plight (Berkowitz & Gibbs, 1983). And because moral development occurs gradually, many peer interaction sessions over weeks or months typically are needed to produce moral change.

■ **Culture.** Individuals in industrialized nations move through Kohlberg's stages more quickly and advance to a higher level than individuals in village societies, who rarely move beyond Stage 3. One explanation of these cultural differences is that in village societies, moral cooperation is based on direct relations between people and does not allow for the development of advanced moral understanding (Stages 4 to 6), which depends on appreciating the role of larger social structures, such as laws and government institutions (Gibbs, Basinger, & Grime, 2005; Snarey, 1995).

A second possible reason for cultural variation is that responses to moral dilemmas in collectivist cultures (including village societies) are often more other-directed than in Western Europe and North America (Miller, 1997). Consistent with this explanation, in both village and industrialized cultures that highly value interdependency, statements portraying the individual as vitally connected to the social group are common. In one study, Japanese male and female adolescents, who almost always integrated caring and justice-based reasoning, placed greater weight on caring, which they regarded as a communal responsibility (Shimizu, 2001). Similarly, in research conducted in India, even highly educated people (expected to have attained Kohlberg's Stages 4 and 5) less often held individuals accountable for moral transgressions. They viewed solutions to moral dilemmas as the responsibility of the entire society, not of a single person (Miller & Bersoff, 1995).

Growing up in an isolated village in India, these adolescents view moral cooperation as based on direct relations between people. Their moral reasoning is likely to emphasize a close connection between individual and group responsibility.

These findings raise the question of whether Kohlberg's highest level represents not a universal way of thinking but a culturally specific one, limited to Western societies that emphasize individualism and an appeal to an inner, private conscience. At the same time, a common justice-based morality is clearly evident in the dilemma responses of people from vastly different cultures.

Moral Reasoning and Behavior

According to Kohlberg, moral thought and action should come together at the higher levels of moral understanding. Mature moral thinkers realize that behaving in line with their beliefs is vital for creating and maintaining a just social world (Gibbs, 2003). Consistent with this idea, higher-stage adolescents more often act prosocially by helping, sharing, and defending victims of injustice (Carlo et al., 1996; Comunian & Gielen, 2000). They also less often engage in cheating, aggression, and other antisocial behaviors (Gregg, Gibbs, & Fuller, 1994; Taylor & Walker, 1997).

Yet the connection between advanced moral reasoning and action is only modest. As we have seen, moral behavior is influenced by many factors besides cognition, including the emotions of empathy, sympathy, and guilt; individual differences in temperament; and a long history of experiences that affect moral decision making. **Moral self-relevance**—the degree to which morality is central to self-concept—also affects moral behavior (Walker, 2004). In a study of low-SES African-American and Hispanic teenagers, those who emphasized moral traits and goals in their self-descriptions displayed exceptional levels of community service (Hart & Fegley, 1995). But these highly prosocial young people did not differ from their agemates in moral reasoning.

Research has yet to discover the origins of a sense of moral self-relevance. Perhaps close relationships with parents, teachers, and friends play vital roles by modeling prosocial behavior and fostering emotional processes of empathy and guilt, which combine with moral cognition to powerfully motivate moral action (Blasi, 1995). Another conjecture is that *just educational environments*—in which teachers guide students in democratic decision making and rule setting, resolving disputes civilly, and taking responsibility for others' welfare—are influential (Atkins, Hart, & Donnelly, 2004). Schools may also foster students' moral self-relevance by expanding opportunities for civic engagement. As the Social Issues box on page 412 reveals, community volunteering can help students see the connection between their personal interests and the public interest—an insight that may enhance all aspects of morality.

Religious Involvement and Moral Development

Recall that in resolving real-life moral dilemmas, many people voice notions of religion and spirituality. Religion is especially important in North American family life. In recent national polls, nearly two-thirds of Americans and about one-half of Canadians reported being religious, compared with one-third of people in Great Britain and Italy and even fewer elsewhere in Europe (Adams, 2003; Jones, 2003). Individuals who regularly attend religious services include many parents with children. But as adolescents search for a personally meaningful identity, formal religious involvement declines—for U.S. youths, from 55 percent at ages 13 to 15 to 40 percent at ages 17 to 18 (Donahue & Benson, 1995; Kerestes & Youniss, 2003).

Nevertheless, teenagers who remain part of a religious community are advantaged in moral values and behavior. Compared with nonaffiliated youths, they are more involved in community service activities aimed at helping the less fortu-

nate (Kerestes, Youniss, & Metz, 2004). And religious involvement promotes responsible academic and social behavior and discourages misconduct (Dowling et al., 2004). It is associated with lower levels of drug and alcohol use, early sexual activity, and delinquency (Regnerus, Smith, & Fritsch, 2003).

A variety of factors probably contribute to these favorable outcomes. In a study of inner-city high school students, religiously involved young people were more likely to report trusting relationships with parents, other adults, and friends who hold similar worldviews. The more activities they shared with this network, the higher they scored in empathy and prosocial behavior (King & Furrow, 2004). Furthermore, religious education and youth activities directly teach concern for others and provide opportunities for moral discussions and civic engagement. And adolescents who feel connected to a higher being may develop certain inner strengths, including moral self-relevance, that help translate their thinking into action (Furrow, King, & White, 2004).

Because most teenagers, regardless of formal affiliation, identify with a religious denomination and say they believe in a higher being, religious institutions may be uniquely suited to foster moral and prosocial commitments. For inner-city youths with few alternative sources of social support, outreach by religious institutions can lead to life-altering involvement (Jang & Johnson, 2001). An exception is seen in religious cults, where rigid indoctrination into the group's beliefs, suppression of individuality, and estrangement from society all work against moral maturity.

Gender Typing

As Sabrina entered adolescence, she began to place more emphasis on excelling in literature, art, and music—traditionally feminine subjects. When with peers, she worried about walking, talking, eating, dressing, laughing, and competing in ways consistent with gender roles.

Early adolescence is a period of **gender intensification**—increased gender stereotyping of attitudes and behavior and movement toward a more traditional gender identity (Basow & Rubin, 1999; Galambos, Almeida, & Petersen, 1990). Gender intensification occurs in both sexes but is stronger for girls, who feel less free to experiment with "other-gender" activities and behavior than they did in middle childhood (Huston & Alvarez, 1990).

What accounts for gender intensification? Biological, social, and cognitive factors are involved. As puberty magnifies sex differences in appearance, teenagers spend more time thinking about themselves in gender-linked ways. Pubertal changes also prompt gender-typed pressures from others. Parents (especially those with traditional gender-role beliefs) may encourage "gender-appropriate" activities and behavior more than they did in middle childhood (Crouter, Manke, & McHale, 1995). When adolescents start to date, they often become more gender-typed as a way of increasing their attractiveness (Maccoby, 1998). Finally, cognitive changes—in particular, greater

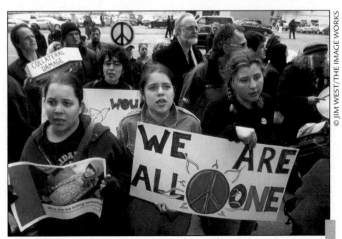

These teenagers gather with other religious groups to protest war and voice their support of world peace. Involvement in a religious community promotes teens' moral values and behavior, encouraging responsible academic work and discouraging early sexual activity and delinquency.

Social Issues

Development of Civic Responsibility

On Thanksgiving day, Jules, Louis, and Sabrina joined their parents at a soup kitchen to serve a holiday dinner to poverty-stricken people. Throughout the year, Sabrina volunteered on Saturday mornings at a nursing home, where she conversed with bedridden elders. In the months before a congressional election, all three young people attended special youth meetings with candidates and raised concerns. "What's your view on preserving our environment?" Louis asked. "How would you prevent the proposed tax cut from mostly benefiting the rich?" Jules chimed in. At school, Louis and his girlfriend Cassie formed an organization devoted to promoting ethnic and racial tolerance.

Already, these young people have a strong sense of civic responsibility—a complex capacity that combines cognition, emotion, and behavior. Civic responsibility involves *knowledge* of political issues and the means through which citizens can resolve differing views fairly; *feelings* of attachment to the community, of wanting to make a difference in its welfare; and *skills* for achieving civic

These adolescents collect food for the needy outside a grocery store on "Make a Difference Day." Involvement in community service grows out of a sense of civic responsibility, which is supported by family, school, and community experiences.

goals, such as how to contact and question public officials and conduct meetings so all participants have a voice (Flanagan & Faison, 2001).

When young people engage in community service that exposes them to people in need or to public issues, they are especially likely to express a commitment to future service and to working toward important societal goals, such as eradicating poverty or ethnic prejudice (Metz, McLellan, & Youniss, 2003). Family, school, and community experiences contribute to adolescents' civic responsibility.

Family Influences. Teenagers whose parents encourage their children to form opinions about controversial issues are more knowledgeable and interested in civic issues and better able to see them from more than one perspective (Santoloupo & Pratt, 1994). Also, adolescents who report that their parents engage in community service and stress compassion for the less fortunate tend to hold socially responsible values. When asked what causes such social ills as unemployment, poverty, and homelessness, these teenagers more often mention situational and societal factors (lack of education, government policies, or the state of the economy) than individual factors (low intelligence or personal problems). Youths who endorse situational and societal causes, in turn, have more altruistic life goals, such as working to eradicate poverty or to preserve the earth for future generations (Flanagan & Tucker, 1999).

School and Community Influences. A democratic climate at school—one in which teachers hold high academic and moral standards for all students, promote discussion of controversial issues, and insist that students listen to and respect one another—fosters a sense of civic responsibility. Teenagers who say their teachers engage in these practices are more aware of political issues, better able to analyze them critically, and more committed to social causes (Flanagan & Faison, 2001).

Participation in extracurricular activities at school and in youth organizations is also associated with civic commitment that persists into adulthood (see Chapter 11, page 394). Two aspects of these involvements seem to account for their lasting impact. First, they introduce adolescents to the vision and skills required for mature civic engagement. Within student government, clubs, teams, and other groups, young people see how their actions affect the wider school and community. They realize that collectively they can achieve results greater than any one person can achieve alone. And they learn to work together, balancing strong convictions with compromise (Atkins, Hart, & Donnelly, 2004; Youniss, McLellan, & Yates, 1997). Second, while producing a weekly newspaper, participating in a dramatic production, or implementing a service project, young people explore political and moral ideals. Often they redefine themselves as having a responsibility to combat others' misfortunes (Wheeler, 2002).

The power of family, school, and community to promote civic responsibility may lie in discussions, educational practices, and activities that jointly foster moral thought, emotion, and behavior. In a comparison of nationally representative samples of 14-year-olds in 28 nations, North American young people excelled at community service, with 50 percent of students reporting membership in organizations devoted to volunteering (Torney-Purta, 2002).

But low-SES, inner-city youths—although they express high interest in contributing to society—score substantially lower than higher-SES youths in civic knowledge and participation (Hart & Atkins, 2002). A broad societal commitment to fostering civic character must pay special attention to supportive school and community experiences for these young people. The Canadian province of Ontario requires 40 hours of community service for high school graduation. Schools arrange these opportunities, helping students select options that match their interests and skills.

© NANCY RICHMOND/THE IMAGE WORKS

Early adolescence is a period of gender intensification. Puberty magnifies differences in appearance, causing teenagers to think more about themselves in gender-linked ways and to participate increasingly in gender-linked activities.

concern with what others think—make young teenagers more responsive to gender-role expectations.

Gender intensification declines by middle to late adolescence, but not all young people move beyond it to the same degree. Teenagers who are encouraged to explore non-gender-typed options and to question the value of gender stereotypes for themselves and society are more likely to build an androgynous gender identity (see Chapter 8, page 227). Overall, androgynous adolescents, especially girls, tend to be psychologically healthier—more self-confident, more willing to speak their own mind, better-liked by peers, and identity-achieved (Dusek, 1987; Harter, 1998).

Ask Yourself

Review

How does an understanding of ideal reciprocity contribute to moral development? Why might Kohlberg's Stages 3 and 4 be morally mature constructions?

Apply

Tam grew up in a small village culture, Lydia in a large industrial city. At age 15, Tam reasons at Kohlberg's Stage 3, Lydia at Stage 4. What factors might account for the difference?

Connect

What experiences that promote mature moral reasoning are also likely to foster identity development?

Reflect

In early adolescence, did you and your friends display gender intensification? Cite examples. When did this concern with gender appropriateness decline?

www.ablongman.com/berk

The Family

Franca and Antonio remember their son Louis's freshman year of high school as a difficult time. Because of a demanding project at work, Franca was away from home many evenings and weekends. In her absence, Antonio took over, but when business picked up at his hardware store, he, too, had less time for the family. That year, Louis and two friends used their computer know-how to crack the code of a long-distance telephone service and, from the family basement, made calls around the country. Louis's grades fell, and he often left the house without saying where he was going. Franca and Antonio began to feel uncomfortable about the long hours Louis was spending in the basement and their lack of contact with him. Finally, when the telephone company traced the illegal calls to their phone number, they knew they had cause for concern.

Development at adolescence involves striving for **autonomy**—a sense of oneself as a separate, self-governing individual. Teenagers strive to rely more on themselves and less on parents for decision making (Steinberg & Silverberg, 1986). Nevertheless, parent–child relationships remain vital for helping adolescents become autonomous, responsible individuals.

Parent–Child Relationships

Adolescent autonomy receives support from a variety of changes within the adolescent. In Chapter 11, we saw that puberty triggers psychological distancing from parents. In addition, as young people look more mature, parents give them more independence and responsibility. Cognitive development also paves the way toward autonomy: Gradually, adolescents solve problems and make decisions more effectively. And an improved ability to reason about social relationships leads teenagers to *deidealize* their parents, viewing them as "just people." Consequently, they no longer bend as easily to parental authority as they did at earlier ages.

Yet as Franca and Antonio's episode with Louis reveals, teenagers still need guidance and, at times, protection from dangerous situations. In diverse ethnic groups, warm, supportive parent–adolescent ties that permit young people to explore ideas and social roles foster autonomy, predicting high self-reliance, work orientation, academic competence, and favorable self-esteem (Slicker & Thornberry, 2002; Vazsonyi, Hibbert, & Snider, 2003). Conversely, parents who are coercive or psychologically controlling interfere with the development of autonomy. Research in Africa, Asia, Europe, the Middle East, and North and South America shows that these tactics are consistently linked to low self-esteem, depression, and antisocial behavior among teenagers—outcomes that persist into early adulthood (Aquilino & Supple, 2001; Barber, Stolz, & Olsen, 2005).

In Chapter 2, we described the family as a *system* that must adapt to changes in its members. The rapid physical and psychological changes of adolescence trigger conflicting expectations in parent–child relationships—a major reason that many parents find rearing teenagers to be stressful.

Earlier we noted that interest in making choices about personal matters strengthens in adolescence. Yet parents and teenagers—especially young teenagers—differ sharply on the appropriate age for granting certain privileges, such as control over clothing, school courses, and going out with friends (Smetana, 2002). Consistent parental monitoring of the young person's daily activities, through a cooperative relationship in which the adolescent willingly discloses information, predicts favorable adjustment. Besides preventing delinquency, it is linked to other positive outcomes—a reduction in sexual activity, improved school performance, and positive psychological well-being (Crouter & Head, 2002; Jacobson & Crockett, 2000; Stattin & Kerr, 2000).

Parents' own development can also lead to friction with teenagers. While their children face a boundless future and a wide array of choices, middle-aged parents must accept the fact that their own possibilities are narrowing (Holmbeck, 1996). Often they can't understand why the adolescent wants to skip family activities to be with peers. And teenagers fail to appreciate that parents want the family to spend as much time together as possible because an important stage in their adult life—child rearing—will soon end.

Throughout adolescence, the quality of the parent–child relationship is the single most consistent predictor of mental health (Steinberg & Silk, 2002). In well-functioning families, teenagers remain attached to parents and seek their advice, but they do so in a context of greater freedom (Steinberg, 2001).

The mild conflict that arises facilitates adolescent identity and autonomy by helping family members express and tolerate disagreement. Conflicts also inform parents of teenagers' changing needs and expectations, signaling that adjustments in the parent–child relationship are necessary.

By middle to late adolescence, most parents and children achieve this mature, mutual relationship, and harmonious interaction is on the rise. The reduced time that Western teenagers spend with parents—for American youths, a drop from 33 percent of waking hours in fifth grade to 14 percent in twelfth grade—has little to do with conflict (Larson et al., 1996). Rather, it results from the large amount of unstructured time available to teenagers in North America and Western Europe—on average, nearly half their waking hours (Larson, 2001). Young people tend to fill these hours with activities that take them away from home—part-time jobs, leisure and volunteer pursuits, and time with friends.

But this drop in family time is not universal. In one study, urban low- and middle-SES African-American youths showed no decline in hours spent at home with family—a pattern typical in cultures with collectivist values (Larson et al., 2001). Furthermore, teenagers living in risky neighborhoods tend to have more trusting relationships with parents and adjust more favorably when parents maintain tighter control and pressure them not to engage in worrisome behaviors (McElhaney & Allen, 2001). In harsh surroundings, young people seem to interpret more measured granting of autonomy as a sign of parental caring.

Family Circumstances

As Franca and Antonio's experience with Louis reminds us, adult life stresses can interfere with warm, involved parenting and, in turn, with children's adjustment at any phase of development. But maternal employment or a dual-earner family does not by itself reduce parental time with teenagers, nor is it harmful to adolescent development (Richards & Duckett, 1994). To the contrary, parents who are financially secure, not overloaded with job pressures, and content with their marriages usually find it easier to grant teenagers appropriate autonomy and experience less conflict with them (Cowan & Cowan, 2002; Crouter & Bumpass, 2001). When Franca and Antonio's work stress eased and they recognized Louis's need for more involvement and guidance, his problems subsided.

Less than 10 percent of families with adolescents have seriously troubled relationships—chronic, escalating levels of conflict and repeated arguments over serious issues. Of these, most have difficulties that began in childhood (Collins & Laursen, 2004). Table 12.2 summarizes family conditions considered in earlier chapters that pose challenges for adolescents. Teenagers who develop well despite family stresses continue to benefit from factors that fostered resilience in earlier years: an appealing, easygoing disposition; a parent who combines warmth with high expectations; and (especially if parental supports are lacking) bonds with prosocial adults outside the family who care deeply about the adolescent's well-being (Masten, 2001).

© STEVE SKJOLD/PHOTOEDIT

A mother congratulates her 15-year-old daughter on winning a track meet event. Consistent parental monitoring of the young person's daily activities, and a cooperative relationship in which the adolescent willingly discloses information, predict favorable adjustment.

Table 12.2	Family Circumstances with Implications for Adolescent Adjustment

Family Circumstance	To Review, Turn to . . .
Type of Family	
Adoptive	Chapter 2, pages 58–59
Divorced single-parent	Chapter 10, pages 346–347
Blended	Chapter 10, pages 348–349
Employed mother and dual-earner	Chapter 10, pages 349–350
Family Conditions	
Child maltreatment	Chapter 8, pages 281–283 Chapter 10, page 351
Economic hardship	Chapter 2, pages 64–65
Adolescent parenthood	Chapter 11, pages 377–379

Siblings

Like parent–child relationships, sibling interactions adapt to change at adolescence. As younger siblings mature and become more self-sufficient, they accept less direction from their older brothers and sisters, and sibling influence declines. Also, as teenagers become more involved in friendships and romantic relationships, they invest less time and energy in siblings, who are part of the family from which they are trying to establish autonomy. As a result, sibling relationships often become less intense, in both positive and negative feelings (Hetherington, Henderson, & Reiss, 1999; Stocker & Dunn, 1994).

Despite a drop in companionship, attachment between siblings remains strong for most young people. Brothers and sisters who established a positive bond in early childhood and whose parents continue to be warm and involved are more likely to express affection and caring (Dunn, Slomkowski, & Beardsall, 1994). Also, mild sibling differences in perceived parental affection no longer trigger jealousy but, instead, predict increasing sibling warmth (Feinberg et al., 2003). Perhaps adolescents interpret a unique parental relationship—as long as it is generally accepting—as a gratifying sign of their own individuality.

Peer Relations

As adolescents spend less time with family members, peers become increasingly important. In industrialized nations, young people spend most of each weekday with agemates in school. Teenagers also spend much out-of-class time together, more in some cultures than others. For example, U.S. young people have about 50 hours of free time per week, Europeans about 45 hours, and East Asians about 33 hours (Larson, 2001). A shorter school year and less demanding academic standards, which lead American youths to spend much less time on schoolwork, account for this difference.

In the following sections, we will see that adolescent peer relations can be both positive and negative. At their best, peers serve as critical bridges between the family and adult social roles.

Friendships

Adolescents report their most favorable moods when in the company of friends (Larson & Richards, 1991). The number of "best friends" declines from about four to six in early adolescence to one or two in adulthood (Hartup & Stevens, 1999). At the same time, the nature of the relationship changes.

■ **Characteristics of Adolescent Friendships.** When asked about the meaning of friendship, teenagers stress two characteristics. The first and most important is *intimacy.* Adolescents seek psychological closeness, trust, and mutual understanding from their friends—the reason that self-disclosure (exchanges of private thoughts and feelings) between friends increases steadily over the adolescent years (see Figure 12.2 on page 416). Second, more than younger children, teenagers want their friends to be *loyal*—to stick up for them and not to leave them for somebody else (Buhrmester, 1996; Hartup & Abecassis, 2004).

As frankness and faithfulness increase, teenage friends get to know each other better as personalities. In addition to the many characteristics that school-age friends share (see page 340 in Chapter 10), adolescent friends tend to be alike in identity status, educational aspirations, political beliefs, and willingness to try drugs and engage in lawbreaking acts. Over time, they become more similar in these ways (Akers, Jones, & Coyl, 1998; Berndt & Murphy, 2002). Occasionally, however, teenagers befriend agemates with differing attitudes and values, which permits them to explore new perspectives within the security of a compatible relationship.

During adolescence, cooperation and mutual affirmation between friends rise—changes that reflect greater effort and skill at preserving the relationship and increased sensitivity to a friend's needs and desires (Phillipsen, 1999). Adolescents also are less possessive of their friends than they were in childhood (Parker et al., 2005). Desiring a certain degree of autonomy for themselves, they recognize that friends need this, too.

■ **Sex Differences in Friendships.** Ask several adolescents to describe their close friendships. You are likely to find a consistent sex difference: Emotional closeness is more common between girls (Markovits, Benenson, & Dolensky, 2001). Girls frequently get together to "just talk," and their interactions contain more *self-disclosure* and supportive statements. In contrast, boys more often gather for an activity—usually sports and competitive games. Boys' discussions usually focus on accomplishments

■ **FIGURE 12.2 Age changes in reported self-disclosure to parents and peers, based on data from several studies.** Self-disclosure to friends increases steadily during adolescence, reflecting intimacy as a major basis of friendship. Self-disclosure to romantic partners also rises. However, not until the college years does it surpass intimacy with friends. Self-disclosure to parents declines in early adolescence, a time of mild parent–child conflict. As family relationships readjust to the young person's increasing autonomy, self-disclosure to parents rises. (From D. Buhrmester, 1996, "Need Fulfillment, Interpersonal Competence, and the Developmental Contexts of Early Adolescent Friendship," in W. M. Bukowski, A. F. Newcomb, & W. W. Hartup, Eds., *The Company They Keep: Friendship in Childhood and Adolescence,* New York: Cambridge University Press, p. 168. Reprinted by permission.)

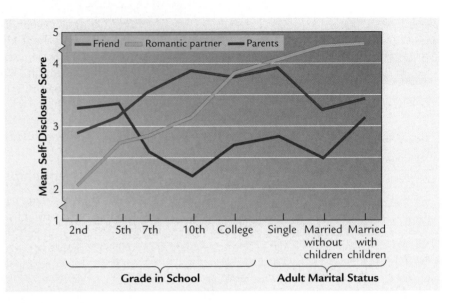

and involve more competition and conflict (Brendgen et al., 2001; Buhrmester, 1998).

In line with gender-role expectations, girls' friendships typically focus on communal concerns, boys' on achievement and status. Boys do form close friendship ties, but the quality of their friendships is more variable than girls'. The intimacy of boys' friendships is related to gender identity: Androgynous boys are just as likely as girls to form intimate same-sex ties, whereas boys with a "masculine" identity are less likely to do so (Jones & Dembo, 1989).

Closeness in friendship, though usually beneficial, can have costs. When focusing on deeper thoughts and feelings, adolescent friends sometimes *coruminate,* or repeatedly mull over problems and negative feelings—an activity that sparks anxiety and depression (Rose, 2002). Also, when conflicts arise between intimate friends, more potential exists for one party to harm the other through relational aggression—for example, by divulging sensitive personal information to outsiders. For this reason, girls' closest same-sex friendships tend to be of shorter duration than boys' (Benenson & Christakos, 2003).

■ **Friendships on the Internet.** Teenagers frequently use the Internet to communicate, and instant messaging—their preferred means of online interaction—seems to support friendship closeness. In one study, as amount of instant messaging increased, so did young people's perceptions of intimacy in the relationship (Hu et al., 2004).

Besides communicating with friends they know, adolescents use the Internet to meet new people. As they strive for autonomy and identity, building relationships in cyberspace is appealing because it opens up vast alternatives beyond their families, schools, and communities. But although online ties give some teens sources of support, they also pose dangers. In a survey of a nationally representative sample of U.S. 10- to 17-year-olds, 14 percent reported online close friendships or romances (Wolak, Mitchell, & Finkelhor, 2003). Although some adolescents who formed these bonds were well-adjusted, many were youths who reported high levels of conflict with parents, peer victimization, depression, and delinquency, and who spent extensive time on the Internet (see Figure 12.3). They also more often had been asked by online friends for face-to-face meetings and had attended those meetings—without telling their parents.

The Internet's value for enabling convenient and satisfying communication among teenage friends must be weighed against its potential for facilitating harmful social experiences. Parents are wise to point out the risks of Internet communication (including harassment and exploitation) and to insist that teenagers follow Internet safety rules (see *www.safeteens.com*).

© ROBERT HARBISON

During adolescence, intimacy and loyalty become defining features of friendship. Compared with boys, girls more often get together to "just talk," and they rate their friendships as higher in self-disclosure and emotional support.

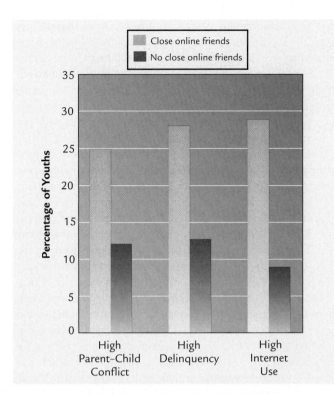

FIGURE 12.3 Association of close online friendships with parent–child conflict, delinquency, and high Internet use. In this survey of a nationally representative sample of 1,500 U.S. Internet-using 10- to 17-year-olds, those who reported that they had formed close online friendships or romances were more likely to be troubled youths who spent much time on the Internet. (Adapted from Wolak, Mitchell, & Finkelhor, 2003.)

■ **Friendships and Adjustment.** As long as adolescent friendships are not characterized by jealousy, relational aggression, or attraction to antisocial behavior, they are related to many aspects of psychological health and competence into early adulthood (Bagwell et al., 2001; Bukowski, 2001). The reasons are several:

🍃 *Close friendships provide opportunities to explore the self and develop a deep understanding of another.* Through open, honest communication, friends become sensitive to each other's strengths and weaknesses, needs and desires, a process that supports the development of self-concept, perspective taking, and identity.

🍃 *Close friendships provide a foundation for future intimate relationships.* Recall from Figure 12.2 that self-disclosure to friends precedes disclosure to romantic partners. Sexuality and romance are common topics of discussion between teenage friends—conversations that, along with the intimacy of friendship itself, may help adolescents establish and work out problems in romantic partnerships (Connolly & Goldberg, 1999).

🍃 *Close friendships help young people deal with the stresses of adolescence.* Because supportive, prosocial friendships enhance sensitivity to and concern for another, they pro-

mote empathy, sympathy, and prosocial behavior. As a result, friendships contribute to involvement in constructive youth activities, avoidance of antisocial acts, and psychological well-being (Lansford et al., 2003; Wentzel, Barry, & Caldwell, 2004).

🍃 *Close friendships can improve attitudes toward and involvement in school.* When teenagers enjoy interacting with friends at school, they may begin to view all aspects of school life more positively (Berndt & Murphy, 2002).

Cliques and Crowds

In early adolescence, *peer groups* become increasingly common and tightly knit (see Chapter 10). They are organized around **cliques,** groups of about five to seven members who are good friends and, therefore, usually resemble one another in family background, attitudes, and values. At first, cliques are limited to same-sex members. Among girls but not boys, being in a clique predicts academic and social competence. Clique membership is more important to girls, who use it as a context for expressing emotional closeness (Henrich et al., 2000). By midadolescence, mixed-sex cliques are common.

Often several cliques with similar values form a larger, more loosely organized group called a **crowd.** Membership in a crowd—unlike the more intimate clique—is based on reputation and stereotype, granting the adolescent an identity within the larger social structure of the school. Prominent crowds in a typical high school might include "brains" (nonathletes who enjoy academics), "jocks" (who are very involved in sports), "populars" (class leaders who are highly social and involved in activities), "partyers" (who value socializing but care little about schoolwork), "nonconformists" (who like unconventional clothing and music), and "burnouts" (who cut school and get into trouble) (Kinney, 1999; Stone & Brown, 1999).

What influences the assortment of teenagers into cliques and crowds? Crowd affiliations are linked to strengths in adolescents' self-concepts, which reflect their interests and abilities (Prinstein & La Greca, 2002). Family factors are important, too. In a study of 8,000 ninth to twelfth graders, adolescents who described their parents as authoritative were members of "brain," "jock," and "popular" groups that accepted both adult and peer reward systems. In contrast, boys with permissive parents aligned themselves with the "partyers" and "burnouts," suggesting lack of identification with adult reward systems (Durbin et al., 1993).

These findings indicate that many peer-group values are extensions of values acquired at home. Once adolescents join a clique or crowd, it can modify their beliefs and behavior. But the positive impact of having academically and socially skilled peers is greatest for teenagers whose own parents are authoritative. And the negative impact of having antisocial, drug-using friends is strongest for teenagers whose parents use less effective child-rearing styles (Mounts & Steinberg, 1995). In sum, family experiences affect the extent to which adolescents become like their peers over time.

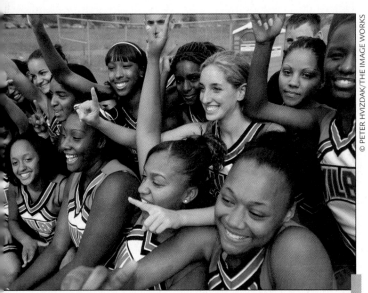

These high school cheerleaders form a crowd. Unlike the more intimate clique, the larger, more loosely organized crowd grants adolescents an identity within the larger social structure of the school.

As interest in dating increases, boys' and girls' cliques come together. Mixed-sex cliques provide boys and girls with models for how to interact and a chance to do so without having to be intimate (Connolly et al., 2004). Gradually, the larger group divides into couples, several of whom spend time going out together. By late adolescence, boys and girls feel comfortable enough about approaching each other directly that the mixed-sex clique disappears (Connolly & Goldberg, 1999).

As adolescents settle on personal values and goals, they no longer feel a need to broadcast who they are through dress, language, and preferred activities, and crowds decline in importance. From tenth to twelfth grade, about half of young people switch crowds, mostly in favorable directions that are associated with rewarding friendships and gains in self-esteem (Strouse, 1999). "Brains" and "normal" crowds grow and deviant crowds lose members as teenagers focus more on their future.

Dating

The hormonal changes of puberty increase sexual interest, but cultural expectations determine when and how dating begins. Asian youths start dating later and have fewer dating partners than young people in Western societies, which tolerate and even encourage romantic involvements between teenagers from middle school on. At age 12 to 14, these relationships last only briefly, but by age 16 they continue, on average, for nearly two years (Carver, Joyner, & Udry, 2003). Young adolescents tend to mention recreation and achieving peer status as reasons for dating. By late adolescence, as young people are ready for greater psychological intimacy, they look for someone who offers companionship, affection, and social support (Furman, 2002; Shulman & Kipnis, 2001).

The achievement of intimacy between dating partners typically lags behind that of friends. Recall from Chapter 6 that according to ethological theory, early attachment bonds lead to an *internal working model,* or set of expectations about attachment figures, that guides later close relationships. Consistent with this idea, in a study of high school seniors, secure models of parental attachment and supportive interactions with parents predicted secure models of friendship. Teenagers' images of friendship security, in turn, were related to the security of their romantic relationships (Furman et al., 2002). These findings suggest that experiences with parents influence the quality of adolescents' friendships. Then teenagers draw on their friendships to transfer what they have learned to the romantic arena.

Perhaps because early adolescent dating relationships are shallow and stereotyped, early dating is related to drug use, delinquency, and poor academic achievement (Brown, Feiring, & Furman, 1999; Zimmer-Gembeck, Siebenbruner, & Collins, 2001). These factors, along with a history of aggression in family and peer relationships, increase the likelihood of dating violence (Arriaga & Foshee, 2004). Young teenagers are better off sticking with group activities, such as parties and dances, before becoming involved with a steady boyfriend or girlfriend.

Homosexual youths face special challenges in initiating and maintaining visible romances. Their first dating relationships seem to be short-lived and to involve little emotional commitment, but for reasons different from those of heterosexuals: They fear peer harassment and rejection. Recall from Chapter 11 that because of intense prejudice, homosexual adolescents often retreat into heterosexual dating. In addition, many have difficulty finding a same-sex partner because their

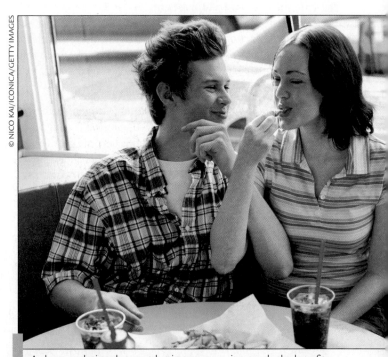

As long as dating does not begin too soon, it extends the benefits of adolescent friendships. Besides being fun, dating promotes sensitivity, empathy, and identity development as teenagers relate to someone whose needs differ from their own.

homosexual peers have not yet come out. Often their first contacts with other sexual minority youths occur in support groups, where they are free to date publicly and can discuss concerns about coming out (Diamond, 2003).

As long as it does not begin too soon, dating provides lessons in cooperation, etiquette, and dealing with people in a wider range of situations. Among older teenagers, close romantic ties promote enhanced sensitivity, empathy, social support, and identity development (Collins, 2003; Furman & Shaffer, 2003). Still, about half of first romances do not survive high school graduation, and those that do become less satisfying (Shaver, Furman, & Buhrmester, 1985). Because young people are still forming their identities, high school couples often find that they have little in common later on.

Peer Conformity

When Franca and Antonio discovered Louis's lawbreaking during his freshman year of high school, they began to worry about the negative side of adolescent peer networks. Although conformity to peer pressure is greater during adolescence than in childhood or early adulthood, it is a complex process, varying with the young person's age, current situation, need for social approval, and culture.

In a study of several hundred American youths, adolescents felt greatest pressure to conform to the most obvious aspects of the peer culture—dress, grooming, and participation in social activities. Peer pressure to engage in proadult behavior, such as cooperating with parents and getting good grades, was also strong (Brown, Lohr, & McClenahan, 1986). Many teenagers said that their friends actively discouraged antisocial acts. In similar research conducted in Singapore, a culture that emphasizes family loyalty, outcomes were similar, except that peer pressure to meet family and school obligations exceeded pressure to join in peer-culture pursuits (Sim & Koh, 2003). As these findings show, peers and parents often act in concert, toward desirable ends!

Perhaps because of greater concern with what their friends think of them, early adolescents are more likely than younger or older individuals to give in to peer pressure (Brown, Clasen, & Eicher, 1986). Yet when parents and peers disagree, even young teenagers do not consistently rebel against the family. Peers exert more influence on teenagers' day-to-day personal choices, such as dress, music, and choice of friends, but parents have more impact on basic life values and educational plans (Steinberg, 2001). And young people who feel competent and worthwhile are less likely to fall in line behind peers.

Finally, authoritative child rearing is related to resistance to peer pressure (Sim, 2000). Teenagers whose parents are supportive and exert appropriate oversight respect their parents and, therefore, usually follow their rules and consider their advice. In contrast, adolescents who experience extremes of parental behavior—either too much or too little control—tend to be highly peer-oriented. They more often rely on friends for advice about their personal lives and future and are more willing to break their parents' rules, ignore their schoolwork, and engage in other problem behaviors.

Problems of Development

Although most young people move through adolescence with little disturbance, we have seen that some encounter major disruptions in development, such as premature parenthood, substance abuse, and school failure. In each instance, biological and psychological changes, families, schools, peers, communities, and culture combine to yield particular outcomes. Serious difficulties rarely occur in isolation but are usually interrelated—as is apparent in three additional problems of the teenage years: depression, suicide, and delinquency.

Depression

Depression—feeling sad, frustrated, and hopeless about life, accompanied by loss of pleasure in most activities and disturbances in sleep, appetite, concentration, and energy—is the most common psychological problem of adolescence. About 15 to 20 percent of teenagers have had one or more major depressive episodes, a rate comparable to that of adults. From 2 to 8 percent are chronically depressed—gloomy and self-critical for many months and sometimes years (Rushton, Forcier, & Schectman, 2002). Serious depression affects only 1 to 2 percent of children, most of whom remain depressed in adolescence. Depressive symptoms increase sharply between ages 13 and 15, when—as Figure 12.4 on page 420 illustrates—sex differences emerge in industrialized nations. Adolescent girls are twice as likely as boys to report persistent depression—a difference sustained throughout the lifespan (Nolen-Hoeksema, 2002). If allowed to continue, depression seriously impairs social, academic, and vocational functioning.

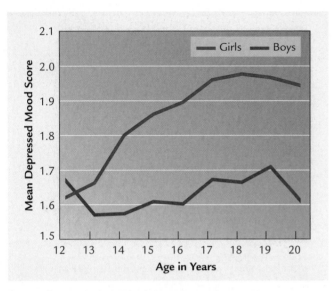

FIGURE 12.4 Change in depressive symptoms from age 12 to age 20 in a cross-sectional study of over 12,000 Norwegian adolescents. Girls showed a more rapid rise in depression around the time of puberty than boys. Similar trends occur in other industrialized nations. (From L. Wichstrøm, 1999, "The Emergence of Gender Difference in Depressed Mood During Adolescence: The Role of Intensified Gender Socialization," *Developmental Psychology, 35,* p. 237. Copyright © 1999 by the American Psychological Association. Reprinted by permission of the publisher and author.)

Unfortunately, because of the popular stereotype of adolescence as a period of storm and stress, teachers and parents tend to minimize the seriousness of adolescents' depressive symptoms. They often misinterpret depression as just a passing phase.

■ **Factors Related to Depression.** The precise combination of biological and environmental factors leading to depression varies from one individual to the next. Kinship studies reveal that heredity plays an important role (Glowinski et al.,

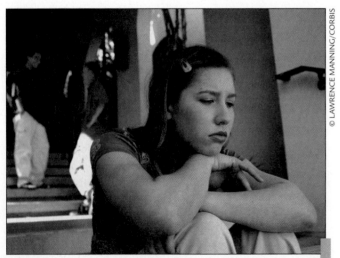

Depression in teenagers should not be dismissed as a temporary side effect of puberty. Adolescent depression can lead to long-term emotional problems, and without treatment, depressed teenagers have a high likelihood of becoming depressed adults.

2003). Genes can induce depression by affecting the balance of neurotransmitters in the brain, the development of brain regions involved in inhibiting negative emotion, or the body's hormonal response to stress (Kaufman & Charney, 2003).

But experience can also activate depression, promoting any of these biological changes. A high incidence of depression and other psychological disorders is seen in parents of depressed children and adolescents. Although a genetic risk may be passed from parent to child, in earlier chapters we saw that depressed or otherwise stressed parents often engage in maladaptive parenting. As a result, their child's emotional self-regulation, attachment, and self-esteem may be impaired, with serious consequences for many cognitive and social skills. Depressed youths usually display a learned-helpless attributional style (see Chapter 10), viewing positive academic and social outcomes as beyond their control (Graber, 2004). In a vulnerable young person, numerous events can spark depression— for example, failing at something important, parental divorce, or the end of a close friendship or romantic partnership.

■ **Sex Differences.** Why are girls more prone to depression than boys? Biological changes associated with puberty cannot be responsible because the gender difference is limited to industrialized nations. In developing countries, rates of depression are similar for males and females and occasionally higher in males (Culbertson, 1997). Even when females do exceed males in depression, the size of the difference varies. For example, it is smaller in China than in North America, perhaps because of decades of efforts by the Chinese government to eliminate gender inequalities (Greenberger et al., 2000).

Instead, stressful life events and gender-typed coping styles seem to be responsible. Early-maturing girls are especially prone to depression (see Chapter 11). And the gender intensification of early adolescence often strengthens girls' passivity and dependency—maladaptive approaches to the tasks expected of teenagers in complex cultures. Consistent with this explanation, adolescents who identify strongly with "feminine" traits are more depressed, regardless of their sex (Wichstrøm, 1999). Girls who repeatedly feel overwhelmed develop an overly reactive physiological stress response and cope more poorly with future challenges (Nolen-Hoeksema, 2002). In this way, stressful experiences and stress reactivity feed on one another, sustaining depression. Profound depression can lead to suicidal thoughts, which all too often are translated into action.

Suicide

The suicide rate increases over the lifespan, from childhood to old age, but it jumps sharply at adolescence. Currently, suicide is the third-leading cause of death (after motor vehicle collisions and homicides) among American youths and the second-leading cause (after motor vehicle collisions) among Canadian youths. Perhaps because North American teenagers experience more stress and fewer supports than in the past, the adolescent suicide rate tripled in both the United States and Canada between the mid-1960s and the mid-1990s, followed by a slight decline. At the same time, rates of adolescent suicide vary widely among industrialized nations—low in Denmark, Greece, Italy, and Spain; intermediate in Australia, Canada, Japan, and the United States; and high in Finland, New Zealand, and Singapore (Lester, 2003). These international differences remain unexplained.

■ **Factors Related to Adolescent Suicide.** Despite girls' higher rates of depression, the number of boys who kill themselves exceeds the number of girls by a ratio of 4 or 5 to 1. Girls make more unsuccessful suicide attempts, using methods from which they are more likely to be revived, such as a sleeping pill overdose. In contrast, boys tend to choose techniques that lead to instant death, such as firearms or hanging. Gender-role expectations may be responsible; less tolerance exists for feelings of helplessness and failed efforts in males than in females (Canetto & Sakinofsky, 1998).

Perhaps because of greater extended family support, African Americans and Hispanics have lower suicide rates than Caucasian Americans. Recently, however, suicide has risen among African-American adolescent males; the current rate approaches that of Caucasian-American males. And Native-American and Canadian-Aboriginal youths commit suicide at rates 2 to 7 times national averages (Health Canada, 2003a; Joe & Marcus, 2003). High rates of profound family poverty, school failure, alcohol and drug use, and depression probably underlie these trends. Gay, lesbian, and bisexual youths are also at high risk, attempting suicide three times as often as other adolescents. Those who have tried to kill themselves report more family conflict, inner turmoil about their sexuality, and peer rejection due to their sexual orientation (Savin-Williams & Ream, 2003b).

Suicide tends to occur in two types of young people. The first group includes highly intelligent adolescents who are solitary, withdrawn, and unable to meet their own high standards or those of important people in their lives. Members of a second, larger group show antisocial tendencies and express their unhappiness through bullying, fighting, stealing, and increased risk taking and drug abuse (Fergusson, Woodward, & Horwood, 2000). Besides being hostile and destructive, they turn their anger and disappointment inward.

Emotional and antisocial disorders are often present in the family backgrounds of suicidal teenagers. In addition, the adolescent is likely to have experienced multiple stressful life events, including economic disadvantage, parental divorce, frequent parent–child conflict, and abuse and neglect. Stressors typically increase during the period preceding a suicide attempt (Beautrais, 2003; Wagner, Silverman, & Martin, 2003). Triggering events include parental blaming of the teenager for family problems, the breakup of an important peer relationship, or the humiliation of having been caught engaging in antisocial acts.

Why does suicide increase in adolescence? Teenagers' improved ability to plan ahead seems to be involved. Although some act impulsively, many young people take purposeful steps toward killing themselves (McKeown et al., 1998). Other cognitive changes also contribute. Belief in the personal fable leads many depressed young people to conclude that no one

could possibly understand their intense pain, and their despair and hopelessness deepen.

■ **Prevention and Treatment.** To prevent suicides, parents and teachers must be trained to pick up on the signals that a troubled teenager sends (see Table 12.3). Schools and recreational and religious organizations can provide sympathetic counselors, peer support groups, and information about telephone hot lines (Spirito et al., 2003). Once a teenager takes steps toward suicide, essential help includes staying with the young person, listening, and expressing compassion and concern until professional help arrives.

Treatments for depressed and suicidal adolescents range from antidepressant medication to individual, family, and group therapy. Until the adolescent improves, removing weapons, knives, razors, scissors, and drugs from the home is vital. On a broader scale, gun-control legislation that limits adolescents' access to the most frequent and deadly suicide method in the United States would greatly reduce both the number of suicides and the high teenage homicide rate. In Canada and other industrialized nations with strict gun-control policies, teenage deaths due to firearms occur, on average, only one-sixteenth as often as in the United States (Fingerhut & Christoffel, 2002).

After a suicide, family and peer survivors need support to help them cope with grief, anger, and guilt over their inability to help the victim. Teenage suicides often occur in clusters, with one death increasing the likelihood of others among peers who knew the young person or heard about the suicide through the media (Bearman & Moody, 2004; Gould, Jamieson, & Romer, 2003). In view of this trend, a watchful eye must

Table 12.3	Warning Signs of Suicide

Efforts to put personal affairs in order—smoothing over troubled relationships, giving away treasured possessions

Verbal cues—saying goodbye to family members and friends, making direct or indirect references to suicide ("I won't have to worry about these problems much longer"; "I wish I were dead")

Feelings of sadness, despondency, "not caring" anymore

Extreme fatigue, lack of energy, boredom

No desire to socialize; withdrawal from friends

Easily frustrated

Emotional outbursts—spells of crying or laughing, bursts of energy

Inability to concentrate, distractible

Decline in grades, absence from school, discipline problems

Neglect of personal appearance

Sleep change—loss of sleep or excessive sleepiness

Appetite change—eating more or less than usual

Physical complaints—stomachaches, backaches, headaches

be kept on vulnerable adolescents after a suicide happens. Restraint by journalists in publicizing teenage suicides also aids prevention.

Delinquency

Juvenile delinquents are children or adolescents who engage in illegal acts. Although North American youth crime has declined since the mid-1990s, U.S. and Canadian 12- to 17-year-olds account for a substantial proportion of police arrests—about 17 percent in the United States and 23 percent in Canada (Statistics Canada, 2004b; U.S. Department of Justice, 2005b). When teenagers are asked directly and confidentially about lawbreaking, almost all admit to having committed an offense of some sort—usually a minor crime, such as petty stealing and disorderly conduct (Flannery et al., 2003).

Both police arrests and self-reports show that delinquency rises over adolescence, then declines into early adulthood (Farrington, 2004). Recall that among young teenagers, antisocial behavior increases as a result of the desire for peer approval. Over time, peers become less influential, moral reasoning improves, and young people enter social contexts (such as marriage, work, and career) that are less conducive to lawbreaking.

For most adolescents, a brush with the law does not forecast long-term antisocial behavior. But repeated arrests are cause for concern. Teenagers are responsible for 13 percent of violent offenses in the United States and for 8 percent in Canada (Statistics Canada, 2004b; U.S. Department of Justice, 2005b). A small percentage become recurrent offenders, who commit most of these crimes, and some enter a life of crime. As the Lifespan Vista box on the following page reveals, childhood-onset conduct problems are far more likely to persist than conduct problems that first appear in adolescence.

■ **Factors Related to Delinquency.** In adolescence, the gender gap in aggression widens (Chesney-Lind, 2001). Although girls account for about 18 percent of adolescent violence—a larger proportion than a decade ago—their offenses are largely limited to simple assault (pushing or spitting), the least serious category. Violent crime, however, continues to be mostly the domain of boys (National Center for Juvenile Justice, 2004). Although SES and ethnicity are strong predictors of arrests, they are only mildly related to teenagers' self-reports of antisocial acts. The difference is due to the tendency to arrest, charge, and punish low-SES ethnic minority youths more often than their higher-SES white and Asian counterparts (U.S. Department of Justice, 2005b).

Difficult temperament, low intelligence, poor school performance, peer rejection in childhood, and association with antisocial peers are linked to delinquency. How do these factors fit together? One of the most consistent findings about delinquent youths is that their families are low in warmth, high in conflict, and characterized by harsh, inconsistent discipline and low monitoring. Because marital transitions often contribute to family discord and disrupted parenting, boys who experience parental separation and divorce are especially prone

Delinquency rises during the early teen years, remains high during middle adolescence, and then declines. Although most of the time it involves petty stealing and disorderly conduct, a small percentage of young people engage in repeated, serious offenses and are at risk for a life of crime.

to delinquency (Farrington, 2004). And youth crime peaks on weekdays between 2:00 and 8:00 P.M., when many teenagers are unsupervised (U.S. Department of Justice, 2005b).

Our discussion on page 271 in Chapter 8 explained how ineffective parenting can promote and sustain children's aggression. Boys are more likely than girls to be targets of angry, inconsistent discipline because they are more active and impulsive and therefore harder to control. When children who are extreme in these characteristics are exposed to inept parenting, aggression rises during childhood, leads to violent offenses in adolescence, and persists into adulthood (again, see the Lifespan Vista box).

Teenagers commit more crimes in poverty-stricken neighborhoods with limited recreational and employment opportunities and high adult criminality. In such neighborhoods, adolescents have easy access to deviant peers, drugs, and firearms and are likely to be recruited into antisocial gangs, whose members commit the vast majority of violent delinquent acts (Thornberry & Krohn, 2001). Furthermore, schools in these locales typically fail to meet students' developmental needs (Flannery et al., 2003). Large classes, weak instruction, and lax enforcement of rules increase teenagers' inclination toward aggression and violence.

■ **Prevention and Treatment.** Because delinquency has roots in childhood and results from events in several contexts, prevention must start early and take place at multiple levels. Positive family relationships, authoritative parenting, high-quality teaching in schools, and communities with healthy economic and social conditions go a long way toward reducing adolescent criminality.

Treating serious offenders also requires an intensive, often lengthy approach that recognizes the multiple determinants of delinquency. The most effective methods include training

A Lifespan Vista

Two Routes to Adolescent Delinquency

Persistent adolescent delinquency follows two paths of development, one with an onset of conduct problems in childhood, the second with an onset in adolescence. Research reveals that the early-onset type is far more likely to lead to a life-course pattern of aggression and criminality (Farrington & Loeber, 2000). The late-onset type usually does not persist beyond the transition to young adulthood.

Both childhood-onset and adolescent-onset delinquent youths engage in serious offenses; associate with deviant peers; participate in substance abuse, unsafe sex, and dangerous driving; and spend time in correctional facilities. Why does antisocial activity more often continue and escalate into violence in the first group than in the second? Longitudinal studies yield similar answers to this question. So far, findings are clearest for boys, who are the focus of most research. But several investigations report that girls who were physically aggressive in childhood are also at risk for later problems—occasionally violent delinquency, but more often other norm-violating behaviors and psychological disorders (Broidy et al., 2003; Chamberlain, 2003). And early relational aggression is linked to adolescent conduct problems as well.

Early-Onset Type. Early-onset youngsters seem to inherit traits that predispose them to aggressiveness (Pettit, 2004). Difficult and fearless temperamental styles characterize physically aggressive boys, who are emotionally negative, restless, and willful as early as age 2. They also show subtle deficits in cognitive functioning that seem to contribute to disruptions in the development of language, memory, and cognitive and emotional self-regulation (Shaw et al., 2003). Some have attention-deficit hyperactivity disorder (ADHD), which compounds their learning and self-control problems (see Chapter 9, page 304).

Yet these biological risks are not sufficient to sustain antisocial behavior: Most early-onset boys do not display serious delinquency followed by adult criminality. Among those who do, inept parenting transforms their undercontrolled style into defiance and persistent aggression (Broidy et al., 2003; Brame, Nagin, & Tremblay, 2001). As they fail academically and are rejected by peers, they befriend other deviant youths, who facilitate one another's violent behavior while relieving loneliness (see Figure 12.5) (Lacourse et al., 2003). Early-onset teenagers' limited cognitive and social skills result in high rates of school dropout and unemployment, contributing further to their antisocial involvements. Often these boys experience their first arrest before age 14—a good indicator that they will be chronic offenders by age 18 (Patterson & Yoerger, 2002).

Preschoolers high in relational aggression also tend to be hyperactive and frequently in conflict with peers and adults (Willoughby, Kupersmidt, & Bryant, 2001). As these behaviors trigger peer rejection, relationally aggressive girls befriend other girls high in relational hostility, and their relational aggression rises (Werner & Crick, 2004). Adolescents high in relational aggression are often angry, vengeful, and defiant of adult rules. Among teenagers who combine physical and relational hostility, these oppositional reactions intensify, increasing the likelihood of serious antisocial activity (Prinstein, Boergers, & Vernberg, 2001).

Late-Onset Type. Other youths begin to display antisocial behavior around the time of puberty, gradually increasing their involvement. Their conduct problems arise from the peer context of early adolescence, not from biological deficits and a history of unfavorable development. For some, quality of parenting may decline for a time, perhaps due to family stresses or the challenges of disciplining an unruly teenager (Moffitt et al., 1996). When age brings gratifying adult privileges, these youths draw on prosocial skills mastered before adolescence and abandon their antisocial ways.

A few late-onset youths, however, continue to engage in antisocial acts. The seriousness of their adolescent offenses seems to trap them in situations that close off opportunities for responsible behavior. In one study, finding a satisfying job and forming positive, close relationships coincided with an end to criminal offending by age 20 (Clingempeel & Henggeler, 2003).

These findings suggest a need for a fresh look at policies aimed at stopping youth crime. Keeping youth offenders locked up for many years disrupts their vocational lives and access to social support during a crucial period of development, committing them to a bleak future.

■ **FIGURE 12.5 Path to chronic delinquency for adolescents with childhood-onset antisocial behavior.** Difficult temperament and cognitive deficits characterize many of these youths in early childhood; some have attention-deficit hyperactivity disorder. Inept parenting transforms biologically based self-control difficulties into hostility and defiance.

parents in communication, monitoring, and discipline strategies and teaching youths cognitive, social, and emotional self-regulation skills for overcoming peer and school difficulties (Elliott & Tolan, 1999).

Yet even these multidimensional treatments can fall short if young people remain embedded in hostile home lives, antisocial peer groups, and fragmented neighborhoods. In a program called Multisystemic Therapy, therapists combined family intervention with integrating violent youths into positive school, work, and leisure activities and disengaging them from violent peers. Compared with typical community services or individual therapy, the intervention led to greater improvement in parent–child relations and a dramatic drop in number of arrests over a four-year period (Huey & Henggeler, 2001). Efforts to create nonaggressive environments—at the family, community, and cultural levels—are needed to help delinquent youths and to foster healthy development of all young people.

Summary

Erikson's Theory: Identity versus Role Confusion

According to Erikson, what is the major personality achievement of adolescence?

■ Erikson's theory regards **identity** as the major personality achievement of adolescence. Young people who successfully resolve the psychological conflict of **identity versus role confusion** construct a solid self-definition consisting of self-chosen values and goals.

Self-Understanding

Describe changes in self-concept and self-esteem during adolescence.

■ Cognitive changes lead adolescents' self-descriptions to become more organized and consistent, and personal and moral values appear as key themes. New dimensions of self-esteem are also added.

■ For most young people, self-esteem rises over the teenage years. Adolescents vary widely in their self-esteem profiles. Of those whose self-esteem drops, most are girls. Authoritative parenting and schools and neighborhoods that respect the young person's ethnicity support positive self-esteem.

Describe the four identity statuses, along with factors that promote identity development.

■ In complex societies, a period of exploration is necessary to form a personally meaningful identity. **Identity achievement** and **identity moratorium** are psychologically healthy identity statuses. Long-term **identity foreclosure** and **identity diffusion** are related to adjustment difficulties.

■ Adolescents who use a flexible, open-minded, rational approach to grappling with competing beliefs and values and who feel attached to parents but free to voice their own opinions are likely to be advanced in identity development. Close friends assist young people in exploring options.

■ Schools and communities that provide rich and varied opportunities also foster identity achievement. Ethnic minority youths who construct a strong, secure **ethnic identity** or a **bicultural identity** are advantaged in many aspects of emotional and social development.

Moral Development

Describe Piaget's theory of moral development and Kohlberg's extension of it, and evaluate the accuracy of each.

■ Piaget identified two stages of moral understanding: (1) **heteronomous morality,** in which moral rules are viewed as fixed dictates of authority figures, and (2) **autonomous morality,** in which rules are seen as flexible, socially agreed-on principles. Although Piaget's theory describes the general direction of moral development, it underestimates young children's moral capacities.

■ According to Kohlberg, moral development is a gradual process that extends into adulthood. Moral reasoning advances through three levels, each of which contains two stages: (1) the **preconventional level,** in which morality is viewed as controlled by rewards, punishments, and the power of authority figures; (2) the **conventional level,** in which conformity to laws and rules is regarded as necessary to preserve positive human relationships and societal order; and (3) the **postconventional level,** in which individuals develop abstract, universal principles of justice.

■ A reexamination of Kohlberg's stages suggests that moral maturity can be found at Stages 3 and 4. The influence of situational factors on moral judgment suggests that Kohlberg's moral stages are best viewed as a loosely organized sequence.

■ Contrary to Gilligan's claim, Kohlberg's theory does not underestimate the morality of females. Both justice and caring moralities coexist but vary in emphasis between males and females, from one situation to the next, and across cultures.

■ Compared with children, teenagers display more subtle reasoning about conflicts between personal choice and community obligation. They are also increasingly aware of the moral implications of following social conventions.

Describe influences on moral reasoning and its relationship to moral behavior.

- Experiences contributing to moral maturity include warm, rational child-rearing practices, years of schooling, and peer discussions of moral issues. Young people in industrialized nations advance to higher levels of moral understanding than those in village societies. Responses to moral dilemmas in collectivist cultures are often more other-directed.

- Maturity of moral reasoning is modestly related to a wide variety of moral behaviors. Other factors affecting moral action include the emotions of empathy and guilt, the individual's history of morally relevant experiences, and **moral self-relevance**—the extent to which morality is central to self-concept.

- Although formal religious involvement declines in adolescence, most teenagers identify with a religious denomination. Adolescents who are part of a religious community are advantaged in moral values and behavior.

Gender Typing

Why is early adolescence a period of gender intensification?

- **Gender intensification** occurs in early adolescence for several reasons. Physical and cognitive changes prompt young teenagers to view themselves in gender-linked ways, and gender-typed pressures from parents and peers increase. Teenagers who eventually build an androgynous gender identity show better psychological adjustment.

The Family

Discuss changes in parent–child and sibling relationships during adolescence.

- Adapting family interaction to meet adolescents' need for **autonomy** is especially challenging. As teenagers deidealize their parents, they often question parental authority. And because both adolescents and parents are undergoing major life transitions, they approach situations from different perspectives. Effective parenting requires an authoritative style that strikes a balance between connection and separation. Consis-

tent parental monitoring, through a cooperative relationship, predicts favorable adjustment.

- Sibling relationships become less intense as adolescents separate from the family and turn toward peers. Still, attachment to siblings remains strong for most young people.

Peer Relations

Describe adolescent friendships, peer groups, and dating relationships and their consequences for development.

- During adolescence, friendship changes, moving toward greater intimacy and loyalty. Girls' friendships place greater emphasis on emotional closeness, boys' on status and mastery.

- As long as they are not based on attraction to antisocial behavior, adolescent friendships promote self-concept, perspective taking, identity, and the capacity for intimate relationships. They also help young people deal with stress and can improve attitudes toward school.

- Adolescent peer groups are organized into **cliques,** small groups of friends with similar family backgrounds, attitudes, and values. Often several cliques form a larger, more loosely organized group called a **crowd** that grants the adolescent an identity within the larger social structure of the school. Parenting styles influence the assortment of teenagers into cliques and crowds. As mixed-sex cliques form, they provide a supportive context for boys and girls to get to know one another.

- Intimacy in dating relationships lags behind that of same-sex friendships, and early, frequent dating is linked to adjustment problems. Positive relationships with parents and friends contribute to warm romantic ties, which enhance emotional and social development in older teenagers.

Discuss conformity to peer pressure in adolescence.

- Peer conformity is greater during adolescence than earlier or later. Young teenagers are most likely to give in to peer pressure for antisocial behavior. Yet most peer pressure is not in conflict with important adult values. Authoritative parenting is related to resistance to unfavorable peer pressure.

Problems of Development

What factors are related to adolescent depression and suicide?

- Depression is the most common psychological problem of the teenage years. Various combinations of biological and environmental factors can lead to depression, and adolescents who are severely depressed are likely to remain so as adults. Depression is more common in girls than in boys—a difference believed to be due to stressful life events and gender-typed coping styles.

- The suicide rate increases dramatically at adolescence. Boys account for most teenage deaths by suicide, while girls make more unsuccessful suicide attempts. Teenagers at risk for suicide may be intelligent, solitary, and withdrawn, but more often, they are antisocial. Family turmoil is common in the backgrounds of suicidal adolescents.

Discuss factors related to delinquency.

- Although almost all teenagers engage in some delinquent activity, only a few are serious repeat offenders. Most are boys with a childhood history of conduct problems.

- A consistent factor related to delinquency is a family environment low in warmth, high in conflict, and characterized by inconsistent discipline. Poverty-stricken neighborhoods with high crime rates and schools that fail to meet adolescents' developmental needs also promote lawbreaking.

Important Terms and Concepts

Milestones

Development in Adolescence

Age	Physical	Cognitive	Emotional/Social
EARLY ADOLESCENCE 11–14 YEARS	• If a girl, reaches peak of growth spurt (363) • If a girl, adds more body fat than muscle (363) • If a girl, motor performance increases gradually, leveling off by age 14 (364) • If a girl, starts to menstruate (365) • If a boy, begins growth spurt (363) • If a boy, starts to ejaculate seminal fluid (366) • Likely to be aware of sexual orientation (375–376) • Synaptic growth and myelination of neural fibers accelerate, especially between the frontal lobes and other brain areas (367) • Neurons in brain become more responsive to excitatory neurotransmitters, heightening stress response and novelty-seeking (367)	• Becomes capable of hypothetico-deductive reasoning and propositional thought (381) • Becomes better at coordinating theory with evidence (383) • Becomes more self-conscious and self-focused (384–385) • Becomes more idealistic and critical (385) • Metacognition and cognitive self-regulation continue to improve (383)	• Moodiness and parent–child conflict tend to increase (368–369, 413) • Is likely to show increased gender stereotyping of attitudes and behavior (411) • Spends more time with peers and less time with parents and siblings (414) • Friendships are based on intimacy and loyalty (415) • Peer groups become organized around cliques (417–418) • Cliques with similar values form crowds (417–418) • Conformity in response to peer pressure increases (419)
MIDDLE ADOLESCENCE 14–16 YEARS	• If a girl, completes growth spurt (363) • If a boy, reaches peak and then completes growth spurt (363) • If a boy, voice deepens (366) • If a boy, adds muscle while body fat declines (363–364)	• Is likely to show scientific, systematic reasoning in familiar situations (381)	• Combines features of the self into an organized self-concept (400) • Self-esteem differentiates further and tends to rise (401)

Age	Physical	Cognitive	Emotional/Social
MIDDLE ADOLESCENCE 14–16 YEARS (continued)	• If a boy, motor performance improves dramatically (364) • May have had sexual intercourse (373)	• Masters scientific reasoning skills in a similar, step-by-step fashion on different types of tasks (383) 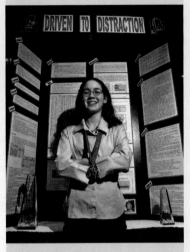 • Becomes less self-conscious and self-focused (384) • Becomes better at everyday decision making (386)	• Is likely to begin constructing an identity (400) • Is likely to engage in societal perspective taking (336) • Increasingly emphasizes ideal reciprocity and societal laws as the basis for resolving moral dilemmas (407) • Engages in more subtle reasoning about conflicts between moral, social-conventional, and personal issues (409) • Gender-stereotyped attitudes and behavior may decline (415) • Has probably started dating (418–419) • Relates more positively with parents (414) • Conformity to peer pressure may decline (419)
LATE ADOLESCENCE 16–18 YEARS	• If a boy, gains in motor performance continue (364)	• Continues to gain in metacognition, scientific reasoning, and decision making	• Continues to construct an identity (400) • Continues to advance in maturity of moral reasoning (407–409) • Cliques and crowds decline in importance (418) • Romantic ties last longer (418)

Note: Numbers in parentheses indicate the page or pages on which each milestone is discussed.

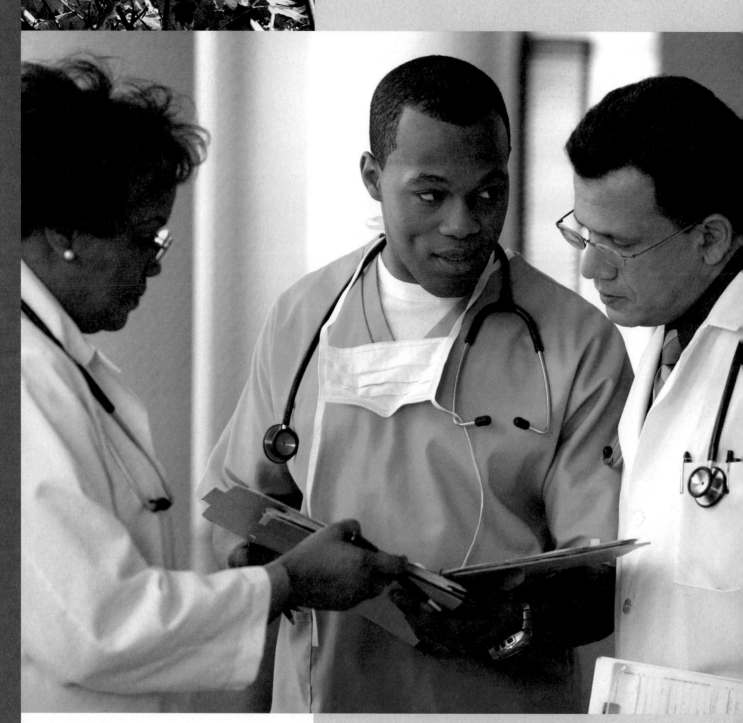

*E*arly adulthood brings momentous life changes—among them, selecting a vocation, completing higher education, starting full-time work, and attaining economic independence. Once young adults embark on a career path, as this young physician has, strong ties with mentors and co-workers are vital for success.

Physical and Cognitive Development in Early Adulthood

© DIGITAL VISION/GETTY IMAGES

T he back seat and trunk piled high with belongings, 23-year-old Sharese hugged her mother and brother goodbye, jumped in the car, and headed toward the interstate with a sense of newfound freedom mixed with apprehension. Three months earlier, the family had watched proudly as Sharese received her bachelor's degree in chemistry from a small university 40 miles from her home. Her college years had been a time of gradual release from economic and psychological dependence on her family. She returned home periodically on weekends and lived there during the summer months. Her mother supplemented Sharese's loans with a monthly allowance. But this day marked a turning point. She was moving to her own apartment in a city 800 miles away, with plans to work on a master's degree. With a teaching assistantship and a student loan, Sharese felt more "on her own" than at any previous time in her life.

During her college years, Sharese made lifestyle changes and settled on a vocational direction. Overweight throughout high school, she lost 20 pounds in her freshman year, revised her diet, and began an exercise regimen by joining the university's Ultimate Frisbee team, eventually becoming its captain. A summer spent as a counselor at a camp for chronically ill children helped convince Sharese to apply her background in science to a career in public health.

Still, two weeks before she was scheduled to leave, Sharese confided to her mother that she was having doubts about her decision. "Sharese," her mother advised, "we never know our life choices are going to suit us just right, and most times they aren't perfect. It's what we make of them—how we view and mold them—that turns them into successes." So Sharese embarked on her journey and found herself face to face with a multitude of exciting challenges and opportunities.

In this chapter, we take up the physical and cognitive sides of early adulthood, which extends from about age 18 to 40. In Chapter 1, we emphasized that the adult years are difficult to divide into discrete periods because the timing of important milestones varies greatly among individuals—much more so than in childhood and adolescence. But for most people, early adulthood involves a common set of tasks: leaving home, completing education, beginning full-time work, attaining economic independence, establishing a long-term sexually and emotionally intimate relationship, and starting a family. These are energetic decades filled with momentous decisions that—more than any other time of life—offer the potential for living to the fullest.

A Gradual Transition: Emerging Adulthood

Take a moment to think about your own development. Do you consider yourself to have reached adulthood? When researchers ask large samples of North American young people this question, the majority of 18- to 25-year-olds answer ambiguously: "Yes and no" (see Figure 13.1). Only after reaching their late twenties and early thirties do most feel that they are truly adult (Arnett, 1997, 2001, 2003).

Compared to a generation ago, today's young people move into widely accepted markers of adulthood—marriage, career,

FIGURE 13.1 North American young people's responses to the question, "Do you feel that you have reached adulthood?" Between ages 18 and 25, the majority answered "yes and no," reflecting their view that they had left adolescence but were not yet fully adult. Even in their late twenties and early thirties, about one-third of young people judged that they had not completed the transition to adulthood. (Adapted from Arnett, 2001.)

and full economic independence—slowly, often vacillating before making lasting commitments. In fact, the transition to adult roles has become so prolonged that it has spawned a new, transitional phase of development, extending from the late teens to the mid-twenties, called **emerging adulthood.** During these years, most people have left adolescence but are still some distance from taking on adult responsibilities. Rather, they explore alternatives more intensely than they did as teenagers (Arnett, 2004, 2006). Frequent changes in love partners, educational paths, and jobs are common.

Notice how emerging adulthood greatly prolongs identity development. Released from the oversight of parents but not yet immersed in adult roles, 18- to 25-year-olds can engage in activities of the widest possible scope. Because so little is normative, or socially expected, routes to adult responsibilities are highly diverse in timing and order across individuals (Côté, 2006). For example, many more college students than in past generations pursue their education in a drawn-out, nonlinear way—changing majors as they explore career options, taking courses while working part-time, or interrupting school to work or travel. About one-third of North American college graduates enter graduate school, taking still more years to settle into a career track (Statistics Canada, 2003f; U.S. Department of Education, 2005b).

Rapid cultural changes explain the recent appearance of this rich, complex bridge between adolescence and adulthood. First, entry-level positions in many fields require more education than in the past, prompting young adults to seek higher education in record numbers. Second, nations with abundant wealth and longer-lived populations have no pressing need for young people's labor. This frees 18- to 25-year-olds for this extended "moratorium." Finally, *globalization*—exchange of ideas, information, trade, and immigration among nations—is promoting the spread of emerging adulthood (Arnett, 2000, 2006). Contact among developed and developing nations fosters economic progress and heightens awareness of events, lifestyles, and practices in faraway places.

In industrialized countries, most young people have access to this time to extend their competencies and to make personally meaningful commitments. Still, emerging adulthood is limited or nonexistent for many low-SES young people who are burdened by early parenthood, did not finish high school, are otherwise academically unprepared for college, or have no avenue to vocational training. Instead of excitement and personal expansion, these individuals encounter a "floundering period," during which they alternate between unemployment and dead-end, low-paying jobs (Cohen et al., 2003; Eccles et al., 2003).

As emerging adults experiment, they often encounter uncertainties and disappointments in relationships, education, and work that require them to adjust, and sometimes radically change, their life path. And their vigorous explorations often extend earlier risks, including sexually transmitted diseases, substance abuse, hazardous driving behavior, and severe psychological stress. But with the help of family, community, and societal contexts, most young adults make the best of wrong turns and surmount the challenges of these years.

Physical Development

We have seen that throughout childhood and adolescence, the body grows larger and stronger, coordination improves, and sensory systems gather information more effectively. Once body structures reach maximum capacity and efficiency, **biological aging,** or **senescence,** begins—genetically influenced declines in the functioning of organs and systems that are universal in all members of our species (Cristofalo et al., 1999). Like physical growth, however, biological aging is *asynchronous* (see Chapter 7, page 217). Change varies widely across parts of the body, and individual differences are great—variation that the *lifespan perspective* helps us understand. A host of contextual factors—including each person's unique genetic makeup, lifestyle, living environment, and historical period—influence biological aging, each of which can accelerate or slow age-related declines (Arking, 1998). As a result, the physical changes of the adult years are, indeed, *multidimensional* and *multidirectional* (see page 9 in Chapter 1).

In the following sections, we examine the process of biological aging. Then we turn to physical and motor changes already under way in early adulthood. As you will see, biological aging is not fixed and immutable. It can be modified substantially through behavioral and environmental interventions. Over the past century, improved nutrition, medical treatment, sanitation, and safety have added 25 to 30 years to *average life expectancy* in industrialized nations (see Chapter 1, page 8). We will take up life expectancy in greater depth in Chapter 17.

Released from the oversight of parents but not yet immersed in adult roles, contemporary 18- to 25-year-olds experience the phase now referred to as *emerging adulthood,* which frees them to engage in activities of the widest possible scope.

© JOHN FEINGERSH/CORBIS

Biological Aging Is Under Way in Early Adulthood

At an intercollegiate tournament, Sharese dashed across the playing field for hours, leaping high to catch Frisbees sailing her way. In her early twenties, she is at her peak in strength, endurance, sensory acuteness, and immune system responsiveness. Yet over the next two decades, she will age and, as she moves into middle and late adulthood, will show more noticeable declines.

Biological aging is the combined result of many causes, some operating at the level of DNA, others at the level of cells, and still others at the level of tissues, organs, and whole organisms. Hundreds of theories exist, indicating that our understanding is still in an early stage (Cristofalo et al., 1999). One popular idea—the *"wear-and-tear" theory*—is that the body wears out from use. But unlike parts of a machine, worn-out parts of the body usually replace or repair themselves. Furthermore, no relationship exists between physical work and early death. To the contrary, regular, moderate-to-vigorous exercise predicts a healthier, longer life for people differing widely in SES and ethnicity (Cockerham et al., 2004; Stessman et al., 2005). We now know that this "wear-and-tear" theory is an oversimplification.

Aging at the Level of DNA and Body Cells

Current explanations of biological aging at the level of DNA and body cells are of two types: (1) those that emphasize the *programmed effects of specific genes* and (2) those that emphasize the *cumulative effects of random events* that damage genetic and cellular material. Support for both views exists, and a combination may eventually prove to be correct.

Genetically programmed aging receives some support from kinship studies indicating that longevity is a family trait. People whose parents had long lives tend to live longer themselves. And greater similarity exists in the lifespans of identical than fraternal twins. But the heritability of longevity is modest, ranging from .15 to .25 for age at death and from .27 to .57 for various measures of current biological age, such as strength of hand grip, respiratory capacity, blood pressure, and bone density (Karasik et al., 2005; Kerber et al., 2001; Mitchell et al., 2001). Rather than inheriting longevity directly, people probably inherit one or more risk factors, which influence their chances of dying earlier or later.

One "genetic programming" theory proposes the existence of "aging genes" that control certain biological changes, such as menopause, gray hair, and deterioration of body cells. The strongest evidence for this view comes from research showing that human cells allowed to divide in the laboratory have a lifespan of 50 divisions, plus or minus 10 (Hayflick, 1965, 1998). With each duplication, a special type of DNA—called

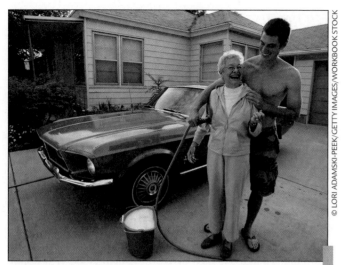

People whose parents had long lives tend to live longer themselves. But genetic factors are not the only influences on longevity. As this grandmother models for her grandson, staying slim and fit and buffering stress by enjoying life also contribute.

telomeres, located at the ends of chromosomes—shortens. Eventually, so little remains that the cells no longer duplicate at all. Telomere shortening acts as a brake against somatic mutations (such as those involved in cancer), which become more likely as cells duplicate (Wright & Shay, 2005). But an increase in the number of senescent cells (ones with short telomeres) also contributes to age-related disease and loss of function (Nakashima et al., 2004).

According to an alternative, "random events" theory, DNA in body cells is gradually damaged through spontaneous or externally caused mutations. As these accumulate, cell repair and replacement become less efficient, or abnormal cancerous cells are produced. Animal studies confirm an increase in DNA breaks and deletions and damage to other cellular material with age. Similar evidence is accruing for humans (Wei & Lee, 2002).

One probable cause of age-related DNA and cellular abnormalities is the release of **free radicals**—naturally occurring, highly reactive chemicals that form in the presence of oxygen. (Radiation and certain pollutants and drugs can trigger similar effects.) When oxygen molecules break down within the cell, the reaction strips away an electron, creating a free radical. As it seeks a replacement from its surroundings, it destroys nearby cellular material, including DNA, proteins, and fats essential for cell functioning. Free radicals are thought to be involved in more than 60 disorders of aging, including cardiovascular disease, neurological disorders, cancer, cataracts, and arthritis (Miguel, 2001; Poon et al., 2004). Although our bodies produce substances that neutralize free radicals, some harm occurs, and it accumulates over time.

Some researchers believe that genes for longevity work by defending against free radicals. In this way, a programmed genetic response may limit random DNA and cellular deterioration. Foods rich in vitamins C and E and beta-carotene also forestall free-radical damage—a reason that improved diet contributes to gains in life expectancy (Harman, 2003).

Aging at the Level of Organs and Tissues

What consequences might the DNA and cellular deterioration just described have for the structure and functioning of organs and tissues? There are many possibilities. Among those with clear support is the **cross-linkage theory of aging.** Over time, protein fibers that make up the body's connective tissue form bonds, or links, with one another. When these normally separate fibers cross-link, tissue becomes less elastic, leading to many negative outcomes, including loss of flexibility in the skin and other organs, clouding of the lens of the eye, clogging of arteries, and damage to the kidneys. Like other aspects of aging, cross-linking can be reduced by external factors, including regular exercise and a vitamin-rich, low-fat diet (Schneider, 1992; Wickens, 2001).

Gradual failure of the endocrine system, which produces and regulates hormones, is yet another route to aging. An obvious example is decreased estrogen production in women, which culminates in menopause. Because hormones affect many body functions, disruptions in the endocrine system can have widespread effects on health and survival. Research on the role of key hormones on aging indicates that a gradual drop in growth hormone (GH) is associated with loss of muscle and bone mass, addition of body fat, thinning of the skin, and decline in cardiovascular functioning. In adults with abnormally low levels of GH, hormone therapy can slow these symptoms, but it has serious side effects, including increased risk of fluid retention in tissues, muscle pain, and cancer (Harman & Blackman, 2004; Toogood, 2004). So far, diet and physical activity are safer ways to limit these aspects of biological aging.

Finally, declines in immune system functioning contribute to many conditions of aging, including increased susceptibility to infectious disease and cancer and changes in blood vessel walls associated with cardiovascular disease. Decreased vigor of the immune response seems to be genetically programmed, but other aging processes we have considered (such as weakening of the endocrine system) can intensify it (Hawkley & Cacioppo, 2004; Malaguarnera et al., 2001). Indeed, combinations of theories—the ones just reviewed as well as others—are needed to explain the complexities of biological aging. With this in mind, let's turn to physical signs and other characteristics of aging.

Physical Changes

During the twenties and thirties, changes in physical appearance and declines in body functioning are so gradual that most are hardly noticeable. Later, they will accelerate. The physical changes of aging are summarized in Table 13.1. We will examine several in detail here and take up others in later chapters. Before we begin, let's note that these trends are derived largely from cross-sectional data. Because younger cohorts have experienced better health care and nutrition, cross-sectional evidence can exaggerate impairments associated with aging. Fortunately, longitudinal evidence is expanding, helping to correct this picture.

Table 13.1	Physical Changes of Aging

Organ or System	Timing of Change	Description
Sensory		
Vision	From age 30	As the lens stiffens and thickens, ability to focus on close objects declines. Yellowing of the lens, weakening of muscles controlling the pupil, and clouding of the vitreous (gelatin-like substance that fills the eye) reduce light reaching the retina, impairing color discrimination and night vision. Visual acuity, or fineness of discrimination, decreases, with a sharp drop between ages 70 and 80.
Hearing	From age 30	Sensitivity to sound declines, especially at high frequencies but gradually extending to all frequencies. Change is more than twice as rapid for men as for women.
Taste	From age 60	Sensitivity to the four basic tastes—sweet, salty, sour, and bitter—is reduced. This may be due to factors other than aging, since number and distribution of taste buds do not change.
Smell	From age 60	Loss of smell receptors reduces ability to detect and identify odors.
Touch	Gradual	Loss of touch receptors reduces sensitivity on the hands, particularly the fingertips.
Cardiovascular	Gradual	As the heart muscle becomes more rigid, maximum heart rate decreases, reducing the heart's ability to meet the body's oxygen requirements when stressed by exercise. As artery walls stiffen and accumulate plaque, blood flow to body cells is reduced.
Respiratory	Gradual	Under physical exertion, respiratory capacity decreases and breathing rate increases. Stiffening of connective tissue in the lungs and chest muscles makes it more difficult for the lungs to expand to full volume.
Immune	Gradual	Shrinking of the thymus limits maturation of T cells and disease-fighting capacity of B cells, impairing the immune response.
Muscular	Gradual	As nerves stimulating them die, fast-twitch muscle fibers (responsible for speed and explosive strength) decline in number and size to a greater extent than slow-twitch fibers (which support endurance). Tendons and ligaments (which transmit muscle action) stiffen, reducing speed and flexibility of movement.
Skeletal	Begins in the late thirties, accelerates in the fifties, slows in the seventies	Cartilage in the joints thins and cracks, leading bone ends beneath it to erode. New cells continue to be deposited on the outer layer of the bones, and mineral content of bone declines. The resulting broader but more porous bones weaken the skeleton and make it more vulnerable to fracture. Change is more rapid in women than in men.
Reproductive	In women, accelerates after age 35; in men, begins after age 40	Fertility problems (including difficulty conceiving and carrying a pregnancy to term) and risk of having a baby with a chromosomal disorder increase.
Nervous	From age 50	Brain weight declines as neurons lose water content and die, mostly in the cerebral cortex, and as ventricles (spaces) within the brain enlarge. Development of new synapses and limited generation of new neurons can, in part, compensate for these declines.
Skin	Gradual	Epidermis (outer layer) is held less tightly to the dermis (middle layer); fibers in the dermis and hypodermis (inner layer) thin; fat cells in the hypodermis decline. As a result, the skin becomes looser, less elastic, and wrinkled. Change is more rapid in women than in men.
Hair	From age 35	Grays and thins.
Height	From age 50	Loss of bone strength leads to collapse of disks in the spinal column, leading to a height loss of as much as 2 inches by the seventies and eighties.
Weight	Increases to age 50; declines from age 60	Weight change reflects a rise in fat and a decline in muscle and bone mineral. Since muscle and bone are heavier than fat, the resulting pattern is weight gain followed by loss. Body fat accumulates on the torso and decreases on the extremities.

Sources: Arking, 1998; Whalley, 2001; Whitbourne, 1996.

Cardiovascular and Respiratory Systems

During her first month in graduate school, Sharese pored over research articles on cardiovascular functioning. In her African-American extended family, her father, an uncle, and three aunts had died of heart attacks in their forties and fifties. The tragedies had prompted Sharese to worry about her own lifespan, reconsider her health-related behaviors, and enter the field of public health in hopes of finding ways to relieve health problems among black Americans. *Hypertension,* or high blood pressure, occurs 12 percent more often in the U.S. black than in the U.S. white population; the rate of death from heart disease among African Americans is 28 percent higher (American Heart Association, 2006a).

Sharese was surprised to learn that fewer age-related changes occur in the heart than we might expect, given that heart disease is a leading cause of death throughout adulthood, responsible for as many as 11 percent of U.S. male and 6 percent of U.S. female deaths between ages 20 and 34—figures that more than double in the following decade and, thereafter, continue to rise steadily with age. In healthy individuals, the heart's ability to meet the body's oxygen requirements under typical conditions (as measured by heart rate in relation to volume of blood pumped) does not change during adulthood. Only during stressful exercise does heart performance decline with age—a change due to a decrease in maximum heart rate and greater rigidity of the heart muscle. Consequently, the heart has difficulty delivering enough oxygen to the body during high activity and bouncing back from strain (Haywood & Getchell, 2001).

One of the most serious diseases of the cardiovascular system is *atherosclerosis,* in which heavy deposits of plaque containing cholesterol and fats collect on the walls of the main arteries. If present, it usually begins early in life, progresses during middle adulthood, and culminates in serious illness. Atherosclerosis is multiply determined, making it hard to separate the contributions of biological aging from individual genetic and environmental influences. The complexity of causes is illustrated by animal research indicating that before puberty, a high-fat diet produces only fatty streaks on the artery walls (Olson, 2000). In sexually mature adults, however, it leads to serious plaque deposits, suggesting that sex hormones may heighten the insults of a high-fat diet.

Heart disease has decreased considerably since the mid-twentieth century, with a larger drop in the last 20 years due to a decline in cigarette smoking, to improved diet and exercise among at-risk individuals, and to better medical detection and treatment of high blood pressure and cholesterol (American Heart Association, 2006a). And as longitudinal research on more than 17,000 Chicago-area 18- to 39-year-olds reveals, young adults at low risk for heart disease—defined by not smoking, absence of diabetes, and normal blood cholesterol, blood pressure, and body weight—had much lower death rates than their higher-risk agemates over the succeeding three decades (Daviglus et al., 2004; Stamler et al., 1999). Later, when we consider health and fitness, we will see why heart attacks

were so common in Sharese's family—and why they occur at especially high rates in the African-American population.

Like the heart, the lungs show few age-related changes in functioning at rest, but during physical exertion, respiratory volume decreases and breathing rate increases with age. Maximum vital capacity (amount of air that can be forced in and out of the lungs) declines by 10 percent per decade after age 25 (Mahanran et al., 1999). Connective tissue in the lungs, chest muscles, and ribs stiffens with age, making it more difficult for the lungs to expand to full volume (Haywood & Getchell, 2001). Fortunately, under normal conditions, we use less than half our vital capacity. Nevertheless, aging of the lungs contributes to older adults' difficulty in meeting the body's oxygen needs while exercising.

Motor Performance

Declines in heart and lung functioning under conditions of exertion, combined with gradual muscle loss, lead to changes in motor performance. In ordinary people, the impact of biological aging on motor skills is difficult to separate from decreases in motivation and practice. Therefore, researchers study outstanding athletes, who try to attain their very best performance in real life (Tanaka & Seals, 2003). As long as athletes continue intensive training, their attainments at each age approach the limits of what is biologically possible.

Many athletic skills peak between ages 20 and 35, then gradually decline. In several investigations, the mean ages for best performance of Olympic and professional athletes in a variety of sports were charted over time. Absolute performance in most events improved over the past century. Athletes continually set new world records, suggesting improved training methods. But ages of best performance remained relatively constant. Athletic tasks that require speed of limb movement,

© ED BOCK/CORBIS

Research on master runners reveals that as long as practice continues, speed drops only slightly from the mid-thirties into the sixties. Here, older adults who have continued to train for many years keep pace with younger adults in a marathon.

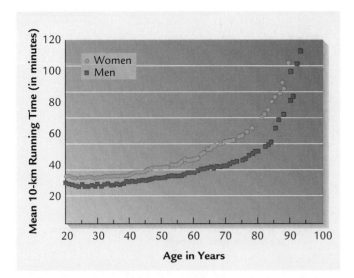

■ **FIGURE 13.2 Ten-kilometer running times with advancing age, based on longitudinal performances of hundreds of master athletes.** Runners maintain their speed into the mid-thirties, followed by modest increases in running times into the sixties, with a progressively steeper increase thereafter. (From H. Tanaka & D. R. Seals, 2003, "Dynamic Exercise Performance in Master Athletes: Insight into the Effects of Primary Human Aging on Physiological Functional Capacity," *Journal of Applied Physiology, 5,* p. 2153. Adapted by permission.)

explosive strength, and gross body coordination—sprinting, jumping, and tennis—typically peak in the early twenties. Those that depend on endurance, arm–hand steadiness, and aiming—long-distance running, baseball, and golf—usually peak in the late twenties and early thirties. Because these skills require either stamina or precise motor control, they take longer to perfect (Schulz & Curnow, 1988).

Research on outstanding athletes tells us that the upper biological limit of motor capacity is reached in the first part of early adulthood. How quickly do athletic skills weaken in later years? Longitudinal research on master runners reveals that as long as practice continues, speed drops only slightly from the mid-thirties into the sixties, when performance falls off at an accelerating pace (see Figure 13.2) (Tanaka & Higuchi, 1998). In the case of long-distance swimming—a non-weight-bearing exercise with a low incidence of injury—the decline in speed with advancing age is even more gradual: The accelerating performance drop-off is delayed until the seventies (Tanaka & Seals, 1997).

Indeed, sustained training leads to adaptations in body structures that minimize motor decline. For example, vital capacity is one-third greater in both younger and older people who participate actively in sports than in healthy inactive age-mates (Pimentel et al., 2003; Tanaka et al., 1997). Training also slows muscle loss, increases speed and force of muscle contraction, and leads fast-twitch muscle fibers to be converted into slow-twitch fibers, which support excellent long-distance running performance and other endurance skills (Trappe, 2001).

In sum, although athletic skills are at their best in early adulthood, biological aging accounts for only a small part of

age-related decline until advanced old age. Lower levels of performance by healthy people into their sixties and seventies largely reflect reduced capacities resulting from adaptation to a less physically demanding lifestyle.

Immune System

The immune response is the combined work of specialized cells that neutralize or destroy antigens (foreign substances) in the body. Two types of white blood cells play vital roles. *T cells,* which originate in the bone marrow and mature in the thymus (a small gland located in the upper part of the chest), attack antigens directly. *B cells,* manufactured in the bone marrow, secrete antibodies into the bloodstream that multiply, capture antigens, and permit the blood system to destroy them. Since receptors on their surfaces recognize only a single antigen, T and B cells come in great variety. They join with additional cells to produce immunity.

The capacity of the immune system to offer protection against disease increases through adolescence and declines after age 20. The trend is partly due to changes in the thymus, which is largest during the teenage years, then shrinks until it is barely detectable by age 50. As a result, production of thymic hormones is reduced, and the thymus is less able to promote full maturity and differentiation of T cells. Because B cells release far more antibodies when T cells are present, the immune response is compromised further (Malaguarnera et al., 2001). Administering thymic hormones can help the aging body fight disease (Goya & Bolognani, 1999).

Withering of the thymus, however, is not the only reason that the body gradually becomes less effective in warding off illness. The immune system interacts with the nervous and endocrine systems. For example, psychological stress can weaken the immune response. During final exams, Sharese was less resistant to colds. And in the month after her father died, she had great difficulty recovering from the flu. Divorce, caring for an ill aging parent, sleep deprivation, and chronic depression can also reduce immunity (Hamer, Wolvers, & Albers, 2004; Robles & Kiecolt-Glaser, 2003). Physical stress—from pollution, allergens, poor nutrition, and rundown housing—also undermines immune functioning throughout adulthood. And when physical and psychological stress combine, the risk of illness is magnified (Friedman & Lawrence, 2002).

The link between stress and illness makes sense when we consider that stress hormones mobilize the body for action, whereas the immune response is fostered by reduced activity. But this also means that increased difficulty coping with physical and psychological stress can contribute to age-related declines in immune system functioning.

Reproductive Capacity

Sharese was born when her mother was in her early twenties— an age at which, a generation later, Sharese was still single and entering graduate school. Many people believe that pregnancy during the twenties is ideal, not only because of lower risk of miscarriage and chromosomal disorders (see Chapter 2) but also because younger parents have more energy to keep up with active children. As Figure 13.3 reveals, however, first births to women in their thirties have increased greatly over the past two decades. Many people are delaying childbearing until their education is complete, their careers are well-established, and they know they can support a child.

Nevertheless, reproductive capacity does decline with age. Fertility problems among women increase from age 15 to 50. Between ages 15 and 29, 8 percent of women surveyed report difficulties, a figure that rises to 14 percent among 30- to 34-year-olds and 18 percent among 35- to 44-year-olds, when the success of reproductive technologies drops sharply (see page 54 in Chapter 2) (U.S. Department of Health and Human Services, 2005e). Since the uterus shows no consistent changes from the late thirties through the forties, the decline in female fertility is largely due to reduced number and quality of ova. In many mammals, including humans, a certain level of reserve ova in the ovaries is necessary for conception. Some women have normal menstrual cycles but do not conceive because their reserve of ova is too low—the major cause of the female age-related decline in fertility (Baird et al., 2005).

In males, semen volume and sperm concentration and motility gradually decrease after age 40, contributing to reduced fertility rates in older men (Kühnert & Nieschlag, 2004). Although there is no best time in adulthood to begin parenthood, individuals who postpone childbearing until their late thirties or their forties risk having fewer children than they desired or none at all.

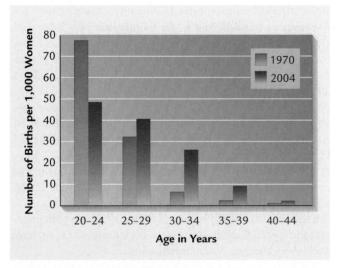

■ **FIGURE 13.3 First births to American women of different ages in 1970 and 2004.** The birthrate decreased during this period for women 20 to 24 years of age, whereas it increased for women 25 years of age and older. For women in their thirties, the birthrate more than doubled. Similar trends have occurred in Canada and other industrialized nations. (Adapted from U. S. Department of Health and Human Services, 2005b.)

Health and Fitness

Figure 13.4 displays leading causes of death in early adulthood in the United States and Canada. Notice that death rates for all causes are lower for Canadians than Americans—a difference believed to be due to a combination of factors, including Canada's lower rates of poverty and extreme obesity, its stricter gun-control policies, and its provision of universal, government-sponsored health insurance (Torrey & Haub, 2004). In later chapters, we will see that unintentional injury (mostly due to auto accidents) and homicide rates decline with age, while disease and physical disability rates rise. Biological aging clearly contributes to this trend. But, as we have noted, wide individual and group differences in physical changes are linked to environmental risks and health-related behaviors.

SES variations in health over the lifespan reflect these influences. Income, education, and occupational status show strong and continuous relationships with almost every disease and health indicator (Adler & Newman, 2002; Alwin & Wray, 2005). Furthermore, when a nationally representative sample of 3,600 Americans were asked about health-related limitations on their daily lives, SES differences widened over early and middle adulthood but contracted during old age, when individuals in the poorest health had died (see Figure 13.5) (House, Lantz, & Herd, 2005). Longitudinal evidence confirms these trends: Economically advantaged and well-educated individuals sustain better health over most of their adult lives, whereas the health of lower-income individuals with limited education steadily declines (Lantz et al., 1998, 2001). SES differences in health-related circumstances and habits—stressful life events, crowding, pollution, diet, exercise, overweight and obesity, substance abuse, availability of supportive social relationships, and (in the United States) access to affordable health

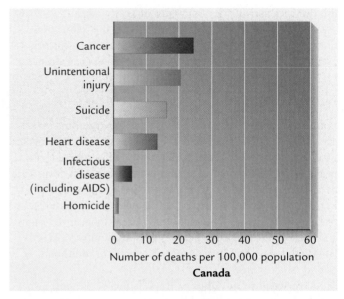

FIGURE 13.4 Leading causes of death between 25 and 44 years of age in the United States and Canada. Death rates are lower in Canada because of a combination of factors. Among these are less widespread poverty, less extreme obesity, stricter gun-control policies, and the availability of universal health insurance. (Adapted from Statistics Canada, 2002d; Torrey & Haub, 2004; U.S. Census Bureau, 2006b).

care—are largely responsible (Evans & Kantrowitz, 2002; Wray, Alwin, & McCammon, 2005). Further, poor health in childhood, which is linked to low SES, affects health in adulthood. The overall influence of childhood factors lessens if SES improves. But in most instances, child and adult SES remain fairly consistent, exerting a cumulative impact that amplifies SES health disparities with age (Dannefer, 2003; Luo & Waite, 2005).

Why are SES disparities in health and mortality larger in the United States than in Canada and other industrialized nations (Mackenbach, 2002)? Besides the lack of universal

health insurance, poverty-stricken U.S. families have lower incomes than their Canadian counterparts. In addition, SES groups are more likely to be segregated by neighborhood in U.S. than in Canadian large cities, resulting in greater inequalities in environmental factors that affect health, such as housing, pollution, and community services.

These findings reveal, once again, that the living conditions that nations and communities provide combine with those that people create for themselves to affect physical aging. Because the incidence of health problems is much lower during

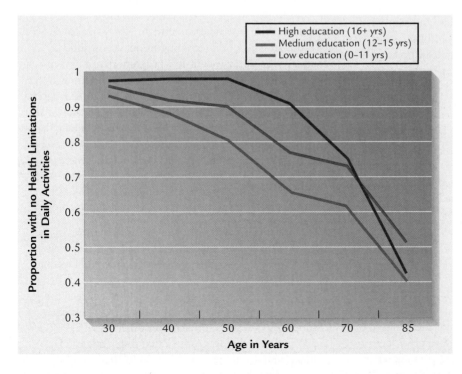

FIGURE 13.5 Age differences in self-reported health status by socioeconomic status (SES), as indexed by education. The figure shows cross-sectional trends. In longitudinal research as well, SES differences in health increase over early and middle adulthood and then contract in old age as people in the poorest health die earlier. Environmental risks and poor health habits contribute to earlier declining health among low-SES adults. (From J. S. House, P. M. Lantz, & P. Herd, 2005, "Continuity and Change in the Social Stratification of Aging and Health Over the Life Course: Evidence from a Nationally Representative Longitudinal Study from 1986 to 2001/2002. *Journal of Gerontology, 60B,* p. 16. Reprinted by permission.)

the twenties and thirties than later on, early adulthood is an excellent time to prevent later problems. In the following sections, we take up a variety of major health concerns—nutrition, exercise, substance abuse, sexuality, and psychological stress.

Nutrition

Bombarded with advertising claims and an extraordinary variety of food choices, adults find it increasingly difficult to make wise dietary decisions. An abundance of food, combined with a heavily scheduled life, means that most North Americans eat because they feel like it or because it is time to do so rather than to maintain the body's functions (Donatelle, 2004). As a result, many eat the wrong types and amounts of food. Overweight and obesity and a high-fat diet are widespread nutritional problems with long-term consequences for health in adulthood.

■ **Overweight and Obesity.** In Chapter 9, we noted that obesity (a greater than 20 percent increase over average body weight, based on age, sex, and physical build) has increased dramatically in many Western nations. Today, 31 percent of U.S. adults and 23 percent of Canadian adults are obese, and the rate rises to 34 percent among Hispanic adults, 38 percent among Canadian-Aboriginal adults, and 40 percent among African-American and Native-American adults. In the United States and Western Europe, 5 to 7 percent more women than men suffer from obesity. In Canada, obesity rates for the two sexes are similar (Tjepkema, 2005; U.S. Department of Health and Human Services, 2005o).

Overweight—a less extreme but nevertheless unhealthy condition—affects an additional 34 percent of Americans and 36 percent of Canadians. Add the rates of overweight and obesity together and Americans, at 65 percent, emerge as the heaviest people in the world, with Canadians, at 59 percent, not far behind. Recall from Chapter 9 that overweight children are very likely to become overweight adults. But a substantial number of people show large weight gains in adulthood, most often between ages 25 and 40. And young adults who were already overweight or obese typically get heavier, leading obesity rates to rise steadily between ages 20 and 60 (Tjepkema, 2005; U.S. Department of Health and Human Services, 2005o).

Causes and Consequences. As noted in Chapter 9, heredity makes some people more vulnerable to obesity than others. But environmental pressures underlie the rising rates of obesity in industrialized nations: With the decline in need for physical labor in the home and workplace, our lives have become more sedentary. Meanwhile, the average number of calories and amount of sugar and fat consumed by North Americans rose over most of the twentieth century, with a sharp increase after 1970 (see the Lifespan Vista box on pages 440–441).

Adding some weight between ages 25 and 50 is a normal part of aging because **basal metabolic rate (BMR),** the amount of energy the body uses at complete rest, gradually declines as the number of active muscle cells (which create the greatest energy demand) drops off. But excess weight is strongly associated with serious health problems—including high blood pres-

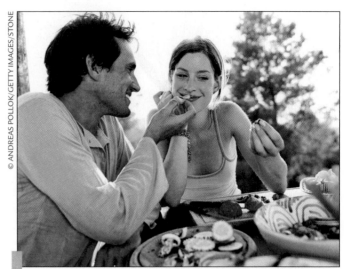

A balanced, low-fat diet promotes physical and psychological well-being and contributes to a normal body weight. These young people enjoy a meal of fresh vegetables, presented in an attractive and appetizing array.

sure, circulatory difficulties, atherosclerosis, stroke, adult-onset diabetes, liver and gallbladder disease, arthritis, sleep and digestive disorders, and most forms of cancer—and with early death (Calle et al., 2003). Furthermore, overweight adults suffer enormous social discrimination. They are less likely than their normal-weight agemates to find mates, to be rented apartments, to be given financial aid for college, and to be offered jobs. And they report frequent mistreatment by family members, peers, co-workers, and health-care professionals (Carr & Friedman, 2005; Rogge, Greenwald, & Golden, 2004).

Treatment. Because obesity climbs in early and middle adulthood, treatment for adults should begin as soon as possible—preferably in the early twenties. Even moderate weight loss reduces health problems substantially (Orzano & Scott, 2004). But successfully intervening in obesity is difficult. Most individuals who start a weight-loss program return to their original weight, and often to a higher weight, within two years (Vogels, Diepvens, & Westerterp-Plantenga, 2005). The high rate of failure is partly due to limited knowledge of just how obesity disrupts the complex neural, hormonal, and metabolic factors that maintain a normal body-weight set point. Until more information is available, researchers are examining the characteristics of treatments and participants associated with greater success. The following elements promote lasting behavior change:

🖋 *A well-balanced diet lower in calories and fat, plus exercise.* To lose weight, Sharese sharply reduced calories, sugar, and fat in her diet and exercised regularly. The precise balance of dietary protein, carbohydrates, and fats that best helps adults lose weight is a matter of heated debate. Although scores of diet books offer different recommendations, no clear-cut evidence exists for the long-term superiority of one approach over others (Tsai & Wadden, 2005). Research does confirm that restricting calorie intake and fat (to no more than 20 to 30 percent of calories) and increasing physical activity are essential for reducing the impact of a genetic tendency toward overweight (Avenell et al., 2004). In addition (as we will see shortly), exercise offers physical and psychological benefits that help prevent overeating. Yet fewer than half of obese American adults are advised by their doctors to control eating and to exercise (Mokdad et al., 2001).

● *Training participants to keep an accurate record of what they eat.* About 30 to 35 percent of obese people sincerely believe they eat less than they do, and from 25 to 45 percent report problems with binge eating (Wadden & Foster, 2000). When Sharese became aware of how often she ate when she was not actually hungry, she was better able to limit her food intake.

● *Social support.* Group or individual counseling and encouragement from friends and relatives help sustain weight-loss efforts by fostering self-esteem (Johnson, 2002). Once Sharese decided to act with the support of her family and a weight-loss counselor, she began to feel better about herself—walking and holding herself differently—even before the first pounds were shed.

● *Teaching problem-solving skills.* Acquiring cognitive and behavioral strategies for coping with tempting situations and periods of slowed progress is associated with long-term change. Weight-loss maintainers are more likely than individuals who relapse to be conscious of their behavior, to use social support, and to confront problems directly (Cooper & Fairburn, 2002).

● *Extended intervention.* Longer treatments (from 25 to 40 weeks) that include the components listed here grant people time to develop new habits.

Although many North Americans on weight-reduction diets are overweight, about one-third are within normal range (Mokdad et al., 2001). Recall from Chapter 11 that the high value placed on thinness creates unrealistic expectations about desirable body weight and contributes to anorexia and bulimia, dangerous eating disorders that remain common in early adulthood (see pages 371–372). Overweight people in weight-loss programs who set too-stringent weight goals are more likely to regain their lost pounds. And people of normal weight on diets often display "starvation syndrome" symptoms, including depression, anxiety, weakness, and preoccupation with food. A sensible body weight—neither too low nor too high—predicts physical and psychological health and longer life. Throughout adulthood, both underweight and obesity are associated with increased mortality (Flegal et al., 2005).

■ **Dietary Fat.** After entering college, Sharese altered the diet of her childhood and adolescent years, sharply limiting red meat, eggs, butter, and fried foods. Although public service announcements about the health risks of a high-fat diet have led to a slight drop in fat consumption by North American adults, about 60 percent of adults still eat too much. U.S. and Canadian national dietary recommendations include reducing dietary fat to 30 percent of total caloric intake, with no more than 10 percent made up of saturated fat (Health Canada, 1999; U.S. Department of Health and Human Services, 2005h). Many researchers believe that fat consumption plays a role in breast cancer and (when it includes large amounts of red meat) is linked to colon cancer (Binukumar & Mathew, 2005; Kono, 2004). But the main reasons for limiting dietary fat are the strong connection of total fat with obesity and of saturated fat with cardiovascular disease.

Fat is a type of molecule made up of carbon atoms dotted with hydrogen atoms. *Saturated fat,* which generally comes from meat and dairy products and is solid at room temperature, has as many hydrogen atoms as it can chemically hold. *Unsaturated fat,* including most liquid vegetable oils, has less than its full complement of hydrogen atoms.

Moderate fat consumption is essential for normal body functioning. But when we consume too much fat, especially saturated fat, some is converted to cholesterol, which accumulates as plaque on the arterial walls in atherosclerosis. Earlier in this chapter, we noted that atherosclerosis is determined by multiple biological and environmental factors. But excess fat consumption (along with other societal conditions) is a major contributor to the high rate of heart disease in the U.S. black population. When researchers compare Africans in West Africa, the Caribbean, and the United States (the historic path of the slave trade), dietary fat increases, and so do high blood pressure and heart disease (see Figure 13.6) (Luke et al., 2001). Indeed, West Africans have one of the lowest rates of heart disease in the world.

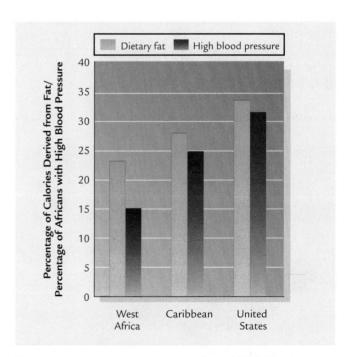

■ **FIGURE 13.6 Dietary fat and prevalence of high blood pressure among black Africans in West Africa, the Caribbean, and the United States.** The three regions represent the historic path of the slave trade and, therefore, have genetically similar populations. As dietary fat increases, high blood pressure and heart disease rise. Both are particularly high among African Americans. (Adapted from Luke et al., 2001.)

A Lifespan Vista

The Obesity Epidemic: How Americans Became the Heaviest People in the World

In the late 1980s, obesity in the United States started to soar. The maps in Figure 13.7 show how quickly it engulfed the nation. The epidemic also spread to other Western nations, including Canada, where (as in the United States) the majority of the adult population is either overweight or obese. But no country matches the United States in prevalence of this life-threatening condition.

A Changing Food Environment and Lifestyle. Several societal factors have encouraged widespread rapid weight gain:

■ *Availability of cheap commercial fat and sugar.* The 1970s saw two massive changes in the U.S. food economy:

(1) the discovery and mass production of high-fructose corn syrup, a sweetener six times as sweet as ordinary sugar, and therefore far less expensive; and (2) the importing from Malaysia of large quantities of palm oil, which is lower in cost and tastier than other vegetable oils because of its high saturated fat content. As food manufacturers relied on corn syrup and palm oil to make soft drinks and calorie-dense convenience foods, the production costs of these items dropped and their variety expanded. A new era of "cheap, abundant, and tasty calories had arrived" (Critser, 2003).

■ *Portion supersizing.* Fast-food chains discovered a successful strategy for attracting customers: increasing por-

tion sizes substantially and prices just a little for foods that had become inexpensive to produce. Customers thronged to buy "value meals," jumbo burgers and burritos, pizza "by the foot," and 20-ounce Cokes (Critser, 2003). And research revealed that when presented with larger portions, individuals 2 years and older increased their intake, on average, by 25 to 30 percent (Fisher, Rolls, & Birch, 2003; Rolls, Morris, & Roe, 2002).

■ *Increasingly busy lives.* Between the 1970s and 1990s, women entered the labor force in record numbers, and the average amount of time North Americans worked increased by 15 percent, or about 350 hours per year (Higgins & Duxbury, 2002; Schor, 2002). As time became scarce, eating out increased. In addition, North Americans became frequent snackers, aided by a growing

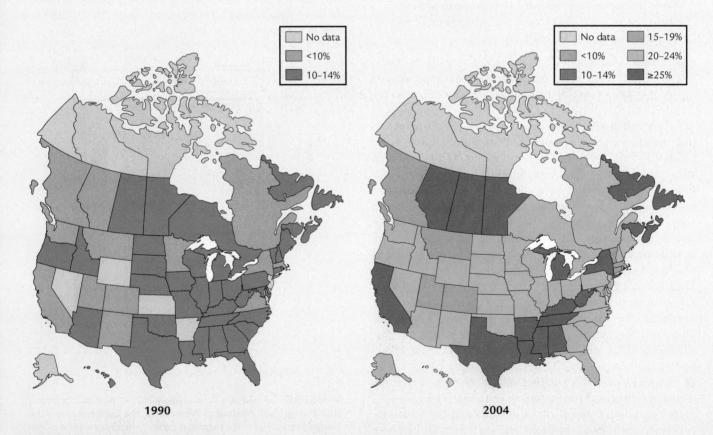

1990

2004

■ **FIGURE 13.7 Obesity trends among U. S. and Canadian adults, 1990 and 2004.** The darkening maps show that obesity has increased sharply in both nations, with the United States more extremely affected. (From Health Canada, 2005d, Mokdad et al., 2001; U.S. Department of Health and Human Services, 2004c.)

diversity of high-calorie snack foods on supermarket shelves. During this period, the number of calories Americans consumed away from home nearly doubled, and dietary fat increased from 19 to 38 percent. Overall, average daily food intake rose by almost 200 calories—enough to add an extra pound every 20 days (Nielsen & Popkin, 2003).

■ *Declining rates of physical activity.* During the 1980s, physical activity, which had risen since the 1960s, started to fall as North Americans spent more time working in sedentary jobs. At home, TV had become their major leisure pursuit—consuming, on average,

about 4 hours per day and linked to weight gain in adults and children alike (Gore et al., 2003).

Combating the Obesity Epidemic. Obesity's toll on society is immense. It is responsible for $90 billion in health expenditures and 300,000 premature deaths per year in the United States alone (Manson et al., 2004). Besides individual treatment, broad societal efforts are needed to combat obesity. Suggestions include

■ Government funding to support massive public education about healthy eating and physical activity

■ A high priority placed on building parks and recreation centers in low-income neighborhoods, where overweight and obesity are highest

■ Laws that mandate prominent posting of the calorie, sugar, and fat content of foods sold in restaurants, movie theaters, and convenience stores

■ A special tax on foods high in calories, sugar, or fat

■ Incentives to schools and workplaces for promoting healthy eating and daily exercise and for offering weight-management programs

The best rule of thumb is to eat less fat of all kinds and to use unsaturated instead of saturated fat whenever possible. Furthermore, regular exercise can reduce the harmful influence of dietary fat because it creates chemical byproducts that help eliminate cholesterol from the body.

Exercise

Three times a week, over the noon hour, Sharese delighted in running, making her way to a wooded trail that cut through a picturesque area of the city. Regular exercise kept her fit and slim. It also limited the number of respiratory illnesses she caught, compared to the days when she had been sedentary and overweight. As Sharese explained to a friend one day, "Exercise gives me a positive outlook and calms me down. Afterward, I feel a burst of energy that gets me through the day. If I don't do it, I get tired in the afternoon."

Although most North Americans are aware of the health benefits of exercise, only one-third engage in at least moderate leisure-time physical activity for 20 minutes or more at least five times a week. About 30 percent in Canada and 38 percent in the United States are inactive, with no regular brief sessions of even light activity (Canadian Fitness and Lifestyle Research Institute, 2002; U.S. Department of Health and Human Services, 2005h). More women than men are inactive. And inactivity is greater among low-SES adults, who live in less safe neighborhoods, have more health problems, experience less social support for exercising regularly, and feel less personal control over their health (Grzywacz & Marks, 2001; Wilson et al., 2004).

Besides reducing body fat and building muscle, exercise fosters resistance to disease. Frequent bouts of moderate-intensity exercise enhance the immune response, lowering the

risk of colds or flu and promoting faster recovery when these illnesses do strike (Nieman, 1994). Furthermore, in several longitudinal studies extending over 10 to 20 years, physical activity was linked to reduced incidence of cancer at all body sites except the skin, with the strongest findings for cancer of the rectum and colon (Albanes, Blair, & Taylor, 1989; Tardon et al., 2005; Wannamethee, Shaper, & Macfarlane, 1993). Physically active people are also less likely to develop diabetes and cardiovascular disease (Bassuk & Manson, 2005). If they do, these illnesses typically occur later and are less severe than among their inactive agemates.

How does exercise help prevent the serious illnesses just mentioned? First, it reduces the incidence of obesity—a risk factor for heart disease, diabetes, and several forms of cancer. In addition, people who exercise probably adopt other healthful behaviors, thereby lowering the risk of diseases associated with high-fat diets, alcohol consumption, and smoking. In animal studies, exercise directly inhibits growth of cancerous tumors—beyond the impact of diet, body fat, and the immune response (MacKinnon, 1999). Exercise also promotes cardiovascular functioning by strengthening the heart muscle, decreasing blood pressure, and producing a form of "good cholesterol" (high-density lipoproteins, or HDLs) that helps remove "bad cholesterol" (low-density lipoproteins, or LDLs) from the artery walls (Donatelle, 2004).

Yet another way that exercise may guard against illness is through its mental health benefits. Many studies show that physical activity reduces anxiety and depression, improves mood, and enhances alertness and energy (Mutrie & Faulkner, 2004; Penedo & Dahn, 2005). The impact of exercise on a "positive outlook," as Sharese expressed it, is most obvious just after a workout and can last for several hours (Chollar, 1995). The stress-reducing properties of exercise undoubtedly strengthen

Regular, moderate-to-vigorous exercise predicts a healthier, longer life. Participants in this kick-boxing class reap both physical and mental health benefits.

© LORI ADAMSKI PEEK/GETTY IMAGES/STONE

immunity to disease. And as physical activity enhances psychological well-being, it promotes self-esteem, ability to cope with stress, on-the-job productivity, and life satisfaction.

When we consider the evidence as a whole, it is not surprising that physical activity is associated with substantially lower death rates from all causes. The contribution of exercise to longevity cannot be accounted for by preexisting illness in inactive people. In a Danish longitudinal study of a nationally representative sample of 7,000 healthy 20- to 79-year-olds followed over several decades, mortality was lower among those who increased their leisure-time physical activity from low to either moderate or high than among those who remained consistently inactive (Schnohr, Scharling, & Jensen, 2003).

How much exercise is recommended for a healthier, happier, and longer life? Moderately intense physical activity—for example, 30 minutes of brisk walking—on most days leads to health benefits for previously inactive people. Adults who exercise at greater intensity—enough to build up a sweat—derive even greater protection against cardiovascular disease, diabetes, colon cancer, and obesity (Hu & Manson, 2001; Yu et al., 2003). Currently, the U.S. government recommends 30 minutes of moderate-intensity physical activity on five or more days per week or 20 or more minutes of vigorous-intensity exercise (for example, jogging, biking uphill, fast swimming) on three or more days per week (U.S. Department of Health and Human Services, 2006). Canadian recommendations are more stringent: at least 30 to 60 minutes of activity every day, with time declining as intensity increases to vigorous effort (Health Canada, 2003d).

Substance Abuse

Drug taking peaks among 19- to 22-year-olds and then declines over the decade of the twenties. Eager to try a wide range of experiences before settling down to the responsibilities of adulthood, young people of this age are more likely than younger or older individuals to smoke cigarettes, chew tobacco, use marijuana, and take stimulants to enhance cognitive or physical performance (U.S. Department of Health and Human Services, 2005k). Binge drinking, experimentation with prescription drugs (such as Oxycontin, a highly addictive painkiller) and "party drugs" (such as LSD and MDMA, or Ecstasy), also increase, at times with tragic consequences. Risks include brain damage, lasting impairments in mental functioning, and unintentional injury and death (Burgess, O'Donohoe, & Gill, 2000; Montoya et al., 2002).

Furthermore, when alcohol and drug taking become chronic, they intensify the psychological problems that underlie addiction. As many as 20 percent of North American 21- to 25-year-olds are substance abusers (Canadian Centre on Substance Abuse, 2004; U.S. Department of Health and Human Services, 2005k). Return to Chapter 11, page 379, to review the factors that lead to alcohol and drug abuse in adolescence. The same personal and situational conditions are predictive in the adult years. Cigarette smoking and alcohol consumption are the most common substance disorders.

■ **Cigarette Smoking.** Dissemination of information on the harmful effects of cigarette smoking has helped reduce its prevalence from 40 percent of North American adults in 1965 to 25 percent in the United States and 19 percent in Canada in 2004 (Shields, 2005; U.S. Department of Health and Human Services, 2005k).

Still, smoking has declined very slowly, and most of the drop is among college graduates, with very little change for those who did not finish high school. Furthermore, although more men than women smoke, the gender gap is much smaller today than in the past, reflecting a sharp increase in smoking among young women who did not finish high school. Smoking among college students has also risen—for students of both sexes and of diverse ethnicities. More than 90 percent of men and 85 percent of women who smoke started before age 21 (Nordstrom et al., 2000; U.S. Department of Health and Human Services, 2005h). And the earlier people start smoking, the greater their daily cigarette consumption and likelihood of continuing, an important reason that preventive efforts with adolescents and young adults are vital.

The ingredients of cigarette smoke—nicotine, tar, carbon monoxide, and other chemicals—leave their damaging mark throughout the body. As smokers inhale, oxygen delivery to tissues is reduced, and heart rate and blood pressure rise. Over time, exposure to toxins and insufficient oxygen result in damage to the retina of the eye; skin abnormalities, including premature aging, poor wound healing, and hair loss; a decline in bone mass; a decrease in reserve ova and earlier menopause in women; and a reduced sperm count and higher rate of sexual impotence in men (American Society for Reproductive Medicine, 2004; Freiman et al., 2004; Thornton et al., 2005). Other deadly outcomes include increased risk of heart attack, stroke, acute leukemia, melanoma, and cancer of the mouth, throat, larynx, esophagus, lungs, stomach, pancreas, kidneys, and bladder. Cigarette smoking is the single most important preventable cause of death in industrialized nations. One of every three young people who become regular smokers will die from a smoking-related disease (U.S. Department of Health and Human Services, 2005a).

The chances of premature death rise with the number of cigarettes consumed. At the same time, the benefits of quitting include return of most disease risks to nonsmoker levels within 3 to 8 years, as well as a healthier living environment. Although millions of people have stopped smoking without help, those who enter treatment programs or use cessation aids (for example, nicotine gum, nasal spray, or patches, designed to reduce dependency gradually) often fail: After one year, 70 to 90 percent start smoking again (Ludvig, Miner, & Eisenberg, 2005).

Unfortunately, too few treatments last long enough or teach skills for avoiding relapse. Sometimes a personal experience or the advice of a doctor is enough to energize quitting. My father, a heavy smoker in his twenties and thirties, sought treatment for chronic bronchitis (inflammation of the bronchial tubes, common among smokers). His doctor told him that if he did not stop smoking, he would not live to see his children grow up. That day marked his last cigarette. He died at age 80, having lived nearly 30 years longer than the average life expectancy for his year of birth.

■ **Alcohol.** National surveys reveal that about 13 percent of men and 3 percent of women in the United States and Canada are heavy drinkers (Canadian Centre on Substance Abuse, 2004; U.S. Department of Health and Human Services, 2005k). About one-third of this group are *alcoholics*—people who cannot limit their alcohol use. In men, alcoholism usually begins in the teens and early twenties and worsens over the following decade. In women, its onset is typically later, in the twenties and thirties, and its course is more variable. Many alcoholics are also addicted to other drugs. About 80 percent are heavy cigarette smokers (John et al., 2003).

Twin studies support a genetic contribution to alcoholism (Tsuang et al., 2001). But whether a person comes to deal with life's problems through drinking is greatly affected by personal characteristics and circumstances: Half of hospitalized alcoholics have no family history of problem drinking (Hawkins, Catalano, & Miller, 1992). Alcoholism crosses SES and ethnic lines but is higher in some groups than others. In cultures where alcohol is a traditional part of religious or ceremonial activities, people are less likely to abuse it. Where access to alcohol is carefully controlled and viewed as a sign of adulthood, dependency is more likely—factors that may, in part, explain why college students drink more heavily than young people not enrolled in college (Slutske et al., 2004). Poverty and hopelessness also promote excessive drinking (Donatelle, 2004; U.S. Department of Health and Human Services, 2005k).

Alcohol acts as a depressant, impairing the brain's ability to control thought and action. In a heavy drinker, it relieves anxiety at first but then induces it as the effects wear off, so the alcoholic drinks again. Chronic alcohol use does widespread

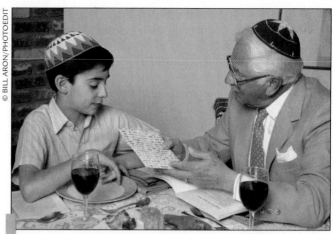

In cultures where alcohol is a traditional part of religious or ceremonial activities, people are less likely to abuse it. This Jewish grandfather teaches his grandson the customs of the Passover Seder, which includes the blessing and drinking of wine.

physical damage. Its best known complication is liver disease, but it is also linked to cardiovascular disease, inflammation of the pancreas, irritation of the intestinal tract, bone marrow problems, disorders of the blood and joints, and some forms of cancer. Over time, alcohol causes brain damage, leading to confusion, apathy, inability to learn, and impaired memory (Brun & Andersson, 2001). The costs to society are enormous. About 40 percent of fatal motor vehicle crashes in the United States and Canada involve drivers who have been drinking (Mayhew, Brown, & Simpson, 2005; Subramanian, 2005). Nearly half of convicted felons are alcoholics, and about half of police activities in large cities involve alcohol-related offenses (McKim, 2002). Alcohol frequently plays a part in sexual coercion, including date rape, and in domestic violence.

The most successful treatments combine personal and family counseling, group support, and aversion therapy (use of medication that produces a physically unpleasant reaction to alcohol, such as nausea and vomiting). Alcoholics Anonymous, a community support approach, helps many people exert greater control over their lives through the encouragement of others with similar problems. Nevertheless, breaking an addiction that has dominated a person's life is difficult; about 50 percent of alcoholics relapse within a few months (Volpicelli, 2001).

Sexuality

By the end of their teenage years, more than 70 percent of young people have had sexual intercourse; by age 22, the figure rises to 90 percent (Michael et al., 1994; U.S. Department of Health and Human Services, 2004d). Compared with earlier generations, contemporary adults display a wider range of sexual choices and lifestyles, including cohabitation, marriage, extramarital experiences, and orientation toward a heterosexual or homosexual partner. In this chapter, we explore the attitudes, behaviors, and health concerns that arise as sexual activity becomes a regular event in young people's lives. In Chapter 14, we focus on the emotional side of close relationships.

■ **Heterosexual Attitudes and Behavior.** One Friday evening, Sharese accompanied her roommate Heather to a young singles bar. Shortly after they arrived, two young men joined them. Faithful to her boyfriend, Ernie, whom she had met in college and who worked in another city, Sharese remained aloof for the next hour. In contrast, Heather was talkative and gave one of the men, Rich, her phone number. The next weekend, Heather went out with Rich. On the second date, they had intercourse, but the romance was short-lived. Within a few weeks, each went in search of a new partner. Aware of Heather's varied sex life, Sharese wondered whether her own was normal. Only after six months of dating exclusively had she and Ernie slept together.

Since the 1950s, public display of sexuality in movies, newspapers, magazines, and books has steadily increased, fostering the impression that North Americans are more sexually active than ever before. This escalation in sexual openness has prompted people whose sexual history falls short of popular images to question whether they might be missing something. What are contemporary adults' sexual attitudes and behaviors really like? Answers were difficult to find until the National Health and Social Life Survey, the first in-depth study of U.S. adults' sex lives based on a nationally representative sample. Nearly 4 out of 5 randomly chosen 18- to 59-year-olds agreed to participate—3,400 in all. Findings were remarkably similar to those of surveys conducted at about the same time in France, Great Britain, and Finland, and to a more recent U.S. survey (Langer, 2004; Laumann et al., 1994; Michael et al., 1994).

Recall from Chapter 11 that the sex lives of most teenagers do not dovetail with exciting media images, and the same is true of adults in Western nations. Although their sexual practices are diverse, they are far less sexually active than we have come to believe. Monogamous, emotionally committed couples like Sharese and Ernie are more typical (and more satisfied) than couples like Heather and Rich.

Sexual partners, whether dating, cohabiting, or married, usually do not select each other arbitrarily. They tend to be alike in age (within 5 years), education, ethnicity, and (to a lesser extent) religion. In addition, people who establish lasting relationships usually meet in conventional ways—either through family members or friends, or at work, school, or social events where people similar to themselves congregate. The powerful influence of social networks on sexual choice is adaptive. Sustaining an intimate relationship is easier when adults share interests and values and people they know approve of the match.

Over the past decade, Internet dating services have become an increasingly popular way to initiate relationships. According to one report, more than 16 million U.S. adults visited these matchmaking websites within a single month (Hollander, 2004). By creating a personal profile and describing the type of person they want to meet, users hope to find a compatible partner quickly. Although success rates are lower than with conventional strategies, adults who form an online relationship and then meet face-to-face often go on to see each other again, with 18 percent of such ties lasting for more than a year (Gavin, Scott, & Duffield, 2005).

Consistent with popular belief, Americans today have more sexual partners over their lifetimes than they did a generation ago. For example, one-third of adults over age 50 have had five or more partners, whereas half of 30- to 50-year-olds have accumulated that many in much less time. But when adults of any age are asked how many partners they have had in the past year, the usual reply (for about 70 percent) is one.

What explains this trend toward more relationships in the context of sexual commitment? In the past, dating several partners was followed by marriage. Today, dating more often gives way to cohabitation, which leads either to marriage or to breakup. In addition, people are marrying later, and the divorce rate remains high. Together, these factors create more opportunities for new sexual partners. Still, surveys of college students reveal that almost all want to settle down with a mutually exclusive sexual partner eventually (Pedersen et al., 2002). In line with this goal, most people spend the majority of their lives with one partner. And only 3 percent of Americans, most of them men, report five or more partners in a single year. (See the Biology and Environment box on the following page for a discussion of sex differences in attitudes toward sexuality.)

How often do Americans have sex? Not nearly as frequently as the media would suggest. One-third of 18- to 59-year-olds have intercourse as often as twice a week, another third have it a few times a month, and the remaining third have it a few times a year or not at all. Three factors affect frequency of sexual activity: age, whether people are cohabiting or married, and how long the couple has been together. Single people have more partners, but this does not translate into more sex! Sexual activity increases through the twenties as people either cohabit or marry. Then, around age 30, it declines, even though hormone levels have not changed much. The demands of daily life—working, commuting, taking care of home and children—are probably responsible. Despite the common assumption that sexual practices vary greatly across social groups, the patterns just described are unaffected by education, SES, or ethnicity.

Nevertheless, most adults are happy with their sex lives. For those in committed relationships, more than 80 percent report feeling "extremely physically and emotionally satisfied," and this figure rises to 88 percent for married couples. In contrast, as number of sex partners increases, satisfaction declines sharply. These findings challenge two stereotypes—that marriage is sexually dull and that people with many partners have the "hottest" sex.

Only a minority of adults—women more often than men—report persistent sexual problems. For women, the two most frequent difficulties are lack of interest in sex (33 percent) and inability to achieve orgasm (24 percent); for men, climaxing too early (29 percent) and anxiety about performance (16 percent). Sexual difficulties are linked to low SES and psychological stress, and are more common among people who are not married, have had more than five partners, and have experienced sexual abuse during childhood or (for women) sexual coercion in adulthood (Laumann, Paik, & Rosen, 1999). As these findings suggest, a history of unfavorable personal

Biology and Environment

Sex Differences in Attitudes Toward Sexuality

Differences between men and women in sexual attitudes and behavior are widely assumed, and contemporary theories offer diverse explanations for them. For example, Nancy Chodorow, a feminist psychoanalytic theorist, and Carol Gilligan, a feminist theorist of moral development (see Chapter 12, page 408), believe that the emotional intensity of the infant–caregiver relationship is carried over into future intimate ties for girls but is disrupted for boys as they form a "masculine" gender identity stressing independence and self-reliance (Chodorow, 1978; Gilligan, 1982).

According to an alternative evolutionary perspective, the desire to have children and ensure their survival powerfully shapes sexuality. Because sperm are far more plentiful than ova, women must be more careful than men to select a partner with the commitment and resources needed to protect children's development (Bjorklund & Shackelford, 1999). Finally, social learning theory attributes sex differences to modeling and reinforcement of gender-role expectations (see Chapter 8, pages 277). Whereas

women receive disapproval for having numerous partners and engaging in casual sex, men are sometimes rewarded with admiration and social status.

Both small-scale studies and large-scale surveys confirm that women are more opposed to casual sex than men and are only half as likely as men to have engaged in it (Cubbins & Tanfer, 2000; Hyde & Oliver, 2000). However, after excluding a small number of men with a great many sexual partners, contemporary men and women differ little in average number of lifetime sexual partners (Langer, 2004). Why is this so? From an evolutionary perspective, more effective contraception has permitted sexual activity with little risk of reproduction, allowing women to have as many partners as men without endangering the welfare of their offspring.

Still, when women complain that the men they meet are not interested in long-term commitments, their laments have a ring of truth. Many more men than women report that they are looking for sexual play and pleasure, not marriage or love. And when infidelity occurs, men are more upset at the thought of their partner having sex with another person,

© YANG LIU/CORBIS

Because of more effective contraception, men and women differ much less in attitudes toward extramarital sex than they once did. And for both genders, satisfying sex is attained in the context of love, affection, and fidelity.

women at the thought of their partner feeling affection for someone else—an outcome that could mean loss of investment in their offspring (Buss, 2004). These conflicting goals and attitudes are greatest for young adults. With age, the two sexes become more similar, regarding a loving relationship as more central to sexuality (Schwartz & Rutter, 1998).

---

relationships and sexual experiences increases the risk of sexual dysfunction.

But overall, a completely untroubled physical experience is not essential for sexual happiness. Surveys of adults repeatedly show that satisfying sex involves more than technique; it is attained in the context of love, affection, and fidelity. In sum, happiness with partnered sex is linked to an emotionally fulfilling relationship, good mental health, and overall contentment with life (Bancroft, 2002; Michael et al., 1994).

■ **Homosexual Attitudes and Behavior.** The majority of North Americans support civil liberties and equal employment opportunities for gay men, lesbians, and bisexuals (Brooks, 2000). And in the past decade, attitudes toward sexual relations between two adults of the same sex have become more accepting: 55 to 65 percent of U.S. 18- to 65-year-olds agree that "it is OK" (Langer, 2004). Homosexuals' political activism and greater openness about their sexual orientation have con-

tributed to slow gains in acceptance. Exposure and interpersonal contact reduce negative attitudes. But perhaps because they are especially concerned with gender-role conformity, heterosexual men judge homosexuals (and especially gay men) more harshly than do heterosexual women (Kite & Whitley, 1998; Lim, 2002).

In the National Health and Social Life Survey, 2.8 percent of men and 1.4 percent of women identified themselves as homosexual or bisexual—figures similar to those of other national surveys conducted in the United States, France, and Great Britain (Black, Gates, & Sanders, 2000; Spira, 1992; Wellings et al., 1994). But an estimated 30 percent of same-sex couples do not report themselves as such in survey research. This unwillingness to answer questions, engendered by a climate of persecution, has limited researchers' access to information about the sex lives of gay men and lesbians. The little evidence available indicates that homosexual sex follows many of the same rules as heterosexual sex: People tend to seek out partners similar in education and background to themselves; partners in committed relationships have sex more often and are more satisfied; and the overall frequency of sex is modest (Laumann et al., 1994; Michael et al., 1994).

Homosexuals tend to live in large cities, where many others share their sexual orientation, or in college towns, where attitudes are more accepting. Living in small communities where prejudice is intense and no social network exists through which to find compatible homosexual partners is isolating, lonely, and predictive of mental health problems (Meyer, 2003).

People who identify themselves as gay or lesbian also tend to be well-educated (Black, Gates, & Sanders, 2000). In the National Health and Social Life Survey, twice as many college-educated as high-school-educated men and 8 times as many college-educated as high-school-educated women stated they were homosexual. Although the reasons for these findings are not clear, they probably reflect greater social and sexual liberalism among the more highly educated and therefore greater willingness to disclose homosexuality.

■ **Sexually Transmitted Diseases.** A large number of North Americans—1 in 4 in the United States and 1 in 12 in Canada—are likely to contract a sexually transmitted disease (STD) at some time in their lives (Health Canada, 2005c; U.S. Department of Health and Human Services, 2005h). Although the incidence is highest in adolescence, STDs continue to be prevalent in early adulthood. During the teens and twenties, people accumulate most of their sexual partners, and they often do not take appropriate precautions to prevent the spread of STDs (see page 375). The overall rate of STDs is higher among women than men because it is at least twice as easy for a man to infect a woman with any STD, including AIDS, than for a woman to infect a man.

Although AIDS, the most deadly STD, remains concentrated among gay men and intravenous drug abusers, many homosexuals have responded to its spread by changing their sexual practices—limiting the number of partners with whom they have sex, choosing partners more carefully, and using latex condoms consistently and correctly. Heterosexuals at high risk due to a history of many partners have done the same. As a result, the number of infections is lower among gay and heterosexual men today than it was in the early 1980s. Still, AIDS remains the fifth-leading cause of death among U.S. young adults (refer to Figure 13.4 on page 437). The incidence of HIV-positive adults is higher in the United States than in any other industrialized nation—2½ times the rate in Canada (Heuveline, 2002). AIDS is spreading most rapidly through heterosexual contact in poverty-stricken minority groups with high rates of intravenous drug abuse combined with poor health, inadequate education, high life stress, and hopelessness. People overwhelmed by these problems are least likely to take preventive measures (Capaldi et al., 2002).

Yet AIDS can be contained and reduced—through sex education extending from childhood into adulthood and through access to health services, condoms, and clean needles and syringes for high-risk individuals. In view of the dramatic

rise in AIDS among women, who currently account for one-fourth of cases in North America, Western Europe, and East Asia, one-third in Latin America, and slightly over half in Africa, a special need exists for female-controlled preventive measures (Quinn & Overbaugh, 2005). The recently developed female condom offers some promise, but its effectiveness and acceptability are not yet established.

■ **Sexual Coercion.** After a long day of classes, Sharese flipped on the TV and caught a talk show discussion on sex without consent. Karen, a 25-year-old woman, described her husband Mike pushing, slapping, verbally insulting, and forcing her to have sex. "It was a control thing," Karen explained tearfully. "He complained that I wouldn't always do what he wanted. I was confused and blamed myself. I didn't leave because I was sure he'd come after me and get more violent."

One day, as Karen was speaking long distance to her mother on the phone, Mike grabbed the receiver and shouted, "She's not the woman I married! I'll kill her if she doesn't shape up!" Alarmed, Karen's parents arrived by plane the next day to rescue her, then helped her start divorce proceedings and get treatment.

An estimated 6 to 15 percent of North American women have endured *rape,* legally defined as intercourse by force, by threat of harm, or when the victim is incapable of giving con-

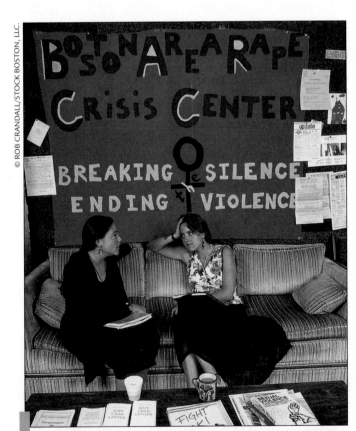

In this rape crisis center, a professional counselor assists a victim in recovering from trauma through social support, validation of her experience, and safety planning. Although some men are also victims of sexual coercion, few treatment services are available for them, and most men are too embarrassed to seek help.

sent (because of mental illness, mental retardation, or alcohol consumption). From 22 to 57 percent of women have experienced other forms of sexual aggression. The majority of victims (8 out of 10) are under age 30 (McGregor et al., 2004; Testa et al. 2003). Women are vulnerable to partners, acquaintances, and strangers, but in most instances their abusers are men they know well. Sexual coercion crosses SES and ethnic lines; people of all walks of life are offenders and victims.

Personal characteristics of the man with whom a woman is involved are far better predictors of her chances of becoming a victim than her own characteristics. Men who engage in sexual assault tend to believe in traditional gender roles, approve of violence against women, and accept rape myths ("Women want to be raped," or "Any healthy woman can resist if she really wants to"). Perpetrators also tend to interpret women's social behavior inaccurately, viewing friendliness as seductiveness, assertiveness as hostility, and resistance as desire. Frequently reasoning that "she brought it on herself," they express little remorse (Abbey & McAuslan, 2004; Scully & Marolla, 1998). Furthermore, sexual abuse in childhood, promiscuity in adolescence, and alcohol abuse in adulthood are associated with sexual coercion. Approximately half of all sexual assaults take place while people are intoxicated (Abbey et al., 2004; Kalof, 2000).

Cultural forces also contribute. When men are taught from an early age to be dominant, competitive, and aggressive and women to be submissive, cooperative, and passive, the themes of rape are reinforced. Under these conditions, men may view a date not as a chance to get to know a partner but as a potential sexual conquest. Societal acceptance of violence also sets the stage for rape, which typically occurs in relationships in which other forms of aggression are commonplace. Exposure to sexually aggressive pornography and other media images, which portray women desiring and enjoying the assault, also promote sexual coercion by dulling sensitivity to its harmful consequences.

About 15 to 30 percent of North American young adult samples report female-initiated coercive sexual behavior against men, with 3 to 10 percent of male responses indicating threats of physical force or actual force. Victimized men often say that women who committed these acts encouraged them to get drunk and threatened to end the relationship unless they complied (Anderson & Savage, 2005). Unfortunately, authorities rarely recognize female-initiated forced sex as illegal, and few men report these crimes.

Consequences. Women's psychological reactions to rape resemble those of survivors of extreme trauma. Immediate responses—shock, confusion, withdrawal, and psychological numbing—eventually give way to chronic fatigue, tension, disturbed sleep, depression, and suicidal thoughts (Stein et al., 2004). When sexual coercion is ongoing, taking any action may seem dangerous, so the victim falls into a pattern of extreme passivity and fear. If she has a history of sexual abuse or received negative feedback after trying to tell someone, she is more likely to blame herself, which strengthens helpless reactions (Briere & Jordan, 2004).

One-third to one-half of female rape victims are physically injured. Some contract sexually transmitted diseases, and pregnancy results in about 5 to 20 percent of cases. Furthermore, women victimized by rape (and other crimes) report more symptoms of illness across almost all body systems. And they are more likely to engage in negative health behaviors, including smoking and alcohol use (McFarlane et al., 2005).

Like their female counterparts, some male victims report psychological and physical consequences, including long-term depression (Struckman-Johnson & Struckman-Johnson, 1998). But female-initiated coercion and its effects are far less often studied.

Prevention and Treatment. Many female rape victims are less fortunate than Karen because anxiety about provoking another attack keeps them from confiding even in trusted family members and friends. If they seek help for other problems, conflict over issues surrounding sexuality may lead a sensitive health professional to detect a possible rape. A variety of community services, including safe houses, crisis hotlines, support groups, and legal assistance, exist to help women take refuge from abusive partners, but most are underfunded and cannot reach out to everyone in need. Practically no services are available for victimized men, who are often too embarrassed to come forward (Anderson & Savage, 2005).

The trauma induced by rape is severe enough that therapy is important. In addition to individual treatment aimed at reducing anxiety and depression, many experts advocate group sessions where contact with other survivors can help counter isolation and self-blame (Neville & Heppner, 2002). Other critical features that foster recovery include

- *Routine screening for victimization* during health-care visits to ensure referral to community services and protection from future harm
- *Validation of the experience,* by acknowledging that many others have been physically and sexually assaulted by intimate partners; that such assaults lead to a wide range of persisting symptoms, are illegal and inappropriate, and should not be tolerated; and that the trauma can be overcome
- *Safety planning,* even when the abuser is no longer present, to prevent recontact and reassault. This includes information about how to obtain police protection, legal intervention, a safe shelter, and other aid should a rape survivor be at risk again.

Finally, many steps can be taken at the level of the individual, the community, and society to prevent sexual coercion. Some are listed in Applying What We Know on page 448.

■ **Menstrual Cycle.** The menstrual cycle is central to women's lives and presents unique health concerns. Although almost all women experience some discomfort during menstruation, others have more severe difficulties. **Premenstrual syndrome (PMS)** refers to an array of physical and psychological symptoms that usually appear 6 to 10 days prior to menstruation. The most common are abdominal cramps, fluid

Preventing Sexual Coercion

Suggestion	Description
Reduce gender stereotyping and gender inequalities.	The roots of men's sexual coercion of women lie in the historically subordinate status of women. Unequal educational and employment opportunities keep many women economically dependent on men and therefore poorly equipped to avoid partner violence. At the same time, there is a need for increased public awareness that women sometimes commit sexually aggressive acts.
Mandate treatment for men and women who physically or sexually assault their partners.	Ingredients of effective intervention include inducing personal responsibility for violent behavior; teaching social awareness, social skills, and anger management; and developing a support system to prevent future attacks.
Expand interventions for children and adolescents who have witnessed violence between their parents.	Although most child witnesses to parental violence do not become involved in abusive relationships as adults, they are at increased risk.
Teach both men and women to take precautions that lower the risk of sexual assault.	Risk of sexual assault can be reduced by communicating sexual limits clearly to a date and, among women, developing neighborhood ties to other women; increasing the safety of the immediate environment (for example, installing deadbolt locks, checking the back seat of the car before entering); avoiding deserted areas; and not walking alone after dark.
Broaden definitions of rape to be gender-neutral.	In some U.S. states, where the definition of rape is limited to vaginal or anal penetration, a woman typically cannot rape a man. A broader definition is needed to encompass women as both receivers and perpetrators of sexual aggression.

Sources: Anderson & Savage, 2005; Smith, 2002.

retention, diarrhea, tender breasts, backache, headache, fatigue, tension, irritability, and depression; the precise combination varies from person to person. Nearly 40 percent of women have some form of PMS, usually beginning sometime after age 20. For most, symptoms are mild, but for 10 to 20 percent, PMS is severe enough to interfere with academic, occupational, and social functioning. PMS affects women of all SES levels and is a worldwide phenomenon—just as common in Italy and the Islamic nation of Bahrain as it is in the United States (Brody, 1992; Halbreich, 2004).

The causes of PMS are not well-established, but evidence for a genetic predisposition is accumulating. Identical twins are twice as likely as fraternal twins to share the syndrome (Freeman & Halbreich, 1998; Treloar, Heath, & Martin, 2002). PMS is related to hormonal changes that follow ovulation and precede menstruation. But hormone therapy is not consistently effective, suggesting that sensitivity of brain centers to these hormones, rather than the hormones themselves, is probably responsible (Dickerson, Mazyck, & Hunter, 2003). Common treatments include analgesics for pain, antidepressant medication, diuretics for fluid buildup, limiting caffeine intake (which can intensify symptoms), a low-fat, high-fiber diet, vitamin/mineral supplements, exercise, and other strategies for reducing stress. Although each of these approaches is helpful in certain cases, no method has been devised for curing PMS.

Psychological Stress

A final health concern, threaded throughout previous sections, has such a broad impact that it merits a comment of its own.

Psychological stress, measured in terms of adverse social conditions, negative life events, or daily hassles, is related to a wide variety of unfavorable health outcomes. In addition to its association with many unhealthy behaviors, stress has clear physical consequences. For example, as it mobilizes the body for action, it elevates blood pressure. Chronic stress resulting from economic hardship and inner-city living is consistently linked to hypertension, a relationship that contributes to the high incidence of heart disease in low-income groups, especially African Americans. Compared with higher-SES individuals, low-SES adults show a stronger cardiovascular response to stress, perhaps because they more often perceive stressors as unsolvable (Almeida et al., 2005; Carroll et al., 2000). Earlier we mentioned that psychological stress interferes with immune system functioning, a link that may underlie its relationship to several forms of cancer. And by reducing digestive activity as blood flows to the brain, heart, and extremities, stress can cause gastrointestinal difficulties, including constipation, diarrhea, colitis, and ulcers (Donatelle, 2004).

The many challenging tasks of early adulthood make it a particularly stressful time of life. Young adults more often report depressive feelings than middle-aged people, many of whom have attained vocational success and financial security and are enjoying more free time as parenting responsibilities decline (Schieman, Gundy, & Taylor, 2001; Wade & Cairney, 1997). Also, as we will see in Chapters 15 and 16, middle-aged adults are better than young adults at coping with stress. Because of their longer life experience and greater sense of personal control over their lives, they are more likely to engage in problem-centered coping when stressful conditions can be

Fostering a Healthy Adult Life

Applying What We Know

Suggestion	Description
Engage in healthy eating behavior.	Educate yourself and those with whom you live about the makeup of a healthy diet. Eat in moderation, and learn to distinguish true hunger from eating due to boredom or stress.
Maintain a reasonable body weight.	If you need to lose weight, make a commitment to a lifelong change in the way you eat, not just a temporary diet. Select a sensible, well-balanced dietary plan, and exercise regularly.
Keep physically fit.	Choose a specific time to exercise, and stick with it. To help sustain physical activity and make it more enjoyable, exercise with your partner or a friend and encourage each other. Set reasonable expectations, and allow enough time to reach your fitness goals; many people become exercise dropouts because their expectations were too high.
Control alcohol intake and do not smoke cigarettes.	Drink moderately or not at all. Do not allow yourself to feel you must drink to be accepted or to enjoy a social event. If you smoke, choose a time that is relatively stress-free to quit. Seek the support of your partner or a friend.
Engage in responsible sexual behavior.	Identify attitudes and behaviors that you need to change to develop a healthy intimate relationship. Educate yourself about sexual anatomy and functioning so you can make sound decisions about contraception and protect yourself against sexually transmitted disease.
Manage stress.	Seek a reasonable balance among work, family, and leisure. Become more aware of stressors, and identify effective ways of coping with them so you are better-prepared when they arise. Engage in regular exercise, and find time each day for relaxation and quiet reflection.

Source: Donatelle, 2004.

changed and emotion-centered coping when nothing can be done about an unpleasant situation (Lazarus, 1999).

In previous chapters, we repeatedly noted the stress-buffering effect of social support, which continues throughout life (Markides & Cooper, 1989). Helping stressed young adults establish and maintain satisfying social ties is as important a health intervention as any we have mentioned. Before we turn to the cognitive side of early adulthood, consult Applying What We Know above for strategies that foster a healthy adult life.

Ask Yourself

Review

List as many factors as you can that may have contributed to heart attacks and early death among Sharese's African-American relatives.

Review

Why are people in committed relationships likely to be more sexually active and satisfied than those who are dating several partners?

Apply

Tom began going to a health club three days a week after work. Soon the pressures of his job convinced him that he no longer had time for regular exercise. Explain to Tom why he should keep up his exercise regimen, and suggest ways to fit it into his busy life.

Connect

Describe history-graded influences that have contributed to the obesity epidemic. (To review this aspect of the lifespan perspective, refer to Chapter 1, page 11.)

🌰 Cognitive Development

How does cognition change with the transition to adulthood? Lifespan theorists have examined this question from three familiar vantage points. First, they have proposed transformations in the structure of thought—new, qualitatively distinct ways of thinking that extend the cognitive-developmental changes of childhood and adolescence. Second, adulthood is a time of attaining advanced knowledge in a particular area, an accomplishment that has important implications for information processing and creativity. Finally, researchers have been interested in the extent to which the diverse mental abilities assessed by intelligence tests remain stable or change during the adult years—a topic we will address in Chapter 15.

Changes in the Structure of Thought

Sharese described her first year in graduate school as a "cognitive turning point." As part of her internship in a public health clinic, she observed firsthand the many factors that affect human health-related behaviors. For a time, she was intensely uncomfortable about the fact that clear-cut solutions to everyday dilemmas were so hard to come by. "Working in this messy reality is so different from the problem solving I did in my undergraduate classes," she told her mother over the phone one day.

Piaget (1967) acknowledged the possibility that important advances in thinking follow the attainment of formal operations. He observed that adolescents place excessive faith in abstract systems, preferring a logical, internally consistent—but inaccurate—perspective on the world to one that is vague, contradictory, and adapted to particular circumstances (see Chapter 11, page 385). Sharese's reflections fit the observations of researchers who have studied **postformal thought**—cognitive development beyond Piaget's formal operations. To clarify how thinking is restructured in adulthood, let's look at some influential theories, along with supportive research. Together, they show how personal effort and social experiences spark increasingly rational, flexible, and practical ways of thinking that accept uncertainties and vary across situations.

Perry's Theory: Epistemic Cognition

William Perry's (1981, 1970/1998) work provided the starting point for a growing research literature on the development of *epistemic cognition*. *Epistemic* means "of or about knowledge," and **epistemic cognition** refers to our reflections on how we arrived at facts, beliefs, and ideas. Mature, rational thinkers consider the justifiability of their conclusions that differ from those of others. When they cannot justify their approach, they revise it, seeking a more balanced, adequate route to acquiring knowledge.

■ **Development of Epistemic Cognition.** Perry wondered why young adults respond in dramatically different ways to the diversity of ideas they encounter in college. To find out, he interviewed Harvard University students at the end of each of their four years of college, asking "what stood out" during the previous year. Responses indicated that students' reflections on knowing changed as they experienced the complexities of university life and moved closer to adult roles—findings confirmed in many subsequent studies (King & Kitchener, 1994, 2002; Magolda, 2002; Moore, 2002).

Younger students regarded knowledge as made up of separate units (beliefs and propositions) whose truth could be determined by comparing them to abstract standards—standards that exist apart from the thinking person and his or her situation. As a result, they engaged in **dualistic thinking,** dividing information, values, and authority into right and wrong, good and bad, we and they. As one college freshman stated, "When I went to my first lecture, what the man said was just like God's word. I believe everything he said because he is a professor . . . and this is a respected position" (Perry, 1981, p. 81). And when asked, "If two people disagree on the interpretation of a poem, how would you decide which one is right?" a sophomore replied, ""You'd have to ask the poet. It's his poem" (Clinchy, 2002, p. 67).

Older students, in contrast, had moved toward **relativistic thinking**—viewing all knowledge as embedded in a framework of thought. Aware of a diversity of opinions on many topics, they gave up the possibility of absolute truth in favor of multiple truths, each relative to its context. As a result, their

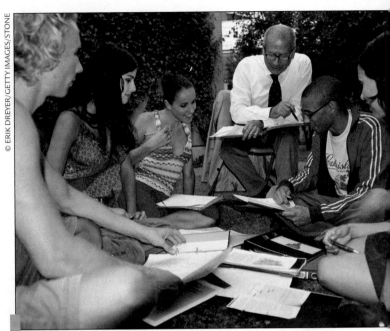

When college students challenge one another's reasoning while tackling realistic, ambiguous problems, they are likely to gain in epistemic cognition. Peer discussion of alternatives encourages reflection on one's own thinking, evaluation of competing ideas and strategies, and coordination of opposing perspectives into a new, more effective structure.

thinking became more flexible and tolerant. As one college senior put it, "Just seeing how [famous philosophers] fell short of an all-encompassing answer, [you realize] that ideas are really individualized. And you begin to have respect for how great their thought could be, without its being absolute" (Perry, 1970/1998, p. 90). Relativistic thinking leads to the realization that one's own beliefs are often subjective, since several frameworks may satisfy the criterion of internal logical consistency (Moore, 2002; Sinnott, 1998, 2003). Thus, the relativistic thinker is acutely aware that each person, in arriving at a position, creates her own "truth"—that is, chooses one of many possible positions, each of which is defensible.

Eventually, the most mature individuals progress to **commitment within relativistic thinking:** Instead of choosing between opposing views, they try to formulate a more satisfying perspective that synthesizes contradictions. When considering which of two theories studied in a college course is better, or which of several movies is most deserving of an Oscar, the individual moves beyond the stance that everything is a matter of opinion and generates rational criteria against which options can be evaluated (Moshman, 2003). Few college students reach this extension of relativism. Adults who attain it often display a more sophisticated approach to learning, in which they actively seek out differing perspectives to advance their knowledge and understanding.

■ **Importance of Peer Interaction and Reflection.** Although many individuals advance in epistemic cognition during early adulthood, progress does not always occur. Development depends on further gains in metacognition, which are likely to occur in situations that challenge young peoples' perspectives and induce them to consider the rationality of their thought processes (Moshman, 2005). In a comparison of the college learning experiences of seniors who scored low and high in Perry's scheme, the high-scoring students frequently reported activities that encouraged them to struggle with realistic but ambiguous problems in a supportive environment, in which faculty offered encouragement and guidance. For example, one engineering major, describing an airplane-design project that required advanced epistemic cognition, noted his discovery that "you can design 30 different airplanes and each one's going to have its benefits and there's going to be problems with each one" (Marra & Palmer, 2004, p. 116). The low-scoring students rarely mentioned such experiences.

When students tackle challenging, ill-structured problems, interaction among individuals who are roughly equal in knowledge and authority is beneficial because it prevents acceptance of another's reasoning simply because of greater power or expertise. In one study, college students were asked to come up with the most effective solution to a difficult logical problem. Only 3 out of 32 students (9 percent) in a "work alone" condition succeeded. But in an "interactive" condition, 15 out of 20 small groups (75 percent) arrived at the correct solution following extensive discussion (Moshman & Geil, 1998). Most groups, but few individuals, reflected on their solution strategies. They engaged in a process of "collective rationality" in which members challenged one another to justify their reasoning and worked out the most defensible strategy collaboratively.

Reflection on one's own thinking can also occur individually. But peer interaction is facilitating because it can foster the necessary type of individual reflection: arguing with oneself over competing ideas and strategies and coordinating opposing perspectives into a new, more effective structure. Recall that research on children supports the importance of peer collaboration (see page 320 in Chapter 9). In adulthood, it continues to spur cognitive development and remains a highly effective basis for education.

Clearly, Perry's theory and the research it stimulated are based on samples of highly educated young adults. These investigators acknowledge that movement from dualism to relativism is probably limited to people confronting the multiplicity of viewpoints typical of a college education, and that the most advanced attainment—commitment within relativism—may require advanced graduate study (King & Kitchener, 2002). But the underlying theme—thought less constrained by the need to find one answer to a question and more responsive to its context—is also evident in another theory of adult cognition.

Labouvie-Vief's Theory: Pragmatic Thought and Cognitive-Emotional Complexity

Gisella Labouvie-Vief's (1980, 1985) portrait of adult cognition echoes features of Perry's theory. Adolescents, she points out, operate within a world of possibility. Adulthood involves

movement from hypothetical to **pragmatic thought,** a structural advance in which logic becomes a tool for solving real-world problems.

According to Labouvie-Vief, the need to specialize motivates this change. As adults select one path out of many alternatives, they become more aware of the constraints of everyday life. And in the course of balancing various roles, they give up their earlier discomfort with contradictions. They accept inconsistencies as part of life and develop ways of thinking that thrive on imperfection and compromise. Sharese's friend Christy, a student and mother of two young children, illustrates:

> I've always been a feminist, and I wanted to remain true to my beliefs in family and career. But this is Gary's first year of teaching high school, and he's saddled with four preparations and coaching the school's basketball team. At least for now, I've had to settle for "give-and-take feminism"—going to school part-time and shouldering most of the responsibility for the kids while he gets used to his new job. Otherwise, we'd never make it financially.

Labouvie-Vief (2003) also points out that young adults' enhanced reflective capacities alter the dynamics of their emotional lives: They become more adept at integrating cognition with emotion and, in doing so, again make sense of discrepancies. Examining the self-descriptions of several hundred 10- to 80-year-olds diverse in SES, Labouvie-Vief found that from adolescence through middle adulthood, people gained in **cognitive-affective complexity**—awareness of positive and negative feelings and coordination of them into a complex, organized structure (see Figure 13.8) (Labouvie-Vief et al.,

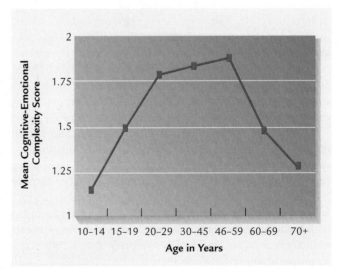

■ **FIGURE 13.8 Changes in cognitive-affective complexity from adolescence to late adulthood.** Performance, based on participants' descriptions of their roles, traits, and emotions, increased steadily from adolescence through early adulthood, peaked in middle age, and fell off in late adulthood when (as we will see in later chapters) basic information-processing skills decline. (From G. Labouvie-Vief, 2004, "Dynamic Integration: Affect, Cognition, and the Self in Adulthood." *Current Directions in Psychological Science, 12,* p. 203. Reprinted by permission.)

1995; Labouvie-Vief, DeVoe, & Bulka, 1989). For example, in describing herself, one 34-year-old combined roles, traits, and diverse emotions into this coherent picture: "With the recent birth of our first child, I find myself more fulfilled than ever, yet struggling in some ways. My elation is tempered by my gnawing concern over meeting all my responsibilities in a satisfying way while remaining an individualized person with needs and desires."

Cognitive-affective complexity promotes greater awareness of one's own and others' perspectives and motivations. As Labouvie-Vief (2003) notes, it is a vital aspect of adult *emotional intelligence* (see page 312 in Chapter 9) and is valuable in solving many pragmatic problems. Individuals high in cognitive-affective complexity view events and people in a tolerant, open-minded fashion. And because cognitive-affective complexity involves accepting and making sense of both positive and negative feelings, it helps people regulate intense emotion and, therefore, in thinking rationally about real-world dilemmas, even those that are laden with negative information (Labouvie-Vief & Gonzalez, 2004).

Awareness of multiple truths, integration of logic with reality, and cognitive-emotional complexity sum up qualitative transformations in thinking under way in early adulthood (Sinnott, 1998, 2003). As we will see next, adults' increasingly specialized and context-bound thought, although it closes off certain options, opens new doors to higher levels of competence.

Expertise and Creativity

In Chapter 9, we noted that children's expanding knowledge improves their ability to remember new information related to what they already know. **Expertise**—acquisition of extensive knowledge in a field or endeavor—is supported by the specialization that begins with selecting a college major or an occupation, since it takes many years for a person to master any complex domain (Horn & Masunaga, 2000). Once attained, expertise has a profound impact on information processing.

Compared with novices, experts remember and reason more quickly and effectively. The expert knows more domain-specific concepts and represents them in richer ways—at a deeper and more abstract level and as having more features that can be linked to other concepts. As a result, unlike novices, whose understanding is superficial, experts approach problems with underlying principles in mind. For example, a highly trained physicist notices when several problems deal with conservation of energy and can therefore be solved similarly. In contrast, a beginning physics student focuses only on surface features—whether the problem contains a disk, a pulley, or a coiled spring (Chi, Glaser, & Farr, 1988). Experts can use what they know to arrive at many solutions automatically—through quick and easy remembering. And when a problem is challenging, they tend to plan ahead, systematically analyzing and categorizing elements and selecting the best from many possibilities, while the novice proceeds more by trial and error.

This member of the Alaskan Tsimshian Nation carves a totem pole for a potlatch ceremony—a celebration that involves sharing food and resources. The sculptor's expertise at his craft enables him to move from problem to solution quickly and effectively.

Expertise is necessary for creativity as well as problem solving. The creative products of adulthood differ from those of childhood in that they are not just original but also directed at a social or aesthetic need. Mature creativity requires a unique cognitive capacity—the ability to formulate new, culturally meaningful problems and to ask significant questions that have not been posed before. According to Patricia Arlin (1989), movement from *problem solving* to *problem finding* is a core feature of postformal thought evident in highly accomplished artists and scientists.

Case studies support the 10-year rule in development of master-level creativity—a decade between initial exposure to a field and sufficient expertise to produce a creative work (Feldman, 1999; Simonton, 2000). Furthermore, a century of research reveals that creative accomplishment rises in early adulthood, peaks in the late thirties or early forties, and gradually declines, though rarely so substantially as to turn a creative person into a noncreative person (Dixon, 2003). And exceptions to this pattern exist. Those who get an early start in creativity tend to peak and drop off sooner, whereas "late bloomers" reach their full stride at older ages. This suggests that creativity is more a function of "career age" than of chronological age.

The course of creativity also varies across disciplines (Simonton, 1991). For example, artists and musicians typically show an early rise in creativity, perhaps because they do not need extensive formal education before they begin to produce. Academic scholars and scientists, who must earn higher academic degrees and spend years doing research to make worthwhile contributions, usually display their achievements later and over a longer time.

Though creativity is rooted in expertise, not all experts are creative. Creativity also requires other qualities—an innovative thinking style, tolerance of ambiguity, a special drive to succeed, and a willingness to experiment and try again after failure (Sternberg & Lubart, 1996; Lubart, 2003). And creativity demands time and energy. For women especially, it can be postponed or disrupted by child rearing, divorce, or an unsupportive partner (Vaillant & Vaillant, 1990). In sum, creativity is multiply determined. When personal and situational factors jointly promote it, creativity can continue for many decades, well into old age.

Ask Yourself

Review

How does expertise affect information processing? Why is expertise necessary for, but not the same as, creativity?

Apply

For her human development course, Marcia wrote a paper in which she discussed differing implications of Piaget's and Vygotsky's theories for education. Then she presented evidence that combining both perspectives yields a more effective approach than either position by itself. Explain how Marcia's reasoning illustrates advanced epistemic cognition.

Connect

Our discussion in Chapter 9 noted that emotional intelligence is associated with life satisfaction and success in the workplace. How might cognitive-emotional complexity contribute to these favorable outcomes?

Reflect

Describe a classroom experience or assignment in one of your college courses that promoted relativistic thinking.

www.ablongman.com/berk

Côté, 2003; Pascarella & Terenzini, 1991). As research inspired by Perry's theory indicates, students become better at reasoning about problems that have no clear solution, identifying the strengths and weaknesses of opposing sides of complex issues, and reflecting on the quality of their thinking. Their attitudes and values also broaden. They show increased interest in literature, the performing arts, and philosophical and historical issues and greater tolerance for ethnic and cultural diversity. Also, as noted in Chapter 12, college leaves its mark on moral reasoning by fostering concern with individual rights and human welfare. Finally, exposure to multiple worldviews encourages young people to look more closely at themselves. During the college years, students develop greater self-understanding, enhanced self-esteem, and a firmer sense of identity.

How do these interrelated changes come about? The type of four-year institution attended—public versus private, highly selective versus relatively open in enrollment—makes little difference in psychological outcomes or even in ultimate career success and earnings (Montgomery & Côté, 2003). And cognitive growth is just as great at two-year community colleges as at four-year institutions (Bohr et al., 1994).

Rather, the impact of college is jointly influenced by the person's involvement in academic and nonacademic activities and the richness and diversity of the campus setting. The more students interact with peers in academic and extracurricular settings, the more they benefit. Residence hall living is one of the most consistent predictors of cognitive change because it maximizes involvement in the educational and social systems of the institution (Terenzini, Pascarella, & Blimling, 1999). These findings underscore the importance of programs that integrate commuting students into out-of-class campus life. Quality of academic experiences also affects college outcomes.

The College Experience

Looking back at the trajectory of their lives, many people view the college years as formative—more influential than any other period of adulthood. This is not surprising. College serves as a "developmental testing ground," a time for devoting full attention to exploring alternative values, roles, and behaviors. To facilitate this exploration, college exposes students to a form of "culture shock"—encounters with new ideas and beliefs, new freedoms and opportunities, and new academic and social demands. About two-thirds of North American high school graduates enroll in an institution of higher education (ACT, 2005; Service Canada, 2005). Besides offering a route to a high-status career and its personal and monetary rewards, colleges and universities have a transforming impact on young people.

Psychological Impact of Attending College

Thousands of studies reveal broad psychological changes from the freshman to the senior year of college (Montgomery &

Residential living enhances the beneficial effects of attending college. Because living on campus increases the likelihood that students will experience the richness and diversity of the institution, it is one of the most consistent predictors of cognitive change.

Psychological benefits increase with students' effort and willingness to participate in class and with challenging teaching—that integrates learning in separate courses, offers extensive contact with faculty, and connects course work with real workplace activities (Franklin, 1995).

Dropping Out

Completing a college education has enduring effects on people's postcollege opportunities and worldview. Yet 45 percent of North American students at two-year institutions and 30 percent of students at four-year institutions drop out, most within the first year and many within the first 6 weeks (ACT, 2005). Dropout rates are higher in colleges with less selective admission requirements; in some, freshmen dropout approaches 50 percent. And ethnic minority students from low-SES families are at increased risk for dropping out (Montgomery & Côté, 2003).

Both personal and institutional factors contribute to college leaving. Most entering freshmen have high hopes for college life but find the transition difficult. Those who have trouble adapting—because of lack of motivation, poor study skills, financial pressures, or emotional dependence on parents—quickly develop negative attitudes toward the college environment. Often these exit-prone students do not meet with their advisors or professors. At the same time, colleges that do little to help high-risk students, through developmental courses and other support services, have a higher percentage of dropouts (Moxley, Najor-Durack, & Dumbrigue, 2001). And when students report experiencing "disrespect" on campus because of their ethnicity or religion, their desire to continue plummets (Zea et al., 1997).

Beginning to prepare young people in early adolescence with the necessary visions and skills can do much to improve college success. In a study that followed up nearly 700 young people from sixth grade until two years after high school graduation, a set of factors—grade point average, academic self-concept, persistence in the face of challenge, parental SES and valuing of a college education, and the individual's plans to attend college—predicted college enrollment at age 20 (Eccles, Vida, & Barber, 2004). Although parental SES is difficult to modify, improving parents' attitudes and behaviors and students' academic motivation and educational aspirations is within reach, through a wide array of strategies considered in Chapters 11 and 12.

Once young people enroll in college, reaching out to them, especially during the early weeks and throughout the first year, is crucial. Programs that forge bonds between teachers and students and that provide academic support, part-time work opportunities, and meaningful extracurricular roles increase retention. Membership in campus-based social and religious organizations is especially helpful in strengthening minority students' sense of belonging (Fashola & Slavin, 1998). Young people who feel that they have entered a college community that is concerned about them as individuals are far more likely to graduate.

Vocational Choice

Young adults, college-bound or not, face a major life decision: the choice of a suitable work role. Being a productive worker calls for many of the same qualities as being an active citizen and a nurturant family member—good judgment, responsibility, dedication, and cooperation. What influences young people's decisions about careers? What is the transition from school to work like, and what factors make it easy or difficult?

Selecting a Vocation

In societies with an abundance of career possibilities, occupational choice is a gradual process that begins long before adolescence. Major theorists view the young person as moving through several periods of vocational development (Gottfredson, 2005; Super, 1990, 1994):

1. The **fantasy period:** In early and middle childhood, children gain insight into career options by fantasizing about them. Their preferences, guided largely by familiarity, glamour, and excitement, bear little relation to the decisions they will eventually make.

2. The **tentative period:** Between ages 11 and 16, adolescents think about careers in more complex ways, at first in terms of their *interests,* and soon—as they become more aware of personal and educational requirements for different vocations—in terms of their *abilities* and *values.* "I like science and the process of discovery," Sharese thought as she neared high school graduation. "But I'm also good with people, and I'd like to do something to help others. So maybe teaching or medicine would suit my needs."

3. The **realistic period:** By the late teens and early twenties, with the economic and practical realities of adulthood just around the corner, young people start to narrow their options. A first step is often further *exploration*—gathering more information about possibilities that blend with their personal characteristics. In the final phase, *crystallization,* they focus on a general vocational category and experiment for a time before settling on a single occupation. As a college sophomore, Sharese pursued her interest in science, but she had not yet selected a major. Once she decided on chemistry, she considered whether to pursue teaching, medicine, or public health.

Factors Influencing Vocational Choice

Most, but not all, young people follow this pattern of vocational development. A few know from an early age just what they want to be and follow a direct path to a career goal. Some decide and later change their minds, and still others remain undecided for an extended period. College students are granted added time to explore various options. In contrast, the life conditions of many low-SES youths restrict their range of choices.

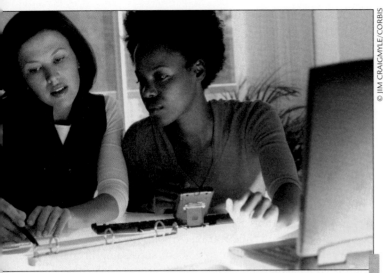

These young women have attained their initial career goals, securing well-paid positions with high responsibility in a corporate setting. Most likely, they came from a college that values the accomplishments of women and that provided opportunities for them to test their abilities in a supportive environment.

Making an occupational choice is not simply a rational process in which young people weigh abilities, interests, and values against career options. Like other developmental milestones, it is the result of a dynamic interaction between person and environment (Van Esbroeck, Tibos, & Zaman, 2005). A great many influences feed into the decision, including personality, family, teachers, and gender stereotypes, among others.

■ **Personality.** People are attracted to occupations that complement their personalities. John Holland (1985, 1997) identified six personality types that affect vocational choice:

🖉 The *investigative person,* who enjoys working with ideas, is likely to select a scientific occupation (for example, anthropologist, physicist, or engineer).

🖉 The *social person,* who likes interacting with people, gravitates toward human services (counseling, social work, or teaching).

🖉 The *realistic person,* who prefers real-world problems and working with objects, tends to choose a mechanical occupation (construction, plumbing, or surveying).

🖉 The *artistic person,* who is emotional and high in need for individual expression, looks toward an artistic field (writing, music, or the visual arts).

🖉 The *conventional person,* who likes well-structured tasks and values material possessions and social status, has traits well suited to certain business fields (accounting, banking, or quality control).

🖉 The *enterprising person,* who is adventurous, persuasive, and a strong leader, is drawn to sales and supervisory positions or to politics.

Research confirms a similar relationship between these six personality types and vocational choice in diverse cultures, but it is only moderate. Many people are blends of several personality types and can do well at more than one kind of occupation (Holland, 1997; Spokane & Cruza-Guet, 2005). Furthermore, career decisions are made in the context of family influences, educational opportunities, and current life circumstances. For example, Sharese's friend Christy scored high on Holland's investigative dimension. But when she married and had children early, she postponed her dream of becoming a college professor and chose a human services career that required fewer years of education. As Christy's case illustrates, personality takes us only partway in understanding vocational choice.

■ **Family Influences.** Young people's vocational aspirations correlate strongly with their parents' jobs. Individuals who grew up in higher-SES homes are more likely to select high-status, white-collar occupations, such as doctor, lawyer, scientist, or engineer. In contrast, those with lower-SES backgrounds tend to choose less prestigious, blue-collar careers—for example, plumber, construction worker, food service employee, or secretary. Parent–child vocational similarity is partly a function of similarity in personality, intellectual abilities, and—especially—educational attainment (Ellis & Bonin, 2003; Schoon & Parsons, 2002). More today than in past generations, number of years of schooling completed powerfully predicts occupational status.

Other factors also promote family resemblance in occupational choice. Higher-SES parents are more likely to give their children important information about the world of work and to have connections with people who can help the young person obtain a high-status position. In a study of African-American mothers' influence on their daughters' academic and career goals, college-educated mothers engaged in a wider range of strategies to promote their daughters' progress, including gathering information on colleges and areas of study and identifying knowledgeable professionals who could help (Kerpelman, Shoffner, & Ross-Griffin, 2002). Parenting practices also shape work-related values. Recall from Chapter 2 that higher-SES parents tend to promote curiosity and self-direction, which are required in many high-status careers. Lower-SES parents, in contrast, are more likely to emphasize conformity and obedience. Eventually, young people may choose careers that dovetail with these differences.

Still, parents can foster higher aspirations. Parental pressure to do well in school and encouragement toward high-status occupations predict vocational attainment beyond SES (Bell et al., 1996).

■ **Teachers.** Young adults preparing for or in careers requiring extensive education often report that teachers influenced their choice (Bright et al., 2005; Reddin, 1997). College-bound high school students tend to have closer relationships with teachers than do other students—relationships that are especially likely to foster high career aspirations in young women (Wigfield et al., 2002). These findings provide yet another reason to promote positive teacher–student relations, especially for high school students from low-SES families. The power of teachers in offering encouragement and acting as role models can serve as an important source of upward mobility for these young people.

■ **Gender Stereotypes.** Over the past three decades, young women have expressed increasing interest in occupations largely held by men (Gottfredson, 2005). Changes in gender-role attitudes along with a dramatic rise in numbers of employed mothers, who serve as career-oriented models for their daughters, are common explanations for women's attraction to nontraditional careers.

But women's progress in entering and excelling at male-dominated professions has been slow. As Table 13.2 shows, although the percentage of women engineers, lawyers, doctors, and business executives increased between 1983 and 2004 in the United States, it still falls far short of equal representation. Women remain concentrated in less well-paid, traditionally feminine professions, such as writing, social work, education, and nursing (U.S. Census Bureau, 2006b). In virtually all fields, their achievements lag behind those of men, who write more books, make more discoveries, hold more positions of leadership, and produce more works of art.

Table 13.2	Percentage of Women in Various Professions in the United States, 1983 and 2005	
Profession	**1983**	**2005**
Engineer	5.8	9.2
Lawyer	15.8	29.4
Doctor	15.8	29.4
Business executive	32.4	36.7[a]
Author, artist, entertainer	42.7	47.8
Social worker	64.3	77.7
Elementary or middle school teacher	93.5	81.3
Secondary school teacher	62.2	55.3
College or university professor	36.3	46.0
Librarian, museum curator	84.4	83.2
Registered nurse	95.8	92.2
Psychologist	57.1	66.7

Source: U.S. Census Bureau, 2006b.

[a]This percentage includes executives and managers at all levels. Women make up only 23 percent of chief executive officers at large corporations, although that figure represents a sixfold increase in the past two decades.

Ability cannot account for these dramatic sex differences. Recall from Chapter 11 that girls are advantaged in reading and writing achievement, and the gender gap favoring boys in math is small. Rather, gender-stereotyped messages play a key role. Although girls' grades are higher than boys', girls begin secondary school less confident of their abilities and are more likely to underestimate their achievement (Wigfield et al., 2002).

During college, the career aspirations of many academically talented women decline further. In one longitudinal study, high school valedictorians were followed over a ten-year period. By their sophomore year of college, women tended to shift their expectations toward less demanding careers because of unresolved questions about their ability and concerns about combining work with child rearing (Arnold, 1994).

Women's low self-confidence about succeeding in male-dominated fields further limits their occupational choices. Research indicates that many mathematically talented college women settle on nonscience majors. And those who remain in the sciences more often choose medicine or another health profession, and less often choose engineering or a math or physical science career, than their male counterparts (Benbow et al., 2000).

These findings reveal a pressing need for programs that sensitize high school and college personnel to the special problems women face in developing and maintaining high vocational aspirations and selecting nontraditional careers. Young women's aspirations rise in response to career guidance that encourages them to set goals that match their abilities, interests, and values. Those who continue to achieve usually have four experiences in common:

🖋 A college environment that values women's accomplishments and attempts to enhance women's experiences in its curriculum

🖋 Frequent interaction with faculty and professionals in their chosen fields

🖋 The opportunity to test their abilities in a supportive environment

🖋 Models of accomplished women who have successfully dealt with family–career role conflict (Pascarella et al., 1997; Swanson & Fouad, 1999)

Compared to women, men have changed little in their interest in nontraditional occupations. See the Social Issues box on the following page for research on the motivations and experiences of men who do choose female-dominated careers.

Vocational Preparation of Non-College-Bound Young Adults

Sharese's younger brother Leon graduated from high school in a vocational track. Like approximately one-third of North American young people with a high school diploma, he had no current plans to go to college. While in school, Leon held a part-time job selling candy at the local shopping mall. He

Social Issues

Masculinity at Work: Men Who Choose Nontraditional Careers

Ross majored in engineering through his sophomore year of college, when he startled his family and friends by switching to nursing. "I've never looked back," Ross said. "I love the work." He noted some benefits of being a male in a female work world, including the high regard of women colleagues and rapid advancement. "But as soon as they learn what I do," Ross remarked with disappointment, "guys on the outside question my abilities and masculinity."

What factors influence the small but increasing number of men who, like Ross, enter careers dominated by women? When several hundred men were assessed in their first year of college and again four years later, those who chose traditionally feminine occupations had more liberal social attitudes, including attitudes about gender roles, than those who chose traditionally masculine occupations. They also less often rated occupational prestige as important in their choice and were less likely to aspire to graduate education (Lease, 2003). Perhaps these men's gender-stereotype flexibility allowed them to choose occupations they found satisfying, even if those jobs were not typically regarded as appropriate for men.

In one study, 40 men who were primary school teachers, nurses, airline stewards, or librarians, when asked how they arrived at their choice, described diverse pathways (Simpson, 2005). Some actively sought the career, others happened on it while exploring possibilities, and still others first spent time in another occupation (usually male-dominated), found it unsatisfying, and then settled into their current career.

The men also confirmed Ross's observations: Because of their male minority status, co-workers often assumed they were more knowledgeable than they actually were. They also had opportunities to move quickly into supervisory positions, although many did not seek advancement (Simpson, 2004). As one teacher commented, "I just want to be a good classroom teacher. What's wrong with that?" Furthermore, while in training and on the job, virtually all the men reported feeling socially accepted—relaxed and comfortable working with women.

But when asked to reflect on how others reacted to their choice, many men expressed anxiety about being stigmatized—by other men, not by women, whom they reported as generally accepting. To reduce these feelings, the men frequently described their job in ways that minimized its feminine image. Several librarians emphasized technical requirements by referring to their title as "information scientist" or "researcher." The teachers often highlighted the sports aspect of their work. And nurses sometimes distanced themselves from a feminine work identity by specializing in "adrenalin-charged" areas such as accident or emergency.

Despite these tensions, the men uniformly derived enjoyment and self-esteem from their nontraditional career choice. As with Ross, their high level of private comfort seemed to prevail over uneasiness about the feminine public image of their work.

© JIM WEST/THE IMAGE WORKS

An increasing number of men—like this flight attendant—are entering nontraditional careers. Although they worry about being stigmatized by other men because of their "feminine" job choice, most report feeling socially accepted on the job. Because of their male minority status, they generally have opportunities to move quickly into supervisory positions.

---

hoped to work in data processing after graduation, but six months later he was still a part-time sales clerk at the candy store. Although Leon had filled out many job applications, he got no interviews or offers. He soon despaired of discovering any relationship between his schooling and a career.

Leon's inability to find a job other than the one he held as a student is typical for North American non-college-bound high school graduates. Although they are more likely to find employment than youths who drop out, they have fewer work opportunities than high school graduates of several decades ago. About 15 percent of Canadian and 20 percent of U.S. recent high school graduates who do not continue their education are unemployed (Statistics Canada, 2004; U.S. Department of Education, 2005b). When they do find work, most are limited to temporary, low-paid, unskilled jobs. In addition, they have few alternatives for vocational counseling and job

Cultural Influences

Work–Study Apprenticeships in Germany

Rolf, an 18-year-old German vocational student, is an apprentice at Brandt, a large industrial firm known worldwide for its high-quality products. Like many German companies, Brandt has a well-developed apprenticeship program that includes a full-time professional training staff, a suite of classrooms, and a lab equipped with the latest learning aids. Apprentices move through at least ten divisions in the company, each carefully selected to meet their learning needs. Rolf has worked in purchasing, inventory, production, personnel, marketing, sales, and finance. Now in cost accounting, he assists Herr Stein, his supervisor, in designing a computerized inventory control system.

Rolf is involved in complex and challenging projects, guided by caring mentors who love their work and want to teach others. Two days a week, he attends the *Berufsschule*, a part-time vocational school. On the job, Rolf applies a wide range of academic skills, including reading, writing, problem solving, and logical thinking. His classroom learning is directly relevant to his daily life (Hamilton & Hamilton, 1999; Shanahan, Mortimer & Krüger, 2002).

Germany has one of the world's most successful apprenticeship systems for preparing young people to enter modern business and industry. About 40 percent of German youths participate. German adolescents who do not attend a *Gymnasium* (college-preparatory high school) usually complete full-time schooling by age 15 or 16, but education remains compulsory until age 18. They fill the two-year gap with part-time vocational schooling combined with apprenticeship. Students are trained for a wide range of blue- and white-collar occupations—more than 400, leading to over 20,000 specialized careers. Educators and employers jointly plan each apprenticeship. Apprentices who complete training and pass a qualifying examination are certified as skilled workers and earn union-set wages for that occupation. Businesses provide training and financial support because they know the apprenticeship program greatly increases workforce competence and dedication (Heinz, 1999b).

The German apprenticeship system offers a smooth and rewarding path from school to career for young people who do not enter higher education. In a longitudinal study of the early career paths of 2,200 German Berufsschule graduates and British high school graduates (who have no national apprenticeship system), German men and women had had far fewer job shifts and periods of unemployment during the first five years after labor market entry (Scherrer, 2001). Many apprentices are hired immediately by the firms that trained them. Most others find jobs elsewhere in the same occupation. For those who change careers, the apprentice certificate is a powerful credential. Employers are willing to invest in further training to adapt the individual's skills to company needs. Beyond this, young employees who excel can get government

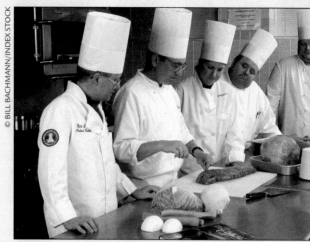

Germany has one of the world's most successful apprenticeship systems for preparing young people who do not go to college to enter well-paid careers in business and industry. These apprentice chefs train in a professional kitchen with high-quality equipment under the guidance of a master chef.

financial aid to extend their vocational education in special promotion programs (Buchman, 2002; Kerckhoff, 2002).

Between ages 18 and 20, German young people establish themselves in well-paid careers with security and advancement possibilities that grant them dignity and full status as adults. The success of the German system—and of similar systems in Austria, Denmark, Switzerland, and several East European countries—suggests that some kind of national apprenticeship program would improve the transition from school to work for young people in Canada and the United States.

placement as they transition from school to work (Shanahan, Mortimer, & Krüger, 2002).

North American employers regard the recent high school graduate as poorly prepared for skilled business and industrial occupations and manual trades. Indeed, there is some truth to this conclusion. As noted in Chapter 11, unlike European nations, the United States and Canada have no widespread training systems for non-college-bound youths. As a result, most graduate without work-related skills and experience a "floundering period" that lasts for several years (Grubb, 1999). Inspired by programs in Austria, Denmark, Switzerland, and several East European countries, youth apprenticeship strategies that coordinate on-the-job training with classroom instruction are being considered as an important dimension of U.S. and Canadian educational reforms. The Cultural Influences box above describes Germany's successful apprenticeship system.

The many benefits of bringing together the worlds of schooling and work include helping non-college-bound young people establish productive lives right after graduation, motivating at-risk youths to stay in school, and contributing to the nation's economic growth. Nevertheless, implementing an apprenticeship system poses major challenges: overcoming the reluctance of employers to assume part of the responsibility for vocational training, ensuring cooperation between schools and businesses, and preventing low-SES youths from being concentrated in the lowest-skilled apprenticeship placements, an obstacle that Germany itself has not yet fully overcome (Hamilton & Hamilton, 2000). Currently, small-scale school-to-work projects in the United States and Canada are attempting to solve these problems and build bridges between learning and working.

Although vocational development is a lifelong process, adolescence and early adulthood are crucial periods for defining occupational goals and launching a career. Young people who are well prepared for an economically and personally satisfying work life are much more likely to become productive citizens, devoted family members, and contented adults. The support of families, schools, businesses, communities, and society as a whole can contribute greatly to a positive outcome. In Chapter 14, we will take up the challenges of establishing a career and integrating it with other life tasks.

Ask Yourself

Review

What student and college-environment characteristics contribute to favorable psychological changes during the college years?

Apply

Diane, a high school senior, knows that she wants to "work with people" but doesn't yet have a specific career in mind. Diane's father is a chemistry professor, her mother a social worker. What steps can Diane's parents take to broaden her awareness of the world of work and help her focus on an occupational goal?

Connect

What have you learned in previous chapters about development of gender stereotypes that helps explain why women's progress in entering and excelling at male-dominant professions has been slow? (*Hint:* See Chapter 10, page 343.)

Reflect

Describe your progress in choosing a vocation. What personal and environmental factors have been influential?

www.ablongman.com/berk

Summary

A Gradual Transition: Emerging Adulthood

What is emerging adulthood, and how has cultural change contributed to the emergence of this period?

■ In **emerging adulthood,** young adults from about age 18 to 25 are released from parental oversight but have not yet taken on adult roles. During these years of extended exploration, young people prolong identity development as they make frequent changes in educational paths, jobs, and love partners.

■ Increased education required for entry-level positions in many fields, gains in economic prosperity, reduced need for young people's labor, and globalization have prompted the appearance and spread of emerging adulthood.

🍂 Physical Development

Biological Aging Is Under Way in Early Adulthood

Describe current theories of biological aging, including those at the level of DNA and body cells and those at the level of tissues and organs.

■ Once body structures reach maximum capacity and efficiency in the teens and twenties, **biological aging,** or **senescence,** begins. The programmed effects of specific genes may control certain age-related biological changes in DNA and body cells. DNA may also be damaged as random mutations accumulate, leading to less efficient cell repair and replacement and to abnormal cancerous cells.

■ Release of highly reactive **free radicals** is a likely cause of age-related DNA and cellular damage. Biological aging may result from a complex combination of programmed effects of specific genes and random events that cause cells to deteriorate.

■ Genetic and cellular deterioration affects organs and tissues. The **cross-linkage theory of aging** suggests that over time, protein fibers form links and become less elastic, producing negative changes in many organs. Declines in the endocrine and immune systems may also contribute to aging.

Physical Changes

Describe the physical changes of aging, paying special attention to the cardiovascular and respi-

ratory systems, motor performance, the immune system, and reproductive capacity.

■ Gradual physical changes take place in early adulthood and later accelerate. Declines in heart and lung performance are evident during exercise. Heart disease is a leading cause of death in adults, although it has decreased considerably in the past half-century due to lifestyle changes and medical advances. Atherosclerosis is a serious, multiply-determined cardiovascular disease involving fatty deposits on artery walls.

■ Athletic skills requiring speed, strength, and gross body coordination peak in the early twenties; those requiring endurance, arm–hand steadiness, and aiming peak in the late twenties and early thirties. Less active lifestyles rather than biological aging account for most of the age-related decline in athletic skill and motor performance.

■ The immune response strengthens through adolescence and declines after age 20. This trend is partly due to shrinking of the thymus gland. Increased difficulty coping with physical and psychological stress also contributes.

■ After age 35, women's reproductive capacity declines dramatically due to reduced quality and quantity of ova. Men show a gradual decrease in amount of semen and concentration of sperm in each ejaculation after age 40.

Health and Fitness

Describe the impact of SES, nutrition, and exercise on health, and discuss obesity in adulthood.

■ Economically advantaged, well-educated individuals tend to sustain good health over most of their adult lives, whereas the health of lower-income individuals with limited education declines. SES differences in health-related living conditions and habits are largely responsible.

■ Overweight and obesity have increased dramatically in Western nations. Today, Americans are the most overweight people in the world. Low-SES ethnic minorities are most affected. Sedentary lifestyles and diets high in sugar and fat contribute to obesity, which is associated with serious health problems, social discrimination, and early death.

■ Some weight gain between ages 25 and 50 results from a decrease in **basal metabolic rate (BMR),** but many young adults show large increases. Successful treatments for obesity typically involve a low-fat diet plus exercise, accurate recording of food consumption, social support, teaching problem-solving skills, and extended intervention.

■ Regular exercise reduces body fat, builds muscle, helps prevent illness (including cardiovascular disease), and enhances psychological well-being. Physical activity is associated with substantially lower death rates from all causes. Moderately intense exercise on most days leads to health benefits, which increase with greater intensity of exercise.

What are the two most common substance disorders, and what health risks do they entail?

■ Cigarette smoking and alcohol consumption are the two most common adult substance disorders. Most adults who smoke began before age 21. They are at increased risk for many health problems, including eye and skin abnormalities, decline in bone mass, fertility problems, heart attack, stroke, numerous cancers, and premature death.

■ About one-third of heavy drinkers suffer from alcoholism, to which both heredity and environment contribute. Alcohol is implicated in liver and cardiovascular disease, certain cancers, numerous other physical disorders, and social problems such as highway fatalities, crime, and sexual coercion.

Describe sexual attitudes and behavior of young adults, and discuss sexually transmitted diseases, sexual coercion, and premenstrual syndrome.

■ Most adults are less sexually active than popular media images suggest, but compared with earlier generations, they display a wider range of sexual choices and lifestyles and have had more sexual partners. Nevertheless, most people spend the majority of their lives with one partner.

■ Adults in committed relationships report high satisfaction with their sex lives. Only a minority of adults report persistent sexual problems—difficulties linked to low SES, stress, having many partners, and a history of childhood sexual abuse or adult sexual coercion.

■ Negative attitudes toward homosexual men and women have begun to change, largely as a result of greater exposure and interpersonal contact. Homosexual relationships, like heterosexual relationships, are characterized by similarity between partners in education and background, greater satisfaction in committed relationships, and modest frequency of sexual activity.

■ Many North Americans are likely to contract a sexually transmitted disease (STD) during their lifetime; women are more vulnerable than men. Although AIDS remains concentrated among gay men and intravenous drug abusers, the incidence among homosexuals is declining. Currently, the disease is spreading most rapidly through heterosexual contact in poverty-stricken minority groups where drug abuse is high. A special need exists for female-controlled preventive measures.

■ Most rape victims have been harmed by men they know well. Men who commit sexual assault typically hold traditional gender roles, approve of violence against women, and have difficulty interpreting women's social behavior accurately. Cultural acceptance of strong gender typing and of violence contributes to sexual coercion, which leads to psychological trauma. Female-initiated coercive sexual behavior also occurs, although it is less often reported and recognized by the legal system.

■ Nearly 40 percent of women experience **premenstrual syndrome (PMS),** usually in mild form. For some, PMS is severe enough to interfere with daily life. Evidence for a genetic predisposition to PMS is accumulating.

How does psychological stress affect health?

■ Chronic psychological stress induces physical responses that contribute to heart disease, several types of cancer, and gastrointestinal problems. Because the many challenges of early adulthood make it a highly stressful time of life, interventions that help stressed young people form supportive social ties are especially important.

🏹 Cognitive Development

Changes in the Structure of Thought

Describe characteristics of adult thought, and explain how thinking changes in adulthood.

■ Cognitive development beyond Piaget's formal operations is known as **postformal thought.** Adult cognition typically reflects an awareness of multiple truths, integrates logic with reality, and tolerates the gap between the ideal and the real.

■ According to Perry's theory of **epistemic cognition,** college students move from **dualistic thinking,** dividing information into right and wrong, to **relativistic thinking,** awareness of multiple truths. Eventually, the most mature individuals progress to **commitment within relativistic thinking,** a perspective that synthesizes contradictions.

■ Epistemic cognition depends on experiences that encourage young people to consider the rationality of their thought processes, resulting in gains in metacognition. Peer collaboration on challenging, ill-structured problems is especially beneficial.

■ According to Labouvie-Vief's theory, the need to specialize motivates adults to progress from the ideal world of possibilities to **pragmatic thought,** which uses logic as a tool to solve real-world problems and accepts inconsistency, imperfection, and the need to compromise. As a result of enhanced reflective capacities, adults also gain in **cognitive-affective complexity**—coordination of positive and negative feelings into a complex, organized structure.

Expertise and Creativity

What roles do expertise and creativity play in adult thought?

■ Specialization in college and in an occupation leads to **expertise**—acquisition of extensive knowledge in a field or endeavor—which enhances problem solving and is necessary for creativity. Mature creativity involves formulating meaningful new problems and questions. Although creativity tends to rise in early adulthood and to peak in the late thirties or early forties, its development varies across disciplines and individuals. In addition to expertise, diverse personal and situational factors jointly promote creativity.

The College Experience

Describe the impact of a college education on young people's lives, and discuss the problem of dropping out.

■ Through involvement in academic programs and campus life, college students engage in exploration that produces gains in knowledge and reasoning ability, revised attitudes and values, enhanced self-esteem and self-knowledge, and preparation for a high-status career.

■ Dropout rates are higher in less selective colleges and for ethnic minority students from low-SES families. Most young people who drop out do so during their freshman year because of both personal and institutional factors. These students benefit from interventions that show concern for them as individuals.

Vocational Choice

Trace the development of vocational choice, and cite factors that influence it.

■ Vocational choice moves through a **fantasy period,** in which children explore career options through play; a **tentative period,** in which teenagers weigh different careers against their interests, abilities, and values; and a **realistic period,** in which young people settle on a vocational category and then a specific occupation.

■ Vocational choice is influenced by personality; parents' provision of educational opportunities, vocational information, and encouragement; and close relationships with teachers. Women's progress in male-dominated professions has been slow, and their achievements lag behind those of men in virtually all fields. Gender-stereotyped messages about women's abilities prevent many from reaching their career potential. Although some men choose careers in female-dominated fields, this is still uncommon.

What problems do North American non-college-bound young people face in preparing for a vocation?

■ North American non-college-bound high school graduates have fewer work opportunities today than they did several decades ago. Most are limited to low-paid, unskilled jobs, and too many are unemployed. To address their need for vocational training, youth apprenticeships inspired by those in Western Europe are being considered as an important dimension of U.S. and Canadian educational reforms.

Important Terms and Concepts

basal metabolic rate (BMR) (p. 438)
biological aging, or senescence (p. 431)
cognitive-affective complexity (p. 451)
commitment within relativistic thinking (p. 450)
cross-linkage theory of aging (p. 432)

dualistic thinking (p. 450)
emerging adulthood (p. 430)
epistemic cognition (p. 450)
expertise (p. 452)
fantasy period (p. 454)
free radicals (p. 432)

postformal thought (p. 450)
pragmatic thought (p. 451)
premenstrual syndrome (PMS) (p. 447)
realistic period (p. 454)
relativistic thinking (p. 450)
tentative period (p. 454)

© ARIEL SKELLEY/CORBIS

*T*he warm communication between this young couple shows that they are passionately in love. Yet many adjustments lie ahead. A lasting intimate partnership requires effort, compromise, sensitivity, and respect.

Emotional and Social Development in Early Adulthood

*A*fter completing her master's degree, Sharese returned to her hometown, where she and Ernie would soon be married. During their year-long engagement, Sharese had vacillated about whether to follow through. At times, she looked with envy at Heather, still unattached and free to pursue career and other options before her.

Sharese also pondered the life circumstances of Christy and her husband, Gary— married their junior year in college and parents of two children born within the next few years. Despite his good teaching performance, Gary's relationship with the high school principal deteriorated, and he quit his job at the end of his first year. Financial pressures and the demands

of parenthood had put Christy's education and career plans on hold. Sharese wondered whether it was really possible to combine family and career.

As her wedding approached, Sharese's ambivalence intensified, and she admitted to Ernie that she didn't feel ready to marry. Ernie's admiration for Sharese had strengthened over their courtship, and he reassured her of his love. His career was launched, and at age 28, he looked forward to starting a family. Uncertain and conflicted, Sharese felt swept toward the altar as relatives, friends, and gifts began to arrive. On the appointed day, she walked down the aisle.

In this chapter, we take up the emotional and social sides of early adulthood. Recall from Chapter 13 that identity development continues to be a central task during the years of *emerging adulthood*. When large, diverse samples of 18- to 25-year-olds were asked what it means to become an adult, most emphasize psychological qualities, especially self-sufficiency: accepting responsibility for one's actions, deciding on personal beliefs and values, establishing equal relationships with parents, and becoming financially independent (Arnett, 2006). Young people from collectivist minority cultures also place special emphasis on attaining certain roles. For example, African-American and Hispanic young adults view supporting and caring for a family as a major marker of adulthood (Arnett, 2001, 2003).

As they achieve a secure identity and independence from parents, young adults seek close, affectionate ties. Yet the decade of the twenties is accompanied by a sharp rise in the extent to which people feel they are personally in control of events in their lives. Indeed, 20- to 29-year-olds report a greater sense of control than they ever will again (Grob, Krings, & Bangerter, 2001). Perhaps for this reason, like Sharese, they often fear losing their freedom.

Once this struggle is resolved, early adulthood leads to new family units and parenthood, accomplished in the context of diverse lifestyles. At the same time, young adults must master the skills and tasks of their chosen career. We will see that identity, love, and work are intertwined. In negotiating these arenas, young adults do more choosing, planning, and changing course than any other age group. When their decisions are in tune with themselves and their social and cultural worlds, they acquire many new competencies, and life is full and rewarding.

Erikson's Theory: Intimacy versus Isolation

Erikson's contributions have energized the study of adult personality development. His vision has influenced all contemporary theories. According to Erikson (1964), each adulthood stage brings both opportunity and risk—"a turning point for better or worse" (p. 139). His psychological conflict of early adulthood is **intimacy versus isolation,** reflected in the young person's thoughts and feelings about making a permanent commitment to an intimate partner.

As Sharese discovered, establishing a mutually gratifying close relationship is challenging. Most young adults are still grappling with identity issues and have only recently attained economic independence. Yet intimacy requires that they give up some of their independence and redefine their identity to include both partners' values and interests. Those in their teens and early twenties frequently say they don't feel ready for a lasting tie (Collins & van Dulmen, 2006). During their first year of marriage, Sharese separated from Ernie twice as she tried to reconcile her desire for self-determination with her desire for intimacy. Maturity involves balancing these forces. Without intimacy, young adults face the negative outcome of Erikson's early adulthood stage: loneliness and self-absorption. Ernie's patience and stability helped Sharese realize that committed love requires generosity and compromise but not total surrender of the self.

Research confirms that—as Erikson emphasized—a secure identity fosters attainment of intimacy. Commitment to per-

sonally meaningful values and goals prepares young adults for interpersonal commitments, which increase as early adulthood progresses (Kroger, 2002). Among large samples of college students, identity achievement was positively correlated with fidelity (loyalty in relationships) and love, for both men and women. In contrast, identity moratorium—a state of searching prior to commitment—was negatively associated with fidelity and love (Markstrom et al., 1997; Markstrom & Kalmanir, 2001). Other studies show that advanced identity development strongly predicts involvement in a deep, committed love partnership or readiness to establish such a partnership (Craig-Bray, Adams, & Dobson, 1988; Montgomery, 2005). Still, the coordination of identity and intimacy is more complex for women, who are more likely than men to consider the impact of their personal goals on important relationships (Archer, 2002b).

In friendships and work ties, too, young people who have achieved intimacy are cooperative, tolerant, and accepting of differences in background and values. They enjoy being with others but are also comfortable when alone. People with a sense of isolation hesitate to form close ties because they fear loss of their own identity, tend to compete rather than cooperate, are not accepting of differences, and are easily threatened when others get too close (Hamachek, 1990; Marcia, 2002).

Erikson believed that successful resolution of intimacy versus isolation prepares the individual for the middle adulthood stage, which focuses on *generativity*—caring for the next generation and helping to improve society. But as noted previously, a fixed series of tasks tied neatly to age does not describe many adults. Childbearing and child rearing (aspects of generativity) usually occur in the twenties and thirties, and contributions to society through work also are under way. Furthermore, as we will see shortly, many combinations of marriage, parenting, and career exist, each with a unique pattern of timing and commitment.

In sum, identity, intimacy and generativity are concerns of early adulthood, with shifts in emphasis that differ among individuals. Recognizing that Erikson's theory provides only a broad sketch of adult personality development, other theorists have expanded and modified his stage approach, adding detail and flexibility.

Other Theories of Adult Psychosocial Development

In the 1970s, growing interest in adult development led to several widely read books on the topic. Daniel Levinson's *The Seasons of a Man's Life* (1978) and George Vaillant's *Adaptation to Life* (1977) and *Aging Well* (2002) present psychosocial theories in the tradition of Erikson. Each is summarized in Table 14.1.

Levinson's Seasons of Life

Seeking an underlying order in the life course, Levinson (1978) conducted in-depth biographical interviews with forty 35- to

Table 14.1	Stages of Adult Psychosocial Development		
Period of Development	**Erikson**	**Levinson**	**Vaillant**
Early adulthood (20–40 years)	Intimacy versus isolation	Early adult transition: 17–22 years Entry life structure for early adulthood: 22–28 years Age-30 transition: 28–33 years Culminating life structure for early adulthood: 33–40 years	Intimacy Career consolidation
Middle adulthood (40–65 years)	Generativity versus stagnation	Midlife transition: 40–45 years Entry life structure for middle adulthood: 45–50 years Age-50 transition (50–55 years) Culminating life structure for middle adulthood (55–60 years)	Generativity Keeper of meanings
Late adulthood (65 years–death)	Ego integrity versus despair	Late adult transition (60–65 years) Late adulthood (65 years–death)	Ego integrity

45-year-old men from four occupational subgroups: hourly workers in industry, business executives, university biologists, and novelists. Later he interviewed forty-five women, also 35 to 45 years of age, from three subgroups: homemakers, business executives, and university professors. His results and those of others reveal a common path of change within which men and women approach developmental tasks in somewhat different ways (Levinson, 1996; Roberts & Newton, 1987).

Like Erikson, Levinson (1978, 1996) saw development as a sequence of qualitatively distinct eras (stages or seasons). In each, biological and social forces introduce new psychological challenges. Each stage begins with a *transition,* lasting about 5 years, which concludes the previous era and prepares the person for the next. Between transitions, people move into stable periods, lasting about 5 to 7 years, in which they build a life structure aimed at harmonizing inner personal and outer societal demands to enhance quality of life. Eventually people question the current structure, and a new transition ensues.

The **life structure,** a key concept in Levinson's theory, is the underlying design of a person's life, consisting of relationships with significant others—individuals, groups, and institutions. Of its many components, usually only a few, relating to marriage/family and occupation, are central. But wide individual differences exist in the weight of central and peripheral components.

Men's and women's accounts of their lives confirm Levinson's description of the life course. They also reveal that early adulthood is the era of "greatest energy and abundance, contradiction and stress" (Levinson, 1986, p. 5). These years can bring rich satisfaction in love, sexuality, family life, occupational advancement, and realization of life goals. But they also involve serious decisions about marriage, children, work, and lifestyle before many people have enough experience to choose wisely.

■ **Dreams and Mentors.** How do young adults cope with the opportunities and hazards of this period? Levinson found

that during the early adult transition (age 17 to 22), most construct a *dream*—an image of themselves in the adult world that guides their decision making. For men, the dream usually emphasizes an independent achiever in an occupational role, while most career-oriented women display "split dreams" in which both marriage and career are prominent. Also, women's dreams tend to define the self in terms of relationships with husband, children, and colleagues. Men's dreams usually are more individualistic: They view significant others, especially wives, as vital supporters of their goals and less often see themselves as supporting others' goals.

Young adults also form a relationship with a *mentor* who facilitates realization of their dream—often a senior colleague at work but occasionally a more experienced friend, neighbor, or relative. Mentors may act as teachers who enhance the

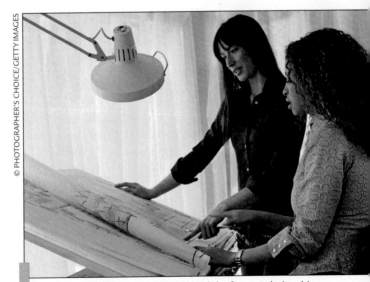

© PHOTOGRAPHER'S CHOICE/GETTY IMAGES

To realize their dreams, most young adults form a relationship with a mentor who fosters their occupational skills and knowledge of workplace values, customs, and characters. This experienced architect advises an intern about a set of plans.

person's occupational skills; guides who acquaint the person with values, customs, and characters in the occupational setting; and sponsors who foster the person's career advancement. As we will see when we take up vocational development, finding a supportive mentor is easier for men than for women.

According to Levinson, men oriented toward high-status careers spend their twenties acquiring professional skills, values, and credentials. Although some women follow this path, for many others career development extends into middle age. Men who serve as primary caregivers of their children also show a delayed career path (Kogan & Vacha-Haase, 2002; Levinson, 1978, 1996).

■ **Age-30 Transition.** During the age-30 transition, young people reevaluate their life structure. Those who were preoccupied with career and are still single usually focus on finding a life partner. But men rarely reverse the relative priority of career and family, whereas career-oriented women sometimes do.

Women who had emphasized marriage and motherhood often develop more individualistic goals. For example, Christy, who had dreamed of becoming a professor, finally earned her doctoral degree in her mid-thirties and secured a college teaching position. Women also become conscious of aspects of their marriage that threaten to inhibit further development of the independent side of their dream. Married women tend to demand that their husbands recognize and accommodate their interests and aspirations beyond the home.

For men and women without a satisfying intimate tie or occupational accomplishments, the age-30 transition can be a crisis. For others who question whether they can create a meaningful life structure, it is a time of considerable conflict and instability.

■ **Settling Down for Men, Continued Instability for Women.** To create the culminating life structure of early adulthood, men usually "settle down" by focusing on certain relationships and aspirations, setting others aside. In doing so, they try to establish a stable niche in society that is consistent with their values, whether those be wealth, power, prestige, artistic or scientific achievement, or forms of family or community participation. In his thirties, Sharese's husband, Ernie, expanded his knowledge of real estate accounting, became a partner in his firm, coached his son's soccer team, and was elected treasurer of his church. He paid less attention to golf, travel, and playing the guitar than he had in his twenties.

"Settling down," however, does not accurately describe women's experiences during their thirties. Many remain unsettled because of the addition of an occupational or relationship commitment. When her two children were born, Sharese felt torn between her research position in the state health department and her family. She took six months off after the arrival of each baby. When she returned to work, she did not pursue attractive administrative openings that required travel and time away from home. And shortly after Christy began teaching, she and Gary divorced. Becoming a single parent while starting her professional life introduced new strains. Not until middle age do many women attain the stability typical of men

in their thirties—reaching career maturity and taking on more authority in the community (Levinson, 1996).

Vaillant's Adaptation to Life

Vaillant (1977) examined the development of nearly 250 men born in the 1920s, selected for study while they were students at a highly competitive liberal arts college, and followed as many as possible over the lifespan. In college, the participants underwent extensive interviews. During each succeeding decade, they answered lengthy questionnaires. Then Vaillant (2002) interviewed the men at ages 47, 60, and 70 about work, family, and physical and mental health.

Other than denying a strict age-related schedule of change, Vaillant's theory is compatible with Levinson's. Both agree that quality of relationships with important people shape the life course. In studying how the men altered themselves and their social world to adapt to life, Vaillant confirmed Erikson's stages but filled gaps between them. After a period in their twenties devoted to intimacy concerns, the men focused on career consolidation in their thirties, working hard and making the grade in their occupations. During their forties, they pulled back from individual achievement and became more generative—giving to and guiding others. In their fifties and sixties, they became "keepers of meaning," or guardians of their culture, expressing concern about the values of the new generation and the state of their society. Many felt a deep need to preserve and pass on cultural traditions by teaching others what they had learned from life experience (Vaillant & Koury, 1994). Finally, in their seventies, the men became more spiritual and reflective, contemplating the meaning of life and accepting its finiteness.

Although Vaillant initially studied only men, eventually he examined the development of a sample of bright, well-educated women who were participants in another lifelong study. His findings, and those of others, suggest that women undergo a series of changes similar to those just described (Block, 1971; Oden & Terman, 1968; Vaillant, 2002).

Limitations of Levinson's and Vaillant's Theories

Although psychosocial theorists express considerable consensus on adult development, their conclusions are based largely on interviews with people born in the first few decades of the twentieth century. The patterns Levinson and Vaillant identified fit the life paths of Sharese, Ernie, Christy, and Gary. Nevertheless, those patterns might not apply as broadly to young adults today as they did to past generations.

Two other factors limit these theorists' conclusions. First, Levinson's sample included only a few non-college-educated, low-income adults, and low-SES women remain almost entirely uninvestigated. Yet SES can profoundly affect the life course. For example, Levinson's blue-collar workers rarely implemented an occupational dream. Perhaps because career advancement is less salient for them, low-SES men perceive "early adulthood" to end and the arrival of "maturity" to begin earlier than their higher-

SES counterparts (Neugarten, 1979). Examining longitudinal archives on low-SES men who had grown up in the 1940s, Vaillant (1993) reported evidence for his stage sequence. Still, he acknowledged that the sample was limited.

Finally, Levinson's participants, interviewed in middle age, might not have remembered all aspects of their early adulthoods accurately. Studies of new generations—both men and women, of diverse backgrounds—are needed before we can conclude that the developmental sequences just described apply to most or all young people.

The Social Clock

As we have seen, changes in society from one generation to the next can affect the life course. Bernice Neugarten (1968a, 1979) pointed out that an important cultural and generational influence on adult development is the **social clock**—age-graded expectations for major life events, such as beginning a first job, getting married, birth of the first child, buying a home, and retiring. All societies have such timetables. Being on time or off time can profoundly affect self-esteem because adults (like children and adolescents) make social comparisons, measuring their progress against that of agemates.

A major source of personality change in adulthood is conformity to or departure from the social clock. In a study of college women born in the 1930s who were followed up at ages 27 and 43, researchers determined how closely participants followed a "feminine" social clock (marriage and parenthood in the early or mid-twenties) or a "masculine" one (entry into a high-status career and advancement by the late twenties). Those who started families on time became more responsible, self-controlled, tolerant, and caring but declined in self-esteem and felt more vulnerable as their lives progressed. Those who followed an occupational timetable typical for men became more dominant, sociable, independent, and intellectually effective, a trend also found in a cohort born a decade later (Vandewater & Stewart, 1997). Women not on a social clock— who had neither married nor begun a career by age 30—were doing especially poorly. They suffered from self-doubt, feelings of incompetence, and loneliness. "My future is a giant question mark," one stated (Helson, 1992; Helson, Mitchell, & Moane, 1984, p. 1090).

As noted in Chapter 1, expectations for appropriate behavior in early, middle, and late adulthood are less definite than in the past. When Australian college students were asked for the best age at which to accomplish various developmental milestones, they mentioned later ages for marriage and grandparenthood and a broader age range for retirement than people did 30 years ago (Peterson, 1996). Still, many adults experience some psychological distress when they are substantially behind in timing of life events (Antonucci & Akiyama, 1997; Rook, Catalano, & Dooley, 1989). Following a social clock of some kind seems to foster confidence during early adulthood because it guarantees that young people will engage in the work of society, develop skills, and increase in understanding of the self and others (Helson, 1997; Helson & Moane, 1987). As Neugarten (1979) suggested, the stability of

An important cultural and generational influence on adult development is the social clock—age-graded expectations for life events. This first-time mother has established herself as a research scientist before having children, a pattern that is now more acceptable, as social-clock expectations have become less rigid than they were in the past.

society depends on having people committed to social-clock patterns. With this in mind, let's take a closer look at how young men and women traverse the major tasks of young adulthood.

Ask Yourself

Review

According to Levinson, how do the life structures of men and women differ?

Apply

Using the concept of the social clock, explain Sharese's conflicted feelings about marrying Ernie after she finished graduate school.

Connect

Return to page 400 in Chapter 12 and review the contributions of exploration and commitment to a mature identity. Using the two criteria, explain why identity achievement is positively related to attainment of intimacy (fidelity and love), whereas identity moratorium is negatively predictive.

Reflect

Describe your early adulthood dream (see page 465). Then ask a friend or classmate of the other gender to describe his or her dream, and compare the two. Are they consistent with Levinson's findings?

Close Relationships

To establish an intimate tie to another person, people must find a partner and build an emotional bond that they sustain over time. Although young adults are especially concerned with romantic love, the need for intimacy is multifaceted: It can also be satisfied through other relationships involving mutual commitment—with friends, siblings, and co-workers.

Romantic Love

During her junior year of college, Sharese found herself noticing Ernie, a senior and one of the top students in her government class. One weekend, Sharese and Ernie ran into each other at a party and struck up a conversation. Sharese discovered that Ernie was as warm and interesting as he had seemed from a distance. And Ernie found Sharese lively, intelligent, and attractive. By the end of the evening, the two realized that they had similar opinions on important social issues and liked the same leisure activities. They began dating steadily. Four years later, they married.

Finding a partner with whom to share one's life is a major milestone of adult development, with profound consequences for self-concept and psychological well-being. As Sharese and Ernie's relationship reveals, it is also a complex process that unfolds over time and is affected by a variety of events.

■ **Selecting a Mate.** Recall from Chapter 13 that intimate partners generally meet in places where they find people of their own age, ethnicity, SES, and religion or (somewhat less often) connect through Internet dating services. People usually select partners who resemble themselves in other ways—attitudes, personality, educational plans, intelligence, physical attractiveness, and even height (Keith & Schafer, 1991; Simpson & Harris, 1994). Romantic partners sometimes have complementary traits—one more gregarious, the other more reserved; one more curious and sensation-seeking, the other preferring consistency and routine. As long as these differences permit each person to satisfy personal preferences and goals, they can contribute to compatibility (Dryer & Horowitz, 1997). But overall, little support exists for the idea that "opposites attract." In fact, many studies confirm that the more similar partners are, the more satisfied they tend to be with their relationship and the more likely they are to stay together (Blackwell & Lichter, 2004; Caspi & Herbener, 1990; Lucas et al., 2004).

Nevertheless, in choosing a long-term partner, men and women differ in the importance they place on certain characteristics. In research carried out in diverse industrialized and developing countries, women assign greater weight to intelligence, ambition, financial status, and moral character, whereas men place more emphasis on physical attractiveness and domestic skills. In addition, women prefer a same-age or slightly older partner, men a younger partner (Buunk, 2002; Cramer, Schaefer, & Reid, 2003; Stewart, Stinnett, & Rosenfeld, 2000).

Evolutionary theory helps us understand these findings. Recall from Chapter 13 that because their capacity to reproduce is limited, women seek a mate with traits, such as earning power and emotional commitment, that help ensure children's survival and well-being. In contrast, men look for a mate with traits that signal youth, health, sexual pleasure, and ability to give birth and care for offspring. As further evidence for this difference, men often want a relationship to move quickly toward physical intimacy, while women typically prefer to take the time to achieve psychological intimacy first (Buss, 2004).

From an alternative, social learning perspective, gender roles profoundly influence criteria for mate selection. Beginning in childhood, men learn to be assertive and independent—behaviors needed for success in the work world. Women acquire nurturant behaviors, which facilitate caregiving. Then each sex learns to value traits in the other that fit with a traditional division of labor (Eagly & Wood, 1999; Wood & Eagly, 2000). In support of this theory, in cultures and in younger generations experiencing greater gender equity, men and women are more alike in their mate preferences. For example, compared with men in China and Japan, North American men place more emphasis on their mate's financial prospects, less on her domestic skills. And both sexes care somewhat less about their mate's age relative to their own. Instead, they place a high value on caring and love—that is, on relationship satisfaction (Buss et al., 2001; Buunk et al., 2001; Toro-Morn & Sprecher, 2003).

Nevertheless, men continue to value physical attractiveness more than women do, and women continue to value earning capacity more than men do. Furthermore, these gender differences—along with gender similarity in desire for a caring, sensitive partner—also characterize homosexual men and women (Regan, Medina, & Joshi, 2001). In sum, both biological and social forces contribute to mate selection.

As the Lifespan Vista box on pages 470–471 reveals, young people's choice of an intimate partner and the quality of their relationship also are affected by memories of their early parent–child bond. Finally, for romance to lead to a lasting partnership, it must happen at the right time. Two people may be right for each other, but if one or both are not ready to marry in terms of their social clock, then the relationship is likely to dissolve.

■ **The Components of Love.** How do we know that we are in love? Robert Sternberg's (1987, 1988, 2000) **triangular theory of love** identifies three components—intimacy, passion, and commitment—that shift in emphasis as romantic relationships develop. *Intimacy,* the emotional component, involves warm, tender communication, expressions of concern about the other's well-being, and a desire for the partner to reciprocate. *Passion,* the desire for sexual activity and romance, is the physical- and psychological-arousal component. *Commitment* is the cognitive component, leading partners to decide that they are in love and to maintain that love.

At the beginning of a relationship, **passionate love**—intense sexual attraction—is strong. Gradually, passion declines in favor of intimacy and commitment, which form the basis for **companionate love**—warm, trusting affection and caregiving (Acker & Davis, 1992; Fehr, 1994). Each aspect of love, however, helps sustain the relationship. Early passionate love is a strong predictor of whether partners keep dating. But without the quiet intimacy, predictability, and shared attitudes and values of companionate love, most romances eventually break up (Hendrick & Hendrick, 2002).

An ongoing relationship requires effort from both partners. Research on newlyweds' feelings and behavior over the first year of marriage reveals that husbands and wives gradually felt less "in love" and pleased with married life. A variety of factors contributed, including a sharp drop in time spent talking to each other and doing things that brought each other pleasure (for example, saying "I love you" or making the other person laugh). Joint leisure pursuits gave way to more household tasks and chores and, therefore, fewer enjoyable times together. Also, when discussing areas of conflict, partners declined in accurate reading of each other's thoughts and feelings. Perhaps after an increasing number of such interactions, they tried less hard to grasp the other's point of view and resorted to well-established habits, such as giving in or withdrawing (Huston, McHale, & Crouter, 1986; Kilpatrick, Bissonnette, & Rusbult, 2002).

But couples whose relationships endure generally report that they love each other more than they did earlier (Sprecher, 1999). In the transformation of romantic involvements from passionate to companionate, *commitment* may be the aspect of love that determines whether a relationship survives. Communicating that commitment—through warmth, attentiveness, empathy, caring, acceptance, and respect—can be of great benefit (Knapp & Taylor, 1994). For example, Sharese's doubts about getting married subsided largely because of Ernie's expressions of commitment. In the most dramatic of these, he painted a large sign, reading "I LOVE SHARESE," and placed it in their front yard on her birthday. Sharese returned Ernie's sentiments, and the intimacy of their bond deepened.

Intimate partners who consistently express their commitment report higher-quality and longer-lasting relationships (Fitzpatrick & Sollie, 1999). An important feature of their communication is constructive conflict resolution—directly expressing wishes and needs, listening patiently, asking for clarification, compromising, accepting responsibility, and avoiding the escalation of negative interaction sparked by criticism, contempt, defensiveness, and stonewalling (Johnson et al., 2005; Schneewind & Gerhard, 2002). In a longitudinal study, newlyweds' negative behavior and, especially, sharp rise in blood levels of stress hormones during conflict predicted eventual marital dissatisfaction and divorce over the following decade (Kiecolt-Glaser et al., 2003). Couples whose relationships dissolved did not show greater initial physiological reactivity. Rather, poor problem solving altered their stress hormone levels, which often remained elevated throughout the day.

How men handle conflict is particularly important because they tend to be less skilled than women at negotiating it, often avoiding discussion (Gayle, Preiss, & Allen, 2002). Applying What We Know below lists ways to help keep the embers of love aglow in a romantic partnership.

Keeping Love Alive in a Romantic Partnership

Applying What We Know

Suggestion	Description
Make time for your relationship.	To foster relationship satisfaction and a sense of being "in love," plan regular times to be together.
Tell your partner of your love.	Express affection and caring, including the powerful words "I love you," at appropriate times. These messages increase perceptions of commitment and encourage your partner to respond in kind.
Be available to your partner in times of need.	Provide emotional support, giving of yourself when your partner is distressed.
Communicate constructively and positively about relationship problems.	When you or your partner is dissatisfied, suggest ways of overcoming difficulties and ask your partner to collaborate in choosing and implementing a course of action. Avoid the four enemies of a gratifying, close relationship: criticism, contempt, defensiveness, and stonewalling.
Show an interest in important aspects of your partner's life.	Ask about your partner's work, friends, family, and hobbies and express appreciation for his or her special abilities and achievements. In doing so, you grant your partner a sense of being valued.
Confide in your partner.	Share innermost feelings, keeping intimacy alive.
Forgive minor offenses and try to understand major offenses.	Whenever possible, overcome feelings of anger through forgiveness. In this way, you acknowledge unjust behavior but avoid becoming preoccupied with it.

Sources: Donatelle, 2004; McCarthy & McCarthy, 2004.

A Lifespan Vista

Childhood Attachment Patterns and Adult Romantic Relationships

Recall from Chapter 6 (page 197) that according to Bowlby's ethological theory of attachment, the early attachment bond leads to the construction of an *internal working model,* or set of expectations about attachment figures, that serves as a guide for close relationships throughout life. We also saw that adults' evaluations of their early attachment experiences are related to their parenting behaviors—specifically, to the quality of attachments they build with their children (see page 205). Additional evidence indicates that recollections of childhood attachment patterns strongly predict romantic relationships in adulthood.

In studies carried out in Australia, Israel, and the United States, researchers asked people to recall and evaluate their early parental bonds (attachment history), their attitudes toward intimate relationships (internal working model), and their actual experiences with romantic partners. In a few studies, investiga-

tors also observed couples' behaviors. Consistent with Bowlby's theory, adults' memories and interpretations of childhood attachment patterns were good indicators of internal working models and relationship experiences. (To review patterns of attachment, see pages 197–198.)

Secure Attachment. Adults who described their attachment history as secure (warm, loving, and supportive) had internal working models that reflected this security. They viewed themselves as likable and easy to get to know, were comfortable with intimacy, and rarely worried about abandonment or someone getting too close to them. In line with these attitudes, they characterized their most important love relationship in terms of trust, happiness, and friendship (Cassidy, 2001). Furthermore, their behaviors toward their partner were supportive and their conflict resolution strategies constructive. They were also at ease in turning to their partner for comfort and assistance and reported mutually initiated, enjoyable sexual activity (Collins & Feeney, 2000; Creasey, 2002; Creasey & Ladd, 2004; Roisman et al., 2002).

Avoidant Attachment. Adults who reported an avoidant attachment history (demanding, disrespectful, and critical parents) displayed internal working models that stressed independence, mistrust of love partners, and anxiety about people getting too close. They were convinced that others disliked them and that romantic love is hard to find and rarely lasts. Jealousy, emotional distance, and little enjoyment of physical contact pervaded their most important love relationship (Collins & Feeney, 2000). Avoidant adults often deny attachment needs through excessive work and brief sexual encounters and affairs (Feeney, 1998). Along with resistant individuals, they endorse many unrealistic beliefs about relationships—for example, that partners cannot change, that males' and females' needs differ, and that "mind reading" is expected (Stackert & Bursik, 2003).

Resistant Attachment. Adults recalling a resistant attachment history (parents who responded unpredictably and unfairly) presented internal working models in which they sought to merge completely with another person and fall

PHOTOS COURTESY OF ELIZABETH NAPOLITANO

How might the internal working model of the 2-year-old seated in her mother's lap (left) have influenced the relationship she forged as a young adult with her husband (center) and with her infant son (right)? Research indicates that early attachment pattern is one among several factors that predict the quality of later intimate ties.

in love quickly (Cassidy, 2001). At the same time, they worried that their intense feelings would overwhelm others, who really did not love them and would not want to stay with them. Their most important love relationship was riddled with jealousy, emotional highs and lows, and desperation about whether the partner would return their affection (Feeney, 1999). Resistant adults are quick to express fear and anger, and they disclose information about themselves at inappropriate times (Brennan & Shaver, 1995).

Are adults' descriptions of their childhood attachment experiences accurate, or are they distorted or even completely invented? In several longitudinal studies, quality of parent–child interactions, observed or assessed through family interviews 5 to 23 years earlier, were good predictors of internal working models and romantic-relationship quality in early adulthood (Allen & Hauser, 1996; Donnellan, Larsen-Rife, & Conger, 2005; Ogawa et al., 1997; Roisman et al., 2001). These findings suggest that adult recollections bear some resemblance to actual parent–child experiences. However, quality of attachment to parents is not the only factor that influences later internal working models and intimate ties. Characteristics of the partner and current life conditions also are important. In one study, adults with an inner sense of security fostered security in their partners as well as in their adolescent and young adult children (Cook, 2000).

In sum, negative parent–child experiences can be carried forward into adult relationships, predisposing people to believe that they are undeserving of love or that their intimate partners cannot be trusted. At the same time, internal working models are continuously "updated." When adults with unhappy love lives have a chance to form more satisfying intimate ties, they may revise their internal working models. As the new partner approaches the relationship with a secure state of mind and sensitive, supportive behavior, the insecure partner reappraises her expectations and responds in kind (Kobak & Hazan, 1991). This reciprocity creates a feedback loop through which a revised, more favorable internal working model, along with mutually gratifying interaction, is sustained over time.

■ **Culture and the Experience of Love.** Passion and intimacy, which form the basis for romantic love, became the dominant basis for marriage in twentieth-century Western nations as the value of individualism strengthened. From this vantage point, mature love is based on autonomy, appreciation of the partner's unique qualities, and intense emotion. Trying to satisfy dependency needs through an intimate bond is regarded as immature (Hatfield, 1993).

This Western view contrasts sharply with the perspectives of Eastern cultures, such as China and Japan. In Japanese, *amae*, or love, means "to depend on another's benevolence." Dependency throughout life is accepted and viewed positively. The traditional Chinese collectivist view defines the self not as independent but through role relationships—son or daughter, brother or sister, husband or wife. Because feelings of affection are distributed across a broad social network, the intensity of any one relationship is reduced.

In choosing a mate, Chinese and Japanese young people are expected to consider obligations to others, especially parents. As one writer summarized, "An American asks, 'How does my heart feel?' A Chinese asks, 'What will other people say?'" (Hsu, 1981, p. 50). College students of Asian heritage are less likely than those of American, Canadian, or European descent to endorse a view of love based on physical attraction and deep emotion (Dion & Dion, 1993; Hatfield & Sprecher, 1995). Instead, they stress companionship and practical matters—similarity of background, career promise, and likelihood of being a good parent. Similarly, compared with American couples, dating couples in China report less passion but equally strong feelings of intimacy and commitment (Gao, 2001).

A young couple poses in traditional Chinese robes on their wedding day in Beijing, China. In collectivist cultures, feelings of affection are distributed across a broad social network, so the intensity of any one relationship is reduced. Couples stress companionship and practical matters rather than deep emotion and physical attraction.

Friendships

Like romantic partners and childhood friends, adult friends are usually similar in age, sex, and SES—factors that contribute to common interests, experiences, and needs and therefore to the pleasure derived from the relationship. As in earlier years, friends in adulthood enhance self-esteem through affirmation and acceptance and provide support in times of stress (Bagwell et al., 2005; Hartup & Stevens, 1999). Friends also make life more interesting by expanding social opportunities and access to knowledge and points of view.

Trust, intimacy, and loyalty continue to be important in adult friendships, as they were in middle childhood and adolescence. Sharing thoughts and feelings is sometimes greater in friendship than in marriage, although commitment is less strong as friends come and go over the life course. Even so, some adult friendships continue for many years, at times throughout life. Friendship continuity is greater for women, who also see their friends more often, which helps sustain the relationship (Sherman, de Vries, & Lansford, 2000).

■ **Same-Sex Friendships.** Throughout life, women have more intimate same-sex friendships than men. Extending a pattern evident in childhood and adolescence, female friends often say they prefer to "just talk," whereas male friends say they like to "do something" such as play sports (see Chapter 12, page 415). Men also report barriers to intimacy with other men. They may feel in competition with male friends and therefore unwilling to disclose weaknesses, or they may worry that if they tell about themselves, their friends will not reciprocate (Reid & Fine, 1992). Because a balance of power and give-and-take is basic to a good friendship, women generally evaluate their same-sex friendships more positively than men do (Veniegas & Peplau, 1997).

Of course, individual differences in friendship quality exist. The longer-lasting men's friendships are, the closer they become and the more they involve disclosure of personal information (Sherman, de Vries, & Lansford, 2000). Furthermore, involvement in family roles affects reliance on friends. For single adults, friends are the preferred companions and confidants. The more intimate young adults' same-sex friendships are in terms of exchange of social support and self-disclosure, the more satisfying and longer-lasting the relationship (Sanderson, Rahm, & Beigbeder, 2005).

As they form romantic ties and marry, young adults—especially men—direct more of their disclosures toward their partners (Carbery & Buhrmester, 1998; Kito, 2005). Still, friendships continue to be vital contexts for personal sharing throughout adulthood. Turn back to Figure 12.2 on page 416 to view developmental trends in self-disclosure to romantic partners and friends.

■ **Other-Sex Friendships.** Other-sex friendships are important to adults, although they occur less often than same-sex friendships and do not last as long. During the college years, these bonds are as common as romantic relationships. After marriage, they decline for men but increase with age for women, who tend to form them in the workplace. Highly educated, employed women have the largest number of other-sex friends. Through these relationships, young adults often gain in companionship and self-esteem and learn a great deal about masculine and feminine styles of intimacy (Bleske & Buss, 2000). Because men confide especially easily in their female friends, such friendships offer them a unique opportunity to broaden their expressive capacity. And women sometimes say male friends offer objective points of view on problems and situations—perspectives not available from female friends (Monsour, 2002).

Many people regulate sexual attraction in other-sex friendships, trying to keep the relationship platonic to safeguard its integrity (Messman et al., 2000). Still, about half of college students engage in sexual activity with an other-sex friend whom they have no intention of dating. Men are more likely than women to feel sexually attracted to an other-sex friend (Kaplan & Keys, 1997). If these feelings persist, the relationship often changes into a romantic bond. Some friends sustain a platonic friendship that includes sexuality. Others find the platonic and sexual aspects incompatible, and the friendship disintegrates (Affifi & Faulkner, 2000). When a solid other-sex friendship does evolve into a romance, it may be more stable and enduring than a romantic relationship formed without a foundation in friendship (Hendrick & Hendrick, 1993).

■ **Siblings as Friends.** Whereas intimacy is essential to friendship, commitment—willingness to maintain a relationship and care about the other—is the defining characteristic of family ties. As young people marry and invest less time in developing a romantic partnership, siblings—especially sisters whose earlier bond was positive—become more frequent companions than in adolescence. Often, friend and sibling roles merge. For example, Sharese described Heather's practical assistance—helping with moving and running errands during an illness—in kinship terms: "She's like a sister to me. I can always turn to her." And adult sibling ties resemble friendships, in which the main concerns are staying in contact, offering social support, and enjoying being together (O'Connor, 1992).

A childhood history of intense parental favoritism and sibling rivalry can disrupt sibling bonds in adulthood (Panish & Stricker, 2002). But when family experiences have been positive,

These brothers enjoy a photographic moment. In early adulthood, siblings often become more frequent companions. Relationships between same-sex siblings can be especially close.

relationships between adult same-sex siblings can be especially close. A shared background promotes similarity in values and perspectives and the possibility of deep mutual understanding.

Warm sibling relationships in adulthood are important sources of psychological well-being (Riggio, 2000). In Vaillant's (1977) study of well-educated men, a close sibling tie in early adulthood was the single best predictor of emotional health at age 65. In another investigation, one-fifth of married women identified a sister as a best friend (Oliker, 1989).

Loneliness

Young adults are at risk for **loneliness**—unhappiness resulting from a gap between the social relationships we currently have and those we desire—when they either do not have an intimate partner or lack gratifying friendships. Though both situations give rise to similar emotions, they are not interchangeable (Brehm, 1992). For example, even though she had several enjoyable friendships, Heather sometimes felt lonely because she was not dating someone she cared about. And although Sharese and Ernie were happily married, they felt lonely after moving to a new town where they did not know anyone.

Loneliness peaks in the late teens and early twenties, then declines steadily into the seventies. Figure 14.1 shows this trend, based on a large Canadian sample ranging in age from 13 to 80 (Rokach, 2001). The rise in loneliness during early adulthood is understandable. Young people must constantly develop new relationships as they move through school and employment settings. Also, young adults may expect more from their intimate ties than older adults, who have learned to live with imperfections. With age, people become better at

accepting loneliness and using it for positive ends—to sharpen awareness of their personal fears and needs (Rokach, 2003).

Loneliness depends in part on circumstances. Separated, divorced, or widowed adults are lonelier than their married, cohabiting, or single counterparts, suggesting that loneliness is intense after loss of an intimate tie. Men not involved in a romantic relationship feel lonelier than women, perhaps because they have fewer alternatives for satisfying intimacy needs (Stroebe et al., 1996). And immigrants from collectivist cultures report higher levels of loneliness than people born in the United States and Canada (DiTommaso, Brannen, & Burgess, 2005). Leaving a large, close-knit family system for an individualistic society seems to prompt intense feelings of isolation.

Personal characteristics also contribute to loneliness. Young adults who are socially anxious or who have insecure working models of attachment to parents are more often intensely lonely (Jackson et al., 2002). When extreme loneliness persists, it is associated with a wide variety of self-defeating attitudes and behaviors. Lonely people evaluate themselves and others more negatively, tend to be socially unresponsive and insensitive, and are slow to develop intimacy because they are reluctant to tell others about themselves (Jones, 1990). These responses, whether cause or consequence of loneliness, promote further isolation.

As long as loneliness is not overwhelming, it can motivate young people to take social risks and reach out to others. It can also encourage them to find ways to be comfortably alone and to use this time to understand themselves better. Healthy personality development involves striking this balance—between "satisfying relationships with others and a secure, internal base of satisfaction within ourselves" (Brehm, 1992, p. 345).

■ FIGURE 14.1 Changes in emotional distress due to loneliness from adolescence to late adulthood. More than 700 Canadian 13- to 80-year-olds responded to a questionnaire assessing the extent to which they experienced emotional distress due to loneliness. Loneliness rose sharply from the teens to the twenties and then declined. (Adapted from Rokach, 2001.)

Ask Yourself

Review

Describe gender differences in traits usually desired in a long-term partner. What findings indicate that *both* biological and social forces contribute to those differences?

Apply

After dating for two years, Mindy and Graham reported greater love and relationship satisfaction than during their first few months of dating. What features of communication probably deepened their bond, and why is it likely to endure?

Apply

Claire and Tom, both married to other partners, got to know each other at work and occasionally have lunch together. What is each likely to gain from this other-sex friendship?

Reflect

Do you have a nonromantic, close other-sex friendship? If so, how has it enhanced your emotional and social development?

The Family Life Cycle

For most young people, the quest for intimacy leads to marriage. Their life course takes shape within the **family life cycle**—a sequence of phases characterizing the development of most families around the world. In early adulthood, people typically live on their own, marry, and bear and rear children. In middle age, as their children leave home, their parenting responsibilities diminish. Late adulthood brings retirement, growing old, and (more often for women) death of one's spouse (Framo, 1994; McGoldrick, Heiman, & Carter, 1993).

But we must be careful not to view the family life cycle as a fixed progression. Recall from Chapter 2 that the family is a dynamic system of relationships embedded in community, cultural, and historical contexts. Today, wide variations exist in the sequence and timing of family life-cycle phases—high rates of out-of-wedlock births, delayed childbearing, divorce, and remarriage, among others. And some people, voluntarily or involuntarily, do not experience all family life-cycle phases.

Still, the family life-cycle model is useful. It offers an organized way of thinking about how the family system changes over time, and the impact of each phase on the family unit and the individuals within it.

Leaving Home

During her first semester of college, Sharese noticed a change in how she related to her mother. She found it more enjoyable to discuss daily experiences and life goals, sought advice and listened with greater openness, and expressed affection more freely. Looking around her childhood bedroom before she moved out permanently, Sharese felt nostalgia for the warmth and security of her childhood days, coupled with a sense of pride at being on her own.

Departure from the parental home is a major step toward assuming adult responsibilities. The average age of leaving has decreased in recent years as more young people live independently before marriage. In 1940, over 80 percent of North Americans in their twenties resided with their parents; today, only about 50 percent of 18- to 25-year-olds do, with residential independence rising steadily with age—a trend evident in most industrialized nations (Cohen et al., 2003; Statistics Canada, 2002h).

Departures for education tend to occur at earlier ages, those for full-time work and marriage later. Because the majority of North American young adults enroll in higher education, many leave home around age 18. Some young people also leave early to escape family friction (Stattin & Magnusson, 1996). Those from divorced, single-parent homes tend to be early leavers, perhaps because of family stress (Cooney & Mortimer, 1999). Compared with the previous generation, fewer North American and Western European young people leave home to marry; more do so just to be "independent"—to express their adult status. But difficult job markets and high housing costs mean that many must take undesirable work or remain financially dependent on parents (Lindsay, Almey, & Normand, 2002).

Nearly half of young adults return home for a brief time after initial leaving. Those who departed to marry are least likely to return. But single, independent living is a fragile arrangement. As people encounter unexpected twists and turns on the road to independence, the parental home offers a safety net and base of operations for launching adult life. Failures in work or marriage can prompt a move back home. Also, young people who left because of family conflict usually return—largely because they were not ready for independent living. Usually, though, role transitions, such as the end of college or military service, bring people back. Contrary to popular belief, returning home is usually not a sign of weakness but a common event among unmarried adults (Graber & Brooks-Gunn, 1996).

Although most high school seniors expect to live on their own before marriage, the extent to which they do so varies with SES and ethnicity. Economically well-off young people are more likely to establish their own residence. Among African-American, Hispanic, Native American, and Canadian Aboriginal groups, poverty and a cultural tradition of extended family living lead to lower rates of leaving home, even among young people in college or working (Fussell & Furstenberg, 2005). Unmarried Asian young adults also tend to live with their parents. But the longer Asian families have lived in North America and thus been exposed to individualistic values, the more likely young people are to move out after finishing high school (Goldscheider & Goldscheider, 1999).

When young adults are prepared for independence and feel securely attached to their parents, departure from the home is linked to more satisfying parent–child interaction and successful transition to adult roles, even among ethnic minorities that strongly emphasize family loyalty and obligations. In a study of middle-SES African-American 17- to 20-year-olds, girls who had moved out of the home to attend college reported fewer negative interactions with their mothers than girls still living at home or in transition to independent living (Smetana, Metzger, & Campione-Barr, 2004). African-American boys (unlike their Caucasian counterparts in other studies) showed no systematic change in frequency of conflict with mothers as a result of autonomous living, perhaps because in adolescence, they had been granted unusually high freedom—considerably more than teenagers of other ethnic groups (Bulcroft, Carmody, & Bulcroft, 1996).

Finally, leaving home very early can contribute to long-term disadvantage because it is associated with job seeking rather than education and with lack of parental financial and social support. Not surprisingly, non-college-bound youths who move out in their late teens have less successful marriages and work lives (White, 1994).

Joining of Families in Marriage

In 1950, the average age of first marriage was about 20 for women and 23 for men. Currently, it is 25 and 27 in the United

States, 27 and 29 in Canada. The number of first and second marriages has declined over the last few decades as more people stay single, cohabit, or do not remarry after divorce. Still, the United States and Canada remain cultures strongly committed to marriage. Nearly 90 percent of North Americans marry at least once. At present, 59 percent of American adults and 47 percent of Canadian adults live together as married couples (Statistics Canada, 2002a; U.S. Census Bureau, 2006b).

Same-sex marriages are recognized nationwide in Belgium, Canada, the Netherlands, and Spain. In the United States, only Massachusetts has legalized same-sex marriages. California, Connecticut, the District of Columbia, Hawaii, Maine, New Jersey, and Vermont grant people in same-sex unions the same legal status as married couples. Because legalization is so recent, research on same-sex couples in the context of marriage is scant. But evidence on cohabiting same-sex couples suggests that the same factors that contribute to happiness in other-sex marriages do so in same-sex unions (Kurdek, 1994).

Although marriage is regarded as the joining of two individuals, it also requires that two systems—the spouses' families—adapt and overlap to create a new subsystem. Consequently, marriage presents complex challenges. This is especially so today because husband–wife roles have only begun to move in the direction of a true partnership—educationally, occupationally, and in emotional connectedness. Among same-sex couples, disclosure of the relationship to parents (even when this sparks disapproval) and inclusion of the partner in family events benefit the relationship. In interviews, gay couples reported that not having to hide their bond is a major advantage (LaSala, 2000).

■ Marital Roles. Their honeymoon over, Sharese and Ernie turned to a multitude of issues that they had previously decided individually or that their families of origin had prescribed—from everyday matters (when and how to eat, sleep, talk, work, relax, have sex, and spend money) to family traditions and rituals (which to retain, which to work out for themselves). And as they related to their social world as a couple, they modified relationships with parents, siblings, extended family, friends, and co-workers.

Recent alterations in the context of marriage, including changing gender roles and living farther away from family members, mean that contemporary couples must work harder to define their relationships. Although husbands and wives are usually similar in religious and ethnic background, "mixed" marriages are more common today than in the past. For example, nearly half of North American Jews who marry today select a non-Jewish spouse (United Jewish Communities, 2004). And other-race unions now account for nearly 4 percent of the married population in the United States and 3 percent in Canada (Statistics Canada, 2003e; U.S. Census Bureau, 2006b). Couples whose backgrounds differ greatly face extra challenges in making the transition to married life.

Because many contemporary couples live together before marriage, it has become less of a turning point in the family life

In an egalitarian marriage, husband and wife share power and authority. And both are equally concerned with the balance between work, children, and their relationship.

cycle. Still, defining marital roles can be difficult. Age of marriage is the most consistent predictor of marital stability. Young people who marry in their teens and early twenties are far more likely to divorce than those who marry later (Heaton, 2002). Most of those who marry early have not developed a secure identity or sufficient independence to form a mature marital bond. Both early marriage followed by childbirth and the reversal of family life-cycle events (childbirth before marriage) are more common among low-SES adults (Leonard & Roberts, 1998; U.S. Census Bureau, 2006b). This acceleration of family formation complicates adjustment to life as a couple.

Despite progress in the area of women's rights, **traditional marriages,** involving a clear division of husband's and wife's roles, still exist in Western nations. The man is the head of household; his primary responsibility is the economic well-being of his family. The woman devotes herself to caring for her husband and children and to creating a nurturant, comfortable home. In recent decades, however, these marriages have changed, with many women who focused on motherhood while their children were young returning to the workforce later on.

In **egalitarian marriages,** husband and wife relate as equals, sharing power and authority. Both partners try to balance the time and energy they devote to their occupations, their children, and their relationship. Most well-educated, career-oriented women expect this form of marriage. And college-student couples who eventually intend to marry often plan in advance how they will coordinate work and family roles, especially if the woman intends to enter a male-dominated career (Botkin, Weeks, & Morris, 2000; Peake & Harris, 2002).

In Western nations, men in *dual-earner marriages* participate much more in child care than in the past, putting in 85 percent as much time as mothers do in the United States,

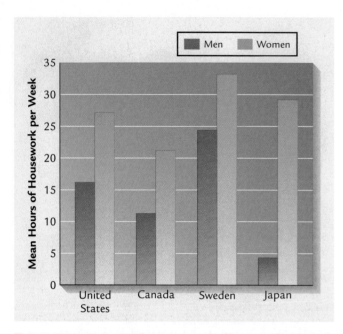

FIGURE 14.2 Average hours per week of housework reported by men and women in four nations. In each nation, women devote considerably more time than men to housework. Men's participation is greater in Sweden, which places a high value on gender equality. In Japan, where traditional gender roles prevail, men devote the least time to housework. (Data for the United States, Sweden, and Japan from Institute for Social Research, 2002; data for Canada derived from Statistics Canada, 2002f.)

75 percent as much in Canada (see page 203 in Chapter 6). But housework—cleaning, shopping, cooking, laundry, picking up clutter—reveals a different story. A recent international study revealed that women in the United States and Canada spend nearly twice as much time as men on housework (see Figure 14.2). In Sweden, which places a high value on gender equality, men do more than in other nations. In contrast, men typically do little housework or child care in Japan, where corporate jobs typically demand long work hours (Institute for Social Research, 2002; Schwalb et al., 2004). In sum, true equality in marriage is still rare, and couples who strive for it usually attain a form of marriage in between traditional and egalitarian.

■ **Marital Satisfaction.** Despite its rocky beginnings, Sharese and Ernie's marriage grew to be especially happy. In contrast, Christy and Gary became increasingly discontented. What distinguishes satisfying marriages from less successful partnerships? Differences between these two couples mirror the findings of a large body of research on personal and contextual factors, summarized in Table 14.2.

Christy and Gary had a brief courtship, married and had children early, and struggled financially. Gary's negative, critical personality led him to get along poorly with Christy's parents and to feel threatened when he and Christy disagreed. Christy tried to offer Gary encouragement and support, but her own needs for nurturance and individuality were not being met. Gary felt threatened by Christy's career aspirations. As she came closer to attaining them, the couple grew farther apart. In contrast, Sharese and Ernie married later, after their educations were complete. They postponed having children until their careers were under way and they had built a sense of togetherness that allowed each to thrive as an individual. Patience, caring, common values, enjoyment of each other's company, sharing of personal experiences through conversation, cooperating in household responsibilities, and good conflict-resolution skills contributed to their compatibility.

Table 14.2	Factors Related to Marital Satisfaction	
Factor	**Happy Marriage**	**Unhappy Marriage**
Family backgrounds	Partners similar in SES, education, religion, and age	Partners very different in SES, education, religion, and age
Age at marriage	After age 23	Before age 23
Length of courtship	At least 6 months	Less than 6 months
Timing of first pregnancy	After first year of marriage	Before or within first year of marriage
Relationship to extended family	Warm and positive	Negative; wish to maintain distance
Marital patterns in extended family	Stable	Unstable; frequent separations and divorces
Financial and employment status	Secure	Insecure
Family responsibilities	Shared; perception of fairness	Largely the woman's responsibility; perception of unfairness
Personality characteristics	Emotionally positive; good conflict-resolution skills	Emotionally negative and impulsive; poor conflict-resolution skills

Note: The more factors present, the greater the likelihood of marital happiness or unhappiness.
Sources: Bradbury, Fincham, & Beach, 2000; Johnson et al., 2005; Waldinger et al., 2004.

Men tend to report feeling slightly happier with their marriages than women do (Dillaway & Broman, 2001; Kurdek, 2005). Although in the past, quality of the marital relationship had a greater impact on women's psychological well-being, today it predicts mental health similarly for both genders (Kurdek, 2005; Williams, 2003). Women, however, feel particularly dissatisfied with marriage when the demands of husband, children, housework, and career are overwhelming (Saginak & Saginak, 2005; Wilkie, Ferree, & Ratcliff, 1998). Research in both Western and non-Western industrialized nations reveals that equal power in the relationship and sharing of family responsibilities usually enhances both men's and women's satisfaction, largely by strengthening marital harmony (Amato & Booth, 1995; Xu & Lai, 2004).

At their worst, marital relationships can become contexts for intense opposition, dominance–submission, and emotional and physical violence. As the Social Issues box on pages 478–479 explains, although women are more often targets of severe partner abuse, both men and women play both roles: perpetrator and victim.

■ **Marital Expectations and Myths.** In a study in which 50 happily married couples were interviewed about their marriages, each participant reported both good times and bad, and many admitted to having moments when they wanted out, when they felt they had made a mistake (Wallerstein & Blakeslee, 1995). Clearly, marital happiness was no "rose garden." Rather, it was grounded in mutual respect, pleasure and comfort in each other's company, and joint problem solving. All couples emphasized the need to reshape their relationship in response to new circumstances and to each partner's changing needs and desires.

Yet cultural expectations work against this view of marriage as an ongoing project requiring both partners' involvement and cooperation. Historically, women had little power in marriage and society; a wife's status came from her husband. This gender gap, with its deep cultural roots, continues to influence marriage today (Brooks, 2000). In a study of college students, more women than men said their partners should be superior to themselves, while more men than women said their partners should be inferior—in intelligence, education, vocational success, and income (Ganong & Coleman, 1992). Under these circumstances, women are likely to play down their abilities, sacrificing part of themselves. And men tend to limit themselves to the provider role rather than participating fully in family life.

Furthermore, many young people have a mythical image of marital bliss—one that resembles TV romantic comedies and dramas, not reality (Segrin & Nabi, 2002). For example, a substantial number of young adults endorse these beliefs, all unsupported by facts:

- ✐ A couple's satisfaction increases through the first year of marriage.

- ✐ The best single predictor of marital satisfaction is the quality of a couple's sex life.

- ✐ If my spouse loves me, he or she should instinctively know what I want and need to be happy.

- ✐ No matter how I behave, my spouse should love me simply because he or she is my spouse. (Larson, 1988, p. 5; McCarthy & McCarthy, 2004)

As these myths are overturned, couples react with disappointment, and marriage becomes less satisfying and more conflict-ridden. Interestingly, young people who hold a religious view of marriage as sacred are less likely to enter it with unrealistic expectations and better able to cope with disagreement (Mahoney et al., 1999). Perhaps because of their reverence for the marital bond, they are highly invested in forging a well-functioning relationship, engaging in more verbal collaboration and less conflict than other couples.

In view of its long-term implications, it is surprising that most couples spend little time before their wedding day reflecting on the decision to marry (McGoldrick, Heiman, & Carter, 1993). High school and college courses in family life education can help dispel marital myths and promote better mate selection. And counseling aimed at helping couples discuss their desires openly and use positive, respectful conflict-resolution strategies are highly effective in easing adjustment to marriage and enhancing relationship quality (Christensen & Heavey, 1999; Gordon, Temple, & Adams, 2005).

Parenthood

In the past, the decision to have children was, for many adults, "a biological given or an unavoidable cultural demand" (Michaels, 1988, p. 23). Today, in Western industrialized nations, parenthood is a matter of true individual choice. Effective birth control techniques enable adults to avoid having children in most instances. And changing cultural values allow people to remain childless with less fear of social criticism and rejection than a generation or two ago.

In 1950, 78 percent of North American married couples were parents. Today, 70 percent bear children, and they tend to be older when they have their first child. Consistent with this pattern of delayed childbearing, family size in industrialized nations has declined. In 1950, the average number of children per couple was 3.1. Currently, it is 2.0 in the United States; 1.8 in Australia; 1.6 in Canada, Great Britain, the Netherlands, and Sweden; 1.3 in Austria, Germany, and Japan; and 1.2 in Italy (U.S. Census Bureau, 2006a). Nevertheless, the vast majority of married people continue to embrace parenthood as one of life's most meaningful experiences. Why do they do so, and how do the challenges of child rearing affect the adult life course?

■ **The Decision to Have Children.** The choice of parenthood is affected by a complex array of factors, including financial circumstances, personal and religious values, and health conditions. Women with traditional gender identities usually decide have children. Whether a woman is employed has less impact on childbearing than her occupation. Women with high-status, demanding careers less often choose parenthood

Social Issues

Partner Abuse

Violence in families is a widespread health and human rights issue, occurring in all cultures and SES groups. Often one form of domestic violence is linked to others. Recall the story of Karen in Chapter 13. Her husband Mike not only assaulted her sexually and physically but also abused her psychologically—isolating, humiliating, and demeaning her (Dutton et al., 2001). Violent adults also break their partner's favorite possessions, punch holes in walls, or throw objects. If children are present, they may become victims.

Partner abuse in which husbands are perpetrators and wives are physically injured is the type most likely to be reported to authorities. But many acts of family violence are not reported. When researchers ask North American couples about fights that led to acts of hostility, men and women report similar rates of assault (Archer, 2002a; Straus, 1999). For example, in a large national survey of Canadians, 7 percent of women and 6 percent of men indicated that they had been physically abused by a spouse within the past five years (Statistics Canada, 2005c). Women, however, are more likely to experience physical assaults that lead to serious injury—beatings, chokings, attempts to drown, and threats with guns. Men are more often targets of kicking, slapping, thrown objects, and threats with knives (Hoff, 2001). And partner abuse occurs at about the same rate in same-sex relationships as in heterosexual relationships (Schwartz & Waldo, 2004).

Although self-defense is a frequent cause of domestic assault by women, North American men and women are equally likely to "strike first" (Carrado et al., 1996; Currie, 1999). "Getting my partner's attention," "gaining control," and "expressing anger" are reasons that partners typically give for abusing each other (Straus, 1999).

Factors Related to Partner Abuse. In abusive relationships, dominance–submission sometimes proceeds from husband to wife, sometimes from wife to husband. In about half of cases, both partners are violent (Cook, 1997). Marvin's and Pat's relationship helps us understand how spouse abuse escalates. Shortly after their wedding, Pat began complaining about the demands of Marvin's work and insisted that he come home early to spend time with her. When he resisted, she hurled epithets, threw objects, and slapped him. One evening, Marvin became so angry at Pat's hostilities that he smashed a dish against the wall, threw his wedding ring at her, and left the house. The next morning, Pat apologized and promised not to attack again. But her outbursts became more frequent and desperate.

These violence–remorse cycles, in which aggression escalates, characterize many abusive relationships. Why do they occur? Personality and developmental history, family circumstances, and cultural factors combine to make partner abuse more likely (Dixon & Browne, 2003).

Many abusers are overly dependent on their spouses as well as jealous, possessive, and controlling. For example, the thought of Karen ever leaving induced such high anxiety in Mike that he monitored all her activities. Depression, anxiety, and low self-esteem also characterize abusers. And because they have great difficulty managing anger, trivial events—such as an unironed shirt or a late meal—can trigger abusive episodes.

When asked to explain their offenses, they attribute greater blame to their partner than to themselves (Henning, Jones, & Holdford, 2005).

A high proportion of spouse abusers grew up in homes where parents engaged in hostile interactions, used coercive discipline, and were abusive toward their children (Bevan & Higgins, 2002; Reitzel-Jaffe & Wolfe, 2001). Perhaps this explains why conduct problems in childhood and violent delinquency in adolescence also predict partner abuse (Magdol et al., 1998). Adults with childhood exposure to domestic violence are not doomed to repeat it. But their parents provided them with negative expectations and behaviors that they often transfer to their close relationships. Stressful life events, such as job loss or financial difficulties, increase the likelihood of partner abuse (Emery & Laumann-Billings, 1998). Because of widespread poverty, African Americans, Native Americans, and Canadian-Aboriginal people report high rates of partner violence (Hoff, 2001; Statistics Canada, 2005c). Alcohol abuse is another related factor.

At a societal level, cultural norms that endorse male dominance and female submissiveness promote partner abuse (World Health Organization, 2000b, 2005b). As Figure 14.3 shows, in countries with widespread poverty that also sanction gender inequality, partner violence against women is especially high,

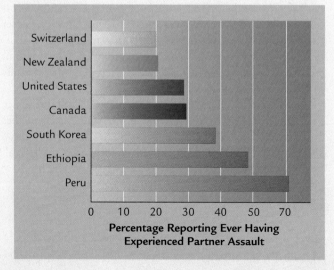

FIGURE 14.3 Assaults by intimate partners against women in seven nations. In each country, samples of women were asked to indicate whether they had ever experienced partner physical abuse. The incidence, always underreported, is high in all nations. It is especially high in countries that endorse traditional gender roles and suffer from widespread poverty. (From World Health Organization, 2000b, 2005b.)

affecting as many as 40 to 50 percent of the female population.

Victims are chronically anxious and depressed and experience frequent panic attacks (Stuart et al., 2006). Why don't they simply leave these destructive relationships? A variety of situational factors discourage them from leaving. A victimized wife may depend on her husband's earning power or fear even worse harm to herself or her children. Extreme assaults, including homicide, tend to occur after partner separation (Statistics Canada, 2005c). And victims of both sexes, but especially men, are deterred by the embarrassment of going to the police. Also, victims may falsely believe that their partner will change (Straus, 1999).

Intervention and Treatment. Community services available to battered women include crisis telephone lines that provide anonymous counseling and social support and shelters that offer protection and treatment (see page 447). Because many women return to their abusive partners several times before making their final move, community agencies usually offer therapy to male batterers. Most rely on several months to a year of group sessions that confront rigid gender stereotyping; teach communication, problem solving, and anger control; and use social support to motivate behavior change (Harway & Hansen, 2004).

Although existing treatments are better than none, most are not effective at dealing with relationship difficulties or alcohol abuse. Consequently, many treated perpetrators repeat their violent behavior with the same or a new partner (Schwartz & Waldo, 2004; Stuart, 2005). At present, few interventions acknowledge that men also are victims. Yet ignoring their needs perpetuates domestic violence. When victims do not want to separate from a violent partner, a whole-family treatment approach that focuses on changing partner interaction and reducing high life stress is crucial.

and, when they do, more often delay it than women with less consuming jobs (Barber, 2001; Tangri & Jenkins, 1997).

When North Americans are asked about their desire to have children, they mention a variety of advantages and disadvantages, listed in Table 14.3. Some ethnic and regional differences exist, but in all groups, the most important reasons for having children include the warm, affectionate relationship and the stimulation and fun that children provide. Also frequently mentioned are growth and learning experiences that children bring to the lives of adults, the desire to have someone carry on after one's own death, and feelings of accomplishment and creativity that come from helping children grow (Cowan & Cowan, 2000; O'Laughlin & Anderson, 2001).

Most young adults also realize that having children means years of extra burdens and responsibilities. Among disadvantages of parenthood, they cite "loss of freedom" most often, followed by "financial strain." Indeed, the cost of child rearing is a major factor in contemporary family planning. According to a conservative estimate, today's new parents will spend about $185,000 in the United States and $168,000 in Canada to rear a

Table 14.3	Advantages and Disadvantages of Parenthood Mentioned by Contemporary Couples
Advantages	**Disadvantages**
Giving and receiving warmth and affection	Loss of freedom, being tied down
Experiencing the stimulation and fun that children add to life	Financial strain
Being accepted as a responsible and mature member of the community	Role overload—not enough time for both family and work responsibilities
Experiencing new growth and learning opportunities that add meaning to life	Interference with mother's employment opportunities
Having someone carry on after one's own death	Worries over children's health, safety, and well-being
Gaining a sense of accomplishment and creativity from helping children grow	Risks of bringing up children in a world plagued by crime, war, and pollution
Learning to become less selfish and to sacrifice	Reduced time to spend with partner
Having offspring who help with parents' work or add their own income to the family's resources	Loss of privacy
	Fear that children will turn out badly, through no fault of one's own

Source: Cowan & Cowan, 2000.

child from birth to age 18, and many will incur substantial additional expense for higher education and financial dependency during emerging adulthood (Child Care Advocacy Association of Canada, 2004; U.S. Department of Agriculture, 2005a).

Greater freedom to choose whether and when to have children makes family planning more challenging today than in the past. As each partner expects to have equal say, childbearing often becomes a matter of delicate negotiation (Cowan & Cowan, 2000). Yet carefully weighing the pros and cons of parenthood means that many more couples are making informed and personally meaningful choices—a trend that should increase the chances that they will have children when ready and that their own lives will be enriched by their decision.

■ **Transition to Parenthood.** The early weeks after a baby enters the family are full of profound changes: new caregiving and household responsibilities, disrupted sleep, less time for the couple's relationship, and added financial responsibilities. In response to these demands, the roles of husband and wife usually become more traditional, even for couples like Sharese and Ernie who are committed to gender equality and accustomed to sharing household tasks (Cowan & Cowan, 2000; Salmela-Aro et al., 2001).

First and Second Births. For most new parents, however, the arrival of a baby does not cause significant marital strain. Marriages that are gratifying and supportive tend to remain so, resembling childless marriages in overall happiness (Feeney et al., 2001; Miller, 2000). But troubled marriages usually become more distressed after a baby is born. In a study of newlyweds who were interviewed annually for six years, the husband's affection, expression of "we-ness" (values and goals similar to

his wife's), and awareness of his wife's daily life predicted mothers' stable or increasing marital satisfaction after childbirth. In contrast, the husband's negativity and the couple's out-of-control conflict predicted a drop in mothers' satisfaction (Shapiro, Gottman, & Carrere, 2000).

Also, violated expectations about division of labor in the home affect new parents' well-being. In dual-earner marriages, the larger the difference in men's and women's caregiving responsibilities, the greater the decline in marital satisfaction after childbirth, especially for women—with negative consequences for parent–infant interaction. In contrast, sharing caregiving predicts greater parental happiness and sensitivity to the baby (Feldman, 2002; Feeney et al., 2001). An exception exists, however, for employed lower-SES women who endorse traditional gender roles. When their husbands help extensively with child care, these mothers tend to report more distress, perhaps because of disappointment at being unable to fulfill their desire to do most of the caregiving (Goldberg & Perry-Jenkins, 2003).

Postponing childbearing until the late twenties or thirties, as more couples do today, eases the transition to parenthood. Waiting permits couples to pursue occupational goals and gain life experience. Under these circumstances, men are more enthusiastic about becoming fathers and therefore more willing to participate. And women whose careers are under way are more likely to encourage their husbands to share housework and child care (Coltrane, 1990).

A second birth typically requires that fathers take an even more active role in parenting—by caring for the firstborn while the mother is recuperating and by sharing in the high demands of tending to both a baby and a young child. Consequently, well-functioning families with a newborn second child typically show a pulling back from the traditional division of responsibilities that occurred after the first birth. In a study that tracked parents from the end of pregnancy through the first year after their second child's birth, fathers' willingness to place greater emphasis on the parenting role was strongly linked to mothers' adjustment after the arrival of a second baby (Stewart, 1990). And the support of family, friends, and spouse are crucial for fathers' well-being.

Interventions. Couples' groups led by counselors are highly effective in easing the transition to parenthood. In one program, first-time expectant couples gathered once a week for six months to discuss their dreams for the family and changes in relationships sparked by the baby's arrival. Eighteen months after the program ended, participating fathers described themselves as more involved with their child than did fathers in a no-intervention condition. Perhaps because of fathers' caregiving assistance, participating mothers maintained their prebirth satisfaction with family and work roles. Three years after the birth, the marriages of all participating couples were intact and just as happy as they had been before parenthood. In contrast, 15 percent of couples receiving no intervention had divorced (Cowan & Cowan, 1997). For high-risk parents struggling with poverty or the birth of a child with disabilities, interventions must be more intensive, focusing on enhancing social support and parenting skills (Cowan & Cowan, 1995).

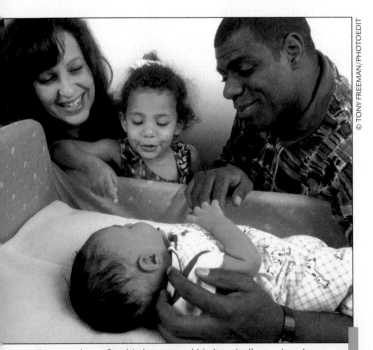

© TONY FREEMAN/PHOTOEDIT

Compared to a first birth, a second birth typically requires that fathers become more actively involved in parenting, sharing in the high demands of tending to both a baby and a young child.

Generous, paid employment leave—widely available in industrialized nations, but not in the United States—is crucial for parents of newborns (see Chapter 3, page 104). But financial pressures mean that many new mothers who are eligible for unpaid work leave take far less than they are guaranteed by U.S. federal law, while new fathers take little or none (Han & Waldfogel, 2003). When favorable workplace policies exist and parents take advantage of them, couples are more likely to support each other and experience family life as gratifying (Feldman, Susssman, & Zigler, 2004). As a result, the stress caused by the birth of a baby stays at manageable levels.

■ **Family Size.** In addition to more effective birth control, a major reason for the steady decline in family size over the past half century is that a smaller family is more compatible with the decision of most women to divide their energies between family and work. Marital instability has also contributed to smaller families: More couples today get divorced before their childbearing plans are complete.

Popular advice to prospective parents often recommends limiting family size in the interests of "child quality"—more parental affection, attention, and material resources per child, which enhances children's intellectual development. But a study that obtained the IQs of a large representative sample of U.S. young people and, 14 years later, measured the IQs of their offspring revealed that this advice is not warranted. The negative relationship between family size and children's IQ was entirely accounted for by the strong trend for parents with lower IQs—as a result of heredity, environment, or both—to have larger families (see Figure 14.4) (Rodgers et al., 2000). In research limited to economically advantaged parents, the family size–IQ correlation disappears (Guo & Van-Wey, 1999).

■ **Families with Young Children.** A year after the birth of their first child, Sharese and Ernie received a phone call from Heather, who asked how they liked parenthood: "Is it a joy, a dilemma, a stressful experience—how would you describe it?"

Chuckling, Sharese and Ernie responded in unison, "All of the above!"

In today's complex world, men and women are less certain about how to rear children than in previous generations. Clarifying child-rearing values and implementing them in warm, involved, and appropriately demanding ways are crucial for the welfare of the next generation and society. Yet cultures do not always place a high priority on parenting, as indicated by the lack of many societal supports for children and families (see Chapter 2, page 68). Furthermore, changing family forms mean that the lives of today's parents differ substantially from those of past generations.

In previous chapters, we discussed a wide variety of influences on child-rearing styles, including personal characteristics of children and parents, SES, and ethnicity. The couple's relationship is also vital. Parents who work together as a *coparenting team,* cooperating and showing solidarity and respect for each other in parenting roles, are more likely to gain in warm marital interaction, feel competent as parents, use effective child-rearing practices, and have children who are developing well (McHale et al., 2002; Schoppe-Sullivan et al., 2004). When parents forge this coparenting alliance within the first few months after childbirth, it is more likely to persist (Fivaz-Depeursinge & Corboz-Warnery, 1999).

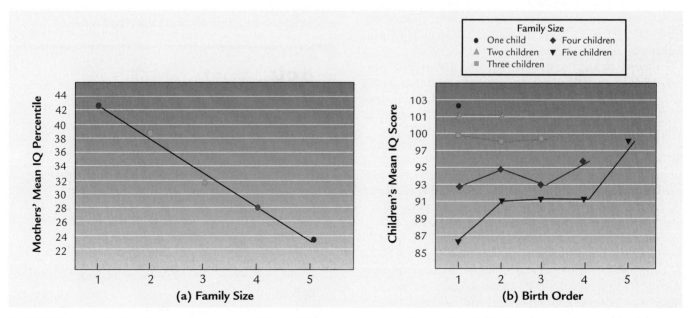

■ **FIGURE 14.4 Relationship of mothers' mental ability to family size.** As maternal IQ declines, family size increases (a). In larger families, all children, regardless of birth order, tend to have lower IQs (b). But notice that children's IQ does not decline with birth order. To the contrary, in larger families, last-born children tend to have higher IQs. So couples who decide to have more children do not reduce later-born children's life chances. Instead, birth rate is higher among young adults with lower IQs—many of whom dropped out of school, live in poverty, and fail to engage in family planning. (From J. L. Rodgers, H. H. Cleveland, E. van den Oord, & D. C. Rowe, 2000, "Resolving the Debate over Birth Order, Family Size, and Intelligence," *American Psychologist, 55,* pp. 607, 609. Copyright © by the American Psychological Association. Reprinted by permission.)

For employed parents, a major struggle is finding good child care and, when their child is ill or otherwise in need of emergency care, taking time off from work or making other urgent arrangements (Lower, 2005). The younger the child, the greater parents' sense of risk and difficulty—especially low-income parents, who must work longer hours to pay bills; who often, in the United States, have no workplace benefits (health insurance or paid sick leave); and who typically cannot afford the cost of child care (Halpern, 2005b). When competent, convenient child care is not available, the woman usually faces added pressures. She must either curtail or give up her work, with profound financial consequences in low-income families, or endure unhappy children, missed workdays, and constant searches for new arrangements.

Despite its challenges, rearing young children is a powerful source of adult development. Parents report that it expands their emotional capacities and enriches their lives. For example, Ernie remarked that through sharing in child rearing, he felt "rounded out" as a person. Other involved parents say that parenthood helped them tune in to others' feelings and needs, required that they become more tolerant, self-confident, and responsible, and broadened their friendship and community ties (Coltrane, 1990; Nomaguchi & Milkie, 2003).

■ **Families with Adolescents.** Adolescence brings sharp changes in parental roles. In Chapters 11 and 12, we noted that parents must establish a revised relationship with their adolescent children—blending guidance with freedom and gradually loosening control. As adolescents gain in autonomy and explore values and goals in their search for identity, parents often complain that their teenager is too focused on peers and no longer cares about being with the family. Heightened parent–child bickering over mundane issues takes a toll, especially on mothers, who do most of the negotiating with teenagers.

Overall, children seem to navigate the challenges of adolescence more easily than parents, many of whom report a dip in marital and life satisfaction. More people seek family therapy during this period of the family life cycle than during any other (Steinberg & Silk, 2002; Young, 1991).

■ **Parent Education.** In the past, family life changed little from one generation to the next, and adults learned what they needed to know about parenting through modeling and direct experience. Today's world confronts adults with a host of factors that impinge on their ability to succeed as parents.

Contemporary parents eagerly seek information on child rearing. New mothers often regard popular parenting books as particularly valuable, second in importance only to their doctors (Deutsch et al., 1988). They also reach out to a network of other women for knowledge and assistance. Fathers, by contrast, rarely have social networks through which they can learn about child care and child rearing. Consequently, they frequently turn to mothers to figure out how to relate to their child, especially if they have a close, confiding marriage (Lamb & Lewis, 2004; McHale, Kuersten-Hogan, & Rao, 2004). Recall from Chapter 6 that marital harmony fosters

Contemporary parents eagerly seek information on child rearing, and women often reach out to their network of friends for knowledge and assistance.

both parents' positive engagement with babies, but it is especially important for fathers.

Parent education courses exist to help parents clarify child-rearing values, improve family communication, understand how children develop, and apply more effective parenting strategies. A variety of programs yield positive outcomes, including improved parent–child interaction, more flexible parenting attitudes, and heightened awareness by parents of their role as educators of their children (Shumow, 1998; Smith, Perou, & Lesesne, 2002). Another benefit is social support—opportunities to discuss concerns with experts and other dedicated parents, who share the view that no job is more important to the future of society than child rearing.

Ask Yourself

Review

What strategies can couples use to ease the transition to parenthood?

Apply

After her wedding, Sharese was convinced she had made a mistake. Cite factors that sustained her marriage and led it to become especially happy.

Connect

What aspects of adolescent development make rearing teenagers stressful for parents, leading to a dip in marital and life satisfaction? (See Chapter 11, pages 368–369 and 385–386, and Chapter 12, page 413.)

Reflect

Do you live with your parents or on your own? What factors contributed to your current living arrangements? If you live independently, has your relationship with your parents changed in ways that match the findings of research?

The Diversity of Adult Lifestyles

The current array of adult lifestyles dates back to the 1960s, when young people began to question the conventional wisdom of previous generations and to ask, "How can I find happiness? What kinds of commitments should I make to live a full and rewarding life?" As the public became more accepting of diverse lifestyles, choices such as staying single, cohabiting, remaining childless, and divorcing seemed more available.

Today, nontraditional family options have penetrated the North American mainstream. Many adults experience not just one but several. As we consider these variations in the following sections, we will see that some adults make a deliberate decision to adopt a lifestyle, whereas others drift into it. The lifestyle may be imposed by society, as is the case for cohabiting same-sex couples in the United States, who cannot marry legally in most states. Or people may choose a certain lifestyle because they feel pushed away from another, such as a marriage gone sour. In sum, the adoption of a lifestyle can be within or beyond the person's control.

Single women usually come to terms with their lifestyle. The social support available to them through intimate same-sex friendships is partly responsible. In comparison, single men have more physical and mental health problems.

Singlehood

On finishing her education, Heather joined the Peace Corps and spent five years in Africa. Though open to a long-term relationship, she had only fleeting romances. When she returned to the United States, she accepted an executive position with an insurance company. Professional challenge and travel preoccupied her. At age 35, over lunch with Sharese, she reflected on her life: "I was open to marriage, but after my career took off, it would have interfered. Now I'm so used to independence that I question whether I could adjust to living with another person. I like being able to pick up and go where I want, when I want, without having to ask anyone or think about caring for anyone. But there's a tradeoff: I sleep alone, eat most of my meals alone, and spend a lot of my leisure time alone."

Singlehood—not living with an intimate partner—has increased in recent years, especially among young adults. For example, rates of never-married North American 30- to 34-year-olds have risen sixfold since 1970, to about one-third of males and one-fourth of females. More people marry later or not at all, and divorce has added to the numbers of single adults. In view of these trends, it is likely that most North Americans will spend a substantial part of their adult lives single, and a growing minority—about 8 to 10 percent—will stay that way (Statistics Canada, 2003e; U.S. Census Bureau, 2006b).

Because they marry later, more young adult men than women are single. But women are far more likely than men to remain single for many years or their entire life. With age, fewer men are available with characteristics that most women seek in a mate—the same age or older, equally or better educated, and professionally successful. In contrast, men can choose partners from a large pool of younger unmarried women. Because of the tendency for women to "marry up" and men to "marry down," men in blue-collar occupations and

women in prestigious careers are overrepresented among singles after age 30.

Ethnic differences also exist. For example, the percentage of never-married African Americans is nearly twice as great as that of Caucasian Americans in early adulthood. As we will see later, high unemployment among black men interferes with marriage. Many African Americans eventually marry in their late thirties and forties, a period in which black and white marriage rates come closer together (U.S. Census Bureau, 2006b).

Singlehood can have a variety of meanings. At one extreme are people who choose it deliberately, at the other those who see themselves as single because of circumstances beyond their control. Most, like Heather, are in the middle—adults who wanted to marry but made choices that took them in a different direction. In interview studies of never-married women, some said they focused on occupational goals instead of marriage. Others reported that they found singlehood preferable to the disappointing relationships they had with men. And still others commented that they just did not meet "the right person" (Baumbusch, 2004; Lewis, 2000).

The most commonly mentioned advantages of singlehood are freedom and mobility. But singles also recognize drawbacks—loneliness, the dating grind, limited sexual and social life, reduced sense of security, and feelings of exclusion from the world of married couples. Single men have more physical and mental health problems than single women, who usually come to terms with their lifestyle, in part because of the greater social support available to women through intimate same-sex friendships (Pinquart, 2003). In addition, never-married men are more likely to have conflict-ridden family backgrounds and personal characteristics that contribute to both their singlehood and their adjustment difficulties (Buunk & van Driel, 1989).

Many single people go through a stressful period in their late twenties, when most of their friends have married. For single women, the mid-thirties is another trying time, as the biological deadline for childbearing approaches. A few decide to become parents through artificial insemination or a love affair. And an increasing number are adopting, often from overseas countries.

Cohabitation

Cohabitation refers to the lifestyle of unmarried couples who have a sexually intimate relationship and who share a residence. Until the 1960s, cohabitation in Western nations was largely limited to low-SES adults. Since then, it has increased in all groups, with an especially dramatic rise among well-educated, economically advantaged young people. As Figure 14.5 shows, today's North American young adults are much more likely than those of a generation ago to form their first conjugal union through cohabitation. Among people in their twenties, cohabitation is now the preferred mode of entry into a committed intimate partnership, chosen by more than 50 percent of couples (Statistics Canada, 2002a; U.S. Census Bureau, 2006b). Cohabitation rates are even higher among adults with failed marriages. Half of cohabiting relationships in the United States and Canada involve at least one partner who is separated or divorced; one-third of these households include children (Cohan & Kleinbaum, 2002).

Like singlehood, cohabitation has various meanings. For some, it serves as *preparation for marriage*—a time to test the relationship and get used to living together. For others, it is an *alternative to marriage,* offering the rewards of sexual intimacy and companionship along with the possibility of easy departure if satisfaction declines. In view of this variation, it is not surprising that cohabiters differ greatly in the extent to which they share money and possessions and take responsibility for each other's children.

Although North Americans are more open to cohabitation than in the past, their attitudes are not yet as positive as those of Western Europeans. In the Netherlands, Norway, and Sweden, cohabitation is thoroughly integrated into society. From 70 to 90 percent of young people cohabit in their first intimate partnership, and cohabiters are nearly as devoted to each other as married people (Fussell & Gauthier, 2005; Ramsøy, 1994). Whereas about 50 percent of cohabiting unions in North America break up within two years, only 6 to 16 percent dissolve in Western Europe (Brown, 2000; Kiernan, 2002). When they decide to marry, Dutch, Norwegian, and Swedish cohabiters more often do so to legalize their relationships, especially for the sake of children. North American cohabiters typically marry to confirm their love and commitment—sentiments that Western Europeans attach to cohabitation.

Furthermore, American and Canadian couples who cohabit before they are engaged to be married are more prone to divorce than couples who wait to live together until after they have made a commitment to one another. But this association is less strong or absent in Western European nations (Kiernan, 2001, 2002; Kline et al., 2004). In North America, people who cohabit prior to engagement tend to have less conventional values. They have had more sexual partners and are more politically liberal, less religious, and more androgynous. In addition, a larger number have parents who divorced (Axinn & Barber, 1997; Cunningham & Antill, 1994).

These personal characteristics may contribute to the negative outcomes associated with cohabitation. The cohabitation experience itself also plays a role. Cohabiters are less likely than married people to pool finances or jointly own a house. In addition, both preengagement cohabiters and formerly cohabiting married couples have poorer-quality relationships (Cohan & Kleinbaum, 2002; Kline et al., 2004). Perhaps the open-ended nature of the cohabiting relationship reduces motivation to develop effective conflict-resolution skills. When cohabiters carry negative communication into marriage, it undermines marital satisfaction. Finally, a history of parental divorce may increase cohabiters' willingness to dissolve a union when it becomes less satisfying.

Certain couples, however, are exceptions to the trends just described. People who cohabit after separation or divorce often test a new relationship carefully to prevent another failure, especially when children are involved. As a result, they cohabit longer and are less likely to move toward marriage (Smock & Gupta, 2002). Similarly, cohabitation is often an alternative to marriage among low-SES couples. Many regard their earning power as too uncertain for marriage and continue living together, sometimes giving birth to children and marrying when their financial status improves (Jayakody & Cabrera,

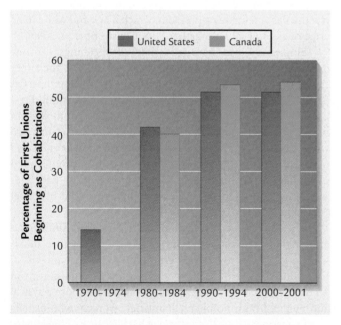

■ **FIGURE 14.5 Generational increase in first conjugal unions beginning as cohabitations in the United States and Canada.** Compared with a generation ago, North American young people are far more likely to choose cohabitation as a way of forming their first conjugal union. (1970–1974 data are available only for the United States.) (From Bumpass & Lu, 2000; Statistics Canada, 2002a; U.S. Census Bureau, 2006h.)

2002). Finally, cohabiting gay and lesbian couples report strong commitment, equal to that of married people. When their relationships become difficult, they end more often than marriages only because of fewer barriers to separating, including children in common, financial dependence on a partner, or concerns about the costs of divorce (Kurdek, 1998).

For people not ready for marriage, cohabitation combines the rewards of a close relationship with the opportunity to remain partially uncommitted. But although most North American couples cohabit to avoid the legal obligations of marriage, they can encounter difficulties precisely because they do not have these obligations (Mahoney, 2002). Bitter fights over property, money, rental contracts, and responsibility for children are the rule rather than the exception when unmarried couples split up.

Childlessness

At work, Sharese got to know Beatrice and Daniel. Married for 7 years and in their mid-thirties, they did not have children and were not planning any. To Sharese, their relationship seemed especially caring and affectionate. "At first, we were open to becoming parents," Beatrice explained, "but eventually we decided to focus on our marriage."

Some people are *involuntarily* childless because they did not find a partner with whom to share parenthood or their efforts at fertility treatments did not succeed. Beatrice and Daniel are in another category—men and women who are *voluntarily* childless.

How many North American couples choose not to have children is a matter of dispute. Some researchers claim the rate has been low for several decades. Others say it rose from 2 percent in the 1980s to 6.5 percent in the mid-1990s, the most recently available figure (Rhone & Fulbright, 2001; Toulemon, 1996). These differing reports may reflect the fact that voluntary childlessness is not always a permanent condition. A few people decide early that they do not want to be parents and stick to their plans. But most, like Beatrice and Daniel, make their decision after they are married and have developed a lifestyle they do not want to give up. Later, some change their minds.

Besides marital satisfaction and freedom from child-care responsibilities, common reasons for not having children include the woman's career and economic security. Consistent with these motives, the voluntarily childless are usually college-educated, have prestigious occupations, and are highly committed to their work (Kemkes-Grottenhaler, 2003). Many were only or firstborn children whose parents encouraged achievement and independence. In cultures that negatively stereotype childlessness, it is not surprising that voluntarily childless women are more self-reliant and assertive (Morell, 1994).

Voluntarily childless adults are just as content with their lives as parents who have warm relationships with their children. In contrast, adults who cannot overcome infertility are likely to be dissatisfied—some profoundly disappointed, others more ambivalent, depending on compensating rewards in other areas of their lives (Letherby, 2002; Nichols & Pace-Nichols, 2000). These findings challenge the stereotype of childless people as lonely and unfulfilled. Childlessness interferes with adjustment and life satisfaction only when it is beyond a person's control.

Divorce and Remarriage

Divorce rates have stabilized since the mid-1980s, partly because of rising age of marriage, which is linked to greater financial stability and marital satisfaction. In addition, the increase in cohabitation has curtailed divorce: Many North American relationships that once would have been marriages now break up before marriage (Bumpass, 2004; Heaton, 2002). Still, 45 percent of U.S. and 30 percent of Canadian marriages dissolve. Because most divorces occur within 7 years of marriage, many involve young children. Divorces are also common during the transition to midlife, when people have adolescent children—a period (as noted earlier) of reduced marital satisfaction.

About two-thirds of divorced people remarry. But marital failure is even greater during the first few years of second marriages—7 percent above that for first marriages. Afterward, the divorce rates for first and second marriages are similar (Coleman, Ganong, & Fine, 2000; Wu & Penning, 1997).

■ **Factors Related to Divorce.** Why do so many marriages fail? As Christy and Gary's divorce illustrates, the most obvious reason is a disrupted husband–wife relationship. Christy and Gary did not argue more than Sharese and Ernie. But their problem-solving style was ineffective. When Christy raised concerns, Gary reacted with resentment, anger, and retreat—a demand–withdraw pattern found in many partners who split up. Another typical style involves little conflict, but partners increasingly lead separate lives because they have different expectations of family life and few shared interests, activities, or friends (Gottman & Levenson, 2000).

What problems underlie these maladaptive communication patterns? In a 9-year longitudinal study, researchers asked a U.S. national sample of 2,000 married people about marital problems and followed up 3, 6, and 9 years later to find out who had separated or divorced (Amato & Rogers, 1997). Wives reported more problems than husbands, with the gender difference largely involving the wife's emotions, such as anger, hurt feelings, and moodiness. Husbands seemed to have difficulty sensing their wife's distress, which contributed to her view of the marriage as unhappy. Regardless of which spouse reported the problem or was judged responsible for it, the strongest predictors of divorce during the following decade were infidelity, spending money foolishly, drinking or using drugs, expressing jealousy, engaging in irritating habits, and moodiness.

Background factors that increase the chances of divorce are younger age at marriage, not attending religious services, being previously divorced, and having parents who had divorced—all of which are linked to marital difficulties. For example, couples who married at younger ages are more likely

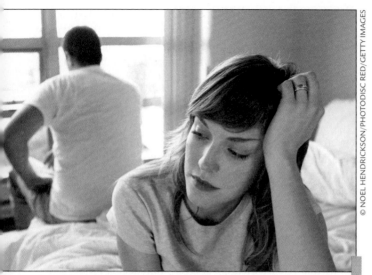

An ineffective problem-solving style can lead to divorce. For example, many partners who split up follow a pattern in which one partner raises concerns, and the other reacts with resentment, anger, and retreat.

© NOEL HENDRICKSON/PHOTODISC RED/GETTY IMAGES

to report infidelity and jealousy. Low religious involvement may raise the odds of divorce by subtracting an influential context for instilling positive marital attitudes and behaviors. And research following families over two decades reveals that parental divorce elevates risk of divorce in at least two succeeding generations, in part because it promotes child adjustment problems and reduces commitment to the norm of lifelong marriage (Amato & Cheadle, 2005; Hetherington & Elmore, 2004). As a result, when adult children marry, they are more likely to engage in inconsiderate behaviors and to have conflict-ridden relationships and less likely to try to work through these difficulties or (if they do try) to have the skills to do so. Marriage to a caring spouse from a stable family background reduces these negative outcomes.

Poorly educated, economically disadvantaged couples who suffer multiple life stresses are especially likely to split up (Amato, 2000). But Christy's case represents another trend—rising marital breakup among well-educated, career-oriented, economically independent women. When a woman's workplace status and income exceed her husband's, the risk of divorce increases—an association explained by differing gender-role beliefs between the spouses (Sayer & Bianchi, 2000). A husband's lack of support for his wife's career can greatly heighten her unhappiness and, therefore, the chances that she will end the marriage. Overall, women are twice as likely as men to initiate divorce proceedings (Popenoe, 2006).

■ **Consequences of Divorce.** Sharese's reaction to the news that Christy and Gary's marriage had dissolved was that it seemed as if "someone had died." Her description is fitting: Divorce involves the loss of a way of life and therefore a part of the self sustained by that way of life. As a result, it provides opportunities for both positive and negative change.

Immediately after separation, both men and women experience disrupted social networks, a decline in social support, and increased anxiety, depression, and impulsive behavior (Amato, 2000). For most, these reactions subside within two years. Women who were in traditional marriages and who organized their identities around their husbands have an especially hard time (Hetherington, Law, & O'Connor, 1994, p. 216). Some noncustodial fathers feel disoriented and rootless as a result of decreased contact with their children. Others distract themselves with a frenzy of social activity (Cherlin, 1992).

Finding a new partner contributes most to the life satisfaction of divorced adults (Forste & Heaton, 2004; Wang & Amato, 2000). But it is more crucial for men, who adjust less well than women to living on their own. Despite loneliness and a drop in income (see Chapter 10), women tend to bounce back more easily from divorce. Christy, for example, developed new friendships and a sense of self-reliance that might not have emerged had she remained married to Gary. However, a few women—especially those who are anxious and fearful or who remain strongly attached to their ex-spouses—experience a drop in self-esteem and persistent depression and tend to enter into unsuccessful relationships repeatedly (Amato, 2000; Ganong & Coleman, 1994). Job training, continued education, career advancement, and social support from family and friends play vital roles in the economic and psychological well-being of many divorced women (DeGarmo & Forgatch, 1997).

■ **Remarriage.** On average, people remarry within four years of divorce, men somewhat faster than women. As noted earlier, remarriages are especially vulnerable to breakup, for several reasons. Although people often remarry for love, practical matters—financial security, help in rearing children, relief from loneliness, and social acceptance—figure more heavily into a second marriage than a first. These concerns do not provide a sound footing for a lasting partnership. Second, some people transfer the negative patterns of interaction and problem solving learned in their first marriage to the second. Third, people with a failed marriage behind them are more likely to view divorce as an acceptable solution when marital difficulties resurface. Finally, remarried couples experience more stress from stepfamily situations (Bray, 1999; Coleman, Ganong, & Fine, 2000). As we will see, stepparent–stepchild ties are powerful predictors of marital happiness.

Divorce and remarriage, like other adult lifestyles, lead to diverse outcomes. It generally takes three to five years for blended families to develop the connectedness and comfort of intact biological families (Ihinger-Tallman & Pasley, 1997). Family life education, couples counseling, and group therapy can help divorced and remarried adults adapt to the complexities of their new circumstances (Forgatch, Patterson, & Ray, 1996).

Variant Styles of Parenthood

Diverse family forms result in varied styles of parenthood. Each type of family—blended, never-married, gay or lesbian, among others—presents unique challenges to parenting competence and adult psychological well-being.

■ Stepparents.

Whether stepchildren live in the household or visit only occasionally, stepparents are in a difficult position. Stepparents enter the family as an outsider and, too often, move into their new parental role too quickly. Lacking a warm attachment bond to build on, their discipline is usually ineffective. Stepparents frequently criticize the biological parent for being too lenient, while the biological parent may view the stepparent as too harsh—differences that can divide the couple (Ganong, Coleman, & Fine, 1995). Compared with first-marriage parents, remarried parents typically report higher levels of tension and disagreement, most centering on child-rearing issues. When both adults have children from prior marriages, rather than only one, more opportunities for conflict exist and relationship quality is poorer (Coleman, Ganong, & Fine, 2000).

Stepmothers are especially likely to experience conflict. Those who have not previously been married and had children may have an idealized image of family life, which is quickly shattered. Expected to be in charge of family relationships, stepmothers quickly find that stepparent–stepchild ties do not develop instantly. After divorce, biological mothers are frequently jealous, uncooperative, and possessive of their children. Even when their husbands do not have custody, stepmothers feel stressed. As stepchildren go in and out of the home, stepmothers compare life with and without resistant children. Many prefer life without them, then feel guilty about their "unmaternal" feelings (Church, 2004; MacDonald & DeMaris, 1996). No matter how hard a stepmother tries to build a close parent–child bond, her efforts are probably doomed to failure in the short run.

Stepfathers with children of their own have an easier time. They tend to establish positive bonds with stepchildren relatively quickly, perhaps because they are experienced in building warm parent–child ties and feel less pressure than stepmothers to plunge into parenting. And stepchildren generally respond favorably to stepfathers' efforts to connect with them through enjoyable activities (Ganong et al., 1999). Stepfathers without biological children (like their stepmother counterparts) can have unrealistic expectations. Or their wives may push them into the father role, sparking negativity from children. After making several overtures that are ignored or rebuffed, these stepfathers often withdraw from parenting (Hetherington & Clingempeel, 1992).

A caring husband–wife relationship, cooperation from the biological parent, and children's willingness to accept their parent's new spouse are crucial for stepparent adjustment. Over time, many couples strengthen their relationship and build a coparenting partnership that improves interactions with stepchildren (Church, 2004). But because stepparent–stepchild bonds are hard to establish, the divorce rate is higher for remarried couples with stepchildren than for those without them (Bray, 1999).

■ Never-Married Single Parents.

About 10 percent of American children and 5 percent of Canadian children live with a single parent who has never married and does not have a partner. Of these parents, about 90 percent are mothers, 10 percent fathers (U.S. Census Bureau, 2006b; Vanier Institute of the Family, 2004a). Earlier we mentioned that single adults occasionally decide to become parents on their own. More single women over age 30 in high-status occupations have become parents in recent years. However, they are still few in number, and little is known about how they and their children fare.

In the United States, the largest group of never-married parents is African-American young women. Over 60 percent of births to black mothers in their twenties are to women without a partner, compared with 13 percent of births to white women (U.S. Census Bureau, 2006b). African-American women postpone marriage more and childbirth less than women in other U.S. ethnic groups. Job loss, persisting unemployment, and consequent inability of many black men to support a family have contributed to the postponement of marriage.

Never-married black mothers tap the extended family, especially their own mothers and sometimes male relatives, for help in rearing children (Gasden, 1999; Jayakody & Kalil, 2002). For about one-third, marriage occurs within 9 years after birth of the first child, not necessarily to the child's biological father (Wu, Bumpass, & Musick, 2001). These couples function much like other first-marriage parents. Their children are often unaware that the father is a stepfather, and parents do not report the child-rearing difficulties typical of blended families (Ganong & Coleman, 1994).

Still, for low-SES women, never-married parenthood generally increases financial hardship. Nearly 50 percent of white mothers and 60 percent of black mothers have a second child while unmarried. And they are far less likely than divorced mothers to receive paternal child support payments (Lipman et al., 2002; Wu, Bumpass, & Musick, 2001). U.S. welfare policies currently mandate that parents find work to sustain welfare benefits. In states where the combination of wages and income supplements is sufficient to lift families out of poverty, children gain in academic performance and social behavior, perhaps because of reduced parental stress. But when welfare programs require parents to take low-paid jobs without counteracting poverty, they do not improve parents' or children's well-being (Gennitian & Morris, 2003; Morris, 2002).

Finally, children of never-married mothers who lack father involvement achieve less well in school and display more antisocial behavior than children in low-SES, first-marriage families—problems that make life more difficult for mothers (Coley, 1998). But marriage to the child's biological father benefits children only when the father provides reliable economic and emotional support. When a mother marries an antisocial father, her child is at greater risk for conduct problems than if she had reared the child alone (Jaffee et al., 2003). Strengthening social support, education, and employment opportunities for low-SES parents would greatly enhance the well-being of unmarried mothers and their children.

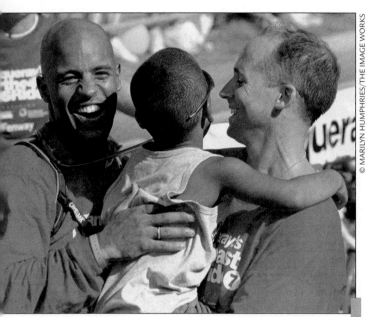

© MARILYN HUMPHRIES/THE IMAGE WORKS

Although research is limited, findings indicate that gay and lesbian parents are as committed to and effective at child rearing as heterosexual parents. Overall, families headed by same-sex partners can be distinguished from other families only by issues related to living in a nonsupportive society.

■ **Gay and Lesbian Parents.** Several million American and tens of thousands of Canadian gay men and lesbians are parents, most through previous heterosexual marriages, some through adoption, and a growing number through reproductive technologies (Ambert, 2003; Patterson, 2002). In the past, laws assuming that homosexuals could not be adequate parents led those who divorced a heterosexual partner to lose custody of their children. Today, some states and the nation of Canada hold that sexual orientation by itself is irrelevant to custody. A few U.S. states, however, ban gay and lesbian adoptions (Laird, 2003).

Research on homosexual parents and children is limited and largely based on small, volunteer samples. Findings of these investigations indicate that gay and lesbian parents are as committed to and effective at child rearing as heterosexual parents (Tasker, 2005). Also, whether born to or adopted by their parents or conceived through donor insemination, children in gay and lesbian families did not differ from the children of heterosexuals in mental health, peer relations, and gender identity (Allen & Burrell, 1996; Flaks et al., 1995; Golombok & Tasker, 1996). Two additional studies, which surmounted the potential bias associated with volunteer samples by including all lesbian-mother families who had conceived children at a fertility clinic, also reported that children were developing favorably (Brewaeys et al., 1997; Chan, Raboy, & Patterson, 1998). And among participants drawn from a representative sample of British mothers and their 7-year-olds, again, children reared in lesbian-mother families did not differ from children reared in heterosexual families in adjustment and gender-role preferences (Golombok et al., 2003). Further-

more, children of gay and lesbian parents do not differ from other children in sexual orientation; the large majority are heterosexual (Tasker, 2005).

When extended-family members have difficulty accepting them, homosexual mothers and fathers often build "families of choice" through friends, who assume the roles of relatives. Usually, however, parents of gays and lesbians cannot endure a permanent rift (Hare, 1994). With time, interactions between homosexual parents and their families of origin become more positive and supportive.

Homosexual couples' joint involvement in parenting varies with the way children entered the family. When partners choose parenthood through adoption or reproductive technologies, they report fairly even division of child-care and household tasks (Chan, Raboy, & Patterson, 1998). When children resulted from a previous heterosexual relationship, the biological parent typically assumes a larger parenting role (Hare & Richards, 1993).

A major concern of gay and lesbian parents is that their children will be stigmatized by their parents' sexual orientation. Most studies indicate that incidents of teasing or bullying are rare because parents and children carefully manage the information they reveal to others (Tasker, 2005). But in an Australian study, even though most third to tenth graders were guarded about discussing their parents' relationship with peers, nearly half reported harassment (Ray & Gregory, 2001). Overall, families headed by homosexuals can be distinguished from other families only by issues related to living in a nonsupportive society.

Ask Yourself

Review

Why is never-married single parenthood especially high among African Americans? What conditions affect parent and child well-being in these families?

Apply

After dating for a year, Wanda and Scott decided to live together. Their parents worried that cohabitation would reduce Wanda and Scott's chances for a successful marriage. Is this fear justified? Why or why not?

Connect

Return to Chapter 10, pages 346–347, and review the impact of divorce and remarriage on children and adolescents. How do those findings resemble outcomes for adults? What might account for the similarities?

Reflect

Do your own experiences or those of your friends match research findings on cohabitation, singlehood, never-married parents, or gay and lesbian parents? Select one instance and discuss.

www.ablongman.com/berk

Career Development

Besides family life, vocational life is a vital domain of social development in early adulthood. After choosing an occupation, young people must learn how to perform its tasks well, get along with co-workers, respond to authority, and protect their own interests. When work experiences go well, adults develop new competencies, feel a sense of personal accomplishment, make new friends, and become financially independent and secure. And as we have seen, especially for women but also for men who support their partners' career development, aspirations and accomplishments in the workplace and the family are interwoven.

Establishing a Career

Our discussion of Levinson's and Vaillant's theories highlighted diverse paths and timetables for career development. Consider, once again, the wide variations among Sharese, Ernie, Christy, and Gary in establishing their careers. As is typical for men, Ernie's and Gary's career lives were long and *continuous,* beginning after completion of formal education and ending with retirement. Like many women, Sharese and Christy had *discontinuous* career paths—ones that were interrupted or deferred by child rearing and other family needs (Hite & McDonald, 2003). Furthermore, not all people embark on the vocation of their dreams. In an Australian study that followed 1,200 young people after they finished their schooling, at any given time during the next 7 years, only 20 percent were working in a field consistent with their greatest interest (Athanasou, 2002).

Even for those who enter their chosen field, initial experiences can be discouraging. At the health department, Sharese discovered that committee meetings and paperwork consumed much of her day. Because each project had a deadline, the pressure of productivity weighed heavily on her. Adjusting to unanticipated disappointments in salary, supervisors, and co-workers is difficult. As new workers become aware of the gap between their expectations and reality, resignations are common. On average, people in their twenties move to a new job every two years; five or six changes are not unusual (Petersen & Gonzales, 1999).

After a period of evaluation and adjustment, young adults generally settle into their work. In careers with opportunities for promotion, high aspirations must often be revised downward because the structure of most work settings resembles a pyramid, with few high-level executive and supervisory jobs. In a longitudinal study of more than 400 lower-level male managers at AT&T, the importance of work in men's lives varied with career advancement and age (Howard & Bray, 1988). For men who advanced very little, "work disengagement" occurred early; family, recreation, and community service assumed greater importance by the early thirties. Men with average levels of career success emphasized nonwork roles at a later age. In contrast, men who were highly successful became more involved in their jobs over time. Although the desire for advancement tends to decline with age, most people still seek challenges and find satisfaction in their work roles.

Besides opportunity, personal characteristics affect career progress. As we will see, a *sense of self-efficacy*—belief in one's own ability to be successful—is influential. (To review this concept, return to page 18 in Chapter 1.) Young people who are very anxious about on-the-job mistakes or failure tend to set their career aspirations either too high or too low. When they encounter obstacles, they quickly conclude that career tasks are too hard and give up (Lent & Brown, 2002). As a result, they achieve far less than their abilities would permit.

Recall from our discussion of Levinson's theory that career success often depends on the quality of a mentoring relationship. Access to an effective mentor—a person with advanced experience and knowledge who is emotionally invested in the junior person's development and who fosters a bond of trust—is jointly affected by the availability of willing people and the individual's capacity to select an appropriate individual (Crosby, 1998). The best mentors are seldom top executives, who tend to be preoccupied and therefore less helpful and sympathetic. Usually, young adults fare better with lower-level mentors—more experienced co-workers or members of their professional associations (Allen & Finkelstein, 2003).

Women and Ethnic Minorities

Although women and ethnic minorities have penetrated nearly all professions, their talents often are not developed to the fullest. Women in general—and those who are members of economically disadvantaged minorities in particular—remain concentrated in occupations that offer little opportunity for advancement, and they are underrepresented in executive and

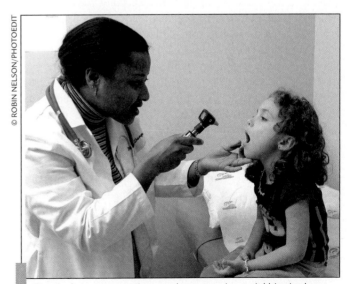

Despite laws guaranteeing equal opportunity, racial bias in the marketplace remains strong. Ethnic minority women face special challenges because of combined racial and gender discrimination. Those who succeed, like this African-American doctor, often display a high sense of self-efficacy, and they cite other women—often their mothers—as mentors and role models.

managerial roles (see Chapter 13, pages 455–456). And although the overall gap between men's and women's earnings is smaller today than 25 years ago, it remains considerable. For every dollar earned by a 25- to 34-year-old man, the average North American same-age woman earns about 82 cents, a gap that increases with age (Prokos & Padavic, 2005). Since men and women with similar work experience and job status differ much less in income, gender disparities in career development largely account for this gap (Venable, 2002).

Especially for women in traditionally feminine occupations, career planning is often short-term and subject to change. Many enter and exit the labor market several times as they give birth to and rear children. Between ages 18 and 34, the typical woman has been out of the labor force 26 percent of the time, in contrast to 11 percent for the typical man (Hynes & Clarkberg, 2005; U.S. Department of Labor, 2004). Time away from a career greatly hinders advancement—a major reason that women in prestigious, male-dominated careers tend to delay or avoid childbearing (Blair-Loy & DeHart, 2003). Yet an increasing number of accomplished professional women are leaving their jobs to devote themselves full-time to child rearing—a trend that has generated much media attention along with mistaken, gender-stereotyped interpretations of their "choice" (see the Social Issues box on the following page).

Low self-efficacy with respect to male-dominated fields also limits women's career progress. Women who pursue nontraditional careers usually have "masculine" traits—high achievement orientation, self-reliance, and belief that their efforts will result in success (Petersen & Gonzales, 1999). But even those with high self-efficacy are less certain than their male counterparts that they can overcome barriers to career success (Lindley, 2005). In addition to family obligations, gender-stereotyped images of women as followers rather than leaders slow advancement into top-level management positions. And because men dominate high-status fields, fewer women are available to serve as mentors. Although amount of mentor support is similar in same-sex and other-sex mentoring relationships, women with female mentors tend to be more productive (Goldstein, 1979; O'Neill, Horton, & Crosby, 1999). Perhaps female mentors are more likely to be perceived as role models and to provide guidance on the unique problems women encounter in the workplace.

Despite laws guaranteeing equal opportunity, racial bias in the labor market remains strong. In one study, researchers responded to more than 1,300 help-wanted newspaper ads with fictitious résumés, some containing higher qualifications and some lower qualifications. Half the résumés were assigned a white-sounding name (Emily Walsh, Brendan Baker) and half a black-sounding name (Lakisha Washington, Jamal Jones). At all job levels, from clerical work to top management, résumés with "white" names evoked 50 percent more callbacks than résumés with "black" names. And although whites received substantially more callbacks in response to high-quality than to low-quality résumés, having a high-quality résumé made little difference for blacks (see Figure 14.6). As the

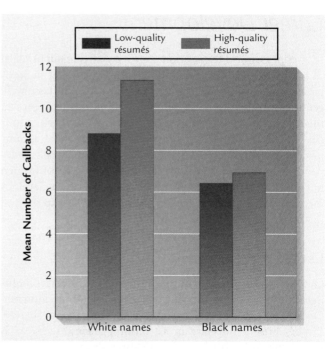

■ **FIGURE 14.6 Relationship of ethnicity of job applicant's name to employer callbacks.** Researchers responded to help-wanted newspaper ads with fictitious résumés, some having white-sounding names and others black-sounding names. Résumés with "white names" evoked many more callbacks than résumés with black names. When résumés were high in quality, callbacks to whites increased, but those to blacks showed little change. (Adapted from Bertrand & Mullainathan, 2004.)

researchers noted, "Discrimination appears to bite twice, making it harder for African Americans to find a job and to improve their employability" (Bertrand & Mullainathan, 2004, p. 3).

Ethnic minority women must surmount combined gender and racial discrimination to realize their career potential. Those who succeed often display an unusually high sense of self-efficacy, attacking problems head-on despite repeated obstacles to achievement (Byars & Hackett, 1998). In an interview study of African-American women who had become leaders in diverse fields, all reported intense persistence, fueled by supportive relationships with other women, including teachers, colleagues, and friends who countered their sense of professional isolation. Many described their mothers as inspiring role models who had set high standards for them. Others mentioned support from their African-American communities, stating that a deep sense of connection to their people had empowered them (Richie et al., 1997).

Despite obstacles to success, young and middle-aged women who have developed rewarding careers generally report higher levels of psychological well-being and life satisfaction (Burke, 2001). This finding suggests that some of the discontent frequently expressed by married women may not be due to marriage per se but, rather, to lack of a gratifying work life. Consistent with this idea, most women prefer to blend work and family (Barnett & Hyde, 2001). And those in financially stressed families must do so.

Social Issues

Women in "Fast-Track" Careers Who Opt to Stay Home

Although the vast majority are employed, women with professional degrees opt out of the labor force at three to four times the rate of similarly accomplished men. In one national survey, 10 years after graduation, 12 percent of women but only 4 percent of men in the field of law were not working. The figures for MDs were 11 versus 3 percent, for MBAs 8 versus 2 percent (Baker, 2002). Women often said they left their careers to attend to family responsibilities.

The apparent contradiction between these women's achievements and their decision to stay home has made them the focus of a growing number of newspaper and magazine features and on-air programs. Often their transformation into full-time mothers is interpreted in gender-stereotyped terms, as the exercise of a personal preference for a traditional role. In fact, it is almost always an agonizing decision—the outcome of multiple constraints in their lives.

In-depth interviews with 43 women—all of whom had left prestigious, well-paid careers after being employed for an average of 13 years to focus full-time on their families—revealed that over 90 percent were ambivalent about quitting (Stone & Lovejoy, 2004). Giving up a solid career identity, pride in accomplishment, and the intrinsic pleasure they derived from work was a painful, protracted process.

Two-thirds of the women had excelled in male-dominated professions such as law, business, medicine, or the sciences. Others had high-powered careers in publishing, marketing, banking, or health. Even though they were professionally and financially successful, a mix of work-, spouse-, and child-related factors led them to hand in their resignations.

Work. For 86 percent, work environments were the most significant reason for leaving. Many, with work weeks of 60 hours or more, had faced extreme time pressures even before they had children. And economic restructuring of their industries—mergers, takeovers, and expansions—often disrupted their existing work–family equilibrium. One former company executive commented after a merger: "I had to travel before, but this was just on a scale like [gesturing with her hands and making sounds to indicate a nuclear explosion]" (p. 71).

More than one-third, citing pervasive workplace inflexibility, characterized their jobs as "all or nothing." Requests to cut back to part-time were often denied. Of those who arranged part-time work, most ended up with part-time positions in name only: Their actual hours expanded. In workplaces where part-time employment was rare, women reported being labeled as on the "mommy track," losing interesting responsibilities, and watching their chances for promotion evaporate. They wondered, "Is this worth it?" and ultimately concluded, "No."

Spouses and Children. Because most participants were married to men in "high-octane" careers like their own, their husbands were usually minimally involved in child care and housework. But despite their own success, few entertained the possibility that their husbands would agree to cut back. Rather, these women implicitly assumed that when the pressures of the dual-earner lifestyle became excessive, they would need to sacrifice. Their husbands, while usually stating, "It's your choice," concurred.

Almost all the women had the financial means to hire in-home help. Yet hav-

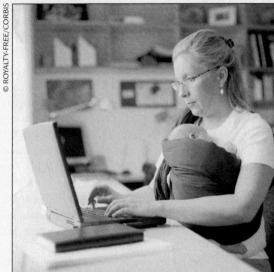

Women in fast-track careers may opt out of the labor force because their workplace is demanding and inflexible, thwarting their efforts to balance work with family. The decision to leave is often painful and protracted, and some women resolve it by bringing their work home.

ing worked for a decade or more and (in many instances) postponed childbearing, they felt uncomfortable, sometimes anguished, about being away from their children. Several who had become first-time mothers in their early forties felt a strong desire to experience motherhood because they did not expect to have more children. Others wanted to be available to support their school-age children's increasingly complex lives—homework, lessons, sports, and other activities. They also viewed childhood as slipping away and worried about "missing out." But though the pull of family was intense, for most, work-related issues cemented their decision.

In sum, few of these professionally successful women freely chose to step off the career track. Rather, their highly demanding, inflexible workplaces thwarted their efforts to balance work and family.

Combining Work and Family

Whether women work because they want to or have to (or both), the dominant family form today is the **dual-earner marriage,** in which both husband and wife are employed. Most dual-earner couples are also parents, since the majority of women with children are in the workforce (see page 349 in Chapter 10). But many more women than men experience moderate to high levels of stress in trying to meet both work and family responsibilities (Cinamon & Rich, 2002; Gilbert & Brownson, 1998).

What are the main sources of strain? When Sharese returned to her job after her children were born, she felt a sense of *role overload,* or conflict between work and family responsibilities. In addition to a demanding career, she also (like most employed women) shouldered most of the household and child-care tasks. And both Sharese and Ernie felt torn between the desire to excel at their jobs and the desire to spend more time with each other, their children, and their friends and relatives. Role overload is linked to a rise in psychological stress, poorer marital relations, less effective parenting, and child behavior problems (Perry-Jenkins, Repetti, & Crouter, 2000; Saginak & Saginak, 2005).

Role overload is greater for women than for men, especially for women in low-status work roles with rigid schedules and little autonomy (Marshall, 1997). Couples in prestigious careers have more control over both work and family domains. For example, Sharese and Ernie devised ways to spend more time with their children. They picked them up at child care early one day a week, compensating by doing certain occupational tasks on evenings and weekends. Like other career-oriented mothers, Sharese coped with role pressures by setting priorities: She decreased the amount of time she spent on household chores, not child rearing (Institute for Social Research, 2002).

As Sharese and Ernie's strategies indicate, workplace supports can greatly reduce role overload, yielding substantial payoffs for employers. Among a large, nationally representative sample of U.S. working adults, the greater the number of time-flexible policies available in their work settings (for example, time off to care for a sick child, choice in start and stop times, and opportunities to work from home), the better their work performance (Halpern, 2005a). Employees with several time-flexible options missed fewer days of work, less often arrived at work late or left early, felt more committed to their employer, and worked harder. They also reported fewer stress-related health symptoms.

Effectively balancing work and family brings many benefits—a better standard of living, improved work productivity, enhanced psychological well-being, greater self-fulfillment, and happier marriages. Ernie took great pride in Sharese's career accomplishments, which contributed to his view of her as an interesting, capable helpmate. Multiple roles also granted both young people expanded contexts for experiencing success and greater similarity in everyday experiences,

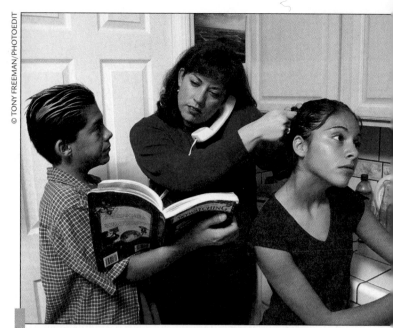

© TONY FREEMAN/PHOTOEDIT

Like most women in dual-earner marriages, this mother takes responsibility for the majority of child-rearing and household tasks. Women are more likely than men to experience role overload, or conflict between work and family responsibilities.

which fostered gratifying communication (Barnett & Hyde, 2001). Applying What We Know on the following page lists strategies that help dual-earner couples combine work and family roles in ways that promote mastery and pleasure in both spheres of life.

Ask Yourself

Review

Why do professionally accomplished women, especially those who are members of economically disadvantaged minorities, typically display high self-efficacy?

Apply

Heather climbed the career ladder of her company quickly, reaching a top-level executive position by her early thirties. In contrast, Sharese and Christy did not attain managerial roles in early adulthood. What factors might account for this disparity in career progress?

Connect

Work and family life are inseparably intertwined. Explain how this is so in early adulthood.

Reflect

Contact a major employer in your area and ask what policies it has to assist workers in combining work and family roles. What improvements would you suggest? Why are family-friendly policies "win-win" situations for both workers and employers?

www.ablongman.com/berk

Strategies That Help Dual-Earner Couples Combine Work and Family Roles

Strategy	Description
Devise a plan for sharing household tasks.	As soon as possible in the relationship, discuss relative commitment to work and family and division of household responsibilities. Decide who does a particular chore on the basis of who has the needed skill and time, not on the basis of gender. Schedule regular times to rediscuss your plan.
Begin sharing child care right after the baby's arrival.	For fathers, strive to spend equal time with the baby early. For mothers, refrain from imposing your standards on your partner. Instead, share the role of "child-rearing expert" by discussing parenting values and concerns often. Attend a parent education course together.
Talk over conflicts about decision making and responsibilities.	Face conflict through communication. Clarify your feelings and needs and express them to your partner. Listen and try to understand your partner's point of view. Then be willing to negotiate and compromise.
Establish a balance between work and family.	Critically evaluate the time you devote to work in view of your values and priorities. If it is too much, cut back.
Make sure your relationship receives regular loving care and attention.	See Applying What We Know on page 469.
Press for workplace and public policies that assist dual-earner-family roles	Difficulties faced by dual-earner couples are partly due to lack of workplace and societal supports. Encourage your employer to provide benefits that help combine work and family, such as flexible work hours, parental leave with pay, and on-site high-quality, affordable child care. Communicate with lawmakers and other citizens about improving public policies for children and families.

Summary

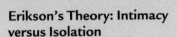

Erikson's Theory: Intimacy versus Isolation

According to Erikson, what personality changes take place during early adulthood?

■ In Erikson's theory, young adults must resolve the conflict of **intimacy versus isolation,** balancing independence and intimacy as they form a close relationship with a partner. Research confirms that a secure identity fosters attainment of intimacy. The negative outcome is loneliness and self-absorption.

■ Young people also focus on aspects of generativity, including contributions to society through work and child rearing.

Other Theories of Adult Psychosocial Development

Describe Levinson's and Vaillant's psychosocial theories of adult personality development.

■ Levinson described a series of eras, each consisting of a transition and a stable

period, in which people revise their **life structure.** Young adults usually construct a dream, typically involving career for men and both marriage and career for women, and form a relationship with a mentor to help them realize their dream. In their thirties, men tend to settle down, whereas many women remain unsettled into middle adulthood.

■ Vaillant refined Erikson's stages, portraying the twenties as devoted to intimacy, the thirties to career consolidation, the forties to guiding others, and the fifties to cultural and philosophical values.

What is the social clock, and how does it affect personality in adulthood?

■ Although societal expectations have become less rigid, conformity to or departure from the **social clock**—the culturally determined timetable for major life events—can be a major source of personality change in adulthood. Following a social clock grants confi-

dence to young adults; deviating from it can bring psychological distress.

Close Relationships

Describe factors affecting mate selection and the role of romantic love in the young adult's quest for intimacy.

■ Establishing an intimate bond is a major milestone of adult development. Romantic partners tend to resemble one another in age, ethnicity, SES, religion, and various personal and physical attributes.

■ According to evolutionary theory, women seek a mate with traits that help ensure children's survival, while men look for characteristics signaling sexual pleasure and ability to bear offspring. An alternative, social learning perspective emphasizes that gender roles profoundly influence criteria for mate selection. Research suggests that both biological and social forces are involved.

■ According to the **triangular theory of love,** the balance among passion, intimacy, and commitment changes as romantic relationships move from the intense sexual attraction of **passionate love** toward more settled **companionate love.** Commitment is key to a satisfying, enduring relationship. The Western emphasis on romantic love in mate selection does not characterize all cultures.

Describe adult friendships and sibling relationships and the role of loneliness in adult development.

■ Adult friendships have characteristics and benefits similar to earlier friendships and are based on trust, intimacy, and loyalty. Women's same-sex friendships tend to be more intimate than men's. Other-sex friendships are beneficial in adulthood but less common and enduring than same-sex friendships. Sibling relationships, especially between same-sex siblings, may become closer in early adulthood than they were in adolescence, often taking on the characteristics of friendship.

■ Young adults are vulnerable to **loneliness,** which declines with age as they form satisfying intimate ties. As long as it is not too intense, loneliness can encourage young people to reach out to others and better understand themselves.

The Family Life Cycle

Trace phases of the family life cycle that are prominent in early adulthood, and cite factors that influence these phases today.

■ Wide variations exist in the sequence and timing of phases of the **family life cycle.** Leaving home is a major step in assuming adult responsibilities. A large percentage of teenagers depart relatively early to go to college. SES and ethnicity influence the likelihood that a young person will live independently before marriage. Many unmarried young adults return home for a period of time.

■ Nearly 90 percent of North Americans marry, although most do so later than in the past. Both **traditional marriages** and

egalitarian marriages are affected by women's participation in the workforce. Husbands and wives today must work harder to define their marital roles. Even in dual-earner families, North American women spend nearly twice as much time on housework as men do.

© 2003 RUSSELL GORDON

■ Quality of the marital relationship predicts mental health similarly for both men and women. Women, however, feel particularly dissatisfied when the combined demands of work and family roles are overwhelming. Many young people enter marriage with unrealistic expectations. Even happy marriages have ups and downs and require adaptability from both partners.

■ Effective birth control techniques and changing cultural values make childbearing a matter of choice in Western industrialized nations. Although most couples become parents, they do so at a later age and have fewer children than in the past.

■ The arrival of a child requires couples to adjust to increased responsibilities and often prompts a shift to more traditional roles, though this may reverse after the birth of a second child. Marriages that are gratifying and supportive tend to remain so after childbirth, but troubled marriages usually become more distressed. Sharing care of the baby is linked to greater parental happiness and positive parent–infant interaction.

■ Decline in family size reflects women's increasing likelihood of dividing their energies between work and child rearing. Contrary to a widespread belief, however, having a larger family does not reduce the quality of children's experiences. Rather, mothers with low IQs bear more children, which accounts for the family size–IQ correlation.

■ Challenges facing families with young children include inadequate preparation for parenthood, lack of societal supports for child rearing, the need for cooperation in the marital relationship, and difficulties in finding good child care. Couples who work together as a coparenting team are more likely to feel competent as parents, use effective child-rearing practices, and have children who are developing well.

■ In families with adolescents, parents must establish new relationships with their increasingly autonomous teenagers, blending guidance with freedom and gradually

loosening control. Marital satisfaction often declines in this phase. Parent education programs can help parents clarify their child-rearing values and use more effective strategies.

The Diversity of Adult Lifestyles

Discuss the diversity of adult lifestyles, focusing on singlehood, cohabitation, and childlessness.

■ Singlehood has risen in recent years because of a trend toward later marriage and a high divorce rate. Women with high-status careers and men in blue-collar occupations are most likely to remain single. Women tend to adjust more favorably than men to singlehood.

■ **Cohabitation** has risen dramatically, especially among well-educated, economically advantaged young adults, for whom it is the preferred mode of entry into a committed intimate partnership. Cohabitation rates are especially high among separated and divorced adults. Compared with their Western European counterparts, North American cohabiters tend to be less conventional in values and behavior and less committed to their partner, and their subsequent marriages are more likely to fail. However, gay and lesbian couples who cohabit because they cannot marry report commitment equal to that of married couples.

■ Voluntarily childless adults tend to be well-educated and career-oriented and are as satisfied with their lives as parents who have good relationships with their children. But when childlessness is beyond a person's control, it interferes with adjustment and life satisfaction.

Discuss today's high rates of divorce and remarriage, and cite factors that contribute to them.

■ Nearly half of American and one-third of Canadian marriages dissolve, often while children are at home. About two-thirds of divorced people remarry, and many divorce again. Maladaptive communication patterns, poverty, a family history of divorce, and the changing status of women all contribute to divorce.

■ Finding a new partner is important to many divorced adults, especially men. Remarriages break up for several reasons, including the prominence of practical concerns rather than love in the decision to remarry, the persistence of negative styles of communication, the acceptance of divorce as a solution to marital difficulties, and problems adjusting to a stepfamily.

© ADRIAN WEINBRECHT/STONE/GETTY IMAGES

Discuss the challenges associated with variant styles of parenthood, including stepparents, never-married parents, and gay and lesbian parents.

■ Establishing stepparent–stepchild ties is difficult, especially for stepmothers and for stepfathers without children of their own. A caring husband–wife relationship, the cooperation of the biological parent, and children's acceptance are crucial for stepparent adjustment.

■ Never-married single parenthood is especially high among low-income African-American women in their twenties. Unemployment among black men contributes to this trend. Although these mothers often receive help from extended family members, they find it difficult to overcome poverty.

■ Gay and lesbian parents are as loving and effective at child rearing as heterosexual parents, and their children are as well-adjusted as those reared by heterosexual parents. Families headed by homosexuals face difficulties related to living in an unsupportive society.

© PETER HVIZDAK/THE IMAGE WORKS

Career Development

Discuss patterns of career development, and cite difficulties faced by women, ethnic minorities, and couples seeking to combine work and family.

■ Men's career paths are usually continuous, whereas women's are often discontinuous because of child rearing and other family needs. After adjusting to the realities of the work world, young adults settle into an occupation. Their progress is affected by opportunities for promotion in their chosen occupations, by personal characteristics such as self-efficacy, and by access to an effective mentor.

■ Women and ethnic minorities have penetrated nearly all professions but have made limited progress in career advancement. Women are hampered by time away from the labor market, low self-efficacy and lack of mentoring in traditionally male-dominated fields, and gender stereotypes of women as followers rather than leaders. Racial bias in the labor market remains strong, and ethnic minority women who succeed display an unusually high sense of self-efficacy.

■ Couples, particularly women, in **dual-earner marriages** often experience role overload and make vocational sacrifices to further their spouse's career. When dual-earner couples cooperate to surmount difficulties, they benefit from higher earnings, a better standard of living, and women's self-fulfillment and improved well-being. Time-flexible workplace policies can help these families effectively balance work and family demands.

Important Terms and Concepts

cohabitation (p. 484)
companionate love (p. 469)
dual-earner marriage (p. 492)
egalitarian marriage (p. 475)

family life cycle (p. 474)
intimacy versus isolation (p. 464)
life structure (p. 465)
loneliness (p. 472)

passionate love (p. 468)
social clock (p. 467)
traditional marriage (p. 475)
triangular theory of love (p. 468)

Milestones

Development in Early Adulthood

Age	Physical	Cognitive	Emotional/Social

20–30 YEARS

Physical

- Athletic skills that require speed of limb movement, explosive strength, and gross-motor coordination peak early in this decade, then decline (434–435)

- Athletic skills that depend on endurance, arm–hand steadiness, and aiming peak at the end of this decade, then decline (434)

- Declines in touch sensitivity; respiratory, cardiovascular, and immune system functioning; and elasticity of the skin begin and continue throughout adulthood (432–435)

- As basal metabolic rate declines, gradual weight gain - begins in the middle of this decade and continues through middle adulthood (438)

- Sexual activity increases (444–446)

Cognitive

- If college educated, dualistic thinking declines in favor of relativistic thinking (450)

- Moves from hypothetical to pragmatic thought (449–453)

- Narrows vocational options and settles on a specific career (454–459)

- Shows gains in cognitive-affective complexity, which continue through middle adulthood (451)

- Develops expertise in a field of endeavor, which enhances problem solving (452–453)

- May increase in creativity (452–453)

Emotional/Social

- Feels increasingly in control of events in one's life (463)

- Is likely to achieve a personally meaningful identity (464)

- Leaves home permanently (474)

- Strives to make a permanent commitment to an intimate partner (464, 468)

- Usually constructs a dream—an image of the self in the adult world that guides decision making (465)

- Usually forms a relationship with a mentor (465–466)

- If in a high-status career, acquires professional skills, values, and credentials (489–491)

- Begins to develop mutually gratifying adult friendships and work ties (441–473)

- May cohabit, marry, and bear children (464, 466–471, 474–482)

- Sibling relationships become more companionate (472)

- Loneliness peaks early in this decade, then declines steadily throughout adulthood (473)

Age	Physical	Cognitive	Emotional/Social
30–40 YEARS	• Declines in vision, hearing, and the skeletal system begin and continue throughout adulthood (433) • In women, fertility problems increase sharply in the middle of this decade (435) • Hair begins to gray and thin in the middle of this decade (433) • Sexual activity declines, probably as a result of the demands of daily life (444)	• May develop commitment within relativistic thinking (450) • Creativity often peaks (452)	• Reevaluates life structure and tries to change components that are inadequate (466) • Establishes a stable niche within society through family, occupation, and community activities (for women, career maturity and authority in the community may be delayed) (466)

Note: Numbers in parentheses indicate the page or pages on which each milestone is discussed.

Middle adulthood is a time of narrowing life options, but it brings compensating gains. Expertise—a wealth of accumulated knowledge that supports high levels of performance in vocational or leisure pursuits—reaches its height. As this professional conductor shares his expertise with young orchestra members during a visit to their school, he transfers knowledge, skill, and passion for music to a new generation.

Physical and Cognitive Development in Middle Adulthood

On a snowy December evening, Devin and Trisha sat down to read the holiday cards piled high on the kitchen counter. Devin's 55th birthday had just passed; Trisha would turn 48 in a few weeks. During the past year, they had celebrated their 24th wedding anniversary. These milestones, along with the annual updates they received from friends, brought the changes of midlife into bold relief.

Instead of new births, children starting school, or a first promotion at work, holiday cards and letters sounded new themes. Jewel's recap of the past year reflected a growing awareness of a finite lifespan, one in which time had become more precious. She wrote:

> My mood has been lighter ever since my birthday. There was some burden I laid down by turning 49. My mother passed away when she was 48, so it all feels like a gift now. Blessed be!

George and Anya reported on their son's graduation from law school and their daughter Michelle's first year of university:

> Anya is filling the gap created by the children's departure by returning to college for a nursing degree. After enrolling this fall, she was surprised to find herself in the same psychology class as Michelle. At first, Anya was worried about handling the academic work, but after a semester of success, she's feeling more confident.

Tim's message reflected continuing robust health, acceptance of physical changes, and a new burden: caring for aging parents—a firm reminder of the limits of the lifespan:

> I used to be a good basketball player in college, but recently I noticed that my 20-year-old nephew Brent can dribble and shoot circles around me. It must be my age! I ran our city marathon in September, coming in seventh in the over-50 division. Brent ran, too, but he opted out a few miles short of the finish line to get

some pizza while I pressed on. That must be my age, too!

The saddest news is that my dad had a bad stroke. His mind is clear, but his body is partially paralyzed. It's really upsetting because he was getting to enjoy the computer I gave him, and it was so upbeat to talk with him about it in the months before the stroke.

Middle age, which begins around age 40 and ends at about 65, is marked by narrowing of life options and a shrinking future as children leave home and career paths become more determined. In other ways, middle adulthood is hard to define because wide variations in attitudes and behaviors exist. Some individuals seem physically and mentally young at age 65—active and optimistic, with a sense of serenity and stability. Others feel old at age 35 or 40—as if their lives had peaked and were on a downhill course.

Another reason that middle age eludes definition is that it is a contemporary phenomenon. Before the twentieth century, only a brief interval separated the tasks of early adulthood from those of old age. Women were often widows by their mid-fifties, before their youngest child left home. And harsh living conditions led people to accept a ravaged body as a natural part of life. As life expectancy—and, with it, health and vigor—increased over the past century, adults became more aware of their own aging and mortality.

In this chapter, we trace physical and cognitive development from the fifth into the seventh decade of life. In both domains, we will encounter not just progressive declines but also sustained performance and compensating gains. As in earlier chapters, we will see that change occurs in manifold ways. Besides heredity and biological aging, our personal approach to passing years combines with family, community, and cultural contexts to affect the way we age.

🍂 Physical Development

Physical development in midlife is a continuation of the gradual changes under way in early adulthood. Even the most vigorous adults notice an older body when looking in the mirror or at family photos. Hair grays and thins, new lines appear on the face, and a fuller, less youthful body shape is evident. During midlife, most individuals begin to experience life-threatening health episodes—if not in themselves,

then in their partners and friends. And a change in time orientation, from "years since birth" to "years left to live," adds to consciousness of aging (Neugarten, 1968b).

These factors lead to a revised physical self-image, with somewhat less emphasis on hoped-for gains and more on feared declines (Bybee & Wells, 2003). Prominent concerns among 40- to 65-year-olds include getting a fatal disease, being too ill to maintain independence, and losing mental capacities. Unfortunately, many middle-aged adults fail to embrace realistic alternatives—becoming more physically fit and developing into healthy, energetic older adults (Hooker & Kaus, 1994).

Although certain aspects of aging cannot be controlled, many positive outcomes can be attained and feared outcomes avoided. People can do much to promote physical vigor and good health in midlife.

Physical Changes

As she dressed for work one morning, Trisha remarked jokingly to Devin, "I think I'll leave the dust on the mirror so I can't see all the wrinkles and gray hairs." Catching sight of her image, she continued in a more serious tone. "I'm certainly not happy about my weight. Look at this fat—it just doesn't want to go! I need to get back to some regular exercise, adjust my life to fit it in." In response, Devin glanced down soberly at his own enlarged midriff.

At breakfast, Devin took his glasses on and off and squinted while reading the paper. "Trish—what's the eye doctor's phone number? I've gotta get these bifocals adjusted again." As they conversed between the kitchen and the adjoining den, Devin sometimes asked Trisha to repeat herself. And he turned the radio and TV volume up so that Trisha frequently asked, "Does it need to be that loud?" Apparently Devin couldn't hear as clearly as before.

In the following sections, we look closely at the major physical changes of midlife. As we do so, you may find it helpful to refer back to Table 13.1 on page 433, which provides a summary.

Vision

By the forties, difficulty reading small print is common, due to growth in size of the lens combined with weakening of the muscle that enables the eye to *accommodate* (adjust its focus) to nearby objects. As new fibers appear on the surface of the lens, they compress older fibers toward the center, creating a thicker, denser, less pliable structure that eventually cannot be transformed at all. By age 50, the accommodative ability of the lens is one-sixth of what it was at age 20. Around age 60, the lens loses its capacity to adjust to objects at varying distances entirely, a condition called **presbyopia** (literally, "old eyes"). As the lens enlarges, the eye rapidly becomes more farsighted between ages 40 and 60 (Strenk, Strenk, & Koretz, 2005). Corrective lenses—or, for nearsighted people, bifocals—ease reading problems.

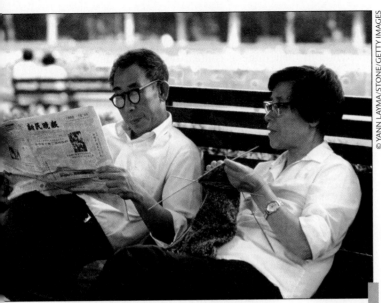

By the forties, the lens of the eye grows in size, thickness, and density, becoming less pliable, while the muscle that enables the eye to adjust its focus to nearby objects weakens. As a result, middle-aged adults commonly have difficulty reading small print and doing detail work. Corrective lenses, such as bifocals, help.

A second set of changes limits ability to see in dim light, which declines at twice the rate of daylight vision (Jackson & Owsley, 2000). Throughout adulthood, the size of the pupil shrinks and the lens yellows. In addition, starting at age 40, the *vitreous* (transparent gelatin-like substance that fills the eye) develops opaque areas, reducing the amount of light reaching the retina. Changes in the lens and vitreous also cause light to scatter within the eye, increasing sensitivity to glare. As a college student, Devin had enjoyed driving at night. Now he sometimes had trouble making out signs and moving objects. And his vision was more disrupted by bright light sources, such as headlights of oncoming cars (Owsley et al., 1998).

Yellowing of the lens and increasing density of the vitreous also limit color discrimination, especially at the green–blue–violet end of the spectrum (Kraft & Werner, 1999). Occasionally, Devin had to ask whether his sport coat, tie, and socks matched.

Besides structural changes in the eye, neural changes in the visual system occur. Gradual loss of rods and cones (light- and color-receptor cells) in the retina and of neurons in the optic nerve (the pathway between the retina and the cerebral cortex) contributes to visual declines. By midlife, half the *rods* (which enable vision in dim light) are lost. And because rods secrete substances necessary for survival of *cones* (which enable daylight and color vision), gradual loss of cones follows (Bonnel, Mohand-Said, & Sahel, 2003).

Middle-aged adults are at increased risk of **glaucoma,** a disease in which poor fluid drainage leads to a buildup of pressure within the eye, damaging the optic nerve. Glaucoma affects nearly 2 percent of people over age 40, more often women than men. It typically progresses without noticeable symptoms and is a leading cause of blindness. Glaucoma runs in families: Siblings of people with glaucoma have a tenfold increased risk, and the disease occurs three to four times as often in African Americans and Hispanics as in Caucasians (Friedman, 2006; Gohdes et al., 2005). Starting in midlife, eye exams should include a glaucoma test, involving an air puff to detect fluid pressure. Drugs that promote release of fluid and surgery to open blocked drainage channels prevent vision loss.

Hearing

An estimated 14 percent of North Americans between ages 45 and 64 suffer from hearing loss, often resulting from adult-onset hearing impairments. Although some conditions run in families and may be hereditary, most are age-related, a condition called **presbycusis** ("old hearing") (Gratton & Vásquez, 2003).

As we age, inner-ear structures that transform mechanical sound waves into neural impulses deteriorate through natural cell death or reduced blood supply caused by atherosclerosis. Processing of neural messages in the auditory cortex also declines. The first sign, at around age 50, is a noticeable hearing loss at high frequencies, which gradually extends to all frequencies. Late in life, human speech becomes more difficult to make out, although hearing loss remains greatest for high tones (Chisolm, Willott, & Lister, 2003). Still, throughout middle adulthood, most people hear reasonably well across a wide frequency range. And African tribal peoples display little age-related hearing loss (Jarvis & van Heerden, 1967; Rosen, Bergman, & Plester, 1962). These findings suggest factors other than biological aging are involved.

Men's hearing declines earlier and more rapidly than women's, a difference associated with cigarette smoking, intense noise in some male-dominated occupations, and (at older ages) high blood pressure and cerebrovascular disease, or strokes that damage brain tissue (Cruickshanks et al., 2003; Heltzner et al., 2005). Government regulations requiring industries to implement such safeguards as noise monitoring, provision of earplugs, and regular hearing tests have greatly reduced hearing damage, but some employers do not comply fully (Sataloff & Sataloff, 2001).

Most middle-aged and elderly people with hearing difficulties benefit from sound amplification with hearing aids. When perception of the human voice is affected, speaking to the person patiently, clearly, and with good eye contact aids understanding.

Skin

Our skin consists of three layers: (1) the *epidermis,* or outer protective layer, where new skin cells are constantly produced; (2) the *dermis,* or middle supportive layer, consisting of connective tissue that stretches and bounces back, giving the skin flexibility; and (3) the *hypodermis,* an inner fatty layer that adds to the soft lines and shape of the skin. As we age, the epidermis becomes less firmly attached to the dermis, fibers in the dermis thin, and fat in the hypodermis diminishes, leading the skin to wrinkle and loosen.

In the thirties, lines develop on the forehead as a result of smiling, furrowing the brow, and other facial expressions. In the forties, these become more pronounced, and "crow's-feet" appear around the eyes. Gradually, the skin loses elasticity and begins to sag, especially on the face, arms, and legs. After age 50, "age spots," collections of pigment under the skin, increase. Blood vessels in the skin become more visible as the fatty layer thins.

Because sun exposure hastens wrinkling and spotting, individuals who have spent much time outdoors without proper skin protection look older than their contemporaries. And partly because the dermis of women is not as thick as that of men, women's skin ages more quickly (Whitbourne, 2001).

Muscle–Fat Makeup

As Trisha and Devin make clear, weight gain—"middle-age spread"—is a concern to both men and women. A common pattern of change is an increase in body fat and a loss of lean body mass (muscle and bone). The rise in fat largely affects the torso and occurs as fatty deposits within the body cavity; as noted earlier, fat beneath the skin on the limbs declines. On average, the size of the abdomen increases 6 to 16 percent in men, 25 to 35 percent in women from early through middle adulthood (Whitbourne, 1996). Sex differences in fat distribution also appear. Men accumulate more on the back and upper abdomen, women around the waist and upper arms. Muscle mass declines very gradually in the forties and fifties, largely due to atrophy of fast-twitch fibers, responsible for speed and explosive strength.

Yet, as indicated in Chapter 13, large weight gain and loss of muscle power are not inevitable. With age, people must gradually reduce caloric intake to adjust for the age-related decline in basal metabolic rate (see page 438). In a longitudinal study of nearly 30,000 U.S. 50- to 79-year-old women diverse in SES and ethnicity, a low-fat diet involving increased consumption of vegetables, fruits, and grains was associated with greater initial weight loss and success at maintaining that loss over a seven-year period (Howard et al., 2006). In nonhuman animals, dietary restraint dramatically increases longevity while sustaining health and vitality. Currently, researchers are trying to identify the biological mechanisms involved and to find out whether these beneficial outcomes apply to humans (see the Biology and Environment box on the following page).

Furthermore, weight-bearing exercise that includes resistance training (a weight-lifting routine that places a moderately stressful load on the muscles) offsets both excess weight and muscle loss. Within the same individual, strength varies between often-used and little-used muscles (Arking, 1998; Macaluso & De Vito, 2004). Consider Devin's 57-year-old friend Tim, who for years has ridden his bike to and from work and jogged on weekends, averaging an hour of vigorous activity per day. Like many endurance athletes, he maintained the same weight and muscular physique throughout early and middle adulthood (Horber et al., 1996).

Skeleton

As new cells accumulate on their outer layers, the bones broaden, but their mineral content declines so they become more porous. This leads to a gradual loss in bone mass that begins in the late thirties and accelerates in the fifties, especially among women (Chan & Duque, 2002). Women's reserve of bone minerals is lower than men's to begin with. And following menopause, the favorable impact of estrogen on bone mineral absorption is lost. Reduction in bone density during adulthood is substantial—about 8 to 12 percent for men and 20 to 30 percent for women (Seeman, 2002).

Loss of bone strength causes the disks in the spinal column to collapse. Consequently, height may drop by as much as 1 inch by age 60, a change that will hasten thereafter. In addition, the weakened bones cannot support as much load: They fracture more easily and heal more slowly. A healthy lifestyle—including weight-bearing exercise, adequate calcium and vitamin D intake, and avoidance of smoking and heavy alcohol consumption—can slow bone loss in postmenopausal women by as much as 30 to 50 percent (Borer, 2005; Dawson-Hughes et al., 1995).

When bone loss is very great, it leads to a debilitating disorder called *osteoporosis*. We will take up this condition shortly when we consider illness and disability.

Reproductive System

The midlife transition in which fertility declines is called the **climacteric.** In women, it brings an end to reproductive capacity; in men, by contrast, fertility diminishes but is retained.

■ **Reproductive Changes in Women.** The changes involved in women's climacteric occur gradually over a 10-year period, during which the production of estrogen drops. As a result, the number of days in a woman's monthly cycle drops from about 28 in her twenties and thirties to perhaps 23 by her late forties, and her cycles become more irregular. In some, ova are not released; when they are, more are defective (see Chapter 2, page 52). The climacteric concludes with **menopause,** the end of menstruation and reproductive capacity. This occurs, on average, in the early fifties among North American, European, and East Asian women, although the age range extends from the late thirties to the late fifties. Women who smoke and who have not borne children tend to reach menopause earlier (Avis, Crawford, & Johannes, 2002; Rossi, 2005).

Following menopause, estrogen declines further, causing the reproductive organs to shrink in size, the genitals to be less easily stimulated, and the vagina to lubricate more slowly during arousal. As a result, complaints about sexual functioning increase, with about 35 to 40 percent of women reporting difficulties, especially among those with health problems or whose partners have sexual performance difficulties (Walsh & Berman, 2004). The drop in estrogen also contributes to decreased elasticity of the skin and loss of bone mass. And estrogen's ability to help protect against accumulation of plaque on the walls of the arteries, by boosting "good cholesterol" (high-density lipoprotein), is lost.

Biology and Environment

Anti-Aging Effects of Dietary Calorie Restriction: Relevant to Humans?

For nearly 70 years, scientists have known that dietary calorie restriction in nonhuman animals slows aging while maintaining good health and body functions. Rats and mice fed 30 to 40 percent fewer calories than they would freely eat beginning in early life show various physiological health benefits, lower incidence of chronic diseases, and a 50 percent increase in length of life (Hursting et al., 2003). Mild to moderate calorie restriction begun after rodents reach physical maturity also slows aging and extends longevity, though to a lesser extent (Roth et al., 2000). Other studies reveal similar dietary-restriction effects in mice, fleas, spiders, worms, fish, and yeast.

Primate Research. Would primates, especially humans, also benefit from a restricted diet? Researchers are tracking health indicators in rhesus monkeys and squirrel monkeys ranging from 1 to 20 years of age, after placing some on regimens of 30 percent reduced calories, supplemented with vitamins and minerals to ensure a healthy diet. More than a decade of longitudinal findings reveals that, compared with freely eating controls, dietary-restricted monkeys are smaller but not overly thin. They accumulate body fat differently—less on the torso, a type of fat distribution that reduces middle-aged humans' risk of heart disease.

Calorie-restricted monkeys also have a lower body temperature and basal metabolic rate—changes that suggest they shift physiological processes away from growth to life-maintaining functions. Consequently, like calorie-restricted rodents, they seem better able to withstand severe physical stress, such as surgery and infectious disease, perhaps because their bodies more easily repair damaged cells (Weindruch et al., 2001). Furthermore, calorie-restricted monkeys sustain youthful levels of the endocrine hormone DHEAS longer. When DHEAS drops in aging primates, cardiovascular disease, diabetes, cancer, and immune-system disorders rise (Mattison et al., 2003).

This 100-year-old Okinawan woman picks fresh vegetables from her garden. Residents of Okinawa consume an average of 20 percent fewer calories than mainland Japanese citizens, while maintaining a healthy diet. Their restricted diet is associated with fewer deaths from cancer and cardiovascular disease and more seniors living to age 100.

Of all physiological processes mediating the benefits of calorie restriction, reduced blood glucose and insulin levels, signaling improved carbohydrate metabolism, seem to be the most powerful. Efficient blood glucose regulation protects against diabetes and cardiovascular disease as primates age. Lower blood pressure and cholesterol and a high ratio of "good" to "bad" cholesterol in calorie-restricted monkeys strengthen these effects (Roth, Ingram, & Lane, 2001).

The earlier monkeys are placed on calorie restriction, the more favorable its physiological consequences. Because most monkeys in the study are still alive, we do not know whether calorie restriction grants them an exceptionally long lifespan (Mattison et al., 2003). But so far, early death rates for calorie-restricted monkeys have been lower than for fully fed controls.

Human Parallels. The laboratory experimental strategies used to study calorie restriction in animals cannot be applied to humans. But two natural experiments indicate that people who limit their food intake may benefit similarly.

Compared with mainland Japanese citizens, residents of the island of Okinawa consume an average of 20 percent fewer calories, while maintaining a healthy diet. This restricted diet is associated with a 60 to 70 percent reduction in incidence of deaths due to cancer and cardiovascular disease and a two- to forty-fold increase in seniors living to age 100 over other regions of Japan (Kagawa, 1978). Although other differences between Okinawans and mainland Japanese may play a role, Okinawans who move away from the island and, presumably, give up their calorie-limited lifestyle show increased mortality rates (Mizushima & Yapori, 1992).

In the early 1990s, eight American men and women ranging in age from 25 to 67 entered the Biosphere, an enclosed three-acre natural habitat, where they

© DAVID MCLAIN/AURORA PHOTOS

lived and raised their own food for two years. Eating 1,800 calories a day and engaging in 3 to 4 hours of daily heavy labor, the Biospherians experienced physiological changes similar to those observed in calorie-restricted rodents and monkeys, including reduced blood glucose, insulin, cholesterol, and blood pressure; a stronger immune-system response; and decreased fat mass (Heilbronn & Ravussin, 2003).

Why might calorie restriction be an anti-aging strategy? Researchers speculate that the body's response to food scarcity evolved to increase the chances of surviving adversity.

Nevertheless, calorie restriction may add only 2 to 3 years to the extended longevity already conferred by human improvements in living conditions and medical treatment (de Grey, 2005). Also, ethical considerations (including risks of malnutrition and insufficient energy to meet the requirements of daily life) argue against attempting to get people to limit their food intake substantially. Finally, very few people would be willing to maintain a drastically reduced diet for most of their lifespan. As a result, scientists have begun to explore *calorie-restriction mimetics*—agents such as natural food substances, herbs, and vigorous exercise regimens that might yield the same benefits as calorie restriction, without dieting (Roth, Lane, & Ingram, 2005; Smith, Heilbronn, & Ravussin, 2004). These investigations are still in their early stages.

The period leading up to and following menopause is often accompanied by emotional and physical symptoms, including mood fluctuations and *hot flashes*—periodic sensations of warmth accompanied by a rise in body temperature and redness in the face, neck, and chest, followed by sweating (Bromberger et al., 2001). Hot flashes—which may occur during the day and also, as *night sweats,* during sleep—affect about 75 percent of women in Western industrialized nations (Bastian, Smith, & Nanda, 2003). But they typically are not severe: Only about 1 in 12 experiences them every day.

Although menopausal women tend to report increased irritability and less satisfying sleep, research using EEG and other physiological measures finds no links between menopause and changes in quantity or quality of sleep (Shaver et al., 1988; Young et al., 2002). Also, many studies reveal no association between menopause and depression in the general population (Avis, 2003; Bosworth et al., 2001; Dennerstein et al., 1999). Rather, women who have a previous history of depression, are physically inactive, or have financial difficulties are more likely to experience depressive episodes during the climacteric. In view of these findings, sleep difficulties or depression should not be dismissed as temporary byproducts of menopause: These problems merit serious evaluation and treatment.

As Figure 15.1 illustrates, compared with North American, European, African, and Middle Eastern women, Asian women report fewer menopausal complaints, including hot flashes.

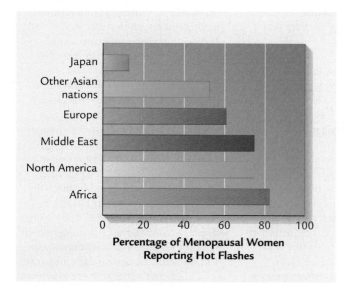

Percentage of Menopausal Women Reporting Hot Flashes

■ **FIGURE 15.1 Percentage of menopausal women in different regions of the world reporting hot flashes.** Findings are derived from interviews with large samples in each region. Women in Asian nations, especially Japanese women, are less likely to suffer from hot flashes, perhaps because they eat soy-based foods, a rich source of plant estrogen. See the Cultural Influences box on page 506 for additional evidence on the low rates of menopausal symptoms among Japanese women. (Adapted from Obermeyer, 2000.)

Asian diets, which are low in fat and high in soy-based foods (a rich source of plant estrogen) may be involved (Obermeyer, 2000).

■ **Hormone Therapy.** To reduce the physical discomforts of menopause, doctors may prescribe **hormone therapy,** or low daily doses of estrogen. Hormone therapy comes in two types: (1) estrogen alone, or *estrogen replacement therapy (ERT),* for women who have had hysterectomies (surgical removal of the uterus); and (2) estrogen plus progesterone, or *hormone replacement therapy (HRT),* for other women. Combining estrogen with progesterone lessens the risk of cancer of the endometrium (lining of the uterus), which has long been known as a serious side effect of hormone therapy.

Hormone therapy is highly successful at counteracting hot flashes and vaginal dryness. Although it has no clear impact on the moods of nondepressed women, for women diagnosed with depression, it may add to the effectiveness of antidepressant medication (Miller, 2003). Hormone therapy also offers some protection against bone deterioration and colon cancer (Nelson et al., 2002).

Nevertheless, a large-scale experiment, in which more than 16,000 50- to 79-year-olds randomly assigned to take HRT or a sugar pill were followed for 5 years, revealed two negative consequences. First, HRT caused a mild increase in heart attacks, stroke, and blood clots. Second, HRT taken for more than 4 years slightly elevated the incidence of breast cancer (Women's Health Initiative, 2002). In other studies, ERT, as well, increased the risk of breast cancer and blood clots (Bhavnani & Strickler, 2005; La Vecchia, 2004).

Furthermore, an additional experiment involving 4,500 65- to 79-year-olds indicated that HRT slightly elevated the risk of mild cognitive declines and nearly doubled the risk of Alzheimer's disease and other dementias (Rapp et al., 2003; Shumaker et al., 2003). But hormone therapy begun much earlier, at menopausal age, may actually reduce the risk of Alzheimer's (Zandi & Breitner, 2003). And research is still needed to verify that the cardiovascular risks of hormone therapy apply to early postmenopausal women.

On the basis of available evidence, women and their doctors should make decisions about hormone therapy carefully. Women with family histories of cardiovascular disease or breast cancer are generally advised against it. Fortunately, the number of alternative treatments is increasing. A relatively safe migraine-headache medication, gabapentin, substantially reduces hot flashes, perhaps by acting on the brain's temperature regulation center. Several new antidepressant drugs and black cohosh, an herbal medication, are effective as well (Guttuso et al., 2003; Osmers et al., 2005). Alternative medications are also available to protect the bones, although their long-term safety is not yet clear.

At present, however, hormone therapy continues to provide the most reliable relief from menopausal symptoms. Therefore, some experts argue that prescribing it to low-risk women on a short-term basis (no longer than 5 years) is justified because it improves quality of life (Col et al., 2004).

■ **Women's Psychological Reactions to Menopause.** How do women react to menopause—a clear-cut signal that their childbearing years are over? The answer lies in how they interpret the event in relation to their past and future lives.

For Jewel, who had wanted marriage and family but never attained these goals, menopause was traumatic. Her sense of physical competence was still bound up with the ability to have children. Physical symptoms can also make menopause a difficult time. And in a society that values a youthful appearance, some women respond to the climacteric with disappointment about a loss of sex appeal (Howell & Beth, 2002).

Many women, however, find menopause to be little or no trouble and regard it as a new beginning (George, 2002). When more than 2,000 U.S. women were asked what their feelings were about no longer menstruating, nearly 50 percent of those currently experiencing changes in their menstrual cycles, and 60 percent of those whose periods had ceased, reported feeling relieved (Rossi, 2005). Most do not want more children and are thankful to be freed from worry about birth control. And highly educated, career-oriented Caucasian-American women with fulfilling lives outside the home usually have more positive attitudes toward menopause than those with less education (Theisen et al., 1995).

Other research suggests that African-American and Mexican-American women hold generally favorable views. In several studies, African Americans experienced less irritability and moodiness than Caucasian Americans (Melby, Lock, & Kaufert, 2005). African-American women rarely spoke of

menopause in terms of physical aging but, instead, regarded it as normal, inevitable, even welcome. One woman explained, "I kind of look forward to it as being something I know I'll go through because I don't think you can go around it" (Holmes-Rovner et al., 1996; Sampselle et al., 2002, p. 359). Several African Americans expressed exasperation at society's readiness to label as "crazy" middle-aged women's authentic reactions to work- or family-based stressors that often coincide with menopause. Among Mexican-American women who have not yet adopted the language (and perhaps certain beliefs) of the larger society, attitudes toward menopause are especially positive (Bell, 1995). And in an investigation of more than 13,000 40- to 55-year-old U.S. women diverse in ethnicity, other factors—SES, physical health, lifestyle factors (smoking, diet, exercise, weight gain), and especially psychological stress—overshadowed menopausal status and three common symptoms (hot flashes, night sweats, and vaginal dryness) in impact on self-rated quality of life (Avis et al., 2004).

The wide variation in physical symptoms and attitudes indicates that menopause is not just a hormonal event; it is also affected by cultural beliefs and practices. The Cultural Influences box on page 506 provides a cross-cultural look at women's experience of menopause.

■ **Reproductive Changes in Men.** Although men also experience a climacteric, no male counterpart to menopause exists. After age 40, quantity of semen and sperm decreases, but sperm production continues throughout life, and men in their nineties have fathered children. Testosterone production declines gradually with age, but the change is minimal in healthy men who continue to engage in sexual activity, which stimulates cells that release testosterone (Hermann et al., 2000).

Nevertheless, because of reduced blood flow to and changes in connective tissue in the penis, more stimulation is required for an erection, and it may be harder to maintain. The inability to attain an erection when desired can occur at any age, but it becomes more common in midlife, affecting about 40 to 50 percent of men by age 60 (Kingsberg, 2002).

An episode or two of impotence is not serious, but frequent bouts can lead some men to fear that their sex life is over and undermine their self-image. Viagra and other drugs that increase blood flow to the penis offer temporary relief from erectile dysfunction. Publicity surrounding these drugs has prompted open discussion of men's sexuality and encouraged more men to seek help. But those taking the medications are often not adequately screened for the host of factors besides declining testosterone that contribute to impotence, including disorders of the nervous, circulatory, and endocrine systems; anxiety and depression; pelvic injury; and loss of interest in one's sexual partner (Montorsi, 2005). Although drugs for impotence are generally safe, a few users have experienced serious vision loss. Whether the medications are at fault is not yet known.

© GERI ENGBERG/THE IMAGE WORKS

African-American women generally speak of menopause as normal, inevitable, even welcome. They also seem to experience less irritability and moodiness during this transition than Caucasian-American women.

Cultural Influences

Menopause as a Biocultural Event

Biology and culture join forces to influence women's response to menopause, making it a *biocultural event*. In Western industrialized nations, menopause is "medicalized"—assumed to be a syndrome requiring treatment. Many women experience physical and emotional symptoms. The more symptoms they report, the more negative their attitude toward menopause tends to be (Theisen et al., 1995).

Yet change the circumstances in which menopause is evaluated, and attitudes change as well. In one study, nearly 600 men and women between ages 19 and 85 described their view of menopause in one of three contexts—as a medical problem, as a life transition, or as a symbol of aging. The medical context evoked many more negative statements than the other contexts (Gannon & Ekstrom, 1993).

Research in non-Western cultures reveals that middle-aged women's social status also affects the experience of menopause. In societies where older women are respected and the mother-in-law and grandmother roles bring new privileges and responsibilities, complaints about menopausal symptoms are rare (Fuh et al., 2005; Patterson & Lynch, 1988). Perhaps in part for this reason, women in Asian nations seldom report discomforts. And when they do, their symptoms usually differ from those of Western women.

For example, although they rarely complain of hot flashes, a small number of Japanese women report shoulder stiffness, back pain, headaches, and fatigue. In midlife, a Japanese woman attains peak respect and responsibility. Typically her days are filled with monitoring the household economy, attending to grandchildren, caring for dependent parents-in-law, and part-time employment (Lock & Kaufert, 2001). The rare woman who experiences menopausal distress seems to interpret it in light of these socially

valued commitments. Neither Japanese women nor their doctors consider menopause to be a significant marker of female middle age. Rather, midlife is viewed as an extended period of "socially recognized, productive maturity" (Menon, 2002, p. 58).

A comparison of rural Mayan women of the Yucatán with rural Greek women on the island of Evia reveals additional biocultural influences on the menopausal experience (Beyene, 1992; Beyene & Martin, 2001). In both societies, old age is a time of increased status, and menopause brings freedom from child rearing and more time for leisure activities. Otherwise, Mayan and Greek women differ greatly.

Mayan women marry as teenagers. By 35 to 40, they have given birth to many children but rarely menstruated because of repeated pregnancies and breast-feeding. Eager for childbearing to end, they welcome menopause, describing it with such phrases as "being happy" and "free like a young girl again."

None report hot flashes or any other symptoms.

Like North Americans, rural Greek women use birth control to limit family size, and most report hot flashes and sweating at menopause. But they regard these as temporary discomforts that will stop on their own, not as medical symptoms requiring treatment. When asked what they do about hot flashes, the Greek women reply, "Pay no attention," "Go outside for fresh air," and "Throw off the covers at night."

Does frequency of childbearing affect menopausal symptoms, as this contrast between Mayan and Greek women suggests? More research is needed to be sure. At the same time, the difference between North American and Greek women in attitudes toward and management of hot flashes is striking. This—along with other cross-cultural findings—highlights the combined impact of biology and culture on menopausal experiences (Melby, Lock, & Kaufert, 2005).

For these rural Mayan women of the Yucatán, old age is a time of increased status, and menopause brings freedom. After decades of childbearing, Mayan women welcome menopause, describing it as "being happy" and "free like a young girl again."

Ask Yourself

Review

Describe cultural influences on the experience of menopause.

Apply

At age 42, Stan began to wear bifocals, and over the next 10 years, he required an adjustment to his corrective lenses almost every year. What physical changes account for Stan's recurring need for new eyewear?

Apply

Between ages 40 and 50, Nancy gained 20 pounds. She also began to have trouble opening tightly closed jars, and her calf muscles ached after she climbed a flight of stairs. "Exchanging muscle for fat must be an inevitable part of aging," Nancy thought. Is she correct? Why or why not?

Reflect

In view of the benefits and risks of hormone therapy, what factors would you consider, or advise others to consider, before taking such medication?

www.ablongman.com/berk

Health and Fitness

In midlife, nearly 85 percent of Americans and 88 percent of Canadians rate their health as either "excellent" or "good"—still a large majority, but considerably lower than the 95 percent figure in early adulthood (Health Canada, 2002b; U.S. Department of Health and Human Services, 2005h). Whereas younger people usually attribute health complaints to temporary infections, middle-aged adults more often point to chronic diseases. Visits to the doctor's office and hospital stays become more frequent. As we will see, among middle-aged adults who rate their health unfavorably, men are more likely to suffer from fatal illnesses, women from nonfatal, limiting health problems.

In addition to typical negative indicators—major diseases and disabling conditions—our discussion takes up sexuality as a positive indicator of health. Before we begin, it is important to note that our understanding of health in middle and late adulthood is limited by insufficient research on women and ethnic minorities. Most studies of illness risk factors, prevention, and treatment have been carried out on men. Fortunately, this situation is changing. For example, the Women's Health Initiative—a 15-year commitment by the U.S. federal government to study the impact of various lifestyle and medical prevention strategies on the health of more than 164,000 postmenopausal women of all ethnic groups and SES levels—has led to important findings, including evidence on cardiovascular disease and breast cancer risks associated with hormone therapy, discussed earlier.

Sexuality

Frequency of sexual activity among married couples tends to decline in middle adulthood, but for most, the drop is slight. Longitudinal research reveals that stability of sexual activity is far more typical than dramatic change. Couples who have sex often in early adulthood continue to do so in midlife (Dennerstein & Lehert, 2004; Walsh & Berman, 2004). And the best predictor of sexual frequency is marital happiness, an association that is probably bidirectional (Edwards & Booth, 1994). Sex is more likely to occur in the context of a good marriage, and couples who have sex often probably view their relationship more positively.

Nevertheless, *intensity* of sexual response declines in midlife due to physical changes of the climacteric. Both men and women take longer to feel aroused and to reach orgasm (Bartlik & Goldstein, 2001; Walsh & Berman, 2004). If partners perceive each other as less attractive, this may contribute to a drop in sexual desire. Yet in the context of a positive outlook, sexual activity can become more satisfying. Devin and Trisha, for example, viewed each other's aging bodies with acceptance and affection—as a sign of their enduring and deepening relationship. And with greater freedom from the demands of work and family, their sex life became more spontaneous. The majority of married people over age 50 say that their sex life is an important component of their relationship, and most find ways to overcome difficulties with sexual functioning. One happily married 52-year-old woman commented, "We know what we are doing, we've had plenty of practice (laughs), and I would never have believed that it gets better as you get older, but it does" (Gott & Hinchliff, 2003, p. 1625; Kingsberg, 2002).

When surveys include both married and unmarried people, a striking gender difference in age-related sexual activity appears. The proportion of men with no sexual partners in the previous year increases only slightly, from 8 percent in the thirties to 11 percent in the late fifties. In contrast, the rise for women is dramatic, from 9 percent to 30 percent—a gender gap that becomes even greater in late adulthood (Avis, 2000). Opportunity, not desire, is responsible. A higher male mortality rate and the value women place on affection and continuity in sexual relations make partners less available to them. Taken as a whole, the evidence reveals that sexual activity in midlife, as in earlier periods, is the combined result of biological, psychological, and social forces.

Illness and Disability

As Figure 15.2 shows, cancer and cardiovascular disease are the leading causes of death in middle age. Unintentional injuries, though still a major health threat, occur at a lower rate than in early adulthood, largely because motor vehicle collisions decline. Despite a rise in vision problems, older adults' many years of driving experience and greater cautiousness may reduce these deaths. In contrast, falls resulting in bone fractures and death nearly double from early to middle adulthood (Statistics Canada, 2002d; U.S. Department of Health and Human Services, 2005h).

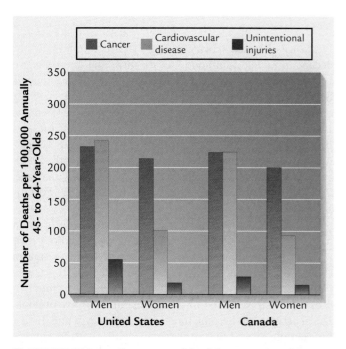

FIGURE 15.2 Leading causes of death between 45 and 64 years of age in the United States and Canada. As in early adulthood, annual death rates are lower in Canada than in the United States. Men are more vulnerable than women to each leading cause of death. Cancer is by far the leading killer of women. For men, death rates due to cancer are similar to those for cardiovascular disease. (Adapted from Statistics Canada, 2002d; U.S. Census Bureau, 2006b.)

Among middle-aged men, rates of cardiovascular disease and cancer are fairly similar. And overall, men are more vulnerable than women to most health problems. Among middle-aged women, cancer is by far the leading cause of death (refer again to Figure 15.2). As in earlier decades, economic disadvantage is a strong predictor of poor health and premature death in midlife. And largely because of more severe poverty and lack of universal health insurance, the United States continues to exceed Canada in death rates from all major causes. Finally, as we take a closer look at illness and disability in the following sections, we will encounter yet another familiar theme: the close connection between emotional and physical well-being. Personality traits that magnify stress—especially hostility and anger—are serious threats to health in midlife.

■ **Cancer.** From early to middle adulthood, the death rate due to cancer multiplies tenfold, accounting for about one-third of all midlife deaths in the United States and one-half in Canada. Although the incidence of many types of cancer is currently leveling off or declining, cancer mortality was on the rise for many decades, largely because of a dramatic increase in lung cancer due to cigarette smoking. In the last 15 years, lung cancer dropped in men; 50 percent fewer smoke today than in the 1950s. In contrast, lung cancer has increased in women, many of whom took up smoking after World War II (U.S. Department of Health and Human Services, 2005h).

Cancer occurs when a cell's genetic program is disrupted, leading to uncontrolled growth and spread of abnormal cells

that crowd out normal tissues and organs. Why does this happen? Mutations of three main kinds contribute to cancer. Some result in *oncogenes* (cancer genes) that directly undergo abnormal cell duplication. Others interfere with the activity of *tumor suppressor genes* so they fail to keep oncogenes from multiplying. And a third type of mutation disrupts the activity of *stability genes,* which normally keep genetic alterations to a minimum by repairing subtle DNA mistakes that occur either during normal cell duplication or as a result of environmental agents (Vogelstein & Kinzler, 2004). When stability genes do not function, mutations in many other genes occur at a higher rate.

Each of these cancer-linked mutations can be either *germline* (due to an inherited predisposition) or *somatic* (occurring in a single cell, which then multiplies) (see page 51 in Chapter 2 to review). Recall from Chapter 13 that according to one theory, error in DNA duplication increases with age, either occurring spontaneously or resulting from the release of free radicals or breakdown of the immune system. Environmental toxins may initiate or intensify this process.

Figure 15.3 shows the incidence of the most common types of cancer. For cancers that affect both sexes, men are generally more vulnerable than women. The difference may be due to genetic makeup, exposure to cancer-causing agents as a result of lifestyle or occupation, and a tendency to delay going to the doctor. Although the relationship of SES to cancer varies with site (for example, lung and stomach cancers are linked to lower SES, breast and prostate cancers to higher SES), cancer death rates increase sharply as SES decreases and are especially high among low-income ethnic minorities (Jemal et al., 2006). Poorer medical care and reduced ability to fight the disease, due to inadequate diet and high life stress, underlie this trend.

Overall, a complex interaction of heredity, biological aging, and environment contributes to cancer. For example, many patients with familial breast cancer who respond poorly to treatment lack a particular tumor-suppressor gene (either BRCA1 or BRCA2). Genetic screening for these mutations is available, permitting prevention efforts to begin early. Even though women with one of these defective genes are at much greater risk for breast cancer than other women, only 35 to 50 percent actually develop the disease. Other genes and lifestyle factors, including alcohol consumption, overweight, number of pregnancies, and use of oral contraceptives, heighten their risk. Women with BRCA1 or BRCA2 mutations are especially likely to develop early-onset breast cancer, before age 30 (Nkondjock & Ghadirian, 2004). But their risk remains elevated throughout middle and late adulthood, when breast cancer rises among women in general.

People often fear cancer because they believe it is incurable. Yet 40 percent of affected individuals are cured (free of the disease for 5 or more years). Breast cancer is the leading malignancy for women, prostate cancer for men. Lung cancer—largely preventable through avoiding tobacco—ranks second for both sexes, followed closely by colon and rectal cancer. Scheduling annual medical checkups that screen for these and other forms of cancer and taking the additional steps listed Applying What We Know on the following page can reduce cancer illness and death rates considerably. An increasing

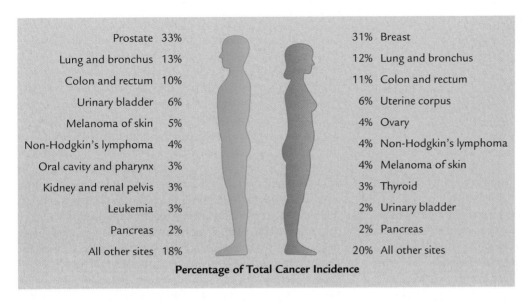

Prostate	33%	31%	Breast
Lung and bronchus	13%	12%	Lung and bronchus
Colon and rectum	10%	11%	Colon and rectum
Urinary bladder	6%	6%	Uterine corpus
Melanoma of skin	5%	4%	Ovary
Non-Hodgkin's lymphoma	4%	4%	Non-Hodgkin's lymphoma
Oral cavity and pharynx	3%	4%	Melanoma of skin
Kidney and renal pelvis	3%	3%	Thyroid
Leukemia	3%	2%	Urinary bladder
Pancreas	2%	2%	Pancreas
All other sites	18%	20%	All other sites

Percentage of Total Cancer Incidence

■ **FIGURE 15.3 Incidence of ten leading cancer types among men and women in the United States.** Although cancer rates are lower in Canada than the United States, the relative incidence of different types of cancers is similar in the two countries. (From A. Jemal et al., 2006, "Cancer Statistics, 2006," *CA: A Cancer Journal for Clinicians, 56,* p. 109. Reprinted by permission of the American Cancer Society.)

number of cancer-promoting mutations are being identified, and promising new therapies targeting these genes are being tested.

Surviving cancer is a triumph, but it also brings emotional challenges. During cancer treatment, relationships focus on the illness. Afterward, they must refocus on health and full participation in daily life. Unfortunately, stigmas associated with cancer exist. Friends, family, and co-workers may need reminders that cancer is not contagious and that with patience and support from supervisors and co-workers, cancer survivors regain their on-the-job productivity (Mains et al., 2005).

■ **Cardiovascular Disease.** Despite a decline during the last few decades (see Chapter 13), each year about 25 percent of middle-aged Americans and Canadians who die succumb to

Reducing the Incidence of Cancer and Cancer Deaths

Intervention	Description
Know the seven warning signs of cancer.	The signs are change in bowel or bladder habits, sore that does not heal, unusual bleeding or discharge, thickening or lump in a breast or elsewhere in your body, indigestion or swallowing difficulty, obvious change in a wart or mole, nagging cough or hoarseness. If you have any of these signs, consult your doctor immediately.
Do self-examination.	Women should self-examine the breasts and men the testicles for lumps and other changes once a month. If detected early, breast and testicular cancers usually can be cured.
Schedule regular medical checkups and cancer-screening tests.	Women should have a mammogram and Pap test every one to two years. Beginning at age 50, men should have an annual prostate screening test. Both men and women should be screened periodically for colon cancer, as recommended by their doctor.
Avoid tobacco.	Cigarette smoking causes 90 percent of lung cancer deaths and 30 percent of all cancer deaths. Smokeless (chewing) tobacco increases risk of cancer of the mouth, larynx, throat, and esophagus.
Avoid excessive sun exposure.	Sun exposure causes many cases of skin cancer. When in the sun for an extended time, use a sun blocker and cover exposed skin.
Avoid unnecessary X-ray exposure.	Excessive exposure to X-rays increases cancer risk. Most medical X-rays are adjusted to deliver the lowest possible dose but should not be used unnecessarily.
Avoid exposure to industrial chemicals and other pollutants.	Exposure to nickel, chromate, asbestos, vinyl chloride, and other industrial agents increases risk of various cancers.
Weigh the benefits versus risks of hormone therapy.	Because estrogen replacement increases risk of uterine and breast cancer, carefully consider hormone therapy with your doctor.
Maintain a healthy diet.	Avoid too much dietary fat and salt-cured, smoked, and nitrite-cured foods; eat vegetables and foods rich in fiber and vitamins A and C.

Applying What We Know

cardiovascular disease (Statistics Canada, 2002d; U.S. Department of Health and Human Services, 2005h). We associate cardiovascular disease with heart attacks, but for Devin (like many middle-aged and older adults), the condition was discovered during an annual checkup. His doctor detected high blood pressure, high blood cholesterol, and *atherosclerosis*—a buildup of plaque in his coronary arteries, which encircle the heart and provide its muscles with oxygen and nutrients. These indicators of cardiovascular disease are known as "silent killers" because they often have no symptoms.

When symptoms *are* evident, they take different forms. The most extreme is a *heart attack*—blockage of normal blood supply to an area of the heart, usually brought on by a blood clot in one or more plaque-filled coronary arteries. Intense pain results as muscle in the affected region dies. A heart attack is a medical emergency; over 50 percent of victims die before reaching the hospital, another 15 percent during treatment, and an additional 15 percent over the next few years (American Heart Association, 2006b). Among other, less extreme symptoms of cardiovascular disease are *arrhythmia,* or irregular heartbeat. When it persists, it can prevent the heart from pumping enough blood and result in faintness. It can also allow clots to form within the heart's chambers, which may

break loose and travel to the brain. In some individuals, indigestion-like pain or crushing chest pain, called *angina pectoris,* reveals an oxygen-deprived heart.

Today, cardiovascular disease can be treated in many ways—including coronary bypass surgery, medication, and pacemakers to regulate heart rhythm. To relieve arterial blockage, Devin had *angioplasty,* a procedure in which a surgeon threaded a needle-thin catheter into his arteries and inflated a balloon at its tip, which flattened fatty deposits to allow blood to flow more freely. Unless Devin took other measures to reduce his risk, his doctor warned, the arteries would clog again within a year. As Applying What We Know below indicates, adults can do much to prevent heart disease or slow its progress.

Some risks, such as heredity, advanced age, and being male, cannot be changed. But cardiovascular disease is so disabling and deadly that people must be alert for it where it is least expected—for example, in women. Because men account for over 70 percent of cases in middle adulthood, doctors often view a heart condition as a "male problem" and frequently overlook women's symptoms, which tend to be milder, more often taking the form of angina than a heart attack (Roger et al., 2000). In one study, researchers had male and female actors present identical symptoms of angina to a sample of over 700

Reducing the Risk of Heart Attack

Applying What We Know

Intervention	Risk Reduction
Quit smoking.	→ 70% 5 years after quitting, up to 70 percent lower risk compared to current smokers
Reduce blood cholesterol level.	→ 60% 2 to 3 percent decline in risk for each 1 percent reduction in blood cholesterol. Reductions in cholesterol average 10 percent with diet therapy and can exceed 20 percent with drug therapy.
Treat high blood pressure.	→ 60% Combined diet and drug therapy can lower blood pressure substantially, leading to as much as a 60 percent risk reduction.
Maintain ideal weight.	→ 55% Up to 55 percent lower risk for people who maintain ideal body weight compared to those who are obese
Exercise regularly.	→ 45% 45 percent lower risk for people who maintain an active rather than a sedentary lifestyle
Drink an occasional glass of wine or beer.[a]	→ 45% Up to 45 percent lower risk for people who consume small-to-moderate amounts of alcohol; believed to promote high-density lipoproteins (a form of "good cholesterol" that reduces "bad cholesterol") and to reduce the risk of clot formation
Take low-dose aspirin.	→ 20% Up to 20 percent lower risk for people who take 162 mg (½ tablet) daily or every other day; reduces the likelihood of blood clots (should be medically recommended; long-term use can have serious side effects)
Reduce hostility and other forms of psychological stress.	Extent of risk reduction not yet known.

[a]Recall from Chapter 13 that heavy alcohol use increases the risk of many diseases, including cardiovascular disease.

Sources: Agarwal, 2002; American Heart Association, 2006b; Ho, Hankey, & Eikelboom, 2004.

doctors. The doctors were far less likely to suspect heart problems in women—especially African-American women, who are at greater risk for heart disease than Caucasian-American women (Schulman et al., 1999). In follow-ups of victims of full-blown heart attacks, once again women—and especially African-American women—were less likely to be offered costly, invasive treatment, such as angioplasty and bypass surgery (Brown, 2002; Watson et al., 2002).

■ **Osteoporosis.** When age-related bone loss is severe, a condition called **osteoporosis** develops. This disorder, affecting more than 25 million Americans and 1.4 million Canadians, greatly magnifies the risk of bone fractures (Osteoporosis Society of Canada, 2006; U.S. Department of Health and Human Services, 2005h). In the largest study of osteoporosis conducted to date, involving more than 200,000 postmenopausal middle-aged women, 40 percent had bone density levels low enough to be of concern, and 7 percent were diagnosed with the disorder (Chestnut, 2001). Osteoporosis affects the majority of people of both sexes over age 70 (Donatelle, 2004). Although we associate it with a slumped-over posture, a shuffling gait, and a "dowager's hump" in the upper back, this extreme is rare. Because the bones gradually become more porous over many years, osteoporosis may not be evident until fractures—typically in the spine, hips, and wrist—occur or are discovered through X-rays.

A major factor related to osteoporosis is the decline in estrogen associated with menopause. In middle and late adulthood, women lose about 50 percent of their bone mass, about half of it in the first 10 years following menopause. The earlier a woman reaches menopause, the greater her chances of developing osteoporosis related to estrogen loss. In men, the age-related decrease in testosterone—though much more gradual than estrogen loss in women—contributes to bone loss because the body converts some to estrogen.

Heredity plays an important role. A family history of osteoporosis increases risk, with identical twins more likely than fraternal twins to share the disorder (Notelovitz, 2002). People with thin, small-framed bodies are more likely to be affected because they typically attain a lower peak bone mass in adolescence. In contrast, higher bone density makes African Americans less susceptible than Asian Americans, Caucasians, and Hispanics. An unhealthy lifestyle also contributes: A calcium-deficient diet and physical inactivity both reduce bone mass, as do cigarette smoking and alcohol consumption, which interfere with the replacement of bone cells (Chakkalakal, 2005; Liu et al., 2001).

When major bone fractures (such as the hip) occur, 10 to 20 percent of patients die within a year (Reginster & Burlet, 2006). Because osteoporosis usually develops earlier in women than in men, it has become known as a "women's disease," and men are far less likely to be screened and treated for it (Kiebzak et al., 2002). Compared with women, men with hip fractures tend to be older and to lack a history of interventions aimed at preserving bone density. Probably for these reasons, the one-year mortality rate after hip fracture is nearly twice as great for men as for women (Campion & Maricic, 2003).

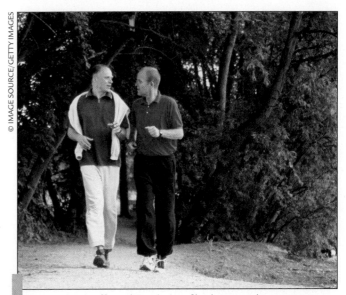

Osteoporosis affects the majority of both men and women over age 70. The best way to reduce the risk is through early prevention: increasing calcium and vitamin D intake and engaging in regular exercise in childhood, adolescence, and early adulthood. This middle-aged father and young adult son enjoy walking—a weight-bearing exercise recommended for bone strengthening.

To treat osteoporosis, doctors recommend a diet enriched with calcium and vitamin D (which promotes calcium absorption), weight-bearing exercise (walking rather than swimming), and bone-strengthening medications. A better way to reduce lifelong risk is through early prevention: maximizing peak bone density by increasing calcium and vitamin D intake and engaging in regular exercise in childhood, adolescence, and early adulthood (NIH Consensus Development Panel, 2001).

Hostility and Anger

Whenever Trisha's sister Dottie called, she seemed like a powder keg ready to explode. Dottie was critical of her boss at work and dissatisfied with the way Trisha, a lawyer, had handled the family's affairs after their father died. All conversations ended with Dottie making demeaning, hurtful remarks as her anger surfaced: "Any lawyer knows that, Trisha. How could you be so stupid! I should have called a *real* lawyer." "You and Devin are so stuck in your privileged lives that you can't think of anyone else. You don't know what work *is*."

Trisha would listen as long as she could bear, then warn, "Dottie, if you continue, I'm going to hang up. . . . Dottie, I'm ending this right now!"

Dottie's life was full of health-related issues. At age 53, she had high blood pressure, difficulty sleeping, and back pain. In the past five years, she had been hospitalized five times—twice for treatment of digestive problems, twice for an irregular heartbeat, and once for a benign tumor on her thyroid gland. Trisha often wondered whether Dottie's personal style was partly responsible for her physical condition.

That hostility and anger might have negative effects on health is a centuries-old idea. Several decades ago, researchers first tested this notion by identifying 35- to 59-year-old men who displayed the **Type A behavior pattern**—extreme competitiveness, ambition, impatience, hostility, angry outbursts, and a sense of time pressure. They found that within the next 8 years, Type As were more than twice as likely as Type Bs (people with a more relaxed disposition) to develop heart disease (Rosenman et al., 1975).

Later studies, however, often failed to confirm these results. Type A is actually a mix of behaviors, only one or two of which affect health. Current evidence pinpoints hostility as the "toxic" ingredient of Type A, since isolating it from global Type A consistently predicts heart disease and other health problems in both men and women (Aldwin et al., 2001; Eaker et al., 2004; Matthews et al., 2004; Williams, 2000). The risk of atherosclerosis is 2½ times higher in adults scoring high on hostility measures than in those who score low (Iribarren et al., 2000).

Recent findings suggest that *expressed hostility* in particular—frequent angry outbursts; rude, disagreeable behavior; critical and condescending nonverbal cues during social interaction, including glares; expressions of contempt and disgust; and a hard, insistent voice—leads to greater cardiovascular arousal, health complaints, and illness (Chesney et al., 1997). As people get angry, heart rate, blood pressure, and stress hormones escalate until the body's response is extreme.

Of course, people who are repeatedly enraged are more likely to be depressed and dissatisfied with their lives, to lack social supports, and to engage in unhealthy behaviors (Siegler et al., 2003). But hostility predicts health problems even after such factors as smoking, alcohol consumption, overweight, general unhappiness, and negative life events are controlled. And because men score higher in hostility than women (Dottie is an exception), emotional style may contribute to the sex differences in heart disease described earlier (Stoney & Engebretson, 1994).

Can Dottie preserve her health by bottling up her hostility instead of expressing it? Repeatedly suppressing overt anger or ruminating about past anger-provoking events is also associated with high blood pressure and heart disease (Hogan & Linden, 2004; Julkunen, 1996). A better alternative, as we will see, is to develop effective ways of handling stress and conflict.

Adapting to the Physical Challenges of Midlife

Middle adulthood is often a productive time of life, when people attain their greatest accomplishments and satisfactions. Nevertheless, it takes considerable stamina to cope with the full array of changes this period can bring. Devin responded to his expanding waistline and cardiovascular symptoms by leaving his desk twice a week to attend a low-impact aerobics class and by reducing job-related stress through daily 10-minute meditation sessions. Aware of her sister Dottie's difficulties, Trisha resolved to handle her own hostile feelings more adaptively. And her generally optimistic outlook enabled her to cope successfully with the physical changes of midlife, the pressures of her legal career, and Devin's chronic illness.

Stress Management

Turn back to Chapter 13, page 448, and review the negative consequences of psychological stress on the cardiovascular, immune, and gastrointestinal systems. As adults encounter problems at home and at work, daily hassles can add up to a serious stress load. Stress management is important at any age, but in middle adulthood it can limit the age-related rise in illness and, when disease strikes, reduce its severity.

Applying What We Know on the following page summarizes effective ways to reduce stress. Even when stressors cannot be eliminated, people can change how they handle some and view others. At work, Trisha focused on problems she could control—not on her boss's irritability, but on ways to delegate routine tasks to her staff so she could focus on problems that required her knowledge and skills. When Dottie phoned, Trisha learned to distinguish normal emotional reactions from unreasonable self-blame. Instead of interpreting Dottie's anger as a sign of her own incompetence, she reminded herself of Dottie's difficult temperament and hard life. And greater life experience helped her accept change as inevitable, so that she was better equipped to deal with the jolt of sudden events, such as Devin's hospitalization for treatment of heart disease.

Notice how Trisha called on two general strategies for coping with stress, discussed in Chapter 10: (1) *problem-centered coping,* in which she appraised the situation as changeable, identified the difficulty, and decided what to do about it, and (2) *emotion-centered coping,* which is internal, private, and aimed at controlling distress when little can be done about a situation. Longitudinal research shows that adults who

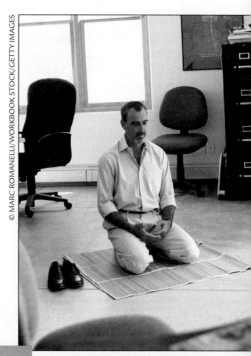

© MARC ROMANELLI/WORKBOOK STOCK/GETTY IMAGES

Stress management is important at any age, but in middle adulthood it can limit the age-related rise in illness and, when disease strikes, reduce its severity. This man has learned to use yoga to calm and center himself while he is at work.

Managing Stress

Strategy	Description
Reevaluate the situation.	Learn to differentiate normal reactions from those based on irrational beliefs.
Focus on events you can control.	Don't worry about things you cannot change or that may never happen; focus on strategies for handling events under your control.
View life as fluid.	Expect change and accept it as inevitable; then many unanticipated changes will have less emotional impact.
Consider alternatives.	Don't rush into action; think before you act.
Set reasonable goals for yourself.	Aim high, but be realistic about your capacities, motivation, and the situation.
Exercise regularly.	A physically fit person can better handle stress, both physically and emotionally.
Master relaxation techniques.	Relaxation helps refocus energies and reduce the physical discomfort of stress. Classes and self-help books teach these techniques.
Use constructive approaches to anger reduction.	Delay responding ("Let me check into that and get back to you"); use mentally distracting behaviors (counting to 10 backwards) and self-instruction (a covert "Stop!") to control anger arousal; then engage in calm, self-controlled problem solving ("I should call him rather than confront him personally").
Seek social support.	Friends, family members, co-workers, and organized support groups can offer information, assistance, and suggestions for coping with stressful situations.

effectively reduce stress move flexibly between problem-centered and emotion-centered techniques, depending on the situation (Zakowski et al., 2001). Their approach is deliberate, thoughtful, and respectful of both themselves and others. In contrast, ineffective coping is largely emotion-centered and either impulsive or escapist (Lazarus, 1991, 1999).

Constructive approaches to anger reduction are a vital health intervention (refer again to Applying What We Know). Teaching people to be assertive rather than hostile and to negotiate rather than explode interrupts the intense physiological response that intervenes between psychological stress and illness. Sometimes it is best to delay responding by simply leaving a provocative situation, as Trisha did when she told Dottie that she would hang up after one more insult (Deffenbacher, 1994).

As noted in Chapter 13, people tend to cope with stress more effectively as they move from early to middle adulthood. They may become more realistic about their ability to change situations and more skilled at anticipating stressful events and taking steps to avoid them (Aldwin & Levenson, 2002). Furthermore, when middle-aged adults surmount a highly stressful experience, they often report lasting personal benefits—for some, a greater sense of mastery as they look back with amazement at what they were able to accomplish under extremely trying conditions. A serious illness and brush with death commonly brings changes in values and perspectives, such as rediscovery of the importance of health-promoting behaviors and of family relationships (Aldwin, Sutton, & Lachman, 1996). In these ways, managing intense stress can serve as a context for positive development.

But for people who do have difficulty handling midlife's challenges, communities provide fewer social supports than for young adults or senior citizens. For example, Jewel had little knowledge of what to expect during the climacteric. "It would have helped to have a support group so I could have learned about menopause and dealt with it more easily," she told Trisha. Community programs addressing typical midlife concerns, such as those of adult learners returning to college and caregivers of elderly parents, can reduce stress during this period.

Exercise

Regular exercise, as noted in Chapter 13, has a range of physical and psychological benefits—among them, equipping adults to handle stress more effectively. Heading for his first aerobics class, Devin wondered, Can starting to exercise at age 50 counteract years of physical inactivity? His question is important: More than half of North American middle-aged adults are sedentary, and half of those who begin an exercise program discontinue it within the first 6 months. Even among those who stay active, fewer than 20 percent exercise at levels that lead to health benefits (Canadian Fitness and Lifestyle Research Institute, 2002; U.S. Department of Health and Human Services, 2005h).

A person beginning to exercise in midlife must overcome initial barriers and ongoing obstacles—lack of time and energy, inconvenience, work conflicts, and health factors (such as overweight). *Self-efficacy*—belief in one's ability to succeed—is just as vital in adopting, maintaining, and exerting oneself in an exercise regimen as it is in career progress (see Chapter 14). An important outcome of starting an exercise program is that sedentary adults gain in self-efficacy, which further promotes physical activity (McAuley & Blissmer, 2000; Wilbur et al., 2005). Enhanced physical fitness, in turn, prompts middle-aged adults to feel better about their physical selves. Over time, their physical self-esteem—sense of body conditioning and attractiveness—rises (McAuley, Mihalko, & Bane, 1997).

The exercise format that works best depends on the beginning exerciser's characteristics. Normal-weight adults are more likely to stick with group classes than are overweight adults, who may feel embarrassed and struggle to keep up with the pace. Overweight people do better with an individualized, home-based routine planned by a consultant (King, 2001). However, adults with highly stressful lives are more likely to persist in group classes, offering a regular schedule and the face-to-face support of others, than in a home-based program (King et al., 1997). Yet when stressed people do manage to sustain a home-based program, it substantially reduces stress—more so than the group format (King, Taylor, & Haskell, 1993). Perhaps succeeding on their own helps stressed adults gain better control over their lives.

Accessible, attractive, and safe exercise environments—parks, walking and biking trails, and community recreation centers—and frequent opportunities to observe others using them also promote physical activity (King et al., 2000). Besides health problems and daily stressors, low-SES adults often mention inconvenient access to facilities, expense, and unsafe neighborhoods as barriers to exercise—important reasons that activity level declines sharply with SES (Burton, Turrell, & Oldenburg, 2003; Wilbur et al., 2003). Interventions aimed at increasing physical activity among low-SES adults must address the availability of low-cost facilities and safe neighborhoods, in addition to lifestyle and motivational factors.

An Optimistic Outlook

What type of individual is likely to cope adaptively with stress brought on by the inevitable changes of life? Researchers interested in this question have identified a set of three personal qualities—control, commitment, and challenge—that, together, they call **hardiness** (Maddi, 1999).

Trisha fit the pattern of a hardy individual. First, she regarded most experiences as *controllable.* "You can't stop all bad things from happening," she advised Jewel after hearing about her menopausal symptoms, "but you can try to do something about them." Second, Trisha displayed a *committed,* involved approach to daily activities, finding interest and meaning in almost all of them. Finally, she viewed change as a *challenge*—a normal part of life and a chance for personal growth.

Research shows that hardiness influences the extent to which people appraise stressful situations as manageable, interesting, and enjoyable. These positive appraisals, in turn, predict health-promoting behaviors, tendency to seek social support, and fewer physical symptoms (Florian, Mikulincer, & Taubman, 1995; Smith, Young, & Lee, 2004). Furthermore,

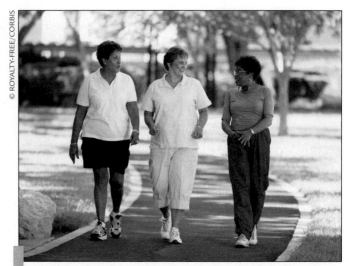

Low-SES adults often mention lack of convenient facilities, expense, and unsafe neighborhoods as barriers to exercise. Attractive, safe parks and trails, and frequent opportunities to observe others using them, promote physical activity.

high-hardy individuals are likely to use active, problem-centered coping strategies in situations they can control. In contrast, low-hardy people more often use emotion-centered and avoidant coping strategies—for example, saying, "I wish I could change how I feel," denying that the stressful event occurred, or eating and drinking to forget about it (Maddi & Hightower, 1999; Soderstrom et al., 2000).

In some studies, hardiness-related positive appraisals were associated with lower physiological arousal to stress—a major means by which hardiness is believed to protect against illness. This link does not always appear, perhaps because a hardy person's active coping sometimes leads to greater physiological arousal. But over time, this increase may be offset by a calm that comes with effective stress management (Wiebe & Williams, 1992). In support of this idea, the optimistic component of hardiness predicts lower average blood pressure, measured over a three-day period (Räikkönen et al., 1999). And in a longitudinal study of more than 400 medical-clinic patients, optimism was positively related to self-reported physical and mental health 30 years later (Maruta et al., 2002).

In this and previous chapters, we have seen that many factors act as stress-resistant resources—among them heredity, diet, exercise, social support, and coping strategies. Research on hardiness adds yet another ingredient: a generally optimistic outlook and zest for life.

Gender and Aging: A Double Standard

Negative stereotypes of aging, which lead many middle-aged adults to fear physical changes, are more likely to be applied to women than to men, yielding a double standard. Though many women in midlife say they have "hit their stride"—feel assertive, confident, versatile, and capable of resolving life's problems—people often rate them as less attractive and as having more negative characteristics than middle-aged men. In some studies, aging men actually gain slightly in positive judgments of appearance, maturity, and power, whereas aging women show a decline. And the sex of the person doing the rating makes a difference: Men judge an aging female much more harshly than women do (Kogan & Mills, 1992).

These effects appear more often when people rate photos as opposed to verbal descriptions of men and women. The ideal of a sexually attractive woman—smooth skin, good muscle tone, lustrous hair—may be at the heart of the double standard of aging. Recall from Chapter 14 that women prefer same-age or slightly older sexual partners, whereas men prefer younger partners. To explain why, evolutionary theory points to sex differences in reproductive capacity, whereas social learning theory emphasizes gender roles (see page 468). Some evidence suggests that the end of a woman's ability to bear children contributes to negative judgments, especially by men (Marcus-Newhall, Thompson, & Thomas, 2001). Yet societal forces exaggerate this view. For example, middle-aged people in media ads are usually male executives, fathers, and grandfathers—images of competence and security. And many more cosmetic products designed to hide signs of aging are offered for women than for men.

At one time in our evolutionary history, this double standard may have been adaptive. Today, as many couples limit childbearing and devote more time to career and leisure pursuits, it has become irrelevant. And new surveys suggest that the double standard is declining—that more people are viewing middle age as a potentially upbeat, satisfying time for both genders (Menon, 2002). Models of older women with lives full of intimacy, accomplishment, hope, and imagination are promoting acceptance of physical aging and a new vision of growing older—one that emphasizes gracefulness, fulfillment, and inner strength.

Ask Yourself

Review

Cite evidence that biological aging, individual heredity, and environmental factors contribute to osteoporosis.

Apply

During a routine physical exam, Dr. Furrow gave 55-year-old Bill a battery of tests for cardiovascular disease but did not assess his bone density. In contrast, when 60-year-old Cara complained of chest pains, Dr. Furrow opted to "wait and see" before initiating further testing. What might account for Dr. Furrow's different approaches to Cara and Bill?

Connect

According to the lifespan perspective, development is multidimensional—affected by biological, psychological, and social forces. Provide examples of how this assumption characterizes health at midlife.

Reflect

Which midlife health problem is of greatest personal concern to you? What steps can you take now to help prevent it?

Cognitive Development

In middle adulthood, the cognitive demands of everyday life extend to new and sometimes more challenging situations. Consider a typical day in the lives of Devin and Trisha. Recently appointed dean of faculty at a small college, Devin was at his desk by 7:00 A.M. In between strategic-planning meetings, he reviewed files of applicants for new positions, worked on the coming year's budget, and spoke at an alumni luncheon. Meanwhile, Trisha prepared for a civil trial, participated in jury selection, and then joined the other top lawyers at her firm for a conference about management issues. That evening, Trisha and Devin advised their 20-year-old son, Mark, who had dropped by to discuss his uncertainty over whether to change his college major. By 7:30 P.M., Trisha was off to an evening meeting of the local school board. And Devin left for a biweekly gathering of an amateur quartet in which he played the cello.

Middle adulthood is a time of expanding responsibilities—on the job, in the community, and at home. To juggle diverse roles effectively, Devin and Trisha called on a wide array of intellectual abilities, including accumulated knowledge, verbal fluency, memory, rapid analysis of information, reasoning, problem solving, and expertise in their areas of specialization. What changes in thinking take place in middle adulthood? How does vocational life—a major arena in which cognition is expressed—influence intellectual skills? And what can be done to support the rising tide of adults who are returning to college in hopes of enhancing their knowledge and quality of life?

Changes in Mental Abilities

At age 50, when he occasionally couldn't recall a name or had to pause in the middle of a lecture or speech to think about what to say next, Devin wondered, Are these signs of an aging mind? Twenty years earlier, he had taken little notice of the same events. His questioning stems from widely held stereotypes of older adults as forgetful, confused, and fragile. Most cognitive aging research has focused on deficits while neglecting cognitive stability and gains.

As we examine changes in thinking in middle adulthood, we will revisit the theme of diversity in development. Different aspects of cognitive functioning show different patterns of change. Although declines occur in some areas, most people display cognitive competence, especially in familiar contexts, and some attain outstanding accomplishment. As we will see, some apparent decrements in cognitive aging result from weaknesses in the research itself! Overall, the evidence supports an optimistic view of adult cognitive potential.

The research we are about to consider brings into bold relief core assumptions of the lifespan perspective: development as *multidimensional,* or the combined result of biological, psychological, and social forces; development as *multidirectional,* or the joint expression of growth and decline, with the precise mix varying across abilities and individuals; and development as *plastic*, or open to change, depending on how a person's biological and environmental history combines with current life conditions. You may find it helpful to return to pages 9–10 in Chapter 1 to review these ideas.

Cohort Effects

Research using intelligence tests sheds light on the widely held belief that intelligence inevitably declines in middle and late adulthood as the brain deteriorates. Many early cross-sectional studies showed this pattern—a peak in performance at age 35 followed by a steep drop into old age. But widespread testing of college students and soldiers in the 1920s provided a convenient opportunity to conduct longitudinal research, retesting participants in middle adulthood. These findings revealed an age-related increase! To explain this contradiction, K. Warner Schaie (1998, 2005) used a sequential design, combining longitudinal and cross-sectional approaches (see page 35 in Chapter 1) in the Seattle Longitudinal Study.

In 1956, people ranging in age from 22 to 70 were tested cross-sectionally. Then, at regular intervals, longitudinal follow-ups were conducted and new samples added, yielding a total of 5,000 participants, five cross-sectional comparisons, and longitudinal data spanning more than 60 years. Findings on five

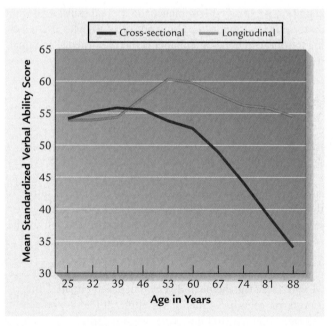

■ **FIGURE 15.4 Cross-sectional and longitudinal trends in verbal ability, illustrating cohort effects.** The steep cross-sectional decline is largely due to better health and education in younger generations. When adults are followed longitudinally, their verbal scores rise during early and middle adulthood and gradually decline during later years. However, this longitudinal trend does not hold for all abilities. (Adapted from K. W. Schaie, 1988, "Variability in Cognitive Functioning in the Elderly," in M. A. Bender, R. C. Leonard, & A. D. Woodhead, Eds., *Phenotypic Variation in Populations,* New York: Plenum, p. 201. Reprinted by permission.)

mental abilities showed the typical cross-sectional drop after the mid-thirties. But longitudinal trends for those abilities revealed modest gains in midlife, sustained into the fifties and the early sixties, after which performance decreased gradually.

Figure 15.4 illustrates Schaie's cross-sectional and longitudinal outcomes for just one intellectual factor: verbal ability. *Cohort effects* are largely responsible for this difference. In cross-sectional research, each new generation experienced better health and education than the one before it. Also, the tests given may tap abilities less often used by older individuals, whose lives no longer require that they learn information for its own sake but, instead, skillfully solve real-world problems.

Crystallized and Fluid Intelligence

A close look at diverse mentally abilities shows that only certain ones follow the longitudinal pattern identified in Figure 15.4. To appreciate this variation, let's consider two broad mental abilities, each of which includes an array of specific intellectual factors.

The first of these broad abilities, **crystallized intelligence,** refers to skills that depend on accumulated knowledge and experience, good judgment, and mastery of social conventions—abilities acquired because they are valued by the individual's culture. Devin made use of crystallized intelligence when he expressed himself articulately at the alumni luncheon and suggested effective ways to save money in budget planning. On intelligence tests, vocabulary, general information, verbal comprehension, and logical reasoning items measure crystallized intelligence.

In contrast, **fluid intelligence** depends more heavily on basic information-processing skills—ability to detect relationships among visual stimuli, speed of analyzing information, and capacity of working memory. Though fluid intelligence often combines with crystallized intelligence to support effective reasoning and problem solving, it is believed to be influenced less by culture than by conditions in the brain and by learning unique to the individual (Horn & Noll, 1997). Intelligence test items reflecting fluid abilities include spatial visualization, digit span, letter-number sequencing, and symbol search. (Refer to page 309 in Chapter 9 for examples.)

Many cross-sectional studies show that crystallized intelligence increases steadily though middle adulthood, whereas fluid intelligence begins to decline in the twenties. These trends have been found repeatedly in investigations in which younger and older participants had similar education and general health status, largely correcting for cohort effects (Horn, Donaldson, & Engstrom, 1981; Kaufman & Horn, 1996; Park et al., 2002). In one such investigation, including nearly 2,500 mentally and physically healthy 16- to 85-year-olds, verbal (crystallized) IQ peaked between ages 45 and 54 and did not decline until the eighties! Nonverbal (fluid) IQ, in contrast, dropped steadily over the entire age range (Kaufman, 2001).

The midlife rise in crystallized abilities makes sense because adults are constantly adding to their knowledge and skills at work, at home, and in leisure activities. In addition, many crystallized skills are practiced almost daily. But does longitudinal evidence confirm the progressive fall-off in fluid intelligence? And if so, how can we explain it?

■ **Schaie's Seattle Longitudinal Study.** Figure 15.5 shows Schaie's longitudinal findings in detail. The five factors that gained in early and middle adulthood—verbal ability, inductive reasoning, verbal memory, spatial orientation, and numeric ability—include both crystallized and fluid skills. Their paths of change confirm that midlife is a time of peak performance on some of the most complex mental abilities (Willis & Schaie, 1999). According to these findings, middle-aged adults are intellectually "in their prime," not—as stereotypes would have it—"over the hill."

Figure 15.5 also shows a sixth ability, *perceptual speed*—a fluid skill in which participants must, for example, identify within a time limit which of five shapes is identical to a model or whether pairs of multidigit numbers are the same or different (Schaie, 1994, 1996, 1998). Perceptual speed decreased from the twenties to the late eighties—a pattern that fits with a wealth of research indicating that cognitive processing slows as people get older. Also notice in Figure 15.5 how, late in life, fluid factors (spatial orientation, numeric ability, and perceptual speed) show greater decrements than crystallized factors (verbal ability, inductive reasoning, and verbal memory). These trends have been confirmed in short-term longitudinal follow-ups of individuals varying widely in age (McArdle et al., 2002).

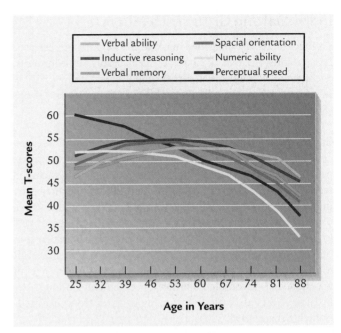

■ **FIGURE 15.5 Longitudinal trends in six mental abilities, from the Seattle Longitudinal Study.** In five abilities, modest gains occurred into the fifties and early sixties, followed by gradual declines. The sixth ability—perceptual speed—decreased steadily from the twenties to the late eighties. And late in life, fluid factors (spatial orientation, perceptual speed, and numeric ability) showed greater decrements than crystallized factors (verbal ability, inductive reasoning, and verbal memory). (From K. W. Schaie, 1994, "The Course of Adult Intellectual Development," *American Psychologist, 49,* p. 308. Copyright © 1994 by the American Psychological Association. Reprinted by permission.)

As this husband and wife paleontologist/paleobotanist team work at an archeological dig site in the Red Deer River badlands of Alberta, Canada, they draw on years of accumulated knowledge and experience. Longitudinal research confirms that midlife is a time of peak performance on some of the most complex mental abilities.

■ **Explaining Changes in Mental Abilities.** Some theorists believe that a general slowing of central nervous system functioning underlies nearly all age-related declines in cognitive performance (Salthouse, 1993, 1996). Many studies offer at least partial support for this idea. For example, Kaufman (2001) reported that scores on speeded tasks mirror the regular, age-related decline in fluid-task performance. Researchers have also identified other important changes in information processing, some of which may be triggered by declines in speed.

But before turning to this evidence, let's clarify why research reveals gains followed by stability in crystallized abilities, despite a much earlier decline in fluid intelligence, or basic information-processing skills. First, the decrease in basic processing, while substantial after age 45, may not be great enough to affect many well-practiced performances until quite late in life. Second, as we will see, adults can often compensate for cognitive limitations by drawing on their cognitive strengths. Finally, as people discover that they are no longer as good as they once were at certain tasks, they accommodate, shifting to activities that depend less on cognitive efficiency and more on accumulated knowledge (Salthouse, 1991). Thus, the basketball player becomes a coach, the once quick-witted salesperson a manager.

Individual and Group Differences

The age trends just described mask large individual differences. Some adults, because of illness or unfavorable environments, decline intellectually much earlier than others. And many show full functioning, even in fluid abilities, at an advanced age (Schaie, 1989).

Adults who use their intellectual skills seem to maintain them longer. In the Seattle Longitudinal Study, declines were delayed for people with above-average education, complex occupations, and stimulating leisure pursuits that included reading, traveling, attending cultural events, and participating in clubs and professional organizations. People with flexible personalities, lasting marriages (especially to a cognitively high-functioning partner), and absence of cardiovascular and other chronic diseases were also likely to maintain mental abilities well into late adulthood. And being economically well-off was linked to favorable cognitive development, undoubtedly because SES is associated with many of the factors just mentioned (Schaie, 1996, 2000).

Several sex differences also emerged, consistent with those obtained in childhood and adolescence. In early and middle adulthood, women outperformed men on verbal tasks and perceptual speed, while men excelled at spatial skills (Maitland et al., 2000). Overall, however, changes in mental abilities over the adult years were remarkably similar for the two sexes, defying the stereotype that older women are less competent than older men.

Furthermore, cohort effects were evident when the baby boom generation, now middle-aged, was compared with the previous generation at the same age. On verbal memory, inductive reasoning, and spatial orientation, the baby boom cohort performed substantially better, reflecting generational advances in education, technology, environmental stimulation, and health care (Willis & Schaie, 1999). These gains are expected to continue in the twenty-first century: Today's children, adolescents, and young adults also attain higher mental test scores than children of past generations (Flynn, 1999, 2003). Interestingly, numeric ability declined in later-born cohorts in the Seattle Longitudinal Study. Reliance on calculators and computers seems to have compromised later generations' calculation skills!

Finally, adults who maintained higher levels of perceptual speed tended to be advantaged in other cognitive capacities. As we turn to information processing in midlife, we will see why a decrement in processing speed affects other aspects of cognitive functioning.

Information Processing

Information-processing researchers interested in adult development usually use the model of the mental system introduced in Chapter 5 (see page 161) to guide their exploration of different aspects of thinking. As processing speed slows, certain aspects of attention and memory decline. Yet

midlife is also a time of great expansion in cognitive competence as adults apply their vast knowledge and life experience to problem solving in the everyday world.

Speed of Processing

Devin watched with fascination as his 20-year-old son, Mark, played a computer game, responding to multiple onscreen cues in rapid-fire fashion. When Devin tried it, although he practiced over several days, his performance remained well behind Mark's. Similarly, on a family holiday in Australia, Mark adjusted quickly to driving on the left side of the road, but after a week, Trisha and Devin still felt confused at intersections, where rapid responses were needed.

These real-life experiences fit with laboratory findings. On both simple reaction-time tasks (pushing a button in response to a light) and complex ones (pushing a left-hand button to a blue light, a right-hand button to a yellow light), response time increases steadily from the early twenties into the nineties. The more complex the situation, the more disadvantaged older adults are. Though small—less than 1 second in most studies—the decline in speed is nevertheless of practical significance (Salthouse, 2000; Deary & Der, 2005).

What causes this age-related slowing of cognitive processing? Researchers agree that changes in the brain are responsible but disagree on the precise explanation. According to the **neural network view,** as neurons in the brain die, breaks in neural networks occur. The brain adapts by forming bypasses—new synaptic connections that go around the breaks but are less efficient (Cerella, 1990). A second hypothesis, the **information-loss view,** suggests that older adults experience greater loss of information as it moves through the cognitive system. As a result, the whole system must slow down to inspect and interpret the information. Imagine making a photocopy, then using it to make another copy. Each subsequent copy is less clear. Similarly, with each step of thinking, information degrades. The older the adult, the more exaggerated this effect. Complex tasks, which have more processing steps, are more affected by information loss (Myerson et al., 1990).

Processing speed predicts adults' performance on many tests of complex abilities. The slower their reaction time, the lower people's scores on memory, reasoning, and problem-solving tasks, with relationships particularly strong for fluid-ability items (Salthouse, 2005). Indeed, as adults get older, correlations between processing speed and other cognitive performances strengthen (see Figure 15.6). This suggests that processing speed is a core ability that contributes broadly to declines in cognitive functioning, which become more widespread and pronounced with aging (Li et al., 2004).

Yet processing speed is far from a perfect predictor of older adults' performances—especially, their everyday activities. Many older adults engage in complex, familiar tasks with considerable proficiency. Devin, for example, played a Mozart quartet on his cello with great speed and dexterity, keeping up with three other players 10 years his junior. How did he manage? Compared with the others, he more often looked ahead in

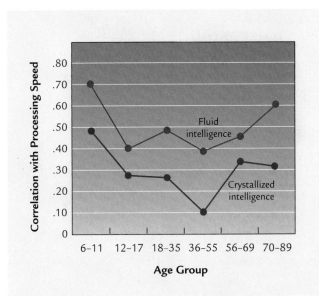

■ FIGURE 15.6 Age-related changes in correlations of processing speed with measures of fluid and crystallized intelligence. Correlations are higher at younger and at older ages. During childhood, gains in processing speed support development of other abilities and are related to mental test performance (see Chapter 9, page 302). As people age, declines in processing speed limit many abilities, but more so for fluid than crystallized skills. Note, however, that even at the oldest ages, correlations between processing speed and other abilities are moderate. (From S.-C. Li et al., 2004, "Transformations in the Couplings Among Intellectual Abilities and Constituent Cognitive Processes Across the Life Span," *Psychological Science, 15*, p. 160. © Association for Psychological Science. Reprinted by permission.)

the score. Using this compensatory approach, he could prepare a response in advance, thereby minimizing the importance of speed. In one study, researchers asked 19- to 72-year-olds to perform a variety of typing tasks and also tested their reaction time. Although reaction time slowed with age, typing speed did not change. Like Devin, older individuals looked further ahead in the material to be typed, anticipating their next keystrokes (Salthouse, 1984).

Knowledge and experience can also compensate for impairments in processing speed. Devin's many years of playing the cello and his familiarity with the Mozart quartet undoubtedly supported his ability to play swiftly and fluidly. Because older adults find ways to compensate for cognitive slowing on familiar tasks, their reaction time is considerably better on verbal items (indicating as quickly as possible whether a string of letters forms a word) than on nonverbal items (responding to a light or other signal) (Hultsch, MacDonald, & Dixon, 2002; Wingfield & Stine-Morrow, 2000).

Attention

Studies of attention focus on how much information adults can take into their mental systems at once; the extent to which they can attend selectively, ignoring irrelevant information;

and the ease with which they can adapt their attention, switching from one task to another as the situation demands. When Dottie telephoned, Trisha sometimes tried to prepare dinner or continue working on a legal brief while talking on the phone. But with age, she found it harder to engage in two activities simultaneously. Consistent with Trisha's experience, laboratory research reveals that sustaining two complex tasks at once becomes more challenging with age (Kausler, 1991; Madden & Plude, 1993). An age-related decrement also occurs in the ability to focus on relevant information and to switch back and forth between mental operations, such as judging one of a pair of numbers as "odd or even" on some trials, "more or less" on others (Kray & Lindenberger, 2000; Radvansky, Zacks, & Hasher, 2005).

These declines in attention might be due to the slowdown in information processing described earlier, which limits the amount of information a person can attend to at once (Plude & Hoyer, 1985). Reduced processing speed may also contribute to a related finding: a decrement with age in the ability to combine many pieces of visual information into a meaningful pattern. When the mind inspects stimuli slowly, they are more likely to remain disconnected. This problem, in turn, can intensify attentional difficulties (Plude & Doussard-Roosevelt, 1989).

As adults get older, *inhibition*—resistance to interference from irrelevant information—is also harder (Hasher, Zacks, & May, 1999). On *continuous performance tasks*, in which participants are shown a series of stimuli on a computer screen and asked to press the space bar only after a particular sequence occurs (for example, the letter K immediately followed by the letter A), performance declines steadily from the thirties into old age, with older adults making more errors of commission (pressing the space bar in response to incorrect letter sequences). And when extraneous noise is introduced, errors of omission (not pressing the space bar after a K–A sequence) also rise with age (Mani, Bedwell, & Miller, 2005). In everyday life, inhibitory difficulties cause older adults to appear

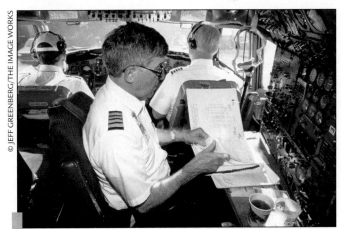

Airline pilots must divide their attention among several tasks, focus on relevant information within a complex field of stimulation, and switch often between mental operations. Because they routinely practice these skills, they show smaller age-related declines in attention than are typical in midlife.

distractible—inappropriately captured by a thought or a feature of the environment and diverted from the task at hand.

Again, adults can compensate for these changes. People highly experienced in attending to critical information and performing several tasks at once, such as air traffic controllers and pilots, know exactly what to look for. As a result, they show smaller age-related attentional declines (Morrow et al., 1994; Tsang & Shaner, 1998). Furthermore, practice can improve the ability to divide attention between two tasks, selectively focus on relevant information, and switch back and forth between mental operations. When older adults receive training in these skills, their performance improves as much as that of younger adults, although training does not close the gap between age groups (Kausler, 1994; Kramer, Hahn, & Gopher, 1998).

Memory

Memory is crucial for all aspects of information processing—an important reason that we place great value on a good memory in middle and late adulthood. From the twenties into the sixties, the amount of information people can retain in working memory diminishes. Whether given lists of words or digits or meaningful prose passages to learn, middle-aged and older adults recall less than young adults, although memory for prose suffers less than memory for list items (Hultsch et al., 1998; Salthouse & Skovronek, 1992).

This change is largely due to a decline in use of memory strategies on these tasks. Older individuals rehearse less than younger individuals—a difference believed to be due to a slower rate of thinking (Salthouse & Babcock, 1991). Older people cannot repeat new information to themselves as quickly as younger people.

Memory strategies of organization and elaboration are also applied less often and less effectively with age. (See Chapter 9, pages 302–303, to review these strategies.) Both require people to link incoming information with already stored information. Older adults are less likely to use organization and elaboration because they find it harder to retrieve information from long-term memory that would help them recall. For example, given a list of words containing *parrot* and *blue jay,* they don't immediately access the category "bird," even though they know it well (Hultsch et al., 1998). Why does this happen? Greater difficulty keeping one's attention on relevant as opposed to irrelevant information seems to be involved. As irrelevant stimuli take up space in working memory, less is available for the memory task at hand (O'Connor & Kaplan, 2003; Radvansky, Zacks, & Hasher, 2005).

But keep in mind that the memory tasks given by researchers require strategies that many adults seldom use and may not be motivated to use, since most are not in school (see Chapter 9, page 303). When a word list has a strong category-based structure, older adults organize as well as younger adults do (Small et al., 1999). And when instructed to organize or elaborate, middle-aged and older people do so willingly, and their performance improves.

Furthermore, tasks can be designed to help older people compensate for age-related declines in working memory—for

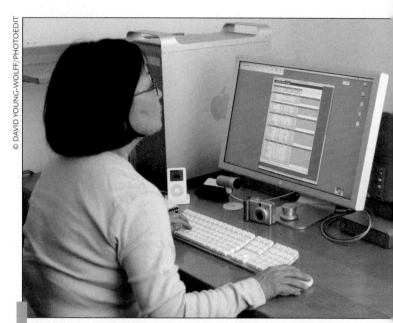

This woman studies information for a job training program, working at home at her own pace. Assessing older adults in highly structured, constrained conditions underestimates what they can remember when allowed to work in contexts that provide ample time to retrieve and apply previous, relevant knowledge.

example, by slowing the pace at which information is presented or cuing the link between new and previously stored information ("To learn these words, try thinking of the category 'bird'") (Hay & Jacoby, 1999; Kausler, 1994). In one study, adults ranging in age from 19 to 68 were shown a video and immediately tested on its content (a pressured, classroomlike condition). Then they were given a packet of information on the same topic as the video to study at their leisure and told to return three days later to be tested (a self-paced condition) (Beier & Ackerman, 2005). Performance declined with age only in the pressured condition, not in the self-paced condition. And although topic-relevant knowledge predicted better recall in both conditions, it did so more strongly in the self-paced condition, which granted participants ample time to retrieve and apply what they already knew.

As these findings illustrate, assessing older adults in highly structured, constrained conditions substantially underestimates what they can remember when given an opportunity to pace their own learning. When we consider the variety of memory skills we call on in daily life, the decrements just described are limited in scope. General *factual knowledge* (such as historical events), *procedural knowledge* (such as how to drive a car or solve a math problem), and knowledge related to one's occupation either remain unchanged or increase into midlife (Baltes, Dittmann-Kohli, & Dixon, 1984). Furthermore, middle-aged people who have trouble recalling something often draw on decades of accumulated *metacognitive knowledge* about how to maximize performance—reviewing major points before an important presentation, organizing notes and files so information can be found quickly, and parking the car in the same area of the parking lot each day. Research suggests that aging has little impact on metacognition (Berg, 2000; Schwartz & Frazier, 2005).

In sum, age-related changes in memory vary widely across tasks and individuals as people use their cognitive capacities to meet the requirements of their everyday worlds. This may remind you of Sternberg's *theory of successful intelligence,* described in Chapter 9—in particular, his notion of *practical intelligence* (see page 309). It emphasizes that intelligent people adapt their information-processing skills to fit with their personal desires and the demands of their environments. To understand memory development (and other aspects of cognition) in adulthood, we must view it in context. As we turn to problem solving, expertise, and creativity, we will encounter this theme again.

Practical Problem Solving and Expertise

One evening, as Devin and Trisha sat in the balcony of the Chicago Opera House awaiting curtain time, the announcement came that 67-year-old Ardis Krainik, the opera company's general director and "life force," had died. After a shocked hush, members of the audience began turning to one another, asking about the woman who had made the opera company into one of the world's greatest.

Starting as a chorus singer and clerk typist, Ardis rose rapidly through the ranks, becoming assistant to the director and developing a reputation for tireless work and unmatched organizational skill. When the opera company fell deeply into debt, Ardis—now the newly appointed general director—erased the deficit within a year and restored the company's sagging reputation. She charmed donors into making large contributions, attracted world-class singers, and filled the house to near capacity. On her office wall hung a sign she had received as a gift. It read, "Wonder Woman" (Rhein, 1997).

Ardis's story is a dramatic one, but all middle-aged adults encounter opportunities to display continued cognitive growth in the realm of **practical problem solving,** which requires people to size up real-world situations and analyze how best to achieve goals that have a high degree of uncertainty. Gains in *expertise*—an extensive, highly organized, and integrated knowledge base that can be used to support a high level of performance—help us understand why practical problem solving takes this leap forward.

The development of expertise is under way in early adulthood and reaches its height in midlife, leading to highly efficient and effective approaches to solving problems that are organized around abstract principles and intuitive judgments. Saturated with experience, the expert intuitively feels when an approach to a problem will work and when it will not. This rapid, implicit application of knowledge is the result of years of learning and experience (Ackerman, 2000; Wagner, 2000). It cannot be assessed by laboratory tasks or mental tests that do not call on this knowledge.

Expertise is not just the province of the highly educated and of those who rise to the top of administrative ladders. In a study of food service workers, researchers identified the diverse ingredients of expert performance in terms of physical skills (strength and dexterity); technical knowledge (of menu items, ordering, and food presentation); organizational skills (setting priorities, anticipating customer needs); and social skills (confident presentation and a pleasant, polished manner). Next, 20- to 60-year-olds with fewer than 2 to more than 10 years of experience were evaluated on these qualities. Although physical strength and dexterity declined with age, job knowledge and practice increased (Perlmutter, Kaplan, & Nyquist, 1990). Compared to younger adults with similar years of experience, middle-aged employees performed more competently, serving customers in especially adept, attentive ways.

Age-related advantages are also evident in solutions to everyday problems (Denney, 1990; Denney & Pearce, 1989). Consider the following dilemma:

> What would you do if you had a landlord who refused to make some expensive repairs you want done because he or she thinks they are too costly?
>
> (a) Try to make the repairs yourself.
>
> (b) Try to understand your landlord's view and decide whether they are necessary repairs.
>
> (c) Try to get someone to settle the dispute between you and your landlord.
>
> (d) Accept the situation and don't dwell on it. (Cornelius & Caspi, 1987, p. 146)

On tasks like these, middle-aged and older adults select better strategies (as rated by independent judges) than young adults.

In the preceding example, the preferred choice is (b), a problem-centered approach that involves seeking information and using it to guide action. From middle age on, adults place greater emphasis on thinking through a practical problem—trying to understand it better, interpret it from different perspectives, and solve it through logical analysis. Perhaps for this reason, middle-aged and older adults are more rational decision makers—less likely than young adults to select attractive-looking options that, on further reflection, are not the best (Kim & Hasher, 2005).

Creativity

As noted in Chapter 13, creative accomplishment tends to peak in the late thirties or early forties and then decline, but with considerable variation across individuals and disciplines. Some people produce highly creative works in later decades: In her early sixties, Martha Graham choreographed *Clytemnestra,* recognized as one of the great full-length modern-dance dramas. Igor Stravinsky composed his last major musical work at age 84. Charles Darwin finished *On the Origin of Species* at age 50 and continued to write groundbreaking books and papers in his sixties and seventies (Tahir & Gruber, 2003). And as with problem solving, the *quality* of creativity may change with advancing age—in at least three ways.

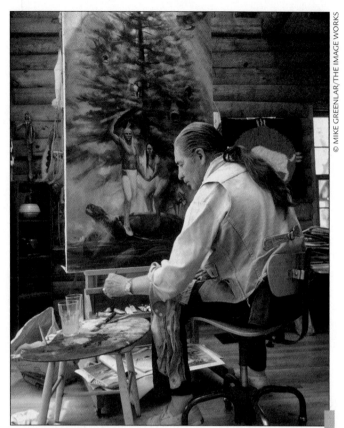

© MIKE GREENLAR/THE IMAGE WORKS

In middle adulthood, creativity becomes more thoughtful, integrative, and altruistic. Oren Lyons, spiritual leader of the Turtle Clan, Onondaga Nation of New York, puts finishing touches on his well-known painting, "Tree of Peace," which captures these qualities.

First, youthful creativity in literature and the arts is often spontaneous and intensely emotional, while creative works produced after age 40 often appear more deliberately thoughtful (Lubart & Sternberg, 1998). Perhaps for this reason, poets produce their most frequently cited works at younger ages than do authors of fiction and nonfiction (Cohen-Shalev, 1986). Poetry depends more on language play and "hot" expression of feelings, whereas story- and book-length works require extensive planning and molding.

Second, with age, many creators shift from generating unusual products to combining extensive knowledge and experience into unique ways of thinking (Abra, 1989; Sasser-Coen, 1993). Creative works by older adults more often sum up or integrate ideas. Mature academics typically devote less energy to new discoveries in favor of writing memoirs, histories of their field, and other reflective works. And in older creators' novels, scholarly writings, paintings, and musical compositions, living with old age and facing death are common themes (Beckerman, 1990; Sternberg & Lubart, 2001).

Finally, creativity in middle adulthood frequently reflects a transition from a largely egocentric concern with self-expression to more altruistic goals (Tahir & Gruber, 2003). As the middle-aged person overcomes the youthful illusion that life is eternal, the desire to contribute to humanity and enrich the lives of others increases.

Taken together, these changes may contribute to an overall decline in creative output in later decades. In reality, however, creativity takes new forms.

Information Processing in Context

Cognitive gains in middle adulthood are especially likely in areas involving experience-based buildup and transformation of knowledge and skills. As the evidence just reviewed confirms, processing speed varies with the situation. When given challenging real-world problems related to their expertise, middle-aged adults are likely to win out in both efficiency and excellence of thinking. Furthermore, on tasks and test items relevant to their real-life endeavors, intelligent, cognitively active older adults respond as quickly and competently as their younger counterparts do!

By middle adulthood, people's past and current experiences vary enormously—more so than in previous decades—and thinking is characterized by an increase in specialization as people branch out in various directions. Yet to reach their cognitive potential, middle-aged adults must have opportunities for continued growth. Let's see how vocational and educational environments can support cognition in midlife.

Ask Yourself

Review
Cite research findings on changes in crystallized and fluid intelligence during adulthood. What accounts for these differing trends?

Review
How does slowing of cognitive processing affect attention and memory in midlife? What can older adults do to compensate for these declines?

Apply
Asked about hiring older sales personnel, a department store manager replied, "They're my best employees!" Why does this manager find older employees desirable, despite the age-related decline in speed of processing?

Connect
In which aspects of cognition did Devin decline, and in which did he gain? How do changes in Devin's thinking reflect assumptions of the lifespan perspective?

www.ablongman.com/berk

Vocational Life and Cognitive Development

Vocational settings are vital contexts for maintaining previously acquired skills and learning new ones. Yet work environments vary in the degree to which they are cognitively stimulating and promote autonomy. And inaccurate, negative stereotypes of age-related problem-solving and decision-making skills can result in older employees being assigned less challenging work.

Recall from Chapter 13 that cognitive and personality characteristics affect occupational choice. Devin, for example, chose college teaching and administration because he enjoyed reading and writing, framing new ideas, and helping others learn. Once a person is immersed in a job, it influences cognition. In a study of over 600 U.S. men representing a wide range of occupations, researchers asked about the task complexity and self-direction of their jobs. During the interview, they also assessed cognitive flexibility, based on logical reasoning, awareness of both sides of an issue, and independence of judgment. A decade later, the job and cognitive variables were remeasured, permitting a look at their effects on each other. As expected, cognitively flexible men sought work that offered challenge and autonomy. But the relationship between vocational life and cognition was reciprocal—complex work also led to gains in cognitive flexibility (Kohn & Schooler, 1978).

These same findings emerged in large-scale studies carried out in Japan and Poland—cultures quite different from the United States (Kohn et al., 1990; Kohn & Slomczynski, 1990). In each nation, having a stimulating, nonroutine job helped explain the relationship between SES and flexible, abstract thinking. Furthermore, learning on the job generalizes to other realms of life. People who do intellectually demanding work seek out stimulating leisure pursuits, which also foster cognitive flexibility (Kohn et al., 2000). And because flexible thinkers come to value self-direction, for themselves and also for their children, they are likely to pass on their cognitive preferences to the next generation.

Is the impact of a challenging job on cognitive growth greatest for young adults, who are in the early phase of career development? In fact, research shows that people in their fifties and early sixties gain as much as those in their twenties and thirties. The relationship also holds for people of different generations and, therefore, widely varying life experiences (Avolio & Sosik, 1999; Miller, Slomczynski, & Kohn, 1985). Once again, we are reminded of the plasticity of development. Cognitive flexibility is responsive to vocational experience well into middle adulthood, and perhaps beyond. This means that more jobs should be designed to promote intellectual stimulation and challenge—factors linked to higher cognitive functioning later in the lifespan.

Adult Learners: Becoming a Student in Midlife

Adults are returning to undergraduate and graduate study in record numbers. During the past quarter-century, students over age 25 in North American colleges and universities increased from 28 to 40 percent of total enrollment, with an especially sharp rise in those over age 35 (Statistics Canada, 2001a; U.S. Department of Education, 2005b). They enroll for various reasons—a career change, a better income, self-enrichment, a sense of personal achievement, or just a degree. Among a sample of African-American women, additional motivations included serving as a role model for children and enriching their ethnic community as a whole (Coker, 2003). Life transitions often trigger a return to formal education, as with Devin and Trisha's friend Anya, who entered a nursing program after her last child left home. Divorce, widowhood, a job layoff, or a youngest child reaching school age are other transitions that commonly precede reentry (Donaldson & Graham, 1999).

Characteristics of Returning Students

About 60 percent of adult learners are women. As Anya's fear of not being able to handle class work suggests (see page 499), first-year reentry women report feeling more self-conscious, inadequate, and hesitant to talk in class than either returning men or traditional-age students (under age 25) (Wilke & Thompson, 1993). Their anxiety is due in part to not having practiced academic learning for many years but is also prompted by negative aging and gender stereotypes—erroneous beliefs that traditional-age students are smarter or that men are more logical and therefore more academically capable. And for minority students, ethnic stereotypes and prejudicial treatment are factors. One African-American mature graduate student commented, "An economics instructor I had used to make me feel stupid if I asked a question he felt I ought to have known the answer to. So eventually I stopped asking questions. I went to the side and got tutoring out of class" (Coker, 2003, p. 668).

Role demands outside of school—from spouses, children, other family members, friends, and employers—pull many returning women in conflicting directions. Those reporting high psychological stress typically have career rather than enrichment goals, young children, limited financial resources,

© TOM STEWART/CORBIS

When support systems are in place, most middle-aged, returning college students reap great personal benefits and do well academically. Success at coordinating education, family, and work demands leads to gains in self-efficacy and admiration from family members, friends, and co-workers.

and nonsupportive husbands (Novak & Thacker, 1991; Padula & Miller, 1999). As a classmate told Anya one day, "I tried keeping the book open and reading, cooking, and talking to the kids. It didn't work. They felt I was ignoring them."

Because of multiple demands on their time, mature-age women tend to take fewer credits, experience more interruptions in their academic programs, and progress at a slower pace than mature-age men. Role overload is the most common reason for not completing their degrees (Jacobs & King, 2002). But many express high motivation to work through those difficulties, referring to the excitement of learning, to the fulfillment academic success brings, and to their hope that a college education will improve both their work and family lives (Chao & Good, 2004).

Supporting Returning Students

As these findings suggest, social supports for returning students can make the difference between continuing in school and dropping out. Adult students need family members and friends who encourage their efforts and help them find time for uninterrupted study. Anya's classmate explained, "My doubts subsided when my husband volunteered, 'I can cook dinner and do the laundry. You take your books and do what you need to do.'" Institutional services for returning students

are also essential. Personal relationships with faculty, peer networks enabling adults to get to know one another, conveniently scheduled evening and Saturday classes, online courses, and financial aid for part-time students (many of whom are returning adults) increase the chances of academic success.

Although nontraditional students rarely require assistance in settling on career goals, they report a strong desire for help in choosing the most appropriate courses and in exploring jobs related to their talents (Luzzo, 1999). Academic advising and professional internship opportunities responsive to their needs are vital. Low-income students often need special assistance, such as academic tutoring, sessions in confidence building and assertiveness, and—in the case of ethnic minorities—help adjusting to styles of learning that are at odds with their cultural background.

Applying What We Know below suggests ways to facilitate adult reentry to college. When support systems are in place, most returning students reap great personal benefits and do well academically. Succeeding at coordinating education, family, and work demands leads to gains in self-efficacy and admiration from family members, friends, and co-workers (Chao & Good, 2004). Nontraditional students especially value forming new relationships, sharing opinions and experiences, and relating subject matter to their own lives. And their greater ability to integrate knowledge results in an enhanced appreciation of

Applying What We Know

Facilitating Adult Reentry to College

Sources of Support	Description
Partner and children	Value and encourage educational efforts.
	Help with household tasks to permit time for uninterrupted study.
Extended family and friends	Value and encourage educational efforts.
Educational institution	Provide orientation programs and literature that inform adult students about services and social supports.
	Provide counseling and intervention addressing academic weaknesses, self-doubts about success, and matching courses to career goals.
	Facilitate peer networks through regular meetings or phone contacts.
	Promote personal relationships with faculty.
	Encourage active engagement and discussion in classes and integration of course content with real-life experiences.
	Offer evening, Saturday, and off-campus classes and online courses.
	Provide financial aid for part-time students.
	Initiate campaigns to recruit returning students, including those from low-income families and ethnic minority groups.
	Help students with young children find child care arrangements and provide on-campus child care.
Workplace	Value and encourage educational efforts.
	Offer flexible work schedules to make possible coordination of work, class, and family responsibilities.

classroom experiences and assignments. Yet another benefit of adult students in college classes is intergenerational contact. As younger students observe the capacities and talents of older classmates, unfavorable stereotypes of aging decline.

In middle adulthood as in earlier years, education transforms development. After finishing her degree, Anya secured a position as a parish nurse with creative opportunities to counsel members of a large congregation about health concerns. Education granted her new life options, financial rewards, and higher self-esteem as she reevaluated her own competencies (Redding & Dowling, 1992). Sometimes, these revised values and increased self-reliance can spark other changes, such as a divorce or a new intimate partnership (Esterberg, Moen, & Dempster-McClain, 1994). In this way too, returning to school can powerfully reshape the life course.

Ask Yourself

Review

In view of the impact of vocational and educational experiences on midlife cognitive development, evaluate the saying "You can't teach an old dog new tricks."

Apply

Marcella completed one year of college in her twenties. Now, at age 42, she has returned to earn a degree. Plan a set of experiences for Marcella's first semester that will increase her chances of success.

Connect

Most high-level government and corporate positions are held by middle-aged and older adults rather than by young adults. What cognitive capacities enable mature adults to perform these jobs well?

Reflect

Interview a nontraditional student in one of your classes about the personal challenges and rewards of working toward a degree at a later age. What services does your institution offer to support returning students?

www.ablongman.com/berk

Summary

✿ Physical Development

Physical Changes

Describe the physical changes of middle adulthood, paying special attention to vision, hearing, the skin, muscle–fat makeup, and the skeleton.

■ The gradual physical changes begun in early adulthood continue in midlife, contributing to a revised physical self-image, with less emphasis on hoped-for gains and more on feared declines.

■ Vision is affected by **presbyopia,** or loss of the accommodative ability of the lens, reduced ability to see in dim light, increased sensitivity to glare, and diminished color discrimination. After age 40, adults are at increased risk of **glaucoma,** a buildup of pressure in the eye that damages the optic nerve.

■ Hearing loss, or **presbycusis,** first affects detection of high frequencies and then spreads to other tones. Presbycusis begins earlier and is more rapid for men, a difference associated in part with cigarette smoking and with intense noise in some male-dominated occupations.

■ The skin wrinkles, loosens, and starts to develop age spots, especially in women and in people exposed to the sun. Muscle mass declines and fat deposits increase, with men and women developing different patterns of fat distribution. A low-fat diet and regular exercise that includes resistance training can offset excess weight and muscle loss.

■ Bone density declines in both sexes, but to a greater extent in women, especially after menopause. Loss in height and bone fractures can result.

Describe reproductive changes in women during middle adulthood, and discuss women's psychological reactions to menopause.

■ The **climacteric** in women, which occurs gradually over a 10-year period as estrogen production drops, concludes with **menopause,** sometimes accompanied by emotional and physical symptoms.

© STEVE SKJOLD/ALAMY

Doctors may recommend **hormone therapy** to reduce the discomforts of menopause and to protect women from other negative effects of estrogen loss. However, hormone therapy remains controversial because of an increased risk of certain cancers, cardiovascular disease, and possibly cognitive decline.

■ Menopause is a biocultural event—affected by societal beliefs and practices as well as hormonal changes. Physical symptoms and psychological reactions vary widely. Whether women find menopause traumatic or liberating depends on how they interpret it in relation to their past and future lives.

Describe reproductive changes in men during middle adulthood.

■ Although men also experience a climacteric, no male counterpart to menopause exists: Men's reproductive capacity merely declines rather than ending. Occasional episodes of impotence are more common in midlife. Although Viagra and other drugs used to treat impotence are generally safe, a few users have experienced serious vision loss, possibly linked to the medication.

Health and Fitness

Discuss sexuality in middle adulthood and its association with psychological well-being.

■ Frequency of sexual activity among married couples declines only slightly in middle adulthood and is associated with marital happiness. Intensity of sexual response declines more, due to physical changes of the climacteric.

■ Most married people over age 50 find ways to overcome difficulties with sexual functioning. Many more women than men are without sexual partners, a trend that continues into late adulthood.

Discuss cancer, cardiovascular disease, and osteoporosis, noting risk factors and interventions.

■ The death rate from cancer increases tenfold from early to middle adulthood. Cancer is the leading killer of middle-aged women. A complex interaction of heredity, biological aging, and environment contributes to cancer. Today 40 percent of people with cancer are cured. Annual screenings and various preventive steps (such as not smoking) can reduce the incidence of cancer and cancer deaths.

■ Although cardiovascular disease has declined in recent decades, it remains a major cause of death in middle adulthood, especially among men. Symptoms include high blood pressure, high blood cholesterol, atherosclerosis, heart attack, arrhythmia, and angina pectoris. Diet, exercise, drug therapy, and stress reduction can reduce risks and aid in treatment. A special concern is accurate diagnosis in women.

■ **Osteoporosis** affects 7 percent of postmenopausal women, and another 40 percent have bone density levels low enough to be of concern. Weight-bearing exercise, calcium and vitamin D, and hormone therapy or other bone-strengthening medications can help prevent and treat osteoporosis.

Discuss the association of hostility and anger with heart disease and other health problems.

■ Hostility is the component of the **Type A behavior pattern** that predicts heart disease and other health problems, largely due to physiological arousal associated with anger. Because inhibiting the expression of emotion is also related to health problems, a better alternative is to develop effective ways of handling stress and conflict.

Adapting to the Physical Challenges of Midlife

Discuss the benefits of stress management, exercise, and an optimistic outlook in dealing effectively with the physical challenges of midlife.

■ The changes and responsibilities of middle adulthood can cause psychological stress, with negative consequences for the cardiovascular, immune, and gastrointestinal systems. Effective stress management includes both problem-centered and emotion-centered coping, depending on the situation; constructive approaches to anger reduction; and social support. In middle adulthood, people tend to cope with stress more effectively, and when they do, they often report lasting personal benefits.

■ Regular exercise confers many physical and psychological advantages, making it worthwhile for sedentary middle-aged people to begin exercising. Developing a sense of self-efficacy and choosing an exercise format that fits the individual's characteristics (home-based for overweight adults, group-based for highly stressed adults) increase the chances that a beginner will stick with an exercise regimen.

■ **Hardiness** is made up of three personal qualities: control, commitment, and challenge. By inducing a generally optimistic outlook on life, hardiness helps people cope with stress adaptively.

Explain the double standard of aging.

■ Although negative stereotypes of aging discourage older adults of both sexes, middle-aged women are more likely to be viewed unfavorably, especially by men. This double standard, which may have been adaptive at an earlier time in our evolutionary history, is irrelevant in an era of limited childbearing and greater involvement in career and leisure pursuits. New surveys suggest that the double standard of aging is declining.

✎ Cognitive Development

Changes in Mental Abilities

Describe cohort effects on intelligence revealed by Schaie's Seattle Longitudinal Study.

■ Early cross-sectional research showed a peak in intelligence test performance around age 35 followed by a steep decline, whereas

© ROBIN SACHS/PHOTOEDIT

longitudinal evidence revealed an age-related increase from early to middle adulthood. Using a sequential design, Schaie found that the cross-sectional, steep drop-off largely resulted from cohort effects, as each new generation experienced better health and education than the previous one.

Describe changes in crystallized and fluid intelligence in middle adulthood, and discuss individual and group differences in intellectual development.

■ In cross-sectional studies that correct for cohort effects, skills that tap **crystallized intelligence** (which depends on accumulated knowledge and experience) gain steadily through middle adulthood. In contrast, **fluid intelligence** (which depends more on basic information-processing skills) declines starting in the twenties.

■ In the Seattle Longitudinal Study, perceptual speed follows a pattern of steady, continuous decline. But other fluid skills, in addition to crystallized abilities, increase through middle adulthood, confirming that midlife is a time of peak performance on a variety of complex abilities.

■ Large individual differences among middle-aged adults remind us that intellectual development is multidimensional, multidirectional, and plastic. Some people, because of illness or unfavorable environments, show early intellectual declines. Those who use their mental abilities are more likely to retain them. Stimulating occupations and leisure pursuits, flexible personalities, lasting marriages, good health, and economic advantage are linked to favorable cognitive development.

■ In early and middle adulthood, women outperform men on verbal tasks and perceptual speed, whereas men excel at spatial skills. Generational gains in certain intellectual skills reflect advances in education, technology, environmental stimulation, and health care.

Information Processing

How does information processing change in midlife?

■ Speed of cognitive processing slows with age, a change explained by either the **neural network view** or the **information-loss view**. As reaction time slows, people perform less well on memory, reasoning, and problem-solving tasks, and especially on fluid-ability items.

- Slower processing speed makes it harder for middle-aged people to divide their attention, focus on relevant stimuli, and switch from one task to another as the situation demands. Cognitive inhibition becomes more difficult, at times prompting distractibility. Adults in midlife retain less information in working memory, largely due to a decline in use of memory strategies.

- Training, practice, improved design of tasks, and metacognitive knowledge enable middle-aged and older adults to compensate for decrements in processing speed, attention, and memory. Assessing older adults in constrained conditions underestimates what they can remember when they are free to pace their own learning.

Discuss the development of practical problem solving, expertise, and creativity in middle adulthood.

- Middle-aged adults in all walks of life often become good at **practical problem solving**, largely due to development of expertise. In midlife, creativity becomes more deliberately thoughtful. It also shifts from generating unusual products to integrating ideas and from concern with self-expression to more altruistic goals.

Vocational Life and Cognitive Development

Describe the relationship between vocational life and cognitive development.

- At all ages and in different cultures, the relationship between vocational life and cognitive development is reciprocal. Stimulating, complex work and flexible, abstract, autonomous thinking support each other.

Adult Learners: Becoming a College Student in Midlife

Discuss the challenges that adults face in returning to college, ways to support returning students, and benefits of earning a degree in midlife.

- Adults are returning to college and graduate school in record numbers. The majority are women, who are often motivated by life transitions. Returning students must cope with a lack of recent practice at academic work, stereotypes of aging, and multiple role demands. Low-income and ethnic minority students need special assistance.

- Social support from family and friends and institutional services suited to their needs can help returning students succeed. Further education results in enhanced competencies, new relationships, intergenerational contact, and reshaped life paths.

Important Terms and Concepts

climacteric (p. 502)
crystallized intelligence (p. 516)
fluid intelligence (p. 516)
glaucoma (p. 501)
hardiness (p. 514)

hormone therapy (p. 504)
information-loss view (p. 518)
menopause (p. 502)
neural network view (p. 518)
osteoporosis (p. 511)

practical problem solving (p. 521)
presbycusis (p. 501)
presbyopia (p. 500)
Type A behavior pattern (p. 512)

© MONIKA GRAFF/THE IMAGE WORKS

Midlife is a time of increased generativity—giving to and guiding younger generations. This grandmother's involved, contented expression illustrates the deep sense of satisfaction that middle-aged adults derive from engaging in generative activities.

Emotional and Social Development in Middle Adulthood

*O*ne weekend when Devin, Trisha, and their 24-year-old son, Mark, were vacationing together, the two middle-aged parents knocked on Mark's hotel room door. "Your dad and I are going off to see a crafts exhibit," Trisha explained. "Feel free to stay behind," she offered, recalling Mark's antipathy toward attending such events as an adolescent. "We'll be back around noon for lunch."

"That exhibit sounds great!" Mark replied. "I'll meet you in the lobby. We've got so little time together as it is."

"Sometimes I forget he's an adult!" exclaimed Trisha as she and Devin returned to their room to grab their coats. "It's been great to have Mark with us these few days—like spending time with a good friend."

In their forties and fifties, Trisha and Devin built on earlier strengths and intensified their commitment to leaving a legacy for those who would come after them. As Mark graduated from college, took his first job, fell in love, and married, they felt a sense of pride at having escorted a member of the next generation into responsible adult roles. Family activities, which had declined during Mark's adolescent and college years, now increased as Trisha and Devin related to their son and daughter-in-law not just as kin but as enjoyable adult companions. Challenging work and more time for community involvement, leisure pursuits, and each other contributed to a richly diverse and gratifying time of life.

The midlife years were not as smooth for two of Trisha and Devin's friends. Fearing that she might grow old alone, Jewel frantically pursued her quest for an intimate partner. She attended singles events, registered with dating services, and traveled in hopes of meeting a like-minded companion. "I can't stand the thought of turning 50. I look like an old bag with big circles under my eyes," she lamented in a letter to Trisha. Jewel also had compensating satisfactions—friendships that had grown more meaningful, a warm relationship with a nephew and niece, and a successful consulting business.

Tim, Devin's best friend from graduate school, had been divorced for over 15 years. Recently, he had met Elena and had come to love her deeply. But Elena was in the midst of major life changes. Besides her own divorce, she was dealing with a troubled daughter, a career change, and a move away from the city that served as a constant reminder of her unhappy past. Whereas Tim had reached the peak of his career and was ready to enjoy life, Elena wanted to recapture much of what she had missed in earlier decades—not just a gratifying intimate relationship, but opportunities to realize her talents. "I don't know where I fit into Elena's plans," Tim wondered aloud on the phone with Trisha.

With the arrival of middle adulthood, half or more of the lifespan is over. Increasing awareness of limited time ahead prompts adults to reevaluate the meaning of their lives, refine and strengthen their identities, and reach out to future generations. Most middle-aged people make modest adjustments in their outlook, goals, and daily lives. But a few experience profound inner turbulence and initiate major changes, often in an effort to make up for lost time. Besides advancing years, family and work transitions contribute greatly to emotional and social development.

Erikson's Theory: Generativity versus Stagnation

Erikson's psychological conflict of midlife is called **generativity versus stagnation.** Generativity involves reaching out to others in ways that give to and guide the next generation. Recall from Chapter 14 that generativity is under way in early adulthood, typically through childbearing and child rearing and establishing a niche in the occupational world. It expands greatly in midlife, when commitment extends beyond oneself (identity) and one's life partner (intimacy) to a larger group—family, community, or society. The generative adult combines the need for self-expression with the need for communion, integrating personal goals with the welfare of the larger social world (McAdams & Logan, 2004). The resulting strength is the capacity to care for others in a broader way than in previous stages.

Erikson (1950) selected the term *generativity* to encompass everything generated that can outlive the self and ensure society's continuity and improvement: children, ideas, products, works of art. Although parenting is a major means of realizing generativity, it is not the only means: Adults can also be generative in other family relationships (as Jewel was with her nephew and niece), as mentors in the workplace, in volunteer endeavors, and through many forms of productivity and creativity.

Notice, from what we have said so far, that generativity brings together personal desires and cultural demands. On the personal side, middle-aged adults feel a need to be needed—to attain symbolic immortality by making a contribution that will survive their death (Kotre, 1984, 1999; McAdams, Hart, & Maruna, 1998). This desire may stem from a deep-seated evolutionary urge to protect and advance the next generation. On the cultural side, society imposes a social clock for generativity in midlife, requiring adults to take responsibility for the next generation through their roles as parents, teachers, mentors, leaders, and coordinators (McAdams & Logan, 2004). And according to Erikson, a culture's "belief in the species"—the conviction that life is good and worthwhile, even in the face of human destructiveness and deprivation—is a major motivator of generative action. Without this optimistic worldview, people would have no hope of improving humanity.

The negative outcome of this stage is *stagnation*. Erikson recognized that once people attain certain life goals, such as marriage, children, and career success, they may become self-centered and self-indulgent. Adults with a sense of stagnation cannot contribute to society's welfare because they place their own comfort and security above challenge and sacrifice (Hamachek, 1990). Their self-absorption is expressed in many ways—through lack of interest in young people (including their own children), through a focus on what they can get from others rather than what they can give, and through taking little interest in being productive at work, developing their talents, or bettering the world in other ways.

Researchers study generativity in diverse ways. Some assess personality traits, such as assertiveness, nurturance, and responsibility. Others ask people to rate themselves on generative characteristics and report on generative activities. Still others look for generative themes in people's narrative descriptions of themselves (Keyes & Ryff, 1998a; McAdams et al., 1997; Ryff & Migdal, 1984). Whichever method is used, generativity increases in midlife (Keyes & Ryff, 1998a; Rossi, 2001). For example, in longitudinal and cross-sectional studies of college-educated women, and in an investigation of middle-aged adults diverse in SES, self-rated generativity rose from the thirties into the forties or fifties (see Figure 16.1 on page 532). At the same time, participants expressed greater concern about aging, increased security with their identities, and a stronger sense of competence (Miner-Rubino, Winter, & Stewart, 2004; Stewart, Ostrove, & Helson, 2001; Zucker, Ostrove, & Stewart, 2002). As the Lifespan Vista box on the following page illustrates, generativity is also a major unifying theme in middle-aged adults' life stories.

Just as Erikson's theory suggests, highly generative people appear especially well-adjusted—low in anxiety and depression, high in self-acceptance and life satisfaction, and more likely to have successful marriages and close friends (Ackerman,

A Lifespan Vista

Generative Adults Tell Their Life Stories

In research aimed at understanding how highly generative adults make sense of their lives, Dan McAdams and his colleagues (1997, 2001) interviewed two groups of midlifers: those who often behave generatively and those who seldom do. Participants were asked to relate their life stories, including a high point, a low point, a turning point, and important scenes from childhood, adolescence, and adulthood. Analyses of story lines and themes revealed that adults high and low in generativity reconstruct their past and anticipate their future in strikingly different ways.

Narratives of highly generative people usually contained an orderly sequence of events that the researchers called a *commitment story,* in which adults give to others as a means of giving back to family, community, and society (McAdams, 1993). The generative storyteller typically describes an early special advantage (such as a good family or a talent), along with early awareness of the suffering of others. This clash between blessing and suffering motivates the person to view the self as "called," or committed, to being good to others. In commitment stories, the *theme of redemption* is prominent. Highly generative adults frequently describe scenes in which extremely negative life events, involving frustration, failure, loss, or death, are followed by good outcomes—personal renewal, improvement, and enlightenment. That is, bad scenes are redeemed, or made better, by what follows.

Consider a story related by Diana, a 49-year-old fourth-grade teacher. Born in a small town to a minister and his wife, Diana was a favorite among the parishioners, who showered her with attention and love. When she was 8, however, her life hit its lowest point: As she looked on in horror, her younger brother ran into the street and was hit by a car; he died later that day. Afterward, Diana, sensing her father's anguish, tried—unsuccessfully—to be the "son" he had lost. But the scene ends on an upbeat note, with Diana marrying a man who forged a warm bond with her father and who became accepted "as his own son." One of Diana's life goals was to improve her teaching, because "I'd like to give something back . . . to grow and help others grow" (McAdams et al., 1997, p. 689). Her interview overflowed with expressions of generative commitment.

Whereas highly generative adults tell stories in which bad scenes turn good, less generative adults relate stories with *themes of contamination,* in which good scenes turn bad. For example, a child gets a treasured musical instrument, which is immediately stolen. A good first year of college turns sour when a professor grades unfairly. A young woman loses weight, looks good, but can't overcome her low self-esteem.

Why is generativity connected to life-story redemption events, in which bad gives way to good? First, some adults may view their generative activities as a way to redeem negative aspects of their lives. In a study of the life stories of ex-convicts who turned away from crime, many spoke of a strong desire to do good works as penance for their transgressions (Maruna, 2001; Maruna, LeBel, & Lanier, 2004). Second, generativity seems to entail the conviction that the imperfections of today can be transformed into a better tomorrow. Through guiding and giving to the next generation, mature adults increase the chances that the mistakes of the past will not happen again. Finally, interpreting one's own life in terms of redemption offers hope that hard work will lead to future benefits—an expectation that may sustain generative efforts of all kinds, from rearing children to advancing communities and societies (Kotre, 1999).

Life stories offer insight into how people imbue their lives with meaning and purpose. Adults high and low in generativity do not differ in the number of positive and negative events included in their narratives. Rather, they interpret those events differently. Commitment stories, filled with redemption, involve a way of thinking about the self that fosters a caring, compassionate approach to others (McAdams & Logan, 2004). Such stories help people realize that although their own personal story will someday end, other stories will follow, due in part to their own generative efforts.

The more redemptive events adults include in their life stories, the higher their life satisfaction, self-esteem, and certainty that the challenges of life are meaningful, manageable, and rewarding (McAdams, 2001). Researchers still have much to learn about factors that lead people to view good as emerging from adversity.

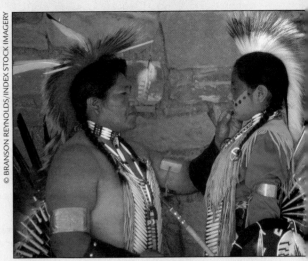

When highly generative adults tell their life stories, they often include themes of redemption, in which good outcomes follow negative life events. Perhaps redemptive experiences contributed to the patience and pleasure with which this Navajo Indian man teaches the art of ceremonial dress to a young member of his culture.

© BRANSON REYNOLDS/INDEX STOCK IMAGERY

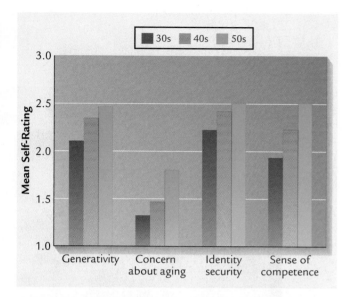

■ FIGURE 16.1 Age-related changes in self-rated generativity, concern about aging, identity security, and sense of competence. In a longitudinal study of college-educated women, self-rated generativity increased from the thirties to the fifties, as did concern about aging. The rise in generativity was accompanied by other indicators of psychological health—greater security with one's identity and sense of competence. (Adapted from Stewart, Ostrove, & Helson, 2001.)

Zuroff, & Moskowitz, 2000; Grossbaum & Bates, 2002; Westermeyer, 2004). They are also more open to differing viewpoints, possess leadership qualities, desire more from work than financial rewards, and care greatly about the welfare of their children, their partner, their aging parents, and the wider society (Peterson, 2002; Peterson, Smirles, & Wentworth, 1997). Furthermore, generativity is associated with more effective child rearing—higher valuing of trust, open communication, transmission of values to children, and an authoritative style (Hart

As this middle-aged woman campaigns for political office, she demonstrates generative values as well as actions and integrates her personal goals with the welfare of the wider social world.

et al., 2001; Pratt et al., 2001). Generative midlifers are also more involved in political activities, including voting, campaigning, and contacting public officials (Cole & Stewart, 1996).

Although these findings characterize adults of all backgrounds, individual differences in contexts for generativity exist. Having children seems to foster men's generative development more than women's. In several studies, fathers scored higher in generativity than childless men (Marks, Bumpass, & Jun, 2004; McAdams & de St. Aubin, 1992; Snarey et al., 1987). In contrast, motherhood is unrelated to women's generativity scores. Perhaps parenting awakens in men a tender, caring attitude toward the next generation that women have opportunities to develop in other ways.

Finally, compared with Caucasians, African Americans more often engage in certain types of generativity. They are more involved in religious groups and activities, offer more social support, and are more likely to view themselves as role models and sources of wisdom for their children (Hart et al., 2001). A life history of strong support from church and extended family may strengthen these generative values and actions. In samples of Caucasian Americans, religiosity and spirituality are also linked to greater generative activity (Dillon & Wink, 2004; Wink & Dillon, 2003). Especially in highly individualistic societies, belonging to a religious community or believing in a higher being may help preserve generative commitments.

Other Theories of Psychosocial Development in Midlife

Erikson's theory provides only a broad sketch of adult personality development. For a closer look at psychosocial change in midlife, let's revisit Levinson's and Vaillant's theories, which were introduced in Chapter 14.

Levinson's Seasons of Life

Return to page 465 to review Levinson's eras (stages or seasons). You will see that like early adulthood, middle adulthood begins with a transitional period (age 40 to 45), followed by the building of an entry life structure (age 45 to 50). This structure is then evaluated and revised (age 50 to 55), resulting in a culminating life structure (age 55 to 60). Among the adults Levinson (1978, 1996) interviewed, the majority displayed these phases. But because of gender stereotypes and differences in opportunity, men and women had somewhat different experiences.

■ **Midlife Transition.** Around age 40, people evaluate their success in meeting early adulthood goals. Realizing that from now on, more time will lie behind than ahead, they regard the remaining years as increasingly precious. Consequently, some people make drastic revisions in family and occupational components of the life structure: divorcing, remarrying, changing careers, or displaying enhanced creativity. Others make smaller

Table 16.1	Levinson's Four Developmental Tasks of Middle Adulthood
Task	**Description**
Young–Old	The middle-aged person must seek new ways of being both young and old. This means giving up certain youthful qualities, retaining and transforming others, and finding positive meaning in being older.
Destruction–Creation	With greater awareness of mortality, the middle-aged person focuses on ways he or she has acted destructively and others have done the same. Past hurtful acts toward parents, intimate partners, children, friends, and rivals are countered by a strong desire to become more creative—by making products of value to the self and others and participating in activities that advance human welfare.
Masculinity–Femininity	The middle-aged person must come to terms with masculine and feminine parts of the self, creating a better balance. For men, this means becoming more empathic and caring; for women, it often means becoming more autonomous, dominant, and assertive.
Engagement–Separateness	The middle-aged person must create a better balance between engagement with the external world and separateness. For men, this generally means pulling back from ambition and achievement and becoming more in touch with the self. Women who have devoted themselves to child rearing or who have unfulfilling jobs typically move in the other direction—toward greater involvement in the work world and wider community.

Sources: Levinson, 1978, 1996.

changes while staying in the same marriage, surroundings, occupation, and workplace.

Whether these years bring a gust of wind or a storm, most people turn inward for a time, focusing on personally meaningful living (Neugarten, 1968b). One reason is that for many middle-aged adults, only limited career advancement and personal growth remain possible. Some are disappointed in not having fully realized their early adulthood dream and want to find a more satisfying path before it is too late. Even people who have reached their goals ask, What good are these accomplishments to others, to society, and to myself?

According to Levinson, for middle-aged adults to reassess their relation to themselves and the external world, they must confront four developmental tasks, summarized in Table 16.1. Each requires the person to reconcile two opposing tendencies within the self, thereby attaining greater internal harmony. Let's see how this happens.

■ **Modifying the Life Structure: Gender Similarities and Differences.** At midlife, adults must give up certain youthful qualities, find age-appropriate ways to express other qualities, and accept being older. Physical changes, personal encounters with illness, and aging parents intensify this task, which often triggers reassessment of what is important. People who can flexibly modify their identities in response to age-related changes yet maintain a sense of self-continuity are more aware of their own thoughts and feelings and higher in self-esteem (Sneed & Whitbourne, 2001, 2003).

Perhaps because of the double standard of aging (see page 514 in Chapter 15), most middle-aged women express concern about appearing less attractive as they grow older (Rossi, 2005). For Jewel, the stereotypical image of an older woman prompted a desperate fear of becoming physically unappealing and unlovable. She tried numerous remedies, from skin creams

to a facelift, to maintain her youth. Although only a small number are as anxious about their looks as Jewel, women are more likely than men to perceive themselves as younger than their chronological age—a difference that increases over middle and late adulthood (Montepare & Lachman, 1989).

But men also receive negative cultural messages about aging, and they, too, express apprehension over their changing appearance. In one study, non-college-educated men showed a greater rise in sensitivity to physical aging over the midlife years than women, both college- and non-college-educated. Women, in turn, were more sensitive than college-educated men (see Figure 16.2 on page 534) (Miner-Rubino, Winter, & Stewart, 2004). Because men who did not attend college often hold blue-collar jobs that require physical strength and stamina, they may worry that physical aging will affect their work capacity.

As middle-aged adults confront their own mortality and the actual or impending death of agemates, they become more aware of ways people can act destructively—to parents, intimate partners, children, friends, and co-workers. Countering this force is a desire to strengthen life-affirming aspects of the self by advancing human welfare and, as a result, leaving a legacy for future generations. The image of a legacy, which flourishes in midlife, can be satisfied in many ways—through charitable gifts, creative products, volunteer service, or mentoring young people.

Middle age is also a time when people must reconcile masculine and feminine parts of the self. For men, this means greater acceptance of "feminine" traits of nurturance and caring, which enhance close relationships and compassionate exercise of authority in the workplace. For women, it generally means being more open to "masculine" characteristics of autonomy, dominance, and assertiveness (Gilligan, 1982; Harris, Ellicott, & Holmes, 1986). Recall from Chapter 8 that people who combine masculine and feminine traits have an androgynous

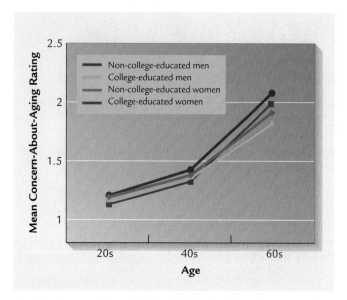

■ **FIGURE 16.2 Age-related change in concern about physical aging, by sex and level of education.** More than 250 men and women in their early sixties retrospectively rated their degree of concern over physical aging in their forties, fifties, and sixties, using a three-point scale. Non-college-educated men reported the greatest rise in sensitivity to physical changes, followed by women, both college- and non-college-educated, and finally college-educated men. (From K. Miner-Rubino, D. G. Winter, & A. J. Stewart, 2004, "Gender, Social Class, and the Subjective Experience of Aging: Self-Perceived Personality Change from Early Adulthood to Midlife," *Personality and Social Psychology Bulletin, 30,* p. 1605. © 2004 by the Society for Personality and Social Psychology, Inc. Reprinted by permission.)

gender identity. Later we will see that androgyny is associated with many favorable personality traits.

Finally, midlife requires a middle ground between engagement with the external world and separateness. Many men must reduce their concern with ambition and achievement and attend more fully to the self. The same is true for women who have had active, successful careers. But women who devoted their early adulthood to child rearing or an unfulfilling job often feel compelled, after a period of self-reflection, to move in the other direction (Levinson, 1996). At age 48, Elena left her position as a reporter for a small-town newspaper, pursued an advanced degree in creative writing, eventually accepted a college teaching position, and began writing a novel. As Tim looked inward, he recognized his overwhelming desire for a gratifying romantic partnership. By scaling back his own career, he realized he could grant Elena the time and space she needed to build a rewarding work life—and that doing so might deepen their attachment to each other.

■ **The Life Structure in Social Context.** Rebuilding the life structure depends on supportive social contexts. When poverty, unemployment, and lack of a respected place in society dominate the life course, energies are directed toward survival rather than pursuit of a satisfying life structure. Even

adults whose jobs are secure and who live in pleasant neighborhoods may find that employment conditions restrict possibilities for growth by placing too much emphasis on productivity and profit and too little on the meaning of work. In her early forties, Trisha left a large law firm, where she felt constant pressure to bring in high-fee clients and received little acknowledgment of her efforts, for a small practice.

Opportunities for advancement ease the transition to middle adulthood by permitting realization of the early adulthood dream. Yet these are far less available to women than to men. Individuals of both sexes in blue-collar jobs also have few possibilities for promotion. The industrial workers in Levinson's (1978) sample made whatever vocational adjustments they could—becoming active union members, shop stewards, or mentors of younger workers. Many found compensating rewards in moving to the senior generation of their families.

Vaillant's Adaptation to Life

Because Levinson interviewed 35- to 45-year-olds, his findings cannot tell us about psychosocial change in the fifties. But Vaillant (1977, 2002), in his longitudinal research on well-educated men and women, followed participants past the half-century mark. Recall from Chapter 14 how adults in their late forties and fifties take on peak responsibility for the functioning of society, eventually becoming "keepers of meaning," or guardians of their culture (see page 466). Vaillant reported that the most-successful and best-adjusted entered a calmer, quieter time of life. "Passing the torch"—concern that the positive aspects of their culture survive—became a major preoccupation.

In societies around the world, older people are guardians of traditions, laws, and cultural values. This stabilizing force holds in check too-rapid change sparked by the questioning and challenging of adolescents and young adults. As people approach the end of middle age, they focus on longer-term, less personal goals, such as the state of human relations in their society. And they become more philosophical, accepting the fact that not all problems can be solved in their lifetime.

Is There a Midlife Crisis?

Levinson (1978, 1996) reported that most men and women in his samples experienced substantial inner turmoil during the transition to middle adulthood. Yet Vaillant (1977) saw few examples of crisis. Instead, change was typically slow and steady. These contrasting findings raise the question of how much personal upheaval actually accompanies entry to midlife. Are self-doubt and stress especially great during the forties, and do they prompt major restructuring of the personality, as the term **midlife crisis** implies?

Think about the reactions of Trisha, Devin, Jewel, Tim, and Elena to middle adulthood. Trisha and Devin moved easily into this period, whereas Jewel, Tim, and Elena displayed greater questioning of their situations and sought alternative life paths. Similarly, wide individual differences exist in

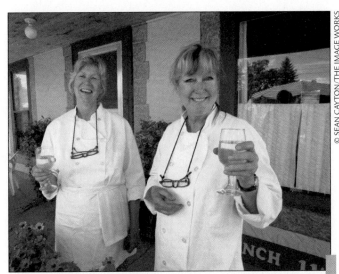

These sisters responded to the midlife transition by opening a new restaurant and cooking school in a small Colorado town. Yet their career change was probably not the result of a crisis. Although wide individual differences exist in response to midlife, sharp disruption and agitation are the exception, not the rule.

response to midlife. Overall, changes for men are more likely to occur in the early forties (in accord with Levinson's timetable). Those for women may be postponed to the late forties and fifties, when a reduction in parenting responsibilities gives them time and freedom to confront personal issues (Harris, Ellicott, & Holmes, 1986; Mercer, Nichols, & Doyle, 1989). In addition, the direction of change for women is more variable. It depends in part on whether they focused as young adults on a "feminine" social clock (marriage and motherhood), a "masculine" social clock (high-status career), or a combination (Helson & Roberts, 1994; Stewart & Vandewater, 1992).

But sharp disruption and agitation are the exception, not the rule. For example, Elena had considered both a divorce and a new career long before she initiated these changes. In her thirties, she separated from her husband; later, she reconciled with him and told him of her desire to return to school, which he firmly opposed. She put her own life on hold because of her daughter's academic and emotional difficulties and her husband's resistance. In a survey of more than 700 adults, only one-fourth reported experiencing a midlife crisis. When asked what they meant by the term, the participants defined it much more loosely than researchers had done. Some reported a crisis well before age 40, others well after age 50. And most attributed it not to age but rather to challenging life events (Wethington, 2000).

Another way of exploring midlife questioning is to ask adults about *life regrets*—attractive opportunities for career or other life-changing activities they did not pursue or lifestyle changes they did not make. In two investigations of women in their early forties, those who acknowledged regret without making life changes, compared to those who modified their lives, reported less favorable psychological well-being and poorer physical health over time (Landman et al., 1995; Stew-

art & Vandewater, 1999). The two groups did not differ in social or financial resources available to effect change. Rather, they differed in personality: Those who made changes were higher in confidence and assertiveness.

By late midlife, with less time ahead to make life changes, people's *interpretation* of regrets plays a major role in their well-being. Among a sample of several hundred 60- to 65-year-olds diverse in SES, about half expressed at least one regret. Compared to those who had not resolved their disappointments, those who had come to terms with them (accepted and identified some eventual benefits) or had "put the best face on things" (identified benefits but still had some lingering regret) reported better physical health and greater life satisfaction (Torges, Stewart, & Miner-Rubino, 2005).

In sum, life evaluation is common during middle age. Most people make changes that are best described as "turning points" rather than drastic alterations of their lives. Those who cannot modify their life paths often look for the "silver lining" in life's difficulties (Lachman & James, 1997; Wethington, Kessler, & Pixley, 2004). The few midlifers who are in crisis typically have had early adulthoods in which gender roles, family pressures, or low income and poverty severely limited their ability to fulfill personal needs and goals, at home or in the wider world.

Stage or Life Events Approach

If crisis and major restructuring in midlife are rare, is middle adulthood actually a *stage* of development, as Erikson's, Levinson's, and Vaillant's theories indicate? Some researchers believe the midadult transition is not stagelike (McCrae & Costa, 1990). Rather, they regard it as simply an adaptation to normative life events, such as children growing up, reaching the crest of a career, and impending retirement.

Yet recall from earlier chapters that life events are no longer as age-graded as they were in the past. Their timing is so variable that they cannot be the sole cause of midlife change. Furthermore, in several studies, people were asked to trace their thoughts, feelings, attitudes, and hopes during early and middle adulthood. Psychosocial change, in terms of personal disruption followed by reassessment, coincided with both family life cycle events and chronological age. For this reason, most experts regard adaptation during midlife as the combined result of growing older and social experiences (Lachman & James, 1997; Whitbourne et al., 1992). Return to our discussion of generativity and the midlife transition, and notice how both factors are involved.

Finally, in describing their lives, the large majority of middle-aged people report troubling moments that prompt new understandings and goals—a finding consistent with the stage approach. As we look closely at emotional and social development in middle adulthood, we will see that this period, like others, is characterized by *both continuity and stagewise change*. With this in mind, let's turn to the diverse inner concerns and outer experiences that contribute to psychological well-being and decision making in midlife.

Ask Yourself

Review

What personal and cultural forces motivate generativity? Why does it increase and contribute vitally to favorable adjustment in midlife?

Apply

After years of experiencing little personal growth at work, 42-year-old Mel looked for a new job and received an attractive offer in another city. Although he felt torn between leaving close friends and pursuing a long-awaited career opportunity, after several weeks of soul searching, he took the new job. Was Mel's dilemma a midlife crisis? Why or why not?

Connect

Review the concept of androgyny on page 277 in Chapter 8. Why might acceptance of both "masculine" and "feminine" parts of the self foster favorable adjustment in middle adulthood?

Reflect

Think of a middle-aged adult whom you admire. Describe the various ways that individual expresses generativity.

www.ablongman.com/berk

Stability and Change in Self-Concept and Personality

Midlife changes in self-concept and personality reflect growing awareness of a finite lifespan, longer life experience, and generative concerns. Yet certain aspects of personality remain stable, revealing the persistence of individual differences established during earlier periods.

Possible Selves

On a business trip, Jewel found a spare afternoon to visit Trisha. Sitting in a coffee shop, the two women reminisced about the past and thought aloud about the future. "It's been tough living on my own and building the business," Jewel said. "What I hope for is to become better at my work, to be more community-oriented, and to stay healthy and available to my friends. Of course, I would rather not grow old alone, but if I don't find that special person, I suppose I can take comfort in the fact that I'll never have to face divorce or widowhood."

Jewel is discussing **possible selves,** future-oriented representations of what one hopes to become and what one is afraid of becoming. Possible selves are the temporal dimension of self-concept—what the individual is striving for and attempting to avoid. To lifespan researchers, these hopes and fears are just as vital in explaining behavior as people's views of their current characteristics. Indeed, possible selves may be an especially strong motivator of action in midlife, as more meaning becomes attached to time. As we age, we may rely less on social

comparisons in judging our self-worth and more on temporal comparisons—how well we are doing in relation to what we had planned.

Throughout adulthood, people's descriptions of their current selves show considerable stability. A 30-year-old who says he is cooperative, competent, outgoing, or successful is likely to report a similar picture at a later age. But reports of possible selves change greatly. Adults in their early twenties mention many possible selves, and their visions are lofty and idealistic—being "perfectly happy," "rich and famous," "healthy throughout life," and not being "down and out" or "a person who does nothing important." With age, possible selves become fewer in number and more modest and concrete. Most middle-aged people no longer desire to be the best or the most successful. Instead, they are largely concerned with performance of roles and responsibilities already begun—"being competent at work," "being a good husband and father," "putting my children through the colleges of their choice," "staying healthy," and not being "a burden to my family" or "without enough money to meet my daily needs" (Bybee & Wells, 2004; Cross & Markus, 1991; Ryff, 1991).

What explains these shifts in possible selves? Because the future no longer holds limitless opportunities, adults preserve mental health by adjusting their hopes and fears. To stay motivated, they must maintain a sense of unachieved possibility; yet they must still manage to feel good about themselves and their lives despite disappointments (Lachman & Bertrand, 2002). For example, Jewel no longer desired to be an executive in a large company, as she had in her twenties. Instead, she wanted to grow in her current occupation. And although she feared loneliness in old age, she reminded herself that marriage can lead to equally negative outcomes, such as divorce and widowhood—possibilities that made not having attained an important interpersonal goal easier to bear.

Unlike current self-concept, which is constantly responsive to others' feedback, possible selves (though influenced by others) can be defined and redefined by the individual, as needed. Consequently, they permit affirmation of the self, even when things are not going well (Cross & Markus, 1991). Researchers believe that possible selves may be the key to continued well-being in adulthood, as people revise these future images to achieve a better match between desired and achieved goals. Many studies reveal that the self-esteem of middle-aged and older individuals equals or surpasses that of younger people, perhaps because of the protective role of possible selves (Bengtson, Reedy, & Gordon, 1985).

Self-Acceptance, Autonomy, and Environmental Mastery

An evolving mix of competencies and experiences leads to changes in certain personality traits during middle adulthood. Middle-aged adults tend to offer more complex, integrated descriptions of themselves than do younger and older individuals (Labouvie-Vief, 2003). And many have reshaped contexts to suit their personal needs and values.

These developments undoubtedly contribute to other gains in personal functioning. In research on well-educated adults ranging in age from the late teens into the seventies, three traits increased from early to middle adulthood and then leveled off:

🍂 *Self-acceptance:* More than young adults, middle-aged people acknowledged and accepted both their good and bad qualities and felt positively about themselves and life.

🍂 *Autonomy:* Middle-aged adults saw themselves as less concerned about others' expectations and evaluations and more concerned with following self-chosen standards.

🍂 *Environmental mastery:* Middle-aged people saw themselves as capable of managing a complex array of tasks easily and effectively (Ryff, 1991, 1995).

In Chapter 15, we noted that midlife brings gains in expertise and practical problem solving. These cognitive changes may support the confidence, initiative, and decisiveness of this period. Overall, midlife is a time of increased comfort with the self, independence, assertiveness, commitment to personal values, psychological well-being, and life satisfaction (Helson, Jones, & Kwan, 2002; Helson & Wink, 1992; Keyes, Shmotkin, & Ryff, 2002; Mitchell & Helson, 1990). Perhaps because of these personal attributes, people sometimes refer to middle age as "the prime of life." Although individual differences exist (see the Biology and Environment box on pages 538–539), middle adulthood is a time when many people report feeling especially happy and functioning at their best.

Notions of happiness, however, vary among cultures. In a comparison of Korean and North American adults in their fifties, the Koreans reported lower levels of psychological well-being, largely because they were less willing to endorse individualistic traits, such as self-acceptance and autonomy, as characteristic of themselves (Keyes & Ryff, 1998b). Consistent with their collectivist orientation, Koreans' highest well-being scores were on positive relations with others. They viewed personal fulfillment as achieved through family, especially the success of children. North American adults also regarded family relations as relevant to well-being but placed greater emphasis on their own traits and accomplishments than on their children's.

Coping Strategies

In Chapter 15, we discussed the importance of stress management in preventing illness. It is also vital for psychological well-being. Interviewing more than 1,000 U.S. adults on eight consecutive evenings, researchers found an early- to mid-adulthood plateau in frequency of daily stressors, followed by a decline over the decade of the sixties as work and family responsibilities ease and leisure time increases (see Figure 16.3) (Almeida & Horn, 2004). Women reported more frequent role overload and family-network and child-related stressors, men more work-related stressors, but both genders experienced all varieties. Compared with older people, young and midlife

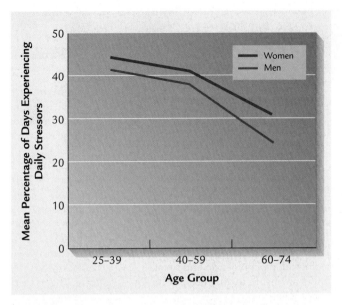

■ **FIGURE 16.3 Age-related change in daily stressors among men and women.** Researchers interviewed a sample of more than 1,000 U.S. adults on eight consecutive evenings. Findings revealed an early- to mid-adulthood plateau, followed by a decline during the decade of the sixties, when work and family responsibilities typically ease and leisure time increases. (From D. M. Almeida & M. C. Horn, 2004, "Is Daily Life More Stressful During Middle Adulthood?" in O. G. Brim, C. D. Ryff, & R. C. Kessler, Eds., *How Healthy Are We? A National Study of Well-Being at Midlife,* Chicago: University of Chicago Press, p. 438. Adapted by permission.)

adults also perceived their stressors as more disruptive and unpleasant, perhaps because they often experienced several at once, and many involved financial risks and children.

But recall, also, from Chapter 15 that midlife brings an increase in effective coping strategies. Middle-aged individuals are more likely to identify the positive side of difficult situations, postpone action to permit evaluation of alternatives, anticipate and plan ways to handle future discomforts, and use humor to express ideas and feelings without offending others (Diehl, Coyle, & Labouvie-Vief, 1996). Notice how these efforts flexibly draw on both problem-centered and emotion-centered strategies.

Why might effective coping increase in middle adulthood? Other personality changes seem to support it. In one study, complex, integrated self-descriptions—which increase in midlife, indicating an improved ability to blend strengths and weaknesses into an organized picture—predicted good coping strategies (Labouvie-Vief & Diehl, 2000). Greater confidence in handling life's problems may also contribute. In a longitudinal investigation of well-educated women, taking initiative to overcome difficult times in early adulthood predicted advanced self-understanding, social and moral maturity, and high life satisfaction at age 43 (Helson & Roberts, 1994). Overall, these findings suggest that years of experience in overcoming stress promote enhanced self-knowledge, which joins with life experience to foster more sophisticated, flexible coping during middle age.

Biology and Environment

What Factors Promote Psychological Well-Being in Midlife?

For Trisha and Devin, midlife brought contentment and high life satisfaction. But the road to happiness was rockier for Jewel, Tim, and Elena. What factors contribute to variations in psychological well-being at midlife? Consistent with the lifespan perspective, biological, psychological, and social forces are involved, and their effects are interwoven.

Good Health and Exercise. Good health affects energy and zest for life. Adults of any age who rate their health as good to excellent are more likely to feel positively about their life circumstances. But during middle and late adulthood, taking steps to improve health and prevent disability becomes a better predictor of psychological well-being. In a study of over 3,000 20- to 64-year-olds, engaging in regular exercise—walking, dancing, jogging, or swimming—was more strongly associated with self-rated health and a positive outlook in older than in younger individuals (Ransford & Palisi, 1996). Middle-aged adults who maintain an exercise regimen are likely to perceive themselves as particularly active for their age and, therefore, to feel a special sense of accomplishment (Netz et al., 2005). And exercise may convey extra psychological benefits by reducing feelings of vulnerability to illness that increase with age. Fear of disease and disability is one of the strongest contributors to poor psychological well-being at midlife (Barsky, Cleary, & Klerman, 1992).

Sense of Control and Personal Life Investment. Middle-aged adults who report a high sense of control over events in various aspects of their lives—health, family, and work—also report more favorable psychological well-being. A sense of control fosters self-efficacy—a belief in one's ability to surmount challenges—and, consequently, helps sustain a positive outlook in the face of health, family, and work difficulties (Lachman & Firth, 2004; Smith et al., 2000).

But beyond feeling in control, personal life investment—firm commitment to goals and involvement in pursuit of those goals—adds to mental health and life satisfaction (Staudinger, Fleeson, & Baltes, 1999). According to Mihaly Csikszentmihalyi, a vital wellspring of happiness is *flow*—the psychological state of being so engrossed in a demanding, meaningful activity that one loses all sense of time and self-awareness. People describe flow as the height of enjoyment, even as an ecstatic state. The more they experience it, the more they judge their lives to be gratifying (Nakamura & Csikszentmihalyi, 2002). Although flow is common in people engaged in creative endeavors, many others report it—students who love studying, employees who like their jobs, adults involved in challenging leisure pursuits, and parents and grandparents engaged in pleasurable learning activities with children. Flow depends on perseverance and skill at complex endeavors that offer potential for growth. These qualities are well developed in middle adulthood.

Positive Social Relationships. Developing gratifying social ties is closely linked to midlife psychological well-being. In a longitudinal study of 90 men selected for good physical and mental health as college students and followed over 32 years, most maintained their physical health status. A good mentor relationship in early adulthood (which fosters high career achievement) and favorable peer ties were among the best predictors of well-being in the late forties and early fifties (Westermeyer, 1998). In a survey of college alumni, those who preferred occupational prestige and high income to close friends were twice as likely as other respondents to describe themselves as "fairly" or "very" unhappy (Perkins, 1991, as cited by Myers, 2000).

A Good Marriage. Although friendships and positive relationships with coworkers are important, a good marriage boosts psychological well-being even more. In both cross-sectional and longitudinal research, the role of marriage as a marker of mental health increases with

While engaged in a vigorous, uplifting recreational activity, this midlifer may be reflecting on ways to surmount health, family, or work challenges. Personal life investment—steadfast pursuit of meaningful goals—fosters psychological well-being in middle age.

age, becoming a powerful predictor by late midlife (Marks, Bumpass, & Jun, 2004; Westermeyer, 1998).

Longitudinal studies tracking people as they move in and out of intimate relationships suggest that marriage actually brings about well-being. For example, when interviews with over 13,000 adults were repeated five years later, people who remained married reported greater happiness than those who remained single. Those who separated or divorced became less happy, reporting considerable depression. Men and women who married for the first time experienced a sharp increase in happiness, those who entered their second marriage a modest increase (Marks & Lambert, 1998).

The link between marriage and well-being is similar in many nations, suggesting that marriage changes people's behavior in ways that make them better off (Diener et al., 2000; Lansford et al., 2005). Married partners monitor each other's health and offer care in times of illness. They also earn and save more money than single people, and higher income is modestly linked to psychological well-being (Myers, 2000; Waite, 1999). Furthermore, sexual satisfaction predicts mental health, and married couples have more satisfying sex lives than unmarried couples and singles (see Chapter 14). Of course, not everyone is better off married. But for many people, the long-term commitment that marriage entails fosters mental health.

Mastery of Multiple Roles. Finally, success in handling multiple roles is linked to psychological well-being. Women are generally happier today than in the past because they now reap satisfactions not just from family relationships but also from vocational achievements. In a study of nearly 300 middle-aged women, researchers asked about feelings of competence and control in four roles: wife, mother, caregiver of an impaired parent, and employee. Participants experienced higher levels of mastery in their work roles than in any other. But competence and control in all four roles predicted life satisfaction and reduced depression (Christensen, Stephens, & Townsend, 1998). Women who occupied several roles—in work and family arenas—seemed to benefit from added opportunities to enhance their sense of mastery.

Gender Identity

In her forties and early fifties, Trisha appeared more assertive at work, speaking out more freely at meetings and taking a leadership role when a team of lawyers worked on an especially complex case. She was also more dominant in family relationships, expressing her opinions to her husband and son more readily than she had 10 or 15 years earlier. In contrast, Devin's sense of empathy and caring became more apparent, and he was less assertive and more accommodating to Trisha's wishes than before.

Many studies report an increase in "masculine" traits in women and "feminine" traits in men across middle age (Huyck, 1990; James et al., 1995). Women become more confident, self-sufficient, and forceful, men more emotionally sensitive, caring, considerate, and dependent. These trends appear in cross-sectional and longitudinal research, in people varying in SES, and in diverse cultures—not just Western industrialized nations but also village societies such as the Mayans of Guatemala, the Navajo of the United States, and the Druze of the Middle East (Fry, 1985; Gutmann, 1977; Turner, 1982). Consistent with Levinson's theory, gender identity in midlife becomes more androgynous—a mixture of "masculine" and "feminine" characteristics.

Although the existence of these changes is well-accepted, explanations for them are controversial. A well-known evolutionary view, **parental imperative theory,** holds that identification with traditional gender roles is maintained during the active parenting years to help ensure the survival of children. Men become more goal-oriented, while women emphasize nurturance. After children reach adulthood, parents are free to express the "other-gender" side of their personalities (Gutmann & Huyck, 1994). A related idea is that the decline in sex hormones associated with aging may contribute to androgyny in later life (Rossi, 1980).

But these biological accounts have been criticized. As we discussed in earlier chapters, parents need both warmth and assertiveness (in the form of firmness and consistency) to rear children effectively. And although children's departure from the home is related to men's openness to the "feminine" side of their personalities, the link to a rise in "masculine" traits among women is less apparent (Huyck, 1996, 1998). In longitudinal research, college-educated women in the labor force became more independent by their early forties, regardless of whether they had children; those who were homemakers did not. Women attaining high status at work gained most in dominance, assertiveness, and outspokenness by their early fifties (Helson & Picano, 1990; Wink & Helson, 1993). Finally, androgyny is not associated with menopause—a finding at odds with a hormonal explanation (Helson & Wink, 1992).

Besides reduced parenting responsibilities, other demands and experiences of midlife may prompt a more androgynous orientation. For example, among men, a need to enrich a marital relationship after children have departed, along with reduced opportunities for career advancement, may be involved in the awakening of emotionally sensitive traits. Compared with men, women are far more likely to face economic and social disadvantages. A greater number remain divorced, are widowed, and encounter discrimination in the workplace. Self-reliance and assertiveness are vital for coping with these circumstances.

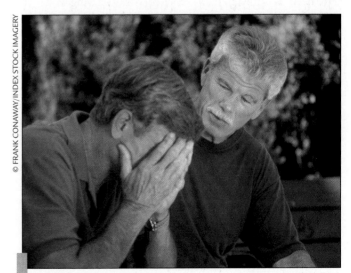

In middle age, gender identity becomes more androgynous for both sexes. Men tend to show an increase in "feminine" traits, becoming more emotionally sensitive, caring, considerate, and dependent.

In sum, androgyny in midlife results from a complex combination of social roles and life conditions. In Chapter 8, we noted that androgyny predicts high self-esteem. In adulthood, it is also associated with advanced moral reasoning and psychosocial maturity (Prager & Bailey, 1985; Waterman & Whitbourne, 1982). People who do not integrate the masculine and feminine sides of their personalities tend to have mental health problems, perhaps because they are unable to adapt flexibly to the challenges of aging (Huyck, 1996).

Individual Differences in Personality Traits

Although Trisha and Jewel both became more self-assured and assertive in midlife, in other respects they differed. Trisha had always been more organized and hardworking, Jewel more gregarious and fun-loving. Once, the two women traveled together. At the end of each day, Trisha was disappointed if she had not kept to a schedule and visited every tourist attraction. Jewel liked to "play it by ear"—wandering through streets, stopping to talk with shopkeepers and residents.

In previous sections, we considered personality changes common to many middle-aged adults, but stable individual differences also exist. The hundreds of personality traits on which people differ have been organized into five basic factors, called the **"big five" personality traits:** neuroticism, extroversion, openness to experience, agreeableness, and conscientiousness. Table 16.2 provides a description of each. Notice that Trisha is high in conscientiousness, whereas Jewel is high in extroversion (Costa & McCrae, 1994; McCrae & Costa, 1990).

Longitudinal and cross-sectional studies of Canadian and U.S. men and women reveal that agreeableness and conscientiousness increase from the teenage years through middle age, whereas neuroticism declines, and extroversion and openness to experience do not change or decrease slightly—changes that reflect "settling down" and greater maturity. Similar trends have been identified in many other countries varying widely in cultural traditions, including Germany, Italy, Japan, Russia, and South Korea (Costa et al., 2000; McCrae et al., 2000;

Roberts et al., 2003; Srivastava et al., 2003). The consistency of these cross-cultural findings has led some researchers to conclude that adult personality change is genetically influenced. They note that individual differences in the "big five" traits are large and highly stable: A person who scores high or low at one age is likely to do the same at another, over intervals ranging from 3 to 30 years (Costa & McCrae, 1994). In a reanalysis of more than 150 longitudinal studies including more than 50,000 participants, personality-trait stability increased during early and middle adulthood, reaching a peak in the decade of the fifties (see Figure 16.4) (Roberts & DelVecchio, 2000).

How can there be high stability in personality traits, yet significant changes in aspects of personality discussed earlier? Studies of the "big five" traits include very large samples and typically do not examine the impact of a host of contextual factors—including life events, the social clock, and cultural values—that shape aspirations, goals, and expectations for appropriate behavior (Caspi & Roberts, 2001). Look closely at the traits in Table 16.2, and you will see that they differ from the attributes considered in previous sections: They do not take into account motivations, preferred tasks, and coping styles, nor do they consider how certain aspects of personality, such as masculinity and femininity, are integrated (Block, 1995; Helson & Stewart, 1994). Theorists concerned with change due to experience focus on how personal needs and life events induce new strategies and goals. In contrast, those who emphasize stability due to heredity measure personality traits on which individuals can easily be compared and that are present at any time of life (Rosenberg, Rosenberg, & Farrell, 1999).

To resolve this apparent contradiction, we can think of adults as changing in overall organization and integration of personality, but doing so on a foundation of basic, enduring dispositions that support a coherent sense of self as people adapt to changing life circumstances. When more than 2,000 individuals in their forties were asked to reflect on their personalities during the previous 6 years, 52 percent said they had "stayed the same," 39 percent said they had "changed a little," and 9 percent said they had "changed a lot" (Herbst et al.,

Table 16.2	The "Big Five" Personality Traits
Trait	**Description**
Neuroticism	Individuals who are high on this trait are worrying, temperamental, self-pitying, self-conscious, emotional, and vulnerable. Individuals who are low are calm, even-tempered, self-content, comfortable, unemotional, and hardy.
Extroversion	Individuals who are high on this trait are affectionate, talkative, active, fun-loving, and passionate. Individuals who are low are reserved, quiet, passive, sober, and emotionally unreactive.
Openness to experience	Individuals who are high on this trait are imaginative, creative, original, curious, and liberal. Individuals who are low are down-to-earth, uncreative, conventional, uncurious, and conservative.
Agreeableness	Individuals who are high on this trait are soft-hearted, trusting, generous, acquiescent, lenient, and good-natured. Individuals who are low are ruthless, suspicious, stingy, antagonistic, critical, and irritable.
Conscientiousness	Individuals who are high on this trait are conscientious, hardworking, well-organized, punctual, ambitious, and persevering. Individuals who are low are negligent, lazy, disorganized, late, aimless, and nonpersistent.

Source: McCrae & Costa, 1990.

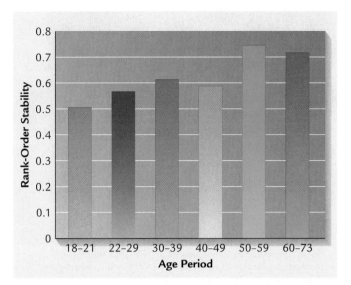

■ **FIGURE 16.4 Increase in stability of the "big five" personality traits across early and middle adulthood.** In a reanalysis of more than 150 longitudinal studies, stability of personality traits was strong at all ages; adults who scored high or low in certain traits largely retained that pattern when retested. Stability reached a peak in the fifties. (Adapted from Roberts & DelVecchio, 2000.)

2000). Again, these findings contradict a view of middle adulthood as a period of great turmoil and change. But they also underscore that personality remains an "open system," responsive to the pressures of life experiences. Indeed, certain midlife personality changes may strengthen trait consistency! Improved self-understanding, self-acceptance, and skill at handling challenging situations may result in less need to modify basic personality dispositions over time (Caspi & Roberts, 2001).

Ask Yourself

Review

> Summarize personality changes at midlife. How can these changes be reconciled with increasing stability of the "big five" personality traits, peaking in the fifties?

Apply

> Jeff, age 46, suggested to his wife, Julia, that they set aside time once a year to discuss their relationship—both positive aspects and ways to improve. Julia reacted with surprise—Jeff had never before expressed interest in working on their marriage. What developments at midlife probably fostered this new concern?

Connect

> List cognitive gains that typically occur during middle adulthood. (See Chapter 15, pages 521–522.) How might they support midlife personality changes?

Reflect

> List your hoped-for and feared possible selves. Then ask your family members in the early and middle adulthood periods to do the same. Are their reports consistent with age-related research findings? Explain.

Relationships at Midlife

The emotional and social changes of midlife take place within a complex web of family relationships and friendships. Although a few middle-aged people live alone, the vast majority—9 out of 10 in the United States and Canada—live in families, most with a spouse (Statistics Canada, 2001b; U.S. Census Bureau, 2006b). Partly because they have ties to older and younger generations in their families and partly because their friendships are well-established, people tend to have a larger number of close relationships during midlife than at any other period (Antonucci, Akiyama, & Takahashi, 2004).

The middle adulthood phase of the family life cycle is often referred to as "launching children and moving on." In the past, it was often called the "empty nest," but this phrase implies a negative transition, especially for women. When adults devote themselves entirely to their children, the end of active parenting can trigger feelings of emptiness and regret. But for many people, middle adulthood is a liberating time, offering a sense of completion and an opportunity to strengthen existing ties and build new ones.

A century ago, most parents reared children for almost all of their active adulthood. A declining birthrate and longer life expectancy mean that many contemporary parents launch children a decade or more before retirement, then seek other rewarding activities. Because this period has lengthened, it is marked by the greatest number of exits and entries of family members. As adult children leave home and marry, middle-aged people must adapt to new roles of parent-in-law and grandparent. At the same time, they must establish a different type of relationship with their aging parents, who may become ill or infirm and die. Let's see how ties within and beyond the family change during this time of life.

Marriage and Divorce

Although not all couples are financially comfortable, middle-aged households are well-off economically compared with other age groups. North Americans between 45 and 54 have the highest average annual income (Statistics Canada, 2002b; U.S. Census Bureau, 2006b). Partly because of increased financial security, and because the time between departure of the last child and retirement has lengthened, the contemporary social view of marriage in midlife is one of expansion and new horizons.

These forces strengthen the need to review and adjust the marital relationship. For Devin and Trisha, this shift was gradual. By middle age, their marriage had permitted satisfaction of family and individual needs, endured many changes, and culminated in deeper feelings of love. Elena's marriage, in contrast, became more conflict-ridden as her teenage daughter's problems introduced added strains and as departure of children made marital difficulties more obvious. Tim's failed marriage revealed yet another pattern. With passing years, the number of problems declined, but so did the love expressed. As less happened in the relationship, good or bad, the couple had little to keep them together (Rokach, Cohen, & Dreman, 2004).

As the Biology and Environment box on pages 538–539 revealed, marital satisfaction is a strong predictor of midlife psychological well-being. Middle-aged men who have focused only on career often realize the limited nature of their pursuits. At the same time, their wives may insist on a more gratifying relationship. And children fully engaged in adult roles remind middle-aged parents that they are in the latter part of their lives, prompting many to decide that the time for improving their marriages is now (Berman & Napier, 2000).

As in early adulthood, divorce is one way of resolving an unsatisfactory marriage in midlife. Although most divorces occur within 5 to 10 years of marriage, about 10 percent take place after 20 years or more (Statistics Canada, 2002a; U.S. Department of Health and Human Services, 2002). Divorce at any age takes a heavy psychological toll, but midlifers seem to adapt more easily than younger people. A survey of more than 13,000 Americans revealed that following divorce, middle-aged men and women reported less decline in psychological well-being than their younger counterparts (Marks & Lambert, 1998). Midlife gains in practical problem solving and effective coping strategies may reduce the stressful impact of divorce.

Because the divorce rate is more than twice as great among remarried couples as among those in first marriages, a substantial number of midlife divorces involve people who have had one or more previous unsuccessful marriages. Highly educated middle-aged adults are more likely to divorce, probably because their more comfortable economic circumstances make it easier to leave an unhappy marriage (Wu & Penning, 1997). Nevertheless, for many women, marital breakup—especially when it is repeated—severely reduces standard of living (see page 346 in Chapter 10). For this reason, in midlife and earlier, it is a strong contributor to the **feminization of poverty**—a trend in which women who support themselves or their families have become the majority of the adult population living in poverty, regardless of age and ethnic group. Because of weak public policies safeguarding families (see Chapter 2), the gender gap in poverty is higher in the United States and Canada than in other Western industrialized nations (Paquet, 2002; U.S. Census Bureau, 2006b).

What do recently divorced middle-aged people say about why their marriages ended? Women frequently mention communication problems, inequality in the relationship, adultery, gradual distancing, substance abuse, physical and verbal abuse, or their own desire for autonomy. Men also bring up poor communication and sometimes admit that their "workaholic" lifestyle or emotional inattentiveness played a major role in their marital failure. Women are more likely than men to initiate divorce, and those who do fare somewhat better in psychological well-being. Men who initiate a split often already have another romantic involvement to turn to (Rokach, Cohen & Dreman, 2004; Sakraida, 2005; Schneller & Arditti, 2004).

Longitudinal evidence reveals that middle-aged women who weather divorce successfully tend to become more tolerant, comfortable with uncertainty, nonconforming, and self-reliant in personality—factors believed to be fostered by divorce-forced independence. And both men and women reevaluate what they consider important in a healthy relation-

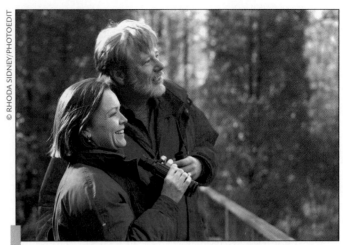

For many middle-aged couples, having forged a relationship that permits satisfaction of both family and individual needs results in deeper feelings of love.

ship, placing greater weight on equal friendship and less on passionate love than they had the first time. As in earlier periods, divorce represents both a time of trauma and a time of growth (Baum, Rahav, & Sharon, 2005; Schneller & Arditti, 2004). Little is known about long-term adjustment following divorce among middle-aged men, perhaps because most enter new relationships and remarry within a short time.

Changing Parent–Child Relationships

Parents' positive relationships with their grown children are the result of a gradual process of "letting go," starting in childhood, gaining momentum in adolescence, and culminating in children's independent living. As mentioned earlier, most middle-aged parents adjust well to the launching phase of the family life cycle; only a minority have difficulty. Investment in nonparental relationships and roles, children's characteristics, parents' marital and economic circumstances, and cultural forces affect the extent to which this transition is expansive and rewarding or sad and distressing.

After moving their son Mark into his college dormitory at the start of his freshman year, Devin and Trisha felt a twinge of nostalgia. Driving home, they recalled his birth, first day of school, and high school graduation and commented on their suddenly tranquil household. Beyond this, they returned to rewarding careers and community participation and delighted in having more time for each other. Parents who have developed gratifying alternative activities typically welcome their children's adult status (Dennerstein, Dudley, & Guthrie, 2002). A strong work orientation, especially, predicts gains in life satisfaction after children depart from the home (Seltzer & Ryff, 1994; Silverberg, 1996).

Whether or not they reside with parents, adolescent and young adult children who are "off-time" in development—not showing expected signs of independence and accomplishment—can prompt parental strain (Aquilino, 1996; Pillemer & Suitor, 2002). Consider Elena, whose daughter was frequently truant from high school and in danger of not graduating. The need for greater parental oversight and guidance caused anxiety and unhappiness for Elena, who was ready to complete the active parenting phase and focus on her own personal and vocational development.

However, wide variations exist in the social clock for launching children. Recall from Chapter 13 that many young people from low-SES homes and with cultural traditions of extended-family living do not leave home early. In the southern European countries of Greece, Italy, and Spain, parents often actively delay their children's departure. In Italy, for example, parents believe that leaving without a "justified" reason signifies that something is wrong in the family (Rossi, 1997). Hence, many more Italian young adults reside with their parents until marriage than in other Western nations. At the same time, Italian adults grant their grown children extensive freedom within the parental home (Rusconi, 2004). Parent–adult-child relationships are usually positive, making living with parents attractive.

With the end of parent–child coresidence comes a substantial decline in parental authority. Devin and Trisha no longer knew of Mark's daily comings and goings or expected him to inform them. Nevertheless, Mark telephoned at regular intervals to report on events in his life and seek advice about major decisions. Although the parental role changes, its continuation is important to middle-aged adults. Departure of children is a relatively minor event when parent–child contact and affection are sustained. When it results in little or no communication, parents' life satisfaction declines (White, 1994). In a large longitudinal study of New Zealand families, parents' relations with adult children were linked to quality of parenting years before. Parents who had been warm and supportive in middle childhood and adolescence were more likely to experience contact and closeness with their child in early adulthood (Belsky et al., 2001).

Throughout middle adulthood, parents continue to give more assistance to children than they receive, especially while children are unmarried or when they face difficulties, such as marital breakup or unemployment (Ploeg et al., 2004; Zarit & Eggebeen, 2002). Providing emotional and financial support while children get their lives under way is related to midlife psychological well-being. Because of their own disrupted relationships and economic need, divorced and remarried parents are less likely than parents in first marriages to offer adult children support, and they are also less content (Marks, 1995). Children's psychological adjustment is more important than their educational and occupational success for midlife parental adjustment (Ryff, Schmutte, & Lee, 1996). When young adult children are relatively free of emotional and social problems, they relate more positively to their parents. Favorable adaptation to the launching phase depends on feeling successful as a parent and on not being estranged from one's children.

When children marry, parents face additional challenges in enlarging the family network to include in-laws. Difficulties occur when parents do not approve of their child's partner or when the young couple adopts a way of life inconsistent with the parents' values. But when warm, supportive relationships endure, intimacy between parents and children increases over the adult years, with great benefits for parents' life satisfaction (Ryff, Singer, & Seltzer, 2002). Once young adults strike out on their own, members of the middle generation, especially mothers, usually take on the role of **kinkeeper,** gathering the family for celebrations and making sure everyone stays in touch.

As children become adults, parents expect a mature relationship with them, marked by tranquility and contentment. Yet many factors—on the child's and the adult's side—affect whether that goal is achieved. Applying What We Know on page 544 suggests ways middle-aged parents can increase the chances that bonds with adult children will be loving and rewarding and serve as contexts for personal growth.

Grandparenthood

Two years after Mark married, Devin and Trisha were thrilled to learn that a granddaughter was on the way. Although the stereotypical image of grandparents as elderly persists, on average American adults become grandparents in their mid- to late forties, Canadian adults in their late forties to early fifties (AARP, 2002; Rosenthal & Gladstone, 2000). A longer life expectancy means that adults will spend as much as one-third of their lifespan in the grandparent role.

■ **Meanings of Grandparenthood.** Why did Trisha and Devin, like many people their age, greet the announcement of a grandchild with such enthusiasm? Most people experience grandparenthood as a significant milestone, mentioning one or more of the following gratifications:

- *Valued elder*—being perceived as a wise, helpful person
- *Immortality through descendants*—leaving behind not just one but two generations after death
- *Reinvolvement with personal past*—being able to pass family history and values to a new generation
- *Indulgence*—having fun with children without major child-rearing responsibilities (AARP, 2002; Miller & Cavanaugh, 1990)

■ **Grandparent–Grandchild Relationships.** Grandparents' styles of relating to grandchildren vary as widely as the meanings they derive from their new role. The grandparent's and grandchild's age and sex make a difference. When their granddaughter was young, Trisha and Devin enjoyed an affectionate, playful relationship with her. As she got older, she looked to them for information and advice in addition to warmth and caring. By the time their granddaughter reached adolescence, Trisha and Devin had become role models, family historians, and conveyers of social, vocational, and religious values (Hurme, 1991).

Typically, relationships are closer between grandparents and grandchildren of the same sex and, especially, between maternal grandmothers and granddaughters—a pattern found in many countries (Brown & Rodin, 2004). Grandmothers also report higher satisfaction with the grandparent role than

Applying What We Know

Ways Middle-Aged Parents Can Promote Positive Ties with Their Adult Children

Suggestion	Description
Emphasize positive communication.	Let adult children know of your respect, support, and interest. This not only communicates affection but also permits conflict to be handled in a constructive context.
Avoid unnecessary comments that are a holdover from childhood.	Adult children, like younger children, appreciate an age-appropriate relationship. Comments that have to do with safety, eating, and cleanliness (for example, "Be careful on the freeway," "Don't eat those foods," and "Make sure you wear a sweater on a cold day") annoy adult children and can stifle communication.
Accept the possibility that some cultural values and practices and aspects of lifestyle will be modified in the next generation.	In constructing a personal identity, most adult children have gone through a process of evaluating the meaning of cultural values and practices for their own lives. Traditions and lifestyles cannot be imposed on adult children.
When an adult child encounters difficulties, resist the urge to "fix" things.	Accept the fact that no meaningful change can take place without the willing cooperation of the adult child. Stepping in and taking over communicates a lack of confidence and respect. Find out whether the adult child wants your help, advice, and decision-making skills.
Be clear about your own needs and preferences.	When it is difficult to arrange for a visit, baby-sit, or provide other assistance, say so and negotiate a reasonable compromise rather than letting resentment build.

Source: Toder, 1994.

grandfathers, perhaps because grandmothers are more likely to participate in recreational, religious, and family activities with grandchildren and therefore have more contact (Silverstein & Marenco, 2001; Somary & Stricker, 1998). The grandparent role may be a vital means through which middle-aged women satisfy their kinkeeping function.

Living nearby made Trisha and Devin's pleasurable interaction with their granddaughter possible. Grandparents who live far from young grandchildren usually have more distant relationships, with little contact except on holidays, birthdays,

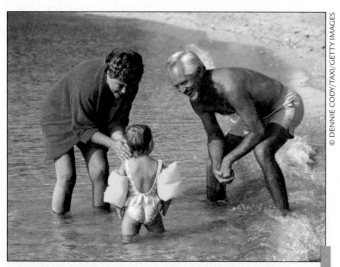

© DENNIE CODY/TAXI/GETTY IMAGES

Many grandparents derive great joy from an affectionate, playful relationship with young grandchildren. As this grandchild gets older, she is likely to look to her grandparents for advice, role models, and family history in addition to warmth and caring.

and other formal occasions. Despite high family mobility in Western industrialized nations, most grandparents live close enough to at least one grandchild to make regular visits possible. And even when grandparents reside far away, a strong desire to affect the development of grandchildren can motivate them to become involved in grandchildren's lives (AARP, 2002). As grandchildren get older, distance has less impact. Instead, the extent to which the adolescent or young adult grandchild believes the grandparent values contact is a good predictor of a close bond (Brussoni & Boon, 1998).

SES and ethnicity also influence grandparent–grandchild ties. In higher-income families, where the grandparent role is not central to family maintenance and survival, it is fairly unstructured and takes many forms. In low-income families, by contrast, grandparents perform essential activities. For example, many single parents live with their families of origin and depend on grandparents' financial and caregiving assistance to reduce the impact of poverty. Compared with grandchildren in intact families, grandchildren in single-parent and stepparent families report engaging in more diverse, higher-quality activities with their grandparents (Kennedy & Kennedy, 1993). As children experience the stress of family transition, bonds with grandparents take on increasing importance.

In some cultures, grandparents are absorbed into an extended-family household and become actively involved in child rearing. When a Chinese, Korean, or Mexican-American maternal grandmother is a homemaker, she is the preferred caregiver while parents of young children are at work (Kamo, 1998; Williams & Torrez, 1998). Similarly, involvement in child care is high among Native-American and Canadian-Aboriginal grandparents. In the absence of a biological grandparent, an unrelated elder may be integrated into the family to serve as a mentor and disciplinarian for children (Werner, 1991). (See Chapter 2, page 67, for a description of the grandmother's role in the African-American extended family.)

■ **Recent Trends in Grandparenting.** Increasingly, grandparents have stepped in as primary caregivers in the face of serious family problems. As the Social Issues box on page 546 reveals, a rising number of North American children live apart from their parents in grandparent-headed households. Despite their willingness to help and their competence at child rearing, grandparents who take full responsibility for young children experience considerable emotional and financial strain. They need much more assistance from community and government agencies than is currently available.

Because parents usually serve as gatekeepers of grandparents' contact with grandchildren, relationships between grandparents and their daughter-in-law or son-in-law strongly affect the closeness of grandparent–grandchild ties. A positive bond with a daughter-in-law seems particularly important in the relationship between grandparents and their son's children (Fingerman, 2004). And after a marital breakup, grandparents related to the custodial parent (typically the mother) have more frequent contact with grandchildren (Johnson, 1998).

A growing concern among grandparents—especially those on the noncustodial side—is maintaining relationships with grandchildren after parental divorce. Currently, all 50 U.S. states and the Canadian province of Québec permit grandparents to seek legal visitation judgments. Yet grandparent visitation rights can add to family difficulties. When parents are divorcing, grandparents' behavior varies greatly, from constructive help to entanglement in parental battles. Unfortunately, intense conflict usually lies behind the legal petitions of grandparents who fail to work out visitation informally (Smith & Drew, 2002). Consequently, courts are wise to exercise restraint in awarding grandparents visitation privileges.

When family relationships are positive, grandparenthood provides an important means of fulfilling personal and societal needs in midlife and beyond. Typically, grandparents are a frequent source of pleasure, support, and knowledge for children, adolescents, and young adults. They also provide the young with firsthand experience in how older people think and function. In return, grandchildren become deeply attached to grandparents and keep them abreast of social change. Clearly, grandparenthood is a vital context for sharing between generations.

Middle-Aged Children and Their Aging Parents

The percentage of North American middle-aged people with living parents has risen dramatically—from 10 percent in 1900 to 50 percent at the beginning of the twenty-first century (U.S. Census Bureau, 2006b; Vanier Institute of the Family, 2004b). A longer life expectancy means that adult children and their parents are increasingly likely to grow old together. What are middle-aged children's relationships with their aging parents

like? And how does life change for adult children when an aging parent's health declines?

■ **Frequency and Quality of Contact.** A widespread myth is that adults of past generations were more devoted to their aging parents than are today's adults. Although adult children spend less time in physical proximity to their parents, the reason is not neglect or isolation. Fewer aging adults live with younger generations now than in the past because of a desire to be independent, made possible by gains in health and financial security. Nevertheless, approximately two-thirds of older adults in the United States and Canada live close to at least one of their children, and frequency of contact is high through both visits and telephone calls (Rosenthal & Gladstone, 2000; U.S. Census Bureau, 2006b). Proximity increases with age: Elders who move usually do so in the direction of kin, and younger people tend to move in the direction of their aging parents.

Middle age is a time when adults reassess relationships with their parents, just as they rethink other close ties (Helson & Moane, 1987). Many adult children become more appreciative of their parents' strengths and generosity. Trisha, for example, marveled at her parents' fortitude in rearing three college-educated children despite limited income. And she recalled her mother's sound advice just before her marriage to Devin nearly three decades earlier: "Build a life together but also forge your own life. You'll be happier." At several turning points, that advice had influenced Trisha's decisions.

As Trisha's rapport with her mother conveys, mother–daughter relationships tend to be closer than other parent–child ties (Fingerman, 2001b). As the tensions of the adolescent years ease, many young-adult daughters and mothers build rewarding, intimate bonds. Daughters benefit greatly from maternal support, and many describe the relationship in glowing terms. As daughters move into middle age, their descriptions of the mother–daughter bond become more complex, reflecting both positive and negative aspects—a change that may stem from daughters' more mature perspective and from

In midlife, many adults become more appreciative of their parents' strengths and generosity. Mother–daughter bonds tend to be closer than other parent–child ties, although daughters' capacity to invest emotionally in the relationship is complicated by many competing demands on their time.

Social Issues

Grandparents Rearing Grandchildren: The Skipped-Generation Family

Nearly 2.4 million U.S. and 75,000 Canadian children—4 to 5 percent of the child population—live with grandparents but apart from parents, in **skipped-generation families** (Statistics Canada, 2003a; U.S. Census Bureau, 2006b). The number of grandparents rearing grandchildren has increased over the past decade. The arrangement occurs in all ethnic groups, though more often in African-American, Hispanic, and Canadian-Aboriginal families than in Caucasian families (Fuller-Thomson, 2005; Minkler & Fuller-Thomson, 2005). Although grandparent caregivers are more likely to be women than men, many grandfathers participate. Often these families take in two or more children.

One grandmother's account illustrates the circumstances in which skipped-generation families form:

> I think [the child's mother] is doing an awful lot of drugs. I don't know if it's serious drugs, but enough that she wasn't doing a good job. They were doing an awful lot of partying, and I just finally went to her one day and said, "Your life is messed up, let me take the baby for a while so you can get your life together." And it was just because we wanted her [the grand-daughter] out of there. She had become our main priority. (Jendrek, 1994, p. 209)

In about half of skipped-generation families, grandparents step in because substance-abuse problems prevent parents, usually the child's mother, from engaging in competent child rearing. In most other instances, parental emotional or physical illness is involved (Pruchno & McKenney, 2000; Weber & Waldrop, 2000). Child abuse and neglect is often a factor. Occasionally child welfare authorities, out of a preference for placing the child with relatives rather than in a foster home, approach the grandparent, who assumes temporary or permanent legal

custody. More often, grandparents offer their assistance, sometimes with and sometimes without legal responsibility. Most say they took action to protect the child only when the parents' situation became intolerable.

Because the skipped-generation family structure is not freely chosen, many custodial grandparents face highly stressful life circumstances. Absent parents' adjustment difficulties strain family relationships (Hirshorn, Van Meter, & Brown, 2000). Unfavorable child-rearing experiences have left their mark on the children, who show high rates of learning difficulties, depression, and antisocial behavior. To make matters worse, some parents interfere by violating the grandparents' behavioral limits, taking grandchildren away without permission, or making promises to children that they do not keep. These youngsters also introduce financial burdens into households that often are already low-income (Mills, Gomez-Smith, & De Leon, 2005; Williamson, Softas-Nall, & Miller, 2003). All these factors heighten grandparents' emotional distress.

Grandparents struggle with daily dilemmas—wanting to be grandparents, not parents; wanting the parent to be present in the child's life but fearing for the child's well-being if the parent returns and does not provide good care. Child-rearing tasks mean that grandparents have less time for spouses, friends, and leisure when they had expected to have more time. Many report feeling emotionally drained, depressed, and worried about what will happen to the children if their own health fails (Hayslip et al., 2002; Kolomer & McCallion, 2005). Some families are extremely burdened. Native-American and Canadian-Aboriginal caregiving grandparents are especially likely to be unemployed, to have a disability, to be caring for several grandchildren, and to be living in extreme poverty (Fuller-Thomson, 2005; Fuller-Thomson & Minkler, 2005).

Skipped-generation families have a tremendous need for social and financial

Vera Saunders, age 71, shown here with her 17-year-old grandson, is tired but proud. In middle age, she took custody of three grand-children. Grandparents in skipped-generation families face shattered dreams of freedom and relaxation and significant financial burdens. To Vera, the sacrifices were worthwhile.

support and intervention services for troubled children. Despite great hardship, these grandparents seem to realize their widespread image as "silent saviors," often forging close emotional bonds with their grandchildren (Fuller-Thomson & Minkler, 2000). A survey of a large, representative sample of U.S. families revealed that compared with children in divorced, single-parent families or in blended families, children reared by grandparents were better-behaved in school, less susceptible to physical illness, and doing just as well academically (Solomon & Marx, 1995).

Although their daily existence is often stressful, many grandparent caregivers report joy from sharing children's lives and helping them grow. Positive outcomes foster feelings of accomplishment and pride, which help compensate for difficult circumstances. And some grandparents view the rearing of grandchildren as a "second chance"—an opportunity to make up for earlier, unfavorable parenting experiences and "do it right" (Minkler & Roe, 1993; Waldrop & Weber, 2001).

growing relationship tensions (Fingerman, 2000). Although middle-aged daughters love their aging mothers and desire their approval, they face many competing demands on their time and energy (Fingerman, 1996). Consequently, older mothers (especially those who are widowed) may be more emotionally invested in their daughters than their middle-aged daughters are able to be in their mothers (Fingerman, 2001a).

In the non-Western world, older adults most often live with their married children. Chinese, Japanese, and Korean elderly, for example, generally move in with a son and his wife and children. This pattern, however, is changing: More elders live with a daughter's family or on their own than in the past (Kamo, 1998; Zhan & Montgomery, 2003; Zhang, 2004). Whether or not coresidence and daily contact are typical, relationship quality usually reflects patterns established earlier: Positive parent–child ties generally remain so, as do conflict-ridden interactions.

Help exchanged between adult children and their aging parents is responsive to past and current family circumstances. The more positive the history of the parent–child tie, the more help given and received (Whitbeck, Hoyt, & Huck, 1994). Also, parents give more to unmarried children and to children with disabilities, whereas children give more to widowed parents and parents in poor health. At the same time, a shift in helping occurs over the adult years. Parent-to-child advice, household aid, gift giving, and financial assistance decline, while child-to-parent help of various kinds increases (Kunemund, Motel-Klingebiel, & Kohli, 2005; Rossi & Rossi, 1990; Zarit & Eggebeen, 2002). But even when parent–child relationships have been emotionally distant, adult children offer more support as their parents age, out of a sense of altruism and family duty (Silverstein et al., 2002).

■ **Caring for Aging Parents.** The burden of caring for aging can be great. In Chapter 2, we noted that as birthrates have declined, the family structure has become more "top-heavy," with more generations alive but fewer younger members. This means that more than one older family member is likely to need assistance, with fewer younger adults available to provide it. About 20 percent of midlifers in the United States and Canada are involved in caring for an aging parent with a chronic illness or disability (Takamura & Williams, 2002; Vanier Institute of the Family, 2004b).

The term **sandwich generation** is widely used to refer to the idea that middle-aged adults must care for multiple generations above and below them at the same time (Riley & Bowen, 2005). Although middle-aged adults who care for elderly parents rarely have young children of their own in their homes, many are providing assistance to young-adult children and to grandchildren—obligations that, when combined with work and community responsibilities, can lead middle-aged caregivers to feel "sandwiched," or squeezed, between the pressures of older and younger generations.

Midlifers living far from aging parents who are in poor health often substitute financial help for direct care, if they have the means. But when parents live nearby and have no spouse to meet their needs, adult children usually engage in direct care. Regardless of family income level, African-American and Hispanic adults give aging parents more financial help and direct care than Caucasian-American adults do (Shuey & Hardy, 2003). Minority families typically build a large and strong support network, with African Americans often drawing on close, family-like relationships with friends and neighbors for financial or caregiving assistance.

In all ethnic groups, responsibility for providing care to aging parents falls more on daughters than on sons (see Figure 16.5). Why are women usually the principal caregivers? Families turn to the person who seems most available—living nearby and with fewer commitments regarded as interfering with the ability to assist. These unstated rules, in addition to parents' preference for same-sex caregivers (aging mothers live longer), lead more women to fill the role. Daughters also feel more obligated than sons to care for aging parents (Stein et al., 1998). And although couples strive to be fair to both sides of the family, they tend to provide more direct care for the wife's parents. This bias, however, is weaker in ethnic minority families and is nonexistent in Asian nations where daughters-in-law are expected to provide care to their husband's parents (Shuey & Hardy, 2003; Zhan & Montgomery, 2003).

About 50 percent of North American women caregivers are employed; another 10 to 30 percent quit their jobs to provide care. And time devoted to caring for a disabled aging parent is substantial, averaging 20 hours per week (Nichols & Junk, 1997; Takamura & Williams, 2002). Nevertheless, as Figure 16.5 shows, men—although doing less than their wives—do contribute. Tim, for example, looked in on his father, a recent stroke victim, every evening, reading to him, running errands, making household repairs, and taking care of finances. His sister, however, provided more hands-on care in her own home—cooking, feeding, and bathing. The care sons and daughters provide tends to be divided along gender-role lines.

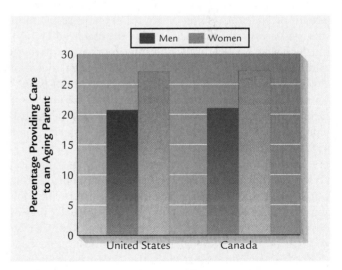

■ **FIGURE 16.5 Percentage of American and Canadian 45- to 54-year-olds providing care to an aging parent.** In both nations, more women than men reported providing care. Still, men make a substantial contribution to care of aging parents. (Adapted from Takamura & Williams, 2002; Vanier Institute of the Family, 2004b.)

About 10 percent of the time—generally when no other family member can do so—sons become primary caregivers, heavily involved in basic-care tasks (Campbell & Martin-Matthews, 2000; Harris, 1998).

As adults move from early to later middle age, the sex difference in parental caregiving declines. Perhaps as men reduce their vocational commitments and feel less need to conform to a "masculine" gender role, they grow more able and willing to provide basic care (Marks, 1996). At the same time, parental caregiving may contribute to men's greater openness to the "feminine" side of their personalities. A man who cared for his mother, severely impaired by Alzheimer's disease, commented on how the experience altered his outlook:

> Having to do personal care, becoming a male nurse, was a great adjustment. It was so difficult to do these tasks; things a man, a son, is not supposed to do. But, I had to alter, since charity must come before maintaining a selfish, conventional view. I have definitely modified my views on conventional expectations. (Hirsch, 1996, p. 112)

Although most adult children help willingly, caring for a chronically ill or disabled parent is highly stressful—and radically different from caring for a young child. The need for parental care typically arises suddenly, after a heart attack, fall, stroke, or diagnosis of cancer, leaving little time for preparation. Whereas children become increasingly independent, the parent usually gets worse, and the caregiving task and its cost escalate. "One of the most difficult aspects is the emotional strain of being such a close observer of my father's physical and mental decline," Tim explained to Devin and Trisha. Tim also felt a sense of grief over the loss of a cherished relationship, as his father no longer seemed to be his former self. Because duration of caregiving is uncertain, caregivers often feel they no longer have control over their lives (Gatz, Bengtson, & Blum, 1990).

Adults who share a household with ill parents—about 10 percent of North American caregivers—experience the most stress. A parent and child who have lived separately for years usually dislike moving in together, and conflicts are likely to arise over routines and lifestyles. But the greatest source of stress is problem behavior, especially for caregivers of parents who have deteriorated mentally (Marks, 1996). Tim's sister reported that their father would wake during the night, ask repetitive questions, follow her around the house, and become agitated and combative.

Parental caregiving often has emotional and physical health consequences. It leads to role overload (conflict among employment, spouse, parent, and elder care roles), high job absenteeism, exhaustion, inability to concentrate, feelings of hostility, anxiety about aging, and rates of depression as high as 30 to 50 percent (Killian, Turner, & Cain, 2005; Stephens et al., 2001). In cultures and subcultures where adult children feel an especially strong sense of obligation to care for aging parents, the toll tends to be greater. In a study of Korean, Korean-American, and Caucasian-American caregivers of parents with mental disabilities, the Koreans and Korean Americans reported the highest levels of family obligation and care burden—and

In all ethnic groups, daughters assume greater responsibility for caring for aging parents than do sons. Often the wife's parents receive more direct care—a bias that is nonexistent in Asian nations. This Korean woman offers sensitive, loving care to her mother-in-law.

also the highest levels of anxiety and depression (Youn et al., 1999). And among African-American caregivers, women who strongly endorsed cultural reasons for providing care ("It's what my people have always done") fared less well in mental health two years later than women who moderately endorsed cultural reasons (Dilworth-Anderson, Goodwin, & Williams, 2004).

Social support is highly effective in reducing caregiver stress. Tim's encouragement, assistance, and willingness to listen helped his sister cope with in-home care of their father so that she could find satisfactions and rewards in it. Despite having more time to care for an ill parent, women who quit work generally fare poorly, probably because of social isolation and financial strain (Pohl et al., 1994). Positive experiences at work can actually reduce the stress of parental care as caregivers bring a favorable self-evaluation and a positive mood home with them (Stephens & Franks, 1999).

In Denmark, Sweden, and Japan, a government-sponsored home helper system eases the burden of parental care by making specially trained nonfamily caregivers available, based on the elder's needs (Blomberg, Edebalk, & Petersson, 2000; Yamanoi, 1993). In the United States and Canada, in-home care by a nonfamily caregiver is too costly for most families; only 10 to 20 percent arrange it (Family Caregiver Alliance, 2002). And unless they must, few people want to place their parents in formal care, such as nursing homes, which also are expensive. Applying What We Know on the following page summarizes ways to relieve the stress of caring for an aging parent—at the individual, family, community, and societal levels. We will address additional elder care options, along with interventions for caregivers, in Chapter 17.

Siblings

As Tim's relationship with his sister reveals, siblings are ideally suited to provide social support. Nevertheless, a survey of a

Applying What We Know

Relieving the Stress of Caring for an Aging Parent

Strategy	Description
Use effective coping strategies.	Use problem-centered coping to manage the parent's behavior and caregiving tasks. Delegate responsibilities to other family members, seek assistance from friends and neighbors, and recognize the parent's limits while calling on capacities the parent does have. Use emotion-centered coping to reinterpret the situation in a positive way, such as emphasizing the opportunity it offers for personal growth and for giving to parents in the last years of their lives. Avoid denial of anger, depression, and anxiety in response to the caregiver work burden, which heightens stress.
Seek social support.	Confide in family members and friends about the stress of caregiving, seeking their encouragement and help. So far as possible, avoid quitting work to care for an ill parent, because doing so leads to social isolation and loss of financial resources.
Make use of community resources.	Contact community organizations to seek information and assistance, in the form of in-home respite help, home-delivered meals, transportation, and adult day care.
Press for workplace and public policies that relieve the emotional and financial burdens of caring for an aging parent.	Encourage your employer to provide elder care benefits, such as flexible work hours and caregiver leave without pay. Communicate with lawmakers and other citizens about the need for additional government funding to help pay for elder care. Emphasize the need for improved health insurance plans that reduce the financial strain of elder care on middle- and low-income families.

large sample of ethnically diverse Americans revealed that sibling contact and support decline from early to middle adulthood, rebounding only after age 70 for siblings living near one another (White, 2001). Decreased midlife contact is probably due to the demands of middle-aged adults' diverse roles. However, most adult siblings report getting together or talking on the phone at least monthly (Antonucci, Akiyama, & Merline, 2002).

Despite reduced contact, many siblings feel closer in midlife, often in response to major life events (Stewart et al., 2001). Launching and marriage of children seem to prompt siblings to think more about one another. As Tim commented, "It helped our relationship when my sister's children were out of the house and married. I'm sure she cared about me. I think she just didn't have time!" When a parent become seriously ill, brothers and sisters who previously had little to do with one another may find themselves in touch about parental care. And when parents die, adult children realize they have become the oldest generation and must look to one another to sustain family ties (Gold, 1996). As in early adulthood, sister–sister relationships are closer than sister–brother and brother–brother ties, a difference apparent in many industrialized nations (Cicirelli, 1995).

Not all sibling bonds improve, of course. Recall Trisha's negative encounters with her sister, Dottie (see Chapter 15, page 511). Dottie's difficult temperament had made her hard to get along with since childhood, and her temper flared when their father died and problems arose over family finances. When siblings do not help with parental caregiving, the child shouldering the burden can unleash powerful negative feelings (Merrill, 1997). As one expert expressed it, "As siblings grow

older, good relationships [often] become better and rotten relationships get worse" (Moyer, 1992, p. 57).

Ethnic background also affects the quality of sibling ties. In one study, Italian-American siblings (especially sisters) had much greater contact and warmer relationships than white Protestant siblings (Johnson, 1985). The researchers speculated that strong parental authority in Italian immigrant families led siblings to turn to one another for support early in life, forming warm bonds that persisted into adulthood.

In industrialized nations, sibling relationships are voluntary. In village societies, they are generally involuntary and basic to family functioning. For example, among Asian Pacific Islanders, family social life is organized around strong brother–sister attachments. A brother–sister pair is often treated as a unit in exchange marriages with another family. After marriage, brothers are expected to protect sisters, and sisters serve as spiritual mentors to brothers. Families not only include biological siblings but also grant other relatives, such as cousins, the status of brother or sister, creating an unusually large network of lifelong sibling support (Cicirelli, 1995).

In village societies, cultural norms reduce sibling conflict, thereby ensuring family cooperation (Weisner, 1993). In industrialized nations, promoting positive sibling interaction in childhood is vital for warm, supportive sibling bonds in later years.

Friendships

As family responsibilities declined in middle age, Devin found he had more time to spend with friends. On Friday afternoons, he met several male friends at a coffee house, and they chatted for a couple of hours. But most of Devin's friendships were

Friendships become more selective in midlife. Compared with younger people, middle-aged adults are less willing to invest in friendships unless they are very rewarding.

couple-based—relationships he shared with Trisha. Compared with Devin, Trisha more often got together with friends on her own (Blieszner & Adams, 1992).

Middle-aged friendships reflect the same trends discussed in Chapter 14. At all ages, men are less expressive than women with friends. Men tend to talk about sports, politics, and business, whereas women focus on feelings and life problems. For this reason, when Trisha and Devin gathered with friends, men often congregated in one area, women in another (Fox, Gibbs, & Auerbach, 1985). Women report a greater number of close friends and say they both receive and provide their friends with more emotional support (Antonucci, 1994).

Nevertheless, for both sexes, number of friends declines with age, probably because people become less willing to invest in nonfamily ties unless they are very rewarding (Carbery & Buhrmester, 1998). As selectivity of friendship increases, older adults express more complex ideas about friendship. They also try harder to get along with friends (Antonucci & Akiyama, 1995). Having chosen a friend, middle-aged people attach great value to the relationship and take extra steps to protect it.

By midlife, family relationships and friendships support different aspects of psychological well-being. Family ties protect against serious threats and losses, offering security within a long-term time frame. In contrast, friendships serve as current sources of pleasure and satisfaction, with women benefiting somewhat more than men (Antonucci, Akiyama, & Merline, 2002). As middle-aged couples renew their sense of companionship, they may combine the best of family and friendship. Indeed, research indicates that viewing a spouse as a best friend contributes greatly to marital happiness (Bengtson, Rosenthal, & Burton, 1990).

Relationships Across Generations

A widely recognized aspiration of families, communities, and society as a whole is that each generation leave the next better off. For more than two centuries, North Americans have achieved this goal. For example, Trisha's high-school-educated parents did everything possible to support her desire to earn a professional degree. And Devin and Trisha reared their son in financially more comfortable circumstances than they had experienced as children.

Yet Trisha and Devin, like many North Americans, often wondered whether the current generation of young people would be as well off as their own. Observing high rates of marital breakup, single-parent families, and youth crime, they questioned whether younger people would continue to respect and care for their elders. Trisha and Devin also worried that improved financial conditions among the elderly, in comparison to the high poverty rate among families with children (see Chapter 2), might fuel intergenerational resentment.

A survey of a large, nationally representative sample of U.S. 18- to 90-year-olds addressed the question of whether solidarity between generations is eroding. Findings showed that despite the social changes just mentioned, supportive ties among younger and older individuals remain strong (Bengtson & Harootyan, 1994; Lawton, Silverstein, & Bengtson, 1994). At the family level, 90 percent of adult children reported feeling close to an aging parent. In fact, adult children described closer ties to their aging parents than aging parents felt toward their adult children (although 80 percent of these ties were strong). And in line with the high rate of help giving noted earlier in this chapter, younger adults expressed a deep sense of commitment toward their parents—more than their parents expected! Furthermore, adult children's willingness to grant time and assistance to aging parents is unaffected by parents' wealth (Wong, Kitayama, & Soldo, 1999).

Young, middle-aged, and older survey respondents reported a wide range of volunteering in their communities. Middle-aged adults frequently devoted time to children and adolescents, usually through religious activities and academic tutoring programs. Older adults, by contrast, more often provided volunteer assistance to the elderly. But they were more likely to do so if they had warm relationships with their adult children. More than 70 percent of the sample described giving some kind of informal assistance to relatives, friends and neighbors, and other community residents (Harootyan & Vorek, 1994).

Finally, in this and other studies, most participants expressed no resentment about government benefits to other age groups. Rather, a *norm of equity* characterized their responses. Adults of all ages supported more funding for younger and older adults than for middle-aged adults, who are, in general, economically better off (Cutler, Whitelaw, & Beattie, 2002; Garstka, Hummert, & Branscombe, 2005). And when people believed the needs of one generation were unmet, they expressed dissatisfaction about government benefits to a less needy age group (Schlesinger & Kronebusch, 1994). In sum, despite public concern over intergenerational conflicts, most people are not guided by self-interest. To the contrary, their values, opinions, and behaviors reveal "hidden bridges" between generations.

www.ablongman.com/berk

Ask Yourself

Review

How do age, sex, proximity, and culture affect grandparent–grandchild ties?

Apply

Raylene and her brother Walter live in the same city as their aging mother, Elsie. When Elsie could no longer live independently, Raylene took primary responsibility for her care. What factors probably contributed to Raylene's involvement in caregiving and Walter's lesser role?

Connect

Cite evidence that early family relationships affect middle-aged adults' bonds with adult children, aging parents, and siblings.

Reflect

Ask a middle-aged couple you know well to describe the number and quality of their friendships today compared to their friendships of early adulthood. Does their report match research findings? Explain.

Vocational Life

As we have seen, the midlife transition typically involves vocational adjustments. For Devin, it resulted in a move up the career ladder to a demanding administrative post as college dean. Trisha reoriented her career from a large to a small law firm, where she felt her efforts were appreciated. Recall from Chapter 15 that after her oldest child left home, Anya earned a college degree and entered the workforce for the first time. Jewel strengthened her commitment to an already successful business, while Elena changed careers. Finally, Tim reduced his career obligations as he prepared for retirement.

Work continues to be a salient aspect of identity and self-esteem in middle adulthood. More so than in earlier or later years, people attempt to increase the personal meaning and self-direction of their vocational lives (Levinson, 1978, 1996). At the same time, certain aspects of job performance improve. Older employees have lower rates of absenteeism, turnover, and accidents and show no change in work productivity (Warr, 1994). Consequently, the value of an older employee ought to be equal to, and possibly even greater than, that of a younger employee.

The post–World War II baby boom, along with the elimination of mandatory retirement age in most industrialized nations, means that the number of older workers will rise dramatically over the next few decades. Yet a favorable transition from adult worker to older worker is hindered by negative stereotypes of aging—incorrect beliefs about limited learning capacity, slower decision making, and resistance to change and supervision (Sterns & Huyck, 2001). Furthermore, gender dis-

crimination continues to restrict the career attainments of many women. Let's take a close look at middle-aged work life.

Job Satisfaction

Job satisfaction has both psychological and economic significance. If people are dissatisfied at work, the consequences include absenteeism, turnover, grievances, and strikes, all of which are costly to employers.

Research shows that job satisfaction increases in midlife at all occupational levels, from executives to hourly workers (see Figure 16.6). The relationship is weaker for women than for men, probably because women's reduced chances for advancement result in a sense of unfairness. It is also weaker for blue-collar than for white-collar workers, perhaps because blue-collar workers have less control over their own work schedules and activities (Avolio & Sosik, 1999; Fotinatos-Ventouratos & Cooper, 1998). When different aspects of jobs are considered, intrinsic satisfaction—happiness with the work itself—shows a strong age-related gain. Extrinsic satisfaction—contentment with supervision, pay, and promotions—changes very little (Hochwarter et al., 2001).

What explains the rise in job satisfaction during middle adulthood? A broader time perspective probably contributes. "When I first started teaching, I complained about a lot of things," remarked Devin. "From my current vantage point, I can tell a big problem from a trivial one." Moving out of unrewarding work roles, as Trisha did, can also boost morale. Key characteristics that predict job well-being include involvement in decision making, reasonable workloads, and good physical working conditions. Older people may have greater access to

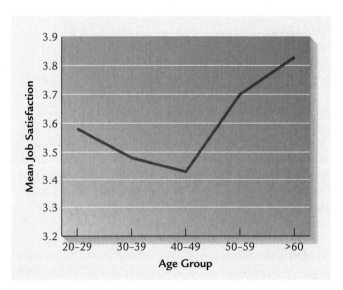

■ FIGURE 16.6 Age-related change in job satisfaction. In this study of more than 2,000 university employees at all levels, from secretary to university president, job satisfaction dropped slightly in early adulthood as people encountered some discouraging experiences (see Chapter 14). In middle age, job satisfaction showed a steady rise. (From W. A. Hochwarter et al., 2001, "A Note on the Nonlinearity of the Age–Job-Satisfaction Relationship," *Journal of Applied Social Psychology, 31,* p. 1232. Reprinted by permission.)

jobs that are attractive in these ways. Furthermore, having fewer alternative positions into which they can move, older workers generally reduce their career aspirations. As the perceived gap between actual and possible achievements declines, work involvement increases (Warr, 1992).

Although emotional engagement with work is usually seen as psychologically healthy, it can also result in **burnout**— a condition in which long-term job stress leads to mental exhaustion, a sense of loss of personal control, and feelings of reduced accomplishment. Burnout occurs more often in the helping professions, including health care, human services, and teaching, which place high emotional demands on employees (Zapf et al., 2001). Although people in interpersonally demanding jobs are as psychologically healthy as other people, sometimes a worker's dedication exceeds his or her coping skills, especially in an unsupportive work environment. Burnout is associated with excessive work assignments for available time and lack of encouragement and feedback from supervisors. It tends to occur more often in North America than in Western Europe, perhaps because of North Americans' greater achievement orientation (Maslach, Schaufeli, & Leiter, 2001).

Burnout is a serious occupational hazard, linked to impaired attention and memory, severe depression, on-the-job injuries, physical illnesses, poor job performance, absenteeism, and turnover (Melamed et al., 1999; Sandström et al., 2005; Wang, 2005; Wright & Bonett, 1997). To prevent burnout, employers can make sure workloads are reasonable, provide opportunities for workers to take time out from stressful situations, limit hours of stressful work, and offer social support. Interventions that enlist employees' participation in designing higher-quality work environments show promise for increasing work engagement and effectiveness and reducing burnout (Leiter & Maslach, 2000). And provisions for work at home may respond to the needs of some people for a calmer, quieter work atmosphere.

Career Development

After several years as a parish nurse, Anya felt a need for additional training to do her job better. Trisha appreciated her firm's generous support of workshop and course attendance, which helped her keep abreast of new legal developments. And as college dean, Devin took several seminars each year on management effectiveness and instructional technology. As these experiences reveal, career development is vital throughout work life.

■ **Job Training.** Anya's 35-year-old supervisor, Roy, was surprised when she asked for time off to upgrade her skills. "You're in your fifties," he replied. "What're you going to do with so much new information at this point in your life?"

Roy's insensitive, narrow-minded response, though usually unspoken, is unfortunately all too common among managers—even some who are older themselves! Research suggests that training and on-the-job career counseling are less available to older workers. And when career development activities are offered, older employees may be less likely to volunteer for

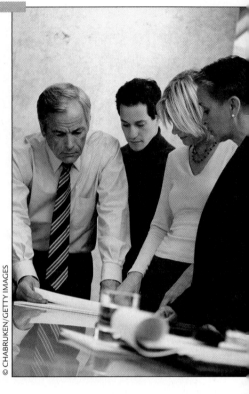

This project team, consisting of two young and two middle-aged adults, works on a challenging assignment. Because team members similar in age communicate more, age-balanced work groups foster on-the-job learning and enhanced performance.

© CHABRUKEN/GETTY IMAGES

them (Hedge, Borman, & Lammlein, 2006; Salthouse & Maurer, 1996). What influences willingness to engage in job training and updating?

Personal characteristics are important, starting with the degree to which an individual wants to change. With age, growth needs give way somewhat to security needs. Consequently, learning and challenge may have less intrinsic value to many older workers. Perhaps for this reason, older employees depend more on co-worker and supervisor encouragement for vocational development. Yet as we have seen, they are less likely to have supportive supervisors. Furthermore, negative stereotypes of aging reduce older workers' self-efficacy, or confidence that they can renew and expand their skills. Self-efficacy is a powerful predictor of employees' efforts to improve career-relevant skills (Maurer, 2001; Maurer, Wrenn, & Weiss, 2003).

Workplace characteristics matter, too. An employee given work that requires new learning must pursue that learning to complete the assignment. Unfortunately, older workers sometimes receive more routine tasks than younger workers. Therefore, some of their reduced motivation to engage in career-relevant learning may be due to the type of assignments they receive. Interaction among co-workers can also have a profound impact. Within project teams, people similar in age communicate more often. Age-balanced work groups (with more than one person in each age range) foster on-the-job learning because communication is a source of support as well as a means of acquiring job-relevant information (Zenger & Lawrence, 1989).

Computer networks facilitate such team interaction and also enhance sharing of information in large companies, helping employees at lower levels develop a broader perspective on their contribution to company goals and feel a part of the larger organization (Avolio & Sosik, 1999). Furthermore, expansion of computer technology compels older workers to upgrade their computer literacy. This, in turn, helps them keep pace with changing aspects of their jobs.

■ **Gender and Ethnicity: The Glass Ceiling.** In her thirties, Jewel became a company president by starting her own business. As a woman, she had decided that her chances of rising to a top executive position in a large corporation were so slim that she didn't even try. In a longitudinal study of more than 1,300 U.S. adults, the probability of attaining a managerial position climbed substantially over 30 years of career experience for white men. By contrast, it rose modestly for white women and black men, and hardly at all for black women. Inequalities at career entry became more pronounced over time—findings that held after work skills and work productivity factors were controlled (see Figure 16.7) (Maume, 2004). When the most prestigious high-level management positions are considered, white men are even more advantaged: They account for 77 percent of chief executive officers at large corporations (U.S. Census Bureau, 2006b).

Women and ethnic minorities face a **glass ceiling,** or invisible barrier to advancement up the corporate ladder. Why is this so? Management is an art and skill that must be taught. Yet women and members of ethnic minorities have less access to mentors, role models, and informal networks that serve as training routes. And because of stereotyped doubts about

Women and ethnic minorities often face a glass ceiling—an invisible barrier to advancement in corporations and government organizations. Marjorie Scardino has succeeded in shattering the glass ceiling. She is chief executive officer of Pearson—an international media company with 32,000 employees worldwide. Pearson's Boston-based company, Allyn and Bacon, publishes this textbook.

© ADRIAN DENNIS/AFP/GETTY IMAGES

women's career commitment and ability to become strong managers, large companies spend less money on formal training programs for their female employees. Furthermore, challenging, high-risk, high-visibility assignments that require leadership and open the door to advancement, such as startup ventures, international experience, and troubleshooting, are rarely granted to women and minorities (Barr, 1996; Lyness & Thompson, 1997). Finally, women who demonstrate qualities linked to leadership and advancement—assertiveness, confidence, forcefulness, and ambition—encounter prejudice because they deviate from traditional gender roles. They are evaluated more negatively than men with these traits (Carli & Eagly, 2000; Eagly & Karau, 2002).

Like Jewel, many women have dealt with the glass ceiling by going around it. Largely because of lack of advancement opportunities, nearly twice as many female as male middle managers quit their jobs in large corporations, with most going into business for themselves (Mergenhagen, 1996). Today, more than half of all start-up businesses in the United States are owned and operated by women. Most are successful entrepreneurs: 72 percent achieve or exceed their expansion and earnings goals (Ahuja, 2005; U.S. Census Bureau, 2006b). But when women and ethnic minorities leave the corporate world to further their careers, companies not only lose valuable talent but also fail to address the leadership needs of an increasingly diverse workforce.

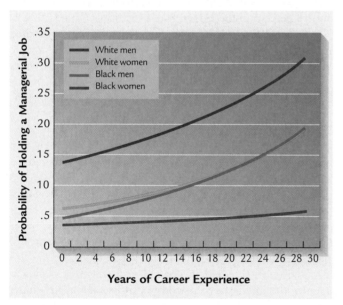

■ **FIGURE 16.7 Probability of attaining a managerial position over 30 years of career experience, by sex and ethnicity.** In a longitudinal study of more than 26,000 U.S. adults, chances of promotion to a managerial position increased steadily with experience for white men. In comparison, women and black men lagged behind in attainment of managerial authority, and black women were nearly shut out of managerial jobs. The trends confirm the existence of a glass ceiling for women and ethnic minorities. (From D. J. Maume, 2004, "Is the Glass Ceiling a Unique Form of Inequality?" *Work and Occupations, 31,* p. 266. © 2004 Sage Publications. Reprinted by permission.)

Career Change at Midlife

Although most people remain in the same vocation through middle age, career change does occur, as with Elena's shift from journalism to teaching and creative writing. Recall that circumstances at home and at work motivated Elena's decision to pursue a new vocation. Like other career changers, she wanted a more satisfying life—a goal she attained by ending an unhappy marriage and initiating a long-awaited vocational move at the same time.

As noted earlier, midlife career changes are seldom radical; they typically involve leaving one line of work for a related one. Elena sought a more stimulating, involving job. But other people move in the reverse direction—to careers that are more relaxing, free of painful decisions, and less demanding in terms of responsibility for others (Juntunen, Wegner, & Matthews, 2002). The decision to change is often difficult. The individual must weigh years invested in one set of skills, current income, and job security against present frustrations and hoped-for gains from a new vocation.

An extreme career shift, by contrast, usually signals a personal crisis (Young & Rodgers, 1997). In a study of professionals who abandoned their well-paid, prestigious positions for routine, poorly paid, semiskilled work, nonwork problems influenced the break with an established career. An eminent 55-year-old TV producer became a school bus driver, a New York banker a waiter in a ski resort. Each was responding to feelings of personal meaninglessness—escaping from family conflict, difficult relationships with colleagues, and work that had become unsatisfying into a freer, more independent lifestyle (Sarason, 1977).

Unemployment

Devin and Trisha's friend George worked in a corporate retirement-planning office, counseling retirees on how to enjoy leisure time or find new work. When he lost his job at age 54, George had to apply his counseling skills to himself. He found unemployment to be a culture shock. For the first two weeks, he spent most of his days in bed, didn't shave, and drank heavily. Even after this initial phase, George was depressed and had frequent bouts of illness.

As companies downsize, eliminating jobs, the majority of people affected are middle-aged and older. Although unemployment is difficult at any time, middle-aged workers show a sharper decline in physical and mental health than their younger counterparts (Breslin & Mustard, 2003). Older workers affected by layoffs remain jobless longer, suffering substantial income loss. In addition, people over age 40 who must reestablish occupational security find themselves "off-time" in terms of the social clock. Consequently, job loss can disrupt major tasks of midlife, including generativity and reappraisal of life goals and accomplishments (Broomhall & Winefield, 1990). Finally, having been more involved in and committed to an occupation, the older unemployed worker has also lost something of greater value.

After a despondent period, George began to follow the advice he had given his clients. He made a list of things he really liked to do, things he didn't want to do again, and the risks he could take given his current financial and life circumstances. He formed his own small business and continued to advise retirees, write articles, and give speeches on all aspects of retirement—but working from home in a T-shirt instead of from an office in a business suit. Effective problem-centered coping strategies enabled George to reestablish a satisfying work life (Kinicki, Prussia, & McKee-Ryan, 2000).

Social support is vital for reducing stress and reassuring middle-aged job seekers of their worth. But not all forms of social support work equally well. Recognition of one's abilities and communication with others who share interests and values—experiences that occur often in relations with co-workers—help the most (Mallinckrodt & Fretz, 1988).

People who lose their jobs in midlife seldom duplicate the status and pay of their previous positions. As they search, they encounter age discrimination and find that they are overqualified for many openings. Counseling that focuses on financial planning, reducing feelings of humiliation due to the stigma of unemployment, and encouraging personal flexibility can help people find gratifying alternative work roles.

Planning for Retirement

One evening, Devin and Trisha met George and Anya for dinner. Halfway through the meal, Devin inquired, "George, tell us what you and Anya are going to do about retirement. You're an expert on the topic—are you planning to close down your business or work part-time? Do you think you'll stay here or move out of town?"

Three or four generations ago, the two couples would not have had this conversation. In 1900, about 70 percent of North American men age 65 and over were in the labor force. By 1970, however, the figure had dropped to 27 percent, and in the early twenty-first century it declined to 9 percent in Canada and 18 percent in the United States (Statistics Canada, 2002c; U.S. Census Bureau, 2006b). Because of government-sponsored retirement benefits—which began in Canada in 1927 and in the United States in 1935—retirement is no longer a privilege reserved for the wealthy. In both countries, the federal governments pay social security to the majority of the aged, and others are covered by employer-based private pension plans (Chappell et al., 2003; Meyer & Bellas, 1995).

Most workers report looking forward to retirement, and an increasing number are leaving full-time work in midlife. The average age of retirement declined during the past two decades. Currently, it is age 62 in Canada and the United States and hovers between 60 and 63 in other Western nations (Statistics Canada, 2002c; U.S. Census Bureau, 2006b). This means that increasing numbers of people spend up to one-fourth of their lives in retirement.

Retirement is a lengthy, complex process that begins as soon as the middle-aged person first thinks about it (Kim & Moen, 2002b). Planning is important because retirement leads to a loss of two important work-related rewards—income and status—and to change in many other aspects of life. Like other life transitions, retirement is often stressful.

"Retirement planning helps you evaluate your options, learn about the availability of resources, and prepare emotionally for the changes ahead," George explained at one of his retirement seminars. Nearly half of middle-aged people engage in no concrete retirement planning, yet research consistently shows that planning results in better retirement adjustment

Applying What We Know

Ingredients of Effective Retirement Planning

Issue	Description
Finances	Ideally, financial planning for retirement should start with the first paycheck; at a minimum, it should begin 10 to 15 years before retirement, since most people spend more than 20 years retired.
Fitness	Starting a fitness program in middle age is important because good health is crucial for well-being in retirement.
Role adjustment	Retirement is harder for people who strongly identify with their work role. Preparing for a radical role adjustment reduces stress.
Where to live	The pros and cons of moving should be considered carefully because where one lives affects access to health care, friends, family, recreation, entertainment, and part-time employment.
Leisure activities	A retiree typically gains an additional 50 hours per week of free time. Careful planning of what to do with that time has a major impact on psychological well-being.
Health insurance	Finding out about government-sponsored health insurance options helps protect quality of life after retirement.
Legal affairs	The preretirement period is an excellent time to finalize a will and begin estate planning.

and satisfaction (Jacobs-Lawson, Hershey, & Neukam, 2004; Quick & Moen, 1998).

Applying What We Know above lists the variety of issues addressed in a typical retirement preparation program. Financial planning is vital, since income typically drops by 50 percent. But although more people engage in financial planning than in other forms of preparation, even those who attend financial education programs often fail to look closely at their financial well-being and to make wise decisions (Hershey et al., 1998). Many could benefit from an expert's financial analysis and counsel.

Retirement leads to ways of spending time that are largely guided by one's interests rather than one's obligations. Individuals who have not thought carefully about how to fill this time may find their sense of purpose in life seriously threatened. Research reveals that planning for an active life has an even greater impact on happiness after retirement than financial planning. Participation in activities promotes many factors essential for psychological well-being, including a structured time schedule, social contact, and self-esteem (Schlossberg, 2004). Carefully considering whether or not to relocate at retirement is related to an active life, since it affects access to family, friends, recreation, entertainment, and part-time work.

Devin retired at age 62, George at age 66. Though several years younger, Trisha and Anya—like many married women—coordinated their retirements with those of their husbands (Ruhm, 1996). In contrast, Jewel—in good health but without an intimate partner to share her life—kept her consulting business going until age 75. Tim took early retirement and moved to be near Elena, where he devoted himself to public service—tutoring second graders in a public school, transporting inner-city children to museums, and coaching after-school and weekend youth sports. For Tim, like many executives, retirement offered a new opportunity to pay attention to the world around him.

Unfortunately, less well-educated people with lower lifetime earnings are least likely to attend retirement preparation programs—yet they stand to benefit the most. And compared with men, women do less planning for retirement, often depending on their husband's preparations—a finding that may change as women increasingly become equal, rather than secondary, family earners (Han & Moen, 1999). Employers must take extra steps to encourage lower-paid workers and women to participate in planning activities (Jacobs-Lawson, Hershey, & Neukam, 2004). In addition, enhancing retirement adjustment among the economically disadvantaged depends on access to better health care, vocational training, and jobs at early ages. Clearly, a lifetime of opportunities and experiences affects the transition to retirement. In Chapter 18, we will consider the decision to retire and retirement adjustment in greater detail.

Ask Yourself

Review
What factors lead job satisfaction to increase with age?

Apply
An executive wonders how his large corporation can foster advancement of women and ethnic minorities to upper management positions. What strategies would you recommend?

Connect
Supervisors sometimes assign only the more routine tasks to older workers, believing that they can no longer handle complex assignments. Cite evidence from this and the previous chapter revealing this assumption to be incorrect.

www.ablongman.com/berk

Summary

Erikson's Theory: Generativity versus Stagnation

According to Erikson, how does personality change in middle age?

■ Generativity begins in early adulthood but expands greatly as middle-aged adults face Erikson's psychological conflict of **generativity versus stagnation.** Highly generative people find fulfillment as they make contributions to society through parenthood, other family relationships, the workplace, and volunteer activities.

■ Personal desires and cultural demands jointly shape adults' generative activities. Highly generative people appear especially well adjusted. The negative outcome, *stagnation*, occurs when people become self-centered and self-indulgent in midlife.

Other Theories of Psychosocial Development in Midlife

Describe Levinson's and Vaillant's views of psychosocial development in middle adulthood, and discuss similarities and differences between men and women.

■ According to Levinson, middle-aged adults reassess their relation to themselves and the external world. They confront four developmental tasks, each requiring them to reconcile two opposing tendencies within the self: young–old, destruction–creation, masculinity–femininity, and engagement–separateness.

■ Perhaps because of the double standard of aging, women express concern about appearing less attractive and are more likely than men to perceive themselves as younger than their chronological age. But non-college-educated men, even more than women, show a rise in sensitivity to physical aging in midlife.

■ Middle-aged men may adopt "feminine" traits of nurturance and caring, while women may take on "masculine" traits of autonomy, dominance, and assertiveness. Men and successful career-oriented women often reduce their focus on ambition and achievement. Women who have devoted themselves to child rearing or an unfulfilling job typically increase their involvement in work and the community.

■ Vaillant found that adults in their late forties and fifties take on responsibility as guardians of their culture, seeking to "pass the torch" to later generations.

Does the term midlife crisis *fit most people's experience of middle adulthood?*

■ Most people respond to midlife with changes that are better described as "turning points" than as a crisis. Only a minority experience a **midlife crisis** characterized by intense self-doubt and inner turmoil and leading to drastic changes in their personal lives and careers.

Characterize middle adulthood using a life events approach and a stage approach.

■ Both continuity and stagewise change characterize emotional and social development in middle adulthood. Some changes are adaptations to external events (such as the family life cycle) that are less age-graded than in the past. Most middle-aged adults also report stagelike development, in which troubling moments prompt new understandings and goals.

Stability and Change in Self-Concept and Personality

Describe changes in self-concept and personality in middle adulthood.

■ Middle-aged individuals maintain self-esteem and stay motivated by revising their **possible selves,** which become fewer in number as well as more modest and concrete as people adjust their hopes and fears to their life circumstances.

■ Midlife typically leads to greater self-acceptance, autonomy, and environmental mastery—changes that lead to greater psychological well-being and life satisfaction. As a result, some people consider middle age the "prime of life." Notions of happiness, however, vary widely among cultures.

© ALAN KEARNEY/GETTY IMAGES/TAXI

■ Daily stressors plateau from early to midlife, then decline in the sixties as work and family responsibilities ease. Coping strategies become more effective as middle-aged adults develop greater confidence in their ability to handle life's problems.

Describe changes in gender identity in midlife.

■ Both men and women become more androgynous in middle adulthood. Biologi-cal explanations, such as **parental imperative theory,** are controversial. A complex combination of social roles and life conditions is probably responsible for midlife changes in gender identity. For men, these changes are often linked to children's departure from the home; for women, to workplace experiences.

Discuss stability and change in the "big five" personality traits in adulthood.

■ Among the **"big five" personality traits,** neuroticism, extroversion, and openness to experience show stability or modest declines during adulthood, while agreeableness and conscientiousness increase. But individual differences in the "big five" traits are large and highly stable: Although adults change in overall organization and integration of personality, they do so on a foundation of basic, enduring dispositions.

Relationships at Midlife

Describe the middle adulthood phase of the family life cycle, including relationships with a marriage partner, adult children, grandchildren, and aging parents.

■ "Launching children and moving on" is the newest and longest phase of the family life cycle. Middle-aged adults must adapt to many entries and exits of family members as their children leave, marry, and produce grandchildren, and as their own parents age and die.

■ Midlife changes prompt many adults to focus on improving their marriages. When divorce occurs, it is more likely to be initiated by the woman, and middle-aged adults seem to adapt more easily than younger people. Many midlife divorces involve couples with one or more previous unsuccessful marriages. For women, marital breakup usually brings significant economic disadvantage, contributing to the **feminization of poverty.**

■ Most middle-aged parents adjust well to the launching phase of the family life cycle, especially if they have a strong work orientation and if parent–child contact and affection are sustained. In Italy and other southern European countries, unmarried adult children commonly continue to live with their parents; in North America, parents often provide emotional and financial support to young-adult children. As children marry and bring in-laws into the family network, middle-aged parents, especially mothers, often become **kinkeepers.**

■ When family relationships are positive, grandparenthood is an important means of fulfilling personal and societal needs. In-law relationships affect the closeness of grandparent–grandchild ties. In low-income families and in some subcultures, grandparents provide essential resources, including financial assistance and child care. When serious family problems exist, grandparents may become primary caregivers in **skipped-generation families.**

■ Middle-aged adults reassess their relationships with aging parents, often becoming more appreciative. Mother-daughter relationships tend to be closer than other parent–child ties. Yet quality of the early parent–child relationship—positive or conflict-ridden—usually persists, affecting help given and received.

■ Middle-aged adults, often caught between caring for ill or frail parents, assisting young-adult children and grandchildren, and meeting work and community responsibilities, are called the **sandwich generation.** The burden of caring for aging parents falls most heavily on adult daughters, though in later middle age, the sex difference declines.

■ Parental caregiving has emotional and health consequences. The toll is greatest in cultures and subcultures where adult children feel an especially strong obligation to provide care. Social support is highly effective in relieving caregiver stress.

Describe midlife sibling relationships and friendships, and discuss relationships across generations.

■ Sibling contact and support decline from early to middle adulthood, probably because of the demands of diverse roles. However,

most middle-aged siblings tend to feel closer, often in response to major life events, such as launching and marriage of children and parents' illness and death. Sister–sister ties are typically closest in industrialized nations. In nonindustrialized societies, where sibling relationships are basic to family functioning, other attachments (such as brother–sister) may be stronger.

■ In midlife, friendships become fewer, more selective, and more deeply valued. Men continue to be less expressive with their friends than women, who have more close friendships. Viewing a spouse as a best friend can contribute greatly to marital happiness.

■ Recent research reveals strong supportive ties across generations in families and communities. Most people support government benefits to other age groups—especially those with greatest need.

Vocational Life

Discuss job satisfaction and career development in middle adulthood, with special attention to sex differences and experiences of ethnic minorities.

■ Vocational readjustments are common as middle-aged people seek to increase the personal meaning and self-direction of their work lives. Certain aspects of job performance improve. Job satisfaction increases at all occupational levels, more so for men than for women.

■ **Burnout** is a serious occupational hazard, especially for those in helping professions. It can be prevented by ensuring reasonable workloads, limiting hours of stressful work, providing workers with social support, and enlisting employees' participation in designing higher-quality work environments.

■ Older workers engage in less career development because of negative stereotypes of aging, which impair self-efficacy; lack of encouragement from supervisors; and less challenging work assignments.

■ Women and ethnic minorities face a **glass ceiling** because of limited access to management training and prejudice against women who demonstrate qualities linked to leader-

ship and advancement. Many women further their careers by leaving the corporate world, often to start their own businesses.

Discuss career change and unemployment in middle adulthood.

■ For most middle-aged people, career change involves leaving one line of work for a related one within the same vocation. Radical career change is unusual and often signals a personal crisis.

■ Unemployment is especially difficult for middle-aged adults, who constitute the majority of workers affected by corporate downsizing and layoffs Counseling can help them find alternative, gratifying work roles, but these rarely duplicate their previous status or pay. Social support is vital for reducing stress.

Discuss the importance of planning for retirement, noting various issues that middle-aged adults should address.

■ An increasing number of North American workers are retiring from full-time work in midlife. Retirement brings stressful changes, including loss of income and status and an increase in free time. Besides financial planning, planning for an active life is vital with an especially strong impact on happiness after retirement. Employers must take extra steps to encourage lower-paid workers and women to participate in retirement preparation programs.

Important Terms and Concepts

"big five" personality traits (p. 540)
burnout (p. 552)
feminization of poverty (p. 542)
generativity versus stagnation (p. 530)
glass ceiling (p. 553)
kinkeeper (p. 543)
midlife crisis (p. 534)
parental imperative theory (p. 539)
possible selves (p. 536)
sandwich generation (p. 547)
skipped-generation family (p. 546)

Milestones
Development in Middle Adulthood

Age	Physical	Cognitive	Emotional/Social

40–50 YEARS

Physical

- Accommodative ability of the lens of the eye, ability to see in dim light, and color discrimination decline; sensitivity to glare increases (500–501)

- Hearing loss at high frequencies occurs (501)

- Hair grays and thins (500)

- Lines on the face become more pronounced; skin loses elasticity and begins to sag (501–502)

- Weight gain continues, accompanied by a rise in fatty deposits in the torso, while fat beneath the skin declines (502)

- Loss of lean body mass (muscle and bone) occurs (502)

- In women, production of estrogen drops, leading to shortening and irregularity of the menstrual cycle (502)

- In men, quantity of semen and sperm declines (505)

- Intensity of sexual response declines, but frequency of sexual activity drops only slightly (507)

- Rates of cancer and cardiovascular disease increase (508–510)

Cognitive

- Consciousness of aging increases (500, 532)

- Crystallized intelligence increases; fluid intelligence declines (516–517)

- Cognitive-processing speed declines, but adults can compensate through experience and practice (518–519)

- On complex tasks, ability to divide and control attention declines, but adults compensate through experience and practice (519–520)

- Amount of information retained in working memory declines, largely because of reduced use of memory strategies (520–521)

- Retrieving information from long-term memory becomes more difficult (520)

- General factual knowledge, procedural knowledge, and knowledge related to one's occupation remain unchanged or may increase (521)

Emotional/Social

- Generativity increases (530)

- Focuses more on personally meaningful living (530, 532)

- Possible selves become fewer in number and more modest and concrete (536)

- Self-acceptance, autonomy, and environmental mastery increase (536–537)

- Coping strategies become more effective (537)

- Gender identity becomes more androgynous; "masculine" traits increase in women, "feminine" traits in men (533–534, 539–540)

- Conscientiousness may increase, while neuroticism may decline (540)

- May launch children (542–543)

- May become a kinkeeper, especially if a mother (543)

- May become a parent-in-law and a grandparent (543–545)

- May care for a parent with a disability or chronic illness (547–548)

Age	Physical	Cognitive	Emotional/Social
40–50 YEARS (continued)		• Practical problem solving and expertise increase (521) • Creativity may emphasize integrating ideas and become more altruistic (521–522) • If in an occupation offering challenge and autonomy, shows gains in cognitive flexibility (523)	• Siblings may feel closer (548–550) • Number of friends generally declines (549–550) • Job satisfaction typically increases (551–552)
50–65 YEARS	• Lens of the eye loses its accommodative ability entirely (500) • Hearing loss extends to all frequencies but remains greatest for highest tones (501) • Skin continues to wrinkle and sag, and "age spots" appear (501) • Menopause occurs (502) • Continued loss of bone mass, leading to high rates of osteoporosis (502, 511) • Collapse of disks in the spinal column causes height to drop by as much as 1 inch (502)	• Changes in cognition listed on the previous page and above continue 	• Emotional and social changes listed on the previous page and above continue • Parent-to-child help-giving declines, and child-to-parent help-giving increases (545–548) • May retire (554–555)

Note: Numbers in parentheses indicate the page or pages on which each milestone is discussed.

Cultures around the world connect age with wisdom. Elders' extensive life experience enhances their ability to solve human problems and fill leadership positions, both important endeavors for the Dalai Lama—head of state and spiritual leader of the Tibetan people.

Physical and Cognitive Development in Late Adulthood

*A*t age 67, Walt gave up his photography business and looked forward to leisure years ahead with 64-year-old Ruth, who retired from her position as a social worker at the same time. This culminating phase of Walt's and Ruth's lives was filled with volunteer work, golfing three times a week, and joint summer vacations with Walt's older brother Dick and his wife, Goldie. Walt also took up activities he had always loved but had little time to pursue—writing poems and short stories, attending theater performances, enrolling in a class on world politics, and cultivating a garden that became the envy of the neighborhood. Ruth read voraciously, served on the board of directors of an adoption agency, and had more time to visit her sister Ida in a nearby city.

© JIM MCGUIRE/INDEX STOCK IMAGERY

Over the next 20 years, Walt's and Ruth's energy and vitality were an inspiration to everyone who met them. Their warmth, concern for others, and generosity with their time led not just their own children and grandchildren, but also nieces, nephews, children of their friends, and former co-workers, to seek them out. On weekends, their home was alive with visitors.

Then, in their early eighties, the couple's lives changed profoundly. Walt had surgery to treat an enlarged, cancerous prostate gland and within 3 months was hospitalized again after a heart attack. He lingered for 6 weeks with Ruth at his side and then died. Ruth's grieving was interrupted by the need to care for Ida. Alert and spry at age 78, Ida deteriorated mentally in her seventy-ninth year, despite otherwise excellent physical health. Meanwhile, Ruth's arthritis worsened, and her vision and hearing weakened.

As Ruth turned 85, certain activities had become more difficult—but not impossible. "It just takes a little adjustment!" Ruth exclaimed in her usual upbeat manner. Reading was harder, so she checked out "talking books" from her local library. Her gait was slower and her eyesight less reliable, so she hesitated to go out alone. At dinner in a noisy restaurant with her daughter and family, Ruth felt overwhelmed and participated very little in the fast-moving conversation. But in one-to-one interactions in a calm environment, she showed the same intelligence, wit, and astute insights that she had displayed all her life.

Late adulthood stretches from age 65 to the end of the lifespan. Unfortunately, popular images of old age fail to capture the quality of these final decades. Instead, many myths prevail—that the elderly are feeble, senile, and sick; that they have little contact with their families, who set them aside in nursing homes; that they are no longer able to learn; and that they have entered a phase of deterioration and dependency. Young people who have little contact with older adults are often surprised that elders like Walt and Ruth even exist—active and involved in the world around them.

As we trace physical and cognitive development in old age, we will see that the balance of gains and declines shifts as death approaches. But in industrialized nations, the typical 65-year-old can anticipate nearly two healthy, rewarding decades before this shift affects everyday life. And as Ruth illustrates, even after older adults become frail, many find ways to surmount physical and cognitive challenges.

Late adulthood is best viewed as an extension of earlier periods, not a break with them. As long as social and cultural contexts give elders support, respect, and purpose in life, these years are a time of continued potential.

🌿 Physical Development

When we say that an older person "looks young" or "looks old" for his or her age, we are acknowledging that chronological age is an imperfect indicator of **functional age,** or actual competence and performance. Because people age biologically at different rates, some 80-year-olds appear younger than many 65-year-olds (Neugarten & Neugarten, 1987). Beyond this gross comparison, recall from Chapter 13 that within each person, change differs across parts of the body. For example, Ruth became infirm physically but remained active mentally, whereas Ida, though physically fit for her age, found it hard to carry on a conversation, keep appointments, or complete familiar tasks.

So much variation exists between and within individuals that researchers have not yet identified any single biological measure that predicts the overall rate at which an elderly person will age. But we do have estimates of how much longer older adults can expect to live, and our knowledge of factors affecting longevity in late adulthood has increased rapidly.

How old are these elders? How old do they look and feel? Because people age biologically at different rates, the 76-year-old woman on the right appears younger than her 74-year-old sister on the left.

Life Expectancy

I wonder how many years I have left," Ruth asked herself each time a major life event, such as retirement and widowhood, occurred. Dramatic gains in **average life expectancy**— the number of years that an individual born in a particular year can expect to live, starting at any given age—provide powerful support for the multiplicity of factors considered in previous chapters that slow biological aging, including improved nutrition, medical treatment, sanitation, and safety. Recall from Chapter 1 that a North American baby born in 1900 had an average life expectancy of just under 50 years. In 2004, this figure reached 77.9 in the United States (75 for men and 80 for women) and 80.1 in Canada (77 for men and 82 for women). Twentieth-century gains in life expectancy were extraordinary— equal to those of the previous 5,000 years! Steady declines in infant mortality (see Chapter 3) are a major contributor to longer life expectancy. But death rates among adults have decreased as well. For example, heart disease, the leading cause of overall adult death in North America, has dropped by nearly 50 percent in the past 30 years, due to declines in risk factors (such as high blood pressure and smoking) and, mostly, advances in medical treatment (Statistics Canada, 2005e; U.S. Department of Health and Human Services, 2005h).

Variations in Life Expectancy

Consistent group differences in life expectancy underscore the joint contribution of heredity and environment to biological aging. As the figures just given reveal, on average, women can look forward to 4 to 7 more years of life than men—a difference found in almost all cultures. The female life expectancy advantage also characterizes several animal species, including rats, mice, and dogs (Shock, 1977). The protective value of the female's extra X chromosome (see Chapter 2) is believed to be responsible. Yet since the early 1970s, the gender gap in life expectancy has narrowed in industrialized nations (Conti et al., 2003; Leung, Zhang, & Zhang, 2004). Because men are at higher risk for disease and early death, they reap somewhat larger generational gains from positive lifestyle changes and new medical discoveries.

Life expectancy varies substantially with SES, ethnicity, and nationality. As education and income increase, so does length of life (De Vogli et al., 2005). And a U.S. white child born in the year 2004 is likely to live 5 to 7 years longer than an African-American child and 4 to 5 years longer than a Native-American child. Similarly, in regions of Canada with an Aboriginal population greater than 20 percent, average life expectancy is 5 to 15 years below that for the nation as a whole (Statistics Canada, 2005e; U.S. Department of Health and Human Services, 2005p). Accounting for these differences are higher rates of infant mortality, unintentional injuries, life-threatening disease, poverty-linked stress, and (in the United States) violent death in low-SES minority groups.

Length of life—and even more important, *quality of life* in old age—can be predicted by a country's health care, housing, and social services, along with lifestyle factors. When researchers estimate **active lifespan,** the number of years of vigorous, healthy life an individual born in a particular year can expect, Japan ranks first, Canada twelfth, and the United States a disappointing twenty-fourth (see Figure 17.1). Japan's low rate of heart disease, linked to its low-fat diet, in combination with favorable health care and other policies for the aged, account for its leading status. Because the United States falls short of other industrialized nations in all these respects, Americans spend somewhat more time disabled and die earlier than elders in most other developed countries. In developing nations with widespread poverty, malnutrition, disease, and armed conflict, average life expectancy hovers around 50 years, and active lifespan is even shorter—44 in Haiti, 38 in Afghanistan, 33 in Rwanda, and 26 in Sierra Leone (World Health Organization, 2000a).

Life Expectancy in Late Adulthood

Although poverty-stricken groups lag behind the economically advantaged, the number of people age 65 and older has risen dramatically in the industrialized world. From 1900 to 2004, the elderly increased from 4 percent to nearly 16 percent of the North American population—a figure expected to reach 23 percent by the middle of the twenty-first century. The fastest-growing segment of senior citizens is the 85-and-older group, who currently make up 1 percent of Americans and 1.4 percent of Canadians. By the year 2020, the proportion of seniors age 85 and older will double, and by 2050 it will quadruple (Statistics Canada, 2005e; U.S. Census Bureau, 2006b).

People reaching age 65 in the early twenty-first century can look forward, on average, to 18 more years of life in the United States and 19 more in Canada. As at earlier ages, life

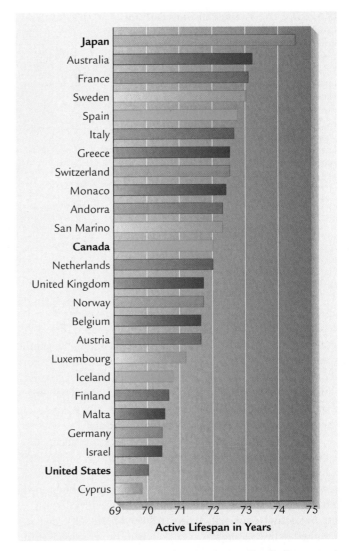

■ **FIGURE 17.1 Active lifespan in 25 nations.** Lifestyle factors and favorable health care and other policies for the aged contribute to active lifespan. Japan ranks first, Canada twelfth, and the United States a disappointing twenty-fourth. (Adapted from World Health Organization, 2000a.)

expectancy continues to be greater for women than for men. Today, the 65- to 69-year age group includes 115 women for every 100 men; for people age 85 and older, this number climbs to 226 (Health Canada, 2002c; U.S. Department of Health and Human Services, 2005p). Discrepancies like these, which occur in all developed countries, are not present in parts of the developing world where death rates of women during childbirth are high or women experience severe discrimination and deprivation (U.S. Census Bureau, 2005).

Although women outnumber men by a greater margin as elders advance in age, differences in average life expectancy between the sexes decline. A North American newborn girl can expect to live about 7 to 8 years longer than a newborn boy. At age 65, the difference narrows to about 3½ years; at age 85, to just over 1 year. Over age 100, the gender gap in life expectancy disappears. Similarly, differences in rates of chronic illness and in life expectancy between higher-SES whites and low-SES

■ FIGURE 17.2 Average life expectancy for Caucasians and African Americans at ages 75 and 85, illustrating the life expectancy cross-over. Below age 85, life expectancy is greater for American whites than blacks. At age 85 and older, this trend reverses; average life expectancy is greater for blacks than whites. Because only the biologically sturdiest members of low-SES minority groups survive into very old age, their life expectancy is slightly longer than that of their higher-SES counterparts. Notice, also, how the gender gap in life expectancy declines with age. (Adapted from U.S. Department of Health and Human Services, 2005h.)

ethnic minorities decline with age. Around age 85, a **life expectancy crossover** occurs—surviving members of low-SES ethnic minority groups live longer than members of the white majority (House, Lantz, & Herd, 2005; Liang et al., 2002). Figure 17.2 illustrates this finding for African Americans. Researchers speculate that among males and members of low-SES groups, only the biologically sturdiest survive into very old age.

Of course, average life expectancy does not tell us how enjoyable living to a ripe old age is likely to be. Most North Americans age 65 and older are capable of living independent, productive lives, although with age, growing numbers need assistance. After age 70, about 10 percent have difficulty carrying out **activities of daily living (ADLs)**—basic self-care tasks required to live on one's own, such as bathing, dressing, getting in and out of bed or a chair, or eating. And about 20 percent cannot carry out **instrumental activities of daily living (IADLs)**—tasks necessary to conduct the business of daily life and also requiring some cognitive competence, such as telephoning, shopping, food preparation, housekeeping, and paying bills. Furthermore, the proportion of elders with these limitations rises sharply with age (Statistics Canada, 2005e; U. S. Department of Health and Human Services, 2005h).

Throughout this book, we have seen that genetic and environmental factors jointly affect aging. With respect to heredity, identical twins typically die within 3 years of each other, whereas fraternal twins of the same sex differ by more than 6 years. Also, longevity runs in families. People with long-lived ancestors tend to survive longer and to be physically healthier in old age. And when both parents survive to age 70 or older, the chances that their children will live to 90 or 100 are double that of the general population (Hayflick, 1994; Mitchell et al., 2001).

At the same time, evidence from twin studies suggests that once people pass 75 to 80 years, the contribution of heredity to length of life decreases in favor of environmental factors—a healthy diet; normal body weight; regular exercise; little or no tobacco, alcohol, and drug use; an optimistic outlook; low psychological stress; and social support (Rowe & Kahn, 1998;

Zaretsky, 2003). The study of centenarians—people who cross the 100-year mark—offers special insights into how biological, psychological, and social influences work together to promote a long, satisfying life. See the Lifespan Vista box on pages 566–567 to find out more about the survival and successful adaptation of these longest-lived individuals.

Maximum Lifespan

Finally, perhaps you are wondering: What is the **maximum lifespan,** or the genetic limit to length of life for a person free of external risk factors? According to current estimates, it varies between 70 and 110 for most people, with 85 about average (Harman, 2002). As you will see in the Lifespan Vista box, the oldest verified age to which an individual has lived is 122 years.

Do these figures reflect the upper bound of human longevity, or can our lifespans be extended further? At present, scientists disagree on the answer. Some believe that about 85 or 90 years is as much as most humans can expect, since gains in average life expectancy are largely the result of reducing health risks in the first 20 or 30 years. Expected life for people age 65 and older has increased very little—only about 5 months—over the past decade (U.S. Department of Health and Human Services, 2005p). Others think we have not yet identified the human genetic limit because the lifespans of several species have been stretched in the laboratory—through selective breeding, genetic engineering, and (as we saw in Chapter 15) dietary calorie restriction (Arking, Novoseltsev, & Novoseltseva, 2004).

The possibility of similar achievements in humans raises another issue: *Should* the lifespan be increased as far as possible? In considering this question, many people respond that quality, not just quantity, of life is the important goal—that is, doing everything possible to extend active lifespan. Most experts agree that only after reducing the high rates of preventable illness and disability among low-SES individuals and wiping out age-related diseases does it make sense to invest in lengthening the maximum lifespan.

Physical Changes

The programmed effects of specific genes and the random cellular events believed to underlie biological aging (see Chapter 13) make physical declines more apparent in late adulthood. More organs and systems of the body are affected. Nevertheless, most body structures can last into our eighties and beyond, if we take good care of them. For an overview of the physical changes we are about to discuss, return to Table 13.1 on page 433.

Nervous System

On a routine office visit, 80-year-old Ruth's doctor asked her how she was getting along. Ruth replied, "During the last two days, I forgot the name of the family that just moved in next door, I couldn't recall where I had put a pile of bills, and I had trouble finding the right words to explain to a delivery service how to get to my house. Am I losing my mind?" Ruth asked anxiously.

"You're much too sharp for that," Dr. Wiley responded. "Ruth, if you were losing your mind, you wouldn't be so concerned about forgetting." Ruth also wondered why extremes of hot and cold weather felt more uncomfortable than in earlier years. And she needed more time to coordinate a series of movements and had become less sure of her balance.

Aging of the central nervous system affects a wide range of complex thoughts and activities. Although brain weight declines throughout adulthood, brain-imaging research and after-death autopsies reveal that the loss becomes greater starting in the sixties and may amount to as much as 5 to 10 percent by age 80, due to death of neurons and enlargement of ventricles (spaces) within the brain (Vinters, 2001).

Neuron loss occurs throughout the cerebral cortex but at different rates among different regions and often inconsistently within parts of those regions. In longitudinal studies, the frontal lobes (responsible for integration of information, judgment, and reflective thought) and the corpus callosum (which connects the two cortical hemispheres) tended to show greater shrinkage than the parietal and temporal lobes, with the occipital lobes changing very little (see page 124 in Chapter 4 for a visual image of these regions) (Raz et al., 2005; Resnick et al., 2003; Sullivan et al., 2002). Besides the cortex, the cerebellum (which controls balance and coordination) loses neurons—in all, about 25 percent. Glial cells, which myelinate neural fibers, decrease as well, contributing to diminished efficiency of the central nervous system (Raz, 2005).

But the brain can overcome some of these declines. In several studies, growth of neural fibers in the brains of older adults unaffected by illness took place at the same rate as in middle-aged people. Aging neurons established new synapses after other neurons had degenerated (Flood & Coleman, 1988). Furthermore, the aging cerebral cortex can, to some degree, generate new neurons (Gould et al., 1999). And fMRI evidence reveals that compared with younger adults, elders who do well on memory and other cognitive tasks sometimes show more widely distributed activity across areas of the cerebral cortex (Gazzaley & D'Esposito, 2005). This suggests that one way older adults compensate for neuron loss is to call on additional brain regions to support cognitive processing (Grady & Craik, 2000).

The autonomic nervous system, involved in many life-support functions, also performs less well in old age, putting the elderly at risk during heat waves and cold spells. For example, Ruth's reduced tolerance for hot weather was due to decreased sweating. And her body found it more difficult to raise its core temperature during cold exposure. However, among physically fit elders who are free of disease, these declines are mild (Whitbourne, 2001). The autonomic nervous system also releases higher levels of stress hormones into the bloodstream than it did earlier, perhaps in an effort to arouse body tissues that have become less responsive to these hormones over the years (Whitbourne, 1999). Later we will see that this change may contribute to decreased immunity and to sleep problems among older adults.

Sensory Systems

Changes in sensory functioning become increasingly noticeable in late life. Older adults see and hear less well, and taste, smell, and touch sensitivity may also decline. As Figure 17.3 shows, in late life, hearing impairments are more common than visual impairments. Extending trends for middle adulthood, more women than men report being visually impaired, more men than women hearing impaired.

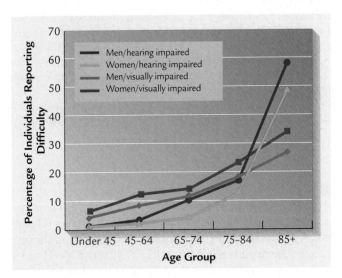

■ **FIGURE 17.3 Rates of visual and hearing impairments among U.S. men and women by age.** Among a large, nationally representative sample, those reporting that they had trouble seeing, even when wearing glasses or contact lenses, were judged visually impaired; those reporting "a lot of trouble" hearing were judged hearing impaired. Women report more visual impairments; men report more hearing impairments, a gap that widens considerably in late adulthood. In late life, hearing impairments become more common than visual impairments. Trends are similar in Canada, although the incidence of sensory impairments is slightly lower. (Adapted from U.S. Department of Health and Human Services, 2005p.)

A Lifespan Vista

What Can We Learn About Aging from Centenarians?

Jeanne Louise Calment, listed in *Guinness World Records* as the longest-lived person whose age could be documented, was born in Arles, France, in 1875 and died there in 1997, 122 years later. Heredity may have contributed to her longevity: Her father lived to age 94, her mother to 86. Her family was middle-SES, and in her twenties, she married a prosperous merchant (Robine & Allard, 1999). As a young woman, she was healthy and energetic; she bicycled, swam, roller-skated, played tennis, and ran up the steps of the cathedral to attend daily Mass.

Jeanne attributed her longevity to a diet rich in olive oil and an occasional glass of port wine. Others credit her easygoing disposition and resistance to stress. "If you can't do anything about it," she once said, "don't worry about it." She took up fencing at age 85 and rode a bicycle until age 100. Shortly thereafter, she moved into assisted living (see page 586), where she blossomed, remaining in good physical and mental health and soon becoming a celebrity, because of both her age and her charming personality. She appeared often before the press and celebrated birthdays on national television. Alert and quick-witted until her final year, she recommended laughter as the best recipe for long life. Asked once about the effects of aging, she quipped, "I've only one wrinkle, and I am sitting on it."

Due to stereotypes of aging and researchers' focus on the very old with the heaviest burden of illness and disability, popular images of the most senior members of the human species are ones of extreme frailty. Yet the past 40 years have seen a tenfold increase in centenarians in the industrialized world—a trend expected to accelerate. Currently, American centenarians number about 67,500, Canadian centenarians about 3,800. These figures are expected to be 12 times greater in 2050 and to double every decade thereafter (Statistics Canada, 2002g; U.S. Census Bureau, 2005).

Women centenarians outnumber men by about 5 to 1. About 60 to 70 percent have physical and mental impairments that interfere with independent functioning. But the rest lead active, autonomous lives (Hagberg et al., 2001; Silver, Jilinskaia, & Perls, 2001). These robust centenarians are of special interest, since they represent the ultimate potential of the human species. What are they like? To find out, several longitudinal studies of centenarians have been initiated. Results reveal that they are diverse in years of education (none to postgraduate), economic well-being (very poor to very rich), and ethnicity. At the same time, their physical condition and life stories reveal common threads.

Health. Longevity runs in centenarians' families, suggesting a genetically based survival advantage. These elders usually have grandparents, parents, and siblings who reached very old age. And their children, most of whom are in their seventies and eighties, appear physically young for their age (Coles, 2004; Perls et al., 2002). Some centenarians share with their siblings a segment of identical DNA on the fourth chromosome, suggesting that a certain gene, or several genes, may increase the likelihood of exceptionally long life (Perls & Terry, 2003).

Most robust centenarians escape age-related chronic illnesses. Genetic testing reveals a low incidence of genes associated with immune-deficiency disorders, cancer, and Alzheimer's disease. Consistent with these findings, robust centenarians typically have efficiently functioning immune systems, and after-death examinations reveal few brain abnormalities (Silver & Perls, 2000). Others live successfully despite underlying chronic illness—typically atherosclerosis and other cardiovascular problems (Berzlanovich et al., 2005). Compared with the general population, about four times as many centenarian women gave birth to healthy children after age 40 (Perls et al., 2000).

■ **Vision.** In Chapter 15 (see pages 500–501), we noted that structural changes in the eye make it harder to focus on nearby objects, see in dim light, and perceive color. In late adulthood, vision diminishes further. The cornea (clear covering of the eye) becomes more translucent and scatters light, which blurs images and increases sensitivity to glare. The lens continues to yellow, leading to further impairment in color discrimination. From middle to old age, cloudy areas in the lens called **cataracts** increase, resulting in foggy vision and (without surgery) eventual blindness. The number of individuals with cataracts increases tenfold from middle to late adulthood; 25 percent of people in their seventies and 50 percent of those in their eighties are affected (Harvey, 2003; U.S. Census Bureau, 2006b). Besides biological aging, heredity, sun exposure, cigarette smoking, and certain diseases (such as diabetes) increase the risk of cataracts (Hammond et al., 2000; Klein et al., 2003). Fortunately, removal of the lens and replacement with an artificial lens implant or corrective eyewear are highly successful in restoring vision.

Impaired eyesight in late adulthood largely results from a reduction in light reaching the retina (caused by yellowing of the lens, shrinking of the pupil, and clouding of the vitreous) and from cell loss in the retina and optic nerve (refer again to Chapter 15). Because dark adaptation—moving from a brightly lit to a dim environment—is harder, entering a movie theater after the show has started becomes a challenge. A decline in binocular vision (the brain's ability to combine images received from both eyes) makes depth perception less reliable (Brabyn et al., 2001). And visual acuity (fineness of discrimination) worsens, with a sharp drop after age 70 (Fozard & Gordon-Salant, 2001).

When light-sensitive cells in the *macula,* or central region of the retina, break down, older adults may develop **macular**

Late childbearing may indicate that the woman's reproductive system is aging slowly—and that the rest of her is doing so as well.

As a group, robust centenarians are of average or slender build and practice moderation in eating. Many have most or all of their own teeth—another sign of unusual physical health. Despite heavy tobacco use in their generation, the large majority have never smoked. And most report lifelong physical activity extending past age 100 (Kropf & Pugh, 1995).

Personality. In personality, these very senior citizens appear highly optimistic. Instead of dwelling on fears and tragedies, they focus on a better tomorrow. The less anxious and fearful centenarians are, the more favorable their self-rated health and their psychological well-being (Quinn et al., 1999). In a study in which robust centenarians retook personality tests after 18 months, they reported more fatigue and depression, perhaps in response to increased frailty at the very end of their lives. But they also scored higher in toughmindedness, independence, emotional security, and openness to experience—traits that may be vital for surviving beyond 100 (Martin, Long, & Poon, 2002). When asked about contributors to their longevity, these extremely long-lived elders often mention close family bonds and a long and happy mar

riage. An unusually large percentage of centenarian men—about one-fourth— are still married (Velkoff, 2000).

Activities. Robust centenarians have a history of community involvement— working for just causes that are central to their growth and happiness. Their current activities often include stimulating work, leisure pursuits, and learning, which may help sustain their good cognition and life satisfaction (Samuelsson et al., 1997). Writing letters, poems, plays, and memoirs; making speeches; teaching music lessons and Sunday school; nursing the sick; chopping wood; selling merchandise, bonds, and insurance; painting; practicing medicine; and preaching sermons are among robust centenarians' varied involvements. In several cases, illiterate centenarians learned to read and write. One of the most impressive was a 105-year-old woman who enrolled in classes four nights a week. Within a short time, she could read road signs, newspaper headlines, and sections of the Bible (Beard, 1991).

Robust centenarians are often regarded as rare curiosities who do not represent the general population. As their numbers increase, they are likely to be viewed less as exceptions and more as people for whom typical development is at its best. These independent, mentally

Jeanne Louise Calment, the longest-lived person on record, died in 1997 at age 122. She defied stereotypes of the very old by taking up fencing at age 85, riding a bicycle until age 100, and maintaining a quick wit until her final year. She is shown here at age 121.

alert, fulfilled 100-year-olds illustrate how a healthy lifestyle, personal resourcefulness, and close ties to family and community can build on biological strengths, thereby pushing the limits of the active lifespan.

---

degeneration, in which central vision blurs and gradually is lost. Macular degeneration is the leading cause of blindness among older adults. If diagnosed early, it can sometimes be treated with laser therapy. As with cataracts, heredity and cigarette smoking increase risk, as does atherosclerosis, because it constricts blood flow to the retina. Protective factors include a diet rich in green, leafy vegetables. These sources of vitamins A, C, and E and carotenoids (yellow and red plant pigments) are believed to exert their beneficial effects by protecting cells in the macula from free-radical damage (Lacour, Kiilgaard, & Nissen, 2002). But vitamin pills, once thought to help reduce the incidence of both cataracts and macular degeneration, show no consistent benefits in carefully designed, experimental studies (Dangour et al., 2004).

Visual difficulties have a profound impact on older people's self-confidence and everyday behavior. Ruth gave up

driving in her mid-seventies, and she worried greatly when Walt had trouble making decisions behind the wheel. He found it hard to shift focus between the road and the dashboard and strained to make out pedestrians at dusk and at night (Wood, 2002). On foot, older adults' problems with depth perception and dark adaptation increase their chances of stumbling.

When vision loss is extensive, it can affect leisure pursuits and be very isolating. Ruth could no longer enjoy museums, movies, playing bridge, and working crossword puzzles. Because of her poor vision, she had to depend on others for help with housekeeping and shopping. Even among people age 85 and older, only 30 percent experience visual impairment severe enough to interfere with daily living (U.S. Department of Health and Human Services, 2005h). For many, however, reduced vision goes undetected (Evans & Rowlands, 2004). Treatment is vital to help them sustain quality of life.

■ **Hearing.** At a Thanksgiving gathering, 85-year-old Ruth had trouble hearing. "Mom, this is Leona, Joe's cousin. I'd like you to meet her," said Ruth's daughter Sybil. In the clamor of boisterous children, banging dishes, television sounds, and nearby conversations, Ruth didn't catch Leona's name or her relationship to Sybil's husband, Joe.

"Tell me your name again?" Ruth asked, adding, "Let's go into the next room, where it's quieter, so we can speak a bit."

Reduced blood supply and natural cell death in the inner ear and auditory cortex, discussed in Chapter 15, along with stiffening of membranes (such as the eardrum), cause hearing to decline in late adulthood. Decrements are greatest at high frequencies, although detection of soft sounds diminishes throughout the frequency range (see page 501). In addition, responsiveness to startling noises lessens, and discriminating complex tone patterns becomes harder (Fitzgibbons & Gordon-Salant, 1998; Hietanen et al., 2004).

Although hearing loss has less impact on self-care than vision loss, it affects safety and enjoyment of life. In the din of traffic on city streets, 80-year-old Ruth didn't always correctly interpret warnings, whether spoken ("Watch it, don't step out yet") or nonspoken (the beep of a horn or a siren). And when she turned up the radio or television volume, she sometimes missed the ring of the telephone or a knock at the door.

As hearing declines, the elderly report lower self-efficacy, more loneliness and depressive symptoms, and a smaller social network than their normally hearing peers (Kramer et al., 2002). Of all hearing difficulties, the age-related decline in speech perception has the greatest impact on life satisfaction. Ability to detect the content and emotionally expressive features of conversation declines after age 70, a difficulty that worsens in noisy settings (Schneider et al., 2000). Although Ruth used problem-centered coping to increase her chances of hearing conversation, she wasn't always successful. And sometimes people were inconsiderate. On a dinner outing, Joe raised his voice impatiently when Ruth asked him to repeat himself, and, in Ruth's presence, said to Sybil, "Be honest, Syb, Ruth's going deaf, isn't she?" This time, Ruth heard every word. At the family's Thanksgiving reunion, fewer relatives took time to talk with Ruth, and she felt some pangs of loneliness.

As with vision, most elders do not suffer from hearing loss great enough to disrupt their daily lives. For those who do, compensating with a hearing aid and minimizing background noise are helpful. Furthermore, recall from Chapter 4 (page 146) that beginning at birth, our perception is *intermodal* (combines information from more than one sensory system). By attending to facial expressions, gestures, and lip movements, older adults can use vision to help interpret the spoken word. When family members and others speak in quiet environments, older people are far more likely to convey an image of alertness and competence than of reduced sensitivity to the surrounding world.

■ **Taste and Smell.** Walt's brother Dick was a heavy smoker. In his sixties, he poured salt and pepper over his food, took his coffee with extra sugar, and asked for "extra hot" in Mexican and Indian restaurants.

Dick's reduced sensitivity to the four basic tastes—sweet, salty, sour, and bitter—is evident in many adults after age 60. Older adults also have greater difficulty recognizing familiar foods by taste alone (Fukunaga, Uematsu, & Sugimoto, 2005; Mojet, Christ-Hazelhof, & Heidema, 2001). But no change in the number or distribution of taste buds occurs late in life, so this drop in taste sensitivity may be due to factors other than aging. Smoking, dentures, medications, and environmental pollutants can affect taste perception. When taste is harder to detect, food is less enjoyable, increasing the likelihood of deficiencies in the elderly person's diet. Flavor additives can help make food more attractive to older adults (Drewnowski & Shultz, 2001).

Besides enhancing enjoyment of food, smell has a self-protective function. An aging person who has difficulty detecting rancid food, gas fumes, or smoke may be in a life-threatening situation. A decrease in the number of smell receptors after age 60 contributes to declines in odor sensitivity. Researchers believe that odor perception not only wanes but becomes distorted, a change that may promote complaints that "food no longer smells and tastes right" (Seiberling & Conley, 2004).

But other factors may make this decline appear greater than it actually is. For example, older adults experiencing greater difficulty with verbal recall, including retrieval of odor labels, have greater difficulty with odor recognition tasks (Larsson & Bäckman, 1998; Larsson, Öberg, & Bäckman, 2005). Furthermore, practicing odor discriminations affects their maintenance (Engen, 1982). In his early eighties, Walt, a lifelong wine enthusiast, could still distinguish the aromas of fine wines.

■ **Touch.** Touch sensitivity is especially crucial for certain adults, such as the severely visually impaired who must read in Braille and people who make fine judgments about texture in their occupations or leisure pursuits—for example, in art and handicraft activities. To measure touch perception, researchers determine how close two stimuli on the skin must be before they are perceived as one. Findings indicate that aging brings a sharp decline on the hands, especially the fingertips, less of a

Aging brings a decline in touch sensitivity in the hands and, especially, the fingertips. Still, many older adults who enjoy art and handicrafts draw on previously acquired expertise to sustain a high level of performance.

drop on the arms and lips. Decreased touch sensitivity may be due to loss of touch receptors in certain regions of the skin and slowing of blood circulation to the extremities. After age 70, nearly all elders are affected (Stevens & Cruz, 1996).

If we consider the spacing among elements of Braille letters, 45 percent of middle-aged and 100 percent of elderly people should have difficulty interpreting them (Stevens, Foulke, & Patterson, 1996). Just as the sighted need new visual aids for reading as they age, so the visually impaired may need new tactile aids—an important consideration in responding to diversity in the aging population.

Cardiovascular and Respiratory Systems

Aging of the cardiovascular and respiratory systems proceeds gradually and usually unnoticed in early and middle adulthood. In late adulthood, signs of change become more apparent, prompting concern among aging individuals, who know these organ systems are vital for quality and length of life. In their sixties, Ruth and Walt noticed that they felt more physically stressed after running to catch a bus or to cross a street before the light changed.

As the years pass, the heart muscle becomes more rigid, and some of its cells die while others enlarge, leading the walls of the left ventricle (the largest heart chamber, from which blood is pumped to the body) to thicken. In addition, artery walls stiffen and accumulate some plaque (cholesterol and fats) due to normal aging (much more in those with atherosclerosis). Finally, the heart muscle becomes less responsive to signals from pacemaker cells within the heart, which initiate each contraction (Whitbourne, 1999).

As a combined result of these changes, the heart pumps with less force, maximum heart rate decreases, and blood flow throughout the circulatory system slows. This means that sufficient oxygen may not be delivered to body tissues during high physical activity. (Recall from Chapter 13 that a healthy heart supports typical levels of exertion well into old age.)

Changes in the respiratory system compound the reduced oxygenation just described. Because lung tissue gradually loses its elasticity, between ages 25 and 80, vital capacity (amount of air that can be forced in and out of the lungs) is reduced by half. As a result, the lungs fill and empty less efficiently, causing the blood to absorb less oxygen and give off less carbon dioxide. This explains why older people increase their breathing rate more and feel more out of breath while exercising.

Cardiovascular and respiratory deficiencies are more extreme in lifelong smokers and in people who have failed to reduce dietary fat or have had many years of exposure to environmental pollutants. As we have seen in previous chapters, exercise is a powerful means of slowing cardiovascular aging. Exercise also facilitates respiratory functioning, as we will see later when we discuss health and fitness.

Immune System

As the immune system ages, T cells, which attack antigens (foreign substances) directly, become less effective (see Chapter 13,

Cuba's national exercise program requires all able-bodied elders to participate in a physical fitness routine for 45 minutes, five days a week. Exercise is a powerful means of slowing cardiovascular aging, and Cuba has the highest average life expectancy in Latin America.

© AP/WIDE WORLD PHOTOS

page 435). In addition, the immune system is more likely to malfunction by turning against normal body tissues in an **autoimmune response.** A less competent immune system can increase the elderly person's risk for a variety of illnesses, including infectious diseases (such as the flu), cardiovascular disease, certain forms of cancer, and various autoimmune disorders, such as rheumatoid arthritis and diabetes (Hasler & Zouali, 2005). But an age-related decline in immune functioning is not the cause of most illnesses among the elderly. It merely permits disease to progress, whereas a stronger immune reaction would have stamped out the disease agent.

Older adults vary greatly in immunity. A few have sturdy immune systems that continue to respond nearly as well as in early adulthood. But most experience some loss of function, ranging from partial to profound (Pawelec et al., 1999). The strength of the aging person's immune system seems to be a sign of overall physical vigor. Certain immune indicators, such as high T cell activity, predict survival over the next two years in very old people (Wikby et al., 1998).

In Chapter 13, we emphasized that other physical changes contribute to impaired immune functioning. Recall that stress hormones undermine immunity. With age, the autonomic nervous system releases higher levels of these into the bloodstream (refer back to page 435). As the immune response declines with age, stress-induced susceptibility to infection rises dramatically (Butcher & Lord, 2004). A healthy diet and exercise help protect the immune response in old age, whereas obesity aggravates the age-related decline (Chandra, 2002b; Drela, Kozdron, & Szczypiorski, 2004; Woods, Lowder, & Keylock, 2002).

Sleep

When Walt went to bed at night, he usually lay awake for a half-hour to an hour before falling asleep, remaining in a drowsy state longer than when he was younger. During the night, he spent less time in the deepest phase of NREM sleep (see Chapter 3, page 108) and awoke several times—again sometimes lying awake for a half-hour or more before drifting back to sleep.

Older adults require about as much total sleep as younger adults: around 7 hours per night. Yet as people age, they have more difficulty falling asleep, staying asleep, and sleeping deeply. Insomnia affects 20 to 40 percent of older adults at least a few nights per month (Ancoli-Israel & Cooke, 2005). The timing of sleep tends to change as well, toward earlier bedtime and earlier morning awakening (Hoch et al., 1997). Changes in brain structures controlling sleep and higher levels of stress hormones in the bloodstream, which have an alerting effect on the central nervous system, are believed to be responsible (Whitbourne, 1996).

Until age 70 or 80, men experience more sleep disturbances than women for several reasons. First, enlargement of the prostate gland, which occurs in almost all aging men, constricts the urethra (the tube draining the bladder) and leads to a need to urinate more often, including during the night. Second, men—especially those who are overweight and use alcohol heavily—are more prone to **sleep apnea,** a condition in which breathing ceases for 10 seconds or longer, resulting in many brief awakenings. An estimated 70 percent of elderly men and 56 percent of elderly women are affected (Quinnell & Smith, 2004). Finally, periodic rapid movement of the legs sometimes accompanies sleep apnea but also occurs at other times of night. Called "restless legs," these movements may be due to muscle tension, reduced circulation, or age-related changes in motor areas of the brain (Martin, Shochat, & Ancoli-Israel, 2000). Though common among the elderly and not dangerous, they do disrupt sleep.

Poor sleep can feed on itself. For example, Walt's nighttime wakings led to daytime fatigue and short naps, which made it harder to fall asleep the following evening. And because Walt expected to have trouble sleeping, he worried about it, which also interfered with sleep.

Fortunately, there are many ways to foster restful sleep, such as establishing a consistent bedtime and waking time, exercising regularly, and using the bedroom only for sleep (not for eating, reading, or watching TV). Explaining that even very healthy older adults have trouble sleeping lets people know that age-related changes in the sleep–wake pattern are normal. The elderly receive more prescription sedatives for sleep complaints than do 40- to 60-year-olds. Used briefly, these drugs can help relieve temporary insomnia. But long-term medication can make matters worse by increasing the frequency and severity of sleep apnea and by inducing rebound insomnia after the drug is discontinued (Feinsilver, 2003). Finally, discomfort due to an enlarged prostate, including frequent urination at night, can be corrected with new laser surgical procedures that relieve symptoms without complications (Aho & Gilling, 2003).

Physical Appearance and Mobility

The inner physical declines we have considered are accompanied by many outward signs of growing older—involving the skin, hair, facial structure, and body build. In earlier chapters, we saw that changes leading to an aged appearance are under way as early as the twenties and thirties. Because these changes occur gradually, older adults may not notice their elderly appearance until its arrival is obvious. Each year during their summer travels, Walt and Ruth observed that Dick's and Goldie's skin appeared more wrinkled. Their hair turned from gray to white as all pigment was lost; their bodies grew rounder and their arms and legs thinner. When they returned home, Walt and Ruth also were more aware that they themselves had aged.

Creasing and sagging of the skin, described in Chapter 15, extends into old age. In addition, oil glands that lubricate the skin become less active, leading to dryness and roughness. "Age spots" increase; in some elderly individuals, the arms, backs of the hands, and face may be dotted with these pigmented marks. Moles and other small skin growths may also appear. Blood vessels can be seen beneath the more transparent skin, which has largely lost its layer of fatty support (Whitbourne, 1999, 2001). This loss further limits the older adult's ability to adapt to hot and cold temperatures.

The face is especially likely to show these effects because it is frequently exposed to the sun, which accelerates aging. Other facial changes occur: The nose and ears broaden as new cells are deposited on the outer layer of the skeleton. Teeth may be yellowed, cracked, and chipped, and gums may recede; with better dental care, these outcomes are likely to be less pronounced in future generations. As hair follicles under the skin's surface die, hair on the head thins in both sexes, and the scalp may be visible. In men with hereditary pattern baldness, follicles do not die but, instead, begin to produce fine, downy hair (Whitbourne, 1996).

Body build changes as well. Height continues to decline, especially in women, as loss of bone mineral content leads to further collapse of the spinal column. Weight generally drops after age 60 because of additional loss of lean body mass (bone density and muscle), which is heavier than the fat deposits accumulating on the torso.

Several factors affect mobility. The first is muscle strength, which generally declines at a faster rate in late adulthood than in middle age. On average, by 60 to 70 years of age, 10 to 20 percent of muscle power has been lost, a figure that climbs to 30 to 50 percent after age 70 to 80 (Whitbourne, 1996, 2001). Second, bone strength deteriorates because of reduced bone mass, and tiny cracks in response to stress weaken the bones further. Third, strength and flexibility of the joints and the tendons and ligaments (which connect muscle to bone) diminish. In her eighties, Ruth's reduced ability to support her body, flex her limbs, and rotate her hips made walking at a steady, moderate pace, climbing stairs, and rising from a chair difficult.

In Chapter 13, we noted that endurance athletes who continue training throughout adulthood retain their muscular physiques and much of their strength into their sixties and seventies. These especially active people, like other aging individuals, lose fast-twitch muscle fibers, but they compensate by strengthening remaining slow-twitch fibers so they work more efficiently. A carefully planned exercise program can also enhance joint flexibility and range of movement. When Ruth complained of joint stiffness and pain, her doctor recommended certain rhythmic and flexing exercises, as well as exercises that strengthen muscles supporting the joints.

Adapting to Physical Changes of Late Adulthood

Great diversity exists in older adults' adaptation to the physical changes of aging. Dick and Goldie took advantage of an enormous industry designed to stave off the appearance of old age, including cosmetics, wigs, plastic surgery, and various "anti-aging" dietary supplements, herbal products, and hormonal medications offered by "longevity" clinics—none of them with any demonstrated benefits and some of them harmful (Olshansky, Hayflick, & Perls, 2004). In contrast, Ruth and Walt gave little thought to their thinning white hair and wrinkled skin. Their identities were less bound up with their appearance than with their ability to remain actively engaged in their surroundings.

People vary in the aspects of physical aging that matter most to them. And because parts of the body age at different rates, older adults' sense of physical aging is multidimensional: They feel older in some domains than in others. Compared with Dick and Goldie, Ruth and Walt approached aging with a more positive outlook and greater peace of mind. Instead of trying to hang on to a youthful identity, they resolved to intervene in those aspects of aging that could be changed and to accept those that could not.

Research shows that the most obvious, outward signs of aging—graying hair, facial wrinkles, and baldness—bear no relationship to sensory, cognitive, and motor functioning or to longevity (Schnohr et al., 1998). In contrast, neurological, sensory, cardiovascular, respiratory, immune-system, and skeletal and muscular health strongly predict cognitive performance and both quality and length of later life (Anstey, Luszcz, & Sanchez, 2001; Reyes-Ortiz et al., 2005). Furthermore, people can do more to prevent declines in the functioning of these internal body systems than they can do to prevent gray hair and baldness!

■ **Effective Coping Strategies.** Think back to our discussion of problem-centered and emotion-centered coping in Chapter 15. It applies here as well. As Walt and Ruth prevented and compensated for age-related changes through diet, exercise, environmental adjustments, and an active, stimulating lifestyle, they felt a sense of personal control over their fates. This prompted additional positive coping and improved physical functioning.

In one study, elders who generated new, problem-centered coping strategies for dealing with vision loss—such as relying

on sound to recognize people, acting more cautiously in risky situations, and exchanging ideas with other visually impaired individuals—adapted more favorably to everyday challenges and felt less depressed (Brennan & Cardinali, 2000). In contrast, older adults who avoid confronting age-related declines—who think these are inevitable and uncontrollable and who ruminate about their damaging effects—tend to be passive when faced with them and to report more physical and psychological adjustment difficulties (Kraaij, Pruymboom, & Garnefski, 2002; Whitbourne & Primus, 1996).

■ **Assistive Technology.** A rapidly expanding **assistive technology,** or array of devices that permit people with disabilities to improve their functioning, is available to help older people cope with physical declines. Computers are the greatest source of these innovative products. People with sensory impairments can use special software to enlarge text or have it read aloud. Phones that can be dialed and answered by voice commands help elders who have difficulty pushing buttons or getting across a room to answer the phone. And for elders who take multiple medications, a tiny computer chip called a "smart cap" can be placed on medicine bottles. It beeps on a programmed schedule to remind the older person to take the drug and tracks how many and at what time pills have been taken.

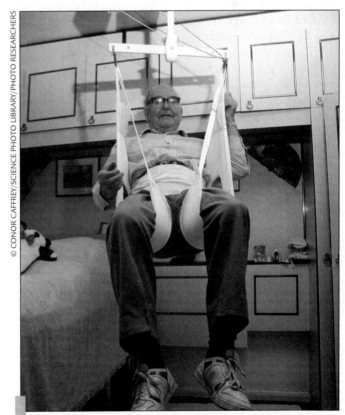

© CONOR CAFFREY/SCIENCE PHOTO LIBRARY/PHOTO RESEARCHERS

Assistive technology expands the functioning of older adults who have physical disabilities. In this "smart" bedroom, an elder who cannot walk sits in a hoist attached to an overhead track. Using a system of color-coded strings, he gets out of bed and moves about the room.

Architects are also designing "smart homes" with a variety of features that promote safety and mobility. For example, sensors in floors can activate room lights when an older person gets up at night to use the bathroom, thereby preventing injuries. Another remarkable device is a harness attached to a track in the ceiling, which carries people with reduced mobility from room to room (Hooyman & Kiyak, 2005). At present, "smart home" systems are beyond the means of most elders. But as the older population increases, future housing may be designed to permit easy and cost-effective installation.

Elders with disabilities who use assistive devices require fewer hours of personal caregiving (Hoenig, Taylor, & Sloan, 2003). Yet in the United States and Canada, government-sponsored health care coverage for assistive technology is largely limited to essential medical equipment. Sweden's health care system, in contrast, covers many assistive devices that promote function and safety (Stone, Staisey, & Sonn, 1991). In this way, Sweden helps older adults remain as independent as possible.

■ **Overcoming Stereotypes of Aging.** Stereotypes of late adulthood, which view "deterioration as inevitable," are widespread in Western nations. Overcoming this pessimistic picture is vital for helping people adapt favorably to late-life physical changes. In a survey of older adults diverse in SES, many reported experiencing prejudice and discrimination. For example, 30 to 40 percent had been ignored, talked down to, or assumed to be unable to hear or understand well because of their age (Palmore, 2001).

Like gender stereotypes, age stereotypes often operate automatically, without awareness; people "see" elders in stereotypical ways, even when they appear otherwise. As seniors encounter these negative messages, they experience *stereotype threat,* which results in diminished performance on tasks related to the stereotype (see page 314 in Chapter 9). In several studies, researchers exposed older adults to words associated with either negative aging stereotypes ("decrepit," "confused") or positive aging stereotypes ("sage," "enlightened"). Those in the negative-stereotype condition displayed a more intense physiological response to stress along with worse handwriting, memory performance, self-efficacy, and will to live (Hess, Hinson, & Statham, 2004; Levy & Banaji, 2002; Levy et al., 2000).

As these findings indicate, negative stereotypes of aging have a stressful, disorganizing impact on elders' functioning, whereas positive stereotypes reduce stress and foster competence. In a longitudinal investigation, people with positive self-perceptions of aging—who, for example, agreed with such statements as "As I get older, things are better than I thought they'd be"—lived, on average, 7½ years longer than those with negative self-perceptions. This survival advantage remained after gender, SES, loneliness, and physical health status were controlled (Levy et al., 2002). Adults with less education are especially susceptible to the detrimental effects of age stereotypes, perhaps because they tend to accept those messages uncritically (Andreoletti & Lachman, 2004).

Elders rarely appear in television programs and, when they do, are typically assigned minor roles. But a positive sign

This Peruvian shaman, or priest, performs a spiritual ceremony that pays tribute to the pre-Columbian earth gods. In cultures where the elderly are treated with deference and respect, an aging appearance can be a source of pride.

is that negative portrayals of seniors on TV and in other media are rare (Miller et al., 1999). In a study examining a sample of more than 1,400 TV commercials broadcast over the past five decades, ads including older adults increased from 2 percent in the 1950s to 5 percent in the 1990s. The overwhelming majority (78 percent) of commercials conveyed positive stereotypes, most commonly an "adventurous golden ager" (lively, fun-loving, sociable, and active), "perfect grandparent" (family-oriented, kind, loving, and generous), or "productive golden ager" (intelligent, capable, successful, and independent). In the 6 percent of ads depicting elders as "mildy impaired," none engaged in ridicule (Miller, Leyell, & Mazachek, 2004). Over time, adventurous golden agers increased, and perfect grandparents decreased—trends reflecting the reality of improved health and vitality among the elderly.

Still, in Western industrialized nations, negative stereotyping of old people is common in everyday social experiences (Ory et al., 2003). In cultures where the elderly are treated with deference and respect, an aging appearance can be a source of pride. In one study, Chinese adults diverse in age were less likely than Canadian adults to stereotype elders, either positively or negatively (Ryan et al., 2004). And in the native language of the Inuit of Canada, the closest word to "elder" is *isumataq,* or "one who knows things"—a high status that begins when a couple becomes head of the extended family unit. When Inuit older adults in a small community on Victoria Island were asked for their thoughts on aging well, they mentioned attitudes—a positive approach to life, interest in transmitting cultural knowledge to young people, and community involvement—nearly twice as often as physical health (Collings, 2001).

Japan honors its elderly citizens with an annual celebration, Respect for the Aged day. Also, a ritual called *kanreki* recognizes the older person's release from the responsibilities of middle age, new freedoms and competencies, and senior place in the family and society. Japanese extended families in the United States and Canada often plan the kanreki as a surprise sixtieth birthday party, incorporating elements of both the traditional ritual (such as dress) and the Western birthday (a special cake) (Doi, 1991; Gelfand, 1994). Cultural valuing of aging prompts a welcoming approach to late adulthood, including some of its physical transitions. (See also the Cultural Influences box on page 574.)

Despite inevitable declines, physical aging can be viewed with either optimism or pessimism. As Walt commented, "You can think of your glass as half full or half empty." Today, a wealth of research supports the "half full" alternative. In the next section, we will encounter additional examples.

Ask Yourself

Review

Cite examples of how older adults can compensate for age-related physical declines.

Apply

"The best way to adjust to this is to learn to like it," thought 65-year-old Herman, inspecting his thinning hair in the mirror. "I remember reading that bald older men are regarded as leaders." What type of coping is Herman using, and why is it effective?

Connect

Review research on stereotype threat on page 314 in Chapter 9. How do stereotypes of aging similarly affect elders' behavior?

Reflect

While watching TV during the coming week, keep a log of portrayals of older adults in programs and commercials. Were elders underrepresented? How many images were positive? How many negative? Compare your observations with research findings.

www.ablongman.com/berk

Health, Fitness, and Disability

At Walt and Ruth's fiftieth wedding anniversary, 77-year-old Walt thanked a roomful of well-wishers for joining in the celebration. Then he announced emotionally, "I'm so grateful Ruth and I are in good health and still able to give to our family, friends, and community."

As Walt's remarks affirm, health is central to psychological well-being in late life. When researchers ask the elderly about possible selves (see Chapter 16, page 536), number of hoped-for physical selves declines with age and number of feared physical selves increases. Nevertheless, older adults are generally optimistic about their health. Because they judge themselves against same-age peers, the majority rate their health

favorably (Statistics Canada, 2005e; U.S. Department of Health and Human Services, 2005h). In an investigation of more than 500 70- to 100-year-olds living in Berlin, Germany, subjective evaluations of one's own health rose in late life, while objective health assessments declined (see Figure 17.4) (Baltes & Smith, 2003). With respect to physical well-being, elders clearly view their glass as at least "half full"! And when it comes to protecting their health, elders' sense of self-efficacy is as high as that of young adults and higher than that of middle-aged people (Frazier, 2002; Hooker, 1992).

The more optimistic elders are about their capacity to cope with physical challenges, the better they are at overcoming threats to health, which promotes further optimism and continued health-enhancing behaviors (Kubzansky et al., 2002; Schwarzer, 1999). Longitudinal research reveals that disability need not follow a path toward further disability and dependency. In several studies, 12 to 20 percent of elders with disabilities showed improvement 2 to 6 years later (Ostir et al., 1999). Furthermore, good health permits older adults to remain socially active, thereby fostering psychological well-being (Heidrich & Ryff, 1993). In this way, physical and mental health are intimately related in late life.

As mentioned earlier, SES and ethnic variations in health diminish in late adulthood. Nevertheless, before age 85, SES continues to predict physical functioning (House, Lantz, & Herd, 2005). African-American and Hispanic elderly (one-fifth of whom live in poverty) remain at greater risk for certain

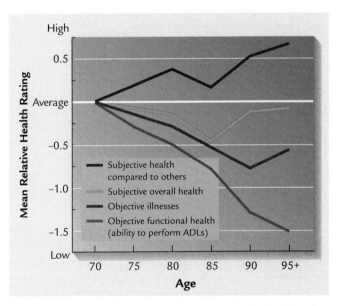

■ **FIGURE 17.4 Changes in subjective and objective health evaluations with age.** In the Berlin Aging Study, 500 70- to 100-year-olds both evaluated their own health and received examinations and assessments by health professionals. Despite declines in objective health, ratings of subjective health—especially comparisons with same-age peers—rose with age. Older adults are generally optimistic about their health, an attitude that helps them cope with physical challenges. (From P. B. Baltes & J. Smith, 2003, "New Frontiers in the Future of Aging: From Successful Aging of the Young Old to the Dilemmas of the Fourth Age," *Gerontology, 49,* p. 127. © 2003 Karger AG, Basel. Reprinted by permission.)

Cultural Influences

Cultural Variations in the Experience of Aging

In a study of diverse communities around the world, a team of anthropologists found that older people fare best when they retain social status and opportunities for community participation, even after they become frail (Fry et al., 1997; Keith et al., 1994). When elders are excluded from important social roles and infirmity brings separation from the community, aging leads to reduced psychological well-being.

Consider the Herero, a pastoral people of Botswana, Africa. Older adults who are strong and active spend their days just as younger adults do, tending the cattle and performing other chores. When elders decline physically, they retain positions of seniority and are treated with respect. A status hierarchy makes the oldest man and his wife village leaders. They are responsible for preserving the sacred flame of the ancestors, who remain significant family members after death. Children are sent to live in the homes of frail elders to provide care—an assignment that is a source of great pride and prestige.

Old age is also a gratifying time of life in Momence, Illinois, a small, working-class farming and manufacturing town. The population is highly stable, so elders are granted positions of authority because of their length of residence and

intimate knowledge of the community. Town, church, and club leaders tend to be older, and past leaders are included in decision making. Furthermore, because frail elders are embedded in family, neighborhood, and church networks that have persisted for many years, other citizens often inquire about them, visit them, and monitor their condition.

In Swarthmore, a middle-SES Philadelphia suburb, life for elders is less certain. Although 25 percent of residents are over age 60, most moved to the community after retirement, and their adult children live elsewhere. As a result, older people are granted no special status due to seniority, and they occupy few valued community roles. Unlike the Herero and the citizens of Momence, Swarthmore elders spend much time in age-segregated settings, such as bridge games and church groups for seniors. Townspeople tend to equate "being older" with chronological age—60 and beyond. In contrast, the Herero and the residents of Momence seldom refer to older adults in terms of their age. Rather, they mention knowledge and social position.

Among the Herero and in Momence, neither age nor physical decline threatens community ties. In Swarthmore, being old limits integration into community life, and frailty has profound, negative consequences, typically bringing social isolation.

© JACOB HALASKA/INDEX STOCK IMAGERY

Among the Herero people of Botswana, Africa, elders continue to participate actively in their community. When these Herero women decline physically, children will be assigned the prestigious task of living in their homes to provide care. And the oldest man and woman will be named leaders of the village.

health problems (see Table 17.1). Native-American and Canadian Aboriginal older adults are even worse off. The majority are poor, and chronic health conditions are so widespread that in the United States, the federal government grants Native Americans special health benefits. These begin as early as age 45, reflecting a much harder and shorter lifespan. Unfortunately, low-SES elders are less likely than their higher-SES counterparts to seek medical treatment. When they do, they often do not comply with the doctor's directions because they are less likely to believe they can control their health and that treatment will work (Hopper, 1993). The absence of a high sense of self-efficacy in these older adults further impairs their physical condition.

The sex differences noted in Chapter 15 extend into late adulthood: Men are more prone to fatal diseases, women to

non-life-threatening disabling conditions. By very old age (80 to 85 and beyond), women are more impaired than men because only the sturdiest men have survived (Murtagh & Hubert, 2004). In addition, with fewer physical limitations, older men are better able to remain independent and to engage in exercise, hobbies, and involvement in the social world, all of which promote better health.

Widespread health-related optimism among the elderly suggests that substantial inroads into preventing disability can be made even in the last few decades of life. Ideally, as life expectancy extends, we want the average period of diminished vigor before death to decrease—a public health goal called the **compression of morbidity.** Several large-scale studies indicate that over the past two decades, compression of morbidity has occurred in industrialized nations despite rising rates of

Table 17.1	Poverty Rates and Health Problems Among Elderly Ethnic Minorities	
Ethnic Minority	**Poverty Rate Age 65 and Over**	**Health Problems Greater than in the General Population of Elderly**
African-American	23%	Cardiovascular disease, a variety of cancers, diabetes
Hispanic	20%	Cardiovascular disease, diabetes
Native-American	Over 80%	Diabetes, kidney disease, liver disease, tuberculosis, hearing and vision impairments
Canadian Aboriginal	Over 63%	Cardiovascular disease, diabetes, liver disease, tuberculosis

Sources: Health Canada, 2002e; U.S. Census Bureau, 2006b.

obesity and sedentary lifestyles, suggesting that medical advances and improved socioeconomic conditions are largely responsible (Fries, 2003; Hessler et al., 2003).

Yet the impact of good health habits on postponement of disability is large, indicating that compression of morbidity can be greatly extended. In a longitudinal investigation following university alumni from their late sixties on, disability was delayed by nearly eight years in those who were lean, who exercised, and who did not smoke compared with those who were obese, sedentary, or addicted to tobacco. Elders with these risks surged to extremely high levels of disability in the two years before death (Hubert et al., 2002; Vita et al., 1998). Researchers believe that the most promising route to further compression of morbidity in developed countries is to reduce negative lifestyle factors. Improved prevention and treatment of chronic diseases, starting early and continuing throughout life, are also vital (Fries, 2003). As we look closely at health, fitness, and disability in late adulthood, we will add to our discussion of health promotion in earlier chapters, taking up additional routes to this objective.

More comprehensive strategies are needed in the developing world, where 70 percent of older people will reside by 2025. In these nations, poverty is rampant, chronic diseases occur earlier, even routine health interventions are unavailable or too costly for all but a few, and most public health programs do not focus on the elderly (Kalache, Aboderin, & Hoskins, 2002). As a result, disability rates among old people are especially high, and as yet, no progress has been made in compression of morbidity.

Nutrition and Exercise

The physical changes of late life lead to an increased need for certain nutrients—calcium and vitamin D to protect the bones; zinc and vitamins B_6, C, and E to protect the immune system; and vitamins A, C, and E to prevent free radicals (see Chapter 13, page 432). Yet declines in physical activity, in the senses of taste and smell, and in ease of chewing (because of deteriorating teeth) can reduce the quantity and quality of food eaten (Morley, 2001). Furthermore, the aging digestive system has greater difficulty absorbing certain nutrients, such as protein, calcium, and vitamin D. And older adults who live alone may have problems shopping or cooking and may feel less like eating by themselves. Together, these physical and environmental conditions increase the risk of dietary deficiencies, which affect 10 to 25 percent of North American elders (High, 2001).

In several studies, a daily vitamin–mineral tablet resulted in an enhanced immune response and a 50 percent drop in days of infectious illness (Chandra, 1992, 2002a; Jain, 2002). But vitamin–mineral supplements do not reduce the incidence of cardiovascular disease, and their impact on cancer prevention is inconclusive. Furthermore, supplemental nutrients and herbs identified as "cognitive enhancers"—including B and E vitamins, folic acid, and ginkgo biloba—do not improve elders' cognitive functioning and neither prevent nor slow the progression of Alzheimer's disease (Gold, Cahill, & Wenk, 2002; Graf et al., 2005; McDaniel, Maier, & Einstein, 2002). At the same time, several surveys suggest that regularly eating fish high in polyunsaturated fatty acids (which promote vascular health) offers some protection against mental disabilities (Barberger-Gateau et al., 2002; Morris et al., 2005).

In addition to a healthy diet, exercise continues to be a powerful health intervention. Sedentary healthy older adults up to age 80 who begin endurance training (walking, cycling, aerobic dance) show gains in vital capacity that compare favorably with those of much younger individuals. And weight-bearing exercise begun in late adulthood—even as late as age 90—promotes muscle size and strength, blood flow to muscles, and ability of muscles to extract oxygen from blood. This translates into improved walking speed, balance, posture, and ability to carry out everyday activities, such as opening a stubborn jar lid, carrying an armload of groceries, or lifting a 30-pound grandchild (deJong & Franklin, 2004; Goldberg, Dengel, & Hagberg, 1996; Pyka et al., 1994).

Exercise also increases blood circulation to the brain, which helps preserve brain structures and behavioral capacities. Brain scans show that, compared with sedentary elders, those who are physically fit experienced less tissue loss—in both neurons and glial cells—in diverse areas of the cerebral cortex (Colcombe et al., 2003). In one study, researchers used fMRI to assess changes in brain activity resulting from a 6-month program of regular brisk walking. Compared to a physically inactive group, 58- to 77-year-old walkers displayed increased activity in areas of the cerebral cortex governing control of attention, as well as improved sustained and selective attention during mental testing (Colcombe et al., 2004).

Although good nutrition and physical activity are most beneficial when they are lifelong, it is never too late to change. Beginning in his sixties and until his death at age 94, Walt's Uncle Louie played tennis for an hour or two every day and went ballroom dancing three nights a week. Exercise led Louie to sustain a high sense of physical self-esteem. As a dancer, he dressed nattily and moved gracefully. He often commented on how dance and other sports could transform an older person's appearance from dowdy to elegant, expressing the beauty of the inner self.

Elders who come to value the intrinsic benefits of exercise—feeling stronger, healthier, and more energetic—are likely to engage in it regularly (Caserta & Gillett, 1998). Yet lack of awareness of the health benefits of exercise and expected discomforts from engaging in it are major barriers to getting older people to take up a fitness routine; 75 percent of men and 80 percent of women are not active enough (Stewart et al., 2001). Furthermore, many with chronic disease symptoms think "taking it easy" is the best treatment and that exercise actually will do harm. In planning exercise programs for older adults, it is important to instill a sense of control over the aging process—by stressing the health-enhancing rewards of physical activity and by changing negative beliefs that interfere with sustained effort (Lachman et al., 1997). Active seniors can serve as positive role models and sources of encouragement.

Sexuality

When Walt turned 60, he asked his 90-year-old Uncle Louie at what age sexual desire and activity cease, if they do. Walt's question stemmed from a widely held myth that sex drive disappears among the elderly (Hillman, 2000). "It's especially important to be reasonably rested and patient during sex," Louie explained to Walt. "I can't do it as often, and it's a quieter experience than it was in my youth, but my sexual interest has never gone away. Rachella and I have led a happy intimate life, and it's still that way."

Although virtually all cross-sectional studies report a decline in sexual desire and frequency of sexual activity in older people, the trend may be exaggerated by cohort effects. A new generation of elders, accustomed to viewing sexuality positively, will probably be more sexually active. In an interview study, all older adults with a current sexual partner attributed at least some importance to sex, and over one-third rated it as "very" or "extremely" important (Gott & Hinchliff, 2003). Consistent with these findings, most healthy older married couples report continued, regular sexual enjoyment (Levy, 1994). The same generalization we discussed for midlife applies to late life: Good sex in the past predicts good sex in the future.

Too often, intercourse is used as the only measure of sexual activity—a circumstance that promotes a narrow view of pleasurable sex. Even at the most advanced ages, there is more

© DAVID YOUNG-WOLFF/PHOTOEDIT

Most healthy older couples report continued, regular sexual enjoyment. And even at the most advanced ages, sexuality involves far more than intercourse. Feeling sensual, enjoying close companionship, and being loved and wanted all are part of sexuality.

to sexuality than the sex act itself—feeling sensual, enjoying close companionship, and being loved and wanted (Hodson & Skeen, 1994). Both older men and older women report that the male partner is usually the one who ceases to interact sexually (Pedersen, 1998). In a culture that emphasizes an erection as necessary for being sexual, a man may withdraw from all erotic activity when he finds that erections are harder to achieve and more time must elapse between them.

Disabilities that disrupt blood flow to the penis—most often, disorders of the autonomic nervous system, cardiovascular disease, and diabetes—are responsible for dampening sexuality in older men. Cigarette smoking, excessive alcohol intake, and a variety of prescription medications also lead to diminished sexual performance. Among women, poor health and absence of a partner are major factors that reduce sexual activity (Gott & Hinchliff, 2003; Kellett, 2000). Because the sex ratio increasingly favors females, aging heterosexual women have fewer and fewer opportunities for sexual encounters.

In most tribal and village cultures, sexual activity among elders is expected and is common for both men and women until very late in life (Winn & Newton, 1982). But in Western nations, sex in old age often meets with disapproval. Educational programs informing older adults about normal, age-related changes in sexual functioning and fostering a view of sex as extending throughout adulthood promote positive sexual attitudes (Hillman & Stricker, 1994). In nursing homes, education for caregivers is vital for ensuring residents' rights to privacy and other living conditions that permit sexual expression (Hajjar & Kamel, 2004).

Physical Disabilities

Illness and disability climb as the end of the lifespan approaches. Compare the death rates shown in Figure 17.5 with those in Figure 15.2 on page 508, and you will see that cardiovascular disease and cancer—illnesses we discussed in Chapter 15—increase dramatically from mid- to late life and remain the leading causes of death. As before, death rates from cardiovascular disease and cancer are higher for men than for women, although the sex difference declines with advancing age (Statistics Canada, 2002g; U.S. Census Bureau, 2006b).

Respiratory diseases also rise sharply in late adulthood. Among them is *emphysema,* caused by extreme loss of elasticity in lung tissue, which results in serious breathing difficulty. Although a few cases of emphysema are inherited, most result from long-term cigarette smoking. In addition, as the longest-lived people escape chronic diseases or weaken because of them, the immune system eventually encounters an infection it cannot fight. Consequently, many of the very old succumb to one of the more than 50 lung inflammations classified as *pneumonia.* Doctors recommend that people age 65 and older be vaccinated against the most common type.

The fourth most common killer among the aged is *stroke.* It is caused by hemorrhage or blockage of blood flow in the brain and is a major cause of disability in late adulthood and, after age 75, of death. Other diseases are less frequent killers, but they limit older adults' ability to live fully and independently. Osteoporosis, discussed in Chapter 15 (see page 511), continues to rise in late adulthood; recall that it affects the majority of men and women after age 70. Yet another bone disorder—*arthritis*—adds to the physical limitations of many elders. And *adult-onset diabetes* and *unintentional injuries* also multiply in late adulthood. In the following sections, we take up these last three conditions.

Finally, an important point must be kept in mind as we discuss physical and mental disabilities of late adulthood: The fact that these conditions are *related to age* does not mean that they are *entirely caused by aging.* To clarify this distinction, some experts distinguish between **primary aging** (another term for *biological aging*), or genetically influenced declines that affect all members of our species and take place even in the context of overall good health, and **secondary aging,** declines due to hereditary defects and negative environmental influences, such as poor diet, lack of exercise, disease, substance abuse, environmental pollution, and psychological stress.

Throughout this book, we have seen that it is difficult to distinguish primary from secondary aging. Undoubtedly you have, at one time or another, encountered a *frail elder*—a person of extreme infirmity who displays wasted muscle mass and strength, weight loss, severe mobility problems, and perhaps cognitive impairment. **Frailty** involves weakened functioning of diverse organs and body systems, which profoundly interferes with everyday competence and leaves the older adult highly vulnerable in the face of an infection, extremely hot or cold weather, or an injury (Fried et al., 2004). Although primary aging contributes to frailty, researchers agree that secondary aging plays a larger role, through genetic disorders, unhealthy lifestyle, and chronic disease (Bortz, 2002; Hogan, MacKnight, & Bergman, 2003). The serious conditions we are about to discuss are major sources of frailty in the elderly.

■ **Arthritis.** Beginning in her fifties, Ruth felt a slight morning stiffness in her neck, back, hips, and knees. In her sixties, she developed bony lumps on the end joints of her fingers. As the years passed, she experienced periodic joint swelling and some loss of flexibility—changes that affected her ability to move quickly and easily.

Arthritis, a condition of inflamed, painful, stiff, and sometimes swollen joints and muscles, becomes more common

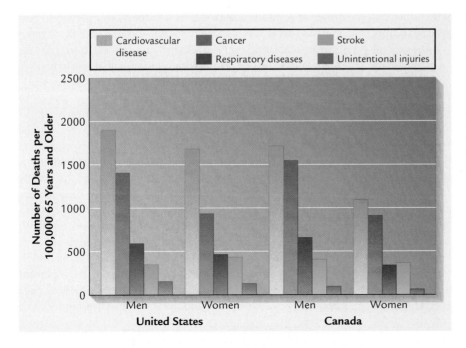

■ FIGURE 17.5 **Leading causes of death among people age 65 and older in the United States and Canada.** In late adulthood, cardiovascular disease is the leading cause of death among men and women, followed by cancer. Respiratory diseases and stroke also claim the lives of many elders. Notice that death rates for all causes, and especially cardiovascular disease, are lower among Canadian than U.S. women. Cardiovascular disease among men shows a similar trend. (Adapted from Statistics Canada, 2002g; U.S. Census Bureau, 2006b.)

© LESTER SLOAN/WOODFIN CAMP & ASSOCIATES

This frail elder suffers from wasted muscle mass and strength, weight loss, severe mobility problems, and perhaps cognitive impairment. Although biological aging contributes to frailty, secondary aging—through genetic disorders, unhealthy lifestyle, and chronic disease—plays a larger role.

in late adulthood. It occurs in several forms. Ruth has **osteoarthritis,** the most common type, which involves deteriorating cartilage on the ends of bones of frequently used joints. Otherwise known as "wear-and-tear arthritis" or "degenerative joint disease," it is one of the few age-related disabilities in which years of use make a difference. Although a genetic proneness seems to exist, the disease usually does not appear until the forties or fifties. In frequently used joints, cartilage on the ends of the bones, which reduces friction during movement, gradually deteriorates. Or obesity places abnormal pressure on the joints and damages cartilage. Almost all older adults show some osteoarthritis on X-rays, although wide individual differences in severity exist (Fajardo & Di Cesare, 2005).

Unlike osteoarthritis, which is limited to certain joints, **rheumatoid arthritis** involves the whole body. An autoimmune response leads to inflammation of connective tissue, particularly the membranes that line the joints, resulting in overall stiffness, inflammation, and aching. Tissue in the cartilage tends to grow, damaging surrounding ligaments, muscles, and bones. The result is deformed joints and often serious loss of mobility. Sometimes other organs, such as the heart and lungs, are affected. Worldwide, about 2 percent of older adults have rheumatoid arthritis (Rasch et al., 2003).

Overall, disability due to arthritis affects 45 percent of U.S and 34 percent of Canadian men over age 65 and rises mod-

estly with age. Among North American women, the incidence is higher and increases sharply with age: About 50 percent of 65- to 84-year-olds and 70 percent of those over age 85 are affected (Health Canada, 2003c; U.S. Census Bureau, 2006b). The reason for the sex difference is unclear. Although rheumatoid arthritis can strike at any age, it rises after age 60. It may be due to a late-appearing genetic defect in the immune system; twin studies reveal a strong hereditary contribution. However, identical twins differ widely in disease severity, indicating that as yet unknown environmental factors make a difference. Early treatment with new, powerful anti-inflammatory medications helps slow the course of the disease (Lee & Weinblatt, 2001).

Managing arthritis requires a balance of rest when the disease flares, pain relief, and physical activity involving gentle stretching of all muscles to maintain mobility. Twice a week, 84-year-old Ruth attended a water-based exercise class. Within two months, her symptoms lessened, and she no longer needed a walker (Kettunen & Kujala, 2004). In obese people, weight loss is also helpful. Although osteoarthritis responds to these interventions more easily than rheumatoid arthritis, the course of each varies greatly. With proper analgesic medication, joint protection, and lifestyle changes, many people with either form of the illness lead long, productive lives. If hip or knee joints are badly damaged or deformed, they can be surgically rebuilt or replaced with plastic or metal devices.

■ **Diabetes.** After a meal, the body breaks down the food, releasing glucose (the primary energy source for cell activity) into the bloodstream. Insulin, produced by the pancreas, keeps the blood concentration of glucose within set limits by stimulating muscle and fat cells to absorb it. When this balance system fails, either because not enough insulin is produced or because body cells become insensitive to it, *adult-onset diabetes* (otherwise known as *diabetes mellitus*) results. Over time, abnormally high blood glucose damages the blood vessels, increasing the risk of stroke, heart attack, circulatory problems in the legs, and injury to the eyes, kidneys, and nerves. In several long-term studies, diabetes was associated with more rapid cognitive declines in the elderly and an elevated risk for Alzheimer's disease—an association we will revisit when we take up Alzheimer's (Arvanitakis et al., 2004; Logroscino, Kang, & Grodstein, 2004; Yaffe et al., 2004a).

From middle to late adulthood, the incidence of adult-onset diabetes doubles; it affects 10 percent of the elderly in the United States and Canada (Lindsay, 1999; U.S. Census Bureau, 2006b). Diabetes runs in families, suggesting that heredity is involved. But inactivity and abdominal fat deposits greatly increase the risk. Higher rates of adult-onset diabetes are found among African-American, Mexican-American, Native-American, and Canadian-Aboriginal minorities for both genetic and environmental reasons, including high-fat diets and obesity associated with poverty. The Pima Indians of Arizona have the world's highest rate of diabetes, with 50 percent of adults affected (Quinn, 2001). Return to Chapter 9, page 292, to review how nature and nurture combine to induce this disease.

Treating adult-onset diabetes requires lifestyle changes, including a carefully controlled diet, regular exercise, and weight loss (Willy & Singh, 2003). By promoting glucose absorption and reducing abdominal fat, physical activity lessens disease symptoms.

■ **Unintentional Injuries.** At age 65 and older, the death rate from unintentional injuries is at an all-time high—more than twice as great as in adolescence and young adulthood. Motor vehicle collisions and falls are largely responsible.

Motor Vehicle Accidents. Motor vehicle collisions account for only one-fourth of injury mortality in late life, compared with one-half in middle adulthood. But a look at individual drivers tells a different story. Older adults have higher rates of traffic violations, accidents, and fatalities per mile driven than any other age group, with the exception of drivers under age 25. The high rate of injury persists, even though many elders limit their driving after noticing that their ability to drive safely is slipping. Women are more likely to take these preventive steps. Deaths due to injuries—motor vehicle and otherwise—continue to be much higher for men than for women in late adulthood (Silvi, 2004; U.S. Census Bureau, 2006b).

Recall that visual declines led Walt to have difficulty seeing the dashboard and identifying pedestrians at night. Most information used in driving is visual. The greater elders' visual processing difficulties, the higher their rate of moving violations and crashes (Wood, 2002). Compared with young drivers, the elderly are less likely to drive quickly and recklessly but more likely to fail to heed signs, yield the right of way, and turn appropriately. They often try to compensate for their difficulties by being more cautious. Slowed reaction time and indecisiveness pose hazards, too. Recall from Chapter 15 that with age, adults find it harder to attend selectively, engage in two activities at once, and switch back and forth between tasks—abilities essential for safe driving (De Raedt & Ponjaert-Kristoffersen, 2000). Elders are at high risk for collisions at busy intersections and in other complex traffic situations.

Nevertheless, elders usually try to drive as long as possible. Giving up driving results in loss of freedom, control over one's life, and self-esteem (Wood, 2002). Specially trained driver rehabilitation consultants—affiliated with hospitals, drivers licensing agencies, or U.S. Area Agencies on Aging (see page 69 in Chapter 2)—can help assess an elder's capacity to continue driving, provide driver retraining, or counsel elders to retire from driving and to arrange other transportation options.

The elderly also account for more than 30 percent of all pedestrian deaths (Transport Canada, 2001; U.S. Census Bureau, 2006b). Confusing intersections, especially crossing signals that do not allow older people enough time to get to the other side of the street, are often involved.

Falls. One day, Ruth fell down the basement steps and lay there with a broken ankle until Walt arrived home an hour later. Ruth's tumble represents the leading type of accident among the elderly. About 30 percent of adults over age 65 and 40 percent over age 80 have experienced a fall within the last year. Declines in vision, hearing, mobility, and cognitive functioning and development of certain chronic illnesses (such as arthritis)—all of which make it harder to avoid hazards and keep one's balance—increase the risk of falling in late adulthood. Because of weakened bones and difficulty breaking a fall, serious injury results about 10 percent of the time. Among the most common is hip fracture (Marks et al., 2003). It increases twentyfold from age 65 to 85 and is associated with a 10 to 20 percent increase in mortality. Of those who survive, half never regain the ability to walk without assistance (U.S. Department of Health and Human Services, 2005d).

Falling can also impair health indirectly, by promoting fear of falling. Almost half of older adults who have fallen admit that they purposefully avoid activities because they are afraid of falling again (Health and Disability Research Institute, 2006). In this way, a fall can limit mobility and social contact, undermining both physical and psychological well-being. Although an active lifestyle may expose the elderly to more situations that can cause a fall, the health benefits of activity far outweigh the risk of serious injury due to falling.

Preventing Unintentional Injuries. Many steps can be taken to reduce unintentional injury in late adulthood. Designing motor vehicles and street signs to accommodate the visual needs of the elderly is a goal for the future. Meanwhile, training that enhances visual and cognitive skills essential for safe driving and that helps older adults avoid high-risk situations (such as busy intersections and rush hour) can save lives.

Similarly, efforts to prevent falls must address risks within the person and the environment—through corrective eyewear, strength and balance training, and improved safety in homes and communities. Applying What We Know on page 580 summarizes ways to protect the elderly from injury.

Mental Disabilities

Normal age-related cell death in the brain, described earlier, does not lead to loss of ability to engage in everyday activities. But when cell death and structural and chemical abnormalities are profound, serious deterioration of mental and motor functions occurs.

Dementia refers to a set of disorders occurring almost entirely in old age in which many aspects of thought and behavior are so impaired that everyday activities are disrupted. Dementia strikes adults of both sexes about equally. Approximately 1 percent of people in their sixties are affected; the rate increases steadily with age, rising sharply after age 75 until it reaches about 50 percent for people age 85 and older—trends that apply to Canada, the United States, and other Western nations (Beers, 2006; Berr, Wancata, & Ritchie, 2005; Matthews & Brayne, 2005). Although dementia rates are similar across SES and most ethnic groups, African Americans are at higher risk—a finding we will take up shortly (Alzheimer's Association, 2006).

Applying What We Know

Preventing Unintentional Injury in Late Adulthood

Suggestion	Description
Motor Vehicle Collisions and Pedestrian Accidents	
Modify driving behavior in accord with visual and other limitations.	Drive fewer miles; reduce or eliminate driving during rush hour, at night, through busy intersections, or in bad weather.
Modify pedestrian behavior in accord with visual and other limitations.	Wear light-colored clothing at night; allow extra time to cross streets; walk with a companion.
Attend training classes for older drivers; if not available, press for them in your community.	Practice tracking vehicles and pedestrians in dim light, judging vehicle speed, and reading signs and dashboard displays; review rules of the road.
Falls	
Schedule regular medical checkups.	Have eye exams to ensure that corrective lenses are up to date; physical exams to identify health risks that increase the chances of falling; do a review of medications for effects on attention and coordination.
Engage in regular exercise.	Take part in strength and balance training to promote coordination and counteract fear of falling.
Use walking aids when necessary.	Use canes and walkers to compensate for poor balance and unsteady gait.
Improve safety of the living environment.	Install extra lighting in dim areas, such as entrances, hallways, and staircases; put handrails in hallways and grab bars in bathrooms; make sure loose rugs are secured to floor or moved and that furniture and other objects are arranged so they are not obstacles.
Be alert and plan ahead in risky situations.	Watch for slippery pavement; carry a flashlight at night; allow extra time to cross streets; become familiar with new settings before moving about freely.

Note: Consult the National Resource Center for Safe Aging, www.safeaging.org, for a wealth of information on senior safety.

About a dozen types of dementia have been identified. Some are reversible with proper treatment, but most are irreversible and incurable. A few forms, such as Parkinson's disease,[1] involve deterioration in subcortical brain regions (primitive structures below the cortex) that often extends to the cerebral cortex and, in many instances, results in brain abnormalities resembling Alzheimer's disease. Some researchers believe that Parkinson's and Alzheimer's are related (Papapetropoulos et al., 2005). But in the large majority of dementia cases, subcortical brain regions are intact, and progressive damage occurs only to the cerebral cortex. *Cortical dementia* comes in two varieties: Alzheimer's disease and cerebrovascular dementia.

■ **Alzheimer's Disease.** When Ruth took 79-year-old Ida to the ballet, an occasion that the two sisters anticipated eagerly each year, she noticed a change in Ida's behavior. Ida, who had forgotten the engagement, reacted angrily when Ruth arrived unannounced at her door. Driving to the theater, which was in

a familiar part of town, Ida got lost—all the while insisting that she knew the way perfectly well. As the lights dimmed and the music began, Ida talked loudly and dug noisily in her purse.

"Shhhhhh," responded a dozen voices from surrounding seats.

"It's just the music!" Ida snapped at full volume. "You can talk all you want until the dancing starts." Ruth was astonished and embarrassed at the behavior of her once socially sensitive sister.

Six months later, Ida was diagnosed with **Alzheimer's disease,** the most common form of dementia, in which structural and chemical brain deterioration is associated with gradual loss of many aspects of thought and behavior. Alzheimer's accounts for 60 percent of all dementia cases and, at older ages, for an even higher percentage. Approximately 8 to 10 percent of people over age 65 have the disorder. Of those over age 80, close to 45 percent are affected. Each year, about 5 percent of all deaths among the elderly—60,000 in the United States and 6,500 in Canada—involve Alzheimer's (U.S. Department of Health and Human Services, 2005p). This makes the disease a leading cause of late-life mortality, although on death certificates, more immediate causes, such as infection and respiratory failure, are usually listed.

---

[1]In Parkinson's disease, neurons in the part of the brain that controls muscle movements deteriorate. Symptoms include tremors, shuffling gait, loss of facial expression, rigidity of limbs, difficulty maintaining balance, and stooped posture.

Symptoms and Course of the Disease. The earliest symptoms are often severe memory problems—forgetting names, dates, appointments, familiar routes of travel, or the need to turn off the kitchen stove. At first, recent memory is most impaired, but as serious disorientation sets in, recall of distant events and such basic facts as time, date, and place evaporates. Faulty judgment puts the person in danger. For example, Ida insisted on driving after she was no longer competent to do so. Personality changes occur—loss of spontaneity and sparkle, anxiety in response to uncertainties created by mental problems, aggressive outbursts, reduced initiative, and social withdrawal. Depression often appears in the early phase of Alzheimer's and other forms of dementia and seems to be part of the disease process (Espiritu et al., 2001; Zubenko et al., 2003). However, depression may worsen as the older adult reacts to disturbing mental changes.

As the disease progresses, skilled and purposeful movements disintegrate. When Ruth took Ida into her home, she had to help her dress, bathe, eat, brush her teeth, and (eventually) walk and use the bathroom. Ida's sleep was disrupted by delusions and imaginary fears. She often awoke in the night and banged on the wall, insisting that it was dinnertime, or cried out that someone was choking her. Over time, Ida lost the ability to comprehend and produce speech. And when her brain ceased to process information, she could no longer recognize objects and familiar people. In the final months, Ida became increasingly vulnerable to infections, lapsed into a coma, and died.

The course of Alzheimer's varies greatly, from a year to as long as 15 years. The average life expectancy for a 70-year-old man with the disease is about 4½ years, for a 70-year-old woman about 8 years (Larson et al., 2004).

Brain Deterioration. A diagnosis of Alzheimer's disease is made through exclusion, after ruling out other causes of dementia by a physical examination and psychological testing—an approach that is more than 90 percent accurate. To confirm Alzheimer's, doctors inspect the brain after death for a set of abnormalities that either cause or result from the disease (Heinz & Blass, 2002). In nearly 90 percent of cases, however, brain-imaging techniques (MRI and PET), which yield three-dimensional pictures of brain volume and activity, predict whether elders who do not yet show symptoms will receive an after-death confirmation of Alzheimer's (Lerch et al., 2005; Rusinek et al., 2004). Researchers are also tracking changes in the chemical makeup of the blood and cerebrospinal fluid to see which ones predict Alzheimer's (de Leon et al., 2004). These procedures offer hope of very early diagnosis, opening the door to more successful interventions.

Two major structural changes in the cerebral cortex, especially in memory and reasoning areas, are associated with Alzheimer's. Inside neurons, **neurofibrillary tangles** appear—bundles of twisted threads that are the product of collapsed neural structures. Outside neurons, **amyloid plaques,** dense deposits of a deteriorated protein called *amyloid,* surrounded by clumps of dead nerve and glial cells, develop. Although

Computer images compare a brain scan of an Alzheimer's patient (left) with one of a healthy older adult (right). The Alzheimer's brain is shrunken, due to massive degeneration and death of neurons. Activity and blood flow (marked by yellow and green coding in the right scan) are also greatly reduced in the Alzheimer's brain.

some neurofibrillary tangles and amyloid plaques are present in the brains of normal middle-aged and older people and increase with age, they are far more abundant in Alzheimer's victims.

Researchers once thought that plaques contributed to the neuronal damage of Alzheimer's. But new findings suggest that they actually reflect the brain's effort to get harmful amyloid away from neurons. Instead, a major culprit may be abnormal breakdown of amyloid remaining *within* neurons (Cleary et al., 2005; National Institute on Aging, 2005). In both Alzheimer's disease and Parkinson's disease, disruptions occur in a key neuronal structure responsible for chopping up and disposing of abnormal proteins (Ding et al., 2004). These damaged proteins (including amyloid) build to toxic levels, causing cell damage and death.

As massive numbers of neurons die and brain volume shrinks, levels of *neurotransmitters*—essential for the brain's communication system—decline. Destruction of neurons that release the neurotransmitter acetylcholine, involved in transporting messages between distant areas of the brain, further disrupt perception, memory, reasoning, and judgment. A drop in serotonin, a neurotransmitter that regulates arousal and mood, may contribute to sleep disturbances, aggressive outbursts, and depression (Lanctot et al., 2002; Mintzer, 2001).

Risk Factors. Alzheimer's disease comes in two types: *familial,* which runs in families, and *sporadic,* which has no obvious family history. Familial Alzheimer's generally has an early onset (before age 65) and progresses more rapidly than the later-appearing sporadic type. Researchers have identified genes on chromosomes 1, 14, and 21, involved in generation of harmful amyloid, that are linked to familial Alzheimer's. In each case, the abnormal gene is dominant; if it is present in only one of the pair of genes inherited from parents, the person will develop early-onset Alzheimer's (Heinz & Blass, 2002; National Institute on Aging, 2005). Recall that chromosome 21 is involved in Down syndrome. Individuals with this chromosomal disorder who live past age 40 almost always have the brain abnormalities and symptoms of Alzheimer's.

Heredity also plays a role in sporadic Alzheimer's, through somatic mutation. About 50 percent of people with this form of the disease have an abnormal gene on chromosome 19, which results in excess levels of *ApoE4,* a blood protein that carries cholesterol throughout the body. Researchers believe that a high blood concentration of ApoE4 affects the expression of a gene involved in regulating insulin. Deficient insulin and resulting glucose buildup in the bloodstream (conditions that, when extreme, lead to diabetes) are linked to brain damage, especially in areas regulating memory, and to abnormally high build-up of amyloid in brain tissue (Convit et al., 2003; National Institute on Aging, 2005; Zhao et al., 2004). In line with these findings, elders with diabetes have a 65 percent increased risk of developing Alzheimer's (Arvanitakis et al., 2004).

At present, the abnormal ApoE4 gene is the most commonly known risk factor for sporadic Alzheimer's. But genetic testing has revealed other regions of the genome with as yet unidentified genes that seem to make an equal or greater contribution to the disease (Blacker et al., 2003; Farrer et al., 2003).

Nevertheless, many sporadic Alzheimer's victims show no currently known genetic marker, and some individuals with the ApoE4 gene do not develop the disease. Evidence is increasing for the role of a variety of other factors in susceptibility to Alzheimer's disease, including excess dietary fat, cardiovascular disease, stroke, and (as noted earlier) diabetes (Koistinaho & Koistinaho, 2005; Korf et al., 2004; Kruman et al., 2005; Schneider et al., 2004; Yaffe et al., 2004b). Head injury, by accelerating deterioration of amyloid, may also increase Alzheimer's risk, especially among people with the ApoE4 gene (Jellinger, 2004).

Alzheimer's disease probably results from different combinations of genetic and environmental factors, each leading to a somewhat different course of the disease. The high incidence of Alzheimer's and other forms of dementia among African-American elderly illustrates the complexity of potential causes. Compared with African Americans, Yoruba village dwellers of Nigeria show a much lower Alzheimer's incidence and no association between the ApoE4 gene and the disease (Gureje et al., 2006). Some investigators speculate that intermarriage with Caucasians heightened genetic risk among African Americans and that environmental factors translated that risk into reality (Hendrie, 2001). Whereas the Yoruba of Nigeria eat a low-fat diet, the African-American diet is high in fat. Eating fatty foods may increase the chances that the ApoE4 gene will lead to Alzheimer's. And even for Yoruba and African Americans without the ApoE4 gene, a high-fat diet is risky. The more fat consumed and the higher the blood level of "bad" cholesterol

(low-density lipoproteins), the greater the incidence of Alzheimer's (Evans et al., 2000; Hall et al., 2006).

Protective Factors. Researchers are testing both drug and nondrug approaches to preventing or slowing the progress of Alzheimer's. Although hormone therapy was previously believed to offer women protection against Alzheimer's, rigorously designed research yielded contrary findings (see Chapter 15, page 504). Vitamins B and E and folate supplements, also once regarded as protective, do not reduce the incidence of the disease or its symptoms (see page 575). Similarly, anti-inflammatory drugs, administered to reduce inflammation of brain tissue caused by amyloid and other abnormalities, did not delay progression of the disease in carefully designed experiments (National Institute on Aging, 2005).

But a "Mediterranean diet" emphasizing fish, unsaturated fat (olive oil), and moderate consumption of red wine is linked to a 60 percent reduced incidence of Alzheimer's disease and also to a reduction in cerebrovascular dementia (which we will turn to next). These foods contain fatty acids and other substances that help maintain the cardiovascular system, and they also promote the health of neural structures and neurotransmitter activity (Panza et al., 2004).

Education and an active lifestyle seem beneficial as well. Compared with their less-educated counterparts, elders with higher education show less than half the rate of Alzheimer's (Qiu et al., 2001). Some researchers speculate that education leads to more synaptic connections, which act as a *cognitive reserve,* giving the aging brain greater tolerance for injury before it crosses the threshold into mental disability. The impact of education, however, is reduced in the presence of the ApoE4 gene (Seeman et al., 2005). Late-life engagement in social and leisure activities also reduces the risk of Alzheimer's and of dementia in general, perhaps by stimulating synaptic growth and thereby preserving cognitive functioning (Verghese et al., 2003; Wang et al., 2002). Finally, intensity and variety of physical activity are associated with decreased risk for Alzheimer's and cerebrovascular dementia, although again, benefits are limited for elders with the ApoE4 gene (Laurin et al., 2001; Podewils et al., 2005).

Helping Alzheimer's Victims and Their Caregivers. As Ida's Alzheimer's worsened, the doctor prescribed a mild sedative and an antidepressant to help control her behavior. Drugs that limit breakdown of the neurotransmitter acetylcholine also reduce dementia symptoms (National Institute on Aging, 2005).

But with no cure available, family interventions ensure the best adjustment possible for the Alzheimer's victim, spouse, and other relatives. Dementia caregivers devote substantially more time to caregiving and experience more stress than do people caring for elders with other disabilities (Ory et al., 2000). They need assistance and encouragement from extended-family members, friends, and community agencies. The Social Issues box on pages 584–585 describes a variety of helpful interventions for family caregivers. In addition to these strategies, avoiding dramatic changes in living conditions, such as moving to a new location, rearranging furniture, or modifying daily routines, helps elders with Alzheimer's disease feel as secure as possible in a cognitive world that is gradually disintegrating.

■ **Cerebrovascular Dementia.** In **cerebrovascular dementia,** a series of strokes leaves areas of dead brain cells, producing step-by-step degeneration of mental ability, with each step occurring abruptly after a stroke. About 20 percent of all cases of dementia in Western nations are cerebrovascular, and about 10 percent are due to a combination of Alzheimer's and repeated strokes (Kalaria, 2002).

Cerebrovascular dementia results from a combination of genetic and environmental forces. The effects of heredity are indirect, through high blood pressure, cardiovascular disease, and diabetes, each of which increases the risk of stroke. And environmental influences—including cigarette smoking, heavy alcohol use, high salt intake, very low dietary protein, obesity, inactivity, and psychological stress—also heighten stroke risk (Román, 2003).

Because of their susceptibility to cardiovascular disease, more men than women have cerebrovascular dementia by their late sixties. Women are not at great risk until after age 75 (Sachdev, Brodaty, & Looi, 1999). The disease also varies among countries. For example, deaths due to stroke are high in Japan. Although a low-fat diet reduces Japanese adults' risk of cardiovascular disease, high intake of alcohol and salt and a diet very low in animal protein increase the risk of stroke. As Japanese consumption of alcohol and salt declined and intake of meat rose in recent decades, rates of cerebrovascular demen-

tia and stroke-caused deaths dropped (Goldman & Takahashi, 1996). However, they remain higher than in other developed nations.

Although Japan presents a unique, contradictory picture (there, cardiovascular disease is low, and stroke is high), in most cases cerebrovascular dementia is caused by atherosclerosis. Prevention is the only effective way to stop the disease. The incidence of cerebrovascular dementia has dropped in the last two decades, largely as a result of the decline in heart disease and more effective stroke prevention methods (U.S. Department of Health and Human Services, 2005h). Signs that a stroke might be coming are weakness, tingling, or numbness in an arm, a leg, or the face; sudden vision loss or double vision; speech difficulty; and severe dizziness and imbalance. Doctors may prescribe drugs to reduce the tendency of the blood to clot. Once strokes occur, paralysis and loss of speech, vision, coordination, memory, and other mental abilities are common.

■ **Misdiagnosed and Reversible Dementia.** Careful diagnosis of dementia is crucial because other disorders can be mistaken for it. And some forms of dementia can be treated and a few reversed.

Depression is the disorder most often misdiagnosed as dementia. The depressed (but not demented) older adult is likely to exaggerate his or her mental difficulties, whereas the demented person minimizes them and is not fully aware of cognitive declines. Fewer than 1 percent of people over age 65 are severely depressed, and another 2 percent are moderately depressed—rates lower than those for young and middle-aged adults (King & Markus, 2000). Most older people have probably learned how to adjust what they expect from life, resulting in fewer feelings of worthlessness. However, as we will see in Chapter 18, depression rises with age. It is often related to physical illness and pain and can lead to cognitive deterioration. As at younger ages, the support of family members and friends, antidepressant medication, and individual, family, and group therapy can help relieve depression. However, the elderly in general and low-SES ethnic minorities in particular are unlikely to seek mental health services (Padgett et al., 1994). This increases the chances that depression will deepen and be confused with dementia.

The older we get, the more likely we are to be taking drugs that might have side effects resembling dementia. For example, some medications for coughs, diarrhea, and nausea inhibit the neurotransmitter acetylcholine, leading to Alzheimer's-like symptoms. Because tolerance for drugs decreases with age, these reactions intensify in late adulthood. In addition, some diseases can cause temporary memory loss and mental symptoms, especially among the elderly, who often become confused and withdrawn when ill. Treatment of the underlying illness relieves the problem. Finally, environmental changes and social isolation can trigger mental declines (Gruetzner, 1992). When supportive ties are restored, cognitive functioning usually bounces back.

© PETER MENZEL/SPL/PHOTO RESEARCHERS, INC.

In this Japanese rehabilitative center, staff provide care for elderly stroke patients. A low-fat diet reduces Japanese adults' risk of cardiovascular disease. But high intake of alcohol and salt coupled with low intake of animal protein increases their risk of stroke.

Social Issues

Interventions for Caregivers of Elders with Dementia

Margaret, wife and caregiver of a 71-year-old Alzheimer's patient, sent a desperate plea to an advice columnist at her local newspaper: "My husband can't feed or bathe himself, or speak to anyone or ask for assistance. I must constantly anticipate his needs and try to meet them. Please help me. I'm at the end of my rope."

The effects of Alzheimer's disease are devastating not just to elderly victims but also to family members who provide care with little or no outside assistance. Caregiving under these conditions has been called the "36-hour day" because of its constant demands. Although the majority of home caregivers are middle-aged, an estimated 15 to 25 percent are elders who care for a spouse or an aging parent. One-third of these elderly caregivers are in poor health themselves, yet the number of hours dedicated to caregiving increases with the age of the caregiver (Chappell et al., 2003; Family Caregiver Alliance, 2005). Family members who exceed their caregiving capacities suffer greatly in physical and mental health and are at risk for early mortality (Schultz & Beach, 1999; Sörensen & Pinquart, 2005). Severity of cognitive impairments and behavior problems in care recipients are strong predictors of weakening caregiver health.

Most communities offer interventions designed to support family caregivers, but these need to be expanded and made more cost-effective. Those that work best begin before caregivers become overwhelmed and address multiple needs: knowledge, coping strategies, caregiving skills, and respite.

Knowledge. Virtually all interventions try to enhance knowledge about the disease, caregiving challenges, and available community assistance. Knowledge is usually delivered through classes. But in one innovative approach, computers were installed in caregivers' homes, enabling them to access a database with wide-ranging information on caregiving (Brennan, Moore, & Smyth, 1991). Gains in knowledge, however, must be combined with other approaches to improve caregivers' well-being.

Coping Strategies. Many interventions teach caregivers everyday problem-solving strategies for managing the dependent elder's behavior, along with techniques for dealing with negative thoughts and feelings, such as resentment about having to provide constant care. Modes of delivery include support groups, individual therapy, and "coping with frustration" classes. In one study, interveners assessed caregivers' current coping strategies and provided individualized training in more effective techniques. Compared with no-intervention controls, trained caregivers felt less burdened and depressed, and their patients engaged in fewer disturbing behaviors—gains still evident three months after the intervention (Marriott et al., 2000).

Caregiving Skills. Caregivers benefit from lessons in how to communicate with elders who can no longer handle everyday tasks—for example, distracting rather than scolding when the person asks the same question over and over; responding patiently with reminders and lists when the person blames others for memory problems; and introducing pleasant activities, such as music and slow-paced children's TV programs, that relieve agitation. Interventions that teach communication skills reduce elders' troublesome behavior and, as a result, may boost caregivers' sense of self-efficacy and reports of positive emotion (Bourgeois et al., 1997).

Respite. Caregivers usually say that *respite*—time away from providing care—is the assistance they most desire. Yet even when communities offer respite services, such as adult day care or tem-

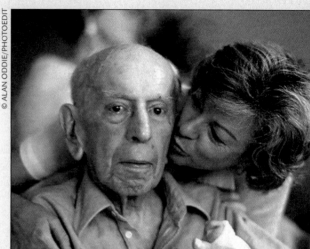

This daughter cares for her father, who has Alzheimer's disease. Although the task has compensating rewards, it is physically demanding and emotionally draining. A great need exists for interventions that support caregivers.

porary placement in a care facility, caregivers are reluctant to use them because of cost, worries about the elder's adjustment, and guilt. Yet respite at least twice a week for several hours improves physical and mental health by permitting caregivers to maintain friendships, engage in enjoyable activities, and sustain a balanced life (Lund & Wright, 2001; Zarit et al., 1998).

Recognizing caregivers' need for relief from unrelenting in-home care, one group of researchers devised a unique tool called Video Respite—a series of videotapes suited to the interests of Alzheimer's patients that provide caregivers with a half-hour to an hour break. On each tape, a professional actor conducts a friendly, slow-paced, simple conversation about familiar experiences, people, and objects, pausing occasionally for the impaired elder to respond. Evaluations of the videos show that they not only capture the attention of people with Alzheimer's but also reduce problem behaviors, such as wandering, agitation, repeated questioning, and aggression (Lund et al., 1995).

No single magic bullet exists for eliminating caregiver stress. But multifaceted interventions that begin early in the caregiving process, that continue for many weeks or months, and that are tailored to caregivers' individual needs make a substantial difference in caregivers' lives. And they usually delay placement of dementia patients in institutions as well (Kennet, Burgio, & Schultz, 2000).

The Resources for Enhancing Alzheimer's Caregiver Health (REACH) initiative is an evaluation of nine "active" intervention programs, each including several to all of the ingredients just described, versus five "passive" interventions providing only information and referral to community agencies. Among more than 1,200 participating caregivers, those receiving six months of active intervention declined more in self-reported burden. And one program providing family therapy in the home— through a telephone system facilitating frequent communication among therapist, caregiver, family members, and other support systems—substantially reduced caregiver depressive symptoms (Gitlin et al., 2003; Schultz et al., 2003). Caregivers with greater care responsibility—women versus men, lower-SES versus higher-SES, spouses versus nonspouses—benefited most from active intervention.

Health Care

Health care professionals and lawmakers in industrialized nations worry about the economic consequences of rapid increase in the elderly population. Rising government-supported health care costs and demand for certain health care services, particularly long-term care, are of greatest concern.

■ **Cost of Health Care for the Elderly.** Adults age 65 and older make up just 12 percent of the North American population but account for 30 percent of government health care expenditures in the United States and 44 percent in Canada (Esmail & Walker, 2005; U.S. Census Bureau, 2006b). According to current estimates, the cost of government-sponsored health insurance, or Medicare, for the elderly will double by 2025 and nearly triple by 2050 as the baby boom generation reaches late adulthood and average life expectancy extends further (Social Security and Medicare Board of Trustees, 2005).

Medicare expenses rise steeply with age. People age 75 and older receive, on average, 70 percent more benefits than younger senior citizens. Most of this increase reflects the need for long-term care—in hospitals and nursing homes—resulting from an age-related rise in disabling chronic diseases and acute illnesses. Because U.S. Medicare funds only about half of older adults' medical needs, American elders spend nearly five times the percentage of their annual incomes on health care as do Canadian elders—19 versus 4 percent (Lindsay, 1999; U.S. Department of Health and Human Services, 2005p). And in both nations, Medicare provides far less support for long-term care than elders with severe disabilities need.

■ **Long-Term Care.** When Ida moved into Ruth's home, Ruth promised never to place Ida in an institution. But as Ida's condition worsened and Ruth faced health problems of her own, she couldn't keep her word. Ida needed round-the-clock monitoring. Reluctantly, Ruth placed her in a nursing home.

As Figure 17.6 reveals, advancing age is strongly associated with use of long-term care services, especially nursing homes.

Among disorders of aging, dementia, especially Alzheimer's disease, most often leads to nursing home placement, followed by arthritis, hip fracture, and stroke (Agüero-Torres et al., 2001). Greater use of nursing homes is also prompted by loss of informal caregiving support through widowhood—which mostly affects women—and aging of adult children and other relatives.

Overall, only 5 percent of Americans and 8 percent of Canadians age 65 and older are institutionalized, about half

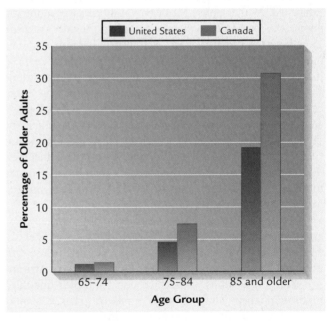

■ FIGURE 17.6 **Increase with age in nursing home care in the United States and Canada.** In both nations, placement in nursing homes rises steeply with age. Canadian elders are generally financially better off than U.S. elders (see Chapter 2, page 69), which helps explain the higher percentages of Canadians in the two older age groups who reside in nursing homes. Another related factor is Canada's longer average life expectancy. (Adapted from Statistics Canada, 2002g; U.S. Department of Health and Human Services, 2005p.)

© MICHAEL VENTURA/PHOTOEDIT

Assisted living is a rapidly expanding alternative for seniors who require more care than can be provided at home but less than is usually provided in nursing homes. It can enhance residents' autonomy, social life, community involvement, and life satisfaction.

the rate in other industrialized nations, such as the Netherlands and Sweden, which provide more generous public financing of institutional care. In the United States, unless nursing home placement follows hospitalization for an acute illness, older adults must pay for it until their resources are exhausted. At that point, Medicaid (health insurance for the poor) takes over. Although most Canadian provinces provide some long-term care coverage, it is limited. Because of spiraling long-term care costs, benefits have been frozen or reduced in recent years, placing large financial burdens on institutionalized Canadian elders and their families (Council on Aging of Ottawa, 2005). As in the United States, only when elders are destitute does the government cover all costs. Consequently, the largest users of nursing homes in the United States and Canada are people with either very low or high incomes. Middle-income elderly and their families are more likely to try to protect their savings from being drained by high nursing home costs.

Nursing home use also varies across ethnic groups. For example, Caucasian Americans are nearly twice as likely as African Americans to be institutionalized. Large, close-knit extended families mean that over 70 percent of African-American older adults do not live alone, and over one-third reside with their adult children. Similarly, Asian, Hispanic, Native-American, and Canadian-Aboriginal elders use nursing homes less often than North-American Caucasians because of families' strong sense of caregiving responsibility (Lindsay, 1999; Yaffe et al., 2002). Overall, families provide at least 60 to 80 percent of all long-term care in Australia, Canada, New Zealand, the United States, and Western Europe. As we have seen, families of diverse ethnic and SES backgrounds willingly step in to care for elders in times of need.

To reduce institutionalized care of the elderly and its associated high cost, some experts have advocated alternatives, such as publicly funded in-home help for family caregivers (see Chapter 16, page 548). Another option rapidly becoming more widely available is *assisted living*—a homelike housing arrangement for seniors who require more care than can be provided at home but less than is usually provided in nursing homes. Assisted living is a cost-effective alternative to nursing homes that prevents unnecessary institutionalization (Maddox, 2001). It also can enhance residents' autonomy, social life, community involvement, and life satisfaction—potential benefits that we will take up in Chapter 18. In Denmark, the combination of a government-sponsored home-helper system and expansion of assisted-living housing resulted in a 30 percent reduction in the need for nursing home beds over the past 15 years. At the same time, the Danish government saved money: Public expenditures for long-term care declined by 8 percent (Stuart & Weinrich, 2001).

When nursing home placement is the best choice, steps can be taken to improve the quality of services. For example, the Netherlands has established separate facilities designed to meet the different needs of patients with mental and physical disabilities. And every elderly person, no matter how disabled, benefits from opportunities to maintain existing strengths and acquire new skills that can compensate for declines. Among institutionalized elderly, health, sense of personal control, gratifying social relationships, and meaningful and enjoyable daily activities strongly predict life satisfaction (Logsdon, 2000). These aspects of living are vital for older people everywhere.

Ask Yourself

Review

Cite evidence that both genetic and environmental factors contribute to Alzheimer's disease and cerebrovascular dementia.

Apply

Marissa complained to a counselor that at age 68, her husband, Wendell, no longer initiated sex or cuddled her. Why might Wendell have ceased to interact sexually? What interventions—both medical and educational—could be helpful to Marissa and Wendell?

Connect

Explain how each level of ecological systems theory (Chapter 1, pages 24–25) contributes to caregiver well-being and quality of home care for elders with dementia.

Reflect

What care and living arrangements have been made for elders needing assistance in your family? How did culture, personal values, financial means, health, and other factors influence those decisions?

✒ Cognitive Development

Ruth's complaints to her doctor about difficulties with memory and verbal expression reflect common concerns about cognitive functioning in late adulthood. Decline in speed of processing, under way throughout the adult years, is believed to affect many aspects of cognition in old age. In Chapter 15, we noted that reduced efficiency of thinking compromises attention, the amount of information that can be held in working memory, the use of memory strategies, and retrieval from long-term memory. These decrements continue in the final decades of life.

Recall that the more a mental ability depends on fluid intelligence (biologically based information-processing skills), the earlier it starts to decline. In contrast, mental abilities that rely on crystallized intelligence (culturally based knowledge) are sustained longer. (Return to Figure 15.5 on page 517 to review these trends.) But maintenance of crystallized intelligence depends on continued opportunities to enhance cognitive skills. When these are available, crystallized abilities—general information and expertise in specific endeavors—can offset losses in fluid intelligence.

Look again at Figure 15.5 on page 517. In advanced old age, decrements in fluid intelligence eventually limit what people can accomplish with the help of cultural supports, including a rich background of experience, knowledge of how to remember and solve problems, and a stimulating daily life. Consequently, crystallized intelligence shows a modest decline (Berg & Sternberg, 2003; Kaufman, 2001).

Overall, loss outweighs improvement and maintenance as people approach the end of life. But plasticity is still possible (Baltes & Carstensen, 1996). Research reveals greater individual variation in cognitive functioning in late adulthood than at any other time of life (Hultsch et al., 1998; Hultsch, MacDonald, & Dixon, 2002). Besides fuller expression of genetic and lifestyle influences, increased freedom to pursue self-chosen courses of action—some that enhance and others that undermine cognitive skills—may be responsible.

How can older adults make the most of their cognitive resources? According to one view, elders who sustain high levels of functioning engage in **selective optimization with compensation:** Narrowing their goals, they *select* personally valued activities to *optimize* (or maximize) returns from their diminishing energy. They also find new ways to *compensate* for losses (Baltes, 1997; Freund & Baltes, 2000). One day, Ruth and Walt watched a public television rebroadcast of an interview with 80-year-old concert pianist Arthur Rubinstein, who was asked how he managed to sustain such extraordinary piano playing at his advanced age. Rubinstein replied that he was *selective;* he played fewer pieces. This enabled him to *optimize* his energy; he could practice each piece more. Finally, he developed new, *compensatory* techniques for a decline in playing speed. For example, before a fast passage, he played extra slowly, so the fast section appeared to his audience to move more quickly.

Elders can sustain high levels of functioning by selective optimization with compensation. This woman does so by focusing her love for gardening on a small area right outside her door and enlisting the help of a grandchild.

As we review major changes in memory, language processing, and problem solving, we will consider ways that older adults can optimize and compensate in the face of declines. We will also see that certain abilities that depend on extensive life experience, not processing efficiency, are sustained or increase in old age. Last, we take up programs that recognize the elderly as lifelong learners empowered by new knowledge, just as they were at earlier periods of development.

Memory

As older adults take in information more slowly and find it harder to apply strategies, inhibit irrelevant information, and retrieve relevant knowledge from long-term memory, the chances of memory failure increase (O'Connor & Kaplan, 2003; Persad et al., 2002). A reduced capacity to hold material in working memory while operating on it means that memory problems are especially evident on complex tasks.

Deliberate versus Automatic Memory

"Ruth, you know that movie we saw—with the little 5-year-old boy who did such a wonderful acting job. I'd like to suggest it to Dick and Goldie. But what was it called?" asked Walt.

"I can't think of it, Walt. We've seen several movies lately, and that one just doesn't ring a bell. Which theater was it at? Who'd we go with? Tell me more about the little boy, and maybe it'll come to me."

Although we all have memory failures like this occasionally, difficulties with recall rise in old age. When Ruth and Walt watched the movie, their slower cognitive processing meant that they retained fewer details. And because their working memories could hold less at once, they attended poorly to *context*—where they saw the movie and who went with them (Craik & Jacoby, 1996; Wegesin et al., 2000). When we try to remember, context serves as an important retrieval cue.

Because older adults take in less about a stimulus and its context, their recall is reduced in relation to that of younger people. For example, they sometimes cannot distinguish an experienced event from one they imagined (Rybash & Hrubi-Bopp, 2000). They also have difficulty remembering the source of information, particularly when potential sources are similar—which member of their bridge club made a certain statement, in what magazine or newspaper they read about a particular news event (Simons et al., 2004). Temporal memory—recall of the order in which events occurred or how recently they happened—suffers as well (Dumas & Hartman, 2003; Hartman & Warren, 2005).

A few days later, when Ruth saw an ad for the movie on TV, she recognized its title immediately. Recognition—a fairly automatic type of memory that demands little mental effort—suffers less than recall in late adulthood because a multitude of environmental supports for remembering are present. Age-related memory declines are greatest on tasks that require deliberate processing (Reuter-Lorenz & Sylvester, 2005).

Consider another automatic form of memory: **implicit memory,** or memory without conscious awareness. In a typical implicit memory task, you would be shown a list of words, then asked to fill in a word fragment (such as *t--k*). You would probably complete the sequence with a word you had just seen (*task*) rather than other words (*took* or *teak*). Without trying to do so, you would engage in recall.

Age differences in implicit memory are much smaller than in explicit, or deliberate, memory. Memory that depends on familiarity rather than on conscious use of strategies is largely spared in old age (Davis, Trussell, & Klebe, 2001; Fleischman et al., 2004). The memory problems elders report—for names of people, places where they put important objects, directions for getting from one place to another, and (as we will see) appointments and medication schedules—all place substantial demands on their more limited working memories.

Associative Memory

The memory deficits just described are part of a general, age-related decline in binding information into complex memories. Researchers call this an **associative memory deficit,** or difficulty creating and retrieving links between pieces of information—for example, two items or an item and its context, such as Ruth trying to remember the name of the movie with the child actor or where she had seen the movie.

To find out whether older adults have greater difficulty with associative memory than younger adults, researchers showed them pairs of unrelated words or pictures of objects (such as *table–overcoat* or *sandwich–radio*) and asked that they study the pairs for an upcoming memory test. During the test, one group of participants was given a page of *single items,* some that had appeared in the study phase and some that had not, and asked to circle the ones they had studied. The other group was given a page of *item pairs,* some intact from the study phase (*table–overcoat*) and some that had been rearranged (*overcoat–radio*), and asked to circle pairs they had studied. As Figure 17.7 shows, older adults did almost as well as younger adults on the single-item memory test. But they performed far worse on the item-pair test—findings that support an associative memory deficit (Naveh-Benjamin, 2000; Naveh-Benjamin et al., 2003).

Notice that the memory tasks in this study relied on recognition. In most cases, recognition memory requires only that we recognize single pieces of information, so elders perform well. When researchers complicate recognition tasks by making them depend on associative memory, elders have difficulty. Providing older adults with repeated presentations of information to be learned and more memory cues improves their associative memory (Naveh-Benjamin et al., 2003; Simons et al., 2004). For example, to associate names with faces, elders profit from mention of relevant facts about those individuals. Enhancing the meaningfulness of names improves recall (Schmidt et al., 1999).

■ **FIGURE 17.7 Young and old adults' performance on single-word and word-pair memory tests, supporting an associative memory deficit in late adulthood.** After studying pairs of unrelated words, some adults were asked to identify single words they had seen. Others were asked to identify word pairs they had seen. Old adults performed almost as well as young adults on the single-word memory test. But they did far worse on the word-pair memory test. These findings support an associative memory deficit in late adulthood. (Adapted from Naveh-Benjamin, 2000.)

Remote Memory

Although older people often say that their **remote memory,** or very long-term recall, is clearer than their memory for recent events, research does not support this conclusion. In several studies, adults ranging in age from their twenties to their seventies were asked to recall names of grade school teachers and high school classmates and Spanish vocabulary from high school—information very well learned early in life. Memory declined rapidly for the first 3 to 6 years, then changed little for the next 20 years. After that, additional modest forgetting occurred (Bahrick, 1984; Bahrick, Bahrick, & Wittlinger, 1975).

How about *autobiographical memory,* or memory for personally meaningful events, such as what you did on your first date or how you celebrated your college graduation? To test for this type of memory, researchers typically give a series of words (such as *book, machine, sorry, surprised*) and ask adults to report a personal memory cued by each. Or they present participants with a time line on a piece of paper, representing birth to present age, and ask them to place important life events on the line and note the age at which each occurred. People between ages 50 and 90 recall both remote and recent events more frequently than intermediate events, with recent events mentioned most often in the word-cue studies (see Figure 17.8). Among remote events recalled using either word-cue or time-line procedures, most happened between ages 10 and 30 (Rubin, 2002; Rubin & Schulkind, 1997; Schroots, van Dijkum, & Assink, 2004).

Why do older adults recall their adolescent and early adulthood experiences more readily than their mid-adulthood lives? Perhaps youthful events are remembered best because they occurred during a period of rapid life change filled with novel experiences that stand out from the humdrum of daily life. Adolescence and early adulthood are also times of identity development, when many personally significant experiences occur. Recall from Chapter 5 that such events are likely to become a lasting part of the individual's life story. Even public events linked to this period—World Series champions, Academy Award winners, and current events—are especially salient to elders (Rubin, Rahhal, & Poon, 1998).

Nevertheless, older adults recall recent personal experiences more readily than remote ones, probably because of interference produced by years of additional experience (Kausler, 1994). As we accumulate more memories, some inevitably resemble others. As a result, certain early memories become less clear than they once were. However, even when asked to recall an important event of the previous year, elders—because of their recall difficulties—provide considerably fewer details than do young adults (Levine et al., 2002).

Prospective Memory

Elderly people often complain that they have become more absent-minded about daily events. Because Ruth and Walt knew they were more likely to forget an appointment, they would ask about it repeatedly. "Sybil, what time is our dinner engagement?" Walt asked several times during the two days before the event. His questioning was not a sign of dementia. He simply wanted to be sure to remember an important date.

So far, we have considered various aspects of *retrospective memory* (remembrance of things past). **Prospective memory** refers to remembering to engage in planned actions in the future. The amount of mental effort required determines whether older adults have trouble with prospective memory. Remembering the dinner date was challenging for Walt because he typically ate dinner with his daughter on Thursday evenings at 6 P.M., but this time, dinner was set for Tuesday at 7:15 P.M.

In the laboratory, older adults do better on *event-based* than on *time-based* prospective memory tasks. In an event-based task, an event (such as a certain word appearing on a computer screen) serves as a cue for remembering to do something (pressing a key) while the participant engages in an ongoing activity (reading paragraphs). As long as the event-based task is not complex, older adults do as well as younger adults. But when researchers introduce extra memory demands (for example, press the key when any one of four cues appears), older adults' performance worsens (Einstein et al., 1997, 2000; Henry et al, 2004). In time-based tasks, the adult must engage in an action after a certain time interval has elapsed, without any obvious external cue (for example, pressing a key every

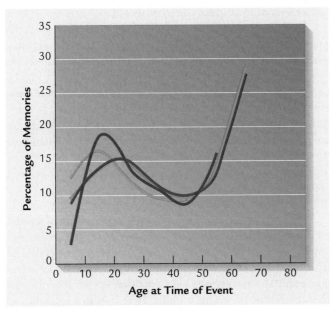

▓ **FIGURE 17.8 Distribution of older adults' autobiographical memories by reported age at time of the event.** In the four studies of 50- to 90-year-olds represented here, later events were remembered better than early events. Among early events, most of those recalled occurred between ages 10 and 30. (Adapted from D. C. Rubin, T. A. Rahhal, & L. W. Poon, 1998, "Things Learned in Early Adulthood Are Remembered Best," *Memory and Cognition, 26,* p. 4. Copyright © 1998 by the Psychonomic Society, Inc. Reprinted by permission.)

10 minutes). Time-based prospective memory requires considerable initiative to keep the planned action in mind, and declines in late adulthood are large (Park et al., 1997; West & Craik, 1999).

But difficulties with prospective memory seen in the laboratory do not appear in real life, where adults are highly motivated to remember and good at setting up reminders for themselves, such as a buzzer ringing in the kitchen or a note tacked up prominently (Henry et al., 2004). In trying to remember a future activity, younger adults rely more on strategies like rehearsal, older adults on external memory aids (Dixon, de Frias, & Bäckman, 2001). In this way, the elderly compensate for their reduced-capacity working memories and the challenge of dividing attention between what they are doing now and what they must do in the future.

Language Processing

Language and memory skills are closely related. In language comprehension (understanding the meaning of spoken or written prose), we recollect what we have heard or read without conscious awareness. Like implicit memory, language comprehension changes very little in late life as long as conversational partners do not speak very quickly and elders are given enough time to process written text accurately (Hultsch et al., 1998; Stine-Morrow & Miller, 1999). In one longitudinal study, 55- to 70-year-olds showed a slight increase over a 6-year period in their recall of written stories! And into their eighties and nineties, elders made good use of story organization to help them recall both main ideas and details (Small et al., 1999).

As this senior of the Apache people of Arizona tells stories to young members of her community, she is likely to enrich her tales with inferences and moral lessons grounded in extensive life experience.

© LAWRENCE MIGDALE/PHOTO RESEARCHERS

In contrast to language comprehension, two aspects of language production show age-related losses. The first is retrieving words from long-term memory. When conversing with others, Ruth and Walt sometimes had difficulty coming up with right words to convey their thoughts—even well-known words they had used many times in the past. Consequently, their speech contained more pronouns and other unclear references than it did at younger ages. They also spoke more slowly and paused more often, partly because they needed time to search their memories for certain words (MacKay & Abrams, 1996). And compared to younger people, they more often reported a *tip-of-the-tongue state*—certainty that they knew a word accompanied by an inability to produce it (Burke & Shafto, 2004).

Second, planning what to say and how to say it is harder in late adulthood. As a result, Walt and Ruth displayed more hesitations, false starts, word repetitions, and sentence fragments as they aged. Their statements were also less well-organized than before (Kemper, Kynette, & Norman, 1992).

What explains these changes? Whereas the meanings elders want to convey have many "mental connections" with other meanings, the sounds of a word have only one mental connection to the word's underlying concept. Consequently, as associative memory declines with age, memory difficulties in everyday conversation are especially apparent in word retrieval (Burke & Shafto, 2004). Also, diminished working-memory capacity is involved. Because less information can be held at once, older adults have difficulty coordinating the multiple tasks required to produce coherent speech.

As with memory, older adults develop compensatory techniques for their language production problems. For example, they simplify their grammatical structures so they can devote more effort to retrieving words and organizing their thoughts. Sacrificing efficiency for greater clarity, they use more sentences to convey their message (Kemper, Thompson, & Marquis, 2001). As elders monitor their word-retrieval failures and try hard to overcome them, they show a greater frequency of tip-of-the-tongue states—but they resolve tip-of-the-tongues at a higher rate than do younger people (Schwartz & Frazier, 2005).

Furthermore, the elderly often compensate by representing information they want to communicate in terms of gist rather than details (Jepson & Labouvie-Vief, 1992). For example, when Walt told his granddaughter Marci fairy tales, he left out many concrete facts while substituting personal inferences and a moral lesson—elements that appear less often in the storytelling of younger adults. Here is Walt's rendition of "Sleeping Beauty": "An evil fairy condemns Sleeping Beauty to death. But a kind fairy changes the curse from death to sleep. Then a handsome prince awakens the girl with a kiss. So you see, Marci, both good and bad exist in the world. The bad things instill in us the need to think of and care for others."

Older adults often make the most of their limited working memories by extracting the essence of a message. Then, drawing on their extensive life experience, they enrich it with symbolic interpretations.

Problem Solving

Problem solving is yet another cognitive skill that illustrates how aging brings not only deterioration but also important adaptive changes. Traditional problem solving, which lacks a real-life context (as in playing Twenty Questions) declines in late adulthood (Sinnott, 1989). Older adults' memory limitations make it hard to keep all relevant facts in mind when dealing with a complex hypothetical problem.

Yet the everyday problematic situations the elderly encounter and care about differ from hypothetical problems devised by researchers—and also from the problems they experienced at earlier ages. Being retired, most do not have to deal with problems in the workplace. Their children are typically grown and living on their own, and their marriages have endured long enough to have fewer difficulties (Berg et al., 1998). Instead, major concerns involve dealing with extended family relationships (desire for more visits from relatives, expectations from adult children that they baby-sit grandchildren) and managing IADLs, such as preparing nutritious meals, handling finances, and attending to health concerns. Surveys in Germany and the United States reveal that older adults spend a third to half of a typical day on IADL issues (Willis, 1996).

How do the elderly solve problems of daily living? Their strategies extend the adaptive problem solving of midlife. As long as they perceive problems as under their control and as important, elders are active and effective in solving them (Artistico, Cervone, & Pezzuti, 2003; Haught et al., 2000). Perhaps because older adults often conclude that they cannot change other people, they usually do what they can to avoid interpersonal conflicts (Blanchard-Fields, Chen, & Norris, 1997). But as we will see in Chapter 18, this strategy often makes sense for elders, who are highly motivated to conserve energy and limit stress.

The health arena, especially salient for elders, illustrates the adaptiveness of everyday problem solving in late adulthood (Sansone & Berg, 1993). Older adults make quicker decisions about whether they are ill and seek medical care sooner. In contrast, young and middle-aged adults are more likely to adopt a "wait and see" approach in favor of gathering more facts, even when the health problem is serious (Leventhal et al., 1993; Meyer, Russo, & Talbot, 1995). This swift response of the elderly is interesting in view of their slower cognitive processing. Perhaps years of experience in coping with illnesses enable them to draw on extensive personal knowledge and move ahead with greater certainty. Acting decisively when faced with health risks is sensible in old age.

Finally, older adults report that they often consult others—generally spouses and adult children, but also friends, neighbors, and members of their religious congregation—for advice about everyday problems (Strough et al., 2003). And compared with younger married couples, older married couples more often collaborate in problem solving, and researchers judge their jointly generated strategies as highly effective (Meegan & Berg, 2002). In jointly solving problems, elders seem to compensate for moments of cognitive difficulty, yielding enhanced accomplishment of life tasks.

Wisdom

We have seen that a wealth of life experience enhances the storytelling and problem solving of the elderly. It also underlies another capacity believed to reach its height in old age: **wisdom.** When researchers ask people to describe wisdom, most mention breadth and depth of practical knowledge, ability to reflect on and apply that knowledge in ways that make life more bearable and worthwhile; emotional maturity, including the ability to listen, evaluate, and give advice; and the altruistic form of creativity discussed in Chapter 15 that involves contributing to humanity and enriching others' lives. One group of researchers summed up the multiple cognitive and personality traits that make up wisdom as "expertise in the conduct and meaning of life" (Baltes & Staudinger, 2000, p. 124; Staudinger, Dörner, & Mickler, 2005).

During her college years, Ruth and Walt's granddaughter Marci telephoned with a pressing personal dilemma. Ruth's advice reflected the features of wisdom just mentioned. Unsure whether her love for her boyfriend Ken would endure, Marci began to date another student after Ken moved to another city to attend medical school. "I can't stand being pulled in two directions. I'm thinking of calling Ken and telling him about Steve," she exclaimed. "Do you think I should?"

"This is not a good time, Marci," Ruth advised. "You'll break Ken's heart before you've had a chance to size up your feelings for Steve. And you said Ken's taking some important exams in two weeks. If you tell him now and he's distraught, it could affect the rest of his life."

Wisdom—whether applied to personal problems or to community, national, and international concerns—requires the "pinnacle of insight into the human condition" (Baltes & Staudinger, 2000; Csikszentmihalyi & Nakamura, 2005). Not surprisingly, cultures around the world assume that age and wisdom go together. In village and tribal societies, the most important social positions, such as chieftain and shaman (religious leader), are reserved for the old. Similarly, in industrialized nations, older adults are chief executive officers of large corporations, high-level religious leaders, members of legislatures, and supreme court justices. What explains this widespread trend? According to an evolutionary view, the genetic program of our species grants health, fitness, and strength to the young. Culture tames this youthful advantage in physical power with the insights of the old, ensuring balance and interdependence between generations (Assmann, 1994; Csikszentmihalyi & Rathunde, 1990).

In the most extensive research to date on development of wisdom, adults ranging in age from 20 to 89 responded to uncertain real-life situations—for example, what to consider and do if a good friend is about to commit suicide or if, after

Former U.S. President Jimmy Carter visited Ethiopia in 2005 as part of a team observing balloting during an election. Carter exemplifies wisdom, applied on an international scale. For decades, he has championed democracy, peaceful conflict resolution, and human rights around the world.

reflecting on your life, you discover that you have not achieved your goals (Staudinger, Dörner, & Mickler, 2005). Responses were rated for five ingredients of wisdom:

- Knowledge about fundamental concerns of life, including human nature, social relations, and emotions

- Effective strategies for applying that knowledge to making life decisions, handling conflict, and giving advice

- A view of people that considers the multiple demands of their life contexts

- A concern with ultimate human values, such as the common good, as well as respect for individual differences in values

- Awareness and management of the uncertainties of life— that many problems have no perfect solution

Results revealed that age was no guarantee of wisdom. A small number of adults of diverse ages ranked among the wise. But type of life experience made a difference. People in human-service careers who had extensive training and practice in grappling with human problems tended to attain high wisdom scores. Other high-scorers held leadership positions (Staudinger, Smith, & Baltes, 1992; Staudinger, 1996). And when age and relevant life experiences were considered together, more older than younger people scored in the top 20 percent. Consistent with this finding, a panel of citizens asked to nominate public figures high in wisdom mostly selected older adults ranging in age from 50 to 70, with an average age of 64 (Baltes et al., 1995).

In addition to age and life experience, having faced and overcome adversity appears to be an important contributor to late-life wisdom. In a longitudinal study of people who were young adults during the Great Depression of the 1930s, those who experienced economic hardship and surmounted it scored especially high in wisdom nearly 40 years later, as indicated by thoughtful interview responses to life events, insights into their own motives and behavior, and warmth and compassion (Ardelt, 1998). Stress-related growth may be one of several as yet unknown paths to the development of wisdom.

Compared to their agemates, older adults with the cognitive, reflective, and emotional qualities that make up wisdom are better educated and physically healthier, forge more positive relations with others, and score higher on the personality dimension of openness to experience (Kramer, 2003). Wisdom is also a strong predictor of psychological well-being (Peterson & Seligman, 2004). Wise elders seem to flourish, even when faced with physical and cognitive challenges. This suggests that finding ways to promote wisdom would be a powerful means of both contributing to human welfare and fostering a gratifying old age (Sternberg, 2001).

Factors Related to Cognitive Change

As in middle adulthood, a mentally active life—above-average education, stimulating leisure pursuits, community participation, and a flexible personality—predicts maintenance of mental abilities into advanced old age (Schaie, 2005). Today's North American elders are better educated than any previous generation. Since 1950, the rate of high school completion has quadrupled, reaching 72 percent. And older adults with at least a bachelor's degree have increased fivefold, to 18 percent (National Institute on Aging, 2006). As the first baby boomers enter late adulthood in 2011, these trends are expected to continue, forecasting improved preservation of cognitive functions and lower rates of mental disabilities among the elderly than in the past.

As noted earlier, health status powerfully predicts older adults' intellectual performance. In several longitudinal studies, cigarette smokers declined cognitively at a faster rate than their nonsmoking counterparts, even after initial health status, SES, and mental test performance were controlled (Ott et al., 2004). And a wide variety of chronic conditions, including vision and hearing impairments, cardiovascular disease, osteoporosis, and arthritis, are strongly associated with cognitive declines (Anstey & Christensen, 2000; Baltes, Lindenberger, & Staudinger, 1998). But we must be cautious in interpreting this link between physical and cognitive deterioration. The relationship may be exaggerated by the fact that brighter adults are more likely to engage in health-protective behaviors, which postpone the onset of serious disease.

Retirement also affects cognitive change, both positively and negatively. When people leave routine jobs for stimulating leisure activities, outcomes are favorable. In contrast, retiring from a highly complex job without developing challenging substitutes accelerates intellectual declines (Schaie, 1996). In fact, complex, challenging work in late adulthood has an even stronger, facilitating impact on intellectual functioning than in middle adulthood (see page 523 in Chapter 15) (Schooler, Mulatu, & Oates, 1999).

As elders grow older, their scores on cognitive tasks become increasingly unstable, showing larger fluctuations from one occasion to the next. This rising inconsistency of performance—especially in speed of response—accelerates in the seventies and is associated with cognitive declines. Researchers speculate that it signals end-of-life deterioration across wide-ranging areas in the brain (Hultsch, MacDonald, & Dixon, 2002; McDonald, Hultsch, & Dixon, 2003). After age 75, cognitive decrements are related to distance to death rather than to chronological age (Small & Bäckman, 1997). In the year before Walt died, those close to him noticed that he had become less active and more withdrawn. In the company of friends, he talked and moved less. At home, he spent more time looking out the window instead of immersing himself in creative writing and gardening.

Terminal decline refers to marked acceleration in deterioration of cognitive functioning prior to death. Some longitudinal studies indicate that it is limited to a few aspects of intelligence, others that it occurs generally, across many areas, signifying general deterioration. Findings also differ greatly in its estimated length. Some report that it lasts only 1 to 3 years, others that it extends for as much as 14 years. The average is 4 to 5 years (Hassing et al., 2002; Lövdén et al., 2005; Small et al., 2003; Wilson et al., 2003). Perhaps the reason for these conflicting findings is that different kinds of terminal decline exist—one type arising from disease processes, another as part of a general biological breakdown due to normal aging (Berg, 1996). What we know for sure is that an extended, steep falloff in cognitive performance is a sign of loss of vitality and impending death.

Cognitive Interventions

For most of late adulthood, cognitive declines are gradual. Although aging of the brain contributes to them, recall from our earlier discussion that the brain can compensate by growing new neural fibers. Furthermore, some cognitive decrements may be due to disuse of particular skills rather than biological aging. If plasticity of development is possible in old age, then interventions that train the elderly in cognitive strategies should at least partially reverse the age-related declines we have discussed.

The Adult Development and Enrichment Project (ADEPT) is the most extensive cognitive intervention program conducted to date. By using participants in the Seattle Longitudinal Study (see Chapter 15, page 516), researchers were able to do what no other investigation has done: assess the effects of cognitive training on long-term development (Schaie, 2005).

Intervention began with adults over age 64, some of whom had maintained their scores on two mental abilities (inductive

reasoning and spatial orientation) over the previous 14 years and others who had shown declines. After just five one-hour training sessions in one of two types of mental-test items, two-thirds of participants improved their performance on the trained skill. Gains for decliners were dramatic. Forty percent returned to the level at which they had been functioning 14 years earlier! A follow-up after 7 years revealed that although scores dropped somewhat, elders remained advantaged in their trained skill over agemates trained in the other ability. Finally, "booster" training at this time led to further gains, although these were smaller than the earlier gains.

In another large-scale intervention study called ACTIVE (Advanced Cognitive Training for Independent and Vital Elderly), more than 2,800 65- to 84-year-olds were randomly assigned to a ten-session training program focusing on one of three abilities—speed of processing, memory, or reasoning—or to a no-intervention control group. Again, trained elders showed an immediate advantage in the trained skill over controls that was still evident—though smaller in magnitude—at one- and two-year follow-ups (Ball et al., 2002).

Clearly, a wide range of cognitive skills can be enhanced in old age. A vital goal is to transfer intervention from the laboratory to the community, weaving it into the daily experiences of elderly people. As we will see in the next section, a promising approach is to provide older adults with well-designed, highly interesting learning experiences in which cognitive training is an integral part.

Lifelong Learning

Think about the competencies that older adults need to live in our complex, changing world. They are the same as those of younger people—communicating effectively through spoken and written systems; locating information, sorting through it, and selecting what is needed; using math strategies such as estimation; planning and organizing activities, including making good use of time and resources; mastering new technologies; and understanding past and current events and the relevance of each to their own lives. The elderly also need to develop new, problem-centered coping strategies—ways to sustain health and operate their households efficiently and safely—and self-employment skills for those who must continue their work lives.

Because of better health and earlier retirement, participation of the elderly in continuing education has increased substantially over the past few decades. Successful programs include a wide variety of offerings responsive to the diversity of senior citizens and teaching methods suited to their developmental needs.

Types of Programs

One summer, Walt and Ruth attended an Elderhostel at a nearby university. After moving into a dormitory room, they

© AP/WIDE WORLD PHOTOS

These seniors call themselves the Silver Stringers Computer Group. They created the website that appears in the foreground, overturning the assumption that seniors and technology do not mix.

joined 30 other seniors for two weeks of morning lectures on Shakespeare, afternoon visits to points of interest, and evening performances of plays at a nearby Shakespeare festival.

Elderhostel programs (in Canada, called Routes to Learning) attract over a quarter million North American older adults annually. Local educational institutions serve as hosts, combining stimulating 1- to 3-week courses with recreational pursuits. Some programs make use of community resources through classes on local ecology or folk life. Others involve travel abroad. Still others focus on innovative topics and experi-

ences—writing one's own life story, discussing contemporary films with screenwriters, whitewater rafting, Chinese painting and calligraphy, and acquiring French language skills.

Other similar educational programs have sprung up in North America and elsewhere. The Bernard Osher Foundation collaborates with more than 80 U.S. universities to establish Osher Lifelong Learning Institutes on campuses. Each offers older adults a wide array of stimulating learning experiences, from auditing regular courses, to forming learning communities that address common interests, to helping to solve community problems. Originating in France, the University of the Third Age[2] provides Western European, British, and Australian elders with university- and community-sponsored courses, workshops on special topics, and excursions. Elders often do the teaching, based on the idea that experts of all kinds retire. Some programs foster intergenerational relations. In Austria, for example, training in academic subjects is offered to grandparents so they can help their grandchildren with schoolwork.

Participants in the programs just mentioned tend to be active, well-educated, and financially well-off (Abraham, 1998). Much less is available for elders with little education and limited income. Community senior centers with inexpensive offerings related to everyday living attract more low-SES people than programs such as Elderhostel (Knox, 1993). Regardless of course content and which seniors attend, using the techniques summarized in Applying What We Know below increases the effectiveness of instruction.

---

[2]The term *third age* refers to the period after the "second age" of midlife, when older people are freed from work and parenting responsibilities and have more time to invest in lifelong learning.

Applying What We Know

Increasing the Effectiveness of Instruction for Older Adults

Technique	Description
Provide a positive learning environment.	Some elders have internalized negative stereotypes of their abilities and come to the learning environment with low self-esteem. A supportive group atmosphere, in which the instructor acts as a colleague, helps convince older adults that they can learn.
Allow ample time to learn new information.	Rate of learning varies widely among older adults, and some master new material at a fairly slow rate. Presenting information over several sessions or allowing for self-paced instruction aids mastery.
Present information in a well-organized fashion.	Older adults do not organize information as effectively as younger adults. Material that is outlined, presented, and then summarized enhances memory and understanding. Digressions make a presentation harder to comprehend.
Relate information to elders' experiences.	Relating new material to what elders have already learned, by drawing on their experiences and giving many vivid examples, enhances recall.

Source: Illeris, 2004.

Benefits of Continuing Education

Elderly participants in continuing education report a rich array of benefits—learning interesting facts, understanding new ideas in many disciplines, making new friends, and developing a broader perspective on the world (Kim & Merriam, 2004; Long & Zoller-Hodges, 1995). Furthermore, seniors come to see themselves differently. Many arrive with ingrained stereotypes of aging, which they abandon when they realize that adults in their seventies and eighties—including themselves—can still engage in complex learning. In Elderhostel courses, participants with the least education report learning the most, an argument for recruiting less economically privileged people into these programs (Brady, 1984).

The educational needs of seniors are likely to be given greater attention in coming decades, as their numbers grow and they assert their right to lifelong learning. Once this happens, false stereotypes—"the elderly are too old to learn" or "education is for the young"—are likely to weaken and, perhaps, disappear.

Summary

🍁 Physical Development

Life Expectancy

Distinguish between chronological age and functional age, and discuss changes in life expectancy over the past century.

■ Because people age biologically at different rates, chronological age is an imperfect indicator of **functional age,** or actual competence and performance. Dramatic twentieth-century gains in **average life expectancy**—resulting from declines in both infant mortality and death rates among adults—confirm that biological aging can be modified by environmental factors, including improved nutrition, medical treatment, sanitation, and safety.

■ Length of life and, even more important, **active lifespan,** can be predicted by a country's health care, housing, and social services, along with lifestyle factors. In developing nations, both total life expectancy and active lifespan are shortened by poverty, malnutrition, disease, and armed conflict.

■ With advancing age, women outnumber men by a greater margin, but the gender gap in average life expectancy declines. Differences between higher-SES whites and low-SES ethnic minorities also diminish until, around age 85, a **life expectancy crossover** occurs, with longer life expectancy for low-SES minority groups.

■ About 10 percent of North Americans age 65 and older have difficulty carrying out **activities of daily living (ADLs),** or basic self-care tasks, and about 20 percent cannot perform **instrumental activities of daily living (IADLs),** which are everyday tasks requiring some cognitive competence. The proportion of elders with these limitations increases sharply with age.

■ Longevity runs in families, but environmental factors become increasingly important with age. Scientists disagree on whether **maximum lifespan** can be extended beyond about 85 to 90 years.

Physical Changes

Describe changes in the nervous system and the senses in late adulthood.

■ Loss of neurons occurs throughout the cerebral cortex, with greater shrinkage in the frontal lobes and the corpus callosum. The cerebellum also loses neurons. However, the brain compensates by forming new synapses and, to some extent, generating new neurons. The autonomic nervous system functions less well in old age and releases more stress hormones.

■ Older adults—more women than men—tend to suffer from impaired vision and may experience **cataracts** and **macular degeneration.** Visual deficits affect elders' self-confidence and everyday behavior and can lead to isolation.

■ In late life, hearing impairments are more common than visual impairments, especially in men, and can lead to loneliness, isolation, and depressive symptoms. Impaired speech perception has the greatest impact on life satisfaction.

■ Taste and odor sensitivity decline, making food less appealing. Touch sensitivity also deteriorates, particularly on the fingertips.

Describe cardiovascular, respiratory, and immune system changes in late adulthood.

■ Reduced capacity of the cardiovascular and respiratory systems becomes more apparent in late adulthood. As at earlier ages, not smoking, reducing dietary fat, avoiding environmental pollutants, and exercising can slow the effects of aging on these systems.

■ The immune system functions less effectively in late life, permitting diseases to progress and making **autoimmune responses** more likely. Consequently, risk of autoimmune disorders and stress-induced infection increase.

Discuss sleep difficulties in late adulthood.

■ Older adults find it harder to fall asleep, stay asleep, and sleep deeply. Until age 70 or 80, men have more trouble sleeping than women because of prostate enlargement (which leads to a need to urinate often), **sleep apnea,** and "restless legs."

Describe changes in physical appearance and mobility in late adulthood, along with effective adaptations to these changes.

■ Outward signs of aging, such as white hair, wrinkled and sagging skin, age spots, and decreased height and weight, become more noticeable, but these bear no relationship to functioning or longevity. Mobility diminishes as muscle and bone strength and joint flexibility decline.

■ "Anti-aging" dietary supplements, herbal products, and hormonal medications have shown no demonstrated benefits and may cause harm. Instead, problem-centered coping strategies yield improved physical functioning in the elderly. A rapidly expanding **assistive technology** is available to help older people cope with physical declines.

■ Negative stereotypes of aging in Western society make adapting to late-life physical changes more difficult. Older people fare best when they have high status and opportunities for social participation.

Health, Fitness, and Disability

Discuss health and fitness in late life, paying special attention to nutrition, exercise, and sexuality.

■ Most elders are optimistic about their health and, with respect to protecting it, have a high sense of self-efficacy. Low-SES ethnic minority elders remain at greater risk for certain health problems and are less likely to believe they can control their health.

■ As in early adulthood, in late life men are more prone to fatal diseases and women to disabling conditions. By very old age,

women are more impaired than surviving men. In industrialized nations, **compression of morbidity** has occurred, largely as a result of medical advances and improved socioeconomic conditions. Good health habits also substantially postpone disability, but more comprehensive strategies will be needed to achieve compression of morbidity in the developing world.

■ Because risk of dietary deficiencies increases, a daily vitamin–mineral supplement is beneficial, preventing infectious illness. But supplements do not reduce the risk of cardiovascular disease, and those labeled as "cognitive enhancers" show no positive effects. Exercise, even when begun in late adulthood, continues to be a powerful health intervention.

■ Compared with other parts of the body, the reproductive organs undergo minimal change in late adulthood. Sexual desire and sexual activity decline but need not disappear.

Discuss physical disabilities common in late adulthood.

■ Illness and disability increase toward the end of life. Cardiovascular disease, cancer, stroke, and emphysema claim many lives. Because of declines in immune system functioning, vaccination against the most common type of pneumonia is advisable.

■ **Primary aging** (species-wide genetically influenced declines) contributes to **frailty** in the elderly. But **secondary aging** (declines due to hereditary defects and negative environmental influences) plays a larger role.

■ **Osteoarthritis** and **rheumatoid arthritis** are widespread among older adults, especially women. Adult-onset diabetes also increases.

■ The death rate from unintentional injuries reaches an all-time high in those age 65 and older, largely due to motor vehicle collisions, pedestrian accidents, and falls. Visual declines and slowed reaction time often contribute. A common, serious injury is hip fracture.

Discuss mental disabilities common in late adulthood.

■ **Alzheimer's disease** is the most common form of **dementia.** Often starting with severe memory problems, it brings personality changes, depression, loss of ability to comprehend and produce speech, disintegration of purposeful movements, and death. Underlying these changes are abundant **neurofibrillary tangles** and **amyloid plaques** and lowered neurotransmitter levels in the brain.

■ Familial Alzheimer's generally has an early onset, progresses rapidly, and is linked to

dominant genes on chromosomes 1, 14, and 21. Although many victims of sporadic Alzheimer's show no known genetic marker, about half have an abnormal ApoE4 gene on chromosome 19, resulting in insulin deficiency that is linked to brain damage.

■ Diverse environmental factors, including head injuries and a high-fat diet, increase the risk of Alzheimer's. A "Mediterranean diet," education, and an active lifestyle are associated with lower incidence.

■ Heredity contributes to **cerebrovascular dementia** indirectly, through high blood pressure, cardiovascular disease, and diabetes. Many environmental influences also heighten stroke risk. Because of their greater susceptibility to cardiovascular disease, men are affected more than women.

■ Treatable problems, such as depression, side effects of medication, and reactions to social isolation, can be mistaken for dementia. Therefore, careful diagnosis is essential.

Discuss health care issues that affect senior citizens.

■ Only a small percentage of North American seniors are institutionalized, a rate about half that of other industrialized nations that offer more generous public financing of nursing home care than the United States and Canada. Family members provide most long-term care, especially among ethnic minorities with close-knit extended families. Publicly funded in-home help and assisted-living arrangements can reduce nursing home placement of the elderly and its associated high cost.

🦊 Cognitive Development

Describe overall changes in cognitive functioning in late adulthood.

■ Individual differences in cognitive functioning are greater in late adulthood than at any other time of life. Although both fluid intelligence and crystallized intelligence decline in advanced old age, plasticity of development is still possible. Older adults can make the most of their cognitive resources through **selective optimization with compensation.**

Memory

How does memory change in late life?

■ Age-related limitations on working memory make memory difficulties more apparent on tasks that are complex and require deliberate processing. Recall of the context, source, and temporal order of events declines. Automatic forms of memory, such as recognition and **implicit memory,** suffer less. In general, an **associative memory deficit,** or difficulty creating and retrieving links between pieces of information, seems to characterize older adults' memory problems.

■ Contrary to what older people sometimes report, **remote memory** is not clearer than recent memory. Autobiographical memory is best for recent experiences, followed by personally meaningful events that happened between ages 10 and 30, a period of rapid life change and identity development. In the laboratory, older adults do better on event-based than on time-based **prospective memory** tasks. In everyday life, they compensate for declines in prospective memory by using external memory aids.

Language Processing

Describe changes in language processing in late adulthood.

■ Although language comprehension changes little in late life, age-related losses occur in two aspects of language production: retrieving words from long-term memory and planning what to say and how to say it. Elders compensate by simplifying their grammatical structures and communicating gist rather than details.

Problem Solving

How does problem solving change in late life?

■ Traditional problem solving declines in late adulthood. But in everyday problem solving, older adults are active and effective as long as they perceive problems as important and under their control. In matters of health, elders make quicker decisions than younger people. And they more often consult others about everyday problems and, if married, collaborate with their spouse, generating highly effective strategies.

Wisdom

What capacities make up wisdom, and how is it affected by age and life experience?

■ **Wisdom** involves extensive practical knowledge, ability to reflect on and apply that knowledge in ways that make life more bearable and worthwhile, emotional maturity, and altruistic creativity. When age and life experience in grappling with human

problems are combined, more older than younger people rank among the wise.

■ Having faced and overcome adversity seems to foster late-life wisdom. And elders who score higher in wisdom tend to be better-educated and physically healthier, to forge more positive relations with others, and to score higher on the personality dimension of openness to experience. Wisdom is a strong predictor of psychological well-being.

Factors Related to Cognitive Change

List factors related to cognitive change in late adulthood.

■ Mentally active people are likely to maintain their cognitive abilities into advanced old age. A wide array of chronic conditions are associated with cognitive decline. Retirement can bring about either positive or negative changes. Stimulating leisure activities and complex, challenging work facilitate intellectual functioning.

© VOISIN/PHOTO RESEARCHERS, INC.

■ As elders grow older, their scores on cognitive tasks become increasingly unstable. As death approaches, **terminal decline**—a marked acceleration in deterioration of cognitive functioning—often occurs.

Cognitive Interventions

Can cognitive interventions help older adults sustain their mental abilities?

■ Large-scale interventions—the Adult Development and Enrichment Project (ADEPT) and Advanced Cognitive Training for Independent and Vital Elderly (ACTIVE)—demonstrate that training can enhance cognitive skills in older adults, with large benefits for those who had experienced cognitive declines. When followed up years after the intervention, trained elders remain advantaged over their agemates.

Lifelong Learning

Discuss types of continuing education and benefits of such programs in late life.

■ Better health and earlier retirement permit increasing numbers of older people to continue their education through university courses, community offerings, and programs such as Elderhostel and Osher Lifelong Learning Institutes. Participants acquire new knowledge, new friends, a broader perspective on the world, and an image of themselves as more competent. Unfortunately, fewer continuing-education opportunities are available to low-SES seniors.

Important Terms and Concepts

active lifespan (p. 563)

activities of daily living (ADLs) (p. 564)

Alzheimer's disease (p. 580)

amyloid plaques (p. 581)

assistive technology (p. 571)

associative memory deficit (p. 588)

autoimmune response (p. 569)

average life expectancy (p. 562)

cataracts (p. 566)

cerebrovascular dementia (p. 583)

compression of morbidity (p. 574)

dementia (p. 579)

frailty (p. 577)

functional age (p. 562)

implicit memory (p. 588)

instrumental activities of daily living (IADLs) (p. 564)

life expectancy crossover (p. 563)

macular degeneration (p. 566)

maximum lifespan (p. 564)

neurofibrillary tangles (p. 581)

osteoarthritis (p. 578)

primary aging (p. 577)

prospective memory (p. 589)

remote memory (p. 589)

rheumatoid arthritis (p. 578)

secondary aging (p. 577)

selective optimization with compensation (p. 587)

sleep apnea (p. 570)

terminal decline (p. 593)

wisdom (p. 591)

*T*hree seniors enjoy a laugh while taking a break on a hiking trip. In late adulthood, high-quality relationships promote mental health. And sociable elders, who more often take advantage of opportunities to interact with others, tend to be high in self-esteem and life satisfaction.

Emotional and Social Development in Late Adulthood

With Ruth at his side, Walt spoke to the guests at their sixtieth-anniversary party. "Even when times were hard," he reflected, "the time of life I was in at the moment was always the one I liked the most. When I was a kid, I adored playing baseball. In my twenties, I loved learning the photography business. And of course," Walt continued, glancing affectionately at Ruth, "our wedding was the most memorable day of all."

© TIM PANNELL/CORBIS

He went on: "Then came the Depression, when professional picture taking was a luxury few people could afford. But we found ways to have fun without money—singing in the church choir and acting in community theater. And then Sybil was born. It meant so much to me to be a father—and now a grandfather and a great-grandfather. Looking back at my parents and grandparents and forward at Sybil, Marci, and Marci's son Jamel, I feel a sense of unity with past and future generations."

Walt and Ruth greeted old age with calm acceptance, grateful for the gift of long life and loved ones. Yet not all older adults find such peace of mind. Walt's brother Dick was contentious, complaining about petty issues and major disappointments alike, from "Goldie, why did you serve cheesecake? No one eats cheesecake on birthdays" to "You know why we've got these financial worries? Uncle Louie wouldn't lend me the money to keep the bakery going, so I *had* to retire."

A mix of gains and losses characterizes these twilight years, extending the multidirectionality of development begun early in life. On one hand, old age is a time of pleasure and tranquility, when children are grown, life's work is nearly done, and responsibilities are lightened. On the other hand, it brings concerns about declining physical functions, unwelcome loneliness, and the growing specter of imminent death.

In this chapter, we consider how older adults reconcile these opposing forces. Although some are weary and discontented, most traverse this phase with poise and calm composure. They attach deeper significance to life and reap great benefits from bonds of family and friendship, leisure activities, and community involvement. We will see how personal attributes and life history combine with home, neighborhood, community, and societal conditions to mold emotional and social development in late life.

Erikson's Theory: Ego Integrity versus Despair

The final psychological conflict of Erikson's (1950) theory, **ego integrity versus despair,** involves coming to terms with one's life. Adults who arrive at a sense of integrity feel whole, complete, and satisfied with their achievements. They have adapted to the mix of triumphs and disappointments that are an inevitable part of love relationships, child rearing, work, friendships, and community participation. They realize that the paths they followed, abandoned, and never selected were necessary for fashioning a meaningful life course.

The capacity to view one's life in the larger context of all humanity—as the chance combination of one person and one segment in history—contributes to the serenity and contentment that accompany integrity. "These last few decades have been the happiest," Walt murmured, clasping Ruth's hand—only weeks before the heart attack that would end his life. At peace with himself, his wife, and his children, Walt had accepted his life course as something that had to be the way it was. In a study of people ranging from 17 to 82, increased age was associated with greater psychosocial maturity, measured in terms of striving for generativity and ego integrity in everyday behavior. Generativity and ego integrity, in turn, largely accounted for the link between age and psychological well-being (Sheldon & Kasser, 2001). As Erikson's theory indicates, the psychosocial maturity of these later years seems to bring increased happiness.

Scanning the newspaper, Walt pondered, "I keep reading these percentages: One out of five people will get heart disease, one out of three will get cancer. But the truth is, one out of one will die. We are all mortal and must accept this fate." The year before, Walt had given his granddaughter, Marci, his collection of prized photos, which had absorbed him for over half a century. With the realization that the integrity of one's own life is part of an extended chain of human existence, death loses its sting (Vaillant, 1994, 2002).

The negative outcome of this stage, despair, occurs when elders feel they have made many wrong decisions, yet time is too short to find an alternate route to integrity. Without another chance, the despairing person finds it hard to accept that death is near and is overwhelmed with bitterness, defeat, and hopelessness. According to Erikson, these attitudes are often expressed as anger and contempt for others, which disguise contempt for oneself. Dick's argumentative, faultfinding behavior, tendency to blame others for his personal failures, and regretful view of his own life reflect this deep sense of despair.

© SARAH PUTNAM/INDEX STOCK

Elders who arrive at a sense of integrity feel whole, complete, and satisfied with their achievements. Erik Erikson and his wife Joan exemplified the ideal of Erikson's final stage. They aged gracefully and could often be seen walking hand in hand, deeply in love.

Other Theories of Psychosocial Development in Late Adulthood

As with Erikson's stages of early and middle adulthood, other theorists have clarified and refined his vision of late adulthood, specifying the tasks and thought processes that contribute to a sense of ego integrity. All agree that successful development in the later years involves greater integration and deepening of the personality.

Peck's Tasks of Ego Integrity and Joan Erikson's Gerotranscendence

According to Robert Peck (1968), Erikson's conflict of ego integrity versus despair comprises three distinct tasks:

● *Ego differentiation versus work-role preoccupation.* After retirement, aging people who have invested heavily in their careers must find other ways of affirming their self-worth—through family, friendship, and community roles that are just as satisfying as work life.

🍂 *Body transcendence versus body preoccupation.* Older adults must *transcend* physical limitations—declines in appearance, physical capacities, and resistance to disease—by emphasizing the compensating rewards of cognitive, emotional, and social powers.

🍂 *Ego transcendence versus ego preoccupation.* As spouse, siblings, friends, and peers die, the elderly must find a way to face the reality of death constructively, through investing in a longer future than their own lifespan. Although the generative years of early and middle adulthood prepare people for a satisfying old age, attaining ego integrity requires a continuing effort to make life more secure, meaningful, and gratifying for those who will go on after one dies.

In Peck's theory, ego integrity requires that older adults move beyond their life's work, their bodies, and their separate identities. Recent evidence suggests that *body transcendence* (focusing on psychological strengths) and *ego transcendence* (orienting toward a larger, more distant future) increase in very old age. In a study of elderly women, those in their eighties and nineties stated with greater certainty than those in their sixties that they "accept the changes brought about by aging," "have moved beyond fear of death," "have a clearer sense of the meaning of life," and "have found new, positive spiritual gifts to explore" (Brown & Lowis, 2003).

Erikson's widow Joan Erikson believes that these attainments actually represent further development beyond ego integrity (which focuses on satisfaction with one's past life) to an additional psychosocial stage that she calls **gerotranscendence**—a cosmic and transcendent perspective directed forward and outward, beyond the self. Drawing on her own experience of aging, her observations of her husband's final years, and the work of others on the positive potential of the years shortly before death, Joan Erikson speculated that success in attaining gerotranscendence is apparent in heightened inner calm and contentment and additional time spent in quiet reflection (Erikson, 1998; Tornstam, 1997, 2000).

Although interviews with people in their ninth and tenth decades reveal that many (but not all) experience this peaceful, contemplative state, more research is needed to confirm the existence of a distinct, transcendent late-life stage. Besides focusing more intently on life's meaning, many of the very old continue to report investments in the real world—visiting friends, keeping up with current events, striving to be a good neighbor, and engaging in pleasurable leisure pursuits (Adams, 2004).

Labouvie-Vief's Emotional Expertise

In Chapter 13, we discussed Gisella Labouvie-Vief's research on development of adults' reasoning about emotion (see page 451). Recall that cognitive-affective complexity (awareness and coordination of positive and negative feelings into an organized self-description) increases from adolescence through middle adulthood, then declines as basic information-processing skills diminish in late adulthood.

But elders display a compensating emotional strength: They improve in **affect optimization,** the ability to maximize positive emotion and dampen negative emotion, which contributes to their remarkable resilience (Labouvie-Vief, 2003; Labouvie-Vief & Medler, 2002). Despite physical declines, increased health problems, a restricted future, and death of loved ones, most older adults sustain a sense of optimism and good psychological well-being (Diehl, Coyle, & Labouvie-Vief, 1996; Mroczek & Kolarz, 1998). And about 30 to 40 percent of elders not only are high in affect optimization but also retain considerable capacity for cognitive-emotional complexity—a combination related to especially effective emotional self-regulation.

Furthermore, when asked to relate personal experiences in which they were happy, angry, fearful, or sad and to indicate how they knew they felt that emotion, many middle-aged and elderly individuals gave more vivid accounts than those of younger people—evidence that they were more in touch with their feelings. Consider this example:

> You have sunshine in your heart. During the wedding the candles were glowing. And that's just how I felt. I was glowing too. It was kind of dull outside. But that isn't how I felt. Everybody in the church felt like they were glowing. It was that kind of feeling. (Labouvie-Vief, DeVoe, & Bulka, 1989, p. 429)

Older adults' emotional perceptiveness helps them separate interpretations from objective aspects of situations. Consequently, their coping strategies often include making sure they fully understand their own feelings before deciding on a course of action. And they readily use emotion-centered coping strategies (controlling distress internally) in negatively charged situations (Blanchard-Fields, 1997; Labouvie-Vief et al., 1995). In sum, a significant late-life psychosocial attainment is becoming expert at processing emotional information and regulating negative affect (Labouvie-Vief & Diehl, 1999; Lawton, 2001b).

Reminiscence and Life Review

We often think of the elderly as engaged in **reminiscence**—telling stories about people and events from their past and reporting associated thoughts and feelings. Indeed, the widespread image of a reminiscing elder ranks among negative stereotypes of aging. In this common view, older people live in the past to escape the realities of a shortened future and the nearness of death. Although we do not yet fully understand why older people reminisce more often than younger people do, current theory and research indicate that reflecting on the past can be positive and adaptive.

In his comments on major events in his life at the beginning of this chapter, Walt was engaging in a special form of reminiscence, **life review,** in which the person calls up, reflects on, and reconsiders past experiences, contemplating their meaning with the goal of achieving greater self-understanding. According to Robert Butler (1968), most older adults engage in life review as part of attaining ego integrity, preventing despair,

A Lifespan Vista

World War II Refugee and Evacuee Children Look Back from the Vantage Point of Old Age

How do elders look back on a traumatic period that occurred early in their lives? To find out, Glen Palmer (1999) interviewed older adults who had come to Australia just before or during World War II as Jewish refugees from Austria, Germany, and Poland or as evacuees from Great Britain. All had been younger than age 16 when their parents put them on boats, giving them up in anguish to protect them. Most parents of the Austrian, Polish, and German children were murdered by the Nazis. After kissing them good-bye, these children never saw their parents again. In contrast, the British evacuees returned to their homeland and families at the end of the war.

Looking back, these elders were largely supportive of their parents' decision to send them away. For the refugees, it meant that their lives had been spared (see Chapter 10, page 352). Beyond this, recollections and assessments of the life-long impact of their experiences varied. Among factors that made a difference were quality of care, age at separation, and temperament.

Care situations included relatives, foster homes, group homes, and boarding schools. For children placed with families, being loved and wanted led to new attachments and pleasant memories, often at the expense of former bonds. As one elder noted, "If you send a child away in the formative years, you take the risk of losing the affection of that child." When relatives and foster families were unkind or outright rejecting, painful memories of an "emotional limbo" emerged. Without new attachments, these children clung to fading images of their families, idealized their parents, and longed to return to them. Separation and inadequate care had a more profound, lasting impact on temperamentally withdrawn, anxious

individuals than on outgoing individuals, who were better able to develop supportive social ties beyond the family.

Compared with interviewees who were children at the time of separation, those who were adolescents were less affected by the absence of close bonds with adults. "I knew in my mind that I had plenty of family support, even though they weren't around," one Polish refugee remarked. On the threshold of adulthood, these young people had little desire for substitute parents. Instead, they fared best in group homes and boarding schools that provided appropriate oversight, balancing security with autonomy. Often their warmest memories were of bonds established with one another. In contrast, when children were placed in group homes and denied family attachments, their sadness was still apparent in old age: "There was a desolation because there was no love. . . . You

need to be able to say to a child, 'You're my special one.' "

By the end of the war, the majority of interviewees had become young adults. The British evacuees were reunited with their families, but rarely with "happily ever after" endings. Children and parents had changed during the intervening years. As one interviewee put it, "It was easier to go than to come back." Still, reunion was vital; its absence usually brings a lifetime of unresolved grief.

For most Polish and German refugees, loss of immediate family was total. More than a half-century later, their searching and sorrow persisted. One commented, "The Holocaust pursues us daily. It is like having a flea in your head." This suggests that rather than healing with the passage of time, the pain of childhood loss and trauma can intensify in later life. Reunions with other refugees helped

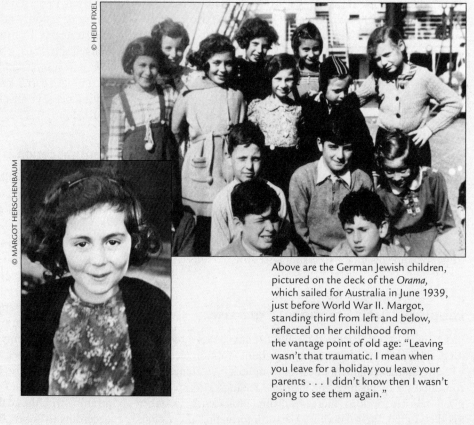

© HEIDI FIXEL

© MARGOT HERSCHENBAUM

Above are the German Jewish children, pictured on the deck of the *Orama*, which sailed for Australia in June 1939, just before World War II. Margot, standing third from left and below, reflected on her childhood from the vantage point of old age: "Leaving wasn't that traumatic. I mean when you leave for a holiday you leave your parents . . . I didn't know then I wasn't going to see them again."

soothe persisting wounds as elders shared experiences with those best able to understand their continued suffering.

Although many refugees and evacuees remained deeply affected by their childhood experiences, few were maladjusted. To the contrary, most found turning points through families, careers, or other interests and led productive, fulfilling lives. When late-life adversities arose, some drew on inner strengths developed during early years of separation. As one Holocaust survivor commented after her husband died, "[W]hen you've been through what I've been through, you can survive anything."

Nevertheless, these victims of genocide—and other similarly traumatized

individuals around the world—probably cannot make a complete recovery. None of the refugees returned to live in Europe, although some visited their countries of birth. Rarely were these journeys comfortable. Almost always, they brought heartaches to the surface—yet another reminder that ethnic and political violence has pervasive effects throughout the lifespan.

Anne was a British evacuee who was reunited with her parents as a young adult at the end of the war. She recalled, "The war years were not always easy or happy, but it was far worse to return to a family I had missed for so long and to find we had grown so far apart."

and accepting the end of life. Butler's ideas have been so influential that many therapists encourage life-review reminiscence among the elderly. Older adults who participate in counselor-led life review report increased self-esteem, greater sense of purpose in life, improved life satisfaction, and reduced depression (Cook, 1998; Lappe, 1987; Watt & Cappeliez, 2000; Westerhof, Bohlmeijer, & Valenkamp, 2004). Life-review interventions can also help bereaved adults find a place for lost loved ones in their emotional lives, reinvest energy in other relationships, and move on with life (Worden, 2002).

Although life review often prompts self-awareness and self-respect, many elders do not spend much time evaluating their pasts. When asked to do so, 10 to 30 percent of older adults in several studies identified one of the decades of late adulthood as the best time of life. Early and middle adulthood received especially high marks, whereas childhood and adolescence ranked as less satisfying (Field, 1997; Mehlson, Platz, & Fromholt, 2003). These findings contradict the widespread belief that older adults inevitably wish to be young again. As the Lifespan Vista box above illustrates, recollections of distant events are colored by many factors, including personality, the timing and nature of the events, and subsequent life experiences.

Besides life review, reminiscence serves other purposes. When it is *self-focused*, engaged in to reduce boredom and revive bitter events, it is linked to adjustment problems. Despairing elders tend to ruminate often, sustaining their negative emotion by dwelling on painful past experiences (Cully, LaVoie, & Gfeller, 2001). In contrast, extraverted elders more often engage in *other-focused* reminiscence directed at social goals, such as solidifying family and friendship ties and reliving relationships with lost loved ones. And at times, older adults—

especially those who score high in openness to experience—engage in *knowledge-based* reminiscence, drawing on their past for effective problem-solving strategies and for teaching younger people. These socially engaged, mentally stimulating forms of reminiscence help make life rich and rewarding (Cappeliez & O'Rourke, 2002). Perhaps because of their strong storytelling traditions, African-American and Chinese immigrant elders are more likely than their Caucasian counterparts to use reminiscence to teach others about the past (Merriam, 1993; Webster, 2002).

Many older adults engage in reminiscence and life review as part of attaining ego integrity. Often, they share their memories to teach younger people about family and cultural history—an activity that makes life richer and more rewarding.

Finally, reminiscence—for young and old alike—often occurs during times of life transition (Parker, 1995). The older adult who has recently retired, been widowed, or moved to a new residence may turn to the past to sustain a sense of personal continuity. Indeed, elders who feel their current lives are adrift reminisce especially often (Fry, 1995). As long as they do not get stuck in mulling over unresolved difficulties, reminiscence probably helps them recapture a sense of meaning.

Stability and Change in Self-Concept and Personality

Longitudinal research reveals continuing stability of the "big five" personality traits from mid- to late life (see Chapter 16, page 540). Yet the ingredients of ego integrity—wholeness, contentment, and image of the self as part of a larger world order—are reflected in several significant late-life changes in both self-concept and personality.

Secure and Multifaceted Self-Concept

Older adults have accumulated a lifetime of self-knowledge, leading to more secure and complex conceptions of themselves than at earlier ages (Labouvie-Vief & Diehl, 1999). Ruth, for example, knew with certainty that she was good at counseling others, growing a flower garden, giving dinner parties, budgeting money, and figuring out who could be trusted and who couldn't. At the same time, she commented wistfully that she couldn't get around the city as easily as before.

The firmness and multifaceted nature of Ruth's self-concept enabled her to compensate for lack of skill in domains she had never tried, had not mastered, or could no longer perform as well as before. Consequently, it allowed for self-acceptance—a key feature of integrity. In a study of old (70 to 84 years) and very old (85 to 103 years) German elders asked to respond to the question "Who am I?," participants mentioned a broad spectrum of life domains, including hobbies, interests, social participation, family, health, and personality traits. Adults in both age groups expressed more positive than negative self-evaluations, although a slight increase in negative comments occurred in the older group. Positive, multifaceted self-definitions predicted psychological well-being (Freund & Smith, 1999).

As the future shortens, most elders, into their eighties and nineties, continue to mention—and actively pursue—hoped-for selves in the areas of good health, personal characteristics, relationships, and social responsibility (Frazier, 2002; Markus & Herzog, 1992). At the same time, possible selves reorganize well into old age. When the German 70- to 103-year-olds just mentioned were followed longitudinally for four years, the majority deleted some possible selves and replaced them with new ones—often related to personal characteristics, social relationships, and health. Elders often characterized hoped-for selves in terms of "improving," "achieving," or "attaining." And

those who sustained desires to strive toward personal goals were more likely to gain in life satisfaction (Smith & Freund, 2002). Clearly, late adulthood is not a time of withdrawal from future planning!

Finally, despite physical and cognitive declines and revisions in personal goals, the majority of older adults retain a coherent sense of self (Troll & Skaff, 1997). They regard themselves as very much the same person they have always been.

Resilience: Agreeableness, Sociability, and Acceptance of Change

During late adulthood, shifts occur in three personality characteristics that, once again, defy stereotypes of the elderly. Old age is not a time in which the personality inevitably becomes rigid and morale declines. Rather, a flexible, optimistic approach to life, which fosters resilience in the face of adversity, is common.

Rating open-ended interviews with elders in their sixties, and again when they reached their eighties and nineties, researchers found that scores on adjectives that make up *agreeableness*—generous, acquiescent, and good-natured—were higher on the second occasion than the first for over one-third of the sample. Similarly, when elders take personality tests, agreeableness rises—especially among men, who initially score lower than women (Weiss et al., 2005). Agreeableness seems to characterize people who have come to terms with life despite its imperfections.

However, participants in the open-ended interview study showed a slight dip in *sociability* as they aged (Field & Millsap, 1991). Perhaps this reflects a narrowing of social contacts as people become more selective about relationships and as family members and friends die—trends we will take up in a later section. Still, older adults who were extraverted throughout their lives tend to remain so—a personality trait associated with greater life satisfaction (Mroczek & Spiro, 2005).

A third, related development is greater *acceptance of change*—an attribute the elderly frequently mention as important to psychological well-being (Ryff, 1989). When asked about dissatisfactions in their lives, many older adults respond that they are not unhappy about anything! Acceptance of change is also evident in most elders' effective coping with the loss of loved ones, including death of a spouse, which they describe as the most stressful event they ever experienced (Lund, Caserta, & Dimond, 1993) The capacity to accept life's twists and turns, many of which are beyond one's control, is vital for positive functioning in late adulthood. Most older adults are resilient, bounding back in the face of adversity—especially if they tended to do so earlier in their lives.

Spirituality and Religiosity

How do older adults manage to accept declines and losses yet still feel whole and complete and anticipate death with calm composure? One possibility, consistent with Peck's and Erikson's emphasis on a transcendent perspective among the elderly, is the development of a more mature sense of spirituality. Spirituality is not the same as religion: An inspirational sense of life's meaning can be found in art, nature, and social relationships. But for many people, religion provides beliefs, symbols, and rituals that guide this quest for meaning.

Older adults attach great value to religious beliefs and behaviors. According to a national survey, 76 percent of Americans age 65 and older say that religion is very important in their lives, and 16 percent describe it as fairly important. Over half attend religious services or other events weekly, nearly two-thirds watch religious TV programs, and about one-fourth pray at least three times a day (Princeton Religion Research Center, 1999). Similarly, 72 percent of Canadian elders consider themselves religious, although they are less involved in organized religion than their U.S. counterparts. But about 30 percent attend religious services weekly, an additional 15 percent monthly (Jones, 2003).

Although health and transportation difficulties reduce organized religious participation in advanced old age, North American elders generally become more religious or spiritual as they age (Argue, Johnson, & White, 1999; Wink & Dillon, 2002). But this trend is far from universal. In a British 20-year longitudinal study, the majority of elders showed stability in religiosity over time, with nearly half indicating that religion was very important to them. One-fourth, however, said they had become less religious, with some citing disappointment at the support they had received from their religious institution during stressful times (such as bereavement) as the reason (Coleman, Ivani-Chalian, & Robinson, 2004). Wide cultural variation also exists that has yet to be explained. For example, the late-life rise in religiosity is even stronger in Japan than in

North America, but in the Netherlands it is minimal (Sasaki & Suzuki, 1987).

Despite these differences, spirituality and faith may advance to a higher level in late life—away from prescribed beliefs toward a more reflective approach that emphasizes links to others and is at ease with mystery and uncertainty. In his theory of the development of faith, James Fowler (1981) posits five stages (summarized in Table 18.1), which have been confirmed in several studies. Notice how adults who reach Stage 4 become aware of their own belief system as one of many possible worldviews, contemplate the deeper significance of religious symbols and rituals, and open themselves to other religious perspectives as sources of inspiration (McFadden, 1996). For example, as a complement to his Catholicism, Walt became intensely interested in Buddhism, especially its focus on attaining perfect peace and happiness by mastering thoughts and feelings, never harming others, and resisting attachment to worldly objects.

Involvement in both organized and informal religious activities is especially high among low-SES ethnic minority elders, including African-American, Hispanic, Native-American, and Canadian-Aboriginal groups. In African-American communities, churches not only provide contexts for deriving meaning from life but also are centers for education, health, social welfare, and political activities aimed at improving life conditions. African-American elders look to religion as a powerful resource for social support beyond the family and for the inner strength to withstand daily stresses and physical impairments (Armstrong & Crowther, 2002; Husaini, Blasi, & Miller, 1999). Compared with their Caucasian agemates, more African-American older adults report collaborating with God

Table 18.1		Fowler's Stages of Faith Development
Stage of Faith	**Period of Development**	**Description**
1. Intuitive-projective	3–7 years	Children's fantasy and imitation lead them to be powerfully influenced by stories, moods, and behaviors demonstrating the faith of adults. They become aware of right and wrong actions.
2. Mythic-literal	7–11 years	Children begin to internalize the stories, beliefs, and observances of their religious community, which they take literally. For example, they often hold concrete images of God living on top of the world and watching over everybody.
3. Synthetic-conventional	Adolescence	Adolescents have a coherent set of deeply felt beliefs and values, which provides a basis for identity. They have not yet examined this ideology systematically.
4. Individuative-reflective	Adulthood	Adults who reach this stage critically reflect on their beliefs and values, recognizing that their worldview is only one of many possible worldviews. They actively shape a personal ideology, forming and re-forming it over time. About religious rituals and symbols, they ask, "What does this really mean?"
5. Conjunctive	Late Adulthood	The few people who attain this stage form an enlarged vision of an all-inclusive human community. They act to bring it about by standing up against persecution and injustice and by promoting a common good that serves the needs of diverse groups. Great religious leaders, such as Mahatma Gandhi and Martin Luther King, Jr., illustrate conjunctive faith.

Source: Fowler, 1981.

These senior choir members are actively involved in their church community. For African-American elders, in addition to providing a context for deriving meaning from life, the church often serves as a center for education, health, political activism, and social support.

to overcome life problems (Krause, 2005). Asked about her philosophy of life, an African-American 65-year-old revealed how faith enabled her to do more than survive:

> We've had lots of misfortunes . . . but we always knew that it could be worse. . . . I know somedays I get up I'd be stiff and my knees aching and my back is aching and my head is hurting and I can get up and go in the bathroom. I say, "Thank you Lord because I have the activities of my limbs. . . ." And then we get a meal on the table and we have . . . at least a portion of health and strength. . . . [I] thank the Lord for things being as well as they are. (Nye, 1993, p. 109)

Sex differences in religious involvement and spirituality are also evident throughout adulthood. Women are more likely than men to belong to a religious congregation, to engage in religious activities, and to report a personal quest for connectedness with a higher power (Levin, Taylor, & Chatters, 1994; Wink & Dillon, 2002). Women's higher rates of poverty, widowhood, and participation in caregiving, including caring for chronically ill family members, expose them to higher levels of stress and anxiety. As with ethnic minorities, they turn to religion for social support and for a larger vision of community that places life's challenges in perspective.

Benefits of religious involvement are as diverse as increased physical and psychological well-being, more time spent exercising, and greater sense of closeness to family and friends (Fry, 2001; Idler & Kasl, 1997; Levin & Chatters, 1998).

In longitudinal research, both organized and informal religious participation predicted longer survival, after family background, health, social, and psychological factors known to affect mortality were controlled (Helm et al., 2000; Strawbridge et al., 2001).

But aspects of religious connection that make a difference in elders' lives are not always clear. In two investigations of Caucasian older adults, religious *activity*—not religiosity or membership in a congregation—was associated with favorable adjustment following loss of a spouse (Lund, Caserta, & Dimond, 1993). The researchers found that increased social engagement brought about by religious participation, rather than the specifically religious nature of the activity, was the influential factor. Other evidence, however, indicates that belief in God's powers contributes substantially to the self-esteem, optimism, and life-satisfaction of low-SES, ethnic minority elders (Krause, 2005; Schieman, Pudrovska, & Milkie, 2005). Older adults who have experienced social and economic disadvantages often turn to their personal relationship with God for help in coping with hardships.

Individual Differences in Psychological Well-Being

As we have seen in this and the previous chapter, most adults adapt well to old age. Yet a few feel dependent, incompetent, and worthless. Identifying personal and environmental influences on late-life psychological well-being is vital for designing interventions that foster positive adjustment.

Control versus Dependency

As Ruth's eyesight, hearing, and mobility declined in her eighties, Sybil visited daily to help with self-care and household tasks. During the hours mother and daughter were together, Sybil interacted most often with Ruth when she asked for help with activities of daily living. When Ruth handled tasks on her own, Sybil usually withdrew.

Observations of people interacting with older adults in both private homes and institutions reveal two highly predictable, complementary behavior patterns. In the first, called the **dependency–support script,** dependent behaviors are attended to immediately. In the second, the **independence–ignore script,** independent behaviors are mostly ignored. Notice how these sequences reinforce dependent behavior at the expense of independent behavior, regardless of the older person's competencies. Even a self-reliant elder like Ruth did not always resist Sybil's unnecessary help, because it brought about social contact (Baltes, 1995, 1996).

Among elders who experience no difficulty with daily activities, opportunities to interact with others are related to high satisfaction with everyday life. In contrast, among elders who have trouble performing daily activities, social contact is

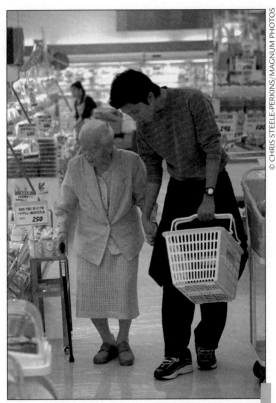

Will this mother become too dependent on her son if she lets him help with her grocery shopping? Not necessarily. If she assumes personal control over her dependency, she can conserve her strength and invest it in highly valued activities.

linked to a less positive everyday existence (Lang & Baltes, 1997). This suggests that social interaction while assisting elders with physical care, household chores, and errands is often not meaningful and rewarding but, rather, demeaning and unpleasant. Consider these typical reactions of care recipients to a spouse's help with daily activities: "felt dependent," "felt indebted," "felt like a weak, incapable person" (Newsom, 1999).

Longitudinal research shows that negative reactions to caregiving can result in persisting depression (Newsom & Schultz, 1998). But whether assistance from others undermines well-being depends on many factors, including the quality of help, the caregiver–elder relationship, and the social and cultural context in which helping occurs. Why do family members and other caregivers often respond in ways that promote excessive dependency in old age? A stereotype of the elderly as passive and incompetent appears to be responsible. Older adults seem well aware of others' low expectations for them. They frequently attribute their dependency to overresponsive social partners (Wahl, 1991).

In Western societies, which highly value independence, many elders fear becoming dependent on others (Frazier, 2002). They may say that when they can no longer care for themselves, it is time to die. Does this mean we should encourage elders to be as independent as possible? According to Mary

Baltes (1996), this alternative is as counterproductive as promoting passivity and incompetence. Aging brings diminished energy at a time when people confront many challenging developmental tasks. Dependency can be adaptive if it permits older people to conserve their strength by investing it in highly valued activities, using a set of strategies we considered in Chapter 17: *selective optimization with compensation.*

Health

As noted in Chapter 16, health is a powerful predictor of psychological well-being in late adulthood. Physical declines and chronic disease can lead to a sense of loss of personal control—a major factor in adult mental health. Furthermore, physical illness resulting in disability is among the strongest risk factors for late-life depression (Geerlings et al., 2001). Although fewer older than young and middle-aged adults are depressed (see Chapter 17), profound feelings of hopelessness rise with age as physical disability and consequent social isolation increase (Roberts et al., 1997).

The relationship between physical and mental health problems can become a vicious cycle, each intensifying the other. At times, the rapid decline of a sick elder is the result of despondency and "giving up" (Penninx et al., 2000). This downward spiral can be hastened by a move to a nursing home, requiring the older person to adjust to distance from family and friends and to a new self-definition as "a person who can survive only in an institution." In the month after admission, many residents deteriorate rapidly and become severely depressed. The stress of illness together with institutionalization is associated with heightened health problems and mortality (Tobin, 1989).

Depression in old age is often lethal. People age 65 and older have the highest suicide rate of all age groups (see the Social Issues box on pages 608–609). What factors enable elders like Ruth to surmount the physical impairment–depression relationship, remaining optimistic and content? Personal characteristics discussed in earlier chapters—effective coping and a sense of self-efficacy—are vitally important. But for frail elders to display these attributes, families and caregivers must grant them autonomy by avoiding the dependency–support script. When older adults remain in charge of personally important areas of their lives, they retain essential aspects of their identity in the face of change, view their past and future more favorably, and are emotionally more upbeat (Brandtstädter & Rothermund, 1994; Kunzmann, Little, & Smith, 2002).

Negative Life Changes

Ruth lost Walt to a heart attack, cared for Ida as her Alzheimer's symptoms worsened, and faced health problems of her own—all within a span of a few years. Elders are at risk for a variety of negative life changes—death of loved ones, illness and physical disabilities, declining income, and greater dependency. Negative life changes are difficult for everyone but may actually

Social Issues

Elder Suicide

When 65-year-old Abe's wife died, he withdrew from life. Living far from his two daughters, he spent his nonworking days alone, watching television and reading mystery novels. As grandchildren were born, Abe visited his daughters' homes from time to time, carrying his despondent behavior with him. "Look at my new pajamas, Grandpa!" Abe's 6-year-old grandson Tony exclaimed on one occasion, but Abe did not respond.

After arthritis made walking difficult, Abe retired. With more empty days, his depression deepened. Gradually, he developed painful digestive difficulties, but he refused to go to the doctor. "Don't need to," he said abruptly when one of his daughters begged him to get medical attention. Answering her invitation to Tony's tenth birthday party, Abe wrote, "Maybe—if I'm still around next month. By the way, when I go, I want my body cremated." Two weeks later, Abe died from an intestinal blockage. His body was found in the living room chair where he habitually spent his days. Although it may seem surprising, Abe's self-destructive acts are a form of suicide.

Factors Related to Elder Suicide. Recall from Chapter 12 that suicide increases over the lifespan. It continues to climb during the elder years, reaching its highest rate among people age 75 and older. Although the incidence of suicide varies among nations, older adults are at increased risk around the world (World Health Organization, 2002).

Recall from Chapter 12 that the suicide rate is much higher among adolescent males than females. This sex difference persists through late adulthood. In the United States and Canada, five times as many elderly men as women take their own lives (Heisel, 2006; U.S. Census Bureau, 2006b). Compared with the white majority, most North American ethnic minority elders have low suicide rates.

What explains these trends? Despite the lifelong pattern of higher rates of depression and more suicide attempts among females, elderly women's closer ties to family and friends, greater willingness to seek social support, and religiosity prevent many from taking their own lives. High levels of social support through extended families and church affiliations may also prevent suicide among ethnic minorities. And within certain groups, such as Alaskan Natives, deep respect for and reliance on older adults to teach cultural traditions foster self-esteem and social integration. This reduces elder suicide, making it nonexistent after age 80 (Kettl, 1998).

As in earlier years, the method favored by elder North American males (firearms) offers less chance of revival than that favored by elder females (poisoning or drug overdose). Nevertheless, failed suicides are much rarer in old age than in adolescence. The ratio of attempts to completions for the young is as high as 300 to 1; for the elderly, it is 4 to 1 or lower (Conwell, Duberstein, & Caine, 2002). When elders decide to die, they seem especially determined to succeed.

Underreporting of suicides probably occurs at all ages, but it is more common in old age. Medical examiners are less likely to pursue suicide as a cause of death when a person is old. And many elders, like Abe, engage in indirect self-destructive acts rarely classified as suicide—deciding not to go to a doctor when ill or refusing to eat or take prescribed medications. Among institutionalized elders, these efforts to hasten death are widespread (Kennedy & Tanenbaum, 2000). Consequently, elder suicide is an even larger problem than official statistics indicate.

---

evoke less stress and depression in older than in younger adults (Gatz, Kasl-Godley, & Karel, 1996). Many elders have learned to cope with hard times and to accept loss as part of human existence.

Still, when negative changes pile up, they test the coping skills of older adults (Kraaij, Arensman, & Spinhoven, 2002). In very old age, such changes are greater for women than for men. Women over age 75 are far less likely to be married, more often have lower incomes, and suffer from more illnesses—especially ones that restrict mobility. Furthermore, elderly women more often say that others depend on them for emotional support: Their social relations, even in very old age, are more often a source of stress. And because of failing health, older women may not be able to meet others' needs for caregiving, with negative consequences for their self-esteem. Not surprisingly, women of very advanced age report a lower sense of psychological well-being than men (Pinquart & Sörensen, 2001).

Social Support and Social Interaction

In late adulthood, social support continues to reduce stress, thereby promoting physical health and psychological well-being. Availability of social support increases the odds of living longer (Liang et al., 1999; Seeman et al., 1993). And it may help explain the relationship of religious participation to survival, noted earlier. Usually, elders receive informal assistance from family members—first from their spouse or, if none exists, from children and then from siblings. If these individuals are not available, other relatives and friends may step in.

Nevertheless, many older adults place such high value on independence that they do not want a great deal of support from people close to them unless they can reciprocate. When assistance is excessive or cannot be returned, it often results in psychological distress (Liang, Krause, & Bennett, 2001). Perhaps for this reason, adult children express a deeper sense of obligation toward their aging parents than their parents expect

Two types of events prompt suicide in late life. Losses—retirement from a highly valued occupation, widowhood, or social isolation—place elders who have difficulty coping with change at risk for persistent depression. Risks of another type arise when chronic and terminal illnesses severely reduce physical functioning or cause intense pain (Conwell, 2004). As comfort and quality of life diminish, feelings of hopelessness and helplessness deepen. Very old people, especially men, are particularly likely to take their own lives under these conditions. The chances are even greater when a sick elder is socially isolated—living alone or in a nursing home with high staff turnover and minimal caregiver support.

Prevention and Treatment. Warning signs of suicide in late adulthood, like those at earlier ages, include efforts to put personal affairs in order, statements about dying, despondency, and sleep and appetite changes. But family members, friends, and caregivers must also watch for indirect self-destructive acts that are unique to old age, such as refusing food or medical treatment. Too often, people in close touch with the elderly incorrectly assume that these symptoms are a "natural" consequence of

aging. More than 70 percent of older suicide victims visited their doctors within a month of taking their lives, and 30 percent did so the same week (Pearson & Brown, 2000). Yet their suicidal risk was not recognized.

When suicidal elders are depressed, the most effective treatment combines antidepressant medication with therapy, including help in coping with role transitions, such as retirement, widowhood, and dependency brought about by illness. Distorted ways of thinking ("I'm old, and nothing can be done about my problems") must be countered and revised. Meeting with the family to find ways to reduce loneliness and desperation is also helpful.

Although youth suicide has risen (see Chapter 12, page 420), elder suicide has declined during the past 50 years, as a result of increased economic security among older adults, improved medical care and social services, and more favorable cultural attitudes toward retirement. Communities are beginning to recognize the importance of additional preventive steps, such as telephone hot lines with trained volunteers who provide emotional support and agencies that arrange for regular home visitors or "buddy system" phone calls. In institutions, providing residents with privacy,

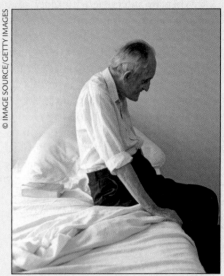

Warning signs of suicide in late adulthood overlap with those at earlier ages. They include efforts to put personal affairs in order, statements about dying, despondency, and sleep and appetite changes.

autonomy, and space helps prevent self-destructive behavior (Conwell & Duberstein, 2001).

Finally, elder suicide raises a controversial ethical issue: Do people with incurable illnesses have the right to take their own lives? We will take up this topic in Chapter 19.

---

from them (see Chapter 16, page 550). Formal support—a paid home helper or agency-provided services—as a complement to informal assistance not only helps relieve caregiving burden but also spares elders from feeling overly dependent in their close relationships (Krause, 1990).

Ethnic minority elders do not readily accept formal assistance. But they are more willing to do so when home helpers are connected to a familiar neighborhood organization, especially the church. Although African-American seniors say they rely more on their families than on the church for assistance, those with support and meaningful roles in both contexts score highest in mental health (Coke, 1992; Walls & Zarit, 1991). Support from religious congregants has psychological benefits for elders of all backgrounds, perhaps because recipients feel that it is motivated by genuine care and concern, not just obligation. Also, the warm atmosphere of religious organizations fosters a sense of social acceptance and belonging (Krause, 2001).

An extraverted personality is also linked to high morale in old age (Adkins, Martin, & Poon, 1996). Sociable elders are more likely to take advantage of opportunities to interact with others, thereby reducing loneliness and depression and fostering self-esteem and life satisfaction. But as we will see in the next section, supportive communication in old age has little to do with quantity of contact. Instead, high-quality relationships, involving expressions of kindness, encouragement, and respect, have the greatest impact on mental health in late life.

Overall, for social support to foster well-being, elders need to assume personal control of it. This means consciously giving up primary control in some areas to remain in control of other, highly valued pursuits. For example, although she could handle dressing, financial matters, shopping, and food preparation for herself, Ruth allowed her daughter Sybil to assist with these activities, leaving Ruth with more stamina for pleasurable reading. To optimize her energies, Ruth selected certain domains in which to become dependent. This permitted her to compensate for poor eyesight by taking extra time to use a magnifying glass while reading or to listen to a book on tape. In this way, social support granted Ruth autonomy—a means for managing her own aging.

When we intervene with older adults, we must ask ourselves, What kind of assistance are we providing? Help that is not wanted or needed or that exaggerates weaknesses can undermine mental health, and—if existing skills fall into disuse—can also accelerate physical disability. In contrast, help that frees up energy for endeavors that are personally satisfying and that lead to growth enhances elders' quality of life. These findings clarify why *perceived social support* (elders' sense of being able to count on family or friends in times of need) is associated with a positive outlook in older adults with disabilities, whereas sheer *amount* of help family and friends provide has little impact (Taylor, Lynch, & Scott, 2004).

Ask Yourself

Review

Many elders adapt effectively to negative life changes. List personal and environmental factors that facilitate this generally positive outcome.

Apply

At age 80, Miriam took a long time to get dressed. Joan, her home helper, suggested, "Wait until I arrive before dressing. Then I can help you, and it won't take so long." What impact is Joan's approach likely to have on Miriam's personality? What alternative approach would you recommend?

Connect

Fowler's stages of faith, summarized in Table 18.1 on page 605, were inspired by Kohlberg's theory of moral development (see Chapter 12, pages 406–408). Cite similarities between Kohlberg's and Fowler's stages.

www.ablongman.com/berk

A Changing Social World

Walt and Ruth's outgoing personalities led many family members and friends to seek them out, and they often reciprocated. In contrast, Dick's stubborn nature meant that he and Goldie, for many years, had had a far more restricted network of social ties.

As noted earlier, extraverts (like Walt and Ruth) continue to interact with a wider range of people than do introverts and people (like Dick) with poor social skills. Nevertheless, both cross-sectional and longitudinal research reveals that size of social networks and, therefore, amount of social interaction decline for virtually everyone (Antonucci, Akiyama, & Takahashi, 2004; Lang, Staudinger, & Carstensen, 1998). This finding presents a curious paradox: If social interaction and social

support are essential for mental health, how is it possible for elders to interact less yet be generally satisfied with life and less depressed than younger adults?

Social Theories of Aging

Social theories of aging offer explanations for changes in elders' social activity. Two older perspectives—disengagement theory and activity theory—interpret declines in social interaction in opposite ways. More recent approaches—continuity theory and socioemotional selectivity theory—account for a wider range of findings.

■ **Disengagement Theory.** According to **disengagement theory,** mutual withdrawal between elders and society takes place in anticipation of death (Cumming & Henry, 1961). Older people decrease their activity levels and interact less frequently, becoming more preoccupied with their inner lives. At the same time, society frees elders from employment and family responsibilities. The result is viewed as beneficial for both sides. Elders are granted a life of tranquility. And once they disengage, their deaths are less disruptive to society.

Clearly, however, not everyone disengages! As we saw in Chapter 17, when we discussed wisdom, older adults in many cultures move into new positions of prestige and power because of their long life experience. Even after retirement, many people sustain aspects of their work; others develop new, rewarding roles in their communities. In tribal and village societies, most elders continue to hold important social positions (Luborsky & McMullen, 1999). Disengagement by the elderly, then, may represent not their personal preference but, rather, a failure of the social world to provide opportunities for engagement. The more social opportunities elders report, the more strongly they believe they can create worthwhile social experiences for themselves (Lang, Featherman, & Nesselroade, 1997). (Return to the Cultural Influences box in Chapter 17, page 574, for some striking community variations in meaningful social roles available to elders.)

As we will see shortly, older adults' retreat from interaction is more complex than disengagement theory implies. Instead of disengaging from all social ties, they let go of unsatisfying contacts and maintain satisfying ones. And sometimes, they put up with less than satisfying relationships to remain engaged! For example, though Ruth often complained about Dick's insensitive behavior, she reluctantly agreed to travel with Dick and Goldie because she wanted to share the experience with Walt.

Finally, disengagement theory has been criticized for overvaluing the survival of society at the expense of individual self-worth and dignity. But paradoxically, by encouraging seniors to withdraw instead of remaining engaged in meaningful activity, acceptance of this perspective risks undermining societal welfare, too! For example, if seniors incorrectly assume a link between aging and disengagement, a rising tide of elders might leave the workforce early and draw on Social Security—with profound negative consequences for both personal well-being and the social system itself.

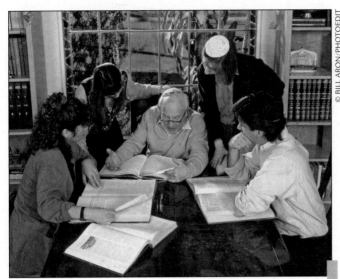

© BILL ARON/PHOTOEDIT

Young people listen intently to a Jewish elder in a religious study group. Because of their long life experience, older adults in many cultures move into new positions of prestige and power—a trend that poses a major challenge to disengagement theory of aging.

■ **Activity Theory.** Attempting to overcome the flaws of disengagement theory, **activity theory** states that social barriers to engagement, not the desires of elders, cause declining rates of interaction. When older people lose certain roles (for example, through retirement or widowhood), they try to find others in an effort to stay about as active and busy as they were in middle age. In this view, elders' life satisfaction depends on conditions that permit them to remain engaged in roles and relationships (Maddox, 1963).

But although people do seek alternative sources of meaning and gratification in response to social losses, activity theory fails to acknowledge any psychological change in old age. Many studies show that merely offering elders opportunities for social contact does not lead to greater social activity. Indeed, most do not take advantage of such opportunities. In nursing homes, for example, where social partners are abundant, social interaction is very low, even among the healthiest residents—a circumstance we will examine when we discuss housing arrangements for the elderly. Especially troubling for activity theory is the repeated finding that when health status is controlled, elders who have larger social networks and engage in more activities are not necessarily happier (Lee & Markides, 1990; Ritchey, Ritchey, & Dietz, 2001). Recall that it is quality, not quantity, of relationships that predicts psychological well-being in old age.

■ **Continuity Theory.** Unlike activity theory, **continuity theory** does not view elders' efforts to remain active in terms of simple replacement of lost social roles with new ones. Rather, according to this view, most aging adults strive to maintain a personal system—an identity and a set of personality dispositions, interests, roles, and skills—that promotes life satisfaction by ensuring consistency between their past and anticipated future. This striving for continuity does not mean that elders' lives are static. To the contrary, aging produces inevitable

change, but most older adults try to minimize stress and disruptiveness by integrating those changes into a coherent, consistent life path. As much as possible, they choose to use familiar skills and engage in familiar activities with familiar people—preferences that provide a secure sense of routine and direction in life.

Research on the daily lives of older adults confirms a high degree of continuity in everyday pursuits and relationships. For most, friends and family members with whom they interact remain much the same, as do work, volunteer, leisure, and social activities. Even after a change (such as retirement), people usually make choices that extend the previous direction of their lives, engaging in new activities but often within familiar domains. For example, a retired manager of a children's bookstore collaborated with friends to build a children's library and donate it to an overseas orphanage. A musician who, because of arthritis, could no longer play the violin arranged regular get-togethers with musically inclined friends to listen to and talk about music. Robert Atchley (1989), originator of continuity theory, noted, "Everyday life for most older people is like long-running improvisational theater in which . . . changes are mostly in the form of new episodes [rather] than entirely new plays" (p. 185).

Elders' reliance on continuity has many benefits. Participation in familiar activities with familiar people provides repeated practice that helps preserve physical and cognitive functioning, fosters self-esteem and mastery, and affirms identity (Finchum & Weber, 2000). Investing in long-standing, close relationships provides comfort, pleasure, and a network of social support. Finally, striving for continuity is essential for attaining Erikson's sense of ego integrity, which depends on preserving a sense of personal history (Atchley, 1999).

As we explore social contexts and relationships of aging, we will encounter many examples of how elders use continuity to experience aging positively, as a "gentle slope." We will also address ways that communities can help them do so.

■ **Socioemotional Selectivity Theory.** A final perspective addresses how people's social networks sustain continuity while also narrowing as they age. According to **socioemotional selectivity theory,** social interaction extends lifelong selection processes. In middle adulthood, marital relationships deepen, siblings feel closer, and number of friendships declines. In old age, contacts with family and long-term friends are sustained until the eighties, when they diminish gradually in favor of a few very close relationships. In contrast, as Figure 18.1 on page 612 shows, contacts with acquaintances and willingness to form new social ties fall off steeply from middle through late adulthood (Carstensen, Fung, & Charles, 2003; Fung, Carstensen, & Lang, 2001).

What explains these changes? Socioemotional selectivity theory states that physical and psychological aspects of aging lead to changes in the functions of social interaction. Consider the reasons you interact with members of your social network. At times, you approach them to get information. At other times, you seek affirmation of your uniqueness and worth as a person. You also choose social partners to regulate emotion, approaching those who evoke positive feelings and avoiding

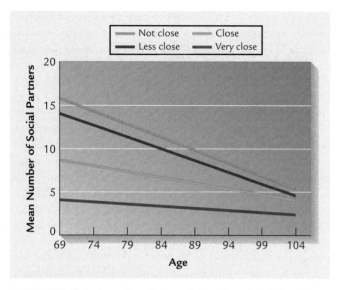

FIGURE 18.1 Age-related change in number of social partners varying in closeness. In interviews with over 500 elders ranging in age from 69 to 104, the number of "not close" and "less close" partners fell off steeply with age, whereas the number of "close" and "very close" partners declined minimally and gradually. (Adapted from F. R. Lang, U. M. Staudinger, & L. L. Carstensen, 1998, "Perspectives on Socioemotional Selectivity in Late Life: How Personality and Social Context Do (and Do Not) Make a Difference," *Journal of Gerontology, 53B,* p. 24. Copyright © 1998 by the Gerontological Society of America. Reprinted by permission.)

those who make you feel sad, angry, or uncomfortable. For older adults, who have gathered a lifetime of information, the information-gathering function becomes less significant. And elders realize it is risky to approach people they do not know for self-affirmation: Stereotypes of aging increase the odds of receiving a condescending, hostile, or indifferent response.

Instead, as physical fragility makes it more important to avoid stress, older adults emphasize the emotion-regulating function of interaction. In one study, younger and older adults were asked to categorize their social partners. Younger people more often sorted them on the basis of information seeking and future contact, while older people emphasized anticipated feelings (Frederickson & Carstensen, 1990). They appeared highly motivated to approach pleasant relationships and avoid unpleasant ones.

Interacting mostly with relatives and friends increases the chances that elders' emotional equilibrium will be preserved. Within these close bonds, older adults apply their emotional expertise to promote harmony. They are less likely than younger people to respond to tensions with destructive tactics (yelling, arguing) and more likely to use constructive strategies, such as expressing affection or calmly letting the situation blow over (Birditt & Fingerman, 2005; Carstensen, Gottman, & Levenson, 1995). Elders also reinterpret conflict in less stressful ways—often by identifying something positive in the situation (Labouvie-Vief, 2003). Consequently, despite their smaller social networks, they are happier than younger people with their number of friends and report fewer problematic relationships (Akiyama et al., 2003; Fingerman & Birditt, 2003).

As the Biology and Environment box on the following page reveals, people's perception of time is strongly linked to their social goals. When remaining time is limited, adults of all ages place more emphasis on the emotional quality of their social experiences. In sum, socioemotional selectivity theory views reduced quantity of social ties in favor of long-standing, high-quality relationships to result from changing life conditions.

Social Contexts of Aging: Communities, Neighborhoods, and Housing

The physical and social contexts in which elders live affect their social experiences and, consequently, their development and adjustment. Communities, neighborhoods, and housing arrangements vary in the extent to which they enable aging residents to satisfy their social needs.

■ **Communities and Neighborhoods.** About half of American and three-fourths of Canadian ethnic minority older adults live in cities, compared with only one-third of Caucasians. The majority of senior citizens reside in suburbs, where they moved earlier in their lives and usually remain after retirement. Suburban elders have higher incomes and report better health than inner-city elders do. But inner-city elders are better off in terms of transportation and proximity to social services, and they are not as disadvantaged in terms of health, income, and availability of services as the one-fourth of American and one-third of Canadian seniors who live in small towns and rural areas. In addition, small-town and rural elderly are less likely to live near their children, who often leave these communities in early adulthood (Statistics Canada, 2003b; U.S. Census Bureau, 2006b).

Yet small-town and rural elderly compensate for distance from family members and social services by interacting more with neighbors and friends (Shaw, 2005). Smaller communities

Like many older adults, these Spanish men reap great satisfaction from residing in a neighborhood with like-minded senior residents. Presence of family is less crucial when neighbors and nearby friends provide social support.

Biology and Environment

Aging, Time Perception, and Social Goals

With whom would you spend time if you knew you would soon be moving away from your community? When asked this question, young people typically choose close friends and relatives, with whom they have enduring, positive relationships. Their response resembles that of older people. Elders view time as precious and perceive it as flying by rapidly (Kennedy, Fung, & Carstensen, 2001). Aware that time is "running out," they don't waste it on unlikely future payoffs. Instead, they opt for emotionally gratifying social experiences in the here and now.

Socioemotional selectivity theory underscores the crucial role our time perspective plays in the social goals we select and pursue (Carstensen, Isaacowitz, & Charles, 1999). People who perceive future time as limited search for meaningful social experiences. Yet tests of the theory documenting an age-related rise in time spent with familiar, highly rewarding social partners do not permit us to separate the influences of age and time orientation on people's social goals. Is time perspective really at the heart of elders' focus on old friends and family members as desired social partners?

To find out, Laura Carstensen and her colleagues uncoupled age from time. In a study that held age constant but varied time left in life, the researchers compared three groups of men in their late thirties. The first group was HIV-negative, the second HIV-positive without AIDS symp-toms, and the third HIV-positive and actively experiencing deadly symptoms of AIDS (Carstensen & Fredrickson, 1998). When asked to categorize a variety of potential social partners, each successive group increasingly emphasized the emotional rewards of the relationship. The men with AIDS symptoms, who had the least time left, focused nearly exclusively on the emotional quality of social ties, just as very old people do.

In another investigation, the researchers permitted age to vary but held time perspective constant by giving participants a hypothetical situation in which their future had expanded. People between ages 11 and 92 were asked to imagine that they had just received a telephone call from their doctor, who told them of a new medical breakthrough that would add 20 years to their life (Fung, Carstensen, & Lutz, 1999). Under these conditions, older people's strong bias for familiar, emotionally close social partners disappeared! Their social preferences were just as diverse as those of younger people.

In further research, the investigators examined the social goals of young and old adults in Taiwan and mainland China. In both cultures, the elderly expressed a stronger desire than young people for familiar social partners likely to provide emotionally satisfying inter-

© RONNIE KAUFMAN/CORBIS

Elders view time as precious. Increasingly aware that it is "running out," they opt for emotionally gratifying social experiences in the here and now, as these grandparents do in a joyous exchange with their grandchildren.

action. But this preference was particularly strong among the mainland Chinese, who perceived future time as more limited. In line with this perception, average life expectancy is 7 years shorter in mainland China than in Taiwan (Fung, Lai, & Ng, 2001).

Finally, the preference for close partners when time is short actually stems from increased desire for emotionally meaningful interactions, not from a need for social support during difficult times. Adults of all ages explain their choice by referring to the emotionally fulfilling quality of the relationship (Fung & Carstensen, 2004).

In sum, the social preferences of old age are an active adaptation to shrinking longevity. When days are numbered, present-oriented goals—social connectedness and emotional depth in relationships—become high priorities.

have features that foster gratifying relationships—stability of residents, shared values and lifestyles, willingness to exchange social support, and frequent social visits as country people "drop in" on one another. And many suburban and rural communities have responded to elder residents' needs by developing transportation programs (such as special buses and vans) to take elders to health and social services, senior centers, and shopping centers.

Both urban and rural older adults report greater life satisfaction when many senior citizens reside in their neighborhood and are available as like-minded companions. Presence

of family is less crucial when neighbors and nearby friends provide social support (Gabriel & Bowling, 2004). This does not mean that neighbors replace family relationships. But elders are content as long as their children and other relatives arrange occasional visits (Hooyman & Kiyak, 2005).

Compared with older adults in urban areas, those in quiet neighborhoods in small and midsized communities are more satisfied with life. The major reason is that smaller communities have lower crime rates (Scheidt & Windley, 1985; Statistics Canada, 2003b). As we will see next, fear of crime has profound, negative consequences for elders' sense of security and comfort.

■ **Victimization and Fear of Crime.** Walt and Ruth's single-family home stood in an urban neighborhood, five blocks from the business district where Walt's photography shop had been prior to his retirement. When leaving home for more than a few hours, Walt and Ruth telephoned their next-door neighbor and asked her to keep an eye on the property. As the neighborhood aged, some homes fell into disrepair, and the population became more transient. Shops were open Thursday and Friday evenings, but Walt and Ruth saved their errands for daylight hours. Although they had never been victimized, crime was on their minds and affected their behavior. In a large, nationally representative Canadian survey, 41 percent of adults age 65 and older said they felt unsafe walking in their neighborhoods, compared with 24 percent of younger adults (Lindsay, 1999).

Media attention has led to a widely held belief that crime against the elderly is common. In reality, older adults are less often targets of crime, especially violent crime, than other age groups. In urban areas, however, purse snatching and pickpocketing are more often committed against elders (especially women) than younger people, probably because perpetrators feel that they can easily overpower older and female victims (U.S. Department of Justice, 2005a). A single incident can strike intense anxiety into the hearts of seniors because of its potential for physical injury and its financial consequences for those with low incomes.

Among frail elders living alone and in inner-city areas, fear of crime, which is sometimes greater than worries about income, health, and housing, restricts activities and undermines morale (Joseph, 1997; Thompson & Krause, 1998). Neighborhood Watch and other programs that encourage residents to look out for one another reduce fear and feelings of isolation from the community. Some cities have established special police units to investigate and prevent crimes against seniors.

■ **Housing Arrangements.** Overwhelmingly, older adults in Western industrialized nations want to stay in the neighborhoods where they spent their adult lives; in fact, 90 percent remain in or near their old home. In the United States and Canada, fewer than 5 percent relocate to other communities (Ostrovsky, 2004; U.S. Department of Health and Human Services, 2005p). These moves are usually motivated by a desire to live closer to children or, among the more economically advantaged and healthy, a desire for a more temperate climate and a place to pursue leisure interests.

Most elder relocations occur within the same town or city; are prompted by declining health, widowhood, or disability; and increase with age (Chappell et al., 2003). As we look at housing arrangements for older adults, we will see that the more a setting deviates from home life, the harder it is for elders to adjust.

Ordinary Homes. For the majority of elders, who are not physically impaired, staying in their own homes affords the greatest possible personal control—freedom to arrange space and schedule daily events as one chooses. More elders in the

Because of improved health and economic well-being, today more older adults than ever before live in their own homes.

United States, Canada, and other Western nations live on their own today than ever before—a trend due to improved health and economic well-being (Lindsay, 1999; U.S. Department of Health and Human Services, 2005h). But when health and mobility problems appear, independent living poses risks. Most homes are designed for younger people. They are seldom modified to suit the physical capacities of their elder residents. And living alone in ill health is linked to social isolation and loneliness (Victor et al., 2000).

When Ruth reached her mid-eighties, Sybil begged her to move into her home. Like many adult children of Southern, Central, and Eastern European descent (Greek, Italian, Polish, and others), Sybil felt an especially strong obligation to care for her frail mother. Older adults of these cultural backgrounds, as well as African Americans, Asians, Hispanics, Native Americans, and Canadian Aboriginals, more often live in extended families (Gabrel, 2000; Hays & George, 2002).

Yet increasing numbers of ethnic minority elders want to live on their own, although poverty often prevents them from doing so. For example, two decades ago, 75 percent of Korean-American older adults were living with their children, whereas today just over 50 percent are (Yoo & Sung, 1997). With sufficient income to keep her home, Ruth refused to move in with Sybil. Continuity theory helps us understand why many elders react this way, even after health problems accumulate. As the site of memorable life events, the home strengthens continuity with the past, sustaining elders' sense of identity in the face of physical declines and social losses. And it permits older adults to adapt to their surroundings in familiar, comfortable ways (Atchley, 1999). Elders also value their independence, privacy, and network of nearby friends and neighbors.

During the past half-century, the number of unmarried, divorced, and widowed elders living alone has risen dramatically. Currently, 33 percent of American and 29 percent of Canadian elders live by themselves, a figure that rises to nearly

50 percent for those age 85 and older. This trend, though evident in all segments of the elderly population, is less pronounced among men, who are far more likely than women to be living with a spouse into advanced old age (Statistics Canada, 2002h; U.S. Census Bureau, 2006b).

Over 40 percent of American and 38 percent of Canadian elders who live alone are poverty-stricken—rates many times greater than among elderly couples. More than 70 percent are widowed women. Because of lower earnings in earlier years, some entered old age this way. Others became poor for the first time, often because they outlived a spouse who suffered a lengthy, costly illness. With age, their financial status worsens as their assets shrink and their own health care costs rise (Government of Canada, 2005; Vartanian & McNamara, 2002). Under these conditions, isolation, loneliness, and depression can pile up. Poverty among lone elderly women is deeper in the United States than Canada because of less generous government-sponsored income and health benefits. Still, in both nations, elderly women living on their own are worse off than their counterparts in Western Europe. Consequently, the feminization of poverty deepens in old age.

Residential Communities. About 5 percent of North American senior citizens live in residential communities, which come in great variety (U.S. Department of Health and Human Services, 2005p). Housing developments for the aged, either single-dwelling or apartment complexes, differ from ordinary homes only in that they have been modified to suit elders' capacities (featuring, for example, single-level living space and grab bars in bathrooms). Some are federally subsidized units for the elderly poor, but most are privately developed retirement villages with adjoining recreational facilities. For elders who need more help with everyday tasks, *assisted-living* arrangements are available (see Chapter 17, page 586). **Congregate housing**—an increasingly popular long-term care option—provides a variety of support services, including meals in a common dining room, along with watchful oversight of residents with physical and mental disabilities. **Life care communities** offer a range of housing alternatives, from independent or congregate housing to full nursing home care. For a large initial payment and additional monthly fees, life care guarantees that elders' changing needs will be met in one place as they age.

Unlike Ruth and Walt, who remained in their own home, Dick and Goldie entered congregate housing in their late sixties. For Dick, the move was a positive turn of events that permitted him to relate to peers on the basis of their current life together, setting aside past failures in the outside world. Dick found gratifying leisure pursuits—leading an exercise class, organizing a charity drive with Goldie, and using his skills as a baker to make cakes for birthday and anniversary celebrations.

Studies of diverse residential communities for the aged reveal that they can have positive effects on physical and mental health. A specially designed physical space and care on an as-needed basis help elders overcome mobility limitations, thereby enabling greater social participation and a more active

Residential communities for the aged can have positive effects on physical and mental health. A specially designed physical space with adjoining recreational facilities and care on an as-needed basis helps elders overcome mobility limitations and lead more active lives.

lifestyle (Fonda, Clipp, & Maddox, 2002; Jenkins, Pienta, & Horgas, 2002). And in societies where old age leads to reduced status, age-segregated living is gratifying to most elders who choose it. It may open up useful roles and leadership opportunities (Ball et al., 2000). And the more older adults perceive the environment as socially supportive, the more they collaborate with one another in coping with stressors of aging and in providing assistance to other residents (Lawrence & Schigelone, 2002). Congregate housing appears to be well-suited to promoting mutually supportive relationships among elder residents.

Yet a collection of elders does not guarantee a comfortable, content community. Shared values and goals among residents with similar backgrounds, a small enough facility to promote frequent communication, and availability of meaningful roles enhance life satisfaction. Older adults who feel socially integrated into the setting are more likely to consider it their home. But those who remain distant and reclusive are unlikely to characterize their apartment or room as home. Citing lack of warmth and like-minded companions as the reason, they are at high risk for loneliness and depression (Adams, Sanders, & Auth, 2004; Young, 1998).

Nursing Homes. The small percentage of North Americans age 65 and older who live in nursing homes experience the most extreme restriction of autonomy. As noted in Chapter 17, sense of personal control and gratifying social relationships are as vital for the mental health of nursing home residents as they are for community-dwelling elders.

Potential social partners are abundant in nursing homes, but interaction is low. To regulate emotion in social interaction (so important to elders), personal control over social experiences is vital. Yet nursing home residents have little opportunity to choose their social partners, and timing of contact is generally determined by staff rather than by elders' preferences. Social withdrawal is an adaptive response to these often overcrowded, hospital-like settings. Although interaction with people in the outside world predicts nursing home residents' life satisfaction, interaction within the institution does not (Baltes, Wahl, & Reichert, 1992). Not surprisingly, nursing home residents with physical but not mental impairments are far more depressed, anxious, and lonely than their community-dwelling counterparts (Guildner et al., 2001).

Designing more homelike nursing homes could help increase residents' sense of security and control over their social experiences. North American nursing homes, usually operated for profit, are often packed with residents and institutional in their operation. In contrast, European facilities are liberally supported by public funds. Residents live in private suites or small apartments furnished in part with their own belongings. Specially adapted parks and gardens draw residents away from passive activities, such as TV viewing, into outdoor communal spaces. When an elder's condition worsens, caregivers modify the existing space rather than move the individual to more medically oriented quarters (Horgas, Wilms, & Baltes, 1998; Schwarz, 1996). In this way, they preserve the person's identity, sense of place, and social relationships as much as possible.

Ask Yourself

Review

Cite features of neighborhoods and residential communities that enhance elders' life satisfaction.

Apply

Sam lives alone in the same home he has occupied for over 30 years. His adult children can't understand why he won't move across town to a modern apartment. Using continuity theory, explain why Sam prefers to stay where he is.

Apply

Vera, a nursing home resident, speaks to her adult children and to a close friend on the phone every day. In contrast, she seldom attends nursing home social events or interacts with her roommate. Using socioemotional selectivity theory, explain Vera's behavior.

Connect

According to socioemotional selectivity theory, when time is limited, adults focus on the emotional quality of their social relationships. How do elders apply their emotional expertise (discussed on page 601) to attain this goal?

Relationships in Late Adulthood

The **social convoy** is an influential model of changes in our social networks as we move through life. Picture yourself in the midst of a cluster of ships traveling together, granting one another safety and support. Ships in the inner circle represent people closest to you, such as a spouse, best friend, parent, or child. Those less close but still important travel on the outside. With age, ships exchange places in the convoy, and some drift off while others join the procession (Antonucci, Akiyama, & Takahashi, 2004). But as long as the convoy continues to exist, you adapt positively.

In the following sections, we examine the ways elders with diverse lifestyles sustain social networks of family members and friends. As ties are lost, older adults draw others closer and occasionally add replacements, though not at the rate they did at younger ages. Tragically, for some older adults the social convoy breaks down. We will also explore the circumstances in which elders experience abuse and neglect at the hands of those close to them.

Marriage

Even with high divorce rates, 1 in every 4 or 5 first marriages in North America is expected to last at least 50 years. Walt's comment to Ruth that "the last few decades have been the happiest" characterizes the attitudes and behaviors of many elderly couples who have spent their adult lives together. Marital satisfaction rises from middle to late adulthood, when it is at its peak (Goodman, 1999; Levenson, Carstensen, & Gottman, 1993). Several changes in life circumstance and couples' communication underlie this trend.

First, late-life marriages involve fewer stressful responsibilities that can negatively affect relationships, such as rearing children and balancing demands of career and family (Kemp & Kemp, 2002). Second, perceptions of fairness in the relationship increase as men participate more in household tasks after retirement. For elders who experienced little social pressure for gender equality in their youth, division of labor in the home still reflects traditional roles (Condie, 1989; Vinick & Ekerdt, 1991). Men take on more home maintenance projects, whereas women's duties—cooking, cleaning, laundry, and shopping—continue as before. Among adults retiring today, "feminine" tasks are more equally shared than they were during work life (Kulik, 2001). In either case, men's increased involvement at home results in a greater sense of equity in marriage than before. Third, with extra time together, the majority of couples engage in more joint leisure activities. Ruth and Walt walked, worked in the garden, played golf, and took frequent day trips. In interviews with a diverse sample of retired couples, women often stated that more time with their husbands enhanced marital closeness (Vinick & Ekerdt, 1991).

Finally, greater emotional understanding and emphasis on regulating emotion in relationships lead to more positive interactions between spouses. Compared to younger couples, elderly couples disagree less often and resolve their differences in

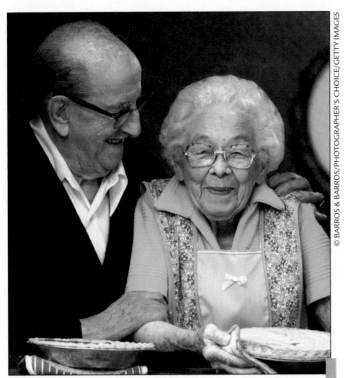

Marital satisfaction peaks in late adulthood. Older couples have more time to enjoy each other's company. And their expertise at understanding and regulating emotion leads to more positive and affectionate interactions.

more constructive ways. Even in unhappy marriages, elders are less likely to let their disagreements escalate into expressions of anger and resentment (Carstensen, Isaacowitz, & Charles, 1999; Hatch & Bulcroft, 2004). For example, when Dick complained about Goldie's cooking, Goldie tried to appease him: "All right, Dick, next birthday I won't make cheesecake." And when Goldie brought up Dick's bickering and criticism, Dick usually said, "I know, dear," and retreated to another room. As in other relationships, the elderly protect themselves from stress by molding marital ties to make them as pleasant as possible.

When marital dissatisfaction exists, it often takes a greater toll on women than on men (Kim & Moen, 2002c). Recall from Chapter 14 that women more often try to work on a troubling relationship. In old age, expending energy in this way is especially taxing, both physically and mentally. Men, in contrast, often protect themselves by avoiding discussion (Levenson, Carstensen, & Gottman, 1993).

Gay and Lesbian Partnerships

Elderly gays and lesbians in long-term partnerships have sustained their relationships through a historical period of hostility and discrimination toward homosexuals. Nevertheless, most report happy, highly fulfilling relationships, pointing to their partner as their most important source of social support. And compared with homosexual elders who live alone, homosexual partners rate their physical and mental health more

favorably (Grossman, D'Augelli, & Hershberger, 2000; Wojciechowski, 1998).

A lifetime of effective coping with an oppressive social environment may have strengthened homosexuals' skill at dealing with late-life physical and social changes, thereby contributing to a satisfying partnership (Gabbay & Wahler, 2002). And greater gender-role flexibility enables gay and lesbian couples to adapt easily to sharing household tasks following retirement. Furthermore, because of imagined or real strain in family relationships when they told others about their homosexuality, gays and lesbians less often assume that family members will provide support in old age. Consequently, many have forged strong friendships to replace or supplement family ties (Kimmel, 2002). Homosexual couples with gratifying friendship networks report high life satisfaction and less fear of aging (Slusher, Mayer, & Dunkle, 1996). These supportive social contexts and positive feelings probably enhance their happiness as aging couples.

Nevertheless, because of continuing prejudice and lack of social recognition of their partnerships, aging gays and lesbians face unique challenges (Woolf, 2001). Health care systems are often unresponsive to their unique needs. And where gay and lesbian unions are not legally recognized (in most U.S. states), if one partner becomes frail or ill, the other may not be welcome in hospitals or nursing homes or be allowed to participate in health care decisions—an issue we will return to in Chapter 19. These circumstances can make late-life declines and losses especially painful.

Divorce, Remarriage, and Cohabitation

When Walt's uncle Louie was 61, he divorced his wife Sandra after 17 years of marriage. Although she knew the marriage was far from perfect, Sandra had lived with Louie long enough that the divorce came as a shock. A year later, Louie married Rachella, a divorcée who shared his enthusiasm for sports and dance.

Couples who divorce in late adulthood constitute less than 1 percent of all divorces in any given year. But the divorce rate among people age 65 and older is increasing as new generations of elders become more accepting of marital breakup and as the divorce risk rises for second and subsequent marriages. When asked about the reasons for divorce, elderly men typically mention lack of shared interests and activities, whereas women frequently cite emotional distance and their partner's refusal to communicate. "We never talked," Sandra said. "I felt isolated" (Weingarten, 1988).

Compared with younger adults, longtime married elders have given their adult lives to the relationship. Following divorce, they find it harder to separate their identity from that of their former spouse, and they suffer more from a sense of personal failure. Relationships with family and friends shift at a time when close bonds are crucial for psychological well-being. Women, overall, suffer more than men because they are more likely to spend their remaining years living alone. The financial consequences are severe—greater than for widowhood because many accumulated assets are lost in property settlements (McDonald & Robb, 2004; Miller, Hemesath, & Nelson, 1997).

In younger individuals, divorce often leads to greater awareness of negative patterns of behavior and determination to change. In contrast, self-criticism in divorced elders heightens guilt and depression because their self-worth depends more on past than on future accomplishments. Louie and Sandra blamed each other. "I was always miserable with Sandra," Louie claimed, even though the couple's earlier days had been reasonably happy. Although blaming the partner may distort the marital history, it is a common coping strategy that enables older adults to preserve integrity and self-esteem (Weingarten, 1989).

Remarriage rates are low in late adulthood and decline with age, although they are considerably higher among divorced than widowed elders. Older men's opportunities for remarriage are far greater than women's. Nevertheless, the gender gap in elder remarriage is much smaller after divorce than after widowhood. Perhaps because their previous relationship was disappointing, divorcées find it easier than widows to enter a new relationship. Also, divorced older women may be more motivated to remarry because of their more extreme economic circumstances. Finally, some divorced elders (like Louie and Rachella) leave their marriages only after a new bond is forming (Huyck, 1995).

Compared with younger people who remarry, elders who do so enter more stable relationships, as their divorce rate is much lower. In Louie and Rachella's case, the second marriage lasted for 32 years! Perhaps late-life remarriages are more successful because they involve more maturity, patience, and a better balance of romantic with practical concerns (Kemp & Kemp, 2002). Older couples who remarry are generally very satisfied with their new relationships, although men tend to be more content than women (Brubaker, 1985). With fewer potential mates, perhaps women who remarry in late life settle for less desirable partners.

Rather than remarrying, today more older adults who enter a new relationship choose cohabitation—a trend expected to continue as younger people, with their greater acceptance of cohabitation, reach late adulthood. Like elder remarriages, cohabitation in late adulthood results in more stable relationships and higher relationship quality than it did at younger ages. But compared with younger people, fewer cohabiting elders have plans to marry. Reasons frequently given are concerns about acceptance of the new partner by adult children and negative financial consequences with respect to taxes, social security or pension benefits, and adult children's inheritance (King & Scott, 2005; Kemp & Kemp, 2002). In addition, older divorced and widowed women often mention unwillingness to give up their newfound independence (Lopata, 1996).

Widowhood

Walt died shortly after Ruth turned 80. Like over 70 percent of widowed elders, Ruth described the loss of her spouse as the most stressful event of her life. As two researchers noted, being widowed means that the survivor has "lost the role and identity of being a spouse (being married and doing things as a couple),

Most widowed elders—especially those with outgoing personalities and high self-esteem—are resilient in the face of loneliness. And because many elderly women share the widowed state, they are likely to seek support and companionship from one another.

which is potentially one of the most pervasive, intense, intimate, and personal roles that they have ever had in their life" (Lund & Caserta, 2004a, p. 29). Ruth felt lonely, anxious, and depressed for several months after the funeral.

Widows make up one-third of the elderly population in the United States and Canada. Because women live longer than men and are less likely to remarry, nearly 50 percent of women age 65 and older are widowed, compared with only 15 percent of U.S. men and 28 percent of Canadian men. Ethnic minorities with high rates of poverty and chronic disease are more likely to be widowed (Statistics Canada, 2002h; U.S. Census Bureau, 2006b).

Earlier we mentioned that most widows and widowers live alone rather than in extended families, a trend that is stronger for whites than for ethnic minorities. Though less well-off financially than married elders, most want to retain control over their time and living space and to avoid disagreements with their adult children. Widowed elders who relocate because they cannot make mortgage payments or keep up their homes usually move closer to family but not into the same residence (Lopata, 1996).

The greatest problem for recently widowed elders is profound loneliness (Lund, 1993). But adaptation varies widely, depending on age, social support, and personality. Elders have fewer lasting problems than younger individuals who are widowed, probably because death in later life is viewed as less unfair (Stroebe & Stroebe, 1993). And most widowed elders—especially those with outgoing personalities and high self-esteem—are resilient in the face of loneliness (Moore & Stratton, 2002; van Baarsen, 2002). To sustain continuity with their past, they try to preserve social relationships that were important before the spouse's death and report that relatives and friends respond in kind, contacting them at least as often as before (Utz et al., 2002). Also, the stronger elders' sense of self-efficacy in handling tasks of daily living, the more favorably they adjust (Fry, 2001).

Nevertheless, widowed individuals must reorganize their lives, reconstructing an identity that is separate from the deceased spouse. The task is harder for wives whose roles depended on their husbands' than for those who developed rewarding roles of their own. But overall, men show more physical and mental health problems and greater risk of mortality, for several reasons (Bennett, Smith, & Hughes, 2005; Pinquart, 2003). First, most men relied on their wives for social connectedness, household tasks, and coping with stressors and, therefore, are less prepared than women for the challenges that accompany widowhood. Second, because of gender-role expectations, men feel less free to express their emotions and to ask for help with meals, household tasks, and social relationships (Lund & Caserta, 2004). Finally, men tend to be less involved in religious activities—a vital source of social support and inner strength (Lee et al., 2001).

In two studies of older widowers, those in their seventies reported the most depression and showed the slowest rate of improvement over the following two years. The death of their wives occurred around the time they were adjusting to retirement, resulting in two major changes at once, with widowhood highly unexpected because most wives outlive their husbands (Lund & Caserta, 2001, 2004a). African-American widowers, however, report less depression than Caucasian widowers, perhaps because of greater support from extended family and church (Balaswamy & Richardson, 2001).

Sex differences in the experience of widowhood contribute to men's higher remarriage rate. Women's kinkeeper role (see Chapter 16, page 543) and ability to form close friendships may lead them to feel less need to remarry. In addition, because many elderly women share the widowed state, they probably offer one another helpful advice and sympathy. In contrast, men often lack skills for maintaining family relationships, forming emotionally satisfying ties outside marriage, and handling the chores of their deceased wives.

Still, most widowed elders fare well within a few years, resembling their married counterparts in psychological well-being. Those who arrive at this traumatic event with high self-esteem and a sense of purpose in life have less difficulty adapting to loss of a spouse. Overall, about 15 to 25 percent have long-term adjustment problems (Lund & Caserta, 2001). Older widows and widowers who participated in several months of weekly classes providing information and support in acquiring daily living skills felt better prepared to manage the challenges of widowed life (Caserta, Lund, & Obray, 2004). Applying What We Know below suggests a variety of ways to foster adaptation to widowhood in old age.

Never-Married, Childless Older Adults

Shortly after Ruth and Walt's marriage in their twenties, Ruth's father died. Her sister Ida continued to live with and care for their mother, who was in ill health until she died 16 years later. When, at age 25, Ida received a marriage proposal, she responded, "I can't marry anybody while my mother is still living. I'm expected to look after her." Ida's decision was not unusual for a daughter of her day. She never married or had children.

About 5 percent of older North Americans have remained unmarried and childless throughout their lives. Almost all are conscious of being different from the norm, but most have developed alternative meaningful relationships. Ida, for example, formed a strong bond with a neighbor's son. In his childhood, she provided emotional support and financial assistance, which helped him overcome a stressful home life. He

Applying What We Know

Fostering Adaptation to Widowhood in Late Adulthood

Suggestion	Description
Family and Friends	
Social support and interaction	Social support and interaction must extend beyond the grieving period to ongoing assistance and caring relationships. Family members and friends can help most by making support available while encouraging the widowed elder to use effective coping strategies.
Community	
Senior centers	Senior centers offer communal meals and other social activities, enabling widowed and other elders to connect with people in similar circumstances and to gain access to other community resources, such as listings of part-time employment and available housing.
Support groups	Support groups can be found in senior centers, churches, and other agencies. Besides new relationships, they offer an accepting atmosphere for coming to terms with loss, effective role models, and assistance with developing skills for daily living.
Religious activities	Involvement in a church, synagogue, or mosque can help relieve the loneliness associated with loss of a spouse and offer social support, new relationships, and meaningful roles.
Volunteer activities	One of the best ways for widowed elders to find meaningful roles is through volunteer activities. Some are sponsored by formal service organizations, such as the Red Cross or the Retired and Senior Volunteer Program. Other volunteer programs exist in hospitals, senior centers, schools, and charitable organizations.

included Ida in family events and visited her regularly until she died. Other nonmarried elders also speak of the centrality of younger people—often nieces and nephews—in their social networks and of influencing them in enduring ways (Rubinstein et al., 1991). In addition, same-sex friendships are key in never-married elderly women's lives. These tend to be unusually close and often involve joint travel, periods of co-residence, and associations with one another's extended families.

In a large, nationally representative sample of Americans over age 70, childless men without marital partners were far more likely than childless women to feel lonely (Zhang & Hayward, 2001). Never-married elderly women report a level of life satisfaction equivalent to that of married elders and greater than that of divorcées and recently widowed elders. Only when they agree with the stereotype that "life is empty without a partner," or when they cannot maintain social contacts because of declining health, do they report feeling lonely (Baumbusch, 2004; Dykstra, 1995). These single women often state that they avoided many problems associated with being a wife and mother, and they view their enhanced friendships as an advantage of not marrying. At the same time, they realize that friendships are not the same as blood ties when it comes to caregiving in old age.

Most unmarried, childless elders say that support is available from friends and family members, and men often rely on a sister for help (Wenger, 2001; Wu & Pollard, 1998). Never-married elderly women are more likely than other older adults to have relatives and nonrelatives living in their households, with whom they form mutually supportive relationships (Stull & Scarisbrick-Hauser, 1989).

Siblings

Nearly 80 percent of North Americans over age 65 have at least one living sibling. Most elder siblings live within 100 miles of each other, communicate regularly, and visit at least several times a year. In one study, 77 percent of a sample of Canadian older adults considered at least one sibling to be a close friend (Connidis, 1989). Both men and women perceive bonds with sisters to be closer than bonds with brothers. Perhaps because of women's greater emotional expressiveness and nurturance, the closer the tie to a sister, the higher elders' psychological well-being (Cicirelli, 1989; O'Bryant, 1988).

Elderly siblings in industrialized nations are more likely to socialize than to provide one another with direct assistance because most older adults turn first to their spouse and children. Nevertheless, siblings seem to be an important "insurance policy" in late adulthood. Figure 18.2 shows the extent to which, in a large, nationally representative U.S. survey, individuals ranging in age from 16 to 85 reported giving or receiving aid from a sibling. As we saw in earlier chapters, sibling support rises in early adulthood and then declines in middle adulthood. After age 70, it increases for siblings living within 25 miles of each other (White, 2001). Most elders say they would turn to a sibling for help in a crisis, less often in other situations (Connidis, 1994).

Widowed and never-married elders have more contacts with siblings, perhaps because they have fewer competing family relationships. They are also more likely to receive sibling

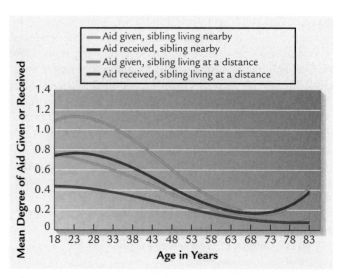

■ **FIGURE 18.2 Age-related change in aid given or received from a sibling.** In a large, nationally representative American survey, adults reported a rise in sibling aid in early adulthood, a decline during middle adulthood, and then a rise after age 70 for siblings living near one another (within 25 miles). In late life, siblings seem to be an important "insurance policy" when help is not available from a spouse or child. (Adapted from L. White, 2001, "Sibling Relationships Over the Life Course: A Panel Analysis," *Journal of Marriage and the Family, 63*, p. 564. Reprinted by permission.)

support during illness (Connidis & Campbell, 1995). For example, when Ida's Alzheimer's symptoms worsened, Ruth came to her aid. Although Ida had many friends, Ruth was her only living relative.

Because siblings share a long and unique history, joint reminiscing about earlier times increases in late adulthood (Cicirelli, 1995). Walt and Dick often talked about their boyhood days, evoking the warmth of early family life. These discussions helped them appreciate the lifelong significance of the sibling bond and contributed to a sense of family continuity and harmony—important aspects of ego integrity.

Friendships

As family responsibilities and vocational pressures lessen, friendships take on increasing importance. Having friends is an especially strong predictor of mental health among the elderly (Nussbaum, 1994; Rawlins, 2004). Older adults report more favorable experiences with friends than with family members, in part because of the pleasurable leisure activities they share with friends (Larson, Mannell, & Zuzanek, 1986). Unique qualities of friendship interaction—openness, spontaneity, mutual caring, and common interests—are also influential.

■ **Functions of Elder Friendships.** The diverse functions of friendship in late adulthood clarify its profound significance:

🖋 *Intimacy and companionship are basic to meaningful elder friendships.* As Ida and her best friend, Rosie, took walks, went shopping, or visited each other, they disclosed their deepest sources of happiness and worry. They also engaged in pleasurable conversation, laughed, and had

Having friends is a strong predictor of mental health among the elderly. Even after declining physical health restricts their mobility, many elders find ways to sustain ties with friends, who offer intimacy and companionship, links to the larger community, and social support in the face of loss.

fun (Crohan & Antonucci, 1989). When elders are asked to describe qualities of their close friendships, their responses reveal that mutual interests, feelings of belongingness, and opportunities to express feelings and confide in another sustain these bonds over time (Field, 1999).

🍂 *Elderly women mention acceptance as a primary aspect of close friendship.* Late-life friends shield one another from others' negative judgments about their capabilities and worth as a person, which frequently stem from stereotypes of aging (Adams, 1985–1986). "Where's your cane, Rosie?" Ida asked when the two women were about to leave for a restaurant. "Come on, don't be self-conscious. When y'get one of those 'you're finished' looks from someone, just remember: In the Greek village where my mother grew up, there was no separation between generations, so the young ones got used to wrinkled skin and weak knees and recognized older women as the wise ones. Why, they were midwives, matchmakers, experts in herbal medicine; they knew about everything!" (Deveson, 1994).

🍂 *Friendships link elderly people to the larger community.* For elders who cannot go out as often, interactions with friends can keep them abreast of events in the wider world. "Rosie," Ida reported, "did you know that the Thompson girl was named high school valedictorian . . . and the business community is supporting Jesse for mayor?" Friends can also open up new experiences that older adults might not take part in alone. Often a first trip to a senior citizens' center takes place within the context of friendship (Nussbaum, 1994).

🍂 *Friendships help protect elders from the psychological consequences of loss.* Older adults in declining health who

remain in contact with friends through phone calls and visits show improved psychological well-being. Similarly, when close relatives die, friends offer compensating social supports (Newsom & Schulz, 1996).

■ **Characteristics of Elder Friendships.** Although older adults prefer familiar, established relationships over new ones, friendship formation continues throughout life. Ties to old and dear friends who live far away are maintained, but practical restrictions promote more frequent interaction with friends in the immediate environment. With age, elders report that the friends they feel closest to are fewer in number and live in the same community. Nevertheless, close elder friendships are not affected by patterns of daily life, such as participation in social groups or volunteerism (Dugan & Kivett, 1998). Many elders find ways to sustain links with friends, even after declining health restricts their mobility.

As in earlier years, elders tend to choose friends whose age, sex, race, ethnicity, and values are like their own. Compared with younger people, fewer report other-sex friendships. But some have them—usually longstanding ones dating back several decades. Elders continue to benefit uniquely from these ties, obtaining an insider's view of the thoughts, feelings, and behavior of members of the other sex (Monsour, 2002). As agemates die, the very old report more intergenerational friends—both same- and other-sex (Johnson & Troll, 1994). In her eighties, Ruth spent time with Margaret, a 55-year-old widow she met while serving on the board of directors of an adoption agency. Two or three times a month, Margaret came to Ruth's home for tea and lively conversation.

Sex differences in friendship, discussed in previous chapters, extend into late adulthood. Women are more likely to have intimate friends; men depend on their wives and, to a lesser extent, their sisters for warm, open communication. Also, older women have more **secondary friends**—people who are not intimates but with whom they spend time occasionally, such as a group that meets for lunch, bridge, or museum tours. Through these associates, elders meet new people, remain socially involved, and gain in psychological well-being (Adams, Bleiszner, & De Vries, 2000).

In elder friendships, affection and emotional support are both given and received to maintain balance in the relationship (Ikkink & van Tilburg, 1998). Although friends call on each other for help with tasks of daily living, they generally do so only in emergencies or for occasional, limited assistance. By avoiding excessive dependency on friends, elders register their own autonomy.

Relationships with Adult Children

About 80 percent of older adults in North America are parents of living children, most of whom are middle-aged. In Chapter 16, we noted that exchanges of help vary with the closeness of the parent–child bond and the needs of the parent and adult child. Recall, also, that over time, parent-to-child help declines, whereas child-to-parent assistance increases. Elders and their adult children are often in touch, even when they live far from each other. But as with other ties, quality rather than quantity of interactions affects older adults' life satisfaction. As people grow older, children usually continue to provide rich rewards, including love, companionship, and stimulation. These warm bonds reduce the negative impact of physical impairments and other losses (such as death of a spouse) on psychological well-being. Alternatively, conflict or unhappiness with adult children contributes to poor physical and mental health (Peterson, 1989; Silverstein & Bengtson, 1991).

Although aging parents and adult children in Western nations provide each other with various forms of help, the level of assistance is typically modest. Older adults in their sixties and seventies—especially those who own their own home and who are married or widowed as opposed to divorced—are more likely to be providers than recipients of help, suggesting SES variations in the balance of support (Grundy, 2005). This balance also shifts as elders age, but well into late adulthood, elders give more than they receive—a circumstance that contradicts stereotypes of older adults as "burdens" on younger generations.

In interviews with a nationally representative U.S. sample, elders reported that help from their adult children most often took the form of emotional support. Only one-third said their children had assisted with household tasks and errands within the past month (Shapiro, 2004). To avoid dependency, older parents expect more emotional support than practical assistance, usually do not seek children's help in the absence of a pressing need, and express annoyance when children are overprotective or help unnecessarily (Spitze & Gallant, 2004). Moderate support, with opportunities to reciprocate, is psychologically beneficial. Extensive support that cannot be returned is linked to poor psychological well-being (Davey & Eggebeen, 1998).

Sex differences in older parent–adult child interaction are evident. As kinkeepers, adult daughters are primary agents of their aging parents' family contacts—telephoning, writing letters, and arranging visits more often than sons. Mother–daughter ties continue to be particularly warm, although competing demands on middle-aged daughters' time may leave less time to devote to their elder mothers than each would like (see page 545 in Chapter 16). Currently, many divorced, non-custodial fathers are reaching late adulthood. Closeness of the parent–child tie affects adult children's sense of obligation to assist an aging parent who had not resided with them for much of their childhood (Ganong & Coleman, 1998). Consequently, in the next few decades, the number of elderly men with limited family contact may increase.

As social networks shrink in size, relationships with adult children become more important sources of family involvement. Elders 85 years and older with children have substantially more contacts with relatives than do those without children (Johnson & Troll, 1992). Why is this so? Consider Ruth, whose daughter Sybil linked her to grandchildren, great-grandchildren, and relatives by marriage. When childless elders reach their eighties, siblings, other same-age relatives, and close friends may have become frail or died and hence may no longer be available as companions.

Relationships with Adult Grandchildren and Great-Grandchildren

Older adults with adult grandchildren and great-grandchildren benefit from a wider potential network of support. Ruth and Walt saw their granddaughter, Marci, and their great-grandson, Jamel, at family gatherings. At other times, Marci telephoned, visited, and sent greeting cards, expressing deep affection for her aging grandparents.

In developed nations, slightly more than half of elders over age 65 have a grandchild who is at least 18 years old (AARP, 2002). In the few studies available on grandparent–adult grandchild relationships, the overwhelming majority of grandchildren felt obligated to assist grandparents in need. Grandparents expected affection (but not practical help) from grandchildren, and in most cases they received it. They regarded the adult grandchild tie as very gratifying—a vital link between themselves and the future (Langer, 1990).

Still, grandparent–adult grandchild relationships vary greatly. Degree of grandparent involvement during childhood strongly predicts the quality of the current relationship. Often, the tie with one grandchild is "special," characterized by more frequent contact, mutual expressions of affection, and enjoyable times together—factors that enhance elders' psychological well-being (Fingerman, 1998). However, longitudinal research reveals that as grandparents and grandchildren move through life, contact declines. Many grandchildren establish distant homes and become immersed in work and family roles that compete for time with extended-family members.

But despite less contact, grandparents' affection for their adult grandchildren strengthens with age, usually exceeding grandchildren's expressed closeness toward their grandparents

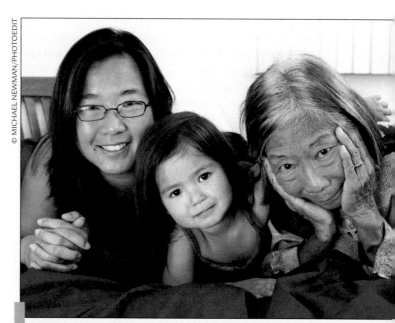

Grandparents regard ties with adult grandchildren as a vital link between themselves and the future. And great-grandparents welcome their new role with enthusiasm, commenting that it reaffirms the continuity of their families.

(which is still strong) (Giarrusso et al., 2001; Harwood, 2001; Silverstein & Long, 1998). This difference in emotional investment reflects each generation's distinct needs and goals—adult grandchildren in establishing independent lives, grandparents in preserving closeness of family relationships and continuity of values across generations. When with their adult grandchildren, grandparents frequently convey information and engage in activities related to family cultural heritage—telling stories about earlier times and discussing family traditions and customs (Wiscott & Kopera-Frye, 2000). Grandchildren become increasingly important sources of emotional meaning for elders in the last decade or two of life.

About 40 percent of older adults have great-grandchildren (Hooyman & Kiyak, 2005). Although most describe their new role as limited and a sign of advancing age, they welcome it with enthusiasm, commenting that it reaffirms the continuity of their families. Parents mediate contact with great-grandchildren, as they did with young grandchildren (see Chapter 16).

Elder Maltreatment

Although the majority of older adults enjoy positive relationships with family members, friends, and professional caregivers, some suffer maltreatment at the hands of these individuals. Through recent media attention, elder maltreatment has become a serious public concern in Western nations.

Reports from many industrialized nations reveal surprisingly similar rates of maltreatment: About 4 to 6 percent of all elders are victims, 1.8 million in the United States and 280,000 in Canada (Brownell & Podnieks, 2005; World Health Organization, 2002). Elder maltreatment crosses ethnic lines, although it is lower in Asian, Hispanic, Native-American, and Canadian-Aboriginal groups with strong traditions of respect for and obligation to the aged (Rittman, Kuzmeskus, & Flum, 2000). Yet all figures underestimate the actual incidence, because most acts take place in private, and victims are often unable or unwilling to complain.

Elder maltreatment usually takes the following forms:

- *Physical abuse.* Intentional infliction of pain, discomfort, or injury, through hitting, cutting, burning, physical force, restraint, and other acts

- *Physical neglect.* Intentional or unintentional failure to fulfill caregiving obligations, resulting in lack of food, medication, or health services or in the elderly person being left alone or isolated

- *Psychological abuse.* Verbal assaults (such as name calling), humiliation (being treated as a child), and intimidation (threats of isolation or placement in a nursing home)

- *Sexual abuse.* Unwanted sexual contact of any kind

- *Financial abuse.* Illegal or improper exploitation of the elder's property or financial resources, through theft or use without the elder's consent

Financial abuse, psychological abuse, and neglect are the most frequently reported types. Often several forms occur in combi-

nation (Anetzberger, 2005; World Health Organization, 2002). The perpetrator is usually a person the older adult trusts and depends on for care and assistance. Most abusers are family members—spouses (usually men), followed by children of both sexes and then by other relatives. Some are friends, neighbors, and in-home caregivers (Hornick, McDonald, & Robertson, 1992). Abuse in nursing homes is a major concern. In one survey, one-third of nurses indicated that they had observed it, and 10 percent admitted to at least one act of physical abuse, 40 percent to at least one act of psychological abuse (Wilber & McNeilly, 2001).

Over the past several decades, another form of neglect—referred to in the media as "granny dumping"—has increased: abandonment of elders with severe disabilities by family caregivers, usually at hospital emergency rooms. According to one U.S. hospital survey, between 100,000 and 200,000 older adults—most suffering from dementia—are left in hospital waiting rooms each year (Tanne, 1992). Overwhelmed, their caregivers seem to have concluded that they have no other option but to take this drastic step. (See page 548 in Chapter 16 and page 584 in Chapter 17 for related research.)

■ **Risk Factors.** Characteristics of the victim, the abuser, their relationship, and its social context are related to the incidence and severity of elder maltreatment. The more of the following risk factors that are present, the greater the likelihood that abuse and neglect will occur.

Dependency of the Victim. Very old, frail, and mentally and physically impaired elders are more vulnerable to maltreatment (Dyer et al., 2000). This does not mean that declines in functioning cause abuse; most older adults with disabilities do not experience it. Rather, when other conditions are ripe for maltreatment, elders with severe disabilities are least able to protect themselves. Those with physical or cognitive impairments may also have personality traits that make them vulnerable—a tendency to lash out when angry or frustrated, a passive or avoidant approach to handling problems, and a low sense of self-efficacy (Comijs et al., 1999).

Dependency of the Perpetrator. Many abusers are dependent, emotionally or financially, on their victims. This dependency, experienced as powerlessness, can lead to aggressive, exploitative behavior. Often the perpetrator–victim relationship is one of mutual dependency (Henderson, Buchanan, & Fisher, 2002). The abuser needs the older person for money or housing, and the older person needs the abuser for assistance with everyday tasks or to relieve loneliness.

Psychological Disturbance and Stress of the Perpetrator. Abusers are more likely than other caregivers to have psychological problems and to be dependent on alcohol or other drugs. Often they are socially isolated, have difficulties at work, or are unemployed, with resulting financial worries. These factors increase the likelihood that they will lash out when caregiving is highly demanding or the behavior of an elder with dementia is irritating or hard to manage.

History of Family Violence. Elder abuse is often part of a long history of family violence. Adults who were abused as children are at increased risk of harming elders (Reay & Browne, 2001). In Chapter 8, we showed how aggressive cycles between family members can easily become self-sustaining, leading to the development of individuals who cope with anger through hostility toward others. In many instances, elder abuse may be an extension of years of partner abuse (Lundy & Grossman, 2004).

Institutional Conditions. Elder maltreatment is more likely to occur in nursing homes that are rundown and overcrowded and that have staff shortages, minimal staff supervision, high staff turnover, and few visitors (Payne & Fletcher, 2005). Highly stressful work conditions combined with minimal oversight of caregiving quality set the stage for abuse and neglect.

■ **Preventing Elder Maltreatment.** Preventing elder maltreatment by family members is especially challenging. Victims may fear retribution, wish to protect abusers who are spouses, sons, or daughters, or feel embarrassed that they cannot control the situation. And they may be intimidated into silence or not know where to turn for help (Henderson, Buchanan, & Fisher, 2002). Once abuse is discovered, intervention involves immediate protection and provision of unmet needs for the elder and of mental health services and social support for the spouse or caregiver.

Prevention programs offer caregivers counseling, education, and respite services, such as elder day care and in-home help. Trained volunteer "buddies" who make visits to the home can combat social isolation among elders and assist them with problem solving to avoid further harm. Support groups help seniors identify abusive acts, practice appropriate responses, and form new relationships. And agencies that provide informal financial services to older adults who are unable to manage on their own, such as writing and cashing checks and holding valuables in a safe, reduce financial abuse (Rabiner, O'Keeffe, & Brown, 2004).

When elder abuse is extreme, legal action offers elders the best protection, yet it is rare. Many victims are reluctant to initiate court procedures or, because of mental impairments, cannot do so. In these instances, social service professionals must help caregivers rethink their role, even if it means that the aging person might be institutionalized. In nursing homes, improving staff selection, training, and working conditions can greatly reduce abuse and neglect.

Combating elder maltreatment also requires efforts at the level of the larger society, including public education to encourage reporting of suspected cases and improved understanding of the needs of older people. As part of this effort, elders benefit from information on how to recognize abusive treatment and where to go for help (Wilber & McNeilly, 2001). Finally, countering negative stereotypes of aging reduces maltreatment because recognizing elders' dignity, individuality, and autonomy is incompatible with acts of physical and psychological harm.

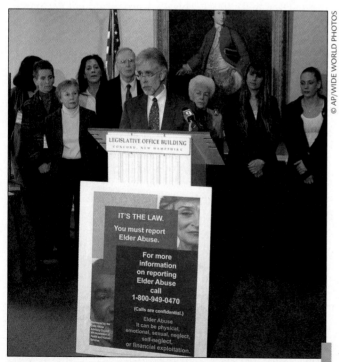

Combating elder abuse requires efforts at the level of the larger society. This news conference on elder-abuse laws helps educate the public about the extent of the problem and encourages reporting of suspected cases.

Ask Yourself

Review

Why is adjustment to late-life divorce usually more difficult for women and adjustment to widowhood more difficult for men?

Apply

At age 51, Mae lost her job and couldn't afford to pay rent. She moved in with her 78-year-old widowed mother, Beryl. Although Beryl welcomed Mae's companionship, Mae grew depressed and drank heavily. When Beryl complained about Mae's failure to look for work, Mae pushed and slapped her. Explain why this mother–daughter relationship led to elder abuse.

Connect

After reviewing sections on sibling relationships in Chapter 14 (page 472) and Chapter 16 (page 549), explain life-course trends in sibling support, shown in Figure 18.2 on page 620.

Reflect

If you have living elderly grandparents, describe your relationship with one or more of them. How have you and your grandparent contributed to each other's development?

www.ablongman.com/berk

Retirement and Leisure

In Chapter 16, we noted that the period of retirement has lengthened because of increased life expectancy and a steady decline in average age of retirement—trends occurring in all Western industrialized nations. These changes have also led to a blurring of the distinction between work and retirement. Because mandatory retirement no longer exists for most workers in Western countries, older adults have more choices about when to retire and how they spend their time. The retirement process may include a planning period, the decision itself, diverse acts of retiring, and continuous adjustment and readjustment of activities for the rest of the life course.

Some older adults retire gradually by cutting down their hours and responsibilities, taking part-time *bridge jobs* that serve as transitions between full-time career and retirement. Others leave their jobs but later return to work both to supplement limited financial resources and to introduce interest and challenge into the retirement years. Recent estimates indicate that 30 to 40 percent of North American retirees reenter the labor force in some capacity, usually part-time, within one year after retirement. With age, however, the likelihood of returning to work declines (Marshall, Clarke, & Ballantyne, 2001; Quinn, 1999).

In the following sections, we examine factors that affect the decision to retire, happiness during the retirement years, and leisure pursuits. We will see that the process of retirement and retired life reflect an increasingly diverse retired population.

The Decision to Retire

When Walt and Ruth retired, both had worked long enough to be eligible for comfortable income-replacement benefits—Walt's through the government-sponsored Social Security program, Ruth's through a private pension plan. In addition, they had planned for retirement (see Chapter 16, pages 554–555) and decided on a date for leaving the workforce. They wanted to retire early enough to pursue leisure activities while they were both in good health and could enjoy them together. In contrast, Walt's brother Dick was forced to retire as the operating costs of his bakery rose and his clientele dropped off. His wife, Goldie, kept her part-time job as a bookkeeper to help cover their living expenses.

Affordability of retirement is usually the first consideration in the decision to retire. Yet despite economic concerns, many preretirees decide to let go of a steady work life in favor of alternative, personally meaningful work or leisure activities. "I was working since I was 10 years old," said one retired automobile worker. "I wanted a rest." Exceptions to this favorable outlook are people like Dick—forced into retirement or anticipating serious financial difficulties (Warr et al., 2004).

Figure 18.3 summarizes personal and workplace factors in addition to income that influence the decision to retire. People in good health, for whom vocational life is central to self-esteem, and whose work environments are pleasant and stimulating are likely to keep on working. For these reasons, individuals in professional occupations usually retire later than those in blue-collar or clerical jobs (Moen, 1996; Moen et al., 2000). Self-employed elders also stay with their jobs longer, probably because they can flexibly adapt their working hours to changing needs. In contrast, people in declining health; who are engaged in routine, boring work; and who have compelling leisure interests often opt for retirement.

Societal factors also affect retirement decisions. When many younger, less costly workers are available to replace older workers, industries are likely to offer added incentives for people to retire, such as increments to pension plans and earlier benefits—a trend that has contributed to more retirements before age 62 in Western nations (United Nations, 2004b). But when

Retire
Adequate retirement benefits
Compelling leisure interests
Low work commitment
Declining health
Spouse retiring
Routine, boring job

Continue Working
Limited or no retirement benefits
Few leisure interests
High work commitment
Good health
Spouse working
Flexible work schedule
Pleasant, stimulating work environment

LEFT: © DAVID YOUNG-WOLFF/PHOTOEDIT
RIGHT: © LARRY DALE GORDON/GETTY IMAGES

■ **FIGURE 18.3 Personal and workplace factors that influence the decision to retire.**

concern increases about the burden on younger generations of an expanding population of retirees, eligibility for retirement benefits may be postponed to a later age.

Retirement decisions vary with gender and ethnicity. On average, women retire earlier than men, largely because family events—a husband's retirement or the need to care for an ill spouse or parent—play larger roles in their decisions (Chappell et al., 2003; Smith & Moen, 1998). Women in or near poverty, however, are an exception. Lacking financial resources to retire, many continue working into old age. This trend is especially pronounced among African-American women, who are more likely to have minimal retirement benefits and to be caring for other family members (Choi, 1994; Flippen & Tienda, 2000).

In many Western nations, generous social security benefits make retirement feasible for the economically disadvantaged and sustain the standard of living of most workers after they retire. In contrast, many U.S. retirees experience falling living standards (Hungerford, 2003). Denmark, France, Germany, Finland, and Sweden have gradual retirement programs in which older employees reduce their work hours, receive a partial pension to make up income loss, and continue to accrue pension benefits. Besides strengthening financial security, this approach introduces a transitional phase that fosters retirement planning (Reday-Mulvey, 2000). And some countries' retirement policies are sensitive to women's more interrupted work lives. In Canada, France, and Germany, for example, time devoted to child rearing is given some credit when figuring retirement benefits (Government of Canada, 1997; O'Grady-LeShane & Williamson, 1992).

In sum, individual preferences shape retirement decisions. At the same time, older adults' opportunities and limitations greatly affect their choices.

Adjustment to Retirement

Because retirement involves giving up roles that are a vital part of identity and self-esteem, it usually is assumed to be a stressful process that contributes to declines in physical and mental health. Yet consider Dick, who reacted to the closing of his bakery with anxiety and depression. His adjustment difficulties resembled those of younger people experiencing job loss (see Chapter 16, page 554). Also, recall that Dick had a cranky, disagreeable personality. In this respect, his psychological well-being after retirement was similar to what it had been before!

We must be careful not to assume a cause-and-effect relationship each time retirement is paired with an unfavorable reaction. For example, a wealth of evidence confirms that physical health problems lead elders to retire, rather than the reverse. And for most people, mental health is fairly stable from the pre- to postretirement years, with little change prompted by retirement itself (Ross & Drentea, 1998).

The widely held belief that retirement inevitably leads to adjustment problems is contradicted by countless research findings indicating that most people adapt well. Contemporary elders view retirement as a time of opportunity and development and describe themselves as active and socially involved—major determinants of retirement satisfaction (Ber-

nard & Phillipson, 2004). Still, about 30 percent mention some adjustment difficulties (Bossé et al., 1990).

Workplace factors—especially financial worries and having to give up one's job— predict stress following retirement. Pressures at work also make a difference. Moving out of a high-stress job is associated with positive adaptation to retirement, whereas leaving a pleasant, low-stress job or a highly satisfying job before one is ready is linked to slightly greater difficulties (Gray & Citera, 1996). And especially for women, a continuous work life leading to consistency between career expectations and actual achievements enhances retirement quality (Quick & Moen, 1998). Perhaps because fewer women than men have continuous careers, women whose husbands heavily influenced their retirement decision are less satisfied. In contrast, men whose wives encourage them to retire are generally happy with retirement (Smith & Moen, 2004).

Among psychological factors, a sense of personal control over life events, including deciding to retire for internally motivated reasons (to do other things), is strongly linked to retirement satisfaction (Kim & Moen, 2002c; Quick & Moen, 1998). At the same time, those who find it hard to give up the predictable schedule and social contacts of the work setting experience discomfort with their less structured way of life. Overall, however, well-educated people in high-status careers adjust more favorably, perhaps because the satisfactions derived from challenging, meaningful work readily transfer to nonwork pursuits (Kim & Moen, 2002a).

As with other major life events, social support reduces stress associated with retirement. Although size of the social network typically shrinks as relationships with co-workers decline, quality of social support (the number of people elders "can count on") remains fairly stable. In Dick's case, entering congregate housing eased a difficult postretirement period, leading to new friends and rewarding leisure pursuits, some of which he shared with Goldie. Besides friends, spouses are a vital source of support in fostering retirement adjustment. The number of leisure activities couples enjoy together predicts retirement satisfaction (Reeves & Darville, 1994).

Finally, earlier in this chapter we noted that marital happiness tends to rise after retirement. When a couple's relationship is positive, it can buffer the uncertainty of retirement. And retirement can enhance marital satisfaction by granting husband and wife more time for companionship (Kim & Moen, 2002a). Consequently, a good marriage not only promotes adjustment to retirement but also benefits from the greater freedom of the retirement years.

In line with continuity theory, people try to sustain earlier lifestyle patterns, self-esteem, and values following retirement and, in favorable economic and social contexts, usually succeed in doing so (Atchley, 2003). Return to Chapter 16, page 555, for ways adults can plan ahead to increase the chances of a favorable transition to retirement.

Leisure Activities

With retirement, most older adults have more time for leisure pursuits than ever before. After a "honeymoon period" of

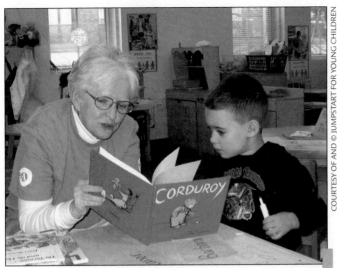

Older adults contribute vitally to their communities through volunteerism. This senior provides one-on-one intervention to a 4-year-old child through Jumpstart, a U.S. nonprofit organization devoted to helping preschoolers from low-income backgrounds acquire the skills they need to succeed in school. The elder reads to the boy and engages in other literacy activities for a total of several hundred hours over the course of a year.

COURTESY OF AND © JUMPSTART FOR YOUNG CHILDREN

trying out new activities, many find that leisure interests and skills do not develop suddenly. Instead, meaningful leisure pursuits are usually formed earlier and sustained or expanded during retirement (Mannell, 1999). For example, Walt's fondness for writing, theater, and gardening dated back to his youth. And Ruth's strong focus on her vocation of social work led her to become an avid community volunteer. The continuity of leisure activities over the lifespan suggests that the best preparation for leisure in late life is to develop rewarding interests at a young age.

Involvement in leisure activities is related to better physical and mental health and reduced mortality (Cutler & Hendricks, 2001). But simply participating does not explain this relationship. Instead, elders select leisure pursuits because they permit self-expression, new achievements, the rewards of helping others, or pleasurable social interaction. These factors account for gains in well-being (Bailey & McLaren, 2005; Guinn, 1999).

With age, the frequency and variety of leisure pursuits tend to decline, especially travel, outdoor recreation, and exercise. After age 75, mobility limitations lead leisure activities to become more sedentary and home-based (Armstrong & Morgan, 1998; Strain et al., 2002). Elders in residential communities participate more than those in ordinary homes because activities are conveniently available. But regardless of living arrangements, older adults do not spend much time in programs designed just for them. Rather, they choose activities on the basis of whether they are personally gratifying. Partly for this reason, organized activities in community senior centers attract only about 15 percent of elders who live nearby (Krout, Cutler, & Coward, 1990). Nevertheless, these structured opportunities are important for elders who have limited incomes or who lack daily companionship.

Older adults make a vital contribution to society through volunteer work—in hospitals, senior centers, schools, charitable organizations, and other community settings. Younger, better-educated, and financially secure elders with social interests are more likely to volunteer, women more often than men. But volunteer work seldom begins in late adulthood. Like other leisure pursuits, it usually originates during the individual's working years. Nevertheless, nonvolunteers are especially receptive to volunteer activities in the first few years after retiring—a prime time to recruit them into these personally rewarding and socially useful pursuits (Mutchler, Burr, & Caro, 2003). Volunteering grants elders a continuing sense of making valuable contributions to society, and many sustain high commitment through their seventies. In a survey of a large, nationally representative U.S. sample, time spent volunteering did not decline until the eighties (see Figure 18.4) (Hendricks & Cutler, 2004). Even then, it remained higher than at any other time of life! In accord with socioemotional selectivity theory, very old adults narrowed their volunteering to fewer roles, concentrating on one or two that meant the most to them.

Finally, when Walt and Ruth got together with Dick and Goldie, the two couples often discussed politics. Older adults report greater awareness of and interest in public affairs and vote at a higher rate than any other age group. Even in late old age, their political knowledge shows no sign of decline. After retiring, elders have more time to keep abreast of current events through reading and watching TV. They also have a

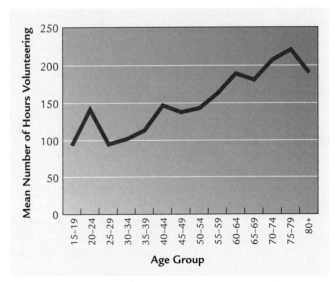

■ FIGURE 18.4 Age-related change in number of hours spent volunteering during the past year. A nationally representative sample of nearly 29,000 U.S. adolescents and adults reported on the amount of time they devoted to each of their volunteer activities. Time devoted to volunteering increased sharply in the early twenties, dipped in the late twenties and thirties as young people focused on establishing families and vocations, then rose steadily, peaking in the seventies. Even in the eighties, when volunteering declined slightly, it remained higher than at any other time of life. (From J. Hendricks and S. J. Cutler, 2004, "Volunteerism and Socioemotional Selectivity in Later Life," *Journal of Gerontology, 59B*, p. S255. Copyright © 2004 by the Gerontological Society of America. Adapted by permission.)

major stake in political debates over policies central to their welfare. But elders' political concerns are far broader than those that serve their own age group, and their voting behavior is not driven by self-interest (Binstock & Quadagno, 2001). Rather, their political involvement may stem from a deep desire for a safer, more secure world for future generations.

Successful Aging

Walt, Ruth, Dick, Goldie, and Ida, and the research findings they illustrate, reveal great diversity in development during the final decades of life. Walt and Ruth fit contemporary experts' view of **successful aging,** in which gains are maximized and losses minimized. Both remained in reasonably good health until advanced old age, coped well with negative life changes, and enjoyed a happy intimate partnership, other close relationships, and daily lives filled with gratifying activities. Ida, too, was a successful ager until the onset of Alzheimer's symptoms overwhelmed her ability to manage life's challenges. As a single adult, she built a rich social network that sustained her into old age, despite the hardship of having spent many years caring for her ailing mother. In contrast, Dick and Goldie reacted with despondency to physical aging and other losses (such as Dick's forced retirement). And Dick's angry outbursts restricted their social contacts, although the couple's move to congregate housing eventually led to an improved social life.

Successful agers are people for whom growth, vitality, and striving limit and, at times, overcome physical, cognitive, and social declines. Researchers want to know more about their characteristics and development so they can help more seniors age well. Yet theorists disagree on the precise ingredients of a satisfying old age. Some focus on easily measurable outcomes, such as excellent cardiovascular functioning, absence of disability, superior cognitive performance, and creative achievements. But this view has been heavily criticized (Baltes & Carstensen, 1996). Not everyone can become an outstanding athlete, an innovative scientist, or a talented artist. And many older adults do not want to keep on accomplishing and producing—the main markers of success in Western nations. Each of us is limited by our genetic potential as it combines with a lifetime of environments we encounter and select for ourselves. Furthermore, outcomes valued in one culture may not be valued in others.

Recent views of successful aging have turned away from specific achievements toward processes people use to reach personally valued goals (Freund & Baltes, 1998; Lund, 1998; Kahana et al., 2005). Instead of identifying one set of standards as "successful," this perspective focuses on how people minimize losses while maximizing gains. In recent research on three samples of adults followed over the lifespan, George Vaillant looked at how various life-course factors contributed to late-life physical and psychological well-being. His findings revealed that factors people could control to some degree (such as health habits, coping strategies, marital stability, and years of education) far outweighed uncontrollable factors (parental SES, family warmth in childhood, early physical health, and longevity of family members) in predicting a happy, active old age (Vaillant & Mukamal, 2001).

Consider the following description of one participant, who in childhood had experienced low SES, parental discord, a depressed mother, and seven siblings crowded into a tenement apartment. Despite these early perils, he became happily married and, through the GI bill, earned an accounting degree. At 70, he was aging well:

> Anthony Pirelli may have been *ill* considering his heart attack and open-heart surgery, but he did not feel *sick*. He was physically active as ever, and he continued to play tennis. Asked what he missed about his work, he exulted, "I'm so busy doing other things that I don't have time to miss work. . . . Life is not boring for me." He did not smoke or abuse alcohol; he loved his wife; he used mature [coping strategies]; he obtained 14 years of education; he watched his waistline; and he exercised regularly. (Adapted from Vaillant, 2002, pp. 12, 305)

Vaillant concluded, "The past often predicts but never determines our old age" (p. 12). Successful aging is an expression of remarkable resilience during this final phase of the lifespan.

In this and the previous chapter, we have considered the many ways that older adults realize their goals. Take a moment to look back and review the most important ones:

- Optimism and sense of self-efficacy in improving health and physical functioning (pages 573–574)

- Selective optimization with compensation to make the most of limited physical energies and cognitive resources (pages 587 and 607)

- Strengthening of self-concept, which promotes self-acceptance and pursuit of hoped-for possible selves (page 604)

- Enhanced emotional understanding and emotional self-regulation, which support meaningful, rewarding social ties (page 601)

- Acceptance of change, which fosters life satisfaction (page 604)

- A mature sense of spirituality and faith, permitting anticipation of death with calmness and composure (pages 604–606)

- Personal control over domains of dependency and independence (pages 606–607, 608–609)

- High-quality relationships, which offer social support and pleasurable companionship (pages 608–609)

Successful aging is facilitated by societal contexts that permit elders to manage life changes effectively. Older adults need well-funded social security plans, good health care, safe housing, and diverse social services. (See, for example, the description of the U.S. Area Agencies on Aging in Chapter 2, page 69.)

Yet because of inadequate funding and difficulties reaching rural communities, many older adults' needs remain unmet. Isolated elders with little education may not know how to access available assistance. Furthermore, the U.S. Medicare system of sharing health care costs with senior citizens strains their financial resources. And in the United States and Canada, housing that adjusts to changes in elders' capacities, permitting them to age in familiar surroundings without disruptive and disorienting moves, is available only to the economically well-off.

Besides improving policies that meet older adults' basic needs, new future-oriented approaches must prepare for increased aging of the population. More emphasis on lifelong learning for workers of all ages would help people maintain and even increase skills as they grow older. Also, reforms that prepare for expected growth in the number of frail elders are vital, including affordable help for family caregivers, adapted housing, and sensitive nursing home care.

All these changes involve recognizing, supporting, and enhancing the contributions that senior citizens make to society—both the elders of today and those of tomorrow. A nation that takes care of its senior citizens and grants them a multitude of opportunities for personal growth maximizes the chances that each of us, when our time comes to be old, will age successfully.

Ask Yourself

Review

What psychological and contextual factors predict favorable adjustment to retirement?

Apply

Nate, happily married to Gladys, adjusted well to retirement. He also found that his marriage became even happier. How can a good marriage ease the transition to retirement? How can retirement enhance marital satisfaction?

Connect

Leisure interests and skills usually form early and persist over the lifespan. Referring back to earlier parts of this book, cite examples of childhood, adolescent, and early adulthood experiences that are likely to foster meaningful leisure pursuits after retirement.

Reflect

Think of someone you know who is aging successfully. What personal qualities led you to select that person?

www.ablongman.com/berk

Summary

Erikson's Theory: Ego Integrity versus Despair

According to Erikson, how does personality change in late adulthood?

- The final psychological conflict of Erikson's theory, **ego integrity versus despair,** involves coming to terms with one's life. Adults who arrive at a sense of integrity feel whole and satisfied with their achievements. Despair occurs when elders feel they have made many wrong decisions, yet time is too short for change.

Other Theories of Psychosocial Development in Late Adulthood

Describe Peck's, Joan Erikson's, and Labouvie-Vief's views of psychosocial development in late adulthood, and discuss the functions of reminiscence and life review in older adults' lives.

- According to Robert Peck, the conflict of ego integrity versus despair comprises three distinct tasks: (1) ego differentiation versus work-role preoccupation, (2) body transcendence versus body preoccupation, and

(3) ego transcendence versus ego preoccupation. The last two increase in very old age. Joan Erikson believes these attainments represent an additional psychosocial stage, which she calls **gerotransccendence,** evident in inner calm and quiet reflection.

- Gisella Labouvie-Vief points out that older adults improve in **affect optimization**—the ability to maximize positive emotion and dampen negative emotion. Older adults are also more in touch with their feelings, which contributes to their expertise in processing emotional information and regulating negative affect.

- **Reminiscence**—telling stories about people and events from one's past—can be positive and adaptive for older people. In a special form called **life review,** elders reflect on past experiences to achieve greater self-understanding. When used to strengthen family and friendship ties, reminiscence serves social goals. And at times, elders use reminiscence to identify effective problem-solving strategies, teach younger people about the past, and cope with life transitions.

Stability and Change in Self-Concept and Personality

Cite stable and changing aspects of self-concept and personality in late adulthood.

- The "big five" personality traits show continuing stability from mid- to late life. With the accumulation of a lifetime of self-knowledge, elders have more secure and complex self-concepts than younger adults. Those who continue to strive toward hoped-for possible selves improve in life satisfaction.

- Shifts in three personality traits occur in late adulthood: Agreeableness and acceptance of change tend to rise, whereas sociability dips slightly.

Discuss spirituality and religiosity in late adulthood, and trace the development of faith.

- Although organized religious participation declines, informal religious activities remain common in late adulthood. North Americans generally become more religious or spiritual as they age, but this trend is not universal: Some elders decline in religiosity.

- According to James Fowler's stage theory, faith and spirituality may advance to a higher level in late adulthood, away from prescribed beliefs toward a more reflective approach that accepts uncertainty.

- Religious involvement is especially high among low-SES ethnic minority elders and women and is linked to improved physical and psychological well-being and longer survival.

Individual Differences in Psychological Well-Being

Discuss individual differences in psychological well-being as older adults respond to increased dependency, declining health, and negative life changes.

- Friends, family members, and caregivers often promote excessive dependency in elders. In patterns of behavior called the **dependency–support script** and the **independence–ignore script,** older adults' dependency behaviors are attended to immediately while their independent behaviors are ignored. But dependency can be adaptive if it permits older people to conserve their strength for highly valued activities.

- Health is a powerful predictor of psychological well-being in late adulthood. The relationship between physical and mental health problems can become a vicious cycle, each intensifying the other. Physical illness resulting in disability often leads to depression, which can be lethal. Older adults have the highest suicide rate of all age groups.

- Although elders are at risk for a variety of negative life changes, these events actually evoke less stress and depression in older than in younger adults. Many seniors have learned to cope with hard times.

Describe the role of social support and social interaction in promoting physical health and psychological well-being in late adulthood.

- In late adulthood, social support from family, friends, and paid helpers reduces stress, thereby promoting physical health and psychological well-being. At the same time, older adults value independence and do not want a great deal of support from people close to them unless they can reciprocate.

- An extraverted personality, which fosters interaction with others, is linked to high morale in old age. However, high-quality relationships have the greatest impact on mental health.

- Help that is not wanted or needed undermines older adults' mental health. This explains why, in elders with disabilities, perceived social support rather than sheer amount of assistance is associated with a positive outlook.

A Changing Social World

Describe social theories of aging, including disengagement theory, activity theory, continuity theory, and socioemotional selectivity theory.

- **Disengagement theory** holds that social interaction declines because of mutual withdrawal between elders and society in anticipation of death. However, not everyone disengages, and elders' retreat from interaction is more complex than this theory implies.

- According to **activity theory,** social barriers to engagement, not the desires of elders, cause declining rates of interaction. Yet offering older adults opportunities for social contact does not guarantee greater social activity.

- **Continuity theory** proposes that most aging adults strive to maintain consistency between their past and anticipated future. By using familiar skills and engaging in familiar activities with familiar people, elders minimize stress and disruptiveness by integrating late-life changes into a coherent, consistent life path.

- **Socioemotional selectivity theory** states that social networks become more selective as we age. Older adults emphasize the emotion-regulating function of interaction by limiting their contacts to familiar partners with whom they have developed pleasurable, rewarding relationships.

How do communities, neighborhoods, and housing arrangements affect elders' social lives and adjustment?

- Elders residing in suburbs are better off in terms of income and health, but those in inner cities have easier access to social services. Elders in small towns and rural areas are least well-off in these ways. Older adults living in neighborhoods with many senior citizens and in small and midsized communities report greater life satisfaction.

- For elders living alone and in inner-city areas, fear of crime may be greater than worries about income, health, and housing.

It restricts their activities and seriously undermines their morale.

- The housing arrangement that offers seniors the greatest personal control is their own home. But for those with health and mobility problems, independent living poses risks. Many older adults who live alone, especially widowed women, are poverty-stricken and suffer from unmet needs.

- Most residential communities for senior citizens are privately developed retirement villages with adjoining recreational facilities. Among assisted-living arrangements, **congregate housing** offers a variety of support services, including meals in a common dining room. **Life care communities** offer a range of options, from independent or congregate housing to full nursing home care. A sense of community in planned housing enhances life satisfaction.

- The small number of North Americans who live in nursing homes experience extreme restriction of autonomy. Typically, social interaction among residents is low. Designing homelike nursing homes could enhance elders' sense of control over their social experiences.

Relationships in Late Adulthood

Describe changes in social relationships in late adulthood, including marriage, divorce, remarriage, and widowhood, and discuss never-married, childless older adults.

- As we move through life, a **social convoy,** or cluster of family members and friends, provides safety and support. With age, some bonds become closer, others more distant, while still others are added or drift away. To preserve personal continuity and security in the face of life changes, elders do their best to sustain social networks of family members and friends.

- Marital satisfaction rises from middle to late adulthood as perceptions of fairness in the relationship increase, couples engage in joint leisure activities, and communication becomes more positive. Most gay and lesbian elders also report happy, highly fulfilling relationships.

- When divorce occurs, stress is higher for older than for younger adults. Because of greater financial hardship and less likelihood of remarrying, women suffer more than men from late-life divorce.

- Although remarriage rates are low in late adulthood, those who do remarry enter into more stable relationships. Increasingly, older adults are choosing cohabitation instead of remarriage, for both financial and personal reasons.

- Wide variation exists in adaptation to widowhood, with age, social support, and personality making a difference. Elders fare better than younger individuals. Efforts to maintain social ties, an outgoing personality, high self-esteem, and a sense of self-efficacy in handling tasks of daily living foster adjustment. Women—especially those who developed rewarding roles outside the marital relationship—fare better than men.

- Most older adults who remain unmarried and childless throughout their lives develop alternative meaningful relationships. Childless men without marital partners are more likely to feel lonely than women. Nevertheless, unmarried, childless elders worry about who will care for them in old age if help is needed.

How do sibling relationships and friendships change in late life?

- In late adulthood, social support from siblings increases, especially when siblings live nearby. Bonds with sisters are closer than bonds with brothers. Because siblings share a long and unique history, joint reminiscing increases in late adulthood, contributing to a sense of family continuity and harmony.

- Friendships serve a variety of functions in late adulthood: intimacy and companionship, acceptance, a link to the larger community, and protection from the psychological consequences of loss. Fewer older than younger people have other-sex friendships, but some do have these ties. Women are more likely than men to have both intimate friends and **secondary friends**—people with whom they spend time occasionally.

Describe older adults' relationships with adult children, adult grandchildren, and great-grandchildren.

- Elders are often in touch with their adult children, who more often provide emotional support than direct assistance to their aging parents. Moderate support, with opportuni-

ties to reciprocate, is psychologically beneficial to elders. Adult daughters are primary agents of elderly parents' family contacts.

- Seniors with adult grandchildren and great-grandchildren benefit from a wider network of support. Most often, grandparents

©JAMES L. AMOS/PHOTO RESEARCHERS INC.

expect and receive affection rather than practical help from their grandchildren. Grandparent–grandchild contact declines over time, but grandparents' affection for their adult grandchildren remains high.

Discuss elder maltreatment, including risk factors and strategies for prevention.

- Some elders suffer maltreatment at the hands of family members, friends, or professional caregivers. Risk factors include a dependent perpetrator–victim relationship, perpetrator psychological disturbance and stress, a history of family violence, and overcrowded nursing homes with staff shortages and turnover. In recent years, abandonment of elders with severe disabilities by family caregivers has increased.

- Elder-abuse prevention programs offer caregivers counseling, education, and respite services. Elders benefit from trained volunteers and support groups that help them avoid future harm. Societal efforts, including public education to encourage reporting of suspected cases and improved understanding of the needs of older people, are also vital.

Retirement and Leisure

Discuss the decision to retire, adjustment to retirement, and involvement in leisure activities.

- The decision to retire depends on affordability, health status, opportunities to pursue meaningful activities, societal factors such as early retirement benefits, gender, and ethnicity. On average, women retire earlier than men because family events play a larger role in their decisions. However, those near poverty may need to continue working, a trend especially pronounced among African-American women.

- Western nations with generous social security benefits make retirement feasible for the economically disadvantaged and sustain the standard of living of most elders. In contrast, many retired Americans experience falling living standards.

- Factors affecting adjustment to retirement include health status, financial stability, a sense of personal control over life events (including the retirement decision), characteristics of the workplace, satisfactions derived from work, social support, and marital happiness.

- Engaging in meaningful and pleasurable leisure activities is related to physical and mental health and to reduced mortality. The best way to prepare for leisure experiences in late life is to develop rewarding interests at a young age.

Successful Aging

Discuss the meaning of successful aging.

- Elders who experience **successful aging** have developed many ways to minimize losses and maximize gains. Social contexts that permit older adults to manage life changes effectively foster successful aging. These include well-funded social security plans, good health care, safe housing that adjusts to changes in elders' capacities, social services, and opportunities for lifelong learning. Reforms are also needed to ensure the well-being of frail elders through affordable in-home help, adapted housing, and sensitive nursing home care.

Important Terms and Concepts

activity theory (p. 611)
affect optimization (p. 601)
congregate housing (p. 615)
continuity theory (p. 611)
dependency–support script (p. 606)
disengagement theory (p. 610)
ego integrity versus despair (p. 600)
gerotranscendence (p. 601)
independence–ignore script (p. 606)
life care communities (p. 615)
life review (p. 601)
reminiscence (p. 601)
secondary friends (p. 621)
social convoy (p. 616)
socioemotional selectivity theory (p. 611)
successful aging (p. 628)

Milestones

Development in Late Adulthood

Age	Physical	Cognitive	Emotional/Social

65–80 YEARS

Physical

- Neurons die at a faster rate, but the brain compensates through growth of new synapses and, to a lesser extent, through generating new neurons (565)

- Performance of autonomic nervous system declines, impairing adaptation to hot and cold weather (565)

- Declines in vision continue, with increased sensitivity to glare and impaired color discrimination, dark adaptation, depth perception, and visual acuity (566–567)

- Declines in hearing continue throughout the frequency range (568)

- Taste and odor sensitivity may decline (568)

- Touch sensitivity declines on the hands, particularly the fingertips, less so on the arms (568–569)

- Declines in cardiovascular and respiratory functioning lead to greater physical stress during exercise (569)

- Aging of the immune system increases risk for a variety of illnesses (569)

Cognitive

- Processing speed continues to decline; crystallized abilities are largely sustained (587–588)

- Amount of information that can be retained in working memory diminishes further; memory problems are greatest on tasks requiring deliberate processing and associative memory (587–588)

- Modest forgetting of remote memories occurs (589)

- Use of external aids for prospective memory increases (589–590)

- Retrieving words from long-term memory and planning what to say and how to say it become more difficult (590)

- Information is more likely to be remembered in terms of gist than details (590)

- Traditional problem solving declines; everyday problem solving remains adaptive (591)

- May hold an important position of leadership in society, such as chief executive officer, religious leader, or Supreme Court justice (591)

Emotional/Social

- Comes to terms with life, developing ego integrity (600)

- Cognitive-affective complexity declines (451, 601)

- Affect optimization, the ability to maximize positive emotion, increases (601)

- May engage in reminiscence and life review (601–603)

- Self-concept strengthens, becoming more secure and complex (604)

- Agreeableness and acceptance of change increase (604)

- Faith and spirituality may advance to a higher level (604–606)

- Size of social network and amount of social interaction decline (610–612)

- Selects social partners on the basis of emotion, pursuing pleasant relationships and avoiding unpleasant ones (611–612)

Age	Physical	Cognitive	Emotional/Social
65–80 YEARS (continued)	• Sleep difficulties increase, especially in men (570) • Graying and thinning of the hair continue; the skin wrinkles further and becomes more transparent as it loses its fatty layer of support (570–571) • Height and weight decline because of loss of lean body mass (570–571) • Loss of bone mass leads to rising rates of osteoporosis (570–571) • Intensity of sexual response and sexual activity decline, although most healthy married couples report regular sexual enjoyment (576)	• May develop wisdom (591–592) • Can improve a wide range of cognitive skills through training (593) 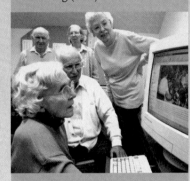	• Marital satisfaction increases (616–617) • May be widowed (618–619) • Sibling closeness and support may increase (620) • Number of friends generally declines (620–621) • May become a great-grandparent (622–623) • May retire (625–628) • More likely to be knowledgeable about politics and to vote (627–628)
80 YEARS AND OLDER	• Physical changes listed on the previous page and above continue • Mobility diminishes because of loss of muscle and bone strength and of joint flexibility (571) 	• Cognitive changes listed on the previous page and above continue • Fluid abilities decline further; crystallized abilities drop as well, though only modestly (587)	• Emotional and social changes listed on the previous page and above continue • May develop gerotranscendence, a cosmic perspective directed beyond the self (600–601) • Relationships with adult children become more important (621) • Frequency and variety of leisure activities decline (626–628)

Note: Numbers in parentheses indicate the page or pages on which each milestone is discussed.

*A*ll cultures have special rituals for celebrating the end of life and helping the bereaved cope with profound loss. Here, mourners in Pakistan toss rose petals—a symbol of mourning—on the coffin as it passes.

Death, Dying, and Bereavement

A s every life is unique, so each death is unique. The final forces of the human spirit separate themselves from the body in manifold ways.

My mother Sofie's death was the culmination of a five-year battle against cancer. In her last months, the disease invaded organs through-out her body, attacking the lungs in its final fury. She withered slowly, with the mixed blessing of time to prepare against certain knowledge that death was just around the cor-ner. My father, Philip, lived another 18 years. At age 80, he was outwardly healthy, active, and about to depart

© PEARSON EDUCATION

on a long-awaited vacation when a heart attack snuffed out his life suddenly, without time for last words or deathbed reconciliations.

As I set to work on this chapter, my 65-year-old neighbor Nicholas gambled for a higher quality of life. To be eligible for a kidney trans-plant, he elected bypass surgery to strengthen his heart. Doctors warned that his body might not withstand the operation. But Nicholas knew that without taking a chance, he would live only a few years, in debilitated condition. Shortly after the surgery, infection set in, travel-ing throughout his system and so weakening him that only extreme measures—a respirator to sustain breathing and powerful drugs to elevate his fading blood pressure—could keep him alive.

"Come on, Dad, you can do it," encouraged Nicholas's daughter Sasha, standing by his bedside and stroking his hand. But Nicholas could not. After two months in intensive care, he experienced brain seizures and slipped into a coma. Three doctors met with his wife, Giselle, to tell her there was no hope. She asked them to disconnect the respirator, and within half an hour Nicholas drifted away.

Death is essential for the survival of our species. We die so that our own children and the children of others may live. When it comes to this fate, nature treats humankind, with all its unique capabilities, just as it treats every other living creature (Nuland, 1993). As hard as it is to accept the reality that we too will die, our greatest solace lies in the knowledge that death is part of ongoing life.

In this chapter, we address the culmination of lifespan development. Over the past century, technology has provided us with so many means to keep death at bay that many people regard it as a forbidden topic. But pressing social and economic dilemmas that are an outgrowth of the dramatic increase in life expectancy are forcing us to attend to life's end—its quality, its timing, and ways to help people adjust to their own and others' final leave taking.

Our discussion addresses the physical changes of dying; understanding of and attitudes toward death in childhood, adolescence, and adulthood; the thoughts and feelings of people as they stand face to face with death; hopelessly ill patients' right to die; and coping with the death of a loved one. The experiences of Sofie, Philip, Nicholas, their families, and others illustrate how each person's life history joins with social and cultural contexts to shape death and dying, lending great diversity to this universal experience.

How We Die

Our vast literature on death is largely aimed at helping people cope with the emotional trauma of dying and its aftermath. Few people in industrialized countries are aware of the physical aspects of death because opportunities to witness it are less available than in previous generations. Today, most people in the developed world die in hospitals, where doctors and nurses, not loved ones, typically attend their last moments. Nevertheless, many want to know how we die, either to anticipate their own end or grasp what is happening to a dying loved one.

Physical Changes

My father's fatal heart attack came suddenly during the night. On being told the news, I longed for reassurance that his death had been swift and without suffering.

When asked how they would like to die, most people say they want "death with dignity"—either a quick, agony-free end during sleep or a clear-minded final few moments in which they can say farewell and review their lives. In reality, death is the culmination of a straightforward biological process. For about 20 percent of people, it is gentle—especially when narcotic drugs ease pain and mask the destructive events taking place (Nuland, 1993). But most of the time it is not.

Recall that unintentional injuries are the leading cause of death in childhood and adolescence, cardiovascular disease and cancer in adulthood. Of the one-quarter of people in industrialized nations who die suddenly, within a few hours of experiencing symptoms, 80 to 90 percent are victims of heart attacks (Winslow, Mehta, & Fuster, 2005). My yearning for a painless death for my father was probably not fulfilled. Undoubtedly he felt the sharp, crushing sensation of a heart deprived of oxygen. As his heart twitched uncontrollably (called *fibrillation*) or stopped entirely, blood circulation slowed and ceased, and he was thrust into unconsciousness. A brain starved of oxygen for more than 2 to 4 minutes is irreversibly damaged—an outcome indicated by the pupils of the eyes becoming unresponsive to light and widening into large, black circles. Other oxygen-deprived organs stop functioning as well.

Death is long and drawn out for three-fourths of people—many more than in times past, as a result of life-saving medical technology (Benoliel & Degner, 1995). They succumb in different ways. Of those with heart disease, most have congestive heart failure, the cause of Nicholas's death. His scarred heart could no longer contract with the force needed to deliver enough oxygen to his tissues. As it tried harder, its muscle weakened further. Without sufficient blood pressure, fluid backed up in Nicholas's lungs. This hampered his breathing and created ideal conditions for inhaled bacteria to multiply, enter the bloodstream, and run rampant in his system, leading many organs to fail.

Cancer also chooses diverse paths to inflict its damage. When it *metastasizes*, bits of tumor travel through the bloodstream and implant and grow in vital organs, disrupting their functioning. Medication made my mother's final days as comfortable as possible, granting a relatively easy death. But the preceding weeks involved physical suffering, including impaired breathing and digestion and turning and twisting to find a comfortable position in bed.

In the days or hours before death, activity declines; the person moves and communicates less and shows little interest in food, water, and surroundings. At the same time, body temperature, blood pressure, and circulation to the limbs fall, so the hands and feet feel cool and skin color changes to a duller, grayish hue (Hospice Foundation of America, 2005). When the transition from life to death is imminent, the person moves through three phases:

1. The **agonal phase.** The Greek word *agon* means "struggle." Here *agonal* refers to gasps and muscle spasms during the first moments in which the body can no longer sustain life.

2. **Clinical death.** A short interval follows in which heartbeat, circulation, breathing, and brain functioning stop but resuscitation is still possible.

3. **Mortality.** The individual passes into permanent death. Within a few hours, the newly lifeless being appears shrunken, not at all like the person he or she was when alive.

Defining Death

Think about what we have said so far, and you will see that death is not an event that happens at a single point in time. Rather, it is a process in which organs stop functioning in a

A Buddhist monk in Japan enacts a purification ritual. Buddhist beliefs about death stress ancestor worship and time for the spirit to leave the corpse. These beliefs may explain the Japanese discomfort with organ donation.

sequence that varies from person to person. Because the dividing line between life and death is fuzzy, societies need a definition of death to help doctors decide when life-saving measures should be terminated, to signal survivors that they must begin to grieve their loss and reorganize their lives, and to establish when donated organs can be removed.

Several decades ago, loss of heartbeat and respiration signified death. But these criteria are no longer adequate, since resuscitation techniques frequently permit vital signs to be restored. Today, **brain death,** irreversible cessation of all activity in the brain and the brain stem (which controls reflexes), is used in most industrialized nations.

But not all countries accept this standard. In Japan, for example, doctors rely on traditional criteria (absence of heartbeat and respiration) that fit with Japanese laypeople's views. This approach stands in the way of a national organ transplant program, since few organs can be salvaged from bodies without artificially maintaining vital signs. Buddhist, Confucian, and Shinto beliefs about death, which stress ancestor worship and time for the spirit to leave the corpse, may be partly responsible for Japan's discomfort with brain death and organ donation. Marring the body to harvest organs violates respect for the deceased. Today, Japanese law allows people who want to be organ donors to choose the standard of brain death, as long as their families do not object (Morioka, 2001). Otherwise, they are considered to be alive until the heart stops beating.

Furthermore, in a great many cases the brain death standard does not solve the dilemma of when to halt treatment. Consider Nicholas, who, though not brain dead, had entered a **persistent vegetative state,** in which the cerebral cortex no longer registered electrical activity but the brain stem remained active. Doctors were certain they could not restore consciousness or body movement. Because thousands of North Americans are in a persistent vegetative state, with health care costs totaling many millions of dollars annually,

some experts believe that absence of activity in the cerebral cortex should be sufficient to declare a person dead. But others point to a few cases in which patients who had been vegetative for months regained cortical responsiveness and consciousness, though usually with very limited functioning (Jennett, 2002; Kotchoubey et al., 2005). In still other instances of illness, a fully conscious but suffering person refuses life-saving measures—an issue we will consider later when we take up the right to die.

Death with Dignity

We have seen that nature rarely delivers the idealized, easy end most people want, nor can medical science guarantee it. Therefore, the greatest dignity in death is in the integrity of the life that precedes it—an integrity we can foster by the way we communicate with and care for the dying person.

First, we can assure the majority of dying people, who succumb gradually, that we will support them through their physical and psychological distress. We can do everything possible to provide the utmost in humane and compassionate care. And we can treat them with esteem and respect—for example, by taking interest in those aspects of their lives that they most value and by addressing their greatest concerns (Chochinov, 2002).

Second, we can be candid about death's certainty. Unless people are aware that they are dying and understand (as far as possible) the likely circumstances of their death, they cannot plan for end-of-life care and decision making and share the sentiments that bring closure to relationships they hold most dear. Because Sofie knew how and when her death would probably take place, she chose a time when she, Philip, and her children could express what their lives had meant to one another.

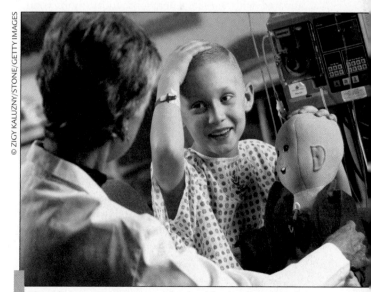

Providing compassionate care for the dying involves taking interest in aspects of their lives that they most value and addressing their greatest concerns. Here a doctor uses a doll to help a young cancer patient understand his illness.

Among those precious bedside exchanges was Sofie's memorable last wish that Philip remarry after her death so he would not live out his final years alone. Openness about impending death granted Sofie a final generative act, helped her let go of the person closest to her, and offered comfort as she faced death.

Finally, doctors and nurses can help dying people learn enough about their condition to make reasoned choices about whether to fight on or say no to further treatment. An understanding of how the normal body works simplifies comprehension of how disease affects it—education that can begin as early as the childhood years.

In sum, although the conditions of illness often do not permit a graceful, serene death, we can ensure the most dignified exit possible by offering the dying person care, affection, and companionship; the truth about diagnosis; and the maximum personal control over this final phase of life (American Hospice Foundation, 2005). These are essential ingredients of a "good death," and we will revisit them throughout this chapter.

Understanding of and Attitudes Toward Death

A century ago, when most deaths occurred at home, people of all ages, including children, helped with care of the dying family member and were present at the moment of death. They saw their loved one buried on family property or in the local cemetery, where the grave could be visited regularly. Because infant and childhood mortality rates were high, all people were likely to know someone their own age, or even younger, who had died. And it was common for children to experience the death of a parent.

Compared with earlier generations, today more young people reach adulthood without having experienced the death of someone they know well. When a death does occur, professionals in hospitals and funeral homes take care of most tasks that involve confronting it directly (Morgan & Laungani, 2005).

This distance from death undoubtedly contributes to a sense of uneasiness about it. Despite frequent images of death in television shows, movies, and news reports of accidents, murders, wars, and natural disasters, we live in a death-denying culture. Adults are often reluctant to talk about death with children and adolescents. And a variety of substitute expressions—"passing away," "going out," "departing"—permit us to avoid acknowledging it candidly. In the following sections, we examine the development of conceptions of and attitudes toward death, along with ways to foster increased understanding and acceptance.

Childhood

Five-year-old Miriam arrived at our university laboratory preschool the day after her dog Pepper died. Instead of joining the other children, she stayed close to her teacher, Leslie, who noticed Miriam's discomfort. "What's wrong?" Leslie asked.

"Daddy said Pepper was so sick the vet had to put him to sleep." For a moment, Miriam looked hopeful. "When I get home, Pepper might wake up."

Leslie answered directly, "No, Pepper won't get up again. He's not asleep. He's dead, and that means he can't sleep, eat, run, or play anymore."

Miriam wandered off but later returned to Leslie and, tears streaming from her eyes, confessed, "I chased Pepper too hard."

Leslie put her arm around Miriam. "Pepper didn't die because you chased him. He was very old and sick," she explained.

Over the next few days, Miriam asked many questions: "When I go to sleep, will I die?" "Can a tummy ache make you die?" "Does Pepper feel better now?" "Will Mommy and Daddy die?"

■ **Development of the Death Concept.** An understanding of death is based on five ideas:

1. *Permanence.* Once a living thing dies, it cannot be brought back to life.

2. *Inevitability.* All living things eventually die.

3. *Cessation.* All living functions, including movement, body processes, thought, and feeling, cease at death.

4. *Applicability.* Death applies only to living things.

5. *Causation.* Death is caused by a breakdown of bodily functioning.

To understand death, children must acquire some basic notions of biology—that animals and plants contain body parts (brain, heart, stomach) essential for maintaining life. They must also break down their global category of "not alive" into dead, inanimate, unreal, and nonexistent (Carey, 1999). Until children grasp these ideas, they interpret death in terms of familiar experiences—as a change in behavior. Consequently, they may believe that they caused a relative's or pet's death; that having a stomachache can cause someone to die; that dead people eat, go to the bathroom, see, and think; and that death is like sleep (Slaughter, Jaakkola, & Carey, 1999; Slaughter & Lyons, 2003).

Permanence is the first understood component of the death concept. Preschoolers accept this fact quickly, perhaps because they have seen it in other situations—for example, in the dead butterflies and beetles they pick up and inspect while playing outside. Appreciation of *inevitability* soon follows. At first, children think that certain people do not die—themselves, people like themselves (other children), and people with whom they have close emotional ties. *Cessation, applicability,* and *causation* are more challenging ideas (Kenyon, 2001). Preschoolers and kindergartners realize that the dead lose the capacity for body processes and perception. But the majority of 10- to 12-year-olds continue to say that the dead are able to think and feel (Bering & Bjorklund, 2004). Many adults, too, believe in some form of personal consciousness after death.

Children who have experienced death generally have a more accurate conception of death. This child grieves over the death of a family member in war-torn Iraq.

dren may take these literally and react with confusion. For example, after a parent told her 5-year-old daughter, "Grandpa went on a long trip," the child wondered, "Why didn't he take me?" (Wolfelt, 1997). Sometimes children ask difficult questions, such as "Will I die? Will you die?" Parents can be truthful as well as comforting by taking advantage of the child's sense of time. "Not for many, many years," they can say. "First I'm going to enjoy you as a grown-up and be a grandparent."

Another way to promote an accurate appreciation of death is to teach young children about the biology of the human body. Three- to 5-year-olds given lessons in the role of the heart, brain, lungs, stomach, and other organs in sustaining life have more advanced death concepts (Slaughter & Lyons, 2003).

Adult–child discussions should also be culturally sensitive. Rather than presenting scientific evidence as counteracting religious beliefs, parents and teachers can help children blend the two sources of knowledge. As children get older, they often combine their appreciation of the death concept with religious and philosophical views, which offer solace in times of bereavement (Cuddy-Casey & Orvaschel, 1997). As we will see later, open, honest discussions with children not only contribute to a realistic understanding of death but also facilitate grieving after a child has experienced a loss.

Adolescence

Recall that teenagers have difficulty integrating logical insights with the realities of everyday life. In this sense, their understanding of death is not yet fully mature.

■ **The Gap Between Logic and Reality.** Teenagers' difficulty applying what they know about death is evident in both their reasoning and their behavior. Although they can explain the permanence and cessation aspects of death, they are attracted to alternatives. For example, teenagers often describe death as an enduring abstract state—"darkness," "eternal light," "transition," or "nothingness" (Brent et al., 1996). They also formulate personal theories about life after death. Besides images of heaven and hell influenced by their religious background, they speculate about reincarnation, transmigration of souls, and spiritual survival on earth or at another level (Noppe & Noppe, 1997; Yang & Chen, 2002).

Although mortality in adolescence is low compared with that in infancy and adulthood, teenage deaths are typically sudden and human-induced; unintentional injuries, homicide, and suicide are leading causes. Adolescents are clearly aware that death happens to everyone and can occur at any time. But this does not make them more safety-conscious. Rather, their high-risk activities suggest that they do not take death personally. In one study, the lower adolescent boys' consciousness of personal mortality, the more they engaged in risky behavior (Word, 1996).

What explains teenagers' difficulty integrating logic with reality in the domain of death? First, adolescence is a period of rapid growth and onset of reproductive capacity—attainments that are the opposite of death! Second, recall the adolescent

■ **Individual and Cultural Variations.** Although children typically attain an adultlike understanding of death in middle childhood, wide individual differences exist (Speece & Brent, 1996). Terminally ill children under age 6 often have a well-developed concept of death. If parents and health professionals have not been forthright, they discover that they are deathly ill in other ways—through nonverbal communication, eavesdropping, and talking with other child patients (O'Halloran & Altmaier, 1996). Children growing up on Israeli kibbutzim (agricultural settlements) who have witnessed terrorist attacks, family members' departure on army tours, and parental anxiety about safety express an adultlike grasp of death by age 6 (Mahon, Goldberg, & Washington, 1999).

Ethnic variations suggest that religious teachings affect children's understanding. In a comparison of four ethnic groups in Israel, Druze and Moslem children's death concepts differed from those of Christian and Jewish children (Florian & Kravetz, 1985). The Druze emphasis on reincarnation and the greater religiosity of both Druze and Moslem groups may have led more of their children to deny that death is permanent and that the body stops functioning. Similarly, children of U.S. Southern Baptist families, who believe in an afterlife, are less likely to endorse permanence than are children of Unitarian families, who focus on achieving peace and justice in today's world (Candy-Gibbs, Sharp, & Petrun, 1985).

■ **Enhancing Children's Understanding.** Parents often worry that discussing death candidly with children will fuel their fears. But children with a good grasp of the facts of death have an easier time accepting it. Direct explanations, like Leslie's, that fit the child's capacity to understand, work best. When adults use clichés or make misleading statements, chil-

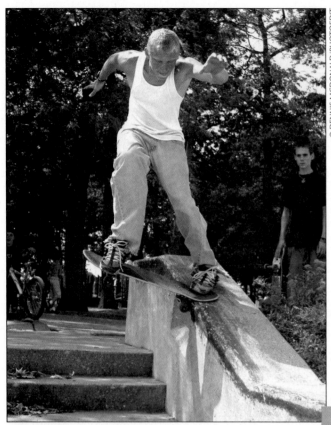

This adolescent knows that death happens to everyone and can occur at any time, but his risk taking suggests otherwise. Teenagers' difficulty integrating logic with reality extends to their understanding of death.

personal fable, which leads teenagers to be so wrapped up in their own uniqueness that they can conclude they are beyond the reach of death. Finally, as teenagers construct a personal identity and experience their first freely chosen love relationships, they may be strongly attracted to romantic notions of death, which challenge logic (Noppe & Noppe, 1991, 1996). Not until early adulthood are young people capable of the relativistic thinking needed to reconcile these conflicting ideas (see Chapter 13, page 450).

■ **Enhancing Adolescents' Understanding.** By encouraging adolescents to discuss concerns about death, adults can help them build a bridge between death as a logical concept and their personal experiences. In Chapter 12, we noted that teenagers with authoritative parents are more likely to turn to adults for guidance on important issues. In one study of 12- to 15-year-olds, most wanted to talk with parents rather than peers about the "meaning of life and death" and "what happens when you die." But 60 percent thought that their parents would not be genuinely interested, and the majority of parents felt inadequately prepared for the task (McNeil, 1986).

Taking up adolescents' thoughts and feelings about death can be part of everyday conversation, sparked by a news report or the death of an acquaintance. Parents can capitalize on these moments to express their own views, listen closely, accept teenagers' feelings, and correct misconceptions. Such mutual sharing deepens bonds of love and provides the basis for further exploration when the need arises. Applying What We Know below suggests ways to discuss concerns about death with children and adolescents.

Discussing Concerns About Death with Children and Adolescents

Applying What We Know

Suggestion	Description
Take the lead.	Be alert to the child's or adolescent's nonverbal behaviors, bringing up the subject sympathetically, especially after a death-related situation has occurred.
Listen perceptively.	Give full attention to the child or adolescent and the feelings underlying his or her words. When adults pretend to listen while thinking about other things, young people quickly pick up this sign of indifference and withdraw their confidence.
Acknowledge feelings.	Accept the child's or adolescent's emotions as real and important; avoid being judgmental. For example, paraphrase sentiments you detect, such as, "I see you're very puzzled about that. Let's talk more about it."
Provide factual information in a candid, culturally sensitive fashion.	For children who do not yet have a realistic understanding of death, provide simple, direct, and accurate explanations. Avoid misleading statements, such as, "Grandpa went away on a long trip." Do not contradict the young person's religious beliefs. Rather, assist him or her in blending scientific with religious sources of knowledge.
Engage in joint problem solving.	When questions do not have easy answers, such as, "Where does your soul go when you die?", convey your belief in the young person's worth by indicating that you do not want to impose a point of view but rather to help him or her come to personally satisfying conclusions. To questions you cannot answer, say, "I don't know." Such honesty shows a willingness to generate and evaluate solutions jointly.

Adulthood

In early adulthood, many people brush aside thoughts of death (Gresser, Wong, & Reker, 1987). This avoidance may be prompted by death anxiety, which we will consider in the next section. Alternatively, it may be due to relative lack of interest in death-related issues, given that young adults typically do not know very many people who have died and (like adolescents) think of their own death as a long way off.

In Chapters 15 and 16, we described midlife as a time of stock taking in which people begin to view the lifespan in terms of time left to live and focus on tasks to be completed. Middle-aged people no longer have a vague conception of their own death. They know that in the not-too-distant future, it will be their turn to grow old and die.

In late adulthood, adults think and talk more about death because it is much closer. Increasing evidence of mortality comes from physical changes, higher rates of illness and disability, and loss of relatives and friends (see Chapter 17). Compared with middle-aged people, older adults spend more time pondering the process and circumstances of dying than the state of death. Nearness to death seems to lead to a practical concern with how and when it might happen (de Vries, Bluck, & Birren, 1993; Kastenbaum, 2007).

Finally, although we have traced overall age-related changes, large individual differences exist. Some people focus on life and death issues early on; others are less reflective, moving into old age without giving these matters much attention.

Death Anxiety

As you read the following statements, do you find yourself agreeing, disagreeing, or reacting neutrally?

"Never feeling anything again after I die upsets me."

"I hate the idea that I will be helpless after I die."

"The total isolation of death is frightening to me."

"The feeling that I will be missing out on so much after I die disturbs me." (Thorson & Powell, 1994, pp. 38–39)

Items like these appear on questionnaires used to measure **death anxiety**—fear and apprehension of death. Even people who are very accepting of the reality of death may be afraid of it (Firestone, 1994).

What predicts whether thoughts of our own demise trigger intense distress, relative calm, or something in between? To answer this question, researchers measure both general death anxiety and a variety of specific factors, including fear of no longer existing, loss of control, a painful death, the body decaying, being separated from loved ones, and the unknown (Neimeyer, 1994). Findings reveal large individual and cultural variations in aspects of death that arouse fear. For example, in a study of devout Islamic Saudi Arabians, certain factors that appear repeatedly in the responses of Westerners, such as fear of the body decaying and of the unknown, were entirely absent (Long, 1985).

Among Westerners, spirituality—a sense of life's meaning—seems to be more important than religious commitment in limiting death anxiety (Rasmussen & Johnson, 1994). People with a well-developed personal philosophy of death are also less fearful. In one study, moderately religious middle-aged and older adults feared death more than those who were high or low in religiosity. And adults whose religious beliefs and behavior were contradictory—who believed in an afterlife but rarely prayed or attended services—were high in death anxiety. Together, these findings suggest that both firmness of beliefs and consistency between beliefs and practices, rather than religiousness itself, reduce fear of death (Wink & Scott, 2005). Death anxiety is especially low among adults with deep faith in some form of higher force or being—faith that may or may not be influenced by religion (Cicirelli, 1999, 2002).

From what you have learned about adult psychosocial development, how do you think death anxiety might change with age? If you predicted it would decline, reaching its lowest level in late adulthood, you are correct (see Figure 19.1) (Thorson & Powell, 2000; Tomer, Eliason, & Smith, 2000). This age-related drop has been found in many cultures and ethnic groups. Recall from Chapter 18 that older adults are especially effective at regulating negative emotion. As a result, most cope with anxieties, including fear of death, effectively. Furthermore, the attainment of ego integrity and a more mature sense of spirituality reduce death anxiety. Elders have had more time to develop *symbolic immortality*—the belief that one will continue to live on through one's children or through one's work or personal influence (see Chapter 16, page 530).

As long as it is not overly intense, death anxiety can motivate people to strive to live up to internalized cultural values—

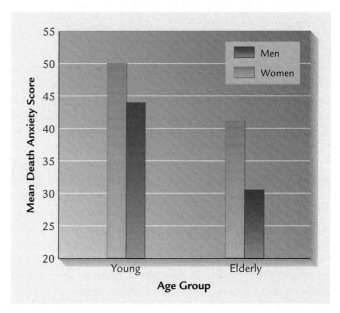

■ **FIGURE 19.1 Relationship of age and gender to death anxiety.** In this study comparing young and elderly adults, death anxiety declined with age. At both ages, women expressed greater fear of death than men. Many other studies show similar findings. (Adapted from Tomer, Eliason, & Smith, 2000.)

Death anxiety declines in old age, and this 81-year-old from the Netherlands seems to have very little! She had this coffin custom made to serve as a bookshelf because, she said, "It's a waste to use a coffin just for burial." The pillow on the top will support her head after she dies.

© MICHEL PORRO/GETTY IMAGES

Death anxiety is largely limited to adolescence and adulthood. Children rarely display it unless they live in high-crime neighborhoods or war-torn areas where they are in constant danger (see the Lifespan Vista box on children of war on page 352 in Chapter 10). Terminally ill children are also at risk for high death anxiety. Compared with other same-age patients, children with cancer express more destructive thoughts and negative feelings about death (Malone, 1982). For those whose parents make the mistake of not telling them they are going to die, loneliness and death anxiety can be extreme (O'Halloran & Altmaier, 1996).

Ask Yourself

Review

Explain why older adults think and talk more about death than do younger people but nevertheless feel less anxious about it.

Apply

When 4-year-old Chloe's aunt died, Chloe asked, "Where's Aunt Susie?" Her mother explained, "Aunt Susie is taking a long, peaceful sleep." For the next two weeks, Chloe refused to go to bed, and, when finally coaxed into her room, lay awake for hours. What is the likely reason for Chloe's behavior? What might be a better way of answering her question?

Connect

How do advances in cognition contribute to adolescents' concepts of death? (Refer to Chapter 11, pages 381–386.)

Reflect

Ask members of earlier generations in your family about their childhood experiences with death. Compare these to your own experiences. What differences did you find, and how would you explain them?

www.ablongman.com/berk

for example, to be kind to others and to work hard to reach one's goals. These efforts increase adults' sense of self-esteem, self-efficacy, and purpose in life—powerful antidotes against the terrifying thought that, in the overall scheme of things, they "are no more important or enduring than any individual potato, pineapple, or porcupine" (Fry, 2003; Pyszczynski et al., 2004, p. 436). In a study of Israeli adults, symbolic immortality predicted reduced fear of death, especially among those with secure attachments (Florian & Mikulincer, 1998). Gratifying, close interpersonal ties seem to help people feel worthwhile and forge a sense of symbolic immortality. And people who view death as an opportunity to pass a legacy to future generations are less likely to fear it (Cicirelli, 2001; Mikulincer, Florian, & Hirschberger, 2003).

Regardless of age, in both Eastern and Western cultures, women appear more anxious about death than men do (refer again to Figure 19.1) (Cicirelli, 1998; Tomer, Eliason, & Smith, 2000). Perhaps women are more likely to admit and men more likely to avoid troubled feelings about mortality—an explanation consistent with females' greater emotional expressiveness throughout the lifespan.

Experiencing some anxiety about death is normal and adaptive. But like other fears, very intense death anxiety can undermine effective adjustment. Although physical health in adulthood is not related to death anxiety, mental health clearly is. In cultures as different as China and the United States, people who are depressed or generally anxious are likely to have more severe death concerns (Neimeyer & Van Brunt, 1995; Wu, Tang, & Kwok, 2002).

Thinking and Emotions of Dying People

In the year before her death, Sofie did everything possible to surmount her illness. In between treatments to control the cancer, she tested her strength. She continued to teach high school, traveled to visit her children, cultivated a garden, and took weekend excursions with Philip. Hope pervaded Sofie's approach to her deadly condition, and she spoke often about the disease—so much so that her friends wondered how she could confront it so directly.

As Sofie deteriorated physically, she moved in and out of various mental and emotional states. She was frustrated, and at times angry and depressed, about her inability to keep on fighting. I recall her lamenting anxiously on a day when she was in pain, "I'm sick, so very sick! I'm trying so hard, but I can't keep on." Once she asked when my husband and I, who were newly married, would have children. "If only I could live long enough to hold them in my arms!" she cried. In the last week, she appeared tired but free of struggle. Occasionally, she spoke of her love for us and commented on the beauty of the hills outside her window. But mostly, she looked and listened rather than actively participating in conversation. One afternoon, she fell permanently unconscious.

Do Stages of Dying Exist?

As dying people move closer to death, are their reactions predictable? Do they go through a series of changes that are the same for everyone, or are their thoughts and feelings unique?

■ **Kübler-Ross's Theory.** Although her theory has been heavily criticized, Elisabeth Kübler-Ross (1969) is credited with awakening society's sensitivity to the psychological needs of dying patients. From interviews with over 200 terminally ill people, she devised a theory of five typical responses—initially proposed as stages—to the prospect of death and the ordeal of dying:

● *Denial.* On learning of the terminal illness, the person denies its seriousness to escape from the prospect of death. While the patient still feels reasonably well, denial is self-protective, allowing the individual to deal with the illness at his or her own pace. Most people move in and out of denial, making great plans one day and, the next, acknowledging that death is near (Smith, 1993). Kübler-Ross recommends that family members and health professionals not prolong denial by distorting the truth about the person's condition. In doing so, they prevent the dying person from adjusting to impending death and hinder necessary arrangements—for social support, for bringing closure to relationships, and for making decisions about medical interventions.

● *Anger.* Recognition that time is short promotes anger at having to die without having had a chance to do all one wants to do. Family members and health professionals may be targets of the patient's rage, resentment, and envy of those who will go on living. Still, they must tolerate rather than lash out at the patient's behavior, recognizing that the underlying cause is the unfairness of death.

● *Bargaining.* Realizing the inevitability of death, the terminally ill person attempts to forestall it by bargaining for extra time—a deal he or she may try to strike with family members, friends, doctors, nurses, or God. The best response to these efforts to sustain hope is to listen sympathetically, as one doctor did to the pleas of a young AIDS-stricken father, whose wish was to live long enough to dance with his daughter—then 8 years old—at her wedding (Selwyn, 1996). Sometimes, bargains are altruistic acts. Tony, a 15-year-old leukemia patient, expressed to his mother:

I don't want to die yet. Gerry [youngest brother] is only 3 and not old enough to understand. If I could live just one more year, I could explain it to him myself and he will understand. Three is just too young. (Komp, 1996, pp. 69–70)

Although many dying patients' bargains are unrealistic and impossible to fulfill, Tony lived for exactly one year—a gift to those who survived him.

● *Depression.* When denial, anger, and bargaining fail to postpone the illness, the person becomes depressed about the loss of his or her life. Unfortunately, many experiences associated with dying, including physical and mental deterioration, pain, lack of control, and being hooked to machines, intensify despondency (Maier & Newman, 1995). Health care that responds humanely to the patient's wishes can limit hopelessness and despair.

● *Acceptance.* Most people who reach acceptance, a state of peace and quiet about upcoming death, do so only in the last weeks or days. The weakened patient yields to death, disengaging from all but a few family members, friends, and caregivers. Some dying people, in an attempt to pull away from all they have loved, withdraw into themselves for long periods of time. "I'm getting my mental and emotional house in order," one patient explained (Samarel, 1995, p. 101).

■ **Evaluation of Kübler-Ross's Theory.** Kübler-Ross cautioned that her five stages should not be viewed as a fixed sequence and that not all people display each response—warnings that might have been better heeded had she not called them "stages." Too often her theory has been interpreted simplistically, as the series of steps a "normal" dying person follows. Some health professionals, unaware of diversity in dying experiences, have insensitively tried to push patients through Kübler-Ross's sequence. And caregivers, through callousness or ignorance, can too easily dismiss a dying patient's legitimate complaints about treatment as "just what you would expect in Stage 2" (Corr, 1993; Kastenbaum, 2007).

Research confirms that, in line with Kübler-Ross's observations, dying people are more likely to display denial after learning of their condition and acceptance shortly before death (Kalish, 1985). But rather than stages, the five reactions Kübler-Ross observed are best viewed as coping strategies that anyone may call on in the face of threat. Furthermore, her list is much too limited. Dying people react in many additional ways—for example, through efforts to conquer the disease, as Sofie displayed; through an overwhelming need to control what happens to their bodies during the dying process; through acts of generosity and caring, as seen in Tony's concern for his 3-year-old brother, Gerry; and through shifting their focus to living in a fulfilling way—"seizing the day" because so little time is left (Silverman, 2004; Wright, 2003).

As these examples suggest, the most serious drawback to Kübler-Ross's theory is that it looks at dying patients' thoughts and feelings outside the contexts that give them meaning. As

Rather than stages, the five responses to dying Kübler-Ross observed are best viewed as possible coping strategies. Dying people react in many different ways, which depend in part on family members' behavior. This terminally ill man seems withdrawn, perhaps trying to come to terms with the limited time he has left.

we will see next, people's adaptations to impending death can be understood only in relation to the multidimensional influences that have contributed to their life course and that also shape this final phase.

Contextual Influences on Adaptations to Dying

From the moment of her diagnosis, Sofie spent little time denying the deadliness of her disease. Instead, she met it head on, just as she had dealt with other challenges of life. Her impassioned plea to hold her grandchildren in her arms was less a bargain with fate than an expression of profound defeat that on the threshold of late adulthood, she would not live to enjoy its rewards. At the end, her quiet, withdrawn demeanor was probably resignation, not acceptance. All her life, she had been a person with a fighting spirit, unwilling to give in to challenge.

According to recent theorists, a single strategy, such as acceptance, is not best for every dying patient. Rather, an **appropriate death** is one that makes sense in terms of the individual's pattern of living and values and, at the same time, preserves or restores significant relationships and is as free of suffering as possible (Samarel, 1995; Worden, 2000). When asked about a "good death," most patients are clear about what, ideally, they would like to happen and mention the following goals:

● Maintaining a sense of identity, or inner continuity with one's past

● Clarifying the meaning of one's life and death

● Maintaining and enhancing relationships

● Achieving a sense of control over the time that remains

● Confronting and preparing for death (Kleespies, 2004; Proulx & Jacelon, 2004)

Research reveals that biological, psychological, and social and cultural forces affect people's coping with dying and, therefore, the extent to which they attain these goals. Let's look at some important influences on how people fare.

■ **Nature of the Disease.** The course of the illness and its symptoms affect the dying person's reactions. For example, the extended nature of Sofie's illness and her doctor's initial optimism about achieving a remission undoubtedly contributed to her attempts to try to conquer the disease. During the final month, when cancer had spread to Sofie's lungs and she could not catch her breath, she was agitated and fearful until oxygen and medication relieved her uncertainty about being able to breathe. In contrast, Nicholas's weakened heart and failing kidneys so depleted his strength that he responded only with passivity.

Because of the toll of the disease, about one-third of cancer patients experience severe depression—reactions distinct from the sadness, grief, and worry that typically accompany the dying process. Profound depression amplifies pain, impairs the immune response, interferes with the patient's capacity for pleasure, meaning, and connection, and is associated with poorer survival (Williams & Dale, 2006). It requires immediate treatment—through therapy, antidepressant medication, and patient and family education.

■ **Personality and Coping Style.** Understanding the way individuals view stressful life events and have coped with them in the past helps us appreciate the way they manage the dying process. In a study in which terminally ill patients discussed their images of dying, responses varied greatly. For example,

● Beth regarded *dying as imprisonment:* "I felt like the clock started ticking . . . like the future has suddenly been taken. . . . In a way, I feel like I'm already dead."

● To Faith, dying was as *a mandate to live ever more fully:* "I have a saying . . . 'You're not ready to live until you're ready to die' . . . It never meant much to me until I . . . looked death in the eye, and now I'm living. . . . This life is a lot better than the one before."

● Dawn viewed dying as *part of life's journey:* "I learned all about my disease . . . I would read, read, read . . . I wanted to know as much as I can about it, and I don't think hiding . . . behind the door . . . could help me at all. And, I realized for the first time in my life—*really, really, really realized* that I could handle anything."

● Patty approached dying as *an experience to be transformed* so as to make it more bearable: "I am an avid, rabid fan of *Star Trek,* a trekkie like there never has been . . . I watch it to the point that I've memorized it . . . [In my mind, I play the various characters so] I'm not [always] thinking about cancer or dying . . . I think that's how I get through it." (Wright, 2003, pp. 442–444, 447)

Each patient's view of dying helps explain her responses to worsening illness. Poorly adjusted individuals—those with conflict-ridden relationships and many disappointments in life—are usually more distressed (Kastenbaum, 2007).

■ Family Members' and Health Professionals' Behavior.

Earlier we noted that a candid approach, in which everyone close to and caring for the dying person acknowledges the terminal illness, is best. Yet this also introduces the burden of participating in the work of dying with the patient—bringing relationships to closure, reflecting on life, and dealing with fears and regrets.

People who find it hard to engage in these tasks may pretend that the disease is not as bad as it is. In patients inclined toward denial, a "game" can be set in motion in which participants are aware that the patient is dying but act as though it were not so. Though this game softens psychological pain for the moment, it makes dying much more difficult. Besides impeding communication, it frequently leads to futile medical interventions, in which the patient has little understanding of what is happening and is subjected to great physical and emotional suffering. One attending physician provided this account of a cancer patient's death:

> The problem was that she had a young husband and parents who were pretty much in complete denial. We were trying to be aggressive up to the end. To the point that we actually hung a new form of chemotherapy about four hours before she died, even though everybody knew except her immediate family that she was going to die within the next four to eight hours. (Jackson et al., 2005, p. 653)

At other times, the patient suspects what he or she has not been told. In one instance, a terminally ill child flew into a rage because his doctor and a nurse spoke to him in ways that denied the fact that he would not grow up. Trying to get the child to cooperate with a medical procedure, the doctor said,

> "I thought you would understand, Sandy. You told me once you wanted to be a doctor."
>
> He screamed back, "I'm not going to be anything!" and threw an empty syringe at her.
>
> The nurse standing nearby asked, "What are you going to be?"
>
> "A ghost," said Sandy, and turned away from them. (Bluebond-Langner, 1977, p. 59)

The behavior of health professionals impeded Sandy's efforts to form a realistic time perspective and intensified his anger at the injustice of his premature death.

When doctors do want to inform patients of their prognosis, they may encounter resistance, especially within certain ethnic groups. Withholding information is common in Southern and Eastern Europe, Central and South America, much of Asia, and the Middle East. Japanese terminally ill cancer patients are seldom told the truth about their condition, partly because dying disrupts important interdependent relationships (Yamamoto, 2004). Many Mexican Americans and Korean Americans believe that informing patients is wrong and will hasten death (Blackhall et al., 1995, 2001). In these instances, providing information is complex. When a family insists that a patient not be told, the doctor can make an offer of information to the patient and, if the patient refuses, ask who should receive information and make health care decisions. The patient's preference can be honored and reassessed at regular intervals (Zane & Yeh, 2002).

Care of the terminally ill is demanding and stressful. In one study, nurses trained to respond to the psychological needs of dying patients and their families consistently provided empathetic and supportive care. Keys to their success were staff meetings aimed at strengthening interpersonal skills, day-to-day mutual support among staff, and development of a personal philosophy of living and dying, which ensured that each nurse did not feel especially threatened by his or her own death (Samarel, 1991). Highly death-anxious health professionals are more likely to delay informing terminal patients of their diagnoses and to prolong life-saving treatment when death is near (Eggerman & Dustin, 1985).

Social support from family members also affects adaptation to dying. Dying patients who feel they have much unfinished business to attend to are more anxious about impending death. But family contact reduces their sense of urgency to prolong life, perhaps because it permits patients to work through at least some incomplete tasks (Mutran et al., 1997).

Effective communication with the dying person is honest, fostering a trusting relationship, yet also oriented toward maintaining hope. Many dying patients move through a hope trajectory—at first, hope for a cure; later, hope for prolonging life; and finally, hope for a peaceful death with as few burdens

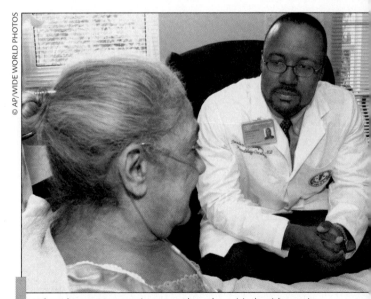

When doctors communicate openly and sensitively with terminally ill patients, they help them prepare for death by bringing relationships to closure, reflecting on life, and dealing with fears and regrets.

Communicating with Dying People

Suggestion	Description
Be truthful about the diagnosis and course of the disease.	Be honest about what the future is likely to hold, thereby permitting the dying person to bring closure to his or her life by expressing sentiments and wishes and participating in decisions about treatment.
Listen perceptively and acknowledge feelings.	Be truly present, focusing full attention on what the dying person has to say and accepting the patient's feelings. Patients who sense another's presence and concern are more likely to relax physically and emotionally and express themselves.
Maintain realistic hope.	Assist the dying person in maintaining hope by encouraging him or her to focus on a realistic goal that might yet be achieved—for example, resolution of a troubled relationship or special moments with a loved one. Knowing the dying person's hope, family members and health professionals can often help fulfill it.
Assist in the final transition.	Assure the dying person that he or she is not alone, offering a sympathetic touch, a caring thought, or just a calm presence. Some patients who struggle may benefit from being given permission to die—the message that giving up and letting go is all right.

Sources: Benoliel & Degner, 1995.

as possible (Fanslow, 1981). Once patients near death stop expressing hope, those close to them must accept this. Family members who find letting go very difficult may benefit from expert, sensitive guidance. Applying What We Know above offers suggestions for communicating with the dying.

■ **Spirituality, Religion, and Culture.** Earlier we noted that a strong sense of spirituality reduces fear of death. Informal reports from health professionals suggest that this is as true for dying patients as for people in general. One experienced nurse commented,

> At the end, those [patients] with a faith—it doesn't really matter in what, but a faith in something—find it easier. Not always, but as a rule. I've seen people with faith panic and I've seen those without faith accept it [death]. But, as a rule, it's much easier for those with faith. (Samarel, 1991, pp. 64–65)

Vastly different cultural beliefs, guided by religious ideas, also shape people's dying experiences:

🖋 Buddhism, widely practiced in China, India, and Southeast Asia, fosters acceptance of death. By reading sutras (teachings of Buddha) to the dying person to calm the mind and emphasizing that dying leads to rebirth in a heaven of peace and relaxation, Buddhists believe that it is possible to reach Nirvana, a state beyond the world of suffering (Kubotera, 2004; Yeung, 1996).

🖋 In many Native-American groups, death is met with stoic self-control, an approach taught at an early age through stories that emphasize a circular, rather than linear, relationship between life and death and the importance of making way for others (Cox, 2002).

🖋 For African Americans, a dying loved one signals a crisis that unites family members in caregiving. The terminally ill person remains an active and vital force within the family until he or she no longer can carry out this role—an attitude of respect that undoubtedly eases the dying process (Sullivan, 1995).

🖋 Among the Maori of New Zealand, relatives and friends gather around the dying person to give spiritual strength and comfort. Elders, clergy, and other experts in tribal customs conduct a *karakia* ceremony, in which they recite prayers asking for peace, mercy, and guidance from the creator. After the ceremony, the patient is encouraged to discuss important matters with those closest to her—giving away of personal belongings, directions for interment, and completion of other unfinished tasks (Ngata, 2004).

In sum, dying prompts a multitude of thoughts, emotions, and coping strategies. Which ones are selected and emphasized depends on a wide array of contextual influences. A vital assumption of the lifespan perspective—that development is multidimensional and multidirectional—is just as relevant to this final phase as to each earlier period.

A Place to Die

Whereas in the past most deaths occurred at home, today about 70 percent in Canada and 80 percent in the United States take place in hospitals (O'Connor, 2003; Wilson, 2002). In the large, impersonal hospital environment, meeting the human needs of dying patients and their families is secondary, not because professionals lack concern, but because the work to be done focuses on saving lives. A dying patient represents a failure.

In the 1960s, a death awareness movement arose as a reaction to hospitals' death-avoiding practices—attachment of complicated machinery to patients with no chance of survival, avoidance of communication with dying patients. This movement led to medical care better suited to the needs of dying people and to hospice programs, which have spread to many countries in the industrialized world. Let's visit each of these settings for dying.

Home

Had Sofie and Nicholas been asked where they wanted to die, undoubtedly each would have responded, "At home"—the preference of about 80 to 90 percent of North Americans (NHPCO, 2005a; O'Connor, 2003; Wade, 2005). The reason is clear: The home offers an atmosphere of intimacy and loving care in which the terminally ill person is unlikely to feel abandoned or humiliated by physical decline or dependence on others.

However, only about one-fourth of Canadians and one-fifth of Americans experience home death (Mezey et al., 2002; Mitchell et al., 2005; Wilson, 2002). And it is important not to romanticize dying at home. Because of dramatic improvements in medicine, dying people tend to be sicker or much older than in the past. Consequently, their bodies may be extremely frail, making ordinary activities—eating, sleeping, taking a pill, toileting, and bathing—major ordeals (Singer et al., 2005). Health problems of elderly spouses, work and other responsibilities of family members, and the physical, psychological, and financial strain of providing home care can make it difficult to honor a terminally ill person's wish to die at home.

For many people, the chance to be with the dying person until the very end is a rewarding tradeoff for the high demands of caregiving. But the advantages and disadvantages of home death should be carefully weighed before undertaking it. Adequate support for the caregiver is essential (Germino, 2003). A home health aide is often necessary—a service (as we will see shortly) that hospice programs have made more accessible. Still, when family relationships are conflict-ridden, a dying patient introduces additional strains, negating the benefits of home death. Finally, even with professional help, most homes are poorly equipped to handle the medical and comfort-care needs of the dying. To make home death possible, hospital-based equipment and technical support often must be transported to the home.

For all these reasons, older adults—although they view home as their ideal place to die—express concerns about quality of care, about burdening family and friends, and about the need for children to engage in unduly intimate caregiving tasks (Gott et al., 2004). And 10 months after a home death, family members continue to report more psychological stress than do family members whose loved one died elsewhere (Addington-Hall, 2000).

Hospital

Hospital dying takes many forms. Each is affected by the physical state of the dying person, the hospital unit in which it takes place, and the goal and quality of care.

Sudden deaths, due to injury or critical illness, typically occur in emergency rooms. Doctors and nurses must evaluate the problem and take action quickly. Little time is available for contact with family members. When staff break the news of death in a sympathetic manner and provide explanations, family members are grateful. Otherwise, feelings of anger, frustration, and confusion can add to their grief. Crisis intervention services are needed to help survivors cope with sudden death (Walsh & McGoldrick, 2004).

Nicholas died on an intensive care ward focused on preventing death in patients whose condition can worsen quickly. Privacy and communication with the family were secondary to monitoring his condition. To prevent disruption of nurses' activities, Giselle and Sasha could be at Nicholas's side only at scheduled times. Dying in intensive care—an experience unique to technologically sophisticated societies—is especially depersonalizing for patients like Nicholas, who linger between life and death while hooked to machines for months.

Cancer patients, who account for most cases of prolonged dying, typically die in general or specialized cancer care hospital units. When hospitalized for a long time, they reach out for help with physical and emotional needs, usually with mixed success. In these hospital settings, as in intensive care, a conflict of values is apparent (Hanson, Danis, & Garrett, 1997). The tasks associated with dying must be performed efficiently so that all patients can be served and health professionals are not drained emotionally by repeated attachments and separations.

Only 14 percent of U.S. hospitals have comprehensive treatment programs aimed at easing physical, emotional, and

Dying in intensive care is a depersonalizing experience unique to technologically sophisticated societies. In such settings, medical responses supersede privacy and communication.

© AP/WIDE WORLD PHOTOS

spiritual suffering at the end of life. Although pain management programs now exist in 42 percent of hospitals, the majority still do not have them. And less than 1 percent of doctors and nurses are specially trained in managing pain in dying people. In sum, many people die in painful, frightening, and depersonalizing hospital conditions, without their wishes being met (Peres, 2002; Open Society Institute, 2003). The hospice approach aims to reduce these profound caregiving failures.

The Hospice Approach

In medieval times, a *hospice* was a place where travelers could find rest and shelter. In the nineteenth and twentieth centuries, the word referred to homes for dying patients. Today, **hospice** is not a place but a comprehensive program of support services for terminally ill people and their families. It aims to provide a caring community sensitive to the dying person's needs so patients and family members can prepare for death in ways that are satisfying to them. Quality of life is central to the hospice approach, which includes these main features:

- The patient and family as a unit of care

- Emphasis on meeting the patient's physical, emotional, social, and spiritual needs, including controlling pain, retaining dignity and self-worth, and feeling cared for and loved

- Care provided by an interdisciplinary team: the patient's doctor, a nurse or nurse's aide, a chaplain, a counselor or social worker, and a pharmacist

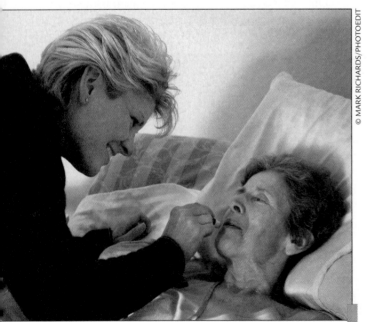

Hospice protects quality of life rather than extending it. This daughter applies lip balm for her mother—an act that increases her mother's comfort and enhances a sense of closeness and connection.

- The patient kept at home or in an inpatient setting with a homelike atmosphere where coordination of care is possible

- Focus on protecting the quality of remaining life with **palliative,** or **comfort, care** that relieves pain and other symptoms (nausea, breathing difficulties, insomnia, and depression) rather than prolonging life

- In addition to regularly scheduled home care visits, on-call services available 24 hours a day, 7 days a week

- Follow-up bereavement services offered to families in the year after a death

Because hospice care is a philosophy, not a facility, it can be applied in diverse ways. In Great Britain, care in a special inpatient unit, sometimes associated with a hospital, is typical. Home care has been emphasized in the United States, where nearly 60 percent of hospice patients die in their own residence, 33 percent in special inpatient units, and 9 percent in typical hospital rooms. In Canada, about half of hospice care is home-based, the other half either hospice unit- or hospital-based (CHPCA, 2004; NHPCO, 2004).

But hospice programs everywhere have expanded to include a continuum of care, from home to inpatient options, including hospitals and nursing homes. Central to the hospice approach is that the dying person and his or her family be offered choices that guarantee an appropriate death. Some programs offer hospice day care, which permits caregivers to continue working or be relieved of the stresses of long-term care (Kernohan et al., 2006). Contact with others facing terminal illness is a supportive byproduct of many hospice arrangements. And to find out about a comforting musical intervention for patients near death, consult the Biology and Environment box on the following page.

Currently, the United States has over 3,200 hospices serving approximately 900,000 terminally ill patients annually; Canada has 650 hospice and palliative care organizations, also reaching thousands of patients. About 50 percent of patients dying of cancer and over 30 percent dying of AIDS choose hospice. Programs also admit patients suffering from a variety of other terminal illnesses (CHPCA, 2004; NHPCO, 2004). Because hospice care is a cost-effective alternative to expensive life-saving treatments, government health care benefits cover it in both the United States and Canada, making it affordable for most dying patients and their families. Hospices also serve dying children—a tragedy so devastating that social support and bereavement intervention are vital.

Research reveals that besides reducing patient physical suffering, hospice care contributes to improved family functioning. The majority of patients and families report improved coping, increased social support, and increased feelings of family closeness after receiving hospice services (Godkin, Krant, & Doster, 1984). In one study, family members experiencing hospice scored higher than nonhospice family members in psychological well-being one to two years after their loved one's death (Ragow-O'Brien, Hayslip, & Guarnaccia, 2000).

Biology and Environment

Music as Palliative Care for Dying Patients

When Peter visits 82-year-old Stuart to play his harp, Stuart reports being transported to an idyllic place with water, children, and trees—far from the lung tumors that will soon take his life "When Peter plays for me . . . I am no longer frightened," Stuart says.

Peter is a specialist in *music thanatology,* an emerging specialty in music therapy that focuses on providing palliative care for the dying through music. He uses his harp, and sometimes his voice, to induce calm and give solace to the dying, their families, and their caregivers. Peter applies music systematically—matching it to each patient's breathing patterns and other responses, delivering different sounds to uplift or comfort, depending on his assessment of the patient's moment-by-moment needs.

Chaplains and counselors informally report that after music vigils, patients' conversations indicate that they more easily come to terms with their own death (Fyfe, 2006). And in a study of 65 dying patients in which pre- and postintervention physiological measures were compared, music vigils averaging an hour in length resulted in decreased agitation and wakefulness and slower, deeper, less effortful breathing (Freeman et al., 2006). These physiological benefits extended to patients who, on the basis of their behavior, were clearly in pain.

Why is music effective in easing the distress of those who are dying? In patients close to death, hearing typically functions longer than other senses. Thus, responsiveness to music may persist until the individual's final moments. Besides reducing anxiety, music can, in some instances, enhance the effects of medica-

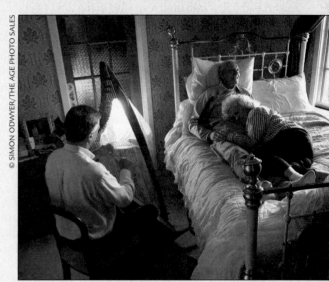

Music thanatology focuses on providing palliative care for the dying through music. This practitioner uses his harp, and sometimes his voice, to induce calm and provide solace.

tion administered to control pain (Starr, 1999). For these reasons, music vigils may be an especially effective end-of-life therapy.

As a long-range goal, hospice organizations are striving for broader acceptance of their patient- and family-centered approach. The majority of North Americans are still unfamiliar with the philosophy, although when it is described to them, nearly 90 percent say it is the type of end-of-life care they want (CHPCA, 2004; NHPCO, 2004). Recently, Canada launched a Web-based hospice outreach service, the Canadian Virtual Hospice *(www.virtualhospice.ca),* to support patients, families, and care providers with information, resources, and connections to others with similar concerns. Culturally sensitive approaches are needed to reach more ethnic minority patients, who are much less likely than white patients to participate in hospice (Crawley et al., 2000).

In developing countries, where millions die of cancer, AIDS, and other devastating illnesses each year, community-based teams working under a nurse's supervision sometimes deliver palliative care. But they face many obstacles, including lack of funding, pain-relieving drugs, and professional and public education about hospice. As a result, they are small "islands of excellence," accessible to only a few families (NHPCO, 2005b).

Ask Yourself

Review

Why is the stage notion an inaccurate account of dying patients' mental and emotional reactions?

Apply

When 5-year-old Timmy's kidney failure was diagnosed as terminal, his parents could not accept the tragic news. Their hospital visits became shorter, and they evaded his anxious questions. Eventually, Timmy blamed himself. He died with little physical pain, but alone, and his parents suffered prolonged guilt. How could hospice care have helped Timmy and his family?

Connect

Reread the description of Sofie's mental and emotional reactions to dying on pages 642–643. Then review the story of Sofie's life on pages 3–4 in Chapter 1. How were Sofie's responses consistent with her personality and lifelong style of coping with adversity?

Reflect

If you were terminally ill, where would you want to die? Explain.

The Right to Die

In 1976, the parents of Karen Ann Quinlan, a young woman who had fallen into an irreversible coma after taking drugs at a party, sued to have her respirator turned off. The New Jersey Supreme Court, invoking Karen's right to privacy and her parents' power as guardians, complied with this request. Although Karen was expected to die quickly, she breathed independently, continued to be fed intravenously, and lived another 10 years in a persistent vegetative state.

In 1990, 26-year-old Terri Schiavo's heart stopped briefly, temporarily cutting off oxygen to her brain. Like Karen, Terri lay in a persistent vegetative state. Her husband and guardian, Michael, claimed that she had earlier told him she would not want to be kept alive artificially, but Terri's parents disagreed. In 1998, the Florida Circuit Court granted Michael's petition to have Terri's feeding tube removed. In 2001, after her parents had exhausted their appeals, the tube was taken out. But on the basis of contradictory medical testimony, Terri's parents convinced a circuit court judge to order the feeding tube reinserted, and the legal wrangling continued. In 2002, Michael won a second judgment to remove the tube.

By that time, publicity over the case and its central question—who should make end-of-life decisions when the patient's wishes are unclear—had made Terri a political issue. In 2003, the Florida legislature passed a law allowing the governor to stay the circuit court's order to keep Terri alive, but on appeal, the law was declared unconstitutional. In 2005, the U.S. Congress entered the fray, passing a bill that transferred Terri's fate to the U.S. District Court. When the judge refused to intervene, the feeding tube was removed for a third time. In 2005—15 years after losing consciousness—Terri Schiavo died. The autopsy confirmed the original persistent vegetative state diagnosis: Her brain was half normal size.

Before the 1950s, the right to die was of little concern, because medical science could do little to extend the lives of terminally ill patients. Today, medical advances mean that the same procedures that preserve life can prolong inevitable death, diminishing both quality of life and personal dignity.

The Quinlan and Schiavo cases—and others like them—have brought right-to-die issues to the forefront of public attention. Today, all U.S. states and most Canadian provinces have laws that honor patients' wishes concerning withdrawal of treatment in cases of terminal illness and, sometimes, in cases of a persistent vegetative state. But in the United States and Canada, no uniform right-to-die policy exists, and heated controversy persists over how to handle the diverse circumstances in which patients and family members make requests.

Euthanasia is the practice of ending the life of a person suffering from an incurable condition. Its various forms are summarized in Table 19.1. As we will see, public acceptance of euthanasia is high, except when it involves ending the life of an anguished, terminally ill patient without his or her expressed permission.

Passive Euthanasia

In **passive euthanasia,** life-sustaining treatment is withheld or withdrawn, permitting a patient to die naturally. Should Terri Schiavo have been allowed to die sooner? Was it right for Nicholas's doctors to turn off his respirator at Giselle's request? Consider an Alzheimer's victim, whose disease has progressed to the point where he has lost all awareness and body functions. Should life support be withheld?

In recent polls, the majority of people answered yes to these questions. When there is no hope of recovery, more three-fourths of North Americans support the patient's or family members' right to end treatment (Angus Reid Group, 1997; Pew Research Center, 2006). In 1986, the American Medical Association endorsed withdrawing all forms of treatment from the terminally ill when death is imminent and from those in a permanent vegetative state. Consequently, passive euthanasia is widely practiced as part of ordinary medical procedure, in which doctors exercise professional judgment.

Still, a minority of citizens do not endorse passive euthanasia. Religious denomination has surprisingly little effect on people's opinions. For example, most Catholics hold favorable views, despite slow official church acceptance because of fears that passive euthanasia might be a first step toward

Table 19.1	Forms of Euthanasia
Form	**Description**
Voluntary passive euthanasia	At the patient's request, the doctor withholds or withdraws treatment, thereby permitting the patient to die naturally. For example, the doctor does not perform surgery or administer medication that could prolong life, or the doctor turns off the respirator of a patient who cannot breathe independently.
Voluntary active euthanasia	The doctor ends a suffering patient's life at the patient's request—for example, by administering a lethal dose of drugs.
Assisted suicide	The doctor helps a suffering patient take his or her own life. For example, the doctor enables the patient to swallow or inject a lethal dose of drugs.
Involuntary active euthanasia	The doctor ends a suffering patient's life without the patient's permission. For example, without obtaining the patient's consent, the doctor administers a lethal dose of drugs.

government-approved mercy killing. However, ethnicity makes a difference: Nearly twice as many African Americans as Caucasian Americans desire all medical means possible, regardless of the patient's condition, and African Americans more often receive life-sustaining intervention, such as feeding tubes (Gessert, Curry, & Robinson, 2001; Hopp & Duffy, 2000). Perhaps this reluctance to forgo treatment reflects strong cultural beliefs about respecting and preserving life.

Because of controversial court cases like Terri Schiavo's, some doctors and health care institutions are unwilling to end treatment without legal protection. In the absence of national consensus on passive euthanasia, people can best ensure that their wishes will be followed by preparing an **advance medical directive**—a written statement of desired medical treatment should they become incurably ill. U.S. states and Canadian provinces recognize two types of advance directives: a *living will* (usually call a *directive* in Canada) and a *durable power of attorney for health care* (CBS News Canada, 2005; U.S. Living Will Registry, 2005). Sometimes they are combined into one document.

In a **living will,** people specify the treatments they do or do not want in case of a terminal illness, coma, or other near-death situation (see Figure 19.2). For example, a person might state that without reasonable expectation of recovery, he or she should not be kept alive through medical intervention of any kind. In addition, living wills sometimes specify that pain-relieving medication be given, even though this may shorten life. In Sofie's case, her doctor administered a powerful narcotic to relieve labored breathing and quiet her fear of suffocation. The narcotic suppressed respiration, causing death to occur hours or days earlier than if the medication had not been prescribed, but without distress. Such palliative care is accepted as appropriate and ethical medical practice.

Although living wills help ensure personal control, they do not guarantee it. Recognition of living wills is usually limited to patients who are terminally ill or are otherwise expected to die shortly. Only a few U.S. states and Canadian provinces cover people in a persistent vegetative state or elders who linger with many chronic problems, including Alzheimer's disease, because these conditions are not classified as terminal. Even when terminally ill patients have living wills, doctors often do not follow them for a variety of reasons, including fear of lawsuits, their own moral beliefs, and failure to inquire about patients' directives (Gorman et al., 2005; Lawton, 2001a).

Because living wills cannot anticipate all future medical conditions and can easily be ignored, a second form of advance directive has become common. The **durable power of attorney for health care** authorizes appointment of another person (usually, though not always, a family member) to make health care decisions on one's behalf. It generally requires only a short signed and witnessed statement like this:

> I hereby appoint [name] as my attorney-in-face (my "agent") to act for me and in my name (in any way I could act in person) to make any and all decisions for me concerning my personal care, medical treatment, hospitalization, and health care and to require, withhold, or withdraw any type of medical treatment or procedure, even though my death may ensue. (Courtesy of Office of the Attorney General, State of Illinois)

The durable power of attorney for health care is more flexible than the living will because it permits a trusted spokesperson to confer with the doctor as medical circumstances arise. Because authority to speak for the patient is not limited to terminal illnesses, more latitude exists for

---

LIVING WILL

THIS DECLARATION is made this _____ day of _____, 20 _____.

I, _____ , being of sound mind, willfully and voluntarily make known my desires that my moment of death shall not be artificially postponed. If at any time I should have an incurable and irreversible injury, disease, or illness judged to be a terminal condition by my attending physician who has personally examined me and has determined that my death is imminent except for death delaying procedures. I direct that such procedures which would only prolong the dying process be withheld or withdrawn, and that I be permitted to die naturally with only the administration of medication, sustenance, or the performance of any medical procedure deemed necessary by my attending physician to provide me with comfort care.

In the absence of my ability to give directions regarding the use of such death delaying procedures, it is my intention that this declaration shall be honored by my family and physician as the final expression of my legal right to refuse medical or surgical treatment and accept the consequences from such refusal.

Signed: _____

City, County and State of Residence: _____

_____

_____

The declarant is personally known to me and I believe him or her to be of sound mind. I saw the declarant sign the declaration in my presence (or the declarant acknowledged in my presence that he or she had signed the declaration) and I signed the declaration as a witness in the presence of the declarant. At the date of this instrument, I am not entitled to any portion of the estate of the declarant according to the laws of intestate succession or, to the best of my knowledge and belief, under any will of declarant or other instrument taking effect at declarant's death, or directly financially responsible for declarant's medical care.

Witness: _____

Witness: _____

■ **FIGURE 19.2 Example of a living will.** This document is legal in the State of Illinois. Each person completing a living will should use a form specific to the U.S. state or Canadian province in which he or she resides because laws vary widely. (Courtesy of Office of the Attorney General, State of Illinois.)

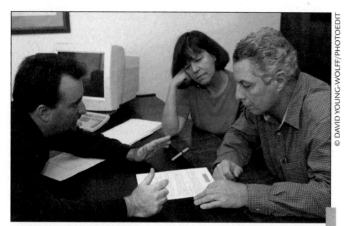

This couple discusses a durable power of attorney with a hospital chaplain. This advance directive authorizes a trusted spokesperson to make health care decisions and helps ensure that one's desires will be granted.

dealing with unexpected situations. And in gay and lesbian and other close relationships not sanctioned by law, the durable power of attorney can ensure the partner's role in decision making and in advocating for the patient's health care needs.

Whether or not a person supports passive euthanasia, it is important to have a living will, durable power of attorney, or both, because most deaths occur in hospitals. Yet fewer than 30 percent of Americans have executed such documents, perhaps because of widespread uneasiness about bringing up the topic of death, especially with relatives (Pew Research Center, 2006). To encourage people to make decisions about potential treatment while they are able, U.S. federal law now requires that all medical facilities receiving federal funds provide information at admission about state laws and institutional policies on patients' rights and advance directives.

As happened with Karen Quinlan and Terri Schiavo, health care professionals—unclear about a patient's intent and fearing liability—will probably decide to continue treatment regardless of cost and a person's prior oral statements. Perhaps for this reason, some U.S. states and Canadian provinces permit appointment of a *health care proxy,* or substitute decision maker, if a patient failed to provide an advance medical directive while competent. Proxies are an important means of covering children and adolescents, who cannot legally execute advance medical directives.

Voluntary Active Euthanasia

In recent years, the right-to-die debate has shifted from withdrawal of treatment for the hopelessly ill to more active alternatives. In **voluntary active euthanasia,** doctors or others act directly, at a patient's request, to end suffering before a natural end to life. The practice, a form of mercy killing, is a criminal offense in most countries, including Canada and almost all U.S. states. But support for voluntary active euthanasia is growing. As Figure 19.3 shows, about 70 to 90 percent of people in Western nations approve of it (World Federation of Right to Die Societies, 2006). When doctors engage in it, U.S. and

Canadian judges are usually lenient, granting suspended sentences or probation—a trend reflecting rising public interest in self-determination in death as in life.

Nevertheless, attempts to legalize voluntary active euthanasia have prompted heated controversy. Supporters believe it represents the most compassionate option for terminally ill people in severe pain. Opponents stress the moral difference between "letting die" and "killing" and point out that at times, even very sick patients recover. They also argue that involving doctors in taking the lives of suffering patients may impair people's trust in health professionals. Finally, a fear exists that legalizing this practice—even when strictly monitored to make sure it does not arise out of depression, loneliness, coercion, or a desire to diminish the burden of illness on others—could lead to a broadening of euthanasia (Loewy, 2004). Initially limited to the terminally ill, it might be applied involuntarily to the frail, demented, or disabled—outcomes that most people find unacceptable and immoral.

Will legalizing voluntary active euthanasia lead us down a "slippery slope" to the killing of vulnerable people who did not ask to die? The Social Issues box on the following page presents lessons from the Australian state of the Northern Territory, where a law allowing voluntary active euthanasia was passed in 1996, and from the Netherlands, where doctors have practiced it for years, even before its recent legalization.

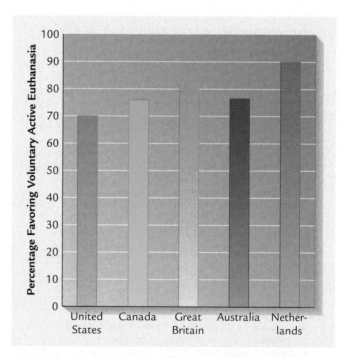

■ **FIGURE 19.3 Public opinion favoring voluntary active euthanasia in five nations.** A struggle exists between public opinion, which has increasingly favored voluntary active euthanasia over the past 30 years, and legal statutes, which prohibit it. The majority of people in Western nations believe that a hopelessly ill, suffering patient who asks for a lethal injection should be granted that request. Public support for voluntary active euthanasia is highest in the Netherlands—the only nation in the world where the practice is legal under certain conditions. (From Pew Research Center, 2006; World Federation of Right to Die Societies, 2006.)

Social Issues

Voluntary Active Euthanasia: Lessons from Australia and the Netherlands

In 1996, Australia's Northern Territory passed legislation allowing a terminally ill patient of sound mind and suffering from pain or other distress to ask a doctor to end his or her life. Two other doctors had to agree that the patient could not be cured, and a psychiatrist had to confirm the absence of treatable depression.

In the months that followed, four deaths occurred under the Northern Territory euthanasia statute, and it was heavily criticized. The Aborigines, valuing harmony and balance with nature, regarded it as culturally inappropriate. Their leaders claimed the law would discourage Aboriginal elders, many of whom have experienced a lifetime of persecution at the hands of European settlers, from seeking medical care (Fleming, 2000). Others considered the law to be a national issue because patients traveled from other states to make use of it. In 1997, the Northern Territory legislation was overturned by the Australian Parliament, which claimed that assemblies do not have the right to legislate intentional killing.

The episode placed Australia at the center of the debate over euthanasia—an issue that continues to spark high passions across the country. Opponents question the mental condition of patients seeking euthanasia and worry about error and abuse of the practice (Fickling, 2004). Supporters emphasize compassion and the right of individuals to control the course of their own lives. June Burns, a 59-year-old Australian woman with bladder cancer who participated in TV ads documenting the course of her illness, responded, "If I were a dog, they would have put me down by

now. I feel life is very precious and . . . I wish I could go on, but I can't and I'd like to die with dignity" (British Broadcasting Corporation, 1999).

For the past several decades, doctors in the Netherlands have engaged in voluntary active euthanasia without criminal prosecution. In 2001, the practice became legal under the following conditions: when physical or mental suffering is severe, with no prospect of relief; when no doubt exists about the patient's desire to die; when the patient's decision is voluntary, well-informed, and stable over time; when all other options for care have been exhausted or refused; and when another doctor has been consulted.

Over 50 percent of Dutch doctors say they perform euthanasia, most often with cancer patients. Despite safeguards, both voluntary and involuntary euthanasia have occurred. A small minority of doctors admit granting the euthanasia requests of physically healthy patients—usually elders who felt "weary of life" (Rurup et al., 2005). And some say they actively caused a death when a patient did not ask for it, defending their action by referring to the impossibility of treating pain, a low quality of life, or drawn-out dying in a patient near death. Although doctors judged most of these patients incompetent to decide for themselves, an estimated 37 percent were deemed competent (Hendin, 1999). When asked why they did not discuss the decision with competent patients, doctors usually said they had previously

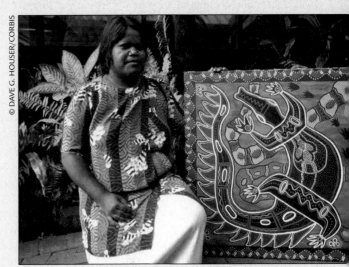
© DAVE G. HOUSER/CORBIS

Australian Aboriginal peoples regard voluntary active euthanasia as contrary to the values of their culture. The priority they place on harmony with nature is reflected in the natural images that permeate their artwork.

done so; they did not express a need to check how the patient felt currently.

Voluntary active euthanasia in the Netherlands has risen steadily over the past decade. Currently, doctors report more than 2,000 cases annually to medical examiners—2.4 percent of all deaths. But anonymous surveys reveal several thousand additional, unreported cases—usually ones in which the attending doctor failed to consult a second doctor (Onwuteaka-Philipsen et al., 2005).

The Northern Territory and Dutch examples reveal that legalizing voluntary active euthanasia can spark both the fear and the reality of death without consent. And the Dutch experience highlights the difficulties in monitoring euthanasia practices. Nevertheless, terminally ill individuals in severe pain continue to plead for such laws. Probably all would agree that when doctors feel compelled to relieve suffering and honor self-determination by assisting a patient in dying, they should be subject to the most stringent professional and legal oversight possible.

Assisted Suicide

After checking Diane's blood count, Dr. Timothy Quill gently broke the news: leukemia. If she were to have any hope of survival, a strenuous course of treatment with only a 25 percent success rate would have to begin immediately. Convinced that she would suffer unspeakably from side effects and lack of control over her body, Diane chose not to undergo chemotherapy and a bone marrow transplant.

Dr. Quill made sure that Diane understood her options. As he adjusted to her decision, Diane raised another issue: She wanted no part of a lingering death. She calmly insisted that when the time came, she desired to take her own life in the least painful way possible—a choice she had discussed with her husband and son, who respected it. Realizing that Diane could get the most out of the time she had left only if her fears of prolonged pain were allayed, Dr. Quill granted her request for sleeping pills, making sure she knew the amounts needed for both sleep and suicide.

Diane's next few months were busy and fulfilling. Her son took leave from college to be with her, and her husband worked at home as much as possible. Gradually, bone pain, fatigue, and fever set in. Saying good-bye to her family and friends, Diane asked to be alone for an hour, took a lethal dose of medication, and died at home (Quill, 1991).

Assisting a suicide is illegal in Canada and in many, but not all, U.S. states. In Western Europe, doctor-assisted suicide is legal in Belgium, Germany, the Netherlands, and Switzerland and is tacitly accepted in many other countries (Hill, 2003; Scherer & Simon, 1999). In North America, Oregon is unique in having passed a law, the Death with Dignity Act, that explicitly allows physicians to prescribe drugs so terminally ill patients can end their lives. To get a prescription, patients must have two doctors agree that they have less than 6 months to live and must request the drugs at least twice, with an interval of at least 15 days. In a 1997 ballot, Oregon residents voted to retain their assisted-suicide law. In January 2006, the U.S. Supreme Court rejected a challenge to the Oregon law, but the Court has also upheld the right of other states to ban assisted suicide.

Only 46 percent of Americans and 55 percent of Canadians approve of assisted suicide (COMPAS, 2002; Pew Research Center, 2006). And a survey of nearly 1,000 terminally ill U.S. patients ranging in age from 22 to 109 revealed that although they largely endorsed the practice, just one-tenth seriously considered asking for it; in a follow-up, many of them had changed their minds (Emanuel, Fairclough, & Emanuel, 2000). People who say they would choose assisted suicide if they were terminally ill tend to be higher in SES and more often Caucasian than African American (Cicirelli, 1997).

The number of Oregon residents dying by assisted suicide has increased since passage of the law, from 16 in 1998 to 38 in 2005. Most had cancer, Lou Gehrig's disease, or AIDS. Still, assisted suicide accounts for only one-tenth of 1 percent of Oregon deaths (Niemeyer, 2006). Ten times as many terminally ill people initiate the qualification process for assisted suicide as engage in it. But hundreds of others have discussed it with their doctors, and thousands of Oregonians say they find comfort in

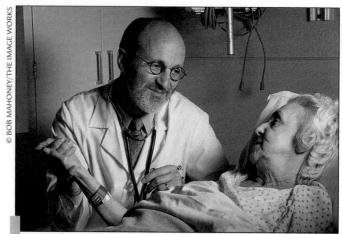

In a prestigious medical journal, Dr. Timothy Quill explained how and why he assisted a terminally ill patient in taking her own life. Doctor-assisted suicide is legal in Oregon and several western European countries. Still, the practice poses grave ethical dilemmas.

knowing the option is available should they suffer while dying (Hedberg, Hopkins, & Kohn, 2003). Doctors report that the most common reasons for assisted-suicide requests are decreasing ability to participate in activities that make life enjoyable, loss of dignity, and loss of autonomy (Niemeyer, 2006).

Public interest in assisted suicide was sparked in the 1990s by Dr. Jack Kevorkian, a proponent of euthanasia who devised "suicide machines" that permitted terminally ill patients, after brief counseling, to self-administer lethal drugs and carbon monoxide. Dr. Kevorkian participated in more than 100 such deaths. Less publicity surrounded Dr. Quill's decision to assist Diane—a patient he knew well after serving for years as her personal doctor. After he told her story in a prestigious medical journal, reactions were mixed, as they currently are toward Oregon's suicide law. Some view doctors who help suffering people who want die as compassionate and respectful of patients' personal choices. Others oppose assisted suicide on religious and moral grounds or believe that the role of doctors should be limited to saving, not taking, lives.

Nevertheless, grave dilemmas, like those we discussed for euthanasia, surround assisted suicide. Analyzing the practice, one group of medical experts concluded that it is warranted only when the following conditions are met:

- The patient requests assisted suicide repeatedly and freely and is suffering intolerably, with no satisfactory options.

- The doctor thoroughly explores comfort-care alternatives with the patient.

- The practice is consistent with the doctor's fundamental values. (If not, the doctor should recommend transfer of care.)

- Even when the doctor and patient agree that there is no other acceptable choice, independent monitoring is crucial for preventing abuse. (Stevens, 1997)

Juries have seldom returned guilty verdicts in cases involving doctor-assisted suicide. Yet in April 1999, Kevorkian—the most vigorous American proponent of assisted suicide—was sentenced to 10 to 25 years in prison for second-degree murder and delivery of a controlled substance. Seven months earlier, he had given a terminally ill man a lethal injection, videotaped the death, and permitted the event to be broadcast on the CBS television program *60 Minutes.* Then he dared prosecutors to charge him. The murder indictment prevented Kevorkian from introducing evidence indicating that the man wanted to kill himself—evidence that would have been permissible had the charge been assisted suicide or voluntary active euthanasia.

Public opinion consistently favors voluntary active euthanasia over assisted suicide. Yet in assisted suicide, the final act is solely the patient's, reducing the possibility of coercion. For this reason, some experts believe that legalizing assisted suicide is preferable to legalizing voluntary active euthanasia. However, in an atmosphere of high family caregiving burdens and intense pressure to contain health care costs (see Chapter 17), legalizing either practice poses risks. The American and Canadian Medical Associations oppose both voluntary active euthanasia and assisted suicide. Helping incurable, suffering patients who yearn for death poses profound moral and legal problems.

Ask Yourself

Review

What benefits and risks does legalizing voluntary active euthanasia pose?

Apply

Thinking ahead to the day she dies, Noreen imagines a peaceful scene in which she says good-bye to loved ones. What social and medical practices are likely to increase Noreen's chances of dying in the manner she desires?

Apply

If he should ever fall terminally ill, Ramón is certain that he wants doctors to halt life-saving treatment. To best ensure that his wish will be granted, what should Ramón do?

Reflect

Do you approve of passive euthanasia, voluntary active euthanasia, or doctor-assisted suicide? If you were terminally ill, would you consider any of these practices? Explain.

www.ablongman.com/berk

Bereavement: Coping with the Death of a Loved One

Loss is an inevitable part of existence throughout the life-span. Even when change is for the better, we must let go of some aspects of experience so we can embrace others. In this way, our development prepares us for profound loss.

Bereavement is the experience of losing a loved one by death. The root of this word means "to be robbed," suggesting unjust and injurious stealing of something valuable. Consistent with this image, we respond to loss with **grief**—intense physical and psychological distress. When we say someone is grief-stricken, we imply that his or her total way of being is affected.

Because grief can be overwhelming, cultures have devised ways of helping their members move beyond it to deal with the life changes demanded by death of a loved one. **Mourning** is the culturally specified expression of the bereaved person's thoughts and feelings. Customs—such as gathering with family and friends, dressing in black, attending the funeral, and observing a prescribed mourning period with special rituals—vary greatly among societies and ethnic groups. But all have in common the goal of helping people work through their grief and learn to live in a world that does not include the deceased.

Clearly, grief and mourning are closely linked—in everyday language, we often use the two words interchangeably. Let's look closely at how people respond to the death of a loved one.

Grief Process

Theorists formerly believed that bereaved individuals—both children and adults—moved through three phases of grieving, each characterized by a different set of responses (Bowlby, 1980; Rando, 1995). In reality, however, people vary greatly in behavior and timing and often move back and forth between these reactions. A more accurate account compares grief to a roller-coaster ride, with many ups and downs and, over time, gradual resolution (Lund, 1996). Rather than phases, grieving process can be conceived as a set of *tasks*—actions that must be taken for the person to recover and return to a fulfilling life: (1) to accept the reality of the loss; (2) to work through the pain of grief; (3) to adjust to a world without the loved one; and (4) and to develop an inner bond with the deceased and move on with life (Worden, 2002). According to this view, people can take active steps to overcome grief—a powerful remedy for the overwhelming feelings of vulnerability that the bereaved often experience.

■ **Avoidance.** On hearing the news, the survivor experiences shock followed by disbelief, which may last from hours to weeks. A numbed feeling serves as "emotional anesthesia" while the person begins the first task of grieving: becoming painfully aware of the loss.

■ **Confrontation.** As the mourner confronts the reality of the death, grief is most intense. The person often experiences a cascade of emotional reactions, including anxiety, sadness, protest, anger, helplessness, frustration, abandonment, and yearning for the loved one. Common responses include obsessively reviewing the circumstances of death, asking how it might have been prevented, and searching for meaning in it (Neimeyer, 2001b). In addition, the grief-stricken person may be absentminded, unable to concentrate, and preoccupied with thoughts of the deceased, and may experience loss of sleep and appetite. Self-destructive behaviors, such as taking drugs or driving too fast, may occur. Most of these responses are symptoms of depression—an invariable component of grieving.

Although confrontation is difficult, it enables the mourner to grapple with the second task: working through the pain of grief. Each surge of anguish that results from an unmet wish to be reunited with the deceased brings the mourner closer to acceptance that the loved one is gone. After hundreds, perhaps thousands, of these painful moments, the grieving person comprehends that a cherished relationship must be transformed from a physical presence to an inner representation. As a result, the mourner makes progress on the third task: adjusting to a world in which the deceased is missing.

■ **Restoration.** Adjusting to the loss is more than an internal, emotional task. The bereaved must also deal with stressors that are secondary outcomes of the death—overcoming loneliness by reaching out to others; mastering skills (such as finances or cooking) that the deceased had performed; reorganizing daily life without the loved one; and revising one's identity from "spouse" to "widow" or from "parent" to "parent of a deceased child."

According to a recent perspective, called the **dual-process model of coping with loss,** effective coping requires people to oscillate between dealing with the emotional consequences of loss and attending to life changes, which—when handled successfully—have restorative, or healing, effects (Stroebe & Schut, 1999, 2001). Moving back and forth offers temporary distraction and relief from painful grieving. Much research indicates that confronting grief without relief has severe negative consequences for physical and mental health (Rimé et al., 1998). Consequently, one 14-session intervention for older adults grieving the loss of a spouse addresses both emotional and life-change issues, alternating between them (Lund et al., 2004).

As grief subsides, emotional energies increasingly shift toward the fourth task—forging a symbolic bond with the deceased and moving on with life by meeting everyday responsibilities, investing in new activities and goals, strengthening old ties, and building new relationships. On certain days, such as family celebrations or the anniversary of death, grief reactions may resurface and require attention, but they do not interfere with a healthy, positive approach to life.

How long does grieving last? No single answer can be given. Sometimes confrontation continues for a few months, at other times for several years. An occasional upsurge of grief may persist for a lifetime and is a common response to losing a much-loved spouse, partner, child, or friend (Sanders, 1999).

Personal and Situational Variations

Like dying, grieving is affected by many factors, including personality, coping style, and religious and cultural background. Sex differences are also evident. Compared with women, men typically express distress and depression less directly and seek social support less readily—factors that may contribute to the much higher mortality rate among bereaved men than women

(Doka & Martin, 2000; Lund & Caserta, 2004b; McGoldrick, 2004). Furthermore, the quality of the mourner's relationship with the deceased is important. An end to a loving, fulfilling bond may lead to anguished grieving, but it is unlikely to leave the residue of guilt and regret that often follows dissolution of a conflict-ridden, ambivalent tie.

Circumstances surrounding the death—whether it is sudden and unanticipated or follows a prolonged illness—also shape mourners' responses. The nature of the lost relationship and the timing of the death within the life course make a difference as well.

■ **Sudden, Unanticipated versus Prolonged, Expected Deaths.** In instances of sudden, unexpected deaths—usually the result of murder, suicide, war, accident, or natural disaster—avoidance may be especially pronounced and confrontation highly traumatic because shock and disbelief are extreme. In a survey of a representative sample of 18- to 45-year-old adults in a large U.S. city, the trauma most often reported as prompting an intense, debilitating stress reaction was the sudden, unanticipated death of a loved one, an event 60 percent of the participants had experienced (Breslau et al., 1998). In contrast, during prolonged dying, the bereaved person has had time to engage in **anticipatory grieving**—acknowledging that the loss is inevitable and preparing emotionally for it.

© PAUL CONKLIN/PHOTOEDIT

Sudden, unanticipated deaths often prompt an intense, debilitating stress reaction. Here teenagers express their feelings for a peer victim of a car accident by constructing a shrine at the site of the crash.

Adjusting to a death is easier when the survivor understands the reasons for it. Without explanations that make sense, mourners often remain anxious and confused. This barrier to confronting loss is tragically apparent in cases of sudden infant death syndrome (SIDS), in which doctors cannot tell parents exactly why their apparently healthy baby died (see Chapter 3, page 109). That death seems "senseless" also complicates grieving after suicides, terrorist attacks, school and drive-by shootings, and natural disasters. In Western societies, people tend to believe that momentous events should be comprehensible and nonrandom. A death that is sudden and unexpected can threaten basic assumptions about a just, benevolent, and controllable world (Gluhoski & Wortman, 1996).

Suicide, particularly that of a young person, is especially hard to bear. Compared with survivors of other sudden deaths, people grieving a suicidal loss are more likely to conclude that they contributed to or could have prevented it—self-blame that can trigger profound guilt and shame. These reactions are likely to be especially intense and persisting when a mourner's culture or religion condemns suicide as immoral (Dunne & Dunne-Maxim, 2004). In one study, college students who had survived a suicide scored higher than those who had experienced any other type of loss in feelings of shame, a sense of rejection by the deceased, and self-destructive behavior (Silverman, Range, & Overholser, 1994). Typically, recovery from grief after a suicide is prolonged.

■ **Parents Grieving the Loss of a Child.** The death of a child, whether unexpected or foreseen, is the most difficult loss an adult can face (Dent & Stewart, 2004). It brings special grieving problems because children are extensions of parents' feelings about themselves—the focus of hopes and dreams, including parents' sense of immortality. Also, since children depend on, admire, and appreciate their parents in a deeply gratifying way, they are an unmatched source of love. Finally, the death of a child is unnatural: Children are not supposed to die before their parents.

Parents who have lost a child often report considerable distress many years later, along with frequent thoughts of the deceased (Kreicbergs et al., 2004). The guilt triggered by outliving their child frequently becomes a tremendous burden, even when parents "know" better. For example, a psychologist who understood that his daughter's cancer was not hereditary nevertheless said to a therapist, "Her genes allowed her to develop cancer. I gave her her genes. Therefore, I killed my daughter" (Rando, 1991, p. 239).

Although a child's death sometimes leads to marital breakup, this is likely to happen only when the relationship was already unsatisfactory (Wheeler, 2001). If parents can reorganize the family system and reestablish a sense of life's meaning through valuing the lost child's impact on their lives and investing in other children and activities, then the result can be firmer family commitments and personal growth. Five years after her son's death, one parent reflected on her progress:

> I was afraid to let go [of my pain, which was] a way of loving him. . . . Finally I had to admit that his life meant

more than pain, it also meant joy and happiness and fun—and living. . . . When we release pain we make room for happiness in our lives. My memories of S. became lighter and more spontaneous. Instead of hurtful, my memories brought comfort, even a chuckle. . . . I realized S. was still teaching me things. (Klass, 2004, p. 87)

■ **Children and Adolescents Grieving the Loss of a Parent or Sibling.** The loss of an attachment figure has long-term consequences for children. When a parent dies, children's basic sense of security and being cared for is threatened. And the death of a sibling not only deprives children of a close emotional tie but also informs them, often for the first time, of their own vulnerability.

Children grieving a family loss describe frequent crying, trouble concentrating in school, sleep difficulties, headaches, and other physical symptoms several months to years after a death. And clinical studies reveal that persistent mild depression, anxiety, and angry outbursts are common (Dowdney, 2000; Silverman & Worden, 1992). At the same time, many children say they have actively maintained mental contact with their dead parent or sibling, dreaming about and speaking to them regularly. In a follow-up 7 to 9 years after sibling loss, thinking about the deceased brother or sister at least once a day was common (Martinson, Davies, & McClowry, 1987; Silverman & Nickman, 1996). These images, sometimes reported by bereaved adults as well, seem to facilitate coping with loss.

Cognitive development contributes to the ability to grieve. For example, children with an immature understanding of death may believe the dead parent left voluntarily, perhaps in anger, and that the other parent may also disappear. For these reasons, young children need careful, repeated explanations assuring them that the parent did not want to die and was not angry at them (Christ, Siegel, & Christ, 2002). Keeping the truth from children isolates them and often leads to profound regrets. One 8-year-old who learned only a half-hour in advance that his sick brother was dying reflected, "If only I'd known, I could have said good-bye."

Regardless of children's level of understanding, honesty, affection, and reassurance help them tolerate painful feelings of loss. Grief-stricken school-age children are usually more willing than adolescents to confide in parents. To appear normal, teenagers tend to keep their grieving from both adults and peers. Consequently, they are more likely than children to become depressed or to escape from grief through acting-out behavior (Granot, 2005).

■ **Adults Grieving the Loss of an Intimate Partner.** Recall from Chapter 18 that after the death of a spouse, adaptation to widowhood varies greatly, with age, social support, and personality making a difference. After a period of intense grieving, most widowed elders in Western nations fare well, while younger individuals display more negative outcomes (see page 618 to review). Loss of a spouse or partner in early or middle adulthood is a nonnormative event that profoundly disrupts life plans. Older widows and widowers have many more contemporaries in similar circumstances. And most have already attained important life goals or adjusted to the fact that some goals will not be attained.

In addition to dealing with feelings of loss, young and middle-aged widows and widowers often must assume a greater role in comforting others, especially children. They also face the stresses of single parenthood and rapid shrinking of the social network established during their life as a couple (Lopata, 1996). Younger widows frequently report that the most valuable support they received came from their mothers, many of whom were also widowed (Bankoff, 1983).

The death of an intimate partner in a gay or lesbian relationship presents unique challenges. When relatives limit or bar the partner from participating in funeral services, the survivor experiences *disenfranchised grief*—a sense of loss without the opportunity to mourn publicly and benefit from others' support—which can profoundly disrupt the grieving process (Lund & Caserta, 2004a). Fortunately, gay and lesbian communities provide helpful alternative support in the form of memorial services and other rituals.

■ **Bereavement Overload.** When a person experiences several deaths at once or in close succession, *bereavement overload* can occur. Multiple losses deplete the coping resources of even well-adjusted people, leaving them emotionally overwhelmed and unable to resolve their grief. For many young adults, especially members of the gay community who have lost partners and friends, AIDS presents this challenge. In a study of over 700 gay men, those experiencing two or more losses in close succession reported more distress, suicidal thoughts, and substance use than did those with only a single loss (Martin & Dean, 1993). Fear of discrimination may prevent sexual minorities overwhelmed by grief from seeking treatment, especially if they are unaware of psychological services, including counseling and social support networks, in the gay community (Springer & Lease, 2000).

Because old age often brings the death of spouse, siblings, and friends in close succession, elders are also at risk for bereavement overload. But recall from Chapter 18 that compared with young people, older adults are often better equipped to handle these losses. They know that decline and death are expected in late adulthood, and they have had a lifetime of experience through which to develop effective coping strategies.

Finally, public tragedies—random murders in schools, terrorist attacks, natural disasters (such as Hurricane Katrina in August 2005), or widely publicized kidnappings—can spark bereavement overload (Corr, 2003). For example, many survivors who lost loved ones, co-workers, or friends in the September 11, 2001, terrorist attacks (including an estimated 15,000 children who lost a parent) experienced repeated images of horror and destruction, which impeded coming to terms with loss. Children and adolescents suffered profoundly—from intense shock, prolonged grief, frequent mental replays of the vicious attack and gruesome outcomes, and fear of the settings in which those events occurred (Nader, 2002; Webb, 2002). The

In the aftermath of the 2004 school siege in Beslan, Russia, with 120 burials scheduled, friends and family weep over the coffins of murdered hostages. A public tragedy like this can spark bereavement overload, and mourners are at risk for prolonged, overwhelming grief.

greater the bereaved individual's exposure to the catastrophic death scene, the more severe these reactions.

Funerals and other bereavement rituals, illustrated in the Cultural Influences box on pages 660–661, assist mourners of all ages in resolving grief with the help of family and friends. Bereaved individuals who remain preoccupied with loss and who have difficulty resuming interest in everyday activities benefit from special interventions designed to help them adjust.

Bereavement Interventions

Sympathy and understanding are sufficient to enable most people to undertake the tasks necessary to recover from grief (see Applying What We Know on the following page). Yet effective support is often difficult to provide, and relatives and friends can benefit from training in how to respond. Sometimes they give advice aimed at hastening recovery, an approach that most bereaved people dislike (Lehman, Ellard, & Wortman, 1986). At other times, mourners are too overcome to acknowledge well-meaning interactions, causing others to withdraw (Stylianos & Vachon, 1993). Listening patiently and "just being there" are among the best ways to help.

Bereavement interventions typically encourage people to draw on their existing social network, while providing additional social support. Self-help groups that bring together mourners who have experienced the same type of loss are highly effective in reducing stress (Lieberman, 1993). In a program for recently widowed elders in which group members

Applying What We Know

Suggestions for Resolving Grief After a Loved One Dies

Suggestion	Description
Give yourself permission to feel the loss.	Permit yourself to confront all thoughts and emotions associated with the death. Make a conscious decision to overcome your grief, recognizing that this will take time.
Accept social support.	In the early part of grieving, let others reach out to you by making meals, running errands, and keeping you company. Be assertive; ask for what you need so people who would like to help will know what to do.
Be realistic about the course of grieving.	Expect to have some negative and intense reactions, such as feeling anguished, sad, and angry, that last from weeks to months and may occasionally resurface years after the death. There is no one way to grieve, so find the best way for you.
Remember the deceased.	Review your relationship to and experiences with the deceased, permitting yourself to see that you can no longer be with him or her as before. Form a new relationship based on memories, keeping it alive through photographs, commemorative donations, prayers, and other symbols and actions.
When ready, invest in new activities and relationships, and master new tasks of daily living.	Determine which roles you must give up and which ones you must assume as a consequence of the death, and take deliberate steps to incorporate these into your life. Set small goals at first, such as a night at the movies, a dinner date with a friend, a cooking or household repair class, or a week's vacation.

helped one another resolve grief and master tasks of daily living, participants readily bonded with one another and gained in sense of self-efficacy at managing their own lives (Caserta, Lund, & Rice, 1999). A widow expressed the many lasting benefits:

> We shared our anger at being left behind, . . . our fright of that aloneness. We shared our favorite pictures, so each of us could know the others' families and the fun we used to have. We shared our feelings of guilt if we had fun . . . and found out that it was okay to keep on living! . . . We cheered when one of us accomplished a new task. We also tried to lend a helping hand and heart when we would have one of our bad days! . . . This group will always be there for me and I will always be there for them. I love you all! (Lund, 2005)

Interventions for children and adolescents following violent deaths must protect them from unnecessary reexposure, help parents and teachers with their own distress so they can effectively offer comfort, and be culturally sensitive. After shootings on the grounds of one school, administrators arranged for a ceremony that removed "angry dead souls." Only then would the large number of Vietnamese Buddhist students return to their classrooms (Nader, Dubrow, & Stamm, 1999).

Sudden, violent, and unexplainable deaths; the loss of a child; a death that the mourner feels he or she could have prevented; or an ambivalent or dependent relationship with the deceased make it harder for bereaved people to overcome their loss. In these instances, grief therapy, or individual counseling with a specially trained professional, is sometimes helpful. An effective approach is to assist bereaved adults in finding some

value in the grieving experience—for example, gaining insight into the meaning of relationships, discovering their own capacity to cope with adversity, or crystallizing a sense of purpose in their lives (Neimeyer, 2001a).

Death Education

Preparatory steps can help people of all ages cope with death more effectively. The death awareness movement that sparked increased sensitivity to the needs of dying patients has also led to the rise of death education. Courses in death, dying, and bereavement are now a familiar part of offerings in colleges and universities. Instruction has been integrated into the training of doctors, nurses, psychologists, and social workers, although most professional offerings are limited to only a few lectures (Wass, 2004). Death education is also found in adult education programs in many communities. And it has filtered down to a few elementary and secondary schools.

Death education at all levels has the following goals:

- Increasing students' understanding of the physical and psychological changes that accompany dying

- Helping students learn how to cope with the death of a loved one

- Preparing students to be informed consumers of medical and funeral services

- Promoting understanding of social and ethical issues involving death

Cultural Influences

Cultural Variations in Mourning Behavior

The ceremonies that commemorated Sofie's and Nicholas's deaths—the first Jewish, the second Quaker—were strikingly different. Yet they served common goals: announcing that a death has occurred, ensuring social support, commemorating the deceased, and conveying a philosophy of life after death.

At the funeral home, Sofie's body was washed and shrouded, a Jewish ritual signifying return to a state of purity. Then it was placed in a plain wooden (not metal) coffin, so as not to impede the natural process of decomposition. To underscore the finality of death, Jewish tradition does not permit viewing of the body; it remains in a closed coffin. Traditionally, the coffin is not left alone until burial; in honor of the deceased, the community maintains a day-and-night vigil.

To return the body quickly to the life-giving earth from which it sprang, Sofie's funeral was scheduled 3 days after death, as soon as relatives could gather. As the service began, Sofie's husband and children symbolized their anguish by cutting a black ribbon and pinning it to their clothing. The rabbi recited psalms of comfort, followed by a eulogy. The service continued at the graveside. Once the coffin had been lowered into the ground, relatives and friends took turns shoveling earth onto it, each participating in the irrevocable act of burial. The service concluded with the "homecoming" prayer called *Kaddish*, which affirms life while accepting death.

The family returned home to light a memorial candle, which burned throughout *shiva*, the seven-day mourning period (Hazell, 2001). A meal of consolation prepared by others followed, creating a warm feeling of community. Jewish custom prescribes that after 30 days, life should gradually return to normal. When a parent dies, the mourning period is extended to 12 months.

In the tradition of Quaker simplicity, Nicholas's death did not require elaborate preparation of the body or a casket;

he was cremated promptly. During the next week, relatives and close friends gathered with Giselle and Sasha at their home. Together, they planned a memorial service uniquely suited to celebrating Nicholas's life.

On the appointed day, people who had known Nicholas sat in chairs arranged in concentric circles. Standing at the center, a clerk of the Friends (Quaker) Meeting extended a welcome and explained to newcomers the custom of worshipping silently, with those who feel moved to speak rising at any time to share thoughts and feelings. During the next hour, many mourners offered personal statements about Nicholas or read poems and selections from Scripture. Giselle and Sasha provided concluding comments. Then everyone joined hands to close the service, and a reception for the family followed.

Variations in mourning behavior are vast—both within and across societies. For most Jews and Christians, extensive ritual accompanies a funeral and burial. In contrast, the Quaker memorial service is among the least ritualized. In some groups, grief is expressed freely. At African-American funerals, for example, venting feelings is common; eulogies and music are usually designed to trigger release of deep emotion (McGoldrick et al., 2004). Other cultures actively discourage any emotional display. The Balinese of Indonesia believe they must remain calm in the face of death if the gods are to hear their prayers. While acknowledging their underlying grief, Balinese mourners—aided by supporters who joke, tease, and distract—work hard to maintain their composure (Rosenblatt, 1993).

Religions also render accounts of the aftermath of death that console both dying and bereaved individuals. Jewish tradition affirms personal survival, although its form is not clearly specified. Greater emphasis is placed on the survival of a people—living on by granting life and care to others. Unlike other Christian faiths, Quakers focus almost exclusively on the here and now—"salvation by character" through working for peace, justice, and a loving community. Little attention is given to fear of hell or hope of heaven. The religions of tribal and village cultures typically include elaborate beliefs about ancestor spirits and the afterlife, and customs designed to ease the journey of the deceased to the spiritual world.

In recent years, a new ritual has arisen: memorials to the deceased on the Internet. These "virtual cemeteries" offer benefits not available through traditional funerals: postings whenever bereaved individuals feel ready to

© DAVID L. RYAN / *THE BOSTON GLOBE*

Venting deep emotion is often part of African-American funerals, particularly in the southern United States. In this Baptist funeral service, a family member weeps openly.

convey their thoughts and feelings, creation of tributes at little or no cost, and continuous, easy access to the memorial. Rather than using the traditional obituary format, most creators of Web tributes choose to tell personal stories, highlighting a laugh, a favorite joke, or a touching moment (Roberts & Vidal, 1999–2000). In addition to celebrating the deceased, some survivors use Web memorials to grieve openly, others to converse with the lost loved one. Visitors can record their feelings in cemetery guestbooks, which enable them to connect with other mourners (Roberts, 2004). Web cemeteries also provide a means for people excluded from traditional death rituals to engage in public mourning. The following "gravesite" message captures the unique qualities of this highly flexible medium for mourning:

I wish I could maintain contact with you, to keep alive the vivid memories of your impact on my life. Perhaps I can do this by sharing my memories in this seemingly unconventional way. Because I cannot visit your grave today, I use this means to tell you how much you are loved.

Educational format varies widely. Some programs simply convey information. Others are experiential and include activities such as role playing, discussions with the terminally ill, visits to mortuaries and cemeteries, and personal awareness exercises. Research reveals that although using a lecture style leads to gains in knowledge, it often leaves students more uncomfortable about death than when they entered. In contrast, experiential programs that help people confront their own mortality are less likely to heighten death anxiety and may sometimes reduce it (Durlak & Riesenberg, 1991; Maglio & Robinson, 1994).

Whether acquired in the classroom or in our daily lives, our thoughts and feelings about death are forged through interactions with others. Becoming more aware of how we die and of our own mortality, we encounter our greatest loss, but we also gain. Dying people have at times confided in those close to them that awareness of the limits of their lifespan permitted them to dispense with superficial distractions and wasted energies and focus on what is truly important in their lives. As one AIDS patient summed up, "[It's] kind of like life, just speeded up"—an accelerated process in which, over a period of weeks to months, one grapples with issues that normally would have taken years or decades to resolve (Selwyn, 1996, p. 36). Applying this lesson to ourselves, we learn that by being in touch with death and dying, we can live ever more fully.

Ask Yourself

Review

What circumstances are likely to induce bereavement overload? Cite examples.

Apply

List features of self-help groups that contribute to their effectiveness in helping people cope with loss.

Connect

Compare grieving individuals' reactions with terminally ill patients' thoughts and feelings as they move closer to death, described on page 643. Can a dying person's reactions be viewed as a form of grieving? Explain.

Reflect

Visit a Web cemetery, such as Virtual Memorials, *virtualmemorials.com,* or EGC Memorials, *www.egcmemorials.com.* Select examples of Web tributes, guestbook entries, and testimonials that illustrate the unique ways in which virtual cemeteries help people cope with death.

www.ablongman.com/berk

Summary

How We Die

Describe the physical changes of dying, along with their implications for defining death and the meaning of death with dignity.

■ Of the one-quarter of people in industrialized nations who die suddenly, 80 to 90 percent are victims of heart attacks. Death is long and drawn-out for three-fourths of people—many more than in times past, as a result of life-saving medical technology.

■ In general, dying takes place in three phases: (1) the **agonal phase,** the gasps and spasms of the first moments in which the body can no longer sustain life; **clinical death,** a short interval in which resuscitation is still possible; and **mortality,** or permanent death.

■ In most industrialized nations, **brain death** is accepted as the definition of death. But for the thousands of patients who remain in a **persistent vegetative state,** the brain death standard does not always solve the dilemma of when to halt treatment of the incurably ill.

■ Most people will not experience an easy death. We can best ensure death with dignity by supporting dying patients through their physical and psychological distress, being candid about death's certainty, and helping them learn enough about their condition to make reasoned choices about treatment.

Understanding of and Attitudes Toward Death

Discuss age-related changes in conceptions of and attitudes toward death, and cite factors that influence death anxiety.

■ Compared with earlier generations, more young people in the industrialized world reach adulthood having had little contact with death, contributing to a sense of unease about it.

■ To understand death, children must have some basic notions of biology and must be able to distinguish between "dead," "inanimate," "unreal," and "nonexistent." During early and middle childhood, most children attain an adultlike concept of death, gradually mastering its various components. Experiences with death and religious teachings affect children's understanding. When parents talk about death candidly, children usually have a good grasp of the facts of death and an easier time accepting it.

© EYEWIRE COLLECTION/GETTY IMAGES

■ Adolescents often fail to apply their understanding of death to everyday life. Though aware that death happens to everyone and can occur at any time, teenagers nevertheless are attracted to alternative views, are high risk takers, and do not take death personally. By discussing concerns about death with adolescents, adults can help them build a bridge between death as a logical concept and their personal experiences.

■ In early adulthood, many people avoid thinking about death, but in midlife, they become more conscious that their own lives are finite. In late adulthood, when death is much closer, people are more apt to ponder the process of dying than the state of death.

■ Wide individual and cultural variations exist in **death anxiety.** People with a sense of spirituality or a well-developed personal philosophy of death experience less fear of death. As part of their greater ability to regulate negative emotion and their sense of symbolic immortality, older adults are less anxious about death than younger adults. Women exhibit more death anxiety than men do, perhaps because they are more open about their feelings.

Thinking and Emotions of Dying People

Describe and evaluate Kübler-Ross's theory of typical responses to dying, citing factors that influence dying patients' responses.

■ According to Elisabeth Kübler-Ross's theory, dying people typically express five responses, which she initially proposed as "stages": denial, anger, bargaining, depression, and acceptance. These reactions do not occur in fixed sequence, and dying people often display other coping strategies.

■ An **appropriate death** is one that makes sense in terms of the individual's pattern of living and values, preserves or restores significant relationships, and is as free of suffering as possible. Many contextual variables—nature of the disease; personality and coping style; family members' and health professionals' truthfulness and sensitivity; and spirituality, religion, and cultural background—affect the way people respond to their own dying and, therefore, the extent to which they attain an appropriate death.

A Place to Die

Evaluate the extent to which homes, hospitals, and the hospice approach meet the needs of dying people and their families.

■ Although the overwhelming majority of people say they want to die at home, even with professional help, caring for a dying patient is highly stressful. To handle the medical and comfort-care needs of the dying, special equipment and technical support often must be brought to the home.

■ Sudden deaths typically occur in hospital emergency rooms, where sympathetic explanations from staff can reduce family members' anger, frustration, and confusion. Intensive care is especially depersonalizing for patients, who may linger between life and death while hooked to machines for months. Even in general or specialized cancer care units, emphasis on efficiency usually interferes with an appropriate death. Most hospitals still do not have comprehensive treatment programs aimed at easing suffering at the end of life.

© ROYALTY-FREE/CORBIS

■ Whether a person dies at home or in a hospital, the **hospice** approach strives to meet the dying person's physical, emotional, social, and spiritual needs by providing **palliative,** or **comfort, care** focused on protecting the quality of remaining life rather than on prolonging life. Hospice programs also offer bereavement services to families in the year after death. Besides reducing patients' physical suffering, hospice care contributes to improved family functioning and better psychological well-being among family survivors in the year or two after the loved one's death.

The Right to Die

Discuss controversies surrounding euthanasia and assisted suicide.

- Modern medical procedures that preserve life can also prolong inevitable death, diminishing quality of life and personal dignity. **Euthanasia**—ending the life of a person suffering from an incurable condition—takes various forms.

- **Passive euthanasia,** withholding or withdrawing life-sustaining treatment from a hopelessly ill patient, is widely accepted and practiced. But in the absence of consensus on end-of-life health care, people can best ensure that their wishes will be followed by preparing a written **advance medical directive.** A **living will** contains instructions for treatment. A more flexible approach, the **durable power of attorney for health care,** authorizes appointment of another person to make health care decisions on one's behalf. When no advance medical directive exists, some U.S. states and Canadian provinces permit appointment of a health care proxy.

- Public support for **voluntary active euthanasia,** in which doctors or others comply with a suffering patient's request to die before a natural end to life, is high. Nevertheless, the practice has sparked heated controversy, fueled by fears that it will undermine trust in health professionals and lead us down a "slippery slope" to the killing of vulnerable people who did not ask to die.

- Less public support exists for assisted suicide. But because the final act is solely the patient's, some experts believe that legalizing assisted suicide is preferable to legalizing voluntary active euthanasia.

Bereavement: Coping with the Death of a Loved One

Describe the phases of grieving, factors that underlie individual variations, and bereavement interventions.

- **Bereavement** refers to the experience of losing a loved one by death, **grief** to the intense

physical and psychological distress that accompanies loss. **Mourning** customs are culturally prescribed expressions of thoughts and feelings designed to help people work through their grief.

- Although many theorists regard grieving as taking place in orderly phases—avoidance, confrontation, and finally restoration—a more accurate image is a roller-coaster ride, with the mourner completing a set of tasks resulting in gradual recovery over time. According to the **dual-process model of coping with loss,** effective coping involves oscillating between dealing with the emotional consequences of loss and attending to life changes, which offer temporary distraction and relief from painful grieving.

- Like dying, grieving is affected by many personal and situational factors. Bereaved men express grief less directly than bereaved women. After a sudden, unanticipated death, avoidance may be especially pronounced and confrontation highly traumatic. In contrast, a prolonged, expected death grants the bereaved person time to engage in **anticipatory grieving.**

- When a parent loses a child or a child loses a parent or sibling, grieving is generally very intense and prolonged. Loss of a spouse or partner in early or middle adulthood profoundly disrupts life plans. Younger widowed individuals usually fare less well than widowed elders. When relatives limit or bar a same-sex partner's participation in funeral services, the mourner experiences *disenfranchised grief,* which can profoundly disrupt the process of grieving.

- People who experience several deaths at once or in close succession may suffer from bereavement overload. Among those at risk are young people who have lost partners and friends to AIDS, the elderly, and people who have witnessed unexpected, violent deaths.

- Sympathy and understanding are sufficient for most people to recover from grief. Self-help groups can provide extra social support. When bereaved individuals find it very hard to overcome loss, professional bereavement interventions can be helpful.

Death Education

Explain how death education can help people cope with death more effectively.

- Today, instruction in death, dying, and bereavement can be found in colleges and universities; in training programs for doctors, nurses, and helping professionals; in adult education programs; and in a few elementary and secondary schools. Courses are more likely to reach students cognitively and emotionally when, in addition to conveying information, they include an experiential component.

Important Terms and Concepts

advance medical directive (p. 651)
agonal phase (p. 636)
anticipatory grieving (p. 656)
appropriate death (p. 644)
bereavement (p. 655)
brain death (p. 637)
clinical death (p. 636)
death anxiety (p. 641)
dual-process model of coping with loss (p. 656)
durable power of attorney for health care (p. 651)

euthanasia (p. 650)
grief (p. 655)
hospice (p. 648)
living will (p. 651)
mortality (p. 636)
mourning (p. 655)
palliative, or comfort, care (p. 648)
passive euthanasia (p. 650)
persistent vegetative state (p. 637)
voluntary active euthanasia (p. 652)

Glossary

Aboriginal Head Start A Canadian federal program that provides First Nations, Inuit, and Métis children younger than age 6 with preschool education and nutritional and health services and that encourages parent involvement in program planning and children's learning. (p. 245)

academic programs Preschools and kindergartens in which teachers structure children's learning, teaching academic skills through formal lessons, often using repetition and drill. Distinguished from *child-centered programs*. (p. 245)

accommodation In Piaget's theory, that part of adaptation in which new schemes are created and old ones adjusted to capture the environment more completely. Distinguished from *assimilation*. (p. 152)

active lifespan The number of years of vigorous, healthy life. Distinguished from *average life expectancy* and *maximum lifespan*. (p. 563)

activities of daily living (ADLs) Basic self-care tasks required to live on one's own, such as bathing, dressing, getting in and out of bed or a chair, or eating. (p. 564)

activity theory A social theory of aging that states that social barriers to engagement, not the desires of elders, cause declining rates of social interaction in late adulthood. When older people lose certain roles, they try to find others in an effort to stay about as active and busy as they were in middle age, so as to preserve life satisfaction. Distinguished from *disengagement theory, continuity theory,* and *socioemotional selectivity theory*. (p. 611)

adaptation In Piaget's theory, the process of building schemes through direct interaction with the environment. Made up of two complementary processes: *assimilation* and *accommodation*. (p. 152)

adolescence The transition between childhood and adulthood. Begins with puberty and involves accepting one's full-grown body, acquiring adult ways of thinking, attaining greater independence from one's family, developing more mature ways of relating to peers of both sexes, and constructing an identity. (p. 361)

advance medical directive A written statement of desired medical treatment should a person become incurably ill. (p. 651)

affect optimization The ability to maximize positive emotion and dampen negative emotion. An emotional strength of late adulthood. (p. 601)

age of viability The age at which the fetus can first survive if born early. Occurs sometime between 22 and 26 weeks. (p. 84)

age-graded influences Influences on lifespan development that are strongly related to age and therefore fairly predictable in when they occur and how long they last. (p. 10)

agonal phase The phase of dying in which gasps and muscle spasms occur during the first moments in which the body can no longer sustain life. Distinguished from *clinical death* and *mortality*. (p. 636)

allele Each form of a gene located at the same place on corresponding pairs of chromosomes. (p. 48)

Alzheimer's disease The most common form of dementia, in which structural and chemical deterioration in the brain is associated with gradual loss of many aspects of thought and behavior, including memory, skilled and purposeful movements, and comprehension and production of speech. (p. 580)

amnion The inner membrane that forms a protective covering around the prenatal organism. (p. 82)

amyloid plaques A structural change in the brain associated with Alzheimer's disease in which dense deposits of a deteriorated protein called amyloid are surrounded by clumps of dead nerve and glial cells. (p. 581)

androgyny A type of gender identity in which the person scores high on both masculine and feminine personality characteristics. (p. 277)

animistic thinking The belief that inanimate objects have lifelike qualities, such as thoughts, wishes, feelings, and intentions. (p. 229)

anorexia nervosa An eating disorder in which young people starve themselves because of a compulsive fear of getting fat. (p. 371)

anoxia Inadequate oxygen supply. (p. 100)

anticipatory grieving Before a prolonged, expected death, acknowledging that the loss is inevitable and preparing emotionally for it. (p. 656)

Apgar Scale A rating used to assess the newborn baby's physical condition immediately after birth. (p. 98)

appropriate death A death that makes sense in terms of the individual's pattern of living and values and, at the same time, preserves or restores significant relationships and is as free of suffering as possible. (p. 644)

assimilation In Piaget's theory, that part of adaptation in which the external world is interpreted in terms of current schemes. Distinguished from *accommodation*. (p. 152)

assistive technology An array of devices that permits people with disabilities, including older adults, to improve their functioning. (p. 571)

associative memory deficit Difficulty creating and retrieving links between pieces of information—for example, two items or an item and its context. (p. 588)

associative play A form of true social participation in which children are engaged in separate activities, but they interact by exchanging toys and comment on one another's behavior. Distinguished from *nonsocial activity, parallel play,* and *cooperative play*. (p. 261)

attachment The strong, affectionate tie that humans have with special people in their lives that leads them to feel pleasure and joy when interacting with them and to be comforted by their nearness during times of stress. (p. 196)

Attachment Q-Sort An alternative method to the Strange Situation, suitable for children between 1 and 4 years, that permits attachment to be assessed through observations in the home. Includes a set of 90 descriptors of child behavior that yield a score ranging from high to low in security. (p. 198)

attention-deficit hyperactivity disorder (ADHD) A childhood disorder involving inattentiveness, impulsivity, and excessive motor activity. Often leads to academic failure and social problems. (p. 304)

authoritarian child-rearing style A child-rearing style that is low in acceptance and involvement, high in coercive and psychological control, and low in autonomy granting. Distinguished from *authoritative, permissive,* and *uninvolved child-rearing styles*. (p. 279)

authoritative child-rearing style A child-rearing style that is high in acceptance and involvement, that emphasizes adaptive control techniques, and that includes appropriate autonomy granting. Distinguished from *authoritarian, permissive,* and *uninvolved child-rearing styles*. (p. 279)

autobiographical memory Representations of special, one-time events that are long lasting because they are imbued with personal meaning. (p. 163)

autoimmune response An abnormal response of the immune system in which it turns against normal body tissues. (p. 569)

autonomous morality Piaget's second stage of moral development, in which children view rules as flexible, socially agreed-on principles that can be revised when necessary. Begins around age 10. (p. 406)

autonomy At adolescence, a sense of oneself as a separate, self-governing individual. Involves relying more on oneself and less on parents for direction and guidance and engaging in careful, well-reasoned decision making. (p. 413)

autonomy versus shame and doubt In Erikson's theory, the psychological conflict of toddlerhood, which is resolved positively if parents provide young children with suitable guidance and appropriate choices. (p. 184)

autosomes The 22 matching chromosome pairs in each human cell. (p. 47)

average life expectancy The number of years an individual born in a particular year can expect to live, starting at any given age. Distinguished from *maximum lifespan* and *active lifespan*. (p. 562)

avoidant attachment The quality of insecure attachment characterizing infants who are usually not distressed by parental separation and who avoid the parent when she or he returns. Distinguished from *secure, resistant,* and *disorganized/disoriented attachment*. (p. 198)

babbling Repetition of consonant–vowel combinations in long strings, beginning around 4 months of age. (p. 174)

basal metabolic rate (BMR) The amount of energy the body uses at complete rest. (p. 438)

basic emotions Emotions that are universal in humans and other primates, have a long evolutionary history of promoting survival, and can be directly inferred from facial expressions. Includes happiness, interest, surprise, fear, anger, sadness, and disgust. (p. 185)

basic trust versus mistrust In Erikson's theory, the psychological conflict of infancy, which is resolved positively if the balance of care, especially during feeding, is sympathetic and loving. (p. 184)

behavior modification Procedures that combine conditioning and modeling to eliminate undesirable behaviors and increase desirable responses. (p. 18)

behaviorism An approach that views directly observable events—stimuli and responses—as the appropriate focus of study and the development of behavior as taking place through classical and operant conditioning. (p. 17)

bereavement The experience of losing a loved one by death. (p. 655)

bicultural identity The identity constructed by adolescents who explore and adopt values from both their subculture and the dominant culture. (p. 404)

"big five" personality traits Five basic factors into which hundreds of personality traits have been organized: neuroticism, extraversion, openness to experience, agreeableness, and conscientiousness. (p. 540)

biological aging, or **senescence** Genetically influenced, age-related declines in the functioning of organs and systems that are universal in all members of our species. Sometimes called *primary aging*. (p. 431)

blended, or reconstituted, family A family structure resulting from cohabitation or remarriage that includes parent, child, and steprelatives. (p. 348)

body image Conception of and attitude toward one's physical appearance. (p. 370)

brain death Irreversible cessation of all activity in the brain and the brain stem. The definition of death accepted in most industrialized nations. (p. 637)

brain plasticity The ability of other parts of the brain to take over functions of damaged regions. Declines as hemispheres of the cerebral cortex lateralize. (p. 124)

breech position A position of the baby in the uterus that would cause the buttocks or feet to be delivered first. (p. 100)

bulimia nervosa An eating disorder in which individuals (mainly females) engage in strict dieting and excessive exercise accompanied by binge eating, often followed by deliberate vomiting and purging with laxatives. (p. 372)

burnout A condition in which long-term job stress leads to mental exhaustion, a sense of loss of personal control, and feelings of reduced accomplishment. (p. 552)

canalization The tendency of heredity to restrict the development of some characteristics to just one or a few outcomes. (p. 73)

cardinality The mathematical principle that the last number in a counting sequence indicates the quantity of items in the set. (p. 243)

carrier A heterozygous individual who can pass a recessive gene to his or her children. (p. 48)

cataracts Cloudy areas in the lens of the eye that increase from middle to old age, resulting in foggy vision and (without surgery) eventual blindness. (p. 566)

categorical self Early categorization of the self according to salient ways in which people differ, such as age, sex, physical characteristics, and goodness and badness. (p. 208)

central executive The conscious part of working memory that directs the flow of information through the mental system by deciding what to attend to, coordinating incoming information with information already in the system, and selecting, applying, and monitoring strategies. (p. 160)

centration The tendency to focus on one aspect of a situation and neglect other important features. (p. 230)

cephalocaudal trend An organized pattern of physical growth and motor control that proceeds from head to tail. Distinguished from *proximodistal trend*. (p. 121)

cerebellum A brain structure that aids in balance and control of body movements. (p. 219)

cerebral cortex The largest structure of the human brain, which accounts for the highly developed intelligence of the human species. (p. 123)

cerebrovascular dementia A form of dementia in which a series of strokes leaves dead brain cells, producing step-by-step degeneration of mental ability, with each step occurring abruptly after a stroke. (p. 583)

cesarean delivery A surgical delivery in which the doctor makes an incision in the mother's abdomen and lifts the baby out of the uterus. (p. 101)

child-centered programs Preschools and kindergartens in which teachers provide a wide variety of activities from which children select, and much learning takes place through play. Distinguished from *academic programs*. (p. 244)

child-directed speech (CDS) A form of language used by adults to speak to infants and toddlers that consists of short sentences with high-pitched, exaggerated expression, clear pronunciation, distinct pauses between speech segments, and repetition of new words in a variety of contexts. (p. 177)

child-rearing styles Combinations of parenting behaviors that occur in a wide range of situations, thereby creating an enduring childrearing climate. (p. 279)

chorion The outer membrane that forms a protective covering around the prenatal organism. It sends out tiny fingerlike villi, from which the placenta begins to emerge. (p. 82)

chromosomes Rodlike structures in the cell nucleus that store and transmit genetic information. (p. 46)

chronosystem In ecological systems theory, temporal changes in environments, which produce new conditions that affect development. These changes can be imposed externally or arise from within the organism, since people select, modify, and create many of their own settings and experiences. (p. 25)

circular reaction In Piaget's theory, a means of building schemes in which infants try to repeat a chance event caused by their own motor activity. (p. 153)

classical conditioning A form of learning that involves associating a neutral stimulus with a stimulus that leads to a reflexive response. Once the person's nervous system makes the connection between the two stimuli, the neutral stimulus will produce the behavior by itself. (p. 133)

climacteric Midlife transition in which fertility declines. Brings an end to reproductive capacity in women and diminished fertility in men. (p. 502)

clinical death The phase of dying in which heartbeat, circulation, breathing, and brain functioning stop, but resuscitation is still possible. Distinguished from *agonal phase* and *mortality*. (p. 636)

clinical interview A method that uses a flexible, conversational style to probe for the participant's point of view. (p. 28)

clinical, or **case study, method** A method in which the researcher tries to understand the unique person by combining interview data, observations, and sometimes test scores. (p. 29)

clique A group of about five to seven members who are good friends and, therefore, resemble one another in family background, attitudes, and values. (p. 417)

cognitive maps Mental representations of familiar large-scale spaces, such as neighborhood or school. (p. 299)

cognitive self-regulation The process of continuously monitoring progress toward a goal, checking outcomes, and redirecting unsuccessful efforts. (p. 306)

cognitive-affective complexity A form of thinking that increases steadily from adolescence through early adulthood, peaking in middle age, that involves awareness of positive and negative feelings and coordination of them into a complex, organized structure. Involves skillful integration of cognition with emotion. (p. 451)

cognitive-developmental theory An approach introduced by Piaget that views children as actively constructing knowledge as they manipulate and explore their world and that considers cognitive development as taking place in stages. (p. 19)

cohabitation The lifestyle of unmarried couples who have an intimate, sexual relationship and share a residence. (p. 484)

cohort effects The effects of history-graded influences on research findings: People born in one period of time are influenced by particular historical and cultural conditions. (p. 35)

collectivist societies Societies in which people define themselves as part of a group and stress group over individual goals. Distinguished from *individualistic societies*. (p. 66)

commitment within relativistic thinking In Perry's theory, the cognitive approach of the most mature adults, who resist choosing between opposing views and, instead, try to formulate a more satisfying perspective that synthesizes contradictions. (p. 450)

companionate love Love based on warm, trusting affection and caregiving. Distinguished from *passionate love*. (p. 469)

compliance Voluntary obedience to requests and commands. (p. 208)

compression of morbidity The public health goal of reducing the average period of diminished vigor before death as life expectancy extends. So far, persistence of poverty and negative lifestyle factors have interfered with progress toward this goal. (p. 574)

concordance rate The percentage of instances in which both twins show a trait when it is present in one twin. Used to study the role of heredity in emotional and behavior disorders, which can be judged as either present or absent. (p. 71)

concrete operational stage Piaget's third stage, during which thought is logical, flexible, and organized in its application to concrete information. However, the capacity for abstract thinking is not yet present. Spans the years from 7 to 11. (p. 298)

conditioned response (CR) In classical conditioning, a new response produced by a conditioned stimulus (CS) that resembles the unconditioned, or reflexive, response (UCR). (p. 133)

conditioned stimulus (CS) In classical conditioning, a neutral stimulus that through pairing with an unconditioned stimulus (UCS) leads to a new response (CR). (p. 133)

congregate housing Housing for the elderly that provides a variety of support services, including meals in a common dining room, along with watchful oversight of elders with physical and mental disabilities (p. 615)

conservation The understanding that certain physical characteristics of objects remain the same, even when their outward appearance changes. (p. 230)

constructivist classroom A classroom that is based on the educational philosophy that students construct their own knowledge. Often grounded in Piaget's theory. Consists of richly equipped learning centers, small groups and individuals solving problems they choose for themselves, and a teacher who guides and supports in response to children's needs. Distinguished from *traditional* and *social-constructivist classrooms*. (p. 319)

contexts Unique combinations of personal and environmental circumstances that can result in markedly different paths of development. (p. 7)

continuity theory A social theory of aging that states that in their choice of everyday activities and social relationships, older adults strive to maintain a personal system—an identity and a set of personality dispositions, interests, roles, and skills—that ensures consistency between their past and anticipated future and, thus, promotes life satisfaction. Distinguished from *disengagement theory, activity theory,* and *socioemotional selectivity theory.* (p. 611)

continuous development A view that regards development as a process of gradually augmenting the same types of skills that were there to begin with. Distinguished from *discontinuous development.* (p. 6)

contrast sensitivity A general principle accounting for early pattern preferences, which states that if babies can detect a difference in contrast between two patterns, they will prefer the one with more contrast. (p. 143)

controversial children Children who get a large number of positive and negative votes on self-report measures of peer acceptance. Distinguished from *popular, neglected,* and *rejected children.* (p. 340)

conventional level Kohlberg's second level of moral development, in which moral understanding is based on conforming to social rules to ensure positive human relationships and societal order. (p. 407)

convergent thinking Thinking that involves arriving at a single correct answer to a problem. The type of cognition emphasized on intelligence tests. Distinguished from *divergent thinking.* (p. 322)

cooing Pleasant vowel-like noises made by infants beginning around 2 months of age. (p. 174)

cooperative play A form of true social participation in which children's actions are directed toward a common goal. Distinguished from *nonsocial activity, parallel play,* and *associative play.* (p. 261)

core knowledge perspective A view that assumes that infants begin life with innate knowledge systems, or core domains of thought, each of which permits a ready grasp of new related information and therefore supports early, rapid development of certain aspects of cognition. (p. 158)

coregulation A transitional form of supervision in which parents exercise general oversight while permitting children to be in charge of moment-by-moment decision making. (p. 344)

corpus callosum A large bundle of fibers that connects the two hemispheres of the brain. (p. 219)

correlation coefficient A number, ranging from +1.00 to −1.00, that describes the strength and direction of the relationship between two variables. The size of the number shows the strength of the relationship. The sign of the number (+ or -) refers to the direction of the relationship. (p. 32)

correlational design A research design that gathers information on individuals, generally in natural life circumstances, without altering their experiences, and that examines relationships between variables. Cannot determine cause and effect. (p. 30)

creativity The ability to produce work that is original yet appropriate—something others have not thought of that is useful in some way. (p. 322)

cross-linkage theory of aging A theory of biological aging asserting that the formation of bonds, or links, between normally separate protein fibers causes the body's connective tissue to become less elastic over time, leading to many negative physical consequences. (p. 432)

cross-sectional design A research design in which groups of participants of different ages are studied at the same point in time. Distinguished from *longitudinal design.* (p. 35)

crowd A large, loosely organized group consisting of several cliques with similar normative characteristics. (p. 417)

crystallized intelligence Intellectual skills that depend on accumulated knowledge and experience, good judgment, and mastery of social conventions—abilities acquired because they are valued by the individual's culture. Distinguished from *fluid intelligence.* (p. 516)

death anxiety Fear and apprehension of death. (p. 641)

deferred imitation The ability to remember and copy the behavior of models who are not present. (p. 155)

delay of gratification Waiting for an appropriate time and place to engage in a tempting act. (p. 208)

dementia A set of disorders occurring almost entirely in old age in which many aspects of thought and behavior are so impaired that everyday activities are disrupted. (p. 579)

deoxyribonucleic acid (DNA) Long, double-stranded molecules that make up chromosomes. (p. 46)

dependency–support script A typical pattern of interaction in which elders' dependency behaviors are attended to immediately, thereby reinforcing those behaviors. Distinguished from *independence–ignore script*. (p. 606)

dependent variable The variable the researcher expects to be influenced by the independent variable in an experiment. Distinguished from *independent* variable. (p. 32)

developmental cognitive neuroscience An area of research that brings together researchers from a variety of disciplines, including psychology, biology, neuroscience, and medicine, to study the relationship between changes in the brain and the developing person's cognitive processing and behavioral capacities. (p. 21)

developmental quotient, or DQ A score on an infant intelligence test, based primarily on perceptual and motor responses. Computed in the same manner as an IQ. (p. 168)

developmentally appropriate practice A set of standards devised by the National Association for the Education of Young Children that specify program characteristics that meet the developmental and individual needs of young children of varying ages, based on current research and the consensus of experts. (p. 170)

differentiation theory The view that perceptual development involves the detection of increasingly fine-grained, invariant features in the environment. (p. 147)

difficult child A child whose temperament is such that he or she is irregular in daily routines, is slow to accept new experiences, and tends to react negatively and intensely. Distinguished from *easy child* and *slow-to-warm-up child*. (p. 190)

discontinuous development A view in which new and different ways of interpreting and responding to the world emerge at particular time periods. Distinguished from *continuous development*. (p. 6)

disengagement theory A social theory of aging that states that the decline in social interaction in late adulthood is due to mutual withdrawal between elders and society in anticipation of death. Distinguished from *activity theory, continuity theory,* and *socioemotional selectivity theory*. (p. 610)

disorganized/disoriented attachment The quality of insecure attachment characterizing infants who respond in a confused, contradictory fashion when reunited with the parent. Distinguished from *secure, avoidant,* and *resistant attachment*. (p. 198)

distributive justice Beliefs about how to divide resources fairly. (p. 337)

divergent thinking The generation of multiple and unusual possibilities when faced with a task or problem. Associated with creativity. Distinguished from *convergent thinking*. (p. 322)

divorce mediation A series of meetings between divorcing adults and a trained professional who tries to help them settle disputes. Aimed at reducing family conflict during the period surrounding divorce. (p. 348)

dominance hierarchy A stable ordering of group members that predicts who will win when conflict arises. (p. 297)

dominant cerebral hemisphere The hemisphere of the brain responsible for skilled motor action. The left hemisphere is dominant in right-handed individuals. In left-handed individuals, the right hemisphere may be dominant, or motor and language skills may be shared between the hemispheres. (p. 218)

dominant–recessive inheritance A pattern of inheritance in which, under heterozygous conditions, the influence of only one gene is apparent. (p. 48)

dual representation Viewing a symbolic object as both an object in its own right and a symbol. (229)

dual-earner marriage A family form in which both husband and wife are employed. (p. 492)

dual-process model of coping with loss A perspective that assumes that effective coping with loss requires people to oscillate between dealing with the emotional consequences of loss and attending to life changes, which—when handled successfully—have restorative, or healing, effects. (p. 656)

dualistic thinking In Perry's theory, the cognitive approach of younger college students who search for absolute truth and therefore divide information, values, and authority into right and wrong, good and bad, we and they. Distinguished from *relativistic thinking*. (p. 450)

durable power of attorney for health care A written statement that authorizes appointment of another person (usually, although not always, a family member) to make health care decisions on one's behalf in case of incompetence. (p. 651)

dynamic systems theory of motor development In motor development, combinations of previously acquired abilities that lead to more advanced ways of exploring and controlling the environment. Each new skill is a joint product of central nervous system development, movement possibilities of the body, environmental supports for the skill, and the goal the child has in mind. (p. 138)

dynamic assessment An approach consistent with Vygotsky's concept of the zone of proximal development, in which purposeful teaching is introduced into the testing situation to find out what the child can attain with social support. (p. 314)

easy child A child whose temperament is such that he or she quickly establishes regular routines in infancy, is generally cheerful, and adapts easily to new experiences. Distinguished from *difficult child* and *slow-to-warm-up child*. (p. 190)

ecological systems theory Bronfenbrenner's approach, which views the person as developing within a complex system of relationships affected by multiple levels of the environment, from immediate settings of family and school to broad cultural values and programs. (p. 24)

educational self-fulfilling prophecy The idea that children may adopt teachers' positive or negative attitudes toward them and start to live up to these views. (p. 321)

effortful control The self-regulatory dimension of temperament that involves voluntarily suppressing a dominant response in order to plan and execute a more adaptive response. Variations in effortful control are evident in how effectively a child can focus and shift attention, inhibit impulses, and engage in problem solving to manage negative emotions. (191)

egalitarian marriage A form of marriage in which husband and wife share power and authority. Both try to balance the time and energy they devote to their occupations, their children, and their relationship. Distinguished from *traditional marriage*. (p. 475)

ego integrity versus despair In Erikson's theory, the psychological conflict of late adulthood, which is resolved positively when elders feel whole, complete, and satisfied with their achievements, having accepted their life course as something that had to be the way it was. (p. 600)

egocentrism Failure to distinguish the symbolic viewpoints of others from one's own. (p. 229)

elaboration The memory strategy of creating a relation between two or more items that are not members of the same category. (p. 303)

embryo The prenatal organism from implantation through the eighth week of pregnancy—the six weeks during which the foundations of all body structures and internal organs are laid down. (p. 82)

emergent literacy Young children's active efforts to construct literacy knowledge through informal experiences. (p. 242)

emerging adulthood A new transitional phase of development, extending from the late teens to the mid-twenties, during which most people have left adolescence but have not yet assumed adult responsibilities. Rather, they explore alternatives more intensely than they did as teenagers. (p. 430)

emotion-centered coping A strategy for managing emotion in which the individual controls distress internally and privately when little can be done about an outcome. Distinguished from *problem-centered coping*. (p. 335)

emotional intelligence Individual differences in the capacity to process and adapt to emotional information. Predicts many aspects of adjustment and life success. (p. 312)

emotional self-regulation Strategies for adjusting our emotional state to a comfortable level of intensity so we can accomplish our goals. (p. 189)

empathy The ability to understand another's emotional state and feel with that person, or respond emotionally in a similar way. (p. 207)

epigenesis Development resulting from ongoing, bidirectional exchanges between heredity and all levels of the environment. (p. 75)

epistemic cognition A form of cognition that typically develops in early adulthood that involves reflecting on how we arrived at facts, beliefs and ideas and, when necessary, revising one's approach in favor of a more balanced, adequate route to knowledge. (p. 450)

ethnic identity An enduring aspect of the self that includes a sense of ethnic group membership and attitudes and feelings associated with that membership. (p. 404)

ethnography A method by which the researcher attempts to understand the unique values and social processes of a culture or a distinct social group through participant observation. The researcher lives with the cultural community for a period of months or years, participating in all aspects of its daily life. (p. 30)

ethological theory of attachment A theory formulated by Bowlby that views the infant's emotional tie to the mother as an evolved response that promotes survival. (p. 196)

ethology An approach concerned with the adaptive, or survival, value of behavior and its evolutionary history. (p. 22)

euthanasia The practice of ending the life of a person suffering from an incurable condition. (p. 650)

evolutionary developmental psychology A new area of research that seeks to understand the adaptive value of species-wide cognitive, emotional, and social competencies as those competencies change with age. (p. 22)

exosystem In ecological systems theory, social settings that do not contain the developing person but nevertheless affect experiences in immediate settings. (p. 25)

expansions Adult responses that elaborate on children's speech, increasing its complexity. (p. 250)

experience-dependent brain growth Additional growth and refinement of established brain structures as a result of specific learning experiences that vary widely across individuals and cultures. Follows experience-expectant brain growth. (p. 127)

experience-expectant brain growth The young brain's rapidly developing organization, which depends on ordinary experiences, such as opportunities to see and touch objects, to hear language and other sounds, and to move about and explore the environment. Provides the foundation for experience-dependent brain growth. (p. 127)

experimental design A research design in which the investigator randomly assigns participants to two or more treatment conditions. Permits inferences about cause and effect. (p. 32)

expertise Acquisition of extensive knowledge in a field or endeavor. (p. 452)

expressive style of language learning A style of early language learning in which toddlers frequently produce pronouns and social formulas, such as "stop it," "thank you," and "I want it." They use language mainly to talk about the feelings and needs of themselves and other people. Distinguished from *referential style*. (p. 176)

extended family household A household in which three or more generations live together. (p. 66)

family life cycle A sequence of phases that characterizes the development of most families around the world. In early adulthood, people typically live on their own, marry, and bear and rear children. During middle age, their parenting responsibilities diminish. Late adulthood brings retirement, growing old, and (mostly for women) death of one's spouse. (p. 474)

fantasy period Period of vocational development in which young children gain insight into career options by fantasizing about them. Distinguished from *tentative period* and *realistic period*. (p. 454)

fast-mapping Connecting a new word with an underlying concept after only a brief encounter. (p. 248)

feminization of poverty A trend in which women who support themselves or their families have become the majority of the adult population living in poverty, regardless of age and ethnic group. (p. 542)

fetal alcohol effects (FAE) The condition of children who display some but not all of the defects of fetal alcohol syndrome. Usually their mothers drank alcohol in smaller quantities during pregnancy than did mothers of children with fetal alcohol syndrome (FAS). (p. 89)

fetal alcohol syndrome (FAS) A set of defects that results when women consume large amounts of alcohol during most or all of pregnancy. Includes mental retardation; impaired motor coordination, attention, memory, and language; overactivity; slow physical growth; and facial abnormalities. (p. 89)

fetal monitors Electronic instruments that track the baby's heart rate during labor. (p. 100)

fetus The prenatal organism from the beginning of the third month to the end of pregnancy, during which time completion of body structures and dramatic growth in size takes place. (p. 83)

fluid intelligence Intellectual skills that largely depend on basic information-processing skills—ability to detect relationships among visual stimuli, speed of analyzing information, and capacity of working memory. Largely influenced by conditions in the brain and by learning unique to the individual. Distinguished from *crystallized intelligence*. (p. 516)

formal operational stage Piaget's final stage, in which adolescents develop the capacity for abstract, systematic, scientific thinking. Begins around 11 years of age. (p. 381)

frailty Weakened functioning of diverse organs and body systems, which profoundly interferes with everyday competence and leaves the older adult highly vulnerable in the face of an infection, extremely hot or cold weather, or an injury. (p. 577)

fraternal, or **dizygotic, twins** Twins resulting from the release and fertilization of two ova. They are genetically no more alike than ordinary siblings. Distinguished from *identical,* or *monozygotic, twins*. (p. 47)

free radicals Naturally occurring, highly reactive chemicals that form in the presence of oxygen and destroy cellular material, including DNA, proteins, and fats essential for cell functioning. (p. 432)

full inclusion Placement of students with learning difficulties in regular classrooms for the entire school day. (p. 321)

functional age Actual competence and performance of an older adult (as distinguished from chronological age). (p. 562)

gametes Human sperm and ova, which contain half as many chromosomes as a regular body cell. (p. 46)

gender constancy The understanding that sex is biologically based and remains the same even if clothing, hairstyle, and play activities change. (p. 277)

gender identity An image of oneself as relatively masculine or feminine in characteristics. (p. 276)

gender intensification Increased gender stereotyping of attitudes and behavior. Occurs in early adolescence. (p. 411)

gender schema theory An information-processing approach to gender typing that combines social learning and cognitive-developmental features to explain how environmental pressures and children's cognitions work together to shape gender-role development. (p. 277)

gender typing Any association of objects, roles, or traits with one sex or the other in ways that conform to cultural stereotypes. (p. 273)

gene A segment of a DNA molecule that contains instructions for production of various proteins that contribute to growth and functioning of the body. (p. 46)

general growth curve A curve that represents overall changes in body size—rapid growth during infancy, slower gains in early and middle childhood, and rapid growth once more during adolescence. (p. 217)

generativity versus stagnation In Erikson's theory, the psychological conflict of midlife, which is resolved positively if the adult can integrate personal goals with the welfare of the larger social environment. The resulting strength is the capacity to give to and guide the next generation. (p. 530)

genetic counseling A communication process designed to help couples assess their chances of giving birth to a baby with a hereditary disorder. (p. 53)

genetic–environmental correlation The idea that heredity influences the environments to which people are exposed. (p. 73)

genetic imprinting A pattern of inheritance in which genes are imprinted, or chemically marked, in such a way that one member of the pair (either the mother's or the father's) is activated, regardless of its makeup. (p. 51)

genotype The genetic makeup of an individual. Distinguished from *phenotype*. (p. 45)

gerotranscendence According to Joan Erikson, a psychosocial stage beyond ego integrity, which characterizes the very old, that involves a cosmic and transcendent perspective directed forward and outward, beyond the self. Evident in heightened inner calm and contentment. (p. 601)

gifted Exceptional intellectual ability. Includes high IQ, high creativity, and specialized talent. (p. 322)

glass ceiling Invisible barrier, faced by women and ethnic minorities, to advancement up the corporate ladder. (p. 553)

glaucoma A disease in which poor fluid drainage leads to a buildup of pressure within the eye, damaging the optic nerve. A leading cause of blindness among older adults. (p. 501)

glial cells Cells serving the function of myelination. (p. 122)

goodness-of-fit model An effective match between child-rearing practices and a child's temperament, leading to favorable adjustment. (p. 194)

grief Intense physical and psychological distress following the loss of a loved one. (p. 655)

growth hormone (GH) A pituitary hormone that from birth on is necessary for development of all body tissues except the central nervous system and genitals. (p. 219)

growth spurt Rapid gain in height and weight during adolescence. (p. 363)

guided participation Shared endeavors between more expert and less expert participants, without specifying the precise features of communication. A broader concept than *scaffolding*. (p. 236)

habituation A gradual reduction in the strength of a response as the result of repetitive stimulation. (p. 134)

hardiness A set of three personal qualities—control, commitment, and challenge—that help people cope with stress adaptively, thereby reducing its impact on illness and mortality. (p. 514)

heritability estimate A statistic that measures the extent to which individual differences in complex traits, such as intelligence or personality, in a specific population are due to genetic factors. (p. 71)

heteronomous morality Piaget's first stage of moral development, in which children view moral rules as permanent features of the external world that are handed down by authorities and cannot be changed. Extends from about 5 to 10 years of age. (p. 406)

heterozygous Having two different alleles at the same place on a pair of chromosomes. Distinguished from *homozygous*. (p. 48)

hierarchical classification The organization of objects into classes and subclasses on the basis of similarities and differences between the groups. (p. 231)

history-graded influences Influences on lifespan development that are unique to a particular historical era and explain why people born around the same time (called a *cohort*) tend to be alike in ways that set them apart from people born at other times. (p. 11)

Home Observation for Measurement of the Environment (HOME) A checklist for gathering information about the quality of children's home lives through observation and parental interview. (p. 168)

homozygous Having two identical alleles at the same place on a pair of chromosomes. Distinguished from *heterozygous*. (p. 48)

hormone therapy Low daily doses of estrogen, aimed at reducing the discomforts of menopause and protecting women from other impairments due to estrogen loss, such as bone deterioration. Comes in two types: (1) estrogen alone, or *estrogen replacement therapy (ERT)*, for women who have had hysterectomies (surgical removal of the uterus), and (2) estrogen plus progesterone, or *hormone replacement therapy (HRT)*, for other women. (p. 504)

hospice A comprehensive program of support services that focuses on meeting terminally ill patients' physical, emotional, social, and spiritual needs and that offers follow-up bereavement services to families. (p. 648)

hostile aggression Aggression intended to harm another individual. Distinguished from *instrumental aggression*. (p. 270)

human development A field of study devoted to understanding constancy and change throughout the lifespan. (p. 5)

hypothetico-deductive reasoning A formal operational problem-solving strategy in which adolescents start with a *hypothesis*, or prediction, about variables that might possibly affect an outcome. Then they *deduce* logical, testable inferences from that hypothesis, systematically isolating and combining variables to see which inferences are confirmed in the real world. (p. 381)

I-self A sense of self as knower and actor, which includes the realization that the self is separate from the surrounding world, remains the same person over time, has a private inner life not accessible to others, and controls its own thoughts and actions. Distinguished from *me-self*. (p. 256)

identical, or **monozygotic, twins** Twins that result when a zygote, during the early stages of cell duplication, divides in two. They have the same genetic makeup. Distinguished from *fraternal,* or *dizygotic, twins*. (p. 48)

identity A well-organized conception of the self, made up of values, beliefs, and goals to which the individual is solidly committed. (p. 400)

identity achievement The identity status of individuals who have explored and committed themselves to self-chosen values and goals. Distinguished from *identity moratorium, identity foreclosure, and identity diffusion*. (p. 402)

identity diffusion The identity status of individuals who lack both exploration and commitment to self-chosen values and goals. Distinguished from *identity achievement, identity moratorium, and identity foreclosure*. (p. 402)

identity foreclosure The identity status of individuals who lack exploration and, instead, are committed to ready-made values and goals that authority figures have chosen for them. Distinguished from *identity achievement, identity moratorium, and identity diffusion*. (p. 402)

identity moratorium The identity status of individuals who are exploring, but are not yet committed to, self-chosen values and goals. Distinguished from *identity achievement, identity foreclosure, and identity diffusion*. (p. 402)

identity versus role confusion In Erikson's theory, the psychological conflict of adolescence, which is resolved positively when adolescents attain an identity after a period of exploration and inner soul-searching. (p. 400)

imaginary audience Adolescents' belief that they are the focus of everyone else's attention and concern. (p. 384)

imitation Learning by copying the behavior of another person. Also called *modeling* or *observational learning*. (p. 135)

implantation Attachment of the blastocyst to the uterine lining 7 to 9 days after fertilization. (p. 82)

implicit memory Memory without conscious awareness. (p. 588)

incomplete dominance A pattern of inheritance in which both alleles are expressed, resulting in a combined trait, or one that is intermediate between the two. (p. 50)

independence–ignore script A typical pattern of interaction in which elders' independent behaviors are mostly ignored, thereby leading them to occur less often. Distinguished from *dependency–support script*. (p. 606)

independent variable In an experiment, the variable the investigator expects to cause changes in another variable and that the researcher manipulates by randomly assigning participants to treatment conditions. Distinguished from *dependent variable*. (p. 32)

individualistic societies Societies in which people think of themselves as separate entities and are largely concerned with their own personal needs. Distinguished from *collectivist societies*. (p. 66)

induction A type of discipline in which the effects of the child's misbehavior on others are communicated to the child. (p. 265)

industry versus inferiority In Erikson's theory, the psychological conflict of middle childhood, which is resolved positively when experiences lead children to develop a sense of competence at useful skills and tasks. (p. 330)

infant mortality The number of deaths in the first year of life per 1,000 live births. (p. 104)

infantile amnesia The inability of most older children and adults to remember events that happened before age 3. (p. 163)

information processing An approach that views the human mind as a symbol-manipulating system through which information flows, that often uses flowcharts to map the precise series of steps individuals use to solve problems and complete tasks, and that regards cognitive development as a continuous process. (p. 20)

information-loss view A view that attributes age-related slowing of cognitive processing to greater loss of information as it moves through the system. As a result, the whole system must slow down to inspect and interpret the information. Distinguished from *neural network view.* (p. 518)

inhibited, or shy, child A child whose temperament is such that he or she reacts negatively to and withdraws from novel stimuli. Distinguished from *uninhibited, or sociable, child.* (p. 191)

initiative versus guilt In Erikson's theory, the psychological conflict of early childhood, which is resolved positively through play experiences that foster a healthy sense of initiative and through development of a superego, or conscience, that is not overly strict and guilt-ridden. (p. 256)

instrumental activities of daily living (IADLs) Tasks necessary to conduct the business of daily life and also requiring some cognitive competence, such as telephoning, shopping, food preparation, housekeeping, and paying bills. (p. 564)

instrumental aggression Aggression aimed at obtaining an object, privilege, or space with no deliberate intent to harm another person. Distinguished from *hostile aggression.* (p. 270)

intelligence quotient, or IQ A score that permits an individual's performance on an intelligence test to be compared to the performances of other individuals of the same age. (p. 168)

intentional, or goal-directed, behavior A sequence of actions in which schemes are deliberately combined to solve a problem. (p. 154)

interactional synchrony A sensitively tuned "emotional dance," in which the caregiver responds to infant signals in a well-timed, appropriate fashion and both partners match emotional states, especially the positive ones. (p. 200)

intermodal perception Perception that combines information from more than one modality, or sensory system. (p. 146)

internal working model A set of expectations derived from early caregiving experiences concerning the availability of attachment figures and their likelihood of providing support during times of stress. Becomes a model, or guide, for all future close relationships. (p. 197)

intimacy versus isolation In Erikson's theory, the psychological conflict of early adulthood, which is resolved positively when young adults give up some of their newfound independence and make a permanent commitment to an intimate partner. (p. 464)

invariant features Features that remain stable in a constantly changing perceptual world. (p. 147)

irreversibility The inability to mentally go through a series of steps in a problem and then reverse direction, returning to the starting point. Distinguished from *reversibility.* (p. 230)

joint attention A state in which the child and the caregiver gaze at the same object or event and the caregiver comments verbally about what the child sees. Supports language development. (p. 174)

joint custody A child custody arrangement following divorce in which the court grants each parent equal say in important decisions about the child's upbringing. (p. 348)

kinkeeper Role assumed by members of the middle generation, especially mothers, who take responsibility for gathering the family for celebrations and making sure everyone stays in touch. (p. 543)

kinship studies Studies comparing the characteristics of family members to determine the importance of heredity in complex human characteristics. (p. 71)

kwashiorkor A disease usually appearing between 1 and 3 years of age that is caused by a diet low in protein. Symptoms include an enlarged belly, swollen feet, hair loss, skin rash, and irritable, listless behavior. (p. 131)

language acquisition device (LAD) In Chomsky's theory, a biologically based innate system that permits children, no matter which language they hear, to understand and speak in a rule-oriented fashion as soon as they have picked up enough words. (p. 173)

lanugo A white, downy hair that covers the entire body of the fetus, helping the vernix stick to the skin. (p. 84)

lateralization Specialization of functions of the two hemispheres of the cerebral cortex. (p. 124)

learned helplessness Attributions that credit success to external factors, such as luck, and failure to low ability. Leads to anxious loss of control in the face of challenging tasks. Distinguished from *mastery-oriented attributions.* (p. 333)

learning disabilities Specific learning disorders that lead children to achieve poorly in school, despite an average or above-average IQ. Believed to be due to faulty brain functioning. (p. 321)

life care communities Housing for the elderly that offers a range of alternatives, from independent or congregate housing to full nursing home care. For a large initial payment and additional monthly fees, guarantees that elders' needs will be met in one place as they age. (p. 615)

life expectancy crossover An age-related reversal in life expectancy of sectors of the population. For example, members of low-SES ethnic minorities who survive to age 85 live longer than members of the white majority. (p. 563)

life review The process of calling up, reflecting on, and reconsidering past experiences, contemplating their meaning with the goal of achieving greater self-understanding. (p. 601)

life structure In Levinson's theory, the underlying pattern or design of a person's life at a given time. Consists of relationships with significant others (the most important of which have to do with marriage/family and occupation) that are reorganized during each period of adult development. (p. 465)

lifespan perspective A balanced perspective that assumes development is lifelong, multidimensional and multidirectional, highly plastic, and influenced by multiple interacting forces. (p. 8)

living will A written statement that specifies the treatments a person does or does not want in case of a terminal illness, coma, or other near-death situation. (p. 651)

loneliness Feelings of unhappiness that result from a gap between actual and desired social relationships. (p. 472)

longitudinal design A research design in which participants are studied repeatedly, and changes are noted as they get older. Distinguished from *cross-sectional design.* (p. 33)

long-term memory In information processing, the part of the mental system that contains our permanent knowledge base. (p. 160)

macrosystem In ecological systems theory, the values, laws, customs, and resources of a culture that influence experiences and interactions at inner levels of the environment. (p. 25)

macular degeneration Blurring and eventual loss of central vision due to a break-down of light-sensitive cells in the macula, or central region of the retina. (p. 566)

mainstreaming Placement of students with learning difficulties into regular classrooms for part of the school day. (p. 321)

make-believe play A type of play in which children pretend, acting out everyday and imaginary activities. (p. 155)

marasmus A disease usually appearing in the first year of life that is caused by a diet low in all essential nutrients. Leads to a wasted condition of the body. (p. 131)

mastery-oriented attributions Attributions that credit success to high ability and failure to insufficient effort. Leads to high self-esteem and a willingness to approach challenging tasks. Distinguished from *learned helplessness.* (p. 333)

matters of personal choice Concerns that do not violate rights, are not socially regulated, and therefore are up to the individual. Distinguished from *moral imperatives* and *social conventions*. (p. 269)

maturation A genetically determined, naturally unfolding course of growth. (p. 13)

maximum lifespan The genetic limit to length of life for a person free of external risk factors. Distinguished from *average life expectancy* and *active lifespan*. (p. 564)

me-self A sense of self as object of knowledge and evaluation, which consists of all qualities that make the self unique: physical characteristics and possessions; psychological characteristics, including desires, attitudes, beliefs, and personality traits; and social characteristics. Distinguished from *I-self*. (p. 256)

meiosis The process of cell division through which gametes are formed and in which the number of chromosomes in each cell is halved. (p. 46)

memory strategies Deliberate mental activities that improve the likelihood of remembering. (p. 227)

menarche First menstruation. (p. 365)

menopause The end of menstruation and, therefore, reproductive capacity in women. Occurs, on average, in the early fifties among North American, European, and East Asian women, although the age range is large—from the late thirties to the late fifties. (p. 502)

mental representation Internal depiction of information that the mind can manipulate. The most powerful mental representations are images and concepts. (p. 154)

mental strategies In information processing, procedures that operate on and transform information, increasing the chances that we will retain information, use it efficiently, and think flexibly, adapting the information to changing circumstances. (p. 160)

mesosystem In ecological systems theory, connections between a person's immediate settings. (p. 24)

metacognition Thinking about thought; awareness of mental activities. (p. 239)

microsystem In ecological systems theory, the activities and interaction patterns in the person's immediate surroundings. (p. 24)

midlife crisis Inner turmoil, self-doubt, and major restructuring of the personality during the transition to middle adulthood. Characterizes the experiences of only a minority of adults. (p. 534)

mild mental retardation Substantially below-average intellectual functioning, resulting in an IQ between 55 and 70 and problems in adaptive behavior, or skills of everyday living. (p. 321)

mitosis The process of cell duplication, in which each new cell receives an exact copy of the original chromosomes. (p. 46)

moral imperatives Standards that protect people's rights and welfare. Distinguished from *social conventions* and *matters of personal choice*. (p. 269)

moral self-relevance The degree to which morality is central to self-concept. (p. 410)

mortality The phase of dying in which the individual passes into permanent death. Distinguished from *agonal phase* and *clinical death*. (p. 636)

mourning The culturally specified expression of the bereaved person's thoughts and feelings through funerals and other rituals. (p. 655)

mutation A sudden change in a segment of DNA. (p. 51)

myelination A process in which neural fibers are coated with an insulating fatty sheath called *myelin* that improves the efficiency of message transfer. (p. 122)

natural, or **prepared, childbirth** An approach designed to reduce pain and medical intervention and to make childbirth a rewarding experience for parents. (p. 99)

naturalistic observation A method in which the researcher goes into the natural environment to record the behavior of interest. Distinguished from *structured observation*. (p. 27)

nature–nurture controversy Disagreement among theorists about whether genetic or environmental factors are more important in development. (p. 7)

neglected children Children who are seldom chosen, either positively or negatively, on self-report measures of peer acceptance. Distinguished from *popular, rejected,* and *controversial children*. (p. 340)

Neonatal Behavioral Assessment Scale (NBAS) A test developed to assess the behavior of the infant during the newborn period. (p. 113)

neural network view A view that attributes age-related slowing of cognitive processing to breaks in neural networks as neurons die. The brain forms bypasses—new synaptic connections that go around the breaks but are less efficient. Distinguished from *information-loss view*. (p. 518)

neural tube The primitive spinal cord that develops from the ectoderm, the top of which swells to form the brain. (p. 83)

neurofibrillary tangles A structural change in the brain associated with Alzheimer's disease in which bundles of twisted threads appear that are the product of collapsed neural structures. (p. 581)

neurons Nerve cells that store and transmit information. (p. 121)

neurotransmitters Chemicals that are released by neurons that send messages across synapses. (p. 121)

niche-picking A type of genetic–environmental correlation in which individuals actively choose environments that complement their heredity. (p. 74)

noble savage Rousseau's view of the child as naturally endowed with an innate plan for orderly, healthy growth. (p. 13)

nonnormative influences Influences on lifespan development that are irregular, in that they happen to just one or a few individuals and do not follow a predictable timetable. (p. 11)

nonorganic failure to thrive A growth disorder usually present by 18 months of age that is caused by lack of affection and stimulation. (p. 132)

non-rapid-eye-movement (NREM) sleep A "regular" sleep state in which the body is quiet and heart rate, breathing, and brain wave activity are slow and regular. Distinguished from *rapid-eye-movement (REM) sleep*. (p. 108)

nonsocial activity Unoccupied, onlooker behavior and solitary play. Distinguished from *parallel, associative,* and *cooperative play*. (p. 261)

normal distribution A bell-shaped distribution that results when individual differences are measured in large samples. Most scores cluster around the mean, or average, and progressively fewer fall toward extremes. (p. 168)

normative approach An approach in which measures of behavior are taken on large numbers of individuals and age-related averages are computed to represent typical development. (p. 14)

obesity A greater-than-20-percent increase over average body weight, based on the individual's age, sex, and physical build. (p. 292)

object permanence The understanding that objects continue to exist when they are out of sight. (p. 154)

operant conditioning A form of learning in which a spontaneous behavior is followed by a stimulus that changes the probability that the behavior will occur again. (p. 133)

ordinality A principle specifying order relationships between quantities, such as three is more than two and two is more than one. (p. 242)

organization In Piaget's theory, the internal rearrangement and linking together of schemes so that they form a strongly interconnected cognitive system. In information processing, the memory strategy of grouping together related items. (p. 152, p. 302)

osteoarthritis A form of arthritis characterized by deteriorating cartilage on the ends of bones of frequently used joints. Leads to swelling, stiffness, and loss of flexibility. Otherwise known as "wear-and-tear" arthritis. Distinguished from *rheumatoid arthritis*. (p. 578)

osteoporosis A severe version of age-related bone loss. Porous bones are easily fractured and when very extreme, lead to a slumped-over posture, a shuffling gait, and a "dowager's hump" in the upper back. (p. 511)

overextension An early vocabulary error in which a word is applied too broadly to a wider collection of objects and events than is appropriate. Distinguished from *underextension*. (p. 175)

overregularization Application of regular grammatical rules to words that are exceptions. (p. 249)

palliative, or **comfort, care** Care for terminally ill, suffering patients that relieves pain and other symptoms (such as breathing difficulties, insomnia, and depression), aimed at protecting the patient's quality of life rather than prolonging life. (p. 648)

parallel play A form of limited social participation in which the child plays near other children with similar materials but does not interact with them. Distinguished from *nonsocial, associative,* and *cooperative play.* (p. 261)

parental imperative theory A theory that claims that traditional gender roles are maintained during the active parenting years to help ensure the survival of children. After children reach adulthood, parents are free to express the "other-gender" side of their personalities. (p. 539)

passionate love Love based on intense sexual attraction. Distinguished from *companionate love.* (p. 468)

passive euthanasia The practice of withholding or withdrawing life-sustaining treatment, permitting a patient to die naturally. Distinguished from *voluntary active euthanasia.* (p. 650)

peer acceptance Likability, or the extent to which a child is viewed by a group of agemates (such as classmates) as a worthy social partner. (p. 340)

peer group Collectives that generate unique values and standards for behavior and a social structure of leaders and followers. (p. 339)

peer victimization A destructive form of peer interaction in which certain children become frequent targets of verbal and physical attacks or other forms of abuse. (p. 342)

permissive child-rearing style A child-rearing style that is high in acceptance but overindulging or inattentive, low in control, and lenient rather than appropriate in autonomy granting. Distinguished from *authoritative, authoritarian,* and *uninvolved child-rearing styles.* (p. 280)

persistent vegetative state A state produced by absence of brain-wave activity in the cortex in which the person is unconscious, displays no voluntary movements, and has no hope of recovery. (p. 637)

personal fable Adolescents' belief that they are special and unique. Leads them to conclude that others cannot possibly understand their thoughts and feelings and may promote a sense of invulnerability to danger. (p. 385)

perspective taking The capacity to imagine what other people may be thinking and feeling. (p. 336)

phenotype The individual's physical and behavioral characteristics, which are determined by both genetic and environmental factors. Distinguished from *genotype.* (p. 45)

phobia An intense, unmanageable fear that leads to persistent avoidance of the feared situation. (p. 351)

phonics approach An approach to beginning reading instruction that emphasizes simplified reading materials and training in the basic rules for translating written symbols into sounds. Distinguished from the *whole-language approach.* (p. 307)

phonological awareness The ability to reflect on and manipulate the sound structure of spoken language, as indicated by sensitivity to changes in sounds within words and to incorrect pronunciation. A strong predictor of reading and spelling achievement. (p. 307)

physical aggression A type of hostile aggression that harms others through physical injury. Includes pushing, hitting, kicking, punching, or destroying another's property. Distinguished from *verbal aggression* and *relational aggression.* (p. 270)

pituitary gland A gland located near the base of the brain that releases hormones that induce physical growth. (p. 219)

placenta The organ that separates the mother's bloodstream from the embryo or fetal bloodstream but permits exchange of nutrients and waste products. (p. 82)

polygenic inheritance A pattern of inheritance in which many genes influence a characteristic. (p. 52)

popular children Children who get many positive votes on self-report measures of peer acceptance. Distinguished from *rejected, controversial,* and *neglected children.* (p. 340)

popular-antisocial children A subgroup of popular children largely made up of "tough" boys who are athletically skilled, aggressive, and poor students. Distinguished from *popular-prosocial children.* (p. 341)

popular-prosocial children A subgroup of popular children who combine academic and social competence. Distinguished from *popular-antisocial children.* (p. 341)

possible selves Future-oriented representations of what one hopes to become and is afraid of becoming. The temporal dimension of self-concept. (p. 536)

postconventional level Kohlberg's highest level of moral development, in which individuals define morality in terms of abstract principles and values that apply to all situations and societies. (p. 407)

postformal thought Cognitive development beyond Piaget's formal operational stage. (p. 450)

practical problem solving Problem solving that requires people to size up real-world situations and analyze how best to achieve goals that have a high degree of uncertainty. (p. 521)

pragmatic thought In Labouvie-Vief's theory, adult thought in which logic becomes a tool to solve real-world problems and inconsistencies and imperfections are accepted. (p. 451)

pragmatics The practical, social side of language that is concerned with how to engage in effective and appropriate communication with others. (p. 250)

preconventional level Kohlberg's first level of moral development, in which moral understanding is based on rewards, punishments, and the power of authority figures. (p. 407)

premenstrual syndrome (PMS) An array of physical and psychological symptoms that usually appear 6 to 10 days prior to menstruation. The most common are abdominal cramps, fluid retention, diarrhea, tender breasts, backache, headache, fatigue, tension, irritability, and depression. (p. 447)

prenatal diagnostic methods Medical procedures that permit detection of developmental problems before birth. (p. 53)

preoperational stage Piaget's second stage, in which rapid growth in representation takes place. However, thought is not yet logical. Spans the years from 2 to 7. (p. 227)

presbycusis Age-related hearing impairments that involve a sharp loss at high frequencies around age 50, which gradually extends to all frequencies. (p. 501)

presbyopia Condition of aging in which, around age 60, the lens of the eye loses its capacity to accommodate entirely to nearby objects. (p. 500)

preterm Infants born several weeks or more before their due date. (p. 102)

primary aging Genetically influenced age-related declines in the functioning of organs and systems that affect all members of our species and take place even in the context of overall good health. Also called *biological aging.* Distinguished from *secondary aging.* (p. 577)

primary sexual characteristics Physical features that involve the reproductive organs directly (ovaries, uterus, and vagina in females; penis, scrotum, and testes in males). Distinguished from *secondary sexual characteristics.* (p. 365)

private speech Self-directed speech that children often use to plan and guide their own behavior. (p. 234)

problem-centered coping A strategy for managing emotion in which the child appraises the situation as changeable, identifies the difficulty, and decides what to do about it. Distinguished from *emotion-centered coping.* (p. 335)

Project Head Start A U.S. federal program that provides poverty-stricken children with a year or two of preschool along with nutritional and health services and that encourages parent involvement in program planning and children's learning. (p. 245)

propositional thought A type of formal operational reasoning in which adolescents evaluate the logic of verbal statements without referring to real-world circumstances. (p. 381)

prosocial, or **altruistic, behavior** Actions that benefit another person without any expected reward for the self. (p. 260)

prospective memory Recall that involves remembering to engage in planned actions at an appropriate time in the future. (p. 589)

proximodistal trend An organized pattern of physical growth and motor control that proceeds from the center of the body outward. Distinguished from *cephalocaudal trend.* (p. 121)

psychoanalytic perspective An approach to personality development introduced by Freud that assumes people move through a series of stages in which they confront conflicts between biological drives and social expectations. The way these conflicts are resolved determines psychological adjustment. (p. 15)

psychological control Parental behaviors that intrude on and manipulate children's verbal expressions, individuality, and attachments to parents. (p. 280)

psychosexual theory Freud's theory, which emphasizes that how parents manage children's sexual and aggressive drives during the first few years is crucial for healthy personality development. (p. 15)

psychosocial dwarfism A growth disorder observed between 2 and 15 years of age. Characterized by very short stature, decreased GH secretion, immature skeletal age, and serious adjustment problems. Caused by emotional deprivation. (p. 220)

psychosocial theory Erikson's theory, which emphasizes that at each Freudian stage, individuals not only develop a unique personality, but also acquire attitudes and skills that help them become active, contributing members of their society. (p. 15)

puberty Biological changes at adolescence that lead to an adult-sized body and sexual maturity. (p. 361)

public policies Laws and government programs designed to improve social problems and current conditions. (p. 67)

punishment In operant conditioning, removing a desirable stimulus or presenting an unpleasant one to decrease the occurrence of a response. (p. 134)

random assignment An evenhanded procedure for assigning participants to treatment groups, such as drawing numbers out of a hat or flipping a coin. Increases the chances that participants' characteristics will be equally distributed across treatment conditions in an experiment. (p. 33)

range of reaction Each person's unique, genetically determined response to a range of environmental conditions. (p. 72)

rapid-eye-movement (REM) sleep An "irregular" sleep state in which brain wave activity is similar to that of the waking state; eyes dart beneath the lids, heart rate, blood pressure, and breathing are uneven, and slight muscle twitches occur. Distinguished from *non-rapid-eye-movement (NREM) sleep.* (p. 108)

realistic period Period of vocational development in which older adolescents and young adults focus on a general vocational category and, slightly later, settle on a single occupation. Distinguished from *fantasy period* and *tentative period.* (p. 454)

recall A type of memory that involves remembering a stimulus that is not present. (p. 162)

recasts Adult responses that restructure children's incorrect speech into a more mature form. (p. 250)

reciprocal teaching An approach to teaching based on Vygotsky's theory in which a teacher and two to four students form a collaborative learning group and take turns leading dialogues on the content of a text passage, using four cognitive strategies: questioning, summarizing, clarifying, and predicting. Creates a zone of proximal development in which reading comprehension improves. (p. 320)

recognition A type of memory that involves noticing whether a stimulus is identical or similar to one previously experienced. (p. 162)

recovery Following habituation, an increase in responsiveness to a new stimulus. (p. 134)

referential style of language learning A style of early language learning in which toddlers produce many words that refer to objects. They use language mainly to name things. Distinguished from *expressive style of language.* (p. 176)

reflex An inborn, automatic response to a particular form of stimulation. (p. 106)

rehearsal The memory strategy of repeating information. (p. 302)

reinforcer In operant conditioning, a stimulus that increases the occurrence of a response. (p. 133)

rejected children Children who are actively disliked and get many negative votes on self-report measures of peer acceptance. Distinguished from *popular, controversial,* and *neglected children.* (p. 340)

rejected-aggressive children A subgroup of rejected children who engage in high rates of conflict, hostility, and hyperactive, inattentive, and impulsive behavior. Distinguished from *rejected-withdrawn children.* (p. 341)

rejected-withdrawn children A subgroup of rejected children who are passive and socially awkward. Distinguished from *rejected-aggressive children.* (p. 341)

relational aggression A form of hostile aggression that damages another's peer relationships through social exclusion, malicious gossip, or friendship manipulation. Distinguished from *physical aggression* and *verbal aggression.* (p. 270)

relativistic thinking In Perry's theory, the cognitive approach of older college students, who favor multiple truths, each relative to its context of evaluation. Distinguished from *dualistic thinking.* (p. 450)

reminiscence The process of telling stories about people and events from the past and reporting associated thoughts and feelings. (p. 601)

remote memory Recall of events that happened long ago. (p. 589)

resilience The ability to adapt effectively in the face of threats to development. (p. 10)

resistant attachment The quality of insecure attachment characterizing infants who remain close to the parent before departure and display angry, resistive behavior when she or he returns. Distinguished from *secure, avoidant,* and *disorganized/disoriented attachment.* (p. 198)

reticular formation A structure in the brain stem that maintains alertness and consciousness. (p. 219)

reversibility The ability to think through a series of steps in a problem and then mentally reverse direction, returning to the starting point. Distinguished from *irreversibility.* (p. 298)

Rh factor incompatibility A condition that arises when the Rh protein, present in the fetus's blood but not in the mother's, causes the mother to build up antibodies. If these return to the fetus's system, they destroy red blood cells, reducing the oxygen supply to organs and tissues. Mental retardation, miscarriage, heart damage, and infant death can occur. (p. 94)

rheumatoid arthritis A form of arthritis in which an autoimmune response leads to inflammation of connective tissue, particularly the membranes that line the joints, resulting in stiffness, inflammation, aching, deformed joints, and serious loss of mobility. Distinguished from *osteoarthritis.* (p. 578)

rough-and-tumble play A form of peer interaction involving friendly chasing and play-fighting that, in our evolutionary past, may have been important for the development of fighting skills. (p. 297)

sandwich generation Today's middle-aged adults, who are "sandwiched," or squeezed, between the needs of ill or frail parents and financially dependent children. (p. 547)

scaffolding Adjusting the quality of support during a teaching session to fit the child's current level of performance. Direct instruction is offered when a task is new; less help is provided as competence increases. (p. 235)

scheme In Piaget's theory, a specific structure, or organized way of making sense of experience, that changes with age. (p. 152)

scripts General descriptions of what occurs and when it occurs in a particular situation. A basic means through which children organize and interpret their everyday experiences. (p. 239)

secondary aging Declines due to hereditary defects and environmental influences, such as poor diet, lack of exercise, substance abuse, environmental pollution, and psychological stress. Distinguished from *primary aging.* (p. 577)

secondary friends People who are not intimates but with whom the individual spends time occasionally, such as a group that meets for lunch, bridge, or museum tours. (p. 621)

secondary sexual characteristics Features visible on the outside of the body that serve as signs of sexual maturity but do not involve the reproductive organs (for example, breast development in females, appearance of underarm and pubic hair in both sexes). Distinguished from *primary sexual characteristics.* (p. 365)

secular trend A change in body size, pubertal timing, or other aspect of development from one generation to the next. (p. 366)

secure attachment The quality of attachment characterizing infants who are distressed by parental separation and easily comforted by the parent when she or he returns. Distinguished from *avoidant, resistant,* and *disorganized/disoriented attachment.* (p. 198)

secure base Infants' use of the familiar caregiver as a point from which to explore the environment and return for emotional support. (p. 188)

selective optimization with compensation A set of strategies that permits the elderly to sustain high levels of functioning. They *select* personally valued activities as a way of *optimizing* returns from their diminishing energies and come up with new ways of *compensating* for losses. (p. 587)

self-care children Children who look after themselves while their parents are at work. (p. 350)

self-concept The sum total of attributes, abilities, attitudes, and values that an individual believes defines who he or she is. (p. 257)

self-conscious emotions Emotions that involve injury to or enhancement of the sense of self. Examples are shame, embarrassment, guilt, envy, and pride. (p. 188)

self-esteem An aspect of self-concept that involves judgments about one's own worth and the feelings associated with those judgments. (p. 257)

self-recognition Identification of the self as a physically unique being. (p. 207)

sensitive caregiving Caregiving involving prompt, consistent, and appropriate responding to infant signals. (p. 200)

sensitive period A time span that is optimal for certain capacities to emerge and in which the individual is especially responsive to environmental influences. (p. 22)

sensorimotor stage Piaget's first stage, in which infants and toddlers "think" with their eyes, ears, hands, and other sensorimotor equipment. Spans the first 2 years of life. (p. 152)

sensory register The part of the information-processing system where sights and sounds are represented directly and stored briefly. (p. 160)

separation anxiety An infant's distressed reaction to the departure of the familiar caregiver. (p. 197)

seriation The ability to order items along a quantitative dimension, such as length or weight. (p. 299)

sequential design A research design in which several similar cross-sectional or longitudinal studies (called *sequences*) are conducted at varying times. (p. 37)

sex chromosomes The twenty-third pair of chromosomes, which determines the sex of the individual. In females, called *XX*; in males, called *XY.* (p. 47)

skipped-generation family A family structure in which children live with grandparents but apart from parents. (p. 546)

sleep apnea A condition during sleep in which breathing ceases for 10 seconds or longer, resulting in many brief awakenings. (p. 570)

slow-to-warm-up child A child whose temperament is such that he or she is inactive, shows mild, low-key reactions to environmental stimuli, is negative in mood, and adjusts slowly when faced with new experiences. Distinguished from *easy child* and *difficult child.* (p. 190)

small for date Infants whose birth weight is below their expected weight when length of pregnancy is taken into account. Some are full term; others are preterm infants who are especially underweight. (p. 102)

social clock Age-graded expectations for life events, such as beginning a first job, getting married, birth of the first child, buying a home, and retiring. (p. 467)

social comparisons Judgments of one's own abilities, behavior, appearance, and other characteristics in relation to those of others. (p. 330)

social conventions Customs determined solely by consensus, such as table manners. Distinguished from *moral imperatives* and *matters of personal choice.* (p. 269)

social constructivist classroom A classroom based on Vygotsky's theory, in which children participate in a wide range of challenging activities with teachers and peers, with whom they jointly construct understandings. As children acquire knowledge, and strategies from working together, they become competent, contributing members of their classroom community and advance in cognitive and social development. (p. 320)

social convoy A model of age-related changes in social networks, which views the individual within a cluster of relationships moving through life. Close ties are in the inner circle, less close ties on the outside. With age, people change places in the convoy, new ties are added, and some are lost entirely. (p. 616)

social learning theory An approach that emphasizes the role of modeling, or observational learning, in the development of behavior. (p. 18)

social referencing Relying on a trusted person's emotional reaction to decide how to respond in an uncertain situation. (p. 188)

social smile The smile evoked by the stimulus of the human face. First appears between 6 and 10 weeks. (p. 186)

sociocultural theory Vygotsky's theory, in which children acquire the ways of thinking and behaving that make up a community's culture through cooperative dialogues with more knowledgeable members of society. (p. 23)

sociodramatic play The make-believe play with others that is under way by age 2½ and increases rapidly during the next few years. (p. 228)

socioeconomic status (SES) A measure of an individual's or a family's social position and economic well-being that combines three interrelated, but not completely overlapping, variables: (1) years of education and (2) the prestige of and skill required by one's job, both of which measure social status; and (3) income, which measures economic status. (p. 61)

socioemotional selectivity theory A social theory of aging that states that the decline in social interaction in late adulthood is due to physical and psychological changes, which lead elders to emphasize the emotion-regulating function of interaction. Consequently, they prefer familiar partners with whom they have developed pleasurable relationships. Distinguished from *disengagement theory, activity theory,* and *continuity theory.* (p. 611)

spermarche First ejaculation of seminal fluid. (p. 366)

stage A qualitative change in thinking, feeling, and behaving that characterizes a specific period of development. (p. 6)

standardization The practice of giving a newly constructed test to a large, representative sample of individuals, which serves as the standard for interpreting individual scores. (p. 168)

states of arousal Different degrees of sleep and wakefulness. (p. 107)

stereotype threat The fear of being judged on the basis of a negative stereotype, which can trigger anxiety that interferes with performance. (p. 314)

Strange Situation A laboratory procedure involving short separations from and reunions with the parent that assesses the quality of the attachment bond. (p. 197)

stranger anxiety The infant's expression of fear in response to unfamiliar adults. Appears in many babies after 6 months of age. (p. 186)

structured interview An interview method in which each participant is asked the same questions in the same way. (p. 29)

structured observation A method in which the investigator sets up a cue for the behavior of interest and observes it in a laboratory. Distinguished from *naturalistic observation.* (p. 27)

subculture A group of people with beliefs and customs that differ from those of the larger culture. (p. 66)

successful aging Aging in which gains are maximized and losses minimized. (p. 628)

sudden infant death syndrome (SIDS) The unexpected death, usually during the night, of an infant under 1 year of age that remains unexplained after thorough investigation. (p. 109)

sympathy Feelings of concern or sorrow for another's plight. (p. 261)

synapses The gaps between neurons, across which chemical messages are sent. (p. 121)

synaptic pruning Loss of connective fibers by seldom-stimulated neurons, thereby returning them to an uncommitted state so they can support the development of future skills. (p. 122)

tabula rasa Locke's view of the child as a blank slate whose character is shaped by experience. (p. 13)

talent Outstanding performance in a specific field. (p. 322)

telegraphic speech Toddlers' two-word utterances that, like a telegram, leave out smaller and less important words. (p. 176)

temperament Early appearing, stable individual differences in reactivity and self-regulation. Reactivity refers to quickness and intensity of emotional arousal, attention, and motor activity. Self-regulation refers to strategies that modify reactivity. (p. 180)

tentative period Period of vocational development in which adolescents think about careers in more complex ways, at first in terms of their interests and, as they become more aware of personal and educational requirements of different vocations, in terms of their abilities and values. Distinguished from *fantasy period* and *realistic period*. (p. 454)

teratogen Any environmental agent that causes damage during the prenatal period. (p. 85)

terminal decline Marked acceleration in deterioration of cognitive functioning prior to death. (p. 593)

theory An orderly, integrated set of statements that describes, explains, and predicts behavior. (p. 5)

theory of multiple intelligences Gardner's theory, which identifies eight independent intelligences on the basis of distinct sets of processing operations that permit individuals to engage in a wide range of culturally valued activities. (p. 310)

thyroid-stimulating hormone (TSH) A pituitary hormone that stimulates the thyroid gland to release thyroxine, which is necessary for brain development and body growth. (p. 219)

time out A form of mild punishment in which children are removed from the immediate setting—for example, sent to their rooms—until they are ready to act appropriately. (p. 267)

traditional classroom A classroom based on the educational philosophy that the teacher is the sole authority for knowledge, rules, and decision-making. Students are relatively passive—listening, responding when called on, and completing teacher-assigned tasks. Their progress is evaluated by how well they keep up with a uniform set of standards for their grade. Distinguished from *constructivist* and *social-constructivist classrooms*. (p. 319)

traditional marriage A form of marriage involving clear division of husband's and wife's roles. The man is the head of household and economic provider. The woman devotes herself to caring for her husband and children and creating a nurturant, comfortable home. Distinguished from *egalitarian marriage*. (p. 475)

transitive inference The ability to seriate—or order items along a quantitative dimension—mentally. (p. 299)

triarchic theory of successful intelligence Sternberg's theory, which states that intelligent behavior involves balancing analytical intelligence, creative intelligence, and practical intelligence to achieve success in life, according to one's personal goals and the requirements of one's cultural community. (p. 309)

triangular theory of love Sternberg's view of love as having three components—intimacy, passion, and commitment—that shift in emphasis as romantic relationships develop. (p. 468)

trimesters Three equal time periods in the prenatal period, each of which lasts three months. (p. 83)

Type A behavior pattern A behavior pattern consisting of extreme competitiveness, ambition, impatience, hostility, angry outbursts, and a sense of time pressure. (p. 512)

umbilical cord The long cord connecting the prenatal organism to the placenta that delivers nutrients and removes waste products. (p. 82)

unconditioned response (UCR) In classical conditioning, a reflexive response that is produced by an unconditioned stimulus (UCS). (p. 133)

unconditioned stimulus (UCS) In classical conditioning, a stimulus that leads to a reflexive response. (p. 133)

underextension An early vocabulary error in which a word is applied too narrowly to a smaller number of objects and events than is appropriate. Distinguished from *overextension*. (p. 175)

uninhibited, or sociable, child A child whose temperament is such that he or she displays positive emotion to and approaches novel stimuli. Distinguished from *inhibited, or shy, child*. (p. 191)

uninvolved child-rearing style A child-rearing style that combines low acceptance and involvement with little control and general indifference to autonomy granting. Distinguished from *authoritative, authoritarian,* and *permissive child-rearing styles*. (p. 280)

verbal aggression A type of hostile aggression that harms others through threats of physical aggression, name-calling, or hostile teasing. Distinguished from *physical aggression* and *relational aggression*. (p. 270)

vernix A white, cheeselike substance covering the fetus and preventing the skin from chapping due to constant exposure to the amniotic fluid. (p. 83)

violation-of-expectation method A method in which researchers habituate infants to a physical event and then determine whether they recover to (look longer at) a possible event (a variation of the first event that conforms to physical laws) or an impossible event (a variation that violates physical laws). Recovery to the impossible event suggests that the infant is surprised at a deviation from reality and is aware of that aspect of the physical world. (p. 155)

visual acuity Fineness of visual discrimination. (p. 113)

voluntary active euthanasia The practice of ending a patient's suffering, at the patient's request, before a natural end to life. A form of mercy killing. Distinguished from *passive euthanasia*. (p. 652)

whole-language approach An approach to beginning reading instruction that parallels children's natural language learning and keeps reading materials whole and meaningful. Distinguished from *phonics approach*. (p. 307)

wisdom A form of cognition that combines breadth and depth of practical knowledge; ability to reflect on and apply that knowledge in ways that make life more bearable and worthwhile; emotional maturity, including the ability to listen, evaluate, and give advice; and altruistic creativity—contributing to humanity and enriching others' lives. (p. 591)

working, or short-term, memory The part of the information-processing system where we "work" on a limited amount of information, actively applying mental strategies so the information will be retained. (p. 160)

X-linked inheritance A pattern of inheritance in which a recessive gene is carried on the X chromosome. Males are more likely to be affected. (p. 50)

zone of proximal development In Vygotsky's theory, a range of tasks that the child cannot yet handle alone but can do with the help of more skilled partners. (p. 165)

zygote The newly fertilized cell formed by the union of sperm and ovum at conception. (p. 46)

✤ References

A

AARP (American Association of Retired Persons). (2002). *The Grandparent Study 2002 report.* Washington, DC: Author.

Abbey, A., & McAuslan, P. (2004). A longitudinal examination of male college students' perpetration of sexual assault. *Journal of Consulting and Clinical Psychology, 72,* 747–756.

Abbey, A., Zawacki, T., Buck, P. O., Clinton, A. M., & McAuslan, P. (2004). Sexual assault and alcohol consumption: What do we know about their relationship and what types of research are still needed? *Aggression and Violent Behavior, 9,* 271–303.

Abbott, S. (1992). Holding on and pushing away: Comparative perspectives on an eastern Kentucky child-rearing practice. *Ethos, 20,* 33–65.

Abel, E. (2004). Paternal contribution to fetal alcohol syndrome. *Addiction Biology, 9,* 127–133.

Abikoff, H. B., Jensen, P. S., Arnold, L. L., & Hoza, B. (2002). Observed classroom behavior of children with ADHD: Relationship to gender and comorbidity. *Journal of Abnormal Child Psychology, 30,* 349–359.

Aboud, F. E. (2003). The formation of in-group favoritism and outgroup prejudice in young children: Are they distinct attitudes? *Developmental Psychology, 39,* 48–60.

Aboud, F. E., & Amato, M. (2001). Developmental and socialization influences on intergroup bias. In R. Brown & S. Gaertner (Eds.), *Blackwell handbook of social psychology: Intergroup processes.* Oxford, UK: Blackwell.

Aboud, F. E., & Doyle, A. (1996). Parental and peer influences on children's racial attitudes. *International Journal of Intercultural Relations, 20,* 371–383.

Abra, J. (1989). Changes in creativity with age: Data, explanations, and further predictions. *International Journal of Aging and Human Development, 28,* 105–126.

Abraham, R. (2005). Emotional intelligence in the workplace: A review and synthesis. In R. Schulze & R. D. Roberts (Eds.), *Emotional intelligence: An international handbook* (pp. 255–270). Göttingen, Germany: Hogrefe & Huber.

Abraham, S. (1998). Satisfaction of participants in university-administered elderhostel programs. *Educational Gerontology, 24,* 529–536.

Achenbach, T. M., Phares, V., Howell, C. T., Rauh, V. A., & Nurcombe, B. (1990). Seven-year outcome of the Vermont program for low-birthweight infants. *Child Development, 61,* 1672–1681.

Acker, M. M., & O'Leary, S. G. (1996). Inconsistency of mothers' feedback and toddlers' misbehavior and negative affect. *Journal of Abnormal Child Psychology, 24,* 703–714.

Acker, M., & Davis, M. H. (1992). Intimacy, passion, and commitment in adult romantic relationships: A test of the triangular love theory. *Journal of Social and Personal Relationships, 9,* 21–50.

Ackerman, P. L. (2000). Domain-specific knowledge as the "dark matter" of adult intelligence: Personality and interest correlates. *Journal of Gerontology, 55B,* P69–P84.

Ackerman, S., Zuroff, D. C., & Moskowitz, D. S. (2000). Generativity in midlife and young adults: Links to agency, communion, and subjective well-being. *International Journal of Aging and Human Development, 50,* 17–41.

ACT (American College Testing). (2005). Retention trends. Retrieved from www.act.org/path/postsec/droptables/index.html

Adams, G. R., & Marshall, S. (1996). A developmental social psychology of identity: Understanding the person in context. *Journal of Adolescence, 19,* 429–442.

Adams, K. B. (2004). Changing investment in activities and interests in elders' lives: Theory and measurement. *International Journal of Aging and Human Development, 58,* 87–108.

Adams, K. B., Sanders, S., & Auth, E. A. (2004). Loneliness and depression in independent living retirement communities: Risk and resilience factors. *Aging and Mental Health, 8,* 475–485.

Adams, M. (2003). *Fire and ice: The United States, Canada, and the myth of converging values.* Toronto: Penguin.

Adams, R. G. (1985–1986). Emotional closeness and physical distance between friends: Implications for elderly women living in age-segregated and age-integrated settings. *International Journal of Aging and Human Development, 22,* 55–76.

Adams, R. G., Bleiszner, R., & De Vries, B. (2000). Definitions of friendship in the third age: Age, gender, and study location effects. *Journal of Aging Studies, 14,* 117–133.

Adams, R., & Laursen, B. (2001). The organization and dynamics of adolescent conflict with parents and friends. *Journal of Marriage and the Family, 63,* 97–110.

Addington-Hall, J. (2000). Do home deaths increase distress in bereavement? *Palliative Medicine, 14,* 161–162.

Adkins, G., Martin, P., & Poon, L. W. (1996). Personality traits and states as predictors of subjective well-being in centenarians, octogenarians, and sexagenarians. *Psychology and Aging, 11,* 408–416.

Adler, N. E., & Newman, K. (2002). Socioeconomic disparities in health: Pathways and policies. *Health Affairs, 21,* 60–76.

Adolph, K. E. (2000). Specificity of learning: Why infants fall over a veritable cliff. *Psychological Science, 11,* 290–295.

Adolph, K. E., & Eppler, M. A. (1998). Development of visually guided locomotion. *Ecological Psychology, 10,* 303–321.

Adolph, K. E., & Eppler, M. A. (1999). Obstacles to understanding: An ecological approach to infant problem solving. In E. Winograd, R. Fivush, & W. Hirst (Eds.), *Ecological approaches to cognition* (pp. 31–58). Mahwah, NJ: Erlbaum.

Adolph, K. E. A., Vereijken, B., & Denny, M. A. (1998). Learning to crawl. *Child Development, 69,* 1299–1312.

Adolph, K. E. A., Vereijken, B., & Shrout, P. E. (2003). What changes in infant walking and why. *Child Development, 74,* 475–497.

Affifi, W. A., & Faulkner, S. L. (2000). On being "just friends": The frequency and impact of sexual activity in cross-sex friendships. *Journal of Social and Personal Relationships, 17,* 205–222.

Agarwal, D. P. (2002). Cardioprotective effects of light-moderate consumption of alcohol: A review of putative mechanisms. *Alcohol and Alcoholism, 37,* 409–415.

Agran, P. F., Winn, D., Anderson, C., Trent, R., & Walton-Haynes, L. (2001). Rates of pediatric and adolescent injuries by year of age. *Pediatrics, 108,* e45.

Agüero-Torres, H., von Strauss, E., Viitanen, M., Winblad, B., & Fratiglioni, L. (2001). Institutionalization in the elderly: The role of chronic diseases and dementia. Cross-sectional and longitudinal data from a population-based study. *Journal of Clinical Epidemiology, 54,* 795–801.

Aguiar, A., & Baillargeon, R. (1999). 2.5-month-old infants' reasoning about when objects should and should not be occluded. *Cognitive Psychology, 39,* 116–157.

Aguiar, A., & Baillargeon, R. (2002). Developments in young infants' reasoning about occluded objects. *Cognitive Psychology, 45,* 267–336.

Ahlgren, M., Melbye, M., Wohlfahrt, J., & Sørensen, T. I. (2004). Growth patterns and the risk of breast cancer in women. *New England Journal of Medicine, 351,* 1619–1626.

Aho, T. F., & Gilling, P. J. (2003). Laser therapy for benign prostatic hyperplasia: A review of recent developments. *Current Opinion in Urology, 13,* 39–44.

Ahuja, J. (2005). *Women's entrepreneurship in the United States.* Kansas City, MO: Kauffman Center for Entrepreneurial Leadership, Clearinghouse on Entrepreneurship Education. Retrieved from www.celcee.edu

Ainsworth, M. D. S., Blehar, M. C., Waters, E., & Wall, S. (1978). *Patterns of attachment.* Hillsdale, NJ: Erlbaum.

Akers, J. F., Jones, R. M., & Coyl, D. D. (1998). Adolescent friendship pairs: Similarities in identity status development, behaviors, attitudes, and intentions. *Journal of Adolescent Research, 13,* 178–201.

Akhtar, N., & Tomasello, M. (2000). The social nature of words and word learning. In R. Golinkoff & K. Hirsh-Pasek (Eds.), *Becoming a word learner: A debate on lexical acquisition.* Oxford, UK: Oxford University Press.

Akimoto, S. A., & Sanbonmatsu, D. M. (1999). Differences in self-effacing behavior between European and Japanese Americans: Effect on competence evaluations. *Journal of Cross-Cultural Psychology, 30,* 159–177.

Akinbami, L. J., & Schoendorf, K. C. (2002). Trends in childhood asthma: Prevalence, health care utilization, and mortality. *Pediatrics, 110,* 315–322.

Akiyama, H., Antonucci, T., Takahashi, K., & Langfahl, E. S. (2003). Negative interactions in close relationships across the lifespan. *Journal of Gerontology, 58B,* P70–P79.

Akshoomoff, N. A., Feroleto, C. C., Doyle, R. E., & Stiles, J. (2002). The impact of early unilateral brain injury on perceptual organization and visual memory. *Neuropsychologia, 40,* 539–561.

Alan Guttmacher Institute. (2001). *Can more progress be made? Teenage sexual and reproductive behavior in developed countries.* New York: Author. Retrieved from www.guttmacher.org

Alan Guttmacher Institute. (2002). Teen pregnancy: Trends and lessons learned. Retrieved from http://www.agi-usa.org/pubs/ib_1-02.html

Alan Guttmacher Institute. (2004). Teen sexuality: Stats & facts. Retrieved from www.fotf.ca/familyfacts/issues/teensexuality/stats.html

Albanes, D., Blair, A., & Taylor, P. R. (1989). Physical activity and risk of cancer in the NHANES I population. *American Journal of Public Health, 79,* 744–750.

Alcohol Concern. (2004). *Advertising alcohol.* Retrieved from www.alcoholconcern.org.uk

Aldridge, M. A., Stillman, R. D., & Bower, T. G. R. (2001). Newborn categorization of vowel-like sounds. *Developmental Science, 4,* 220–232.

Aldwin, C. M., & Levenson, M. (2002). Stress, coping, and health at midlife: A developmental perspective. In M. E. Lachman (Ed.), *Handbook of midlife development* (pp. 188–214). New York: Wiley.

Aldwin, C. M., Spiro, A., III, Levenson, M. R., & Cupertino, A. P. (2001). Longitudinal findings from The Normative Aging Study: III. Personality, individual health trajectories, and mortality. *Psychology and Aging, 16,* 450–465.

Aldwin, C. M., Sutton, K. J., & Lachman, M. (1996). The development of coping resources in adulthood. *Journal of Personality, 64,* 91–113.

Alessandri, S. M., Bendersky, M., & Lewis, M. (1998). Cognitive functioning in 8- to 18-month-old drug-exposed infants. *Developmental Psychology, 34,* 565–573.

Alessandri, S. M., Sullivan, M. W., & Lewis, M. (1990). Violation of expectancy and frustration in early infancy. *Developmental Psychology, 26,* 738–744.

Alexander, J. M., Fabricius, W. V., Fleming, V. M., Zwahr, M., & Brown, S. A. (2003). The development of metacognitive causal explanations. *Learning and Individual Differences, 13,* 227–238.

Alexandre-Bidon, K. L., & Lett, D. (1997). *Les enfants au Moyen Age, Ve–XVe siecles.* Paris: Hachette.

Ali, L., & Scelfo, J. (2002, December 9). Choosing virginity. *Newsweek,* pp. 60–65.

Alibali, M. W. (1999). How children change their minds: Strategy change can be gradual or abrupt. *Developmental Psychology, 35,* 127–145.

Allen, J. P., & Hauser, S. T. (1996). Autonomy and relatedness in adolescent–family interactions as predictors of young adults' states of mind regarding attachment. *Development and Psychopathology, 8,* 793–809.

Allen, J. P., Philliber, S., Herrling, S., & Kuperminc, G. P. (1997). Preventing teen pregnancy and academic failure: Experimental evaluation of a developmentally based approach. *Child Development, 64,* 729–742.

Allen, M., & Burrell, N. (1996). Comparing the impact of homosexual and heterosexual parents on children: Meta-analysis of existing research. *Journal of Homosexuality, 32,* 19–35.

Allen, S. E. M., & Crago, M. B. (1996). Early passive acquisition in Inukitut. *Journal of Child Language, 23,* 129–156.

Allen, T. D., & Finkelstein, L. M. (2003). Beyond mentoring: Alternative sources and functions of developmental support. *Career Development Quarterly, 51,* 346–355.

Allison, B. N., & Schultz, J. B. (2004). Parent–adolescent conflict in early adolescence. *Adolescence, 39,* 101–119.

Almeida, D. M., & Horn, M. C. (2004). Is daily life more stressful during middle adulthood? In O. G. Brim, C. D. Ryff, & R. C. Kessler (Eds.), *How healthy are we? A national study of well-being at midlife* (pp. 425–451). Chicago: University of Chicago Press.

Almeida, D. M., Neupert, S. D., Banks, S. R., & Serido, J. (2005). Do daily stress processes account for socioeconomic health disparities? *Journal of Gerontology, 60B,* 34–39.

Alpert-Gillis, L. J., & Connell, J. P. (1989). Gender and sex-role influences on children's self-esteem. *Journal of Personality, 57,* 97–114.

Alsaker, F. D. (1995). Timing of puberty and reactions to pubertal changes. In M. Rutter (Ed.), *Psychosocial disturbances in young people* (pp. 37–82). New York: Cambridge University Press.

Alwin, D. F., & Wray, L. A. (2005). A life-span developmental perspective on social status and health. *Journal of Gerontology, 60B*(Special Issue II), 7–14.

Alzheimer's Association. (2006). *African Americans and Alzheimer's disease: The silent epidemic.* Chicago: Author.

Amato, P. R. (2000). The consequences of divorce for adults and children. *Journal of Marriage and the Family, 62,* 1269–1287.

Amato, P. R. (2001). Children of divorce in the 1990s: An update of the Amato and Keith (1991) meta-analysis. *Journal of Family Psychology, 15,* 355–370.

Amato, P. R., & Booth, A. (1995). Change in gender role attitudes and perceived marital quality. *American Sociological Review, 60,* 58–66.

Amato, P. R., & Cheadle, J. (2005). The long reach of divorce: Divorce and child well-being across three generations. *Journal of Marriage and Family, 67,* 191–206.

Amato, P. R., & Fowler, F. (2002). Parenting practices, child adjustment, and family diversity. *Journal of Marriage and the Family, 64,* 703–716.

Amato, P. R., & Rogers, S. J. (1997). A longitudinal study of marital problems and subsequent divorce. *Journal of Marriage and the Family, 59,* 612–624.

Amato, P. R., & Sobolewski, J. M. (2004). The effects of divorce on fathers and children: Nonresidential fathers and stepfathers. In M. E. Lamb (Ed.), *The role of the father in child development* (4th ed., pp. 341–367). Hoboken, NJ: Wiley.

Ambert, A.-M. (2003). *Same-sex couples and same-sex parent families: Relationships, parenting, and issues of marriage.* Ottawa: Vanier Institute of the Family.

American Academy of Pediatrics, Subcommittee on Attention-Deficit Hyperactivity Disorder. (2005a). Treatment of attention-deficit hyperactivity disorder. *Pediatrics, 115,* e749–e757.

American Academy of Pediatrics. (2005b). Use of performance-enhancing substances. *Pediatrics, 115,* 1103–1106.

American Heart Association. (2006a). Heart attack and angina statistics. Retrieved from www.americanheart.org

American Heart Association. (2006b). *Heart disease and stroke statistics: 2006 update.* Dallas, TX: Author.

American Hospice Foundation. (2005). *Talking about hospice: Tips for physicians.* Washington, DC: Author.

American Psychiatric Association. (1994). *Diagnostic and statistical manual of mental disorders* (4th ed.). Washington, DC: Author.

American Psychological Association. (2002). Ethical principles of psychologists and code of conduct. *American Psychologist, 57,* 1060–1073.

American Society for Reproductive Medicine. (2004). Smoking and infertility. *Fertility and Sterility, 81,* 1181–1186.

Ames, E. W., & Chisholm, K. (2001). Social and emotional development in children adopted from institutions. In D. B. Bailey, Jr., J. T. Bruer, F. J. Symons, & J. W. Lichtman (Eds.), *Critical thinking about critical periods* (pp. 129–148). Baltimore, MD: Brookes.

Anand, S. S., Yusuf, S., Jacobs, R., Davis, A. D., Yi, Q., & Gerstein, H. (2001). Risk factors, atherosclerosis, and cardiovascular disease among Aboriginal people in Canada: The study of health assessment and risk evaluation in Aboriginal peoples (SHARE-AP). *Lancet, 358,* 1147–1153.

Anaya, H. D., Cantwell, S. M., & Rothman-Borus, M. J. (2003). Sexual risk behaviors among adolescents. In A. Biglan & M. C. Wang (Eds.), *Preventing youth problems* (pp. 113–143). New York: Kluwer Academic.

Ancoli-Israel, S., & Cooke, J. R. (2005). Prevalence and comorbidity of insomnia and effect on functioning in elderly populations. *Journal of the American Geriatric Society, 53,* S264–S271.

Anderman, E. M., Eccles, J. S., Yoon, K. S., Roeser, R., Wigfield, A., & Blumenfeld, P. (2001). Learning to value mathematics and reading: Relations to mastery and performance-oriented instructional practices. *Contemporary Educational Psychology, 26,* 76–95.

Anderman, E. M., & Midgley, C. (1997). Changes in achievement goal orientations, perceived academic competence, and grades across the transition to middle-level schools. *Contemporary Educational Psychology, 22,* 269–298.

Anderson, C. A., Berkowitz, L., Donnerstein, E., Huesmann, R., Johnson, J. D., Linz, D., Malamuth, N. M., & Wartella, E. (2003). The influence of media violence on youth. *Psychological Science in the Public Interest, 4*(3), 81–106.

Anderson, D. M., Huston, A. C., Schmitt, K. L., Linebarger, D. L., & Wright, J. C. (2001). Early childhood television viewing and adolescent behavior. *Monographs of the Society for Research in Child Development, 66*(1, Serial No. 264).

Anderson, E. (1992). *Speaking with style: The sociolinguistic skills of children.* London: Routledge.

Anderson, E. (2000). Exploring register knowledge: The value of "controlled improvisation." In L. Menn & N. B. Ratner (Eds.), *Methods for studying language production* (pp. 225–248). Mahwah, NJ: Erlbaum.

Anderson, J. L., Morgan, J. L., & White, K. S. (2003). A statistical basis for speech sound discrimination. *Language and Speech, 46,* 155–182.

Anderson, M. E., Johnson, D. C., & Batal, H. A. (2005). Sudden infant death syndrome and prenatal maternal smoking: Rising attributed risk in the Back to Sleep era. *BMC Medicine, 3,* 4.

Anderson, P. B., & Savage, J. S. (2005). Social, legal, and institutional context of heterosexual aggression by college women.

Trauma, Violence, and Abuse, 6, 130–140.

Anderson, S. E., Dallal, G. E., & Must, A. (2003). Relative weight and race influence average age at menarche: Results from two nationally representative surveys of U.S. girls studied 25 years apart. *Pediatrics, 111,* 844–850.

Andersson, B.-E. (1989). Effects of public day care—A longitudinal study. *Child Development, 60,* 857–866.

Andersson, B.-E. (1992). Effects of day care on cognitive and socio-emotional competence of thirteen-year-old Swedish schoolchildren. *Child Development, 63,* 20–36.

Andersson, T., & Magnusson, D. (1990). Biological maturation in adolescence and the development of drinking habits and alcohol abuse among young males: A prospective longitudinal study. *Journal of Youth and Adolescence, 19,* 33–41.

Andre, T., Whigham, M., Hendrickson, A., & Chambers, S. (1999). Competence beliefs, positive affect, and gender stereotypes of elementary students and their parents about science versus other school subjects. *Journal of Research in Science Teaching, 36,* 719–747.

Andreoletti, C., & Lachman, M. E. (2004). Susceptibility and resilience to memory aging stereotypes: Education matters more than age. *Experimental Aging Research, 30,* 129–148.

Andrews, G., & Halford, G. S. (1998). Children's ability to make transitive inferences: The importance of premise integration and structural complexity. *Cognitive Development, 13,* 479–513.

Andrews, G., & Halford, G. S. (2002). A cognitive complexity metric applied to cognitive development. *Cognitive Psychology, 45,* 475–506.

Anetzberger, G. J. (2005). The reality of elder abuse. *Clinical Gerontologist, 28,* 2–25.

Anglin, J. M. (1993). Vocabulary development: A morphological analysis. *Monographs of the Society for Research in Child Development, 58*(10, Serial No. 238).

Angus Reid Group. (1997). *Canadians' views on euthanasia.* Retrieved from www.dyingwithdignity.ca/angus.html

Anisfeld, M., Turkewitz, G., Rose, S. A., Rosenberg, F. R., Shelber, F. J., Couturier-Fagan, D. A., Ger, J. S., & Sommer, I. (2001). No compelling evidence that newborns imitate oral gestures. *Infancy, 2,* 111–122.

Annett, M. (2002). *Handedness and brain asymmetry: The right shift theory.* Hove, UK: Psychology Press.

Anslow, P. (1998). Birth asphyxia. *European Journal of Radiology, 26,* 148–153.

Anstey, K., & Christensen, H. (2000). Education, activity, health, blood pressure, and apolipoprotein E as predictors of cognitive change in old age: A review. *Gerontology, 46,* 163–177.

Anstey, K. J., Luszcz, M. A., & Sanchez, L. (2001). Two-year decline in vision but not hearing is associated with memory decline in very old adults in a population-based sample. *Gerontology, 47,* 289–293.

Antonucci, T. C. (1994). A life-span view of women's social relations. In B. F. Turner & L. E. Troll (Eds.), *Women growing older* (pp. 239–269). Thousand Oaks, CA: Sage.

Antonucci, T. C., & Akiyama, H. (1995). Convoys of social relations: Family and friendships within a life span context. In R. Blieszner & V. H. Bedford (Eds.), *Handbook of aging and the family* (pp. 355–371). Westport, CT: Greenwood Press.

Antonucci, T. C., & Akiyama, H. (1997). Concern with others at midlife: Care, comfort, or compromise? In M. E. Lachman & J. B. James (Eds.), *Multiple paths of midlife development* (pp. 145–169). Chicago: University of Chicago Press.

Antonucci, T. C., Akiyama, H., & Merline, A. (2002). Dynamics of social relationships in midlife. In M. E. Lachman (Ed.), *Handbook of midlife development* (pp. 571–598). New York: Wiley.

Antonucci, T. C., Akiyama, H., & Takahashi, K. (2004). Attachment and close relationships across the lifespan. *Attachment and Human Development, 6,* 353–370.

Antshel, K. M. (2003). Timing is everything: Executive functions in children exposed to elevated levels of phenylalanine. *Neuropsychology, 17,* 458–468.

Apgar, V. (1953). A proposal for a new method of evaluation in the newborn infant. *Current Research in Anesthesia and Analgesia, 32,* 260–267.

Aquilino, W. S. (1996). The returning adult child and parental experience at midlife. In C. D. Ryff & M. M. Seltzer (Eds.), *The parental experience in midlife* (pp. 423–458). Chicago: University of Chicago Press.

Aquilino, W. S., & Supple, A. J. (2001). Long-term effects of parenting practices during adolescence on well-being outcomes in young adulthood. *Journal of Family Issues, 22,* 289–308.

Archer, J. (2002a). Sex differences in aggression between heterosexual partners: A meta-analytic review. *Psychological Bulletin, 126,* 651–681.

Archer, S. L. (2002b). Commentary on "Feminist Perspectives on Erikson's Theory: Their Relevance for Contemporary Identity Development Research." *Identity, 2,* 267–270.

Archer, S. L., & Waterman, A. S. (1990). Varieties of identity diffusions and foreclosures: An exploration of subcategories of the identity statuses. *Journal of Adolescent Research, 5,* 96–111.

Ardelt, M. (1998). Social crisis and individual growth: The long-term effects of the Great Depression. *Journal of Aging Studies, 12,* 291–314.

Ardila-Rey, A., & Killen, M. (2001). Middle-class Colombian children's evaluations of personal, moral, and social-conventional interactions in the classroom. *International Journal of Behavioral Development, 25,* 246–255.

Argue, A., Johnson, D. R., & White, L. K. (1999). Age and religiosity: Evidence from a three-wave panel analysis. *Journal for the Scientific Study of Religion, 38,* 423–435.

Arking, R. (1998). *Biology of aging* (2nd ed.). Sunderland, MA: Sinaur Associates.

Arking, R., Novoseltsev, V., & Novoseltseva, J. (2004). The human life span is not that limited: The effect of multiple longevity phenotypes. *Journal of Gerontology, 59A,* 697–704.

Arlin, P. K. (1989). Problem solving and problem finding in young artists and young scientists. In M. L. Commons, J. D. Sinnott, F. A. Richards, & C. Armon (Eds.), *Adult development: Vol 1. Comparisons and applications of developmental models* (pp. 197–216). New York: Praeger.

Armstrong, G. K., & Morgan, K. (1998). Stability and change in levels of habitual physical activity in later life. *Age and Ageing, 27*(Suppl. 3), 17–23.

Armstrong, T. D., & Crowther, M. R. (2002). Spirituality among older African Americans. *Journal of Adult Development, 9,* 3–12.

Arnett, J. J. (1997). Young people's conceptions of the transition to adulthood. *Youth and Society, 29,* 1–23.

Arnett, J. J. (2000). Emerging adulthood: A theory of development from the late teens through the twenties. *American Psychologist, 55,* 469–480.

Arnett, J. J. (2001). Conceptions of the transition to adulthood: Perspectives from adolescence to midlife. *Journal of Adult Development, 8,* 133–143.

Arnett, J. J. (2003). Conceptions of the transition to adulthood among emerging adults in American ethnic groups. In J. J. Arnett & N. L. Galambos (Eds.), *New directions for child and adolescent development* (No. 100, pp. 63–75). San Francisco: Jossey-Bass.

Arnett, J. J. (2004). *Emerging adulthood: The winding road from the late teens through the twenties.* New York: Oxford University Press.

Arnett, J. J. (2006). Emerging adulthood: Understanding the new way of coming of age. In J. J. Arnett & J. L. Tanner (Eds.), *Emerging adults in America: Coming of age in the 21st century* (pp. 3–19). Washington, DC: American Psychological Association.

Arnold, D. H., Fisher, P. H., Doctoroff, G. L., & Dobbs, J. (2002). Accelerating math development in Head Start classrooms. *Journal of Educational Psychology, 94,* 762–770.

Arnold, D. H., McWilliams, L., & Harvey-Arnold, E. (1998). Teacher discipline and child misbehavior in daycare: Untangling causality with correlational data. *Developmental Psychology, 34,* 276–287.

Arnold, K. (1994). The Illinois Valedictorian Project: Early adult careers of academically talented male and female high school students. In R. F. Subotnik & K. D. Arnold (Eds.), *Beyond Terman: Contemporary longitudinal studies of giftedness and talent* (pp. 24–51). Norwood, NJ: Ablex.

Arnold, P. (1999). Emotional disorders in deaf children. In V. L. Schwean & D. H. Saklofske (Eds.), *Handbook of psychosocial characteristics of exceptional children* (pp. 493–522). New York: Kluwer.

Arora, S., McJunkin, C., Wehrer, J., & Kuhn, P. (2000). Major factors influencing breastfeeding rates: Mother's perception of father's attitude and milk supply. *Pediatrics, 106,* e67.

Arriaga, X. B., & Foshee, V. A. (2004). Adolescent dating violence: Do adolescents follow in their friends' or their parents' footsteps? *Journal of Interpersonal Violence, 19,* 162–184.

Artistico, D., Cervone, D., & Pezzuti, L. (2003). Perceived self-efficacy and everyday problem solving among young and older adults. *Psychology and Aging, 18,* 68–79.

Artman, L., & Cahan, S. (1993). Schooling and the development of transitive inference. *Developmental Psychology, 29,* 753–759.

Arvanitakis, Z., Wilson, R. S., Bienias, J. L., Evans, D. A., & Bennett, D. A. (2004). Diabetes mellitus and risk of Alzheimer disease and decline in cognitive function. *Archives of Neurology, 61,* 661–666.

Asakawa, K. (2001). Family socialization practices and their effects on the internationalization of educational values for Asian and white American adolescents. *Applied Developmental Science, 5,* 184–194.

Asher, S. R., & Rose, A. J. (1997). Promoting children's social-emotional adjustment with peers. In P. Salovey & D. J. Sluyter (Eds.), *Emotional development and emotional intelligence* (pp. 193–195). New York: Basic Books.

Aslin, R. N. (1993). Perception of visual direction in human infants. In C. E. Granrud (Ed.), *Visual perception and cognition in infancy* (pp. 91–119). Hillsdale, NJ: Erlbaum.

Aslin, R. N., Jusczyk, P. W., & Pisoni, D. B. (1998). Speech and auditory processing during infancy: Constraints on and precursors to language. In D. Kuhn & R. S. Siegler (Eds.), *Handbook of child psychology: Vol. 2. Cognition, perception, and language* (5th ed., pp. 147–198). New York: Wiley.

Assmann, A. (1994). Wholesome knowledge: Concepts of wisdom in a historical and cross-cultural perspective. In D. L. Featherman, R. M. Lerner, & M. Perlmutter (Eds.), *Lifespan development and behavior* (pp. 187–224). Hillsdale, NJ: Erlbaum.

Astington, J. W., Pelletier, J., & Homer, B. (2002). Theory of mind and epistemological development: The relation between children's second-order false belief understanding and their ability to reason about evidence. *New Ideas in Psychology, 20,* 131–144.

Atchley, R. C. (1989). A continuity theory of normal aging. *Gerontologist, 29,* 183–190.

Atchley, R. C. (1999). *Continuity and adaptation in aging: Creating positive experiences.* Baltimore, MD: Johns Hopkins University Press.

Atchley, R. C. (2003). Why people cope well with retirement. In J. L. Ronch & J. A. Goldfield (Eds.), *Mental wellness in aging: Strengths-based approaches* (pp. 123–138). Baltimore, MD: Health Professions Press.

Aten, M. J., Siegel, D. M., Enaharo, M., & Auinger, P. (2002). Keeping middle school students abstinent: Outcomes of a primary prevention intervention. *Journal of Adolescent Health, 31,* 70–78.

Athanasou, J. A. (2002). Vocational pathways in the early part of a career: An Australian study. *Career Development Quarterly, 52,* 78–88.

Atkins, R., Hart, D., & Donnelly, T. M. (2004). Moral identity development and school attachment. In D. Lapsley & D. Narvaez (Eds.), *Moral development, self, and identity* (pp. 65–82). Mahwah, NJ: Erlbaum.

Atkinson, J. (2000). *The developing visual brain.* Oxford: Oxford University Press.

Atkinson, R. C., & Shiffrin, R. M. (1968). Human memory: A proposed system and its control processes. In K. W. Spence & J. T. Spence (Eds.), *Advances in the psychology of learning and motivation* (Vol. 2, pp. 90–195). New York: Academic Press.

Au, T. K., Sidle, A. L., & Rollins, K. B. (1993). Developing an intuitive understanding of conservation and contamination: Invisible particles as a plausible mechanism. *Developmental Psychology, 29,* 286–299.

Aunola, K., Stattin, H., & Nurmi, J.-E. (2000). Parenting styles and adolescents' achievement strategies. *Journal of Adolescence, 23,* 205–222.

Australian Bureau of Statistics. (2004). Divorce rates. Retrieved from www.abus.gov.au

Avenell, A., Broom, J., Brown, T. J., Poobalan, A., Aucott, L., & Stearns, S. C. (2004). Systematic review of the long-term effects and economic consequences of treatments for obesity and implications for health improvement. *Health Technology Assessment, 8,* 1–182.

Averhart, C. J., & Bigler, R. S. (1997). Shades of meaning: Skin tone, racial attitudes, and constructive memory in African-American children. *Journal of Experimental Child Psychology, 67,* 368–388.

Avis, N. E. (2000). Sexual function and aging in men and women: Community and population-based studies. *Journal of Gender-Specific Medicine, 3,* 37–41.

Avis, N. E. (2003). Depression during the menopausal transition. *Psychology of Women Quarterly, 27,* 91–100.

Avis, N. E., Assmann, S. F., Kravitz, H. M., Ganz, P.A., & Ory, M. (2004). Quality of life in diverse groups of midlife women: Assessing the influence of menopause, health status and psychosocial and demographic factors. *Quality of Life Research, 13,* 933–946.

Avis, N. E., Crawford, S., & Johannes, C. B. (2002). Menopause. In G. M. Wingood & R. J. DeClemente (Eds.), *Handbook of women's sexual and reproductive health* (pp. 367–391). New York: Kluwer.

Avolio, B. J., & Sosik, J. J. (1999). A lifespan framework for assessing the impact of work on white-collar workers. In S. L. Willis & J. D. Reid (Eds.), *Life in the middle*

(pp. 249–274). San Diego, CA: Academic Press.

AWC (American Women's Club) Oslo. (2005). Health care in Norway. Retrieved from www.awcoslo.org/Sections/LivingInOslo/health_care_in_norway.htm

Axia, G., & Baroni, R. (1985). Linguistic politeness at different age levels. *Child Development, 56,* 918–927.

Axia, G., Bonichini, S., & Benini, F. (1999). Attention and reaction to distress in infancy: A longitudinal study. *Developmental Psychology, 35,* 500–504.

Axinn, W. G., & Barber, J. S. (1997). Living arrangements and family formation attitudes in early adulthood. *Journal of Marriage and the Family, 59,* 595–611.

B

Bach-y-Rita, P. (2001). Theoretical and practical considerations in the restoration of function after stroke. *Topics in Stroke Rehabilitation, 8,* 1–15.

Baddeley, A. (1993). Working memory and conscious awareness. In A. F. Collins, S. E. Gathercole, M. A. Conway, & P. E. Morris (Eds.), *Theories of memory* (pp. 11–28). Hove, UK: Erlbaum.

Baddeley, A. (2000). Short-term and working memory. In E. Tulving & R. I. M. Craik (Eds.), *The Oxford handbook of memory* (pp. 77–92). New York: Oxford University Press.

Baenninger, M., & Newcombe, N. (1995). Environmental input to the development of sex-related differences in spatial and mathematical ability. *Learning and Individual Differences, 7,* 363–379.

Baer, J. S., Sampson, P. D., Barr, H. M., Connor, P. D., & Streissguth, A. P. (2003). A 21-year longitudinal analysis of the effects of prenatal alcohol exposure on young adult drinking. *Archives of General Psychiatry, 60,* 377–385.

Bagwell, C. L., Bender, S. E., Andreassi, C. L., Kinoshita, T. L., Montarello, S. A., & Muller, J. G. (2005). Friendship quality and perceived relationship changes predict psychosocial adjustment in early adulthood. *Journal of Social and Personal Relationships, 22,* 235–254.

Bagwell, C. L., & Coie, J. D. (2004). The best friendships of aggressive boys: Relationship quality, conflict management, and rule-breaking behavior. *Journal of Experimental Child Psychology, 88,* 5–24.

Bagwell, C. L., Newcomb, A. F., & Bukowski, W. M. (1998). Preadolescent friendship and peer rejection as predictors of adult

adjustment. *Child Development, 69,* 140–153.

Bagwell, C. L., Schmidt, M. E., Newcomb, A. F., & Bukowski, W. M. (2001). Friendship and peer rejection as predictors of adult adjustment. In D. W. Nangle & C. A. Erdley (Eds.), *The role of friendship in psychological adjustment* (pp. 25–49). San Francisco: Jossey-Bass.

Bahrick, H. P. (1984). Semantic memory content in permastore: Fifty years of memory for Spanish learned in school. *Journal of Experimental Psychology: General, 113,* 1–29.

Bahrick, H. P., Bahrick, P. O., & Wittlinger, R. P. (1975). Fifty years of memory for names and faces: A cross-sectional approach. *Journal of Experimental Psychology: General, 104,* 54–75.

Bahrick, L. E. (2001). Increasing specificity in perceptual development: Infants' detection of nested levels of multimodal stimulation. *Journal of Experimental Child Psychology, 79,* 253–270.

Bahrick, L. E., Gogate, L. J., & Ruiz, I. (2002). Attention and memory for faces and actions in infancy: The salience of actions over faces in dynamic events. *Child Development, 73,* 1629–1643.

Bahrick, L. E., Hernandez-Reif, M., & Flom, R. (2005). The development of infant learning about specific face–voice relations. *Developmental Psychology, 41,* 541–552.

Bahrick, L. E., Hernandez-Reif, M., & Pickens, J. N. (1997). The effect of retrieval cues on visual preferences and memory in infancy: Evidence for a four-phase attention function. *Journal of Experimental Child Psychology, 67,* 1–20.

Bahrick, L. E., Lickliter, R., & Flom, R. (2004). Intersensory redundancy guides the development of selective attention, perception, and cognition in infancy. *Current Directions in Psychological Science, 13,* 99–102.

Bahrick, L. E., Netto, D., & Hernandez-Reif, M. (1998). Intermodal perception of adult and child faces and voices by infants. *Child Development, 69,* 1263–1275.

Bahrick, L. E., & Pickens, J. N. (1995). Infant memory for object motion across a period of three months: Implications for a four-phase attention function. *Journal of Experimental Child Psychology, 59,* 343–371.

Bai, D. L., & Bertenthal, B. I. (1992). Locomotor status and the development of spatial search skills. *Child Development, 63,* 215–226.

Bailey, J. M., Bobrow, D., Wolfe, M., & Mikach, S. (1995). Sexual orientation of adult sons of gay fathers.

Developmental Psychology, 31, 124–129.

Bailey, J. M., Dunne, M. P., & Martin, N. G. (2000). Genetic and environmental influences on sexual orientation and its correlates in an Australian twin sample. *Journal of Personality and Social Psychology, 78,* 524–536.

Bailey, M., & McLaren, S. (2005). Physical activity alone and with others as predictors of sense of belonging and mental health in retirees. *Aging and Mental Health, 9,* 82–90.

Baillargeon, R. (2000). Reply to Bogartz, Shinskey, and Schilling; Schilling; and Cashon and Cohen. *Infancy, 1,* 447–462.

Baillargeon, R. (2004). Infants' reasoning about hidden objects: Evidence for event-general and event-specific expectations. *Developmental Science, 7,* 391–424.

Baillargeon, R., & DeVos, J. (1991). Object permanence in young infants: Further evidence. *Child Development, 62,* 1227–1246.

Baird, D. T., Collins, J., Egozcue, J., Evers, L. H., Gianaroli, L., & Leridon, H. (2005). Fertility and ageing. *Human Reproduction Update, 11,* 261–276.

Baker, J. G. (2002). The influx of women into legal professions: An economic analysis. *Monthly Labor Review, 125,* 14–24.

Baker, J. L., Michaelsen, K. F., Rasmussen, K. M., & Sørensen, T. I. (2004). Maternal prepregnant body mass index, duration of breastfeeding, and timing of complementary food introduction are associated with infant weight gain. *American Journal of Clinical Nutrition, 80,* 1579–1588.

Bakermans-Kranenburg, M. J., van IJzendoorn, M. H., & Juffer, F. (2003). Less is more: Meta-analyses of sensitivity and attachment interventions in early childhood. *Psychological Bulletin, 129,* 195–215.

Balaswamy, S., & Richardson, V. E. (2001). The cumulative effects of life event, personal, and social resources on subjective well-being of elderly widowers. *International Journal of Aging and Human Development, 53,* 311–327.

Ball, K., Berch, D. B., Helmers, K. F., Jobe, J. B., Leveck, M. D., & Marsiske, M. (2002). Effects of cognitive training interventions with older adults: A randomized controlled trial. *Journal of the American Medical Association, 288,* 2271–2281.

Ball, M. M., Whittington, F. J., Perkins, M. M., Patterson, V. L., Hollingsworth, C., King, S. V., & Combs, B. L. (2000). Quality of life in assisted living facilities: Viewpoints of residents. *Journal of Applied Gerontology, 19,* 304–325.

Baltes, M. M. (1995, February). Dependency in old age: Gains and losses. *Psychological Science, 4*(1), 14–19.

Baltes, M. M. (1996). *The many faces of dependency in old age.* New York: Cambridge University Press.

Baltes, M. M., & Carstensen, L. L. (1996). The process of successful ageing. *Ageing and Society, 16,* 397–422.

Baltes, M. M., Wahl, H.-W., & Reichert, M. (1992). Successful aging in long-term care institutions. In K. W. Schaie & M. P. Lawton (Eds.), *Annual review of gerontology and geriatrics* (pp. 311–337). New York: Springer.

Baltes, P. B. (1997). On the incomplete architecture of human ontogeny: Selection, optimization, and compensation as foundation of developmental theory. *American Psychologist, 52,* 366–380.

Baltes, P. B., Dittmann-Kohli, F., & Dixon, R. A. (1984). New perspectives on the development of intelligence in adulthood: Toward a dual-process conception and a model of selective optimization with compensation. In P. B. Baltes & O. G. Brim, Jr. (Eds.), *Life-span development and behavior* (Vol. 6, pp. 33–76). San Diego, CA: Academic Press.

Baltes, P. B., Lindenberger, U., & Staudinger, U. M. (1998). Life-span theory in developmental psychology. In R. M. Lerner (Ed.), *Handbook of child psychology: Vol. 1. Theoretical models of human development* (5th ed., pp. 1029–1143). New York: Wiley.

Baltes, P. B., & Smith, J. (2003). New frontiers in the future of aging: From successful aging of the young old to the dilemmas of the fourth age. *Gerontology, 49,* 123–135.

Baltes, P. B., & Staudinger, U. M. (2000). Wisdom: A metaheuristic (pragmatic) to orchestrate mind and virtue toward excellence. *American Psychologist, 55,* 122–136.

Baltes, P. B., Staudinger, U. M., Maercker, A., & Smith, J. (1995). People nominated as wise: A comparative study of wisdom-related knowledge. *Psychology and Aging, 10,* 155–166.

Bancroft, J. (2002). The medicalization of female sexual dysfunction: The need for caution. *Archives of Sexual Behavior, 31,* 451–455.

Band, G. P. H., van der Molen, M. W., Overtoom, C. C. E., & Verbaten, M. N. (2000). The ability to activate and inhibit speeded responses: Separate developmental trends. *Journal of Experimental Child Psychology, 75,* 263–290.

Bandura, A. (1977). *Social learning theory.* Englewood Cliffs, NJ: Prentice-Hall.

Bandura, A. (1992). Perceived self-efficacy in cognitive development and functioning. *Educational Psychologist, 28,* 117–148.

Bandura, A. (1999). Social cognitive theory of personality. In L. A. Pervin (Ed.), *Handbook of personality: Theory and research* (2nd ed., pp. 154–196). New York: Guilford.

Bandura, A. (2001). Social cognitive theory: An agentic perspective. *Annual Review of Psychology, 52,* 1–26.

Banish, M. T., & Heller, W. (1998). Evolving perspectives on lateralization of function. *Current Directions in Psychological Science, 7,* 1–2.

Bankoff, E. A. (1983). Aged parents and their widowed daughters: A support relationship. *Journal of Gerontology, 38,* 226–230.

Banks, M. S. (1980). The development of visual accommodation during early infancy. *Child Development, 51,* 646–666.

Banks, M. S., & Ginsburg, A. P. (1985). Early visual preferences: A review and new theoretical treatment. In H. W. Reese (Ed.), *Advances in child development and behavior* (Vol. 19, pp. 207–246). New York: Academic Press.

Banta, D. H., & Thacker, S. B. (2001). Historical controversy in health technology assessment: The case of electronic fetal monitoring. *Obstetrical and Gynecological Survey, 56,* 707–719.

Barakat, L. P., & Kazak, A. E. (1999). Family issues. In R. T. Brown (Ed.), *Cognitive aspects of chronic illness in children* (pp. 333–354). New York: Guilford.

Barber, B. K. (1996). Parental psychological control: Revisiting a neglected construct. *Child Development, 67,* 3296–3319.

Barber, B. K., & Harmon, E. L. (2002). Violating the self: Parental psychological control of children and adolescents. In B. K. Barber (Ed.), *Intrusive parenting: How psychological control affects children and adolescents* (pp. 15–52). Washington, DC: American Psychological Association.

Barber, B. K., & Olsen, J. A. (1997). Socialization in context: Connection, regulation, and autonomy in the family, school, and neighborhood, and with peers. *Journal of Adolescent Research, 12,* 287–315.

Barber, B. K., Stolz, H. E., & Olsen, J. A. (2005). Parental support, psychological control, and behavioral control: Assessing relevance across time, culture, and method. *Monographs of the Society for Research in Child Development, 70*(4, Serial No. 282).

Barber, J. S. (2001). Ideational influences on the transition to parenthood: Attitudes toward childbearing and competing alternatives. *Social Psychology Quarterly, 64,* 101–127.

Barberger-Gateau, P., Letenneur, L., Deschamps, V., Peres, K., Dartigues, J. F., & Renaud, S. (2002). Fish, meat, and risk of dementia: Cohort study. *British Medical Journal, 325,* 932–933.

Barenbaum, J., Ruchkin, V., & Schwab-Stone, M. (2004). The psychosocial aspects of children exposed to war: Practice and policy initiatives. *Journal of Child Psychology and Psychiatry, 45,* 41–62.

Barker, D. (2002). Fetal programming of coronary heart disease. *Trends in Endocrinology and Metabolism, 13,* 364.

Barker, D. J. P. (1994). *Mothers, babies, and disease in later life.* London: British Medical Journal Publishing.

Barkley, R. A. (2002a). Psychosocial treatments of attention-deficit/hyperactivity disorder in children. *Journal of Clinical Psychology, 63*(Suppl. 12), 36–43.

Barkley, R. A. (2002b). Major life activity and health outcomes associated with attention-deficit/hyperactivity disorder. *Journal of Clinical Psychiatry, 63*(Suppl. 12), 10–15.

Barkley, R. A. (2003a). Attention-deficit/hyperactivity disorder. In E. J. Mash & R. A. Barkley (Eds.), *Child psychopathology* (2nd ed., pp. 75–143). New York: Guilford Press.

Barkley, R. A. (2003b). Issues in the diagnosis of attention-deficit hyperactivity disorder in children. *Brain and Development, 25,* 77–83.

Barnet, B., Arroyo, C., Devoe, M., & Duggan, A. K. (2004). Reduced school dropout rates among adolescent mothers receiving school-based prenatal care. *Archives of Pediatric and Adolescent Medicine, 158,* 262–268.

Barnett, D., & Vondra, J. I. (1999). Atypical patterns of early attachment: Theory, research, and current directions. In J. I Vondra & D. Barnett (Eds.), Atypical attachment in infancy and early childhood among children at developmental risk. *Monographs of the Society for Research in Child Development, 64*(3, Serial No. 258), 1–24.

Barnett, R. C., & Hyde, J. S. (2001). Women, men, work, family: An expansionist theory. *American Psychologist, 56,* 781–796.

Baron-Cohen, S., Baldwin, D. A., & Crowson, M. (1997). Do children with autism use the speaker's direction of gaze strategy to crack the code of language? *Child Development, 68,* 48–57.

Baron-Cohen, S., & Belmonte, M. K. (2005). Autism: A window onto the development of the social and the analytic brain. *Annual Review of Neuroscience, 28,* 109–126.

Barr, H. M., Streissguth, A. P., Darby, B. L., & Sampson, P. D. (1990). Prenatal exposure to alcohol, caffeine, tobacco, and aspirin: Effects on fine and gross motor performance in 4-year-old children. *Developmental Psychology, 26,* 339–348.

Barr, R. G. (2001). "Colic" is something infants do, rather than a condition they "have": A developmental approach to crying phenomena patterns, pacification and (patho)genesis. In R. G. Barr, I. St. James-Roberts, & M. R. Keefe (Eds.), *New evidence on unexplained infant crying* (pp. 87–104). St. Louis: Johnson & Johnson Pediatric Institute.

Barr, R. G., & Gunnar, M. (2000). Colic: The 'transient responsivity' hypothesis. In R. G. Barr, B. Hopkins, & J. A. Green (Eds.), *Crying as a sign, a symptom, and a signal* (pp. 41–66). Cambridge, UK: Cambridge University Press.

Barr, R., & Hayne, H. (1999). Developmental changes in imitation from television during infancy. *Child Development, 70,* 1067–1081.

Barr, R., & Hayne, H. (2003). It's not what you know, it's who you know: Older siblings facilitate imitation during infancy. *International Journal of Early Years Education, 11,* 7–21.

Barr, R., Marrott, H., & Rovee-Collier, C. (2003). The role of sensory preconditioning in memory retrieval by preverbal infants. *Learning and Behavior, 31,* 111–123.

Barr, S. (1996, September). Up against the glass. *Management Review, 85*(9), 12–17.

Barratt, M. S., Roach, M. A., & Leavitt, L. A. (1996). The impact of low-risk prematurity on maternal behaviour and toddler outcomes. *International Journal of Behavioral Development, 19,* 581–602.

Barrett, K. C. (1998). The origins of guilt in early childhood. In J. Bybee (Ed.), *Guilt and children* (pp. 75–90). San Diego: Academic Press.

Barsky, A. J., Cleary, P. D., & Klerman, G. L. (1992). Determinants of perceived health status of medical outpatients. *Social Science and Medicine, 34,* 1147–1154.

Bartlik, B., & Goldstein, M. Z. (2001). Men's sexual health after midlife. *Practical Geriatrics, 52,* 291–306.

Bartrip, J., Morton, J., & de Schonen, S. (2001). Responses to mother's face in 3-week- to 5-month-old infants. *British Journal of Developmental Psychology, 19,* 219–232.

Bartsch, K., & Wellman, H. (1995). *Children talk about the mind.* New York: Oxford University Press.

Basow, S. A., & Rubin, L. R. (1999). Gender influences on adolescent development. In N. G. Johnson & M. C. Roberts (Eds.), *Beyond appearance: A new look at adolescent girls* (pp. 25–52). Washington, DC: American Psychological Association.

Bassuk, S. S., & Manson, J. E. (2005). Epidemiological evidence for the role of physical activity in reducing risk of type 2 diabetes and cardiovascular disease. *Journal of Applied Physiology, 99,* 1193–1204.

Bastian, L. A., Smith, C. M., & Nanda, K. (2003). Is this woman perimenopausal? *Journal of the American Medical Association, 289,* 895–902.

Bates, E. (1999). Plasticity, localization, and language development. In S. H. Broman & J. M. Fletcher (Eds.), *The changing nervous system: Neurobehavioral consequences of early brain disorders* (pp. 214–247). New York: Oxford University Press.

Bates, E., Marchman, V., Thal, D., Fenson, L., Dale, P., Reznick, J. S., Reilly, J., & Hartung, J. (1994). Developmental and stylistic variation in the composition of early vocabulary. *Journal of Child Language, 21,* 85–123.

Bates, E., Wilson, S. M., Saygin, A. P., Dick, F., Sereno, M. I., Knight, R. T., & Dronkers, N. F. (2003). Voxel-based lesion-symptom mapping. *Nature Neuroscience, 6,* 448–450.

Bates, J. E., Wachs, T. D., & Emde, R. N. (1994). Toward practical uses for biological concepts. In J. E. Bates & T. D. Wachs (Eds.), *Temperament: Individual differences at the interface of biology and behavior* (pp. 275–306). Washington, DC: American Psychological Association.

Bauer, C. R., Langer, J. C., Shakaran, S., Bada, H. S., & Lester, B. (2005). Acute neonatal effects of cocaine exposure during pregnancy. *Archives of Pediatrics and Adolescent Medicine, 159,* 824–834.

Bauer, P. J. (1997). Development of memory in early childhood. In N. Cowan (Ed.), *The development of memory in childhood* (pp. 83–111). Hove, UK: Psychology Press.

Bauer, P. J. (2002). Early memory development. In U. Goswami (Ed.), *Blackwell handbook of child cognitive development* (pp. 127–150). Malden, MA: Blackwell.

Baum, N., Rahav, G., & Sharon, D. (2005). Changes in the self-concepts of divorced women. *Journal of Divorce and Remarriage, 43,* 47–67.

Baumbusch, J. L. (2004). Unclaimed treasures: Older women's reflections on lifelong singlehood. *Journal of Women and Aging, 16,* 105–121.

Baumeister, R. F. (1998). Inducing guilt. In J. Bybee (Ed.), *Guilt and children* (pp. 185–213). San Diego: Academic Press.

Baumeister, R. F., Campbell, J. D., Krueger, J. I., & Vohs, K. D. (2003). Does high self-esteem cause better performance, interpersonal success, happiness, or healthier lifestyles? *Psychological Science in the Public Interest, 4*(1), 1–44.

Baumrind, D. (1971). Current patterns of parental authority. *Developmental Psychology Monograph, 4*(No. 1, Pt. 2).

Baumrind, D. (1991). The influence of parenting style on adolescent competence and substance use. *Journal of Early Adolescence, 11,* 56–95.

Baumrind, D. (1997). Necessary distinctions. *Psychological Inquiry, 8,* 176–182.

Baumwell, L., Tamis-LeMonda, C. S., & Bornstein, M. H. (1997). Maternal verbal sensitivity and child language comprehension. *Infant Behavior and Development, 20,* 247–258.

Bauserman, R. (2002). Child adjustment in joint-custody versus sole-custody arrangements: A meta-analytic review. *Journal of Family Psychology, 16,* 91–102.

Baydar, N., Greek, A., & Brooks-Gunn, J. (1997). A longitudinal study of the effects of the birth of a sibling during the first 6 years of life. *Journal of Marriage and the Family, 59,* 939–956.

Bayer, A., & Tadd, W. (2000). Unjustified exclusion of elderly people from studies submitted to research ethics committee for approval: Descriptive study. *British Medical Journal, 321,* 992–993.

Bayley, N. (1969). *Bayley Scales of Infant Development.* New York: Psychological Corporation.

Bayley, N. (2005). *Bayley Scales of Infant and Toddler Development, Third Edition* (Bayley-III). San Antonio, TX: Harcourt Assessment.

Beals, D. E. (2001). Eating and reading: Links between family conversations with preschoolers and later language and literacy. In D. K. Kickinson & P. O. Tabors (Eds.), *Beginning literacy with home and school* (pp. 75–92). Baltimore, MD: Paul H. Brookes.

Beard, B. B. (1991). *Centenarians: The new generation.* New York: Greenwood Press.

Bearison, D. J. (1998). Pediatric psychology and children's medical problems. In I. G. Sigel & K. A. Renninger (Eds.), *Handbook of child psychology: Vol. 4. Child psychology in practice* (5th ed., pp. 635–711). New York: Wiley.

Bearman, P. S., & Moody, J. (2004). Suicide and friendships among American adolescents. *American Journal of Public Health, 94,* 89–95.

Beatty, W. W. (1992). Gonadal hormones and sex differences in non-reproductive behaviors. In A. A. Gerall, H. Moltz, & I. L. Ward (Eds.), *Handbook of behavioral neurobiology: Vol. 11. Sexual differentiation* (pp. 85–128). New York: Plenum.

Beautrais, A. L. (2003). Life course factors associated with suicidal behaviors in young people. *American Behavioral Scientist, 46,* 1137–1156.

Becker, G., Beyene, Y., Newsome, E., & Mayen, N. (2003). Creating continuity through mutual assistance: Intergenerational reciprocity in four ethnic groups. *Journal of Gerontology, 38B,* S151–S159.

Beckerman, M. B. (1990). Leos Janácek and "the late style" in music. *Gerontologist, 30,* 632–635.

Bedford, O. A. (2004). The individual experience of guilt and shame in Chinese culture. *Culture and Psychology, 10,* 29–52.

Beers, M. H. (2006). Dementia. In M. H. Beers & T. V. Jones (Eds.), *Merck manual of geriatrics.* Whitehouse Station, NJ: Merck & Co. Retrieved from www.merck.com/mrkshared/mmg/sec5/ch40/ch40a.jsp

Behnke, M., Eyler, F. D., Garvan, C. W., & Wobie, K. (2001). The search for congenital malformations in newborns with fetal cocaine exposure. *Pediatrics, 107,* e74.

Behrman, R. E., Kliegman, R. M., & Arvin, A. M. (Eds.). (1996). *Nelson textbook of pediatrics* (15th ed.). Philadelphia: Saunders.

Behrman, R. E., Kliegman, R. M., & Jenson, H. B. (2000). *Nelson textbook of pediatrics* (16th ed.). Philadelphia: Saunders.

Beier, M. E., & Ackerman, P. L. (2005). Age, ability, and the role of prior knowledge on the acquisition of new domain knowledge: Promising results in a real-world learning environment. *Psychology and Aging, 20,* 341–355.

Beilin, H. (1992). Piaget's enduring contribution to developmental psychology. *Developmental Psychology, 28,* 191–204.

Beitel, A. H., & Parke, R. D. (1998). Paternal involvement in infancy:

The role of maternal and paternal attitudes. *Journal of Family Psychology, 12,* 268–288.

Bell, J. H., & Bromnick, R. D. (2003). The social reality of the imaginary audience: A grounded theory approach. *Adolescence, 38,* 205–219.

Bell, K. L., Allen, J. P., Hauser, S. T., & O'Connor, T. G. (1996). Family factors and young adult transitions: Educational attainment and occupational prestige. In J. A. Graber, J. Brooks-Gunn, & A. C. Petersen (Eds.), *Transitions through adolescence: Interpersonal domains and context* (pp. 345–366). Mahwah, NJ: Erlbaum.

Bell, M. A. (1998). Frontal lobe function during infancy: Implications for the development of cognition and attention. In J. E. Richards (Ed.), *Cognitive neuroscience of attention: A developmental perspective* (pp. 327–362). Mahwah, NJ: Erlbaum.

Bell, M. A., & Fox, N. A. (1996). Crawling experience is related to changes in cortical organization during infancy: Evidence from EEG coherence. *Developmental Psychobiology, 29,* 551–561.

Bell, M. L. (1995). Attitudes toward menopause among Mexican American women. *Health Care for Women International, 16,* 425–435.

Bellamy, C. (2004). *The state of the world's children: 2004.* New York: UNICEF.

Bellamy, C. (2005). *The state of the world's children: 2005.* New York: UNICEF.

Bellinger, D. C. (2005). Teratogen update: Lead and pregnancy. *Birth Defects Research: Part A, Clinical and Molecular Teratology, 73,* 409–420.

Belsky, J. (1992). Consequences of child care for children's development: A deconstructionist view. In A. Booth (Ed.), *Child care in the 1990s: Trends and consequences* (pp. 83–85). Hillsdale, NJ: Erlbaum.

Belsky, J. (2001). Developmental risks (still) associated with child care. *Journal of Child Psychology and Psychiatry, 42,* 845–859.

Belsky, J., Campbell, S. B., Cohn, J. F., & Moore, G. (1996). Instability of infant–parent attachment security. *Developmental Psychology, 32,* 921–924.

Belsky, J., & Fearon, R. M. P. (2002). Early attachment security, subsequent maternal sensitivity, and later child development: Does continuity in development depend on caregiving? *Attachment and Human Development, 4,* 361–387.

Belsky, J., Jaffee, S., Hsieh, K., & Silva, P. A. (2001) Child-rearing antecedents of intergenerational relations in young adulthood: A prospective study. *Developmental Psychology, 37,* 801–813.

Bempechat, J., & Drago-Severson, E. (1999). Cross-national differences in academic achievement: Beyond etic conceptions of children's understandings. *Review of Educational Research, 69,* 287–314.

Benbow, C. P., Lubinski, D., Shea, D. L., & Eftekhara-Sanjani, H. (2000). Sex differences in mathematical reasoning ability at age 13: Their status 20 years later. *Psychological Science, 11,* 474–480.

Benbow, C. P., & Stanley, J. C. (1983). Sex differences in mathematical reasoning: More facts. *Science, 222,* 1029–1031.

Benenson, J. F., & Christakos, A. (2003). The greater fragility of females' versus males' closest same-sex friendships. *Child Development, 74,* 1123–1129.

Benenson, J. F., Nicholson, C., Waite, A., Roy, R., & Simpson, A. (2001). The influence of group size on children's competitive behavior. *Child Development, 72,* 921–928.

Bengtson, V. L., & Harootyan, R. A. (1994). *Intergenerational linkages: Hidden connections in American society.* New York: Springer.

Bengtson, V. L., Reedy, M. N., & Gordon, C. (1985). Aging and self-conceptions: Personality processes and social contexts. In J. E. Birren & K. W. Schaie (Eds.), *Handbook of the psychology of aging* (pp. 544–593). New York: Van Nostrand Reinhold.

Bengtson, V. L., Rosenthal, C. L., & Burton, L. (1990). Families and aging: Diversity and heterogeneity. In R. H. Binstock & L. K. George (Eds.), *Handbook of aging and the social sciences* (3rd ed., pp. 263–287). San Diego: Academic Press.

Bengtsson, H. (2005). Children's cognitive appraisal of others' distressful and positive experiences. *International Journal of Behavioral Development, 29,* 457–466.

Bennett, K. M., Smith, P. T., & Hughes, G. M. (2005). Coping depressive feelings and gender differences in late life widowhood. *Aging and Mental Health, 9,* 348–353.

Benoliel, J. Q., & Degner, L. F. (1995). Institutional dying: A convergence of cultural values, technology, and social organization. In H. Wass & R. A. Neimeyer (Eds.), *Dying: Facing the facts* (pp. 117–162). Washington, DC: Taylor and Francis.

Ben-Zeev, T., Carrasquillo, C. M., Ching, A. M. L., Patton, G. E., Stewart, T. D., & Stoddard, T. (2005). "Math is hard!" (Barbie™, 1994): Responses of threat vs. challenge-mediated arousal to stereotypes alleging intellectual inferiority. In A. M. Gallagher & J. C. Kaufman (Eds.), *Gender differences in mathematics: An integrative psychological approach* (pp. 189–206). New York: Cambridge University Press.

Berenbaum, S. A. (2001). Cognitive function in congenital adrenal hyperplasia. *Endocrinology and Metabolism Clinics of North America, 30,* 173–192.

Berg, C. A. (2000). Intellectual development in adulthood. In R. J. Sternberg (Ed.), *Handbook of intelligence* (pp. 117–137). New York: Cambridge University Press.

Berg, C. A., & Sternberg, R. J. (2003). Multiple perspectives on the development of adult intelligence. In J. Demick & C. Andreoletti (Eds.), *Handbook of adult development* (pp. 103–119). New York: Springer.

Berg, C. A., Strough, J., Calderone, K. S., Sansone, C., & Weir, C. (1998). The role of problem definitions in understanding age and context effects on strategies for solving everyday problems. *Psychology and Aging, 13,* 29–44.

Berg, S. (1996). Aging, behavior, and terminal decline. In J. E. Birren & K. W. Schaie (Eds.), *Handbook of the psychology of aging* (4th ed., pp. 323–337). San Diego: Academic Press.

Bergen, D., & Mauer, D. (2000). Symbolic play, phonological awareness, and literacy skills at three age levels. In K. A. Roskos & J. F. Christie (Eds.), *Play and literacy in early childhood: Research from multiple perspectives* (pp. 45–62). Mahwah, NJ: Erlbaum.

Bergman, R. (2004). Identity as motivation. In D. K. Lapsley & D. Narvaez (Eds.), *Moral development, self, and identity* (pp. 21–46). Mahwah, NJ: Erlbaum.

Bering, J. M., & Bjorklund, D. F. (2004). The natural emergence of reasoning about the afterlife as a developmental regularity. *Developmental Psychology, 40,* 217–233.

Berk, L. E. (1992). The extracurriculum. In P. W. Jackson (Ed.), *Handbook of research on curriculum* (pp. 1003–1043). New York: Macmillan.

Berk, L. E. (2001). *Awakening children's minds: How parents and teachers can make a difference.* New York: Oxford University Press.

Berk, L. E. (2003). Vygotsky, Lev. In L. Nadel (Ed.), *Encyclopedia of cognitive science* (Vol. 6). London: Macmillan.

Berk, L. E. (2005). Why parenting matters. In S. Olfman (Ed.), *Childhood lost: How American culture is failing our kids* (pp. 19–53). New York: Guilford.

Berk, L. E. (2006a). Play=learning. In D. Singer, K. Hirsh-Pasek, & R. Golinkoff (Eds.), *Play=learning.* New York: Oxford University Press.

Berk, L. E. (2006b). Who is the kindergarten child? In D. Gullo (Ed.), *Kindergarten and beyond.* Washington, DC: National Association for the Education of Young Children

Berk, L. E., & Harris, S. (2003). Vygotsky, Lev. In L. Nadel (Ed.), *Encyclopedia of cognitive science.* London: Macmillan.

Berk, L. E., Mann, T., & Ogan, A. (2006). Make-believe play: Wellspring for development of self-regulation. In D. Singer, K. Hirsh-Pasek, & R. Golinkoff (Eds.), *Play=learning.* New York: Oxford University Press.

Berk, L. E., & Spuhl, S. (1995). Maternal interaction, private speech, and task performance in preschool children. *Early Childhood Research Quarterly, 10,* 145–169.

Berkowitz, C. M. (2004). Talking to your kids about sex. Somerville, NJ: Somerset Medical Center. Retrieved from www.somerset medicalcenter.com/1817.cfm

Berkowitz, M. W., & Gibbs, J. C. (1983). Measuring the developmental features of moral discussion. *Merrill-Palmer Quarterly, 29,* 399–410.

Berkowitz, R. J., & Stunkard, A. J. (2002). Development of childhood obesity. In T. A. Wadden & A. J. Stunkard (Eds.), *Handbook of obesity treatment* (pp. 515–531). New York: Guilford.

Berman, E., & Napier, A. Y. (2000). The midlife family: Dealing with adolescents, young adults, and the marriage in transition. In W. C. Nichols, M. A. Pace-Nichols, D. S. Becvar, & A. Y. Napier (Eds.), *Handbook of family development and intervention* (pp. 208–234). New York: Wiley.

Berman, P. W. (1980). Are women more responsive than men to the young? A review of developmental and situational variables. *Psychological Bulletin, 88,* 668–695.

Bernard, M., & Phillipson, C. (2004). Retirement and leisure. In J. F. Nussbaum & J. Coupland (Eds.), *Handbook of communication and aging research* (2nd ed., pp. 353–378). Mahwah, NJ: Erlbaum.

Berndt, T. J., & Keefe, K. (1995). Friends' influence on adolescents' adjustment to school. *Child Development, 66,* 1312–1329.

Berndt, T. J., & Murphy, L. M. (2002). Influences of friends and friendships: Myths, truths, and research recommendations. In R. V. Kail (Ed.), *Advances in child develop-*

ment and behavior* (Vol. 30, pp. 275–310). San Diego, CA: Academic Press.

Bernier, J. C., & Siegel, D. H. (1994). Attention-deficit hyperactivity disorder: A family ecological systems perspective. *Families in Society, 75,* 142–150.

Berninger, V. W., Vermeulen, K., Abbortt, R. D., McCutchen, D., Cotton, S., & Cude, J. (2003). Naming speed and phonological awareness as predictors of reading development. *Journal of Educational Psychology, 95,* 452–464.

Berr, C., Wancata, J., & Ritchie, K. (2005). Prevalence of dementia in the elderly in Europe. *European Neuropsychopharmacology, 15,* 463–471.

Bertenthal, B. I. (1993). Infants' perception of biomechanical motions: Instrinsic image and knowledge-based constraints. In C. Granrud (Ed.), *Visual perception and cognition in infancy* (pp. 175–214). Hillsdale, NJ: Erlbaum.

Bertrand, M., & Mullainathan, S. (2004). Are Emily and Brendan more employable than Lakisha and Jamal? *A field experiment on labor market discrimination.* Unpublished manuscript, University of Chicago.

Berzlanovich, A. M., Keil, W. W., Sim, T., Fasching, P., & Fazeny-Dorner, B. (2005). Do centenarians die healthy? An autopsy study. *Journal of Gerontology, 60A,* 862–865.

Berzonsky, M. D. (2003). Identity style and well-being: Does commitment matter? *Identity: An International Journal of Theory and Research, 3,* 131–142.

Berzonsky, M. D. (2004). Identity style, parental authority, and identity commitment. *Journal of Youth and Adolescence, 33,* 213–220.

Berzonsky, M. D., & Kuk, L. S. (2000). Identity status, identity processing style, and the transition to university. *Journal of Adolescent Research, 15,* 81–98.

Best, D. L. (2001). Gender concepts: Convergence in cross-cultural research and methodologies. *Cross-cultural Research: The Journal of Comparative Social Science, 35,* 23–43.

Bevan, E., & Higgins, D. J. (2002). Is domestic violence learned? The contribution of five forms of child maltreatment to men's violence and adjustment. *Journal of Family Violence, 17,* 223–245.

Beyene, Y. (1992). Menopause: A bio-cultural event. In A. J. Dan & L. L. Lewis (Eds.), *Menstrual health in women's lives* (pp. 169– 177). Urbana, IL: University of Illinois Press.

Beyene, Y., & Martin, M. C. (2001). Menopausal experiences and bone density of Mayan women in Yucatan, Mexico. *American Journal of Human Biology, 13,* 47–71.

Beyers, J. M., Bates, J. E., Pettit, G. S., & Dodge, K. A. (2003). Neighborhood structure, parenting processes, and the development of youths' externalizing behaviors: A multilevel analysis. *American Journal of Community Psychology, 31,* 35–53.

Beyth-Marom, R., & Fischhoff, B. (1997). Adolescents' decisions about risks: A cognitive perspective. In J. Schulenberg, J. L. Maggs, & K. Hurrelmann (Eds.), *Health risks and developmental transitions during adolescence* (pp. 110–135). New York: Cambridge University Press.

Bhandari, N., Bahl, R., Taneja, S., Strand, T., & Mølbak, K. (2002). Substantial reduction in severe diarrheal morbidity by daily zinc supplementation in young North Indian children. *Pediatrics, 109,* e86–e92.

Bhatt, R. S., Rovee-Collier, C., & Weiner, S. (1994). Developmental changes in the interface between perception and memory retrieval. *Developmental Psychology, 30,* 151–162.

Bhatt, R. S., Wilk, A., Hill, D., & Rovee-Collier, C. (2004). Correlated attributes and categorization in the first half-year of life. *Developmental Psychobiology, 44,* 103–115.

Bhavnani, B. R., & Strickler, R. C. (2005). Menopausal hormone therapy. *Journal of Obstetrics and Gynaecology Canada, 27,* 137–162.

Bhutta, A. T., Cleves, M. A., Casey, P. H., Cradock, M. M., & Anand, K. J. S. (2002). Cognitive and behavioral outcomes of school-aged children who were born preterm. *Journal of the American Medical Association, 288,* 728–737.

Bialystok, E. (1999). Cognitive complexity and attentional control in the bilingual mind. *Child Development, 70,* 636–644.

Bialystok, E. (2001). *Bilingualism in development: Language, literacy, and cognition.* New York: Cambridge University Press.

Bialystok, E., & Herman, J. (1999). Does bilingualism matter for early literacy? *Language and Cognition, 2,* 35–44.

Bialystok, E., & Martin, M. M. (2003). Notation to symbol: Development in children's understanding of print. *Journal of Experimental Child Psychology, 86,* 223–243.

Bialystok, E., McBride-Chang, C., & Luk, G. (2005). Bilingualism, language proficiency, and learning to read in two writing systems. *Journal of Educational Psychology, 97,* 580–590.

Bialystok, E., & Senman, L. (2004). Executive processes in appearance–reality tasks: The role of inhibition of attention and symbolic representation. *Child Development, 75,* 562–579.

Bianco, A., Stone, J., Lynch, L., Lapinski, R., Berkowitz, G., & Berkowitz, R. L. (1996). Pregnancy outcome at age 40 and older. *Obstetrics and Gynecology, 87,* 917–922.

Biederman, J., Kwon, A., Aleardi, M., Chouinard, V.-A., Marino, T., & Cole, H. (2005). Absence of gender effects on attention-deficit hyperactivity disorder: Findings in nonreferred subjects. *American Journal of Psychiatry, 162,* 1083–1089.

Biederman, J., & Spencer, T. J. (2000). Genetics of childhood disorders: XIX, ADHD, part 3: Is ADHD a noradrenergic disorder? *Journal of the American Academy of Child and Adolescent Psychiatry, 39,* 1330–1333.

Bielinski, J., & Davison, M. L. (1998). Gender differences by item difficulty interactions in multiple-choice mathematics items. *American Educational Research Journal, 35,* 455–476.

Bigelow, A. (1992). Locomotion and search behavior in blind infants. *Infant Behavior and Development, 15,* 179–189.

Bigelow, A. E. (2003). The development of joint attention in blind infants. *Development and Psychopathology, 15,* 179–189.

Bigler, R. S. (1995). The role of classification skill in moderating environmental influences on children's gender stereotyping: A study of the functional use of gender in the classroom. *Child Development, 66,* 1072–1087.

Bigler, R. S., Brown, C. S., & Markell, M. (2001). When groups are not created equal: Effects of group status on the formation of intergroup attitudes in children. *Child Development, 72,* 1151–1162.

Bigler, R. S., & Liben, L. S. (1992). Cognitive mechanisms in children's gender stereotyping: Theoretical and educational implications of a cognitive-based intervention. *Child Development, 63,* 1351–1363.

Binstock, R. H., & Quadagno, J. (2001). Aging and politics. In R. H. Binstock & L. K. George (Eds.), *Handbook of aging and the social sciences* (5th ed., pp. 333–351). San Diego, CA: Academic Press.

Binukumar, B., & Mathew, A. (2005). Dietary fat and risk of breast cancer. *World Journal of Surgical Oncology, 3,* 45.

Bioethics Consultative Committee. (2003). *Comparison of ethics legislation in Europe.* Retrieved from www.synapse.net.mt/bioethics/euroleg1.htm

Birch, E. E. (1993). Stereopsis in infants and its developmental relation to visual acuity. In K. Simons (Ed.), *Early visual development: Normal and abnormal* (pp. 224–236). New York: Oxford University Press.

Birch, L. L., & Fisher, J. A. (1995). Appetite and eating behavior in children. *Pediatric Clinics of North America, 42,* 931–953.

Birch, L. L., Fisher, J. O., & Davison, K. K. (2003). Learning to overeat: Maternal use of restrictive feeding practices promotes girls' eating in the absence of hunger. *American Journal of Clinical Nutrition, 78,* 215–220.

Birch, L. L., Zimmerman, S., & Hind, H. (1980). The influence of social–affective context on preschool children's food preferences. *Child Development, 51,* 856–861.

Birch, S. A. J., & Bloom, P. (2003). Children are cursed: An asymmetric bias in mental-state attribution. *Psychological Science, 14,* 283–285.

Birditt, K. S., & Fingerman, K. L. (2005). Do we get better at picking our battles? Age group differences in descriptions of behavioral reactions to interpersonal tensions. *Journal of Gerontology, 60B,* P121–P128.

Biringen, Z., Emde, R. N., Campos, J. J., & Appelbaum, M. I. (1995). Affective reorganization in the infant, the mother, and the dyad: The role of upright locomotion and its timing. *Child Development, 66,* 499–514.

Birney, D. P., Citron-Pousty, J. H., Lutz, D. J., & Sternberg, R. J. (2005). The development of cognitive and intellectual abilities. In M. H. Bornstein & M. E. Lamb (Eds.), *Developmental science: An advanced textbook* (5th ed., pp. 327–358). Mahwah, NJ: Erlbaum.

Bjorklund, D. F. (2004). *Children's thinking* (4th ed.). Belmont, CA: Wadsworth.

Bjorklund, D. F., & Douglas, R. N. (1997). The development of memory strategies. In N. Cowan (Ed.), *The development of memory in childhood* (pp. 83–111). Hove, UK: Psychology Press.

Bjorklund, D. F., Schneider, W., Cassel, W. S., & Ashley, E. (1994). Training and extension of a memory strategy: Evidence for utilization deficiencies in high- and low-IQ children. *Child Development, 65,* 951–965.

Bjorklund, D. F., & Shackelford, T. K. (1999). Differences in parental investment contribute to important differences between men and women. *Current Directions in Psychological Science, 8,* 86–89.

Black, D., Gates, G., & Sanders, S. (2000). Demographics of the gay and lesbian population in the United States: Evidence from available systematic data sources. *Demography, 37,* 139–154.

Black, R. E., Williams, S. M., Jones, I. E., & Goulding, A. (2002). Children who avoid drinking cow milk have low dietary calcium intakes and poor bone health. *American Journal of Clinical Nutrition, 76,* 675–680.

Blacker, D., Bertram, L., Saunders, A. J., Moscarillo, T. J., Albert, M. S., & Wiener, H. (2003). Results of a high-resolution genome screen of 437 Alzheimer's disease families. *Human Molecular Genetics, 12,* 23–92.

Blackhall, L. J., Frank, G., Murphy, S., & Michel, V. (2001). Bioethics in a different tongue: The case of truth-telling. *Journal of Urban Health, 78,* 59–71.

Blackhall, L. J., Murphy, S. T., Frank, G., Michel, V., & Azen, S. (1995). Ethnicity and attitudes toward patient autonomy. *Journal of the American Medical Association, 274,* 820–825.

Blackwell, D. L., & Lichter, D. T. (2004). Homogamy among dating, cohabiting, and married couples. *Sociological Quarterly, 45,* 719–737.

Blair-Loy, M., & DeHart, G. (2003). Family and career trajectories among African-American female attorneys. *Journal of Family Issues, 24,* 908–933.

Blakemore, J. E. O. (2003). Children's beliefs about violating gender norms: Boys shouldn't look like girls, and girls shouldn't act like boys. *Sex Roles, 48,* 411–419.

Blanchard, R., & Bogaert, A. F. (2004). Proportion of homosexual men who owe their sexual orientation to fraternal birth order: An estimate based on two national probability samples. *American Journal of Human Biology, 16,* 151–157.

Blanchard-Fields, F. (1997). The role of emotion in social cognition across the adult life span. In K. W. Schaie & M. P. Lawton (Eds.), *Annual review of gerontology and geriatrics* (Vol. 17, pp. 325–352). New York: Springer.

Blanchard-Fields, F., Chen, Y., & Norris, L. (1997). Everyday problem solving across the adult life span: Influence of domain specificity and cognitive appraisal. *Psychology and Aging, 12,* 684–693.

Blasi, A. (1994). Moral identity: Its role in moral functioning. In B. Puka (Ed.), *Fundamental research in moral development: A*

compendium (Vol. 2, pp. 123–167). New York: Garland.

Blasi, A. (1995). Moral understanding and the moral personality: The process of moral integration. In W. Kurtines & J. L. Gewirtz (Eds.), *Moral development: An introduction* (pp. 229–253). Boston: Allyn and Bacon.

Blasi, C. H., & Bjorklund, D. F. (2003). Evolutionary developmental psychology: A new tool for better understanding human ontogeny. *Human Development, 46,* 259–281.

Blass, E. M. (1999). Savoring sucrose and suckling milk: Easing pain, saving calories, and learning about mother. In M. Lewis & D. Ramsay (Eds.), *Soothing and stress* (pp. 79–107). Mahwah, NJ: Erlbaum.

Blass, E. M., Ganchrow, J. R., & Steiner, J. E. (1984). Classical conditioning in newborn humans 2–48 hours of age. *Infant Behavior and Development, 7,* 223–235.

Blatchford, P., Bassett, P., Goldstein, H., & Martin, C. (2003). Are class size differences related to pupils' educational progress and classroom processes? Findings from the Institute of Education Class Size Study of Children Aged 5–7 years. *British Educational Research Journal, 29,* 709–730.

Bleeker, M. M., & Jacobs, J. E. (2004). Achievement in math and science: Do mothers' beliefs matter 12 years later? *Journal of Educational Psychology, 96,* 97–109.

Bleske, A. L., & Buss, D. M. (2000). Can men and women be just friends? *Personal Relationships, 7,* 131–151.

Blieszner, R., & Adams, R. G. (1992). *Adult friendship.* Newbury Park, CA: Sage.

Bliss, L. S., McCabe, A., & Miranda, A. E. (1998). Narrative assessment profile: Discourse analysis for school-age children. *Journal of Communication Disorders, 31,* 347–363.

Block, J. (1971). *Lives through time.* Berkeley, CA: Bancroft.

Block, J. (1995). A contrarian view of the five-factor approach to personality description. *Psychological Bulletin, 117,* 187–215.

Blomberg, S., Edebalk, P. G., & Petersson, J. (2000). The withdrawal of the welfare state: Elderly care in Sweden in the 1990s. *European Journal of Social Work, 3,* 151–163.

Bloom, L. (1998). Language acquisition in its developmental context. In D. Kuhn & R. S. Siegler (Eds.), *Handbook of child psychology: Vol. 2. Cognition, perception, and language* (5th ed., pp. 309–370). New York: Wiley.

Bloom, L. (2000). The intentionality model of language development: How to learn a word, any word. In R. Golinkoff, K. Hirsh-Pasek, N. Akhtar, L. Bloom, G. Hollich, L. Smith, M. Tomasello, & A. Woodward (Eds.), *Becoming a word learner: A debate on lexical acquisition.* New York: Oxford University Press.

Bloom, P. (1999). The role of semantics in solving the bootstrapping problem. In R. Jackendoff & P. Bloom (Eds.), *Language, logic, and concepts* (pp. 285–309). Cambridge, MA: Cambridge University Press.

Blotner, R., & Bearison, D. J. (1984). Developmental consistencies in socio-moral knowledge: Justice reasoning and altruistic behavior. *Merrill-Palmer Quarterly, 30,* 349–367.

Bluebond-Langner, M. (1977). Meanings of death to children. In H. Feifel (Ed.), *New meanings of death* (pp. 47–66). New York: McGraw-Hill.

Bluestone, C., & Tamis-LeMonda, C. S. (1999). Correlates of parenting styles in predominantly working- and middle-class African American mothers. *Journal of Marriage and the Family, 61,* 881–893.

Blum, M. (2000). Embryos and the new reproductive technologies. Retrieved from http://www.surrogacy.com/ legals/embryotech.html

Boardman, J. D. (2004). Stress and physical health: The role of neighborhoods as mediating and moderating mechanisms. *Social Science and Medicine, 58,* 2473–2483.

Bogartz, R. S., Shinskey, J. L., & Schilling, T. H. (2000). Object permanence in five-and-a-half-month-old infants. *Infancy, 1,* 403–428.

Bogin, B. (2001). *The growth of humanity.* New York: Wiley-Liss.

Bohannon, J. N., & Bonvillian, J. D. (2005). Theoretical approaches to language acquisition. In J. B. Gleason (Ed.), *The development of language* (6th ed., pp. 230–291). Boston: Allyn and Bacon.

Bohannon, J. N., III, & Stanowicz, L. (1988). The issue of negative evidence: Adult responses to children's language errors. *Developmental Psychology, 24,* 684–689.

Bohman, M. (1996) Predispositions to criminality: Swedish adoption studies in retrospect. In G. R. Bock & J. A. Goode (Eds.), *Genetics of criminal and antisocial behavior, Ciba Foundation Symposium 194* (pp. 99–114). Chichester, UK: Wiley.

Bohman, M., & Sigvardsson, S. (1990). Outcome in adoption: Lessons from longitudinal studies. In D. M. Brodzinsky & M. D.

Schechter (Eds.), *The psychology of adoption* (pp. 93–106). New York: Oxford University Press.

Bohnert, A. M., Crnic, K., & Lim, K. G. (2003). Emotional competence and aggressive behavior in school-age children. *Journal of Abnormal Child Psychology, 31,* 79–91.

Bohr, L., Pascarella, E., Nora, A., Zusman, B., Jacobs, M., Desler, M., & Bulakowski, C. (1994). Cognitive effects of two-year and four-year institutions: A preliminary study. *Community College Review, 22,* 4–11.

Boldizar, J. P. (1991). Assessing sex typing and androgyny in children: The children's sex role inventory. *Developmental Psychology, 27,* 505–515.

Bolen, R. M. (2001). *Child sexual abuse.* New York: Kluwer Academic.

Bolzani, L. H., Messinger, D. S., Yale, M., & Dondi, M. (2002). Smiling in infancy. In M. H. Abel (Ed.), *An empirical reflection on the smile* (pp. 111–136). Lewiston, NY: Edwin Mellen Press.

Bonnel, S., Mohand-Said, S., & Sahel, J.-A. (2003). The aging of the retina. *Experimental Gerontology, 38,* 825–831.

Bono, M. A., & Stifter, C. A. (2003). Maternal attention-directing strategies and infant focused attention during problem solving. *Infancy, 4,* 235–250.

Bookstein, F. L., Sampson, P. D., Connor, P. D., & Streissguth, A. P. (2002). Midline corpus callosum is a neuroanatomical focus of fetal alcohol damage. *Anatomical Record, 269,* 162–174.

Borer, K. T. (2005). Physical activity in the prevention and amelioration of osteoporosis in women: Interaction of mechanical, hormonal and dietary factors. *Sports Medicine, 35,* 779–830.

Borke, H. (1975). Piaget's mountains revisited: Changes in the egocentric landscape. *Developmental Psychology, 11,* 240–243.

Bornstein, M. H. (1989). Sensitive periods in development: Structural characteristics and causal interpretations. *Psychological Bulletin, 105,* 179–197.

Bornstein, M. H., & Arteberry, M. E. (1999). Perceptual development. In M. H. Bornstein & M. E. Lamb (Eds.), *Developmental psychology: An advanced textbook* (pp. 231–274). Mahwah, NJ: Erlbaum.

Bornstein, M. H., & Arterberry, M. E. (2003). Recognition, discrimination, and categorization of smiling by 5-month-old infants. *Developmental Science, 6,* 585–599.

Bornstein, M. H., Selmi, A. M. Haynes, O. M., Painter, K. M., & Marx, E. S. (1999). Representational abilities and the hearing status of child/mother dyads. *Child Development, 70,* 833–852.

Bornstein, M. H., Vibbert, M., Tal, J., & O'Donnell, K. (1992). Toddler language and play in the second year: Stability, covariation, and influences of parenting. *First Language, 12,* 323–338.

Borst, C. G. (1995). *Catching babies: The professionalization of childbirth, 1870–1920.* Cambridge, MA: Harvard University Press.

Bortolus, R., Parazzini, F., Chatenoud, L., Benzi, G., Bianchi, M. M., & Marini, A. (1999). The epidemiology of multiple births. *Human Reproduction Update, 5,* 179–187.

Bortz, W. M., II. (2002). A conceptual framework of frailty: A review. *Journal of Gerontology, 57A,* M283–M288.

Bosacki, S. L., & Moore, C. (2004). Preschoolers' understanding of simple and complex emotions: Links with gender and language. *Sex Roles, 50,* 659–675.

Bossé, R., Aldwin, C. M., Levenson, M. R., Workman-Daniels, K., & Ekerdt, D. J. (1990). Differences in social support among retirees and workers: Findings from the Normative Aging Study. *Psychology and Aging, 5,* 41–47.

Bosworth, H. B., Bastian, L. A., Kuchlbhatia, M. N., Steffens, D. C., McBride, C. M., & Sinner, C. S. (2001). Depressive symptoms, menopausal status, and climacteric symptoms in women at midlife. *Psychosomatic Medicine, 63,* 603–608.

Botkin, D. R., Weeks, M. O., & Morris, J. E. (2000). Changing marriage role expectations: 1961–1996. *Sex Roles, 42,* 933–942.

Bouchard, T. J., & McGue, M. (2003). Genetic and environmental influences on human psychological differences. *Journal of Neurobiology, 54,* 4–45.

Boukydis, C. F. Z., & Lester, B. M. (1998). Infant crying, risk status and social support in families of preterm and term infants. *Early Development and Parenting, 7,* 31–39.

Boulton, M. J. (1999). Concurrent and longitudinal relations between children's playground behavior and social preference, victimization, and bullying. *Child Development, 70,* 944–954.

Bourgeois, M., Burgio, L., Schulz, R., Beach, S., & Palmer, B. (1997). Modifying repetitive verbalization of community dwelling patients with AD. *Gerontologist, 37,* 30–39.

Bowen, N. K., Bowen, G. L., & Ware, W. B. (2002). Neighborhood social disorganization, families, and the educational behavior of adoles-

cents. *Journal of Adolescent Research, 17,* 468–490.

Bower-Russa, M. E., Knutson, J. F., & Winebarger, A. (2001). Disciplinary history, adult disciplinary attitudes, and risk for abusive parenting. *Journal of Community Psychology, 29,* 219–240.

Bowlby, J. (1969). *Attachment and loss: Vol. 1. Attachment.* New York: Basic Books.

Bowlby, J. (1979). *The making and breaking of affectional bonds.* London: Tavistock.

Bowlby, J. (1980). *Attachment and loss: Vol. 3. Loss: Sadness and depression.* New York: Basic Books.

Bowlby, J. W., & McMullen, K. (2002). *At a crossroads: First results for the 18- to 20-year-old cohort of the Youth in Transition Survey.* Ottawa: Human Resources Development Canada.

Bowman, S. A., Gortmaker, S. L., Ebbeling, C. B., Pereira, M. A., & Ludwig, D. S. (2004). Effects of fast-food consumption on energy intake and diet quality among children in a national household survey. *Pediatrics, 113,* 112–113.

Boyce, W., Doherty, M., Fortin, C., & MacKinnon, D. (2003*). Canadian youth, sexual health and HIV/AIDS study.* Toronto: Council of Ministers of Education, Canada.

Boyer, K., & Diamond, A. (1992). Development of memory for temporal order in infants and young children. In A. Diamond (Ed.), *Development and neural bases of higher cognitive function* (pp. 267–317). New York: New York Academy of Sciences.

Boyes, M. C., & Chandler, M. (1992). Cognitive development, epistemic doubt, and identity formation in adolescence. *Journal of Youth and Adolescence, 21,* 277–304.

Boysson-Bardies, B. de, & Vihman, M. M. (1991). Adaptation to language: Evidence from babbling and first words in four languages. *Language, 67,* 297–319.

Brabyn, J., Schneck, M., Haegerstrom-Portnoy, G., & Lott, L. (2001). The Smith-Kettlewell Institute (SKI) longitudinal study of vision function and its impact among the elderly: An overview. *Optometry & Vision Science, 78,* 264–269.

Brackbill, Y., McManus, K., & Woodward, L. (1985). *Medication in maternity: Infant exposure and maternal information.* Ann Arbor: University of Michigan Press.

Bracken, B. A. (2000). Maximizing construct relevant assessment: The optimal preschool testing situation. In B. A. Bracken (Ed.), *The psychoeducational assessment of preschool children* (3rd ed., pp. 33–44). Upper Saddle River, NJ: Prentice-Hall.

Bradbury, T. N., Fincham, F. D., & Beach, S. R. H. (2000). Research on the nature and determinants of marital satisfaction: A decade in review. *Journal of Marriage and the Family, 62,* 964–980.

Bradford, K., Barber, B. K., Olsen, J. A., Maughan, S. L., Erickson, L. D., Ward, D., & Stolz, H. E. (2003). A multi-national study of interparental conflict, parenting, and adolescent functioning: South Africa, Bangladesh, China, India, Bosnia, Germany, Palestine, Colombia, and the United States. *Marriage and Family Review, 35,* 107–137.

Bradley, P. J., & Bray, K. H. (1996). The Netherlands' Maternal–Child Health Program: Implications for the United States. *Journal of Obstetric, Gynecologic, and Neonatal Nursing, 25,* 471–475.

Bradley, R. H. (1994). The HOME Inventory: Review and reflections. In H. W. Reese (Ed.), *Advances in child development and behavior* (Vol. 25, pp. 241–288). San Diego, CA: Academic Press.

Bradley, R. H., & Caldwell, B. M. (1982). The consistency of the home environment and its relation to child development. *International Journal of Behavioral Development, 5,* 445–465.

Bradley, R. H., & Corwyn, R. F. (2003). Age and ethnic variations in family process mediators of SES. In M. H. Bornstein & R. H. Bradley (Eds.), *Socioeconomic status, parenting, and child development* (pp. 161–188). Mahwah, NJ: Erlbaum.

Bradley, R. H., Corwyn, R. F., McAdoo, H. P., & Garcia-Coll, C. (2001). The home environments of children in the United States. Part I: Variations by age, ethnicity, and poverty status. *Child Development, 72,* 1844–1867.

Bradley, R. H., Whiteside, L., Mundfrom, D. J., Casey, P. H., Kelleher, K. J., & Pope, S. K. (1994). Early indications of resilience and their relation to experiences in the home environments of low birthweight, premature children living in poverty. *Child Development, 65,* 346–360.

Bradshaw, R. A., & Burlingame, A. L. (2005). From proteins to proteomics. *IUBMB Life, 57,* 267–272.

Brady, E. M. (1984). Demographic and educational correlates of self-reported learning among older students. *Educational Gerontology, 10,* 27–38.

Braet, C., & Crombez, G. (2003). Cognitive interference due to food cues in childhood obesity. *Journal of Clinical Child and Adolescent Psychology, 32,* 32–39.

Braine, L. G., Schauble, L., Kugelmass, S., & Winter, A. (1993). Rep-

resentation of depth by children: Spatial strategies and lateral biases. *Developmental Psychology, 29,* 466–479.

Brainerd, C. J. (2003). Jean Piaget, learning, research, and American education. In B. J. Zimmerman (Ed.), *Educational psychology: A century of contributions* (pp. 251–287). Mahwah, NJ: Erlbaum.

Brame, B., Nagin, D. S., & Tremblay, R. E. (2001). Developmental trajectories of physical aggression from school entry to late adolescence. *Journal of Child Psychology and Psychiatry, 42,* 503–512.

Branca, F., & Ferrari, M. (2002). Impact of micronutrient deficiencies on growth: The stunting syndrome. *Annals of Nutrition and Metabolism, 46*(Suppl. 1), 8–17.

Brandtstädter, J., & Rothermund, K. (1994). Self-percepts of control in middle and later adulthood: Buffering losses by rescaling goals. *Psychology and Aging, 9,* 265–273.

Branje, S. J. T., van Lieshout, C. F. M., van Aken, M. A. G., & Haselager, G. J. T. (2004). Perceived support in sibling relationships and adolescent adjustment. *Journal of Child Psychology and Psychiatry, 45,* 1385–1396.

Braswell, G. S., & Callanan, M. A. (2003). Learning to draw recognizable graphic representations during mother–child interactions. *Merrill-Palmer Quarterly, 49,* 471–494.

Bratt, R. G. (2002). Housing: The foundation of family life. In F. Jacobs, D. Wertlieb, & R. M. Lerner (Eds.), *Handbook of applied developmental science* (Vol. 2, pp. 445–468). Thousand Oaks, CA: Sage.

Bray, J. H. (1999). From marriage to remarriage and beyond: Findings from the Developmental Issues in Stepfamilies Research Project. In E. M. Hetherington (Ed.), *Coping with divorce, single parenting, and remarriage: A risk and resiliency perspective* (pp. 295–319). Mahwah, NJ: Erlbaum.

Braybyn, J., Schneck, M., Haegerstrom-Portnoy, G., & Lott, L. (2001). The Smith-Kettlewell Institute (SKI) longitudinal study of vision function and its impact among the elderly: An overview. *Optometry and Vision Science, 78,* 264–269.

Brazelton, T. B., Koslowski, B., & Tronick, E. (1976). Neonatal behavior among urban Zambians and Americans. *Journal of the American Academy of Child Psychiatry, 15,* 97–107.

Brazelton, T. B., & Nugent, J. K. (1995). *Neonatal Behavioral Assessment Scale.* London, Mac Keith Press.

Brazelton, T. B., Nugent, J. K., & Lester, B. M. (1987). Neonatal Behavioral Assessment Scale. In J. D. Osofsky (Ed.), *Handbook of infant development* (2nd ed., pp. 780–817). New York: Wiley.

Bredekamp, S., & Copple, C. (Eds.). (1997). *Developmentally appropriate practice in early childhood programs* (rev. ed.). Washington, DC: National Association for the Education of Young Children.

Brehm, S. S. (1992). *Intimate relationships* (2nd ed.). New York: McGraw-Hill.

Bremner, A. J., & Mareschal, D. (2004). Reasoning . . . what reasoning? *Developmental Science, 7,* 419–421.

Brendgen, M., Markiewicz, D., Doyle, A. B., & Bukowski, W. M. (2001). The relations between friendship quality, ranked-friendship preference, and adolescents' behavior with their friends. *Merrill-Palmer Quarterly, 47,* 395–415.

Brennan, K. A., & Shaver, P. R. (1995). Dimensions of adult attachment, affect regulation, and romantic relationship functioning. *Personality and Social Psychology Bulletin, 21,* 267–283.

Brennan, M., & Cardinali, G. (2000). The use of preexisting and novel coping strategies in adapting to age-related vision loss. *Gerontologist, 40,* 327–334.

Brennan, P. F., Moore, S. M., & Smyth, K. A. (1991). Computer-Link: Electronic support for the home caregiver. *Advances in Nursing Science, 13,* 14–27.

Brennan, R. T., Kim, J., Wenz-Gross, M., & Siperstein, G. N. (2001). The relative equitability of high-stakes testing versus teacher-assigned grades: An analysis of the Massachusetts Comprehensive Assessment System (MCAS). *Harvard Educational Review, 71,* 173–216.

Brennan, W. M., Ames, E. W., & Moore, R. W. (1966). Age differences in infants' attention to patterns of different complexities. *Science, 151,* 354–356.

Brenner, E., & Salovey, P. (1997). Emotional regulation during childhood: Developmental, interpersonal, and individual considerations. In P. Salovey & D. Sluyter (Eds.), *Emotional literacy and emotional development* (pp. 168–192). New York: Basic Books.

Brenner, R. A. (2003). Prevention of drowning in infants, children, and adolescents. *Pediatrics, 112,* 440–445.

Brenner, R. A., Simons-Morton, B. G., Bhaskar, B., Revenis, M., Das, A., & Clemens, J. D. (2003). Infant–parent bed sharing in an inner-city population. *Archives of Pediatrics and Adolescent Medicine, 157,* 33–39.

Brent, S. B., Speece, M. W., Lin, C., Dong, Q., & Yang, C. (1996). The development of the concept of death among Chinese and U.S. children 3–17 years of age: From binary to "fuzzy" concepts? *Omega, 33,* 67–83.

Breslau, N., Kessler, R. C., Chilcoat, H. D., Schultz, L. R., Davis, G. C., & Andreski, P. (1998). Trauma and posttraumatic stress disorder in the community: The 1996 Detroit Area Survey of Trauma. *Archives of General Psychiatry, 55,* 626–632.

Breslin, F. C., & Mustard, C. (2003). Factors influencing the impact of unemployment on mental health among young and older adults in a longitudinal, population-based survey. *Scandinavian Journal of Work, Environment, and Health, 29,* 5–14.

Bretherton, I., Fritz, J., Zahn-Waxler, C., & Ridgeway, D. (1986). Learning to talk about emotions: A functionalist perspective. *Child Development, 57,* 529–548.

Bretherton, I., & Munholland, K. A. (1999). Internal working models in attachment relationships: A construct revisited. In J. Cassidy & P. R. Shaver (Eds.), *Handbook of attachment* (pp. 89–111). New York: Guilford.

Brewaeys, A., Ponjaert, I., Van Hall, E. V., & Golombok, S. (1997). Donor insemination: Child development and family functioning in lesbian mother families. *Human Reproduction, 12,* 1349–1359.

Brezina, T. (1999). Teenage violence toward parents as an adaptation to family strain: Evidence from a national survey of male adolescents. *Youth and Society, 30,* 416–444.

Briefel, R. R., Reidy, K., Karwe, V., & Devaney, B. (2004). Feeding Infants and Toddlers Study: Improvements needed in meeting infant feeding recommendations. *Journal of the American Dietetic Association, 104*(Suppl. 1), s31–s37.

Briere, J., & Jordan, C. E. (2004). Violence against women: Outcome complexity and implications for assessment and treatment. *Journal of Interpersonal Violence, 19,* 1252–1276.

Briggs, F. (2002). *To what extent can Keeping Ourselves Safe protect children?* Wellington, NZ: New Zealand Police.

Bright, J. E. H., Pryor, R. G. L., Wilkenfeld, S., & Earl, J. (2005). The role of social context and serendipitous events in career decision making. *International Journal for Educational and Vocational Guidance, 5,* 19–36.

British Broadcasting Corporation. (1999, May 11). *Euthanasia special report: Lessons from down under.* London: Author.

British Columbia Reproductive Care Program. (2003). Guidelines for perinatal care manual: Perinatal cocaine use: Care of the newborn. Retrieved from mdm.ca/cpgsnew/cpgs-f/search/french/help/2bcrcp.htm

Broberg, A. G., Wessels, H., Lamb, M. E., & Hwang, C. P. (1997). Effects of day care on the development of cognitive abilities in 8-year-olds: A longitudinal study. *Developmental Psychology, 33,* 62–69.

Brody, G. H. (2004). Siblings' direct and indirect contributions to child development. *Current Directions in Psychological Science, 13,* 124–126.

Brody, G. H., & Flor, D. L. (1998). Maternal resources, parenting practices, and child competence in rural, single-parent African American families. *Child Development, 69,* 803–816.

Brody, G. H., Ge, X., Kim, S. Y., Murry, V. M., Simons, R. L., & Gibbons, F. X. (2003). Neighborhood disadvantage moderates associations of parenting and older sibling problem attitudes and behavior with conduct disorders in African American children. *Journal of Consulting and Clinical Psychology, 71,* 211–222.

Brody, G. H., Stoneman, Z., & McCoy, J. K. (1992). Associations of maternal and paternal direct and differential behavior with sibling relationships: Contemporaneous and longitudinal analyses. *Child Development, 63,* 82–92.

Brody, G. H., Stoneman, Z., & McCoy, J. K. (1994). Forecasting sibling relationships in early adolescence from child temperaments and family processes in middle childhood. *Child Development, 65,* 771–784.

Brody, J. E. (1992, November 11). PMS is a worldwide phenomenon. *The New York Times,* p. C14.

Brody, L. (1999). *Gender, emotion, and the family.* Cambridge, MA: Harvard University Press.

Brody, L. R. (1997). Gender and emotion: Beyond stereotypes. *Journal of Social Issues, 53,* 369–393.

Brody, M. (2006). Child psychiatry, drugs, and the corporation. In S. Olfman (Ed.), *No child left different* (pp. 89–105). Westport, CT: Praeger.

Brodzinsky, D. M., & Pinderhughes, E. (2002). Parenting and child development in adoptive families. In M. H. Bornstein (Ed.), *Handbook of parenting: Vol. 1* (2nd ed., pp. 279–311). Mahwah, NJ: Erlbaum.

Broidy, L. M., Nagin, D. S., Tremblay, R. E., Bates, J. E., Brame, B., Dodge, K. A., Fergusson, D., Horwood, J. L., Loeber, R., Laird, R., Lynam, D. R., Moffitt, T. E., Pettit, G. S., & Vitaro, F. (2003). Developmental trajectories of childhood disruptive behaviors and adolescent delinquency: A six-site, cross-national study. *Developmental Psychology, 39,* 222–245.

Bromberger, J. T., Meyer, P. M., Kravitz, H. M., Sommer, B., Cordal, A., & Powell, L. (2001). Psychologic distress and natural menopause: A multiethnic community study. *American Journal of Public Health, 91,* 1435–1442.

Bronfenbrenner, U., & Evans, G. W. (2000). Developmental science in the 21st century: Emerging theoretical models, research designs, and empirical findings. *Social Development, 9,* 115–125.

Bronfenbrenner, U., & Morris, P. A. (1998). The ecology of developmental processes. In R. M. Lerner (Ed.), *Handbook of child psychology: Vol. 1. Theoretical models of human development* (5th ed., pp. 535–584). New York: Wiley.

Bronson, G. W. (1994). Infants' transitions toward adult-like scanning. *Child Development, 65,* 1243–1261.

Brooks, C. (2000). Civil rights, liberalism, and the suppression of a Republican political realignment in the United States, 1972 to 1996. *American Sociological Review, 65,* 483–505.

Brooks, D., & Barth, R. P. (1999). Adult transracial and inracial adoptees: Effects of race, gender, adoptive family structure, and placement history on adjustment outcomes. *American Journal of Orthopsychiatry, 69,* 87–99.

Brooks, P. J., Hanauere, J. B., Padowska, B., & Rosman, H. (2003). The role of selective attention in preschoolers' rule use in a novel dimensional card sort. *Cognitive Development, 18,* 195–215.

Brooks, R., & Meltzoff, A. N. (2005). The development of gaze following and its relation to language. *Developmental Science, 8,* 535–543.

Brooks-Gunn, J. (1988). Antecedents and consequences of variations in girls' maturational timing. *Journal of Adolescent Health Care, 9,* 365–373.

Brooks-Gunn, J. (2003). Do you believe in magic? What we can expect from early childhood intervention programs. *Social Policy Report of the Society for Research in Child Development, 17,* 3–14.

Brooks-Gunn, J. (2004). Intervention and policy as change agents for young children. In P. L. Chase-Lansdale, K. Kiernan, & R. J. Friedman (Eds.), *Human development across lives and generations: The potential for change* (pp. 293–340). New York: Cambridge University Press.

Brooks-Gunn, J., Han, W.-J., & Waldfogel, J. (2002). Maternal employment and child cognitive outcomes in the first three years of life: The NICHD study of early child care. *Child Development, 73*, 1052–1072.

Brooks-Gunn, J., Klebanov, P. K., Smith, J., Duncan, G. J., & Lee, K. (2003). The black–white test score gap in young children. Contributions of test and family characteristics. *Applied Developmental Science, 7*, 239–252.

Brooks-Gunn, J., & Ruble, D. N. (1983). The experience of menarche from a developmental perspective. In J. Brooks-Gunn & A. C. Petersen (Eds.), *Girls at puberty* (pp. 155–177). New York: Plenum.

Brooks-Gunn, J., Schley, S., & Hardy, J. (2002). Marriage and the baby carriage: Historical change and intergenerational continuity in early parenthood. In L. J. Crockett & R. K. Sibereisen (Eds.), *Negotiating adolescence in times of social change* (pp. 36–57). New York: Cambridge University Press.

Broomhall, H. S., & Winefield, A. H. (1990). A comparison of the affective well-being of young and middle-aged unemployed men matched for length of employment. *British Journal of Medical Psychology, 63*, 43–52.

Brown, A. M., & Miracle, J. A. (2003). Early binocular vision in human infants: Limitations on the generality of the Superposition Hypothesis. *Vision Research, 43*, 1563–1574.

Brown, A. S., & Susser, E. S. (2002). In utero infection and adult schizophrenia. *Mental Retardation and Developmental Disabilities Research Reviews, 8*, 51–57.

Brown, B. B., Clasen, D., & Eicher, S. (1986). Perceptions of peer pressure, peer conformity dispositions, and self-reported behavior among adolescents. *Developmental Psychology, 22*, 521–530.

Brown, B. B., Feiring, C., & Furman, W. (1999). Missing the love boat: Why researchers have shied away from adolescent romance. In W. Furman, B. B. Brown, & C. Feiring (Eds.), *The development of romantic relationships in adolescence* (pp. 1–16). New York: Cambridge University Press.

Brown, B. B., Lohr, M. J., & McClenahan, E. L. (1986). Early adolescents' perceptions of peer pressure. *Journal of Early Adolescence, 6*, 139–154.

Brown, C., & Lowis, M. J. (2003). Psychosocial development in the elderly: An investigation into Erikson's ninth stage. *Journal of Aging Studies, 17*, 415–426.

Brown, C. S., & Bigler, R. S. (2004). Children's perceptions of gender discrimination. *Developmental Psychology, 40*, 714–726.

Brown, J. R., Donelan-McCall, N., & Dunn, J. (1996). Why talk about mental states? The significance of children's conversations with friends, siblings, and mothers. *Child Development, 67*, 836–849.

Brown, L. H., & Rodin, P. A. (2004). Grandparent–grandchild relationships and the life course perspective. In J. Demick & C. Andreoletti (Eds.), *Handbook of adult development* (pp. 459–474). New York: Springer.

Brown, R. T., Reynolds, C. R., & Whitaker, J. S. (1999). Bias in mental testing since Bias in Mental Testing. *School Psychology Quarterly, 14*, 208–238.

Brown, R. W. (1973). *A first language: The early stages.* Cambridge, MA: Harvard University Press.

Brown, S. L. (2000). Union transitions among cohabitors: The significance of relationship assessments and expectations. *Journal of Marriage and the Family, 62*, 833–846.

Brown, S. L. (2002). Race and sex differences in the use of cardiac procedures for patients with ischemic heart disease. *Journal of Health Care for the Poor and Underserved, 13*, 526–537.

Brownell, C. A., & Carriger, M. S. (1990). Changes in cooperation and self-other differentiation during the second year. *Child Development, 61*, 1164–1174.

Brownell, P., & Podnieks, E. (2005). Long-overdue recognition for the critical issue of elder abuse and neglect: A global policy and practice perspective. *Brief Treatment and Crisis Intervention, 5*, 187–191.

Brubaker, T. (1985). *Later life families.* Beverly Hills, CA: Sage.

Bruce, D., Dolan, A., & Phillips-Grant, K. (2000). On the transition from childhood amnesia to recall of personal memories. *Psychological Science, 11*, 360–364.

Bruch, H. (2001). *The golden cage: The enigma of anorexia nervosa.* Cambridge, MA: Harvard University Press.

Bruck, M., & Ceci, S. J. (2004). Forensic developmental psychology: Unveiling four common misconceptions. *Current Directions in Psychological Science, 13*, 229–232.

Bruer, J. T. (1999). *The myth of the first three years.* New York: Free Press.

Brun, A., & Andersson, J. (2001). Frontal dysfunction and frontal cortical synapse loss in alcoholism: The main cause of alcohol dementia? *Dementia and Geriatric Cognitive Disorders, 12*, 289–294.

Brussoni, M. J., and Boon, S. D. (1998). Grandparental impact in young adults' relationships with their closest grandparents: The role of relationship strength and emotional closeness. *International Journal of Aging and Human Development, 45*, 267–286.

Bruzzese, J.-M., & Fisher, C. B. (2003). Assessing and enhancing the research consent capacity of children and youth. *Applied Developmental Science, 7*, 13–26.

Bryant, P., & Nunes, T. (2002). Children's understanding of mathematics. In U. Goswami (Ed.), *Blackwell handbook of childhood cognitive development* (pp. 412–439). Malden, MA: Blackwell.

Buchanan, A. (1996). *Cycles of child maltreatment.* Chichester, UK: Wiley.

Buchanan, C. M., Eccles, J. S., & Becker, J. B. (1992). Are adolescents the victims of raging hormones? Evidence for activational effects of hormones on moods and behavior at adolescence. *Psychological Bulletin, 111*, 62–107.

Buchanan, C. M., & Holmbeck, G. N. (1998). Measuring beliefs about adolescent personality and behavior. *Journal of Youth and Adolescence, 27*, 609–629.

Buchanan, C. M., Maccoby, E. E., & Dornbusch, S. M. (1996). *Adolescents after divorce.* Cambridge, MA: Harvard University Press.

Buchanan-Barrow, E., & Barrett, M. (1998). Children's rule discrimination within the context of the school. *British Journal of Developmental Psychology, 16*, 539–551.

Buchman, M. (2002). Labour market entry and beyond: Some reflections on the changing structure of work. *Education + Training, 44*, 217–223.

Buescher, E. S. (2001). Anti-inflammatory characteristics of human milk: How, where, why. *Advances in Experimental Medicine and Biology, 501*, 207–222.

Bugental, D. B., & Happaney, K. (2004). Predicting infant maltreatment in low-income families: The interactive effects of maternal attributions and child status at birth. *Developmental Psychology, 40*, 234–243.

Buhrmester, D. (1996). Need fulfillment, interpersonal competence, and the developmental contexts of early adolescent friendship. In W. M. Bukowski, A. F. Newcomb, & W. W. Hartup (Eds.), *The company they keep: Friendship during childhood and adolescence* (pp. 158–185). New York: Cambridge University Press.

Buhrmester, D. (1998). Need fulfillment, interpersonal competence, and the developmental contexts of early adolescent friendship. In W. M. Bukowski, A. F. Newcomb, & W. W. Hartup (Eds.), *The company they keep: Friendship during childhood and adolescence* (pp. 158–185). New York: Cambridge University Press.

Buhrmester, D., & Furman, W. (1990). Perceptions of sibling relationships during middle childhood and adolescence. *Child Development, 61*, 1387–1398.

Buhs, E. S., & Ladd, G. W. (2001). Peer rejection as antecedent of young children's school adjustment: An examination of mediating processes. *Developmental Psychology, 37*, 550–560.

Bukowski, W. M. (2001). Friendship and the worlds of childhood. In D. W. Nangle & C. A. Erdley (Eds.), *The role of friendship in psychological adjustment* (pp. 93–105). San Francisco: Jossey-Bass.

Bulcroft, R. A., Carmody, D. C., & Bulcroft, K. A. (1996). Patterns of independence giving to adolescents: Variations by race, age, and gender of child. *Journal of Marriage and the Family, 58*, 866–883.

Bullock, M., & Lutkenhaus, P. (1990). Who am I? The development of self-understanding in toddlers. *Merrill-Palmer Quarterly, 36*, 217–238.

Bumpass, L. L. (2004). Social change and the American family. *Annals of the New York Academy of Sciences, 1038*, 213–219.

Bumpass, L. L., & Lu, H. H. (2000). Trends in cohabitation and implications for children's family contexts in the United States. *Population Studies, 54*, 29–41.

Burgess, C., O'Donohoe, A., & Gill, M. (2000). Agony and ecstasy: A review of MDMA effects and toxicity. *European Psychiatry, 15*, 287–294.

Burhans, K. K., & Dweck, C. S. (1995). Helplessness in early childhood: The role of contingent worth. *Child Development, 66*, 1719–1738.

Burke, D. M., & Shafto, M. A. (2004). Aging and language production. *Current Directions in Psychological Science, 13*, 21–24.

Burke, R. J. (2001). Organizational values, work experiences, and satisfactions among managerial and professional women. *Journal of Management Development, 20*, 346–354.

Burke, W., et al. (2002). Genetic test evaluation: Information needs of clinicians, policy makers, and the public. *American Journal of Epidemiology, 156,* 311-318.

Burton, N. W., Turrell, G., & Oldenburg, B. (2003). Participation in recreational physical activity: Why do socioeconomic groups differ? *Health Education and Behavior, 30,* 225–244.

Burts, D.C., Hart, C. H., Charlesworth, R., Fleege, P. O., Mosely, J., & Thomasson, R. H. (1992). Observed activities and stress behaviors of children in developmentally appropriate and inappropriate kindergarten classrooms. *Early Childhood Research Quarterly, 7,* 297–318.

Bushman, B. J., & Huesmann, L. R. (2001). Effects of televised violence on aggression. In D. G. Singer & J. L. Singer (Eds.), *Handbook of children and the media* (pp. 223–254). Thousand Oaks, CA: Sage.

Bushnell, E. W., & Boudreau, J. P. (1993). Motor development and the mind: The potential role of motor abilities as a determinant of aspects of perceptual development. *Child Development, 64,* 1005–1021.

Bushnik, T., Barr-Telford, L., & Bussiére, P. (2004). *In and out of high school: First results from the second cycle of the Youth in Transition Survey, 2002.* Ottawa, ON: Statistics Canada.

Buss, D. M. (2004). *Evolutionary psychology: The new science of the mind* (2nd ed.). Boston: Allyn and Bacon.

Buss, D. M., Shackelford, T. K., Kirkpatrick, L. A., & Larsen, R. J. (2001). A half century of mate preferences: The cultural evolution of values. *Journal of Marriage and the Family, 63,* 491–503.

Bussey, K. (1992). Lying and truthfulness: Children's definitions, standards, and evaluative reactions. *Child Development, 63,* 129–137.

Bussey, K. (1999). Children's categorization and evaluation of different types of lies and truths. *Child Development, 70,* 1338–1347.

Butcher, S. K., & Lord, J. M. (2004). Stress responses and innate immunity: Aging as a contributory factor. *Aging Cell, 10,* 151–160.

Butler, R. (1998). Age trends in the use of social and temporal comparison for self-evaluation: Examination of a novel developmental hypothesis. *Child Development, 69,* 1054–1073.

Butler, R. N. (1968). The life review: An interpretation of reminiscence in the aged. In B. Neugarten (Ed.), *Middle age and aging* (pp.

486–496). Chicago: University of Chicago Press.

Buunk, B. P. (2002). Age and gender differences in mate selection criteria for various involvement levels. *Personal Relationships, 9,* 271–278.

Buunk, B. P., Dijkstra, P., Kenrick, D. T., & Warntjes, A. (2001). Age preferences for mates as related to gender, own age, and involvement level. *Evolution and Human Behavior, 22,* 241–250.

Buunk, B. P., & van Driel, B. (1989). *Variant lifestyles and relationships.* Newbury Park, CA: Sage.

Byard, R. W., & Krous, H. F. (2003). Sudden infant death syndrome: Overview and update. *Perspectives on Pediatric Pathology, 6,* 112–127.

Byars, A. M., & Hackett, G. (1998). Applications of social cognitive theory to the career development of women of color. *Applied and Preventive Psychology, 7,* 255–267.

Bybee, J. A., & Wells, Y. V. (2003). The development of possible selves during adulthood. In J. Demick & C. Andreoletti (Eds.), *Handbook of adult development* (pp. 257–270). New York: Springer.

Byrnes, J. P. (2003). Cognitive development during adolescence. In G. R. Adams & M. D. Berzonsky (Eds.), *Blackwell handbook of adolescence* (pp. 227–246). Malden, MA: Blackwell.

C

Cabeza, R., Nyberg, L., & Park, D. (2005). *Cognitive neuroscience of aging: Linking cognitive and cerebral aging.* New York: Oxford University Press.

Cabrera, N. J., & Garcia-Coll, C. (2004). Latino fathers: Uncharted territory in need of much exploration. In M. E. Lamb (Ed.), *The role of the father in child development* (4th ed., pp. 98–120). Hoboken, NJ: Wiley.

Cabrera, N. J., Tamis-LeMonda, C. S., Bradley, R. H., Hoferth, S., & Lamb, M. E. (2000). Fatherhood in the twenty-first century. *Child Development, 71,* 127–136.

Cain, K. M., & Dweck, C. S. (1995). The relation between motivational patterns and achievement cognitions through the elementary school years. *Merrill-Palmer Quarterly, 41,* 25–52.

Caine, N. (1986). Behavior during puberty and adolescence. In G. Mitchell & J. Erwin (Eds.), *Comparative primate biology: Vol. 2A. Behavior, conservation, and ecology* (pp. 327–361). New York: Liss.

Cairns, R., Xie, H., & Leung, M.-C. (1998). The popularity of friendship and the neglect of social networks: Toward a new balance. In W. M. Bukowski & A. H. Cillessen (Eds.), *Sociometry then and now:*

Building on six decades of measuring children's experiences with the peer group (pp. 25–53). San Francisco: Jossey-Bass.

Caldwell, B. M., & Bradley, R. H. (1994). Environmental issues in developmental follow-up research. In S. L. Friedman & H. C. Haywood (Eds.), *Developmental follow-up* (pp. 235–256). San Diego: Academic Press.

Caldwell, J. (1999). Paths to lower fertility. *British Medical Journal, 319,* 985–987.

Calkins, S. D. (2002). Does aversive behavior during toddlerhood matter? The effects of difficult temperament on maternal perceptions and behavior. *Infant Mental Health Journal, 23,* 381–402.

Calkins, S. D., Fox, N. A., & Marshall, T. R. (1996). Behavioral and physiological antecedents of inhibited and uninhibited behavior. *Child Development, 67,* 523–540.

Callaghan, T., Rochat, P., Lillard, A., Claux, M. L., Odden, H., Itakura, S., Tapanya, S., & Singh, S. (2005). Synchrony in the onset of mental-state reasoning: Evidence from five cultures. *Psychological Science, 16,* 378–384.

Callanan, M. A., & Sabbagh, M. A. (2004). Multiple labels for objects in conversations with young children: Parents' language and children's developing expectations about word meanings. *Developmental Psychology, 40,* 746–763.

Calle, E. E., Rodriguez, C., Walker-Thurmond, K., & Thun, M. J. (2003). Overweight, obesity, and mortality from cancer in a prospectively studied cohort of U.S. adults. *New England Journal of Medicine, 348,* 1625–1638.

Cameron, C. A., & Lee, K. (1997). The development of children's telephone communication. *Journal of Applied Developmental Psychology, 18,* 55–70.

Cameron-Faulkner, T., Lieven, E., & Tomasello, M. (2003). A construction based analysis of child-directed speech. *Cognitive Science, 27,* 843–873.

Camodeca, M., Goossens, F. A., Terwogt, M. M., & Schuengel, C. (2002). Bullying and victimization among school-age children: Stability and links to proactive and reactive aggression. *Social Development, 11,* 332–345.

Campbell, F. A., Pungello, E. P., Miller-Johnson, S., Burchinal, M., & Ramey, C. T. (2001). The development of cognitive and academic abilities: Growth curves from an early childhood educational experiment. *Developmental Psychology, 37,* 231–242.

Campbell, F. A., Ramey, C. T., Pungello, E. P., Sparling, J., & Miller-Johnson, S. (2002). Early

childhood education: Young adult outcomes from the Abecedarian Project. *Applied Developmental Science, 6,* 42–57.

Campbell, J. R., Hombo, C. M., & Mazzeo, J. (2000). *NAEP 1999: Trends in academic progress.* Washington, DC: U.S. Department of Education.

Campbell, L. D., & Martin-Matthews, A. (2000). Caring sons: Exploring men's involvement in filial care. *Canadian Journal on Aging, 19,* 57–97.

Campbell, S. B., Brownell, C. A., Hungerford, A., Spieker, S. J., Mohan, R., & Blessing, J. S. (2004). The course of maternal depressive symptoms and maternal sensitivity as predictors of attachment security at 36 months. *Development and Psychopathology, 16,* 231–252.

Campion, J. M., & Maricic, M. J. (2003). Osteoporosis in men. *American Family Physician, 67,* 1521–1526.

Campos, J. J., Anderson, D. I., Barbu-Roth, M. A., Hubbard, E. M., Hertenstein, J. J., & Witherington, D. (2000). Travel broadens the mind. *Infancy, 1,* 149–219.

Campos, J. J., Kermoian, R., & Zumbahlen, M. R. (1992). Socioemotional transformation in the family system following infant crawling onset. In N. Eisenberg & R. A. Fabes (Eds.), *New directions for child development* (No. 55, pp. 25–40). San Francisco: Jossey-Bass.

Campos, R. G. (1989). Soothing pain-elicited distress in infants with swaddling and pacifiers. *Child Development, 60,* 781–792.

Camras, L. A., Oster, H., Campos, J. J., & Bakeman, R. (2003). Emotional facial expressions in European-American, Japanese, and Chinese infants. *Annals of the New York Academy of Sciences, 1000,* 1–17.

Camras, L. A., Oster, H., Campos, J. J., Campos, R., Ujie, T., Miyake, K., Wang, L., & Meng, Z. (1998). Production of emotional and facial expressions in European American, Japanese, and Chinese infants. *Developmental Psychology, 34,* 616–628.

Camras, L. A., & Sachs, V. B. (1991). Social referencing and caretaker expressive behavior in a day care setting. *Infant Behavior and Development, 14,* 27–36.

Camras, L. A., Oster, H., Campos, J. J., Miyake, K., & Bradshaw, D. (1992). Japanese and American infants' responses to arm restraint. *Developmental Psychology, 28,* 578–583.

Canada Campaign 2000. (2003a). *Diversity or disparity? Early childhood education and care in*

Canada. Retrieved from www.campaign2000.ca

Canada Campaign 2000. (2003b). *Poverty amidst prosperity—building a Canada for all children: 2002 report card.* Ottawa, ON: Author.

Canada Campaign 2000. (2004). *The real facts about child and poverty in Canada.* Ottawa, ON: Author. Retrieved from www.campaign 2000.ca

Canadian Broadcast Standards Council. (2003). *Voluntary code regarding violence in television programming.* Retrieved from www .cbsc.ca/english/codes/violence/ violence.htm

Canadian Centre on Substance Abuse. (2004). Alcohol and illicit drug dependence. *Health Reports,* 15(Supplement), 9–19.

Canadian Fitness and Lifestyle Research Institute. (2002). *Physical activity monitor 2002.* Retrieved from www.cflri.ca

Canadian Fitness and Lifestyle Research Institute. (2003). A case for daily physical education. Retrieved from www.cflri.ca/cflri/ tips/95/LT95_09.html

Canadian Fitness and Lifestyle Research Institute. (2005). *Survey of physical activity in Canadian schools.* Retrieved from www.cflri .ca/cflri/pa/surveys/2001survey/ 2001survey.html

Canadian Institute for Health Information. (2005). Proportion of deliveries by caesarean section, excluding stillbirths. Retrieved from www.cihi.ca

Canadian Psychological Association. (2000). *Canadian code of ethics for psychologists.* Ottawa, ON: Author. Retrieved from www.cpa.ca/ethics 2000.html

Candy-Gibbs, S., Sharp, K., & Petrun, C. (1985). The effects of age, object, and cultural/religious background on children's concepts of death. *Omega, 154,* 329–345.

Canetto, S. S., & Sakinofsky, I. (1998). The gender paradox in suicide. *Suicide and Life-Threatening Behavior, 28,* 1–23.

Canobi, K. H. (2004). Individual differences in children's addition and subtraction knowledge. *Cognitive Development, 19,* 81–93.

Canobi, K. H., Reeve, R. A., & Pattison, P. E. (1998). The role of conceptual understanding in children's addition problem solving. *Developmental Psychology, 34,* 882–891.

Canobi, K. H., Reeve, R. A., & Pattison, P. E. (2003). The role of conceptual understanding in children's addition problem solving. *Developmental Psychology, 39,* 521–534.

Capaldi, D., DeGarmo, D., Patterson, G. R., & Forgatch, M. (2002). Contextual risk across the early life span and association with antisocial behavior. In J. B. Reid, G. R. Patterson, & J. Snyder (Eds.), *Antisocial behavior in children and adolescents* (pp. 123–145). Washington, DC: American Psychological Association.

Capaldi, D. M., Stoolmiller, M., Clark, S., & Owen, L. D. (2002). Heterosexual risk behaviors in at-risk young men from early adolescence to young adulthood: Prevalence, prediction, and association with STD contraction. *Developmental Psychology, 38,* 394–406.

Caplan, M., Vespo, J., Pedersen, J., & Hay, D. F. (1991). Conflict and its resolution in small groups of one- and two-year-olds. *Child Development, 62,* 1513–1524.

Cappeliez, P., & O'Rourke, N. (2002). Personality traits and existential concerns as predictors of the functions of reminiscence in older adults. *Journal of Gerontology, 57B,* P116–P123.

Carbery, J., & Buhrmester, D. (1998). Friendship and need fulfillment during three phases of young adulthood. *Journal of Social and Personal Relationships, 15,* 393–409.

Carey, S. (1999). Sources of conceptual change. In E. K. Scholnick, K. Nelson, S. A. Gelman, & P. H. Miller (Eds.), *Conceptual development: Piaget's legacy* (pp. 293–326). Mahwah, NJ: Erlbaum.

Carey, S., & Markman, E. M. (1999). Cognitive development. In B. M. Bly & D. E. Rumelhart (Eds.), *Cognitive science* (pp. 201–254). San Diego: Academic Press.

Carli, L. L., & Eagly, A. H. (2000). Gender effects on influence and emergent leadership. In G. N. Powell (Ed.), *Handbook of gender in organizations* (pp. 203–222). Newbury Park, CA: Sage.

Carlo, G., Koller, S. H., Eisenberg, N., Da Silva, M., & Frohlich, C. (1996). A cross-national study on the relations among prosocial moral reasoning, gender role orientations, and prosocial behaviors. *Developmental Psychology, 32,* 231–240.

Carlson, C., Uppal, S., & Prosser, E. (2000). Ethnic differences in processes contributing to the self-esteem of early adolescent girls. *Journal of Early Adolescence, 20,* 44–67.

Carlson, S. M., & Moses, L. J. (2001). Individual differences in inhibitory control and children's theory of mind. *Child Development, 72,* 1032–1053.

Carlson, S. M., Moses, L. J., & Claxton, S. J. (2004). Individual differences in executive functioning and theory of mind: An investigation of inhibitory control and planning ability. *Journal of Experimental Child Psychology, 87,* 299–319.

Carlson, V. J., & Harwood, R. L. (2003). Attachment, culture, and the caregiving system: The cultural patterning of everyday experiences among Anglo and Puerto Rican mother–infant pairs. *Infant Mental Health Journal, 24,* 53–73.

Carmichael, S. L., & Shaw, G. M. (2000). Maternal life stress and congenital abnormalities. *Epidemiology, 11,* 30–35.

Caroll, D., Harrison, L. K., Johnston, D. W., Ford, G., Hunt, K., Der, G., & West, P. (2000). Cardiovascular reactions to psychological stress: The influence of demographic variables. *Journal of Epidemiological Community Health, 54,* 876–877.

Carpendale, J. I., & Chandler, M. J. (1996). On the distinction between false belief understanding and subscribing to an interpretive theory of mind. *Child Development, 67,* 1686–1706.

Carpenter, C. J. (1983). Activity structure and play: Implications for socialization. In M. Liss (Eds.), *Social and cognitive skills: Sex roles and children's play* (pp. 117–145). New York: Academic Press.

Carpenter, M., Akhtar, N., & Tomasello, M. (1998). Fourteen-through eighteen-month-old infants differentially imitate intentional and accidental actions. *Infant Behavior and Development, 21,* 315–330.

Carpenter, M., Nagell, K., & Tomasello, M. (1998). Social cognition, joint attention, and communicative competence. *Monographs of the Society for Research in Child Development, 63*(4, Serial No. 255).

Carpenter, T. P., Fennema, E., Fuson, K., Hiebert, J., Human, P., & Murray, H. (1999). Learning basic number concepts and skills as problem solving. In E. Fennema & T. A. Romberg (Eds.), *Mathematics classrooms that promote understanding: Studies in mathematical thinking and learning series* (pp. 45–61). Mahwah, NJ: Erlbaum.

Carr, D., & Friedman, M. A. (2005). Is obesity stigmatizing? Body weight, perceived discrimination, and psychological well-being in the United States. *Journal of Health and Social Behavior, 46,* 244–259.

Carr, J. (2002). Down syndrome. In P. Howlin & O. Udwin (Eds.), *Outcomes in neurodevelopmental and genetic disorders* (pp. 169–197). New York: Cambridge University Press.

Carrado, M., George, M. J., Loxam, E., Jones, L., & Templar, D. (1996). Aggression in British heterosexual relationships: A descriptive analysis. *Aggressive Behavior, 22,* 401–415.

Carroll, D., Harrison, L. K., Johnston, D. W., Ford, G., Hunt, K., Der, G., & West, P. (2000). Cardiovascular reactions to psychological stress: The influence of demographic variables. *Journal of Epidemiology and Community Health, 54,* 876–877.

Carskadon, M. A., Harvey, K., Duke, P., Anders, T. F., Litt, I. F., & Dement, W. C. (2002). Pubertal changes in daytime sleepiness. *Sleep, 25,* 525–605.

Carstensen, L. L., & Fredrickson, B. F. (1998). Socioemotional selectivity in healthy older people and younger people living with the human immunodeficiency virus: The centrality of emotion when the future is constrained. *Health Psychology, 17,* 1–10.

Carstensen, L. L., Fung, H. H., & Charles, S. T. (2003). Socioemotional selectivity theory and the regulation of emotion in the second half of life. *Motivation and Emotion, 27,* 103–123.

Carstensen, L. L., Gottman, J. M., & Levenson, R. W. (1995). Emotional behavior in long-term marriage. *Psychology and Aging, 10,* 140–149.

Carstensen, L. L., Isaacowitz, D. M., & Charles, S. T. (1999). Taking time seriously: A theory of socioemotional selectivity. *American Psychologist, 54,* 165–181.

Carta, J. J., Atwater, J. B., Greenwood, C. R., McConnell, S. R., & McEvoy, M. A. (2001). Effects of cumulative prenatal substance exposure and environmental risks on children's developmental trajectories. *Journal of Clinical Psychology, 30,* 327–337.

Carus, F. A. (1808). *Psychologie. Zweiter Teil: Specialpsychologie.* Leipzig: Barth & Kummer.

Carver, K., Joyner, K., & Udry, J. R. (2003). National estimates of adolescent romantic relationships. In P. Florsheim (Ed.), *Adolescent romantic relations and sexual behavior: Theory, research, and practical implications* (pp. 23–56). Mahwah, NJ: Erlbaum.

Carver, P. R., Egan, S. K., & Perry, D. G. (2004). Children who question their heterosexuality. *Developmental Psychology, 40,* 43–53.

Casasola, M., Cohen, L. B., & Chiarello, E. (2003). Six-month-old infants' categorization of containment spatial relations. *Child Development, 74,* 679–693.

Case, R. (1992). *The mind's staircase: Exploring the conceptual underpinnings of children's thought and knowledge.* Hillsdale, NJ: Erlbaum.

Case, R. (1996). Introduction: Reconceptualizing the nature of children's conceptual structures and their development in middle childhood. In R. Case & Y. Okamoto (Eds.), The role of central conceptual structures in the development of children's thought. *Monographs of the Society for Research in Child Development, 246*(61, Serial No. 246), pp. 1–26.

Case, R. (1998). The development of central conceptual structures. In D. Kuhn & R. Siegler (Eds.), *Handbook of child psychology: Vol. 2. Cognition, perception, and language* (5th ed., pp. 745–800). New York: Wiley.

Case, R., & Okamoto, Y. (Eds.). (1996). The role of central conceptual structures in the development of children's thought. *Monographs of the Society for Research in Child Development, 61*(1–2, Serial No. 246).

Caselli, M. C., Bates, E., Casadio, P., Fenson, J., Fenson, L., Sanderl, L., & Weir, J. (1995). A crosslinguistic study of early lexical development. *Cognitive Development, 10,* 159–199.

Caserta, M. S., & Gillett, P. A. (1998). Older women's feelings about exercise and their adherence to an aerobic regimen over time. *Gerontologist, 38,* 602–609.

Caserta, M. S., Lund, D. A., & Obray, S. J. (2004). Promoting self-care and daily living skills among older widows and widowers: Evidence from the Pathfinders Demonstration Project. *Omega, 49,* 217–236.

Caserta, M. S., Lund, D. A., & Rice, S. J. (1999). Pathfinders: A selfcare and health education program for older widows and widowers. *Gerontologist, 39,* 615–620.

Casey, B. J., Thomas, K. M., Davidson, M. C., Kunz, K., & Franzen, P. L. (2002). Dissociating striatal and hippocampal function developmentally with a stimulusresponse compatibility task. *Journal of Cognitive Neuroscience, 22,* 8647–8652.

Casey, M. B. (1986). Individual differences in selective attention among prereaders: A key to mirror-image confusions. *Developmental Psychology, 22,* 824–831.

Casey, M. B., Nuttall, R. L., & Pezaris, E. (1997). Mediators of gender differences in mathematics college entrance test scores: A comparison of spatial skills with internalized beliefs and anxieties.

Developmental Psychology, 33, 669–680.

Casey, M. B., Nuttall, R. L., & Pezaris, E. (2001). Spatialmechanical reasoning skills versus mathematics self-confidence as mediators of gender differences on mathematics subtests using cross-national gender-based items. *Journal for Research in Mathematics Education, 32,* 28–57.

Cashon, C. H., & Cohen, L. B. (2000). Eight-month-old infants' perceptions of possible and impossible events. *Infancy, 1,* 429–446.

Casper, L. M., & Smith, K. E. (2002). Dispelling the myths: Self-care, class, and race. *Journal of Family Issues, 23,* 716–727.

Caspi, A. (1998). Personality development across the life course. In N. Eisenberg (Ed.), *Handbook of child psychology: Vol. 3. Social, emotional, and personality development* (5th ed., pp. 311–388). New York: Wiley.

Caspi, A. (2000). The child is father of the man: Personality continuities from childhood to adulthood. *Journal of Personality and Social Psychology, 78,* 158–172.

Caspi, A., Elder, G. H., Jr., & Bem, D. J. (1987). Moving against the world: Life-course patterns of explosive children. *Developmental Psychology, 23,* 308–313.

Caspi, A., Elder, G. H., Jr., & Bem, D. J. (1988). Moving away from the world: Life-course patterns of shy children. *Developmental Psychology, 24,* 824–831.

Caspi, A., Harrington, H., Milne, B., Amell, J. W., Theodore, R. F., & Moffitt, T. E. (2003). Children's behavioral styles at age 3 are linked to their adult personality traits at age 26. *Journal of Personality, 71,* 495–513.

Caspi, A., & Herbener, E. (1990). Continuity and change: Assortative marriage and the consistency of personality in adulthood. *Journal of Personality and Social Psychology, 58,* 250–258.

Caspi, A., Lynam, D., Moffitt, T. E., & Silva, P. A. (1993). Unraveling girls' delinquency: Biological, dispositional, and contextual contributions to adolescent misbehavior. *Developmental Psychology, 29,* 19–30.

Caspi, A., Moffitt, T. E., Morgan, J., Rutter, M., Taylor, A., KimCohen, J., & Polo-Tomas, M. (2004). Maternal expressed emotion predicts children's antisocial behavior problems: Using monozygotic-twin differences to identify environmental effects on behavioral development. *Developmental Psychology, 40,* 149–161.

Caspi, A., & Roberts, B. W. (2001). Personality development across the life course: The argument for

change and continuity. *Psychological Inquiry, 12,* 49–66.

Cassidy, J. (2001). Adult romantic attachments: A developmental perspective on individual differences. *Review of General Psychology, 4,* 111–131.

Cassidy, J., & Berlin, L. J. (1994). The insecure/ambivalent pattern of attachment: Theory and research. *Child Development, 65,* 971–991.

Castellanos, F. X., Lee, P. P., Sharp, W., Jeffries, N. O., Greenstein, D. K., & Clasen, L. S. (2002). Developmental trajectories of brain volume abnormalities in children and adolescents with attentiondeficit/hyperactivity disorder. *Journal of the American Medical Association, 288,* 1740–1748.

Castellanos, F. X., Sharp, W. S., Gottesman, R. F., Greenstein, D. K., Giedd, J. N., & Rapoport, J. L. (2003). Anatomic brain abnormalities in monozygotic twins discordant for attentiondeficit hyperactivity disorder. *American Journal of Psychiatry, 160,* 1693–1695.

Catalano, R. A. (2003). Sex ratios in the two Germanies: A test of the economic stress hypothesis. *Human Reproduction, 18,* 1972–1975.

Caton, D., Corry, M. P., Frigoletto, F. D., Hokins, D. P., Liberman, E., & Mayberry, L. (2002). The nature and management of labor pain: Executive summary. *American Journal of Obstetrics and Gynecology, 186,* S1–S15.

Catsambis, S. (1994). The path to math: Gender and racial-ethnic differences in mathematics participation from middle school to high school. *Sociology of Education, 67,* 199–215.

Cavadini, C., Siega-Riz, A. M., & Popkin, B. M. (2000). U.S. adolescent food intake trends from 1965 to 1996. *Archives of Diseases in Childhood, 83,* 18–24.

CBS News Canada. (2005). *Living wills: FAQs.* Retrieved from www .cbc.ca/news/background/wills

Ceci, S. J. (1991). How much does schooling influence general intelligence and its cognitive components? A reassessment of the evidence. *Developmental Psychology, 27,* 703–722.

Ceci, S. J. (1999). Schooling and intelligence. In S. J. Ceci & W. M. Williams (Eds.), *The naturenurture debate: The essential readings* (pp. 168–175). Oxford, UK: Blackwell.

Ceci, S. J., & Bruck, M. (1998). Children's testimony: Applied and basic issues. In I. Sigel & K. A. Renninger (Eds.), *Handbook of child psychology: Vol. 4. Child psychology in practice* (5th ed., pp. 713–774). New York: Wiley.

Ceci, S. J., Bruck, M., & Battin, D. B. (2000). The suggestibility of children's testimony. In D. F. Bjorklund (Ed.), *False-memory creation in children and adults* (pp. 169–201). Mahwah, NJ: Erlbaum.

Ceci, S. J., Fitneva, S. A., & Gilstrap, L. L. (2003). Memory development and eyewitness testimony. In A. Slater & G. Bremner (Eds.), *An introduction to developmental psychology* (pp. 283–310). Malden, MA: Blackwell.

Ceci, S. J., Rosenblum, T. B., & Kumpf, M. (1998). The shrinking gap between high- and lowscoring groups: Current trends and possible causes. In U. Neisser (Ed.), *The rising curve* (pp. 287–302). Washington, DC: American Psychological Association.

Ceci, S. J., & Williams, W. M. (1997). Schooling, intelligence, and income. *American Psychologist, 52,* 1051–1058.

Center for Communication and Social Policy. (Ed.). (1998). *National Television Violence Study* (Vol. 2). Newbury Park, CA: Sage.

Center for Effective Discipline. (2005). Worldwide bans on corporal punishment. Retrieved from www.stophitting.com/ disatschool/facts.php

Cerella, J. (1990). Aging and information processing rate. In J. E. Birren & K. W. Schaie (Eds.), *Handbook of the psychology of aging* (3rd ed., pp. 201–221). San Diego: Academic Press.

Cernoch, J. M., & Porter, R. H. (1985). Recognition of maternal axillary odors by infants. *Child Development 56,* 1593–1598.

Chakkalakal, D. A. (2005). Alcoholinduced bone loss and deficient bone repair. *Alcoholism, Clinical and Experimental Research, 29,* 2077–2090.

Chalmers, J. B., & Townsend, M. A. R. (1990). The effects of training in social perspective taking on socially maladjusted girls. *Child Development, 61,* 178–190.

Chamberlain, P. (2003). Antisocial behavior and delinquency in girls. In P. Chamberlain (Ed.), *Treating chronic juvenile offenders* (pp. 109–127). Washington, DC: American Psychological Association.

Champion, T. B. (2003a). "A matter of vocabulary": Performances of low-income African-American Head Start children on the Peabody Picture Vocabulary Test. *Communication Disorders Quarterly, 24,* 121–127.

Champion, T. B. (2003b). *Understanding storytelling among African-American children: A journey from Africa to America.* Mahwah, NJ: Erlbaum.

Chan, G. K., & Duque, G. (2002). Age-related bone loss: Old bone, new facts. *Gerontology, 48,* 62–71.

Chan, R. W., Raboy, B., & Patterson, C. J. (1998). Psychosocial adjustment among children conceived via donor insemination by lesbian and heterosexual mothers. *Child Development, 69,* 443–457.

Chandra, R. K. (1991). Interactions between early nutrition and the immune system. In *Ciba Foundation Symposium No. 156* (pp. 77–92). Chichester, UK: Wiley.

Chandra, R. K. (1992). Effect of vitamin and trace-element supplementation on immune responses and infection in elderly subjects. *Lancet, 340,* 1124–1127.

Chandra, R. K. (2002a). Influence of multinutrient supplement on immune response and infection-related illness in 50–65 year old individuals. *Nursing Research, 22,* 5–11.

Chandra, R. K. (2002b). Nutrition and the immune system from birth to old age. *European Journal of Clinical Nutrition, 56*(Suppl. 3), S73–S76.

Chang, L., Schwartz, D., Dodge, D. A., & McBride-Chang, C. (2003). Harsh parenting in relation to child emotion regulation and aggression. *Journal of Family Psychology, 17,* 598–606.

Chao, R., & Good, G. E. (2004). Nontraditional students' perspectives on college education: A qualitative study. *Journal of College Counseling, 7,* 5–12.

Chao, R. K. (1994). Beyond parental control and authoritarian parenting style: Understanding Chinese parenting through the cultural notion of training. *Child Development, 65,* 1111–1119.

Chapman, R. S. (2000). Children's language learning: An interactionist perspective. *Journal of Child Psychology and Psychiatry, 41,* 33–54.

Chappell, N., Gee, E., McDonald, L., & Stones, M. (2003). *Aging in contemporary Canada.* Toronto: Pearson Education Canada.

Charman, T., Baron-Cohen, S., Swettenham, J., Baird, G., Cox, A., & Drew, A. (2001). Testing joint attention, imitation, and play as infancy precursors to language and theory of mind. *Cognitive Development, 15,* 481–49.

Charpak, N., Ruiz-Peláez, J. G., & Figueroa, Z. (2005). Influence of feeding patterns and other factors on early somatic growth of healthy, preterm infants in home-based kangaroo mother care: A cohort study. *Journal of Pediatric Gastroenterology and Nutrition, 41,* 430–437.

Chase-Lansdale, P. L., Brooks-Gunn, J., & Zamsky, E. S. (1994). Young African-American multigenerational families in poverty: Quality of mothering and grandmothering. *Child Development, 65,* 373–393.

Chase-Lansdale, P. L., Gordon, R., Brooks-Gunn, J., & Klebanov, P. K. (1997). Neighborhood and family influences on the intellectual and behavioral competence of preschool and early school-age children. In J. Brooks-Gunn, G. Duncan, & J. L. Aber (Eds.), *Neighborhood poverty: Context and consequences for development* (pp. 79–118). New York: Russell Sage Foundation.

Chassin, L., & Ritter, J. (2001). Vulnerability to substance use disorders in childhood and adolescence. In R. E. Ingram & J. M. Price (Eds.), *Vulnerability to psychopathology: Risk across the lifespan* (pp. 107–134). New York: Guilford.

Chavajay, P., & Rogoff, B. (1999). Cultural variation in management of attention by children and their caregivers. *Developmental Psychology, 35,* 1079–1090.

Chavajay, P., & Rogoff, B. (2002). Schooling and traditional collaborative social organization of problem solving by Mayan mothers and children. *Developmental Psychology, 38,* 55–66.

Chavous, T. M., Bernat, D. H., Schmeelk-Cone, K., Caldwell, C. H., Kohn-Wood, L., & Zimmerman, M. A. (2003). Racial identity and academic attainment among African-American adolescents. *Child Development, 74,* 1076–1090.

Chazottes, D. (2004). Use of memory compensation strategies is related to psychosocial and health indicators. *Journal of Gerontology, 58B,* P12–P22.

Chen, M. (2003). Wombs for rent: An examination of prohibitory and regulatory approaches to governing preconception arrangements. *Health Law in Canada, 23,* 33–50.

Chen, X., Cen, G., Li, D., & He, Y. (2005). Social functioning and adjustment in Chinese children: The imprint of historical time. *Child Development, 76,* 182–195.

Chen, X., Hastings, P. D., Rubin, K. H., Chen, H., Cen, G., & Stewart, S. L. (1998). Childrearing attitudes and behavioral inhibition in Chinese and Canadian toddlers: A cross-cultural study. *Developmental Psychology, 34,* 677–686.

Chen, X., Rubin, K. H., & Li, Z. (1995). Social functioning and adjustment in Chinese children: A longitudinal study. *Developmental Psychology, 31,* 531–539.

Chen, X., Wu, H., Chen, H., Wang, L., & Cen, G. (2001). Parenting practices and aggressive behavior in Chinese children. *Parenting: Science and Practice, 1,* 159–184.

Chen, Y.-C., Yu, M.-L., Rogan, W., Gladen, B., & Hsu, C.-C. (1994). A 6-year follow-up of behavior and activity disorders in the Taiwan Yu-cheng children. *American Journal of Public Health, 84,* 415–421.

Chen, Y.-J., & Hsu, C.-C. (1994). Effects of prenatal exposure to PCBs on the neurological function of children: A neuropsychological and neurophysiological study. *Developmental Medicine and Child Neurology, 36,* 312–320.

Chen, Z., Sanchez, R. P., & Campbell, T. (1997). From beyond to within their grasp: The rudiments of analogical problem solving in 10- to 13-month-olds. *Developmental Psychology, 33,* 790–801.

Cherlin, A. J. (1992). *Marriage, divorce, remarriage* (rev. ed.). Cambridge, MA: Harvard University Press.

Chesney, M. A., Ekman, P., Friesen, W. V., Black, G. W., & Hecker, M. H. L. (1997). Type A behavior pattern: Facial behavior and speech components. In P. Ekman & E. L. Rosenberg (Eds.*), What the face reveals* (pp. 453–468). New York: Oxford University Press.

Chesney-Lind, M. (2001). Girls, violence, and delinquency: Popular myths and persistent problems. In S. O. White (Ed.), *Handbook of youth and justice* (pp. 135–158). New York: Kluwer Academic.

Chess, S., & Thomas, A. (1984). *Origins and evolution of behavior disorders.* New York: Brunner/Mazel.

Chestnut, C. H., III. (2001). Osteoporosis, an underdiagnosed disease. *Journal of the American Medical Association, 286,* 2865–2866.

Chi, M. T. H., Glaser, R., & Farr, M. J. (Eds.). (1988). *The nature of expertise.* Hillsdale, NJ: Erlbaum.

Child Care Advocacy Association of Canada. (2004). Family living costs in Manitoba, 2004, and cost of raising a child. Retrieved from www.action.web.ca/home/ccaac/alerts.shtm?x=67753

Child Trends. (2005a). *Facts at a glance.* Washington, DC: Author.

Child Trends. (2005b). *Late or no prenatal care.* Retreived from www.childtrendsdatabank.org

Children's Defense Fund. (2005). *The state of America's children: 2005.* Washington, DC: Author.

Chisholm, J. S. (1989). Biology, culture, and the development of temperament: A Navajo example. In J. K. Nugent, B. M. Lester, & T. B. Brazelton (Eds.), *Biology, culture, and development* (Vol. 1, pp. 341–364). Norwood, NJ: Ablex.

Chisolm, T. H., Willott, J. F., & Lister, J. J. (2003). The aging auditory system: Anatomic and physiologic changes and implications for rehabilitation. *International Journal of Audiology, 42,* 2S3–2S10.

Chochinov, H. M. (2002). Dignity-conserving care: A new model for palliative care. Helping the patient feel valued. *Journal of the American Medical Association, 287,* 2253–2260.

Chodirker, B., Cadrin, C., Davies, G., Summers, A., Wilson, R., Winsor, E., & Young, D. (2001). Genetic indications for prenatal diagnosis. *Journal of the Society of Obstetricians and Gynaecologists of Canada, 23,* 525–531.

Chodorow, N. (1978). *The reproduction of mothering.* Berkeley: University of California Press.

Choi, J., & Silverman, I. (2003). Processes underlying sex differences in route-learning strategies in children and adolescents. *Personality and Individual Differences, 34,* 1153–1166.

Choi, N. G. (1994). Racial differences in timing and factors associated with retirement. *Journal of Sociology and Social Welfare, 21,* 31–52.

Choi, S., & Gopnik, A. (1995). Early acquisition of verbs in Korean: A cross-linguistic study. *Journal of Child Language, 22,* 497–529.

Chollar, S. (1995, June). The psychological benefits of exercise. *American Health, 14*(5), 72–75.

Chomsky, C. (1969). *The acquisition of syntax in children from five to ten.* Cambridge, MA: MIT Press.

Chomsky, N. (1957). *Syntactic structures.* The Hague: Mouton.

Chouinard, M. M., & Clark, E. V. (2003). Adult reformulations of child errors as negative evidence. *Journal of Child Language, 30,* 637–669.

CHPCA (Canadian Hospice Palliative Care Association). (2004). *Fact sheet: Hospice palliative care in Canada.* Ottawa: Author.

Christ, G. H., Siegel, K., & Christ, A. E. (2002). "It never really hit me . . . until it actually happened." *Journal of the American Medical Association, 288,* 1269–1278.

Christensen, A., & Heavey, C. L. (1999). Interventions for couples. *Annual Review of Psychology, 50,* 165–190.

Christensen, K. A., Stephens, M. A. P., & Townsend, A. L. (1998). Mastery in women's multiple roles and well-being: Adult daughters providing care to impaired parents. *Health Psychology, 17,* 163–171.

Christenson, S. L., & Sheridan, S. M. (2001). *Schools and families.* New York: Guilford.

Chumlea, W. C., Schubert, C. M., Roche, A. F., Kulin, H. E., Lee, P. A., Himes, J. H., & Sun, S. S. (2003). Age at menarche and racial comparisons in U.S. girls. *Pediatrics, 111,* 110–113.

Church, E. (2004). *Understanding stepmothers: Women share their struggles, successes, and insights.* Toronto: HarperCollins.

Cicchetti, D. (2003). Neuroendocrine functioning in maltreated children. In D. Cicchetti & E. F. Walker (Eds.), *Neurodevelopmental mechanisms in psychopathology* (pp. 345–365). New York: Cambridge University Press.

Cicchetti, D., & Toth, S. L. (2000). Developmental processes in maltreated children. In. D. J. Hansen (Ed.), *Nebraska Symposium on Motivation* (Vol. 46, pp. 85–160). Lincoln: University of Nebraska Press.

Cicirelli, V. G. (1989). Feelings of attachment to siblings and well-being in later life. *Psychology and Aging, 4,* 211–216.

Cicirelli, V. G. (1995). *Sibling relationships across the life span.* New York: Plenum.

Cicirelli, V. G. (1997). Relationship of psychosocial and background variables to older adults' end-of-life decisions. *Psychology and Aging, 12,* 72–83.

Cicirelli, V. G. (1998). Personal meanings of death in relation to fear of death. *Death Studies, 22,* 713–733.

Cicirelli, V. G. (1999). Personality and demographic factors in older adults' fear of death. *Gerontologist, 39,* 569–579.

Cicirelli, V. G. (2001). Personal meanings of death in older adults and young adults in relation to their fears of death. *Death Studies, 25,* 663–683.

Cicirelli, V. G. (2002). *Older adults' views on death.* New York: Springer.

Cillessen, A. H. N., & Bellmore, A. D. (2004). Social skills and interpersonal perception in early and middle childhood. In P. K. Smith & C. H. Hart (Eds.), *Blackwell handbook of childhood social development* (pp. 355–374). Malden, MA: Blackwell.

Cillessen, A. H. N., & Mayeux, L. (2004). From censure to reinforcement: Developmental changes in the association between aggression and social status. *Child Development, 75,* 147–163.

Cinamon, R. G., & Rich, Y. (2002). Gender differences in the importance of work and family roles: Implications for work–family conflict. *Sex Roles, 47,* 531–541.

Clapp, J. F., III, Kim, H., Burciu, B., Schmidt, S., Petry, K., & Lopez, B. (2002). Continuing regular exercise during pregnancy: Effect of exercise volume on fetoplacental growth. *American Journal of Obstetrics and Gynecology, 186,* 142–147.

Clark, E. V. (1995). The lexicon and syntax. In J. L. Miller & P. D. Eimas (Eds.), *Speech, language, and communication* (pp. 303–337). San Diego: Academic Press.

Clark, K. E., & Ladd, G. W. (2000). Connectedness and autonomy support in parent–child relationships: Links to children's socioemotional orientation and peer relationships. *Developmental Psychology, 36,* 485–498.

Clark, R., Hyde, J. S., Essex, M. J., & Klein, M. H. (1997). Length of maternity leave and quality of mother–infant interaction. *Child Development, 68,* 364–383.

Clarke-Stewart, A., Althusen, V., & Goosens, F. (2001). Day care and the Strange Situation. In A. Göncu & E. L. Klein (Eds.), *Children in play, story, and school* (pp. 241–266). New York: Guilford.

Clarke-Stewart, K. A. (1998). Historical shifts and underlying themes in ideas about rearing young children in the United States: Where have we been? Where are we going? *Early Development and Parenting, 7,* 101–117.

Clarke-Stewart, K. A., & Hayward, C. (1996). Advantages of father custody and contact for the psychological well-being of school-age children. *Journal of Applied Developmental Psychology, 17,* 239–270.

Clarkson, T. W., Magos, L., & Myers, G. J. (2003). The toxicology of mercury—current exposures and clinical manifestations. *New England Journal of Medicine, 349,* 1731–1737.

Clausen, J. A. (1975). The social meaning of differential physical and sexual maturation. In S. E. Dragastin & G. H. Elder (Eds.), *Adolescence in the life cycle: Psychological change and the social context* (pp. 25–47). New York: Halsted.

Claxton, L. J., Keen, R., & McCarty, M. E. (2003). Evidence of motor planning in infant reaching behavior. *Psychological Science, 14,* 354–356.

Cleary, J. P., Walsh, D. M., Hofmeister, J. J., Shankar, G. M., Kuskowski, M. A., Selkoe, D. J., & Ashe, K. H. (2005). Natural oligomers of the amyloid-beta protein specifically disrupt cognitive function. *Nature Neuroscience, 8,* 79–84.

Clements, D. H. (1995). Teaching creativity with computers. *Educational Psychology, Review, 7,* 141—149.

Clements, D. H., & Sarama, J. (2003). Young children and technology: What does the research say? *Young Children, 58*(6), 34–40.

Clifton, R. K., Rochat, P., Robin, D. J., & Berthier, N. E. (1994). Multimodal perception in the control of infant reaching. *Journal of Experimental Psychology: Human Perception and Performance, 20,* 876–886.

Clinchy, B. M. (2002). Revisiting women's ways of knowing. In B. K. Hofer & P. R. Pintrich (Eds.), *Personal epistemology: The psychological beliefs about knowledge and knowing* (pp. 63–87). Mahwah, NJ: Erlbaum.

Clingempeel, W. G., & Henggeler, S. W. (2003). Aggressive juvenile offenders transitioning into emerging adulthood: Factors discriminating persistors and desistors. *American Journal of Orthopsychiatry, 73,* 310–323.

Cloud, N., Genesee, F., & Humayan, E. (2000). *Dual language instruction: A handbook for enriched education.* Boston, MA: Heinle & Heinle.

Cockerham, W. C., Hinote, B. P., Abbott, P., & Haerpfer, C. (2004). Healthy lifestyles in central Asia: The case of Kazakhstan and Kyrgyzstan. *Social Science and Medicine, 59,* 1409–1421.

Cohan, C. L., & Kleinbaum, S. (2002). Toward a greater understanding of the cohabitation effect: Premarital cohabitation and marital communication. *Journal of Marriage and the Family, 64,* 180–192.

Cohen, L. B. (2003). Commentary on Part I: Unresolved issues in infant categorization. In D. H. Rakison & L. M. Oakes (Eds.), *Early category and concept development: Making sense of the blooming, buzzing confusion* (pp. 193–209). New York: Oxford University Press.

Cohen, P., Kasen, S., Chen, H., Hartmark, C., & Gordon, K. (2003). Variations in patterns of developmental transitions in the emerging adulthood period. *Developmental Psychology, 39,* 657–669.

Cohen, S., & Herbert, T. B. (1996). Health psychology: Psychological factors and physical disease from the perspective of human psychoneuroimmunology. *Annual Review of Psychology, 47,* 113–142.

Cohen-Shalev, A. (1986). Artistic creativity across the adult life span: An alternative approach. *Interchange, 17*(4), 1–16.

Coholl, A., Kassotis, J., Parks, R., Vaughan, R., Bannister, H., & Northridge, M. (2001). Adolescents in the age of AIDS: Myths, misconceptions, and misunderstandings regarding sexually transmitted diseases. *Journal of the National Medical Association, 93,* 64–69.

Coie, J. D., & Dodge, K. A. (1998). Aggression and antisocial behavior. In N. Eisenberg (Ed.), *Handbook of child psychology: Vol. 3. Social, emotional, and personality development* (5th ed., pp. 779–862). New York: Wiley.

Coie, J. D., Dodge, K. A., & Coppotelli, H. (1982). Dimensions and types of social status: A cross-age perspective. *Developmental Psychology, 18,* 557–570.

Coke, M. M. (1992). Correlates of life satisfaction among elderly African Americans. *Journal of Gerontology, 47,* P316–P320.

Coker, A. D. (2003). African American female adult learners: Motivations, challenges, and coping strategies. *Journal of Black Studies, 33,* 654–674.

Col, N. F., Weber, G., Stiggelbout, A., Chuo, J., D'Agostino, R., & Corso, P. (2004). Short-term menopausal hormone therapy for symptom relief. *Archives of Internal Medicine, 164,* 1634–1640.

Colapinto, J. (2001). *As nature made him: The boy who was raised as a girl.* New York: Perennial.

Colby, A., Kohlberg, L., Gibbs, J., & Lieberman, M. (1983). A longitudinal study of moral judgment. *Monographs of the Society for Research in Child Development, 48*(1–2, Serial No. 200).

Colcombe, S. J., Erickson, K. I., Raz, N., Webb, A. G., Cohen, N. J., & McAuley, E. (2003). Aerobic fitness reduces brain tissue loss in aging humans. *Journal of Gerontology, 58,* M176–M180.

Colcombe, S. J., Kramer, A. F., Erickson, K. I., Scalf, P., McAuley, E., & Cohen, N. J. (2004). Cardiovascular fitness, cortical plasticity, and aging. *Proceedings of the National Academy of Sciences, 101,* 3316–3321.

Cole, D. A., Martin, J. M., Peeke, L. A., Seroczynski, A. D., & Fier, J. (1999). Children's over- and underestimation of academic competence: A longitudinal study of gender differences, depression, and anxiety. *Child Development, 70,* 459–473.

Cole, D. A., Maxwell, S. E., Martin, J. M., Peeke, L. G., Seroczynski, A. D., & Tram, J. M. (2001). The development of multiple domains of child and adolescent self-concept: A cohort sequential longitudinal design. *Child Development, 72,* 1723–1746.

Cole, E. R., & Stewart, A. J. (1996). Meanings of political participation among black and white women: Political identity and social responsibility. *Journal of Personality and Social Psychology, 71,* 130–140.

Cole, M. (1990). Cognitive development and formal schooling: The evidence from cross-cultural research. In L. C. Moll (Ed.), *Vygotsky and education* (pp. 89–110). New York: Cambridge University Press.

Cole, M. (2005). Culture in development. In M. H. Bornstein & M. E. Lamb (Eds.), *Developmental science: An advanced textbook* (5th ed., pp. 45–102). Mahwah, NJ: Erlbaum.

Coleman, M., Ganong, L., & Fine, M. (2000). Reinvestigating remarriage: Another decade of progress. *Journal of Marriage and the Family, 62,* 1288–1307.

Coleman, P. G., Ivani-Chalian, C., & Robinson, M. (2004). Religious attitudes among British older people: Stability and change in a 20-year longitudinal study. *Ageing and Society, 24,* 167–188.

Coleman, P. K. (2003). Perceptions of parent–child attachment, social self-efficacy, and peer relationships in middle childhood. *Infant and Child Development, 12,* 351–368.

Coles, L. (2004). Demography of human supercentenarians. *Journal of Gerontology, 59A,* 579–586.

Coley, R. L. (1998). Children's socialization experiences and functioning in single-mother households: The importance of fathers and other men. *Child Development, 69,* 219–230.

Coley, R. L., Morris, J. E., & Hernandez, D. (2004). Out-of-school care and problem behavior trajectories among low-income adolescents: Individual, family, and neighborhood characteristics as added risks. *Child Development, 75,* 948–965.

Collings, P. (2001). "If you got everything, it's good enough": Perspectives on successful aging in a Canadian Inuit community. *Journal of Cross-Cultural Gerontology, 16,* 127–155.

Collins, F. S. (2003). *A brief primer on genetic testing.* Washington, DC: National Human Genome Research Institute.

Collins, N. L., & Feeney, B. C. (2000). A safe haven: An attachment theory perspective on support-seeking and caregiving in intimate relationships. *Journal of Personality and Social Psychology, 78,* 1053–1073.

Collins, W. A. (2003). More than myth: The developmental significance of romantic relationships during adolescence. *Journal of Research on Adolescence, 13,* 1–24.

Collins, W. A., & Laursen, B. (2004). Parent–adolescent relationships and influences. In R. M. Lerner & L. Steinberg (Eds.), *Handbook of adolescent psychology* (2nd ed., pp. 331–361). New York: Wiley.

Collins, W. A., Maccoby, E. E., Steinberg, L., Hetherington, E. M., & Bornstein, M. H. (2000). Contemporary research on parenting: The case for nature and nurture. *American Psychologist, 55,* 218–232.

Collins, W. A., Madsen, S. D., & Susman-Stillman, A. (2002). Parenting during middle childhood. In M. H. Bornstein (Ed.), *Handbook of parenting: Vol. 1* (2nd ed., pp. 73–101). Mahwah, NJ: Erlbaum.

Collins, W. A., & Russell, G. (1991). Mother–child and father–child interactions in middle childhood and adolescence. *Developmental Review, 11,* 99–136.

Collins, W. A., & van Dulmen, M. (2006). Friendships and romance in emerging adulthood: Assessing distinctiveness in close relationships. In J. J. Arnett & J. L. Tanner (Eds.), *Emerging adults in America: Coming of age in the 21st century* (pp. 219–234). Washington, DC: American Psychological Association.

Colman, L. L., & Colman, A. D. (1991). *Pregnancy: The psychological experience.* New York: Noonday Press.

Colombo, J. (1995). On the neural mechanism underlying developmental and individual differences in visual fixation in infancy. *Developmental Review, 15,* 97–135.

Colombo, J. (2002). Infant attention grows up: The emergence of a developmental cognitive neuroscience perspective. *Current Directions in Psychological Science, 11,* 196–199.

Coltrane, S. (1990). Birth timing and the division of labor in dual-earner families. *Journal of Family Issues, 11,* 157–181.

Coltrane, S. (1996). *Family man.* New York: Oxford University Press.

Comijs, H. C., Jonker, C., van Tilberg, W., and Smit, J. H. (1999). Hostility and coping capacity as risk factors of elder mistreatment. *Social Psychiatry and Psychiatric Epidemiology, 34,* 48–52.

COMPAS. (2002). *Freedom cherished, but not unfettered: A COMPAS/National Post poll.* Retrieved from www.compas.ca/html/archivesdocument.asp?compasID=373

Comstock, G. A., & Scharrer, E. (2001). The use of television and other film-related media. In D. G. Singer & J. L. Singer (Eds.), *Handbook of children and the media* (pp. 47–72). Thousand Oaks, CA: Sage.

Comunian, A. L., & Gielen, U. P. (2000). Sociomoral reflection and prosocial and antisocial behavior: Two Italian studies. *Psychological Reports, 87,* 161–175.

Condie, S. J. (1989). Older married couples. In S. J. Bahr & E. T. Peterson (Eds.), *Aging and the family* (pp. 143–158). Lexington, MA: Lexington Books.

Conger, R. D., & Conger, K. J. (2002). Resilience in Midwestern families: Selected findings from the first decade of a prospective, longitudinal study. *Journal of Marriage and the Family, 64,* 361–373.

Conner, D. B., & Cross, D. R. (2003). Longitudinal analysis of the presence, efficacy, and stability of maternal scaffolding during informal problem-solving interactions. *British Journal of Developmental Psychology, 21,* 315–334.

Connidis, I. A. (1989). Siblings as friends in later life. *American Behavioral Scientist, 33,* 81–93.

Connidis, I. A. (1994). Sibling support in older age. *Journal of Gerontology, 49,* S309–S317.

Connidis, I. A., & Campbell, L. D. (1995). Closeness, confiding, and contact among siblings in middle and late adulthood. *Journal of Family Issues, 16,* 722–745.

Connolly, J. A., & Doyle, A. B. (1984). Relations of social fantasy play to social competence in preschoolers. *Developmental Psychology, 20,* 797–806.

Connolly, J., Craig, W., Goldberg, A., & Pepler, D. (2004). Mixed-gender groups, dating, and romantic relationships in early adolescence. *Journal of Research on Adolescence, 14,* 185–207.

Connolly, J., & Goldberg, A. (1999). Romantic relationships in adolescence: The role of friends and peers in their emergence and development. In W. Furman, B. B. Brown, & C. Feiring (Eds.), *The development of romantic relationships in adolescence* (pp. 266–290). New York: Cambridge University Press.

Connor, J. M. (2003). Physical activity and well-being. In M. H. Bornstein, L. Davidson, C. L. M. Keyes, K. A. Moore, & the Center for Child Well-Being (Eds.), *Well-being: Positive development across the life course* (pp. 65–79). Mahwah, NJ: Erlbaum.

Connor, P. D., Sampson, P. D., Bookstein, F. L., Barr, H. M., & Streissguth, A. P. (2001). Direct and indirect effects of prenatal alcohol damage on executive function. *Developmental Neuropsychology, 18,* 331–354.

Conti, S., Farchi, G., Masocco, M., Minelli, G., Toccaceli, V., & Vichi, M. (2003). Gender differentials in life expectancy in Italy. *European Journal of Epidemiology, 18,* 107–112.

Conti-Ramsden, G., & Pérez-Pereira, M. (1999). Conversational interactions between mothers and their infants who are congenitally blind, have low vision, or are sighted. *Journal of Visual Impairment and Blindness, 93,* 691–703.

Convit, A., Wolf, O. T., Harshish, C., & de Leon, M. J. (2003). Reduced glucose tolerance is associated with poor memory performance and hippocampal atrophy among normal elderly. *Proceedings of the National Academy of Sciences, 100,* 2019–2022.

Conwell, Y. (2004). Suicide. In S. P. Roose & H.A. Sackeim (Ed.), *Late-life depression* (pp. 95–106). New York: Oxford University Press.

Conwell, Y., & Duberstein, P. R. (2001). Suicide in elders. *Annals of the New York Academy of Sciences, 932,* 132–150.

Conwell, Y., Duberstein, P. R., & Caine, E. D. (2002). Risk factors for suicide in later life. *Biological Psychiatry, 52,* 193–204.

Conyers, C., Miltenberger, R., Maki, A., Barenz, R., Jurgens, M., Sailer, A., Haugen, M., & Kopp, B. (2004). A comparison of response cost and differential reinforcement of other behaviors to reduce disruptive behavior in a preschool classroom. *Journal of Applied Behavior Analysis, 37,* 411–415.

Cook, E. A. (1998). Effects of reminiscence on life satisfaction of elderly female nursing home residents. *Health Care for Women International, 19,* 109–118.

Cook, P. W. (1997). *Abused men: the hidden side of domestic violence.* Westport, CT: Praeger.

Cook, W. L. (2000). Understanding attachment security in family context. *Journal of Personality and Social Psychology, 78,* 285–294.

Cooney, T. M., & Mortimer, J. T. (1999). Family structure differences in the timing of leaving home: Exploring mediating factors. *Journal of Research on Adolescence, 9,* 367–393.

Cooper, C. R. (1998). *The weaving of maturity: Cultural perspectives on adolescent development.* New York: Oxford University Press.

Cooper, Z., & Fairburn, C. G. (2002). Cognitive-behavioral treatment of obesity. In T. A. Wadden & A. J. Stunkard (Eds.), *Handbook of obesity treatment* (3rd ed., pp. 465–479). New York: Guilford.

Cope-Farrar, K. M., & Kunkel, D. (2002). Sexual messages in teens' favorite prime-time television programs. In J. D. Brown, J. R. Steele, & K. Walsh-Childers (Eds.), *Sexual teens, sexual media* (pp. 59–78). Mahwah, NJ: Erlbaum.

Coplan, R. J., Bowker, A., & Cooper, S. M. (2003). Parenting daily hassles, child temperament, and social adjustment in preschool. *Early Childhood Research Quarterly, 18,* 376–395.

Coplan, R. J., Gavinsky-Molina, M. H., Lagace-Seguin, D., & Wichmann, C. (2001). When girls versus boys play alone: Gender differences in the associates of nonsocial play in kindergarten.

Developmental Psychology, 37, 464–474.

Coplan, R. J., Prakash, K., O'Neil, K., & Armer, M. (2004). Do you "want" to play? Distinguishing between conflicted shyness and social disinterest in early childhood. *Developmental Psychology, 40,* 244–258.

Corenblum, B. (2003). What children remember about ingroup and outgroup peers: Effects of stereotypes on children's processing of information about group members. *Journal of Experimental Child Psychology, 86,* 32–66.

Cornelius, J. R., Maisto, S. A., Pollock, N. K., Martin, C. S., Salloum, I. M., Lynch, K. G., & Clark, D. B. (2003). Rapid relapse generally follows treatment for substance use disorders among adolescents. *Addictive Behaviors, 28,* 381–386.

Cornelius, M. D., Ryan, C. M., Day, N. L., Goldschmidt, L., & Willford, J. A. (2001). Prenatal tobacco effects on neuropsychological outcomes among preadolescents. *Developmental and Behavioral Pediatrics, 22,* 217–225.

Cornelius, S. W., & Caspi, A. (1987). Everyday problem solving in adulthood and old age. *Psychology and Aging, 2,* 144–153.

Corr, C. A. (1993). Coping with dying: Lessons that we should and should not learn from the work of Elisabeth Kübler-Ross. *Death Studies, 17,* 69–83.

Corr, C. A. (2003). Loss, grief, and trauma in public tragedy. In M. Lattanzi-Licht & K. J. Doka (Eds.), *Living with grief: Coping with public tragedy* (pp. 63–76). New York: Brunner-Routledge.

Correa-Chavez, M., Rogoff, B., & Arauz, R. M. (2005). Cultural patterns in attending to two events at once. *Child Development, 76,* 664–678.

Cortese, D. A., & Smith, H. C. (2003). Mayo Clinic family health book (3rd ed.). New York: Harper-Collins.

Cosden, M., Peerson, S., & Elliott, K. (1997). Effects of prenatal drug exposure on birth outcomes and early child development. *Journal of Drug Issues, 27,* 525–539.

Costa, P. T., Jr., & McCrae, R. R. (1994). Set like plaster? Evidence for the stability of adult personality. In T. F. Heatherton & J. L. Weinberger (Eds.), *Can personality change?* (pp. 21–40). Washington, DC: American Psychological Association.

Costa, P. T., Jr., McCrae, R. R., Martin, T. A., Oryol, V. E., Senin, I. G., & Rukavishnikow, A. A. (2000). Personality development from adolescence through adulthood: Further cross-cultural comparisons of age differences. In V. J.

Molfese & D. L. Molfese (Eds.), *Temperament and personality development across the life span* (pp. 235–252). Mahwah, NJ: Erlbaum.

Costei, A. M., Kozer, E., Ho, T., Ito, S., & Koren, G. (2002). Perinatal outcome following third trimester exposure to paroxetine. *Archives of Pediatrics and Adolescent Medicine, 156,* 1129–1132.

Costello, E. J., & Angold, A. (1995). Developmental epidemiology. In D. Cicchetti & D. Cohen (Eds.), *Developmental psychopathology: Vol. 1. Theory and method* (pp. 23–56). New York: Wiley.

Costigan, C. L., Cox, M. J., & Cauce, A. M. (2003). Work–parenting linkages among dual-earner couples at the transition to parenthood. *Journal of Family Psychology, 17,* 397–408.

Costos, D., Ackerman, R., & Paradis, L. (2002). Recollections of menarche: Communication between mothers and daughters regarding menstruation. *Sex Roles, 46,* 49–59.

Côté, J. E. (2006). Emerging adulthood as an institutional moratorium. In J. J. Arnett & J. L. Tanner (Eds.), *Emerging adults in America: Coming of age in the 21st century* (pp. 85–116). Washington, DC: American Psychological Association.

Coté, S., Zoccolillo, M., Tremblay, R., Nagin, D., & Vitaro, F. (2001). Predicting girls' conduct disorder in adolescence from childhood trajectories of disruptive behaviors. *Journal of the American Academy of Child and Adolescent Psychiatry, 40,* 678–684.

Coulton, C. J., Korbin, J. E., & Su, M. (1999). Neighborhoods and child maltreatment: A multi-level study. *Child Abuse and Neglect, 23,* 1019–1040.

Council on Aging of Ottawa. (2005). *Long-term care insurance in Canada: What is it and do I need it?* Ottawa: Author. Retrieved from www.coaottawa.ca

Courage, M. L., & Howe, M. L. (1998). The ebb and flow of infant attentional preferences: Evidence for long-term recognition memory in 3-month-olds. *Journal of Experimental Child Psychology, 18,* 98–106.

Courage, M. L., & Howe, M. L. (2002). From infant to child: They dynamics of cognitive change in the second year of life. *Psychological Bulletin, 128,* 250–277.

Courchesne, E., Carper, R., & Akshoomoff, N. (2003). Evidence of brain overgrowth in the first year of life in autism. *Journal of the American Medical Association, 290,* 337–344.

Cournoyer, M., Solomon, C. R., & Trudel, M. (1998). I speak then I expect: Language and self-control in the young child at home. *Canadian Journal of Behavioural Science, 30,* 69–81.

Covington, C. Y., Nordstrom-Klee, B., Ager, J., Sokol, R., & Delaney-Black, V. (2002). Birth to age 7 growth of children prenatally exposed to drugs: A prospective cohort study. *Neurotoxicology and Teratology, 24,* 489–496.

Cowan, C. P., & Cowan, P. A. (1995). Interventions to ease the transition to parenthood: Why they are needed and what they can do. *Family Relations, 44,* 412–423.

Cowan, C. P., & Cowan, P. A. (1997). Working with couples during stressful transitions. In S. Dreman (Ed.), *The family on the threshold of the 21st century* (pp. 17–47). Mahwah, NJ: Erlbaum.

Cowan, C. P., & Cowan, P. A. (2000). Working with couples during stressful transitions. In S. Dreman (Ed.), *The family on the threshold of the 21st century* (pp. 17–47). Mahwah, NJ: Erlbaum.

Cowan, P. A., & Cowan, C. P. (2002). Interventions as tests of family systems theories: Marital and family relationships in children's development and psychopathology. *Development and Psychopathology, 14,* 731–759.

Cowan, P. A., & Cowan, C. P. (2004). From family relationships to peer rejection to antisocial behavior in middle childhood. In J. B. Kupersmidt & K. A. Dodge (Eds.), *Children's peer relations: From development to intervention* (pp. 159–177). Washington, DC: American Psychological Association.

Cox, C. E., Kotch, J. B., & Everson, M. D. (2003). A longitudinal study of modifying influences in the relationship between domestic violence and child maltreatment. *Journal of Family Violence, 18,* 5–17.

Cox, G. (2002). The Native American patient. In R. B. Gilbert (Ed.), *Health care and spirituality: Listening, assessing, caring* (pp. 107–127). Amityville, NY: Baywood.

Cox, M., & Littlejohn, K. (1995). Children's use of converging obliques in their perspective drawings. *Educational Psychology, 15,* 127–139.

Cox, M. J., Owen, M. T., Henderson, V. K., & Margand, N. A. (1992). Prediction of infant–father and infant–mother attachment. *Developmental Psychology, 28,* 474–483.

Cox, M. J., Paley, B., & Harter, K. (2001). Interparental conflict and parent–child relationships. In J. H. Grych & F. D. Fincham (Eds.),

Interparental conflict and child development: Theory, research, and applications (pp. 249–272). New York: Cambridge University Press.

Cox, S. M., Hopkins, J., & Hans, S. L. (2000). Attachment in preterm infants and their mothers: Neonatal risk status and maternal representations. *Infant Mental Health Journal, 21,* 464–480.

Crago, M. B., Annahatak, B., & Ningiuruvik, L. (1993). Changing patterns of language socialization in Inuit homes. *Anthropology and Education Quarterly, 24,* 205–223.

Craig, C. M., & Lee, D. N. (1999). Neonatal control of sucking pressure: Evidence for an intrinsic tauguide. *Experimental Brain Research, 124,* 371–382.

Craig, W. M., Pepler, D., & Atlas, R. (2000). Observations of bullying in the playground and in the classroom. *School Psychology International, 21,* 22–36.

Craig-Bray, L., Adams, G. R., & Dobson, W. R. (1988). Identity formation and social relations during late adolescence. *Journal of Youth and Adolescence, 17,* 173–187.

Craik, F. I. M., & Jacoby, L. L. (1996). Aging and memory: Implications for skilled performance. In W. A. Rogers, A. D. Fisk, & N. Walker (Eds.), *Aging and skilled performance* (pp. 113–137). Mahwah, NJ: Erlbaum.

Crain, W. (2005). *Theories of development* (5th ed.). Upper Saddle River, NJ: Prentice-Hall.

Crair, M. C., Gillespie, D. C., & Stryker, M. P. (1998). The role of visual experience in the development of columns in cat visual cortex. *Science, 279,* 566–570.

Cramer, R. E., Schaefer, J. T., & Reid, S. (2003). Identifying the ideal mate: More evidence for male–female convergence. In N. J. Pallone (Ed.), *Love, romance, sexual interaction: Research perspectives from current psychology* (pp. 61–73). New Brunswick, NJ: Transaction Publishers.

Cratty, B. J. (1986). *Perceptual and motor development in infants and children* (3rd ed.). Englewood Cliffs, NJ: Prentice-Hall.

Crawford, J. (1997). *Best evidence: Research foundations of the bilingual education act.* Washington, DC: National Clearinghouse for Bilingual Education.

Crawley, L., Payne, R., Bolden, J., Payne, T., Washington, P., & Williams, S. (2000). Palliative and end-of-life care in the African American community. *Journal of the American Medical Association, 284,* 2518–2521.

Creasey, G. (2002). Associations between working models of attachment and conflict management behavior in romantic couples. *Journal of Counseling Psychology, 49,* 365–375.

Creasey, G., & Ladd, A. (2004). Negative mood regulation expectancies and conflict behaviors in late adolescent college student romantic relationships: The moderating role of generalized attachment representations. *Journal of Research on Adolescence, 14,* 235–255.

Creasey, G. L., Jarvis, P. A., & Berk, L. E. (1998). Play and social competence. In O. N. Saracho & B. Spodek (Eds.), *Multiple perspectives on play in early childhood education* (pp. 116–143). Albany: State University of New York Press.

Crick, N. R. (1996). The role of overt aggression, relational aggression, and prosocial behavior in the prediction of children's future social adjustment. *Child Development, 67,* 2317–2327.

Crick, N. R., Casas, J. F., & Nelson, D. A. (2002). Toward a more comprehensive understanding of peer maltreatment: Studies of relational victimization. *Current Directions in Psychological Science, 11,* 98–101.

Crick, N. R., & Nelson, D. A. (2002). Relational and physical victimization within friendships: Nobody told me there'd be friends like these. *Journal of Abnormal Child Psychology, 30,* 599–607.

Cristofalo, V. J., Tresini, M., Francis, M. K., & Volker, C. (1999). Biological theories of senescence. In V. L. Bengtson & K. W. Schaie (Eds.), *Handbook of theories of aging* (pp. 98–112). New York: Springer.

Critser, G. (2003). *Fat land.* Boston: Houghton Mifflin.

Crockenberg, S., & Leerkes, E. (2000). Infant social and emotional development in family context. In C. H. Zeanah, Jr., *Handbook of infant mental health* (2nd ed., pp. 60–90). New York: Guilford.

Crockenberg, S., & Leerkes, E. (2003). Infant negative emotionality, caregiving, and family relationships. In A. C. Crouter & A. Booth (Eds.), *Children's influence on family dynamics* (pp. 57–78). Mahwah, NJ: Erlbaum.

Crohan, S. E., & Antonucci, T. C. (1989). Friends as a source of social support in old age. In R. G. Adams & R. Blieszner (Eds.), *Older adult friendship* (pp. 129–146). Newbury Park, CA: Sage.

Croninger, R. G., & Lee, V. E. (2001). Social capital and dropping out of high school: Benefits to at-risk students of teachers' support and guidance. *Teachers College Record, 103,* 548–581.

Crosby, F. J. (1998). The developing literature on developmental rela-

tionships. In A. J. Murrell, F. J. Crosby, & R. J. Ely (Eds.), *Mentoring dilemmas* (pp. 3–20). Mahwah, NJ: Erlbaum.

Crosno, R., Kirkpatrick, M., & Elder, G. H., Jr. (2004). Intergenerational bonding in school: The behavioral and contextual correlates of student–teacher relationships. *Sociology of Education, 77,* 60–81.

Cross, S., & Markus, H. (1991). Possible selves across the life span. *Human Development, 34,* 230–255.

Crouter, A. C., & Bumpass, M. F. (2001). Linking parents' work stress to children's and adolescents' psychological adjustment. *Current Directions in Psychological Science, 10,* 156–159.

Crouter, A. C., & Head, M. R. (2002). Parental monitoring and knowledge of children. In M. H. Bornstein (Ed.), *Handbook of parenting: Vol. 3. Being and becoming a parent* (2nd ed., pp. 461–483). Mahwah, NJ: Erlbaum.

Crouter, A. C., Helms-Erikson, H., Updegraff, K., & McHale, S. M. (1999). Conditions underlying parents' knowledge about children's daily lives in middle childhood: Between- and within-family comparisons. *Child Development, 70,* 246–259.

Crouter, A. C., Manke, B. A., & McHale, S. M. (1995). The family context of gender intensification in early adolescence. *Child Development, 66,* 317–329.

Cruickshanks, K. J., Tweed, T. S., Wiley, T. L., Klein, B. E. K., Klein, R., Chappell, R., Nondahl, D. M., & Dalton, D. S. (2003). The 5-year incidence and progression of hearing loss: The epidemiology of hearing loss study. *Archives of Otolaryngology—Head and Neck Surgery, 129,* 1041–1046.

Csikszentmihalyi, M. (1999). Implications of a systems perspective for the study of creativity. In R. J. Sternberg (Ed.), *Handbook of creativity* (pp. 313–335). Cambridge, UK: Cambridge University Press.

Csikszentmihalyi, M., & Nakamura, J. (2005). The role of emotions in the development of wisdom. In R. J. Sternbeerg & J. Jordan (Eds.), *A handbook of wisdom: Psychological perspectives* (pp. 220–242). New York: Cambridge University Press.

Csikszentmihalyi, M., & Rathunde, K. (1990). The psychology of wisdom: An evolutionary interpretation. In R. J. Sternberg (Ed.), *Wisdom: Its nature, origins, and development* (pp. 25–51). New York: Cambridge University Press.

Csoti, M. (2003). *School phobia, panic attacks, and anxiety in children.* London: Jessica Kingsley.

Cubbins, L. A., & Tanfer, K. (2000). The influence of gender on sex: A study of men's and women's self-reported high-risk sexual behavior. *Archives of Sexual Behavior, 29,* 229–257.

Cuddy-Casey, M., & Orvaschel, H. (1997). Children's understanding of death in relation to child suicidality and homicidality. *Clinical Psychology Review, 17,* 33–45.

Cuijpers, P. (2002). Effective ingredients of school-based drug prevention programs: A systematic review. *Addictive Behaviors, 27,* 1009–1023.

Culbertson, F. M. (1997). Depression and gender: An international review. *American Psychologist, 52,* 25–51.

Cully, J. A., LaVoie, D., & Gfeller, J. D. (2001). Reminiscence, personality, and psychological functioning in older adults. *Gerontologist, 41,* 89–95.

Culnane, M., Fowler, M. G., Lee, S. S., McSherry, G., Brady, M., & O'Donnell, K. (1999). Lack of long-term effects of in utero exposure to zidovudine among uninfected children born to HIV-infected women. *Journal of the American Medical Association, 281,* 151–157.

Cumming, E., & Henry, W. E. (1961). *Growing old: The process of disengagement.* New York: Basic Books.

Cummings, E. M., & Cummings, J. S. (2002). Parenting and attachment. In M. H. Bornstein (Ed.), *Handbook of parenting* (2nd ed., pp. 35–58). Mahwah, NJ: Erlbaum.

Cummings, E. M., & Davies, P. T. (1994). Maternal depression and child development. *Journal of Child Psychology and Psychiatry, 35,* 73–112.

Cunningham, A. E., & Stanovich, K. E. (1998, Spring/Summer). What reading does for the mind. *American Educator,* 8–15.

Cunningham, J. D., & Antill, J. K. (1994). Cohabitation and marriage: Retrospective and predictive comparisons. *Journal of Social and Personal Relationships, 11,* 77–93.

Currie, D. H. (1999). Violent men or violent women? Whose definition counts? In R. K. Bergen (Ed.), *Issues in intimate violence* (pp. 97–111). Thousand Oaks, CA: Sage.

Curtin, S. C., & Park, M. M. (1999). Trends in the attendant, place, and timing of births and in the use of obstetric interventions: United States, 1989–1997. *National Vital Statistics Report, 47*(27), 1–12.

Cutler, N. E., Whitelaw, N. A., & Beattie, B. L. (2002). *American perceptions of aging in the 21st century.* Washington, DC: National Council on the Aging.

Cutler, S. J., & Hendricks, J. (2001). Emerging social trends. In R. H. Binstock & L. K. George (Eds.), *Handbook of aging and the social sciences* (5th ed., pp. 462–480). San Diego, CA: Academic Press.

Cutrona, C. E., Hessling, R. M., Bacon, P. L., & Russell, D. W. (1998). Predictors and correlates of continuing involvement with the baby's father among adolescent mothers. *Journal of Family Psychology, 12,* 369–387.

D

Dabrowska, E. (2000). From formula to schema: The acquisition of English questions. *Cognitive Linguistics, 11,* 1–20.

D'Agostino, J. A., & Clifford, P. (1998). Neurodevelopmental consequences associated with the premature neonate. *AACN Clinical Issues, 9,* 11–24.

Dahl, R. E., & Lewin, D. S. (2002). Pathways to adolescent healthy sleep regulation and behavior. *Journal of Adolescent Health, 31,* 175–184.

Dahl, R. E., Scher, M. S., Williamson, D. E., Robles, N., & Day, N. (1995). A longitudinal study of prenatal marijuana use: Effects on sleep and arousal at age 3 years. *Archives of Pediatric and Adolescent Medicine, 149,* 145–150.

Dal Santo, J. A., Goodman, R. M., Glik, D., & Jackson, K. (2004). Childhood unintentional injuries: Factors predicting injury risk among preschoolers. *Journal of Pediatric Psychology, 29,* 273–283.

Dales, L., Hammer, S. J., & Smith, N. J. (2001). Time trends in autism and MMR immunization coverage in California. *Journal of the American Medical Association, 285,* 1183–1185.

Daley, K. C. (2004). Update on sudden infant death syndrome. *Current Opinion in Pediatrics, 16,* 227–232.

Damon, W. (1977). *The social world of the child.* San Francisco: Jossey-Bass.

Damon, W. (1988). *Self-understanding in childhood and adolescence.* New York: Cambridge University Press.

Damon, W. (1990). Self-concept, adolescent. In R. M. Lerner, A. C. Petersen, & J. Brooks-Gunn (Eds.), *The encyclopedia of adolescence* (Vol. 2, pp. 87–91). New York: Garland.

Damon, W. (1995). *Greater expectations: Overcoming the culture of indulgence in America's homes and schools.* New York: Free Press.

Damon, W., & Hart, D. (1988). *Self-understanding in childhood and adolescence.* New York: Cambridge University Press.

Dangour, A. D., Sibson, V. L., & Fletcher, A. E. (2004). Micronutrient supplementation in later life: Limited evidence for benefit. *Journal of Gerontology, 59A,* 659–673.

Daniels, D. H., Kalkman, D. L., & McCombs, B. L. (2001). Young children's perspectives on learning and teacher practices in different classroom contexts: Implications for motivation. *Early Education and Development, 12,* 253–273.

Dannefer, D. (2003). Cumulative advantage/disadvantage and the life course: Cross-fertilizing age and social science theory. *Journal of Gerontology, 58B,* P327–P337.

Dannemiller, J. L., & Stephens, B. R. (1988). A critical test of infant pattern preference models. *Child Development, 59,* 210–216.

Dapretto, M., & Bjork, E. L. (2000). The development of word retrieval abilities in the second year and its relation to early vocabulary growth. *Child Development, 71,* 635–648.

Darroch, J. E., Frost, J. J., & Singh, S. (2001). *Teenage sexual and reproductive behavior in developed countries: Can more progress be made?* New York: Alan Guttmacher Institute.

Darwin, C. (1936). *On the origin of species by means of natural selection.* New York: Modern Library. (Original work published 1859)

D'Augelli, A. R. (2002). Mental health problems among lesbian, gay, and bisexual youths ages 14 to 21. *Clinical Child Psychology and Psychiatry, 7,* 433–456.

D'Augelli, A. R. (2006). Developmental and contextual factors and mental health among lesbian, gay, and bisexual youths. In A. M. Omoto & H. S. Howard (Eds.), *Sexual orientation and mental health: Examining identity and development in lesbian, gay, and bisexual people* (pp. 37–53). Washington, DC: American Psychological Association.

Davey, A., & Eggebeen, D. J. (1998). Patterns of intergenerational exchange and mental health. *Journal of Gerontology, 53B,* P86–P95.

Davidson, R. J. (1994). Asymmetric brain function, affective style, and psychopathology: The role of early experience and plasticity. *Development and Psychopathology, 6,* 741–758.

Davies, P. A., & Lindsay, L. L. (2004). Everyday marital conflict and child aggression. *Journal of Abnormal Child Psychology, 32,* 191–202.

Daviglus, M. L., Stamler, J., Pirzada, A., Yan, L. L., Garside, D. B., & Liu, K. (2004). Favorable cardiovascular risk profile in young women and long-term risk of cardiovascular and all-cause mortality. *Journal of the American Medical Association, 292,* 1588–1592.

Davis, D. W. (2003). Cognitive outcomes in school-age children born prematurely. *Neonatal Network, 22*(3), 27–38.

Davis, H. A. (2003). Conceptualizing the role and influence of student–teacher relationships on children's social and cognitive development. *Educational Psychologist, 38,* 207–234.

Davis, H. P., Trussell, L. H., & Klebe, K. J. (2001). A ten-year longitudinal examination of repetition priming, incidental recall, free recall, and recognition in young and elderly. *Brain and Cognition, 46,* 99–104.

Davis, K. F., Parker, K. P., & Montgomery, G. L. (2004). Sleep in infants and young children. Part 1: Normal sleep. *Journal of Pediatric Health Care, 18,* 65–71.

Dawson, G., Ashman, S. B., Panagiotides, H., Hessl, D., Self, J., Yamada, E., & Embry, L. (2003). Preschool outcomes of children of depressed mothers: Role of maternal behavior, contextual risk, and children's brain activity. *Child Development, 74,* 1158–1175.

Dawson, T. L. (2002). New tools, new insights: Kohlberg's moral judgment stages revisited. *International Journal of Behavioral Development, 26,* 154–166.

Dawson-Hughes, B., Harris, S. S., Krall, E. A., Dallal, G. E., Falconer, G., & Green, C. L. (1995). Rates of bone loss in postmenopausal women randomly assigned to one of two dosages of vitamin D. *American Journal of Clinical Nutrition, 61,* 1140–1145.

Day, N. L., Leach, S. L., Richardson, G. A., Cornelius, M. D., Robles, N., & Larkby, C. (2002). Prenatal alcohol exposure predicts continued deficits in offspring size at 14 years of age. *Alcoholism: Clinical and Experimental Research, 26,* 1584–1591.

Deafness Research Foundation. (2005). Hear us: Incidence of deafness in newborns. Retrieved from www.hearinghealth.com

Deák, G. O. (2000). Hunting the fox of word learning: Why "constraints" fail to capture it. *Developmental Review, 20,* 29–80.

Deák, G. O., Ray, S. D., & Brenneman, K. (2003). Children's perseverative appearance–reality errors are related to emerging language skills. *Child Development, 74,* 944–964.

Deary, I. J. (2001). *g* and cognitive elements of information progressing: An agnostic view. In R. J. Sternberg & E. L. Grigorenko (Eds.), *The general factor of intelligence: How general is it?* (pp. 447–479). Mahwah, NJ: Erlbaum.

Deary, I. J., & Der, G. (2005). Reaction time, age, and cognitive abil-ity: Longitudinal findings from age 16 to 63 years in representative population samples. *Aging, Neuropsychology, and Cognition, 12,* 187–215.

Deater-Deckard, K., Lansford, J. E., Dodge, K. A., Pettit, G. S., & Bates, J. E. (2003). The development of attitudes about physical punishment: An 8-year longitudinal study. *Journal of Family Psychology, 17,* 351–360.

Deater-Deckard, K., Pickering, K., Dunn, J. F., & Golding, J. (1998). Family structure and depressive symptoms in men preceding and following the birth of a child. *American Journal of Psychiatry, 155,* 818–823.

Deater-Deckard, K., Pike, A., Petrill, S. A., Cutting, A. L., Hughes, C., & O'Connor, T. G. (2001). Nonshared environmental processes in social-emotional development: An observational study of identical twin differences in the preschool period. *Developmental Science, 4,* F1–F6.

DeBerry, K. M., Scarr, S., & Weinberg, R. (1996). Family racial socialization and ecological competence: Longitudinal assessments of African-American transracial adoptees. *Child Development, 67,* 2375–2399.

DeCasper, A. J., & Spence, M. J. (1986). Prenatal maternal speech influences newborns' perception of speech sounds. *Infant Behavior and Development, 9,* 133–150.

Deffenbacher, J. L. (1994). Anger reduction: Issues, assessment, and intervention strategies. In A. W. Siegman & T. W. Smith (Eds.), *Anger, hostility, and the heart* (pp. 239–269). Hillsdale, NJ: Erlbaum.

DeGarmo, D. S., & Forgatch, M. S. (1997). Determinants of observed confidant support for divorced mothers. *Journal of Personality and Social Psychology, 72,* 336–345.

de Grey, A. D. N. J. (2005). The unfortunate influence of the weather on the rate of ageing: Why human caloric restriction or its emulation may only extend life expectancy by 2–3 years. *Gerontology, 51,* 73–82.

de Haan, M., & Johnson, M. H. (2003). Mechanisms and theories of brain development. In M. de Haan & M. H. Johnson (Eds.), *The cognitive neuroscience of development* (pp. 1–18). Hove, UK: Psychology Press.

deJong, A., & Franklin, B. A. (2004). Prescribing exercise for the elderly: Current research and recommendations. *Current Sports Medicine Reports, 3,* 337–343.

Deković, M., & Buist, K. L. (2005). Multiple perspectives within the family: Family relationship pat-terns. *Journal of Family Issues, 26,* 467–490.

Deković, M., Noom, M. J., & Meeus, W. (1997). Expectations regarding development during adolescence: Parent and adolescent perceptions. *Journal of Youth and Adolescence, 26,* 253–271.

Delemarre-van de Waal, H. A. (2002). Regulation of puberty. *Best Practice and Research in Clinical Endocrinology and Metabolism, 16,* 1–12.

Delemarre-van de Waal, H. A., van Coeverden, S. C., & Rotteveel, J. (2001). Hormonal determinants of pubertal growth. *Journal of Pediatric Endocrinology and Metabolism, 14,* 1521–1526.

de Leon, M. J., Desanti, S., Zinkowski, R., Mehta, P. D., Pratico, D., & Segal, S. (2004). MRI and CSF studies in the early diagnosis of Alzheimer's disease. *Journal of Internal Medicine, 256,* 205–223.

Delgado-Gaitan, C. (1994). Socializing young children in Mexican-American families: An intergenerational perspective. In P. Greenfield & R. Cocking (Eds.), *Cross-cultural roots of minority child development* (p. 55–86). Hillsdale, NJ: Erlbaum.

De Lisi, R., & Gallagher, A. M. (1991). Understanding gender stability and constancy in Argentinean children. *Merrill-Palmer Quarterly, 37,* 483–502.

Dell, D. L. (2001). Adolescent pregnancy. In N. L. Stotland & D. E. Stewart (Eds.), *Psychological aspects of women's health care* (pp. 95–116). Washington, DC: American Psychiatric Association.

DeLoache, J. S. (1987). Rapid change in symbolic functioning of very young children. *Science, 238,* 1556–1557.

DeLoache, J. S. (2000). Dual representation and children's use of scale models. *Child Development, 71,* 329–338.

DeLoache, J. S. (2002). The symbol-mindedness of young children. In W. Hartup & R. A. Weinberg (Eds.), *Minnesota Symposia on Child Psychology* (Vol. 32, pp. 73–101). Mahwah, NJ: Erlbaum.

Demetriou, A., Christou, C., Spanoudis, G., & Platsidou, M. (2002). The development of mental processing: Efficiency, working memory, and thinking. *Monographs of the Society for Research in Child Development, 67*(1, Serial No. 268).

Demetriou, A., Efklides, A., Papadaki, M., Papantoniou, G., & Economou, A. (1993). Structure and development of causal–experimental thought: From early adolescence to youth. *Developmental Psychology, 29,* 480–497.

Demetriou, A., & Kazi, S. (2001). *Unity and modularity in the mind and the self: Studies on the relationships between self-awareness, personality, and intellectual development from childhood to adolescence.* London: Routledge.

Demetriou, A., Pachaury, A., Metallidou, Y., & Kazi, S. (1996). Universals and specificities in the structure and development of quantitative-relational throught: A cross-cultural study in Greece and India. *International Journal of Behavioral Development, 19,* 255–290.

Dempster, F. N., & Corkill, A. J. (1999). Interference and inhibition in cognition and behavior: Unifying themes for educational psychology. *Educational Psychology Review, 11,* 1–88.

Denham, S. A. (2005). Emotional competence counts: Assessment as support for school readiness. In K. Hirsh-Pasek, A. Kochanoff, N. S. Newcombe, & J. de Villiers (Eds.), Using scientific knowledge to inform preschool assessment. *Social Policy Report of the Society for Research in Child Development, 19*(No.1), 12.

Denham, S. A., Blair, K., Schmidt, M., & DeMulder, E. (2002). Compromised emotional competence: Seeds of violence sown early? *American Journal of Orthopsychiatry, 72,* 70–82.

Denham, S. A., & Burton, R. (2003). *Social and emotional prevention and intervention programming for preschoolers.* New York: Kluwer-Plenum.

Denham, S., & Kochanoff, A. T. (2002). Parental contributions to preschoolers' understanding of emotion. *Marriage and Family Review, 34,* 311–343.

Dennerstein, L., & Lehert, P. (2004). Modeling mid-aged women's sexual functioning: A prospective, population-based study. *Journal of Sex and Marriage Therapy, 30,* 173–183.

Dennerstein, L., Dudley, E., & Guthrie, J. (2002). Empty nest or revolving door? A prospective study of women's quality of life in midlife during the phase of children leaving and re-entering the home. *Psychological Medicine, 32,* 545–550.

Dennerstein, L., Lehert, P., Burger, H., & Dudley, E. (1999). Mood and the menopausal transition. *Journal of Nervous and Mental Disease, 187,* 685–691.

Denney, N. W. (1990). Adult age differences in traditional and practical problem solving. *Advances in Psychology, 72,* 329–349.

Denney, N. W., & Pearce, K A. (1989). A developmental study of practi-

cal problem solving in adults. *Psychology and Aging, 4,* 438–442.

Dennis, W. (1960). Causes of retardation among institutionalized children: Iran. *Journal of Genetic Psychology, 96,* 47–59.

Dennison, B. A., Straus, J. H., Mellits, D., & Charney, E. (1998). Childhood physical fitness tests: Predictor of adult physical activity levels? *Pediatrics, 82,* 342–350.

Dent, A., & Stewart, A. (2004). *Sudden death in childhood: Support for the bereaved family.* London: Butterworth-Heinemann.

de Pree-Geerlings, B., de Pree, I. M., & Bulk-Bunschoten, A. M. (2001). 1901–2001: 100 years of physicians of infant and toddler welfare centers in the Netherlands. *Netherlands Tijdschrift Voor Geneeskunde, 145,* 2461–2465.

De Raedt, R., & Ponjaert-Kristoffersen, I. (2000). The relationship between cognitive/neuropsychological factors and car driving performance in older adults. *Journal of the American Geriatrics Society, 48,* 1664–1668.

Derom, C., Thiery, E., Vlietinck, R., Loos, R., & Derom, R. (1996). Handedness in twins according to zygosity and chorion type: A preliminary report. *Behavior Genetics, 26,* 407–408.

DeRosier, M. E., & Thomas, J. M. (2003). Strengthening sociometric prediction: Scientific advances in the assessment of children's peer relations. *Child Development, 75,* 1379–1392.

De Schipper, J. C., Tavecchio, L. W. C., van IJzendoorn, M. H., & van Zeijl, J. (2004). Goodness-of-fit in center day care: Relations of temperament, stability, and quality of care with the child's adjustment. *Early Childhood Research Quarterly, 19,* 257–272.

De Schipper, J. C., van IJzendoorn, M. H., & Tavecchio, L. W. C. (2004). Stability in center day care: Relations with children's well-being and problem behavior in day care. *Social Development, 13,* 531–550.

Deutsch, F. M., Ruble, D. N., Fleming, A., Brooks-Gunn, J., & Stangor, C. (1988). Information-seeking and maternal self-definition during the transition to motherhood. *Journal of Personality and Social Psychology, 55,* 420–431.

Deutsch, W., & Pechmann, T. (1982). Social interaction and the development of definite descriptions. *Cognition, 11,* 159–184.

Deveson, A. (1994). *Coming of age: Twenty-one interviews about growing older.* Newham, Australia: Scribe.

de Villiers, J. G., & de Villiers, P. A. (1973). A cross-sectional study of

the acquisition of grammatical morphemes in child speech. *Journal of Psycholinguistic Research, 2,* 267–278.

de Villiers, J. G., & de Villiers, P. A. (1999). Language development. In M. H. Bornstein & M. E. Lamb (Eds.), *Developmental psychology: An advanced textbook* (4th ed., pp. 313–373). Mahwah, NJ: Erlbaum.

de Villiers, J. G., & de Villiers, P. A. (2000). Linguistic determinism and the understanding of false beliefs. In P. Metchell & K. J. Riggs (Eds.), *Children's reasoning and the mind* (pp. 87–99). Hove, UK: Psychology Press.

De Vogli, R., Mistry, R., Gnesolto, R., & Cornia, G. A. (2005). Has the relation between income inequality and life expectancy disappeared? Evidence from Italy and top industrialized countries. *Journal of Epidemiology and Community Health, 59,* 158–162.

de Vries, B., Bluck, S., & Birren, J. E. (1993). The understanding of death and dying in a life-span perspective. *Gerontologist, 33,* 366–372.

DeVries, R. (2001). Constructivist education in preschool and elementary school: The sociomoral atmosphere as the first educational goal. In S. L. Golbeck (Ed.), *Psychological perspectives on early childhood education* (pp. 153–180). Mahwah, NJ: Erlbaum.

de Waal, F. B. M. (1993). Sex differences in chimpanzee (and human) behavior: A matter of social values? In M. Hechter, L. Nadel, & R. E. Michod (Eds.), *The origin of values* (pp. 285–303). New York: Aldine de Gruyter.

De Weerd, A. W., & van den Bossche, A. S. (2003). The development of sleep during the first months of life. *Sleep Medicine Reviews, 7,* 179–191.

de Winter, M., Balledux, M., & de Mare, J. (1997). A critical evaluation of Dutch preventive child health care. *Child: Care, Health and Development, 23,* 437–446.

De Wolff, M. S., & van IJzendoorn, M. H. (1997). Sensitivity and attachment: A meta-analysis on parental antecedents of infant attachment. *Child Development, 68,* 571–591.

Dexter, E., LeVine, S., & Velasco, P. (1998). Maternal schooling and health-related language and literacy skills in rural Mexico. *Comparative Education Review, 42,* 139–162.

Diamond, A. (2000). Close interrelation of motor development and cognitive development and of the cerebellum and prefrontal cortex. *Child Development, 71,* 44–56.

Diamond, A. (2004). Normal development of prefrontal cortex from

birth to young adulthood: Cognitive functions, anatomy, and biochemistry. In D. T. Stuff & R. T. Knight (Eds.), *Principles of frontal lobe function* (pp. 466–503). New York: Oxford University Press.

Diamond, A., Cruttenden, L., & Neiderman, D. (1994). AB with multiple wells: 1. Why are multiple wells sometimes easier than two wells? 2. Memory or memory + inhibition. *Developmental Psychology, 30,* 192–205.

Diamond, A., & Taylor, C. (1996). Development of an aspect of executive control: Development of the abilities to remember what I said and to "do as I say, not as I do." *Developmental Psychobiology, 29,* 315–334.

Diamond, L. M. (1998). Development of sexual orientation among adolescent and young adult women. *Developmental Psychology, 34,* 1085–1095.

Diamond, L. M. (2003). Love matters: Romantic relationships among sexual-minority adolescents. In P. Florsheim (Ed.), *Adolescent romantic relations and sexual behavior* (pp. 85–108). Mahwah, NJ: Erlbaum.

Diamond, M., & Sigmundson, H. K. (1999). Sex reassignment at birth. In S. J. Ceci & W. M. Williams (Eds.), *The nature–nurture debate* (pp. 55–75). Malden, MA: Blackwell.

Dias, M. G., & Harris, P. (1988). The effect of make-believe play on deductive reasoning. *British Journal of Developmental Psychology, 6,* 207–221.

Dias, M. G., & Harris, P. L. (1990). The influence of the imagination on reasoning by young children. *British Journal of Developmental Psychology, 8,* 305–318.

DiCenso, A., Guyatt, G., Willan, A., & Griffith, L. (2002). Interventions to reduce unintended pregnancies among adolescents: Systematic review of randomized controlled trials. *British Medical Journal, 324,* 1426–1430.

Dick, D. M., Rose, R. J., Viken, R. J., & Kaprio, J. (2000). Pubertal timing and substance use: Associations between and within families across late adolescence. *Developmental Psychology, 36,* 180–189.

Dick, F., Dronkers, N. F., Pizzamiglio, L., Saygin, A. P., Small, S. L., Wilson, S. (2004). Language and the brain. In M. Tomasello & D. I. Slobin (Eds.), *Beyond nature–nurture: Essays in honor of Elizabeth Bates* (pp. 237–260). Mahwah, NJ: Erlbaum.

Dickerson, L. M., Mazyck, P. J., & Hunter, M. H. (2003). Premenstrual syndrome. *American Family Physician, 67,* 1743–1752.

Dickinson, D. K., & McCabe, A. (2001). Bringing it all together: The multiple origins, skills, and environmental supports of early literacy. *Learning Disabilities Research and Practice, 16,* 186–202.

Dickinson, D. K., McCabe, A., Anastasopoulos, L., Peisner-Feinberg, E. S., & Poe, M. D. (2003). The comprehensive language approach to early literacy: The interrelationships among vocabulary, phonological sensitivity, and print knowledge among preschool-age children. *Journal of Educational Psychology, 95,* 465–481.

Dick-Read, G. (1959). *Childbirth without fear.* New York: Harper & Row.

Dickson, K. L., Fogel, A., & Messinger, D. (1998). The development of emotion from a social process view. In M. F. Mascolo (Ed.), *What develops in emotional development?* (pp. 253–271). New York: Plenum.

Dickson, S. V., Collins, V. L., Simmons, D. C., & Dameenui, E. J. (1998). Metacognitive strategies: Research bases. In D. C. Simmons & E. J. Kameenui (Eds.), *What reading research tells us about children with diverse learning needs: Bases and basics* (pp. 295–360). Mahwah, NJ: Erlbaum.

Diehl, M., Coyle, N., & Labouvie-Vief, G. (1996). Age and sex differences in strategies of coping and defense across the life span. *Psychology and Aging, 11,* 127–139.

Diener, E., Gohm, C. L., Suh, E., & Oishi, S. (2000). Similarity of the relations between marital status and subjective well-being across cultures. *Journal of Cross-Cultural Psychology, 31,* 419–436.

DiLalla, L. F., Kagan, J., & Reznick, J. S. (1994). Genetic etiology of behavioral inhibition among 2-year-old children. *Infant Behavior and Development, 17,* 405–412.

Dildy, G. A., Jackson, G. M., Fowers, G. K., Oshiro, B. T., Varner, M. W., & Clark, S. L. (1996). Very advanced maternal age. Pregnancy after age 45. *American Journal of Obstetrics and Gynecology, 175,* 668–674.

Dillaway, H., & Broman, C. (2001). Race, class, and gender differences in marital satisfaction and divisions of household labor among dual-earner couples. *Journal of Family Issues, 22,* 309–327.

Dillon, M., & Wink, P. (2004). American religion, generativity, and the therapeutic culture. In E. de St. Aubin & D. P. McAdams (Eds.), *The generative society: Caring for future generations* (pp. 15–31). Washington, DC: American Psychological Association.

Dilworth-Anderson, P., Goodwin, P. Y., & Williams, S. W. (2004). Can culture help explain the physical health effects of caregiving over time among African American caregivers? *Journal of Gerontology, 59B,* S138–S145.

Ding, Q., Bruce-Keller, A. J., Chen, Q., & Keller, J. N. (2004). Analysis of gene expression in neural cells subject to chronic proteasome inhibition. *Free Radical Biology and Medicine, 36,* 445–455.

DiNitto, D. M. (2002). *Social welfare: Politics and public policy* (2nd ed.). Boston: Allyn and Bacon.

DiNitto, D. M., & Cummins, L. (2005). *Social welfare: Politics and public policy* (6th ed.). Boston: Allyn and Bacon.

Dion, K. L., & Dion, K. K. (1993). Gender and ethnocultural comparisons in styles of love. *Journal of Social Issues, 49,* 53–69.

DiPietro, J. A., Bornstein, M. H., Costigan, K. A., Pressman, E. K., Hahn, C.-S., & Painter, K. (2002). What does fetal movement predict about behavior during the first two years of life? *Developmental Psychobiology, 40,* 358–371.

DiPietro, J. A., Hodgson, D. M., Costigan, K. A., & Hilton, S. C. (1996). Fetal neurobehavioral development. *Child Development, 67,* 2553–2567.

Dirks, J. (1982). The effect of a commercial game on children's Block Design scores on the WISC–R test. *Intelligence, 6,* 109–123.

Dishion, T. J., Andrews, D. W., & Crosby, L. (1995). Antisocial boys and their friends in early adolescence: Relationship characteristics, quality, and interactional processes. *Child Development, 66,* 139–151.

DiTommaso, E., Brannen, C., & Burgess, M. (2005). The universality of relationship characteristics: A cross-cultural comparison of different types of attachment and loneliness in Canadian and visiting Chinese students. *Social Behavior and Personality, 33,* 57–68.

Dixon, L., & Browne, K. (2003). The heterogeneity of spouse abuse: A review. *Aggression and Violent Behavior, 8,* 107–130.

Dixon, R. A. (2003). Themes in the aging of intelligence: Robust decline with intriguing possibilities. In R. J. Sternberg, J. Lautrey, & T. I. Lubart (Eds.), *Models of intelligence: International perspectives* (pp. 151–167). Washington, DC: American Psychological Association.

Dixon, R. A., de Frias, C. M., & Bäckman, L. (2001). Characteristics of self-reported memory compensation in older adults. *Journal of* *Clinical and Experimental Neuropsychology, 23,* 650–661.

Doeker, B., Simic-Schleicher, A., Hauffa, B. P., & Andler, W. (1999). Psychosozialer Kleinwuchs maskiert als Wachstumshormonmangel [Psychosocially stunted growth masked as growth hormone deficiency]. *Klinisch Padiatrie, 211,* 394–398.

Doherty, G., Lero, D. S., Goelman, H., Tougas, J., & LaGrange, A. (2000). *You bet I care! Caring and learning environments: Quality in regulated family child care across Canada.* Guelph, ON: Centre for Families, Work and Well-Being, University of Guelph.

Doherty, N. N., & Hepper, P. G. (2000). Habituation in fetuses of diabetic mothers. *Early Human Development, 59,* 85–93.

Doi, M. (1991). A transformation of ritual: The Nisei 60th birthday. *Journal of Cross-Cultural Gerontology, 6,* 153–161.

Doka, K., & Martin, T. (2000). Take it like a man: Masculine response to loss. In D. A. Lund (Ed.), *Men coping with grief* (pp. 37–47). Amityville, NY: Baywood.

Dombrowski, K. J., Lantz, P. M., & Freed, G. L. (2004). Risk factors for delay in age-appropriate vaccination. *Public Health Reports, 119,* 144–155.

Donahue, M. J., & Benson, P. L. (1995). Religion and the well-being of adolescents. *Journal of Social Issues, 51,* 145–160.

Donaldson, J. F., & Graham, S. (1999). A model of college outcomes for adults. *Adult Education Quarterly, 50,* 24–40.

Donatelle, R. (2004). Health: *The basics* (6th ed.). San Francisco: Benjamin Cummings.

Dondi, M., Simion, F., & Caltran, G. (1999). Can newborns discriminate between their own cry and the cry of another newborn infant? *Developmental Psychology, 35,* 418–426.

Donnellan, M. B., Larsen-Rife, D., & Conger, R. D. (2005). Personality, family history, and competence in early adult romantic relationships. *Journal of Personality and Social Psychology, 88,* 562–576.

Donnerstein, E., Slaby, R. G., & Eron, L. D. (1994). The mass media and youth aggression. In L. D. Eron, J. H. Gentry, & P. Schlegel (Eds.), *Reason to hope: A psychosocial perspective on violence and youth* (pp. 219–250). Washington, DC: American Psychological Association.

Dornbusch, S. M., Glasgow, K. L., & Lin, I.-C. (1996). The social structure of schooling. *Annual Review of Psychology, 47,* 401–427.

Dornbusch, S. M., Ritter, P. L., Mont-Reynaud, R., & Chen, Z. (1990). Family decision making and academic performance in a diverse high school population. *Journal of Adolescent Research, 5,* 143–160.

Dorris, M. (1989). *The broken cord.* New York: Harper & Row.

Dowdney, L. (2000). Annotation: Childhood bereavement following parental death. *Journal of Child Psychology and Psychiatry and Allied Disciplines, 41,* 819–830.

Dowling. E. M., Gestsdottir, S., Anderson, P. M., von Eye, A., Almerigi, J., & Lerner, R. M. (2004). Structural relations among spirituality, religiosity, and thriving in adolescence. *Applied Developmental Psychology, 8,* 7–16.

Downs, A. C., & Fuller, M. J. (1991). Recollections of spermarche: An exploratory investigation. *Current Psychology: Research and Reviews, 10,* 93–102.

Dozier, M., Stovall, K. C., Albus, K. E., & Bates, B. (2001). Attachment for infants in foster care: The role of caregiver state of mind. *Child Development, 72,* 1467–1477.

Drabman, R. S., Cordua, G. D., Hammer, D., Jarvie, G. J., & Horton, W. (1979). Developmental trends in eating rates of normal and overweight preschool children. *Child Development, 50,* 211–216.

Drela, N., Kozdron, E., & Szczypiorski, P. (2004). Moderate exercise may attenuate some aspects of immunosenscence. *BMC Geriatrics, 4,* 8.

Drewnowski, A., & Shultz, J. M. (2001). Impact of aging on eating behaviors, food choices, nutrition, and health status. *Journal of Nutrition, Health, and Aging, 5,* 75–79.

Drotar, D., Pallotta, J., & Eckerle, D. (1994). A prospective study of family environments of children hospitalized for nonorganic failure-to-thrive. *Developmental and Behavioral Pediatrics, 15,* 78–85.

Dryburgh, H. (2001). Teenage pregnancy. *Health Reports, 12*(1), Statistics Canada, Cat. No. 82–003.

Dryer, D. C., & Horowitz, L. M. (1997). When do opposites attract? Interpersonal complementarity versus similarity. *Journal of Personality and Social Psychology, 72,* 592–603.

Dubé, E. M., Savin-Williams, R. C., & Diamond, L. M. (2001). Intimacy development, gender, and ethnicity among sexual-minority youths. In A. R. D'Augelli & C. J. Patterson (Eds.), *Lesbian, gay, and bisexual identities and youth* (pp. 129–152). New York: Oxford University Press.

DuBois, D. L., Burk-Braxton, C., Swenson, L. P., Tevendale, H. D.,

Lockerd, E. M., & Moran, B. L. (2002). Getting by with a little help from self and others: Self-esteem and social support as resources during early adolescence. *Developmental Psychology, 38,* 822–939.

DuBois, D. L., Felner, R. D., Brand, S., & George, G. R. (1999). Profiles of self-esteem in early adolescence: Identification and investigation of adaptive correlates. *American Journal of Community Psychology, 27,* 899–932.

Duckworth, A. L., & Seligman, M. E. P. (2005). Self-discipline outdoes IQ in predicting academic performance of adolescents. *Psychological Science, 12,* 939–944.

Dugan, E., & Kivett, V. R. (1998). Implementing the Adams and Blieszner conceptual model: Predicting interactive friendship processes of older adults. *Journal of Social and Personal Relationships, 15,* 607–622.

Dumas, J. A., & Hartman, M. (2003). Age differences in temporal and item memory. *Psychology and Aging, 18,* 573–586.

Duncan, G. J., & Magnuson, K. A. (2003). Off with Hollingshead: Socioeconomic resources, parenting, and child development. In M. H. Bornstein & R. H. Bradley (Eds.), *Socioeconomic status, parenting, and child development* (pp. 83–106). Mahwah, NJ: Erlbaum.

Duniz, M., Scheer, P. J., Trojovsky, A., Kaschnitz, W., Kvas, E., & Macari, S. (1996). *European Child and Adolescent Psychiatry, 5,* 93–100.

Dunn, J. (1989). Siblings and the development of social understanding in early childhood. In P. G. Zukow (Ed.), *Sibling interaction across cultures* (pp. 106–116). New York: Springer-Verlag.

Dunn, J. (1994). Temperament, siblings, and the development of relationships. In W. B. Carey & S. C. McDevitt (Eds.), *Prevention and early intervention* (pp. 50–58). New York: Brunner/Mazel.

Dunn, J. (2002). The adjustment of children in stepfamilies: Lessons from community studies. *Child and Adolescent Mental Health, 7,* 154–161.

Dunn, J. (2004). Sibling relationships. In P. K. Smith & C. H. Hart (Eds.), *Handbook of childhood social development* (pp. 223–237). Malden, MA: Blackwell.

Dunn, J., Cheng, H., O'Connor, T. G., & Bridges, L. (2004). Children's perspectives on their relationships with their nonresident fathers: Influences, outcomes and implications. *Journal of Child Psychology and Psychiatry, 45,* 553–566.

Dunn, J., Slomkowski, C., & Beardsall, L. (1994). Sibling relationships from the preschool period through middle childhood and early adolescence. *Developmental Psychology, 30,* 315–324.

Dunne, E. J., & Dunne-Maxim, K. (2004). Working with families in the aftermath of suicide. In F. Walsh & M. McGoldrick (Eds.), *Living beyond loss: Death in the family* (2nd ed., pp. 272–284). New York: Norton.

Durbin, D. L., Darling, N., Steinberg, L., & Brown, B. B. (1993). Parenting style and peer group membership among European-American adolescents. *Journal of Research on Adolescence, 3,* 87–100.

Durlak, J. A., & Riesenberg, L. A. (1991). The impact of death education. *Death Studies, 15,* 39–58.

Durrant, J., Broberg, A., & Rose-Krasnor, L. (2000). Predicting use of physical punishment during mother–child conflicts in Sweden and Canada. In P. Hastings & C. Piotrowski (Eds.), *Conflict as a context for understanding maternal beliefs about child rearing and children's misbehavior: New directions for child development.* San Francisco: Jossey-Bass.

Durston, S., Pol, H. E. H., Schnack, H. G., Buitelaar, J. K., Steenhuis, M. P., & Minderaa, R. B. (2004). Magnetic resonance imaging of boys with attention-deficit/hyperactivity disorder and their unaffected siblings. *Journal of the American Academy of Child and Adolescent Psychiatry, 43,* 332–340.

Dusek, J. B. (1987). Sex roles and adjustment. In D. B. Carter (Ed.), *Current conceptions of sex roles and sex typing* (pp. 211–222). New York: Praeger.

Dutton, D. G., Landolt, M. A., Starzomski, A., & Bodnarchuk, M. (2001). Validation of the propensity for abusiveness scale in diverse male populations. *Journal of Family Violence, 16,* 59–73.

Dweck, C. S. (2002). Messages that motivate: How praise molds students' beliefs, motivation, and performance (in surprising ways). In J. Aronson (Ed.), *Improving academic achievement: Impact of psychological factors on education* (pp. 37–60). San Diego, CA: Academic Press.

Dworkin, J. B., Larson, R., & Hansen, D. (1993). Adolescents' accounts of growth experiences in youth activities. *Journal of Youth and Adolescence, 32,* 17–26.

Dyer, C. B., Pavlik, V. N., Murphy, K. P., & Hyman, D. J. (2000). The high prevalence of depression and dementia in elder abuse and neglect. *Journal of the American Geriatrics Society, 48,* 205–208.

Dykman, R., Casey, P. H., Ackerman, P. T., & McPherson, W. B. (2001). Behavioral and cognitive status in school-aged children with a history of failure to thrive during early childhood. *Clinical Pediatrics, 40,* 63–70.

Dykstra, P. A. (1995). Loneliness among the never and formerly married: The importance of supportive friendships and a desire for independence. *Journal of Gerontology, 50B,* S321–S329.

E

Eagly, A. H., & Karau, S. J. (2002). Role congruity theory of prejudice toward female leaders. *Psychological Review, 109,* 573–598.

Eagly, A. H., & Wood, W. (1999). The origins of sex differences in human behavior: Evolved dispositions versus social roles. *American Psychologist, 54,* 408–423.

Eaker, E. D., Sullivan, L. M., Kelly-Hayes, M., D'Agostino, R. B., & Benjamin, E. J. (2004). Anger and hostility predict the development of atrial fibrillation in men in the Framingham Offspring Study. *Circulation, 109,* 1267–1271.

East, P. L., & Felice, M. E. (1996). *Adolescent pregnancy and parenting: Findings from a racially diverse sample.* Mahwah, NJ: Erlbaum.

Ebeling, K. S., & Gelman, S. A. (1994). Children's use of context in interpreting "big" and "little." *Child Development, 65,* 1178–1192.

Eberhart-Phillips, J. E., Frederick, P. D., & Baron, R. C. (1993). Measles in pregnancy: A descriptive study of 58 cases. *Obstetrics and Gynecology, 82,* 797–801.

Eccles, J. S. (2004). Schools, academic motivation, and stage–environment fit. In R. M. Lerner & L. Steinberg (Eds.), *Handbook of Adolescent Psychology* (2nd ed., pp. 125–154). Hoboken, N. J.: Wiley.

Eccles, J. S., & Harold, R. D. (1991). Gender differences in sport involvement: Applying the Eccles' expectancy-value model. *Journal of Applied Sport Psychology, 3,* 7–35.

Eccles, J. S., Jacobs, J. E., & Harold, R. D. (1990). Gender-role stereotypes, expectancy effects, and parents' role in the socialization of gender differences in self-perceptions and skill acquisition. *Journal of Social Issues, 46,* 183–201.

Eccles, J. S., Templeton, J., Barber, B., & Stone, M. (2003). Adolescence and emerging adulthood: The critical passage ways to adulthood. In M. H. Bornstein, L. Davidson, C. L. M., Keyes, K. A. Moore, & the Center for Child Well-Being (Eds.), *Well-being: Positive devel-*opment across the life course (pp. 383–406). Mahwah, NJ: Erlbaum.

Eccles, J. S., Vida, M. N., & Barber, B. (2004). The relation of early adolescents' college plans and both academic ability and task-value beliefs to subsequent college enrollment. *Journal of Early Adolescence, 24,* 63–77.

Eccles, J. S., Wigfield, A., & Schiefele, U. (1998). Motivation to succeed. In N. Eisenberg (Ed.), *Handbook of child psychology: Vol. 3. Social, emotional, and personality development* (5th ed., pp. 1017–1095). New York: Wiley.

Eckenrode, J., Zielinski, D., Smith, E., Marcynyszyn, L. A., Henderson, C. R., Jr., & Kitzman, H. (2001). Child maltreatment and the early onset of problem behaviors: Can a program of nurse home visitation break the link? *Development and Psychopathology, 13,* 873–890.

Eder, R. A., & Mangelsdorf, S. C. (1997). The emotional basis of early personality development: Implications for the emergent self-concept. In R. Hogan, J. Johnson, & S. Briggs (Eds.), *Handbook of personality psychology* (pp. 209–240). San Diego, CA: Academic Press.

Edwards, J. N., & Booth, A. (1994). Sexuality, marriage, and well-being: The middle years. In A. S. Rossi (Ed.), *Sexuality across the life course* (pp. 233–259). Chicago: University of Chicago Press.

Egan, S. K., & Perry, D. G. (2001). Gender identity: A multidimensional analysis with implications for psychosocial adjustment. *Developmental Psychology, 37,* 451–463.

Egeland, B., Jacobvitz, D., & Sroufe, L. A. (1988). Breaking the cycle of abuse. *Child Development, 59,* 1080–1088.

Eggerman, S., & Dustin, D. (1985). Death orientation and communication with the terminally ill. *Omega, 16,* 255–265.

Eichstedt, J. A., Serbin, L. A., Poulin-Dubois, D., & Sen, M. G. (2002). Of bears and men: Infants' knowledge of conventional and metaphorical gender stereotypes. *Infant Behavior and Development, 25,* 296–310.

Eiden, R. D., & Reifman, A. (1996). Effects of Brazelton demonstrations on later parenting: A meta-analysis. *Journal of Pediatric Psychology, 21,* 857–868.

Einstein, G. O., McDaniel, M. A., Manzi, M., Cochran, B., & Baker, M. (2000). Prospective memory and aging: Forgetting intentions over short delays. *Psychology and Aging, 15,* 671–683.

Einstein, G. O., Smith, R. E., McDaniel, M. A., & Shaw, P. (1997). Aging and prospective memory: The influence of increased task demands at encoding and retrieval. *Psychology and Aging, 12,* 479–488.

Eisenberg, N. (2003). Prosocial behavior, empathy, and sympathy. In M. H. Bornstein & L. Davidson (Eds.), *Well-being: Positive development across the life course* (pp. 253–265). Mahwah, NJ: Erlbaum.

Eisenberg, N. (2005). The development of empathy-related responding. In G. Carlo & C. P. Edwards (Eds.), *Moral motivation through the life span* (pp. 73–117). Lincoln, NE: University of Nebraska Press.

Eisenberg, N., & Fabes, R. A. (1998). Prosocial development. In N. Eisenberg (Ed.), *Handbook of child psychology: Vol. 3. Social, emotional, and personality development* (5th ed., pp. 701–778). New York: Wiley.

Eisenberg, N., Fabes, R. A., Murphy, B., Maszk, P., Smith, M., & Karbon, M. (1995). The role of emotionality and regulation in children's social functioning: A longitudinal study. *Child Development, 66,* 1360–1384.

Eisenberg, N., Fabes, R. A., Shepard, S. A., Murphy, B. C., Jones, S., & Guthrie, I. K. (1998). Contemporaneous and longitudinal prediction of children's sympathy from dispositional regulation and emotionality. *Developmental Psychology, 34,* 910–924.

Eisenberg, N., Gershoff, E. T., Fabes, R. A., Shepard, S. A., Cumberland, A. J., & Losoya, S. H. (2001). Mothers' emotional expressivity and children's behavior problems and social competence: Mediation through children's regulation. *Developmental Psychology, 37,* 475–490.

Eisenberg, N., & McNally, S. (1993). Socialization and mothers' and adolescents' empathy-related characteristics. *Journal of Research on Adolescence, 3,* 171–191.

Eisenberg, N., & Morris, A. S. (2002). Children's emotion-related regulation. In R. Kail (Ed.), *Advances in child development and behavior* (Vol. 30, pp. 190–229). San Diego, CA: Elsevier.

Eisenberg, N., & Spinrad, T. L. (2004). Emotion-related regulation: Sharpening the definition. *Child Development, 75,* 334–339.

Ekman, P. (2003). *Emotions revealed.* New York: Times Books.

Ekman, P., & Friesen, W. (1972). Constants across culture in the face of emotion. *Journal of Personality and Social Psychology, 17,* 124–129.

Elder, G. H. Jr. (1998). The life course and human development. In R. M. Lerner (Ed.), *Handbook of child psychology: Vol. 1. Theoretical models of human development* (5th ed., pp. 939–991). New York: Wiley.

Elder, G. H., Jr. (1999). *Children of the Great Depression* (25th anniversary ed.). Boulder, CO: Westview.

Elder, G. H., Jr., & Caspi, A. (1988). Human development and social change: An emerging perspective on the life course. In N. Bolger, A. Caspi, G. Downey, & M. Moorehouse (Eds.), *Persons in context: Developmental processes* (pp. 77–113). Cambridge, UK: Cambridge University Press.

Elder, G. H., Jr., & Conger, R. (2000). *Children of the land: Adversity and success in rural America.* Chicago: University of Chicago Press.

Elder, G. H., Jr., & Hareven, T. K. (1993). Rising above life's disadvantage: From the Great Depression to war. In G. H. Elder, Jr., J. Modell, & R. D. Parke (Eds.), *Children in time and place* (pp. 47–72). Cambridge, UK: Cambridge University Press.

Elder, G. H., Jr., Liker, J. K., & Cross, C. E. (1984). Parent–child behavior in the Great Depression: Life course and intergenerational influences. In P. B. Baltes & O. G. Brim (Eds.), *Life-span development and behavior* (Vol. 6, pp. 109–158). New York: Academic Press.

Elder, G. H., Jr., Nguyen, T. V., & Caspi, A. (1985). Linking family hardship to children's lives. *Child Development, 56,* 361–375.

Elfenbein, D. S., & Felice, M. E. (2003). Adolescent pregnancy. *Pediatric Clinics of North America, 50,* 781–800.

Eliakim, A., Friedland, O., Kowen, G., Wolach, B., & Nemet, D. (2004). Parental obesity and higher pre-intervention BMI reduce the likelihood of a multidisciplinary childhood obesity program to succeed: A clinical observation. *Journal of Pediatric Endocrinology and Metabolism, 17,* 1055–1061.

Elias, C. L., & Berk, L. E. (2002). Self-regulation in young children: Is there a role for sociodramatic play? *Early Childhood Research Quarterly, 17,* 1–17.

Elicker, J., Englund, M., & Sroufe, L. A. (1992). Predicting peer competence and peer-relationships in childhood from early parent–child relationships. In R. D. Parke & G. W. Ladd (Eds.), *Family–peer relationships: Modes of linkage* (pp. 77–106). Hillsdale, NJ: Erlbaum.

Elkind, D. (1994). *A sympathetic understanding of the child: Birth to sixteen* (3rd ed.). Boston: Allyn and Bacon.

Elkind, D., & Bowen, R. (1979). Imaginary audience behavior in children and adolescents. *Developmental Psychology, 15,* 33–44.

Ellingson, S., & Fuller, J. D. (2001). A good death? Finding a balance between the interests of patients and caregivers. In M. B. Holstein & P. B. Mitzen (Eds.), *Ethics in community-based elder care* (pp. 200–207). New York: Springer.

Elliott, D., & Tolan, P. (1999). Youth violence prevention, intervention, and social policy: An overview. In D. J. Flannery & C. R. Huff (Eds.), *Youth violence: Prevention, intervention, and social policy* (pp. 3–45). Washington, DC: American Psychiatric Press.

Elliott, D. S., Wilson, W. J., Huizinga, D., Sampson, R. J., Elliott, A., & Rankin, B. (1996). The effects of neighborhood disadvantage on adolescent development. *Journal of Research in Crime and Delinquency, 33,* 389–426.

Elliott, J. G. (1999). School refusal: Issues of conceptualization, assessment, and treatment. *Journal of Child Psychology and Psychiatry and Allied Disciplines, 40,* 1001–1012.

Ellis, B. J., Bates, J. E., Dodge, K. A., Fergusson, D. M., Horwood, L. J., Pettit, G. S., & Woodward, L. (2003). Does father absence place daughters at special risk for early sexual activity and teenage pregnancy? *Child Development, 74,* 801–821.

Ellis, B. J., & Garber, J. (2000). Psychosocial antecedents of variation in girls' pubertal timing: Maternal depression, stepfather presence, and marital and family stress. *Child Development, 71,* 485–501.

Ellis, B. J., McFadyen-Ketchum, S., Dodge, K. A., Pettit, G. S., & Bates, J. E. (1999). Quality of early family relationships and individual differences in the timing of pubertal maturation in girls: A longitudinal test of an evolutionary model. *Journal of Personality and Social Psychology, 77,* 933–952.

Ellis, L., & Bonin, S. L. (2003). Genetics and occupation-related preferences: Evidence from adoptive and non-adoptive families. *Personality and Individual Differences, 35,* 929–937.

Elman, J. L. (2001). Connectionism and language acquisition. In M. Tomasello & E. Bates (Eds.), *Language development* (pp. 295–306). Oxford, UK: Blackwell.

El-Sheikh, M., Cummings, E. M., & Reiter, S. (1996). Preschoolers' responses to ongoing interadult conflict: The role of prior exposure to resolved versus unresolved arguments. *Journal of Abnormal Child Psychology, 24,* 665–679.

Eltzschig, H. K., Lieberman, E. S., & Camann, W. R. (2003). Regional anesthesia and analgesia for labor and delivery. *New England Journal of Medicine, 384,* 319–332.

Ely, R. (2005). Language development in the school years. In J. B. Gleason (Ed.), *The development of language* (6th ed., pp. 395–443). Boston: Allyn and Bacon.

Emanuel, E. J., Fairclough, D. L., & Emanuel, L. L. (2000). Attitudes and desires related to euthanasia and physician-assisted suicide among terminally ill patients and their caregivers. *Journal of the American Medical Association, 284,* 2460–2468.

Emde, R. N., Plomin, R., Robinson, J., Corley, R., DeFries, J., Fulker, D. W., Reznick, J. S., Campos, J., Kagan, J., & Zahn-Waxler, C. (1992). Temperament, emotion, and cognition at fourteen months: The MacArthur Longitudinal Twin Study. *Child Development, 63,* 1437–1455.

Emery, R. E. (2001). Interparental conflict and social policy. In J. H. Grych & F. D. Fincham (2001). *Interparental conflict and child development: Theory, research, and applications* (pp. 417–439). New York: Cambridge University Press.

Emery, R. E., & Laumann-Billings, L. (1998). An overview of the nature, causes, and consequences of abusive family relationships: Toward differentiating maltreatment and violence. *American Psychologist, 53,* 121–135.

Emory, E. K., Schlackman, L. J., & Fiano, K. (1996). Drug–hormone interactions on neurobehavioral responses in human neonates. *Infant Behavior and Development, 19,* 213–220.

Engen, T. (1982). *The perception of odors.* New York: Academic Press.

Entwisle, D. R., Alexander, K. L., & Olson, L. S. (2005). First grade and educational attainment by age 22: A new story. *American Journal of Sociology, 110,* 1458–1502.

Epstein, J. L. (2001). *School, family, and community partnerships: Preparing educators and improving schools.* Bolder, CO: Westview.

Epstein, J. L., & Sanders, M. G. (2002). Family, school, and community partnerships. In M. H. Bornstein (Ed.), *Handbook of parenting: Vol. 5* (2nd ed., pp. 407–437). Mahwah, NJ: Erlbaum.

Epstein, L. H., Roemmich, J. N., & Raynor, H. A. (2001). Behavioral therapy in the treatment of pediatric obesity. *Pediatric Clinics of North America, 48,* 981–983.

Erden, F., & Wolfgang, C. H. (2004). An exploration of the differences in prekindergarten, kindergarten, and first-grade teachers' beliefs related to discipline when dealing with male and female students. *Early Child Development and Care, 174,* 3–11.

Erikson, E. H. (1950). *Childhood and society*. New York: Norton.

Erikson, E. H. (1964). *Insight and responsibility*. New York: Norton.

Erikson, E. H. (1968). *Identity, youth, and crisis*. New York: Norton.

Erikson, E. H. (1998). *The life cycle completed. Extended version with new chapters on the ninth stage by Joan M. Erikson*. New York: Norton.

Ernst, M., Moolchan, E. T., & Robinson, M. L. (2001). Behavioral and neural consequences of prenatal exposure to nicotine. *Journal of the American Academy of Child and Adolescent Psychiatry, 40*, 630–641.

Esmail, N., & Walker, M. (2005). *How good is Canadian health care? 2005 report*. Vancouver: Fraser Institute.

Espiritu, D. A. V., Rashid, H., Mast, B. T., Fitzgerald, J., Steinberg, J., & Lichtenberg, P. A. (2001). Depression, cognitive impairment and function in Alzheimer's disease. *International Journal of Geriatric Psychiatry, 16*, 1098–1103.

Espy, K. A., Molfese, V. J., & DiLalla, L. F. (2001). Effects of environmental measures on intelligence in young children: Growth curve modeling of longitudinal data. *Merrill-Palmer Quarterly, 47*, 42–73.

Esterberg, K. G., Moen, P., & Dempster-McClain, D. (1994). Transition to divorce: A life-course approach to women's marital duration and dissolution. *Sociological Quarterly, 35*, 289–307.

Ethier, K. A., Kershaw, T., Niccolai, L., Lewis, J. B., & Ickovics, J. R. (2003). Adolescent women underestimate their susceptibility to sexually transmitted infections. *Sexually Transmitted Infections, 79*, 408–411.

Evans, B. J., & Rowlands, G. (2004). Correctable visual impairment in older people: A major unmet need. *Ophthalmic and Physiological Optics, 24*, 161–180.

Evans, G. W. (2004). The environment of child poverty. *American Psychologist, 59*, 77–92.

Evans, G. W., & Kantrowitz, E. (2002). Socioeconomic status and health: The potential role of environmental risk exposure. *Annual Review of Public Health, 23*, 303–331.

Evans, G. W., Maxwell, L. E., & Hart, B. (1999). Parental language and verbal responsiveness to children in crowded homes. *Developmental Psychology, 35*, 1020–1023.

Evans, R. M., Emsley, C. L., Gao, S., Sahota, A., Farlow, M. R., & Hendrie, H. C. (2000). Serum cholesterol, ApoE gene type and the risk of Alzheimer's disease: A population-based study of African Americans. *Neurology, 54*, 95–99.

Everman, D. B., & Cassidy, S. B. (2000). Genetics of childhood disorders: XII. Genomic imprinting: Breaking the rules. *Journal of the American Academy of Child and Adolescent Psychiatry, 38*, 386–389.

F

Fabes, R. A., Eisenberg, N., Hanish, L. D., & Spinrad, T. L. (2001). Preschoolers' spontaneous emotion vocabulary: Relations to likeability. *Early Education and Development, 12*, 11–27.

Fabes, R. A., Eisenberg, N., McCormick, S. E., & Wilson, M. S. (1988). Preschoolers' attributions of the situational determinants of others' naturally occurring emotions. *Developmental Psychology, 24*, 376–385.

Fabes, R. A., Martin, C. L., & Hanish, L. D. (2003). Young children's play qualities in same-, other-, and mixed-sex peer groups. *Child Development, 74*, 921–932.

Fagan, J. F., III. (1973). Infants' delayed recognition memory and forgetting. *Journal of Experimental Child Psychology, 16*, 424–450.

Fagard, J., & Pezé, A. (1997). Age changes in interlimb coupling and the development of bimanual coordination. *Journal of Motor Behavior, 29*, 199–208.

Fagot, B. I. (1984). The child's expectations of differences in adult male and female interactions. *Sex Roles, 11*, 593–600.

Fagot, B. I. (1985). Changes in thinking about early sex role development. *Developmental Review, 5*, 83–98.

Fagot, B. I., & Hagan, R. I. (1991). Observations of parent reactions to sex-stereotyped behaviors: Age and sex effects. *Child Development, 62*, 617–628.

Fagot, B. I., & Leinbach, M. D. (1989). The young child's gender schema: Environmental input, internal organization. *Child Development, 60*, 663–672.

Fagot, B. I., Leinbach, M. D., & O'Boyle, C. (1992). Gender labeling, gender stereotyping, and parenting behaviors. *Developmental Psychology, 28*, 225–230.

Fahrmeier, E. D. (1978). The development of concrete operations among the Hausa. *Journal of Cross-Cultural Psychology, 9*, 23–44.

Fairburn, C. G. (2005). Evidence-based treatment of anorexia nervosa. *International Journal of Eating Disorders, 37*, S26–S30.

Fairburn, C. G., & Harrison, P. J. (2003). Eating disorders. *Lancet, 361*, 407–416.

Fajardo, M., & Di Cesare, P. E. (2005). Disease-modifying therapies for osteoarthritis. *Drugs and Aging, 22*, 141–161.

Falbo, T. (1992). Social norms and the one-child family: Clinical and policy implications. In F. Boer & J. Dunn (Eds.), *Children's sibling relationships* (pp. 71–82). Hillsdale, NJ: Erlbaum.

Falbo, T., & Poston, D. L., Jr. (1993). The academic, personality, and physical outcomes of only children in China. *Child Development, 64*, 18–35.

Falbo, T., Poston, D. L., Jr., Triscari, R. S., & Zhang, X. (1997). Self-enhancing illusions among Chinese schoolchildren. *Journal of Cross-Cultural Psychology, 28*, 172–191.

Family Caregiver Alliance. (2002). *Fact sheet: Selected caregiver statistics*. Retrieved from www.nlm.nih.gov/medlineplus/caregivers.html

Family Caregiver Alliance. (2005). *Fact sheet: Selected caregiver statistics*. Retrieved from www.caregiver.org/factsheets/selected_caregiver_statisticsC.html

Fanslow, C. A. (1981). Death: A natural facet of the life continuum. In D. Krieger (Ed.), *Foundations for holistic health nursing practices: The renaissance nurse* (pp. 249–272). Philadelphia: Lippincott.

Fantz, R. L. (1961, May). The origin of form perception. *Scientific American, 204* (5), 66–72.

Farrant, K., & Reese, E. (2000). Maternal style and children's participation in reminiscing: Stepping stones in children's autobiological memory development. *Journal of Cognition and Development, 1*, 193–225.

Farrer, L. A., Bowirrat, A., Friedland, R. P., Waraska, K., Korczyn, A. D., & Baldwin, C. T. (2003). Identification of multiple loci for Alzheimer disease in a consanguineous Israeli-Arab community. *Human Molecular Genetics, 12*, 415–422.

Farrington, D. P. (2004). Conduct disorder, aggression, and delinquency. In R. M. Lerner & L. Steinberg (Eds.), *Handbook of adolescent psychology* (2nd ed., pp. 627–664). New York: Wiley.

Farrington, D. P., & Loeber, R. (2000). Epidemiology of juvenile violence. *Juvenile Violence, 9*, 733–748.

Farver, J. M., & Branstetter, W. H. (1994). Preschoolers' prosocial responses to their peers' distress. *Developmental Psychology, 30*, 334–341.

Farver, J. M., Kim, Y. K., & Lee, Y. (1995). Cultural differences in Korean- and Anglo-American preschoolers' social interaction and play behaviors. *Child Development, 66*, 1088–1099.

Farver, J., & Wimbarti, S. (1995). Indonesian toddlers' social play with their mothers and older siblings. *Child Development, 66*, 1493–1503.

Fashola, O. S., & Slavin, R. E. (1998). Effective dropout prevention and college attendance programs for students placed at risk. *Journal of Education for Students Placed at Risk, 3*, 159–183.

Fasig, L. G. (2000). Toddlers' understanding of ownership: Implications for self-concept development. *Social Development, 9*, 370–382.

Fasouliotis, S. J., & Schenker, J. G. (2000). Ethics and assisted reproduction. *European Journal of Obstetrics, Gynecology, and Reproductive Biology, 90*, 171–180.

Fattibene, P., Mazzei, F., Nuccetelli, C., & Risica, S. (1999). Prenatal exposure to ionizing radiation: Sources, effects, and regulatory aspects. *Acta Paediatrica, 88*, 693–702.

Federal Interagency Forum on Child and Family Statistics. (2005). *America's children: Key national indicators of well-being: 2005*. Washington, DC: U.S. Government Printing Office.

Federenko, I. S., & Wadhwa, P. D. (2004). Women's mental health during pregnancy influences fetal and infant developmental and health outcomes. *CNS Spectrums, 9*, 198–206.

Federico, M. J., & Liu, A. H. (2003). Overcoming childhood asthma disparities of the inner-city poor. *Pediatric Clinics of North America, 50*, 655–675.

Feeney, J. A. (1998). Adult attachment and relationship-centered anxiety: Responses to physical and emotional distancing. In J. A. Simpson & W. S. Rholes (Eds.), *Attachment theory and close relationships* (pp. 189–218). New York: Guilford.

Feeney, J. A. (1999). Adult romantic attachment and couple relationships. In J. Cassidy & P. R. Shaver (Eds.), *Handbook of attachment* (pp. 355–377). New York: Guilford.

Feeney, J. A., Hohaus, L., Noller, P., & Alexander, R. P. (2001). *Becoming parents: Exploring the bonds between mothers, fathers, and their infants*. New York: Cambridge University Press.

Fehr, B. (1994). Prototype based assessment of laypeoples' views of love. *Personal Relationships, 1*, 309–331.

Feinberg, M. E., McHale, S. M., Crouter, A. C., & Cumsille, P. (2003). Sibling differentiation: Sibling and parent relationship trajectories in adolescence. *Child Development, 74*, 1261–1274.

Feinsilver, S. H. (2003). Sleep in the elderly: What is normal? *Clinical Geriatric Medicine, 19,* 177–188.

Feiring, C., & Taska, L. S. (1996). Family self-concept: Ideas on its meaning. In B. Bracken (Ed.), *Handbook of self-concept* (pp. 317–373). New York: Wiley.

Feiring, C., Taska, L., & Lewis, M. (1999). Age and gender differences in children's and adolescents' adaptation to sexual abuse. *Child Abuse and Neglect, 23,* 115–128.

Feldkámper, M., & Schaeffel, F. (2003). Interactions of genes and environment in myopia. *Developmental Ophthalmology, 37,* 34–49.

Feldman, D. H. (1999). The development of creativity. In R. J. Sternberg (Ed.), *Handbook of creativity* (pp. 169–186). Cambridge, UK: Cambridge University Press.

Feldman, P. J., & Steptoe, A. (2004). How neighborhoods and physical functioning are related: The roles of neighborhood socioeconomic status, perceived neighborhood strain, and individual health risk factors. *Annals of Behavioral Medicine, 27,* 91–99.

Feldman, R. (2002). Parents' convergence on sharing marital satisfaction, father involvement, and parent–child relationship in the transition to parenthood. *Infant Mental Health Journal, 21,* 171–191.

Feldman, R. (2003). Infant–mother and infant–father synchrony: The coregulation of positive arousal. *Infant Mental Health Journal, 24,* 1–23.

Feldman, R., & Eidelman, A. I. (2003). Skin-to-skin contact (kangaroo care) accelerates autonomic and neurobehavioral maturation in preterm infants. *Developmental Medicine and Child Neurology, 45,* 274–281.

Feldman, R., Eidelman, A. R., & Rotenberg, N. (2004). Parenting stress, infant emotion regulation, maternal sensitivity, and the cognitive development of triplets: A model for parent and child influences in a unique ecology. *Child Development, 75,* 1774–1791.

Feldman, R., Eidelman, A., Sirota, L., & Weller, A. (2002). Comparison of skin-to-skin (kangaroo) and traditional care: Parenting outcomes and preterm infant development. *Pediatrics, 110,* 16–26.

Feldman, R., & Klein, P. S. (2003). Toddlers' self-regulated compliance to mothers, caregivers, and fathers: Implications for theories of socialization. *Developmental Psychology, 39,* 680–692.

Feldman, R., Sussman, A. L., & Zigler, E. (2004). Parental leave and work adaptation at the transition to parenthood: Individual, marital, and social correlates. *Applied Developmental Psychology, 25,* 459–479.

Feldman, R., Weller, A., Sirota, L., & Eidelman, A. I. (2003). Testing a family intervention hypothesis: The contribution of mother–infant skin-to-skin contact (kangaroo care) to family interaction, proximity, and touch. *Journal of Family Psychology, 17,* 94–107.

Felner, R. D., Favazza, A., Shim, M., Brand, S., Gu, K., & Noonan, N. (2002). Whole school improvement and restructuring as prevention and promotion: Lessons from STEP and the Project on High Performance Learning Communities. *Journal of School Psychology, 39,* 177–202.

Felsman, D. E., & Blustein, D. L. (1999). The role of peer relatedness in late adolescent career development. *Journal of Vocational Behavior, 54,* 279–295.

Feng, Q. (2005). Postnatal consequences of prenatal cocaine exposure and myocardial apoptosis: Does cocaine in utero imperil the adult heart? *British Journal of Pharmacology, 144,* 887–888.

Fennema, E., Carpenter, T. P., Jacobs, V. R., Franke, M. L., & Levi, L. W. (1998). A longitudinal study of gender differences in young children's mathematical thinking. *Educational Researcher, 27,* 6–11.

Fenson, L., Dale, P. S., Reznick, J. S., Bates, E., Thal, D. J., & Pethick, S. J. (1994). Variability in early communicative development. *Monographs of the Society for Research in Child Development, 59*(5, Serial No. 242).

Fergus, M. A. (1995, March 19). 99 years and . . . a joy to be around. *The Pantagraph,* pp. C1–C2.

Ferguson, T. J., Stegge, H., & Damhuis, I. (1991). Children's understanding of guilt and shame. *Child Development, 62,* 827–839.

Ferguson, T. J., Stegge, H., Miller, E. R., & Olsen, M. E. (1999). Guilt, shame, and symptoms in children. *Developmental Psychology, 35,* 347–357.

Fergusson, D. M., & Horwood, J. (2003). Resilience to childhood adversity: Results of a 21-year study. In S. S. Luthar (Ed.), *Resilience and vulnerability* (pp. 130–155). New York: Cambridge University Press.

Fergusson, D. M., & Woodward, L. J. (1999). Breast-feeding and later psychosocial adjustment. *Paediatric and Perinatal Epidemiology, 13,* 144–157.

Fergusson, D. M., Woodward, L. J., & Horwood, L. J. (2000). Risk factors and life processes associated with the onset of suicidal behaviour during adolescence and early adulthood. *Psychological Medicine, 30,* 23–39.

Fernald, A., Taeschner, T., Dunn, J., Papousek, M., Boyssen-Bardies, B., & Fukui, I. (1989). A cross-language study of prosodic modifications in mothers' and fathers' speech to preverbal infants. *Journal of Child Language, 16,* 477–502.

Fernald, L. C., & Grantham-McGregor, S. M. (1998). Stress response in school-age children who have been growth-retarded since early childhood. *American Journal of Clinical Nutrition, 68,* 691–698.

Ficca, G., Fagioli, I., Giganti, F., & Salzarulo, P. (1999). Spontaneous awakenings from sleep in the first year of life. *Early Human Development, 55,* 219–228.

Fickling, D. (2004). A happy ending? *Lancet, 364,* 831–832.

Field, D. (1997). "Looking back, what period of your life brought you the most satisfaction?" *International Journal of Aging and Human Development, 45,* 169–194.

Field, D. (1999). Stability of older women's friendships: A commentary on Roberto. *International Journal of Aging and Human Development, 48,* 81–83.

Field, D., & Millsap, R. E. (1991). Personality in advanced old age: Continuity or change? *Journal of Gerontology, 46,* 299–308.

Field, T. (2001). Massage therapy facilitates weight gain in preterm infants. *Current Directions in Psychological Science, 10,* 51–54.

Field, T., Hernandez-Reif, M., & Freedman, J. (2004). Stimulation programs for preterm infants. *Social Policy Report of the Society for Research in Child Development, 18*(1).

Field, T. M. (1998). Massage therapy effects. *American Psychologist, 53,* 1270–1281.

Field, T. M., Woodson, R., Greenberg, R., & Cohen, D. (1982). Discrimination and imitation of facial expressions by neonates. *Science, 218,* 179–181.

Finchum, T., & Weber, J. A. (2000). Applying continuity theory to elder adult friendships. *Journal of Aging and Identity, 5,* 159–168.

Fingerhut, L. S., & Christoffel, K. K. (2002). Firearm-related death and injury among children and adolescents. *Future of Children, 12,* 25–37.

Fingerman, K. L. (1996). Sources of tension in the aging mother and adult daughter relationship. *Psychology and Aging, 11,* 591–606.

Fingerman, K. L. (1998). The good, the bad, and the worrisome: Emotional complexities in grandparents' experiences with individual grandchildren. *Family Relations, 47,* 403–414.

Fingerman, K. L. (2000). "We had a nice little chat": Age and generational differences in mothers' and daughters' descriptions of enjoyable visits. *Journal of Gerontology, 55B,* P95–P106.

Fingerman, K. L. (2001a). A distant closeness: Intimacy between parents and their children in later life. *Generations, 25,* 26–33.

Fingerman, K. L. (2001b). *Aging mothers and their adult daughters: A study in mixed emotions.* New York: Springer.

Fingerman, K. L. (2004). The role of offspring and in-laws in grandparents' ties to their grandchildren. *Journal of Family Issues, 25,* 1026–1049.

Fingerman, K. L., & Birditt, K. S. (2003). Do we get better at picking our battles? Age group differences in descriptions of behavioral reactions to interpersonal tensions. *Journal of Gerontology, 60B,* P121–P128.

Finn, J. D., Pannozzo, G. M., & Achilles, C. M. (2003). The "why's" of class size: Student behavior in small classes. *Review of Educational Research, 73,* 321–368.

Finnilä, K., Mahlberga, N., Santtilia, P., & Niemib, P. (2003). Validity of a test of children's suggestibility for predicting responses to two interview situations differing in degree of suggestiveness. *Journal of Experimental Child Psychology, 85,* 32–49.

Fins, A. I., & Wohlgemuth, W. K. (2001). Sleep disorders in children and adolescents. In H. Orvaschel & J. Faust (Eds.), *Handbook of conceptualization and treatment of child psychopathology* (pp. 437–448). Amsterdam: Pergamon.

Firestone, R. W. (1994). Psychological defenses against death anxiety. In R. A. Neimeyer (Ed.), *Death anxiety handbook* (pp. 217–241). Washington, DC: Taylor & Francis.

Fisch, H., Hyun, G., Golden, R., Hensle, T. W., Olsson, C. A., & Liberson, G. L. (2003). The influence of paternal age on Down syndrome. *Journal of Urology, 169,* 2275–2278.

Fisch, S. M., Truglio, R. T., & Cole, C. F. (1999). The impact of *Sesame Street* on preschool children: A review and synthesis of 30 years' research. *Media Psychology, 1,* 165–190.

Fischer, K., & Bidell, T. (1991). Constraining nativist inferences about cognitive capacities. In S. Carey & R. Gelman (Eds.), *The epigenesis of mind: Essays on biology and cognition* (pp. 199–235). Hillsdale, NJ: Erlbaum.

Fischer, K. W., & Bidell, T. R. (1998). Dynamic development of psychological structures in action and thought. In R. M. Lerner (Ed.), *Handbook of child psychology: Vol. 1. Theoretical models of human development* (5th ed., pp. 467–562). New York: Wiley.

Fischman, M. G., Moore, J. B., & Steele, K. H. (1992). Children's one-hand catching as a function of age, gender, and ball location. *Research Quarterly for Exercise and Sport, 63,* 349–355.

Fisher, C. B. (1993, Winter). Integrating science and ethics in research with high-risk children and youth. *Social Policy Report of the Society for Research in Child Development, 4*(4).

Fisher, J. O., Rolls, B. J., & Birch, L. L. (2003). Children's bite size and intake of an entrée are greater with large portions than with age-appropriate or self-selected portions. *American Journal of Clinical Nutrition, 77,* 1164–1170.

Fisher, M., Barkley, R. A., Smallish, L., & Fletcher, K. (2002). Young adult follow-up of hyperactive children: Self-reported psychiatric disorders, comorbidity, and the role of childhood conduct problems and teen CD. *Journal of Abnormal Child Psychology, 39,* 463–475.

FitzGerald, D. P., & White, K. J. (2003). Linking children's social worlds: Perspective-taking in parent–child and peer contexts. *Social Behavior and Personality, 31,* 509–522.

Fitzgibbons, P. J., & Gordon-Salant, S. (1998). Auditory temporal order perception in younger and older adults. *Journal of Speech, Language, and Hearing Research, 41,* 1052–1060.

Fitzpatrick, J., & Sollie, D. L. (1999). Influence of individual and interpersonal factors on satisfaction and stability in romantic relationships. *Personal Relationships, 6,* 337–350.

Fivaz-Depeursinge, E., & Corboz-Warnery, A. (1999). *The primary triangle: A developmental systems view of mothers, fathers, and infants.* New York: Basic Books.

Fivush, R., & Reese, E. (2002). Reminiscing and relating: The development of parent–child talk about the past. In J. D. Webster & B. K. Haight (Eds.), *Critical advances in reminiscence work: From theory to application* (pp. 109–122). New York: Springer.

Flake, A. W. (2003). Surgery in the human fetus: The future. *Journal of Physiology, 547,* 45–51.

Flaks, D. K., Ficher, I., Masterpasqua, F., & Joseph, G. (1995). Lesbians choosing motherhood: A comparative study of lesbian and heterosexual parents and their children. *Developmental Psychology, 31,* 105–114.

Flanagan, C. A., & Faison, N. (2001). Youth civic development: Implications of research for social policy and programs. *Social Policy Report of the Society for Research in Child Development, 15*(1).

Flanagan, C. A., & Tucker, C. J. (1999). Adolescents' explanations for political issues: Concordance with their views of self and society. *Developmental Psychology, 35,* 1198–1209.

Flannery, D. J., Hussey, D. L., Biebelhausen, L., & Wester, K. L. (2003). Crime, delinquency, and youth gangs. In G. R. Adams & M. D. Berzonsky (Eds.), *Blackwell handbook of adolescence* (pp. 502–522). Malden, MA: Blackwell.

Flannery, K. A., & Liederman, J. (1995). Is there really a syndrome involving the co-occurrence of neurodevelopmental disorder, talent, non–right handedness and immune disorder among children? *Cortex, 31,* 503–515.

Flavell, J. H., Flavell, E. R., & Green, F. L. (2001). Development of children's understanding of connections between thinking and feeling. *Psychological Science, 12,* 430–432.

Flavell, J. H., Green, F. L., & Flavell, E. R. (1987). Development of knowledge about the appearance–reality distinction. *Monographs of the Society for Research in Child Development, 51*(1, Serial No. 212).

Flavell, J. H., Green, F. L., & Flavell, E. R. (1993). Children's understanding of the stream of consciousness. *Child Development, 64,* 387–398.

Flavell, J. H., Green, F. L., & Flavell, E. R. (1995). Young children's knowledge about thinking. *Monographs of the Society for Research in Child Development, 60*(1, Serial No. 243).

Flegal, K. M., Graubard, B. I., Williamson, D. F., & Gail, M. H. (2005). Excess deaths associated with underweight, overweight, and obesity. *Journal of the American Medical Association, 293,* 1861–1867.

Fleischman, D. A., Wilson, R. S., Gabrieli, J. D. E., Bienias, J. L., & Bennett, D. A. (2004). A longitudinal study of implicit and explicit memory in old persons. *Psychology and Aging, 19,* 617–625.

Fleming, J. I. (2000). Death, dying, and euthanasia: Australia versus the Northern Territory. *Issues in Law and Medicine, 15,* 291–305.

Fletcher, A. C., Nickerson, P., & Wright, K. L. (2003). Structured leisure activities in middle childhood: Links to well-being. *Journal of Community Psychology, 31,* 641–659.

Flippen, C., & Tienda, M. (2000). Pathways to retirement: Patterns of labor force participation and labor market exit among the pre-retirement population by race, Hispanic origins, and sex. *Journal of Gerontology, 55B,* S14–S27.

Floccia, C., Christophe, A., & Bertoncini, J. (1997). High-amplitude sucking and newborns: The quest for underlying mechanisms. *Journal of Experimental Child Psychology, 64,* 175–198.

Flom, R., & Pick, A. D. (2003). Verbal encouragement and joint attention in 18-month-old infants. *Infant Behavior and Development, 26,* 121–134.

Flood, D. G., & Coleman, P. D. (1988). Cell type heterogeneity of changes in dendritic extent in the hippocampal region of the human brain in normal aging and in Alzheimer's disease. In T. L. Petit & G. O. Ivy (Ed.), *Neural plasticity: A lifespan approach* (pp. 265–281). New York: Alan R. Liss.

Florian, V., & Kravetz, S. (1985). Children's concepts of death: A cross-cultural comparison among Muslims, Druze, Christians, and Jews in Israel. *Journal of Cross-Cultural Psychology, 16,* 174–179.

Florian, V., & Mikulincer, M. (1998). Symbolic immortality and the management of the terror of death: The moderating role of attachment style. *Journal of Personality and Social Psychology, 74,* 725–734.

Florian, V., Mikulincer, M., & Taubman, O. (1995). Does hardiness contribute to mental health during a stressful real-life situation? The roles of appraisal and coping. *Journal of Personality and Social Psychology, 68,* 687–695.

Florsheim, P., & Smith, A. (2005). Expectant adolescent couples' relations and subsequent parenting behavior. *Infant Mental Health Journal, 26,* 533–548.

Flouri, E., & Buchanan, A. (2004). Early father's and mother's involvement and child's later educational outcomes. *British Journal of Educational Psychology, 74,* 141–153.

Flynn, J. R. (1999). Searching for justice: The discovery of IQ gains over time. *American Psychologist, 54,* 5–20.

Flynn, J. R. (2003). Movies about intelligence: The limitations of g. *Current Directions in Psychological Science, 12,* 95–99.

Focus on the Family Canada. (2004). Substance abuse: What every family should know. Retrieved from www.fotf.ca/familyfacts/analysis/010902.html

Fogel, A. (1993). *Developing through relationships: Origins of communi-cation, self and culture.* New York: Harvester Wheatsheaf.

Fomon, S. J., & Nelson, S. E. (2002). Body composition of the male and female reference infants. *Annual Review of Nutrition, 22,* 1–17.

Fonda, S. J., Clipp, E. C., & Maddox, G. L. (2002). Patterns in functioning among residents of an affordable assisted living housing facility. *Gerontologist, 42,* 178–187.

Forgatch, M. S., Patterson, G. R., & Ray, J. A. (1996). Divorce and boys' adjustment problems: Two paths with a single model. In E. M. Hetherington (Ed.), *Stress, coping, and resiliency in children and the family* (pp. 67–105). Hillsdale, NJ: Erlbaum.

Forste, R., & Heaton, T. B. (2004). The divorce generation: Well-being, family attitudes, and socioeconomic consequences of marital disruption. *Journal of Divorce and Remarriage, 42,* 95–114.

Fotinatos-Ventouratos, R., & Cooper, C. L. (1998). Social class differences and occupational stress. *International Journal of Stress Management, 5,* 211–222.

Fowden, A. L., Giussani, D. A., & Forhead, A. J. (2005). Endocrine and metabolic programming during intrauterine development. *Early Human Development, 81,* 723–734.

Fowler, J. W. (1981). *Stages of faith.* San Francisco: Harper & Row.

Fowles, D. C., & Kochanska, G. (2000). Temperament as a moderator of pathways to conscience in children: The contribution of electrodermal activity. *Psychophysiology, 37,* 788–795.

Fox, M., Gibbs, M., & Auerbach, D. (1985). Age and gender dimensions of friendship. *Psychology of Women Quarterly, 9,* 489–501.

Fox, N. A. (1991). If it's not left, it's right: Electroencephalograph asymmetry and the development of emotion. *American Psychologist, 46,* 863–872.

Fox, N. A., & Calkins, S. D. (2003). The development of self-control of emotion: Intrinsic and extrinsic influences. *Motivation and Emotion, 27,* 7–26.

Fox, N. A., & Davidson, R. J. (1986). Taste-elicited changes in facial signs of emotion and the asymmetry of brain electrical activity in newborn infants. *Neuropsychologia, 24,* 417–422.

Foy, J. G., & Mann, V. (2003). Home literacy environment and phonological awareness in preschool children: Differential effects for rhyme and phoneme awareness. *Applied Psycholinguistics, 24,* 59–88.

Fozard, J. L., & Gordon-Salant, S. (2001). Changes in vision and hearing with aging. In J. E. Birren & K. W. Schaie (Eds.), *Handbook of the psychology of aging* (pp. 241–266). San Diego: Academic Press.

Framo, J. L. (1994). The family life cycle: Impressions. *Contemporary Family Therapy, 16,* 87–117.

Franco, M. C., Danias, A. P., Akamine, E. H., Kawamoto, E. M., Fortes, Z. B., Scavone, C., Tostes, R. C., Carvalho, M. H., & Nigro, D. (2002). Enhanced oxidative stress as a potential mechanism underlying the programming of hypertension in utero. *Journal of Cardiovascular Pharmacology, 40,* 501–509.

Franco, P., Chabanski, S., Szliwowski, H., Dramaiz, M., & Kahn, A. (2000). Influence of maternal smoking on autonomic nervous system in healthy infants. *Pediatric Research, 47,* 215–220.

Frank, D. A., Rose-Jacobs, R., Beeghly, M., Wilbur, M., Bellinger, D., & Cabral, H. (2005). Level of prenatal cocaine exposure and 48-month IQ: Importance of preschool enrichment. *Neurotoxicology and Teratology, 27,* 15–28.

Franklin, M. (1995). The effects of differential college environments on academic learning and student perceptions of cognitive development. *Research in Higher Education, 36,* 127–153.

Frazier, L. D. (2002). Perceptions of control over health: Implications for sense of self in healthy and ill older adults. In S. P. Shohov (Ed.), *Advances in psychology research* (Vol. 10, pp. 145–163). Huntington, NY: Nova Science Publishers.

Frederickson, B. L., & Carstensen, L. L. (1990). Relationship classification using grade of membership analysis: A typology of sibling relationships in later life. *Journal of Gerontology, 45,* S43–S51.

Frederiksen-Goldsen, K. I., & Sharlach, A. E. (2000). *Families and work: New directions in the twenty-first century.* New York: Oxford University Press.

Fredricks, J. A., & Eccles, J. S. (2002). Children's competence and value beliefs from childhood through adolescence: Growth trajectories in two male-sex-typed domains. *Developmental Psychology, 38,* 519–533.

Freedman-Doan, C., Wigfield, A., Eccles, J. S., Blumenfeld, P., Arbreton, A., & Harold, R. D. (2000). What am I best at? Grade and gender differences in children's beliefs about ability improvement. *Journal of Applied Developmental Psychology, 21,* 379–402.

Freeman, C. E. (2004). *Trends in educational equity of girls and women: 2004.* U.S. Department of Education, National Center for Educa-

tion Statistics. Washington, DC: U.S. Government Printing Office.

Freeman, D. (1983). *Margaret Mead and Samoa: The making and unmaking of an anthropological myth.* Cambridge, MA: Harvard University Press.

Freeman, E. W., & Halbreich, U. (1998). Premenstrual syndromes. *Psychopharmacological Bulletin, 34,* 291–295.

Freeman, L., Caserta, M., Lund, D., Rossa, S., Dowdy, A., & Partenheimer, A. (2006). Music thanatology: Prescriptive harp music as palliative care for the dying patient. *American Journal of Hospice and Palliative Care, 23,* 100–104.

Freiman, A., Bird, G., Metelitsa, A. I., Barankin, B., & Lauzon, G. J. (2004). Cutaneous effects of smoking. *Journal of Cutaneous Medicine and Surgery, 8,* 415–423.

Freud, A. (1969). Adolescence as a developmental disturbance. In G. Caplan & S. Lebovici (Eds.), *Adolescence* (pp. 5–10). New York: Basic Books.

Freud, S. (1973). *An outline of psychoanalysis.* London: Hogarth. (Original work published 1938)

Freud, S. (1974). *The ego and the id.* London: Hogarth. (Original work published 1923)

Freund, A. M., & Baltes, P. B. (1998). Selection, optimization, and compensation as strategies of life management: Correlations with subjective indicators of successful aging. *Psychology and Aging, 13,* 531–543.

Freund, A. M., & Baltes, P. B. (2000). The orchestration of selection, optimization and compensation: An action-theoretical conceptualization of a theory of developmental regulation. In W. J. Perrig & A. Grob (Eds.), *Control of human behavior, mental processes, and consciousness* (pp. 35–58). Mahwah, NJ: Erlbaum.

Freund, A. M., & Smith, J. (1999). Content and function of the self-definition in old and very old age. *Journal of Gerontology, 54B,* P55–P67.

Fried, L. P., Ferrucci, L., Darer, J., Williamson, J. D., & Anderson, G. (2004). Untangling the concepts of disability, frailty, and comorbidity: Implications for improved targeting and care. *Journal of Gerontology, 59A,* B255–B263.

Fried, P. A. (1993). Prenatal exposure to tobacco and marijuana: Effects during pregnancy, infancy, and early childhood. *Clinical Obstetrics and Gynecology, 36,* 319–337.

Fried, P. A., Watkinson, B., & Gray, R. (2003). Differential effects on cognitive functioning in 13- to 16-year-olds prenatally exposed to

cigarettes and marijuana. *Neurotoxicology and Teratology, 25,* 427–436.

Friedman, D. S. (2006, January). Understanding who is at high risk of having glaucoma. *Gleams,* pp. 1–2. Retrieved from www.umm.edu/patiented/articles/who_gets_glaucoma_000025_5.htm

Friedman, E. M., & Lawrence, D. A. (2002). Environmental stress mediates changes in neuroimmunological interactions. *Toxicological Sciences, 67,* 4–10.

Friedman, J. M. (1996). *The effects of drugs on the fetus and nursing infant: A handbook for health care professionals.* Baltimore: Johns Hopkins University Press.

Friedman, S. L., & Scholnick, E. K. (1997). An evolving "blueprint" for planning: Psychological requirements, task characteristics, and social–cultural influences. In S. L. Friedman & E. K. Scholnick (Eds.), *The developmental psychology of planning: Why, how, and when do we plan?* (pp. 3–22). Mahwah, NJ: Erlbaum.

Friedrich, W. N., Grambusch, P., Damon, L., & Hewitt, S. K. (2001). Child sexual behavior inventory: Normative and clinical comparisons. *Child Maltreatment, 6,* 37–49.

Fries, J. F. (2003). Measuring and monitoring success in compressing morbidity. *Annals of Internal Medicine, 139,* 455–459.

Frijda, N. (2000). The psychologist's point of view. In M. Lewis & J. M. Haviland-Jones (Eds.), *Handbook of emotions* (pp. 59–74). New York: Guilford.

Frith, L. (2001). Gamete donation and anonymity: The ethical and legal debate. *Human Reproduction, 16,* 818–824.

Frith, U. (2003). *Autism: Explaining the enigma* (2nd ed.). Malden, MA: Blackwell.

Fry, C. L. (1985). Culture, behavior, and aging in the comparative perspective. In J. E. Birren & K. W. Schaie (Eds.), *Handbook of the psychology of aging* (2nd ed., pp. 216–244). New York: Van Nostrand Reinhold.

Fry, C., Dickerson-Putman, J., Draper, P., Ikels, C., Keith, J., Glascock, A. P., & Harpending, H. C. (1997). Culture and the meaning of a good old age. In J. Sokolovsky (Ed.), *The cultural context of aging: Worldwide perspectives* (2nd ed., pp. 99–124). New York: Bergin & Garvey.

Fry, P. M. (1995). Individual differences in reminiscence among older adults: Predictors of frequency and pleasantness ratings of reminiscence activity. In J. Hendricks (Ed.), *The meaning of remi-*

niscence and life review (pp. 83–97). Amityville, NY: Baywood.

Fry, P. M. (2001). Predictors of health-related quality of life perspectives, self-esteem, and life satisfactions of older adults following spousal loss: An 18-month follow-up study of widows and widowers. *Gerontologist, 41,* 787–798.

Fry, P. S. (2003). Perceived self-efficacy domains as predictors of fear of the unknown and fear of dying among older adults. *Psychology and Aging, 18,* 474–486.

Fuchs, D., Fuchs, L. S., Mathes, P. G., Martinez, E. A. (2002a). Preliminary evidence on the standing of students with learning disabilities in PALS and No-PALS classrooms. *Learning Disabilities Research and Practice, 17,* 205–215.

Fuchs, L. S., Fuchs, D., Yazkian, L., & Powell, S. R. (2002b). Enhancing first-grade children's mathematical development with peer-assisted learning strategies. *School Psychology Review, 31,* 569–583.

Fuh, M.-H., Wang, S.-J., Wang, P.-H., & Fuh, J.-L. (2005). Attitudes toward menopause among middle-aged women: A community survey in an island of Taiwan. *Maturitas, 52,* 348–355.

Fukunaga, A., Uematsu, H., & Sugimoto, K. (2005). Influences of aging on taste perception and oral somatic sensation. *Journal of Gerontology, 60A,* 109–113.

Fulhan, J., Collier, S., & Duggan, C. (2003). Update on pediatric nutrition: Breastfeeding, infant nutrition, and growth. *Current Opinion in Pediatrics, 15,* 323–332.

Fuligni, A. J. (1997). The academic achievement of adolescents from immigrant families: The roles of family background, attitudes, and behavior. *Child Development, 68,* 261–273.

Fuligni, A. J. (1998). The adjustment of children from immigrant families. *Current Directions in Psychological Science, 7,* 99–103.

Fuligni, A. J. (2001). A comparative longitudinal approach to acculturation among children from immigrant families. *Harvard Educational Review, 71,* 566–578.

Fuligni, A. J., Yip, T., & Tseng, V. (2002). The impact of family obligation on the daily activities and psychological well-being of Chinese-American adolescents. *Child Development, 73,* 302–314.

Fuligni, A. J., & Yoshikawa, H. (2003). Socioeconomic resources, parenting, and child development among immigrant families. In M. H. Bornstein & R. H. Bradley (Eds.), *Socioeconomic status, parenting, and child development* (pp. 107–124). Mahwah, NJ: Erlbaum.

Fuller-Thomson, E. (2005). Canadian First Nations grandparents

inequity. *Journal of Social Issues, 61,* 321–342.

Gartstein, M. A., & Rothbart, M. K. (2003). Studying infant temperament via the revised infant behavior questionnaire. *Infant Behavior and Development, 26,* 64–86.

Gartstein, M. A., Slobodskaya, H. R., & Kinsht, I. A. (2003). Cross-cultural differences in temperament in the first year of life: United States of America (U.S.) and Russia. *International Journal of Behavioral Development, 27,* 316–328.

Gasden, V. (1999). Black families in intergenerational and cultural perspective. In M. E. Lamb (Ed.), *Parenting and child development in "nontraditional" families* (pp. 221–246). Mahwah, NJ: Erlbaum.

Gaskins, S. (1999). Children's daily lives in a Mayan village: A case study of culturally constructed roles and activities. In R. Göncü (Ed.), *Children's engagement in the world: Sociocultural perspectives* (pp. 25–61). Cambridge, UK: Cambridge University Press.

Gaskins, S. (2000). Children's daily activities in a Mayan village: A culturally grounded description. *Cross-Cultural Research, 34,* 375–389.

Gathercole, S. E., Adams, A.-M., & Hitch, G. (1994). Do young children rehearse? An individual-differences analysis. *Memory and Cognition, 22,* 201–207.

Gathercole, V., Sebastián, E., & Soto, P. (1999). The early acquisition of Spanish verb morphology: Across-the-board or piecemeal knowledge? *International Journal of Bilingualism, 3,* 133–182.

Gatz, M., Bengtson, V. L., & Blum, M. J. (1990). Caregiving families. In J. E. Birren & K. W. Schaie (Eds.), *Handbook of the psychology of aging* (3rd ed., pp. 404–426). San Diego, CA: Academic Press.

Gatz, M., Kasl-Godley, J. E., & Karel, M. J. (1996). Aging and mental disorders. In J. E. Birren & K. W. Schaie (Eds.), *Handbook of the psychology of aging* (pp. 365–382). Sand Diego: Academic Press.

Gauvain, M. (2004). Bringing culture into relief: Cultural contributions to the development of children's planning skills. In R. V. Kail (Ed.), *Advances in child development and behavior* (pp. 39–71). San Diego, CA: Elsevier.

Gauvain, M., de la Ossa, J. L., & Hurtado-Ortiz, M. T. (2001). Parental guidance as children learn to use cultural tools: The case of pictorial plans. *Cognitive Development, 16,* 551–575.

Gauvain, M., & Huard, R. D. (1999). Family interaction, parenting style, and the development of planning: A longitudinal analysis

using archival data. *Journal of Family Psychology, 13,* 75–92.

Gauvain, M., & Rogoff, B. (1989). Ways of speaking about space: The development of children's skill in communicating spatial knowledge. *Cognitive Development, 4,* 295–307.

Gavin, J., Scott, A., & Duffield, J. (2005). *Internet dating more successful than thought.* Retrieved from www.sciencedaily.com/releases/2005/02/050218125144.htm

Gayle, B. M., Preiss, R. W., & Allen, M. (2002). A meta-analytic interpretation of nonintimate interpersonal conflict. In M. Allen & R. W. Preiss (Eds.), *Interpersonal communication research: Advances through meta-analysis* (pp. 345–368). Mahwah, NJ: Erlbaum.

Gazzaley, A. H., & D'Esposito, M. (2005). BOLD functional MRI and cognitive aging. In R. Cabeza, L. Nyberg, & D. Park (Eds.), *Cognitive neuroscience of aging: Linking cognitive and cerebral aging* (pp. 107–131). New York: Oxford University Press.

Ge, X., Brody, G. H., Conger, R. D., Simons, R. L., & Murry, V. (2002). Contextual amplification of the effects of pubertal transition on African American children's deviant peer affiliation and externalized behavioral problems. *Developmental Psychology, 38,* 42–54.

Ge, X., Conger, R. D., & Elder, G. H., Jr. (1996). Coming of age too early: Pubertal influences on girls' vulnerability to psychological distress. *Child Development, 67,* 3386–3400.

Ge, X., Conger, R. D., & Elder, G. H., Jr. (2001). The relation between puberty and psychological distress in adolescent boys. *Journal of Research on Adolescence, 11,* 49–70.

Ge, X., Kim, I. J., Brody, G. H., Conger, R. D., & Simons, R. L. (2003). It's about timing and change: Pubertal transition effects on symptoms of major depression among African American youths. *Developmental Psychology, 39,* 430–439.

Geary, D. C. (1999). Evolution and developmental sex differences. *Current Directions in Psychological Science, 8,* 115–120.

Geary, D. C., Bow-Thomas, C. C., Liu, F., & Siegler, R. S. (1996). Development of arithmetical competencies in Chinese and American children: Influence of age, language, and schooling. *Child Development, 67,* 2022–2044.

Gee, C. B., & Rhodes, J. E. (2003). Adolescent mothers' relationship with their children's biological

fathers: Social support, social strain, and relationship continuity. *Journal of Family Psychology, 17,* 370–383.

Geerlings, S. W., Beekman, A. T. F., Deeg, D. J. H., Twisk, J. W. R., & van Tilburg, W. (2001). The longitudinal effect of depression on functional limitations and disability in older adults: An eight-wave prospective community-based study. *Psychological Medicine, 31,* 1361–1371.

Gelfand, D. E. (1994). *Aging and ethnicity.* New York: Springer.

Gelman, R. (1972). Logical capacity of very young children: Number invariance rules. *Child Development, 43,* 75–90.

Gelman, R., & Shatz, M. (1978). Appropriate speech adjustments: The operation of conversational constraints on talk to two-year-olds. In M. Lewis & L. A. Rosenblum (Eds.), *Interaction, conversation, and the development of language* (pp. 27–61). New York: Wiley.

Gelman, S. A., Coley, J. D., Rosengren, K. S., Hartman, E., & Pappas, A. (1998). Beyond labeling: The role of maternal input in the acquisition of richly structured categories. *Monographs of the Society for Research in Child Development, 63*(1, Serial No. 253).

Gelman, S. A., & Koenig, M. A. (2003). Theory-based categorization in early childhood. In D. H. Rakison & L. M. Oakes (Eds.), *Early category and concept development* (pp. 330–359). New York: Oxford University Press.

Gelman, S. A., & Opfer, J. E. (2002). Development of the animate–inanimate distinction. In U. Goswami (Ed.), *Blackwell handbook of childhood cognitive development* (pp. 151–166). Malden, MA: Blackwell.

Gelman, S. A., Taylor, M. G., & Nguyen, S. P. (2004). Mother–child conversations about gender. *Monographs of the Society for Research in Child Development, 69*(1, Serial No. 275), pp. 1–127.

Genesee, F. (2001). Portrait of the bilingual child. In V. Cook (Ed.), *Portraits of the second language user* (pp. 170–196). Clevedon, UK: Multilingual Matters.

Gennitian, L. A., & Morris, P. A. (2003). The effects of time limits and make-work-pay strategies on the well-being of children: Experimental evidence from two welfare reform programs. *Children and Youth Services Review, 25,* 17–54.

George, S. A. (2002). The menopause experience: A woman's perspective. *Journal of Obstetric, Gynecologic, and Neonatal Nursing, 31,* 71–85.

Gerardi-Caulton, G. (2000). Sensitivity to spatial conflict and the development of self-regulation in children 24–36 months of age. *Developmental Science, 3,* 397–404.

Gergely, G., Bekkering, H., & Király, I. (2003). Rational imitation in preverbal infants. *Nature, 415,* 755.

Gergely, G., & Watson, J. (1999). Early socio-emotional development: Contingency perception and the social-biofeedback model. In P. Rochat (Ed.), *Early social cognition: Understanding others in the first months of life* (pp. 101–136). Mahwah, NJ: Erlbaum.

Germino, B. B. (2003). Dying at home. In I. Corless, B. B. Germino, & M. A. Pittman (Eds.), *Dying, death, and bereavement: A challenge for the living* (pp. 105–116). New York: Springer.

Gershoff, E. T. (2002a). Corporal punishment by parents and associated child behaviors and experiences: A meta-analytic and theoretical review. *Psychological Bulletin, 128,* 539–579.

Gershoff, E. T. (2002b). Corporal punishment, physical abuse, and the burden of proof: Reply to Baumrind, Larzelere, and Cowan (2002), Holden (2002), and Parke (2002). *Psychological Bulletin, 128,* 602–611.

Gershoff-Stowe, L., & Smith, L. B. (1997). A curvilinear trend in naming errors as a function of early vocabulary growth. *Cognitive Psychology, 34,* 37–71.

Gerten, K. A., Coonrod, D. V., Bay, R. C., & Chambliss, L. R. (2005). Cesarean delivery and respiratory distress syndrome: Does labor make a difference? *American Journal of Obstetrics and Gynecology, 193,* 1061–1064.

Gertner, S., Greenbaum, C. W., Sadeh, A., Dolfin, Z., Sirota, L., & Ben-Nun, Y. (2002). Sleep-wake patterns in preterm infants and 6 month's home environment: Implications for early cognitive development. *Early Human Development, 68,* 93–102.

Geschwind, D. H., Boone, K. B., Miller, B. L., & Swerdloff, R. S. (2000). Neurobehavioral phenotype of Klinefelter syndrome. *Mental Retardation and Developmental Disabilities Research Reviews, 6,* 107–116.

Gesell, A. (1933). Maturation and patterning of behavior. In C. Murchison (Ed.), *A handbook of child psychology.* Worcester, MA: Clark University Press.

Gessert, C. E., Curry, N. M., & Robinson, A. (2001). Ethnicity and end-of-life care: The use of feeding tubes. *Ethnicity and Disease, 11,* 97–106.

Gest, S. D., Graham-Bermann, S. A., & Hartup, W. W. (2001). Peer experience: Common and unique features of number of friendships, social network, centrality, and socioeconomic status. *Social Development, 10,* 23–40.

Geurts, H. M., Verte, S., Oosterlaan, J., Roeyers, H., Sergeant, J. A., & Geurts, H. M. (2004). How specific are executive functioning deficits in attention-deficit hyperactivity disorder and autism? *Journal of Child Psychology and Psychiatry, 45,* 836–854.

Ghim, H. R. (1990). Evidence for perceptual organization in infants: Perception of subjective contours by young infants. *Infant Behavior and Development, 13,* 221–248.

Giarrusso, R., Feng, D., Silverstein, M., & Bengtson, V. L. (2001). Grandparent–adult grandchild affection and consensus. *Journal of Family Issues, 22,* 456–477.

Gibbons, R., Dugaiczyk, L. J., Girke, T., Duistermars, B., Zielinski, R., & Dugaiczyk, A. (2004). Distinguishing humans from great apes with AluYb8 repeats. *Journal of Molecular Biology, 339,* 721–729.

Gibbs, J. C. (1991). Toward an integration of Kohlberg's and Hoffman's theories of morality. In W. M. Kurtines & J. L. Gewirtz (Eds.), *Handbook of moral behavior and development* (Vol. 1, pp. 183–222). Hillsdale, NJ: Erlbaum.

Gibbs, J. C. (2003). *Moral development and reality: Beyond the theories of Kohlberg and Hoffman.* Thousand Oaks, CA: Sage.

Gibbs, J. C., Basinger, K. S., & Grime, R. L. (2005, August). Cross-cultural research using the SRM–SF. In J. Comunian (Chair), *Cross-cultural research on morality using different assessment instruments.* Symposium conducted at the meeting of the American Psychological Association, Washington, DC.

Gibson, E. J. (1970). The development of perception as an adaptive process. *American Scientist, 58,* 98–107.

Gibson, E. J. (2000). Perceptual learning in development: Some basic concepts. *Ecological Psychology, 12,* 295–302.

Gibson, E. J. (2003). The world is so full of a number of things: On specification and perceptual learning. *Ecological Psychology, 15,* 283–287.

Gibson, E. J., & Walk, R. D. (1960). The "visual cliff." *Scientific American, 202,* 64–71.

Gibson, J. J. (1979). *The ecological approach to visual perception.* Boston: Houghton Mifflin.

Giedd, J. N., Blumenthal, J., Jeffries, N. O., Castellanos, F. X., Liu, H., & Zijdenbos, A. (1999). Brain development during childhood and adolescence: A longitudinal MRI study. *Nature Neuroscience, 2,* 861–863.

Gilbert, L. A., & Brownson, C. (1998). Current perspectives on women's multiple roles. *Journal of Career Assessment, 6,* 433–448.

Gillies, R. M. (2003). The behaviors, interactions, and perceptions of junior high school students during small-group learning. *Journal of Educational Psychology, 95,* 137–147.

Gillies, R. M., & Ashman, A. F. (1996). Teaching collaborative skills to primary school children in classroom-based workgroups. *Learning and Instruction, 6,* 187–200.

Gilligan, C. F. (1982). *In a different voice.* Cambridge, MA: Harvard University Press.

Gilliom, M., Shaw, D. S., Beck, J. E., Schonberg, M. A., & Lukon, J. L. (2002). Anger regulation in disadvantaged preschool boys: Strategies, antecedents, and the development of self-control. *Developmental Psychology, 38,* 222–235.

Ginsburg, H. P. (1997). *Entering the child's mind: The clinical interview in psychological research and practice.* New York: Cambridge University Press.

Gitlin, L. N., Belle, S. H., Burgio, L. D., Szaja, S. J., Mahoney, D., & Gallagher-Thompson, D. (2003). Effect of multicomponent interventions on caregiver burden and depression: the REACH multisite initiative at 6-month follow-up. *Psychology and Aging, 18,* 361–374.

Giuliani, A., Schöll, W. M., Basver, A., & Tasmussino, K. F. (2002). Mode of delivery and outcome of 699 term singleton breech deliveries at a single center. *American Journal of Obstetrics and Gynaecology, 187,* 1649–1698.

Gladwell, M. (1998, February 2). The Pima paradox. *The New Yorker,* pp. 44–57.

Glasgow, K. L., Dornbusch, S. M., Troyer, L., Steinberg, L., & Ritter, P. L. (1997). Parenting styles, adolescents' attributions, and educational outcomes in nine heterogeneous high schools. *Child Development, 68,* 507–523.

Gleitman, L. R., & Newport, E. (1996). *The invention of language by children.* Cambridge, MA: MIT Press.

Glowinski, A. L., Madden, P. A. F., Bucholz, K. K., Lynskey, M. T., & Heath, A. C. (2003). Genetic epidemiology of self-reported lifetime DSM-IV major depressive disorder in a population-based twin sample of female adolescents. *Journal of Child Psychology and Psychiatry and Allied Disciplines, 44,* 988–996.

Gluckman, P. D., Sizonenko, S. V., & Bassett, N. S. (1999). The transition from fetus to neonate—an endocrine perspective. *Acta Paediatrica Supplement, 88*(428), 7–11.

Gluhoski, V. L., & Wortman, C. B. (1996). The impact of trauma on world views. *Journal of Social and Clinical Psychology, 15,* 417–429.

Gnepp, J. (1983). Children's social sensitivity: Inferring emotions from conflicting cues. *Developmental Psychology, 19,* 805–814.

Godfrey, K. M., & Barker, D. J. (2000). Fetal nutrition and adult disease. *American Journal of Clinical Nutrition, 71,* 1344S–1352S.

Godfrey, K. M., & Barker, D. J. (2001). Fetal programming and adult health. *Public Health Nutrition, 4,* 611–624.

Godkin, M., Krant, M., & Doster, N. (1984). The impact of hospice care on families. *International Journal of Psychiatry in Medicine, 13,* 153–165.

Goelman, H., Doherty, G., Lero, D., LaGrange, A., & Tougas, J. (2000). *You bet I care! Caring and learning environments: Quality in child care centers across Canada.* Guelph, Ontario: Centre for Families, Work and Well-Being, University of Guelph.

Goering, J. (Ed.). (2003). *Choosing a better life? How public housing tenants selected a HUD experiment to improve their lives and those of their children: The Moving to Opportunity Demonstration Program.* Washington, DC: Urban Institute Press.

Goetz, T., Frenzel, A. C., Pekrun, R., & Hall, N. (2005). Emotional intelligence in the context of learning and achievement. In R. Schulze & R. D. Roberts (Eds.), *Emotional intelligence: An international handbook* (pp. 233–253). Göttingen, Germany: Hogrefe & Huber.

Gogate, L. J., & Bahrick, L. E. (2001). Intersensory redundancy and 7-month-old infants' memory for arbitrary syllable–object relations. *Infancy, 2,* 219–231.

Gohdes, D. M., Balamurugan, A., Larsen, B. A., & Maylahn, C. (2005). Age-related eye diseases: An emerging challenge for public health professionals. *Public Health Research, Practice, and Policy, 2,* 1545–1551.

Gold, D. T. (1996). Continuities and discontinuities in sibling relationships across the life span. In V. L. Bengtson (Ed.), *Adulthood and aging: Research on continuities and discontinuities* (pp. 228–243). New York: Springer.

Gold, P. E., Cahill, L., & Wenk, G. L. (2002). Ginkgo biloba: A cognitive enhancer? *Psychological Science in the Public Interest, 3,* 3–11.

Goldbaum, S., Craig, W. M., Pepler, D., & Connolly, J. (2003). Developmental trajectories of victimization: Identifying risk and protective factors. *Journal of Applied School Psychology, 19,* 139–156.

Goldberg, A. E., & Perry-Jenkins, M. (2003). Division of labor and working-class women's well-being across the transition to parenthood. *Journal of Family Psychology, 18,* 225–236.

Goldberg, A. P., Dengel, D. R., & Hagberg, J. M. (1996). Exercise physiology and aging. In E. L. Schneider & J. W. Rowe (Eds.), *Handbook of the biology of aging* (pp. 331–354). San Diego: Academic Press.

Goldberg, M. C., Maurer, D., & Lewis, T. L. (2001). Developmental changes in attention: The effects of endogenous cueing and of distracters. *Developmental Science, 4,* 209–219.

Goldberg, S., Benoit, D., Blokland, K., & Madigan, S. (2003). Atypical maternal behavior, maternal representations, and infant disorganized attachment. *Development and Psychopathology, 15,* 239–257.

Goldenberg, C., Gallimore, R., Reese, L., & Garnier, H. (2001). Cause or effect? Immigrant Latino parents' aspirations and expectations, and their children's school performance. *American Educational Research Journal, 38,* 547–582.

Goldfield, B. A. (1987). The contributions of child and caregiver to referential and expressive language. *Applied Psycholinguistics, 8,* 267–280.

Goldin-Meadow, S., & Butcher, S. (2003). Pointing toward two-word speech in young children. In S. Kita (Ed.), *Pointing: Where language, culture, and cognition meet* (pp. 85–107). Mahwah, NJ: Erlbaum.

Goldman, N., & Takahashi, S. (1996). Old-age mortality in Japan: Demographic and epidemiological perspectives. In G. Caselli & A. D. Lopez (Eds.), *Health and mortality among elderly populations* (pp. 157–181). New York: Oxford University Press.

Goldscheider, F., & Goldscheider, C. (1999). *The changing transition to adulthood: Leaving and returning home.* Thousand Oaks, CA: Sage.

Goldschmidt, L., Richardson, G. A., Cornelius, M. D., & Day, N. L. (2004). Prenatal marijuana and alcohol exposure and academic achievement at age 10. *Neurotoxicology and Teratology, 26,* 521–532.

Goldsmith, H. H., Lemery, K. S., Buss, K. A., & Campos, J. J. (1999). Genetic analyses of focal aspects of infant temperament. *Developmental Psychology, 35,* 972–985.

Goldsmith, L. T. (2000). Tracking trajectories of talent: Child prodigies growing up. In R. C. Friedman & B. M. Shore (Eds.), *Talents unfolding: Cognition and development* (pp. 89–122). Washington, DC: American Psychological Association.

Goldstein, E. (1979). Effect of same-sex and cross-sex role models on the subsequent academic productivity of scholars. *American Psychologist, 34,* 407–410.

Goleman, D. (1995). *Emotional intelligence.* New York: Bantam.

Goleman, D. (1998). *Working with emotional intelligence.* New York: Bantam.

Golomb, C. (2004). *The child's creation of a pictorial world* (2nd ed.). Mahwah, NJ: Erlbaum.

Golombok, S., & MacCallum, F. (2003). Practitioner review: Outcomes for parents and children following non-traditional conception: What do clinicians need to know? *Journal of Child Psychology and Psychiatry, 44,* 303–315.

Golombok, S., Perry, B., Burston, A., Murray, C., Mooney-Somers, J., Stevens, M., & Golding, J. (2003). Children with lesbian parents: A community study. *Developmental Psychology, 39,* 20–33.

Golombok, S., & Tasker, F. L. (1996). Do parents influence the sexual orientation of their children? Findings from a longitudinal study of lesbian families. *Developmental Psychology, 32,* 3–11.

Golub, M. S. (1996). Labor analgesia and infant brain development. *Pharmacology, Biochemistry and Behavior, 55,* 619–628.

Gómez-Sanchiz, M., Canete, R., Rodero, I., Baeza, J. E., & Avilo, O. (2003). Influence of breast-feeding on mental and psychomotor development. *Clinical Pediatrics, 42,* 35–42.

Göncü, A. (1993). Development of intersubjectivity in the dyadic play of preschoolers. *Early Childhood Research Quarterly, 8,* 99–116.

Gonzales, N. A., Cauce, A. M., Friedman, R. J., & Mason, C. A. (1996). Family, peer, and neighborhood influences on academic achievement among African-American adolescents: One-year prospective effects. *American Journal of Community Psychology, 24,* 365–387.

Good, T. L., & Brophy, J. (2003). *Looking in classrooms* (9th ed.). Boston: Allyn and Bacon.

Goodlin-Jones, B. L., Burnham, M. M., & Anders, T. F. (2000). Sleep and sleep disturbances: Regulatory processes in infancy. In A. J. Sameroff, M. Lewis, & S. M. Miller (Eds.), *Handbook of developmental psychology* (2nd ed., pp. 309–325). New York: Kluwer.

Goodlin-Jones, B. L., Tassone, F., Gane, L. W., & Hagerman, R. J. (2004). Autistic spectrum disorder and the fragile X permutation. *Journal of Developmental and Behavioral Pediatrics, 25,* 392–398.

Goodman, C. (1999). Intimacy and autonomy in long-term marriage. *Journal of Gerontological Social Work, 32,* 83–97.

Goodman, G. S., Quas, J. A., Bulkley, J., & Shapiro, C. (1999). Innovations for child witnesses: A national survey. *Psychology, Public Policy, and Law, 5,* 255, 281.

Gootman, E. (2005, January 16). New York City: The politics of promotion. *New York Times.* Retrieved from www.nytimes.com/2005/01/16/education/edlife/EDGOOT.html

Gopnik, A., & Choi, S. (1990). Do linguistic differences lead to cognitive differences? A cross-linguistic study of semantic and cognitive development. *First Language, 11,* 199–215.

Gopnik, A., & Meltzoff, A. N. (1986). Relations between semantic and cognitive development in the one-word stage: The specificity hypothesis. *Child Development, 57,* 1040–1053.

Gopnik, A., & Meltzoff, A. N. (1987). The development of categorization in the second year and its relation to other cognitive and linguistic developments. *Child Development, 58,* 1523–1531.

Gopnik, A., & Nazzi, T. (2003). Words, kinds, and causal powers: A theory theory perspective on early naming and categorization. In D. H. Rakison & L. M. Oakes (Eds.), *Early category and concept development* (p. 303–329). New York: Oxford University Press.

Gordon, D. (2003). *The distribution of child poverty in the developing world: Report to UNICEF.* Bristol, UK: Centre for International Poverty Research, University of Bristol.

Gordon, L. H., Temple, R. R., & Adams, D. W. (2005). Premarital counseling from the PAIRS perspective. In M. Harway (Ed.), *Handbook of couples therapy* (pp. 7–27). Hoboken, NJ: Wiley.

Gordon, R. A., Chase-Lansdale, P. L., & Brooks-Gunn, J. (2004). Extended households and the life course of young mothers: Understanding the associations using a sample of mothers with premature, low-birth-weight babies.

Child Development, 75, 1013–1038.

Gore, S. A., Foster, J. A., DiLillo, V. G., Kirk, K., & West, D. S. (2003). Television viewing and snacking. *Eating Behaviors, 4,* 399–405.

Gormally, S., Barr, R. G., Wertheim, L., Alkawaf, R., Calinoiu, N., & Young, S. N. (2001). Contact and nutrient caregiving effects on newborn infant pain responses. *Developmental Medicine and Child Neurology, 43,* 28–38.

Gorman, T. E., Ahern, S. P., Wiseman, J., & Skrobik, Y. (2005). Residents' end-of-life decision making with adult hospitalized patients: A review of the literature. *Academic Medicine, 80,* 622–633.

Goswami, U. (1996). Analogical reasoning and cognitive development. In H. Reese (Ed.), *Advances in child development and behavior* (Vol. 26, pp. 91–138). New York: Academic Press.

Gott, M., & Hinchliff, S. (2003). How important is sex in later life? The views of older people. *Social Science and Medicine, 56,* 1617–1628.

Gott, M., Seymour, J., Bellamy, G., Clark, D., & Ahmedzai, S. (2004). Older people's views about home as a place of care at the end of life. *Palliative Medicine, 18,* 460–467.

Gott, V. L. (1998). Antoine Marfan and his syndrome: One hundred years later. *Maryland Medical Journal, 47,* 247–252.

Gottesman, I. I. (1963). Genetic aspects of intelligent behavior. In N. Ellis (Ed.), *Handbook of mental deficiency* (pp. 253–296). New York: McGraw-Hill.

Gottesman, I. I. (1991). *Schizophrenia genetics: The origins of madness.* New York: Freeman.

Gottfredson, L. S. (2005). Applying Gottfredson's theory of circumscription and compromise in career guidance and counseling. In S. D. Brown & R. W. Lent (Eds.), *Career development and counseling* (pp. 71–100). Hoboken, NJ: Wiley.

Gottfried, A. E., Gottfried, A. W., & Bathurst, K. (2002). Maternal and dual-earner employment status and parenting. In M. H. Bornstein (Ed.), *Handbook of parenting. Vol. 2: Biology and ecology of parenting* (2nd ed., pp. 207–229). Mahwah, NJ: Erlbaum.

Gottlieb, B., Beitel, L. K., & Trifiro, M. A. (2001). Somatic mosaicism and variable expressivity. *Trends in Genetics, 11,* 70–82.

Gottlieb, G. (1998). Normally occurring environmental and behavioral influences on gene activity: From central dogma to probabilistic epigenesis. *Psychological Review, 105,* 792–802.

Gottlieb, G. (2000). Environmental and behavioral influences on gene activity. *Current Directions in Psychological Science, 9,* 93–97.

Gottlieb, G. (2002). *Individual development and evolution: The genesis of novel behavior.* New York: Oxford University Press.

Gottlieb, G. (2003). On making behavioral genetics truly developmental. *Human Development, 46,* 337–355.

Gottman, J. M., Katz, L. F., & Hooven, C. (1997). *Meta-emotion: How families communicate emotionally.* Mahwah, NJ: Erlbaum.

Gottman, J. M., & Levenson, R. W. (2000). The timing of divorce: Predicting when a couple will divorce over a 14-year period. *Journal of Marriage and the Family, 62,* 737–745.

Gould, E., Reeves, A. J., Graziano, M. S. A., & Gross, C. G. (1999). Neurogenesis in the neocortex of adult primates. *Science, 286,* 548–552.

Gould, J. L., & Keeton, W. T. (1996). *Biological science* (6th ed.). New York: Norton.

Gould, M., Jamieson, P., & Romer, D. (2003). Media contagion and suicide among the young. *American Behavioral Scientist, 46,* 1269–1284.

Government of Canada. (1997). *Canada Pension Plan Phase III evaluation.* Ottawa: Author.

Government of Canada. (2004). Food insecurity in Canada, 1998–May 2001. Retrieved from www11.sdc.gc.ca/en/cs/sp/arb/publications/research/2001-000066/page00.shtml

Government of Canada. (2005). *Aging in poverty in Canada.* Ottawa: National Advisory Council on Aging.

Goya, R. G., & Bolognani, F. (1999). Homeostatis, thymic hormones, and aging. *Gerontology, 45,* 174–178.

Graber, J. A. (2003). Puberty in context. In C. Hayward (Ed.), *Gender differences at puberty* (pp. 307–325). New York: Cambridge University Press.

Graber, J. A. (2004). Internalizing problems during adolescence. In R. M. Lerner & L. Steinberg (Eds.), *Handbook of adolescent psychology* (2nd ed., pp. 587–626). Hoboken, NJ: Wiley.

Graber, J. A., & Brooks-Gunn, J. (1996). Expectations for and precursors to leaving home in young women. In J. A. Graber & J. S. Dubas (Eds.), *New directions for child development* (No. 71, pp. 21–38). San Francisco: Jossey-Bass.

Graber, J. A., Lewinsohn, P. M., Seeley, J. R., & Brooks-Gunn, J. (1997). Is psychopathology associated with timing of pubertal development? *Journal of the American Academy of Child and Adolescent Psychiatry, 36,* 1768–1776.

Graber, J. A., Seeley, J. R., Brooks-Gunn, J., & Lewinsohn, P. M. (2004). Is pubertal timing associated with psychopathology in young adulthood? *Journal of the American Academy of Child and Adolescent Psychiatry, 43,* 718–726.

Graczyk, P. A., Weikssberg, R. P., Payton, J. W., Elias, M. J., Greenberg, M. T., & Zins, J. E. (2000). Criteria for evaluating the quality of school-based social and emotional learning programs. In R. Bar-On & J. D. A. Parker (Eds.), *Handbook of emotional intelligence* (pp. 391–410). San Francisco: Jossey-Bass.

Grady, C. L., & Craik, F. I M. (2000). Changes in memory processing with age. *Current Opinion in Neurobiology, 10,* 224–231.

Graf, M., Ecker, D., Horowski, R., Kramer, B., Riederer, P., & Gerlach, M. (2005). High-dose vitamin E therapy in amyotrophic lateral sclerosis as add-on therapy to riluzole: Results of a placebo-controlled double-blind study. *Journal of Neural Transmission, 112,* 649–660.

Gralinski, J. H., & Kopp, C. B. (1993). Everyday rules for behavior: Mothers' requests to young children. *Developmental Psychology, 29,* 573–584.

Granot, M., Spitzer, A., Aroian, K. J., Ravid, C., Tamir, B., & Noam, R. (1996). Pregnancy and delivery practices and beliefs of Ethiopian immigrant women in Israel. *Western Journal of Nursing Research, 18,* 299–313.

Granot, T. (2005). *Without you: Children and young people growing up with loss and its effects.* London: Jessica Kingsley.

Grant, K., O'Koon, J., Davis, T., Roache, N., Poindexter, L., & Armstrong, M. (2000). Protective factors affecting low-income urban African American youth exposed to stress. *Journal of Early Adolescence, 20,* 388–418.

Grantham-McGregor, S., Powell, C., Walker, S., Chang, S., & Fletcher, P. (1994). The long-term follow-up of severely malnourished children who participated in an intervention program. *Child Development, 65,* 428–439.

Grantham-McGregor, S., Schofield, W., & Powell, C. (1987). Development of severely malnourished children who received psychosocial stimulation: Six-year follow-up. *Pediatrics, 79,* 247–254.

Grantham-McGregor, S., Walker, S. P., & Chang, S. (2000). Nutritional deficiencies and later behav-ioral development. *Proceedings of the Nutrition Society, 59,* 47–54.

Gratton, M. A., & Vásquez, A. E. (2003). Age-related hearing loss: Current research. *Current Opinion in Otolaryngology—Head and Neck Surgery, 11,* 367–371.

Graue, M. E., & DiPerna, J. (2000). Redshirting and early retention: Who gets the "gift of time" and what are its outcomes? *American Educational Research Journal, 37,* 509–534.

Gray, J. H., & Citera, M. (1996). *A meta-analytical review of the relation between work attitudes and retirement attitudes.* Paper presented at the annual meeting of the Society for Industrial and Organizational Psychology, San Diego, CA.

Gray, K. A., Day, N. L., Leech, S., & Richardson, G. A. (2005). Prenatal marijuana exposure: Effect on child depressive symptoms at ten years of age. *Neurotoxicology and Teratology, 27,* 439–448.

Gray, M. R., & Steinberg, L. (1999). Unpacking authoritative parenting: Reassessing a multidimensional construct. *Journal of Marriage and the Family, 61,* 574–587.

Gray-Little, B., & Carels, R. (1997). The effects of racial and socioeconomic consonance on self-esteem and achievement in elementary, junior high, and high school students. *Journal of Research on Adolescence, 7,* 109–131.

Gray-Little, B., & Hafdahl, A. R. (2000). Factors influencing racial comparisons of self-esteem: A quantitative review. *Psychological Bulletin, 126,* 26–54.

Graziano, A. M., & Hamblen, J. L. (1996). Subabusive violence in child rearing in middle-class American families. *Pediatrics, 98,* 845–848.

Green, G. E., Irwin, J. R., & Gustafson, G. E. (2000). Acoustic cry analysis, neonatal status and long-term developmental outcomes. In R. G. Barr, B. Hopkins, & J. A. Green (Eds.), *Crying as a sign, a symptom, and a signal* (pp. 137–156). Cambridge, UK: Cambridge University Press.

Greenberg, S. A. (2005). *A profile of older Americans: 2004.* Washington, DC: National Institute on Aging.

Greenberger, E., Chen, C., Tally, S. R., & Dong, Q. (2000). Family, peer, and individual correlates of depressive symptomatology among U.S. and Chinese adolescents. *Journal of Counseling and Clinical Psychology, 68,* 209–219.

Greenberger, E., O'Neil, R., & Nagel, S.K. (1994). Linking workplace and homeplace: Relations between the nature of adults' work and their parenting behavior. *Developmental Psychology, 30,* 990–1002.

Greendorfer, S. L., Lewko, J. H., & Rosengren, K. S. (1996). Family and gender-based socialization of children and adolescents. In F. L. Smoll & R. E. Smith (Eds.), *Children and youth in sport: A biopsychological perspective* (pp. 89–111). Dubuque, IA: Brown & Benchmark.

Greene, K., Krcmar, M., Walters, L. H., Rubin, D. L., Hale, J., & Hale, L. (2000). Targeting adolescent risk-taking behaviors: The contributions of egocentrism and sensation-seeking. *Journal of Adolescence, 23,* 439–461.

Greene, S. M., Anderson, E., Hetherington, E. M., Forgath, M. S., & DeGarmo, D. S. (2003). Risk and resilience after divorce. In R. Walsh (Ed.), *Normal family processes* (pp. 96–120). New York: Guilford.

Greenfield, P. (1992, June). *Notes and references for developmental psychology.* Conference on Making Basic Texts in Psychology More Culture-Inclusive and Culture-Sensitive, Western Washington University, Bellingham, WA.

Greenfield, P. M., Keller, H., Fuligni, A., & Maynard, A. (2003). Cultural pathways through universal development. *Annual Review of Psychology, 54,* 461–490.

Greenfield, P. M., Maynard, A. E., & Childs, C. P. (2000). History, culture, learning, and development. *Cross-Cultural Research, 34,* 351–374.

Greenfield, P. M., Quiroz, B., & Raeff, C. (2000). Cross-cultural conflict and harmony in the social construction of the child. In S. Harkness, C. Raeff, & C. M. Super (Eds.), *Variability in the social construction of the child* (pp. 93–108). San Francisco: Jossey-Bass.

Greenhill, L. L., Halperin, J. M., & Abikoff, H. (1999). Stimulant medications. *Journal of the American Academy of Child and Adolescent Psychiatry, 38,* 503–512.

Greenough, W. T., & Black, J. E. (1992). Induction of brain structure by experience: Substrates for cognitive development. In M. R. Gunnar & C. A. Nelson (Eds.), *Minnesota Symposia on Child Psychology* (pp. 155–200). Hillsdale, NJ: Erlbaum.

Greenough, W. T., Wallace, C. S., Alcantara, A. A., Anderson, B. J., Hawrylak, N., Sirevaag, A. M., Weiler, I. J., & Withers, G. S. (1993). Experience affects the structure of neurons, glia, and blood vessels. In N. J. Anastasiow & S. Harel (Eds.), *At-risk infants: Interventions, family, and research* (pp. 175–185). Baltimore: Paul H. Brookes.

Greenspan, S. I., & Shanker, S. G. (2004). *The first idea: how symbols, language, and intelligence evolved from our primate ancestors to modern humans.* Cambridge, MA: Da Capo Press.

Gregg, V., Gibbs, J. C., & Fuller, D. (1994). Patterns of developmental delay in moral judgment by male and female delinquents. *Merrill-Palmer Quarterly, 40,* 538–553.

Gresham, F. M., & MacMillan, D. L. (1997). Social competence and affective characteristics of students with mild disabilities. *Review of Educational Research, 67,* 377–415.

Gresser, G., Wong, P., & Reker, G. (1987). Death attitudes across the life-span: The development and validation of the Death Attitude Profile (DAP). *Omega, 18,* 113–128.

Grief, G. L., Hrabowski, F. A., & Maton, K. I. (1998). African-American fathers of high-achieving sons: Using outstanding members of an at-risk population to guide intervention. *Families in Society, 79,* 45–52.

Grigorenko, E. L. (2000). Heritability and intelligence. In R. J. Sternberg (Ed.), *Handbook of intelligence* (pp. 53–91). Cambridge, UK: Cambridge University Press.

Grigorenko, E. L., & Sternberg, R. J. (1998). Dynamic testing. *Psychological Bulletin, 124,* 75–111.

Grob, A., & Flammer, A. (1999). Macrosocial context and adolescents' perceived control. In F. D. Alsaker & A. Flammer (Eds.), *The adolescent experience* (pp. 99–114). Mahwah, NJ: Erlbaum.

Grob, A., Krings, F., & Bangerter, A. (2001). Life markers in biographical narratives of people from three cohorts: A life span perspective in its historical context. *Human Development, 44,* 171–190.

Grody, W. W. (1999). Cystic fibrosis: Molecular diagnosis, population screening, and public policy. *Archives of Pathology and Laboratory Medicine, 123,* 1041–1046.

Grolnick, W. S., Bridges, L. J., & Connell, J. P. (1996). Emotion regulation in two-year-olds: Strategies and emotional expression in four contexts. *Child Development, 67,* 928–941.

Grolnick, W. S., Kurowski, C. O., Dunlap, K. G., & Hevey, C. (2000). Parental resources and the transition to junior high. *Journal of Research on Adolescence, 10,* 466–488.

Groome, L. J., Swiber, M. J., Atterbury, J. L., Bentz, L. S., & Holland, S. B. (1997). Similarities and differences in behavioral state organization during sleep periods in the perinatal infant before and after birth. *Child Development, 68,* 1–11.

Gross, M. (1993). *Exceptionally gifted children.* London: Routledge.

Grossbaum, M. F., & Bates, G. W. (2002). Correlates of psychological well-being at midlife: The role of generativity, agency and communion, and narrative themes. *International Journal of Behavioral Development, 26,* 120–127.

Grossman, A. H., D'Augelli, A. R., & Hershberger, S. L. (2000). Social support networks of lesbian, gay, and bisexual adults 60 years of age and older. *Journal of Gerontology, 55B,* P171–179.

Grossmann, K., Grossmann, K. E., Fremmer-Bombik, E., Kindler, H., Scheuerer-Englisch, H., & Zimmermann, P. (2002). The uniqueness of the child–father attachment relationship: Fathers' sensitive and challenging play as a pivotal variable in a 16-year longitudinal study. *Social Development, 11,* 307–331.

Grossmann, K., Grossmann, K. E., Spangler, G., Suess, G., & Unzner, L. (1985). Maternal sensitivity and newborns' orientation responses as related to quality of attachment in Northern Germany. In I. Bretherton & E. Waters (Eds.), Growing points of attachment theory and research. *Monographs of the Society for Research in Child Development, 50*(1–2, Serial No. 209).

Grotevant, H. D. (1998). Adolescent development in family contexts. In N. Eisenberg (Ed.), *Handbook of child psychology: Vol. 3. Social, emotional, and personality development* (5th ed., pp. 1097–1149). New York: Wiley.

Grotevant, H. D., & Cooper, C. R. (1998). Individuality and connectedness in adolescent development: Review and prospects for research on identity, relationships, and context. In E. Skoe & A. von der Lippe (Eds.), *Personality development in adolescence* (pp. 3–37). London: Routledge & Kegan Paul.

Grotpeter, J. K., & Crick, N. R. (1996). Relational aggression, overt aggression, and friendship. *Child Development, 67,* 2328–2338.

Grow-Maienza, J., Hahn, D.-D., & Joo, C.-A. (2001). Mathematics instruction in Korean primary schools: Structure, processes, and a linguistic analysis of questioning. *Journal of Educational Psychology, 93,* 363–376.

Grubb, W. N. (1999). The subbaccalaureate labor market in the United States: Challenges for the school-to-work transition. In W. R. Heinz (Ed.), *From education to work: Cross-national perspectives* (pp. 171–193). New York: Cambridge University Press.

Gruetzner, H. (1992). *Alzheimer's.* New York: Wiley.

Grundy, E. (2005). Reciprocity in relationships: Socio-economic and health influences on intergenerational exchanges between Third Age parents and their adult children in Great Britain. *British Journal of Sociology, 56,* 233–255.

Grusec, J. E. (1988). *Social development: History, theory, and research.* New York: Springer.

Grusec, J. E., & Goodnow, J. J. (1994). Impact of parental discipline methods on the child's internalization of values: A reconceptualization of current points of view. *Developmental Psychology, 30,* 4–19.

Grych, J. H., & Clark, R. (1999). Maternal employment and development of the father–infant relationship in the first year. *Developmental Psychology, 35,* 893–903.

Grzywacz, J. G., & Marks, N. F. (2001). Social inequalities and exercise during adulthood: Toward an ecological perspective. *Journal of Health and Social Behavior, 42,* 202–220.

Guay, F., La Rose, S., & Boivin, M. (2004). Academic self-concept and educational attainment level: A ten-year longitudinal study. *Self and Identity, 3,* 53–68.

Guay, F., Marsh, H. W., & Boivin, M. (2003). Academic self-concept and academic achievement: Developmental perspectives on their causal ordering. *Journal of Educational Psychology, 95,* 124–136.

Guildner, S. H., Loeb, S., Morris, D., Penrod, J., Bramlett, M., Johnston, L., & Schlotzhauer, P. (2001). A comparison of life satisfaction and mood in nursing home residents and community-dwelling elders. *Archives of Psychiatric Nursing, 15,* 232–240.

Guilford, J. P. (1985). The structure-of-intellect model. In B. B. Wolman (Ed.), *Handbook of intelligence* (pp. 225–266). New York: Wiley.

Guinn, B. (1999). Leisure behavior motivation and the life satisfaction of retired persons. *Activities, Adaptation, and Aging, 23,* 13–20.

Gullone, E. (2000). The development of normal fear: A century of research. *Clinical Psychology Review, 20,* 429–451.

Gunnar, M. R., & Cheatham, C. L. (2003). Brain and behavior interfaces: Stress and the developing brain. *Infant Mental Health Journal, 24,* 195–211.

Gunnar, M. R., Morison, S. J., Chisholm, K., & Schuder, M. (2001). Salivary cortisol levels in children adopted from Romanian orphanages. *Development and Psychopathology, 13,* 611–628.

Gunnar, M. R., & Nelson, C. A. (1994). Event-related potentials in year-old infants: Relations with emotionality and cortisol. *Child Development, 65,* 80–94.

Gunnoe, M. L., & Mariner, C. L. (1997). Toward a developmental-contextual model of the effects of parental spanking on children's aggression. *Archives of Pediatrics and Adolescent Medicine, 151,* 768–775.

Guo, G., & VanWey, L. K. (1999). Sibship size and intellectual development: Is the relationship causal? *American Sociological Review, 64,* 169–187.

Gureje, O., Ogunniyi, A., Baiyewu, O., Price, B., Unverzagt, F. W., & Evans, R. M. (2006). APOE epsilon4 is not associated with Alzheimer's disease in elderly Nigerians. *Annals of Neurology, 59,* 182–185.

Gustafson, G. E., Green, J. A., & Cleland, J. W. (1994). Robustness of individual identity in the cries of human infants. *Developmental Psychobiology, 27,* 1–9.

Gustafson, G. E., Wood, R. M., & Green, J. A. (2000). Can we hear the causes of infants' crying? In R. G. Barr & B. Hopkins (Eds.), *Crying as a sign, a symptom, and a signal: Clinical, emotional, and developmental aspects of infant and toddler crying* (p.p. 8–22). New York: Cambridge University Press.

Gutman, L. M., Sameroff, A. J., & Cole, R. (2003). Academic growth curve trajectories from 1st grade to 12th grade: Effects of multiple social risk factors and preschool child factors. *Developmental Psychology, 39,* 777–790.

Gutmann, D. (1977). The cross-cultural perspective: Notes toward a comparative psychology of aging. In J. E. Birren & K. W. Schaie (Eds.), *Handbook of the psychology of aging* (pp. 302–326). New York: Van Nostrand Reinhold.

Gutmann, D. L., & Huyck, M. H. (1994). Development and pathology in post-parental men: A community study. In E. Thompson, Jr. (Ed.), *Older men's lives* (pp. 65–84). Thousand Oaks, CA: Sage.

Guttuso, T., Jr., Kurlan, R., McDermott, M. P., & Kieburtz, K. (2003). Gabapentin's effects on hot flashes in postmenopausal women: A randomized controlled trial. *Obstetrics and Gynecology, 101,* 337–345.

Gwiazda, J., & Birch, E. E. (2001). Perceptual development: Vision. In E. B. Goldstein (Ed.), *Blackwell handbook of perception* (pp. 636–668). Oxford, UK: Blackwell.

H

Haden, C. A., Haine, R. A., & Fivush, R. (1997). Developing narrative structure in parent–child reminiscing across the preschool years. *Developmental Psychology, 33,* 295–307.

Hagberg, B., Alfredson, B. B., Poon, L. W., & Homma, A. (2001). Cognitive functioning in centenarians: A coordinated analysis of results from three countries. *Journal of Gerontology, 56B,* P141–P151.

Hagekull, B., Bohlin, G., & Rydell, A. (1997). Maternal sensitivity, infant temperament, and the development of early feeding problems. *Infant Mental Health Journal, 18,* 92–106.

Haight, W. L., & Miller, P. J. (1993). *Pretending at home: Early development in a sociocultural context.* Albany, NY: State University of New York Press.

Hainline, L. (1998). The development of basic visual abilities. In A. Slater (Ed.), *Perceptual development: Visual, auditory, and speech perception in infancy* (pp. 37–44). Hove, UK: Psychology Press.

Hajjar, R. R., & Kamel, H. K. (2004). Sexuality in the nursing home, Part 1: Attitudes and barriers to sexual expression. *Journal of the American Medical Directors Association, 5,* S43–S47.

Hakuta, K. (1999). The debate on bilingual education. *Developmental and Behavioral Pediatrics, 20,* 36–37.

Hakuta, K., Bialystok, E., & Wiley, E. (2003). Critical evidence: A test of the critical-period hypothesis for second-language acquisitions. *Psychological Science, 14,* 31–38.

Halberstadt, A., Denham, S. A., & Dunsmore, J. (2001). Affective social competence. *Social Development, 10,* 79–119.

Halbreich, U. (2004). The diagnosis of premenstrual syndromes and premenstrual dysphoric disorder—clinical procedures and research perspectives. *Gynecological Endocrinology, 19,* 320–334.

Hale, C. M., & Tager-Flusberg, H. (2003). The influence of language on theory of mind: A training study. *Developmental Science, 6,* 346–359.

Hales, C. N., & Ozanne, S. E. (2003). The dangerous road of catch-up growth. *Journal of Physiology, 547,* 5–10.

Halfon, N., & McLearn, K. T. (2002). Families with children under 3: What we know and implications for results and policy. In N. Halfon & K. T. McLearn (Eds.), *Child rearing in America: Challenges facing parents with young children* (pp. 367–412). New York: Cambridge University Press.

Halford, G. S. (2002). Information-processing models of cognitive development. In U. Goswami (Ed.), *Blackwell handbook of childhood cognitive development* (pp. 555–574). Malden, MA: Blackwell.

Halford, G. S., & Andrews, G. (2006). Reasoning and problem solving. In D. Kuhn & R. S. Siegler (Eds.), *Handbook of child psychology: Vol. 2. Cognition, perception, and language* (6th ed.). Hoboken, NJ: Wiley.

Hall, D. G., & Graham, S. A. (1999). Lexical form class information guides word-to-object mapping in preschoolers. *Child Development, 70,* 78–91.

Hall, G. S. (1904). *Adolescence.* New York: Appleton.

Hall, K., Murrell, J., Ogunniyi, A., Deeg, M., Baiyewu, O., & Gao, S. (2006). Cholesterol, APOE genotype, and Alzheimer disease: An epidemiologic study of Nigerian Yoruba. *Neurology, 66,* 223–227.

Halle, T. G. (2003). Emotional development and well-being. In M. H. Bornstein, L. Davidson, C. L. M. Keyes, K. A. Moore, & the Center for Child Well-Being (Eds.), *Well-being: Positive development across the life course* (pp. 125–138). Mahwah, NJ: Erlbaum.

Hallett, M. (2000). Brain plasticity and recovery from hemiplegia. *Journal of Medical Speech-Language Pathology, 9,* 107–115.

Halliday, J. L., Watson, L. F., Lumley, J., Danks, D. M., & Sheffield, L. S. (1995). New estimates of Down syndrome risks of chorionic villus sampling, amniocentesis, and live birth in women of advanced maternal age from a uniquely defined population. *Prenatal Diagnosis, 15,* 455–465.

Hallinan, M. T., & Kubitschek, W. N. (1999). Curriculum differentiation and high school achievement. *Social Psychology of Education, 3,* 41–62.

Halpern, C. T., Udry, J. R., & Suchindran, C. (1997). Testosterone predicts initiation of coitus in adolescent females. *Psychosomatic Medicine, 59,* 161–171.

Halpern, D. F. (1997). Sex differences in intelligence. *American Psychologist, 52,* 1091–1102.

Halpern, D. F. (2000*). Sex differences in cognitive abilities* (3rd ed.). Mahwah, NJ: Erlbaum.

Halpern, D. F. (2004). A cognitive-process taxonomy for sex differences in cognitive abilities. *Current Directions in Psychological Science, 13,* 135–139.

Halpern, D. F. (2005a). How time-flexible work policies can reduce stress, improve health, and save money. *Stress and Health, 21,* 157–168.

Halpern, D. F. (2005b). Psychology at the intersection of work and family: Recommendations for employers, working families, and policymakers. *American Psychologist, 60,* 397–409.

Halpern, D. F., Wai, J., & Saw, A. (2005). A psychobiological model: Why females are sometimes greater than and sometimes less than males in math achievement. In D. F. Halpern, J. Wai, & A. Saw (Eds.), *Gender differences in mathematics: An integrative psychological approach* (pp. 48–72). New York: Cambridge University Press.

Halpern-Felsher, B. L., & Cauffman, E. (2001). Costs and benefits of a decision: Decision-making competence in adolescents and adults. *Journal of Applied Developmental Psychology, 22,* 257–273.

Hamachek, D. (1990). Evaluating self-concept and ego status in Erikson's last three psychosocial stages. *Journal of Counseling and Development, 68,* 677–683.

Hamer, D. H., Hu, S., Magnuson, V. L., Hu, N., & Pattatucci, A. M. L. (1993). A linkage between DNA markers on the X chromosome and male sexual orientation. *Science, 261,* 321–327.

Hamer, M., Wolvers, D., & Albers, R. (2004). Using stress models to evaluate immuno-modulating effects of nutritional intervention in healthy individuals. *Journal of the American College of Nutrition, 23,* 637–646.

Hamilton, B. E., Ventura, S. J., Martin, J. A., & Sutton, P. D. (2005). Preliminary births for 2004. *Health E-Stats.* Retrieved from www.cdc.gov/nchs/products/pubs/pubd/hestats/prelim_births/prelim_births04.htm

Hamilton, H. A. (2005). Extended families and adolescent well-being. *Journal of Adolescent Health, 36,* 260–266.

Hamilton, S. F., & Hamilton, M. A. (1999). Creating new pathways to adulthood by adapting German apprenticeship in the United States. In W. R. Heinz (Ed.), *From education to work: Cross-national perspectives* (pp. 194–213). New York: Cambridge University Press.

Hamilton, S. F., & Hamilton, M. A. (2000). Research, intervention, and social change: Improving adolescents' career opportunities. In L. J. Crockett & R. K., Silbereisen (Eds.), *Negotiating adolescence in times of social change* (pp. 267–283). New York: Cambridge University Press.

Hammes, B., & Laitman, C. J. (2003). Diethylstilbestrol (DES) update: Recommendations for the identification and management of DES-exposed individuals. *Journal of Midwifery and Women's Health, 48,* 19–29.

Hammond, C. J., Snieder, H., Spector, T. D., & Gilbert, C. E. (2000). Genetic and environmental factors in age-related nuclear cataracts in monozygotic and dizygotic twins. *New England Journal of Medicine, 342,* 1786–1790.

Han, J. J., Leichtman, M. D., & Wang, Q. (1998). Autobiographical memory in Korean, Chinese, and American children. *Developmental Psychology, 34,* 701–713.

Han, S. K., & Moen, P. (1999). Clocking out: Temporal patterning of retirement. *American Journal of Sociology, 105,* 191–236.

Han, W.-J., & Waldfogel, J. (2003). Parental leave: The impact of recent legislation on parents' leave taking. *Demography, 40,* 191–200.

Hanawalt, B. A. (2003). The child in the Middle Ages and the Renaissance. In W. Koops & M. Zuckerman (Eds.), *Beyond the century of childhood: Cultural history and developmental psychology.* Philadelphia: University of Pennsylvania Press.

Hanke, W., Sobala, W., & Kalinka, J. (2004). Environmental tobacco smoke exposure among pregnant women: Impact on fetal biometry at 20–24 weeks of gestation and newborn child's birth weight. *International Archives of Occupational and Environmental Health, 77,* 47–52.

Hannon, T. S., Rao, G., & Arslanian, S. A. (2005). Childhood obesity and Type 2 diabetes mellitus. *Pediatrics, 116,* 473–480.

Hansen, M., Janssen, I., Schiff, A., Zee, P. C., & Dubocovich, M. L. (2005). The impact of school daily schedule on adolescent sleep. *Pediatrics, 115,* 1555–1561.

Hansen, M., Kurinczuk, J. J., Bower, C., & Webb, S. (2002). The risk of major birth defects after intracytoplasmic sperm injection and in vitro fertilization. *New England Journal of Medicine, 346,* 725–730.

Hanson, L. C., Danis, M., & Garrett, J. (1997). What is wrong with end-of-life care? Opinions of bereaved family members. *Journal of the American Geriatric Society, 45,* 1339–1344.

Hanson, T. L. (1999). Does parental conflict explain why divorce is negatively associated with child welfare? *Social Forces, 77,* 1283–1316.

Hanvey, L., & Kunz, J. L. (2000). *Immigrant youth in Canada.* Toronto, ON: Canadian Council on Social Development.

Hardre, P. L., & Reeve, J. (2003). A motivational model of rural students' intentions to persist in, versus drop out of, high school. *Journal of Educational Psychology, 95,* 347–356.

Hare, J. (1994). Concerns and issues faced by families headed by a lesbian couple. *Families in Society, 43,* 27–35.

Hare, J., & Richards, L. (1993). Children raised by lesbian couples: Does context of birth affect father and partner involvement? *Family Relations, 42,* 249–255.

Harley, B., & Jean, G. (1999). Vocabulary skills of French immersion students in their second language. *Zeitschrift für Interkulturellen Fremdsprachenunterricht, 4*(2). Retrieved from http://www.ualberta.ca

Harley, K., & Reese, E. (1999). Origins of autobiographical memory. *Developmental Psychology, 35,* 1338–1348.

Harlow, H. F., & Zimmerman, R. (1959). Affectional responses in the infant monkey. *Science, 130,* 421–432.

Harman, D. (2002). Aging: Overview. *Annals of the New York Academy of Sciences, 959,* 1–21.

Harman, D. (2003). The free radical theory of aging. *Antioxidants and Redox Signaling, 5,* 557–561.

Harman, S. M., & Blackman, M. R. (2004). Use of growth hormone for prevention or treatment of effects of aging. *Journal of Gerontology, 59,* 652–658.

Harold, G. T., Shelton, K. H., Goeke-Morey, M. C., & Cummings, E. M. (2004). Marital conflict, child emotional security about family relationships, and child adjustment. *Social Development, 13,* 350–376.

Harootyan, R. A., & Vorek, R. E. (1994). Volunteering, helping and gift giving in families and communities. In V. L. Bengtson & R. A. Harootyan (Eds.), *Intergenerational linkages: Hidden connections in American society* (pp. 77–111). New York: Springer.

Harris, G. (1997). Development of taste perception and appetite regulation. In G. Bremner, A. Slater, & G. Butterworth (Eds.), *Infant development: Recent advances* (pp. 9–30). East Sussex, UK: Erlbaum.

Harris, J. R. (1998). *The nurture assumption: Why children turn out the way they do.* New York: Free Press.

Harris, P. B. (1998). Listening to caregiving sons: Misunderstood realities. *Gerontologist, 38,* 342–352.

Harris, P. L., & Leevers, H. J. (2000). Reasoning from false premises. In P. Mitchell & K. J. Riggs (Eds.), *Children's reasoning and the mind* (pp. 67–99). Hove, UK: Psychology Press.

Harris, R. L., Ellicott, A. M., & Holmes, D. S. (1986). The timing of psychosocial transitions and changes in women's lives: An examination of women aged 45 to 60. *Journal of Personality and Social Psychology, 51,* 409–416.

Harrison, A. O., Wilson, M. N., Pine, C. J., Chan, S. Q., & Buriel, R. (1994). Family ecologies of ethnic minority children. In G. Handel & G. G. Whitchurch (Eds.), *The psychosocial interior of the family* (pp. 187–210). New York: Aldine de Gruyter.

Harrist, A. W., Zaia, A. F., Bates, J. E., Dodge, K. A., & Pettit, G. S. (1997). Subtypes of social withdrawal in early childhood: Sociometric status and social–cognitive differences across four years. *Child Development, 68,* 278–294.

Hart, B. (2004). What toddlers talk about. *First Language, 24,* 91–106.

Hart, B., & Risley, T. R. (1995). *Meaningful differences in the everyday experience of young American children.* Baltimore: Paul H. Brookes.

Hart, C. H., Burts, D. C., Durland, M. A., Charlesworth, R., DeWolf, M., & Fleege, P. O. (1998). Stress behaviors and activity type participation of preschoolers in more and less developmentally appropriate classrooms: SES and sex differences. *Journal of Research in Childhood Education, 13,* 176–196.

Hart, C. H., Nelson, D. A., Robinson, C. C., Olsen, S. F., & McNeilly-Choque, M. K. (1998). Overt and relational aggression in Russian nursery-school-age children: Parenting style and marital linkages. *Developmental Psychology, 34,* 687–697.

Hart, C. H., Newell, L. D., & Olsen, S. F. (2003). Parenting skills and social–communicative competence in childhood. In J. O. Greene & B. R. Burleson (Eds.), *Handbook of communication and social interaction skills* (pp. 753–797). Mahwah, NJ: Erlbaum.

Hart, C. H., Yang, C., Charlesworth, R., & Burts, D. C. (2003, April). *Kindergarten teaching practices: Associations with later child academic and social/emotional adjustment to school.* Paper presented at the biennial meeting of the Society for Research in Child Development, Tampa, FL.

Hart, C. H., Yang, C., Nelson, L. J., Robinson, C. C., Olsen, J. A., Nelson, D. A., Porter, C. L., Jin, S., Olsen, S. F., & Wu, P. (2000). Peer acceptance in early childhood and subtypes of socially withdrawn behavior in China, Russia, and the United States. *International Journal of Behavioral Development, 24,* 73–81.

Hart, D., & Atkins, R. (2002). Civic competence in urban youth. *Applied Developmental Science, 6,* 227–236.

Hart, D., & Fegley, S. (1995). Prosocial behavior and caring in adolescence: Relations to self-understanding and social judgment. *Child Development, 66,* 1346–1359.

Hart, H. M., McAdams, D. P., Hirsch, B. J., & Bauer, J. J. (2001). Generativity and social involvement among African Americans and white adults. *Journal of Research in Personality, 35,* 208–230.

Hart, S., Field, T., & Roitfarb, M. (1999). Depressed mothers' assessments of their neonates' behaviors. *Infant Mental Health Journal, 20,* 200–210.

Harter, S. (1990). Issues in the assessment of the self-concept of children and adolescents. In A. LaGreca (Ed.), *Through the eyes of a child* (pp. 292–325). Boston: Allyn and Bacon.

Harter, S. (1996). Developmental changes in self-understanding across the 5 to 7 shift. In A. J. Sameroff & M. M. Haith (Eds.), *The five to seven year shift* (pp. 207–236). Chicago: University of Chicago Press.

Harter, S. (1998). The development of self-representations. In N. Eisenberg (Ed.), *Handbook of child psychology: Vol. 3. Social, emotional, and personality development* (5th ed., pp. 553–618). New York: Wiley.

Harter, S. (1999). *The construction of self: A developmental perspective.* New York: Guilford.

Harter, S. (2003). The development of self-representations during childhood and adolescence. In M. R. Leary & J. P. Tangney (Eds.), *Handbook of self and identity* (pp. 610–642). New York: Guilford.

Harter, S., & Whitesell, N. (1989). Developmental changes in children's understanding of simple, multiple, and blended emotion concepts. In C. Saarni & P. Harris (Eds.), *Children's understanding of emotion* (pp. 81–116). Cambridge, UK: Cambridge University Press.

Hartman, J., & Warren, L. H. (2005). Explaining age differences in temporal working memory. *Psychology and Aging, 20,* 645–656.

Hartshorn, K., Rovee-Collier, C., Gerhardstein, P., Bhatt, R. S., Wondoloski, T. L., Klein, P., Gilch, J., Wurtzel, N., & Campos-de-Carvalho, M. (1998). The ontogeny of long-term memory over the first year-and-a-half of life. *Developmental Psychobiology, 32,* 69–89.

Hartup, W. W. (1996). The company they keep: Friendships and their developmental significance. *Child Development, 67,* 1–13.

Hartup, W. W., & Abecassis, M. (2004). Friends and enemies. In P. K. Smith & C. H. Hart (Eds.), *Blackwell handbook of childhood social development* (pp. 285–306). Malden, MA: Blackwell.

Hartup, W. W., & Stevens, N. (1999). Friendships and adaptation across the life span. *Current Directions in Psychological Science, 8,* 76–79.

Harvey, P. T. (2003). Common eye diseases of elderly people: Identifying and treating causes of vision loss. *Gerontology, 49,* 1–11.

Harway, M., & Hansen, M. (2004). *Spouse abuse: Assessing and treating battered women, batterers, and their children* (2nd ed.). Sarasota, FL: Professional Resource Press.

Harwood, J. (2001). Comparing grandchildren's and grandparents' stake in their relationship. *International Journal of Aging and Human Development, 53,* 195–210.

Hasher, L., Zacks, R. T., & May, C. P. (1999). Inhibitory control, circadian arousal, and age. In D. Gopher & A. Koriat (Eds.), *Attention and performance* (Vol. 17, pp. 653–675). Cambridge, MA: MIT Press.

Haskett, M. E., Scott, S. S., Grant, R., Ward, C. S., & Robinson, C. (2003). Child-related cognitions and affective functioning of physically abusive and comparison parents. *Child Abuse and Neglect, 27,* 663–686.

Hasler, P., & Zouali, M. (2005). Immune receptor signaling, aging, and autoimmunity. *Cellular Immunology, 233,* 102–108.

Hassing, L. B., Johansson, B., Berg, S., Nilsson, S. E., Pedersen, N. L., Hofer, S. M., & McClearn, G. (2002). Terminal decline and markers of cerebro- and cardiovascular disease: Findings from a longitudinal study of the oldest old. *Journal of Gerontology, 57B,* P268–P276.

Hatch, L. R., & Bulcroft, K. (2004). Does long-term marriage bring less frequent disagreements? *Journal of Family Issues, 25,* 465–495.

Hatfield, E. (1993). *Love, sex, and intimacy: Their psychology, biology, and history.* New York: Harper-Collins.

Hatfield, E., & Sprecher, S. (1995). Men's and women's mate preferences in the United States, Russia, and Japan. *Journal of Cross-Cultural Psychology, 26,* 728–750.

Hatton, D. D., Bailey, D. B., Jr., Burchinal, M. R., & Ferrell, K. A. (1997). Developmental growth curves of preschool children with vision impairments. *Child Development, 68,* 788–806.

Hauck, F. R., Herman, S. M., Donovan, M., Iyasu, S., Moore, C. M., & Donoghue, E. (2003). Sleep environment and the risk of sudden infant death syndrome in an urban population: The Chicago Infant Mortality Study. *Pediatrics, 111,* 1207–1214.

Hauck, F. R., Omojokun, O. O., & Siadaty, M. S. (2005). Do pacifiers reduce the risk of sudden infant death syndrome? A meta-analysis. *Pediatrics, 116,* e716–e723.

Haught, P. A., Hill, L. A., Nardi, A. H., & Walls, R. T. (2000). Perceived ability and level of education as predictors of traditional and practical adult problem solving. *Experimental Aging Research, 36,* 89–101.

Hausfather, A., Toharia, A., LaRoche, C., & Engelsmann, F. (1997). Effects of age of entry, day-care quality, and family characteristics on preschool behavior. *Journal of Child Psychology and Psychiatry, 38,* 441–448.

Hauth, J. C., Goldenberg, R. L., Parker, C. R., Cutter, G. R., & Cliver, S. P. (1995). Low-dose aspirin—Lack of association with an increase in abruptio placentae or perinatal mortality. *Obstetrics and Gynecology, 85,* 1055–1058.

Hawkins, J. D., Catalano, R. F., & Miller, J. Y. (1992). Risk and protective factors for alcohol and other drug problems in adolescence and early adulthood: Implications for substance abuse prevention. *Psychological Bulletin, 112,* 64–105.

Hawkins, J. N. (1994). Issues of motivation in Asian education. In H. F. O'Neil, Jr., & M. Drillings (Eds.), *Motivation: Theory and research* (pp. 101–115). Hillsdale, NJ: Erlbaum.

Hawkley, L. C., & Cacioppo, J. T. (2004). Stress and the aging immune system. *Brain, Behavior and Immunity, 18,* 114–119.

Hay, D. F., Pawlby, S., Angold, A., Harold, G. T., & Sharp, D. (2003). Pathways to violence in the children of mothers who were depressed postpartum. *Developmental Psychology, 39,* 1983–1094.

Hay, J. F., & Jacoby, L. L. (1999). Separating habit and recollection in young and older adults: Effects of elaborative processing and distinctiveness. *Psychology and Aging, 14,* 122–134.

Hay, P., & Bacaltchuk, J. (2004). Bulimia nervosa. *Clinical Evidence, 12,* 1326–1347.

Hayflick, L. (1965). The limited in vitro lifetime of human diploid cell strains. *Experimental Cell Research, 37,* 614–636.

Hayflick, L. (1994). *How and why we age.* New York: Ballantine.

Hayflick, L. (1998). How and why we age. *Experimental Gerontology, 33,* 639–653.

Hayne, H. (2002). Thoughts from the crib: Meltzoff and Moore (1994) alter our views of mental representation during infancy. *Infant Behavior and Development, 25,* 62–64.

Hayne, H. (2004). Infant memory development: Implications for childhood amnesia. *Developmental Review, 24,* 33–73.

Hayne, H., Boniface, J., & Barr, R. (2000). The development of declarative memory in human infants: Age-related changes in deferred imitation. *Behavioral Neuroscience, 114,* 77–83.

Hayne, H., Rovee-Collier, C., & Perris, E. E. (1987). Categorization and memory retrieval by three-month-olds. *Child Development, 58,* 750–767.

Hays, J. C., & George, L. K. (2002). The life-course trajectory toward living alone: Racial differences. *Research on Aging, 24,* 283–307.

Hayslip, B., Emick, M. A., Henderson, C. E., & Elias, K. (2002). Temporal variations in the experience of custodial grandparenting: A short-term longitudinal study. *Journal of Applied Gerontology, 21,* 139–156.

Haywood, K. M., & Getchell, N. (2001). *Life span motor development* (3rd ed.). Champaign, IL: Human Kinetics.

Hazell, L. V. (2001). Multicultural aftercare issues. In O. D. Weeks & C. Johnson (Eds.), *When all the friends have gone: Guide for aftercare providers* (pp. 57–71). Amityville, NY: Baywood.

Head Start Bureau. (2005). 2005 Head Start fact sheet. Retrieved from www.acf.dhhs.gov/programs/opa/facts/headst/htm

Health and Disability Research Institute. (2006). *Fear of falling: A matter of balance.* Boston: Author.

Health Canada. (1999). *Canadian dietary guidelines, recommendations and standards.* Retrieved from www.sfu.ca

Health Canada. (2002a). *Canada's aging population.* Ottawa, ON: Author.

Health Canada. (2002b). *Canadian Community Health Survey: A first look.* Retrieved from www.statcan.ca/english/concepts/health/

Health Canada. (2002c). Healthy Canadians: A federal report on comparable health indicators. Retrieved from www.hc-sc.gc.ca/iacb-dgiac/arad-draa/english/accountability/indicators/html#high

Health Canada. (2002d). Proceedings of a meeting of the Expert Advisory Group on Rubella in Canada. Retrieved from www.hc-sc.gc.ca/pphb-dgspsp/publicat/ccdr-rmtc/02vol28/28s4

Health Canada. (2002e). Statistical report on the health of Canadians. Retrieved from www.statcan.ca:80/english/freepub/82-570-XIE/partb.htm

Health Canada. (2003a). *Acting on what we know: Preventing youth suicide in first nations.* Ottawa, CA: Author.

Health Canada. (2003b). Alcohol and pregnancy. Retrieved from www.hc-sc.gc.ca/pphb-dgspsp/rhs-ssg/factshts/alcprg_e.html

Health Canada. (2003c). *Arthritis in Canada: An ongoing challenge.* Ottawa: Author.

Health Canada. (2003d). *Physical activity guide to healthy, active living.* Retrieved from www.phac-aspc.gc.ca/pau-uap/paguide/index.html

Health Canada. (2003e). Rate of breastfeeding. *Canadian Perinatal Health Report, 2003.* Retrieved from www.phac-aspc.gc.ca/publicat/cphr-rspc03/index.html

Health Canada. (2004a). *Aboriginal Head Start: Program overview.* Retrieved from www.phac-aspc.gc.ca/dca-dea/programs-mes/cpnp_main_e.html

Health Canada. (2004b). *Canadian perinatal health report 2004.* Ottawa, ON: Minister of Public Works and Government Services.

Health Canada. (2004c). *Exclusive breastfeeding duration—2004 Health Canada recommendation.* Retrieved from www.hc-sc.gc.ca/hpfb-dgpsa/onpp-bppn/exclusive_breastfeeding_duration_e.html

Health Canada. (2004d). Healthy Canadians: A federal report on comparable health indicators. Retrieved from www.hc-sc.gc.ca/iacb-dgiac/arad-draa/english/accountability/indicators/html#high

Health Canada. (2005a). Canada Prenatal Nutrition Program (CPNP). Retrieved from www.phac-aspc.gc.ca/dea/programs-mes/cpnp_main_e.html

Health Canada. (2005b). Childhood injury: Deaths and hospitalizations in Canada. Retrieved from www.hc-sc.ca

Health Canada. (2005c). Supplement: 2002 Canadian sexually transmitted infections surveillance report. *Canada Communicable Disease Report, 31S2,* 1–39.

Health Canada. (2005d, July 5). 2004 Canadian Community Health Survey: Nutrition. *The Daily.* Retrieved from www.statcan.ca/Daily/English/050706/d050706a.htm

Heath, S. B. (1990). The children of Trackton's children: Spoken and written in social change. In J. Stigler, G. Herdt, & R. A. Shweder (Eds.), *Cultural psychology: Essays on comparative human development* (pp. 496–519). New York: Cambridge University Press.

Heaton, T. B. (2002). Factors contributing to increasing marital stability in the United States. *Journal of Family Issues, 23,* 392–409.

Heckman, J. J., & Masterov, D. V. (2004). *The productivity argument for investing in young children.* Working Paper 5, Invest in Kids Working Group, Committee for Economic Development. Retrieved from jenni.uchicago.edu/Invest

Hedberg, K., Hopkins, D., & Kohn, M. (2003). Five years of legal physician-assisted suicide in Oregon. *New England Journal of Medicine, 348,* 961–964.

Hedge, J. W., Borman, W. C., & Lammlein, S. E. (2006). *The aging workforce: Realities, myths, and implications for organizations.* Washington, DC: American Psychological Association.

Hedges, L. V., & Nowell, A. (1995). Sex differences in mental scores, variability, and numbers of high-scoring individuals. *Science, 269,* 41–45.

Hediger, M. L., Overpeck, M. D., Ruan, W. J., & Troendle, J. F. (2002). Birthweight and gestational age effects on motor and social development. *Paediatric and Perinatal Epidemiology, 16,* 33–46.

Heidrich, S. M., & Ryff, C. D. (1993). Physical and mental health in later life: The self-system as mediator. *Psychology and Aging, 8,* 327–338.

Heilbronn, L. K., & Ravussin, E. (2003). Calorie restriction and aging: Review of the literature and implications for studies in humans. *American Journal of Clinical Nutrition, 78,* 361–369.

Heiman, N., Stallings, M. C., Hofer, S. M., & Hewitt, J. K. (2003). Investigating age differences in the genetic and environmental structure of the tridimensional personality questionnaire in later adulthood. *Behavior Genetics, 33,* 171–180.

Heinz, A., & Blass, J. P. (2002). *Alzheimer's disease: A status report for 2002.* New York: American Council on Science and Health.

Heinz, W. R. (1999a). Introduction: Transitions to employment in a cross-national perspective. In W. R. Heinz (Ed.), *From education to work: Cross-national perspectives* (pp. 1–21). New York: Cambridge University Press.

Heinz, W. R. (1999b). Job entry patterns in life-course perspective. In W. R. Heinz (Ed.), *From education to work: Cross-national perspectives* (pp. 214–231). New York: Cambridge University Press.

Heisel, M. J. (2006). Suicide and its prevention among older adults. *Canadian Journal of Psychiatry, 51,* 143–154.

Helburn, S. W. (Ed.). (1995). *Cost, quality and child outcomes in child care centers.* Denver: University of Colorado.

Helm, H. M., Hays, J. C., Flint, E. P., Koenig, H. G., & Blazer, D. G. (2000). Does private religious activity prolong survival? A six-year follow-up study of 3,851 older adults. *Journal of Gerontology, 55A,* M400–M405.

Helson, R. (1992). Women's difficult times and the rewriting of the life story. *Psychology of Women Quarterly, 16,* 331–347.

Helson, R. (1997). The self in middle age. In M. E. Lachman & J. B. James (Eds.), *Multiple paths of midlife development* (pp. 21–43). Chicago: University of Chicago Press.

Helson, R., Jones, C. J., & Kwan, V. S. Y. (2002). Personality change over 40 years of adulthood: Hierarchical linear modeling analyses of two longitudinal samples. *Journal of Personality and Social Psychology, 83,* 752–766.

Helson, R., Mitchell, V., & Moane, G. (1984). Personality and patterns of adherence and nonadherence to the social clock. *Journal of Personality and Social Psychology, 46,* 1079–1096.

Helson, R., & Moane, G. (1987). Personality change in women from college to midlife. *Journal of Personality and Social Psychology, 53,* 176–186.

Helson, R., & Picano, J. (1990). Is the traditional role bad for women? *Journal of Personality and Social Psychology, 59,* 311–320.

Helson, R., & Roberts, B. W. (1994). Ego development and personality change in adulthood. *Journal of Personality and Social Psychology, 66,* 911–920.

Helson, R., & Stewart, A. (1994). Personality change in adulthood. In T. F. Heatherton & J. L. Weinberger (Eds.), *Can personality change?* (pp. 201–225). Washington, DC: American Psychological Association.

Helson, R., & Wink, P. (1992). Personality change in women from the early 40s to the early 50s. *Psychology and Aging, 7,* 46–55.

Heltzner, E. P., Cauley, J. A., Pratt, S. R., Wisniewski, S. R., Zmuda, J. M., & Talbott, E. O. (2005). Race and sex differences in age-related hearing loss: The health, aging and body composition study. *Journal of the American Geriatrics Society, 53,* 2119–2127.

Helwig, C. C. (1995). Adolescents' and young adults conceptions of civil liberties: Freedom of speech and religion. *Child Development, 66,* 152–166.

Helwig, C. C., & Jasiobedzka, U. (2001). The relation between law and morality: Children's reasoning about socially beneficial and unjust laws. *Child Development, 72,* 1382–1393.

Helwig, C. C., & Prencipe, A. (1999). Children's judgments of flags and flag-burning. *Child Development, 70,* 132–143.

Helwig, C. C., & Turiel, E. (2002a). Children's social and moral reasoning. In P. K. Smith & C. H. Hart (Eds.), *Blackwell handbook of childhood social development* (pp. 476–490). Malden, MA: Blackwell.

Helwig, C. C., & Turiel, E. (2002b). Civil liberties, autonomy, and democracy: Children's perspective. *International Journal of Law and Psychiatry, 25,* 253–270.

Helwig, C. C., Zelazo, P. D., & Wilson, M. (2001). Children's judgments of psychological harm in normal and canonical situations. *Child Development, 72,* 66–81.

Henderson, D., Buchanan, J. A., & Fisher, J. E. (2002). Violence and the elderly population: Issues for prevention. In P.A. Schewe (Ed.), *Preventing violence in relationships: Interventions across the life span* (pp. 223–245). Washington, DC: American Psychological Association.

Henderson, H. A., Marshall, P. J., Fox, N. A., & Rubin, K. H. (2004). Psychophysiological and behavioral evidence for varying forms and functions of nonsocial behavior in preschoolers. *Child Development, 75,* 251–263.

Hendin, H. (1999). Suicide, assisted suicide, and euthanasia. In D. G. Jacobs (Ed.), *The Harvard Medical School guide to suicide assessment and intervention* (pp. 540–560). San Francisco: Jossey-Bass.

Hendrick, S. S., & Hendrick, C. (1993). Lovers as friends. *Journal of Social and Personal Relationships, 10,* 459–466.

Hendrick, S. S., & Hendrick, C. (2002). Love. In C. R. Snyder & S. J. Lopez (Eds.), *Handbook of positive psychology* (pp. 472–484). New York: Oxford University Press.

Hendricks, J., & Cutler, S. J. (2004). Volunteerism and socioemotional selectivity in later life. *Journal of Gerontology, 59B,* S251–S257.

Hendrie, H. H. (2001). Exploration of environmental and genetic risk factors for Alzheimer's disease: The value of cross-cultural studies. *Current Directions in Psychological Science, 10,* 98–101.

Henning, K., Jones, A. R., & Holdford, R. (2005). Attributions of blame among male and female domestic violence offenders. *Journal of Family Violence, 20,* 131–139.

Henrich, C. C., Kuperminc, G. P., Sack, A., Blatt, S. J., & Leadbeater, B. J. (2000). Characteristics and homogeneity of early adolescent friendship groups: A comparison of male and female clique and nonclique members. *Applied Developmental Science, 4,* 15–26.

Henricsson, L., & Rydell, A.-M. (2004). Elementary school children with behavior problems: Teacher–child relations and self-perception. A prospective study. *Merrill-Palmer Quarterly, 50,* 111–138.

Henry, J. D., MacLeod, M. S., Phillips, L. H., & Crawford, J. R. (2004). A meta-analytic review of prospective memory and aging. *Psychology and Aging, 19,* 27–39.

Herbst, J. H., McCrae, R. R., Costa, P. T., Jr., Feaganes, J. R., & Siegler, I. C. (2000). Self-perceptions of stability and change in personality at midlife: The UNC Alumni Heart Study. *Assessment, 7,* 379–388.

Herman, M. (2004). Forced to choose: Some determinants of racial identification in multiracial adolescents. *Child Development, 75,* 730–748.

Hermann, M., Untergasser, G., Rumpold, H., & Berger, P. (2000). Aging of the male reproductive system. *Experimental Gerontology, 35,* 1267–1279.

Herrera, E., Reissland, N., & Shepherd, J. (2004). Maternal touch and maternal child-directed speech: Effects of depressed mood in the postnatal period. *Journal of Affective Disorders, 81,* 29–39.

Herrnstein, R. J., & Murray, C. (1994). *The bell curve.* New York: Free Press.

Hershey, D. A., Walsh, D. A., Brougham, R., & Carter, S. (1998). Challenges of training pre-retirees to make sound financial planning decisions. *Educational Gerontology, 24,* 447–470.

Hespos, S. J., & Baillargeon, R. (2001). Reasoning about containment events in very young infants. *Cognition, 78,* 207–245.

Hess, T. M., Hinson, J. T., & Statham, J. A. (2004). Explicit and implicit stereotype activation effects on memory: Do age and awareness moderate the impact of priming? *Psychology and Aging, 19,* 495–505.

Hesse, E., & Main, M. (2000). Disorganized infant, child, and adult attachment: Collapse in behavioral and attentional strategies. *Journal of the American Psychoanalytic Association, 48,* 1097–1127.

Hessler, R. M., Eriksson, B. G., Dey, D., Steen, G., Sundh, V., & Steen, B. (2003). The compression of morbidity debate in aging: An empirical test using the gerontological and geriatric population studies in Göteborg, Sweden. *Archives of Gerontology and Geriatrics, 37,* 213–222.

Hetherington, E. M. (1999). Should we stay together for the sake of the children? In E. M. Hetherington (ed.), *Coping with divorce, single-parenting, and remarriage: A risk and resiliency perspective* (pp. 93–116). Hillsdale, NJ: Erlbaum.

Hetherington, E. M. (2003). Social support and the adjustment of children in divorced and remarried families. *Childhood, 10,* 237–254

Hetherington, E. M., & Clingempeel, W. G. (1992). Coping with marital transitions: A family systems perspective. *Monographs of the Society for Research in Child Development, 57*(2–3, Serial No. 227).

Hetherington, E. M., & Elmore, A. M. (2004). The intergenerational transmission of couple instability. In P. L. Chase-Landsdale, K. Kiernan, & R. J. Friedman (Eds.), *Human development across lives and generations: The potential for change* (pp. 171–203). New York: Cambridge University Press.

Hetherington, E. M., Henderson, S. H., & Reiss, D. (1999). Adolescent siblings in stepfamilies: Family functioning and adolescent adjustment. *Monographs of the Society for Research in Child Development, 64*(4, Serial No. 259).

Hetherington, E. M., & Jodl, K. M. (1994). Stepfamilies as settings for child development. In A. Booth & J. Dunn (Eds.), *Stepfamilies: Who benefits? Who does not?* (pp. 55–79). Hillsdale, NJ: Erlbaum.

Hetherington, E. M., & Kelly, J. (2002). *For better or for worse: Divorce reconsidered.* New York: Norton.

Hetherington, E. M., Law, T. C., & O'Connor, T. G. (1994). Divorce: Challenges, changes, and new chances. In F. Walsh (Ed.), *Normal family processes* (2nd ed., pp. 208–234). New York: Guilford.

Hetherington, E. M., & Stanley-Hagan, M. (1999). The adjustment of children with divorced parents: A risk and resiliency perspective. *Journal of Child Psychology and Psychiatry, 40,* 129–140.

Hetherington, E. M., & Stanley-Hagan, M. (2000). Diversity among stepfamilies. In D. H. Demo, K. R. Allen, & M. A. Fine (Eds.), *Handbook of family diversity* (pp. 173–196). New York: Oxford University Press.

Hetherington, E. M., & Stanley-Hagan, M. (2002). Parenting in divorced and remarried families. In M. H. Bornstein (Ed.), *Handbook of parenting* (2nd ed., Vol. 3, pp. 287–315). Mahwah, NJ: Erlbaum.

Heuveline, P. (2002). An international comparison of adolescent and young adult morality. *Annals of the American Association of Political and Social Science, 580,* 172–200.

Hewlett, B. S. (1992). Husband–wife reciprocity and the father–infant relationship among Aka pygmies. In B. S. Hewlett (Ed.), *Father–child relations: Cultural and biosocial contexts* (pp. 153–176). New York: Aldine de Gruyter.

Hewlett, B. S. (2004). Fathers in forager, farmer, and pastoral cultures. In M. E. Lamb (Ed.), *The role of the father in child development* (4th ed., pp. 182–195). Hoboken, NJ: Wiley.

Heyman, G. D., & Dweck, C. S. (1998). Children's thinking about traits: Implications for judgments of the self and others. *Child Development, 69,* 391–403.

Heyman, G. D., & Gelman, S. A. (1999). The use of trait labels in making psychological inferences. *Child Development, 70,* 604–619.

Heyman, G. D., & Legare, C. H. (2004). Children's beliefs about gender differences in the academic and social domains. *Sex Roles, 50,* 227–239.

Heyman, G. D., Dweck, C. S., & Cain, K. M. (1992). Young children's vulnerability to self-blame and helplessness: Relationship to beliefs about goodness. *Child Development, 63,* 401–415.

Hibell, B. (2001). *European School Survey Project on Alcohol and Drugs.* Stockholm: Swedish Council for Information on Alcohol and Other Drugs.

Hickling, A. K., & Wellman, H. M. (2001). The emergence of children's causal explanations and theories: Evidence from everyday conversation. *Developmental Psychology, 37,* 668–683.

Hietanen, A., Era, P., Sorri, M., & Heikkinen, E. (2004). Changes in hearing in 80-year-old people: A 10-year follow-up study. *International Journal of Audiology, 43,* 126–135.

Higgins, C., & Duxbury, L. (2002). *The 2001 National Work-Life Conflict Study: Report One.* Retrieved from www.phac-aspc.gc.ca/publicat/work-travail/report1/index.html

High, K. P. (2001). Nutritional strategies to boost immunity and prevent infection in elderly individuals. *Aging and Infectious Diseases, 33,* 1892–1900.

High, P. C., LaGasse, L., Becker, S., Ahlgren, I., & Gardner, A. (2000). Literacy promotion in primary care pediatrics: Can we make a difference? *Pediatrics, 105,* 927–934.

Hildreth, K., & Rovee-Collier, C. (2002). Forgetting functions of reactivated memories over the first year of life. *Developmental Psychobiology, 41,* 277–288.

Hildreth, K., Sweeney, B., & Rovee-Collier, C. (2003). Differential memory-preserving effects of reminders at 6 months. *Journal of Experimental Child Psychology, 84,* 41–62.

Hill, D. (2003). Europe: When dying seems better than living. New York: Radio Free Europe. Retrieved from http://www. rferl .org/nca/features/2003/01/ 22012003154227.as

Hill, J. L., Brooks-Gunn, J., & Waldfogel, J. (2003). Sustained effects of high participation in an early intervention for low-birth-weight premature infants. *Developmental Psychology, 39,* 730–744.

Hill, N. E., & Taylor, I. C. (2004). Parental school involvement and children's academic achievement: Pragmatics and issues. *Current Directions in Psychological Science, 13,* 161–164.

Hillis, S. D., Anda, R. F., Dube, S. R., Felitti, V. J., Marchbanks, P. A., & Marks, J. S. (2004). The association between adverse childhood experiences and adolescent pregnancy, long-term psychosocial consequences, and fetal death. *Pediatrics, 113,* 320–327.

Hillman, J. L. (2000). *Clinical perspectives on elderly sexuality.* New York: Kluwer Academic.

Hillman, J. L., & Stricker, G. (1994). A linkage of knowledge and attitudes toward elderly sexuality: Not necessarily a uniform relationship. *Gerontologist, 34,* 256–260.

Hilt, L. M. (2004). Attribution retaining for therapeutic change: Theory, practice, and future directions. *Imagination, Cognition, and Personality, 23,* 289–307.

Hinde, R. A. (1992). Ethological relationships and approaches. In R. Vasta (Ed.), *Six theories of child development* (pp. 251–285). Philadelphia, PA: Jessica Kingsley.

Hinojosa, T., Sheu, C.-F., & Michael, G. F. (2003). Infant hand-use preference for grasping objects contributes to the development of a hand-use preference for manipulating objects. *Developmental Psychobiology, 43,* 328–334.

Hirsch, C. (1996). Understanding the influence of gender role identity on the assumption of family caregiving roles by men. *International Journal of Aging and Human Development, 42,* 103–121.

Hirshberg, L. M., & Svejda, M. (1990). When infants look to their parents: I. Infants' social referencing of mothers compared to fathers. *Child Development, 61,* 1175–1186.

Hirshorn, B. A., Van Meter, J. V., & Brown, D. R. (2000). When grandparents raise grandchildren due to substance abuse: Responding to a uniquely destabilizing factor. In B. Hayslip, Jr., & R. Goldberg-Glen (Eds.), *Grandparents raising grandchildren: Theoretical, empirical, and clinical perspectives* (pp. 269–288). New York: Springer.

Hirsh-Pasek, K., & Golinkoff, R. M. (2003). *Einstein never used flash cards.* New York: Rodale.

Hite, L. M., & McDonald, K. S. (2003). Career aspirations of nonmanagerial women: Adjustment and adaptation. *Journal of Career Development, 29,* 221–235.

Ho, W. K., Hankey, G. J., & Eikelboom, J. W. (2004). Prevention of coronary heart disease with aspirin and clopidogrel: Efficacy, safety, and cost-effectiveness. *Expert Opinion on Pharmacotherapy, 5,* 493–503.

Hoch, C. C., Dew, M. A., Reynolds, C. F., III, Buysse, D. J., Nowell, P. D., Monk, T. H., Mazumdar, S., Borland, M. D., Miewald, J., & Kupfer, D. J. (1997). Longitudinal changes in diary- and laboratory-based sleep measures in healthy "old old" and "young old" subjects: A three-year follow-up. *Sleep, 20,* 192–202.

Hochwarter, W. A., Ferris, G. R., Perrewe, P. L., Witt, L. A., & Kiewitz, C. (2001). A note on the nonlinearity of the age–job satisfaction relationship. *Journal of Applied Social Psychology, 31,* 1223–1237.

Hock, H. S., Park, C. L., & Bjorklund, D. F. (1998). Temporal organization in children's strategy formation. *Journal of Experimental Child Psychology, 70,* 187–206.

Hodges, J., & Tizard, B. (1989). Social and family relationships of ex-institutional adolescents. *Journal of Child Psychology and Psychiatry, 30,* 77–97.

Hodges, R. M., & French, L. A. (1988). The effect of class and collection labels on cardinality, class-inclusion, and number conservation tasks. *Child Development, 59,* 1387–1396.

Hodgson, J., & Spriggs, M. (2005). A practical account of autonomy: Why genetic counseling is especially well suited to the facilitation of informed autonomous decision making. *Journal of Genetic Counseling, 14,* 89–97.

Hodson, D. S., & Skeen, P. (1994). Sexuality and aging: The hammerlock of myths. *Journal of Applied Gerontology, 13,* 219–235.

Hoenig, H., Taylor, D. H., Jr., & Sloan, F. A. (2003). Does assistive technology substitute for personal assistance among the disabled elderly? *American Journal of Public Health, 93,* 330–337.

Hoff, B. (2001). *Full report of the prevalence, incidence, and consequences of violence against women.* Washington, DC: U.S. Department of Justice.

Hoff, E. (2004). The specificity of environmental influence: Socioeconomic status affects early vocabulary development via maternal speech. *Child Development, 74,* 1368–1378.

Hoff, E., Laursen, B., & Tardif, T. (2002). Socioeconomic status and parenting. In M. H. Bornstein (Ed.), *Handbook of parenting* (pp. 231–252). Mahwah, NJ: Erlbaum.

Hoff, E., & Naigles, L. (2002). How children use input to acquire a lexicon. *Child Development, 73,* 418–433.

Hoffman, L. W. (2000). Maternal employment: Effects of social context. In R. D. Taylor & M. C. Wang (Eds.), *Resilience across contexts: Family, work, culture, and community* (pp. 147–176). Mahwah, NJ: Erlbaum.

Hoffman, L. W., & Youngblade, L. M. (1999). *Mothers at work: Effects on children's well-being.* New York: Cambridge University Press.

Hoffman, M. L. (2000). *Empathy and moral development.* New York: Cambridge University Press.

Hoffman, S., & Hatch, M. C. (1996). Stress, social support and pregnancy outcome: A reassessment based on research. *Paediatric and Perinatal Epidemiology, 10,* 380–405.

Hoffmann, W. (2001). Fallout from the Chernobyl nuclear disaster and congenital malformations in Europe. *Archives of Environmental Health, 56,* 478–483.

Hoffner, C., & Badzinski, D. M. (1989). Children's integration of facial and situational cues to emotion. *Child Development, 60,* 411–422.

Hogan, B. E., & Linden, W. (2004). Anger response styles and blood pressure: At least don't ruminate about it! *Annals of Behavioral Medicine, 27,* 38–49.

Hogan, D. B., MacKnight, C., & Bergman, H. (2003). Models, definitions, and criteria of frailty. *Aging Clinical and Experimental Research, 15* (Suppl. to No. 3), 3–29.

Hogan, J. D. (2003). G. Stanley Hall: Educator, organizer, and pioneer developmental psychologist. In G. A. Kimble & M. Wertheimer (Eds.), *Portraits of pioneers in psychology* (Vol. 5, pp. 19–35). Mahwah, NJ: Erlbaum.

Hokoda, A., & Fincham, F. D. (1995). Origins of children's helpless and mastery achievement patterns in the family. *Journal of Educational Psychology, 87,* 375–385.

Holden, G. W., Coleman, S. M., & Schmidt, K. L. (1995). Why 3-year-old children get spanked: Determinants as reported by college-educated mothers. *Merrill-Palmer Quarterly, 41,* 431–452.

Holland, J. L. (1985). *Making vocational choices: A theory of vocational personalities and work environments.* Englewood Cliffs, NJ: Prentice-Hall.

Holland, J. L. (1997). *Making vocational choices: A theory of vocational personalities and work environments* (3rd ed.). Odessa, FL: Psychological Assessment Resources.

Hollander, P. (2004). The counterculture of the heart. *Society, 41,* 69–77.

Hollich, G. J., Hirsh-Pasek, K., & Golinkoff, R. M. (2000). Breaking the language barrier: An emergentist coalition model for the origins of word learning. *Monographs of the Society for Research in Child Development, 65*(3, Serial No. 262).

Holliday, R. E. (2003). Reducing misinformation effects in children with cognitive interviews: Dissociating recollection and familiarity. *Child Development, 74,* 728–751.

Holmbeck, G. N. (1996). A model of family relational transformations during the transition to adolescence: Parent–adolescent conflict and adaptation. In J. A. Graber, J. Brooks-Gunn, & A. C. Petersen (Eds.), *Transitions through adolescence* (pp. 167–199). Mahwah, NJ: Erlbaum.

Holmes-Rovner, M., Rovner, D. R., Padonu, G., Talarczyk, G., Kroll, J. Rothert, M., & Breer, L. (1996). African-American women's attitudes and expectations of menopause. *American Journal of Preventive Medicine, 12,* 420–423.

Holobow, N., Genesee, F., & Lambert, W. (1991). The effectiveness of a foreign language immersion program for children from different ethnic and social class backgrounds: Report 2. *Applied Psycholinguistics, 12,* 179–198.

Honein, M. A., Paulozzi, L. J., & Erickson, J. D. (2001). Continued occurrence of Accutane-exposed pregnancies. *Teratology, 64,* 142–147.

Hong, Z.-R., Veach, P. M., & Lawrenz, F. (2003). An investigation of the gender stereotyped thinking of Taiwanese secondary school boys and girls. *Sex Roles, 48,* 495–504.

Hood, B. M. (2004). Is looking good enough or does it beggar belief?

Developmental Science, 7, 415–417.

Hood, B. M., Atkinson, J., & Braddick, O. J. (1998). Selection-for-action and the development of orienting and visual attention. In J. E. Richards (Ed.), *Cognitive neuroscience of attention: A developmental perspective* (pp. 219– 251). Mahwah, NJ: Erlbaum.

Hooker, K. (1992). Possible selves and perceived health in older adults and college students. *Journal of Gerontology, 47,* P85–P89.

Hooker, K., & Kaus, C. R. (1994). Health-related possible selves in young and middle adulthood. *Psychology and Aging, 9,* 126–133.

Hooyman, N. B., & Kiyak, H. A. (2005). *Social gerontology* (7th ed.). Boston: Allyn and Bacon.

Hope, S., Power, C., & Rodgers, B. (1999). Does financial hardship account for elevated psychological distress in lone mothers? *Social Science and Medicine, 29,* 381–389.

Hopkins, B., & Butterworth, G. (1997). Dynamical systems approaches to the development of action. In G. Bremner, A. Slater, & G. Butterworth (Eds.), *Infant development: Recent advances* (pp. 75–100). East Sussex, UK: Psychology Press.

Hopkins, B., & Westra, T. (1988). Maternal handling and motor development: An intracultural study. *Genetic, Social and General Psychology Monographs, 14,* 377–420.

Hopp, F. P., & Duffy, S. A. (2000). Racial variations in end-of-life care. *Journal of the American Geriatrics Society, 48,* 658–663.

Hopper, S. V. (1993). The influence of ethnicity on the health of older women. *Clinics in Geriatric Medicine, 9,* 231–259.

Horber, F. F., Kohler, S. A., Lippuner, K., & Jaeger, P. (1996). Effect of regular physical training on age-associated alteration of body composition in men. *European Journal of Clinical Investigation, 26,* 279–285.

Horgan, D. (1978). The development of the full passive. *Journal of Child Language, 5,* 65–80.

Horgas, A. L., Wilms, H., & Baltes, M. M. (1998). Daily life in very old age: Everyday activities as expression of successful living. *Gerontologist, 38,* 556–568.

Horn, J. L., & Donaldson, G. (1980). Cognitive development in adulthood. In O. G. Brim, Jr., & J. Kagan (Eds.), *Constancy and change in human development* (pp. 445–529). Cambridge, MA: Harvard University Press.

Horn, J. L., Donaldson, G., & Engstrom, R. (1981). Apprehension, memory, and fluid intelligence decline through the "vital years"

of adulthood. *Research on Aging, 3,* 33–84.

Horn, J. L., & Masunaga, H. (2000). New directions for research into aging and intelligence: The development of expertise. In T. J. Perfect & E. A. Maylor (Eds.), *Models of cognitive aging* (pp. 125–159). New York: Oxford University Press.

Horn, J. L., & Noll, J. (1997). Human cognitive capabilities: Gf–Gc theory. In D. P. Flanagan, J. L., Genshaft, & P. L. Harrison (Eds.), *Beyond traditional intellectual assessment* (pp. 53–91). New York: Guilford.

Horner, S. L., & Gaither, S. M. (2004). Attribution retraining instruction with a second-grade class. *Early Childhood Education Journal, 31,* 165–170.

Horner, T. M. (1980). Two methods of studying stranger reactivity in infants: A review. *Journal of Child Psychology and Psychiatry, 21,* 203–219.

Hornick, J. P., McDonald, L., & Robertson, G. B. (1992). Elder abuse in Canada and the United States: Prevalence, legal, and service issues. In R. D. Peters, R. J. McMahon, & V. L. Quinsey (Eds.), *Aggression and violence throughout the life span* (pp. 301– 335). Newbury Park, CA: Sage.

Hospice Foundation of America. (2005). *The dying process: A guide for caregivers.* Washington, DC: Author.

Houlihan, J., Kropp. T., Wiles, R., Gray, S., & Campbell, C. (2005). *Body burden: The pollution in newborns.* Washington, DC: Environmental Working Group.

House, J. S., Lantz, P. M., & Herd, P. (2005). Continuity and change in the social stratification of aging and health over the life course: Evidence from a nationally representative longitudinal study from 1986 to 2001/2002 (Americans' Changing Lives Study). *Journal of Gerontology, 60B*(Special Issue II), 15–26.

Hovdestad, W., Tonmyr, L., Hubka, D., & De Marco, R. (2005). The Canadian Incidence Study of Reported Child Abuse and Neglect: Implications for federal responses to child maltreatment. *International Journal of Mental Health Promotion, 7,* 6–13.

Hoven, C. W., Mandell, D., & Duarte, C. S. (2003). Mental health of New York City public school children after 9/11: An epidemiologic investigation. In S. W. Coates & J. L. Rosenthal (Eds.), *September 11: Trauma and human bonds* (pp. 51–74). Hillsdale, NJ: Analytic Press.

Howard, A., & Bray, D. W. (1988). *Managerial lives in transition:*

Advancing age and changing times. New York: Guilford Press.

Howard, A. W. (2002). Automobile restraints for children: A review for clinicians. *Canadian Medical Association Journal, 167,* 769–773.

Howard, B. V., Manson, J. E., Stefanick, M. L., Beresford, S. A., Frank, G., & Jones, B. (2006). Low-fat dietary pattern and weight change over 7 years: The Women's Health Initiative Dietary Modification Trial. *Journal of the American Medical Association, 295,* 39–49.

Howard, D. E., & Wang, M. Q. (2004). Multiple sexual-partner behavior among sexually active U.S. adolescent girls. *American Journal of Health Behavior, 28,* 3–12.

Howe, N., Aquan-Assee, J., & Bukowski, W. M. (2001). Predicting sibling relations over time: Synchrony between maternal management styles and sibling relationship quality. *Merrill-Palmer Quarterly, 47,* 121–141.

Howell, L. C., & Beth, A. (2002). Midlife myths and realities: Women reflect on their experiences. *Journal of Women and Aging, 14,* 189–204.

Howes, C., & James, J. (2002). Children's social development within the socialization context of child care and early childhood education. In P. Smith & C. H. Hart (Eds.), *Blackwell Handbook of childhood social development* (pp. 137–155). New York: Blackwell.

Howes, C., & Matheson, C. C. (1992). Sequences in the development of competent play with peers: Social and social pretend play. *Developmental Psychology, 28,* 961–974.

Hsu, F. L. K. (1981). *Americans and Chinese: Passage to difference* (3rd ed.). Honolulu: University of Hawaii Press.

Hu, F. B., & Manson, J. E. (2001). Diet, lifestyle, and the risk of type 2 diabetes mellitus in women. *New England Journal of Medicine, 345,* 790–797.

Hu, Y., Wood, J. F., Smith, V., & Westbrook, N. (2004). Friendships through IM: Examining the relationship between instant messaging and intimacy. *Journal of Computer-Mediated Communication, 10*(1). Retrieved from jcmc .indiana.edu/vol10/issue1

Hubert, H. B., Bloch, D. A., Oehlert, J. W., & Fries, J. F. (2002). Lifestyle habits and compression of morbidity. *Journal of Gerontology, 57A,* M347–351.

Hudson, J. A., Fivush, R., & Kuebli, J. (1992). Scripts and episodes: The development of event memory. *Applied Cognitive Psychology, 6,* 483–505.

Hudson, J. A., Sosa, B. B., & Shapiro, L. R. (1997). Scripts and plans: The development of preschool children's event knowledge and event planning. In S. L. Friedman & E. K. Scholnick (Eds.), *The developmental psychology of planning* (pp. 77–102). Mahwah, NJ: Erlbaum.

Huesmann, L. R. (1986). Psychological processes promoting the relation between exposure to media violence and aggressive behavior by the viewer. *Journal of Social Issues, 42,* 125–139.

Huesmann, L. R., Moise-Titus, J., Podolski, C. & Eron, L. D. (2003). Longitudinal relations between children's exposure to TV violence and their aggressive and violent behavior in young adulthood: 1977–1992. *Developmental Psychology, 39,* 201–221.

Huey, S. J., Jr., & Henggeler, S. W. (2001). Effective community-based interventions for antisocial and delinquent adolescents. In J. N. Hughes & A. M. La Greca (Eds.), *Handbook of psychological services for children and adolescents* (pp. 301–322). London: Oxford University Press.

Hughes, C. (1998). Finding your marbles: Does preschoolers' strategic behavior predict later understanding of mind? *Developmental Psychology, 34,* 1326–1339.

Hughes, C., & Dunn, J. (1998). Understanding mind and emotion: Longitudinal associations with mental-state talk between young friends. *Developmental Psychology, 34,* 1026–1037.

Hughes, D. C., & Ng, S. (2003). Reducing health disparities among children. *Future of Children, 13,* 153–167.

Hughes, J. N., Cavell, T. A., & Grossman, P. B. (1997). A positive view of self: Risk or protection for aggressive children? *Development and Psychopathology, 9,* 75–94.

Hultsch, D. F., Hertzog, C., Dixon, R. A., & Small, B. J. (1998). *Memory change in the aged.* New York: Cambridge University Press.

Hultsch, D. F., MacDonald, S. W. S., & Dixon, R. A. (2002). Variability in reaction time performance of younger and older adults. *Journal of Gerontology, 57B,* P101–P115.

Human Genome Program. (2004). SNP Fact Sheet. Retrieved from www.ornl.gov/hgmis

Human Resources Development Canada. (2000). *Dropping out of high school: Definitions and costs.* Hull, Quebec: Author.

Humphrey, T. (1978). Function of the nervous system during prenatal life. In U. Stave (Ed.), *Perinatal physiology* (pp. 651–683). New York: Plenum.

Hungerford, T. L. (2003). Is there an American way of aging? Income dynamics of the elderly in the United States and Germany. *Research on Aging, 25,* 435–455.

Hunnius, S., & Geuze, R. H. (2004a). Developmental changes in visual scanning of dynamic faces and abstract stimuli in infants: A longitudinal study. *Infancy, 6,* 231–255.

Hunnius, S., & Geuze, R. H. (2004b). Gaze shifting in infancy: A longitudinal study using dynamic faces and abstract stimuli. *Infant Behavior and Development, 27,* 397–416.

Hurme, H. (1991). Dimensions of the grandparent role in Finland. In P. K. Smith (Ed.), *The psychology of grandparenthood: An international perspective* (pp. 19–31). London: Routledge.

Hursti, U. K. (1999). Factors influencing children's food choice. *Annals of Medicine, 31,* 26–32.

Hursting, S. D., Lavigne, J. A., Berrigan, D., Perkins, S. N., & Barrett, J. C. (2003). Calorie restriction, aging, and cancer prevention: Mechanisms of action and applicability to humans. *Annual Review of Medicine, 54,* 131–152.

Hurt, H., Brodsky, N. L., Roth, H., Malmud, E., & Giannetta, J. M. (2005). School performance of children with gestational cocaine exposure. *Neurotoxicology and Teratology, 27,* 203–211.

Husain, G., Thompson, W. F., & Schellenberg, E. G. (2002). Effects of musical tempo and mode on arousal, mood, and spatial abilities. *Music Perception, 20,* 151–171.

Husaini, B. A., Blasi, A. J., & Miller, O. (1999). Does public and private religiosity have a moderating effect on depression? A bi-racial study of elders in the American south. *International Journal of Aging and Human Development, 48,* 63–72.

Huston, A. C., & Alvarez, M. M. (1990). The socialization of gender role development in early adolescence. In R. Montemayor, G. R. Adams, & T. P. Gullotta (Eds.), *From childhood to adolescence: A transitional period?* (pp. 156–179). Newbury Park, CA: Sage.

Huston, A. C., Wright, J. C., Marquis, J., & Green, S. B. (1999). How young children spend their time: Television and other activities. *Developmental Psychology, 35,* 912–925.

Huston, P., McHale, S., & Crouter, A. (1986). When the honeymoon's over: Changes in the marriage relationship over the first year. In R. Gilmour & S. Duck (Eds.), *The emerging field of personal relationships* (pp. 109– 132). Hillsdale, NJ: Erlbaum.

Huttenlocher, P. R. (2002). *Neural plasticity: The effects of environment on the development of the cerebral cortex.* Cambridge, MA: Harvard University Press.

Huyck, M. H. (1990). Gender differences in aging. In J. E. Birren & K. W. Schaie (Eds.), *Handbook of the psychology of aging* (3rd ed., pp. 124–134). New York: Academic Press.

Huyck, M. H. (1995). Marriage and close relationships of the marital kind. In R. Blieszner & V. H. Bedford (Eds.), *Handbook of aging and the family* (pp. 181– 200). Westport, CT: Greenwood Press.

Huyck, M. H. (1996). Continuities and discontinuities in gender identity. In V. L. Bengtson (Ed.), *Adulthood and aging* (pp. 98–121). New York: Springer-Verlag.

Huyck, M. H. (1998). Gender roles and gender identity in midlife. In S. L. Willis & J. D. Reid (Eds.), *Life in the middle* (pp. 209–232). San Diego: Academic Press.

Hyde, J. S., Essex, M. J., Clark, R., & Klein, M. H. (2001). Maternity leave, women's employment, and marital incompatibility. *Journal of Family Psychology, 15,* 476–491.

Hyde, J. S., & Oliver, M. B. (2000). Gender differences in sexuality: Results from meta-analysis. In C. B. Travis & J. W. White (Eds.), *Sexuality, society, and feminism* (pp. 57–77). Washington, DC: American Psychological Association.

Hymel, S., LeMare, L., Ditner, E., & Woody, E. Z. (1999). Assessing self-concept in children: Variations across self-concept domains. *Merrill-Palmer Quarterly, 45,* 602–623.

Hynes, K., & Clarkberg, M. (2005). Women's employment patterns during early parenthood: A group-based trajectory analysis. *Journal of Marriage and Family, 67,* 222–239.

Hyppönen, E., Power, C., & Smith, G. D. (2003). Prenatal growth, BMI, and risk of type 2 diabetes by early midlife. *Diabetes Care, 26,* 2512–2517.

I

Ianni, F. A. J., & Orr, M. T. (1996). Dropping out. In J. A. Graber, J. Brooks-Gunn, & A. C. Petersen (Eds.), *Transitions through adolescence: Interpersonal domains and context* (pp. 285–322). Mahwah, NJ: Erlbaum.

Idler, E. L., & Kasl, S. V. (1997). Religion among disabled and nondisabled persons I: Cross-sectional patterns in health practices, social activities, and well-being. *Journal of Gerontology, 52B,* S294–S305.

Iglowstein, I., Jenni, O. G., Molinari, L., & Largo, R. H.

(2003). Sleep duration from infancy to adolescence: Reference values and generational trends. *Pediatrics, 111,* 302–307.

Ihinger-Tallman, M., & Pasley, K. (1997). Stepfamilies in 1984 and today—A scholarly perspective. *Marriage and Family Review, 26,* 19–40.

Ikkink, K. K., & van Tilburg, T. (1998). Do older adults' network members continue to provide instrumental support in unbalanced relationships? *Journal of Social and Personal Relationships, 15,* 59–75.

Illeris, K. (2004). *Adult education and adult learning.* Melbourne, FL: Krieger Publishing.

Inhelder, B., & Piaget, J. (1958). *The growth of logical thinking from childhood to adolescence: An essay on the construction of formal operational structures.* New York: Basic Books. (Original work published 1955)

Institute for Social Research. (2002). U.S. husbands do more housework. Ann Arbor: Author. Retrieved from: http://www .newswise.com/articles/2002/3/ timeuse.umi.html

International Human Genome Sequencing Consortium. (2004). Finishing the euchronmatic sequence of the human genome. *Nature, 21,* 931–945.

Iocaboni, M., Molnar-Szakacs, I., Gallese, V., Buccino, G., & Mazziotta, J. C. (2005). Grasping the intentions of others with one's own mirror neuron system. *Public Library of Science: Biology, 3*(3), e79.

Iribarren, C., Sidney, S., Bild, D. E., Liu, K., Markowitz, J. H., Roseman, J. M., & Matthews, K. (2000). Association of hostility with coronary artery calcification in young adults. *Journal of the American Medical Association, 283,* 2546–2551.

Isabella, R. (1993). Origins of attachment: Maternal interactive behavior across the first year. *Child Development, 64,* 605–621.

Isabella, R., & Belsky, J. (1991). Interactional synchrony and the origins of infant–mother attachment: A replication study. *Child Development, 62,* 373–384.

Izard, C. E., & Ackerman, B. P. (2000). Motivational, organizational, and regulatory functions of discrete emotions. In M. Lewis & J. M. Haviland-Jones (Eds.), *Handbook of emotions* (2nd ed., pp. 253–264). New York: Guilford.

Izard, C. E., Hembree, E. A., & Huebner, R. R. (1987). Infants' emotional expressions to acute pain. *Developmental Psychology, 23,* 105–113.

Izard, C. E., Trentacosta, C. J., King, K. A., & Mostow, A. J. (2004). An emotion-based prevention program for Head Start children. *Early Education and Development, 15,* 407–422.

J

Jaakkola, J. J., & Gissler, M. (2004). Maternal smoking in pregnancy, fetal development, and childhood asthma. *American Journal of Public Health, 94,* 136–140.

Jaccard, J., Dodge, T., & Dittus, P. (2002). Parent–adolescent communication about sex and birth control: A conceptual framework. In S. S. Feldman & D. A. Rosenthal (Eds.), *Talking sexuality: Parent–adolescent communication* (pp. 9–41). San Francisco: Jossey-Bass.

Jaccard, J., Dodge, T., & Dittus, P. (2003). Maternal discussions about pregnancy and adolescents' attitudes toward pregnancy. *Journal of Adolescent Health, 33,* 84–87.

Jackson, G. R., & Owsley, C. (2000). Scotopic sensitivity during adulthood. *Vision Research, 40,* 2467–2473.

Jackson, R. A., Gibson, K. A., & Wu, Y. W. (2004). Perinatal outcomes in singletons following in vitro fertilization: A meta-analysis. *Obstetrics and Gynecology, 103,* 551–563.

Jackson, T., Fritch, A., Nagaska, T., & Gunderson, J. (2002). Towards explaining the association between shyness and loneliness: A path analysis with American college students. *Social Behavior and Personality, 30,* 263–270.

Jackson, V. A., Sullivan, A. M., Gadmer, N. M., Seltzer, J., Mitchell, A. M., & Lakoma, M. D. (2005). "It was haunting . . .": Physicians' descriptions of emotionally powerful patient deaths. *Academic Medicine, 80,* 648–656.

Jacobs, J. A., & King, R. B. (2002). Age and college completion: A life-history analysis of women aged 15–44. *Sociology of Education, 75,* 211–230.

Jacobs, J. E., & Klaczynski, P. A. (2002). The development of judgment and decision making during childhood and adolescence. *Current Directions in Psychological Science, 11,* 145–149.

Jacobs, J. E., Lanza, S., Osgood, D. W., Eccles, J. S., & Wigfield, A. (2002). Changes in children's self-competence and values: Gender and domain differences across grades one through twelve. *Child Development, 73,* 509–527.

Jacobs, J. E., & Weisz, V. (1994). Gender stereotypes: Implications for gifted education. *Roeper Review, 16,* 152–155.

Jacobs-Lawson, J. M., Hershey, D. A., & Neukam, K. A. (2004). Gender differences in factors that influence time spent planning for retirement. *Journal of Women and Aging, 16,* 55–69.

Jacobson, J. L., & Jacobson, S. W. (2003). Prenatal exposure to polychlorinated biphenyls and attention at school age. *Journal of Pediatrics, 143,* 780–788.

Jacobson, K. C., & Crockett, L. J. (2000). Parental monitoring and adolescent adjustment: An ecological perspective. *Journal of Research on Adolescence, 10,* 65–97.

Jacobson, S. W., Jacobson, J. L., Sokol, R. J., Chiodo, L. M., & Corobana, R. (2004). Maternal age, alcohol abuse history, and quality of parenting as moderators of the effects of prenatal alcohol exposure on 7.5-year intellectual function. *Alcoholism: Clinical and Experimental Research, 28,* 1732–1745.

Jacquet, P. (2004). Sensitivity of germ cells and embryos to ionizing radiation. *Journal of Biological Regulators and Homeostatic Agents, 18,* 106–114.

Jadack, R. A., Hyde, J. S., Moore, C. F., & Keller, M. L. (1995). Moral reasoning about sexually transmitted diseases. *Child Development, 66,* 167–177.

Jaffe, J., Beebe, B., Feldstein, S., Crown, C. L., & Jasnow, M. D. (2001). Rhythms of dialogue in infancy. *Monographs of the Society for Research in Child Development, 66* (2, Serial No. 265).

Jaffee, S. R., Caspi, A., Moffitt, T. E., Belsky, J., & Silva, P. (2001). Why are children born to teen mothers at risk for adverse outcomes in young adulthood? Results of a 20-year longitudinal study. *Development and Psychopathology, 13,* 377–397.

Jaffee, S. R., & Hyde, J. S. (2000). Gender differences in moral orientation: A meta-analysis. *Psychological Bulletin, 126,* 703–706.

Jaffee, S. R., Moffitt, T. E., Caspi, A., & Taylor, A. (2003). Life with (or without) father: The benefits of living with two biological parents depend on the father's antisocial behavior. *Child Development, 74,* 109–126.

Jain, A. (2002). Influence of vitamins and trace-elements on the incidence of respiratory infection in the elderly. *Nutrition Research, 22,* 85–87.

Jain, A., Concat, J., & Leventhal, J. M. (2002). How good is the evidence linking breastfeeding and intelligence? *Pediatrics, 109,* 1044–1053.

Jambunathan, S., Burts, D. C., & Pierce, S. (2000). Comparisons of parenting attitudes among five ethnic groups in the United States.

Journal of Comparative Family Studies, 31, 395–406.

James, D. (1998). Recent advances in fetal medicine. *British Medical Journal, 316,* 1580–1583.

James, J. B., Lewkowicz, C., Libhaber, J., & Lachman, M. (1995). Rethinking the gender identity crossover hypothesis: A test of a new model. *Sex Roles, 32,* 185–207.

James, W. (1963). *Psychology.* New York: Fawcett. (Original work published 1890)

Jamieson, J. R. (1995). Interactions between mothers and children who are deaf. *Journal of Early Intervention, 19,* 108–117.

Jang, S. J., & Johnson, B. R. (2001). Neighborhood disorder, individual religiosity, and adolescent use of illicit drugs: A test of multilevel hypotheses. *Criminology, 39,* 109–143.

Janosz, M., Le Blanc, M., Boulerice, B., & Tremblay, R. E. (2000). Predicting different types of school dropouts: A typological approach with two longitudinal samples. *Journal of Educational Psychology, 92,* 171–190.

Jansen, A., Theunissen, N., Slechten, K., Nederkoorn, C., Boon, B., Mulkens, S., & Roefs, A. (2003). Overweight children overeat after exposure to food cues. *Eating Behaviors, 4,* 197–209.

Janssen, P. A., Lee, S. K., Ryan, E. M., Etches, D. J., Farquharson, D. F., & Peacock, D. (2002). Outcomes of planned home births versus planned hospital births after regulation of midwifery in British Columbia. *Canadian Medical Association Journal, 166,* 315–323.

Janssens, J. M. A. M., & Deković, M. (1997). Child rearing, prosocial moral reasoning, and prosocial behaviour. *International Journal of Behavioral Development, 20,* 509–527.

Jarvis, J. F., & van Heerden, H. G. (1967). The acuity of hearing in the Kalahari Bushman: A pilot study. *Journal of Laryngology and Otology, 81,* 63–68.

Jayakody, R., & Cabrera, N. (2002). What are the choices for low-income families? Cohabitation, marriage, and remaining single. In A. Booth & A. C. Crouter (Eds.), *Just living together* (pp. 85–96). Mahwah, NJ: Erlbaum.

Jayakody, R., & Kalil, A. (2002). Social fathering in low-income, African-American families with preschool children. *Journal of Marriage and Family, 64,* 504–516.

Jeffrey, J. (2004, November). Parents often blind to their kids' weight. *British Medical Journal Online.* Retrieved from content.health .msn.com/content/article/97/ 104292.htm

Jellinger, K. A. (2004). Head injury and dementia. *Current Opinion in Neurology, 17,* 719–723.

Jemal, A., Siegel, R., Ward, E., Murray, T., Xu, J., Smigal, C., & Thun, M. J. (2006). Cancer statistics, 2006. *CA: A Cancer Journal for Clinicians, 56,* 106–130.

Jendrek, M. P. (1994). Grandparents who parent their grandchildren: Circumstances and decisions. *Gerontologist, 34,* 206–216.

Jenkins, J. M., & Astington, J. W. (2000). Theory of mind and social behavior: Causal models tested in a longitudinal study. *Merrill-Palmer Quarterly, 46,* 203–220.

Jenkins, J. M., Rasbash, J., & O'Connor, T. G. (2003). The role of the shared family context in differential parenting. *Developmental Psychology, 39,* 99–113.

Jenkins, J. M., Turrell, S. L., Kogushi, Y., Lollis, S., & Ross, H. S. (2003). A longitudinal investigation of the dynamics of mental state talk in families. *Child Development, 74,* 905–920.

Jenkins, K. R., Pienta, A. M., & Horgas, A. L. (2002). Activity and health-related quality of life in continuing care retirement communities. *Research on Aging, 24,* 124–149.

Jennett, B. (2002). The vegetative state. *Journal of Neurology and Neurosurgical Psychiatry, 73,* 355–356.

Jensen, A. R. (1969). How much can we boost IQ and scholastic achievement? *Harvard Educational Review, 39,* 1–123.

Jensen, A. R. (1985). The nature of the black–white difference on various psychometric tests: Spearman's hypothesis. *Behavioral and Brain Sciences, 8,* 193–219.

Jensen, A. R. (1998). *The g factor: The science of mental ability.* New York: Praeger.

Jensen, A. R. (2001). Spearman's hypothesis. In J. M. Collis & S. Messick (Eds.), *Intelligence and personality: Bridging the gap in theory and measurement* (pp. 3–24). Mahwah, NJ: Erlbaum.

Jensen, A. R. (2002). Galton's legacy to research on intelligence. *Journal of Biosocial Science, 34,* 145–172.

Jepson, K. L., & Labouvie-Vief, G. (1992). Symbolic processing of youth and elders. In R. L. West and J. D. Sinnott (Eds.), *Everyday memory and aging* (pp. 124–137). New York: Springer.

Jiao, S., Ji, G., & Jing, Q. (1996). Cognitive development of Chinese urban only children and children with siblings. *Child Development, 67,* 387–395.

Joe, S., & Marcus, S. C. (2003). Data-points: Trends by race and gender in suicide attempts among U.S.

adolescents. *Psychiatric Services, 54,* 454.

John, U., Meyer, C., Rumpf, H. J., & Hapke, U. (2003). Probabilities of alcohol high-risk drinking, abuse or dependence estimating on grounds of tobacco smoking and nicotine dependence. *Addiction, 98,* 805–814.

Johnson, C. (2002). Obesity, weight management, and self-esteem. In T. A. Wadden & A. J. Stunkard (Eds.), *Handbook of obesity treatment* (pp. 480–493). New York: Guilford.

Johnson, C. L. (1985). *Growing up and growing old in Italian-American families.* New Brunswick, NJ: Rutgers University Press.

Johnson, C. L. (1998). Effects of adult children's divorce on grandparenthood. In M. E. Szinovacz (Ed.), *Handbook on grandparenthood* (pp. 87–96). Westport, CT: Greenwood Press.

Johnson, C. L., & Troll, L. (1992). Family functioning in late life. *Journal of Gerontology, 47,* S66–S72.

Johnson, C. L., & Troll, L. E. (1994). Constraints and facilitators to friendships in late life. *Gerontologist, 34,* 79–87.

Johnson, D. E. (2000). Medical and developmental sequelae of early childhood institutionalization in Eastern European adoptees. In C. A. Nelson (Ed.), *Minnesota symposia on child psychology* (Vol. 31, pp. 113–162). Mahwah, NJ: Erlbaum.

Johnson, D. E. (2002). Adoption and the effect on children's development. *Early Human Development, 68,* 39–54.

Johnson, J. G., Cohen, P., Smailes, E. M., Kasen, S., & Brook, J. S. (2002). Television viewing and aggressive behavior during adolescence and adulthood. *Science, 295,* 2468–2471.

Johnson, M. D., Cohan, C. L., Davila, J., Lawrence, E., Rogge, R. D., Karney, B. R., Sullivan, K. T., & Bradbury, T. N. (2005). Problem-solving skills and affective expressions as predictors of change in marital satisfaction. *Journal of Consulting and Clinical Psychology, 73,* 15–27.

Johnson, M. H. (1999). Ontogenetic constraints on neural and behavioral plasticity: Evidence from imprinting and face processing. *Canadian Journal of Experimental Psychology, 55,* 77–90.

Johnson, M. H. (2001). The development and neural basis of face recognition: Comment and speculation. *Infant and Child Development, 10,* 31–33.

Johnson, M. H. (2005). Developmental neuroscience, psychophysiology, and genetics. In M. H.

Bornstein & M. E. Lamb (Eds.), *Developmental science: An advanced textbook* (5th ed., pp. 187–222). Mahwah, NJ: Erlbaum.

Johnson, S. P., Bremner, J. G., Slater, A., Mason, U., Foster, K., & Cheshire, A. (2003). Infants' perception of object trajectories. *Child Development, 74,* 94–108.

Johnson, S. P., Slemmer, J. A., & Amso, D. (2004). Where infants look determines how they see: Eye movements and object perception performance in 3-month-olds. *Infancy, 6,* 185–201.

Johnston, M. V., Nishimura, A., Harum, K., Pekar, J., & Blue, M. E. (2001). Sculpting the developing brain. *Advances in Pediatrics, 48,* 1–38.

Jones, C. M., Braithwaite, V. A., & Healy, S. D. (2003). The evolution of sex differences in spatial ability. *Behavioral Neuroscience, 117,* 403–411.

Jones, E. F., & Thompson, N. R. (2001). Action perception and outcome valence: Effects on children's inferences of intentionality and moral and liking judgments. *Journal of Genetic Psychology, 162,* 154–166.

Jones, F. (2003). *Religious commitment in Canada, 1997 and 2000. Religious Commitment Monograph No. 3.* Ottawa: Christian Commitment Research Institute.

Jones, G. P., & Dembo, M. H. (1989). Age and sex role differences in intimate friendships during childhood and adolescence. *Merrill-Palmer Quarterly, 35,* 445–462.

Jones, J., Lopez, A., & Wilson, M. (2003). Congenital toxoplasmosis. *American Family Physician, 67,* 2131–2137.

Jones, M. C. (1965). Psychological correlates of somatic development. *Child Development, 36,* 899–911.

Jones, M. C., & Mussen, P. H. (1958). Self-conceptions, motivations, and interpersonal attitudes of early- and late-maturing girls. *Child Development, 29,* 491–501.

Jones, R. K., Purcell, A., Singh, S., & Finer, L. B. (2005). Adolescents' reports of parental knowledge of adolescents' use of sexual health services and their reactions to mandated parental notification for prescription contraceptives. *Journal of the American Medical Association, 293,* 340–348.

Jones, W. H. (1990). Loneliness and social exclusion. *Journal of Social and Clinical Psychology, 9,* 214–220.

Jongbloet, P. H., Zielhuis, G. A., Groenewoud, H. M., & Pasker-De Jong, P. C. (2001). The secular trends in male:female ratio at birth in postwar industrialized countries. *Environmental Health Perspectives, 109,* 749–752.

Jordan, B. (1993). *Birth in four cultures.* Prospect Heights, IL: Waveland.

Jorgensen, K. M. (1999). Pain assessment and management in the newborn infant. *Journal of Peri-Anesthesia Nursing, 14,* 349–356.

Jose, P., Huntsinger, C., Huntsinger, P., & Liaw, F.-R. (2000). Parental values and practices relevant to young children's social development in Taiwan and the United States. *Journal of Cross-Cultural Psychology, 31,* 677–702.

Joseph, J. (1997). Fear of crime among black elderly. *Journal of Black Studies, 27,* 698–717.

Joseph, R. M., & Tager-Flusberg, H. (2004). The relationship of theory of mind and executive functions to symptom type and severity in children with autism. *Development and Psychopathology, 16,* 137–155.

Joyner, M. H., & Kurtz-Costes, B. (1997). Metamemory development. In W. Schneider & F. E. Weinert (Eds.), *Memory performance and competencies: Issues in growth and development* (pp. 275–300). Hillsdale, NJ: Erlbaum.

Julkunen, J. (1996). Suppressing your anger: Good manners, bad health? In C. D. Spielberger & I. G. Sarason (Eds.), *Stress and emotion: Anxiety, anger, and curiosity* (Vol. 16, pp. 227–240). Washington, DC: Taylor & Francis.

Juntunen, C. L., Wegner, K. E., & Matthews, L. G. (2002). Promoting positive career change in midlife. In C. L. Juntunen & D. R. Atkinson (Eds.), *Counseling across the lifespan* (pp. 329–347). Thousand Oaks, CA: Sage.

Jusczyk, P. W. (2002). Some critical developments in acquiring native language sound organization. *Annals of Otology, Rhinology and Laryngology, 189,* 11–15.

Jusczyk, P. W., & Luce, P. A. (2002). Speech perception. In H. Pashler & S. Yantis (Eds.), *Steven's handbook of experimental psychology: Vol. 1. Sensation and perception* (3rd ed., pp. 493–536). New York: Wiley.

Justice for Children and Youth. (2003). *Corporal punishment.* Toronto: Canadian Foundation for Children, Youth, and the Law. Retrieved from www.jfcy.org/corporalp/corporalp.html

K

Kagan, J. (1998). Biology and the child. In N. Eisenberg (Ed.), *Handbook of child psychology: Vol. 3. Social, emotional, and personality development* (5th ed., pp. 177–236). New York: Wiley.

Kagan, J. (2003). Behavioral inhibition as a temperamental category. In R. J. Davidson, K. R. Scherer, & H. H. Goldsmith (Eds.), *Handbook of affective science* (pp. 320–331). New York: Oxford University Press.

Kagan, J., Arcus, D., Snidman, N., Feng, W. Y. Hendler, J., & Greene, S. (1994). Reactivity in infants: A cross-national comparison. *Developmental Psychology, 30,* 342–345.

Kagan, J., & Saudino, K. J. (2001). Behavioral inhibition and related temperaments. In R. N. Emde & J. K. Hewitt (Eds.), *Infancy to early childhood: Genetic and environmental influences on developmental change* (pp. 111–119). New York: Oxford University Press.

Kagan, J., Snidman, N., Zentner, M., & Peterson, E. (1999). Infant temperament and anxious symptoms in school-age children. *Development and Psychopathology, 11,* 209–224.

Kagawa, Y. (1978). Impact of westernization on the nutrition of Japanese: Changes in physique, cancer, longevity, and centenarians. *Preventive Medicine, 7,* 205–217.

Kahana, E., King, C., Kahana, B., Menne, H., Webster, N. J., & Dan, A. (2005). Successful aging in the face of chronic disease. In M. L. Wykle, P. J. Whitehouse, & D. L. Morris (Eds.), *Successful aging through the life span* (pp. 101–126). New York: Springer.

Kahn, P. H., Jr. (1992). Children's obligatory and discretionary moral judgments. *Child Development, 63,* 416–430.

Kail, R. V. (2003). Information processing and memory. In M. H. Bornstein, L. Davidson, C. L. M. Keyes, K. A. Moore, and the Center for Child Well-Being (Eds.), *Well-being: Positive development across the life course* (pp. 269–280). Mahwah, NJ: Erlbaum.

Kail, R., & Park, Y. (1992). Global developmental change in processing time. *Merrill-Palmer Quarterly, 38,* 525–541.

Kail, R., & Park, Y. (1994). Processing time, articulation time, and memory span. *Journal of Experimental Child Psychology, 57,* 281–291.

Kaisa, A., Stattin, H., & Nurmi, J. (2000). Parenting styles and adolescents' achievement strategies. *Journal of Adolescence, 23,* 205–222.

Kalache, A., Aboderin, I., & Hoskins, I. (2002). Compression of morbidity and active ageing: Key priorities for public health policy in the 21st century. *Bulletin of the World Health Organization, 80,* 243–244.

Kalaria, R. (2002). Similarities between Alzheimer's disease and vascular dementia. *Journal of the Neurological Sciences, 15,* 203–204.

Kalies, H., Heinrich, J., Borte, N., Schaaf, B., von Berg, A., & von Kries, R. (2005). The effect of breastfeeding on weight gain in infants: Results of a birth cohort study. *European Journal of Medical Research, 10,* 36–42.

Kalish, R. A. (1985). The social context of death and dying. In R. H. Binstock & E. Shanas (Eds.), *Handbook of aging and the social sciences* (2nd ed., pp. 149–170). New York: Van Nostrand Reinhold.

Kalof, L. (2000). Ethnic differences in female sexual victimization. *Sexuality and Culture, 2,* 75–97.

Kaltiala-Heino, R., Kosunen, E., & Rimpelä, M. (2003). Pubertal timing, sexual behaviour and self-reported depression in middle adolescence. *Journal of Adolescence, 26,* 531–545.

Kamerman, S. B. (1993). International perspectives on child care policies and programs. *Pediatrics, 91,* 248–252.

Kamo, Y. (1998). Asian grandparents. In M. E. Szinovacz (Ed.), *Handbook on grandparenthood* (pp. 97–112). Westport, CT: Greenwood Press.

Kandall, S. R., Gaines, J., Habel, L., Davidson, G., & Jessop, D. (1993). Relationship of maternal substance abuse to subsequent sudden infant death syndrome in offspring. *Journal of Pediatrics, 123,* 120–126.

Kane, C. M. (2000). African-American family dynamics as perceived by family members. *Journal of Black Studies, 30,* 691–702.

Kane, P., & Garber, J. (2004). The relations among depression in fathers, children's psychopathology, and father–child conflict: A meta-analysis. *Clinical Psychology Review, 24,* 339–360.

Kao, G., & Tienda, M. (1995). Optimism and achievement: The educational performance of immigrant youth. *Social Science Quarterly, 76,* 1–19.

Kaplan, D. L., & Keys, C. B. (1997). Sex and relationship variables as predictors of sexual attraction in cross-sex platonic friendships between young heterosexual adults. *Journal of Social and Personal Relationships, 14,* 191–206.

Kaprio, J., Rimpela, A., Winter, T., Viken, R. J., Pimpela, M., & Rose, R. J. (1995). Common genetic influence on BMI and age at menarche. *Human Biology, 67,* 739–753.

Karadsheh, R. (1991, April). *This room is a junkyard!: Children's* comprehension of metaphorical language. Paper presented at the biennial meeting of the Society for Research in Child Development, Seattle, WA.

Karasik, D., Demissie, S., Cupples, L. A., & Kiel, D. P. (2005). Disentangling the genetic determinants of human aging: Biological age as an alternative to the use of survival measures. Journal of Gerontology, 60A, 574–587.

Karpati, A. M., Rubin, C. H., Kieszak, S. M., Marcus, M., & Troiano, R. P. (2002). Stature and pubertal stage assessment in American boys: The 1988–1994 Third National Health and Nutrition Examination Survey. Journal of Adolescent Health, 30, 205–212.

Karpov, Y. (2005). The neo-Vygotskian approach to child development. New York: Cambridge University Press.

Kastenbaum, R. (2007). Death, society, and human experience (9th ed.). Boston: Allyn and Bacon.

Kato, I., Franco, P., Groswasser, J., Scaillet, S., Kelmanson, I., Togari, H., & Kahn, A. (2003). Incomplete arousal processes in infants who were victims of sudden death. American Journal of Respiratory and Critical Care, 168, 1298–1303.

Katz, L. F., & Windecker-Nelson, B. (2004). Parental meta-emotion philosophy in families with conduct-problem children: Links with peer relations. Journal of Abnormal Child Psychology, 32, 385–398.

Katzman, D. K. (2005). Medical complications in adolescents with anorexia nervosa: A review of the literature. International Journal of Eating Disorders, 37, S52–S59.

Kaufman, A. S. (2001). WAIS-III IQs, Horn's theory, and generational changes from young adulthood to old age. Intelligence, 29, 131-167.

Kaufman, A. S., & Horn, J. L. (1996). Age changes on tests of fluid and crystallized intelligence for females and males on the Kaufman Adolescent and Adult Intelligence Test (KAIT) at ages 17 to 94 years. Archives of Clinical Neuropsychology, 11, 97–121.

Kaufman, J., & Charney, D. (2001). Effects of early stress on brain structure and function: Implications for understanding the relationship between child maltreatment and depression. Development and Psychopathology, 13, 451–471.

Kaufman, J., & Charney, D. (2003). The neurobiology of child and adolescent depression: Current knowledge and future directions. In D. Cicchetti & E. Walker (Eds.), Neurodevelopmental mechanisms in psychopathology (pp. 461–490).

New York: Cambridge University Press.

Kausler, D. H. (1991). Experimental psychology, cognition, and human aging. New York: Springer.

Kausler, D. H. (1994). Learning and memory in normal aging. San Diego: Academic Press.

Kavanaugh, R. D., & Engel, S. (1998). The development of pretense and narrative in early childhood. In O. N. Saracho & B. Spodek (Eds.), Multiple perspectives on play in early childhood education (pp. 80–99). Albany: State University of New York Press.

Kaye, K., & Marcus, J. (1981). Infant imitation: The sensory-motor agenda. Developmental Psychology, 17, 258–265.

Kaye, W. H., Frank, G. K., Bailer, U. F., & Henry, S. E. (2005). Neurobiology of anorexia nervosa: Clinical implications of alterations of the function of serotonin and other neuronal systems. International Journal of Eating Disorders, 37, S15–S19.

Kazdin, A. E., & Whitley, M. E. (2003). Treatment of parental stress to enhance therapeutic change among children referred for aggressive and antisocial behavior. Journal of Consulting and Clinical Psychology, 71, 504–515.

Kearins, J. M. (1981). Visual spatial memory in Australian aboriginal children of desert regions. Cognitive Psychology, 13, 434–460.

Keating, D. (1979). Adolescent thinking. In J. Adelson (Ed.), Handbook of adolescent psychology (pp. 211–246). New York: Wiley.

Keating, D. P. (1990). Adolescent thinking. In S. S. Feldman & G. R. Elliott (Eds.), At the threshold (pp. 54–89). Cambridge, MA: Harvard University Press.

Keating, D. P. (2004). Cognitive and brain development. In R. M. Lerner & L. Steinberg (Eds.), Handbook of adolescent psychology (2nd ed., pp. 45–84). Hoboken, NJ: Wiley.

Keil, F. C. (1986). Conceptual domains and the acquisition of metaphor. Cognitive Development, 1, 73–96.

Keil, F. C., & Lockhart, K. L. (1999). Explanatory understanding in conceptual development. In E. K. Scholnick, K. Nelson, S. A. Gelman, & P. H. Miller (Eds.), Conceptual development: Piaget's legacy (pp. 103–130). Mahwah, NJ: Erlbaum.

Keith, J., Fry, C. L., Glascock, A. P., Ikels, C., Dickerson-Putman, J., Harpending, H. C., & Draper, P. (1994). The aging experience: Diversity and commonality across cultures. Thousand Oaks, CA: Sage.

Keith, P. M., & Schafer, R. B. (1991). Relationships and well-being over the life stages. New York: Praeger.

Keith, T. Z., Keith, P. B., Quirk, K. J., Sperduto, J., Santillo, S., & Killings, S. (1998). Longitudinal effects of parent involvement on high school grades: Similarities and differences across gender and ethnic groups. Journal of School Psychology, 36, 335–363.

Keller, H. (2003). Socialization for competence: Cultural models of infancy. Human Development, 46, 288–311.

Kellett, J. M. (2000). Older adult sexuality. In L. T. Szuchman & F. Muscarella (Eds.), Psychological perspectives on human sexuality (pp. 355–379). New York: Wiley.

Kelley, S. A., Brownell, C. A., & Campbell, S. B. (2000). Mastery motivation and self-evaluative affect in toddlers: Longitudinal relations with maternal behavior. Child Development, 71, 1061–1071.

Kelley, S. S., Borawski, E. A., Flocke, S. A., & Keen, K. J. (2003). The role of sequential and concurrent sexual relationships in the risk of sexually transmitted diseases among adolescents. Journal of Adolescent Health, 32, 296–305.

Kelly, S. J., Day, N., & Streissguth, A. P. (2000). Effects of prenatal alcohol exposure on social behavior in humans and other species. Neurotoxicology and Teratology, 22, 143–149.

Kemeny, M. E. (2003). The psychobiology of stress. Current Directions in Psychological Science, 12, 124–129.

Kemkes-Grottenhaler, A. (2003). Postponing or rejecting parenthood? Results of a survey among female academic professionals. Journal of Biosocial Science, 35, 213–226.

Kemp, E. A., & Kemp, J. E. (2002). Older couples: New romances. Berkeley, CA: Celestial Arts.

Kempe, C. H., Silverman, B. F., Steele, P. W., Droegemueller, P. W., & Silver, H. K. (1962). The battered-child syndrome. Journal of the American Medical Association, 181, 17–24.

Kemper, S., Kynette, D., & Norman, S. (1992). Age differences in spoken language. In R. L. West & J. D. Sinnott (Eds.), Everyday memory and aging (pp. 138–152). New York: Springer-Verlag.

Kemper, S., Thompson, M., & Marquis, J. (2001). Longitudinal change in language production: Effects of aging and dementia on grammatical complexity and prepositional content. Psychology and Aging, 16, 600–614.

Kendler, K. S., Thornton, L. M., Gilman, S. E., & Kessler, R. C.

(2000). Sexual orientation in a U.S. national sample of twin and non-twin sibling pairs. American Journal of Psychiatry, 157, 1843–1846.

Kennedy, C. M. (1998). Childhood nutrition. Annual Review of Nursing Research, 16, 3–38.

Kennedy, G. E., & Kennedy, C. E. (1993). Grandparents: A special resource for children in stepfamilies. Journal of Divorce and Remarriage, 19, 45–68.

Kennedy, G. J., & Tanenbaum, S. (2000). Suicide and aging: International perspectives. Psychiatric Quarterly, 71, 345–362.

Kennedy, Q., Fung, H. H., & Carstensen, L. L. (2001). Aging, time estimation, and emotion. In S. H. McFadden & R. C. Atchley (Eds.), Aging and the meaning of time: A multidisciplinary exploration (pp. 51–73). New York: Springer.

Kennell, J., Klaus, M., McGrath, S., Robertson, S., & Hinkley, C. (1991). Continuous emotional support during labor in a U.S. hospital. Journal of the American Medical Association, 265, 2197–2201.

Kennet, J., Burgio, L., & Schultz, R. (2000). Interventions for in-home caregivers: A review of research 1990 to present. In R. Schulz (Ed.), Handbook on dementia caregiving (pp. 61–126). New York: Springer.

Kenyon, B. L. (2001). Current research in children's conceptions of death: A critical review. Omega, 43, 63–91.

Kerber, R. A., O'Brien, E., Smith, K. R., & Cawthon, R. M. (2001). Familial excess longevity in Utah genealogies. Journals of Gerontology, 567, B130–B139.

Kerckhoff, A. C. (2002). The transition from school to work. In J. T. Mortimer & R. Larson (Eds.), The changing adolescent experience (pp. 52–87). New York: Cambridge University Press.

Keren, M., Feldman, R., Namdari-Weinbaum, I., Spitzer, S., & Tyano, S. (2005). Relations between parents' interactive style in dyadic and triadic play and toddlers' symbolic capacity. American Journal of Orthopsychiatry, 75, 599–607.

Kerestes, M., & Youniss, J. E. (2003). Rediscovering the importance of religion in adolescent development. In R. M. Lerner, F. Jacobs, & D. Wertlieb (Eds.), Handbook of applied developmental science (Vol. 1, pp. 165–184). Thousand Oaks, CA: Sage.

Kerestes, M., Youniss, J., & Metz, E. (2004). Longitudinal patterns of religious perspective and civic integration. Applied Developmental Science, 8, 39–46.

Kernis, M. H. (2002). Self-esteem as a multifaceted construct. In T. M. Brinthaupt & R. P. Lipka (Eds.), *Understanding early adolescent self and identity* (pp. 57–88). Albany, NY: State University of New York Press.

Kernohan, W. G., Hasson, F., Hutchison, P., & Cochrane, B. (2006). Patient satisfaction with hospice day care. *Supportive Care in Cancer, 14*, 462–468.

Kerpelman, J. L., Shoffner, M. F., & Ross-Griffin, S. (2002). African American mothers' and daughters' beliefs about possible selves and their strategies for reaching the adolescent's future academic and career goals. *Journal of Youth and Adolescence, 31*, 289–302.

Kerr, D. C. R., Lopez, N. L., Olson, S. L., & Sameroff, A. J. (2004). Parental discipline and externalizing behavior problems in early childhood: The roles of moral regulation and child gender. *Journal of Abnormal Child Psychology, 32*, 369–383.

Kettl, P. (1998). Alaska Native suicide: Lessons for elder suicide. *International Psychogeriatrics, 10*, 205–211.

Kettunen, J. A., & Kujala, U. M. (2004). Exercise therapy for people with rheumatoid arthritis and osteoarthritis. *Scandinavian Journal of Medicine and Science in Sports, 14*, 138–142.

Keyes, C. L. M., & Ryff, C. D. (1998a). Generativity and adult lives: Social structural contours and quality of life consequences. In D. P. McAdams & E. de St. Aubin (Eds.), *Generativity and adult development: How and why we care for the next generation* (pp. 227–263). Washington, DC: American Psychological Association.

Keyes, C. L. M., & Ryff, C. D. (1998b). Psychological well-being in midlife. In S. L. Willis & J. D. Reid (Eds.), *Life in the middle* (pp. 161–180). San Diego: Academic Press.

Keyes, C. L. M., Shmotkin, D., & Ryff, C. D. (2002). Optimizing well-being: The empirical encounter of two traditions. *Journal of Personality and Social Psychology, 82*, 1007–1022.

Kidd, S. A., & Scrimenti, K. (2004). Evaluating child and youth homelessness: The example of New Haven, Connecticut. *Evaluation Review, 28*, 325–341.

Kiebzak, G. M., Beinart, G. A., Perser, K., Ambrose, C. G., Siff, S. J., & Heggeness, M. H. (2002). Undertreatment of osteoporosis in men with hip fracture. *Archives of Internal Medicine, 162*, 2217–2222.

Kiecolt-Glaser, J. K., Bane, C., Glaser, R., & Malarkey, W. B. (2003). Love, marriage, and divorce: Newlyweds' stress hormones foreshadow relationship changes. *Journal of Consulting and Clinical Psychology, 71*, 176–188.

Kiernan, K. (2001). European perspectives on nonmarital childbearing. In L. L. Wu & B. Wolfe (Eds.), *Out of wedlock: Causes and consequences of nonmarital fertility* (pp. 77–108). New York: Russell Sage Foundation.

Kiernan, K. (2002). Cohabitation in Western Europe: Trends, issues, and implications. In A. Booth & A. C. Crouter (Eds.), *Just living together* (pp. 3–32). Mahwah, NJ: Erlbaum.

Kihlstrom, J. F., & Cantor, N. (2000). Social intelligence. In R. J. Sternberg (Ed.), *Handbook of intelligence* (pp. 359–379). Cambridge, UK: Cambridge University Press.

Killen, M., & Nucci, L. P. (1995). Morality, autonomy, and social conflict. In M. Killen & D. Hart (Eds.), *Morality in everyday life: Developmental perspectives* (pp. 52–86). Cambridge, UK: Cambridge University Press.

Killen, M., & Smetana, J. G. (1999). Social interactions in preschool classrooms and the development of young children's conceptions of the personal. *Child Development, 70*, 486–501.

Killen, M., Lee-Kim, J., McGlothlin, H., & Stangor, C. (2002). How children and adolescents evaluate gender and racial exclusion. *Monographs of the Society for Research in Child Development, 67*(4, Serial No. 271).

Killian, T., Turner, J., & Cain, R. (2005). Depressive symptoms of caregiving women in midlife: The role of physical health. *Journal of Women and Aging, 17*, 115–127.

Kilpatrick, S. D., Bissonnette, V. L., & Rusbult, C. E. (2002). Empathic accuracy and accommodative behavior among newly married couples. *Personal Relationships, 9*, 369–393.

Kilpatrick, S. W., & Sanders, D. M. (1978). Body image stereotypes: A developmental comparison. *Journal of Genetic Psychology, 132*, 87–95.

Kim, A., & Merriam, S. B. (2004). Motivations for learning among older adults in a learning retirement institute. *Educational Gerontology, 30*, 441–455.

Kim, J. E., & Moen, P. (2002a). Is retirement good or bad for subjective well-being? *Current Directions in Psychological Science, 10*, 83–86.

Kim, J. E., & Moen, P. (2002b). Moving into retirement: Preparation and transitions in late midlife. In M. E. Lachman (Ed.), *Handbook of midlife development* (pp. 487–527). New York: Wiley.

Kim, J. E., & Moen, P. (2002c). Retirement transitions, gender, and psychological well-being: A life-course, ecological model. *Journal of Gerontology, 57B*, P212–P222.

Kim, J. M. (1998). Korean children's concepts of adult and peer authority and moral reasoning. *Developmental Psychology, 34*, 947–955.

Kim, J. M., & Turiel, E. (1996). Korean children's concepts of adult and peer authority. *Social Development, 5*, 310–329.

Kim, M., McGregor, K. K., & Thompson, C. K. (2000). Early lexical development in English- and Korean-speaking children: Language-general and language-specific patterns. *Journal of Child Language, 27*, 225–254.

Kim, S. Y. H., Appelbaum, P. S. J., Olin, D. V., & Jason, T. (2004). Proxy and surrogate consent in geriatric neuropsychiatric research: Update and recommendations. *American Journal of Psychiatry, 161*, 797–806.

Kim, S. Y. S., Barton, D. A., Obarzanek, E., McMahon, R. P., Kronsberg, S., & Waclawiw, M. A. (2002). Obesity development during adolescence in a biracial cohort: The NHLBI Growth and Health Study. *Pediatrics, 110*, 354–358.

Kim, S., & Hasher, L. (2005). The attraction effect in decision making: Superior performance by older adults. *Quarterly Journal of Experimental Psychology, 58A*, 120–133.

Kim, W. J. (2002). Benefits and risks of intercountry adoption. *Lancet, 360*, 423–424.

Kimmel, D. C. (2002). Aging and sexual orientation. In B. E. Jones & M. J. Hill (Eds.), *Mental health issues in lesbian, gay, bisexual, and transgender communities. (Review of psychiatry, Vol. 21*, pp. 17–36). Washington, DC: American Psychiatric Publishing.

King, A. C. (2001). Interventions to promote physical activity by older adults. *Journal of Gerontology, 56A*, 36A–46A.

King, A. C., Castro, C., Wilcox, S., Eyler, A. A., Sallis, J. F., & Brownson, R. C. (2000). Personal and environmental factors associated with physical inactivity among different racial–ethnic groups of U.S. middle-aged and older-aged women. *Health Psychology, 19*, 354–364.

King, A. C., Kiernan, M., Oman, R. F., Kraemer, H., Hull, M., & Ahn, D. (1997). Can we identify who will adhere to long-term physical activity? Signal detection methodology as a potential aid to clinical decision making. *Health Psychology, 16*, 380–389.

King, A. C., Taylor, C. B., & Haskell, W. L. (1993). Effects of differing intensities and formats of 12 months of exercise training on psychological outcomes in older adults. *Health Psychology, 12*, 292–300.

King, D. A., & Markus, H. E. (2000). Mood disorders in older adults. In S. K. Whitbourne (Ed.), *Psychopathology in later adulthood* (pp. 141–172). New York: Wiley.

King, E. M., & Mason, A. D. (2001). *Engendering development: Through gender equality in rights, resources, and voice.* Washington, DC: UNICEF.

King, P. E., & Furrow, J. L. (2004). Religion as a resource for positive youth development: Religion, social capital, and moral outcomes. *Developmental Psychology, 40*, 703–713.

King, P. M., & Kitchener, K. S. (1994). *Developing reflective judgment: Understanding and promoting intellectual growth and critical thinking in adolescents and adults.* San Francisco: Jossey-Bass.

King, P. M., & Kitchener, K. S. (2002). The reflective judgment model: Twenty years of research on epistemic cognition. In B. K. Hofer & P. R. Pintrich (Eds.), *Personal epistemology: The psychological beliefs about knowledge and knowing* (pp. 37–61). Mahwah, NJ: Erlbaum.

King, V., & Scott, M. E. (2005). A comparison of cohabiting relationships among older and younger adults. *Journal of Marriage and the Family, 67*, 271–285.

Kingsberg, S. A. (2002). The impact of aging on sexual function in women and their partners. *Archives of Sexual Behavior, 31*, 431–437.

Kinicki, A. J., Prussia, G. E., & McKee-Ryan, F. M. (2000). A panel study of coping with involuntary job loss. *Academy of Management Journal, 43*, 90–100.

Kinney, D. (1999). From "headbangers" to "hippies": Delineating adolescents' active attempts to form an alternative peer culture. In J. A. McLellan & M. J. V. Pugh (Eds.), *The role of peer groups in adolescent social identity: Exploring the importance of stability and change* (pp. 21–35). San Francisco: Jossey-Bass.

Kinney, H. C., Randall, L. L. Sleeper, L. A., Willinger, M., Belliveau, R. A., & Zec, N. (2003). Serotonergic brainstem abnormalities in Northern Plains Indians with the sudden infant death syndrome. *Journal of Neuropathology and Experimental Neurology, 62*, 1178–1191.

Kirby, D. (2002a). Antecedents of adolescent initiation of sex, contraceptive use, and pregnancy. *American Journal of Health Behavior, 26,* 473–485.

Kirby, D. (2002b). Effective approaches to reducing adolescent unprotected sex, pregnancy, and childbearing. *Journal of Sex Research, 39,* 51–57.

Kirby, D. (2002c). The impact of schools and school programs upon adolescent sexual behavior. *Journal of Sex Research, 39,* 27–33.

Kirchner, G. (2000). *Children's games from around the world.* Boston: Allyn and Bacon.

Kirk, K. M., Bailey, J. M., Dunne, M. P., & Martin, N. G. (2000). Measurement models for sexual orientation in a community twin sample. *Behavior Genetics, 30,* 345–356.

Kirkham, N. Z., Cruess, L., & Diamond, A. (2003). Helping children apply their knowledge to their behavior on a dimension-switching task. *Developmental Science, 6,* 449–476.

Kirkham, N. Z., Slemmer, J. A., & Johnson, S. P. (2002). Visual statistical learning in infancy: Evidence for a domain general learning mechanism. *Cognition, 83,* B35–B42.

Kisilevsky, B. S., Hains, S. M. J., Lee, K., Xie, X., Huang, H., Ye, H. H., Zhang, K., & Wang, Z. (2003). Effects of experience on fetal voice recognition. *Psychological Science, 14,* 220–224.

Kisilevsky, B. S., & Low, J. A. (1998). Human fetal behvior: 100 years of study. *Developmental Review, 18,* 1–29.

Kite, M. E., & Whitley, B. E., Jr. (1998). Do heterosexual women and men differ in their attitudes toward homosexuality? In G. M. Herek (Ed.), *Stigma and sexual orientation* (pp. 39–61). Thousand Oaks, CA: Sage.

Kito, M. (2005). Self-disclosure in romantic relationships and friendships among American and Japanese college students. *Journal of Social Psychology, 145,* 127–145.

Kitzmann, K. M., Cohen, R., & Lockwood, R. L. (2002). Are only children missing out? Comparison of the peer-related social competence of only children and siblings. *Journal of Social and Personal Relationships, 19,* 299–316.

Klaczynski, P. A. (1997). Bias in adolescents' everyday reasoning and its relationships with intellectual ability, personal theories, and self-serving motivation. *Developmental Psychology, 33,* 273–283.

Klaczynski, P. A. (2001). Framing effects on adolescent task representations, analytic and heuristic processing, and decision making: Implications for the normative/descriptive gap. *Applied Developmental Psychology, 22,* 289–309.

Klaczynski, P. A., & Narasimham, G. (1998). Development of scientific reasoning biases: Cognitive versus ego-protective explanations. *Developmental Psychology, 34,* 175–187.

Klaczynski, P. A., Schuneman, M. J., & Daniel, D. B. (2004). Theories of conditional reasoning: A developmental examination of competing hypotheses. *Developmental Psychology, 40,* 559–571.

Klahr, D., & MacWhinney, B. (1998). Information processing. In D. Kuhn & R. S. Siegler (Eds.), *Handbook of child psychology: Vol. 2. Cognition, perception, and language* (5th ed., pp. 631–678). New York: Wiley.

Klahr, D., & Nigam, M. (2004). The equivalence of learning paths in early science instruction: Effects of direct instruction and discovery learning. *Psychological Science, 15,* 661–667.

Klass, D. (2004). The inner representation of the dead child in the psychic and social narratives of bereaved parents. In R. A. Neimeyer (Ed.), *Meaning reconstruction and the experience of loss* (pp. 77–94). Washington, DC: American Psychological Association.

Klaw, E. L., Rhodes, J. E., & Fitzgerald, L. F. (2003). Natural mentors in the lives of African-American adolescent mothers: Tracking relationships over time. *Journal of Youth and Adolescence, 32,* 223–232.

Klebanoff, M. A., Levine, R. J., Clemens, J. D., & Wilkins, D. G. (2002). Maternal serum caffeine metabolites and small-for-gestational-age birth. *American Journal of Epidemiology, 155,* 32–37.

Klebanov, P. K., Brooks-Gunn, J., McCarton, C., & McCormick, M. C. (1998). The contribution of neighborhood and family income to developmental test scores over the first three years of life. *Child Development, 69,* 1420–1436.

Kleespies, P. M. (2004). Concluding thoughts on suffering, dying and choice. In P. M. Kleespies (Ed.), *Life and death decisions: Psychological and ethical considerations in end-of-life care* (pp. 163–167). Washington, DC: American Psychological Association.

Klein, B. E., Klein, R., Lee, K. E., & Meuer, S. M. (2003). Socioeconomic and lifestyle factors and the 10-year incidence of age-related cataracts. *American Journal of Ophthalmology, 136,* 506–512.

Klein, P. J., & Meltzoff, A. N. (1999). Long-term memory, forgetting, and deferred imitation in 12-month-old infants. *Developmental Science, 2,* 102–113.

Klesges, L., M., Johnson, K. C., Ward, K. D. & Barnard, M. (2001). Smoking cessation in pregnant women. *Obstetrics and Gynecology Clinics of North America, 28,* 269–282.

Kliewer, W., Fearnow, M. D., & Miller, P. A. (1996). Coping socialization in middle childhood: Tests of maternal and paternal influences. *Child Development, 67,* 2339–2357.

Klimes-Dougan, B., & Kistner, J. (1990). Physically abused preschoolers' responses to peers' distress. *Developmental Psychology, 26,* 599–602.

Kline, G. H., Stanley, S. M., Markman, H. J., Olmos-Gallo, P. A., St. Peters, M., Whitton, S. W., & Prado, L. M. (2004). Timing is everything: Pre-engagement cohabitation and increased risk for poor marital outcomes. *Journal of Family Psychology, 18,* 311–318.

Klingner, J. K., Vaughn, S., Hughes, M. T., Schumm, J. S., & Elbaum, B. (1998). Outcomes for students with and without learning disabilities in inclusive classrooms. *Learning Disabilities Research and Practice, 13,* 153–161.

Klomsten, A. T., Skaalvik, E. M., & Espnes, G. A. (2004). Physical self-concept and sports: Do gender differences exist? *Sex Roles, 50,* 119–127.

Klump, K. L., Kaye, W. H., & Strober, M. (2001). The evolving foundations of eating disorders. *Psychiatric Clinics of North America, 24,* 215–225.

Knapp, M. L., & Taylor, E. H. (1994). Commitment and its communication in romantic relationships. In A. L. Weber & J. H. Harvey (Eds.), *Perspectives on close relationships* (pp. 153–175). Boston: Allyn and Bacon.

Knobloch, H., & Pasamanick, B. (Eds.). (1974). *Gesell and Amatruda's Developmental Diagnosis.* Hagerstown, MD: Harper & Row.

Knoers, N., van den Ouweland, A., Dreesen, J., Verdijk, M., Monnens, L. S., & van Oost, B. A. (1993). Nephrogenic diabetes insipidus: Identification of the genetic defect. *Pediatric Nephrology, 7,* 685–688.

Knox, A. B. (1993). *Strengthening adult and continuing education.* San Francisco: Jossey-Bass.

Kobak, R. R., & Hazan, C. (1991). Attachment in marriage: Effects of security and accuracy of working models. *Journal of Personality and Social Psychology, 60,* 861–869.

Kobayashi, T., Hiraki, K., & Hasegawa, T. (2005). Auditory-visual intermodal matching of small numerosities in 6-month-old infants. *Developmental Science, 8,* 409–419.

Kobayashi, T., Kazuo, H., Ryoko, M., & Hasegawa, T. (2004). Baby arithmetic: One object plus one tone. *Cognition, 91,* B23–B34.

Kobayashi, Y. (1994). Conceptual acquisition and change through social interaction. *Human Development, 37,* 233–241.

Kochanska, G. (1991). Socialization and temperament in the development of guilt and conscience. *Child Development, 62,* 1379–1392.

Kochanska, G. (1993). Toward a synthesis of parental socialization and child temperament in early development of conscience. *Child Development, 64,* 325–347.

Kochanska, G., Aksan, N., & Nichols, K. E. (2003). Maternal power assertion in discipline and moral discourse contexts: Commonalities, differences, and implications for children's moral conduct and cognition. *Developmental Psychology, 39,* 949–963.

Kochanska, G., Casey, R. J., & Fukumoto, A. (1995). Toddlers' sensitivity to standard violations. *Child Development, 66,* 643–656.

Kochanska, G., Gross, J. N., Lin, M.-H., & Nichols, K. E. (2002). Guilt in young children: Development, determinants, and relations with broader system standards. *Child Development, 73,* 461–482.

Kochanska, G., & Knaack, A. (2003). Effortful control as a personality characteristic of young children: Antecedents, correlates, and consequences. *Journal of Personality, 71,* 1087–1112.

Kochanska, G., & Murray, K. T. (2000). Mother–child mutually responsive orientation and conscience development: From toddler to early school age. *Child Development, 71,* 417–431.

Kochanska, G., Murray, K. T., & Harlan, E. T. (2000). Effortful control in early childhood: Continuity and change, antecedents, and implications for social development. *Developmental Psychology, 36,* 220–232.

Kochenderfer-Ladd, B. (2003). Identification of aggressive and asocial victims and the stability of their peer victimization. *Merrill-Palmer Quarterly, 49,* 401–425.

Kochenderfer-Ladd, B., & Wardrop, J. L. (2001). Chronicity and instability of children's peer victimization experiences as predictors of loneliness and social satisfaction trajectories. *Child Development, 72,* 134–151.

Koestner, R., Franz, C., & Weinberger, J. (1990). The family origins of empathic concern: A 26-year longitudinal study. *Journal of Personality and Social Psychology, 58,* 709–717.

Kogan, L. R., & Vacha-Haase, T. (2002). Supporting adaptation to new family roles in middle age. In C. L. Juntunen & D. R. Atkinson (Eds.), *Counseling across the life-span* (pp. 299–347). Thousand Oaks, CA: Sage.

Kogan, N., & Mills, M. (1992). Gender influences on age cognitions and preferences: Sociocultural or sociobiological? *Psychology and Aging, 7,* 98–106.

Kohen, D., Hunter, T., Pence, A., & Goelman, H. (2000). The Victoria Day Care Research Project: Overview of a longitudinal study of child care and human development in Canada. *Canadian Journal of Research in Early Childhood Education, 8,* 49–54.

Kohen, D. E., Brooks-Gunn, J., Leventhal, T., & Hertzman, C. (2002). Neighborhood income and physical and social disorder in Canada: Associations with young children's competencies. *Child Development, 73,* 1844–1860.

Kohlberg, L. (1966). A cognitive-developmental analysis of children's sex-role concepts and attitudes. In E. E. Maccoby (Ed.), *The development of sex differences* (pp. 82–173). Stanford, CA: Stanford University Press.

Kohlberg, L. (1969). Stage and sequence: The cognitive-developmental approach to socialization. In D. A. Goslin (Ed.), *Handbook of socialization theory and research* (pp. 347–480). Chicago: Rand McNally.

Kohlberg, L., Levine, C., & Hewer, A. (1983). *Moral stages: A current formulation and a response to critics.* Basel, Switzerland: Karger.

Kohn, M. L., & Schooler, C. (1978). The reciprocal effects of the substantive complexity of work and intellectual flexibility: A longitudinal assessment. *American Journal of Sociology, 84,* 24–52.

Kohn, M. L., & Slomczynski, D. M. (1990). *Social structure and self-direction: A comparative analysis of the United States and Poland.* Cambridge, MA: Blackwell.

Kohn, M. L., Naoi, A., Schoenbach, C., Schooler, C., & Slomczynski, K. M. (1990). Position in the class structure and psychological functioning in the United States, Japan, and Poland. *American Journal of Sociology, 95,* 964–1008.

Kohn, M. L., Zaborowski, W., Janicka, K., Mach, B. W., Khmelko, V., Slomczynski, K. M., Heyman, C., & Podobnik, B. (2000). *Social Psychology Quarterly, 63,* 187–208.

Koistinaho, M., & Koistinaho, J. (2005). Interactions between Alzheimer's disease and cerebral ischemia—focus on inflammation. *Brain Research Reviews, 48,* 240–250.

Kojima, H. (1986). Childrearing concepts as a belief–value system of the society and the individual. In H. Steveson, H. Azuma, & K. Hakuta (Eds.), *Child development and education in Japan* (pp. 39–54). New York: Freeman.

Kolb, B., & Gibb, R. (2001). Early brain injury, plasticity, and behavior. In C. A. Nelson & M. Luciana (Eds.), *Handbook of developmental cognitive neuroscience* (pp. 175–190). Cambridge, MA: MIT Press.

Kolomer, S. R., & McCallion, P. (2005). Depression and caregiver mastery in grandfathers caring for their grandchildren. *International Journal of Aging and Human Development, 60,* 283–294.

Kolominsky, Y., Igumnov, S., & Drozdovitch, V. (1999). The psychological development of children from Belarus exposed in the prenatal period to radiation from the Chernobyl atomic power plant. *Journal of Child Psychology and Psychiatry, 40,* 299–305.

Kolvin, I., & Trowell, J. (1996). Child sexual abuse. In I. Rosen (Ed.), *Sexual deviation* (3rd ed., pp. 337–360). Oxford, UK: Oxford University Press.

Komp, D. M. (1996). The changing face of death in children. In H. M. Spiro, M. G. M. Curnen, & L. P. Wandel (Eds.), *Facing death: Where culture, religion, and medicine meet* (pp. 66–76). New Haven: Yale University Press.

Kono, S. (2004). Secular trend of colon cancer incidence and mortality in relation to fat and meat intake in Japan. *European Journal of Cancer Prevention, 13,* 127–132.

Kopp, C. B., & Neufeld, S. J. (2003). Emotional development during infancy. In R. Davidson, K. R. Scherer, & H. H. Goldsmith (Eds.), *Handbook of affective sciences* (pp. 347–374). Oxford, UK: Oxford University Press.

Korf, E. S. C., Scheltens, P., Barkhof, F., & de Leeuw, F.-E. (2004). Blood pressure, white matter lesions and medial temporal lobe atrophy: Closing the gap between vascular pathology and Alzheimer's disease? *Dementia, 20,* 331–337.

Korkman, M., Kettunen, S., & Autti-Raemoe, I. (2003). Neurocognitive impairment in early adolescence following prenatal alcohol exposure of varying duration. *Child Neurology, 9,* 117–128.

Kornhaber, M. L. (2004). Using multiple intelligences to overcome cultural barriers to identification for gifted education. In D. Boothe & J. C. Stanley (Eds.), *In the eyes of the beholder: Critical issues for diversity in gifted education* (pp. 215–225). Waco, TX: Prufrock Press.

Kornhaber, M., Orfield, G., & Kurlaender, M. (2001). *Raising standards or raising barriers? Inequality and high-stakes testing in public education.* New York: Century Foundation Press.

Kotchoubey, B., Lang, S., Mezger, G., Schmalohr, D., Schneck, M., & Semmler, A. (2005). Information processing in severe disorders of consciousness: Vegetative state and minimally conscious state. *Clinical Neurophysiology, 116,* 2441–2453.

Kotre, J. (1984). *Outliving the self: Generativity and the interpretation of lives.* Baltimore: Johns Hopkins University Press.

Kotre, J. (1999). *Make it count: How to generate a legacy that gives meaning to your life.* New York: Free Press.

Kouvonen, A., & Kivivuori, J. (2001). Part-time jobs, delinquency, and victimization among Finnish adolescents. *Journal of Scandinavian Studies in Criminology and Crime Prevention, 2,* 191–212.

Kraaij, V., Arensman, E., & Spinhoven, P. (2002). Negative life events and depression in elderly persons: A meta-analysis. *Journal of Gerontology, 57B,* P87–P94.

Kraaij, V., Pruymboom, E., & Garnefski, N. (2002). Cognitive coping and depressive symptoms in the elderly: A longitudinal study. *Aging and Mental Health, 6,* 275–281.

Kraemer, H. C., Yesavage, J. A., Taylor, J. L., & Kupfer, D. (2000). How can we learn about developmental processes from cross-sectional studies, or can we? *American Journal of Psychiatry, 157,* 163–171.

Krafft, K., & Berk, L. E. (1998). Private speech in two preschools: Significance of open-ended activities and make-believe play for verbal self-regulation. *Early Childhood Research Quarterly, 13,* 637–658.

Kraft, J. M., & Werner, J. S. (1999). Aging and the saturation of colors. 2. Scaling of color appearance. *Journal of the Optical Society of America, 16,* 231–235.

Kramer, A. F., Hahn, S., & Gopher, D. (1998). Task coordination and aging: Explorations of executive control processes in the task switching paradigm. *Acta Psychologica, 101,* 339–378.

Kramer, D. A. (2003). The ontogeny of wisdom in its variations. In J. Demick & C. Andreoletti (Eds.), *Handbook of adult development* (pp. 131–151). New York: Springer.

Kramer, M. S., Guo, T., Platt, R. W., Sevkowskaya, Z., Dzikovich, I., & Collet, J. P. (2003). Infant growth and health outcomes associated with 3 compared with 6 mo. of exclusive breastfeeding. *American Journal of Clinical Nutrition, 78,* 291–295.

Kramer, M. S., Guo, T., Platt, R. W., Shapiro, S., Collet, J. P., & Chalmers, B. (2002). Breastfeeding and infant growth: Biology or bias? *Pediatrics, 110,* 343–347.

Kramer, S. E., Kapteyn, T. S., Kuik, D. J., & Deeg, D. J. (2002). The association of hearing impairment and chronic diseases with psychosocial health status in older age. *Journal of Aging and Health, 14,* 122–137.

Krascum, R. M., & Andrews, S. (1998). The effects of theories on children's acquisition of family-resemblance categories. *Child Development, 69,* 333–346.

Krause, N. (1990). Perceived health problems, formal/informal support, and life satisfaction among older adults. *Journal of Gerontology, 45,* S193–S205.

Krause, N. (2001). Social support. In R. H. Binstock & L. K. George (Eds.), *Handbook of aging and the social sciences* (5th ed., pp. 272–294). San Diego, CA: Academic Press.

Krause, N. (2005). God-mediated control and psychological well-being in late life. *Research on Aging, 27,* 136–164.

Kray, J., & Lindenberger, U. (2000). Adult age differences in task switching. *Psychology and Aging, 15,* 126–147.

Krebs, N. F., & Jacobson, M. S. (2003). Prevention of pediatric overweight and obesity. *Pediatrics, 112,* 424–430.

Kreicbergs, U., Valdimarsdottir, U., Onelov, E., Henter, J.-I., & Steineck, G. (2004). Anxiety and depression in parents 4–9 years after the loss of a child owing to a malignancy: A population-based follow-up. *Psychological Medicine, 34,* 1431–1441.

Krevans, J., & Gibbs, J. C. (1996). Parents' use of inductive discipline: Relations to children's empathy and prosocial behavior. *Child Development, 67,* 3263–3277.

Kroger, J. (2000). *Identity development: Adolescence through adulthood.* Thousand Oaks, CA: Sage.

Kroger, J. (2001). What transits in an identity status transition: A rejoinder to commentaries. *Identity, 3,* 291–304.

Kroger, J. (2002). *Identity development: Adolescence through adulthood.* Thousand Oaks, CA: Sage.

Kroger, J. (2005). *Identity in adolescence: The balance between self and other*. New York: Routledge.

Kropf, N. P., & Pugh, K. L. (1995). Beyond life expectancy: Social work with centenarians. *Journal of Gerontological Social Work, 23*, 121–137.

Krout, J., Cutler, S. J., & Coward, R. T. (1990). Correlates of senior center participation: A national analysis. *Gerontologist, 30*, 72–79.

Kruman, I. I., Mouton, P. R., Emokpae, R., Jr., Cutler, R. G., & Mattson, M. P. (2005). Folate deficiency inhibits proliferation of adult hippocampal progenitors. *Neuroreport, 16*, 1055–1059.

Krumhansl, C. L., & Jusczyk, P. W. (1990). Infants' perception of phrase structure in music. *Psychological Science, 1*, 70–73.

Kubik, M. Y., Lytle, L. A., Hannan, P. J., Perry, C. L., & Story, M. (2003). The association of the school food environment with dietary behaviors of young adolescents. *American Journal of Public Health, 93*, 1168–1173.

Kübler-Ross, E. (1969). *On death and dying*. New York: Macmillan.

Kubotera, T. (2004). Japanese religion in changing society: The spirits of the dead. In J. D. Morgan & P. Laungani (Eds.), *Death and bereavement around the world: Vol. 4. Asia, Australia, and New Zealand* (pp. 95–99). Amityville, NY: Baywood Publishing Company.

Kubzansky, L. D., Wright, R. J., Cohen, S., Weiss, S., Rosner, B., & Sparrow, D. (2002). Breathing easy: A prospective study of optimism and pulmonary function in the Normative Aging Study. *Annals of Behavioral Medicine, 24*, 345–353.

Kuchner, J. (1989, April). *Chinese-American and European-American mothers and infants: Cultural influences in the first three months of life*. Paper presented at the biennial meeting of the Society for Research in Child Development, Kansas City, MO.

Kuczynski, L. (1984). Socialization goals and mother–child interaction: Strategies for long-term and short-term compliance. *Developmental Psychology, 20*, 1061–1073.

Kuczynski, L. (2003). Beyond bidirectionality. In L. Kuczynski (Ed.), *Handbook of dynamics in parent–child relations* (pp. 3–24). Thousand Oaks, CA: Sage.

Kuczynski, L., & Lollis, S. (2002). Four foundations for a dynamic model of parenting. In J. R. M. Gerris (Ed.), *Dynamics of parenting*. Hillsdale, NJ: Erlbaum.

Kuebli, J., Butler, S., & Fivush, R. (1995). Mother–child talk about past emotions: Relations of maternal language and child gender over time. *Cognition and Emotion, 9*, 265–283.

Kuhl, P. K. (2000). A new view of language acquisition. *Proceedings of the National Academy of Sciences, 97*, 11850–11857.

Kuhn, D. (1993). Connecting scientific and informal reasoning. *Merrill-Palmer Quarterly, 39*, 74–103.

Kuhn, D. (1999). Metacognitive development. *Current Directions in Psychological Science, 9*, 178–181.

Kuhn, D. (2000). Theory of mind, metacognition, and reasoning: A life-span perspective. In P. Mitchell & K. J. Riggs (Eds.), *Children's reasoning and the mind* (pp. 301–326). Hove, UK: Psychology Press.

Kuhn, D. (2002). What is scientific thinking, and how does it develop? In U. Goswami (Ed.), *Blackwell handbook of childhood cognitive development* (pp. 371–393). Malden, MA: Blackwell.

Kuhn, D., Amsel, E., & O'Loughlin, M. (1988). *The development of scientific thinking skills*. Orlando, FL: Academic Press.

Kuhn, D., & Dean, D. (2004). Connecting scientific reasoning and causal inference. *Journal of Cognition and Development, 5*, 261–288.

Kuhn, D., & Franklin, S. (2006). The second decade: What develops (and how)? In D. Kuhn & R. S. Siegler (Eds.), *Handbook of child psychology: Vol. 2. Cognition, perception, and language* (6th ed.). Hoboken, NJ: Wiley.

Kuhn, D., & Pearsall, S. (2000). Developmental origins of scientific thinking. *Journal of Cognition and Development, 1*, 113–129.

Kühnert, B., & Nieschlag, E. (2004). Reproductive functions of the ageing male. *Human Reproduction Update, 10*, 327–339.

Kuklinski, M. R., & Weinstein, R. S. (2001). Classroom and developmental differences in a path model of teacher expectancy effects. *Child Development, 72*, 1554–1578.

Kulik, K. (2001). Marital relationships in late adulthood: Synchronous versus asynchronous couples. *International Journal of Aging and Human Development, 52*, 323–339.

Kumar, S., & O'Brien, A. (2004). Recent developments in fetal medicine. *British Medical Journal, 328*, 1002–1006.

Kumpfer, K. L., & Alvarado, R. (2003). Family-strengthening approaches for the prevention of youth problem behaviors. *American Psychologist, 58*, 457–465.

Kunemund, H., Motel-Klingebiel, A., & Kohli, M. (2005). Do intergenerational transfers from elderly parents increase social inequality among their middle-aged children? Evidence from the German Aging Survey. *Journal of Gerontology, 60B*, S30-S36.

Kunnen, E. S., & Bosma, H. A. (2003). Fischer's skill theory applied to identity development: A response to Kroger. *Identity, 3*, 247–270.

Kunzinger, E. L., III. (1985). A short-term longitudinal study of memorial development during early grade school. *Developmental Psychology, 21*, 642–646.

Kunzmann, U., Little, T., & Smith, J. (2002). Perceiving control: A double-edged sword in old age. *Journal of Gerontology, 57B*, P484–P491.

Kurdek, L. A. (1994). Conflict resolution styles in gay, lesbian, heterosexual nonparent, and heterosexual parent couples. *Journal of Marriage and the Family, 56*, 705–722.

Kurdek, L. A. (1998). Relationship outcomes and their predictors: Longitudinal evidence from heterosexual married, gay cohabiting, and lesbian cohabiting couples. *Journal of Marriage and the Family, 60*, 553–568.

Kurdek, L. A. (2005). Gender and marital satisfaction early in marriage: A growth curve approach. *Journal of Marriage and Family, 67*, 68–84.

Kurdek, L. A., & Fine, M. A. (1994). Family acceptance and family control as predictors of adjustment in young adolescents: Linear, curvilinear, or interactive effects? *Child Development, 65*, 1137–1146.

L

Laberge, L. Petit, D., Simard, C., Vitaro, F., Tremblay, R. E., & Montplaisir, J. (2001). Development of sleep patterns in early adolescence. *Journal of Sleep Research, 10*, 59–67.

Labouvie-Vief, G. (1980). Beyond formal operations: Uses and limits of pure logic in life-span development. *Human Development, 23*, 141–160.

Labouvie-Vief, G. (1985). Logic and self-regulation from youth to maturity: A model. In M. Commons, F. Richards, & C. Armon (Eds.), *Beyond formal operations: Late adolescent and adult cognitive development* (pp. 158–180). New York: Praeger.

Labouvie-Vief, G. (2003). Dynamic integration: Affect, cognition, and the self in adulthood. *Current Directions in Psychological Science, 12*, 201–206.

Labouvie-Vief, G., & Diehl, M. (1999). Self and personality development. In J. C. Kavanaugh &

S. K. Whitbourne (Eds.), *Gerontology: An interdisciplinary perspective* (pp. 238–268). New York: Oxford University Press.

Labouvie-Vief, G., & Diehl, M. (2000). Cognitive complexity and cognitive-affective integration: Related or separate domains of adult development? *Psychology and Aging, 15*, 490–504.

Labouvie-Vief, G., Chiodo, L. M., Goguen, L. A., Diehl, M., & Orwoll, L. (1995). Representations of self across the life span. *Psychology and Aging, 10*, 404–415.

Labouvie-Vief, G., DeVoe, M., & Bulka, D. (1989). Speaking about feelings: Conceptions of emotion across the life span. *Psychology and Aging, 4*, 425–437.

Labouvie-Vief, G., & Gonzalez, M. M. (2004). Dynamic integration: Affect optimization and differentiation in development. In D. Y. Dai & R. J. Sternberg (Eds.), *Motivation, emotion, and cognition: Integrative perspectives on intellectual functioning and development* (pp. 237–272). Mahwah, NJ: Erlbaum.

Labouvie-Vief, G., & Medler, M. (2002). Affect optimization and affect complexity: Modes and styles of regulation in adulthood. *Psychology and Aging, 17*, 571–588.

Lachman, M. E., & Bertrand, R. M. (2002). Personality and self in midlife. In M. E. Lachman (Ed.), *Handbook of midlife development* (pp. 279–309). New York: Wiley.

Lachman, M. E., & Firth, K. M. P. (2004). The adaptive value of feeling in control during midlife. In O. G. Brim, C. D. Ryff, & R. C. Kessler (Eds.), *How healthy are we? A national study of well-being at midlife* (pp. 320–349). Chicago: University of Chicago Press.

Lachman, M. E., & James, J. B. (1997). Charting the course of midlife development: An overview. In M. E. Lachman & J. B. James (Eds.), *Multiple paths of midlife development* (pp. 1–17). Chicago: University of Chicago Press.

Lacour, M., Kiilgaard, J. F., & Nissen, M. H. (2002). Age-related macular degeneration: Epidemiology and optimal treatment. *Drugs and Aging, 19*, 101–133.

Lacourse, E., Nagin, D., Tremblay, R. E., Vitaro, F., & Claes, M. (2003). Developmental trajectories of boys' delinquent group membership and facilitation of violent behaviors during adolescence. *Development and Psychopathology, 15*, 183–197.

Ladd, G. W., Birch, S. H., & Buhs, E. S. (1999). Children's social and scholastic lives in kindergarten: Related spheres of influence?

Child Development, 70, 1373–1400.

Ladd, G. W., & Burgess, K. B. (1999). Charting the relationship trajectories of aggressive, withdrawn, and aggressive/withdrawn children during early grade school. *Child Development, 70,* 910–929.

Ladd, G. W., LeSieur, K., & Profilet, S. M. (1993). Direct parental influences on young children's peer relations. In S. Duck (Ed.), *Learning about relationships* (Vol. 2, pp. 152–183). London: Sage.

Ladd, G. W., & Pettit, G. S. (2002). Parenting and the development of children's peer relationships. In M. Bornstein (Ed.), *Handbook of parenting* (2nd ed.). Mahwah, NJ: Erlbaum.

Ladd, G. W., & Price, J. M. (1987). Predicting children's social and school adjustment following the transition from preschool to kindergarten. *Child Development, 58,* 1168–1189.

Ladd, G. W., & Troop-Gordon, W. (2003). The role of chronic peer difficulties in the development of children's psychological adjustment problems. *Child Development, 74,* 1344–1367.

LaFontana, K. M., & Cillessen, A. H. N. (1999). Children's interpersonal perceptions as a function of sociometric and peer perceived popularity. *Journal of Genetic Psychology, 160,* 225–242.

Lagattuta, K. H., Wellman, H. M., & Flavell, J. H. (1997). Preschoolers' understanding of the link between thinking and feeling: Cognitive cuing and emotional change. *Child Development, 68,* 1081–1104.

Lagercrantz, H., & Slotkin, T. A. (1986). The "stress" of being born. *Scientific American, 254,* 100–107.

Lagnado, L. (2001, November 2). Kids confront Trade Center trauma. *Wall Street Journal,* pp. B1, B6.

Laible, D. J., & Thompson, R. A. (2000). Mother–child discourse, attachment security, shared positive affect, and early conscience development. *Child Development, 71,* 1424–1440.

Laible, D. J., & Thompson, R. A. (2002). Mother–child conflict in the toddler years: Lessons in emotion, morality, and relationships. *Child Development, 73,* 1187–1203.

Laird, J. (2003). Lesbian and gay families. In F. Walsh (Ed.), *Normal family processes* (pp. 176–209). New York: Guilford.

Laird, R. D., Jordan, K. Y., Dodge, K. A., Pettit, G. S., & Bates, J. E. (2001). Peer rejection in childhood, involvement with antisocial peers in early adolescence, and the development of externalizing

behavior problems. *Development and Psychopathology, 13,* 337–354.

Lalonde, C., & Chandler, M. (2005). Culture, selves, and time: Theories of personal persistence in native and non-native youth. In C. Lightfoot, C. Lalonde, & M. Chandler (Eds.), *Changing conceptions of psychological life* (pp. 207–229). Mahwah, NJ: Erlbaum.

Lamaze, F. (1958). *Painless childbirth.* London: Burke.

Lamb, M. E. (1997). The development of father–infant relationships. In M. E. Lamb (Ed.), *The role of the father in child development* (3rd ed., pp. 104–120). New York: Wiley.

Lamb, M. E. (1998). Nonparental child care: Context, quality, correlates, and consequences. In I. E. Sigel & K. A. Renninger (Eds.), *Handbook of child psychology: Vol. 4. Child psychology in practice* (5th ed., pp. 73–133). New York: Wiley.

Lamb, M. E., & Lewis, C. (2004). The development and significance of father–child relationships in two-parent families. In M. E. Lamb (Ed.), *The role of the father in child development* (4th ed., pp. 272–306). Hoboken, NJ: Wiley.

Lamb, M. E., & Oppenheim, D. (1989). Fatherhood and father–child relationships: Five years of research. In S. H. Cath, A. Gurwitt, & L. Gunsberg (Eds.), *Fathers and their families* (pp. 11–26). Hillsdale, NJ: Erlbaum.

Lamb, M. E., Sternberg, K. J., & Prodromidis, M. (1992). Nonmaternal care and the security of infant–mother attachment: A reanalysis of the data. *Infant Behavior and Development, 15,* 71–83.

Lamb, M. E., Thompson, R. A., Gardner, W., Charnov, E. L., & Connell, J. P. (1985). Infant–mother attachment: The origins and developmental significance of individual differences in the Strange Situation: Its study and biological interpretation. *Behavioral and Brain Sciences, 7,* 127–147.

Lampl, M. (1993). Evidence of saltatory growth in infancy. *American Journal of Human Biology, 5,* 641–652.

Lampl, M., Veldhuis, J. D., & Johnson, M. L. (1992). Saltation and stasis: A model of human growth. *Science, 258,* 801–803.

Lanctot, K. L., Herrmann, N., Eryavec, G., van Reekum, R., Reed, K., & Naranjo, C. A. (2002). Central serotonergic activity is related to the aggressive behaviors of Alzheimer's disease. *Neuropsychopharmacology, 27,* 646–654.

Landman, J., Vandewater, E. A., Stewart, A. J., & Malley, J. E. (1995). Missed opportunities: Psychological ramifications of counterfactual

thought in midlife women. *Journal of Adult Development, 2,* 87–97.

Lang, F. R., & Baltes, M. M. (1997). Being with people and being alone in later life: Costs and benefits for everyday functioning. *International Journal of Behavioral Development, 21,* 729–749.

Lang, F. R., Featherman, D. L., & Nesselroade, J. R. (1997). Social self-efficacy and short-term variability in social relationships: The MacArthur Successful Aging Studies. *Psychology and Aging, 12,* 657–666.

Lang, F. R., Staudinger, U. M., & Carstensen, L. L. (1998). Perspectives on socioemotional selectivity in late life: How personality and social context do (and do not) make a difference. *Journal of Gerontology, 53B,* P21–P30.

Langer, G. (2004). *ABC New Prime Time Live Poll: The American Sex Survey.* Retrieved from abcnews .go.com/Primetime/News/story?id =174461&page=1

Langer, J., Gillette, P., & Arriaga, R. I. (2003). Toddlers' cognition of adding and subtracting objects in action and in perception. *Cognitive Development, 18,* 233–246.

Langer, N. (1990). Grandparents and adult grandchildren: What do they do for one another? *International Journal of Aging and Human Development, 31,* 101–110.

Lansford, J. E., Antonucci, T. C., Akiyama, H., & Takahashi, K. (2005). A quantitative and qualitative approach to social relationships and well-being in the United States and Japan. *Journal of Comparative Family Studies, 36,* 1–22.

Lansford, J. E., Criss, M. M., Pettit, G. S., Dodge, K. A., & Bates, J. E. (2003). Friendship quality, peer group affiliation, and peer antisocial behavior as moderators of the link between negative parenting and adolescent externalizing behavior. *Journal of Research on Adolescence, 13,* 161–184.

Lansford, J. E., Deater-Deckard, K., Dodge, K. A., Bates, J. E., & Pettit, G. S. (2004). Ethnic differences in the link between physical discipline and later adolescent externalizing behaviors. *Journal of Child Psychology and Psychiatry, 45,* 801–812.

Lantz, P. M., House, J. S., Lepkowski, J. M., Williams, D. R., Mero, R. P., & Chen, J. (1998). Socioeconomic factors, health behaviors, and mortality. *Journal of the American Medical Association, 279,* 1703–1708.

Lantz, P. M., Lynch, J. W., House, J. S., Lepkowski, J. M., Mero, R. P., & Musick, M. (2001). Socioeconomic disparities in health change in a longitudinal study of U.S.

adults: The role of health risk behaviors. *Social Science and Medicine, 53,* 29–40.

Lappe, J. M. (1987). Reminiscing: The life review therapy. *Journal of Gerontological Nursing, 13,* 12–16.

Lapsley, D. K., Jackson, S., Rice, K., & Shadid, G. (1988). Self-monitoring and the "new look" at the imaginary audience and personal fable: An ego-developmental analysis. *Journal of Adolescent Research, 3,* 17–31.

Larson, E. B., Shadlen, M. F., Wang, L., McCormick, W. C., Bowen, J. D., Teri, L., & Kukull, W. A. (2004). Survival after initial diagnosis of Alzheimer disease. *Annals of Internal Medicine, 140,* 501–509.

Larson, J. H. (1988). The marriage quiz: College students' beliefs about selected myths about marriage. *Family Relations, 37,* 3–11.

Larson, R., & Ham, M. (1993). Stress and "storm and stress" in early adolescence: The relationship of negative events with dysphoric affect. *Developmental Psychology, 29,* 130–140.

Larson, R., & Lampman-Petraitis, C. (1989). Daily emotional states as reported by children and adolescents. *Child Development, 60,* 1250–1260.

Larson, R., & Richards, M. (1998). Waiting for the weekend: Friday and Saturday night as the emotional climax of the week. In A. C. Crouter & R. Larson (Eds.), *Temporal rhythms in adolescence: Clocks, calendars, and the coordination of daily life* (pp. 37–51). San Francisco: Jossey-Bass.

Larson, R., & Richards, M. H. (1991). Daily companionship in late childhood and early adolescence: Changing developmental contexts. *Child Development, 62,* 284–300.

Larson, R., Mannell, R., & Zuzanek, J. (1986). Daily well-being of older adults with friends and family. *Psychology and Aging, 1,* 117–126.

Larson, R. W. (2001). How U.S. children and adolescents spend time: What it does (and doesn't) tell us about their development. *Current Directions in Psychological Science, 10,* 160–164.

Larson, R. W., Moneta, G., Richards, M. H., & Wilson, S. (2002). Continuity, stability, and change in daily emotional experience across adolescence. *Child Development, 73,* 1151–1165.

Larson, R. W., Richards, M. H., Moneta, G., Holmbeck, G., & Duckett, E. (1996). Changes in adolescents' daily interactions with their families from ages 10 to 18: Disengagement and transformation. *Developmental Psychology, 32,* 744–754.

Larson, R. W., Richards, M. H., Sims, B., & Dworkin, J. (2001). How urban African-American young adolescents spend their time: Time budgets for locations, activities, and companionship. *American Journal of Community Psychology, 29,* 565–597.

Larsson, M., & Bäckman, L. (1998). Modality memory across the adult life span: Evidence for selective age-related olfactory deficits. *Experimental Aging Research, 24,* 63–82.

Larsson, M., Öberg, C., & Bäckman, L. (2005). Odor identification in old age: Demographic, sensory and cognitive correlates. *Aging, Neuropsychology, and Cognition, 12,* 231–244.

Larzelere, R. E., Schneider, W. N., Larson, D. B., & Pike, P. L. (1996). The effects of discipline responses in delaying toddler misbehavior recurrences. *Child and Family Behavior Therapy, 18,* 35–57.

LaSala, M. C. (2000). Gay male couples: The importance of coming out and being out to parents. *Journal of Homosexuality, 39,* 47–71.

Latz, S., Wolf, A. W., & Lozoff, B. (1999). Sleep practices and problems in young children in Japan and the United States. *Archives of Pediatric and Adolescent Medicine, 153,* 339–346.

Laucht, M., Esser, G., & Schmidt, M. H. (1997). Developmental outcome of infants born with biological and psychosocial risks. *Journal of Child Psychology and Psychiatry, 38,* 843–853.

Laumann, E. O., Gagnon, J. H., Michael, R. T., & Michaels, S. (1994). *The social organization of sexuality.* Chicago: University of Chicago Press.

Laumann, E. O., Paik, A., & Rosen, R. C. (1999). Sexual dysfunction in the United States: Prevalence and predictors. *Journal of the American Medical Association, 281,* 537–544.

Laurin, D., Verreault, R., Lindsay, J., MacPherson, K., & Rockwood, K. (2001). Physical activity and risk of cognitive impairment and dementia in elderly persons. *Archives of Neurology, 58,* 498–504.

Laursen, B., Coy, K., & Collins, W. A. (1998). Reconsidering changes in parent–child conflict across adolescence: A meta-analysis. *Child Development, 69,* 817–832.

La Vecchia, C. (2004). Estrogen and combined estrogen-progestogen therapy in the menopause and breast cancer. *Breast, 13,* 515–518.

Law, K. L., Stroud, L. R., Niaura, R., LaGasse, L. L., Giu, J., & Lester, B. M. (2003). Smoking during pregnancy and newborn neurobehavior. *Pediatrics, 111,* 1318–1323.

Law, K. S., Wong, C.-S., Song, L., J., & Law, K. S. (2004). The construct and criterion validity of emotional intelligence and its potential utility for management studies. *Journal of Applied Psychology, 89,* 483–496.

Lawrence, A. R., & Schigelone, A. R. S. (2002). Reciprocity beyond dyadic relationships: Aging-related communal coping. *Research on Aging, 24,* 684–704.

Lawrence, K., Kuntsi, J., Coleman, M., Campbell, R., & Skuse, D. (2003). Face and emotion recognition deficits in Turner syndrome: A possible role for X-linked genes in amygdala development. *Neuropsychology, 17,* 39–49.

Lawton, L., Silverstein, M., & Bengtson, V. L. (1994). Solidarity between generations in families. In V. L. Bengtson & R. A. Harootyan (Eds.), *Intergenerational linkages: Hidden connections in American society* (pp. 19– 42). New York: Springer-Verlag.

Lawton, M. P. (2001a). *Annual review of gerontology and geriatrics: Vol. 20. Focus on the end of life: Scientific and social issues.* New York: Springer.

Lawton, M. P. (2001b). Emotion in later life. *Current Directions in Psychological Science, 10,* 120–123.

Lazar, I., & Darlington, R. (1982). Lasting effects of early education: A report from the Consortium for Longitudinal Studies. *Monographs of the Society for Research in Child Development, 47*(2–3, Serial No. 195).

Lazarus, R. S. (1991). *Emotion and adaptation.* New York: Oxford University Press.

Lazarus, R. S. (1999). *Stress and emotion: A new synthesis.* New York: Springer.

Lazarus, R. S., & Lazarus, B. N. (1994). *Passion and reason.* New York: Oxford University Press.

Leadbeater, B. J., Kuperminc, G. P., Blatt, S. J., & Herzog, C. (1999). A multivariate model of gender differences in adolescents' internalizing and externalizing problems. *Developmental Psychology, 35,* 1268–1282.

Leaper, C. (1994). Exploring the correlates and consequences of gender segregation: Social relationships in childhood, adolescence, and adulthood. In C. Leaper (Ed.), *New directions for child development* (No. 65, pp. 67–86). San Francisco: Jossey-Bass.

Leaper, C. (2000). Gender, affiliation, assertion, and the interactive context of parent–child play. *Developmental Psychology, 36,* 381–393.

Leaper, C., Anderson, K. J., & Sanders, P. (1998). Moderators of gender effects on parents' talk to their children: A meta-analysis. *Developmental Psychology, 34,* 3–27.

Leaper, C., Leve, L., Strasser, T., & Schwartz, R. (1995). Mother–child communication sequences: Play activity, child gender, and marital status effects. *Merrill-Palmer Quarterly, 41,* 307–327.

Leaper, C., Tenenbaum, H. R., & Shaffer, T. G. (1999). Communication patterns of African-American girls and boys from low-income, urban backgrounds. *Child Development, 70,* 1489–1503.

Lease, S. H. (2003). Testing a model of men's nontraditional occupational choices. *Career Development Quarterly, 51,* 244–258.

LeBlanc, L. A., Goldsmith, T., & Patel, D. R. (2003). Behavioral aspects of chronic illness in children and adolescents. *Pediatric Clinics of North America, 50,* 859–878.

Lecanuet, J.-P., Granier-Deferre, C., Jacquet, A.-Y., Capponi, I., & Ledru, L. (1993). Prenatal discrimination of a male and female voice uttering the same sentence. *Early Development and Parenting, 2,* 217–228.

Lederer, J. M. (2000). Reciprocal teaching of social studies in inclusive elementary classrooms. *Journal of Learning Disabilities, 33,* 91–106.

Lee, D. J., & Markides, K. S. (1990). Activity and morality among aged persons over an eight-year period. *Journal of Gerontology, 45,* S39–S42.

Lee, D. M., & Weinblatt, M. E. (2001). Rheumatoid arthritis. *Lancet, 358,* 903–911.

Lee, G. R., DeMaris, A., Bavin, S., & Sullivan, R. (2001). Gender differences in the depressive effect of widowhood in later life. *Journal of Gerontology, 56B,* S56–S61.

Lee, K., Cameron, C., Xu, F., Fu, G., & Board, J. (1997). Chinese and Canadian children's evaluations of lying and truth telling: Similarities and differences in the context of pro- and antisocial behaviors. *Child Development, 68,* 924–934.

Lee, S. J., Ralston, H. J., Partridge, J. C., & Rosen, M. A. (2005). Fetal pain: A systematic multidisciplinary review of the evidence. *Journal of the American Medical Association, 294,* 947–954.

Lee, V. E., & Burkam, D. T. (2002). *Inequality at the starting gate.* Washington, DC: Economic Policy Institute.

Lee, V. E., & Burkam, D. T. (2003). Dropping out of high school: The role of school organization and structure. *American Educational Research Journal, 40,* 353–393.

Lehman, D., Ellard, J., & Wortman, C. (1986). Social support for the bereaved: Recipients' and providers' perspectives on what is helpful. *Journal of Consulting and Clinical Psychology, 54,* 438–446.

Lehman, D. R., & Nisbett, R. E. (1990). A longitudinal study of the effects of undergraduate training on reasoning. *Developmental Psychology, 26,* 952–960.

Lehman, E. B., Steier, A., Guidash, K. M., & Wanna, S. Y. (2002). Predictors of compliance in toddlers: Child temperament, maternal personality, and emotional availability. *Early Child Development and Care, 172,* 301–310.

Leiferman, J. A., & Evenson, K. R. (2003). The effect of regular leisure physical activity on birth outcomes. *Maternal and Child Health Journal, 7,* 59–64.

Leiter, M. P., & Maslach, C. (2000). *Preventing burnout and building engagement: A complete program for organizational renewal.* San Francisco: Jossey-Bass.

Lemche, E., Lennertz, I., Orthmann, C., Ari, A., Grote, K., Hafker, J., & Klann-Delius, G. (2003). Emotion-regulatory process in evoked play narratives: Their relation with mental representations and family interactions. *Praxis der Kinderpsychologie und Kinderpsychiatrie, 52,* 156–171.

Lemery, K. S., Goldsmith, H. H., Klinnert, M. D., & Mrazek, D. A. (1999). Developmental models of infant and childhood temperament. *Developmental Psychology, 35,* 189–204.

Lemme, B. H. (2006). *Development in adulthood* (4th ed.). Boston: Allyn and Bacon.

Lempert, H. (1990). Acquisition of passives: The role of patient animacy, salience, and lexical accessibility. *Journal of Child Language, 17,* 677–696.

Lent, R. W., & Brown, S. D. (2002). Social cognitive career theory and adult career development. In R. W. Lent & S. D. Brown (Eds.), *Adult career development: Concepts, issues, and practices* (3rd ed., pp. 76–97). Columbus, OH: National Career Development Association.

Leon, K. (2003). Risk and protective factors in young children's adjustment to parental divorce: A review of the research. *Family Relations, 52,* 258–270.

Leonard, K. E., & Roberts, L. J. (1998). Marital aggression, quality, and stability in the first year of marriage: Findings from the Buffalo Newlywed Study. In T. N. Bradbury (Ed.), *The developmental course of marital dysfunction* (pp. 44–73). New York: Cambridge University Press.

Lerch, J. P., Pruessner, J. C., Zijdenbosl, A., Hampel, H., Teipel, S. J., & Evans, A. C. (2005). Focal decline of cortical thickness in Alzheimer's disease identified by computational neuroanatomy. *Cerebral Cortex, 15,* 995–1001.

Lerner, R. M., Fisher, C. B., & Weinberg, R. A. (2000). Toward a science for and of the people: Promoting civil society through the application of developmental science. *Child Development, 71,* 11–20.

Lerner, R. M., Rothbaum, F., Boulos, S., & Castellino, D. R. (2002). Developmental systems perspective on parenting. In M. H. Bornstein (Ed.), *Handbook of parenting: Vol. 2* (2nd ed., pp. 315–344). Mahwah, NJ: Erlbaum.

Lerner, R. M., Theokas, C., & Bobek, D. L. (2005). Concepts and theories of human development: Historical and contemporary dimensions. In M. H. Bornstein & M. E. Lamb (Eds.), *Developmental science: An advanced textbook* (pp. 3–43). Mahwah, NJ: Erlbaum.

Lester, B. M. (1985). Introduction: There's more to crying than meets the ear. In B. M. Lester & C. F. Z. Boukydis (Eds.), *Infant crying* (pp. 1–27). New York: Plenum.

Lester, B. M., ElSohly, M., Wright, L. L., Smeriglio, V. L., Verter, J., & Bauer, C. R. (2001). The maternal lifestyle study: Drug use by meconium toxicology and maternal self-report. *Pediatrics, 107,* 309–317.

Lester, B. M., LaGasse, L., Seifer, R., Tronick, E. Z., Bauer, C., & Shankaran, S. (2003). The maternal lifestyle study (MLS): Effects of prenatal cocaine and/or opiate exposure on auditory brain response at one month. *Journal of Pediatrics, 142,* 279–285.

Lester, D. (2003). Adolescent suicide from an international perspective. *American Behavioral Scientist, 46,* 1157–1170.

Letherby, G. (2002). Childless and bereft? Stereotypes and realities in relation to "voluntary" and "involuntary" childlessness and womanhood. *Sociological Inquiry, 72,* 7–20.

Leung, M. C. M., Zhang, J., & Zhang, J. (2004). An economic analysis of life expectancy by gender with application to the United States. *Journal of Health Economics, 23,* 737–759.

LeVay, S. (1993). *The sexual brain.* Cambridge, MA: MIT Press.

Levenson, R. W., Carstensen, L. L., & Gottman, J. M. (1993). Long-term marriage: Age, gender, and satisfaction. *Psychology and Aging, 8,* 301–313.

Leventhal, E. A., Leventhal, H., Schaefer, P. M., & Easterling, D. (1993). Conservation of energy, uncertainty reduction, and swift utilization of medical care among the elderly. *Journal of Gerontology, 48,* P78–P86.

Leventhal, T., & Brooks-Gunn, J. (2003). Children and youth in neighborhood contexts. *Current Directions in Psychological Science, 12,* 27–31.

Levin, I., & Bus, A. G. (2003). How is emergent writing based on drawing? Analyses of children's products and their sorting by children and mothers. *Developmental Psychology, 39,* 891–905.

Levin, J. S., & Chatters, L. M. (1998). Religion, health, and psychological well-being in older adults. *Journal of Aging and Health, 10,* 504–531.

Levin, J. S., Taylor, R. J., & Chatters, L. M. (1994). Race and gender differences in religiosity among older adults: Findings from four national surveys. *Journal of Gerontology, 49,* S137–S145.

Levine, B., Svoboda, E., Hay, J. F., Winocur, G., & Moscovitch, M. (2002). Aging and autobiographical memory: Dissociating episodic from semantic retrieval. *Psychology and Aging, 17,* 677–689.

Levine, L. E. (1983). Mine: Self-definition in 2-year-old boys. *Developmental Psychology, 19,* 544–549.

Levine, L. J. (1995). Young children's understanding of the causes of anger and sadness. *Child Development, 66,* 697–709.

LeVine, R. A., Dixon, S., LeVine, S., Richman, A., Leiderman, P. H., Keefer, C. H., & Brazelton, T. B. (1994). *Child care and culture: Lessons from Africa.* New York: Cambridge University Press.

LeVine, R. A., LeVine, S.E., Richman, A., Tapia Uribe, M. R., Suderland Correa, C., & Miller, P. M. (1991). Women's schooling and child care in the demographic transition: A Mexican case study. *Population and Development Review, 17,* 459–496.

LeVine, R. A., LeVine, S. E., Rowe, M. L., & Schnell-Anzola, B. (2004). Maternal literacy and health behavior: A Nepalese case study. *Social Science and Medicine, 58,* 863–877.

LeVine, R. A., LeVine, S. E., & Schnell, B. (2001). "Improve the women": Mass schooling, female literacy, and worldwide social change. *Harvard Educational Review, 71,* 1–50.

Levine, S. C., Huttenlocher, J., Taylor, A., & Langrock, A. (1999). Early sex differences in spatial skill. *Developmental Psychology, 35,* 940–949.

Levinson, D. J. (1978). *The seasons of a man's life.* New York: Knopf.

Levinson, D. J. (1986). A conception of adult development. *American Psychologist, 41,* 3–13.

Levinson, D. J. (1996). *The seasons of a woman's life.* New York: Knopf.

Levtzion-Korach, O., Tennenbaum, A., Schnitzer, R., & Ornoy, A. (2000). Early motor development of blind children. *Journal of Paediatric and Child Health, 36,* 226–229.

Levy, B. R., & Banaji, M. R. (2002). Implicit ageism. In T. D. Nelson (Ed.), *Ageism: Stereotyping and prejudice against older persons* (pp. 49–75). Cambridge, MA: MIT Press.

Levy, B. R., Hausdorff, J., Hencke, R., & Wei, J. Y. (2000). Reducing cardiovascular stress with positive self-stereotypes of aging. *Journal of Gerontology, 55B,* P205–P213.

Levy, B. R., Slade, M. D., Kunkel, S. R., & Kasl, S. V. (2002). Longevity increased by positive self-perceptions of aging. *Journal of Personality and Social Psychology, 83,* 261–270.

Levy, G. D., Taylor, M. G., & Gelman, S. A. (1995). Traditional and evaluative aspects of flexibility in gender roles, social conventions, moral rules, and physical laws. *Child Development, 66,* 515–531.

Levy, J. A. (1994). Sex and sexuality in later life stages. In A. S. Rossi (Ed.), *Sexuality across the life course* (pp. 287–309). Chicago: University of Chicago Press.

Levy, S. R., & Dweck, C. S. (1999). The impact of children's static vs. dynamic conceptions of people on stereotype formation. *Child Development, 70,* 1163–1180.

Levy-Shiff, R., & Israelashvili, R. (1988). Antecedents of fathering: Some further exploration. *Developmental Psychology, 24,* 434–440.

Lewis, C., Freeman, N. H., Kyriadidou, C., Maridakikassotaki, K., & Berridge, D. M. (1996). Social influences on false belief access—specific sibling influences or general apprenticeship? *Child Development, 67,* 2930–2947.

Lewis, K. G. (2000). *With or without a man: Single women taking control of their lives.* New York: Bull Publishing.

Lewis, M. (1992). *Shame: The exposed self.* New York: Free Press.

Lewis, M. (1995). Embarrassment: The emotion of self-exposure and evaluation. In J. P. Tangney & K. W. Fischer (Eds.), *Self-conscious emotions* (pp. 198–218). New York: Guilford Press.

Lewis, M. (1997). *Altering fate: Why the past does not predict the future.* New York: Guilford.

Lewis, M. (1998). Emotional competence and development. In D. Pushkar, W. M. Bukowski, A. E. Schwartzman, E. M. Stack, & D. R. White (Eds.), *Improving competence across the lifespan* (pp. 27–36). New York: Plenum.

Lewis, M., & Brooks-Gunn, J. (1979). *Social cognition and the acquisition of self.* New York: Plenum.

Lewis, M., Ramsay, D. S., & Kawakami, K. (1993). Differences between Japanese infants and Caucasian American infants in behavioral and cortisol response to inoculation. *Child Development, 64,* 1722–1731.

Lewis, M., Sullivan, M. W., Stanger, C., & Weiss, M. (1989). Self development and self-conscious emotions. *Child Development, 60,* 146–156.

Li, S.-C., Lindenberger, U., Hommel, B., Aschersleben, G., Prinz, W., & Baltes, P. B. (2004). Transformations in the couplings among intellectual abilities and constituent cognitive processes across the life span. *Psychological Science, 15,* 155–163.

Liang, J., Bennett, J., Krause, N., Kobayashi, E., Kim, H., Brown, J. W., Akiyama, H., Sugiawa, H., & Jain, A. (2002). Old age mortality in Japan: Does the socioeconomic gradient interact with gender and age? *Journal of Gerontology, 57,* S294–S307.

Liang, J., Bennett, J. M., Krause, N. M., Chang, M., Lin, S., Chuang, Y. L., & Wo, S. (1999). Stress, social relationships, and old age mortality in Taiwan. *Journal of Clinical Epidemiology, 52,* 983–995.

Liang, J., Krause, N. M., & Bennett, J. M. (2001). Social exchange and well-being: Is giving better than receiving? *Psychology and Aging, 16,* 511–523.

Liben, L. S. (1999). Developing an understanding of external spatial representations. In I. E. Sigel (Ed.), *Development of mental representation* (pp. 297–321). Mahwah, NJ: Erlbaum.

Liben, L. S., & Bigler, R. S. (2002). The developmental course of gender differentiation: Conceptualizing, measuring, and evaluating constructs and pathways. *Monographs of the Society for Research in Child Development, 6* (4, Serial No. 271).

Liben, L. S., Bigler, R. S., & Krogh, H. R. (2001). Pink and blue collar jobs: Children's judgments of job status and job aspirations in relation to sex of worker. *Journal of Experimental Child Psychology, 79,* 346–363.

Liben, L. S., & Downs, R. M. (1993). Understanding person–space–map relations: Cartographic and developmental perspectives. *Developmental Psychology, 29,* 739–752.

Liben, L. S., & Signorella, M. L. (1993). Gender-schematic processing in children: The role of initial interpretations of stimuli.

Developmental Psychology, 29, 141–149.

Lickliter, R., & Bahrick, L. E. (2000). The development of infant intersensory perception: Advantages of a comparative convergent-operations approach. *Psychological Bulletin, 126,* 260–280.

Lickliter, R., Bahrick, L. E., & Honeycutt, H. (2002). Intersensory redundancy facilitates prenatal perceptual learning in bobwhite quail *(Colinus virginianus)* embryos. *Developmental Psychology, 38,* 15–23.

Lidz, C. S. (2001). Multicultural issues and dynamic assessment. In L. A. Suzuki & J. G. Ponterotto (Eds.), *Handbook of multicultural assessment: Clinical, psychological, and educational applications* (2nd ed., pp. 523–539). San Francisco: Jossey-Bass.

Lieberman, M. A. (1993). Bereavement self-help groups: A review of conceptual and methodological issues. In M. S. Stroebe, W. Stroebe, & R. O. Hansson (Eds.), *Handbook of bereavement* (pp. 427–453). New York: Cambridge University Press.

Lieven, E., Pine, J., & Baldwin, G. (1997). Lexically based learning and early grammatical development. *Journal of Child Language, 24,* 187–220.

Light, P., & Perrett-Clermont, A.-N. (1989). Social context effects in learning and testing. In A. Gellatly, D. Rogers, & J. Sloboda (Eds.), *Cognition and social worlds* (pp. 99–112). Oxford, UK: Clarendon Press.

Lillard, A. S. (1998). Playing with a theory of mind. In O. N. Saracho & B. Spodek (Eds.), *Multiple perspectives on play in early childhood education* (pp. 11–33). Albany: State University of New York Press.

Lillard, A. S. (2001). Pretending, understanding pretense, and understanding minds. In S. Reifel (Ed.), *Play and culture studies* (Vol. 3). Norwood, NJ: Ablex.

Lim, V. K. G. (2002). Gender differences and attitudes toward homosexuality. *Journal of Homosexuality, 43,* 85–97.

Lin, C. C., Hsiao, C. K., & Chen, W. J. (1999). Development of sustained attention assessed using the continuous performance test among children 6–15 years. *Journal of Abnormal Child Psychology, 27,* 403–412.

Lindley, L. D. (2005). Perceived barriers to career development in the context of social-cognitive career theory. *Journal of Career Assessment, 13,* 271–287.

Lindsay, C. (1999). *A portrait of seniors in Canada* (3rd ed.). Ottawa: Statistics Canada.

Lindsay, C., Almey, M., & Normand, J. (2002). *Youth in Canada.* Retrieved from http://www.statcan.ca/english/IPS/Data/85-511-XPE.htm

Lindsay-Hartz, J., de Rivera, J., & Mascolo, M. F. (1995). Differentiating guilt and shame and their effects on motivation. In J. P. Tangney & K. W. Fischer (Eds.), *Self-conscious emotions* (pp. 274–300). New York: Guilford.

Lindsey, E. W., & Colwell, M. J. (2003). Preschoolers' emotional competence: Links to pretend and physical play. *Child Study Journal, 33,* 39–52.

Lindsey, E. W., & Mize, J. (2000). Parent–child physical and pretense play: Links to children's social competence. *Merrill-Palmer Quarterly, 46,* 565–591.

Link, S. C., & Ancoli-Israel, S. (1995). Sleep and the teenager. *Sleep Research, 24a,* 184.

Linn, M. C., & Petersen, A. C. (1985). Emergence and characterization of sex differences in spatial ability: A meta-analysis. *Child Development, 56,* 1479–1498.

Lipman, E. L., Boyle, M. H., Dooley, M. D., & Offord, D. R. (2002). Child well-being in single-mother families. *Journal of the American Academy of Child and Adolescent Psychiatry, 41,* 75–82.

Lipsitt, L. P. (2003). Crib death: A biobehavioral phenomenon? *Psychological Science, 12,* 164–170.

Liston, R., Crane, J., Hamilton, E., Hughes, O., Kuling, S., & MacKinnon, C. (2002). Fetal health surveillance during labour. *Journal of Obstetrics and Gynecology of Canada, 24,* 250–276.

Litovsky, R. Y., & Ashmead, D. H. (1997). Development of binaural and spatial hearing in infants and children. In R. H. Gilkey & T. R. Anderson (Eds.), *Binaural and spatial hearing in real and virtual environments* (pp. 571–592). Mahwah, NJ: Erlbaum.

Liu, J., Raine, A., Venables, P. H., Dalais, C., & Mednick, S. A. (2003). Malnutrition at age 3 years and lower cognitive ability at age 11 years. *Archives of Paediatric and Adolescent Medicine, 157,* 593–600.

Liu, X. D., Zhu, Y. K., Umino, T., Spurzem, J. R., Romberger, D. J., & Wang, H. (2001). Cigarette smoke inhibits osteogenic differentiation and proliferation of human osteoprogenitor cells in monolayer and three-dimensional collagen gel culture. *Journal of Laboratory and Clinical Medicine, 137,* 208–219.

Lloyd, L. (1999). Multi-age classes and high ability students. *Review of Educational Research, 69,* 187–212.

Lochman, J. E., & Dodge K. A. (1998). Distorted perceptions in dyadic interactions of aggressive and nonaggressive boys: Effects of prior expectations, context, and boys' age. *Development and Psychopathology, 10,* 495–512.

Lock, M., & Kaufert, P. (2001). Menopause, local biologies, and cultures of aging. *American Journal of Human Biology, 13,* 494–504.

Locke, J. (1892). Some thoughts concerning education. In R. H. Quick (Ed.), *Locke on education* (pp. 1–236). Cambridge, UK: Cambridge University Press. (Original work published 1690)

Lockhart, R. S., & Craik, F. I. M. (1990). Levels of processing: A retrospective commentary on a framework for memory research. *Canadian Journal of Psychology, 44,* 87–112.

Loeb, S., Fuller, B., Kagan, S. L., & Carrol, B. (2004). Child care in poor communities: Early learning effects of type, quality, and stability. *Child Development, 75,* 47–65.

Loehlin, J. C. (2000). Group differences in intelligence. In R. J. Sternberg (Ed.), *Handbook of intelligence* (pp. 176–193). New York: Cambridge University Press.

Loehlin, J. C., Horn, J. M., & Willerman, L. (1997). Heredity, environment, and IQ in the Texas Adoption Project. In R. J. Sternberg & E. L. Grigorenko (Eds.), *Intelligence, heredity, and environment* (pp. 105–125). New York: Cambridge University Press.

Loehlin, J. C., Jonsson, E. G., Gustavsson, J. P., Stallings, M. C., Gillespie, N. A., Wright, M. J., & Martin, N. G. (2005). Psychological masculinity–femininity via the gender diagnosticity approach: Heritability and consistency across ages and populations. *Journal of Personality, 73,* 1295–1319.

Loehlin, J. C., & Martin, N. G. (2001). Age changes in personality traits and their heritabilities during the adult years: Evidence from Australian twin registry samples. *Personality and Individual Differences, 30,* 1147–1160.

Loewy, E. H. (2004). Euthanasia, physician assisted suicide and other methods of helping along death. *Health Care Analysis, 12,* 181–191.

Loganovskaja, T. K., & Loganovsky, K. N. (1999). EEG, cognitive and psychopathological abnormalities in children irradiated in utero. *International Journal of Psychophysiology, 34,* 211–224.

Logroscino, G., Kang, J. H., & Grodstein, F. (2004). Prospective study of type 2 diabetes and cognitive decline in women aged 70–81 years. *British Medical Journal, 328,* 548.

Logsdon, R. G. (2000). *Enhancing quality of life in long term care: A comprehensive guide.* New York: Hatherleigh Press.

Lohman, D. F. (2000). Measures of intelligence: Cognitive theories. In A. E. Kazdin (Ed.), *Encyclopedia of psychology: Vol. 5* (pp. 147–150). Washington, DC: American Psychological Association.

Long, D. D. (1985). A cross-cultural examination of fears of death among Saudi Arabians. *Omega, 16,* 43–50.

Long, H. B., & Zoller-Hodges, D. (1995). Outcomes of Elderhostel participation. *Educational Gerontology, 21,* 113–127.

Looker, D., & Thiessen, V. (2003). *The digital divide in Canadian schools: Factors affecting student access to and use of information technology.* Ottawa: Canadian Education Statistics Council.

Loots, G., & Devise, I. (2003). The use of visual-tactile communication strategies by deaf and hearing fathers and mothers of deaf infants. *Journal of Deaf Studies and Deaf Education, 8,* 31–42.

Lopata, H. Z. (1996). *Current widowhood: Myths and realities.* Thousand Oaks, CA: Sage.

Lorenz, K. (1952). *King Solomon's ring.* New York: Crowell.

Louie, V. (2001). Parents' aspirations and investment: The role of social class in the educational experiences of 1.5- and second generation Chinese Americans. *Harvard Educational Review, 71,* 438–474.

Louis, J., Cannard, C., Bastuji, H., & Challemel, M.-J. (1997). Sleep ontogenesis revisited: A longitudinal 24-hour home polygraphic study on 15 normal infants during the first two years of life. *Sleep, 20,* 323–333.

Lourenco, O. (2003). Making sense of Turiel's dispute with Kohlberg: The case of the child's moral competence. *New Ideas in Psychology, 21,* 43–68.

Lövdén, M., Bergman, L., Adolfsson, R., Lindenberger, U., & Nilsson, L.-G. (2005). Studying individual aging in an interindividual context: Typical paths of age-related, dementia-related, and mortality-related cognitive development in old age. *Psychology and Aging, 20,* 303–316.

Love, J. M., Harrison, L., Sagi-Schwartz, A., van IJzendoorn, M. H., Ross, C., & Ungerer, J. A. (2003). Child care quality matters: How conclusions may vary with context. *Child Development, 74,* 1021–1033.

Love, J. M., Kisker, E. E., Ross, C., Raikes, H., Constantine, J., Boller, K., & Brooks-Gunn, J.

(2005). The effectiveness of early Head Start for 3-year-old children and their parents: Lessons for policy and programs. *Developmental Psychology, 41,* 885–901.

Lower, L. M. (2005). Couples with young children. In M. Harway (Ed.), *Handbook of couples therapy* (pp. 44–60). New York: Wiley.

Lubart, T. I. (2003). In search of creative intelligence. In R. J. Sternberg, J. Lautrey, & T. I. Lubart (Eds.), *Models of intelligence: International perspectives* (pp. 279–292). Washington, DC: American Psychological Association.

Lubart, T. I., & Sternberg, R. J. (1998). Life span creativity: An investment theory approach. In C. E. Adams-Price (Ed.), *Creativity and successful aging.* New York: Springer.

Luborsky, M. R., & McMullen, K. (1999). Culture and aging. In J. C. Kavanaugh & S. K. Whitbourne (Eds.), *Gerontology: An interdisciplinary perspective* (pp. 65–90). New York: Oxford University Press.

Lucas, S. R., & Behrends, M. (2002). Sociodemographic diversity, correlated achievement, and de facto tracking. *Sociology of Education, 75,* 328–348.

Lucas, T. W., Wendorf, C. A., Imamoglu, E. O., Shen, J., Parkhill, M. R., Weisfeld, C. C. & Weisfeld, G. E. (2004). Marital satisfaction in four cultures as a function of homogamy, male dominance, and female attractiveness. *Sexualities, Evolution and Gender, 6,* 97–130.

Luciana, M., Sullivan, J., & Nelson, C. A. (2001). Associations between phenylalanine-to-tyrosine ratios and performance on tests of neuropsychological function in adolescents treated early and continuously for phenylketonuria. *Child Development, 72,* 1637–1652.

Ludemann, P. M. (1991). Generalized discrimination of positive facial expressions by seven- and ten-month-old infants. *Child Development, 62,* 55–67.

Ludvig, J., Miner, B., & Eisenberg, M. J. (2005). Smoking cessation in patients with coronary artery disease. *American Heart Journal, 149,* 565–572.

Luke, A., Cooper, R. S., Prewitt, T. E., Adeyemo, A. A., & Forrester, T. E. (2001). Nutritional consequences of the African diaspora. *Annual Review of Nutrition, 21,* 47–71.

Luna, B., Garver, K. E., Urban, T. A., Lazar, N. A., & Sweeney, J. A. (2004). Maturation of cognitive processes from late childhood to adulthood. *Child Development, 75,* 1357–1372.

Luna, B., Thulborn, K. R., Monoz, D. P., Merriam, E. P., Garver, K. E., Minshew, N. J., Keshavan, M. S., Genovese, C. R., Eddy, W. F., & Sweeney, J. A. (2001). Maturation of widely distributed brain function subserves cognitive development. *Neuroimage, 13,* 786–793.

Lund, D. (2005). *My journey* [Sue's letter]. Unpublished document. Salt Lake City, UT: University of Utah.

Lund, D. A. (1993). Widowhood: The coping response. In R. Kastenbaum (Ed.), *Encyclopedia of adult development* (pp. 537–541). Phoenix, AZ: Oryx Press.

Lund, D. A. (1996). Bereavement and loss. In J. E. Birren (Ed.), *Encyclopedia of gerontology* (pp. 173–183). San Diego: Academic Press.

Lund, D. A. (1998). Statements and perspectives from leaders in the field of aging in Utah. In *Utah sourcebook on aging.* Salt Lake City: Empire Publishing.

Lund, D. A., & Caserta, M. S. (2001). When the unexpected happens: Husbands coping with the deaths of their wives. In D. Lund (Ed.), *Men coping with grief* (pp. 147–166). Amityville, NY: Baywood.

Lund, D. A., & Caserta, M. S. (2004a). Facing life alone: Loss of a significant other in later life. In D. Doda (Ed), *Living with grief: Loss in later life* (pp. 207–223). Washington, DC: Hospice Foundation of America.

Lund, D. A., & Caserta, M. S. (2004b). Older men coping with widowhood. *Geriatrics and Aging, 7*(6), 29–33.

Lund, D. A., Caserta, M. S., de Vries, B., & Wright, S. (2004). Restoration after bereavement. *Generations Review, 14,* 9–15.

Lund, D. A., Caserta, M. S., & Dimond, M. F. (1993). The course of spousal bereavement in later life. In M. S. Stroebe, W. Stroebe, & R. O. Hansson (Eds.), *Handbook of bereavement* (pp. 240–245). New York: Cambridge University Press.

Lund, D. A., Hill, R. D., Caserta, M. S., & Wright, S. D. (1995). Video Respite™: An innovative resource for family, professional cargivers, and persons with dementia. *Gerontologist, 35,* 683–687.

Lund, D. A., & Wright, S. D. (2001). Respite services: Enhancing the quality of daily life for caregivers and persons with dementia. Retrieved from http://www.nurs.utah.edu/Gerontology

Lundy, B. L. (2002). Paternal socio-psychological factors and infant attachment: The mediating role of synchrony in father–infant interactions. *Infant Behavior and Development, 25,* 221–236.

Lundy, B. L. (2003). Father– and mother–infant face-to-face interactions: Differences in mind-related comments and infant attachment? *Infant Behavior and Development, 26,* 200–212.

Lundy, M., & Grossman, S. F. (2004). Elder abuse: Spouse/intimate partner abuse and family violence among elders. *Journal of Elder Abuse and Neglect, 16,* 85–102.

Luo, Y., & Baillargeon, R. (2005). When the ordinary seems unexpected: Evidence for incremental physical knowledge in young infants. *Cognition, 95,* 297–328.

Luo, Y., & Waite, L. J. (2005). The impact of childhood and adult SES on physical, mental, and cognitive well-being in later life. *Journal of Gerontology, 60B,* S93–S101.

Lussier, G., Deater-Deckard, K., Dunn, J., & Davies, L. (2002). Support across two generations: Children's closeness to grandparents following parental divorce and remarriage. *Journal of Family Psychology, 16,* 363–376.

Luster, T., & McAdoo, H. (1996). Family and child influences on educational attainment: A secondary analysis of the High/Scope Perry Preschool data. *Developmental Psychology, 32,* 26–39.

Luthar, S. S., & Becker, B. E. (2002). Privileged but pressured: A study of affluent youth. *Child Development, 73,* 1593–1610.

Luthar, S. S., & Latendresse, S. J. (2005a). Children of the affluent: Challenges to well-being. *Current Directions in Psychological Science, 14,* 49–53.

Luthar, S. S., & Latendresse, S. J. (2005b). Comparable "risks" at the socioeconomic status extremes: Preadolescents' perceptions of parenting. *Development and Psychopathology, 17,* 207–230.

Luthar, S. S., & Sexton, C. (2004). The high price of affluence. In R. V. Kail (Ed.), *Advances in child development* (Vol. 32, pp. 126–162). San Diego, CA: Academic Press.

Luxembourg Income Study. (2005). *Household income surveys, 2000.* Retrieved from www.lisproject.org

Luzzo, D. A. (1999). Identifying the career decision-making needs of nontraditional college students. *Journal of Counseling and Development, 77,* 135–140.

Lyness, K., & Thompson, D. (1997). Above the glass ceiling? A comparison of matched samples of female and male executives. *Journal of Applied Psychology, 82,* 359–375.

Lyon, G. R., Fletcher, J. M., & Barnes, M. C. (2002). Learning disabilities. In E. J. Mash & R. A. Barkley (Eds.), *Child psychopathology* (2nd ed., pp. 520–586). New York: Guilford.

Lyon, T. D., & Flavell, J. H. (1994). Young children's understanding of "remember" and "forget." *Child Development, 65,* 1357–1371.

Lyons-Ruth, K. (1996). Attachment relationships among children with aggressive behavior problems: The role of disorganized early attachment patterns. *Journal of Consulting and Clinical Psychology, 64,* 64–73.

Lyons-Ruth, K., Bronfman, E., & Parsons, E. (1999). Maternal frightened, frightening, or atypical behavior and disorganized infant attachment patterns. *Monographs of the Society for Research in Child Development, 64*(3, Serial No. 258), 67–96.

Lyons-Ruth, K., Easterbrooks, A., & Cibelli, C. (1997). Infant attachment strategies, infant mental lag, and maternal depressive symptoms: Predictors of internalizing and externalizing problems at age 7. *Developmental Psychology, 33,* 681–692.

Lytton, H., & Gallagher, L. (2002). Parenting twins and the genetics of parenting. In M. H. Bornstein (Ed.), *Handbook of parenting* (Vol. 1, pp. 227–253). Mahwah, NJ: Erlbaum.

M

Macaluso, A., & De Vito, G. (2004). Muscle strength, power and adaptations to resistance training in older people. *European Journal of Applied Physiology, 91,* 450–472.

Maccoby, E. E. (1984). Socialization and developmental change. *Child Development, 55,* 317–328.

Maccoby, E. E. (1998). *The two sexes: Growing up apart, coming together.* Cambridge, MA: Belknap.

Maccoby, E. E. (2000). Perspectives on gender development. *International Journal of Behavioral Development, 24,* 398–406.

Maccoby, E. E. (2002). Gender and group process: A developmental perspective. *Current Directions in Psychological Science, 11,* 54–58.

MacDonald, S. W. S., Hultsch, D. F., & Dixon, R. A. (2003). Performance variability is related to change in cognition: Evidence from the Victoria Longitudinal Study. *Psychology and Aging, 18,* 510–523.

MacDonald, W. L., & DeMaris, A. (1996). The effects of stepparent's gender and new biological children. *Journal of Family Issues, 17,* 5–25.

MacKay, D. G., & Abrams, L. (1996). Language, memory, and aging: Distributed deficits and the structure of new-versus-old connections. In J. E. Birren & K. W. Schaie (Eds.), *Handbook of the psychology of aging* (pp. 251–265). San Diego: Academic Press.

Mackenbach, J. P. (2002). Income inequality and population health. *British Medical Journal, 324,* 1–2.

Mackey, K., Arnold, M. K., & Pratt, M. W. (2001). Adolescents' stories of decision making in more and less authoritative families: Representing the voices of parents in narrative. *Journal of Adolescent Research, 16,* 243–268.

MacKinnon, L. T. (1999). *Exercise and immunology.* Champaign, IL: Human Kinetics.

MacLean, K. (2003). The impact of institutionalization on child development. *Development and Psychopathology, 15,* 853–884.

MacWhinney, B. (2005). Language development. In M. H. Bornstein & M. E. Lamb (Eds.), *Developmental science: An advanced textbook* (5th ed., pp. 359–387). Mahwah, NJ: Erlbaum.

Madden, D. J., & Plude, D. J. (1993). Selective preservation of selective attention. In J. Cerella & J. M. Rybash (Eds.), *Adult information processing: Limits on loss* (pp. 273–300). San Diego: Academic Press.

Maddi, S. R. (1999). The personality construct of hardiness: I. Effects on experiencing, coping, and strain. *Consulting Psychology Journal: Practice and Research, 51,* 83–94.

Maddi, S. R., & Hightower, M. (1999). Hardiness and optimism as expressed in coping patterns. *Consulting Psychology Journal: Practice and Research, 51,* 95–105.

Maddox, G. L. (1963). Activity and morale: A longitudinal study of selected elderly subjects. *Social Forces, 42,* 195–204.

Maddox, G. L. (2001). Housing and living arrangements. In R. H. Binstock & L. K. George (Eds.), *Handbook of aging and the social sciences* (5th ed., pp. 426–443). San Diego: Academic Press.

Madon, S., Jussim, L., & Eccles, J. (1997). In search of the powerful self-fulfilling prophecy. *Journal of Personality and Social Psychology, 72,* 791–809.

Magdol, L., Moffitt, T. E., Caspi, A., & Silva, P. A. (1998). Developmental antecedents of partner abuse: A prospective-longitudinal study. *Journal of Abnormal Psychology, 107,* 375–389.

Maglio, C. J., & Robinson, S. E. (1994). The effects of death education on death anxiety: A meta-analysis. *Omega, 29,* 319–335.

Magnuson, K. A., & Duncan, G. J. (2002). Parents in poverty. In M. H. Bornstein (Ed.), *Handbook of parenting* (Vol. 4, pp. 95–122). Mahwah, NJ: Erlbaum.

Magnusson, D. (1999). Holistic interactionism: A perspective for research on personality development. In L. A. Pervin & O. P. John (Eds.), *Handbook of personality: Theory and research* (2nd ed., pp. 219–247). New York: Guilford.

Magolda, M. B. B. (2002). Epistemological reflection: The evolution of epistemological assumptions from age 18 to 30. In B. K. Hofer & P. R. Pintrich (Eds.), *Personal epistemology* (pp. 89–102). Mahwah, NJ: Erlbaum.

Mahanran, L. G., Bauman, P. A., Kalman, D., Skolnik, H., & Pele, S. M. (1999). Master athletes: Factors affecting performance. *Sports Medicine, 28,* 273–285.

Mahon, M. M., Goldberg, E. Z., & Washington, S. K. (1999). Concept of death in a sample of Israeli kibbutz children. *Death Studies, 23,* 43–59.

Mahoney, A., Pargament, K. I., Jewell, T., Swank, A. B., Scott, E., Emery, E., & Rye, M. (1999). Marriage and the spiritual realm: The role of proximal and distal religious constructs in marital functioning. *Journal of Family Psychology, 13,* 321–338.

Mahoney, J. L. (2000). Participation in school extracurricular activities as a moderator in the development of antisocial patterns. *Child Development, 71,* 502–516.

Mahoney, J. L., & Magnuson, D. (2001). Parent participation in community activities and the persistence of criminality. *Development and Psychopathology, 13,* 123–139.

Mahoney, J. L., Schweder, A. E., & Stattin, H. (2002). Structured after-school activities as a moderator of depressed mood for adolescents with detached relations to their parents. *Journal of Community Psychology, 30,* 69–86.

Mahoney, J. L., & Stattin, H. (2000). Leisure activities and antisocial behavior: The role of structure and social context. *Journal of Adolescence, 23,* 113–127.

Mahoney, J. L., Stattin, H., & Magnusson, D. (2001). Youth recreation centre participation and criminal offending: A 20-year longitudinal study of Swedish boys. *International Journal of Behavioral Development, 25,* 509–520.

Mahoney, M. M. (2002). The economic rights and responsibilities of unmarried cohabitants. In A. Booth & A. C. Crouter (Eds.), *Just living together* (pp. 247–254). Mahwah, NJ: Erlbaum.

Maier, D. M., & Newman, M. J. (1995). Legal and psychological considerations in the development of a euthanasia statute for adults in the United States. *Behavioral Sciences and the Law, 13,* 3–25.

Main, M. (2000). The organized categories of infant, child, and adult attachment: Flexible vs. inflexible attention under attachment-related stress. *Journal of the American Psychoanalytic Association, 48,* 1055–1096.

Main, M., & Goldwyn, R. (1998). *Adult attachment classification system.* London: University College.

Main, M., & Solomon, J. (1990). Procedures for identifying infants as disorganized/disoriented during the Ainsworth Strange Situation. In M. Greenberg, D. Cicchetti, & M. Cummings (Eds.), *Attachment in the preschool years: Theory, research, and intervention* (pp. 121–160). Chicago: University of Chicago Press.

Mains, D. S., Nowels, C. T., Cavender, T. A., Etschmaier, M., & Steiner, J. F. (2005). A qualitative study of work and work return in cancer survivors. *Psycho-Oncology, 14,* 992–1004.

Maitland, S. B., Intrieri, R. C., Schaie, K. W., & Willis, S. L. (2000). Gender differences and changes in cognitive abilities across the adult life span. *Aging, Neuropsychology, and Cognition, 7,* 32–53.

Majnemer, A., & Barr, R. G. (2005). Influence of supine sleep positioning on early motor milestone acquisition. *Developmental Medicine and Child Neurology, 47,* 370–376.

Major, B., Spencer, S., Schmader, T., Wolfe, C., & Crocker, J. (1998). Coping with negative stereotypes about intellectual performance: The role of psychological disengagement. *Personality and Social Psychology Bulletin, 24,* 34–50.

Makin, J., Fried, P. A., & Watkinson, B. (1991). A comparison of active and passive smoking during pregnancy: Long-term effects. *Neurotoxicology and Teratology, 13,* 5–12.

Malaguarnera, L., Ferlito, L., Imbesi, R. M., Gulizia, G. S., Di Mauro, S., Maugeri, D., Malaguarnera, M., & Messina, A. (2001). Immunosenescence: A review. *Archives of Gerontology and Geriatrics, 32,* 1–14.

Malatesta, C. Z., Grigoryev, P., Lamb, C., Albin, M., & Culver, C. (1986). Emotion socialization and expressive development in preterm and full-term infants. *Child Development, 57,* 316–330.

Malina, R. M., & Bouchard, C. (1991). *Growth, maturation, and physical activity.* Champaign, IL: Human Kinetics.

Mallinckrodt, B., & Fretz, B. R. (1988). Social support and the impact of job loss on older professionals. *Journal of Counseling Psychology, 35,* 281–286.

Malone, M. M. (1982). Consciousness of dying and projective fantasy of young children with malignant disease. *Developmental and Behavioral Pediatrics, 3,* 55–60.

Mandler, J. M. (2004). Thought before language. *Trends in Cognitive Sciences, 8,* 508–513.

Mandler, J. M., & McDonough, L. (1998). On developing a knowledge base in infancy. *Developmental Psychology, 34,* 1274–1288.

Mange, E. J., & Mange, A. P. (1998). *Basic human genetics* (2nd ed.). Sunderland, MA: Sinauer Associates.

Mangelsdorf, S. C., Schoppe, S. J., & Burr, H. (2000). The meaning of parental reports: A contextual approach to the study of temperament and behavior problems. In V. J. Molfese & D. L. Molfese (Eds.), *Temperament and personality across the life span* (pp. 121–140). Mahwah, NJ: Erlbaum.

Mani, T. M., Bedwell, J. S., & Miller, L. S. (2005). Age-related decrements in performance on a brief continuous performance task. *Archives of Clinical Neuropsychology, 20,* 575–586.

Manlove, J., Ryan, S., & Franzetta, K. (2003). Patterns of contraceptive use within teenagers' first sexual relationships. *Perspectives on Sexual and Reproductive Health, 35,* 246–255.

Mannell, R. C. (1999). Older adults, leisure, and wellness. *Journal of Leisurability, 26*(2), 3–10.

Manson, J. E., Skerrett, P. J., Greenland, P., & VanItallie, T. B. (2004). The escalating pandemics of obesity and sedentary lifestyle: A call to action for clinicians. *Archives of Internal Medicine, 164,* 249–258.

Maratsos, M. (1998). The acquisition of grammar. In D. Kuhn & R. S. Siegler (Eds.), *Handbook of child psychology: Vol. 2. Cognition, perception, and language* (5th ed., pp. 421–466). New York: Wiley.

Maratsos, M. (2000). More overregularizations after all: New data and discussion on Marcus, Pinker, Ullman, Hollander, Rosen, & Xu. *Journal of Child Language, 27,* 183–212.

Marchman, V. A., & Thal, D. J. (2005). Words and grammar. In M. Tomasello & D. I. Slobin (Eds.), *Beyond nature–nurture: Essays in honor of Elizabeth Bates* (pp. 141–164). Mahwah, NJ: Erlbaum.

Marcia, J. E. (1980). Identity in adolescence. In J. Adelson (Ed.), *Handbook of adolescent psychology* (pp. 159–187). New York: Wiley.

Marcia, J. E. (2002). Identity and psychosocial development in adulthood. *Identity, 2,* 7–28.

Marcon, R. A. (1999a). Differential impact of preschool models on development and early learning of inner-city children: A three-cohort study. *Developmental Psychology, 35,* 358–375.

Marcon, R. A. (1999b). Positive relationships between parent–school involvement and public school inner-city preschoolers' development and academic performance. *School Psychology Review, 28,* 395–412.

Marcus, G. F. (1995). Children's overregularization of English plurals: A quantitative analysis. *Journal of Child Language, 22,* 447–459.

Marcus-Newhall, A., Thompson, S., & Thomas, C. (2001). Examining a gender stereotype: Menopausal women. *Journal of Applied Social Psychology, 31,* 698–719.

Mardh, P. A. (2002). Influence of infection with *Chlamydia trachomatis* on pregnancy outcome, infant health and life-long sequelae in infected offspring. *Best Practice and Research in Clinical Obstetrics and Gynaecology, 16,* 847–964.

Markides, K. S., & Cooper, C. L. (1989). Aging, stress, social support and health: An overview. In K. S. Markides & C. L. Cooper (Eds.), *Aging, stress and health* (pp. 1–10). Chicester: Wiley.

Markman, E. M. (1992). Constraints on word learning: Speculations about their nature, origins, and domain specificity. In M. R. Gunnar & M. P. Maratsos (Eds.), *Minnesota Symposia on Child Psychology* (Vol. 25, pp. 59–101). Hillsdale, NJ: Erlbaum.

Markovits, H., Benenson, J., & Dolensky, E. (2001). Evidence that children and adolescents have internal models of peer interactions that are gender differentiated. *Child Development, 72,* 879–886.

Markovits, H., & Vachon, R. (1990). Conditional reasoning, representation, and level of abstraction. *Developmental Psychology, 26,* 942–951.

Marks, N. (1995). Midlife marital status differences in social support relationships with adult children and psychological well-being. *Journal of Family Issues, 16,* 5–28.

Marks, N. F. (1996). Caregiving across the lifespan: National prevalence and predictors. *Family Relations, 45,* 27–36.

Marks, N. F., & Lambert, J. D. (1998). Marital status continuity and change among young and midlife adults. *Journal of Family Issues, 19,* 652–686.

Marks, N. F., Bumpass, L. L., & Jun, H. (2004). Family roles and well-being during the middle life course. In O. G. Brim, C. D. Ryff, & R.C. Kessler (Eds.), *How healthy are we? A national study of well-being at midlife* (pp. 514–549).

Chicago: University of Chicago Press.

Marks, R., Allegrante, J. P., MacKenzie, C. R., & Lane, J. M. (2003). Hip fractures among the elderly: Causes, consequences, and control. *Ageing Research Reviews, 2,* 57–97.

Markson, L., & Bloom, P. (1997). Evidence against a dedicated system for word learning in children. *Nature, 385,* 813–815.

Markstrom, C. A., & Kalmanir, H. M. (2001). Linkages between the psychosocial stages of identity and intimacy and the ego strengths of fidelity and love. *Identity, 1,* 179–196.

Markstrom, C. A., Sabino, V., Turner, B., & Berman, R. (1997). The Psychosocial Inventory of Ego Strengths: Development and validation of a new Eriksonian measure. *Journal of Youth and Adolescence, 26,* 705–732.

Markstrom-Adams, C., & Adams, G. R. (1995). Gender, ethnic group, and grade differences in psychosocial functioning during middle adolescence? *Journal of Youth and Adolescence, 24,* 397–417.

Markus, H. R., & Herzog, A. R. (1992). The role of self-concept in aging. In K. W. Schaie & M. P. Lawton (Eds.), *Annual review of gerontology and geriatrics* (pp. 110–143). New York: Springer.

Marlier, L., & Schaal, B. (1997). La perception de la familiarité olfactive chez le nouveau-né: Influence différentielle du mode d'alimentation? [The perception of olfactory familiarity in the neonate: Differential influence of the mode of feeding] *Enfance, 1,* 47–61.

Marlier, L., Schaal, B., & Soussignan, R. (1998). Neonatal responsiveness to the odor of amniotic and lacteal fluids: A test of perinatal chemosensory continuity. *Child Development, 69,* 611–623.

Marra, R., & Palmer, B. (2004). Encouraging intellectual growth: Senior college student profiles. *Journal of Adult Development, 11,* 111–122.

Marriott, A., Donaldson, C., Tarrier, N., & Burns, A. (2000). Effectiveness of cognitive-behavioural family intervention in reducing the burden of care in carers of patients with Alzheimer's disease. *British Journal of Psychiatry, 176,* 557–562.

Marsh, H. W. (1990). The structure of academic self-concept: The Marsh/Shavelson model. *Journal of Educational Psychology, 82,* 623–636.

Marsh, H. W., & Ayotte, V. (2003). Do multiple dimensions of self-concept become more differenti-

ated with age? The differential distinctiveness hypothesis. *Journal of Educational Psychology, 95,* 687–706.

Marsh, H. W., Craven, R., & Debus, R. (1998). Structure, stability, and development of young children's self-concepts: A multicohort–multioccasion study. *Child Development, 69,* 1030–1053.

Marsh, H. W., Ellis, L. A., & Craven, R. G. (2002). How do preschool children feel about themselves? Unraveling measurement and multidimensional self-concept structure. *Developmental Psychology, 38,* 376–393.

Marsh, H., & Kleitman, S. (2005). Consequences of employment during high school: Character building, subversion of academic goals, or a threshold? *American Educational Research Journal, 42,* 331–369.

Marsh, J. S., & Daigneault, J. P. (1999). The young athlete. *Current Opinion in Pediatrics, 11,* 84–88.

Marsh, M. W., Parada, R. H., & Ayotte, V. (2004). A multidimensional perspective of relations between self-concept (Self Description Questionnaire II) and adolescent mental health (Youth Self Report). *Psychological Assessment, 16,* 27–41.

Marshall, N. L. (1997). Combining work and family. In S. J. Gallant, G. P. Keita, & R. Royak-Schaler (Eds.), *Health care for women* (pp. 163–174). Washington, DC: American Psychological Association.

Marshall, V. W., Clarke, P. J., & Ballantyne, P. J. (2001). Instability in the retirement transition: Effects on health and well-being in a Canadian study. *Research on Aging, 23,* 379–409.

Marshall-Baker, A., Lickliter, R., & Cooper, R. P. (1998). Prolonged exposure to a visual pattern may promote behavioral organization in preterm infants. *Journal of Perinatal and Neonatal Nursing, 12,* 50–62.

Martin, C. L., & Fabes, C. A. (2001). The stability and consequences of young children's same-sex peer interactions. *Developmental Psychology, 37,* 431–446.

Martin, C. L., Fabes, R. A., Evans, S. M., & Wyman, H. (1999). Social cognition on the playground: Children's beliefs about playing with girls versus boys and their relations to sex segregated play. *Journal of Social and Personal Relationships, 16,* 751–771.

Martin, C. L., & Halverson, C. F. (1987). The role of cognition in sex role acquisition. In D. B. Carter (Ed.), *Current conceptions of sex roles and sex typing: Theory and*

research (pp. 123–137). New York: Praeger.

Martin, C. L., Ruble, D. N., & Szkrybalo, J. (2002). Cognitive theories of early gender development. *Psychological Bulletin, 128,* 903–933.

Martin, J., Shochat, T., & Ancoli-Israel, S. (2000). Assessment and treatment of sleep disturbances in older adults. *Clinical Psychology Review, 20,* 783–805.

Martin, J. A., Hamilton, B. E., Sutton, P. D., Ventura, S. J., Menacker, F., & Munson, M. L. (2005). Births: Final data for 2003. *National Vital Statistics Report, 54*(2), 1–116.

Martin, J. E., & Dean, L. (1993). Bereavement following death from AIDS: Unique problems, reactions, and special needs. In M. S. Stroebe, W. Stroebe, & R. O. Hansson (Eds.), *Handbook of bereavement* (pp. 317–330). Cambridge, UK: Cambridge University Press.

Martin, P., Long, M. V., & Poon, L. W. (2002). Age changes and differences in personality traits and states of the old and very old. *Journal of Gerontology, 57B,* P144–P152.

Martinez, C. R., & Forgatch, M. S. (2002). Adjusting to change: Linking family structure transitions with parenting and boys' adjustment. *Journal of Family Psychology, 16,* 107–117.

Martins, C., & Gaffan, E. A. (2000). Effects of maternal depression on patterns of infant–mother attachment: A meta-analytic investigation. *Journal of Child Psychology and Psychiatry, 41,* 737–746.

Martins, P. A., Hoffman, D. J., Fernandes, M. T., Nascimento, C. R., Roberts, S. B., Sesso, R., & Sawaya, A. L. (2004). Stunted children gain less lean body mass and more fat mass than their non-stunted counterparts: A prospective study. *British Journal of Nutrition, 92,* 819–825.

Martinson, I. M., Davies, E., & McClowry, S. G. (1987). The long-term effect of sibling death on self-concept. *Journal of Pediatric Nursing, 2,* 227–235.

Martlew, M., & Connolly, K. J. (1996). Human figure drawings by schooled and unschooled children in Papua New Guinea. *Child Development, 67,* 2743–2762.

Martyn, C. N., Barker, D. J. P., & Osmond, C. (1996). Mothers' pelvic size, fetal growth, and death from stroke and coronary heart disease in men in the UK. *Lancet, 348,* 1264–1268.

Maruna, S. (2001). *Making good: How ex-convicts reform and rebuild their lives.* Washington, DC: American Psychological Association.

Maruna, S., LeBel, T. P., & Lanier, C. S. (2004). Generativity behind bars: Some "redemptive truths" about prison society. In E. de St. Aubin, D. P. McAdams, & T.-C. Kim (Eds.), *The generative society* (pp. 131–151). Washington, DC: American Psychological Association.

Maruta, T., Colligan, R. C., Malinchoc, M., & Offord, K. P. (2002). Optimism–pessimism assessed in the 1960s and self-reported health status 30 years later. *Mayo Clinic Proceedings, 77*, 748–753.

Marzolf, D. P., & DeLoache, J. S. (1994). Transfer in young children's understanding of spatial representations. *Child Development, 65*, 1–15.

Masataka, N. (1996). Perception of motherese in a signed language by 6-month-old deaf infants. *Developmental Psychology, 32*, 874–879.

Maslach, C., Schaufeli, W. B., & Leiter, M. P. (2001). Job burnout. *Annual Review of Psychology, 52*, 397–422.

Mason, M. G., & Gibbs, J. C. (1993a). Role-taking opportunities and the transition to advanced moral judgment. *Moral Education Forum, 18*, 1–12.

Mason, M. G., & Gibbs, J. C. (1993b). Social perspective taking and moral judgment among college students. *Journal of Adolescent Research, 8*, 109–123.

Masten, A. S. (2001). Ordinary magic: Resilience processes in development. *American Psychologist, 56*, 227–238.

Masten, A. S., & Coatsworth, J. D. (1998). The development of competence in favorable and unfavorable environments: Lessons from research on successful children. *American Psychologist, 53*, 205–220.

Masten, A. S., Coatsworth, J. D., Neemann, J., Gest, S. D., Tellegen, A., & Garmezy, N. (1995). The structure and coherence of competence from childhood through adolescence. *Child Development, 66*, 1635–1659.

Masten, A. S., Hubbard, J. J., Gest, S. D., Tellegen, A., Garmezy, N., & Ramirez, M. (1999). Adaptation in the context of adversity: Pathways to resilience and maladaptation from childhood to late adolescence. *Development and Psychopathology, 11*, 143–169.

Masten, A. S., & Powell, J. L. (2003). A resilience framework for research, policy, and practice. In S. S. Luthar (Ed.), *Resilience and vulnerability* (pp. 1–25). New York: Cambridge University Press.

Masten, A. S., & Reed, M. J. (2002). Resilience in development. In C. R. Snyder & S. J. Lopez (Eds.), *Handbook of positive psychology* (pp. 74–88). New York: Oxford University Press.

Mastropieri, D., & Turkewitz, G. (1999). Prenatal experience and neonatal responsiveness to vocal expression of emotion. *Developmental Psychobiology, 35*, 204–214.

Masur, E. F., McIntyre, C. W., & Flavell, J. H. (1973). Developmental changes in apportionment of study time among items in a multi-trial free recall task. *Journal of Experimental Child Psychology, 15*, 237–246.

Masur, E. F., & Rodemaker, J. E. (1999). Mothers' and infants' spontaneous vocal, verbal, and action imitation during the second year. *Merrill-Palmer Quarterly, 45*, 392–412.

Matas, L., Arend, R., & Sroufe, L. A. (1978). Continuity of adaptation in the second year: The relationship between quality of attachment and later competence. *Child Development, 49*, 547–556.

Matheny, A. P., Jr. (1991). Children's unintentional injuries and gender: Differentiation and psychosocial aspects. *Children's Environment Quarterly, 8*, 51–61.

Maticka-Tyndale, E. (2001). Sexual health and Canadian youth: How do we measure up? *Canadian Journal of Human Sexuality, 10*(1–2), 1–17.

Matthews, F., & Brayne, C. (2005). The incidence of dementia in England and Wales: Findings from the five identical sites of the MRC CFA Study. *PLoS Medicine, 2*, e193.mmg/sec5/ch40/ch40a.jsp

Matthews, K. A., Gump, B. B., Harris, K. F., Haney, T. L., & Barefoot, J. C. (2004). Hostile behaviors predict cardiovascular mortality among men enrolled in the Multiple Risk Factor Intervention Trial. *Circulation, 109*, 66–70.

Mattison, J. A., Lane, M. A., Roth, G. S., & Ingram, D. K. (2003). Calorie restriction in rhesus monkeys. *Experimental Gerontology, 38*, 35–46.

Matute-Bianchi, M. E. (1986). Ethnic identities and patterns of school success and failure among Mexican-descent and Japanese-American students in a California high school: An ethnographic analysis. *American Journal of Education, 95*, 233–255.

Maume, D. J., Jr. (2004). Is the glass ceiling a unique form of inequality? *Work and Occupations, 31*, 250–274.

Maupin, R., Lyman, R., Fatsis, J., Prystowiski, E., Nguyen, A., & Wright, C. (2004). Characteristics of women who deliver with no prenatal care. *Journal of Maternal-Fetal and Neonatal Medicine, 16*, 45–50.

Maurer, T. J. (2001). Career-relevant learning and development, worker age, and beliefs about self-efficacy for development. *Journal of Management, 27*, 123–140.

Maurer, T. J., Wrenn, K. A., & Weiss, E. M. (2003). Toward understanding and managing stereotypical beliefs about older workers' ability and desire for learning and development. In J. J. Martocchio & G. R. Ferris (Eds.), *Research in personnel and human resources management* (Vol. 22, pp. 253–285). Stamford, CT: JAI Press.

Mayberry, R. I. (1994). The importance of childhood to language acquisition: Evidence from American Sign Language. In J. C. Goodman & H. C. Nusbaum (Eds.), *The development of speech perception: The transition from speech sounds to spoken words* (pp. 57–90). Cambridge, MA: MIT Press.

Mayeux, L., & Cillessen, A. H. N. (2003). Development of social problem solving in early childhood: Stability, change, and associations with social competence. *Journal of Genetic Psychology, 164*, 153–173.

Mayer, J. D., Salovey, P., & Caruso, D. R. (2003). *Mayer–Salovey–Caruso Emotional Intelligence Test (MSCEIT): User's manual.* Toronto, Ontario: Multi-Health Systems.

Mayes, L. C. (1999). Reconsidering the concept of vulnerability in children using the model of prenatal cocaine exposure. In T. B. Cohen & E. M. Hossein (Eds.), *The vulnerable child* (Vol. 3, pp. 35–54). Madison, CT: International Universities Press.

Mayes, L. C., & Zigler, E. (1992). An observational study of the affective concomitants of mastery in infants. *Journal of Child Psychology and Psychiatry, 33*, 659–667.

Mayhew, D. R., Brown, S. W., & Simpson, H. M. (2005). *The alcohol-crash problem in Canada: 2003.* Ottawa: The Traffic Injury Research Foundation of Canada.

Maynard, A. E. (2002). Cultural teaching: The development of teaching skills in Maya sibling interactions. *Child Development, 73*, 969–982.

Maynard, A. E., & Greenfield, P. M. (2003). Implicit cognitive development in cultural tools and children: Lessons from Maya Mexico. *Cognitive Development, 18*, 489–510.

McAdams, D. (1993). *The stories we live by: Personal myths and the making of the self.* New York: William Morrow.

McAdams, D. P. (2001). Generativity in midlife. In M. E. Lachman (Ed.), *Handbook of midlife development* (pp. 395–443). New York: Wiley.

McAdams, D. P., & de St. Aubin, E. (1992). A theory of generativity and its assessment through self-report, behavioral acts, and narrative themes in autobiography. *Journal of Personality and Social Psychology, 62*, 1003–1015.

McAdams, D. P., de St. Aubin, E., & Logan, R. L. (1993). Generativity among young, midlife, and older adults. *Psychology and Aging, 8*, 221–230.

McAdams, D. P., Diamond, A., de St. Aubin, E., & Mansfield, E. (1997). Stories of commitment: The psychosocial construction of generative lives. *Journal of Personality and Social Psychology, 72*, 678–694.

McAdams, D. P., Hart, H. M., & Maruna, S. (1998). The anatomy of generativity. In D. P. McAdams & E. de St. Aubin (Eds.), *Generativity and adult development* (pp. 7–43). Washington, DC: American Psychological Association.

McAdams, D. P., & Logan, R. L. (2004). What is generativity? In E. de St. Aubin & D. P. McAdams (Eds.), *The generative society: Caring for future generations* (pp. 15–31). Washington, DC: American Psychological Association.

McAdams, D. P., Reynolds, J., Lewis, M., Patten, A. H., & Bowman, P. J. (2001). When bad things turn good and good things turn bad: Sequences of redemption and contamination in life narrative and their relation to psychosocial adaptation in midlife adults and children. *Personality and Social Psychology Bulletin, 27*, 474–485.

McArdle, J. J., Ferrer-Caja, E., Hamagami, F., & Woodcock, R. W. (2002). Comparative longitudinal structural analyses of the growth and decline of multiple intellectual abilities over the life span. *Developmental Psychology, 38*, 115–142.

McAuley, E., & Blissmer, B. (2000). Self-efficacy determinants and consequences of physical activity. *Exercise and Sport Sciences Reviews, 28*, 85–88.

McAuley, E., Mihalko, S. L., & Bane, S. M. (1997). Exercise and self-esteem in middle-aged adults: Multidimensional relationships and physical fitness and self-efficacy influences. *Journal of Behavioral Medicine, 20*, 67–83.

McBride-Chang, C., & Kail, R. V. (2002). Cross-cultural similarities in the predictors of reading acquisition. *Child Development, 73*, 1392–1407.

McCabe, A. (1997). Developmental and cross-cultural aspects of children's narration. In M. Bamberg (Ed.), *Narrative development: Six approaches* (pp. 137–174). Mahwah, NJ: Erlbaum.

McCall, R. B. (1993). Developmental functions for general mental performance. In D. K. Detterman (Ed.), *Current topics in human intelligence* (Vol. 3, pp. 3–29). Norwood, NJ: Ablex.

McCall, R. B., & Carriger, M. S. (1993). A meta-analysis of infant habituation and recognition memory performance as predictors of later IQ. *Child Development, 64,* 57–79.

McCarthy, B., & McCarthy, E. J. (2004). *Getting it right the first time: Creating a healthy marriage.* New York: Brunner-Routledge.

McCartney, K., Harris, M. J., & Bernieri, F. (1990). Growing up and growing apart: A developmental meta-analysis of twin studies. *Psychological Bulletin, 107,* 226–237.

McCarton, C. (1998). Behavioral outcomes in low birth weight infants. *Pediatrics, 102,* 1293–1297.

McCarty, M. E., & Ashmead, D. H. (1999). Visual control of reaching and grasping in infants. *Developmental Psychology, 35,* 620–631.

McCarty, M. E., & Keen, R. (2005). Facilitating problem-solving performance among 9- and 12-month-old infants. *Journal of Cognition and Development, 6,* 209–228.

McClearn, G. E., Johansson, B., Berg, S., & Pedersen, N. L. (1997). Substantial genetic influence on cognitive abilities in twins 80 or more years old. *Science, 276,* 1560–1563.

McConaghy, M. J. (1979). Gender permanence and the genital basis of gender: Stages in the development of constancy of gender identity. *Child Development, 50,* 1223–1226.

McCormack, V. A., dos Santos Silva, I., Koupil, I., Leon, D. A., & Lithell, H. O. (2005). Birth characteristics and adult cancer incidence: Swedish cohort of over 11,000 men and women. *International Journal of Cancer, 115,* 611–617.

McCrae, R. R., & Costa, P. T., Jr. (1990). *Personality in adulthood.* New York: Guilford.

McCrae, R. R., Costa, P. T., Jr., Ostendorf, F., Angleitner, A., Hrebickov, M., & Avia, M. D. (2000). Nature over nurture: Temperament, personality, and life span development. *Journal of Personality and Social Psychology, 78,* 173–186.

McCune, L. (1993). The development of play as the development of consciousness. In M. H. Bornstein & A. O'Reilly (Eds.), *New directions for child development*

(No. 59, pp. 67–79). San Francisco: Jossey-Bass.

McDaniel, J., Purcell, D., & D'Augelli, A. R. (2001). The relationship between sexual orientation and risk for suicide: Research findings and future directions for research and prevention. *Suicide and Life-Threatening Behavior, 31,* 84–105.

McDaniel, M. A., Maier, S. F., & Einstein, G. O. (2002). "Brain-specific" nutrients: A memory cure? *Psychological Science in the Public Interest, 3,* 12–38.

McDonagh, M. S., Osterweil, P., & Guise, J. M. (2005). The benefits and risks of inducing labour in patients with prior cesarean delivery: A systematic review. *BJOG, 112,* 1007–1015.

McDonald, L., & Robb, A. L. (2004). The economic legacy of divorce and separation for women in old age. *Canadian Journal on Aging, 23*(Suppl. 1), S83–S97.

McDonald, S. W. S., Hultsch, D. F., & Dixon, R. A. (2003). Performance variability is related to change in cognition: Evidence from the Victoria Longitudinal Study. *Psychology and Aging, 18,* 510–523.

McDonough, L. (1999). Early declarative memory for location. *British Journal of Developmental Psychology, 17,* 381–402.

McDowell, D. J., & Parke, R. D. (2000). Differential knowledge of display rules for positive and negative emotions: Influences from parents, influences on peers. *Social Development, 9,* 415–432.

McElhaney, K. B., & Allen, J. P. (2001). Autonomy and adolescent social functioning: The moderating effect of risk. *Child Development, 72,* 220–235.

McFadden, S. H. (1996). Religion, spirituality, and aging. In J. E. Birren & K. W. Schaie (Eds.), *Handbook of the psychology of aging* (pp. 162–177). San Diego: Academic Press.

McFarlane, J., Malecha, A., Watson, K., Gist, J., Batten, E., Hall, I., & Smith, S. (2005). Intimate partner assault against women: Frequency, health consequences, and treatment outcomes. *Obstetrics and Gynecology, 105,* 99–108.

McGee, G. (1997). Legislating gestation. *Human Reproduction, 12,* 407–408.

McGee, L. M., & Richgels, D. J. (2004). *Literacy's beginnings* (4th ed.). Boston: Allyn and Bacon.

McGillicuddy-De Lisi, A. V., Watkins, C., & Vinchur, A. J. (1994). The effect of relationship on children's distributive justice reasoning. *Child Development, 65,* 1694–1700.

McGoldrick, M. (2004). Echoes from the past: Helping families deal

with their ghosts. In F. Walsh & M. McGoldrick (Eds.), *Living beyond loss* (pp. 99–118). New York: Norton.

McGoldrick, M., Heiman, M., & Carter, B. (1993). The changing family life cycle: A perspective on normalcy. In F. Walsh (Ed.), *Normal family processes* (pp. 405–443). New York: Guilford.

McGoldrick, M., Schlesinger, J. M., Lee, E., Hines, P. M., Chan, J., & Almeida, R. (2004). Mourning in different cultures. In F. Walsh & M. McGoldrick (Eds.), *Living beyond loss* (pp. 1119–1160). New York: Norton.

McGregor, M. J., Janssen, P. A., Ericksen, J., Van Vliet, A., Ronald, L. A., & Schulzer, M. (2004). Rising incidence of hospital-reported drug-facilitated sexual assault in a large urban community in Canada. *Canadian Journal of Public Health, 95,* 441–445.

McGue, M., & Bouchard, T. J., Jr. (1998). Genetic and environmental influences on human behavioral differences. *Annual Review of Neuroscience, 21,* 1–24.

McGue, M., & Christensen, K. (2002). The heritability of level and rate-of-change in cognitive functioning in Danish twins aged 70 years and older. *Experimental Aging Research, 28,* 435–451.

McGuffin, P., & Sargeant, M. P. (1991). Major affective disorder. In P. McGuffin & R. Murray (Eds.), *The new genetics of mental illness* (pp. 165–181). London: Butterworth-Heinemann.

McHale, J., Khazan, I., Erera, P., Rotman, T., DeCourcey, W., & McConnell, M. (2002). Coparenting in diverse family systems. In M. H. Bornstein (Ed.), *Handbook of parenting: Vol. 3* (2nd ed., pp. 75–107). Mahwah, NJ: Erlbaum.

McHale, J. P., Kuersten-Hogan, R., & Rao, N. (2004). Growing points for coparenting theory and research. *Journal of Adult Development, 11,* 221–234.

McHale, J. P., Lauretti, A., Talbot, J., & Pouquette, C. (2002). Retrospect and prospect in the psychological study of coparenting and family group process. In J. P. McHale & W. S. Grolnick (Eds.), *Retrospect and prospect in the psychological study of families* (pp. 127–165). Mahwah, NJ: Erlbaum.

McIntyre, T. M., & Ventura, M. (2003). Children of war: Psychosocial sequelae of war trauma in Angolan adolescents. In S. Krippner & T. M. McIntyre (Eds.), *The psychological impact of war trauma on civilians: An international perspective* (pp. 39–53). Westport, CT: Praeger.

McKelvie, P., & Low, J. (2002). Listening to Mozart does not improve

children's spatial ability: Final curtains for the Mozart effect. *British Journal of Developmental Psychology, 20,* 241–258.

McKenna, J. J. (2001). Why we never ask "Is it safe for infants to sleep alone?" *Academy of Breast Feeding Medicine News and Views, 7*(4), 32, 38.

McKenna, J. J. (2002, September/October). Breastfeeding and bedsharing still useful (and important) after all these years. *Mothering, 114.* Retrieved from www.mothering.com/articles/new_baby/sleep/mckenna.html

McKenna, J. J., & McDade, T. (2005). Why babies should never sleep alone: A review of the co-sleeping controversy in relation to SIDS, bedsharing, and breastfeeding. *Paediatric Respiratory Reviews, 6,* 134–152.

McKeown, R. E., Garrison, C. Z., Cuffe, S. P., Waller, J. L., Jackson, K. L., & Addy, C. L. (1998). Incidence and predictors of suicidal behaviors in a longitudinal sample of young adolescents. *Journal of the American Academy of Child and Adolescent Psychiatry, 37,* 612–619.

McKim, W. A. (2002). *Drugs and behavior* (5th ed.). Upper Saddle River, NJ: Prentice-Hall.

McKown, C., & Weinstein, R. S. (2002). Modeling the role of child ethnicity and gender in children's differential response to teacher expectations. *Journal of Applied Social Psychology, 32,* 159–184.

McKown, C., & Weinstein, R. S. (2003). The development and consequences of stereotype consciousness in middle childhood. *Child Development, 74,* 498–515.

McKusick, V. A. (2002). *Online Mendelian inheritance in man: A catalog of human genes and genetic disorders.* Baltimore: Johns Hopkins University Press. Retrieved from www.ncbi.nlm.nih.gov/entrez/query.fcgi?db=OMIM

McLanahan, S. (1999). Father absence and the welfare of children. In E. M. Hetherington (Ed.), *Coping with divorce, single parenting, and remarriage: A risk and resiliency perspective* (pp. 117–145). Mahwah, NJ: Erlbaum.

McLoyd, V. C., & Smith, J. (2002). Physical discipline and behavior problems in African-American, European-American, and Hispanic children: Emotional support as a moderator. *Journal of Marriage and the Family, 64,* 40–53.

McNamee, S., & Peterson, J. (1986). Young children's distributive justice reasoning, behavior, and role taking: Their consistency and relationship. *Journal of Genetic Psychology, 146,* 399–404.

McNeil, J. N. (1986). Talking about death: Adolescents, parents, and peers. In C. A. Corr & J. N. McNeil (Eds.), *Adolescence and death* (pp. 185–201). New York: Springer.

MCR Vitamin Study Research Group. (1991). Prevention of neural tube defects: Results of the Medical Research Council Vitamin Study. *Lancet, 338,* 131–137.

Mead, G. H. (1934). *Mind, self, and society.* Chicago: University of Chicago Press.

Mead, M. (1928). *Coming of age in Samoa.* Ann Arbor, MI: Morrow.

Mead, M., & Newton, N. (1967). Cultural patterning of perinatal behavior. In S. Richardson & A. Guttmacher (Eds.), *Childbearing: Its social and psychological aspects* (pp. 142–244). Baltimore: Williams & Wilkins.

Media Awareness Network. (2001). Parental awareness of Canadian children's Internet use. Retrieved from www.media-awareness.ca

Meegan, S. P., & Berg, C. A. (2002). Contexts, functions, forms, and processes of collaborative everyday problem solving in older adulthood. *International Journal of Behavioral Development, 26,* 6–15.

Meehan, B. T., Hughes, J. N. & Cavell, T. A. (2003). Teacher–student relationships as compensatory resources for aggressive children. *Child Development, 74,* 1145–1157.

Meeus, W. (1996). Studies on identity development in adolescence: An overview of research and some new data. *Journal of Youth and Adolescence, 25,* 569–598.

Meeus, W., Iedema, J., Helsen, M., & Vollebergh, W. (1999). Patterns of adolescent identity development: Review of literature and longitudinal analysis. *Developmental Review, 19,* 419–461.

Meeus, W., Oosterwegel, A., & Vollebergh, W. (2002). Parental and peer attachment and identity development in adolescence. *Journal of Adolescence, 25,* 93–106.

Mehlmadrona, L., & Madrona, M. M. (1997). Physician- and midwife-attended home births—effects of breech, twin, and post-dates outcome data on mortality rates. *Journal of Nurse-Midwifery, 42,* 91–98.

Mehlson, M., Platz, M., & Fromholt, P. (2003). Life satisfaction across the life course: Evaluations of the most and least satisfying decades of life. *International Journal of Aging and Human Development, 57,* 217–236.

Meins, E., Fernyhough, C., Russell, J., & Clark-Carter, D. (1998). Security of attachment as a predictor of symbolic and mentalizing abilities: A longitudinal study. *Social Development, 7,* 1–24.

Meins, E., Fernyhough, C., Wainwright, R., Gupta, M. D., Fradley, E., & Tukey, M. (2002). Maternal mind-mindedness and attachment security as predictors of theory of mind understanding. *Child Development, 73,* 1715–1716.

Melamed, S., Yekutieli, D., Froom, P., Kristal-Boneh, E., & Ribak, J. (1999). Adverse work and environmental conditions predict occupational injuries. The Israeli Cardiovascular Occupational Risk Factors Determination in Israel (CORDIS) Study. *American Journal of Epidemiology, 150,* 18–26.

Melby, M. K., Lock, M., & Kaufert, P. (2005). Culture and symptom reporting at menopause. *Human Reproduction Update, 11,* 495–512.

Meltzoff, A. N. (1995). Understanding the intentions of others: Re-enactment of intended acts by 18-month-old children. *Developmental Psychology, 31,* 838–850.

Meltzoff, A. N., & Decety, J. (2003). What imitation tells us about social cognition: A rapprochement between developmental psychology and cognitive neuroscience. *Philosophical Transactions of the Royal Society of London, Series B, Biological Sciences, 358,* 491–500.

Meltzoff, A. N., & Kuhl, P. K. (1994). Faces and speech: Intermodal processing of biologically relevant signals in infants and adults. In D. J. Lewkowicz & R. Lickliter (Eds.), *The development of intersensory perception* (pp. 335– 369). Hillsdale, NJ: Erlbaum.

Meltzoff, A. N., & Moore, M. K. (1977). Imitation of facial and manual gestures by human neonates. *Science, 198,* 75–78.

Meltzoff, A. N., & Moore, M. K. (1994). Imitation, memory, and the representation of persons. *Infant Behavior and Development, 17,* 83–99.

Meltzoff, A. N., & Moore, M. K. (1999). Persons and representations: Why infant imitation is important for theories of human development. In J. Nadel & G. Butterworth (Eds.), *Imitation in infancy* (pp. 9–35). Cambridge, UK: Cambridge University Press.

Mennella, J. A., & Beauchamp, G. K. (1998). Early flavor experiences: Research update. *Nutrition Reviews, 56,* 205–211.

Menon, U. (2002). Middle adulthood in cultural perspective: The imagined and the experienced in three cultures. In M. E. Lachman (Ed.), *Handbook of midlife development* (pp. 40–74). New York: Wiley.

Ment, L. R., Vohr, B., Allan, W., Katz, K. H., Schneider, K. C., Westerveld, M., Cuncan, C. C., & Makuch, R. W. (2003). Change in cognitive function over time in

very low-birth-weight infants. *Journal of the American Medical Association, 289,* 705–711.

Mercer, R. T., Nichols, E. G., & Doyle, G. C. (1989). *Transitions in a woman's life: Major life events in developmental context.* New York: Springer-Verlag.

Mergenhagen, P. (1996). Her own boss. *American Demographics, 18,* 36–41.

Merriam, S. B. (1993). The uses of reminiscence in older adulthood. *Educational Gerontology, 8,* 275–290.

Merrill, D. M. (1997). *Caring for elderly parents.* Westport, CT: Auburn House.

Mervis, C. B., Pani, J. R., & Pani, A. M. (2003). Transaction of child cognitive-linguistic abilities and adult input in the acquisition of lexical categories at the basic and subordinate levels. In D. H. Rakison & L. M. Oakes (Eds.), *Early category and concept development* (pp. 242–274). New York: Oxford University Press.

Messman, S. J., Canary, D. J., & Hause, K. S. (2000). Motives to remain platonic, equity, and the use of maintenance strategies in opposite-sex friendships. *Journal of Social and Personal Relationships, 17,* 67–94.

Metz, E., McLellan, J., & Youniss, J. (2003). Types of voluntary service and adolescents' civic development. *Journal of Adolescent Research, 18,* 188–203.

Meyer, B. J. F., Russo, C., & Talbot, A. (1995). Discourse comprehension and problem solving: Decisions about the treatment of breast cancer by women across the lifespan. *Psychology and Aging, 10,* 84–103.

Meyer, I. H. (2003). Prejudice, social stress, and mental health in lesbian, gay, and bisexual populations: Conceptual issues and research evidence. *Psychological Bulletin, 129,* 674–697.

Meyer, M. H., & Bellas, M. L. (1995). U.S. old-age policy and the family. In R. Blieszner & V. H. Bedford (Eds.), *Handbook of aging and the family* (pp. 263– 283). Westport, CT: Greenwood Press.

Meyer-Bahlburg, H. F. L., Ehrhardt, A. A., Rosen, L. R., Gruen, R. S., Veridiano, N. P., Vann, F. H., & Neuwalder, H. F. (1995). Prenatal estrogens and the development of homosexual orientation. *Developmental Psychology, 31,* 12–21.

Meyers, C., Adam, R., Dungan, J., & Prenger, V. (1997). Aneuploidy in twin gestations: When is maternal age advanced? *Obstetrics and Gynecology, 89,* 248–251.

Mezey, M., Dubler, N. N., Mitty, E., & Brody, A. A. (2002). What impact do setting and transitions have on the quality of life at the end of life

and the quality of the dying process? *Gerontologist, 42*(Special Issue III), 54–76.

Mezulis, A. H., Hyde, J. S., & Clark, R. (2004). Father involvement moderates the effect of maternal depression during a child's infancy on child behavior problems in kindergarten. *Journal of Family Psychology, 18,* 575–588.

Miceli, P. J., Whitman, T. L., Borkowski, J. G., Braungart-Riekder, J., & Mitchell, D. W. (1998). Individual differences in infant information processing: The role of temperamental and maternal factors. *Infant Behavior and Development, 21,* 119–136.

Michael, R. T., Gagnon, J. H., Laumann, E. O., & Kolata, G. (1994). *Sex in America.* Boston: Little, Brown.

Michaels, G. Y. (1988). Motivational factors in the decision and timing of pregnancy. In G. Y. Michaels & W. A. Goldberg (Eds.), *The transition to parenthood: Current theory and research* (pp. 23–61). New York: Cambridge University Press.

Miguel, J. (2001). Nutrition and aging. *Public Health Nutrition, 4,* 1385–1388.

Mikulincer, M., Florian, V., & Hirschberger, G. (2003). The existential function of close relationships: Introducing death into the science of love. *Personality and Social Psychology Review, 7,* 20–40.

Milberger, S., Biederman, J., Faraone, S. V., Guite, J., & Tsuang, M. T. (1997). Pregnancy, delivery and infancy complications and attention deficit hyperactivity disorder: Issues of gene–environment interaction. *Biological Psychiatry, 41,* 65–75.

Millar, W. J., & Hill, G. (2004). Pregnancy and smoking. *Health Reports, 15,* 53–56.

Miller, D. W., Leyell, T. S., & Mazachek, J. (2004). Stereotypes of the elderly in U.S. television commercials from the 1950s to the 1990s. *International Journal of Aging and Human Development, 58,* 315–340.

Miller, J., Slomczynski, K. M., & Kohn, M. L. (1985). Continuity of learning-generalization: The effect of job on men's intellective process in the United States and Poland. *American Journal of Sociology, 91,* 593–615.

Miller, J. G. (1997). Culture and self: Uncovering the cultural grounding of psychological theory. In J. G. Snodgrass & R. L. Thompson (Eds.), *Annals of the New York Academy of Sciences* (Vol. 18, pp. 217–231). New York: New York Academy of Sciences.

Miller, J. G., & Bersoff, D. M. (1995). Development in the context of everyday family relationships:

Culture, interpersonal morality, and adaptation. In M. Killen & D. Hart (Eds.), *Morality in everyday life: Developmental perspectives* (pp. 259–282). Cambridge: Cambridge University Press.

Miller, K. J. (2003). The other side of estrogen replacement therapy: Outcome study results of mood improvement in estrogen users and nonusers. *Current Psychiatry Reports, 5,* 439–444.

Miller, K. S., Forehand, R., & Kotchick, B. (1999). Adolescent sexual behavior in two ethnic minority samples: The role of family variables. *Journal of Marriage and the Family, 61,* 85–98.

Miller, L. T., & Vernon, P. A. (1992). The general factor in short-term memory, intelligence, and reaction time. *Intelligence, 16,* 5–29.

Miller, P. A., Eisenberg, N., Fabes, R. A., & Shell, R. (1996). Relations of moral reasoning and vicarious emotion to young children's prosocial behavior toward peers and adults. *Developmental Psychology, 32,* 210–219.

Miller, P. H., & Bigi, L. (1979). The development of children's understanding of attention. *Merrill-Palmer Quarterly, 25,* 235–250.

Miller, P. J., Fung, H., & Mintz, J. (1996). Self-construction through narrative practices: A Chinese and American comparison of early socialization. *Ethos, 24,* 1–44.

Miller, P. J., Hengst, J. A., & Wang, S. (2003). Ethnographic methods: Applications from developmental cultural psychology. In P. M. Carnic & J. E. Rhodes (Eds.), *Qualitative research in psychology* (pp. 219–242). Washington, DC: American Psychological Association.

Miller, P. J., Wang, S., Sandel, T., & Cho, G. E. (2002). Self-esteem as folk theory: A comparison of European American and Taiwanese mothers' beliefs. *Parenting: Science and Practice, 2,* 209–239.

Miller, P. J., Wiley, A. R., Fung, H., & Liang, C.-H. (1997). Personal storytelling as a medium of socialization in Chinese and American families. *Child Development, 68,* 557–568.

Miller, P. N., Miller, D. W., McKibbin, E. M., & Pettyes, G. D. (1999). Stereotypes of the elderly in print advertisements 1956–1996. *International Journal of Aging and Human Development, 49,* 319–337.

Miller, R. B. (2000). Do children make a marriage unhappy? *Family Science Review, 13,* 60–73.

Miller, R. B., Hemesath, K., & Nelson, B. (1997). Marriage in middle and later life. In T. D. Hargrave & S. M. Hanna (Eds.), *The*

aging family (pp. 178–198). New York: Brunner/Mazel.

Miller, S. A., Hardin, C. A., & Montgomery, D. E. (2003). Young children's understanding of the conditions for knowledge acquisition. *Journal of Cognition and Development, 4,* 325–356.

Miller, S. S., & Cavanaugh, J. C. (1990). The meaning of grandparenthood and its relationship to demographic, relationship, and social participation variables. *Journal of Gerontology, 45,* P244–P246.

Mills, D. L., Coffey-Corina, S., & Neville, H. J. (1997). Language comprehension and cerebral specialization from 13 to 20 months. *Developmental Neuropsychology, 13,* 397–445.

Mills, R., & Grusec, J. (1989). Cognitive, affective, and behavioral consequences of praising altruism. *Merrill-Palmer Quarterly, 35,* 299–326.

Mills, R. S. L. (2005). Taking stock of the developmental literature on shame. *Developmental Review, 25,* 26–63.

Mills, T. L., Gomez-Smith, Z., & De Leon, J. M. (2005). Skipped generation families: Sources of psychological distress among grandmothers of grandchildren who live in homes where neither parent is present. *Marriage and Family Review, 37,* 191–212.

Miner-Rubino, K., Winter, D. G., & Stewart, A. J. (2004). Gender, social class, and the subjective experience of aging: Self-perceived personality change from early adulthood to late midlife. *Personality and Social Psychology Bulletin, 30,* 1599–1610.

Minkler, M., & Fuller-Thomson, E. (2005). African American grandparents raising grandchildren: A national study using the Census 2000 American Community Survey. *Journal of Gerontology, 60B,* S82–S92.

Minkler, M., & Roe, K. M. (1993). *Grandmothers as caregivers: Raising children of the crack cocaine epidemic.* Newbury Park, CA: Sage.

Mintzer, J. E. (2001). Underlying mechanisms of psychosis and aggression in patients with Alzheimer's disease. *Journal of Clinical Psychiatry, 62*(Suppl. 21), 23–25.

Mischel, W., & Liebert, R. M. (1966). Effects of discrepancies between observed and imposed reward criteria on their acquisition and transmission. *Journal of Personality and Social Psychology, 3,* 45–53.

Mitchell, A., & Boss, B. J. (2002). Adverse effects of pain on the nervous systems of newborns and young children: A review of the

literature. *Journal of Neuroscience Nursing, 34,* 228–235.

Mitchell, B. D., Hsueh, W. C., King, T. M., Pollin, T. I., Sorkin, J., Agarwala, R., Schäffer, A. A., & Shuldiner, A. R. (2001). Heritability of life span in the Old Order Amish. *American Journal of Medical Genetics, 102,* 346–352.

Mitchell, S. L., Teno, J. M., Miller, S. C., & Mor, V. (2005). A national study of the location of death for older persons with dementia. *Journal of the American Geriatrics Society, 53,* 299–305.

Mitchell, V., & Helson, R. (1990). Women's prime of life. *Psychology of Women Quarterly, 14,* 451–470.

Miura, I. T., & Okamoto, Y. (2003). Language supports for mathematics understanding and performance. In A. J. Baroody & A. Dowker (Eds.), *The development of arithmetic concepts and skills* (pp. 229–242). Mahwah, NJ: Erlbaum.

Mize, J., & Pettit, G. S. (1997). Mothers' social coaching, mother–child relationship style, and children's peer competence: Is the medium the message? *Child Development, 68,* 312–332.

Mizushima, S., & Yapori, Y. (1992). Nutritional improvement, cardiovascular diseases and longevity in Japan. *Nutrition and Health, 8,* 97–105.

Mocarelli, P., Gerthoux, P., Ferrari, E., Patterson, D. G., Jr., Kieszak, S. M., & Brambilla, P. (2000). Paternal concentrations of dioxin and sex ratio of offspring. *Lancet, 355,* 1858–1862.

Moen, P. (1996). Gender, age, and the life course. In R. H. Binstock & L. K. George (Eds.), *Handbook of aging and the social sciences* (pp. 171–187). San Diego: Academic Press.

Moen, P., Fields, V., Quick, H. E., & Hofmeister, H. (2000). A life-course approach to retirement and social integration. In K. Pillemer, P. Moen, E. Wethington, & N. Glasgow (Eds.), *Social integration in the second half of life* (pp. 75–107). Baltimore: Johns Hopkins University Press.

Moerk, E. L. (1992). *A first language taught and learned.* Baltimore: Paul H. Brookes.

Moffitt, T. E., Caspi, A., Dickson, N., Silva, P., & Stanton, W. (1996). Childhood-onset versus adolescent-onset antisocial conduct problems in males: Natural history from ages 3 to 18 years. *Development and Psychopathology, 8,* 399–424.

Mogford-Bevan, K. (1999). Twins and their language development. In A. C. Sandbank (Ed.), *Twin and triplet psychology.* New York: Routledge.

Mojet, J., Christ-Hazelhof, E., & Heidema, J. (2001). Taste perception with age: Generic or specific losses in threshold sensitivity to the five basic tastes? *Chemical Senses, 26,* 845–860.

Mokdad, A. H., Bowman, B. A., Ford, E. S., Vinicor, F., Marks, J. S., & Koplan, J. P. (2001). The continuing epidemics of obesity and diabetes in the United States. *Journal of the American Medical Association, 286,* 1195–1200.

Moll, I. (1994). Reclaiming the natural line in Vygotsky's theory of cognitive development. *Human Development, 37,* 333–342.

Monastersky, R. (2005, March 4). Primed for numbers: Are boys born better at math? Experts try to divide the influences of nature and nurture. *Chronicle of Higher Education,* pp. A1, A12–A14.

Mondloch, C. J., Lewis, T., Budreau, D. R., Maurer, D., Dannemiller, J. L., Stephens, B. R., & Kleiner-Gathercoal, K. A. (1999). Face perception during early infancy. *Psychological Science, 10,* 419–422.

Monk, C., Fifer, W. P., Myers, M. M., Sloan, R. P., Trien, L., & Hurtado, A. (2000). Maternal stress responses and anxiety during pregnancy: Effects on fetal heart rate. *Developmental Psychobiology, 36,* 67–77.

Monk, C., Sloan, R., Myers, M. M., Ellman, L., Werner, E., Jeon, J., Tager, F., & Fifer, W. P. (2004). Fetal heart rate reactivity differs by women's psychiatric status: An early marker for developmental risk? *Journal of the American Academy of Child and Adolescent Psychiatry, 43,* 283–290.

Monsour, M. (2002). *Women and men as friends.* Mahwah, NJ: Erlbaum.

Montague, D. P. F., & Walker-Andrews, A. S. (2001). Peekaboo: A new look at infants' perception of emotion expressions. *Developmental Psychology, 37,* 826–838.

Montemayor, R., & Eisen, M. (1977). The development of self-conceptions from childhood to adolescence. *Developmental Psychology, 37,* 826–838.

Montepare, J., & Lachman, M. (1989). "You're only as old as you feel": Self-perceptions of age, fears of aging, and life satisfaction from adolescence to old age. *Psychology and Aging, 4,* 73–78.

Montgomery, M. J. (2005). Psychosocial intimacy and identity: From early adolescence to emerging adulthood. *Journal of Adolescent Research, 20,* 346–374.

Montgomery, M. J., & Côté, J. E. (2003). College as a transition to adulthood. In G. R. Adams & M. D. Berzonsky (Eds.), *Blackwell handbook of adolescence* (pp. 150–172). Malden, MA: Blackwell.

Montorsi, F. (2005). Assessment, diagnosis, and investigation of erectile dysfunction. *Clinical Cornerstone, 7,* 29–35.

Montoya, A. G., Sorrentino, R., Lukas, S. E., & Price, B. H. (2002). Long-term neuropsychiatric consequences of "ecstasy" (MDMA): A review. *Harvard Review of Psychiatry, 10,* 212–220.

Moon, C., Cooper, R. P., & Fifer, W. P. (1993). Two-day-old infants prefer their native language. *Infant Behavior and Development, 16,* 495–500.

Moon, S. M., & Feldhusen, J. F. (1994). The Program for Academic and Creative Enrichment (PACE): A follow-up study ten years later. In R. F. Subotnik & K. D. Arnold (Eds.), *Beyond Terman: Contemporary longitudinal studies of giftedness and talent* (pp. 375–400). Norwood, NJ: Ablex.

Moore, A., & Stratton, D. C. (2002). *Resilient widowers.* New York: Springer.

Moore, D. R., & Florsheim, P. (2001). Interpersonal processes and psychopathology among expectant and nonexpectant adolescent couples. *Journal of Consulting and Clinical Psychology, 69,* 101–113.

Moore, E. G. J. (1986). Family socialization and the IQ test performance of traditionally and transracially adopted black children. *Developmental Psychology, 22,* 317–326.

Moore, K. A., Myers, D. E., Morrison, D. R., Nord, C. W., Brown, B., & Edmonston, B. (1993). Age at first childbirth and later poverty. *Journal of Research on Adolescence, 3,* 393–422.

Moore, K. L., & Persaud, T. V. N. (2003). *Before we are born* (6th ed.). Philadelphia: Saunders.

Moore, M. K., & Meltzoff, A. N. (1999). New findings on object permanence: A developmental difference between two types of occlusion. *British Journal of Developmental Psychology, 17,* 563–584.

Moore, M. K., & Meltzoff, A. N. (2004). Object permanence after a 24-hr delay and leaving the locale of disappearance: The role of memory, space, and identity. *Developmental Psychology, 40,* 606–620.

Moore, W. S. (2002). Understanding learning in a postmodern world: Reconsidering the Perry scheme of ethical and intellectual development. In B. K. Hofer & P. R. Pintrich (Eds.), *Personal epistemology* (pp. 17–36). Mahwah, NJ: Erlbaum.

Morell, C. M. (1994). *Unwomanly conduct: The challenges of inten-*

tional childlessness. New York: Routledge.

Morelli, G. A., Rogoff, B., & Angelillo, C. (2003). Cultural variation in young children's access to work or involvement in specialized child-focused activities. *International Journal of Behavioral Development, 27,* 264–274.

Morelli, G., Rogoff, B., Oppenheim, D., & Goldsmith, D. (1992). Cultural variation in infants' sleeping arrangements: Questions of independence. *Developmental Psychology, 28,* 604–613.

Morgan, B., Maybery, M., & Durkin, K. (2003). Weak central coherence, poor joint attention, and low verbal ability: Independent deficits in early autism. *Developmental Psychology, 39,* 646–656.

Morgan, J. D., & Laungani, P. (2005). General introduction. In J. D. Morgan & P. Laungani (Eds.), *Death and bereavement around the world* (pp. 1–4). Amityville, NY: Baywood.

Morgane, P. J., Austin-LaFrance, R., Bronzino, J., Tonkiss, J., Diaz-Cintra, S., Cintra, L., Kemper, T., & Galler, J. R. (1993). Prenatal malnutrition and development of the brain. *Neuroscience and Biobehavioral Reviews, 17,* 91–128.

Morioka, M. (2001). Reconsidering brain death: A lesson from Japan's fifteen years of experience. *Hastings Center Report, 31*(4), 41–46.

Morley, J. E. (2001). Decreased food intake with aging. *Journal of Gerontology, 56A,* 81–88.

Morris, M. C., Evans, D. A., Tangney, C. C., Bienias, J. L., & Wilson, R. S. (2005). Fish consumption and cognitive decline with age in a large community study. *Archives of Neurology, 62,* 1849–1853.

Morris, P. A. (2002). The effects of welfare reform policies on children. *Social Policy Report of the Society for Research in Child Development, 16*(1).

Morrongiello, B. A., Fenwick, K. D., & Chance, G. (1998). Crossmodal learning in newborn infants: Inferences about properties of auditory-visual events. *Infant Behavior and Development, 21,* 543–554.

Morrongiello, B. A., Midgett, C., & Shields, R. (2001). Don't run with scissors: Young children's knowledge of home safety rules. *Journal of Pediatric Psychology, 26,* 105–115.

Morrow, D., Leirer, V., Altieri, P., & Fitzsimmons, C. (1994). When expertise reduces age differences in performance. *Psychology and Aging, 9,* 134–148.

Mosby, L., Rawls, A. W., Meehan, A. J., Mays, E., & Pettinari, C. J.

(1999). Troubles in interracial talk about discipline: An examination of African American child rearing narratives. *Journal of Comparative Family Studies, 30,* 489–521.

Mosely-Howard, G. S., & Evans, C. B. (2000). Relationships and contemporary experiences of the African-American family: An ethnographic case study. *Journal of Black Studies, 30,* 428–451.

Moses, L. J., Baldwin, D. A., Rosicky, J. G., & Tidball, G. (2001). Evidence for referential understanding in the emotions domain at twelve and eighteen months. *Child Development, 72,* 718–735.

Moshman, D. (1998). Identity as a theory of oneself. *Genetic Epistemologist, 26*(3), 1–9.

Moshman, D. (1999). *Adolescent psychological development: Rationality, morality, and identity.* Mahwah, NJ: Erlbaum.

Moshman, D. (2003). Developmental change in adulthood. In J. Demick & C. Andreoletti (Eds.), *Handbook of adult development* (pp. 43–61). New York: Plenum.

Moshman, D. (2005). *Adolescent psychological development: Rationality, morality, and identity* (2nd ed.). Mahwah, NJ: Erlbaum.

Moshman, D., & Franks, B. A. (1986). Development of the concept of inferential validity. *Child Development, 57,* 153–165.

Moshman, D., & Geil, M. (1998). Collaborative reasoning: Evidence for collective rationality. *Thinking and Reasoning, 4,* 231–248.

Mosko, S., Richard, C., & McKenna, J. J. (1997). Maternal sleep and arousals during bedsharing with infants. *Sleep, 20,* 142–150.

Mosteller, F. (1995, Fall). The Tennessee Study of Class Size in the Early School Grades. *Future of Children, 5*(2), 113–127.

Mounts, N. S., & Steinberg, L. (1995). An ecological analysis of peer influence on adolescent grade point average and drug use. *Developmental Psychology, 31,* 915–922.

Moxley, D. P., Najor-Durack, A., & Dumbrigue, C. (2001). *Keeping students in higher education.* London: Kogan Page.

Moyer, M. S. (1992). Sibling relationships among older adults. *Generations, 16*(3), 55–58.

Mroczek, D. K., & Kolarz, C. M. (1998). The effect of age on positive and negative affect: A developmental perspective on happiness. *Journal of Personality and Social Psychology, 75,* 1333–1349.

Mroczek, D. K., & Spiro, A., III. (2005). Change in life satisfaction during adulthood: Findings from the Veterans Affairs Normative Aging Study. *Journal of Personal-*

ity and Social Psychology, 88, 189–202.

Mrug, S., Hoza, B., & Gerdes, A. C. (2001). Children with attention-deficit/hyperactivity disorder: Peer relationships and peer-oriented interventions. In D. W. Nangle & C. A. Erdley (Eds.), *The role of friendship in psychological adjustment* (pp. 51–77). San Francisco: Jossey-Bass.

Mueller, C. M., & Dweck, C. S. (1998). Intelligence praise can undermine motivation and performance. *Journal of Personality and Social Psychology, 75,* 33–52.

Mulder, E. J. H., Robles de Medina, P. G., Huizink, A. C., Van den Bergh, B. R. H., Buitelaar, J. K., & Visser, G. H. A. (2002). Prenatal maternal stress: Effects on pregnancy and the (unborn) child. *Early Human Development, 70,* 3–14.

Muller, F., Rebiff, M., Taillandier, A., Qury, J. F., & Mornet, E. (2000). Parental origin of the extra chromosome in prenatally diagnosed fetal trisomy. *Human Genetics, 106,* 340–344.

Müller, U., Overton, W. F., & Reese, K. (2001). Development of conditional reasoning: A longitudinal study. *Journal of Cognition and Development, 2,* 27–49.

Munakata, Y. (2001). Task-dependency in infant behavior: Toward an understanding of the processes underlying cognitive development. In F. Lacerda, C. von Hofsten, & M. Heimann (Eds.), *Emerging cognitive abilities in early infancy* (pp. 29–52). Mahwah, NJ: Erlbaum.

Munakata, Y., Casey, B. J., & Diamond, A. (2004). Developmental cognitive neuroscience: progress and potential. *Trends in Cognitive Sciences, 8,* 122–128.

Mundy, P. (2003). The neural basis of social impairments in autism: The role of the dorsal medial-frontal cortex and anterior cingulate system. *Journal of Child Psychology and Psychiatry and Allied Disciplines, 44,* 793–809.

Mundy, P., & Stella, J. (2000). Joint attention, social orienting, and nonverbal communication in autism. In A. M. Wetherby & B. M. Prizant (Eds.), *Autism spectrum disorders* (Vol. 9, pp. 55–77). Baltimore, MD: Paul H. Brookes.

Muret-Wagstaff, S., & Moore, S. G. (1989). The Hmong in America: Infant behavior and rearing practices. In J. K. Nugent, B. M. Lester, & T. B. Brazelton (Eds.), *Biology, culture, and development* (Vol. 1, pp. 319–339). Norwood, NJ: Ablex.

Muris, P., Merckelbach, H., Gadet, B., & Moulaert, V. (2000). Fears, worries, and scary dreams in 4- to 12-

year-old children: Their content, developmental pattern, and origins. *Journal of Clinical Child Psychology, 29,* 43–52.

Muris, P., Merckelbach, H., Ollendick, T. H., King, N. J., & Bogie, N. (2001). Children's nighttime fears: Parent–child ratings of frequency, content, origins, coping behaviors, and severity. *Behaviour Research and Therapy, 39,* 13–28.

Murray, A. D. (1985). Aversiveness is in the mind of the beholder. In B. M. Lester & C. F. Z. Boukydis (Eds.), *Infant crying* (pp. 217–239). New York: Plenum.

Murtagh, K. N., & Hubert, H. B. (2004). Gender differences in physical disability among an elderly cohort. *American Journal of Public Health, 94,* 1406–1411.

Mussen, P., & Eisenberg-Berg, N. (1977). *Roots of caring, sharing, and helping.* San Francisco: Freeman.

Mustillo, S., Worthman, C., Erkanli, A., Keeler, G., Angold, A., & Costello, E. J. (2003). Obesity and psychiatric disorder: Developmental trajectories. *Pediatrics, 111,* 851–859.

Mutchler, J. E., Burr, J. A., & Caro, F. G. (2003). From paid worker to volunteer: Leaving the paid workforce and volunteering in later life. *Social Forces, 81,* 1267–1293.

Mutran, E. J., Danis, M., Bratton, K. A., Sudha, S., & Hanson, L. (1997). Attitudes of the critically ill toward prolonging life: The role of social support. *Gerontologist, 37,* 192–199.

Mutrie, N., & Faulkner, G. (2004). Physical activity: Positive psychology in motion. In P. A. Linley & S. Joseph (Eds.), *Positive psychology in practice* (pp. 146–164). Hoboken, NJ: Wiley.

Mutti, D. O., Mitchell, G. L., Moeschberger, M. L., Jones, L. A., & Zadnik, K. (2002). Parental myopia, near work, school achievement, and children's refractive error. *Investigative Ophthalmology and Visual Science, 43,* 3633–3640.

Myers, D. G. (2000). The funds, friends, and faith of happy people. *American Psychologist, 55,* 56–67.

Myers, M. G., Brown, S. A., Tate, S., Abrantes, A., & Tomlinson, K. (2001). *Adolescents, alcohol, and substance abuse* (pp. 275–296). New York: Guilford.

Myerson, J., Hale, S., Wagstaff, D., Poon, L. W., & Smith, G. A. (1990). The information-loss model: A mathematical theory of age-related cognitive slowing. *Psychological Review, 97,* 475–487.

Myowa-Yamakoshi, M., Tomonaga, M., Tanaka, M., & Matsuzawa, T. (2004). Imitation in neonatal chimpanzees (*Pan*

troglodytes). *Developmental Science, 7,* 437–442.

N

Nader, K. (2002). Treating children after violence in schools and communities. In N. B. Webb (Ed.), *Helping bereaved children: A handbook for practitioners* (pp. 214–244). New York: Guilford.

Nader, K., Dubrow, N., & Stamm, B. H. (1999). *Honoring differences: Cultural issues in the treatment of trauma and loss.* Washington, DC: Taylor & Francis.

Nagy, W. E., & Scott, J. A. (2000). Vocabulary processes. In M. L. Kamil & P. B. Mosenthal (Eds.), *Handbook of reading research* (Vol. 3, pp. 269–284). Mahwah, NJ: Erlbaum.

Naigles, L. G., & Gelman, S. A. (1995). Overextensions in comprehension and production revisited: Preferential-looking in a study of dog, cat, and cow. *Journal of Child Language, 22,* 19–46.

Nakamura, J., & Csikszentmihalyi, M. (2002). The concept of flow. In C. R. Snyder & S. J. Lopez (Eds.), *Handbook of positive psychology* (pp. 89–105). New York: Oxford University Press.

Nakashima, H., Ozono, R., Suyama, C., Sueda, T., Kambe, M., & Oshima, T. (2004). Telomere attrition in white blood cell correlating with cardiovascular damage. *Hypertension Research, 27,* 319–325.

Namy, L. L., & Waxman, S. R. (1998). Words and gestures: Infants' interpretations of different forms of symbolic reference. *Child Development, 69,* 295–308.

Nánez, J., Sr., & Yonas, A. (1994). Effects of luminance and texture motion on infant defensive reactions to optical collision. *Infant Behavior and Development, 17,* 165–174.

Narayan, D., Chambers, R., Shah, M. K., & Petesch, P. (2000). *Voices of the poor: Crying out for change.* New York: Oxford University Press for the World Bank.

Nastasi, B. K., & Clements, D. H. (1994). Effectance motivation, perceived scholastic competence, and higher-order thinking in two cooperative computer environments. *Journal of Educational Computing Research, 10,* 249–275.

National Association for the Education of Young Children. (1998). *Accreditation criteria and procedures of the National Academy of Early Childhood Programs* (2nd ed.). Washington, DC: Author.

National Center for Biotechnology Information. (2004). SNPs: Variations on a theme. Retrieved from www.ncbi.nlm.nih.gov/About/primer/snps.html

National Center for Juvenile Justice. (2004, September). Juvenile arrests 2002. *Juvenile Justice Bulletin.* Washington, DC: Author.

National Coalition on Health Care. (2005). Facts on health care costs. Washington, DC: Author. Retrieved from www.agingstats.gov/chartbook2004/healthcare.html

National Council of Youth Sports. (2002). *Report on trends and participation in youth sports.* Stuart, FL: Author.

National Federation of State High School Associations. (2004). *High school athletic participation survey.* Kansas City, MO: Author.

National Human Genome Research Institute. (2005). Genetic discrimination in health insurance. Retrieved from www.genome.gov/page.cfm?pageID=10002328

National Institute on Aging. (2005). *Progress report on Alzheimer's disease 2004–2005: New discoveries, new insights.* Bethesda, MD: Author.

National Institute on Aging. (2006). *65+ in the United States: 2005.* Bethesda, MD: Author.

National Institutes of Health. (2005). Genes and disease. Retrieved from www.ncbi.nlm.nih.gov/books/bv.fcgi?call=bv.view

National Safe Kids Campaign. (2005). *Report to the nation: Trends in unintentional childhood injury mortality: 1987–2000.* Washington, DC: Author.

Navarrete, C., Martinez, I., & Salamanca, F. (1994). Paternal line of transmission in chorea of Huntington with very early onset. *Genetic Counseling, 5,* 175–178.

Naveh-Benjamin, M. (2000). Adult age differences in memory performance: Tests of an associative deficit hypothesis. *Journal of Experimental Psychology: Learning, Memory, and Cognition, 26,* 1170–1187.

Naveh-Benjamin, M., Hussain, Z., Guez, J., & Bar-On, M. (2003). Adult age differences in episodic memory: Further support for an associative-deficit hypothesis. *Journal of Experimental Psychology: Learning, Memory, and Cognition, 29,* 826–837.

Neff, K. D., & Helwig, C. C. (2002). A constructivist approach to understanding the development of reasoning about rights and authority within cultural contexts. *Cognitive Development, 17,* 1429–1450.

Neimeyer, R. A. (Ed.). (1994). *Death anxiety handbook.* Washington, DC: Taylor & Francis.

Neimeyer, R. A. (2001a). Meaning reconstruction and loss. In R. A. Neimeyer (Ed.), *Meaning reconstruction and the experience of loss*

(pp. 1–9). Washington, DC: American Psychological Association.

Neimeyer, R. A. (2001b). The language of loss: Grief therapy as a process of meaning reconstruction. In R. A. Neimeyer (Ed.), *Meaning reconstruction and the experience of loss* (pp. 261–292). Washington, DC: American Psychological Association.

Neimeyer, R. A., & Van Brunt, D. (1995). Death anxiety. In H. Waas & R. A. Neimeyer (Eds.), *Dying: Facing the facts* (3rd ed., pp. 49–88). Washington, DC: Taylor & Francis.

Neitzel, C., & Stright, A. D. (2003). Mothers' scaffolding of children's problem solving: Establishing a foundation of academic self-regulatory competence. *Journal of Family Psychology, 17,* 147–159.

Nelson, C. A. (2000). Neural plasticity and human development: The role of early experience sculpting memory systems. *Developmental Science, 3,* 115–130.

Nelson, C. A. (2001). The development and neural bases of face recognition. *Infant and Child Development, 10,* 3–18.

Nelson, C. A. (2002). Neural development and lifelong plasticity. In R. M. Lerner, F. Jacobs, & D. Wertlieb (Eds.), *Handbook of applied developmental science* (Vol. 1, pp. 31–60). Thousand Oaks, CA: Sage.

Nelson, C. A., & Bosquet, M. (2000). Neurobiology of fetal and infant development: Implications for infant mental health. In C. H. Zeanah, Jr. (Ed.), *Handbook of infant mental health* (2nd ed., pp. 37–59). New York: Guilford.

Nelson, D. A., Nelson, L. J., Hart, C. H., Yang, C., & Jin, S. (2005). Parenting and peer-group behavior in cultural context. In X. Chen, B. Schneider, & D. French (Eds.), *Peer relations in cultural context.* New York Cambridge University Press.

Nelson, D. A., Robinson, C. C., & Hart, C. H. (2005). Relational and physical aggression of preschool-age children: Peer status linkages across informants. *Early Education and Development, 16,* 115–139.

Nelson, E. A. S., Schiefenhoevel, W., & Haimerl, F. (2000). Child care practices in nonindustrialized societies. *Pediatrics, 105,* e75.

Nelson, G., Westhues, A., & MacLeod, J. (2003). A meta-analysis of longitudinal research on preschool prevention programs for children. *Prevention and Treatment, 6.* Retrieved from www.apa.org

Nelson, H. D., Humphrey, L. L., Nygren, P., Teutsch, S. M., & Allan, J. D. (2002). Postmenopausal hormone replacement therapy: Scientific review. *Journal of the American Medical Association, 288,* 872–881.

Nelson, K. (1973). Structure and strategy in learning to talk. *Monographs of the Society for Research in Child Development, 38*(1–2, Serial No. 149).

Nelson, K., & Fivush, R. (2004). The emergence of autobiographical memory: A social cultural developmental theory. *Developmental Review, 111,* 486–511.

Nemet, D., Barkan, S., Epstein, Y., Friedland, O., Kowen, G., & Eliakim, A. (2005). Short- and long-term beneficial effects of a combined dietary–behavioral–physical activity intervention for the treatment of childhood obesity. *Pediatrics, 115,* e443–e449.

Nesdale, D., Durkin, K., Maass, A., & Griffiths, J. (2004). Group status, outgroup ethnicity, and children's ethnic attitudes. *Applied Developmental Psychology, 25,* 237–251.

Netz, Y., Wu, M.-J., Becker, B. J., & Tenenbaum, G. (2005). Physical activity and psychological well-being in advanced age: A meta-analysis of intervention studies. *Psychology and Aging, 20,* 272–284.

Neugarten, B. L. (1968a). Adult personality: Toward a psychology of the life cycle. In B. Neugarten (Ed.), *Middle age and aging* (pp. 137–147). Chicago: University of Chicago Press.

Neugarten, B. L. (1968b). The awareness of middle aging. In B. L. Neugarten (Ed.), *Middle age and aging* (pp. 93–98). Chicago: University of Chicago Press.

Neugarten, B. L. (1979). Time, age, and the life cycle. *American Journal of Psychiatry, 136,* 887–894.

Neugarten, B., & Neugarten, D. (1987, May). The changing meanings of age. *Psychology Today, 21*(5), 29–33.

Neuman, S. B. (1999). Books make a difference: A study of access to literacy. *Reading Research Quarterly, 34,* 286–311.

Neuman, S. B. (2003). From rhetoric to reality: The case for high-quality compensatory prekindergarten programs. *Phi Delta Kappan, 85*(4), pp. 286–291.

Neumark-Sztainer, D., Hannan, P. J., Story, M., Croll, J., & Perry, C. (2003). Family meal patterns: Associations with sociodemographic characteristics and improved dietary intake among adolescents. *Journal of the American Dietetic Association, 103,* 317–322.

Neville, H. A., & Heppner, M. J. (2002). Prevention and treatment of violence against women: An examination of sexual assault. In

C. L. Juntunen & D. R. Atkinson (Eds.), *Counseling across the life-span: Prevention and treatment* (pp. 261–277). Thousand Oaks, CA: Sage.

Neville, H. J., & Bavelier, D. (2002). Human brain plasticity: Evidence from sensory deprivation and altered language experience. In M. A. Hofman, G. J. Boer, A. J. G. D. Holtmaat, E. J. W. van Someren, J. Berhaagen, & D. F. Swaab (Eds.), *Plasticity in the adult brain: From genes to neurotherapy* (pp. 177–188). Amsterdam: Elsevier Science.

Newachek, P., Hung, Y.-Y., Hochstein, M., & Halfon, N. (2002). Access to health care for disadvantaged young children. *Journal of Early Intervention, 25,* 1–11.

Newborg, J., Stock, J. R., & Wnek, L. (1984). *Batelle Developmental Inventory.* Allen, TX: LINC Associates.

Newcomb, A. F., Bukowski, W. M., & Pattee, L. (1993). Children's peer relations: A meta-analytic review of popular, rejected, neglected, controversial, and average sociometric status. *Psychological Bulletin, 113,* 99–128.

Newcomb, M. D., Abbott, R. D., Catalano, R. F., Hawkins, J. D., Battin-Pearson, S., & Hill, K. (2002). Mediational and deviance theories of late high school failure: Process roles of structural strains, academic competence, and general versus specific problem behavior. *Journal of Counseling Psychology, 49,* 172–186.

Newcombe, N., & Huttenlocher, J. (1992). Children's early ability to solve perspective-taking problems. *Developmental Psychology, 28,* 635–643.

Newcombe, N. S., Sluzenski, J., & Huttenlocher, J. (2005). Preexisting knowledge versus on-line learning: What do young infants really know about spatial location? *Psychological Science, 16,* 222–227.

Newman, C., Atkinson, J., & Braddick, O. (2001). The development of reaching and looking preferences in infants to objects of different sizes. *Developmental Psychology, 37,* 561–572.

Newnham, J. P., Evans, S. F., Michael, C. A., Stanley, F. J., & Landau, L. I. (1993). Effects of frequent ultrasound during pregnancy: A randomized control trial. *Lancet, 342,* 887–890.

Newport, E. L. (1991). Contrasting conceptions of the critical period for language. In S. Cary & R. Gelman (Eds.), *The epigenesis of mind: Essays on biology and cognition* (pp. 111–130). Hillsdale, NJ: Erlbaum.

Newport, E. L., & Aslin, R. N. (2000). Innately constrained learning: Blending old and new approaches to language acquisition. In S. C. Howell, S. A. Fish, & T. Keith-Lucas (Eds.), *Proceedings of the 24th Annual Boston University Conference on Language Development* (pp. 1–21). Somerville, MA: Cascadilla Press.

Newsom, J. T. (1999). Another side to caregiving: Negative reactions to being helped. *Current Directions in Psychological Science, 8,* 183–187.

Newsom, J. T., & Schulz, R. (1996). Social support as a mediator in the relation between functional status and quality of life in older adults. *Psychology and Aging, 11,* 34–44.

Ngata, P. (2004). Death, dying, and grief: A Maori perspective. In J. D. Morgan & P. Laungani (Eds.), *Death and bereavement around the world: Vol. 4. Asia, Australia, and New Zealand* (pp. 95–99). Amityville, NY: Baywood.

NHPCO (National Hospice and Palliative Care Organization). (2004). *Facts and figures.* Alexandria, VA: Author.

NHPCO (National Hospice and Palliative Care Organization). (2005a). 83% of Americans want to die at home. Retrieved from www.nhpco.org/templates/1/homepage.cfm

NHPCO (National Hospice and Palliative Care Organization). (2005b). *Hospice and palliative care worldwide.* Retrieved from www.hospiceinformation.info/factsandfigures.asp

Ni, Y. (1998). Cognitive structure, content knowledge, and classificatory reasoning. *Journal of Genetic Psychology, 159,* 280–296.

Niccolai, L. M., Ethier, K. A., Kershaw, T. S., Lewis, J. B., Meade, C. S., & Ickovics, J. R. (2004). New sex partner acquisition and sexually transmitted disease risk among adolescent females. *Journal of Adolescent Health, 34,* 216–223.

NICHD (National Institute of Child Health and Human Development) Early Child Care Research Network. (1997). The effects of infant child care on infant–mother attachment security: Results of the NICHD Study of Early Child Care. *Child Development, 68,* 860–879.

NICHD (National Institute of Child Health and Human Development) Early Child Care Research Network. (1999). Child care and mother–child interaction in the first 3 years of life. *Developmental Psychology, 35,* 1399–1413.

NICHD (National Institute of Child Health and Human Development) Early Child Care Research Network. (2000a). Characteristics and quality of child care for toddlers

and preschoolers. *Applied Developmental Science, 4,* 116–135.

NICHD (National Institute of Child Health and Human Development) Early Child Care Research Network. (2000b). The relation of child care to cognitive and language development. *Child Development, 71,* 960–980.

NICHD (National Institute of Child Health and Human Development) Early Child Care Research Network. (2001). Before Head Start: Income and ethnicity, family characteristics, child care experiences, and child development. *Early Education and Development, 12,* 545–575.

NICHD (National Institute of Child Health and Human Development) Early Child Care Research Network. (2002a). Child-care structure → process → outcome: Direct and indirect effects of child-care quality on young children's development. *Psychological Science, 13,* 199–206.

NICHD (National Institute of Child Health and Human Development) Early Child Care Research Network. (2002b). The interaction of child care and family risk in relation to child development at 24 and 36 months. *Applied Developmental Science, 6,* 144–156.

NICHD (National Institute of Child Health and Human Development) Early Child Care Research Network. (2003a). Does amount of time spent in child care predict socioemotional adjustment during the transition to kindergarten? *Child Development, 74,* 976–1005.

NICHD (National Institute of Child Health and Human Development) Early Child Care Research Network. (2003b). Does quality of child care affect child outcomes at age 4½? *Developmental Psychology, 39,* 451–469.

NICHD (National Institute of Child Health and Human Development) Early Child Care Research Network. (2004). Type of child care and children's development at 54 months. *Early Childhood Research Quarterly, 19,* 203–230.

Nichols, L. S., & Junk, V. W. (1997). The sandwich generation: Dependency, proximity, and task assistance needs of parents. *Journal of Family and Economic Issues, 18,* 299–326.

Nichols, W. C., & Pace-Nichols, M. A. (2000). Childless married couples. In W. C. Nichols, M. A. Pace-Nichols, D. S. Becvar, & A. Y. Napier (Eds.), *Handbook of family development and prevention* (pp. 171–188). New York: Wiley.

Nickman, S. L., Rosenfeld, A. A., & Fine, P. (2005). Children in adoptive families: Overview and update. *Journal of the American*

Academy of Child and Adolescent Psychiatry, 44, 987–995.

Nielsen, S. J., & Popkin, B. M. (2003). Patterns and trends in food portion sizes. *Journal of the American Medical Association, 289*, 450–453.

Nieman, D. (1994). Exercise: Immunity from respiratory infections. *Swimming Technique, 31*(2), 38–43.

Niemeyer, D. (2006). *Eighth annual report on Oregon's Death with Dignity Act*. Portland: Oregon Department of Human Services.

NIH Consensus Development Panel on Osteoporosis Prevention, Diagnosis, and Therapy. (2001). Osteoporosis prevention, diagnosis, and therapy. *Journal of the American Medical Association, 285*, 785–795.

Nippold, M. A., Taylor, C. L., & Baker, J. M. (1996). Idiom understanding in Australian youth: A cross-cultural comparison. *Journal of Speech and Hearing Research, 39*, 442–447.

Nkondjock, A., & Ghadirian, P. (2004). Epidemiology of breast cancer among BRCA mutation carriers: An overview. *Cancer Letters, 205*, 1–8.

Noland, J. S., Singer, L. T., Short, E. J., Minnes, S., Arendt, R. E., & Krichner, H. L. (2005). Prenatal drug exposure and selective attention in preschoolers. *Neurotoxicology and Teratology, 27*, 429–438.

Nolen-Hoeksema, S. (2002). Gender differences in depression. In I. H. Gotlib & C. L. Hammen (Eds.), *Handbook of depression* (pp. 492–509). New York: Guilford.

Nomaguchi, K. M., & Milkie, M. A. (2003). Costs and rewards of children: The effects of becoming a parent on adults' lives. *Journal of Marriage and Family, 65*, 356–374.

Noppe, I. C., & Noppe, L. D. (1997). Evolving meanings of death during early, middle, and later adolescence. *Death Studies, 21*, 253–275.

Noppe, L. D., & Noppe, I. C. (1991). Dialectical themes in adolescent conceptions of death. *Journal of Adolescent Research, 6*, 28–42.

Nordstrom, B. L., Kinnunen, T. U., Krall, C. H., & Et, E. A. (2000). Predictors of continued smoking over 25 years of follow-up in the normative aging study. *American Journal of Public Health, 90*, 404–406.

Notelovitz, M. (2002). Overview of bone mineral density in post-menopausal women. *Journal of Reproductive Medicine, 47*(Suppl.), 71–81.

Noterdaeme, M., Mildenberger, K., Minow, F., & Amorosa, H. (2002). Evaluation of neuromotor deficits in children with autism and children with a specific speech and language disorder. *European Child and Adolescent Psychiatry, 11*, 219–225.

Novak, M., & Thacker, C. (1991). Satisfaction and strain among middle-aged women who return to school: Replication and extension of findings in a Canadian context. *Educational Gerontology, 17*, 323–342.

Nucci, L. P. (1996). Morality and the personal sphere of action. In E. Reed, E. Turiel, & T. Brown (Eds.), *Values and knowledge* (pp. 41–60). Hillsdale, NJ: Erlbaum.

Nucci, L. P. (2001). *Education in the moral domain*. New York: Cambridge University Press.

Nucci, L. P. (2002). The development of moral reasoning. In U. Goswami (Ed.), *Blackwell handbook of childhood cognitive development* (pp. 303–325). Malden, MA: Blackwell.

Nuland, S. B. (1993). *How we die*. New York: Random House.

Nussbaum, J. F. (1994). Friendship in older adulthood. In M. L. Hummer, J. M. Wiemann, & J. F. Nussbaum (Eds.), *Interpersonal communication in older adulthood* (pp. 209–225). Thousand Oaks, CA: Sage.

Nuttal, R. L., Casey, M. B., & Pezaris, E. (2005). Spatial ability as a mediator of gender differences on mathematics tests: A biological–environmental framework. In A. M. Gallagher & J. C. Kaufman (Eds.), *Gender differences in mathematics: An integrated psychological approach* (pp. 121–142). New York: Cambridge University Press.

Nyberg, L. (2005). Cognitive training in healthy aging: A cognitive neuroscience perspective. In R. Cabeza, L. Nyberg, & D. Park (Eds.), *Cognitive neuroscience of aging: Linking cognitive and cerebral aging* (pp. 309–321). New York: Oxford University Press.

Nye, B., Hedges, L. V., & Konstantopoulos, S. (2001). Are effects of small classes cumulative? Evidence from a Tennessee experiment. *Journal of Educational Research, 94*, 336–345.

Nye, W. P. (1993). Amazing grace: Religion and identity among elderly black individuals. *International Journal of Aging and Human Development, 36*, 103–114.

O

Oakes, L. M., Coppage, D. J., & Dingel, A. (1997). By land or by sea: The role of perceptual similarity in infants' categorization of animals. *Developmental Psychology, 33*, 396–407.

Oakes, L. M., & Madole, K. L. (2003). Principles of developmental change in infants' category formation. In D. H. Rakison & L. M. Oakes (Eds.), *Early category and concept development: Making sense of the blooming, buzzing confusion* (pp. 132–158). New York: Oxford University Press.

Obermeyer, C. M. (2000). Menopause across cultures: A review of the evidence. *Menopause, 7*, 184–192.

O'Bryant, S. L. (1988). Sibling support and older widows' well-being. *Journal of Marriage and the Family, 50*, 173–183.

O'Callaghan, M. J., Burn, Y. R., Mohay, H. A., Rogers, Y., & Tudehope, D. I. (1993). The prevalence and origins of left hand preference in high risk infants, and its implications for intellectual, motor, and behavioral performance at four and six years. *Cortex, 29*, 617–627.

O'Connor, A. R., Stephenson, T., Johnson, A., Tobin, M. J., Ratib, S., Ng, Y., & Fielder, A. R. (2002). Long-term ophthalmic outcome of low birth weight children with and without retinopathy of prematurity. *Pediatrics, 109*, 12–18.

O'Connor, C. (1997). Dispositions toward (collective) struggle and educational resilience in the inner city: A case analysis of six African-American high school students. *American Educational Research Journal, 34*, 593–629.

O'Connor, M. G., & Kaplan, E. F. (2003). Age-related changes in memory. In J. Demick & C. Andreoletti (Eds.), *Handbook of adult development* (pp. 121–130). New York: Springer.

O'Connor, P. (1992). *Friendships between women*. New York: Guilford.

O'Connor, P. (2003). Dying in the hospital. In I. Corless, B. B. Germino, & M. A. Pitman (Eds.), *Dying, death, and bereavement: A challenge for the living* (2nd ed., pp. 87–103). New York: Springer.

O'Connor, T. G., & Croft, C. M. (2001). A twin study of attachment in preschool children. *Child Development, 72*, 1501–1511.

O'Connor, T. G., Marvin, R. S., Rutter, M., Olrich, J. T., Britner, P. A., & the English and Romanian Adoptees Study Team. (2003). Child–parent attachment following early institutional deprivation. *Development and Psychopathology, 15*, 19–38.

O'Connor, T. G., Rutter, M., Beckett, C., Keaveney, L., Dreppner, J. M., & the English and Romanian Adoptees Study Team. (2000). The effects of global severe privation on cognitive competence: Extension and longitudinal follow-up. *Child Development, 71*, 376–390.

Oden, M. H., & Terman, L. M. (1968). The fulfillment of promise—40-year follow-up of the Terman gifted group. *Genetic Psychology Monographs, 77*, 3–93.

OECD (Organisation for Economic Cooperation and Development). (2004*)*. *Education at a glance*. OECD Indicator 2004. Paris: Author.

OECD (Organisation of Economic Cooperation and Development). (2005). *Education at a glance: OECD indicators 2005*. Paris: Author.

Ogawa, J. R., Sroufe, L. A., Weinfield, N. S., Carlson, E. A., & Egeland, B. (1997). Development and the fragmented self: Longitudinal study of dissociative symptomatology in a nonclinical sample. *Development and Psychopathology, 9*, 855–879.

Ogbu, J. U. (2003). *Black American students in an affluent suburb: A study of academic disengagement*. Mahwah, NJ: Erlbaum.

O'Grady-LeShane, R., & Williamson, J. B. (1992). Family provisions in old-age pensions. In M. E. Szinovacz, D. J. Ekerdt, & B. H. Vinick (Eds.), *Families and retirement* (pp. 64–77). Newbury Park, CA: Sage.

O'Halloran, C. M., & Altmaier, E. M. (1996). Awareness of death among children: Does a life-threatening illness alter the process of discovery? *Journal of Counseling and Development, 74*, 259–262.

Ohgi, S., Arisawa, K., Takahashi, T., Kusumoto, T., Goto, Y., Akiyama, T., & Saito, H. (2003a). Neonatal behavioral assessment scale as a predictor of later developmental disabilities of low-birth-weight and/or premature infants. *Brain and Development, 25*, 313–321.

Ohgi, S., Takahashi, T., Nugent, J. K., Arisawa, K., & Akiyama, T. (2003b). Neonatal behavioral characteristics and later behavioral problems. *Clinical Pediatrics, 42*, 679–686.

Okagaki, L., & Frensch, P. A. (1996). Effects of video game playing on measures of spatial performance: Gender effects in late adolescence. In P. M. Greenfield & R. R. Cocking (Eds.), *Interacting with video* (pp. 115–140). Norwood, NJ: Ablex.

Okagaki, L., & Sternberg, R. J. (1993). Parental beliefs and children's school performance. *Child Development, 64*, 36–56.

Okami, P., Weisner, T., & Olmstead, R. (2002). Outcome correlates of parent–child bed-sharing: An eighteen-year longitudinal study. *Developmental and Behavioral Pediatrics, 23*, 244–253.

O'Keefe, M. J., O'Callaghan, M., Williams, G. M., Najman, J. M., & Bor, W. (2003). Learning, cognitive, and attentional problems in adolescents born small for gestational age. *Pediatrics, 112,* 301–307.

Oken, E., & Lightdale, J. R. (2000). Updates in pediatric nutrition. *Current Opinion in Pediatrics, 12,* 282–290.

Olafson, E., & Boat, B. W. (2000). Long-term management of the sexually abused child: Considerations and challenges. In R. M. Reece (Ed.), *Treatment of child abuse: Common ground for mental health, medical, and legal practitioners* (pp. 14–35). Baltimore: Johns Hopkins University Press.

O'Laughlin, E. M., & Anderson, V. N. (2001). Perceptions of parenthood among young adults: Implications for career and family planning. *American Journal of Family Therapy, 29,* 95–108.

Oliker, S. J. (1989). *Best friends and marriage: Exchange among women.* Berkeley: University of California Press.

Ollendick, T. H., King, N. J., & Muris, P. (2002). Fears and phobias in children: Phenomenology, epidemiology, and aetiology. *Child and Adolescent Mental Health, 7,* 98–106.

Oller, D. K. (2000). *The emergence of the speech capacity.* Mahwah, NJ: Erlbaum.

Oller, D. K., Eilers, R. E., Neal, A. R., & Schwartz, H. K. (1999). Precursors to speech in infancy: The prediction of speech and language disorders. *Journal of Communication Disorders, 32,* 223–245.

Olshansky, S. J., Hayflick, L., & Perls, T. T. (2004). Antiaging medicine: The hype and the reality—Part II. *Journal of Gerontology, 59A,* 649–651.

Olson, R. E. (2000). Is it wise to restrict fat in the diets of children? *Journal of the American Dietetic Association, 100,* 28–32.

Olson, S. L., Bates, J. E., Sandy, J. M., & Lantheir, R. (2000). Early development precursors of externalizing behavior in middle childhood and adolescence. *Journal of Abnormal Child Psychology, 28,* 119–133.

Omar, H., McElderry, D., & Zakharia, R. (2003). Educating adolescents about puberty: What are we missing? *International Journal of Adolescent Medicine and Health, 15,* 79–83.

Ondrusek, N., Abramovitch, R., Pencharz, P., & Koren, G. (1998). Empirical examination of the ability of children to consent to clinical research. *Journal of Medical Ethics, 24,* 158–165.

O'Neill, R., Welsh, M., Parke, R. D., Wang, S., & Strand, C. (1997). A longitudinal assessment of the academic correlates of early peer acceptance and rejection. *Journal of Clinical Child Psychology, 26,* 290–303.

O'Neill, R. M., Horton, S., & Crosby, F. J. (1999). *Mentoring dilemmas* (pp. 63–80). Mahwah, NJ: Erlbaum.

Ong, W., Allison, J., & Haladyna, T. M. (2000). Student achievement of third graders in comparable single-age and multiage classrooms. *Journal of Research in Childhood Education, 14,* 205–215.

Onwuteaka-Philipsen, B. D., van der Heide, A., Muller, M. T., Rurup, M., Rietjens, J. A. C., & Georges, J.-J. (2005). Dutch experience of monitoring euthanasia. *British Medical Journal, 331,* 691–693.

Oosterwegel, A., & Oppenheimer, L. (1993). *The self-system: Developmental changes between and within self-concepts.* Hillsdale, NJ: Erlbaum.

Open Society Institute. (2003). *Project on death in America.* New York: Author.

O'Rahilly, R., & Müller, F. (2001). *Human embryology and teratology.* New York: Wiley-Liss.

Orbio de Castro, B., Veerman, J. W., Koops, W., Bosch, J. D., & Monshouwer, H. J. (2002). Hostile attribution of intent and aggressive behavior: A meta-analysis. *Child Development, 73,* 916–934.

O'Reilly, A. W. (1995). Using representations: Comprehension and production of actions with imagined objects. *Child Development, 66,* 999–1010.

Ory, M., Hoffman, M. K., Hawkins, M., Sanner, B., & Mockenhaupt, R. (2003). Challenging aging stereotypes: Strategies for creating a more active society. *American Journal of Preventive Medicine, 25,* 164–171.

Ory, M. G., Yee, J. L., Tennstedt, S. L., & Schulz, R. (2000). The extent and impact of dementia care: Unique challenges experienced by family caregivers. In R. Schulz (Ed.), *Handbook on dementia caregiving* (pp. 1–32). New York: Springer.

Orzano, A. J., & Scott, J. G. (2004). Diagnosis and treatment of obesity in adults: An applied evidence-based review. *Journal of the American Board of Family Practice, 17,* 359–369.

Osborne, J. (1994). Academics, self-esteem, and race: A look at the underlying assumption of the disidentification hypothesis. *Personality and Social Psychology Bulletin, 21,* 449–455.

Osherson, D. N., & Markman, E. M. (1975). Language and the ability to evaluate contradictions and tautologies. *Cognition, 2,* 213–226.

Osmers, R., Friede, M., Liske, E., Schnitker, J., Freudenstein, J., & Henneicke-von Zepelin, H. H. (2005). Efficacy and safety of isopropanolic black cohosh extract for climacteric symptoms. *Obstetrics and Gynecology, 105,* 1074–1083.

OSSTF (Ontario Secondary School Teachers' Federation). *Grade 10 literacy test continues to take its toll on students.* Retrieved from www.newswire.ca/en/releases/archive/April2004/29/c6966.html

Osteoporosis Society of Canada. (2006). *About osteoporosis.* Retrieved from www.osteoporosis.ca

Ostir, G. V., Carlson, J. E., Black, S. A., Rudkin, L., Goodwin, J. S., & Markides, K. S. (1999). Disability in older adults 1: Prevalence, causes, and consequences. *Behavioral Medicine, 24,* 147–156.

Ostrovsky, Y. (2004). Life cycle theory and the residential mobility of older Canadians. *Canadian Journal of Aging, 23*(Suppl.), s23–s37.

Ott, A., Andersen, K., Dewey, M. E., Letenneur, L., Brayne, C., & Copeland, J. R. (2004). Effect of smoking on global cognitive function in nondemented elderly. *Neurology, 23,* 920–924.

Ovando, C. J., & Collier, V. P. (1998). *Bilingual and ESL classrooms: Teaching in multicultural contexts.* Boston: McGraw-Hill.

Owens, R. E. (2005). *Language development: An introduction.* Boston: Allyn and Bacon.

Owsley, C., Ball, K., McGwin, G., Jr., Sloane, M. E., Roenker, D. L., White, M. F., & Overley, E. T. (1998). Visual processing impairment and risk of motor vehicle crash among older adults. *Journal of the American Medical Association, 279,* 1083–1088.

P

Pacella, R., McLellan, M., Grice, K., Del Bono, E. A., Wiggs, J. L., & Gwiazda, J. E. (1999). Role of genetic factors in the etiology of juvenile-onset myopia based on a longitudinal study of refractive error. *Optometry and Vision Science, 76,* 381–386.

Padgett, D. K., Patrick, C., Bruns, B. J., & Schlesinger, H. J. (1994). Women and outpatient mental health services: Use by black, Hispanic, and white women in a national insured population. *Journal of Mental Health Administration, 2,* 347–360.

Padula, M. A., & Miller, D. L. (1999). Understanding graduate women's reentry experiences. *Psychology of Women Quarterly, 23,* 327–343.

Palincsar, A. S. (2003). Advancing a theoretical model of learning and instruction. In B. J. Zimmerman (Ed.), *Educational psychology: A century of contributions* (pp. 459–475). Mahwah, NJ: Erlbaum.

Palincsar, A. S., & Herrenkohl, L. R. (1999). Designing collaborative contexts: Lessons from three research programs. In A. M. O'Donnell & A. King (Eds.), *Cognitive perspectives on peer learning. The Rutgers Invitational Symposium on Education Series* (pp. 151–177). Mahwah, NJ: Erlbaum.

Palmer, G. (1999). *Reluctant refugee.* Sydney: Kangaroo Press.

Palmer, J. R., Hatch, E. E., Rao, R. S., Kaufman, R. H., Herbst, A. L., & Noller, K. L. (2001). Infertility among women exposed prenatally to diethylstilbestrol. *American Journal of Epidemiology, 154,* 316–321.

Palmore, E. (2001). The ageism survey: First findings. *Gerontologist, 41,* 572–575.

Pan, B. A., & Snow, C. E. (1999). The development of conversation and discourse skills. In M. Barrett (Ed.), *The development of language* (pp. 229–249). Hove, UK: Psychology Press.

Pan, H. W. (1994). Children's play in Taiwan. In J. L. Roopnarine, J. E. Johnson, & F. H. Hooper (Eds.), *Children's play in diverse cultures* (pp. 31–50). Albany, NY: SUNY Press.

Panish, J. B., & Stricker, G. (2002). Perceptions of childhood and adult sibling relationships. *NYS Psychologist, 14,* 33–36.

Panza, F., Solfrizzi, V., Colacicco, A. M., D'Introno, A., Capurso, C., & Torres, F. (2004). Mediterranean diet and cognitive decline. *Public Health Nutrition, 7,* 959–963.

Papapetropoulos, S., Lieberman, A., Gonzales, J., & Mash, D. C. (2005). Can Alzheimer's type pathology influence the clinical phenotype of Parkinson's disease? *Acta Neuologica Scandinavica, 111,* 353–359.

Paquet, B. (2002). *Low-income cutoffs from 1992–2001 and low-income measures from 1991–2000.* Ottawa: Minister of Industry.

Paquette, D. (2004). Theorizing the father–child relationship: Mechanisms and developmental outcomes. *Human Development, 47,* 193–219.

Parameswaran, G. (2003). Experimenter instructions as a mediator in the effects of culture on mapping one's neighborhood. *Journal of Environmental Psychology, 23,* 409–417.

Pardeck, J. T. (2005). An exploration of child maltreatment among homeless families: Implications for family policy. *Early Child Development and Care, 175,* 335–342.

Parent, A., Teilmann, G., Juul, A., Skakkebaek, N. E., Toppari, J., & Bourguingnon, J. (2003). The timing of normal puberty and the age limits of sexual precocity: Variations around the world, secular trends, and changes after migration. *Endocrine Reviews, 24,* 668–693.

Park, D. C., Hertzog, C., Kidder, D. P., Morrell, R. W., & Mayhorn, C. B. (1997). Effect of age on event-based and time-based prospective memory. *Psychology and Aging, 12,* 314–327.

Park, D. C., Lautenschlager, G., Hedden, T., Davidson, N. S., Smith, A. D., & Smith, P. K. (2002). Models of visuospatial and verbal memory across the adult life span. *Psychology and Aging, 17,* 299–320.

Parke, R. D., & Buriel, R. (1998). Socialization in the family: Ethnic and ecological perspectives. In N. Eisenberg (Ed.), *Handbook of child psychology: Vol. 3. Social, emotional, and personality development* (pp. 463–552). New York: Wiley.

Parke, R. D., Coltrane, S., Fabricius, W., Powers, J., & Adams, M. (2004). Assessing father involvement in Mexican-American families. In R. Day & M. E. Lamb (Eds.), *Conceptualizing and measuring paternal involvement* (pp. 17–38). Mahwah, NJ: Erlbaum.

Parke, R. D., Simpkins, S. D., McDowell, D. J., Kim, M., Killian, C., Dennis, J., Flyr, M. L., Wild, M., & Rah, Y. (2004). Relative contributions of families and peers to children's social development. In P. K. Smith & C. H. Hart (Eds.), *Blackwell handbook of childhood social development* (pp. 156–177). Malden, MA: Blackwell.

Parker, F. L., Boak, A. Y., Griffin, K. W., Ripple, C., & Peay, L. (1999). Parent–child relationship, home learning environment, and school readiness. *School Psychology Review, 28,* 413–425.

Parker, J. G., Low, C. M., Walker, A. R., & Gamm, B. K. (2005). Friendship jealousy in young adolescents: Individual differences and links to sex, self-esteem, aggression, and social adjustment. *Developmental Psychology, 41,* 235–250.

Parker, J. G., Rubin, K. H., Price, J., & DeRosier, M. E. (1995). Peer relationships, child development, and adjustment: A developmental psychopathology perspective. In D. Cicchetti & D. Cohen (Eds.), *Developmental psychopathology: Vol. 2. Risk, disorder, and adaptation* (pp. 96–161). New York: Wiley.

Parker, R. G. (1995). Reminiscence: A continuity theory framework. *Gerontologist, 35,* 515–525.

Parmelee, P. A., & Lawton, M. P. (1990). The design of special environments for the aged. In J. E. Birren & K. W. Schaie (Eds.), *Handbook of the psychology of aging* (3rd ed., pp. 464–488). San Diego, CA: Academic Press.

Parten, M. (1932). Social participation among preschool children. *Journal of Abnormal and Social Psychology, 27,* 243–269.

Pascalis, O., de Haan, M., & Nelson, C. A. (1998). Long-term recognition memory for faces assessed by visual paired comparison in 3- and 6-month-old infants. *Journal of Experimental Psychology: Learning, Memory, and Cognition, 24,* 249–260.

Pascarella, E. T., & Terenzini, P. T. (1991). *How college affects students.* San Francisco: Jossey-Bass.

Pascarella, E. T., Whitt, E. J., Edison, M. I., Nora, A., Hagedorn, L. S., Yeager, P. M., & Terenzini, P. T. (1997). Women's perceptions of a "chilly climate" and their cognitive outcomes during the first year of college. *Journal of College Student Development, 38,* 109–124.

Patrick, E., & Abravanel, E. (2000). The self-regulatory nature of preschool children's private speech in a naturalistic setting. *Applied Psycholinguistics, 21,* 45–61.

Patterson, C. J. (2002). Lesbian and gay parenthood. In M. H. Bornstein (Ed.), *Handbook of parenting* (Vol. 3, pp. 317–338). Mahwah, NJ: Erlbaum.

Patterson, G. R., DeBaryshe, B. D., & Ramsey, E. (1989). A developmental perspective on antisocial behavior. *American Psychologist, 44,* 329–335.

Patterson, G. R., & Fisher, P. A. (2002). Recent developments in our understanding of parenting: Bidirectional effects, causal models, and the search for parsimony. In M. H. Bornstein (Ed.), *Handbook of parenting* (Vol. 5, pp. 59–88). Mahwah, NJ: Erlbaum.

Patterson, G. R., & Yoerger, K. (2002). A developmental model for early- and late-onset delinquency. In J. B. Reid & G. R. Patterson (Eds.), *Antisocial behavior in children and adolescents* (pp. 147–172). Washington, DC: American Psychological Association.

Patterson, M. L., & Werker, J. F. (2002). Infants' ability to match dynamic phonetic and gender information in the face and voice. *Journal of Experimental Child Psychology, 81,* 93–115.

Patterson, M. M., & Lynch, A. Q. (1988). Menopause: Salient issues for counselors. *Journal of Counseling and Development, 67,* 185–188.

Patton, G. C., Selzer, R., Coffey, C., Carlin, J. B., & Wolfe, R. (1999). Onset of adolescent eating disorders: Population based cohort study over 3 years. *British Medical Journal, 318,* 765–768.

Paul, J. J., & Cillessen, A. H. N. (2003). Dynamics of peer victimization in early adolescence: Results from a four-year longitudinal study. *Journal of Applied School Psychology, 19,* 25–43.

Pawelec, G., Wagner, W., Adibzadeh, M., & Engel, A. (1999). T cell immunosenescence in vitro and in vivo. *Experimental Gerontology, 34,* 419–429.

Payne, B. K., & Fletcher, L. B. (2005). Elder abuse in nursing homes: Prevention and resolution strategies and barriers. *Journal of Criminal Justice, 33,* 119–125.

Peake, A., & Harris, K. L. (2002). Young adults' attitudes toward multiple role planning: The influence of gender, career traditionality, and marriage plans. *Journal of Vocational Behavior, 60,* 405–421.

Pearson, J. L., & Brown, G. K. (2000). Suicide prevention in late life: Directions for science and practice. *Clinical Psychology Review, 20,* 685–705.

Pebody, R. G., Edmunds, W. J., Conyn-van Spaendonck, M., Olin, P., Berbers, G., & Rebiere, I. (2000). The seroepidemiology of rubella in western Europe. *Epidemiology and Infections, 125,* 347–357.

Peck, R. C. (1968). Psychological developments in the second half of life. In B. L. Neugarten (Ed.), *Middle age and aging* (pp. 88–92). Chicago: University of Chicago Press.

Pedersen, J. B. (1998). Sexuality and aging. In I. H. Nordhus, G. R. VandenBos, S. Berg, & P. Fromholt (Eds.), *Clinical geropsychology* (pp. 141–145). Washington, DC: American Psychological Association.

Pedersen, W. C., Miller, L. C., Putcha-Bhagavatula, A. D., & Yang, Y. (2002). Evolved sex differences in the number of partners desired? The long and the short of it. *Psychological Science, 13,* 157–161.

Pederson, D. R., & Moran, G. (1995). A categorical description of infant–mother relationships in the home and its relation to Q-sort measures of infant–mother interaction. In E. Waters, B. E.Vaughn, G. Posada, & K. Kondo-Ikemura (Eds.), Caregiving, cultural, and cognitive perspectives on secure-base behavior and working models: New growing points of attachment theory and research. *Monographs of the Society for Research in Child Development, 60*(2–3, Serial No. 244).

Pederson, D. R., & Moran, G. (1996). Expressions of the attachment relationship outside of the Strange Situation. *Child Development, 67,* 915–927.

Pedlow, R., Sanson, A., Prior, M., & Oberklaid, F. (1993). Stability of maternally reported temperament from infancy to 8 years. *Developmental Psychology, 29,* 998–1007.

Peisner-Feinberg, E. S. (1999). *The children of the Cost, Quality, and Outcomes Study go to school.* Chapel Hill, NC: University of North Carolina.

Peisner-Feinberg, E. S., Burchinal, M. R., Clifford, R. M., Culkin, M. L., Howes, C., Kagan, S. L., & Yazijian, N. (2001). The relation of preschool child-care quality to children's cognitive and social developmental trajectories through second grade. *Child Development, 72,* 1534–1553.

Pellegrini, A. D. (2003). Perceptions and functions of play and real fighting in early adolescence. *Child Development, 74,* 1522–1533.

Pellegrini, A. D. (2004). Rough-and-tumble play from childhood through adolescence: Development and possible functions. In P. K. Smith & C. H. Hart (Eds.), *Blackwell handbook of childhood social development* (pp. 438–453). Malden, MA: Blackwell.

Pellegrini, A. D., & Smith, P. K. (1998). Physical activity play: The nature and function of a neglected aspect of play. *Child Development, 69,* 577–598.

Peña, R., Wall, S., & Person, L. (2000). The effect of poverty, social inequality, and maternal education on infant mortality in Nicaragua, 1988–1993. *American Journal of Public Health, 90,* 64–69.

Penedo, F. J., & Dahn, J. R. (2005). Exercise and well-being: A review of mental and physical health benefits associated with physical activity. *Current Opinion in Psychiatry, 18,* 189–193.

Penninx, B. W., Deeg, D. J., van Eijk, J. T., Beekman, A. T., & Guralnik, J. M. (2000). Changes in depression and physical decline in older adults: A longitudinal perspective. *Journal of Affective Disorders, 61,* 1–12.

Pepler, D., Craig, W., Yuile, A., & Connolly, J. (2004). Girls who bully: A developmental and relational perspective. In M. Putallaz & K. L. Bierman (Eds.), *Aggression, antisocial behavior, and violence among girls: A developmental perspective* (pp. 90–109). New York: Guilford.

Peralta de Mendoza, O. A., & Salsa, A. M. (2003). Instruction in early comprehension and use of a symbol–referent relation. *Cognitive Development, 18,* 269–284.

Peres, J. R. (2002). *Means to a better end: A report on dying in America today.* Princeton, NJ: Robert Wood Johnson Foundation.

Perfect, T. J., & Maylor, E. A. (2000). Rejecting the dull hypothesis: The relation between method and theory in cognitive aging research. In T. J. Perfect & E. A. Maylor (Eds.), *Models of cognitive aging* (pp. 1–18). New York: Oxford University Press.

Perie, M., Sherman, J. D., Phillips, G., & Riggan, M. (2000). Elementary and secondary education: An international perspective. *Education Statistics Quarterly.* Retrieved from http://nces.ed.gov/pubs2000/quarterly/summer/5int/q51.html

Perkins, H. W. (1991). Religious commitment, yuppie values, and well-being in post-collegiate life. *Review of Religious Research, 32,* 244–251.

Perlmutter, M. (1984). Continuities and discontinuities in early human memory: Paradigms, processes, and performances. In R. V. Kail, Jr., & N. R. Spear (Eds.), *Comparative perspectives on the development of memory* (pp. 253–287). Hillsdale, NJ: Erlbaum.

Perlmutter, M., Kaplan, M., & Nyquist, L. (1990). Development of adaptive competence in adulthood. *Human Development, 33,* 185–197.

Perls, T., & Terry, D. (2003). Understanding the determinants of exceptional longevity. *Annals of Internal Medicine, 139,* 445–449.

Perls, T., Levenson, R., Regan, M., & Puca, A. (2002). What does it take to live to 100? *Mechanisms of Ageing and Development, 123,* 231–242.

Perls, T., Terry, D. F., Silver, M., Shea, M., Bowen, J., & Joyce, E. (2000). Centenarians and the genetics of longevity. *Results and Problems in Cell Differentiation, 29,* 1–20.

Perry, W. G. (1998). *Forms of intellectual and ethical development in the college years: A scheme.* San Francisco: Jossey-Bass. (Originally published 1970.)

Perry, W. G., Jr. (1981). Cognitive and ethical growth. In A. Chickering (Ed.), *The modern American college* (pp. 76–116). San Francisco: Jossey-Bass.

Perry-Jenkins, M., Repetti, R. L., & Crouter, A. C. (2000). Work and family in the 1990s. *Journal of Marriage and the Family, 62,* 981–998.

Persad, C. C., Abeles, N., Zacks, R. T., & Denburg, N. L. (2002). Inhibitory changes after age 60 and their relationship to measures of attention and memory. *Journal of Gerontology, 57B,* P223–P232.

Peshkin, A. (1978). *Growing up American: Schooling and the survival of the community.* Chicago: University of Chicago Press.

Peshkin, A. (1997). *Places of memory: Whiteman's schools and native American communities.* Mahwah, NJ: Erlbaum.

Peters, R. D., Petrunka, K., & Arnold, R. (2003). The Better Beginnings, Better Futures Project: A universal, comprehensive, community-based prevention approach for primary school children and their families. *Journal of Clinical Child and Adolescent Psychology, 32,* 215–227.

Petersen, N., & Gonzales, R. C. (1999). *Career counseling models for diverse populations.* Belmont, CA: Wadsworth.

Peterson, B. E. (2002). Longitudinal analysis of midlife generativity, intergenerational roles, and caregiving. *Psychology and Aging, 17,* 161–168.

Peterson, B. E., Smirles, K. A., & Wentworth, P. A. (1997). Generativity and authoritarianism: Implications for personality, political involvement, and parenting. *Journal of Personality and Social Psychology, 72,* 1202–1216.

Peterson, C., & Rideout, R. (1998). Memory for medical emergencies experienced by 1- and 2-year-olds. *Developmental Psychology, 34,* 1059–1072.

Peterson, C., & Roberts, C. (2003). Like mother, like daughter: Similarities in narrative style. *Developmental Psychology, 39,* 551–562.

Peterson, C., & Seligman, M. E. (2004). *Character strengths and virtues.* New York: Oxford University Press.

Peterson, C. C. (1996). The ticking of the social clock: Adults' beliefs about the timing of transition events. *International Journal of Aging and Human Development, 42,* 189–203.

Peterson, C. C. (2001). Influence of siblings' perspectives on theory of mind. *Cognitive Development, 15,* 435-455.

Peterson, L. (1989). Latchkey children's preparation for self-care: Overestimated, underrehearsed, and unsafe. *Journal of Clinical Child Psychology, 18,* 36–43.

Petitto, L. A., Holowka, S., Sergio, L. E., Levy, B., & Ostry, D. J. (2004). Baby hands that move to the rhythm of language: Hearing babies acquiring sign languages babble silently on the hands. *Cognition, 93,* 43–73.

Petitto, L. A., Holowka, S., Sergio, L. E., & Ostry, D. (2001, September 6). Language rhythms in babies' hand movements. *Nature, 413,* 35–36.

Petitto, L. A., & Marentette, P. F. (1991). Babbling in the manual mode: Evidence for the ontogeny of language. *Science, 251,* 1493–1496.

Pettigrew, T. (1998). Intergroup contact theory. *American Review of Psychology, 49,* 65–85.

Pettit, G. S. (2004). Violent children in developmental perspective. *Current Directions in Psychological Science, 13,* 194–197.

Pettit, G. S., Brown, E. G., Mize, J., & Lindsey, E. (1998). Mothers' and fathers' socializing behaviors in three contexts: Links with children's peer competence. *Merrill-Palmer Quarterly, 44,* 173–193.

Pew Research Center. (2006). *Strong public support for right to die.* Retrieved from http://people-press.org/reports

Phillips, M. (1997). What makes schools effective? A comparison of the relationships of communitarian climate and academic climate to mathematics achievement and attendance during middle school. *American Educational Research Journal, 34,* 633–662.

Phillipsen, L. C. (1999). Associations between age, gender, and group acceptance and three components of friendship quality. *Journal of Early Adolescence, 19,* 438–464.

Phinney, J. S., & Chavira, V. (1995). Parental ethnic socialization and adolescent outcomes in ethnic minority families. *Journal of Research on Adolescence, 5,* 31–53.

Phinney, J. S., Horenczyk, G., Liebkind, K., & Vedder, P. (2001a). Ethnic identity, immigration, and well-being: An interactional perspective. *Journal of Social Issues, 57,* 493–510.

Phinney, J. S., & Kohatsu, E. L. (1997). Ethnic and racial identity development and mental health. In J. Schulenberg, J. L. Maggs, & K. Hurrelmann (Eds.), *Health risks and developmental transitions during adolescence* (pp. 420–443). Cambridge, UK: Cambridge University Press.

Phinney, J. S., Ong, A., & Madden, T. (2000). Cultural values and intergenerational value discrepancies in immigrant and non-immigrant families. *Child Development, 71,* 528–539.

Phinney, J. S., Romero, I., Nava, M., & Huang, D. (2001b). The role of language, parents, and peers in ethnic identity among adolescents in immigrant families. *Journal of Youth and Adolescence, 30,* 135–153.

Piaget, J. (1926). *The language and thought of the child.* New York: Harcourt, Brace & World. (Original work published 1923)

Piaget, J. (1930). *The child's conception of the world.* New York: Harcourt, Brace, & World. (Original work published 1926)

Piaget, J. (1951). *Play, dreams, and imitation in childhood.* New York: Norton. (Original work published 1945)

Piaget, J. (1952). *The origins of intelligence in children.* New York: International Universities Press. (Original work published 1936)

Piaget, J. (1965). *The moral judgment of the child.* New York: Free Press. (Original work published 1932)

Piaget, J. (1967). *Six psychological studies.* New York: Vintage.

Piaget, J. (1971). *Biology and knowledge.* Chicago: University of Chicago Press.

Pianta, R., Egeland, B., & Erickson, M. F. (1989). The antecedents of maltreatment: Results of the Mother–Child Interaction Research Project. In D. Cicchetti & V. Carlson (Eds.), *Child maltreatment* (pp. 203–253). New York: Cambridge University Press.

Pianta, R. C., Hamre, B., & Stuhlman, M. (2003). Relationships between teachers and children. In W. M. Reynolds & G. E. Miller (Eds.), *Handbook of psychology: Educational psychology* (Vol. 7, pp. 199–234). New York: Wiley.

Pickens, J., Field, T., & Nawrocki, T. (2001). Frontal EEG asymmetry in response to emotional vignettes in preschool age children. *International Journal of Behavioral Development, 25,* 105–112.

Pickett, K. E., Luo, Y., & Lauderdale, D. S. (2005). Widening social inequalities in risk for sudden infant death syndrome. *American Journal of Public Health, 95,* 1976–1981.

Pierce, K. M., Hamm, J. V., & Vandell, D. L. (1999). Experiences in after-school programs and children's adjustment in first-grade classrooms. *Child Development, 70,* 756–767.

Pierce, S. H., & Lange, G. (2000). Relationships among metamemory, motivation and memory performance in young school-age children. *British Journal of Developmental Psychology, 18,* 121–135.

Pillemer, K., & Suitor, J. (2002). Explaining mothers' ambivalence toward their adult children. *Journal of Marriage and Family, 64,* 602–613.

Pillow, B. (2002). Children's and adults' evaluation of the certainty of deductive inferences, inductive inferences, and guesses. *Child Development, 73,* 779–792.

Pimentel, A. E., Gentiel, C. L., Tanaka, H., Seals, D. R., & Gates, P. E. (2003). Greater rate of decline in maximal aerobic capacity with age in endurance-trained vs. sedentary men. *Journal of Applied Physiology, 94,* 2406–2413.

Pinderhughes, E. E., Dodge, K. A., Bates, J. E., Pettit, G. S., & Zelli, A. (2000). Discipline responses:

Influences of parents' socioeconomic status, ethnicity, beliefs about parenting, stress, and cognitive-emotional processes. *Journal of Family Psychology, 14,* 380–400.

Pinderhughes, E. E., Nix, R., Foster, E. M., Jones, D., & the Conduct Problems Prevention Research Group. (2001). Parenting in context: Impact of neighborhood poverty, residential stability, public services, social networks, and danger on parental behaviors. *Journal of Marriage and Family, 63,* 941–953.

Pinker, S. (1999). *Words and rules: The ingredients of language.* New York: Basic Books.

Pinker, S., Lebeaux, D. S., & Frost, L. A. (1987). Productivity and constraints in the acquisition of the passive. *Cognition, 26,* 195–267.

Pinquart, M. (2003). Loneliness in married, widowed, divorced, and never-married older adults. *Journal of Social and Personal Relationships, 20,* 31–53.

Pinquart, M., & Sörensen, S. (2001). Gender differences in self-concept and psychological well-being in old age: A meta-analysis. *Journal of Gerontology, 56B,* P195–P213.

Pipp, S., Easterbrooks, M. A., & Harmon, R. J. (1992). The relation between attachment and knowledge of self and mother in one-year-old infants to three-year-old infants. *Child Development, 63,* 738–750.

Pivarnik, J. M. (1998). Potential effects of maternal physical activity on birth weight: Brief review. *Medicine and Science in Sports and Exercise, 30,* 407–414.

Plassman, B. L., & Breitner, C. S. (1996). Recent advances in the genetics of Alzheimer's disease and vascular dementia with an emphasis on gene–environment interactions. *Journal of the American Genetics Society, 44,* 1242–1250.

Pleck, J. H., & Masciadrelli, B. P. (2004). Paternal involvement by U.S. residential fathers: Levels, sources, and consequences. In M. E. Lamb (Ed.), *The role of the father in child development* (4th ed., pp. 222–271). Hoboken, NJ: Wiley.

Pless, B., & Millar, W. (2000). *Unintentional injuries in childhood: Results from Canadian health surveys.* Ottawa, ON: Public Health Agency of Canada.

Ploeg, J., Campbell, L., Denton, M., Joshi, A., & Davies, S. (2004). Helping to build and rebuild secure lives and futures: Financial transfers from parents to adult children and grandchildren. *Canadian Journal on Aging, 23,* S131–S143.

Plomin, R. (1994). *Genetics and experience: The interplay between nature and nurture.* Thousand Oaks, CA: Sage.

Plomin, R. (2003). General cognitive ability. In R. Plomin & J. C. DeFries (Eds.), *Behavioral genetics in the postgenomic era* (pp. 183–201). Washington, DC: American Psychological Association.

Plomin, R. (2005). *Finding genes in child psychology and psychiatry: When are we going to be there?* Unpublished manuscript. London: King's College.

Plomin, R., DeFries, J. C., Craig, I. W., & McGuffin, P. (2003). Behavioral genomics. In R. Plomin, J. C. DeFries, I. W. Craig, & P. McGuffin (Eds.), *Behavioral genetics in the postgenomic era* (pp. 531–540). Washington, DC: American Psychological Association.

Plomin, R., DeFries, J. C., McClearn, G. E., & McGuffin, P. (2001). *Behavioral genetics* (4th ed.). New York: Worth.

Plomin, R., Fulker, D. W., Corley, R., & DeFries, J. C. (1997). Nature, nurture and cognitive development from 1 to 16 years: A parent–offspring study. *Psychological Science, 8,* 442–447.

Plomin, R., & Spinath, F. M. (2004). Intelligence: Genetics, genes, and genomics. *Journal of Personality and Social Psychology, 86,* 112–129.

Plude, D. J., & Doussard-Roosevelt, J. A. (1989). Aging, selective attention, and feature integration. *Psychology and Aging, 4,* 98–105.

Plude, D. J., & Hoyer, W. J. (1985). Attention and performance: Identifying and localizing age deficits. In N. Charness (Ed.), *Aging and human performance* (pp. 47–99). Chichester, England: Wiley.

Podewils, L. J., Guallar, E., Kuller, L. H., Fried, L. P., Lopez, O. L., Carlson, M., & Lyketsos, C. G. (2005). Physical activity, APOE genotype, and dementia risk: Findings from the Cardiovascular Health Cognition Study. *American Journal of Epidemiology, 161,* 639–651.

Pohl, J. M., Given, C. W., Collins, C. E., & Given, B. A. (1994). Social vulnerability and reactions to caregiving in daughters and daughters-in-law caring for disabled aging parents. *Health Care for Women International, 15,* 385–395.

Pohl, R. (2002). *Poverty in Canada.* Ottawa, ON: Innercity Ministries.

Polka, L., & Werker, J. F. (1994). Developmental changes in perception of non-native vowel contrasts. *Journal of Experimental Psychology: Human Perception and Performance, 20,* 421–435.

Pollitt, E. (1996). A reconceptualization of the effects of undernutrition on children's biological, psychosocial, and behavioral development. *Social Policy Report of the Society for Research in Child Development, 10*(5).

Pomerantz, E. M., & Eaton, M. M. (2000). Developmental differences in children's conceptions of parental control: "They love me, but they make me feel incompetent." *Merrill-Palmer Quarterly, 46,* 140–167.

Pomerantz, E. M., & Ruble, D. N. (1998). The multidimensional nature of control: Implications for the development of sex differences in self-evaluation. In J. Heckhausen & C. S. Dweck (Eds.), *Motivation and self-regulation across the lifespan* (pp. 159–184). New York: Cambridge University Press.

Pomerantz, E. M., & Saxon, J. L. (2001). Conceptions of ability as stable and self-evaluative processes: A longitudinal examination. *Child Development, 72,* 152–173.

Pomerleau, A., Scuccimarri, C., & Malcuit, G. (2003). Mother–infant behavioral interactions in teenage and adult mothers during the first six months postpartum: Relations with infant development. *Infant Mental Health Journal, 24,* 495–509.

Pons, F., Lawson, J., Harris, P. L., & de Rosnay, M. (2003). Individual differences in children's emotion understanding: Effects of age and language. *Scandinavian Journal of Psychology, 44,* 347–353.

Poon, H. F., Calabrese, V., Scapagnini, G., & Butterfield. D. A. (2004). Free radicals: Key to brain aging and heme oxygenase as a cellular response to oxidative stress. *Journal of Gerontology, 59A,* 478–493.

Popenoe, D. (2006). *Debunking divorce myths.* Retrieved from health.discovery.com/centers/love relationships/articles/divorce.html

Porter, R. H., Makin, J. W., Davis, L. B., & Christensen, K. M. (1992). An assessment of the salient olfactory environment of formula-fed infants. *Physiology and Behavior, 50,* 907–911.

Posada, G., Carbonell, O. A., Alzate, G., & Plata, S. J. (2004). Through Colombian lenses: Ethnographic and conventional analyses of maternal care and their associations with secure base behavior. *Developmental Psychology, 40,* 508–518.

Posada, G., Jacobs, A., Richmond, M. K., Carbonell, O. A., Alzate, G., Bustamante, M. R., & Quiceno, J. (2002). Maternal caregiving and infant security in two cultures.

Developmental Psychology, 38, 67–78.

Posner, J. K., & Vandell, D. L. (1994). Low-income children's after-school care: Are there beneficial effects of after-school programs? *Child Development, 58,* 568–595.

Poulin-Dubois, D., Serbin, L. A., Eichstedt, J. A., Sen, M. G., & Beissel, C. F. (2002). Men don't put on make-up: Toddlers' knowledge of the gender stereotyping of household activities. *Social Development, 11,* 166–181.

Poulton, R., Caspi, A., Milne, B. J., Thomson, W. M., Taylor, A., Sears, M. R., & Moffitt, T. E. (2002). Association between children's experience of socioeconomic disadvantage and adult health: A life-course study. *Lancet, 360,* 1640–1645.

Povinelli, D. J. (2001). The self—Elevated in consciousness and extended in time. In C. Moore & K. Lemmon (Eds.), *The self in time: Developmental perspectives* (pp. 75–95. Mahwah, NJ: Erlbaum.

Power, T. G. (2000). *Play and exploration in children and animals.* Mahwah, NJ: Erlbaum.

Powlishta, K. K., Serbin, L. A., & Moller, L. C. (1993). The stability of individual differences in gender typing: Implications for understanding gender segregation. *Sex Roles, 29,* 723–737.

Powls, A., Botting, N., Cooke, R. W. I., & Marlow, N. (1996). Handedness in very-low-birth-weight (VLBW) children at 12 years of age: Relation to perinatal and outcome variables. *Developmental Medicine and Child Neurology, 38,* 594–602.

Prager, K. J., & Bailey, J. M. (1985). Androgyny, ego development, and psychological crisis resolution. *Sex Roles, 13,* 525–535.

Pratt, M. W., Danso, H. A., Arnold, M. L., Norris, J. E., & Filyer, R. (2001). Adult generativity and the socialization of adolescents: Relations to mothers' and fathers' parenting beliefs, styles, and practices. *Journal of Personality, 69,* 89–120.

Pratt, M. W., Skoe, E. E., & Arnold, M. L. (2004). Care reasoning development and family socialization patterns in later adolescence: A longitudinal analysis. *International Journal of Behavioral Development, 28,* 139–147.

Prechtl, H. F. R., & Beintema, D. (1965). *The neurological examination of the full-term newborn infant.* London: Heinemann Medical Books.

Preisler, G. M. (1991). Early patterns of interaction between blind infants and their sighted mothers. *Child: Care, Health and Development, 17,* 65–90.

Preisler, G. M. (1993). A descriptive study of blind children in nurseries with sighted children. *Child: Care, Health and Development, 19,* 295–315.

Preissler, M. A., & Carey, S. (2004). Do both pictures and words function as symbols for 18- and 24-month-old children? *Journal of Cognition and Development, 5,* 185–212.

Pressley, M., Wharton-McDonald, R., Raphael, L. M., Bogner, K., & Roehrig, A. (2002). Exemplary first-grade teaching. In B. M. Taylor & P. D. Pearson (Eds.), *Teaching reading: Effective schools, accomplished teachers* (pp. 73–88). Mahwah, NJ: Erlbaum.

Prevatt, F. (2003). Dropping out of school: A review of intervention programs. *Journal of School Psychology, 41,* 377–399.

Previc, F. H. (1991). A general theory concerning the prenatal origins of cerebral lateralization. *Psychological Review, 98,* 299–334.

Princeton Religion Research Center. (1999). *Religious Practices in the United States.* Princeton, NJ: Author.

Prinstein, M. J., Boergers, J., & Spirito, A. (2001). Adolescents' and their friends' health-risk behavior: Factors that alter or add to peer influences. *Journal of Pediatric Psychology, 26,* 287–298.

Prinstein, M. J., Boergers, J., & Vernberg, E. M. (2001). Overt and relational aggression in adolescents: Social–psychological adjustment of aggressors and victims. *Journal of Clinical Child Psychology, 30,* 479–491.

Prinstein, M. J., & La Greca, A. (2004). Childhood peer rejection and aggression as predictors of adolescent girls' externalizing and health risk behaviors: A 6-year longitudinal study. *Journal of Consulting and Clinical Psychology, 72,* 103–112.

Prinstein, M. J., & La Greca, A. M. (2002). Peer crowd affiliation and internalizing distress in childhood and adolescence: A longitudinal follow-back study. *Journal of Research on Adolescence, 12,* 325–351.

Prior, M., Smart, D., Sanson, A., & Oberklaid, F. (2000). Does shy-inhibited temperament in childhood lead to anxiety problems in adolescence? *Journal of the American Academy of Child and Adolescent Psychiatry, 39,* 461–468.

Privacy Commissioner of Canada. (2005). *Genetic testing and privacy.* Ottawa, ON: Author.

Proctor, M. H., Moore, L. L., Gao, D., Cupples, L. A., Bradlee, M. L., Hood, M. Y., & Ellison, R. C. (2003). Television viewing and change in body fat from preschool to early adolescence: The Framingham Children's Study. *International Journal of Obesity, 27,* 827–833.

Programme for International Student Assessment. (2003). *Learning for tomorrow's world: First results from Program for International Student Assessment 2003.* Retrieved from www.pisa.oecd.org

Programme for International Student Assessment. (2005). *School factors related to quality and equity.* Retrieved from www.pisa.oecd.org

Prokos, A., & Padavic, I. (2005). An examination of competing explanations for the pay gap among scientists and engineers. *Gender and Society, 19,* 523–543.

Proulx, K., & Jacelon, C. (2004). Dying with dignity: The good patient versus the good death. *American Journal of Hospice and Palliative Care, 21,* 116–120.

Provins, K. A. (1997). Handedness and speech: A critical reappraisal of the role of genetic and environmental factors in the cerebral lateralization of function. *Psychological Review, 104,* 554–571.

Pruchno, R., & McKenney, D. (2000). The effects of custodial and coresident households on the mental health of grandmothers. *Journal of Mental Health and Aging, 6,* 291–310.

Pruett, M. K., Williams, T. Y., Insabella, G., & Little, T. D. (2003). Family and legal indicators of child adjustment to divorce among families with young children. *Journal of Family Psychology, 17,* 169–180.

Pryor, J., & Rodgers, B. (2001). *Children in changing families: Life after parental separation.* Oxford, UK: Blackwell.

Prysak, M., Lorenz, R. P., & Kisly, A. (1995). Pregnancy outcome in nulliparous women 35 years and older. *Obstetrics and Gynecology, 85,* 65–70.

Purcell-Gates, V. (1996). Stories, coupons, and the TV Guide: Relationships between home literacy experiences and emergent literacy knowledge. *Reading Research Quarterly, 31,* 406–428.

Putnam, F. W. (2003). Ten-year research update review: Child sexual abuse. *Journal of the American Academy of Child and Adolescent Psychiatry, 42,* 269–278.

Putnam, S. P., Samson, A. V., & Rothbart, M. K. (2000). Child temperament and parenting. In V. J. Molfese & D. L. Molfese (Eds.), *Temperament and personality across the life span* (pp. 255–277). Mahwah, NJ: Erlbaum.

Pyeritz, R. E. (1998). Sex: What we make of it. *Journal of the American Medical Association, 279,* 269.

Pyka, G., Lindenberger, E., Charette, S., & Marcus, R. (1994). Muscle strength and fiber adaptations to a year-long resistance training program in elderly men and women. *Journal of Gerontology, 49,* M22–27.

Pyszczynski, T., Greenberg, J., Solomon, S., Arndt, J., & Schimel, J. (2004). Why do people need self-esteem? A theoretical and empirical view. *Psychological Bulletin, 130,* 435–468.

Q

Qiu, C., Bäckman, L., Winblad, B., Agüero-Torres, H., & Fratiglioni, L. (2001). The influence of education on clinically diagnosed dementia incidence and mortality data from the Kungsholmen Project. *Archives of Neurology, 58,* 2034–2039.

Quick, H. E., & Moen, P. (1998). Gender, employment, and retirement quality: A life course approach to the differential experiences of men and women. *Journal of Occupational Health Psychology, 3,* 44–64.

Quill, T. E. (1991). Death and dignity: A case of individualized decision making. *New England Journal of Medicine, 324,* 691–694.

Quinn, C. T., Rogers, Z. R., & Buchanan, G. R. (2004). Survival of children with sickle cell disease. *Blood, 103,* 4023–4027.

Quinn, J. F. (1999). Retirement patterns and bridge jobs in the 1990s. *EBRI Issue Brief, 206,* 1–22.

Quinn, L. (2001). Type 2 diabetes. *Nursing Clinics of North America, 36,* 175–192.

Quinn, M. E., Johnson, M. A., Poon, L. W., & Martin, P. (1999). Psychosocial correlates of subjective health in sexagenarians, octogenarians, and centenarians. *Issues in Mental Health Nursing, 20,* 151–171.

Quinn, T. C., & Overbaugh, J. (2005). HIV/AIDS in women: An expanding epidemic. *Science, 308,* 1582–1583.

Quinnell, T. G., & Smith, I. E. (2004). Obstructive sleep apnoea in the elderly: Recognition and management considerations. *Drugs and Aging, 21,* 307–322.

Quist, J. F., & Kennedy, J. L. (2001). Genetics of childhood disorders: XXIII. ADHD, part 7: The serotonin system. *Journal of the American Academy of Child and Adolescent Psychiatry, 40,* 253–256.

Quyen, G. T., Bird, H. R., Davies, M., Hoven, C., Cohen, P., Jensen, P. S., & Goodman, S. (1998). Adverse life events and resilience. *Journal of the American Academy of Child and Adolescent Psychiatry, 37,* 1191–1200.

R

Rabiner, D. J., O'Keeffe, J., & Brown, D. (2004). A conceptual framework of financial exploitation of older persons. *Journal of Elder Abuse and Neglect, 16,* 53–73.

Radvansky, G. A., Zacks, R. T., & Hasher, L. (2005). Age and inhibition: The retrieval of situation models. *Journal of Gerontology, 60B,* P276–P278.

Ragow-O'Brien, D., Hayslip, B., Jr., & Guarnaccia, C. A. (2000). The impact of hospice on attitudes toward funerals and subsequent bereavement adjustment. *Omega, 41,* 291–305.

Rahman, Q., & Wilson, G. D. (2003). Born gay? The psychobiology of human sexual orientation. *Personality and Individual Differences, 34,* 1337–1382.

Räikkönen, K., Matthews, K. A., Flory, J. D., Owens, J. F., & Gump, B. B. (1999). Effects of optimism, pessimism, and trait anxiety on ambulatory blood pressure and mood during everyday life. *Journal of Personality and Social Psychology, 76,* 104–113.

Rakoczy, H., Tomasello, M., & Striano, T. (2004). Young children know that trying is not pretending: A test of the "behaving-as-if" construal of children's early concept of pretense. *Developmental Psychology, 40,* 388–399.

Ralph, K., Harrington, K., & Pandha, H. (2004). Recent developments and current status of gene therapy using viral vectors in the United Kingdom. *British Medical Journal, 329,* 839–842.

Ramchandani, P., Stein, A., Evans, J., O'Connor, T. G., & the ALSPAC Study Team. (2005). Paternal depression in the postnatal period and child development: A prospective population study. *Lancet, 365,* 2201–2205.

Ramey, S. L., & Ramey, C. T. (1999). Early experience and early intervention for children "at risk" for developmental delay and mental retardation. *Mental Retardation and Developmental Disabilities, 5,* 1–10.

Ramos, E., Frontera, W. R., Llorpart, A., & Feliciano, D. (1998). Muscle strength and hormonal levels in adolescents: Gender related differences. *International Journal of Sports Medicine, 19,* 526–531.

Ramos, M. C., Guerin, D. W., Gottfried, A. W., Bathurst, K., & Oliver, P. H. (2005). Family conflict and children's behavior problems: The moderating role of child temperament. *Structural Equation Modeling, 12,* 278–298.

Ramsay, L. J., Moreton, G., Gorman, D. R., Blake, E., Goh, D., & Elton, R. A. (2003). Unintentional home injury in preschool-aged children: Looking for the key—an exploration of the inter-relationship and relative importance of potential risk factors. *Public Health, 117,* 404–411.

Ramsøy, N. R. (1994). Non-marital cohabitation and change in norms: The case of Norway. *Acta Sociologica, 37,* 23–37.

Rando, T. A. (1991). Parental adjustment to the loss of a child. In D. Papadatou & C. Papadatos (Eds.), *Children and death* (pp. 233–253). New York: Hemisphere.

Rando, T. A. (1995). Grief and mourning: Accommodating to loss. In H. Wass & R. A. Neimeyer (Eds.), *Dying: Facing the facts* (3rd ed., pp. 211–241). Washington, DC: Taylor & Francis.

Ransford, H. E., & Palisi, B. J. (1996). Aerobic exercise, subjective health and psychological well-being within age and gender subgroups. *Social Science and Medicine, 42,* 1555–1559.

Rapp, S. R., Espeland, M. A., Shumaker, S. A., Henderson, V. W., Brunner, R. L., & Manson, J. E. (2003). Effect of estrogen plus progestin on global cognitive function in postmenopausal women: The Women's Health Initiative Memory Study: A randomized controlled trial. *Journal of the American Medical Association, 289,* 2663–2672.

Rasch, E. K., Hirsch, R., Paulose-Ram, R., & Hochberg, M. C. (2003). Prevalence of rheumatoid arthritis in persons 60 years of age and older in the United States: Effect of different methods of classification. *Arthritis and Rheumatism, 48,* 917–926.

Rasmussen, C., Ho, E., & Bisanz, J. (2003). Use of the mathematical principle of inversion in young children. *Journal of Experimental Child Psychology, 85,* 89–102.

Rasmussen, C. H., & Johnson, M. E. (1994). Spirituality and religiosity: Relative relationships to death anxiety. *Omega, 29,* 313–318.

Rasmussen, E. R., Neuman, R. J., Heath, A. C., Levy, F., Hay, D. A., & Todd, R. D. (2004). Familial clustering of latent class and DSM-IV defined attention-deficit hyperactivity disorder (ADHD) subtypes. *Journal of Child Psychology and Psychiatry, 45,* 589–598.

Rauscher, F. H., Shaw, G. L., & Ky, K. N. (1993). Music and spatial task performance. *Nature, 365,* 611.

Raver, C. C. (2003). Does work pay psychologically as well as economically? The role of employment in predicting depressive symptoms and parenting among low-income families. *Child Development, 74,* 1720–1736.

Ravid, D., & Tolchinsky, L. (2002). Developing linguistic literacy: A comprehensive model. *Journal of Child Language, 29,* 417–447.

Rawlins, W. K. (2004). Friendships in later life. In J. F. Nussbaum & J. Coupland (Eds.), *Handbook of communication and aging research* (2nd ed., pp. 273–299). Mahwah, NJ: Erlbaum.

Ray, V., & Gregory, R. (2001). School experiences of the children of lesbian and gay parents. *Family Matters, 59,* 28–35.

Rayner, K., & Pollatsek, A. (1989). *The psychology of reading.* Englewood Cliffs, NJ: Prentice-Hall.

Rayner, K., Pollatsek, A., & Starr, M. S. (2003). Reading. In A. F. Healy & R. W. Proctor (Eds.), *Handbook of psychology: Experimental psychology* (Vol. 4, pp. 549–574). New York: Wiley.

Raz, N. (2005). The aging brain observed in vivo: Differential changes and their modifiers. In R. Cabeza, L. Nyberg, & D. Park (Eds.), *Cognitive neuroscience of aging: Linking cognitive and cerebral aging* (pp. 19–57). New York: Oxford University Press.

Raz, N., Lindenberger, U., Rodriguez, K. M., Kennedy, K. M., Head, D., Williamson, A., Dahle, C., & Acker, J. D. (2005). Regional brain changes in aging healthy adults: General trends, individual differences and modifiers. *Cerebral Cortex, 15,* 1676–1689.

Reay, A. M., & Browne, K. D. (2001). Risk factor characteristics in carers who physically abuse or neglect their elderly dependents. *Aging and Mental Health, 5,* 56–62.

Reday-Mulvey, G. (2000). Gradual retirement in Europe. *Journal of Aging and Social Policy, 11,* 49–60.

Reddin, J. (1997). High-achieving women: Career development patterns. In H. S. Farmer (Ed.), *Diversity and women's career development* (pp. 95–126). Thousand Oaks, CA: Sage.

Redding, N. P., & Dowling, W. D. (1992). Rites of passage among women reentering higher education. *Adult Education Quarterly, 42,* 221–236.

Reese, E., Haden, C. A., & Fivush, R. (1993). Mother–child conversations about the past: Relationships of style and memory over time. *Cognitive Development, 8,* 403–430.

Reeves, J. B., & Darville, R. L. (1994). Social contact patterns and satisfaction with retirement of women in dual-career/earner families. *International Journal of Aging and Human Development, 39,* 163–175.

Regan, P. C., Medina, R., Joshi, A. (2001). Partner preferences among homosexual men and women: What is desirable in a sex partner is not necessarily desirable in a romantic partner. *Social Behavior and Personality, 29,* 625–634.

Reginster, J. Y., & Burlet, N. (2006). Osteoporosis: A still increasing prevalence. *Bone, 38,* 4–9.

Regnerus, M., Smith, C., & Fritsch, M. (2003). *Religion in the lives of American adolescents: A review of the literature.* Chapel Hill, NC: National Study of Youth and Religion.

Reid, H. M., & Fine, A. (1992). Self-disclosure in men's friendships: Variations associated with intimate relations. In P. M. Nardi (Ed.), *Men's friendships* (pp. 153–171). Newbury Park, CA: Sage.

Reilly, J. S., Bates, E. A., & Marchman, V. A. (1998). Narrative discourse in children with early focal brain injury. *Brain and Language, 61,* 335–375.

Reis, O., & Youniss, J. (2004). Patterns in identity change and development in relationships with mothers and friends. *Journal of Adolescent Research, 19,* 31–44.

Reisman, J. E. (1987). Touch, motion, and proprioception. In P. Salapatek & L. Cohen (Eds.), *Handbook of infant perception: Vol. 1. From sensation to perception* (pp. 265–303). Orlando, FL: Academic Press.

Reiss, A. L., & Dant, C. C. (2003). The behavioral neurogenetics of fragile X syndrome: Analyzing gene–brain–behavior relationships in child developmental psychopathologies. *Development and Psychopathology, 15,* 927–968.

Reiss, D. (2003). Child effects on family systems: Behavioral genetic strategies. In A. C. Crouter & A. Booth (Eds.), *Children's influence on family dynamics: The neglected side of family relationships* (pp. 3–36). Mahwah, NJ: Erlbaum.

Reitzel-Jaffe, D., & Wolfe, D. A. (2001). Predictors of relationship abuse among young men. *Journal of Interpersonal Violence, 16,* 99–115.

Repacholi, B. M. (1998). Infants' use of attentional cues to identify the referent of another person's emotional expression. *Developmental Psychology, 33,* 12–21.

Repacholi, B. M., & Gopnik, A. (1997). Early reasoning about desires: Evidence from 14- and 18-month-olds. *Developmental Psychology, 33,* 12–21.

Resnick, M. B., Gueorguieva, R. V., Carter, R. L., Ariet, M., Sun, Y., Roth, J., Bucciarelli, R. L., Curran, J. S., & Mahan, C. S. (1999). The impact of low birth weight, perinatal conditions, and sociodemographic factors on educational outcome in kindergarten. *Pediatrics, 104,* e74.

Resnick, S. M., Pham, D. L., Kraut, M. A., Zonderman, A. B., & Davatzikos, C. (2003). Longitudinal magnetic resonance imaging studies of older adults: A shrinking brain. *Journal of Neuroscience, 23,* 3295–3301.

Rest, J. R. (1979). *Development in judging moral issues.* Minneapolis: University of Minnesota Press.

Reuter-Lorenz, P. A., & Sylvester, C.-Y. C. (2005). The cognitive neuroscience of working memory and aging. In R. Cabeza, L. Nyberg, & D. Park (Eds.), *Cognitive neuroscience of aging* (pp. 186–217). New York: Oxford University Press.

Reyes-Ortiz, C. A., Kuo, Y.-F., DiNuzzo, A. R., Ray, L. A., Raji, M. A., & Markides, K. S. (2005). Near vision impairment predicts cognitive decline: Data from the Hispanic established populations for epidemiologic studies of the elderly. *Journal of the American Geriatric Society, 53,* 681–686.

Reynolds, C. R., & Kaiser, S. M. (1990). Test bias in psychological assessment. In T. B. Gutkin & C. R. Reynolds (Eds.), *The handbook of school psychology* (pp. 487–525). New York: Wiley.

Reynolds, M. A., Schieve, L. A., Martin, J. A., Meng, G., & Macaluso, M. (2003). Trends in multiple births conceived using assisted reproductive technology, United States, 1997–2000. *Pediatrics, 111,* 1159–1162.

Rhein, J. von (1997, January 19). Ardis Krainik, Lyric Opera's life force, dies. *Chicago Tribune,* pp. 1, 16.

Rhone, S. S., & Fulbright, L. (2001, November 1). Childless by choice—childless couples an emerging demographic. *American Demographics.* Retrieved from www.findarticles.com/p/articles/mi_m4021/is_2001_Oct_1/ai_79052844

Richards, J. E., & Holley, F. B. (1999). Infant attention and the development of smooth pursuit tracking. *Developmental Psychology, 35,* 856–867.

Richards, M. H., & Duckett, E. (1994). The relationship of maternal employment to early adolescent daily experience with and without parents. *Child Development, 65,* 225–236.

Richie, B. S., Fassinger, R. E., Linn, S. G., Johnson, J., Prosser, J., & Robinson, S. (1997). Persistence, connection, and passion: A qualitative study of the career development of highly achieving African American–black and white women. *Journal of Counseling Psychology, 44,* 133–148.

Rietvelt, M. J. H., Hudziak, J. J., Bartels, M., van Beijsterveldt, C. E. M., & Boomsma, D. I. (2004). Heritability of attention problems in children: Longitudinal results from a study of twins, age 3 to 12. *Journal of Child Psychology and Psychiatry, 45,* 577–588.

Rigby, K. (2004). Bullying in childhood. In P. K. Smith & C. H. Hart (Eds.), *Blackwell handbook of childhood social development* (pp. 549–568). Malden, MA: Blackwell.

Riggio, H. R. (2000). Measuring attitudes toward adult sibling relationships: The lifespan sibling relationship scale. *Journal of Social and Personal Relationships, 17,* 707–728.

Riley, E. P., McGee, C. L., & Sowell, E. R. (2004). Teratogenic effects of alcohol: A decade of brain imaging. *American Journal of Medical Genetics: Part C, Seminars in Medical Genetics, 127,* 35–41.

Riley, L. D., & Bowen, C. P. (2005). The sandwich generation: Challenges and coping strategies of multigenerational families. *Counseling and Therapy for Couples and Families, 13,* 52–58.

Rimé, B., Finkenauer, C., Luminet, O., Zech, E., & Philippot, P. (1998). Social sharing of emotion: New evidence and new questions. In W. Stroebe & M. Hewstone (Eds.), *European review of social psychology* (Vol. 9). Chichester, UK: Wiley.

Riordan, J., Gross, A., Angeron, J., Drumwiede, B., & Melin, J. (2000). The effect of labor pain relief medication on neonatal suckling and breastfeeding duration. *Journal of Human Lactation, 16,* 7–12.

Ripple, C. H., & Zigler, E. (2003). Research, policy, and the federal role in prevention initiatives for children. *American Psychologist, 58,* 482–490.

Ritchey, L. H., Ritchey, P. N., & Dietz, B. E. (2001). Clarifying the measurement of activity. *Activities, Adaptation, and Aging, 26,* 1–21.

Rittman, M., Kuzmeskus, L. B., & Flum, M. A. (2000). A synthesis of current knowledge on minority elder abuse. In T. Tatara (Ed.), *Understanding elder abuse in minority populations* (pp. 221–238). Philadelphia: Brunner/Mazel.

Riva, D., & Giorgi, C. (2000). The cerebellum contributes to higher functions during development: Evidence from a series of children surgically treated for posterior fossa tumours. *Brain, 123,* 1051–1061.

Rivera, S. M., Wakeley, A., & Langer, J. (1999). The drawbridge phenomenon: Representational reasoning or perceptual preference? *Developmental Psychology, 35,* 427–435.

Rizzolatti, G., & Craighero, L. (2004). The mirror-neuron system. *Annual Review of Neuroscience, 27,* 169–192.

Robb, A. S., & Dadson, M. J. (2002). Eating disorders in males. *Child and Adolescent Psychiatric Clinics of North America, 11,* 399–418.

Roberton, M. A. (1984). Changing motor patterns during childhood. In J. R. Thomas (Ed.), *Motor development during childhood and adolescence* (pp. 48–90). Minneapolis: Burgess.

Roberts, B. W., & DelVecchio, W. E. (2000). The rank-order consistency of personality traits from childhood to old age: A quantitative review of longitudinal studies. *Psychological Bulletin, 126,* 3–25.

Roberts, B. W., Robins, R. W., Caspi, A., & Trzesniewski, K. H. (2003). Personality trait development in adulthood. In J. L. Mortimer & M. Shanahan (Eds.), *Handbook of the life course* (pp. 579–598). New York: Plenum.

Roberts, D. F., Foehr, U. G., & Rideout, V. (2005). *Generation M: Media in the lives of 8–18 year olds.* Menlo Park, CA: Henry J. Kaiser Family Foundation.

Roberts, D. F., Henriksen, L., & Foehr, U. G. (2004). Adolescents and media. In R. M. Lerner & L. Steinberg (Eds.), *Handbook of adolescent psychology* (2nd ed., pp. 627–664). Hoboken, NJ: Wiley.

Roberts, J. E., Burchinal, M. R., & Durham, M. (1999). Parents' report of vocabulary and grammatical development of American preschoolers: Child and environment associations. *Child Development, 70,* 92–106.

Roberts, P. (2004). The living and the dead: Community in the virtual cemetery. *Omega: Journal of Death and Dying, 49,* 57–76.

Roberts, P., & Newton, P. M. (1987). Levinsonian studies of women's adult development. *Psychology and Aging, 2,* 154–163.

Roberts, P., & Vidal, L. A. (1999–2000). Perpetual care in cyberspace: A portrait of memorials on the Web. *Omega, 40,* 521–545.

Roberts, R. E., Kaplan, G. A., Shema, S. J., & Strawbridge, W. J. (1997). Prevalence and correlates of depression in an aging cohort: The Alameda County Study. *Journal of Gerontology, 52B,* S252–S258.

Robine, J.-M., & Allard, M. (1999). Jeanne Louise Calment: Validation of the duration of her life. In B. Jeune & J. W. Vaupel (Ed.), *Validation of exceptional longevity.* Odense, Denmark: Odense University Press.

Robins, R. W., Tracy, J. L., Trzesniewski, K., Potter, J., & Gosling, S. D. (2001). Personality correlates of self-esteem. *Journal of Research in Personality, 35,* 463–482.

Robinson, C. C., Anderson, G. T., Porter, C. L., Hart, C. H., & Wouden-Miller, M. (2003). Sequential transition patterns of preschoolers' social interactions during child-initiated play: Is parallel-aware play a bi-directional bridge to other play states? *Early Childhood Research Quarterly, 18,* 3–21.

Robles, T. F., & Kiecolt-Glaser, J. K. (2003). The physiology of marriage: Pathways to health. *Physiology and Behavior, 79,* 409–416.

Rochat, P. (1989). Object manipulation and exploration in 2- to 5-month-old infants. *Developmental Psychology, 25,* 871–884.

Rochat, P. (1998). Self-perception and action in infancy. *Experimental Brain Research, 123,* 102–109.

Rochat, P. (2001). The infant's world. Cambridge, MA: Harvard University Press.

Rochat, P. (2003). Five levels of self-awareness as they unfold early in life. *Consciousness and Cognition, 12,* 717–731.

Rochat, P., & Goubet, N. (1995). Development of sitting and reaching in 5- to 6-month-old infants. *Infant Behavior and Development, 18,* 53–68.

Rochat, P., & Hespos, S. J. (1997). Differential rooting responses by neonates: Evidence for an early sense of self. *Early Development and Parenting, 6,* 105–112.

Rochat, P, Querido, J. G., & Striano, T. (1999). Emerging sensitivity to the timing and structure of proto-conversation. *Developmental Psychology, 35,* 950–957.

Rochat, P., & Striano, T. (2002). Who's in the mirror? Self–other discrimination in specular images by four- and nine-month-old infants. *Infant and Child Development, 11,* 289–303.

Rochat, P., Striano, T., & Blatt, L. (2002). Differential effects of happy, neutral, and sad still-faces on 2-, 4-, and 6-month-old infants. *Infant and Child Development, 11,* 289–303.

Rodgers, J. L., Cleveland, H. H., van den Oord, E., & Rowe, D. C. (2000). Resolving the debate over birth order, family size, and intelligence. *American Psychologist, 55,* 599–612.

Rodkin, P. C., Farmer, T. W., Pearl, R., & Van Acker, R. (2000). Heterogeneity of popular boys: Antisocial and prosocial configurations. *Developmental Psychology, 36,* 14–24.

Roebers, C. M., & Schneider, W. (2001). Individual differences in children's eyewitness recall: The influence of intelligence and shyness. *Applied Developmental Science, 5,* 9–20.

Roelfsema, N. M., Hop, W. C., Boito, S. M., & Wladimiroff, J. W. (2004). Three-dimensional sonographic measurement of normal fetal brain volume during the second half of pregnancy. *American Journal of Obstetrics and Gynecology, 190,* 275–280.

Roeser, R. W., Eccles, J. S., & Freedman-Doan, C. (1999). Academic functioning and mental health in adolescence: Patterns, progressions, and routes from childhood. *Journal of Adolescent Research, 14,* 135–174.

Roeser, R. W., Eccles, J. S., & Sameroff, A. J. (2000). School as a context of early adolescents' academic and social-emotional development: A summary of research findings. *Elementary School Journal, 100,* 443–471.

Roger, V. L., Farkouh, M. E., Weston, S. A., Reeder, G. S., Jacobsen, S. J., Zinsmeister, A. R., Yawn, B. P., Kopeky, S. L., & Gabriel, S. E. (2000). Sex differences in evaluation and outcome of unstable angina. *Journal of the American Medical Association, 283,* 646–652.

Rogers, C., & Shiff, M. (1996). Early versus late prenatal care in New Mexico: Barriers and motivators. *Birth, 23,* 26–30.

Rogers, L. J. (2000). Evolution of hemispheric specialization: Advantages and disadvantages. *Brain and Language, 73,* 236–253.

Rogers, L., Resnick, M. D., Mitchell, J. E., & Blum, R. W. (1997). The relationship between socioeconomic status and eating disordered behaviors in a community sample of adolescent girls. *International Journal of Eating Disorders, 22,* 15–23.

Rogge, M. M., Greenwald, M., & Golden, A. (2004). Obesity, stigma, and civilized oppression. *Advances in Nursing Science, 27,* 301–315.

Roggman, L. A., Langlois, J. H., Hubbs-Tait, L., & Rieser-Danner, L. A. (1994). Infant day-care, attachment, and the "file drawer problem." *Child Development, 65,* 1429–1443.

Rogler, L. H. (2002). Historical generations and psychology. *American Psychologist, 57,* 1013–1023.

Rogoff, B. (1986). The development of strategic use of context in spatial memory. In M. Perlmutter (Ed.), *Perspectives on intellectual development* (pp. 107–123). Hillsdale, NJ: Erlbaum.

Rogoff, B. (1996). Developmental transitions in children's participation in sociocultural activities. In A. J. Sameroff & M. M. Haith (Eds.), *The five to seven year shift: The age of reason and responsibility* (pp. 273–294). Chicago: University of Chicago Press.

Rogoff, B. (1998). Cognition as a collaborative process. In D. Kuhn & R. S. Siegler (Eds.), *Handbook of child psychology: Vol. 2. Cognition, perception, and language* (5th ed., pp. 679–744). New York: Wiley.

Rogoff, B. (2003). *The cultural nature of human development.* New York: Oxford University Press.

Rogoff, B., & Chavajay, P. (1995). What's become of research on the cultural basis of cognitive development? *American Psychologist, 50,* 859–877.

Rogoff, B., Paradise, R., Arauz, R. M., Correa-Chávez, M., & Angelillo, C. (2003). Firsthand learning through intent participation. *Annual Review of Psychology, 54,* 175–203.

Rogol, A. D., Roemmich, J. N., & Clark, P. A. (2002). Growth at puberty. *Journal of Adolescent Health, 31,* 192–200.

Rohner, R., & Brothers, S. (1999). Perceived parental rejection, psychological maladjustment, and borderline personality disorder. *Journal of Emotional Abuse, 1,* 81–95.

Rohner, R. P., & Veneziano, R. A. (2001). The importance of father love: History and contemporary evidence. *Review of General Psychology, 5,* 382–405.

Roid, G. (2003). *The Stanford-Binet Intelligence Scales, Fifth Edition, interpretive manual.* Itasca, IL: Riverside Publishing.

Roisman, G. I., Madsen, S. D., Hennighausen, K. H., Sroufe, L. A., & Collins, W. A. (2001). The coherence of dyadic behavior across parent–child and romantic relationships as mediated by the internalized representation of experience. *Attachment and Human Development, 3,* 156–172.

Roisman, G. I., Padron, E., Sroufe, L. A., & Egeland, B. (2002). Earned-secure attachment status in retrospect and prospect. *Child Development, 73,* 1204–1219.

Roizen, N. J., & Patterson, D. (2003). Down's syndrome. *Lancet, 361,* 1281–1289.

Rokach, A. (2001). Perceived causes of loneliness in adulthood. *Journal of Social Behavior and Personality, 15,* 67–84.

Rokach, A. (2003). Strategies of coping with loneliness throughout the lifespan. In N. J. Pallone (Ed.), *Love, romance, sexual interaction: Research perspectives from current psychology* (pp. 225–344). New Brunswick, NJ: Transaction.

Rokach, R., Cohen, O., & Dreman, S. (2004). Who pulls the trigger? Who initiates divorce among over 45-year-olds. *Journal of Divorce and Remarriage, 42,* 61–83.

Rolls, B. J., Morris, E. L., & Roe, L. S. (2002). Portion size of food affects energy intake in normal-weight and overweight men and women. *American Journal of Clinical Nutrition, 6,* 1207–1213.

Román, G. C. (2003). Vascular dementia: Distinguishing characteristics, treatment, and prevention. *Journal of the American Geriatrics Society, 51,* S296–S304.

Romans, S. E., Martin, M., Gendall, K., & Herbison, G. P. (2003). Age of menarche: The role of some psychosocial factors. *Psychological Medicine, 33,* 933–939.

Rome-Flanders, T., & Cronk, C. (1995). A longitudinal study of infant vocalizations during mother–infant games. *Journal of Child Language, 22,* 259–274.

Romero, A. J., & Roberts, R. E. (2003). The impact of multiple dimensions of ethnic identity on discrimination and adolescents' self-esteem. *Journal of Applied Social Psychology, 33,* 2288–2305.

Rook, K. S., Catalano, R., & Dooley, D. (1989). The timing of major life events: Effects of departing from the social clock. *American Journal of Community Psychology, 17,* 233–258.

Roopnarine, J. L., Hossain, Z., Gill, P., & Brophy, H. (1994). Play in the East Indian context. In J. L. Roopnarine, J. E. Johnson, & F. H. Hooper (Eds.), *Children's play in diverse cultures* (pp. 9–30). Albany: State University of New York Press.

Roopnarine, J. L., Lasker, J., Sacks, M., & Stores, M. (1998). The cultural contexts of children's play. In O. N. Saracho & B. Spodek (Eds.), *Multiple perspectives on play in early childhood education* (pp. 194–219). Albany: State University of New York Press.

Roopnarine, J. L., Talukder, E., Jain, D., Joshi, P., & Srivastav, P. (1990). Characteristics of holding, patterns of play, and social behaviors between parents and infants in New Delhi, India. *Developmental Psychology, 26,* 667–673.

Rose, A. J. (2002). Co-rumination in the friendships of girls and boys. *Child Development, 73,* 1830–1843.

Rose, A. J., & Asher, S. R. (1999). Children's goals and strategies in response to conflicts within a friendship. *Developmental Psychology, 35,* 69–79.

Rose, A. J., Swenson, L. P., & Waller, E. M. (2004). Overt and relational aggression and perceived popularity: Developmental differences in concurrent and prospective relations. *Developmental Psychology, 40,* 378–387.

Rose, S. A., & Feldman, J. F. (1997). Memory and speed: Their role in the relation of infant information processing to later IQ. *Child Development, 68,* 610–620.

Rose, S. A., Jankowski, J. J., & Senior, G. J. (1997). Infants' recognition of contour-deleted figures. *Journal of Experimental Psychology: Human Perception and Performance, 23,* 1206–1216.

Rosen, A. B., & Rozin, P. (1993). Now you see it, now you don't: The preschool child's conception of invisible particles in the context of dissolving. *Developmental Psychology, 29,* 300–311.

Rosen, S., Bergman, M., & Plester, D. (1962). Presbycusis study of a relatively noise-free population in the Sudan. *Transactions of the American Otological Society, 50,* 135–152.

Rosen, S., Bergman, M., Plester, D., El-Mofty, A., & Satti, M. H. (1962). Presbycusis study of a relatively noise-free population in the Sudan. *Annals of Otology, Rhinology, and Laryngology, 71,* 727–743.

Rosenberg, S. D., Rosenberg, H. J., & Farrell, M. P. (1999). The midlife crisis revisited. In S. L. Willis & J. D. Reid (Eds.), *Life in the middle* (pp. 47–73). San Diego: Academic Press.

Rosenblatt, P. C. (1993). Cross-cultural variation in the experience, expression, and understanding of grief. In D. P. Irish, K. F. Lundquist, & V. J. Nelsen (Eds.), *Ethnic variations in dying, death, and grief* (pp. 13–19). Washington, DC: Taylor & Francis.

Rosengren, K. S., & Hickling, A. K. (2000). The development of children's thinking about possible events and plausible mechanisms. In K. S. Rosengren, C. N. Johnson, & P. L. Harris (Eds.), *Imagining the impossible* (pp. 75–98). Cambridge, UK: Cambridge University Press.

Rosenman, R. H., Brand, R. J., Jenkins, C. D., Friedman, M., Strauss, R., & Wurm, M. (1975). Coronary heart disease in the Western Collaborative Group Study: Final follow-up experience of 8½ years. *Journal of the American Medical Association, 223,* 872–877.

Rosenshine, B., & Meister, C. (1994). Reciprocal teaching: A review of nineteen experimental studies. *Review of Educational Research, 64,* 479–530.

Rosenthal, C. J., & Gladstone, J. (2000). *Grandparenthood in Canada.* Ottawa: Vanier Institute of the Family.

Ross, C. E., & Drentea, P. (1998). Consequences of retirement activities for distress and the sense of personal control. *Journal of Health and Social Behavior, 39,* 317–334.

Rossi, A. S. (1980). Life-span theories and women's lives. *Signs: Journal of Women in Culture and Society, 6,* 4–32.

Rossi, A. S. (2001). (Ed.). *Caring and doing for others: Social responsibility in the domains of family, work, and community.* Chicago: University of Chicago Press.

Rossi, A. S. (2005). The menopausal transition and aging processes. In O. G. Brim, C. D. Ryff, & R. C. Kessler (Eds.), *How healthy are we? A national study of well-being at midlife* (pp. 153–201). Chicago: University of Chicago Press.

Rossi, A. S., & Rossi, P. H. (1990). *Of human bonding: Parent–child relations across the life course.* New York: Aldine de Gruyter.

Rossi, G. (1997). The nestling. Why young adults stay at home longer: The Italian case. *Journal of Family Issues, 18,* 627–644.

Roth, G. S., Ingram, D. K., Black, A., & Lane, M. A. (2000). Effects of reduced energy intake on the biology of aging: The primate model. *European Journal of Clinical Nutrition, 54*(Suppl. 3), S15–S20.

Roth, G. S., Ingram, D. K., & Lane, M. A. (2001). Caloric restriction in primates and relevance to humans. *Annals of the New York Academy of Sciences, 928,* 305–315.

Roth, G. S., Lane, M. A., & Ingram, D. K. (2005). Caloric restriction mimetics: The next phase. *Annals of the New York Academy of Sciences, 1057,* 365–371.

Roth, J., Brooks-Gunn, J., Murray, L., & Foster, W. (1998). Promoting healthy adolescents: Synthesis of youth development program evaluations. *Journal of Research on Adolescence, 8,* 423–459.

Rothbart, M. K. (2003). Temperament and the pursuit of an integrated developmental psychology. *Merrill-Palmer Quarterly, 50,* 492–505.

Rothbart, M. K. (2004). Emotion-related regulation: Sharpening the definition. *Child Development, 75,* 334–339.

Rothbart, M. K., Ahadi, S. A., & Evans, D. E. (2000). Temperament and personality: Origins and outcome. *Journal of Personality and Social Psychology, 78,* 122–135.

Rothbart, M. K., & Bates, J. E. (1998). Temperament. In N. Eisenberg (Ed.), *Handbook of child psychology: Vol. 3. Social, emotional, and personality development* (5th ed., pp. 105–176). New York: Wiley.

Rothbart, M. K., Ellis, L. K., Rueda, M. R., & Posner, M. I. (2003). Developing mechanisms of temperamental effortful control. *Journal of Personality, 71,* 1113–1143.

Rothbart, M. K., & Mauro, J. A. (1990). Questionnaire approaches to the study of infant temperament. In J. W. Fagen & J. Colombo (Eds.), *Individual differences in infancy: Reliability, stability and prediction* (pp. 411–429). Hillsdale, NJ: Erlbaum.

Rothbaum, F., Pott, M., Azuma, H., Miyake, K., & Weisz, J. (2000a). The development of close relationships in Japan and the United States: Paths of symbiotic harmony and generative tension. *Child Development, 71,* 1121–1142.

Rothbaum, F., Weisz, J., Pott, M., Miyake, K., & Morelli, G. (2000b). Attachment and culture: Security in the United States and Japan. *American Psychologist, 55,* 1093–1104.

Rousseau, J. J. (1955). *Emile.* New York: Dutton. (Original work published 1762)

Rovee-Collier, C. K. (1999). The development of infant memory. *Current Directions in Psychological Science, 8,* 80–85.

Rovee-Collier, C. K., & Barr, R. (2001). Infant learning and memory. In G. Bremner & A. Fogel (Eds.), *Blackwell handbook of infant development* (pp. 139–168). Oxford, UK: Blackwell.

Rovee-Collier, C. K., & Bhatt, R. S. (1993). Evidence of long-term memory in infancy. *Annals of Child Development, 9,* 1–45.

Rowe, D. C. (1994). *The limits of family influence: Genes, experience, and behavior.* New York: Guilford.

Rowe, J. W., & Kahn, R. L. (1998). *Successful aging.* New York: Random House.

Rowe, S., & Wertsch, J. V. (2002). Vygotsky's model of cognitive development. In G. Bremner & A. Fogel (Eds.), *Blackwell handbook of infant development* (pp. 538–554). Oxford, UK: Blackwell.

Rowland, C., & Pine, J. M. (2000). Subject-auxiliary inversion errors and wh-question acquisition: "What children do know?" *Journal of Child Language, 27,* 157–181.

Rubin, D. C. (2002). Autobiographical memory across the lifespan. In P. Graf & N. Ohta (Eds.), *Lifespan development of human memory* (pp. 159–184). Cambridge, MA: MIT Press.

Rubin, D. C., Rahhal, T. A., & Poon, L. W. (1998). Things learned in early adulthood are remembered best. *Memory and Cognition, 26,* 3–19.

Rubin, D. C., & Schulkind, M. D. (1997). Distribution of important and word-cued autobiographical memories in 20-, 35-, and 70-year-old adults. *Psychology and Aging, 12,* 524–535.

Rubin, K. H., & Coplan, R. J. (1998). Social and nonsocial play in childhood: An individual differences perspective. In O. N. Saracho &

B. Spodek (Eds.), *Multiple perspectives on play in early childhood education* (pp. 144–170). Albany: State University of New York Press.

Rubin, K. H., Burgess, K. B., & Coplan, R. (2002). Social withdrawal and shyness. In P. K. Smith & C. H. Hart (Eds.), *Blackwell handbook of child social development* (pp. 329–352). Oxford, UK: Blackwell.

Rubin, K. H., Burgess, K. B., Dwyer, K. M., & Hastings, P. D. (2003). Predicting preschoolers' externalizing behaviors from toddler temperament, conflict, and maternal negativity. *Developmental Psychology, 39,* 164–176.

Rubin, K. H., Burgess, K. B., & Hastings, P. D. (2002). Stability and social-behavioral consequences of toddlers' inhibited temperament and parenting behaviors. *Child Development, 73,* 483–495.

Rubin, K. H., Coplan, J., Chen, X., Buskirk, A. A., & Wojslawowicz, J. C. (2005). Peer relationships in childhood. In M. H. Bornstein & M. E. Lamb (Eds.), *Developmental science: An advanced textbook* (pp. 469–512). Mahwah, NJ: Erlbaum.

Rubin, K. H., Fein, G. G., & Vandenberg, B. (1983). Play. In E. M. Hetherington (Ed.), *Handbook of child psychology: Vol. 4. Socialization, personality, and social development* (4th ed., pp. 693–744). New York: Wiley.

Rubin, K. H., Hastings, P. D., Stewart, S. L., Henderson, H. A., & Chen, X. (1997). The consistency and concomitants of inhibition: Some of the children, all of the time. *Child Development, 68,* 467–483.

Rubin, K. H., Watson, K. S., & Jambor, T. W. (1978). Free-play behaviors in preschool and kindergarten children. *Child Development, 49,* 539–536.

Rubinstein, R. L. (1987). Never married elderly as a social type: Re-evaluating some images. *Gerontologist, 27,* 108–113.

Rubinstein, R. L., Alexander, B. B., Goodman, M., & Luborsky, M. (1991). Key relationships of never married, childless older women: A cultural analysis. *Journal of Gerontology, 46,* S270–S277.

Ruble, D. N., Alvarez, J., Bachman, M., Cameron, J., Fuligni, A., Garcia-Coll, C., & Rhee, E. (2004). The development of a sense of "we": The emergence and implications of children's collective identity. In M. Bennett & F. Sani (Eds.), *The development of the social self* (pp. 29–76). Hove, UK: Psychology Press.

Ruble, D. N., & Martin, C. L. (1998). Gender development. In N. Eisenberg (Ed.), *Handbook of child psy-*

chology: Vol. 3. Social, emotional, and personality development* (5th ed., pp. 933–1016). New York: Wiley.

Rudolph, D. K., Lambert, S. F., Clark, A. G., & Kurlakowsky, K. D. (2001). Negotiating the transition to middle school: The role of self-regulatory processes. *Child Development, 72,* 929–946.

Ruff, H. A., & Capozzoli, M. C. (2003). Development of attention and distractibility in the first 4 years of life. *Developmental Psychology, 39,* 877–890.

Ruff, H. A., & Rothbart, M. K. (1996). *Attention in early development.* New York: Oxford University Press.

Ruffman, T. (1999). Children's understanding of logical inconsistency. *Child Development, 70,* 887–895.

Ruffman, T., & Langman, L. (2002). Infants' reaching in a multi-well A not B task. *Infant Behavior and Development, 25,* 237–246.

Ruffman, T., Perner, J., Olson, D. R., & Doherty, M. (1993). Reflecting on scientific thinking: Children's understanding of the hypothesis–evidence relation. *Child Development, 64,* 1617–1636.

Ruhm, C. J. (1996). Gender differences in employment behavior during late middle age. *Journal of Gerontology, 51B,* S11–S17.

Runco, M. A. (1992). Children's divergent thinking and creative ideation. *Developmental Review, 12,* 233–264.

Rurup, M. L., Muller, M. T., Onwuteaka-Philipsen, B. D., van der Heide, A., van der Wal, G., & van der Maas, P. J. (2005). Requests for euthanasia or physician-assisted suicide from older persons who do not have a severe disease: An interview study. *Psychological Medicine, 35,* 665–671.

Rusconi, A. (2004). Different pathways out of the parental home: A comparison of West Germany and Italy. *Journal of Comparative Family Studies, 35,* 627–649.

Rushton, J. L., Forcier, M., & Schectman, R. M. (2002). Epidemiology of depressive symptoms in the National Longitudinal Study of Adolescent Health. *Journal of the American Academy of Child and Adolescent Psychiatry, 41,* 199–205.

Rushton, J. P., & Bons, T. A. (2005). Mate choice and friendship in twins. *Psychological Science, 16,* 555–559.

Rushton, J. P., & Jensen, A. R. (2003). African–white IQ differences from Zimbabwe on the Wechsler Intelligence Scale for Children–Revised are mainly on the *g* factor. *Personality and Individual Differences, 34,* 177–183.

Rusinek, H., Endo, Y., De Santi, S., Frid, D., Tsui, W.-H., & Segal, S. (2004). Atrophy rate in medial temporal lobe during progression of Alzheimer disease. *Neurology, 63,* 2354–2359.

Russell, A., Mize, J., & Bissaker, K. (2004). Parent–child relationships. In P. K. Smith & C. H. Hart (Eds.), *Blackwell handbook of childhood social development* (pp. 204–222). Malden, MA: Blackwell.

Russell, J. A. (1990). The preschooler's understanding of the causes and consequences of emotion. *Child Development, 61,* 1872–1881.

Russell, J. A., Douglas, A. J., & Ingram, C. D. (2001). Brain preparations for maternity—adaptive changes in behavioral and neuroendocrine systems during pregnancy and lactation. *Progress in Brain Research, 133,* 1–38.

Russell, R. B., Petrini, J. R., Damus, K., Mattison, D. R., & Schwarz, R. H. (2003). The changing epidemiology of multiple births in the United States. *Obstetrics and Gynecology, 101,* 129–135.

Rutter, M. (1996). Maternal deprivation. In M. H. Bornstein (Ed.), *Handbook of parenting: Vol. 4. Applied and practical parenting* (pp. 3–31). Mahwah, NJ: Erlbaum.

Rutter, M. (2002). Nature, nurture, and development: From evangelism through science toward policy and practice. *Child Development, 73,* 1–21.

Rutter, M., & the English and Romanian Adoptees Study Team. (1998). Developmental catch-up, and deficit, following adoption after severe global early privation. *Journal of Child Psychology and Psychiatry, 39,* 465–476.

Rutter, M., O'Connor, T. G., and the English and Romanian Adoptees Study Team. (2004). Are there biological programming effects for psychological development? Findings from a study of Romanian adoptees. *Developmental Psychology, 40,* 81–94.

Rutter, M., Pickles, A., Murray, R., & Eaves, L. (2001). Testing hypotheses on specific environmental causal effects on behavior. *Psychological Bulletin, 127,* 291–324.

Ryan, A. M., & Patrick, H. (2001). The classroom social environment and changes in adolescents' motivation and engagement during middle school. *American Educational Research Journal, 38,* 437–460.

Ryan, E. B., Jin, Y., Anas, A. P., & Luh, J. J. (2004). Communication beliefs about youth and old age in Asia and Canada. *Journal of Cross-Cultural Gerontology, 19,* 343–360.

Rybash, J. M., & Hrubi-Bopp, K. L. (2000). Isolating the neural mechanisms of age-related changes in human working memory. *Nature Neuroscience, 3,* 509–515.

Ryding, M., Konradsson, K., Kalm, O., & Prellner, K. (2002). Auditory consequences of recurrent acute purulent otitis media. *Annals of Otology, Rhinology, and Laryngology, 111*(3, Pt. 1), 261–266.

Ryff, C. D. (1989). In the eye of the beholder: Views of psychological well-being among middle-aged and older adults. *Psychology and Aging, 4,* 195–210.

Ryff, C. D. (1991). Possible selves in adulthood and old age: A tale of shifting horizons. *Psychology and Aging, 6,* 286–295.

Ryff, C. D. (1995). Psychological well-being in adult life. *Current Directions in Psychological Science, 4,* 99–104.

Ryff, C. D., & Migdal, S. (1984). Intimacy and generativity: Self-perceived transitions. *Signs: Journal of Women in Culture and Society, 9,* 470–481.

Ryff, C. D., Schmutte, P. S., & Lee, Y. H. (1996). How children turn out: Implications for parental self-evaluation. In C. D. Ryff & M. M. Seltzer (Eds.), *The parental experience in midlife* (pp. 383– 422). Chicago: University of Chicago Press.

Ryff, C. D., & Singer, B. H. (2005). Social environments and the genetics of aging: Advancing knowledge of protective health mechanisms. *Journal of Gerontology, 60B,* 12–23.

Ryff, C. D., Singer, B. H., & Seltzer, M. M. (2002). Pathways through challenge: Implications for well-being and health. In L. Pulkkinen & A. Caspi (Eds.), *Paths to successful development* (pp. 302–328). Cambridge, UK: Cambridge University Press.

S

Saarni, C. (1999). *The development of emotional competence.* New York: Guilford.

Saarni, C. (2000). Emotional competence: A developmental perspective. In R. Bar-On & J. D. A. Parker (Eds.), *Handbook of emotional intelligence* (pp. 68–91). San Francisco: Jossey-Bass.

Saarni, C., Mumme, D. L., & Campos, J. J. (1998). Emotional development: Action, communication, and understanding. In N. Eisenberg (Ed.), *Handbook of child psychology: Vol. 3. Social, emotional, and personality development* (5th ed., pp. 237–309). New York: Wiley.

Sachdev, P. S., Brodaty, H., & Looi, J. C. L. (1999). Vascular dementia: Diagnosis, management, and pos-sible prevention. *Medical Journal of Australia, 170,* 81–85.

Sacks, P. (1999). *Standardized minds: The high price of America's testing culture and what we can do to change it.* Cambridge, MA: Perseus.

Sadeh, A. (1997). Sleep and melatonin in infants: A preliminary study. *Sleep, 20,* 185–191.

Sadler, T. W. (2003). *Langman's medical embryology* (9th ed.). Baltimore: William & Wilkins.

Saenger, P. (2003). Dose effects of growth hormone during puberty. *Hormone Research, 60*(Suppl. 1), 52–57.

Safe Kids Worldwide. (2002). Childhood injury worldwide: Meeting the challenge. Retrieved from http://www.safekidsworldwide .org

Saffran, J. R., Aslin, R. N., & Newport, E. L. (1996). Statistical learning by 8-month-old infants. *Science, 27,* 1926–1928.

Saffran, J. R., & Thiessen, E. D. (2003). Pattern induction by infant language learners. *Developmental Psychology, 39,* 484–494.

Saginak, K. A., & Saginak, M. A. (2005). Balancing work and family: Equity, gender, and marital satisfaction. *Counseling and Therapy for Couples and Families, 13,* 162–166.

Saha, C., Riner, M. E., & Liu, G. (2005). Individual and neighborhood-level factors in predicting asthma. *Archives of Pediatrics and Adolescent Medicine, 159,* 759–763.

Sakraida, T. J. (2005). Divorce transition differences of midlife women. *Issues in Mental Health Nursing, 26,* 225–249.

Salbe, A. D., Weyer, C., Lindsay, R. S., Ravussin, E., & Tataranni, P. A. (2002). Assessing risk factors for obesity between childhood and adolescence: I. Birth weight, childhood adiposity, parental obesity, insulin, and leptin. *Pediatrics, 110,* 299–306.

Salerno, M., Micillo, M., Di Maio, S., Capalbo, D., Ferri, P., & Lettiero, T. (2001). Longitudinal growth, sexual maturation and final height in patients with congenital hypothyroidism detected by neonatal screening. *European Journal of Endocrinology, 145,* 377–383.

Salihu, H. M., Shumpert, M. N., Slay, M., Kirby, R. S., & Alexander, G. R. (2003). Childbearing beyond maternal age 50 and fetal outcomes in the United States. *Obstetrics and Gynecology, 102,* 1006–1014.

Salmela-Aro, K., Nurmi, J.-E., Saisto, T., & Halmesmaki, E. (2001). Goal reconstruction and depressive symptoms during the transition to motherhood: Evi-dence from two cross-lagged longitudinal studies. *Journal of Personality and Social Psychology, 81,* 1144–1159.

Salmivalli, C., Kaukiainen, A., & Lagerspetz, K. (2000). Aggression and sociometric status of adolescents' self-concept and its relation to their social behavior. *Journal of Research on Adolescence, 8,* 333–354.

Salmivalli, C., & Voeten, M. (2004). Connections between attitudes, group norms, and behaviour in bullying situations. *International Journal of Behavioral Development, 28,* 246–258.

Salovey, P., & Pizzaro, D. A. (2003). The value of emotional intelligence. In R. J. Sternberg, J. Lautrey, & T. I. Lubart (Eds.), *Models of intelligence: International perspectives* (pp. 263–278). Washington, DC: American Psychological Association.

Salter, D., McMillan, D., Richards, M., Talbot, T., Hodges, J., Bentovim, A., & Hastings, R. (2003). Development of sexually abusive behavior in sexually victimized males: A longitudinal study. *Lancet, 361,* 471–476.

Salthouse, T. A. (1984). Effects of age and skill in typing. *Journal of Experimental Psychology: General, 113,* 345–371.

Salthouse, T. A. (1991). *Theoretical perspectives in cognitive aging.* Hillsdale, NJ: Erlbaum.

Salthouse, T. A. (1993). Speed mediation of adult age differences in cognition. *Developmental Psychology, 29,* 722–738.

Salthouse, T. A. (1996). Constraints on theories of cognitive aging. *Psychonomic Bulletin and Review, 3,* 287–299.

Salthouse, T. A. (2000). Aging and measures of processing speed. *Biological Psychology, 54,* 35–54.

Salthouse, T. A. (2005). Relations between cognitive abilities and measures of executive functioning. *Neuropsychology, 19,* 532–545.

Salthouse, T. A., & Babcock, R. L. (1991). Decomposing adult age differences in working memory. *Developmental Psychology, 27,* 763–776.

Salthouse, T. A., & Maurer, T. J. (1996). Aging, job performance, and career development. In J. E. Birren & K. W. Schaie (Eds.), *Handbook of the psychology of aging* (pp. 353–364). San Diego, CA: Academic Press.

Salthouse, T. A., & Skovronek, E. (1992). Within-context assessment of working memory. *Journal of Gerontology, 47,* P110–P129.

Samarel, N. (1991). *Caring for life and death.* Washington, DC: Hemisphere.

Samarel, N. (1995). The dying process. In H. Wass & R. A. Neimeyer (Eds.), *Dying: Facing the facts* (3rd ed., pp. 89–116). Washington, DC: Taylor & Francis.

Sampselle, C. M., Harris, V., Harlow, S. D., & Sowers, M. (2002). Midlife development and menopause in African-American and Caucasian women. *Health Care for Women International, 23,* 351–363.

Samuels, M. (2003). Viruses and sudden infant death. *Peaediatric Respiratory Review, 4,* 178–183.

Samuelsson, S. M., Alfredson, B. B., Hagberg, B., Anonymous, Nordbeck, B., Brun, A., Gustafson, L., & Risberg, J. (1997). The Swedish Centenarian Study: A multidisciplinary study of five consecutive cohorts at the age of 100. *International Journal of Aging and Human Development, 45,* 223–253.

Sandberg, J. F., & Hofferth, S. L. (2001). Changes in children's time with parents: United States, 1981–1997. *Demography, 38,* 423–436.

Sanders, C. M. (1999). *Grief: The mourning after* (2nd ed.). New York: Wiley.

Sanderson, C. A., Rahm, K. B., & Beigbeder, S. A. (2005). The link between the pursuit of intimacy goals and satisfaction in close same-sex friendships: An examination of the underlying processes. *Journal of Social and Personal Relationships, 22,* 75–98.

Sanderson, J. A., & Siegal, M. (1988). Conceptions of moral and social rules in rejected and nonrejected preschoolers. *Journal of Clinical Child Psychology, 17,* 66–72.

Sandnabba, N. K., & Ahlberg, C. (1999). Parents' attitudes and expectations about children's cross-gender behavior. *Sex Roles, 40,* 249–263.

Sandström, A., Rhodin, N., Lundberg, M., Olsson, T., & Nyberg, L. (2005). Impaired cognitive performance in patients with chronic burnout syndrome. *Biological Psychology, 69,* 271–279.

Sandstrom, M. J., & Coie, J. D. (1999). A developmental perspective on peer rejection: Mechanisms of stability and change. *Child Development, 70,* 955–966.

Sansavini, A., Bertoncini, J., & Giovanelli, G. (1997). Newborns discriminate the rhythm of multisyllabic stressed words. *Developmental Psychology, 33,* 3–11.

Sansone, C., & Berg, C. A. (1993). Adapting to the environment across the life span: Different process or different inputs? *International Journal of Behavioral Development, 16,* 215–241.

Santoloupo, S., & Pratt, M. (1994). Age, gender, and parenting style variations in mother–adolescent dialogues and adolescent reasoning about political issues. *Journal of Adolescent Research, 9,* 241–261.

Santoro, M. L., Mobili, L., Mesoraca, A., & Giorlandino, C. (2003). First report of prenatal diagnosis of genetic congenital deafness in a routine prenatal genetic test. *Prenatal Diagnosis, 23,* 1083–1085.

Sapp, F., Lee, K., & Muir, D. (2000). Three-year-olds' difficulty with the appearance–reality distinction: Is it real or is it apparent? *Developmental Psychology, 36,* 547–560.

Sarason, S. B. (1977). *Work, aging, and social change.* New York: Free Press.

Sarnecka, B. W., & Gelman, S. A. (2004). Six does not just mean a lot: Preschoolers see number words as specific. *Cognition, 92,* 329–352.

Sasaki, M., & Suzuki, T. (1987). Changes in religious commitment in the United States, Holland and Japan. *American Journal of Sociology, 92,* 1055–1076.

Sasser-Coen, J. A. (1993). Qualitative changes in creativity in the second half of life: A life-span developmental perspective. *Journal of Creative Behavior, 27,* 18–27.

Sataloff, R. T., & Sataloff, J. (2001). A monumental achievement. *Occupational Health and Safety, 70,* 122–125.

Saucier, J. F., Sylvestre, R., Doucet, H., Lambert, J., Frappier, J. Y., Charbonneau, L., & Malus, M. (2002). Cultural identity and adaptation to adolescence in Montreal. In F. J. C. Azima & N. Grizenko (Eds.), *Immigrant and refugee children and their families: Clinical, research, and training issues* (pp. 133–154). Madison, WI: International Universities Press.

Saudino, K. J. (2003). Parent ratings of infant temperament: Lessons from twin studies. *Infant Behavior and Development, 26,* 100–107.

Saudino, K. J., & Cherny, S. S. (2001). Sources of continuity and change in observed temperament. In R. N. Emde & J. K. Hewitt (Eds.), *Infancy to early childhood: Genetic and environmental influences on developmental change* (pp. 89–110). New York: Oxford University Press.

Saudino, K. J., & Plomin, R. (1997). Cognitive and temperamental mediators of genetic contributions to the home environment during infancy. *Merrill-Palmer Quarterly, 43,* 1–23.

Sauls, D. J. (2002). Effects of labor support on mothers, babies, and birth outcomes. *Journal of Obstetric, Gynecologic, and Neonatal Nursing, 31,* 733–741.

Savage, A. R., Petersen, M. B., Pettay, D., Taft, L., Allran, K., Freeman, S. B., Karadima, G., Avramopoulos, D., Torfs, C., Mikkelsen, M., & Hassold, T. J. (1998). Elucidating the mechanisms of paternal non-disjunction of chromosome 21 in humans. *Human Molecular Genetics, 7,* 1221–1227.

Savin-Williams, R. C. (2001). A critique of research on sexual-minority youths. *Journal of Adolescence, 24,* 5–13.

Savin-Williams, R. C. (2003). Lesbian, gay, and bisexual youths' relationships with their parents. In L. D. Garnets & D. C. Kimmel (Eds.), *Psychological perspectives on lesbian, gay, and bisexual experiences* (2nd ed., pp. 299–326). New York: Columbia University Press.

Savin-Williams, R. C., & Diamond, L. M. (2004). Sex. In R. M. Lerner & L. Steinberg (Eds.), *Handbook of adolescent development* (2nd ed., pp. 189–231). Hoboken, NJ: Wiley.

Savin-Williams, R. C., & Ream, G. L. (2003a). Sex variations in the disclosure to parents of same-sex attractions. *Journal of Family Psychology, 17,* 429–438.

Savin-Williams, R. C., & Ream, G. L. (2003b). Suicide attempts among sexual-minority male youth. *Journal of Clinical Child and Adolescent Psychology, 32,* 509–522.

Saw, S. M., Carkeet, A., Chia, K. S., Stone, R. A., & Tan, D. T. (2002). Component dependent risk factors for ocular parameters in Singapore Chinese children. *Ophthalmology, 109,* 2065–2071.

Saxe, G. B. (1988, August–September). Candy selling and math learning. *Educational Researcher, 17(6),* 14–21.

Sayer, L. C., & Bianchi, S. M. (2000). Women's economic independence and the probability of divorce: A review and reexamination. *Journal of Family Issues, 21,* 906–943.

Saygin, A. P., Wilson, S. M., Dronkers, N. F., & Bates, E. (2004). Action comprehension in aphasia: Linguistic and non-linguistic deficits and their lesion correlates. *Neuropsychologia, 42,* 1788–1804.

Saylor, C. F., Cowart, B. L., Lipovsky, J. A., Jackson, C., & Finch, A. J., Jr. (2003). Media exposure to September 11: Elementary school students' experiences and post-traumatic symptoms. *American Behavioral Scientist, 46,* 1622–1642.

Saylor, M. M., Baldwin, D. A., & Sabbagh, M. A. (2005). Word learning: A complex product. In G. Hall & S. Waxman (Eds.), *Weaving a lexicon.* Cambridge, MA: MIT Press.

Saylor, M. M., Sabbagh, M. A., & Baldwin, D. A. (2002). Children use whole–part juxtaposition as a pragmatic cue to word meaning. *Developmental Psychology, 38,* 993–1003.

Saywitz, K. J., Goodman, G. S., & Lyon, T. D. (2002). Interviewing children in and out of court: Current research and practice implications. In J. E. B. Myers & L. Berliner (Eds.), *The APSAC handbook on child maltreatment* (2nd ed., pp. 349–377). Thousand Oaks, CA: Sage.

Scarr, S., & McCartney, K. (1983). How people make their own environments: A theory of genotype environment effects. *Child Development, 54,* 424–435.

Scarr, S., & Weinberg, R. A. (1983). The Minnesota Adoption Studies: Genetic differences and malleability. *Child Development, 54,* 260–267.

Schaal, B., Marlier, L., & Soussignan, R. (2000). Human fetuses learn odours from their pregnant mother's diet. *Chemical Senses, 25,* 729–737.

Schaie, K. W. (1988). Variability in cognitive functioning in the elderly. In M. A. Bender, R. C. Leonard, & A. D. Woodhead (Eds.), *Phenotypic variation in populations* (p. 201). New York: Plenum.

Schaie, K. W. (1989). Individual differences in rate of cognitive change in adulthood. In V. L. Bengtson & K. W. Schaie (Eds.), *The course of later life: Research and reflections* (pp. 68–83). New York: Springer.

Schaie, K. W. (1994). The course of adult intellectual development. *American Psychologist, 49,* 304–313.

Schaie, K. W. (1996). *Intellectual development in adulthood: The Seattle Longitudinal Study.* New York: Cambridge University Press.

Schaie, K. W. (1998). The Seattle Longitudinal Studies of Adult Intelligence. In M. P. Lawton & T. A. Salthouse (Eds.), *Essential papers on the psychology of aging* (pp. 263–271). New York: New York University Press.

Schaie, K. W. (2000). The impact of longitudinal studies on understanding development from young adulthood to old age. *International Journal of Behavioral Development, 24,* 257–266.

Schaie, K. W. (2005). *Developmental influences on adult intelligence: The Seattle Longitudinal Study.* New York: Oxford University Press.

Scharrer, E., & Comstock, G. (2003). Entertainment televisual media: Content patterns and themes. In E. L. Palmer & B. M. Young (Eds.), *The faces of televisual media: Teaching, violence, selling to children* (pp. 161–193). Mahwah, NJ: Erlbaum.

Scheidt, R. J., & Windley, P. G. (1985). The ecology of aging. In J. E. Birren & K. W. Schaie (Eds.), *Handbook of the psychology of aging* (pp. 245–258). New York: Van Nostrand Reinhold.

Schellenberg, E. G. (2004). Music lessons enhance IQ. *Psychological Science, 15,* 511–514.

Scher, A., Epstein, R., & Tirosh, E. (2004). Stability and changes in sleep regulation: A longitudinal study from 3 months to 3 years. *International Journal of Behavioral Development, 28,* 268–274.

Scher, A., Tirosh, E., Jaffe, M., Rubin, L., Sadeh, A., & Lavie, P. (1995). Sleep patterns of infants and young children in Israel. *International Journal of Behavioral Development, 18,* 701–711.

Scherer, J. M., & Simon, R. J. (1999). *Euthanasia and the right to die: A comparative view.* Lanham, MD: Rowman & Littlefield.

Scherrer, S. (2001). Early career patterns: A comparison of Great Britain and West Germany. *European Sociological Review, 17,* 119–144.

Schieber, R. A., & Sacks, J. J. (2001). Measuring community bicycle helmet use among children. *Public Health Reports, 116,* 113–121.

Schieman, S., Gundy, V., & Taylor, K. (2001). Status, role, and resource explanations for age patterns in psychological distress. *Journal of Health and Social Behavior, 42,* 80–96.

Schieman, S., Pudrovska, T., & Milkie, M. A. (2005). The sense of divine control and the self-concept: A study of race differences in late life. *Research on Aging, 27,* 165–196.

Schilling, T. (2000). Infants' looking at possible and impossible screen rotations: The role of familiarization. *Infancy, 1,* 389–402.

Schlagmüller, M., & Schneider, W. (2002). The development of organizational strategies in children: Evidence from a microgenetic longitudinal study. *Journal of Experimental Child Psychology, 81,* 298–319.

Schlegel, A., & Barry, H., III (1991). *Adolescence: An anthropological inquiry.* New York: Free Press.

Schlesinger, M., & Kronebusch, K. (1994). The sources of intergenerational burdens and tensions. In V. L. Bengtson & R. A. Harootyan (Eds.), *Intergenerational linkages: Hidden connections in American society* (pp. 185–209). New York: Springer.

Schlossberg, N. (2004). *Retire smart, retire happy: Finding your true path in life.* Washington, DC:

American Psychological Association.

Schmidt, I. W., Berg, I. J., Deelman, B. G., & Pelemans, W. (1999). Memory training for remembering names in older adults. *Clinical Gerontologist, 20,* 57–73.

Schmitz, S., Fulker, D. W., Plomin, R., Zahn-Waxler, C., Emde, R. N., & DeFries, J. C. (1999). Temperament and problem behaviour during early childhood. *International Journal of Behavioural Development, 23,* 333–355.

Schneewind, K. A., & Gerhard, A. (2002). Relationship personality, conflict resolution, and marital satisfaction in the first 5 years of marriage. *Family Relations, 51,* 63–71.

Schneider, B. A., Daneman, M., Murphy, D. R., & See, S. K. (2000). Listening to discourse in distracting settings: The effects of aging. *Psychology and Aging, 15,* 110–125.

Schneider, B. H., Atkinson, L., & Tardif, C. (2001). Child–parent attachment and children's peer relations: A quantitative review. *Developmental Psychology, 37,* 87–100.

Schneider, E. L. (1992). Biological theories of aging. *Generations, 16*(4), 7–10.

Schneider, J. A., Wilson, R. S., Bienias, J. L., Evans, D. A., & Bennett, D. A. (2004). Cerebral infarctions and the likelihood of dementia from Alzheimer disease pathology. *Neurology, 62,* 1148–1155.

Schneider, W. (2002). Memory development in childhood. In U. Goswami (Ed.), *Blackwell handbook of childhood cognitive development* (pp. 236–256). Malden, MA: Blackwell.

Schneider, W., & Bjorklund, D. F. (1992). Expertise, aptitude, and strategic remembering. *Child Development, 63,* 461–473.

Schneider, W., & Bjorklund, D. F. (1998). Memory. In D. Kuhn & R. S. Siegler (Eds.), *Handbook of child psychology: Vol. 2. Cognition, perception, and language* (5th ed., pp. 467–521). New York: Wiley.

Schneider, W., & Pressley, M. (1997). *Memory development between two and twenty* (2nd ed.). Mahwah, NJ: Erlbaum.

Schneller, D. P., & Arditti, J.A. (2004). After the breakup: Interpreting divorce and rethinking intimacy. *Journal of Divorce and Remarriage, 42,* 1–37.

Schnohr, P., Nyboe, J., Lange, P., & Jensen, G. (1998). Longevity and gray hair, baldness, facial wrinkles, and arcus senilis in 13,000 men and women: The Copenhagen City Heart Study. *Journal of Gerontology, 53,* M347–350.

Schnohr, P., Scharling, H., & Jensen, J. S. (2003). Changes in leisure-time physical activity and risk of death: An observational study of 7,000 men and women. *American Journal of Epidemiology, 158,* 639–644.

Scholl, B. J., & Leslie, A. M. (2000). Minds, modules, and meta-analysis. *Child Development, 72,* 696–701.

Scholl, T. O., Heidiger, M. L., & Belsky, D. H. (1996). Prenatal care and maternal health during adolescent pregnancy: A review and meta-analysis. *Journal of Adolescent Health, 15,* 444–456.

Scholnick, E. K. (1995, Fall). Knowing and constructing plans. *SRCD Newsletter,* pp. 1–2, 17.

Schonert-Reichl, K. A. (1999). Relations of peer acceptance, friendship adjustment, and social behavior to moral reasoning during early adolescence. *Journal of Early Adolescence, 19,* 249–279.

Schooler, C., Mulatu, M. S., & Oates, G. (1999). The continuing effects of substantively complex work on the intellectual functioning of older workers. *Psychology and Aging, 14,* 483–506.

Schoon, L., & Parsons, S. (2002). Teenage aspirations for future careers and occupational outcomes. *Journal of Vocational Behavior, 60,* 262–288.

Schoppe-Sullivan, S. J., Mangelsdorf, S. C., Frosch, C. A., & McHale, J. (2004). Associations between coparenting and marital behavior from infancy to the preschool years. *Journal of Family Psychology, 18,* 194–207.

Schor, J. B. (2002). Time crunch among American parents. In S. A. Hewlett, N. Rankin, & C. West (Eds.), *Taking parenting public* (pp. 83–102). Boston: Rowman & Littlefield.

Schott, J. M., & Rossor, M. N. (2003). The grasp and other primitive reflexes. *Journal of Neurological and Neurosurgical Psychiatry, 74,* 558–560.

Schroots, J. J. F., van Dijkum, C., & Assink, M. H. J. (2004). Autobiographical memory from a life span perspective. *International Journal of Aging and Human Development, 58,* 69–85.

Schull, W. J. (2003). The children of atomic bomb survivors: A synopsis. *Journal of Radiological Protection, 23,* 369–394.

Schulman, J. D., & Black, S. H. (1997). Screening for Huntington disease and certain other dominantly inherited disorders: A case for preimplantation genetic testing. *Journal of Medical Screening, 4,* 58–59.

Schulman, K. A., Berlin, J. A., Harless, W., Kerner, J. F., Sistrunk, S., & Gersh, B. J. (1999). The effect of race and sex on physicians' recommendations for cardiac catheterization. *New England Journal of Medicine, 340,* 618–626.

Schultz, R., & Beach, S. (1999). Caregiving as a risk factor for mortality: The caregiver health effects study. *Journal of the American Medical Association, 282,* 2215–2219.

Schultz, R., Burgio, L., Burns, R., Eisdorfer, C., Gallagher-Thompson, D., Gitlin, L. N., & Mahoney, D. F. (2003). Resources for enhancing Alzheimer's caregiver health (REACH): Overview, site-specific outcomes, and future directions. *Gerontologist, 43,* 514–520.

Schulz, R., & Curnow, C. (1988). Peak performance and age among superathletes: Track and field, swimming, baseball, tennis, and golf. *Journal of Gerontology, 43,* P113–P120.

Schunk, D. H., & Zimmerman, B. J. (2003). Self-regulation and learning. In W. M. Reynolds & G. E. Miller (Eds.), *Handbook of psychology* (Vol. 7, pp. 59–78). New York: Wiley.

Schwalb, D. W., Nakawaza, J., Yamamoto, T., & Hyun, J.-H. (2004). Fathering in Japanese, Chinese, and Korean cultures: A review of the research literature. In M. E. Lamb (Ed.), *The role of the father in child development* (4th ed., pp. 146–181). Hoboken, NJ: Wiley.

Schwanenflugel, P. J., Henderson, R. L., & Fabricius, W. V. (1998). Developing organization of mental verbs and theory of mind in middle childhood: Evidence from extensions. *Developmental Psychology, 34,* 512–524.

Schwartz, B. L., & Frazier, L. D. (2005). Tip-of-the-tongue states and aging: Contrasting psycholinguistic and metacognitive perspectives. *Journal of General Psychology, 132,* 377–391.

Schwartz, C. E., Wright, C. I., Shin, L. M., Kagan, J., & Rauch, S. L. (2003). Inhibited and uninhibited infants "grown up": Adult amygdalar response to novelty. *Science, 300,* 1952–1953.

Schwartz, D., Proctor, L. J., & Chien, D. H. (2001). The aggressive victim of bullying: Emotional and behavioral dysregulation as a pathway to victimization by peers. In J. Juonen & S. Graham (Eds.), *Peer harassment in school: The plight of the vulnerable and victimized* (pp. 147–174). New York: Guilford.

Schwartz, J. P., & Waldo, M. (2004). Group work with men who have committed partner abuse. In J. L. DeLucia-Waack, D. A. Gerrity, C. R. Kalodner, & M. T. Riva (Eds.), *Handbook of group counseling and psychotherapy* (pp. 576–592). Thousand Oaks, CA: Sage.

Schwartz, P., & Rutter, V. (1998). *The gender of sexuality.* Thousand Oaks, CA: Pine Forge.

Schwarz, B. (1996). *Nursing home design: Consequences of employing the medical model.* New York: Garland.

Schwarz, N. (1999). Self-reports: How the questions shape the answers. *American Psychologist, 54,* 93–105.

Schwarzer, R. (1999). Self-regulatory processes in the adoption and maintenance of health behaviors. *Journal of Health Psychology, 4,* 115–127.

Schwebel, D. C., & Bounds, M. L. (2003). The role of parents and temperament on children's estimation of physical ability: Links to unintentional injury prevention. *Journal of Pediatric Psychology, 28,* 505–516.

Schwebel, D. C., Brezausek, C. M., Ramey, S. L., & Ramey, C. T. (2004). Interactions between child behavior patterns and parenting: Implications for children's unintentional injury risk. *Journal of Pediatric Psychology, 29,* 93–104.

Schweiger, W. K., & O'Brien, M. (2005). Special needs adoption: An ecological systems approach. *Family Relations, 54,* 512–522.

Schweinhart, L. J., Montie, J., Xiang, Z., Barnett, W. S., & Belfield, C. R. (2004). *Lifetime effects: The High/Scope Perry Preschool Study through age 40.* Boston, MA: Strategies for Children. Retrieved from www.highscope.org/Research/PerryProject/perrymain.htm

Schwimmer, J. B., Burwinkle, T. M., & Varni, J. W. (2003). Health-related quality of life of severely obese children and adolescents. *Journal of the American Medical Association, 289,* 1813–1819.

Scrutton, D. (2005). Influence of supine sleep positioning on early motor milestone acquisition. *Developmental Medicine and Child Neurology, 47,* 364.

Scully, D., & Marolla, J. (1998). "Riding the bull at Gilley's": Convicted rapists describe the rewards of rape. In M. E. Odem & J. Clay-Warner (Eds.), *Confronting rape and sexual assault* (pp. 181–198). Wilmington, DE: Scholarly Resources.

Seccombe, K. (2002). "Beating the odds" versus "changing the odds": Poverty, resilience, and family policy. *Journal of Marriage and the Family, 64,* 384–394.

Seeman, E. (2002). Pathogenesis of bone fragility in women and men. *Lancet, 359,* 1841–1850).

Seeman, T. E., Berkman, L. F., Kohout, F., Lacroix, A., Glynn, R., & Blazer, D. (1993). Intercommunity variations in the association between social ties and mortality in the elderly. *Annals of Epidemiology, 3*, 325–335.

Seeman, T. E., Huang, M.-H., Bretsky, P., Crimmins, E., Launer, L., & Guralnik, J. M. (2005). Education and APOE-e4 in longitudinal cognitive decline: MacAurthur Studies of Successful Aging. *Journal of Gerontology, 60B*, P74–P83.

Segrin, C., & Nabi, R. L. (2002). Does television viewing cultivate unrealistic expectations about marriage? *Journal of Communication, 52*, 247–263.

Seiberling, K. A., & Conley, D. B. (2004). Aging and olfactory and taste function. *Otolaryngologic Clinics of North America, 37*, 1209–1228.

Seidman, E., Aber, J. L., & French, S. E. (2004). Assessing the transitions to middle and high school. *Journal of Adolescent Research, 19*, 3–30.

Seidman, E., Lambert, L. E., Allen, L., & Aber, J. L. (2003). Urban adolescents' transition to junior high school and protective family transactions. *Journal of Early Adolescence, 23*, 166–193.

Seifer, R., & Schiller, M. (1995). The role of parenting sensitivity, infant temperament, and dyadic interaction in attachment theory and assessment. In E. Waters, B. E. Vaughn, G. Posada, & K. Kondo-Ikemura (Eds.), Caregiving, cultural, and cognitive perspectives on secure-base behavior and working models: New growing points of attachment theory and research. *Monographs of the Society for Research in Child Development, 60*(2–3, Serial No. 244).

Seitz, V., & Apfel, N. H. (1993). Adolescent mothers and repeated childbearing: Effects of a school-based intervention program. *American Journal of Orthopsychiatry, 63*, 572–581.

Seitz, V., & Apfel, N. H. (1994). Effects of a school for pregnant students on the incidence of low-birthweight deliveries. *Child Development, 65*, 666–676.

Selman, R. L. (1976). Social-cognitive understanding: A guide to educational and clinical practice. In T. Lickona (Ed.), *Moral development and behavior: Theory, research, and social issues* (pp. 299–316). New York: Holt, Rinehart and Winston.

Selman, R. L. (1980). *The growth of interpersonal understanding.* New York: Academic Press.

Selman, R. L., & Byrne, D. F. (1974). A structural-developmental analysis of levels of role taking in mid-dle childhood. *Child Development, 45*, 803–806.

Seltzer, M. M., & Ryff, C. D. (1994). Parenting across the life span: The normative and nonnormative cases. In D. L. Featherman, R. M. Lerner, & M. Perlmutter (Eds.), *Lifespan development and behavior* (pp. 1–40). Hillsdale, NJ: Erlbaum.

Selwyn, P. A. (1996). Before their time: A clinician's reflections on death and AIDS. In H. M. Spiro, M. G. M. Curnen, & L. P. Wandel (Eds.), *Facing death: Where culture, religion, and medicine meet* (pp. 33–37). New Haven, CT: Yale University Press.

Sen, M. G., Yonas, A., & Knill, D. C. (2001). Development of infants' sensitivity to surface contour information for spatial layout. *Perception, 30*, 167–176.

Serafini, T. E., & Adams, G. R. (2002). Functions of identity: Scale construction and validation. Identity: *An International Journal of Theory and Research, 2*, 361–389.

Serbin, L. A., Powlishta, K. K., & Gulko, J. (1993). The development of sex typing in middle childhood. *Monographs of the Society for Research in Child Deelopment, 58*(2, Serial No. 232).

Sermon, K., Van Steirteghem, A., & Liebaers, I. (2004). Preimplantation genetic diagnosis. *Lancet, 363*, 1633–1641.

Serpell, R., Sonnenschein, S., Baker, L., & Ganapathy, H. (2002). Intimate culture of families in the early socialization of literacy. *Journal of Family Psychology, 16*, 391–405.

Service Canada. (2005). *Canadian youth: Who are they and what do they want?* Retrieved from www.youth.gc.ca

Sesame Workshop. (2005). Sesame workshop. Retrieved from www.sesameworkshop.org

Seward, R. R., Yeats, D. E., & Zottarelli, L. K. (2002). Parental leave and father involvement in child care: Sweden and the United States. *Journal of Comparative Family Studies, 33*, 387–399.

Seymour, S. C. (1999). *Women, family, and child care in India.* Cambridge, UK: Cambridge University Press.

Shainess, N. (1961). A re-evaluation of some aspects of femininity through a study of menstruation: A preliminary report. *Comparative Psychiatry, 2*, 20–26.

Shanahan, M. J., Mortimer, J. T., & Krüger, H. (2002). Adolescence and adult work in the twenty-first century. *Journal of Research on Adolescence, 12*, 99–120.

Shapiro, A. (2004). Revisiting the generation gap: Exploring the relationships of parent/adult-child dyads. *International Journal of Aging and Human Development, 58*, 127–146.

Shapiro, A. E., Gottman, J. M., & Carrere, S. (2000). The baby and the marriage: Identifying factors that buffer against decline in marital satisfaction after the first baby arrives. *Journal of Family Psychology, 14*, 59–70.

Sharma, S. K., & Leveno, K. J. (2003). Regional analgesia and progress of labor. *Clinical Obstetrics and Gynecology, 46*, 633–645.

Shaver, J., Giblin, E., Lentz, M., & Lee, K. (1988). Sleep patterns and stability in perimenopausal women. *Sleep*, 556–561.

Shaver, P., Furman, W., & Buhrmester, D. (1985). Transition to college: Network changes, social skills, and loneliness. In S. Duck & D. Perlman (Eds.), *Understanding personal relationships: An interdisciplinary approach* (pp. 193–219). London: Sage.

Shaw, B. A. (2005). Anticipated support from neighbors and physical functioning during later life. *Research on Aging, 27*, 503–525.

Shaw, D. S., Gilliom, M., Ingoldsby, E. M., & Nagin, D. S. (2003). Trajectories leading to school-age conduct problems. *Developmental Psychology, 39*, 189–200.

Shedler, J., & Block, J. (1990). Adolescent drug use and psychological health: A longitudinal inquiry. *American Psychologist, 45*, 612–630.

Sheehy, A., Gasser, T., Molinari, L., & Largo, R. H. (1999). An analysis of variance of the pubertal and midgrowth spurts for length and width. *Annals of Human Biology, 26*, 309–331.

Sheldon, K. M., & Kasser, T. (2001). Getting older, getting better? Personal strivings and psychological maturity across the life span. *Developmental Psychology, 37*, 491–501.

Shenkin, J. D., Broffitt, B., Levy, S. M., & Warren, J. J. (2004). The association between environmental tobacco smoke and primary tooth caries. *Journal of Public Health Dentistry, 64*, 184–186.

Sherman, A. M., de Vries, B., & Lansford, J. E. (2000). Friendship in childhood and adulthood: Lessons across the life span. *International Journal of Aging and Human Development, 51*, 31–51.

Sherrill, C. L., & Pinderhughes, E. E. (1999). Conceptions of family and adoption among older adoptees. *Adoption Quarterly, 2*, 21–48.

Sherry, B., McDivitt, J., Brich, L. L., Cook, F. H., Sanders, S., Prish, J. L., Francis, L. A., & Scanlon, K. S. (2004). Attitudes, practices, and concerns about child feeding and child weight status among socioeconomically diverse white, His-panic, and African-American mothers. *Journal of the American Dietetic Association, 104*, 215–221.

Shields, A., Dickstein, S., Siefer, R., Giusti, L., Magee, K. D., & Spritz, B. (2001). Emotional competence and early school adjustment: A study of preschoolers at risk. *Early Education and Development, 12*, 73–96.

Shields, G., King, W., Fulks, S., & Fallon, L. F. (2002). Determinants of perceived safety among the elderly: An exploratory study. *Journal of Gerontological Social Work, 38*, 73–83.

Shields, M. (2005). The journey to quitting smoking. *Health Reports, 16*, 19–36.

Shimizu, H. (2001). Japanese adolescent boys' senses of empathy (omoiyari) and Carol Gilligan's perspectives on the morality of care: A phenomenological approach. *Culture and Psychology, 7*, 453–475.

Shipman, K. L., Zeman, J., Nesin, A. E., & Fitzgerald, M. (2003). Children's strategies for displaying anger and sadness: What works with whom? *Merrill-Palmer Quarterly, 49*, 100–122.

Shock, N. W. (1977). Biological theories of aging. In J. E. Birren & K. W. Schaie (Eds.), *Handbook of the psychology of aging* (pp. 103–115). New York: Van Nostrand Reinhold.

Shonk, S. M., & Cicchetti, D. (2001). Maltreatment, competency deficits, and risk for academic and behavioral maladjustment. *Developmental Psychology, 37*, 3–17.

Shonkoff, J., & Phillips, D. (Eds.). (2001). *Neurons to neighborhoods: The science of early childhood development.* Washington, DC: National Academy Press.

Shuey, K., & Hardy, M. A. (2003). Assistance to aging parents and parents-in-law: Does lineage affect family allocation decisions? *Journal of Marriage and Family, 65*, 418–431.

Shulman, S., Elicker, J., & Sroufe, A. (1994). Stages of friendship growth in preadolescence as related to attachment history. *Journal of Social and Personal Relationships, 11*, 341–361.

Shulman, S., & Kipnis, O. (2001). Adolescent romantic relationships: A look from the future. *Journal of Adolescence, 24*, 337–351.

Shumaker, S. A., Legault, C., Thal, L., Wallace, R. B., Ockene, J. K., & Hendrix, S. L. (2003). Estrogen plus progestin and the incidence of dementia and mild cognitive impairment in postmenopausal women: The Women's Health Initiative Memory Study: A randomized controlled trial. *Journal of the*

American Medical Association, 289, 2651–2662.

Shumow, L. (1998). Contributions of parent education to adult development. In C. M. Smith & T. Pourchot (Eds.), *Adult learning and development: Perspectives from educational psychology* (pp. 239–255). Mahwah, NJ: Erlbaum.

Shure, M. B. (2001). I Can Problem Solve (ICPS): An interpersonal cognitive problem solving program for children. *Residential Treatment for Children and Youth, 18,* 3–14.

Shweder, R. A. (1996). True ethnography: The lore, the law, and the lure. In R. Jessor, A. Colby, & R. A. Shweder (Eds.), *Ethnography and human development* (pp. 15–52). Chicago: University of Chicago Press.

Sidebotham, P., Heron, J., & the ALSPAC Study Team. (2003). Child maltreatment in the "children of the nineties:" The role of the child. *Child Abuse and Neglect, 27,* 337–352.

Siegler, I., Costa, P. T., Brummett, B. H., Helms, M. J., Barefoot, J. C., Williams, R. B., & Dahlstrom W. G. (2003). Patterns of change in hostility from college to midlife in the UNC Alumni Heart Study predict high-risk status. *Psychosomatic Medicine, 65,* 738–745.

Siegler, R. S. (1996). *Emerging minds: The process of change in children's thinking.* New York: Oxford University Press.

Siegler, R. S. (1998). *Children's thinking* (3rd ed.). Upper Saddle River, NJ: Prentice-Hall.

Siervogel, R. M., Maynard, L. M., Wisemandle, W. A., Roche, A. F., Guo, S. S., Chumlea, W. C., & Towne, B. (2000). Annual changes in total body fat and fat-free mass in children from 8 to 18 years in relation to changes in body mass index: The Fels Longitudinal Study. *Annals of the New York Academy of Sciences, 904,* 420–423.

Sigman, M. (1995). Nutrition and child development: More food for thought. *Current Directions in Psychological Science, 4,* 52–55.

Sigman, M. (1999). Developmental deficits in children with Down syndrome. In H. Tager-Flusberg (Ed.), *Neurodevelopmental disorders: Developmental cognitive neuroscience* (pp. 179–195). Cambridge, MA: MIT Press.

Sigman, M., Cohen, S. E., & Beckwith, L. (1997). Why does infant attention predict adolescent intelligence? *Infant Behavior and Development, 20,* 133–140.

Silberg, J., Rutter, M., D'Onofrio, B., & Eaves, L. (2003). Genetic and environmental risk factors in adolescent substance use. *Journal of Child Psychology and Psychiatry*

and Allied Disciplines, 44, 664–676.

Silk, J. S., Morris, A. S., Kanaya, T., & Steinberg, L. (2003). Psychological control and autonomy granting: Opposite ends of a continuum or distinct constructs? *Journal of Research on Adolescence, 13,* 113–128.

Silva, I. dos Santos, De Stavola, B. L., Hardy, R. J., Kuh, D. J., McCormack, V. A., & Wadsworth, M. E. J. (2004). Is the association of birth weight with premenopausal breast cancer risk mediated through childhood growth? *British Journal of Cancer, 91,* 519–524.

Silvén, M. (2001). Attention in very young infants predicts learning of first words. *Infant Behavior and Development, 24,* 229–237.

Silver, M. H., Jilinskaia, E., & Perls, T. T. (2001). Cognitive functional status of age-confirmed centenarians in a population-based study. *Journal of Gerontology, 56B,* P134–P140.

Silver, M. H., & Perls, T. T. (2000). Is dementia the price of a long life? An optimistic report from centenarians. *Journal of Geriatric Psychiatry, 33,* 71–79.

Silverberg, S. B. (1996). Parents' well-being at their children's transition to adolescence. In C. D. Ryff & M. M. Seltzer (Eds.), *The parental experience in midlife* (pp. 215–254). Chicago: University of Chicago Press.

Silverman, B. E., Goodine, W. M., Adouceur, M. G., & Quinn, J. (2003). Learning needs of nurses working in Canada's First Nations communities. *Journal of Continuing Education in Nursing, 32,* 38–45.

Silverman, E., Range, L., & Overholser, J. (1994). Bereavement from suicide as compared to other forms of bereavement. *Omega, 30,* 41–51.

Silverman, P. R. (2004). Dying and bereavement in historical perspective. In J. Berzoff & P. R. Silverman (Eds.), *Living with dying: A handbook for end-of-life healthcare practitioners* (pp. 128–149). New York: Columbia University Press.

Silverman, P. R., & Nickman, S. L. (1996). Children's construction of their dead parents. In D. Klass, P. R. Silverman, & S. L. Nickman (Ed.), *Continuing bonds: New understandings of grief* (pp. 73–86). Washington, DC: Taylor & Francis.

Silverman, P. R., & Worden, J. M. (1992). Children's reactions in the early months after the death of a parent. *American Journal of Orthopsychiatry, 62,* 93–104.

Silverman, W. K., La Greca, A. M., & Wasserstein, S. (1995). What do children worry about? Worries

and their relation to anxiety. *Child Development, 66,* 671–686.

Silverstein, M., & Bengtson, V. L. (1991). Do close parent–child relations reduce the mortality risk of older parents? *Journal of Health and Social Behavior, 32,* 382–395.

Silverstein, M., Conroy, S., Wang, H., Giarrusso, R., & Bengtson, V. L. (2002). Reciprocity in parent–child relations over the adult life course. *Journal of Gerontology, 57B,* S3–S13.

Silverstein, M., & Long, J. D. (1998). Trajectories of grandparents' perceived solidarity with adult grandchildren: A growth curve analysis over 23 years. *Journal of Marriage and the Family, 60,* 912–923.

Silverstein, M., & Marenco, A. (2001). How Americans enact the grandparent role across the family life course. *Journal of Family Issues, 22,* 493–522.

Silvi, J. (2004). Deaths from motor vehicle traffic accidents in selected countries of the Americas, 1985–2001. *Epidemiological Bulletin, 25,* 2–5.

Sim, T. N. (2000). Adolescent psychosocial competence: The importance and role of regard for parents. *Journal of Research on Adolescence, 10,* 49–64.

Sim, T. N., & Koh, S. F. (2003). A domain conceptualization of adolescent susceptibility to peer pressure. *Journal of Research on Adolescence, 13,* 57–80.

Simcock, G., & Hayne, H. (2002). Breaking the barrier? Children fail to translate their preverbal memories into language. *Psychological Science, 13,* 225–231.

Simcock, G., & Hayne, H. (2003). Age-related changes in verbal and nonverbal memory during early childhood. *Developmental Psychology, 39,* 805–814.

Simoneau, M., & Markovits, H. (2003). Reasoning with premises that are not empirically true: Evidence for the role of inhibition and retrieval. *Developmental Psychology, 39,* 964–975.

Simons, J. S., Dodson, C. S., Bell, D., & Schachter, D. L. (2004). Specific- and partial-source memory: Effects of aging. *Psychology and Aging, 19,* 689–694.

Simons, R. L., & Chao, W. (1996). Conduct problems. In R. L. Simons & Associates (Eds.), *Understanding differences between divorced and intact families* (pp. 125–143). Thousand Oaks, CA: Sage.

Simons, R. L., Whitbeck, L. B., Conger, R. D., & Wu, C.-I. (1991). Intergenerational transmission of harsh parenting. *Developmental Psychology, 27,* 159–171.

Simons-Morton, B. G., & Haynie, D. L. (2003). Growing up drug

free: A developmental challenge. In M. H. Bornstein, L. Davidson, C. L. M. Keyes, K. A. Moore, & the Center for Child Well-Being (Eds.), *Well-being: Positive development across the life course* (pp. 109–122). Mahwah, NJ: Erlbaum.

Simonton, D. K. (1991). Creative productivity through the adult years. *Generations, 15*(2), 13–16.

Simonton, D. K. (2000). Creativity: Cognitive, personal, developmental, and social aspects. *American Psychologist, 55,* 151–158.

Simpson, J. A., & Harris, B. A. (1994). Interpersonal attraction. In A. L. Weber & J. H. Harvey (Eds.), *Perspectives on close relationships* (pp. 45–66). Boston: Allyn and Bacon.

Simpson, J. A., Rholes, W. S., Campbell, L., Tran, S., & Wilson, C. L. (2003). Adult attachment, the transition to parenthood, and depressive symptoms. *Journal of Personality and Social Psychology, 84,* 1172–1187.

Simpson, J. L., de la Cruz, F., Swerdloff, R. S., Samango-Sprouse, C., Skakkebaek, N. E., & Graham, J. M., Jr. (2003). Klinefelter syndrome: Expanding the phenotype and identifying new research directions. *Genetic Medicine, 5,* 460–468.

Simpson, J. M. (2001). Infant stress and sleep deprivation as an aetiological basis for the sudden infant death syndrome. *Early Human Development, 61,* 1–43.

Simpson, R. (2004). Masculinity at work: The experiences of men in female dominated occupations. *Work, Employment and Society, 18,* 349–368.

Simpson, R. (2005). Men in non-traditional occupations: Career entry, career orientation and experience of role strain. *Gender, Work and Organization, 12,* 363–380.

Singer, D. G., & Singer, J. L. (2005). *Imagination and play in the electronic age.* Cambridge, MA: Harvard University Press.

Singer, L. T., Arendt, R., Minnes, S., Farkas, K., Salvator, A., Kirchner, H. L., & Kliegman, R. (2002). Cognitive and motor outcomes of cocaine-exposed infants. *Journal of the American Medical Association, 287,* 1952–1960.

Singer, L. T., Minnes, S., Short, E., Arendt, R., Farkas, K., Lewis, B., & Klein, N. (2004). Cognitive outcomes of preschool children with prenatal cocaine exposure. *Journal of the American Medical Association, 291,* 2448–2456.

Singer, Y., Bachner, Y. G., & Shvartzman, P., & Carmel, S. (2005). Home death—the caregivers' experiences. *Journal of Pain and Symptom Management, 30,* 70–74.

Singh, S., & Darroch, J. E. (2000). Adolescent pregnancy and childbearing: Levels and trends in developed countries. *Family Planning Perspectives, 32,* 14–23.

Singleton, J. L., & Newport, E. L. (2004). When learners surpass their models: The acquisition of American Sign Language from inconsistent input. *Cognitive Psychology, 49,* 370–407.

Sinkkonen, J., Anttila, R., & Siimes, M. A. (1998). Pubertal maturation and changes in self-image in early adolescent Finnish boys. *Journal of Youth and Adolescence, 27,* 209–218.

Sinnott, J. D. (1989). A model for solution of ill-structured problems: Implications for everyday and abstract problem solving. In J. D. Sinnott (Ed.), *Everyday problem solving: Theory and applications* (pp. 72–99). New York: Praeger.

Sinnott, J. D. (1998). *The development of logic in adulthood: Postformal thought and its applications.* New York: Plenum.

Sinnott, J. D. (2003). Postformal thought and adult development: Living in balance. In J. Demick & C. Andreoletti (Eds.), *Handbook of adult development* (pp. 221–238). New York: Kluwer Academic.

Skinner, B. F. (1957). *Verbal behavior.* New York: Appleton-Century-Crofts.

Skinner, E. A., Zimmer-Gembeck, M. J., & Connell, J. P. (1998). Individual differences and the development of perceived control. *Monographs of the Society for Research in Child Development, 63*(2–3, Serial No. 254).

Skoe, E. S. A. (1998). The ethic of care: Issues in moral development. In E. E. A. Skoe & A. L. von der Lippe (Eds.), *Personality development in adolescence* (pp. 143–171). London: Routledge.

Slade, A., Belsky, J., Aber, J. L., & Phelps, J. L. (1999). Mothers' representations of their relationships with their toddlers: Links to adult attachment and observed mothering. *Developmental Psychology, 35,* 611–619.

Slater, A. (2001). Visual perception. In G. Bremner & A. Fogel (Eds.), *Blackwell handbook of infant development* (pp. 5–34). Malden, MA: Blackwell.

Slater, A., Bremner, G., Johnson, S. P., Sherwood, P., Hayes, R., & Brown, E. (2000). Newborn infants' preference for attractive faces: The role of internal and external facial features. *Infancy, 1,* 265–274.

Slater, A., Brown, E., Mattock, A., & Bornstein, M. H. (1996). Continuity and change in habituation in the first 4 months from birth. *Journal of Reproductive and Infant Psychology, 14,* 187–194.

Slater, A., & Quinn, P. C. (2001). Face recognition in the newborn infant. *Infant and Child Development, 10,* 21–24.

Slaughter, V., Jaakkola, R., & Carey, S. (1999). Constructing a coherent theory: Children's biological understanding of life and death. In M. Siegel & C. C. Petersen (Eds.), *Children's understanding of biology and health* (pp. 71–96). Cambridge, UK: Cambridge University Press.

Slaughter, V., & Lyons, M. (2003). Learning about life and death in early childhood. *Cognitive Psychology, 46,* 1–30.

Slavin, R. E., & Cooper, R. (1999). Improving intergroup relations: Lessons learned from cooperative learning programs. *Journal of Social Issues, 55,* 647–633.

Sleet, D. A., & Mercy, J. A. (2003). Promotion of safety, security, and well-being. In M. H. Bornstein, L. Davidson, C. M. M. Keyes, K. A. Moore, & the Center for Child Well-Being (Eds.), *Well-being: Positive development across the life course* (pp. 81–97). Mahwah, NJ: Erlbaum.

Slicker, E. K., & Thornberry, I. (2002). Older adolescent well-being and authoritative parenting. *Adolescent and Family Health, 3,* 9–19.

Slobin, D. I. (1985). Crosslinguistic evidence for the language-making capacity. In D. I. Slobin (Ed.), *The crosslinguistic study of language acquisition: Vol. 2. Theoretical issues.* Hillsdale, NJ: Erlbaum.

Slobin, D. I. (1997). *The crosslinguistic study of language acquisition: Vol. 5. Expanding the contexts.* Mahwah, NJ: Erlbaum.

Slusher, M. P., Mayer, C. J., & Dunkle, R. E. (1996). Gays and lesbians older and wiser (GLOW): A support group for older gay people. *Gerontologist, 36,* 118–123.

Slutske, W. S., Hunt-Carter, E. E., Nabors-Oberg, R. E., Sher, K. J., Bucholz, K. K., & Madden, P. A. F. (2004). Do college students drink more than their non-college-attending peers? Evidence from a population-based longitudinal female twin study. *Journal of Abnormal Psychology, 113,* 530–540.

Small, B. J., & Bäckman, L. (1997). Cognitive correlates of mortality: Evidence from a population-based sample of very old adults. *Psychology and Aging, 12,* 309–313.

Small, B. J., Dixon, R. A., Hultsch, D. F., & Hertzog, C. (1999). Longitudinal changes in quantitative and qualitative indicators of word and story recall in young–old and old–old adults. *Journal of Gerontology, 54B,* P107–P115.

Small, B. J., Fratiglioni, L., von Strauss, E., & Bäckman, L. (2003). Terminal decline and cognitive performance in very old age: Does cause of death matter? *Psychology and Aging, 18,* 193–202.

Small, M. (1998). *Our babies, ourselves.* New York: Anchor.

Smetana, J. G. (1995). Morality in context: Abstractions, ambiguities, and applications. In R. Vasta (Ed.), *Annals of child development* (Vol. 10, p. 83–130). London: Jessica Kingsley.

Smetana, J. G. (2002). Culture, autonomy, and personal jurisdiction in adolescent–parent relationships. In R. V. Kail & H. W. Reese (Eds.), *Advances in child development and behavior* (Vol. 29, pp. 51–87). San Diego, CA: Academic Press.

Smetana, J. G., Metzger, A., & Campione-Barr, N. (2004). African-American late adolescents' relationships with parents: Developmental transitions and longitudinal patterns. *Child Development, 75,* 932–947.

Smith, A. E., Jussim, L., Eccles, J., VanNoy, M., Madon, S., & Palumbo, P. (1998). Self-fulfilling prophecies, perceptual biases, and accuracy at the individual and group levels. *Journal of Experimental Social Psychology, 34,* 530–561.

Smith, C., Perou, R., & Lesesne, C. (2002). Parent education. M. H. Bornstein (Ed.), *Handbook of parenting.* (Vol. 4, pp. 389–410). Mahwah, NJ: Erlbaum.

Smith, D. B., & Moen, P. (1998). Spousal influence on retirement: His, her, and their perceptions. *Journal of Marriage and the Family, 60,* 734–744.

Smith, D. B., & Moen, P. (2004). Retirement satisfaction for retirees and their spouses: Do gender and the retirement decision-making process matter? *Journal of Family Issues, 25,* 262–285.

Smith, D. C. (1993). The terminally ill patient's right to be in denial. *Omega, 27,* 115–121.

Smith, E. P., Walker, K., Fields, L., Brookins, C. C., & Seay, R. C. (1999). Ethnic identity and its relationship to self-esteem, perceived efficacy, and prosocial attitudes in early adolescence. *Journal of Adolescence, 22,* 867–880.

Smith, G. C., Kohn, S. J., Savage-Stevens, S. E., Finch, J. J., Ingate, R., & Lim, Y. (2000). The effects of interpersonal and personal agency on perceived control and psychological well-being in adulthood. *Gerontologist, 40,* 458–468.

Smith, J., & Baltes, P. B. (1999). Lifespan perspectives on development. In M. H. Bornstein & M. E. Lamb (Eds.), *Developmental psychology: An advanced textbook* (4th ed., pp. 275–311). Mahwah, NJ: Erlbaum.

Smith, J., Duncan, G. J., & Lee, K. (2003). The black–white test score gap in young children: Contributions of test and family characteristics. *Applied Developmental Science, 7,* 239–252.

Smith, J., & Freund, A. M. (2002). The dynamics of possible selves in old age. *Journal of Gerontology, 57B,* P492–P500.

Smith, J. V., Heilbronn, L. K., & Ravussin, E. (2004). Energy restriction and aging. *Current Opinion in Clinical Nutrition and Metabolic Care, 7,* 615–622.

Smith, K. E., Landry, S. H., Swank, P. R., Baldwin, C. D., Denson, S. E., & Wildin, S. (1996). The relation of medical risk and maternal stimulation with preterm infants' development of cognitive, language and daily living skills. *Journal of Child Psychology and Psychiatry, 37,* 855–864.

Smith, L. B., Thelen, E., Titzer, R., & McLin, D. (1999). Knowing in the context of acting: The task dynamics of the A-not-B error. *Psychological Review, 106,* 235–260.

Smith, M. (Ed.). (2002). *Sex without consent.* New York: New York University Press.

Smith, N., Young, A., & Lee, C. (2004). Optimism, health-related hardiness and well-being among older Australian women. *Journal of Health Psychology, 9,* 741–752.

Smith, P., Perrin, S., Yule, W., & Rabe-Hesketh, S. (2001). War exposure and maternal reactions in the psychological adjustment of children from Bosnia-Hercegovina. *Journal of Child Psychology and Psychiatry and Allied Disciplines, 42,* 395–404.

Smith, P. B., Buzi, R. S., & Weinman, M. L. (2002). Programs for young fathers: Essential components and evaluation issues. *North American Journal of Psychology, 4,* 81–92.

Smith, P. K., Ananiadou, K., & Cowie, H. (2003). Interventions to reduce school bullying. *Canadian Journal of Psychiatry, 48,* 591–599.

Smith, P. K., & Drew, L. M. (2002). Grandparenthood. In M. H. Bornstein (Ed.), *Handbook of parenting, Vol. 3* (2nd ed., pp. 141–172). Mahwah, NJ: Erlbaum.

Smock, P. J., & Gupta, S. (2002). *Cohabitation in contemporary North America.* In A. Booth & A. C. Crouter (Eds.), *Just living together* (pp. 53–84). Mahwah, NJ: Erlbaum.

Smylie, J. (2001). A guide for health professionals working with Aboriginal peoples. *Journal SOGC, 100,* 2–15.

Snarey, J. (1995). In a communitarian voice: The sociological expansion of Kohlbergian theory, research, and practice. In W. M. Kurtines & J. L. Gewirtz (Eds.), *Moral development: An introduction* (pp. 109–134). Boston: Allyn and Bacon.

Snarey, J., Son, L., Kuehne, V. S., Hauser, S., & Vaillant, G. (1987). The role of parenting in men's psychosocial development: A longitudinal study of early adulthood infertility and midlife generativity. *Developmental Psychology, 23,* 593–603.

Sneed, J. R., & Whitbourne, S. K. (2001). Identity processing styles and the need for self-esteem in middle-aged and older adults. *International Journal of Aging and Human Development, 52,* 311–321.

Sneed, J. R., & Whitbourne, S. K. (2003). Identity processing and self-consciousness in middle and later adulthood. *Journal of Gerontology, 58B,* P313–P319.

Snidman, N., Kagan, J., Riordan, L., & Shannon, D. C. (1995). Cardiac function and behavioral reactivity. *Psychophysiology, 32,* 199–207.

Snyder, J., Brooker, M., Patrick, M. R., Snyder, A., Schrepferman, L., & Stoolmiller, M. (2003). Observed peer victimization during early elementary school: Continuity, growth, and relation to risk for child antisocial and depressive behavior. *Child Development, 74,* 1881–1898.

Social Security and Medicare Board of Trustees. (2005). *Financial status of Social Security and Medicare.* Retrieved from www.ssa.gov/OACT/TRSUM/trsummary.html

Society for Research in Child Development (1993). Ethical standards for research with children. In *Directory of Members* (pp. 337–339). Ann Arbor, MI: Author.

Soderstrom, M., Dolbier, C., Leiferman, J., & Steinhardt, M. (2000). The relationship of hardiness, coping strategies, and perceived stress to symptoms of illness. *Journal of Behavioral Medicine, 23,* 311–328.

Soderstrom, M., Seidl, A., Nelson, D. G. K., & Jusczyk, P. W. (2003). The prosodic bootstrapping of phrases: Evidence from prelinguistic infants. *Journal of Memory and Language, 49,* 249–267.

SOGC (Society of Obstetricians and Gynaecologists of Canada). (2005). Multiple births. Retrieved from www.sogc.org/multiple/facts–e.shtml

Sokol, R. J., Delaney-Black, V., & Nordstrom, B. (2003). Fetal alcohol spectrum disorder. *Journal of the American Medical Association, 290,* 2996–2999.

Solomon, G. B., & Bredemeier, B. J. L. (1999). Children's moral conceptions of gender stratification in sport. *International Journal of Sport Psychology, 30,* 350–368.

Solomon, J. C., & Marx, J. (1995). "To grandmother's house we go": Health and school adjustment of children raised solely by grandparents. *Gerontologist, 35,* 386–394.

Somary, K., & Stricker, G. (1998). Becoming a grandparent: A longitudinal study of expectations and early experiences as a function of sex and lineage. *Gerontologist, 38,* 53–61.

Sondergaard, C., Henriksen, T. B., Obel, C., & Wisborg, K. (2002). Smoking during pregnancy and infantile colic. *Journal of the American Academy of Child and Adolescent Psychiatry, 41,* 147.

Sophian, C. (1995). Representation and reasoning in early numerical development: Counting, conservation, and comparisons between sets. *Child Development, 66,* 559–577.

Sörensen, S., & Pinquart, M. (2005). Racial and ethnic differences in the relationship of caregiving stressors, resources, and sociodemographic variables to caregiver depression and perceived physical health. *Aging and Mental Health, 9,* 482–495.

Sørensen, T. I., Holst, C., & Stunkard, A. J. (1998). Adoption study of environmental modifications of the genetic influences on obesity. *International Journal of Obesity and Related Metabolic Disorders, 22,* 73–81.

Sosa, R., Kennell, J., Klaus, M., Robertson, S., & Urrutia, J. (1980). The effect of a supportive companion on perinatal problems, length of labor, and mother–infant interaction. *New England Journal of Medicine, 303,* 597–600.

Sowell, E. R., Trauner, D. A., Gamst, A., & Jernigan, T. (2002). Development of cortical and subcortical brain structures in childhood and adolescence: A structural MRI study. *Developmental Medicine and Child Neurology, 44,* 4–16.

Spear, L. P. (2003). Neurodevelopment during adolescence. In D. Cicchetti & E. Walker (Eds.), *Neurodevelopmental mechanisms in psychopathology* (pp. 62–83). New York: Cambridge University Press.

Speece, M. W., & Brent, S. B. (1996). The development of children's understanding of death. In C. A. Corr & D. M. Corr (Eds.), *Handbook of childhood death and bereavement* (pp. 29–50). New York: Springer.

Speicher, B. (1994). Family patterns of moral judgment during adolescence and early adulthood. *Developmental Psychology, 30,* 624–632.

Spelke, E. (2000). Core knowledge. *American Psychologist, 55,* 1233–1242.

Spelke, E. S., & Newport, E. L. (1998). Nativism, empiricism, and the development of knowledge. In R. M. Lerner (Ed.), *Handbook of child psychology: Vol. 1. Theoretical models of human development* (5th ed., pp. 199–254). New York: Wiley.

Spence, M. J., & DeCasper, A. J. (1987). Prenatal experience with low-frequency maternal voice sounds influences neonatal perception of maternal voice samples. *Infant Behavior and Development, 10,* 133–142.

Spencer, J. P., & Schöner, G. (2003). Bridging the representational gap in the dynamic systems approach to development. *Developmental Science, 6,* 392–412.

Spencer, J. P., Verejiken, B., Diedrich, F. J., & Thelen, E. (2000). Posture and the emergence of manual skills. *Developmental Science, 3,* 216–233.

Spencer, P. E. (2000). Looking without listening: Is audition a prerequisite for normal development of visual attention in infancy? *Journal of Deaf Studies and Education, 5,* 291–302.

Spencer, P. E., & Lederberg, A. (1997). Different modes, different models: Communication and language of young deaf children and their mothers. In L. B. Adamson & M. Romski (Eds.), *Communication and language acquisition: Discoveries from atypical development* (pp. 203–230). Baltimore, MD: Paul H. Brookes.

Spencer, P. E., & Meadow-Orlans, K. P. (1996). Play, language, and maternal responsiveness: A longitudinal study of deaf and hearing infants. *Child Development, 67,* 3176–3191.

Spera, C. (2005). A review of the relationship among parenting practices, parenting styles, and adolescent school achievement. *Educational Psychology Review, 17,* 125–146.

Spere, K. A., Schmidt, L. A., Theall-Honey, L. A., & Martin-Chang, S. (2004). Expressive and receptive language skills of temperamentally shy preschoolers. *Infant and Child Development, 13,* 123–133.

Spira, A. (1992). *Les comportements sexuels en France.* Paris: La documentation Française.

Spirito, A., Valeri, S., Boergers, J., & Donaldson, D. (2003). Predictors of continued suicidal behavior in adolescents following a suicide attempt. *Journal of Clinical Child and Adolescent Psychology, 32,* 284–289.

Spitz, R. A. (1946). Anaclitic depression. *Psychoanalytic Study of the Child, 2,* 313–342.

Spitze, G., & Gallant, M. P. (2004). "The bitter with the sweet": Older adults' strategies for handling ambivalence in relations with their adult children. *Research on Aging, 26,* 387–412.

Spock, B., & Needlman, R. (2004). *Dr. Spock's baby and child care* (8th ed.). New York: Pocket.

Spokane, A. R., & Cruza-Guet, M. C. (2005). Holland's theory of vocational personalities in work environments. In S. D. Brown & R. W. Lent (Eds.), *Career development and counseling* (pp. 24–41). Hoboken, NJ: Wiley.

Sprecher, S. (1999). "I love you more today than yesterday": Romantic partners' perceptions of changes in love and related affect over time. *Journal of Personality and Social Psychology, 76,* 46–53.

Springer, C. A., & Lease, S. H. (2000). The impact of multiple AIDS-related bereavement in the gay male population. *Journal of Counseling and Development, 78,* 297–304.

Spruijt-Metz, D., Lindquist, C. H., Birch, L. L., Fisher, J. O., & Goran, M. I. (2002). Relation between mothers' child-feeding practices and children's adiposity. *American Journal of Clinical Nutrition, 75,* 581–586.

Sridhar, D., & Vaughn, S. (2001). Social functioning of students with learning disabilities. In D. P. Hallahan & B. K. Keogh (Eds.), *Research and global perspectives in learning disabilities* (pp. 65–91). Mahwah, NJ: Erlbaum.

Srivastava, S., John, O. P., Gosling, S. D., & Potter, J. (2003). Development of personality in early and middle adulthood: Set like plaster or persistent change? *Journal of Personality and Social Psychology, 84,* 1041–1053.

Sroufe, L. A., Egeland, B., & Kreutzer, T. (1990). The fate of early experience following developmental change: Longitudinal approaches to individual adaptation. *Child Development, 61,* 1363–1373.

Sroufe, L. A., & Waters, E. (1976). The ontogenesis of smiling and laughter: A perspective on the organization of development in infancy. *Psychological Review, 83,* 173–189.

Sroufe, L. A., & Wunsch, J. P. (1972). The development of laughter in the first year of life. *Child Development, 43,* 1324–1344.

St James-Roberts, I., Goodwin, J., Peter, B., Adams, D., & Hunt, S. (2003). Individual differences in responsivity to a neurobehavioural examination predict crying patterns of 1-week-old infants at home. *Developmental Medicine and Child Neurology, 45,* 400–407.

Stackert, R. A., & Bursik, K. (2003). Why am I unsatisfied? Adult attachment style, gendered irrational relationship beliefs, and young adult romantic relationship satisfaction. *Personality and Individual Differences, 34,* 1419–1429.

Staff, J., & Uggen, C. (2003). The fruits of good work: Early work experiences and adolescent deviance. *Journal of Research in Crime and Delinquency, 40,* 263–290.

Stamler, J., Stamler, R., Neaton, J. D., Wentworth, D., Daviglus, M. L., Garside, D., Dyer, A. R., Liu, K. A., & Greenland, P. (1999). Low risk-factor profile and long-term cardiovascular and noncardiovascular mortality and life expectancy: Findings for five large cohorts of young adult and middle-aged men and women. *Journal of the American Medical Association, 282,* 2012–2018.

Stams, G. J. M., Juffer, F., & van IJzendoorn, M. H. (2002). Maternal sensitivity, infant attachment, and temperament in early childhood predict adjustment in middle childhood: The case of adopted children and their biologically unrelated parents. *Developmental Psychology, 38,* 806–821.

Standley, J. M. (1998). The effect of music and multimodal stimulation on responses of premature infants in neonatal intensive care. *Pediatric Nursing, 24,* 532–538.

Stanley, C., Murray, L., & Stein, A. (2004). The effect of postnatal depression on mother–infant interaction, infant response to the still-face perturbation, and performance on an instrumental learning task. *Development and Psychopathology, 16,* 1–18.

Stanovich, K. E. (2004). *How to think straight about psychology* (7th ed.). Boston: Allyn and Bacon.

Starr, R. J. (1999). Music therapy in hospice care. *American Journal of Hospice and Palliative Care, 16,* 739–742.

Statistics Canada. (1999). Education indicators in Canada: Equity. Retrieved from www.cmec.ca/stats/pceip/1999old/indicatorsite.n4/english/pages/page26e.html

Statistics Canada. (2001a). *Education in Canada.* Ottawa: Statistics Canada.

Statistics Canada. (2001b). *Families and household living arrangements: Highlight tables 2001.* Ottawa: Census Operations Division.

Statistics Canada. (2002a). *Changing conjugal life in Canada.* Ottawa: Author.

Statistics Canada. (2002b, December 2). Divorces. *The Daily.* Retrieved from www.statcan.ca

Statistics Canada. (2002c). *Labour force historical review.* Catalogue No. 71F0004. Ottawa: Author.

Statistics Canada. (2002d). *Mortality, summary list of causes—shelf tables.* Ottawa: Health Statistics Division.

Statistics Canada. (2002e). *Number of income recipients and their average income in constant dollars by sex and age groups, for Canada, provinces and territories.* Retrieved from www.statcan.ca/english/census96/may12/tl.htm

Statistics Canada. (2002f). Population 15 years and over by hours spent on unpaid housework. Retrieved from http://www.statcan.ca/english/Pgdb/famil56a.htm

Statistics Canada. (2002g). *Statistical report on the health of Canadians.* Retrieved from www.statcan.ca:80/english/freepub/82-570-XIE/partb.htm

Statistics Canada. (2002h). 2001 Census. Retrieved from www12.statcan.ca/English/census01/products/analytic/companion/fam/provs.cfm

Statistics Canada. (2003a). *Age groups, number of grandparents, and sex for grandchildren living with grandparents with no parent present, 2001.* Retrieved from www12.statcan.ca/English/census01

Statistics Canada. (2003b). Aging in rural communities and small towns. *Expression, 9*(1). Retrieved from www.hc-sc.gc.ca/seniors-aines/pubs/expression/9-1/exp–9-1-e.htm

Statistics Canada. (2003c). *The gap in achievement between boys and girls.* Retrieved from www.statcan.ca/english/freepub/81-004-XIE/200410/mafe.htm

Statistics Canada. (2003d). *National Longitudinal Survey of Children and Youth: Challenges of late adolescence.* Retrieved from www.statcan.ca/Daily/English/030616/d030616a.htm

Statistics Canada. (2003e). Population 15 years and over by marital status, showing selected age groups and sex, for Canada, provinces, and territories. Retrieved from www.statcan.ca/english/census01/oct14/mar1.htm

Statistics Canada. (2003f). Who goes to postsecondary education and when: Pathways chosen by 20-year-olds. Retrieved from www.statcan.ca/english/IPS/Data/81-595-MIE2003006.htm

Statistics Canada. (2003g). Women in Canada: Work chapter updates. Retrieved from www.statcan.ca/cgi-bin/downpub/freepub.cgi

Statistics Canada. (2004a). Canadian vital statistics, births. Retrieved from www.statcan.ca/english/freepub/84F0210XIE/free.htm

Statistics Canada. (2004b, July 28). Crime statistics increasing. *The Daily.* Retrieved from www.statcan.ca/Daily/English/040728/d040728a.htm

Statistics Canada. (2004c, July 8). Household Internet use survey. *The Daily.* Retrieved from www.statcan.ca/Daily/English/040708/d040708a.htm

Statistics Canada. (2004d, June 16). Youth in Transition Survey: Education and labour market pathways of young adults. *The Daily.* Retrieved from www.statcan.ca/Daily/English/040616b.htm

Statistics Canada. (2005a, February 7). Child care. *The Daily.* Retrieved from www.statcan.ca/Daily/English/050207/d050207b.htm

Statistics Canada. (2005b) Divorces. Retrieved from www.statcan.ca

Statistics Canada. (2005c). *Family violence in Canada: A statistical profile.* Ottawa: National Clearinghouse on Family Violence.

Statistics Canada. (2005d). Infant mortality rates. Retrieved from www.statcan.ca/english/Pgdb/health21.htm

Statistics Canada. (2005e). Population. Retrieved from www.statcan.ca

Statistics Canada. (2005f). Statistics Canada data bank and analysis of television viewing in Canada. Retrieved from www.ctatcan.ca/english/freepub/87-008-GIE/sect/tvmain.htm

Statistics Canada. (2005g, October 11). University enrolment. *The Daily.* Retrieved from www.statcan.ca/Daily/English/051011/d051011b.htm

Stattin, H., & Kerr, M. (2000). Parental monitoring: A reinterpretation. *Child Development, 71,* 1072–1085.

Stattin, H., & Magnusson, D. (1990). *Pubertal maturation in female development.* Hillsdale, NJ: Erlbaum.

Stattin, H., & Magnusson, D. (1996). Leaving home at an early age among females. In J. A. Graber & J. S. Dubas (Eds.), *New directions for child development* (No. 71, pp. 53–69). San Francisco: Jossey-Bass.

Staudinger, L. (1996). Wisdom and the social-interactive foundation of the mind. In P. B. Baltes & U. M. Staudinger (Eds.), *Interactive minds: Life-span perspectives on the social foundation of cognition* (pp. 276–315). New York: Cambridge University Press.

Staudinger, U. M., Dörner, J., & Mickler, C. (2005). Wisdom and personality. In R. J. Sternberg & J. Jordan (Eds.), *A handbook of wisdom: Psychological perspectives* (pp 191–219). New York: Cambridge University Press.

Staudinger, U. M., Fleeson, W., & Baltes, P. B. (1999). Predictors of subjective physical health and global well-being: Similarities and differences between the United States and Germany. *Journal of Personality and Social Psychology, 76,* 305–319.

Staudinger, U. M., & Lindenberger, U. (2003). Understanding human development takes a metatheory and multiple disciplines. In U. M. Staudinger & U. Lindenberger (Eds.), *Understanding human development: Dialogues with life-span psychology* (pp. 1–13). Norwell, MA: Kluwer.

Staudinger, U. M., Smith, J., & Baltes, P. B. (1992). Wisdom-related knowledge in a life-review task: Age differences and the role of professional specialization. *Psychology and Aging, 7,* 271–281.

Steele, C. M. (1997). A threat in the air: How stereotypes shape intellectual identity and performance. *American Psychologist, 52,* 613–629.

Steele, S., Joseph, R. M., & Tager-Flusberg, H. (2003). Developmental change in theory of mind abilities in children with autism. *Journal of Autism and Developmental Disorders, 33,* 461–467.

Stehr-Green, P., Tull, P., Stellfeld, M., Mortenson, P. B., & Simpson, D. (2003). Autism and thimerosal-containing vaccines: Lack of consistent evidence for an association. *American Journal of Preventive Medicine, 25,* 101–106.

Stein, C. H., Wemmerus, V. A., Ward, M., Gaines, M. E., Freeberg, A. L., & Jewell, T. C. (1998). "Because they're my parents": An intergenerational study of felt obligation and parental caregiving. *Journal of Marriage and the Family, 60,* 611–622.

Stein, J. H., & Reiser, L. W. (1994). A study of white middle-class adolescent boys' responses to "semenarche" (the first ejaculation). *Journal of Youth and Adolescence, 23,* 373–384.

Stein, M. B., Lang, A. J., Laffaye, C., Satz, L. E., Lenox, R. J., & Dresselhaus, T. R. (2004). Relationship of sexual assault history to somatic symptoms and health anxiety in women. *General Hospital Psychiatry, 26,* 178–183.

Stein, N., & Levine, L. J. (1999). The early emergence of emotional understanding and appraisal: Implications for theories of development. In T. Dalgleish & M. J.

Power (Eds.), *Handbook of cognition and emotion* (pp. 383–408). Chichester, UK: Wiley.

Steinberg, L. D. (1986). Latchkey children and susceptibility to peer pressure: An ecological analysis. *Developmental Psychology, 22,* 433–439.

Steinberg, L. D. (2001). We know some things: Parent–adolescent relationships in retrospect and prospect. *Journal of Research on Adolescence, 11,* 1–19.

Steinberg, L. D., Darling, N. E., & Fletcher, A. C. (1995). Authoritative parenting and adolescent development: An ecological journey. In P. Moen, G. H. Elder, Jr., & K. Luscher (Eds.), *Examining lives in context* (pp. 423–466). Washington, DC: American Psychological Association.

Steinberg, L. D., & Morris, A. S. (2001). Adolescent development. *Annual Review of Psychology, 52,* 83–110.

Steinberg, L. D., & Silk, J. S. (2002). Parenting adolescents. In M. H. Bornstein (Ed.), *Handbook of parenting* (Vol. 1, pp. 103–134). Mahwah, NJ: Erlbaum.

Steinberg, L. D., & Silverberg, S. (1986). The vicissitudes of autonomy in early adolescence. *Child Development, 57,* 841–851.

Steinberg, S., & Bellavance, F. (1999). Characteristics and treatment of women with antenatal and postpartum depression. *International Journal of Psychiatry and Medicine, 29,* 209–233.

Steiner, J. E. (1979). Human facial expression in response to taste and smell stimulation. In H. W. Reese & L. P. Lipsitt (Eds.), *Advances in child development and behavior* (Vol. 13, pp. 257–295). New York: Academic Press.

Steiner, J. E., Glaser, D., Hawilo, M. E., & Berridge, D. C. (2001). Comparative expression of hedonic impact: Affective reactions to taste by human infants and other primates. *Neuroscience and Biobehavioral Review, 25,* 53–74.

Steinlein, O. K. (2004). Genes and mutations in human idiopathic epilepsy. *Brain Development, 26,* 213–218.

Stenberg, C. (2003). Effects of maternal inattentiveness on infant social referencing. *Infant and Child Development, 12,* 399–419.

Stenberg, C., & Campos, J. (1990). The development of anger expressions in infancy. In N. Stein, B. Leventhal, & T. Trabasso (Eds.), *Psychological and biological approaches to emotion* (pp. 247–282). Hillsdale, NJ: Erlbaum.

Stephens, M. A. P., & Franks, M. M. (1999). Parent care in the context of women's multiple roles. *Current*

Directions in Psychological Science, 8, 149–152.

Stephens, M. A. P., Townsend, A. L., Martire, L. M., & Druley, A. (2001). Balancing parent care with other roles: Interrole conflict of adult daughter caregivers. *Journal of Gerontology, 56B,* P24–P34.

Stern, M., & Karraker, K. H. (1989). Sex stereotyping of infants: A review of gender labeling studies. *Sex Roles, 20,* 501–522.

Sternberg, R. J. (1987). Liking versus loving: A comparative evaluation of theories. *Psychological Bulletin, 102,* 331–345.

Sternberg, R. J. (1988). Triangulating love. In R. J. Sternberg & M. L. Barnes (Eds.), *The psychology of love* (pp. 119–138). New Haven, CT: Yale University Press.

Sternberg, R. J. (1997). *Successful intelligence.* New York: Plume.

Sternberg, R. J. (1999). A triarchic approach to understanding and assessment of intelligence in multicultural populations. *Journal of School Psychology, 37,* 145–159.

Sternberg, R. J. (2000). *Cupid's arrow: The course of love through time.* Cambridge, UK: Cambridge University Press.

Sternberg, R. J. (2001). Why schools should teach for wisdom: The balance theory of wisdom in educational settings. *Educational Psychologist, 36,* 227–245.

Sternberg, R. J. (2002). Intelligence is not just inside the head: The theory of successful intelligence. In J. Aronson (Ed.), *Improving academic achievement* (pp. 227–244). San Diego, CA: Academic Press.

Sternberg, R. J. (2003a). A broad view of intelligence: The theory of successful intelligence. *Consulting Psychology Journal: Practice and Research, 55,* 139–154.

Sternberg, R. J. (2003b). The development of creativity as a decision-making process. In R. K. Sawyer, V. John-Steiner, S. Moran, R. J. Sternberg, D. H. Feldman, J. Nakamura, & M. Csikszentmihalyi (Eds.), *Creativity and development* (pp. 91–138). New York: Oxford University Press.

Sternberg, R. J., Forsythe, G. B., Hedlund, J., Horvath, J. A., Wagner, R. K., Williams, W. M., Snook, S. A., & Grigorenko, E. L. (2000). *Practical intelligence in everyday life.* Cambridge, UK: Cambridge University Press.

Sternberg, R. J., & Grigorenko, E. L. (2002). *Dynamic testing.* New York: Cambridge University Press.

Sternberg, R. J., & Lubart, T. I. (1996). Investing in creativity. *American Psychologist, 51,* 677–688.

Sternberg, R. J., & Lubart, T. I. (2001). Wisdom and creativity. In J. E. Birren & K. W. Schaie (Eds.),

Handbook of the psychology of aging (pp. 500–522). San Diego: Academic Press.

Sterns, H. L., & Huyck, M. H. (2001). The role of work in midlife. In M. E. Lachman (Ed.), *Handbook of midlife development* (pp. 447–486). New York: Wiley.

Stessman, J., Hammerman-Rozenberg, R., Maaravi, Y., Azoulai, D., & Cohen, A. (2005). Strategies to enhance longevity and independent function: The Jerusalem Longitudinal Study. *Mechanisms of Ageing and Development, 126,* 327–331.

Stettler, N., Stallings, V. A., Troxel, A. B., Zhao, J., Schinnar, R., Nelson, S. E., Ziegler, E. E., & Strom, B. L. (2005). Weight gain in the first week of life and overweight in adulthood: A cohort study of European American subjects fed infant formula. *Circulation, 111,* 1897–1903.

Stevens, J. C., & Cruz, L. A. (1996). Spatial acuity of touch: Ubiquitous decline with aging revealed by repeated threshold testing. *Somatosensory and Motor Research, 13,* 1–10.

Stevens, J. C., Foulke, E., & Patterson, M. Q. (1996). Tactile acuity, aging, and Braille reading in long-term blind adults. *Journal of Experimental Psychology: Applied, 2,* 91–106.

Stevens, M. L. T. (1997, March–April). What Quinlan can tell Kevorkian about the right to die. *The Humanist, 57*(2), 10–14.

Stevenson, H. W., Lee, S., & Mu, X. (2000). Successful achievement in mathematics: China and the United States. In C. F. M. van Lieshout & P. G. Heymans (Eds.), *Developing talent across the lifespan* (pp. 167–183). Philadelphia: Psychology Press.

Stevenson, R., & Pollitt, C. (1987). The acquisition of temporal terms. *Journal of Child Language, 14,* 533–545.

Steward, D. K. (2001). Behavioral characteristics of infants with nonorganic failure to thrive during a play interaction. *American Journal of Maternal Child Nursing, 26,* 79–85.

Stewart, A. J., & Vandewater, E. A. (1992, August). *Combining tough and tender methods to study women's lives.* Paper presented at the annual meeting of the American Psychological Association, Washington, DC.

Stewart, A. J., & Vandewater, E. A. (1999). "If I had to do over again . . .": Midlife review, midcourse corrections, and women's well-being in midlife. *Journal of Personality and Social Psychology, 76,* 270–283.

Stewart, A. J., Ostrove, J. M., & Helson, R. (2001). Middle aging in women: Patterns of personality change from the 30s to the 50s. *Journal of Adult Development, 8,* 23–37.

Stewart, A. L., Verboncoeur, C. J., McLellan, B. Y., Gillis, D. E., Rush, S., & Mills, K. M. (2001). Physical activity outcomes of CHAMPS II: A physical activity promotion program for older adults. *Journal of Gerontology, 56A,* M465–M470.

Stewart, R. B., Jr. (1990). *The second child: Family transition and adjustment.* Newbury Park, CA: Sage.

Stewart, R. B., Kozak, A. L., Tingley, L. M., Goddard, J. M., Blake, E. M., & Cassel, W. A. (2001). Adult sibling relationships: Validation of a typology. *Personal Relationships, 8,* 299–324.

Stewart, S., Stinnett, H., & Rosenfeld, L. B. (2000). Sex differences in desired characteristics of short-term and long-term relationship partners. *Journal of Social and Personal Relationships, 17,* 843–853.

Stifter, C. A., Coulehan, C. M., & Fish, M. (1993). Linking employment to attachment: The mediating effects of maternal separation anxiety and interactive behavior. *Child Development, 64,* 1451–1460.

Stiles, J. (2001a). Neural plasticity in cognitive development. *Developmental Neuropsychology, 18,* 237–272.

Stiles, J. (2001b). Spatial cognitive development. In C. A. Nelson & M. Luciana (Eds.), *Handbook of developmental cognitive neuroscience* (pp. 399–414). Cambridge, MA: MIT Press.

Stiles, J., Bates, E. A., Thal, D., Trauner, D. A., & Reilly, J. (2002). Linguistic and spatial cognitive development in children with pre- and perinatal focal brain injury: A ten-year overview from the San Diego longitudinal project. In M. H. Johnson & Y. Munakata (Eds.), *Brain development and cognition: A reader* (2nd ed., pp. 272–291). Malden, MA: Blackwell.

Stiles, J., Moses, P., Roe, K., Akshoomoff, N. A., Trauner, D., & Hesselink, J. (2003). Alternative brain organization after prenatal cerebral injury: Convergent fMRI and cognitive data. *Journal of the International Neuropsychological Society, 9,* 604–622.

Stilson, S. R., & Harding, C. G. (1997). Early social context as it relates to symbolic play: A longitudinal investigation. *Merrill-Palmer Quarterly, 43,* 682–693.

Stine-Morrow, E. A. L., & Miller, L. M. S. (1999). Basic cognitive processes. In J. C. Cavanaugh & S. K. Whitbourne (Eds.), *Gerontol-*

ogy: An interdisciplinary perspective (pp.186–212). New York: Oxford University Press.

Stipek, D. (1995). The development of pride and shame in toddlers. In J. P. Tangney & K. W. Fischer (Eds.), Self-conscious emotions (pp. 237–252). New York: Guilford.

Stipek, D. (2002). At what age should children enter kindergarten? A question for policy makers and parents. Social Policy Report of the Society for Research in Child Development, 16(3).

Stipek, D., & Byler, P. (2001). Academic achievement and social behaviors associated with age of entry into kindergarten. Journal of Applied Developmental Psychology, 22, 175–189.

Stipek, D. J., Feiler, R., Daniels, D., & Milburn, S. (1995). Effects of different instructional approaches on young children's achievement and motivation. Child Development, 66, 209–223.

Stipek, D. J., Gralinski, J. H., & Kopp, C. B. (1990). Self-concept development in the toddler years. Developmental Psychology, 26, 972–977.

Stith, S. M., & Farley, S. C. (1993). A predictive model of male spousal violence. Journal of Family Violence, 8, 183–201.

Stoch, M. B., Smythe, P. M., Moodie, A. D., & Bradshaw, D. (1982). Psychosocial outcome and CT findings after growth undernourishment during infancy: A 20-year developmental study. Developmental Medicine and Child Neurology, 24, 419–436

Stocker, C., & Dunn, J. (1994). Sibling relationships in childhood and adolescence. In J. C. DeFries, R. Plomin, & D. W. Fulker (Eds.), Nature and nurture in middle childhood (pp. 214–232). Cambridge, MA: Blackwell.

Stocker, C. J., Arch, J. R., & Cawthorne, M. A. (2005). Fetal origins of insulin resistance and obesity. Proceedings of the Nutrition Society, 64, 143–151.

Stone, M. R., & Brown, B. B. (1999). Identity claims and projections: Descriptions of self and crowds in secondary school. In J. A. McLellan & M. J. V. Pugh (Eds.), The role of peer groups in adolescent social identity: Exploring the importance of stability and change (pp. 7–20). San Francisco: Jossey-Bass.

Stone, P., & Lovejoy, M. (2004). Fast-track women and the "choice" to stay home. Annals of the American Academy of Political and Social Science, 596, 62–83.

Stone, R. G., Staisey, N., & Sonn, U. (1991). Systems for delivery of assistive equipment to elders in Canada, Sweden, and the United States. International Journal of Technology and Aging, 4, 129–140.

Stoney, C. M., & Engebretson, T. O. (1994). Anger and hostility: Potential mediators of the gender difference in coronary artery disease. In A. W. Siegman & T. W. Smith (Eds.), Anger, hostility, and the heart (pp. 215–238). Hillsdale, NJ: Erlbaum.

Storey, A. E., Walsh, C. J., Quinton, R. L., & Wynn-Edwards, K. E. (2000). Hormonal correlates of paternal responsiveness in new and expectant fathers. Evolution and Human Behavior, 21, 79–95.

Stormshak, E. A., Bierman, K. L., McMahon, R. J., Lengua, L. J., & the Conduct Problems Prevention Research Group. (2000). Parenting practices and child disruptive behavior problems in early elementary school. Journal of Clinical Child Psychology, 29, 17–29.

Strachan, T., & Read, A. (2004). Human molecular genetics (3rd ed.). New York: Garland Science.

Strain, L. A., Grabusic, C. C., Searle, M. S., & Dunn, N. J. (2002). Continuing and ceasing leisure activities in later life: A longitudinal study. Gerontologist, 42, 217–223.

Strapp, C. M., & Federico, A. (2000). Imitations and repetitions: What do children say following recasts? First Language, 20, 273–290.

Straus, M. A. (1999). The controversy over domestic violence by women: A methodological, theoretical, and sociology of science analysis. In X. B. Arriaga & S. Oskamp (Eds.), Violence in intimate relationships (pp.17–44). Thousand Oaks, CA: Sage.

Straus, M. A., & Stewart, J. H. (1999). Corporal punishment by American parents: National data on prevalence, chronicity, severity, and duration, in relation to child and family characteristics. Clinical Child and Family Psychology Review, 2, 55–70.

Strauss, R. S., & Pollack, H. A. (2003). Social marginalization of overweight children. Archives of Pediatric and Adolescent Medicine, 157, 746–752.

Strawbridge, W. J., Shema, S. J., Cohen, R. D., & Kaplan, G. A. (2001). Religious attendance increases survival by improving and maintaining good health behaviors. Annals of Behavioral Medicine, 23, 68–74.

Strayer, J., & Roberts, W. (2004). Children's anger, emotional expressiveness, and empathy: Relations with parents' empathy, emotional expressiveness, and parenting practices. Social Development, 13, 229–254.

Streissguth, A. P., Barr, H. M., Sampson, P. D., & Bookstein, F. L. (1994). Prenatal alcohol and offspring development: The first fourteen years. Drug and Alcohol Dependence, 36, 89–99.

Streissguth, A. P., Treder, R., Barr, H. M., Shepard, T., Bleyer, W. A., Sampson, P. D., & Martin, D. (1987). Aspirin and acetaminophen use by pregnant women and subsequent child IQ and attention decrements. Teratology, 35, 211–219.

Strenk, S. A., Strenk, L. M., & Koretz, J. F. (2005). The mechanism of presbyopia. Progress in Retinal and Eye Research, 24, 379–393.

Striano, T., & Rochat, P. (2000). Emergence of selective social referencing in infancy. Infancy, 1, 253–264.

Striano, T., Tomasello, M., & Rochat, P. (2001). Social and object support for early symbolic play. Developmental Science, 4, 442–455.

Stright, A. D., Neitzel, C., Sears, K. G., & Hoke-Sinex, L. (2002). Instruction begins in the home: Relations between parental instruction and children's self-regulation in the classroom. Journal of Educational Psychology, 93, 456–466.

Stroebe, M., & Schut, H. (1999). The dual process model of coping with bereavement: Rationale and description. Death Studies, 23, 197–224.

Stroebe, M., & Schut, H. (2001). Models of coping with bereavement: A review. In M. S. Stroebe, R. O. Hansson, W. Stroebe, & H. Schut (Eds.), Handbook of bereavement research (pp. 375–403). Washington, DC: American Psychological Association.

Stroebe, W., & Stroebe, M. S. (1993). Determinants of adjustment to bereavement in younger widows and widowers. In M. S. Stroebe, W. Stroebe, & R. O. Hansson (Eds.), Handbook of bereavement (pp. 208–226). New York: Cambridge University Press.

Stroebe, W., Stroebe, M., Abakoumkin, G., & Schut, H. (1996). The role of loneliness and social support in adjustment to loss: A test of attachment versus stress theory. Journal of Personality and Social Psychology, 70, 1241–1249.

Strough, J., Hicks, P. J., Swenson, L. M., Cheng, S., & Barnes, K. A. (2003). Collaborative everyday problem solving: Interpersonal relationships and problem dimensions. International Journal of Aging and Human Development, 56, 43–66.

Strouse, D. L. (1999). Adolescent crowd orientations: A social and temporal analysis. In J. A. McLellan & M. J. V. Pugh (Eds.), The role of peer groups in adolescent social identity: Exploring the importance of stability and change (pp. 37–54). San Francisco: Jossey-Bass.

Struckman-Johnson, C. J., & Struckman-Johnson, D. L. (1998). The dynamics and impact of sexual coercion of men by women. In P. B. Anderson & C. J. Struckman-Johnson (Eds.), Sexually aggressive women: Current perspectives and controversies (pp. 121–143). New York: Guilford.

Stuart, G. L., Moore, T. M., Gordon, K. C., Ramsey, S. E., & Kahler, C. W. (2006). Psychopathology in women arrested for domestic violence. Journal of Interpersonal Violence, 21, 376–389.

Stuart, M., & Weinrich, M. (2001). Home- and community-based long-term care: Lessons from Denmark. Gerontologist, 41, 474–480.

Stuart, R. B. (2005). Treatment for partner abuse: Time for a paradigm shift. Professional Psychology: Research and Practice, 36, 254–263.

Stull, D., & Scarisbrick-Hauser, A. (1989). Never-married elderly. Research on Aging, 11, 124–139.

Stylianos, S. K., & Vachon, M. L. S. (1993). The role of social support in bereavement. In M. S. Stroebe, W. Stroebe, & R. O. Hansson (Eds.), Handbook of bereavement (pp. 397–410). New York: Cambridge University Press.

Styne, D. M. (2003). The regulation of pubertal growth. Hormone Research, 60(Suppl. 1), 22–26.

Suárez-Orozco, C., & Suárez-Orozco, M. M. (2001). Children of immigration. Cambridge, MA: Harvard University Press.

Subbotsky, E. (2004). Magical thinking in judgments of causation: Can anomalous phenomena affect ontological causal beliefs in children and adults? British Journal of Developmental Psychology, 22, 123–152.

Subbotsky, E. V. (1994). Early rationality and magical thinking in preschoolers: Space and time. British Journal of Developmental Psychology, 12, 97–108.

Subrahmanyam, K., & Greenfield, P. M. (1996). Effect of video game practice on spatial skills in girls and boys. In P. M. Greenfield & R. R. Cocking (Eds.), Interacting with video (pp. 95–114). Norwood, NJ: Ablex.

Subramanian, R. (2003). Alcohol involvement in fatal motor vehicle traffic crashes, 2003. Springfield, VA: U.S. Department of Transportation.

Sullivan, E. V., Pfefferbaum, A., Adasteinsson, E., Swan, G. E., & Carmelli, D. (2002). Differential rates of regional brain change in callosal and ventricular size: A 4-year longitudinal MRI study of elderly men. *Cerebral Cortex, 12,* 438–445.

Sullivan, M. A. (1995). May the circle be unbroken: The African-American experience of death, dying, and spirituality. In J. K. Parry & A. S. Ryan (Eds.), *A cross-cultural look at death, dying, and religion* (pp. 160–171). Chicago: Nelson-Hall.

Sullivan, M. W., & Lewis, M. (2003). Contextual determinants of anger and other negative expressions in young infants. *Developmental Psychology, 39,* 693–705.

Super, D. E. (1990). A life span, life space approach to career development. In D. Brown & L. Brooks (Eds.), *Career choice and development* (2nd ed., pp. 197–261). San Francisco: Jossey-Bass.

Super, D. E. (1994). A life span, life space perspective on convergence. In M. L. Savikas & R. W. Lent (Eds.), *Convergence in career development theories* (pp. 62–71). Palo Alto, CA: Consulting Psychologists Press.

Sureau, C. (1997). Trials and tribulations of surrogacy: From surrogacy to parenthood. *Human Reproduction, 12,* 410–411.

Susman, E. J., & Rogol, A. (2004). Puberty and psychological development. In R. M. Lerner & L. Steinberg (Eds.), *Handbook of adolescent psychology* (2nd ed., pp.15–44). Hoboken, NJ: Wiley.

Sutcliffe, A. G. (2002). Health risks in babies born after assisted reproduction. *British Medical Journal, 325,* 117–118.

Svensson, A. (2000). Computers in school: Socially isolating or a tool to promote collaboration? *Journal of Educational Computing Research, 22,* 437–453.

Swanson, J. L., & Fouad, N. A. (1999). Applying theories of person–environment fit to the transition from school to work. *Career Development Quarterly, 47,* 337–347.

Symons, D. K. (2001). A dyad-oriented approach to distress and mother–child relationship outcomes in the first 24 months. *Parenting: Science and Practice, 1,* 101–122.

Szaflarski, J. P., Binder, J. R., Possing, E. T., McKiernan, K. A., Ward, B. D., & Hammeke, T. A. (2002). Language lateralization in left-handed and ambidextrous people: fMRI data. *Neurology, 59,* 238–244.

Szkrybalo, J., & Ruble, D. N. (1999). "God made me a girl": Sex-category constancy judgments and explanations revisited. *Developmental Psychology, 35,* 392–402.

T

Tacon, A., & Caldera, Y. (2001). Attachment and parental corre-lates in late adolescent Mexican American women. *Hispanic Journal of Behavioral Sciences, 23,* 71–88.

Tager-Flusberg, H. (2005). Putting words together: Morphology and syntax in the preschool years. In J. B. Gleason (Ed.), *The development of language* (5th ed., pp. 148–190). Boston: Allyn and Bacon.

Tahir, L., & Gruber, H. E. (2003). Developmental trajectories and creative work in late life. In J. Demick & C. Andreoletti (Eds.), *Handbook of adult development* (pp. 239–255). New York: Springer.

Takahashi, K. (1990). Are the key assumptions of the "Strange Situation" procedure universal? A view from Japanese research. *Human Development, 33,* 23–30.

Takamura, J., & Williams, B. (2002). *Informal caregiving: Compassion in action.* Arlington, TX: Arc of the United States.

Tamis-LeMonda, C. S., & Bornstein, M. H. (1989). Habituation and maternal encouragement of attention in infancy as predictors of toddler language, play, and representational competence. *Child Development, 60,* 738–751.

Tammelin, T., Näyhä, S., Hills, A. P., & Järvelin, M. (2003). Adolescent participation in sports and adult physical activity. *American Journal of Preventive Medicine, 24,* 22–28.

Tanaka, H., DeSouza, C. A., Jones, P. P., Stevenson, E. T., Davy, K. P., & Seals, D. R. (1997). Greater rate of decline in maximal aerobic capacity with age in physically active vs. sedentary healthy women. *Journal of Applied Physiology, 83,* 1947–1953.

Tanaka, H., & Higuchi, M. (1998). Age, exercise performance, and physiological functional capacities. *Advances in Exercise Sports Physiology, 4,* 51–56.

Tanaka, H., & Seals, D. R. (1997). Age and gender interactions in physiological functional capacity: Insight from swimming performance. *Journal of Applied Physiology, 82,* 846–851.

Tanaka, H., & Seals, D. R. (2003). Dynamic exercise performance in master athletes: Insight into the effects of primary human aging on physiological functional capacity. *Journal of Applied Physiology, 95,* 2152–2162.

Tangney, J. P. (2001). Constructive and destructive aspects of shame and guilt. In A. C. Bohart & D. J. Stipek (Eds.), *Constructive and destructive behavior* (pp. 127–145). Washington, DC: American Psychological Association.

Tangri, S. S., & Jenkins, S. R. (1997). Why expecting conflict is good. *Sex Roles, 36,* 725–746.

Tanne, J. H. (1992). "Granny dumping" in the U.S. *British Medical Journal, 304,* 333–334.

Tanner, J. M. (1990). *Foetus into man* (2nd ed.). Cambridge, MA: Harvard University Press.

Tanner, J. M., Healy, M., & Cameron, N. (2001). *Assessment of skeletal maturity and prediction of adult height* (3rd ed.). Philadelphia: Saunders.

Tardif, T., Gelman, S. A., & Xu, F. (1999). Putting the "noun bias" in context: A comparison of English and Mandarin. *Child Development, 70,* 620–635.

Tardif, T., Wellman, H. M., & Cheung, K. M. (2004). False belief understanding in Cantonese-speaking children. *Journal of Child Language, 31,* 779–800.

Tardon, A., Lee, W. J., Delgado-Rodriguez, M., Dosemeci, M., Albanese, D., Hoover, R., & Blair, A. (2005). Leisure-time physical activity and lung cancer: A meta-analysis. *Cancer Causes and Control, 16,* 389–397.

Tasker, F. (2005). Lesbian mothers, gay fathers, and their children: A review. *Developmental and Behavioral Pediatrics, 26,* 224–240.

Taylor, E. (2004). ADHD is best understood as a cultural construct: Against, *British Journal of Psychiatry, 184,* 9.

Taylor, J. H., & Walker, L. J. (1997). Moral climate and the development of moral reasoning: The effects of dyadic discussions between young offenders. *Journal of Moral Education, 26,* 21–43.

Taylor, M. C., & Hall, J. A. (1982). Psychological androgyny: Theories, methods, and conclusions. *Psychological Bulletin, 92,* 347–366.

Taylor, M. G., Lynch, S. M., & Scott, M. (2004). Trajectories of impairment, social support, and depressive symptoms in later life. *Journal of Gerontology, 59B,* S238–S246.

Taylor, R. D., & Roberts, D. (1995). Kinship support and maternal and adolescent well-being in economically disadvantaged African-American families. *Child Development, 66,* 1585–1597.

Taylor, R. L. (2000). Diversity within African-American families. In D. H. Demo & K. R. Allen (Eds.), *Handbook of family diversity* (pp. 232–251). New York: Oxford University Press.

Teller, D. Y. (1998). Spatial and temporal aspects of infant color vision. *Vision Research, 38,* 3275–3282.

Tellings, A. (1999). Psychoanalytical and genetic-structuralistic approaches to moral development: Incompatible views? *Psychoanalytic Review, 86,* 903–914.

Temple, C. M., & Carney, R. A. (1995). Patterns of spatial functioning in Turner's syndrome. *Cortex, 31,* 109–118.

ten Tusscher, G. W., & Koppe, J. G. (2004). Perinatal dioxin exposure and later effects—a review. *Chemosphere, 54,* 1329–1336.

Tenenbaum, H. R., & Leaper, C. (2003). Parent–child conversations about science: The socialization of gender inequities? *Developmental Psychology, 39,* 34–47.

Tenenbaum, H. R., Snow, C. E., Roach, K. A., & Kurland, B. (2005). Talking and reading science: Longitudinal data on sex differences in mother–child conversations in low-income families. *Journal of Applied Developmental Psychology, 26,* 1–19.

Terenzini, P. T., Pascarella, E. T., & Blimling, G. S. (1999). Students' out-of-class experiences and their influence on learning and cognitive development: A literature review. *Journal of College Student Development, 40,* 610–623.

Terwel, J., Gillies, R. M., van den Eeden, P., & Hoek, D. (2001). Cooperative learning processes of students: A longitudinal multilevel perspective. *British Journal of Educational Psychology, 71,* 619–645.

Tessier, R., Cristo, M., Velez, S., Giron, M., Nadeau, L., & Figueroa de Calume, Z. (2003). Kangaroo mother care: A method of protecting high-risk premature infants against developmental delay. *Infant Behavior and Development, 26,* 384–397.

Testa, M., Livingston, J. A., Vanzile-Tamsen, C., & Frone, M. R. (2003). The role of women's substance use in vulnerability to forcible and incapacitated rape. *Journal of Studies in Alcohol, 64,* 756–764.

Tetens, J. N. (1777). *Philosophische Versuche über die menschliche Natur und ihre Entwicklung.* Leipzig: Weidmanns Erben & Reich.

Teti, D. M., Saken, J. W., Kucera, E., & Corns, K. M. (1996). And baby makes four: Predictors of attachment security among preschool-age firstborns during the transition to siblinghood. *Child Development, 67,* 579–596.

Teyber, E. (2001). *Helping children cope with divorce* (rev. ed.). San Francisco: Jossey-Bass.

Thacker, S. B., & Stroup, D. F. (2003). Revisiting the use of the electronic fetal monitor. *Lancet, 361,* 445–446.

Thapar, A., Fowler, T., Rice, F., Scourfield, J., van den Bree, M., Thomas, H., Harold, G., & Hay, D.

(2003). Maternal smoking during pregnancy and attention deficit hyperactivity disorder symptoms in offspring. *American Journal of Psychiatry, 160,* 1985–1989.

Tharpar, N., & Sanderson, I. R. (2004). Diarrhea in children: An interface between developing and developed countries. *Lancet, 363,* 641–653.

Tharpe, A. M., & Ashmead, D. H. (2001). A longitudinal investigation of infant auditory sensitivity. *American Journal of Audiology, 10,* 104–112.

Thatcher, R. W., Lyon, G. R., Rumsey, J., & Krasnegor, J. (1996). *Developmental neuroimaging.* San Diego, CA: Academic Press.

Thatcher, R. W., Walker, R. A., & Giudice, S. (1987). Human cerebral hemispheres develop at different rates and ages. *Science, 236,* 1110–1113.

Theisen, S. C., Mansfield, P. K., Seery, B. L., & Voda, A. (1995). Predictors of midlife women's attitudes toward menopause. *Health Values, 19,* 22–31.

Thelen, E. (1989). The (re)discovery of motor development: Learning new things from an old field. *Developmental Psychology, 25,* 946–949.

Thelen, E. (2001). Dynamic mechanisms of change in early perceptual–motor development. In J. L. McClelland & R. S. Siegler (Eds.), *Mechanisms of cognitive development: Behavioral and neural perspectives* (pp. 161– 184). Mahwah, NJ: Erlbaum.

Thelen, E., & Adolph, K. E. (1992). Arnold Gesell: The paradox of nature and nurture. *Developmental Psychology, 28,* 368–380.

Thelen, E., Fisher, D. M., & Ridley-Johnson, R. (1984). The relationship between physical growth and a newborn reflex. *Infant Behavior and Development, 7,* 479–493.

Thelen, E., & Smith, L. B. (1994). *A dynamic systems approach to the development of cognition and action.* Cambridge, MA: Cambridge University Press.

Thelen, E., & Smith, L. B. (1998). Dynamic systems theories. In R. M. Lerner (Ed.), *Handbook of child psychology: Vol. 1. Theoretical models of human development* (5th ed., pp. 563–634). New York: Wiley.

Théoret, E., Halligan, M., Kobayashi, F., Fregni, H., Tager-Flusberg, H.,& Pascual-Leone, A. (2005). Impaired motor facilitation during action observation in individuals with autism spectrum disorder, *Current Biology, 15,* R84–R85.

Thomas, A., & Chess, S. (1977). *Temperament and development.* New York: Brunner/Mazel.

Thomas, A., Chess, S., & Birch, H. G. (1968). *Temperament and behavior disorders in children.* New York: New York University Press.

Thomas, J. R., & French, K. E. (1985). Gender differences across age in motor performance: A meta-analysis. *Psychological Bulletin, 98,* 260–282.

Thomas, R. M. (2005). *Comparing theories of child development* (6th ed.). Belmont, CA: Wadsworth.

Thompson, A., Hollis, C., & Richards, D. (2003). Authoritarian parenting attitudes as a risk for conduct problems: Results of a British national cohort study. *European Child and Adolescent Psychiatry, 12,* 84–91.

Thompson, E. E., & Krause, N. (1998). Living alone and neighborhood characteristics as predictors of social support in late life. *Journal of Gerontology, 53,* S354–S364.

Thompson, G., & Foth, D. (2005). Cognitive-training programs for older adults: What are they and can they enhance mental fitness? *Educational Gerontology, 31,* 603–626.

Thompson, P. M., Giedd, J. N., Woods, R. P., MacDonald, D., Evans, A. C., & Toga, A. W. (2000a). Growth patterns in the developing brain detected by using continuum mechanical tensor maps. *Nature, 404,* 190–192.

Thompson, P. M., Giedd, J. N., Woods, R. P., MacDonald, D., Evans, A. C., & Toga, A. W. (2000b). Is more neonatal intensive care always better? Insights from a cross-sectional comparison of reproductive care. *Pediatrics, 109,* 1036–1043.

Thompson, R. A. (1990). On emotion and self-regulation. In R. A. Thompson (Ed.), *Nebraska Symposia on Motivation* (Vol. 36, pp. 383–483). Lincoln: University of Nebraska Press.

Thompson, R. A. (1998). Early sociopersonality development. In N. Eisenberg (Ed.), *Handbook of child psychology: Vol. 3. Social, emotional, and personality development* (5th ed., pp. 25–104). New York: Wiley.

Thompson, R. A. (2000). The legacy of early attachments. *Child Development, 71,* 145–152.

Thompson, R. A., Easterbrooks, M. A., & Padilla-Walker, L. M. (2003). Social and emotional development in infancy. In R. M. Lerner & M. A. Easterbrooks (Eds.), *Social and emotional development in infancy* (pp. 91–112). New York: Wiley.

Thompson, R. A., & Leger, D. W. (1999). From squalls to calls: The cry as a developing socioemotional signal. In B. Lester, J. New-man, & F. Pedersen (Eds.), *Biological and social aspects of infant crying.* New York: Plenum.

Thompson, R. A., & Limber, S. (1991). "Social anxiety" in infancy: Stranger wariness and separation distress. In H. Leitenberg (Ed.), *Handbook of social and evaluation anxiety* (pp. 85–137). New York: Plenum.

Thompson, R. A., & Nelson C. A. (2001). Developmental science and the media. *American Psychologist, 56,* 5–15.

Thompson, R. A., & Raikes, H. A. (2003). Toward the next quarter-century: Conceptual and methodological challenges for attachment theory. *Development and Psychopathology, 15,* 691–718.

Thompson, W. F., Schellenberg, E. G., & Husain, G. (2001). Arousal, mood and the Mozart effect. *Psychological Science, 12,* 248–251.

Thornberry, T., & Krohn, M. D. (2001). The development of delinquency: An interactional perspective. In S. O. White (Ed,), *Handbook of youth and justice* (pp. 289–305). Dordrecht, Netherlands: Kluwer.

Thornton, J., Edwards, R., Mitchell, P., Harrison, R. A., Buchan, I., & Kelly, S. P. (2005). Smoking and age-related macular degeneration: A review of association. *Eye, 19,* 935–944.

Thornton, S. (1999). Creating conditions for cognitive change: The interaction between task structures and specific strategies. *Child Development, 70,* 588–603.

Thorson, J. A., & Powell, F. C. (1994). A Revised Death Anxiety Scale. In R. A. Neimeyer (Ed.), *Death anxiety handbook* (pp. 31–43). Washington, DC: Taylor & Francis.

Thorson, J. A., & Powell, F. C. (2000). Death anxiety in younger and older adults. In A. Tomer (Ed.), *Death attitudes and the older adult: Theories, concepts, and applications* (pp. 123–136). Philadelphia: Taylor & Francis.

Tienari, P., Wynne, L. C., Lasky, K., Moring, J., Nieminen, P., & Sorri, A. (2003). Genetic boundaries of the schizophrenia spectrum: Evidence from the Finnish adoptive family study of schizophrenia. *American Journal of Psychiatry, 160,* 1587–1594.

Tiggemann, M., & Anesbury, T. (2000). Negative stereotyping of obesity in children: The role of controllability beliefs. *Journal of Applied Social Psychology, 30,* 1977–1993.

Tincoff, R., & Jusczyk, P. W. (1999). Some beginnings of word comprehension in 6-month-olds. *Psychological Science, 10,* 172–175.

Tizard, B., & Rees, J. (1975). The effect of early institutional rearing on the behaviour problems and affectional relationships of four-year-old children. *Journal of Child Psychology and Psychiatry, 16,* 61–73.

Tjepkema, M. (2005). Insomnia. *Health Reports, 17,* 9–25.

Tobin, S. S. (1989). The effects of institutionalization. In K. S. Markides & C. L. Cooper (Eds.), *Aging, stress and health* (pp. 139–164). Chichester: Wiley.

Tocci, S. (2000). *Down syndrome.* New York: Franklin Watts.

Toder, F. A. (1994). *Your kids are grown: Moving on with and without them.* New York: Plenum.

Tofler, I. R., Knapp, P. K., & Drell, M. J. (1998). The achievement by proxy spectrum in youth sports: Historical perspective and clinical approach to pressured and high-achieving children and adolescents. *Child and Adolescent Psychiatric Clinics of North America, 7,* 803–820.

Tomasello, M. (1992). *First verbs: A case study of early grammatical development.* New York: Cambridge University Press.

Tomasello, M. (1999). Having intentions, understanding intentions, and understanding communicative intentions. In P. D. Zelazo, J. W. Astington, & J. Wilde (Eds.), *Developing theories of intention: Social understanding and self-control* (pp. 63–75). Mahwah, NJ: Erlbaum.

Tomasello, M. (2000). Do young children have adult syntactic competence? *Cognition, 74,* 209–253.

Tomasello, M. (2003). *Constructing a language: A usage-based theory of language acquisition.* Cambridge, MA: Harvard University Press.

Tomasello, M., & Akhtar, N. (1995). Two-year-olds use pragmatic cues to differentiate reference to objects and actions. *Cognitive Development, 10,* 201–224.

Tomasello, M., & Brooks, P. (1999). Early syntactic development: A construction grammar approach. In M. Barrett (Ed.), *The development of language* (pp. 161–190). Philadelphia: Psychology Press.

Tomasello, M., Call, J., & Hare, B. (2003). Chimpanzees understand psychological states—the question is which ones and to what extent. *Trends in Cognitive Sciences, 7,* 153–156.

Tomasello, M., & Rakoczy, H. (2003). What makes human cognition unique? From individual to shared to collective intentionality. *Mind and Language, 18,* 121–147.

Tomasello, M., Striano, T., & Rochat, P. (1999). Do young children use objects as symbols? *British Journal of Developmental Psychology, 17,* 563–584.

Tomer, A., Eliason, G., & Smith, J. (2000). Beliefs about the self, life, and death: Testing aspects of a comprehensive model of death anxiety and death attitudes. *Death attitudes and the older adult: Theories, concepts, and applications* (pp. 109–122). Philadelphia: Taylor & Francis.

Toogood, A. A. (2004). The somatopause: An indication for growth hormone therapy? *Treatments in Endocrinology, 3,* 201–209.

Toomela, A. (2002). Drawing as a verbally mediated activity: A study of relationships between verbal, motor, visuospatial skills and drawing in children. *International Journal of Behavioral Development, 26,* 234–247.

Torff, B., & Gardner, H. (1999). The vertical mind—The case for multiple intelligences. In M. Anderson (Ed.), *The development of intelligence* (pp. 139–159). Hove, UK: Psychology Press.

Torges, C. M., Stewart, A. J., & Miner-Rubino, K. (2005). Personality after the prime of life: Men and women coming to terms with regrets. *Journal of Research in Personality, 39,* 148–165.

Torney-Purta, J. (2002). The school's role in developing civic engagement: A study of adolescents in twenty-eight countries. *Applied Developmental Science, 6,* 203–212.

Tornstam, L. (1997). Gero-transcendence: A reformulation of disengagement theory. *Aging, 1,* 55–63.

Tornstam, L. (2000). Transcendence in later life. *Generations, 23*(10), 10–14.

Toro-Morn, M., & Sprecher, S. (2003). A cross-cultural comparison of mate preferences among university students: The United States vs. the People's Republic of China (PRC). *Journal of Comparative Family Studies, 34,* 151–170.

Torrance, E. P. (1988). The nature of creativity as manifest in its testing. In R. J. Sternberg (Ed.), *The nature of creativity: Contemporary psychological perspectives* (pp. 43–75). New York: Cambridge University Press.

Torrey, B. B., & Haub, C. (2004). A comparison of U.S. and Canadian mortality in 1998. *Population and Development Review, 30,* No. 3.

Toulemon, L. (1996). Very few couples remain voluntarily childless. *Population, 8,* 1–27.

Trahms, C. M., & Pipes, P. L. (1997). *Nutrition in infancy and childhood* (6th ed.). New York: McGraw-Hill.

Transport Canada. (2001). Pedestrian fatalities and injuries, 1988–1997. Retrieved from http://www.tc.gc.ca/roadsafety/tp2436/rs200101/en/menu.htm

Trappe, S. (2001). Master athletes. *International Journal of Sport Nutrition and Exercise Metabolism, 11,* S196–S207.

Trautner, H. M., Gervai, J., & Nemeth, R. (2003). Appearance–reality distinction and development of gender constancy understanding in children. *International Journal of Behavioral Development, 27,* 275–283.

Treasure, J., & Schmidt, U. (2005). Anorexia nervosa. *Clinical Evidence, 13,* 1148–1157.

Trehub, S. E. (2001). Musical predispositions in infancy. *Annals of the New York Academy of Sciences, 930,* 1–16.

Treloar, S. A., Heath, A. C., & Martin, N. G. (2002). Genetic and environmental influences on premenstrual symptoms in an Australian twin sample. *Psychological Medicine, 32,* 25–38.

Tremblay, M. S., & Willms, J. D. (2000). Secular trends in the body mass index of Canadian children. *Canadian Medical Association Journal, 163,* 1429–1433.

Tremblay, R. E. (2000). The development of aggressive behaviour during childhood: What have we learned in the past century? *International Journal of Behavioral Development, 24,* 129–141.

Tremblay, R. E. (2002). Prevention of injury by early socialization of aggressive behavior. *Injury Prevention, 8*(Suppl. IV), 17–21.

Tremblay, R. E., Japel, C., Perusse, D., Voivin, M., Zoccolillo, M., Montplaisir, J., & McDuff, P. (1999). The search for the age of "onset" of physical aggression: Rousseau and Bandura revisited. *Criminal Behavior and Mental Health, 9,* 8–23.

Trent, K., & Harlan, S. L. (1994). Teenage mothers in nuclear and extended households. *Journal of Family Issues, 15,* 309–337.

Triandis, H. C. (1995). *Individualism and collectivism.* Boulder, CO: Westview Press.

Triandis, H. C. (1998, May). *Cross-cultural versus cultural psychology: A synthesis?* Colloquium presented at Illinois Wesleyan University, Bloomington, IL.

Trickett, P., Noll, J., Reiffman, A., & Putnam, F. (2001). Variants of intrafamilial sexual abuse experience: Implications for short- and long-term development. *Development and Psychopathology, 13,* 1001–1019.

Trickett, P. K., & Putnam, F. W. (1998). Developmental consequences of child sexual abuse. In P. K. Trickett & C. J. Schellenbach (Eds.), *Violence against children in the family and community* (pp. 39–56). Washington, DC: American Psychological Association.

Trocomé, N., & Wolfe, D. (2002). *Child maltreatment in Canada: The Canadian Incidence Study of Reported Child Abuse and Neglect.* Retrieved from www.hc-sc.gc.ca/pphb-dgspsp/cm-vee

Troll, L. E., & Skaff, M. M. (1997). Perceived continuity of self in very old age. *Psychology and Aging, 12,* 162–169.

Tronick, E., Morelli, G., & Ivey, P. (1992). The Efe forager infant and toddler's pattern of social relationships: Multiple and simultaneous. *Developmental Psychology, 28,* 568–577.

Tronick, E. Z., Thomas, R. B., & Daltabuit, M. (1994). The Quechua manta pouch: A caretaking practice for buffering the Peruvian infant against the multiple stressors of high altitude. *Child Development, 65,* 1005–1013.

True, M. M., Pisani, L., & Oumar, F. (2001). Infant–mother attachment among the Dogon of Mali. *Child Development, 72,* 1451–1466.

Trusty, J. (1999). Effects of eighth-grade parental involvement on late adolescents' educational expectations. *Journal of Research and Development in Education, 32,* 224–233.

Trzesniewski, K. H., Donnellan, M. B., & Robins, R. W. (2003). Stability of self-esteem across the life span. *Journal of Personality and Social Psychology, 84,* 205–220.

Tsai, A. G., & Wadden, T. A. (2005). Systematic review: An evaluation of major commercial weight loss programs in the United States. *Annals of Internal Medicine, 142,* 56–66.

Tsang, P. S., & Shaner, T. L. (1998). Age, attention, expertise, and time-sharing performance. *Psychology and Aging, 13,* 323–347.

Tsuang, M. T., Bar, J. L., Harley, R. M., & Lyons, M. J. (2001). The Harvard Twin Study of Substance Abuse: What we have learned. *Harvard Review of Psychiatry, 9,* 267–279.

Tuchfarber, B. S., Zins, J. E., & Jason, L. A. (1997). Prevention and control of injuries. In R. Weissberg, T. P. Gullotta, R. L. Hampton, B. A. Ryan, & G. R. Adams (Eds.), *Enhancing children's wellness* (pp. 250–277). Thousand Oaks, CA: Sage.

Tucker, C. J., McHale, S. M., & Crouter, A. C. (2001). Conditions of sibling support in adolescence. *Journal of Family Psychology, 15,* 254–271.

Tudge, J., & Scrimsher, S. (2003). Lev S. Vygotsky on education: A cultural-historical, interpersonal, and individual approach to development. In B. J. Zimmerman & D. H. Schunk (Eds.), *Educational*

psychology: A century of contributions (pp. 207–228). Mahwah, NJ: Erlbaum.

Tudge, J. R. H. (1992). Processes and consequences of peer collaboration: A Vygotskian analysis. *Child Development, 63,* 1364–1397.

Tudge, J. R. H., Hogan, D. M., Snezhkova, I. A., Kulakova, N. N., & Etz, K. E. (2000). Parents' child-rearing values and beliefs in the United States and Russia: The impact of culture and social class. *Infant and Child Development, 9,* 105–121.

Turati, C. (2004). Why faces are not special to newborns: An account of the face preference. *Current Directions in Psychological Science, 13,* 5–8.

Turiel, E. (1998). The development of morality. In N. Eisenberg (Ed.), *Handbook of child psychology: Vol. 3. Social, emotional, and personality development* (5th ed., pp. 863–932). New York: Wiley.

Turiel, E., Smetana, J. G., & Killen, M. (1991). Social contexts in social cognitive development. In W. M. Kurtines & J. L. Gewirtz (Eds.), *Handbook of moral behavior and development* (Vol. 2, pp. 307–332). Hillsdale, NJ: Erlbaum.

Turkheimer, E., Haley, A., Waldron, M., D'Onofrio, B., & Gottesman, I. I. (2003). Socioeconomic status modifies heritability of IQ in young children. *Psychological Science, 14,* 623–628.

Turnbull, M., Hart, D., & Lapkin, S. (2003). Grade 6 French immersion students' performance on large-scale reading, writing, and mathematics tests: Building explanations. *Alberta Journal of Educational Research, 49,* 6–23.

Turner, B. F. (1982). Sex-related differences in aging. In B. B. Wolman (Ed.), *Handbook of developmental psychology* (pp. 912–936). Englewood Cliffs, NJ: Prentice-Hall.

Turner, P. J., & Gervai, J. (1995). A multidimensional study of gender typing in preschool children and their parents: Personality, attitudes, preferences, behavior, and cultural differences. *British Journal of Developmental Psychology, 11,* 323–342.

Tuyen, J. M., & Bisgard, K. (2003). Community setting: Pertussis outbreak. Atlanta, GA: U.S. Centers for Disease Control and Prevention. Retrieved from www.cdc.gov/nip/publications/pertussis/chapter10.pdf

Twenge, J. M., & Campbell, W. K. (2001). Age and birth cohort differences in self-esteem: A cross-temporal meta-analysis. *Personality and Social Psychology Review, 5,* 321–344.

Twenge, J. M., & Crocker, J. (2002). Race and self-esteem: Meta-analyses comparing whites, blacks, Hispanics, Asians, and America Indians and comment on Gray-Little and Hafdahl (2000). *Psychological Bulletin, 128,* 371–408.

Tyrka, A. R., Graber, J. A., & Brooks-Gunn, J. (2000). The development of disordered eating: Correlates and predictors of eating problems in the context of adolescence. In A. J. Sameroff & M. Lewis (Eds.), *Handbook of developmental psychopathology* (2nd ed., pp. 607–624). New York: Kluwer.

U

Underwood, M. K. (2003). *Social aggression among girls.* New York: Guilford.

Underwood, M. K., Galen, B. R., & Paquette, J. (2001). Top ten challenges for understanding aggression and gender: Why can't we all just get along? *Social Development, 10,* 248–266.

UNICEF (United Nations Children's Fund). (2001). *Teenage births in rich nations. Innocenti Report Card No. 3.* Florence, Italy: UNICEF Innocenti Research Centre.

UNICEF (United Nations Children's Fund). (2005a). *Child poverty in rich countries 2005.* Florence, Italy: UNICEF Innocenti Research Centre.

UNICEF (United Nations Children's Fund). (2005b). *Children under threat.* New York: Author.

United Jewish Communities. (2004). *The national Jewish population survey 2000–2001. Strength, challenge, and diversity in the American Jewish population.* New York: Author.

United Nations. (2001). *World social situation.* New York: Author.

United Nations. (2002). *Human development report 2001.* New York: Author.

United Nations. (2004a). Women, girls, HIV and AIDS. Retrieved from www.un.org/events/aids

United Nations. (2004b). *World demographic trends.* Florence, Italy: Economic and Social Council of the UN.

United Nations Development Programme. (2002). *Human development report 2002.* New York: Oxford University Press.

U.S. Census Bureau. (2005). *Residential population.* Retrieved from www.census.gov/ipc/www/usinterimproj

U.S. Census Bureau. (2006a). International data base. Retrieved from www.census.gov/ipc/www/idbnew.html

U.S. Census Bureau. (2006b). *Statistical abstract of the United States* (125th ed.). Washington, DC: U.S. Government Printing Office.

U.S. Department of Agriculture. (2005a). Expenditures on children by families, 2004. Retrieved from www.cnpp.usda.gov

U.S. Department of Agriculture. (2005b). *Food insecurity in households with children.* Washington, DC: Author.

U.S. Department of Agriculture. (2005c). Frequently asked questions about the Special Supplemental Nutrition Program for Women, Infants, and Children (WIC). Retrieved from www.ers.usda.gov/Briefing/WIC

U.S. Department of Education. (2003). The Nation's Report Card: National Assessment of Educational Progress: 2003 results. Retrieved from nces.ed.gov/nationsreportcard/mathematics

U.S. Department of Education. (2005a). *The condition of education, 2000–2005.* Washington, DC: U.S. Government Printing Office.

U.S. Department of Education. (2005b). *Digest of education statistics 2004.* Washington, DC: U.S. Government Printing Office.

U.S. Department of Education. (2005c). Long-term trend: Trends in average mathematics scale scores by gender. *The Nation's Report Card.* Retrieved from nces.ed.gov/nationsreportcard/ltt/results2004/sub-mathematics-gender.asp

U.S. Department of Education. (2005d). Long-term trend: Trends in average mathematics scale scores by race/ethnicity. *The Nation's Report Card.* Retrieved from nces.ed.gov/nationsreportcard/ltt/results2004/sub_mathematics_race2.asp

U.S. Department of Education. (2005e). Long-term trend: Trends in average reading scale scores by gender. *The Nation's Report Card.* Retrieved from nces.ed.gov/nationsreportcard/ltt/results2004/sub-reading-gender.asp

U.S. Department of Education. (2005f). Long-term trend: Trends in average reading scale scores by race/ethnicity. *The Nation's Report Card.* Retrieved from nces.ed.gov/nationsreportcard/ltt/results2004/sub_reading_race2.asp

U.S. Department of Education. (2005g). Long-term trend: Trends in average writing scale scores by gender. *The Nation's Report Card.* Retrieved from nces.ed.gov/nationsreportcard/ ltt/results2004/sub-writing-gender.asp

U.S. Department of Education. (2005h). *Trial urban district report cards in reading and mathematics, 2005.* Retrieved from nces.ed.gov/nationsreportcard/nrc/tuda_reading_mathematics_2005

U.S. Department of Health and Human Services. (2002). Cohabitation, marriage, divorce, and remarriage in the United States. *Vital and Health Statistics,* Series Report 23, Number 22. Washington, DC: U.S. Government Printing Office.

U.S. Department of Health and Human Services. (2004a). Breastfeeding: Frequently asked questions. Retrieved from www.cdc.gov/breastfeeding.faq/index.htm

U.S. Department of Health and Human Services. (2004b). *Health United States and injury chartbook.* Washington, DC: U.S. Government Printing Office.

U.S. Department of Health and Human Services. (2004c). *Overweight and obesity: U.S. obesity trends 1985–2004.* Retrieved from ww.cdc.gov/nccdphp/dnpa/obesity/trend/maps

U.S. Department of Health and Human Services. (2004d). Youth risk behavior surveillance— United States, 2003. *Morbidity and Mortality Weekly Report, 53* (S-52), 1–29.

U.S. Department of Health and Human Services. (2005a). Annual smoking-attributable mortality, years of potential life lost, and productivity losses—United States, 1997–2001. *Morbidity and Mortality Weekly Report, 54,* 625–628.

U.S. Department of Health and Human Services. (2005b, December 20). Births: Preliminary data for 2004. *National Vital Statistics Report, 54,* 1–20.

U.S. Department of Health and Human Services. (2005c). *Child maltreatment 2003: Summary of key findings.* Retrieved from nccanch.acf.hhs.gov/pubs/factsheets/canstats.cfm

U.S. Department of Health and Human Services. (2005d). *Fact sheet: Falls and hip fractures among older adults.* Retrieved from www.cdc.gov/ncipc/factsheets/falls.htm

U.S. Department of Health and Human Services. (2005e). Fertility, family planning, and reproductive health of U.S. women: Data from the 2002 National Survey of Family Growth. *Vital and Health Statistics,* Series 23, No. 25 (DHHS Publication No. PHS 2006-1977). Hyattsville, MD: Author.

U.S. Department of Health and Human Services. (2005f). Fetal alcohol syndrome. Retrieved from www.cdc.gov/ncbddd/fas/fasask.htm

U.S. Department of Health and Human Services. (2005g). *Health United States.* Washington, DC: U.S. Government Printing Office.

U.S. Department of Health and Human Services. (2005h). *Health, United States, with chartbook on trends in the health of Americans.* Hyattsville. MD: National Center for Health Statistics.

U.S. Department of Health and Human Services. (2005i). Medical privacy: National standards to protect the privacy of personal health information. Retrieved from www.hhs.gov/ocr/hipaa/finalreg.html

U.S. Department of Health and Human Services. (2005j). National, state, and urban area vaccination levels among children aged 19 to 35 months: United States 2005. *Morbidity and Mortality Weekly Report, 54,* 717–721.

U.S. Department of Health and Human Services. (2005k). *National survey on drug use and health.* Retrieved from www.drugabusestatistics.samhsa.gov/nhsda.htm

U.S. Department of Health and Human Services. (2005l). *National survey results on drug use from the Monitoring the Future Study. Vol. 1. Secondary school students.* Washington, DC: U.S. Government Printing Office.

U.S. Department of Health and Human Services. (2005m). Nurse-Family Partnership Program, SAMHSA model program. Retrieved from www.samhsa.gov

U.S. Department of Health and Human Services. (2005n). Prenatal care. Retrieved from www.cdc.gov/nchs/fastats/prenatal.htm

U.S. Department of Health and Human Services. (2005o). *Prevalence of overweight and obesity among adults: United States, 1999–2002.* Hyattsville, MD: National Center for Health Statistics.

U.S. Department of Health and Human Services. (2005p). *Profile of older Americans 2004.* Retrieved from www.aoa.dhhs.gov/aoa/stats/profile/2004/default

U.S. Department of Health and Human Services. (2005q). SHPPS 2000 fact sheets: Physical education and activity 2000. Retrieved from www.cdc.gov/HealthyYouth/shpps/factsheets/pe.htm

U.S. Department of Health and Human Services. (2006). *Physical activity for everyone: Recommendations.* Retrieved from www.cdc.gov/nccdphp/dnpa/physical/recommendations/index.htm

U.S. Department of Justice. (2005a). *Crime in the United States.* Washington, DC: U.S. Government Printing Office.

U.S. Department of Justice. (2005b). *Uniform crime reports: Preliminary semiannual report, January–June 2005.* Retrieved from www.fbi.gov/ucr/ucr.htm

U.S. Department of Labor. (2004, August 25). Number of jobs held, labor market activity, and earnings growth among younger baby boomers: Recent results from a longitudinal survey. *News* USDL04-1678. Washington DC: Bureau of Labor Statistics.

U.S. Living Will Registry. (2005). *Advance directive forms.* Retrieved from www.uslivingwillregistry .com/forms.shtm

Updegraff, K. A., McHale, S. M., & Crouter, A. C. (1996). Gender roles in marriage: What do they mean for girls' and boys' school achievement? *Journal of Youth and Adolescence, 25,* 73–88.

Utz, R. L., Carr, D., Nesse, R., & Wortman, C. B. (2002). The effect of widowhood on older adults' social participation: An evaluation of activity, disengagement, and continuity theories. *Gerontologist, 42,* 522–533.

V

Vaillancourt, T., Brendgen, M., Boivin, M., & Tremblay, R. E. (2003). A longitudinal confirmatory factor analysis of indirect and physical aggression: Evidence of two factors over time? *Child Development, 74,* 1628–1638.

Vaillancourt, T., Hymel, S., & McDougall, P. (2003). Bullying is power: Implications for school-based intervention strategies. *Journal of Applied Social Psychology, 19,* 157–176.

Vaillant, G. E. (1977). *Adaptation to life.* Boston: Little, Brown.

Vaillant, G. E. (1993). *The wisdom of the ego.* Cambridge, MA: Harvard University Press.

Vaillant, G. E. (1994). "Successful aging" and psychosocial well-being. In E. H. Thompson, Jr. (Ed.), *Older men's lives* (pp. 22–41). Thousand Oaks, CA: Sage.

Vaillant, G. E. (2002). *Aging well.* Boston: Little, Brown.

Vaillant, G. E., & Koury, S. H. (1994). Late midlife development. In G. H. Pollock & S. I. Greenspan (Eds.), *The course of life* (pp. 1–22). Madison, CT: International Universities Press.

Vaillant, G. E., & Mukamal, K. (2001). Successful aging. *American Journal of Psychiatry, 158,* 839–847.

Vaillant, G. E., & Vaillant, C. O. (1990). Determinants and consequences of creativity in a cohort of gifted women. *Psychology of Women Quarterly, 14,* 607–616.

Vaish, A., & Striano, T. (2004). Is visual reference necessary? Contributions of facial versus vocal cues in 12-month-olds' social referencing behavior. *Developmental Science, 7,* 261–269.

Valdés, G. (1998). The world outside and inside schools: Language and immigrant children. *Educational Researcher, 27*(6), 4–18.

Valentine, J. C., DuBois, D. L., & Cooper, H. (2004). The relation between self-beliefs and academic achievement: A meta-analytic review. *Educational Psychologist, 39,* 111–133.

Valian, V. V. (1996). *Parental replies: Linguistic status and didactic roles.* Cambridge, MA: MIT Press.

van Baarsen, B. (2002). Theroies on coping with loss: The impact of social support and self-esteem on adjustment to emotional and social loneliness following a partner's death in later life. *Journal of Gerontology, 57B,* S33–S42.

Vandell, D. L. (1999). When school is out: Analysis and recommendations. *The Future of Children, 9*(2). Retrieved from http:// www .futureofchildren.org

Vandell, D. L., & Posner, J. K. (1999). Conceptualization and measurement of children's after-school environments. In S. L. Friedman & T. D. Wachs (Eds.), *Measuring environment across the life span* (pp. 167–196). Washington, DC: American Psychological Association.

Vandell, D. L., & Shumow, L. (1999). After-school child care programs. *Future of Children, 9*(2), 64–80.

Van den Bergh, B. R. H. (2004). High antenatal maternal anxiety is related to ADHD symptoms, externalizing problems, and anxiety in 8- and 9-year-olds. *Child Development, 75,* 1085–1097.

Van den Bergh, B. R. H., & De Rycke, L. (2003). Measuring the multidimensional self-concept and global self-worth of 6- to 8-year-olds. *Journal of Genetic Psychology, 164,* 201–225.

van den Boom, D. (2002). First attachments: Theory and research. In G. Bremner & A. Fogel (Eds.), *Blackwell handbook of infant development* (pp. 296–325). Oxford, UK: Blackwell.

van der Woerd, K. A., & Cox, D. N. (2001, August). *Assessing academic competence and the well-being of Aboriginal students in British Columbia.* Poster presented at the annual meeting of the American Psychological Association, Atlanta.

Vandewater, E. A., & Stewart, A. J. (1997). Women's career commitment patterns and personality development. In M. E. Lachman & J. B. James (Eds.), *Multiple paths of midlife development* (pp. 375–410). Chicago: University of Chicago Press.

Van Doesum, K. T. M., Hosman, C. M. H., & Riksen-Walraven, J. M. (2005). A model-based intervention for depressed mothers and their infants. *Infant Mental Health Journal, 26,* 157–176.

Van Esbroeck, R., Tibos, K., & Zaman, M. (2005). A dynamic model of career choice development. *International Journal for Educational and Vocational Guidance, 5,* 5–18.

Van Goozen, S. H. M., Cohen-Kettenis, P. T., Gooren, I. J. G., Frijda, N. H., & Van De Poll, N. E. (1995). Gender differences in behaviour: Activating effects of cross-sex hormones. *Psychoneuroendocrinology, 20,* 171–177.

Vanier Institute of the Family. (2004a). *Profiling Canada's families II.* Retrieved from www .vifamily.ca/profiling/3d.htm

Vanier Institute of the Family. (2004b). *Profiling Canada's families III.* Retrieved from www.vifamily.ca/profiling/3d.htm

van IJzendoorn, M. H. (1995). Adult attachment representations, parental responsiveness, and infant attachment: A meta-analysis on the predictive validity of the Adult Attachment Interview. *Psychological Bulletin, 117,* 387–403.

van IJzendoorn, M. H., & Hubbard, F. O. A. (2000). Are infant crying and maternal responsiveness during the first year related to infant–mother attachment at 15 months? *Attachment and Human Development, 2,* 371–391.

van IJzendoorn, M. H., & Kroonenberg, P. M. (1988). Cross-cultural patterns of attachment: A meta-analysis of the Strange Situation. *Child Development, 59,* 147–156.

van IJzendoorn, M. H., & Sagi, A. (1999). Cross-cultural patterns of attachment. In J. Cassidy & P. R. Shaver (Eds.), *Handbook of attachment: Theory, research, and clinical applications* (pp. 713–734). New York: Guilford.

van IJzendoorn, M. H., Schuengel, C., & Bakermans-Kranenburg, M. J. (1999). Disorganized attachment in early childhood: Meta-analysis of precursors, concomitants, and sequelae. *Development and Psychopathology, 11,* 225–249.

van IJzendoorn, M. H., Vereijken, C. M. J. L., Bakermans-Kranenburg, M. J., & Riksen-Walraven, J. M. (2004). Assessing attachment security with the Attachment Q Sort: Meta-analytic evidence for the validity of the Observer AQS. *Child Development, 75,* 1188–1213.

Van Keer, H. (2004). Fostering reading comprehension in fifth grade by explicit instruction in reading strategies and peer tutoring. *British Journal of Educational Psychology, 74,* 37–70.

Varendi, H., Christensson, K., Porter, R. H., & Winberg, J. (1998). Soothing effect of amniotic fluid smell in newborn infants. *Early Human Development, 51,* 47–55.

Varendi, H., & Porter, R. H. (2001). Breast odour as the only maternal stimulus elicits crawling toward the odour source. *Acta Paediatrica, 90,* 372–375.

Vartanian, L. R. (1997). Separation–individuation, social support, and adolescent egocentrism: An exploratory study. *Journal of Early Adolescence, 17,* 245–270.

Vartanian, T. P., & McNamara, J. M. (2002). Older women in poverty: The impact of midlife factors. *Journal of Marriage and the Family, 64,* 532–547.

Vartanian, L. R., & Powlishta, K. K. (1996). A longitudinal examination of the social-cognitive foundations of adolescent egocentrism. *Journal of Early Adolescence, 16,* 157–178.

Vatten, L. J., Maehle, B. O., Lund, N. T., Treti, S., Hsieh, C. C., Trichopoulos, D., & Stuver, S. O. (2002). Birth weight as a predictor of breast cancer: A case-control study in Norway. *British Journal of Cancer, 86,* 89–91.

Vaughn, B. E., & Bost, K. K. (1999). Attachment and temperament: Redundant, independent, or interacting influences on interpersonal adaptation and personality development? In J. Cassidy & P. Shaver (Eds.), *Handbook of attachment: Theory, research, and clinical applications* (pp. 265–286). New York: Guilford.

Vaughn, B. E., Colvin, T. N., Azria, M. R., Caya, L., & Krzysik, L. (2001). Dyadic analyses of friendship in a sample of preschool-age children attending Head Start: Correspondence between measures and implications for social competence. *Child Development, 72,* 862–878.

Vaughn, B. E., Kopp, C. B., & Krakow, J. B. (1984). The emergence and consolidation of self-control from eighteen to thirty months of age: Normative trends and individual differences. *Child Development, 55,* 990–1004.

Vaughn, S., & Klingner, J. K. (1998). Students' perceptions of inclusion and resource room settings. *Journal of Special Education, 32,* 79–88.

Vazsonyi, A. T., Hibbert, J. R., & Snider, J. B. (2003). Exotic enterprise no more? Adolescent reports of family and parenting processes from youth in four countries. *Journal of Research on Adolescence, 13,* 129–160.

Vedam, S. (2003). Home birth versus hospital birth: Questioning the quality of the evidence on safety. *Birth, 30,* 57–63.

Velkoff, V. (2000, January–March). Centenarians in the United States, 1990 and beyond. *Statistical Bulletin, U.S. Bureau of the Census.*

Washington, DC: U.S. Government Printing Office.

Venable, D. (2002). *The wage gap myth.* Dallas: National Center for Policy Analysis.

Venet, M., & Markovits, H. (2001). Understanding uncertainty with abstract conditional premises. *Merrill-Palmer Quarterly, 47,* 74–99.

Veneziano, R. A. (2003). The importance of paternal warmth. *Cross-Cultural Research, 37,* 265–281.

Veniegas, R., & Peplau, L. A. (1997). Power and the quality of same-sex friendships. *Psychology of Women Quarterly, 21,* 279–297.

Verghese, J., Lipston, R. B., Katz, M. J., Hall, C. B., Derby, C. A., & Kuslansky, G. (2003). Leisure activities and the risk of dementia in the elderly. *New England Journal of Medicine, 348,* 2508–2516.

Victor, C., Scambler, S., Bond, J., & Bowling, A. (2000). Being alone in later life: Loneliness, social isolation, and living alone. *Reviews in Clinical Gerontology, 10,* 407–417.

Vidaeff, A. C., Carroll, M. A., & Ramin, S. M. (2005). Acute hypertensive emergencies in pregnancy. *Critical Care Medicine, 33,* S307–S312.

Videon, T. M., & Manning, C. K. (2003). Influences on adolescent eating patterns: The importance of family meals. *Journal of Adolescent Health, 32,* 365–373.

Vijg, J. (2000). Somatic mutations and aging: A re-evaluation. *Mutation Research, 447,* 117–135.

Vik, T., Bakketeig, L. S., Trygg, K. U., Lund-Larsen, K., & Jacobsen, G. (2003). High caffeine consumption in the third trimester of pregnancy: Gender-specific effects on fetal growth. *Paediatric and Perinatal Epidemiology, 17,* 324–331.

Vinden, P. G. (1996). Junín Quechua children's understanding of mind. *Child Development, 67,* 1707–1716.

Vinden, P. G. (2002). Understanding minds and evidence for belief: A study of Mofu children in Cameroon. *International Journal of Behavioral Development, 26,* 445–452.

Vinick, B. H., & Ekerdt, D. J. (1991). Retirement: What happens to husband–wife relationships? *Journal of Geriatric Psychiatry, 24,* 23–40.

Vinters, H. V. (2001). Aging and the human nervous system. In J. E. Birren & K. W. Schaie (Eds.), *Handbook of the psychology of aging* (pp. 135–160). San Diego: Academic Press.

Visher, E. B., Visher, J. S., & Pasley, K. (2003). Remarriage families and stepparenting. In F. Walsh (Ed.), *Normal family processes* (pp. 153–175). New York: Guilford.

Vita, A. J., Terry, R. B., Hubert, H. B., & Fries, J. F. (1998). Aging, health risks, and cumulative disability. *New England Journal of Medicine, 338,*1035–1041.

Vogel, D. A., Lake, M. A., Evans, S., & Karraker, H. (1991). Children's and adults' sex-stereotyped perceptions of infants. *Sex Roles, 24,* 605–616.

Vogels, N., Diepvens, K., & Westerterp-Plantenga, M. S. (2005). Predictors of long-term weight maintenance. *Obesity Research, 13,* 2162–2168.

Vogelstein, B., & Kinzler, K. (2004). Cancer genes and the pathways they control. *Nature Medicine, 10,* 789–799.

Volling, B. L. (2001). Early attachment relationships as predictors of preschool children's emotion regulation with a distressed sibling. *Early Education and Development, 12,* 185–207.

Volling, B. L., & Belsky, J. (1992). Contribution of mother–child and father–child relationships to the quality of sibling interaction: A longitudinal study. *Child Development, 63,* 1209–1222.

Volpicelli, J. R. (2001). Alcohol abuse and alcoholism. *Journal of Clinical Psychiatry, 62*(Suppl. 20), 4–10.

Vondra, J. I., Hommerding, K. D., & Shaw, D. S. (1999). Stability and change in infant attachment in a low-income sample. In J. I. Vondra & D. Barnett (Eds.), *Atypical attachment in infancy and early childhood among children at developmental risk. Monographs of the Society for Research in Child Development, 64*(3, Serial No. 258), 119–144.

Vondra, J. I., Shaw, D. S., Searingen, L., Cohen, M., & Owens, E. B. (2001). Attachment stability and emotional and behavioral regulation from infancy to preschool age. *Development and Psychopathology, 13,* 13–33.

von Hofsten, C. (2004). An action perspective on motor development. *Trends in Cognitive Sciences, 8,* 266–272.

von Hofsten, C., & Rosander, K. (1998). The establishment of gaze control in early infancy. In S. Simion & S. G. Butterworth (Eds.), *The development of sensory, motor and cognitive capacities in early infancy* (pp. 49–66). Hove, UK: Psychology Press.

Voss, L. D., Mulligan, J., & Betts, P. R. (1998). Short stature at school entry—an index of social deprivation? (The Wessex Growth Study). *Child: Care, Health and Development, 24,* 145–156.

Vostanis, P., Grattan, E., & Cumella, S. (1997). Psychosocial functioning of homeless children. *Journal of the American Academy of Child and Adolescent Psychiatry, 36,* 881–889.

Vouloumanos, A., & Werker, J. F. (2004). Tuned to the signal: The privileged status of speech for young infants. *Developmental Science, 7,* 270–276.

Voyer, D., Voyer, S., & Bryden, M. P. (1995). Magnitude of sex differences in spatial abilities: A meta-analysis and consideration of critical variables. *Psychological Bulletin, 117,* 250–270

Vygotsky, L. S. (1978). *Mind in society: The development of higher mental processes.* Cambridge, MA: Harvard University Press. (Original works published 1930, 1933, and 1935)

Vygotsky, L. S. (1987). Thinking and speech. In R. W. Rieber, & A. S. Carton (Eds.), & N. Minick (Trans.), *The collected works of L. S. Vygotsky: Vol. 1. Problems of general psychology* (pp. 37–285). New York: Plenum. (Original work published 1934)

W

Wachs, T. D. (1999). The what, why, and how of temperament: A piece of the action. In L. Balter & C. S. Tamis-LeMonda (Eds.), *Child psychology: A handbook of contemporary issues* (pp. 23-44). Philadelphia: Psychology Press.

Wachs, T. D., & Bates, J. E. (2001). Temperament. In G. Bremner & A. Fogel (Eds.), *Blackwell handbook of infant development* (pp. 465–501). Oxford, UK: Blackwell.

Wadden, T. A., & Foster, G. D. (2000). Behavioral treatment of obesity. *Medical Clinics of North America, 84,* 441–461.

Waddington, C. H. (1957). *The strategy of the genes.* London: Allen & Unwin.

Wade, P. J. (2005). *Canadian residential hospices: A home-away-from-home.* Retrieved from www.realtytimes.com/printrtpages/ 20050419_hospices.htm

Wade, T. J., & Cairney, J. (1997). Age and depression in a nationally representative sample of Canadians: A preliminary look at the National Population Health Survey. *Canadian Journal of Public Health, 88,* 297–302.

Wadhwa, P. D., Sandman, C. A., & Garite, T. J. (2001). The neurobiology of stress in human pregnancy: Implications for prematurity and development of the fetal central nervous system. *Progress in Brain Research, 133,* 131–142.

Wagner, B. M., Silverman, M. A. C., & Martin, C. E. (2003). Family factors in youth suicidal behaviors. *American Behavioral Scientist, 46,* 1171–1191.

Wagner, R. K. (2000). Practical intelligence. In R. J. Sternberg (Ed.), *Handbook of intelligence* (pp. 380–395). New York: Cambridge University Press.

Wahl, H.-W. (1991). Dependence in the elderly from an interactional point of view: Verbal and observational data. *Psychology and Aging, 6,* 238–246.

Wahlsten, D. (1994). The intelligence of heritability. *Canadian Psychology, 35,* 244–259.

Wainryb, C. (1997). The mismeasure of diversity: Reflections on the study of cross-cultural differences. In H. D. Saltzstein (Ed.), *New directions for child development* (No. 76, pp. 51–65). San Francisco: Jossey-Bass.

Waite, L. J. (1999, July). *Debunking the marriage myth: It works for women, too.* Paper presented at the annual Smart Marriages Conference, Washington, DC.

Wakeley, A., Rivera, S., & Langer, J. (2000). Can young infants add and subtract? *Child Development, 71,* 1477–1720.

Walberg, H. J. (1986). Synthesis of research on teaching. In M. C. Wittrock (Ed.), *Handbook of research on teaching* (3rd ed., pp. 214–229). New York: Macmillan.

Waldfogel, J. (2001). International policies toward parental leave and child care. *Future of Children 11,* 52–61.

Waldinger, R. J., Schulz, M. S., Hauser, S. T., Allen, J. P., & Crowell, J. A. (2004). Reading others' emotions: The role of intuitive judgments in predicting marital satisfaction, quality, and stability. *Journal of Family Psychology, 18,* 58–71.

Waldman, I. D., Weinberg, R. A., & Scarr, S. (1994). Racial-group differences in IQ in the Minnesota Transracial Adoption Study: A reply to Levin and Lynn. *Intelligence, 19,* 29–44.

Waldrop, D. P., & Weber, J. A. (2001). From grandparent to caregiver: The stress and satisfaction of raising grandchildren. *Families in Society, 82,* 461–472.

Walker, A., Rosenberg, M., & Balaban-Gil, K. (1999). Neurodevelopmental and neurobehavioral sequelae of selected substances of abuse and psychiatric medications in utero. *Neurological Disorders: Developmental and Behavioral Sequelae, 8,* 845–867.

Walker, L. (1995). Sexism in Kohlberg's moral psychology? In W. M. Kurtines & J. L. Gewirtz (Eds.), *Moral development: An introduction* (pp. 83–107). Boston: Allyn and Bacon.

Walker, L. J. (2004). Progress and prospects in the psychology of moral development. *Merrill-Palmer Quarterly, 50,* 546–557.

Walker, L. J., Pitts, R. C., Hennig, K. H., & Matsuba, M. K. (1995). Reasoning about morality and real-life moral problems. In M. Killen & D. Hart (Eds.), *Morality in everyday life* (pp. 371–407). New York: Cambridge University Press.

Walker, L. J., & Taylor, J. H. (1991a). Family interactions and the development of moral reasoning. *Child Development, 62,* 264–283.

Walker, L. J., & Taylor, J. H. (1991b). Stage transitions in moral reasoning: A longitudinal study of developmental processes. *Developmental Psychology, 27,* 330–337.

Walker-Andrews, A. (1997). Infants' perception of expressive behaviors: Differentiation of multimodal information. *Psychological Bulletin, 121,* 437–456.

Walkowiak, J., Wiener, J., Fastabend, A., Heinzow, B., Krämer, U., & Schmidt, E. (2001). Environmental exposure to polychlorinated biphenyls and quality of the home environment: Effects on psychodevelopment in early childhood. *Lancet, 358,* 1602–1607.

Wall, E. J. (2000). Practical primary pediatric orthopedics. *Nursing Clinics of North America, 35,* 95–113.

Wallace, J. M., Jr., Bachman,, J. G., O'Malley, P. M., Schulenberg, J. E., Cooper, S. M., & Johnston, L. D. (2003). Gender and ethnic differences in smoking, drinking, and illicit drug use among American 8th, 10th, and 12th grade students, 1976–2000. *Addiction, 98,* 225–234.

Wallerstein, J. S., & Blakeslee, S. (1995). *The good marriage.* Boston: Houghton Mifflin.

Walls, C. T., & Zarit, S. H. (1991). Informal support from black churches and the well-being of elderly blacks. *Gerontologist, 31,* 490–495.

Walsh, F., & McGoldrick, M. (2004). Loss and the family: A systemic perspective. In F. Walsh & M. McGoldrick (Eds.), *Living beyond loss: Death in the family* (2nd ed., pp. 3–26). New York: Norton.

Walsh, K. E., & Berman, J. R. (2004). Sexual dysfunction in the older woman: An overview of the current understanding and management. *Therapy in Practice, 21,* 655–675.

Wang, H., & Amato, P. R. (2000). Predictors of divorce adjustment: Stressors, resources, and definitions. *Journal of Marriage and the Family, 62,* 655–668.

Wang, H. X., Karp, A., Winblad, B., & Fratiglioni, L. (2002). Late-life engagement in social and leisure activities is associated with a decreased risk of dementia: A longitudinal study from the Kungsholmen project. *American Journal of Epidemiology, 155,* 1081–1087.

Wang, J. (2005). Work stress as a risk factor for major depressive episode(s). *Psychological Medicine, 35,* 865–871.

Wang, S., Baillargeon, R., & Paterson, S. (2005). Detecting continuity violations in infancy: A new account and new evidence from covering and tube events. *Cognition, 95,* 129–173.

Wannamethee, G., Shaper, A. G., & Macfarlane, P. W. (1993). Heart rate, physical activity, and mortality from cancer and other noncardiovascular diseases. *American Journal of Epidemiology, 137,* 735–748.

Wark, G. R., & Krebs, D. L. (1996). Gender and dilemma differences in real-life moral judgment. *Developmental Psychology, 32,* 220–230.

Warnock, F., & Sandrin, D. (2004). Comprehensive description of newborn distress behavior in response to acute pain (newborn male circumcision). *Pain, 107,* 242–255.

Warr, P. B. (1992). Age and occupational well-being. *Psychology and Aging, 7,* 37–45.

Warr, P. B. (1994). Age and employment. In M. D. Dunnette, L. Hough, & H. Triandis (Eds.), *Handbook of industrial and organizational psychology* (pp. 485–550). Palo Alto, CA: Consulting Psychologists Press.

Warr, P., Butcher, V., Robertson, I., & Callinan, M. (2004). Older people's well-being as a function of employment, retirement, environmental characteristics, and role preference. *British Journal of Psychology, 95,* 297–324.

Warren, A. R., & Tate, C. S. (1992). Egocentrism in children's telephone conversations. In R. M. Diaz & L. E. Berk (Eds.), *Private speech: From social interaction to self-regulation* (pp. 245–264). Hillsdale, NJ: Erlbaum.

Warren, D. H. (1994). *Blindness and children: An individual difference approach.* New York: Cambridge University Press.

Warren, S. L., & Simmens, S. J. (2005). Predicting toddler anxiety/depressive symptoms: Effects of caregiver sensitivity of temperamentally vulnerable children. *Infant Mental Health Journal, 26,* 40–55.

Wasik, B. A., & Bond, M. A. (2001). Beyond the pages of a book: Interactive book reading and language development in preschool classrooms. *Journal of Educational Psychology, 93,* 243–250.

Wass, H. (2004). A perspective on the current state of death education. *Death Studies, 28,* 289–308.

Wasserman, E. A., & Rovee-Collier, C. (2001). Pick the flowers and mind your As and 2s! Categorization by pigeons and infants. In M. E. Carroll & J. B. Overmier (Eds.), *Animal research and human health: Advancing human welfare through behavioral science* (pp. 263–279). Washington, DC: American Psychological Association.

Watamura, S. E., Donzella, B., Alwin, J., & Gunnar, M. R. (2003). Morning-to-afternoon increases in cortisol concentrations for infants and toddlers at child care: Age differences and behavioral correlates. *Child Development, 74,* 1006–1020.

Waterman, A. S., & Whitbourne, S. K. (1982). Androgyny and psychosocial development among college students and adults. *Journal of Personality, 50,* 121–133.

Waters, E., & Cummings, E. M. (2000). A secure base from which to explore close relationships. *Child Development, 71,* 164–172.

Waters, E., Merrick, S., Treboux, D., Crowell, J., & Albersheim, L. (2000). Attachment security in infancy and early adulthood: A twenty-year longitudinal study. *Child Development, 71,* 684–689.

Waters, E., Vaughn, B. E., Posada, G., & Kondo-Ikemura, K. (Eds.). (1995). Caregiving, cultural, and cognitive perspectives on secure-base behavior and working models: New growing points of attachment theory and research. *Monographs of the Society for Research in Child Development, 60*(2–3, Serial No. 244).

Watkins, W. E., & Pollitt, E. (1998). Iron deficiency and cognition among school-age children. In S. G. McGregor (Ed.), *Recent advances in research on the effects of health and nutrition on children's development and school achievement in the Third World.* Washington, DC: Pan American Health Organization.

Watson, A. C., Nixon, C. L., Wilson, A., & Capage, L. (1999). Social interaction skills and theory of mind in young children. *Developmental Psychology, 35,* 386–391.

Watson, D. J. (1989). Defining and describing whole language. *Elementary School Journal, 90,* 129–141.

Watson, J. B., & Raynor, R. (1920). Conditioned emotional reactions. *Journal of Experimental Psychology, 3,* 1–14.

Watson, M. (1990). Aspects of self development as reflected in children's role playing. In D. Cicchetti & M. Beeghly (Eds.), *The self in transition: Infancy to childhood* (pp. 281–307). Chicago: University of Chicago Press.

Watson, R. E., Stein, A. D., Dwamena, F. C., Krlj, M. M., & McIntosh, B. A. (2002). Do race and gender influence the use of invasive procedures? *Internal Medicine, 16,* 227–234.

Watt, L. M., & Cappeliez, P. (2000). Integrative and instrumental reminiscence therapies for depression in older adults: Intervention strategies and treatment effectiveness. *Aging and Mental Health, 4,* 166–177.

Waxman, S. R. (2003). Links between object categorization and naming: Origins and emergence in human infants. In D. H. Rakison & L. M. Oakes (Eds.), *Early category and concept development: Making sense of the blooming, buzzing confusion* (pp. 193–209). New York: Oxford University Press.

Waxman, S. R., & Senghas, A. (1992). Relations among word meanings in early lexical development. *Developmental Psychology, 28,* 862–873.

Webb, N. B. (2002). September 11, 2001. In N. B. Webb (Ed.), *Helping bereaved children: A handbook for practitioners* (pp. 365–384). New York: Guilford.

Webb, S. J., Monk, C. S., & Nelson, C. A. (2001). Mechanisms of postnatal neurobiological development: Implications for human development. *Developmental Neuropsychology, 19,* 147–171.

Weber, C., Hahne, A., Friedrich, M., & Friederici, A. (2004). Discrimination of word stress in early infant perception: Electrophysiological evidence. *Cognitive Brain Research, 18,* 149–161.

Weber, J. A., & Waldrop, D. P. (2000). Grandparents raising grandchildren: Families in transition. *Journal of Gerontological Social Work, 33,* 27–46.

Webster, J. D. (2002). Reminiscence function in adulthood: Age, ethnic, and family dynamics correlates. In J. D. Webster & B. K. Haight (Eds.), *Critical advances in reminiscence work* (pp. 140–142). New York: Springer.

Wechsler, D. (2002). *WPPSI-III: Wechsler Preschool and Primary Scale of Intelligence* (3rd ed.). San Antonio, TX: Psychological Corporation.

Wechsler, D. (2003). *WISC-IV: Wechsler Intelligence Scale for Children* (4th ed.). San Antonio, TX: Psychological Corporation.

Wegesin, D. J., Jacobs, D. M., Zubin, N. R., & Ventura, P. R. (2000). Source memory and encoding strategy in normal aging. *Journal of Clinical and Experimental Neuropsychology, 22,* 455–464.

Wehren, A., De Lisi, R., & Arnold, M. (1981). The development of noun definition. *Journal of Child Language, 8,* 165–175.

Wei, Y. H., & Lee, H. C. (2002). Oxidative stress, mitochondrial DNA mutation, and impairment of antioxidant enzymes in aging. *Experimental Biology and Medicine, 227,* 671–682.

Weikart, D. P. (1998). Changing early childhood development through educational intervention. *Preventive Medicine, 27,* 233–237.

Weinberg, M. K., & Tronick, E. Z. (1994). Beyond the face: An empirical study of infant affective configurations of facial, vocal, gestural, and regulatory behaviors. *Child Development, 65,* 1503–1515.

Weinberg, M. K., Tronick, E. Z., Cohn, J. F., & Olson, K. L. (1999). Gender differences in emotional expressivity and self-regulation during early infancy. *Developmental Psychology, 35,* 175–188.

Weindruch, R., Keenan, K. P., Carney, J. M., Fernandes, G., Feuers, R. J., & Floyd, R. A. (2001). Caloric restriction mimetics: Metabolic interventions. *Journal of Gerontology, 56A,* 20–33.

Weiner, J., & Tardif, C. (2004). Social and emotional functioning of children with learning disabilities: Does special education placement make a difference? *Learning Disabilities Research and Practice, 19,* 20–32.

Weinert, F. E., & Hany, E. A. (2003). The stability of individual differences in intellectual development: Empirical evidence, theoretical problems, and new research questions. In R. J. Sternberg & J. Lautrey (Eds.), *Models of intelligence: International perspectives* (pp. 169–181). Washington, DC: American Psychological Association.

Weinfield, N. S., Sroufe, L. A., & Egeland, B. (2000). Attachment from infancy to early adulthood in a high-risk sample: Continuity, discontinuity, and their correlates. *Child Development, 71,* 695–702.

Weinfield, N. S., Whaley, G. J. L., & Egeland, B. (2004). Continuity, discontinuity, and coherence in attachment from infancy to late adolescence: Sequelae of organization and disorganization. *Attachment and Human Development, 6,* 73–97.

Weingarten, H. R. (1988). Late life divorce and the life review. *Journal of Gerontological Social Work, 12*(3–4), 83–97.

Weingarten, H. R. (1989). The impact of late life divorce: A conceptual and empirical study. *Journal of Divorce, 12,* 21–38.

Weinstein, R. S. (2002). *Reaching higher: The power of expectations in schooling.* Cambridge, MA: Harvard University Press.

Weinstock, H., Berman, S., & Cates, W., Jr. (2004). Sexually transmitted diseases among American youth: Incidence and prevalence estimates, 2000. *Perspectives on Sexual and Reproductive Health, 36,* 6–10.

Weisfeld, G. E. (1997). Puberty rites as clues to the nature of human adolescence. *Cross-Cultural Research, 31,* 27–54.

Weisner, T. S. (1993). Ethnographic and ecocultural perspectives on sibling relationships. In Z. Stoneman & P. W. Berman (Eds.), *The effects of mental retardation, disability, and illness on sibling relationships* (pp. 51–83). Baltimore: Paul H. Brookes.

Weisner, T. S. (1996). The 5 to 7 year transition as an ecocultural project. In A. J. Sameroff & M. M. Haith (Eds.), *The five to seven year shift* (pp. 295–326). Chicago: University of Chicago Press.

Weisner, T. S., & Wilson-Mitchell, J. E. (1990). Nonconventional family life-styles and sex typing in six-year-olds. *Child Development, 61,* 1915–1933.

Weiss, A., Costa, P. T., Jr., Karuza, J., Duberstein, P. R., Friedman, B., & McCrae, R. M. (2005). Cross-sectional age differences in personality among Medicare patients aged 65 to 100. *Psychology and Aging, 20,* 182–185.

Weiss, K. M. (2005). Cryptic causation of human disease: Reading between the germ lines. *Trends in Genetics, 21,* 82–88.

Weisz. A. N., & Black, B. M. (2002). Gender and moral reasoning: African American youths respond to dating dilemmas. *Journal of Human Behavior in the Social Environment, 6,* 17–34.

Weizman, Z. O., & Snow, C. E. (2001). Lexical output as related to children's vocabulary acquisition: Effects of sophisticated exposure and support for meaning. *Developmental Psychology, 37,* 265–279.

Wekerle, C., & Wolfe, D. A. (2003). Child maltreatment. In E. J. Mash & R. A. Barkley (Eds.), *Child psychopathology* (2nd ed., pp. 632–684). New York: Guilford.

Wellings, K., Field, J., Johnson, A., & Wadsworth, J. (1994). *Sexual behavior in Britain: The National Survey of Sexual Attitudes and Lifestyles.* New York: Penguin.

Wellman, H. M. (1990). *The child's theory of mind.* Cambridge, MA: MIT Press.

Wellman, H. M. (2002). Understanding the psychological world: Developing a theory of mind. In U. Goswami (Ed.), *Blackwell handbook of child cognitive development* (pp. 167–187). Malden, MA: Blackwell.

Wellman, H. M., Cross, D., & Watson, J. (2001). Meta-analysis of theory-of-mind development: The truth about false belief. *Child Development, 72,* 655–684.

Wellman, H. M., & Hickling, A. K. (1994). The mind's "I": Children's conception of the mind as an active agent. *Child Development, 65,* 1564–1580.

Wellman, H. M., Somerville, S. C., & Haake, R. J. (1979). Development of search procedures in real-life spatial environments. *Developmental Psychology, 15,* 530–542.

Wendland-Carro, J., Piccinini, C. A., & Millar, W. S. (1999). The role of an early intervention on enhancing the quality of mother-infant interaction. *Child Development, 70,* 713–731.

Wenger, G. C. (2001). Ageing without children: Rural Wales. *Journal of Cross-Cultural Gerontology, 16,* 79–109.

Wentworth, N., Benson, J. B., & Haith, M. M. (2000). The development of infants' reaches for stationary and moving targets. *Child Development, 71,* 576–601.

Wentzel, K. R., Barry, C. M., & Caldwell, K. A. (2004). Friendships in middle school: Influences on motivation and school adjustment. *Journal of Educational Psychology, 96,* 195–203.

Werner, E. (2001). *Journeys from childhood to midlife: Risk, resilience, and recovery.* Ithaca, NY: Cornell University Press.

Werner, E. E. (1989, April). Children of the garden island. *Scientific American, 260*(4), 106–111.

Werner, E. E. (1991). Grandparent–grandchild relationships amongst U.S. ethnic groups. In P. K. Smith (Ed.), *The psychology of grandparenthood: An international perspective* (pp. 68–82). London: Routledge.

Werner, E. E., & Smith, R. S. (1982). *Vulnerable but invincible.* New York: McGraw-Hill.

Werner, E. E., & Smith, R. S. (1992). *Overcoming the odds: High-risk children from birth to adulthood.* Ithaca, NY: Cornell University Press.

Werner, E. E., & Smith, R. S. (2001). *Journeys from childhood to midlife: Risk, resilience, and recovery.* Ithaca, NY: Cornell University Press.

Werner, N. E., & Crick, N. R. (2004). Maladaptive peer relationships and the development of relational and physical aggression during middle childhood. *Social Development, 13,* 495–514.

West, R. L., & Craik, F. I. M. (1999). Age-related decline in prospective memory: The roles of cue accessibility and cue sensitivity. *Psychology and Aging, 14,* 264–272.

Westerhof, G. J., Bohlmeijer, E., & Valenkamp, M. W. (2004). In search of meaning: A reminiscence program for older persons. *Educational Gerontology, 30,* 751–766.

Westermeyer, J. F. (1998). Predictors and characteristics of mental health among men at midlife: A 32-year longitudinal study. *American Journal of Orthopsychiatry, 68,* 265–273.

Westermeyer, J. F. (2004). Predictors and characteristics of Erikson's life cycle model among men: A 32-year longitudinal study. *International Journal of Aging and Human Development, 58,* 29–48.

Wethington, E. (2000). Expecting stress: Americans and the "midlife crisis." *Motivation and Emotion, 24,* 85–103.

Wethington, E., Kessler, R. C., & Pixley, J. E. (2004). Turning points in adulthood. In O. G. Brim & C. D. Ryff (Eds.), *How healthy are we?: A national study of well-being at midlife* (pp. 586–613). Chicago: University of Chicago Press.

Whalley, L. (2001). *The aging brain.* London: Weidenfeld & Nicolson.

Wheeler, I. (2001). Parental bereavement: The crisis of meaning. *Death Studies, 25,* 51–66.

Wheeler, W. (2002). Youth leadership for development: Civic activism as a component of youth development programming and a strategy for strengthening civil society. In R. M. Lerner, F. Jacobs, & D. Wertlieb (Eds.), *Handbook of applied developmental science* (Vol. 2, pp. 491–506). Thousand Oaks, CA: Sage.

Whitaker, D. J., & Miller, K. S. (2000). Parent–adolescent discussions about sex and condoms: Impact on peer influences of sexual risk behavior. *Journal of Adolescent Research, 15,* 251–273.

Whitbeck, L., Hoyt, D. R., & Huck, S. M. (1994). Early family relationships, intergenerational solidarity, and support provided to parents by their adult children. *Journal of Gerontology, 49,* 585–594.

Whitbourne, S. K. (1996). *The aging individual: Physical and psychological perspectives.* New York: Springer.

Whitbourne, S. K. (1999). Physical changes. In J. C. Kavanaugh & S. K. Whitbourne (Eds.), *Gerontology: An interdisciplinary perspective* (pp. 33–64). New York: Oxford University Press.

Whitbourne, S. K. (2001). The physical aging process in midlife: Interactions with psychological and sociocultural factors. In M. E. Lachman (Ed.), *Handbook of midlife development* (pp. 109–155). New York: Wiley.

Whitbourne, S. K., & Primus, L. (1996). Identity, physical. In J. E. Birren (Ed.), *Encyclopedia of aging* (pp. 733–742). San Diego: Academic Press.

Whitbourne, S. K., Zuschlag, M. K., Elliot, L. B., & Waterman, A. S. (1992). Psychosocial development in adulthood: A 22-year sequential study. *Journal of Personality and Social Psychology, 63,* 260–271.

White, L. (2001). Sibling relationships over the life course: A panel analysis. *Journal of Marriage and the Family, 63,* 555–568.

White, L., & Gilbreth, J. G. (2001). When children have two fathers: Effects of relationships with stepfathers and noncustodial fathers on adolescent outcomes. *Journal of Marriage and the Family, 63,* 155–167.

White, L. K. (1994). Coresidence and leaving home: Young adults and their parents. *Annual Review of Sociology, 20,* 81–102.

Whiteside-Mansell, L., Bradley, R. H., Owen, M. T., Randolph, S. M., & Cauce, A. M. (2003). Parenting and children's behavior at 36 months: Equivalence between African-American and European-American mother–child dyads. *Parenting: Science and Practice, 3,* 197–234.

Whiting, B., & Edwards, C. P. (1988). A cross-cultural analysis of sex differences in the behavior of children aged 3 through 11. In G. Handel (Ed.), *Childhood socialization* (pp. 281–297). New York: Aldine de Gruyter.

Wichmann, C., Coplan, R. J., & Daniels, T. (2004). The social cognitions of socially withdrawn children. *Social Development, 13,* 377–392.

Wichstrøm, L. (1999). The emergence of gender difference in depressed mood: The role of intensified gender socialization. *Developmental Psychology, 35,* 232–245.

Wickens, A. P. (2001). Aging and the free radical theory. *Respiration Physiology, 128,* 379–391.

Wideen, M. F., O'Shea, T., Pye, I., & Ivany, G. (1997). High-stakes testing and the teaching of science. *Canadian Journal of Education, 22,* 428–444.

Wiebe, D. J., & Williams, P. G. (1992). Hardiness and health: A social psychophysiological perspective on stress and adaptation. *Journal of Social and Clinical Psychology, 11,* 238–262.

Wierenga, K. J., Hambleton, I. R., & Lewis, N. A. (2001). Survival estimates for patients with homozygous sickle-cell disease in Jamaica: A clinic-based population study. *Lancet, 357,* 680–683.

Wigfield, A., Battle, A., Keller, L. B., & Eccles, J. S. (2002). Sex differences in motivation, self-concept, career aspiration, and career choice: Implications for cognitive development. In A. McGillicudy-De Lisi & R. De Lisi (Eds.), *Biology, society, and behavior: The development of sex differences in cognition* (pp. 93–124). Westport, CT: Ablex.

Wigfield, A., & Eccles, J. S. (1994). Children's competence beliefs, achievement values, and general self-esteem change across elementary and middle school. *Journal of Early Adolescence, 14,* 107–138.

Wigfield, A., Eccles, J. S., Yoon, K. S., Harold, R. D., Arbreton, A. J., Freedman-Doan, C., & Blumenfeld, P. C. (1997). Changes in children's competence beliefs and subjective task values across the elementary school years: A three-year study. *Journal of Educational Psychology, 89,* 451–469.

Wikby, A., Maxson, P., Olsson, J., Johansson, B., & Ferguson, F. G. (1998). Changes in CD8 and CD4 lymphocyte subsets, T cell proliferation responses and nonsurvival in the very old: The Swedish longitudinal OCTO-immune study. *Mechanisms of Ageing and Development, 102,* 187–198.

Wilber, K. H., & McNeilly, D. P. (2001). Elder abuse and victimization. In J. E. Birren (Ed.), *Handbook of the psychology of aging* (pp. 569–591). San Diego: Academic Press.

Wilbur, J., Chandler, P. J., Dancy, B., & Lee, H. (2003). Correlates of physical activity in urban Midwestern African-American women. *American Journal of Preventive Medicine, 25,* 45–52.

Wilbur, J., Vassalo, A., Chandler, P., McDevitt, J., & Miller, A. M. (2005). Midlife women's adherence to home-based walking during maintenance. *Nursing Research, 54,* 33–40.

Wilcox, A. J., Weinberg, C. R., & Baird, D. D. (1995). Timing of sexual intercourse in relation to ovulation: Effects on the probability of conception, survival of the pregnancy, and sex of the baby. *New England Journal of Medicine, 333,* 1517–1519.

Wilcox, W. B. (2002). Religion, convention, and paternal involvement. *Journal of Marriage and the Family, 64,* 780–792.

Wildes, J. E., Emery, R. E., & Simons, A. D. (2001). The roles of ethnicity and culture in the development of eating disturbance and body dissatisfaction: A meta-analytic review. *Clinical Psychology Review, 21,* 521–551.

Wilhelm, O. (2005). Measures of emotional intelligence: Practice and standards. In R. Schulze & R. D. Roberts (Eds.), *Emotional intelligence: An international handbook* (pp. 131–154). Göttingen, Germany: Hogrefe & Huber.

Wilke, C. J., & Thompson, C. A. (1993). First-year reentry women's perceptions of their classroom experiences. *Journal of the Freshman Year Experience, 5,* 69–90.

Wilkie, J. R., Ferree, M. M., & Ratcliff, K. S. (1998). Gender and fairness: Marital satisfaction and two-earner couples. *Journal of Marriage and the Family, 60,* 577–594.

Wilkinson, K., Ross, E., & Diamond, A. (2003). Fast mapping of multiple words: Insights into when "the information provided" does and does not equal "the information perceived." *Applied Developmental Psychology, 24,* 739–762.

Willatts, P. (1999). Development of means–end behavior in young infants: Pulling a support to retrieve a distant object. *Developmental Psychology, 35,* 651–667.

Wille, D. E. (1991). Relation of preterm birth with quality of infant–mother attachment at one year. *Infant Behavior and Development, 14,* 227–240.

Wille, M. C., Weitz, B., Kerper, P., & Frazier, S. (2004). Advances in preconception genetic counseling. *Journal of Perinatal and Neonatal Nursing, 18,* 28–40.

Williams, J. M., & Currie, C. (2000). Self-esteem and physical development in early adolescence: Pubertal timing and body image. *Journal of Early Adolescence, 20,* 129–149.

Williams, K. (2003). Has the future of marriage arrived? A contemporary examination of gender, marriage, and psychological well-being. *Journal of Health and Social Relationships, 44,* 470–487.

Williams, N., & Torrez, D. J. (1998). Grandparenthood among Hispanics. In M. E. Szinovacz (Ed.), *Handbook on grandparenthood* (pp. 87–96). Westport, CT: Greenwood Press.

Williams, P. E., Weis, L. G., & Rolfhus, E. (2003). *WISC-IV: Theoretical model and test blueprint.* San Antonio, TX: Psychological Corporation.

Williams, R. B. (2000). Psychological factors, health, and disease: The impact of aging and the life cycle. In S. B. Manuck, R. Jennings, B. S. Rabin, & A. Baum (Eds.), *Behavior, health, and aging* (pp. 135–151). Mahwah, NJ: Erlbaum.

Williams, S., & Dale, J. (2006). The effectiveness of treatment for depression/depressive symptoms in adults with cancer: A systematic review. *British Journal of Cancer, 94,* 372–390.

Williamson, J., Softas-Nall, B., & Miller, J. (2003). Grandmothers raising grandchildren: An exploration of their experiences and emotions. *Counseling and Therapy for Couples with Families, 11,* 23–32.

Willinger, M., Ko, C.-W., Hoffman, H. J., Kessler, R. C., & Corwin, M. J. (2003). Trends in infant bed sharing in the United States. *Archives of Pediatrics and Adolescent Medicine, 157,* 43–49.

Willis, S. (1996). Everyday problem solving. In J. E. Birren & K. W. Schaie (Eds.), *Handbook of the psychology of aging* (4th ed., pp. 287–307). San Diego: Academic Press.

Willis, S. L., & Schaie, K. W. (1999). Intellectual functioning in midlife. In S. L. Willis & J. D. Reid (Eds.), *Life in the middle* (pp. 105–146). San Diego: Academic Press.

Willms, J. D., Tremblay, M. S., & Katzmarzyk, P. T. (2003). Geographic and demographic variation in the prevalence of overweight Canadian children. *Obesity Research, 11,* 668–673.

Willoughby, J., Kupersmidt, J. B., & Bryant, D. (2001). Overt and covert dimensions of antisocial behavior. *Journal of Abnormal Child Psychology, 29,* 177–187.

Willy, K. A., & Singh, M. A. (2003). Battling insulin resistance in elderly obese people with type 2 diabetes: Bring on the heavy weights. *Diabetes Care, 26,* 1580–1588.

Wilson, D. K., Kirtland, K. A., Ainsworth, B. E., & Addy, C. L. (2004). Socioeconomic status and perceptions of access and safety for physical activity. *Annals of Behavioral Medicine, 28,* 20–28.

Wilson, D. M. (2002). Addressing myths about end-of-life care: Research into the use of acute care hospitals over the last five years of life. *Journal of Palliative Care, 18,* 29–38.

Wilson, R. S., Beckett, L. A., Evans, D. A., & Bennett, D. A. (2003). Terminal decline in cognitive function. *Neurology, 60,* 1782–1787.

Wingfield, A., & Stine-Morrow, E. A. L. (2000). Language and speech. In F. I. M. Craik & T. A. Salthouse (Eds.), *Handbook of aging and cognition* (2nd ed., pp. 359–416). Mahwah, NJ: Erlbaum.

Wink, P., & Dillon, M. (2002). Spiritual development across the adult life course: Findings from a longitudinal study. *Journal of Adult Development, 9,* 79–94.

Wink, P., & Dillon, M. (2003). Religiousness, spirituality, and psychosocial functioning in late adulthood: Findings from a longitudinal study. *Psychology and Aging, 18,* 916–924.

Wink, P., & Helson, R. (1993). Personality change in women and their partners. *Journal of Personality and Social Psychology, 65,* 597–605.

Wink, P., & Scott, J. (2005). Does religiousness buffer against the fear of death and dying in late adulthood? Findings from a longitudinal study. *Journal of Gerontology, 60B,* P207–P214.

Winn, R., & Newton, N. (1982). Sexual activity in aging: A study of 106 cultures. *Archives of Sexual Behavior, 11,* 283–298.

Winner, E. (1986, August). Where pelicans kiss seals. *Psychology Today, 20*(8), 25–35.

Winner, E. (1988). *The point of words: Children's understanding of metaphor and irony.* Cambridge, MA: Harvard University Press.

Winner, E. (1996). *Gifted children: Myths and realities.* New York: Basic Books.

Winner, E. (2000). The origins and ends of giftedness. *American Psychologist, 55,* 159–169.

Winner, E. (2003). Creativity and talent. In M. H. Bornstein, L. Davidson, C. L. M. Keyes, K. A. Moore, & the Center for Child Well-Being (Eds.), *Well-being: Positive development across the life course* (pp. 371–380). Mahwah, NJ: Erlbaum.

Winsler, A., & Naglieri, J. (2003). Overt and covert verbal problem-solving strategies: Developmental trends in use, awareness, and relations with task performance in children aged 5 to 17. *Child Development, 74,* 659–678.

Winsler, A., Diaz, R. M., & Montero, I. (1997). The role of private speech in the transition from collaborative to independent task performance in young children. *Early Childhood Research Quarterly, 12,* 59–79.

Winslow, R. D., Mehta, D., & Fuster, V. (2005). Sudden cardiac death: Mechanisms, therapies and challenges. *Cardiovascular Medicine, 2,* 352–360.

Wiscott, R., & Kopera-Frye, K. (2000). Sharing of culture: Adult grandchildrens' perceptions of intergenerational relations. *International Journal of Aging and Human Development, 5,* 199–215.

Wojciechowski, W. C. (1998). Issues in caring for older lesbians. *Journal of Gerontological Nursing, 24,* 28–33.

Wolak, J., Mitchell, K. J., & Finkelhor, D. (2003). Escaping or connecting? Characteristics of youth who form close online relationships. *Journal of Adolescence, 26,* 105–119.

Wolchik, S. A., Wilcox, K. L., Tein, J.-Y. & Sandler, I. N. (2000).

Maternal acceptance and consistency of discipline as buffers of divorce stressors on children's psychological adjustment problems. *Journal of Abnormal Child Psychology, 28,* 87–102.

Wolfe, D. A. (1999). *Child abuse* (2nd ed.). Thousand Oaks, CA: Sage.

Wolfe, D. A., Scott, K., Wekerle, C., & Pittman, A. (2001). Child maltreatment: Risk of adjustment problems and dating violence in adolescence. *Journal of the American Academy of Child and Adolescent Psychiatry, 40,* 282–289.

Wolfelt, A. D. (1997). Death and grief in the school setting. In T. N. Fairchild (Ed.), *Crisis intervention strategies for school-based helpers* (pp. 199–244). Springfield, IL: Charles C. Thomas.

Wolff, P. H. (1966). The causes, controls and organization of behavior in the neonate. *Psychological Issues, 5*(1, Serial No. 17).

Wolff, P. H., & Fesseha, G. (1999). The orphans of Eritrea: A five-year follow-up study. *Journal of Child Psychology and Psychiatry and Allied Disciplines, 40,* 1231–1237.

Wolfinger, N. H. (2000). Beyond the intergenerational transmission of divorce: Do people replicate the patterns of marital instability they grew up with? *Journal of Family Issues, 21,* 1061–1086.

Wolpe, J., & Plaud, J. J. (1997). Pavlov's contributions to behavior therapy: The obvious and not so obvious. *American Psychologist, 52,* 966–972.

Women's Health Initiative. (2002). Risks and benefits of estrogen plus progestin in healthy postmenopausal women: Principal results from the Women's Health Initiative randomized control trial. *Journal of the American Medical Association, 288,* 321–333.

Wong, C. A., Eccles, J. S., & Sameroff, A. (2003). The influence of ethnic discrimination and ethnic identification on African American adolescents' school and socioemotional adjustment. *Journal of Personality, 71,* 1197–1232.

Wong, R., Kitayama, K. E., & Soldo, B. J. (1999). Ethnic differences in time transfers from adult children to elderly parents: Unobserved heterogeneity across families? *Research on Aging, 21,* 144–175.

Wood, E., Desmarais, S., & Gugula, S. (2002). The impact of parenting experience on gender stereotyped toy play of children. *Sex Roles, 47,* 39–49.

Wood, J. J., Emmerson, N. A., & Cowan, P. A. (2004). Is early attachment security carried forward into relationships with preschool peers? *British Journal of Developmental Psychology, 22,* 245–253.

Wood, J. M. (2002). Aging, driving and vision. *Clinical and Experimental Optometry, 85,* 214–220.

Wood, S. (2001). Interview. *Frontline.* Retrieved from http://www. pbs .org/wgbh/pages/frontline/ shows/fertility/interviews/ wood.html

Wood, W., & Eagly, A. H. (2000). Once again, the origins of sex differences. *American Psychologist, 55,* 1062–1063.

Woods, J. A., Lowder, T. W., & Keylock, K. T. (2002). Can exercise training improve immune function in the aged? *Annals of the New York Academy of Sciences, 959,* 117–127.

Woodward, A. L., & Markman, E. M. (1998). Early word learning. In D. Kuhn & R. S. Siegler (Eds.), *Handbook of child psychology: Vol. 2. Cognition, perception, and language* (5th ed., pp. 371–420). New York: Wiley.

Woodward, J., & Ono, Y. (2004). Mathematics and academic diversity in Japan. *Journal of Learning Disabilities, 37,* 74–82.

Woolf, L. M. (2001). Gay and lesbian aging. *SIECUS Report, 30,* 16–21.

Woolley, J. D. (1997). Thinking about fantasy: Are children fundamentally different thinkers and believers from adults? *Child Development, 68,* 991–1011.

Woolley, J. D. (2000). The development of beliefs about direct mental–physical causality in imagination, magic, and religion. In K. S. Rosengren, C. N. Johnson, & P. L. Harris (Eds.), *Imagining the impossible* (pp. 99–156). Cambridge, UK: Cambridge University Press.

Wooster, D. M. (1999). Assessment of nonorganic failure to thrive. *Infant–Toddler Intervention, 9,* 353–371.

Word, S. (1996). Mortality awareness and risk-taking in late adolescence. *Death Studies, 20,* 133–148.

Worden, J. W. (2000). Toward an appropriate death. In T. A. Rando (Ed.), *Clinical dimensions of anticipatory mourning* (pp. 267–277). Champaign, IL: Research Press.

Worden, J. W. (2002). *Grief counseling and grief therapy* (3rd ed.). New York: Springer.

World Education Services. (2005). World education database. Retrieved from www.wes.org

World Federation of Right to Die Societies. (2006). Public opinion. Retrieved from www.worldrtd.net

World Health Organization. (2000a). *Healthy life expectancy rankings.* Geneva: Author.

World Health Organization. (2000b). Violence against women information pack. Retrieved from http://www.who.int/frh-whd/ VAW/infopack/English

World Health Organization. (2002). *World report on violence and health.* Geneva: Author.

World Health Organization. (2003). *Oral Health Country/Area Profile Program.* Retrieved from www .whocollab.od.mah.se/index.html

World Health Organization. (2005a). *The world health report, 2005.* Geneva, Switzerland: Author.

World Health Organization. (2005b). *WHO Multi-Country Study on Women's Health and Domestic Violence Against Women.* Geneva: Author.

World Press Review. (2004). Obesity: A worldwide issue. Retrieved from www.worldpress.org/Africa/1961 .cfm

Wray, L. A., Alwin, D. F., & McCammon, R. J. (2005). Social status and risky health behaviors: Results from the health and retirement study. *Journal of Gerontology, 60B,* S85–S92.

Wright, B. C., & Dowker, A. D. (2002). The role of cues to differential absolute size in children's transitive inferences. *Journal of Experimental Child Psychology, 81,* 249–275.

Wright, J. C., Huston, A. C., Murphy, K. C., St. Peters, M., Pinon, M., Scantlin, R., & Kotler, J. (2001). The relations of early television viewing to school readiness and vocabulary of children from low-income families: The Early Window Project. *Child Development, 72,* 1347–1366.

Wright, J. W. (Ed.). (1999). *The universal almanac 1999.* Kansas City: Andrews and McMeel.

Wright, K. (2003). Relationships with death: The terminally ill talk about dying. *Journal of Marital and Family Therapy, 29,* 439–454.

Wright, T. A., & Bonett, D. G. (1997). The contribution of burnout to work performance. *Journal of Organizational Behavior, 18,* 491–499.

Wright, V. C., Schieve, L. A., Reynolds, M. A., Jeng, G., & Kissin, D. (2004). Assisted reproductive technology surveillance— United States 2001. *Morbidity and Mortality Weekly Report, 53,* 1–20.

Wright, W. E., & Shay, J. W. (2005). Telomere biology in aging and cancer. *Journal of the American Geriatric Society, 53,* S292–S294.

Wrotniak, B. H., Epstein, L. H., Raluch, R. A., & Roemmich, J. N. (2004). Parent weight change as a predictor of child weight change in family-based behavioral obesity treatment. *Archives of Pediatric and Adolescent Medicine, 158,* 342–347.

Wu, A. M. S., Tang, C. S. K., & Kwok, T. C. Y. (2002). Death anxiety among Chinese elderly people in

Hong Kong. *Journal of Aging and Health, 14,* 42–56.

Wu, G., Bazer, F. W., Cudd, T. A., Meininger, C. J., & Spencer, T. E. (2004). Maternal nutrition and fetal development. *Journal of Nutrition, 134,* 2169–2172.

Wu, L. L., Bumpass, L. L., & Musick, K. (2001). Historical and life course trajectories of nonmarital childbearing. In L. L. Wu & B. Wolfe (Eds.), *Out of wedlock: Causes and consequences of non-marital fertility* (pp. 3–48). New York: Russell Sage Foundation.

Wu, P., Robinson, C. C., Yang, C., Hart, C. H., Olsen, S. F., Porter, C. L., Jin, S., Wo, J., & Wu, X. (2002). Similarities and differences in mothers' parenting of preschoolers in China and the United States. *International Journal of Behavioral Development, 26,* 481–491.

Wu, T., Mendola, P., & Buck, G. M. (2002). Ethnic differences in the presence of secondary sex characteristics and menarche among U.S. girls: The Third National Health and Nutrition Examination Survey, 1988–1994. *Pediatrics, 110,* 752–757.

Wu, Z., & Penning, M. J. (1997). Marital instability after midlife. *Journal of Family Issues, 18,* 459–478.

Wu, Z., & Pollard, M. S. (1998). Social support among unmarried childless elderly persons. *Journal of Gerontology, 53B,* S324–S335.

Wust, S., Entringer, S., Federenko, I. S., Schlotz, W., Helhammer, D. H. (2005). Birth weight is associated with salivary cortisol responses to psychosocial stress in adult life. *Psychoneuroendocrinology, 30,* 591–598.

Wyatt, J. M., & Carlo, G. (2002). What will my parents think? Relations among adolescents' expected parental reactions, prosocial moral reasoning, and prosocial and antisocial behaviors. *Journal of Adolescent Research, 16,* 646–666.

Wyman, P. A., Cowen, E. L., Work, W. C., Hoyt-Meyers, L., Magnus, K. B., & Fagen, D. B. (1999). Caregiving and developmental factors differentiating young at-risk urban children showing resilient versus stress-affected outcomes: A replication and extension. *Child Development, 70,* 645–659.

Wynn, K. (1992). Addition and subtraction by human infants. *Nature, 358,* 749–750.

Wynn, K., Bloom, P., & Chiang, W.-C. (2002). Enumeration of collective entities by 5-month-old infants. *Cognition, 83,* B55–B62.

Wynne-Edwards, K. E. (2001). Hormonal changes in mammalian fathers. *Hormones and Behavior, 40,* 139–145.

X

Xu, X., & Lai, S.-C. (2004). Gender ideologies, marital roles, and marital quality in Taiwan. *Journal of Family Issues, 25,* 318–355.

Xu, X., & Peng, L. (2001). Reflection on parents' educational beliefs in the new century. *Theory and Practice of Education, 21,* 62–63.

Xue, Y., & Meisels, S. J. (2004). Early literacy instruction and learning in kindergarten: Evidence from the early childhood longitudinal study—kindergarten classes of 1998–1999. *American Educational Research Journal, 41,* 191–229.

Y

Yaffe, K., Blackwell, T., Kanaya, A. M., Davidowitz, N., Barrett-Connor, E., & Krueger, K. (2004a). Diabetes, impaired fasting glucose, and development of cognitive impairment in older women. *Neurology, 63,* 658–663.

Yaffe, K., Fox, P., Newcomer, R., Sands, L., Lindquist, K., Dane, K., & Covinsky, K. E. (2002). Patient and caregiver characteristics and nursing home placement in patients with dementia. *Journal of the American Medical Association, 287,* 2090–2097.

Yaffe, K., Kanaya, A., Lindquist, K., Simonsick, E. M., Harris, T., Shorr, R. I., Tyulavsky, F. A., & Newman, A. B. (2004b). The metabolic syndrome, inflammation, and risk of cognitive decline. *Journal of the American Medical Association, 292,* 2237–2242.

Yale, M. E., Messinger, D. S., Cobo-Lewis, A. B., Oller, D. K., & Eilers, R. E. (1999). An event-based analysis of the coordination of early infant vocalizations and facial actions. *Developmental Psychology, 35,* 505–513.

Yamamoto, K. (2004). The care of the dying and the grieving in Japan. In J. D. Morgan & P. Laungani (Eds.), *Death and bereavement around the world: Vol. 4. Death and bereavement in Asia, Australia, and New Zealand* (pp. 101–107). Amityville, NY: Baywood Publishing Company.

Yamanoi, K. (1993). Care for the elderly in Sweden and Japan. Retrieved from http://www.wao.or.jp/yamanoi/report/lunds/index.htm

Yan, J., & Smetana, J. G. (2003). Conceptions of moral, social-conventional, and personal events among Chinese preschoolers in Hong Kong. *Child Development, 74,* 647–658.

Yang, B., Ollendick, T. H., Dong, Q., Xia, Y., & Lin, L. (1995). Only children and children with siblings in the People's Republic of China: Levels of fear, anxiety, and depression. *Child Development, 66,* 1301–1311.

Yang, C., Hart, C. H., Nelson, D. A., Porter, C. L., Olsen, S. F., Robinson, C. C., & Jin, S. (2003). Fathering in a Beijing Chinese sample: Associations with boys' and girls' negative emotionality and aggression. In R. D. Day & M. E. Lamb (Eds.), *Conceptualizing and measuring father involvement* (pp. 185–215). Mahwah, NJ: Erlbaum.

Yang, C.-K., & Hahn, H.-M. (2002). Cosleeping in young Korean children. *Developmental and Behavioral Pediatrics, 23,* 151–157.

Yang, S. C., & Chen, S.-F. (2002). A phenomenographic approach to the meaning of death: A Chinese perspective. *Death Studies, 26,* 143–175.

Yanovski, J. A. (2003). Rapid weight gain during infancy as a predictor of adult obesity. *American Journal of Clinical Nutrition, 77,* 1350–1351.

Yarrow, M. R., Scott, P. M., & Waxler, C. Z. (1973). Learning concern for others. *Developmental Psychology, 8,* 240–260.

Yates, T. M., Egeland, B., & Sroufe, L. A. (2003). Rethinking resilience: A developmental process perspective. In S. S. Luthar (Ed.), *Resilience and vulnerability: Adaptation in the context of childhood adversities* (pp. 243–266). New York: Cambridge University Press.

Yates, W. R., Cadoret, R. J., & Troughton, E. P. (1999). The Iowa adoption studies: Methods and results. In M. C. LaBuda & E. L. Grigorenko (Eds.), *On the way to individuality: Current methodological issues in behavioral genetics* (pp. 95–125). Commack, NY: Nova Science Publishers.

Yehuda, R., Engel, S. M., Brand, S. R., Seckl, J., Marcus, S. M., & Berkowitz, G. S. (2005). Transgenerational effects of posttraumatic stress disorder in babies of mothers exposed to the World Trade Center attacks during pregnancy. *Journal of Clinical Endocrinology and Metabolism, 90,* 4115–4118.

Yeung, W. (1996). Buddhism, death, and dying. In J. K. Parry & A. S. Ryan (Eds.), *A cross-cultural look at death, dying, and religion* (pp. 74–83). Chicago: Nelson-Hall.

Yip, R., Scanlon, K., & Trowbridge, F. (1993). Trends and patterns in height and weight status of low-income U.S. children. *Critical Reviews in Food Science and Nutrition, 33,* 409–421.

Yirmiya, N., Erel, O., Shaked, M., & Solomonica-Levi, D. (1998). Meta-analyses comparing theory of mind abilities of individuals with autism, individuals with mental retardation, and normally developing individuals. *Psychological Bulletin, 124,* 283–307.

Yogman, M. W. (1981). Development of the father–infant relationship. In H. Fitzgerald, B. Lester, & M. W. Yogman (Eds.), *Theory and research in behavioral pediatrics* (Vol. 1, pp. 221–279). New York: Plenum.

Yonas, A., Granrud, E. C., Arterberry, M. E., & Hanson, B. L. (1986). Infants' distance perception from linear perspective and texture gradients. *Infant Behavior and Development, 9,* 247–256.

Yoo, S. H., & Sung, K.-T. (1997). Elderly Koreans' tendency to live independently from their adult children: Adaptation to cultural differences in America. *Journal of Cross-Cultural Gerontology, 12,* 225–244.

Yoon, D. P. (2004). Intercountry adoption: The importance of ethnic socialization and subjective well-being for Korean-born adopted children. *Journal of Ethnic and Cultural Diversity in Social Work, 13,* 71–89.

Yoshinaga-Itano, C. (2003). Early intervention after universal neonatal hearing screening: Impact on outcomes. *Mental Retardation and Developmental Disabilities Research and Reviews, 9,* 252–266.

Youn, G., Knight, B. G., Jeon, H., & Benton, D. (1999). Differences in familism values and caregiving outcomes among Korean, Korean American, and White American dementia caregivers. *Psychology and Aging, 14,* 355–364.

Young, H. M. (1998). Moving to congregate housing: The last chosen home. *Journal of Aging Studies, 12,* 149–165.

Young, J. B., & Rodgers, R. F. (1997). A model of radical career change in the context of psychosocial development. *Journal of Career Assessment, 5,* 167–172.

Young, J. F., & Mroczek, D. K. (2003). Predicting intraindividual self-concept trajectories during adolescence. *Journal of Adolescence, 26,* 589–603.

Young, L. R., & Nestle, M. (2002). The contribution of expanding portion sizes to the U.S. obesity epidemic. *American Journal of Public Health, 92,* 246–249.

Young, P. (1991). Families with adolescents. In F. H. Brown (Ed.), *Reweaving the family tapestry* (pp. 131–168). New York: Norton.

Young, T., Rabago, D., Zgierska, A., Austin, D., & Finn, L. (2002). Objective and subjective sleep quality in premenopausal, peri-menopausal, and postmenopausal women in the Wisconsin Sleep

Cohort Study. *Epidemiology, 26,* 667–672.

Youngblade, L. M., & Dunn, J. (1995). Individual differences in young children's pretend play with mother and sibling: Links to relationships and understanding of other people's feelings and beliefs. *Child Development, 66,* 1472–1492.

Youniss, J., McLellan, J. A., & Yates, M. (1997). What we know about engendering civic identity. *American Behavioral Scientist, 40,* 620–631.

Yu, R. (2002). On the reform of elementary school education in China. *Educational Exploration, 129,* 56–57.

Yu, S., Yarnell, J. W. G., Sweetnam, P. M., & Murray, L. (2003). What level of physical activity protects against premature cardiovascular death? The Caerphilly Study. *Heart, 89,* 502–506.

Yunger, J. L., Carver, P. R., & Perry, D. G. (2004). Does gender identity influence children's psychological well-being? *Developmental Psychology, 40,* 572–582.

Z

Zach, T., Pramanik, A., & Ford, S. P. (2001). Multiple births. *eMedicine.* Retrieved from www.mypage.direct.ca/csamson/multiples/2twinningrates.html

Zafeiriou, D. I. (2000). Plantar grasp reflex in high-risk infants during the first year of life. *Pediatric Neurology, 22,* 75–76.

Zahn-Waxler, C., Kochanska, G., Krupnick, J., & McKnew, D. (1990). Patterns of guilt in children of depressed and well mothers. *Developmental Psychology, 26,* 51–59.

Zahn-Waxler, C., Radke-Yarrow, M., & King, R. M. (1979). Childrearing and children's prosocial initiations toward victims of distress. *Child Development, 50,* 319–330.

Zahn-Waxler, C., & Robinson, J. (1995). Empathy and guilt: Early origins of feelings of responsibility. In J. P. Tangney & K. W. Fischer (Eds.), *Self-conscious emotions* (pp. 143–173). New York: Guilford.

Zahn-Waxler, C., Schiro, K., Robinson, J. L., Emde, R. N., & Schmitz, S. (2001). Empathy and prosocial patterns in young MZ and DZ twins: Development and genetic and environmental influences. In R. N. Emde & J. K.

Hewitt (Eds.), *Infancy to early childhood: Genetic and environmental influences on developmental change* (pp. 141–162). New York: Oxford University Press.

Zakowski, S. G., Hall, M. H., Klein, L. C., & Baum, A. (2001). Appraised control, coping, and stress in a community sample: A test of the goodness-of-fit hypothesis. *Annals of Behavioral Medicine, 23,* 158–165.

Zandi, P. P., & Breitner, J. C. (2003). Estrogen replacement and risk of Alzheimer's disease. *Journal of the American Medical Association, 289,* 1100–1102.

Zane, N., & Yeh, M. (2002). The use of culturally based variables in assessment: Studies on loss of face. In K. Kurasaki, S. Okazaki, & S. Sue (Eds.), *Asian American mental health: Assessment theories and methods* (pp. 123–138). Dordrecht, Netherlands: Kluwer Academic.

Zapf, D., Seifert, C., Schmutte, B., Mertini, H., & Hotz, M. (2001). Emotion work and job stressors and their effects on burnout. *Psychology and Health, 16,* 527–545.

Zaretsky, M. D. (2003). Communication between identical twins: Health behavior and social factors are associated with longevity that is greater among identical than fraternal U.S. World War II veteran twins. *Journal of Gerontology, 58,* 566–572.

Zarit, S. H., & Eggebeen, D. J. (2002). Parent–child relationships in adulthood and later years. In M. H. Bornstein (Ed.), *Handbook of parenting, Vol. 1* (2nd ed., pp. 135–161). Mahwah, NJ: Erlbaum.

Zarit, S. H., Stephens, M. A. P., Townsend, A., & Greene, R. (1998). Stress reduction for family caregivers: Effects of adult day care use. *Journal of Gerontology, 53B,* S267–S277.

Zea, M. C., Reisen, C. A., Beil, C., & Caplan, R. D. (1997). Predicting intention to remain in college among ethnic minority and nonminority students. *Journal of Social Psychology, 137,* 149–160.

Zelazo, N. A., Zelazo, P. R., Cohen, K. M., & Zelazo, P. D. (1993). Specificity of practice effects on elementary neuromotor patterns. *Developmental Psychology, 29,* 686–691.

Zelazo, P. D., Frye, D., & Rapus, T. (1996). An age-related dissociation between knowing rules and

using them. *Cognitive Development, 11,* 37–63.

Zelazo, P. D., Muller, U., Frye, D., & Marcovitch, S. (2003). The development of executive function: Cognitive complexity and control—revised. *Monographs of the Society for Research in Child Development, 68*(3), 93–119.

Zeman, J., Shipman, K., & Suveg, C. (2002). Anger and sadness regulation: Predictions to internalizing and externalizing symptoms in children. *Journal of Clinical Child and Adolescent Psychology, 31,* 393–398.

Zenger, T., & Lawrence, B. (1989). Organizational demography: The differential effects of age and tenure distributions on technical communication. *Academy of Management Journal, 32,* 353–376.

Zeskind, P. S., & Barr, R. G. (1997). Acoustic characteristics of naturally occurring cries of infants with "colic." *Child Development, 68,* 394–403.

Zeskind, P. S., & Lester, B. M. (2001). Analysis of infant crying. In L. T. Singer & P. S. Zeskind (Eds.), *Biobehavioral assessment of the infant* (pp. 149–166). New York: Guilford.

Zhan, H. J., & Montgomery, R. J. V. (2003). Gender and elder care in China: The influence of filial piety and structural constraints. *Gender and Society, 17,* 209–229.

Zhang, Q. F. (2004). Economic transition and new patterns of parent–adult child coresidence in urban China. *Journal of Marriage and Family, 66,* 1231–1245.

Zhang, Z., & Hayward, M. D. (2001). Childlessness and the psychological well-being of older persons. *Journal of Gerontology, 56B,* S311–S320.

Zhao, L., Teter, B., Horihara, T., Lim, G. P., Ambegaokar, S. S., & Ubeda, O. J. (2004). Insulin-degrading enzyme as a downstream target of insulin receptor signaling cascade: Implications for Alzheimer's disease intervention. *Journal of Neuroscience, 24,* 11120–11126.

Zhou, M., & Bankston, C. L. (1998). *Growing up American: How Vietnamese children adapt to life in the United States.* New York: Russell Sage Foundation.

Zigler, E. F., & Gilman, E. (1998). The legacy of Jean Piaget. In G. A. Kimble & M. Wertheimer (Eds.),

Portraits of pioneers in psychology (Vol. 3, pp. 145–160). Washington, DC: American Psychological Association.

Zimmer-Gembeck, M. J., Siebenbruner, J., & Collins, W. A. (2001). Diverse aspects of dating: Associations with psychosocial functioning from early to middle adolescence. *Journal of Adolescence, 24,* 313–336.

Zimmerman, B. J., & Risemberg, R. (1997). Self-regulatory dimensions of academic learning and motivation. In G. D. Phye (Ed.), *Handbook of academic learning: Construction of knowledge* (pp. 105–125). San Diego: Academic Press.

Zimmerman, P., & Becker-Stoll, F. (2002). Stability of attachment representations during adolescence: The influence of ego-identity status. *Journal of Adolescence, 25,* 107–124.

Zins, J. E., Garcia, V. F., Tuchfarber, B. S., Clark, K. M., & Laurence, S. C. (1994). Preventing injury in children and adolescents. In R. J. Simeonsson (Ed.), *Risk, resilience, and prevention: Promoting the well-being of all children* (pp. 183–202). Baltimore: Paul H. Brookes.

Zubenko, G. S., Zubenko, W. N., McPherson, S., Spoor, E., Marin, D. B., & Farlow, M. R. (2003). A collaborative study of the emergence and clinical features of the major depressive syndrome of Alzheimer's disease. *American Journal of Psychiatry, 160,* 857–866.

Zucker, A. N., Ostrove, J. M., & Stewart, A. J. (2002). College-educated women's personality development in adulthood: Perceptions and age differences. *Psychology and Aging, 17,* 236–244.

Zukow-Goldring, P. (2002). Sibling caregiving. In M. H. Bornstein (Ed.), *Handbook of parenting: Vol. 3* (2nd ed., pp. 253–286). Hillsdale, NJ: Erlbaum.

Zur, O., & Gelman, R. (2004). Young children can add and subtract by predicting and checking. *Early Childhood Research Quarterly, 19,* 121–137.

Zuzanek, J. (2000). *The effects of time use and time pressure on child–parent relationships.* Waterloo, ON: Otium.

Name Index

Italic *n* following page number indicates source for an illustration or figure.

Subject Index

Alphabetization is letter-by-letter (e.g., "Egocentrism" precedes "Ego differentiation").

Mount San Antonio College

Child Growth and Development

- **Observations**
- **Interviews**
- **Child Study**

Instructions for the Observation Assignment

Preliminary Steps

1: T.B Test—

According to state law, all employees and volunteers to early childhood programs are required to have proof of being clear of tuberculosis. Therefore, the first step in preparing for your observation assignment should be to make an appointment for a TB test. TB tests are given at the campus health center. Call for their hours, fees, and to make an appointment at (909) 594-5611 extension 4400. TB tests are also given at Walnut Medical Group, 19687 E. Valley Blvd. in Walnut. Their number is (909) 598-5228. TB tests re of two kinds, a skin test or a chest X-ray. The skin test takes three days to get a result. The X-ray results can be read immediately, but must be done off campus.

You can use the campus health center or your private health care provider for the test. Some students may require an X-Ray examine, but most will be given the Manitou skin test. Your instructor must be shown this verification before issuing you a "letter of introduction." Without a signed letter of introduction, no credit will be given for completed observations and the child study.

2: Observation Appointment—

Arrange a time for observation visits with the director of an early childhood program. Tell the director you are taking a child development class in which observation of children is required. Assure the director that the information contained in these observations will be used for no purpose other than for your class assignment. When you meet for the first time, present your letter of introduction show the director your TB test result and the observation packet. The recommended time for this assignment is four visits at two hours each; however, you have some discretion is arranging the observation time. Observations three, four, five, and six are ideally done on different days with enough time on each visit to absorb the context of the day. You will need to select one child who attends the class regularly. This child will be the "focus child" of your child study. Your focus child should be between three and four years old.

3: Observation Forms—

Carry out your observations, using the forms provided by your instructor. Your role during the observations is to remain inconspicuous. Some observations can be done from a distance (observing what large motor skills the child engages in while playing outdoors) while others will require closer proximity (recording samples of the language the child uses). At no time are you expected to participate in the class activities, indoors or out. If children question your presence, just say you are doing a school assignment. Cameras, video tape recorders and audio tape recorders are prohibited in most centers. Any rules particular to the center you choose should be communicated to you by the director before you begin your observations. The duration, timing and other specific details about the observations Is up to the individual instructors, and should be discussed with him or her before proceeding.

The Observations

Observation 1:   Infants—Newborn to 12 months
Observation 2:   Toddlers—12 months to 24 months
Observation 3:   Play Years—Physical Growth and Motor Skills
Observation 4:   Play Years—Cognitive Development and Language Development
Observation 5:   Play Years—Emotional and Social Development
Observation 6:   Play Years—Emotional and Social Development

Observations 3-6 must be completed at an early childhood education and care center. You must observe a group of three- or four-year-old children and choose one child to be the subject of your observations. This child will be the focus child of your child study. Observations 3-6 provide the data you will use to write your child study.

Hints for Quality Observations

- Use first names only to ensure confidentiality.

- Use the format (4-3) to indicate age—4 years, three months old.

- Provide a context when describing specific behaviors and language.
  Provide details. (WHO? WHAT? WHEN? WHAT WAS THE STIMULUS?)

- Do not use vague terms such as: object or toy [instead, identify it such as "the blue, plastic hammer" or "the red, blue, and green plush ball"]; or playing [instead, state "Rosa (3 years, 10 months) places all the red legos in a pile and then places all the blue legos in a separate pile and then proceeds to place them in a line lengthwise alternating the red legos with the blue legos." or "John (4 years, 2 months) rolls a ball of yellow playdough between his hands in a circular motion and then places the ball in his right hand and squeezes it with a tightly clenched fist and watches it squish out between his fingers"

- Do not use terms that imply a value judgment—words that are judgmental usually are vague and have very little value or meaning in objective behavioral descriptions. Examples: good, bad, nice, naughty, normal, very well, or hyper.

- Relate observed characteristics to developmental stages when appropriate. For example comments about cognitive skills can be related to Piaget's stages. Comments about social and emotional skills can be related to Erikson's stages.

- Use language found in the textbook glossary. This improves the vocabulary of the observation and incorporates concepts with text material.

- Respond to all components in the questions with complete sentences as much as possible. Avoid unnecessary words.

- You are making statements based on limited data. Don't use words that imply a definite, potentially irrevocable conclusion. Instead of "is," use "it seemed" or "it appears." Don't use "I" statements such as "I feel…" or "In my opinion…" unless a personal opinion is clearly requested in the question.

- Observations should be written in the present tense and objectively.

Evaluation Criteria

Each instructor will have his or her particular criteria for grading your observations. Be sure you are aware of these before you begin. Some typical elements of evaluation are as follows:

- format (spelling, organization, neatness)
- clear descriptions, specific detail, completeness
- ability to relate observations to text
- use of objective and professional language

Instructions for the Interview Assignment

The interview assignment consists of four interviews, one each for a school age child and adolescent, and two for the middle-aged or older adult. The questions are provided for you in the forms included in this packet. Be sure to pay careful attention to the summary section that follows each set of interview questions. In this section, you will make conclusions based on your subject's answers to the interview questions. Always support your conclusions with evidence from the interview. There is no requirement for who you can interview. You can interview a friend, neighbor of family member, if you so desire.

Evaluation Criteria

Each instructor will have his or her particular criteria for grading your observations. Be sure you are aware of these before you begin. Some typical elements of evaluation are as follows:

- format (spelling, organization, neatness)
- clear descriptions, specific detail, completeness
- conclusions supported by information from the answers ot the interview questions
- thorough answers to each summary question

Instructions for the Child Study

General Guidelines

The child study is based on the data you gather in observations 3 through 6. It is a summary of your focus child's development in all domains. It is the intention of this guide to provide the basic framework and outline of the assignment. Each instructor will provide his or her particular requirements.

Elements of the child study to be determined by the instructor include:
Page limit
Content and style of cover page
Presentation format
Bibliography style
Reference style
Inclusion of TB test results

Elements of the child study that are essential to the assignment include:
Signed letter of introduction with hours verified by the teacher or director
Completed observations 3 thorough 6
The written child study

Elements of the Child Study

Introduction: Include information about the site where you observed. Provide a context for the observation. Identify your focus child's first name. Describe some of the salient features and qualities of your focus child, including a physical description. Explain what about this child motivated you to choose him or her instead of another child.

Body: Each section should include an introductory statement related to that area of development. You will express your observations about this child's development, and then follow this with supporting examples of behavior from your observations. For example, suppose you write "Graciela is an active child who enjoys playing outdoors." You would support this with something like "As noted on observation 3, question 3, she spends the majority of her free play time climbing on the jungle gym and riding the tricycle as opposed to playing quietly in the sand."

Compare and contrast the behavior, growth and development of your focus child to information in the text. References to the text are an essential part of each section of your child study. You may also make reference to other books on human development. The particular style you will use for making these references will be left to your instructor's discretion. Regardless of the style you use, all references to published work must be properly credited. Direct quotes and paraphrases are common elements of academic writing. Their correct use should be discussed with your instructor prior to writing your child study.

Conclusion: In this part of the paper, you will briefly summarize what you have observed about the strengths of your focus child as well as areas where he or she has yet to develop. Here you will offer your opinion as to your focus child's current level and projected future development.

Reference/Bibliography Page: On this page, quoted or paraphrased work will be given credit. The style of reference is left to the discretion of your instructor. Most academic work in the social sciences uses American Psychological Association (APA) style referencing.

Outline of the Child Study

Introduction

A. Biosocial Development: Physical Description

Size, height, weight, activity level and abilities compared to others. Evidence of health status as compared to norms. Description of body build.

B. Motor Skills

Use of gross and fine motor skills. Favorite activities, favorite games, and table activities.

C. Cognition

Evidence of characteristics of Piaget's Preoperational Stage with specific examples. Include activities which show classification, seriation, and symbolism. Also imitation, role play, memory, ideas about reality and special interests.

D. Communication

Gestures, body language, facial expressions, motions. Examples of vocabulary used with peers and adults (language samples). Ability to use humor, slang.

E. Emotions

Stage of personality development-Erikson's theory. Evidence of autonomy, initiative, guilt, etc. Temperament and child's characteristic way of expressing feelings. Mood, range of emotions expressed, evidence of feelings.

F. Social Interaction

Attachment, pro-social behavior, size of play groups preferred. Interaction with age mates, parents, siblings, adults. Favorite roles, small group play, large group play, types of play.

G. Self Esteem

Indication of how child thinks and feels about himself. Motivation, self direction, dependent and independent behaviors.

Conclusion:

Evaluation Criteria

Each instructor will have his or her particular criteria for grading your Child Study. Be sure you are aware of these before you begin. Some typical elements of evaluation are as follows:

- format (spelling, organization, neatness)
- clear descriptions, specific detail, completeness
- ability to relate observations to text
- use of objective and professional language
- connection of your conclusions with evidence from your observations

The Observations

Observation 1: The Infant (birth to 12 months)

Indicate for each question the first name and age (years-months) of the infant you are observing.

Biosocial Development: Physical Growth
1. How does the infant compare in height and weight to developmental norms?
    Consult the height and weight chart at the rear of this manual.
    What are the body proportions of the infant?

Perception: (pp. 134-135)
2. What evidence did you see of visual preference? Is there evidence of habituation?
    Explain.

Motor Development: (pp. 106-107 and 137-140)
3. What kinds of reflexes do you see? Describe and name.

4. Describe how the infant controls his or her head.
    Can this be done independently or is support required?

5. Is the child able to reach a sitting position alone? Describe how this is done.
    If the child cannot reach a seated position independently, when places in a seated
    position can he or she maintain this posture?

6. Describe the grasp the infant uses when holding an object. (p. 140)
   - <u>ulnar grasp</u>: palm, fourth and fifth fingers
   - <u>radial grasp</u>: index finger and side of palm
   - <u>pincer grasp</u>: thumb and forefinger together
   - <u>palmar grasp</u>: middle fingers and center of palm

Cognitive Development: (Chapter 5)
7. What evidence did you see of object permanence or that the infant has not yet attained object permanence. (pp. 155-156)

8. What substage of sensorimotor development does the child seem to be in now? Describe the sensorimotor activity observed that supports this inference. (p. 153)

Language Development: (pp. 172-177)
9. Describe the vocalizations of the infant. Provide the context.
   Was there a clear stimulus?

10. Describe the responses to language that the infant demonstrates.

Emotional and Social Development:
11. Does the infant show evidence of basic emotions (happiness, interest, surprise, fear, anger, sadness, disgust)? How does the infant show this? What is the stimulus? (pp. 185-188)

12. How does the infant react to being approached by a stranger (stranger wariness)? How does the infant react to being separated from the significant adult? (p. 186)

Observation 2: The Toddler (12 – 24 months)

Indicate for each question the first name and age (years-months) of the toddler you are observing.

Biosocial Development

1. How does the toddler compare in height and weight to developmental norms? Consult the height and weight chart at the rear of this manual.

Motor Development: (pp. 137-140)

2. Describe the physical movement involved when the toddler throws a ball, pounds a toy with a hammer or pushes or pulls a toy.

3. Describe how the toddler picks up toys from the floor. Indicate the type of grasp the child uses

4. Describe how the toddler climbs on a chair and sits in it.

5. Describe how the toddler moves from one part of the room to another. Compare this with another toddler's walking locomotor ability.

Cognitive Development:

6. What substage of sensorimotor development does the child seem to be in? What do you observe that supports your conclusion? (p. 153)

7. Describe two examples of ways that a toddler solved a problem.

Language Development: (pp. 174-177)
8. Listen for evidence of pre-linguistic speech (babbling), and linguistic speech (holophrase, multi-word sentences, underextension, overextension). Write the examples you heard. Indicate if the toddler was speaking to a child, adult, or vocalizing to no one in particular; indicate the type of speech you heard.
Be sure to use quotation marks for direct quotes.

Emotional and Social Development:
9. Describe the ways the toddler approaches or interacts with other children.

10. How does the toddler react to being approached by a stranger (stranger wariness)? How does the toddler react to being separated from the significant adult? (p.186)

11. Describe evidence of attachment.

12. Describe observed evidence of autonomous and/or dependent behavior showing self-confidence or shame and doubt.   (p. 184)

Observation 3: The Preschool Child (3 – 4 years)

Beginning with observation 3, you will focus your attention on one child, which will henceforth be referred to as the "focus child" of your observations and child study. Indicate the first name and age (years-months) of the child you are observing here:

Biosocial Development

1. How does your focus child compare in height and weight to developmental norms? Consult the height and weight chart at the rear of this manual.

2. Observe the child's fine and gross motor activities both indoors and outdoors. List the skills your focus child demonstrates. (pp. 224-225)

Gross Motor   Fine Motor

a. _____   a. _____

b. _____   b. _____

c. _____   c. _____

d. _____   d. _____

3. What activities does your focus child choose? Confine your remarks to activities in which the child has a choice. Include both indoor and outdoor periods in your analysis. Indicate after each activity whether fine or gross motor activity predominates.

4. Describe examples of your focus child's participation in the following type of play: Sensorimotor, Mastery, Rough and Tumble. Include an entry for each type of play, even if only a definition.

Definitions:

Sensorimotor Play: play that emphasizes sensory experience. This type of play has no objective other than to experience the medium. Examples of sensorimoror play are water play, finger painting, rubbing hands in shaving cream, squeezing play dough (without constructing anything).

Mastery Play: play that emphasizes the mastery of some physical or cognitive skill. Examples of mastery play include shooting a basketball over and over through a hoop, riding a scooter to gain control of its capabilities, making a puzzle over and over, watching a video over and over.

Rough and Tumble Play: play that emphasizes physical contact or pretend fighting. Examples of rough and tumble play are pretend wrestling and pretend Kung Fu fighting.

5. Describe an instance of your focus child's drawing or painting. Describe in detail the child's manipulation of the instrument and the medium. Provide a facsimile of the child's creation in the space provided. How does the child's physical development influence his or her drawing or painting? (pp. 225-226)

6. Describe 4 observable indications of the health of your focus child.

Observation 4: The Preschool Child (3 – 4 years)

Cognitive Skills and Language

1. Listen carefully to your focus child's sentence length and vocabulary. Quote the child directly. Circle the nouns (naming words), underline the verbs (action words), and highlight the adjectives (describing words). (pp. 248-251)

2. What cognitive activities does your focus child choose when he or she is free to choose? Name the activity and describe the associated cognitive skill. (pp. 223 Table 7.2)

3. What evidence do you see of your focus child's use of scripts? (pp. 238-239)

4. Record (in minutes) the length of time your focus child remains engaged in a activity during free choice time. Indicate the activity and the duration of involvement.

5. Describe how your focus child solves a problem. This can be a social problem or a physical problem. Provide the context and a detailed description.

6. Record your focus child's speech that includes concepts of mathematics. Listen for the use of comparative terms such as less-more, big-smaller, light-heavy, close-far, full-empty, and so on. Listen for the use of operational terms such as adding to or taking from. (pp. 242-243)

7. Describe an instance of your focus child showing centration in his or her speech or actions. (p. 230)

8. Describe an instance of your focus child showing egocentric thinking in his or her speech or actions. (p. 229)

9. Describe an instance of your focus using classification or seriation in an activity or in play. (p. 232)

10. How does your focus child's cognitive development influence his or her drawing or painting?

11. Record your focus child's use of the following pragmatics of language.

- Private Speech (pp. 234-235)

- Overregularization   (p. 249)

- Vocabulary Development (p. 248-249)

Observation 5: The Preschool Child (3 – 4 years)

Social and Emotional Development

1. Listen to the child's social conversations carefully. Record 5 sentences. Indicate the purpose of each sentence. (Gaining information, giving information, commanding, getting needs met)

    1.

    2.

    3.

    4.

    5.

2. How does your focus child express emotion? Include both verbal and nonverbal means of expression. Cite at least two examples. (pp. 259-260)

    1.

    2.

3. Which of the following types of play did your focus child engage in? (p. 261)

    <u>Unoccupied</u>: disengaged from play, daydreaming alone

    <u>Onlooker</u>: watches other children play

    <u>Solitary</u>: plays alone, seemingly unaware of other children nearby

    <u>Parallel</u>: children play with similar toys, but they don't interact

    <u>Associative</u>: children interact, share materials-but aren't playing the same game

    <u>Cooperative</u>: children play together, helping and taking turns with each other

4. Describe how your focus child shows aggression, if at all. (pp. 270-273)

5. Using Chess and Thomas' Model of Temperament, (p. 191) describe 3 temperament traits of your focus child. Cite the behavior that supports these inferences.

6. What evidence do you see of your focus child being in Erikson's "Initiative vs Guilt" stage of development? (p. 17 and p. 256)

7. What is your focus child's favorite make-believe play role during inside or outside play time? (p. 262)

8. What signs of gender-role awareness did you observe in your focus child? (pp. 273-278)

Observation 6: The Preschool Child (3 – 4 years)

Emotional and Social Development: Self-Concept

1. Describe signs of self-awareness and self-understanding. How does your focus child refer to himself or herself? Is your focus child proud of doing the right thing and following the rules or does he or she seem to lack confidence? Include the behavior that lead to your conclusion. (p. 256-258)

2. Does your focus child accept responsibility for small jobs or does he or she avoid responsibility? Cite an example to support this inference.

3. Describe a situation where your focus child shows empathy for another child. (pp. 260-261)

4. Describe an observed associative or cooperative play experience of your focus child. Include the context for the play and your focus child's role in it. Does this appear to you to be typical or atypical for your focus child?

The Interviews

Interview 1: The School Age Child (Ages 7-11)

Subject's First Name_____   **Age**_____   **Grade**_____

1. Describe yourself. If you met a fairy and were granted one wish that you could change anything about yourself that you wanted— but only one thing— what would that thing be?

2. What are your special interests or hobbies outside of school? Do you take lessons, attend special interest classes, or play on any teams? Do you belong to any organizations such as Boy Scouts or Girl Scouts?

3. What are you good at?

4. Who is your best friend? How long have you known him (her)?   What do you like about this friend? What do you think your best friend would say he (she) likes about you?

5. If I asked the other kids in your class what you are good at, what do you think they would tell me?

6. What do you think it is about someone that makes other people like him (her)? (What makes a person popular?)

7. What do you think it is about someone that could make other people not like him (her) and not want to be his (her) friend? (What makes a child unpopular?)

8. What is your favorite subject in school? What is your least favorite? How do feel about school?

9. Do you have any special tricks or techniques that help you remember information in school?

10. What responsibilities do you have at home?

11. What is your place in the birth order of your family?
    What do you like about it or dislike about it?

12. If you could be like any other person, who would you be like? What do you admire about this person?

13. What do you feel is the greatest challenge or problem in the world today? What can we do about it?

14. Imagine you are at the grocery store, and there on the floor in the soft drinks aisle, you see a wallet. You can see that this wallet has money in it: some of the bills are showing at the corners. No one else is in this aisle but you.

What would you do? Why?

Interview 1 Summary:

1. Which of Piaget's periods of cognitive development do you believe this child is in? Support your conclusion. (p. 20 and pp. 298-301

2. Which of Erikson's psychosocial stages of development do you believe this child is in? Support your conclusion. (p. 17 and p. 330)

3. Where do you see this child being in his or her moral development? Support your conclusion. (pp. 336-339)

4. What is this child's social status among his or her peers? Support your conclusion. (pp. 340-341)

Interview 2: Adolescent Development (Ages 14-17)

Subject's First Name_____   **Age**_____   **Grade**_____

1. Describe yourself.

2. What do you like best about yourself? What would you like to change?

3. What kinds of activities do you enjoy? Do you have any special interests or hobbies?

4. Do you have a best friend? Is your best friend a boy or a girl?

5. What do you enjoy doing with your best friend?

6. How did you come to know each other and how did you come to be best friends?

7. How much time do you spend together? Do you talk on the phone often?
    How long are the typical conversations? Do you have a beeper or cell phone?

8. What is your favorite subject in school? What is your least favorite?

9. Do you spend more time thinking about how you look or about your school work?

10. Who is the most popular girl at school? How do you feel about her? Why?

11. Who is the most popular boy at school? How do you feel about him? Why?

12. What do you want to do when you finish high school?

13. What is the purpose of punishment?

14. What is the most important thing in your life? How does this help or support you?

15. Do you have a job? If so, how do you feel about it?

16. What responsibilities do you have at home?

17. How do you feel about your parents and family? How much time do you spend with them each week? What do you talk about most?

18. Do you have a boyfriend or a girlfriend? What is the most difficult part of this relationship? What is the best part?

19. Of all the people in the world, who would you choose to be like? What do you admire about this person?

20. What dreams do you have for your future? Are you looking forward to having a career? Are you looking forward to starting a family?

21. What do you think we left out that is important to you?

Interview 2 Summary:

1. Which of Piaget's cognitive stages does this adolescent seem to be in? Support your conclusions (pp. 381-383)

2. Which of Erikson's psychosocial stages does this adolescent seem to be in? Support your conclusions. (p. 400)

2. What does this person think about himself or herself? (pp. 400-401)

3. Where does this person seem to be in terms of identity formation?   (p. 402)

2. Using the Chess and Thomas Model of Temperament (p. 191), describe 3 aspects of this adolescent's temperament.   Support your conclusion.

3. What do you remember about your teen years that is similar or different from this adolescent's experience?

PLEASE NOTE: *Turn in interviews 3 and 4 together.*

Interview 3: Adult Development— Middle Age or Late Adulthood -- Male

Reference: Chapters 15 and16 or 17 and 18

1. Describe yourself briefly.

2 How do you feel about your work? How do you feel about your hobbies or special interests?

3. What is your opinion of today's youth?

4. What changes have taken place in society since the time you were a teenager?

5. Do you have any special philosophy that guides your life?

6. What are your immediate goals? What are your long-range goals?

7. What were you doing 5 years ago? Have you attained some of the goals that you set for yourself since that time?

8. In what ways are you a different person than you were in your early 20's?

9. Have you had a mentor in your adult life?

10. If you had your life to live over again, what would you do differently?

11. What do you look forward to most in the future?

12. How do you feel about marriage? How do you feel about sex?

13. How do you feel about children? (Whether a parent or not.)

14. How do you feel about grandchildren? (Whether a grandparent or not.)

15. Do you think children should be raised in a permissive, authoritarian, or authoritative manner? (Whether a parent or not.)

16. How do your friendships today compare to those during your teens? Do you have the same friends?

17. How do you feel about old age?

18 What else do you think is relevant to your personality and development as an adult?

Interview 4: Adult Development— Middle Age or Late Adulthood -- Female

Reference: Chapters 15 and 16 or 17 and 18

1. Describe yourself briefly.

2   How do you feel about your work?   How do you feel about your hobbies or special interests?

3. What is your opinion of today's youth?

4. What changes have taken place in society since the time you were a teenager?

5. Do you have any special philosophy that guides your life?

6. What are your immediate goals? What are your long range goals?

7. What were you doing 5 years ago? Have you attained some of the goals that you set for yourself since that time?

8. In what ways are you a different person than you were in your early 20's?

9. Have you had a mentor in your adult life?

10. If you had your life to live over again, what would you do differently?

11. What do you look forward to most in the future?

12. How do you feel about marriage? How do you feel about sex?

13. How do you feel about children? (Whether a parent or not.)

14. How do you feel about grandchildren? (Whether a grandparent or not.)

15. Do you think children should be raised in a permissive, authoritarian, or authoritative manner? (Whether a parent or not.)

16. How do your friendships today compare to those during your teens? Do you have the same friends?

17. How do you feel about old age?

18. What else do you think is relevant to your personality and development as an adult?

<u>**Interviews 3 and 4 Summary:**</u>

PLEASE NOTE:
Turn in the Summary and Comparison of the adult interviews (3 and 4) together.

1. Explain what stage of life the adults you interviewed are in according to the theories of Erikson (pages 16-18) and Levinson (pages 447 and 515-516). Describe what you have discovered about the adults that you have interviewed. What factors may contribute to the similarities and differences in the life stages of the adults you interviewed? Use the format provided. Use complete sentences in paragraphs.

Stages of Development: <u>Erikson's Stages of Pychosocial Development</u>
                                 EXAMPLE: Integrity vs. Despair

                                 <u>Levinson's Stages of Adulthood</u>
                                 EXAMPLE: Midlife Transition

Male: Include the specific responses to the interview questions that suggest these stages.

<u>Erikson's Stages of Pychosocial Development</u>:   (p. 530)

<u>Levison's Stages of Adulthood</u>:   (p. 533)

Female: Include the specific responses to the interview questions that suggest these stages.

Erikson's Stages of Pychosocial Development: (p. 530)

Levinson's Stages of Adulthood: (p. 533)

2. What factors may contribute to the similarities and differences in the life stages and personal characteristics of the adults you interviewed?

Similarities:

Differences:

3. Did you notice a sense of fulfillment in life or a sense of dissatisfaction in life in these adults? Compare and contrast your current sense of fulfillment or dissatisfaction in life with theirs.

Birth to 36 months: Boys
Length-for-age and Weight-for-age percentiles

NAME _____

RECORD # _____

AGE (MONTHS)

Birth 3 6 9 **12** 15 18 21 **24** 27 30 33 **36**

LENGTH

in	cm		cm	in
41	100		100	41
40		95		40
39	95	90		39
38		75	95	38
37		50		37
36	90	25		36
35		10 5	90	35
34	85			
33				
32	80	95		38
31		90	17	36
30	75			
29		75	16	34
28	70		15	
27				32
26	65	50	14	
25				30
24	60	25	13	
23				28
22	55	10	12	
21		5		26
20	50		11	24
19				
18	45		10	22
17				
16	40		9	20
15				18

WEIGHT

AGE (MONTHS)

12 15 18 21 **24** 27 30 33 **36** kg lb

8 — 18

lb	kg
16	7
14	6
12	5
10	4
8	3
6	2
lb	**kg**

Birth 3 6 9

Mother's Stature _____		Gestational		
Father's Stature _____		Age: _____ Weeks		Comment
Date	Age	Weight	Length	Head Circ.
	Birth			

Published May 30, 2000 (modified 4/20/01).
SOURCE: Developed by the National Center for Health Statistics in collaboration with
the National Center for Chronic Disease Prevention and Health Promotion (2000).
http://www.cdc.gov/growthcharts

SAFER · HEALTHIER · PEOPLE™

Birth to 36 months: Girls
Length-for-age and Weight-for-age percentiles

NAME _____

RECORD # _____

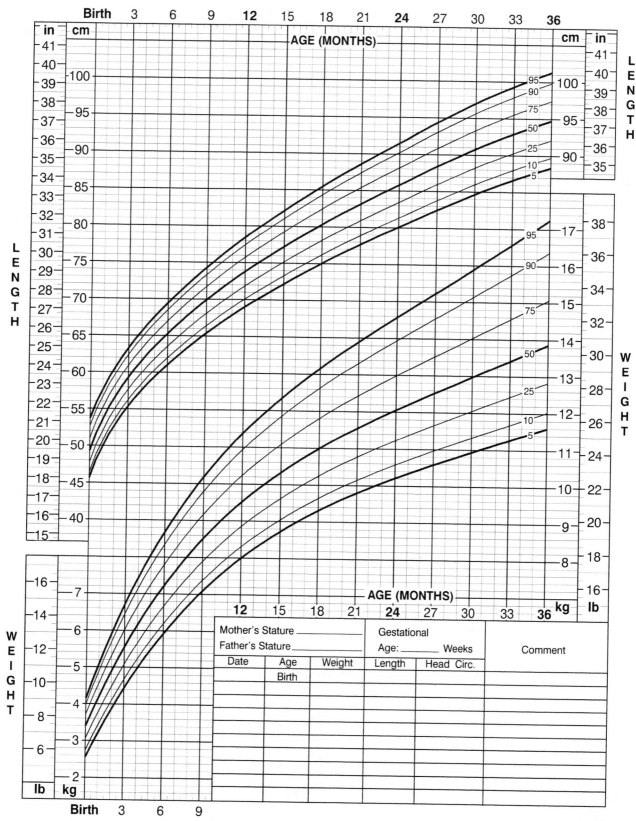

AGE (MONTHS)

Mother's Stature _____			Gestational		Comment
Father's Stature _____			Age: _____ Weeks		
Date	Age	Weight	Length	Head Circ.	
	Birth				

Published May 30, 2000 (modified 4/20/01).
SOURCE: Developed by the National Center for Health Statistics in collaboration with
the National Center for Chronic Disease Prevention and Health Promotion (2000).
http://www.cdc.gov/growthcharts

SAFER · HEALTHIER · PEOPLE™